Holy Cow! 250,000 Graphics

Holy Cow! 250,000 Graphics

Trademarks and Copyrights

A portion of the photographs provided by:

Painet Stock Photo Agency
(Photographic Arts & Illustration NETwork)
email: macmillan@painetworks.com
tel: 1-800-645-9877
http://painetworks.com

All Painet's images are dated 5/5/97. Contact them for high-resolution versions of their images.

Special thanks to:

Travis Bartlett

Carol Blankenbeckler

Bruce Clingaman

Alonez Cox

Mike Dietsch

Bryan Flores

Cheryl Fridley

Paul Gilchrist

Stephen Graham

Randy Jarrett

Kitty Jarrett

Wendy Layton

Chris Lowell

Eric Morgan

Grant Munroe

James Nelson

Mike Opincar

Deborah Petro

Casey Price

Dave Sechrist

Michael Shafer

Ian Smith

Rebecca Tapley

Marvin Van Tiem

Mark Walchle

Skip Whiting

Macmillan Digital Publishing License Agreement

YOU SHOULD CAREFULLY READ THE FOLLOWING TERMS AND CONDITIONS BEFORE INSTALLING OR USING THIS SOFTWARE. AMONG OTHER THINGS, THIS AGREEMENT LICENSES THE ENCLOSED SOFTWARE TO YOU AND CONTAINS WARRANTY AND LIABILITY DISCLAIMERS. BY USING THE DISC(S) AND/OR INSTALLING THE SOFTWARE, YOU ARE ACCEPTING AND AGREEING TO THE TERMS AND CONDITIONS OF THIS AGREEMENT. IF YOU DO NOT AGREE TO THE TERMS OF THIS AGREEMENT, DO NOT USE THE DISCS. YOU SHOULD PROMPTLY RETURN THE PACKAGE UNUSED.

LICENSE

Macmillan Digital Publishing USA, Simon & Schuster, Inc., and its licensers (the "Company") provides this Software to you and grants to you a non-exclusive, non-transferable license to:

a. use the Software on a single computer of the type identified on the package;

b. make one copy of the Software in machine readable-form solely for back-up purposes; and

c. use the Software for your personal use or in your business or profession.

This disk may contain the proprietary property of the Company, or of others which has been licensed to the Company, such as fonts, sound effects, music, animations, and clip art ("ClipMedia"). There are no additional usage fees for the ClipMedia, provided, however, that you may reproduce the ClipMedia only as a graphic design element of a personal or professional Web site or other multimedia application. Republication, reproduction or any other distribution or sale of the ClipMedia in any other way, whether in print or electronic form, is strictly prohibited.

TERM

This license is effective until terminated. You may terminate it at any time by destroying the Software and ClipMedia together with all copies in any form. This license will also terminate upon conditions set forth elsewhere in this agreement or if you fail to comply with any term or condition of this agreement. You agree that upon such termination you will destroy the Software and ClipMedia together with all copies in any form.

LIMITED WARRANTY

The Company warrants the physical CD-ROM or diskette(s) on which the Software is furnished to be free from defects in materials and workmanship under normal use for a period of sixty (60) days from the date of purchase as evidenced by a copy of your receipt.

DISCLAIMER AND LIMITATIONS OF REMEDIES

THE SOFTWARE IS PROVIDED 'AS IS' AND COMPANY SPECIFICALLY DISCLAIMS ALL WARRANTIES OF ANY KIND, EITHER EXPRESS OR IMPLIED, INCLUDING, BUT NOT LIMITED TO, THE IMPLIED WARRANTIES OF MERCHANTABILITY AND FITNESS FOR A PARTICULAR PURPOSE. IN NO EVENT WILL COMPANY BE LIABLE TO YOU FOR ANY DAMAGES, INCLUDING ANY LOSS OF PROFIT OR OTHER INCIDENTAL, SPECIAL OR CONSEQUENTIAL DAMAGES EVEN IF COMPANY HAS BEEN ADVISED OF THE POSSIBILITY OF SUCH DAMAGES.

COMPANY DOES NOT WARRANT, GUARANTY OR MAKE ANY REPRESENTATIONS REGARDING THE USE, OR THE RESULTS OF THE USE, OF THE SOFTWARE IN TERMS OF CORRECTNESS, ACCURACY, RELIABILITY, CURRENTNESS, OR OTHERWISE AND DOES NOT WARRANT THAT THE OPERATION OF ANY SOFTWARE WILL BE UNINTERRUPTED OR ERROR FREE. COMPANY EXPRESSLY DISCLAIMS ANY WARRANTIES NOT STATED HEREIN. NO ORAL OR WRITTEN INFORMATION OR ADVICE GIVEN COMPANY OR OTHERS SHALL CREATE A WARRANTY OR IN ANY WAY INCREASE THE SCOPE OF THE FOREGOING WARRANTY, AND NEITHER SUBLICENSEE NOR PURCHASER MAY RELY ON ANY SUCH INFORMATION OR ADVICE.

SOME JURISDICTIONS DO NOT ALLOW THE EXCLUSION OF IMPLIED WARRANTIES OR LIMITATION OR EXCLUSION OF LIABILITY FOR INCIDENTAL OR CONSEQUENTIAL DAMAGES, SO THE ABOVE EXCLUSIONS AND/OR LIMITATIONS MAY NOT APPLY TO YOU.

The Company's entire liability and your exclusive remedy shall be:

1. the replacement of such CD-ROM or diskette if you return a defective diskette during the limited warranty period, or

2. if the Company is unable to deliver a replacement CD-ROM or diskette that is free of defects in materials or workmanship, you may terminate this Agreement by returning the Software.

GENERAL

The Software is owned or licensed by the Company and is protected by United States copyright laws and international treaty provisions. You may not sublicense, assign, or transfer the license or the Software or make or distribute copies of the Software. Any attempt to sublicense, assign, or transfer any of the rights, duties, or obligations hereunder is void. As licensee, you own the media on which the Software is recorded or fixed, but the Company or its licensors retain ownership of the Software. You may not translate, reverse engineer, decompile, disassemble, modify or create derivative works based on, the Software, and except for the single backup copy permitted hereunder, you may not copy the Software. Further, you may not copy the written materials accompanying the Software.

Should you have any questions concerning this Agreement or technical support, you may contact the Company by writing to:

Macmillan Digital Publishing USA
201 W. 103rd Street
Indianapolis, IN 46290-1097
Attention: Software Licensing

YOU ACKNOWLEDGE THAT YOU HAVE READ THIS AGREEMENT, UNDERSTAND IT, AND AGREE TO BE BOUND BY ITS TERMS AND CONDITIONS. YOU FURTHER AGREE THAT IT IS THE COMPLETE AND EXCLUSIVE STATEMENT OF THE AGREEMENT BETWEEN US THAT SUPERSEDES ANY PROPOSAL OR PRIOR AGREEMENT, ORAL OR WRITTEN, AND ANY OTHER COMMUNICATIONS BETWEEN US RELATING TO THE SUBJECT MATTER OF THIS AGREEMENT.

Thank you for purchasing *Holy Cow! 250,000 Graphics.*

Welcome to one of the largest collections of graphics ever assembled, with 17 CD-ROMs of graphics and media clips in the most popular formats:

- Scalable vector clip art in WMF format
- Photos in JPG format
- Bitmap images in TIF and JPG formats
- Web graphics and animations in GIF and JPG formats
- Sound effects and music in MIDI and WAV formats
- And more…

Product Registration

Be sure to complete and mail in your product registration card. To save time and save stamps, register on our Web site. Open your Web browser and connect with this address:

`www.MacmillanSoftware.com`

Click on the Register link to reach our online registration page. When you register, you become eligible for product support.

Product Support

Our support team can help you if you experience problems with installation of the included software, or with any of the images themselves. We cannot help you with editing images or with using other programs that are not included on these discs. If you contact us, please be prepared to give us the following information:

- Complete name of this product
- Version number on the CD-ROM, if any
- Specific details of the problem you're having
- Complete information on your computer system setup, including operating system version, amount of RAM, type of processor, and type of graphics card.

Email (best method): `support@mcp.com`

Telephone: (317) 581-3833

Fax: (317) 581-4773

Mail: Macmillan Publishing
Attention: Support Department
201 West 103rd Street
Indianapolis, IN 46290

Usage Guidelines

This product contains clip art images, photographs, Web graphics, and sounds which are either owned by Macmillan Digital Publishing or licensed from various third parties. You are free to use, modify, and publish the images in this collection, subject to the following conditions:

1. You may not use any of these files to create scandalous, obscene, illegal, or immoral works.
2. You may not redistribute or sell any portion of these files as a collection of graphics or media clips.
3. You may not use any images related to identifiable individuals or entities in a manner which suggests their association with or endorsement of any product or service.
4. You may not use these files to create a product which is similar to or competes with any Macmillan Publishing product.
5. You may not use more than fifty (50) of these images in commercial products, documents, Web pages, online content, or other commercial applications without contacting us first for licensing approval.
6. You must also comply with any third-party conditions listed on the *Trademarks and Copyrights* page in the front of this book.

Include the following credit in documents, multimedia applications, Web pages, or other uses that include our images. You do not need to include this notice if your use is strictly personal.

Some images are from "Holy Cow! 250,000 Graphics", by Macmillan Digital Publishing USA

If you have any questions about use of these images, send an email to `swfeedback@mcp.com`, or write to:

Macmillan Digital Publishing
Image Licensing
201 W. 103rd Street
Indianapolis, IN 46290

About This Catalog

This printed catalog contains thumbnail representations of all the scalable vector clip art on the CD-ROMs. The header at the top of the page shows the category and subcategory for each page. For example:

Africa • Miscellaneous (MISC)

The name on the left is the main category, which corresponds to the folder name on the CD-ROM. We can only use 8-character filenames on the CD-ROM; if the category name is different from the actual folder name, we've indicated the actual folder name in parentheses.

The photographs, bitmaps, and web graphics are not included in this printed catalog. Each CD-ROM contains a full-color electronic catalog of every image on that disc. See the *Using the Electronic Catalogs* section for more information on these image catalogs.

Organization of the CD-ROMs

The CD-ROMs are organized by type of graphic. For example, the *Photos 2* disc contains photographs. The information below shows you what's on each disc.

Master Disc

Contains the ThumbsCD program, miscellaneous bitmap images, and demo programs from PictureWorks. For more information on the PictureWorks programs, run the *PictureWorks Demos* program from the *Holy Cow 250000 Graphics* program group. The PictureWorks demos are only compatible with Windows 95.

Vector 1 through Vector 5

Contains scalable vector clip art in WMF format.

Vector 1: Advertising to Borders/Corners 2

Vector 2: Borders/Frames1 to Entertainment

Vector 3: Fantasy & Mythology to Maps

Vector 4: Men to Sports/Racquets

Vector 5: Sports/Signs to Zodiac, plus additional Classic Images bitmaps (CLASSIC folder) and 3D Objects bitmaps (3DOBJECT folder).

Photos 1 through Photos 5

Contains photographs in JPG format.

Photos 1: Activity to Buildings/Cities

Photos 2: Buildings/Cities2 to Ireland

Photos 3: Kid Stuff to People

Photos 4: Plants to Transportation

Photos 5: Trash to Western

Bitmap 1 through Bitmap 5

Contains Classic Images from the Dover collections in TIF bitmap format. You'll also find additional Classic Images on the Vector 5 and Master discs.

Bitmap 1 Images	Folder Name
Ad Spots 1-20's & 30's	ADSPTIL1
Ad Spots 2-20's & 30's	ADSPTIL2
Amish Quilts	AMSHQULT
Chinese Lattice Designs 1	CHINALAT
Chinese Lattice Designs 2	CHLATDES
Deco Mortise Cuts	DECMRTCT
Early Advertising Cuts	EAADVCTS
Geometric Designs	GEOMDSGN
Isometric Perspectives	ISOMPERS
Lively Ad Cuts-20's & 30's	LVLYADCT
Printer Ornamentation	PRNTORNM
Spot Illustrations-20's & 30's	SPTILL20
Vintage Spot Illustrations-Children	VNTSPCHL

Bitmap 2 Images	Folder Name
Animals	ANIMALS
Dinosaurs	DINOSAUR
Insects	INSECTS
Misc. Life Images	XTRALIFE

Bitmap 3 Images	Folder Name
America	AMERICA
Autos	AUTOS
Children	CHILDREN
Costumes	COSTUMES
Cultures	CULTURES
Deco Cuts	DECOCUTS
Sorcery	DEVDEMWT
Early Advertising Art	EAADVART
Hands	HANDS
Oceans	OCEANS
Snowflakes	SNOWFLAK
Treasury of Design	TREADSGN
Women's Magazines, early 20th Cent.	WMNSMAGS

Bitmap 4 Images	Folder Name
Eating & Drinking	EATDRNK
Holidays	HOLIDAYS
Humor	HUMOR
Miscellaneous	MEN
Men	MISC
Music	MUSIC
Office	OFFICE
Old Fashioned	OLDFASH
Romance	ROMANCE
Sports	SPORTS
Woodcuts	WOODCUTS

Bitmap 5 Images	Folder Name
Plants	PLANTS
Silhouettes	SILHOUET
Styles of Ornaments	STYLORNM
Women	WOMEN

Web Graphics

Contains Web graphics in JPG and GIF formats. You'll find everything from animated GIF images to buttons, banners, backgrounds and dividers.

Getting Started

To setup the software and the thumbnails browser, insert the CD-ROM labeled *Master Disc* into your drive and follow these steps.

1. Windows 3.1x or NT 3.51 users, choose File + Run from the Program Manager menu. Windows 95 or Windows NT 4 users, click on the Start menu and choose Run.
2. Type **D:\CDSetup** and press Enter. If your CD-ROM drive is not drive D, substitute the correct drive letter. For example, if your CD-ROM drive is actually drive F, type **F:\CDSetup**.
3. The setup program for the disc will start and an opening screen will appear. Click the Next button to proceed and follow the instructions on screen.
4. **Windows 3.1 Users:** When the main setup is complete, the Microsoft Win32s setup program will begin. The graphics viewer program requires these software drivers. When the Win32s setup is complete, you need to restart Windows to allow the changes to take effect.

A program group named *Holy Cow 250000 Graphics* will be created.

Using the Electronic Catalogs

To make viewing and finding images easier, we've included the ThumbsCD program. Each disc is catalogued with small "thumbnail" previews of every image on the disc. With the ThumbsCD program, you can also view the images full-size, edit files, convert to other formats, view "slide shows" of images, apply special effects to the images, and much more.

Once you've installed the software from the *Master Disc*, here's how to view the color thumbnails catalog for any disc:

1. Insert the disc into your CD-ROM drive.
2. Run the *View Graphics* program in the *Holy Cow 250000 Graphics* program group.

This starts the ThumbsCD image browser, and opens up the thumbnails catalog for that disc. The first time you start ThumbsCD, you may have to double-click the icon for your CD-ROM drive in the ThumbsCD folder window. For example, if your CD-ROM drive is D, and you have the Vector 1 disc inserted, double-click on the icon labeled **D:** or **D: Vector1**. The figure at the top of the next page shows an example of what you'll see.

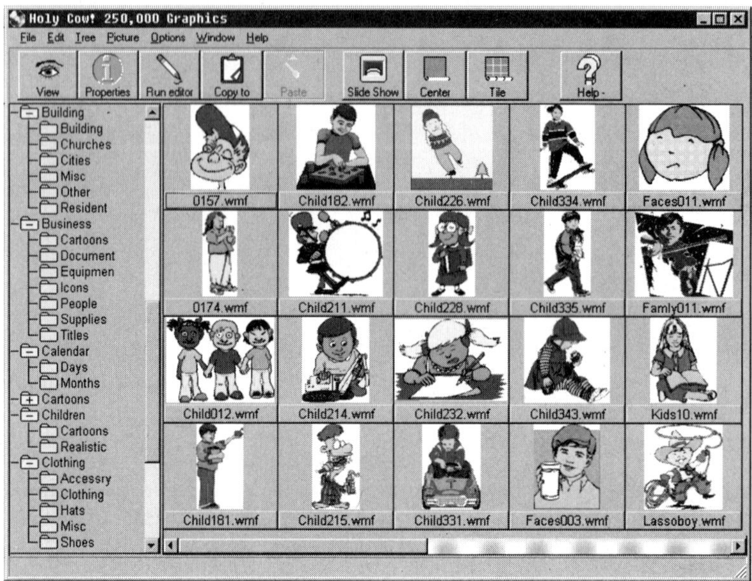

The left window shows the directory folders on the CD-ROM. The right window shows small "thumbnail" previews of the graphics within a particular folder.

> **Tip:** Click and drag the divider between these two windows to change the width of the windows.

A + symbol on a folder indicates that there are other sub-folders beneath it. Double-click on a folder to display the folders beneath it, or to hide the subfolders that are already displayed. The folders are also color-coded. Blue indicates that there are sub-folders beneath that folder. Green indicates that there are only images in that folder, and no folders beneath it.

If you click on a folder and don't see any images, wait a few seconds. With folders that contain a large amount of images, it takes a little time for the images to be displayed on your screen, depending on the speed of your computer and the speed of your CD-ROM drive. You can see the status of what's happening in the status bar at the bottom of the ThumbsCD screen.

If you still don't see any images, that's because you're at a top-level category that has subcategories beneath it. Double-click on the folder to display the subcategory folders, and click on any of these folders to view thumbnail images.

Using Images

Once you've located an image you like, it's easy to use it in your graphics-capable Windows program. There are several ways to use the images; perhaps the easiest methods are copy-and-paste or drag-and-drop, outlined below.

Copy and Paste Into Your Program

Highlight an image, then select Edit + Copy from the ThumbsCD menu. Switch to the program where you want to use the image, and select Edit + Paste from that program's menu. This will paste the image directly into your application.

Drag-and-Drop Into Your Program

With many Windows programs, you can also click on an image in ThumbsCD and drag it into your program. This pastes the full-size image into your application.

Copy the Image to Your Hard Drive

To copy one or several images to your hard drive, highlight the thumbnails you want with your mouse. To highlight more than one image, hold down the Control key as you select each file. Then, Select File + Copy File from the menu. You'll be prompted where to copy the files. Choose a location on your hard drive and click OK.

Editing Images

To edit an image before using it in your application, double-click on a thumbnail and the actual image will appear. If the image is too large to fit on your screen, press the F6 key and the entire image will be displayed.

You can use the Image menu in ThumbsCD to resize, rotate, add special effects, change the number of colors, convert, and much more.

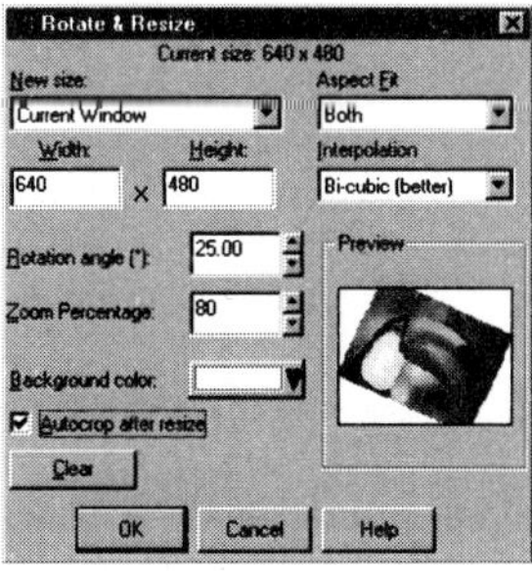

You can also apply a wide variety of effects filters to an image. To browse through the range of effects, open an image and chose Image + Filter + Select Filter... from the menu. You can preview the results of any change you make before applying the filter to the image.

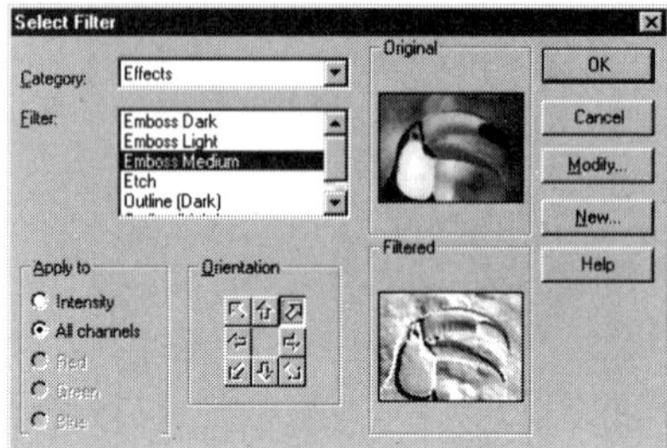

See the online help for more details on using ThumbsCD to view and edit images.

Troubleshooting Common Problems

When the ThumbsCD browser starts, I don't see any folders or images displayed.

- Do you have the CD-ROM in the drive? If you start the *View Graphics* program without one of the discs in the drive, you'll see an error message.
- If you have a Holy Cow CD-ROM inserted, double-click on the icon for your CD-ROM drive in the folder view of ThumbsCD. For example, if your CD-ROM drive is D, double-click on the icon labeled **D:**.

I'm running Windows 3.1 and the ThumbsCD browser won't start.

- Did you allow the CDSetup program to install the Win32s drivers? These drivers are needed by the ThumbsCD program. Re-run the CDSetup program on the disc, allow the Win32s installation to proceed, and restart your computer.

Some of the thumbnails are hard to see.

- The thumbnails are reproduced in 256 colors, and many of the graphics have thousands of colors. To view the actual graphic in its full resolution, double-click on any thumbnail image.
- If you're viewing the thumbnails at a screen size of 800x600, 1024x768, or higher, temporarily switch to a lower screen size. This will make the thumbnail pictures larger.

When I click on a folder, the images take a really long time to appear.

- If you have a slow (1x, 2x, or 3x) CD-ROM drive, the images may be displayed slowly. The faster your CD-ROM drive, and the faster your system, the quicker the images will display.
- If you're running Windows 3.1x and MS-DOS 6.0 or higher, make sure you have SmartDrive installed and enabled for your CD-ROM drive. See your Windows manual for information on how to configure SmartDrive.

Using Graphics in Common Windows Programs

If you want to, you can bypass the ThumbsCD program and bring a graphic directly into your program. Once you've identified an image from this printed catalog, or from the electronic thumbnails catalog, make a note of the image name and the folder on the CD-ROM where it's located.

The following sections show you how to import an image into many common Windows programs. If you need additional information, see your program's user manual.

Lotus Amí Pro

File types supported

JPG, TIF, WMF

Importing instructions

1. In an open document, choose **Create Frame** from the **Frame** menu.
2. Use the mouse to draw a frame, the size of the frame determines the size of the imported graphic.
3. Choose **Import Picture** from the **File** menu.
4. Select the drive, directory, and file name for the graphic you want to import. Click **OK**.

ClarisWorks

File types supported

JPG, WMF

Importing instructions

1. Choose **Import** from the **File** menu to place an image into an open document in the word processing module.
2. Select the drive, directory, and file name for the graphic you want to import. Click **OK**.

   Choose **Open** from the **File** menu to open and edit TIF graphic files.

CorelDRAW!

File types supported

JPG, WMF

Importing instructions

1. Choose **Import** from the **File** menu to place an image into an open document.
2. Select the drive, directory, and file name for the graphic you want to import. Click **OK**.

MacroMedia Freehand

File types supported

TIF

Importing instructions

1. For TIF images, choose **Place** from the **File** menu to place an image into an open document.
2. Select the drive, directory, and file name for the graphic you want to import. Click **OK**.
3. A TIF image can be used a background template, see the user's guide for more information.

Adobe Illustrator

File types supported

TIF

Importing instructions

1. For TIF images, choose **Import** from the **File** menu to place an image into an open document.
2. Select the drive, directory, and file name for the graphic you want to import. Click **OK**.

Adobe Pagemaker

File types supported

TIF, WMF

Importing instructions

1. Choose **Place** from the **File** menu to place an image into an open document.
2. Select the drive, directory, and file name for the graphic you want to import. Click **OK**.
3. Click in the document where you want the graphic to be.

Adobe PhotoShop

File types supported

TIF, WMF, JPG, GIF

Importing instructions

1. Choose **Open** from the **File** menu to open an image.
2. Select the drive, directory, and file name for the graphic you want to import. Click **OK**.
3. Vector images will need to be rasterized for use in PhotoShop, click **OK** in the Rasterize dialogue box to accept the settings.

Microsoft Publisher

File types supported

TIF, WMF

Importing instructions

1. Choose **Import Picture** from the **File** menu to place an image into an open document.
2. Select the drive, directory, and file name for the graphic you want to import. Click **OK**.

PrintShop Deluxe

File types supported

TIF, WMF

Importing instructions

1. Choose **Add** + **Import** from the **Object** menu to place an image into an open document.
2. Select the drive, directory, and file name for the graphic you want to import. Click **OK**.

Quark Xpress

File types supported

TIF, WMF

Importing instructions

1. In an open document draw a picture box with the Picture Box tool.
2. Select the 'Hand' tool from the toolbox.
3. Choose **Get Picture** from the **File** menu to place an image.
4. Select the drive, directory, and file name for the graphic you want to import. Click **OK**.

Microsoft Word

File types supported

TIF, WMF, JPG, GIF

Importing instructions

1. Choose **Picture** from the **Insert** menu to place an image into an open document.
2. Select the drive, directory, and file name for the graphic you want to import. If some graphics files are not showing up in the dialogue box, make sure 'All Graphics Files' is checked. Click **OK**.

WordPerfect

File types supported

TIF, WMF

Importing instructions

1. Choose **Figure** from the **Graphic** menu to place an image into an open document.
2. Select the drive, directory, and file name for the graphic you want to import. Click **OK**.

Microsoft Works

File types supported

TIF, WMF

Importing instructions

1. Choose **Drawing** from the **Insert** menu to begin Microsoft Drawing.
2. Choose **Import Picture** from the **File** menu.
3. Select the drive, directory, and file name for the graphic you want to import. If some graphics files are not showing up in the dialogue box, make sure 'All Graphics Files' is checked. Click **OK**.

Web Graphics

When you find an image (or several images) that you like, follow these steps within ThumbsCD to copy them to your hard drive. You can then use your favorite Web page editor to include the files in your Web pages. All Web images are in ready-to-use formats—no image editing required.

1. Highlight the images you want with your mouse. To highlight more than one image, hold down the Control key as you select each file.
2. Select File + Copy File from the menu. You'll be prompted where to copy the files. Choose a location on your hard drive and click OK.

Animated GIF Images

The **AnimGIFs** folder contains more than 10,000 animated GIF images. You can view the animations within your favorite Web browser. You can also view the images within the ThumbsCD thumbnails catalog. If you double-click on an animated image within ThumbsCD, you can see a brief preview of the animation. However, ThumbsCD does not properly display many types of animated files.

If you're using Windows 95, you can use the included GIF Explorer program to view the animated GIF images. GIF Explorer allows you to play with animation rates, view individual frames, start-and-stop animations, and permanently change the animation rate.

Run the **\GIFE** program on the **Web Graphics** disc to start GIF Explorer. To view animated GIF images from the CD-ROM, choose any folder within **\AnimGIFs** on the CD-ROM. The left window lists the drives and folders. Then, choose any of the GIF files in the list in the upper-right window. The animation will display in the lower-right window.

To permanently change the speed of an animation, change the speed with the animation speed slider on the toolbar. When you're happy with the rate, choose File + Save As from the menu, select a location on your hard drive, name the file and click OK.

Categories Of Web Graphics

AnimGIFs: Animated GIF images

Arrows: Misc. arrows (left, right, up, and down)

Banners: Medium-to-large images suitable for banners

Bullets: Small objects suitable for bullets (part 1)

Bullets2: Small objects suitable for bullets (part 2)

Buttons: Buttons in various styles (part 1)

Buttons2: Buttons in various styles (part 2)

Controls: Unusually-shaped "control pads"

Dividers: Horizontal dividers

Flags: Non-animated U.S. and World flags (see AnimGIFs folder for animated flags)

Frames: Picture frames type images

Icons: Simple icons

Rbuttons: Round buttons

Sbuttons: Square buttons

Sidebars: Sidebar-style backgrounds

Styles1: Coordinated styles (part 1)

Styles2: Coordinated styles (part 2)

Styles3: Coordinated styles (part 3)

Texture1: Background textures organized by style (part 1)

Texture2: Background textures organized by style (part 2)

Things: Images of animals and objects

Tiles: Misc. background textures organized by size (part 1)

Tiles2: Misc. background textures organized by size (part 2)

Overview of Graphics Formats

The graphics on *Holy Cow! 250,000 Graphics* come in several different formats: WMF, TIF, JPG, and GIF. Each format has its own advantages, and is used for certain types of images.

Vector Graphics vs. Bitmap graphics.

Vector and **bitmap** are types of graphic formats. WMF images are a vector format; TIF, JPG and GIF images are bitmap formats.

A **vector** graphic is made up of mathematical equations for geometric shapes, like circles or squares. Because the image is defined by an equation, it is *resolution independent*, which means that you can enlarge or reduce a vector image to any size and it will always be crisp and sharp. Vector graphics are usually line art, or "draw" images.

A **bitmap** graphic is made up of lines of tiny dots, or *pixels*. A vector graphic saves a graphic of a square as one equation, but a bitmap graphic will save a graphic of a square as many rows of many pixels, each pixel a specific color. When a bitmap image is reduced, the pixels get smaller, but if the graphic is enlarged too much, each pixel gets bigger, which may make the image appear jagged. Bitmap images are usually reproductions of original art or photographs, or "paint" images.

Graphic Formats

WMF, or Windows Metafile, is a vector graphic format. It is a 16-bit file, widely used by Windows applications. Vector images on the Vector 1 through Vector 5 discs are in this format.

TIF, or Tagged Image File Format, is a bitmap graphic format that is platform independent. It is one of the most popular graphic file formats. The Classic Images are in this format.

JPG, or Joint Photographic Expert Group compressed file, is a bitmap graphic format that is very common for photographic images, especially images to be used on the world wide web. JPG, also known as JPEG, is a compressed graphic format. JPEG images must be 24-bit color (16 million colors); all photographs, some bitmap images, and many of the Web graphics are in this format.

GIF, or Graphics Interchange Format file, is an 8-bit bitmap graphic format that is platform independent. GIF images are widely used for non-photographic images on the World Wide Web, such as buttons, headers, and icons. The GIF format also allows for one of the colors in a file to be read as transparent. Many of the graphics on the Web Graphics disc are in this format.

2178.WMF 2182.WMF 2184.WMF 2185.WMF 2190.WMF 2191.WMF 2193.WMF ACCOMMOD.WMF AMERICAN.WMF ANTIQUES.WMF
APARTMEN.WMF APPLIANC.WMF AUTOMOB1.WMF AUTOMOBI.WMF AUTOMOTI.WMF BACK175.WMF BIRTHANN.WMF BUILDIN1.WMF BUILDING.WMF BUSINES1.WMF
BUSINESS.WMF CAMPSRES.WMF CARDSOFT.WMF CATERING.WMF CHILDCAR.WMF COMMERCI.WMF COMPUTER.WMF CONDOMIN.WMF DANCEINS.WMF DRIVAWA.WMF
ELECTRIC.WMF EMPLOYM1.WMF EMPLOYME.WMF ENTERTAI.WMF FARMEQUI.WMF FARMSAFE.WMF FINANCIA.WMF FLOORCOV.WMF FOOD.WMF FOREHEAD.WMF
GIFTSFO1.WMF GIFTSFOR.WMF HEALTHSU.WMF HOMEFURN.WMF HOMEIMPR.WMF HOMESFO1.WMF HOMESFOR.WMF ICON080.WMF IMPORTED.WMF INSTRUCT.WMF
LANDSCAP.WMF LAWNSERV.WMF LIVESTOC.WMF LOSTFOUD.WMF LOTSFORS.WMF MARINESU.WMF MASONRYB.WMF MERCHAND.WMF MOTORCYC.WMF MOVINGSE.WMF
MUSICALI.WMF N21440.WMF OFFICESU.WMF PESTCONT.WMF PETS_SPL.WMF PHOTOGRA.WMF PLUMBING.WMF PNTS154.WMF POOLSALE.WMF PRINTNG2.WMF
RESTAURA.WMF RVSALES.WMF SAVINGSA.WMF SNOWMOBI.WMF SPORTING.WMF STEREOEQ.WMF STIR_FRY.WMF SUMMERS2.WMF TICKETEX.WMF TRAVELSE.WMF
V7_01.WMF V7_02.WMF V7_03.WMF V7_04.WMF V7_05.WMF V7_06.WMF V7_07.WMF V7_09.WMF V7_10.WMF V7_11.WMF
V7_12.WMF VACATIN5.WMF WAVE_MAK.WMF WINNERSC.WMF

0102BULC.WMF 1350.WMF 1379.WMF 3D_FC.WMF 3D_HEAD2.WMF 3D_HEAD3.WMF 3D_HEAD4.WMF 3D_HEAD5.WMF 3D_HEAD6.WMF 3D_PS.WMF

3D_TF.WMF ACTION.WMF AGGRWHL2.WMF BACK088.WMF BACK169.WMF BACK170.WMF BACK194.WMF BACK221.WMF BACK245.WMF BANG.WMF

BEARING1.WMF BENIFITS.WMF BSNSS145.WMF BUSI172D.WMF CAA0414.WMF CELEBRAT.WMF COOKOUTH.WMF EDCN104.WMF EDCN116.WMF ENERGY.WMF

ENJOYTHE.WMF ENSI010M.WMF ENSI016D.WMF F57.WMF F58.WMF FREE_DIA.WMF FRESHFAS.WMF HEADER07.WMF HEADER20.WMF HEADER22.WMF

HEADER23.WMF HEADER_5.WMF HEADER_7.WMF HHGC008D.WMF ITSHOT.WMF ITSMAGIC.WMF JUSTSAY.WMF KABOOM01.WMF LICENSE.WMF MADEUSA.WMF

MARCHHEA.WMF MIDHEAD1.WMF N21434.WMF N21435.WMF N21436.WMF N21437.WMF N21438.WMF NEEDKNOW.WMF NEWHEADI.WMF O21509.WMF

OPEN.WMF PICNIC1.WMF PICNICHE.WMF PNTS034.WMF PNTS035.WMF PNTS036.WMF PNTS037.WMF PNTS038.WMF PNTS041.WMF PNTS128.WMF

PNTS129.WMF PNTS130.WMF PNTS131.WMF PNTS132.WMF PNTS133.WMF PNTS134.WMF PNTS135.WMF PNTS136.WMF PNTS137.WMF PNTS140.WMF

PNTS141.WMF PNTS142.WMF PNTS153.WMF PNTS155.WMF PNTS157.WMF PNTS159.WMF PNTS160.WMF PNTS161.WMF POW.WMF S21724.WMF

SHAPE102.WMF SHAPE103.WMF SHAPE279.WMF SHAPE281.WMF SOCA007J.WMF SPLASH01.WMF SPLASHEX.WMF SPRIHEAD.WMF SPRINGCL.WMF STOCKH02.WMF

STOCKH03.WMF STOCKH04.WMF STOCKH17.WMF SUMMER.WMF TCHRCERT.WMF THAWOUTH.WMF THISWAYT.WMF VICTORY3.WMF Z21937.WMF

1382.WMF 1383.WMF 1384.WMF 1385.WMF 1386.WMF 1387.WMF 1388.WMF 1STSALEO.WMF ACTIONIS.WMF ACTNOW.WMF

AFTRTHNX.WMF AFTRXMAS.WMF ALL_AMER.WMF AMERICN2.WMF ANNIVER1.WMF ANNIVER2.WMF ANNIVER3.WMF ANNOUNCE.WMF ANVERSAY.WMF ATTENT.WMF

ATTENTON.WMF AUTUMN.WMF B20089.WMF BACK112.WMF BACK138.WMF BACK142.WMF BACK143.WMF BANNER1.WMF BARGAINS.WMF BEWITCH.WMF

BIGBUYS.WMF BIGTOP.WMF BIGTOPSA.WMF BOOKGIFT.WMF BUSIWEEK.WMF BUYERS.WMF BUYERS2.WMF BUYERS3.WMF BUYNOW.WMF BUYNOWHE.WMF

C20792.WMF CAINE.WMF CAREER.WMF CARNIVAL.WMF CELEBRA1.WMF CHALKUP.WMF CHECKERE.WMF CLASSIF2.WMF CLASSIF3.WMF CLASSIFI.WMF

CLASSY.WMF CLEARAN1.WMF CLEARANC.WMF CLIPSAVE.WMF COUPONSH.WMF COUPONST.WMF DAYS.WMF DEATHNOT.WMF DISCOUNT.WMF DOGDAY.WMF

DOGDAYDE.WMF DOGDAYS1.WMF DOGDAYS2.WMF ELECTRON.WMF ELEPHANT.WMF EVRYTHNG.WMF EXTRAVAG.WMF EYE_OPEN.WMF FAIRDAYS.WMF FILLPOCK.WMF

FLAGDAYH.WMF FRESPICK.WMF G21054.WMF G21055.WMF G21056.WMF G21057.WMF GARAGESA.WMF GARGSAL2.WMF GARGSALE.WMF GOFORTHE.WMF

GOING.WMF GRADE.WMF GRAND2.WMF GRANDOP2.WMF GRANDOP3.WMF GRANDOP4.WMF GRANDOP5.WMF GRANDOPE.WMF GREATBUY.WMF GREATDEA.WMF

GREATVAL.WMF HARVEST.WMF HITMARK.WMF HOLIDAY.WMF HOLIDAYE.WMF HOMEIS.WMF HOMESHOP.WMF HOMESWET.WMF HOTDEALS.WMF HOTTESTD.WMF

HPI024G.WMF HPI028A.WMF HUNTTRES.WMF ICEDPRIC.WMF INCREAS.WMF INCREDIB.WMF INDNSUMR.WMF INVCLEAR.WMF ITSALL.WMF JOBHUNT.WMF

JOBS.WMF KICK_OF1.WMF LASTMINT.WMF LEPRECHN.WMF LIQUIDAT.WMF MAKECENT.WMF MAKESALE.WMF MARCHMA1.WMF MARCHMA2.WMF MARCHMAD.WMF

MARCHSAV.WMF NAW1.WMF NAW2.WMF OKTOBERF.WMF OPENHOUS.WMF OPENING.WMF OPPORT.WMF PERSONAL.WMF PET.WMF PLACEBE.WMF

PNTS139.WMF PNTS143.WMF PNTS144.WMF PNTS145.WMF PNTS146.WMF PNTS147.WMF PNTS149.WMF PNTS150.WMF PNTS158.WMF PRESIDE1.WMF

PRESIDEN.WMF PRICESEL.WMF PURSE_PL.WMF RAKESAVE.WMF REALESTA.WMF REDWHITE.WMF RESULTS.WMF RUFFLEFE.WMF S21634.WMF S21635.WMF

S21636.WMF S21637.WMF S21638.WMF S21643.WMF S21644.WMF S21645.WMF S21646.WMF S21647.WMF SALE.WMF SALE0.WMF

SALE1.WMF SALE2.WMF SALE22.WMF SALE3.WMF SALE4.WMF SALECONF.WMF SALEHEA1.WMF SALEHEA3.WMF SALEHEA4.WMF SALEHEA5.WMF

SALES.WMF SAVE.WMF SAVEHEA1.WMF SAVEHEAD.WMF SAYHELLO.WMF SHOUTABO.WMF SIDEWAL1.WMF SIZZLING.WMF SOLD.WMF SPECIALP.WMF

SPECTACU.WMF SPINWHEL.WMF SPRINGSP.WMF SPRINGTM.WMF STOCKH01.WMF STOPSAVE.WMF SUCCESS.WMF SUMMEREX.WMF SUMMERTI.WMF SUMRCLER.WMF

SUMRSALE.WMF SUPERSAV.WMF SUPERSPO.WMF SUPERSUM.WMF SUREBET.WMF SURESALE.WMF TAGDAYHE.WMF TAKEAIMH.WMF TEMPTAT.WMF TENTSAL1.WMF

TENTSAL2.WMF TESTDRIV.WMF THANXVAL.WMF TIMETOSA.WMF V7_08.WMF VETERAN1.WMF VETERANS.WMF WALKING.WMF WHATNEED.WMF WHELDEAL.WMF

WHYWISHH.WMF WINTERCA.WMF WINTRCLE.WMF YARDSALE.WMF

0154THEC.WMF 0161COOC.WMF 1115DAYC.WMF 1129DRUC.WMF 1147GIFC.WMF 1148GIFC.WMF 1151GRAC.WMF 1342.WMF 1343.WMF 1344.WMF

1345.WMF 1346.WMF 1347.WMF 1348.WMF 1349.WMF 2142.WMF 2143.WMF 2164.WMF 2165.WMF 2168.WMF

2169.WMF 2172.WMF 2196.WMF 2211.WMF 2213.WMF 2216.WMF 2219.WMF 2220.WMF 2221.WMF 2225.WMF

2229.WMF 2230.WMF 2233.WMF 2237.WMF 2251.WMF 2256.WMF ANNOUNC1.WMF ANNOUNCI.WMF ANOUNCNG.WMF B20091.WMF

BACK101.WMF BACK107.WMF BACK108.WMF BACK128.WMF BACK131.WMF BACK219.WMF BACK220.WMF BACK249.WMF BANNER2.WMF BILLBORD.WMF

BUSIWEEK.WMF C20770.WMF C20807.WMF CAA0007.WMF CAA0009.WMF CAA0010.WMF CAA0011.WMF CAA0014.WMF CAA0015.WMF CAA0016.WMF

CAA0019.WMF CAA0021.WMF CAA0321.WMF CAA0322.WMF CAA0412.WMF CAA0413.WMF CELEBRAT.WMF CELEBRT2.WMF CHAMPAGN.WMF COMEDINE.WMF

COOKOUT.WMF CUSTOMER.WMF D20860.WMF D20873.WMF E20939.WMF F21007.WMF FALL043.WMF FALL045.WMF FAMILYRE.WMF FANTASTI.WMF

GASI114M.WMF GIFTIDEA.WMF GIFTSLIS.WMF HIGHTECH.WMF HPI024H.WMF KABOOM.WMF L21188.WMF MAGCXMAS.WMF MAKEAGOA.WMF PASTAHEA.WMF

PNTS126.WMF PNTS138.WMF PNTS148.WMF PNTS151.WMF PNTS152.WMF PNTS156.WMF PNTS162.WMF POCKETBO.WMF PROGRESS.WMF PRSNMIN.WMF

R21610.WMF R21611.WMF ROOMMATE.WMF S21686.WMF S21805.WMF SAFETYFI.WMF SIGN01.WMF TRSI005D.WMF VISITTHE.WMF W21875.WMF

0052.WMF 0672.WMF 1378.WMF 1380.WMF 1381.WMF 1389.WMF 1390.WMF 1391.WMF 1392.WMF 1393.WMF

1394.WMF 1395.WMF 1396.WMF 1397.WMF 1398.WMF 1399.WMF 1400.WMF 2147.WMF 2148.WMF 2149.WMF

2150.WMF 2152.WMF 2153.WMF 2154.WMF 2155.WMF 2156.WMF 2157.WMF 2158.WMF 2159.WMF 2160.WMF

2162.WMF 2163.WMF 2166.WMF 2167.WMF 2170.WMF 2171.WMF 2173.WMF 2174.WMF 2175.WMF 2176.WMF

2177.WMF 2180.WMF 2183.WMF 2186.WMF 2187.WMF 2188.WMF 2189.WMF 2192.WMF 2194.WMF 2195.WMF

2197.WMF 2198.WMF 2199.WMF 2200.WMF 2201.WMF 2202.WMF 2204.WMF 2205.WMF 2206.WMF 2207.WMF

2210.WMF 2212.WMF 2214.WMF 2215.WMF 2218.WMF 2223.WMF 2226.WMF 2227.WMF 2228.WMF 2232.WMF

2234.WMF 2235.WMF 2236.WMF 2238.WMF 2239.WMF 2240.WMF 2241.WMF 2242.WMF 2243.WMF 2244.WMF

2245.WMF 2246.WMF 2247.WMF 2249.WMF 2250.WMF 2252.WMF 2253.WMF 2254.WMF 2255.WMF 3001.WMF

3002.WMF 3003.WMF 3004.WMF 3005.WMF 3006.WMF 3007.WMF 3008.WMF 3009.WMF 3010.WMF 3011.WMF

3012.WMF 3013.WMF 3014.WMF 3015.WMF 3016.WMF 3017.WMF 3018.WMF 3019.WMF 3020.WMF 3021.WMF

3022.WMF 3023.WMF 3024.WMF 3025.WMF 3026.WMF 3027.WMF 3028.WMF 3029.WMF 3030.WMF 3031.WMF

Ziemsvētkus	Lieldienas	Vesels	Kudsut	Esi Gaidits Ievienats	Pääsiäistä	Vuotta	Tervetullut	Juhla	Uutta
3032.WMF	3033.WMF	3034.WMF	3035.WMF	3036.WMF	3037.WMF	3038.WMF	3039.WMF	3040.WMF	3041.WMF
Maljasi	Hyvää	Joulu	Kemut	Pidot	Inbjudan	Geburtstag	Bröllop	Födelsedags	Einladung
3042.WMF	3043.WMF	3044.WMF	3045.WMF	3046.WMF	3047.WMF	3048.WMF	3049.WMF	3050.WMF	3051.WMF
Einladen	Invitation	Wedding	Birthday	Kalas	Hochzeit	Prosit			
3052.WMF	3053.WMF	3054.WMF	3055.WMF	3056.WMF	3057.WMF	3058.WMF			

BEAST.WMF
BIRD.WMF
BIRD04.WMF
BIRD05.WMF
BIRD06.WMF
BIRD07.WMF
BIRD1.WMF
BIRD2.WMF
BIRD3.WMF
BUCK.WMF
BUCK1.WMF
BUCK2.WMF
CAMEL.WMF
CAMELEO2.WMF
CAMELEON.WMF
CRAB.WMF
CRITTR01.WMF
CRITTR02.WMF
CRITTR03.WMF
CRITTR04.WMF
CRITTR05.WMF
CRITTR06.WMF
CRITTR07.WMF
CRITTR08.WMF
CRITTR09.WMF
CRITTR10.WMF
CRITTR11.WMF
CRITTR12.WMF
CRITTR13.WMF
CRITTR14.WMF
CRITTR15.WMF
CRITTR16.WMF
CRITTR17.WMF
CRITTR18.WMF
DRAGON.WMF
ELEPHAN2.WMF
ELEPHANT.WMF
FISH.WMF
FROG.WMF
GIRAFFE.WMF
GIRAFFE2.WMF
GOAT.WMF
HEDGEHOG.WMF
HORSE.WMF
JAGUAR01.WMF
LEGUAAN.WMF
LEOPARD.WMF
LIZZARD.WMF
MONKEY01.WMF
OX.WMF
RHINO.WMF
SNAKE.WMF
TORTOISE.WMF
WHALE.WMF
WILDBOAR.WMF

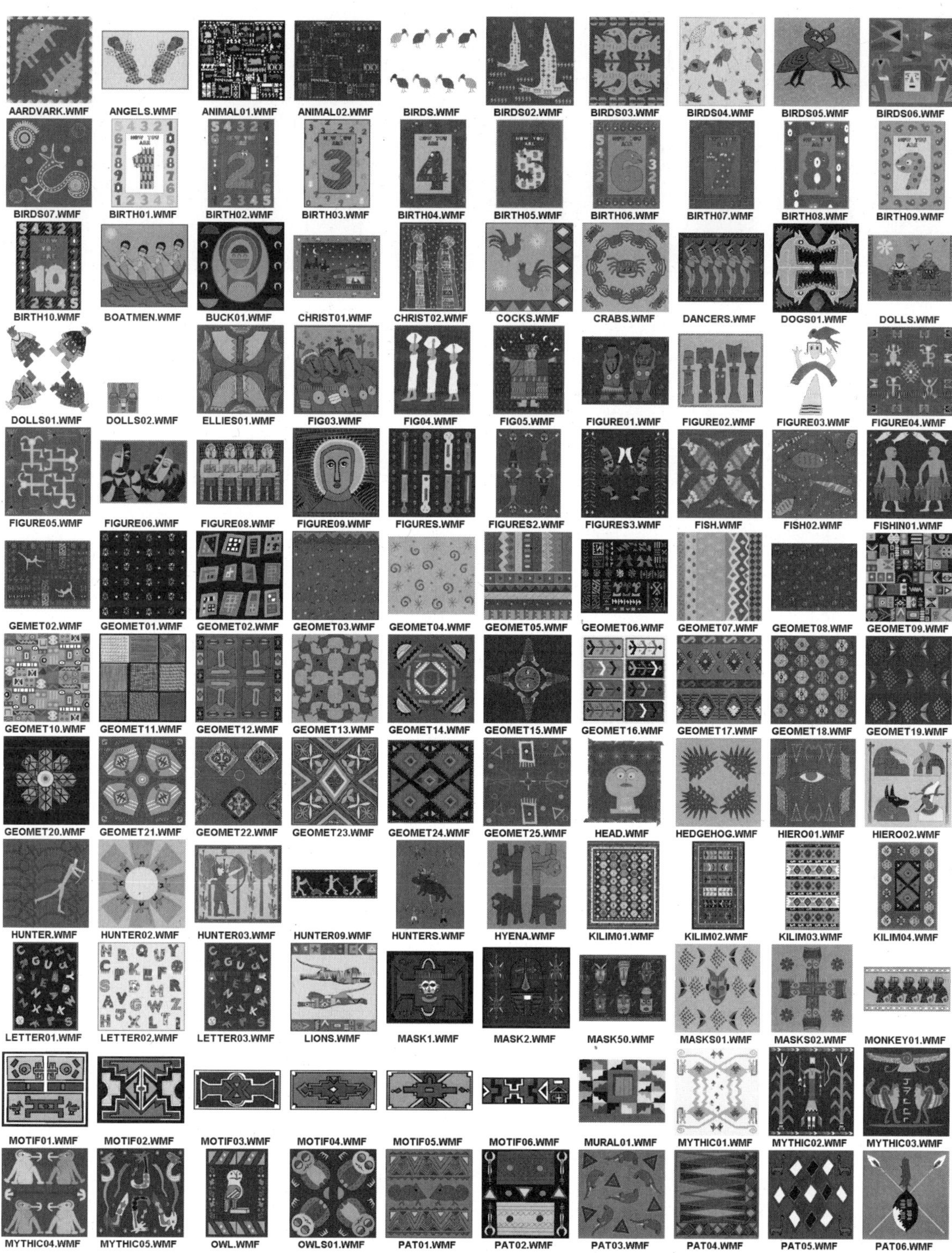

AARDVARK.WMF ANGELS.WMF ANIMAL01.WMF ANIMAL02.WMF BIRDS.WMF BIRDS02.WMF BIRDS03.WMF BIRDS04.WMF BIRDS05.WMF BIRDS06.WMF

BIRDS07.WMF BIRTH01.WMF BIRTH02.WMF BIRTH03.WMF BIRTH04.WMF BIRTH05.WMF BIRTH06.WMF BIRTH07.WMF BIRTH08.WMF BIRTH09.WMF

BIRTH10.WMF BOATMEN.WMF BUCK01.WMF CHRIST01.WMF CHRIST02.WMF COCKS.WMF CRABS.WMF DANCERS.WMF DOGS01.WMF DOLLS.WMF

DOLLS01.WMF DOLLS02.WMF ELLIES01.WMF FIG03.WMF FIG04.WMF FIG05.WMF FIGURE01.WMF FIGURE02.WMF FIGURE03.WMF FIGURE04.WMF

FIGURE05.WMF FIGURE06.WMF FIGURE08.WMF FIGURE09.WMF FIGURES.WMF FIGURES2.WMF FIGURES3.WMF FISH.WMF FISH02.WMF FISHIN01.WMF

GEMET02.WMF GEOMET01.WMF GEOMET02.WMF GEOMET03.WMF GEOMET04.WMF GEOMET05.WMF GEOMET06.WMF GEOMET07.WMF GEOMET08.WMF GEOMET09.WMF

GEOMET10.WMF GEOMET11.WMF GEOMET12.WMF GEOMET13.WMF GEOMET14.WMF GEOMET15.WMF GEOMET16.WMF GEOMET17.WMF GEOMET18.WMF GEOMET19.WMF

GEOMET20.WMF GEOMET21.WMF GEOMET22.WMF GEOMET23.WMF GEOMET24.WMF GEOMET25.WMF HEAD.WMF HEDGEHOG.WMF HIERO01.WMF HIERO02.WMF

HUNTER.WMF HUNTER02.WMF HUNTER03.WMF HUNTER09.WMF HUNTERS.WMF HYENA.WMF KILIM01.WMF KILIM02.WMF KILIM03.WMF KILIM04.WMF

LETTER01.WMF LETTER02.WMF LETTER03.WMF LIONS.WMF MASK1.WMF MASK2.WMF MASK50.WMF MASKS01.WMF MASKS02.WMF MONKEY01.WMF

MOTIF01.WMF MOTIF02.WMF MOTIF03.WMF MOTIF04.WMF MOTIF05.WMF MOTIF06.WMF MURAL01.WMF MYTHIC01.WMF MYTHIC02.WMF MYTHIC03.WMF

MYTHIC04.WMF MYTHIC05.WMF OWL.WMF OWLS01.WMF PAT01.WMF PAT02.WMF PAT03.WMF PAT04.WMF PAT05.WMF PAT06.WMF

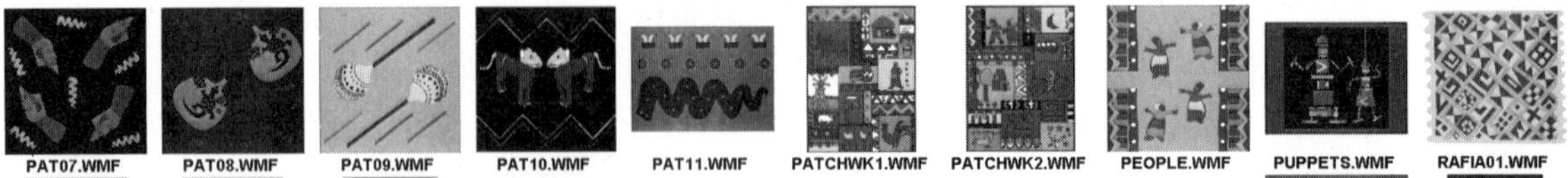

PAT07.WMF PAT08.WMF PAT09.WMF PAT10.WMF PAT11.WMF PATCHWK1.WMF PATCHWK2.WMF PEOPLE.WMF PUPPETS.WMF RAFIA01.WMF

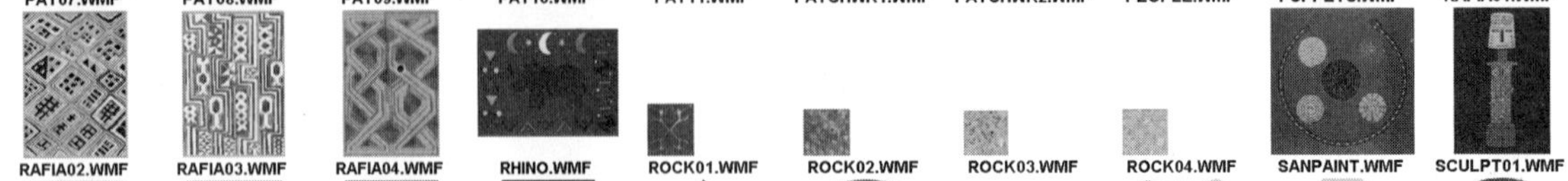

RAFIA02.WMF RAFIA03.WMF RAFIA04.WMF RHINO.WMF ROCK01.WMF ROCK02.WMF ROCK03.WMF ROCK04.WMF SANPAINT.WMF SCULPT01.WMF

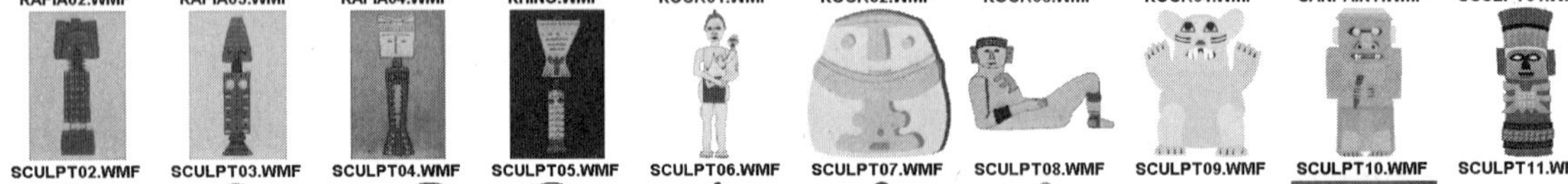

SCULPT02.WMF SCULPT03.WMF SCULPT04.WMF SCULPT05.WMF SCULPT06.WMF SCULPT07.WMF SCULPT08.WMF SCULPT09.WMF SCULPT10.WMF SCULPT11.WMF

SCULPT12.WMF SCULPT13.WMF SCULPT14.WMF SCULPT15.WMF SCULPT16.WMF SCULPT17.WMF SCULPT18.WMF SERPNT01.WMF SNAKE.WMF SPIRIT01.WMF

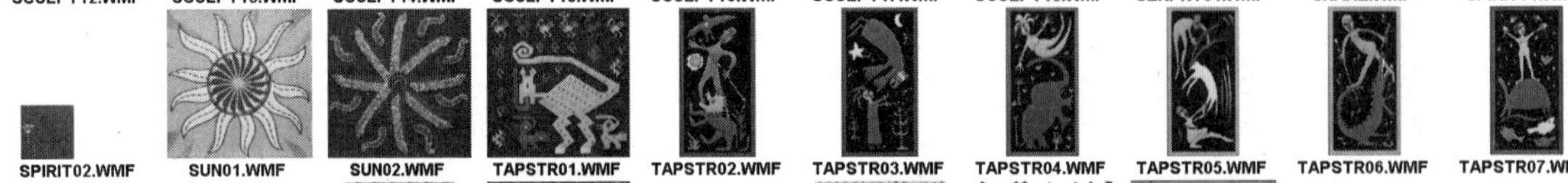

SPIRIT02.WMF SUN01.WMF SUN02.WMF TAPSTR01.WMF TAPSTR02.WMF TAPSTR03.WMF TAPSTR04.WMF TAPSTR05.WMF TAPSTR06.WMF TAPSTR07.WMF

TOTEM01.WMF TOTEM02.WMF TOTEM03.WMF TRACTOR.WMF WARIOR01.WMF WARIOR03.WMF WEAVE.WMF WINDMILL.WMF WISEMEN.WMF WOODCUT1.WMF

WOODCUT2.WMF

WOODCUT3.WMF

Africa • Houses

GHANAHUT.WMF

MURAL02.WMF

MURAL03.WMF

MURAL04.WMF

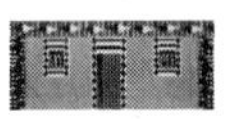
MURAL05.WMF

MURAL06.WMF

MURAL07.WMF

MURAL08.WMF

MURAL09.WMF

MURAL10.WMF

MUSGUHUT.WMF

NDEBELE.WMF

XHOSAHUT.WMF

ZULUHUT.WMF

Africa • Masks

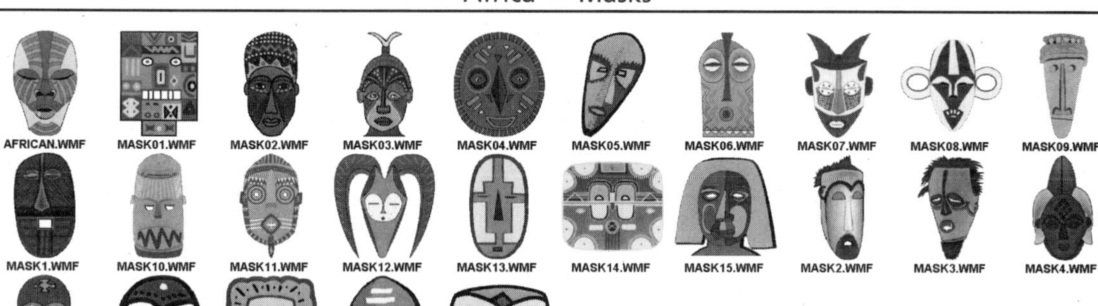

BUTT01.WMF BUTT02.WMF BUTT03.WMF BUTT04.WMF BUTT05.WMF BUTT06.WMF BUTT07.WMF BUTT08.WMF BUTT09.WMF BUTT10.WMF

BUTT11.WMF BUTT12.WMF BUTT13.WMF BUTT14.WMF BUTT15.WMF BUTT16.WMF BUTT17.WMF BUTT18.WMF BUTT19.WMF BUTT20.WMF

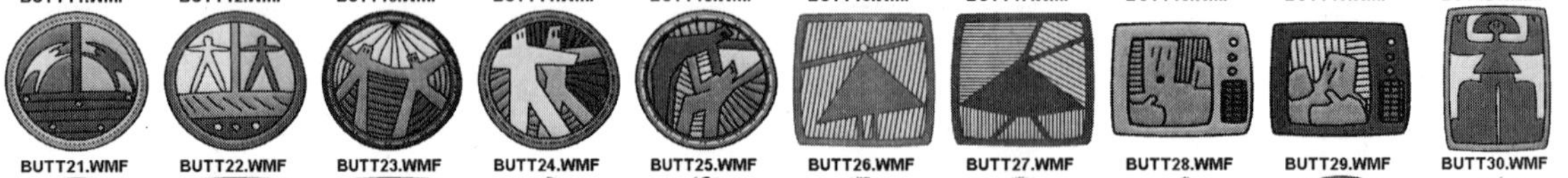

BUTT21.WMF BUTT22.WMF BUTT23.WMF BUTT24.WMF BUTT25.WMF BUTT26.WMF BUTT27.WMF BUTT28.WMF BUTT29.WMF BUTT30.WMF

BUTT31.WMF BUTT32.WMF BUTT33.WMF DOLL01.WMF DOLL02.WMF DOLL05.WMF DOLL06.WMF DOLL07.WMF DOLL08.WMF DOLL09.WMF

DOLL10.WMF EASTEG01.WMF EASTEG02.WMF EASTEG03.WMF EASTEG04.WMF EASTEG05.WMF EASTEG06.WMF EASTEG07.WMF EASTEG08.WMF EASTEG09.WMF

EASTEG10.WMF EASTEG11.WMF EASTEG12.WMF EASTEG13.WMF EASTEG14.WMF EASTEG15.WMF EASTEG16.WMF EASTEG17.WMF EASTEG18.WMF PUPPET01.WMF

PUPPET02.WMF PUPPET03.WMF PUPPET04.WMF PUPPET05.WMF PUPPET06.WMF PUPPET07.WMF PUPPET08.WMF PUPPET09.WMF PUPPET10.WMF PUPPET11.WMF

PUPPET12.WMF

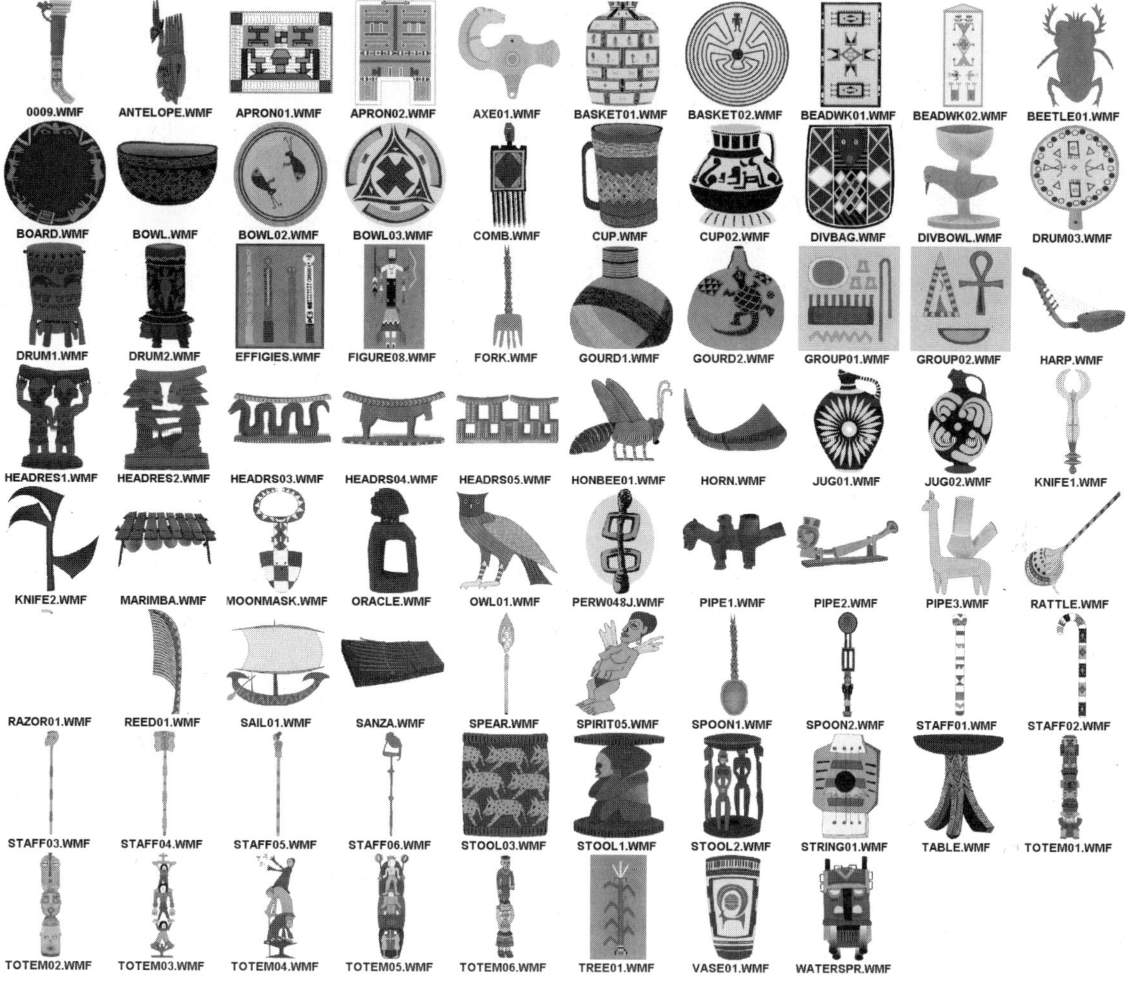
0009.WMF
ANTELOPE.WMF
APRON01.WMF
APRON02.WMF
AXE01.WMF
BASKET01.WMF
BASKET02.WMF
BEADWK01.WMF
BEADWK02.WMF
BEETLE01.WMF
BOARD.WMF
BOWL.WMF
BOWL02.WMF
BOWL03.WMF
COMB.WMF
CUP.WMF
CUP02.WMF
DIVBAG.WMF
DIVBOWL.WMF
DRUM03.WMF
DRUM1.WMF
DRUM2.WMF
EFFIGIES.WMF
FIGURE08.WMF
FORK.WMF
GOURD1.WMF
GOURD2.WMF
GROUP01.WMF
GROUP02.WMF
HARP.WMF
HEADRES1.WMF
HEADRES2.WMF
HEADRS03.WMF
HEADRS04.WMF
HEADRS05.WMF
HONBEE01.WMF
HORN.WMF
JUG01.WMF
JUG02.WMF
KNIFE1.WMF
KNIFE2.WMF
MARIMBA.WMF
MOONMASK.WMF
ORACLE.WMF
OWL01.WMF
PERW048J.WMF
PIPE1.WMF
PIPE2.WMF
PIPE3.WMF
RATTLE.WMF
RAZOR01.WMF
REED01.WMF
SAIL01.WMF
SANZA.WMF
SPEAR.WMF
SPIRIT05.WMF
SPOON1.WMF
SPOON2.WMF
STAFF01.WMF
STAFF02.WMF
STAFF03.WMF
STAFF04.WMF
STAFF05.WMF
STAFF06.WMF
STOOL03.WMF
STOOL1.WMF
STOOL2.WMF
STRING01.WMF
TABLE.WMF
TOTEM01.WMF
TOTEM02.WMF
TOTEM03.WMF
TOTEM04.WMF
TOTEM05.WMF
TOTEM06.WMF
TREE01.WMF
VASE01.WMF
WATERSPR.WMF

ACCOUNT.WMF ARTIST.WMF BORDER13.WMF CAMERA.WMF CANDLE.WMF CARRYING.WMF CATERER.WMF CONSERVE.WMF CONSULT.WMF CRUSHING.WMF
DANCING.WMF DIVINER.WMF DOMEST1.WMF DOMEST2.WMF DRESS01.WMF DRESS02.WMF DRESS03.WMF DRESS04.WMF DRESS05.WMF DRUMMING.WMF
FACTORY.WMF FIGURE01.WMF FIGURE04.WMF FIGURE05.WMF FIGURE06.WMF FIGURE07.WMF FIREMAKE.WMF FUELPUMP.WMF GAMESHOW.WMF GIANT.WMF
HOEING.WMF HUTMAKER.WMF INTERPRE.WMF IT.WMF LIBRARY.WMF MANAGER.WMF MATMAKER.WMF MECHANIC.WMF MEETING1.WMF MEETING3.WMF
MINER.WMF MUSIC1.WMF MUSIC2.WMF NURSERY.WMF PAINTER1.WMF PAINTING.WMF PAPER.WMF PLANNER.WMF POTTER.WMF PRESENT.WMF
FREEDOM
PRODLINE.WMF RALLY.WMF REMOVAL.WMF SANGOMA.WMF SCULPTOR.WMF SEWING.WMF SHUSHINE.WMF SIGNING.WMF SITTING.WMF SMOKING.WMF
TRADE UNION
VOTE HERE
STAMPING.WMF STANDING.WMF SURVEY.WMF TAXI2.WMF THERAPY.WMF TRAIN.WMF UNION.WMF VOTER.WMF WAITER.WMF WARRIOR.WMF
WELD.WMF WINDRESS.WMF WOMAN.WMF WOMAN01.WMF WOMAN02.WMF WOMBABE.WMF WOMN01.WMF

1012.WMF
1041.WMF
1042.WMF
1047.WMF
1065.WMF
AGR001.WMF
AGR003.WMF
AGR007.WMF
AGR008.WMF
AGR009.WMF
B20069.WMF
BARN.WMF
BARNMORT.WMF
CAA0417.WMF
CAA0424.WMF
CAA0426.WMF
CAA0427.WMF
EAA001H.WMF
FARM.WMF
FARM_SUN.WMF
FARMSCE1.WMF
FOSI004J.WMF
GRAINBIN.WMF
HARVEST2.WMF
HAY_BAIL.WMF
INDIANCO.WMF
MSL077G.WMF
MSL078H.WMF
OFS042A.WMF
PD027EBW.WMF
PD027FBW.WMF
PD027JBW.WMF
PD027KBW.WMF
PD050KCU.WMF
REAL11.WMF
REAL12.WMF
S21649.WMF
TRACSIL.WMF
TRACTOR.WMF
TRACTOR2.WMF
TRACTOR5.WMF
TRACTOR8.WMF
TRACTORC.WMF
TRACTR.WMF
TRACTR01.WMF
TRACTR2.WMF
TRCA023J.WMF
TRSI013D.WMF
WINDMILL.WMF

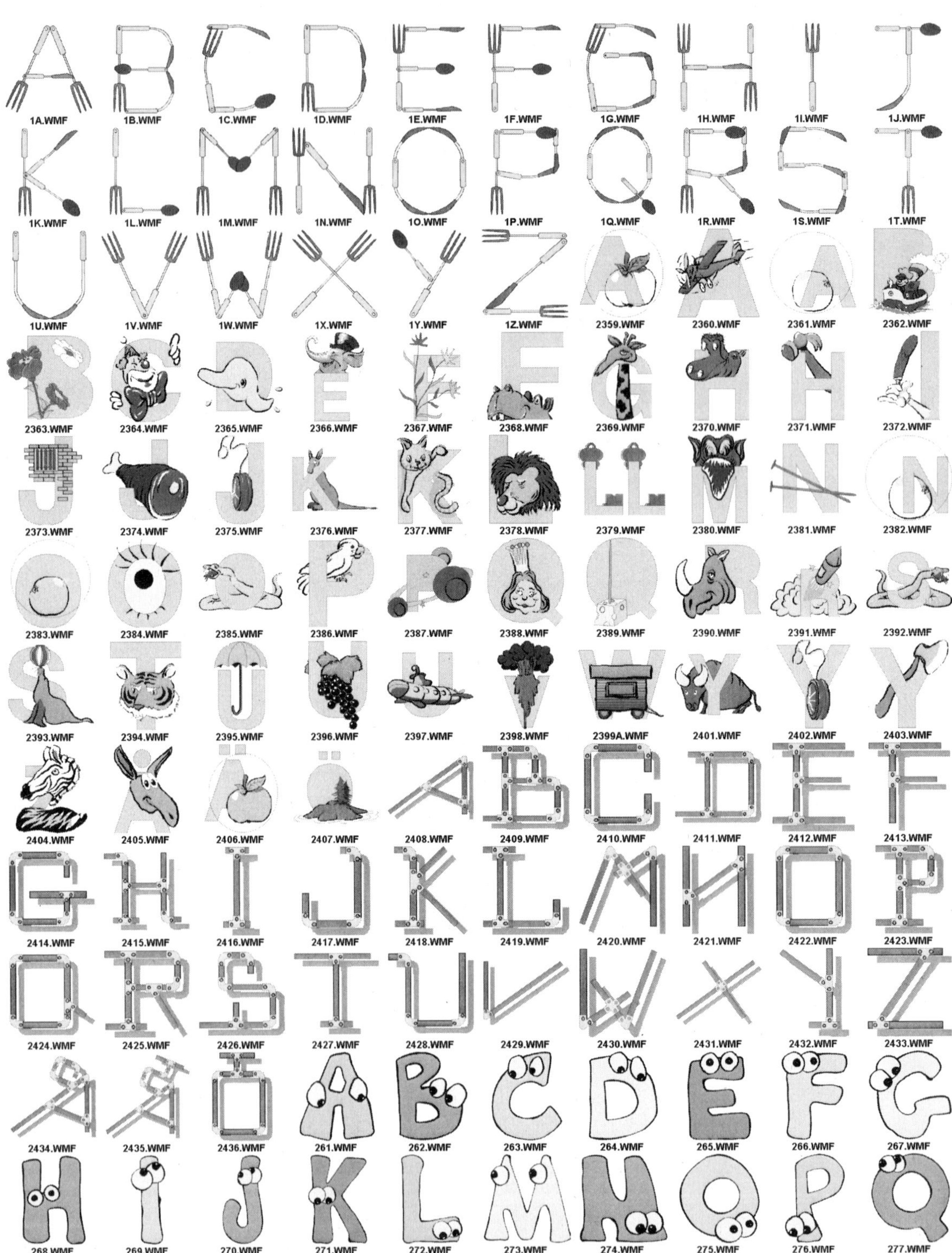
1A.WMF 1B.WMF 1C.WMF 1D.WMF 1E.WMF 1F.WMF 1G.WMF 1H.WMF 1I.WMF 1J.WMF
1K.WMF 1L.WMF 1M.WMF 1N.WMF 1O.WMF 1P.WMF 1Q.WMF 1R.WMF 1S.WMF 1T.WMF
1U.WMF 1V.WMF 1W.WMF 1X.WMF 1Y.WMF 1Z.WMF 2359.WMF 2360.WMF 2361.WMF 2362.WMF
2363.WMF 2364.WMF 2365.WMF 2366.WMF 2367.WMF 2368.WMF 2369.WMF 2370.WMF 2371.WMF 2372.WMF
2373.WMF 2374.WMF 2375.WMF 2376.WMF 2377.WMF 2378.WMF 2379.WMF 2380.WMF 2381.WMF 2382.WMF
2383.WMF 2384.WMF 2385.WMF 2386.WMF 2387.WMF 2388.WMF 2389.WMF 2390.WMF 2391.WMF 2392.WMF
2393.WMF 2394.WMF 2395.WMF 2396.WMF 2397.WMF 2398.WMF 2399A.WMF 2401.WMF 2402.WMF 2403.WMF
2404.WMF 2405.WMF 2406.WMF 2407.WMF 2408.WMF 2409.WMF 2410.WMF 2411.WMF 2412.WMF 2413.WMF
2414.WMF 2415.WMF 2416.WMF 2417.WMF 2418.WMF 2419.WMF 2420.WMF 2421.WMF 2422.WMF 2423.WMF
2424.WMF 2425.WMF 2426.WMF 2427.WMF 2428.WMF 2429.WMF 2430.WMF 2431.WMF 2432.WMF 2433.WMF
2434.WMF 2435.WMF 2436.WMF 261.WMF 262.WMF 263.WMF 264.WMF 265.WMF 266.WMF 267.WMF
268.WMF 269.WMF 270.WMF 271.WMF 272.WMF 273.WMF 274.WMF 275.WMF 276.WMF 277.WMF

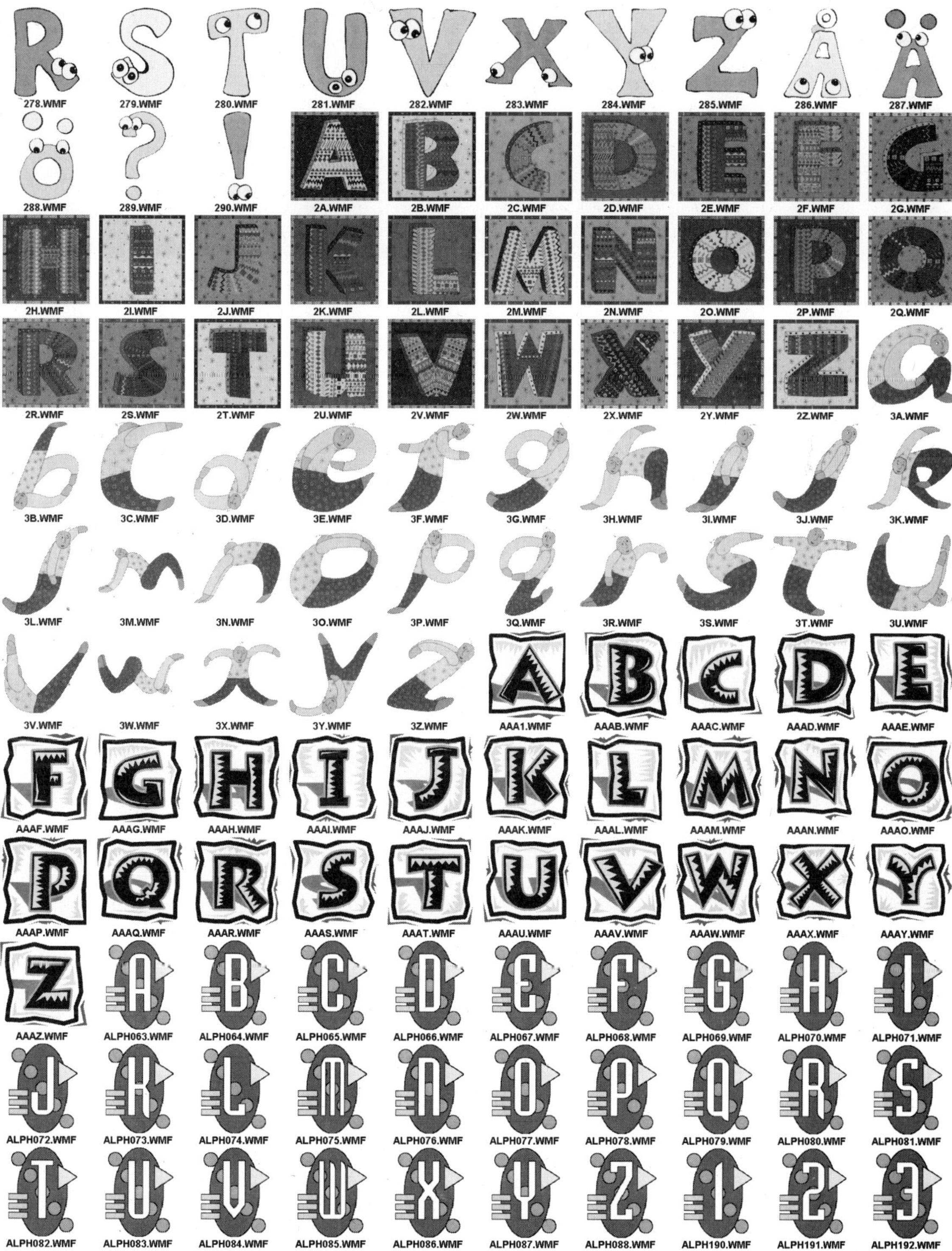

278.WMF 279.WMF 280.WMF 281.WMF 282.WMF 283.WMF 284.WMF 285.WMF 286.WMF 287.WMF

288.WMF 289.WMF 290.WMF 2A.WMF 2B.WMF 2C.WMF 2D.WMF 2E.WMF 2F.WMF 2G.WMF

2H.WMF 2I.WMF 2J.WMF 2K.WMF 2L.WMF 2M.WMF 2N.WMF 2O.WMF 2P.WMF 2Q.WMF

2R.WMF 2S.WMF 2T.WMF 2U.WMF 2V.WMF 2W.WMF 2X.WMF 2Y.WMF 2Z.WMF 3A.WMF

3B.WMF 3C.WMF 3D.WMF 3E.WMF 3F.WMF 3G.WMF 3H.WMF 3I.WMF 3J.WMF 3K.WMF

3L.WMF 3M.WMF 3N.WMF 3O.WMF 3P.WMF 3Q.WMF 3R.WMF 3S.WMF 3T.WMF 3U.WMF

3V.WMF 3W.WMF 3X.WMF 3Y.WMF 3Z.WMF AAA1.WMF AAAB.WMF AAAC.WMF AAAD.WMF AAAE.WMF

AAAF.WMF AAAG.WMF AAAH.WMF AAAI.WMF AAAJ.WMF AAAK.WMF AAAL.WMF AAAM.WMF AAAN.WMF AAAO.WMF

AAAP.WMF AAAQ.WMF AAAR.WMF AAAS.WMF AAAT.WMF AAAU.WMF AAAV.WMF AAAW.WMF AAAX.WMF AAAY.WMF

AAAZ.WMF ALPH063.WMF ALPH064.WMF ALPH065.WMF ALPH066.WMF ALPH067.WMF ALPH068.WMF ALPH069.WMF ALPH070.WMF ALPH071.WMF

ALPH072.WMF ALPH073.WMF ALPH074.WMF ALPH075.WMF ALPH076.WMF ALPH077.WMF ALPH078.WMF ALPH079.WMF ALPH080.WMF ALPH081.WMF

ALPH082.WMF ALPH083.WMF ALPH084.WMF ALPH085.WMF ALPH086.WMF ALPH087.WMF ALPH088.WMF ALPH190.WMF ALPH191.WMF ALPH192.WMF

ALPH193.WMF
ALPH194.WMF
ALPH195.WMF
ALPH196.WMF
ALPH197.WMF
ALPH198.WMF
ALPH199.WMF
ALPHA0.WMF
ALPHA1.WMF
ALPHA10.WMF
ALPHA11.WMF
ALPHA12.WMF
ALPHA13.WMF
ALPHA14.WMF
ALPHA15.WMF
ALPHA16.WMF
ALPHA17.WMF
ALPHA18.WMF
ALPHA19.WMF
ALPHA2.WMF
ALPHA20.WMF
ALPHA21.WMF
ALPHA22.WMF
ALPHA23.WMF
ALPHA24.WMF
ALPHA25.WMF
ALPHA26.WMF
ALPHA27.WMF
ALPHA28.WMF
ALPHA3.WMF
ALPHA4.WMF
ALPHA5.WMF
ALPHA6.WMF
ALPHA7.WMF
ALPHA8.WMF
ALPHA9.WMF
ANIM_A.WMF
ANIM_B.WMF
ANIM_C.WMF
ANIM_D.WMF
ANIM_E.WMF
ANIM_F.WMF
ANIM_G.WMF
ANIM_H.WMF
ANIM_I.WMF
ANIM_J.WMF
ANIM_K.WMF
ANIM_L.WMF
ANIM_M.WMF
ANIM_N.WMF
ANIM_O.WMF
ANIM_P.WMF
ANIM_Q.WMF
ANIM_R.WMF
ANIM_S.WMF
ANIM_T.WMF
ANIM_U.WMF
ANIM_V.WMF
ANIM_W.WMF
ANIM_X.WMF
ANIM_Y.WMF
ANIM_Z.WMF
BLKA.WMF
BLKB.WMF
BLKC.WMF
BLKD.WMF
BLKE.WMF
BLKF.WMF
BLKG.WMF
BLKH.WMF
BLKI.WMF
BLKJ.WMF
BLKK.WMF
BLKL.WMF
BLKM.WMF
BLKN.WMF
BLKO.WMF
BLKP.WMF
BLKQ.WMF
BLKR.WMF
BLKS.WMF
BLKT.WMF
BLKU.WMF
BLKV.WMF
BLKW.WMF
BLKX.WMF
BLKY.WMF
BLKZ.WMF
BUTT0.WMF
BUTT1.WMF
BUTT2.WMF
BUTT3.WMF
BUTT4.WMF
BUTT5.WMF
BUTT6.WMF
BUTT7.WMF
BUTT8.WMF
BUTT9.WMF
BUTT_.WMF
BUTTA.WMF
BUTTB.WMF
BUTTC.WMF
BUTTD.WMF
BUTTE.WMF
BUTTF.WMF
BUTTG.WMF
BUTTH.WMF
BUTTI.WMF
BUTTJ.WMF
BUTTK.WMF
BUTTL.WMF
BUTTM.WMF
BUTTN.WMF
BUTTO.WMF
BUTTP.WMF
BUTTQ.WMF
BUTTR.WMF
BUTTS.WMF
BUTTT.WMF
BUTTU.WMF

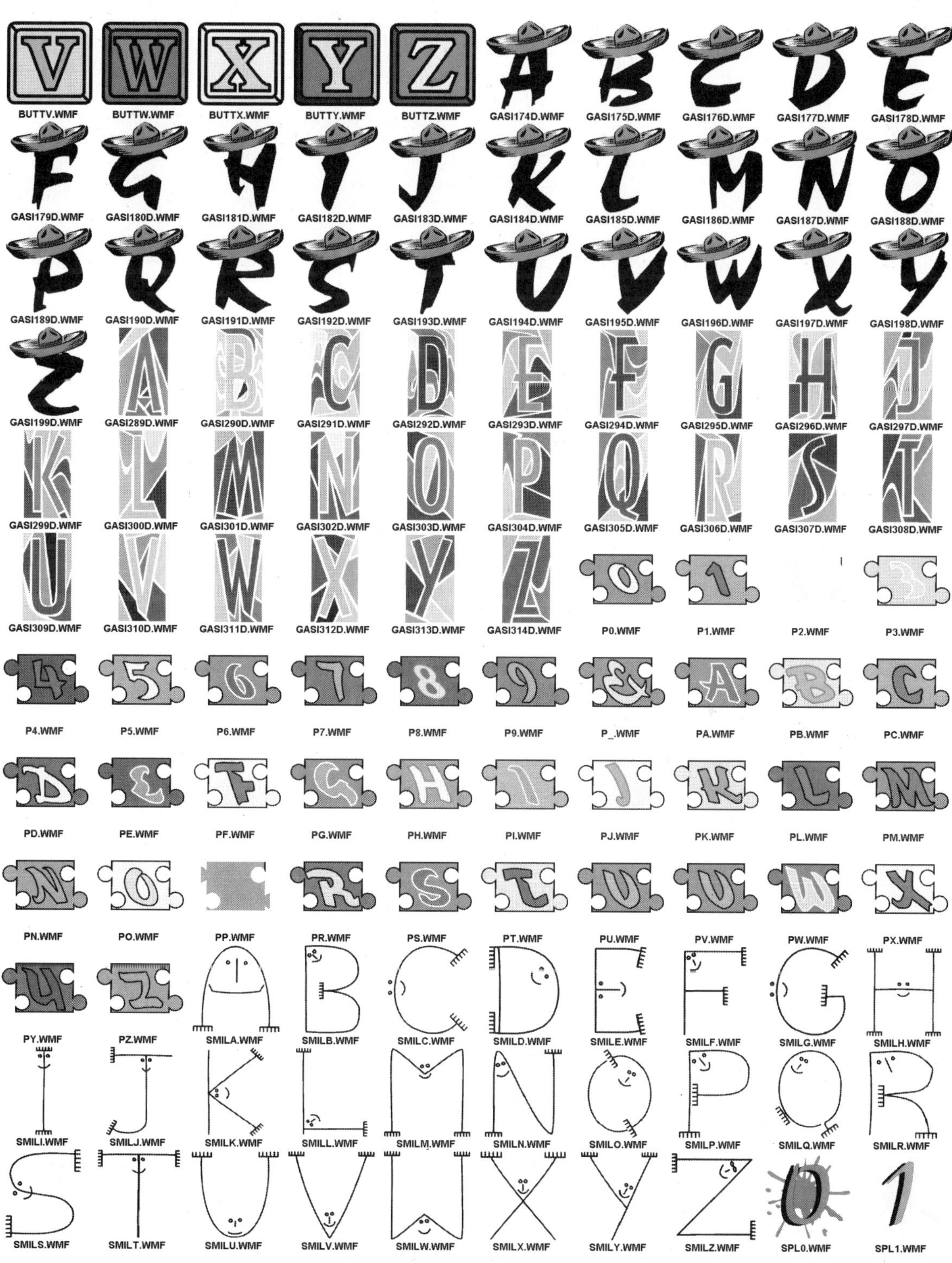

BUTTV.WMF BUTTW.WMF BUTTX.WMF BUTTY.WMF BUTTZ.WMF GASI174D.WMF GASI175D.WMF GASI176D.WMF GASI177D.WMF GASI178D.WMF
GASI179D.WMF GASI180D.WMF GASI181D.WMF GASI182D.WMF GASI183D.WMF GASI184D.WMF GASI185D.WMF GASI186D.WMF GASI187D.WMF GASI188D.WMF
GASI189D.WMF GASI190D.WMF GASI191D.WMF GASI192D.WMF GASI193D.WMF GASI194D.WMF GASI195D.WMF GASI196D.WMF GASI197D.WMF GASI198D.WMF
GASI199D.WMF GASI289D.WMF GASI290D.WMF GASI291D.WMF GASI292D.WMF GASI293D.WMF GASI294D.WMF GASI295D.WMF GASI296D.WMF GASI297D.WMF
GASI299D.WMF GASI300D.WMF GASI301D.WMF GASI302D.WMF GASI303D.WMF GASI304D.WMF GASI305D.WMF GASI306D.WMF GASI307D.WMF GASI308D.WMF
GASI309D.WMF GASI310D.WMF GASI311D.WMF GASI312D.WMF GASI313D.WMF GASI314D.WMF P0.WMF P1.WMF P2.WMF P3.WMF
P4.WMF P5.WMF P6.WMF P7.WMF P8.WMF P9.WMF P_.WMF PA.WMF PB.WMF PC.WMF
PD.WMF PE.WMF PF.WMF PG.WMF PH.WMF PI.WMF PJ.WMF PK.WMF PL.WMF PM.WMF
PN.WMF PO.WMF PP.WMF PR.WMF PS.WMF PT.WMF PU.WMF PV.WMF PW.WMF PX.WMF
PY.WMF PZ.WMF SMILA.WMF SMILB.WMF SMILC.WMF SMILD.WMF SMILE.WMF SMILF.WMF SMILG.WMF SMILH.WMF
SMILI.WMF SMILJ.WMF SMILK.WMF SMILL.WMF SMILM.WMF SMILN.WMF SMILO.WMF SMILP.WMF SMILQ.WMF SMILR.WMF
SMILS.WMF SMILT.WMF SMILU.WMF SMILV.WMF SMILW.WMF SMILX.WMF SMILY.WMF SMILZ.WMF SPL0.WMF SPL1.WMF

SPL2.WMF
SPL3.WMF
SPL4.WMF
SPL5.WMF
SPL6.WMF
SPL7.WMF
SPL8.WMF
SPL9.WMF
SPL_.WMF
SPLA.WMF
SPLB.WMF
SPLC.WMF
SPLD.WMF
SPLE.WMF
SPLF.WMF
SPLG.WMF
SPLH.WMF
SPLI.WMF
SPLJ.WMF
SPLK.WMF
SPLL.WMF
SPLM.WMF
SPLN.WMF
SPLO.WMF
SPLP.WMF
SPLQ.WMF
SPLR.WMF
SPLS.WMF
SPLT.WMF
SPLU.WMF
SPLV.WMF
SPLW.WMF
SPLX.WMF
SPLY.WMF
SPLZ.WMF

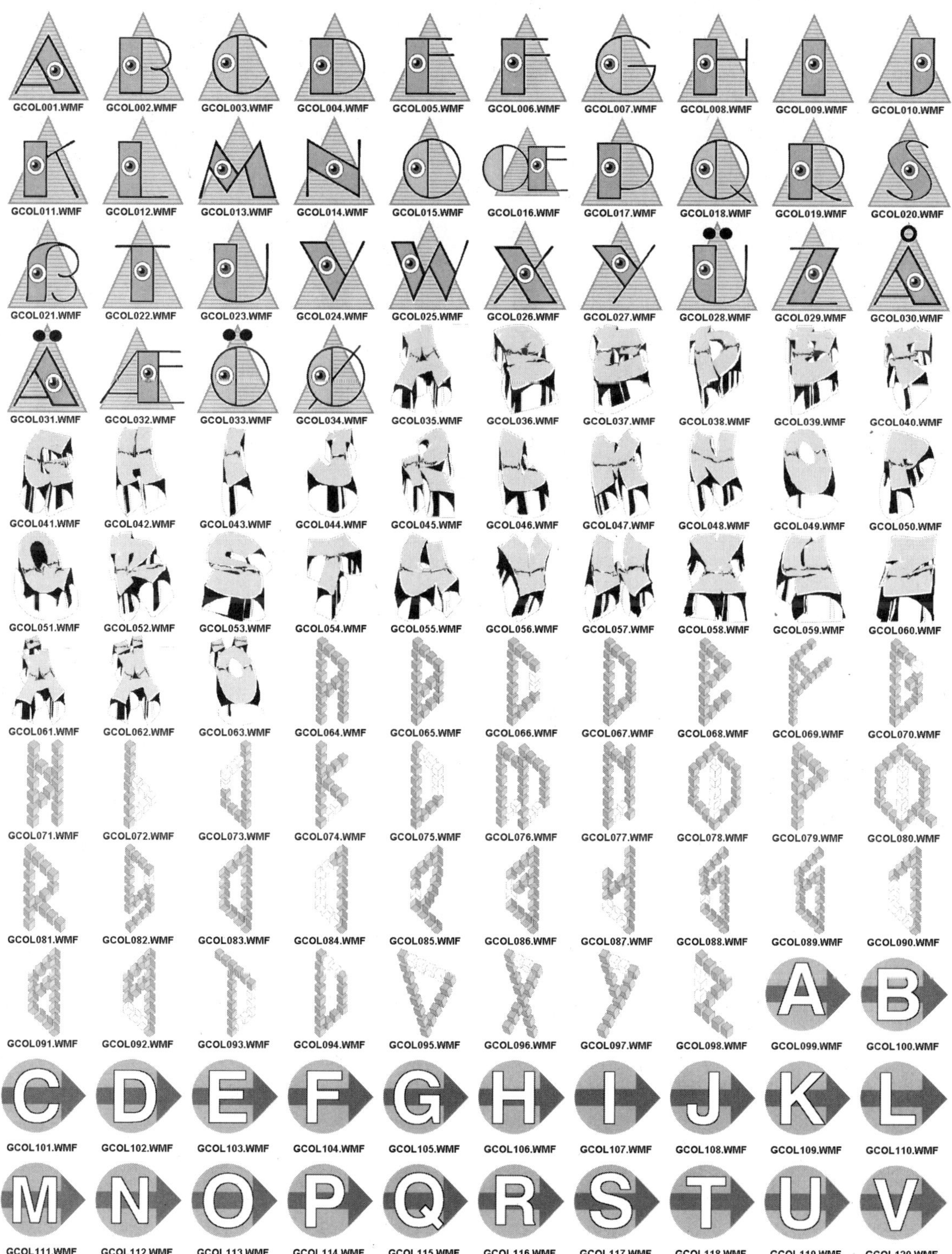
GCOL001.WMF
GCOL002.WMF
GCOL003.WMF
GCOL004.WMF
GCOL005.WMF
GCOL006.WMF
GCOL007.WMF
GCOL008.WMF
GCOL009.WMF
GCOL010.WMF
GCOL011.WMF
GCOL012.WMF
GCOL013.WMF
GCOL014.WMF
GCOL015.WMF
GCOL016.WMF
GCOL017.WMF
GCOL018.WMF
GCOL019.WMF
GCOL020.WMF
GCOL021.WMF
GCOL022.WMF
GCOL023.WMF
GCOL024.WMF
GCOL025.WMF
GCOL026.WMF
GCOL027.WMF
GCOL028.WMF
GCOL029.WMF
GCOL030.WMF
GCOL031.WMF
GCOL032.WMF
GCOL033.WMF
GCOL034.WMF
GCOL035.WMF
GCOL036.WMF
GCOL037.WMF
GCOL038.WMF
GCOL039.WMF
GCOL040.WMF
GCOL041.WMF
GCOL042.WMF
GCOL043.WMF
GCOL044.WMF
GCOL045.WMF
GCOL046.WMF
GCOL047.WMF
GCOL048.WMF
GCOL049.WMF
GCOL050.WMF
GCOL051.WMF
GCOL052.WMF
GCOL053.WMF
GCOL054.WMF
GCOL055.WMF
GCOL056.WMF
GCOL057.WMF
GCOL058.WMF
GCOL059.WMF
GCOL060.WMF
GCOL061.WMF
GCOL062.WMF
GCOL063.WMF
GCOL064.WMF
GCOL065.WMF
GCOL066.WMF
GCOL067.WMF
GCOL068.WMF
GCOL069.WMF
GCOL070.WMF
GCOL071.WMF
GCOL072.WMF
GCOL073.WMF
GCOL074.WMF
GCOL075.WMF
GCOL076.WMF
GCOL077.WMF
GCOL078.WMF
GCOL079.WMF
GCOL080.WMF
GCOL081.WMF
GCOL082.WMF
GCOL083.WMF
GCOL084.WMF
GCOL085.WMF
GCOL086.WMF
GCOL087.WMF
GCOL088.WMF
GCOL089.WMF
GCOL090.WMF
GCOL091.WMF
GCOL092.WMF
GCOL093.WMF
GCOL094.WMF
GCOL095.WMF
GCOL096.WMF
GCOL097.WMF
GCOL098.WMF
GCOL099.WMF
GCOL100.WMF
GCOL101.WMF
GCOL102.WMF
GCOL103.WMF
GCOL104.WMF
GCOL105.WMF
GCOL106.WMF
GCOL107.WMF
GCOL108.WMF
GCOL109.WMF
GCOL110.WMF
GCOL111.WMF
GCOL112.WMF
GCOL113.WMF
GCOL114.WMF
GCOL115.WMF
GCOL116.WMF
GCOL117.WMF
GCOL118.WMF
GCOL119.WMF
GCOL120.WMF

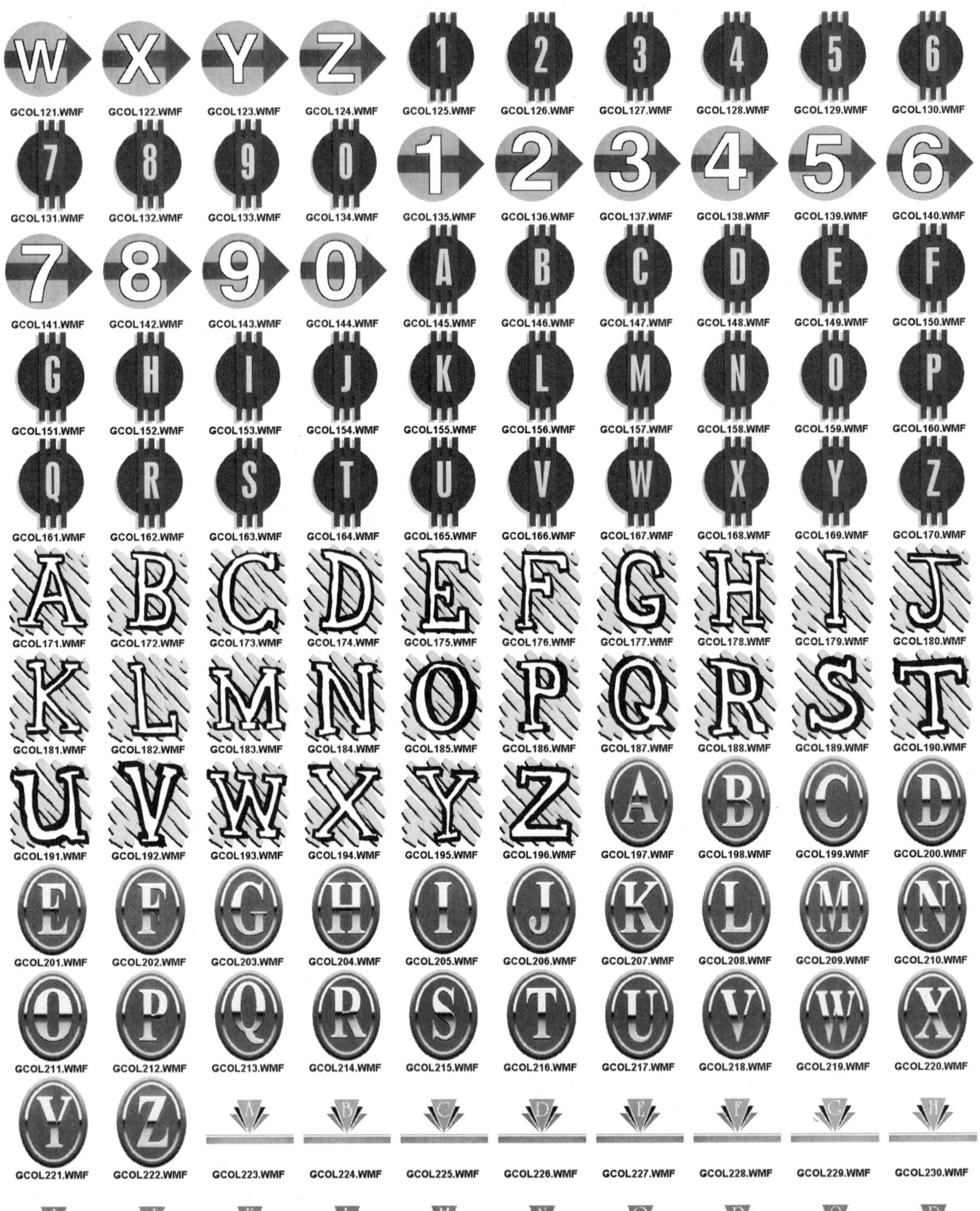
GCOL121.WMF GCOL122.WMF GCOL123.WMF GCOL124.WMF GCOL125.WMF GCOL126.WMF GCOL127.WMF GCOL128.WMF GCOL129.WMF GCOL130.WMF
GCOL131.WMF GCOL132.WMF GCOL133.WMF GCOL134.WMF GCOL135.WMF GCOL136.WMF GCOL137.WMF GCOL138.WMF GCOL139.WMF GCOL140.WMF
GCOL141.WMF GCOL142.WMF GCOL143.WMF GCOL144.WMF GCOL145.WMF GCOL146.WMF GCOL147.WMF GCOL148.WMF GCOL149.WMF GCOL150.WMF
GCOL151.WMF GCOL152.WMF GCOL153.WMF GCOL154.WMF GCOL155.WMF GCOL156.WMF GCOL157.WMF GCOL158.WMF GCOL159.WMF GCOL160.WMF
GCOL161.WMF GCOL162.WMF GCOL163.WMF GCOL164.WMF GCOL165.WMF GCOL166.WMF GCOL167.WMF GCOL168.WMF GCOL169.WMF GCOL170.WMF
GCOL171.WMF GCOL172.WMF GCOL173.WMF GCOL174.WMF GCOL175.WMF GCOL176.WMF GCOL177.WMF GCOL178.WMF GCOL179.WMF GCOL180.WMF
GCOL181.WMF GCOL182.WMF GCOL183.WMF GCOL184.WMF GCOL185.WMF GCOL186.WMF GCOL187.WMF GCOL188.WMF GCOL189.WMF GCOL190.WMF
GCOL191.WMF GCOL192.WMF GCOL193.WMF GCOL194.WMF GCOL195.WMF GCOL196.WMF GCOL197.WMF GCOL198.WMF GCOL199.WMF GCOL200.WMF
GCOL201.WMF GCOL202.WMF GCOL203.WMF GCOL204.WMF GCOL205.WMF GCOL206.WMF GCOL207.WMF GCOL208.WMF GCOL209.WMF GCOL210.WMF
GCOL211.WMF GCOL212.WMF GCOL213.WMF GCOL214.WMF GCOL215.WMF GCOL216.WMF GCOL217.WMF GCOL218.WMF GCOL219.WMF GCOL220.WMF
GCOL221.WMF GCOL222.WMF GCOL223.WMF GCOL224.WMF GCOL225.WMF GCOL226.WMF GCOL227.WMF GCOL228.WMF GCOL229.WMF GCOL230.WMF
GCOL231.WMF GCOL232.WMF GCOL233.WMF GCOL234.WMF GCOL235.WMF GCOL236.WMF GCOL237.WMF GCOL238.WMF GCOL239.WMF GCOL240.WMF

GCOL241.WMF GCOL242.WMF GCOL243.WMF GCOL244.WMF GCOL245.WMF GCOL246.WMF GCOL247.WMF GCOL248.WMF GCOL249.WMF GCOL250.WMF

GCOL251.WMF GCOL252.WMF GCOL253.WMF GCOL254.WMF GCOL255.WMF GCOL256.WMF GCOL257.WMF GCOL258.WMF GCOL259.WMF GCOL260.WMF

GCOL261.WMF GCOL262.WMF GCOL263.WMF GCOL264.WMF GCOL265.WMF GCOL266.WMF GCOL267.WMF GCOL268.WMF GCOL269.WMF GCOL270.WMF

GCOL271.WMF GCOL272.WMF GCOL273.WMF GCOL274.WMF GCOL275.WMF GCOL276.WMF GCOL277.WMF GCOL278.WMF GCOL279.WMF GCOL280.WMF

GCOL281.WMF GCOL282.WMF GCOL283.WMF GCOL284.WMF GCOL285.WMF GCOL286.WMF GCOL287.WMF GCOL288.WMF GCOL289.WMF GCOL290.WMF

GCOL291.WMF GCOL292.WMF GCOL293.WMF GCOL294.WMF GCOL295.WMF GCOL296.WMF GCOL297.WMF GCOL298.WMF GCOL299.WMF GCOL300.WMF

GCOL301.WMF GCOL302.WMF GCOL303.WMF GCOL304.WMF GCOL305.WMF GCOL306.WMF GCOL307.WMF GCOL308.WMF GCOL309.WMF GCOL310.WMF

GCOL311.WMF GCOL312.WMF GCOL313.WMF GCOL314.WMF GCOL315.WMF GCOL316.WMF GCOL317.WMF GCOL318.WMF GCOL319.WMF GCOL320.WMF

GCOL321.WMF GCOL322.WMF GCOL323.WMF GCOL324.WMF GCOL325.WMF GCOL326.WMF GCOL327.WMF GCOL328.WMF GCOL329.WMF GCOL330.WMF

GCOL331.WMF GCOL332.WMF GCOL333.WMF GCOL334.WMF GCOL335.WMF GCOL336.WMF GCOL337.WMF GCOL338.WMF GCOL339.WMF GCOL340.WMF

GCOL341.WMF GCOL342.WMF GCOL343.WMF GCOL344.WMF GCOL345.WMF GCOL346.WMF GCOL347.WMF GCOL348.WMF GCOL349.WMF GCOL350.WMF

GCOL351.WMF GCOL352.WMF GCOL353.WMF GCOL354.WMF GCOL355.WMF GCOL356.WMF GCOL357.WMF GCOL358.WMF GCOL359.WMF GCOL360.WMF

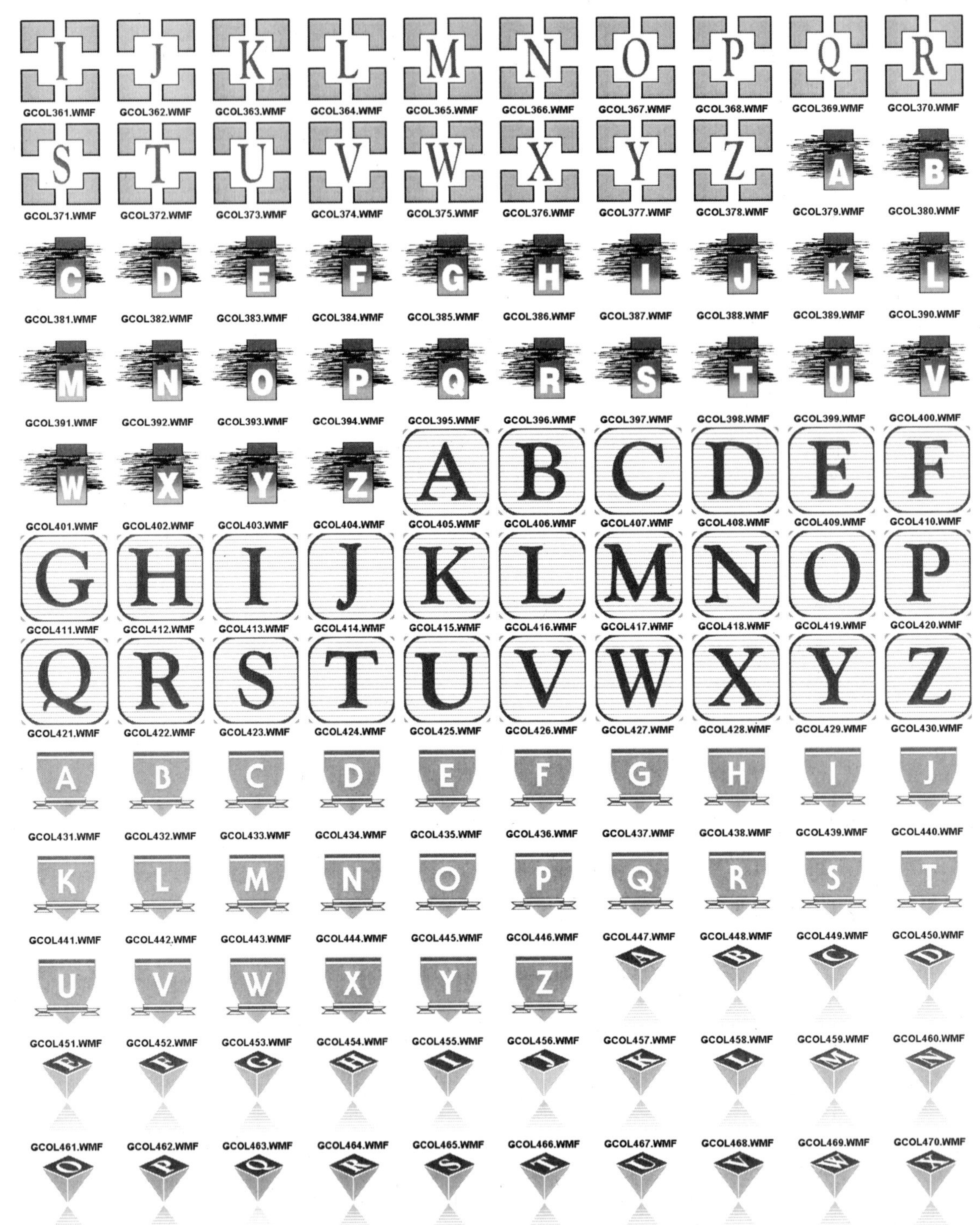
GCOL361.WMF GCOL362.WMF GCOL363.WMF GCOL364.WMF GCOL365.WMF GCOL366.WMF GCOL367.WMF GCOL368.WMF GCOL369.WMF GCOL370.WMF
GCOL371.WMF GCOL372.WMF GCOL373.WMF GCOL374.WMF GCOL375.WMF GCOL376.WMF GCOL377.WMF GCOL378.WMF GCOL379.WMF GCOL380.WMF
GCOL381.WMF GCOL382.WMF GCOL383.WMF GCOL384.WMF GCOL385.WMF GCOL386.WMF GCOL387.WMF GCOL388.WMF GCOL389.WMF GCOL390.WMF
GCOL391.WMF GCOL392.WMF GCOL393.WMF GCOL394.WMF GCOL395.WMF GCOL396.WMF GCOL397.WMF GCOL398.WMF GCOL399.WMF GCOL400.WMF
GCOL401.WMF GCOL402.WMF GCOL403.WMF GCOL404.WMF GCOL405.WMF GCOL406.WMF GCOL407.WMF GCOL408.WMF GCOL409.WMF GCOL410.WMF
GCOL411.WMF GCOL412.WMF GCOL413.WMF GCOL414.WMF GCOL415.WMF GCOL416.WMF GCOL417.WMF GCOL418.WMF GCOL419.WMF GCOL420.WMF
GCOL421.WMF GCOL422.WMF GCOL423.WMF GCOL424.WMF GCOL425.WMF GCOL426.WMF GCOL427.WMF GCOL428.WMF GCOL429.WMF GCOL430.WMF
GCOL431.WMF GCOL432.WMF GCOL433.WMF GCOL434.WMF GCOL435.WMF GCOL436.WMF GCOL437.WMF GCOL438.WMF GCOL439.WMF GCOL440.WMF
GCOL441.WMF GCOL442.WMF GCOL443.WMF GCOL444.WMF GCOL445.WMF GCOL446.WMF GCOL447.WMF GCOL448.WMF GCOL449.WMF GCOL450.WMF
GCOL451.WMF GCOL452.WMF GCOL453.WMF GCOL454.WMF GCOL455.WMF GCOL456.WMF GCOL457.WMF GCOL458.WMF GCOL459.WMF GCOL460.WMF
GCOL461.WMF GCOL462.WMF GCOL463.WMF GCOL464.WMF GCOL465.WMF GCOL466.WMF GCOL467.WMF GCOL468.WMF GCOL469.WMF GCOL470.WMF
GCOL471.WMF GCOL472.WMF GCOL473.WMF GCOL474.WMF GCOL475.WMF GCOL476.WMF GCOL477.WMF GCOL478.WMF GCOL479.WMF GCOL480.WMF

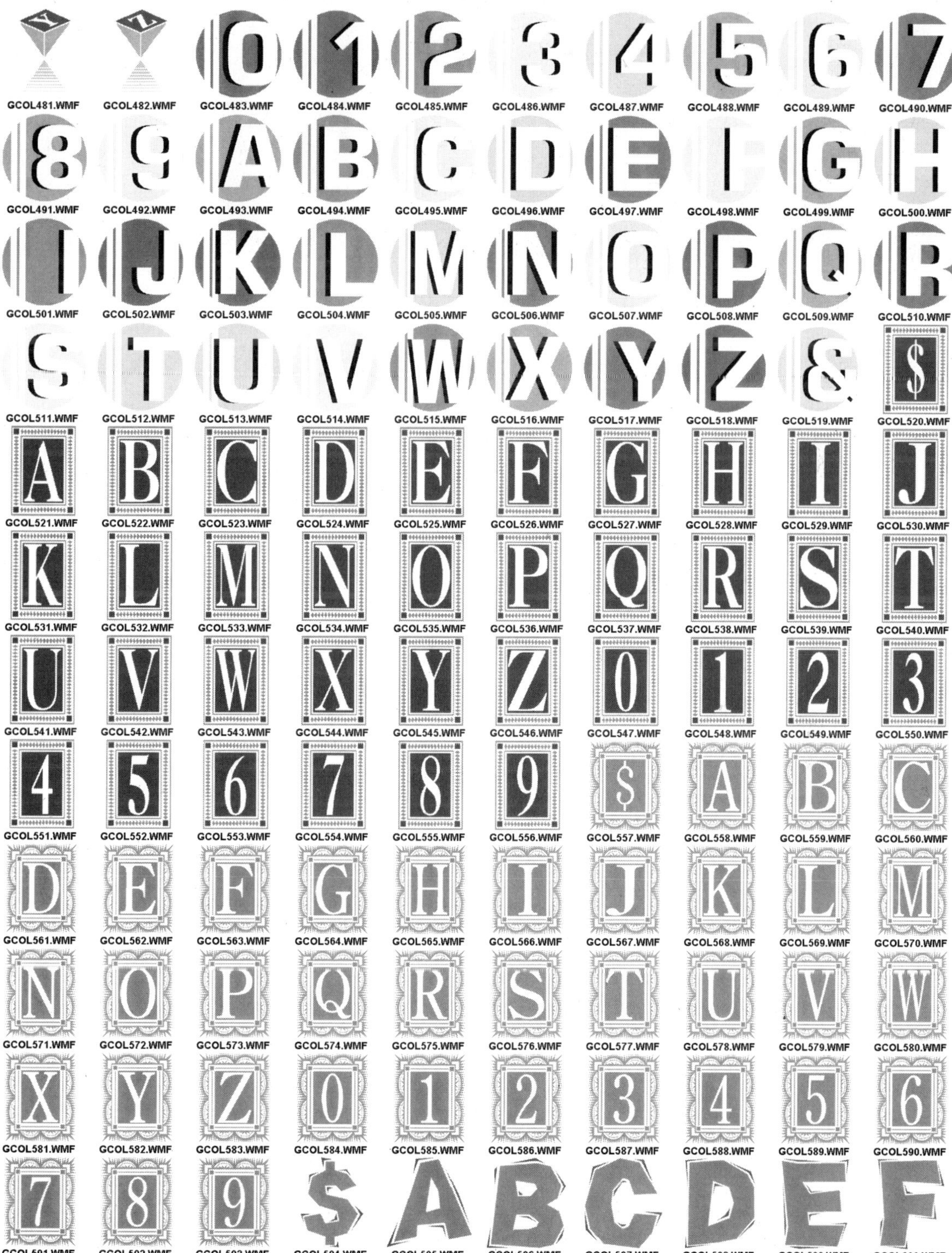
GCOL481.WMF GCOL482.WMF GCOL483.WMF GCOL484.WMF GCOL485.WMF GCOL486.WMF GCOL487.WMF GCOL488.WMF GCOL489.WMF GCOL490.WMF
GCOL491.WMF GCOL492.WMF GCOL493.WMF GCOL494.WMF GCOL495.WMF GCOL496.WMF GCOL497.WMF GCOL498.WMF GCOL499.WMF GCOL500.WMF
GCOL501.WMF GCOL502.WMF GCOL503.WMF GCOL504.WMF GCOL505.WMF GCOL506.WMF GCOL507.WMF GCOL508.WMF GCOL509.WMF GCOL510.WMF
GCOL511.WMF GCOL512.WMF GCOL513.WMF GCOL514.WMF GCOL515.WMF GCOL516.WMF GCOL517.WMF GCOL518.WMF GCOL519.WMF GCOL520.WMF
GCOL521.WMF GCOL522.WMF GCOL523.WMF GCOL524.WMF GCOL525.WMF GCOL526.WMF GCOL527.WMF GCOL528.WMF GCOL529.WMF GCOL530.WMF
GCOL531.WMF GCOL532.WMF GCOL533.WMF GCOL534.WMF GCOL535.WMF GCOL536.WMF GCOL537.WMF GCOL538.WMF GCOL539.WMF GCOL540.WMF
GCOL541.WMF GCOL542.WMF GCOL543.WMF GCOL544.WMF GCOL545.WMF GCOL546.WMF GCOL547.WMF GCOL548.WMF GCOL549.WMF GCOL550.WMF
GCOL551.WMF GCOL552.WMF GCOL553.WMF GCOL554.WMF GCOL555.WMF GCOL556.WMF GCOL557.WMF GCOL558.WMF GCOL559.WMF GCOL560.WMF
GCOL561.WMF GCOL562.WMF GCOL563.WMF GCOL564.WMF GCOL565.WMF GCOL566.WMF GCOL567.WMF GCOL568.WMF GCOL569.WMF GCOL570.WMF
GCOL571.WMF GCOL572.WMF GCOL573.WMF GCOL574.WMF GCOL575.WMF GCOL576.WMF GCOL577.WMF GCOL578.WMF GCOL579.WMF GCOL580.WMF
GCOL581.WMF GCOL582.WMF GCOL583.WMF GCOL584.WMF GCOL585.WMF GCOL586.WMF GCOL587.WMF GCOL588.WMF GCOL589.WMF GCOL590.WMF
GCOL591.WMF GCOL592.WMF GCOL593.WMF GCOL594.WMF GCOL595.WMF GCOL596.WMF GCOL597.WMF GCOL598.WMF GCOL599.WMF GCOL600.WMF

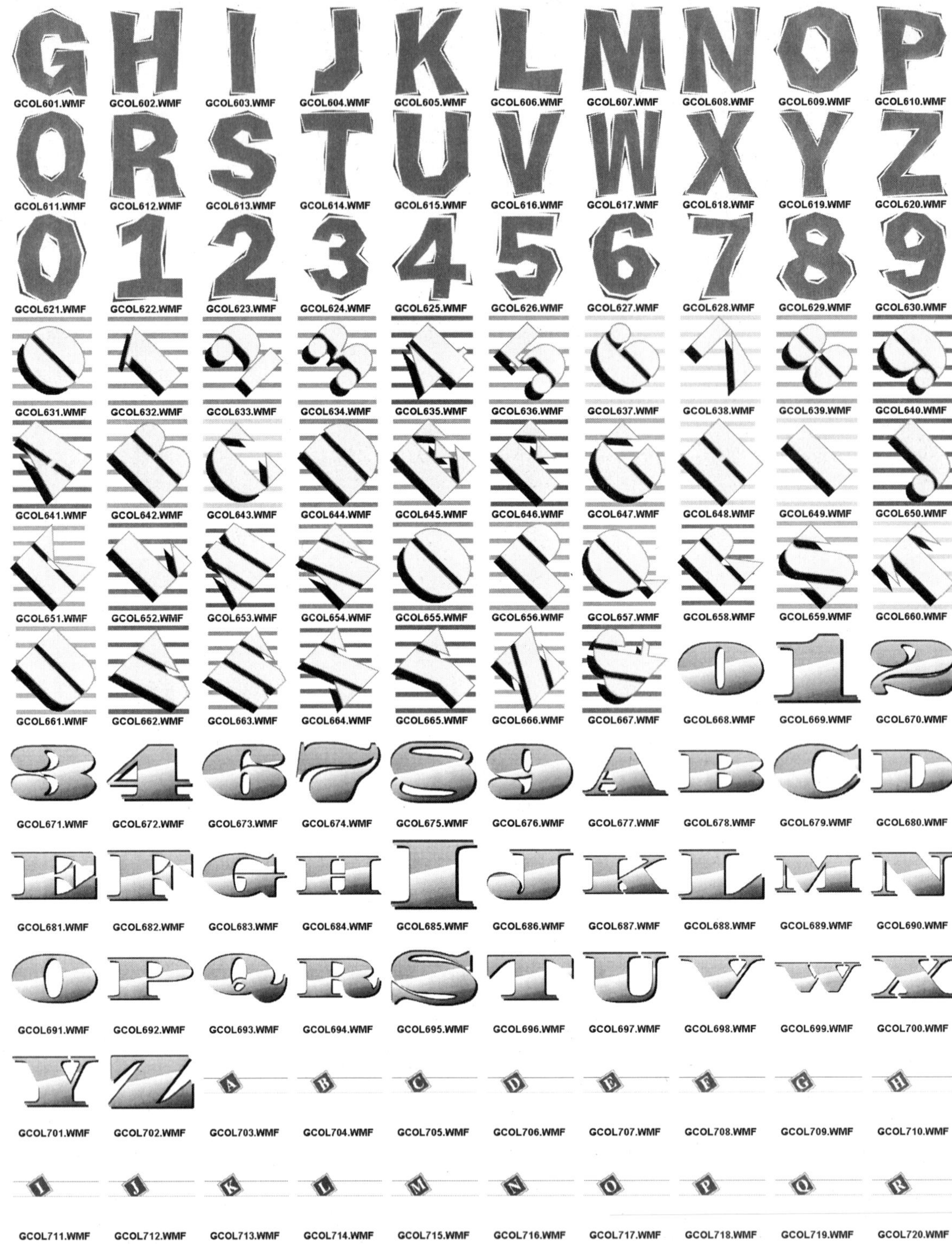
GCOL601.WMF
GCOL602.WMF
GCOL603.WMF
GCOL604.WMF
GCOL605.WMF
GCOL606.WMF
GCOL607.WMF
GCOL608.WMF
GCOL609.WMF
GCOL610.WMF
GCOL611.WMF
GCOL612.WMF
GCOL613.WMF
GCOL614.WMF
GCOL615.WMF
GCOL616.WMF
GCOL617.WMF
GCOL618.WMF
GCOL619.WMF
GCOL620.WMF
GCOL621.WMF
GCOL622.WMF
GCOL623.WMF
GCOL624.WMF
GCOL625.WMF
GCOL626.WMF
GCOL627.WMF
GCOL628.WMF
GCOL629.WMF
GCOL630.WMF
GCOL631.WMF
GCOL632.WMF
GCOL633.WMF
GCOL634.WMF
GCOL635.WMF
GCOL636.WMF
GCOL637.WMF
GCOL638.WMF
GCOL639.WMF
GCOL640.WMF
GCOL641.WMF
GCOL642.WMF
GCOL643.WMF
GCOL644.WMF
GCOL645.WMF
GCOL646.WMF
GCOL647.WMF
GCOL648.WMF
GCOL649.WMF
GCOL650.WMF
GCOL651.WMF
GCOL652.WMF
GCOL653.WMF
GCOL654.WMF
GCOL655.WMF
GCOL656.WMF
GCOL657.WMF
GCOL658.WMF
GCOL659.WMF
GCOL660.WMF
GCOL661.WMF
GCOL662.WMF
GCOL663.WMF
GCOL664.WMF
GCOL665.WMF
GCOL666.WMF
GCOL667.WMF
GCOL668.WMF
GCOL669.WMF
GCOL670.WMF
GCOL671.WMF
GCOL672.WMF
GCOL673.WMF
GCOL674.WMF
GCOL675.WMF
GCOL676.WMF
GCOL677.WMF
GCOL678.WMF
GCOL679.WMF
GCOL680.WMF
GCOL681.WMF
GCOL682.WMF
GCOL683.WMF
GCOL684.WMF
GCOL685.WMF
GCOL686.WMF
GCOL687.WMF
GCOL688.WMF
GCOL689.WMF
GCOL690.WMF
GCOL691.WMF
GCOL692.WMF
GCOL693.WMF
GCOL694.WMF
GCOL695.WMF
GCOL696.WMF
GCOL697.WMF
GCOL698.WMF
GCOL699.WMF
GCOL700.WMF
GCOL701.WMF
GCOL702.WMF
GCOL703.WMF
GCOL704.WMF
GCOL705.WMF
GCOL706.WMF
GCOL707.WMF
GCOL708.WMF
GCOL709.WMF
GCOL710.WMF
GCOL711.WMF
GCOL712.WMF
GCOL713.WMF
GCOL714.WMF
GCOL715.WMF
GCOL716.WMF
GCOL717.WMF
GCOL718.WMF
GCOL719.WMF
GCOL720.WMF

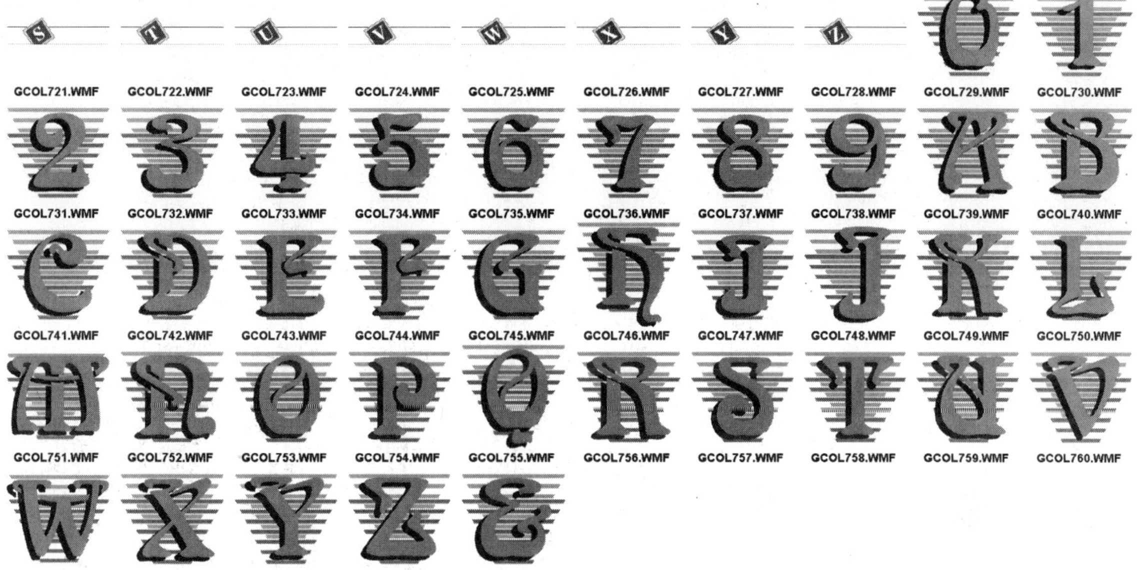

GCOL721.WMF GCOL722.WMF GCOL723.WMF GCOL724.WMF GCOL725.WMF GCOL726.WMF GCOL727.WMF GCOL728.WMF GCOL729.WMF GCOL730.WMF

GCOL731.WMF GCOL732.WMF GCOL733.WMF GCOL734.WMF GCOL735.WMF GCOL736.WMF GCOL737.WMF GCOL738.WMF GCOL739.WMF GCOL740.WMF

GCOL741.WMF GCOL742.WMF GCOL743.WMF GCOL744.WMF GCOL745.WMF GCOL746.WMF GCOL747.WMF GCOL748.WMF GCOL749.WMF GCOL750.WMF

GCOL751.WMF GCOL752.WMF GCOL753.WMF GCOL754.WMF GCOL755.WMF GCOL756.WMF GCOL757.WMF GCOL758.WMF GCOL759.WMF GCOL760.WMF

GCOL761.WMF GCOL762.WMF GCOL763.WMF GCOL764.WMF GCOL765.WMF

GBW001.WMF
GBW002.WMF
GBW003.WMF
GBW004.WMF
GBW005.WMF
GBW006.WMF
GBW007.WMF
GBW008.WMF
GBW009.WMF
GBW010.WMF
GBW011.WMF
GBW012.WMF
GBW013.WMF
GBW014.WMF
GBW015.WMF
GBW016.WMF
GBW017.WMF
GBW018.WMF
GBW019.WMF
GBW020.WMF
GBW021.WMF
GBW022.WMF
GBW023.WMF
GBW024.WMF
GBW025.WMF
GBW026.WMF
GBW027.WMF
GBW028.WMF
GBW029.WMF
GBW030.WMF
GBW031.WMF
GBW032.WMF
GBW033.WMF
GBW034.WMF
GBW035.WMF
GBW036.WMF
GBW037.WMF
GBW038.WMF
GBW039.WMF
GBW040.WMF
GBW041.WMF
GBW042.WMF
GBW043.WMF
GBW044.WMF
GBW045.WMF
GBW046.WMF
GBW047.WMF
GBW048.WMF
GBW049.WMF
GBW050.WMF
GBW051.WMF
GBW052.WMF
GBW053.WMF
GBW054.WMF
GBW055.WMF
GBW056.WMF
GBW057.WMF
GBW058.WMF
GBW059.WMF
GBW060.WMF
GBW061.WMF
GBW062.WMF
GBW063.WMF
GBW064.WMF
GBW065.WMF
GBW066.WMF
GBW067.WMF
GBW068.WMF
GBW069.WMF
GBW070.WMF
GBW071.WMF
GBW072.WMF
GBW073.WMF
GBW074.WMF
GBW075.WMF
GBW076.WMF
GBW077.WMF
GBW078.WMF
GBW079.WMF
GBW080.WMF
GBW081.WMF
GBW082.WMF
GBW083.WMF
GBW084.WMF
GBW085.WMF
GBW086.WMF
GBW087.WMF
GBW088.WMF
GBW089.WMF
GBW090.WMF
GBW091.WMF
GBW092.WMF
GBW093.WMF
GBW094.WMF
GBW095.WMF
GBW096.WMF
GBW097.WMF
GBW098.WMF
GBW099.WMF
GBW100.WMF
GBW101.WMF
GBW102.WMF
GBW103.WMF
GBW104.WMF
GBW105.WMF
GBW106.WMF
GBW107.WMF
GBW108.WMF
GBW109.WMF
GBW110.WMF
GBW111.WMF
GBW112.WMF
GBW113.WMF
GBW114.WMF
GBW115.WMF
GBW116.WMF
GBW117.WMF
GBW118.WMF
GBW119.WMF
GBW120.WMF

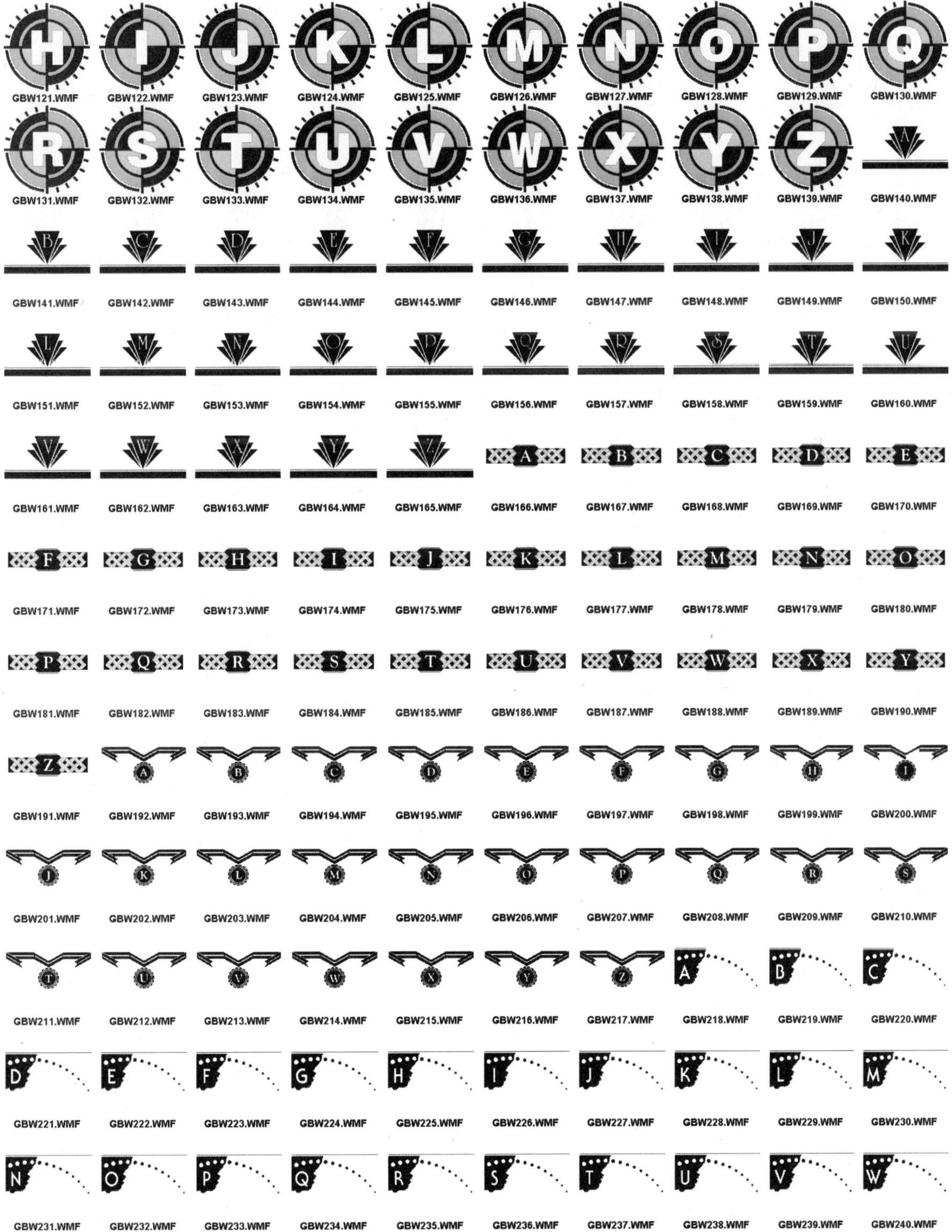
GBW121.WMF GBW122.WMF GBW123.WMF GBW124.WMF GBW125.WMF GBW126.WMF GBW127.WMF GBW128.WMF GBW129.WMF GBW130.WMF
GBW131.WMF GBW132.WMF GBW133.WMF GBW134.WMF GBW135.WMF GBW136.WMF GBW137.WMF GBW138.WMF GBW139.WMF GBW140.WMF
GBW141.WMF GBW142.WMF GBW143.WMF GBW144.WMF GBW145.WMF GBW146.WMF GBW147.WMF GBW148.WMF GBW149.WMF GBW150.WMF
GBW151.WMF GBW152.WMF GBW153.WMF GBW154.WMF GBW155.WMF GBW156.WMF GBW157.WMF GBW158.WMF GBW159.WMF GBW160.WMF
GBW161.WMF GBW162.WMF GBW163.WMF GBW164.WMF GBW165.WMF GBW166.WMF GBW167.WMF GBW168.WMF GBW169.WMF GBW170.WMF
GBW171.WMF GBW172.WMF GBW173.WMF GBW174.WMF GBW175.WMF GBW176.WMF GBW177.WMF GBW178.WMF GBW179.WMF GBW180.WMF
GBW181.WMF GBW182.WMF GBW183.WMF GBW184.WMF GBW185.WMF GBW186.WMF GBW187.WMF GBW188.WMF GBW189.WMF GBW190.WMF
GBW191.WMF GBW192.WMF GBW193.WMF GBW194.WMF GBW195.WMF GBW196.WMF GBW197.WMF GBW198.WMF GBW199.WMF GBW200.WMF
GBW201.WMF GBW202.WMF GBW203.WMF GBW204.WMF GBW205.WMF GBW206.WMF GBW207.WMF GBW208.WMF GBW209.WMF GBW210.WMF
GBW211.WMF GBW212.WMF GBW213.WMF GBW214.WMF GBW215.WMF GBW216.WMF GBW217.WMF GBW218.WMF GBW219.WMF GBW220.WMF
GBW221.WMF GBW222.WMF GBW223.WMF GBW224.WMF GBW225.WMF GBW226.WMF GBW227.WMF GBW228.WMF GBW229.WMF GBW230.WMF
GBW231.WMF GBW232.WMF GBW233.WMF GBW234.WMF GBW235.WMF GBW236.WMF GBW237.WMF GBW238.WMF GBW239.WMF GBW240.WMF

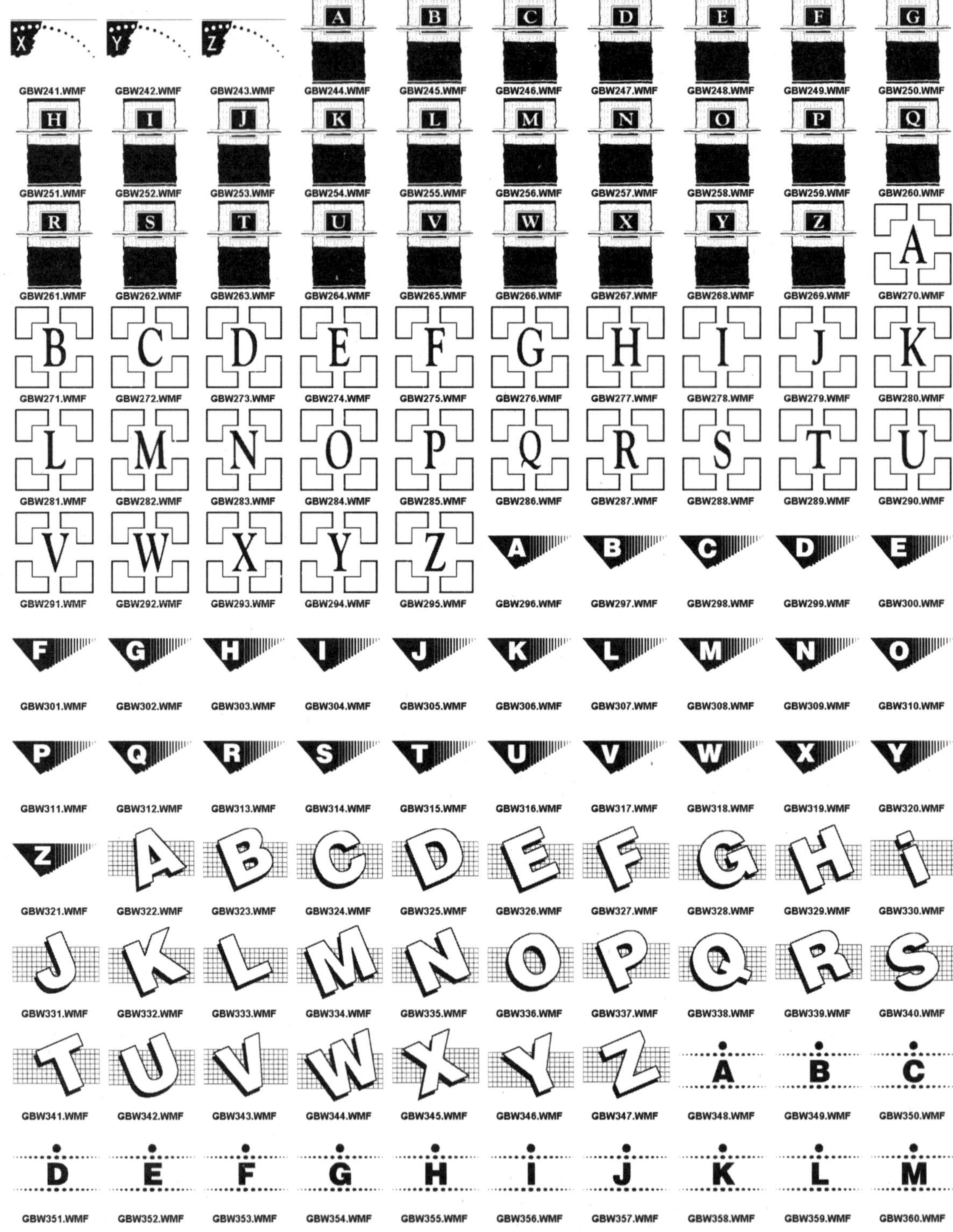
GBW241.WMF
GBW242.WMF
GBW243.WMF
GBW244.WMF
GBW245.WMF
GBW246.WMF
GBW247.WMF
GBW248.WMF
GBW249.WMF
GBW250.WMF
GBW251.WMF
GBW252.WMF
GBW253.WMF
GBW254.WMF
GBW255.WMF
GBW256.WMF
GBW257.WMF
GBW258.WMF
GBW259.WMF
GBW260.WMF
GBW261.WMF
GBW262.WMF
GBW263.WMF
GBW264.WMF
GBW265.WMF
GBW266.WMF
GBW267.WMF
GBW268.WMF
GBW269.WMF
GBW270.WMF
GBW271.WMF
GBW272.WMF
GBW273.WMF
GBW274.WMF
GBW275.WMF
GBW276.WMF
GBW277.WMF
GBW278.WMF
GBW279.WMF
GBW280.WMF
GBW281.WMF
GBW282.WMF
GBW283.WMF
GBW284.WMF
GBW285.WMF
GBW286.WMF
GBW287.WMF
GBW288.WMF
GBW289.WMF
GBW290.WMF
GBW291.WMF
GBW292.WMF
GBW293.WMF
GBW294.WMF
GBW295.WMF
GBW296.WMF
GBW297.WMF
GBW298.WMF
GBW299.WMF
GBW300.WMF
GBW301.WMF
GBW302.WMF
GBW303.WMF
GBW304.WMF
GBW305.WMF
GBW306.WMF
GBW307.WMF
GBW308.WMF
GBW309.WMF
GBW310.WMF
GBW311.WMF
GBW312.WMF
GBW313.WMF
GBW314.WMF
GBW315.WMF
GBW316.WMF
GBW317.WMF
GBW318.WMF
GBW319.WMF
GBW320.WMF
GBW321.WMF
GBW322.WMF
GBW323.WMF
GBW324.WMF
GBW325.WMF
GBW326.WMF
GBW327.WMF
GBW328.WMF
GBW329.WMF
GBW330.WMF
GBW331.WMF
GBW332.WMF
GBW333.WMF
GBW334.WMF
GBW335.WMF
GBW336.WMF
GBW337.WMF
GBW338.WMF
GBW339.WMF
GBW340.WMF
GBW341.WMF
GBW342.WMF
GBW343.WMF
GBW344.WMF
GBW345.WMF
GBW346.WMF
GBW347.WMF
GBW348.WMF
GBW349.WMF
GBW350.WMF
GBW351.WMF
GBW352.WMF
GBW353.WMF
GBW354.WMF
GBW355.WMF
GBW356.WMF
GBW357.WMF
GBW358.WMF
GBW359.WMF
GBW360.WMF

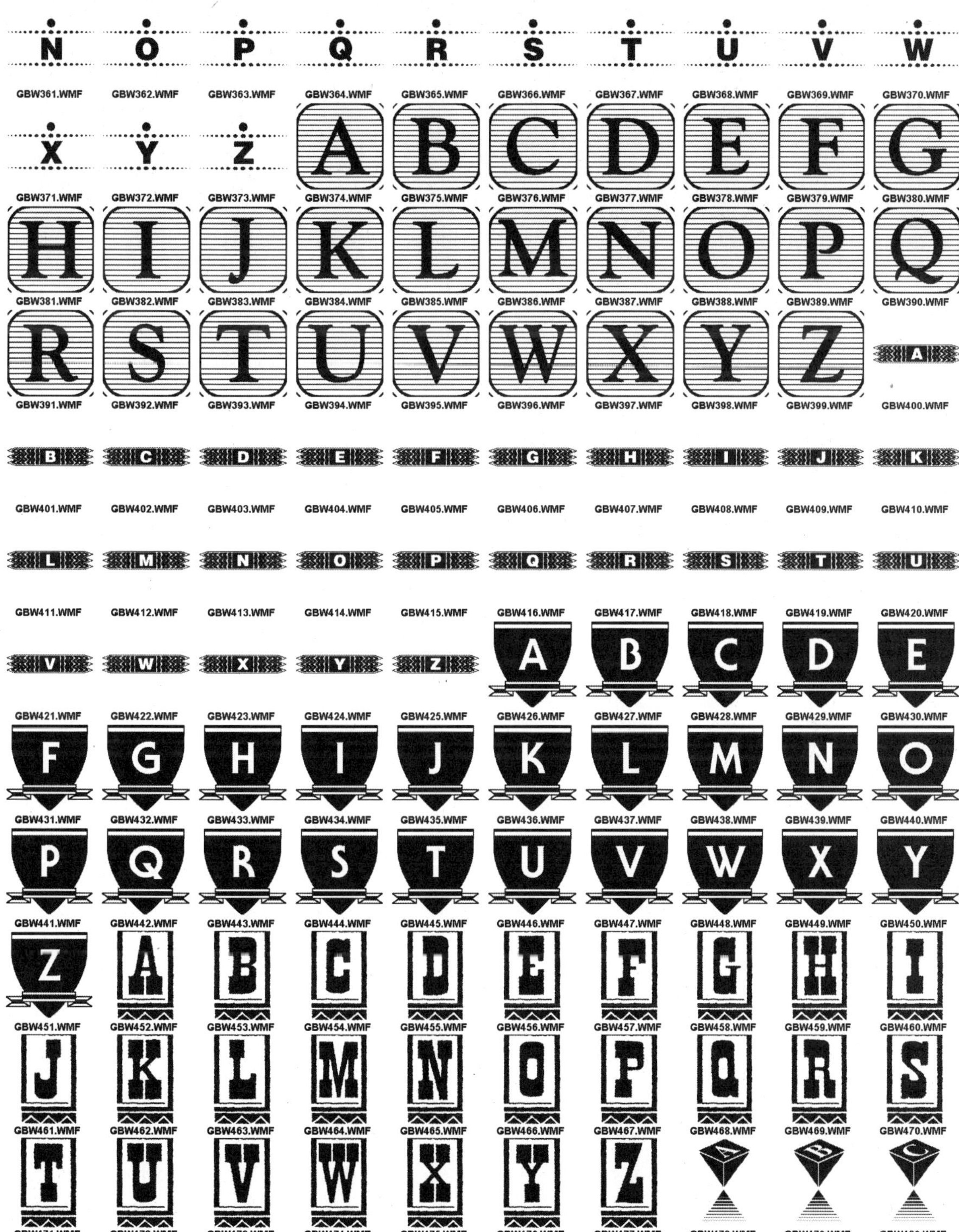
GBW361.WMF GBW362.WMF GBW363.WMF GBW364.WMF GBW365.WMF GBW366.WMF GBW367.WMF GBW368.WMF GBW369.WMF GBW370.WMF
GBW371.WMF GBW372.WMF GBW373.WMF GBW374.WMF GBW375.WMF GBW376.WMF GBW377.WMF GBW378.WMF GBW379.WMF GBW380.WMF
GBW381.WMF GBW382.WMF GBW383.WMF GBW384.WMF GBW385.WMF GBW386.WMF GBW387.WMF GBW388.WMF GBW389.WMF GBW390.WMF
GBW391.WMF GBW392.WMF GBW393.WMF GBW394.WMF GBW395.WMF GBW396.WMF GBW397.WMF GBW398.WMF GBW399.WMF GBW400.WMF
GBW401.WMF GBW402.WMF GBW403.WMF GBW404.WMF GBW405.WMF GBW406.WMF GBW407.WMF GBW408.WMF GBW409.WMF GBW410.WMF
GBW411.WMF GBW412.WMF GBW413.WMF GBW414.WMF GBW415.WMF GBW416.WMF GBW417.WMF GBW418.WMF GBW419.WMF GBW420.WMF
GBW421.WMF GBW422.WMF GBW423.WMF GBW424.WMF GBW425.WMF GBW426.WMF GBW427.WMF GBW428.WMF GBW429.WMF GBW430.WMF
GBW431.WMF GBW432.WMF GBW433.WMF GBW434.WMF GBW435.WMF GBW436.WMF GBW437.WMF GBW438.WMF GBW439.WMF GBW440.WMF
GBW441.WMF GBW442.WMF GBW443.WMF GBW444.WMF GBW445.WMF GBW446.WMF GBW447.WMF GBW448.WMF GBW449.WMF GBW450.WMF
GBW451.WMF GBW452.WMF GBW453.WMF GBW454.WMF GBW455.WMF GBW456.WMF GBW457.WMF GBW458.WMF GBW459.WMF GBW460.WMF
GBW461.WMF GBW462.WMF GBW463.WMF GBW464.WMF GBW465.WMF GBW466.WMF GBW467.WMF GBW468.WMF GBW469.WMF GBW470.WMF
GBW471.WMF GBW472.WMF GBW473.WMF GBW474.WMF GBW475.WMF GBW476.WMF GBW477.WMF GBW478.WMF GBW479.WMF GBW480.WMF

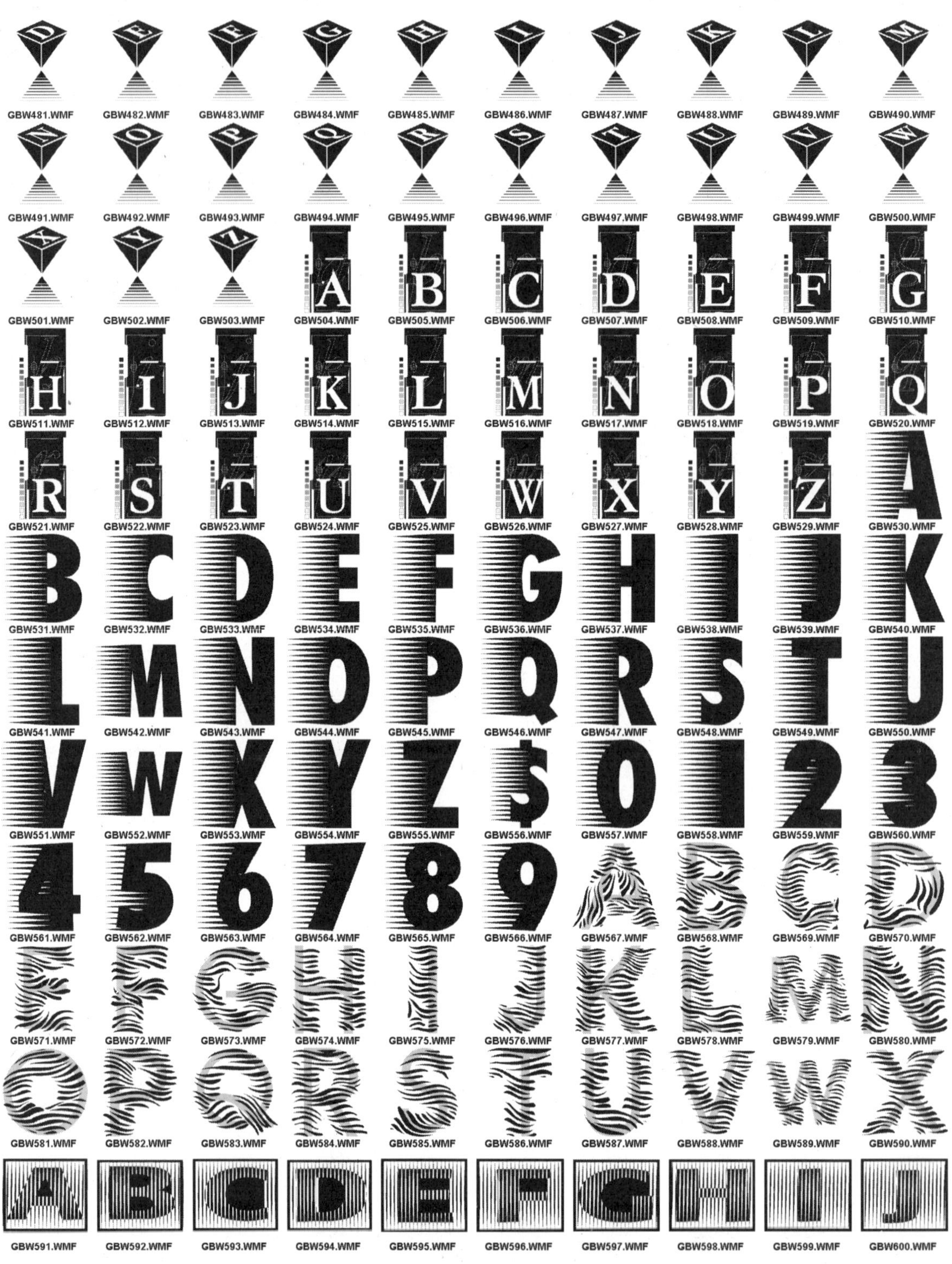
GBW481.WMF GBW482.WMF GBW483.WMF GBW484.WMF GBW485.WMF GBW486.WMF GBW487.WMF GBW488.WMF GBW489.WMF GBW490.WMF
GBW491.WMF GBW492.WMF GBW493.WMF GBW494.WMF GBW495.WMF GBW496.WMF GBW497.WMF GBW498.WMF GBW499.WMF GBW500.WMF
GBW501.WMF GBW502.WMF GBW503.WMF GBW504.WMF GBW505.WMF GBW506.WMF GBW507.WMF GBW508.WMF GBW509.WMF GBW510.WMF
GBW511.WMF GBW512.WMF GBW513.WMF GBW514.WMF GBW515.WMF GBW516.WMF GBW517.WMF GBW518.WMF GBW519.WMF GBW520.WMF
GBW521.WMF GBW522.WMF GBW523.WMF GBW524.WMF GBW525.WMF GBW526.WMF GBW527.WMF GBW528.WMF GBW529.WMF GBW530.WMF
GBW531.WMF GBW532.WMF GBW533.WMF GBW534.WMF GBW535.WMF GBW536.WMF GBW537.WMF GBW538.WMF GBW539.WMF GBW540.WMF
GBW541.WMF GBW542.WMF GBW543.WMF GBW544.WMF GBW545.WMF GBW546.WMF GBW547.WMF GBW548.WMF GBW549.WMF GBW550.WMF
GBW551.WMF GBW552.WMF GBW553.WMF GBW554.WMF GBW555.WMF GBW556.WMF GBW557.WMF GBW558.WMF GBW559.WMF GBW560.WMF
GBW561.WMF GBW562.WMF GBW563.WMF GBW564.WMF GBW565.WMF GBW566.WMF GBW567.WMF GBW568.WMF GBW569.WMF GBW570.WMF
GBW571.WMF GBW572.WMF GBW573.WMF GBW574.WMF GBW575.WMF GBW576.WMF GBW577.WMF GBW578.WMF GBW579.WMF GBW580.WMF
GBW581.WMF GBW582.WMF GBW583.WMF GBW584.WMF GBW585.WMF GBW586.WMF GBW587.WMF GBW588.WMF GBW589.WMF GBW590.WMF
GBW591.WMF GBW592.WMF GBW593.WMF GBW594.WMF GBW595.WMF GBW596.WMF GBW597.WMF GBW598.WMF GBW599.WMF GBW600.WMF

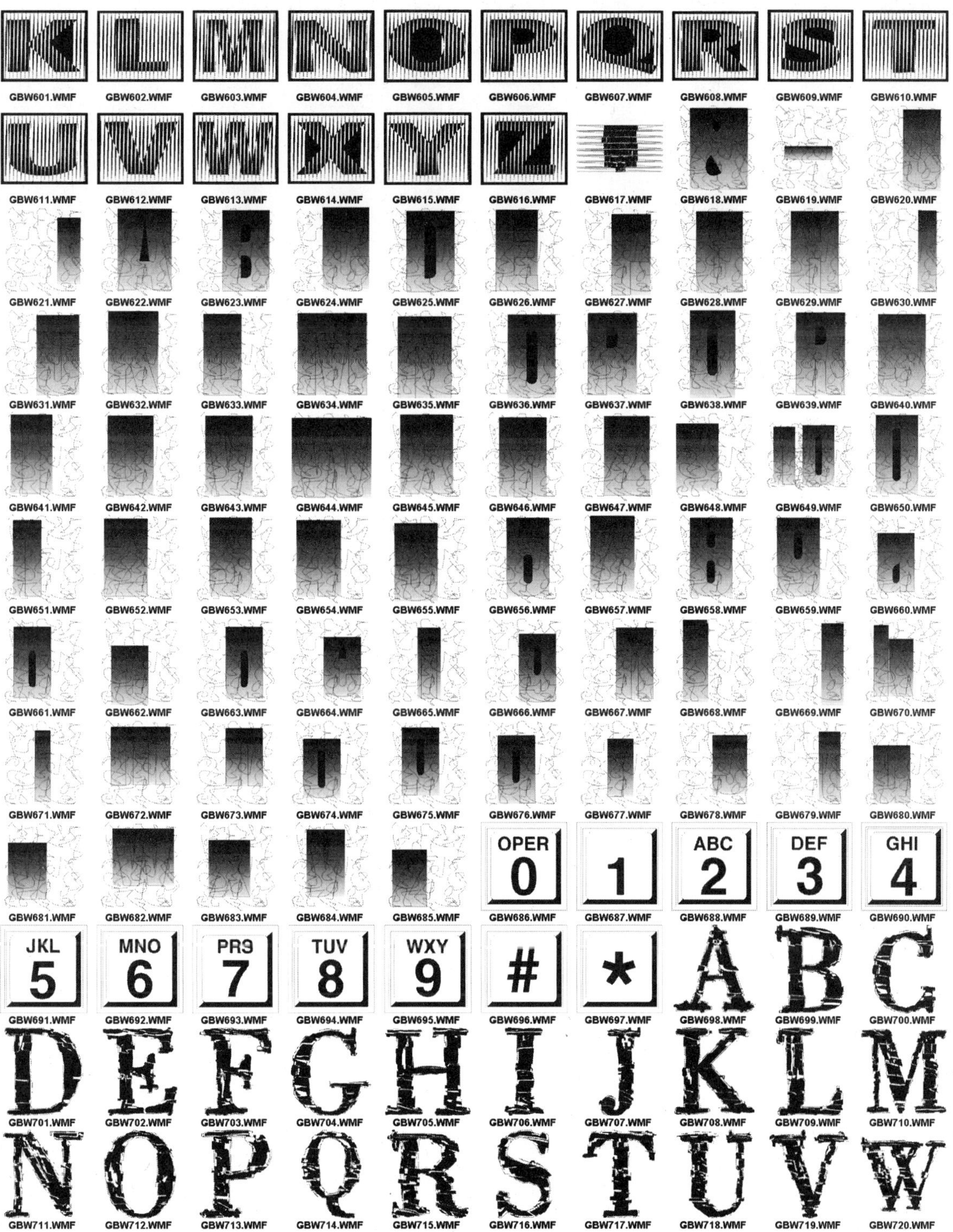

GBW601.WMF GBW602.WMF GBW603.WMF GBW604.WMF GBW605.WMF GBW606.WMF GBW607.WMF GBW608.WMF GBW609.WMF GBW610.WMF
GBW611.WMF GBW612.WMF GBW613.WMF GBW614.WMF GBW615.WMF GBW616.WMF GBW617.WMF GBW618.WMF GBW619.WMF GBW620.WMF
GBW621.WMF GBW622.WMF GBW623.WMF GBW624.WMF GBW625.WMF GBW626.WMF GBW627.WMF GBW628.WMF GBW629.WMF GBW630.WMF
GBW631.WMF GBW632.WMF GBW633.WMF GBW634.WMF GBW635.WMF GBW636.WMF GBW637.WMF GBW638.WMF GBW639.WMF GBW640.WMF
GBW641.WMF GBW642.WMF GBW643.WMF GBW644.WMF GBW645.WMF GBW646.WMF GBW647.WMF GBW648.WMF GBW649.WMF GBW650.WMF
GBW651.WMF GBW652.WMF GBW653.WMF GBW654.WMF GBW655.WMF GBW656.WMF GBW657.WMF GBW658.WMF GBW659.WMF GBW660.WMF
GBW661.WMF GBW662.WMF GBW663.WMF GBW664.WMF GBW665.WMF GBW666.WMF GBW667.WMF GBW668.WMF GBW669.WMF GBW670.WMF
GBW671.WMF GBW672.WMF GBW673.WMF GBW674.WMF GBW675.WMF GBW676.WMF GBW677.WMF GBW678.WMF GBW679.WMF GBW680.WMF
GBW681.WMF GBW682.WMF GBW683.WMF GBW684.WMF GBW685.WMF GBW686.WMF GBW687.WMF GBW688.WMF GBW689.WMF GBW690.WMF
GBW691.WMF GBW692.WMF GBW693.WMF GBW694.WMF GBW695.WMF GBW696.WMF GBW697.WMF GBW698.WMF GBW699.WMF GBW700.WMF
GBW701.WMF GBW702.WMF GBW703.WMF GBW704.WMF GBW705.WMF GBW706.WMF GBW707.WMF GBW708.WMF GBW709.WMF GBW710.WMF
GBW711.WMF GBW712.WMF GBW713.WMF GBW714.WMF GBW715.WMF GBW716.WMF GBW717.WMF GBW718.WMF GBW719.WMF GBW720.WMF

GBW721.WMF GBW722.WMF GBW723.WMF GBW724.WMF GBW725.WMF GBW726.WMF GBW727.WMF GBW728.WMF GBW729.WMF GBW730.WMF

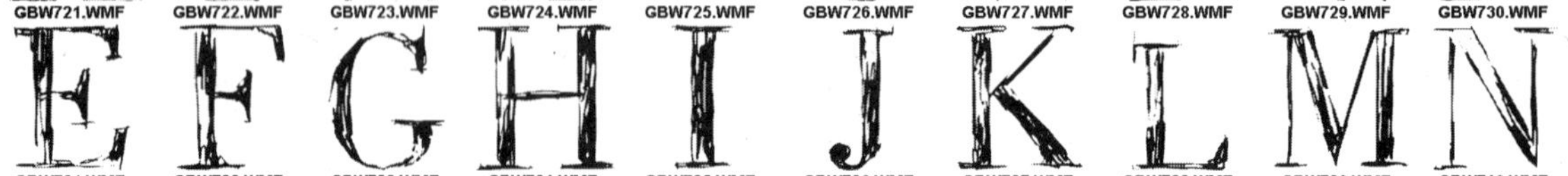

GBW731.WMF GBW732.WMF GBW733.WMF GBW734.WMF GBW735.WMF GBW736.WMF GBW737.WMF GBW738.WMF GBW739.WMF GBW740.WMF

GBW741.WMF GBW742.WMF GBW743.WMF GBW744.WMF GBW745.WMF GBW746.WMF GBW747.WMF GBW748.WMF GBW749.WMF GBW750.WMF

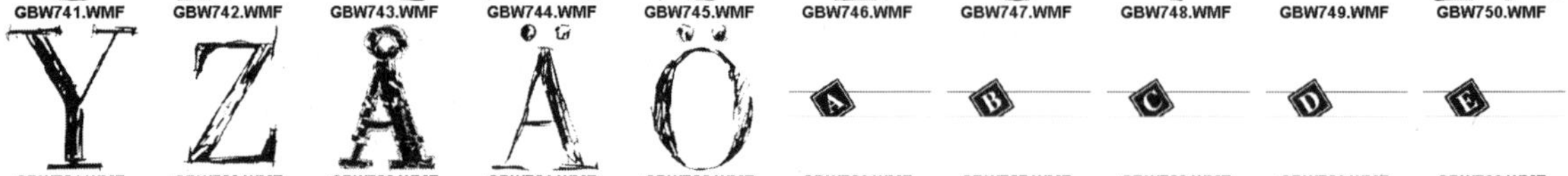

GBW751.WMF GBW752.WMF GBW753.WMF GBW754.WMF GBW755.WMF GBW756.WMF GBW757.WMF GBW758.WMF GBW759.WMF GBW760.WMF

GBW761.WMF GBW762.WMF GBW763.WMF GBW764.WMF GBW765.WMF GBW766.WMF GBW767.WMF GBW768.WMF GBW769.WMF GBW770.WMF

GBW771.WMF GBW772.WMF GBW773.WMF GBW774.WMF GBW775.WMF GBW776.WMF GBW777.WMF GBW778.WMF GBW779.WMF GBW780.WMF

GBW781.WMF

Alphabet • Groups

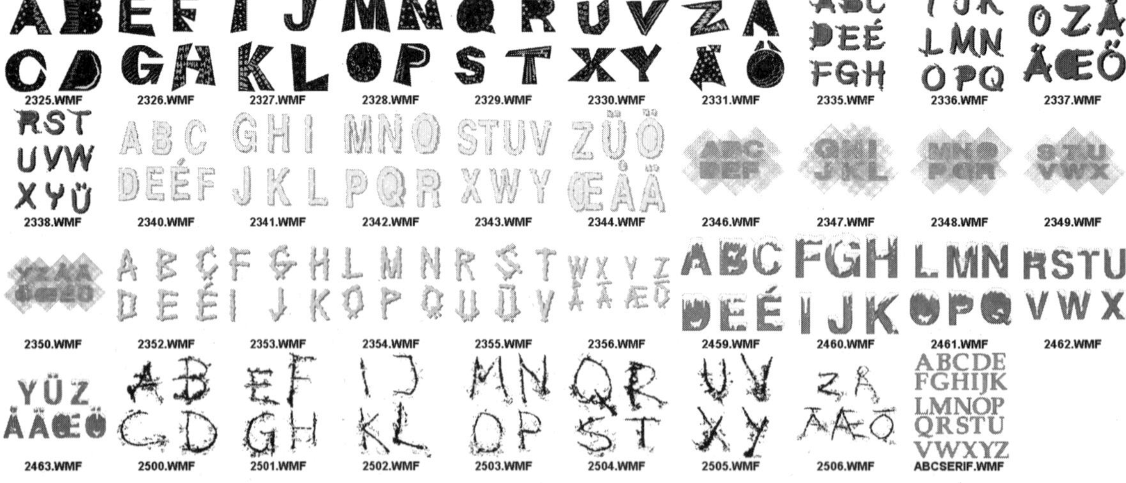

2325.WMF 2326.WMF 2327.WMF 2328.WMF 2329.WMF 2330.WMF 2331.WMF 2335.WMF 2336.WMF 2337.WMF

2338.WMF 2340.WMF 2341.WMF 2342.WMF 2343.WMF 2344.WMF 2346.WMF 2347.WMF 2348.WMF 2349.WMF

2350.WMF 2352.WMF 2353.WMF 2354.WMF 2355.WMF 2356.WMF 2459.WMF 2460.WMF 2461.WMF 2462.WMF

2463.WMF 2500.WMF 2501.WMF 2502.WMF 2503.WMF 2504.WMF 2505.WMF 2506.WMF ABCSERIF.WMF

A01.WMF A02.WMF A03.WMF A04.WMF A05.WMF A06.WMF A07.WMF A08.WMF A09.WMF A10.WMF
A11.WMF A12.WMF A13.WMF A14.WMF A15.WMF A16.WMF A17.WMF A18.WMF A19.WMF A20.WMF
A21.WMF A22.WMF A23.WMF A24.WMF A25.WMF A26.WMF A27.WMF A28.WMF A29.WMF A30.WMF
A31.WMF A32.WMF A33.WMF A34.WMF A35.WMF A36.WMF A37.WMF A38.WMF A39.WMF A4.WMF
A40.WMF A41.WMF A42.WMF A43.WMF A44.WMF A45.WMF A46.WMF A47.WMF A48.WMF A49.WMF
A5.WMF A50.WMF AZTCA.WMF AZTCE.WMF AZTCI.WMF AZTCO.WMF AZTCU.WMF B01.WMF B02.WMF B03.WMF
B04.WMF B05.WMF B06.WMF B07.WMF B08.WMF B09.WMF B10.WMF B11.WMF B12.WMF B13.WMF
B14.WMF B15.WMF B16.WMF B17.WMF B18.WMF B19.WMF B20.WMF B21.WMF B22.WMF B23.WMF
B24.WMF B25.WMF C01.WMF C02.WMF C03.WMF C04.WMF C05.WMF C06.WMF C07.WMF C08.WMF
C09.WMF C10.WMF C11.WMF C12.WMF C13.WMF C14.WMF C15.WMF C16.WMF C17.WMF C18.WMF
C19.WMF C20.WMF C21.WMF C22.WMF D01.WMF D02.WMF D03.WMF D04.WMF D05.WMF D06.WMF
D07.WMF D08.WMF D09.WMF D10.WMF D11.WMF D12.WMF D13.WMF D14.WMF D15.WMF D16.WMF

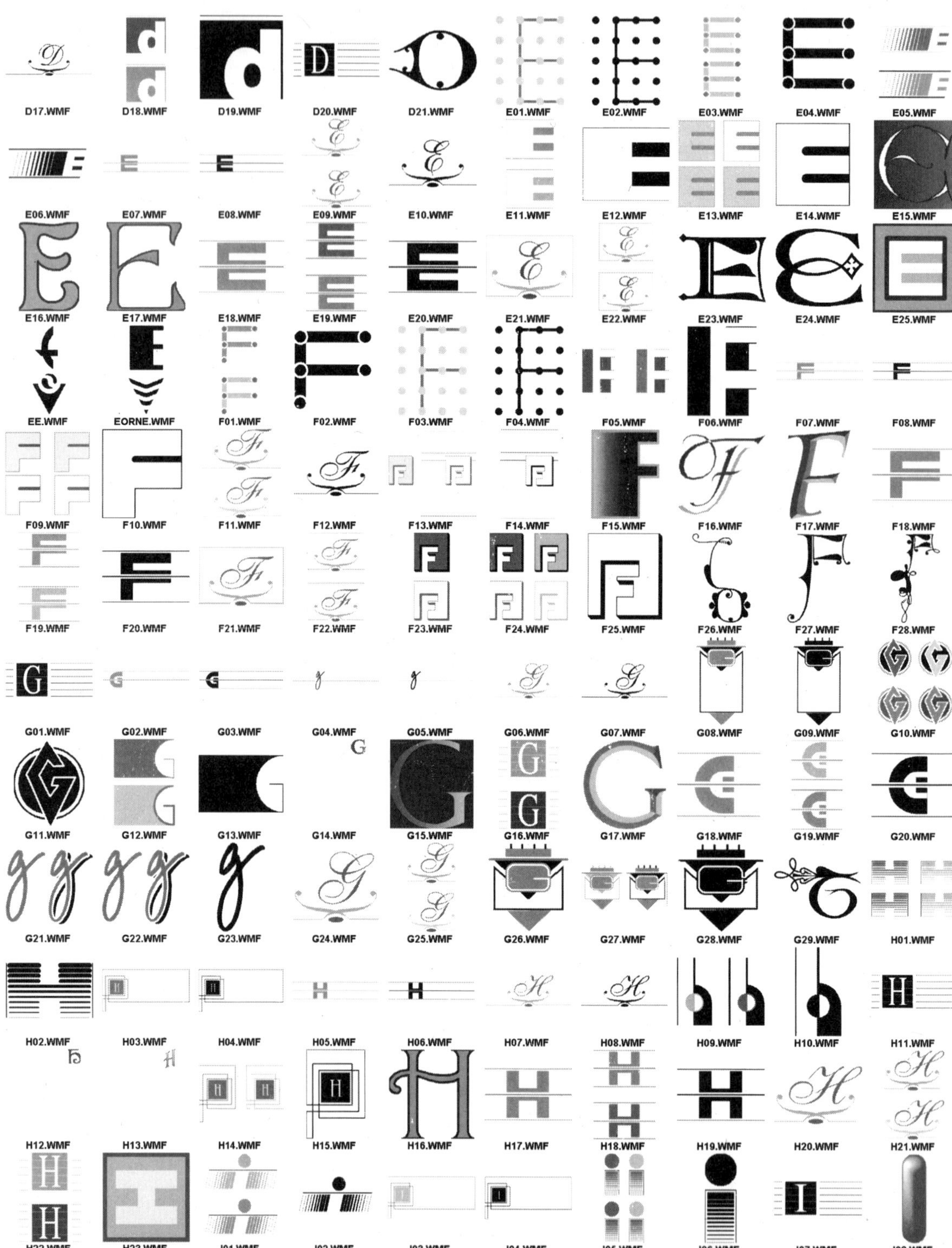

D17.WMF D18.WMF D19.WMF D20.WMF D21.WMF E01.WMF E02.WMF E03.WMF E04.WMF E05.WMF

E06.WMF E07.WMF E08.WMF E09.WMF E10.WMF E11.WMF E12.WMF E13.WMF E14.WMF E15.WMF

E16.WMF E17.WMF E18.WMF E19.WMF E20.WMF E21.WMF E22.WMF E23.WMF E24.WMF E25.WMF

EE.WMF EORNE.WMF F01.WMF F02.WMF F03.WMF F04.WMF F05.WMF F06.WMF F07.WMF F08.WMF

F09.WMF F10.WMF F11.WMF F12.WMF F13.WMF F14.WMF F15.WMF F16.WMF F17.WMF F18.WMF

F19.WMF F20.WMF F21.WMF F22.WMF F23.WMF F24.WMF F25.WMF F26.WMF F27.WMF F28.WMF

G01.WMF G02.WMF G03.WMF G04.WMF G05.WMF G06.WMF G07.WMF G08.WMF G09.WMF G10.WMF

G11.WMF G12.WMF G13.WMF G14.WMF G15.WMF G16.WMF G17.WMF G18.WMF G19.WMF G20.WMF

G21.WMF G22.WMF G23.WMF G24.WMF G25.WMF G26.WMF G27.WMF G28.WMF G29.WMF H01.WMF

H02.WMF H03.WMF H04.WMF H05.WMF H06.WMF H07.WMF H08.WMF H09.WMF H10.WMF H11.WMF

H12.WMF H13.WMF H14.WMF H15.WMF H16.WMF H17.WMF H18.WMF H19.WMF H20.WMF H21.WMF

H22.WMF H23.WMF I01.WMF I02.WMF I03.WMF I04.WMF I05.WMF I06.WMF I07.WMF I08.WMF

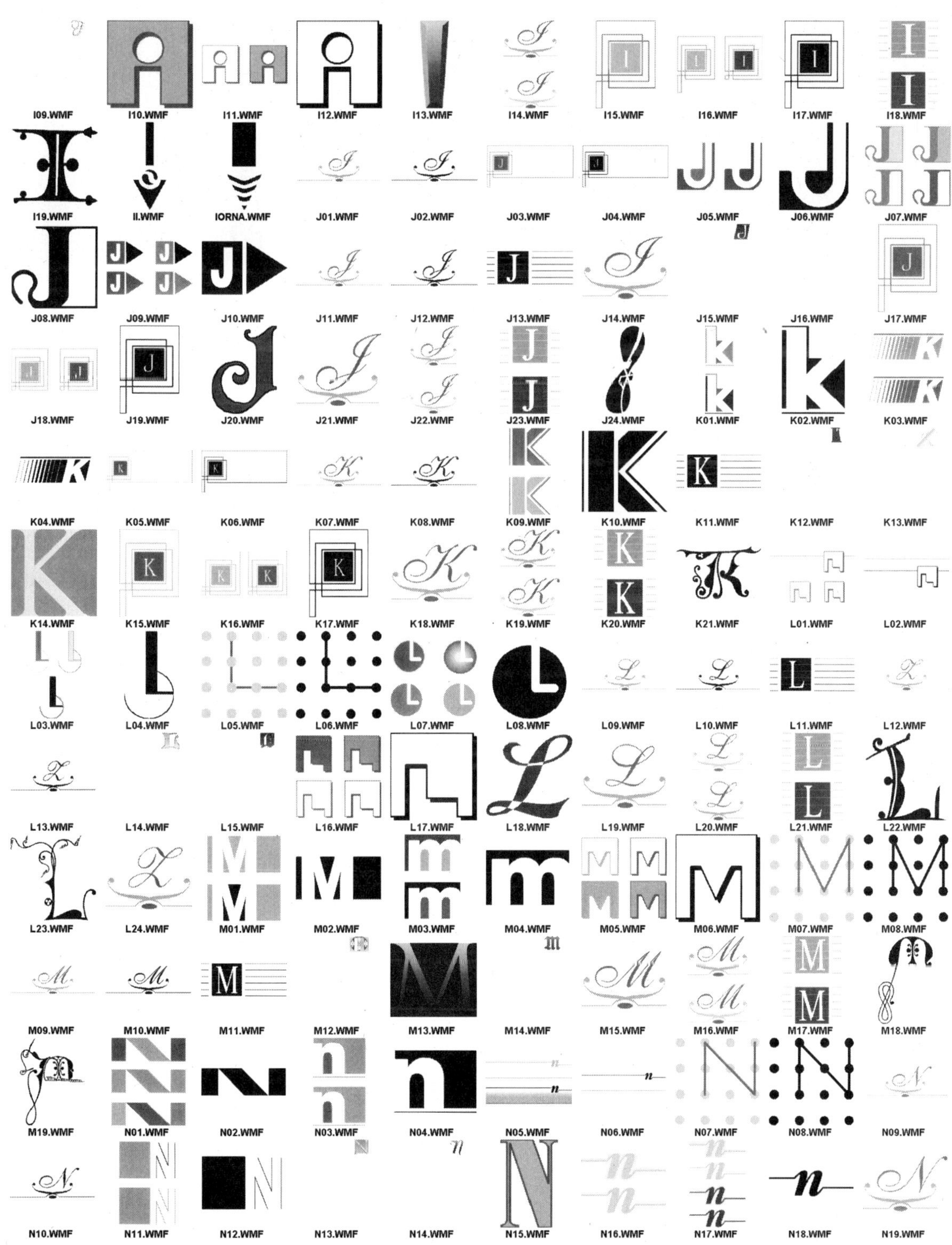
I09.WMF
I10.WMF
I11.WMF
I12.WMF
I13.WMF
I14.WMF
I15.WMF
I16.WMF
I17.WMF
I18.WMF
I19.WMF
II.WMF
IORNA.WMF
J01.WMF
J02.WMF
J03.WMF
J04.WMF
J05.WMF
J06.WMF
J07.WMF
J08.WMF
J09.WMF
J10.WMF
J11.WMF
J12.WMF
J13.WMF
J14.WMF
J15.WMF
J16.WMF
J17.WMF
J18.WMF
J19.WMF
J20.WMF
J21.WMF
J22.WMF
J23.WMF
J24.WMF
K01.WMF
K02.WMF
K03.WMF
K04.WMF
K05.WMF
K06.WMF
K07.WMF
K08.WMF
K09.WMF
K10.WMF
K11.WMF
K12.WMF
K13.WMF
K14.WMF
K15.WMF
K16.WMF
K17.WMF
K18.WMF
K19.WMF
K20.WMF
K21.WMF
L01.WMF
L02.WMF
L03.WMF
L04.WMF
L05.WMF
L06.WMF
L07.WMF
L08.WMF
L09.WMF
L10.WMF
L11.WMF
L12.WMF
L13.WMF
L14.WMF
L15.WMF
L16.WMF
L17.WMF
L18.WMF
L19.WMF
L20.WMF
L21.WMF
L22.WMF
L23.WMF
L24.WMF
M01.WMF
M02.WMF
M03.WMF
M04.WMF
M05.WMF
M06.WMF
M07.WMF
M08.WMF
M09.WMF
M10.WMF
M11.WMF
M12.WMF
M13.WMF
M14.WMF
M15.WMF
M16.WMF
M17.WMF
M18.WMF
M19.WMF
N01.WMF
N02.WMF
N03.WMF
N04.WMF
N05.WMF
N06.WMF
N07.WMF
N08.WMF
N09.WMF
N10.WMF
N11.WMF
N12.WMF
N13.WMF
N14.WMF
N15.WMF
N16.WMF
N17.WMF
N18.WMF
N19.WMF

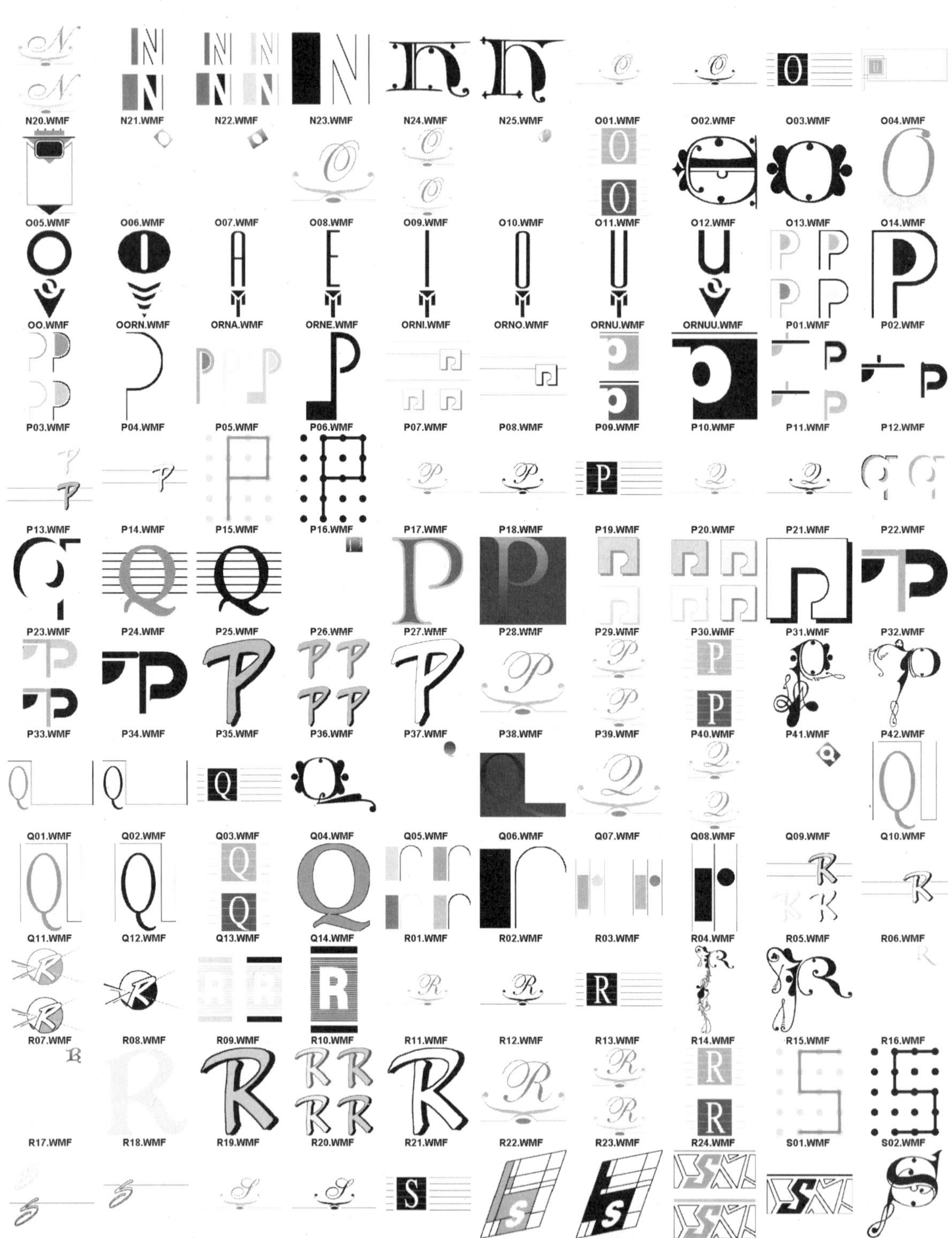
N20.WMF N21.WMF N22.WMF N23.WMF N24.WMF N25.WMF O01.WMF O02.WMF O03.WMF O04.WMF
O05.WMF O06.WMF O07.WMF O08.WMF O09.WMF O10.WMF O11.WMF O12.WMF O13.WMF O14.WMF
OO.WMF OORN.WMF ORNA.WMF ORNE.WMF ORNI.WMF ORNO.WMF ORNU.WMF ORNUU.WMF P01.WMF P02.WMF
P03.WMF P04.WMF P05.WMF P06.WMF P07.WMF P08.WMF P09.WMF P10.WMF P11.WMF P12.WMF
P13.WMF P14.WMF P15.WMF P16.WMF P17.WMF P18.WMF P19.WMF P20.WMF P21.WMF P22.WMF
P23.WMF P24.WMF P25.WMF P26.WMF P27.WMF P28.WMF P29.WMF P30.WMF P31.WMF P32.WMF
P33.WMF P34.WMF P35.WMF P36.WMF P37.WMF P38.WMF P39.WMF P40.WMF P41.WMF P42.WMF
Q01.WMF Q02.WMF Q03.WMF Q04.WMF Q05.WMF Q06.WMF Q07.WMF Q08.WMF Q09.WMF Q10.WMF
Q11.WMF Q12.WMF Q13.WMF Q14.WMF R01.WMF R02.WMF R03.WMF R04.WMF R05.WMF R06.WMF
R07.WMF R08.WMF R09.WMF R10.WMF R11.WMF R12.WMF R13.WMF R14.WMF R15.WMF R16.WMF
R17.WMF R18.WMF R19.WMF R20.WMF R21.WMF R22.WMF R23.WMF R24.WMF S01.WMF S02.WMF
S03.WMF S04.WMF S05.WMF S06.WMF S07.WMF S08.WMF S09.WMF S10.WMF S11.WMF S12.WMF

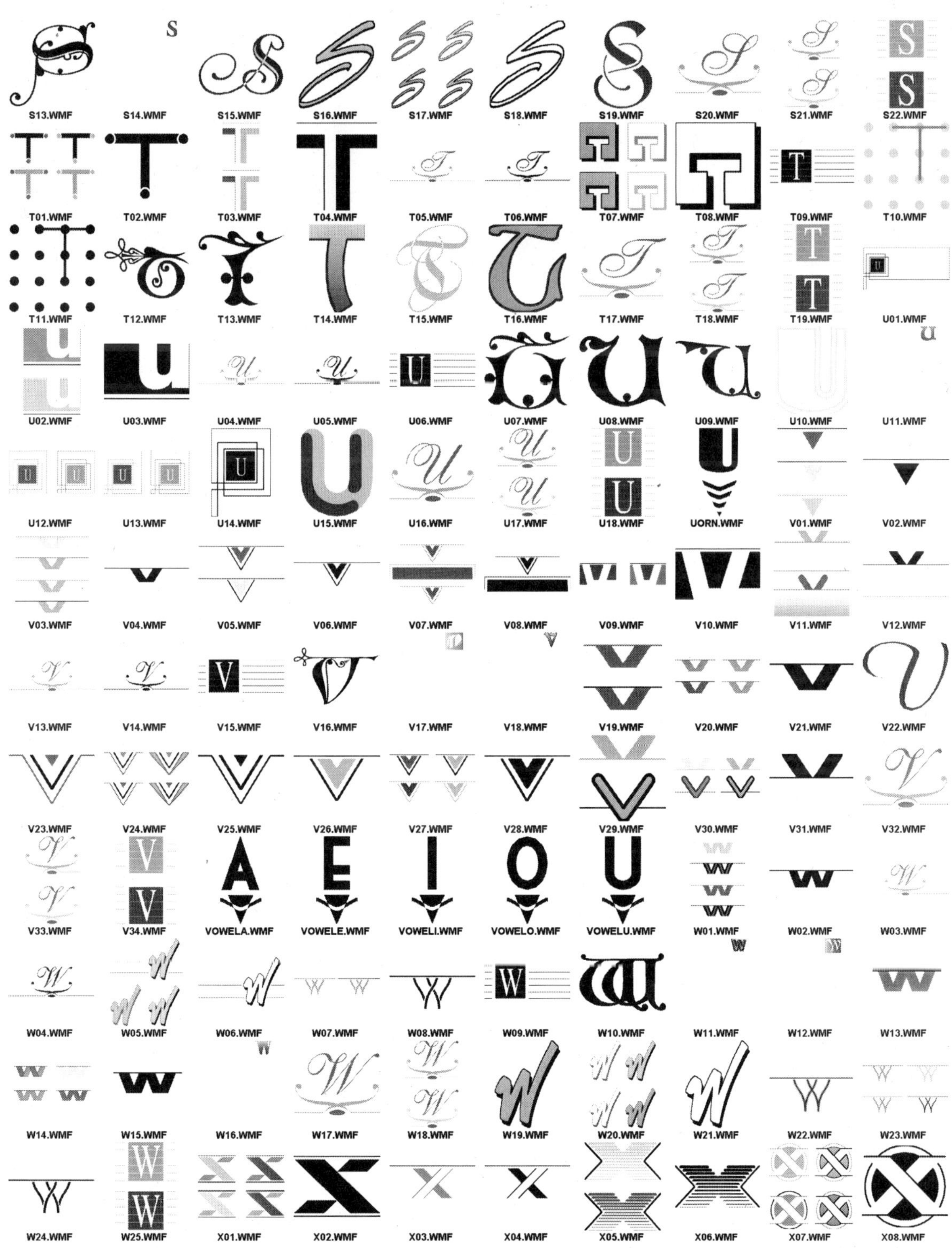
S13.WMF S14.WMF S15.WMF S16.WMF S17.WMF S18.WMF S19.WMF S20.WMF S21.WMF S22.WMF
T01.WMF T02.WMF T03.WMF T04.WMF T05.WMF T06.WMF T07.WMF T08.WMF T09.WMF T10.WMF
T11.WMF T12.WMF T13.WMF T14.WMF T15.WMF T16.WMF T17.WMF T18.WMF T19.WMF U01.WMF
U02.WMF U03.WMF U04.WMF U05.WMF U06.WMF U07.WMF U08.WMF U09.WMF U10.WMF U11.WMF
U12.WMF U13.WMF U14.WMF U15.WMF U16.WMF U17.WMF U18.WMF UORN.WMF V01.WMF V02.WMF
V03.WMF V04.WMF V05.WMF V06.WMF V07.WMF V08.WMF V09.WMF V10.WMF V11.WMF V12.WMF
V13.WMF V14.WMF V15.WMF V16.WMF V17.WMF V18.WMF V19.WMF V20.WMF V21.WMF V22.WMF
V23.WMF V24.WMF V25.WMF V26.WMF V27.WMF V28.WMF V29.WMF V30.WMF V31.WMF V32.WMF
V33.WMF V34.WMF VOWELA.WMF VOWELE.WMF VOWELI.WMF VOWELO.WMF VOWELU.WMF W01.WMF W02.WMF W03.WMF
W04.WMF W05.WMF W06.WMF W07.WMF W08.WMF W09.WMF W10.WMF W11.WMF W12.WMF W13.WMF
W14.WMF W15.WMF W16.WMF W17.WMF W18.WMF W19.WMF W20.WMF W21.WMF W22.WMF W23.WMF
W24.WMF W25.WMF X01.WMF X02.WMF X03.WMF X04.WMF X05.WMF X06.WMF X07.WMF X08.WMF

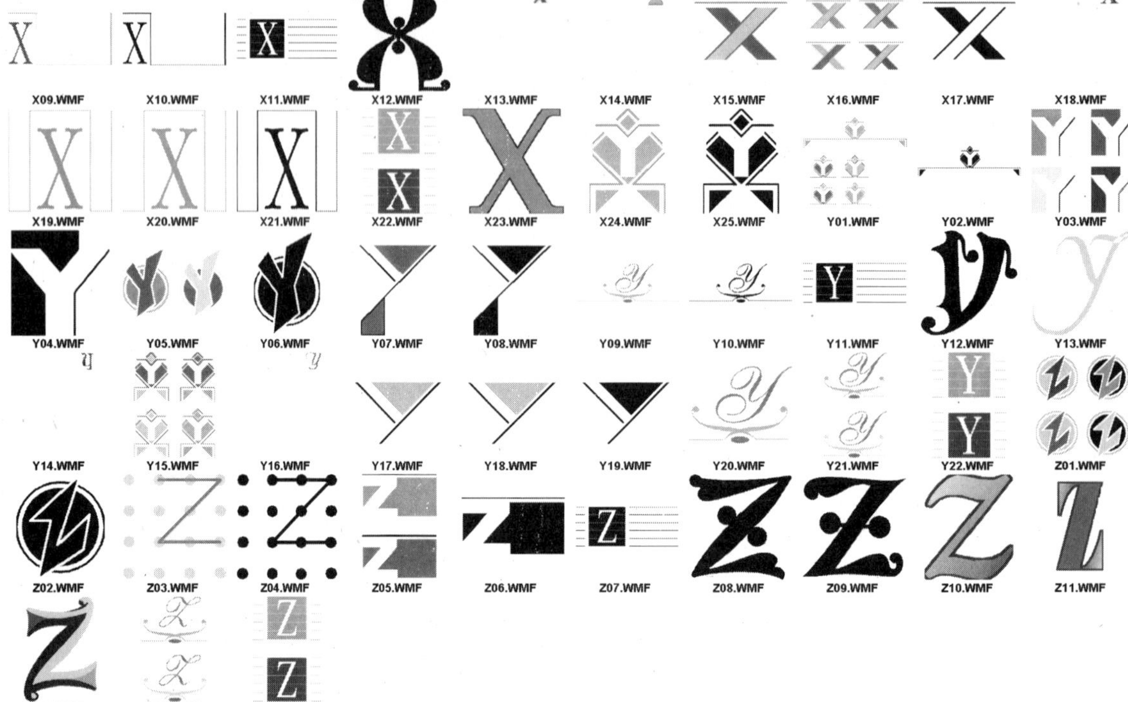
X09.WMF X10.WMF X11.WMF X12.WMF X13.WMF X14.WMF X15.WMF X16.WMF X17.WMF X18.WMF
X19.WMF X20.WMF X21.WMF X22.WMF X23.WMF X24.WMF X25.WMF Y01.WMF Y02.WMF Y03.WMF
Y04.WMF Y05.WMF Y06.WMF Y07.WMF Y08.WMF Y09.WMF Y10.WMF Y11.WMF Y12.WMF Y13.WMF
Y14.WMF Y15.WMF Y16.WMF Y17.WMF Y18.WMF Y19.WMF Y20.WMF Y21.WMF Y22.WMF Z01.WMF
Z02.WMF Z03.WMF Z04.WMF Z05.WMF Z06.WMF Z07.WMF Z08.WMF Z09.WMF Z10.WMF Z11.WMF
Z12.WMF Z13.WMF Z14.WMF

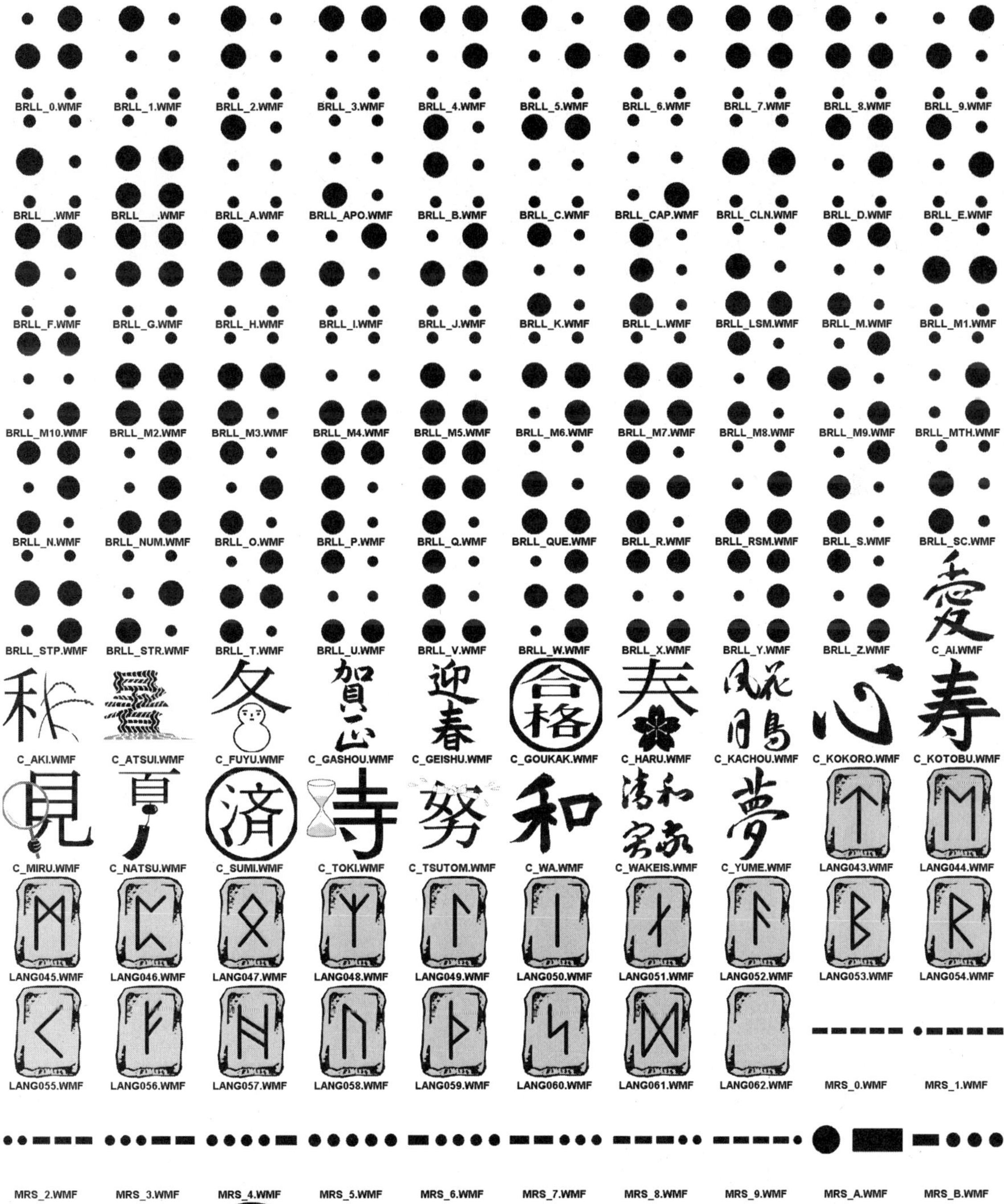

MRS_C.WMF MRS_D.WMF MRS_E.WMF MRS_F.WMF MRS_G.WMF MRS_H.WMF MRS_I.WMF MRS_J.WMF MRS_K.WMF MRS_L.WMF

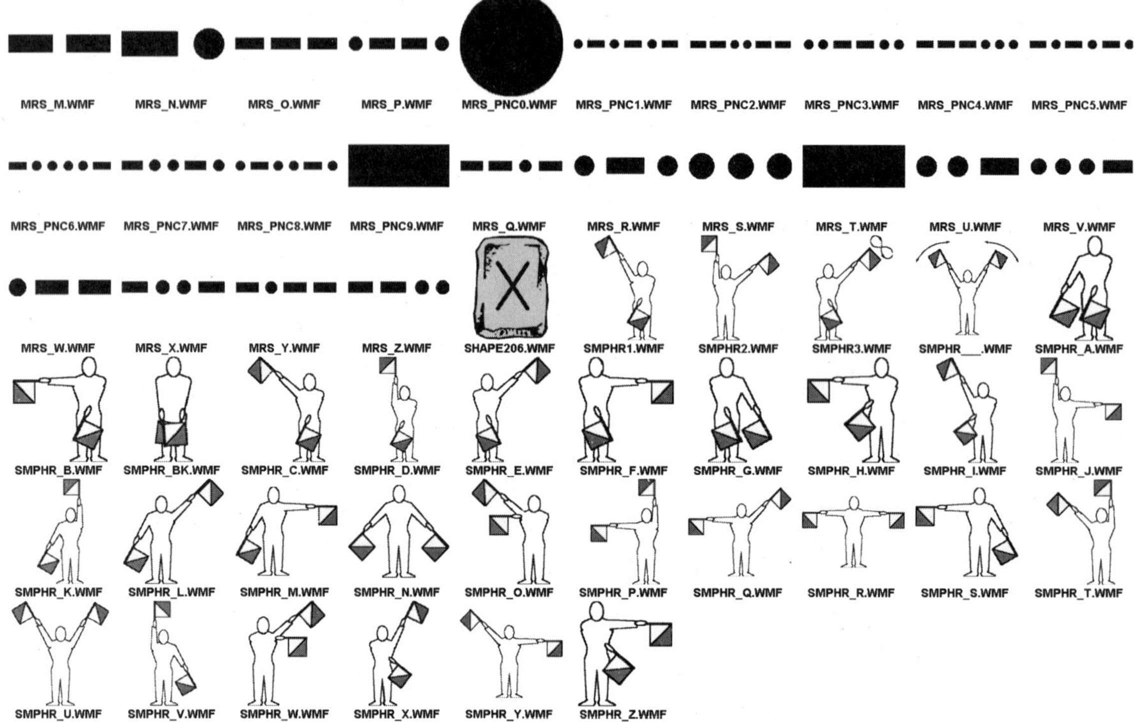

MRS_M.WMF
MRS_N.WMF
MRS_O.WMF
MRS_P.WMF
MRS_PNC0.WMF
MRS_PNC1.WMF
MRS_PNC2.WMF
MRS_PNC3.WMF
MRS_PNC4.WMF
MRS_PNC5.WMF
MRS_PNC6.WMF
MRS_PNC7.WMF
MRS_PNC8.WMF
MRS_PNC9.WMF
MRS_Q.WMF
MRS_R.WMF
MRS_S.WMF
MRS_T.WMF
MRS_U.WMF
MRS_V.WMF
MRS_W.WMF
MRS_X.WMF
MRS_Y.WMF
MRS_Z.WMF
SHAPE206.WMF
SMPHR1.WMF
SMPHR2.WMF
SMPHR3.WMF
SMPHR___.WMF
SMPHR_A.WMF
SMPHR_B.WMF
SMPHR_BK.WMF
SMPHR_C.WMF
SMPHR_D.WMF
SMPHR_E.WMF
SMPHR_F.WMF
SMPHR_G.WMF
SMPHR_H.WMF
SMPHR_I.WMF
SMPHR_J.WMF
SMPHR_K.WMF
SMPHR_L.WMF
SMPHR_M.WMF
SMPHR_N.WMF
SMPHR_O.WMF
SMPHR_P.WMF
SMPHR_Q.WMF
SMPHR_R.WMF
SMPHR_S.WMF
SMPHR_T.WMF
SMPHR_U.WMF
SMPHR_V.WMF
SMPHR_W.WMF
SMPHR_X.WMF
SMPHR_Y.WMF
SMPHR_Z.WMF

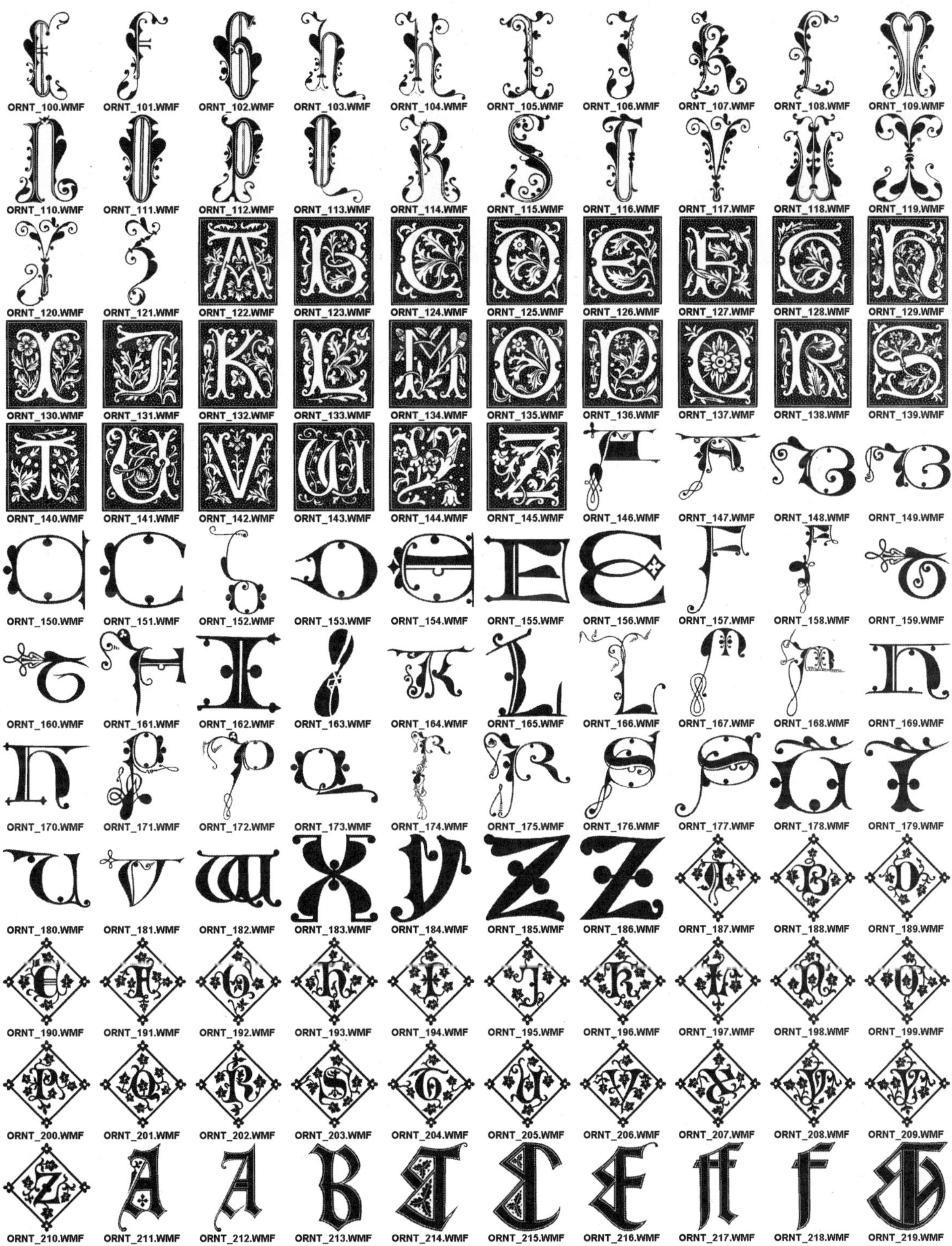
ORNT_100.WMF ORNT_101.WMF ORNT_102.WMF ORNT_103.WMF ORNT_104.WMF ORNT_105.WMF ORNT_106.WMF ORNT_107.WMF ORNT_108.WMF ORNT_109.WMF
ORNT_110.WMF ORNT_111.WMF ORNT_112.WMF ORNT_113.WMF ORNT_114.WMF ORNT_115.WMF ORNT_116.WMF ORNT_117.WMF ORNT_118.WMF ORNT_119.WMF
ORNT_120.WMF ORNT_121.WMF ORNT_122.WMF ORNT_123.WMF ORNT_124.WMF ORNT_125.WMF ORNT_126.WMF ORNT_127.WMF ORNT_128.WMF ORNT_129.WMF
ORNT_130.WMF ORNT_131.WMF ORNT_132.WMF ORNT_133.WMF ORNT_134.WMF ORNT_135.WMF ORNT_136.WMF ORNT_137.WMF ORNT_138.WMF ORNT_139.WMF
ORNT_140.WMF ORNT_141.WMF ORNT_142.WMF ORNT_143.WMF ORNT_144.WMF ORNT_145.WMF ORNT_146.WMF ORNT_147.WMF ORNT_148.WMF ORNT_149.WMF
ORNT_150.WMF ORNT_151.WMF ORNT_152.WMF ORNT_153.WMF ORNT_154.WMF ORNT_155.WMF ORNT_156.WMF ORNT_157.WMF ORNT_158.WMF ORNT_159.WMF
ORNT_160.WMF ORNT_161.WMF ORNT_162.WMF ORNT_163.WMF ORNT_164.WMF ORNT_165.WMF ORNT_166.WMF ORNT_167.WMF ORNT_168.WMF ORNT_169.WMF
ORNT_170.WMF ORNT_171.WMF ORNT_172.WMF ORNT_173.WMF ORNT_174.WMF ORNT_175.WMF ORNT_176.WMF ORNT_177.WMF ORNT_178.WMF ORNT_179.WMF
ORNT_180.WMF ORNT_181.WMF ORNT_182.WMF ORNT_183.WMF ORNT_184.WMF ORNT_185.WMF ORNT_186.WMF ORNT_187.WMF ORNT_188.WMF ORNT_189.WMF
ORNT_190.WMF ORNT_191.WMF ORNT_192.WMF ORNT_193.WMF ORNT_194.WMF ORNT_195.WMF ORNT_196.WMF ORNT_197.WMF ORNT_198.WMF ORNT_199.WMF
ORNT_200.WMF ORNT_201.WMF ORNT_202.WMF ORNT_203.WMF ORNT_204.WMF ORNT_205.WMF ORNT_206.WMF ORNT_207.WMF ORNT_208.WMF ORNT_209.WMF
ORNT_210.WMF ORNT_211.WMF ORNT_212.WMF ORNT_213.WMF ORNT_214.WMF ORNT_215.WMF ORNT_216.WMF ORNT_217.WMF ORNT_218.WMF ORNT_219.WMF

ORNT_220.WMF
ORNT_221.WMF
ORNT_222.WMF
ORNT_223.WMF
ORNT_224.WMF
ORNT_225.WMF
ORNT_226.WMF
ORNT_227.WMF
ORNT_228.WMF
ORNT_229.WMF
ORNT_230.WMF
ORNT_231.WMF
ORNT_232.WMF
ORNT_233.WMF
ORNT_234.WMF
ORNT_235.WMF
ORNT_236.WMF
ORNT_237.WMF
ORNT_238.WMF
ORNT_239.WMF
ORNT_240.WMF
ORNT_241.WMF
ORNT_242.WMF
ORNT_243.WMF
ORNT_244.WMF
ORNT_245.WMF
ORNT_246.WMF
ORNT_247.WMF
ORNT_248.WMF
ORNT_249.WMF
ORNT_250.WMF
ORNT_251.WMF
ORNT_252.WMF
ORNT_253.WMF
ORNT_254.WMF
ORNT_255.WMF
ORNT_256.WMF
ORNT_257.WMF
ORNT_258.WMF
ORNT_259.WMF
ORNT_260.WMF
ORNT_261.WMF
ORNT_262.WMF
ORNT_263.WMF
ORNT_264.WMF
ORNT_265.WMF
ORNT_266.WMF
ORNT_267.WMF
ORNT_268.WMF
ORNT_269.WMF
ORNT_270.WMF
ORNT_271.WMF
ORNT_272.WMF
ORNT_273.WMF
ORNT_274.WMF
ORNT_275.WMF
ORNT_276.WMF
ORNT_277.WMF
ORNT_278.WMF
ORNT_279.WMF
ORNT_280.WMF
ORNT_281.WMF
ORNT_282.WMF
ORNT_283.WMF
ORNT_284.WMF
ORNT_285.WMF
ORNT_286.WMF
ORNT_287.WMF
ORNT_288.WMF
ORNT_289.WMF
ORNT_290.WMF
ORNT_291.WMF
ORNT_292.WMF
ORNT_293.WMF
ORNT_294.WMF
ORNT_295.WMF
ORNT_296.WMF
ORNT_297.WMF
ORNT_298.WMF
ORNT_299.WMF
ORNT_300.WMF
ORNT_301.WMF
ORNT_302.WMF
ORNT_303.WMF
ORNT_304.WMF
ORNT_305.WMF
ORNT_306.WMF
ORNT_307.WMF
ORNT_308.WMF
ORNT_309.WMF
ORNT_310.WMF
ORNT_311.WMF
ORNT_312.WMF
ORNT_313.WMF
ORNT_314.WMF
ORNT_315.WMF
ORNT_316.WMF
ORNT_317.WMF
ORNT_318.WMF
ORNT_319.WMF
ORNT_320.WMF
ORNT_321.WMF
ORNT_322.WMF
ORNT_323.WMF
ORNT_324.WMF
ORNT_325.WMF
ORNT_326.WMF
ORNT_327.WMF
ORNT_328.WMF
ORNT_329.WMF
ORNT_330.WMF
ORNT_331.WMF
ORNT_332.WMF
ORNT_333.WMF
ORNT_334.WMF
ORNT_335.WMF
ORNT_336.WMF
ORNT_337.WMF
ORNT_338.WMF
ORNT_339.WMF

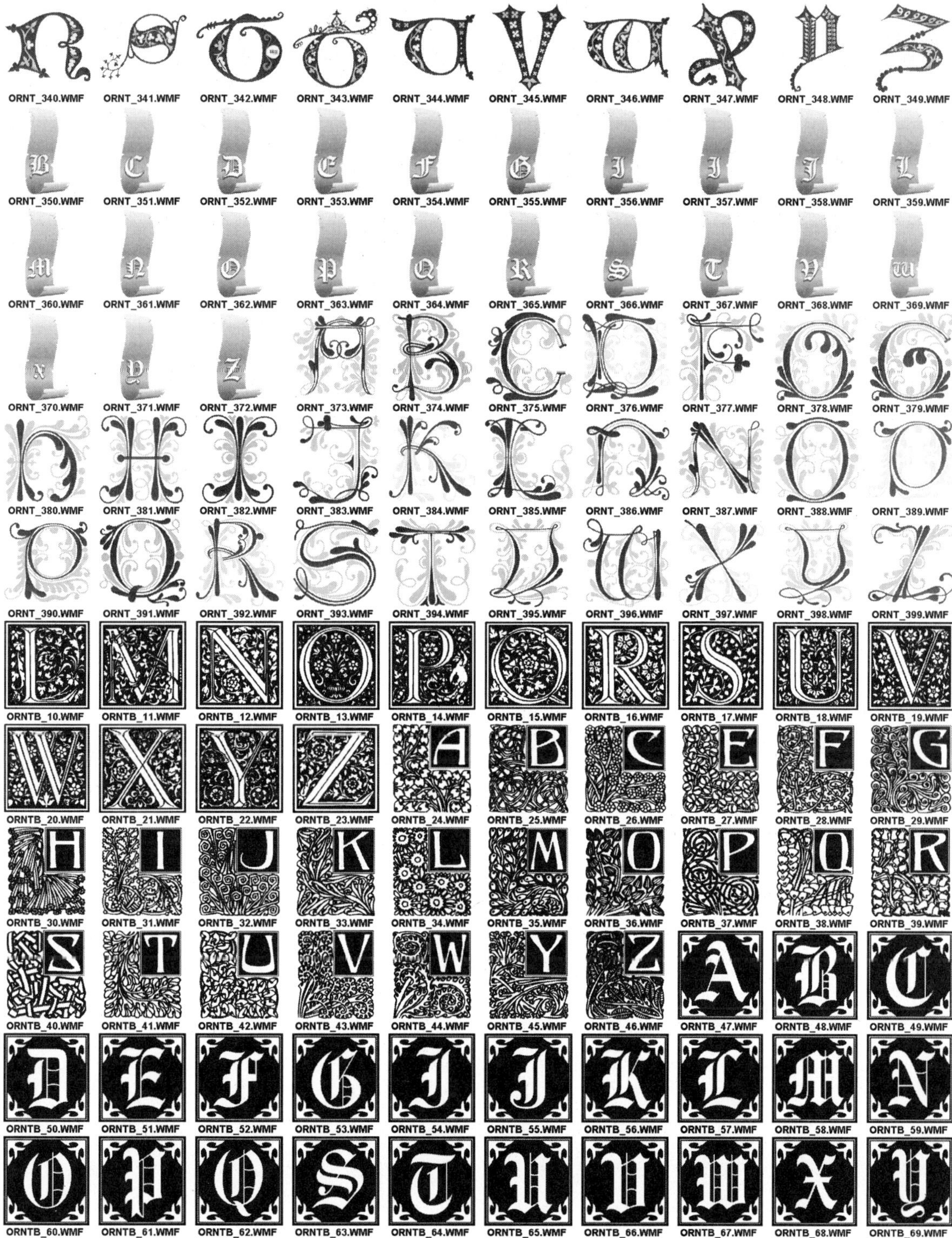

ORNT_340.WMF ORNT_341.WMF ORNT_342.WMF ORNT_343.WMF ORNT_344.WMF ORNT_345.WMF ORNT_346.WMF ORNT_347.WMF ORNT_348.WMF ORNT_349.WMF
ORNT_350.WMF ORNT_351.WMF ORNT_352.WMF ORNT_353.WMF ORNT_354.WMF ORNT_355.WMF ORNT_356.WMF ORNT_357.WMF ORNT_358.WMF ORNT_359.WMF
ORNT_360.WMF ORNT_361.WMF ORNT_362.WMF ORNT_363.WMF ORNT_364.WMF ORNT_365.WMF ORNT_366.WMF ORNT_367.WMF ORNT_368.WMF ORNT_369.WMF
ORNT_370.WMF ORNT_371.WMF ORNT_372.WMF ORNT_373.WMF ORNT_374.WMF ORNT_375.WMF ORNT_376.WMF ORNT_377.WMF ORNT_378.WMF ORNT_379.WMF
ORNT_380.WMF ORNT_381.WMF ORNT_382.WMF ORNT_383.WMF ORNT_384.WMF ORNT_385.WMF ORNT_386.WMF ORNT_387.WMF ORNT_388.WMF ORNT_389.WMF
ORNT_390.WMF ORNT_391.WMF ORNT_392.WMF ORNT_393.WMF ORNT_394.WMF ORNT_395.WMF ORNT_396.WMF ORNT_397.WMF ORNT_398.WMF ORNT_399.WMF
ORNTB_10.WMF ORNTB_11.WMF ORNTB_12.WMF ORNTB_13.WMF ORNTB_14.WMF ORNTB_15.WMF ORNTB_16.WMF ORNTB_17.WMF ORNTB_18.WMF ORNTB_19.WMF
ORNTB_20.WMF ORNTB_21.WMF ORNTB_22.WMF ORNTB_23.WMF ORNTB_24.WMF ORNTB_25.WMF ORNTB_26.WMF ORNTB_27.WMF ORNTB_28.WMF ORNTB_29.WMF
ORNTB_30.WMF ORNTB_31.WMF ORNTB_32.WMF ORNTB_33.WMF ORNTB_34.WMF ORNTB_35.WMF ORNTB_36.WMF ORNTB_37.WMF ORNTB_38.WMF ORNTB_39.WMF
ORNTB_40.WMF ORNTB_41.WMF ORNTB_42.WMF ORNTB_43.WMF ORNTB_44.WMF ORNTB_45.WMF ORNTB_46.WMF ORNTB_47.WMF ORNTB_48.WMF ORNTB_49.WMF
ORNTB_50.WMF ORNTB_51.WMF ORNTB_52.WMF ORNTB_53.WMF ORNTB_54.WMF ORNTB_55.WMF ORNTB_56.WMF ORNTB_57.WMF ORNTB_58.WMF ORNTB_59.WMF
ORNTB_60.WMF ORNTB_61.WMF ORNTB_62.WMF ORNTB_63.WMF ORNTB_64.WMF ORNTB_65.WMF ORNTB_66.WMF ORNTB_67.WMF ORNTB_68.WMF ORNTB_69.WMF

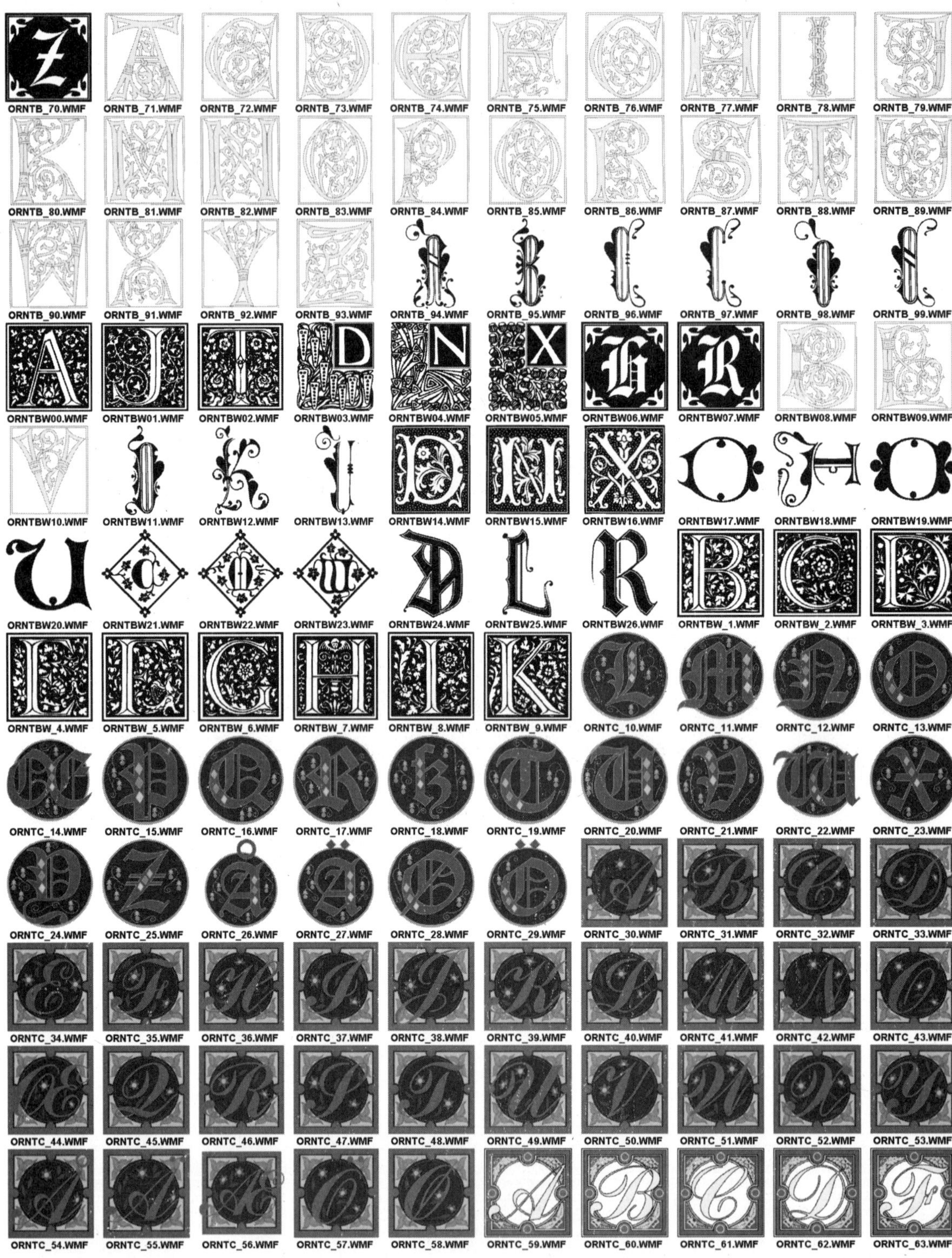
ORNTB_70.WMF ORNTB_71.WMF ORNTB_72.WMF ORNTB_73.WMF ORNTB_74.WMF ORNTB_75.WMF ORNTB_76.WMF ORNTB_77.WMF ORNTB_78.WMF ORNTB_79.WMF
ORNTB_80.WMF ORNTB_81.WMF ORNTB_82.WMF ORNTB_83.WMF ORNTB_84.WMF ORNTB_85.WMF ORNTB_86.WMF ORNTB_87.WMF ORNTB_88.WMF ORNTB_89.WMF
ORNTB_90.WMF ORNTB_91.WMF ORNTB_92.WMF ORNTB_93.WMF ORNTB_94.WMF ORNTB_95.WMF ORNTB_96.WMF ORNTB_97.WMF ORNTB_98.WMF ORNTB_99.WMF
ORNTBW00.WMF ORNTBW01.WMF ORNTBW02.WMF ORNTBW03.WMF ORNTBW04.WMF ORNTBW05.WMF ORNTBW06.WMF ORNTBW07.WMF ORNTBW08.WMF ORNTBW09.WMF
ORNTBW10.WMF ORNTBW11.WMF ORNTBW12.WMF ORNTBW13.WMF ORNTBW14.WMF ORNTBW15.WMF ORNTBW16.WMF ORNTBW17.WMF ORNTBW18.WMF ORNTBW19.WMF
ORNTBW20.WMF ORNTBW21.WMF ORNTBW22.WMF ORNTBW23.WMF ORNTBW24.WMF ORNTBW25.WMF ORNTBW26.WMF ORNTBW_1.WMF ORNTBW_2.WMF ORNTBW_3.WMF
ORNTBW_4.WMF ORNTBW_5.WMF ORNTBW_6.WMF ORNTBW_7.WMF ORNTBW_8.WMF ORNTBW_9.WMF ORNTC_10.WMF ORNTC_11.WMF ORNTC_12.WMF ORNTC_13.WMF
ORNTC_14.WMF ORNTC_15.WMF ORNTC_16.WMF ORNTC_17.WMF ORNTC_18.WMF ORNTC_19.WMF ORNTC_20.WMF ORNTC_21.WMF ORNTC_22.WMF ORNTC_23.WMF
ORNTC_24.WMF ORNTC_25.WMF ORNTC_26.WMF ORNTC_27.WMF ORNTC_28.WMF ORNTC_29.WMF ORNTC_30.WMF ORNTC_31.WMF ORNTC_32.WMF ORNTC_33.WMF
ORNTC_34.WMF ORNTC_35.WMF ORNTC_36.WMF ORNTC_37.WMF ORNTC_38.WMF ORNTC_39.WMF ORNTC_40.WMF ORNTC_41.WMF ORNTC_42.WMF ORNTC_43.WMF
ORNTC_44.WMF ORNTC_45.WMF ORNTC_46.WMF ORNTC_47.WMF ORNTC_48.WMF ORNTC_49.WMF ORNTC_50.WMF ORNTC_51.WMF ORNTC_52.WMF ORNTC_53.WMF
ORNTC_54.WMF ORNTC_55.WMF ORNTC_56.WMF ORNTC_57.WMF ORNTC_58.WMF ORNTC_59.WMF ORNTC_60.WMF ORNTC_61.WMF ORNTC_62.WMF ORNTC_63.WMF

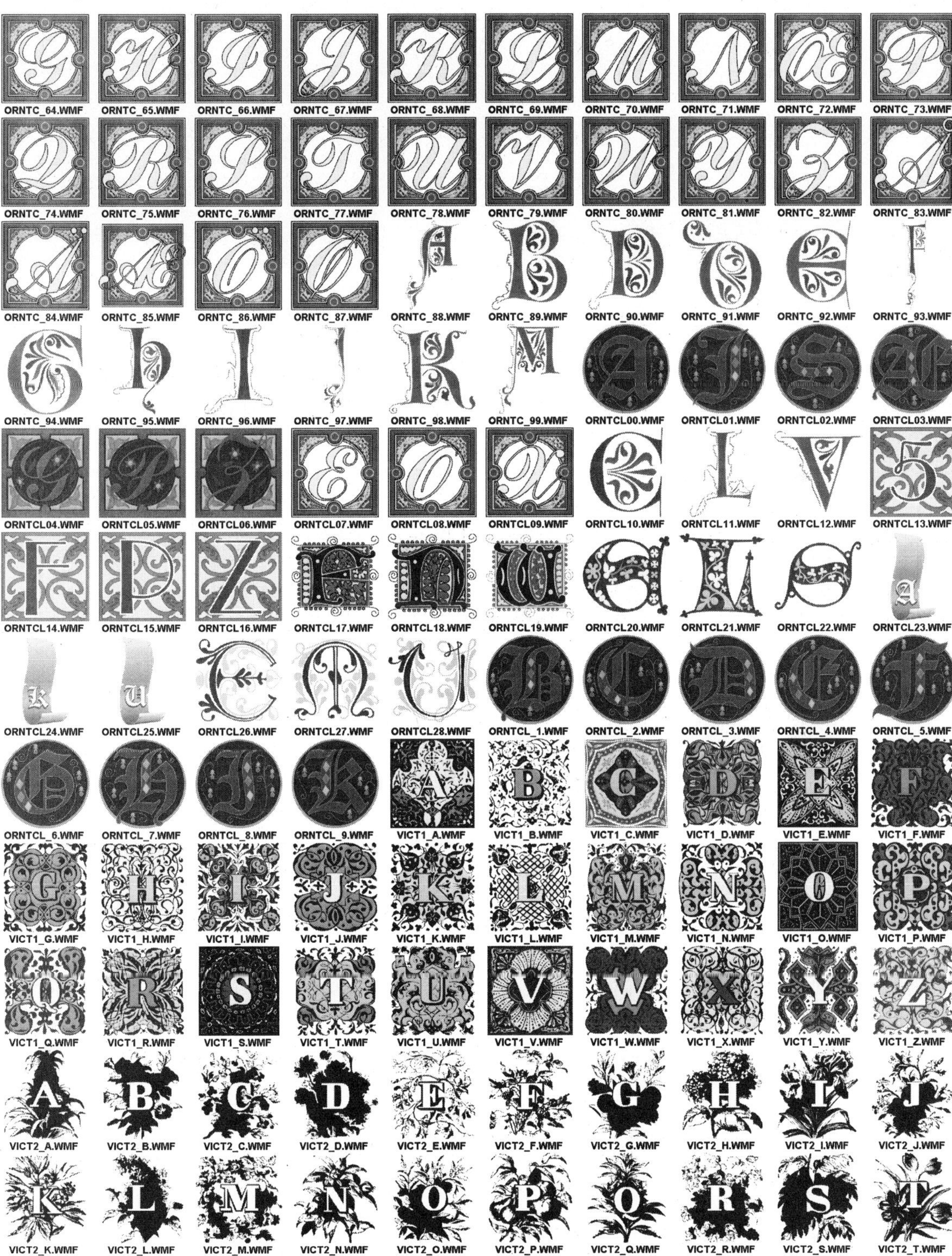
ORNTC_64.WMF
ORNTC_65.WMF
ORNTC_66.WMF
ORNTC_67.WMF
ORNTC_68.WMF
ORNTC_69.WMF
ORNTC_70.WMF
ORNTC_71.WMF
ORNTC_72.WMF
ORNTC_73.WMF
ORNTC_74.WMF
ORNTC_75.WMF
ORNTC_76.WMF
ORNTC_77.WMF
ORNTC_78.WMF
ORNTC_79.WMF
ORNTC_80.WMF
ORNTC_81.WMF
ORNTC_82.WMF
ORNTC_83.WMF
ORNTC_84.WMF
ORNTC_85.WMF
ORNTC_86.WMF
ORNTC_87.WMF
ORNTC_88.WMF
ORNTC_89.WMF
ORNTC_90.WMF
ORNTC_91.WMF
ORNTC_92.WMF
ORNTC_93.WMF
ORNTC_94.WMF
ORNTC_95.WMF
ORNTC_96.WMF
ORNTC_97.WMF
ORNTC_98.WMF
ORNTC_99.WMF
ORNTCL00.WMF
ORNTCL01.WMF
ORNTCL02.WMF
ORNTCL03.WMF
ORNTCL04.WMF
ORNTCL05.WMF
ORNTCL06.WMF
ORNTCL07.WMF
ORNTCL08.WMF
ORNTCL09.WMF
ORNTCL10.WMF
ORNTCL11.WMF
ORNTCL12.WMF
ORNTCL13.WMF
ORNTCL14.WMF
ORNTCL15.WMF
ORNTCL16.WMF
ORNTCL17.WMF
ORNTCL18.WMF
ORNTCL19.WMF
ORNTCL20.WMF
ORNTCL21.WMF
ORNTCL22.WMF
ORNTCL23.WMF
ORNTCL24.WMF
ORNTCL25.WMF
ORNTCL26.WMF
ORNTCL27.WMF
ORNTCL28.WMF
ORNTCL_1.WMF
ORNTCL_2.WMF
ORNTCL_3.WMF
ORNTCL_4.WMF
ORNTCL_5.WMF
ORNTCL_6.WMF
ORNTCL_7.WMF
ORNTCL_8.WMF
ORNTCL_9.WMF
VICT1_A.WMF
VICT1_B.WMF
VICT1_C.WMF
VICT1_D.WMF
VICT1_E.WMF
VICT1_F.WMF
VICT1_G.WMF
VICT1_H.WMF
VICT1_I.WMF
VICT1_J.WMF
VICT1_K.WMF
VICT1_L.WMF
VICT1_M.WMF
VICT1_N.WMF
VICT1_O.WMF
VICT1_P.WMF
VICT1_Q.WMF
VICT1_R.WMF
VICT1_S.WMF
VICT1_T.WMF
VICT1_U.WMF
VICT1_V.WMF
VICT1_W.WMF
VICT1_X.WMF
VICT1_Y.WMF
VICT1_Z.WMF
VICT2_A.WMF
VICT2_B.WMF
VICT2_C.WMF
VICT2_D.WMF
VICT2_E.WMF
VICT2_F.WMF
VICT2_G.WMF
VICT2_H.WMF
VICT2_I.WMF
VICT2_J.WMF
VICT2_K.WMF
VICT2_L.WMF
VICT2_M.WMF
VICT2_N.WMF
VICT2_O.WMF
VICT2_P.WMF
VICT2_Q.WMF
VICT2_R.WMF
VICT2_S.WMF
VICT2_T.WMF

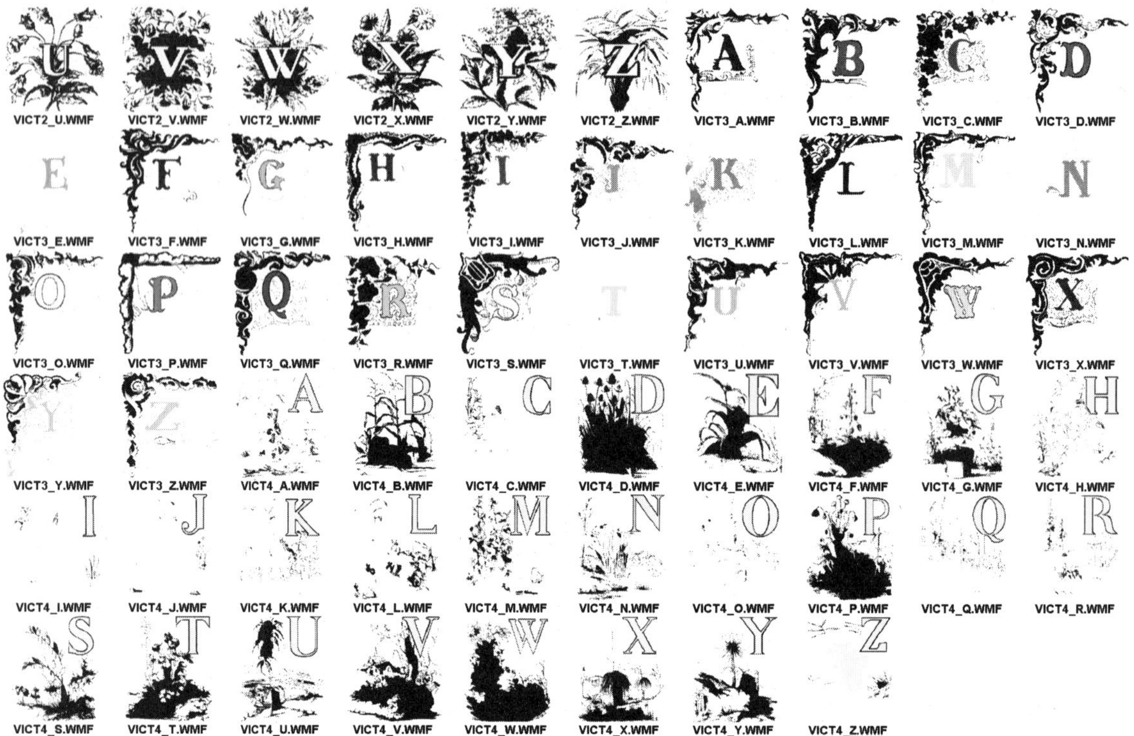
VICT2_U.WMF
VICT2_V.WMF
VICT2_W.WMF
VICT2_X.WMF
VICT2_Y.WMF
VICT2_Z.WMF
VICT3_A.WMF
VICT3_B.WMF
VICT3_C.WMF
VICT3_D.WMF
VICT3_E.WMF
VICT3_F.WMF
VICT3_G.WMF
VICT3_H.WMF
VICT3_I.WMF
VICT3_J.WMF
VICT3_K.WMF
VICT3_L.WMF
VICT3_M.WMF
VICT3_N.WMF
VICT3_O.WMF
VICT3_P.WMF
VICT3_Q.WMF
VICT3_R.WMF
VICT3_S.WMF
VICT3_T.WMF
VICT3_U.WMF
VICT3_V.WMF
VICT3_W.WMF
VICT3_X.WMF
VICT3_Y.WMF
VICT3_Z.WMF
VICT4_A.WMF
VICT4_B.WMF
VICT4_C.WMF
VICT4_D.WMF
VICT4_E.WMF
VICT4_F.WMF
VICT4_G.WMF
VICT4_H.WMF
VICT4_I.WMF
VICT4_J.WMF
VICT4_K.WMF
VICT4_L.WMF
VICT4_M.WMF
VICT4_N.WMF
VICT4_O.WMF
VICT4_P.WMF
VICT4_Q.WMF
VICT4_R.WMF
VICT4_S.WMF
VICT4_T.WMF
VICT4_U.WMF
VICT4_V.WMF
VICT4_W.WMF
VICT4_X.WMF
VICT4_Y.WMF
VICT4_Z.WMF

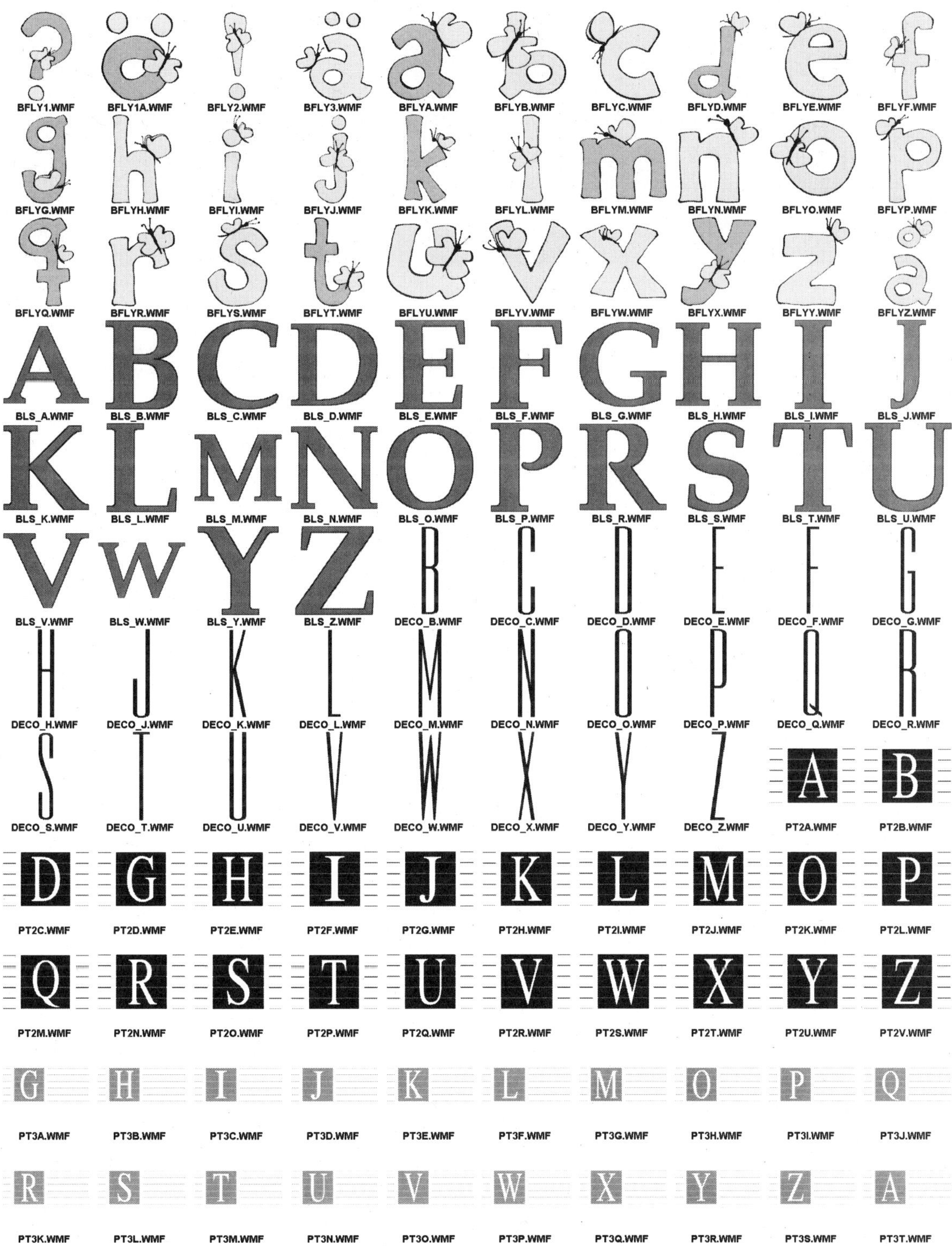
BFLY1.WMF BFLY1A.WMF BFLY2.WMF BFLY3.WMF BFLYA.WMF BFLYB.WMF BFLYC.WMF BFLYD.WMF BFLYE.WMF BFLYF.WMF
BFLYG.WMF BFLYH.WMF BFLYI.WMF BFLYJ.WMF BFLYK.WMF BFLYL.WMF BFLYM.WMF BFLYN.WMF BFLYO.WMF BFLYP.WMF
BFLYQ.WMF BFLYR.WMF BFLYS.WMF BFLYT.WMF BFLYU.WMF BFLYV.WMF BFLYW.WMF BFLYX.WMF BFLYY.WMF BFLYZ.WMF
BLS_A.WMF BLS_B.WMF BLS_C.WMF BLS_D.WMF BLS_E.WMF BLS_F.WMF BLS_G.WMF BLS_H.WMF BLS_I.WMF BLS_J.WMF
BLS_K.WMF BLS_L.WMF BLS_M.WMF BLS_N.WMF BLS_O.WMF BLS_P.WMF BLS_R.WMF BLS_S.WMF BLS_T.WMF BLS_U.WMF
BLS_V.WMF BLS_W.WMF BLS_Y.WMF BLS_Z.WMF DECO_B.WMF DECO_C.WMF DECO_D.WMF DECO_E.WMF DECO_F.WMF DECO_G.WMF
DECO_H.WMF DECO_J.WMF DECO_K.WMF DECO_L.WMF DECO_M.WMF DECO_N.WMF DECO_O.WMF DECO_P.WMF DECO_Q.WMF DECO_R.WMF
DECO_S.WMF DECO_T.WMF DECO_U.WMF DECO_V.WMF DECO_W.WMF DECO_X.WMF DECO_Y.WMF DECO_Z.WMF PT2A.WMF PT2B.WMF
PT2C.WMF PT2D.WMF PT2E.WMF PT2F.WMF PT2G.WMF PT2H.WMF PT2I.WMF PT2J.WMF PT2K.WMF PT2L.WMF
PT2M.WMF PT2N.WMF PT2O.WMF PT2P.WMF PT2Q.WMF PT2R.WMF PT2S.WMF PT2T.WMF PT2U.WMF PT2V.WMF
PT3A.WMF PT3B.WMF PT3C.WMF PT3D.WMF PT3E.WMF PT3F.WMF PT3G.WMF PT3H.WMF PT3I.WMF PT3J.WMF
PT3K.WMF PT3L.WMF PT3M.WMF PT3N.WMF PT3O.WMF PT3P.WMF PT3Q.WMF PT3R.WMF PT3S.WMF PT3T.WMF

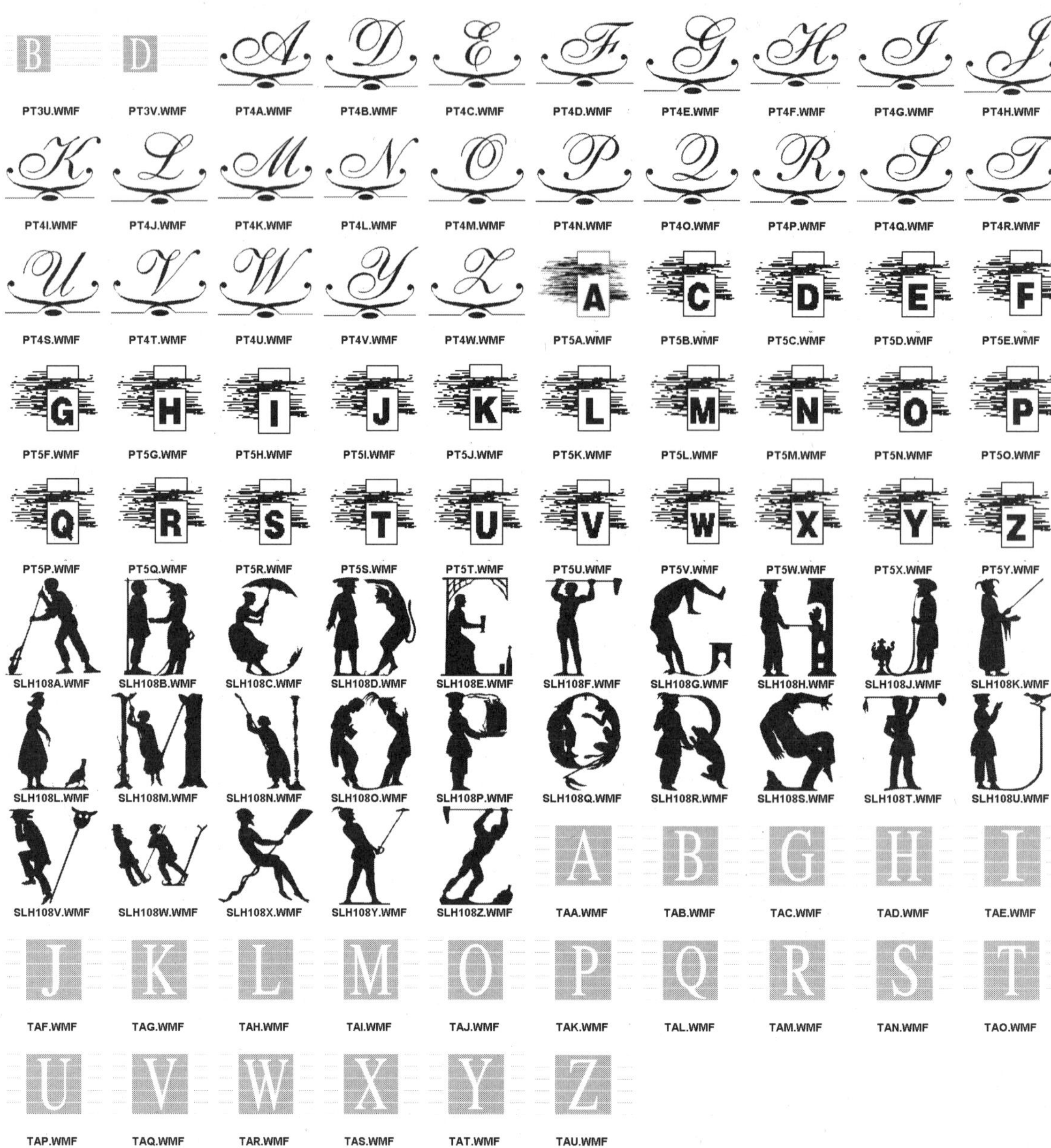
PT3U.WMF PT3V.WMF PT4A.WMF PT4B.WMF PT4C.WMF PT4D.WMF PT4E.WMF PT4F.WMF PT4G.WMF PT4H.WMF
PT4I.WMF PT4J.WMF PT4K.WMF PT4L.WMF PT4M.WMF PT4N.WMF PT4O.WMF PT4P.WMF PT4Q.WMF PT4R.WMF
PT4S.WMF PT4T.WMF PT4U.WMF PT4V.WMF PT4W.WMF PT5A.WMF PT5B.WMF PT5C.WMF PT5D.WMF PT5E.WMF
PT5F.WMF PT5G.WMF PT5H.WMF PT5I.WMF PT5J.WMF PT5K.WMF PT5L.WMF PT5M.WMF PT5N.WMF PT5O.WMF
PT5P.WMF PT5Q.WMF PT5R.WMF PT5S.WMF PT5T.WMF PT5U.WMF PT5V.WMF PT5W.WMF PT5X.WMF PT5Y.WMF
SLH108A.WMF SLH108B.WMF SLH108C.WMF SLH108D.WMF SLH108E.WMF SLH108F.WMF SLH108G.WMF SLH108H.WMF SLH108J.WMF SLH108K.WMF
SLH108L.WMF SLH108M.WMF SLH108N.WMF SLH108O.WMF SLH108P.WMF SLH108Q.WMF SLH108R.WMF SLH108S.WMF SLH108T.WMF SLH108U.WMF
SLH108V.WMF SLH108W.WMF SLH108X.WMF SLH108Y.WMF SLH108Z.WMF TAA.WMF TAB.WMF TAC.WMF TAD.WMF TAE.WMF
TAF.WMF TAG.WMF TAH.WMF TAI.WMF TAJ.WMF TAK.WMF TAL.WMF TAM.WMF TAN.WMF TAO.WMF
TAP.WMF TAQ.WMF TAR.WMF TAS.WMF TAT.WMF TAU.WMF

3208.WMF
3209.WMF
3210.WMF
3211.WMF
3212.WMF
3213.WMF
3214.WMF
3215.WMF
3216.WMF
3217.WMF
3218.WMF
3219.WMF
3220.WMF
3221.WMF
3222.WMF
3223.WMF
3224.WMF
3225.WMF
3226.WMF
3227.WMF
3228.WMF
3229.WMF
3230.WMF
3231.WMF
3232.WMF
3233.WMF
3234.WMF
3235.WMF
3236.WMF
DECOA.WMF
DECOB.WMF
DECOC.WMF
DECOD.WMF
DECOE.WMF
DECOF.WMF
DECOG.WMF
DECOH.WMF
DECOI.WMF
DECOJ.WMF
DECOK.WMF
DECOL.WMF
DECOM.WMF
DECON.WMF
DECOO.WMF
DECOP.WMF
DECOQ.WMF
DECOR.WMF
DECOS.WMF
DECOT.WMF
DECOU.WMF
DECOV.WMF
DECOW.WMF
DECOX.WMF
DECOY.WMF
DECOZ.WMF
WAA1.WMF
WAA2.WMF
WAB.WMF
WAC1.WMF
WAC2.WMF
WAD.WMF
WAE.WMF
WAF1.WMF
WAF2.WMF
WAG1.WMF
WAG2.WMF
WAH.WMF
WAI.WMF
WAJ.WMF
WAK.WMF
WAL.WMF
WAM1.WMF
WAM2.WMF
WAM3.WMF
WAN.WMF
WAO1.WMF
WAO2.WMF
WAP.WMF
WAQ1.WMF
WAQ2.WMF
WAR.WMF
WAS.WMF
WAT1.WMF
WAT2.WMF
WAU.WMF
WAV.WMF
WAW.WMF
WAX.WMF
WAY.WMF
WAZ.WMF
ZONT1.WMF
ZONT1_0.WMF
ZONT1_1.WMF
ZONT1_2.WMF
ZONT1_3.WMF
ZONT1_4.WMF
ZONT1_5.WMF
ZONT1_6.WMF
ZONT1_7.WMF
ZONT1_8.WMF
ZONT1_9.WMF
ZONT1A.WMF
ZONT1B.WMF
ZONT1C.WMF
ZONT1D.WMF
ZONT1E.WMF
ZONT1F.WMF
ZONT1G.WMF
ZONT1H.WMF
ZONT1I.WMF
ZONT1J.WMF
ZONT1K.WMF
ZONT1L.WMF
ZONT1M.WMF
ZONT1N.WMF
ZONT1O.WMF
ZONT1P.WMF
ZONT1Q.WMF
ZONT1R.WMF
ZONT1S.WMF

ZONT1T.WMF

ZONT1U.WMF

ZONT1V.WMF

ZONT1W.WMF

ZONT1X.WMF

ZONT1Y.WMF

ZONT1Z.WMF

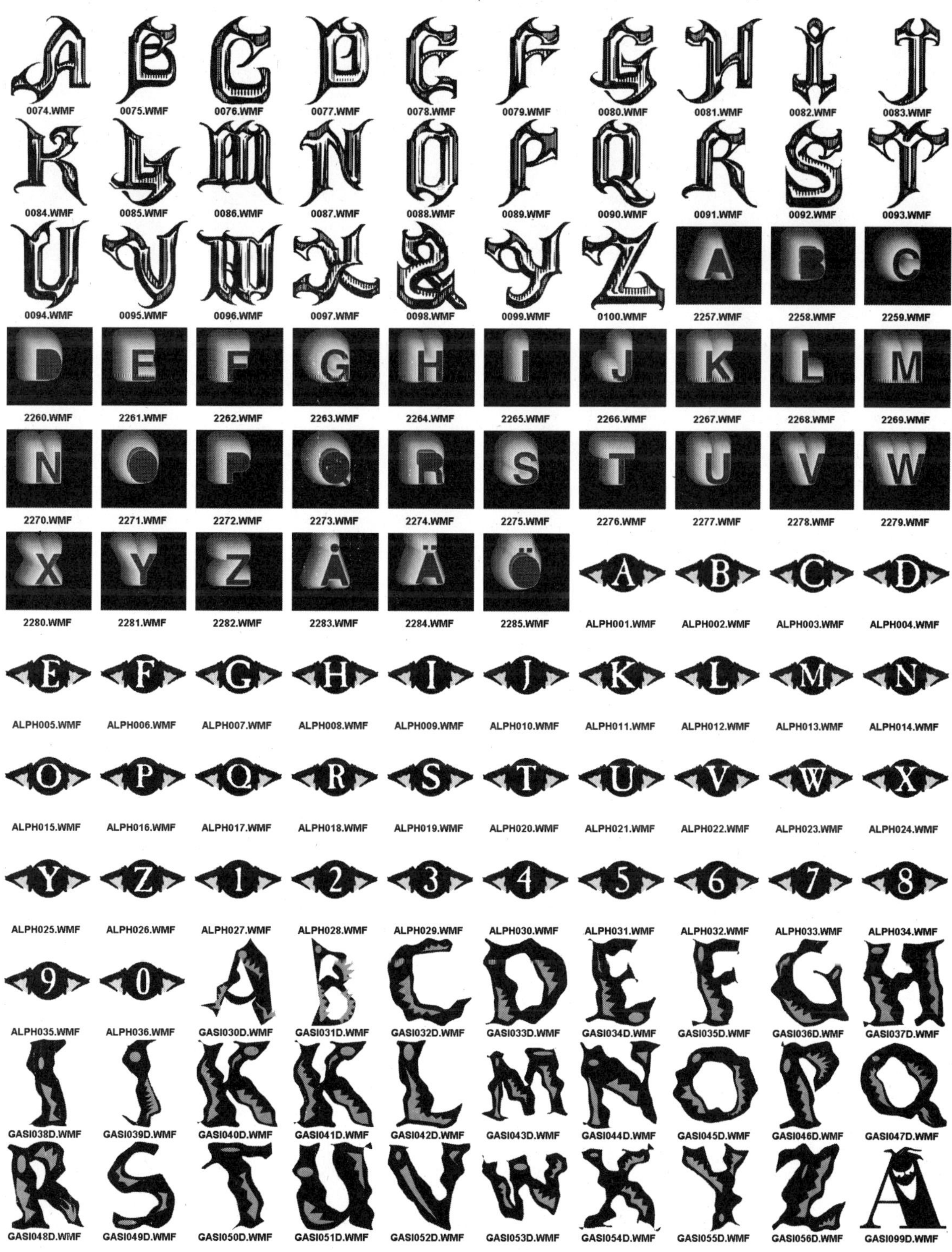
0074.WMF 0075.WMF 0076.WMF 0077.WMF 0078.WMF 0079.WMF 0080.WMF 0081.WMF 0082.WMF 0083.WMF
0084.WMF 0085.WMF 0086.WMF 0087.WMF 0088.WMF 0089.WMF 0090.WMF 0091.WMF 0092.WMF 0093.WMF
0094.WMF 0095.WMF 0096.WMF 0097.WMF 0098.WMF 0099.WMF 0100.WMF 2257.WMF 2258.WMF 2259.WMF
2260.WMF 2261.WMF 2262.WMF 2263.WMF 2264.WMF 2265.WMF 2266.WMF 2267.WMF 2268.WMF 2269.WMF
2270.WMF 2271.WMF 2272.WMF 2273.WMF 2274.WMF 2275.WMF 2276.WMF 2277.WMF 2278.WMF 2279.WMF
2280.WMF 2281.WMF 2282.WMF 2283.WMF 2284.WMF 2285.WMF ALPH001.WMF ALPH002.WMF ALPH003.WMF ALPH004.WMF
ALPH005.WMF ALPH006.WMF ALPH007.WMF ALPH008.WMF ALPH009.WMF ALPH010.WMF ALPH011.WMF ALPH012.WMF ALPH013.WMF ALPH014.WMF
ALPH015.WMF ALPH016.WMF ALPH017.WMF ALPH018.WMF ALPH019.WMF ALPH020.WMF ALPH021.WMF ALPH022.WMF ALPH023.WMF ALPH024.WMF
ALPH025.WMF ALPH026.WMF ALPH027.WMF ALPH028.WMF ALPH029.WMF ALPH030.WMF ALPH031.WMF ALPH032.WMF ALPH033.WMF ALPH034.WMF
ALPH035.WMF ALPH036.WMF GASI030D.WMF GASI031D.WMF GASI032D.WMF GASI033D.WMF GASI034D.WMF GASI035D.WMF GASI036D.WMF GASI037D.WMF
GASI038D.WMF GASI039D.WMF GASI040D.WMF GASI041D.WMF GASI042D.WMF GASI043D.WMF GASI044D.WMF GASI045D.WMF GASI046D.WMF GASI047D.WMF
GASI048D.WMF GASI049D.WMF GASI050D.WMF GASI051D.WMF GASI052D.WMF GASI053D.WMF GASI054D.WMF GASI055D.WMF GASI056D.WMF GASI099D.WMF

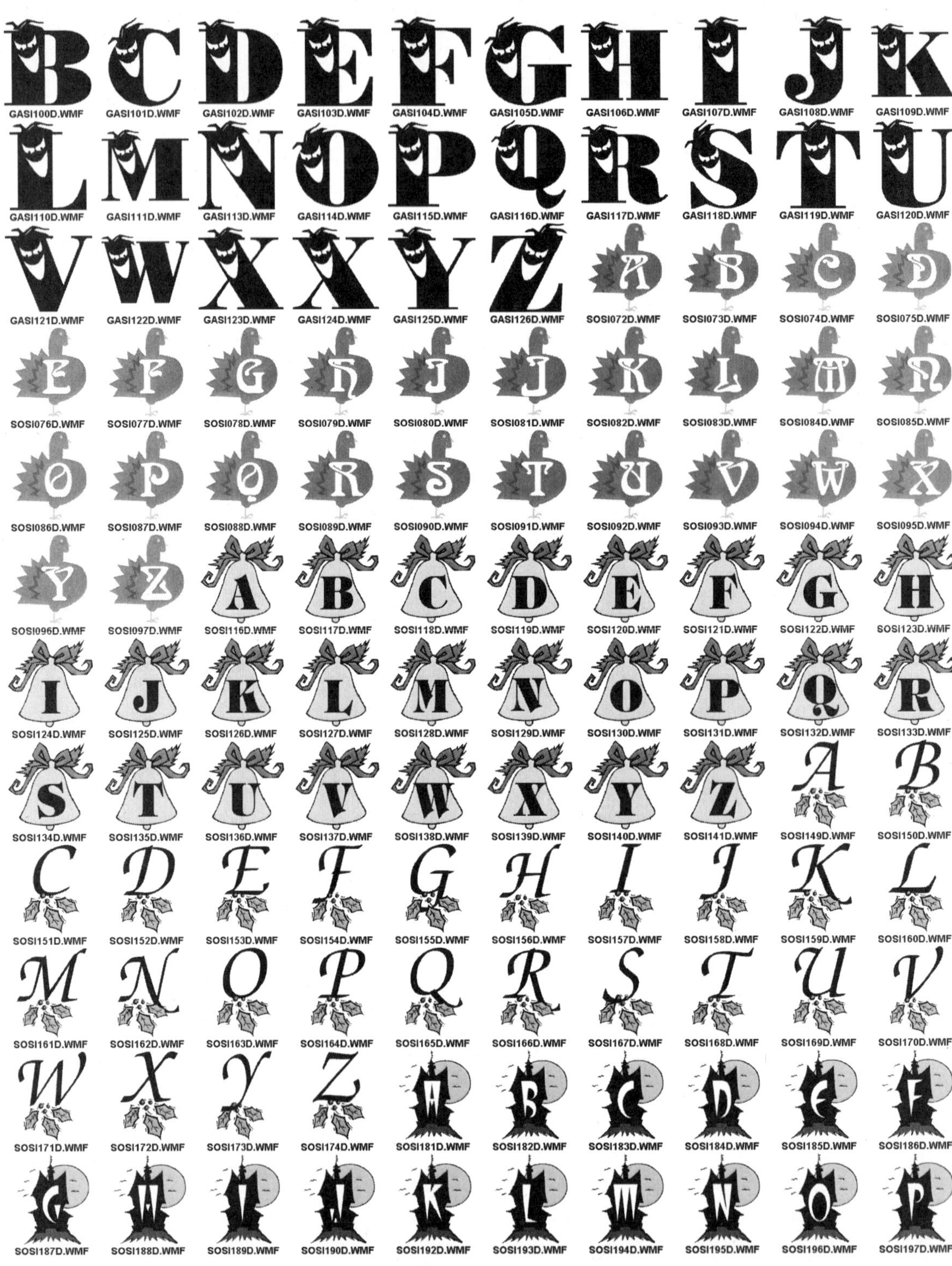
GASI100D.WMF
GASI101D.WMF
GASI102D.WMF
GASI103D.WMF
GASI104D.WMF
GASI105D.WMF
GASI106D.WMF
GASI107D.WMF
GASI108D.WMF
GASI109D.WMF
GASI110D.WMF
GASI111D.WMF
GASI113D.WMF
GASI114D.WMF
GASI115D.WMF
GASI116D.WMF
GASI117D.WMF
GASI118D.WMF
GASI119D.WMF
GASI120D.WMF
GASI121D.WMF
GASI122D.WMF
GASI123D.WMF
GASI124D.WMF
GASI125D.WMF
GASI126D.WMF
SOSI072D.WMF
SOSI073D.WMF
SOSI074D.WMF
SOSI075D.WMF
SOSI076D.WMF
SOSI077D.WMF
SOSI078D.WMF
SOSI079D.WMF
SOSI080D.WMF
SOSI081D.WMF
SOSI082D.WMF
SOSI083D.WMF
SOSI084D.WMF
SOSI085D.WMF
SOSI086D.WMF
SOSI087D.WMF
SOSI088D.WMF
SOSI089D.WMF
SOSI090D.WMF
SOSI091D.WMF
SOSI092D.WMF
SOSI093D.WMF
SOSI094D.WMF
SOSI095D.WMF
SOSI096D.WMF
SOSI097D.WMF
SOSI116D.WMF
SOSI117D.WMF
SOSI118D.WMF
SOSI119D.WMF
SOSI120D.WMF
SOSI121D.WMF
SOSI122D.WMF
SOSI123D.WMF
SOSI124D.WMF
SOSI125D.WMF
SOSI126D.WMF
SOSI127D.WMF
SOSI128D.WMF
SOSI129D.WMF
SOSI130D.WMF
SOSI131D.WMF
SOSI132D.WMF
SOSI133D.WMF
SOSI134D.WMF
SOSI135D.WMF
SOSI136D.WMF
SOSI137D.WMF
SOSI138D.WMF
SOSI139D.WMF
SOSI140D.WMF
SOSI141D.WMF
SOSI149D.WMF
SOSI150D.WMF
SOSI151D.WMF
SOSI152D.WMF
SOSI153D.WMF
SOSI154D.WMF
SOSI155D.WMF
SOSI156D.WMF
SOSI157D.WMF
SOSI158D.WMF
SOSI159D.WMF
SOSI160D.WMF
SOSI161D.WMF
SOSI162D.WMF
SOSI163D.WMF
SOSI164D.WMF
SOSI165D.WMF
SOSI166D.WMF
SOSI167D.WMF
SOSI168D.WMF
SOSI169D.WMF
SOSI170D.WMF
SOSI171D.WMF
SOSI172D.WMF
SOSI173D.WMF
SOSI174D.WMF
SOSI181D.WMF
SOSI182D.WMF
SOSI183D.WMF
SOSI184D.WMF
SOSI185D.WMF
SOSI186D.WMF
SOSI187D.WMF
SOSI188D.WMF
SOSI189D.WMF
SOSI190D.WMF
SOSI192D.WMF
SOSI193D.WMF
SOSI194D.WMF
SOSI195D.WMF
SOSI196D.WMF
SOSI197D.WMF

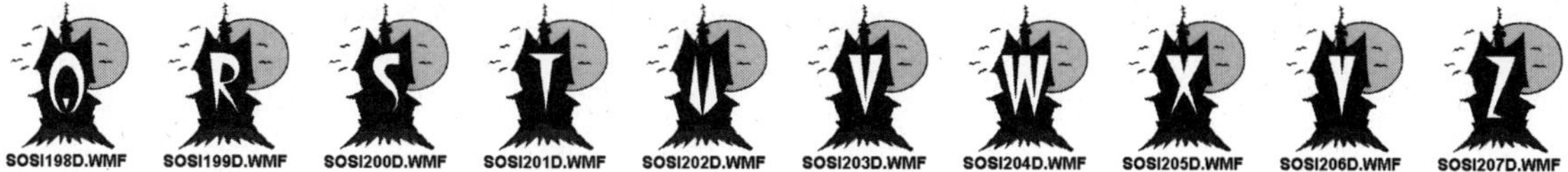

SOSI198D.WMF SOSI199D.WMF SOSI200D.WMF SOSI201D.WMF SOSI202D.WMF SOSI203D.WMF SOSI204D.WMF SOSI205D.WMF SOSI206D.WMF SOSI207D.WMF

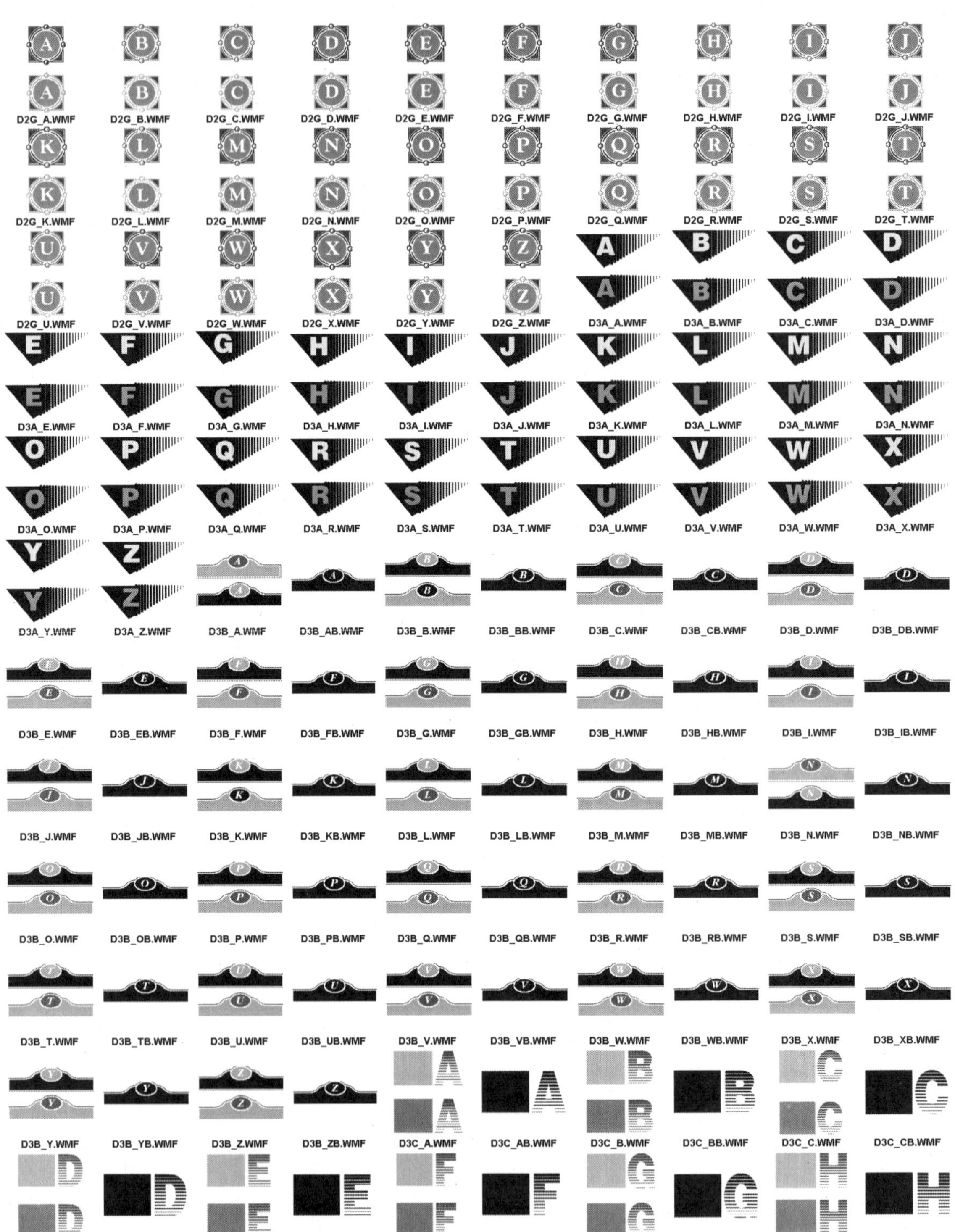
D2G_A.WMF D2G_B.WMF D2G_C.WMF D2G_D.WMF D2G_E.WMF D2G_F.WMF D2G_G.WMF D2G_H.WMF D2G_I.WMF D2G_J.WMF
D2G_K.WMF D2G_L.WMF D2G_M.WMF D2G_N.WMF D2G_O.WMF D2G_P.WMF D2G_Q.WMF D2G_R.WMF D2G_S.WMF D2G_T.WMF
D2G_U.WMF D2G_V.WMF D2G_W.WMF D2G_X.WMF D2G_Y.WMF D2G_Z.WMF D3A_A.WMF D3A_B.WMF D3A_C.WMF D3A_D.WMF
D3A_E.WMF D3A_F.WMF D3A_G.WMF D3A_H.WMF D3A_I.WMF D3A_J.WMF D3A_K.WMF D3A_L.WMF D3A_M.WMF D3A_N.WMF
D3A_O.WMF D3A_P.WMF D3A_Q.WMF D3A_R.WMF D3A_S.WMF D3A_T.WMF D3A_U.WMF D3A_V.WMF D3A_W.WMF D3A_X.WMF
D3A_Y.WMF D3A_Z.WMF D3B_A.WMF D3B_AB.WMF D3B_B.WMF D3B_BB.WMF D3B_C.WMF D3B_CB.WMF D3B_D.WMF D3B_DB.WMF
D3B_E.WMF D3B_EB.WMF D3B_F.WMF D3B_FB.WMF D3B_G.WMF D3B_GB.WMF D3B_H.WMF D3B_HB.WMF D3B_I.WMF D3B_IB.WMF
D3B_J.WMF D3B_JB.WMF D3B_K.WMF D3B_KB.WMF D3B_L.WMF D3B_LB.WMF D3B_M.WMF D3B_MB.WMF D3B_N.WMF D3B_NB.WMF
D3B_O.WMF D3B_OB.WMF D3B_P.WMF D3B_PB.WMF D3B_Q.WMF D3B_QB.WMF D3B_R.WMF D3B_RB.WMF D3B_S.WMF D3B_SB.WMF
D3B_T.WMF D3B_TB.WMF D3B_U.WMF D3B_UB.WMF D3B_V.WMF D3B_VB.WMF D3B_W.WMF D3B_WB.WMF D3B_X.WMF D3B_XB.WMF
D3B_Y.WMF D3B_YB.WMF D3B_Z.WMF D3B_ZB.WMF D3C_A.WMF D3C_AB.WMF D3C_B.WMF D3C_BB.WMF D3C_C.WMF D3C_CB.WMF
D3C_D.WMF D3C_DB.WMF D3C_E.WMF D3C_EB.WMF D3C_F.WMF D3C_FB.WMF D3C_G.WMF D3C_GB.WMF D3C_H.WMF D3C_HB.WMF

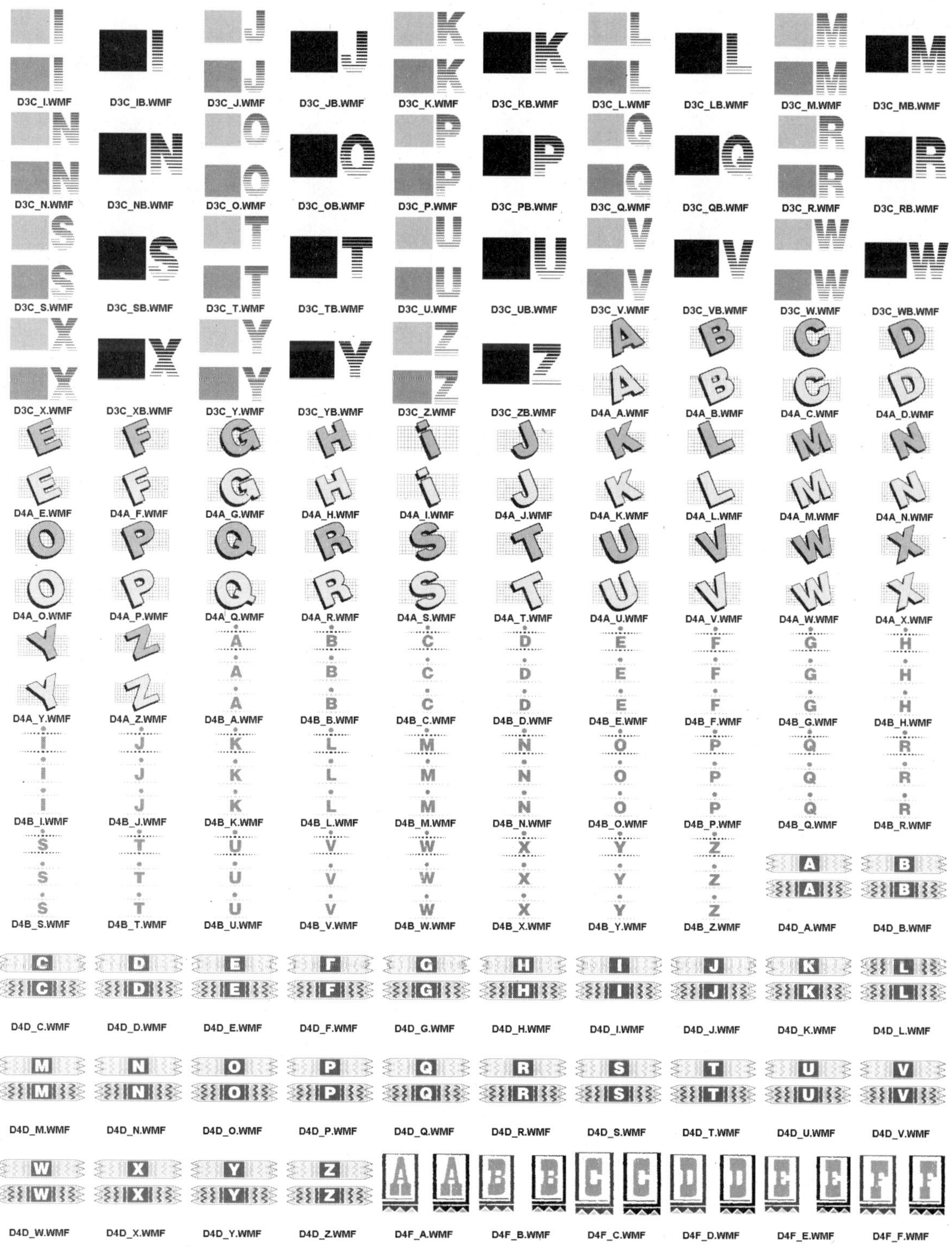
D3C_I.WMF
D3C_IB.WMF
D3C_J.WMF
D3C_JB.WMF
D3C_K.WMF
D3C_KB.WMF
D3C_L.WMF
D3C_LB.WMF
D3C_M.WMF
D3C_MB.WMF
D3C_N.WMF
D3C_NB.WMF
D3C_O.WMF
D3C_OB.WMF
D3C_P.WMF
D3C_PB.WMF
D3C_Q.WMF
D3C_QB.WMF
D3C_R.WMF
D3C_RB.WMF
D3C_S.WMF
D3C_SB.WMF
D3C_T.WMF
D3C_TB.WMF
D3C_U.WMF
D3C_UB.WMF
D3C_V.WMF
D3C_VB.WMF
D3C_W.WMF
D3C_WB.WMF
D3C_X.WMF
D3C_XB.WMF
D3C_Y.WMF
D3C_YB.WMF
D3C_Z.WMF
D3C_ZB.WMF
D4A_A.WMF
D4A_B.WMF
D4A_C.WMF
D4A_D.WMF
D4A_E.WMF
D4A_F.WMF
D4A_G.WMF
D4A_H.WMF
D4A_I.WMF
D4A_J.WMF
D4A_K.WMF
D4A_L.WMF
D4A_M.WMF
D4A_N.WMF
D4A_O.WMF
D4A_P.WMF
D4A_Q.WMF
D4A_R.WMF
D4A_S.WMF
D4A_T.WMF
D4A_U.WMF
D4A_V.WMF
D4A_W.WMF
D4A_X.WMF
D4A_Y.WMF
D4A_Z.WMF
D4B_A.WMF
D4B_B.WMF
D4B_C.WMF
D4B_D.WMF
D4B_E.WMF
D4B_F.WMF
D4B_G.WMF
D4B_H.WMF
D4B_I.WMF
D4B_J.WMF
D4B_K.WMF
D4B_L.WMF
D4B_M.WMF
D4B_N.WMF
D4B_O.WMF
D4B_P.WMF
D4B_Q.WMF
D4B_R.WMF
D4B_S.WMF
D4B_T.WMF
D4B_U.WMF
D4B_V.WMF
D4B_W.WMF
D4B_X.WMF
D4B_Y.WMF
D4B_Z.WMF
D4D_A.WMF
D4D_B.WMF
D4D_C.WMF
D4D_D.WMF
D4D_E.WMF
D4D_F.WMF
D4D_G.WMF
D4D_H.WMF
D4D_I.WMF
D4D_J.WMF
D4D_K.WMF
D4D_L.WMF
D4D_M.WMF
D4D_N.WMF
D4D_O.WMF
D4D_P.WMF
D4D_Q.WMF
D4D_R.WMF
D4D_S.WMF
D4D_T.WMF
D4D_U.WMF
D4D_V.WMF
D4D_W.WMF
D4D_X.WMF
D4D_Y.WMF
D4D_Z.WMF
D4F_A.WMF
D4F_B.WMF
D4F_C.WMF
D4F_D.WMF
D4F_E.WMF
D4F_F.WMF

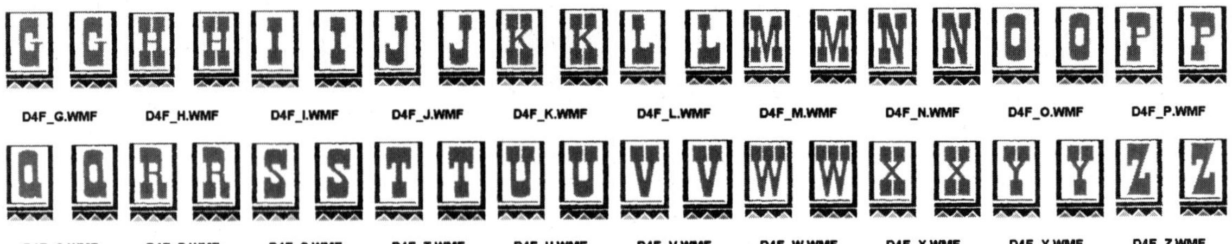

D4F_G.WMF D4F_H.WMF D4F_I.WMF D4F_J.WMF D4F_K.WMF D4F_L.WMF D4F_M.WMF D4F_N.WMF D4F_O.WMF D4F_P.WMF

D4F_Q.WMF D4F_R.WMF D4F_S.WMF D4F_T.WMF D4F_U.WMF D4F_V.WMF D4F_W.WMF D4F_X.WMF D4F_Y.WMF D4F_Z.WMF

ALPH099.WMF ALPH100.WMF ALPH101.WMF ALPH102.WMF ALPH103.WMF ALPH104.WMF ALPH105.WMF ALPH106.WMF ALPH107.WMF ALPH108.WMF

ALPH109.WMF ALPH110.WMF ALPH111.WMF ALPH112.WMF ALPH113.WMF ALPH114.WMF ALPH115.WMF ALPH116.WMF ALPH117.WMF ALPH118.WMF

ALPH119.WMF ALPH120.WMF ALPH121.WMF ALPH122.WMF ALPH123.WMF ALPH124.WMF BLIMP_A.WMF BLIMP_B.WMF BLIMP_C.WMF BLIMP_D.WMF

BLIMP_E.WMF BLIMP_F.WMF BLIMP_G.WMF BLIMP_H.WMF BLIMP_I.WMF BLIMP_J.WMF BLIMP_K.WMF BLIMP_L.WMF BLIMP_M.WMF BLIMP_N.WMF

BLIMP_O.WMF BLIMP_P.WMF BLIMP_Q.WMF BLIMP_R.WMF BLIMP_S.WMF BLIMP_T.WMF BLIMP_U.WMF BLIMP_V.WMF BLIMP_W.WMF BLIMP_X.WMF

BLIMP_Y.WMF BLIMP_Z.WMF BLOCK_A.WMF BLOCK_B.WMF BLOCK_C.WMF BLOCK_D.WMF BLOCK_E.WMF BLOCK_F.WMF BLOCK_G.WMF BLOCK_H.WMF

BLOCK_I.WMF BLOCK_J.WMF BLOCK_K.WMF BLOCK_L.WMF BLOCK_M.WMF BLOCK_N.WMF BLOCK_O.WMF BLOCK_P.WMF BLOCK_Q.WMF BLOCK_R.WMF

BLOCK_S.WMF BLOCK_T.WMF BLOCK_U.WMF BLOCK_V.WMF BLOCK_W.WMF BLOCK_X.WMF BLOCK_Y.WMF CHIS1_A.WMF CHIS1_B.WMF CHIS1_C.WMF

CHIS1_D.WMF CHIS1_E.WMF CHIS1_F.WMF CHIS1_G.WMF CHIS1_H.WMF CHIS1_I.WMF CHIS1_J.WMF CHIS1_K.WMF CHIS1_L.WMF CHIS1_M.WMF

CHIS1_N.WMF CHIS1_O.WMF CHIS1_P.WMF CHIS1_Q.WMF CHIS1_R.WMF CHIS1_S.WMF CHIS1_T.WMF CHIS1_U.WMF CHIS1_V.WMF CHIS1_W.WMF

CHIS1_X.WMF CHIS1_Y.WMF CHIS1_Z.WMF CHIS2_A.WMF CHIS2_B.WMF CHIS2_C.WMF CHIS2_D.WMF CHIS2_E.WMF CHIS2_F.WMF CHIS2_G.WMF

CHIS2_H.WMF CHIS2_I.WMF CHIS2_J.WMF CHIS2_K.WMF CHIS2_L.WMF CHIS2_M.WMF CHIS2_N.WMF CHIS2_O.WMF CHIS2_P.WMF CHIS2_Q.WMF

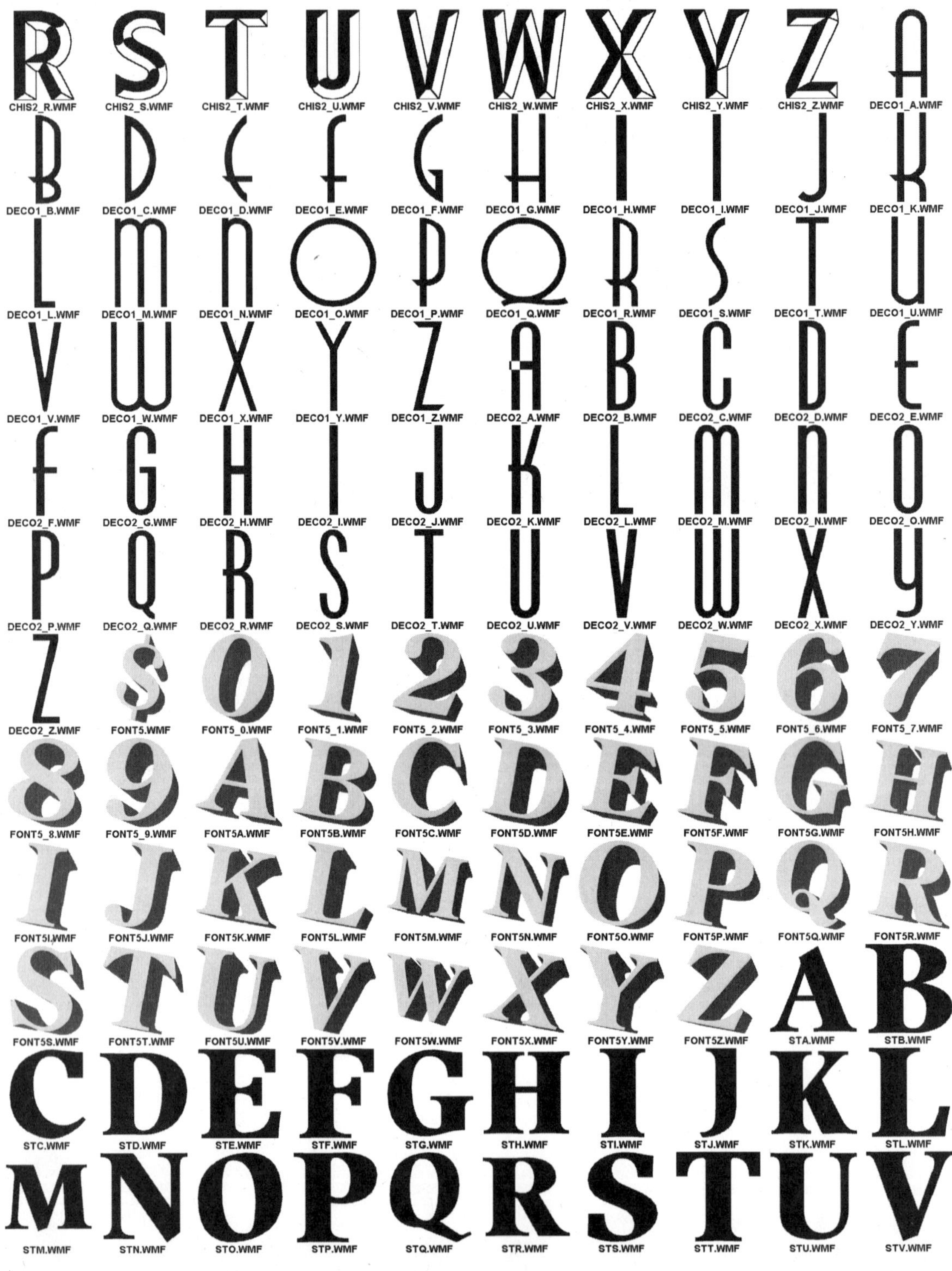
CHIS2_R.WMF
CHIS2_S.WMF
CHIS2_T.WMF
CHIS2_U.WMF
CHIS2_V.WMF
CHIS2_W.WMF
CHIS2_X.WMF
CHIS2_Y.WMF
CHIS2_Z.WMF
DECO1_A.WMF
DECO1_B.WMF
DECO1_C.WMF
DECO1_D.WMF
DECO1_E.WMF
DECO1_F.WMF
DECO1_G.WMF
DECO1_H.WMF
DECO1_I.WMF
DECO1_J.WMF
DECO1_K.WMF
DECO1_L.WMF
DECO1_M.WMF
DECO1_N.WMF
DECO1_O.WMF
DECO1_P.WMF
DECO1_Q.WMF
DECO1_R.WMF
DECO1_S.WMF
DECO1_T.WMF
DECO1_U.WMF
DECO1_V.WMF
DECO1_W.WMF
DECO1_X.WMF
DECO1_Y.WMF
DECO1_Z.WMF
DECO2_A.WMF
DECO2_B.WMF
DECO2_C.WMF
DECO2_D.WMF
DECO2_E.WMF
DECO2_F.WMF
DECO2_G.WMF
DECO2_H.WMF
DECO2_I.WMF
DECO2_J.WMF
DECO2_K.WMF
DECO2_L.WMF
DECO2_M.WMF
DECO2_N.WMF
DECO2_O.WMF
DECO2_P.WMF
DECO2_Q.WMF
DECO2_R.WMF
DECO2_S.WMF
DECO2_T.WMF
DECO2_U.WMF
DECO2_V.WMF
DECO2_W.WMF
DECO2_X.WMF
DECO2_Y.WMF
DECO2_Z.WMF
FONT5.WMF
FONT5_0.WMF
FONT5_1.WMF
FONT5_2.WMF
FONT5_3.WMF
FONT5_4.WMF
FONT5_5.WMF
FONT5_6.WMF
FONT5_7.WMF
FONT5_8.WMF
FONT5_9.WMF
FONT5A.WMF
FONT5B.WMF
FONT5C.WMF
FONT5D.WMF
FONT5E.WMF
FONT5F.WMF
FONT5G.WMF
FONT5H.WMF
FONT5I.WMF
FONT5J.WMF
FONT5K.WMF
FONT5L.WMF
FONT5M.WMF
FONT5N.WMF
FONT5O.WMF
FONT5P.WMF
FONT5Q.WMF
FONT5R.WMF
FONT5S.WMF
FONT5T.WMF
FONT5U.WMF
FONT5V.WMF
FONT5W.WMF
FONT5X.WMF
FONT5Y.WMF
FONT5Z.WMF
STA.WMF
STB.WMF
STC.WMF
STD.WMF
STE.WMF
STF.WMF
STG.WMF
STH.WMF
STI.WMF
STJ.WMF
STK.WMF
STL.WMF
STM.WMF
STN.WMF
STO.WMF
STP.WMF
STQ.WMF
STR.WMF
STS.WMF
STT.WMF
STU.WMF
STV.WMF

STW.WMF
STX.WMF
STY.WMF
STZ.WMF

0163.WMF 0164.WMF 0165.WMF 0166.WMF 0167.WMF 0168.WMF 0169.WMF 0170.WMF 0171.WMF 0172.WMF
0173.WMF 0174.WMF 0175.WMF 0176.WMF 0177.WMF 0178.WMF 0179.WMF 0180.WMF 0181.WMF 0182.WMF
0183.WMF 0184.WMF 0185.WMF 0186.WMF 0187.WMF 0188.WMF 0189.WMF 0190.WMF 0220.WMF 0221.WMF
0222.WMF 0223.WMF 0224.WMF 0225.WMF 0226.WMF 0227.WMF 0228.WMF 0229.WMF 0230.WMF 0231.WMF
0232.WMF 0233.WMF 0234.WMF 0235.WMF 0236.WMF 0237.WMF 0238.WMF 0239.WMF 0240.WMF 0241.WMF
0242.WMF 0243.WMF 0244.WMF 0245.WMF 0246.WMF 0247.WMF 0248.WMF 0249.WMF 0250.WMF 0251.WMF
0252.WMF ALPH125.WMF ALPH126.WMF ALPH127.WMF ALPH128.WMF ALPH129.WMF ALPH130.WMF ALPH131.WMF ALPH132.WMF ALPH133.WMF
ALPH134.WMF ALPH135.WMF ALPH136.WMF ALPH137.WMF ALPH138.WMF ALPH139.WMF ALPH140.WMF ALPH141.WMF ALPH142.WMF ALPH143.WMF
ALPH144.WMF ALPH145.WMF ALPH146.WMF ALPH147.WMF ALPH148.WMF B0.WMF B1.WMF B2.WMF B3.WMF B4.WMF
B5.WMF B6.WMF B7.WMF B8.WMF B9.WMF B_.WMF BA.WMF BB.WMF BC.WMF BD.WMF
BE.WMF BF.WMF BG.WMF BH.WMF BI.WMF BJ.WMF BK.WMF BL.WMF BM.WMF BN.WMF
BO.WMF BP.WMF BQ.WMF BR.WMF BS.WMF BT.WMF BU.WMF BV.WMF BW.WMF BX.WMF

BY.WMF BZ.WMF FONT4.WMF FONT4_0.WMF FONT4_1.WMF FONT4_2.WMF FONT4_3.WMF FONT4_4.WMF FONT4_5.WMF FONT4_6.WMF
FONT4_7.WMF FONT4_8.WMF FONT4_9.WMF FONT4A.WMF FONT4B.WMF FONT4C.WMF FONT4D.WMF FONT4E.WMF FONT4F.WMF FONT4G.WMF
FONT4H.WMF FONT4I.WMF FONT4J.WMF FONT4K.WMF FONT4L.WMF FONT4M.WMF FONT4N.WMF FONT4O.WMF FONT4P.WMF FONT4Q.WMF
FONT4R.WMF FONT4S.WMF FONT4T.WMF FONT4U.WMF FONT4V.WMF FONT4W.WMF FONT4X.WMF FONT4Y.WMF FONT4Z.WMF FONT6.WMF
FONT6_0.WMF FONT6_1.WMF FONT6_2.WMF FONT6_3.WMF FONT6_4.WMF FONT6_5.WMF FONT6_6.WMF FONT6_7.WMF FONT6_8.WMF FONT6_9.WMF
FONT6A.WMF FONT6B.WMF FONT6C.WMF FONT6D.WMF FONT6E.WMF FONT6F.WMF FONT6G.WMF FONT6H.WMF FONT6I.WMF FONT6J.WMF
FONT6K.WMF FONT6L.WMF FONT6M.WMF FONT6N.WMF FONT6O.WMF FONT6P.WMF FONT6Q.WMF FONT6R.WMF FONT6S.WMF FONT6T.WMF
FONT6U.WMF FONT6V.WMF FONT6W.WMF FONT6X.WMF FONT6Y.WMF FONT6Z.WMF FONT8.WMF FONT8_0.WMF FONT8_1.WMF FONT8_2.WMF
FONT8_3.WMF FONT8_4.WMF FONT8_5.WMF FONT8_6.WMF FONT8_7.WMF FONT8_8.WMF FONT8_9.WMF FONT8A.WMF FONT8B.WMF FONT8C.WMF
FONT8D.WMF FONT8E.WMF FONT8F.WMF FONT8G.WMF FONT8H.WMF FONT8I.WMF FONT8J.WMF FONT8K.WMF FONT8L.WMF FONT8M.WMF
FONT8N.WMF FONT8O.WMF FONT8P.WMF FONT8Q.WMF FONT8R.WMF FONT8S.WMF FONT8T.WMF FONT8U.WMF FONT8V.WMF FONT8W.WMF
FONT8X.WMF FONT8Y.WMF FONT8Z.WMF GASI137D.WMF GASI138D.WMF GASI139D.WMF GASI140D.WMF GASI141D.WMF GASI142D.WMF GASI143D.WMF

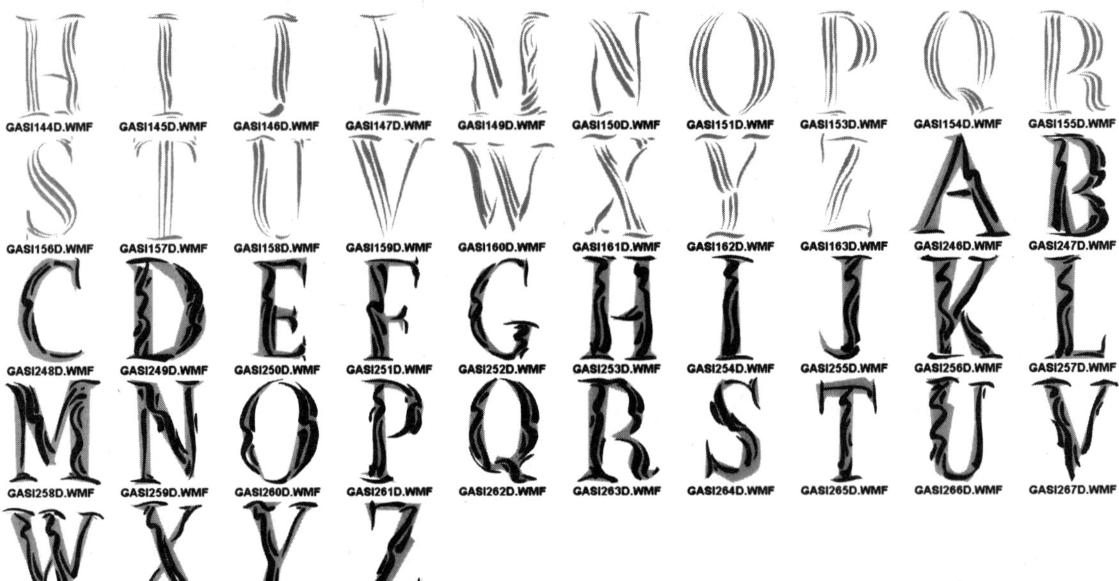
GASI144D.WMF
GASI145D.WMF
GASI146D.WMF
GASI147D.WMF
GASI149D.WMF
GASI150D.WMF
GASI151D.WMF
GASI153D.WMF
GASI154D.WMF
GASI155D.WMF
GASI156D.WMF
GASI157D.WMF
GASI158D.WMF
GASI159D.WMF
GASI160D.WMF
GASI161D.WMF
GASI162D.WMF
GASI163D.WMF
GASI246D.WMF
GASI247D.WMF
GASI248D.WMF
GASI249D.WMF
GASI250D.WMF
GASI251D.WMF
GASI252D.WMF
GASI253D.WMF
GASI254D.WMF
GASI255D.WMF
GASI256D.WMF
GASI257D.WMF
GASI258D.WMF
GASI259D.WMF
GASI260D.WMF
GASI261D.WMF
GASI262D.WMF
GASI263D.WMF
GASI264D.WMF
GASI265D.WMF
GASI266D.WMF
GASI267D.WMF
GASI268D.WMF
GASI269D.WMF
GASI270D.WMF
GASI271D.WMF

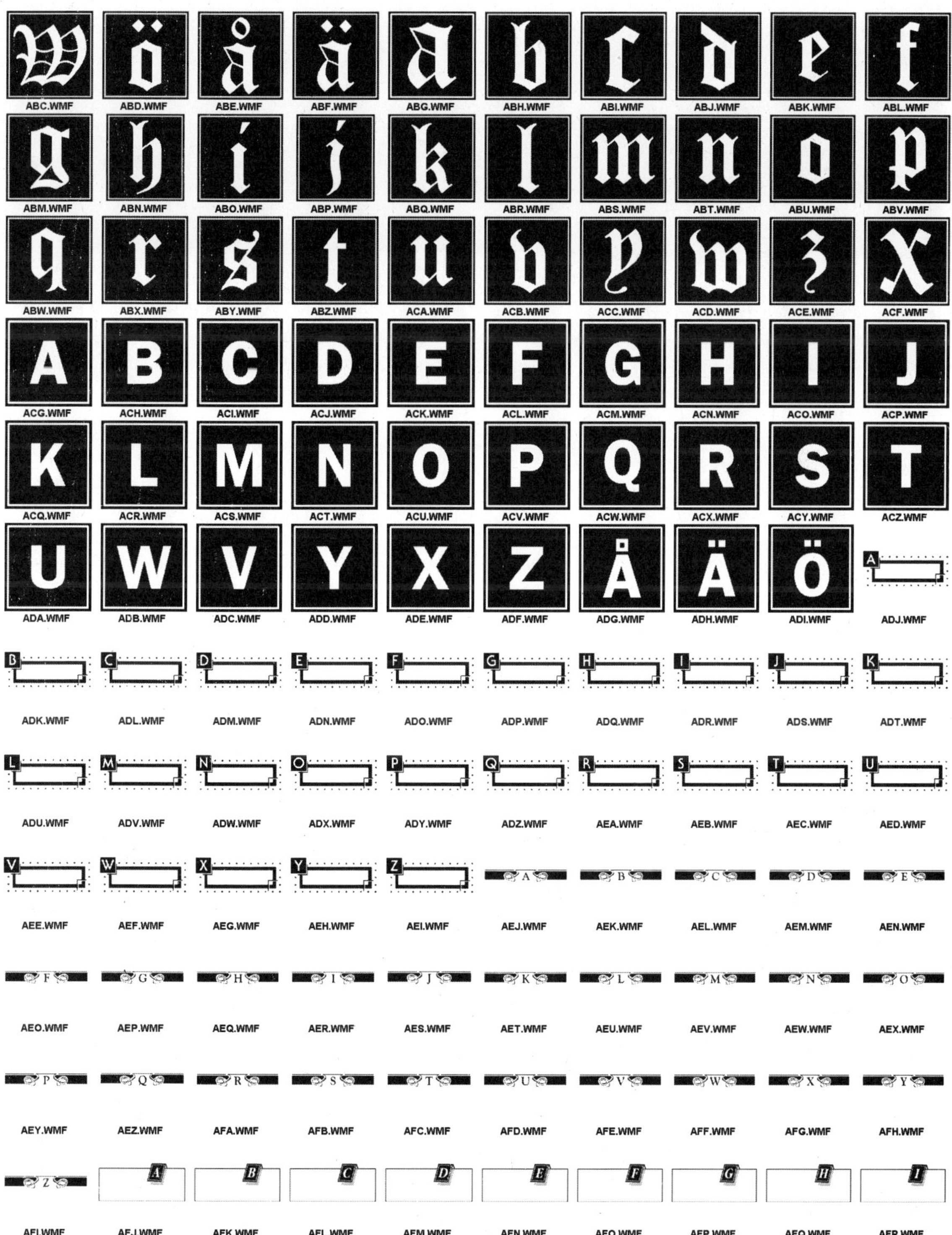
ABC.WMF ABD.WMF ABE.WMF ABF.WMF ABG.WMF ABH.WMF ABI.WMF ABJ.WMF ABK.WMF ABL.WMF
ABM.WMF ABN.WMF ABO.WMF ABP.WMF ABQ.WMF ABR.WMF ABS.WMF ABT.WMF ABU.WMF ABV.WMF
ABW.WMF ABX.WMF ABY.WMF ABZ.WMF ACA.WMF ACB.WMF ACC.WMF ACD.WMF ACE.WMF ACF.WMF
ACG.WMF ACH.WMF ACI.WMF ACJ.WMF ACK.WMF ACL.WMF ACM.WMF ACN.WMF ACO.WMF ACP.WMF
ACQ.WMF ACR.WMF ACS.WMF ACT.WMF ACU.WMF ACV.WMF ACW.WMF ACX.WMF ACY.WMF ACZ.WMF
ADA.WMF ADB.WMF ADC.WMF ADD.WMF ADE.WMF ADF.WMF ADG.WMF ADH.WMF ADI.WMF ADJ.WMF
ADK.WMF ADL.WMF ADM.WMF ADN.WMF ADO.WMF ADP.WMF ADQ.WMF ADR.WMF ADS.WMF ADT.WMF
ADU.WMF ADV.WMF ADW.WMF ADX.WMF ADY.WMF ADZ.WMF AEA.WMF AEB.WMF AEC.WMF AED.WMF
AEE.WMF AEF.WMF AEG.WMF AEH.WMF AEI.WMF AEJ.WMF AEK.WMF AEL.WMF AEM.WMF AEN.WMF
AEO.WMF AEP.WMF AEQ.WMF AER.WMF AES.WMF AET.WMF AEU.WMF AEV.WMF AEW.WMF AEX.WMF
AEY.WMF AEZ.WMF AFA.WMF AFB.WMF AFC.WMF AFD.WMF AFE.WMF AFF.WMF AFG.WMF AFH.WMF
AFI.WMF AFJ.WMF AFK.WMF AFL.WMF AFM.WMF AFN.WMF AFO.WMF AFP.WMF AFQ.WMF AFR.WMF

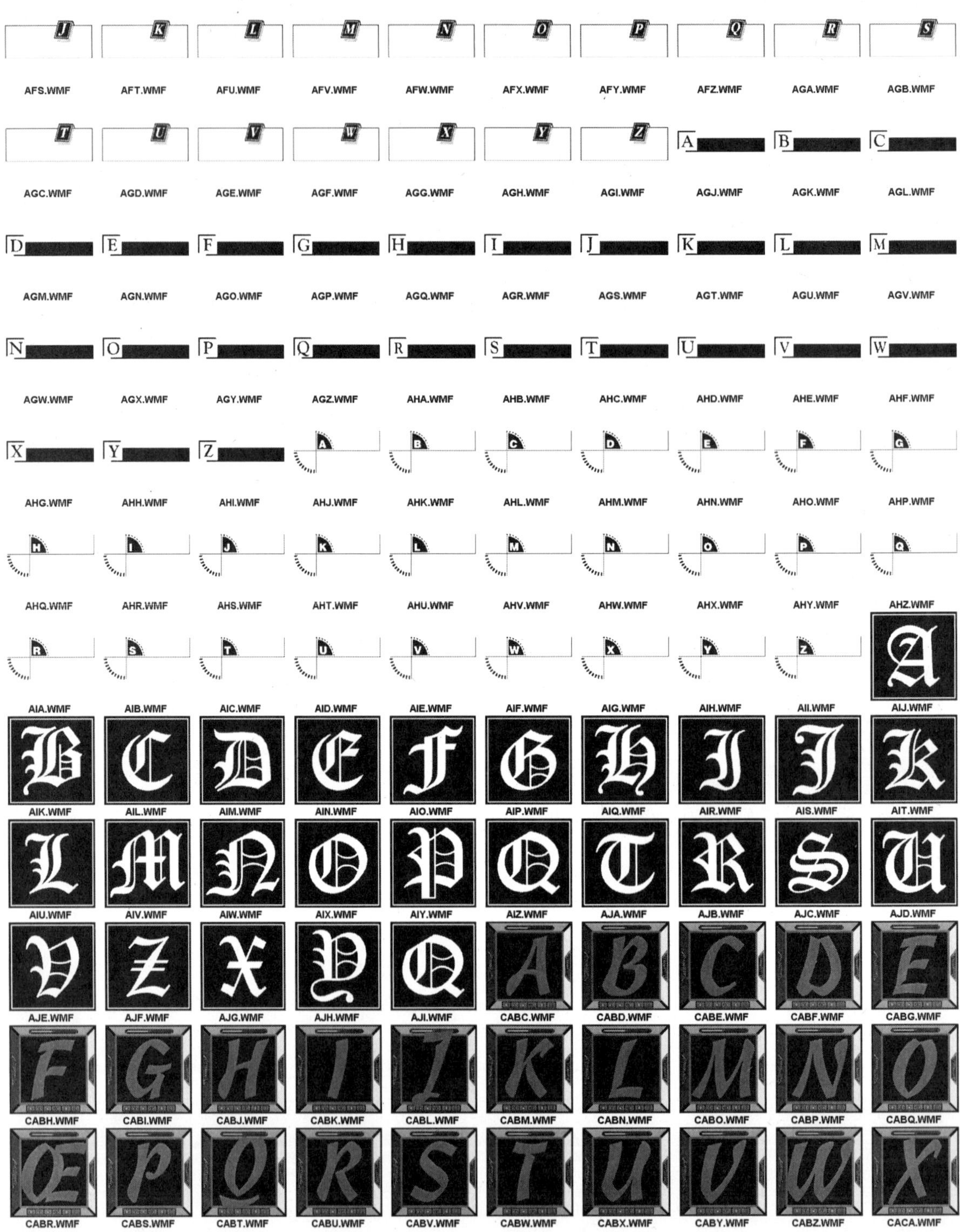
AFS.WMF
AFT.WMF
AFU.WMF
AFV.WMF
AFW.WMF
AFX.WMF
AFY.WMF
AFZ.WMF
AGA.WMF
AGB.WMF
AGC.WMF
AGD.WMF
AGE.WMF
AGF.WMF
AGG.WMF
AGH.WMF
AGI.WMF
AGJ.WMF
AGK.WMF
AGL.WMF
AGM.WMF
AGN.WMF
AGO.WMF
AGP.WMF
AGQ.WMF
AGR.WMF
AGS.WMF
AGT.WMF
AGU.WMF
AGV.WMF
AGW.WMF
AGX.WMF
AGY.WMF
AGZ.WMF
AHA.WMF
AHB.WMF
AHC.WMF
AHD.WMF
AHE.WMF
AHF.WMF
AHG.WMF
AHH.WMF
AHI.WMF
AHJ.WMF
AHK.WMF
AHL.WMF
AHM.WMF
AHN.WMF
AHO.WMF
AHP.WMF
AHQ.WMF
AHR.WMF
AHS.WMF
AHT.WMF
AHU.WMF
AHV.WMF
AHW.WMF
AHX.WMF
AHY.WMF
AHZ.WMF
AIA.WMF
AIB.WMF
AIC.WMF
AID.WMF
AIE.WMF
AIF.WMF
AIG.WMF
AIH.WMF
AII.WMF
AIJ.WMF
AIK.WMF
AIL.WMF
AIM.WMF
AIN.WMF
AIO.WMF
AIP.WMF
AIQ.WMF
AIR.WMF
AIS.WMF
AIT.WMF
AIU.WMF
AIV.WMF
AIW.WMF
AIX.WMF
AIY.WMF
AIZ.WMF
AJA.WMF
AJB.WMF
AJC.WMF
AJD.WMF
AJE.WMF
AJF.WMF
AJG.WMF
AJH.WMF
AJI.WMF
CABC.WMF
CABD.WMF
CABE.WMF
CABF.WMF
CABG.WMF
CABH.WMF
CABI.WMF
CABJ.WMF
CABK.WMF
CABL.WMF
CABM.WMF
CABN.WMF
CABO.WMF
CABP.WMF
CABQ.WMF
CABR.WMF
CABS.WMF
CABT.WMF
CABU.WMF
CABV.WMF
CABW.WMF
CABX.WMF
CABY.WMF
CABZ.WMF
CACA.WMF

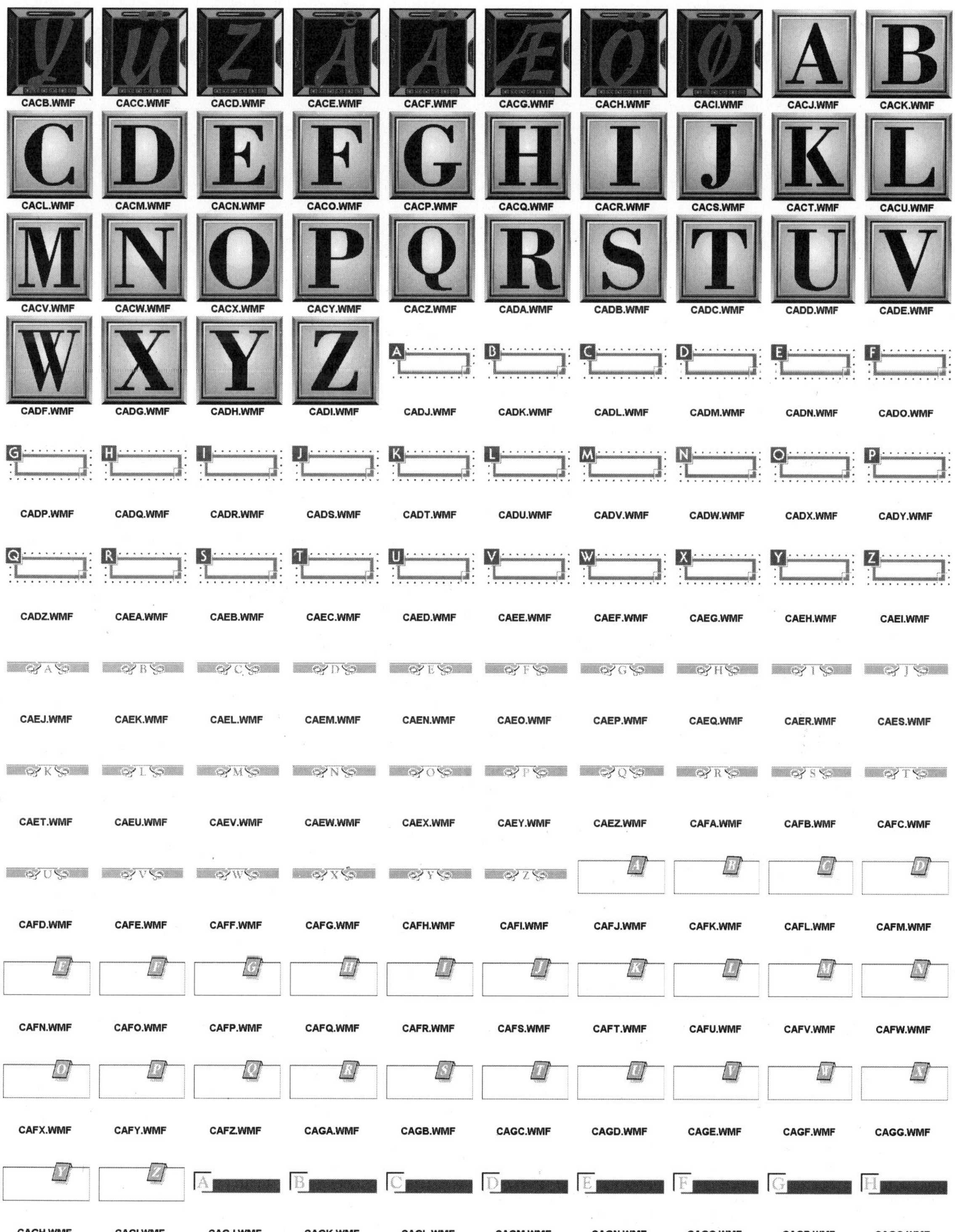
CACB.WMF
CACC.WMF
CACD.WMF
CACE.WMF
CACF.WMF
CACG.WMF
CACH.WMF
CACI.WMF
CACJ.WMF
CACK.WMF
CACL.WMF
CACM.WMF
CACN.WMF
CACO.WMF
CACP.WMF
CACQ.WMF
CACR.WMF
CACS.WMF
CACT.WMF
CACU.WMF
CACV.WMF
CACW.WMF
CACX.WMF
CACY.WMF
CACZ.WMF
CADA.WMF
CADB.WMF
CADC.WMF
CADD.WMF
CADE.WMF
CADF.WMF
CADG.WMF
CADH.WMF
CADI.WMF
CADJ.WMF
CADK.WMF
CADL.WMF
CADM.WMF
CADN.WMF
CADO.WMF
CADP.WMF
CADQ.WMF
CADR.WMF
CADS.WMF
CADT.WMF
CADU.WMF
CADV.WMF
CADW.WMF
CADX.WMF
CADY.WMF
CADZ.WMF
CAEA.WMF
CAEB.WMF
CAEC.WMF
CAED.WMF
CAEE.WMF
CAEF.WMF
CAEG.WMF
CAEH.WMF
CAEI.WMF
CAEJ.WMF
CAEK.WMF
CAEL.WMF
CAEM.WMF
CAEN.WMF
CAEO.WMF
CAEP.WMF
CAEQ.WMF
CAER.WMF
CAES.WMF
CAET.WMF
CAEU.WMF
CAEV.WMF
CAEW.WMF
CAEX.WMF
CAEY.WMF
CAEZ.WMF
CAFA.WMF
CAFB.WMF
CAFC.WMF
CAFD.WMF
CAFE.WMF
CAFF.WMF
CAFG.WMF
CAFH.WMF
CAFI.WMF
CAFJ.WMF
CAFK.WMF
CAFL.WMF
CAFM.WMF
CAFN.WMF
CAFO.WMF
CAFP.WMF
CAFQ.WMF
CAFR.WMF
CAFS.WMF
CAFT.WMF
CAFU.WMF
CAFV.WMF
CAFW.WMF
CAFX.WMF
CAFY.WMF
CAFZ.WMF
CAGA.WMF
CAGB.WMF
CAGC.WMF
CAGD.WMF
CAGE.WMF
CAGF.WMF
CAGG.WMF
CAGH.WMF
CAGI.WMF
CAGJ.WMF
CAGK.WMF
CAGL.WMF
CAGM.WMF
CAGN.WMF
CAGO.WMF
CAGP.WMF
CAGQ.WMF

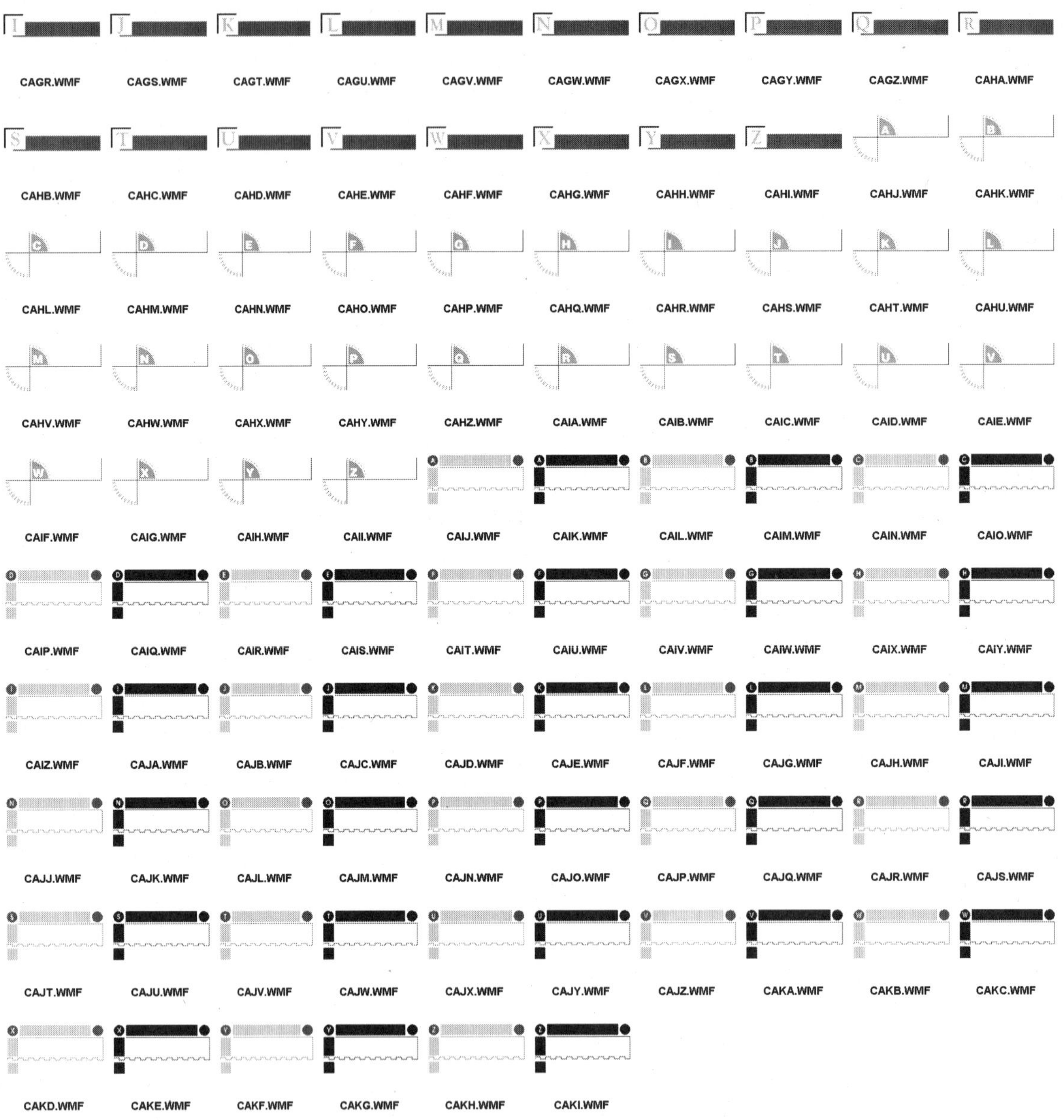
CAGR.WMF
CAGS.WMF
CAGT.WMF
CAGU.WMF
CAGV.WMF
CAGW.WMF
CAGX.WMF
CAGY.WMF
CAGZ.WMF
CAHA.WMF
CAHB.WMF
CAHC.WMF
CAHD.WMF
CAHE.WMF
CAHF.WMF
CAHG.WMF
CAHH.WMF
CAHI.WMF
CAHJ.WMF
CAHK.WMF
CAHL.WMF
CAHM.WMF
CAHN.WMF
CAHO.WMF
CAHP.WMF
CAHQ.WMF
CAHR.WMF
CAHS.WMF
CAHT.WMF
CAHU.WMF
CAHV.WMF
CAHW.WMF
CAHX.WMF
CAHY.WMF
CAHZ.WMF
CAIA.WMF
CAIB.WMF
CAIC.WMF
CAID.WMF
CAIE.WMF
CAIF.WMF
CAIG.WMF
CAIH.WMF
CAII.WMF
CAIJ.WMF
CAIK.WMF
CAIL.WMF
CAIM.WMF
CAIN.WMF
CAIO.WMF
CAIP.WMF
CAIQ.WMF
CAIR.WMF
CAIS.WMF
CAIT.WMF
CAIU.WMF
CAIV.WMF
CAIW.WMF
CAIX.WMF
CAIY.WMF
CAIZ.WMF
CAJA.WMF
CAJB.WMF
CAJC.WMF
CAJD.WMF
CAJE.WMF
CAJF.WMF
CAJG.WMF
CAJH.WMF
CAJI.WMF
CAJJ.WMF
CAJK.WMF
CAJL.WMF
CAJM.WMF
CAJN.WMF
CAJO.WMF
CAJP.WMF
CAJQ.WMF
CAJR.WMF
CAJS.WMF
CAJT.WMF
CAJU.WMF
CAJV.WMF
CAJW.WMF
CAJX.WMF
CAJY.WMF
CAJZ.WMF
CAKA.WMF
CAKB.WMF
CAKC.WMF
CAKD.WMF
CAKE.WMF
CAKF.WMF
CAKG.WMF
CAKH.WMF
CAKI.WMF

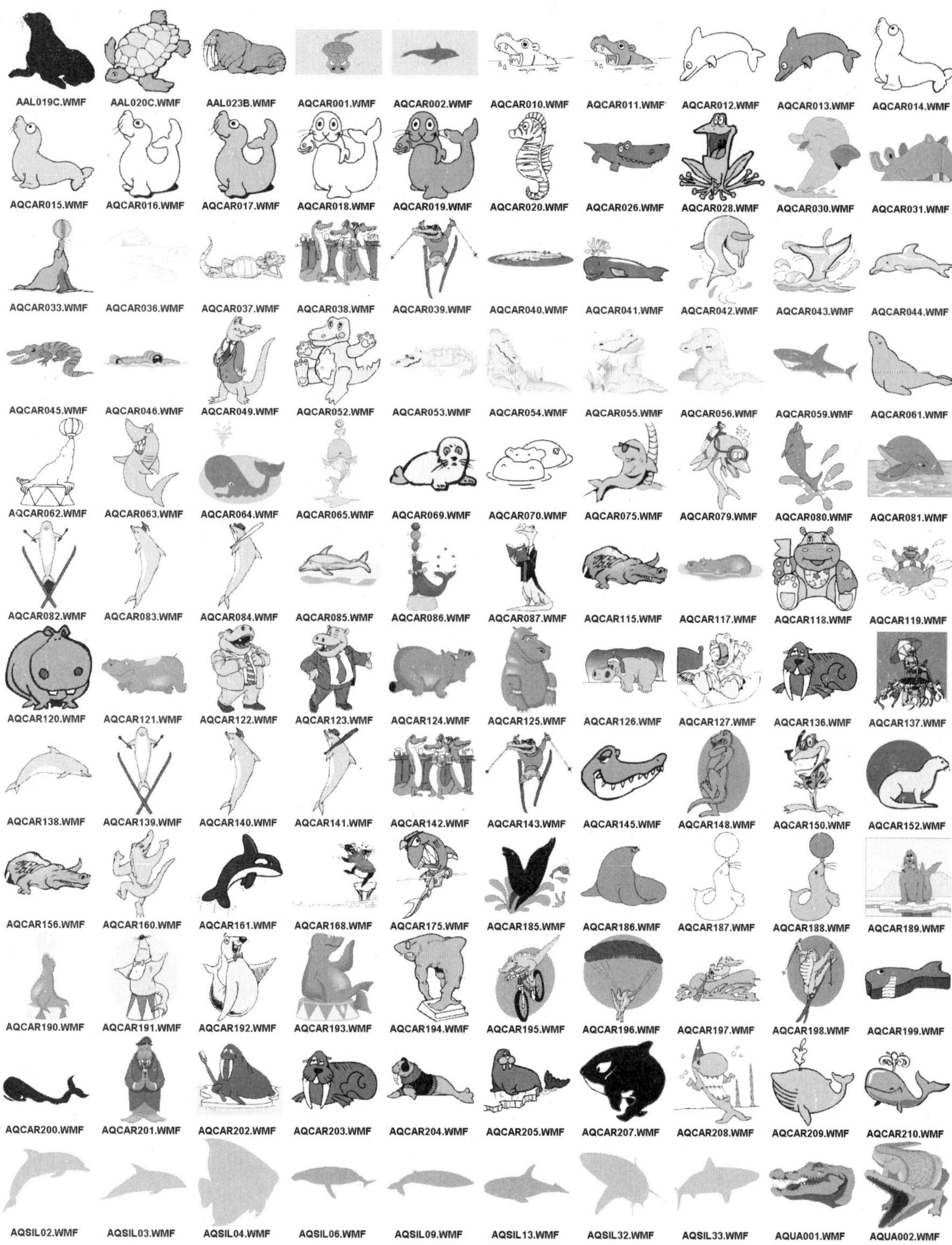

AAL019C.WMF AAL020C.WMF AAL023B.WMF AQCAR001.WMF AQCAR002.WMF AQCAR010.WMF AQCAR011.WMF AQCAR012.WMF AQCAR013.WMF AQCAR014.WMF

AQCAR015.WMF AQCAR016.WMF AQCAR017.WMF AQCAR018.WMF AQCAR019.WMF AQCAR020.WMF AQCAR026.WMF AQCAR028.WMF AQCAR030.WMF AQCAR031.WMF

AQCAR033.WMF AQCAR036.WMF AQCAR037.WMF AQCAR038.WMF AQCAR039.WMF AQCAR040.WMF AQCAR041.WMF AQCAR042.WMF AQCAR043.WMF AQCAR044.WMF

AQCAR045.WMF AQCAR046.WMF AQCAR049.WMF AQCAR052.WMF AQCAR053.WMF AQCAR054.WMF AQCAR055.WMF AQCAR056.WMF AQCAR059.WMF AQCAR061.WMF

AQCAR062.WMF AQCAR063.WMF AQCAR064.WMF AQCAR065.WMF AQCAR069.WMF AQCAR070.WMF AQCAR075.WMF AQCAR079.WMF AQCAR080.WMF AQCAR081.WMF

AQCAR082.WMF AQCAR083.WMF AQCAR084.WMF AQCAR085.WMF AQCAR086.WMF AQCAR087.WMF AQCAR115.WMF AQCAR117.WMF AQCAR118.WMF AQCAR119.WMF

AQCAR120.WMF AQCAR121.WMF AQCAR122.WMF AQCAR123.WMF AQCAR124.WMF AQCAR125.WMF AQCAR126.WMF AQCAR127.WMF AQCAR136.WMF AQCAR137.WMF

AQCAR138.WMF AQCAR139.WMF AQCAR140.WMF AQCAR141.WMF AQCAR142.WMF AQCAR143.WMF AQCAR145.WMF AQCAR148.WMF AQCAR150.WMF AQCAR152.WMF

AQCAR156.WMF AQCAR160.WMF AQCAR161.WMF AQCAR168.WMF AQCAR175.WMF AQCAR185.WMF AQCAR186.WMF AQCAR187.WMF AQCAR188.WMF AQCAR189.WMF

AQCAR190.WMF AQCAR191.WMF AQCAR192.WMF AQCAR193.WMF AQCAR194.WMF AQCAR195.WMF AQCAR196.WMF AQCAR197.WMF AQCAR198.WMF AQCAR199.WMF

AQCAR200.WMF AQCAR201.WMF AQCAR202.WMF AQCAR203.WMF AQCAR204.WMF AQCAR205.WMF AQCAR207.WMF AQCAR208.WMF AQCAR209.WMF AQCAR210.WMF

AQSIL02.WMF AQSIL03.WMF AQSIL04.WMF AQSIL06.WMF AQSIL09.WMF AQSIL13.WMF AQSIL32.WMF AQSIL33.WMF AQUA001.WMF AQUA002.WMF

AQUA004.WMF AQUA005.WMF AQUA006.WMF AQUA008.WMF AQUA009.WMF AQUA010.WMF AQUA012.WMF AQUA013.WMF AQUA014.WMF AQUA016.WMF
AQUA018.WMF AQUA019.WMF AQUA021.WMF AQUA022.WMF AQUA023.WMF AQUA024.WMF AQUA025.WMF AQUA026.WMF AQUA039.WMF AQUA040.WMF
AQUA041.WMF AQUA042.WMF AQUA045.WMF AQUA046.WMF AQUA051.WMF AQUA052.WMF AQUA056.WMF AQUA058.WMF AQUA060.WMF AQUA061.WMF
AQUA062.WMF AQUA063.WMF AQUA064.WMF AQUA065.WMF AQUA068.WMF AQUA069.WMF AQUA072.WMF AQUA073.WMF AQUA074.WMF AQUA075.WMF
AQUA076.WMF AQUA077.WMF AQUA079.WMF AQUA080.WMF AQUA081.WMF AQUA082.WMF AQUA087.WMF AQUA088.WMF AQUA089.WMF AQUA090.WMF
AQUA091.WMF AQUA092.WMF AQUA093.WMF AQUA094.WMF AQUA095.WMF AQUA096.WMF AQUA097.WMF AQUA100.WMF AQUA102.WMF AQUA111.WMF
AQUA113.WMF AQUA114.WMF AQUA115.WMF AQUA117.WMF AQUA118.WMF AQUA119.WMF AQUA120.WMF AQUA121.WMF AQUA122.WMF AQUA123.WMF
AQUA124.WMF AQUA126.WMF AQUA128.WMF AQUA129.WMF AQUA130.WMF AQUA131.WMF AQUA132.WMF AQUA135.WMF AQUA136.WMF AQUA137.WMF
AQUA146.WMF AQUA147.WMF AQUA148.WMF AQUA149.WMF AQUA150.WMF AQUA151.WMF AQUA153.WMF AWH011C.WMF AWH017A.WMF AWP032A.WMF
AWP035E.WMF CROCODIL.WMF DOLPHIN.WMF FCP036E.WMF FCP042G.WMF FSW006D.WMF FSW013C.WMF FSW029A.WMF FSW034B.WMF HIPPO.WMF
LAC013F.WMF LAC013I.WMF MAR023A.WMF MAR024B.WMF NAU010D.WMF NPC025A.WMF PLATYPC.WMF SEAL1.WMF SEAL2.WMF SHARK.WMF
SPA004E.WMF TOD071W.WMF VSC069I.WMF WAG002A.WMF WHALE.WMF WHD005A.WMF WHD010A.WMF WHD034A.WMF

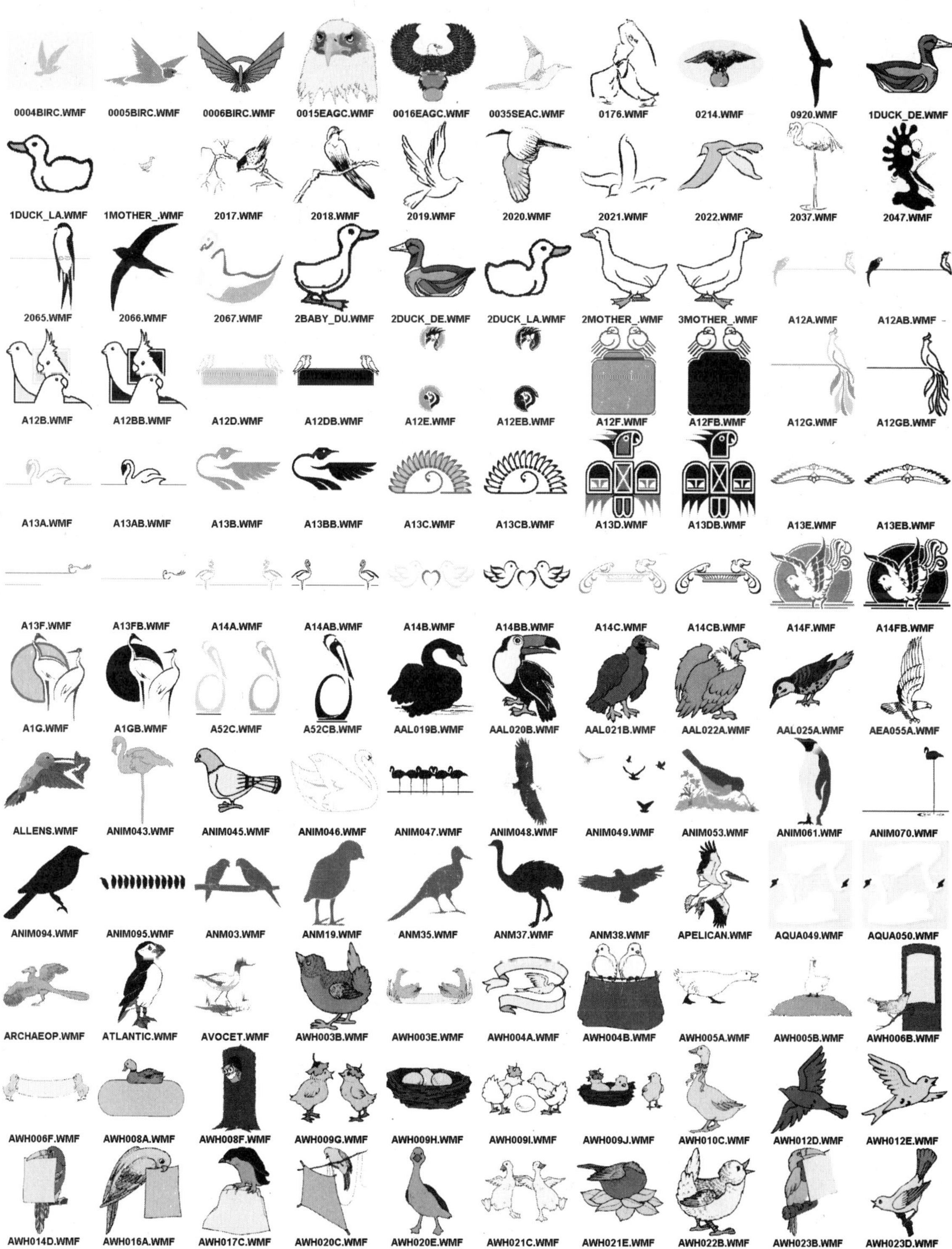
0004BIRC.WMF 0005BIRC.WMF 0006BIRC.WMF 0015EAGC.WMF 0016EAGC.WMF 0035SEAC.WMF 0176.WMF 0214.WMF 0920.WMF 1DUCK_DE.WMF
1DUCK_LA.WMF 1MOTHER_.WMF 2017.WMF 2018.WMF 2019.WMF 2020.WMF 2021.WMF 2022.WMF 2037.WMF 2047.WMF
2065.WMF 2066.WMF 2067.WMF 2BABY_DU.WMF 2DUCK_DE.WMF 2DUCK_LA.WMF 2MOTHER_.WMF 3MOTHER_.WMF A12A.WMF A12AB.WMF
A12B.WMF A12BB.WMF A12D.WMF A12DB.WMF A12E.WMF A12EB.WMF A12F.WMF A12FB.WMF A12G.WMF A12GB.WMF
A13A.WMF A13AB.WMF A13B.WMF A13BB.WMF A13C.WMF A13CB.WMF A13D.WMF A13DB.WMF A13E.WMF A13EB.WMF
A13F.WMF A13FB.WMF A14A.WMF A14AB.WMF A14B.WMF A14BB.WMF A14C.WMF A14CB.WMF A14F.WMF A14FB.WMF
A1G.WMF A1GB.WMF A52C.WMF A52CB.WMF AAL019B.WMF AAL020B.WMF AAL021B.WMF AAL022A.WMF AAL025A.WMF AEA055A.WMF
ALLENS.WMF ANIM043.WMF ANIM045.WMF ANIM046.WMF ANIM047.WMF ANIM048.WMF ANIM049.WMF ANIM053.WMF ANIM061.WMF ANIM070.WMF
ANIM094.WMF ANIM095.WMF ANM03.WMF ANM19.WMF ANM35.WMF ANM37.WMF ANM38.WMF APELICAN.WMF AQUA049.WMF AQUA050.WMF
ARCHAEOP.WMF ATLANTIC.WMF AVOCET.WMF AWH003B.WMF AWH003E.WMF AWH004A.WMF AWH004B.WMF AWH005A.WMF AWH005B.WMF AWH006B.WMF
AWH006F.WMF AWH008A.WMF AWH008F.WMF AWH009G.WMF AWH009H.WMF AWH009I.WMF AWH009J.WMF AWH010C.WMF AWH012D.WMF AWH012E.WMF
AWH014D.WMF AWH016A.WMF AWH017C.WMF AWH020C.WMF AWH020E.WMF AWH021C.WMF AWH021E.WMF AWH022B.WMF AWH023B.WMF AWH023D.WMF

AWH024A.WMF AWH025D.WMF AWH027I.WMF AWH028E.WMF AWP030.WMF AWP030B.WMF AWP030D.WMF AWP031A.WMF AWP037B.WMF B20098.WMF
B_RD.WMF B_RDS.WMF BANTAM.WMF BARBET.WMF BARNOWL.WMF BBOOBY.WMF BELLM.WMF BELTED.WMF BF03.WMF BIRD.WMF
BIRD1.WMF BIRD1A.WMF BIRD1C.WMF BIRD2.WMF BIRD22.WMF BIRD23.WMF BIRD23B.WMF BIRD26.WMF BIRD26B.WMF BIRD28.WMF
BIRD28B.WMF BIRD2A.WMF BIRD3.WMF BIRD3B.WMF BIRD4.WMF BIRD42.WMF BIRD4B.WMF BIRD5.WMF BIRD7.WMF BIRD7B.WMF
BIRD8.WMF BIRD8B.WMF BIRD_BRA.WMF BIRD_S_N.WMF BIRDCAGE.WMF BIRDNEST.WMF BIRDPP.WMF BIRDS.WMF BIRDS1.WMF BIRDS10.WMF
BIRDS3.WMF BIRDS5.WMF BIRDS6.WMF BIRDSITT.WMF BIRDWLAR.WMF BIT0626.WMF BIT0876.WMF BIT0931.WMF BIT1114.WMF BIT1115.WMF
BIT1116.WMF BIT1117.WMF BIT1118.WMF BIT1119.WMF BIT1120.WMF BIT1121.WMF BIT1122.WMF BIT1132.WMF BIT1133.WMF BIT1134.WMF
BIT1135.WMF BIT1139.WMF BKCPLORY.WMF BLACKBD.WMF BLACKBR.WMF BLKITE.WMF BLUBIRD8.WMF BLUE_BIR.WMF BLUEBIRD.WMF BLUEHEN.WMF
BLUEJAY.WMF BLUETIT.WMF BLWREN.WMF BNEST.WMF BOBWHITE.WMF BOWER.WMF BRFCAT.WMF BRNOWL.WMF BROWNBAT.WMF BROWNBOO.WMF
BROWNPEL.WMF BSD004A.WMF BSD017A.WMF BSD023B.WMF BSD039A.WMF BSD047A.WMF BSD050B.WMF BSD055B.WMF BSWAN.WMF BTHRSHER.WMF
BUDGIE.WMF BUDGIE1.WMF BUNTING.WMF BUSTARD.WMF BUSTARD1.WMF BUTCHR.WMF CAA0253.WMF CAA0254.WMF CAA0255.WMF CAA0256.WMF
CAA0264.WMF CAA0292.WMF CAA0300.WMF CACTWREN.WMF CANADAGO.WMF CANARY.WMF CANARY8.WMF CAPTIMUL.WMF CAQUAIL.WMF CARDI.WMF

CARDIN_1.WMF
CARDINA1.WMF
CARDINA2.WMF
CARDINA3.WMF
CARDINA4.WMF
CARDINAL.WMF
CARDNAL8.WMF
CAROWREN.WMF
CASSO.WMF
CASUARIS.WMF
CATTAILS.WMF
CDS002A.WMF
CDS002D.WMF
CDS008C.WMF
CDS034D.WMF
CDS034E.WMF
CDS035C.WMF
CHAFFNCH.WMF
CHICK.WMF
CHICKADE.WMF
CHICKEN.WMF
CHICKEN_.WMF
CHICKN.WMF
CHUKAR.WMF
CHW016F.WMF
CLREAGL.WMF
CM13.WMF
COAST1.WMF
COCK.WMF
COCKAT.WMF
COCKATOO.WMF
COCKEREL.WMF
COCKOO.WMF
COFTROCK.WMF
CONDOR.WMF
COOT.WMF
CORMORNT.WMF
CRANE.WMF
CRANE22.WMF
CROW.WMF
CROWNED.WMF
CS61_.WMF
CS62_.WMF
CS63_.WMF
CS64_.WMF
CS65_.WMF
CS66_.WMF
CS67_.WMF
CS68_.WMF
CS69_.WMF
CS70_.WMF
CS71_.WMF
CTANI060.WMF
CUCKOO.WMF
CURLEW.WMF
DABCHCK.WMF
DACELO.WMF
DEC082M.WMF
DEC083C.WMF
DEC084CC.WMF
DEC084FF.WMF
DEC084U.WMF
DEC084X.WMF
DEC085J.WMF
DEC086J.WMF
DEC086N.WMF
DEC087D.WMF
DEC087L.WMF
DEC087X.WMF
DEC087Y.WMF
DEC088A.WMF
DEC088K.WMF
DEC088R.WMF
DEC089G.WMF
DESIGN20.WMF
DOVE.WMF
DOVE1.WMF
DOVE10.WMF
DOVE13.WMF
DOVE2.WMF
DOVE20.WMF
DOVE3.WMF
DOVE4.WMF
DOVE5.WMF
DOVE6.WMF
DOVEPP.WMF
DUCK.WMF
DUCK1.WMF
DUCK10.WMF
DUCK2.WMF
DUCK2P.WMF
DUCK3.WMF
DUCKC.WMF
DUCKPP.WMF
DUNNOCK.WMF
E20927.WMF
E20928.WMF
E20929.WMF
EAG_HEA.WMF
EAGL.WMF
EAGL2.WMF
EAGL3.WMF
EAGL44.WMF
EAGLE.WMF
EAGLE1.WMF
EAGLE10.WMF
EAGLE12.WMF
EAGLE1A.WMF
EAGLE1C.WMF
EAGLE2.WMF
EAGLE20.WMF
EAGLE22.WMF
EAGLE2A.WMF
EAGLE3.WMF
EAGLE32.WMF
EAGLE35.WMF
EAGLE8.WMF
EAGLE_4C.WMF
EAGLEFAC.WMF
EAGLEHEA.WMF

EAGLEOWL.WMF
EAGLEPER.WMF
EAGLPP.WMF
EARLYBRD.WMF
EASTRLIL.WMF
EGLEFLY1.WMF
EGLEFLY2.WMF
EGRET.WMF
EGRET1.WMF
EGRET32.WMF
EMPEROR.WMF
EMU.WMF
EMU5.WMF
EMUC.WMF
FALCO.WMF
FALCON.WMF
FCCKOO.WMF
FEATHER.WMF
FEMALEAL.WMF
FINCH.WMF
FKING.WMF
FLAM44.WMF
FLAM_.WMF
FLAMIN_1.WMF
FLAMING.WMF
FLAMINGO.WMF
FLICKER.WMF
FLMINGO.WMF
FLMINGO0.WMF
FLOR_FLA.WMF
FLYCATCH.WMF
FLYEAGL1.WMF
FLYEAGL2.WMF
FLYFOX.WMF
FPIGEON.WMF
FROGM.WMF
FSW006C.WMF
FSW031E.WMF
FWN022A.WMF
FWN022B.WMF
FWN022C.WMF
FWN022D.WMF
FWN022E.WMF
FWN022F.WMF
FWN022G.WMF
FWN022H.WMF
FWN022I.WMF
FWN022J.WMF
FWN022K.WMF
FWN022L.WMF
FWN022M.WMF
FWN022N.WMF
FWN022O.WMF
FWN022P.WMF
FWN022Q.WMF
FWN022R.WMF
FWN022S.WMF
FWN022T.WMF
FWN032A.WMF
FWN032B.WMF
FWN032C.WMF
FWN032D.WMF
FWN032E.WMF
FWN032F.WMF
FWN032G.WMF
FWN032H.WMF
FWN032J.WMF
FWN032K.WMF
FWN032L.WMF
FWN032M.WMF
FWN032N.WMF
FWN032O.WMF
FWN032P.WMF
GALAH.WMF
GAMEHEN.WMF
GBOWER.WMF
GCGREBE.WMF
GEESE.WMF
GEESE30.WMF
GENTOO.WMF
GHERON.WMF
GOO44.WMF
GOOSE.WMF
GOOSE0.WMF
GOOSE1.WMF
GOOSE2.WMF
GREATIT.WMF
GREATOWL.WMF
GREBE.WMF
GRIFFON.WMF
GRIFNVUL.WMF
GROSBEAK.WMF
GROUSE.WMF
GRSOWL.WMF
GTHRSH.WMF
GUILLMOT.WMF
GUINEA.WMF
GULL.WMF
GULL1.WMF
GULLS.WMF
HAWK.WMF
HAWK45.WMF
HEATH3.WMF
HEN.WMF
HERON.WMF
HIGOOSE.WMF
HOOHOE.WMF
HOOPOE.WMF
HORNBILL.WMF
HOUSREPS.WMF
HPI016A.WMF
HPI016C.WMF
HSEMARTN.WMF
HSPARROW.WMF
HTHRUSH.WMF
HUMING.WMF
HUMMBIRD.WMF
HUMMING.WMF
HUMMINGB.WMF
HUMMINGR.WMF

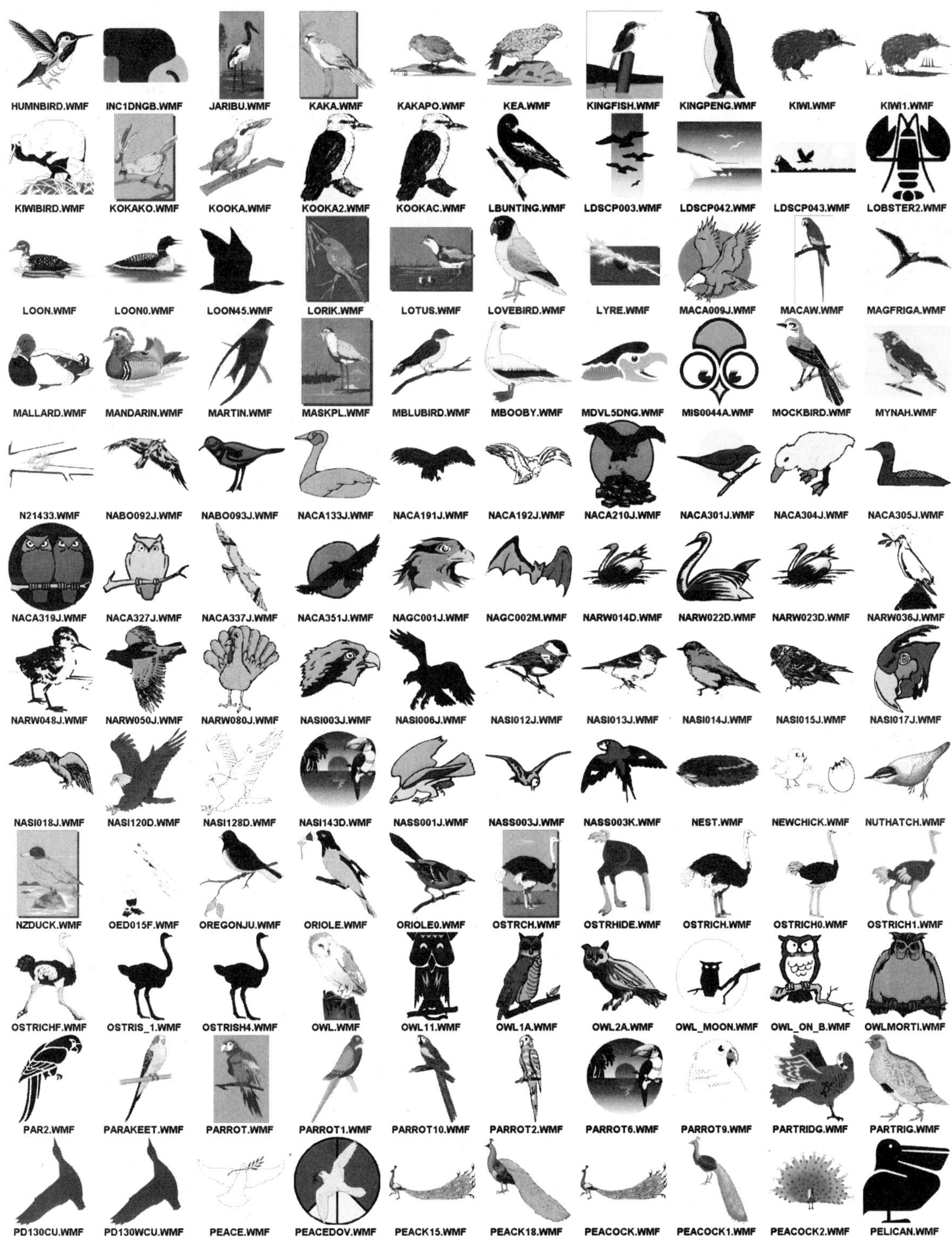
HUMNBIRD.WMF INC1DNGB.WMF JARIBU.WMF KAKA.WMF KAKAPO.WMF KEA.WMF KINGFISH.WMF KINGPENG.WMF KIWI.WMF KIWI1.WMF
KIWIBIRD.WMF KOKAKO.WMF KOOKA.WMF KOOKA2.WMF KOOKAC.WMF LBUNTING.WMF LDSCP003.WMF LDSCP042.WMF LDSCP043.WMF LOBSTER2.WMF
LOON.WMF LOON0.WMF LOON45.WMF LORIK.WMF LOTUS.WMF LOVEBIRD.WMF LYRE.WMF MACA009J.WMF MACAW.WMF MAGFRIGA.WMF
MALLARD.WMF MANDARIN.WMF MARTIN.WMF MASKPL.WMF MBLUBIRD.WMF MBOOBY.WMF MDVL5DNG.WMF MIS0044A.WMF MOCKBIRD.WMF MYNAH.WMF
N21433.WMF NABO092J.WMF NABO093J.WMF NACA133J.WMF NACA191J.WMF NACA192J.WMF NACA210J.WMF NACA301J.WMF NACA304J.WMF NACA305J.WMF
NACA319J.WMF NACA327J.WMF NACA337J.WMF NACA351J.WMF NAGC001J.WMF NAGC002M.WMF NARW014D.WMF NARW022D.WMF NARW023D.WMF NARW036J.WMF
NARW048J.WMF NARW050J.WMF NARW080J.WMF NASI003J.WMF NASI006J.WMF NASI012J.WMF NASI013J.WMF NASI014J.WMF NASI015J.WMF NASI017J.WMF
NASI018J.WMF NASI120D.WMF NASI128D.WMF NASI143D.WMF NASS001J.WMF NASS003J.WMF NASS003K.WMF NEST.WMF NEWCHICK.WMF NUTHATCH.WMF
NZDUCK.WMF OED015F.WMF OREGONJU.WMF ORIOLE.WMF ORIOLE0.WMF OSTRCH.WMF OSTRHIDE.WMF OSTRICH.WMF OSTRICH0.WMF OSTRICH1.WMF
OSTRICHF.WMF OSTRIS_1.WMF OSTRISH4.WMF OWL.WMF OWL11.WMF OWL1A.WMF OWL2A.WMF OWL_MOON.WMF OWL_ON_B.WMF OWLMORTI.WMF
PAR2.WMF PARAKEET.WMF PARROT.WMF PARROT1.WMF PARROT10.WMF PARROT2.WMF PARROT6.WMF PARROT9.WMF PARTRIDG.WMF PARTRIG.WMF
PD130CU.WMF PD130WCU.WMF PEACE.WMF PEACEDOV.WMF PEACK15.WMF PEACK18.WMF PEACOCK.WMF PEACOCK1.WMF PEACOCK2.WMF PELICAN.WMF

PELICAN1.WMF
PELICAN2.WMF
PELICAN9.WMF
PELICN.WMF
PELICN_1.WMF
PENGUIN.WMF
PENGUIN1.WMF
PENGUIN6.WMF
PENGUIN9.WMF
PENGUINS.WMF
PENGUN1.WMF
PEREGRIN.WMF
PETREL.WMF
PFINCH.WMF
PHEA44.WMF
PHEAS.WMF
PHEASA44.WMF
PHEASANT.WMF
PHEASNT.WMF
PIGEON.WMF
PIGEON15.WMF
PILINGS.WMF
PODICEPS.WMF
PRIN0019.WMF
PRIN0020.WMF
PRIN0021.WMF
PRIN0022.WMF
PRIN0023.WMF
PRIN0024.WMF
PRIN0029.WMF
PRIN0030.WMF
PRIN0031.WMF
PRIN0032.WMF
PRIN0033.WMF
PRIN0034.WMF
PRIN0035.WMF
PRIN0036.WMF
PRIN0039.WMF
PRIN0040.WMF
PRIN0041.WMF
PRIN0042.WMF
PRROT15.WMF
QUAIL.WMF
RAIL.WMF
RAINBW.WMF
RBGULL.WMF
REDHEAD.WMF
REDWING.WMF
ROBIN.WMF
ROBIN1.WMF
ROBIN30.WMF
ROCKHOPP.WMF
ROCKW.WMF
ROO.WMF
ROOST_R5.WMF
ROOSTER.WMF
ROOSTERH.WMF
ROSELA.WMF
ROSERING.WMF
RUNNER.WMF
SAWOWL.WMF
SBLUEWRN.WMF
SCARLETI.WMF
SEAG44.WMF
SEAGUL42.WMF
SEAGUL_L.WMF
SEAGUL_R.WMF
SEAGULL.WMF
SEAGULLS.WMF
SECRETRY.WMF
SGOOSE.WMF
SNOWYOWL.WMF
SONGTHR.WMF
SOSI009D.WMF
SPA003F.WMF
SPA009E.WMF
SPA010F.WMF
SPA014B.WMF
SPA018A.WMF
SPA021D.WMF
SPA022A.WMF
SPA026E.WMF
SPARR_W5.WMF
SPARROW.WMF
SPARROW1.WMF
SPOONBIL.WMF
SPOTTED2.WMF
SPOTTED3.WMF
STARLI_1.WMF
STARLING.WMF
STO.WMF
STORK.WMF
STORK_SI.WMF
SUNBIRD.WMF
SWA45.WMF
SWALL_W5.WMF
SWALLOW.WMF
SWALLOW1.WMF
SWAN.WMF
SWAN1.WMF
SWAN10.WMF
SWAN15.WMF
SWAN2TO.WMF
SWAN9.WMF
SWANTO.WMF
SWEEP.WMF
SWNDGBT1.WMF
SWNDNGBT.WMF
SWNSKT1.WMF
SWNSKT2.WMF
SYMBL101.WMF
SYMBL102.WMF
SYMBL103.WMF
SYMBL104.WMF
SYMBL105.WMF
SYMBL106.WMF
SYMBL107.WMF
SYMBL108.WMF
SYMBL109.WMF
SYMBL1_1.WMF

SYMBL1_2.WMF SYMBL1_3.WMF SYMBL1_4.WMF SYMBL1_5.WMF SYMBL1_6.WMF SYMBL1_7.WMF SYMBL1_8.WMF SYMBL1_9.WMF SYMBL1A2.WMF SYMBL1A3.WMF

SYMBL1A4.WMF SYMBL1A5.WMF SYMBL1A6.WMF SYMBL1A7.WMF SYMBL1A9.WMF TAILOR.WMF TAKAHE.WMF TANAGER.WMF TERN.WMF THNKPARR.WMF

TOUCAN.WMF TOUCAN1.WMF TOUCAN15.WMF TOUKAN.WMF TOWHEE.WMF TUFTEDCK.WMF TURKEY.WMF TURKEY1.WMF TURKEY15.WMF TURKEY2.WMF

TURKEY3.WMF TURKEY8.WMF UGUISU.WMF UPLAND2.WMF VIOLET.WMF VULCHR.WMF WDPECK15.WMF WETLAND2.WMF WHIP.WMF WHIST.WMF

WHISTLE.WMF WILDDUCK.WMF WILGOLD.WMF WILPTMGN.WMF WILSONS.WMF WMEADLRK.WMF WOODDUCK.WMF WOODLND2.WMF WOODPE_1.WMF WOODPECK.WMF

YHAMMER.WMF

AQCAR058.WMF AQCAR072.WMF AQCAR088.WMF AQCAR089.WMF AQCAR090.WMF AQCAR092.WMF AQCAR162.WMF AQCAR163.WMF AQCAR164.WMF AQCAR165.WMF

AQCAR166.WMF AQCAR167.WMF AQCAR169.WMF AQCAR170.WMF AQCAR171.WMF AQCAR172.WMF AQCAR183.WMF AWH001C.WMF AWH006B.WMF AWH008B.WMF

AWH008D.WMF AWH016A.WMF BIRCR001.WMF BIRCR002.WMF BIRCR003.WMF BIRCR004.WMF BIRCR005.WMF BIRCR006.WMF BIRCR007.WMF BIRCR008.WMF

BIRCR009.WMF BIRCR010.WMF BIRCR011.WMF BIRCR012.WMF BIRCR013.WMF BIRCR014.WMF BIRCR015.WMF BIRCR016.WMF BIRCR017.WMF BIRCR018.WMF

BIRCR019.WMF BIRCR020.WMF BIRCR021.WMF BIRCR022.WMF BIRCR023.WMF BIRCR024.WMF BIRCR025.WMF BIRCR026.WMF BIRCR027.WMF BIRCR028.WMF

BIRCR029.WMF BIRCR030.WMF BIRCR031.WMF BIRCR032.WMF BIRCR033.WMF BIRCR034.WMF BIRCR035.WMF BIRCR036.WMF BIRCR037.WMF BIRCR038.WMF

BIRCR039.WMF BIRCR040.WMF BIRCR041.WMF BIRCR042.WMF BIRCR043.WMF BIRCR044.WMF BIRCR045.WMF BIRCR046.WMF BIRCR047.WMF BIRCR048.WMF

BIRCR049.WMF BIRCR050.WMF BIRCR051.WMF BIRCR052.WMF BIRCR053.WMF BIRCR054.WMF BIRCR055.WMF BIRCR056.WMF BIRCR057.WMF BIRCR058.WMF

BIRCR059.WMF BIRCR060.WMF BIRCR061.WMF BIRCR062.WMF BIRCR063.WMF BIRCR064.WMF BIRCR065.WMF BIRCR066.WMF BIRCR067.WMF BIRCR068.WMF

BIRCR069.WMF BIRCR070.WMF BIRCR071.WMF BIRCR072.WMF BIRCR073.WMF BIRCR074.WMF BIRCR075.WMF BIRCR076.WMF BIRCR077.WMF BIRCR078.WMF

BIRCR079.WMF BIRCR080.WMF BIRCR081.WMF BIRCR082.WMF BIRCR083.WMF BIRCR084.WMF BIRCR085.WMF BIRCR086.WMF BIRCR087.WMF BIRCR088.WMF

BIRCR089.WMF BIRCR090.WMF BIRCR091.WMF BIRCR092.WMF BIRCR093.WMF BIRCR094.WMF BIRCR095.WMF BIRCR096.WMF BIRCR097.WMF BIRCR098.WMF

BIRCR099.WMF BIRCR100.WMF BIRCR101.WMF BIRCR102.WMF BIRCR103.WMF BIRCR104.WMF BIRCR105.WMF BIRCR106.WMF BIRCR107.WMF BIRCR108.WMF

BIRCR109.WMF BIRCR110.WMF BIRCR111.WMF BIRCR112.WMF BIRCR113.WMF BIRCR114.WMF BIRCR115.WMF BIRCR116.WMF BIRCR117.WMF BIRCR118.WMF

BIRCR119.WMF BIRCR120.WMF BIRCR121.WMF BIRCR122.WMF BIRCR123.WMF BIRCR124.WMF BIRCR125.WMF BIRCR126.WMF BIRCR127.WMF BIRCR128.WMF

BIRCR129.WMF BIRCR130.WMF BIRCR131.WMF BIRCR132.WMF BIRCR133.WMF BIRCR134.WMF BIRCR135.WMF BIRCR136.WMF BIRCR137.WMF BIRCR138.WMF

BIRCR139.WMF BIRCR140.WMF BIRCR141.WMF BIRCR142.WMF BIRCR143.WMF BIRCR144.WMF BIRCR145.WMF BIRCR146.WMF BIRCR147.WMF BIRCR148.WMF

BIRCR149.WMF BIRCR150.WMF BIRCR151.WMF BIRCR152.WMF BIRCR153.WMF BIRCR154.WMF BIRCR155.WMF BIRCR156.WMF BIRCR157.WMF BIRCR158.WMF

BIRCR159.WMF BIRCR160.WMF BIRCR161.WMF BIRCR162.WMF BIRCR163.WMF BIRCR164.WMF BIRCR165.WMF BIRCR166.WMF BIRCR167.WMF BIRCR168.WMF

BIRCR169.WMF BIRCR170.WMF BIRCR171.WMF BIRCR172.WMF BIRCR173.WMF BIRCR174.WMF BIRCR175.WMF BIRCR176.WMF BIRCR177.WMF BIRCR178.WMF

BIRCR179.WMF BIRCR180.WMF BIRCR181.WMF BIRCR182.WMF BIRCR183.WMF BIRCR184.WMF BIRCR185.WMF BIRCR186.WMF BIRCR187.WMF BIRCR188.WMF

BIRCR189.WMF BIRCR190.WMF BIRCR191.WMF BIRCR192.WMF BIRCR193.WMF BIRCR194.WMF BIRCR195.WMF BIRCR196.WMF BIRCR197.WMF BIRCR198.WMF

BIRCR199.WMF BIRCR200.WMF BIRCR201.WMF BIRCR202.WMF BIRCR203.WMF BIRCR204.WMF BIRCR205.WMF BIRCR206.WMF BIRCR207.WMF BIRCR208.WMF

BIRCR209.WMF BIRCR210.WMF BIRCR211.WMF BIRCR212.WMF BIRCR213.WMF BIRCR214.WMF BIRCR215.WMF BIRCR216.WMF BIRCR217.WMF BIRCR218.WMF

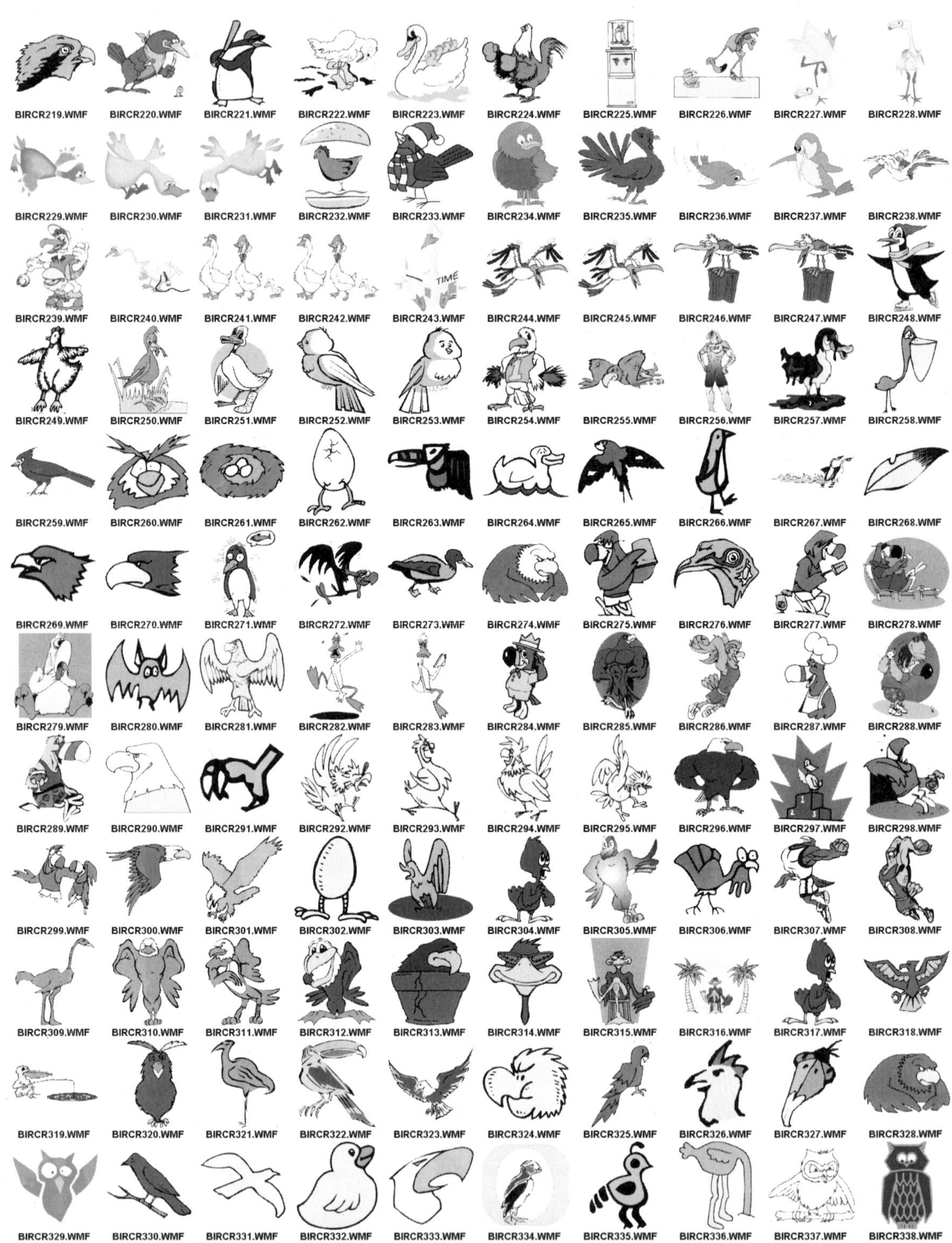

BIRCR219.WMF BIRCR220.WMF BIRCR221.WMF BIRCR222.WMF BIRCR223.WMF BIRCR224.WMF BIRCR225.WMF BIRCR226.WMF BIRCR227.WMF BIRCR228.WMF
BIRCR229.WMF BIRCR230.WMF BIRCR231.WMF BIRCR232.WMF BIRCR233.WMF BIRCR234.WMF BIRCR235.WMF BIRCR236.WMF BIRCR237.WMF BIRCR238.WMF
BIRCR239.WMF BIRCR240.WMF BIRCR241.WMF BIRCR242.WMF BIRCR243.WMF BIRCR244.WMF BIRCR245.WMF BIRCR246.WMF BIRCR247.WMF BIRCR248.WMF
BIRCR249.WMF BIRCR250.WMF BIRCR251.WMF BIRCR252.WMF BIRCR253.WMF BIRCR254.WMF BIRCR255.WMF BIRCR256.WMF BIRCR257.WMF BIRCR258.WMF
BIRCR259.WMF BIRCR260.WMF BIRCR261.WMF BIRCR262.WMF BIRCR263.WMF BIRCR264.WMF BIRCR265.WMF BIRCR266.WMF BIRCR267.WMF BIRCR268.WMF
BIRCR269.WMF BIRCR270.WMF BIRCR271.WMF BIRCR272.WMF BIRCR273.WMF BIRCR274.WMF BIRCR275.WMF BIRCR276.WMF BIRCR277.WMF BIRCR278.WMF
BIRCR279.WMF BIRCR280.WMF BIRCR281.WMF BIRCR282.WMF BIRCR283.WMF BIRCR284.WMF BIRCR285.WMF BIRCR286.WMF BIRCR287.WMF BIRCR288.WMF
BIRCR289.WMF BIRCR290.WMF BIRCR291.WMF BIRCR292.WMF BIRCR293.WMF BIRCR294.WMF BIRCR295.WMF BIRCR296.WMF BIRCR297.WMF BIRCR298.WMF
BIRCR299.WMF BIRCR300.WMF BIRCR301.WMF BIRCR302.WMF BIRCR303.WMF BIRCR304.WMF BIRCR305.WMF BIRCR306.WMF BIRCR307.WMF BIRCR308.WMF
BIRCR309.WMF BIRCR310.WMF BIRCR311.WMF BIRCR312.WMF BIRCR313.WMF BIRCR314.WMF BIRCR315.WMF BIRCR316.WMF BIRCR317.WMF BIRCR318.WMF
BIRCR319.WMF BIRCR320.WMF BIRCR321.WMF BIRCR322.WMF BIRCR323.WMF BIRCR324.WMF BIRCR325.WMF BIRCR326.WMF BIRCR327.WMF BIRCR328.WMF
BIRCR329.WMF BIRCR330.WMF BIRCR331.WMF BIRCR332.WMF BIRCR333.WMF BIRCR334.WMF BIRCR335.WMF BIRCR336.WMF BIRCR337.WMF BIRCR338.WMF

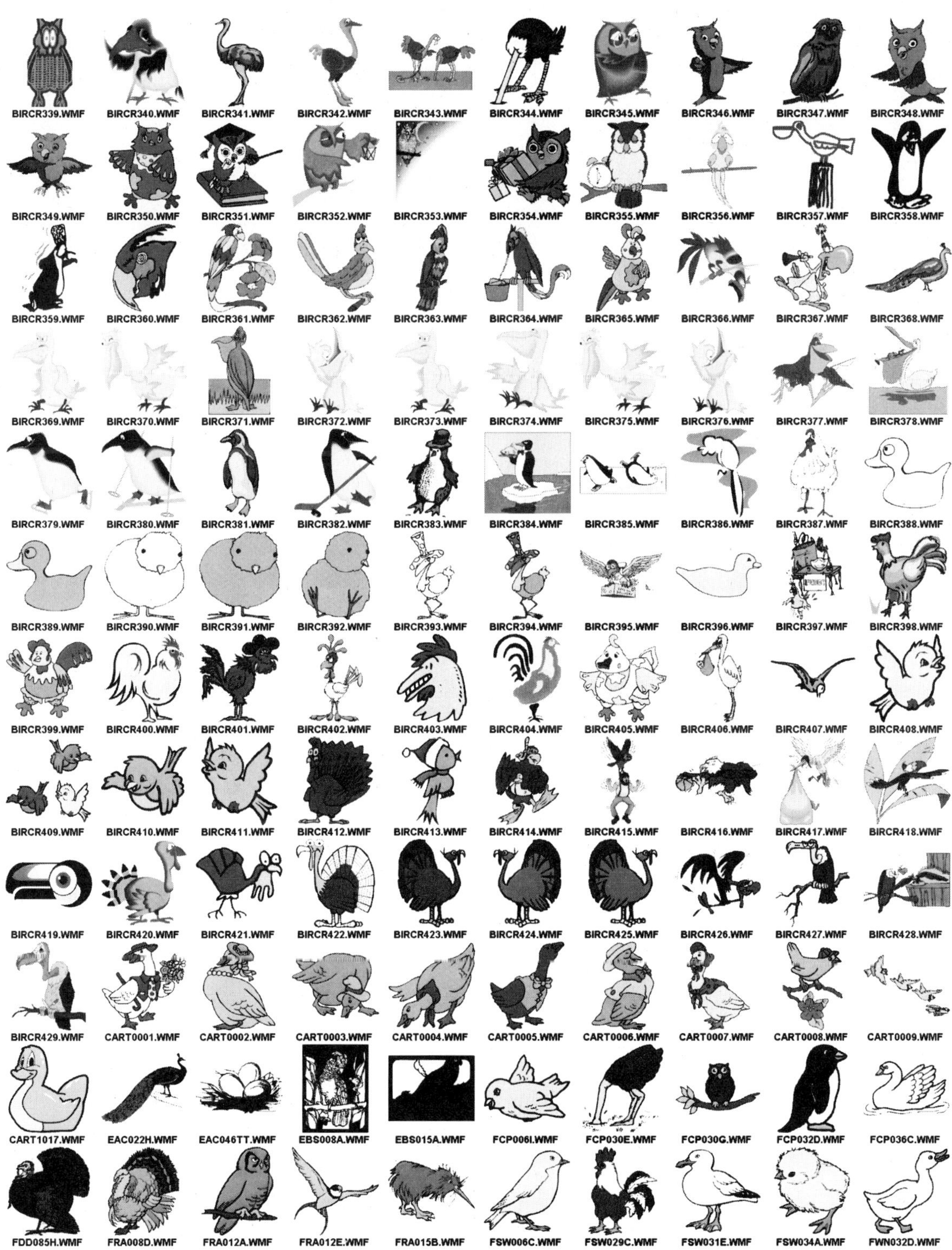
BIRCR339.WMF
BIRCR340.WMF
BIRCR341.WMF
BIRCR342.WMF
BIRCR343.WMF
BIRCR344.WMF
BIRCR345.WMF
BIRCR346.WMF
BIRCR347.WMF
BIRCR348.WMF
BIRCR349.WMF
BIRCR350.WMF
BIRCR351.WMF
BIRCR352.WMF
BIRCR353.WMF
BIRCR354.WMF
BIRCR355.WMF
BIRCR356.WMF
BIRCR357.WMF
BIRCR358.WMF
BIRCR359.WMF
BIRCR360.WMF
BIRCR361.WMF
BIRCR362.WMF
BIRCR363.WMF
BIRCR364.WMF
BIRCR365.WMF
BIRCR366.WMF
BIRCR367.WMF
BIRCR368.WMF
BIRCR369.WMF
BIRCR370.WMF
BIRCR371.WMF
BIRCR372.WMF
BIRCR373.WMF
BIRCR374.WMF
BIRCR375.WMF
BIRCR376.WMF
BIRCR377.WMF
BIRCR378.WMF
BIRCR379.WMF
BIRCR380.WMF
BIRCR381.WMF
BIRCR382.WMF
BIRCR383.WMF
BIRCR384.WMF
BIRCR385.WMF
BIRCR386.WMF
BIRCR387.WMF
BIRCR388.WMF
BIRCR389.WMF
BIRCR390.WMF
BIRCR391.WMF
BIRCR392.WMF
BIRCR393.WMF
BIRCR394.WMF
BIRCR395.WMF
BIRCR396.WMF
BIRCR397.WMF
BIRCR398.WMF
BIRCR399.WMF
BIRCR400.WMF
BIRCR401.WMF
BIRCR402.WMF
BIRCR403.WMF
BIRCR404.WMF
BIRCR405.WMF
BIRCR406.WMF
BIRCR407.WMF
BIRCR408.WMF
BIRCR409.WMF
BIRCR410.WMF
BIRCR411.WMF
BIRCR412.WMF
BIRCR413.WMF
BIRCR414.WMF
BIRCR415.WMF
BIRCR416.WMF
BIRCR417.WMF
BIRCR418.WMF
BIRCR419.WMF
BIRCR420.WMF
BIRCR421.WMF
BIRCR422.WMF
BIRCR423.WMF
BIRCR424.WMF
BIRCR425.WMF
BIRCR426.WMF
BIRCR427.WMF
BIRCR428.WMF
BIRCR429.WMF
CART0001.WMF
CART0002.WMF
CART0003.WMF
CART0004.WMF
CART0005.WMF
CART0006.WMF
CART0007.WMF
CART0008.WMF
CART0009.WMF
CART1017.WMF
EAC022H.WMF
EAC046TT.WMF
EBS008A.WMF
EBS015A.WMF
FCP006I.WMF
FCP030E.WMF
FCP030G.WMF
FCP032D.WMF
FCP036C.WMF
FDD085H.WMF
FRA008D.WMF
FRA012A.WMF
FRA012E.WMF
FRA015B.WMF
FSW006C.WMF
FSW029C.WMF
FSW031E.WMF
FSW034A.WMF
FWN032D.WMF

IHO026I.WMF KPPFRZN.WMF LAC007A.WMF LAC007F.WMF LAC007J.WMF LAC008A.WMF LAC008C.WMF LAC008E.WMF LAC008F.WMF LAC008G.WMF

LAC008I.WMF LAC008K.WMF LAC012B.WMF LAC015A.WMF LAC015C.WMF LAC015G.WMF MAR002A.WMF MAR010C.WMF MAR012C.WMF MOD022N.WMF

MOD026K.WMF MOD031L.WMF MSL080F.WMF MSL094D.WMF NAU006C.WMF OEC021J.WMF OEC022I.WMF OFS033F.WMF OFS034J.WMF OFS035G.WMF

OFS035H.WMF OFS039J.WMF OFS040E.WMF OTS014F.WMF OTS017E.WMF OTS064A.WMF OTS064E.WMF OTS065B.WMF OTS068P.WMF PENGUIN.WMF

POC100F.WMF POC113K.WMF SAC007C.WMF SIT074L.WMF SIT077B.WMF SIT080F.WMF SIT081C.WMF SPA009E.WMF SWA001A.WMF SWA027A.WMF

TAD083C.WMF TOD071L.WMF TOD074C.WMF TPB009A.WMF TPB028A.WMF TPB033A.WMF TPB040A.WMF VSI002A.WMF VSI002E.WMF WMG031G.WMF

WMG033B.WMF WMG033I.WMF WMG033Q.WMF

AWH001F.WMF AWH003D.WMF AWH008C.WMF AWH009A.WMF AWH011D.WMF AWH012C.WMF AWH012G.WMF AWH013F.WMF AWH015B.WMF AWH018B.WMF

AWH018F.WMF AWH024B.WMF AWH024C.WMF AWH026A.WMF CART18E.WMF CART18F.WMF CART1E.WMF CAT01.WMF CAT02.WMF CAT029I.WMF

CAT029J.WMF CAT03.WMF CAT030I.WMF CAT031J.WMF CAT031M.WMF CAT032D.WMF CAT04.WMF CAT05.WMF CAT06.WMF CAT07.WMF

CAT08.WMF CAT09.WMF CAT10.WMF CAT11.WMF CAT12.WMF CAT13.WMF CAT14.WMF CAT15.WMF CAT16.WMF CAT17.WMF

CAT18.WMF CAT19.WMF CAT20.WMF CAT21.WMF CAT22.WMF CAT23.WMF CAT24.WMF CAT25.WMF CAT26.WMF CAT27.WMF

CAT28.WMF CAT29.WMF CAT30.WMF CAT31.WMF CAT32.WMF CAT33.WMF CAT34.WMF CAT35.WMF CAT36.WMF CAT37.WMF

CAT38.WMF CAT39.WMF CAT40.WMF CAT41.WMF CAT42.WMF CAT43.WMF CAT44.WMF CAT45.WMF CAT46.WMF CAT47.WMF

CAT48.WMF CAT49.WMF CAT50.WMF CAT51.WMF CAT52.WMF CAT53.WMF CAT54.WMF CAT55.WMF CAT56.WMF CAT57.WMF

CAT58.WMF CAT59.WMF CAT60.WMF CAT61.WMF CAT62.WMF CAT63.WMF CAT64.WMF CAT65.WMF CAT66.WMF CAT67.WMF

CAT68.WMF CAT69.WMF CAT70.WMF CAT71.WMF CAT72.WMF CAT73.WMF CAT74.WMF CAT75.WMF CAT76.WMF CAT77.WMF

CAT78.WMF CAT79.WMF CAT80.WMF CAT81.WMF CAT82.WMF CAT83.WMF CAT84.WMF CAT85.WMF CATCR001.WMF CATCR002.WMF

CATCR003.WMF CATCR004.WMF CATCR005.WMF CATCR006.WMF CATCR007.WMF CATCR008.WMF CATCR009.WMF CATCR010.WMF CATCR011.WMF CATCR012.WMF

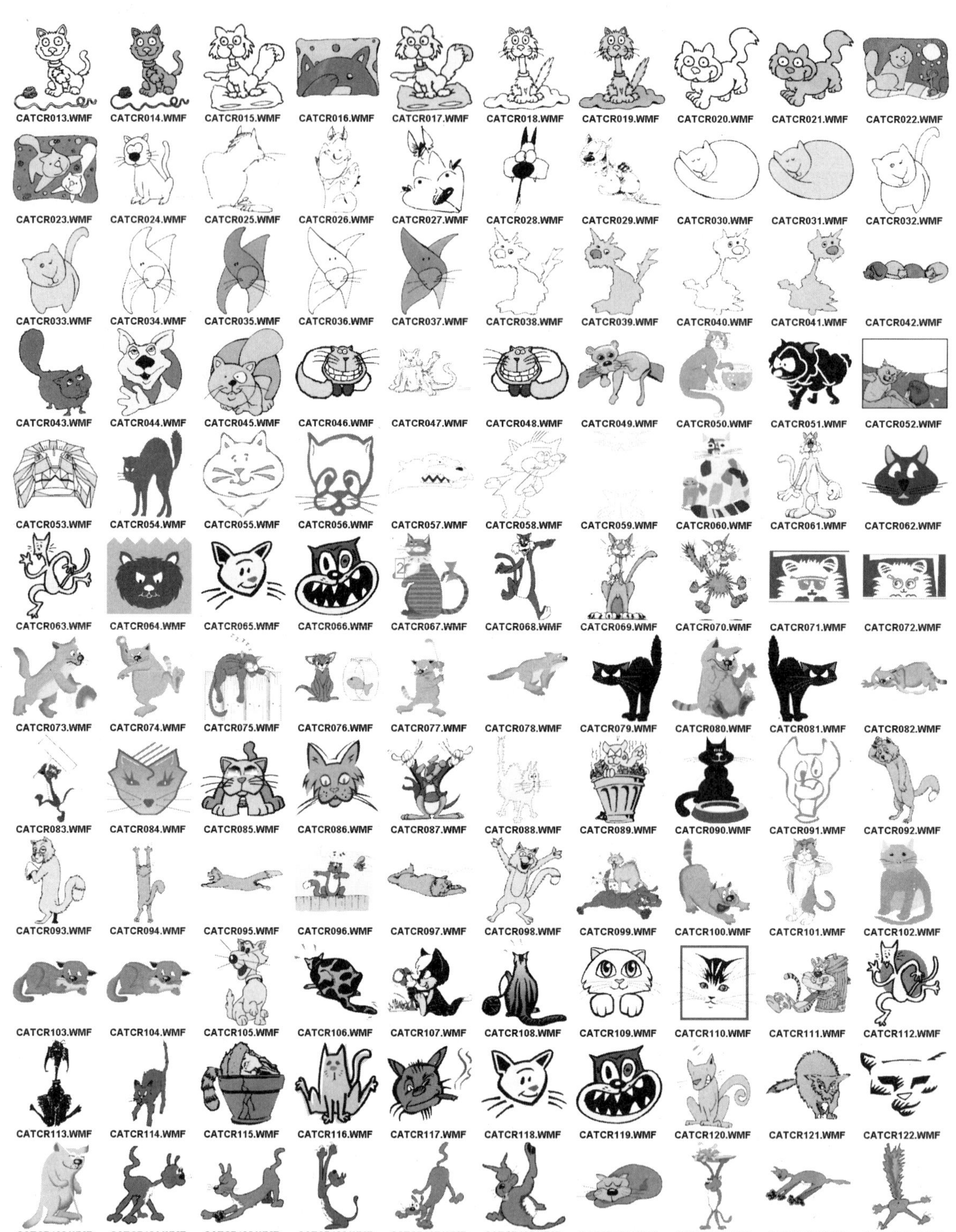

CATCR013.WMF CATCR014.WMF CATCR015.WMF CATCR016.WMF CATCR017.WMF CATCR018.WMF CATCR019.WMF CATCR020.WMF CATCR021.WMF CATCR022.WMF

CATCR023.WMF CATCR024.WMF CATCR025.WMF CATCR026.WMF CATCR027.WMF CATCR028.WMF CATCR029.WMF CATCR030.WMF CATCR031.WMF CATCR032.WMF

CATCR033.WMF CATCR034.WMF CATCR035.WMF CATCR036.WMF CATCR037.WMF CATCR038.WMF CATCR039.WMF CATCR040.WMF CATCR041.WMF CATCR042.WMF

CATCR043.WMF CATCR044.WMF CATCR045.WMF CATCR046.WMF CATCR047.WMF CATCR048.WMF CATCR049.WMF CATCR050.WMF CATCR051.WMF CATCR052.WMF

CATCR053.WMF CATCR054.WMF CATCR055.WMF CATCR056.WMF CATCR057.WMF CATCR058.WMF CATCR059.WMF CATCR060.WMF CATCR061.WMF CATCR062.WMF

CATCR063.WMF CATCR064.WMF CATCR065.WMF CATCR066.WMF CATCR067.WMF CATCR068.WMF CATCR069.WMF CATCR070.WMF CATCR071.WMF CATCR072.WMF

CATCR073.WMF CATCR074.WMF CATCR075.WMF CATCR076.WMF CATCR077.WMF CATCR078.WMF CATCR079.WMF CATCR080.WMF CATCR081.WMF CATCR082.WMF

CATCR083.WMF CATCR084.WMF CATCR085.WMF CATCR086.WMF CATCR087.WMF CATCR088.WMF CATCR089.WMF CATCR090.WMF CATCR091.WMF CATCR092.WMF

CATCR093.WMF CATCR094.WMF CATCR095.WMF CATCR096.WMF CATCR097.WMF CATCR098.WMF CATCR099.WMF CATCR100.WMF CATCR101.WMF CATCR102.WMF

CATCR103.WMF CATCR104.WMF CATCR105.WMF CATCR106.WMF CATCR107.WMF CATCR108.WMF CATCR109.WMF CATCR110.WMF CATCR111.WMF CATCR112.WMF

CATCR113.WMF CATCR114.WMF CATCR115.WMF CATCR116.WMF CATCR117.WMF CATCR118.WMF CATCR119.WMF CATCR120.WMF CATCR121.WMF CATCR122.WMF

CATCR123.WMF CATCR124.WMF CATCR125.WMF CATCR126.WMF CATCR127.WMF CATCR128.WMF CATCR129.WMF CATCR130.WMF CATCR131.WMF CATCR132.WMF

CATCR133.WMF CATCR134.WMF CATCR135.WMF CATCR136.WMF CATCR137.WMF CATCR138.WMF CATCR139.WMF CATCR140.WMF CATCR141.WMF CATCR142.WMF

CATCR143.WMF CATCR144.WMF CATCR145.WMF CATCR146.WMF CATCR147.WMF CATCR148.WMF CATCR149.WMF CATCR150.WMF CATCR151.WMF CATCR152.WMF

CATCR153.WMF CATCR154.WMF CATCR155.WMF CATCR156.WMF CATCR157.WMF CATCR158.WMF CATCR159.WMF CATCR160.WMF CATCR161.WMF CATCR162.WMF

CATCR163.WMF CATCR164.WMF CATCR165.WMF CATCR166.WMF CATCR167.WMF CATCR168.WMF CATCR169.WMF CATCR170.WMF CATCR171.WMF CATCR172.WMF

DEC083F.WMF DEC089Q.WMF FCP008I.WMF FSW038C.WMF FWN016A.WMF FWN018A.WMF FWN018B.WMF FWN018C.WMF FWN018D.WMF FWN018G.WMF

FWN018H.WMF FWN018I.WMF FWN018J.WMF FWN018K.WMF FWN018L.WMF FWN018M.WMF FWN018N.WMF FWN018O.WMF FWN018P.WMF FWN019A.WMF

HPI016D.WMF LAC001C.WMF LAC001K.WMF MSL090B.WMF MSL090I.WMF MSL092E.WMF OFS032G.WMF OFS034G.WMF OFS038G.WMF OTS015I.WMF

OTS061C.WMF OTS066F.WMF SMR028D.WMF SPA010E.WMF VSC061C.WMF

DINO01.WMF DINO02.WMF DINO03.WMF DINO04.WMF DINO05.WMF DINO06.WMF DINO07.WMF DINO08.WMF DINO09.WMF DINO10.WMF
DINO11.WMF DINO12.WMF DINO13.WMF DINO14.WMF DINO15.WMF DINO16.WMF DINO17.WMF DINO18.WMF DINO19.WMF DINO20.WMF
DINO21.WMF DINO22.WMF DINO23.WMF DINO24.WMF DINO25.WMF DINO26.WMF DINO27.WMF DINO28.WMF DINO29.WMF DINO30.WMF
DINO31.WMF DINO32.WMF DINO33.WMF DINO34.WMF DINO35.WMF DINO36.WMF DINO37.WMF DINO38.WMF DINO39.WMF DINO40.WMF
DINO41.WMF DINO42.WMF DINO43.WMF DINO44.WMF DINO45.WMF DINO46.WMF DINO47.WMF DINO48.WMF DINO49.WMF DINO50.WMF
DINO51.WMF DINO52.WMF DINO53.WMF DINO54.WMF DINO55.WMF DINO56.WMF DINO57.WMF DINO58.WMF DINO59.WMF DINO60.WMF
DINO61.WMF DINO62.WMF DINO63.WMF DINO64.WMF DINO65.WMF DINO66.WMF DINO67.WMF DINO68.WMF DINO69.WMF DINOCR01.WMF
DINOCR02.WMF DINOCR03.WMF DINOCR04.WMF DINOCR05.WMF DINOCR06.WMF DINOCR07.WMF DINOCR08.WMF DINOCR09.WMF DINOCR10.WMF DINOCR11.WMF
DINOCR12.WMF DINOCR13.WMF DINOCR14.WMF DINOCR15.WMF DINOCR16.WMF DINOCR17.WMF DINOCR18.WMF DINOCR19.WMF DINOCR20.WMF DINOCR21.WMF
DINOCR22.WMF DINOCR23.WMF DINOCR24.WMF DINOCR25.WMF DINOCR26.WMF DINOCR27.WMF DINOCR28.WMF DINOCR29.WMF DINOCR30.WMF DINOCR31.WMF
DINOCR32.WMF DINOCR33.WMF DINOCR34.WMF DINOCR35.WMF DINOCR36.WMF DINOCR37.WMF DINOCR38.WMF DINOCR39.WMF DINOCR40.WMF DINOCR41.WMF
DINOCR42.WMF DINOCR43.WMF DINOCR44.WMF DINOCR45.WMF DINOCR46.WMF DINOCR47.WMF DINOCR48.WMF DINOCR49.WMF DINOCR50.WMF DINOCR51.WMF

DLA004E.WMF DLA004N.WMF DLA013B.WMF DLA030B.WMF DLA030F.WMF DLA039B.WMF DLA039C.WMF DPM006B.WMF DPM007B.WMF DPM024B.WMF

DPM025B.WMF TDG002A.WMF

2031.WMF 2032.WMF A11A.WMF A11AB.WMF A11B.WMF A11BB.WMF A11C.WMF A11CB.WMF A11D.WMF A11DB.WMF
A11E.WMF A11EB.WMF A11F.WMF A11FB.WMF A11G.WMF A11GB.WMF A44B.WMF AAL025D.WMF AFGHAN.WMF AIL023A.WMF
ANGLSXND.WMF ANIM006.WMF ANIM062.WMF ANIM063.WMF ANIM066.WMF ANIM096.WMF APRICOTM.WMF AWH004E.WMF AWH004F.WMF AWH006D.WMF
AWH012H.WMF AWH013A.WMF AWH016B.WMF AWH016B1.WMF AWH026B.WMF AWH027C.WMF AWP030C.WMF BAS_HOUN.WMF BEAGLE.WMF BEGGING.WMF
BIT0305.WMF BIT0372.WMF BIT0755.WMF BIT0756.WMF BIT0757.WMF BIT0758.WMF BLOODHOU.WMF BONE.WMF BULLDOG.WMF CAA0226.WMF
CAA0227.WMF CAA0228.WMF CAA0229.WMF CAA0230.WMF CAA0231.WMF CAA0232.WMF CAA0233.WMF CAA0235.WMF CAA0236.WMF CAA0237.WMF
CAA0238.WMF CAA0239.WMF CAA0240.WMF CAA0241.WMF CAA0242.WMF CAA0243.WMF CAA0244.WMF CAA0245.WMF CAA0246.WMF CAA0247.WMF
CANINE.WMF COLLIE.WMF CTANI005.WMF CTANI006.WMF CTANI073.WMF CTANI074.WMF CTANI080.WMF CTANI081.WMF CTANI082.WMF CTANI086.WMF
CTANI102.WMF D20880.WMF DACHSHND.WMF DALMATIA.WMF DALMATIN.WMF DALMATIO.WMF DEC089P.WMF DEC091H.WMF DINGO.WMF DINGOC.WMF
DOBERMAN.WMF DOG.WMF DOG1.WMF DOG15.WMF DOG15A.WMF DOG15B.WMF DOG17.WMF DOG1B.WMF DOG1G.WMF DOG2.WMF
DOG2A.WMF DOG2G.WMF DOG3.WMF DOG3G.WMF DOG4.WMF DOG45.WMF DOG4G.WMF DOG5.WMF DOG5A.WMF DOGATEIT.WMF
DOGBONE.WMF DOGBONE2.WMF DOGBONEM.WMF DOGCR001.WMF DOGCR002.WMF DOGCR003.WMF DOGCR004.WMF DOGCR005.WMF DOGCR006.WMF DOGCR007.WMF

DOGCR008.WMF DOGCR009.WMF DOGCR010.WMF DOGCR011.WMF DOGCR012.WMF DOGCR013.WMF DOGCR014.WMF DOGCR015.WMF DOGCR016.WMF DOGCR017.WMF

DOGCR018.WMF DOGCR019.WMF DOGCR020.WMF DOGCR021.WMF DOGCR022.WMF DOGCR023.WMF DOGCR024.WMF DOGCR025.WMF DOGCR026.WMF DOGCR027.WMF

DOGCR028.WMF DOGCR029.WMF DOGCR030.WMF DOGCR031.WMF DOGCR032.WMF DOGCR033.WMF DOGCR034.WMF DOGCR035.WMF DOGCR036.WMF DOGCR037.WMF

DOGCR038.WMF DOGCR039.WMF DOGCR040.WMF DOGCR041.WMF DOGCR042.WMF DOGCR043.WMF DOGCR044.WMF DOGCR045.WMF DOGCR046.WMF DOGCR047.WMF

DOGCR048.WMF DOGCR049.WMF DOGCR050.WMF DOGCR051.WMF DOGCR052.WMF DOGCR053.WMF DOGCR054.WMF DOGCR055.WMF DOGCR056.WMF DOGCR057.WMF

DOGCR058.WMF DOGCR059.WMF DOGCR060.WMF DOGCR061.WMF DOGCR062.WMF DOGCR063.WMF DOGCR064.WMF DOGCR065.WMF DOGCR066.WMF DOGCR067.WMF

DOGCR068.WMF DOGCR069.WMF DOGCR070.WMF DOGCR071.WMF DOGCR072.WMF DOGCR073.WMF DOGCR074.WMF DOGCR075.WMF DOGCR076.WMF DOGCR077.WMF

DOGCR078.WMF DOGCR079.WMF DOGCR080.WMF DOGCR081.WMF DOGCR082.WMF DOGCR083.WMF DOGCR084.WMF DOGCR085.WMF DOGCR086.WMF DOGCR087.WMF

DOGCR088.WMF DOGCR089.WMF DOGCR090.WMF DOGCR091.WMF DOGCR092.WMF DOGCR093.WMF DOGCR094.WMF DOGCR095.WMF DOGCR096.WMF DOGCR097.WMF

DOGCR098.WMF DOGCR099.WMF DOGCR100.WMF DOGCR101.WMF DOGCR102.WMF DOGCR103.WMF DOGCR104.WMF DOGCR105.WMF DOGCR106.WMF DOGCR107.WMF

DOGCR108.WMF DOGCR109.WMF DOGCR110.WMF DOGCR111.WMF DOGCR112.WMF DOGCR113.WMF DOGCR114.WMF DOGCR115.WMF DOGCR116.WMF DOGCR117.WMF

DOGCR118.WMF DOGCR119.WMF DOGCR120.WMF DOGCR121.WMF DOGCR122.WMF DOGCR123.WMF DOGCR124.WMF DOGCR125.WMF DOGCR126.WMF DOGCR127.WMF

DOGCR128.WMF DOGCR129.WMF DOGCR130.WMF DOGCR131.WMF DOGCR132.WMF DOGCR133.WMF DOGCR134.WMF DOGCR135.WMF DOGCR136.WMF DOGCR137.WMF
DOGCR138.WMF DOGCR139.WMF DOGCR140.WMF DOGCR141.WMF DOGCR142.WMF DOGCR143.WMF DOGCR144.WMF DOGCR145.WMF DOGCR146.WMF DOGCR147.WMF
DOGCR148.WMF DOGCR149.WMF DOGCR150.WMF DOGCR151.WMF DOGCR152.WMF DOGCR153.WMF DOGCR154.WMF DOGCR155.WMF DOGCR156.WMF DOGCR157.WMF
DOGCR158.WMF DOGCR159.WMF DOGCR160.WMF DOGCR161.WMF DOGCR162.WMF DOGCR163.WMF DOGCR164.WMF DOGCR165.WMF DOGCR166.WMF DOGCR167.WMF
DOGCR168.WMF DOGCR169.WMF DOGCR170.WMF DOGCR171.WMF DOGCR172.WMF DOGCR173.WMF DOGCR174.WMF DOGCR175.WMF DOGCR176.WMF DOGCR177.WMF
DOGCR178.WMF DOGCR179.WMF DOGCR180.WMF DOGCR181.WMF DOGCR182.WMF DOGCR183.WMF DOGCR184.WMF DOGCR185.WMF DOGCR186.WMF DOGCR187.WMF
DOGCR188.WMF DOGCR189.WMF DOGCR190.WMF DOGCR191.WMF DOGCR192.WMF DOGCR193.WMF DOGCR194.WMF DOGCR195.WMF DOGCR196.WMF DOGCR197.WMF
DOGCR198.WMF DOGCR199.WMF DOGCR200.WMF DOGCR201.WMF DOGCR202.WMF DOGCR203.WMF DOGCR204.WMF DOGCR205.WMF DOGCR206.WMF DOGCR207.WMF
DOGCR208.WMF DOGCR209.WMF DOGCR210.WMF DOGCR211.WMF DOGCR212.WMF DOGCR213.WMF DOGCR214.WMF DOGCR215.WMF DOGCR216.WMF DOGCR217.WMF
DOGCR218.WMF DOGCR219.WMF DOGCR220.WMF DOGCR221.WMF DOGCR222.WMF DOGCR223.WMF DOGCR224.WMF DOGCR225.WMF DOGCR226.WMF DOGCR227.WMF
DOGCR228.WMF DOGCR229.WMF DOGCR230.WMF DOGCR231.WMF DOGCR232.WMF DOGCR233.WMF DOGCR234.WMF DOGCR235.WMF DOGCR236.WMF DOGCR237.WMF
DOGCR238.WMF DOGCR239.WMF DOGCR240.WMF DOGCR241.WMF DOGCR242.WMF DOGCR243.WMF DOGCR244.WMF DOGCR245.WMF DOGCR246.WMF DOGCR247.WMF

DOGCR248.WMF
DOGCR249.WMF
DOGCR250.WMF
DOGCR251.WMF
DOGCR252.WMF
DOGCR253.WMF
DOGCR254.WMF
DOGCR255.WMF
DOGCR256.WMF
DOGCR257.WMF
DOGCR258.WMF
DOGCR259.WMF
DOGCR260.WMF
DOGCR261.WMF
DOGCR262.WMF
DOGCR263.WMF
DOGCR264.WMF
DOGDISH.WMF
DOGFITE.WMF
DOGFOOD.WMF
DOGGIE.WMF
DOGH_USE.WMF
DOGHOLDI.WMF
DOGHOUSE.WMF
DOGPOUND.WMF
DOGSLED.WMF
DOGWFRIS.WMF
EAA020H.WMF
EAC020X.WMF
ET2_INU.WMF
FSW039A.WMF
FSW039B.WMF
FSW039C.WMF
FSW039D.WMF
GREYHUND.WMF
GUIDEDOG.WMF
HOSPDOG.WMF
HPI008J.WMF
IGB021C.WMF
IGB021D.WMF
LAC001A.WMF
LAC001D.WMF
LAC001H.WMF
LAC001I.WMF
LAC001L.WMF
LAC003G.WMF
LAC004G.WMF
LAC017C.WMF
LAZYDOG.WMF
MOD019C.WMF
NAAB001J.WMF
NAGC002D.WMF
NAGC031J.WMF
NAGC176J.WMF
NARW059J.WMF
NARW071J.WMF
NASI133D.WMF
OAN007P.WMF
OAN007S.WMF
OAN007X.WMF
OAN007Y.WMF
OAN007Z.WMF
OEC040C.WMF
OFS034F.WMF
OFS037G.WMF
OFS038C.WMF
OTS061B.WMF
OTS061E.WMF
PET1.WMF
PET1B.WMF
POC112O.WMF
POINTER.WMF
POODLE.WMF
PRIN0007.WMF
PRIN0008.WMF
PRIN0009.WMF
PRIN0010.WMF
PRIN0011.WMF
PRIN0012.WMF
PRIN0619.WMF
PRIN0620.WMF
PUP_Y.WMF
PUPPBOOT.WMF
PUPPY.WMF
PUPPYRUN.WMF
PUPPYSIT.WMF
PUPPYWSL.WMF
ROCKHOU.WMF
ROTTWEIL.WMF
RUNAWAY.WMF
SALTYDOG.WMF
SCOTTISH.WMF
SHAGGY_D.WMF
SHARPEI.WMF
SIL121K.WMF
SIL122F.WMF
SIL122G.WMF
SIT084C.WMF
SIT085D.WMF
SLEEPD_G.WMF
SPA021E.WMF
SYMBL061.WMF
SYMBL062.WMF
SYMBL063.WMF
SYMBL064.WMF
SYMBL065.WMF
SYMBL61.WMF
SYMBL62.WMF
SYMBL63.WMF
SYMBL64.WMF
SYMBL65.WMF
SYMBOL61.WMF
SYMBOL62.WMF
SYMBOL63.WMF
SYMBOL64.WMF
SYMBOL65.WMF
TIRED_DG.WMF
TOYPOODL.WMF
VSI080M.WMF
WHIPPET.WMF

0341.WMF
0342.WMF
0343.WMF
0344.WMF
0766.WMF
2024.WMF
2025.WMF
2026.WMF
2044.WMF
2045.WMF
2046.WMF
2070.WMF
2071.WMF
3303.WMF
3304.WMF
3305.WMF
3306.WMF
3307.WMF
3308.WMF
3309.WMF
3310.WMF
3416.WMF
3417.WMF
AIL022D.WMF
ANIM020.WMF
ANIM026.WMF
ANIM027.WMF
ANMO5.WMF
ASI008N.WMF
AWH002E.WMF
AWH003A.WMF
AWH003C.WMF
AWH006E.WMF
AWH011B.WMF
AWH011E.WMF
AWH013D.WMF
AWH015D.WMF
AWH019D.WMF
AWH019E.WMF
AWH020B.WMF
AWH025B.WMF
AWH025C.WMF
AWH025G.WMF
AWP036A.WMF
AWP038C.WMF
BACK094.WMF
BIT1153.WMF
BIT1154.WMF
BIT1155.WMF
BIT1157.WMF
BIT1158.WMF
BIT1159.WMF
BUL1.WMF
BULL.WMF
BULL02.WMF
BULL1.WMF
BULL2.WMF
BULL3.WMF
BULLMORT.WMF
BULLSYM.WMF
BULLY.WMF
CAA0215.WMF
CAA0216.WMF
CALF.WMF
CART001.WMF
CART002.WMF
CART003.WMF
CART004.WMF
CART005.WMF
CART006.WMF
CART007.WMF
CART008.WMF
CART009.WMF
CART010.WMF
CART1002.WMF
CHICKHN.WMF
CHIK.WMF
CHW027D.WMF
CLYDESDA.WMF
CO_W.WMF
COW.WMF
COW2.WMF
COW22.WMF
COW45.WMF
COW_SILH.WMF
COWC.WMF
COWHEAD.WMF
DAIRYCO1.WMF
DAIRYCOW.WMF
DAIRYCW2.WMF
DEC085A.WMF
DEC086A.WMF
DONKEY.WMF
DONKEY2.WMF
DONKY20.WMF
EAA006F.WMF
EAA011A.WMF
EAA011H.WMF
EAC023I.WMF
EAC023M.WMF
EAC023Q.WMF
EAC023S.WMF
ET2_HITS.WMF
ET2_TORI.WMF
ET2_UMA.WMF
ET2_USHI.WMF
FACR001.WMF
FACR002.WMF
FACR003.WMF
FACR004.WMF
FACR005.WMF
FACR006.WMF
FACR007.WMF
FACR008.WMF
FACR009.WMF
FACR010.WMF
FACR011.WMF
FACR012.WMF
FACR013.WMF
FACR014.WMF

FACR015.WMF FACR016.WMF FACR017.WMF FACR018.WMF FACR019.WMF FACR020.WMF FACR021.WMF FACR022.WMF FACR023.WMF FACR024.WMF
FACR025.WMF FACR026.WMF FACR027.WMF FACR028.WMF FACR029.WMF FACR030.WMF FACR031.WMF FACR032.WMF FACR033.WMF FACR034.WMF
FACR035.WMF FACR036.WMF FACR037.WMF FACR038.WMF FACR039.WMF FACR040.WMF FACR041.WMF FACR042.WMF FACR043.WMF FACR044.WMF
FACR045.WMF FACR046.WMF FACR047.WMF FACR048.WMF FACR049.WMF FACR050.WMF FACR051.WMF FACR052.WMF FACR053.WMF FACR054.WMF
FACR055.WMF FACR056.WMF FACR057.WMF FACR058.WMF FACR059.WMF FACR060.WMF FACR061.WMF FACR062.WMF FACR063.WMF FACR064.WMF
FACR065.WMF FACR066.WMF FACR067.WMF FACR068.WMF FACR069.WMF FACR070.WMF FACR071.WMF FACR072.WMF FACR073.WMF FACR074.WMF
FACR075.WMF FACR076.WMF FACR077.WMF FACR078.WMF FACR079.WMF FACR080.WMF FACR081.WMF FACR082.WMF FACR083.WMF FACR084.WMF
FACR085.WMF FACR086.WMF FACR087.WMF FACR088.WMF FACR089.WMF FACR090.WMF FACR091.WMF FACR092.WMF FACR093.WMF FACR094.WMF
FACR095.WMF FACR096.WMF FACR097.WMF FACR098.WMF FACR099.WMF FACR100.WMF FACR101.WMF FACR102.WMF FACR103.WMF FACR104.WMF
FACR105.WMF FACR106.WMF FACR107.WMF FACR108.WMF FACR109.WMF FACR110.WMF FACR111.WMF FACR112.WMF FACR113.WMF FACR114.WMF
FACR115.WMF FACR116.WMF FACR117.WMF FACR118.WMF FACR119.WMF FACR120.WMF FACR121.WMF FACR122.WMF FACR123.WMF FACR124.WMF
FACR125.WMF FACR126.WMF FACR127.WMF FACR128.WMF FACR129.WMF FACR130.WMF FACR131.WMF FACR132.WMF FACR133.WMF FACR134.WMF

FACR135.WMF
FACR136.WMF
FACR137.WMF
FACR138.WMF
FACR139.WMF
FACR140.WMF
FACR141.WMF
FACR142.WMF
FACR143.WMF
FACR144.WMF
FACR145.WMF
FACR146.WMF
FACR147.WMF
FACR148.WMF
FACR149.WMF
FACR150.WMF
FACR151.WMF
FACR152.WMF
FACR153.WMF
FACR154.WMF
FACR155.WMF
FACR156.WMF
FACR157.WMF
FACR158.WMF
FACR159.WMF
FACR160.WMF
FACR161.WMF
FACR162.WMF
FACR163.WMF
FACR164.WMF
FACR165.WMF
FACR166.WMF
FACR167.WMF
FACR168.WMF
FACR169.WMF
FACR170.WMF
FACR171.WMF
FACR172.WMF
FACR173.WMF
FACR174.WMF
FACR175.WMF
FCP008J.WMF
FCP032C.WMF
FDD085E.WMF
FDD085F.WMF
FDD085G.WMF
FSW013D.WMF
FSW024B.WMF
FSW024C.WMF
FSW024D.WMF
FSW024E.WMF
FSW029C.WMF
FSW034A.WMF
GOAT.WMF
GOAT22.WMF
GOATFACE.WMF
HEREFORD.WMF
HOG.WMF
HOG1.WMF
HPI001M.WMF
LAC005B.WMF
LAC005E.WMF
LAC005H.WMF
LAC006A.WMF
LAC006D.WMF
LAC006L.WMF
LAC007K.WMF
LAC010C.WMF
LAC010D.WMF
LAC010F.WMF
LAMB.WMF
LAMB18.WMF
LAMBS.WMF
MILKCOW.WMF
MILKGOAT.WMF
MSL087M.WMF
MSL087O.WMF
MSL094H.WMF
MULE.WMF
NAAB005J.WMF
NAAB006J.WMF
NAAB007J.WMF
NABO029J.WMF
NACA292J.WMF
NAGC035D.WMF
NASI153D.WMF
OFF001A.WMF
OFS037I.WMF
OXCART.WMF
PIG.WMF
PIG18.WMF
PIG44.WMF
PIG4A.WMF
PIG_1.WMF
PIG_2.WMF
PIG_SILH.WMF
PIGA2.WMF
PIGFLYER.WMF
PIGLET.WMF
PIGLET18.WMF
PIGNTIE.WMF
PRIN0037.WMF
PRIN0634.WMF
RABBIT.WMF
RABBIT2.WMF
RABBIT22.WMF
RAM.WMF
SCENE.WMF
SHEEP.WMF
SHEEP1.WMF
SHEEP22.WMF
SHEEP_SI.WMF
SHIRE.WMF
SHPDOG.WMF
SIT075D.WMF
SIT075E.WMF
SIT077I.WMF
SIT078C.WMF
SIT078J.WMF
SIT078P.WMF

SIT078Q.WMF
SIT085F.WMF
SIT085H.WMF
SLAMB.WMF
SMR020K.WMF
SOW.WMF
SOW18.WMF
SPA006E.WMF
SPA010B.WMF
SPA019A.WMF
SPA020B.WMF
SPA027E.WMF
STEER.WMF
STEERTO.WMF
SYMBL146.WMF
SYMBL147.WMF
SYMBL149.WMF
SYMBL1_1.WMF
SYMBL1_2.WMF
SYMBL1_3.WMF
SYMBL1_4.WMF
SYMBL1_5.WMF
TOD074B.WMF
TURKEY.WMF
TURKEYMO.WMF
WMG033G.WMF

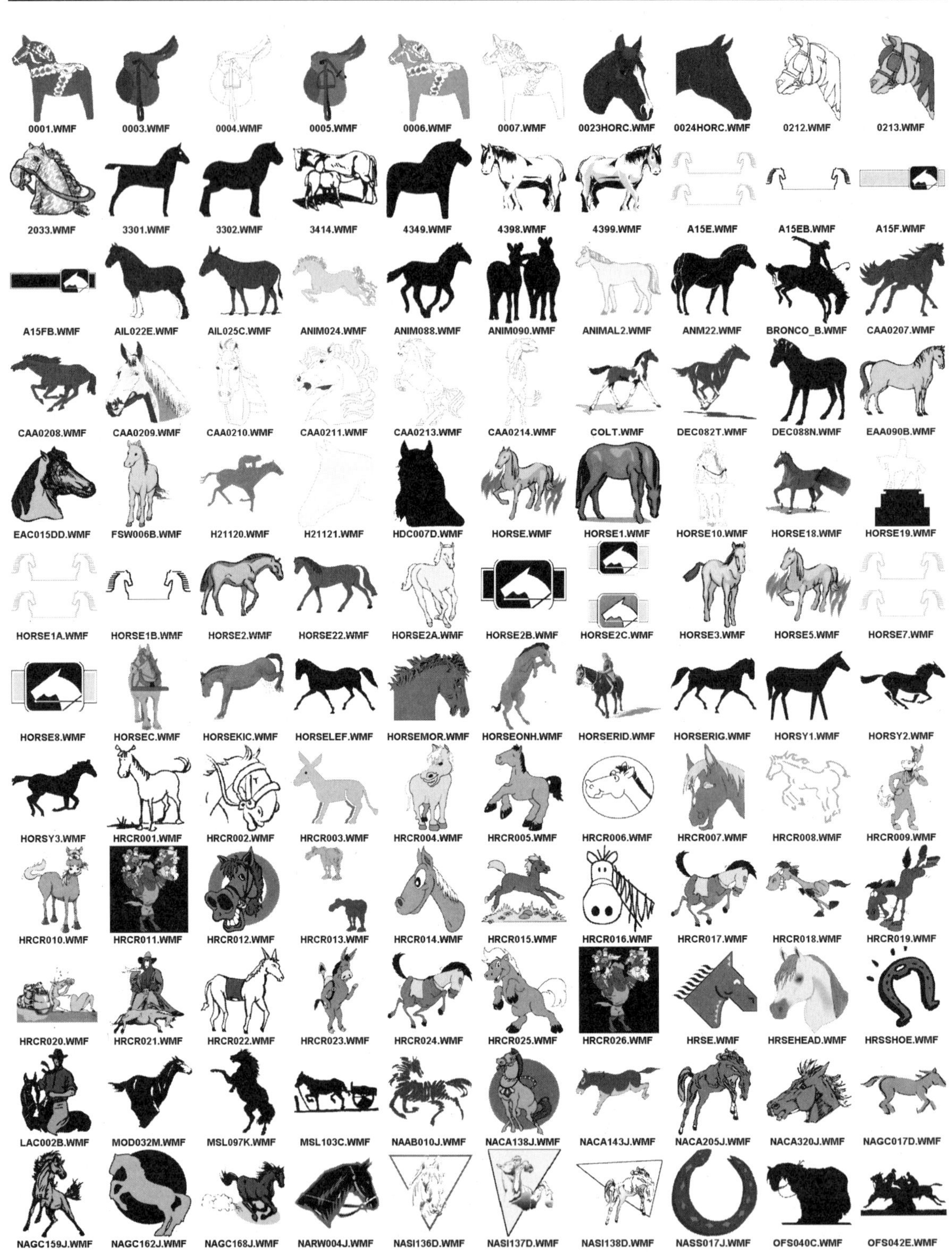
0001.WMF 0003.WMF 0004.WMF 0005.WMF 0006.WMF 0007.WMF 0023HORC.WMF 0024HORC.WMF 0212.WMF 0213.WMF
2033.WMF 3301.WMF 3302.WMF 3414.WMF 4349.WMF 4398.WMF 4399.WMF A15E.WMF A15EB.WMF A15F.WMF
A15FB.WMF AIL022E.WMF AIL025C.WMF ANIM024.WMF ANIM088.WMF ANIM090.WMF ANIMAL2.WMF ANM22.WMF BRONCO_B.WMF CAA0207.WMF
CAA0208.WMF CAA0209.WMF CAA0210.WMF CAA0211.WMF CAA0213.WMF CAA0214.WMF COLT.WMF DEC082T.WMF DEC088N.WMF EAA090B.WMF
EAC015DD.WMF FSW006B.WMF H21120.WMF H21121.WMF HDC007D.WMF HORSE.WMF HORSE1.WMF HORSE10.WMF HORSE18.WMF HORSE19.WMF
HORSE1A.WMF HORSE1B.WMF HORSE2.WMF HORSE22.WMF HORSE2A.WMF HORSE2B.WMF HORSE2C.WMF HORSE3.WMF HORSE5.WMF HORSE7.WMF
HORSE8.WMF HORSEC.WMF HORSEKIC.WMF HORSELEF.WMF HORSEMOR.WMF HORSEONH.WMF HORSERID.WMF HORSERIG.WMF HORSY1.WMF HORSY2.WMF
HORSY3.WMF HRCR001.WMF HRCR002.WMF HRCR003.WMF HRCR004.WMF HRCR005.WMF HRCR006.WMF HRCR007.WMF HRCR008.WMF HRCR009.WMF
HRCR010.WMF HRCR011.WMF HRCR012.WMF HRCR013.WMF HRCR014.WMF HRCR015.WMF HRCR016.WMF HRCR017.WMF HRCR018.WMF HRCR019.WMF
HRCR020.WMF HRCR021.WMF HRCR022.WMF HRCR023.WMF HRCR024.WMF HRCR025.WMF HRCR026.WMF HRSE.WMF HRSEHEAD.WMF HRSSHOE.WMF
LAC002B.WMF MOD032M.WMF MSL097K.WMF MSL103C.WMF NAAB010J.WMF NACA138J.WMF NACA143J.WMF NACA205J.WMF NACA320J.WMF NAGC017D.WMF
NAGC159J.WMF NAGC162J.WMF NAGC168J.WMF NARW004J.WMF NASI136D.WMF NASI137D.WMF NASI138D.WMF NASS017J.WMF OFS040C.WMF OFS042E.WMF

OFS054E.WMF PD112ECU.WMF PLOWHRSE.WMF PONY.WMF PONY1.WMF RIDER.WMF SIT075H.WMF SIT086M.WMF SMR016O.WMF SMR020I.WMF

SPA005A.WMF SYMBL7.WMF SYMBL7S.WMF SYMBL8.WMF SYMBL8S.WMF SYMBL9.WMF SYMBL9S.WMF SYMBOL7B.WMF SYMBOL8B.WMF SYMBOL9B.WMF

TSD031D.WMF

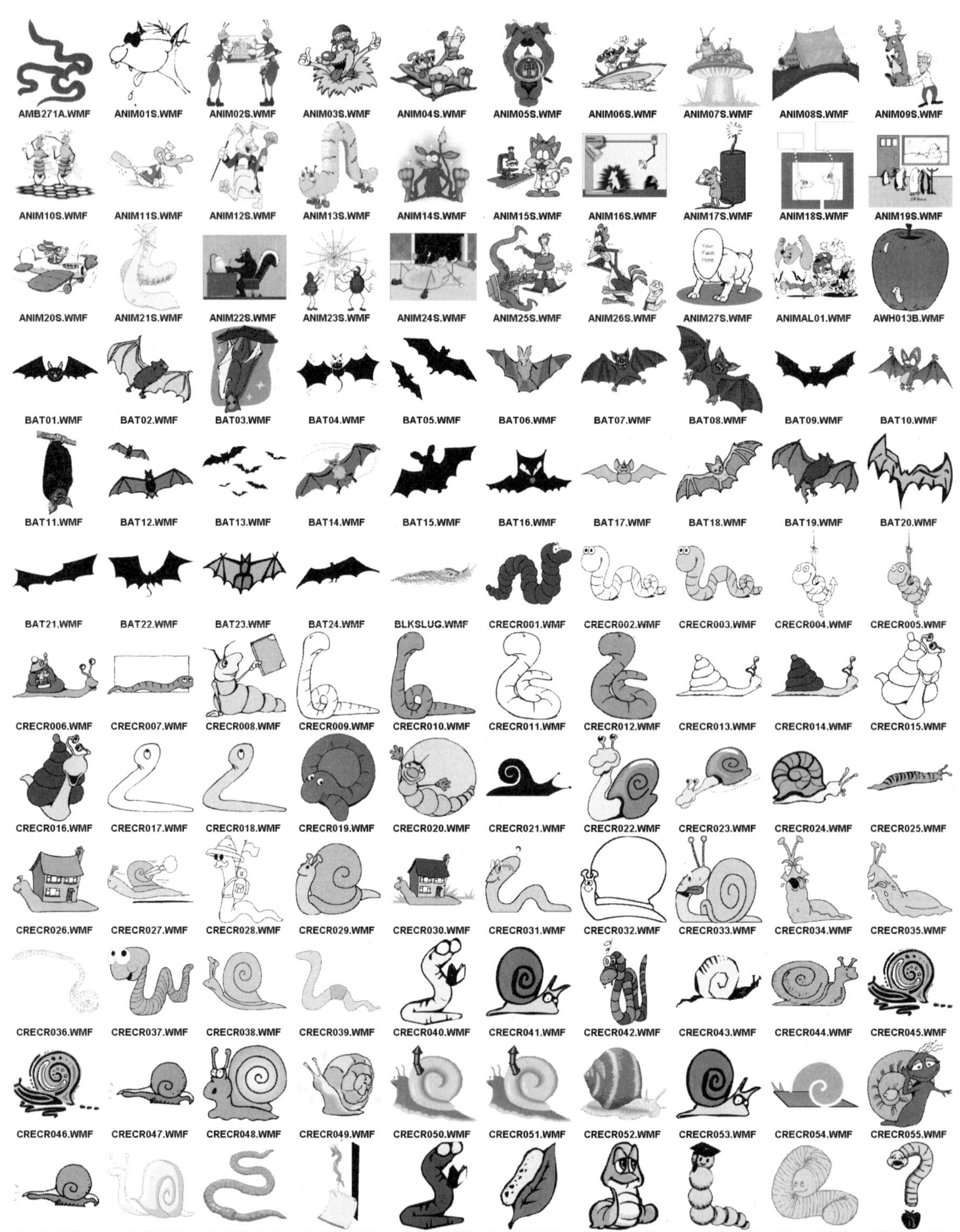
AMB271A.WMF
ANIM01S.WMF
ANIM02S.WMF
ANIM03S.WMF
ANIM04S.WMF
ANIM05S.WMF
ANIM06S.WMF
ANIM07S.WMF
ANIM08S.WMF
ANIM09S.WMF
ANIM10S.WMF
ANIM11S.WMF
ANIM12S.WMF
ANIM13S.WMF
ANIM14S.WMF
ANIM15S.WMF
ANIM16S.WMF
ANIM17S.WMF
ANIM18S.WMF
ANIM19S.WMF
ANIM20S.WMF
ANIM21S.WMF
ANIM22S.WMF
ANIM23S.WMF
ANIM24S.WMF
ANIM25S.WMF
ANIM26S.WMF
ANIM27S.WMF
ANIMAL01.WMF
AWH013B.WMF
BAT01.WMF
BAT02.WMF
BAT03.WMF
BAT04.WMF
BAT05.WMF
BAT06.WMF
BAT07.WMF
BAT08.WMF
BAT09.WMF
BAT10.WMF
BAT11.WMF
BAT12.WMF
BAT13.WMF
BAT14.WMF
BAT15.WMF
BAT16.WMF
BAT17.WMF
BAT18.WMF
BAT19.WMF
BAT20.WMF
BAT21.WMF
BAT22.WMF
BAT23.WMF
BAT24.WMF
BLKSLUG.WMF
CRECR001.WMF
CRECR002.WMF
CRECR003.WMF
CRECR004.WMF
CRECR005.WMF
CRECR006.WMF
CRECR007.WMF
CRECR008.WMF
CRECR009.WMF
CRECR010.WMF
CRECR011.WMF
CRECR012.WMF
CRECR013.WMF
CRECR014.WMF
CRECR015.WMF
CRECR016.WMF
CRECR017.WMF
CRECR018.WMF
CRECR019.WMF
CRECR020.WMF
CRECR021.WMF
CRECR022.WMF
CRECR023.WMF
CRECR024.WMF
CRECR025.WMF
CRECR026.WMF
CRECR027.WMF
CRECR028.WMF
CRECR029.WMF
CRECR030.WMF
CRECR031.WMF
CRECR032.WMF
CRECR033.WMF
CRECR034.WMF
CRECR035.WMF
CRECR036.WMF
CRECR037.WMF
CRECR038.WMF
CRECR039.WMF
CRECR040.WMF
CRECR041.WMF
CRECR042.WMF
CRECR043.WMF
CRECR044.WMF
CRECR045.WMF
CRECR046.WMF
CRECR047.WMF
CRECR048.WMF
CRECR049.WMF
CRECR050.WMF
CRECR051.WMF
CRECR052.WMF
CRECR053.WMF
CRECR054.WMF
CRECR055.WMF
CRECR056.WMF
CRECR057.WMF
CRECR058.WMF
CRECR059.WMF
CRECR060.WMF
CRECR061.WMF
CRECR062.WMF
CRECR063.WMF
CRECR064.WMF
CRECR065.WMF

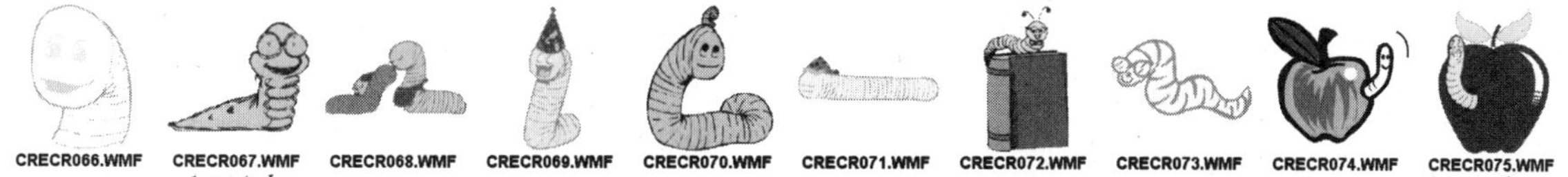

CRECR066.WMF CRECR067.WMF CRECR068.WMF CRECR069.WMF CRECR070.WMF CRECR071.WMF CRECR072.WMF CRECR073.WMF CRECR074.WMF CRECR075.WMF

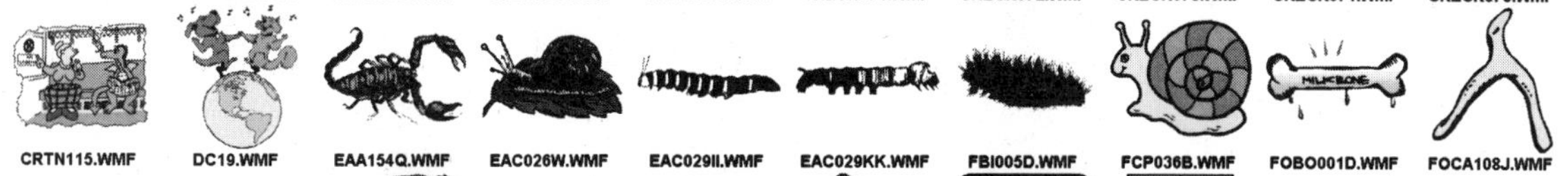

CRTN115.WMF DC19.WMF EAA154Q.WMF EAC026W.WMF EAC029II.WMF EAC029KK.WMF FBI005D.WMF FCP036B.WMF FOBO001D.WMF FOCA108J.WMF

GASI024M.WMF GDNSNAIL.WMF GRZZLBR.WMF HHSI034J.WMF HHSI048M.WMF LEECH.WMF LIVEANI1.WMF LIVEANI2.WMF MINER_AN.WMF MOD021L.WMF

NAAB002D.WMF NACA004D.WMF NACA037J.WMF NACA052J.WMF NACA144J.WMF NACA207J.WMF NACA290J.WMF NACA342J.WMF NAGC012D.WMF NAGC013D.WMF

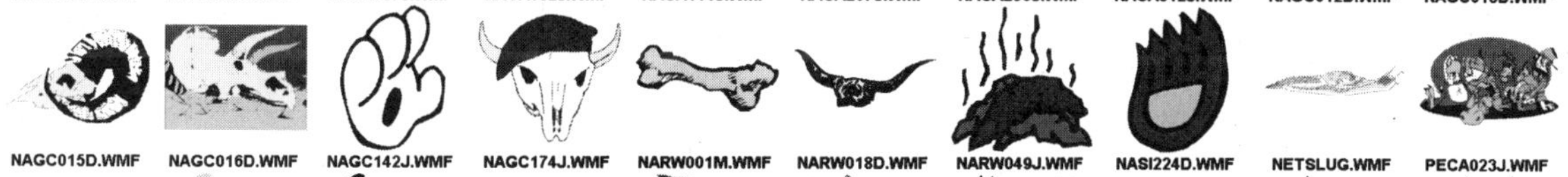

NAGC015D.WMF NAGC016D.WMF NAGC142J.WMF NAGC174J.WMF NARW001M.WMF NARW018D.WMF NARW049J.WMF NASI224D.WMF NETSLUG.WMF PECA023J.WMF

PET1.WMF PET6.WMF PET6B.WMF PET7.WMF PET7B.WMF PRTYANML.WMF SCORPION.WMF SNAIL.WMF SPA003C.WMF SPIDER.WMF

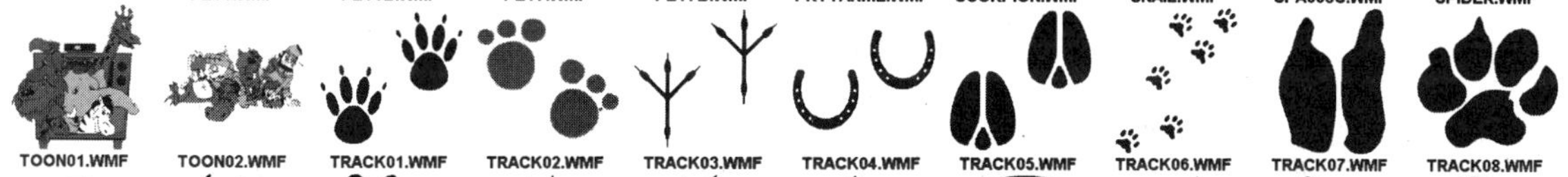

TOON01.WMF TOON02.WMF TRACK01.WMF TRACK02.WMF TRACK03.WMF TRACK04.WMF TRACK05.WMF TRACK06.WMF TRACK07.WMF TRACK08.WMF

TRACK09.WMF TRACK10.WMF TRACK11.WMF TRACK12.WMF TRACK13.WMF TRACK14.WMF TRACK15.WMF TRACK16.WMF TRACK17.WMF TRACK18.WMF

TRACK19.WMF TRACK20.WMF TRACK21.WMF TRACK22.WMF TRACK23.WMF TRACK24.WMF TRACK25.WMF TRACK26.WMF TRACK27.WMF TRACK28.WMF

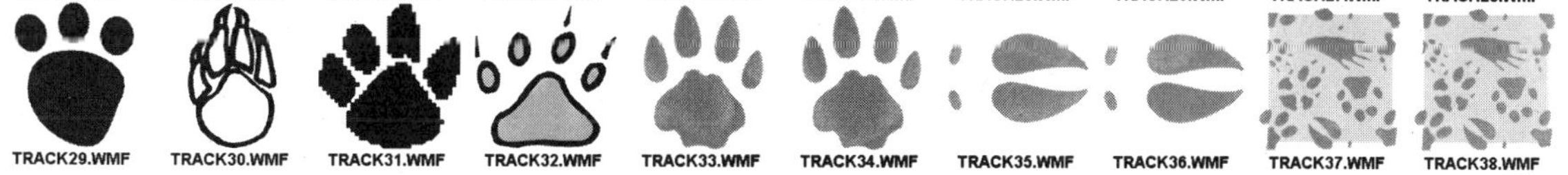

TRACK29.WMF TRACK30.WMF TRACK31.WMF TRACK32.WMF TRACK33.WMF TRACK34.WMF TRACK35.WMF TRACK36.WMF TRACK37.WMF TRACK38.WMF

WHLSNAIL.WMF

AAL020F.WMF AQCAR067.WMF AQCAR071.WMF AQCAR174.WMF AQUA007.WMF AQUA027.WMF AQUA028.WMF AQUA029.WMF AQUA030.WMF AQUA036.WMF

AQUA037.WMF AQUA038.WMF AQUA053.WMF AQUA054.WMF AQUA055.WMF AQUA059.WMF AQUA066.WMF AQUA070.WMF AQUA071.WMF AQUA101.WMF

AQUA105.WMF AQUA106.WMF AQUA107.WMF AQUA108.WMF AQUA109.WMF AQUA110.WMF AQUA112.WMF AQUA125.WMF AQUA127.WMF AQUA134.WMF

CART0001.WMF CART0002.WMF CART0003.WMF CART0004.WMF CART0005.WMF CART0006.WMF CART0007.WMF CART0008.WMF CART0009.WMF CART0010.WMF

CART0011.WMF CART0012.WMF CART0013.WMF CART0014.WMF CART0015.WMF CART0016.WMF CART0017.WMF CART0018.WMF CART0019.WMF CART0020.WMF

CART0021.WMF CART0022.WMF CART0023.WMF CART0024.WMF CART0025.WMF CART0026.WMF CART0027.WMF CART0028.WMF CART0029.WMF CART0030.WMF

CART0031.WMF CART0032.WMF CART0033.WMF CART0034.WMF CART0035.WMF CART0036.WMF CART0037.WMF CART0038.WMF CART0039.WMF CART0040.WMF

CART0041.WMF CART0042.WMF CART0043.WMF CART0044.WMF CART0045.WMF CART0046.WMF CART0047.WMF CART0048.WMF CART0049.WMF CART0050.WMF

CART0051.WMF CART0052.WMF CART0053.WMF CART0054.WMF CART0055.WMF CART0056.WMF CART0057.WMF CART0058.WMF CART0059.WMF CART0060.WMF

CART0061.WMF CART0062.WMF CART0063.WMF CART0064.WMF CART0065.WMF CART0066.WMF CART0067.WMF CART0068.WMF CART0069.WMF CART0070.WMF

CART0071.WMF CART0072.WMF CART0073.WMF CART0074.WMF CART0075.WMF CART0076.WMF CART0077.WMF CART0078.WMF CART0079.WMF CART0080.WMF

CART0081.WMF CART0082.WMF CART0083.WMF CART0084.WMF CART0085.WMF CART0086.WMF CART0087.WMF CART0088.WMF CART0089.WMF CART0090.WMF

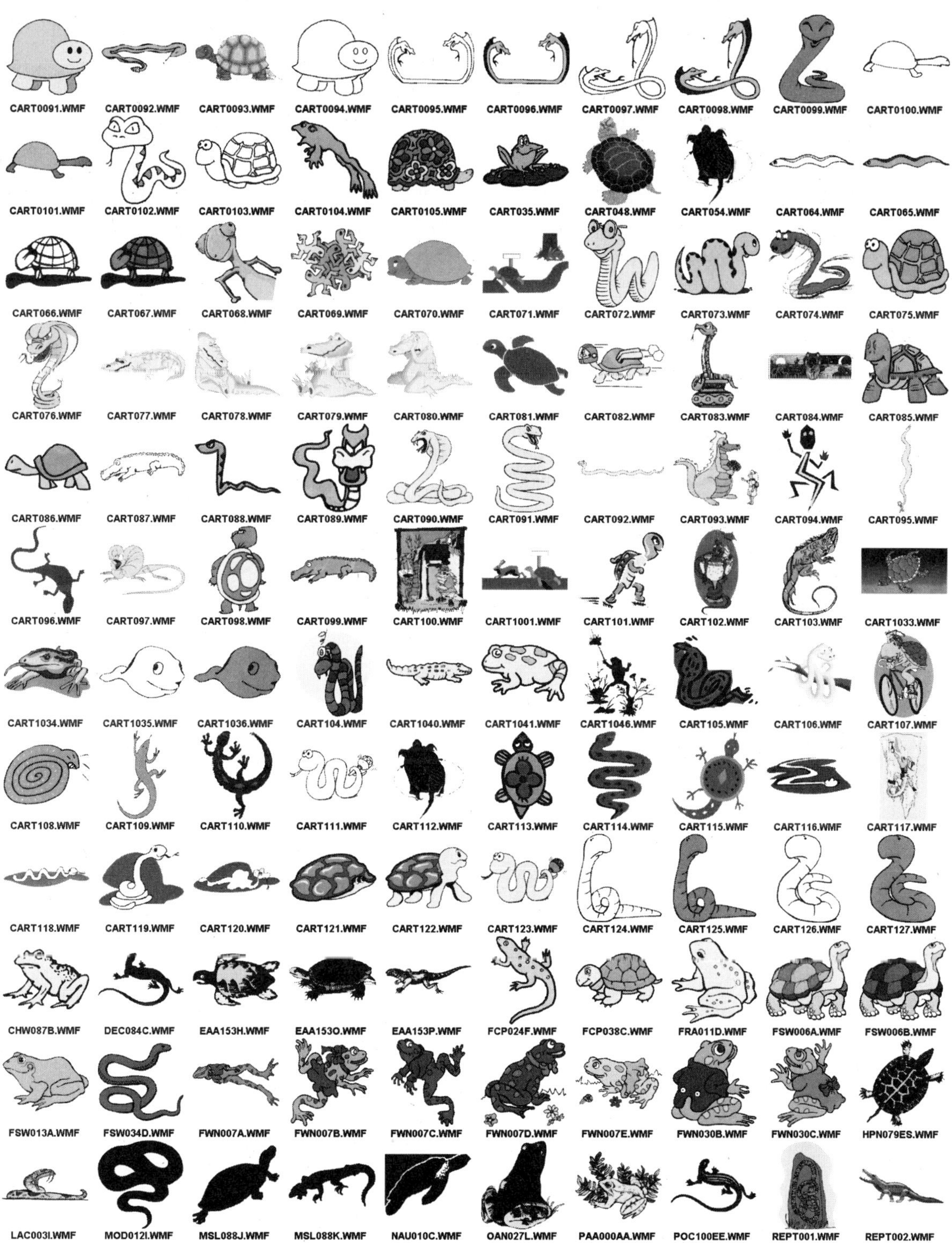
CART0091.WMF CART0092.WMF CART0093.WMF CART0094.WMF CART0095.WMF CART0096.WMF CART0097.WMF CART0098.WMF CART0099.WMF CART0100.WMF
CART0101.WMF CART0102.WMF CART0103.WMF CART0104.WMF CART0105.WMF CART035.WMF CART048.WMF CART054.WMF CART064.WMF CART065.WMF
CART066.WMF CART067.WMF CART068.WMF CART069.WMF CART070.WMF CART071.WMF CART072.WMF CART073.WMF CART074.WMF CART075.WMF
CART076.WMF CART077.WMF CART078.WMF CART079.WMF CART080.WMF CART081.WMF CART082.WMF CART083.WMF CART084.WMF CART085.WMF
CART086.WMF CART087.WMF CART088.WMF CART089.WMF CART090.WMF CART091.WMF CART092.WMF CART093.WMF CART094.WMF CART095.WMF
CART096.WMF CART097.WMF CART098.WMF CART099.WMF CART100.WMF CART1001.WMF CART101.WMF CART102.WMF CART103.WMF CART1033.WMF
CART1034.WMF CART1035.WMF CART1036.WMF CART104.WMF CART1040.WMF CART1041.WMF CART1046.WMF CART105.WMF CART106.WMF CART107.WMF
CART108.WMF CART109.WMF CART110.WMF CART111.WMF CART112.WMF CART113.WMF CART114.WMF CART115.WMF CART116.WMF CART117.WMF
CART118.WMF CART119.WMF CART120.WMF CART121.WMF CART122.WMF CART123.WMF CART124.WMF CART125.WMF CART126.WMF CART127.WMF
CHW087B.WMF DEC084C.WMF EAA153H.WMF EAA153O.WMF EAA153P.WMF FCP024F.WMF FCP038C.WMF FRA011D.WMF FSW006A.WMF FSW006B.WMF
FSW013A.WMF FSW034D.WMF FWN007A.WMF FWN007B.WMF FWN007C.WMF FWN007D.WMF FWN007E.WMF FWN030B.WMF FWN030C.WMF HPN079ES.WMF
LAC003I.WMF MOD012I.WMF MSL088J.WMF MSL088K.WMF NAU010C.WMF OAN027L.WMF PAA000AA.WMF POC100EE.WMF REPT001.WMF REPT002.WMF

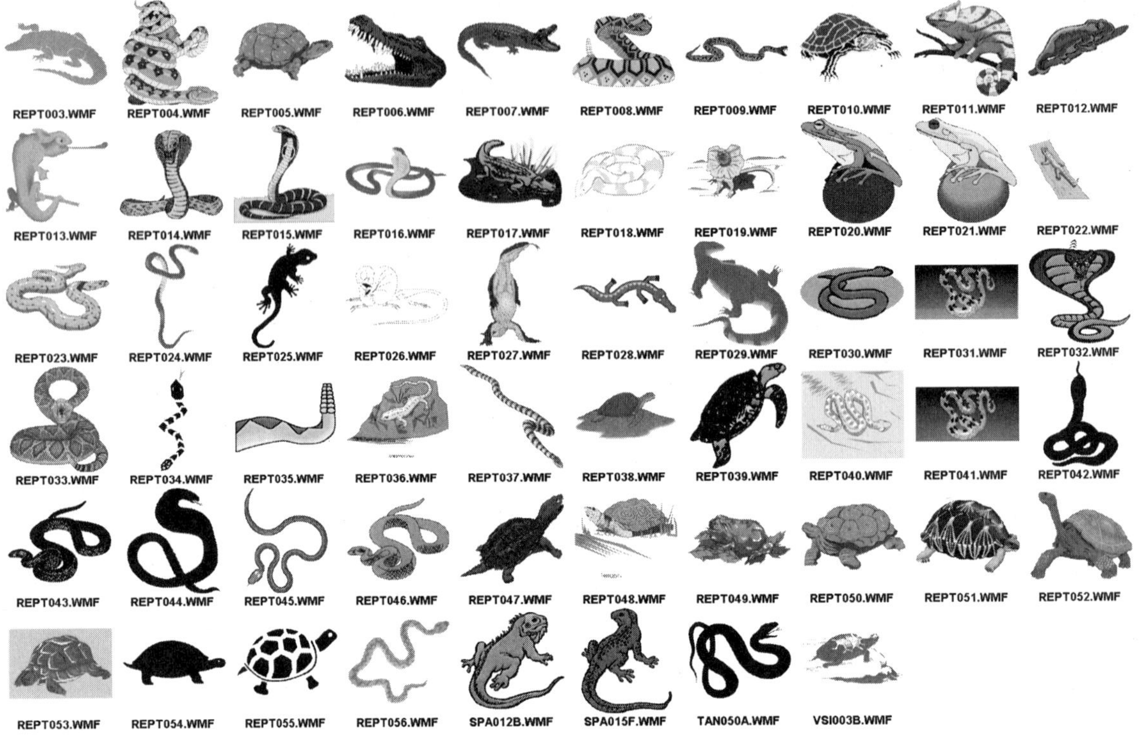
REPT003.WMF
REPT004.WMF
REPT005.WMF
REPT006.WMF
REPT007.WMF
REPT008.WMF
REPT009.WMF
REPT010.WMF
REPT011.WMF
REPT012.WMF
REPT013.WMF
REPT014.WMF
REPT015.WMF
REPT016.WMF
REPT017.WMF
REPT018.WMF
REPT019.WMF
REPT020.WMF
REPT021.WMF
REPT022.WMF
REPT023.WMF
REPT024.WMF
REPT025.WMF
REPT026.WMF
REPT027.WMF
REPT028.WMF
REPT029.WMF
REPT030.WMF
REPT031.WMF
REPT032.WMF
REPT033.WMF
REPT034.WMF
REPT035.WMF
REPT036.WMF
REPT037.WMF
REPT038.WMF
REPT039.WMF
REPT040.WMF
REPT041.WMF
REPT042.WMF
REPT043.WMF
REPT044.WMF
REPT045.WMF
REPT046.WMF
REPT047.WMF
REPT048.WMF
REPT049.WMF
REPT050.WMF
REPT051.WMF
REPT052.WMF
REPT053.WMF
REPT054.WMF
REPT055.WMF
REPT056.WMF
SPA012B.WMF
SPA015F.WMF
TAN050A.WMF
VSI003B.WMF

AAL020A.WMF
AWH014A.WMF
AWP038D.WMF
CART001.WMF
CART002.WMF
CART003.WMF
CART004.WMF
CART005.WMF
CART006.WMF
CART007.WMF
CART008.WMF
CART009.WMF
CART010.WMF
CART011.WMF
CART012.WMF
CART013.WMF
CART014.WMF
CART015.WMF
CART016.WMF
CART017.WMF
CART018.WMF
CART019.WMF
CART020.WMF
CART021.WMF
CART022.WMF
CART023.WMF
CART024.WMF
CART025.WMF
CART026.WMF
CART027.WMF
CART028.WMF
CART029.WMF
CART030.WMF
CART031.WMF
CART032.WMF
CART033.WMF
CART034.WMF
CART035.WMF
CART036.WMF
CART037.WMF
CART038.WMF
CART039.WMF
CART040.WMF
CART041.WMF
CART042.WMF
CART043.WMF
CART044.WMF
CART045.WMF
CART046.WMF
CART047.WMF
CART048.WMF
CART049.WMF
CART050.WMF
CART051.WMF
CART052.WMF
CART053.WMF
CART054.WMF
CART055.WMF
CART056.WMF
CART057.WMF
CART058.WMF
CART059.WMF
CART060.WMF
CART061.WMF
CART062.WMF
CART063.WMF
CART064.WMF
CART065.WMF
CART066.WMF
CART067.WMF
CART068.WMF
CART069.WMF
CART070.WMF
CART071.WMF
CART072.WMF
CART073.WMF
CART074.WMF
CART075.WMF
CART076.WMF
CART077.WMF
CART078.WMF
CART079.WMF
CART080.WMF
CART081.WMF
CART082.WMF
CART083.WMF
CART084.WMF
CART085.WMF
CART086.WMF
CART087.WMF
CART088.WMF
CART089.WMF
CART090.WMF
CART091.WMF
CART092.WMF
CART093.WMF
CART094.WMF
CART095.WMF
CART096.WMF
CART097.WMF
CAT001.WMF
CAT002.WMF
CAT003.WMF
CAT004.WMF
CAT005.WMF
CAT006.WMF
CAT007.WMF
CAT008.WMF
CAT009.WMF
CAT010.WMF
CAT011.WMF
CAT012.WMF
CAT013.WMF
CAT014.WMF
CAT015.WMF
CAT016.WMF
CAT017.WMF
CAT018.WMF
CAT019.WMF
CAT020.WMF

CAT021.WMF CAT022.WMF CAT023.WMF CAT024.WMF CAT025.WMF CAT026.WMF CAT027.WMF CAT028.WMF CAT029.WMF CAT030.WMF
CAT031.WMF CAT032.WMF CAT033.WMF CAT034.WMF CAT035.WMF CAT036.WMF CAT037.WMF CAT038.WMF CAT039.WMF CAT040.WMF
CAT041.WMF CAT042.WMF CAT043.WMF CAT044.WMF CAT045.WMF CAT046.WMF CAT047.WMF CAT048.WMF CAT049.WMF CAT050.WMF
CAT051.WMF CAT052.WMF CAT053.WMF CAT054.WMF CAT055.WMF CAT056.WMF CAT057.WMF CAT058.WMF CAT059.WMF CAT060.WMF
CAT061.WMF CAT062.WMF CAT063.WMF CAT064.WMF CAT065.WMF CAT066.WMF CAT067.WMF CAT068.WMF CAT069.WMF CAT070.WMF
CAT071.WMF CAT072.WMF CAT073.WMF CAT074.WMF CAT075.WMF CAT076.WMF CAT077.WMF CAT078.WMF CAT079.WMF CAT080.WMF
CAT081.WMF CAT082.WMF CAT083.WMF CAT084.WMF CAT085.WMF CAT086.WMF CAT087.WMF CAT088.WMF CAT089.WMF CAT090.WMF
CAT091.WMF CAT092.WMF CAT093.WMF CAT094.WMF CAT095.WMF CAT096.WMF CAT097.WMF CAT098.WMF CAT099.WMF CAT100.WMF
CAT101.WMF CAT102.WMF CAT103.WMF CAT104.WMF CAT105.WMF CAT106.WMF CAT107.WMF CAT108.WMF CAT109.WMF CAT110.WMF
CAT111.WMF CAT112.WMF CAT113.WMF CAT114.WMF CAT115.WMF CAT116.WMF CAT117.WMF CAT118.WMF CAT119.WMF DEC084P.WMF
DEC084T.WMF DEC085Z.WMF DEC088M.WMF FCP024E.WMF FSW038A.WMF FSW038B.WMF FSW038D.WMF HFS004D.WMF HPI016G.WMF HPI016H.WMF
HRC294A.WMF MOD010L.WMF MOD015G.WMF MSL087F.WMF MSL089B.WMF OEC044H.WMF OTS028C.WMF POC100X.WMF POC100Y.WMF SPA015B.WMF

SPA025F.WMF

WAG009A.WMF

WAG015A.WMF

WCW010A.WMF

WCW018A.WMF

WSG011A.WMF

AAL026A.WMF
AIL005A.WMF
AIL019A.WMF
AIL022A.WMF
ANIMLCON.WMF
AWH001E.WMF
AWH002C.WMF
AWH020A.WMF
AWH021A.WMF
AWH021B.WMF
AWH023C.WMF
AWH023E.WMF
AWH027A.WMF
AWP035D.WMF
AWP037E.WMF
AWP038B.WMF
CART001.WMF
CART002.WMF
CART003.WMF
CART004.WMF
CART005.WMF
CART006.WMF
CART007.WMF
CART008.WMF
CART009.WMF
CART010.WMF
CART011.WMF
CART012.WMF
CART013.WMF
CART014.WMF
CART015.WMF
CART016.WMF
CART017.WMF
CART018.WMF
CART019.WMF
CART020.WMF
CART021.WMF
CART022.WMF
CART023.WMF
CART024.WMF
CART025.WMF
CART026.WMF
CART027.WMF
CART028.WMF
CART029.WMF
CART030.WMF
CART031.WMF
CART032.WMF
CART033.WMF
CART034.WMF
CART035.WMF
CART036.WMF
CART037.WMF
CART038.WMF
CART039.WMF
CART040.WMF
CART041.WMF
CART042.WMF
CART043.WMF
CART044.WMF
CART045.WMF
CART046.WMF
CART047.WMF
CART048.WMF
CART049.WMF
CART050.WMF
CART051.WMF
CART052.WMF
CART053.WMF
CART054.WMF
CART055.WMF
CART056.WMF
CART057.WMF
CART058.WMF
CART059.WMF
CART060.WMF
CART061.WMF
CART062.WMF
CART063.WMF
CART064.WMF
CART065.WMF
CART066.WMF
CART067.WMF
CART068.WMF
CART069.WMF
CART070.WMF
CART071.WMF
CART072.WMF
CART073.WMF
CART074.WMF
CART075.WMF
CART076.WMF
CART077.WMF
CART078.WMF
CART079.WMF
CART080.WMF
CART081.WMF
CART082.WMF
CART083.WMF
CART084.WMF
CART085.WMF
CART086.WMF
CART087.WMF
CART088.WMF
CART089.WMF
CART090.WMF
CART091.WMF
CART092.WMF
CART093.WMF
CART094.WMF
CART095.WMF
CART096.WMF
CART097.WMF
CART098.WMF
CART099.WMF
CART100.WMF
CART101.WMF
CART102.WMF
CART103.WMF
CART104.WMF

CART105.WMF CART106.WMF CART107.WMF CART108.WMF CART109.WMF CART110.WMF CART111.WMF CART112.WMF CART113.WMF CART114.WMF
CART115.WMF CART116.WMF CART117.WMF CART118.WMF CART119.WMF CART120.WMF CART121.WMF CART122.WMF CART123.WMF CART124.WMF
CART125.WMF CART126.WMF CART127.WMF CART128.WMF CART129.WMF CART130.WMF CART131.WMF CART132.WMF CART133.WMF CART134.WMF
CART135.WMF CART136.WMF CART137.WMF CART138.WMF CART139.WMF CART140.WMF CART141.WMF CART142.WMF CART143.WMF CART144.WMF
CART145.WMF CART146.WMF CART147.WMF CART148.WMF CART149.WMF CART150.WMF CART151.WMF CART152.WMF CART153.WMF CART154.WMF
CART155.WMF CART156.WMF CART157.WMF CART158.WMF CART159.WMF CART160.WMF CART161.WMF CART162.WMF CART163.WMF CART164.WMF
CART165.WMF CART166.WMF CART167.WMF CART168.WMF CART169.WMF CART170.WMF CART171.WMF CART172.WMF CART173.WMF CART174.WMF
CART175.WMF CART176.WMF CART177.WMF CART178.WMF CART179.WMF CART180.WMF CART181.WMF CART182.WMF CART183.WMF CART184.WMF
CART185.WMF CART186.WMF CART187.WMF CART188.WMF CART189.WMF CART190.WMF CART191.WMF CART192.WMF CART193.WMF CART194.WMF
CART195.WMF CART196.WMF CART197.WMF CART198.WMF CART199.WMF CART200.WMF CART201.WMF CART202.WMF CART203.WMF CART204.WMF
CART205.WMF CART206.WMF CART207.WMF CART208.WMF CART209.WMF CART210.WMF CART211.WMF CART212.WMF CART213.WMF CART214.WMF
CART215.WMF CART216.WMF CART217.WMF CART218.WMF CART219.WMF CART220.WMF CART221.WMF CART222.WMF CART223.WMF CART224.WMF

CART225.WMF CART226.WMF CART227.WMF CART228.WMF CART229.WMF CART230.WMF CART231.WMF CART232.WMF CART233.WMF CART234.WMF
CART235.WMF CART236.WMF CART237.WMF CART238.WMF CART239.WMF CART240.WMF CART241.WMF CART242.WMF CART243.WMF CART244.WMF
CART245.WMF CART246.WMF CART247.WMF CART248.WMF CART249.WMF CART250.WMF CART251.WMF CART252.WMF CART253.WMF CART254.WMF
CART255.WMF CART256.WMF CART257.WMF CART258.WMF CART259.WMF CART260.WMF CART261.WMF CART262.WMF CART263.WMF CART264.WMF
CART265.WMF CART266.WMF CART267.WMF CART268.WMF CART269.WMF CART270.WMF CART271.WMF CART272.WMF CART273.WMF CART274.WMF
CART275.WMF CART276.WMF CART277.WMF CART278.WMF CART279.WMF CART280.WMF CART281.WMF CART282.WMF CART283.WMF CART284.WMF
CART285.WMF CART286.WMF CART287.WMF CART288.WMF CART289.WMF CART290.WMF CDS023B.WMF CDS023C.WMF CDS023F.WMF DEC070L.WMF
DEC071Y.WMF DEC085E.WMF DONK45.WMF EAA014B.WMF EAA014G.WMF EAA016F.WMF EAA019K.WMF EAC013A.WMF EAC013J.WMF EAC013K.WMF
EAC014N.WMF EAC014Q.WMF FCP008C.WMF FCP016H.WMF FCP022G.WMF FCP044K.WMF FRA009F.WMF FRA015E.WMF FSW013B.WMF FSW029B.WMF
FSW029C.WMF HFS029A.WMF HPI016B.WMF HRC295B.WMF LAC003C.WMF LAC003F.WMF LAC003H.WMF LAC011D.WMF LAC012A.WMF LAC012I.WMF
MAR017B.WMF MOD003I.WMF MSL083G.WMF MSL086E.WMF MSL086J.WMF MSL088Q.WMF NPC023A.WMF NPC035A.WMF NPC041A.WMF OEC024E.WMF
OFS032B.WMF OFS033A.WMF OFS035A.WMF OFS038H.WMF OFS039H.WMF OTS063F.WMF POC113M.WMF SIT071G.WMF SIT072J.WMF SIT085E.WMF

SIT086A.WMF SMR023I.WMF SPA008F.WMF SPA013A.WMF SPA016C.WMF SPA019C.WMF SPA020E.WMF SPA025B.WMF SPA028C.WMF SPA030A.WMF
TVA087F.WMF VSC069E.WMF VSI001E.WMF WAG003A.WMF WAG004A.WMF WAG005A.WMF WAG006A.WMF WAG007A.WMF WAG008A.WMF WAG010A.WMF
WAG011A.WMF WAG012A.WMF WAG013A.WMF WAG014A.WMF WILD001.WMF WILD002.WMF WILD003.WMF WILD004.WMF WILD005.WMF WILD006.WMF
WILD007.WMF WILD008.WMF WILD009.WMF WILD010.WMF WILD011.WMF WILD012.WMF WILD013.WMF WILD014.WMF WILD015.WMF WILD016.WMF
WILD017.WMF WILD018.WMF WILD019.WMF WILD020.WMF WILD021.WMF WILD022.WMF WILD023.WMF WILD024.WMF WILD025.WMF WILD026.WMF
WILD027.WMF WILD028.WMF WILD029.WMF WILD030.WMF WILD031.WMF WILD032.WMF WILD033.WMF WILD034.WMF WILD035.WMF WILD036.WMF
WILD037.WMF WILD038.WMF WILD039.WMF WILD040.WMF WILD041.WMF WILD042.WMF WILD043.WMF WILD044.WMF WILD045.WMF WILD046.WMF
WILD047.WMF WILD048.WMF WILD049.WMF WILD050.WMF WILD051.WMF WILD052.WMF WILD053.WMF WILD054.WMF WILD055.WMF WILD056.WMF
WILD057.WMF WILD058.WMF WILD059.WMF WILD060.WMF WILD061.WMF WILD062.WMF WILD063.WMF WILD064.WMF WILD065.WMF WILD066.WMF
WILD067.WMF WILD068.WMF WILD069.WMF WILD070.WMF WILD071.WMF WILD072.WMF WILD073.WMF WILD074.WMF WILD075.WMF WILD076.WMF
WILD077.WMF WILD078.WMF WILD079.WMF WILD080.WMF WILD081.WMF WILD082.WMF WILD083.WMF WILD084.WMF WILD085.WMF WILD086.WMF
WILD087.WMF WILD088.WMF WILD089.WMF WILD090.WMF WILD091.WMF WILD092.WMF WILD093.WMF WILD094.WMF WILD095.WMF WILD096.WMF

WILD097.WMF WILD098.WMF WILD099.WMF WILD100.WMF WILD101.WMF WILD102.WMF WILD103.WMF WILD104.WMF WILD105.WMF WILD106.WMF
WILD107.WMF WILD108.WMF WILD109.WMF WILD110.WMF WILD111.WMF WILD112.WMF WILD113.WMF WILD114.WMF WILD115.WMF WILD116.WMF
WILD117.WMF WILD118.WMF WILD119.WMF WILD120.WMF WILD121.WMF WILD122.WMF WILD123.WMF WILD124.WMF WILD125.WMF WILD126.WMF
WILD127.WMF WILD128.WMF WILD129.WMF WILD130.WMF WILD131.WMF WILD132.WMF WILD133.WMF WILD134.WMF WILD135.WMF WILD136.WMF
WILD137.WMF WILD138.WMF WILD139.WMF WILD140.WMF WILD141.WMF WILD142.WMF WILD143.WMF WILD144.WMF WILD145.WMF WILD146.WMF
WILD147.WMF WILD148.WMF WILD149.WMF WILD150.WMF WILD151.WMF WILD152.WMF WILD153.WMF WILD154.WMF WILD155.WMF WILD156.WMF
WILD157.WMF WILD158.WMF WILD159.WMF WILD160.WMF WILD161.WMF WILD162.WMF WILD163.WMF WILD164.WMF WILD165.WMF WILD166.WMF
WILD167.WMF WILD168.WMF WILD169.WMF WILD170.WMF WILD171.WMF WILD172.WMF WILD173.WMF WILD174.WMF WILD175.WMF WILD176.WMF
WILD177.WMF WILD178.WMF WILD179.WMF WILD180.WMF WILD181.WMF WILD182.WMF WILD183.WMF WILD184.WMF WILD185.WMF WILD186.WMF
WILD187.WMF WILD188.WMF WILD189.WMF WILD190.WMF WILD191.WMF WILD192.WMF WILD193.WMF WILD194.WMF WILD195.WMF WILD196.WMF
WILD197.WMF WILD198.WMF WILD199.WMF WILD200.WMF WILD201.WMF WILD202.WMF WILD203.WMF WILD204.WMF WILD205.WMF WILD206.WMF
WILD207.WMF WILD208.WMF WILD209.WMF WILD210.WMF WILD211.WMF WILD212.WMF WILD213.WMF WILD214.WMF WILD215.WMF WILD216.WMF

WILD217.WMF
WILD218.WMF
WILD219.WMF
WILD220.WMF
WILD221.WMF
WILD222.WMF
WILD223.WMF
WILD224.WMF
WILD225.WMF
WILD226.WMF
WILD227.WMF
WILD228.WMF
WILD229.WMF
WILD230.WMF
WILD231.WMF
WILD232.WMF
WILD233.WMF
WILD234.WMF
WILD235.WMF
WILD236.WMF
WILD237.WMF
WILD238.WMF
WILD239.WMF
WILD240.WMF
WILD241.WMF
WILD242.WMF
WILD243.WMF
WILD244.WMF
WILD245.WMF
WILD246.WMF
WSG002A.WMF
WSG004A.WMF
WSG006A.WMF
WSG009A.WMF
WSG012A.WMF
WSG014A.WMF
WSG015A.WMF

AAL019A.WMF AAL019E.WMF AAL021A.WMF AAL022C.WMF AAL023E.WMF AAL023F.WMF AIL002B.WMF AIL003A.WMF AIL011D.WMF AIL022C.WMF
AIL026D.WMF AWH001A.WMF AWH002A.WMF AWH002A1.WMF AWH002B.WMF AWH002B1.WMF AWH002D.WMF AWH002F.WMF AWH004C.WMF AWH005C.WMF
AWH005D.WMF AWH006A.WMF AWH006C.WMF AWH007A.WMF AWH007B.WMF AWH007C.WMF AWH007D.WMF AWH008E.WMF AWH009B.WMF AWH009C.WMF
AWH009D.WMF AWH009E.WMF AWH009F.WMF AWH010A.WMF AWH010B.WMF AWH011A.WMF AWH012A.WMF AWH012F.WMF AWH013C.WMF AWH013E.WMF
AWH014B.WMF AWH014B1.WMF AWH014C.WMF AWH015A.WMF AWH015C.WMF AWH015E.WMF AWH016D.WMF AWH016E.WMF AWH017B.WMF AWH017D.WMF
AWH017E.WMF AWH017F.WMF AWH018A.WMF AWH018C.WMF AWH018D.WMF AWH018G.WMF AWH019A.WMF AWH019B.WMF AWH019C.WMF AWH019F.WMF
AWH020D.WMF AWH020F.WMF AWH021D.WMF AWH022A.WMF AWH022C.WMF AWH022D.WMF AWH022E.WMF AWH023A.WMF AWH024D.WMF AWH024E.WMF
AWH024F.WMF AWH025A.WMF AWH025I.WMF AWH026C.WMF AWH026D.WMF AWH026E.WMF AWH027B.WMF AWH027E.WMF AWH027F.WMF AWH027G.WMF
AWH027H.WMF AWH028A.WMF AWH028B.WMF AWH028C.WMF AWH028D.WMF AWH028F.WMF AWH028G.WMF AWP037A.WMF CART001.WMF CART002.WMF
CART003.WMF CART004.WMF CART005.WMF CART006.WMF CART007.WMF CART008.WMF CART009.WMF CART010.WMF CART011.WMF CART012.WMF
CART013.WMF CART014.WMF CART015.WMF CART016.WMF CART017.WMF CART018.WMF CART019.WMF CART020.WMF CART021.WMF CART022.WMF
CART023.WMF CART024.WMF CART025.WMF CART026.WMF CART027.WMF CART028.WMF CART029.WMF CART030.WMF CART031.WMF CART032.WMF

CART033.WMF CART034.WMF CART035.WMF CART036.WMF CART037.WMF CART038.WMF CART039.WMF CART040.WMF CART041.WMF CART042.WMF

CART043.WMF CART044.WMF CART045.WMF CART046.WMF CART047.WMF CART048.WMF CART049.WMF CART050.WMF CART051.WMF CART052.WMF

CART053.WMF CART054.WMF CART055.WMF CART056.WMF CART057.WMF CART058.WMF CART059.WMF CART060.WMF CART061.WMF CART062.WMF

CART063.WMF CART064.WMF CART065.WMF CART066.WMF CART067.WMF CART068.WMF CART069.WMF CART070.WMF CART071.WMF CART072.WMF

CART073.WMF CART074.WMF CART075.WMF CART076.WMF CART077.WMF CART078.WMF CART079.WMF CART080.WMF CART081.WMF CART082.WMF

CART083.WMF CART084.WMF CART085.WMF CART086.WMF CART087.WMF CART088.WMF CART089.WMF CART090.WMF CART091.WMF CART092.WMF

CART093.WMF CART094.WMF CART095.WMF CART097.WMF CART098.WMF CART099.WMF CART100.WMF CART1001.WMF CART1002.WMF CART1003.WMF

CART1004.WMF CART1005.WMF CART1006.WMF CART1007.WMF CART1008.WMF CART1009.WMF CART101.WMF CART1010.WMF CART1011.WMF CART1012.WMF

CART1013.WMF CART1014.WMF CART1015.WMF CART102.WMF CART103.WMF CART104.WMF CART105.WMF CART106.WMF CART107.WMF CART108.WMF

CART109.WMF CART110.WMF CART111.WMF CART112.WMF CART113.WMF CART114.WMF CART115.WMF CART116.WMF CART117.WMF CART118.WMF

CART119.WMF CART120.WMF CART121.WMF CART122.WMF CART123.WMF CART124.WMF CART125.WMF CART126.WMF CART127.WMF CART128.WMF

CART129.WMF CART130.WMF CART131.WMF CART132.WMF CART133.WMF CART134.WMF CART135.WMF CART136.WMF CART137.WMF CART138.WMF

CART139.WMF
CART140.WMF
CART141.WMF
CART142.WMF
CART143.WMF
CART144.WMF
CART145.WMF
CART146.WMF
CART147.WMF
CART148.WMF
CART149.WMF
CART150.WMF
CART151.WMF
CART152.WMF
CART153.WMF
CART154.WMF
CART155.WMF
CART156.WMF
CART157.WMF
CART158.WMF
CART159.WMF
CART160.WMF
CART161.WMF
CART162.WMF
CART163.WMF
CART164.WMF
CART165.WMF
CART166.WMF
CART167.WMF
CART168.WMF
CART169.WMF
CART170.WMF
CART171.WMF
CART172.WMF
CART173.WMF
CART174.WMF
CART175.WMF
CART176.WMF
CART177.WMF
CART178.WMF
CART179.WMF
CART180.WMF
CART181.WMF
CART182.WMF
CART183.WMF
CART184.WMF
CART185.WMF
CART186.WMF
CART187.WMF
CART188.WMF
CART189.WMF
CART190.WMF
CART191.WMF
CART192.WMF
CART193.WMF
CART194.WMF
CART195.WMF
CART196.WMF
CART197.WMF
CART198.WMF
CART199.WMF
CART200.WMF
CART201.WMF
CART202.WMF
CART203.WMF
CART204.WMF
CART205.WMF
CART206.WMF
CART207.WMF
CART208.WMF
CART209.WMF
CART210.WMF
CART211.WMF
CART212.WMF
CART213.WMF
CART214.WMF
CART215.WMF
CART216.WMF
CART217.WMF
CART218.WMF
CART219.WMF
CART220.WMF
CART221.WMF
CART222.WMF
CART223.WMF
CART224.WMF
CART225.WMF
CART226.WMF
CART227.WMF
CART228.WMF
CART229.WMF
CART230.WMF
CART231.WMF
CART232.WMF
CART233.WMF
CART234.WMF
CART235.WMF
CART236.WMF
CART237.WMF
CART238.WMF
CART239.WMF
CART240.WMF
CART241.WMF
CART242.WMF
CART243.WMF
CART244.WMF
CART245.WMF
CART246.WMF
CART247.WMF
CART248.WMF
CART249.WMF
CART250.WMF
CART251.WMF
CART252.WMF
CART253.WMF
CART254.WMF
CART255.WMF
CART256.WMF
CART257.WMF
CART258.WMF

CART259.WMF CART260.WMF CART261.WMF CART262.WMF CART263.WMF CART264.WMF CART265.WMF CART266.WMF CART267.WMF CART268.WMF
CART269.WMF CART270.WMF CART271.WMF CART272.WMF CART273.WMF CART274.WMF CART275.WMF CART276.WMF CART277.WMF CART278.WMF
CART279.WMF CART280.WMF CART281.WMF CART282.WMF CART283.WMF CART284.WMF CART285.WMF CART286.WMF CART287.WMF CART288.WMF
CART289.WMF CART290.WMF CART291.WMF CART292.WMF CART293.WMF CART294.WMF CART295.WMF CART296.WMF CART297.WMF CART298.WMF
CART299.WMF CART300.WMF CART301.WMF CART302.WMF CART303.WMF CART304.WMF CART305.WMF CART306.WMF CART307.WMF CART308.WMF
CART309.WMF CART310.WMF CART311.WMF CART312.WMF CART313.WMF CART314.WMF CART315.WMF CART316.WMF CART317.WMF CART318.WMF
CART319.WMF CART320.WMF CART321.WMF CART322.WMF CART323.WMF CART324.WMF CART325.WMF CART326.WMF CART327.WMF CART328.WMF
CART329.WMF CART330.WMF CART331.WMF CART332.WMF CART333.WMF CART334.WMF CART335.WMF CART336.WMF CART337.WMF CART338.WMF
CART339.WMF CART340.WMF CART341.WMF CART342.WMF CART343.WMF CART344.WMF CART345.WMF CART346.WMF CART347.WMF CART348.WMF
CART349.WMF CART350.WMF CART351.WMF CART352.WMF CART353.WMF CART354.WMF CART355.WMF CART356.WMF CART357.WMF CART358.WMF
CART359.WMF CART360.WMF CART361.WMF CART362.WMF CART363.WMF CART364.WMF CART365.WMF CART366.WMF CART367.WMF CART368.WMF
CART369.WMF CART370.WMF CART371.WMF CART372.WMF CART373.WMF CART374.WMF CART375.WMF CART376.WMF CART377.WMF CART378.WMF

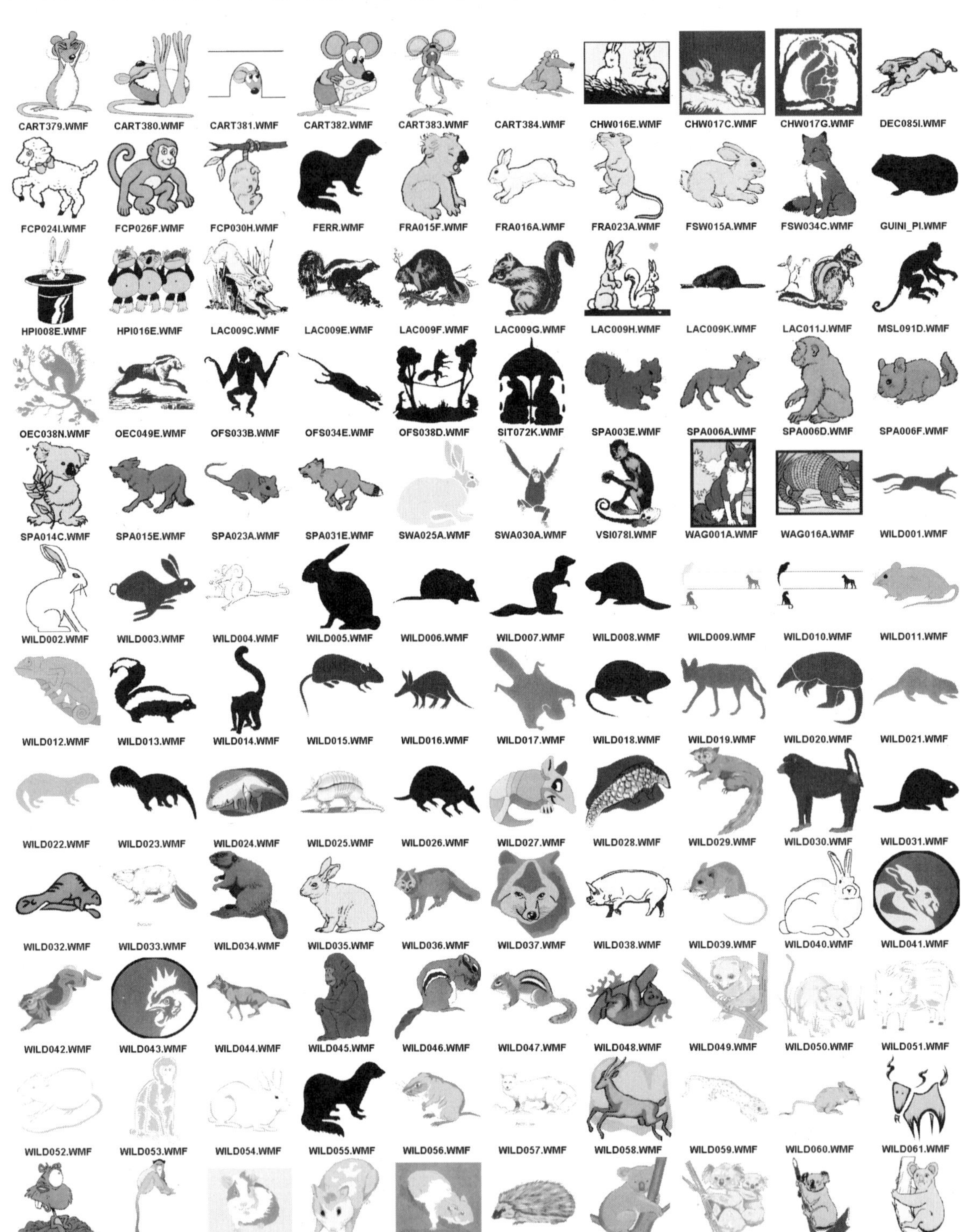
CART379.WMF
CART380.WMF
CART381.WMF
CART382.WMF
CART383.WMF
CART384.WMF
CHW016E.WMF
CHW017C.WMF
CHW017G.WMF
DEC085I.WMF
FCP024I.WMF
FCP026F.WMF
FCP030H.WMF
FERR.WMF
FRA015F.WMF
FRA016A.WMF
FRA023A.WMF
FSW015A.WMF
FSW034C.WMF
GUINI_PI.WMF
HPI008E.WMF
HPI016E.WMF
LAC009C.WMF
LAC009E.WMF
LAC009F.WMF
LAC009G.WMF
LAC009H.WMF
LAC009K.WMF
LAC011J.WMF
MSL091D.WMF
OEC038N.WMF
OEC049E.WMF
OFS033B.WMF
OFS034E.WMF
OFS038D.WMF
SIT072K.WMF
SPA003E.WMF
SPA006A.WMF
SPA006D.WMF
SPA006F.WMF
SPA014C.WMF
SPA015E.WMF
SPA023A.WMF
SPA031E.WMF
SWA025A.WMF
SWA030A.WMF
VSI078I.WMF
WAG001A.WMF
WAG016A.WMF
WILD001.WMF
WILD002.WMF
WILD003.WMF
WILD004.WMF
WILD005.WMF
WILD006.WMF
WILD007.WMF
WILD008.WMF
WILD009.WMF
WILD010.WMF
WILD011.WMF
WILD012.WMF
WILD013.WMF
WILD014.WMF
WILD015.WMF
WILD016.WMF
WILD017.WMF
WILD018.WMF
WILD019.WMF
WILD020.WMF
WILD021.WMF
WILD022.WMF
WILD023.WMF
WILD024.WMF
WILD025.WMF
WILD026.WMF
WILD027.WMF
WILD028.WMF
WILD029.WMF
WILD030.WMF
WILD031.WMF
WILD032.WMF
WILD033.WMF
WILD034.WMF
WILD035.WMF
WILD036.WMF
WILD037.WMF
WILD038.WMF
WILD039.WMF
WILD040.WMF
WILD041.WMF
WILD042.WMF
WILD043.WMF
WILD044.WMF
WILD045.WMF
WILD046.WMF
WILD047.WMF
WILD048.WMF
WILD049.WMF
WILD050.WMF
WILD051.WMF
WILD052.WMF
WILD053.WMF
WILD054.WMF
WILD055.WMF
WILD056.WMF
WILD057.WMF
WILD058.WMF
WILD059.WMF
WILD060.WMF
WILD061.WMF
WILD062.WMF
WILD063.WMF
WILD064.WMF
WILD065.WMF
WILD066.WMF
WILD067.WMF
WILD068.WMF
WILD069.WMF
WILD070.WMF
WILD071.WMF

WILD072.WMF
WILD073.WMF
WILD074.WMF
WILD075.WMF
WILD076.WMF
WILD077.WMF
WILD078.WMF
WILD079.WMF
WILD080.WMF
WILD081.WMF
WILD082.WMF
WILD083.WMF
WILD084.WMF
WILD085.WMF
WILD086.WMF
WILD087.WMF
WILD088.WMF
WILD089.WMF
WILD090.WMF
WILD091.WMF
WILD092.WMF
WILD093.WMF
WILD094.WMF
WILD095.WMF
WILD096.WMF
WILD097.WMF
WILD098.WMF
WILD099.WMF
WILD100.WMF
WILD101.WMF
WILD102.WMF
WILD103.WMF
WILD104.WMF
WILD105.WMF
WILD106.WMF
WILD107.WMF
WILD108.WMF
WILD109.WMF
WILD110.WMF
WILD111.WMF
WILD112.WMF
WILD113.WMF
WILD114.WMF
WILD115.WMF
WILD116.WMF
WILD117.WMF
WILD118.WMF
WILD119.WMF
WILD120.WMF
WILD121.WMF
WSG001A.WMF
WSG003A.WMF
WSG005A.WMF
WSG007A.WMF
WSG008A.WMF
WSG010A.WMF
WSG013A.WMF

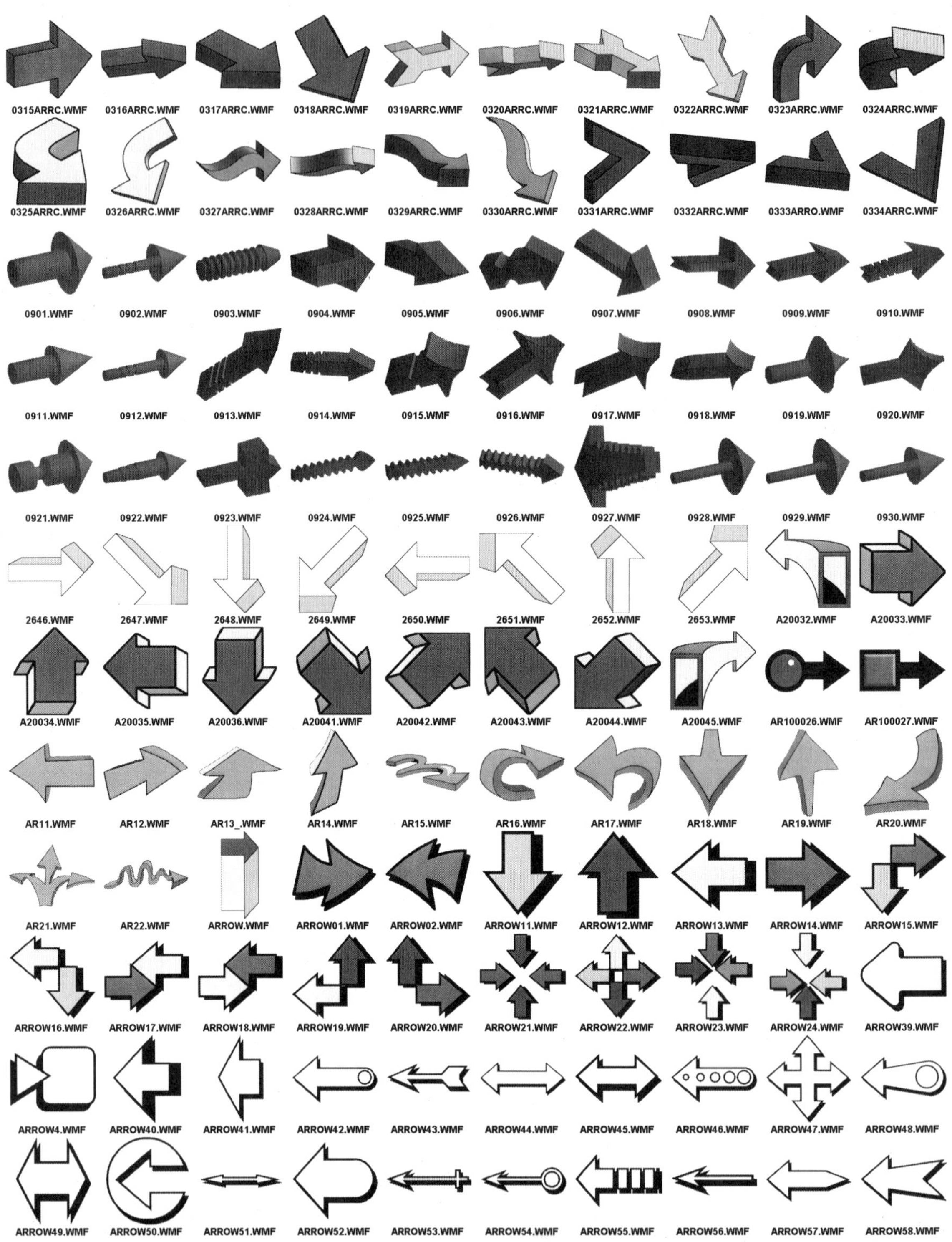
0315ARRC.WMF 0316ARRC.WMF 0317ARRC.WMF 0318ARRC.WMF 0319ARRC.WMF 0320ARRC.WMF 0321ARRC.WMF 0322ARRC.WMF 0323ARRC.WMF 0324ARRC.WMF
0325ARRC.WMF 0326ARRC.WMF 0327ARRC.WMF 0328ARRC.WMF 0329ARRC.WMF 0330ARRC.WMF 0331ARRC.WMF 0332ARRC.WMF 0333ARRO.WMF 0334ARRC.WMF
0901.WMF 0902.WMF 0903.WMF 0904.WMF 0905.WMF 0906.WMF 0907.WMF 0908.WMF 0909.WMF 0910.WMF
0911.WMF 0912.WMF 0913.WMF 0914.WMF 0915.WMF 0916.WMF 0917.WMF 0918.WMF 0919.WMF 0920.WMF
0921.WMF 0922.WMF 0923.WMF 0924.WMF 0925.WMF 0926.WMF 0927.WMF 0928.WMF 0929.WMF 0930.WMF
2646.WMF 2647.WMF 2648.WMF 2649.WMF 2650.WMF 2651.WMF 2652.WMF 2653.WMF A20032.WMF A20033.WMF
A20034.WMF A20035.WMF A20036.WMF A20041.WMF A20042.WMF A20043.WMF A20044.WMF A20045.WMF AR100026.WMF AR100027.WMF
AR11.WMF AR12.WMF AR13_.WMF AR14.WMF AR15.WMF AR16.WMF AR17.WMF AR18.WMF AR19.WMF AR20.WMF
AR21.WMF AR22.WMF ARROW.WMF ARROW01.WMF ARROW02.WMF ARROW11.WMF ARROW12.WMF ARROW13.WMF ARROW14.WMF ARROW15.WMF
ARROW16.WMF ARROW17.WMF ARROW18.WMF ARROW19.WMF ARROW20.WMF ARROW21.WMF ARROW22.WMF ARROW23.WMF ARROW24.WMF ARROW39.WMF
ARROW4.WMF ARROW40.WMF ARROW41.WMF ARROW42.WMF ARROW43.WMF ARROW44.WMF ARROW45.WMF ARROW46.WMF ARROW47.WMF ARROW48.WMF
ARROW49.WMF ARROW50.WMF ARROW51.WMF ARROW52.WMF ARROW53.WMF ARROW54.WMF ARROW55.WMF ARROW56.WMF ARROW57.WMF ARROW58.WMF

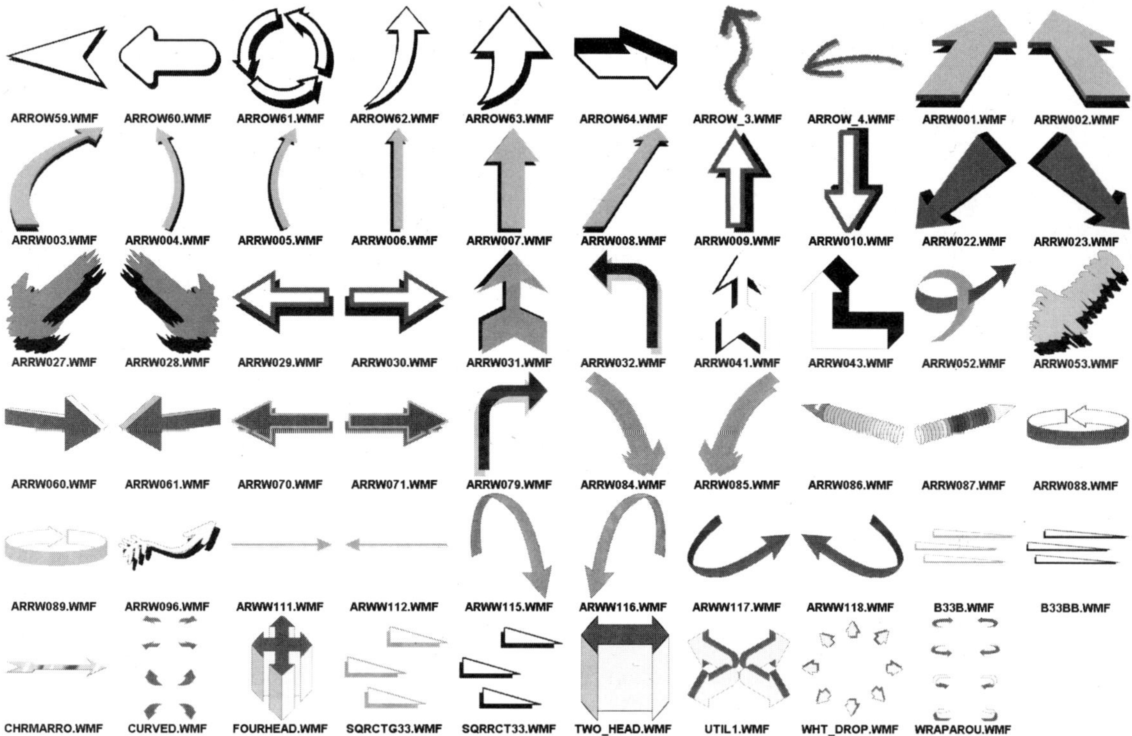
ARROW59.WMF
ARROW60.WMF
ARROW61.WMF
ARROW62.WMF
ARROW63.WMF
ARROW64.WMF
ARROW_3.WMF
ARROW_4.WMF
ARRW001.WMF
ARRW002.WMF
ARRW003.WMF
ARRW004.WMF
ARRW005.WMF
ARRW006.WMF
ARRW007.WMF
ARRW008.WMF
ARRW009.WMF
ARRW010.WMF
ARRW022.WMF
ARRW023.WMF
ARRW027.WMF
ARRW028.WMF
ARRW029.WMF
ARRW030.WMF
ARRW031.WMF
ARRW032.WMF
ARRW041.WMF
ARRW043.WMF
ARRW052.WMF
ARRW053.WMF
ARRW060.WMF
ARRW061.WMF
ARRW070.WMF
ARRW071.WMF
ARRW079.WMF
ARRW084.WMF
ARRW085.WMF
ARRW086.WMF
ARRW087.WMF
ARRW088.WMF
ARRW089.WMF
ARRW096.WMF
ARWW111.WMF
ARWW112.WMF
ARWW115.WMF
ARWW116.WMF
ARWW117.WMF
ARWW118.WMF
B33B.WMF
B33BB.WMF
CHRMARRO.WMF
CURVED.WMF
FOURHEAD.WMF
SQRCTG33.WMF
SQRRCT33.WMF
TWO_HEAD.WMF
UTIL1.WMF
WHT_DROP.WMF
WRAPAROU.WMF

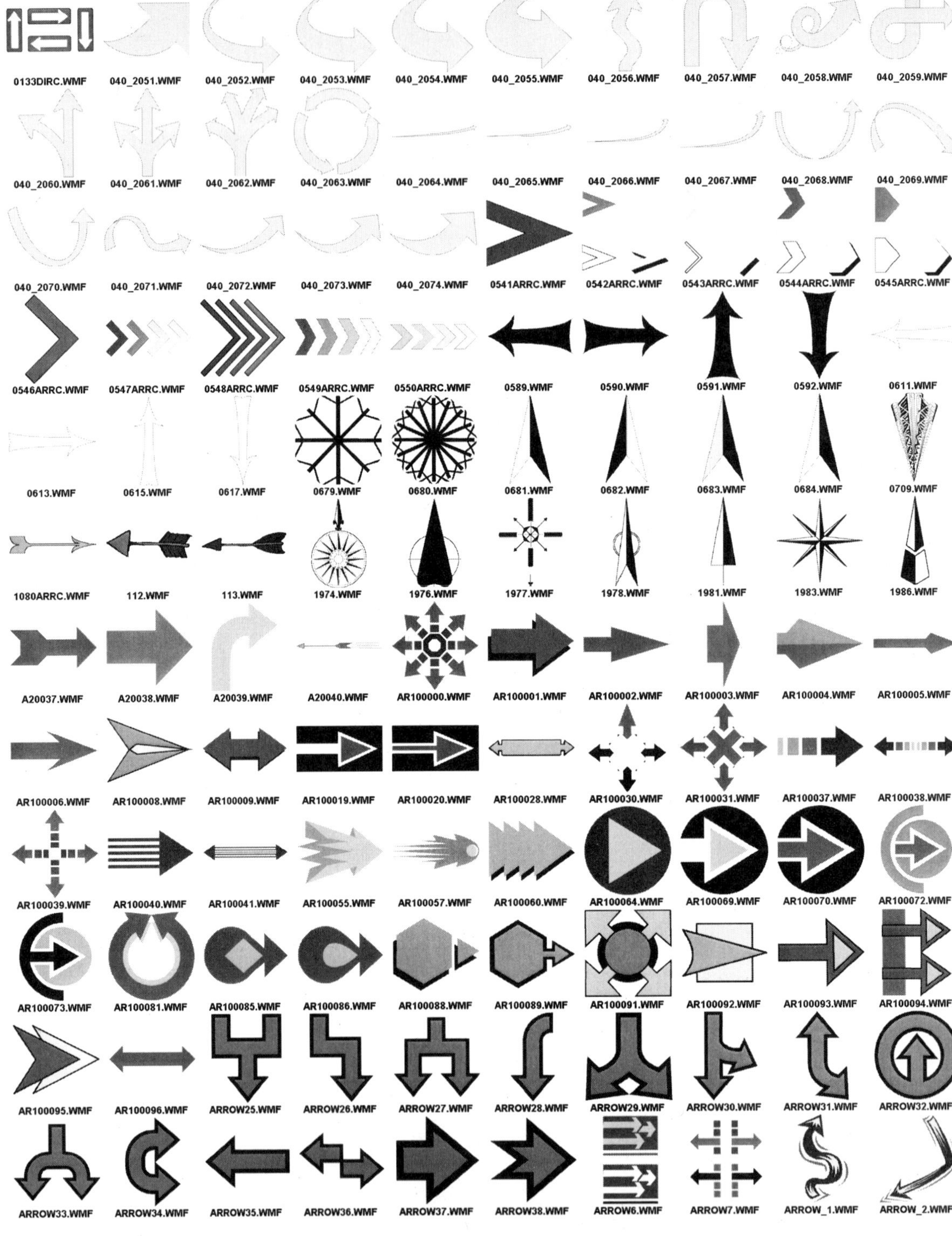
0133DIRC.WMF 040_2051.WMF 040_2052.WMF 040_2053.WMF 040_2054.WMF 040_2055.WMF 040_2056.WMF 040_2057.WMF 040_2058.WMF 040_2059.WMF
040_2060.WMF 040_2061.WMF 040_2062.WMF 040_2063.WMF 040_2064.WMF 040_2065.WMF 040_2066.WMF 040_2067.WMF 040_2068.WMF 040_2069.WMF
040_2070.WMF 040_2071.WMF 040_2072.WMF 040_2073.WMF 040_2074.WMF 0541ARRC.WMF 0542ARRC.WMF 0543ARRC.WMF 0544ARRC.WMF 0545ARRC.WMF
0546ARRC.WMF 0547ARRC.WMF 0548ARRC.WMF 0549ARRC.WMF 0550ARRC.WMF 0589.WMF 0590.WMF 0591.WMF 0592.WMF 0611.WMF
0613.WMF 0615.WMF 0617.WMF 0679.WMF 0680.WMF 0681.WMF 0682.WMF 0683.WMF 0684.WMF 0709.WMF
1080ARRC.WMF 112.WMF 113.WMF 1974.WMF 1976.WMF 1977.WMF 1978.WMF 1981.WMF 1983.WMF 1986.WMF
A20037.WMF A20038.WMF A20039.WMF A20040.WMF AR100000.WMF AR100001.WMF AR100002.WMF AR100003.WMF AR100004.WMF AR100005.WMF
AR100006.WMF AR100008.WMF AR100009.WMF AR100019.WMF AR100020.WMF AR100028.WMF AR100030.WMF AR100031.WMF AR100037.WMF AR100038.WMF
AR100039.WMF AR100040.WMF AR100041.WMF AR100055.WMF AR100057.WMF AR100060.WMF AR100064.WMF AR100069.WMF AR100070.WMF AR100072.WMF
AR100073.WMF AR100081.WMF AR100085.WMF AR100086.WMF AR100088.WMF AR100089.WMF AR100091.WMF AR100092.WMF AR100093.WMF AR100094.WMF
AR100095.WMF AR100096.WMF ARROW25.WMF ARROW26.WMF ARROW27.WMF ARROW28.WMF ARROW29.WMF ARROW30.WMF ARROW31.WMF ARROW32.WMF
ARROW33.WMF ARROW34.WMF ARROW35.WMF ARROW36.WMF ARROW37.WMF ARROW38.WMF ARROW6.WMF ARROW7.WMF ARROW_1.WMF ARROW_2.WMF

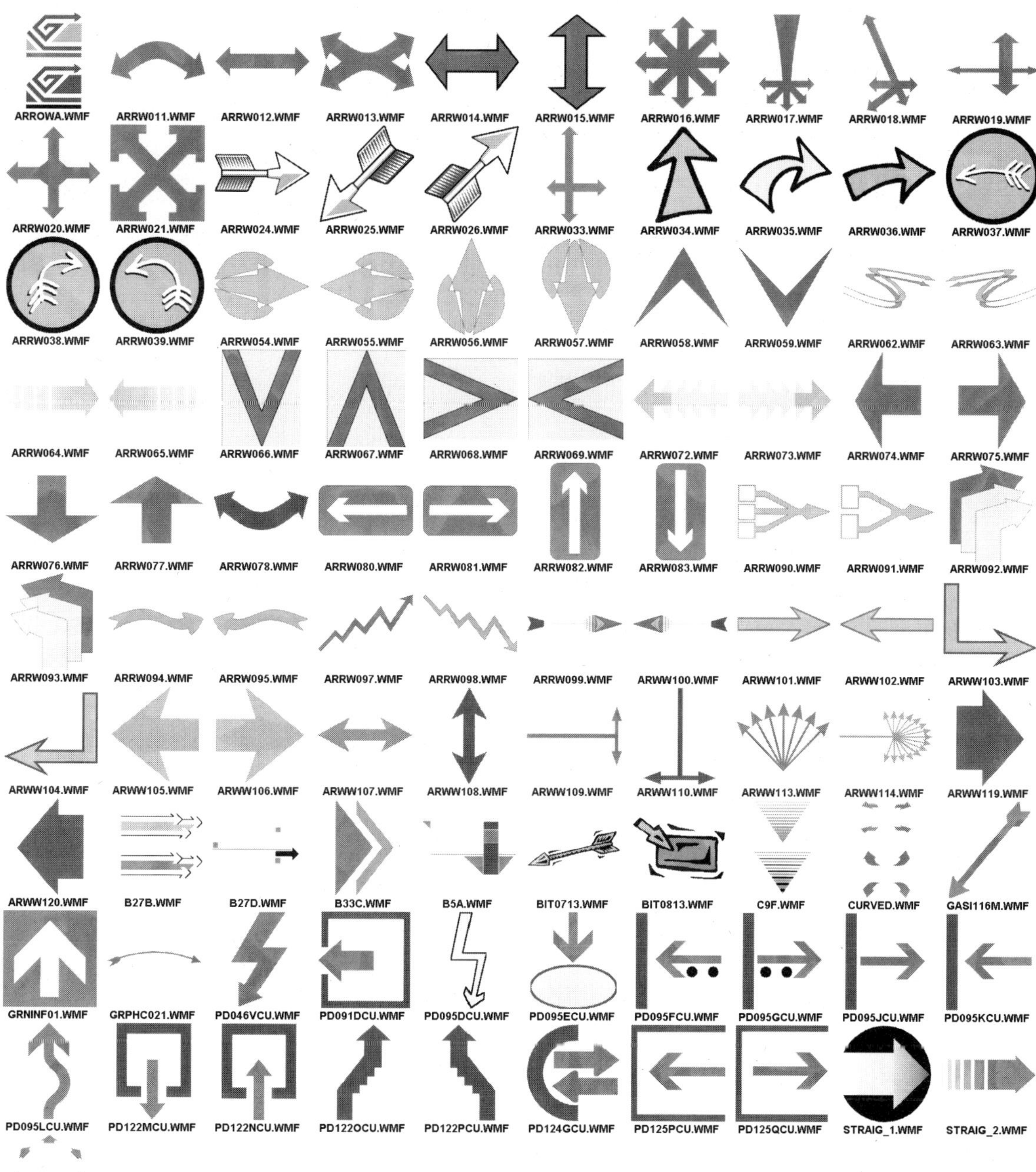
ARROWA.WMF ARRW011.WMF ARRW012.WMF ARRW013.WMF ARRW014.WMF ARRW015.WMF ARRW016.WMF ARRW017.WMF ARRW018.WMF ARRW019.WMF
ARRW020.WMF ARRW021.WMF ARRW024.WMF ARRW025.WMF ARRW026.WMF ARRW033.WMF ARRW034.WMF ARRW035.WMF ARRW036.WMF ARRW037.WMF
ARRW038.WMF ARRW039.WMF ARRW054.WMF ARRW055.WMF ARRW056.WMF ARRW057.WMF ARRW058.WMF ARRW059.WMF ARRW062.WMF ARRW063.WMF
ARRW064.WMF ARRW065.WMF ARRW066.WMF ARRW067.WMF ARRW068.WMF ARRW069.WMF ARRW072.WMF ARRW073.WMF ARRW074.WMF ARRW075.WMF
ARRW076.WMF ARRW077.WMF ARRW078.WMF ARRW080.WMF ARRW081.WMF ARRW082.WMF ARRW083.WMF ARRW090.WMF ARRW091.WMF ARRW092.WMF
ARRW093.WMF ARRW094.WMF ARRW095.WMF ARRW097.WMF ARRW098.WMF ARRW099.WMF ARWW100.WMF ARWW101.WMF ARWW102.WMF ARWW103.WMF
ARWW104.WMF ARWW105.WMF ARWW106.WMF ARWW107.WMF ARWW108.WMF ARWW109.WMF ARWW110.WMF ARWW113.WMF ARWW114.WMF ARWW119.WMF
ARWW120.WMF B27B.WMF B27D.WMF B33C.WMF B5A.WMF BIT0713.WMF BIT0813.WMF C9F.WMF CURVED.WMF GASI116M.WMF
GRNINF01.WMF GRPHC021.WMF PD046VCU.WMF PD091DCU.WMF PD095DCU.WMF PD095ECU.WMF PD095FCU.WMF PD095GCU.WMF PD095JCU.WMF PD095KCU.WMF
PD095LCU.WMF PD122MCU.WMF PD122NCU.WMF PD122OCU.WMF PD122PCU.WMF PD124GCU.WMF PD125PCU.WMF PD125QCU.WMF STRAIG_1.WMF STRAIG_2.WMF
STRAIG_3.WMF

01DOWN.WMF
01LEFT.WMF
01RIGHT.WMF
01UP.WMF
02DOWN.WMF
02LEFT.WMF
02RIGHT.WMF
02UP.WMF
03LEFT.WMF
03RIGHT.WMF
04LEFT.WMF
04RIGHT.WMF
0540.WMF
0559.WMF
0560.WMF
0561.WMF
0562.WMF
0564.WMF
0565.WMF
0566.WMF
05DOWN.WMF
05LEFT.WMF
05RIGHT.WMF
05UP.WMF
0610.WMF
0612.WMF
0614.WMF
0616.WMF
0618.WMF
0620.WMF
0622.WMF
0624.WMF
0639.WMF
0654.WMF
0655.WMF
0656.WMF
0657.WMF
0658.WMF
0659.WMF
0660.WMF
0667.WMF
0668.WMF
06DOWN.WMF
06LEFT.WMF
06RIGHT.WMF
06UP.WMF
07DOWN.WMF
07LEFT.WMF
07RIGHT.WMF
07UP.WMF
0863.WMF
0865.WMF
0867.WMF
0869.WMF
0871.WMF
0873.WMF
0875.WMF
0877.WMF
0879.WMF
0881.WMF
0883.WMF
0885.WMF
0887.WMF
0889.WMF
0891.WMF
0893.WMF
0895.WMF
0897.WMF
0899.WMF
0900.WMF
09LEFT.WMF
09RIGHT.WMF
10LEFT.WMF
10RIGHT.WMF
11LEFT.WMF
11RIGHT.WMF
1220.WMF
1221.WMF
1243.WMF
1244.WMF
1245.WMF
1246.WMF
1285.WMF
1286.WMF
1287.WMF
1288.WMF
1289.WMF
1290.WMF
1291.WMF
1292.WMF
1293.WMF
1294.WMF
1295.WMF
1296.WMF
1297.WMF
1298.WMF
1299.WMF
12LEFT.WMF
12RIGHT.WMF
1300.WMF
13DOWN.WMF
13UP.WMF
14DOWN.WMF
14UP.WMF
15LEFT.WMF
15RIGHT.WMF
16LEFT.WMF
16RIGHT.WMF
17DOWN.WMF
17UP.WMF
18DOWN.WMF
18UP.WMF
1901.WMF
1902.WMF
1903.WMF
1904.WMF
1905.WMF
1906.WMF
1907.WMF
1908.WMF

1909.WMF 1910.WMF 1911.WMF 1912.WMF 1913.WMF 1914.WMF 1915.WMF 1916.WMF 1929.WMF 1930.WMF
1931.WMF 1932.WMF 1933.WMF 1934.WMF 1935.WMF 1936.WMF 1979.WMF 1980.WMF 1982.WMF 1984.WMF
1987.WMF 1988.WMF 1989.WMF 1990.WMF 1991.WMF 1992.WMF 1993.WMF 1994.WMF 1995.WMF 1997.WMF
1998.WMF 1999.WMF 19DOWN.WMF 19LEFT.WMF 19RIGHT.WMF 19UP.WMF 20LEFT.WMF 20RIGHT.WMF 2109.WMF 2110.WMF
2111.WMF 2112.WMF 2113.WMF 2114.WMF 2115.WMF 2116.WMF 2117.WMF 2118.WMF 2119.WMF 2120.WMF
2121.WMF 2122.WMF 2123.WMF 2124.WMF 2125.WMF 2126.WMF 2127.WMF 2128.WMF 2129.WMF 2130.WMF
2131.WMF 2132.WMF 2133.WMF 2134.WMF 2135.WMF 2136.WMF 2137.WMF 2138.WMF 2139.WMF 2140.WMF
21LEFT.WMF 21RIGHT.WMF 2241.WMF 2242.WMF 2243.WMF 2244.WMF 2297.WMF 2298.WMF 2299.WMF 22LEFT.WMF
22RIGHT.WMF 2300.WMF 2349.WMF 2350.WMF 2351.WMF 2352.WMF 2353.WMF 2354.WMF 2355.WMF 2356.WMF
2379.WMF 2380.WMF 2381.WMF 2382.WMF 2383.WMF 2384.WMF 2385.WMF 2386.WMF 23DOWN.WMF 23LEFT.WMF
23RIGHT.WMF 23UP.WMF 24DOWN.WMF 24LEFT.WMF 24RIGHT.WMF 24UP.WMF 2510.WMF 2511.WMF 2512.WMF 2513.WMF
2514.WMF 2515.WMF 2516.WMF 2517.WMF 25DOWN.WMF 25LEFT.WMF 25RIGHT.WMF 25UP.WMF 2654.WMF 2655.WMF

2656.WMF
2657.WMF
2658.WMF
2659.WMF
2660.WMF
2661.WMF
26_2_WAY.WMF
26_4_WAY.WMF
27LEFT.WMF
27RIGHT.WMF
28LEFT.WMF
28RIGHT.WMF
29DOWN.WMF
29LEFT.WMF
29RIGHT.WMF
29UP.WMF
30DOWN.WMF
30LEFT.WMF
30RIGHT.WMF
30UP.WMF
31DOWN.WMF
31LEFT.WMF
31RIGHT.WMF
31UP.WMF
32DOWN.WMF
32LEFT.WMF
32RIGHT.WMF
32UP.WMF
33DOWN.WMF
33LEFT.WMF
33RIGHT.WMF
33UP.WMF
34DOWN.WMF
34LEFT.WMF
34RIGHT.WMF
34UP.WMF
35DOWN.WMF
35LEFT.WMF
35RIGHT.WMF
35UP.WMF
36DOWN.WMF
36LEFT.WMF
36RIGHT.WMF
36UP.WMF
37LEFT.WMF
37RIGHT.WMF
38LEFT.WMF
38RIGHT.WMF
39DOWN.WMF
39LEFT.WMF
39RIGHT.WMF
39UP.WMF
40DOWN.WMF
40LEFT.WMF
40RIGHT.WMF
40UP.WMF
41DOWN.WMF
41LEFT.WMF
41RIGHT.WMF
41UP.WMF
42DOWN.WMF
42LEFT.WMF
42RIGHT.WMF
42UP.WMF
43LEFT.WMF
43RIGHT.WMF
44LEFT.WMF
44RIGHT.WMF
45LEFT.WMF
45RIGHT.WMF
46LEFT.WMF
46RIGHT.WMF
47_3_WAY.WMF
48LEFT.WMF
48RIGHT.WMF
49LEFT.WMF
49RIGHT.WMF
50LEFT.WMF
50RIGHT.WMF
51LEFT.WMF
51RIGHT.WMF
52DOWN.WMF
52LEFT.WMF
52RIGHT.WMF
52UP.WMF
53DOWN.WMF
53LEFT.WMF
53RIGHT.WMF
53UP.WMF
54LEFT.WMF
54RIGHT.WMF
55LEFT.WMF
55RIGHT.WMF
56LEFT.WMF
56RIGHT.WMF
57LEFT.WMF
57RIGHT.WMF
58LEFT.WMF
58RIGHT.WMF
59DOWN.WMF
59LEFT.WMF
59RIGHT.WMF
59UP.WMF
60LEFT.WMF
60RIGHT.WMF
61DOWN.WMF
61LEFT.WMF
61RIGHT.WMF
61UP.WMF
62DOWN.WMF
62LEFT.WMF
62RIGHT.WMF
62UP.WMF
63_4_WAY.WMF
64DOWN.WMF
64LEFT.WMF
64RIGHT.WMF
64UP.WMF
65DOWN.WMF
65LEFT.WMF

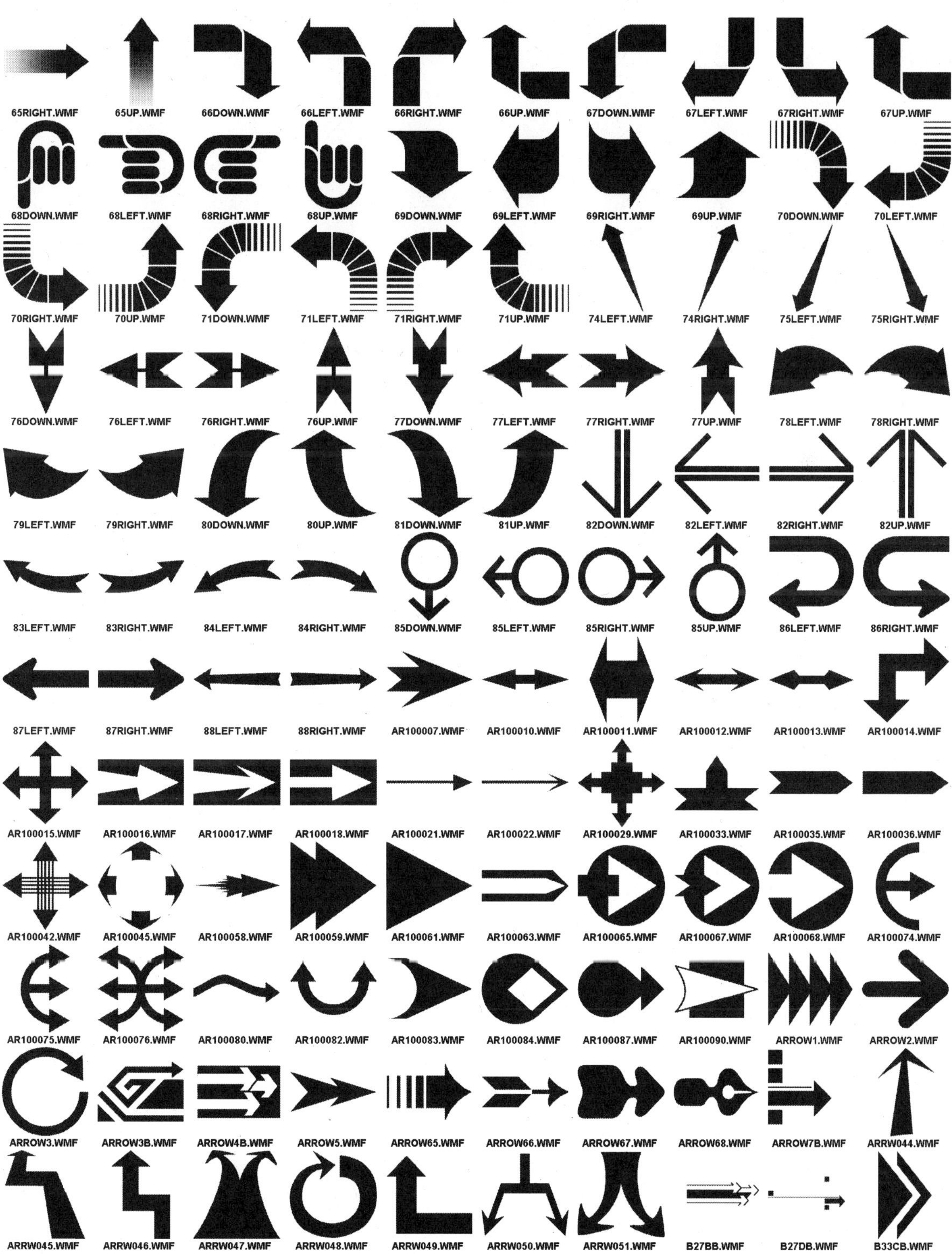
65RIGHT.WMF
65UP.WMF
66DOWN.WMF
66LEFT.WMF
66RIGHT.WMF
66UP.WMF
67DOWN.WMF
67LEFT.WMF
67RIGHT.WMF
67UP.WMF
68DOWN.WMF
68LEFT.WMF
68RIGHT.WMF
68UP.WMF
69DOWN.WMF
69LEFT.WMF
69RIGHT.WMF
69UP.WMF
70DOWN.WMF
70LEFT.WMF
70RIGHT.WMF
70UP.WMF
71DOWN.WMF
71LEFT.WMF
71RIGHT.WMF
71UP.WMF
74LEFT.WMF
74RIGHT.WMF
75LEFT.WMF
75RIGHT.WMF
76DOWN.WMF
76LEFT.WMF
76RIGHT.WMF
76UP.WMF
77DOWN.WMF
77LEFT.WMF
77RIGHT.WMF
77UP.WMF
78LEFT.WMF
78RIGHT.WMF
79LEFT.WMF
79RIGHT.WMF
80DOWN.WMF
80UP.WMF
81DOWN.WMF
81UP.WMF
82DOWN.WMF
82LEFT.WMF
82RIGHT.WMF
82UP.WMF
83LEFT.WMF
83RIGHT.WMF
84LEFT.WMF
84RIGHT.WMF
85DOWN.WMF
85LEFT.WMF
85RIGHT.WMF
85UP.WMF
86LEFT.WMF
86RIGHT.WMF
87LEFT.WMF
87RIGHT.WMF
88LEFT.WMF
88RIGHT.WMF
AR100007.WMF
AR100010.WMF
AR100011.WMF
AR100012.WMF
AR100013.WMF
AR100014.WMF
AR100015.WMF
AR100016.WMF
AR100017.WMF
AR100018.WMF
AR100021.WMF
AR100022.WMF
AR100029.WMF
AR100033.WMF
AR100035.WMF
AR100036.WMF
AR100042.WMF
AR100045.WMF
AR100058.WMF
AR100059.WMF
AR100061.WMF
AR100063.WMF
AR100065.WMF
AR100067.WMF
AR100068.WMF
AR100074.WMF
AR100075.WMF
AR100076.WMF
AR100080.WMF
AR100082.WMF
AR100083.WMF
AR100084.WMF
AR100087.WMF
AR100090.WMF
ARROW1.WMF
ARROW2.WMF
ARROW3.WMF
ARROW3B.WMF
ARROW4B.WMF
ARROW5.WMF
ARROW65.WMF
ARROW66.WMF
ARROW67.WMF
ARROW68.WMF
ARROW7B.WMF
ARRW044.WMF
ARRW045.WMF
ARRW046.WMF
ARRW047.WMF
ARRW048.WMF
ARRW049.WMF
ARRW050.WMF
ARRW051.WMF
B27BB.WMF
B27DB.WMF
B33CB.WMF

B5AB.WMF C9FB.WMF GRPHC023.WMF

Arrows • Outline

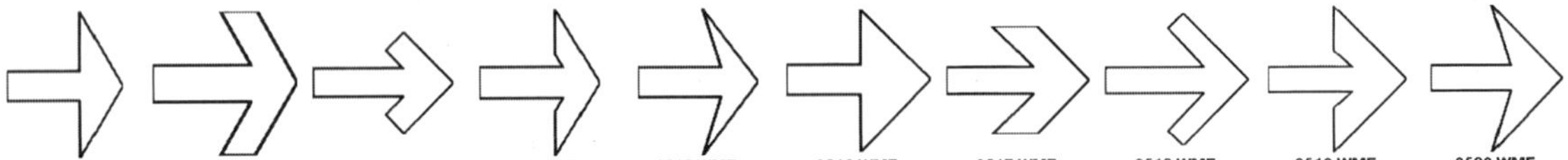

0511.WMF 0512.WMF 0513.WMF 0514.WMF 0515.WMF 0516.WMF 0517.WMF 0518.WMF 0519.WMF 0520.WMF

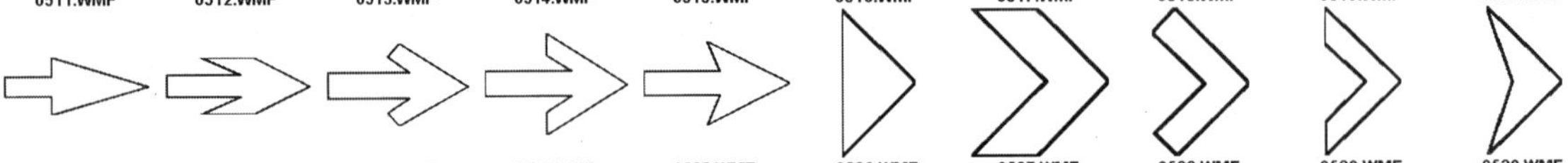

0521.WMF 0522.WMF 0523.WMF 0524.WMF 0525.WMF 0526.WMF 0527.WMF 0528.WMF 0529.WMF 0530.WMF

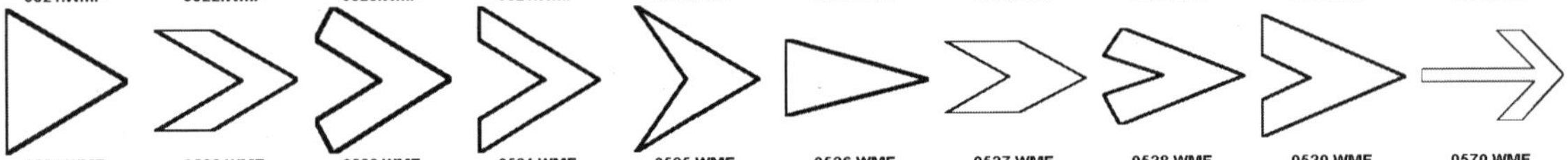

0531.WMF 0532.WMF 0533.WMF 0534.WMF 0535.WMF 0536.WMF 0537.WMF 0538.WMF 0539.WMF 0570.WMF

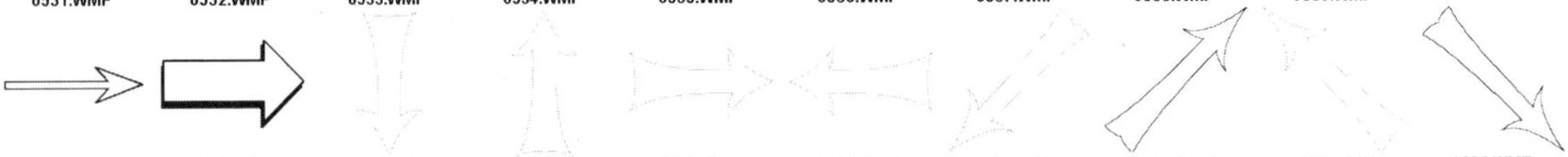

0572.WMF 0583.WMF 0593.WMF 0594.WMF 0595.WMF 0596.WMF 0619.WMF 0621.WMF 0623.WMF 0625.WMF

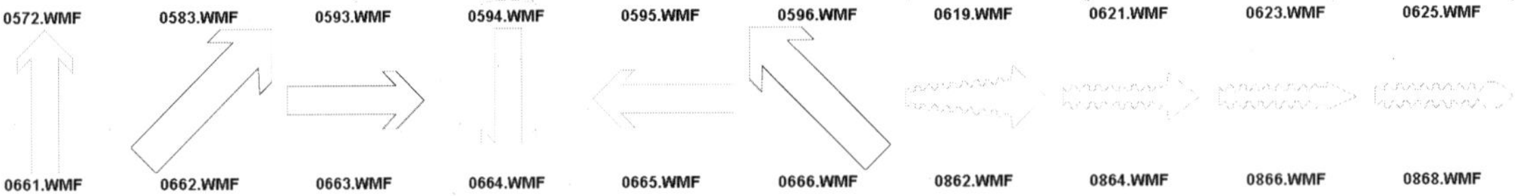

0661.WMF 0662.WMF 0663.WMF 0664.WMF 0665.WMF 0666.WMF 0862.WMF 0864.WMF 0866.WMF 0868.WMF

0870.WMF 0872.WMF 0874.WMF 0876.WMF 0878.WMF 0880.WMF 0882.WMF 0884.WMF 0886.WMF 0888.WMF

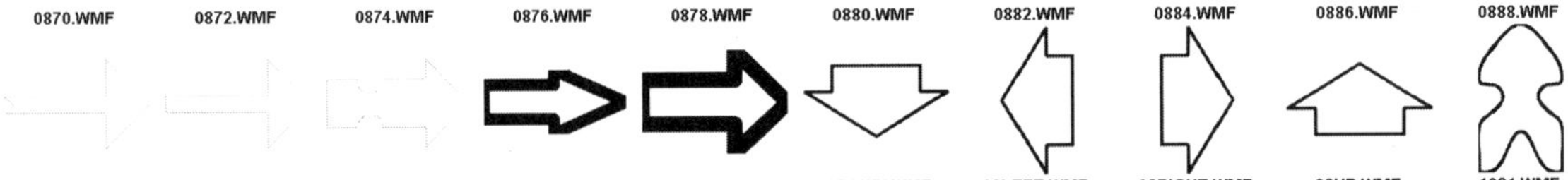

0890.WMF 0892.WMF 0894.WMF 0896.WMF 0898.WMF 08DOWN.WMF 08LEFT.WMF 08RIGHT.WMF 08UP.WMF 1921.WMF

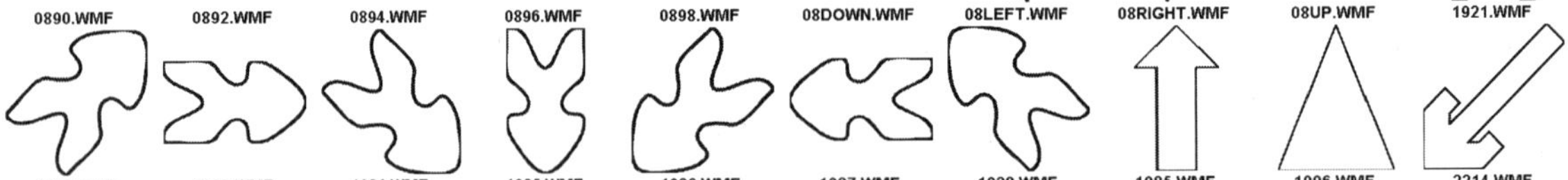

1922.WMF 1923.WMF 1924.WMF 1925.WMF 1926.WMF 1927.WMF 1928.WMF 1985.WMF 1996.WMF 2214.WMF

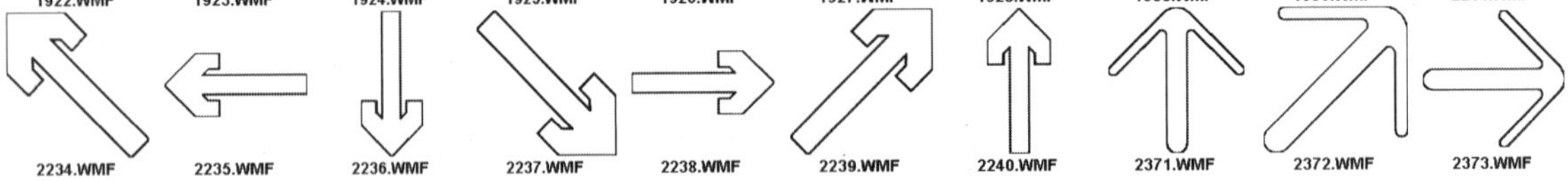

2234.WMF 2235.WMF 2236.WMF 2237.WMF 2238.WMF 2239.WMF 2240.WMF 2371.WMF 2372.WMF 2373.WMF

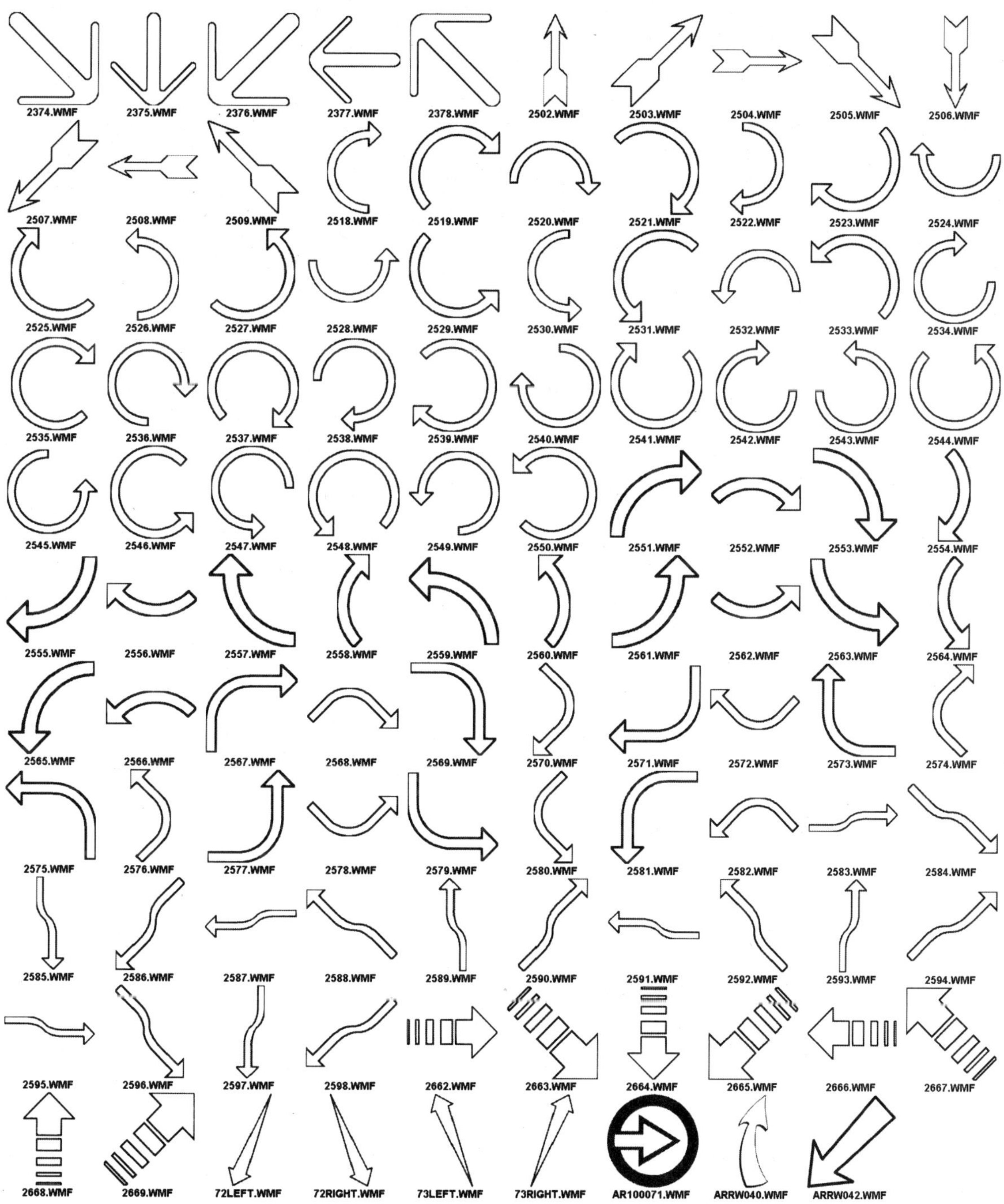
2374.WMF 2375.WMF 2376.WMF 2377.WMF 2378.WMF 2502.WMF 2503.WMF 2504.WMF 2505.WMF 2506.WMF
2507.WMF 2508.WMF 2509.WMF 2518.WMF 2519.WMF 2520.WMF 2521.WMF 2522.WMF 2523.WMF 2524.WMF
2525.WMF 2526.WMF 2527.WMF 2528.WMF 2529.WMF 2530.WMF 2531.WMF 2532.WMF 2533.WMF 2534.WMF
2535.WMF 2536.WMF 2537.WMF 2538.WMF 2539.WMF 2540.WMF 2541.WMF 2542.WMF 2543.WMF 2544.WMF
2545.WMF 2546.WMF 2547.WMF 2548.WMF 2549.WMF 2550.WMF 2551.WMF 2552.WMF 2553.WMF 2554.WMF
2555.WMF 2556.WMF 2557.WMF 2558.WMF 2559.WMF 2560.WMF 2561.WMF 2562.WMF 2563.WMF 2564.WMF
2565.WMF 2566.WMF 2567.WMF 2568.WMF 2569.WMF 2570.WMF 2571.WMF 2572.WMF 2573.WMF 2574.WMF
2575.WMF 2576.WMF 2577.WMF 2578.WMF 2579.WMF 2580.WMF 2581.WMF 2582.WMF 2583.WMF 2584.WMF
2585.WMF 2586.WMF 2587.WMF 2588.WMF 2589.WMF 2590.WMF 2591.WMF 2592.WMF 2593.WMF 2594.WMF
2595.WMF 2596.WMF 2597.WMF 2598.WMF 2662.WMF 2663.WMF 2664.WMF 2665.WMF 2666.WMF 2667.WMF
2668.WMF 2669.WMF 72LEFT.WMF 72RIGHT.WMF 73LEFT.WMF 73RIGHT.WMF AR100071.WMF ARRW040.WMF ARRW042.WMF

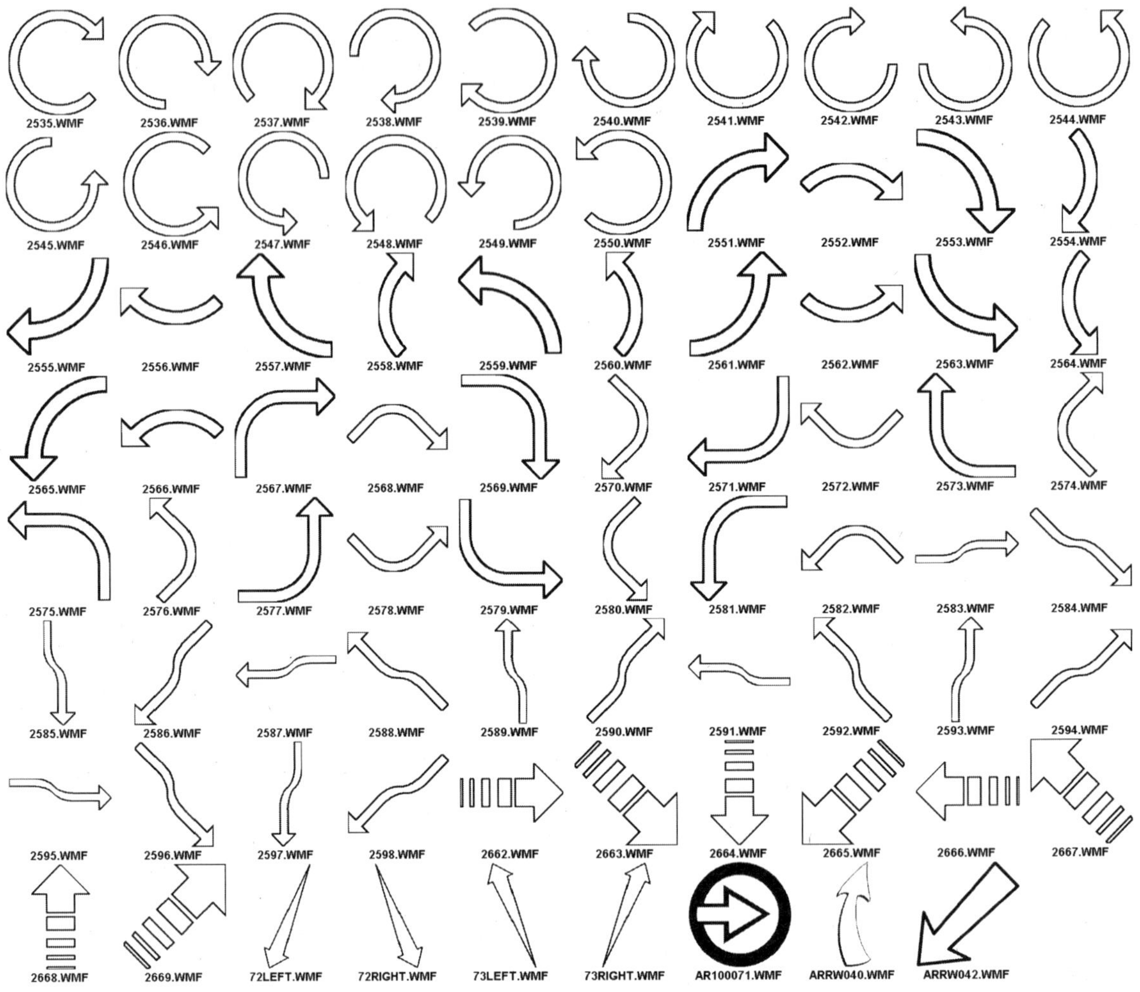
2535.WMF
2536.WMF
2537.WMF
2538.WMF
2539.WMF
2540.WMF
2541.WMF
2542.WMF
2543.WMF
2544.WMF
2545.WMF
2546.WMF
2547.WMF
2548.WMF
2549.WMF
2550.WMF
2551.WMF
2552.WMF
2553.WMF
2554.WMF
2555.WMF
2556.WMF
2557.WMF
2558.WMF
2559.WMF
2560.WMF
2561.WMF
2562.WMF
2563.WMF
2564.WMF
2565.WMF
2566.WMF
2567.WMF
2568.WMF
2569.WMF
2570.WMF
2571.WMF
2572.WMF
2573.WMF
2574.WMF
2575.WMF
2576.WMF
2577.WMF
2578.WMF
2579.WMF
2580.WMF
2581.WMF
2582.WMF
2583.WMF
2584.WMF
2585.WMF
2586.WMF
2587.WMF
2588.WMF
2589.WMF
2590.WMF
2591.WMF
2592.WMF
2593.WMF
2594.WMF
2595.WMF
2596.WMF
2597.WMF
2598.WMF
2662.WMF
2663.WMF
2664.WMF
2665.WMF
2666.WMF
2667.WMF
2668.WMF
2669.WMF
72LEFT.WMF
72RIGHT.WMF
73LEFT.WMF
73RIGHT.WMF
AR100071.WMF
ARRW040.WMF
ARRW042.WMF

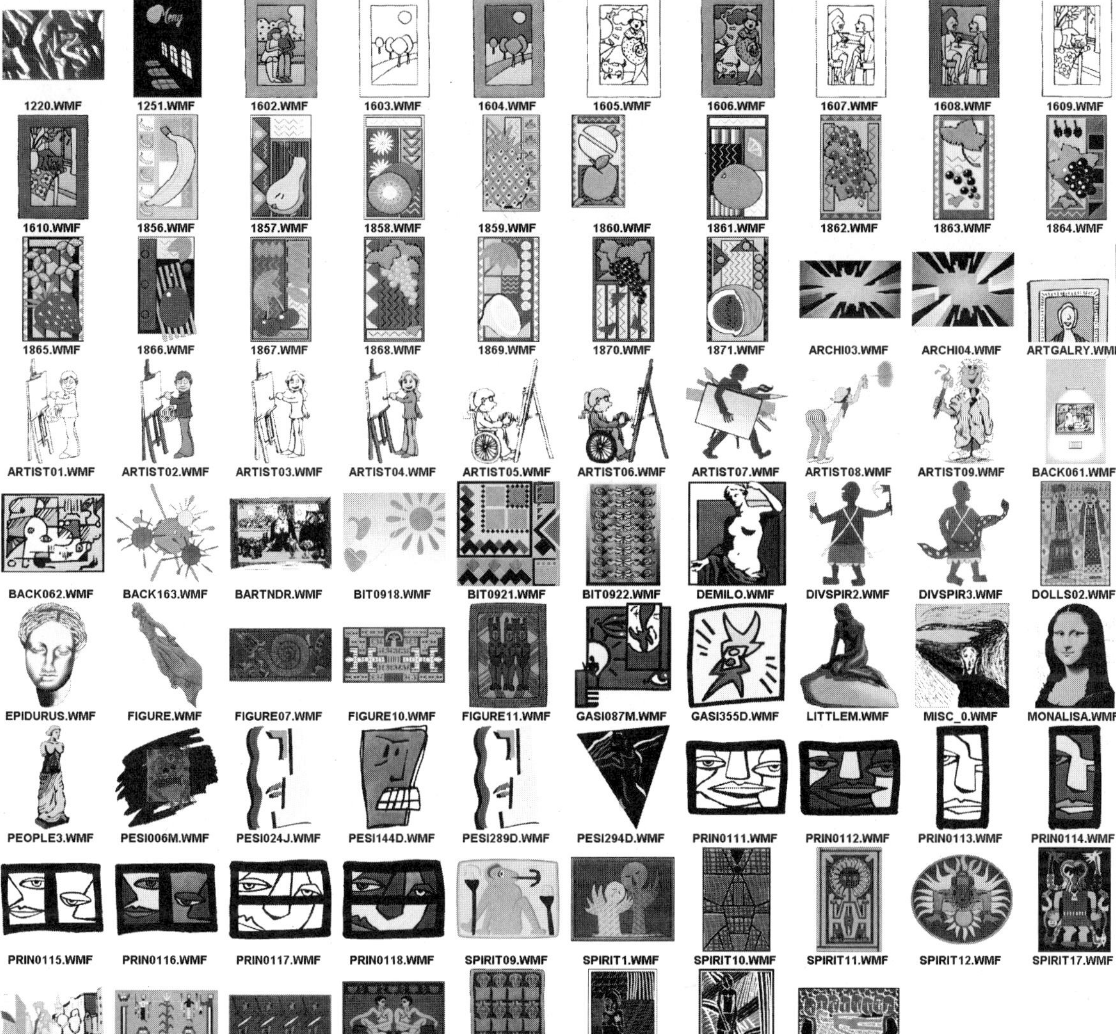

1220.WMF 1251.WMF 1602.WMF 1603.WMF 1604.WMF 1605.WMF 1606.WMF 1607.WMF 1608.WMF 1609.WMF
1610.WMF 1856.WMF 1857.WMF 1858.WMF 1859.WMF 1860.WMF 1861.WMF 1862.WMF 1863.WMF 1864.WMF
1865.WMF 1866.WMF 1867.WMF 1868.WMF 1869.WMF 1870.WMF 1871.WMF ARCHI03.WMF ARCHI04.WMF ARTGALRY.WMF
ARTIST01.WMF ARTIST02.WMF ARTIST03.WMF ARTIST04.WMF ARTIST05.WMF ARTIST06.WMF ARTIST07.WMF ARTIST08.WMF ARTIST09.WMF BACK061.WMF
BACK062.WMF BACK163.WMF BARTNDR.WMF BIT0918.WMF BIT0921.WMF BIT0922.WMF DEMILO.WMF DIVSPIR2.WMF DIVSPIR3.WMF DOLLS02.WMF
EPIDURUS.WMF FIGURE.WMF FIGURE07.WMF FIGURE10.WMF FIGURE11.WMF GASI087M.WMF GASI355D.WMF LITTLEM.WMF MISC_0.WMF MONALISA.WMF
PEOPLE3.WMF PESI006M.WMF PESI024J.WMF PESI144D.WMF PESI289D.WMF PESI294D.WMF PRIN0111.WMF PRIN0112.WMF PRIN0113.WMF PRIN0114.WMF
PRIN0115.WMF PRIN0116.WMF PRIN0117.WMF PRIN0118.WMF SPIRIT09.WMF SPIRIT1.WMF SPIRIT10.WMF SPIRIT11.WMF SPIRIT12.WMF SPIRIT17.WMF
STREET4.WMF TAPSTR08.WMF WARIOR02.WMF WOMAN02.WMF WOODCUT4.WMF WOODCUT5.WMF WOODCUT6.WMF WOODCUT7.WMF

Art & Design (Artstuff) • Photography

1635.WMF
1636.WMF
1637.WMF
1638.WMF
1639.WMF
1640.WMF
1641.WMF
1642.WMF
1643.WMF
1644.WMF
1645.WMF
1646.WMF
BABOONS.WMF
BIRD01.WMF
BUCK01.WMF
BUCK02.WMF
BUCK03.WMF
BUCK04.WMF
CAVEART.WMF
DANCING.WMF
ELAND01.WMF
ELAND02.WMF
ENSI049D.WMF
GAGC013D.WMF
GASI284D.WMF
GASI286D.WMF
GATHERER.WMF
GRBO014J.WMF
HHSI112D.WMF
HIPPO.WMF
HORSEMAN.WMF
HORSMN02.WMF
HUNTER01.WMF
HUNTER02.WMF
HUNTER03.WMF
HUNTER04.WMF
HUNTER05.WMF
HUNTER06.WMF
HUNTER07.WMF
HUNTER08.WMF
LION.WMF
NABO107J.WMF
NABO109J.WMF
NABO110J.WMF
NABO111J.WMF
NABO113J.WMF
NABO114J.WMF
NABO115J.WMF
NABO116J.WMF
NABO117J.WMF
NABO118J.WMF
NABO119J.WMF
NABO120J.WMF
NABO121J.WMF
NABO122J.WMF
NASI006M.WMF
NASI014M.WMF
NASI016J.WMF
NASI161D.WMF
NASI162D.WMF
NASI163D.WMF
NASI200D.WMF
NASI201D.WMF
NASI202D.WMF
NASI204D.WMF
NASI205D.WMF
NASI206D.WMF
NASI208D.WMF
NASI209D.WMF
NASI210D.WMF
NASI211D.WMF
NASI212D.WMF
NASI213D.WMF
NASI214D.WMF
NASI215D.WMF
NASI216D.WMF
NASI218D.WMF
NASI219D.WMF
NASI221D.WMF
NASI222D.WMF
NASI226D.WMF
NASI228D.WMF
NASI232D.WMF
NASI233D.WMF
NASI234D.WMF
NASI235D.WMF
NASI236D.WMF
NASI237D.WMF
NASI239D.WMF
NASI240D.WMF
NASI241D.WMF
NASI242D.WMF
NASI243D.WMF
NASI244D.WMF
NASI245D.WMF
NASI249D.WMF
NASI251D.WMF
NASI252D.WMF
NASI253D.WMF
NASI254D.WMF
NASS011J.WMF
NASS012J.WMF
NASS020J.WMF
NASS022J.WMF
NASS023J.WMF
PEBO048J.WMF
PEBO049J.WMF
PEBO057J.WMF
PEBO063J.WMF
PEBO064J.WMF
PEBO067J.WMF
PECA038J.WMF
PEJB017J.WMF
PERW049J.WMF
PESI003J.WMF
PESI137D.WMF
PESI140D.WMF
PESI141D.WMF
PESI345D.WMF
PESI346D.WMF

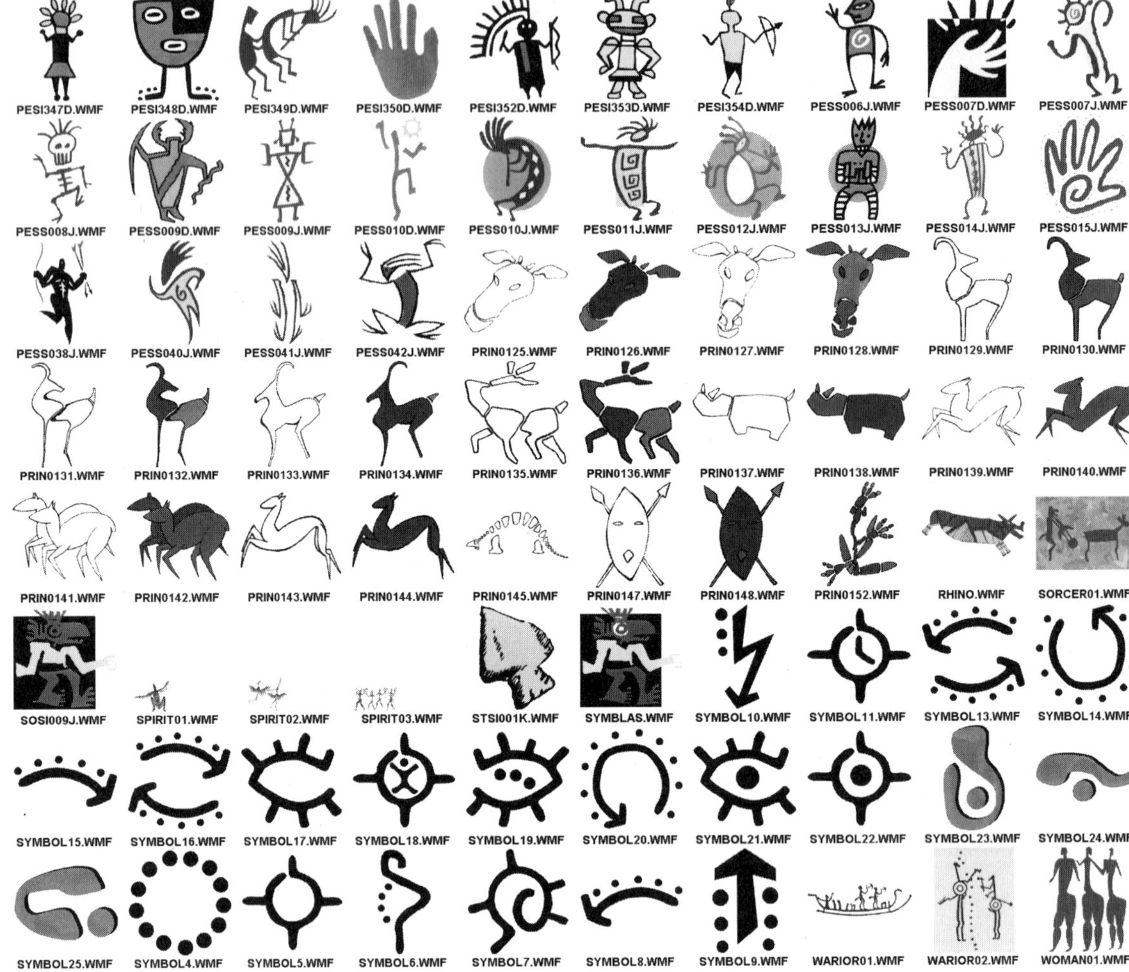
PESI347D.WMF PESI348D.WMF PESI349D.WMF PESI350D.WMF PESI352D.WMF PESI353D.WMF PESI354D.WMF PESS006J.WMF PESS007D.WMF PESS007J.WMF
PESS008J.WMF PESS009D.WMF PESS009J.WMF PESS010D.WMF PESS010J.WMF PESS011J.WMF PESS012J.WMF PESS013J.WMF PESS014J.WMF PESS015J.WMF
PESS038J.WMF PESS040J.WMF PESS041J.WMF PESS042J.WMF PRIN0125.WMF PRIN0126.WMF PRIN0127.WMF PRIN0128.WMF PRIN0129.WMF PRIN0130.WMF
PRIN0131.WMF PRIN0132.WMF PRIN0133.WMF PRIN0134.WMF PRIN0135.WMF PRIN0136.WMF PRIN0137.WMF PRIN0138.WMF PRIN0139.WMF PRIN0140.WMF
PRIN0141.WMF PRIN0142.WMF PRIN0143.WMF PRIN0144.WMF PRIN0145.WMF PRIN0147.WMF PRIN0148.WMF PRIN0152.WMF RHINO.WMF SORCER01.WMF
SOSI009J.WMF SPIRIT01.WMF SPIRIT02.WMF SPIRIT03.WMF STSI001K.WMF SYMBLAS.WMF SYMBOL10.WMF SYMBOL11.WMF SYMBOL13.WMF SYMBOL14.WMF
SYMBOL15.WMF SYMBOL16.WMF SYMBOL17.WMF SYMBOL18.WMF SYMBOL19.WMF SYMBOL20.WMF SYMBOL21.WMF SYMBOL22.WMF SYMBOL23.WMF SYMBOL24.WMF
SYMBOL25.WMF SYMBOL4.WMF SYMBOL5.WMF SYMBOL6.WMF SYMBOL7.WMF SYMBOL8.WMF SYMBOL9.WMF WARIOR01.WMF WARIOR02.WMF WOMAN01.WMF

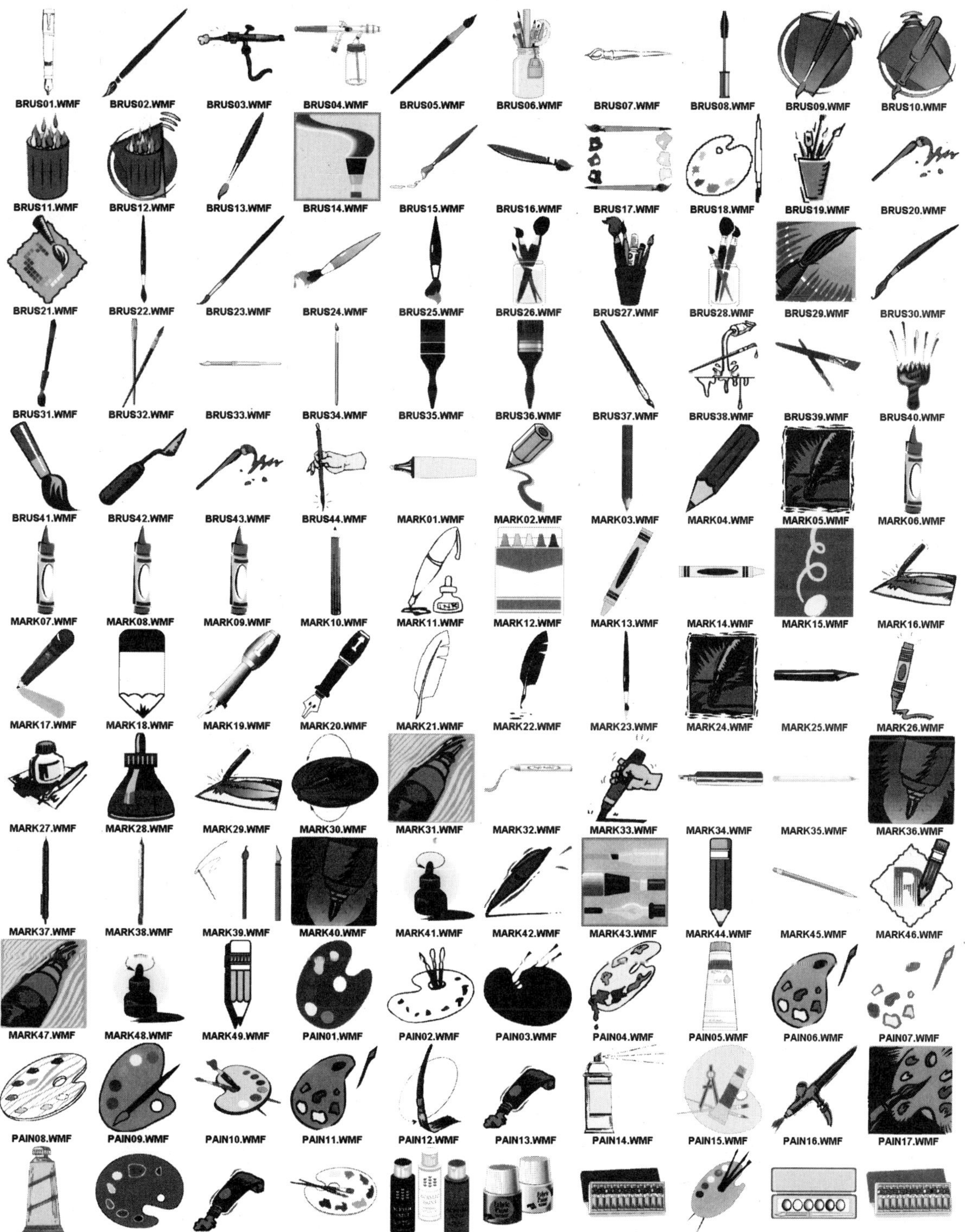
BRUS01.WMF BRUS02.WMF BRUS03.WMF BRUS04.WMF BRUS05.WMF BRUS06.WMF BRUS07.WMF BRUS08.WMF BRUS09.WMF BRUS10.WMF
BRUS11.WMF BRUS12.WMF BRUS13.WMF BRUS14.WMF BRUS15.WMF BRUS16.WMF BRUS17.WMF BRUS18.WMF BRUS19.WMF BRUS20.WMF
BRUS21.WMF BRUS22.WMF BRUS23.WMF BRUS24.WMF BRUS25.WMF BRUS26.WMF BRUS27.WMF BRUS28.WMF BRUS29.WMF BRUS30.WMF
BRUS31.WMF BRUS32.WMF BRUS33.WMF BRUS34.WMF BRUS35.WMF BRUS36.WMF BRUS37.WMF BRUS38.WMF BRUS39.WMF BRUS40.WMF
BRUS41.WMF BRUS42.WMF BRUS43.WMF BRUS44.WMF MARK01.WMF MARK02.WMF MARK03.WMF MARK04.WMF MARK05.WMF MARK06.WMF
MARK07.WMF MARK08.WMF MARK09.WMF MARK10.WMF MARK11.WMF MARK12.WMF MARK13.WMF MARK14.WMF MARK15.WMF MARK16.WMF
MARK17.WMF MARK18.WMF MARK19.WMF MARK20.WMF MARK21.WMF MARK22.WMF MARK23.WMF MARK24.WMF MARK25.WMF MARK26.WMF
MARK27.WMF MARK28.WMF MARK29.WMF MARK30.WMF MARK31.WMF MARK32.WMF MARK33.WMF MARK34.WMF MARK35.WMF MARK36.WMF
MARK37.WMF MARK38.WMF MARK39.WMF MARK40.WMF MARK41.WMF MARK42.WMF MARK43.WMF MARK44.WMF MARK45.WMF MARK46.WMF
MARK47.WMF MARK48.WMF MARK49.WMF PAIN01.WMF PAIN02.WMF PAIN03.WMF PAIN04.WMF PAIN05.WMF PAIN06.WMF PAIN07.WMF
PAIN08.WMF PAIN09.WMF PAIN10.WMF PAIN11.WMF PAIN12.WMF PAIN13.WMF PAIN14.WMF PAIN15.WMF PAIN16.WMF PAIN17.WMF
PAIN18.WMF PAIN19.WMF PAIN20.WMF PAIN21.WMF PAIN22.WMF PAIN23.WMF PAIN24.WMF PAIN25.WMF PAIN26.WMF PAIN27.WMF

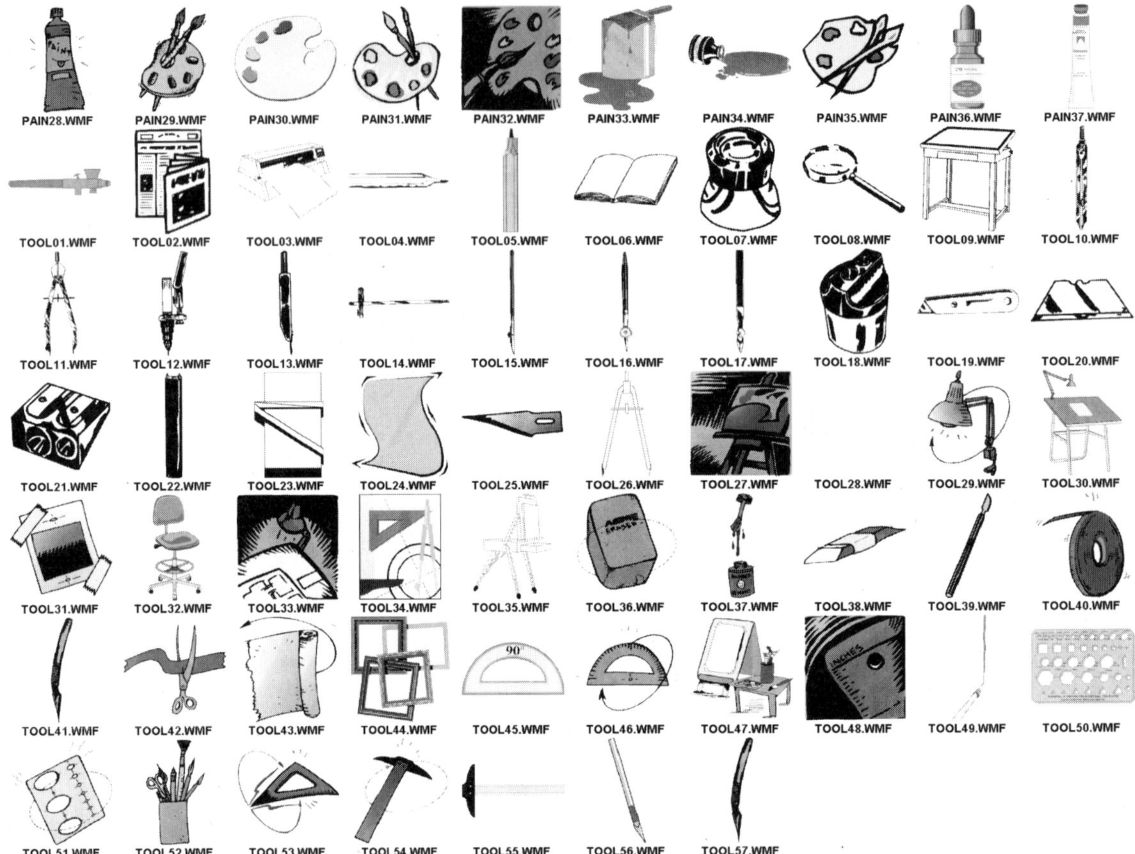
PAIN28.WMF PAIN29.WMF PAIN30.WMF PAIN31.WMF PAIN32.WMF PAIN33.WMF PAIN34.WMF PAIN35.WMF PAIN36.WMF PAIN37.WMF
TOOL01.WMF TOOL02.WMF TOOL03.WMF TOOL04.WMF TOOL05.WMF TOOL06.WMF TOOL07.WMF TOOL08.WMF TOOL09.WMF TOOL10.WMF
TOOL11.WMF TOOL12.WMF TOOL13.WMF TOOL14.WMF TOOL15.WMF TOOL16.WMF TOOL17.WMF TOOL18.WMF TOOL19.WMF TOOL20.WMF
TOOL21.WMF TOOL22.WMF TOOL23.WMF TOOL24.WMF TOOL25.WMF TOOL26.WMF TOOL27.WMF TOOL28.WMF TOOL29.WMF TOOL30.WMF
TOOL31.WMF TOOL32.WMF TOOL33.WMF TOOL34.WMF TOOL35.WMF TOOL36.WMF TOOL37.WMF TOOL38.WMF TOOL39.WMF TOOL40.WMF
90°
TOOL41.WMF TOOL42.WMF TOOL43.WMF TOOL44.WMF TOOL45.WMF TOOL46.WMF TOOL47.WMF TOOL48.WMF TOOL49.WMF TOOL50.WMF
TOOL51.WMF TOOL52.WMF TOOL53.WMF TOOL54.WMF TOOL55.WMF TOOL56.WMF TOOL57.WMF

010.WMF 0517.WMF 0518.WMF 1042BLUC.WMF 1345TROC.WMF 1ST.WMF 1STPLACE.WMF 2ND.WMF 3RD.WMF 4TH.WMF

AWARD.WMF AWARDBDR.WMF AWARDRIB.WMF B20107.WMF B20108.WMF BACK125.WMF BACK159.WMF BACK160.WMF BACK162.WMF BANNER7.WMF

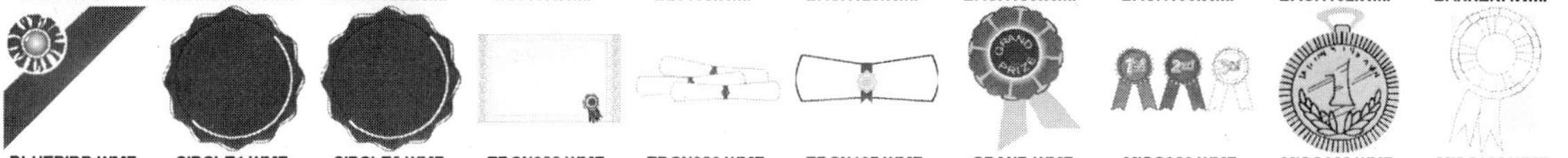

BLUERIBB.WMF CIRCLE1.WMF CIRCLE5.WMF EDCN088.WMF EDCN089.WMF EDCN197.WMF GRAND.WMF MISC059.WMF MISC063.WMF MISC065.WMF

NUMBER1.WMF O21505.WMF R21614.WMF R21615.WMF R21616.WMF RIBBON.WMF RIBBON1.WMF RIBBON11.WMF RIBBON2.WMF RIBBON3.WMF

RIBBON5.WMF SEAL2.WMF SECBADGE.WMF SHAPE242.WMF SOSI017M.WMF SPORT100.WMF SPORT101.WMF SPORT102.WMF SPORT107.WMF SPORT108.WMF

SPORT109.WMF SPORT110.WMF SPORTS9.WMF SPSI002D.WMF T21844.WMF TROPHY.WMF TROPHY05.WMF TROPHY15.WMF TROPHY5.WMF TROPYKIS.WMF

WEWON2.WMF

ABSTR001.WMF ABSTR002.WMF ABSTR003.WMF ABSTR004.WMF ABSTR005.WMF ABSTR006.WMF ABSTR007.WMF ABSTR008.WMF ABSTR009.WMF ABSTR010.WMF

ABSTR011.WMF ABSTR012.WMF ABSTR013.WMF ABSTR014.WMF ABSTR015.WMF ABSTR016.WMF ABSTR017.WMF ABSTR018.WMF ABSTR019.WMF ABSTR020.WMF

ABSTR021.WMF ABSTR022.WMF ABSTR023.WMF ABSTR024.WMF ABSTR025.WMF ABSTR026.WMF ABSTR027.WMF ABSTR028.WMF ABSTR029.WMF ABSTR030.WMF

ABSTR031.WMF ABSTR032.WMF ABSTR033.WMF ABSTR034.WMF ABSTR035.WMF ABSTR036.WMF ABSTR037.WMF ABSTR038.WMF ABSTR039.WMF ABSTR040.WMF

ABSTR041.WMF ABSTR042.WMF ABSTR043.WMF ABSTR044.WMF ABSTR045.WMF ABSTR046.WMF ABSTR047.WMF ABSTR048.WMF ABSTR049.WMF ABSTR050.WMF

ABSTR051.WMF ABSTR052.WMF ABSTR053.WMF ABSTR054.WMF ABSTR055.WMF ABSTR056.WMF ABSTR057.WMF ABSTR058.WMF ABSTR059.WMF ABSTR060.WMF

ABSTR061.WMF ABSTR062.WMF ABSTR063.WMF ABSTR064.WMF ABSTR065.WMF ABSTR066.WMF ABSTR067.WMF ABSTR068.WMF ABSTR069.WMF ABSTR070.WMF

ABSTR071.WMF ABSTR072.WMF ABSTR073.WMF ABSTR074.WMF ABSTR075.WMF ABSTR076.WMF ABSTR077.WMF ABSTR078.WMF ABSTR079.WMF ABSTR080.WMF

ABSTR081.WMF ABSTR082.WMF ABSTR083.WMF ABSTR084.WMF ABSTR085.WMF ABSTR086.WMF ABSTR087.WMF ABSTR088.WMF ABSTR089.WMF ABSTR090.WMF

ABSTR091.WMF ABSTR092.WMF ABSTR093.WMF ABSTR094.WMF ABSTR095.WMF ABSTR096.WMF ABSTR097.WMF ABSTR098.WMF ABSTR099.WMF ABSTR100.WMF

ABSTR101.WMF ABSTR102.WMF ABSTR103.WMF ABSTR104.WMF ABSTR105.WMF ABSTR106.WMF ABSTR107.WMF ABSTR108.WMF ABSTR109.WMF ABSTR110.WMF

ABSTR111.WMF ABSTR112.WMF ABSTR113.WMF ABSTR114.WMF ABSTR115.WMF ABSTR116.WMF ABSTR117.WMF ABSTR118.WMF ABSTR119.WMF ABSTR120.WMF

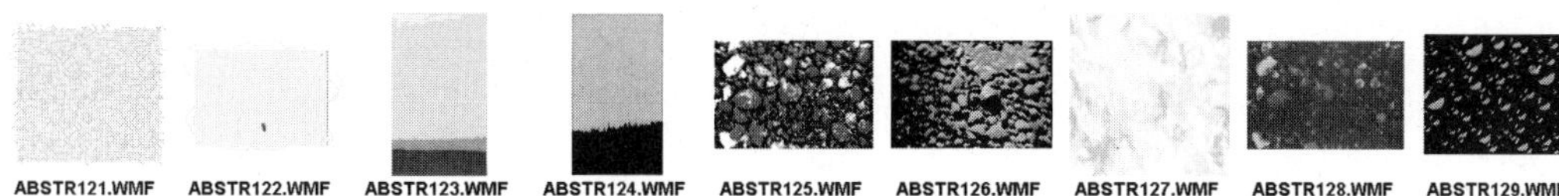

ABSTR121.WMF ABSTR122.WMF ABSTR123.WMF ABSTR124.WMF ABSTR125.WMF ABSTR126.WMF ABSTR127.WMF ABSTR128.WMF ABSTR129.WMF

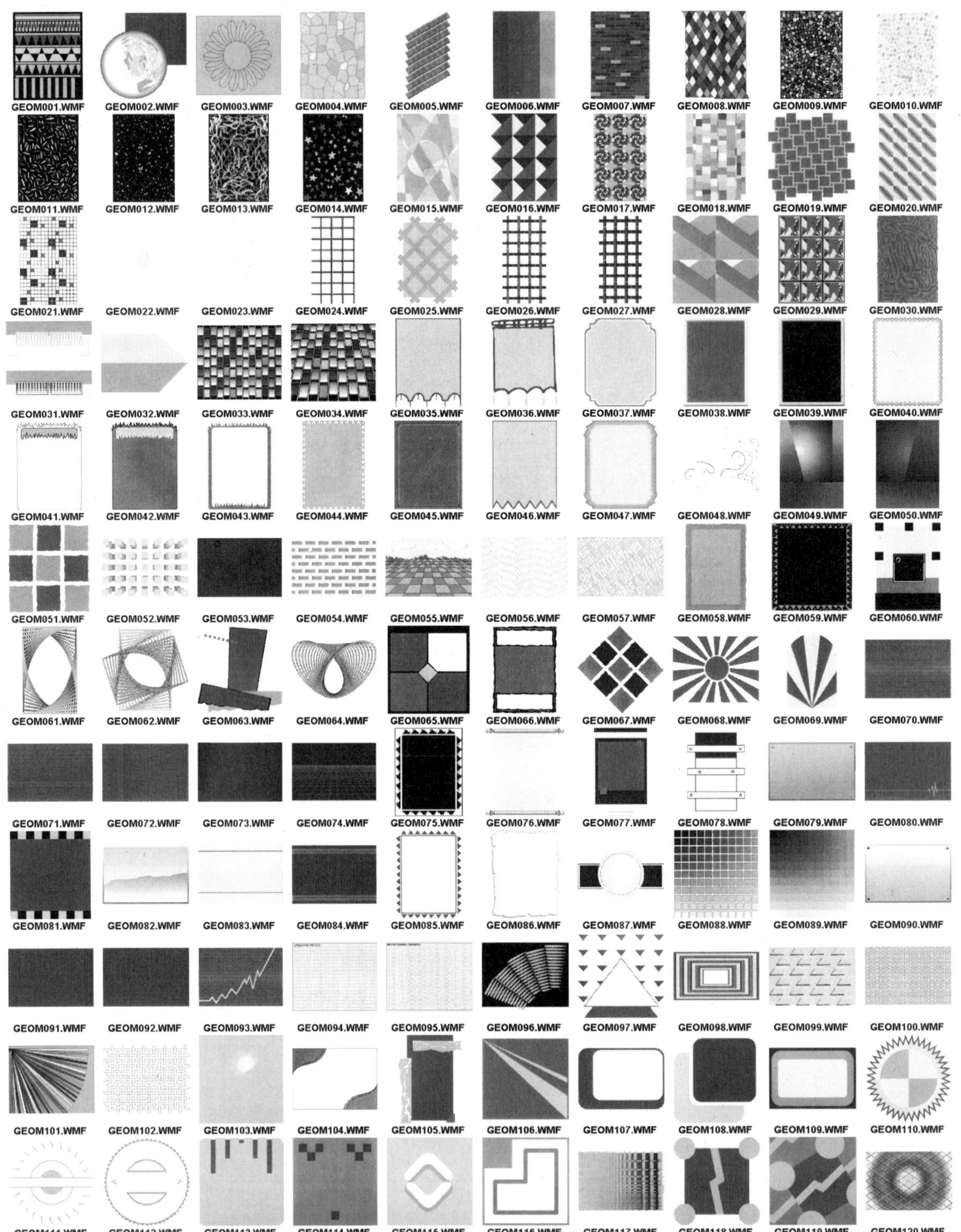
GEOM001.WMF GEOM002.WMF GEOM003.WMF GEOM004.WMF GEOM005.WMF GEOM006.WMF GEOM007.WMF GEOM008.WMF GEOM009.WMF GEOM010.WMF
GEOM011.WMF GEOM012.WMF GEOM013.WMF GEOM014.WMF GEOM015.WMF GEOM016.WMF GEOM017.WMF GEOM018.WMF GEOM019.WMF GEOM020.WMF
GEOM021.WMF GEOM022.WMF GEOM023.WMF GEOM024.WMF GEOM025.WMF GEOM026.WMF GEOM027.WMF GEOM028.WMF GEOM029.WMF GEOM030.WMF
GEOM031.WMF GEOM032.WMF GEOM033.WMF GEOM034.WMF GEOM035.WMF GEOM036.WMF GEOM037.WMF GEOM038.WMF GEOM039.WMF GEOM040.WMF
GEOM041.WMF GEOM042.WMF GEOM043.WMF GEOM044.WMF GEOM045.WMF GEOM046.WMF GEOM047.WMF GEOM048.WMF GEOM049.WMF GEOM050.WMF
GEOM051.WMF GEOM052.WMF GEOM053.WMF GEOM054.WMF GEOM055.WMF GEOM056.WMF GEOM057.WMF GEOM058.WMF GEOM059.WMF GEOM060.WMF
GEOM061.WMF GEOM062.WMF GEOM063.WMF GEOM064.WMF GEOM065.WMF GEOM066.WMF GEOM067.WMF GEOM068.WMF GEOM069.WMF GEOM070.WMF
GEOM071.WMF GEOM072.WMF GEOM073.WMF GEOM074.WMF GEOM075.WMF GEOM076.WMF GEOM077.WMF GEOM078.WMF GEOM079.WMF GEOM080.WMF
GEOM081.WMF GEOM082.WMF GEOM083.WMF GEOM084.WMF GEOM085.WMF GEOM086.WMF GEOM087.WMF GEOM088.WMF GEOM089.WMF GEOM090.WMF
GEOM091.WMF GEOM092.WMF GEOM093.WMF GEOM094.WMF GEOM095.WMF GEOM096.WMF GEOM097.WMF GEOM098.WMF GEOM099.WMF GEOM100.WMF
GEOM101.WMF GEOM102.WMF GEOM103.WMF GEOM104.WMF GEOM105.WMF GEOM106.WMF GEOM107.WMF GEOM108.WMF GEOM109.WMF GEOM110.WMF
GEOM111.WMF GEOM112.WMF GEOM113.WMF GEOM114.WMF GEOM115.WMF GEOM116.WMF GEOM117.WMF GEOM118.WMF GEOM119.WMF GEOM120.WMF

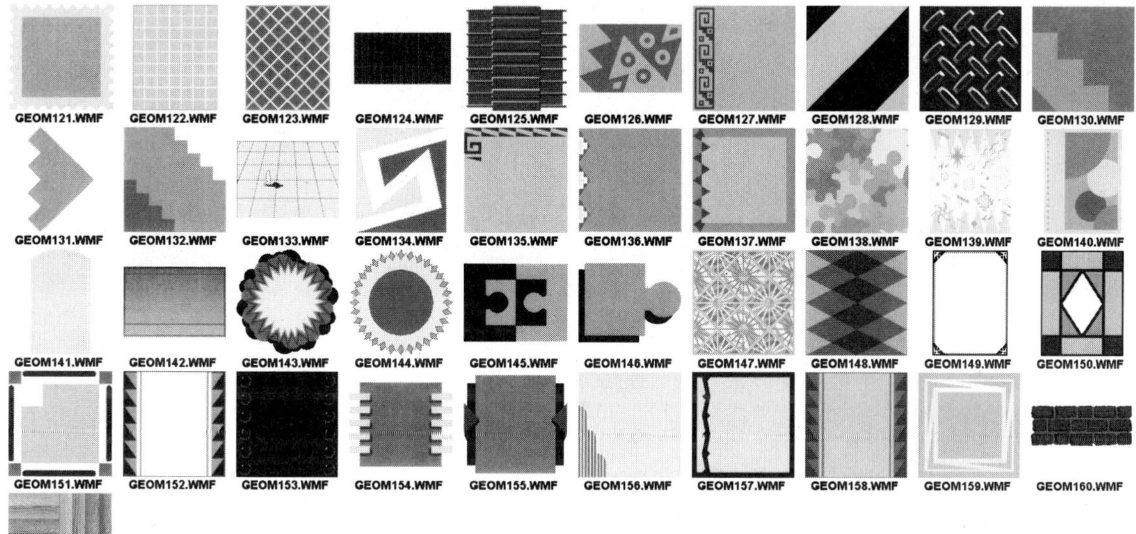
GEOM121.WMF
GEOM122.WMF
GEOM123.WMF
GEOM124.WMF
GEOM125.WMF
GEOM126.WMF
GEOM127.WMF
GEOM128.WMF
GEOM129.WMF
GEOM130.WMF
GEOM131.WMF
GEOM132.WMF
GEOM133.WMF
GEOM134.WMF
GEOM135.WMF
GEOM136.WMF
GEOM137.WMF
GEOM138.WMF
GEOM139.WMF
GEOM140.WMF
GEOM141.WMF
GEOM142.WMF
GEOM143.WMF
GEOM144.WMF
GEOM145.WMF
GEOM146.WMF
GEOM147.WMF
GEOM148.WMF
GEOM149.WMF
GEOM150.WMF
GEOM151.WMF
GEOM152.WMF
GEOM153.WMF
GEOM154.WMF
GEOM155.WMF
GEOM156.WMF
GEOM157.WMF
GEOM158.WMF
GEOM159.WMF
GEOM160.WMF
GEOM161.WMF

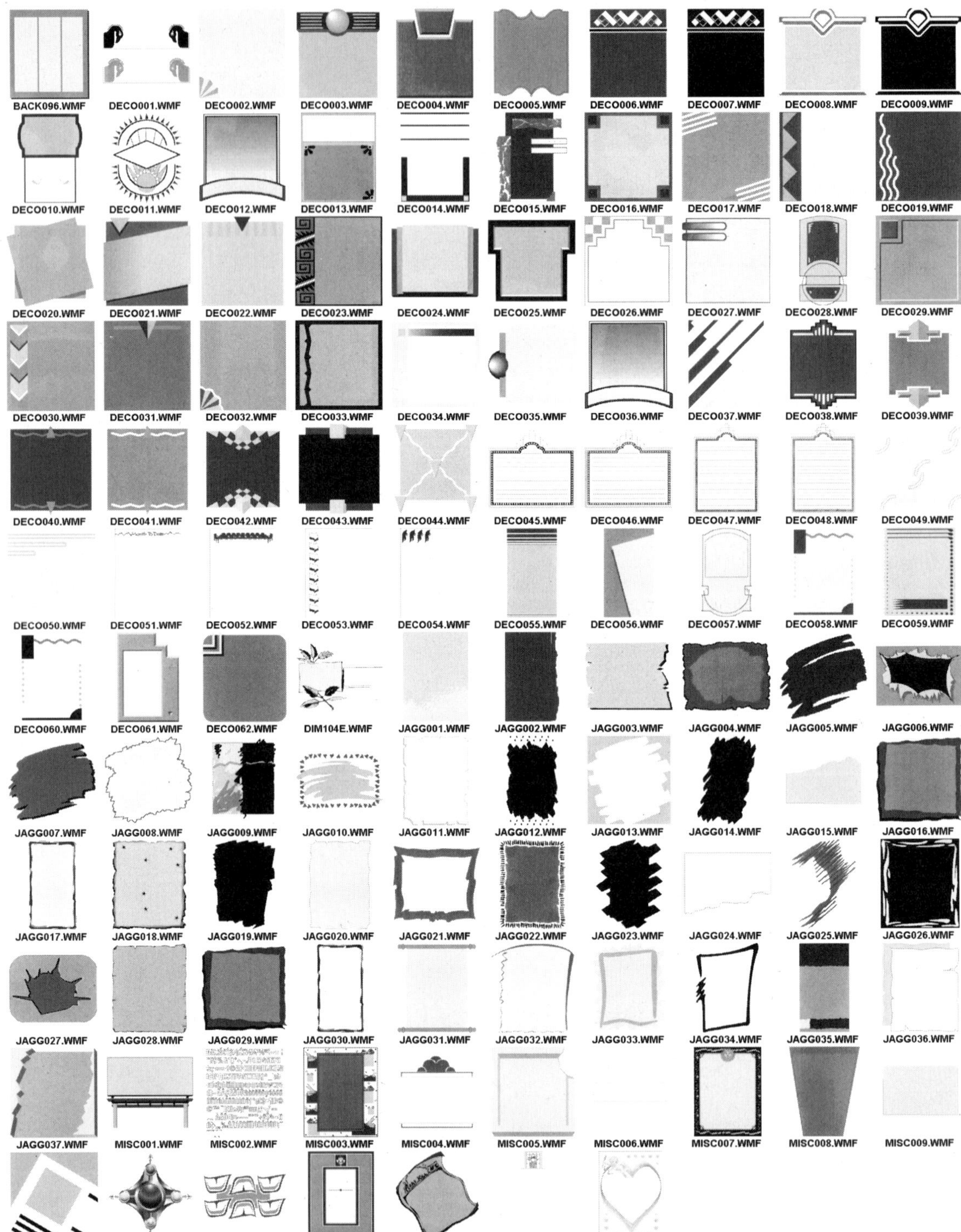

BACK096.WMF
DECO001.WMF
DECO002.WMF
DECO003.WMF
DECO004.WMF
DECO005.WMF
DECO006.WMF
DECO007.WMF
DECO008.WMF
DECO009.WMF
DECO010.WMF
DECO011.WMF
DECO012.WMF
DECO013.WMF
DECO014.WMF
DECO015.WMF
DECO016.WMF
DECO017.WMF
DECO018.WMF
DECO019.WMF
DECO020.WMF
DECO021.WMF
DECO022.WMF
DECO023.WMF
DECO024.WMF
DECO025.WMF
DECO026.WMF
DECO027.WMF
DECO028.WMF
DECO029.WMF
DECO030.WMF
DECO031.WMF
DECO032.WMF
DECO033.WMF
DECO034.WMF
DECO035.WMF
DECO036.WMF
DECO037.WMF
DECO038.WMF
DECO039.WMF
DECO040.WMF
DECO041.WMF
DECO042.WMF
DECO043.WMF
DECO044.WMF
DECO045.WMF
DECO046.WMF
DECO047.WMF
DECO048.WMF
DECO049.WMF
DECO050.WMF
DECO051.WMF
DECO052.WMF
DECO053.WMF
DECO054.WMF
DECO055.WMF
DECO056.WMF
DECO057.WMF
DECO058.WMF
DECO059.WMF
DECO060.WMF
DECO061.WMF
DECO062.WMF
DIM104E.WMF
JAGG001.WMF
JAGG002.WMF
JAGG003.WMF
JAGG004.WMF
JAGG005.WMF
JAGG006.WMF
JAGG007.WMF
JAGG008.WMF
JAGG009.WMF
JAGG010.WMF
JAGG011.WMF
JAGG012.WMF
JAGG013.WMF
JAGG014.WMF
JAGG015.WMF
JAGG016.WMF
JAGG017.WMF
JAGG018.WMF
JAGG019.WMF
JAGG020.WMF
JAGG021.WMF
JAGG022.WMF
JAGG023.WMF
JAGG024.WMF
JAGG025.WMF
JAGG026.WMF
JAGG027.WMF
JAGG028.WMF
JAGG029.WMF
JAGG030.WMF
JAGG031.WMF
JAGG032.WMF
JAGG033.WMF
JAGG034.WMF
JAGG035.WMF
JAGG036.WMF
JAGG037.WMF
MISC001.WMF
MISC002.WMF
MISC003.WMF
MISC004.WMF
MISC005.WMF
MISC006.WMF
MISC007.WMF
MISC008.WMF
MISC009.WMF
MISC010.WMF
MISC011.WMF
MISC012.WMF
MISC013.WMF
MISC014.WMF
MISC015.WMF
MISC016.WMF

0015.WMF
0510.WMF
1221.WMF
1222.WMF
1223.WMF
1224.WMF
1226.WMF
1229.WMF
1236.WMF
1240.WMF
1247.WMF
1289.WMF
1294.WMF
1298.WMF
1299.WMF
1341.WMF
1343.WMF
1345.WMF
1346.WMF
1347.WMF
1348.WMF
1349.WMF
1351.WMF
1352.WMF
1354.WMF
1356.WMF
1357.WMF
1358.WMF
1359.WMF
1360.WMF
1361.WMF
1363.WMF
1364.WMF
1365.WMF
1367.WMF
1368.WMF
1369.WMF
1371.WMF
1372.WMF
1373.WMF
1375.WMF
1376.WMF
1377.WMF
1378.WMF
1379.WMF
1380.WMF
1381.WMF
1382.WMF
1383.WMF
1384.WMF
1385.WMF
1386.WMF
1387.WMF
1388.WMF
1389.WMF
1390.WMF
1391.WMF
1392.WMF
1393.WMF
1394.WMF
1395.WMF
1396.WMF
1397.WMF
1398.WMF
1399.WMF
1401.WMF
1404.WMF
1407.WMF
1408.WMF
1409.WMF
1410.WMF
1412.WMF
1413.WMF
1414.WMF
1418.WMF
1419.WMF
1424.WMF
1425.WMF
1426.WMF
1427.WMF
1428.WMF
1429.WMF
1430.WMF
1431.WMF
1432.WMF
1433.WMF
1434.WMF
1435.WMF
1436.WMF
1437.WMF
1438.WMF
1439.WMF
1440.WMF
1441.WMF
1442.WMF
1443.WMF
1444.WMF
1445.WMF
1446.WMF
1447.WMF
1448.WMF
1449.WMF
1450.WMF
1451.WMF
1452.WMF
1453.WMF
1454.WMF
1456.WMF
1457.WMF
1458.WMF
1459.WMF
1460.WMF
1461.WMF
1463.WMF
1464.WMF
1465.WMF
1467.WMF
1468.WMF
1469.WMF
1471.WMF

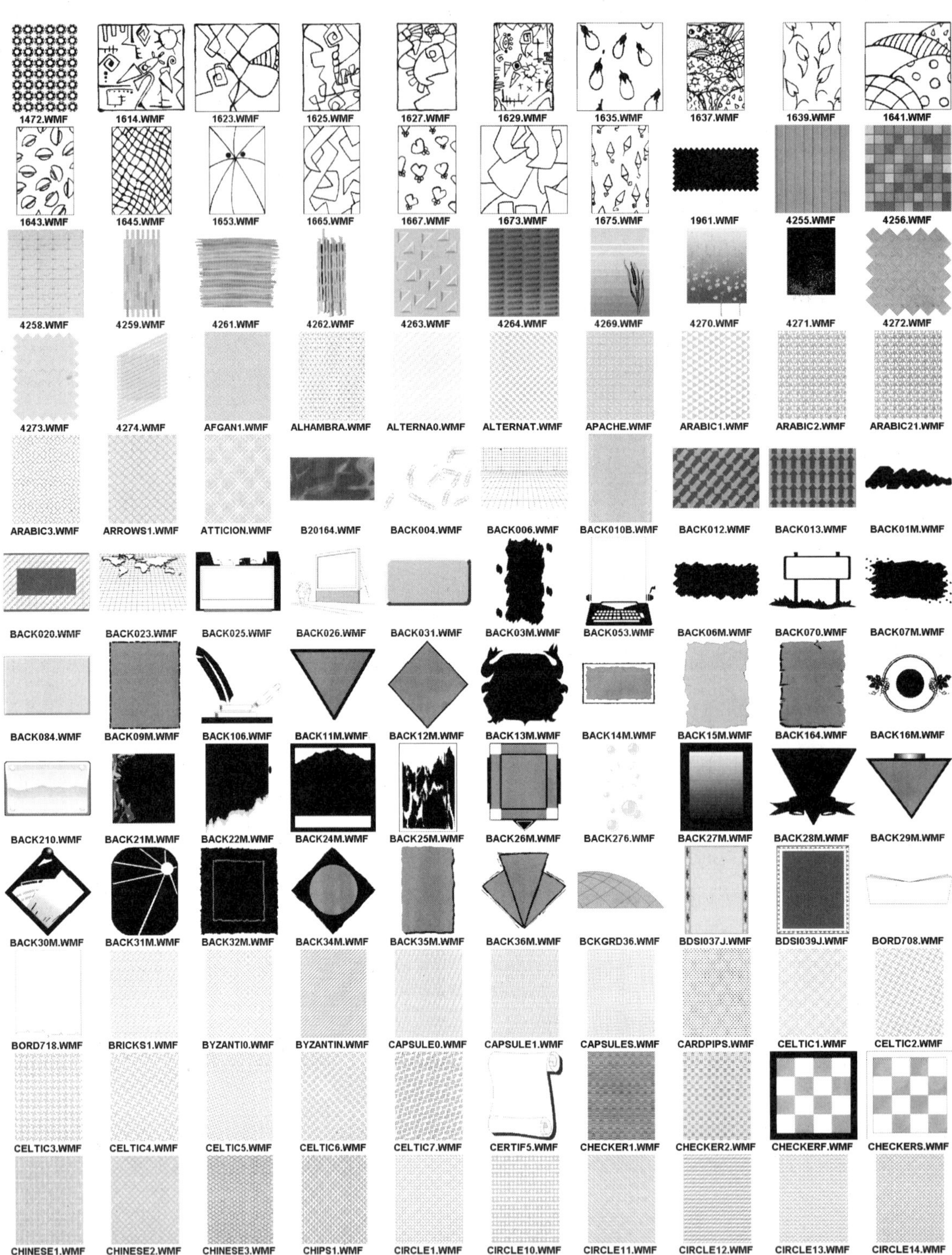

1472.WMF 1614.WMF 1623.WMF 1625.WMF 1627.WMF 1629.WMF 1635.WMF 1637.WMF 1639.WMF 1641.WMF

1643.WMF 1645.WMF 1653.WMF 1665.WMF 1667.WMF 1673.WMF 1675.WMF 1961.WMF 4255.WMF 4256.WMF

4258.WMF 4259.WMF 4261.WMF 4262.WMF 4263.WMF 4264.WMF 4269.WMF 4270.WMF 4271.WMF 4272.WMF

4273.WMF 4274.WMF AFGAN1.WMF ALHAMBRA.WMF ALTERNA0.WMF ALTERNAT.WMF APACHE.WMF ARABIC1.WMF ARABIC2.WMF ARABIC21.WMF

ARABIC3.WMF ARROWS1.WMF ATTICION.WMF B20164.WMF BACK004.WMF BACK006.WMF BACK010B.WMF BACK012.WMF BACK013.WMF BACK01M.WMF

BACK020.WMF BACK023.WMF BACK025.WMF BACK026.WMF BACK031.WMF BACK03M.WMF BACK053.WMF BACK06M.WMF BACK070.WMF BACK07M.WMF

BACK084.WMF BACK09M.WMF BACK106.WMF BACK11M.WMF BACK12M.WMF BACK13M.WMF BACK14M.WMF BACK15M.WMF BACK164.WMF BACK16M.WMF

BACK210.WMF BACK21M.WMF BACK22M.WMF BACK24M.WMF BACK25M.WMF BACK26M.WMF BACK276.WMF BACK27M.WMF BACK28M.WMF BACK29M.WMF

BACK30M.WMF BACK31M.WMF BACK32M.WMF BACK34M.WMF BACK35M.WMF BACK36M.WMF BCKGRD36.WMF BDSI037J.WMF BDSI039J.WMF BORD708.WMF

BORD718.WMF BRICKS1.WMF BYZANTI0.WMF BYZANTIN.WMF CAPSULE0.WMF CAPSULE1.WMF CAPSULES.WMF CARDPIPS.WMF CELTIC1.WMF CELTIC2.WMF

CELTIC3.WMF CELTIC4.WMF CELTIC5.WMF CELTIC6.WMF CELTIC7.WMF CERTIF5.WMF CHECKER1.WMF CHECKER2.WMF CHECKERF.WMF CHECKERS.WMF

CHINESE1.WMF CHINESE2.WMF CHINESE3.WMF CHIPS1.WMF CIRCLE1.WMF CIRCLE10.WMF CIRCLE11.WMF CIRCLE12.WMF CIRCLE13.WMF CIRCLE14.WMF

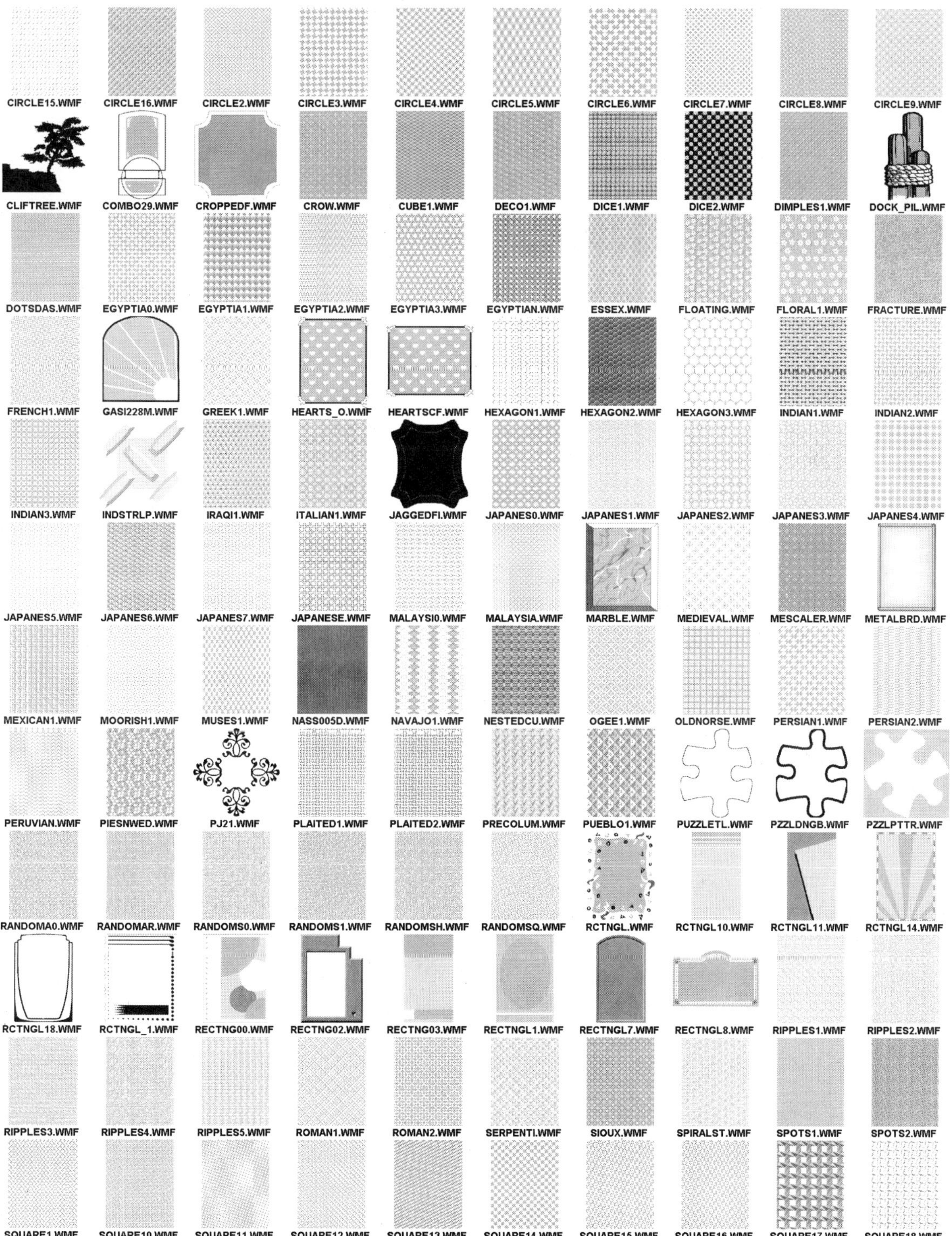
CIRCLE15.WMF
CIRCLE16.WMF
CIRCLE2.WMF
CIRCLE3.WMF
CIRCLE4.WMF
CIRCLE5.WMF
CIRCLE6.WMF
CIRCLE7.WMF
CIRCLE8.WMF
CIRCLE9.WMF
CLIFTREE.WMF
COMBO29.WMF
CROPPEDF.WMF
CROW.WMF
CUBE1.WMF
DECO1.WMF
DICE1.WMF
DICE2.WMF
DIMPLES1.WMF
DOCK_PIL.WMF
DOTSDAS.WMF
EGYPTIA0.WMF
EGYPTIA1.WMF
EGYPTIA2.WMF
EGYPTIA3.WMF
EGYPTIAN.WMF
ESSEX.WMF
FLOATING.WMF
FLORAL1.WMF
FRACTURE.WMF
FRENCH1.WMF
GASI228M.WMF
GREEK1.WMF
HEARTS_O.WMF
HEARTSCF.WMF
HEXAGON1.WMF
HEXAGON2.WMF
HEXAGON3.WMF
INDIAN1.WMF
INDIAN2.WMF
INDIAN3.WMF
INDSTRLP.WMF
IRAQI1.WMF
ITALIAN1.WMF
JAGGEDFI.WMF
JAPANES0.WMF
JAPANES1.WMF
JAPANES2.WMF
JAPANES3.WMF
JAPANES4.WMF
JAPANES5.WMF
JAPANES6.WMF
JAPANES7.WMF
JAPANESE.WMF
MALAYSI0.WMF
MALAYSIA.WMF
MARBLE.WMF
MEDIEVAL.WMF
MESCALER.WMF
METALBRD.WMF
MEXICAN1.WMF
MOORISH1.WMF
MUSES1.WMF
NASS005D.WMF
NAVAJO1.WMF
NESTEDCU.WMF
OGEE1.WMF
OLDNORSE.WMF
PERSIAN1.WMF
PERSIAN2.WMF
PERUVIAN.WMF
PIESNWED.WMF
PJ21.WMF
PLAITED1.WMF
PLAITED2.WMF
PRECOLUM.WMF
PUEBLO1.WMF
PUZZLETL.WMF
PZZLDNGB.WMF
PZZLPTTR.WMF
RANDOMA0.WMF
RANDOMAR.WMF
RANDOMS0.WMF
RANDOMS1.WMF
RANDOMSH.WMF
RANDOMSQ.WMF
RCTNGL.WMF
RCTNGL10.WMF
RCTNGL11.WMF
RCTNGL14.WMF
RCTNGL18.WMF
RCTNGL_1.WMF
RECTNG00.WMF
RECTNG02.WMF
RECTNG03.WMF
RECTNGL1.WMF
RECTNGL7.WMF
RECTNGL8.WMF
RIPPLES1.WMF
RIPPLES2.WMF
RIPPLES3.WMF
RIPPLES4.WMF
RIPPLES5.WMF
ROMAN1.WMF
ROMAN2.WMF
SERPENTI.WMF
SIOUX.WMF
SPIRALST.WMF
SPOTS1.WMF
SPOTS2.WMF
SQUARE1.WMF
SQUARE10.WMF
SQUARE11.WMF
SQUARE12.WMF
SQUARE13.WMF
SQUARE14.WMF
SQUARE15.WMF
SQUARE16.WMF
SQUARE17.WMF
SQUARE18.WMF

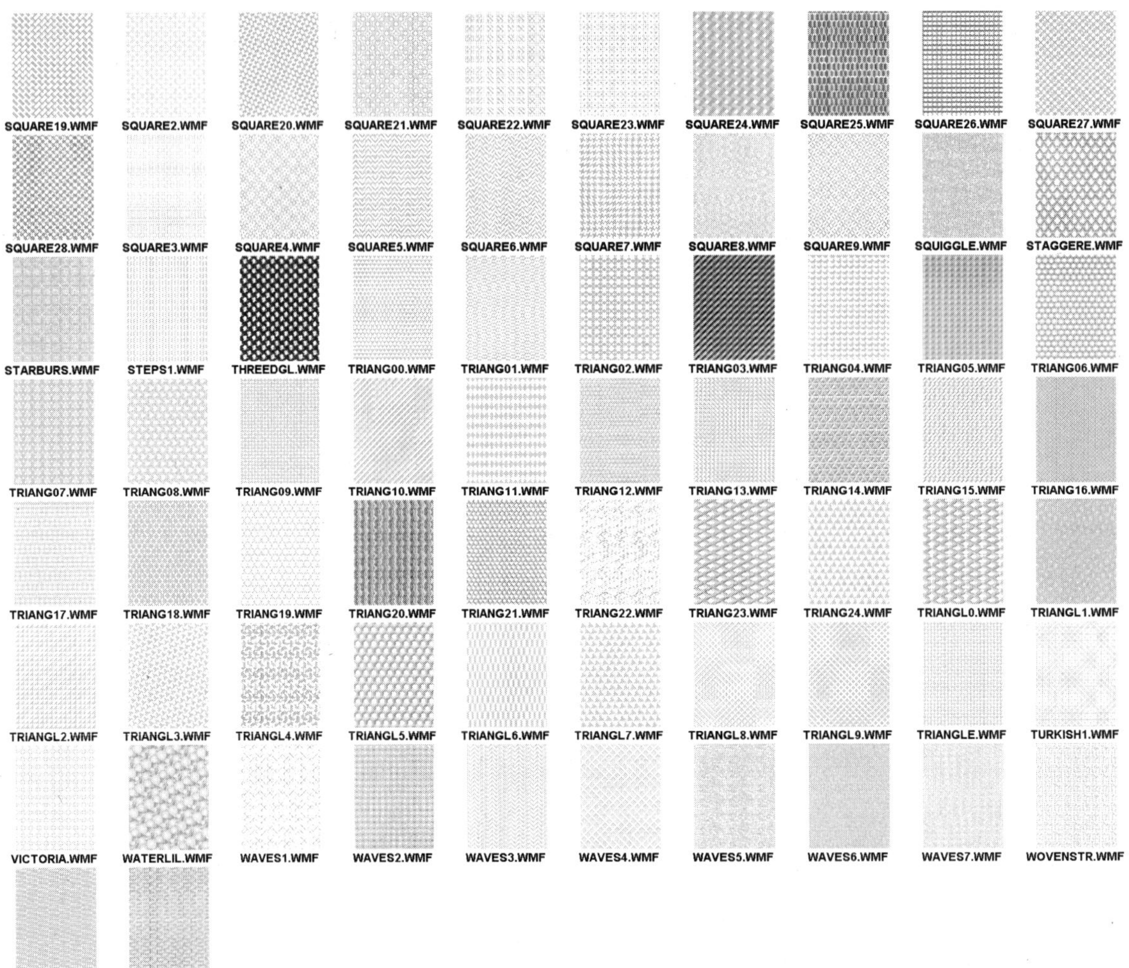
SQUARE19.WMF
SQUARE2.WMF
SQUARE20.WMF
SQUARE21.WMF
SQUARE22.WMF
SQUARE23.WMF
SQUARE24.WMF
SQUARE25.WMF
SQUARE26.WMF
SQUARE27.WMF
SQUARE28.WMF
SQUARE3.WMF
SQUARE4.WMF
SQUARE5.WMF
SQUARE6.WMF
SQUARE7.WMF
SQUARE8.WMF
SQUARE9.WMF
SQUIGGLE.WMF
STAGGERE.WMF
STARBURS.WMF
STEPS1.WMF
THREEDGL.WMF
TRIANG00.WMF
TRIANG01.WMF
TRIANG02.WMF
TRIANG03.WMF
TRIANG04.WMF
TRIANG05.WMF
TRIANG06.WMF
TRIANG07.WMF
TRIANG08.WMF
TRIANG09.WMF
TRIANG10.WMF
TRIANG11.WMF
TRIANG12.WMF
TRIANG13.WMF
TRIANG14.WMF
TRIANG15.WMF
TRIANG16.WMF
TRIANG17.WMF
TRIANG18.WMF
TRIANG19.WMF
TRIANG20.WMF
TRIANG21.WMF
TRIANG22.WMF
TRIANG23.WMF
TRIANG24.WMF
TRIANGL0.WMF
TRIANGL1.WMF
TRIANGL2.WMF
TRIANGL3.WMF
TRIANGL4.WMF
TRIANGL5.WMF
TRIANGL6.WMF
TRIANGL7.WMF
TRIANGL8.WMF
TRIANGL9.WMF
TRIANGLE.WMF
TURKISH1.WMF
VICTORIA.WMF
WATERLIL.WMF
WAVES1.WMF
WAVES2.WMF
WAVES3.WMF
WAVES4.WMF
WAVES5.WMF
WAVES6.WMF
WAVES7.WMF
WOVENSTR.WMF
ZIGZAG1.WMF
ZIGZAG2.WMF

1253.WMF
1317.WMF
1331.WMF
1332.WMF
1333.WMF
1340.WMF
1473.WMF
1474.WMF
4267.WMF
A40A.WMF
A40AB.WMF
ALAD.WMF
ARCH.WMF
B20171.WMF
BACK001B.WMF
BACK003.WMF
BACK006B.WMF
BACK007.WMF
BACK032.WMF
BACK033.WMF
BACK034.WMF
BACK035.WMF
BACK038.WMF
BACK040.WMF
BACK041.WMF
BACK042.WMF
BACK043B.WMF
BACK044.WMF
BACK049B.WMF
BACK054B.WMF
BACK056.WMF
BACK059.WMF
BACK063.WMF
BACK065B.WMF
BACK067B.WMF
BACK068.WMF
BACK069B.WMF
BACK071B.WMF
BACK073.WMF
BACK074.WMF
JUNGLE
BACK075.WMF
BACK082.WMF
BACK092.WMF
BACK094.WMF
BACK095.WMF
BACK097.WMF
BACK098.WMF
BACK100.WMF
BACK105A.WMF
BACK107.WMF
BACK111.WMF
BACK112.WMF
BACK114.WMF
BACK119.WMF
BACK120.WMF
BACK126.WMF
BACK127.WMF
BACK131.WMF
BACK134.WMF
BACK145.WMF
RECIEPTS
BACK149.WMF
BACK175.WMF
BACK177.WMF
BACK179.WMF
BACK181.WMF
BACK195.WMF
BACK206.WMF
BACK236.WMF
BACK237.WMF
BACK246.WMF
BACK251.WMF
BACK275.WMF
BALONBNR.WMF
BANNER8.WMF
BCKGRD37.WMF
BCKGRD41.WMF
BCKGRD42.WMF
BCKGRD43.WMF
BCKGRD44.WMF
BCKGRD45.WMF
BCKGRD46.WMF
BCKGRD48.WMF
BCKGRD58.WMF
BCKGRD59.WMF
BCKGRD60.WMF
BDEDUCAT.WMF
BDSI096J.WMF
BISI012M.WMF
BISI016M.WMF
BIT0925.WMF
BOSS' DAY
$AVINGS
BLNKPAGE.WMF
BOATING.WMF
BORD083.WMF
BORD616.WMF
BORD617.WMF
BORDER12.WMF
BORDR008.WMF
BOSSDAY2.WMF
BOYGHOUL.WMF
BQUILL.WMF
BREADMT.WMF
BRITIDEA.WMF
BULBS_HO.WMF
BULBSHOL.WMF
BULTNBRD.WMF
BUSI054D.WMF
CANADATH.WMF
CANDLE.WMF
CANDYCA1.WMF
CANDYCA2.WMF
CASHIN
CANDYCN2.WMF
CANDYHRT.WMF
CARPRTMT.WMF
CARSNOMT.WMF
CASHIN.WMF
CAT_MOUS.WMF
CELEBRAT.WMF
CERTIF6.WMF
CHIEF.WMF
CHRISTM3.WMF

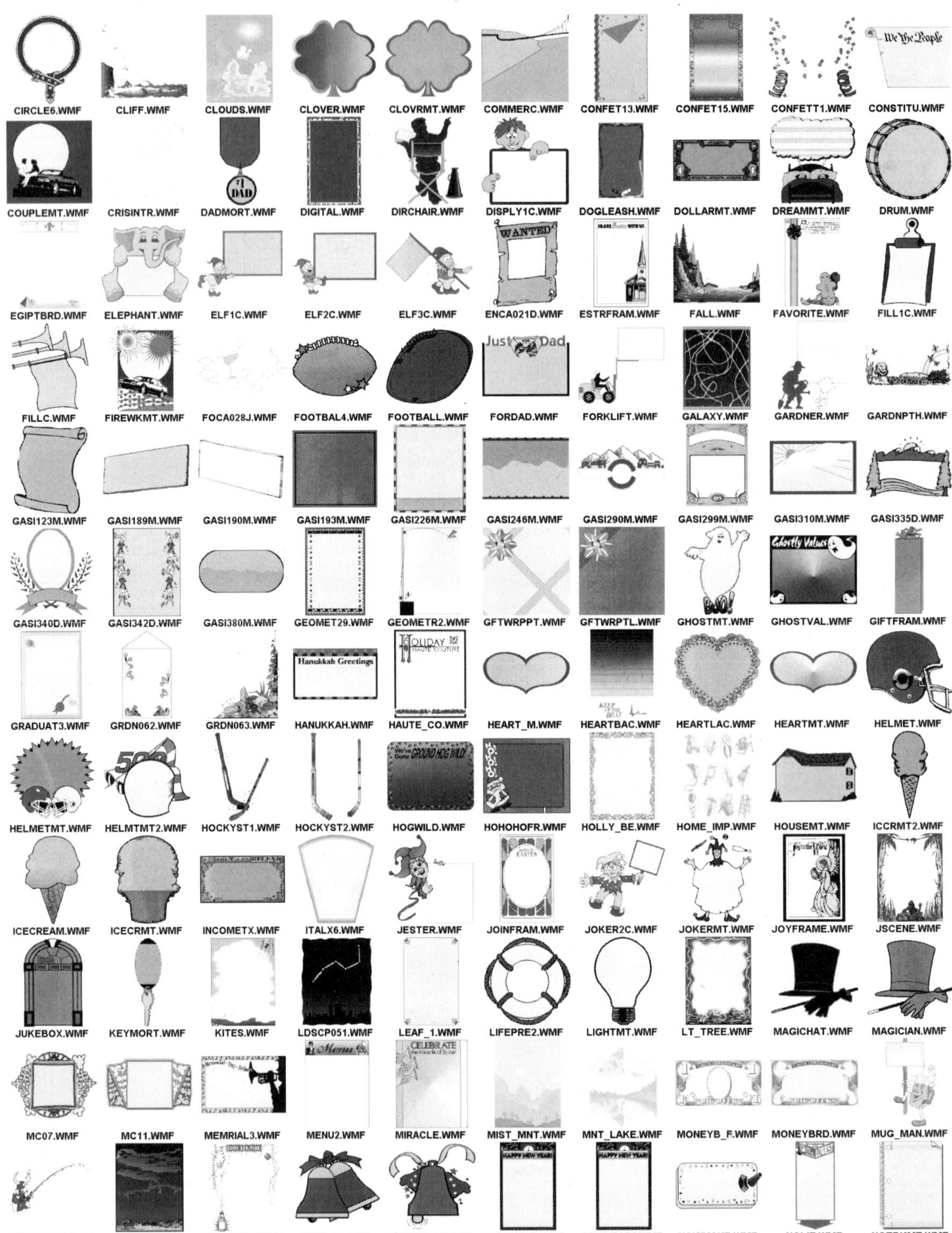
We the People
CIRCLE6.WMF
CLIFF.WMF
CLOUDS.WMF
CLOVER.WMF
CLOVRMT.WMF
COMMERC.WMF
CONFET13.WMF
CONFET15.WMF
CONFETT1.WMF
CONSTITU.WMF
#1 DAD
COUPLEMT.WMF
CRISINTR.WMF
DADMORT.WMF
DIGITAL.WMF
DIRCHAIR.WMF
DISPLY1C.WMF
DOGLEASH.WMF
DOLLARMT.WMF
DREAMMT.WMF
DRUM.WMF
WANTED
EGIPTBRD.WMF
ELEPHANT.WMF
ELF1C.WMF
ELF2C.WMF
ELF3C.WMF
ENCA021D.WMF
ESTRFRAM.WMF
FALL.WMF
FAVORITE.WMF
FILL1C.WMF
Just Dad
FILLC.WMF
FIREWKMT.WMF
FOCA028J.WMF
FOOTBAL4.WMF
FOOTBALL.WMF
FORDAD.WMF
FORKLIFT.WMF
GALAXY.WMF
GARDNER.WMF
GARDNPTH.WMF
GASI123M.WMF
GASI189M.WMF
GASI190M.WMF
GASI193M.WMF
GASI226M.WMF
GASI246M.WMF
GASI290M.WMF
GASI299M.WMF
GASI310M.WMF
GASI335D.WMF
Ghostly Values
BOO!
GASI340D.WMF
GASI342D.WMF
GASI380M.WMF
GEOMET29.WMF
GEOMETR2.WMF
GFTWRPPT.WMF
GFTWRPTL.WMF
GHOSTMT.WMF
GHOSTVAL.WMF
GIFTFRAM.WMF
Hanukkah Greetings
HOLIDAY
HAUTE COUTURE
KEEP TO THE BEAT
GRADUAT3.WMF
GRDN062.WMF
GRDN063.WMF
HANUKKAH.WMF
HAUTE_CO.WMF
HEART_M.WMF
HEARTBAC.WMF
HEARTLAC.WMF
HEARTMT.WMF
HELMET.WMF
500
We've Gone GROUND HOG WILD
HELMETMT.WMF
HELMTMT2.WMF
HOCKYST1.WMF
HOCKYST2.WMF
HOGWILD.WMF
HOHOHOFR.WMF
HOLLY_BE.WMF
HOME_IMP.WMF
HOUSEMT.WMF
ICCRMT2.WMF
EASTER
ICECREAM.WMF
ICECRMT.WMF
INCOMETX.WMF
ITALX6.WMF
JESTER.WMF
JOINFRAM.WMF
JOKER2C.WMF
JOKERMT.WMF
JOYFRAME.WMF
JSCENE.WMF
JUKEBOX.WMF
KEYMORT.WMF
KITES.WMF
LDSCP051.WMF
LEAF_1.WMF
LIFEPRE2.WMF
LIGHTMT.WMF
LT_TREE.WMF
MAGICHAT.WMF
MAGICIAN.WMF
Menu
CELEBRATE
MC07.WMF
MC11.WMF
MEMRIAL3.WMF
MENU2.WMF
MIRACLE.WMF
MIST_MNT.WMF
MNT_LAKE.WMF
MONEYB_F.WMF
MONEYBRD.WMF
MUG_MAN.WMF
HAPPY NEW YEAR
HAPPY NEW YEAR
NACA075D.WMF
NASI177D.WMF
NEW_YEAR.WMF
NEWBELL.WMF
NEWBELL2.WMF
NEWYEAR.WMF
NEWYEAR2.WMF
NOISMAKR.WMF
NOLIE.WMF
NOTBKMT.WMF

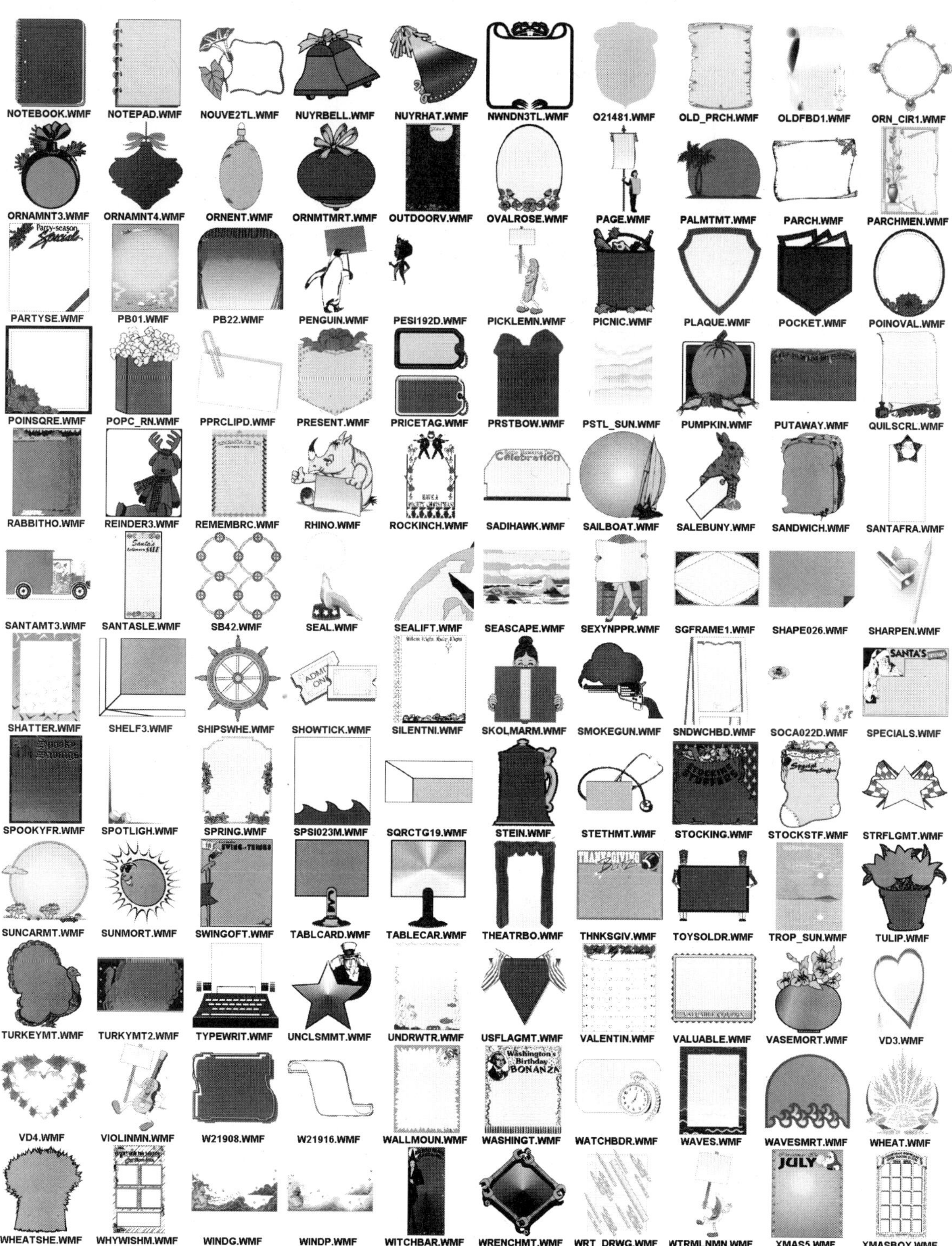
NOTEBOOK.WMF NOTEPAD.WMF NOUVE2TL.WMF NUYRBELL.WMF NUYRHAT.WMF NWNDN3TL.WMF O21481.WMF OLD_PRCH.WMF OLDFBD1.WMF ORN_CIR1.WMF
ORNAMNT3.WMF ORNAMNT4.WMF ORNENT.WMF ORNMTMRT.WMF OUTDOORV.WMF OVALROSE.WMF PAGE.WMF PALMTMT.WMF PARCH.WMF PARCHMEN.WMF
PARTYSE.WMF PB01.WMF PB22.WMF PENGUIN.WMF PESI192D.WMF PICKLEMN.WMF PICNIC.WMF PLAQUE.WMF POCKET.WMF POINOVAL.WMF
POINSQRE.WMF POPC_RN.WMF PPRCLIPD.WMF PRESENT.WMF PRICETAG.WMF PRSTBOW.WMF PSTL_SUN.WMF PUMPKIN.WMF PUTAWAY.WMF QUILSCRL.WMF
RABBITHO.WMF REINDER3.WMF REMEMBRC.WMF RHINO.WMF ROCKINCH.WMF SADIHAWK.WMF SAILBOAT.WMF SALEBUNY.WMF SANDWICH.WMF SANTAFRA.WMF
SANTAMT3.WMF SANTASLE.WMF SB42.WMF SEAL.WMF SEALIFT.WMF SEASCAPE.WMF SEXYNPPR.WMF SGFRAME1.WMF SHAPE026.WMF SHARPEN.WMF
SHATTER.WMF SHELF3.WMF SHIPSWHE.WMF SHOWTICK.WMF SILENTNI.WMF SKOLMARM.WMF SMOKEGUN.WMF SNDWCHBD.WMF SOCA022D.WMF SPECIALS.WMF
SPOOKYFR.WMF SPOTLIGH.WMF SPRING.WMF SPSI023M.WMF SQRCTG19.WMF STEIN.WMF STETHMT.WMF STOCKING.WMF STOCKSTF.WMF STRFLGMT.WMF
SUNCARMT.WMF SUNMORT.WMF SWINGOFT.WMF TABLCARD.WMF TABLECAR.WMF THEATRBO.WMF THNKSGIV.WMF TOYSOLDR.WMF TROP_SUN.WMF TULIP.WMF
TURKEYMT.WMF TURKYMT2.WMF TYPEWRIT.WMF UNCLSMMT.WMF UNDRWTR.WMF USFLAGMT.WMF VALENTIN.WMF VALUABLE.WMF VASEMORT.WMF VD3.WMF
VD4.WMF VIOLINMN.WMF W21908.WMF W21916.WMF WALLMOUN.WMF WASHINGT.WMF WATCHBDR.WMF WAVES.WMF WAVESMRT.WMF WHEAT.WMF
WHEATSHE.WMF WHYWISHM.WMF WINDG.WMF WINDP.WMF WITCHBAR.WMF WRENCHMT.WMF WRT_DRWG.WMF WTRMLNMN.WMF XMAS5.WMF XMASBOX.WMF

XMASCLER.WMF

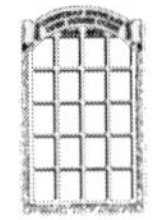
XMASGUID.WMF

XMASTRE.WMF

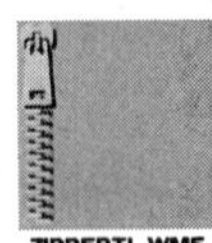
ZIPPERTL.WMF

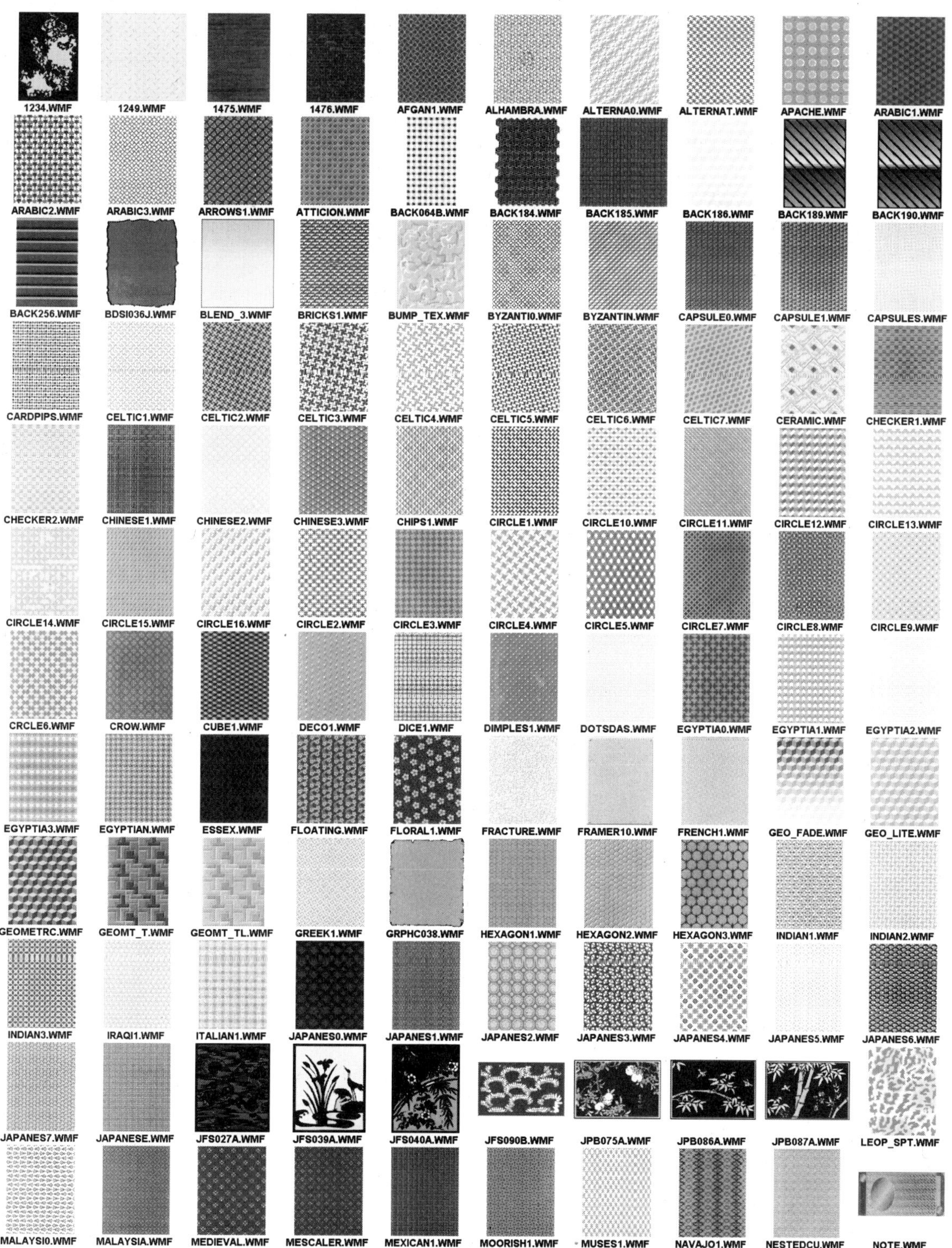
1234.WMF
1249.WMF
1475.WMF
1476.WMF
AFGAN1.WMF
ALHAMBRA.WMF
ALTERNA0.WMF
ALTERNAT.WMF
APACHE.WMF
ARABIC1.WMF
ARABIC2.WMF
ARABIC3.WMF
ARROWS1.WMF
ATTICION.WMF
BACK064B.WMF
BACK184.WMF
BACK185.WMF
BACK186.WMF
BACK189.WMF
BACK190.WMF
BACK256.WMF
BDSI036J.WMF
BLEND_3.WMF
BRICKS1.WMF
BUMP_TEX.WMF
BYZANTI0.WMF
BYZANTIN.WMF
CAPSULE0.WMF
CAPSULE1.WMF
CAPSULES.WMF
CARDPIPS.WMF
CELTIC1.WMF
CELTIC2.WMF
CELTIC3.WMF
CELTIC4.WMF
CELTIC5.WMF
CELTIC6.WMF
CELTIC7.WMF
CERAMIC.WMF
CHECKER1.WMF
CHECKER2.WMF
CHINESE1.WMF
CHINESE2.WMF
CHINESE3.WMF
CHIPS1.WMF
CIRCLE1.WMF
CIRCLE10.WMF
CIRCLE11.WMF
CIRCLE12.WMF
CIRCLE13.WMF
CIRCLE14.WMF
CIRCLE15.WMF
CIRCLE16.WMF
CIRCLE2.WMF
CIRCLE3.WMF
CIRCLE4.WMF
CIRCLE5.WMF
CIRCLE7.WMF
CIRCLE8.WMF
CIRCLE9.WMF
CRCLE6.WMF
CROW.WMF
CUBE1.WMF
DECO1.WMF
DICE1.WMF
DIMPLES1.WMF
DOTSDAS.WMF
EGYPTIA0.WMF
EGYPTIA1.WMF
EGYPTIA2.WMF
EGYPTIA3.WMF
EGYPTIAN.WMF
ESSEX.WMF
FLOATING.WMF
FLORAL1.WMF
FRACTURE.WMF
FRAMER10.WMF
FRENCH1.WMF
GEO_FADE.WMF
GEO_LITE.WMF
GEOMETRC.WMF
GEOMT_T.WMF
GEOMT_TL.WMF
GREEK1.WMF
GRPHC038.WMF
HEXAGON1.WMF
HEXAGON2.WMF
HEXAGON3.WMF
INDIAN1.WMF
INDIAN2.WMF
INDIAN3.WMF
IRAQI1.WMF
ITALIAN1.WMF
JAPANES0.WMF
JAPANES1.WMF
JAPANES2.WMF
JAPANES3.WMF
JAPANES4.WMF
JAPANES5.WMF
JAPANES6.WMF
JAPANES7.WMF
JAPANESE.WMF
JFS027A.WMF
JFS039A.WMF
JFS040A.WMF
JFS090B.WMF
JPB075A.WMF
JPB086A.WMF
JPB087A.WMF
LEOP_SPT.WMF
MALAYSI0.WMF
MALAYSIA.WMF
MEDIEVAL.WMF
MESCALER.WMF
MEXICAN1.WMF
MOORISH1.WMF
MUSES1.WMF
NAVAJO1.WMF
NESTEDCU.WMF
NOTE.WMF

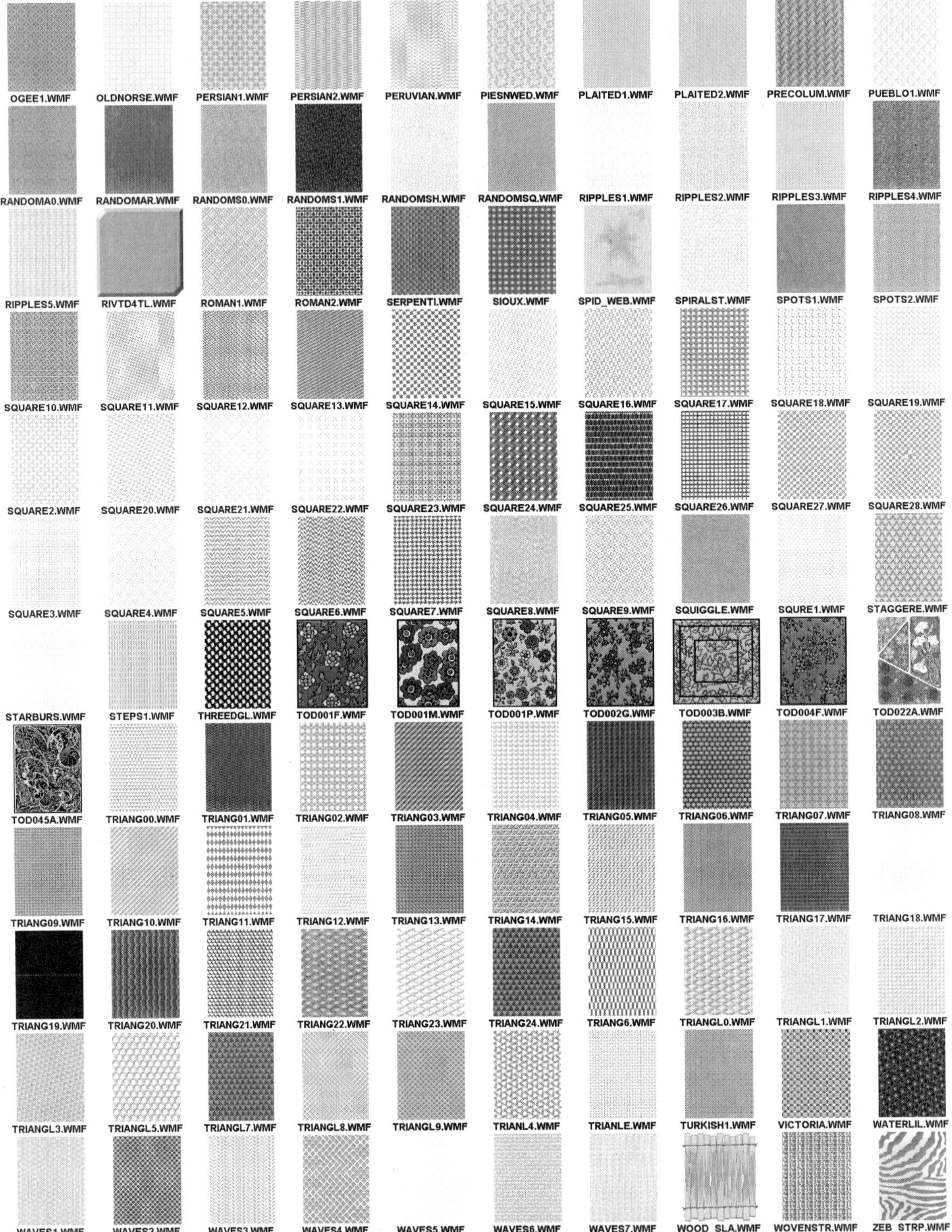

OGEE1.WMF
OLDNORSE.WMF
PERSIAN1.WMF
PERSIAN2.WMF
PERUVIAN.WMF
PIESNWED.WMF
PLAITED1.WMF
PLAITED2.WMF
PRECOLUM.WMF
PUEBLO1.WMF
RANDOMA0.WMF
RANDOMAR.WMF
RANDOMS0.WMF
RANDOMS1.WMF
RANDOMSH.WMF
RANDOMSQ.WMF
RIPPLES1.WMF
RIPPLES2.WMF
RIPPLES3.WMF
RIPPLES4.WMF
RIPPLES5.WMF
RIVTD4TL.WMF
ROMAN1.WMF
ROMAN2.WMF
SERPENTI.WMF
SIOUX.WMF
SPID_WEB.WMF
SPIRALST.WMF
SPOTS1.WMF
SPOTS2.WMF
SQUARE10.WMF
SQUARE11.WMF
SQUARE12.WMF
SQUARE13.WMF
SQUARE14.WMF
SQUARE15.WMF
SQUARE16.WMF
SQUARE17.WMF
SQUARE18.WMF
SQUARE19.WMF
SQUARE2.WMF
SQUARE20.WMF
SQUARE21.WMF
SQUARE22.WMF
SQUARE23.WMF
SQUARE24.WMF
SQUARE25.WMF
SQUARE26.WMF
SQUARE27.WMF
SQUARE28.WMF
SQUARE3.WMF
SQUARE4.WMF
SQUARE5.WMF
SQUARE6.WMF
SQUARE7.WMF
SQUARE8.WMF
SQUARE9.WMF
SQUIGGLE.WMF
SQURE1.WMF
STAGGERE.WMF
STARBURS.WMF
STEPS1.WMF
THREEDGL.WMF
TOD001F.WMF
TOD001M.WMF
TOD001P.WMF
TOD002G.WMF
TOD003B.WMF
TOD004F.WMF
TOD022A.WMF
TOD045A.WMF
TRIANG00.WMF
TRIANG01.WMF
TRIANG02.WMF
TRIANG03.WMF
TRIANG04.WMF
TRIANG05.WMF
TRIANG06.WMF
TRIANG07.WMF
TRIANG08.WMF
TRIANG09.WMF
TRIANG10.WMF
TRIANG11.WMF
TRIANG12.WMF
TRIANG13.WMF
TRIANG14.WMF
TRIANG15.WMF
TRIANG16.WMF
TRIANG17.WMF
TRIANG18.WMF
TRIANG19.WMF
TRIANG20.WMF
TRIANG21.WMF
TRIANG22.WMF
TRIANG23.WMF
TRIANG24.WMF
TRIANG6.WMF
TRIANGL0.WMF
TRIANGL1.WMF
TRIANGL2.WMF
TRIANGL3.WMF
TRIANGL5.WMF
TRIANGL7.WMF
TRIANGL8.WMF
TRIANGL9.WMF
TRIANL4.WMF
TRIANLE.WMF
TURKISH1.WMF
VICTORIA.WMF
WATERLIL.WMF
WAVES1.WMF
WAVES2.WMF
WAVES3.WMF
WAVES4.WMF
WAVES5.WMF
WAVES6.WMF
WAVES7.WMF
WOOD_SLA.WMF
WOVENSTR.WMF
ZEB_STRP.WMF

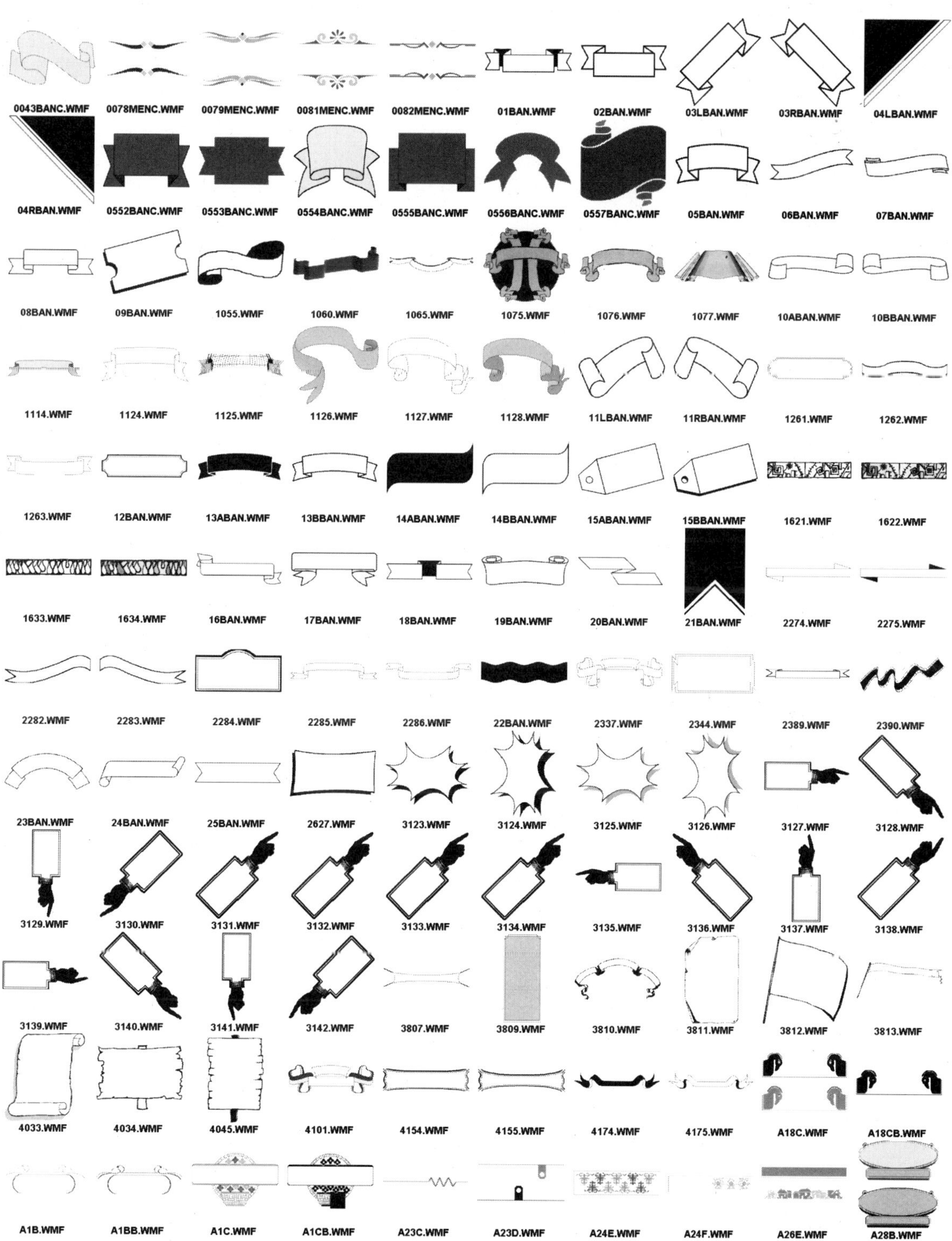
0043BANC.WMF
0078MENC.WMF
0079MENC.WMF
0081MENC.WMF
0082MENC.WMF
01BAN.WMF
02BAN.WMF
03LBAN.WMF
03RBAN.WMF
04LBAN.WMF
04RBAN.WMF
0552BANC.WMF
0553BANC.WMF
0554BANC.WMF
0555BANC.WMF
0556BANC.WMF
0557BANC.WMF
05BAN.WMF
06BAN.WMF
07BAN.WMF
08BAN.WMF
09BAN.WMF
1055.WMF
1060.WMF
1065.WMF
1075.WMF
1076.WMF
1077.WMF
10ABAN.WMF
10BBAN.WMF
1114.WMF
1124.WMF
1125.WMF
1126.WMF
1127.WMF
1128.WMF
11LBAN.WMF
11RBAN.WMF
1261.WMF
1262.WMF
1263.WMF
12BAN.WMF
13ABAN.WMF
13BBAN.WMF
14ABAN.WMF
14BBAN.WMF
15ABAN.WMF
15BBAN.WMF
1621.WMF
1622.WMF
1633.WMF
1634.WMF
16BAN.WMF
17BAN.WMF
18BAN.WMF
19BAN.WMF
20BAN.WMF
21BAN.WMF
2274.WMF
2275.WMF
2282.WMF
2283.WMF
2284.WMF
2285.WMF
2286.WMF
22BAN.WMF
2337.WMF
2344.WMF
2389.WMF
2390.WMF
23BAN.WMF
24BAN.WMF
25BAN.WMF
2627.WMF
3123.WMF
3124.WMF
3125.WMF
3126.WMF
3127.WMF
3128.WMF
3129.WMF
3130.WMF
3131.WMF
3132.WMF
3133.WMF
3134.WMF
3135.WMF
3136.WMF
3137.WMF
3138.WMF
3139.WMF
3140.WMF
3141.WMF
3142.WMF
3807.WMF
3809.WMF
3810.WMF
3811.WMF
3812.WMF
3813.WMF
4033.WMF
4034.WMF
4045.WMF
4101.WMF
4154.WMF
4155.WMF
4174.WMF
4175.WMF
A18C.WMF
A18CB.WMF
A1B.WMF
A1BB.WMF
A1C.WMF
A1CB.WMF
A23C.WMF
A23D.WMF
A24E.WMF
A24F.WMF
A26E.WMF
A28B.WMF

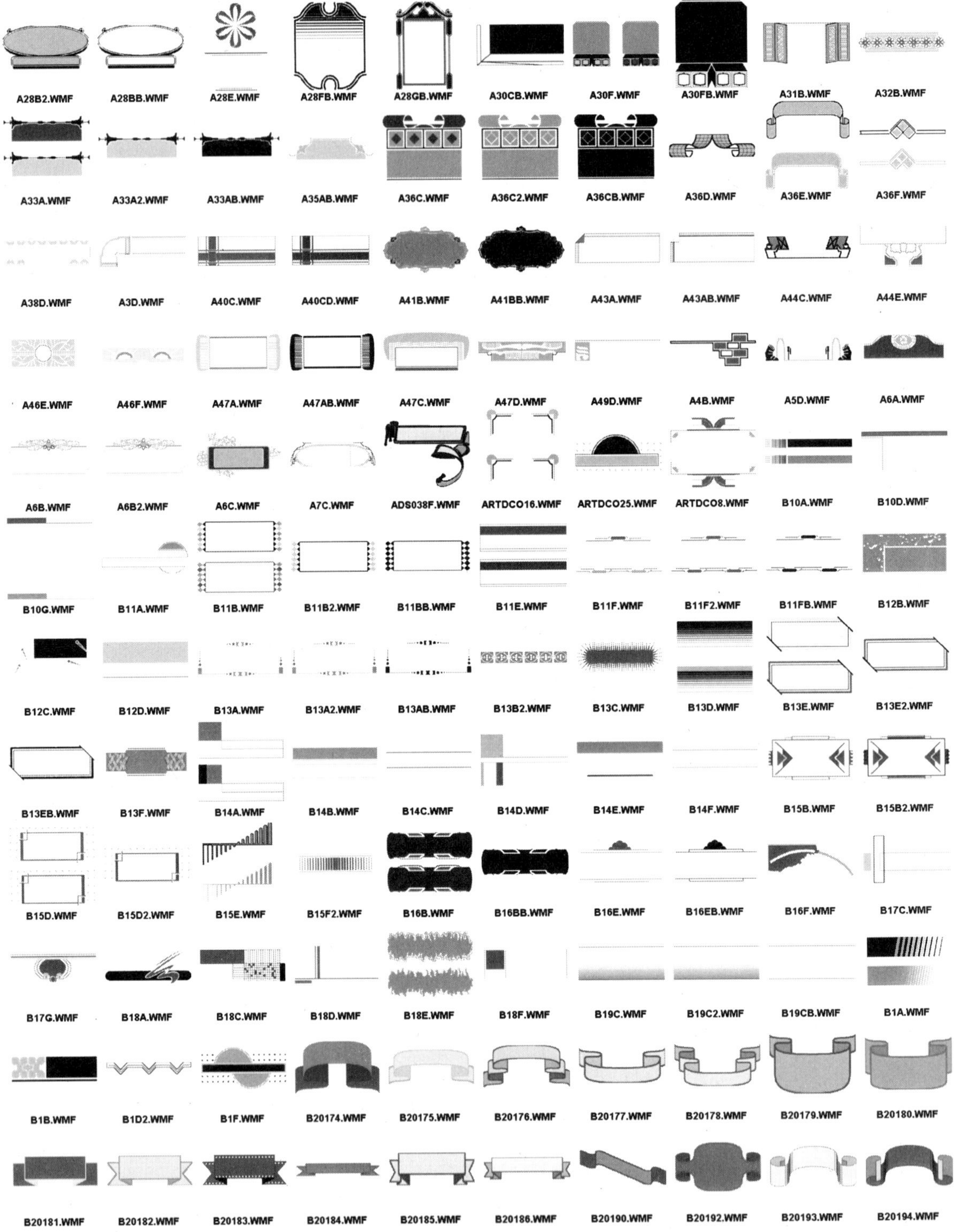
A28B2.WMF
A28BB.WMF
A28E.WMF
A28FB.WMF
A28GB.WMF
A30CB.WMF
A30F.WMF
A30FB.WMF
A31B.WMF
A32B.WMF
A33A.WMF
A33A2.WMF
A33AB.WMF
A35AB.WMF
A36C.WMF
A36C2.WMF
A36CB.WMF
A36D.WMF
A36E.WMF
A36F.WMF
A38D.WMF
A3D.WMF
A40C.WMF
A40CD.WMF
A41B.WMF
A41BB.WMF
A43A.WMF
A43AB.WMF
A44C.WMF
A44E.WMF
A46E.WMF
A46F.WMF
A47A.WMF
A47AB.WMF
A47C.WMF
A47D.WMF
A49D.WMF
A4B.WMF
A5D.WMF
A6A.WMF
A6B.WMF
A6B2.WMF
A6C.WMF
A7C.WMF
ADS038F.WMF
ARTDCO16.WMF
ARTDCO25.WMF
ARTDCO8.WMF
B10A.WMF
B10D.WMF
B10G.WMF
B11A.WMF
B11B.WMF
B11B2.WMF
B11BB.WMF
B11E.WMF
B11F.WMF
B11F2.WMF
B11FB.WMF
B12B.WMF
B12C.WMF
B12D.WMF
B13A.WMF
B13A2.WMF
B13AB.WMF
B13B2.WMF
B13C.WMF
B13D.WMF
B13E.WMF
B13E2.WMF
B13EB.WMF
B13F.WMF
B14A.WMF
B14B.WMF
B14C.WMF
B14D.WMF
B14E.WMF
B14F.WMF
B15B.WMF
B15B2.WMF
B15D.WMF
B15D2.WMF
B15E.WMF
B15F2.WMF
B16B.WMF
B16BB.WMF
B16E.WMF
B16EB.WMF
B16F.WMF
B17C.WMF
B17G.WMF
B18A.WMF
B18C.WMF
B18D.WMF
B18E.WMF
B18F.WMF
B19C.WMF
B19C2.WMF
B19CB.WMF
B1A.WMF
B1B.WMF
B1D2.WMF
B1F.WMF
B20174.WMF
B20175.WMF
B20176.WMF
B20177.WMF
B20178.WMF
B20179.WMF
B20180.WMF
B20181.WMF
B20182.WMF
B20183.WMF
B20184.WMF
B20185.WMF
B20186.WMF
B20190.WMF
B20192.WMF
B20193.WMF
B20194.WMF

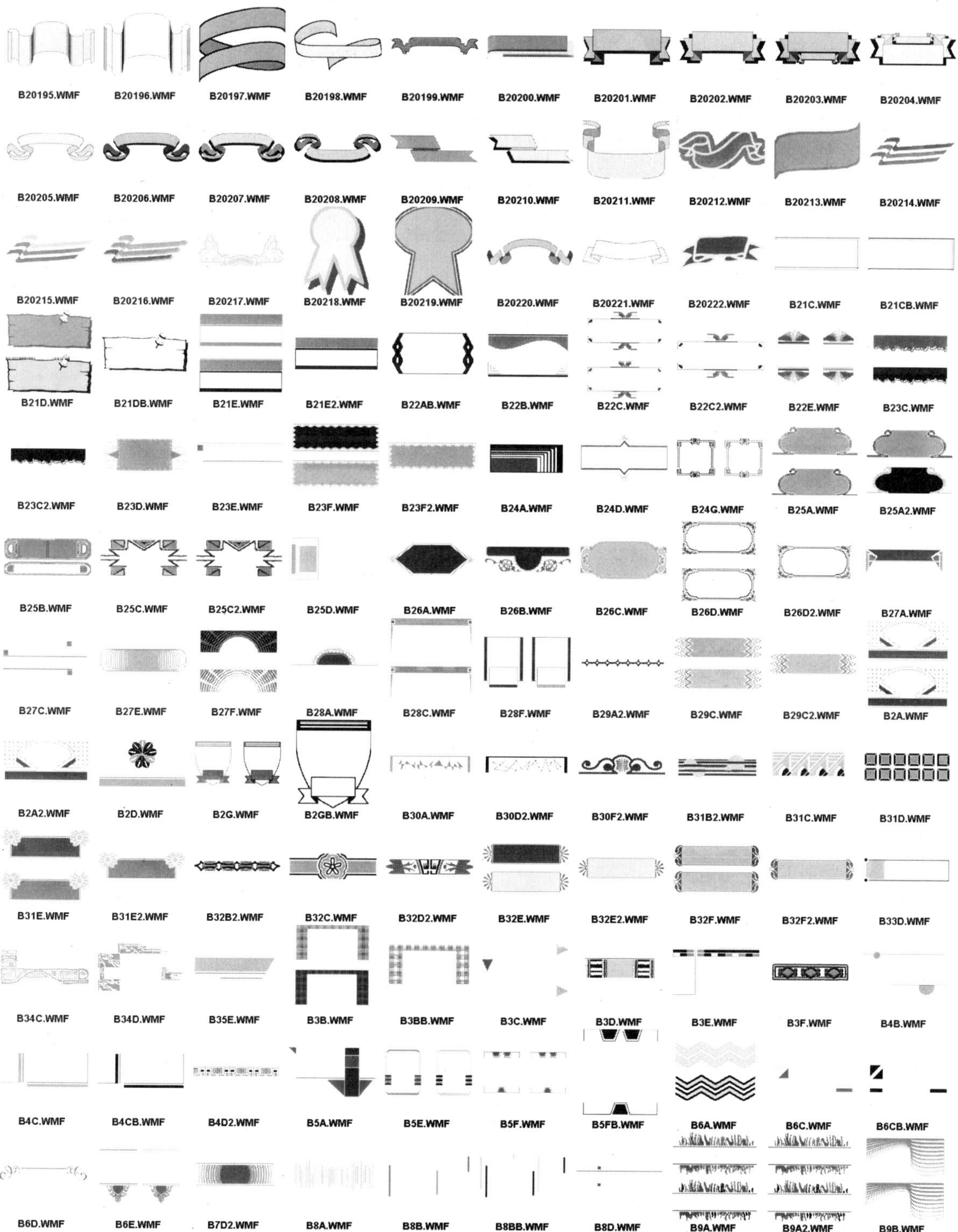
B20195.WMF
B20196.WMF
B20197.WMF
B20198.WMF
B20199.WMF
B20200.WMF
B20201.WMF
B20202.WMF
B20203.WMF
B20204.WMF
B20205.WMF
B20206.WMF
B20207.WMF
B20208.WMF
B20209.WMF
B20210.WMF
B20211.WMF
B20212.WMF
B20213.WMF
B20214.WMF
B20215.WMF
B20216.WMF
B20217.WMF
B20218.WMF
B20219.WMF
B20220.WMF
B20221.WMF
B20222.WMF
B21C.WMF
B21CB.WMF
B21D.WMF
B21DB.WMF
B21E.WMF
B21E2.WMF
B22AB.WMF
B22B.WMF
B22C.WMF
B22C2.WMF
B22E.WMF
B23C.WMF
B23C2.WMF
B23D.WMF
B23E.WMF
B23F.WMF
B23F2.WMF
B24A.WMF
B24D.WMF
B24G.WMF
B25A.WMF
B25A2.WMF
B25B.WMF
B25C.WMF
B25C2.WMF
B25D.WMF
B26A.WMF
B26B.WMF
B26C.WMF
B26D.WMF
B26D2.WMF
B27A.WMF
B27C.WMF
B27E.WMF
B27F.WMF
B28A.WMF
B28C.WMF
B28F.WMF
B29A2.WMF
B29C.WMF
B29C2.WMF
B2A.WMF
B2A2.WMF
B2D.WMF
B2G.WMF
B2GB.WMF
B30A.WMF
B30D2.WMF
B30F2.WMF
B31B2.WMF
B31C.WMF
B31D.WMF
B31E.WMF
B31E2.WMF
B32B2.WMF
B32C.WMF
B32D2.WMF
B32E.WMF
B32E2.WMF
B32F.WMF
B32F2.WMF
B33D.WMF
B34C.WMF
B34D.WMF
B35E.WMF
B3B.WMF
B3BB.WMF
B3C.WMF
B3D.WMF
B3E.WMF
B3F.WMF
B4B.WMF
B4C.WMF
B4CB.WMF
B4D2.WMF
B5A.WMF
B5E.WMF
B5F.WMF
B5FB.WMF
B6A.WMF
B6C.WMF
B6CB.WMF
B6D.WMF
B6E.WMF
B7D2.WMF
B8A.WMF
B8B.WMF
B8BB.WMF
B8D.WMF
B9A.WMF
B9A2.WMF
B9B.WMF

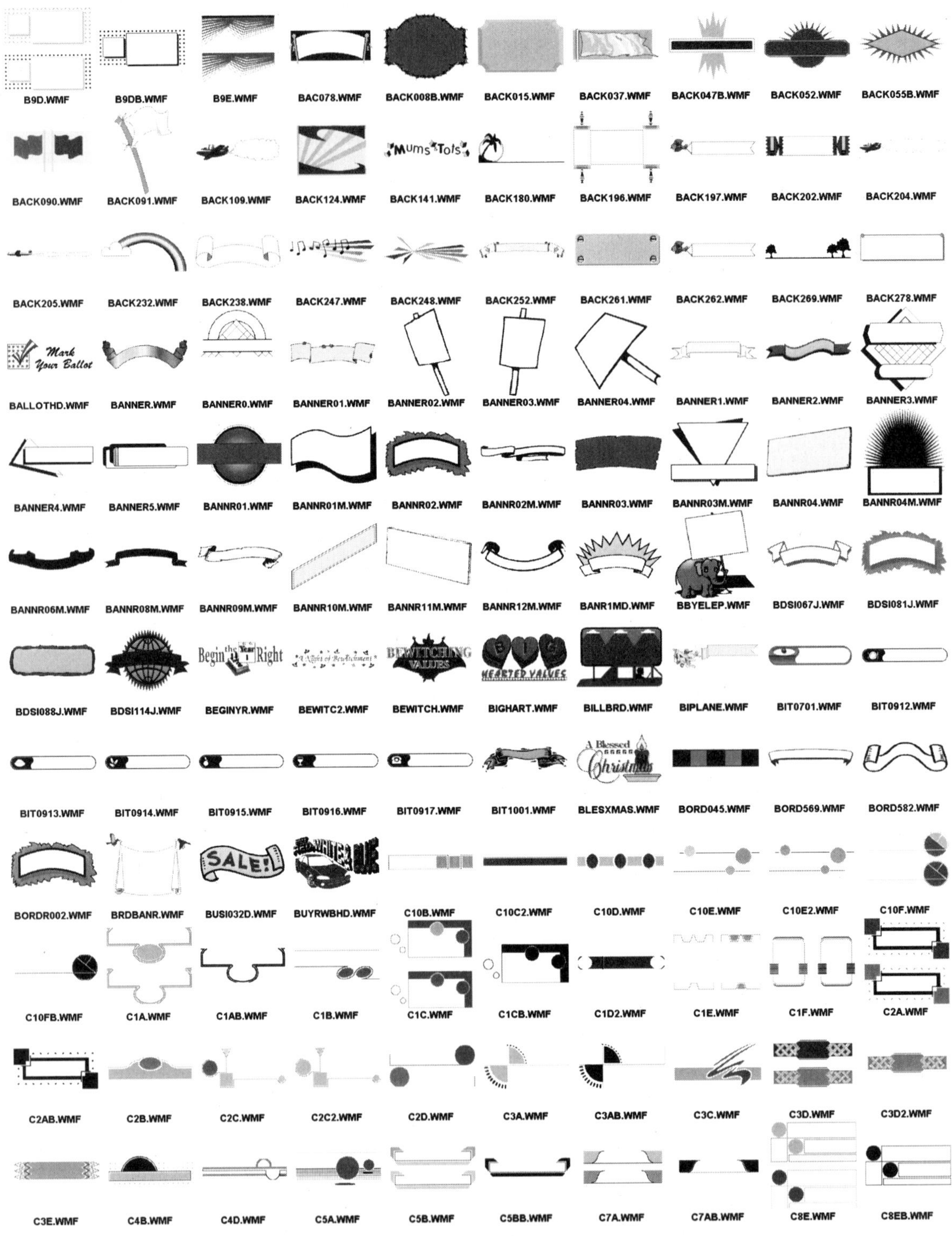
B9D.WMF
B9DB.WMF
B9E.WMF
BAC078.WMF
BACK008B.WMF
BACK015.WMF
BACK037.WMF
BACK047B.WMF
BACK052.WMF
BACK055B.WMF
BACK090.WMF
BACK091.WMF
BACK109.WMF
BACK124.WMF
BACK141.WMF
BACK180.WMF
BACK196.WMF
BACK197.WMF
BACK202.WMF
BACK204.WMF
BACK205.WMF
BACK232.WMF
BACK238.WMF
BACK247.WMF
BACK248.WMF
BACK252.WMF
BACK261.WMF
BACK262.WMF
BACK269.WMF
BACK278.WMF
BALLOTHD.WMF
BANNER.WMF
BANNER0.WMF
BANNER01.WMF
BANNER02.WMF
BANNER03.WMF
BANNER04.WMF
BANNER1.WMF
BANNER2.WMF
BANNER3.WMF
BANNER4.WMF
BANNER5.WMF
BANNR01.WMF
BANNR01M.WMF
BANNR02.WMF
BANNR02M.WMF
BANNR03.WMF
BANNR03M.WMF
BANNR04.WMF
BANNR04M.WMF
BANNR06M.WMF
BANNR08M.WMF
BANNR09M.WMF
BANNR10M.WMF
BANNR11M.WMF
BANNR12M.WMF
BANR1MD.WMF
BBYELEP.WMF
BDSI067J.WMF
BDSI081J.WMF
BDSI088J.WMF
BDSI114J.WMF
BEGINYR.WMF
BEWITC2.WMF
BEWITCH.WMF
BIGHART.WMF
BILLBRD.WMF
BIPLANE.WMF
BIT0701.WMF
BIT0912.WMF
BIT0913.WMF
BIT0914.WMF
BIT0915.WMF
BIT0916.WMF
BIT0917.WMF
BIT1001.WMF
BLESXMAS.WMF
BORD045.WMF
BORD569.WMF
BORD582.WMF
BORDR002.WMF
BRDBANR.WMF
BUSI032D.WMF
BUYRWBHD.WMF
C10B.WMF
C10C2.WMF
C10D.WMF
C10E.WMF
C10E2.WMF
C10F.WMF
C10FB.WMF
C1A.WMF
C1AB.WMF
C1B.WMF
C1C.WMF
C1CB.WMF
C1D2.WMF
C1E.WMF
C1F.WMF
C2A.WMF
C2AB.WMF
C2B.WMF
C2C.WMF
C2C2.WMF
C2D.WMF
C3A.WMF
C3AB.WMF
C3C.WMF
C3D.WMF
C3D2.WMF
C3E.WMF
C4B.WMF
C4D.WMF
C5A.WMF
C5B.WMF
C5BB.WMF
C7A.WMF
C7AB.WMF
C8E.WMF
C8EB.WMF

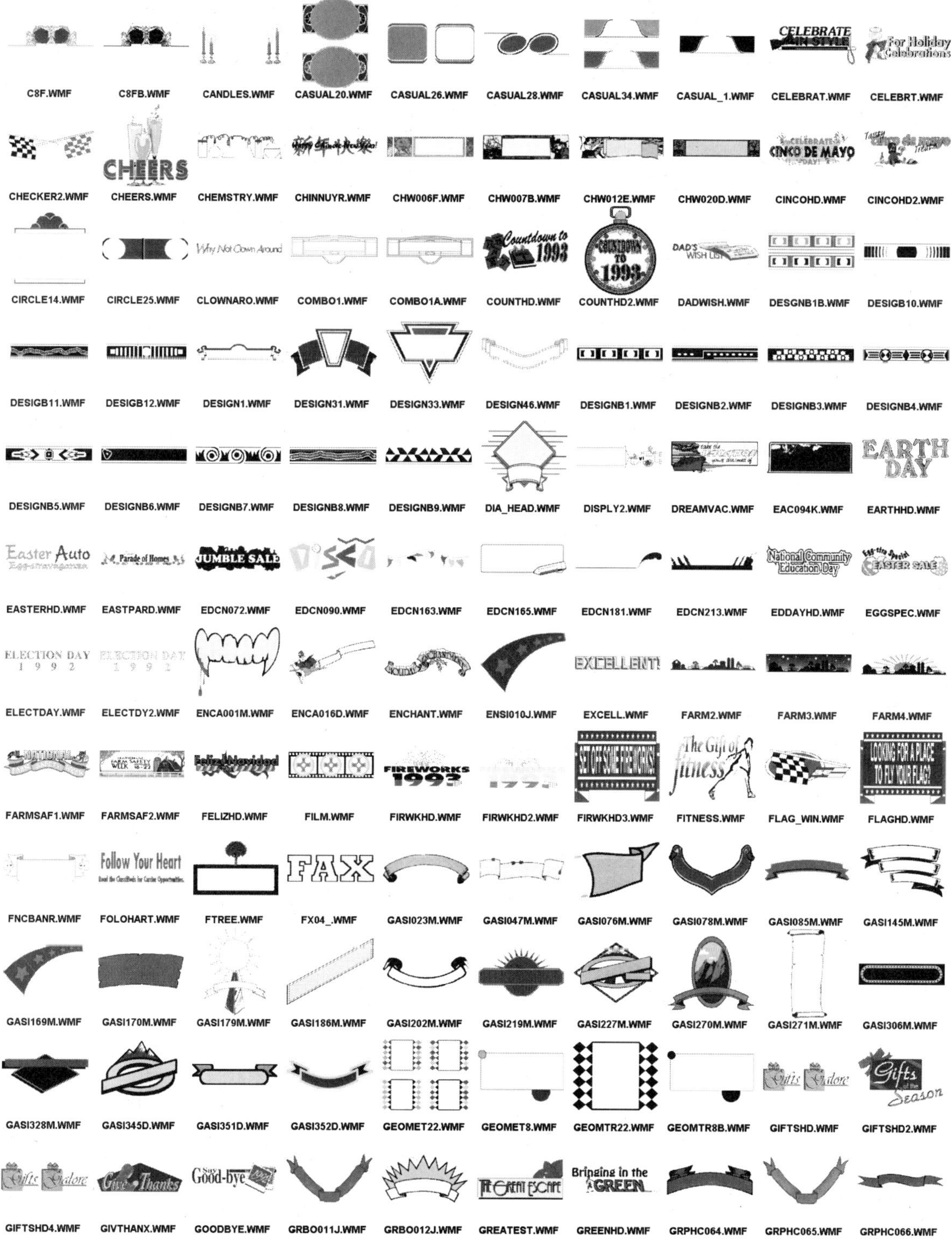

C8F.WMF C8FB.WMF CANDLES.WMF CASUAL20.WMF CASUAL26.WMF CASUAL28.WMF CASUAL34.WMF CASUAL_1.WMF CELEBRAT.WMF CELEBRT.WMF

CHECKER2.WMF CHEERS.WMF CHEMSTRY.WMF CHINNUYR.WMF CHW006F.WMF CHW007B.WMF CHW012E.WMF CHW020D.WMF CINCOHD.WMF CINCOHD2.WMF

CIRCLE14.WMF CIRCLE25.WMF CLOWNARO.WMF COMBO1.WMF COMBO1A.WMF COUNTHD.WMF COUNTHD2.WMF DADWISH.WMF DESGNB1B.WMF DESIGB10.WMF

DESIGB11.WMF DESIGB12.WMF DESIGN1.WMF DESIGN31.WMF DESIGN33.WMF DESIGN46.WMF DESIGNB1.WMF DESIGNB2.WMF DESIGNB3.WMF DESIGNB4.WMF

DESIGNB5.WMF DESIGNB6.WMF DESIGNB7.WMF DESIGNB8.WMF DESIGNB9.WMF DIA_HEAD.WMF DISPLY2.WMF DREAMVAC.WMF EAC094K.WMF EARTHHD.WMF

EASTERHD.WMF EASTPARD.WMF EDCN072.WMF EDCN090.WMF EDCN163.WMF EDCN165.WMF EDCN181.WMF EDCN213.WMF EDDAYHD.WMF EGGSPEC.WMF

ELECTDAY.WMF ELECTDY2.WMF ENCA001M.WMF ENCA016D.WMF ENCHANT.WMF ENSI010J.WMF EXCELL.WMF FARM2.WMF FARM3.WMF FARM4.WMF

FARMSAF1.WMF FARMSAF2.WMF FELIZHD.WMF FILM.WMF FIRWKHD.WMF FIRWKHD2.WMF FIRWKHD3.WMF FITNESS.WMF FLAG_WIN.WMF FLAGHD.WMF

FNCBANR.WMF FOLOHART.WMF FTREE.WMF FX04_.WMF GASI023M.WMF GASI047M.WMF GASI076M.WMF GASI078M.WMF GASI085M.WMF GASI145M.WMF

GASI169M.WMF GASI170M.WMF GASI179M.WMF GASI186M.WMF GASI202M.WMF GASI219M.WMF GASI227M.WMF GASI270M.WMF GASI271M.WMF GASI306M.WMF

GASI328M.WMF GASI345D.WMF GASI351D.WMF GASI352D.WMF GEOMET22.WMF GEOMET8.WMF GEOMTR22.WMF GEOMTR8B.WMF GIFTSHD.WMF GIFTSHD2.WMF

GIFTSHD4.WMF GIVTHANX.WMF GOODBYE.WMF GRBO011J.WMF GRBO012J.WMF GREATEST.WMF GREENHD.WMF GRPHC064.WMF GRPHC065.WMF GRPHC066.WMF

GRPHC067.WMF GRPHC068.WMF GRPHC069.WMF GRPHC070.WMF GRPHC071.WMF GRPHC072.WMF GRPHC073.WMF GRPHC074.WMF GRPHC075.WMF GRPHC076.WMF
GRRQ001J.WMF GRRW009J.WMF GRRW010J.WMF GRSI046J.WMF GRSI100J.WMF GRSI101J.WMF GRSI102J.WMF GRSI104J.WMF GRSI118J.WMF GRSI119J.WMF
GRSI122J.WMF GRSI123J.WMF GRSI130J.WMF GRSI132J.WMF HAG015C.WMF HALLOWEN.WMF HALOWEN2.WMF HANDSHAK.WMF HANDSSHA.WMF HANUKKAH.WMF
HAPPY93.WMF HAPPYNU.WMF HAPYHOLI.WMF HARTCNVR.WMF HARTTHRB.WMF HARVEST.WMF HEADING.WMF HEALTHY.WMF HEARTSHD.WMF HEROES.WMF
HOHOHOHD.WMF HOLIBLES.WMF HOLICOOK.WMF HOLIDAY.WMF HOLIDAY2.WMF HOLIDAYS.WMF HOLIDGR.WMF HOLIGRET.WMF HOLIMEM.WMF HOLISAF2.WMF
HOLISAFE.WMF HOLISPRT.WMF HOLITHNX.WMF HOLIWISH.WMF HONRVETS.WMF HPI001P.WMF HPI006B.WMF IHO013I.WMF INK_PEN.WMF INLUVHD.WMF
IRISHHD.WMF ISLAND.WMF ITSPARTY.WMF JOYBEGIN.WMF JOYEUXHD.WMF JOYHD.WMF JOYHOLI.WMF JOYOUSHD.WMF LABORDAY.WMF LABORDY2.WMF
LABORDY3.WMF LAC010A.WMF LASTMINU.WMF LETRING.WMF LIGHTHD.WMF MAKLIST.WMF MARDIGR2.WMF MARDIGRA.WMF MAYFLOWR.WMF MC39.WMF
MEMORIAL.WMF MEMRIAL2.WMF MERIXMAS.WMF MERIXMS2.WMF MERIXMS3.WMF MERIXMS4.WMF MERIXMS5.WMF MERYXMAS.WMF METALPLT.WMF MODERN32.WMF
MODERN_1.WMF MOMDAYHD.WMF MORTIS1B.WMF MORTIS3B.WMF MORTIS4B.WMF MORTISE.WMF MORTISE1.WMF MORTISE2.WMF MORTISE3.WMF MORTISE4.WMF
MORTISE5.WMF MORTISE7.WMF MORTISE8.WMF MORTSE8.WMF MRYXMAS2.WMF NATVAM13.WMF NATVEA13.WMF NEXTXMAS.WMF NOELHD.WMF NOV2HFRM.WMF
NUYEAR.WMF NUYEAR2.WMF NUYEAR3.WMF NUYEAR4.WMF NUYEARHD.WMF NUYRDEAL.WMF OKTBRFHD.WMF OLDCB.WMF OPENHOUS.WMF OPENLAB.WMF

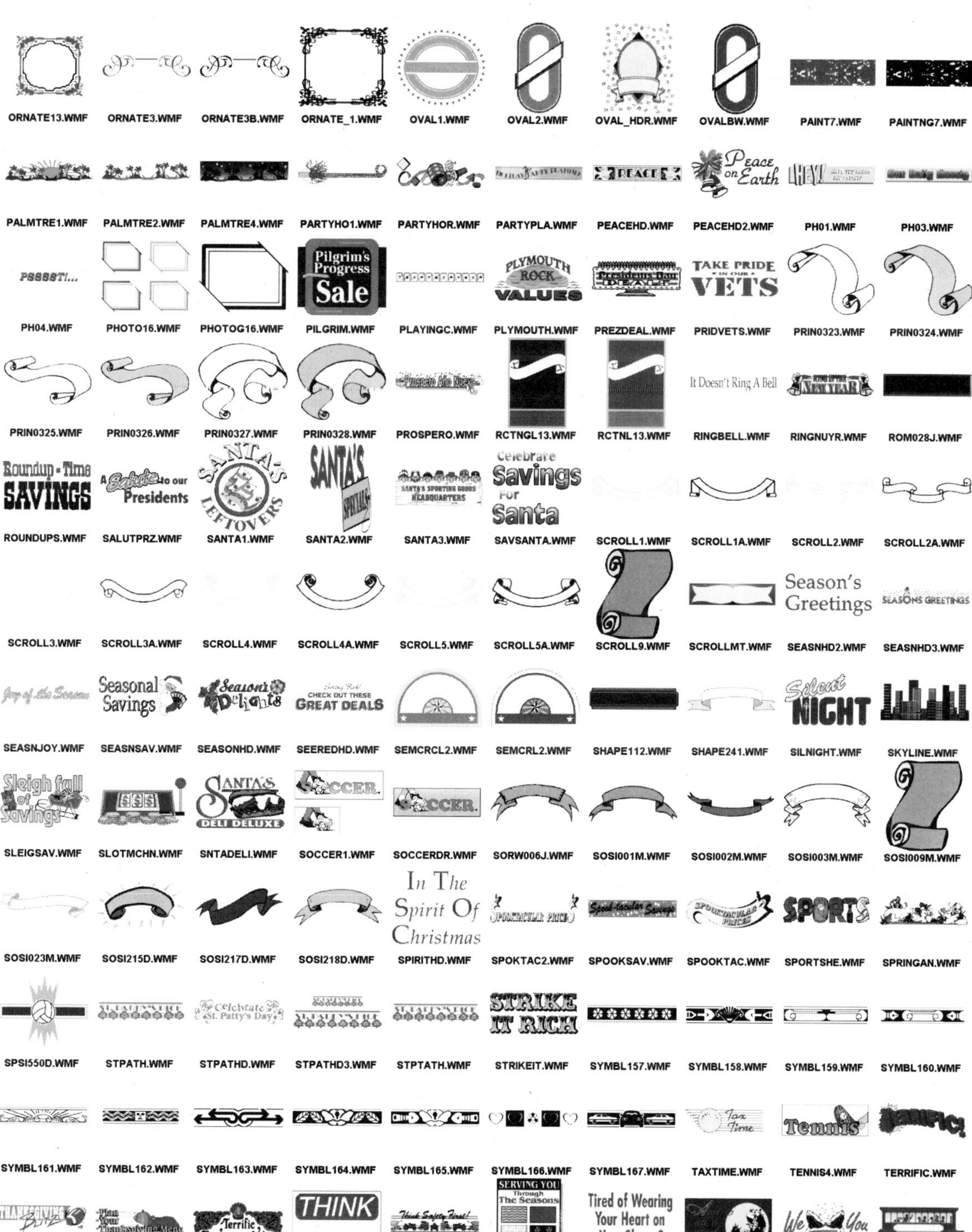

ORNATE13.WMF ORNATE3.WMF ORNATE3B.WMF ORNATE_1.WMF OVAL1.WMF OVAL2.WMF OVAL_HDR.WMF OVALBW.WMF PAINT7.WMF PAINTNG7.WMF

PALMTRE1.WMF PALMTRE2.WMF PALMTRE4.WMF PARTYHO1.WMF PARTYHOR.WMF PARTYPLA.WMF PEACEHD.WMF PEACEHD2.WMF PH01.WMF PH03.WMF

PH04.WMF PHOTO16.WMF PHOTOG16.WMF PILGRIM.WMF PLAYINGC.WMF PLYMOUTH.WMF PREZDEAL.WMF PRIDVETS.WMF PRIN0323.WMF PRIN0324.WMF

PRIN0325.WMF PRIN0326.WMF PRIN0327.WMF PRIN0328.WMF PROSPERO.WMF RCTNGL13.WMF RCTNL13.WMF RINGBELL.WMF RINGNUYR.WMF ROM028J.WMF

ROUNDUPS.WMF SALUTPRZ.WMF SANTA1.WMF SANTA2.WMF SANTA3.WMF SAVSANTA.WMF SCROLL1.WMF SCROLL1A.WMF SCROLL2.WMF SCROLL2A.WMF

SCROLL3.WMF SCROLL3A.WMF SCROLL4.WMF SCROLL4A.WMF SCROLL5.WMF SCROLL5A.WMF SCROLL9.WMF SCROLLMT.WMF SEASNHD2.WMF SEASNHD3.WMF

SEASNJOY.WMF SEASNSAV.WMF SEASONHD.WMF SEEREDHD.WMF SEMCRCL2.WMF SEMCRL2.WMF SHAPE112.WMF SHAPE241.WMF SILNIGHT.WMF SKYLINE.WMF

SLEIGSAV.WMF SLOTMCHN.WMF SNTADELI.WMF SOCCER1.WMF SOCCERDR.WMF SORW006J.WMF SOSI001M.WMF SOSI002M.WMF SOSI003M.WMF SOSI009M.WMF

SOSI023M.WMF SOSI215D.WMF SOSI217D.WMF SOSI218D.WMF SPIRITHD.WMF SPOKTAC2.WMF SPOOKSAV.WMF SPOOKTAC.WMF SPORTSHE.WMF SPRINGAN.WMF

SPSI550D.WMF STPATH.WMF STPATHD.WMF STPATHD3.WMF STPTATH.WMF STRIKEIT.WMF SYMBL157.WMF SYMBL158.WMF SYMBL159.WMF SYMBL160.WMF

SYMBL161.WMF SYMBL162.WMF SYMBL163.WMF SYMBL164.WMF SYMBL165.WMF SYMBL166.WMF SYMBL167.WMF TAXTIME.WMF TENNIS4.WMF TERRIFIC.WMF

THANKS.WMF THANKS3.WMF THANKS4.WMF THINK.WMF THINKSAF.WMF THRUSEAS.WMF TIREDHRT.WMF TOALLHD.WMF TOASTU.WMF TRAINCAR.WMF

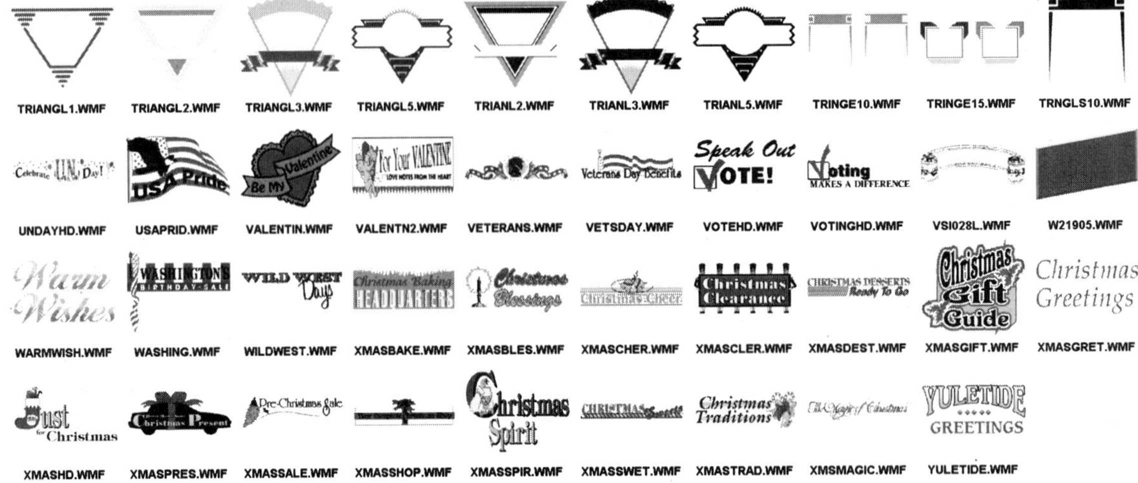

TRIANGL1.WMF TRIANGL2.WMF TRIANGL3.WMF TRIANGL5.WMF TRIANL2.WMF TRIANL3.WMF TRIANL5.WMF TRINGE10.WMF TRINGE15.WMF TRNGLS10.WMF

UNDAYHD.WMF USAPRID.WMF VALENTIN.WMF VALENTN2.WMF VETERANS.WMF VETSDAY.WMF VOTEHD.WMF VOTINGHD.WMF VSI028L.WMF W21905.WMF

WARMWISH.WMF WASHING.WMF WILDWEST.WMF XMASBAKE.WMF XMASBLES.WMF XMASCHER.WMF XMASCLER.WMF XMASDEST.WMF XMASGIFT.WMF XMASGRET.WMF

XMASHD.WMF XMASPRES.WMF XMASSALE.WMF XMASSHOP.WMF XMASSPIR.WMF XMASSWET.WMF XMASTRAD.WMF XMSMAGIC.WMF YULETIDE.WMF

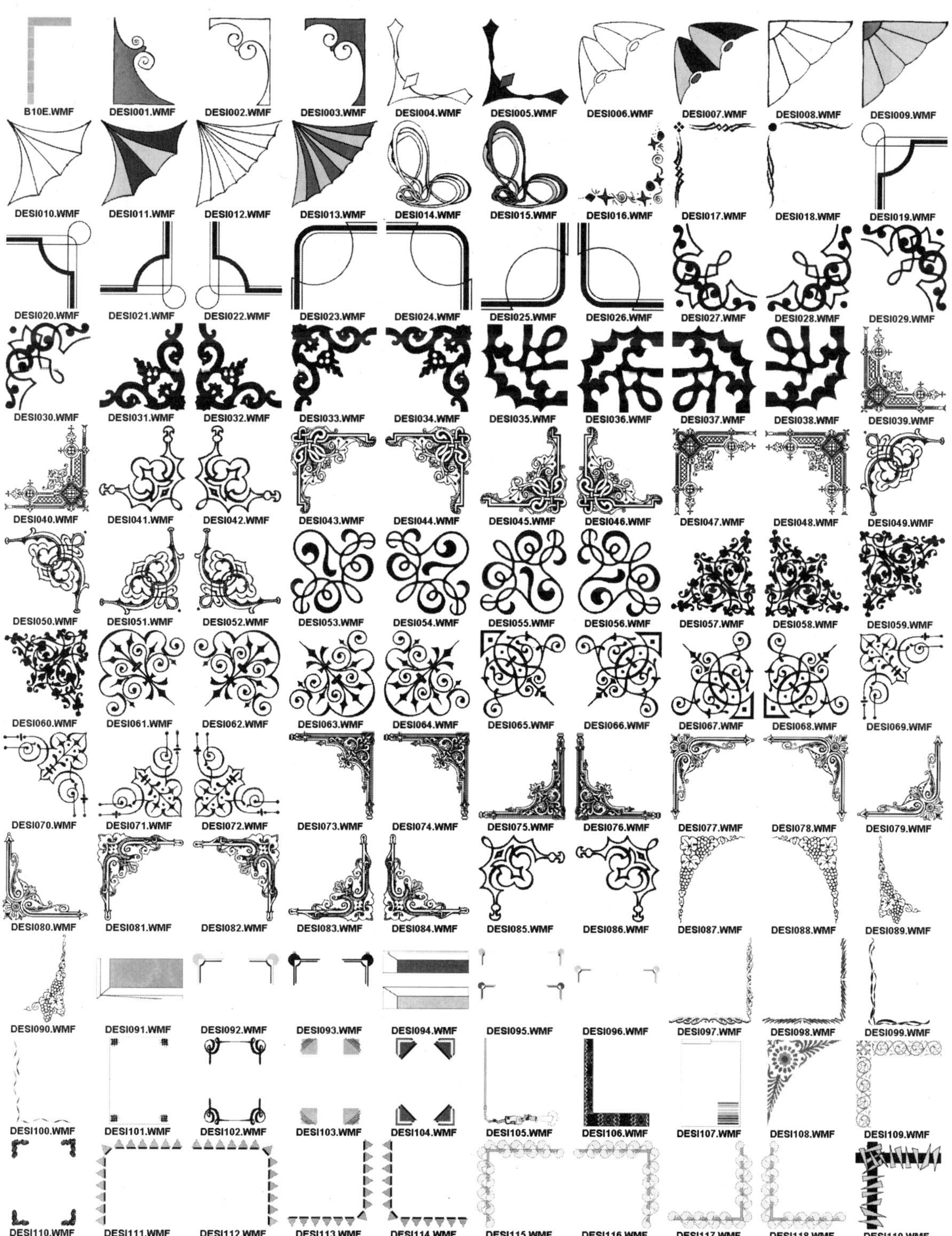
B10E.WMF DESI001.WMF DESI002.WMF DESI003.WMF DESI004.WMF DESI005.WMF DESI006.WMF DESI007.WMF DESI008.WMF DESI009.WMF
DESI010.WMF DESI011.WMF DESI012.WMF DESI013.WMF DESI014.WMF DESI015.WMF DESI016.WMF DESI017.WMF DESI018.WMF DESI019.WMF
DESI020.WMF DESI021.WMF DESI022.WMF DESI023.WMF DESI024.WMF DESI025.WMF DESI026.WMF DESI027.WMF DESI028.WMF DESI029.WMF
DESI030.WMF DESI031.WMF DESI032.WMF DESI033.WMF DESI034.WMF DESI035.WMF DESI036.WMF DESI037.WMF DESI038.WMF DESI039.WMF
DESI040.WMF DESI041.WMF DESI042.WMF DESI043.WMF DESI044.WMF DESI045.WMF DESI046.WMF DESI047.WMF DESI048.WMF DESI049.WMF
DESI050.WMF DESI051.WMF DESI052.WMF DESI053.WMF DESI054.WMF DESI055.WMF DESI056.WMF DESI057.WMF DESI058.WMF DESI059.WMF
DESI060.WMF DESI061.WMF DESI062.WMF DESI063.WMF DESI064.WMF DESI065.WMF DESI066.WMF DESI067.WMF DESI068.WMF DESI069.WMF
DESI070.WMF DESI071.WMF DESI072.WMF DESI073.WMF DESI074.WMF DESI075.WMF DESI076.WMF DESI077.WMF DESI078.WMF DESI079.WMF
DESI080.WMF DESI081.WMF DESI082.WMF DESI083.WMF DESI084.WMF DESI085.WMF DESI086.WMF DESI087.WMF DESI088.WMF DESI089.WMF
DESI090.WMF DESI091.WMF DESI092.WMF DESI093.WMF DESI094.WMF DESI095.WMF DESI096.WMF DESI097.WMF DESI098.WMF DESI099.WMF
DESI100.WMF DESI101.WMF DESI102.WMF DESI103.WMF DESI104.WMF DESI105.WMF DESI106.WMF DESI107.WMF DESI108.WMF DESI109.WMF
DESI110.WMF DESI111.WMF DESI112.WMF DESI113.WMF DESI114.WMF DESI115.WMF DESI116.WMF DESI117.WMF DESI118.WMF DESI119.WMF

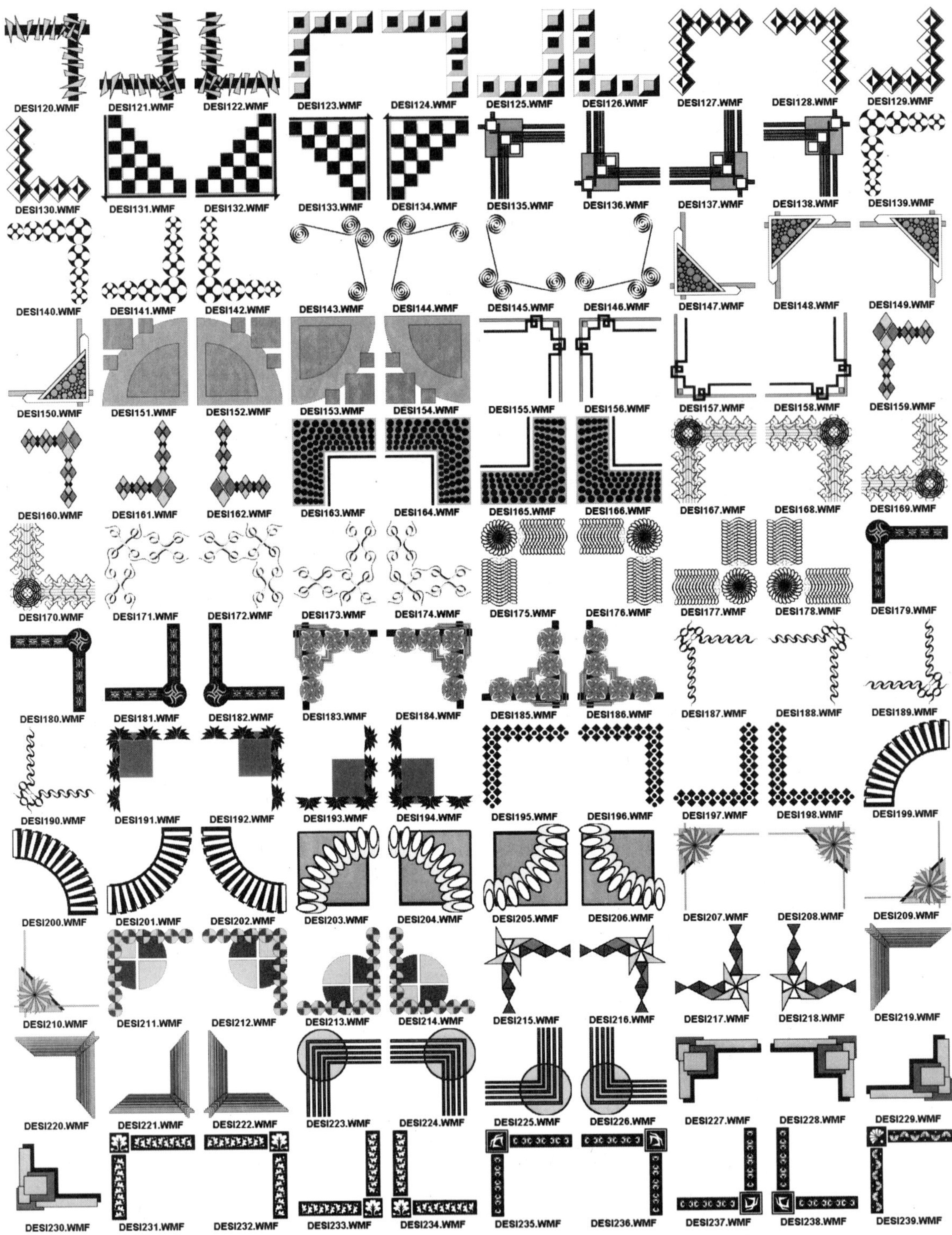
DESI120.WMF
DESI121.WMF
DESI122.WMF
DESI123.WMF
DESI124.WMF
DESI125.WMF
DESI126.WMF
DESI127.WMF
DESI128.WMF
DESI129.WMF
DESI130.WMF
DESI131.WMF
DESI132.WMF
DESI133.WMF
DESI134.WMF
DESI135.WMF
DESI136.WMF
DESI137.WMF
DESI138.WMF
DESI139.WMF
DESI140.WMF
DESI141.WMF
DESI142.WMF
DESI143.WMF
DESI144.WMF
DESI145.WMF
DESI146.WMF
DESI147.WMF
DESI148.WMF
DESI149.WMF
DESI150.WMF
DESI151.WMF
DESI152.WMF
DESI153.WMF
DESI154.WMF
DESI155.WMF
DESI156.WMF
DESI157.WMF
DESI158.WMF
DESI159.WMF
DESI160.WMF
DESI161.WMF
DESI162.WMF
DESI163.WMF
DESI164.WMF
DESI165.WMF
DESI166.WMF
DESI167.WMF
DESI168.WMF
DESI169.WMF
DESI170.WMF
DESI171.WMF
DESI172.WMF
DESI173.WMF
DESI174.WMF
DESI175.WMF
DESI176.WMF
DESI177.WMF
DESI178.WMF
DESI179.WMF
DESI180.WMF
DESI181.WMF
DESI182.WMF
DESI183.WMF
DESI184.WMF
DESI185.WMF
DESI186.WMF
DESI187.WMF
DESI188.WMF
DESI189.WMF
DESI190.WMF
DESI191.WMF
DESI192.WMF
DESI193.WMF
DESI194.WMF
DESI195.WMF
DESI196.WMF
DESI197.WMF
DESI198.WMF
DESI199.WMF
DESI200.WMF
DESI201.WMF
DESI202.WMF
DESI203.WMF
DESI204.WMF
DESI205.WMF
DESI206.WMF
DESI207.WMF
DESI208.WMF
DESI209.WMF
DESI210.WMF
DESI211.WMF
DESI212.WMF
DESI213.WMF
DESI214.WMF
DESI215.WMF
DESI216.WMF
DESI217.WMF
DESI218.WMF
DESI219.WMF
DESI220.WMF
DESI221.WMF
DESI222.WMF
DESI223.WMF
DESI224.WMF
DESI225.WMF
DESI226.WMF
DESI227.WMF
DESI228.WMF
DESI229.WMF
DESI230.WMF
DESI231.WMF
DESI232.WMF
DESI233.WMF
DESI234.WMF
DESI235.WMF
DESI236.WMF
DESI237.WMF
DESI238.WMF
DESI239.WMF

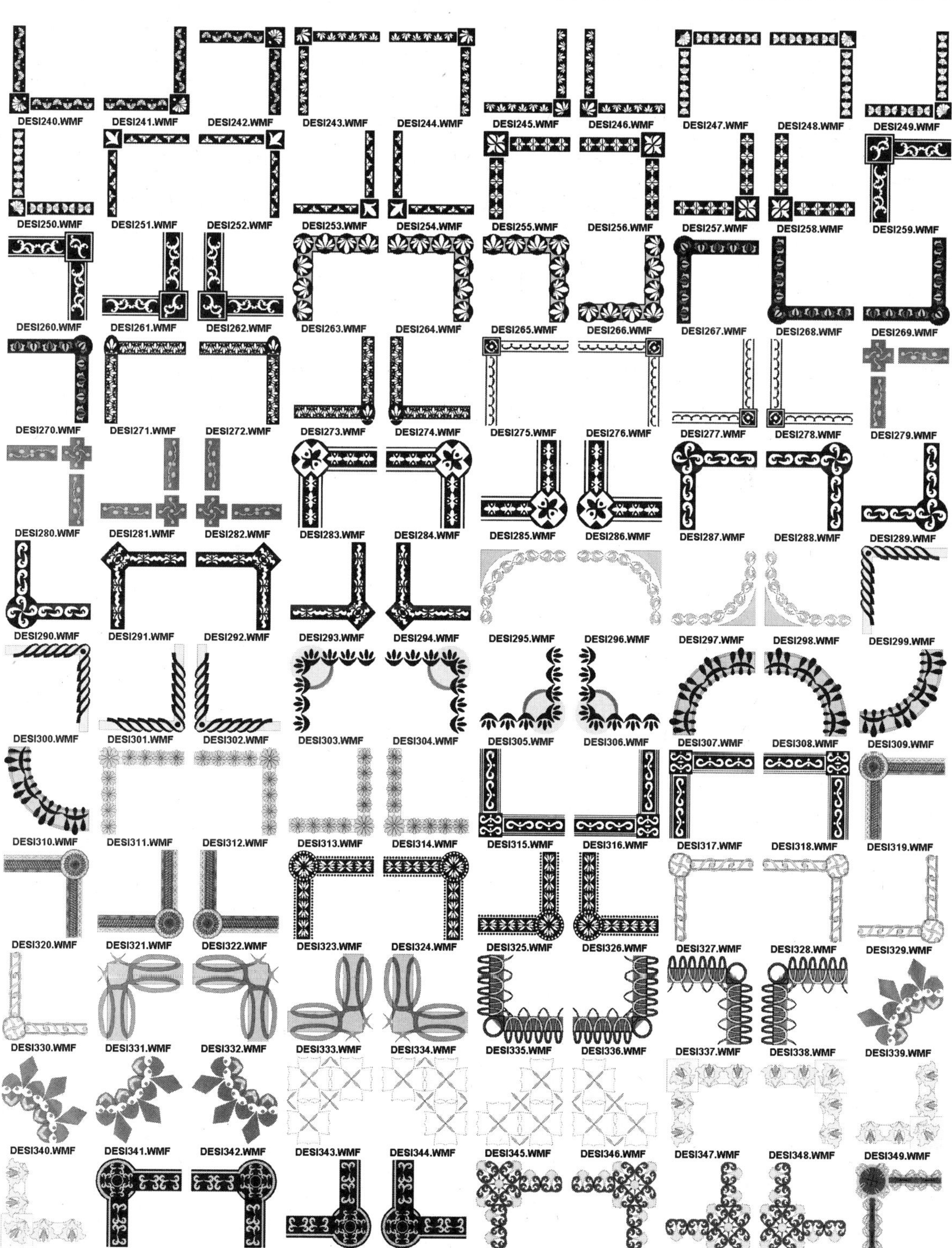
DESI240.WMF
DESI241.WMF
DESI242.WMF
DESI243.WMF
DESI244.WMF
DESI245.WMF
DESI246.WMF
DESI247.WMF
DESI248.WMF
DESI249.WMF
DESI250.WMF
DESI251.WMF
DESI252.WMF
DESI253.WMF
DESI254.WMF
DESI255.WMF
DESI256.WMF
DESI257.WMF
DESI258.WMF
DESI259.WMF
DESI260.WMF
DESI261.WMF
DESI262.WMF
DESI263.WMF
DESI264.WMF
DESI265.WMF
DESI266.WMF
DESI267.WMF
DESI268.WMF
DESI269.WMF
DESI270.WMF
DESI271.WMF
DESI272.WMF
DESI273.WMF
DESI274.WMF
DESI275.WMF
DESI276.WMF
DESI277.WMF
DESI278.WMF
DESI279.WMF
DESI280.WMF
DESI281.WMF
DESI282.WMF
DESI283.WMF
DESI284.WMF
DESI285.WMF
DESI286.WMF
DESI287.WMF
DESI288.WMF
DESI289.WMF
DESI290.WMF
DESI291.WMF
DESI292.WMF
DESI293.WMF
DESI294.WMF
DESI295.WMF
DESI296.WMF
DESI297.WMF
DESI298.WMF
DESI299.WMF
DESI300.WMF
DESI301.WMF
DESI302.WMF
DESI303.WMF
DESI304.WMF
DESI305.WMF
DESI306.WMF
DESI307.WMF
DESI308.WMF
DESI309.WMF
DESI310.WMF
DESI311.WMF
DESI312.WMF
DESI313.WMF
DESI314.WMF
DESI315.WMF
DESI316.WMF
DESI317.WMF
DESI318.WMF
DESI319.WMF
DESI320.WMF
DESI321.WMF
DESI322.WMF
DESI323.WMF
DESI324.WMF
DESI325.WMF
DESI326.WMF
DESI327.WMF
DESI328.WMF
DESI329.WMF
DESI330.WMF
DESI331.WMF
DESI332.WMF
DESI333.WMF
DESI334.WMF
DESI335.WMF
DESI336.WMF
DESI337.WMF
DESI338.WMF
DESI339.WMF
DESI340.WMF
DESI341.WMF
DESI342.WMF
DESI343.WMF
DESI344.WMF
DESI345.WMF
DESI346.WMF
DESI347.WMF
DESI348.WMF
DESI349.WMF
DESI350.WMF
DESI351.WMF
DESI352.WMF
DESI353.WMF
DESI354.WMF
DESI355.WMF
DESI356.WMF
DESI357.WMF
DESI358.WMF
DESI359.WMF

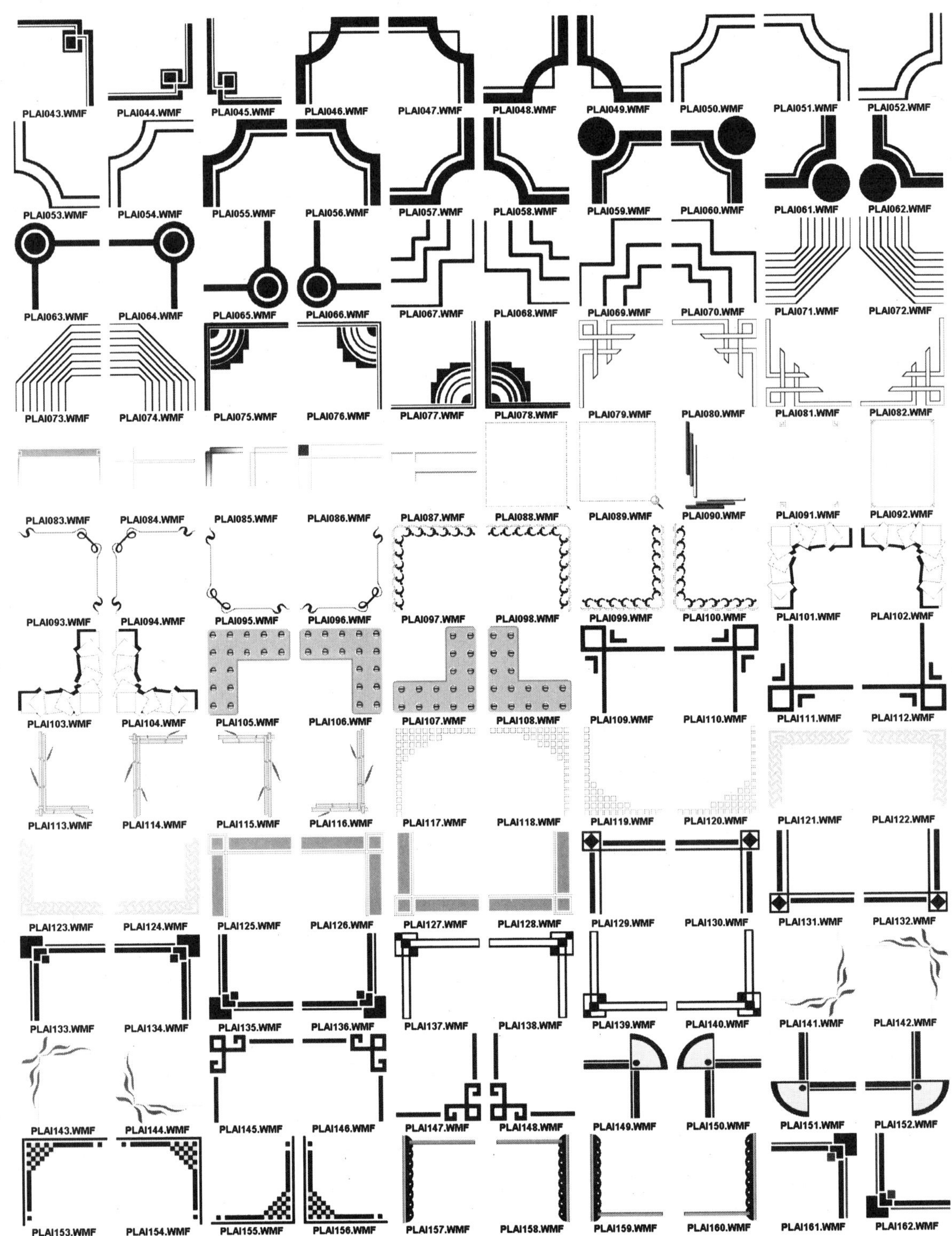
PLAI043.WMF
PLAI044.WMF
PLAI045.WMF
PLAI046.WMF
PLAI047.WMF
PLAI048.WMF
PLAI049.WMF
PLAI050.WMF
PLAI051.WMF
PLAI052.WMF
PLAI053.WMF
PLAI054.WMF
PLAI055.WMF
PLAI056.WMF
PLAI057.WMF
PLAI058.WMF
PLAI059.WMF
PLAI060.WMF
PLAI061.WMF
PLAI062.WMF
PLAI063.WMF
PLAI064.WMF
PLAI065.WMF
PLAI066.WMF
PLAI067.WMF
PLAI068.WMF
PLAI069.WMF
PLAI070.WMF
PLAI071.WMF
PLAI072.WMF
PLAI073.WMF
PLAI074.WMF
PLAI075.WMF
PLAI076.WMF
PLAI077.WMF
PLAI078.WMF
PLAI079.WMF
PLAI080.WMF
PLAI081.WMF
PLAI082.WMF
PLAI083.WMF
PLAI084.WMF
PLAI085.WMF
PLAI086.WMF
PLAI087.WMF
PLAI088.WMF
PLAI089.WMF
PLAI090.WMF
PLAI091.WMF
PLAI092.WMF
PLAI093.WMF
PLAI094.WMF
PLAI095.WMF
PLAI096.WMF
PLAI097.WMF
PLAI098.WMF
PLAI099.WMF
PLAI100.WMF
PLAI101.WMF
PLAI102.WMF
PLAI103.WMF
PLAI104.WMF
PLAI105.WMF
PLAI106.WMF
PLAI107.WMF
PLAI108.WMF
PLAI109.WMF
PLAI110.WMF
PLAI111.WMF
PLAI112.WMF
PLAI113.WMF
PLAI114.WMF
PLAI115.WMF
PLAI116.WMF
PLAI117.WMF
PLAI118.WMF
PLAI119.WMF
PLAI120.WMF
PLAI121.WMF
PLAI122.WMF
PLAI123.WMF
PLAI124.WMF
PLAI125.WMF
PLAI126.WMF
PLAI127.WMF
PLAI128.WMF
PLAI129.WMF
PLAI130.WMF
PLAI131.WMF
PLAI132.WMF
PLAI133.WMF
PLAI134.WMF
PLAI135.WMF
PLAI136.WMF
PLAI137.WMF
PLAI138.WMF
PLAI139.WMF
PLAI140.WMF
PLAI141.WMF
PLAI142.WMF
PLAI143.WMF
PLAI144.WMF
PLAI145.WMF
PLAI146.WMF
PLAI147.WMF
PLAI148.WMF
PLAI149.WMF
PLAI150.WMF
PLAI151.WMF
PLAI152.WMF
PLAI153.WMF
PLAI154.WMF
PLAI155.WMF
PLAI156.WMF
PLAI157.WMF
PLAI158.WMF
PLAI159.WMF
PLAI160.WMF
PLAI161.WMF
PLAI162.WMF

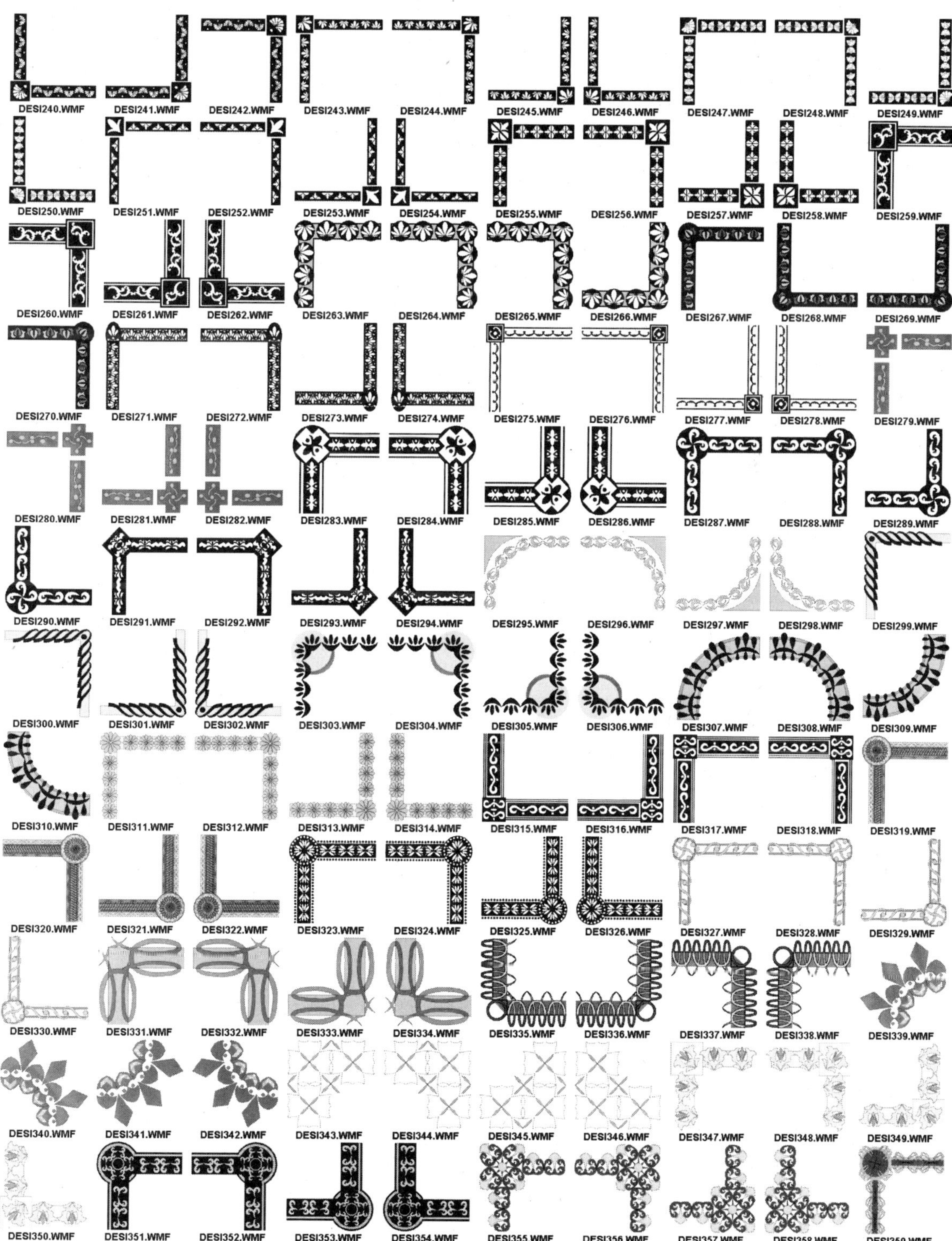
DESI240.WMF
DESI241.WMF
DESI242.WMF
DESI243.WMF
DESI244.WMF
DESI245.WMF
DESI246.WMF
DESI247.WMF
DESI248.WMF
DESI249.WMF
DESI250.WMF
DESI251.WMF
DESI252.WMF
DESI253.WMF
DESI254.WMF
DESI255.WMF
DESI256.WMF
DESI257.WMF
DESI258.WMF
DESI259.WMF
DESI260.WMF
DESI261.WMF
DESI262.WMF
DESI263.WMF
DESI264.WMF
DESI265.WMF
DESI266.WMF
DESI267.WMF
DESI268.WMF
DESI269.WMF
DESI270.WMF
DESI271.WMF
DESI272.WMF
DESI273.WMF
DESI274.WMF
DESI275.WMF
DESI276.WMF
DESI277.WMF
DESI278.WMF
DESI279.WMF
DESI280.WMF
DESI281.WMF
DESI282.WMF
DESI283.WMF
DESI284.WMF
DESI285.WMF
DESI286.WMF
DESI287.WMF
DESI288.WMF
DESI289.WMF
DESI290.WMF
DESI291.WMF
DESI292.WMF
DESI293.WMF
DESI294.WMF
DESI295.WMF
DESI296.WMF
DESI297.WMF
DESI298.WMF
DESI299.WMF
DESI300.WMF
DESI301.WMF
DESI302.WMF
DESI303.WMF
DESI304.WMF
DESI305.WMF
DESI306.WMF
DESI307.WMF
DESI308.WMF
DESI309.WMF
DESI310.WMF
DESI311.WMF
DESI312.WMF
DESI313.WMF
DESI314.WMF
DESI315.WMF
DESI316.WMF
DESI317.WMF
DESI318.WMF
DESI319.WMF
DESI320.WMF
DESI321.WMF
DESI322.WMF
DESI323.WMF
DESI324.WMF
DESI325.WMF
DESI326.WMF
DESI327.WMF
DESI328.WMF
DESI329.WMF
DESI330.WMF
DESI331.WMF
DESI332.WMF
DESI333.WMF
DESI334.WMF
DESI335.WMF
DESI336.WMF
DESI337.WMF
DESI338.WMF
DESI339.WMF
DESI340.WMF
DESI341.WMF
DESI342.WMF
DESI343.WMF
DESI344.WMF
DESI345.WMF
DESI346.WMF
DESI347.WMF
DESI348.WMF
DESI349.WMF
DESI350.WMF
DESI351.WMF
DESI352.WMF
DESI353.WMF
DESI354.WMF
DESI355.WMF
DESI356.WMF
DESI357.WMF
DESI358.WMF
DESI359.WMF

DESI360.WMF DESI361.WMF DESI362.WMF DESI363.WMF DESI364.WMF DESI365.WMF DESI366.WMF DESI367.WMF DESI368.WMF DESI369.WMF
DESI370.WMF DESI371.WMF DESI372.WMF DESI373.WMF DESI374.WMF DESI375.WMF DESI376.WMF DESI377.WMF DESI378.WMF DESI379.WMF
DESI380.WMF DESI381.WMF DESI382.WMF DESI383.WMF DESI384.WMF DESI385.WMF DESI386.WMF DESI387.WMF DESI388.WMF DESI389.WMF
DESI390.WMF DESI391.WMF DESI392.WMF DESI393.WMF DESI394.WMF DESI395.WMF DESI396.WMF DESI397.WMF DESI398.WMF DESI399.WMF
DESI400.WMF DESI401.WMF DESI402.WMF DESI403.WMF DESI404.WMF DESI405.WMF DESI406.WMF DESI407.WMF DESI408.WMF DESI409.WMF
DESI410.WMF DESI411.WMF DESI412.WMF DESI413.WMF DESI414.WMF DESI415.WMF DESI416.WMF DESI417.WMF DESI418.WMF DESI419.WMF
DESI420.WMF DESI421.WMF DESI422.WMF DESI423.WMF DESI424.WMF DESI425.WMF DESI426.WMF DESI427.WMF DESI428.WMF DESI429.WMF
DESI430.WMF DESI431.WMF DESI432.WMF DESI433.WMF DESI434.WMF DESI435.WMF DESI436.WMF DESI437.WMF DESI438.WMF DESI439.WMF
DESI440.WMF DESI441.WMF DESI442.WMF DESI443.WMF DESI444.WMF DESI445.WMF DESI446.WMF DESI447.WMF DESI448.WMF DESI449.WMF
DESI450.WMF DESI451.WMF DESI452.WMF DESI453.WMF DESI454.WMF DESI455.WMF DESI456.WMF DESI457.WMF DESI458.WMF DESI459.WMF
DESI460.WMF DESI461.WMF DESI462.WMF DESI463.WMF DESI464.WMF DESI465.WMF DESI466.WMF DESI467.WMF DESI468.WMF DESI469.WMF
DESI470.WMF DESI471.WMF DESI472.WMF DESI473.WMF DESI474.WMF DESI475.WMF DESI476.WMF DESI477.WMF DESI478.WMF DESI479.WMF

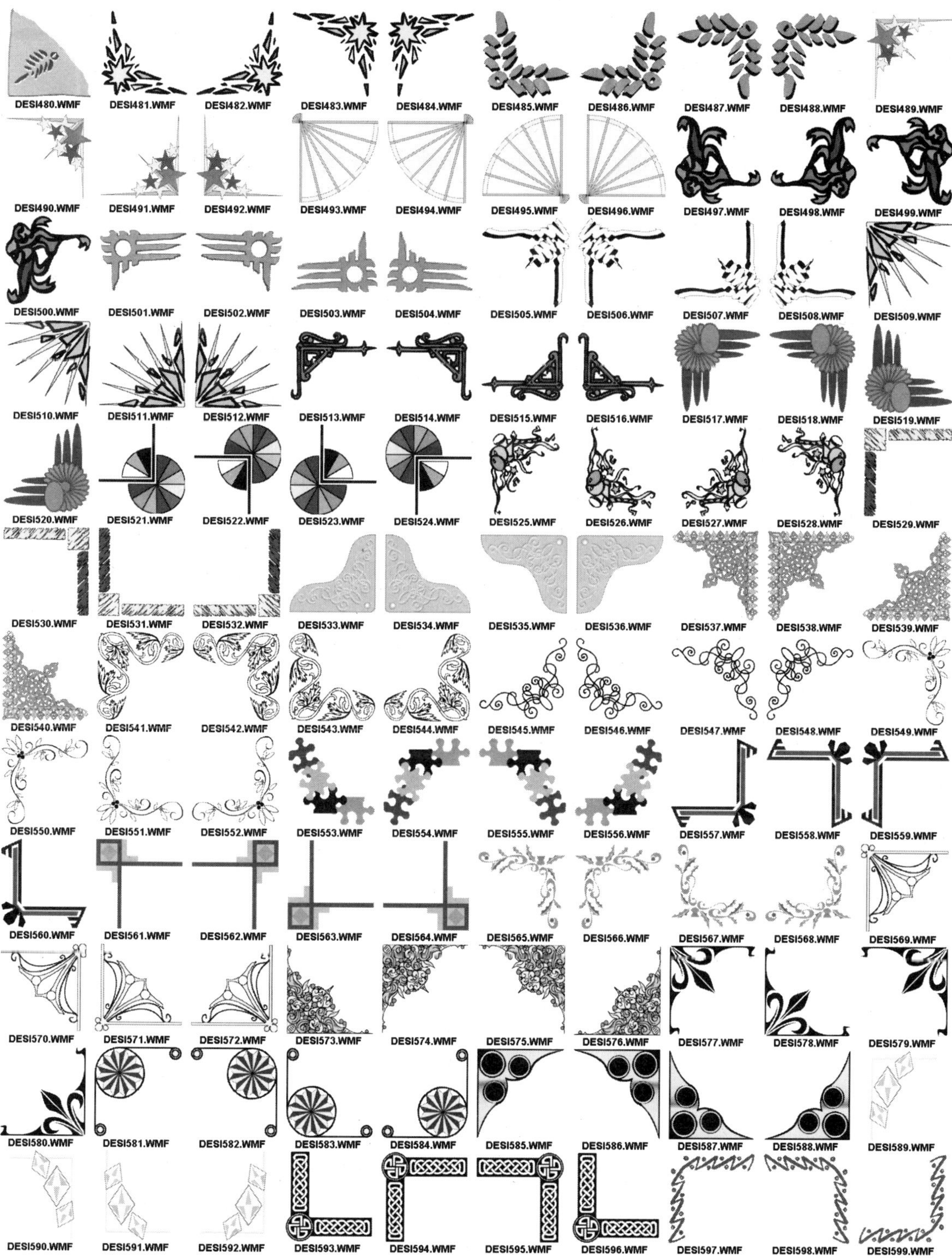
DESI480.WMF
DESI481.WMF
DESI482.WMF
DESI483.WMF
DESI484.WMF
DESI485.WMF
DESI486.WMF
DESI487.WMF
DESI488.WMF
DESI489.WMF
DESI490.WMF
DESI491.WMF
DESI492.WMF
DESI493.WMF
DESI494.WMF
DESI495.WMF
DESI496.WMF
DESI497.WMF
DESI498.WMF
DESI499.WMF
DESI500.WMF
DESI501.WMF
DESI502.WMF
DESI503.WMF
DESI504.WMF
DESI505.WMF
DESI506.WMF
DESI507.WMF
DESI508.WMF
DESI509.WMF
DESI510.WMF
DESI511.WMF
DESI512.WMF
DESI513.WMF
DESI514.WMF
DESI515.WMF
DESI516.WMF
DESI517.WMF
DESI518.WMF
DESI519.WMF
DESI520.WMF
DESI521.WMF
DESI522.WMF
DESI523.WMF
DESI524.WMF
DESI525.WMF
DESI526.WMF
DESI527.WMF
DESI528.WMF
DESI529.WMF
DESI530.WMF
DESI531.WMF
DESI532.WMF
DESI533.WMF
DESI534.WMF
DESI535.WMF
DESI536.WMF
DESI537.WMF
DESI538.WMF
DESI539.WMF
DESI540.WMF
DESI541.WMF
DESI542.WMF
DESI543.WMF
DESI544.WMF
DESI545.WMF
DESI546.WMF
DESI547.WMF
DESI548.WMF
DESI549.WMF
DESI550.WMF
DESI551.WMF
DESI552.WMF
DESI553.WMF
DESI554.WMF
DESI555.WMF
DESI556.WMF
DESI557.WMF
DESI558.WMF
DESI559.WMF
DESI560.WMF
DESI561.WMF
DESI562.WMF
DESI563.WMF
DESI564.WMF
DESI565.WMF
DESI566.WMF
DESI567.WMF
DESI568.WMF
DESI569.WMF
DESI570.WMF
DESI571.WMF
DESI572.WMF
DESI573.WMF
DESI574.WMF
DESI575.WMF
DESI576.WMF
DESI577.WMF
DESI578.WMF
DESI579.WMF
DESI580.WMF
DESI581.WMF
DESI582.WMF
DESI583.WMF
DESI584.WMF
DESI585.WMF
DESI586.WMF
DESI587.WMF
DESI588.WMF
DESI589.WMF
DESI590.WMF
DESI591.WMF
DESI592.WMF
DESI593.WMF
DESI594.WMF
DESI595.WMF
DESI596.WMF
DESI597.WMF
DESI598.WMF
DESI599.WMF

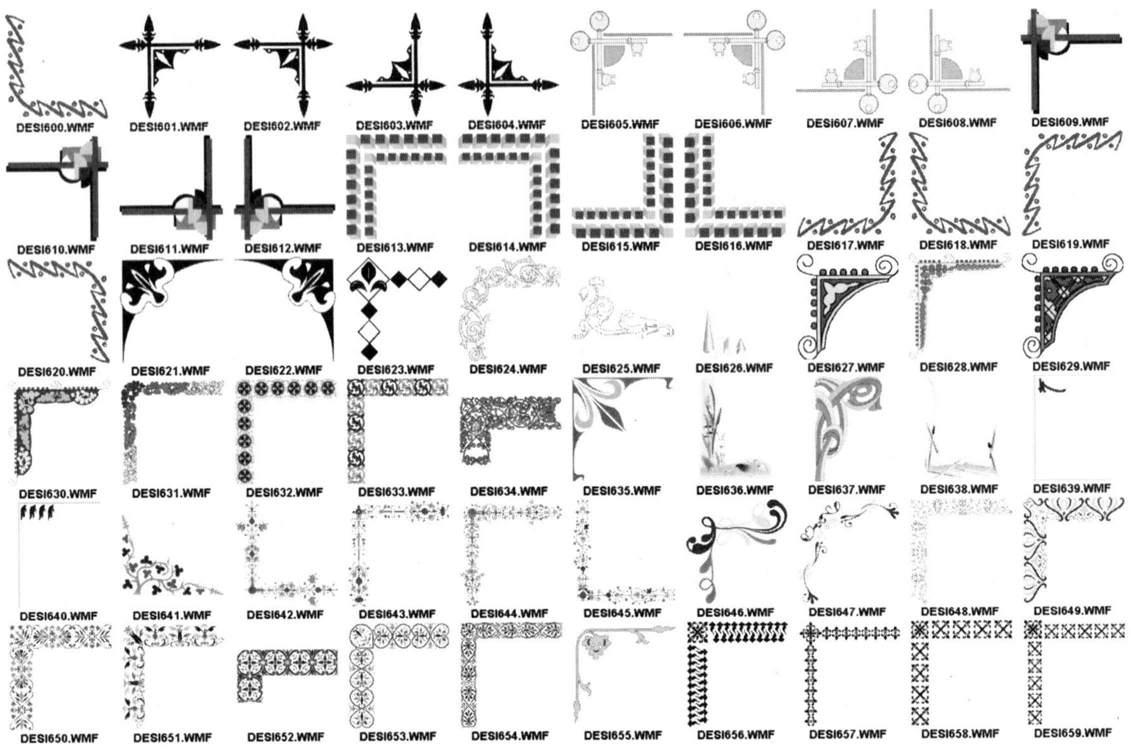
DESI600.WMF
DESI601.WMF
DESI602.WMF
DESI603.WMF
DESI604.WMF
DESI605.WMF
DESI606.WMF
DESI607.WMF
DESI608.WMF
DESI609.WMF
DESI610.WMF
DESI611.WMF
DESI612.WMF
DESI613.WMF
DESI614.WMF
DESI615.WMF
DESI616.WMF
DESI617.WMF
DESI618.WMF
DESI619.WMF
DESI620.WMF
DESI621.WMF
DESI622.WMF
DESI623.WMF
DESI624.WMF
DESI625.WMF
DESI626.WMF
DESI627.WMF
DESI628.WMF
DESI629.WMF
DESI630.WMF
DESI631.WMF
DESI632.WMF
DESI633.WMF
DESI634.WMF
DESI635.WMF
DESI636.WMF
DESI637.WMF
DESI638.WMF
DESI639.WMF
DESI640.WMF
DESI641.WMF
DESI642.WMF
DESI643.WMF
DESI644.WMF
DESI645.WMF
DESI646.WMF
DESI647.WMF
DESI648.WMF
DESI649.WMF
DESI650.WMF
DESI651.WMF
DESI652.WMF
DESI653.WMF
DESI654.WMF
DESI655.WMF
DESI656.WMF
DESI657.WMF
DESI658.WMF
DESI659.WMF

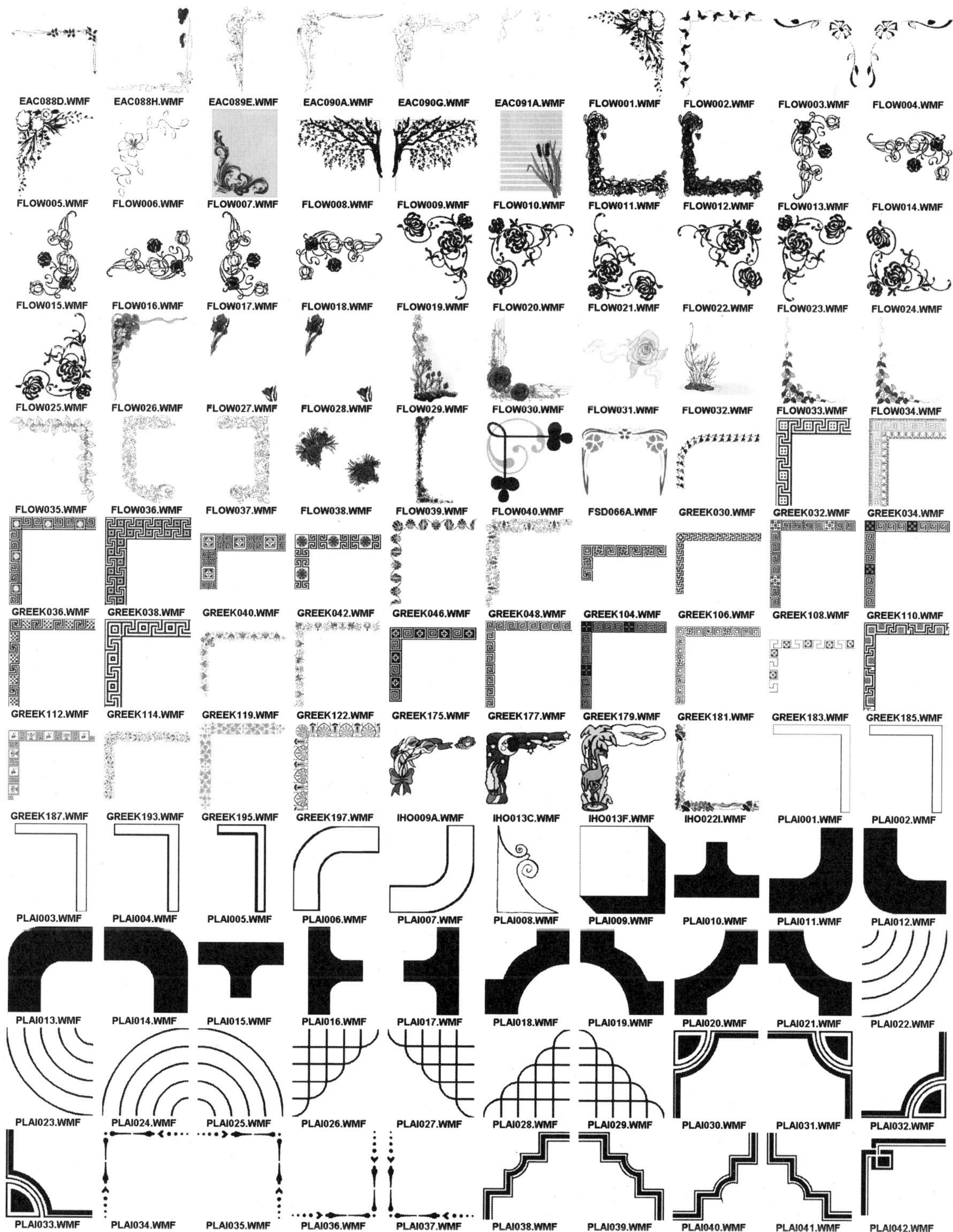
EAC088D.WMF
EAC088H.WMF
EAC089E.WMF
EAC090A.WMF
EAC090G.WMF
EAC091A.WMF
FLOW001.WMF
FLOW002.WMF
FLOW003.WMF
FLOW004.WMF
FLOW005.WMF
FLOW006.WMF
FLOW007.WMF
FLOW008.WMF
FLOW009.WMF
FLOW010.WMF
FLOW011.WMF
FLOW012.WMF
FLOW013.WMF
FLOW014.WMF
FLOW015.WMF
FLOW016.WMF
FLOW017.WMF
FLOW018.WMF
FLOW019.WMF
FLOW020.WMF
FLOW021.WMF
FLOW022.WMF
FLOW023.WMF
FLOW024.WMF
FLOW025.WMF
FLOW026.WMF
FLOW027.WMF
FLOW028.WMF
FLOW029.WMF
FLOW030.WMF
FLOW031.WMF
FLOW032.WMF
FLOW033.WMF
FLOW034.WMF
FLOW035.WMF
FLOW036.WMF
FLOW037.WMF
FLOW038.WMF
FLOW039.WMF
FLOW040.WMF
FSD066A.WMF
GREEK030.WMF
GREEK032.WMF
GREEK034.WMF
GREEK036.WMF
GREEK038.WMF
GREEK040.WMF
GREEK042.WMF
GREEK046.WMF
GREEK048.WMF
GREEK104.WMF
GREEK106.WMF
GREEK108.WMF
GREEK110.WMF
GREEK112.WMF
GREEK114.WMF
GREEK119.WMF
GREEK122.WMF
GREEK175.WMF
GREEK177.WMF
GREEK179.WMF
GREEK181.WMF
GREEK183.WMF
GREEK185.WMF
GREEK187.WMF
GREEK193.WMF
GREEK195.WMF
GREEK197.WMF
IHO009A.WMF
IHO013C.WMF
IHO013F.WMF
IHO022I.WMF
PLAI001.WMF
PLAI002.WMF
PLAI003.WMF
PLAI004.WMF
PLAI005.WMF
PLAI006.WMF
PLAI007.WMF
PLAI008.WMF
PLAI009.WMF
PLAI010.WMF
PLAI011.WMF
PLAI012.WMF
PLAI013.WMF
PLAI014.WMF
PLAI015.WMF
PLAI016.WMF
PLAI017.WMF
PLAI018.WMF
PLAI019.WMF
PLAI020.WMF
PLAI021.WMF
PLAI022.WMF
PLAI023.WMF
PLAI024.WMF
PLAI025.WMF
PLAI026.WMF
PLAI027.WMF
PLAI028.WMF
PLAI029.WMF
PLAI030.WMF
PLAI031.WMF
PLAI032.WMF
PLAI033.WMF
PLAI034.WMF
PLAI035.WMF
PLAI036.WMF
PLAI037.WMF
PLAI038.WMF
PLAI039.WMF
PLAI040.WMF
PLAI041.WMF
PLAI042.WMF

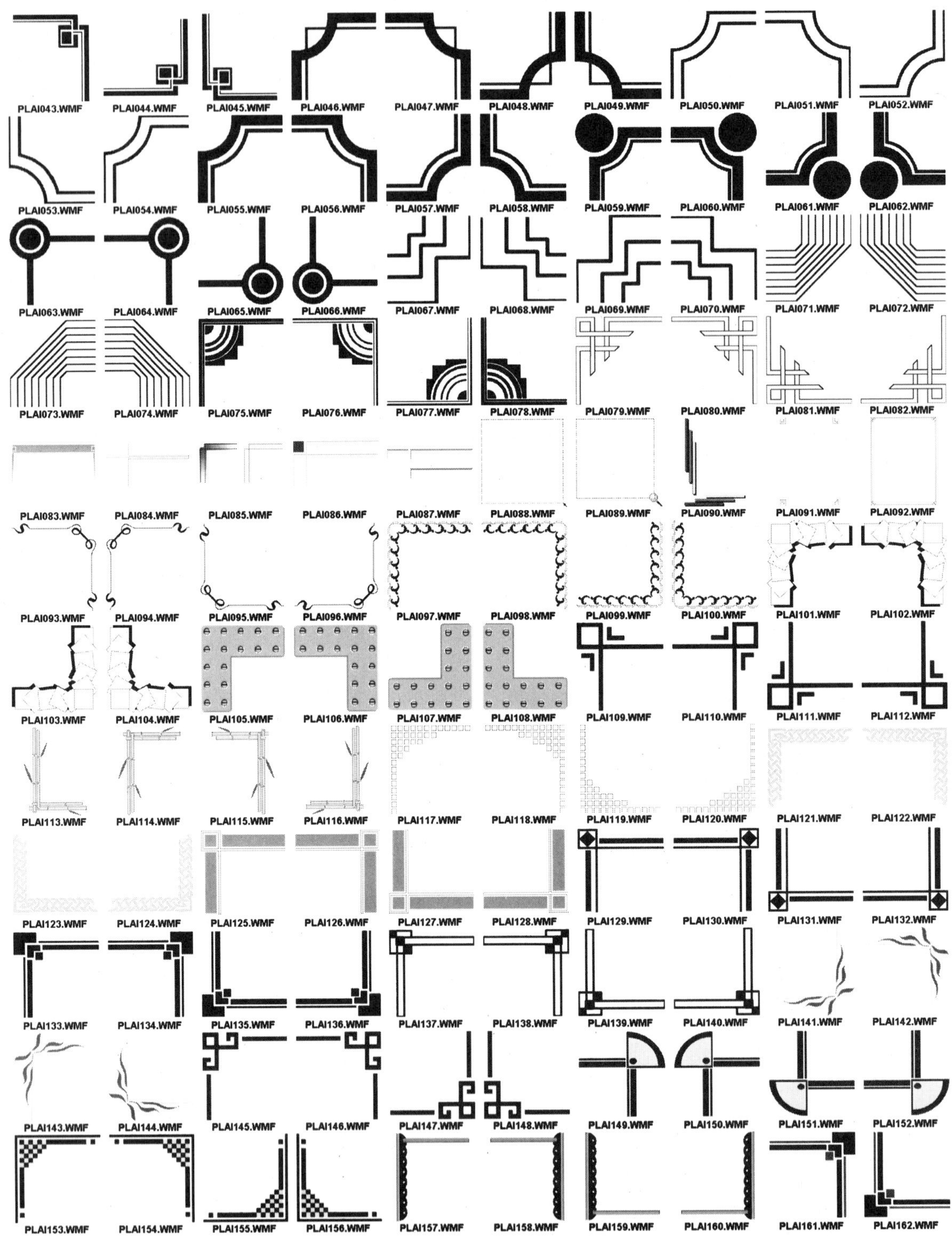
PLAI043.WMF
PLAI044.WMF
PLAI045.WMF
PLAI046.WMF
PLAI047.WMF
PLAI048.WMF
PLAI049.WMF
PLAI050.WMF
PLAI051.WMF
PLAI052.WMF
PLAI053.WMF
PLAI054.WMF
PLAI055.WMF
PLAI056.WMF
PLAI057.WMF
PLAI058.WMF
PLAI059.WMF
PLAI060.WMF
PLAI061.WMF
PLAI062.WMF
PLAI063.WMF
PLAI064.WMF
PLAI065.WMF
PLAI066.WMF
PLAI067.WMF
PLAI068.WMF
PLAI069.WMF
PLAI070.WMF
PLAI071.WMF
PLAI072.WMF
PLAI073.WMF
PLAI074.WMF
PLAI075.WMF
PLAI076.WMF
PLAI077.WMF
PLAI078.WMF
PLAI079.WMF
PLAI080.WMF
PLAI081.WMF
PLAI082.WMF
PLAI083.WMF
PLAI084.WMF
PLAI085.WMF
PLAI086.WMF
PLAI087.WMF
PLAI088.WMF
PLAI089.WMF
PLAI090.WMF
PLAI091.WMF
PLAI092.WMF
PLAI093.WMF
PLAI094.WMF
PLAI095.WMF
PLAI096.WMF
PLAI097.WMF
PLAI098.WMF
PLAI099.WMF
PLAI100.WMF
PLAI101.WMF
PLAI102.WMF
PLAI103.WMF
PLAI104.WMF
PLAI105.WMF
PLAI106.WMF
PLAI107.WMF
PLAI108.WMF
PLAI109.WMF
PLAI110.WMF
PLAI111.WMF
PLAI112.WMF
PLAI113.WMF
PLAI114.WMF
PLAI115.WMF
PLAI116.WMF
PLAI117.WMF
PLAI118.WMF
PLAI119.WMF
PLAI120.WMF
PLAI121.WMF
PLAI122.WMF
PLAI123.WMF
PLAI124.WMF
PLAI125.WMF
PLAI126.WMF
PLAI127.WMF
PLAI128.WMF
PLAI129.WMF
PLAI130.WMF
PLAI131.WMF
PLAI132.WMF
PLAI133.WMF
PLAI134.WMF
PLAI135.WMF
PLAI136.WMF
PLAI137.WMF
PLAI138.WMF
PLAI139.WMF
PLAI140.WMF
PLAI141.WMF
PLAI142.WMF
PLAI143.WMF
PLAI144.WMF
PLAI145.WMF
PLAI146.WMF
PLAI147.WMF
PLAI148.WMF
PLAI149.WMF
PLAI150.WMF
PLAI151.WMF
PLAI152.WMF
PLAI153.WMF
PLAI154.WMF
PLAI155.WMF
PLAI156.WMF
PLAI157.WMF
PLAI158.WMF
PLAI159.WMF
PLAI160.WMF
PLAI161.WMF
PLAI162.WMF

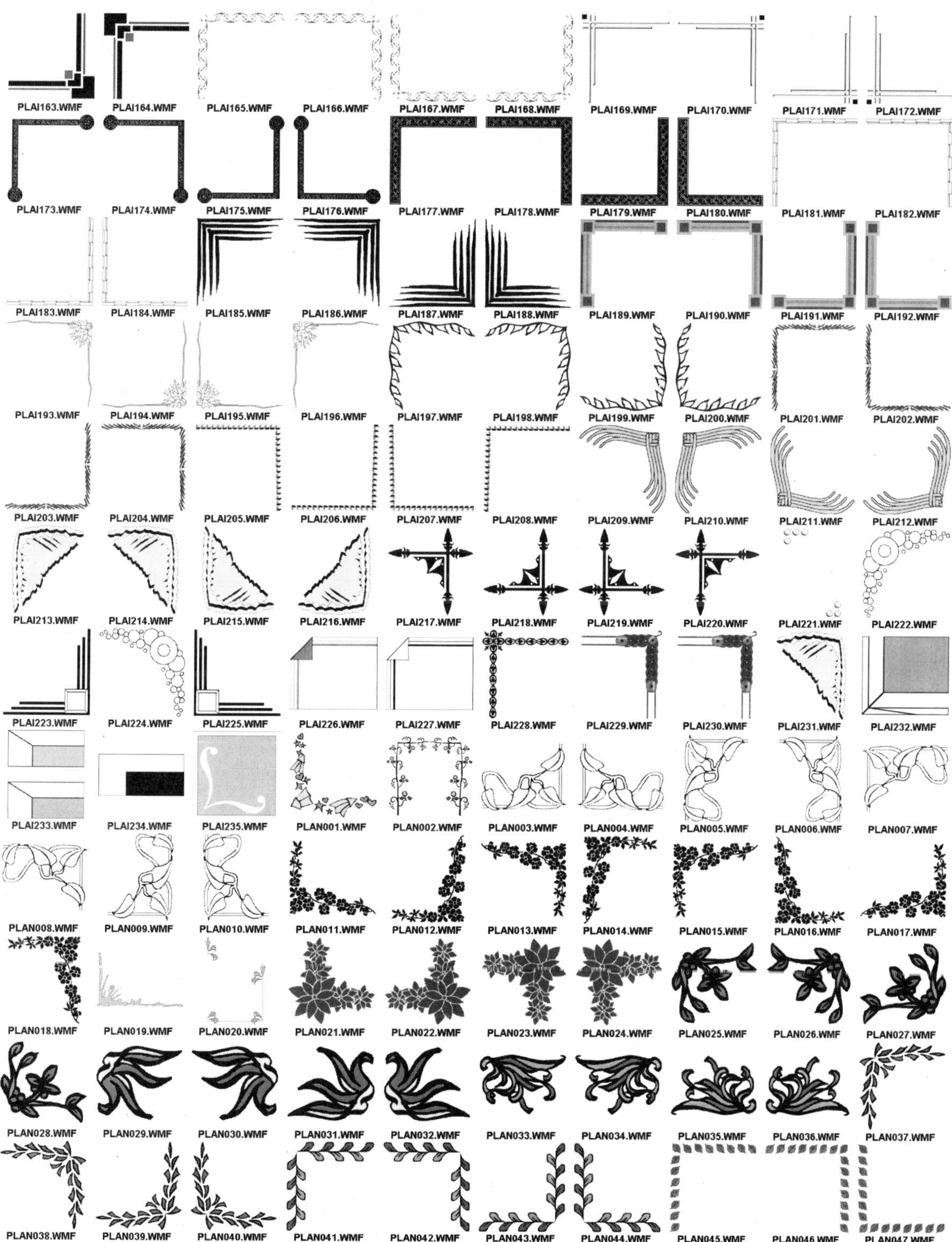
PLAI163.WMF
PLAI164.WMF
PLAI165.WMF
PLAI166.WMF
PLAI167.WMF
PLAI168.WMF
PLAI169.WMF
PLAI170.WMF
PLAI171.WMF
PLAI172.WMF
PLAI173.WMF
PLAI174.WMF
PLAI175.WMF
PLAI176.WMF
PLAI177.WMF
PLAI178.WMF
PLAI179.WMF
PLAI180.WMF
PLAI181.WMF
PLAI182.WMF
PLAI183.WMF
PLAI184.WMF
PLAI185.WMF
PLAI186.WMF
PLAI187.WMF
PLAI188.WMF
PLAI189.WMF
PLAI190.WMF
PLAI191.WMF
PLAI192.WMF
PLAI193.WMF
PLAI194.WMF
PLAI195.WMF
PLAI196.WMF
PLAI197.WMF
PLAI198.WMF
PLAI199.WMF
PLAI200.WMF
PLAI201.WMF
PLAI202.WMF
PLAI203.WMF
PLAI204.WMF
PLAI205.WMF
PLAI206.WMF
PLAI207.WMF
PLAI208.WMF
PLAI209.WMF
PLAI210.WMF
PLAI211.WMF
PLAI212.WMF
PLAI213.WMF
PLAI214.WMF
PLAI215.WMF
PLAI216.WMF
PLAI217.WMF
PLAI218.WMF
PLAI219.WMF
PLAI220.WMF
PLAI221.WMF
PLAI222.WMF
PLAI223.WMF
PLAI224.WMF
PLAI225.WMF
PLAI226.WMF
PLAI227.WMF
PLAI228.WMF
PLAI229.WMF
PLAI230.WMF
PLAI231.WMF
PLAI232.WMF
PLAI233.WMF
PLAI234.WMF
PLAI235.WMF
PLAN001.WMF
PLAN002.WMF
PLAN003.WMF
PLAN004.WMF
PLAN005.WMF
PLAN006.WMF
PLAN007.WMF
PLAN008.WMF
PLAN009.WMF
PLAN010.WMF
PLAN011.WMF
PLAN012.WMF
PLAN013.WMF
PLAN014.WMF
PLAN015.WMF
PLAN016.WMF
PLAN017.WMF
PLAN018.WMF
PLAN019.WMF
PLAN020.WMF
PLAN021.WMF
PLAN022.WMF
PLAN023.WMF
PLAN024.WMF
PLAN025.WMF
PLAN026.WMF
PLAN027.WMF
PLAN028.WMF
PLAN029.WMF
PLAN030.WMF
PLAN031.WMF
PLAN032.WMF
PLAN033.WMF
PLAN034.WMF
PLAN035.WMF
PLAN036.WMF
PLAN037.WMF
PLAN038.WMF
PLAN039.WMF
PLAN040.WMF
PLAN041.WMF
PLAN042.WMF
PLAN043.WMF
PLAN044.WMF
PLAN045.WMF
PLAN046.WMF
PLAN047.WMF

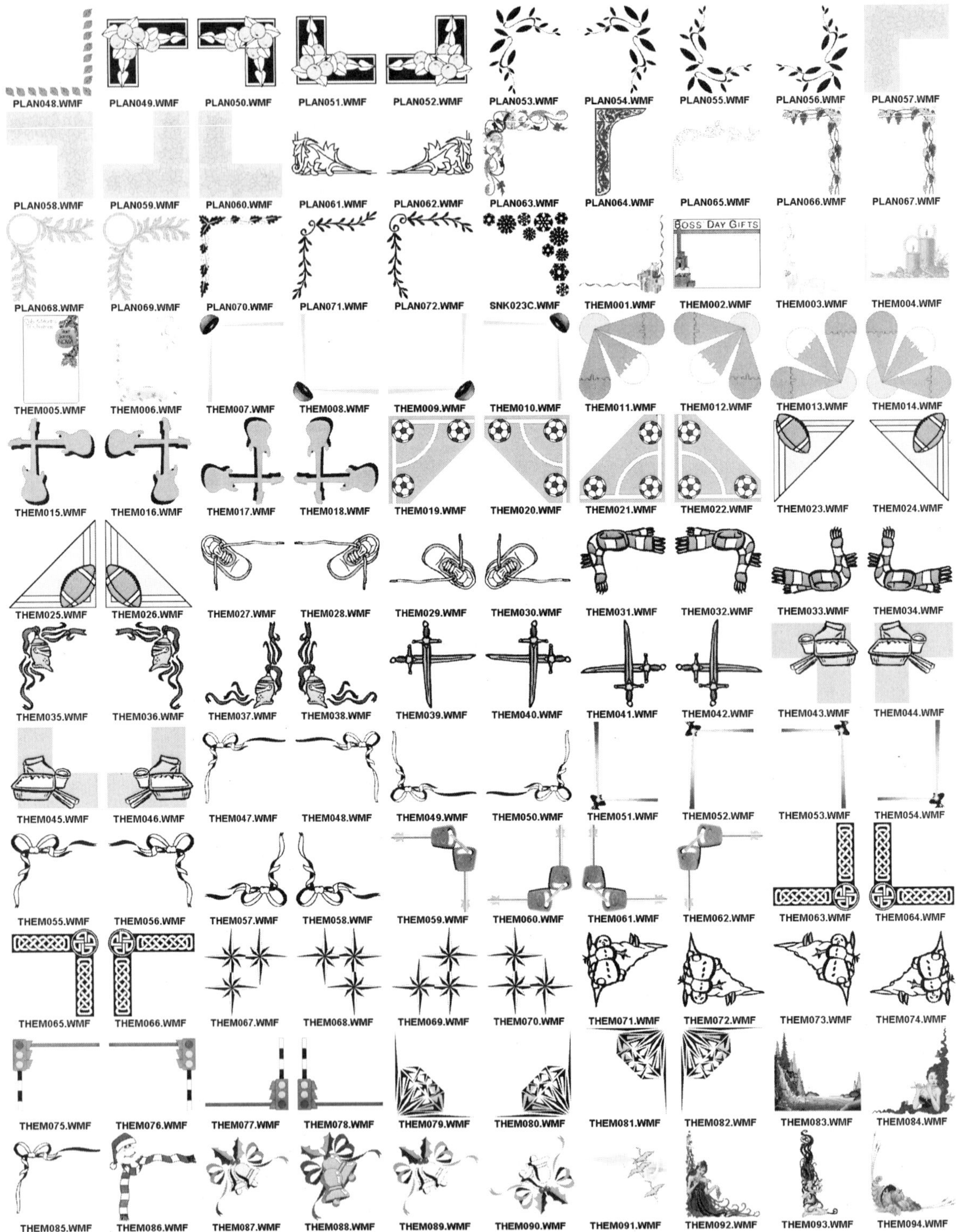

PLAN048.WMF PLAN049.WMF PLAN050.WMF PLAN051.WMF PLAN052.WMF PLAN053.WMF PLAN054.WMF PLAN055.WMF PLAN056.WMF PLAN057.WMF

PLAN058.WMF PLAN059.WMF PLAN060.WMF PLAN061.WMF PLAN062.WMF PLAN063.WMF PLAN064.WMF PLAN065.WMF PLAN066.WMF PLAN067.WMF

PLAN068.WMF PLAN069.WMF PLAN070.WMF PLAN071.WMF PLAN072.WMF SNK023C.WMF THEM001.WMF THEM002.WMF THEM003.WMF THEM004.WMF

THEM005.WMF THEM006.WMF THEM007.WMF THEM008.WMF THEM009.WMF THEM010.WMF THEM011.WMF THEM012.WMF THEM013.WMF THEM014.WMF

THEM015.WMF THEM016.WMF THEM017.WMF THEM018.WMF THEM019.WMF THEM020.WMF THEM021.WMF THEM022.WMF THEM023.WMF THEM024.WMF

THEM025.WMF THEM026.WMF THEM027.WMF THEM028.WMF THEM029.WMF THEM030.WMF THEM031.WMF THEM032.WMF THEM033.WMF THEM034.WMF

THEM035.WMF THEM036.WMF THEM037.WMF THEM038.WMF THEM039.WMF THEM040.WMF THEM041.WMF THEM042.WMF THEM043.WMF THEM044.WMF

THEM045.WMF THEM046.WMF THEM047.WMF THEM048.WMF THEM049.WMF THEM050.WMF THEM051.WMF THEM052.WMF THEM053.WMF THEM054.WMF

THEM055.WMF THEM056.WMF THEM057.WMF THEM058.WMF THEM059.WMF THEM060.WMF THEM061.WMF THEM062.WMF THEM063.WMF THEM064.WMF

THEM065.WMF THEM066.WMF THEM067.WMF THEM068.WMF THEM069.WMF THEM070.WMF THEM071.WMF THEM072.WMF THEM073.WMF THEM074.WMF

THEM075.WMF THEM076.WMF THEM077.WMF THEM078.WMF THEM079.WMF THEM080.WMF THEM081.WMF THEM082.WMF THEM083.WMF THEM084.WMF

THEM085.WMF THEM086.WMF THEM087.WMF THEM088.WMF THEM089.WMF THEM090.WMF THEM091.WMF THEM092.WMF THEM093.WMF THEM094.WMF

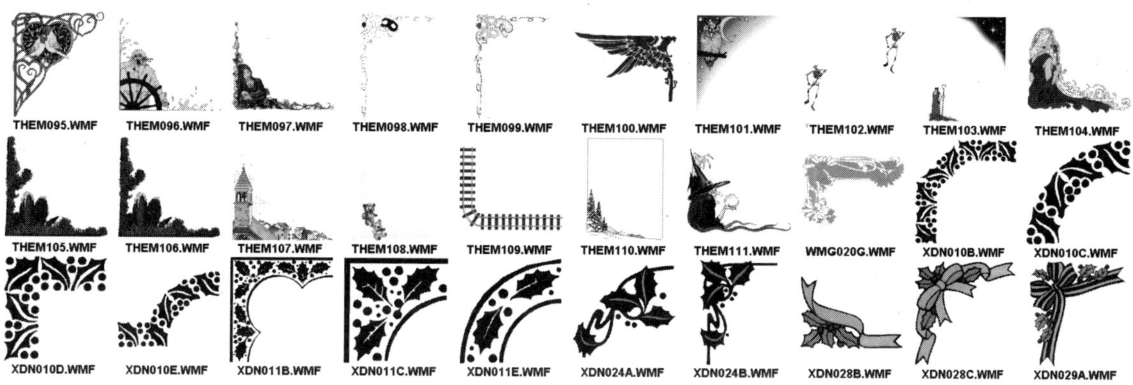
THEM095.WMF THEM096.WMF THEM097.WMF THEM098.WMF THEM099.WMF THEM100.WMF THEM101.WMF THEM102.WMF THEM103.WMF THEM104.WMF
THEM105.WMF THEM106.WMF THEM107.WMF THEM108.WMF THEM109.WMF THEM110.WMF THEM111.WMF WMG020G.WMF XDN010B.WMF XDN010C.WMF
XDN010D.WMF XDN010E.WMF XDN011B.WMF XDN011C.WMF XDN011E.WMF XDN024A.WMF XDN024B.WMF XDN028B.WMF XDN028C.WMF XDN029A.WMF

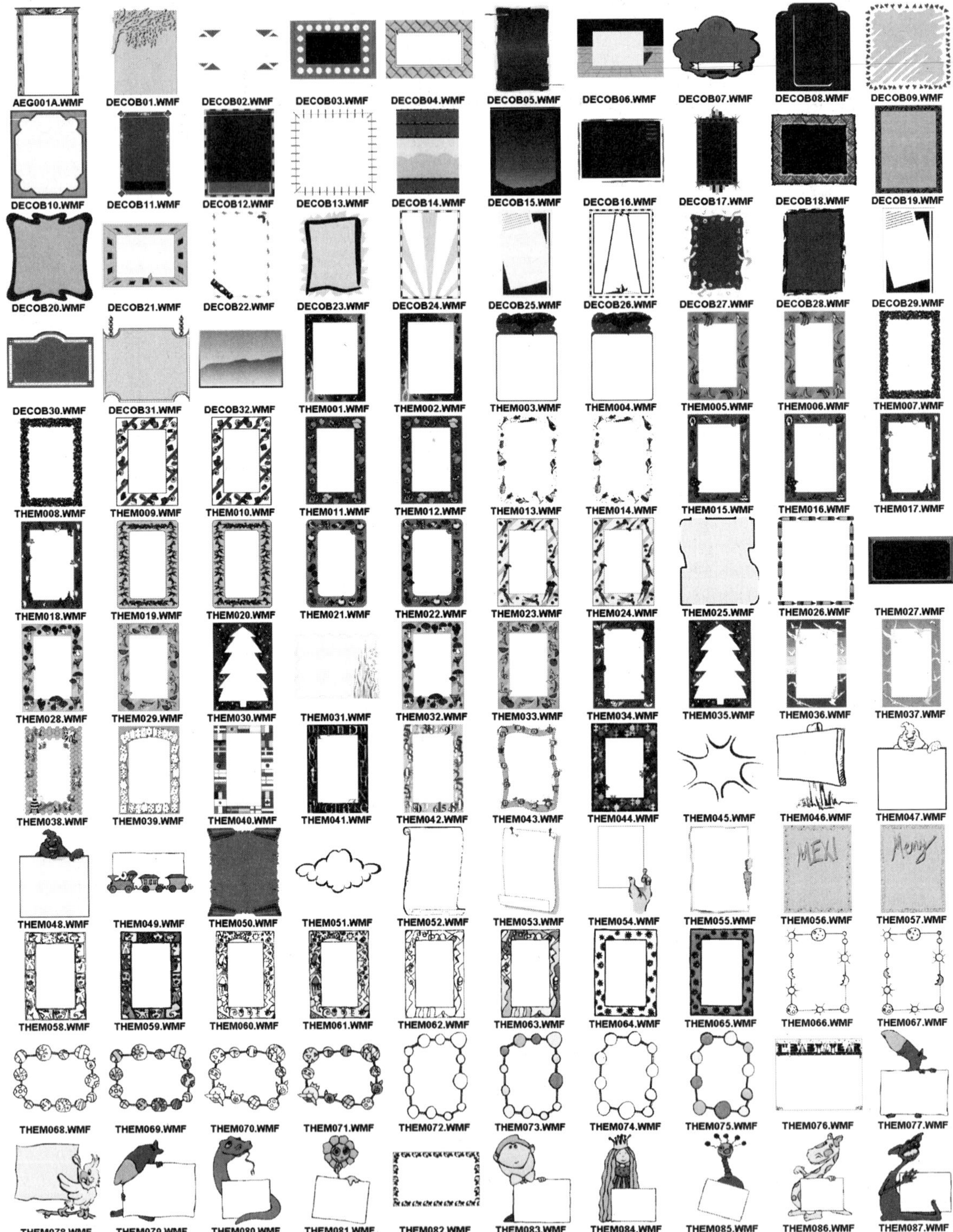
AEG001A.WMF DECOB01.WMF DECOB02.WMF DECOB03.WMF DECOB04.WMF DECOB05.WMF DECOB06.WMF DECOB07.WMF DECOB08.WMF DECOB09.WMF
DECOB10.WMF DECOB11.WMF DECOB12.WMF DECOB13.WMF DECOB14.WMF DECOB15.WMF DECOB16.WMF DECOB17.WMF DECOB18.WMF DECOB19.WMF
DECOB20.WMF DECOB21.WMF DECOB22.WMF DECOB23.WMF DECOB24.WMF DECOB25.WMF DECOB26.WMF DECOB27.WMF DECOB28.WMF DECOB29.WMF
DECOB30.WMF DECOB31.WMF DECOB32.WMF THEM001.WMF THEM002.WMF THEM003.WMF THEM004.WMF THEM005.WMF THEM006.WMF THEM007.WMF
THEM008.WMF THEM009.WMF THEM010.WMF THEM011.WMF THEM012.WMF THEM013.WMF THEM014.WMF THEM015.WMF THEM016.WMF THEM017.WMF
THEM018.WMF THEM019.WMF THEM020.WMF THEM021.WMF THEM022.WMF THEM023.WMF THEM024.WMF THEM025.WMF THEM026.WMF THEM027.WMF
THEM028.WMF THEM029.WMF THEM030.WMF THEM031.WMF THEM032.WMF THEM033.WMF THEM034.WMF THEM035.WMF THEM036.WMF THEM037.WMF
THEM038.WMF THEM039.WMF THEM040.WMF THEM041.WMF THEM042.WMF THEM043.WMF THEM044.WMF THEM045.WMF THEM046.WMF THEM047.WMF
THEM048.WMF THEM049.WMF THEM050.WMF THEM051.WMF THEM052.WMF THEM053.WMF THEM054.WMF THEM055.WMF THEM056.WMF THEM057.WMF
THEM058.WMF THEM059.WMF THEM060.WMF THEM061.WMF THEM062.WMF THEM063.WMF THEM064.WMF THEM065.WMF THEM066.WMF THEM067.WMF
THEM068.WMF THEM069.WMF THEM070.WMF THEM071.WMF THEM072.WMF THEM073.WMF THEM074.WMF THEM075.WMF THEM076.WMF THEM077.WMF
THEM078.WMF THEM079.WMF THEM080.WMF THEM081.WMF THEM082.WMF THEM083.WMF THEM084.WMF THEM085.WMF THEM086.WMF THEM087.WMF

THEM088.WMF THEM089.WMF THEM090.WMF THEM091.WMF THEM092.WMF THEM093.WMF THEM094.WMF THEM095.WMF THEM096.WMF THEM097.WMF
THEM098.WMF THEM099.WMF THEM100.WMF THEM101.WMF THEM102.WMF THEM103.WMF THEM104.WMF THEM105.WMF THEM106.WMF THEM107.WMF
THEM108.WMF THEM109.WMF THEM110.WMF THEM111.WMF THEM112.WMF THEM113.WMF THEM114.WMF THEM115.WMF THEM116.WMF THEM117.WMF
THEM118.WMF THEM119.WMF THEM120.WMF THEM121.WMF THEM122.WMF THEM123.WMF THEM124.WMF THEM125.WMF THEM126.WMF THEM127.WMF
THEM128.WMF THEM129.WMF THEM130.WMF THEM131.WMF THEM132.WMF THEM133.WMF THEM134.WMF THEM135.WMF THEM136.WMF THEM137.WMF
THEM138.WMF THEM139.WMF THEM140.WMF THEM141.WMF THEM142.WMF THEM143.WMF THEM144.WMF THEM145.WMF THEM146.WMF THEM147.WMF
THEM148.WMF THEM149.WMF THEM150.WMF THEM151.WMF THEM152.WMF THEM153.WMF THEM154.WMF THEM155.WMF THEM156.WMF THEM157.WMF
THEM158.WMF THEM159.WMF THEM160.WMF THEM161.WMF THEM162.WMF THEM163.WMF THEM164.WMF THEM165.WMF THEM166.WMF THEM167.WMF
THEM168.WMF THEM169.WMF THEM170.WMF THEM171.WMF THEM172.WMF THEM173.WMF THEM174.WMF THEM175.WMF THEM176.WMF THEM177.WMF
THEM178.WMF THEM179.WMF THEM180.WMF THEM181.WMF THEM182.WMF THEM183.WMF THEM184.WMF THEM185.WMF THEM186.WMF THEM187.WMF
THEM188.WMF THEM189.WMF THEM190.WMF THEM191.WMF THEM192.WMF THEM193.WMF THEM194.WMF THEM195.WMF THEM196.WMF THEM197.WMF
THEM198.WMF THEM199.WMF THEM200.WMF THEM201.WMF THEM202.WMF THEM203.WMF THEM204.WMF THEM205.WMF THEM206.WMF THEM207.WMF

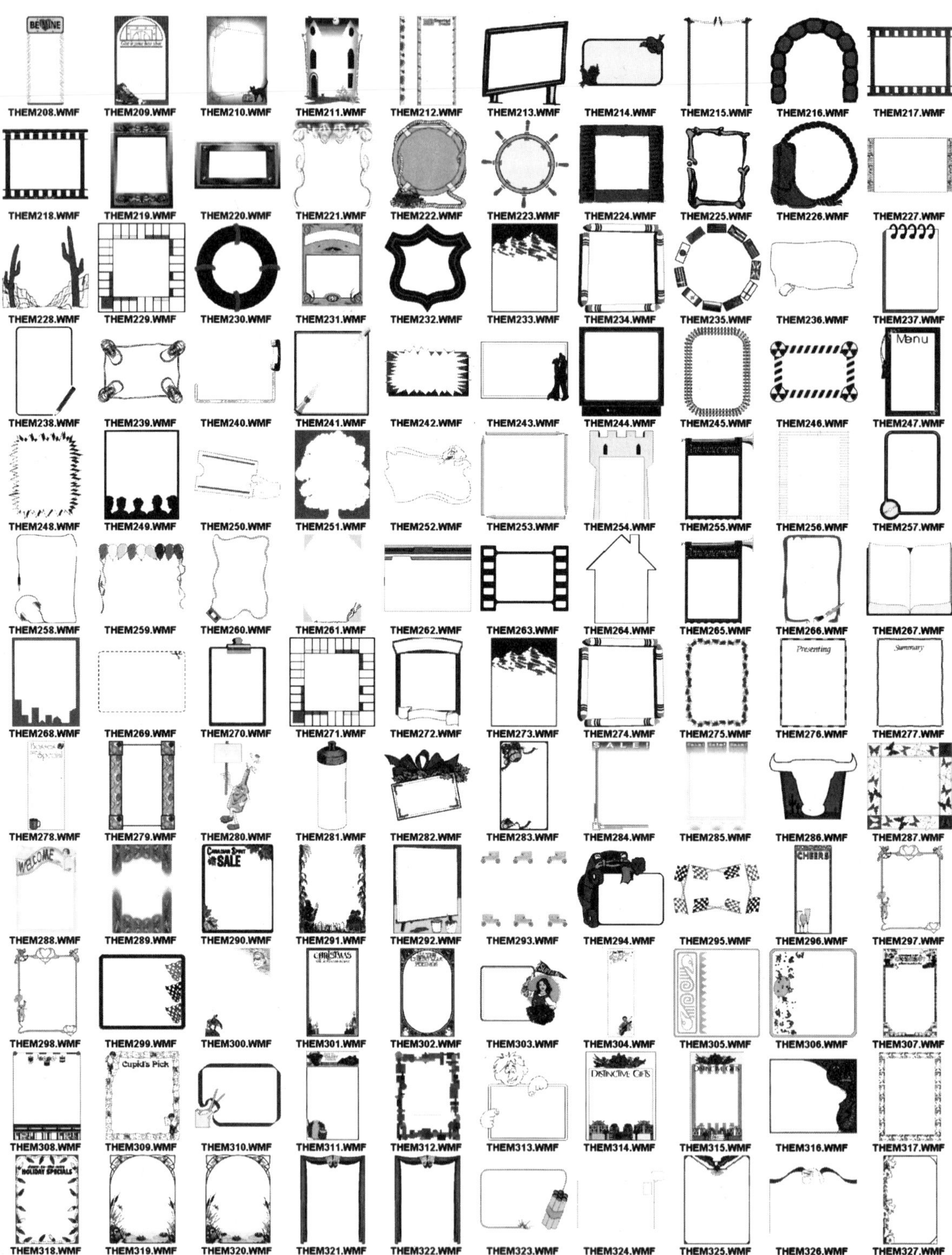
THEM208.WMF THEM209.WMF THEM210.WMF THEM211.WMF THEM212.WMF THEM213.WMF THEM214.WMF THEM215.WMF THEM216.WMF THEM217.WMF
THEM218.WMF THEM219.WMF THEM220.WMF THEM221.WMF THEM222.WMF THEM223.WMF THEM224.WMF THEM225.WMF THEM226.WMF THEM227.WMF
THEM228.WMF THEM229.WMF THEM230.WMF THEM231.WMF THEM232.WMF THEM233.WMF THEM234.WMF THEM235.WMF THEM236.WMF THEM237.WMF
Menu
THEM238.WMF THEM239.WMF THEM240.WMF THEM241.WMF THEM242.WMF THEM243.WMF THEM244.WMF THEM245.WMF THEM246.WMF THEM247.WMF
THEM248.WMF THEM249.WMF THEM250.WMF THEM251.WMF THEM252.WMF THEM253.WMF THEM254.WMF THEM255.WMF THEM256.WMF THEM257.WMF
THEM258.WMF THEM259.WMF THEM260.WMF THEM261.WMF THEM262.WMF THEM263.WMF THEM264.WMF THEM265.WMF THEM266.WMF THEM267.WMF
Presenting
Summary
THEM268.WMF THEM269.WMF THEM270.WMF THEM271.WMF THEM272.WMF THEM273.WMF THEM274.WMF THEM275.WMF THEM276.WMF THEM277.WMF
SALE!
THEM278.WMF THEM279.WMF THEM280.WMF THEM281.WMF THEM282.WMF THEM283.WMF THEM284.WMF THEM285.WMF THEM286.WMF THEM287.WMF
WELCOME
SALE
CHEERS
THEM288.WMF THEM289.WMF THEM290.WMF THEM291.WMF THEM292.WMF THEM293.WMF THEM294.WMF THEM295.WMF THEM296.WMF THEM297.WMF
CHRISTMAS
THEM298.WMF THEM299.WMF THEM300.WMF THEM301.WMF THEM302.WMF THEM303.WMF THEM304.WMF THEM305.WMF THEM306.WMF THEM307.WMF
Cupid's Pick
DISTINCTIVE GIFTS
THEM308.WMF THEM309.WMF THEM310.WMF THEM311.WMF THEM312.WMF THEM313.WMF THEM314.WMF THEM315.WMF THEM316.WMF THEM317.WMF
HOLIDAY SPECIALS
THEM318.WMF THEM319.WMF THEM320.WMF THEM321.WMF THEM322.WMF THEM323.WMF THEM324.WMF THEM325.WMF THEM326.WMF THEM327.WMF

THEM328.WMF THEM329.WMF THEM330.WMF THEM331.WMF THEM332.WMF THEM333.WMF THEM334.WMF THEM335.WMF THEM336.WMF THEM337.WMF

THEM338.WMF THEM339.WMF THEM340.WMF THEM341.WMF THEM342.WMF THEM343.WMF THEM344.WMF THEM345.WMF THEM346.WMF THEM347.WMF

THEM348.WMF THEM349.WMF THEM350.WMF THEM351.WMF THEM352.WMF THEM353.WMF THEM354.WMF THEM355.WMF THEM356.WMF THEM357.WMF

THEM358.WMF THEM359.WMF THEM360.WMF THEM361.WMF THEM362.WMF THEM363.WMF THEM364.WMF THEM365.WMF THEM366.WMF THEM367.WMF

THEM368.WMF THEM369.WMF THEM370.WMF THEM371.WMF THEM372.WMF THEM373.WMF THEM374.WMF THEM375.WMF THEM376.WMF THEM377.WMF

THEM378.WMF THEM379.WMF THEM380.WMF THEM381.WMF THEM382.WMF THEM383.WMF THEM384.WMF THEM385.WMF THEM386.WMF THEM387.WMF

THEM388.WMF THEM389.WMF THEM390.WMF THEM391.WMF THEM392.WMF THEM393.WMF THEM394.WMF THEM395.WMF THEM396.WMF THEM397.WMF

THEM398.WMF THEM399.WMF THEM400.WMF THEM401.WMF THEM402.WMF THEM403.WMF THEM404.WMF THEM405.WMF THEM406.WMF THEM407.WMF

THEM408.WMF THEM409.WMF THEM410.WMF THEM411.WMF THEM412.WMF THEM413.WMF THEM414.WMF THEM415.WMF THEM416.WMF THEM417.WMF

THEM418.WMF THEM419.WMF THEM420.WMF THEM421.WMF THEM422.WMF THEM423.WMF THEM424.WMF THEM425.WMF THEM426.WMF THEM427.WMF

THEM428.WMF THEM429.WMF THEM430.WMF THEM431.WMF THEM432.WMF THEM433.WMF THEM434.WMF THEM435.WMF THEM436.WMF THEM437.WMF

THEM438.WMF THEM439.WMF THEM440.WMF THEM441.WMF THEM442.WMF THEM443.WMF THEM444.WMF THEM445.WMF THEM446.WMF THEM447.WMF

THEM448.WMF THEM449.WMF THEM450.WMF THEM451.WMF THEM452.WMF THEM453.WMF THEM454.WMF THEM455.WMF THEM456.WMF THEM457.WMF
THEM458.WMF THEM459.WMF THEM460.WMF THEM461.WMF THEM462.WMF THEM463.WMF THEM464.WMF THEM465.WMF THEM466.WMF THEM467.WMF
THEM468.WMF THEM469.WMF THEM470.WMF THEM471.WMF THEM472.WMF THEM473.WMF THEM474.WMF THEM475.WMF THEM476.WMF THEM477.WMF
THEM478.WMF THEM479.WMF THEM480.WMF THEM481.WMF THEM482.WMF THEM483.WMF THEM484.WMF THEM485.WMF THEM486.WMF THEM487.WMF
THEM488.WMF THEM489.WMF THEM490.WMF THEM491.WMF THEM492.WMF THEM493.WMF THEM494.WMF THEM495.WMF THEM496.WMF THEM497.WMF
THEM498.WMF THEM499.WMF THEM500.WMF THEM501.WMF THEM502.WMF THEM503.WMF THEM504.WMF THEM505.WMF THEM506.WMF THEM507.WMF
THEM508.WMF THEM509.WMF THEM510.WMF THEM511.WMF THEM512.WMF THEM513.WMF THEM514.WMF THEM515.WMF THEM516.WMF THEM517.WMF
THEM518.WMF THEM519.WMF THEM520.WMF THEM521.WMF THEM522.WMF THEM523.WMF THEM524.WMF THEM525.WMF THEM526.WMF THEM527.WMF
THEM528.WMF THEM529.WMF THEM530.WMF THEM531.WMF THEM532.WMF THEM533.WMF THEM534.WMF THEM535.WMF THEM536.WMF THEM537.WMF
THEM538.WMF THEM539.WMF THEM540.WMF THEM541.WMF THEM542.WMF THEM543.WMF THEM544.WMF THEM545.WMF THEM546.WMF THEM547.WMF
THEM548.WMF THEM549.WMF THEM550.WMF THEM551.WMF THEM552.WMF THEM553.WMF THEM554.WMF THEM555.WMF THEM556.WMF THEM557.WMF
THEM558.WMF THEM559.WMF THEM560.WMF THEM561.WMF THEM562.WMF THEM563.WMF THEME201.WMF THEME202.WMF THEME203.WMF THEME204.WMF

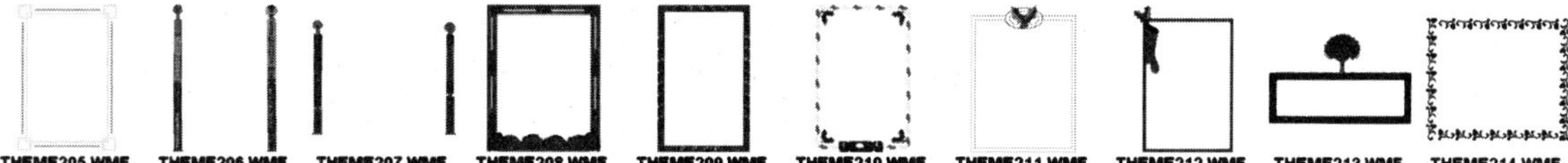

THEME205.WMF THEME206.WMF THEME207.WMF THEME208.WMF THEME209.WMF THEME210.WMF THEME211.WMF THEME212.WMF THEME213.WMF THEME214.WMF

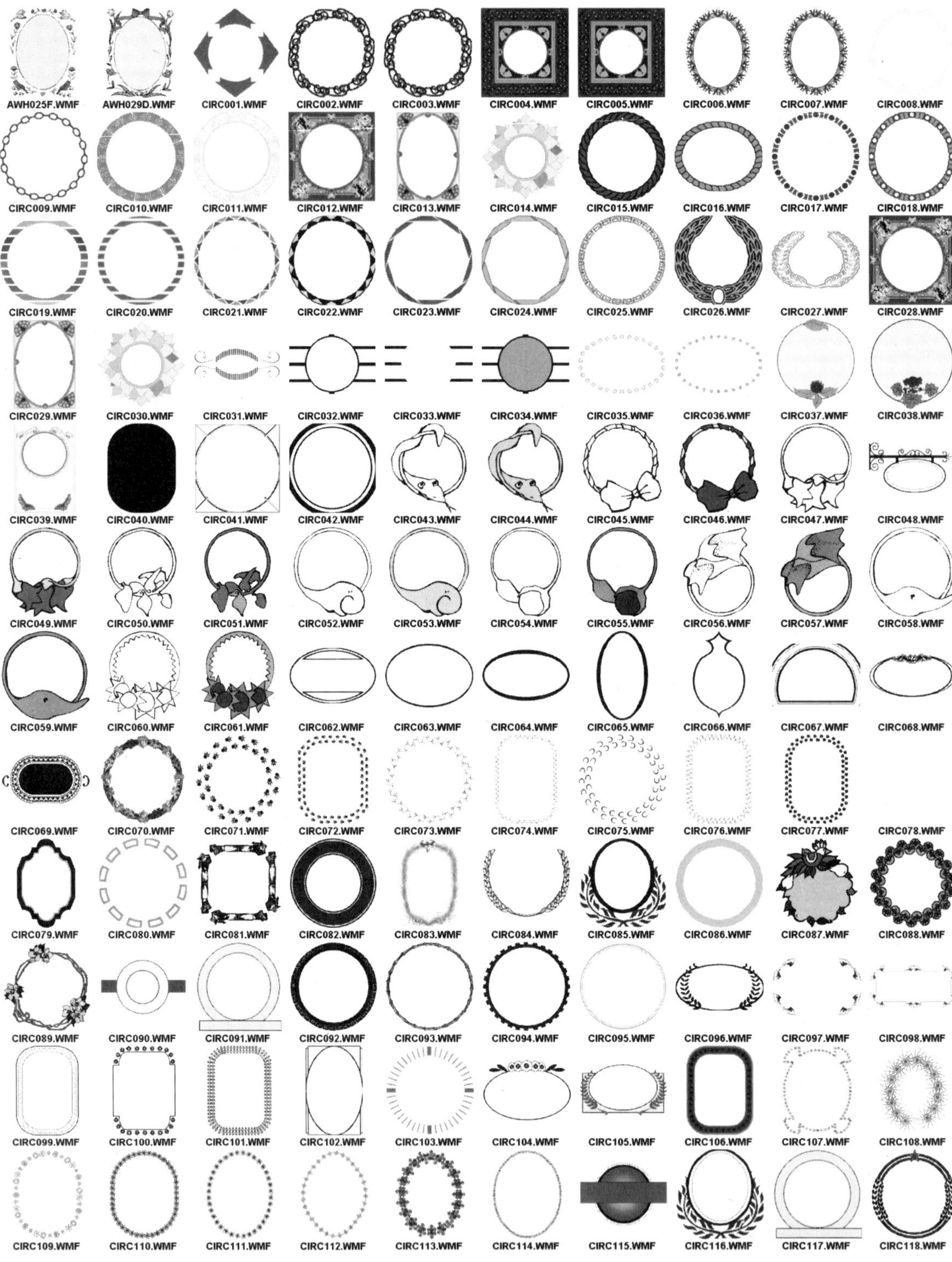
AWH025F.WMF
AWH029D.WMF
CIRC001.WMF
CIRC002.WMF
CIRC003.WMF
CIRC004.WMF
CIRC005.WMF
CIRC006.WMF
CIRC007.WMF
CIRC008.WMF
CIRC009.WMF
CIRC010.WMF
CIRC011.WMF
CIRC012.WMF
CIRC013.WMF
CIRC014.WMF
CIRC015.WMF
CIRC016.WMF
CIRC017.WMF
CIRC018.WMF
CIRC019.WMF
CIRC020.WMF
CIRC021.WMF
CIRC022.WMF
CIRC023.WMF
CIRC024.WMF
CIRC025.WMF
CIRC026.WMF
CIRC027.WMF
CIRC028.WMF
CIRC029.WMF
CIRC030.WMF
CIRC031.WMF
CIRC032.WMF
CIRC033.WMF
CIRC034.WMF
CIRC035.WMF
CIRC036.WMF
CIRC037.WMF
CIRC038.WMF
CIRC039.WMF
CIRC040.WMF
CIRC041.WMF
CIRC042.WMF
CIRC043.WMF
CIRC044.WMF
CIRC045.WMF
CIRC046.WMF
CIRC047.WMF
CIRC048.WMF
CIRC049.WMF
CIRC050.WMF
CIRC051.WMF
CIRC052.WMF
CIRC053.WMF
CIRC054.WMF
CIRC055.WMF
CIRC056.WMF
CIRC057.WMF
CIRC058.WMF
CIRC059.WMF
CIRC060.WMF
CIRC061.WMF
CIRC062.WMF
CIRC063.WMF
CIRC064.WMF
CIRC065.WMF
CIRC066.WMF
CIRC067.WMF
CIRC068.WMF
CIRC069.WMF
CIRC070.WMF
CIRC071.WMF
CIRC072.WMF
CIRC073.WMF
CIRC074.WMF
CIRC075.WMF
CIRC076.WMF
CIRC077.WMF
CIRC078.WMF
CIRC079.WMF
CIRC080.WMF
CIRC081.WMF
CIRC082.WMF
CIRC083.WMF
CIRC084.WMF
CIRC085.WMF
CIRC086.WMF
CIRC087.WMF
CIRC088.WMF
CIRC089.WMF
CIRC090.WMF
CIRC091.WMF
CIRC092.WMF
CIRC093.WMF
CIRC094.WMF
CIRC095.WMF
CIRC096.WMF
CIRC097.WMF
CIRC098.WMF
CIRC099.WMF
CIRC100.WMF
CIRC101.WMF
CIRC102.WMF
CIRC103.WMF
CIRC104.WMF
CIRC105.WMF
CIRC106.WMF
CIRC107.WMF
CIRC108.WMF
CIRC109.WMF
CIRC110.WMF
CIRC111.WMF
CIRC112.WMF
CIRC113.WMF
CIRC114.WMF
CIRC115.WMF
CIRC116.WMF
CIRC117.WMF
CIRC118.WMF

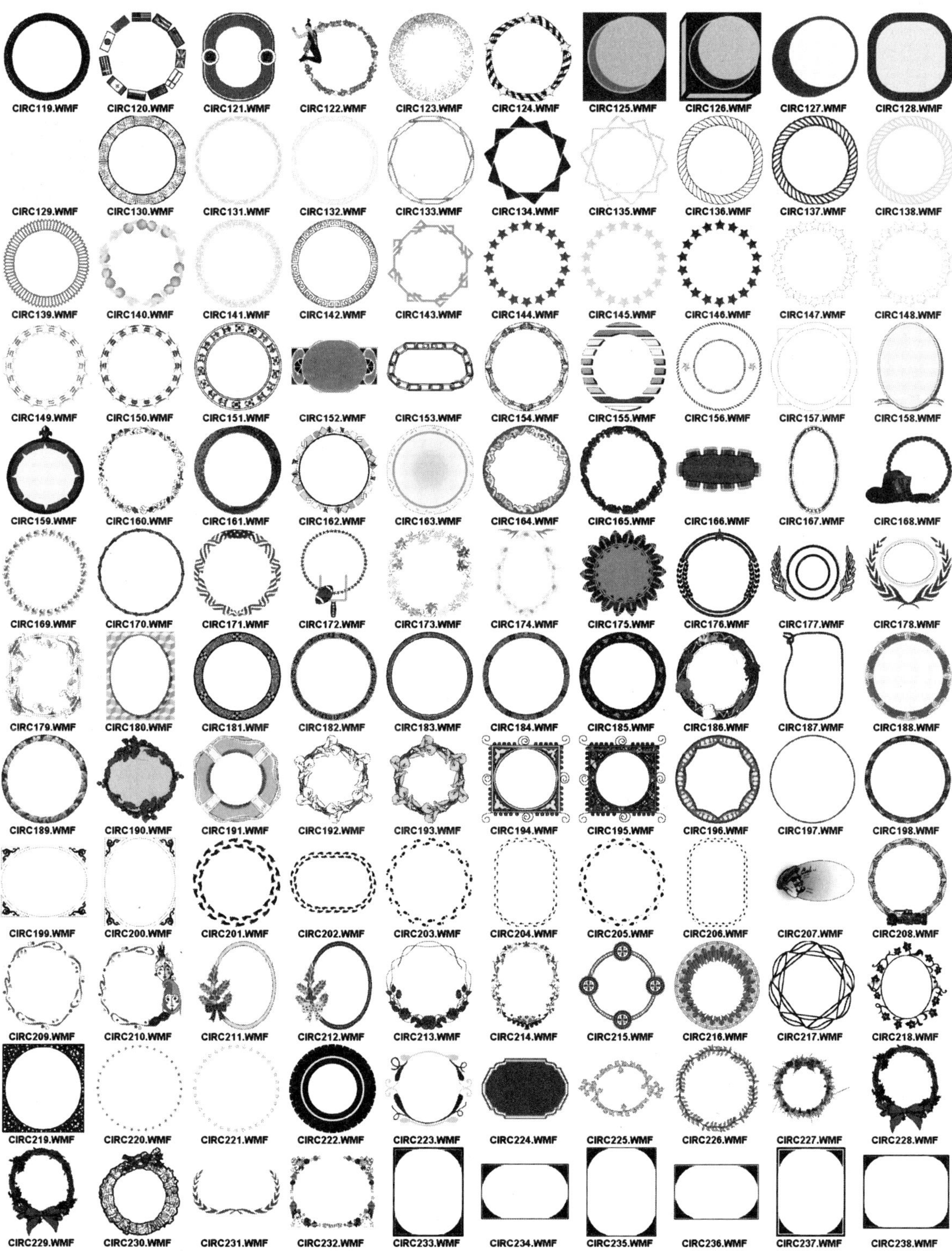
CIRC119.WMF CIRC120.WMF CIRC121.WMF CIRC122.WMF CIRC123.WMF CIRC124.WMF CIRC125.WMF CIRC126.WMF CIRC127.WMF CIRC128.WMF
CIRC129.WMF CIRC130.WMF CIRC131.WMF CIRC132.WMF CIRC133.WMF CIRC134.WMF CIRC135.WMF CIRC136.WMF CIRC137.WMF CIRC138.WMF
CIRC139.WMF CIRC140.WMF CIRC141.WMF CIRC142.WMF CIRC143.WMF CIRC144.WMF CIRC145.WMF CIRC146.WMF CIRC147.WMF CIRC148.WMF
CIRC149.WMF CIRC150.WMF CIRC151.WMF CIRC152.WMF CIRC153.WMF CIRC154.WMF CIRC155.WMF CIRC156.WMF CIRC157.WMF CIRC158.WMF
CIRC159.WMF CIRC160.WMF CIRC161.WMF CIRC162.WMF CIRC163.WMF CIRC164.WMF CIRC165.WMF CIRC166.WMF CIRC167.WMF CIRC168.WMF
CIRC169.WMF CIRC170.WMF CIRC171.WMF CIRC172.WMF CIRC173.WMF CIRC174.WMF CIRC175.WMF CIRC176.WMF CIRC177.WMF CIRC178.WMF
CIRC179.WMF CIRC180.WMF CIRC181.WMF CIRC182.WMF CIRC183.WMF CIRC184.WMF CIRC185.WMF CIRC186.WMF CIRC187.WMF CIRC188.WMF
CIRC189.WMF CIRC190.WMF CIRC191.WMF CIRC192.WMF CIRC193.WMF CIRC194.WMF CIRC195.WMF CIRC196.WMF CIRC197.WMF CIRC198.WMF
CIRC199.WMF CIRC200.WMF CIRC201.WMF CIRC202.WMF CIRC203.WMF CIRC204.WMF CIRC205.WMF CIRC206.WMF CIRC207.WMF CIRC208.WMF
CIRC209.WMF CIRC210.WMF CIRC211.WMF CIRC212.WMF CIRC213.WMF CIRC214.WMF CIRC215.WMF CIRC216.WMF CIRC217.WMF CIRC218.WMF
CIRC219.WMF CIRC220.WMF CIRC221.WMF CIRC222.WMF CIRC223.WMF CIRC224.WMF CIRC225.WMF CIRC226.WMF CIRC227.WMF CIRC228.WMF
CIRC229.WMF CIRC230.WMF CIRC231.WMF CIRC232.WMF CIRC233.WMF CIRC234.WMF CIRC235.WMF CIRC236.WMF CIRC237.WMF CIRC238.WMF

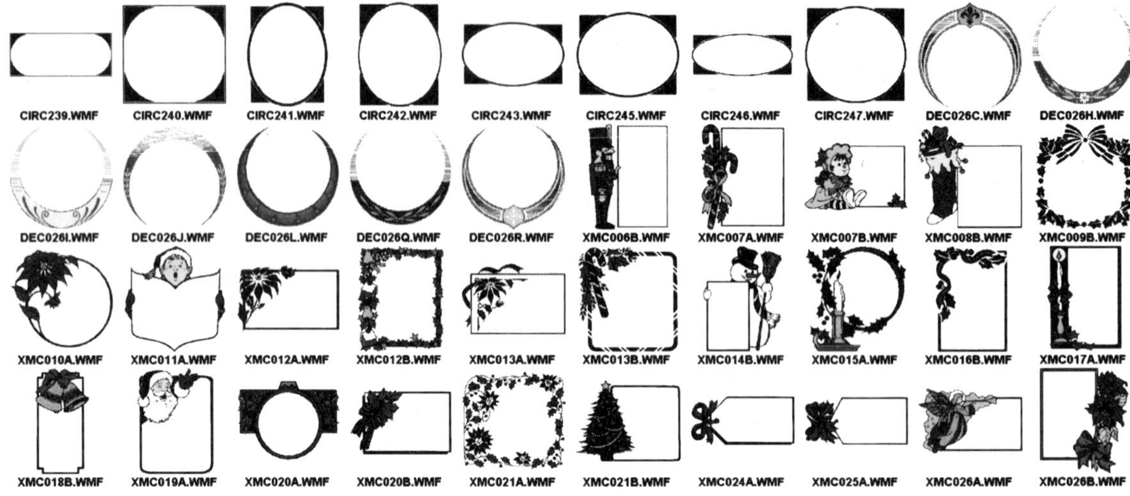
CIRC239.WMF
CIRC240.WMF
CIRC241.WMF
CIRC242.WMF
CIRC243.WMF
CIRC245.WMF
CIRC246.WMF
CIRC247.WMF
DEC026C.WMF
DEC026H.WMF
DEC026I.WMF
DEC026J.WMF
DEC026L.WMF
DEC026Q.WMF
DEC026R.WMF
XMC006B.WMF
XMC007A.WMF
XMC007B.WMF
XMC008B.WMF
XMC009B.WMF
XMC010A.WMF
XMC011A.WMF
XMC012A.WMF
XMC012B.WMF
XMC013A.WMF
XMC013B.WMF
XMC014B.WMF
XMC015A.WMF
XMC016B.WMF
XMC017A.WMF
XMC018B.WMF
XMC019A.WMF
XMC020A.WMF
XMC020B.WMF
XMC021A.WMF
XMC021B.WMF
XMC024A.WMF
XMC025A.WMF
XMC026A.WMF
XMC026B.WMF

XMC027A.WMF

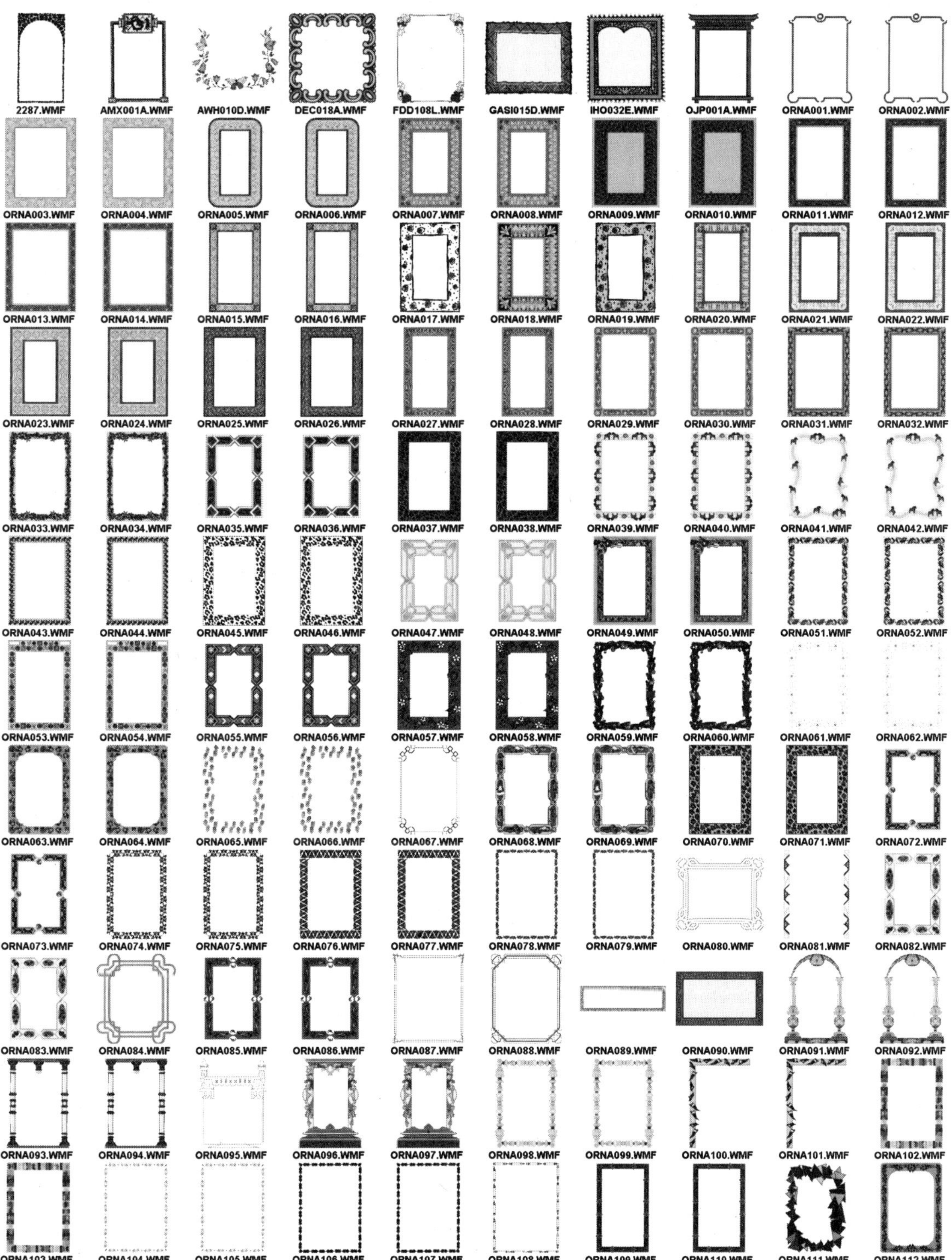
2287.WMF
AMX001A.WMF
AWH010D.WMF
DEC018A.WMF
FDD108L.WMF
GASI015D.WMF
IHO032E.WMF
OJP001A.WMF
ORNA001.WMF
ORNA002.WMF
ORNA003.WMF
ORNA004.WMF
ORNA005.WMF
ORNA006.WMF
ORNA007.WMF
ORNA008.WMF
ORNA009.WMF
ORNA010.WMF
ORNA011.WMF
ORNA012.WMF
ORNA013.WMF
ORNA014.WMF
ORNA015.WMF
ORNA016.WMF
ORNA017.WMF
ORNA018.WMF
ORNA019.WMF
ORNA020.WMF
ORNA021.WMF
ORNA022.WMF
ORNA023.WMF
ORNA024.WMF
ORNA025.WMF
ORNA026.WMF
ORNA027.WMF
ORNA028.WMF
ORNA029.WMF
ORNA030.WMF
ORNA031.WMF
ORNA032.WMF
ORNA033.WMF
ORNA034.WMF
ORNA035.WMF
ORNA036.WMF
ORNA037.WMF
ORNA038.WMF
ORNA039.WMF
ORNA040.WMF
ORNA041.WMF
ORNA042.WMF
ORNA043.WMF
ORNA044.WMF
ORNA045.WMF
ORNA046.WMF
ORNA047.WMF
ORNA048.WMF
ORNA049.WMF
ORNA050.WMF
ORNA051.WMF
ORNA052.WMF
ORNA053.WMF
ORNA054.WMF
ORNA055.WMF
ORNA056.WMF
ORNA057.WMF
ORNA058.WMF
ORNA059.WMF
ORNA060.WMF
ORNA061.WMF
ORNA062.WMF
ORNA063.WMF
ORNA064.WMF
ORNA065.WMF
ORNA066.WMF
ORNA067.WMF
ORNA068.WMF
ORNA069.WMF
ORNA070.WMF
ORNA071.WMF
ORNA072.WMF
ORNA073.WMF
ORNA074.WMF
ORNA075.WMF
ORNA076.WMF
ORNA077.WMF
ORNA078.WMF
ORNA079.WMF
ORNA080.WMF
ORNA081.WMF
ORNA082.WMF
ORNA083.WMF
ORNA084.WMF
ORNA085.WMF
ORNA086.WMF
ORNA087.WMF
ORNA088.WMF
ORNA089.WMF
ORNA090.WMF
ORNA091.WMF
ORNA092.WMF
ORNA093.WMF
ORNA094.WMF
ORNA095.WMF
ORNA096.WMF
ORNA097.WMF
ORNA098.WMF
ORNA099.WMF
ORNA100.WMF
ORNA101.WMF
ORNA102.WMF
ORNA103.WMF
ORNA104.WMF
ORNA105.WMF
ORNA106.WMF
ORNA107.WMF
ORNA108.WMF
ORNA109.WMF
ORNA110.WMF
ORNA111.WMF
ORNA112.WMF

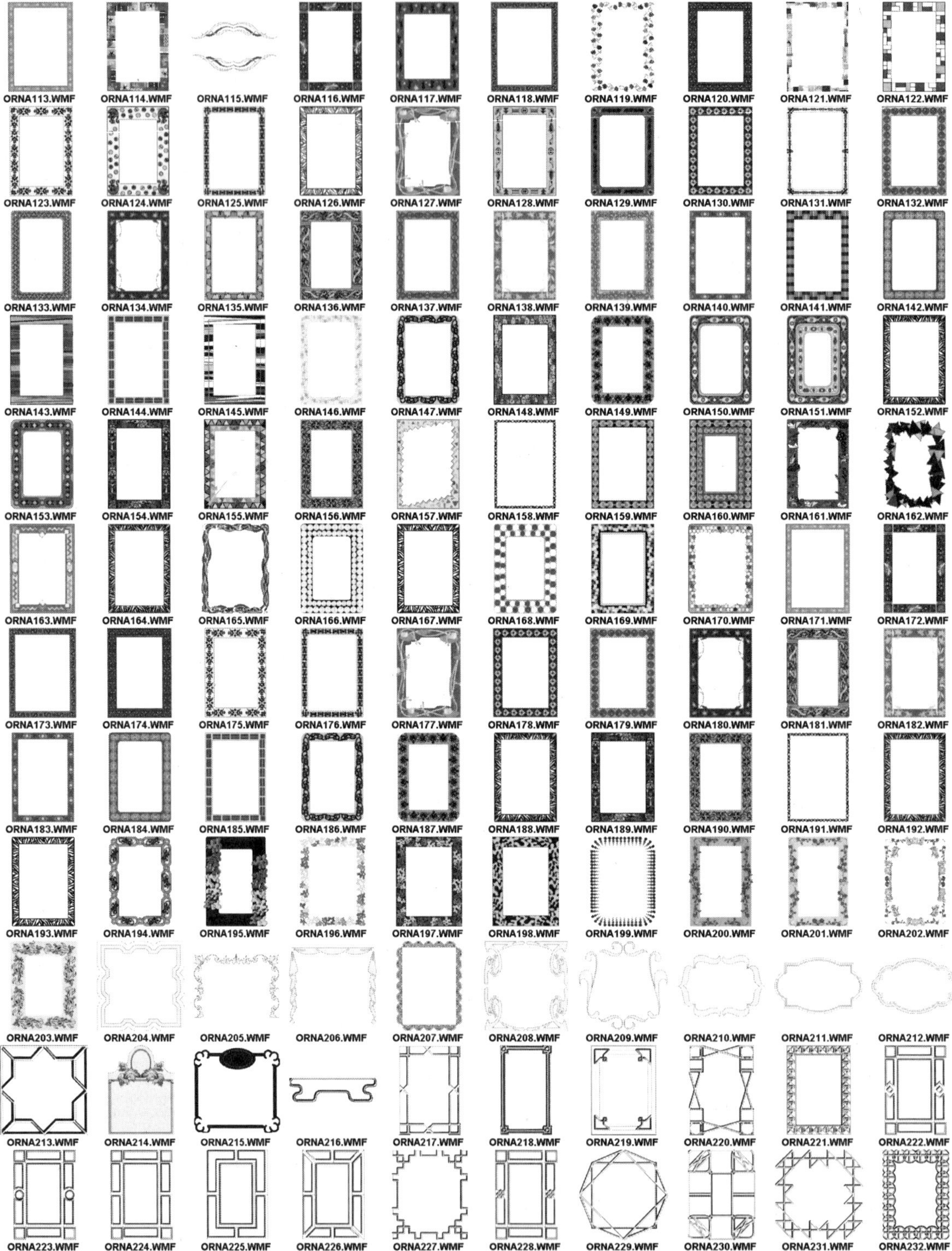
ORNA113.WMF
ORNA114.WMF
ORNA115.WMF
ORNA116.WMF
ORNA117.WMF
ORNA118.WMF
ORNA119.WMF
ORNA120.WMF
ORNA121.WMF
ORNA122.WMF
ORNA123.WMF
ORNA124.WMF
ORNA125.WMF
ORNA126.WMF
ORNA127.WMF
ORNA128.WMF
ORNA129.WMF
ORNA130.WMF
ORNA131.WMF
ORNA132.WMF
ORNA133.WMF
ORNA134.WMF
ORNA135.WMF
ORNA136.WMF
ORNA137.WMF
ORNA138.WMF
ORNA139.WMF
ORNA140.WMF
ORNA141.WMF
ORNA142.WMF
ORNA143.WMF
ORNA144.WMF
ORNA145.WMF
ORNA146.WMF
ORNA147.WMF
ORNA148.WMF
ORNA149.WMF
ORNA150.WMF
ORNA151.WMF
ORNA152.WMF
ORNA153.WMF
ORNA154.WMF
ORNA155.WMF
ORNA156.WMF
ORNA157.WMF
ORNA158.WMF
ORNA159.WMF
ORNA160.WMF
ORNA161.WMF
ORNA162.WMF
ORNA163.WMF
ORNA164.WMF
ORNA165.WMF
ORNA166.WMF
ORNA167.WMF
ORNA168.WMF
ORNA169.WMF
ORNA170.WMF
ORNA171.WMF
ORNA172.WMF
ORNA173.WMF
ORNA174.WMF
ORNA175.WMF
ORNA176.WMF
ORNA177.WMF
ORNA178.WMF
ORNA179.WMF
ORNA180.WMF
ORNA181.WMF
ORNA182.WMF
ORNA183.WMF
ORNA184.WMF
ORNA185.WMF
ORNA186.WMF
ORNA187.WMF
ORNA188.WMF
ORNA189.WMF
ORNA190.WMF
ORNA191.WMF
ORNA192.WMF
ORNA193.WMF
ORNA194.WMF
ORNA195.WMF
ORNA196.WMF
ORNA197.WMF
ORNA198.WMF
ORNA199.WMF
ORNA200.WMF
ORNA201.WMF
ORNA202.WMF
ORNA203.WMF
ORNA204.WMF
ORNA205.WMF
ORNA206.WMF
ORNA207.WMF
ORNA208.WMF
ORNA209.WMF
ORNA210.WMF
ORNA211.WMF
ORNA212.WMF
ORNA213.WMF
ORNA214.WMF
ORNA215.WMF
ORNA216.WMF
ORNA217.WMF
ORNA218.WMF
ORNA219.WMF
ORNA220.WMF
ORNA221.WMF
ORNA222.WMF
ORNA223.WMF
ORNA224.WMF
ORNA225.WMF
ORNA226.WMF
ORNA227.WMF
ORNA228.WMF
ORNA229.WMF
ORNA230.WMF
ORNA231.WMF
ORNA232.WMF

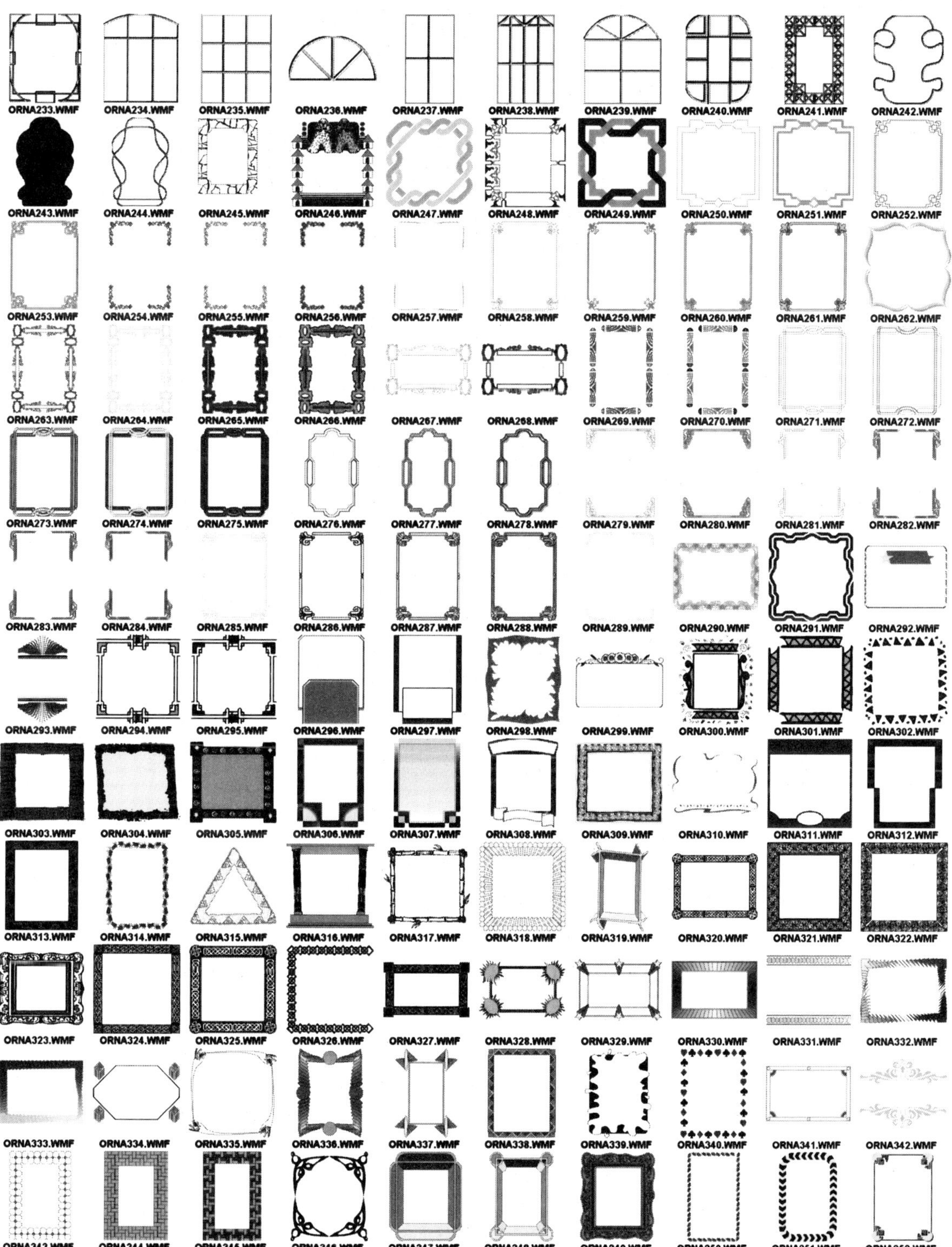
ORNA233.WMF ORNA234.WMF ORNA235.WMF ORNA236.WMF ORNA237.WMF ORNA238.WMF ORNA239.WMF ORNA240.WMF ORNA241.WMF ORNA242.WMF
ORNA243.WMF ORNA244.WMF ORNA245.WMF ORNA246.WMF ORNA247.WMF ORNA248.WMF ORNA249.WMF ORNA250.WMF ORNA251.WMF ORNA252.WMF
ORNA253.WMF ORNA254.WMF ORNA255.WMF ORNA256.WMF ORNA257.WMF ORNA258.WMF ORNA259.WMF ORNA260.WMF ORNA261.WMF ORNA262.WMF
ORNA263.WMF ORNA264.WMF ORNA265.WMF ORNA266.WMF ORNA267.WMF ORNA268.WMF ORNA269.WMF ORNA270.WMF ORNA271.WMF ORNA272.WMF
ORNA273.WMF ORNA274.WMF ORNA275.WMF ORNA276.WMF ORNA277.WMF ORNA278.WMF ORNA279.WMF ORNA280.WMF ORNA281.WMF ORNA282.WMF
ORNA283.WMF ORNA284.WMF ORNA285.WMF ORNA286.WMF ORNA287.WMF ORNA288.WMF ORNA289.WMF ORNA290.WMF ORNA291.WMF ORNA292.WMF
ORNA293.WMF ORNA294.WMF ORNA295.WMF ORNA296.WMF ORNA297.WMF ORNA298.WMF ORNA299.WMF ORNA300.WMF ORNA301.WMF ORNA302.WMF
ORNA303.WMF ORNA304.WMF ORNA305.WMF ORNA306.WMF ORNA307.WMF ORNA308.WMF ORNA309.WMF ORNA310.WMF ORNA311.WMF ORNA312.WMF
ORNA313.WMF ORNA314.WMF ORNA315.WMF ORNA316.WMF ORNA317.WMF ORNA318.WMF ORNA319.WMF ORNA320.WMF ORNA321.WMF ORNA322.WMF
ORNA323.WMF ORNA324.WMF ORNA325.WMF ORNA326.WMF ORNA327.WMF ORNA328.WMF ORNA329.WMF ORNA330.WMF ORNA331.WMF ORNA332.WMF
ORNA333.WMF ORNA334.WMF ORNA335.WMF ORNA336.WMF ORNA337.WMF ORNA338.WMF ORNA339.WMF ORNA340.WMF ORNA341.WMF ORNA342.WMF
ORNA343.WMF ORNA344.WMF ORNA345.WMF ORNA346.WMF ORNA347.WMF ORNA348.WMF ORNA349.WMF ORNA350.WMF ORNA351.WMF ORNA352.WMF

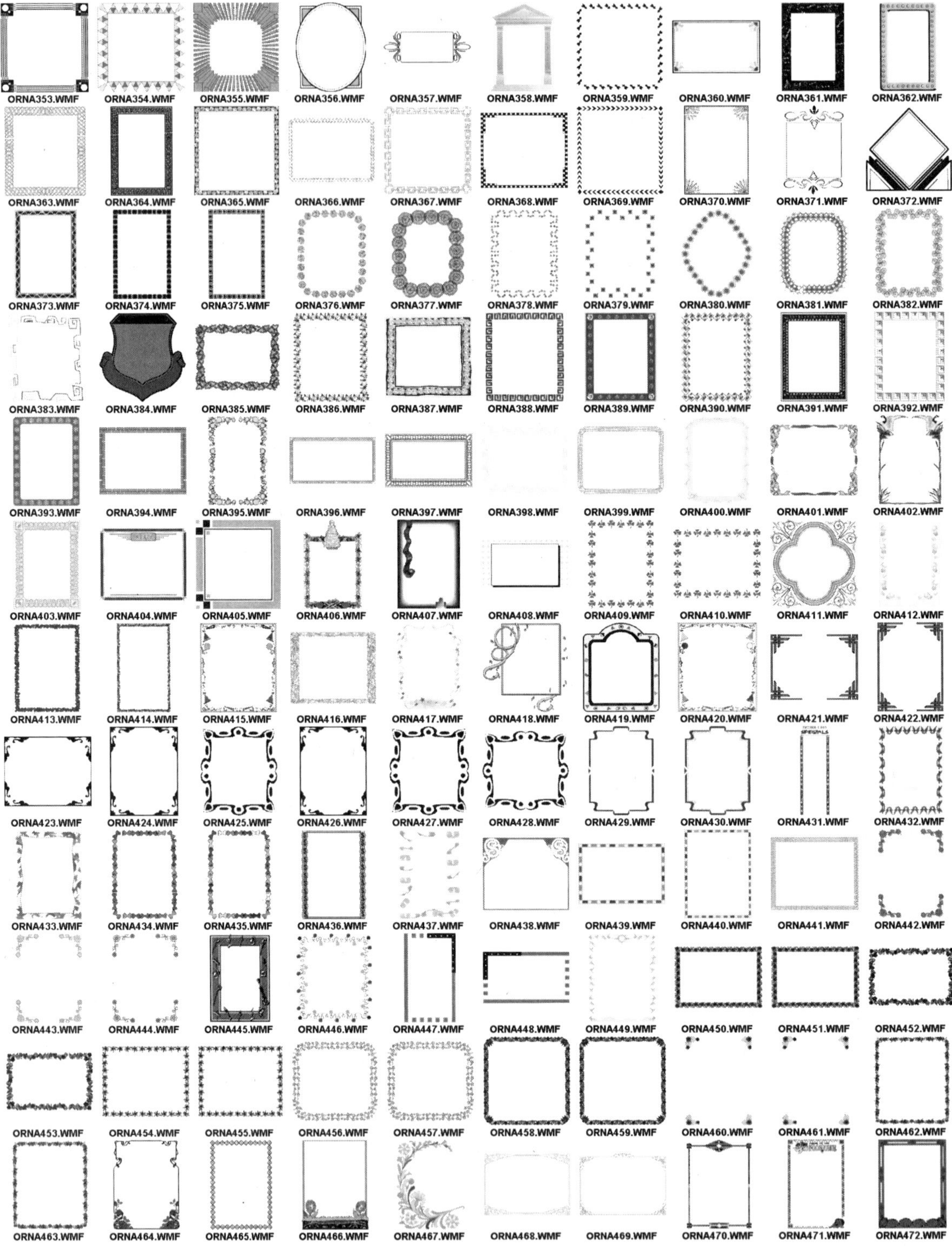
ORNA353.WMF ORNA354.WMF ORNA355.WMF ORNA356.WMF ORNA357.WMF ORNA358.WMF ORNA359.WMF ORNA360.WMF ORNA361.WMF ORNA362.WMF
ORNA363.WMF ORNA364.WMF ORNA365.WMF ORNA366.WMF ORNA367.WMF ORNA368.WMF ORNA369.WMF ORNA370.WMF ORNA371.WMF ORNA372.WMF
ORNA373.WMF ORNA374.WMF ORNA375.WMF ORNA376.WMF ORNA377.WMF ORNA378.WMF ORNA379.WMF ORNA380.WMF ORNA381.WMF ORNA382.WMF
ORNA383.WMF ORNA384.WMF ORNA385.WMF ORNA386.WMF ORNA387.WMF ORNA388.WMF ORNA389.WMF ORNA390.WMF ORNA391.WMF ORNA392.WMF
ORNA393.WMF ORNA394.WMF ORNA395.WMF ORNA396.WMF ORNA397.WMF ORNA398.WMF ORNA399.WMF ORNA400.WMF ORNA401.WMF ORNA402.WMF
ORNA403.WMF ORNA404.WMF ORNA405.WMF ORNA406.WMF ORNA407.WMF ORNA408.WMF ORNA409.WMF ORNA410.WMF ORNA411.WMF ORNA412.WMF
ORNA413.WMF ORNA414.WMF ORNA415.WMF ORNA416.WMF ORNA417.WMF ORNA418.WMF ORNA419.WMF ORNA420.WMF ORNA421.WMF ORNA422.WMF
ORNA423.WMF ORNA424.WMF ORNA425.WMF ORNA426.WMF ORNA427.WMF ORNA428.WMF ORNA429.WMF ORNA430.WMF ORNA431.WMF ORNA432.WMF
ORNA433.WMF ORNA434.WMF ORNA435.WMF ORNA436.WMF ORNA437.WMF ORNA438.WMF ORNA439.WMF ORNA440.WMF ORNA441.WMF ORNA442.WMF
ORNA443.WMF ORNA444.WMF ORNA445.WMF ORNA446.WMF ORNA447.WMF ORNA448.WMF ORNA449.WMF ORNA450.WMF ORNA451.WMF ORNA452.WMF
ORNA453.WMF ORNA454.WMF ORNA455.WMF ORNA456.WMF ORNA457.WMF ORNA458.WMF ORNA459.WMF ORNA460.WMF ORNA461.WMF ORNA462.WMF
ORNA463.WMF ORNA464.WMF ORNA465.WMF ORNA466.WMF ORNA467.WMF ORNA468.WMF ORNA469.WMF ORNA470.WMF ORNA471.WMF ORNA472.WMF

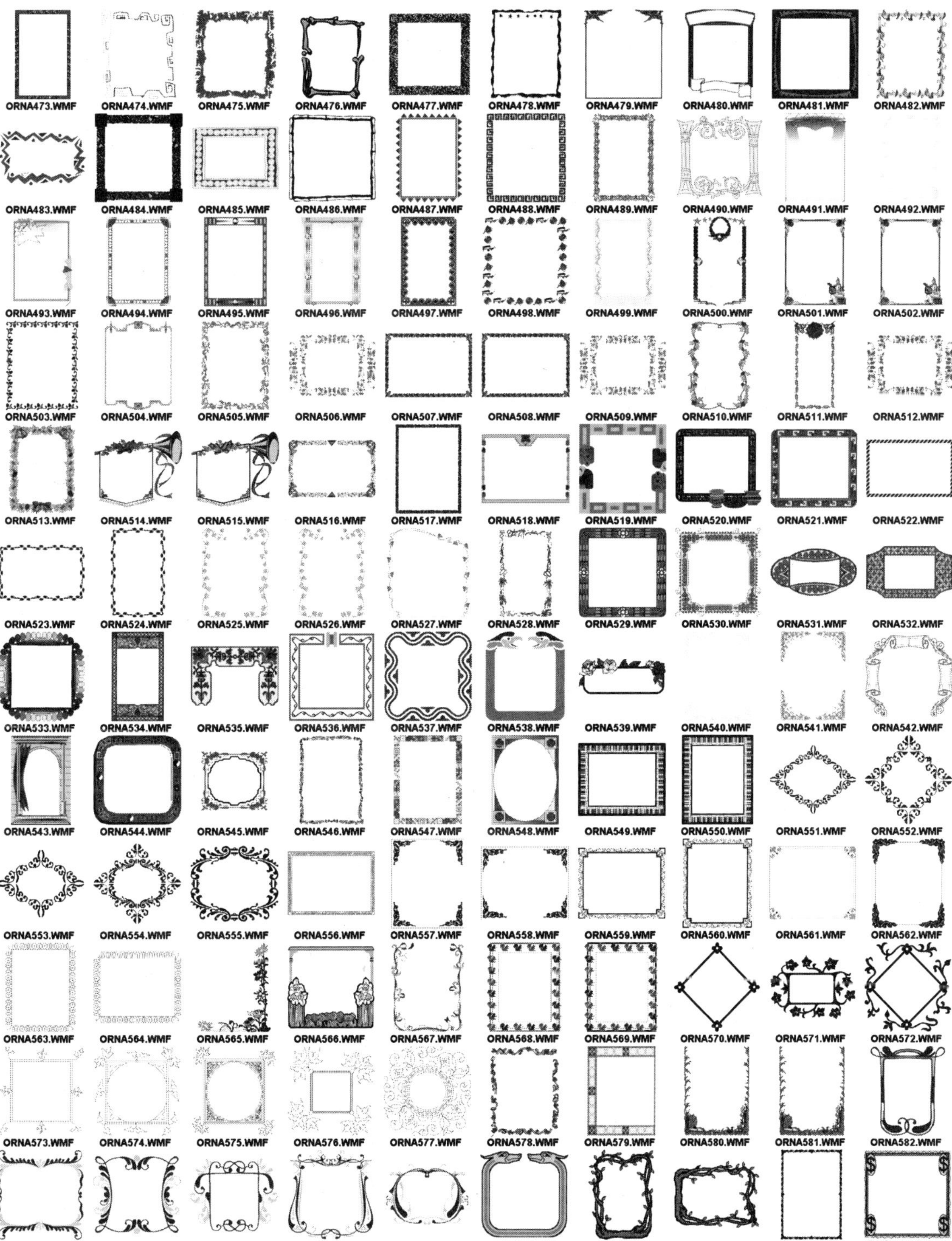
ORNA473.WMF
ORNA474.WMF
ORNA475.WMF
ORNA476.WMF
ORNA477.WMF
ORNA478.WMF
ORNA479.WMF
ORNA480.WMF
ORNA481.WMF
ORNA482.WMF
ORNA483.WMF
ORNA484.WMF
ORNA485.WMF
ORNA486.WMF
ORNA487.WMF
ORNA488.WMF
ORNA489.WMF
ORNA490.WMF
ORNA491.WMF
ORNA492.WMF
ORNA493.WMF
ORNA494.WMF
ORNA495.WMF
ORNA496.WMF
ORNA497.WMF
ORNA498.WMF
ORNA499.WMF
ORNA500.WMF
ORNA501.WMF
ORNA502.WMF
ORNA503.WMF
ORNA504.WMF
ORNA505.WMF
ORNA506.WMF
ORNA507.WMF
ORNA508.WMF
ORNA509.WMF
ORNA510.WMF
ORNA511.WMF
ORNA512.WMF
ORNA513.WMF
ORNA514.WMF
ORNA515.WMF
ORNA516.WMF
ORNA517.WMF
ORNA518.WMF
ORNA519.WMF
ORNA520.WMF
ORNA521.WMF
ORNA522.WMF
ORNA523.WMF
ORNA524.WMF
ORNA525.WMF
ORNA526.WMF
ORNA527.WMF
ORNA528.WMF
ORNA529.WMF
ORNA530.WMF
ORNA531.WMF
ORNA532.WMF
ORNA533.WMF
ORNA534.WMF
ORNA535.WMF
ORNA536.WMF
ORNA537.WMF
ORNA538.WMF
ORNA539.WMF
ORNA540.WMF
ORNA541.WMF
ORNA542.WMF
ORNA543.WMF
ORNA544.WMF
ORNA545.WMF
ORNA546.WMF
ORNA547.WMF
ORNA548.WMF
ORNA549.WMF
ORNA550.WMF
ORNA551.WMF
ORNA552.WMF
ORNA553.WMF
ORNA554.WMF
ORNA555.WMF
ORNA556.WMF
ORNA557.WMF
ORNA558.WMF
ORNA559.WMF
ORNA560.WMF
ORNA561.WMF
ORNA562.WMF
ORNA563.WMF
ORNA564.WMF
ORNA565.WMF
ORNA566.WMF
ORNA567.WMF
ORNA568.WMF
ORNA569.WMF
ORNA570.WMF
ORNA571.WMF
ORNA572.WMF
ORNA573.WMF
ORNA574.WMF
ORNA575.WMF
ORNA576.WMF
ORNA577.WMF
ORNA578.WMF
ORNA579.WMF
ORNA580.WMF
ORNA581.WMF
ORNA582.WMF
ORNA583.WMF
ORNA584.WMF
ORNA585.WMF
ORNA586.WMF
ORNA587.WMF
ORNA588.WMF
ORNA589.WMF
ORNA590.WMF
ORNA591.WMF
ORNA592.WMF

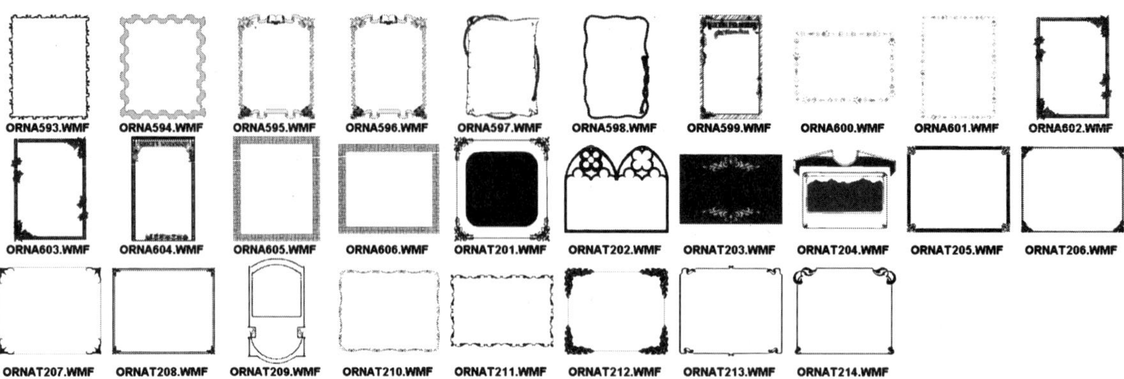
ORNA593.WMF
ORNA594.WMF
ORNA595.WMF
ORNA596.WMF
ORNA597.WMF
ORNA598.WMF
ORNA599.WMF
ORNA600.WMF
ORNA601.WMF
ORNA602.WMF
ORNA603.WMF
ORNA604.WMF
ORNA605.WMF
ORNA606.WMF
ORNAT201.WMF
ORNAT202.WMF
ORNAT203.WMF
ORNAT204.WMF
ORNAT205.WMF
ORNAT206.WMF
ORNAT207.WMF
ORNAT208.WMF
ORNAT209.WMF
ORNAT210.WMF
ORNAT211.WMF
ORNAT212.WMF
ORNAT213.WMF
ORNAT214.WMF

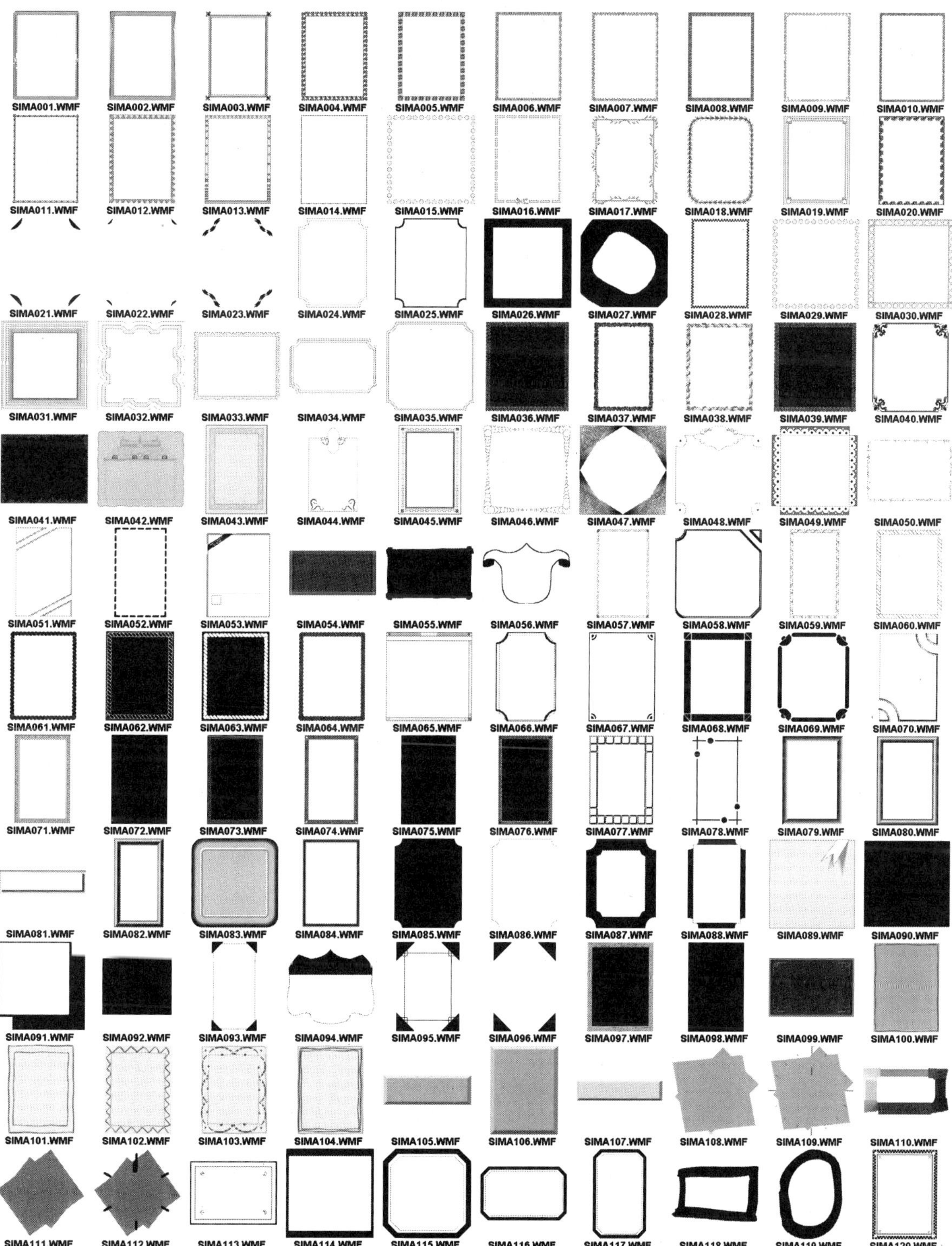
SIMA001.WMF
SIMA002.WMF
SIMA003.WMF
SIMA004.WMF
SIMA005.WMF
SIMA006.WMF
SIMA007.WMF
SIMA008.WMF
SIMA009.WMF
SIMA010.WMF
SIMA011.WMF
SIMA012.WMF
SIMA013.WMF
SIMA014.WMF
SIMA015.WMF
SIMA016.WMF
SIMA017.WMF
SIMA018.WMF
SIMA019.WMF
SIMA020.WMF
SIMA021.WMF
SIMA022.WMF
SIMA023.WMF
SIMA024.WMF
SIMA025.WMF
SIMA026.WMF
SIMA027.WMF
SIMA028.WMF
SIMA029.WMF
SIMA030.WMF
SIMA031.WMF
SIMA032.WMF
SIMA033.WMF
SIMA034.WMF
SIMA035.WMF
SIMA036.WMF
SIMA037.WMF
SIMA038.WMF
SIMA039.WMF
SIMA040.WMF
SIMA041.WMF
SIMA042.WMF
SIMA043.WMF
SIMA044.WMF
SIMA045.WMF
SIMA046.WMF
SIMA047.WMF
SIMA048.WMF
SIMA049.WMF
SIMA050.WMF
SIMA051.WMF
SIMA052.WMF
SIMA053.WMF
SIMA054.WMF
SIMA055.WMF
SIMA056.WMF
SIMA057.WMF
SIMA058.WMF
SIMA059.WMF
SIMA060.WMF
SIMA061.WMF
SIMA062.WMF
SIMA063.WMF
SIMA064.WMF
SIMA065.WMF
SIMA066.WMF
SIMA067.WMF
SIMA068.WMF
SIMA069.WMF
SIMA070.WMF
SIMA071.WMF
SIMA072.WMF
SIMA073.WMF
SIMA074.WMF
SIMA075.WMF
SIMA076.WMF
SIMA077.WMF
SIMA078.WMF
SIMA079.WMF
SIMA080.WMF
SIMA081.WMF
SIMA082.WMF
SIMA083.WMF
SIMA084.WMF
SIMA085.WMF
SIMA086.WMF
SIMA087.WMF
SIMA088.WMF
SIMA089.WMF
SIMA090.WMF
SIMA091.WMF
SIMA092.WMF
SIMA093.WMF
SIMA094.WMF
SIMA095.WMF
SIMA096.WMF
SIMA097.WMF
SIMA098.WMF
SIMA099.WMF
SIMA100.WMF
SIMA101.WMF
SIMA102.WMF
SIMA103.WMF
SIMA104.WMF
SIMA105.WMF
SIMA106.WMF
SIMA107.WMF
SIMA108.WMF
SIMA109.WMF
SIMA110.WMF
SIMA111.WMF
SIMA112.WMF
SIMA113.WMF
SIMA114.WMF
SIMA115.WMF
SIMA116.WMF
SIMA117.WMF
SIMA118.WMF
SIMA119.WMF
SIMA120.WMF

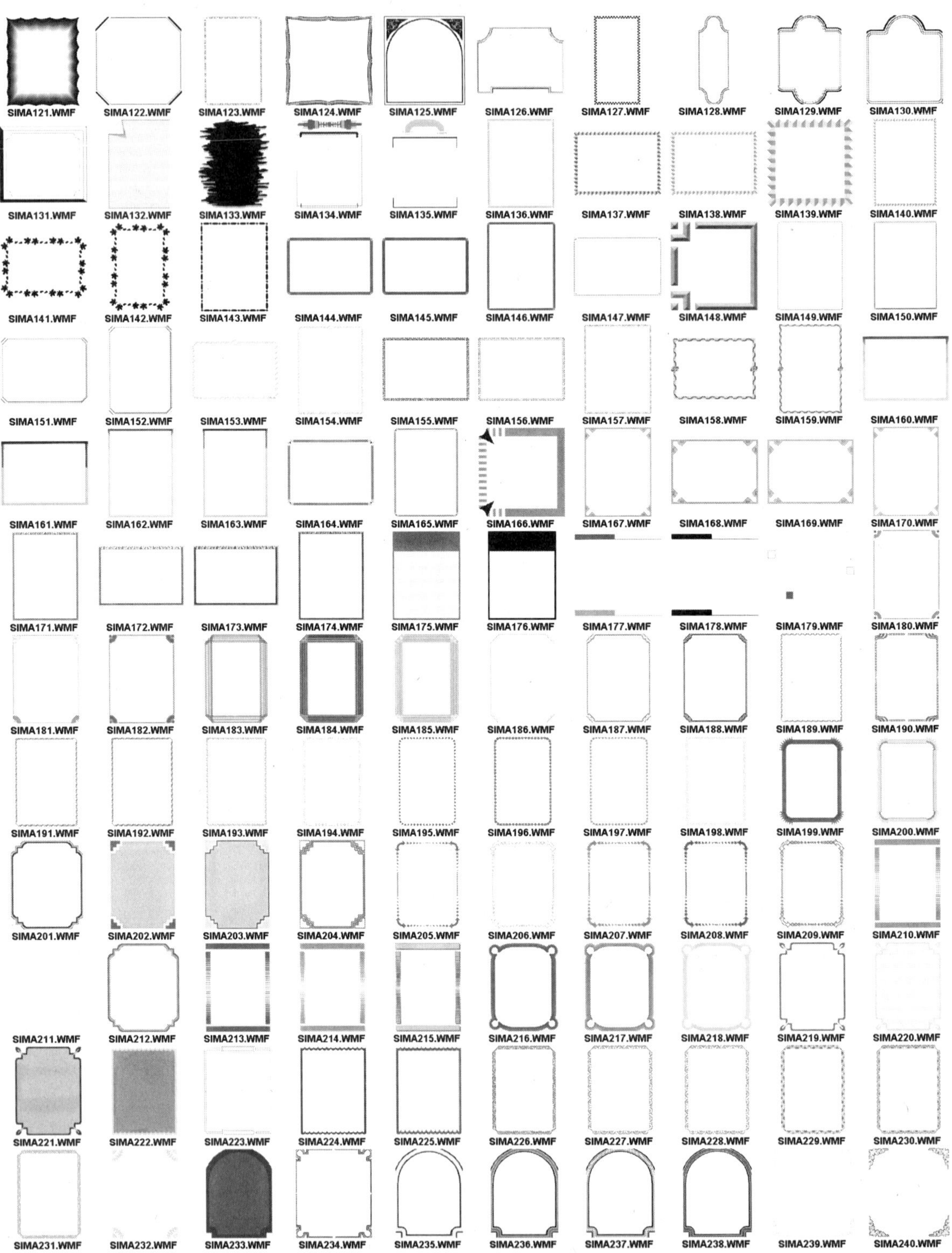
SIMA121.WMF
SIMA122.WMF
SIMA123.WMF
SIMA124.WMF
SIMA125.WMF
SIMA126.WMF
SIMA127.WMF
SIMA128.WMF
SIMA129.WMF
SIMA130.WMF
SIMA131.WMF
SIMA132.WMF
SIMA133.WMF
SIMA134.WMF
SIMA135.WMF
SIMA136.WMF
SIMA137.WMF
SIMA138.WMF
SIMA139.WMF
SIMA140.WMF
SIMA141.WMF
SIMA142.WMF
SIMA143.WMF
SIMA144.WMF
SIMA145.WMF
SIMA146.WMF
SIMA147.WMF
SIMA148.WMF
SIMA149.WMF
SIMA150.WMF
SIMA151.WMF
SIMA152.WMF
SIMA153.WMF
SIMA154.WMF
SIMA155.WMF
SIMA156.WMF
SIMA157.WMF
SIMA158.WMF
SIMA159.WMF
SIMA160.WMF
SIMA161.WMF
SIMA162.WMF
SIMA163.WMF
SIMA164.WMF
SIMA165.WMF
SIMA166.WMF
SIMA167.WMF
SIMA168.WMF
SIMA169.WMF
SIMA170.WMF
SIMA171.WMF
SIMA172.WMF
SIMA173.WMF
SIMA174.WMF
SIMA175.WMF
SIMA176.WMF
SIMA177.WMF
SIMA178.WMF
SIMA179.WMF
SIMA180.WMF
SIMA181.WMF
SIMA182.WMF
SIMA183.WMF
SIMA184.WMF
SIMA185.WMF
SIMA186.WMF
SIMA187.WMF
SIMA188.WMF
SIMA189.WMF
SIMA190.WMF
SIMA191.WMF
SIMA192.WMF
SIMA193.WMF
SIMA194.WMF
SIMA195.WMF
SIMA196.WMF
SIMA197.WMF
SIMA198.WMF
SIMA199.WMF
SIMA200.WMF
SIMA201.WMF
SIMA202.WMF
SIMA203.WMF
SIMA204.WMF
SIMA205.WMF
SIMA206.WMF
SIMA207.WMF
SIMA208.WMF
SIMA209.WMF
SIMA210.WMF
SIMA211.WMF
SIMA212.WMF
SIMA213.WMF
SIMA214.WMF
SIMA215.WMF
SIMA216.WMF
SIMA217.WMF
SIMA218.WMF
SIMA219.WMF
SIMA220.WMF
SIMA221.WMF
SIMA222.WMF
SIMA223.WMF
SIMA224.WMF
SIMA225.WMF
SIMA226.WMF
SIMA227.WMF
SIMA228.WMF
SIMA229.WMF
SIMA230.WMF
SIMA231.WMF
SIMA232.WMF
SIMA233.WMF
SIMA234.WMF
SIMA235.WMF
SIMA236.WMF
SIMA237.WMF
SIMA238.WMF
SIMA239.WMF
SIMA240.WMF

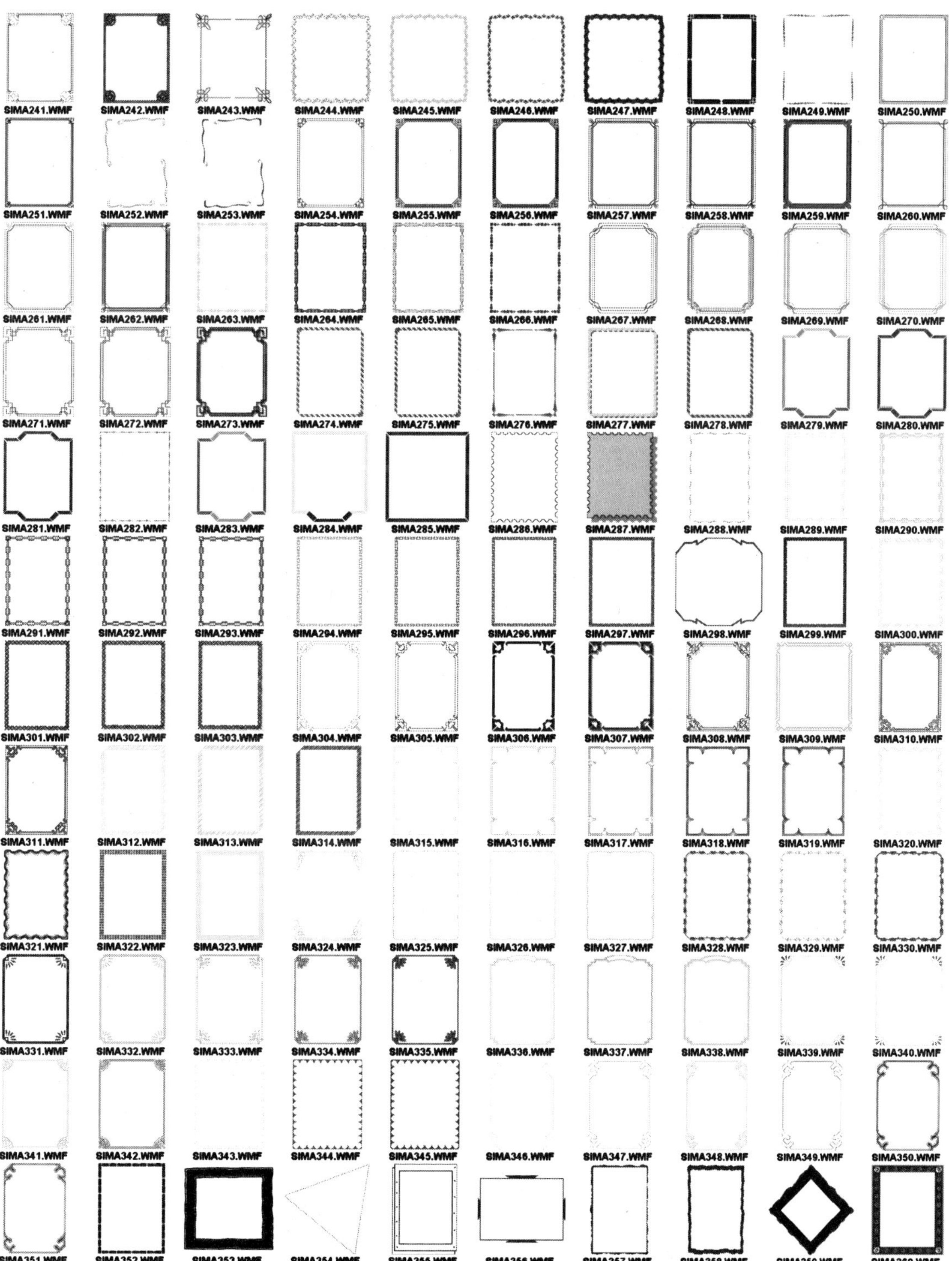
SIMA241.WMF
SIMA242.WMF
SIMA243.WMF
SIMA244.WMF
SIMA245.WMF
SIMA246.WMF
SIMA247.WMF
SIMA248.WMF
SIMA249.WMF
SIMA250.WMF
SIMA251.WMF
SIMA252.WMF
SIMA253.WMF
SIMA254.WMF
SIMA255.WMF
SIMA256.WMF
SIMA257.WMF
SIMA258.WMF
SIMA259.WMF
SIMA260.WMF
SIMA261.WMF
SIMA262.WMF
SIMA263.WMF
SIMA264.WMF
SIMA265.WMF
SIMA266.WMF
SIMA267.WMF
SIMA268.WMF
SIMA269.WMF
SIMA270.WMF
SIMA271.WMF
SIMA272.WMF
SIMA273.WMF
SIMA274.WMF
SIMA275.WMF
SIMA276.WMF
SIMA277.WMF
SIMA278.WMF
SIMA279.WMF
SIMA280.WMF
SIMA281.WMF
SIMA282.WMF
SIMA283.WMF
SIMA284.WMF
SIMA285.WMF
SIMA286.WMF
SIMA287.WMF
SIMA288.WMF
SIMA289.WMF
SIMA290.WMF
SIMA291.WMF
SIMA292.WMF
SIMA293.WMF
SIMA294.WMF
SIMA295.WMF
SIMA296.WMF
SIMA297.WMF
SIMA298.WMF
SIMA299.WMF
SIMA300.WMF
SIMA301.WMF
SIMA302.WMF
SIMA303.WMF
SIMA304.WMF
SIMA305.WMF
SIMA306.WMF
SIMA307.WMF
SIMA308.WMF
SIMA309.WMF
SIMA310.WMF
SIMA311.WMF
SIMA312.WMF
SIMA313.WMF
SIMA314.WMF
SIMA315.WMF
SIMA316.WMF
SIMA317.WMF
SIMA318.WMF
SIMA319.WMF
SIMA320.WMF
SIMA321.WMF
SIMA322.WMF
SIMA323.WMF
SIMA324.WMF
SIMA325.WMF
SIMA326.WMF
SIMA327.WMF
SIMA328.WMF
SIMA329.WMF
SIMA330.WMF
SIMA331.WMF
SIMA332.WMF
SIMA333.WMF
SIMA334.WMF
SIMA335.WMF
SIMA336.WMF
SIMA337.WMF
SIMA338.WMF
SIMA339.WMF
SIMA340.WMF
SIMA341.WMF
SIMA342.WMF
SIMA343.WMF
SIMA344.WMF
SIMA345.WMF
SIMA346.WMF
SIMA347.WMF
SIMA348.WMF
SIMA349.WMF
SIMA350.WMF
SIMA351.WMF
SIMA352.WMF
SIMA353.WMF
SIMA354.WMF
SIMA355.WMF
SIMA356.WMF
SIMA357.WMF
SIMA358.WMF
SIMA359.WMF
SIMA360.WMF

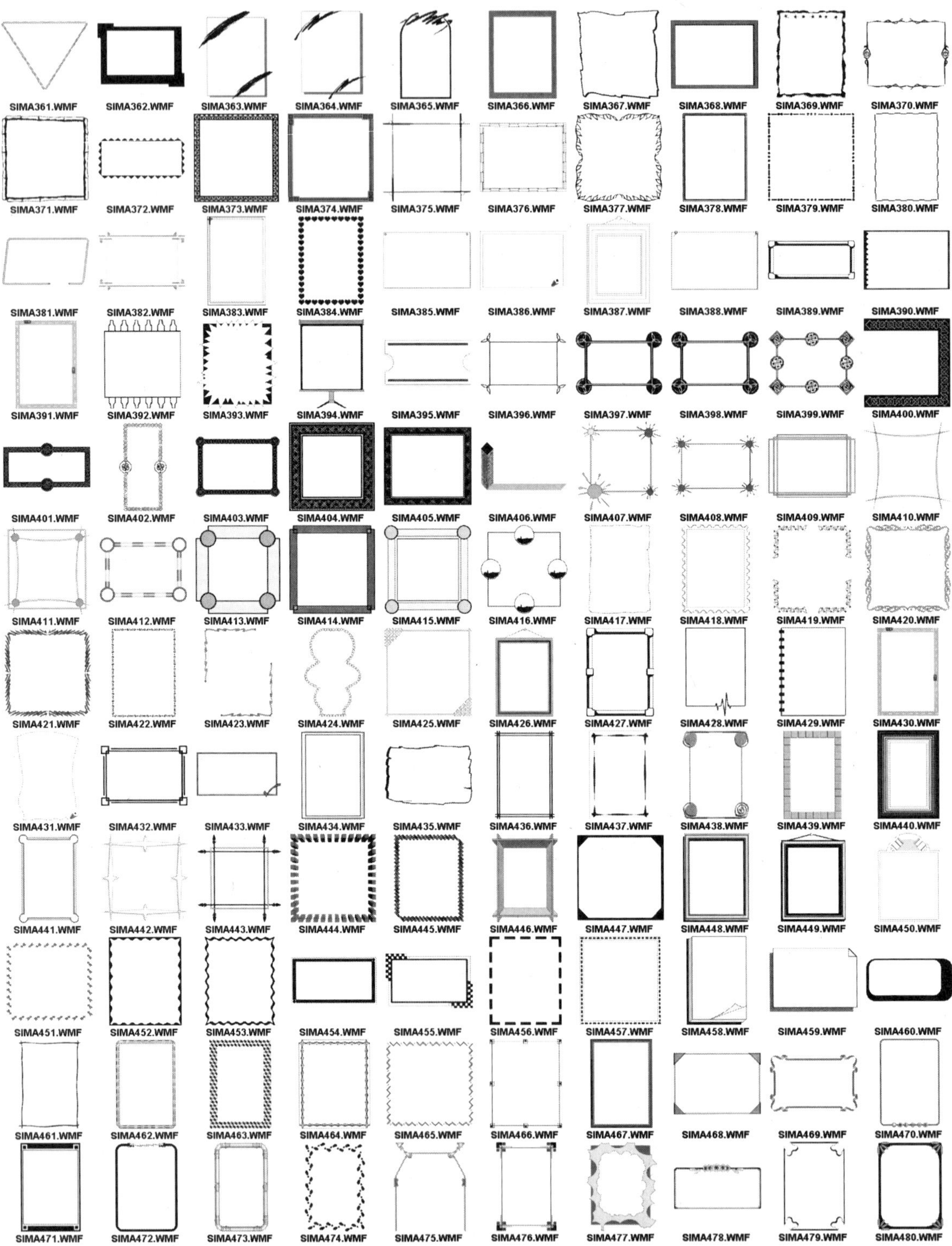
SIMA361.WMF
SIMA362.WMF
SIMA363.WMF
SIMA364.WMF
SIMA365.WMF
SIMA366.WMF
SIMA367.WMF
SIMA368.WMF
SIMA369.WMF
SIMA370.WMF
SIMA371.WMF
SIMA372.WMF
SIMA373.WMF
SIMA374.WMF
SIMA375.WMF
SIMA376.WMF
SIMA377.WMF
SIMA378.WMF
SIMA379.WMF
SIMA380.WMF
SIMA381.WMF
SIMA382.WMF
SIMA383.WMF
SIMA384.WMF
SIMA385.WMF
SIMA386.WMF
SIMA387.WMF
SIMA388.WMF
SIMA389.WMF
SIMA390.WMF
SIMA391.WMF
SIMA392.WMF
SIMA393.WMF
SIMA394.WMF
SIMA395.WMF
SIMA396.WMF
SIMA397.WMF
SIMA398.WMF
SIMA399.WMF
SIMA400.WMF
SIMA401.WMF
SIMA402.WMF
SIMA403.WMF
SIMA404.WMF
SIMA405.WMF
SIMA406.WMF
SIMA407.WMF
SIMA408.WMF
SIMA409.WMF
SIMA410.WMF
SIMA411.WMF
SIMA412.WMF
SIMA413.WMF
SIMA414.WMF
SIMA415.WMF
SIMA416.WMF
SIMA417.WMF
SIMA418.WMF
SIMA419.WMF
SIMA420.WMF
SIMA421.WMF
SIMA422.WMF
SIMA423.WMF
SIMA424.WMF
SIMA425.WMF
SIMA426.WMF
SIMA427.WMF
SIMA428.WMF
SIMA429.WMF
SIMA430.WMF
SIMA431.WMF
SIMA432.WMF
SIMA433.WMF
SIMA434.WMF
SIMA435.WMF
SIMA436.WMF
SIMA437.WMF
SIMA438.WMF
SIMA439.WMF
SIMA440.WMF
SIMA441.WMF
SIMA442.WMF
SIMA443.WMF
SIMA444.WMF
SIMA445.WMF
SIMA446.WMF
SIMA447.WMF
SIMA448.WMF
SIMA449.WMF
SIMA450.WMF
SIMA451.WMF
SIMA452.WMF
SIMA453.WMF
SIMA454.WMF
SIMA455.WMF
SIMA456.WMF
SIMA457.WMF
SIMA458.WMF
SIMA459.WMF
SIMA460.WMF
SIMA461.WMF
SIMA462.WMF
SIMA463.WMF
SIMA464.WMF
SIMA465.WMF
SIMA466.WMF
SIMA467.WMF
SIMA468.WMF
SIMA469.WMF
SIMA470.WMF
SIMA471.WMF
SIMA472.WMF
SIMA473.WMF
SIMA474.WMF
SIMA475.WMF
SIMA476.WMF
SIMA477.WMF
SIMA478.WMF
SIMA479.WMF
SIMA480.WMF

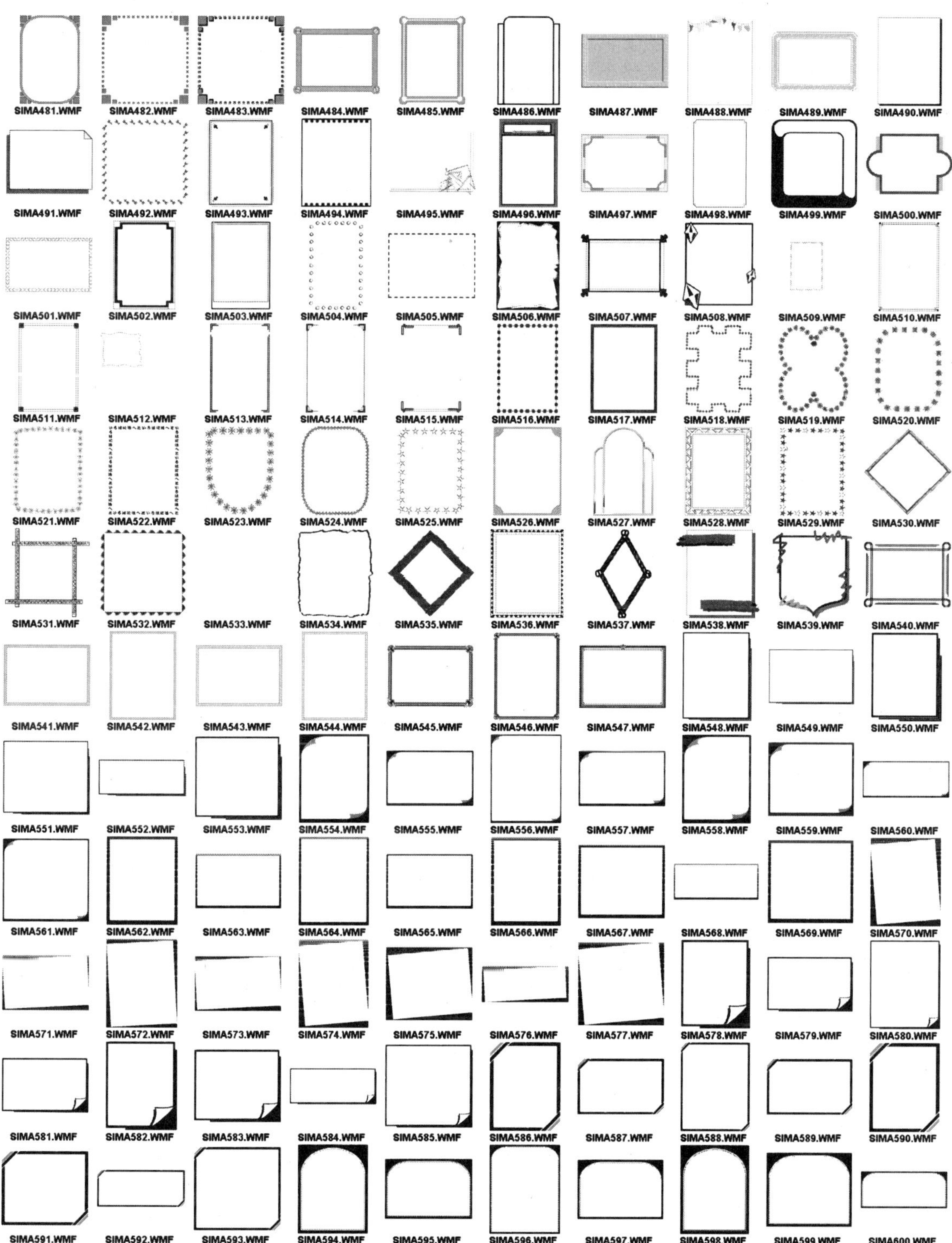
SIMA481.WMF
SIMA482.WMF
SIMA483.WMF
SIMA484.WMF
SIMA485.WMF
SIMA486.WMF
SIMA487.WMF
SIMA488.WMF
SIMA489.WMF
SIMA490.WMF
SIMA491.WMF
SIMA492.WMF
SIMA493.WMF
SIMA494.WMF
SIMA495.WMF
SIMA496.WMF
SIMA497.WMF
SIMA498.WMF
SIMA499.WMF
SIMA500.WMF
SIMA501.WMF
SIMA502.WMF
SIMA503.WMF
SIMA504.WMF
SIMA505.WMF
SIMA506.WMF
SIMA507.WMF
SIMA508.WMF
SIMA509.WMF
SIMA510.WMF
SIMA511.WMF
SIMA512.WMF
SIMA513.WMF
SIMA514.WMF
SIMA515.WMF
SIMA516.WMF
SIMA517.WMF
SIMA518.WMF
SIMA519.WMF
SIMA520.WMF
SIMA521.WMF
SIMA522.WMF
SIMA523.WMF
SIMA524.WMF
SIMA525.WMF
SIMA526.WMF
SIMA527.WMF
SIMA528.WMF
SIMA529.WMF
SIMA530.WMF
SIMA531.WMF
SIMA532.WMF
SIMA533.WMF
SIMA534.WMF
SIMA535.WMF
SIMA536.WMF
SIMA537.WMF
SIMA538.WMF
SIMA539.WMF
SIMA540.WMF
SIMA541.WMF
SIMA542.WMF
SIMA543.WMF
SIMA544.WMF
SIMA545.WMF
SIMA546.WMF
SIMA547.WMF
SIMA548.WMF
SIMA549.WMF
SIMA550.WMF
SIMA551.WMF
SIMA552.WMF
SIMA553.WMF
SIMA554.WMF
SIMA555.WMF
SIMA556.WMF
SIMA557.WMF
SIMA558.WMF
SIMA559.WMF
SIMA560.WMF
SIMA561.WMF
SIMA562.WMF
SIMA563.WMF
SIMA564.WMF
SIMA565.WMF
SIMA566.WMF
SIMA567.WMF
SIMA568.WMF
SIMA569.WMF
SIMA570.WMF
SIMA571.WMF
SIMA572.WMF
SIMA573.WMF
SIMA574.WMF
SIMA575.WMF
SIMA576.WMF
SIMA577.WMF
SIMA578.WMF
SIMA579.WMF
SIMA580.WMF
SIMA581.WMF
SIMA582.WMF
SIMA583.WMF
SIMA584.WMF
SIMA585.WMF
SIMA586.WMF
SIMA587.WMF
SIMA588.WMF
SIMA589.WMF
SIMA590.WMF
SIMA591.WMF
SIMA592.WMF
SIMA593.WMF
SIMA594.WMF
SIMA595.WMF
SIMA596.WMF
SIMA597.WMF
SIMA598.WMF
SIMA599.WMF
SIMA600.WMF

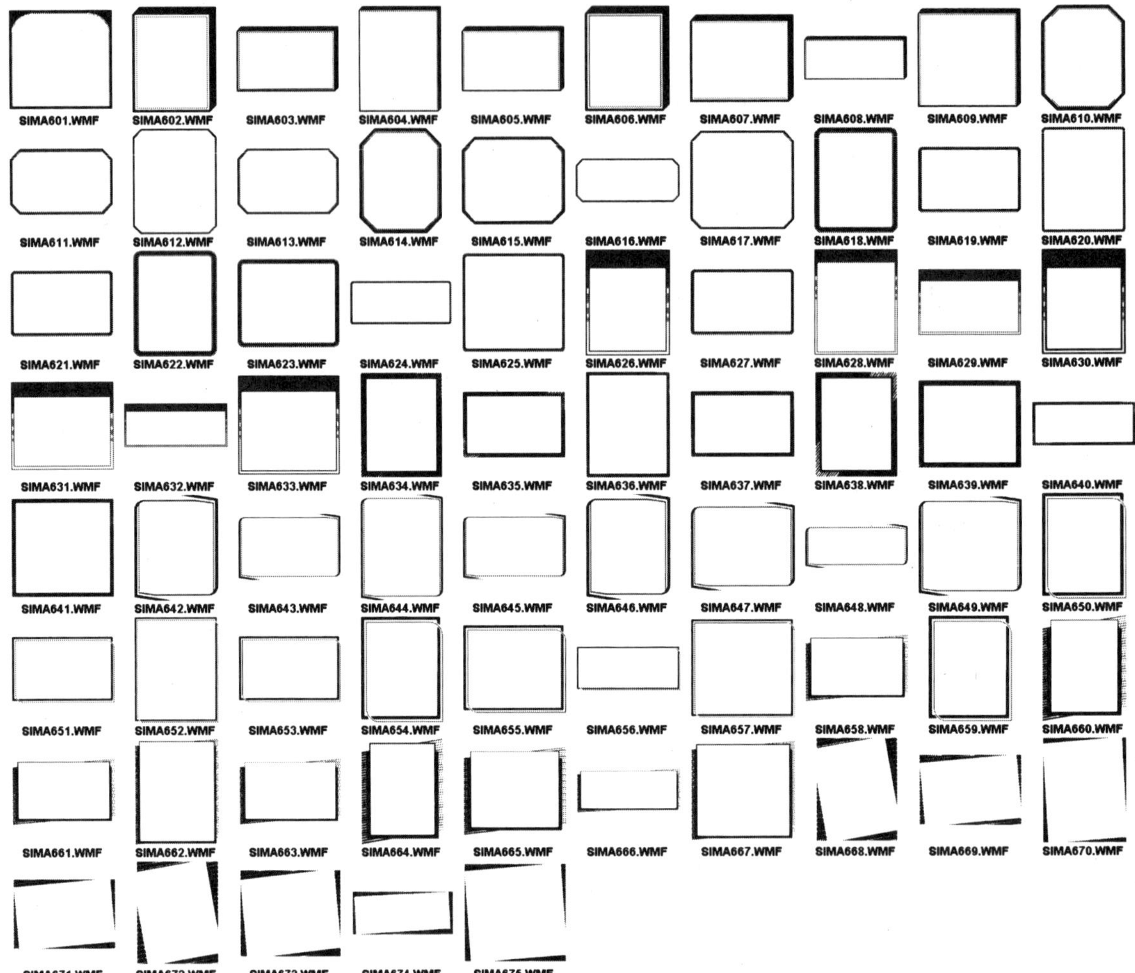
SIMA601.WMF
SIMA602.WMF
SIMA603.WMF
SIMA604.WMF
SIMA605.WMF
SIMA606.WMF
SIMA607.WMF
SIMA608.WMF
SIMA609.WMF
SIMA610.WMF
SIMA611.WMF
SIMA612.WMF
SIMA613.WMF
SIMA614.WMF
SIMA615.WMF
SIMA616.WMF
SIMA617.WMF
SIMA618.WMF
SIMA619.WMF
SIMA620.WMF
SIMA621.WMF
SIMA622.WMF
SIMA623.WMF
SIMA624.WMF
SIMA625.WMF
SIMA626.WMF
SIMA627.WMF
SIMA628.WMF
SIMA629.WMF
SIMA630.WMF
SIMA631.WMF
SIMA632.WMF
SIMA633.WMF
SIMA634.WMF
SIMA635.WMF
SIMA636.WMF
SIMA637.WMF
SIMA638.WMF
SIMA639.WMF
SIMA640.WMF
SIMA641.WMF
SIMA642.WMF
SIMA643.WMF
SIMA644.WMF
SIMA645.WMF
SIMA646.WMF
SIMA647.WMF
SIMA648.WMF
SIMA649.WMF
SIMA650.WMF
SIMA651.WMF
SIMA652.WMF
SIMA653.WMF
SIMA654.WMF
SIMA655.WMF
SIMA656.WMF
SIMA657.WMF
SIMA658.WMF
SIMA659.WMF
SIMA660.WMF
SIMA661.WMF
SIMA662.WMF
SIMA663.WMF
SIMA664.WMF
SIMA665.WMF
SIMA666.WMF
SIMA667.WMF
SIMA668.WMF
SIMA669.WMF
SIMA670.WMF
SIMA671.WMF
SIMA672.WMF
SIMA673.WMF
SIMA674.WMF
SIMA675.WMF

SIMB001.WMF	SIMB002.WMF	SIMB003.WMF	SIMB004.WMF	SIMB005.WMF	SIMB006.WMF	SIMB007.WMF	SIMB008.WMF	SIMB009.WMF	SIMB010.WMF
SIMB011.WMF	SIMB012.WMF	SIMB013.WMF	SIMB014.WMF	SIMB015.WMF	SIMB016.WMF	SIMB017.WMF	SIMB018.WMF	SIMB019.WMF	SIMB020.WMF
SIMB021.WMF	SIMB022.WMF	SIMB023.WMF	SIMB024.WMF	SIMB025.WMF	SIMB026.WMF	SIMB027.WMF	SIMB028.WMF	SIMB029.WMF	SIMB030.WMF
SIMB031.WMF	SIMB032.WMF	SIMB033.WMF	SIMB034.WMF	SIMB035.WMF	SIMB036.WMF	SIMB037.WMF	SIMB038.WMF	SIMB039.WMF	SIMB040.WMF
SIMB041.WMF	SIMB042.WMF	SIMB043.WMF	SIMB044.WMF	SIMB045.WMF	SIMB046.WMF	SIMB047.WMF	SIMB048.WMF	SIMB049.WMF	SIMB050.WMF
SIMB051.WMF	SIMB052.WMF	SIMB053.WMF	SIMB054.WMF	SIMB055.WMF	SIMB056.WMF	SIMB057.WMF	SIMB058.WMF	SIMB059.WMF	SIMB060.WMF
SIMB061.WMF	SIMB062.WMF	SIMB063.WMF	SIMB064.WMF	SIMB065.WMF	SIMB066.WMF	SIMB067.WMF	SIMB068.WMF	SIMB069.WMF	SIMB070.WMF
SIMB071.WMF	SIMB072.WMF	SIMB073.WMF	SIMB074.WMF	SIMB075.WMF	SIMB076.WMF	SIMB077.WMF	SIMB078.WMF	SIMB079.WMF	SIMB080.WMF
SIMB081.WMF	SIMB082.WMF	SIMB083.WMF	SIMB084.WMF	SIMB085.WMF	SIMB086.WMF	SIMB087.WMF	SIMB088.WMF	SIMB089.WMF	SIMB090.WMF
SIMB091.WMF	SIMB092.WMF	SIMB093.WMF	SIMB094.WMF	SIMB095.WMF	SIMB096.WMF	SIMB097.WMF	SIMB098.WMF	SIMB099.WMF	SIMB100.WMF
SIMB101.WMF	SIMB102.WMF	SIMB103.WMF	SIMB104.WMF	SIMB105.WMF	SIMB106.WMF	SIMB107.WMF	SIMB108.WMF	SIMB109.WMF	SIMB110.WMF
SIMB111.WMF	SIMB112.WMF	SIMB113.WMF	SIMB114.WMF	SIMB115.WMF	SIMB116.WMF	SIMB117.WMF	SIMB118.WMF	SIMB119.WMF	SIMB120.WMF

SIMB121.WMF SIMB122.WMF SIMB123.WMF SIMB124.WMF SIMB125.WMF SIMB126.WMF SIMB127.WMF SIMB128.WMF SIMB129.WMF SIMB130.WMF

SIMB131.WMF SIMB132.WMF SIMB133.WMF SIMB134.WMF SIMB135.WMF SIMB136.WMF SIMB137.WMF SIMB138.WMF SIMB139.WMF SIMB140.WMF

SIMB141.WMF SIMB142.WMF SIMB143.WMF SIMB144.WMF SIMB145.WMF SIMB146.WMF SIMB147.WMF SIMB148.WMF SIMB149.WMF SIMB150.WMF

SIMB151.WMF SIMB152.WMF SIMB153.WMF SIMB154.WMF SIMB155.WMF SIMB156.WMF SIMB157.WMF SIMB158.WMF SIMB159.WMF SIMB160.WMF

SIMB161.WMF SIMB162.WMF SIMB163.WMF SIMB164.WMF SIMB165.WMF SIMB166.WMF SIMB167.WMF SIMB168.WMF SIMB169.WMF SIMB170.WMF

SIMB171.WMF SIMB172.WMF SIMB173.WMF SIMB174.WMF SIMB175.WMF SIMB176.WMF SIMB177.WMF SIMB178.WMF SIMB179.WMF SIMB180.WMF

SIMB181.WMF SIMB182.WMF SIMB183.WMF SIMB184.WMF SIMB185.WMF SIMB186.WMF SIMB187.WMF SIMB188.WMF SIMB189.WMF SIMB190.WMF

SIMB191.WMF SIMB192.WMF SIMB193.WMF SIMB194.WMF SIMB195.WMF SIMB196.WMF SIMB197.WMF SIMB198.WMF SIMB199.WMF SIMB200.WMF

SIMB201.WMF SIMB202.WMF SIMB203.WMF SIMB204.WMF SIMB205.WMF SIMB206.WMF SIMB207.WMF SIMB208.WMF SIMB209.WMF SIMB210.WMF

SIMB211.WMF SIMB212.WMF SIMB213.WMF SIMB214.WMF SIMB215.WMF SIMB216.WMF SIMB217.WMF SIMB218.WMF SIMB219.WMF SIMB220.WMF

SIMB221.WMF SIMB222.WMF SIMB223.WMF SIMB224.WMF SIMB225.WMF SIMB226.WMF SIMB227.WMF SIMB228.WMF SIMB229.WMF SIMB230.WMF

SIMB231.WMF SIMB232.WMF SIMB233.WMF SIMB234.WMF SIMB235.WMF SIMB236.WMF SIMB237.WMF SIMB238.WMF SIMB239.WMF SIMB240.WMF

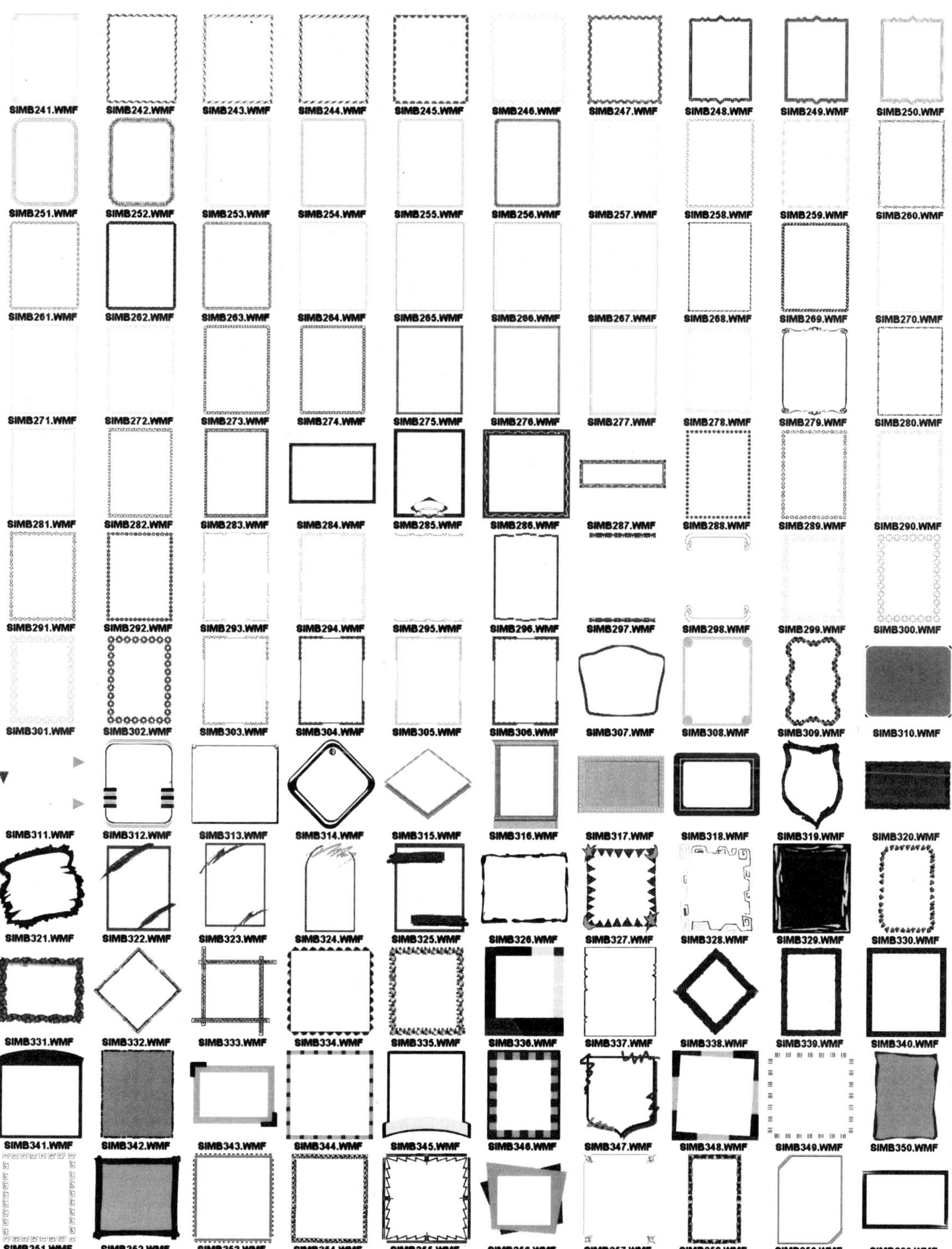
SIMB241.WMF
SIMB242.WMF
SIMB243.WMF
SIMB244.WMF
SIMB245.WMF
SIMB246.WMF
SIMB247.WMF
SIMB248.WMF
SIMB249.WMF
SIMB250.WMF
SIMB251.WMF
SIMB252.WMF
SIMB253.WMF
SIMB254.WMF
SIMB255.WMF
SIMB256.WMF
SIMB257.WMF
SIMB258.WMF
SIMB259.WMF
SIMB260.WMF
SIMB261.WMF
SIMB262.WMF
SIMB263.WMF
SIMB264.WMF
SIMB265.WMF
SIMB266.WMF
SIMB267.WMF
SIMB268.WMF
SIMB269.WMF
SIMB270.WMF
SIMB271.WMF
SIMB272.WMF
SIMB273.WMF
SIMB274.WMF
SIMB275.WMF
SIMB276.WMF
SIMB277.WMF
SIMB278.WMF
SIMB279.WMF
SIMB280.WMF
SIMB281.WMF
SIMB282.WMF
SIMB283.WMF
SIMB284.WMF
SIMB285.WMF
SIMB286.WMF
SIMB287.WMF
SIMB288.WMF
SIMB289.WMF
SIMB290.WMF
SIMB291.WMF
SIMB292.WMF
SIMB293.WMF
SIMB294.WMF
SIMB295.WMF
SIMB296.WMF
SIMB297.WMF
SIMB298.WMF
SIMB299.WMF
SIMB300.WMF
SIMB301.WMF
SIMB302.WMF
SIMB303.WMF
SIMB304.WMF
SIMB305.WMF
SIMB306.WMF
SIMB307.WMF
SIMB308.WMF
SIMB309.WMF
SIMB310.WMF
SIMB311.WMF
SIMB312.WMF
SIMB313.WMF
SIMB314.WMF
SIMB315.WMF
SIMB316.WMF
SIMB317.WMF
SIMB318.WMF
SIMB319.WMF
SIMB320.WMF
SIMB321.WMF
SIMB322.WMF
SIMB323.WMF
SIMB324.WMF
SIMB325.WMF
SIMB326.WMF
SIMB327.WMF
SIMB328.WMF
SIMB329.WMF
SIMB330.WMF
SIMB331.WMF
SIMB332.WMF
SIMB333.WMF
SIMB334.WMF
SIMB335.WMF
SIMB336.WMF
SIMB337.WMF
SIMB338.WMF
SIMB339.WMF
SIMB340.WMF
SIMB341.WMF
SIMB342.WMF
SIMB343.WMF
SIMB344.WMF
SIMB345.WMF
SIMB346.WMF
SIMB347.WMF
SIMB348.WMF
SIMB349.WMF
SIMB350.WMF
SIMB351.WMF
SIMB352.WMF
SIMB353.WMF
SIMB354.WMF
SIMB355.WMF
SIMB356.WMF
SIMB357.WMF
SIMB358.WMF
SIMB359.WMF
SIMB360.WMF

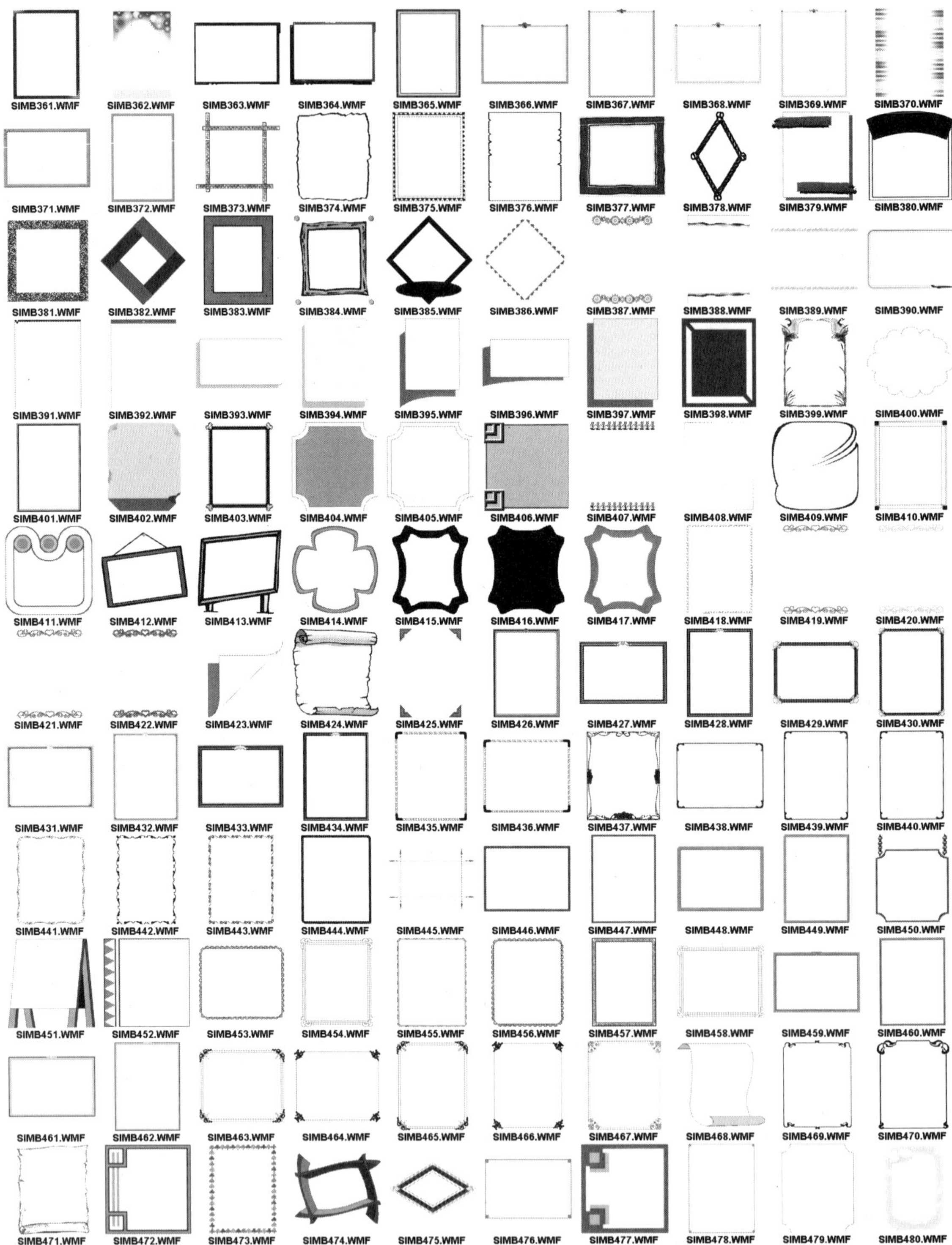
SIMB361.WMF
SIMB362.WMF
SIMB363.WMF
SIMB364.WMF
SIMB365.WMF
SIMB366.WMF
SIMB367.WMF
SIMB368.WMF
SIMB369.WMF
SIMB370.WMF
SIMB371.WMF
SIMB372.WMF
SIMB373.WMF
SIMB374.WMF
SIMB375.WMF
SIMB376.WMF
SIMB377.WMF
SIMB378.WMF
SIMB379.WMF
SIMB380.WMF
SIMB381.WMF
SIMB382.WMF
SIMB383.WMF
SIMB384.WMF
SIMB385.WMF
SIMB386.WMF
SIMB387.WMF
SIMB388.WMF
SIMB389.WMF
SIMB390.WMF
SIMB391.WMF
SIMB392.WMF
SIMB393.WMF
SIMB394.WMF
SIMB395.WMF
SIMB396.WMF
SIMB397.WMF
SIMB398.WMF
SIMB399.WMF
SIMB400.WMF
SIMB401.WMF
SIMB402.WMF
SIMB403.WMF
SIMB404.WMF
SIMB405.WMF
SIMB406.WMF
SIMB407.WMF
SIMB408.WMF
SIMB409.WMF
SIMB410.WMF
SIMB411.WMF
SIMB412.WMF
SIMB413.WMF
SIMB414.WMF
SIMB415.WMF
SIMB416.WMF
SIMB417.WMF
SIMB418.WMF
SIMB419.WMF
SIMB420.WMF
SIMB421.WMF
SIMB422.WMF
SIMB423.WMF
SIMB424.WMF
SIMB425.WMF
SIMB426.WMF
SIMB427.WMF
SIMB428.WMF
SIMB429.WMF
SIMB430.WMF
SIMB431.WMF
SIMB432.WMF
SIMB433.WMF
SIMB434.WMF
SIMB435.WMF
SIMB436.WMF
SIMB437.WMF
SIMB438.WMF
SIMB439.WMF
SIMB440.WMF
SIMB441.WMF
SIMB442.WMF
SIMB443.WMF
SIMB444.WMF
SIMB445.WMF
SIMB446.WMF
SIMB447.WMF
SIMB448.WMF
SIMB449.WMF
SIMB450.WMF
SIMB451.WMF
SIMB452.WMF
SIMB453.WMF
SIMB454.WMF
SIMB455.WMF
SIMB456.WMF
SIMB457.WMF
SIMB458.WMF
SIMB459.WMF
SIMB460.WMF
SIMB461.WMF
SIMB462.WMF
SIMB463.WMF
SIMB464.WMF
SIMB465.WMF
SIMB466.WMF
SIMB467.WMF
SIMB468.WMF
SIMB469.WMF
SIMB470.WMF
SIMB471.WMF
SIMB472.WMF
SIMB473.WMF
SIMB474.WMF
SIMB475.WMF
SIMB476.WMF
SIMB477.WMF
SIMB478.WMF
SIMB479.WMF
SIMB480.WMF

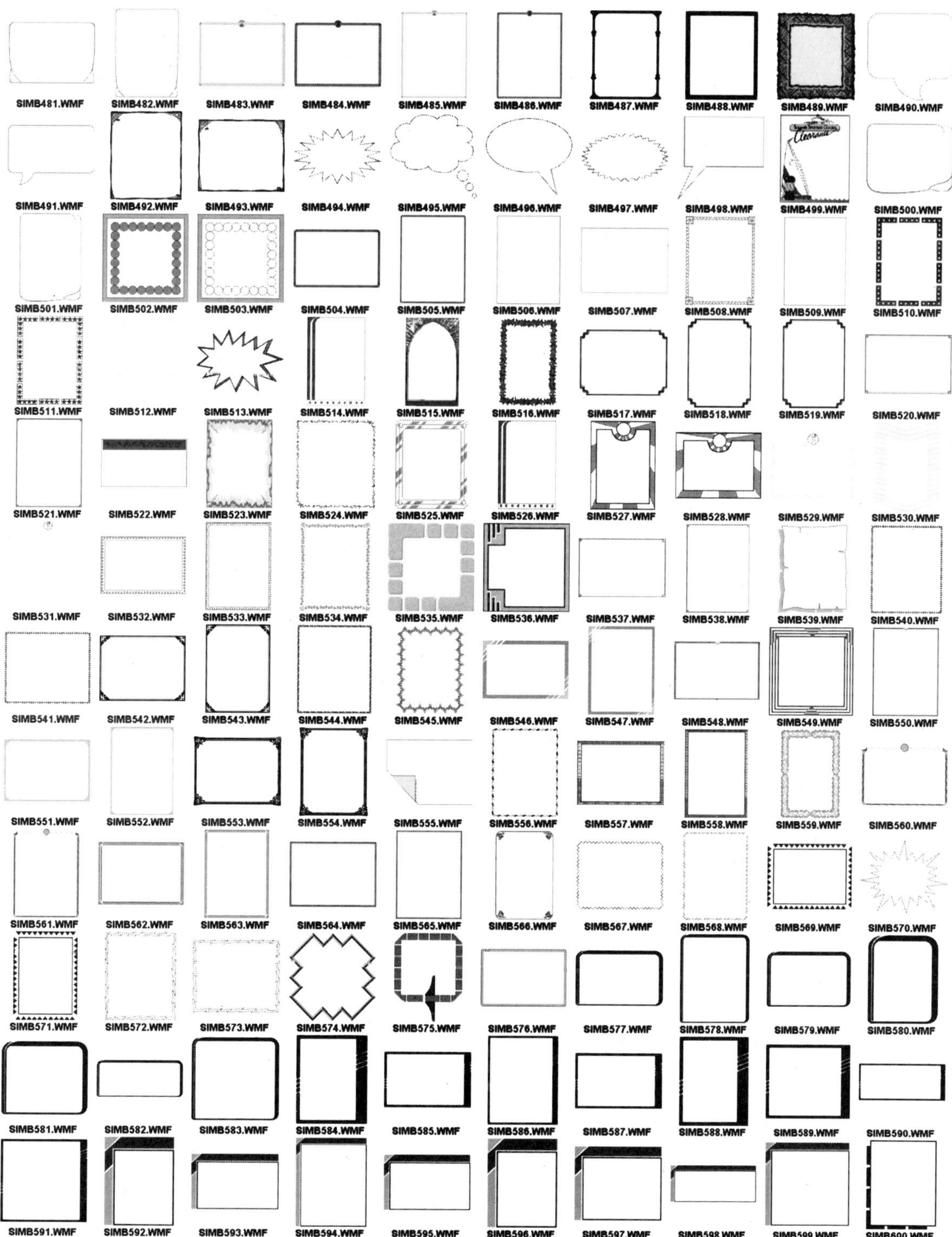
SIMB481.WMF
SIMB482.WMF
SIMB483.WMF
SIMB484.WMF
SIMB485.WMF
SIMB486.WMF
SIMB487.WMF
SIMB488.WMF
SIMB489.WMF
SIMB490.WMF
SIMB491.WMF
SIMB492.WMF
SIMB493.WMF
SIMB494.WMF
SIMB495.WMF
SIMB496.WMF
SIMB497.WMF
SIMB498.WMF
SIMB499.WMF
SIMB500.WMF
SIMB501.WMF
SIMB502.WMF
SIMB503.WMF
SIMB504.WMF
SIMB505.WMF
SIMB506.WMF
SIMB507.WMF
SIMB508.WMF
SIMB509.WMF
SIMB510.WMF
SIMB511.WMF
SIMB512.WMF
SIMB513.WMF
SIMB514.WMF
SIMB515.WMF
SIMB516.WMF
SIMB517.WMF
SIMB518.WMF
SIMB519.WMF
SIMB520.WMF
SIMB521.WMF
SIMB522.WMF
SIMB523.WMF
SIMB524.WMF
SIMB525.WMF
SIMB526.WMF
SIMB527.WMF
SIMB528.WMF
SIMB529.WMF
SIMB530.WMF
SIMB531.WMF
SIMB532.WMF
SIMB533.WMF
SIMB534.WMF
SIMB535.WMF
SIMB536.WMF
SIMB537.WMF
SIMB538.WMF
SIMB539.WMF
SIMB540.WMF
SIMB541.WMF
SIMB542.WMF
SIMB543.WMF
SIMB544.WMF
SIMB545.WMF
SIMB546.WMF
SIMB547.WMF
SIMB548.WMF
SIMB549.WMF
SIMB550.WMF
SIMB551.WMF
SIMB552.WMF
SIMB553.WMF
SIMB554.WMF
SIMB555.WMF
SIMB556.WMF
SIMB557.WMF
SIMB558.WMF
SIMB559.WMF
SIMB560.WMF
SIMB561.WMF
SIMB562.WMF
SIMB563.WMF
SIMB564.WMF
SIMB565.WMF
SIMB566.WMF
SIMB567.WMF
SIMB568.WMF
SIMB569.WMF
SIMB570.WMF
SIMB571.WMF
SIMB572.WMF
SIMB573.WMF
SIMB574.WMF
SIMB575.WMF
SIMB576.WMF
SIMB577.WMF
SIMB578.WMF
SIMB579.WMF
SIMB580.WMF
SIMB581.WMF
SIMB582.WMF
SIMB583.WMF
SIMB584.WMF
SIMB585.WMF
SIMB586.WMF
SIMB587.WMF
SIMB588.WMF
SIMB589.WMF
SIMB590.WMF
SIMB591.WMF
SIMB592.WMF
SIMB593.WMF
SIMB594.WMF
SIMB595.WMF
SIMB596.WMF
SIMB597.WMF
SIMB598.WMF
SIMB599.WMF
SIMB600.WMF

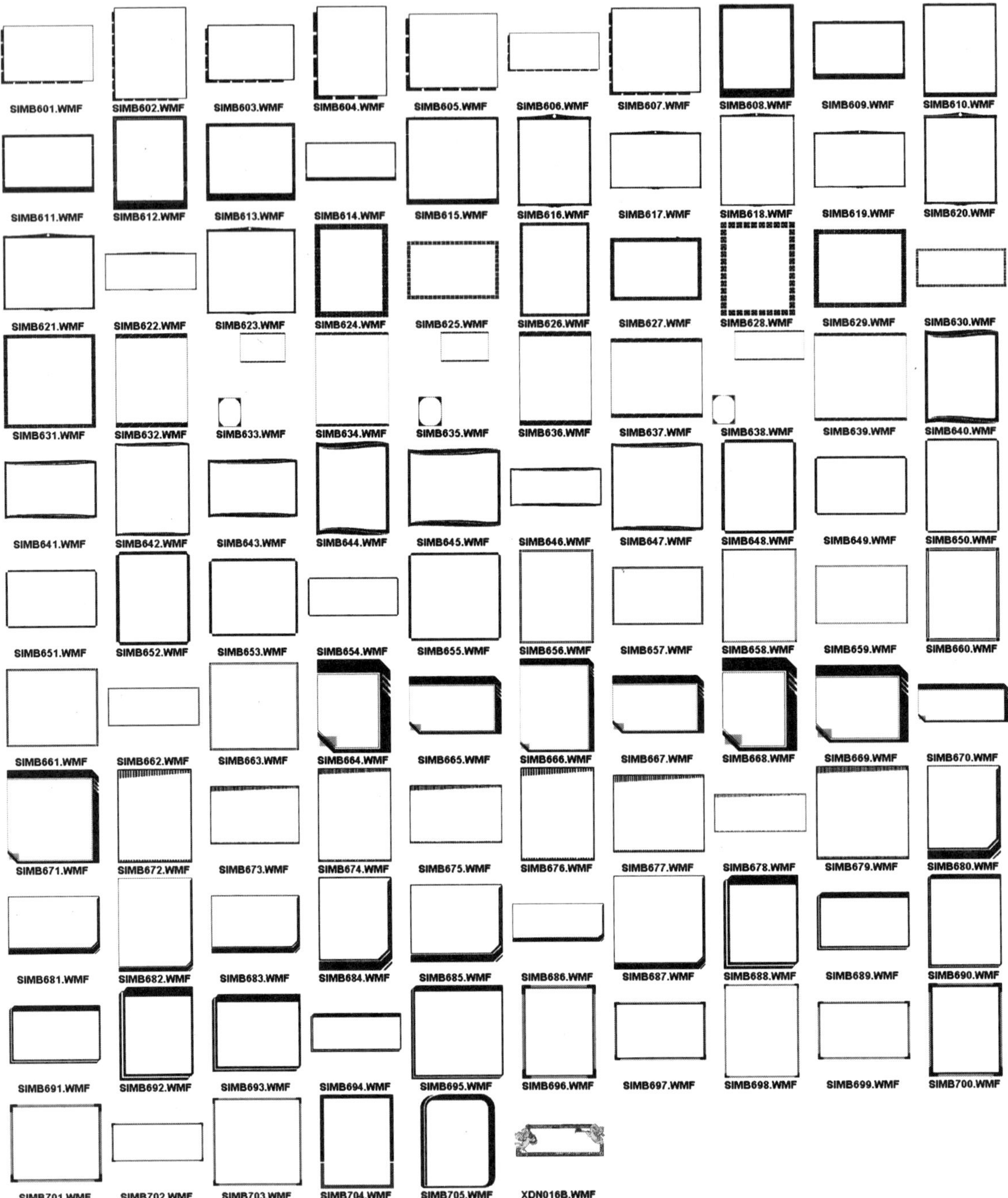
SIMB601.WMF SIMB602.WMF SIMB603.WMF SIMB604.WMF SIMB605.WMF SIMB606.WMF SIMB607.WMF SIMB608.WMF SIMB609.WMF SIMB610.WMF
SIMB611.WMF SIMB612.WMF SIMB613.WMF SIMB614.WMF SIMB615.WMF SIMB616.WMF SIMB617.WMF SIMB618.WMF SIMB619.WMF SIMB620.WMF
SIMB621.WMF SIMB622.WMF SIMB623.WMF SIMB624.WMF SIMB625.WMF SIMB626.WMF SIMB627.WMF SIMB628.WMF SIMB629.WMF SIMB630.WMF
SIMB631.WMF SIMB632.WMF SIMB633.WMF SIMB634.WMF SIMB635.WMF SIMB636.WMF SIMB637.WMF SIMB638.WMF SIMB639.WMF SIMB640.WMF
SIMB641.WMF SIMB642.WMF SIMB643.WMF SIMB644.WMF SIMB645.WMF SIMB646.WMF SIMB647.WMF SIMB648.WMF SIMB649.WMF SIMB650.WMF
SIMB651.WMF SIMB652.WMF SIMB653.WMF SIMB654.WMF SIMB655.WMF SIMB656.WMF SIMB657.WMF SIMB658.WMF SIMB659.WMF SIMB660.WMF
SIMB661.WMF SIMB662.WMF SIMB663.WMF SIMB664.WMF SIMB665.WMF SIMB666.WMF SIMB667.WMF SIMB668.WMF SIMB669.WMF SIMB670.WMF
SIMB671.WMF SIMB672.WMF SIMB673.WMF SIMB674.WMF SIMB675.WMF SIMB676.WMF SIMB677.WMF SIMB678.WMF SIMB679.WMF SIMB680.WMF
SIMB681.WMF SIMB682.WMF SIMB683.WMF SIMB684.WMF SIMB685.WMF SIMB686.WMF SIMB687.WMF SIMB688.WMF SIMB689.WMF SIMB690.WMF
SIMB691.WMF SIMB692.WMF SIMB693.WMF SIMB694.WMF SIMB695.WMF SIMB696.WMF SIMB697.WMF SIMB698.WMF SIMB699.WMF SIMB700.WMF
SIMB701.WMF SIMB702.WMF SIMB703.WMF SIMB704.WMF SIMB705.WMF XDN016B.WMF

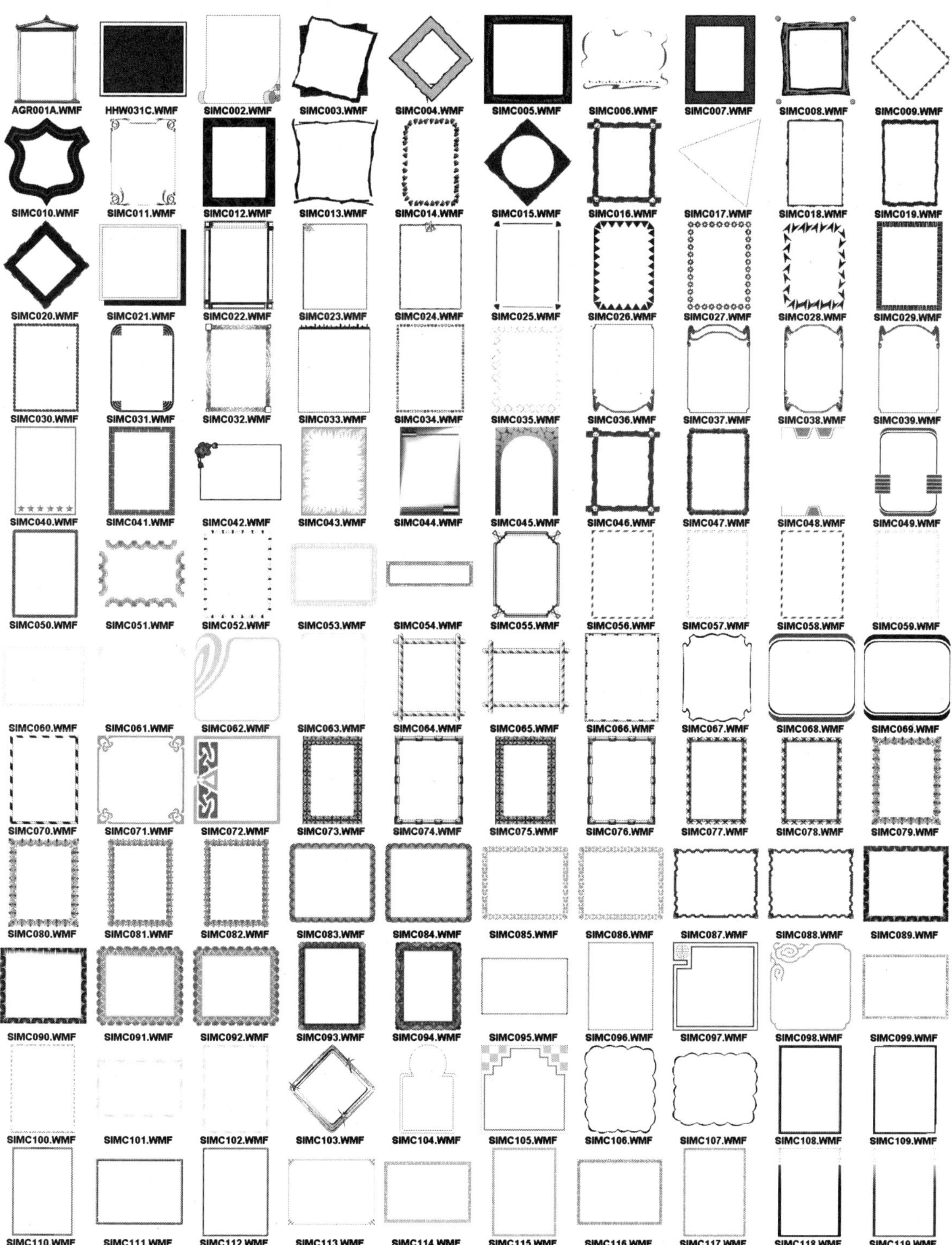
AGR001A.WMF
HHW031C.WMF
SIMC002.WMF
SIMC003.WMF
SIMC004.WMF
SIMC005.WMF
SIMC006.WMF
SIMC007.WMF
SIMC008.WMF
SIMC009.WMF
SIMC010.WMF
SIMC011.WMF
SIMC012.WMF
SIMC013.WMF
SIMC014.WMF
SIMC015.WMF
SIMC016.WMF
SIMC017.WMF
SIMC018.WMF
SIMC019.WMF
SIMC020.WMF
SIMC021.WMF
SIMC022.WMF
SIMC023.WMF
SIMC024.WMF
SIMC025.WMF
SIMC026.WMF
SIMC027.WMF
SIMC028.WMF
SIMC029.WMF
SIMC030.WMF
SIMC031.WMF
SIMC032.WMF
SIMC033.WMF
SIMC034.WMF
SIMC035.WMF
SIMC036.WMF
SIMC037.WMF
SIMC038.WMF
SIMC039.WMF
SIMC040.WMF
SIMC041.WMF
SIMC042.WMF
SIMC043.WMF
SIMC044.WMF
SIMC045.WMF
SIMC046.WMF
SIMC047.WMF
SIMC048.WMF
SIMC049.WMF
SIMC050.WMF
SIMC051.WMF
SIMC052.WMF
SIMC053.WMF
SIMC054.WMF
SIMC055.WMF
SIMC056.WMF
SIMC057.WMF
SIMC058.WMF
SIMC059.WMF
SIMC060.WMF
SIMC061.WMF
SIMC062.WMF
SIMC063.WMF
SIMC064.WMF
SIMC065.WMF
SIMC066.WMF
SIMC067.WMF
SIMC068.WMF
SIMC069.WMF
SIMC070.WMF
SIMC071.WMF
SIMC072.WMF
SIMC073.WMF
SIMC074.WMF
SIMC075.WMF
SIMC076.WMF
SIMC077.WMF
SIMC078.WMF
SIMC079.WMF
SIMC080.WMF
SIMC081.WMF
SIMC082.WMF
SIMC083.WMF
SIMC084.WMF
SIMC085.WMF
SIMC086.WMF
SIMC087.WMF
SIMC088.WMF
SIMC089.WMF
SIMC090.WMF
SIMC091.WMF
SIMC092.WMF
SIMC093.WMF
SIMC094.WMF
SIMC095.WMF
SIMC096.WMF
SIMC097.WMF
SIMC098.WMF
SIMC099.WMF
SIMC100.WMF
SIMC101.WMF
SIMC102.WMF
SIMC103.WMF
SIMC104.WMF
SIMC105.WMF
SIMC106.WMF
SIMC107.WMF
SIMC108.WMF
SIMC109.WMF
SIMC110.WMF
SIMC111.WMF
SIMC112.WMF
SIMC113.WMF
SIMC114.WMF
SIMC115.WMF
SIMC116.WMF
SIMC117.WMF
SIMC118.WMF
SIMC119.WMF

SIMC120.WMF	SIMC121.WMF	SIMC122.WMF	SIMC123.WMF	SIMC124.WMF	SIMC125.WMF	SIMC126.WMF	SIMC127.WMF	SIMC128.WMF	SIMC129.WMF
SIMC130.WMF	SIMC131.WMF	SIMC132.WMF	SIMC133.WMF	SIMC134.WMF	SIMC135.WMF	SIMC136.WMF	SIMC137.WMF	SIMC138.WMF	SIMC139.WMF
SIMC140.WMF	SIMC141.WMF	SIMC142.WMF	SIMC143.WMF	SIMC144.WMF	SIMC145.WMF	SIMC146.WMF	SIMC147.WMF	SIMC148.WMF	SIMC149.WMF
SIMC150.WMF	SIMC151.WMF	SIMC152.WMF	SIMC153.WMF	SIMC154.WMF	SIMC155.WMF	SIMC156.WMF	SIMC157.WMF	SIMC158.WMF	SIMC159.WMF
SIMC160.WMF	SIMC161.WMF	SIMC162.WMF	SIMC163.WMF	SIMC164.WMF	SIMC165.WMF	SIMC166.WMF	SIMC167.WMF	SIMC168.WMF	SIMC169.WMF
SIMC170.WMF	SIMC171.WMF	SIMC172.WMF	SIMC173.WMF	SIMC174.WMF	SIMC175.WMF	SIMC176.WMF	SIMC177.WMF	SIMC178.WMF	SIMC179.WMF
SIMC180.WMF	SIMC181.WMF	SIMC182.WMF	SIMC183.WMF	SIMC184.WMF	SIMC185.WMF	SIMC186.WMF	SIMC187.WMF	SIMC188.WMF	SIMC189.WMF
SIMC190.WMF	SIMC191.WMF	SIMC192.WMF	SIMC193.WMF	SIMC194.WMF	SIMC195.WMF	SIMC196.WMF	SIMC197.WMF	SIMC198.WMF	SIMC199.WMF
SIMC200.WMF	SIMC201.WMF	SIMC202.WMF	SIMC203.WMF	SIMC204.WMF	SIMC205.WMF	SIMC206.WMF	SIMC207.WMF	SIMC208.WMF	SIMC209.WMF
SIMC210.WMF	SIMC211.WMF	SIMC212.WMF	SIMC213.WMF	SIMC214.WMF	SIMC215.WMF	SIMC216.WMF	SIMC217.WMF	SIMC218.WMF	SIMC219.WMF
SIMC220.WMF	SIMC221.WMF	SIMC222.WMF	SIMC223.WMF	SIMC224.WMF	SIMC225.WMF	SIMC226.WMF	SIMC227.WMF	SIMC228.WMF	SIMC229.WMF
SIMC230.WMF	SIMC231.WMF	SIMC232.WMF	SIMC233.WMF	SIMC234.WMF	SIMC235.WMF	SIMC236.WMF	SIMC237.WMF	SIMC238.WMF	SIMC239.WMF

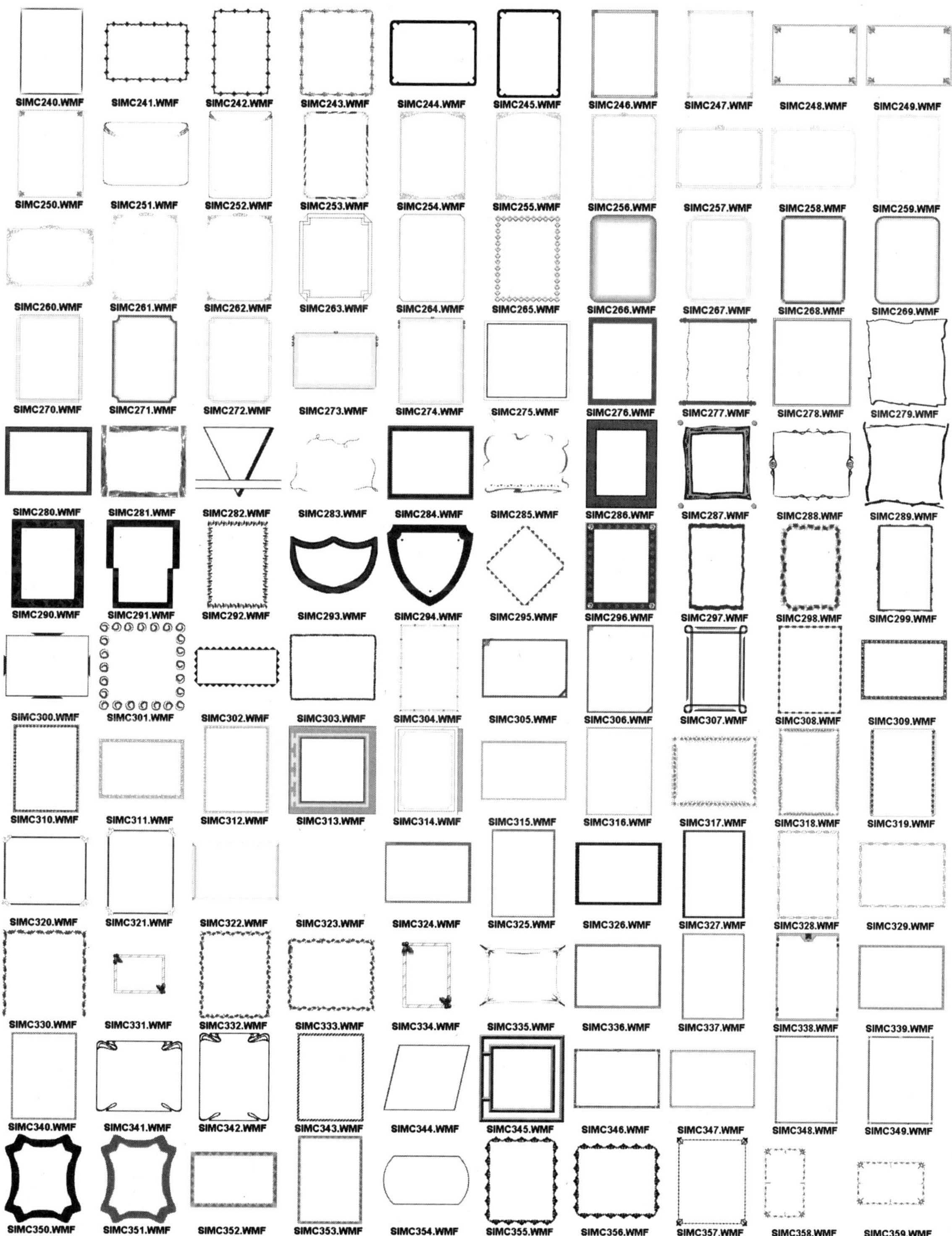
SIMC240.WMF SIMC241.WMF SIMC242.WMF SIMC243.WMF SIMC244.WMF SIMC245.WMF SIMC246.WMF SIMC247.WMF SIMC248.WMF SIMC249.WMF
SIMC250.WMF SIMC251.WMF SIMC252.WMF SIMC253.WMF SIMC254.WMF SIMC255.WMF SIMC256.WMF SIMC257.WMF SIMC258.WMF SIMC259.WMF
SIMC260.WMF SIMC261.WMF SIMC262.WMF SIMC263.WMF SIMC264.WMF SIMC265.WMF SIMC266.WMF SIMC267.WMF SIMC268.WMF SIMC269.WMF
SIMC270.WMF SIMC271.WMF SIMC272.WMF SIMC273.WMF SIMC274.WMF SIMC275.WMF SIMC276.WMF SIMC277.WMF SIMC278.WMF SIMC279.WMF
SIMC280.WMF SIMC281.WMF SIMC282.WMF SIMC283.WMF SIMC284.WMF SIMC285.WMF SIMC286.WMF SIMC287.WMF SIMC288.WMF SIMC289.WMF
SIMC290.WMF SIMC291.WMF SIMC292.WMF SIMC293.WMF SIMC294.WMF SIMC295.WMF SIMC296.WMF SIMC297.WMF SIMC298.WMF SIMC299.WMF
SIMC300.WMF SIMC301.WMF SIMC302.WMF SIMC303.WMF SIMC304.WMF SIMC305.WMF SIMC306.WMF SIMC307.WMF SIMC308.WMF SIMC309.WMF
SIMC310.WMF SIMC311.WMF SIMC312.WMF SIMC313.WMF SIMC314.WMF SIMC315.WMF SIMC316.WMF SIMC317.WMF SIMC318.WMF SIMC319.WMF
SIMC320.WMF SIMC321.WMF SIMC322.WMF SIMC323.WMF SIMC324.WMF SIMC325.WMF SIMC326.WMF SIMC327.WMF SIMC328.WMF SIMC329.WMF
SIMC330.WMF SIMC331.WMF SIMC332.WMF SIMC333.WMF SIMC334.WMF SIMC335.WMF SIMC336.WMF SIMC337.WMF SIMC338.WMF SIMC339.WMF
SIMC340.WMF SIMC341.WMF SIMC342.WMF SIMC343.WMF SIMC344.WMF SIMC345.WMF SIMC346.WMF SIMC347.WMF SIMC348.WMF SIMC349.WMF
SIMC350.WMF SIMC351.WMF SIMC352.WMF SIMC353.WMF SIMC354.WMF SIMC355.WMF SIMC356.WMF SIMC357.WMF SIMC358.WMF SIMC359.WMF

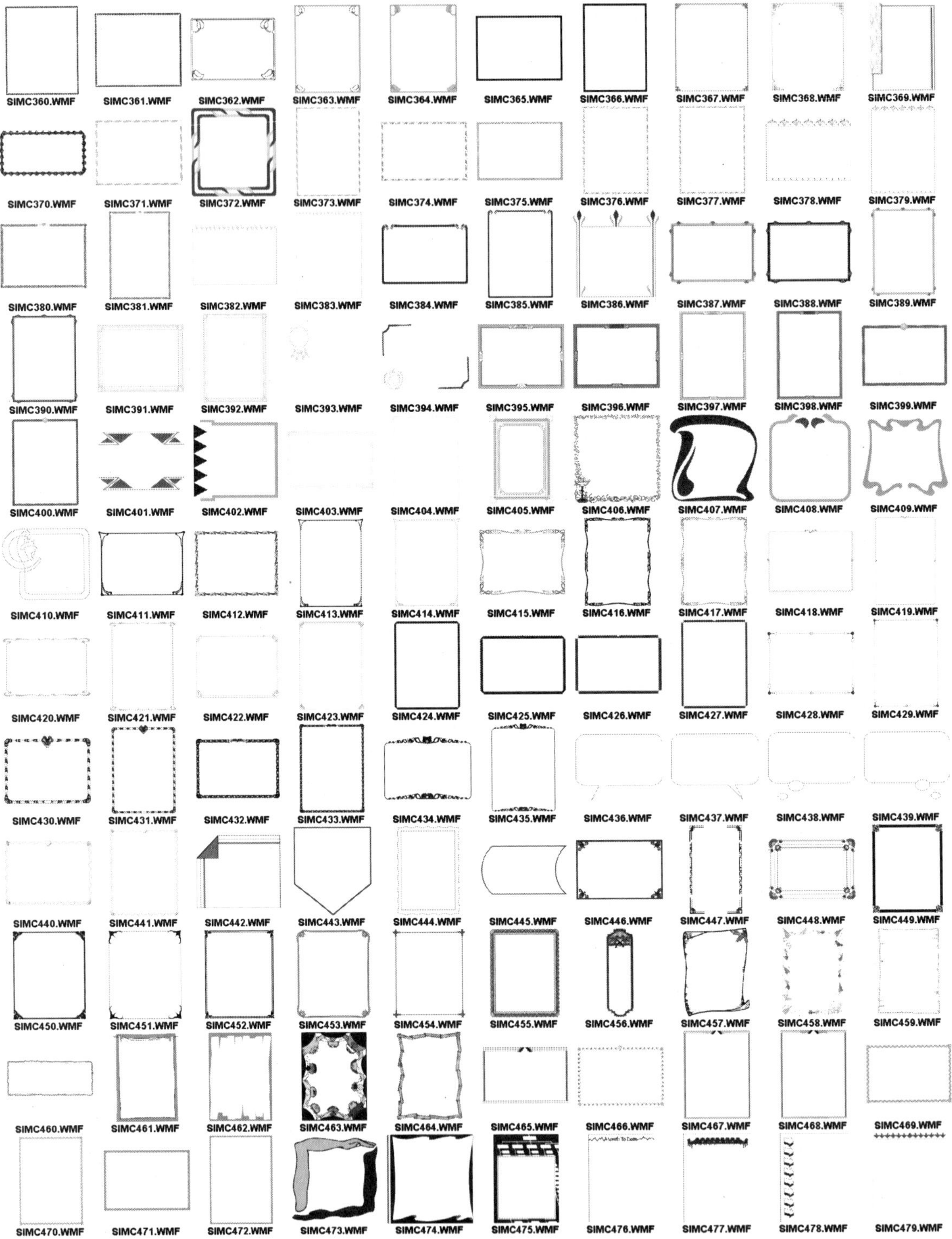

SIMC360.WMF SIMC361.WMF SIMC362.WMF SIMC363.WMF SIMC364.WMF SIMC365.WMF SIMC366.WMF SIMC367.WMF SIMC368.WMF SIMC369.WMF
SIMC370.WMF SIMC371.WMF SIMC372.WMF SIMC373.WMF SIMC374.WMF SIMC375.WMF SIMC376.WMF SIMC377.WMF SIMC378.WMF SIMC379.WMF
SIMC380.WMF SIMC381.WMF SIMC382.WMF SIMC383.WMF SIMC384.WMF SIMC385.WMF SIMC386.WMF SIMC387.WMF SIMC388.WMF SIMC389.WMF
SIMC390.WMF SIMC391.WMF SIMC392.WMF SIMC393.WMF SIMC394.WMF SIMC395.WMF SIMC396.WMF SIMC397.WMF SIMC398.WMF SIMC399.WMF
SIMC400.WMF SIMC401.WMF SIMC402.WMF SIMC403.WMF SIMC404.WMF SIMC405.WMF SIMC406.WMF SIMC407.WMF SIMC408.WMF SIMC409.WMF
SIMC410.WMF SIMC411.WMF SIMC412.WMF SIMC413.WMF SIMC414.WMF SIMC415.WMF SIMC416.WMF SIMC417.WMF SIMC418.WMF SIMC419.WMF
SIMC420.WMF SIMC421.WMF SIMC422.WMF SIMC423.WMF SIMC424.WMF SIMC425.WMF SIMC426.WMF SIMC427.WMF SIMC428.WMF SIMC429.WMF
SIMC430.WMF SIMC431.WMF SIMC432.WMF SIMC433.WMF SIMC434.WMF SIMC435.WMF SIMC436.WMF SIMC437.WMF SIMC438.WMF SIMC439.WMF
SIMC440.WMF SIMC441.WMF SIMC442.WMF SIMC443.WMF SIMC444.WMF SIMC445.WMF SIMC446.WMF SIMC447.WMF SIMC448.WMF SIMC449.WMF
SIMC450.WMF SIMC451.WMF SIMC452.WMF SIMC453.WMF SIMC454.WMF SIMC455.WMF SIMC456.WMF SIMC457.WMF SIMC458.WMF SIMC459.WMF
SIMC460.WMF SIMC461.WMF SIMC462.WMF SIMC463.WMF SIMC464.WMF SIMC465.WMF SIMC466.WMF SIMC467.WMF SIMC468.WMF SIMC469.WMF
SIMC470.WMF SIMC471.WMF SIMC472.WMF SIMC473.WMF SIMC474.WMF SIMC475.WMF SIMC476.WMF SIMC477.WMF SIMC478.WMF SIMC479.WMF

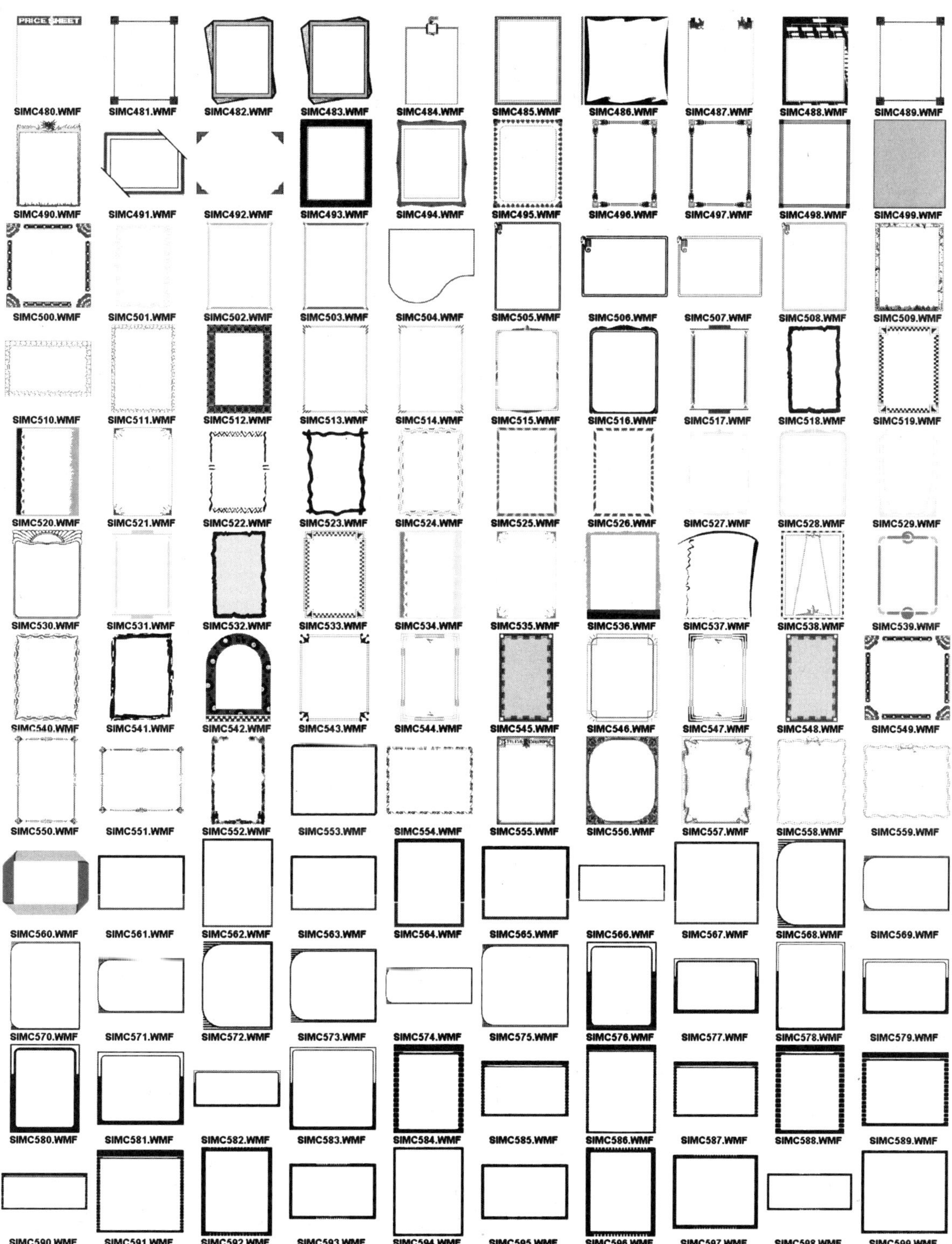
SIMC480.WMF
SIMC481.WMF
SIMC482.WMF
SIMC483.WMF
SIMC484.WMF
SIMC485.WMF
SIMC486.WMF
SIMC487.WMF
SIMC488.WMF
SIMC489.WMF
SIMC490.WMF
SIMC491.WMF
SIMC492.WMF
SIMC493.WMF
SIMC494.WMF
SIMC495.WMF
SIMC496.WMF
SIMC497.WMF
SIMC498.WMF
SIMC499.WMF
SIMC500.WMF
SIMC501.WMF
SIMC502.WMF
SIMC503.WMF
SIMC504.WMF
SIMC505.WMF
SIMC506.WMF
SIMC507.WMF
SIMC508.WMF
SIMC509.WMF
SIMC510.WMF
SIMC511.WMF
SIMC512.WMF
SIMC513.WMF
SIMC514.WMF
SIMC515.WMF
SIMC516.WMF
SIMC517.WMF
SIMC518.WMF
SIMC519.WMF
SIMC520.WMF
SIMC521.WMF
SIMC522.WMF
SIMC523.WMF
SIMC524.WMF
SIMC525.WMF
SIMC526.WMF
SIMC527.WMF
SIMC528.WMF
SIMC529.WMF
SIMC530.WMF
SIMC531.WMF
SIMC532.WMF
SIMC533.WMF
SIMC534.WMF
SIMC535.WMF
SIMC536.WMF
SIMC537.WMF
SIMC538.WMF
SIMC539.WMF
SIMC540.WMF
SIMC541.WMF
SIMC542.WMF
SIMC543.WMF
SIMC544.WMF
SIMC545.WMF
SIMC546.WMF
SIMC547.WMF
SIMC548.WMF
SIMC549.WMF
SIMC550.WMF
SIMC551.WMF
SIMC552.WMF
SIMC553.WMF
SIMC554.WMF
SIMC555.WMF
SIMC556.WMF
SIMC557.WMF
SIMC558.WMF
SIMC559.WMF
SIMC560.WMF
SIMC561.WMF
SIMC562.WMF
SIMC563.WMF
SIMC564.WMF
SIMC565.WMF
SIMC566.WMF
SIMC567.WMF
SIMC568.WMF
SIMC569.WMF
SIMC570.WMF
SIMC571.WMF
SIMC572.WMF
SIMC573.WMF
SIMC574.WMF
SIMC575.WMF
SIMC576.WMF
SIMC577.WMF
SIMC578.WMF
SIMC579.WMF
SIMC580.WMF
SIMC581.WMF
SIMC582.WMF
SIMC583.WMF
SIMC584.WMF
SIMC585.WMF
SIMC586.WMF
SIMC587.WMF
SIMC588.WMF
SIMC589.WMF
SIMC590.WMF
SIMC591.WMF
SIMC592.WMF
SIMC593.WMF
SIMC594.WMF
SIMC595.WMF
SIMC596.WMF
SIMC597.WMF
SIMC598.WMF
SIMC599.WMF

SIMC600.WMF SIMC601.WMF SIMC602.WMF SIMC603.WMF SIMC604.WMF SIMC605.WMF SIMC606.WMF SIMC607.WMF SIMC608.WMF SIMC609.WMF

SIMC610.WMF SIMC611.WMF SIMC612.WMF SIMC613.WMF SIMC614.WMF SIMC615.WMF SIMC616.WMF SIMC617.WMF SIMC618.WMF SIMC619.WMF

SIMC620.WMF SIMC621.WMF SIMC622.WMF SIMC623.WMF SIMC624.WMF SIMC625.WMF SIMC626.WMF SIMC627.WMF SIMC628.WMF SIMC629.WMF

SIMC630.WMF SIMC631.WMF SIMC632.WMF SIMC633.WMF SIMC634.WMF SIMC635.WMF SIMC636.WMF SIMC637.WMF SIMC638.WMF SIMC639.WMF

SIMC640.WMF SIMC641.WMF SIMC642.WMF SIMC643.WMF SIMC644.WMF SIMC645.WMF SIMC646.WMF SIMC647.WMF SIMC648.WMF SIMC649.WMF

SIMC650.WMF SIMC651.WMF SIMC652.WMF SIMC653.WMF SIMC654.WMF SIMC655.WMF SIMC656.WMF SIMC657.WMF SIMC658.WMF SIMC659.WMF

SIMC660.WMF SIMC661.WMF SIMC662.WMF SIMC663.WMF SIMC664.WMF SIMC665.WMF SIMC666.WMF SIMC667.WMF SIMC668.WMF SIMC669.WMF

SIMC670.WMF SIMC671.WMF SIMC672.WMF SIMC673.WMF SIMC674.WMF SIMC675.WMF SIMC676.WMF SIMC677.WMF SIMC678.WMF SIMC679.WMF

SIMC680.WMF SIMC681.WMF SIMC682.WMF SIMC683.WMF SIMC684.WMF SIMC685.WMF SIMC686.WMF SIMC687.WMF SIMC688.WMF SIMC689.WMF

SIMP01.WMF SIMP02.WMF SIMP03.WMF SIMP04.WMF SIMP05.WMF SIMP06.WMF SIMP07.WMF SIMP08.WMF SIMP09.WMF SIMP10.WMF

SIMP11.WMF SIMP12.WMF SIMP13.WMF SIMP14.WMF SIMP15.WMF SIMP16.WMF SIMP17.WMF SIMP18.WMF SIMP19.WMF SIMP20.WMF

SIMP21.WMF SIMP22.WMF SIMP23.WMF SIMP24.WMF SIMP25.WMF SIMP26.WMF SIMP27.WMF SIMP28.WMF SIMP29.WMF SIMP30.WMF

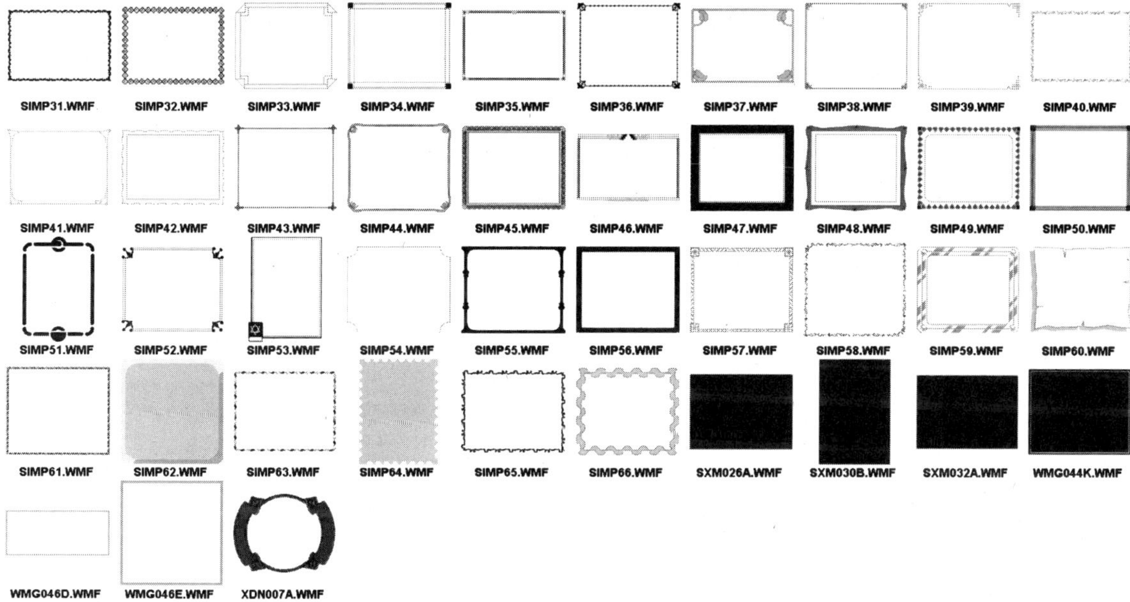
SIMP31.WMF
SIMP32.WMF
SIMP33.WMF
SIMP34.WMF
SIMP35.WMF
SIMP36.WMF
SIMP37.WMF
SIMP38.WMF
SIMP39.WMF
SIMP40.WMF
SIMP41.WMF
SIMP42.WMF
SIMP43.WMF
SIMP44.WMF
SIMP45.WMF
SIMP46.WMF
SIMP47.WMF
SIMP48.WMF
SIMP49.WMF
SIMP50.WMF
SIMP51.WMF
SIMP52.WMF
SIMP53.WMF
SIMP54.WMF
SIMP55.WMF
SIMP56.WMF
SIMP57.WMF
SIMP58.WMF
SIMP59.WMF
SIMP60.WMF
SIMP61.WMF
SIMP62.WMF
SIMP63.WMF
SIMP64.WMF
SIMP65.WMF
SIMP66.WMF
SXM026A.WMF
SXM030B.WMF
SXM032A.WMF
WMG044K.WMF
WMG046D.WMF
WMG046E.WMF
XDN007A.WMF

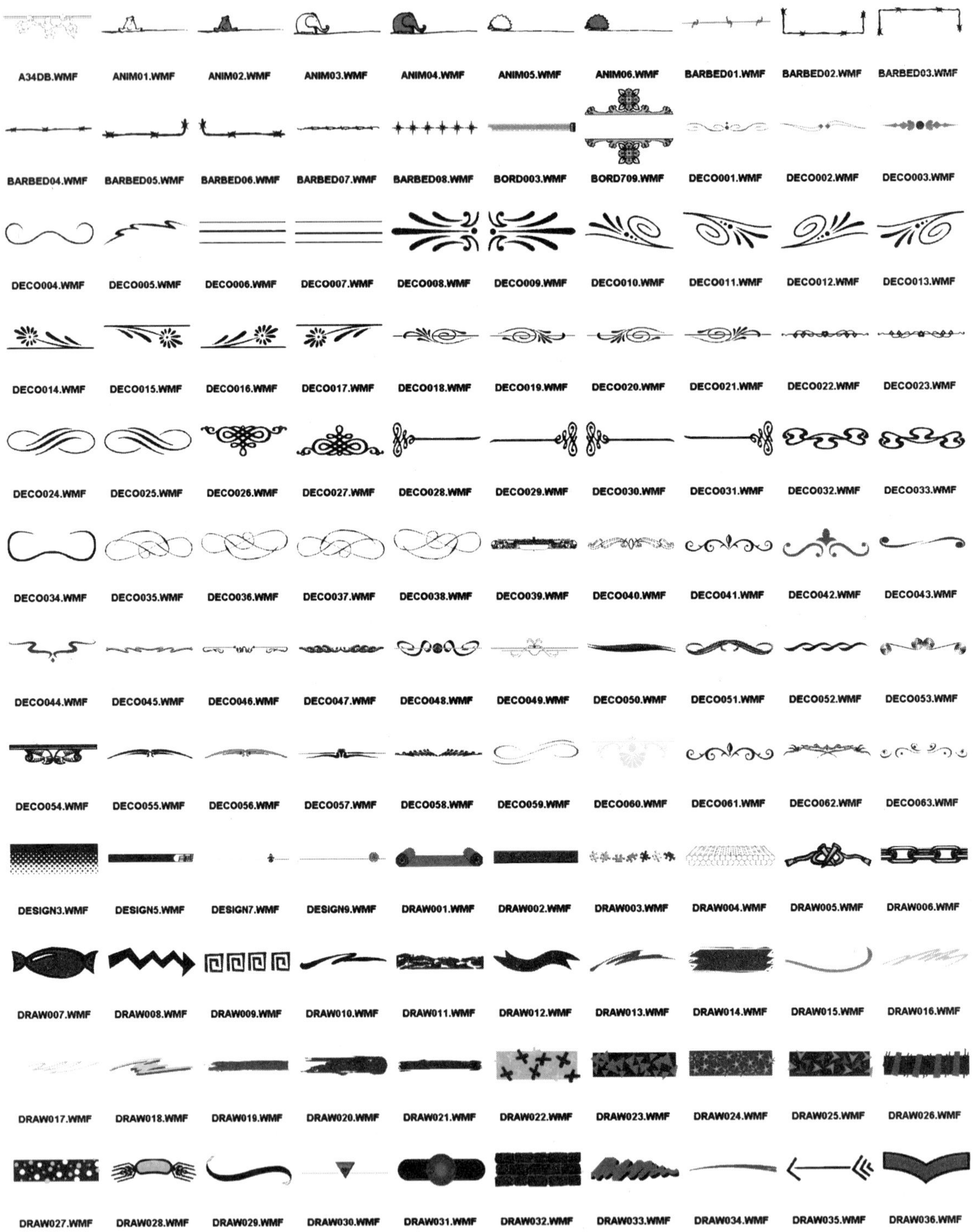
A34DB.WMF
ANIM01.WMF
ANIM02.WMF
ANIM03.WMF
ANIM04.WMF
ANIM05.WMF
ANIM06.WMF
BARBED01.WMF
BARBED02.WMF
BARBED03.WMF
BARBED04.WMF
BARBED05.WMF
BARBED06.WMF
BARBED07.WMF
BARBED08.WMF
BORD003.WMF
BORD709.WMF
DECO001.WMF
DECO002.WMF
DECO003.WMF
DECO004.WMF
DECO005.WMF
DECO006.WMF
DECO007.WMF
DECO008.WMF
DECO009.WMF
DECO010.WMF
DECO011.WMF
DECO012.WMF
DECO013.WMF
DECO014.WMF
DECO015.WMF
DECO016.WMF
DECO017.WMF
DECO018.WMF
DECO019.WMF
DECO020.WMF
DECO021.WMF
DECO022.WMF
DECO023.WMF
DECO024.WMF
DECO025.WMF
DECO026.WMF
DECO027.WMF
DECO028.WMF
DECO029.WMF
DECO030.WMF
DECO031.WMF
DECO032.WMF
DECO033.WMF
DECO034.WMF
DECO035.WMF
DECO036.WMF
DECO037.WMF
DECO038.WMF
DECO039.WMF
DECO040.WMF
DECO041.WMF
DECO042.WMF
DECO043.WMF
DECO044.WMF
DECO045.WMF
DECO046.WMF
DECO047.WMF
DECO048.WMF
DECO049.WMF
DECO050.WMF
DECO051.WMF
DECO052.WMF
DECO053.WMF
DECO054.WMF
DECO055.WMF
DECO056.WMF
DECO057.WMF
DECO058.WMF
DECO059.WMF
DECO060.WMF
DECO061.WMF
DECO062.WMF
DECO063.WMF
DESIGN3.WMF
DESIGN5.WMF
DESIGN7.WMF
DESIGN9.WMF
DRAW001.WMF
DRAW002.WMF
DRAW003.WMF
DRAW004.WMF
DRAW005.WMF
DRAW006.WMF
DRAW007.WMF
DRAW008.WMF
DRAW009.WMF
DRAW010.WMF
DRAW011.WMF
DRAW012.WMF
DRAW013.WMF
DRAW014.WMF
DRAW015.WMF
DRAW016.WMF
DRAW017.WMF
DRAW018.WMF
DRAW019.WMF
DRAW020.WMF
DRAW021.WMF
DRAW022.WMF
DRAW023.WMF
DRAW024.WMF
DRAW025.WMF
DRAW026.WMF
DRAW027.WMF
DRAW028.WMF
DRAW029.WMF
DRAW030.WMF
DRAW031.WMF
DRAW032.WMF
DRAW033.WMF
DRAW034.WMF
DRAW035.WMF
DRAW036.WMF

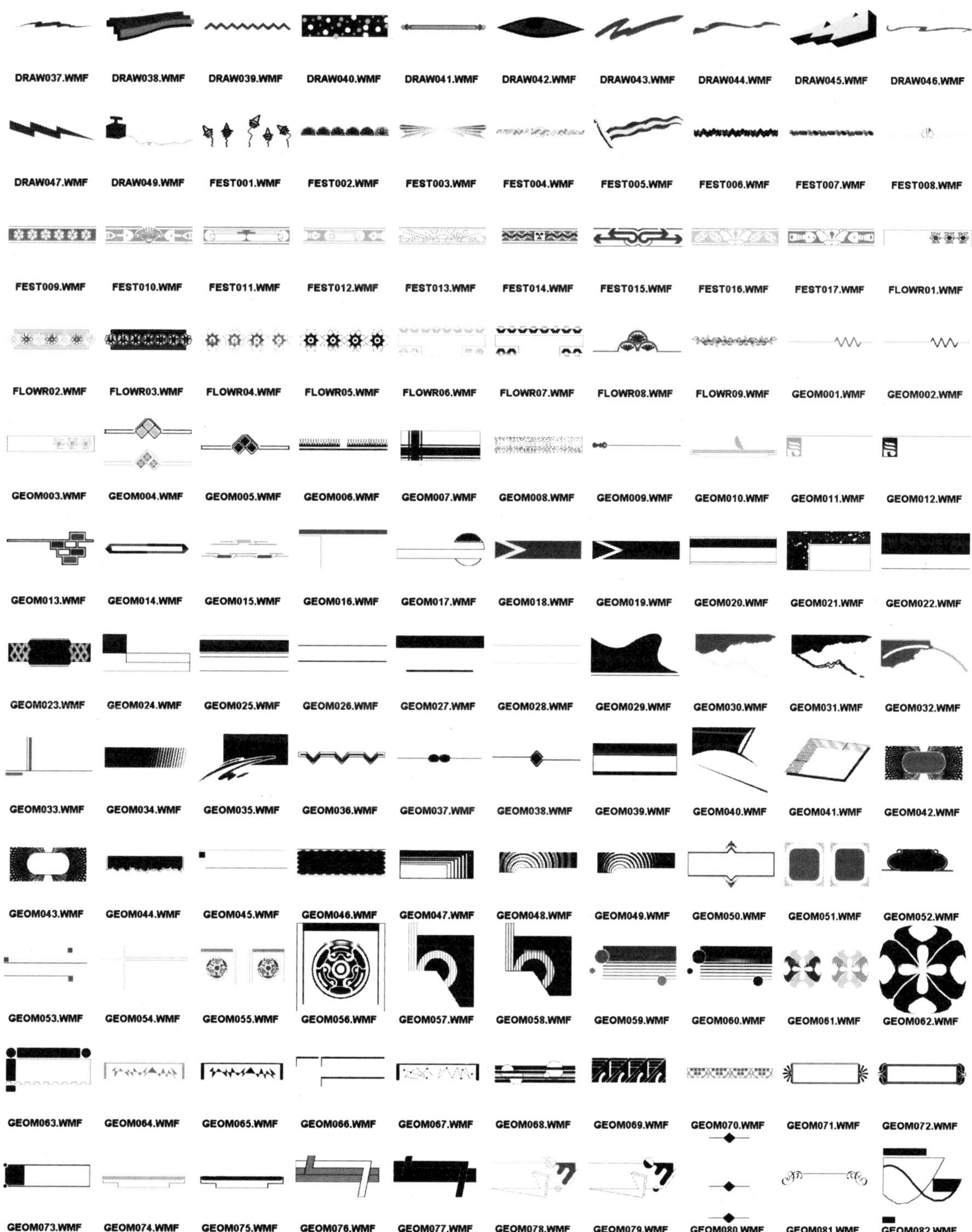
DRAW037.WMF
DRAW038.WMF
DRAW039.WMF
DRAW040.WMF
DRAW041.WMF
DRAW042.WMF
DRAW043.WMF
DRAW044.WMF
DRAW045.WMF
DRAW046.WMF
DRAW047.WMF
DRAW049.WMF
FEST001.WMF
FEST002.WMF
FEST003.WMF
FEST004.WMF
FEST005.WMF
FEST006.WMF
FEST007.WMF
FEST008.WMF
FEST009.WMF
FEST010.WMF
FEST011.WMF
FEST012.WMF
FEST013.WMF
FEST014.WMF
FEST015.WMF
FEST016.WMF
FEST017.WMF
FLOWR01.WMF
FLOWR02.WMF
FLOWR03.WMF
FLOWR04.WMF
FLOWR05.WMF
FLOWR06.WMF
FLOWR07.WMF
FLOWR08.WMF
FLOWR09.WMF
GEOM001.WMF
GEOM002.WMF
GEOM003.WMF
GEOM004.WMF
GEOM005.WMF
GEOM006.WMF
GEOM007.WMF
GEOM008.WMF
GEOM009.WMF
GEOM010.WMF
GEOM011.WMF
GEOM012.WMF
GEOM013.WMF
GEOM014.WMF
GEOM015.WMF
GEOM016.WMF
GEOM017.WMF
GEOM018.WMF
GEOM019.WMF
GEOM020.WMF
GEOM021.WMF
GEOM022.WMF
GEOM023.WMF
GEOM024.WMF
GEOM025.WMF
GEOM026.WMF
GEOM027.WMF
GEOM028.WMF
GEOM029.WMF
GEOM030.WMF
GEOM031.WMF
GEOM032.WMF
GEOM033.WMF
GEOM034.WMF
GEOM035.WMF
GEOM036.WMF
GEOM037.WMF
GEOM038.WMF
GEOM039.WMF
GEOM040.WMF
GEOM041.WMF
GEOM042.WMF
GEOM043.WMF
GEOM044.WMF
GEOM045.WMF
GEOM046.WMF
GEOM047.WMF
GEOM048.WMF
GEOM049.WMF
GEOM050.WMF
GEOM051.WMF
GEOM052.WMF
GEOM053.WMF
GEOM054.WMF
GEOM055.WMF
GEOM056.WMF
GEOM057.WMF
GEOM058.WMF
GEOM059.WMF
GEOM060.WMF
GEOM061.WMF
GEOM062.WMF
GEOM063.WMF
GEOM064.WMF
GEOM065.WMF
GEOM066.WMF
GEOM067.WMF
GEOM068.WMF
GEOM069.WMF
GEOM070.WMF
GEOM071.WMF
GEOM072.WMF
GEOM073.WMF
GEOM074.WMF
GEOM075.WMF
GEOM076.WMF
GEOM077.WMF
GEOM078.WMF
GEOM079.WMF
GEOM080.WMF
GEOM081.WMF
GEOM082.WMF

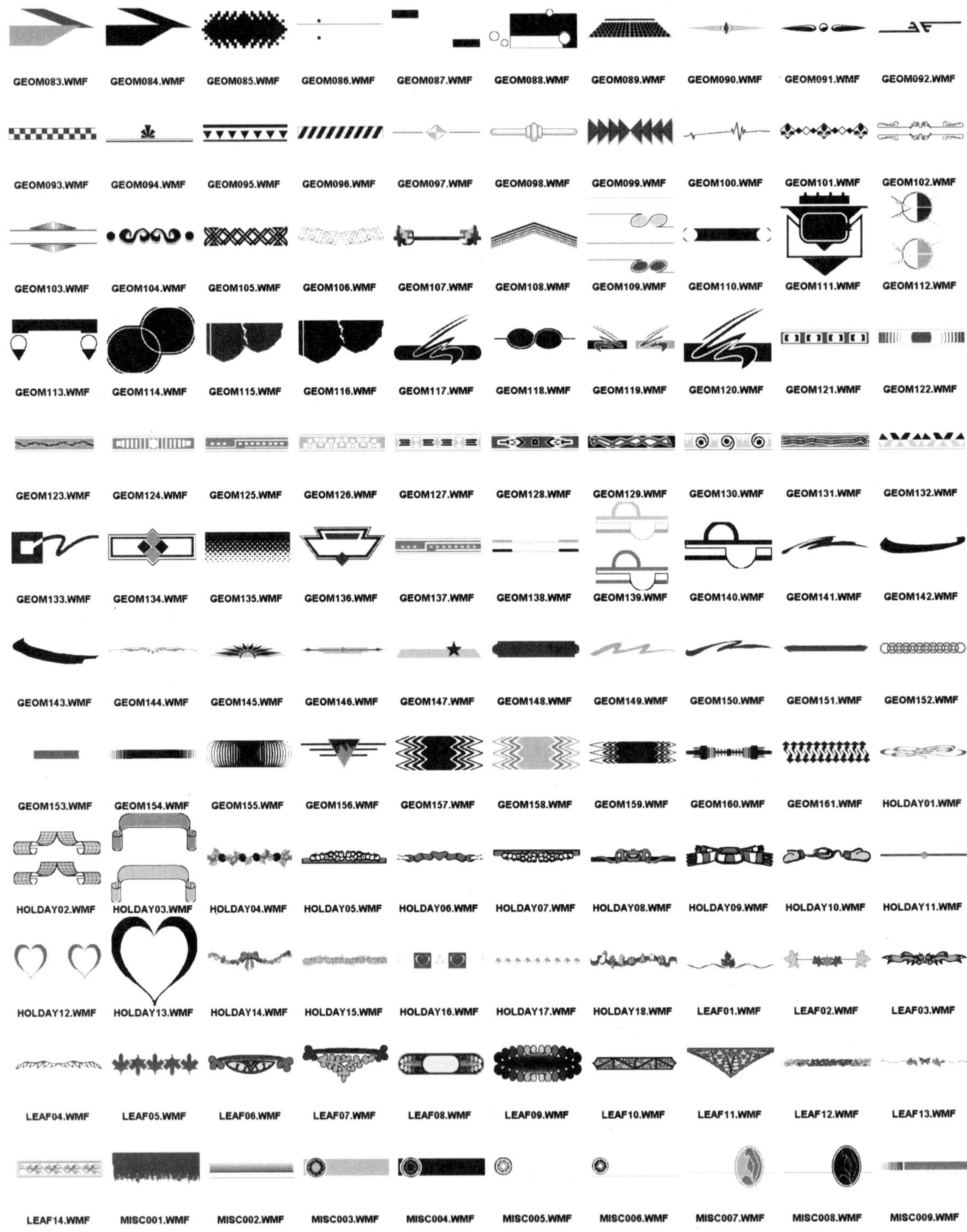
GEOM083.WMF
GEOM084.WMF
GEOM085.WMF
GEOM086.WMF
GEOM087.WMF
GEOM088.WMF
GEOM089.WMF
GEOM090.WMF
GEOM091.WMF
GEOM092.WMF
GEOM093.WMF
GEOM094.WMF
GEOM095.WMF
GEOM096.WMF
GEOM097.WMF
GEOM098.WMF
GEOM099.WMF
GEOM100.WMF
GEOM101.WMF
GEOM102.WMF
GEOM103.WMF
GEOM104.WMF
GEOM105.WMF
GEOM106.WMF
GEOM107.WMF
GEOM108.WMF
GEOM109.WMF
GEOM110.WMF
GEOM111.WMF
GEOM112.WMF
GEOM113.WMF
GEOM114.WMF
GEOM115.WMF
GEOM116.WMF
GEOM117.WMF
GEOM118.WMF
GEOM119.WMF
GEOM120.WMF
GEOM121.WMF
GEOM122.WMF
GEOM123.WMF
GEOM124.WMF
GEOM125.WMF
GEOM126.WMF
GEOM127.WMF
GEOM128.WMF
GEOM129.WMF
GEOM130.WMF
GEOM131.WMF
GEOM132.WMF
GEOM133.WMF
GEOM134.WMF
GEOM135.WMF
GEOM136.WMF
GEOM137.WMF
GEOM138.WMF
GEOM139.WMF
GEOM140.WMF
GEOM141.WMF
GEOM142.WMF
GEOM143.WMF
GEOM144.WMF
GEOM145.WMF
GEOM146.WMF
GEOM147.WMF
GEOM148.WMF
GEOM149.WMF
GEOM150.WMF
GEOM151.WMF
GEOM152.WMF
GEOM153.WMF
GEOM154.WMF
GEOM155.WMF
GEOM156.WMF
GEOM157.WMF
GEOM158.WMF
GEOM159.WMF
GEOM160.WMF
GEOM161.WMF
HOLDAY01.WMF
HOLDAY02.WMF
HOLDAY03.WMF
HOLDAY04.WMF
HOLDAY05.WMF
HOLDAY06.WMF
HOLDAY07.WMF
HOLDAY08.WMF
HOLDAY09.WMF
HOLDAY10.WMF
HOLDAY11.WMF
HOLDAY12.WMF
HOLDAY13.WMF
HOLDAY14.WMF
HOLDAY15.WMF
HOLDAY16.WMF
HOLDAY17.WMF
HOLDAY18.WMF
LEAF01.WMF
LEAF02.WMF
LEAF03.WMF
LEAF04.WMF
LEAF05.WMF
LEAF06.WMF
LEAF07.WMF
LEAF08.WMF
LEAF09.WMF
LEAF10.WMF
LEAF11.WMF
LEAF12.WMF
LEAF13.WMF
LEAF14.WMF
MISC001.WMF
MISC002.WMF
MISC003.WMF
MISC004.WMF
MISC005.WMF
MISC006.WMF
MISC007.WMF
MISC008.WMF
MISC009.WMF

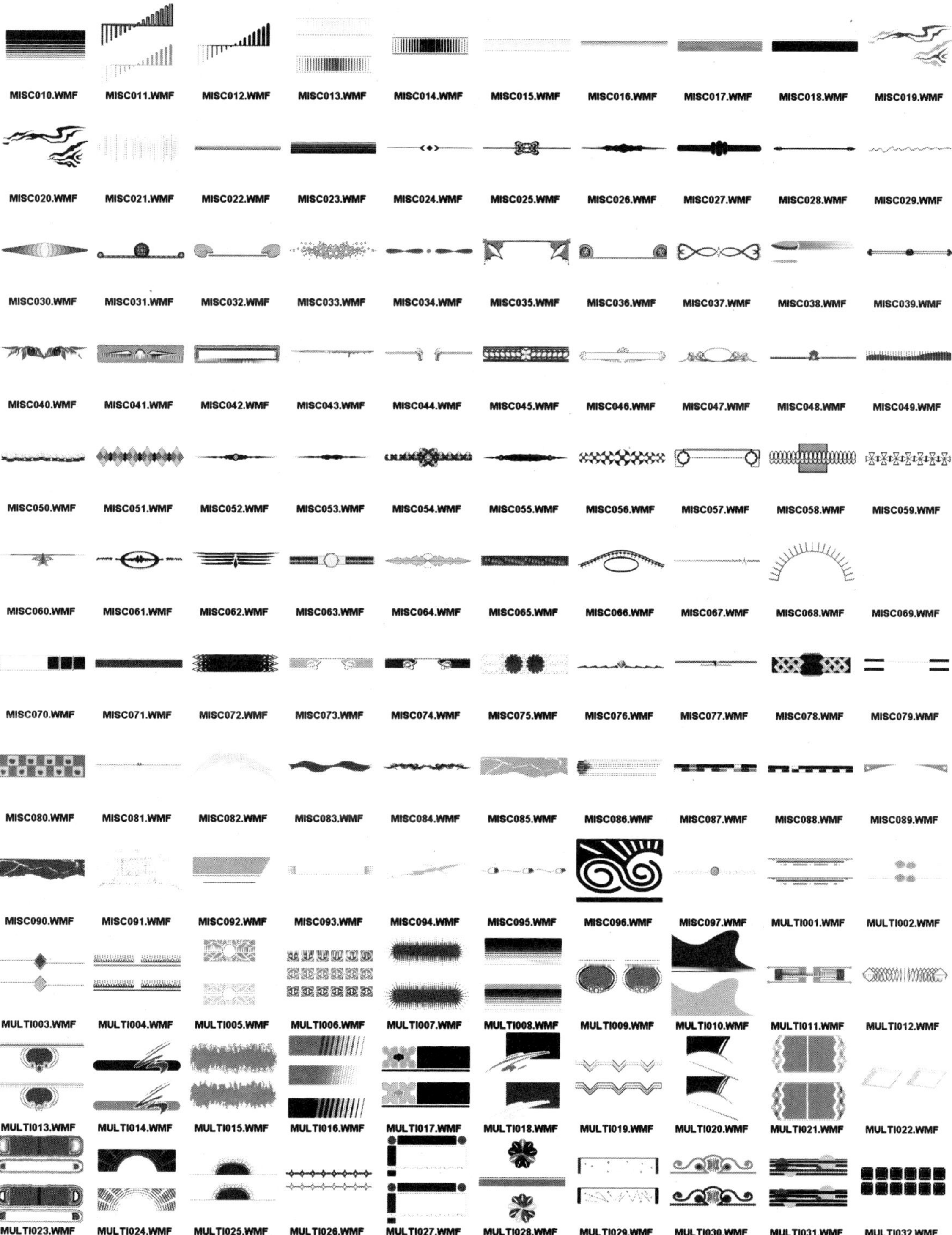
MISC010.WMF
MISC011.WMF
MISC012.WMF
MISC013.WMF
MISC014.WMF
MISC015.WMF
MISC016.WMF
MISC017.WMF
MISC018.WMF
MISC019.WMF
MISC020.WMF
MISC021.WMF
MISC022.WMF
MISC023.WMF
MISC024.WMF
MISC025.WMF
MISC026.WMF
MISC027.WMF
MISC028.WMF
MISC029.WMF
MISC030.WMF
MISC031.WMF
MISC032.WMF
MISC033.WMF
MISC034.WMF
MISC035.WMF
MISC036.WMF
MISC037.WMF
MISC038.WMF
MISC039.WMF
MISC040.WMF
MISC041.WMF
MISC042.WMF
MISC043.WMF
MISC044.WMF
MISC045.WMF
MISC046.WMF
MISC047.WMF
MISC048.WMF
MISC049.WMF
MISC050.WMF
MISC051.WMF
MISC052.WMF
MISC053.WMF
MISC054.WMF
MISC055.WMF
MISC056.WMF
MISC057.WMF
MISC058.WMF
MISC059.WMF
MISC060.WMF
MISC061.WMF
MISC062.WMF
MISC063.WMF
MISC064.WMF
MISC065.WMF
MISC066.WMF
MISC067.WMF
MISC068.WMF
MISC069.WMF
MISC070.WMF
MISC071.WMF
MISC072.WMF
MISC073.WMF
MISC074.WMF
MISC075.WMF
MISC076.WMF
MISC077.WMF
MISC078.WMF
MISC079.WMF
MISC080.WMF
MISC081.WMF
MISC082.WMF
MISC083.WMF
MISC084.WMF
MISC085.WMF
MISC086.WMF
MISC087.WMF
MISC088.WMF
MISC089.WMF
MISC090.WMF
MISC091.WMF
MISC092.WMF
MISC093.WMF
MISC094.WMF
MISC095.WMF
MISC096.WMF
MISC097.WMF
MULTI001.WMF
MULTI002.WMF
MULTI003.WMF
MULTI004.WMF
MULTI005.WMF
MULTI006.WMF
MULTI007.WMF
MULTI008.WMF
MULTI009.WMF
MULTI010.WMF
MULTI011.WMF
MULTI012.WMF
MULTI013.WMF
MULTI014.WMF
MULTI015.WMF
MULTI016.WMF
MULTI017.WMF
MULTI018.WMF
MULTI019.WMF
MULTI020.WMF
MULTI021.WMF
MULTI022.WMF
MULTI023.WMF
MULTI024.WMF
MULTI025.WMF
MULTI026.WMF
MULTI027.WMF
MULTI028.WMF
MULTI029.WMF
MULTI030.WMF
MULTI031.WMF
MULTI032.WMF

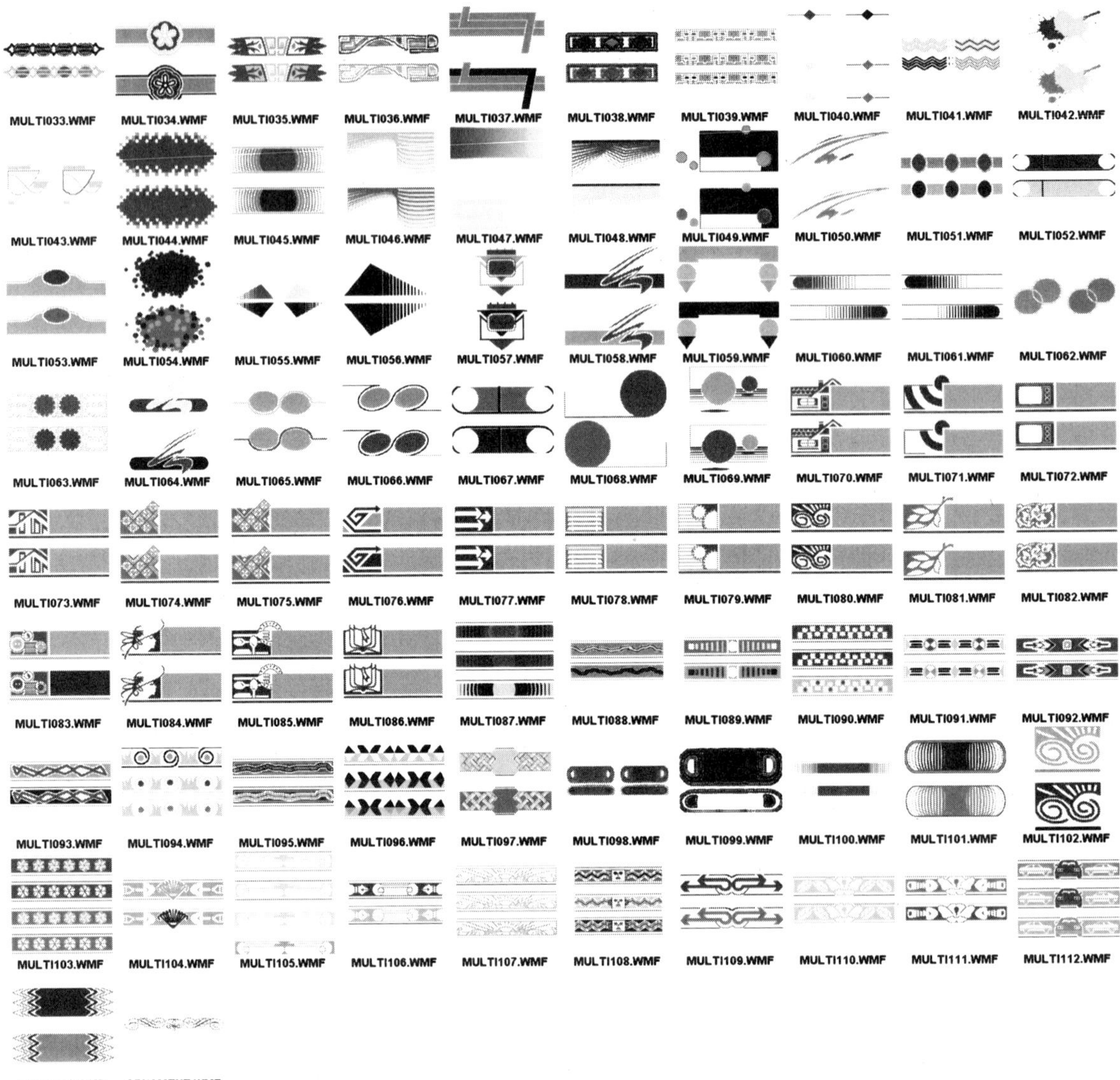
MULTI033.WMF
MULTI034.WMF
MULTI035.WMF
MULTI036.WMF
MULTI037.WMF
MULTI038.WMF
MULTI039.WMF
MULTI040.WMF
MULTI041.WMF
MULTI042.WMF
MULTI043.WMF
MULTI044.WMF
MULTI045.WMF
MULTI046.WMF
MULTI047.WMF
MULTI048.WMF
MULTI049.WMF
MULTI050.WMF
MULTI051.WMF
MULTI052.WMF
MULTI053.WMF
MULTI054.WMF
MULTI055.WMF
MULTI056.WMF
MULTI057.WMF
MULTI058.WMF
MULTI059.WMF
MULTI060.WMF
MULTI061.WMF
MULTI062.WMF
MULTI063.WMF
MULTI064.WMF
MULTI065.WMF
MULTI066.WMF
MULTI067.WMF
MULTI068.WMF
MULTI069.WMF
MULTI070.WMF
MULTI071.WMF
MULTI072.WMF
MULTI073.WMF
MULTI074.WMF
MULTI075.WMF
MULTI076.WMF
MULTI077.WMF
MULTI078.WMF
MULTI079.WMF
MULTI080.WMF
MULTI081.WMF
MULTI082.WMF
MULTI083.WMF
MULTI084.WMF
MULTI085.WMF
MULTI086.WMF
MULTI087.WMF
MULTI088.WMF
MULTI089.WMF
MULTI090.WMF
MULTI091.WMF
MULTI092.WMF
MULTI093.WMF
MULTI094.WMF
MULTI095.WMF
MULTI096.WMF
MULTI097.WMF
MULTI098.WMF
MULTI099.WMF
MULTI100.WMF
MULTI101.WMF
MULTI102.WMF
MULTI103.WMF
MULTI104.WMF
MULTI105.WMF
MULTI106.WMF
MULTI107.WMF
MULTI108.WMF
MULTI109.WMF
MULTI110.WMF
MULTI111.WMF
MULTI112.WMF
MULTI113.WMF
ORNAMENT.WMF

1250.WMF 1251.WMF A38BB.WMF BAMBOO_N.WMF BEACH.WMF DESIGN26.WMF DESIGN28.WMF DESIGN38.WMF FSTV037.WMF ORN_02.WMF
ORN_03.WMF ORN_05.WMF ORN_09.WMF ORN_11.WMF ORN_13.WMF ORN_14.WMF ORNAT001.WMF ORNAT002.WMF ORNAT003.WMF ORNAT004.WMF
ORNAT005.WMF ORNAT006.WMF ORNAT007.WMF ORNAT008.WMF ORNAT009.WMF ORNAT010.WMF ORNAT011.WMF ORNAT012.WMF ORNAT013.WMF ORNAT014.WMF
ORNAT015.WMF ORNAT016.WMF ORNAT017.WMF ORNAT018.WMF ORNAT019.WMF ORNAT020.WMF ORNAT021.WMF ORNAT022.WMF ORNAT023.WMF ORNAT024.WMF
ORNAT025.WMF ORNAT026.WMF ORNAT027.WMF ORNAT028.WMF ORNAT029.WMF ORNAT030.WMF ORNAT031.WMF ORNAT032.WMF ORNAT033.WMF ORNAT034.WMF
ORNAT035.WMF ORNAT036.WMF ORNAT037.WMF ORNAT038.WMF ORNAT039.WMF ORNAT040.WMF ORNAT041.WMF ORNAT042.WMF ORNAT043.WMF ORNAT044.WMF
ORNAT045.WMF ORNAT046.WMF ORNAT047.WMF ORNAT048.WMF ORNAT049.WMF ORNAT050.WMF ORNAT051.WMF ORNAT052.WMF ORNAT053.WMF ORNAT054.WMF
ORNAT055.WMF ORNAT056.WMF ORNAT057.WMF ORNAT058.WMF ORNAT059.WMF ORNAT060.WMF ORNAT061.WMF PALMTREE.WMF PATT001.WMF PATT002.WMF
PATT003.WMF PATT004.WMF PATT005.WMF PATT006.WMF PATT007.WMF PATT008.WMF PATT009.WMF PATT010.WMF PATT011.WMF PATT012.WMF
PATT013.WMF PATT014.WMF PATT015.WMF PATT016.WMF PATT017.WMF PATT018.WMF PATT019.WMF PATT020.WMF PATT021.WMF PATT022.WMF
PATT023.WMF PATT024.WMF PATT025.WMF PATT026.WMF PATT027.WMF PATT028.WMF PATT029.WMF PATT030.WMF PATT031.WMF PATT032.WMF
PATT033.WMF PATT034.WMF PATT035.WMF PATT036.WMF PATT037.WMF PATT038.WMF PATT039.WMF PATT040.WMF PATT041.WMF PATT042.WMF

PATT043.WMF	PATT044.WMF	PATT045.WMF	PATT046.WMF	PATT047.WMF	PATT048.WMF	PATT049.WMF	PATT050.WMF	PATT051.WMF	PATT052.WMF
PATT053.WMF	PATT054.WMF	PATT055.WMF	PATT056.WMF	PATT057.WMF	PATT058.WMF	PATT059.WMF	PATT060.WMF	PATT061.WMF	PATT062.WMF
PATT063.WMF	PATT064.WMF	PATT065.WMF	PATT066.WMF	PATT067.WMF	PATT068.WMF	PATT069.WMF	PATT070.WMF	PATT071.WMF	PATT072.WMF
PATT073.WMF	PATT074.WMF	PATT075.WMF	PATT076.WMF	PATT077.WMF	PATT078.WMF	PATT079.WMF	PATT080.WMF	PATT081.WMF	PATT082.WMF
PATT083.WMF	PATT084.WMF	PATT085.WMF	PATT086.WMF	PATT087.WMF	PATT088.WMF	PATT089.WMF	PATT090.WMF	PATT091.WMF	PATT092.WMF
PATT093.WMF	PATT094.WMF	PATT095.WMF	PATT096.WMF	PATT097.WMF	PATT098.WMF	PATT099.WMF	PATT100.WMF	PATT101.WMF	PATT102.WMF
PATT103.WMF	PATT104.WMF	PATT105.WMF	PATT106.WMF	PATT107.WMF	PATT108.WMF	PATT109.WMF	PATT110.WMF	PATT111.WMF	PATT112.WMF
PATT113.WMF	PATT114.WMF	PATT115.WMF	PATT116.WMF	PATT117.WMF	PATT118.WMF	PATT119.WMF	PATT120.WMF	PATT121.WMF	PATT122.WMF
PATT123.WMF	PATT124.WMF	PATT125.WMF	PATT126.WMF	PATT127.WMF	PATT128.WMF	PATT129.WMF	PATT130.WMF	PATT131.WMF	PATT132.WMF
PATT133.WMF	PATT134.WMF	PATT135.WMF	PATT136.WMF	PATT137.WMF	PATT138.WMF	PATT139.WMF	PATT140.WMF	PATT141.WMF	PATT142.WMF
PATT143.WMF	PATT144.WMF	PATT145.WMF	PATT146.WMF	PATT147.WMF	PATT148.WMF	PATT149.WMF	PATT150.WMF	PATT151.WMF	PATT152.WMF
PATT153.WMF	PATT154.WMF	PATT155.WMF	PATT156.WMF	PATT157.WMF	PATT158.WMF	PATT159.WMF	PATT160.WMF	PATT161.WMF	PATT162.WMF

PATT163.WMF PATT164.WMF PATT165.WMF PATT166.WMF PATT167.WMF PATT168.WMF PATT169.WMF PATT170.WMF PATT171.WMF PATT172.WMF

PATT173.WMF PATT174.WMF PATT175.WMF PATT176.WMF PATT177.WMF PATT178.WMF PATT179.WMF PATT180.WMF PATT181.WMF PATT182.WMF

PATT183.WMF PATT184.WMF PATT185.WMF PATT186.WMF PATT187.WMF PATT188.WMF PATT189.WMF PATT190.WMF PATT191.WMF PATT192.WMF

PATT193.WMF PATT194.WMF PATT195.WMF PATT196.WMF PATT197.WMF PATT198.WMF PATT199.WMF PATT200.WMF PATT201.WMF PATT202.WMF

PATT203.WMF PATT204.WMF PATT205.WMF PATT206.WMF PATT207.WMF PATT208.WMF PATT209.WMF PATT210.WMF PATT211.WMF PATT212.WMF

PATT213.WMF PATT214.WMF PATT215.WMF PATT216.WMF PATT217.WMF PATT218.WMF PATT219.WMF PATT220.WMF PATT221.WMF PATT222.WMF

PATT223.WMF PATT224.WMF PATT225.WMF PATT226.WMF PATT227.WMF PATT228.WMF PATT229.WMF PATT230.WMF PATT231.WMF PATT232.WMF

PATT233.WMF PATT234.WMF PATT235.WMF PATT236.WMF PATT237.WMF PATT238.WMF PATT239.WMF PEOPL001.WMF PEOPL002.WMF PEOPL003.WMF

PEOPL004.WMF PEOPL005.WMF PEOPL006.WMF PEOPL007.WMF PEOPL008.WMF PEOPL009.WMF PEOPL010.WMF PEOPL011.WMF PEOPL012.WMF PEOPL013.WMF

RIBBN001.WMF RIBBN002.WMF RIBBN003.WMF RIBBN004.WMF RIBBN005.WMF RIBBN006.WMF RIBBN007.WMF RIBBN008.WMF RIBBN009.WMF RIBBN010.WMF

RIBBN011.WMF RIBBN012.WMF RIBBN013.WMF RIBBN014.WMF RIBBN015.WMF RIBBN016.WMF RIBBN017.WMF RIBBN018.WMF RIBBN019.WMF RIBBN020.WMF

RIBBN021.WMF RIBBN022.WMF RIBBN023.WMF RIBBN024.WMF RIBBN025.WMF RIBBN026.WMF RIBBN027.WMF RIBBN028.WMF RIBBN029.WMF RIBBN030.WMF

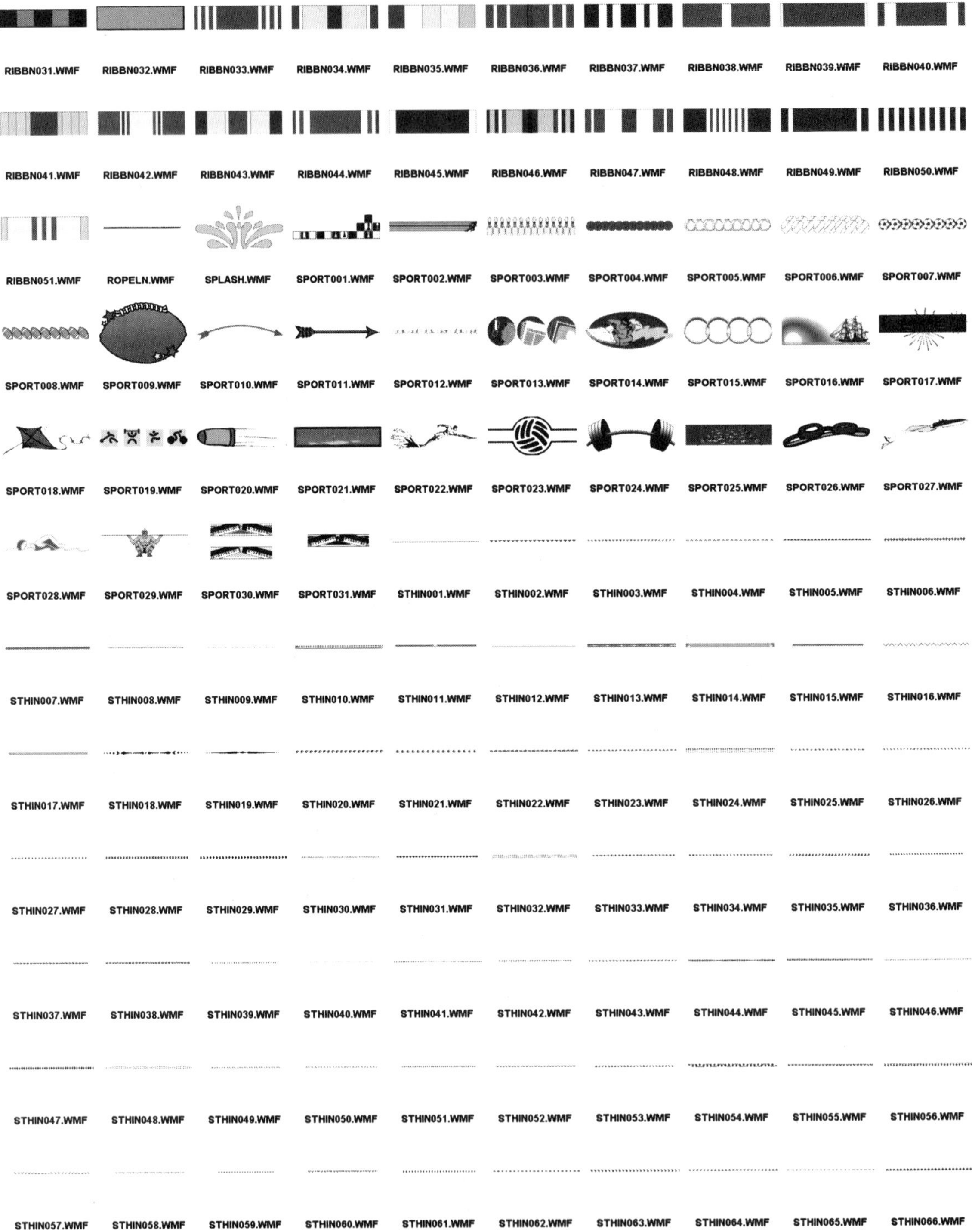
RIBBN031.WMF
RIBBN032.WMF
RIBBN033.WMF
RIBBN034.WMF
RIBBN035.WMF
RIBBN036.WMF
RIBBN037.WMF
RIBBN038.WMF
RIBBN039.WMF
RIBBN040.WMF
RIBBN041.WMF
RIBBN042.WMF
RIBBN043.WMF
RIBBN044.WMF
RIBBN045.WMF
RIBBN046.WMF
RIBBN047.WMF
RIBBN048.WMF
RIBBN049.WMF
RIBBN050.WMF
RIBBN051.WMF
ROPELN.WMF
SPLASH.WMF
SPORT001.WMF
SPORT002.WMF
SPORT003.WMF
SPORT004.WMF
SPORT005.WMF
SPORT006.WMF
SPORT007.WMF
SPORT008.WMF
SPORT009.WMF
SPORT010.WMF
SPORT011.WMF
SPORT012.WMF
SPORT013.WMF
SPORT014.WMF
SPORT015.WMF
SPORT016.WMF
SPORT017.WMF
SPORT018.WMF
SPORT019.WMF
SPORT020.WMF
SPORT021.WMF
SPORT022.WMF
SPORT023.WMF
SPORT024.WMF
SPORT025.WMF
SPORT026.WMF
SPORT027.WMF
SPORT028.WMF
SPORT029.WMF
SPORT030.WMF
SPORT031.WMF
STHIN001.WMF
STHIN002.WMF
STHIN003.WMF
STHIN004.WMF
STHIN005.WMF
STHIN006.WMF
STHIN007.WMF
STHIN008.WMF
STHIN009.WMF
STHIN010.WMF
STHIN011.WMF
STHIN012.WMF
STHIN013.WMF
STHIN014.WMF
STHIN015.WMF
STHIN016.WMF
STHIN017.WMF
STHIN018.WMF
STHIN019.WMF
STHIN020.WMF
STHIN021.WMF
STHIN022.WMF
STHIN023.WMF
STHIN024.WMF
STHIN025.WMF
STHIN026.WMF
STHIN027.WMF
STHIN028.WMF
STHIN029.WMF
STHIN030.WMF
STHIN031.WMF
STHIN032.WMF
STHIN033.WMF
STHIN034.WMF
STHIN035.WMF
STHIN036.WMF
STHIN037.WMF
STHIN038.WMF
STHIN039.WMF
STHIN040.WMF
STHIN041.WMF
STHIN042.WMF
STHIN043.WMF
STHIN044.WMF
STHIN045.WMF
STHIN046.WMF
STHIN047.WMF
STHIN048.WMF
STHIN049.WMF
STHIN050.WMF
STHIN051.WMF
STHIN052.WMF
STHIN053.WMF
STHIN054.WMF
STHIN055.WMF
STHIN056.WMF
STHIN057.WMF
STHIN058.WMF
STHIN059.WMF
STHIN060.WMF
STHIN061.WMF
STHIN062.WMF
STHIN063.WMF
STHIN064.WMF
STHIN065.WMF
STHIN066.WMF

STHIN067.WMF	STHIN068.WMF	STHIN069.WMF	STHIN070.WMF	STHIN071.WMF	STHIN072.WMF	STHIN073.WMF	STHIN074.WMF	STHIN075.WMF	STHIN076.WMF
STHIN077.WMF	STHIN078.WMF	STHIN079.WMF	STHIN080.WMF	STHIN081.WMF	STHIN082.WMF	STHIN083.WMF	STHIN084.WMF	STHIN085.WMF	STHIN086.WMF
STHIN087.WMF	STHIN088.WMF	STHIN089.WMF	STHIN090.WMF	STHIN091.WMF	STHIN092.WMF	STHIN093.WMF	STHIN094.WMF	STHIN095.WMF	STHIN096.WMF
STHIN097.WMF	STHIN098.WMF	STHIN099.WMF	STHIN100.WMF	STHIN101.WMF	STHIN102.WMF	STHIN103.WMF	STHIN104.WMF	STHIN105.WMF	STHIN106.WMF
STHIN107.WMF	STHIN108.WMF	STHIN109.WMF	STHIN110.WMF	STHIN111.WMF	STHIN112.WMF	STHIN113.WMF	STHIN114.WMF	STHIN115.WMF	STHIN116.WMF
STHIN117.WMF	STHIN118.WMF	STHIN119.WMF	STHIN120.WMF	STHIN121.WMF	STHIN122.WMF	STHIN123.WMF	STHIN124.WMF	STHIN125.WMF	STHIN126.WMF
STHIN127.WMF	STHIN128.WMF	STHIN129.WMF	STHIN130.WMF	STHIN131.WMF	STHIN132.WMF	STHIN133.WMF	STHIN134.WMF	STHIN135.WMF	STHIN136.WMF
STHIN137.WMF	STHIN138.WMF	STHIN139.WMF	STHIN140.WMF	STHIN141.WMF	STHIN142.WMF	STHIN143.WMF	STHIN144.WMF	STHIN145.WMF	STHIN146.WMF
STHIN147.WMF	STHIN148.WMF	STHIN149.WMF	STHIN150.WMF	STHIN151.WMF	STHIN152.WMF	STHIN153.WMF	STHIN154.WMF	STHIN155.WMF	STHIN156.WMF
STHIN157.WMF	STHIN158.WMF	STHIN159.WMF	STHIN160.WMF	STHIN161.WMF	STHIN162.WMF	STHIN163.WMF	WKSHP017.WMF		

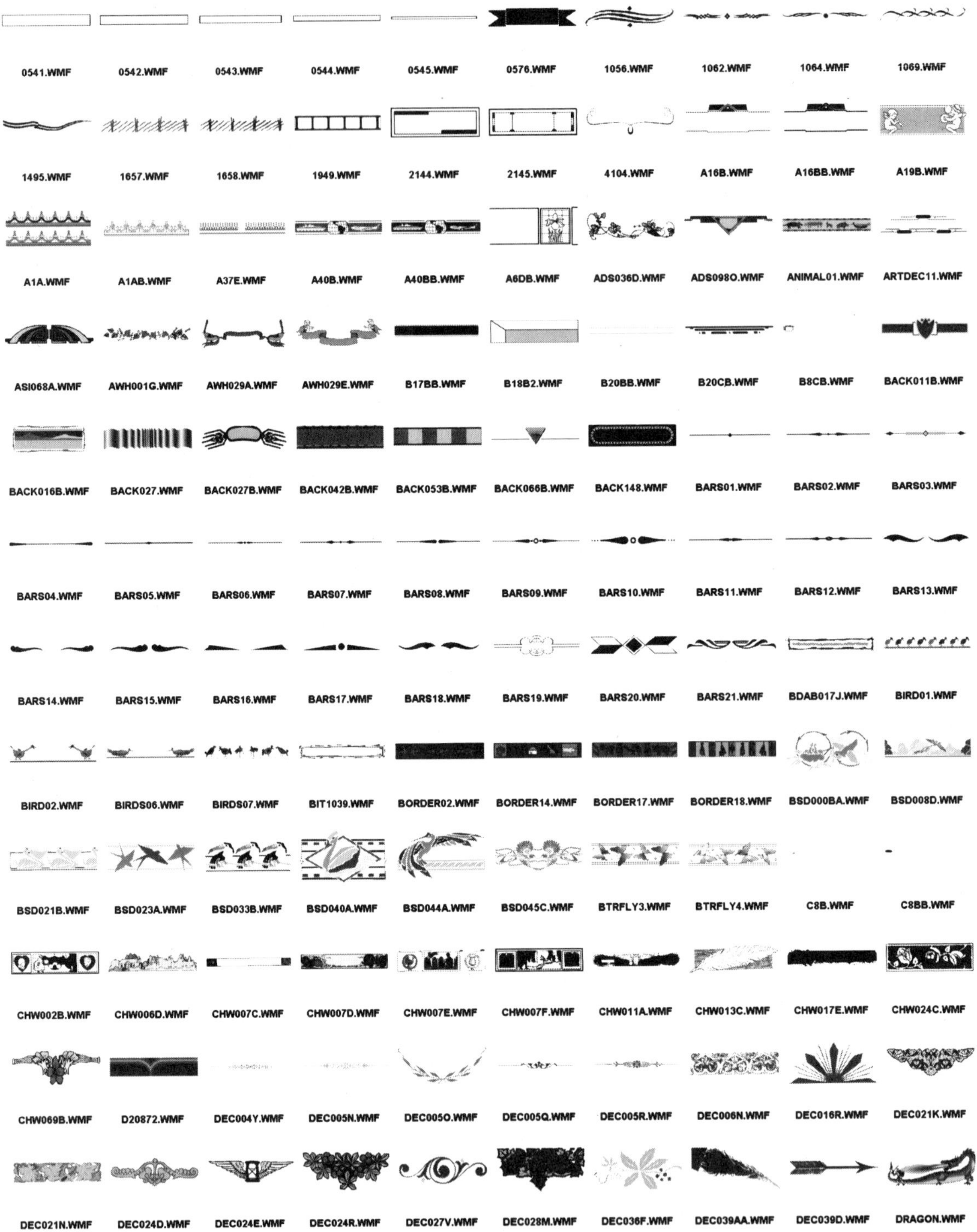
0541.WMF
0542.WMF
0543.WMF
0544.WMF
0545.WMF
0576.WMF
1056.WMF
1062.WMF
1064.WMF
1069.WMF
1495.WMF
1657.WMF
1658.WMF
1949.WMF
2144.WMF
2145.WMF
4104.WMF
A16B.WMF
A16BB.WMF
A19B.WMF
A1A.WMF
A1AB.WMF
A37E.WMF
A40B.WMF
A40BB.WMF
A6DB.WMF
ADS036D.WMF
ADS098O.WMF
ANIMAL01.WMF
ARTDEC11.WMF
ASI068A.WMF
AWH001G.WMF
AWH029A.WMF
AWH029E.WMF
B17BB.WMF
B18B2.WMF
B20BB.WMF
B20CB.WMF
B8CB.WMF
BACK011B.WMF
BACK016B.WMF
BACK027.WMF
BACK027B.WMF
BACK042B.WMF
BACK053B.WMF
BACK066B.WMF
BACK148.WMF
BARS01.WMF
BARS02.WMF
BARS03.WMF
BARS04.WMF
BARS05.WMF
BARS06.WMF
BARS07.WMF
BARS08.WMF
BARS09.WMF
BARS10.WMF
BARS11.WMF
BARS12.WMF
BARS13.WMF
BARS14.WMF
BARS15.WMF
BARS16.WMF
BARS17.WMF
BARS18.WMF
BARS19.WMF
BARS20.WMF
BARS21.WMF
BDAB017J.WMF
BIRD01.WMF
BIRD02.WMF
BIRDS06.WMF
BIRDS07.WMF
BIT1039.WMF
BORDER02.WMF
BORDER14.WMF
BORDER17.WMF
BORDER18.WMF
BSD000BA.WMF
BSD008D.WMF
BSD021B.WMF
BSD023A.WMF
BSD033B.WMF
BSD040A.WMF
BSD044A.WMF
BSD045C.WMF
BTRFLY3.WMF
BTRFLY4.WMF
C8B.WMF
C8BB.WMF
CHW002B.WMF
CHW006D.WMF
CHW007C.WMF
CHW007D.WMF
CHW007E.WMF
CHW007F.WMF
CHW011A.WMF
CHW013C.WMF
CHW017E.WMF
CHW024C.WMF
CHW069B.WMF
D20872.WMF
DEC004Y.WMF
DEC005N.WMF
DEC005O.WMF
DEC005Q.WMF
DEC005R.WMF
DEC006N.WMF
DEC016R.WMF
DEC021K.WMF
DEC021N.WMF
DEC024D.WMF
DEC024E.WMF
DEC024R.WMF
DEC027V.WMF
DEC028M.WMF
DEC036F.WMF
DEC039AA.WMF
DEC039D.WMF
DRAGON.WMF

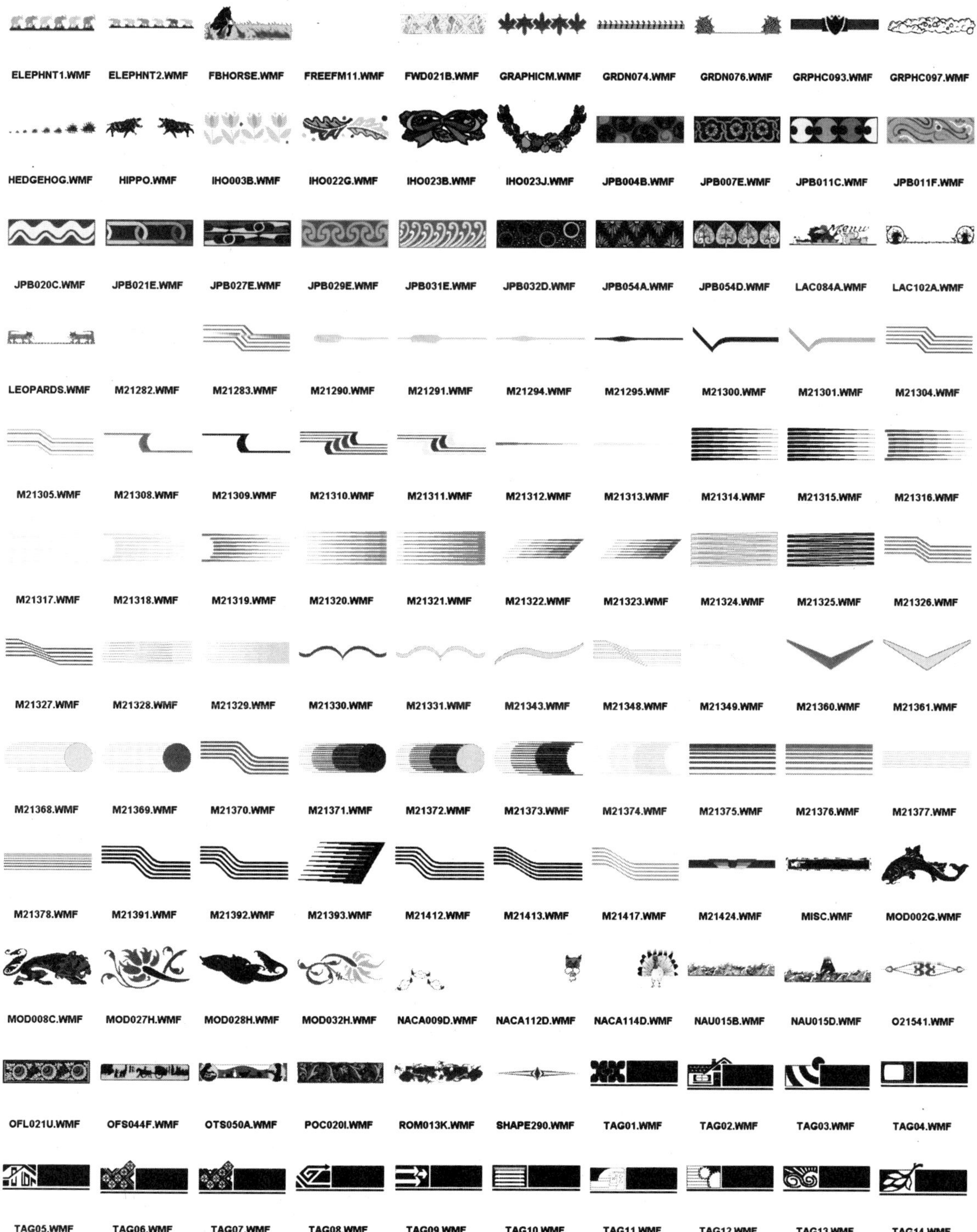
ELEPHNT1.WMF
ELEPHNT2.WMF
FBHORSE.WMF
FREEFM11.WMF
FWD021B.WMF
GRAPHICM.WMF
GRDN074.WMF
GRDN076.WMF
GRPHC093.WMF
GRPHC097.WMF
HEDGEHOG.WMF
HIPPO.WMF
IHO003B.WMF
IHO022G.WMF
IHO023B.WMF
IHO023J.WMF
JPB004B.WMF
JPB007E.WMF
JPB011C.WMF
JPB011F.WMF
JPB020C.WMF
JPB021E.WMF
JPB027E.WMF
JPB029E.WMF
JPB031E.WMF
JPB032D.WMF
JPB054A.WMF
JPB054D.WMF
LAC084A.WMF
LAC102A.WMF
LEOPARDS.WMF
M21282.WMF
M21283.WMF
M21290.WMF
M21291.WMF
M21294.WMF
M21295.WMF
M21300.WMF
M21301.WMF
M21304.WMF
M21305.WMF
M21308.WMF
M21309.WMF
M21310.WMF
M21311.WMF
M21312.WMF
M21313.WMF
M21314.WMF
M21315.WMF
M21316.WMF
M21317.WMF
M21318.WMF
M21319.WMF
M21320.WMF
M21321.WMF
M21322.WMF
M21323.WMF
M21324.WMF
M21325.WMF
M21326.WMF
M21327.WMF
M21328.WMF
M21329.WMF
M21330.WMF
M21331.WMF
M21343.WMF
M21348.WMF
M21349.WMF
M21360.WMF
M21361.WMF
M21368.WMF
M21369.WMF
M21370.WMF
M21371.WMF
M21372.WMF
M21373.WMF
M21374.WMF
M21375.WMF
M21376.WMF
M21377.WMF
M21378.WMF
M21391.WMF
M21392.WMF
M21393.WMF
M21412.WMF
M21413.WMF
M21417.WMF
M21424.WMF
MISC.WMF
MOD002G.WMF
MOD008C.WMF
MOD027H.WMF
MOD028H.WMF
MOD032H.WMF
NACA009D.WMF
NACA112D.WMF
NACA114D.WMF
NAU015B.WMF
NAU015D.WMF
O21541.WMF
OFL021U.WMF
OFS044F.WMF
OTS050A.WMF
POC020I.WMF
ROM013K.WMF
SHAPE290.WMF
TAG01.WMF
TAG02.WMF
TAG03.WMF
TAG04.WMF
TAG05.WMF
TAG06.WMF
TAG07.WMF
TAG08.WMF
TAG09.WMF
TAG10.WMF
TAG11.WMF
TAG12.WMF
TAG13.WMF
TAG14.WMF

TAG15.WMF	TAG16.WMF	TAG17.WMF	TAG18.WMF	TAG19.WMF	TAG20.WMF	TAG21.WMF	TAG22.WMF	TAG23.WMF	TAG24.WMF
TAG25.WMF	TAG26.WMF	TAG27.WMF	TAG28.WMF	TAG29.WMF	TAG30.WMF	TAG31.WMF	TAG32.WMF	TAG33.WMF	TAG34.WMF
TAG35.WMF	TAG36.WMF	THIN001.WMF	THIN002.WMF	THIN003.WMF	THIN004.WMF	THIN005.WMF	THIN006.WMF	THIN007.WMF	THIN008.WMF
THIN009.WMF	THIN010.WMF	THIN011.WMF	THIN012.WMF	THIN013.WMF	THIN014.WMF	THIN015.WMF	THIN016.WMF	THIN017.WMF	THIN018.WMF
THIN019.WMF	THIN020.WMF	THIN021.WMF	THIN022.WMF	THIN023.WMF	THIN024.WMF	THIN025.WMF	THIN026.WMF	THIN027.WMF	THIN028.WMF
THIN029.WMF	THIN030.WMF	THIN031.WMF	THIN032.WMF	THIN033.WMF	THIN034.WMF	THIN035.WMF	THIN036.WMF	THIN037.WMF	THIN038.WMF
THIN039.WMF	THIN040.WMF	THIN041.WMF	THIN042.WMF	THIN043.WMF	THIN044.WMF	THIN045.WMF	THIN046.WMF	THIN047.WMF	THIN048.WMF
THIN049.WMF	THIN050.WMF	THIN051.WMF	THIN052.WMF	THIN053.WMF	THIN054.WMF	THIN055.WMF	THIN056.WMF	THIN057.WMF	THIN058.WMF
THIN059.WMF	THIN060.WMF	THIN061.WMF	THIN062.WMF	THIN063.WMF	THIN064.WMF	THIN065.WMF	THIN066.WMF	THIN067.WMF	THIN068.WMF
THIN069.WMF	THIN070.WMF	THIN071.WMF	THIN072.WMF	THIN073.WMF	THIN074.WMF	THIN075.WMF	THIN076.WMF	THIN077.WMF	THIN078.WMF
THIN079.WMF	THIN080.WMF	THIN081.WMF	THIN082.WMF	THIN083.WMF	THIN084.WMF	THIN085.WMF	THIN086.WMF	THIN087.WMF	THIN088.WMF
THIN089.WMF	THIN090.WMF	THIN091.WMF	THIN092.WMF	THIN093.WMF	THIN094.WMF	THIN095.WMF	THIN096.WMF	THIN097.WMF	THIN098.WMF

THIN099.WMF THIN100.WMF THIN101.WMF THIN102.WMF THIN103.WMF THIN104.WMF THIN105.WMF THIN106.WMF THIN107.WMF THIN108.WMF

THIN109.WMF THIN110.WMF THIN111.WMF THIN112.WMF THIN113.WMF THIN114.WMF THIN115.WMF THIN116.WMF THIN117.WMF THIN118.WMF

THIN119.WMF THIN120.WMF THIN121.WMF THIN122.WMF THIN123.WMF THIN124.WMF THIN125.WMF THIN126.WMF THIN127.WMF THIN128.WMF

THIN129.WMF THIN130.WMF THIN131.WMF THIN132.WMF THIN133.WMF THIN134.WMF THIN135.WMF THIN136.WMF THIN137.WMF THIN138.WMF

THIN139.WMF THIN140.WMF THIN141.WMF THIN142.WMF THIN143.WMF THIN144.WMF THIN145.WMF THIN146.WMF THIN147.WMF THIN148.WMF

THIN149.WMF THIN150.WMF THIN151.WMF THIN152.WMF THIN153.WMF THIN154.WMF THIN155.WMF THIN156.WMF THIN157.WMF THIN158.WMF

THIN159.WMF THIN160.WMF THIN161.WMF THIN162.WMF THIN163.WMF THIN164.WMF THIN165.WMF THIN166.WMF THIN167.WMF THIN168.WMF

THIN169.WMF THIN170.WMF THIN171.WMF THIN172.WMF THIN173.WMF THIN174.WMF THIN175.WMF THIN176.WMF THIN177.WMF THIN178.WMF

THIN179.WMF THIN180.WMF THIN181.WMF THIN182.WMF THIN183.WMF THIN184.WMF THIN185.WMF THIN186.WMF THIN187.WMF THIN188.WMF

THIN189.WMF THIN190.WMF THIN191.WMF THIN192.WMF THIN193.WMF THIN194.WMF THIN195.WMF THIN196.WMF THIN197.WMF THIN198.WMF

THIN199.WMF THIN200.WMF THIN201.WMF THIN202.WMF THIN203.WMF THIN204.WMF THIN205.WMF THIN206.WMF THIN207.WMF THIN208.WMF

THIN209.WMF THIN210.WMF THIN211.WMF THIN212.WMF THIN213.WMF THIN214.WMF THIN215.WMF THIN216.WMF THIN217.WMF THIN218.WMF

THIN219.WMF	THIN220.WMF	THIN221.WMF	THIN222.WMF	THIN223.WMF	THIN224.WMF	THIN225.WMF	THIN226.WMF	THIN227.WMF	THIN228.WMF
THIN229.WMF	THIN230.WMF	THIN231.WMF	THIN232.WMF	THIN233.WMF	THIN234.WMF	THIN235.WMF	THIN236.WMF	THIN237.WMF	THIN238.WMF
THIN239.WMF	THIN240.WMF	THING001.WMF	THING002.WMF	THING003.WMF	THING004.WMF	THING005.WMF	THING006.WMF	THING007.WMF	THING008.WMF
THING009.WMF	THING010.WMF	THING011.WMF	THING012.WMF	THING013.WMF	THING014.WMF	THING015.WMF	THING016.WMF	THING017.WMF	THING018.WMF
THING019.WMF	THING020.WMF	THING021.WMF	THING022.WMF	THING023.WMF	THING024.WMF	THING025.WMF	THING026.WMF	THING027.WMF	THING028.WMF
THING029.WMF	THING030.WMF	THING031.WMF	THING032.WMF	THING033.WMF	THING034.WMF	THING035.WMF	THING036.WMF	THING037.WMF	THING038.WMF
THING039.WMF	THING040.WMF	THING041.WMF	THING042.WMF	THING043.WMF	THING044.WMF	THING045.WMF	THING046.WMF	THING047.WMF	THING048.WMF
THING049.WMF	THING050.WMF	THING051.WMF	THING052.WMF	THING053.WMF	THING054.WMF	THING055.WMF	THING056.WMF	THING057.WMF	THING058.WMF
THING059.WMF	THING060.WMF	THING061.WMF	THING062.WMF	THING063.WMF	THING064.WMF	THING065.WMF	THING066.WMF	THING067.WMF	THING068.WMF
THING069.WMF	THING070.WMF	THING071.WMF	THING072.WMF	THING073.WMF	THING074.WMF	THING075.WMF	THING076.WMF	THING077.WMF	THING078.WMF
THING079.WMF	THING080.WMF	THING081.WMF	THING082.WMF	THING083.WMF	THING084.WMF	THING085.WMF	THING086.WMF	THING087.WMF	THING088.WMF
THING089.WMF	THING090.WMF	THING091.WMF	THING092.WMF	THING093.WMF	THING094.WMF	THING095.WMF	THING096.WMF	THING097.WMF	THING098.WMF

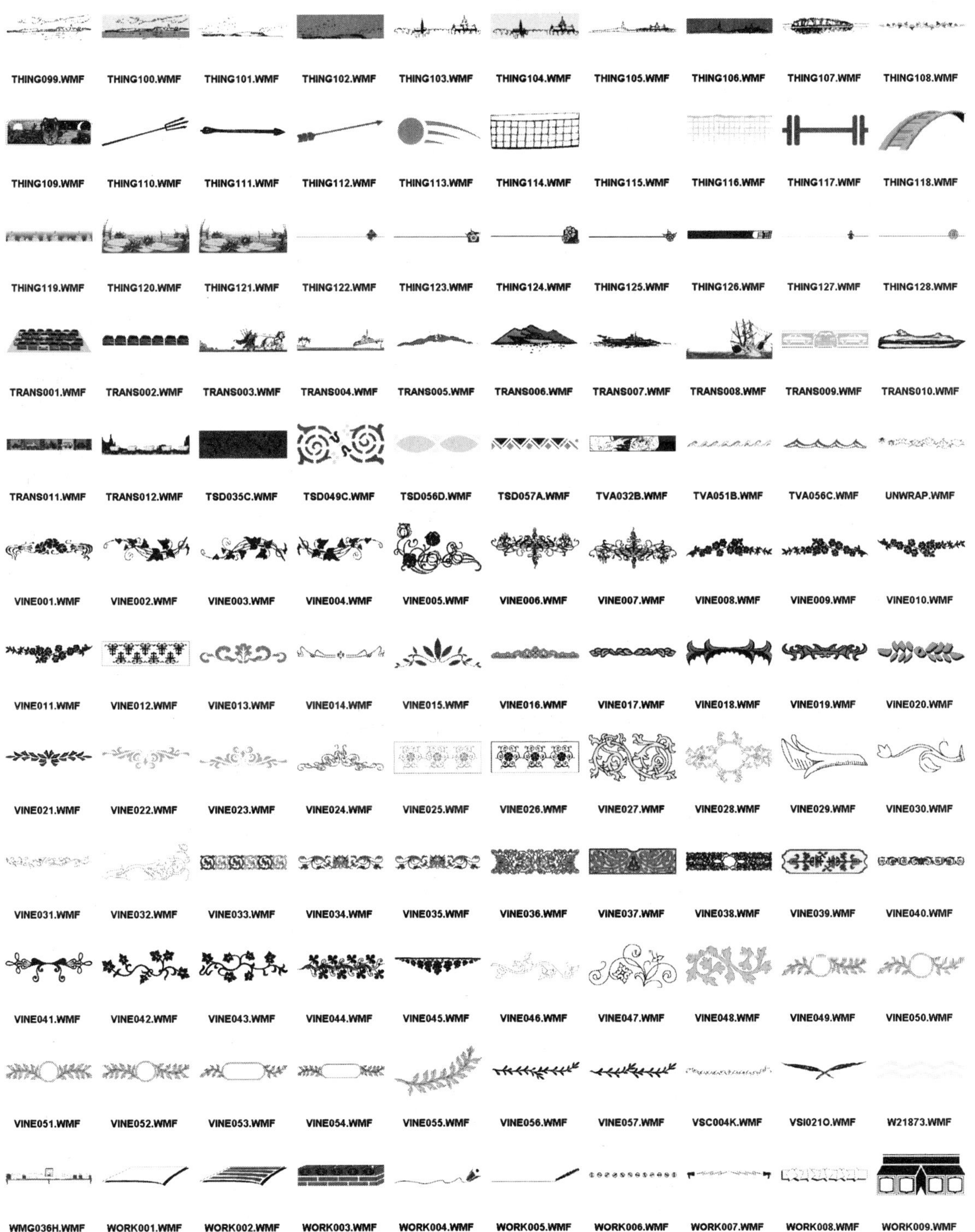
THING099.WMF
THING100.WMF
THING101.WMF
THING102.WMF
THING103.WMF
THING104.WMF
THING105.WMF
THING106.WMF
THING107.WMF
THING108.WMF
THING109.WMF
THING110.WMF
THING111.WMF
THING112.WMF
THING113.WMF
THING114.WMF
THING115.WMF
THING116.WMF
THING117.WMF
THING118.WMF
THING119.WMF
THING120.WMF
THING121.WMF
THING122.WMF
THING123.WMF
THING124.WMF
THING125.WMF
THING126.WMF
THING127.WMF
THING128.WMF
TRANS001.WMF
TRANS002.WMF
TRANS003.WMF
TRANS004.WMF
TRANS005.WMF
TRANS006.WMF
TRANS007.WMF
TRANS008.WMF
TRANS009.WMF
TRANS010.WMF
TRANS011.WMF
TRANS012.WMF
TSD035C.WMF
TSD049C.WMF
TSD056D.WMF
TSD057A.WMF
TVA032B.WMF
TVA051B.WMF
TVA056C.WMF
UNWRAP.WMF
VINE001.WMF
VINE002.WMF
VINE003.WMF
VINE004.WMF
VINE005.WMF
VINE006.WMF
VINE007.WMF
VINE008.WMF
VINE009.WMF
VINE010.WMF
VINE011.WMF
VINE012.WMF
VINE013.WMF
VINE014.WMF
VINE015.WMF
VINE016.WMF
VINE017.WMF
VINE018.WMF
VINE019.WMF
VINE020.WMF
VINE021.WMF
VINE022.WMF
VINE023.WMF
VINE024.WMF
VINE025.WMF
VINE026.WMF
VINE027.WMF
VINE028.WMF
VINE029.WMF
VINE030.WMF
VINE031.WMF
VINE032.WMF
VINE033.WMF
VINE034.WMF
VINE035.WMF
VINE036.WMF
VINE037.WMF
VINE038.WMF
VINE039.WMF
VINE040.WMF
VINE041.WMF
VINE042.WMF
VINE043.WMF
VINE044.WMF
VINE045.WMF
VINE046.WMF
VINE047.WMF
VINE048.WMF
VINE049.WMF
VINE050.WMF
VINE051.WMF
VINE052.WMF
VINE053.WMF
VINE054.WMF
VINE055.WMF
VINE056.WMF
VINE057.WMF
VSC004K.WMF
VSI021O.WMF
W21873.WMF
WMG036H.WMF
WORK001.WMF
WORK002.WMF
WORK003.WMF
WORK004.WMF
WORK005.WMF
WORK006.WMF
WORK007.WMF
WORK008.WMF
WORK009.WMF

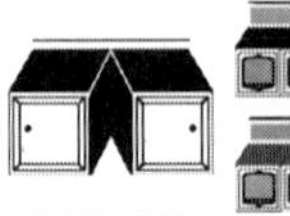
WORK010.WMF

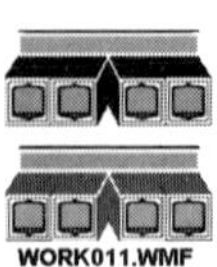
WORK011.WMF

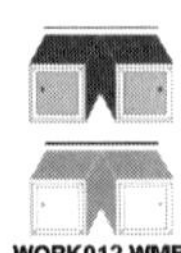
WORK012.WMF

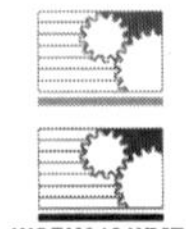
WORK013.WMF

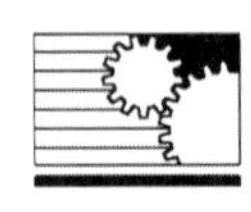
WORK014.WMF

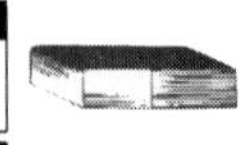
WORK015.WMF

WORK016.WMF

XDN024D.WMF

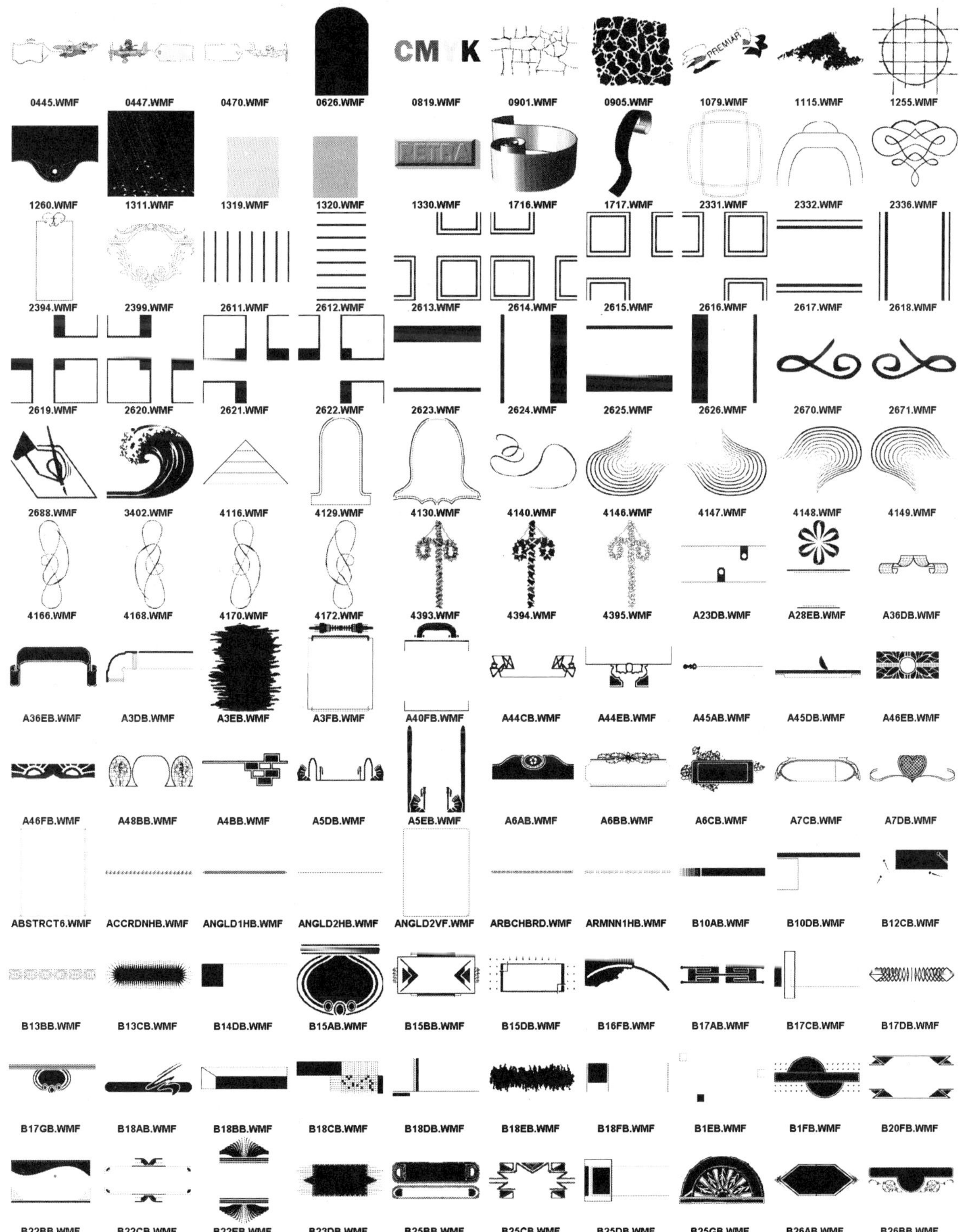
0445.WMF 0447.WMF 0470.WMF 0626.WMF 0819.WMF 0901.WMF 0905.WMF 1079.WMF 1115.WMF 1255.WMF
1260.WMF 1311.WMF 1319.WMF 1320.WMF 1330.WMF 1716.WMF 1717.WMF 2331.WMF 2332.WMF 2336.WMF
2394.WMF 2399.WMF 2611.WMF 2612.WMF 2613.WMF 2614.WMF 2615.WMF 2616.WMF 2617.WMF 2618.WMF
2619.WMF 2620.WMF 2621.WMF 2622.WMF 2623.WMF 2624.WMF 2625.WMF 2626.WMF 2670.WMF 2671.WMF
2688.WMF 3402.WMF 4116.WMF 4129.WMF 4130.WMF 4140.WMF 4146.WMF 4147.WMF 4148.WMF 4149.WMF
4166.WMF 4168.WMF 4170.WMF 4172.WMF 4393.WMF 4394.WMF 4395.WMF A23DB.WMF A28EB.WMF A36DB.WMF
A36EB.WMF A3DB.WMF A3EB.WMF A3FB.WMF A40FB.WMF A44CB.WMF A44EB.WMF A45AB.WMF A45DB.WMF A46EB.WMF
A46FB.WMF A48BB.WMF A4BB.WMF A5DB.WMF A5EB.WMF A6AB.WMF A6BB.WMF A6CB.WMF A7CB.WMF A7DB.WMF
ABSTRCT6.WMF ACCRDNHB.WMF ANGLD1HB.WMF ANGLD2HB.WMF ANGLD2VF.WMF ARBCHBRD.WMF ARMNN1HB.WMF B10AB.WMF B10DB.WMF B12CB.WMF
B13BB.WMF B13CB.WMF B14DB.WMF B15AB.WMF B15BB.WMF B15DB.WMF B16FB.WMF B17AB.WMF B17CB.WMF B17DB.WMF
B17GB.WMF B18AB.WMF B18BB.WMF B18CB.WMF B18DB.WMF B18EB.WMF B18FB.WMF B1EB.WMF B1FB.WMF B20FB.WMF
B22BB.WMF B22CB.WMF B22EB.WMF B23DB.WMF B25BB.WMF B25CB.WMF B25DB.WMF B25GB.WMF B26AB.WMF B26BB.WMF

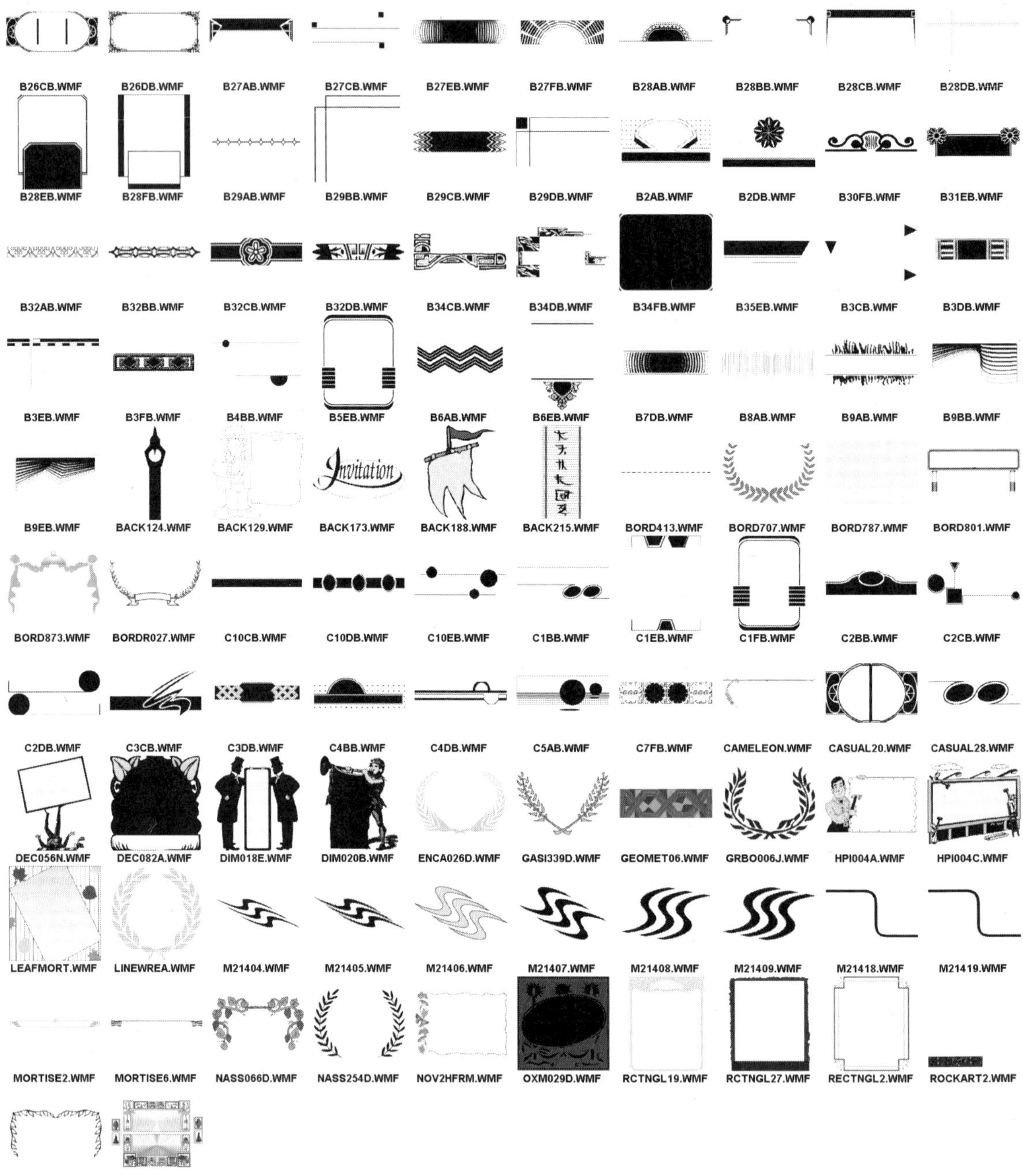
B26CB.WMF
B26DB.WMF
B27AB.WMF
B27CB.WMF
B27EB.WMF
B27FB.WMF
B28AB.WMF
B28BB.WMF
B28CB.WMF
B28DB.WMF
B28EB.WMF
B28FB.WMF
B29AB.WMF
B29BB.WMF
B29CB.WMF
B29DB.WMF
B2AB.WMF
B2DB.WMF
B30FB.WMF
B31EB.WMF
B32AB.WMF
B32BB.WMF
B32CB.WMF
B32DB.WMF
B34CB.WMF
B34DB.WMF
B34FB.WMF
B35EB.WMF
B3CB.WMF
B3DB.WMF
B3EB.WMF
B3FB.WMF
B4BB.WMF
B5EB.WMF
B6AB.WMF
B6EB.WMF
B7DB.WMF
B8AB.WMF
B9AB.WMF
B9BB.WMF
Invitation
B9EB.WMF
BACK124.WMF
BACK129.WMF
BACK173.WMF
BACK188.WMF
BACK215.WMF
BORD413.WMF
BORD707.WMF
BORD787.WMF
BORD801.WMF
BORD873.WMF
BORDR027.WMF
C10CB.WMF
C10DB.WMF
C10EB.WMF
C1BB.WMF
C1EB.WMF
C1FB.WMF
C2BB.WMF
C2CB.WMF
C2DB.WMF
C3CB.WMF
C3DB.WMF
C4BB.WMF
C4DB.WMF
C5AB.WMF
C7FB.WMF
CAMELEON.WMF
CASUAL20.WMF
CASUAL28.WMF
DEC056N.WMF
DEC082A.WMF
DIM018E.WMF
DIM020B.WMF
ENCA026D.WMF
GASI339D.WMF
GEOMET06.WMF
GRBO006J.WMF
HPI004A.WMF
HPI004C.WMF
LEAFMORT.WMF
LINEWREA.WMF
M21404.WMF
M21405.WMF
M21406.WMF
M21407.WMF
M21408.WMF
M21409.WMF
M21418.WMF
M21419.WMF
MORTISE2.WMF
MORTISE6.WMF
NASS066D.WMF
NASS254D.WMF
NOV2HFRM.WMF
OXM029D.WMF
RCTNGL19.WMF
RCTNGL27.WMF
RECTNGL2.WMF
ROCKART2.WMF
SIMC001.WMF
TOYBORD1.WMF

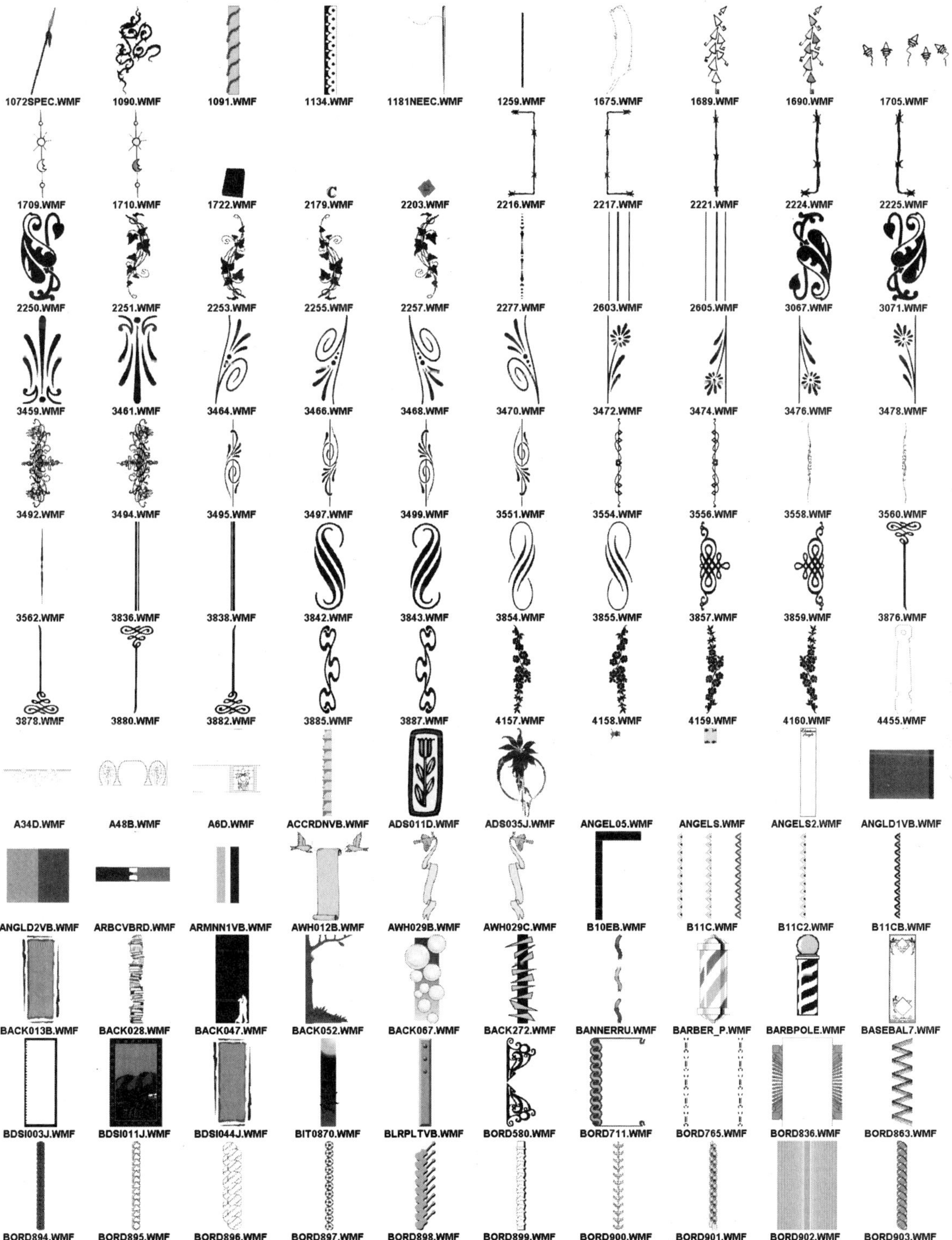
1072SPEC.WMF
1090.WMF
1091.WMF
1134.WMF
1181NEEC.WMF
1259.WMF
1675.WMF
1689.WMF
1690.WMF
1705.WMF
1709.WMF
1710.WMF
1722.WMF
2179.WMF
2203.WMF
2216.WMF
2217.WMF
2221.WMF
2224.WMF
2225.WMF
2250.WMF
2251.WMF
2253.WMF
2255.WMF
2257.WMF
2277.WMF
2603.WMF
2605.WMF
3067.WMF
3071.WMF
3459.WMF
3461.WMF
3464.WMF
3466.WMF
3468.WMF
3470.WMF
3472.WMF
3474.WMF
3476.WMF
3478.WMF
3492.WMF
3494.WMF
3495.WMF
3497.WMF
3499.WMF
3551.WMF
3554.WMF
3556.WMF
3558.WMF
3560.WMF
3562.WMF
3836.WMF
3838.WMF
3842.WMF
3843.WMF
3854.WMF
3855.WMF
3857.WMF
3859.WMF
3876.WMF
3878.WMF
3880.WMF
3882.WMF
3885.WMF
3887.WMF
4157.WMF
4158.WMF
4159.WMF
4160.WMF
4455.WMF
A34D.WMF
A48B.WMF
A6D.WMF
ACCRDNVB.WMF
ADS011D.WMF
ADS035J.WMF
ANGEL05.WMF
ANGELS.WMF
ANGELS2.WMF
ANGLD1VB.WMF
ANGLD2VB.WMF
ARBCVBRD.WMF
ARMNN1VB.WMF
AWH012B.WMF
AWH029B.WMF
AWH029C.WMF
B10EB.WMF
B11C.WMF
B11C2.WMF
B11CB.WMF
BACK013B.WMF
BACK028.WMF
BACK047.WMF
BACK052.WMF
BACK067.WMF
BACK272.WMF
BANNERRU.WMF
BARBER_P.WMF
BARBPOLE.WMF
BASEBAL7.WMF
BDSI003J.WMF
BDSI011J.WMF
BDSI044J.WMF
BIT0870.WMF
BLRPLTVB.WMF
BORD580.WMF
BORD711.WMF
BORD765.WMF
BORD836.WMF
BORD863.WMF
BORD894.WMF
BORD895.WMF
BORD896.WMF
BORD897.WMF
BORD898.WMF
BORD899.WMF
BORD900.WMF
BORD901.WMF
BORD902.WMF
BORD903.WMF

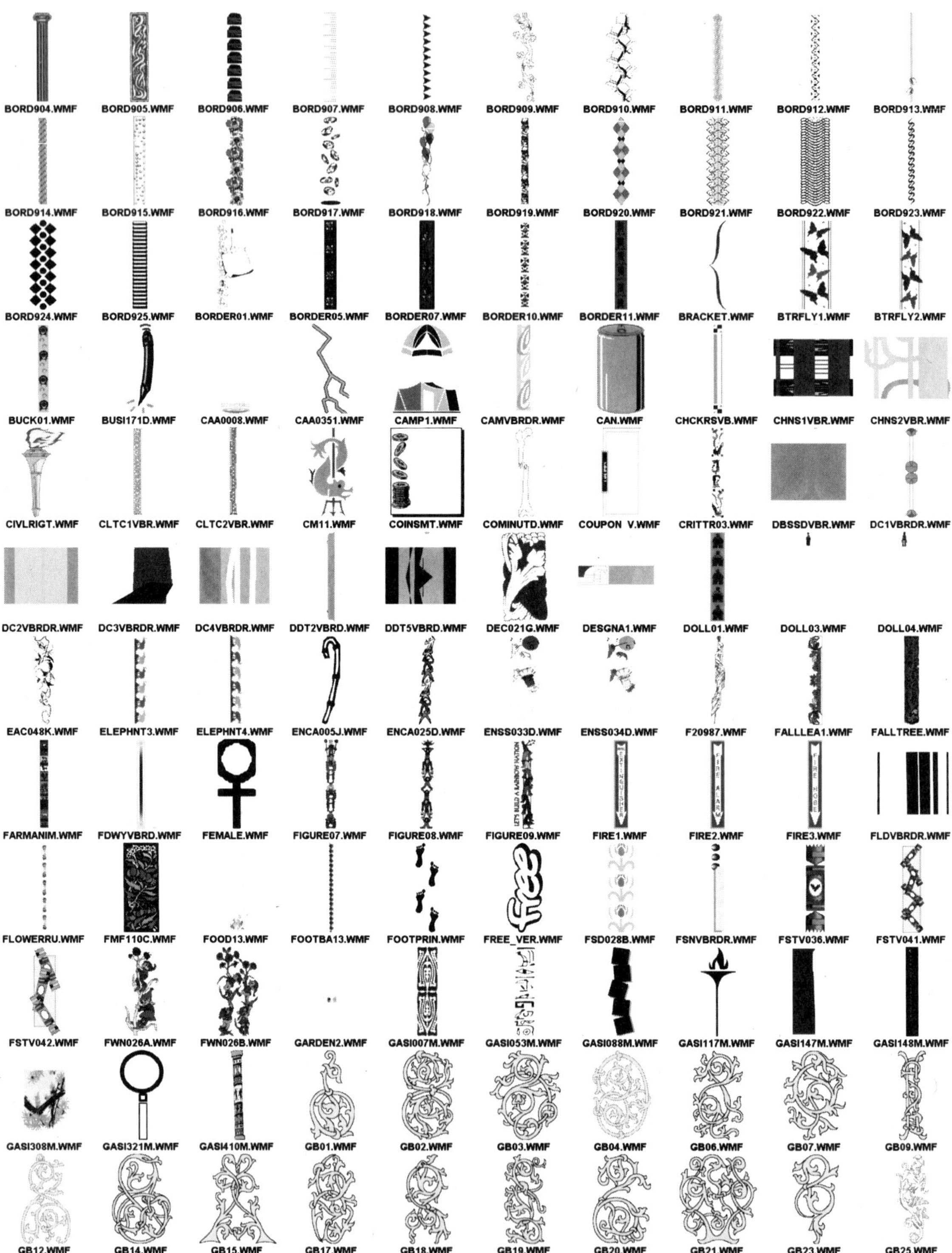
BORD904.WMF BORD905.WMF BORD906.WMF BORD907.WMF BORD908.WMF BORD909.WMF BORD910.WMF BORD911.WMF BORD912.WMF BORD913.WMF
BORD914.WMF BORD915.WMF BORD916.WMF BORD917.WMF BORD918.WMF BORD919.WMF BORD920.WMF BORD921.WMF BORD922.WMF BORD923.WMF
BORD924.WMF BORD925.WMF BORDER01.WMF BORDER05.WMF BORDER07.WMF BORDER10.WMF BORDER11.WMF BRACKET.WMF BTRFLY1.WMF BTRFLY2.WMF
BUCK01.WMF BUSI171D.WMF CAA0008.WMF CAA0351.WMF CAMP1.WMF CAMVBRDR.WMF CAN.WMF CHCKRSVB.WMF CHNS1VBR.WMF CHNS2VBR.WMF
CIVLRIGT.WMF CLTC1VBR.WMF CLTC2VBR.WMF CM11.WMF COINSMT.WMF COMINUTD.WMF COUPON V.WMF CRITTR03.WMF DBSSDVBR.WMF DC1VBRDR.WMF
DC2VBRDR.WMF DC3VBRDR.WMF DC4VBRDR.WMF DDT2VBRD.WMF DDT5VBRD.WMF DEC021G.WMF DESGNA1.WMF DOLL01.WMF DOLL03.WMF DOLL04.WMF
EAC048K.WMF ELEPHNT3.WMF ELEPHNT4.WMF ENCA005J.WMF ENCA025D.WMF ENSS033D.WMF ENSS034D.WMF F20987.WMF FALLLEA1.WMF FALLTREE.WMF
FARMANIM.WMF FDWYVBRD.WMF FEMALE.WMF FIGURE07.WMF FIGURE08.WMF FIGURE09.WMF FIRE1.WMF FIRE2.WMF FIRE3.WMF FLDVBRDR.WMF
FLOWERRU.WMF FMF110C.WMF FOOD13.WMF FOOTBA13.WMF FOOTPRIN.WMF FREE_VER.WMF FSD028B.WMF FSNVBRDR.WMF FSTV036.WMF FSTV041.WMF
FSTV042.WMF FWN026A.WMF FWN026B.WMF GARDEN2.WMF GASI007M.WMF GASI053M.WMF GASI088M.WMF GASI117M.WMF GASI147M.WMF GASI148M.WMF
GASI308M.WMF GASI321M.WMF GASI410M.WMF GB01.WMF GB02.WMF GB03.WMF GB04.WMF GB06.WMF GB07.WMF GB09.WMF
GB12.WMF GB14.WMF GB15.WMF GB17.WMF GB18.WMF GB19.WMF GB20.WMF GB21.WMF GB23.WMF GB25.WMF

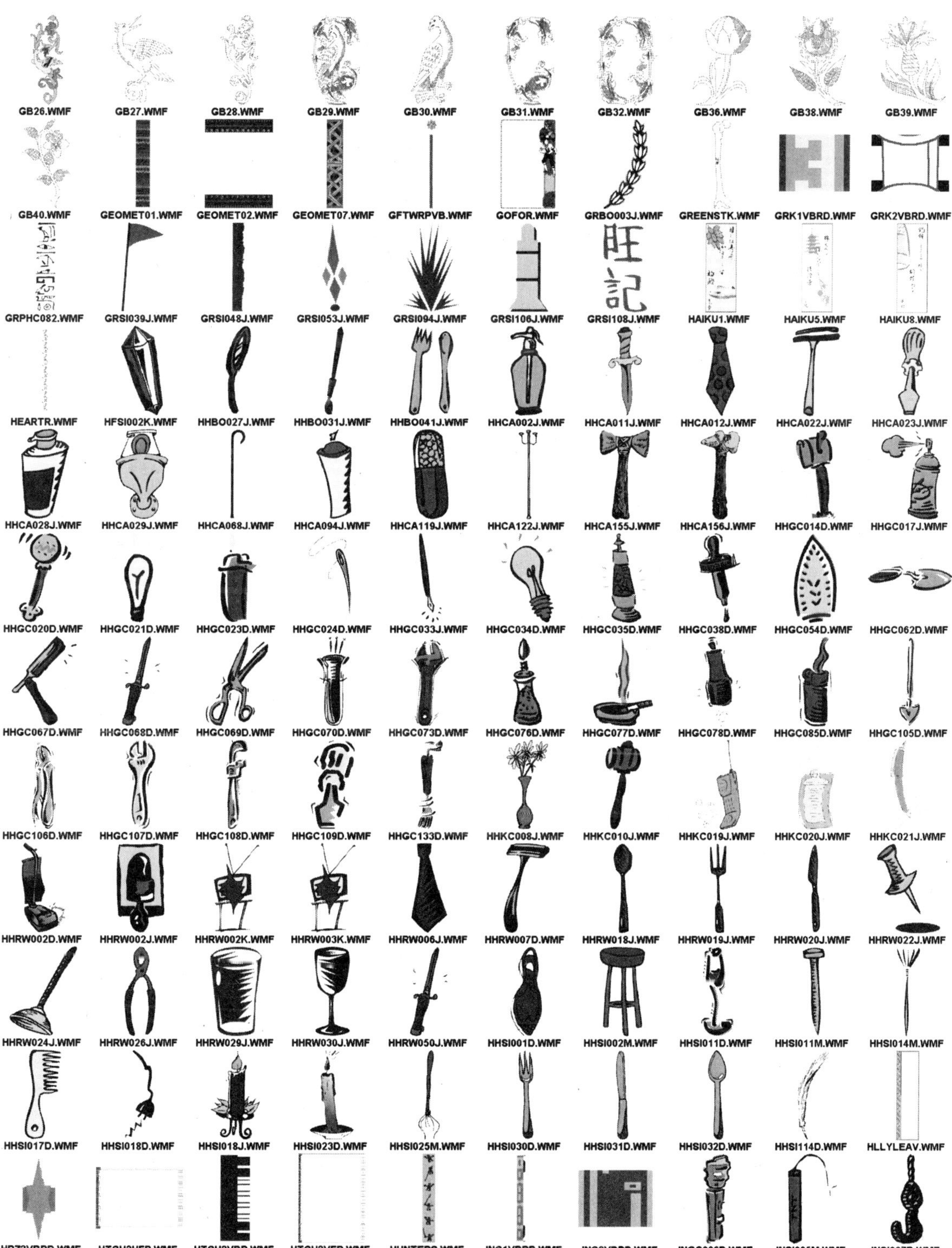
GB26.WMF
GB27.WMF
GB28.WMF
GB29.WMF
GB30.WMF
GB31.WMF
GB32.WMF
GB36.WMF
GB38.WMF
GB39.WMF
GB40.WMF
GEOMET01.WMF
GEOMET02.WMF
GEOMET07.WMF
GFTWRPVB.WMF
GOFOR.WMF
GRBO003J.WMF
GREENSTK.WMF
GRK1VBRD.WMF
GRK2VBRD.WMF
GRPHC082.WMF
GRSI039J.WMF
GRSI048J.WMF
GRSI053J.WMF
GRSI094J.WMF
GRSI106J.WMF
GRSI108J.WMF
HAIKU1.WMF
HAIKU5.WMF
HAIKU8.WMF
HEARTR.WMF
HFSI002K.WMF
HHBO027J.WMF
HHBO031J.WMF
HHBO041J.WMF
HHCA002J.WMF
HHCA011J.WMF
HHCA012J.WMF
HHCA022J.WMF
HHCA023J.WMF
HHCA028J.WMF
HHCA029J.WMF
HHCA068J.WMF
HHCA094J.WMF
HHCA119J.WMF
HHCA122J.WMF
HHCA155J.WMF
HHCA156J.WMF
HHGC014D.WMF
HHGC017J.WMF
HHGC020D.WMF
HHGC021D.WMF
HHGC023D.WMF
HHGC024D.WMF
HHGC033J.WMF
HHGC034D.WMF
HHGC035D.WMF
HHGC038D.WMF
HHGC054D.WMF
HHGC062D.WMF
HHGC067D.WMF
HHGC068D.WMF
HHGC069D.WMF
HHGC070D.WMF
HHGC073D.WMF
HHGC076D.WMF
HHGC077D.WMF
HHGC078D.WMF
HHGC085D.WMF
HHGC105D.WMF
HHGC106D.WMF
HHGC107D.WMF
HHGC108D.WMF
HHGC109D.WMF
HHGC133D.WMF
HHKC008J.WMF
HHKC010J.WMF
HHKC019J.WMF
HHKC020J.WMF
HHKC021J.WMF
HHRW002D.WMF
HHRW002J.WMF
HHRW002K.WMF
HHRW003K.WMF
HHRW006J.WMF
HHRW007D.WMF
HHRW018J.WMF
HHRW019J.WMF
HHRW020J.WMF
HHRW022J.WMF
HHRW024J.WMF
HHRW026J.WMF
HHRW029J.WMF
HHRW030J.WMF
HHRW050J.WMF
HHSI001D.WMF
HHSI002M.WMF
HHSI011D.WMF
HHSI011M.WMF
HHSI014M.WMF
HHSI017D.WMF
HHSI018D.WMF
HHSI018J.WMF
HHSI023D.WMF
HHSI025M.WMF
HHSI030D.WMF
HHSI031D.WMF
HHSI032D.WMF
HHSI114D.WMF
HLLYLEAV.WMF
HRZ3VBRD.WMF
HTCH3HFR.WMF
HTCH3VBR.WMF
HTCH3VFR.WMF
HUNTERS.WMF
INC1VBRD.WMF
INC2VBRD.WMF
INGC006D.WMF
INSI005M.WMF
INSI007D.WMF

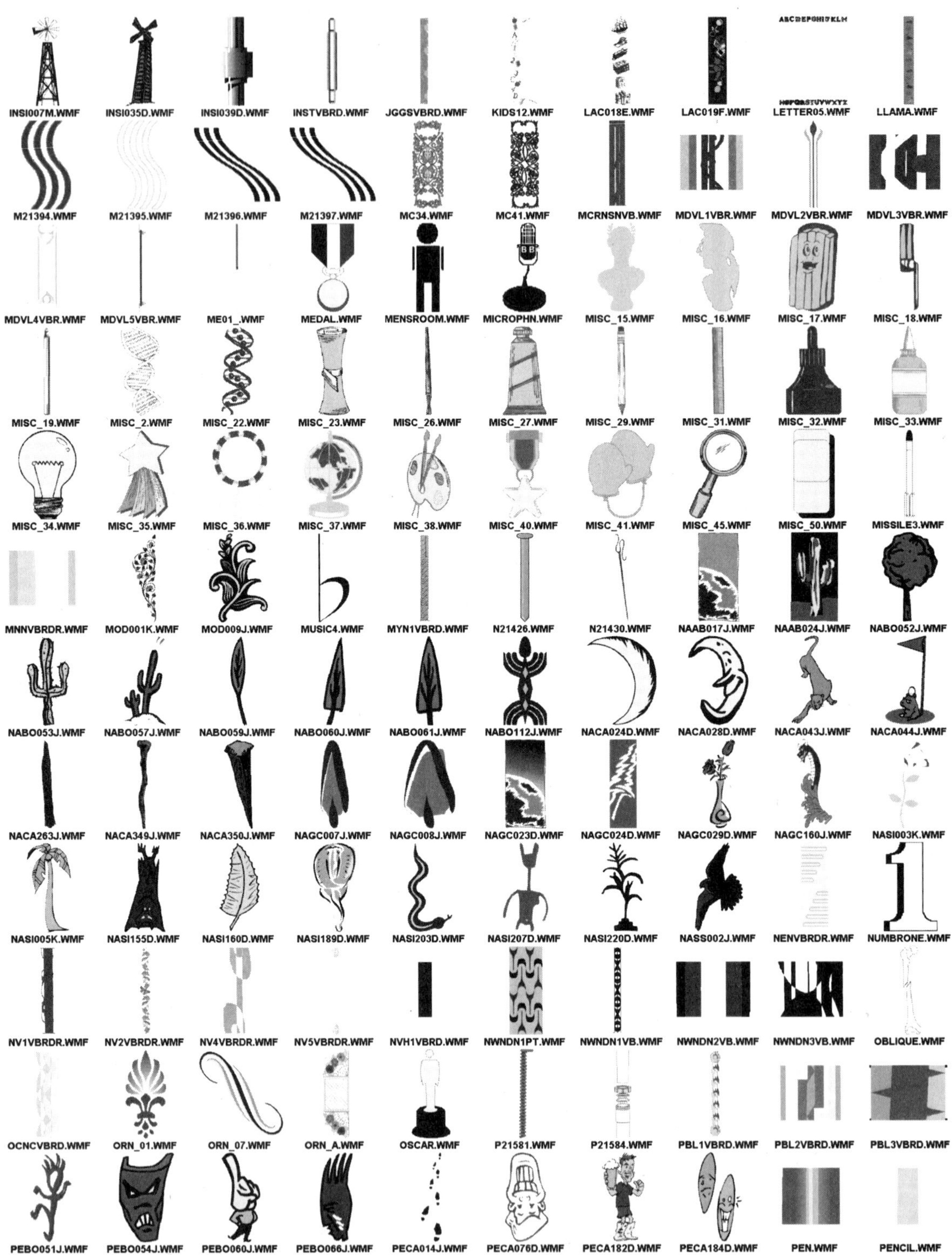
INSI007M.WMF
INSI035D.WMF
INSI039D.WMF
INSTVBRD.WMF
JGGSVBRD.WMF
KIDS12.WMF
LAC018E.WMF
LAC019F.WMF
LETTER05.WMF
LLAMA.WMF
M21394.WMF
M21395.WMF
M21396.WMF
M21397.WMF
MC34.WMF
MC41.WMF
MCRNSNVB.WMF
MDVL1VBR.WMF
MDVL2VBR.WMF
MDVL3VBR.WMF
MDVL4VBR.WMF
MDVL5VBR.WMF
ME01_.WMF
MEDAL.WMF
MENSROOM.WMF
MICROPHN.WMF
MISC_15.WMF
MISC_16.WMF
MISC_17.WMF
MISC_18.WMF
MISC_19.WMF
MISC_2.WMF
MISC_22.WMF
MISC_23.WMF
MISC_26.WMF
MISC_27.WMF
MISC_29.WMF
MISC_31.WMF
MISC_32.WMF
MISC_33.WMF
MISC_34.WMF
MISC_35.WMF
MISC_36.WMF
MISC_37.WMF
MISC_38.WMF
MISC_40.WMF
MISC_41.WMF
MISC_45.WMF
MISC_50.WMF
MISSILE3.WMF
MNNVBRDR.WMF
MOD001K.WMF
MOD009J.WMF
MUSIC4.WMF
MYN1VBRD.WMF
N21426.WMF
N21430.WMF
NAAB017J.WMF
NAAB024J.WMF
NABO052J.WMF
NABO053J.WMF
NABO057J.WMF
NABO059J.WMF
NABO060J.WMF
NABO061J.WMF
NABO112J.WMF
NACA024D.WMF
NACA028D.WMF
NACA043J.WMF
NACA044J.WMF
NACA263J.WMF
NACA349J.WMF
NACA350J.WMF
NAGC007J.WMF
NAGC008J.WMF
NAGC023D.WMF
NAGC024D.WMF
NAGC029D.WMF
NAGC160J.WMF
NASI003K.WMF
NASI005K.WMF
NASI155D.WMF
NASI160D.WMF
NASI189D.WMF
NASI203D.WMF
NASI207D.WMF
NASI220D.WMF
NASS002J.WMF
NENVBRDR.WMF
NUMBRONE.WMF
NV1VBRDR.WMF
NV2VBRDR.WMF
NV4VBRDR.WMF
NV5VBRDR.WMF
NVH1VBRD.WMF
NWNDN1PT.WMF
NWNDN1VB.WMF
NWNDN2VB.WMF
NWNDN3VB.WMF
OBLIQUE.WMF
OCNCVBRD.WMF
ORN_01.WMF
ORN_07.WMF
ORN_A.WMF
OSCAR.WMF
P21581.WMF
P21584.WMF
PBL1VBRD.WMF
PBL2VBRD.WMF
PBL3VBRD.WMF
PEBO051J.WMF
PEBO054J.WMF
PEBO060J.WMF
PEBO066J.WMF
PECA014J.WMF
PECA076D.WMF
PECA182D.WMF
PECA184D.WMF
PEN.WMF
PENCIL.WMF

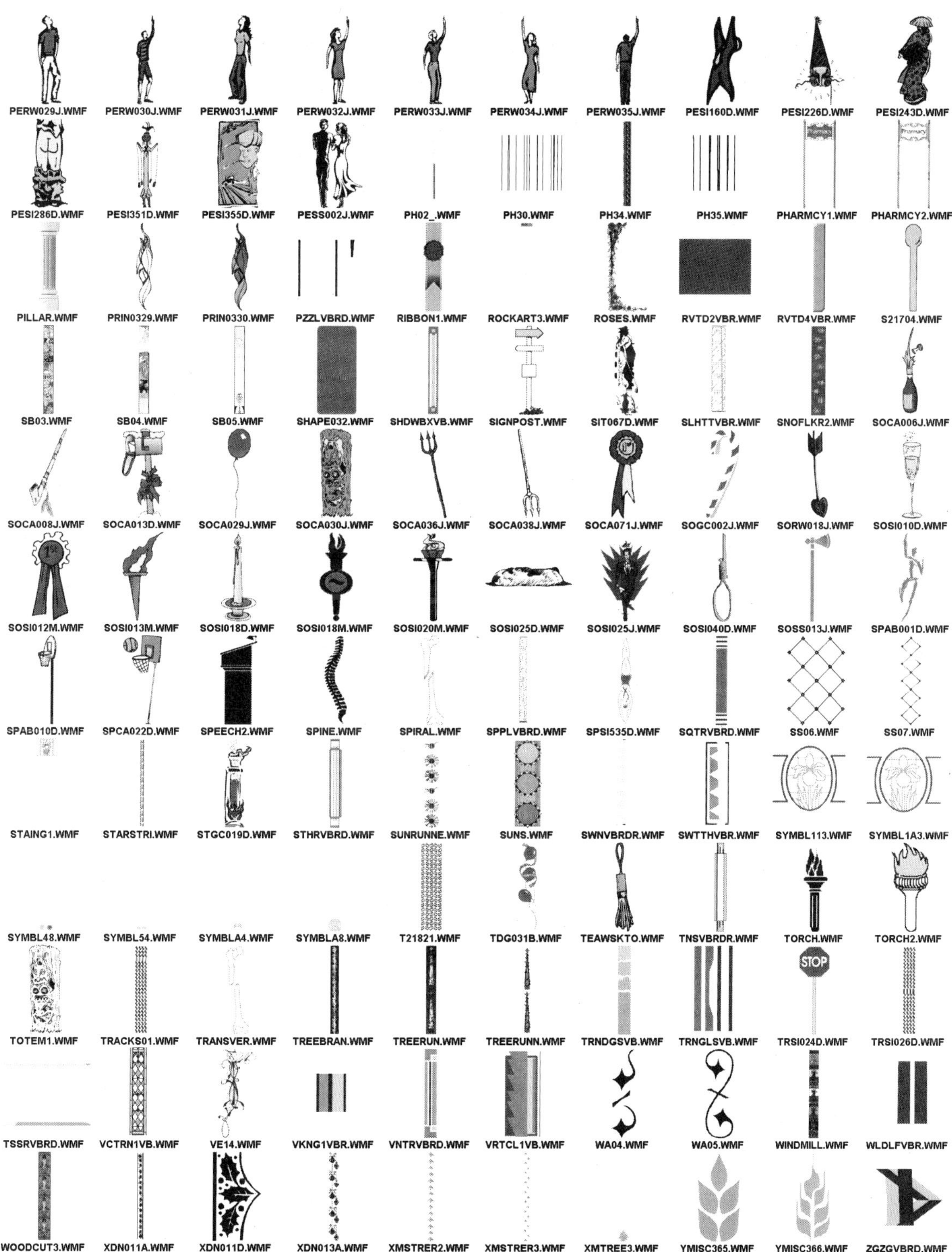
PERW029J.WMF PERW030J.WMF PERW031J.WMF PERW032J.WMF PERW033J.WMF PERW034J.WMF PERW035J.WMF PESI160D.WMF PESI226D.WMF PESI243D.WMF
PESI286D.WMF PESI351D.WMF PESI355D.WMF PESS002J.WMF PH02_.WMF PH30.WMF PH34.WMF PH35.WMF PHARMCY1.WMF PHARMCY2.WMF
PILLAR.WMF PRIN0329.WMF PRIN0330.WMF PZZLVBRD.WMF RIBBON1.WMF ROCKART3.WMF ROSES.WMF RVTD2VBR.WMF RVTD4VBR.WMF S21704.WMF
SB03.WMF SB04.WMF SB05.WMF SHAPE032.WMF SHDWBXVB.WMF SIGNPOST.WMF SIT067D.WMF SLHTTVBR.WMF SNOFLKR2.WMF SOCA006J.WMF
SOCA008J.WMF SOCA013D.WMF SOCA029J.WMF SOCA030J.WMF SOCA036J.WMF SOCA038J.WMF SOCA071J.WMF SOGC002J.WMF SORW018J.WMF SOSI010D.WMF
SOSI012M.WMF SOSI013M.WMF SOSI018D.WMF SOSI018M.WMF SOSI020M.WMF SOSI025D.WMF SOSI025J.WMF SOSI040D.WMF SOSS013J.WMF SPAB001D.WMF
SPAB010D.WMF SPCA022D.WMF SPEECH2.WMF SPINE.WMF SPIRAL.WMF SPPLVBRD.WMF SPSI535D.WMF SQTRVBRD.WMF SS06.WMF SS07.WMF
STAING1.WMF STARSTRI.WMF STGC019D.WMF STHRVBRD.WMF SUNRUNNE.WMF SUNS.WMF SWNVBRDR.WMF SWTTHVBR.WMF SYMBL113.WMF SYMBL1A3.WMF
SYMBL48.WMF SYMBL54.WMF SYMBLA4.WMF SYMBLA8.WMF T21821.WMF TDG031B.WMF TEAWSKTO.WMF TNSVBRDR.WMF TORCH.WMF TORCH2.WMF
STOP
TOTEM1.WMF TRACKS01.WMF TRANSVER.WMF TREEBRAN.WMF TREERUN.WMF TREERUNN.WMF TRNDGSVB.WMF TRNGLSVB.WMF TRSI024D.WMF TRSI026D.WMF
TSSRVBRD.WMF VCTRN1VB.WMF VE14.WMF VKNG1VBR.WMF VNTRVBRD.WMF VRTCL1VB.WMF WA04.WMF WA05.WMF WINDMILL.WMF WLDLFVBR.WMF
WOODCUT3.WMF XDN011A.WMF XDN011D.WMF XDN013A.WMF XMSTRER2.WMF XMSTRER3.WMF XMTREE3.WMF YMISC365.WMF YMISC366.WMF ZGZGVBRD.WMF

4095.WMF
ARC023.WMF
ARC024.WMF
ASI103O.WMF
BICA003M.WMF
BICA038J.WMF
BICA039J.WMF
BICA040J.WMF
BIGC005J.WMF
BIGC008J.WMF
BIGC009J.WMF
BIGC010J.WMF
BIGC011J.WMF
BUIL022.WMF
BUIL024.WMF
CHAPEL.WMF
CHRCH.WMF
CHRCH2.WMF
CHRCH3.WMF
CHRCHOUS.WMF
CHUCHINR.WMF
CHURC1.WMF
CHURCAS.WMF
CHURCH.WMF
CHURCH01.WMF
CHURCH02.WMF
CHURCH03.WMF
CHURCH04.WMF
CHURCH05.WMF
CHURCH1.WMF
CHURCH2.WMF
CHURCH3.WMF
CHURCH33.WMF
CHURCH4.WMF
CHURCH5.WMF
CHURCH5C.WMF
CHURCH_1.WMF
CHURCHAS.WMF
COMUNITY.WMF
COUNTRY.WMF
CTMISC50.WMF
DEC071DD.WMF
DOME.WMF
GCHURCH.WMF
RCHURCH.WMF
RLGN034.WMF
RLGN048.WMF
RLGN049.WMF
RLGN050.WMF
RLGN051.WMF
RLGN169.WMF
SOFIA.WMF
SPA012E.WMF
STEEP.WMF
STEEPLE.WMF
TVA017F.WMF
WOODCHRH.WMF

1321.WMF 1663.WMF 1665.WMF 1667.WMF 1668.WMF 4427.WMF ASI102B.WMF ASI102L.WMF ASI103I.WMF ASI103N.WMF

ASI104C.WMF ASI104K.WMF ASI105A.WMF BUIL031.WMF BUIL038.WMF BUIL040.WMF BUIL041.WMF BUIL042.WMF BUIL043.WMF CART001.WMF

CART002.WMF CART003.WMF CART004.WMF CART005.WMF CART006.WMF CART007.WMF CART008.WMF CART009.WMF CART010.WMF CART011.WMF

CART012.WMF CART013.WMF CART014.WMF CART015.WMF CART016.WMF CART017.WMF CART018.WMF CART019.WMF CART020.WMF CART021.WMF

CART022.WMF CART023.WMF CART024.WMF CART025.WMF CART026.WMF CART027.WMF CART028.WMF CART029.WMF CART030.WMF CART031.WMF

CART032.WMF CART033.WMF CART034.WMF CART035.WMF CART036.WMF CART037.WMF CART038.WMF CART039.WMF CART040.WMF CART041.WMF

CART042.WMF CART043.WMF CART044.WMF CART045.WMF CART046.WMF CART047.WMF CITY001.WMF CITY002.WMF CITY003.WMF CITY004.WMF

CITY005.WMF CITY006.WMF CITY007.WMF CITY008.WMF CITY009.WMF CITY01.WMF CITY010.WMF CITY011.WMF CITY012.WMF CITY013.WMF

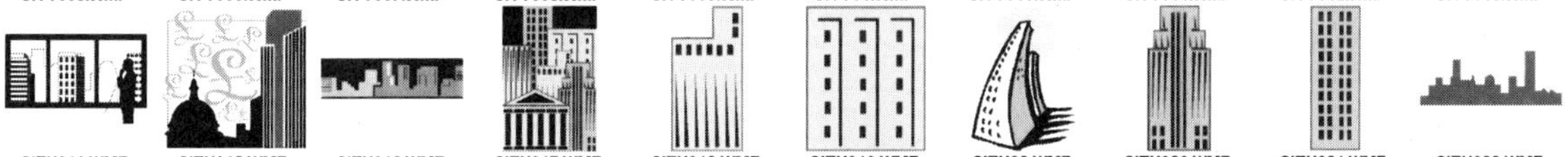

CITY014.WMF CITY015.WMF CITY016.WMF CITY017.WMF CITY018.WMF CITY019.WMF CITY02.WMF CITY020.WMF CITY021.WMF CITY022.WMF

CITY023.WMF CITY024.WMF CITY025.WMF CITY026.WMF CITY027.WMF CITY028.WMF CITY029.WMF CITY03.WMF CITY030.WMF CITY031.WMF

CITY032.WMF CITY033.WMF CITY034.WMF CITY035.WMF CITY036.WMF CITY037.WMF CITY038.WMF CITY039.WMF CITY04.WMF CITY040.WMF

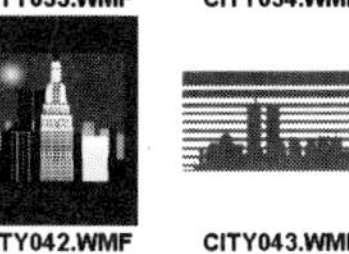

CITY041.WMF CITY042.WMF CITY043.WMF CITY044.WMF CITY045.WMF CITY046.WMF CITY047.WMF CITY048.WMF CITY049.WMF CITY05.WMF

CITY050.WMF CITY051.WMF CITY052.WMF CITY06.WMF CITY07.WMF CITY08.WMF CITY09.WMF CITY10.WMF CITY11.WMF CITY12.WMF

CITY13.WMF CITY14.WMF CITY15.WMF CITY16.WMF CITY17.WMF CITY18.WMF CITY19.WMF CITYGLOB.WMF CITYSKY.WMF LDSCP001.WMF

LDSCP004.WMF LDSCP017.WMF LDSCP034.WMF NDAK_3.WMF PD035FBW.WMF PRIN0063.WMF PRIN0081.WMF SKYLINE.WMF SKYLINE1.WMF SKYLINE2.WMF

SKYLINE3.WMF SKYLINE4.WMF SKYLINE5.WMF SKYLINE6.WMF SRI028B.WMF SRI029A.WMF

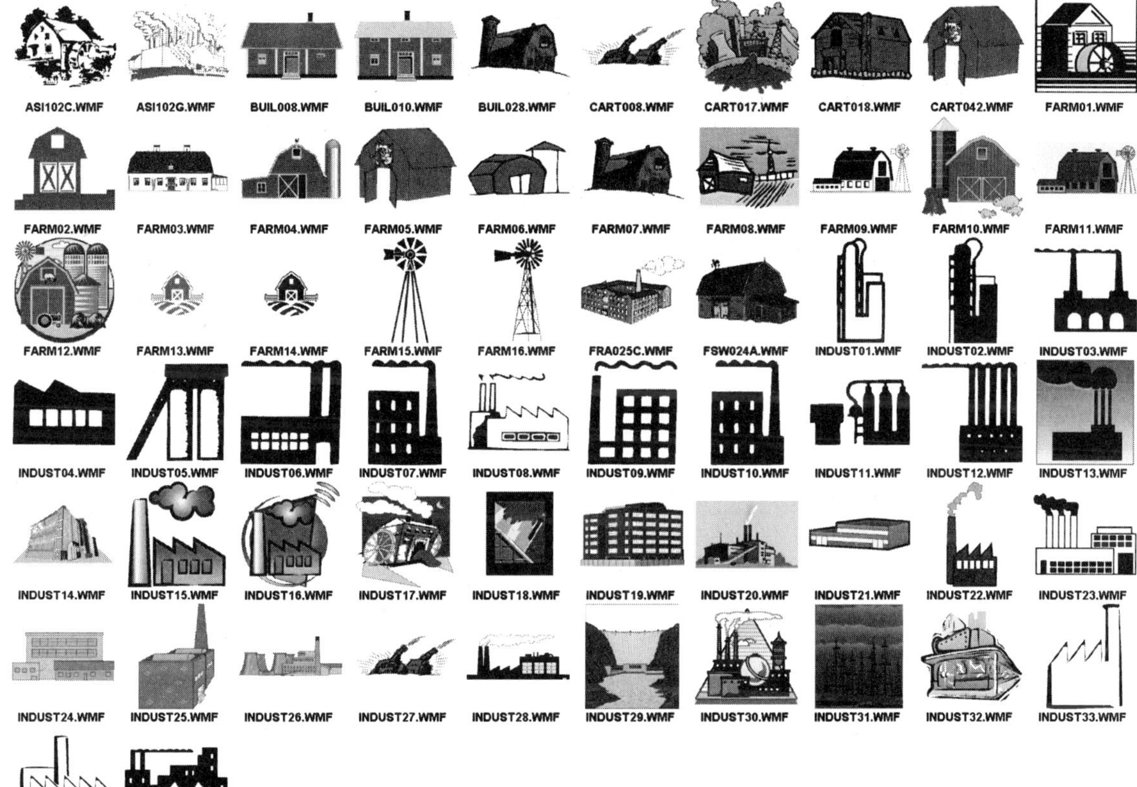

ASI102C.WMF ASI102G.WMF BUIL008.WMF BUIL010.WMF BUIL028.WMF CART008.WMF CART017.WMF CART018.WMF CART042.WMF FARM01.WMF

FARM02.WMF FARM03.WMF FARM04.WMF FARM05.WMF FARM06.WMF FARM07.WMF FARM08.WMF FARM09.WMF FARM10.WMF FARM11.WMF

FARM12.WMF FARM13.WMF FARM14.WMF FARM15.WMF FARM16.WMF FRA025C.WMF FSW024A.WMF INDUST01.WMF INDUST02.WMF INDUST03.WMF

INDUST04.WMF INDUST05.WMF INDUST06.WMF INDUST07.WMF INDUST08.WMF INDUST09.WMF INDUST10.WMF INDUST11.WMF INDUST12.WMF INDUST13.WMF

INDUST14.WMF INDUST15.WMF INDUST16.WMF INDUST17.WMF INDUST18.WMF INDUST19.WMF INDUST20.WMF INDUST21.WMF INDUST22.WMF INDUST23.WMF

INDUST24.WMF INDUST25.WMF INDUST26.WMF INDUST27.WMF INDUST28.WMF INDUST29.WMF INDUST30.WMF INDUST31.WMF INDUST32.WMF INDUST33.WMF

INDUST34.WMF PD035EBW.WMF

d:\BUILDING\OTHER
0498.WMF
0804.WMF
1064.WMF
1674.WMF
1675.WMF
1676.WMF
1691.WMF
3619.WMF
A29B.WMF
A29B2.WMF
A29BB.WMF
AFACDMY.WMF
ARC042.WMF
ARCHES.WMF
ASI041A.WMF
ASI041B.WMF
ASI042G.WMF
BERLNWAL.WMF
BIBO003J.WMF
BIBO011D.WMF
BICA001M.WMF
BICA005J.WMF
BICA029J.WMF
BIGC012J.WMF
BIGC013J.WMF
BIRW001J.WMF
BIRW001K.WMF
BIRW003J.WMF
BIRW006J.WMF
BIRW008J.WMF
BIRW022J.WMF
BIRW023J.WMF
BIRW025J.WMF
BISI002M.WMF
BISI011J.WMF
BISI014J.WMF
BISI014M.WMF
BISI015J.WMF
BISI016J.WMF
BISI017J.WMF
BISI019J.WMF
BISI019M.WMF
BISI020J.WMF
BISI021J.WMF
BISI024J.WMF
BISI030J.WMF
BISW001J.WMF
BIT0145.WMF
BIT0146.WMF
BIT0549.WMF
BIT0550.WMF
BIT0901.WMF
BIT0903.WMF
BIT0904.WMF
BIT0906.WMF
BLDG02.WMF
BLDG02M.WMF
BLDG05.WMF
BLDG10M.WMF
BLDG12M.WMF
BLDG13M.WMF
BRIDGE01.WMF
BSNSS154.WMF
BUIL001.WMF
BUIL002.WMF
BUIL003.WMF
BUIL004.WMF
BUIL005.WMF
BUIL007.WMF
BUIL009.WMF
BUIL011.WMF
BUIL012.WMF
BUIL013.WMF
BUIL014.WMF
BUIL015.WMF
BUIL016.WMF
BUIL017.WMF
BUIL018.WMF
BUIL019.WMF
BUIL020.WMF
BUIL021.WMF
BUIL023.WMF
BUIL025.WMF
BUIL026.WMF
BUIL027.WMF
BUIL029.WMF
Green Earth
BUIL032.WMF
BUIL033.WMF
BUIL034.WMF
BUIL035.WMF
BUIL036.WMF
BUIL037.WMF
BUIL039.WMF
BUIL045.WMF
BUIL046.WMF
BUIL047.WMF
BUIL048.WMF
BUIL049.WMF
BUIL050.WMF
BUIL051.WMF
BUIL052.WMF
BUIL053.WMF
BUIL054.WMF
BUILD01.WMF
BUILD02.WMF
BUILD03.WMF
BUILD04.WMF
BUILD05.WMF
BUILD06.WMF
BUILD07.WMF
BUILD08.WMF
BUILD09.WMF
BUILD11.WMF
BUILD12.WMF
BUILD13.WMF
BUILD14.WMF
BUILD15.WMF
BUILD16.WMF
BUILD17.WMF
BUILD18.WMF

BUILDS6.WMF
BUSI024M.WMF
BUSI034M.WMF
C20727.WMF
CAMPDAVD.WMF
CAPITOLB.WMF
CART006.WMF
CART010.WMF
CART013.WMF
CART014.WMF
CART015.WMF
CART016.WMF
CART020.WMF
CART021.WMF
CART022.WMF
CART027.WMF
CART028.WMF
CART029.WMF
CART032.WMF
CART033.WMF
CART039.WMF
CART043.WMF
CART044.WMF
CART046.WMF
CART047.WMF
CART048.WMF
CART049.WMF
CART050.WMF
CART052.WMF
CART053.WMF
CART054.WMF
CART055.WMF
CART057.WMF
CART058.WMF
CART059.WMF
CART061.WMF
CART063.WMF
CART064.WMF
CASTLE.WMF
CASTLE1.WMF
CASTLE2.WMF
CASTLE2C.WMF
CHW081C.WMF
CTMISC79.WMF
CVBRIDGE.WMF
DISNEY.WMF
EDISON.WMF
EMPIRE.WMF
FRA009B.WMF
FRA013E.WMF
FRA015D.WMF
FTCITY.WMF
GASI337M.WMF
GASI375M.WMF
GAZEBO.WMF
GOJUU1.WMF
HIMEJIJO.WMF
HOSPITAL.WMF
HUT.WMF
HUTTO.WMF
INGC027D.WMF
KIYOMIZU.WMF
KOKKAI.WMF
LITHO_SE.WMF
LITHOUSE.WMF
LTHOUS01.WMF
LTHOUS02.WMF
MA03.WMF
MSL076B.WMF
MUSEUM.WMF
MYKONAS.WMF
021539.WMF
OAST.WMF
OTS065A.WMF
OUTHOUSE.WMF
PAGODA.WMF
PLCA004J.WMF
PLSI009D.WMF
PMI050PP.WMF
PRO_BALL.WMF
PUERTO.WMF
SCHOOL
SCHOOLHS.WMF
SHOP.WMF
SOR051F.WMF
SOR051P.WMF
SPA008A.WMF
SPA012A.WMF
STADIUM1.WMF
SUPER.WMF
SUSPENBR.WMF
SYMBL12.WMF
SYMBOL12.WMF
TEEPEE2.WMF
TENTS01.WMF
THEATRE.WMF
TOWER.WMF
TOWER2MD.WMF
TVA066B.WMF
TVA075F.WMF
VSI064C.WMF
WELL.WMF
WINDMIL2.WMF
WINDMIL8.WMF
WINDMILL.WMF
WMG025M.WMF
ZONING.WMF

0812.WMF 0814.WMF 0889.WMF 1140FRAC.WMF 1660.WMF 1661.WMF 1684.WMF 1686.WMF 1689.WMF 1692.WMF
1694.WMF 1696.WMF 1699.WMF 1701.WMF 1703.WMF 4344.WMF 4367.WMF 4368.WMF 4369.WMF 4370.WMF
A25F.WMF A25F2.WMF A25FB.WMF A4A.WMF A4AB.WMF A4E.WMF A4EB.WMF A4F.WMF A4FB.WMF A_FRAME.WMF
ARC002.WMF ARC003.WMF ARC004.WMF ARC005.WMF ARC007.WMF ARC008.WMF ARC020.WMF ARC025.WMF ARC027.WMF ARC028.WMF
ARC046.WMF ARC050.WMF ARC053.WMF ASI103F.WMF ASI103J.WMF ASI106J.WMF ASI107G.WMF BICA015J.WMF BICA028J.WMF BICA037J.WMF
BIGC002J.WMF BIRW007J.WMF BISI001M.WMF BISI015M.WMF BISI021M.WMF BISI027J.WMF BISI029J.WMF BIT0152.WMF BIT0905.WMF BLDG01M.WMF
BLDG04M.WMF BLDG10.WMF BLDG15M.WMF BUIL006.WMF BUIL030.WMF BUILD2.WMF BUILD3.WMF BUILD4.WMF C20787.WMF C20788.WMF
CABIN1MD.WMF CAPE1.WMF CAPE2.WMF CAPE3.WMF CART001.WMF CART002.WMF CART026.WMF CART030.WMF CART031.WMF CART034.WMF
CART051.WMF CART056.WMF CART060.WMF CHALET.WMF CHURCH.WMF COLNIAL1.WMF COLNIAL2.WMF CONTEMP1.WMF CONTEMP2.WMF COTAGE2.WMF
COTTAGE.WMF DEC070D.WMF DUPLEX.WMF EAA041E.WMF EXPCAPE.WMF FRA017E.WMF FRNCHCAP.WMF FWN011A.WMF FWN011B.WMF FWN011C.WMF
FWN011D.WMF FWN011E.WMF FWN011F.WMF FWN011G.WMF FWN011H.WMF FWN011I.WMF FWN027A.WMF FWN027B.WMF FWN027C.WMF FWN027D.WMF
GEORGCOL.WMF H21126.WMF H21129.WMF H21130.WMF H21133.WMF H21134.WMF HFSI001D.WMF HIGHRISE.WMF HOUS1MD.WMF HOUS2.WMF

HOUS3AS.WMF HOUS57.WMF HOUSE.WMF HOUSE01.WMF HOUSE02.WMF HOUSE04.WMF HOUSE05.WMF HOUSE1.WMF HOUSE10.WMF HOUSE11.WMF

HOUSE12.WMF HOUSE17.WMF HOUSE17B.WMF HOUSE18.WMF HOUSE18B.WMF HOUSE1A.WMF HOUSE1C.WMF HOUSE1K.WMF HOUSE2.WMF HOUSE2A.WMF

HOUSE2AS.WMF HOUSE2B.WMF HOUSE2C.WMF HOUSE2K.WMF HOUSE3.WMF HOUSE3A.WMF HOUSE3AS.WMF HOUSE3B.WMF HOUSE4.WMF HOUSE4A.WMF

HOUSE55.WMF HOUSE56.WMF HOUSE59.WMF HOUSE5AS.WMF HOUSE6.WMF HOUSE6B.WMF HOUSE8.WMF HOUSE_EM.WMF HOUSEA.WMF HOUSEB.WMF

HOUSEC.WMF HOUSES12.WMF HOUSESNW.WMF HOWSE1.WMF HOWSE1C.WMF HOWSE2.WMF HOWSE2C.WMF HOWSE3.WMF HUOS1AS.WMF ICONA09.WMF

LAC095C.WMF LAC104F.WMF LAC105F.WMF LITHSEC.WMF LOG_CABI.WMF MEDITERR.WMF MIS00141.WMF MIS00142.WMF MIS00143.WMF MIS0014A.WMF

MIS0014C.WMF MOBLHOME.WMF MSL076A.WMF NEIHBORS.WMF OEC047J.WMF OTS002B.WMF OXM010I.WMF OXM011F.WMF OXM018H.WMF PD035VCU.WMF

PD035WCU.WMF PD035XCU.WMF PD035YCU.WMF PD036ACU.WMF PD036BCU.WMF PD036CCU.WMF PD036DCU.WMF PD036ECU.WMF PD036FCU.WMF PD036GCU.WMF

PD036HCU.WMF PD036ICU.WMF PD036JCU.WMF PD036KCU.WMF PD036LCU.WMF PD036MCU.WMF PD036PCU.WMF PD129DCU.WMF PD129ECU.WMF PD129FCU.WMF

PRECINCT.WMF QLDHSE.WMF QLDHSEC.WMF RAISRAN.WMF RANCH.WMF SALTBOX.WMF SEV11.WMF SIT091G.WMF SIT091I.WMF SOUTHCOL.WMF

SPA005E.WMF SPLITLVL.WMF SRI001A.WMF SRI001B.WMF SRI001C.WMF SRI006A.WMF SRI006B.WMF SRI010A.WMF SRI010B.WMF SRI015A.WMF

SRI015B.WMF SRI018A.WMF SRI032B.WMF SSP007A.WMF STREET1.WMF STREET2.WMF SUBURB.WMF SYMBL145.WMF SYMBL25.WMF SYMBL60.WMF

SYMBOL25.WMF

TOWN01.WMF

TOWNHSES.WMF

TWOSTOR1.WMF

TWOSTOR2.WMF

VACATION.WMF

WMSBURG.WMF

0056.WMF 0057.WMF 0058.WMF 0059.WMF 0060.WMF 0062.WMF 0063.WMF 0064.WMF 0065.WMF 0066.WMF
0067.WMF 0084.WMF 0099.WMF 0105.WMF 0106.WMF 0116.WMF 0137.WMF 0141.WMF 0142.WMF 0143.WMF
0144.WMF 0145.WMF 0153.WMF 0154.WMF 079.WMF 080.WMF 081.WMF 083.WMF 092.WMF 094.WMF
095.WMF 098.WMF 099.WMF 100.WMF 101.WMF 102.WMF 1499.WMF 1500.WMF ACTNPLAN.WMF AD01.WMF
AD02.WMF AD03.WMF AD04.WMF AD05.WMF AD06.WMF AD07.WMF APPOINT.WMF BACK104.WMF BADMOOD.WMF BADNEWS.WMF
BADNEWSC.WMF BBROTHER.WMF BEARISH.WMF BELTTIGH.WMF BIAB001J.WMF BIAB002J.WMF BICA002D.WMF BICA002M.WMF BICA003D.WMF BRAIN_1.WMF
BRAIN_2.WMF BRFCSE01.WMF BSNSS144.WMF BUBO001J.WMF BUBO004J.WMF BUCA006D.WMF BUCA006J.WMF BUCA007J.WMF BUCA008D.WMF BUCA008J.WMF
BUCA009D.WMF BUCA009J.WMF BUGC002J.WMF BUGC003J.WMF BUGC004J.WMF BUGC012D.WMF BUGC014D.WMF BUGC015D.WMF BUGC022D.WMF BUGC028D.WMF
BUGC030D.WMF BUGC036D.WMF BUGC037D.WMF BUGC040D.WMF BUGC051D.WMF BUGC056D.WMF BUGC057D.WMF BUGC062D.WMF BUGC074D.WMF BUGC079D.WMF
BUGC082D.WMF BUGC088D.WMF BUGC089D.WMF BUGC098D.WMF BUKC001J.WMF BULLISH.WMF BUSI002J.WMF BUSI004D.WMF BUSI004M.WMF BUSI008D.WMF
BUSI010D.WMF BUSI011D.WMF BUSI015M.WMF BUSI025D.WMF BUSI026M.WMF BUSI030M.WMF BUSI031D.WMF BUSI036D.WMF BUSI050D.WMF BUSI053D.WMF
BUSI056D.WMF BUSI059D.WMF BUSI061D.WMF BUSI062D.WMF BUSI088D.WMF BUSI127D.WMF BUSI143D.WMF BUSI151D.WMF BUSI161D.WMF BUSI163D.WMF

BUSI166D.WMF
BUSI174D.WMF
BUSI175D.WMF
BUSI185D.WMF
BUSI190D.WMF
BUSI194D.WMF
BUSI202D.WMF
BUSY.WMF
CC01.WMF
CC53.WMF
COMPASS.WMF
COMPASSC.WMF
CONSULT.WMF
COOLOFFC.WMF
COPIERPR.WMF
CRTN082.WMF
CRTN083.WMF
CRTN086.WMF
CRTN096.WMF
CRTN097.WMF
CRTN111.WMF
CRTN112.WMF
CRTN113.WMF
CRTN114.WMF
CRTN173.WMF
CRTN176.WMF
CTOFF001.WMF
CTOFF002.WMF
CTOFF003.WMF
CTOFF004.WMF
CTOFF005.WMF
CTOFF006.WMF
CTOFF007.WMF
CTOFF008.WMF
CTOFF009.WMF
CTOFF010.WMF
CTOFF011.WMF
CTOFF012.WMF
CTOFF013.WMF
CTOFF014.WMF
CTOFF015.WMF
CTOFF016.WMF
CTOFF017.WMF
CTOFF018.WMF
CTOFF019.WMF
CTOFF020.WMF
CTOFF021.WMF
CTOFF022.WMF
CTOFF023.WMF
CTOFF024.WMF
CTOFF025.WMF
CTOFF026.WMF
CTOFF027.WMF
CTOFF028.WMF
CTOFF029.WMF
CTOFF030.WMF
CTOFF031.WMF
CTOFF032.WMF
CTOFF033.WMF
CTOFF034.WMF
CTOFF035.WMF
CTOFF036.WMF
CTOFF037.WMF
CTOFF038.WMF
CTOFF039.WMF
CTOFF040.WMF
CTOFF041.WMF
CTOFF042.WMF
CTOFF043.WMF
CTOFF044.WMF
CTOFF045.WMF
CTOFF046.WMF
CTOFF047.WMF
CTOFF048.WMF
CTOFF049.WMF
CTOFF050.WMF
CTOFF051.WMF
CTOFF052.WMF
CTOFF053.WMF
CTOFF054.WMF
CTOFF055.WMF
CTOFF056.WMF
CTOFF057.WMF
CTOFF058.WMF
CTOFF061.WMF
CTOFF062.WMF
CTOFF063.WMF
CTOFF064.WMF
CTOFF066.WMF
CTOFF067.WMF
CTOFF068.WMF
CTOFF069.WMF
CTOFF071.WMF
CTOFF072.WMF
CTOFF073.WMF
CTOFF074.WMF
CTOFF075.WMF
CTOFF076.WMF
CTOFF077.WMF
CTOFF078.WMF
CTOFF079.WMF
CTOFF080.WMF
CTOFF081.WMF
CTOFF082.WMF
CTOFF083.WMF
CTOFF084.WMF
CTOFF085.WMF
CTOFF086.WMF
CTOFF087.WMF
CTOFF088.WMF
CTOFF089.WMF
CTOFF090.WMF
CTOFF091.WMF
CTOFF092.WMF
CTOFF093.WMF
CTOFF094.WMF
CTOFF095.WMF
CTOFF096.WMF
CTOFF097.WMF
CTOFF098.WMF

CTOFF099.WMF CTOFF100.WMF CTOFF101.WMF CTOFF102.WMF CTOFF103.WMF CTOFF104.WMF CTOFF105.WMF CTOFF106.WMF CTOFF107.WMF CTOFF108.WMF

CTOFF109.WMF CTOFF110.WMF CTOFF111.WMF CTOFF112.WMF CTOFF113.WMF CTOFF114.WMF CTOFF115.WMF CTOFF116.WMF CTOFF117.WMF CTOFF118.WMF

CTOFF119.WMF CTOFF120.WMF CTOFF121.WMF CTOFF122.WMF CTOFF123.WMF CTOFF124.WMF CTOFF125.WMF CTOFF126.WMF CTOFF127.WMF CTOFF128.WMF

CTOFF129.WMF CTOFF130.WMF CTOFF131.WMF CTOFF132.WMF CTOFF133.WMF CTOFF134.WMF CTOFF135.WMF CTOFF136.WMF CTOFF137.WMF CTOFF138.WMF

CTOFF139.WMF CTOFF140.WMF CTOFF141.WMF CTOFF142.WMF CTOFF143.WMF CTOFF144.WMF CTOFF145.WMF CTOFF146.WMF CTOFF147.WMF CTOFF148.WMF

CTOFF149.WMF CTOFF150.WMF CTOFF151.WMF CTOFF152.WMF CTOFF153.WMF CTOFF154.WMF CTOFF155.WMF CTOFF156.WMF CTOFF157.WMF CTOFF158.WMF

CTOFF159.WMF CTOFF160.WMF CTOFF161.WMF CTOFF162.WMF CTOFF163.WMF CTOFF164.WMF CTOFF165.WMF CTOFF166.WMF CTOFF167.WMF CTOFF168.WMF

CTOFF169.WMF CTOFF170.WMF CTOFF171.WMF CTOFF172.WMF CTOFF173.WMF CTOFF174.WMF CTOFF175.WMF CTOFF176.WMF CTOFF177.WMF CTOFF178.WMF

CTOFF179.WMF CTOFF180.WMF CTOFF181.WMF CTOFF182.WMF CTOFF183.WMF CTOFF184.WMF CTOFF185.WMF CTOFF186.WMF CTOFF187.WMF CTOFF188.WMF

CTOFF189.WMF CTOFF190.WMF CTOFF191.WMF CTOFF192.WMF CTOFF193.WMF CTOFF194.WMF CTOFF195.WMF CTOFF196.WMF CTOFF197.WMF CTOFF198.WMF

CTOFF199.WMF CTOFF200.WMF CTOFF201.WMF CTOFF202.WMF CTOFF203.WMF CUPPA.WMF CUPPAC.WMF DECISION.WMF DESK.WMF DOLLARS.WMF

DONTBANG.WMF DOWNOUT.WMF DREAMER.WMF EDCN094.WMF EDCN106.WMF ENGC019D.WMF ENTOURAG.WMF EVESDROP.WMF EW01.WMF EW02.WMF

F48.WMF F49.WMF F68.WMF FD13.WMF FD14.WMF FD15.WMF FD17.WMF FD18.WMF FD20.WMF FD21.WMF

FD22.WMF FD24.WMF FS73.WMF FS73A.WMF FS74.WMF FS74A.WMF FS75.WMF FS75A.WMF FS76.WMF FS76A.WMF

FS77.WMF FS77A.WMF FS78.WMF FS78A.WMF FS79.WMF FS79A.WMF FS80.WMF FS80A.WMF GOODNEWS.WMF GREEDYMN.WMF

GUN1.WMF GUN1C.WMF HOLDINGC.WMF HPI012B.WMF HPI012C.WMF HPI012D.WMF HPI012E.WMF HPI012F.WMF HPI012G.WMF HPI024I.WMF

HPI026C.WMF HPI026D.WMF HPI026E.WMF HPI026F.WMF HPI026G.WMF HPI026H.WMF HPI032E.WMF IB01.WMF IB02.WMF IB08.WMF

IB10.WMF INGC011D.WMF INTERVEW.WMF JMDCPYR.WMF JUNKMAIL.WMF KISSBOSS.WMF LATEAGAI.WMF LIFTING.WMF LISTEN.WMF MANBILL.WMF

MANBILLC.WMF MANFEET.WMF MANICURE.WMF ME04_.WMF MENTREAC.WMF MNDESK.WMF MNDESKC.WMF MONDAYS.WMF MONEY2.WMF MONEY2C.WMF

MR_CALC.WMF MRCOFEE.WMF MURPHYNO.WMF NOTEPAD1.WMF OM07.WMF OM13.WMF OM20.WMF OM21.WMF OS01.WMF OS02.WMF

OS07.WMF OS23.WMF OS24.WMF OS25.WMF OS26.WMF OS27.WMF OS30.WMF OS32.WMF PAPERBLI.WMF PECA011J.WMF

PEERINGC.WMF PENCIL.WMF PHONE.WMF PHONECAL.WMF PLBO001D.WMF PNC.WMF PS09.WMF RD12.WMF RISKYBUS.WMF SALEUP.WMF

SALEUPC.WMF SCISSORS.WMF SICKCOLO.WMF SIZZS.WMF SNAILCOL.WMF SPEECH.WMF SPEECHC.WMF TANGLED.WMF TC01.WMF TC03.WMF

TC04.WMF TC05.WMF TC06.WMF TC07.WMF THEBOOT.WMF THERULES.WMF TIEDUP.WMF TIMEFLIE.WMF TIMERCOL.WMF TRSI014D.WMF

UPTOASS.WMF

WELCOMEB.WMF

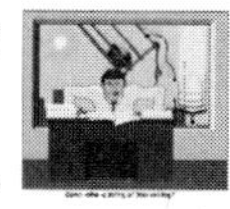
WINDOW.WMF

WORKERS.WMF

0287.WMF
0288.WMF
0290.WMF
0291.WMF
0292.WMF
0293.WMF
0294.WMF
0296.WMF
0297.WMF
0711.WMF
1748.WMF
BALSHET1.WMF
BIT128.WMF
BSNSS041.WMF
BSNSS131.WMF
BSNSS132.WMF
BSNSS133.WMF
BSNSS134.WMF
BSNSS135.WMF
BSNSS136.WMF
BSNSS137.WMF
BSNSS138.WMF
BSNSS139.WMF
BSNSS140.WMF
BSNSS167.WMF
BSNSS168.WMF
BSNSS178.WMF
BSNSS180.WMF
BSNSS189.WMF
BUSLETR1.WMF
C20769.WMF
C20774.WMF
CHECK.WMF
CLIPPED.WMF
CONTRACT.WMF
CONTROLR.WMF
DEED.WMF
DOCMNT01.WMF
EDCN182.WMF
EDCN183.WMF
EDCN184.WMF
EDCN189.WMF
FILING.WMF
FX01_.WMF
FX07_.WMF
INSURNCE.WMF
INVOICE.WMF
LEASE.WMF
LETRSTKD.WMF
LETTER1.WMF
LETTER2.WMF
LETTER3.WMF
M21239.WMF
MESSGPAD.WMF
MISC061.WMF
MISC080.WMF
MONYPAPR.WMF
NOTE.WMF
NOTEC.WMF
O21465.WMF
OFCA002J.WMF
P21555.WMF
PAYCHECK.WMF
PLAN024.WMF
PLAN025.WMF
PLAN062.WMF
PLANABC.WMF
PO.WMF
REPORT.WMF
S21651.WMF
S21652.WMF
S21653.WMF
SECRET01.WMF
TAXFORM.WMF
WILL.WMF

0128CLCC.WMF 0715.WMF 1501.WMF 1503.WMF 1606.WMF 1607.WMF 1623.WMF 1635.WMF 1636.WMF 1640.WMF
1641.WMF 1642.WMF 1643.WMF 1644.WMF 1652.WMF 1653.WMF 1658.WMF 1659.WMF 1697.WMF 1699.WMF
1700.WMF 1731.WMF 1732.WMF 1746.WMF 1750.WMF 3COMPUTE.WMF A20006.WMF A20056.WMF ADDING.WMF ADDMAC.WMF
ADDMACHN.WMF AFBUDGET.WMF B20129.WMF BANKSAFE.WMF BCASE_.WMF BCASEC_.WMF BIT0451.WMF BOOK.WMF BOX.WMF BREFCAS.WMF
BRFCAS01.WMF BRFCSE01.WMF BRIEF.WMF BRIEFCAS.WMF BSNSS033.WMF BSNSS039.WMF BSNSS043.WMF BSNSS079.WMF BSNSS080.WMF BSNSS082.WMF
BSNSS083.WMF BSNSS084.WMF BSNSS085.WMF BSNSS086.WMF BSNSS087.WMF BSNSS088.WMF BSNSS090.WMF BSNSS091.WMF BSNSS092.WMF BSNSS093.WMF
BSNSS096.WMF BSNSS101.WMF BSNSS105.WMF BSNSS106.WMF BSNSS107.WMF BSNSS108.WMF BSNSS109.WMF BSNSS113.WMF BSNSS114.WMF BSNSS115.WMF
BSNSS116.WMF BSNSS117.WMF BSNSS127.WMF BSNSS157.WMF BSNSS169.WMF BSNSS170.WMF BSNSS171.WMF BSNSS172.WMF BSNSS173.WMF BSNSS177.WMF
BSNSS184.WMF BSNSS187.WMF BSNSS191.WMF BSNSS192.WMF BUSI010J.WMF BUSNS14.WMF C20728.WMF C20729.WMF C20730.WMF CALCLTR.WMF
CALCULAT.WMF CALCULTR.WMF CALLBELL.WMF CARPHONE.WMF CLOCK01.WMF CLOCK02.WMF COLRCOPY.WMF COMM033.WMF COPIER.WMF COPIER2.WMF
COPYCOMP.WMF CORDLESS.WMF CTOFF070.WMF CW43.WMF D20893.WMF DESK.WMF DESKLAMP.WMF DESKPHON.WMF DIGPHON1.WMF DIGPHON2.WMF
EDCN013.WMF FAX.WMF FAX5.WMF FCAB01.WMF FCAB01C.WMF FIL_CAB.WMF FILE.WMF FILECAB.WMF FILECAB1.WMF FILECBNT.WMF

FILMPROJ.WMF
FIRE_XTG.WMF
FOUNTAIN.WMF
G21036.WMF
GLASS01M.WMF
H21085.WMF
HAN005.WMF
HAN044.WMF
HAN051.WMF
HAN052.WMF
HAN053.WMF
HAN060.WMF
HAN063.WMF
HAN069.WMF
HAN070.WMF
HAN076.WMF
HANDTRK.WMF
HANDTRK2.WMF
HESI005D.WMF
HLTH106.WMF
HOLDER.WMF
INRW003D.WMF
L21207.WMF
LAMP.WMF
LAMP2.WMF
LAMPS.WMF
LASERWRI.WMF
LCHBX01M.WMF
LIGHT01.WMF
M21242.WMF
MC01.WMF
MC02.WMF
MESI005D.WMF
O21472.WMF
O21473.WMF
OF01.WMF
OF04.WMF
OF11.WMF
OF12.WMF
OF13.WMF
OFFICE.WMF
OFFICE1.WMF
OFFICE19.WMF
OFFICE25.WMF
OFICE1.WMF
OFSI001D.WMF
OFSI009D.WMF
OHT.WMF
OHTC.WMF
OM01.WMF
OM02.WMF
OM03.WMF
OM04.WMF
OM05.WMF
OM06.WMF
OM08.WMF
OM10.WMF
OM18.WMF
OM22.WMF
OM24.WMF
OPENSAFE.WMF
OVERHEAD.WMF
OVHDPROJ.WMF
PAGER.WMF
PAINT01.WMF
PAP_CUT.WMF
PAPRCLP.WMF
PB27.WMF
PENSET.WMF
PHONE1.WMF
PHONE1C.WMF
PHONEREC.WMF
PLAN004.WMF
PLAN005.WMF
PLAN009.WMF
PLAN013.WMF
PLAN014.WMF
PLAN015.WMF
PLAN017.WMF
PLAN018.WMF
PLAN019.WMF
PLAN023.WMF
PLAN029.WMF
PLAN030.WMF
PLAN031.WMF
PLAN032.WMF
PLAN033.WMF
PLAN034.WMF
PLAN035.WMF
PLAN036.WMF
PLAN040.WMF
PLAN043.WMF
PLAN045.WMF
PLAN046.WMF
PLAN086.WMF
PLAN087.WMF
PLAN088.WMF
PLAN093.WMF
PLAN135.WMF
POCKET.WMF
POSTSCAL.WMF
PRNT001.WMF
PRNT002.WMF
PRNT003.WMF
PRNT005.WMF
PRNT008.WMF
PRNT009.WMF
PRNT010.WMF
PRNT011.WMF
PRNT012.WMF
PRNT013.WMF
PRNT014.WMF
PRNT015.WMF
PRNT016.WMF
PRNT029.WMF
PROJECTR.WMF
PRPHL026.WMF
PS01.WMF
REGISTER.WMF
ROLODEX.WMF

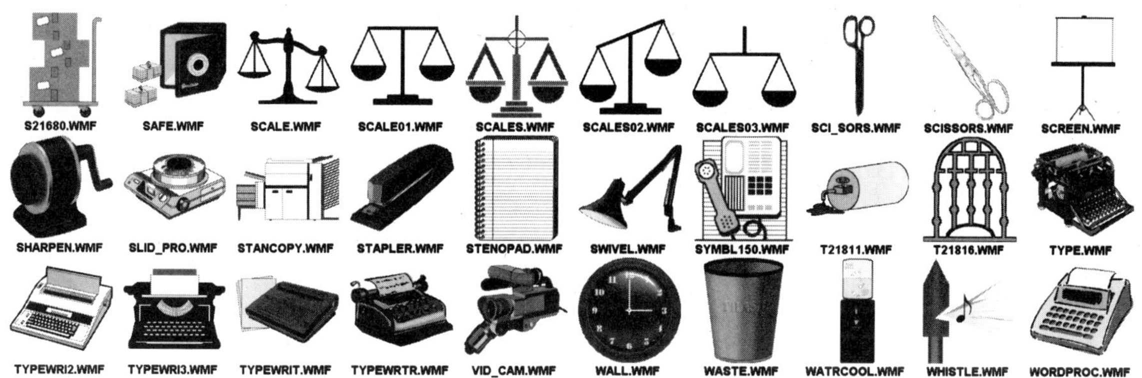
S21680.WMF
SAFE.WMF
SCALE.WMF
SCALE01.WMF
SCALES.WMF
SCALES02.WMF
SCALES03.WMF
SCI_SORS.WMF
SCISSORS.WMF
SCREEN.WMF
SHARPEN.WMF
SLID_PRO.WMF
STANCOPY.WMF
STAPLER.WMF
STENOPAD.WMF
SWIVEL.WMF
SYMBL150.WMF
T21811.WMF
T21816.WMF
TYPE.WMF
TYPEWRI2.WMF
TYPEWRI3.WMF
TYPEWRIT.WMF
TYPEWRTR.WMF
VID_CAM.WMF
WALL.WMF
WASTE.WMF
WATRCOOL.WMF
WHISTLE.WMF
WORDPROC.WMF

ACCOUNT.WMF
AIRCOND1.WMF
AIRCOND2.WMF
AIRMAIL.WMF
ANSSERV.WMF
ANTIQUES.WMF
APPLIANC.WMF
mon tues wed
APPOINT.WMF
ARTIST.WMF
ATM.WMF
SOLD
AUCTION.WMF
AWARDS.WMF
BABYSITT.WMF
BAKERY.WMF
BARBER.WMF
BEAUTY1.WMF
BEAUTY2.WMF
BOOKSTR1.WMF
BOOKSTR2.WMF
BRIDAL.WMF
BROADCS1.WMF
BROADCS2.WMF
BUILDG1.WMF
BUILDG2.WMF
BUILDG3.WMF
BUILDG4.WMF
BUSFORMS.WMF
CABINETS.WMF
CARPENTR.WMF
CARPET.WMF
CARPETCL.WMF
CHIMSWEP.WMF
COMP.WMF
COMPSUP1.WMF
COMPSUP2.WMF
COMPSUP3.WMF
CONSTR1.WMF
CONSTR2.WMF
COPIER.WMF
COSMETIC.WMF
CRIME.WMF
DELIV1.WMF
DELIV2.WMF
DETECT.WMF
DJ.WMF
DRAFTNG1.WMF
DRAFTNG2.WMF
DRAPERY.WMF
DRYWALL.WMF
EDUCATN1.WMF
EDUCATN2.WMF
EDUCATN3.WMF
EDUCATN4.WMF
EDUCATN5.WMF
ELECTR1.WMF
ELECTR2.WMF
ELECTR3.WMF
ELECTR4.WMF
ENGINEER.WMF
EXPRESS SHIPPING
EXPRSHIP.WMF
FAX
FACS1.WMF
FACS2.WMF
FACS3.WMF
FAX
FACS4.WMF
FARM.WMF
FINANC1.WMF
FINANC2.WMF
FLORIST1.WMF
FLORIST2.WMF
FORMWEAR.WMF
FORTELLR.WMF
FURNITUR.WMF
GLASS.WMF
GOVMENT.WMF
GOVMENT2.WMF
GOVMENT3.WMF
HANDSHAK.WMF
HARDWRE1.WMF
HARDWRE2.WMF
HEATING.WMF
INSURANC.WMF
JANITOR1.WMF
JANITOR2.WMF
JANITOR3.WMF
LANDSCP1.WMF
LANDSCP2.WMF
LANGUAGE.WMF
LAUNDMAT.WMF
LOCKSMIT.WMF
LUMBER1.WMF
LUMBER2.WMF
MANAGMNT.WMF
MARINE.WMF
MARKETG1.WMF
MARKETG2.WMF
MASONRY.WMF
NEWS
MEDIA.WMF
MOVIES1.WMF
MOVIES2.WMF
MOVIES3.WMF
EXTRA!!
NEWSPAPR.WMF
NOSOLIC.WMF
OFFFURN.WMF
OFFSUP1.WMF
OFFSUP2.WMF
24
OPEN24HR.WMF
PAINT1.WMF
PAINT2.WMF
PAINT3.WMF
PAINT4.WMF
PAPER.WMF
PAVING.WMF
PAWNSHP1.WMF
PAWNSHP2.WMF
PHOTO1.WMF
PHOTO2.WMF
PHOTO3.WMF
PHOTO4.WMF
PHOTO5.WMF
PIANOTUN.WMF

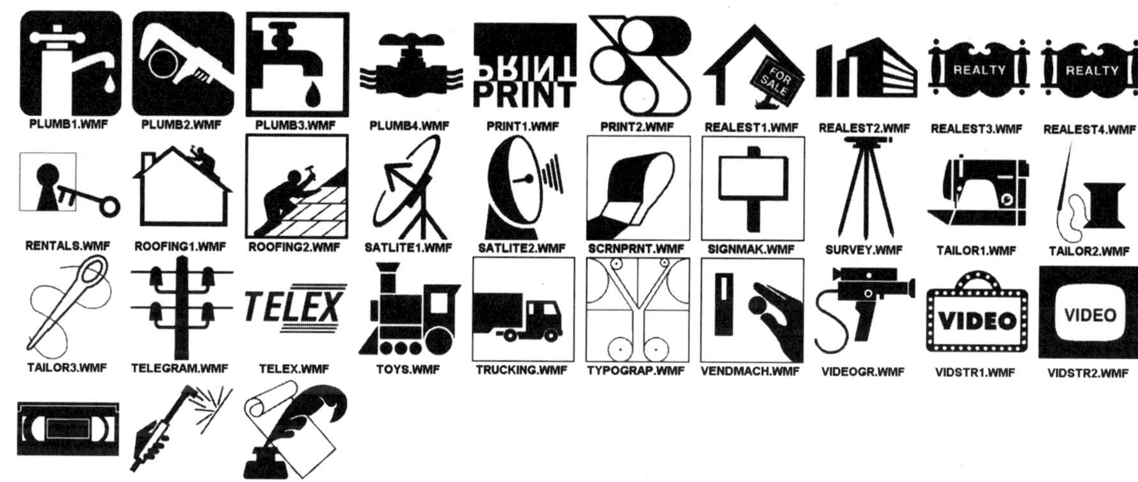

PLUMB1.WMF PLUMB2.WMF PLUMB3.WMF PLUMB4.WMF PRINT1.WMF PRINT2.WMF REALEST1.WMF REALEST2.WMF REALEST3.WMF REALEST4.WMF

RENTALS.WMF ROOFING1.WMF ROOFING2.WMF SATLITE1.WMF SATLITE2.WMF SCRNPRNT.WMF SIGNMAK.WMF SURVEY.WMF TAILOR1.WMF TAILOR2.WMF

TAILOR3.WMF TELEGRAM.WMF TELEX.WMF TOYS.WMF TRUCKING.WMF TYPOGRAP.WMF VENDMACH.WMF VIDEOGR.WMF VIDSTR1.WMF VIDSTR2.WMF

VIDSTR3.WMF WELDING.WMF WRITER.WMF

0020.WMF 004.WMF 005.WMF 007.WMF 008.WMF 0191.WMF 020.WMF 0200.WMF 021.WMF 025.WMF

026.WMF 027.WMF 028.WMF 029.WMF 030.WMF 031.WMF 032.WMF 033.WMF 034.WMF 035.WMF

036.WMF 037.WMF 038.WMF 039.WMF 040.WMF 041.WMF 042.WMF 043.WMF 045.WMF 047.WMF

048.WMF 049.WMF 050.WMF 051.WMF 052.WMF 053.WMF 054.WMF 059.WMF 060.WMF 061.WMF

064.WMF 066.WMF 067.WMF 068.WMF 075.WMF 077.WMF 078.WMF 085.WMF A007.WMF A010.WMF

AGREEMNT.WMF ARGUE.WMF AUCTION.WMF BACK102.WMF BACK103.WMF BIGSTIK.WMF BSNSS044.WMF BSNSS048.WMF BSNSS049.WMF BSNSS050.WMF

BSNSS051.WMF BSNSS052.WMF BSNSS053.WMF BSNSS054.WMF BSNSS055.WMF BSNSS056.WMF BSNSS057.WMF BSNSS058.WMF BSNSS059.WMF BSNSS066.WMF

BSNSS067.WMF BSNSS068.WMF BSNSS069.WMF BSNSS070.WMF BSNSS071.WMF BSNSS072.WMF BSNSS073.WMF BSNSS074.WMF BSNSS075.WMF BSNSS076.WMF

BUDGET2.WMF BURDENED.WMF BUS_DISC.WMF BUSIMAN.WMF BUSWOMN1.WMF BUSWOMN2.WMF BUSWOMN3.WMF CAR_PHON.WMF CC10.WMF CHK_TIME.WMF

COFFEEBK.WMF COMM012.WMF CRSFNGR.WMF EW13.WMF EW14.WMF EW16.WMF EW17.WMF EW22.WMF HAND_OVR.WMF HANDSHAK.WMF

HN05.WMF HN06.WMF HN07.WMF IB03.WMF IB04.WMF IB05.WMF IB06.WMF IB07.WMF IB09.WMF IB11.WMF

IB12.WMF IB13.WMF LATENITE.WMF LATEWORK.WMF LISTEN.WMF LOOKING.WMF MAKER.WMF MAN_GLAS.WMF MAN_POD.WMF MANCAR.WMF

MANCHART.WMF
MANCOMP1.WMF
MANCOMP2.WMF
MENTREA.WMF
NIGHTER.WMF
OF06.WMF
OF07.WMF
OF09.WMF
OF10.WMF
OM12.WMF
OM25.WMF
ONTHEGO.WMF
OPERATOR.WMF
OUTCAST.WMF
OVERWORK.WMF
PAPERWRK.WMF
PD01.WMF
PD02.WMF
PD04.WMF
PD05.WMF
PECA021J.WMF
POLICIES.WMF
PRESENTA.WMF
PROFCPLE.WMF
PROPOSL.WMF
PS06.WMF
RD01.WMF
RD02.WMF
RD03.WMF
RD04.WMF
RD05.WMF
RD06.WMF
RD07.WMF
RD08.WMF
RD09.WMF
RD10.WMF
RD16.WMF
RD21.WMF
RECEPTIO.WMF
REPORT.WMF
SALES_GI.WMF
SALESMAN.WMF
SCHEDUL.WMF
SE02.WMF
SE03.WMF
SE04.WMF
SE05.WMF
SLOWDAY.WMF
SERVICES
SMGOV1.WMF
SPEECH.WMF
SS10.WMF
SS12.WMF
STRESS.WMF
TEAMWORK.WMF
THINKING.WMF
TYPIST.WMF
VACATION.WMF
WOMAN_1.WMF
WOMNCOMP.WMF
WOMNCORD.WMF
WOMNPH_2.WMF
WOMNRE_3.WMF
WORK.WMF
WORK1.WMF
WORK2.WMF
WORK3.WMF
ZZ09.WMF

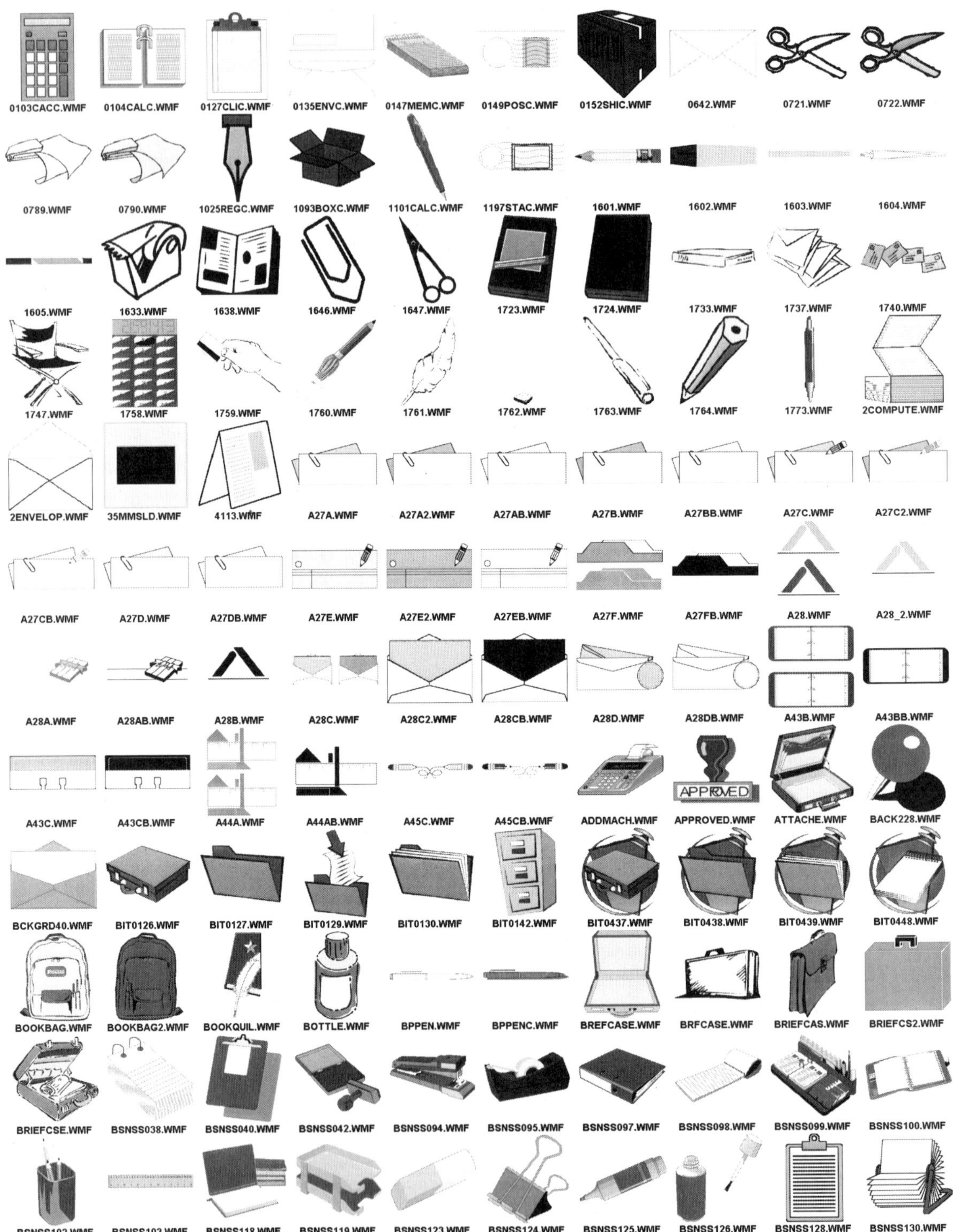
0103CACC.WMF
0104CALC.WMF
0127CLIC.WMF
0135ENVC.WMF
0147MEMC.WMF
0149POSC.WMF
0152SHIC.WMF
0642.WMF
0721.WMF
0722.WMF
0789.WMF
0790.WMF
1025REGC.WMF
1093BOXC.WMF
1101CALC.WMF
1197STAC.WMF
1601.WMF
1602.WMF
1603.WMF
1604.WMF
1605.WMF
1633.WMF
1638.WMF
1646.WMF
1647.WMF
1723.WMF
1724.WMF
1733.WMF
1737.WMF
1740.WMF
1747.WMF
1758.WMF
1759.WMF
1760.WMF
1761.WMF
1762.WMF
1763.WMF
1764.WMF
1773.WMF
2COMPUTE.WMF
2ENVELOP.WMF
35MMSLD.WMF
4113.WMF
A27A.WMF
A27A2.WMF
A27AB.WMF
A27B.WMF
A27BB.WMF
A27C.WMF
A27C2.WMF
A27CB.WMF
A27D.WMF
A27DB.WMF
A27E.WMF
A27E2.WMF
A27EB.WMF
A27F.WMF
A27FB.WMF
A28.WMF
A28_2.WMF
A28A.WMF
A28AB.WMF
A28B.WMF
A28C.WMF
A28C2.WMF
A28CB.WMF
A28D.WMF
A28DB.WMF
A43B.WMF
A43BB.WMF
A43C.WMF
A43CB.WMF
A44A.WMF
A44AB.WMF
A45C.WMF
A45CB.WMF
ADDMACH.WMF
APPROVED
APPROVED.WMF
ATTACHE.WMF
BACK228.WMF
BCKGRD40.WMF
BIT0126.WMF
BIT0127.WMF
BIT0129.WMF
BIT0130.WMF
BIT0142.WMF
BIT0437.WMF
BIT0438.WMF
BIT0439.WMF
BIT0448.WMF
BOOKBAG.WMF
BOOKBAG2.WMF
BOOKQUIL.WMF
BOTTLE.WMF
BPPEN.WMF
BPPENC.WMF
BREFCASE.WMF
BRFCASE.WMF
BRIEFCAS.WMF
BRIEFCS2.WMF
BRIEFCSE.WMF
BSNSS038.WMF
BSNSS040.WMF
BSNSS042.WMF
BSNSS094.WMF
BSNSS095.WMF
BSNSS097.WMF
BSNSS098.WMF
BSNSS099.WMF
BSNSS100.WMF
BSNSS102.WMF
BSNSS103.WMF
BSNSS118.WMF
BSNSS119.WMF
BSNSS123.WMF
BSNSS124.WMF
BSNSS125.WMF
BSNSS126.WMF
BSNSS128.WMF
BSNSS130.WMF

BSNSS156.WMF
BSNSS166.WMF
BSNSS182.WMF
BSNSS183.WMF
BSNSS188.WMF
BUBO002J.WMF
BUGC018J.WMF
BUGC024J.WMF
BUGC038D.WMF
BUGC045D.WMF
BUGC048D.WMF
BUGC049D.WMF
BUGC050D.WMF
BUGC064D.WMF
BUGC080D.WMF
BUGC081D.WMF
BUSI003M.WMF
BUSI024D.WMF
BUSI027D.WMF
BUSI039D.WMF
BUSI043D.WMF
BUSI048D.WMF
BUSI049D.WMF
BUSI124D.WMF
BUSI144D.WMF
BUSI147D.WMF
BUSI149D.WMF
BUSI150D.WMF
BUSI177D.WMF
BUSI178D.WMF
BUSI188D.WMF
BUSI200D.WMF
BUSNS0.WMF
BUSNS10.WMF
BUSNS12.WMF
BUSNS16.WMF
BUSNS17.WMF
BUSNS18.WMF
BUSNS19.WMF
BUSNS2.WMF
BUSNS20.WMF
BUSNS21.WMF
BUSNS25.WMF
BUSNS3.WMF
BUSNS5.WMF
BUSNS6.WMF
BUSNS8.WMF
BUSNS9.WMF
C20793.WMF
C20817.WMF
CALCLAT1.WMF
CALCLAT3.WMF
CALCU.WMF
CALCULAT.WMF
CALENDAR.WMF
CALL_BEL.WMF
CANCELED.WMF
CART.WMF
CLIPBD.WMF
CLIPBRD.WMF
CLIPBRD2.WMF
CLIPBRD8.WMF
CLIPS.WMF
CMPPAPER.WMF
CRATE01.WMF
CRAYON_1.WMF
CRAYONS.WMF
DCALENDR.WMF
DESKCAL.WMF
DESKPHON.WMF
DIPPING_.WMF
DIVIDER.WMF
DRAFTING.WMF
EMAIL1.WMF
ENV.WMF
ENVE1.WMF
ENVELOP.WMF
ENVELOP2.WMF
ENVELOPE.WMF
ENVELPE2.WMF
ENVLOPE.WMF
ENVLOPES.WMF
F20997.WMF
FIL_FDR1.WMF
FIL_FDR2.WMF
FILE.WMF
FILECARD.WMF
FILECBNT.WMF
FILEFLD2.WMF
FILEFLDR.WMF
FILES.WMF
FILFLDR.WMF
FLOPPY.WMF
FLPYDK01.WMF
FNTPNTO.WMF
FOLDER.WMF
FOLDS.WMF
FOUNTNPN.WMF
G21047.WMF
G21048.WMF
GAVEL.WMF
GLUEGUN.WMF
HHCA092J.WMF
HHGC041D.WMF
HHGC100D.WMF
HHRW069J.WMF
HHSI020M.WMF
HOLEPNCH.WMF
HOURGLAS.WMF
ID.WMF
INBOX.WMF
INGC012D.WMF
INK.WMF
INK4.WMF
INK_BOTT.WMF
INK_BTTL.WMF
INKPEN.WMF
INSI032D.WMF
LAMPS.WMF
LASERWRI.WMF

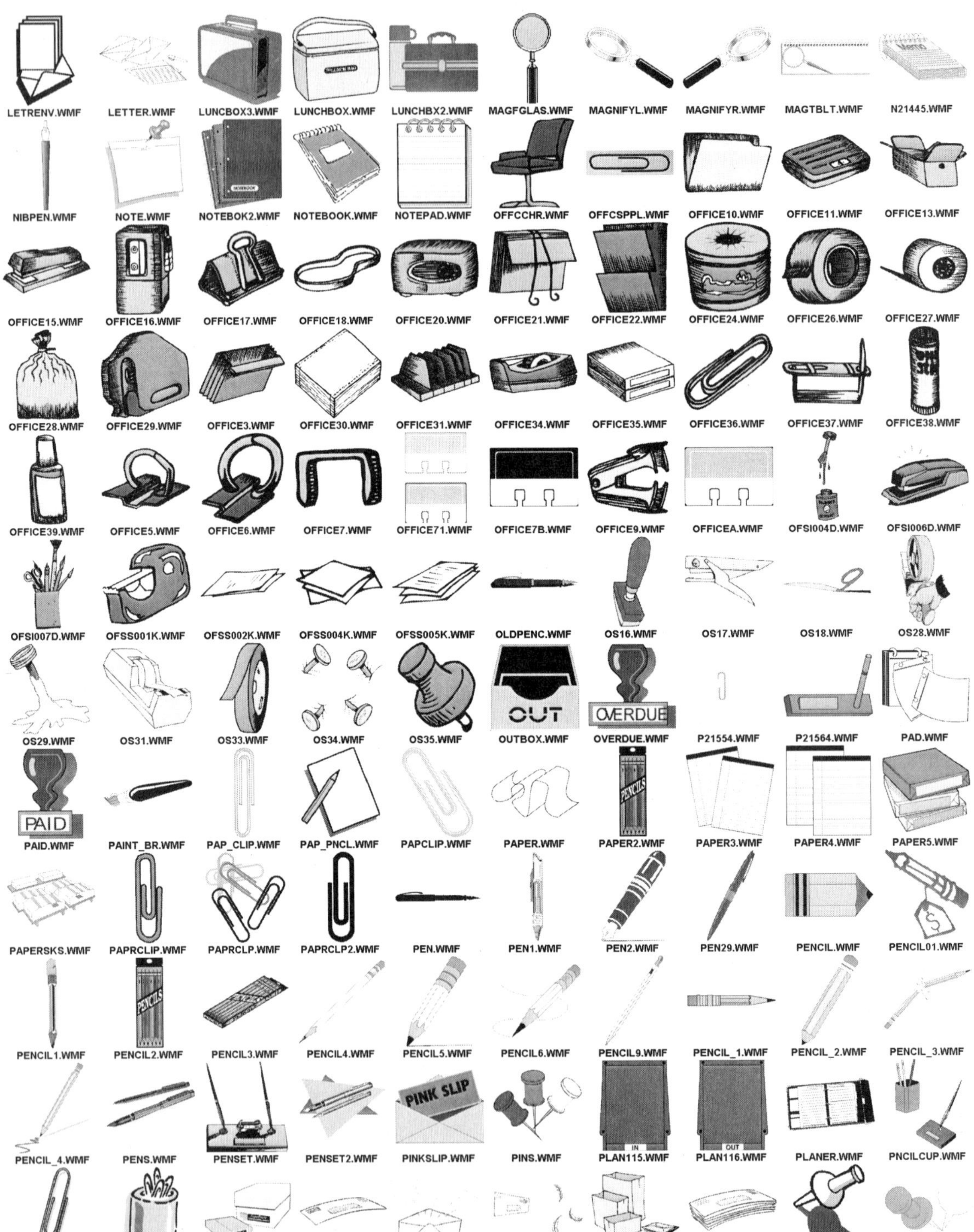
LETRENV.WMF LETTER.WMF LUNCBOX3.WMF LUNCHBOX.WMF LUNCHBX2.WMF MAGFGLAS.WMF MAGNIFYL.WMF MAGNIFYR.WMF MAGTBLT.WMF N21445.WMF
NIBPEN.WMF NOTE.WMF NOTEBOK2.WMF NOTEBOOK.WMF NOTEPAD.WMF OFFCCHR.WMF OFFCSPPL.WMF OFFICE10.WMF OFFICE11.WMF OFFICE13.WMF
OFFICE15.WMF OFFICE16.WMF OFFICE17.WMF OFFICE18.WMF OFFICE20.WMF OFFICE21.WMF OFFICE22.WMF OFFICE24.WMF OFFICE26.WMF OFFICE27.WMF
OFFICE28.WMF OFFICE29.WMF OFFICE3.WMF OFFICE30.WMF OFFICE31.WMF OFFICE34.WMF OFFICE35.WMF OFFICE36.WMF OFFICE37.WMF OFFICE38.WMF
OFFICE39.WMF OFFICE5.WMF OFFICE6.WMF OFFICE7.WMF OFFICE71.WMF OFFICE7B.WMF OFFICE9.WMF OFFICEA.WMF OFSI004D.WMF OFSI006D.WMF
OFSI007D.WMF OFSS001K.WMF OFSS002K.WMF OFSS004K.WMF OFSS005K.WMF OLDPENC.WMF OS16.WMF OS17.WMF OS18.WMF OS28.WMF
OUT
OVERDUE
OS29.WMF OS31.WMF OS33.WMF OS34.WMF OS35.WMF OUTBOX.WMF OVERDUE.WMF P21554.WMF P21564.WMF PAD.WMF
PAID
PENCILS
PAID.WMF PAINT_BR.WMF PAP_CLIP.WMF PAP_PNCL.WMF PAPCLIP.WMF PAPER.WMF PAPER2.WMF PAPER3.WMF PAPER4.WMF PAPER5.WMF
PAPERSKS.WMF PAPRCLIP.WMF PAPRCLP.WMF PAPRCLP2.WMF PEN.WMF PEN1.WMF PEN2.WMF PEN29.WMF PENCIL.WMF PENCIL01.WMF
PENCILS
PENCIL1.WMF PENCIL2.WMF PENCIL3.WMF PENCIL4.WMF PENCIL5.WMF PENCIL6.WMF PENCIL9.WMF PENCIL_1.WMF PENCIL_2.WMF PENCIL_3.WMF
PINK SLIP
IN
OUT
PENCIL_4.WMF PENS.WMF PENSET.WMF PENSET2.WMF PINKSLIP.WMF PINS.WMF PLAN115.WMF PLAN116.WMF PLANER.WMF PNCILCUP.WMF
PPRCLP1.WMF PPRCLPHL.WMF PRNTRPPR.WMF PS03.WMF PS04.WMF PS05.WMF PS07.WMF PS10.WMF PUSH_PIN.WMF PUSHPIN.WMF

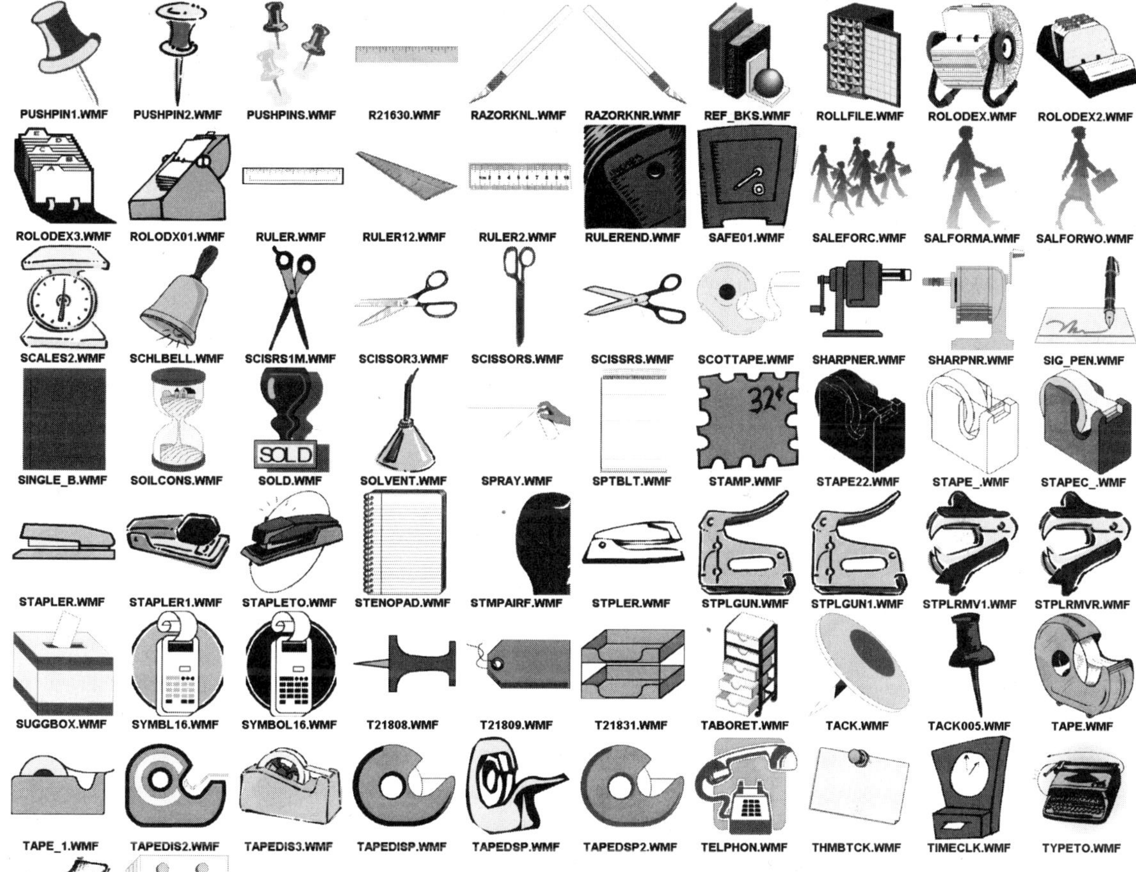

PUSHPIN1.WMF PUSHPIN2.WMF PUSHPINS.WMF R21630.WMF RAZORKNL.WMF RAZORKNR.WMF REF_BKS.WMF ROLLFILE.WMF ROLODEX.WMF ROLODEX2.WMF

ROLODEX3.WMF ROLODX01.WMF RULER.WMF RULER12.WMF RULER2.WMF RULEREND.WMF SAFE01.WMF SALEFORC.WMF SALFORMA.WMF SALFORWO.WMF

SCALES2.WMF SCHLBELL.WMF SCISRS1M.WMF SCISSOR3.WMF SCISSORS.WMF SCISSRS.WMF SCOTTAPE.WMF SHARPNER.WMF SHARPNR.WMF SIG_PEN.WMF

SINGLE_B.WMF SOILCONS.WMF SOLD.WMF SOLVENT.WMF SPRAY.WMF SPTBLT.WMF STAMP.WMF STAPE22.WMF STAPE_.WMF STAPEC_.WMF

STAPLER.WMF STAPLER1.WMF STAPLETO.WMF STENOPAD.WMF STMPAIRF.WMF STPLER.WMF STPLGUN.WMF STPLGUN1.WMF STPLRMV1.WMF STPLRMVR.WMF

SUGGBOX.WMF SYMBL16.WMF SYMBOL16.WMF T21808.WMF T21809.WMF T21831.WMF TABORET.WMF TACK.WMF TACK005.WMF TAPE.WMF

TAPE_1.WMF TAPEDIS2.WMF TAPEDIS3.WMF TAPEDISP.WMF TAPEDSP.WMF TAPEDSP2.WMF TELPHON.WMF THMBTCK.WMF TIMECLK.WMF TYPETO.WMF

TYPEWRTR.WMF WALLCAL.WMF

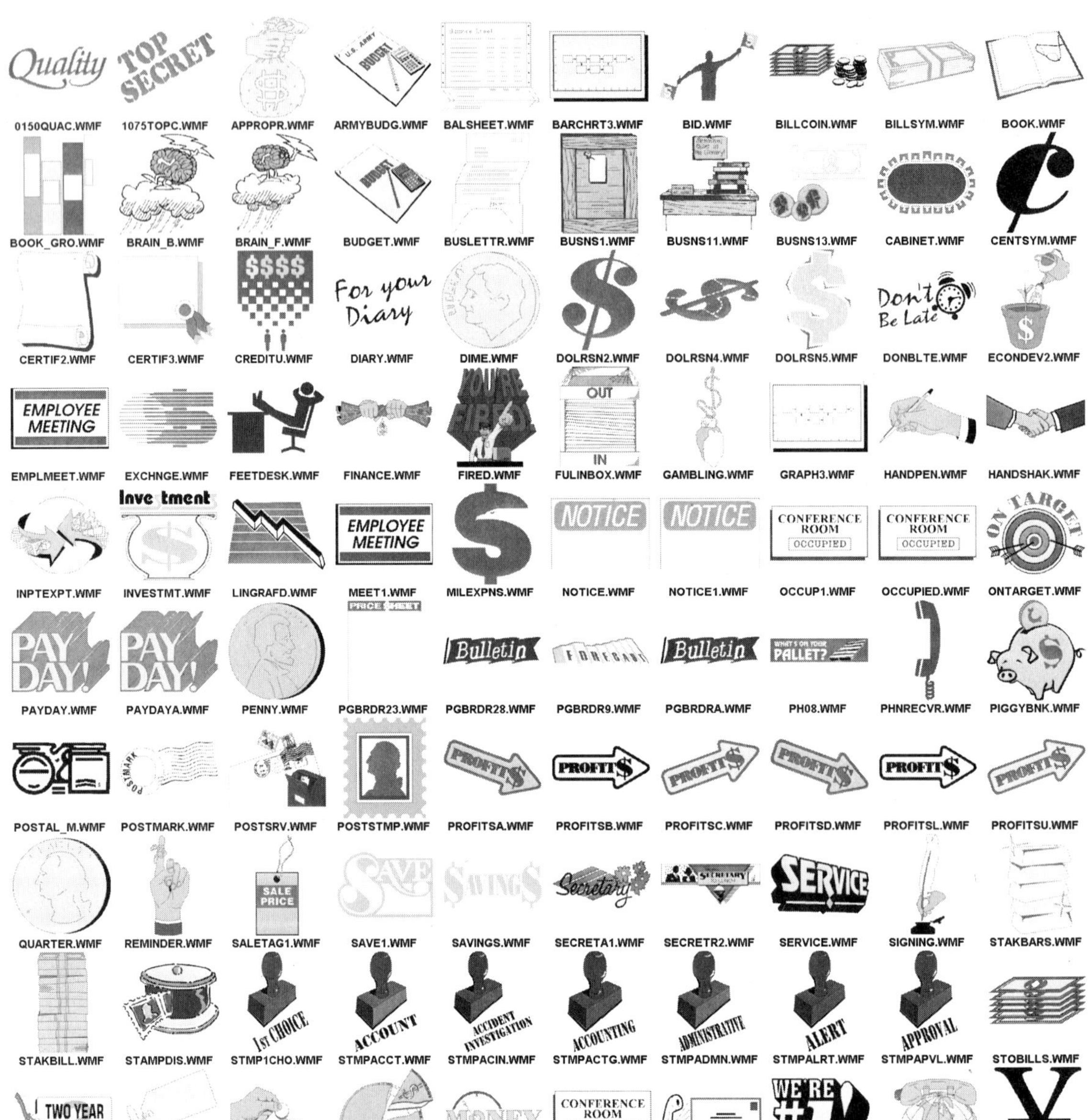

0150QUAC.WMF 1075TOPC.WMF APPROPR.WMF ARMYBUDG.WMF BALSHEET.WMF BARCHRT3.WMF BID.WMF BILLCOIN.WMF BILLSYM.WMF BOOK.WMF

BOOK_GRO.WMF BRAIN_B.WMF BRAIN_F.WMF BUDGET.WMF BUSLETTR.WMF BUSNS1.WMF BUSNS11.WMF BUSNS13.WMF CABINET.WMF CENTSYM.WMF

CERTIF2.WMF CERTIF3.WMF CREDITU.WMF DIARY.WMF DIME.WMF DOLRSN2.WMF DOLRSN4.WMF DOLRSN5.WMF DONBLTE.WMF ECONDEV2.WMF

EMPLMEET.WMF EXCHNGE.WMF FEETDESK.WMF FINANCE.WMF FIRED.WMF FULINBOX.WMF GAMBLING.WMF GRAPH3.WMF HANDPEN.WMF HANDSHAK.WMF

INPTEXPT.WMF INVESTMT.WMF LINGRAFD.WMF MEET1.WMF MILEXPNS.WMF NOTICE.WMF NOTICE1.WMF OCCUP1.WMF OCCUPIED.WMF ONTARGET.WMF

PAYDAY.WMF PAYDAYA.WMF PENNY.WMF PGBRDR23.WMF PGBRDR28.WMF PGBRDR9.WMF PGBRDRA.WMF PH08.WMF PHNRECVR.WMF PIGGYBNK.WMF

POSTAL_M.WMF POSTMARK.WMF POSTSRV.WMF POSTSTMP.WMF PROFITSA.WMF PROFITSB.WMF PROFITSC.WMF PROFITSD.WMF PROFITSL.WMF PROFITSU.WMF

QUARTER.WMF REMINDER.WMF SALETAG1.WMF SAVE1.WMF SAVINGS.WMF SECRETA1.WMF SECRETR2.WMF SERVICE.WMF SIGNING.WMF STAKBARS.WMF

STAKBILL.WMF STAMPDIS.WMF STMP1CHO.WMF STMPACCT.WMF STMPACIN.WMF STMPACTG.WMF STMPADMN.WMF STMPALRT.WMF STMPAPVL.WMF STOBILLS.WMF

TAG.WMF TAGFINGR.WMF TAXES.WMF TAXPIE.WMF TIMESMON.WMF UNOCCUPD.WMF VOICMAIL.WMF WERE1.WMF WOLDWIDE.WMF YEN.WMF

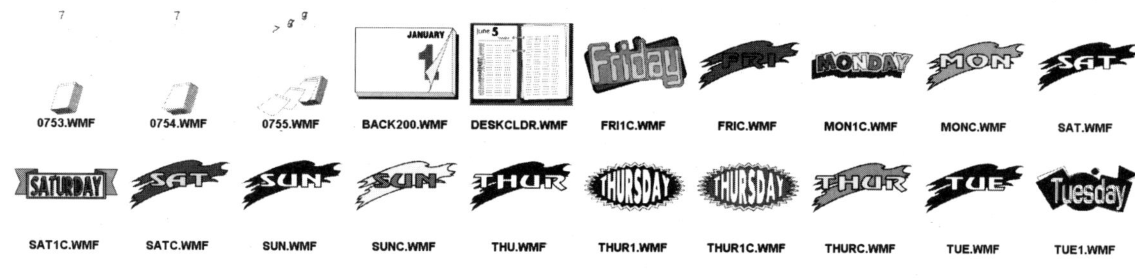

0753.WMF 0754.WMF 0755.WMF BACK200.WMF DESKCLDR.WMF FRI1C.WMF FRIC.WMF MON1C.WMF MONC.WMF SAT.WMF

SAT1C.WMF SATC.WMF SUN.WMF SUNC.WMF THU.WMF THUR1.WMF THUR1C.WMF THURC.WMF TUE.WMF TUE1.WMF

TUEC.WMF

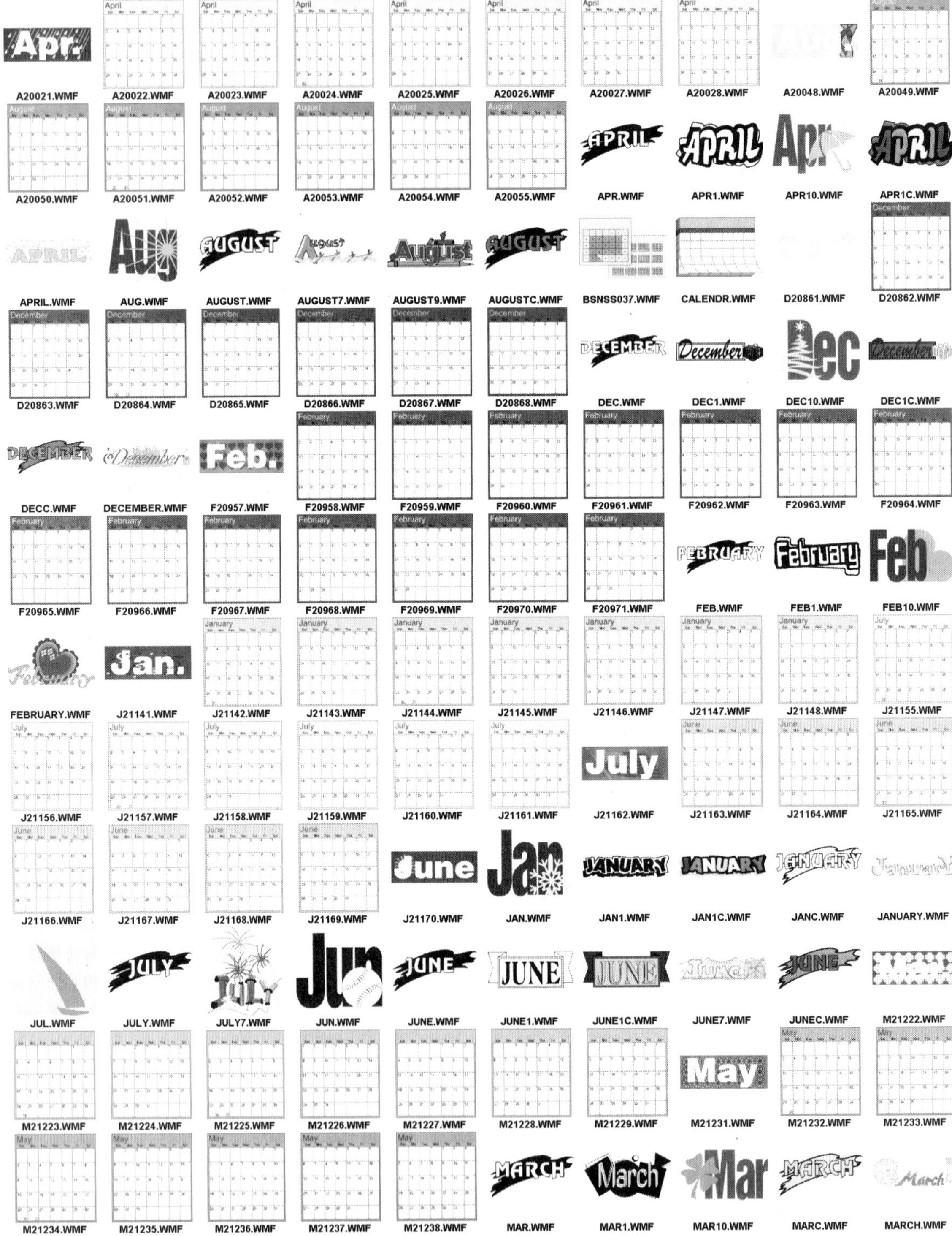

A20021.WMF A20022.WMF A20023.WMF A20024.WMF A20025.WMF A20026.WMF A20027.WMF A20028.WMF A20048.WMF A20049.WMF

A20050.WMF A20051.WMF A20052.WMF A20053.WMF A20054.WMF A20055.WMF APR.WMF APR1.WMF APR10.WMF APR1C.WMF

APRIL.WMF AUG.WMF AUGUST.WMF AUGUST7.WMF AUGUST9.WMF AUGUSTC.WMF BSNSS037.WMF CALENDR.WMF D20861.WMF D20862.WMF

D20863.WMF D20864.WMF D20865.WMF D20866.WMF D20867.WMF D20868.WMF DEC.WMF DEC1.WMF DEC10.WMF DEC1C.WMF

DECC.WMF DECEMBER.WMF F20957.WMF F20958.WMF F20959.WMF F20960.WMF F20961.WMF F20962.WMF F20963.WMF F20964.WMF

F20965.WMF F20966.WMF F20967.WMF F20968.WMF F20969.WMF F20970.WMF F20971.WMF FEB.WMF FEB1.WMF FEB10.WMF

FEBRUARY.WMF J21141.WMF J21142.WMF J21143.WMF J21144.WMF J21145.WMF J21146.WMF J21147.WMF J21148.WMF J21155.WMF

J21156.WMF J21157.WMF J21158.WMF J21159.WMF J21160.WMF J21161.WMF J21162.WMF J21163.WMF J21164.WMF J21165.WMF

J21166.WMF J21167.WMF J21168.WMF J21169.WMF J21170.WMF JAN.WMF JAN1.WMF JAN1C.WMF JANC.WMF JANUARY.WMF

JUL.WMF JULY.WMF JULY7.WMF JUN.WMF JUNE.WMF JUNE1.WMF JUNE1C.WMF JUNE7.WMF JUNEC.WMF M21222.WMF

M21223.WMF M21224.WMF M21225.WMF M21226.WMF M21227.WMF M21228.WMF M21229.WMF M21231.WMF M21232.WMF M21233.WMF

M21234.WMF M21235.WMF M21236.WMF M21237.WMF M21238.WMF MAR.WMF MAR1.WMF MAR10.WMF MARC.WMF MARCH.WMF

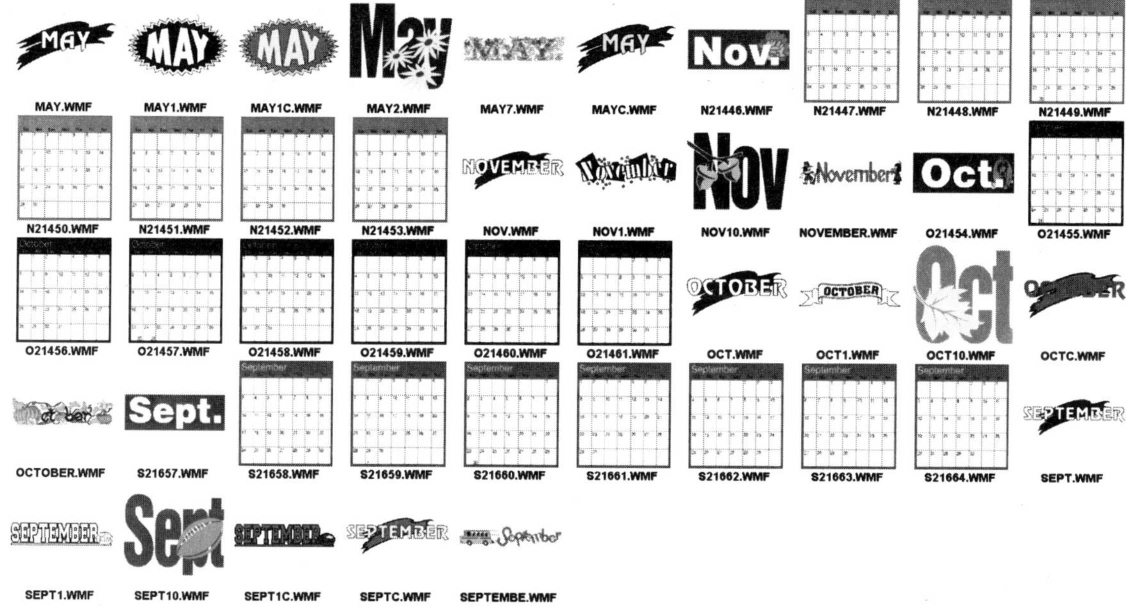

MAY.WMF MAY1.WMF MAY1C.WMF MAY2.WMF MAY7.WMF MAYC.WMF N21446.WMF N21447.WMF N21448.WMF N21449.WMF

N21450.WMF N21451.WMF N21452.WMF N21453.WMF NOV.WMF NOV1.WMF NOV10.WMF NOVEMBER.WMF O21454.WMF O21455.WMF

O21456.WMF O21457.WMF O21458.WMF O21459.WMF O21460.WMF O21461.WMF OCT.WMF OCT1.WMF OCT10.WMF OCTC.WMF

OCTOBER.WMF S21657.WMF S21658.WMF S21659.WMF S21660.WMF S21661.WMF S21662.WMF S21663.WMF S21664.WMF SEPT.WMF

SEPT1.WMF SEPT10.WMF SEPT1C.WMF SEPTC.WMF SEPTEMBE.WMF

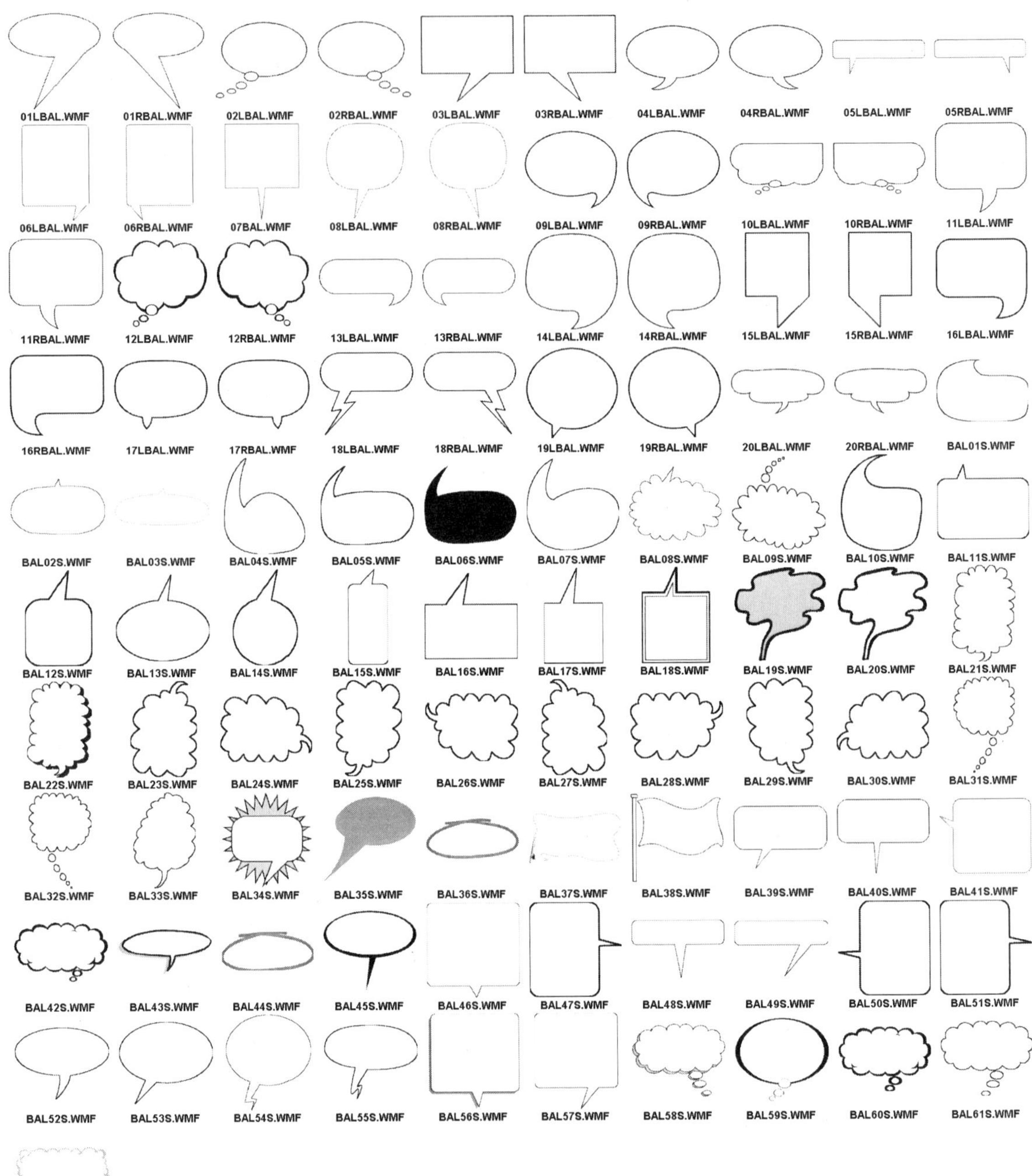
01LBAL.WMF
01RBAL.WMF
02LBAL.WMF
02RBAL.WMF
03LBAL.WMF
03RBAL.WMF
04LBAL.WMF
04RBAL.WMF
05LBAL.WMF
05RBAL.WMF
06LBAL.WMF
06RBAL.WMF
07BAL.WMF
08LBAL.WMF
08RBAL.WMF
09LBAL.WMF
09RBAL.WMF
10LBAL.WMF
10RBAL.WMF
11LBAL.WMF
11RBAL.WMF
12LBAL.WMF
12RBAL.WMF
13LBAL.WMF
13RBAL.WMF
14LBAL.WMF
14RBAL.WMF
15LBAL.WMF
15RBAL.WMF
16LBAL.WMF
16RBAL.WMF
17LBAL.WMF
17RBAL.WMF
18LBAL.WMF
18RBAL.WMF
19LBAL.WMF
19RBAL.WMF
20LBAL.WMF
20RBAL.WMF
BAL01S.WMF
BAL02S.WMF
BAL03S.WMF
BAL04S.WMF
BAL05S.WMF
BAL06S.WMF
BAL07S.WMF
BAL08S.WMF
BAL09S.WMF
BAL10S.WMF
BAL11S.WMF
BAL12S.WMF
BAL13S.WMF
BAL14S.WMF
BAL15S.WMF
BAL16S.WMF
BAL17S.WMF
BAL18S.WMF
BAL19S.WMF
BAL20S.WMF
BAL21S.WMF
BAL22S.WMF
BAL23S.WMF
BAL24S.WMF
BAL25S.WMF
BAL26S.WMF
BAL27S.WMF
BAL28S.WMF
BAL29S.WMF
BAL30S.WMF
BAL31S.WMF
BAL32S.WMF
BAL33S.WMF
BAL34S.WMF
BAL35S.WMF
BAL36S.WMF
BAL37S.WMF
BAL38S.WMF
BAL39S.WMF
BAL40S.WMF
BAL41S.WMF
BAL42S.WMF
BAL43S.WMF
BAL44S.WMF
BAL45S.WMF
BAL46S.WMF
BAL47S.WMF
BAL48S.WMF
BAL49S.WMF
BAL50S.WMF
BAL51S.WMF
BAL52S.WMF
BAL53S.WMF
BAL54S.WMF
BAL55S.WMF
BAL56S.WMF
BAL57S.WMF
BAL58S.WMF
BAL59S.WMF
BAL60S.WMF
BAL61S.WMF
BAL62S.WMF

CAP0001S.WMF
CAP0002S.WMF
CAP0003S.WMF
CAP0004S.WMF
CAP0005S.WMF
CAP0006S.WMF
CAP0007S.WMF
CAP0008S.WMF
CAP0009S.WMF
CAP0010S.WMF
CAP0011S.WMF
CAP0012S.WMF
CAP0013S.WMF
CAP0014S.WMF
CAP0015S.WMF
CAP0016S.WMF
CAP0017S.WMF
CAP0018S.WMF
CAP0019S.WMF
CAP0020S.WMF
CAP0021S.WMF
CAP0022S.WMF
CAP0023S.WMF
CAP0024S.WMF
CAP0025S.WMF
CAP0026S.WMF
CAP0027S.WMF
CAP0028S.WMF
CAP0029S.WMF
CAP0030S.WMF
CAP0031S.WMF
CAP0032S.WMF
CAP0033S.WMF
CAP0034S.WMF
CAP0035S.WMF
CAP0036S.WMF
CAP0037S.WMF
CAP0038S.WMF
CAP0039S.WMF
CAP0040S.WMF
CAP0041S.WMF
CAP0042S.WMF
CAP0043S.WMF
CAP0044S.WMF
CAP0045S.WMF
CAP0046S.WMF
CAP0047S.WMF
CAP0048S.WMF
CAP0049S.WMF
CAP0050S.WMF
CAP0051S.WMF
CAP0052S.WMF
CAP0053S.WMF
CAP0054S.WMF
CAP0055S.WMF
CAP0056S.WMF
CAP0057S.WMF
CAP0058S.WMF
CAP0059S.WMF
CAP0060S.WMF
CAP0061S.WMF
CAP0062S.WMF
CAP0063S.WMF
CAP0064S.WMF
CAP0065S.WMF
CAP0066S.WMF
CAP0067S.WMF
CAP0068S.WMF
CAP0069S.WMF
CAP0070S.WMF
CAP0071S.WMF
CAP0072S.WMF
CAP0073S.WMF
CAP0074S.WMF
CAP0075S.WMF
CAP0076S.WMF
CAP0077S.WMF
CAP0078S.WMF
CAP0079S.WMF
CAP0080S.WMF
CAP0081S.WMF
CAP0082S.WMF
CAP0083S.WMF
CAP0084S.WMF
CAP0085S.WMF
CAP0086S.WMF
CAP0087S.WMF
CAP0088S.WMF
CAP0089S.WMF
CAP0090S.WMF
CAP0091S.WMF
CAP0092S.WMF
CAP0093S.WMF
CAP0094S.WMF
CAP0095S.WMF
CAP0096S.WMF
CAP0097S.WMF
CAP0098S.WMF
CAP0099S.WMF
CAP0100S.WMF
CAP0101S.WMF
CAP0102S.WMF
CAP0103S.WMF
CAP0104S.WMF
CAP0105S.WMF
CAP0106S.WMF
CAP0107S.WMF
CAP0108S.WMF
CAP0109S.WMF
CAP0110S.WMF
CAP0111S.WMF
CAP0112S.WMF
CAP0113S.WMF
CAP0114S.WMF
CAP0115S.WMF
CAP0116S.WMF
CAP0117S.WMF
CAP0118S.WMF
CAP0119S.WMF
CAP0120S.WMF

CAP0121S.WMF CAP0122S.WMF CAP0123S.WMF CAP0124S.WMF CAP0125S.WMF CAP0126S.WMF CAP0127S.WMF CAP0128S.WMF CAP0129S.WMF CAP0130S.WMF

CAP0131S.WMF CAP0132S.WMF CAP0133S.WMF CAP0134S.WMF CAP0135S.WMF CAP0136S.WMF CAP0137S.WMF CAP0138S.WMF CAP0139S.WMF CAP0140S.WMF

CAP0141S.WMF CAP0142S.WMF CAP0143S.WMF CAP0144S.WMF CAP0145S.WMF CAP0146S.WMF CAP0147S.WMF CAP0148S.WMF CAP0149S.WMF CAP0150S.WMF

CAP0151S.WMF CAP0152S.WMF CAP0153S.WMF CAP0154S.WMF CAP0155S.WMF CAP0156S.WMF CAP0157S.WMF CAP0158S.WMF CAP0159S.WMF CAP0160S.WMF

CAP0161S.WMF CAP0162S.WMF CAP0163S.WMF CAP0164S.WMF CAP0165S.WMF CAP0166S.WMF CAP0167S.WMF CAP0168S.WMF CAP0169S.WMF CAP0170S.WMF

CAP0171S.WMF CAP0172S.WMF CAP0173S.WMF CAP0174S.WMF CAP0175S.WMF CAP0176S.WMF CAP0177S.WMF CAP0178S.WMF CAP0179S.WMF CAP0180S.WMF

CAP0181S.WMF CAP0182S.WMF CAP0183S.WMF CAP0184S.WMF CAP0185S.WMF CAP0186S.WMF CAP0187S.WMF CAP0188S.WMF CAP0189S.WMF CAP0190S.WMF

CAP0191S.WMF CAP0192S.WMF CAP0193S.WMF CAP0194S.WMF CAP0195S.WMF CAP0196S.WMF CAP0197S.WMF CAP0198S.WMF CAP0199S.WMF CAP0200S.WMF

CAP0201S.WMF CAP0202S.WMF CAP0203S.WMF CAP0204S.WMF CAP0205S.WMF CAP0206S.WMF CAP0207S.WMF CAP0208S.WMF CAP0209S.WMF CAP0210S.WMF

CAP0211S.WMF CAP0212S.WMF CAP0213S.WMF CAP0214S.WMF CAP0215S.WMF CAP0216S.WMF CAP0217S.WMF CAP0218S.WMF CAP0219S.WMF CAP0220S.WMF

CAP0221S.WMF CAP0222S.WMF HPI012A.WMF HPI012I.WMF HPI014D.WMF HPI014G.WMF HPI016F.WMF HPI018A.WMF HPI018D.WMF HPI026B.WMF

HPI032A.WMF HPI032B.WMF HPI032C.WMF HPI032D.WMF HPI032F.WMF HPI032G.WMF HPI032H.WMF HPI032I.WMF

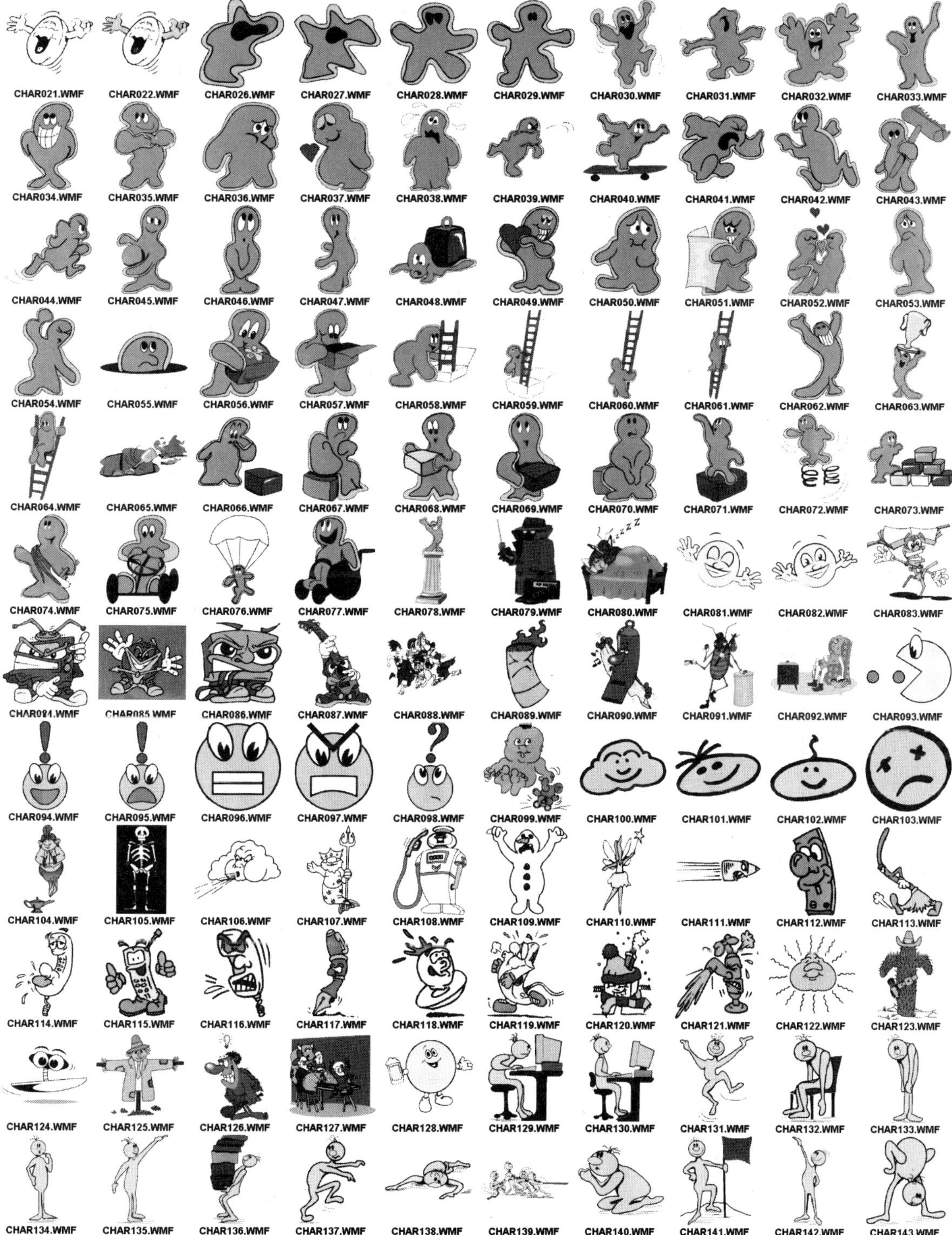
CHAR021.WMF CHAR022.WMF CHAR026.WMF CHAR027.WMF CHAR028.WMF CHAR029.WMF CHAR030.WMF CHAR031.WMF CHAR032.WMF CHAR033.WMF
CHAR034.WMF CHAR035.WMF CHAR036.WMF CHAR037.WMF CHAR038.WMF CHAR039.WMF CHAR040.WMF CHAR041.WMF CHAR042.WMF CHAR043.WMF
CHAR044.WMF CHAR045.WMF CHAR046.WMF CHAR047.WMF CHAR048.WMF CHAR049.WMF CHAR050.WMF CHAR051.WMF CHAR052.WMF CHAR053.WMF
CHAR054.WMF CHAR055.WMF CHAR056.WMF CHAR057.WMF CHAR058.WMF CHAR059.WMF CHAR060.WMF CHAR061.WMF CHAR062.WMF CHAR063.WMF
CHAR064.WMF CHAR065.WMF CHAR066.WMF CHAR067.WMF CHAR068.WMF CHAR069.WMF CHAR070.WMF CHAR071.WMF CHAR072.WMF CHAR073.WMF
CHAR074.WMF CHAR075.WMF CHAR076.WMF CHAR077.WMF CHAR078.WMF CHAR079.WMF CHAR080.WMF CHAR081.WMF CHAR082.WMF CHAR083.WMF
CHAR084.WMF CHAR085.WMF CHAR086.WMF CHAR087.WMF CHAR088.WMF CHAR089.WMF CHAR090.WMF CHAR091.WMF CHAR092.WMF CHAR093.WMF
CHAR094.WMF CHAR095.WMF CHAR096.WMF CHAR097.WMF CHAR098.WMF CHAR099.WMF CHAR100.WMF CHAR101.WMF CHAR102.WMF CHAR103.WMF
CHAR104.WMF CHAR105.WMF CHAR106.WMF CHAR107.WMF CHAR108.WMF CHAR109.WMF CHAR110.WMF CHAR111.WMF CHAR112.WMF CHAR113.WMF
CHAR114.WMF CHAR115.WMF CHAR116.WMF CHAR117.WMF CHAR118.WMF CHAR119.WMF CHAR120.WMF CHAR121.WMF CHAR122.WMF CHAR123.WMF
CHAR124.WMF CHAR125.WMF CHAR126.WMF CHAR127.WMF CHAR128.WMF CHAR129.WMF CHAR130.WMF CHAR131.WMF CHAR132.WMF CHAR133.WMF
CHAR134.WMF CHAR135.WMF CHAR136.WMF CHAR137.WMF CHAR138.WMF CHAR139.WMF CHAR140.WMF CHAR141.WMF CHAR142.WMF CHAR143.WMF

CHAR144.WMF CHAR145.WMF CHAR146.WMF CHAR147.WMF CHAR148.WMF CHAR149.WMF CHAR150.WMF CHAR151.WMF CHAR152.WMF CHAR153.WMF
CHAR154.WMF CHAR155.WMF CHAR156.WMF CHAR157.WMF CHAR158.WMF CHAR159.WMF CHAR160.WMF CHAR161.WMF CHAR162.WMF CHAR163.WMF
STOP
GO
CHAR164.WMF CHAR165.WMF CHAR166.WMF CHAR167.WMF CHAR168.WMF CHAR169.WMF CHAR170.WMF CHAR171.WMF CHAR172.WMF CHAR173.WMF
CHAR174.WMF CHAR175.WMF CHAR176.WMF CHAR177.WMF CHAR178.WMF CHAR179.WMF CHAR180.WMF CHAR181.WMF CHAR182.WMF CHAR183.WMF
CHAR184.WMF CHAR185.WMF CHAR186.WMF CHAR187.WMF CHAR188.WMF CHAR189.WMF CHAR190.WMF CHAR191.WMF CHAR192.WMF CHAR193.WMF
CHAR194.WMF CHAR195.WMF CHAR196.WMF CHAR197.WMF CHAR198.WMF CHAR199.WMF CHAR200.WMF CHAR201.WMF CHAR202.WMF CHAR203.WMF
CHAR204.WMF CHAR205.WMF CHAR206.WMF CHAR207.WMF CHAR208.WMF CHAR209.WMF CHAR210.WMF CHAR211.WMF CHAR212.WMF CHAR216.WMF
CHAR234.WMF CHAR235.WMF CHAR236.WMF CHAR237.WMF CHAR239.WMF CHAR240.WMF CHAR241.WMF CHAR242.WMF EV001.WMF EV002.WMF
EV003.WMF EV004.WMF EV005.WMF EV006.WMF EV007.WMF EV008.WMF EV009.WMF EV010.WMF EV011.WMF EV012.WMF
EV013.WMF EV014.WMF EV015.WMF EV016.WMF EV017.WMF EV018.WMF EV019.WMF EV020.WMF EV021.WMF EV022.WMF
EV023.WMF EV024.WMF FACE01.WMF FACE02.WMF FACE03.WMF FACE04.WMF FACE05.WMF FACE06.WMF FACE07.WMF FACE08.WMF
FACE09.WMF FACE10.WMF FACE11.WMF FACE12.WMF FACE13.WMF FACE14.WMF FACE15.WMF FACE16.WMF FACE17.WMF FACE18.WMF

FACE19.WMF FACE20.WMF

FACE21.WMF FACE22.WMF

RNDP01.WMF

RNDP02.WMF

RNDP03.WMF

RNDP04.WMF

RNDP05.WMF

RNDP06.WMF

RNDP07.WMF RNDP08.WMF RNDP09.WMF RNDP10.WMF RNDP11.WMF RNDP12.WMF RNDP13.WMF

RNDP14.WMF

RNDP15.WMF

RNDP16.WMF

RNDP17.WMF RNDP18.WMF

RNDP19.WMF

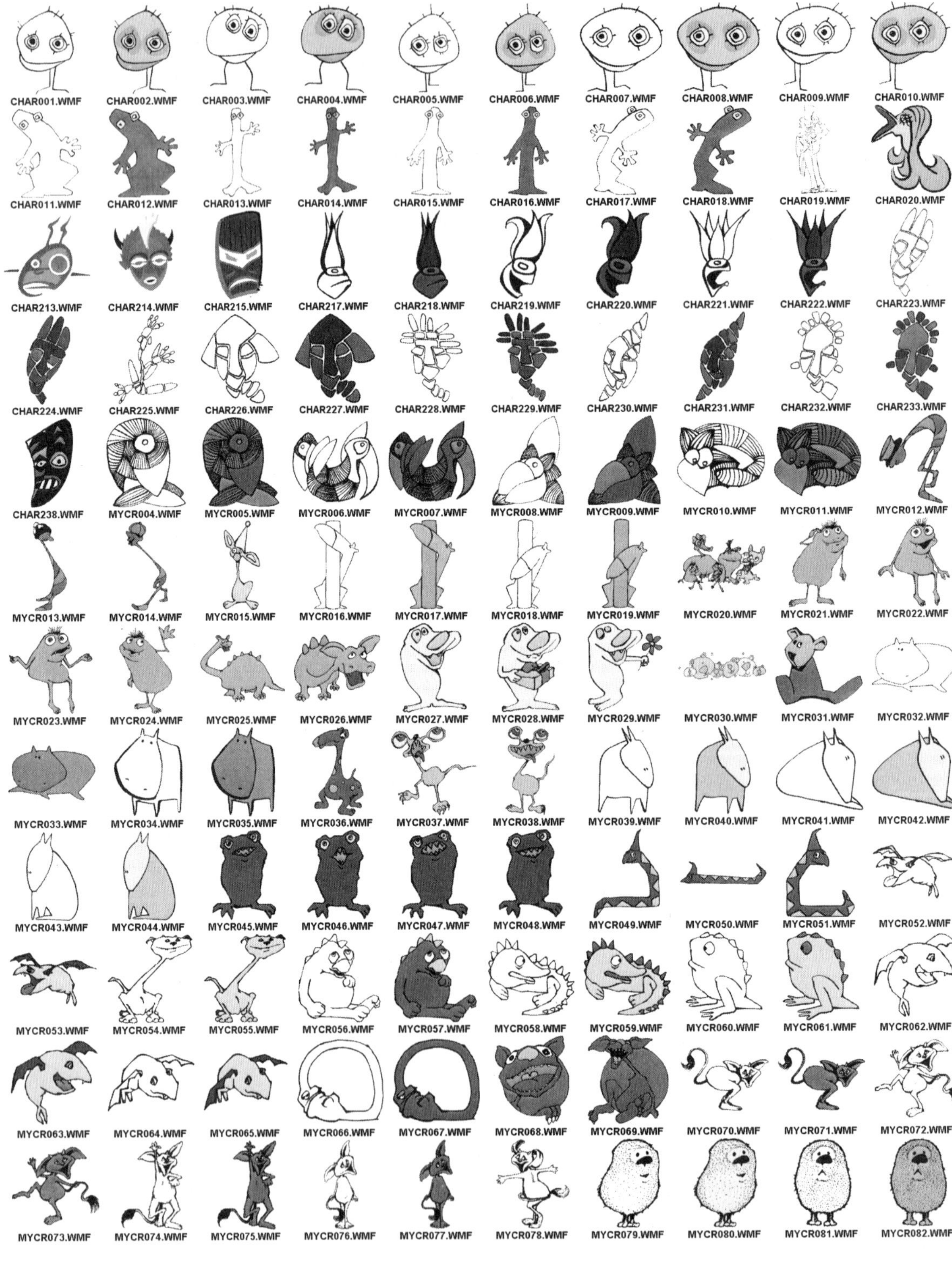
CHAR001.WMF CHAR002.WMF CHAR003.WMF CHAR004.WMF CHAR005.WMF CHAR006.WMF CHAR007.WMF CHAR008.WMF CHAR009.WMF CHAR010.WMF
CHAR011.WMF CHAR012.WMF CHAR013.WMF CHAR014.WMF CHAR015.WMF CHAR016.WMF CHAR017.WMF CHAR018.WMF CHAR019.WMF CHAR020.WMF
CHAR213.WMF CHAR214.WMF CHAR215.WMF CHAR217.WMF CHAR218.WMF CHAR219.WMF CHAR220.WMF CHAR221.WMF CHAR222.WMF CHAR223.WMF
CHAR224.WMF CHAR225.WMF CHAR226.WMF CHAR227.WMF CHAR228.WMF CHAR229.WMF CHAR230.WMF CHAR231.WMF CHAR232.WMF CHAR233.WMF
CHAR238.WMF MYCR004.WMF MYCR005.WMF MYCR006.WMF MYCR007.WMF MYCR008.WMF MYCR009.WMF MYCR010.WMF MYCR011.WMF MYCR012.WMF
MYCR013.WMF MYCR014.WMF MYCR015.WMF MYCR016.WMF MYCR017.WMF MYCR018.WMF MYCR019.WMF MYCR020.WMF MYCR021.WMF MYCR022.WMF
MYCR023.WMF MYCR024.WMF MYCR025.WMF MYCR026.WMF MYCR027.WMF MYCR028.WMF MYCR029.WMF MYCR030.WMF MYCR031.WMF MYCR032.WMF
MYCR033.WMF MYCR034.WMF MYCR035.WMF MYCR036.WMF MYCR037.WMF MYCR038.WMF MYCR039.WMF MYCR040.WMF MYCR041.WMF MYCR042.WMF
MYCR043.WMF MYCR044.WMF MYCR045.WMF MYCR046.WMF MYCR047.WMF MYCR048.WMF MYCR049.WMF MYCR050.WMF MYCR051.WMF MYCR052.WMF
MYCR053.WMF MYCR054.WMF MYCR055.WMF MYCR056.WMF MYCR057.WMF MYCR058.WMF MYCR059.WMF MYCR060.WMF MYCR061.WMF MYCR062.WMF
MYCR063.WMF MYCR064.WMF MYCR065.WMF MYCR066.WMF MYCR067.WMF MYCR068.WMF MYCR069.WMF MYCR070.WMF MYCR071.WMF MYCR072.WMF
MYCR073.WMF MYCR074.WMF MYCR075.WMF MYCR076.WMF MYCR077.WMF MYCR078.WMF MYCR079.WMF MYCR080.WMF MYCR081.WMF MYCR082.WMF

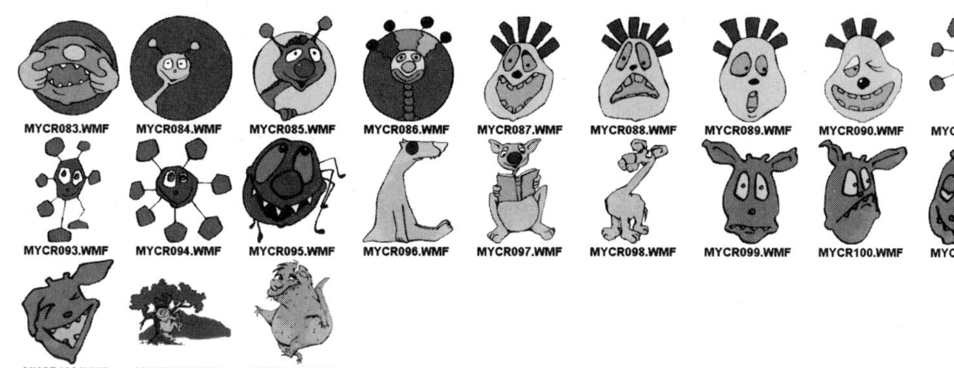
MYCR083.WMF
MYCR084.WMF
MYCR085.WMF
MYCR086.WMF
MYCR087.WMF
MYCR088.WMF
MYCR089.WMF
MYCR090.WMF
MYCR091.WMF
MYCR092.WMF
MYCR093.WMF
MYCR094.WMF
MYCR095.WMF
MYCR096.WMF
MYCR097.WMF
MYCR098.WMF
MYCR099.WMF
MYCR100.WMF
MYCR101.WMF
MYCR102.WMF
MYCR103.WMF
MYCR104.WMF
MYCR105.WMF

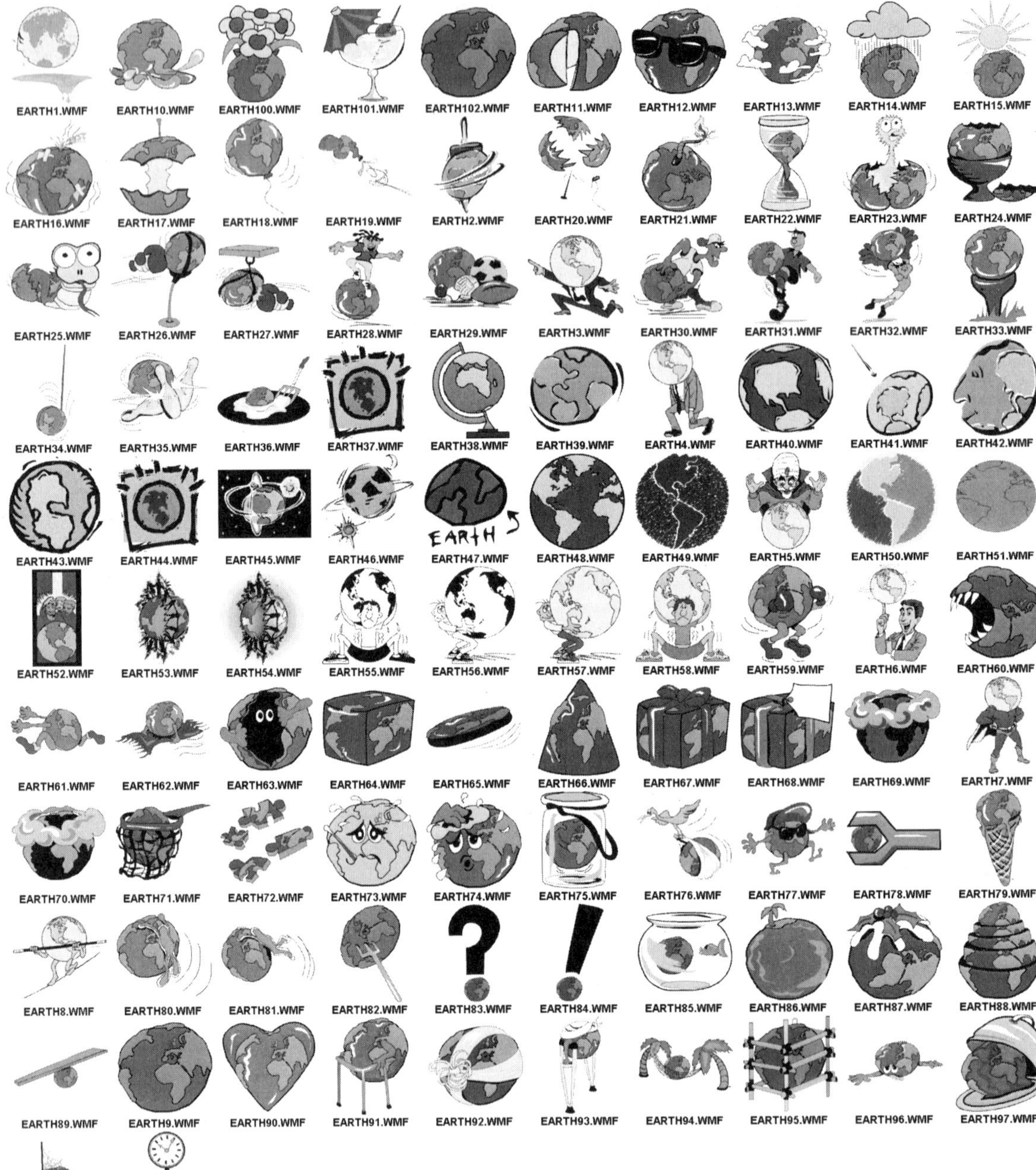
EARTH1.WMF
EARTH10.WMF
EARTH100.WMF
EARTH101.WMF
EARTH102.WMF
EARTH11.WMF
EARTH12.WMF
EARTH13.WMF
EARTH14.WMF
EARTH15.WMF
EARTH16.WMF
EARTH17.WMF
EARTH18.WMF
EARTH19.WMF
EARTH2.WMF
EARTH20.WMF
EARTH21.WMF
EARTH22.WMF
EARTH23.WMF
EARTH24.WMF
EARTH25.WMF
EARTH26.WMF
EARTH27.WMF
EARTH28.WMF
EARTH29.WMF
EARTH3.WMF
EARTH30.WMF
EARTH31.WMF
EARTH32.WMF
EARTH33.WMF
EARTH34.WMF
EARTH35.WMF
EARTH36.WMF
EARTH37.WMF
EARTH38.WMF
EARTH39.WMF
EARTH4.WMF
EARTH40.WMF
EARTH41.WMF
EARTH42.WMF
EARTH43.WMF
EARTH44.WMF
EARTH45.WMF
EARTH46.WMF
EARTH
EARTH47.WMF
EARTH48.WMF
EARTH49.WMF
EARTH5.WMF
EARTH50.WMF
EARTH51.WMF
EARTH52.WMF
EARTH53.WMF
EARTH54.WMF
EARTH55.WMF
EARTH56.WMF
EARTH57.WMF
EARTH58.WMF
EARTH59.WMF
EARTH6.WMF
EARTH60.WMF
EARTH61.WMF
EARTH62.WMF
EARTH63.WMF
EARTH64.WMF
EARTH65.WMF
EARTH66.WMF
EARTH67.WMF
EARTH68.WMF
EARTH69.WMF
EARTH7.WMF
EARTH70.WMF
EARTH71.WMF
EARTH72.WMF
EARTH73.WMF
EARTH74.WMF
EARTH75.WMF
EARTH76.WMF
EARTH77.WMF
EARTH78.WMF
EARTH79.WMF
EARTH8.WMF
EARTH80.WMF
EARTH81.WMF
EARTH82.WMF
?
EARTH83.WMF
!
EARTH84.WMF
EARTH85.WMF
EARTH86.WMF
EARTH87.WMF
EARTH88.WMF
EARTH89.WMF
EARTH9.WMF
EARTH90.WMF
EARTH91.WMF
EARTH92.WMF
EARTH93.WMF
EARTH94.WMF
EARTH95.WMF
EARTH96.WMF
EARTH97.WMF
EARTH98.WMF
EARTH99.WMF

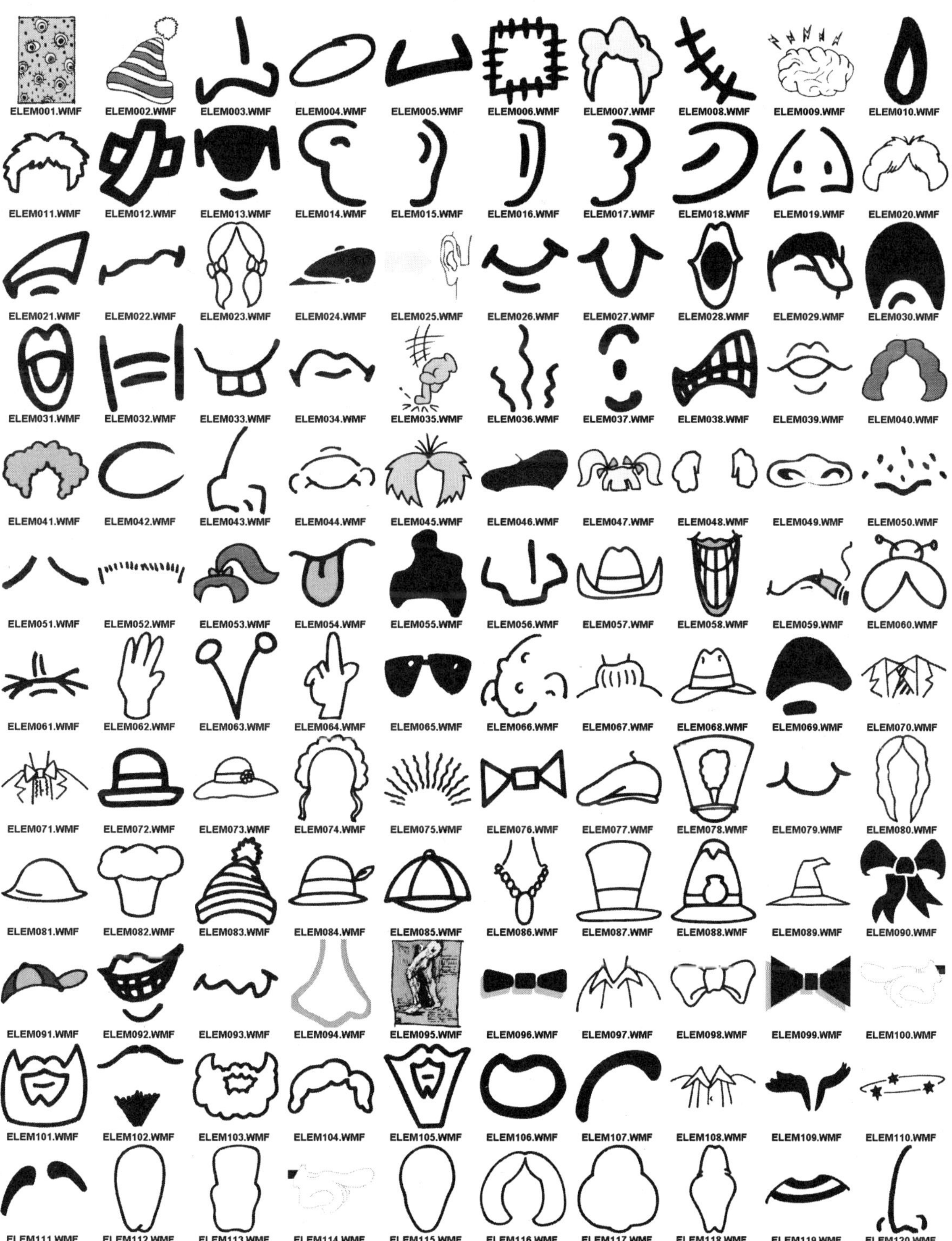

ELEM001.WMF ELEM002.WMF ELEM003.WMF ELEM004.WMF ELEM005.WMF ELEM006.WMF ELEM007.WMF ELEM008.WMF ELEM009.WMF ELEM010.WMF
ELEM011.WMF ELEM012.WMF ELEM013.WMF ELEM014.WMF ELEM015.WMF ELEM016.WMF ELEM017.WMF ELEM018.WMF ELEM019.WMF ELEM020.WMF
ELEM021.WMF ELEM022.WMF ELEM023.WMF ELEM024.WMF ELEM025.WMF ELEM026.WMF ELEM027.WMF ELEM028.WMF ELEM029.WMF ELEM030.WMF
ELEM031.WMF ELEM032.WMF ELEM033.WMF ELEM034.WMF ELEM035.WMF ELEM036.WMF ELEM037.WMF ELEM038.WMF ELEM039.WMF ELEM040.WMF
ELEM041.WMF ELEM042.WMF ELEM043.WMF ELEM044.WMF ELEM045.WMF ELEM046.WMF ELEM047.WMF ELEM048.WMF ELEM049.WMF ELEM050.WMF
ELEM051.WMF ELEM052.WMF ELEM053.WMF ELEM054.WMF ELEM055.WMF ELEM056.WMF ELEM057.WMF ELEM058.WMF ELEM059.WMF ELEM060.WMF
ELEM061.WMF ELEM062.WMF ELEM063.WMF ELEM064.WMF ELEM065.WMF ELEM066.WMF ELEM067.WMF ELEM068.WMF ELEM069.WMF ELEM070.WMF
ELEM071.WMF ELEM072.WMF ELEM073.WMF ELEM074.WMF ELEM075.WMF ELEM076.WMF ELEM077.WMF ELEM078.WMF ELEM079.WMF ELEM080.WMF
ELEM081.WMF ELEM082.WMF ELEM083.WMF ELEM084.WMF ELEM085.WMF ELEM086.WMF ELEM087.WMF ELEM088.WMF ELEM089.WMF ELEM090.WMF
ELEM091.WMF ELEM092.WMF ELEM093.WMF ELEM094.WMF ELEM095.WMF ELEM096.WMF ELEM097.WMF ELEM098.WMF ELEM099.WMF ELEM100.WMF
ELEM101.WMF ELEM102.WMF ELEM103.WMF ELEM104.WMF ELEM105.WMF ELEM106.WMF ELEM107.WMF ELEM108.WMF ELEM109.WMF ELEM110.WMF
ELEM111.WMF ELEM112.WMF ELEM113.WMF ELEM114.WMF ELEM115.WMF ELEM116.WMF ELEM117.WMF ELEM118.WMF ELEM119.WMF ELEM120.WMF

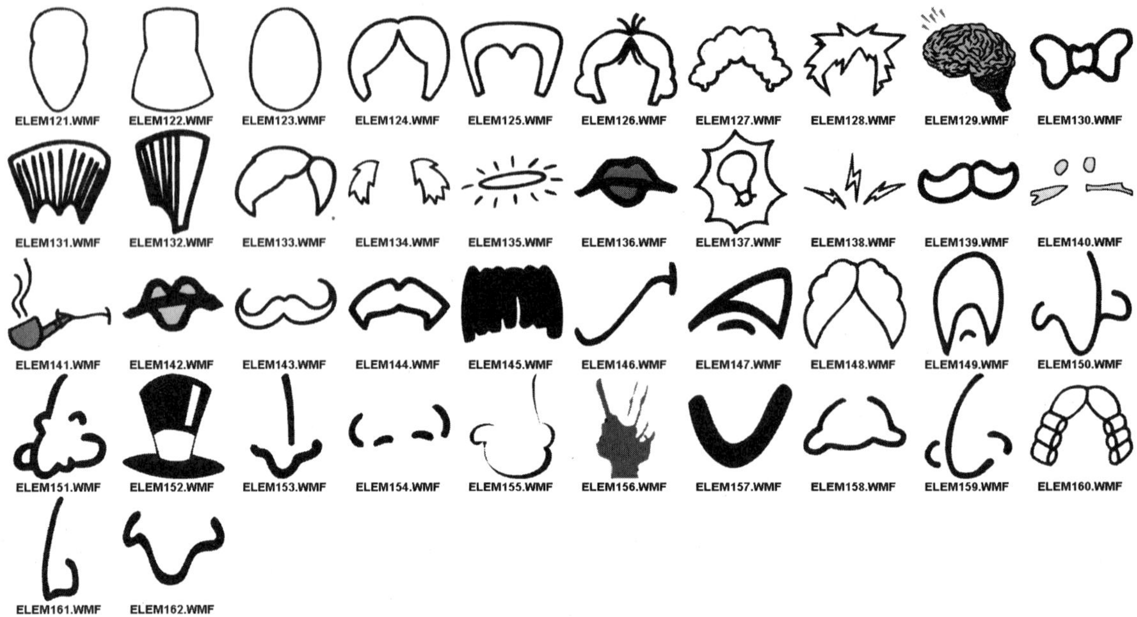

Cartoons • Miscellaneous (MISC)

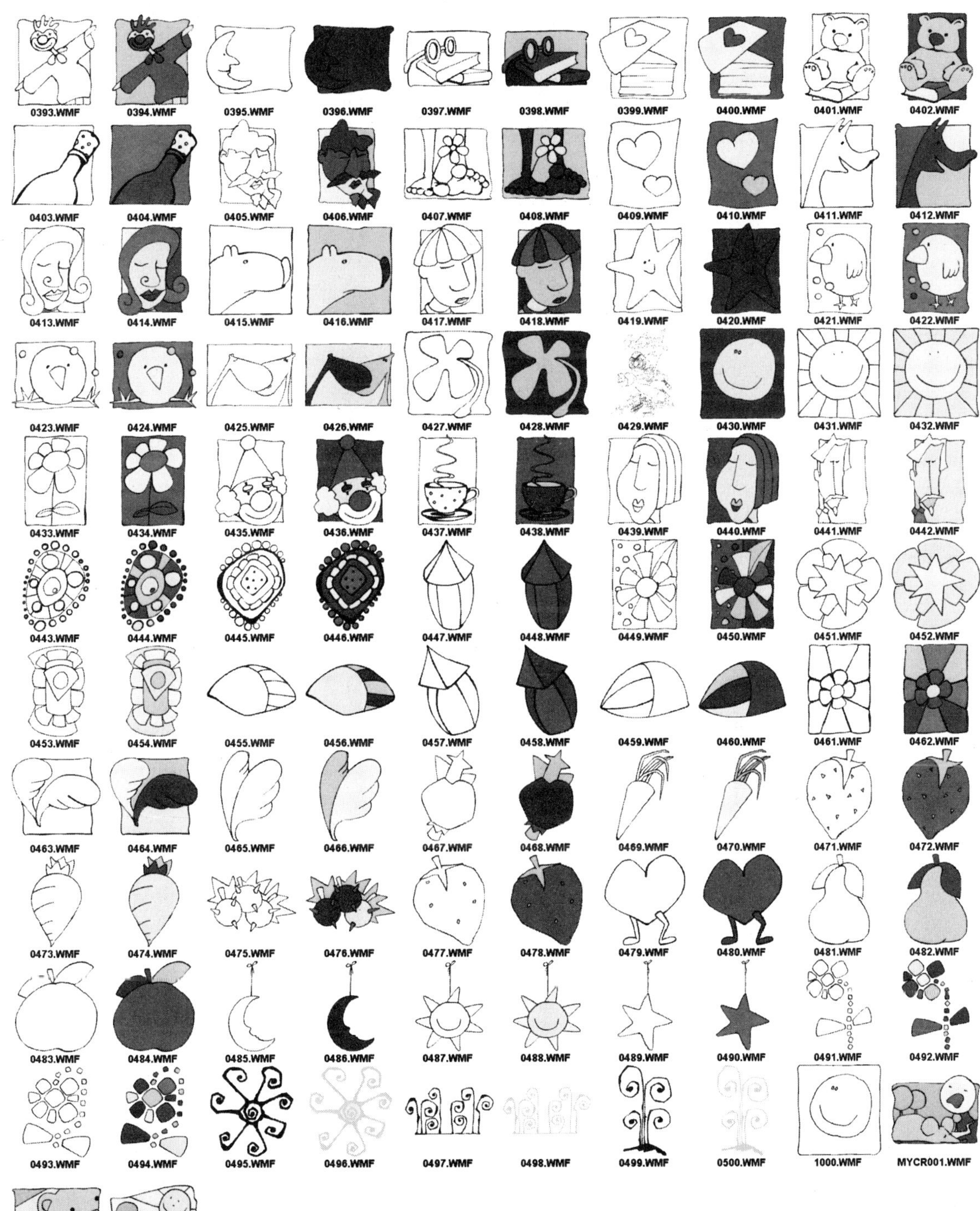

0393.WMF 0394.WMF 0395.WMF 0396.WMF 0397.WMF 0398.WMF 0399.WMF 0400.WMF 0401.WMF 0402.WMF

0403.WMF 0404.WMF 0405.WMF 0406.WMF 0407.WMF 0408.WMF 0409.WMF 0410.WMF 0411.WMF 0412.WMF

0413.WMF 0414.WMF 0415.WMF 0416.WMF 0417.WMF 0418.WMF 0419.WMF 0420.WMF 0421.WMF 0422.WMF

0423.WMF 0424.WMF 0425.WMF 0426.WMF 0427.WMF 0428.WMF 0429.WMF 0430.WMF 0431.WMF 0432.WMF

0433.WMF 0434.WMF 0435.WMF 0436.WMF 0437.WMF 0438.WMF 0439.WMF 0440.WMF 0441.WMF 0442.WMF

0443.WMF 0444.WMF 0445.WMF 0446.WMF 0447.WMF 0448.WMF 0449.WMF 0450.WMF 0451.WMF 0452.WMF

0453.WMF 0454.WMF 0455.WMF 0456.WMF 0457.WMF 0458.WMF 0459.WMF 0460.WMF 0461.WMF 0462.WMF

0463.WMF 0464.WMF 0465.WMF 0466.WMF 0467.WMF 0468.WMF 0469.WMF 0470.WMF 0471.WMF 0472.WMF

0473.WMF 0474.WMF 0475.WMF 0476.WMF 0477.WMF 0478.WMF 0479.WMF 0480.WMF 0481.WMF 0482.WMF

0483.WMF 0484.WMF 0485.WMF 0486.WMF 0487.WMF 0488.WMF 0489.WMF 0490.WMF 0491.WMF 0492.WMF

0493.WMF 0494.WMF 0495.WMF 0496.WMF 0497.WMF 0498.WMF 0499.WMF 0500.WMF 1000.WMF MYCR001.WMF

MYCR002.WMF MYCR003.WMF

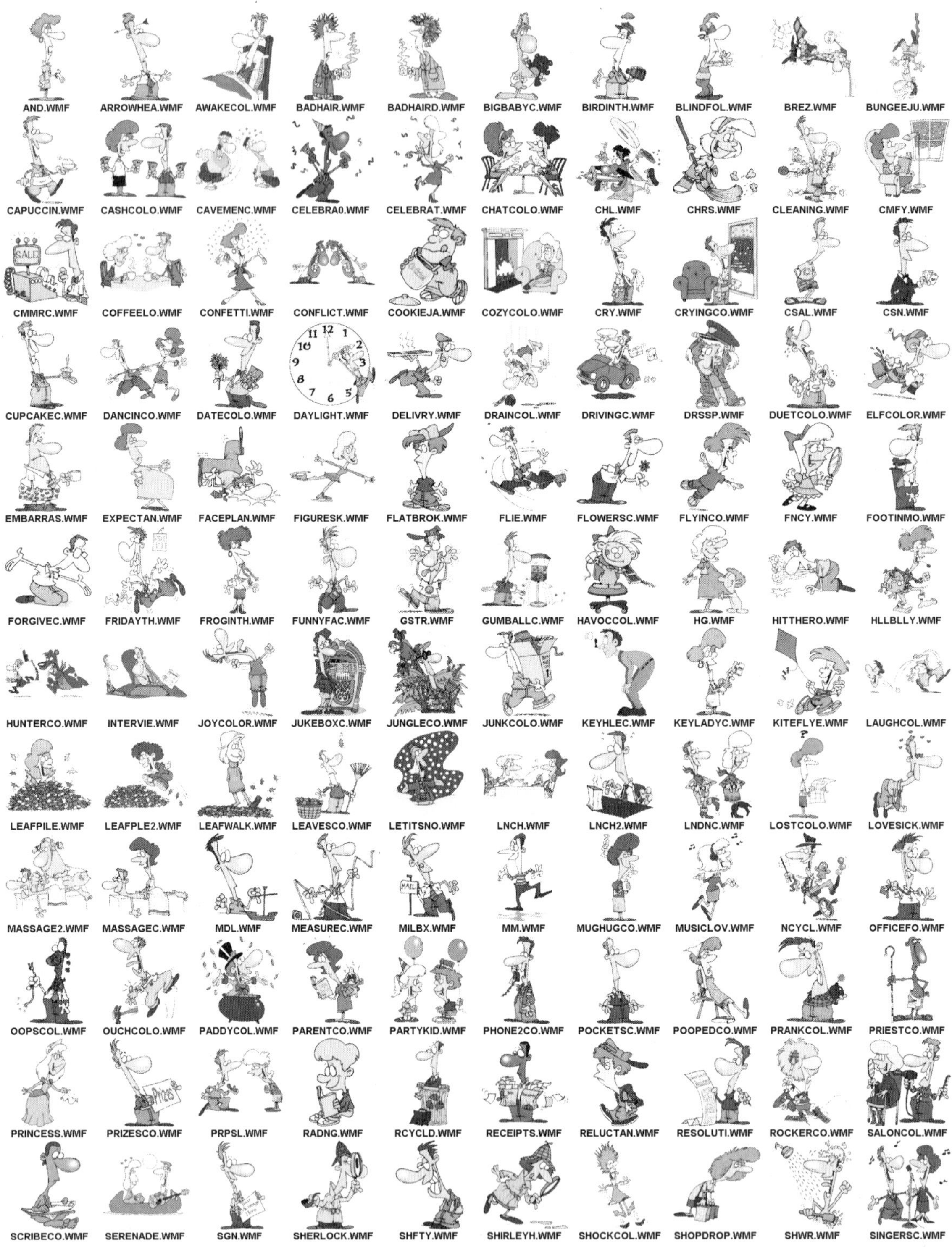
AND.WMF ARROWHEA.WMF AWAKECOL.WMF BADHAIR.WMF BADHAIRD.WMF BIGBABYC.WMF BIRDINTH.WMF BLINDFOL.WMF BREZ.WMF BUNGEEJU.WMF
CAPUCCIN.WMF CASHCOLO.WMF CAVEMENC.WMF CELEBRA0.WMF CELEBRAT.WMF CHATCOLO.WMF CHL.WMF CHRS.WMF CLEANING.WMF CMFY.WMF
SALE
CMMRC.WMF COFFEELO.WMF CONFETTI.WMF CONFLICT.WMF COOKIEJA.WMF COZYCOLO.WMF CRY.WMF CRYINGCO.WMF CSAL.WMF CSN.WMF
11 12 1 2 3 10 9 8 7 6 5
CUPCAKEC.WMF DANCINCO.WMF DATECOLO.WMF DAYLIGHT.WMF DELIVRY.WMF DRAINCOL.WMF DRIVINGC.WMF DRSSP.WMF DUETCOLO.WMF ELFCOLOR.WMF
EMBARRAS.WMF EXPECTAN.WMF FACEPLAN.WMF FIGURESK.WMF FLATBROK.WMF FLIE.WMF FLOWERSC.WMF FLYINCO.WMF FNCY.WMF FOOTINMO.WMF
FORGIVEC.WMF FRIDAYTH.WMF FROGINTH.WMF FUNNYFAC.WMF GSTR.WMF GUMBALLC.WMF HAVOCCOL.WMF HG.WMF HITTHERO.WMF HLLBLLY.WMF
HUNTERCO.WMF INTERVIE.WMF JOYCOLOR.WMF JUKEBOXC.WMF JUNGLECO.WMF JUNKCOLO.WMF KEYHLEC.WMF KEYLADYC.WMF KITEFLYE.WMF LAUGHCOL.WMF
LEAFPILE.WMF LEAFPLE2.WMF LEAFWALK.WMF LEAVESCO.WMF LETITSNO.WMF LNCH.WMF LNCH2.WMF LNDNC.WMF LOSTCOLO.WMF LOVESICK.WMF
MAIL
MASSAGE2.WMF MASSAGEC.WMF MDL.WMF MEASUREC.WMF MILBX.WMF MM.WMF MUGHUGCO.WMF MUSICLOV.WMF NCYCL.WMF OFFICEFO.WMF
OOPSCOL.WMF OUCHCOLO.WMF PADDYCOL.WMF PARENTCO.WMF PARTYKID.WMF PHONE2CO.WMF POCKETSC.WMF POOPEDCO.WMF PRANKCOL.WMF PRIESTCO.WMF
Prizes
PRINCESS.WMF PRIZESCO.WMF PRPSL.WMF RADNG.WMF RCYCLD.WMF RECEIPTS.WMF RELUCTAN.WMF RESOLUTI.WMF ROCKERCO.WMF SALONCOL.WMF
SCRIBECO.WMF SERENADE.WMF SGN.WMF SHERLOCK.WMF SHFTY.WMF SHIRLEYH.WMF SHOCKCOL.WMF SHOPDROP.WMF SHWR.WMF SINGERSC.WMF

SLIPUPCO.WMF SMITTENC.WMF SPRING2C.WMF SPRINGCL.WMF SPRINGCO.WMF SPRINGFE.WMF SPRINGMA.WMF SPT.WMF STORYTIM.WMF STROLLCO.WMF

STRSS.WMF STTR.WMF SURVEYCO.WMF TERRORCO.WMF THINKERC.WMF TOGACOLO.WMF TONGUETI.WMF TRAT.WMF TRKCKR.WMF TTTO.WMF

TWOFACEC.WMF WALLPAPE.WMF WESTERNW.WMF WHELS.WMF WHITEWAT.WMF WINDFALL.WMF WINTERCO.WMF YOYOMAST.WMF YUCKCOLO.WMF

Cartoons • Style 3

PEBO041J.WMF PEBO042J.WMF PEBO043J.WMF PEBO044J.WMF PEBO045J.WMF PEBO047J.WMF PEBO058J.WMF PEBO059J.WMF PEBO061J.WMF PEBO062J.WMF

PESS016J.WMF PESS017J.WMF PESS019J.WMF PESS020J.WMF PESS021J.WMF PESS022J.WMF PESS023J.WMF PESS024J.WMF PESS026J.WMF PESS027J.WMF

Cartoons • Style 4

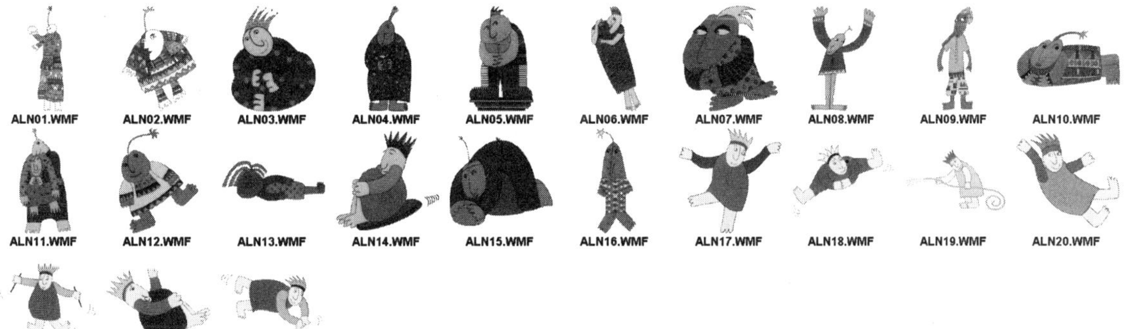

ALN01.WMF ALN02.WMF ALN03.WMF ALN04.WMF ALN05.WMF ALN06.WMF ALN07.WMF ALN08.WMF ALN09.WMF ALN10.WMF

ALN11.WMF ALN12.WMF ALN13.WMF ALN14.WMF ALN15.WMF ALN16.WMF ALN17.WMF ALN18.WMF ALN19.WMF ALN20.WMF

ALN21.WMF ALN22.WMF ALN23.WMF

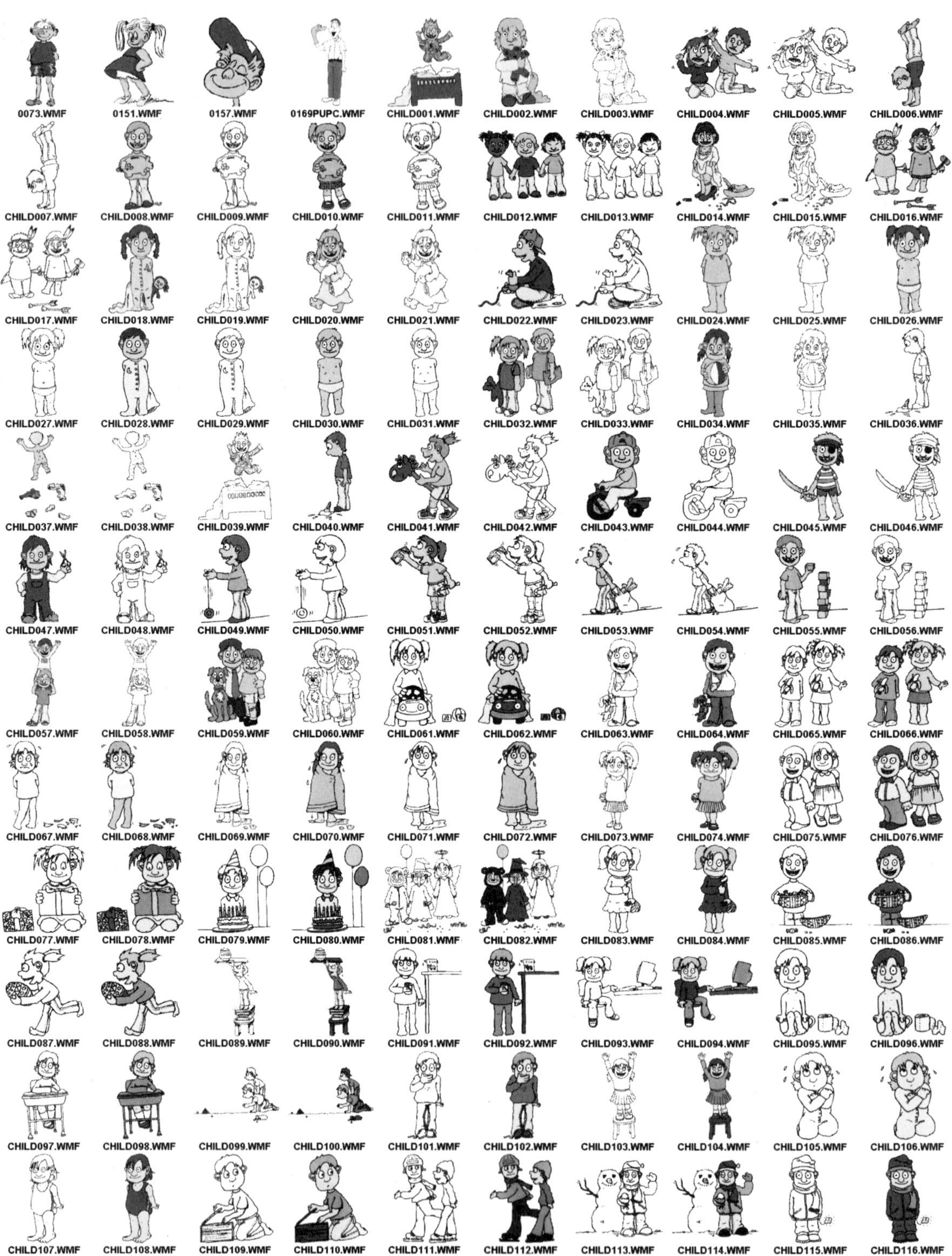
0073.WMF
0151.WMF
0157.WMF
0169PUPC.WMF
CHILD001.WMF
CHILD002.WMF
CHILD003.WMF
CHILD004.WMF
CHILD005.WMF
CHILD006.WMF
CHILD007.WMF
CHILD008.WMF
CHILD009.WMF
CHILD010.WMF
CHILD011.WMF
CHILD012.WMF
CHILD013.WMF
CHILD014.WMF
CHILD015.WMF
CHILD016.WMF
CHILD017.WMF
CHILD018.WMF
CHILD019.WMF
CHILD020.WMF
CHILD021.WMF
CHILD022.WMF
CHILD023.WMF
CHILD024.WMF
CHILD025.WMF
CHILD026.WMF
CHILD027.WMF
CHILD028.WMF
CHILD029.WMF
CHILD030.WMF
CHILD031.WMF
CHILD032.WMF
CHILD033.WMF
CHILD034.WMF
CHILD035.WMF
CHILD036.WMF
CHILD037.WMF
CHILD038.WMF
CHILD039.WMF
CHILD040.WMF
CHILD041.WMF
CHILD042.WMF
CHILD043.WMF
CHILD044.WMF
CHILD045.WMF
CHILD046.WMF
CHILD047.WMF
CHILD048.WMF
CHILD049.WMF
CHILD050.WMF
CHILD051.WMF
CHILD052.WMF
CHILD053.WMF
CHILD054.WMF
CHILD055.WMF
CHILD056.WMF
CHILD057.WMF
CHILD058.WMF
CHILD059.WMF
CHILD060.WMF
CHILD061.WMF
CHILD062.WMF
CHILD063.WMF
CHILD064.WMF
CHILD065.WMF
CHILD066.WMF
CHILD067.WMF
CHILD068.WMF
CHILD069.WMF
CHILD070.WMF
CHILD071.WMF
CHILD072.WMF
CHILD073.WMF
CHILD074.WMF
CHILD075.WMF
CHILD076.WMF
CHILD077.WMF
CHILD078.WMF
CHILD079.WMF
CHILD080.WMF
CHILD081.WMF
CHILD082.WMF
CHILD083.WMF
CHILD084.WMF
CHILD085.WMF
CHILD086.WMF
CHILD087.WMF
CHILD088.WMF
CHILD089.WMF
CHILD090.WMF
CHILD091.WMF
CHILD092.WMF
CHILD093.WMF
CHILD094.WMF
CHILD095.WMF
CHILD096.WMF
CHILD097.WMF
CHILD098.WMF
CHILD099.WMF
CHILD100.WMF
CHILD101.WMF
CHILD102.WMF
CHILD103.WMF
CHILD104.WMF
CHILD105.WMF
CHILD106.WMF
CHILD107.WMF
CHILD108.WMF
CHILD109.WMF
CHILD110.WMF
CHILD111.WMF
CHILD112.WMF
CHILD113.WMF
CHILD114.WMF
CHILD115.WMF
CHILD116.WMF

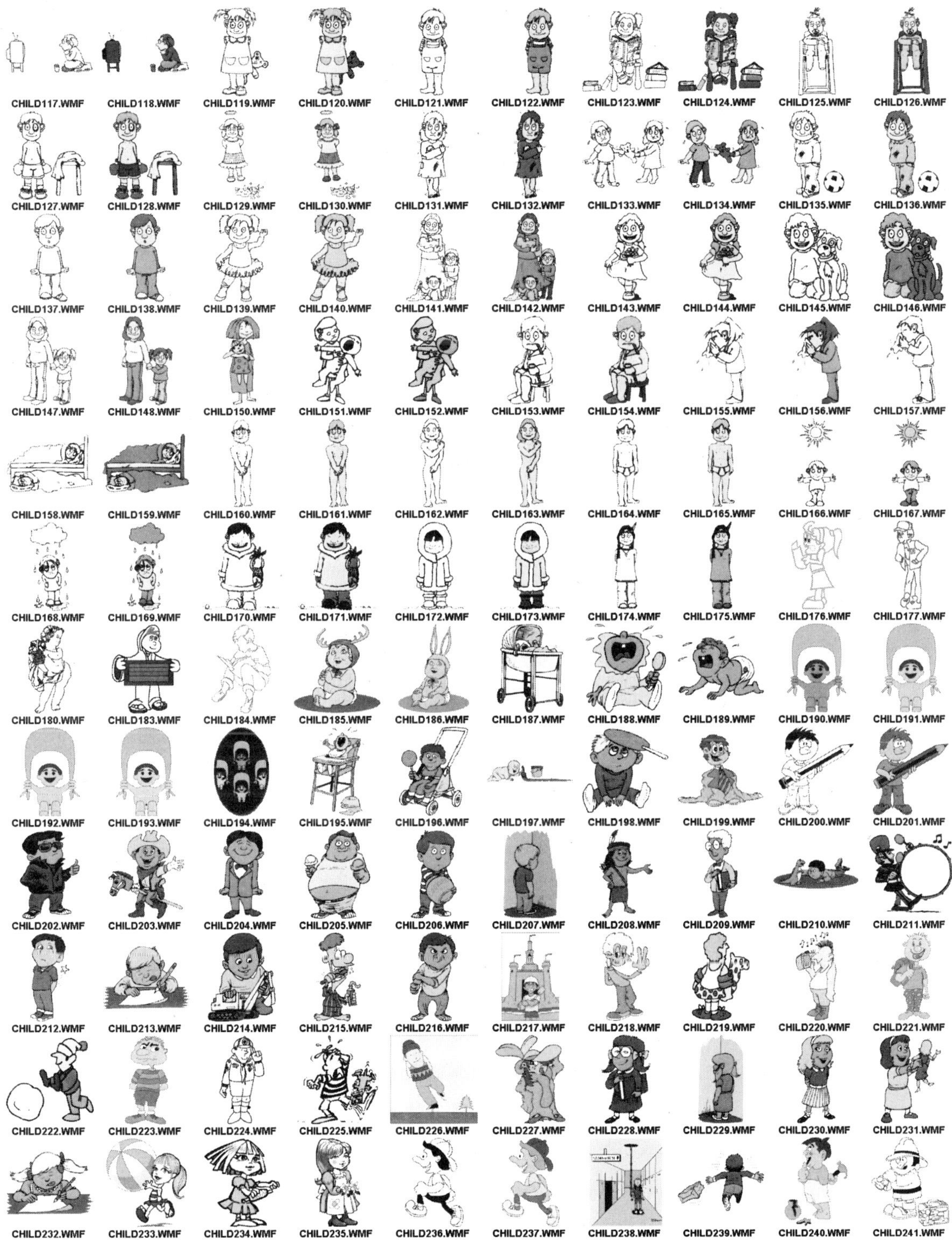

CHILD117.WMF CHILD118.WMF CHILD119.WMF CHILD120.WMF CHILD121.WMF CHILD122.WMF CHILD123.WMF CHILD124.WMF CHILD125.WMF CHILD126.WMF

CHILD127.WMF CHILD128.WMF CHILD129.WMF CHILD130.WMF CHILD131.WMF CHILD132.WMF CHILD133.WMF CHILD134.WMF CHILD135.WMF CHILD136.WMF

CHILD137.WMF CHILD138.WMF CHILD139.WMF CHILD140.WMF CHILD141.WMF CHILD142.WMF CHILD143.WMF CHILD144.WMF CHILD145.WMF CHILD146.WMF

CHILD147.WMF CHILD148.WMF CHILD150.WMF CHILD151.WMF CHILD152.WMF CHILD153.WMF CHILD154.WMF CHILD155.WMF CHILD156.WMF CHILD157.WMF

CHILD158.WMF CHILD159.WMF CHILD160.WMF CHILD161.WMF CHILD162.WMF CHILD163.WMF CHILD164.WMF CHILD165.WMF CHILD166.WMF CHILD167.WMF

CHILD168.WMF CHILD169.WMF CHILD170.WMF CHILD171.WMF CHILD172.WMF CHILD173.WMF CHILD174.WMF CHILD175.WMF CHILD176.WMF CHILD177.WMF

CHILD180.WMF CHILD183.WMF CHILD184.WMF CHILD185.WMF CHILD186.WMF CHILD187.WMF CHILD188.WMF CHILD189.WMF CHILD190.WMF CHILD191.WMF

CHILD192.WMF CHILD193.WMF CHILD194.WMF CHILD195.WMF CHILD196.WMF CHILD197.WMF CHILD198.WMF CHILD199.WMF CHILD200.WMF CHILD201.WMF

CHILD202.WMF CHILD203.WMF CHILD204.WMF CHILD205.WMF CHILD206.WMF CHILD207.WMF CHILD208.WMF CHILD209.WMF CHILD210.WMF CHILD211.WMF

CHILD212.WMF CHILD213.WMF CHILD214.WMF CHILD215.WMF CHILD216.WMF CHILD217.WMF CHILD218.WMF CHILD219.WMF CHILD220.WMF CHILD221.WMF

CHILD222.WMF CHILD223.WMF CHILD224.WMF CHILD225.WMF CHILD226.WMF CHILD227.WMF CHILD228.WMF CHILD229.WMF CHILD230.WMF CHILD231.WMF

CHILD232.WMF CHILD233.WMF CHILD234.WMF CHILD235.WMF CHILD236.WMF CHILD237.WMF CHILD238.WMF CHILD239.WMF CHILD240.WMF CHILD241.WMF

CHILD242.WMF CHILD244.WMF CHILD245.WMF CHILD246.WMF CHILD247.WMF CHILD248.WMF CHILD249.WMF CHILD250.WMF CHILD251.WMF CHILD252.WMF
CHILD253.WMF CHILD254.WMF CHILD255.WMF CHILD256.WMF CHILD257.WMF CHILD258.WMF CHILD259.WMF CHILD260.WMF CHILD261.WMF CHILD262.WMF
CHILD263.WMF CHILD264.WMF CHILD265.WMF CHILD266.WMF CHILD267.WMF CHILD268.WMF CHILD269.WMF CHILD270.WMF CHILD271.WMF CHILD272.WMF
CHILD273.WMF CHILD274.WMF CHILD275.WMF CHILD276.WMF CHILD277.WMF CHILD278.WMF CHILD279.WMF CHILD280.WMF CHILD281.WMF CHILD282.WMF
CHILD283.WMF CHILD284.WMF CHILD285.WMF CHILD286.WMF CHILD287.WMF CHILD288.WMF CHILD289.WMF CHILD290.WMF CHILD291.WMF CHILD292.WMF
CHILD293.WMF CHILD294.WMF CHILD295.WMF CHILD296.WMF CHILD297.WMF CHILD298.WMF CHILD299.WMF CHILD300.WMF CHILD301.WMF CHILD302.WMF
CHILD303.WMF CHILD304.WMF CHILD305.WMF CHILD306.WMF CHILD307.WMF CHILD308.WMF CHILD309.WMF CHILD310.WMF CHILD311.WMF CHILD312.WMF
CHILD313.WMF CHILD314.WMF CHILD315.WMF CHILD316.WMF CHILD317.WMF CHILD318.WMF CHILD319.WMF CHILD320.WMF CHILD321.WMF CHILD322.WMF
CHILD323.WMF CHILD324.WMF CHILD325.WMF CHILD326.WMF CHW027C.WMF CHW069E.WMF CHW089D.WMF FACES001.WMF FACES002.WMF FACES003.WMF
FACES004.WMF FACES005.WMF FACES006.WMF FACES007.WMF FACES008.WMF FACES009.WMF FACES010.WMF FACES011.WMF FACES012.WMF FACES013.WMF
FACES014.WMF FACES015.WMF FACES016.WMF FACES017.WMF FACES018.WMF FACES019.WMF FACES020.WMF FACES021.WMF FACES022.WMF FACES023.WMF
FACES024.WMF FACES025.WMF FACES026.WMF FACES028.WMF FACES029.WMF FACES030.WMF FSW011B.WMF FWN004A.WMF FWN017A.WMF FWN032I.WMF

HMC002B.WMF HMC004A.WMF HPI020B.WMF HPI020C.WMF ICH003A.WMF ICH006A.WMF ICP003A.WMF LAC021D.WMF LASSOBOY.WMF PEGC001M.WMF
PEGC010J.WMF PEGC011D.WMF PEJB016J.WMF PESI052D.WMF PESI073D.WMF PESI074D.WMF PESI075D.WMF PESI076D.WMF PESI077D.WMF PESI078D.WMF
PESI095D.WMF PESI194D.WMF PESI195D.WMF PONYRIDE.WMF SIT036E.WMF SPA022B.WMF SPCA007J.WMF SPCA028J.WMF SPCA062J.WMF SPSI580D.WMF
TOONBOY2.WMF VSC008I.WMF VSC008N.WMF VSC009B.WMF VSC009H.WMF VSC019R.WMF VSC033A.WMF VSC033D.WMF VSC034C.WMF VSC035G.WMF
VSC042D.WMF VSC066F.WMF VSC066J.WMF

0174.WMF
0175.WMF
ADS070L.WMF
ADS073C.WMF
ADS075A.WMF
CFS016G.WMF
CHILD149.WMF
CHILD178.WMF
CHILD179.WMF
CHILD181.WMF
CHILD182.WMF
CHILD243.WMF
CHILD327.WMF
CHILD328.WMF
CHILD329.WMF
CHILD330.WMF
CHILD331.WMF
CHILD332.WMF
CHILD333.WMF
CHILD334.WMF
CHILD335.WMF
CHILD336.WMF
CHILD337.WMF
CHILD338.WMF
CHILD339.WMF
CHILD340.WMF
CHILD341.WMF
CHILD342.WMF
CHILD343.WMF
CHILD344.WMF
CHILD345.WMF
CHILD346.WMF
CHILD347.WMF
CHILD348.WMF
CHILD349.WMF
CHILD350.WMF
CHILD351.WMF
CHILD352.WMF
CHILD353.WMF
CHILD354.WMF
CHILD355.WMF
CHILD356.WMF
CHW040A.WMF
DIM017E.WMF
FACES001.WMF
FACES002.WMF
FACES003.WMF
FACES004.WMF
FACES005.WMF
FAMLY011.WMF
FSW020E.WMF
FSW033B.WMF
ICH001B.WMF
ICH004A.WMF
ICH005A.WMF
ICH008C.WMF
ICH012A.WMF
ICP005B.WMF
ICP006C.WMF
ICP014A.WMF
ICP018B.WMF
IIN009B.WMF
KICKING.WMF
KIDS10.WMF
KIDS11.WMF
KIDS13.WMF
KIDS19.WMF
KIDS3.WMF
KIDS4.WMF
KIDS6.WMF
KIDS7.WMF
KIDS9.WMF
LAC027I.WMF
OXM021F.WMF
SPA001A.WMF
SPA005C.WMF
SPA018E.WMF
SPA031B.WMF

ADS015H.WMF
ADS090L.WMF
ADS093J.WMF
LAC025E.WMF
LAC026J.WMF
MOD001H.WMF
MSL020G.WMF
MSL023D.WMF
MSL023I.WMF
MSL025H.WMF
MSL028E.WMF
MSL031H.WMF
MSL046A.WMF
MSL046C.WMF
MSL046D.WMF
MSL101C.WMF
OTS030K.WMF
OTS032E.WMF
OTS059K.WMF
SCT004B.WMF
SMR004A.WMF
SMR013H.WMF
VSC014B.WMF
VSC021K.WMF
VSC021L.WMF
WMG057O.WMF
WMG060B.WMF

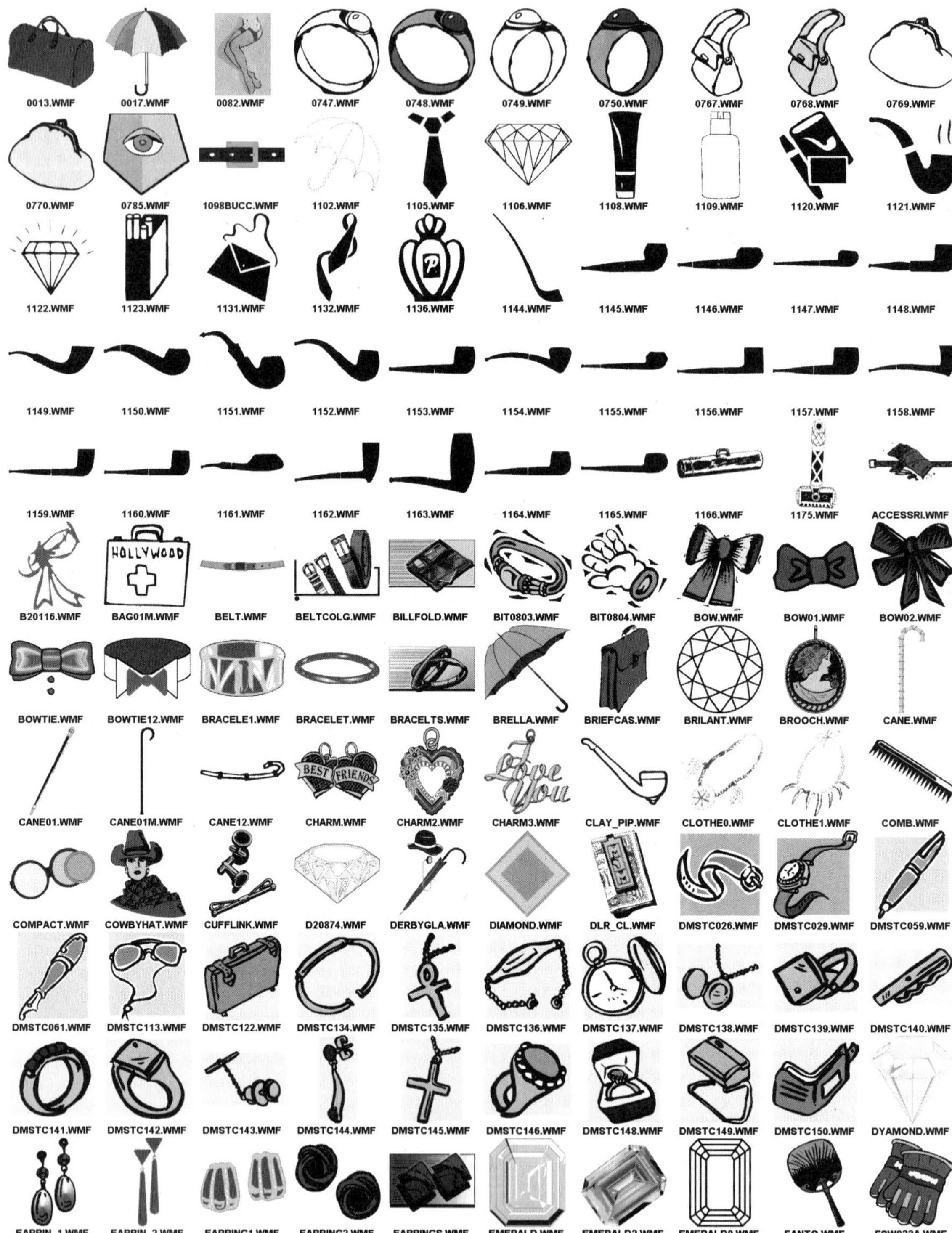

HOLLYWOOD
BEST FRIENDS
I Love You
0013.WMF 0017.WMF 0082.WMF 0747.WMF 0748.WMF 0749.WMF 0750.WMF 0767.WMF 0768.WMF 0769.WMF
0770.WMF 0785.WMF 1098BUCC.WMF 1102.WMF 1105.WMF 1106.WMF 1108.WMF 1109.WMF 1120.WMF 1121.WMF
1122.WMF 1123.WMF 1131.WMF 1132.WMF 1136.WMF 1144.WMF 1145.WMF 1146.WMF 1147.WMF 1148.WMF
1149.WMF 1150.WMF 1151.WMF 1152.WMF 1153.WMF 1154.WMF 1155.WMF 1156.WMF 1157.WMF 1158.WMF
1159.WMF 1160.WMF 1161.WMF 1162.WMF 1163.WMF 1164.WMF 1165.WMF 1166.WMF 1175.WMF ACCESSRI.WMF
B20116.WMF BAG01M.WMF BELT.WMF BELTCOLG.WMF BILLFOLD.WMF BIT0803.WMF BIT0804.WMF BOW.WMF BOW01.WMF BOW02.WMF
BOWTIE.WMF BOWTIE12.WMF BRACELE1.WMF BRACELET.WMF BRACELTS.WMF BRELLA.WMF BRIEFCAS.WMF BRILANT.WMF BROOCH.WMF CANE.WMF
CANE01.WMF CANE01M.WMF CANE12.WMF CHARM.WMF CHARM2.WMF CHARM3.WMF CLAY_PIP.WMF CLOTHE0.WMF CLOTHE1.WMF COMB.WMF
COMPACT.WMF COWBYHAT.WMF CUFFLINK.WMF D20874.WMF DERBYGLA.WMF DIAMOND.WMF DLR_CL.WMF DMSTC026.WMF DMSTC029.WMF DMSTC059.WMF
DMSTC061.WMF DMSTC113.WMF DMSTC122.WMF DMSTC134.WMF DMSTC135.WMF DMSTC136.WMF DMSTC137.WMF DMSTC138.WMF DMSTC139.WMF DMSTC140.WMF
DMSTC141.WMF DMSTC142.WMF DMSTC143.WMF DMSTC144.WMF DMSTC145.WMF DMSTC146.WMF DMSTC148.WMF DMSTC149.WMF DMSTC150.WMF DYAMOND.WMF
EARRIN_1.WMF EARRIN_2.WMF EARRING1.WMF EARRING2.WMF EARRINGS.WMF EMERALD.WMF EMERALD2.WMF EMERALD9.WMF FANTO.WMF FSW033A.WMF

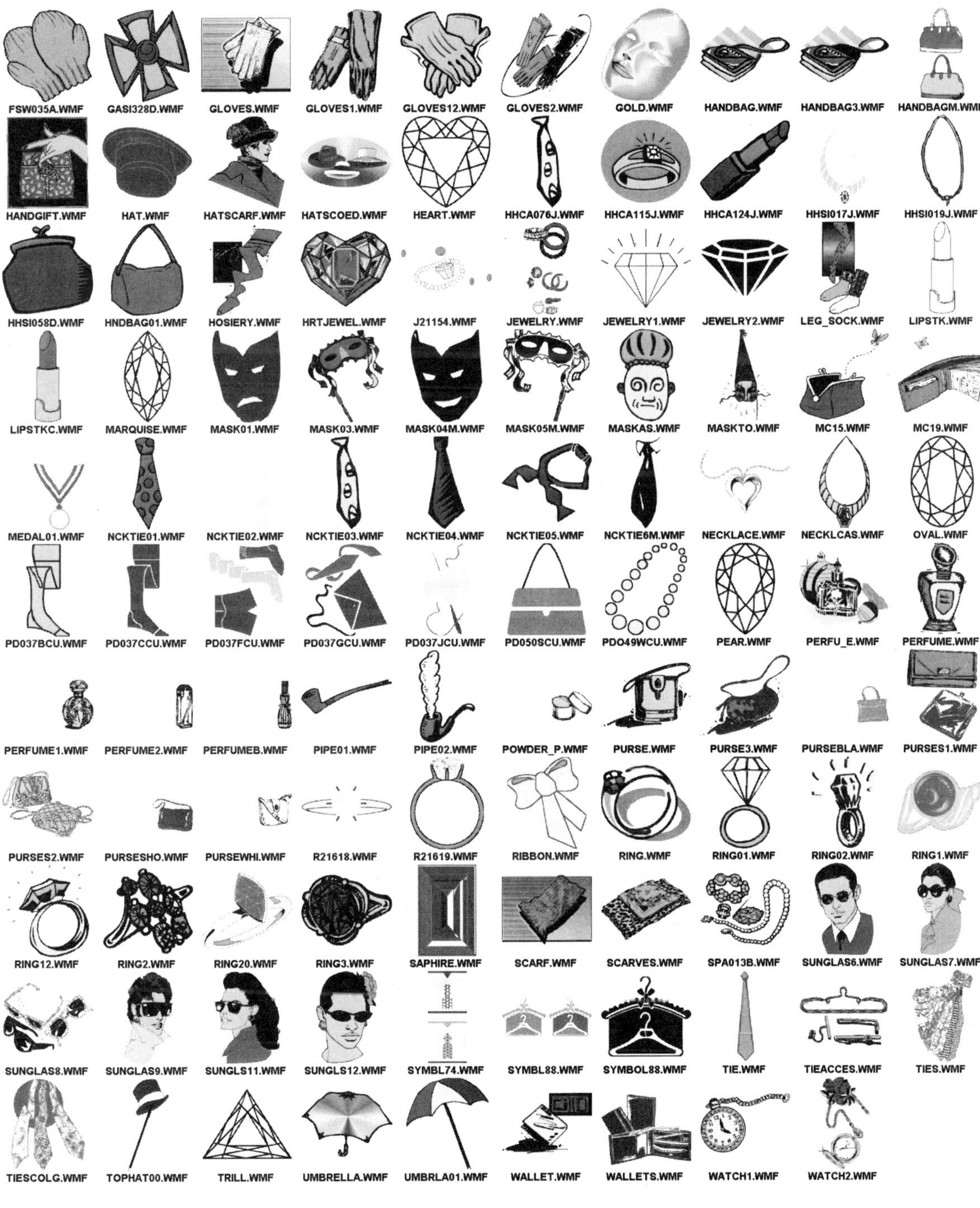

FSW035A.WMF
GASI328D.WMF
GLOVES.WMF
GLOVES1.WMF
GLOVES12.WMF
GLOVES2.WMF
GOLD.WMF
HANDBAG.WMF
HANDBAG3.WMF
HANDBAGM.WMF
HANDGIFT.WMF
HAT.WMF
HATSCARF.WMF
HATSCOED.WMF
HEART.WMF
HHCA076J.WMF
HHCA115J.WMF
HHCA124J.WMF
HHSI017J.WMF
HHSI019J.WMF
HHSI058D.WMF
HNDBAG01.WMF
HOSIERY.WMF
HRTJEWEL.WMF
J21154.WMF
JEWELRY.WMF
JEWELRY1.WMF
JEWELRY2.WMF
LEG_SOCK.WMF
LIPSTK.WMF
LIPSTKC.WMF
MARQUISE.WMF
MASK01.WMF
MASK03.WMF
MASK04M.WMF
MASK05M.WMF
MASKAS.WMF
MASKTO.WMF
MC15.WMF
MC19.WMF
MEDAL01.WMF
NCKTIE01.WMF
NCKTIE02.WMF
NCKTIE03.WMF
NCKTIE04.WMF
NCKTIE05.WMF
NCKTIE6M.WMF
NECKLACE.WMF
NECKLCAS.WMF
OVAL.WMF
PD037BCU.WMF
PD037CCU.WMF
PD037FCU.WMF
PD037GCU.WMF
PD037JCU.WMF
PD050SCU.WMF
PDO49WCU.WMF
PEAR.WMF
PERFU_E.WMF
PERFUME.WMF
PERFUME1.WMF
PERFUME2.WMF
PERFUMEB.WMF
PIPE01.WMF
PIPE02.WMF
POWDER_P.WMF
PURSE.WMF
PURSE3.WMF
PURSEBLA.WMF
PURSES1.WMF
PURSES2.WMF
PURSESHO.WMF
PURSEWHI.WMF
R21618.WMF
R21619.WMF
RIBBON.WMF
RING.WMF
RING01.WMF
RING02.WMF
RING1.WMF
RING12.WMF
RING2.WMF
RING20.WMF
RING3.WMF
SAPHIRE.WMF
SCARF.WMF
SCARVES.WMF
SPA013B.WMF
SUNGLAS6.WMF
SUNGLAS7.WMF
SUNGLAS8.WMF
SUNGLAS9.WMF
SUNGLS11.WMF
SUNGLS12.WMF
SYMBL74.WMF
SYMBL88.WMF
SYMBOL88.WMF
TIE.WMF
TIEACCES.WMF
TIES.WMF
TIESCOLG.WMF
TOPHAT00.WMF
TRILL.WMF
UMBRELLA.WMF
UMBRLA01.WMF
WALLET.WMF
WALLETS.WMF
WATCH1.WMF
WATCH2.WMF

1101.WMF
1118.WMF
1119.WMF
1124.WMF
1130.WMF
1134.WMF
1150GLOC.WMF
1209T_SC.WMF
1248TEXC.WMF
4097.WMF
ATHSUP1M.WMF
BICA001D.WMF
BIKINI1.WMF
BIT0129.WMF
BOWTIE.WMF
BUGC010J.WMF
CAA0349.WMF
CAA0355.WMF
CAA0356.WMF
CAA0357.WMF
CAA0358.WMF
CAA0359.WMF
CLOTHE3.WMF
CLOTHE5.WMF
DRESS.WMF
DRESS9.WMF
DRESSRAK.WMF
DRESSSHI.WMF
DRESSTO.WMF
FRA015C.WMF
FSW005A.WMF
FSW005B.WMF
FSW005D.WMF
FSW017D.WMF
FURCOATM.WMF
FURN01.WMF
GLOVE.WMF
GLOVES.WMF
GLOVES01.WMF
HHCA033J.WMF
HHCA036J.WMF
HHCA037J.WMF
HHCA055J.WMF
HHCA065J.WMF
HHCA086J.WMF
HHCA088J.WMF
HHCA108J.WMF
HHCA110J.WMF
HHCA113J.WMF
HHCA116J.WMF
HHGC047D.WMF
HHRW008D.WMF
HHSI007D.WMF
HHSI029J.WMF
HHSI045D.WMF
HHSI052J.WMF
HHSI055J.WMF
HHSI056J.WMF
HHSI070D.WMF
JACKET.WMF
JACKET01.WMF
JACKET02.WMF
JACKET2.WMF
JEANS.WMF
JEANS01.WMF
JEANSF.WMF
LAC057C.WMF
N21429.WMF
PD036C_1.WMF
PD036CU.WMF
PD036YCU.WMF
PD036ZCU.WMF
PD037ACU.WMF
PD037HCU.WMF
PD037PCU.WMF
PD047MCU.WMF
PD048UCU.WMF
PD099PCU.WMF
PD117LCU.WMF
S21681.WMF
SCARF1.WMF
SCARF2.WMF
SHIRT.WMF
SHIRT01.WMF
SHIRT02.WMF
SHIRT03.WMF
SHIRT1.WMF
SHIRTTIE.WMF
SHIRTTO.WMF
SHRT1.WMF
SHRT10.WMF
SHRT11.WMF
SHRT13.WMF
SHRT14.WMF
SHRT15.WMF
SHRT2.WMF
SHRT4.WMF
SHRT5.WMF
SHRT6.WMF
SHRT7.WMF
SHRT8.WMF
SHRT9.WMF
SORW002J.WMF
SOSI051D.WMF
SPA005F.WMF
SPA006C.WMF
SPA009F.WMF
SPA010D.WMF
SPA014A.WMF
SPA014E.WMF
SPA021C.WMF
SUIT.WMF
SYMBL74.WMF
SYMBL87.WMF
SYMBOL74.WMF
T21820.WMF
T21852.WMF
TEESHIRT.WMF
TROUSERS.WMF
TSHIRT.WMF

TSHIRT1A.WMF

TSHIRTM.WMF

TUXEDO.WMF

UNDRWR1M.WMF

Z21939.WMF

ZIPPER.WMF

ZIPPER9.WMF

ZIPPR01M.WMF

0358.WMF 0359.WMF 0360.WMF 0361.WMF 0362.WMF 0363.WMF 0364.WMF 0367.WMF 0368.WMF 0369.WMF
0370.WMF 0371.WMF 0372.WMF 0373.WMF 0374.WMF 0375.WMF 0376.WMF 0377.WMF 0378.WMF 0379.WMF
0755.WMF 0756.WMF 1103.WMF 1104.WMF 1112.WMF 1113.WMF 1115.WMF 1128.WMF 1129.WMF BIT0731.WMF
BIT0782.WMF BIT0783.WMF BIT0784.WMF BIT0821.WMF BIT0835.WMF BUSI195D.WMF CAA0343.WMF CAP.WMF CAP01.WMF CAP02.WMF
CAP03M.WMF CLOTHE2.WMF CROWN.WMF CRWN.WMF CTMISC76.WMF EAA056T.WMF FSW005C.WMF FTHRS.WMF G21051.WMF H21087.WMF
H21088.WMF HAT.WMF HAT01.WMF HAT02.WMF HAT03.WMF HAT04.WMF HAT05.WMF HAT06.WMF HAT07.WMF HAT08.WMF
HAT09.WMF HAT1.WMF HAT10.WMF HAT11.WMF HAT1173.WMF HAT12.WMF HAT13.WMF HAT14.WMF HAT15.WMF HAT16.WMF
HAT17.WMF HAT18.WMF HAT19.WMF HAT1A.WMF HAT2.WMF HAT20.WMF HAT21.WMF HAT213.WMF HAT214.WMF HAT215.WMF
HAT216.WMF HAT217.WMF HAT218.WMF HAT219.WMF HAT22.WMF HAT220.WMF HAT23.WMF HAT24.WMF HAT25.WMF HAT26.WMF
HAT27.WMF HAT28.WMF HAT29.WMF HAT292.WMF HAT2A.WMF HAT2AS.WMF HAT3.WMF HAT30.WMF HAT31.WMF HAT32.WMF
HAT33.WMF HAT34.WMF HAT35.WMF HAT36.WMF HAT37.WMF HAT38.WMF HAT39.WMF HAT4.WMF HAT40.WMF HAT41.WMF
HAT42.WMF HAT43.WMF HAT44.WMF HAT45.WMF HAT46M.WMF HAT47M.WMF HAT48M.WMF HAT49M.WMF HAT50M.WMF HAT51M.WMF

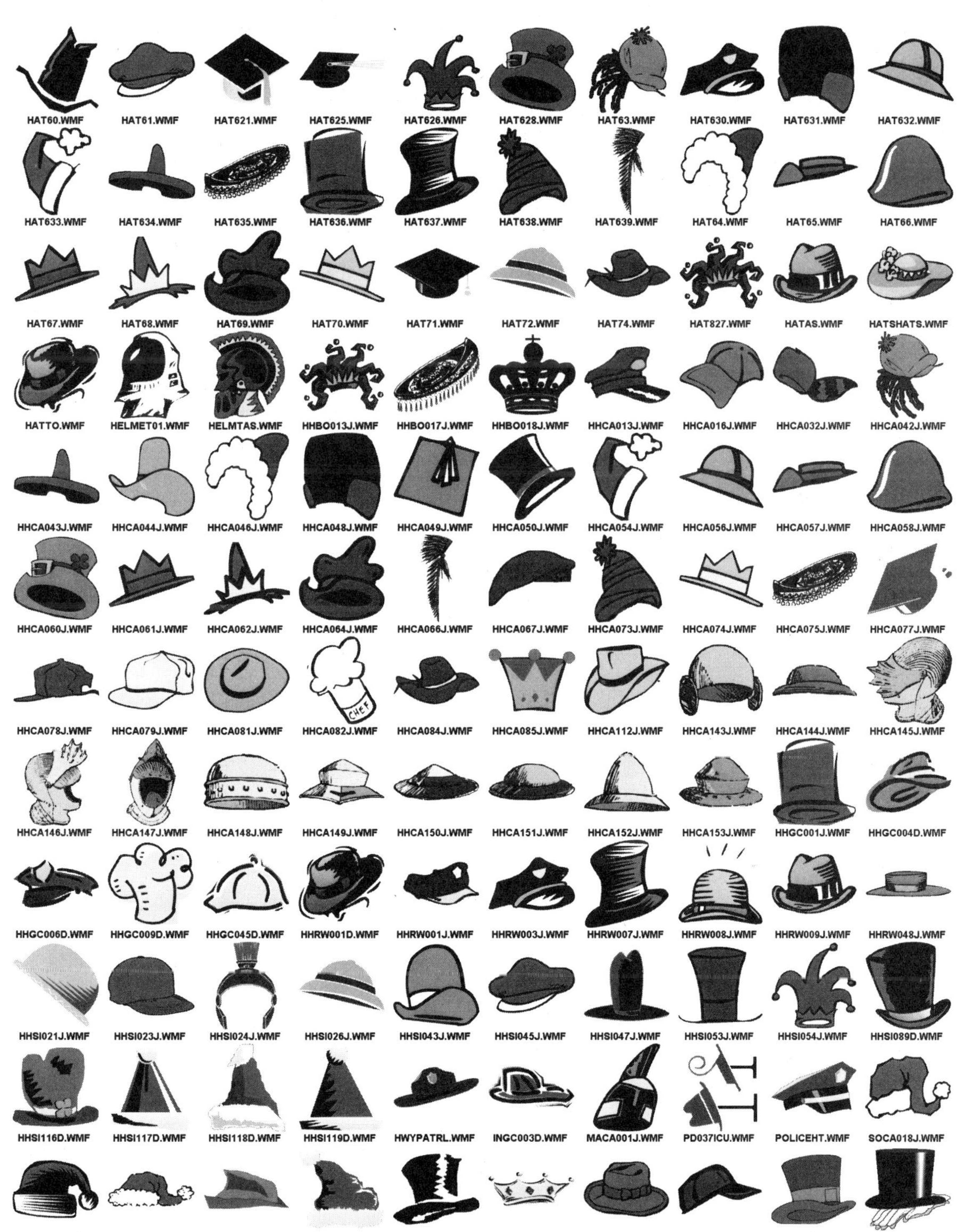
HAT60.WMF
HAT61.WMF
HAT621.WMF
HAT625.WMF
HAT626.WMF
HAT628.WMF
HAT63.WMF
HAT630.WMF
HAT631.WMF
HAT632.WMF
HAT633.WMF
HAT634.WMF
HAT635.WMF
HAT636.WMF
HAT637.WMF
HAT638.WMF
HAT639.WMF
HAT64.WMF
HAT65.WMF
HAT66.WMF
HAT67.WMF
HAT68.WMF
HAT69.WMF
HAT70.WMF
HAT71.WMF
HAT72.WMF
HAT74.WMF
HAT827.WMF
HATAS.WMF
HATSHATS.WMF
HATTO.WMF
HELMET01.WMF
HELMTAS.WMF
HHBO013J.WMF
HHBO017J.WMF
HHBO018J.WMF
HHCA013J.WMF
HHCA016J.WMF
HHCA032J.WMF
HHCA042J.WMF
HHCA043J.WMF
HHCA044J.WMF
HHCA046J.WMF
HHCA048J.WMF
HHCA049J.WMF
HHCA050J.WMF
HHCA054J.WMF
HHCA056J.WMF
HHCA057J.WMF
HHCA058J.WMF
HHCA060J.WMF
HHCA061J.WMF
HHCA062J.WMF
HHCA064J.WMF
HHCA066J.WMF
HHCA067J.WMF
HHCA073J.WMF
HHCA074J.WMF
HHCA075J.WMF
HHCA077J.WMF
HHCA078J.WMF
HHCA079J.WMF
HHCA081J.WMF
CHEF
HHCA082J.WMF
HHCA084J.WMF
HHCA085J.WMF
HHCA112J.WMF
HHCA143J.WMF
HHCA144J.WMF
HHCA145J.WMF
HHCA146J.WMF
HHCA147J.WMF
HHCA148J.WMF
HHCA149J.WMF
HHCA150J.WMF
HHCA151J.WMF
HHCA152J.WMF
HHCA153J.WMF
HHGC001J.WMF
HHGC004D.WMF
HHGC006D.WMF
HHGC009D.WMF
HHGC045D.WMF
HHRW001D.WMF
HHRW001J.WMF
HHRW003J.WMF
HHRW007J.WMF
HHRW008J.WMF
HHRW009J.WMF
HHRW048J.WMF
HHSI021J.WMF
HHSI023J.WMF
HHSI024J.WMF
HHSI026J.WMF
HHSI043J.WMF
HHSI045J.WMF
HHSI047J.WMF
HHSI053J.WMF
HHSI054J.WMF
HHSI089D.WMF
HHSI116D.WMF
HHSI117D.WMF
HHSI118D.WMF
HHSI119D.WMF
HWYPATRL.WMF
INGC003D.WMF
MACA001J.WMF
PD037ICU.WMF
POLICEHT.WMF
SOCA018J.WMF
SORW014J.WMF
SORW056J.WMF
SOSI035D.WMF
SOSI050D.WMF
SOSI058D.WMF
SOSI213D.WMF
SPA024F.WMF
SPCA025D.WMF
T21824.WMF
TOP_HAT_.WMF

TOPHAT.WMF TOPHAT1A.WMF TOPHATTO.WMF V21865.WMF YACHTHAT.WMF

AGITATE.WMF BABYCLS.WMF BEDTABLE.WMF COOLIRON.WMF CUPBOARD.WMF CURTAINS.WMF DAINTY.WMF DONTIRN1.WMF DONTIRN2.WMF DRESSES.WMF
DRIPROFF.WMF DRYCLN.WMF DRYCLNG.WMF DRYHEAT.WMF DRYING.WMF FABRIC.WMF FAD_TAST.WMF FASHIONF.WMF FASHIONH.WMF GLASS01.WMF
GLASS02.WMF GLASS03.WMF GLASS04.WMF GLASS05.WMF GLASS06.WMF GLASS07.WMF GLASS08.WMF GLASS09.WMF GLASS10.WMF GLASS11.WMF
GLASS12.WMF GLASS13.WMF GLASS14.WMF GLASS15.WMF GLASS16.WMF GLASS17.WMF GLASS18.WMF GLASS19.WMF GLASS20.WMF GLASS21.WMF
GLASS22.WMF GLASS23.WMF GLASS24.WMF GLASS25.WMF GLASS26.WMF GLASS27.WMF GLASS28.WMF GLASS29.WMF GLASS30.WMF GLASS31.WMF
GLASS32.WMF GLASS33.WMF GLASS34.WMF GLASS35.WMF GLASS36.WMF GLASS37.WMF GLASS38.WMF GLASS39.WMF GLASS40.WMF GLASS41.WMF
GLASS42.WMF GLASS43.WMF GLASS44.WMF GLASS45.WMF GLASS46.WMF GLASS47.WMF GLASS48.WMF GLASS49.WMF GLASS50.WMF HANDWASH.WMF
HANGDRY.WMF HOSIERY.WMF JUSTYOUR.WMF LINGERIE.WMF LOOKYOUR.WMF MACHWASH.WMF MENSHIRT.WMF NOCHLOR.WMF NODRYCLN.WMF NOMACHWA.WMF
OUTRGMT1.WMF OUTRGMT2.WMF SEASONYO.WMF SEW01.WMF SEW02.WMF SEW03.WMF SEW04.WMF SEW05.WMF SEW06.WMF SEW07.WMF
SEW08.WMF SEW09.WMF SEW10.WMF SEW11.WMF SEW12.WMF SEW13.WMF SEW14.WMF SEW15.WMF SEW16.WMF SEW17.WMF
SEW18.WMF SEW19.WMF SEW20.WMF SEW21.WMF SEW22.WMF SEW23.WMF SEW24.WMF SEW25.WMF SEW26.WMF SEW27.WMF
SEW28.WMF SEW29.WMF SEW30.WMF SEW31.WMF SEW32.WMF SHIRTS.WMF SOCKS.WMF SPINDRY.WMF SPLASHPR.WMF SPRINGFA.WMF

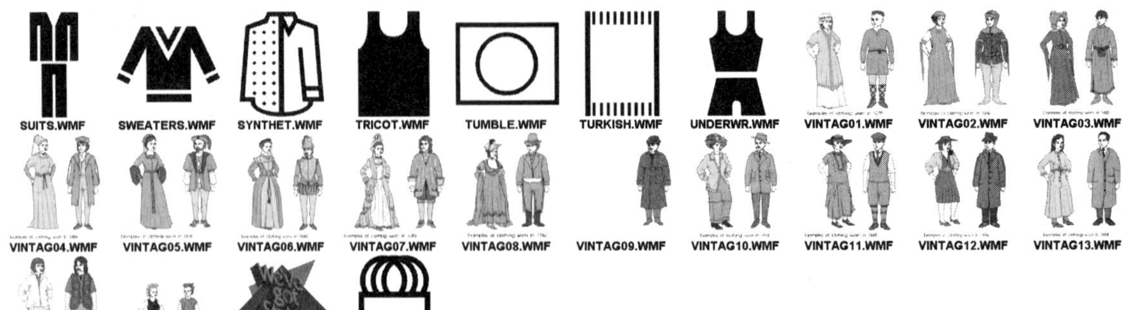

Clothing & Accessories (CLOTHING) • Shoes & Socks (SHOES)

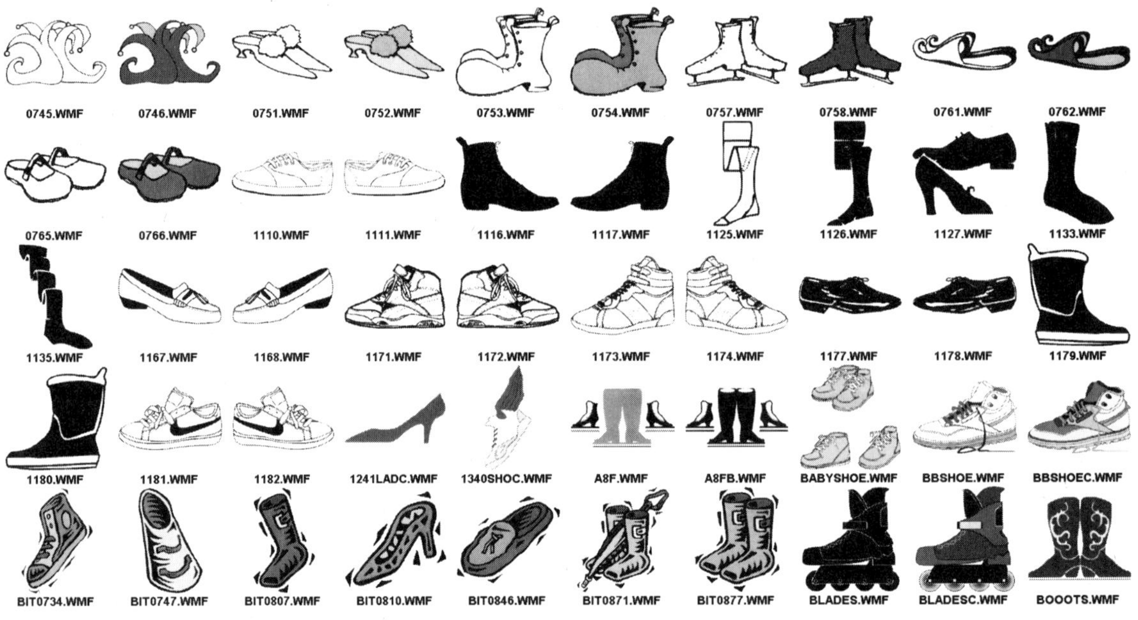

BOOT.WMF	BOOT01.WMF	BOOT02.WMF	BOOT03.WMF	BOOT05.WMF	BOOT06.WMF	BOOT1MD.WMF	BOOTAS.WMF	BOOTS.WMF	BOOTS1.WMF
BOOTS2.WMF	BOOTS29.WMF	BOOTS4.WMF	BOOTS5.WMF	BORD602.WMF	CLIP0008.WMF	FCP036H.WMF	FSW017B.WMF	FTPRNT01.WMF	FTPRNT1M.WMF
GETA.WMF	HFSI001K.WMF	HHCA001J.WMF	HHCA027J.WMF	HHCA038J.WMF	HHCA039J.WMF	HHCA040J.WMF	HHCA051J.WMF	HHCA052J.WMF	HHCA080J.WMF
HHCA087J.WMF	HHCA089J.WMF	HHCA106J.WMF	HHCA107J.WMF	HHGC007D.WMF	HHRW006D.WMF	HHRW059J.WMF	HHRW077J.WMF	HHSI009D.WMF	HHSI010D.WMF
HHSI044J.WMF	HHSI046J.WMF	HHSI048J.WMF	HHSI051J.WMF	HHSI058J.WMF	HHSI063D.WMF	HHSI064D.WMF	HHSI082D.WMF	HHSI126D.WMF	HHSI129D.WMF
HHSI130D.WMF	HPI001A.WMF	JOGNG05.WMF	JOGNG35.WMF	PD037DCU.WMF	PD037ECU.WMF	PD047NCU.WMF	PD048LCU.WMF	PD050NCU.WMF	REDHEELT.WMF
SHOE01.WMF	SHOE02.WMF	SHOE03.WMF	SHOE04.WMF	SHOE05M.WMF	SHOE06M.WMF	SHOE07M.WMF	SHOE08M.WMF	SHOE KEY.WMF	SHOEPRIN.WMF
SHOES.WMF	SHOES12.WMF	SHOES22.WMF	SHOES29.WMF	SHOETO.WMF	SOCKS.WMF	SOCKS01.WMF	SOCKS12.WMF	SOCKS1A.WMF	SOSI052D.WMF
SOSI053D.WMF	SPA031C.WMF	SPSI281D.WMF	SPSI385D.WMF	SPSI401D.WMF	SYMBL23.WMF	SYMBL72.WMF	SYMBL81.WMF	SYMBOL23.WMF	SYMBOL72.WMF

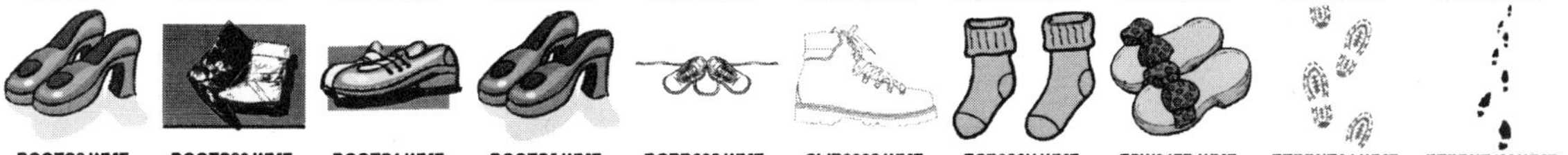

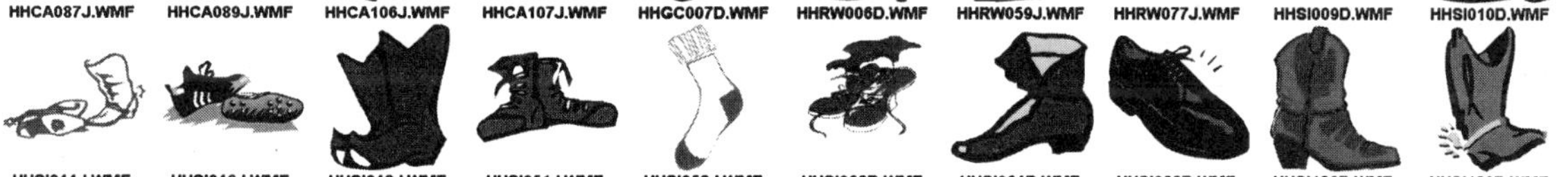

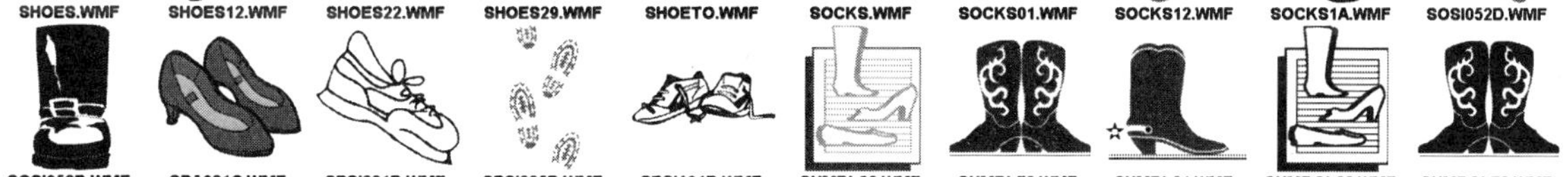

SYMBOL81.WMF TRAINERS.WMF

006.WMF 0092.WMF 0093.WMF 013.WMF 014.WMF 015.WMF 065.WMF 069.WMF 070.WMF 0703.WMF

071.WMF 0718.WMF 072.WMF 073.WMF 074.WMF 076.WMF 084.WMF 086.WMF 087.WMF 088.WMF

091.WMF 093.WMF 096.WMF 097.WMF 1719.WMF 1720.WMF 1721.WMF 1738.WMF 1752.WMF 1COMPUTE.WMF

4COMPUTE.WMF AHYESCO.WMF ALRIGHTC.WMF BACK071.WMF BOMBED.WMF BOYCOMP.WMF BOYNCMP.WMF BROWSER.WMF BUBO005J.WMF BUCA007D.WMF

BUCA011J.WMF BUCA012J.WMF BUGC052D.WMF BUGC053D.WMF BUGC054D.WMF BUGC055D.WMF BUGC058D.WMF BUGC059D.WMF BUGC066D.WMF BUGC068D.WMF

BUGC070D.WMF BUGC073D.WMF BUGC075D.WMF BUGC077D.WMF BUGC085D.WMF BULLETIN.WMF BUSI020M.WMF BUSI026D.WMF BUSI040D.WMF BUSI042D.WMF

BUSI058D.WMF BUSI079D.WMF BUSI142D.WMF BYTES.WMF C20805.WMF CHATLINE.WMF CMPTR01.WMF COMP072.WMF COMP073.WMF COMP074.WMF

COMP075.WMF COMP077.WMF COMP078.WMF COMP079.WMF COMP080.WMF COMP081.WMF COMP082.WMF COMP083.WMF COMP084.WMF COMP085.WMF

COMP086.WMF COMP087.WMF COMP088.WMF COMP089.WMF COMP22.WMF COMPEYES.WMF COMPGIRL.WMF COMPINST.WMF COMPKIDS.WMF COMPMAN.WMF

COMPSUP.WMF COMPTER.WMF COMPTR04.WMF COMPTR4.WMF COMPUT.WMF COMPUT_1.WMF COMPUTE0.WMF COMPUTER.WMF COMPUTIN.WMF COMPUTR2.WMF

COMPUTR3.WMF COMPWOMN.WMF CONNECT.WMF CONNECT1.WMF COPUTER.WMF CRTN094.WMF CT02.WMF CT03.WMF CT04.WMF CT06.WMF

CT07.WMF CT08.WMF CT09.WMF CT10.WMF CT11.WMF CT12.WMF CT13.WMF CT14.WMF CT15.WMF CT16.WMF

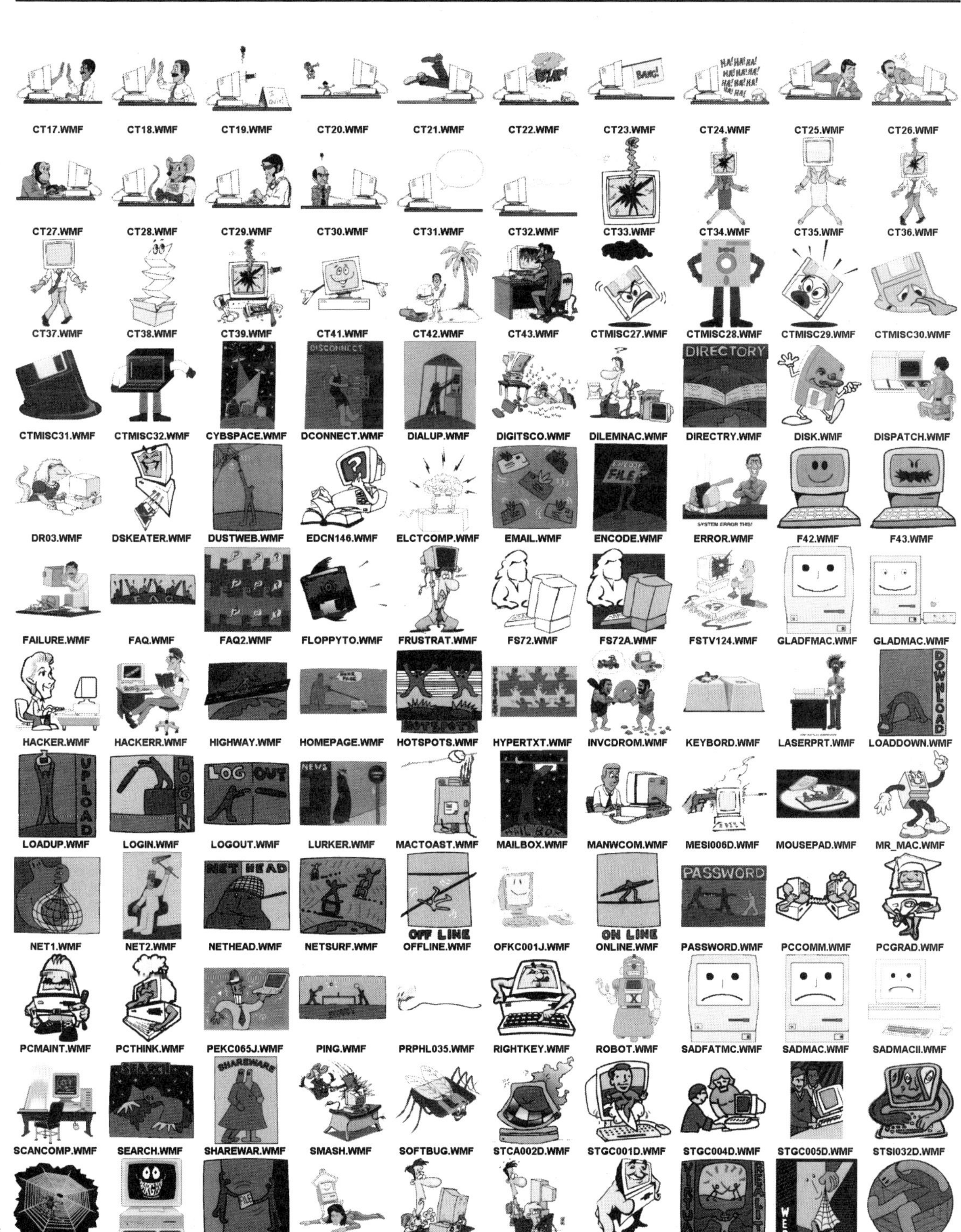

CT17.WMF CT18.WMF CT19.WMF CT20.WMF CT21.WMF CT22.WMF CT23.WMF CT24.WMF CT25.WMF CT26.WMF

CT27.WMF CT28.WMF CT29.WMF CT30.WMF CT31.WMF CT32.WMF CT33.WMF CT34.WMF CT35.WMF CT36.WMF

CT37.WMF CT38.WMF CT39.WMF CT41.WMF CT42.WMF CT43.WMF CTMISC27.WMF CTMISC28.WMF CTMISC29.WMF CTMISC30.WMF

CTMISC31.WMF CTMISC32.WMF CYBSPACE.WMF DCONNECT.WMF DIALUP.WMF DIGITSCO.WMF DILEMNAC.WMF DIRECTRY.WMF DISK.WMF DISPATCH.WMF

DR03.WMF DSKEATER.WMF DUSTWEB.WMF EDCN146.WMF ELCTCOMP.WMF EMAIL.WMF ENCODE.WMF ERROR.WMF F42.WMF F43.WMF

FAILURE.WMF FAQ.WMF FAQ2.WMF FLOPPYTO.WMF FRUSTRAT.WMF FS72.WMF FS72A.WMF FSTV124.WMF GLADFMAC.WMF GLADMAC.WMF

HACKER.WMF HACKERR.WMF HIGHWAY.WMF HOMEPAGE.WMF HOTSPOTS.WMF HYPERTXT.WMF INVCDROM.WMF KEYBORD.WMF LASERPRT.WMF LOADDOWN.WMF

LOADUP.WMF LOGIN.WMF LOGOUT.WMF LURKER.WMF MACTOAST.WMF MAILBOX.WMF MANWCOM.WMF MESI006D.WMF MOUSEPAD.WMF MR_MAC.WMF

NET1.WMF NET2.WMF NETHEAD.WMF NETSURF.WMF OFFLINE.WMF OFKC001J.WMF ONLINE.WMF PASSWORD.WMF PCCOMM.WMF PCGRAD.WMF

PCMAINT.WMF PCTHINK.WMF PEKC065J.WMF PING.WMF PRPHL035.WMF RIGHTKEY.WMF ROBOT.WMF SADFATMC.WMF SADMAC.WMF SADMACII.WMF

SCANCOMP.WMF SEARCH.WMF SHAREWAR.WMF SMASH.WMF SOFTBUG.WMF STCA002D.WMF STGC001D.WMF STGC004D.WMF STGC005D.WMF STSI032D.WMF

SURFING.WMF TALKING.WMF TRANSFER.WMF TRICOMP.WMF UHOHCOLO.WMF UNPLUGGE.WMF UZRFRND.WMF VIRTUAL.WMF WEB01.WMF WEB1.WMF

WEB2.WMF

WEBCRAWL.WMF

WEBSITE.WMF

ZIP.WMF

1328.WMF	1477.WMF	1478.WMF	1479.WMF	1480.WMF	1481.WMF	1483.WMF	1489.WMF	1495.WMF	CKEY0.WMF
CKEY1.WMF	CKEY2.WMF	CKEY3.WMF	CKEY4.WMF	CKEY5.WMF	CKEY6.WMF	CKEY7.WMF	CKEY8.WMF	CKEY9.WMF	CKEYA.WMF
CKEYALT.WMF	CKEYAPOS.WMF	CKEYB.WMF	CKEYBKSP.WMF	CKEYBRKL.WMF	CKEYBRKR.WMF	CKEYBSLA.WMF	CKEYC.WMF	CKEYCAPS.WMF	CKEYCOMA.WMF
CKEYCPLK.WMF	CKEYCTRL.WMF	CKEYD.WMF	CKEYDASH.WMF	CKEYDEL.WMF	CKEYDELE.WMF	CKEYDOWN.WMF	CKEYE.WMF	CKEYEND.WMF	CKEYENT1.WMF
CKEYENT2.WMF	CKEYEQUL.WMF	CKEYESCP.WMF	CKEYF.WMF	CKEYF1.WMF	CKEYF10.WMF	CKEYF11.WMF	CKEYF12.WMF	CKEYF2.WMF	CKEYF3.WMF
CKEYF4.WMF	CKEYF5.WMF	CKEYF6.WMF	CKEYF7.WMF	CKEYF8.WMF	CKEYF9.WMF	CKEYFSLA.WMF	CKEYG.WMF	CKEYH.WMF	CKEYHOME.WMF
CKEYHYPH.WMF	CKEYI.WMF	CKEYINST.WMF	CKEYJ.WMF	CKEYK.WMF	CKEYL.WMF	CKEYLEFT.WMF	CKEYM.WMF	CKEYN.WMF	CKEYNUM1.WMF
CKEYNUM2.WMF	CKEYO.WMF	CKEYP.WMF	CKEYPAUS.WMF	CKEYPERD.WMF	CKEYPGDN.WMF	CKEYPGUP.WMF	CKEYPLUS.WMF	CKEYPRNS.WMF	CKEYQ.WMF
CKEYR.WMF	CKEYRGHT.WMF	CKEYS.WMF	CKEYSCR1.WMF	CKEYSCR2.WMF	CKEYSEMI.WMF	CKEYSHFT.WMF	CKEYSLSH.WMF	CKEYSPCE.WMF	CKEYSTAR.WMF
CKEYT.WMF	CKEYTAB.WMF	CKEYTILD.WMF	CKEYU.WMF	CKEYUP.WMF	CKEYV.WMF	CKEYW.WMF	CKEYX.WMF	CKEYY.WMF	CKEYZ.WMF
CNKEY0.WMF	CNKEY1.WMF	CNKEY2.WMF	CNKEY3.WMF	CNKEY4.WMF	CNKEY5.WMF	CNKEY6.WMF	CNKEY7.WMF	CNKEY8.WMF	CNKEY9.WMF
COMP040.WMF	COMP041.WMF	COMP042.WMF	COMP043.WMF	COMP044.WMF					

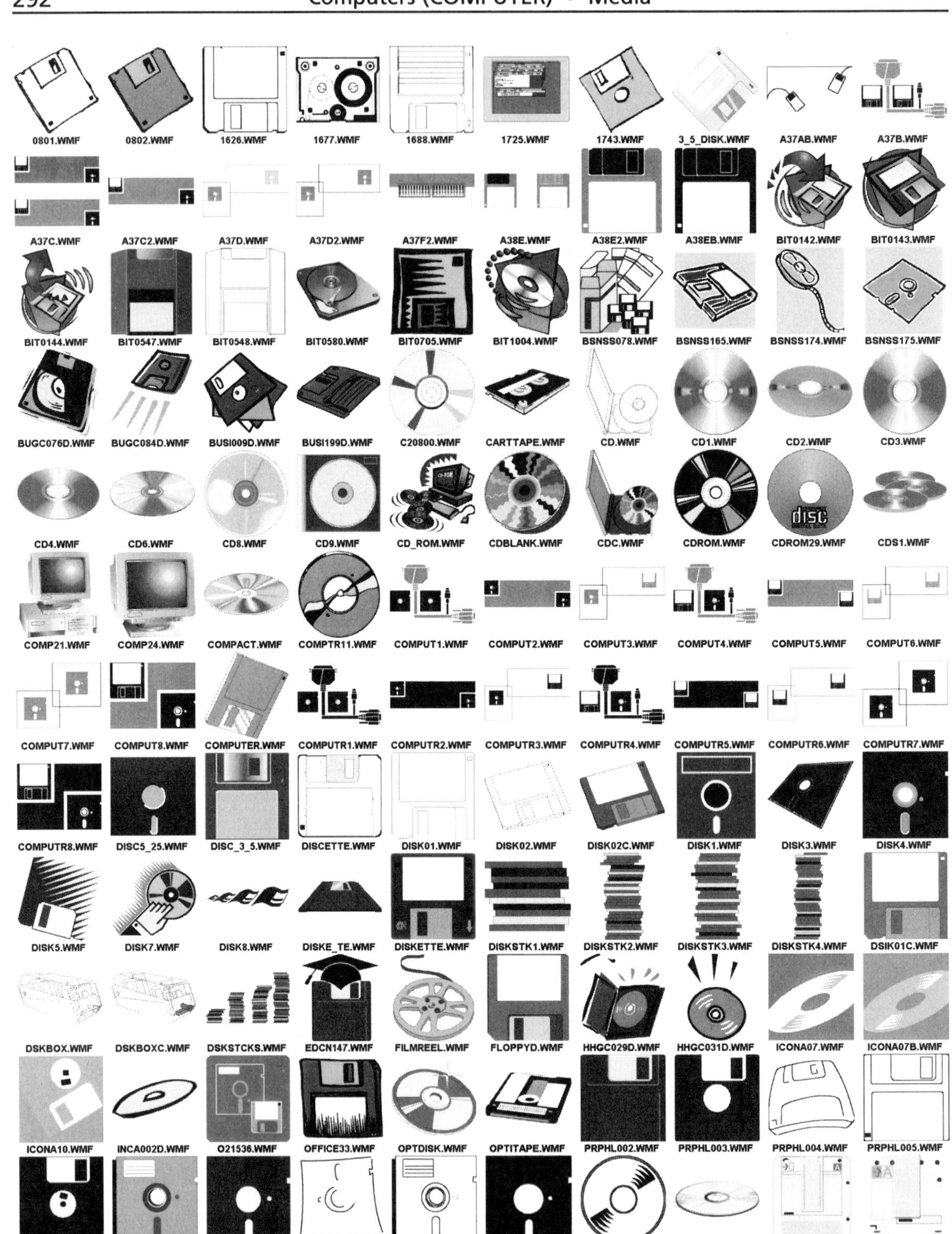
0801.WMF 0802.WMF 1626.WMF 1677.WMF 1688.WMF 1725.WMF 1743.WMF 3_5_DISK.WMF A37AB.WMF A37B.WMF
A37C.WMF A37C2.WMF A37D.WMF A37D2.WMF A37F2.WMF A38E.WMF A38E2.WMF A38EB.WMF BIT0142.WMF BIT0143.WMF
BIT0144.WMF BIT0547.WMF BIT0548.WMF BIT0580.WMF BIT0705.WMF BIT1004.WMF BSNSS078.WMF BSNSS165.WMF BSNSS174.WMF BSNSS175.WMF
BUGC076D.WMF BUGC084D.WMF BUSI009D.WMF BUSI199D.WMF C20800.WMF CARTTAPE.WMF CD.WMF CD1.WMF CD2.WMF CD3.WMF
CD4.WMF CD6.WMF CD8.WMF CD9.WMF CD_ROM.WMF CDBLANK.WMF CDC.WMF CDROM.WMF CDROM29.WMF CDS1.WMF
COMP21.WMF COMP24.WMF COMPACT.WMF COMPTR11.WMF COMPUT1.WMF COMPUT2.WMF COMPUT3.WMF COMPUT4.WMF COMPUT5.WMF COMPUT6.WMF
COMPUT7.WMF COMPUT8.WMF COMPUTER.WMF COMPUTR1.WMF COMPUTR2.WMF COMPUTR3.WMF COMPUTR4.WMF COMPUTR5.WMF COMPUTR6.WMF COMPUTR7.WMF
COMPUTR8.WMF DISC5_25.WMF DISC_3_5.WMF DISCETTE.WMF DISK01.WMF DISK02.WMF DISK02C.WMF DISK1.WMF DISK3.WMF DISK4.WMF
DISK5.WMF DISK7.WMF DISK8.WMF DISKE_TE.WMF DISKETTE.WMF DISKSTK1.WMF DISKSTK2.WMF DISKSTK3.WMF DISKSTK4.WMF DSIK01C.WMF
DSKBOX.WMF DSKBOXC.WMF DSKSTCKS.WMF EDCN147.WMF FILMREEL.WMF FLOPPYD.WMF HHGC029D.WMF HHGC031D.WMF ICONA07.WMF ICONA07B.WMF
ICONA10.WMF INCA002D.WMF O21536.WMF OFFICE33.WMF OPTDISK.WMF OPTITAPE.WMF PRPHL002.WMF PRPHL003.WMF PRPHL004.WMF PRPHL005.WMF
PRPHL006.WMF PRPHL007.WMF PRPHL008.WMF PRPHL009.WMF PRPHL010.WMF PRPHL011.WMF PRPHL030.WMF PRPHL031.WMF PRPHL039.WMF PRPHL040.WMF

PRPHL041.WMF

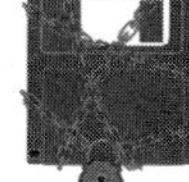
PRPHL048.WMF

PRPHL049.WMF

PRPHL050.WMF

PRPHL051.WMF

PRPHL053.WMF

PRPHL054.WMF

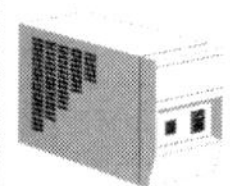
PWRSUPLY.WMF

REELTAPE.WMF

STRW001D.WMF

VIDDISC.WMF

Computers (COMPUTER) • Miscellaneous (MISC)

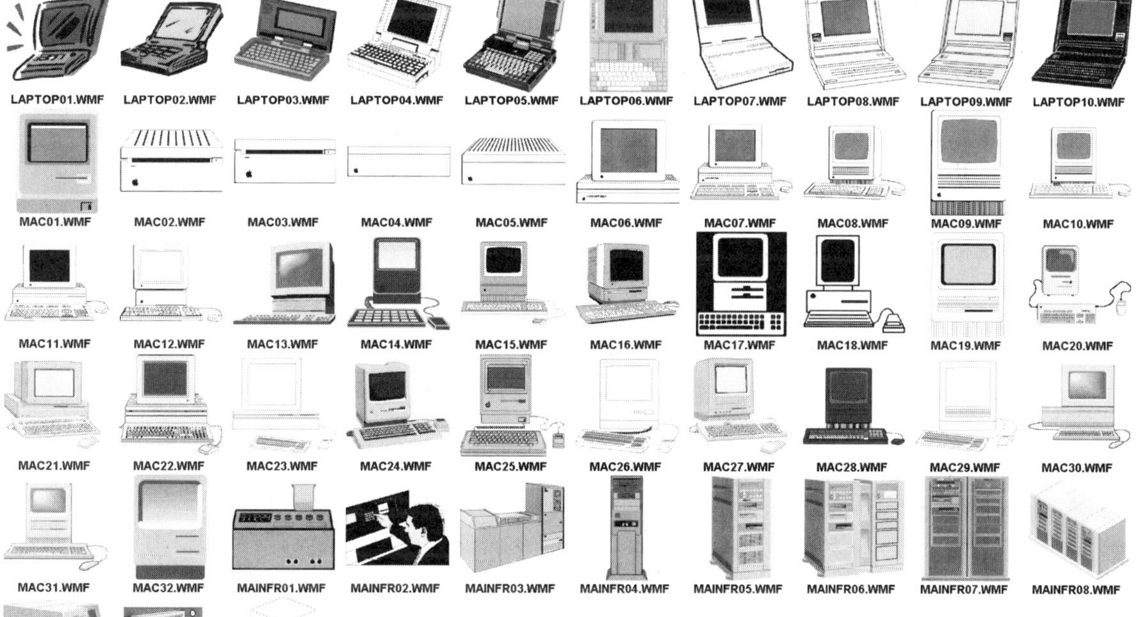
LAPTOP01.WMF LAPTOP02.WMF LAPTOP03.WMF LAPTOP04.WMF LAPTOP05.WMF LAPTOP06.WMF LAPTOP07.WMF LAPTOP08.WMF LAPTOP09.WMF LAPTOP10.WMF

MAC01.WMF MAC02.WMF MAC03.WMF MAC04.WMF MAC05.WMF MAC06.WMF MAC07.WMF MAC08.WMF MAC09.WMF MAC10.WMF

MAC11.WMF MAC12.WMF MAC13.WMF MAC14.WMF MAC15.WMF MAC16.WMF MAC17.WMF MAC18.WMF MAC19.WMF MAC20.WMF

MAC21.WMF MAC22.WMF MAC23.WMF MAC24.WMF MAC25.WMF MAC26.WMF MAC27.WMF MAC28.WMF MAC29.WMF MAC30.WMF

MAC31.WMF MAC32.WMF MAINFR01.WMF MAINFR02.WMF MAINFR03.WMF MAINFR04.WMF MAINFR05.WMF MAINFR06.WMF MAINFR07.WMF MAINFR08.WMF

MAINFR09.WMF

MAINFR10.WMF

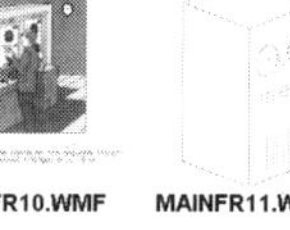
MAINFR11.WMF

0131COMC.WMF
0145KEYC.WMF
1609.WMF
1627.WMF
1628.WMF
1629.WMF
1679.WMF
1680.WMF
1681.WMF
1682.WMF
1684.WMF
1685.WMF
1686.WMF
1687.WMF
1692.WMF
1739.WMF
A37A.WMF
A37A2.WMF
BACK093.WMF
BARCODE.WMF
BIT0131.WMF
BIT0440.WMF
BIT0578.WMF
BIT0579.WMF
CHIP.WMF
CHIP20.WMF
CIRCTBD.WMF
CIRCTBD2.WMF
COMP010.WMF
COMP014.WMF
COMP026.WMF
COMP037.WMF
COMP051.WMF
COMP053.WMF
COMP064.WMF
COMP069.WMF
COMP070.WMF
COMP071.WMF
COMPTR2.WMF
COMPTR3.WMF
DIGIPNT.WMF
HANDSCAN.WMF
HND_KEY.WMF
HND_MOUS.WMF
ICONA03.WMF
INKEYBRD.WMF
INTERACT.WMF
K21173.WMF
KEY_DRAW.WMF
KEYIN1.WMF
LINO.WMF
M21263.WMF
M21269.WMF
MONITOR.WMF
MOUSE.WMF
OPTISTRG.WMF
POINTER.WMF
PRINT01.WMF
PRINT02.WMF
PRINT03.WMF
PRINT04.WMF
PRINT05.WMF
PRINT06.WMF
PRINT07.WMF
PRINT08.WMF
PRINT09.WMF
PRINT10.WMF
PRINT11.WMF
PRINT12.WMF
PRINT13.WMF
PRINT14.WMF
PRINT15.WMF
PRINT16.WMF
PRINT17.WMF
PRINT18.WMF
PRINT19.WMF
PRINT20.WMF
PRINT21.WMF
PRINT22.WMF
PRINT23.WMF
PRINT24.WMF
PRINT25.WMF
PRINT26.WMF
PRINT27.WMF
PRINT28.WMF
PRINT29.WMF
PRINT30.WMF
PRINT31.WMF
PRINT32.WMF
PRINT33.WMF
PRINT34.WMF
PRINT35.WMF
PRINT36.WMF
PRINT37.WMF
PRINT38.WMF
PRINT39.WMF
PRINT40.WMF
PRINT41.WMF
PRINT42.WMF
PRINT43.WMF
PRINT44.WMF
PRINT45.WMF
PRINT46.WMF
PRINT47.WMF
PRINT48.WMF
PRINT49.WMF
PRINT50.WMF
PRINT51.WMF
PRINT52.WMF
PRINT53.WMF
PRINT54.WMF
PRINT55.WMF
PRINT56.WMF
PRINT57.WMF
PRINT58.WMF
PRINT59.WMF
PRINT60.WMF
PRINT61.WMF
PRPHL001.WMF
PRPHL012.WMF

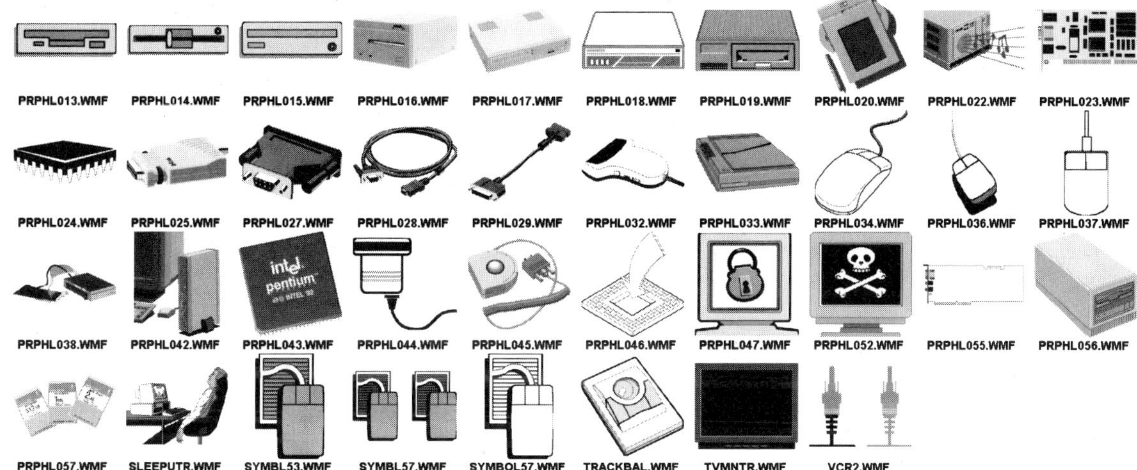
PRPHL013.WMF
PRPHL014.WMF
PRPHL015.WMF
PRPHL016.WMF
PRPHL017.WMF
PRPHL018.WMF
PRPHL019.WMF
PRPHL020.WMF
PRPHL022.WMF
PRPHL023.WMF
PRPHL024.WMF
PRPHL025.WMF
PRPHL027.WMF
PRPHL028.WMF
PRPHL029.WMF
PRPHL032.WMF
PRPHL033.WMF
PRPHL034.WMF
PRPHL036.WMF
PRPHL037.WMF
PRPHL038.WMF
PRPHL042.WMF
intel
pentium
PRPHL043.WMF
PRPHL044.WMF
PRPHL045.WMF
PRPHL046.WMF
PRPHL047.WMF
PRPHL052.WMF
PRPHL055.WMF
PRPHL056.WMF
PRPHL057.WMF
SLEEPUTR.WMF
SYMBL53.WMF
SYMBL57.WMF
SYMBOL57.WMF
TRACKBAL.WMF
TVMNTR.WMF
VCR2.WMF

0130COMC.WMF
1622.WMF
1625.WMF
1630.WMF
1678.WMF
1683.WMF
1690.WMF
1691.WMF
1696.WMF
1730.WMF
1771.WMF
4115.WMF
4345.WMF
4401.WMF
4402.WMF
AVLAB.WMF
BCKGRD57.WMF
BIT1008.WMF
BIT1009.WMF
BLACK_PC.WMF
BSNSS077.WMF
BSNSS149.WMF
BUSI028M.WMF
BUSI187D.WMF
BUSI201D.WMF
C20804.WMF
C_MPUTER.WMF
CLEANRM.WMF
COM_ABC.WMF
COM_NETW.WMF
COM_PERI.WMF
COM_TERM.WMF
COMP001.WMF
COMP003.WMF
COMP004.WMF
COMP005.WMF
COMP007.WMF
COMP01.WMF
COMP011.WMF
COMP012.WMF
COMP013.WMF
COMP016.WMF
COMP017.WMF
COMP018.WMF
COMP019.WMF
COMP02.WMF
COMP020.WMF
COMP021.WMF
COMP022.WMF
COMP023.WMF
COMP024.WMF
COMP025.WMF
COMP028.WMF
COMP029.WMF
COMP03.WMF
COMP030.WMF
COMP031.WMF
COMP032.WMF
COMP033.WMF
COMP034.WMF
COMP035.WMF
COMP036.WMF
COMP039.WMF
COMP045.WMF
COMP046.WMF
COMP047.WMF
COMP048.WMF
COMP049.WMF
COMP052.WMF
COMP055.WMF
COMP057.WMF
COMP06.WMF
COMP063.WMF
COMP065.WMF
COMP066.WMF
COMP067.WMF
COMP068.WMF
COMP1.WMF
COMP3.WMF
COMP_DIA.WMF
COMPTR8.WMF
COMPUTER.WMF
COMTR22.WMF
CT05.WMF
DESKPUB.WMF
DESKTOP8.WMF
GRAPHICS.WMF
HALFBW.WMF
IBM.WMF
IBM_PC.WMF
LAN.WMF
LAPTOP2.WMF
MODEMSYM.WMF
MONITOR.WMF
MONITOR1.WMF
NET01.WMF
NEXT.WMF
OVERCOMP.WMF
PC.WMF
PC2.WMF
PC29.WMF
PC_DESK.WMF
PCDSKTOP.WMF
PCSYML.WMF
PCTOWER.WMF
PGBRDR12.WMF
PLAN006.WMF
PLAN007.WMF
PLAN008.WMF
PLAN010.WMF
PRPHL021.WMF
PS2CMPTR.WMF
REMOTWRK.WMF
SERVBURE.WMF
SERVER1.WMF
SERVER3.WMF
SYMBL53.WMF
SYMBL58.WMF
SYMBOL58.WMF
WDPRCSR.WMF

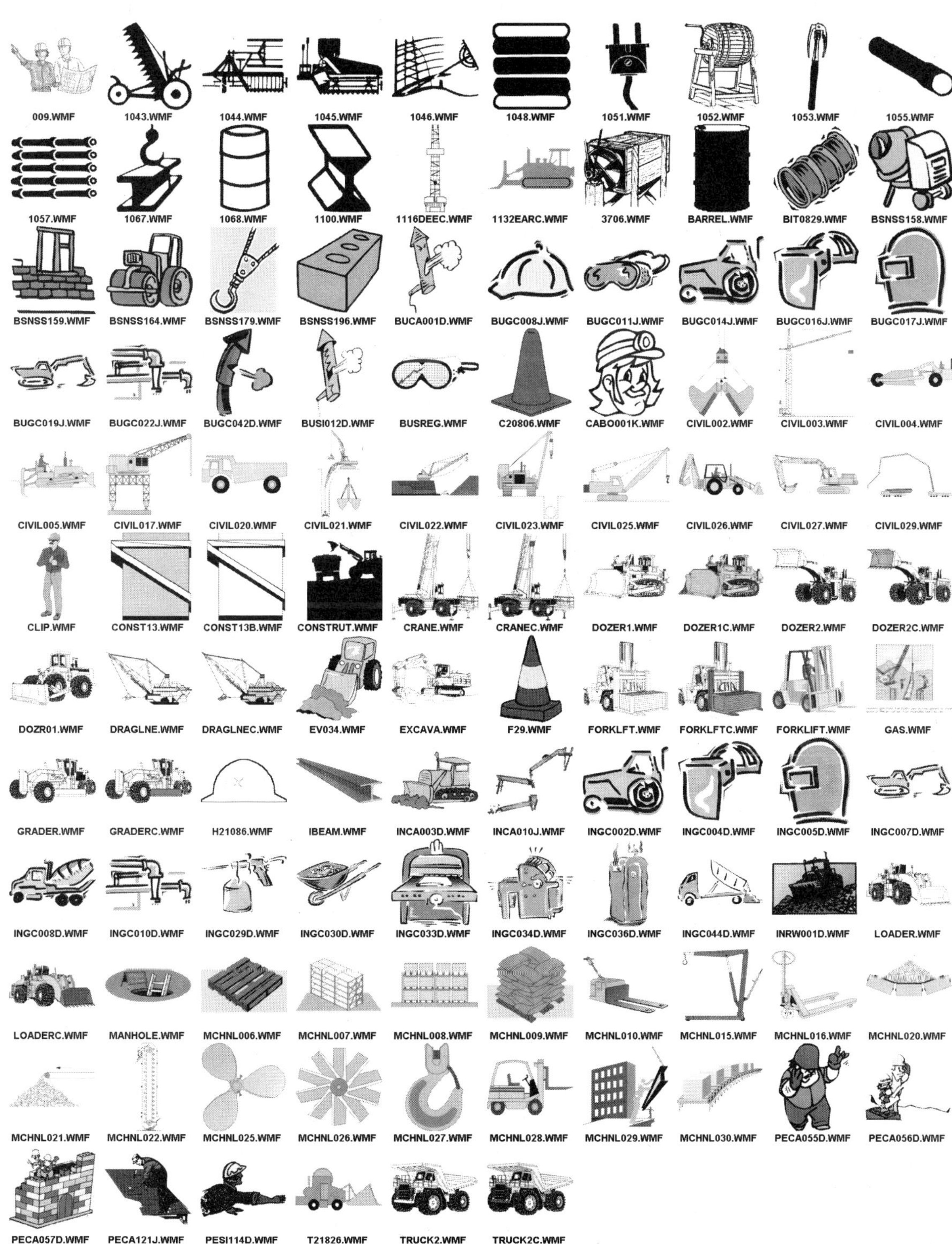
009.WMF 1043.WMF 1044.WMF 1045.WMF 1046.WMF 1048.WMF 1051.WMF 1052.WMF 1053.WMF 1055.WMF
1057.WMF 1067.WMF 1068.WMF 1100.WMF 1116DEEC.WMF 1132EARC.WMF 3706.WMF BARREL.WMF BIT0829.WMF BSNSS158.WMF
BSNSS159.WMF BSNSS164.WMF BSNSS179.WMF BSNSS196.WMF BUCA001D.WMF BUGC008J.WMF BUGC011J.WMF BUGC014J.WMF BUGC016J.WMF BUGC017J.WMF
BUGC019J.WMF BUGC022J.WMF BUGC042D.WMF BUSI012D.WMF BUSREG.WMF C20806.WMF CABO001K.WMF CIVIL002.WMF CIVIL003.WMF CIVIL004.WMF
CIVIL005.WMF CIVIL017.WMF CIVIL020.WMF CIVIL021.WMF CIVIL022.WMF CIVIL023.WMF CIVIL025.WMF CIVIL026.WMF CIVIL027.WMF CIVIL029.WMF
CLIP.WMF CONST13.WMF CONST13B.WMF CONSTRUT.WMF CRANE.WMF CRANEC.WMF DOZER1.WMF DOZER1C.WMF DOZER2.WMF DOZER2C.WMF
DOZR01.WMF DRAGLNE.WMF DRAGLNEC.WMF EV034.WMF EXCAVA.WMF F29.WMF FORKLFT.WMF FORKLFTC.WMF FORKLIFT.WMF GAS.WMF
GRADER.WMF GRADERC.WMF H21086.WMF IBEAM.WMF INCA003D.WMF INCA010J.WMF INGC002D.WMF INGC004D.WMF INGC005D.WMF INGC007D.WMF
INGC008D.WMF INGC010D.WMF INGC029D.WMF INGC030D.WMF INGC033D.WMF INGC034D.WMF INGC036D.WMF INGC044D.WMF INRW001D.WMF LOADER.WMF
LOADERC.WMF MANHOLE.WMF MCHNL006.WMF MCHNL007.WMF MCHNL008.WMF MCHNL009.WMF MCHNL010.WMF MCHNL015.WMF MCHNL016.WMF MCHNL020.WMF
MCHNL021.WMF MCHNL022.WMF MCHNL025.WMF MCHNL026.WMF MCHNL027.WMF MCHNL028.WMF MCHNL029.WMF MCHNL030.WMF PECA055D.WMF PECA056D.WMF
PECA057D.WMF PECA121J.WMF PESI114D.WMF T21826.WMF TRUCK2.WMF TRUCK2C.WMF

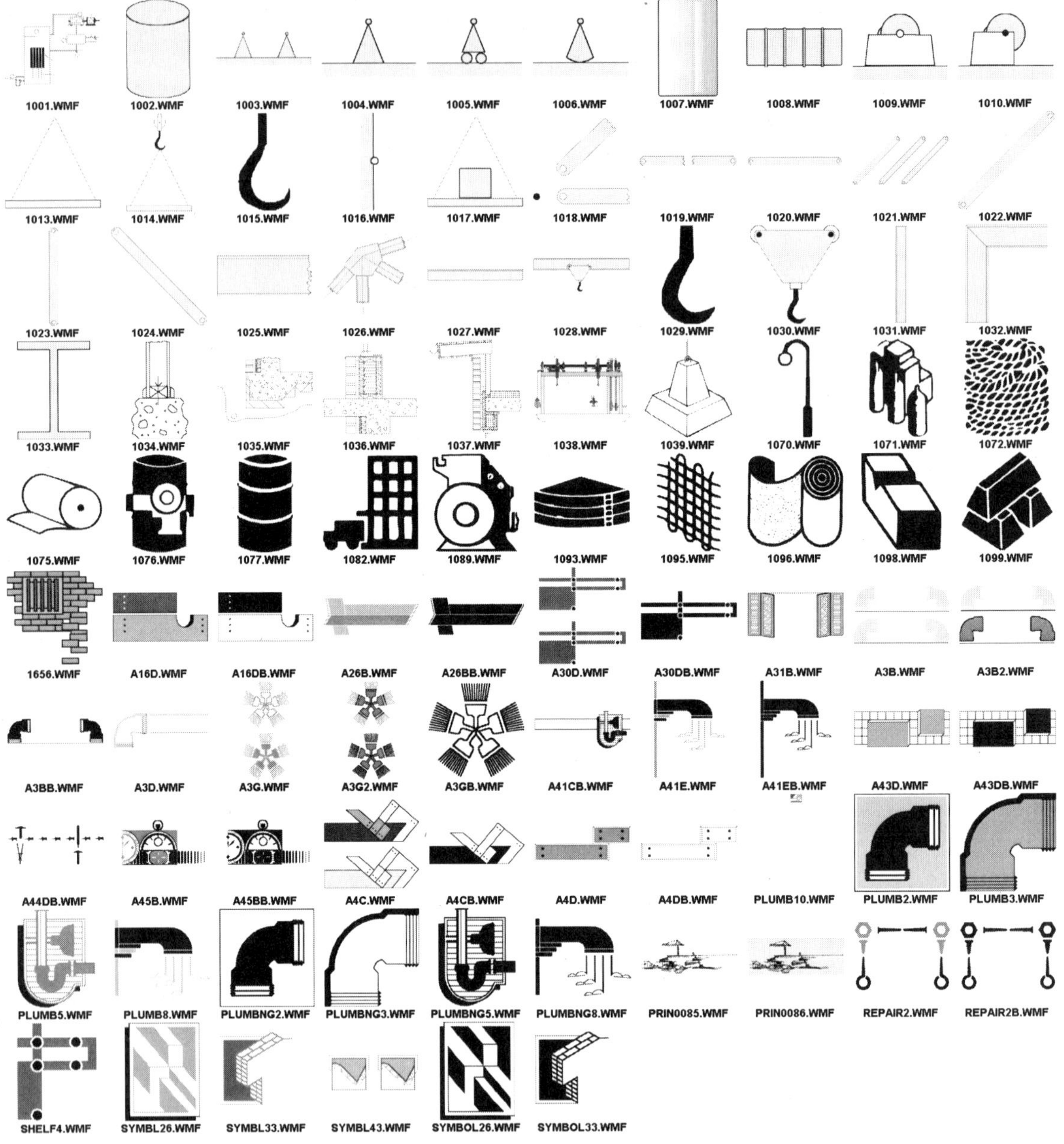
1001.WMF
1002.WMF
1003.WMF
1004.WMF
1005.WMF
1006.WMF
1007.WMF
1008.WMF
1009.WMF
1010.WMF
1013.WMF
1014.WMF
1015.WMF
1016.WMF
1017.WMF
1018.WMF
1019.WMF
1020.WMF
1021.WMF
1022.WMF
1023.WMF
1024.WMF
1025.WMF
1026.WMF
1027.WMF
1028.WMF
1029.WMF
1030.WMF
1031.WMF
1032.WMF
1033.WMF
1034.WMF
1035.WMF
1036.WMF
1037.WMF
1038.WMF
1039.WMF
1070.WMF
1071.WMF
1072.WMF
1075.WMF
1076.WMF
1077.WMF
1082.WMF
1089.WMF
1093.WMF
1095.WMF
1096.WMF
1098.WMF
1099.WMF
1656.WMF
A16D.WMF
A16DB.WMF
A26B.WMF
A26BB.WMF
A30D.WMF
A30DB.WMF
A31B.WMF
A3B.WMF
A3B2.WMF
A3BB.WMF
A3D.WMF
A3G.WMF
A3G2.WMF
A3GB.WMF
A41CB.WMF
A41E.WMF
A41EB.WMF
A43D.WMF
A43DB.WMF
A44DB.WMF
A45B.WMF
A45BB.WMF
A4C.WMF
A4CB.WMF
A4D.WMF
A4DB.WMF
PLUMB10.WMF
PLUMB2.WMF
PLUMB3.WMF
PLUMB5.WMF
PLUMB8.WMF
PLUMBNG2.WMF
PLUMBNG3.WMF
PLUMBNG5.WMF
PLUMBNG8.WMF
PRIN0085.WMF
PRIN0086.WMF
REPAIR2.WMF
REPAIR2B.WMF
SHELF4.WMF
SYMBL26.WMF
SYMBL33.WMF
SYMBL43.WMF
SYMBOL26.WMF
SYMBOL33.WMF

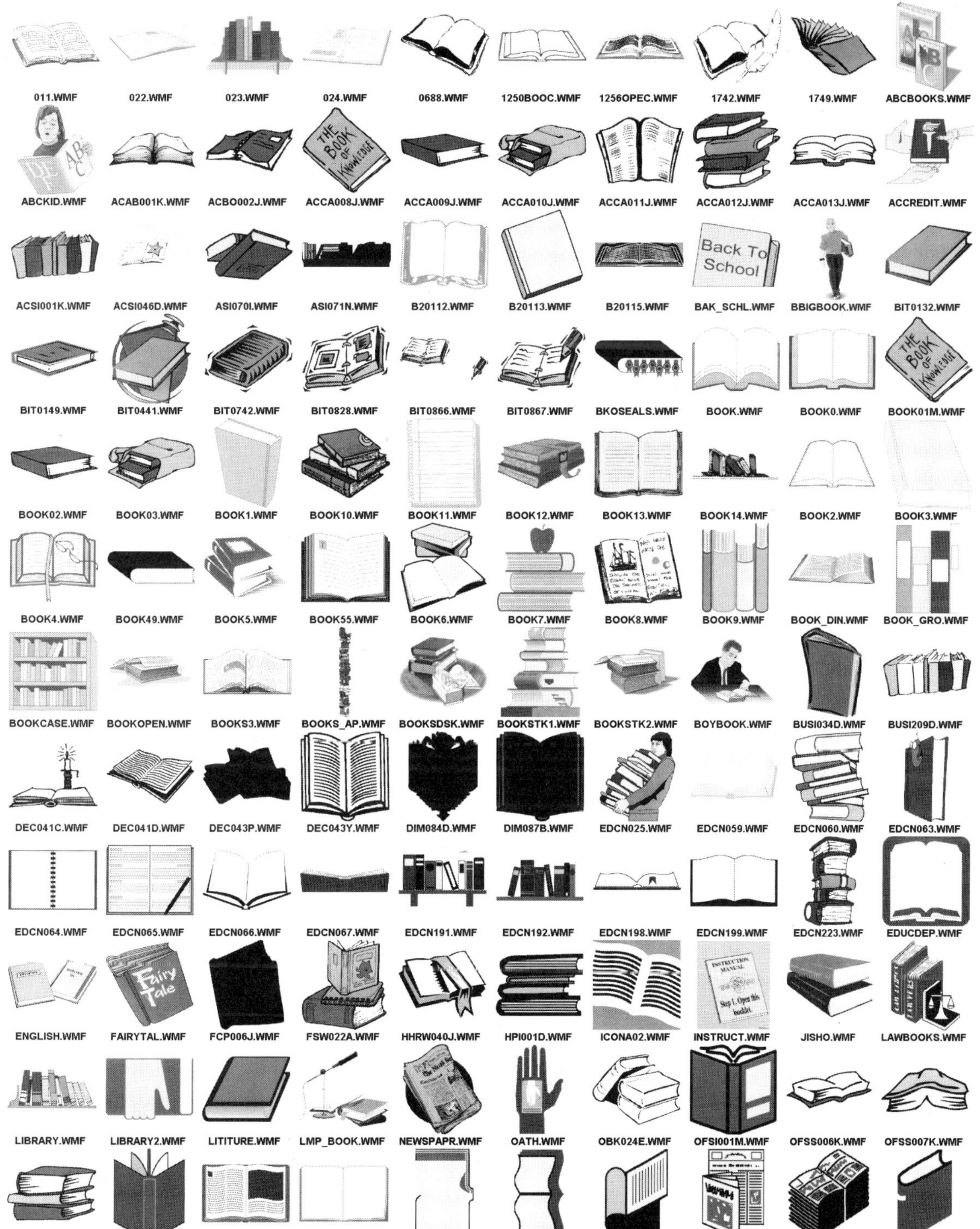
011.WMF
022.WMF
023.WMF
024.WMF
0688.WMF
1250BOOC.WMF
1256OPEC.WMF
1742.WMF
1749.WMF
ABCBOOKS.WMF
ABCKID.WMF
ACAB001K.WMF
ACBO002J.WMF
ACCA008J.WMF
ACCA009J.WMF
ACCA010J.WMF
ACCA011J.WMF
ACCA012J.WMF
ACCA013J.WMF
ACCREDIT.WMF
ACSI001K.WMF
ACSI046D.WMF
ASI070I.WMF
ASI071N.WMF
B20112.WMF
B20113.WMF
B20115.WMF
BAK_SCHL.WMF
BBIGBOOK.WMF
BIT0132.WMF
BIT0149.WMF
BIT0441.WMF
BIT0742.WMF
BIT0828.WMF
BIT0866.WMF
BIT0867.WMF
BKOSEALS.WMF
BOOK.WMF
BOOK0.WMF
BOOK01M.WMF
BOOK02.WMF
BOOK03.WMF
BOOK1.WMF
BOOK10.WMF
BOOK11.WMF
BOOK12.WMF
BOOK13.WMF
BOOK14.WMF
BOOK2.WMF
BOOK3.WMF
BOOK4.WMF
BOOK49.WMF
BOOK5.WMF
BOOK55.WMF
BOOK6.WMF
BOOK7.WMF
BOOK8.WMF
BOOK9.WMF
BOOK_DIN.WMF
BOOK_GRO.WMF
BOOKCASE.WMF
BOOKOPEN.WMF
BOOKS3.WMF
BOOKS_AP.WMF
BOOKSDSK.WMF
BOOKSTK1.WMF
BOOKSTK2.WMF
BOYBOOK.WMF
BUSI034D.WMF
BUSI209D.WMF
DEC041C.WMF
DEC041D.WMF
DEC043P.WMF
DEC043Y.WMF
DIM084D.WMF
DIM087B.WMF
EDCN025.WMF
EDCN059.WMF
EDCN060.WMF
EDCN063.WMF
EDCN064.WMF
EDCN065.WMF
EDCN066.WMF
EDCN067.WMF
EDCN191.WMF
EDCN192.WMF
EDCN198.WMF
EDCN199.WMF
EDCN223.WMF
EDUCDEP.WMF
ENGLISH.WMF
FAIRYTAL.WMF
FCP006J.WMF
FSW022A.WMF
HHRW040J.WMF
HPI001D.WMF
ICONA02.WMF
INSTRUCT.WMF
JISHO.WMF
LAWBOOKS.WMF
LIBRARY.WMF
LIBRARY2.WMF
LITITURE.WMF
LMP_BOOK.WMF
NEWSPAPR.WMF
OATH.WMF
OBK024E.WMF
OFSI001M.WMF
OFSS006K.WMF
OFSS007K.WMF
OFSS008K.WMF
OPENBOOK.WMF
OPNBOOK.WMF
OPNBOOK2.WMF
PD042XCU.WMF
PD042YCU.WMF
PD042ZCU.WMF
PD043ACU.WMF
PD043BCU.WMF
PD043CCU.WMF

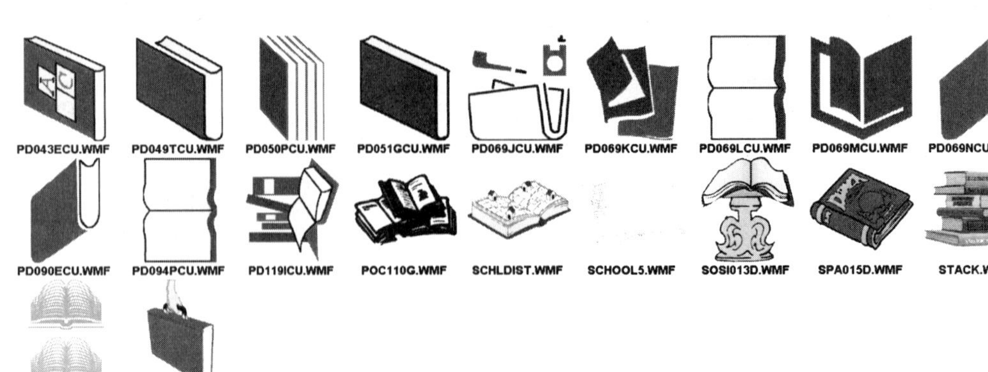
PD043ECU.WMF
PD049TCU.WMF
PD050PCU.WMF
PD051GCU.WMF
PD069JCU.WMF
PD069KCU.WMF
PD069LCU.WMF
PD069MCU.WMF
PD069NCU.WMF
PD069OCU.WMF
PD090ECU.WMF
PD094PCU.WMF
PD119ICU.WMF
POC110G.WMF
SCHLDIST.WMF
SCHOOL5.WMF
SOSI013D.WMF
SPA015D.WMF
STACK.WMF
STUDY2.WMF
SYMBL51.WMF
VOCA_ED.WMF

1756.WMF
1757.WMF
1MOUSE_W.WMF
1WORM_PR.WMF
2MOUSE_W.WMF
2WORM_PR.WMF
3WORM_PR.WMF
A20009.WMF
ACCA001J.WMF
ACCA007J.WMF
ACCA015J.WMF
ACSI005D.WMF
APPLE_BO.WMF
APPLEFOR.WMF
APPLENOT.WMF
BACKTOSC.WMF
BLACKBRD.WMF
BOARD.WMF
BOOKBAGS.WMF
BOOKPILE.WMF
CALCULAT.WMF
CHALKBO1.WMF
CLASS.WMF
CRAM.WMF
DEMONIC.WMF
DESKBOUN.WMF
DRIVER.WMF
DUNCE.WMF
EDCN001.WMF
EDCN002.WMF
EDCN003.WMF
EDCN061.WMF
EDCN062.WMF
EDCN087.WMF
EDCN091.WMF
EDCN092.WMF
EDCN093.WMF
EDCN095.WMF
EDCN096.WMF
EDCN098.WMF
EDCN099.WMF
EDCN102.WMF
EDCN103.WMF
EDCN105.WMF
EDCN107.WMF
EDCN108.WMF
EDCN109.WMF
EDCN110.WMF
EDCN111.WMF
EDCN112.WMF
EDRILL.WMF
ENSI012D.WMF
FCHILD.WMF
FROG_MEA.WMF
GRADUATE.WMF
HARRIED.WMF
HEARNGEX.WMF
HM.WMF
HOMEWORK.WMF
JUVENILE.WMF
LATCLASS.WMF
LEARNING.WMF
MORON.WMF
ORCHESTR.WMF
OS03.WMF
OS04.WMF
OS06.WMF
OS09.WMF
OS10.WMF
OS11.WMF
OS12.WMF
OS14.WMF
OS15.WMF
OS20.WMF
OS21.WMF
OSS05.WMF
PADDLING.WMF
POWER.WMF
PULLING.WMF
SCHLKIDS.WMF
SCHOOL.WMF
SCHOOL10.WMF
SCHOOL17.WMF
SCHOOL18.WMF
SCHOOL3.WMF
SCHOOL9.WMF
SCHOOLGI.WMF
SCHOOLS.WMF
SCOLOUT.WMF
SCOLOUTC.WMF
STRCTCHR.WMF
STUDEN01.WMF
TAKETEST.WMF
TEACHE01.WMF
TEACHERC.WMF
TEXTSCOL.WMF
THINKING.WMF

0700.WMF ADJOURN.WMF ADS073B.WMF ADS073O.WMF APPLEBRD.WMF ATEACHER.WMF BACKSCHL.WMF BLACKBRD.WMF BUSI156D.WMF C20776.WMF

CHALK4.WMF CHALKB.WMF CHALKBOA.WMF CHALKE.WMF CHEAT.WMF CHLBRD01.WMF CLASS1.WMF CSTUDENT.WMF DESK.WMF DOING.WMF

EDCN004.WMF EDCN005.WMF EDCN010.WMF EDCN011.WMF EDCN012.WMF EDCN014.WMF EDCN015.WMF EDCN016.WMF EDCN017.WMF EDCN018.WMF

EDCN019.WMF EDCN020.WMF EDCN021.WMF EDCN023.WMF EDCN024.WMF EDCN026.WMF EDCN027.WMF EDCN028.WMF EDCN029.WMF EDCN101.WMF

EDCN124.WMF EDCN125.WMF EDCN126.WMF EDCN129.WMF EDCN156.WMF ENAB002K.WMF FSW022C.WMF FSW022E.WMF GIRL_ON_.WMF GIRLBRD.WMF

GRADING.WMF HOLDING.WMF HOMEWORK.WMF HTEACH.WMF KIDS0.WMF KIDS14.WMF KIDS2.WMF KIDS_CO1.WMF KIDS_COM.WMF LANGUAGE.WMF

LIBRYSCN.WMF MAJORITY.WMF MARKINGP.WMF MINORITY.WMF NOTE.WMF PD005JCU.WMF PD005KCU.WMF PD005LCU.WMF PD005MCU.WMF PD005NCU.WMF

PD005OCU.WMF PD005PCU.WMF PD005QCU.WMF PD005RCU.WMF PD005SCU.WMF PD005VCU.WMF PD005WCU.WMF PD005YCU.WMF READGIRL.WMF REPORT.WMF

S21698.WMF S21723.WMF SCH002C.WMF SCHCLOCK.WMF SCHOOL.WMF SCHOOL0.WMF SCHOOL11.WMF SCHOOL16.WMF SCHOOL19.WMF SCHOOL21.WMF

SCHOOL41.WMF SCHOOL42.WMF SCHOOL_H.WMF SCHOOL_T.WMF SEI002A.WMF SEI003A.WMF SEI018A.WMF SEI018B.WMF SEI032B.WMF SQUINT.WMF

STUDNT1.WMF STUDNT10.WMF STUDNT2.WMF STUDNT3.WMF STUDNT5.WMF STUDNT9.WMF SUDDEN.WMF TAKING.WMF TALKING.WMF TEACH.WMF

TEACHERF.WMF TEACHERS.WMF TEACHR1.WMF TEACHR2.WMF TEACHR4.WMF TEACHR6.WMF TEACHR7.WMF TEACHR8.WMF THEORY.WMF UNVRSITY.WMF

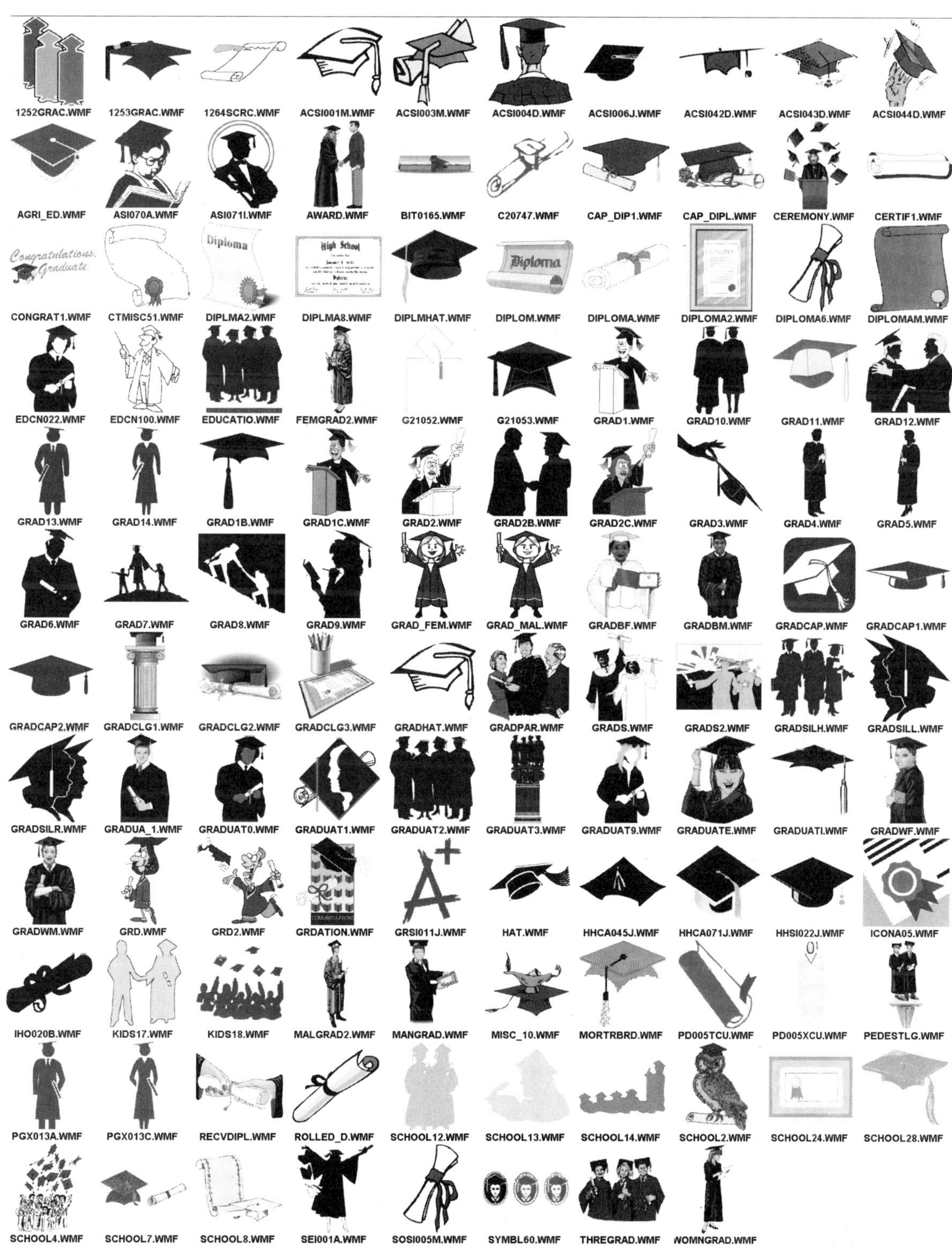
1252GRAC.WMF
1253GRAC.WMF
1264SCRC.WMF
ACSI001M.WMF
ACSI003M.WMF
ACSI004D.WMF
ACSI006J.WMF
ACSI042D.WMF
ACSI043D.WMF
ACSI044D.WMF
AGRI_ED.WMF
ASI070A.WMF
ASI071I.WMF
AWARD.WMF
BIT0165.WMF
C20747.WMF
CAP_DIP1.WMF
CAP_DIPL.WMF
CEREMONY.WMF
CERTIF1.WMF
Congratulations, Graduate
CONGRAT1.WMF
CTMISC51.WMF
Diploma
DIPLMA2.WMF
High School
DIPLMA8.WMF
DIPLMHAT.WMF
Diploma
DIPLOM.WMF
DIPLOMA.WMF
DIPLOMA2.WMF
DIPLOMA6.WMF
DIPLOMAM.WMF
EDCN022.WMF
EDCN100.WMF
EDUCATIO.WMF
FEMGRAD2.WMF
G21052.WMF
G21053.WMF
GRAD1.WMF
GRAD10.WMF
GRAD11.WMF
GRAD12.WMF
GRAD13.WMF
GRAD14.WMF
GRAD1B.WMF
GRAD1C.WMF
GRAD2.WMF
GRAD2B.WMF
GRAD2C.WMF
GRAD3.WMF
GRAD4.WMF
GRAD5.WMF
GRAD6.WMF
GRAD7.WMF
GRAD8.WMF
GRAD9.WMF
GRAD_FEM.WMF
GRAD_MAL.WMF
GRADBF.WMF
GRADBM.WMF
GRADCAP.WMF
GRADCAP1.WMF
GRADCAP2.WMF
GRADCLG1.WMF
GRADCLG2.WMF
GRADCLG3.WMF
GRADHAT.WMF
GRADPAR.WMF
GRADS.WMF
GRADS2.WMF
GRADSILH.WMF
GRADSILL.WMF
GRADSILR.WMF
GRADUA_1.WMF
GRADUAT0.WMF
GRADUAT1.WMF
GRADUAT2.WMF
GRADUAT3.WMF
GRADUAT9.WMF
GRADUATE.WMF
GRADUATI.WMF
GRADWF.WMF
GRADWM.WMF
GRD.WMF
GRD2.WMF
CONGRATULATIONS
GRDATION.WMF
GRSI011J.WMF
HAT.WMF
HHCA045J.WMF
HHCA071J.WMF
HHSI022J.WMF
ICONA05.WMF
IHO020B.WMF
KIDS17.WMF
KIDS18.WMF
MALGRAD2.WMF
MANGRAD.WMF
MISC_10.WMF
MORTRBRD.WMF
PD005TCU.WMF
PD005XCU.WMF
PEDESTLG.WMF
PGX013A.WMF
PGX013C.WMF
RECVDIPL.WMF
ROLLED_D.WMF
SCHOOL12.WMF
SCHOOL13.WMF
SCHOOL14.WMF
SCHOOL2.WMF
SCHOOL24.WMF
SCHOOL28.WMF
SCHOOL4.WMF
SCHOOL7.WMF
SCHOOL8.WMF
SEI001A.WMF
SOSI005M.WMF
SYMBL60.WMF
THREGRAD.WMF
WOMNGRAD.WMF

1260SCHC.WMF 1263SCHC.WMF 1265SCRC.WMF 1266STAC.WMF ABC.WMF ABC_GRAY.WMF ABCKIDS.WMF ADULT_ED.WMF APLNEW.WMF ASI071H.WMF

ASI100A.WMF ASI100B.WMF ASI100J.WMF BACK_TO2.WMF BACK_TO3.WMF BACK_TO_.WMF BKCLAS1.WMF BKCLAS2.WMF BKSCHOL.WMF BKTOSCHL.WMF

CELEBRAT.WMF CHALKUPS.WMF CHECKMRK.WMF CONGRATU.WMF DEC043FF.WMF DECALIT.WMF DECAMTR.WMF DECILITR.WMF DIM085G.WMF DRIPPY_Q.WMF

EDCN006.WMF EDCN007.WMF EDCN008.WMF EDCN009.WMF EDCN030.WMF EDCN054.WMF EDCN055.WMF EDCN056.WMF EDCN057.WMF EDCN058.WMF

EDCN083.WMF EDCN084.WMF EDCN134.WMF EDCN142.WMF EDCN212.WMF EDCN230.WMF ELASTIC.WMF EXPRMNT1.WMF FAMLY009.WMF FOOT.WMF

FSW022D.WMF GALLON.WMF GIFTGR1.WMF GIFTSFOR.WMF GRADES.WMF GRADGIFT.WMF HANDCHLK.WMF HANDPEN1.WMF HECTOLIT.WMF HECTOMTR.WMF

HITBOOKS.WMF HITTHEBO.WMF ICP028C.WMF IHD029C.WMF INGC035D.WMF KIDS1.WMF KIDS8.WMF KILOLIT.WMF KILOMTR.WMF LITER.WMF

LNK_BLOT.WMF LUNCHSPC.WMF MATH.WMF MATH1.WMF MATH2.WMF MATH3.WMF MESSY_IN.WMF METER.WMF MILE.WMF MISC_21.WMF

MOD009B.WMF OBK015I.WMF OBK019G.WMF OTS038A.WMF OUNCE.WMF PECK.WMF PENCIL0.WMF PGX013E.WMF PINT.WMF PLYMTH.WMF

QUART.WMF QUILLINK.WMF RECESS.WMF SCH019D.WMF SCH025B.WMF SCH027B.WMF SCHLBD.WMF SCHOLHDG.WMF SCHOLSPL.WMF SCHOLSU2.WMF

SCHOOL34.WMF SCHOOL35.WMF SCHOOL38.WMF SCHOOL40.WMF SCOLLAG3.WMF SEI001B.WMF SEI002B.WMF SEI003B.WMF SEI010B.WMF SRVIVHDG.WMF

STGC010D.WMF STGC013D.WMF TEACHER1.WMF TEACHER2.WMF TEACHERM.WMF TESTSCOR.WMF W21877.WMF W21886.WMF WRTNTLS.WMF YARD.WMF

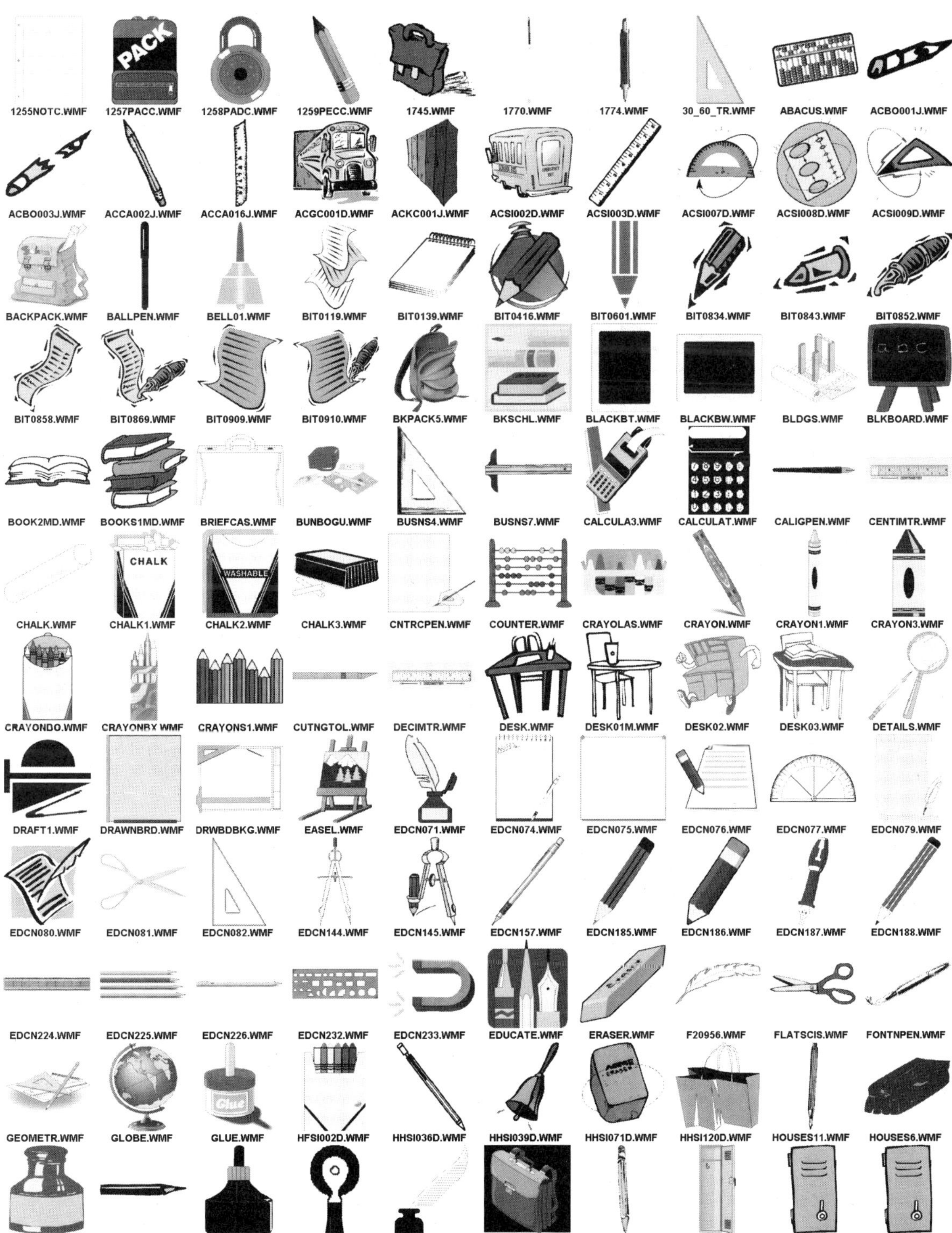
1255NOTC.WMF
1257PACC.WMF
1258PADC.WMF
1259PECC.WMF
1745.WMF
1770.WMF
1774.WMF
30_60_TR.WMF
ABACUS.WMF
ACBO001J.WMF
ACBO003J.WMF
ACCA002J.WMF
ACCA016J.WMF
ACGC001D.WMF
ACKC001J.WMF
ACSI002D.WMF
ACSI003D.WMF
ACSI007D.WMF
ACSI008D.WMF
ACSI009D.WMF
BACKPACK.WMF
BALLPEN.WMF
BELL01.WMF
BIT0119.WMF
BIT0139.WMF
BIT0416.WMF
BIT0601.WMF
BIT0834.WMF
BIT0843.WMF
BIT0852.WMF
BIT0858.WMF
BIT0869.WMF
BIT0909.WMF
BIT0910.WMF
BKPACK5.WMF
BKSCHL.WMF
BLACKBT.WMF
BLACKBW.WMF
BLDGS.WMF
BLKBOARD.WMF
BOOK2MD.WMF
BOOKS1MD.WMF
BRIEFCAS.WMF
BUNBOGU.WMF
BUSNS4.WMF
BUSNS7.WMF
CALCULA3.WMF
CALCULAT.WMF
CALIGPEN.WMF
CENTIMTR.WMF
CHALK.WMF
CHALK1.WMF
CHALK2.WMF
CHALK3.WMF
CNTRCPEN.WMF
COUNTER.WMF
CRAYOLAS.WMF
CRAYON.WMF
CRAYON1.WMF
CRAYON3.WMF
CRAYONDO.WMF
CRAYONBX.WMF
CRAYONS1.WMF
CUTNGTOL.WMF
DECIMTR.WMF
DESK.WMF
DESK01M.WMF
DESK02.WMF
DESK03.WMF
DETAILS.WMF
DRAFT1.WMF
DRAWNBRD.WMF
DRWBDBKG.WMF
EASEL.WMF
EDCN071.WMF
EDCN074.WMF
EDCN075.WMF
EDCN076.WMF
EDCN077.WMF
EDCN079.WMF
EDCN080.WMF
EDCN081.WMF
EDCN082.WMF
EDCN144.WMF
EDCN145.WMF
EDCN157.WMF
EDCN185.WMF
EDCN186.WMF
EDCN187.WMF
EDCN188.WMF
EDCN224.WMF
EDCN225.WMF
EDCN226.WMF
EDCN232.WMF
EDCN233.WMF
EDUCATE.WMF
ERASER.WMF
F20956.WMF
FLATSCIS.WMF
FONTNPEN.WMF
GEOMETR.WMF
GLOBE.WMF
GLUE.WMF
HFSI002D.WMF
HHSI036D.WMF
HHSI039D.WMF
HHSI071D.WMF
HHSI120D.WMF
HOUSES11.WMF
HOUSES6.WMF
HOUSES7.WMF
HSEHLD22.WMF
INK.WMF
INKERASR.WMF
INKQUILL.WMF
KNAPSACK.WMF
LEADPNCL.WMF
LOCKER.WMF
LOCKER01.WMF
LOCKER1M.WMF

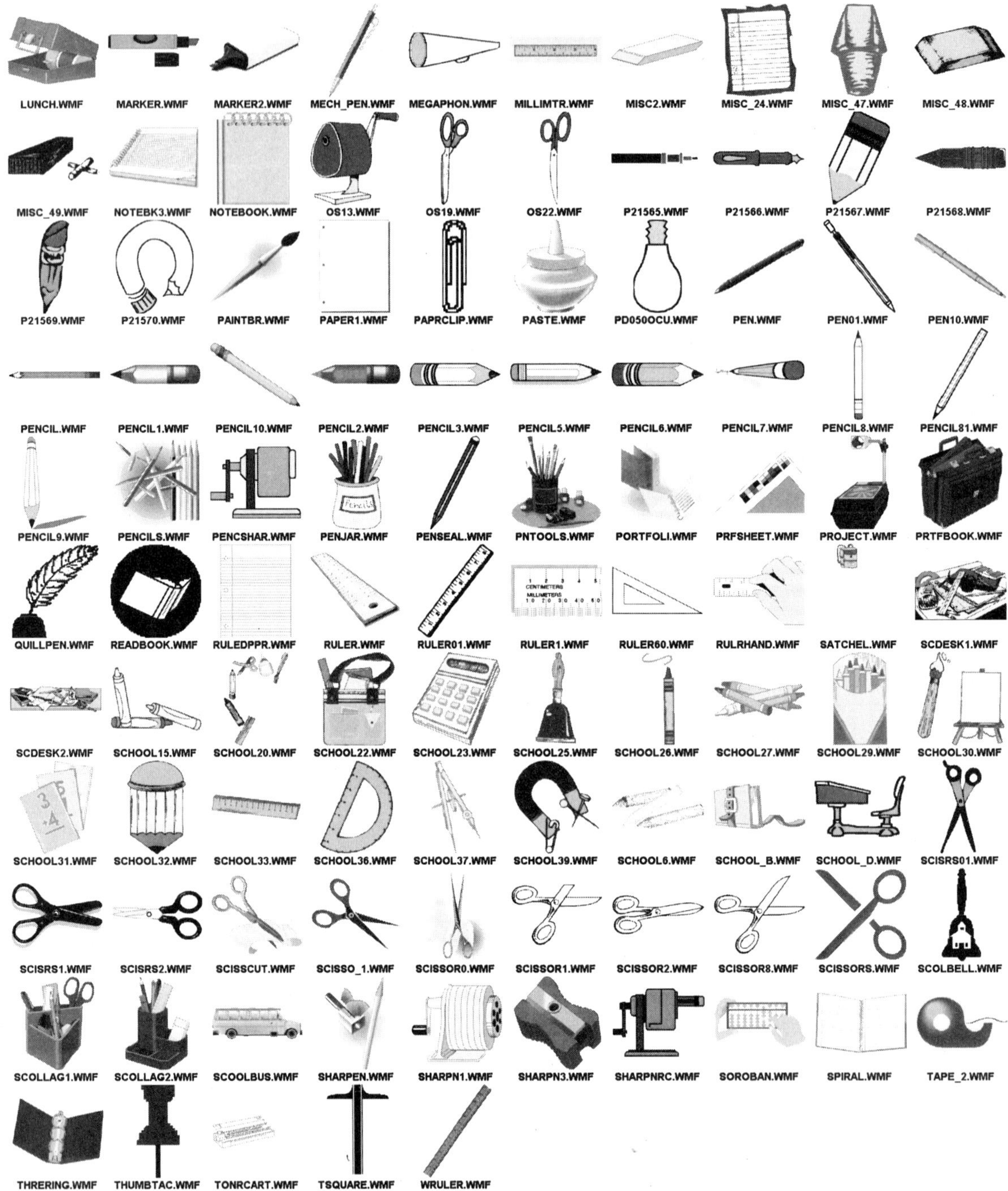
LUNCH.WMF
MARKER.WMF
MARKER2.WMF
MECH_PEN.WMF
MEGAPHON.WMF
MILLIMTR.WMF
MISC2.WMF
MISC_24.WMF
MISC_47.WMF
MISC_48.WMF
MISC_49.WMF
NOTEBK3.WMF
NOTEBOOK.WMF
OS13.WMF
OS19.WMF
OS22.WMF
P21565.WMF
P21566.WMF
P21567.WMF
P21568.WMF
P21569.WMF
P21570.WMF
PAINTBR.WMF
PAPER1.WMF
PAPRCLIP.WMF
PASTE.WMF
PD0500CU.WMF
PEN.WMF
PEN01.WMF
PEN10.WMF
PENCIL.WMF
PENCIL1.WMF
PENCIL10.WMF
PENCIL2.WMF
PENCIL3.WMF
PENCIL5.WMF
PENCIL6.WMF
PENCIL7.WMF
PENCIL8.WMF
PENCIL81.WMF
PENCIL9.WMF
PENCILS.WMF
PENCSHAR.WMF
PENJAR.WMF
PENSEAL.WMF
PNTOOLS.WMF
PORTFOLI.WMF
PRFSHEET.WMF
PROJECT.WMF
PRTFBOOK.WMF
QUILLPEN.WMF
READBOOK.WMF
RULEDPPR.WMF
RULER.WMF
RULER01.WMF
RULER1.WMF
RULER60.WMF
RULRHAND.WMF
SATCHEL.WMF
SCDESK1.WMF
SCDESK2.WMF
SCHOOL15.WMF
SCHOOL20.WMF
SCHOOL22.WMF
SCHOOL23.WMF
SCHOOL25.WMF
SCHOOL26.WMF
SCHOOL27.WMF
SCHOOL29.WMF
SCHOOL30.WMF
SCHOOL31.WMF
SCHOOL32.WMF
SCHOOL33.WMF
SCHOOL36.WMF
SCHOOL37.WMF
SCHOOL39.WMF
SCHOOL6.WMF
SCHOOL_B.WMF
SCHOOL_D.WMF
SCISRS01.WMF
SCISRS1.WMF
SCISRS2.WMF
SCISSCUT.WMF
SCISSO_1.WMF
SCISSOR0.WMF
SCISSOR1.WMF
SCISSOR2.WMF
SCISSOR8.WMF
SCISSORS.WMF
SCOLBELL.WMF
SCOLLAG1.WMF
SCOLLAG2.WMF
SCOOLBUS.WMF
SHARPEN.WMF
SHARPN1.WMF
SHARPN3.WMF
SHARPNRC.WMF
SOROBAN.WMF
SPIRAL.WMF
TAPE_2.WMF
THRERING.WMF
THUMBTAC.WMF
TONRCART.WMF
TSQUARE.WMF
WRULER.WMF

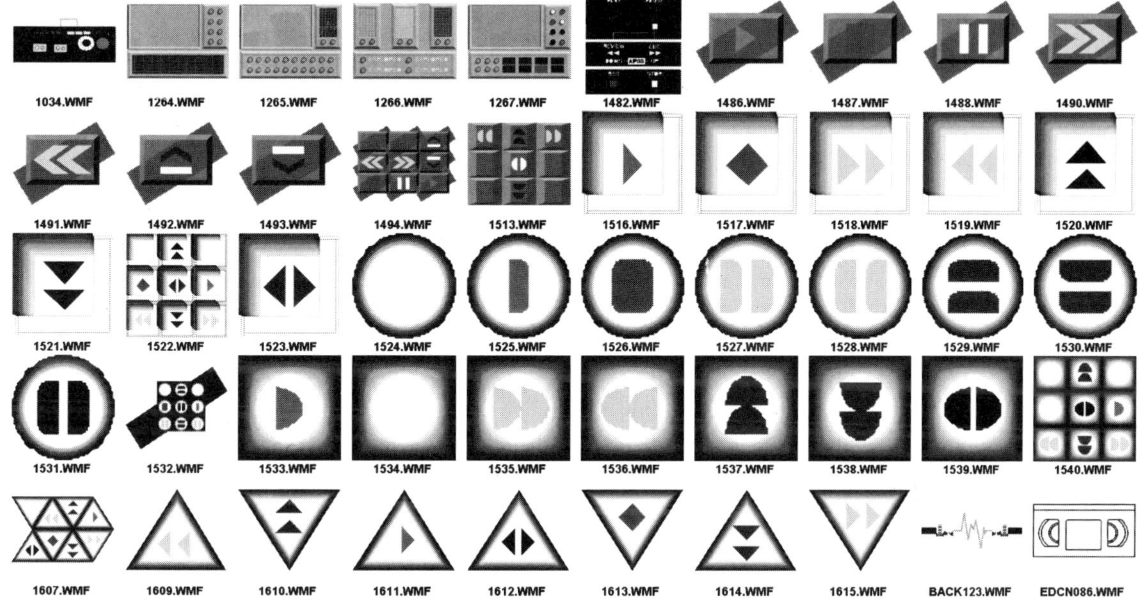
1034.WMF
1264.WMF
1265.WMF
1266.WMF
1267.WMF
1482.WMF
1486.WMF
1487.WMF
1488.WMF
1490.WMF
1491.WMF
1492.WMF
1493.WMF
1494.WMF
1513.WMF
1516.WMF
1517.WMF
1518.WMF
1519.WMF
1520.WMF
1521.WMF
1522.WMF
1523.WMF
1524.WMF
1525.WMF
1526.WMF
1527.WMF
1528.WMF
1529.WMF
1530.WMF
1531.WMF
1532.WMF
1533.WMF
1534.WMF
1535.WMF
1536.WMF
1537.WMF
1538.WMF
1539.WMF
1540.WMF
1607.WMF
1609.WMF
1610.WMF
1611.WMF
1612.WMF
1613.WMF
1614.WMF
1615.WMF
BACK123.WMF
EDCN086.WMF

1484.WMF
1485.WMF
1735.WMF
1736.WMF
4109.WMF
4412.WMF
4424.WMF
4428.WMF
4456.WMF
4457.WMF
4465.WMF
4467.WMF
A37BB.WMF
A3A.WMF
A3F.WMF
ANSMACH.WMF
ANSRMACH.WMF
AUDIOSYS.WMF
BIT0365.WMF
BIT0463.WMF
BIT1001.WMF
BIT1001B.WMF
BIT1003.WMF
BIT1010.WMF
BORD605.WMF
BSNSS190.WMF
BUGC060D.WMF
BUSI001D.WMF
BUSI003D.WMF
BUSI005D.WMF
BUSI044D.WMF
C20756.WMF
CABLE.WMF
CAMCORD3.WMF
CAMCORDR.WMF
CAMCRDR2.WMF
CAMERA2.WMF
CASETTE.WMF
CASSETTE.WMF
CASSPLAY.WMF
CDCASPLA.WMF
CELTELE2.WMF
CORDLESS.WMF
CTMISC23.WMF
EDCN070.WMF
ELECTRO1.WMF
ENCA001J.WMF
ENGC001D.WMF
ENGC007D.WMF
ENGC016D.WMF
ENGC018D.WMF
ENGC021D.WMF
ENGC022D.WMF
ENKC001J.WMF
ENSI018D.WMF
ENSS011D.WMF
EQ02.WMF
HDPHONES.WMF
HEADPHON.WMF
HHCA005J.WMF
HHCA025J.WMF
HHGC094D.WMF
HHRW037J.WMF
HHRW056J.WMF
HHSI067D.WMF
HPI001E.WMF
INCA001J.WMF
INDTY1.WMF
LOUDMUSC.WMF
LOUDSPKR.WMF
MCROPHN.WMF
MIC.WMF
MIKE1.WMF
MIKE2.WMF
MIKE3.WMF
MIKEDIZ.WMF
MIKEYELL.WMF
OVERHEAD.WMF
PAGER.WMF
PHONE2.WMF
PWRSTRIP.WMF
R21620.WMF
RADIOMUS.WMF
RPLAYER1.WMF
RPLAYER2.WMF
RPLAYER3.WMF
RPLAYER4.WMF
SIREN6.WMF
STEREO.WMF
STEREO1.WMF
STEREO2.WMF
STEREO3.WMF
STEREO7.WMF
STEREOSP.WMF
STERO.WMF
STERO3.WMF
TELEPHON.WMF
TVMONITR.WMF
VCR.WMF
VCR2B.WMF
VCR3.WMF
VCR3B.WMF
VCRTAPE.WMF
VIDEO.WMF
WALKMAN.WMF
WALKMAN3.MF

0018.WMF
0039.WMF
2801.WMF
4200.WMF
ACSI002M.WMF
B20125.WMF
BACK135.WMF
BACK170.WMF
BDCA006J.WMF
BDCA007J.WMF
BDRW002J.WMF
BDSI013J.WMF
BLNKBADG.WMF
BLURIBON.WMF
COPPER.WMF
D20870.WMF
EDCN227.WMF
EDCN228.WMF
EDCN234.WMF
EDCN235.WMF
EDCN236.WMF
EDCN237.WMF
EDCN238.WMF
EDCN239.WMF
EDCN240.WMF
EDCN241.WMF
EDCN242.WMF
EDCN243.WMF
EDCN244.WMF
EDCN245.WMF
EDCN246.WMF
EDCN247.WMF
EDCN248.WMF
EDCN249.WMF
EDCN250.WMF
EDCN251.WMF
EDCN252.WMF
EDCN253.WMF
EDCN254.WMF
EDCN255.WMF
EDCN256.WMF
EDCN257.WMF
EDCN258.WMF
EDCN259.WMF
EDCN260.WMF
EDCN261.WMF
EDCN262.WMF
EDCN263.WMF
EDCN264.WMF
EDCN265.WMF
EDCN266.WMF
EDCN267.WMF
EDCN268.WMF
EDCN269.WMF
EDCN270.WMF
EDCN271.WMF
EDCN272.WMF
EDCN273.WMF
EMBLEM01.WMF
F21009.WMF
F21010.WMF
F21011.WMF
F21012.WMF
F21013.WMF
GASI052M.WMF
GASI134M.WMF
GASI140M.WMF
GRPHC055.WMF
GRPHC114.WMF
GRPHC115.WMF
GRPHC116.WMF
GRSI131J.WMF
GRSI157J.WMF
HAMPTON.WMF
HLDAY021.WMF
INTRSTAT.WMF
KNIGHTCR.WMF
M21245.WMF
MOD001J.WMF
MOD017E.WMF
MODOO11.WMF
NACA011J.WMF
NACA141J.WMF
NASS009J.WMF
O21540.WMF
PB19.WMF
PH43.WMF
PLAQUE.WMF
SHIELD01.WMF
SHIELD02.WMF
SHIELD03.WMF
SHIELD04.WMF
SHIELD05.WMF
SHIELD06.WMF
SHIELD07.WMF
SHIELD08.WMF
SHIELD09.WMF
SHIELD10.WMF
SHIELD11.WMF
SHIELD12.WMF
SHIELD13.WMF
SHIELD14.WMF
SHIELD15.WMF
SHIELD16.WMF
SHIELD17.WMF
SHIELD18.WMF
SHIELD19.WMF
SHIELD2.WMF
SHIELD20.WMF
SHIELD21.WMF
SHIELD22.WMF
SHIELD23.WMF
SHIELD24.WMF
SHIELD25.WMF
SHIELD26.WMF
SHIELD27.WMF
SHLD01.WMF
SHLD02.WMF
SHLD03.WMF
SHLD04.WMF

SHLD05.WMF
SHLD06.WMF
SHLD07.WMF
SHLD08.WMF
SHLD09.WMF
SHLD10.WMF
SHLD11.WMF
SHLD12.WMF
SHLD13.WMF
SHLD14.WMF
SHLD15.WMF
SHLD16.WMF
SHLD17.WMF
SOSI210D.WMF
SOSI211D.WMF
W21901.WMF
W21902.WMF
W21903.WMF
W21904.WMF

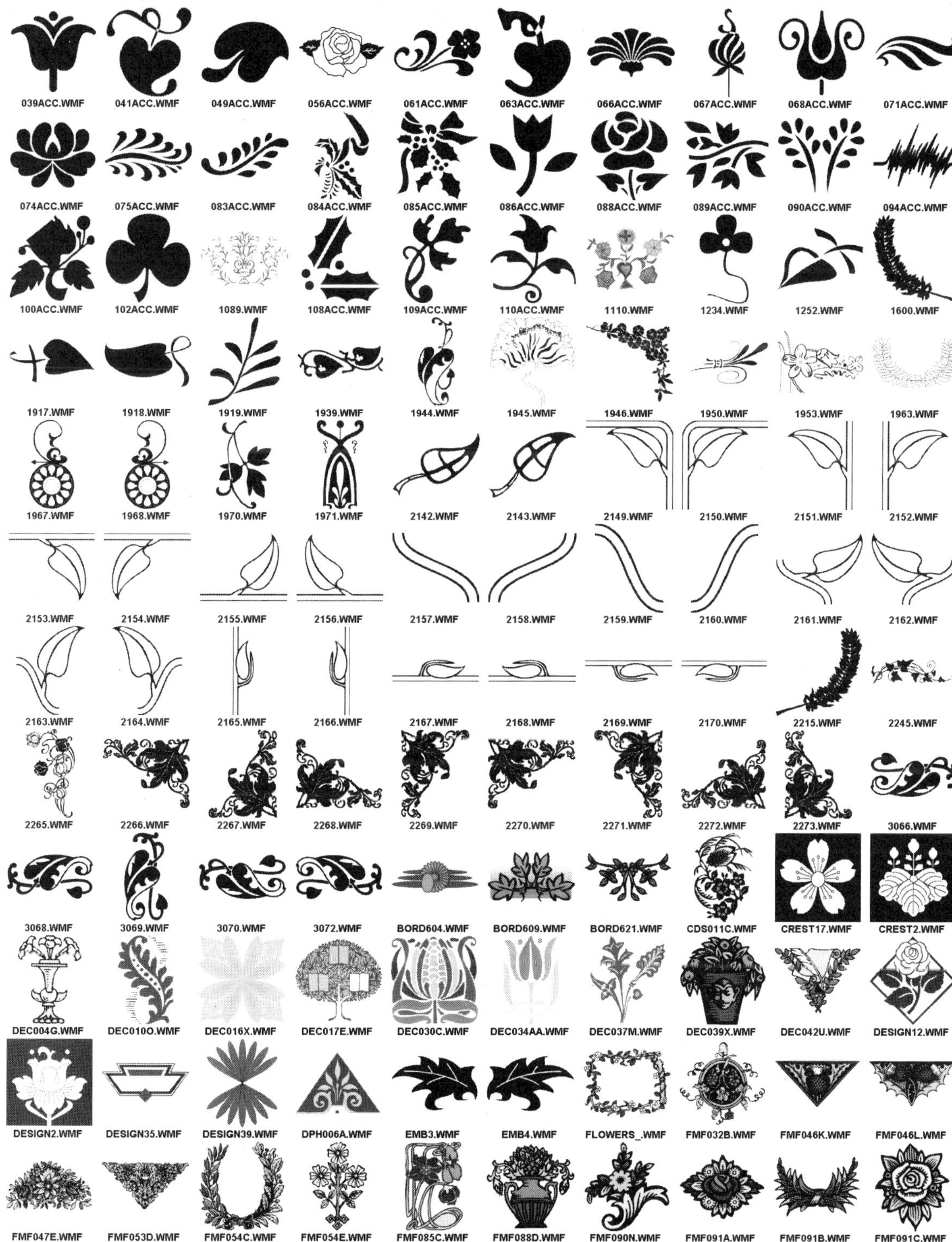
039ACC.WMF 041ACC.WMF 049ACC.WMF 056ACC.WMF 061ACC.WMF 063ACC.WMF 066ACC.WMF 067ACC.WMF 068ACC.WMF 071ACC.WMF
074ACC.WMF 075ACC.WMF 083ACC.WMF 084ACC.WMF 085ACC.WMF 086ACC.WMF 088ACC.WMF 089ACC.WMF 090ACC.WMF 094ACC.WMF
100ACC.WMF 102ACC.WMF 1089.WMF 108ACC.WMF 109ACC.WMF 110ACC.WMF 1110.WMF 1234.WMF 1252.WMF 1600.WMF
1917.WMF 1918.WMF 1919.WMF 1939.WMF 1944.WMF 1945.WMF 1946.WMF 1950.WMF 1953.WMF 1963.WMF
1967.WMF 1968.WMF 1970.WMF 1971.WMF 2142.WMF 2143.WMF 2149.WMF 2150.WMF 2151.WMF 2152.WMF
2153.WMF 2154.WMF 2155.WMF 2156.WMF 2157.WMF 2158.WMF 2159.WMF 2160.WMF 2161.WMF 2162.WMF
2163.WMF 2164.WMF 2165.WMF 2166.WMF 2167.WMF 2168.WMF 2169.WMF 2170.WMF 2215.WMF 2245.WMF
2265.WMF 2266.WMF 2267.WMF 2268.WMF 2269.WMF 2270.WMF 2271.WMF 2272.WMF 2273.WMF 3066.WMF
3068.WMF 3069.WMF 3070.WMF 3072.WMF BORD604.WMF BORD609.WMF BORD621.WMF CDS011C.WMF CREST17.WMF CREST2.WMF
DEC004G.WMF DEC010O.WMF DEC016X.WMF DEC017E.WMF DEC030C.WMF DEC034AA.WMF DEC037M.WMF DEC039X.WMF DEC042U.WMF DESIGN12.WMF
DESIGN2.WMF DESIGN35.WMF DESIGN39.WMF DPH006A.WMF EMB3.WMF EMB4.WMF FLOWERS_.WMF FMF032B.WMF FMF046K.WMF FMF046L.WMF
FMF047E.WMF FMF053D.WMF FMF054C.WMF FMF054E.WMF FMF085C.WMF FMF088D.WMF FMF090N.WMF FMF091A.WMF FMF091B.WMF FMF091C.WMF

FMF091D.WMF
FMF091F.WMF
FMF091G.WMF
FMF091H.WMF
FMF091I.WMF
FMF097D.WMF
FMF105D.WMF
FSD004A.WMF
FSD058A.WMF
FWD026A.WMF
FWD045B.WMF
GASI326D.WMF
GB34.WMF
GB35.WMF
GB37.WMF
GRSI124J.WMF
GRSI125J.WMF
GRSI158J.WMF
IHO016A.WMF
MDVL2DNG.WMF
MDVL2PTT.WMF
MIS0034A.WMF
MIS0040A.WMF
MIS0047A.WMF
MOD002E.WMF
MOD006E.WMF
MOD021E.WMF
MOD025J.WMF
MOD032C.WMF
MOD032I.WMF
MOD032J.WMF
MSL104A.WMF
MYN1PTTR.WMF
NASS125D.WMF
NV2DNGBT.WMF
OFL005F.WMF
OFL006Q.WMF
OFL007F.WMF
OFL007M.WMF
ORN_I.WMF
OXM016I.WMF
PD027MBW.WMF
PD027WBW.WMF
PH01.WMF
PH02.WMF
PH03.WMF
PH04.WMF
PH05.WMF
PH06.WMF
PH07.WMF
PH08.WMF
PH09.WMF
PH10.WMF
PH11.WMF
PH12.WMF
PH13.WMF
PH14.WMF
PH15.WMF
PH16.WMF
PH17.WMF
PH18.WMF
PH19.WMF
PH20.WMF
PH21.WMF
PH22.WMF
PH23.WMF
PH24.WMF
PH25.WMF
PH26.WMF
POC001P.WMF
POC094D.WMF
POC098G.WMF
POC098I.WMF
POC099F.WMF
POC102I.WMF
POC112F.WMF
ROM025I.WMF
SB23.WMF
SB24.WMF
SB29.WMF
SHAPE093.WMF
SHAPE277.WMF
SS11.WMF
SS15.WMF
SS18.WMF
SS19.WMF
SS20.WMF
SS21.WMF
SS22.WMF
SS23.WMF
SS24.WMF
SS25.WMF
SS26.WMF
SS27.WMF
SS28.WMF
SS29.WMF
SS30.WMF
SS31.WMF
SS32.WMF
SS37.WMF
SS38.WMF
SS42.WMF
TJP000AA.WMF
TOD019A.WMF
TOD019B.WMF
TOD019C.WMF
TOD019D.WMF
TOD020A.WMF
TOD020B.WMF
TOD020C.WMF
TOD021A.WMF
TOD021B.WMF
TOD021C.WMF
TOD021D.WMF
TOD023A.WMF
TOD053E.WMF
TSD016C.WMF
WA09.WMF
XDN007B.WMF
XDN011F.WMF

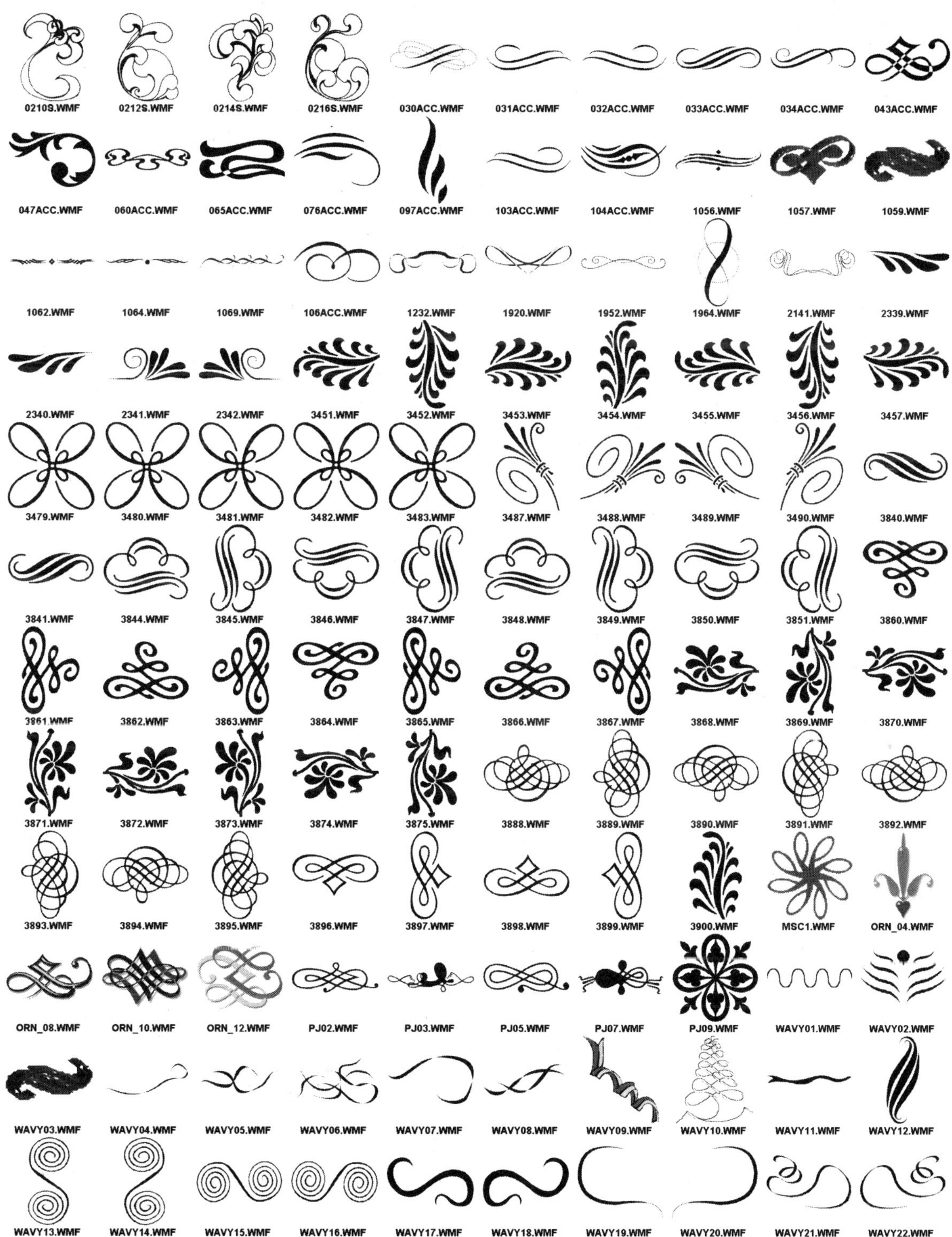
0210S.WMF
0212S.WMF
0214S.WMF
0216S.WMF
030ACC.WMF
031ACC.WMF
032ACC.WMF
033ACC.WMF
034ACC.WMF
043ACC.WMF
047ACC.WMF
060ACC.WMF
065ACC.WMF
076ACC.WMF
097ACC.WMF
103ACC.WMF
104ACC.WMF
1056.WMF
1057.WMF
1059.WMF
1062.WMF
1064.WMF
1069.WMF
106ACC.WMF
1232.WMF
1920.WMF
1952.WMF
1964.WMF
2141.WMF
2339.WMF
2340.WMF
2341.WMF
2342.WMF
3451.WMF
3452.WMF
3453.WMF
3454.WMF
3455.WMF
3456.WMF
3457.WMF
3479.WMF
3480.WMF
3481.WMF
3482.WMF
3483.WMF
3487.WMF
3488.WMF
3489.WMF
3490.WMF
3840.WMF
3841.WMF
3844.WMF
3845.WMF
3846.WMF
3847.WMF
3848.WMF
3849.WMF
3850.WMF
3851.WMF
3860.WMF
3861.WMF
3862.WMF
3863.WMF
3864.WMF
3865.WMF
3866.WMF
3867.WMF
3868.WMF
3869.WMF
3870.WMF
3871.WMF
3872.WMF
3873.WMF
3874.WMF
3875.WMF
3888.WMF
3889.WMF
3890.WMF
3891.WMF
3892.WMF
3893.WMF
3894.WMF
3895.WMF
3896.WMF
3897.WMF
3898.WMF
3899.WMF
3900.WMF
MSC1.WMF
ORN_04.WMF
ORN_08.WMF
ORN_10.WMF
ORN_12.WMF
PJ02.WMF
PJ03.WMF
PJ05.WMF
PJ07.WMF
PJ09.WMF
WAVY01.WMF
WAVY02.WMF
WAVY03.WMF
WAVY04.WMF
WAVY05.WMF
WAVY06.WMF
WAVY07.WMF
WAVY08.WMF
WAVY09.WMF
WAVY10.WMF
WAVY11.WMF
WAVY12.WMF
WAVY13.WMF
WAVY14.WMF
WAVY15.WMF
WAVY16.WMF
WAVY17.WMF
WAVY18.WMF
WAVY19.WMF
WAVY20.WMF
WAVY21.WMF
WAVY22.WMF

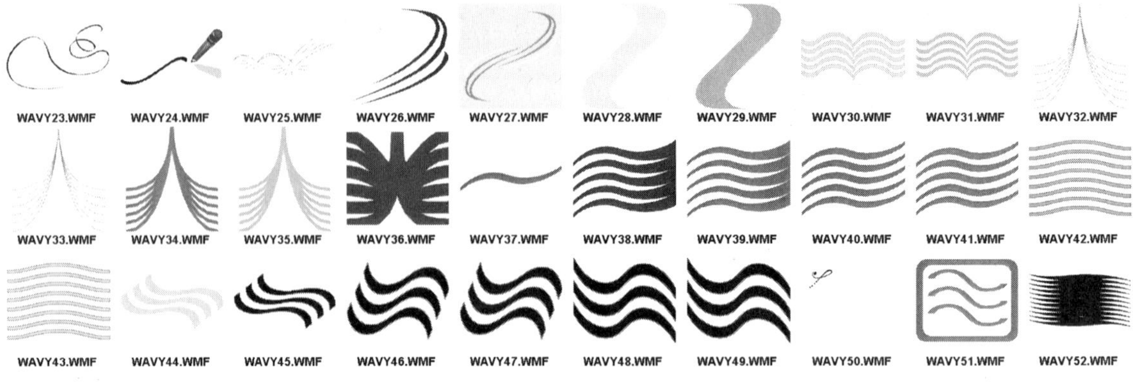

WAVY23.WMF WAVY24.WMF WAVY25.WMF WAVY26.WMF WAVY27.WMF WAVY28.WMF WAVY29.WMF WAVY30.WMF WAVY31.WMF WAVY32.WMF

WAVY33.WMF WAVY34.WMF WAVY35.WMF WAVY36.WMF WAVY37.WMF WAVY38.WMF WAVY39.WMF WAVY40.WMF WAVY41.WMF WAVY42.WMF

WAVY43.WMF WAVY44.WMF WAVY45.WMF WAVY46.WMF WAVY47.WMF WAVY48.WMF WAVY49.WMF WAVY50.WMF WAVY51.WMF WAVY52.WMF

WAVY53.WMF

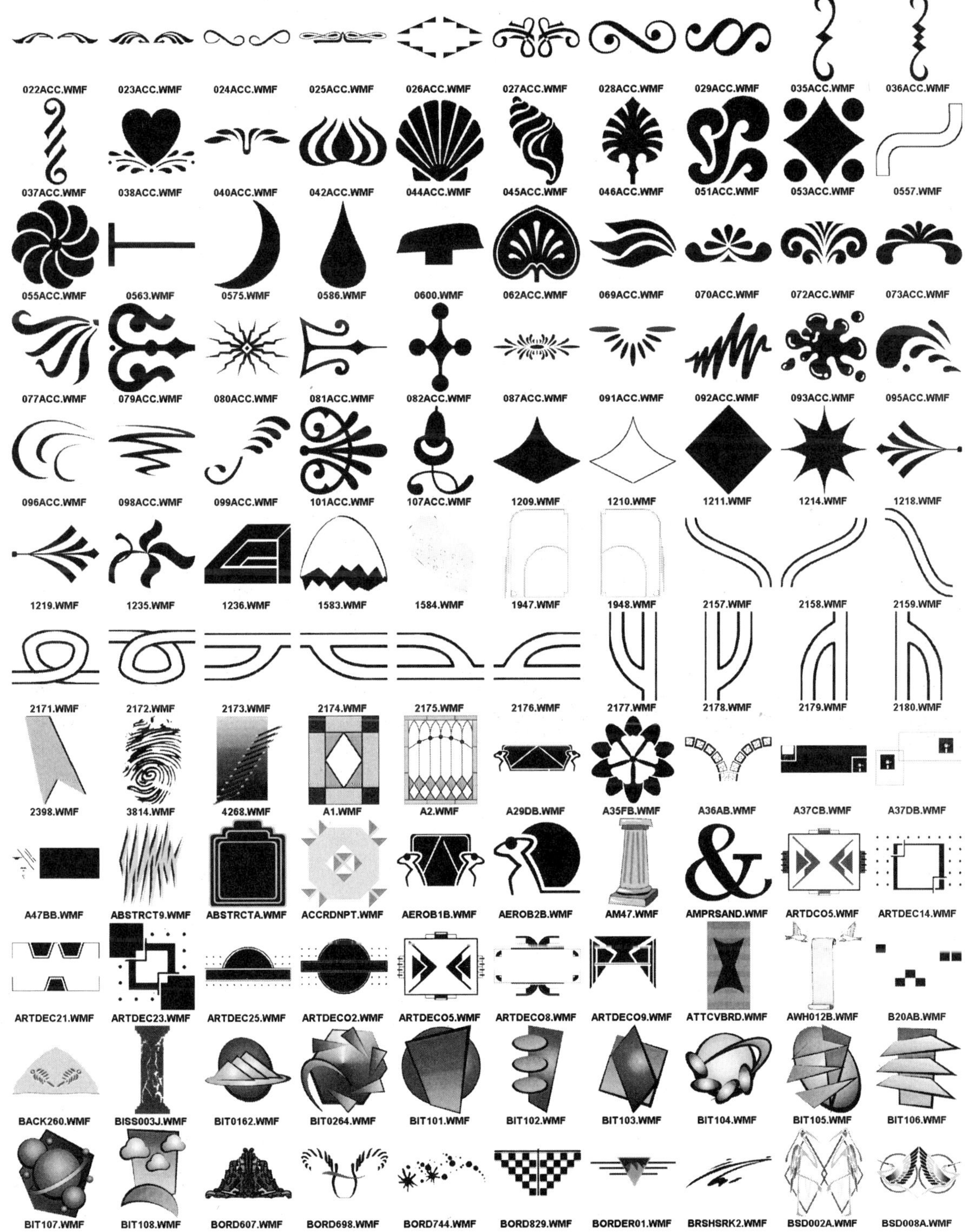
022ACC.WMF 023ACC.WMF 024ACC.WMF 025ACC.WMF 026ACC.WMF 027ACC.WMF 028ACC.WMF 029ACC.WMF 035ACC.WMF 036ACC.WMF
037ACC.WMF 038ACC.WMF 040ACC.WMF 042ACC.WMF 044ACC.WMF 045ACC.WMF 046ACC.WMF 051ACC.WMF 053ACC.WMF 0557.WMF
055ACC.WMF 0563.WMF 0575.WMF 0586.WMF 0600.WMF 062ACC.WMF 069ACC.WMF 070ACC.WMF 072ACC.WMF 073ACC.WMF
077ACC.WMF 079ACC.WMF 080ACC.WMF 081ACC.WMF 082ACC.WMF 087ACC.WMF 091ACC.WMF 092ACC.WMF 093ACC.WMF 095ACC.WMF
096ACC.WMF 098ACC.WMF 099ACC.WMF 101ACC.WMF 107ACC.WMF 1209.WMF 1210.WMF 1211.WMF 1214.WMF 1218.WMF
1219.WMF 1235.WMF 1236.WMF 1583.WMF 1584.WMF 1947.WMF 1948.WMF 2157.WMF 2158.WMF 2159.WMF
2171.WMF 2172.WMF 2173.WMF 2174.WMF 2175.WMF 2176.WMF 2177.WMF 2178.WMF 2179.WMF 2180.WMF
2398.WMF 3814.WMF 4268.WMF A1.WMF A2.WMF A29DB.WMF A35FB.WMF A36AB.WMF A37CB.WMF A37DB.WMF
A47BB.WMF ABSTRCT9.WMF ABSTRCTA.WMF ACCRDNPT.WMF AEROB1B.WMF AEROB2B.WMF AM47.WMF AMPRSAND.WMF ARTDCO5.WMF ARTDEC14.WMF
ARTDEC21.WMF ARTDEC23.WMF ARTDEC25.WMF ARTDECO2.WMF ARTDECO5.WMF ARTDECO8.WMF ARTDECO9.WMF ATTCVBRD.WMF AWH012B.WMF B20AB.WMF
BACK260.WMF BISS003J.WMF BIT0162.WMF BIT0264.WMF BIT101.WMF BIT102.WMF BIT103.WMF BIT104.WMF BIT105.WMF BIT106.WMF
BIT107.WMF BIT108.WMF BORD607.WMF BORD698.WMF BORD744.WMF BORD829.WMF BORDER01.WMF BRSHSRK2.WMF BSD002A.WMF BSD008A.WMF

BSD009A.WMF BSD010B.WMF BSD013B.WMF BSD030A.WMF BSD057B.WMF BSD060A.WMF BUTN005.WMF BUTN006.WMF CAA0346.WMF CDS002C.WMF

CDS007D.WMF CDS024E.WMF CHECKERF.WMF CHNS2DNG.WMF CHW050A.WMF CHW068A.WMF CHW092C.WMF CLSSCS10.WMF CLSSCS12.WMF CLSSCS20.WMF

CLSSCS21.WMF CLSSCS22.WMF CLSSCS23.WMF CLTC1DNG.WMF CLTC2DNG.WMF COLUMN01.WMF D28B.WMF D28BB.WMF D31D.WMF D31DB.WMF

DEC042DD.WMF DEC043J.WMF DEC061O.WMF DEC087W.WMF DEC088G.WMF DEC089G.WMF DECO30N.WMF DESIGN29.WMF DESIGN30.WMF DESIGN32.WMF

DIM103E.WMF DPH006C.WMF EAA081K.WMF EAC016Z.WMF EDCN152.WMF EGYPTN1P.WMF EMBSSD5D.WMF FDD114Q.WMF FLEUR01.WMF FLEUR02.WMF

FLEUR03.WMF FLEUR04.WMF FLEUR05.WMF FLEUR06.WMF FLEUR07.WMF FLEUR08.WMF FLEUR09.WMF FLEUR10.WMF FLEUR11.WMF FLEUR12.WMF

FLEUR13.WMF FLEUR14.WMF FLEUR15.WMF FLEUR16.WMF FMF084I.WMF FMI065F.WMF FREEFM6.WMF GAGC002D.WMF GASI240M.WMF GASI288D.WMF

GASI351M.WMF GASI397M.WMF GB41.WMF GB42.WMF GDO014E.WMF GDO020C.WMF GDO020J.WMF GDO020L.WMF GDO027H.WMF GOA022A.WMF

GOA023F.WMF GOA024G.WMF GOA077C.WMF GRBO016J.WMF GRPHC094.WMF GRSI141J.WMF GRSI142J.WMF GRSI160J.WMF HEART1.WMF HEART2.WMF

HEART3.WMF HEART5.WMF HRC268L.WMF HRC294O.WMF IIN010A.WMF IIN021A.WMF INC2PTTR.WMF ISP002B.WMF ISP002C.WMF ISP003A.WMF

ISP003B.WMF ISP004K.WMF ISP005C.WMF ISP005I.WMF ISP005J.WMF ISP008A.WMF ISP008B.WMF ISP008D.WMF ISP041A.WMF ISP041B.WMF

ISP041E.WMF ISP043A.WMF ISP043C.WMF ISP043E.WMF ISP043F.WMF ISP047B.WMF ISP047C.WMF ISP047G.WMF JPB093A.WMF LAC019C.WMF

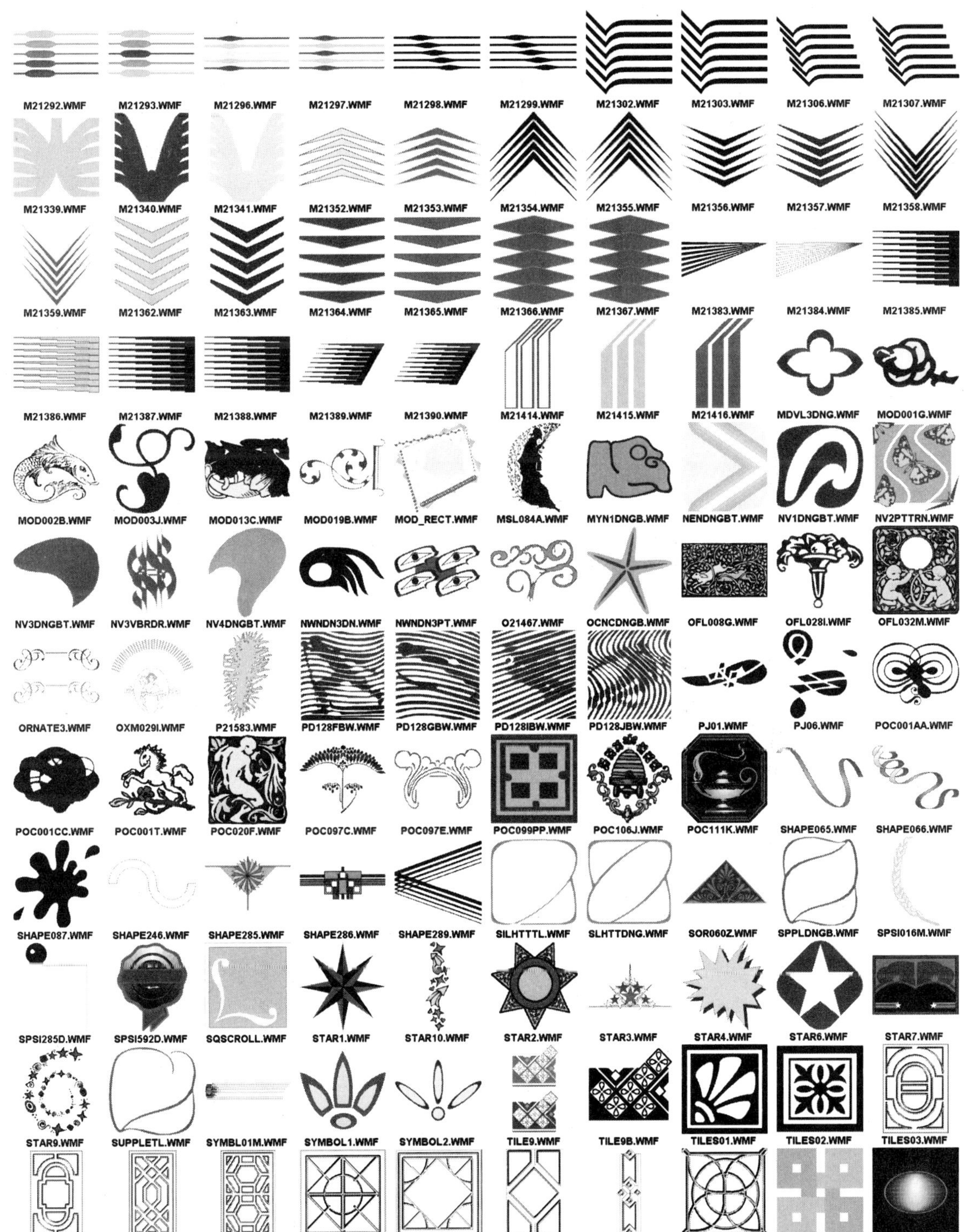
M21292.WMF M21293.WMF M21296.WMF M21297.WMF M21298.WMF M21299.WMF M21302.WMF M21303.WMF M21306.WMF M21307.WMF
M21339.WMF M21340.WMF M21341.WMF M21352.WMF M21353.WMF M21354.WMF M21355.WMF M21356.WMF M21357.WMF M21358.WMF
M21359.WMF M21362.WMF M21363.WMF M21364.WMF M21365.WMF M21366.WMF M21367.WMF M21383.WMF M21384.WMF M21385.WMF
M21386.WMF M21387.WMF M21388.WMF M21389.WMF M21390.WMF M21414.WMF M21415.WMF M21416.WMF MDVL3DNG.WMF MOD001G.WMF
MOD002B.WMF MOD003J.WMF MOD013C.WMF MOD019B.WMF MOD_RECT.WMF MSL084A.WMF MYN1DNGB.WMF NENDNGBT.WMF NV1DNGBT.WMF NV2PTTRN.WMF
NV3DNGBT.WMF NV3VBRDR.WMF NV4DNGBT.WMF NWNDN3DN.WMF NWNDN3PT.WMF O21467.WMF OCNCDNGB.WMF OFL008G.WMF OFL028I.WMF OFL032M.WMF
ORNATE3.WMF OXM029I.WMF P21583.WMF PD128FBW.WMF PD128GBW.WMF PD128IBW.WMF PD128JBW.WMF PJ01.WMF PJ06.WMF POC001AA.WMF
POC001CC.WMF POC001T.WMF POC020F.WMF POC097C.WMF POC097E.WMF POC099PP.WMF POC106J.WMF POC111K.WMF SHAPE065.WMF SHAPE066.WMF
SHAPE087.WMF SHAPE246.WMF SHAPE285.WMF SHAPE286.WMF SHAPE289.WMF SILHTTTL.WMF SLHTTDNG.WMF SOR060Z.WMF SPPLDNGB.WMF SPSI016M.WMF
SPSI285D.WMF SPSI592D.WMF SQSCROLL.WMF STAR1.WMF STAR10.WMF STAR2.WMF STAR3.WMF STAR4.WMF STAR6.WMF STAR7.WMF
STAR9.WMF SUPPLETL.WMF SYMBL01M.WMF SYMBOL1.WMF SYMBOL2.WMF TILE9.WMF TILE9B.WMF TILES01.WMF TILES02.WMF TILES03.WMF
TILES04.WMF TILES05.WMF TILES06.WMF TILES07.WMF TILES08.WMF TILES09.WMF TILES10.WMF TILES11.WMF TILES12.WMF TILES13.WMF

TILES14.WMF
TILES15.WMF
TILES16.WMF
TILES17.WMF
TILES18.WMF
TILES19.WMF
TILES20.WMF
TILES21.WMF
TILES22.WMF
TILES23.WMF
TILES24.WMF
TILES25.WMF
TILES26.WMF
TILES27.WMF
TILES28.WMF
TILES29.WMF
TILES30.WMF
TILES31.WMF
TILES32.WMF
TILES33.WMF
TILES34.WMF
TILES35.WMF
TILES36.WMF
TILES37.WMF
TILES38.WMF
TILES39.WMF
TILES40.WMF
TILES41.WMF
TILES42.WMF
TILES43.WMF
TILES44.WMF
TILES45.WMF
TILES46.WMF
TILES47.WMF
TILES48.WMF
TILES49.WMF
TILES50.WMF
TILES51.WMF
TILES52.WMF
TILES53.WMF
TILES54.WMF
TILES55.WMF
TILES56.WMF
TILES57.WMF
TILES58.WMF
TILES59.WMF
TILES60.WMF
TILES61.WMF
TJP000BA.WMF
TJP087A.WMF
TOD026D.WMF
TOD028A.WMF
TOD051DD.WMF
TOD093C.WMF
TOD093E.WMF
TOD093G.WMF
TOD093H.WMF
TOD093I.WMF
TOD093J.WMF
TOI013A.WMF
TOI056F.WMF
TOI061A.WMF
TORCHSYM.WMF
TSD007C.WMF
TSD011C.WMF
TSD036D.WMF
TVA001D.WMF
WA35.WMF
WMG039L.WMF
YOKE.WMF
ZGZGDNGB.WMF
ZPPRDNGB.WMF

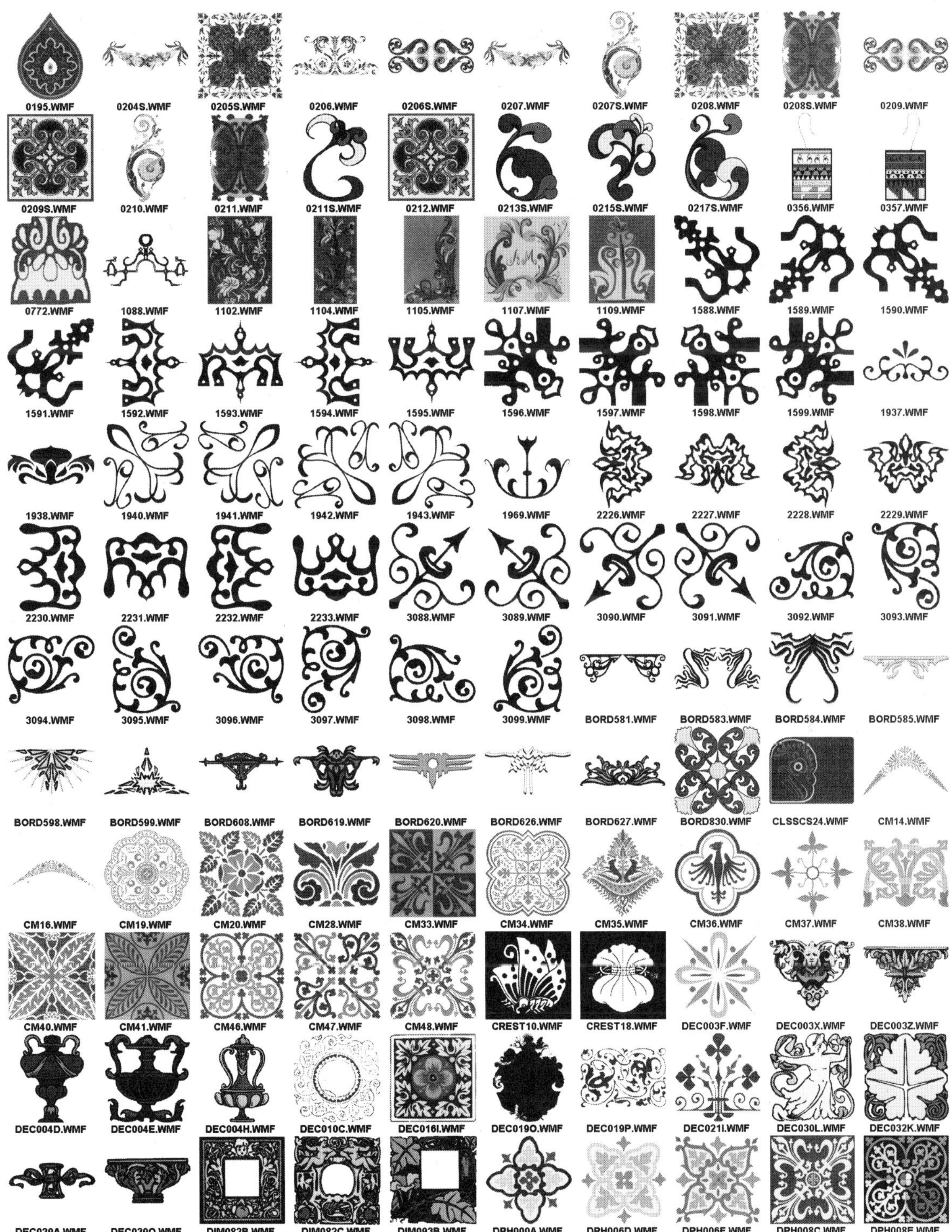
0195.WMF 0204S.WMF 0205S.WMF 0206.WMF 0206S.WMF 0207.WMF 0207S.WMF 0208.WMF 0208S.WMF 0209.WMF
0209S.WMF 0210.WMF 0211.WMF 0211S.WMF 0212.WMF 0213S.WMF 0215S.WMF 0217S.WMF 0356.WMF 0357.WMF
0772.WMF 1088.WMF 1102.WMF 1104.WMF 1105.WMF 1107.WMF 1109.WMF 1588.WMF 1589.WMF 1590.WMF
1591.WMF 1592.WMF 1593.WMF 1594.WMF 1595.WMF 1596.WMF 1597.WMF 1598.WMF 1599.WMF 1937.WMF
1938.WMF 1940.WMF 1941.WMF 1942.WMF 1943.WMF 1969.WMF 2226.WMF 2227.WMF 2228.WMF 2229.WMF
2230.WMF 2231.WMF 2232.WMF 2233.WMF 3088.WMF 3089.WMF 3090.WMF 3091.WMF 3092.WMF 3093.WMF
3094.WMF 3095.WMF 3096.WMF 3097.WMF 3098.WMF 3099.WMF BORD581.WMF BORD583.WMF BORD584.WMF BORD585.WMF
BORD598.WMF BORD599.WMF BORD608.WMF BORD619.WMF BORD620.WMF BORD626.WMF BORD627.WMF BORD830.WMF CLSSCS24.WMF CM14.WMF
CM16.WMF CM19.WMF CM20.WMF CM28.WMF CM33.WMF CM34.WMF CM35.WMF CM36.WMF CM37.WMF CM38.WMF
CM40.WMF CM41.WMF CM46.WMF CM47.WMF CM48.WMF CREST10.WMF CREST18.WMF DEC003F.WMF DEC003X.WMF DEC003Z.WMF
DEC004D.WMF DEC004E.WMF DEC004H.WMF DEC010C.WMF DEC016I.WMF DEC019O.WMF DEC019P.WMF DEC021I.WMF DEC030L.WMF DEC032K.WMF
DEC039A.WMF DEC039O.WMF DIM082B.WMF DIM082C.WMF DIM093B.WMF DPH000A.WMF DPH006D.WMF DPH006F.WMF DPH008C.WMF DPH008E.WMF

DPH008F.WMF
DPH009A.WMF
DPH009B.WMF
DPH009C.WMF
DPH009D.WMF
DPH009E.WMF
DPH009F.WMF
DPH015D.WMF
DPH018H.WMF
DPH027E.WMF
DPH036C.WMF
DPH036D.WMF
DPH036E.WMF
DPH037A.WMF
DPH037C.WMF
DPH037E.WMF
DPH037F.WMF
GASI344D.WMF
GB05.WMF
GB24.WMF
GREEK045.WMF
GREEK055.WMF
GREEK056.WMF
GREEK059.WMF
GREEK060.WMF
GREEK062.WMF
GREEK117.WMF
GREEK118.WMF
GREEK121.WMF
GREEK132.WMF
GREEK133.WMF
GREEK191.WMF
GRK2PTTR.WMF
GRSI110J.WMF
ORN_06.WMF
ORN_F.WMF
ORN_H.WMF
ORN_J.WMF
ORN_K.WMF
ORN_L.WMF
PH27.WMF
PH29.WMF
PH31.WMF
PH33.WMF
PH37.WMF
PH38.WMF
PH39.WMF
PH40.WMF
PH41.WMF
PJ12.WMF
PJ13.WMF
PJ15.WMF
PJ22.WMF
PJ23.WMF
PJ24.WMF
PJ25.WMF
PJ27.WMF
PJ28.WMF
PJ30.WMF
PJ31.WMF
PJ32.WMF
POC094C.WMF
POC094F.WMF
SOR055C.WMF
SOR286E.WMF
TOD034A.WMF
TOD034B.WMF
TOD034C.WMF
TOD034D.WMF
TOD034E.WMF
TOD034F.WMF
TOD034G.WMF
TOD034H.WMF
TOD034I.WMF
TOD034J.WMF
TOD034K.WMF
TOD034L.WMF
TOD034M.WMF
TOD034N.WMF
TOD034O.WMF
TOD034P.WMF
TOD035A.WMF
TOD035B.WMF
TOD035C.WMF
TOD035D.WMF
TOD036A.WMF
TOD036B.WMF
TOD036C.WMF
TOD036D.WMF
TOD036E.WMF
TOD037A.WMF
TOD037D.WMF
TOD037E.WMF
TOD037F.WMF
TOD038A.WMF
TOD038B.WMF
TOD038C.WMF
TOD038D.WMF
TOD039A.WMF
TOD039B.WMF
TOD039C.WMF
TOD040A.WMF
VKNG1PTT.WMF
XDN030A.WMF
XDN030B.WMF
XDN030C.WMF

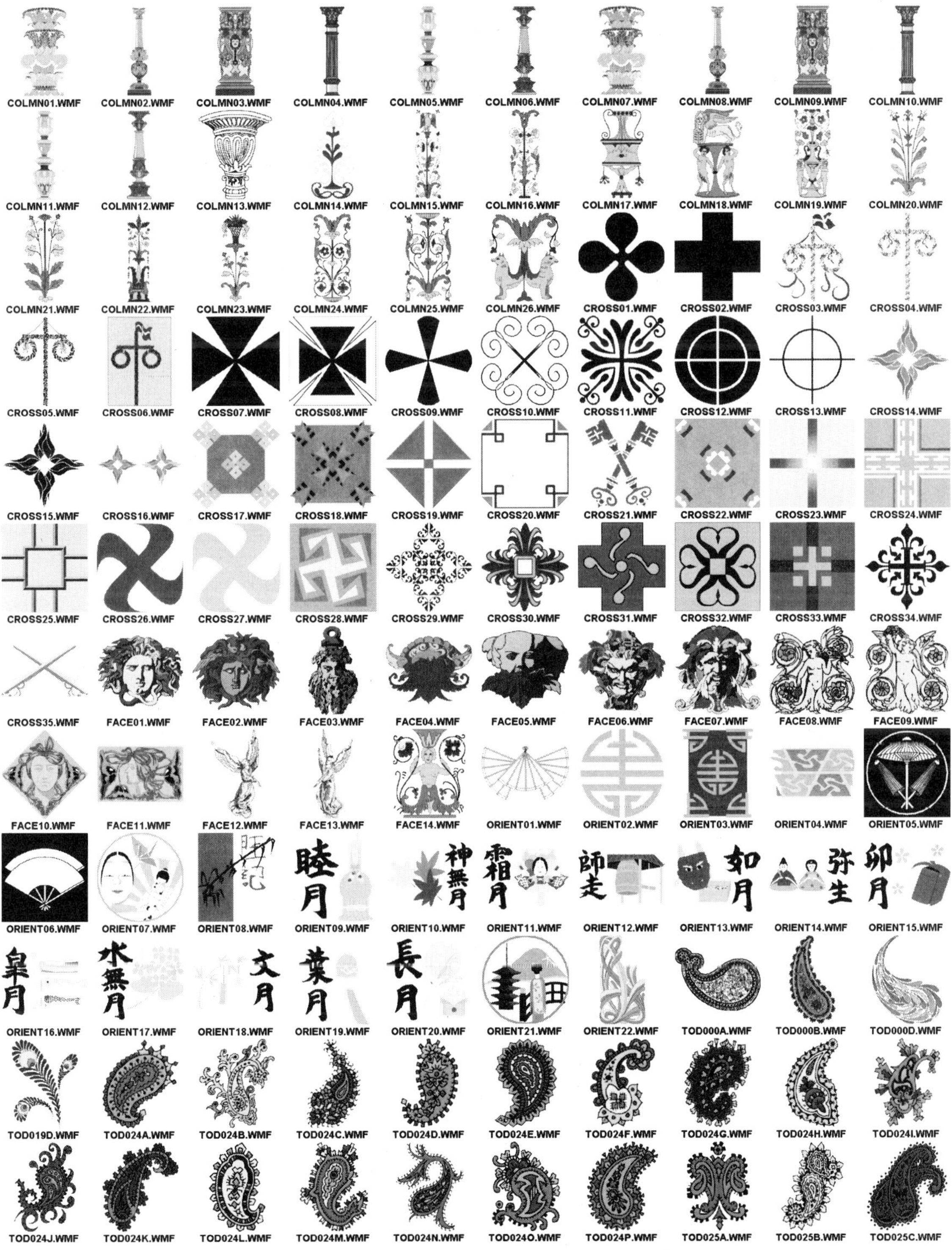
COLMN01.WMF COLMN02.WMF COLMN03.WMF COLMN04.WMF COLMN05.WMF COLMN06.WMF COLMN07.WMF COLMN08.WMF COLMN09.WMF COLMN10.WMF
COLMN11.WMF COLMN12.WMF COLMN13.WMF COLMN14.WMF COLMN15.WMF COLMN16.WMF COLMN17.WMF COLMN18.WMF COLMN19.WMF COLMN20.WMF
COLMN21.WMF COLMN22.WMF COLMN23.WMF COLMN24.WMF COLMN25.WMF COLMN26.WMF CROSS01.WMF CROSS02.WMF CROSS03.WMF CROSS04.WMF
CROSS05.WMF CROSS06.WMF CROSS07.WMF CROSS08.WMF CROSS09.WMF CROSS10.WMF CROSS11.WMF CROSS12.WMF CROSS13.WMF CROSS14.WMF
CROSS15.WMF CROSS16.WMF CROSS17.WMF CROSS18.WMF CROSS19.WMF CROSS20.WMF CROSS21.WMF CROSS22.WMF CROSS23.WMF CROSS24.WMF
CROSS25.WMF CROSS26.WMF CROSS27.WMF CROSS28.WMF CROSS29.WMF CROSS30.WMF CROSS31.WMF CROSS32.WMF CROSS33.WMF CROSS34.WMF
CROSS35.WMF FACE01.WMF FACE02.WMF FACE03.WMF FACE04.WMF FACE05.WMF FACE06.WMF FACE07.WMF FACE08.WMF FACE09.WMF
FACE10.WMF FACE11.WMF FACE12.WMF FACE13.WMF FACE14.WMF ORIENT01.WMF ORIENT02.WMF ORIENT03.WMF ORIENT04.WMF ORIENT05.WMF
ORIENT06.WMF ORIENT07.WMF ORIENT08.WMF ORIENT09.WMF ORIENT10.WMF ORIENT11.WMF ORIENT12.WMF ORIENT13.WMF ORIENT14.WMF ORIENT15.WMF
ORIENT16.WMF ORIENT17.WMF ORIENT18.WMF ORIENT19.WMF ORIENT20.WMF ORIENT21.WMF ORIENT22.WMF TOD000A.WMF TOD000B.WMF TOD000D.WMF
TOD019D.WMF TOD024A.WMF TOD024B.WMF TOD024C.WMF TOD024D.WMF TOD024E.WMF TOD024F.WMF TOD024G.WMF TOD024H.WMF TOD024I.WMF
TOD024J.WMF TOD024K.WMF TOD024L.WMF TOD024M.WMF TOD024N.WMF TOD024O.WMF TOD024P.WMF TOD025A.WMF TOD025B.WMF TOD025C.WMF

TOD025D.WMF TOD025E.WMF TOD025F.WMF TOD025G.WMF TOD025H.WMF TOD025I.WMF TOD025J.WMF TOD025K.WMF TOD025L.WMF TOD025M.WMF
TOD025N.WMF TOD025O.WMF TOD025P.WMF TOD026A.WMF TOD026B.WMF TOD026C.WMF TOD026D.WMF TOD027A.WMF TOD027B.WMF TOD027C.WMF
TOD027D.WMF TOD027E.WMF TOD027F.WMF TOD028A.WMF TOD028B.WMF TOD028C.WMF TOD028D.WMF TOD029A.WMF TOD029B.WMF TOD029C.WMF
TOD029D.WMF TOD030A.WMF TOD030B.WMF TOD030C.WMF TOD031A.WMF TOD031B.WMF TOD031C.WMF TOD031D.WMF TOD032A.WMF TOD033A.WMF
TOD040B.WMF TOD040C.WMF TOD040D.WMF TOD041A.WMF TOD041B.WMF TOD042A.WMF TOD042B.WMF TOD042C.WMF TOD042D.WMF TOD043A.WMF
TOD043B.WMF TOD043C.WMF TOD043D.WMF TOD044A.WMF TOD046A.WMF TOD046B.WMF TOD046C.WMF TOD046D.WMF TOD047A.WMF TOD047B.WMF
TOD047C.WMF TOD047D.WMF TOD048A.WMF TOD048B.WMF TOD048C.WMF TOD049A.WMF TOD049B.WMF TOD050A.WMF TOD050B.WMF TOD050C.WMF
TOD051_1.WMF TOD051_2.WMF TOD051_3.WMF TOD051_4.WMF TOD051_5.WMF TOD051_6.WMF TOD051_7.WMF TOD051_8.WMF TOD051_9.WMF TOD051A.WMF
TOD051AA.WMF TOD051B.WMF TOD051BB.WMF TOD051C.WMF TOD051CC.WMF TOD051D.WMF TOD051DD.WMF TOD051E.WMF TOD051EE.WMF TOD051F.WMF
TOD051FF.WMF TOD051G.WMF TOD051GG.WMF TOD051H.WMF TOD051HH.WMF TOD051I.WMF TOD051II.WMF TOD051J.WMF TOD051JJ.WMF TOD05_10.WMF

0014.WMF 0015.WMF 0201S.WMF 0204.WMF 052ACC.WMF 054ACC.WMF 0551.WMF 0552.WMF 0553.WMF 0554.WMF
0555.WMF 0568.WMF 057ACC.WMF 0597.WMF 0599.WMF 059ACC.WMF 0687.WMF 095.WMF 1058.WMF 1083.WMF
1084.WMF 1092.WMF 1093.WMF 1094.WMF 1101.WMF 1106.WMF 1108.WMF 1173.WMF 1176.WMF 1177.WMF
1222.WMF 1223.WMF 1972.WMF 1975.WMF 203.WMF 2121.WMF 2122.WMF 3458.WMF 3815.WMF 4266.WMF
4396.WMF ADS098B.WMF B15A.WMF B20165.WMF B20168.WMF B20169.WMF B20170.WMF B25G.WMF BACK187.WMF BCKGRD52.WMF
BCKGRD53.WMF BDSI087J.WMF BIT0161.WMF BIT0930.WMF BIT0934.WMF BIT0935.WMF BLRPLTDN.WMF BORD603.WMF CDS007C.WMF CIRCLE1.WMF
CIRCLE2.WMF CIRCLE3.WMF CIRCLE4.WMF CIRCLE5.WMF CIRCLE6.WMF CIRCLE_I.WMF CIRCLE_O.WMF CLASSCS8.WMF CLSSCS2D.WMF CLTC1PTT.WMF
CM31.WMF CM32.WMF CM42.WMF CM43.WMF CM44.WMF CM49.WMF CREST4.WMF DC1DNGBT.WMF DEC004L.WMF DEC016DD.WMF
DEC016EE.WMF DEC019F.WMF DEC023A.WMF DESIGN24.WMF DESIGN27.WMF DESIGN36.WMF DESIGN42.WMF DESIGN43.WMF DPH018E.WMF FLASH02.WMF
FLASH03.WMF FLASH04.WMF FLASH05.WMF FOODSYM.WMF FSNDNGBT.WMF FWD023A.WMF GASI335M.WMF GASI353D.WMF GASI363M.WMF GASI386M.WMF
GASI396M.WMF GASI404M.WMF GASI405M.WMF GDO021L.WMF GDO023B.WMF GDO026C.WMF GDO026G.WMF GDO027C.WMF GDO029D.WMF GRK2DNGB.WMF
GRSI013J.WMF GRSI021J.WMF GRSI038J.WMF GRSI074J.WMF INDIANAZ.WMF INDSYM.WMF KYOTOSYM.WMF LEAF_2.WMF LEAFCI1.WMF M21288.WMF

M21289.WMF
M21381.WMF
M21382.WMF
M21410.WMF
M21411.WMF
M21420.WMF
M21421.WMF
M21422.WMF
M21423.WMF
MC22.WMF
MC23.WMF
MC24.WMF
MC29.WMF
MC30.WMF
MC38.WMF
MC42.WMF
MCRNSNDN.WMF
MIS0026A.WMF
MIS0036A.WMF
MIS0037A.WMF
MIS0051B.WMF
MIS0052B.WMF
MOD_CIR1.WMF
MOD_CIR2.WMF
MSC00036.WMF
MSC00037.WMF
NASS005K.WMF
NASS018J.WMF
NV4PTTRN.WMF
NV5DNGBT.WMF
NV5PTTRN.WMF
ORN_C.WMF
ORN_G.WMF
OVAL1.WMF
PBL1DNGB.WMF
PBL1PTTR.WMF
PLACESYM.WMF
PRODSYM.WMF
PSTL_SP1.WMF
PSTL_SP2.WMF
RNDCREST.WMF
SB40.WMF
SEMCRCL1.WMF
SHAPE085.WMF
SHAPE086.WMF
SHAPE247.WMF
SHAPE248.WMF
SHAPE253.WMF
SHAPE254.WMF
SHAPE255.WMF
SHAPE256.WMF
SHAPE259.WMF
SHAPE260.WMF
SHAPE268.WMF
SHAPE269.WMF
SHAPE270.WMF
SHAPE273.WMF
SHAPE274.WMF
SHAPE278.WMF
TOD051_1.WMF
TOD051CC.WMF
TOD051X.WMF
TOD051XX.WMF
TOI050E.WMF
TOKYOSYM.WMF
TSD000A.WMF
TSD002B.WMF
TSD054D.WMF
TSD054E.WMF
TSUBA1.WMF
TSUBA2.WMF
TSUBA3.WMF
VKNG1DNG.WMF

0666.WMF
0668.WMF
0810.WMF
1036.WMF
4379.WMF
AMETER.WMF
AMETERC.WMF
B23E.WMF
B23E2.WMF
B23EB.WMF
B23F.WMF
B23F2.WMF
B23FB.WMF
BIT0147.WMF
BIT0354.WMF
BIT0456.WMF
BIT0518.WMF
BIT0519.WMF
BIT0520.WMF
BIT0521.WMF
BIT0563.WMF
BIT0564.WMF
COALPOWR.WMF
CONECT01.WMF
CONECT02.WMF
CONECT03.WMF
CONECT04.WMF
CONECT05.WMF
CONECT06.WMF
CONECT07.WMF
CONECT08.WMF
CONECT09.WMF
CONECT10.WMF
CONECT11.WMF
CONECT12.WMF
CONECT13.WMF
CONECT14.WMF
CONECT15.WMF
CONECT16.WMF
CONECT17.WMF
CONECT18.WMF
CONECT19.WMF
CONECT20.WMF
CONECT21.WMF
CONECT22.WMF
CONECT23.WMF
CONECT24.WMF
CONECT25.WMF
CONECT26.WMF
CONECT27.WMF
CONECT28.WMF
CONECT29.WMF
CONECT30.WMF
CONECT31.WMF
CONECT32.WMF
CONECT33.WMF
CONECT34.WMF
CONECT35.WMF
CW18.WMF
CW19.WMF
ON. OFF.
DIAL.WMF
EDCN069.WMF
EDCN229.WMF
ELECTR01.WMF
ELECTR2.WMF
ELECTR2B.WMF
ELECTR4.WMF
ELECTR4B.WMF
ELECTRC1.WMF
ELECTRC2.WMF
FUSE.WMF
GASRIG.WMF
FUEL GAUGE
GAUGE.WMF
HANDPLUG.WMF
HHBO005J.WMF
HHBO067J.WMF
HHGC001D.WMF
HHGC030D.WMF
HHRW068J.WMF
HYDROE.WMF
IHD032E.WMF
INGC028D.WMF
INSI009D.WMF
LANTERN.WMF
LGHTBLB.WMF
LIGHBULB.WMF
LITE1.WMF
METER.WMF
MISC108.WMF
MISC114.WMF
MTRGAGE.WMF
NARW067J.WMF
NUC_PLNT.WMF
NUC_PWR.WMF
NUCLEARP.WMF
NUCPLANT.WMF
ON
OFF
OFFON.WMF
OIL_WELL.WMF
OILPIPES.WMF
OILRIG.WMF
OUTLET.WMF
P21591.WMF
PD043PCU.WMF
PD047TCU.WMF
PD048TCU.WMF
PD049DCU.WMF
PD115RCU.WMF
220 V~
PD123ACU.WMF
PD129WCU.WMF
PIGGYBAK.WMF
PLUG.WMF
POWER2.WMF
POWERS1.WMF
POWERS2.WMF
POWERST.WMF
PPOINT1.WMF
PPOINT2.WMF
PWRLINE.WMF
QUICKDIS.WMF
REFINERY.WMF

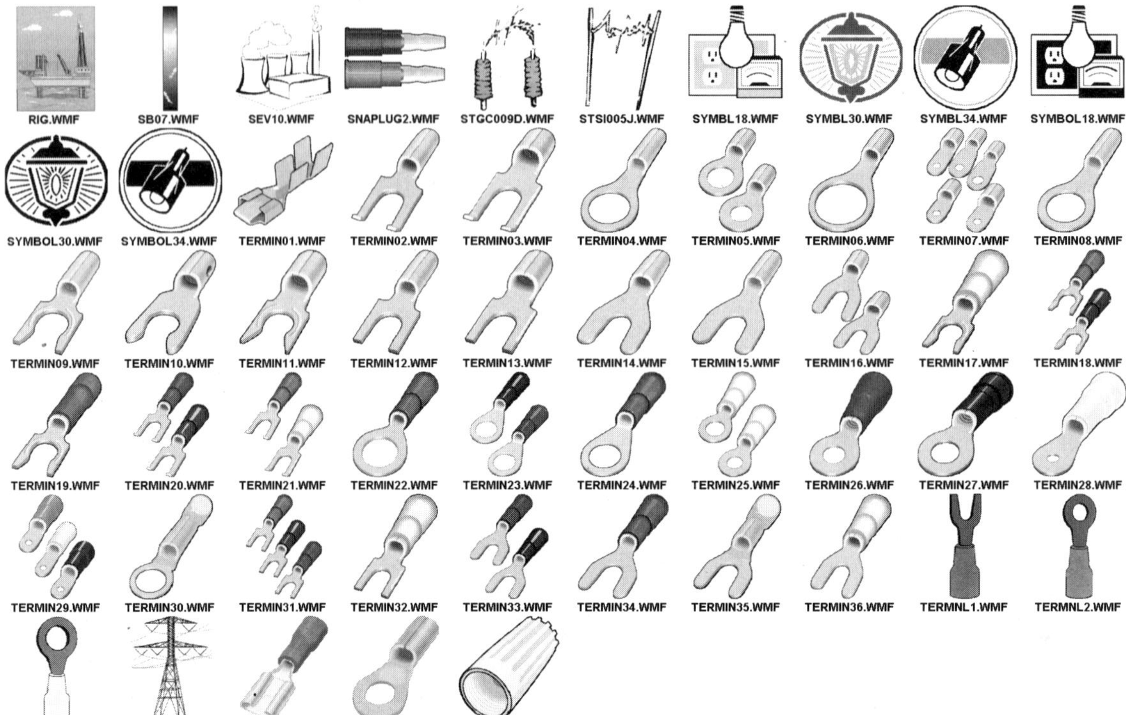
RIG.WMF
SB07.WMF
SEV10.WMF
SNAPLUG2.WMF
STGC009D.WMF
STSI005J.WMF
SYMBL18.WMF
SYMBL30.WMF
SYMBL34.WMF
SYMBOL18.WMF
SYMBOL30.WMF
SYMBOL34.WMF
TERMIN01.WMF
TERMIN02.WMF
TERMIN03.WMF
TERMIN04.WMF
TERMIN05.WMF
TERMIN06.WMF
TERMIN07.WMF
TERMIN08.WMF
TERMIN09.WMF
TERMIN10.WMF
TERMIN11.WMF
TERMIN12.WMF
TERMIN13.WMF
TERMIN14.WMF
TERMIN15.WMF
TERMIN16.WMF
TERMIN17.WMF
TERMIN18.WMF
TERMIN19.WMF
TERMIN20.WMF
TERMIN21.WMF
TERMIN22.WMF
TERMIN23.WMF
TERMIN24.WMF
TERMIN25.WMF
TERMIN26.WMF
TERMIN27.WMF
TERMIN28.WMF
TERMIN29.WMF
TERMIN30.WMF
TERMIN31.WMF
TERMIN32.WMF
TERMIN33.WMF
TERMIN34.WMF
TERMIN35.WMF
TERMIN36.WMF
TERMNL1.WMF
TERMNL2.WMF
TERMNL3.WMF
TOWER.WMF
WIRECON1.WMF
WIRECON2.WMF
WIRENUT.WMF

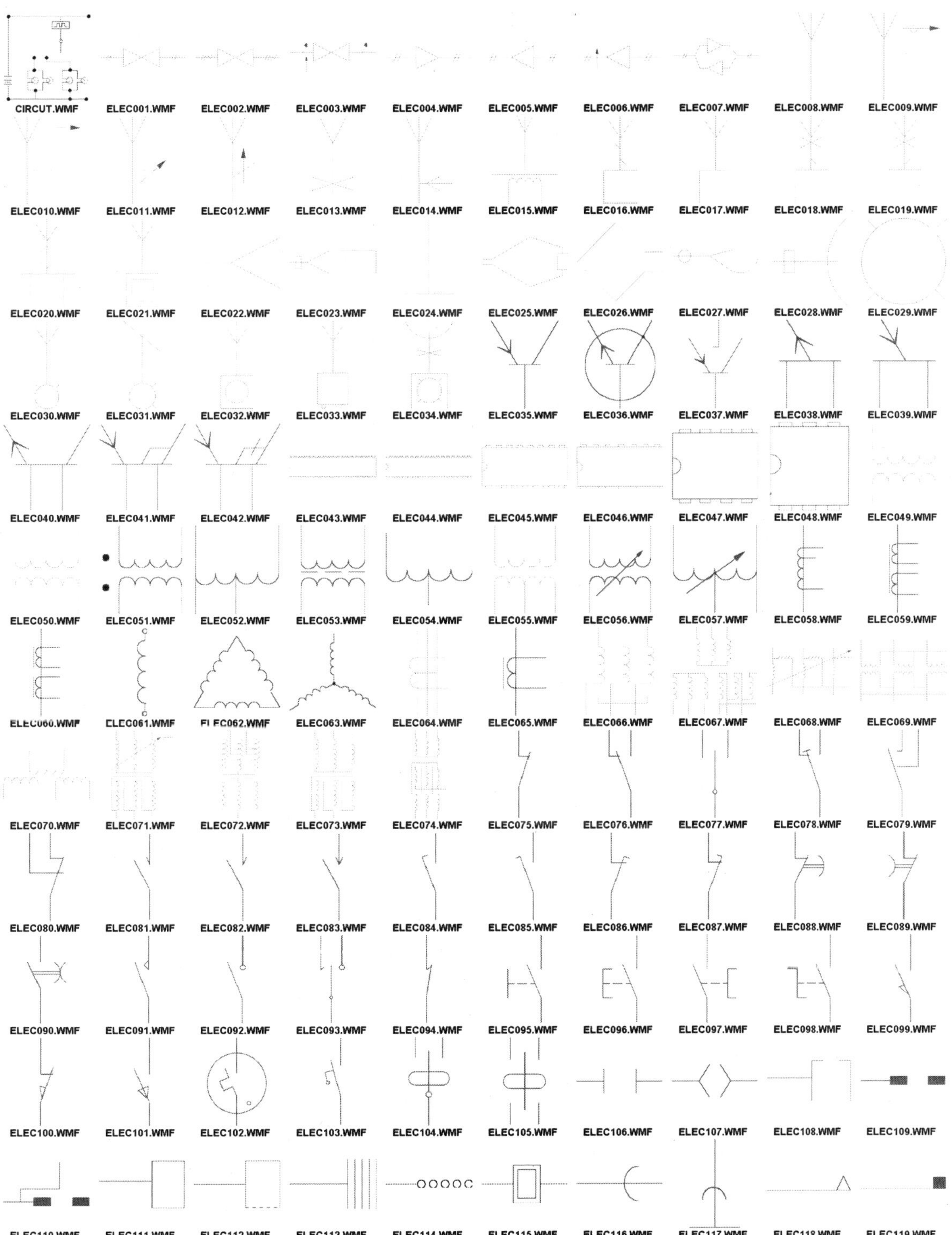
CIRCUT.WMF
ELEC001.WMF
ELEC002.WMF
ELEC003.WMF
ELEC004.WMF
ELEC005.WMF
ELEC006.WMF
ELEC007.WMF
ELEC008.WMF
ELEC009.WMF
ELEC010.WMF
ELEC011.WMF
ELEC012.WMF
ELEC013.WMF
ELEC014.WMF
ELEC015.WMF
ELEC016.WMF
ELEC017.WMF
ELEC018.WMF
ELEC019.WMF
ELEC020.WMF
ELEC021.WMF
ELEC022.WMF
ELEC023.WMF
ELEC024.WMF
ELEC025.WMF
ELEC026.WMF
ELEC027.WMF
ELEC028.WMF
ELEC029.WMF
ELEC030.WMF
ELEC031.WMF
ELEC032.WMF
ELEC033.WMF
ELEC034.WMF
ELEC035.WMF
ELEC036.WMF
ELEC037.WMF
ELEC038.WMF
ELEC039.WMF
ELEC040.WMF
ELEC041.WMF
ELEC042.WMF
ELEC043.WMF
ELEC044.WMF
ELEC045.WMF
ELEC046.WMF
ELEC047.WMF
ELEC048.WMF
ELEC049.WMF
ELEC050.WMF
ELEC051.WMF
ELEC052.WMF
ELEC053.WMF
ELEC054.WMF
ELEC055.WMF
ELEC056.WMF
ELEC057.WMF
ELEC058.WMF
ELEC059.WMF
ELEC060.WMF
ELEC061.WMF
ELEC062.WMF
ELEC063.WMF
ELEC064.WMF
ELEC065.WMF
ELEC066.WMF
ELEC067.WMF
ELEC068.WMF
ELEC069.WMF
ELEC070.WMF
ELEC071.WMF
ELEC072.WMF
ELEC073.WMF
ELEC074.WMF
ELEC075.WMF
ELEC076.WMF
ELEC077.WMF
ELEC078.WMF
ELEC079.WMF
ELEC080.WMF
ELEC081.WMF
ELEC082.WMF
ELEC083.WMF
ELEC084.WMF
ELEC085.WMF
ELEC086.WMF
ELEC087.WMF
ELEC088.WMF
ELEC089.WMF
ELEC090.WMF
ELEC091.WMF
ELEC092.WMF
ELEC093.WMF
ELEC094.WMF
ELEC095.WMF
ELEC096.WMF
ELEC097.WMF
ELEC098.WMF
ELEC099.WMF
ELEC100.WMF
ELEC101.WMF
ELEC102.WMF
ELEC103.WMF
ELEC104.WMF
ELEC105.WMF
ELEC106.WMF
ELEC107.WMF
ELEC108.WMF
ELEC109.WMF
ELEC110.WMF
ELEC111.WMF
ELEC112.WMF
ELEC113.WMF
ELEC114.WMF
ELEC115.WMF
ELEC116.WMF
ELEC117.WMF
ELEC118.WMF
ELEC119.WMF

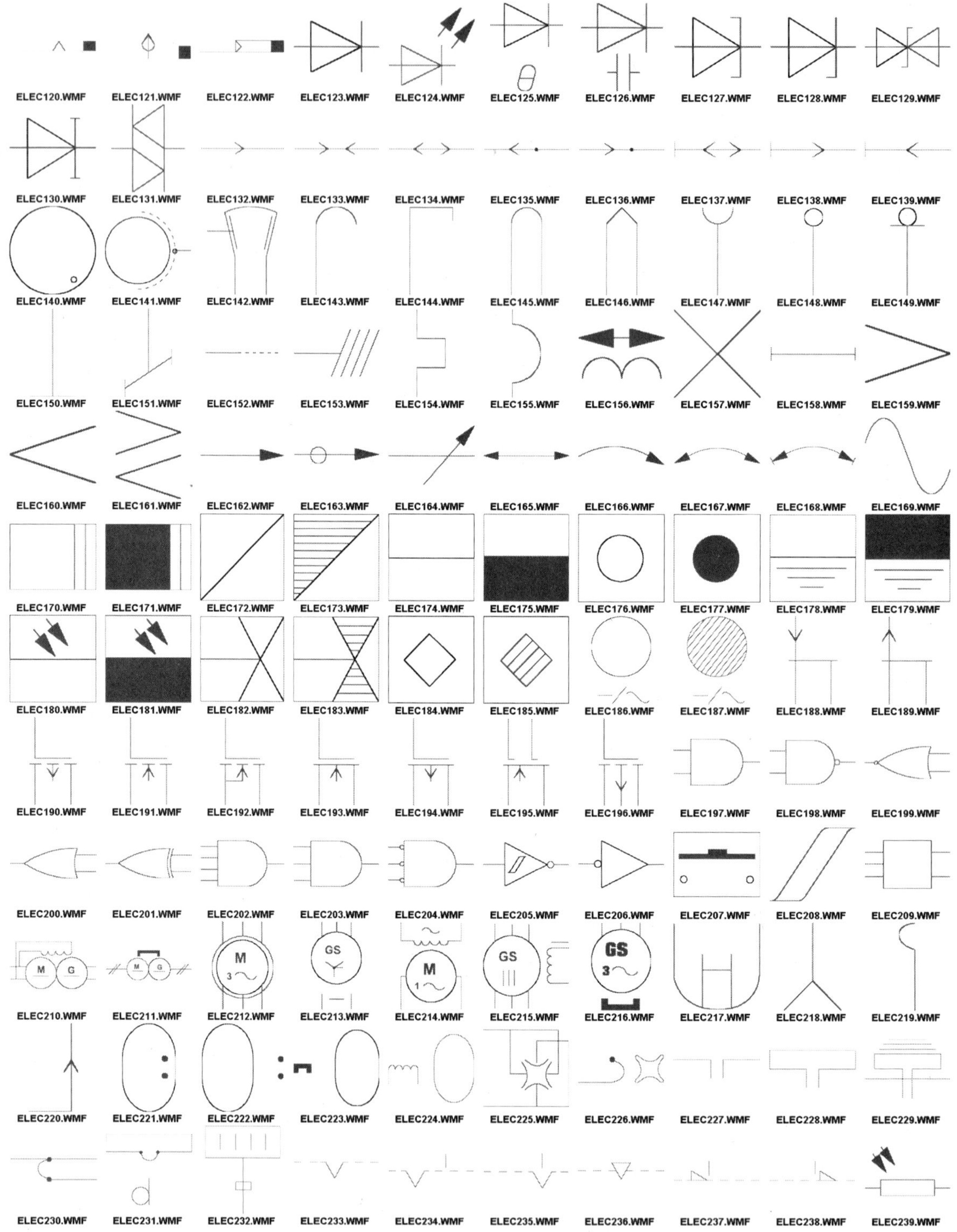
ELEC120.WMF
ELEC121.WMF
ELEC122.WMF
ELEC123.WMF
ELEC124.WMF
ELEC125.WMF
ELEC126.WMF
ELEC127.WMF
ELEC128.WMF
ELEC129.WMF
ELEC130.WMF
ELEC131.WMF
ELEC132.WMF
ELEC133.WMF
ELEC134.WMF
ELEC135.WMF
ELEC136.WMF
ELEC137.WMF
ELEC138.WMF
ELEC139.WMF
ELEC140.WMF
ELEC141.WMF
ELEC142.WMF
ELEC143.WMF
ELEC144.WMF
ELEC145.WMF
ELEC146.WMF
ELEC147.WMF
ELEC148.WMF
ELEC149.WMF
ELEC150.WMF
ELEC151.WMF
ELEC152.WMF
ELEC153.WMF
ELEC154.WMF
ELEC155.WMF
ELEC156.WMF
ELEC157.WMF
ELEC158.WMF
ELEC159.WMF
ELEC160.WMF
ELEC161.WMF
ELEC162.WMF
ELEC163.WMF
ELEC164.WMF
ELEC165.WMF
ELEC166.WMF
ELEC167.WMF
ELEC168.WMF
ELEC169.WMF
ELEC170.WMF
ELEC171.WMF
ELEC172.WMF
ELEC173.WMF
ELEC174.WMF
ELEC175.WMF
ELEC176.WMF
ELEC177.WMF
ELEC178.WMF
ELEC179.WMF
ELEC180.WMF
ELEC181.WMF
ELEC182.WMF
ELEC183.WMF
ELEC184.WMF
ELEC185.WMF
ELEC186.WMF
ELEC187.WMF
ELEC188.WMF
ELEC189.WMF
ELEC190.WMF
ELEC191.WMF
ELEC192.WMF
ELEC193.WMF
ELEC194.WMF
ELEC195.WMF
ELEC196.WMF
ELEC197.WMF
ELEC198.WMF
ELEC199.WMF
ELEC200.WMF
ELEC201.WMF
ELEC202.WMF
ELEC203.WMF
ELEC204.WMF
ELEC205.WMF
ELEC206.WMF
ELEC207.WMF
ELEC208.WMF
ELEC209.WMF
M
G
ELEC210.WMF
M
G
ELEC211.WMF
M
3
ELEC212.WMF
GS
ELEC213.WMF
M
1
ELEC214.WMF
GS
ELEC215.WMF
GS
3
ELEC216.WMF
ELEC217.WMF
ELEC218.WMF
ELEC219.WMF
ELEC220.WMF
ELEC221.WMF
ELEC222.WMF
ELEC223.WMF
ELEC224.WMF
ELEC225.WMF
ELEC226.WMF
ELEC227.WMF
ELEC228.WMF
ELEC229.WMF
ELEC230.WMF
ELEC231.WMF
ELEC232.WMF
ELEC233.WMF
ELEC234.WMF
ELEC235.WMF
ELEC236.WMF
ELEC237.WMF
ELEC238.WMF
ELEC239.WMF

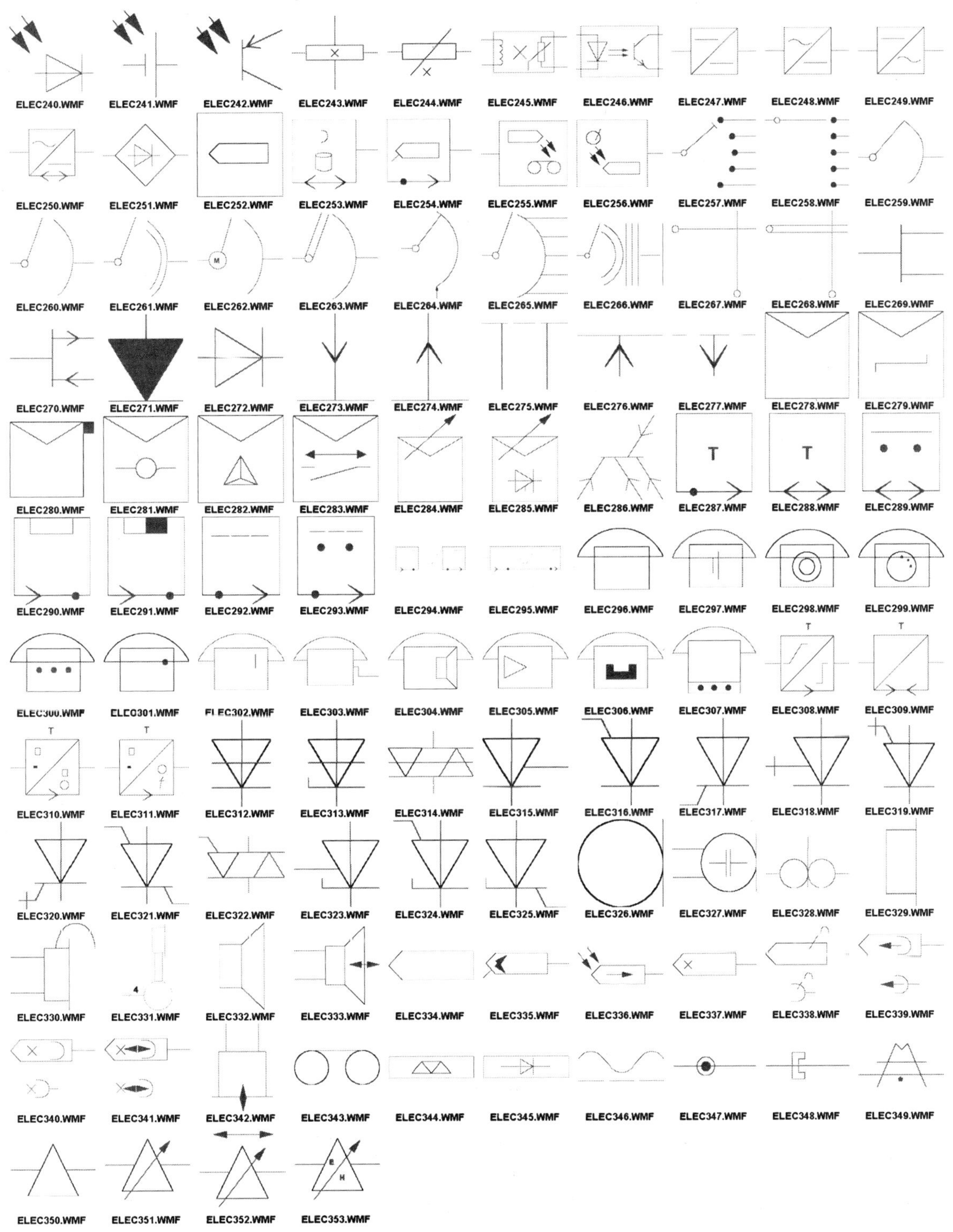
ELEC240.WMF
ELEC241.WMF
ELEC242.WMF
ELEC243.WMF
ELEC244.WMF
ELEC245.WMF
ELEC246.WMF
ELEC247.WMF
ELEC248.WMF
ELEC249.WMF
ELEC250.WMF
ELEC251.WMF
ELEC252.WMF
ELEC253.WMF
ELEC254.WMF
ELEC255.WMF
ELEC256.WMF
ELEC257.WMF
ELEC258.WMF
ELEC259.WMF
ELEC260.WMF
ELEC261.WMF
ELEC262.WMF
ELEC263.WMF
ELEC264.WMF
ELEC265.WMF
ELEC266.WMF
ELEC267.WMF
ELEC268.WMF
ELEC269.WMF
ELEC270.WMF
ELEC271.WMF
ELEC272.WMF
ELEC273.WMF
ELEC274.WMF
ELEC275.WMF
ELEC276.WMF
ELEC277.WMF
ELEC278.WMF
ELEC279.WMF
T
T
ELEC280.WMF
ELEC281.WMF
ELEC282.WMF
ELEC283.WMF
ELEC284.WMF
ELEC285.WMF
ELEC286.WMF
ELEC287.WMF
ELEC288.WMF
ELEC289.WMF
ELEC290.WMF
ELEC291.WMF
ELEC292.WMF
ELEC293.WMF
ELEC294.WMF
ELEC295.WMF
ELEC296.WMF
ELEC297.WMF
ELEC298.WMF
ELEC299.WMF
T
T
ELEC300.WMF
ELEC301.WMF
ELEC302.WMF
ELEC303.WMF
ELEC304.WMF
ELEC305.WMF
ELEC306.WMF
ELEC307.WMF
ELEC308.WMF
ELEC309.WMF
T
T
ELEC310.WMF
ELEC311.WMF
ELEC312.WMF
ELEC313.WMF
ELEC314.WMF
ELEC315.WMF
ELEC316.WMF
ELEC317.WMF
ELEC318.WMF
ELEC319.WMF
ELEC320.WMF
ELEC321.WMF
ELEC322.WMF
ELEC323.WMF
ELEC324.WMF
ELEC325.WMF
ELEC326.WMF
ELEC327.WMF
ELEC328.WMF
ELEC329.WMF
ELEC330.WMF
ELEC331.WMF
ELEC332.WMF
ELEC333.WMF
ELEC334.WMF
ELEC335.WMF
ELEC336.WMF
ELEC337.WMF
ELEC338.WMF
ELEC339.WMF
ELEC340.WMF
ELEC341.WMF
ELEC342.WMF
ELEC343.WMF
ELEC344.WMF
ELEC345.WMF
ELEC346.WMF
ELEC347.WMF
ELEC348.WMF
ELEC349.WMF
ELEC350.WMF
ELEC351.WMF
ELEC352.WMF
ELEC353.WMF

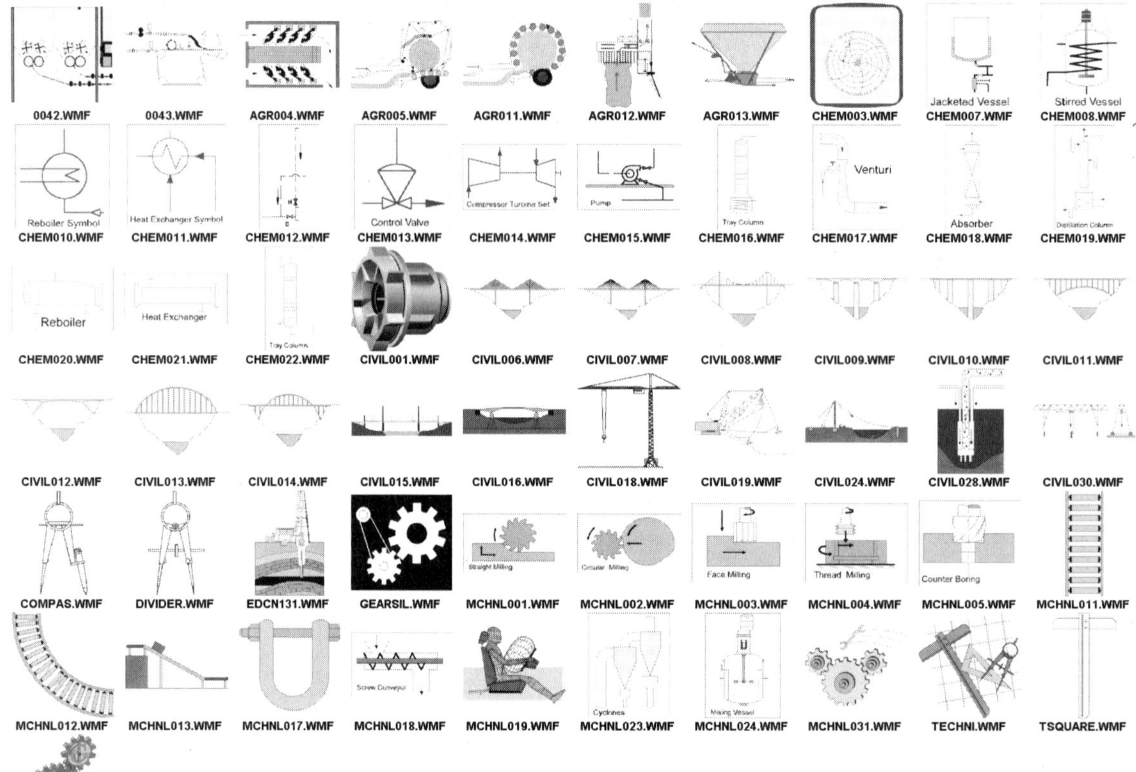
0042.WMF
0043.WMF
AGR004.WMF
AGR005.WMF
AGR011.WMF
AGR012.WMF
AGR013.WMF
CHEM003.WMF
Jacketed Vessel
CHEM007.WMF
Stirred Vessel
CHEM008.WMF
Reboiler Symbol
CHEM010.WMF
Heat Exchanger Symbol
CHEM011.WMF
CHEM012.WMF
Control Valve
CHEM013.WMF
Compressor Turbine Set
CHEM014.WMF
Pump
CHEM015.WMF
Tray Column
CHEM016.WMF
Venturi
CHEM017.WMF
Absorber
CHEM018.WMF
Distillation Column
CHEM019.WMF
Reboiler
CHEM020.WMF
Heat Exchanger
CHEM021.WMF
Tray Column
CHEM022.WMF
CIVIL001.WMF
CIVIL006.WMF
CIVIL007.WMF
CIVIL008.WMF
CIVIL009.WMF
CIVIL010.WMF
CIVIL011.WMF
CIVIL012.WMF
CIVIL013.WMF
CIVIL014.WMF
CIVIL015.WMF
CIVIL016.WMF
CIVIL018.WMF
CIVIL019.WMF
CIVIL024.WMF
CIVIL028.WMF
CIVIL030.WMF
COMPAS.WMF
DIVIDER.WMF
EDCN131.WMF
GEARSIL.WMF
Straight Milling
MCHNL001.WMF
Circular Milling
MCHNL002.WMF
Face Milling
MCHNL003.WMF
Thread Milling
MCHNL004.WMF
Counter Boring
MCHNL005.WMF
MCHNL011.WMF
MCHNL012.WMF
MCHNL013.WMF
MCHNL017.WMF
Screw Conveyor
MCHNL018.WMF
MCHNL019.WMF
Cyclones
MCHNL023.WMF
Mixing Vessel
MCHNL024.WMF
MCHNL031.WMF
TECHNI.WMF
TSQUARE.WMF
WHEELS.WMF

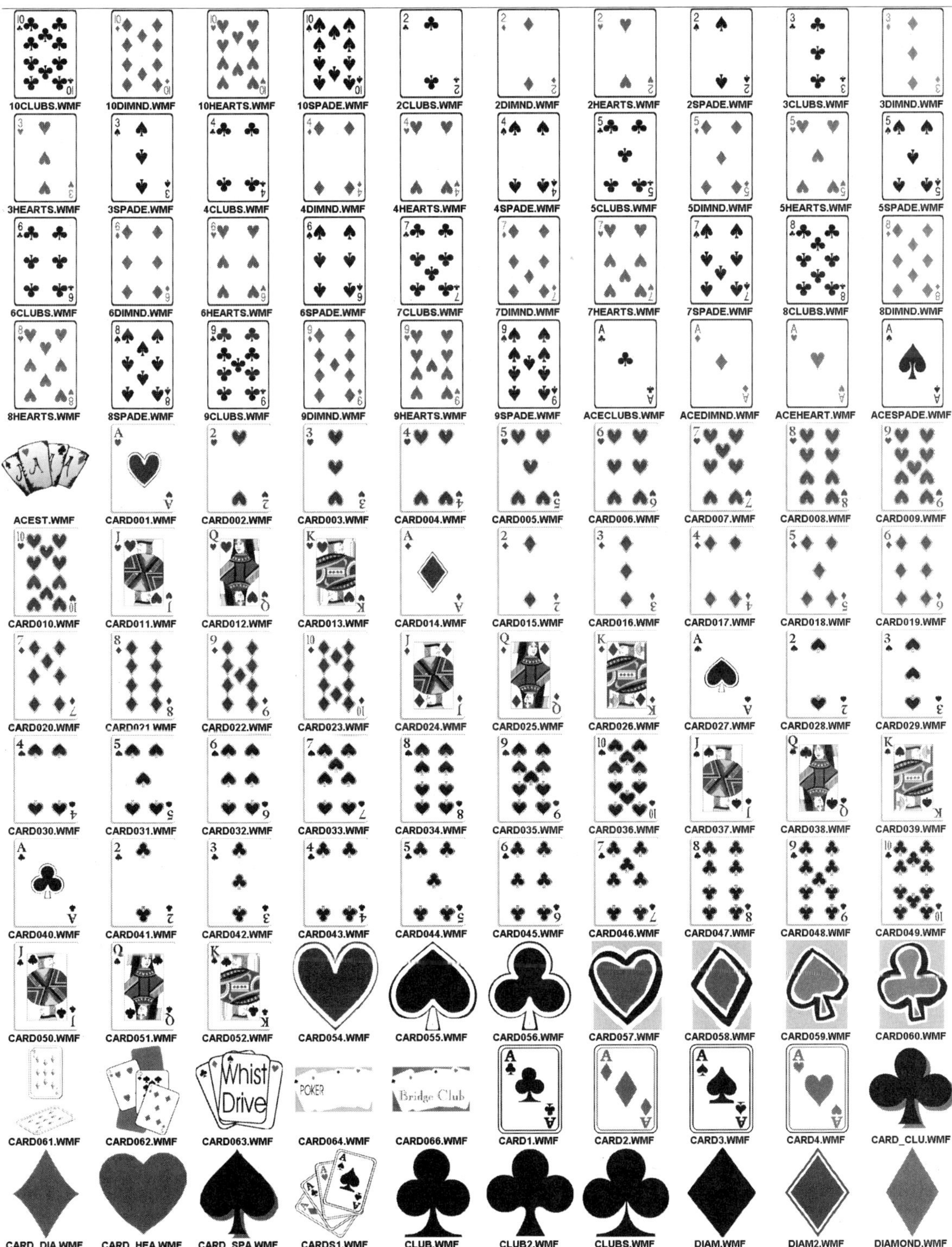

10CLUBS.WMF 10DIMND.WMF 10HEARTS.WMF 10SPADE.WMF 2CLUBS.WMF 2DIMND.WMF 2HEARTS.WMF 2SPADE.WMF 3CLUBS.WMF 3DIMND.WMF

3HEARTS.WMF 3SPADE.WMF 4CLUBS.WMF 4DIMND.WMF 4HEARTS.WMF 4SPADE.WMF 5CLUBS.WMF 5DIMND.WMF 5HEARTS.WMF 5SPADE.WMF

6CLUBS.WMF 6DIMND.WMF 6HEARTS.WMF 6SPADE.WMF 7CLUBS.WMF 7DIMND.WMF 7HEARTS.WMF 7SPADE.WMF 8CLUBS.WMF 8DIMND.WMF

8HEARTS.WMF 8SPADE.WMF 9CLUBS.WMF 9DIMND.WMF 9HEARTS.WMF 9SPADE.WMF ACECLUBS.WMF ACEDIMND.WMF ACEHEART.WMF ACESPADE.WMF

ACEST.WMF CARD001.WMF CARD002.WMF CARD003.WMF CARD004.WMF CARD005.WMF CARD006.WMF CARD007.WMF CARD008.WMF CARD009.WMF

CARD010.WMF CARD011.WMF CARD012.WMF CARD013.WMF CARD014.WMF CARD015.WMF CARD016.WMF CARD017.WMF CARD018.WMF CARD019.WMF

CARD020.WMF CARD021.WMF CARD022.WMF CARD023.WMF CARD024.WMF CARD025.WMF CARD026.WMF CARD027.WMF CARD028.WMF CARD029.WMF

CARD030.WMF CARD031.WMF CARD032.WMF CARD033.WMF CARD034.WMF CARD035.WMF CARD036.WMF CARD037.WMF CARD038.WMF CARD039.WMF

CARD040.WMF CARD041.WMF CARD042.WMF CARD043.WMF CARD044.WMF CARD045.WMF CARD046.WMF CARD047.WMF CARD048.WMF CARD049.WMF

CARD050.WMF CARD051.WMF CARD052.WMF CARD054.WMF CARD055.WMF CARD056.WMF CARD057.WMF CARD058.WMF CARD059.WMF CARD060.WMF

CARD061.WMF CARD062.WMF CARD063.WMF CARD064.WMF CARD066.WMF CARD1.WMF CARD2.WMF CARD3.WMF CARD4.WMF CARD_CLU.WMF

CARD_DIA.WMF CARD_HEA.WMF CARD_SPA.WMF CARDS1.WMF CLUB.WMF CLUB2.WMF CLUBS.WMF DIAM.WMF DIAM2.WMF DIAMOND.WMF

DIAMONDS.WMF
EAC173W.WMF
ENGC006D.WMF
ENSI003J.WMF
ENSI035D.WMF
FOURACES.WMF
HEART.WMF
HEARTS.WMF
IHD014B.WMF
JACK.WMF
JACKCLUB.WMF
JACKDMND.WMF
JACKHRTS.WMF
JACKSPAD.WMF
KING.WMF
KINGCLUB.WMF
KINGDMND.WMF
KINGHRTS.WMF
KINGSPAD.WMF
OSP031F.WMF
OSP032K.WMF
PD043TCU.WMF
QUEEN.WMF
QUENCLUB.WMF
QUENDMND.WMF
QUENHRTS.WMF
QUENSPAD.WMF
SOSI020J.WMF
SPADE.WMF
SPADE01.WMF
SPADE2.WMF
SPADES.WMF
SPSI016J.WMF

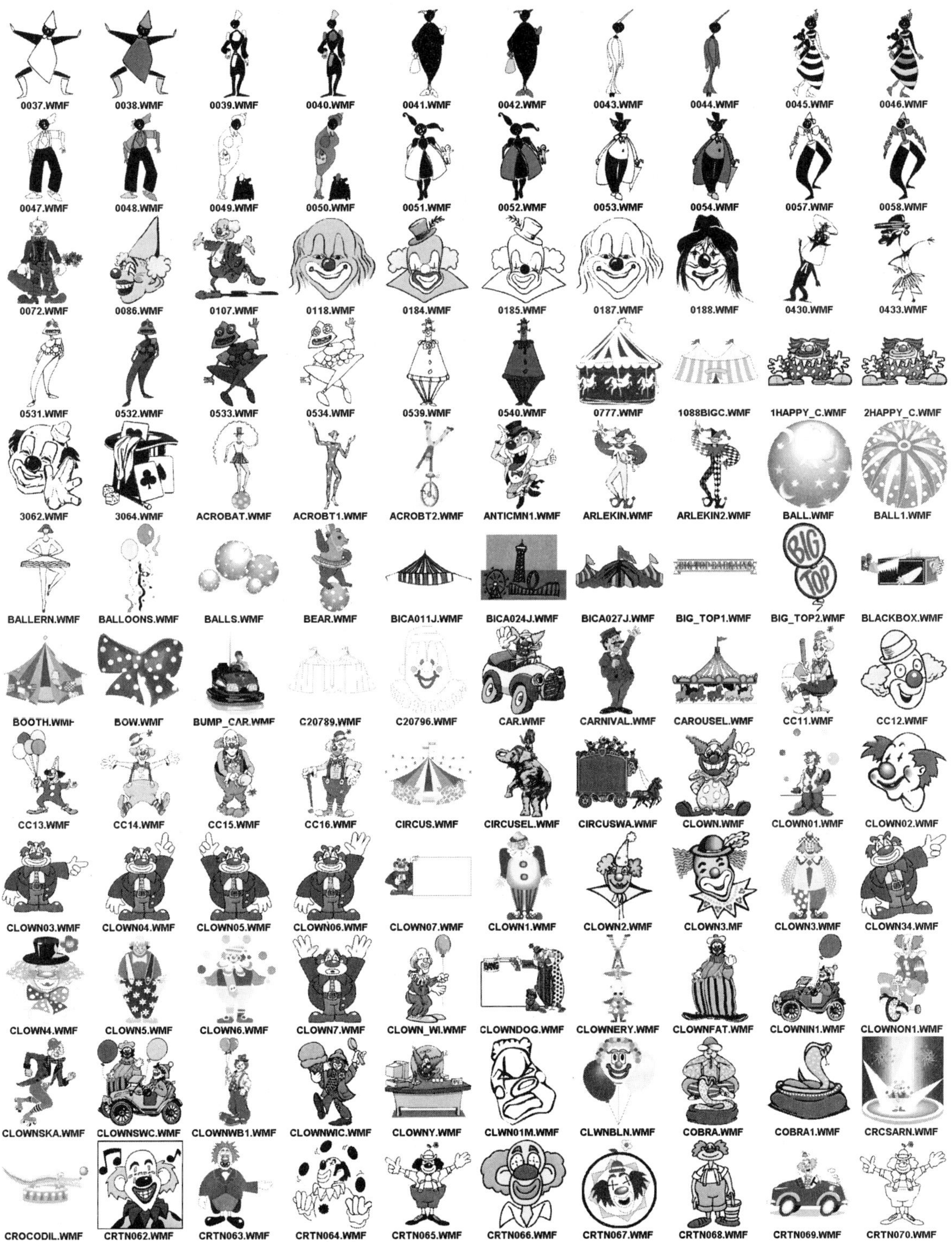
0037.WMF
0038.WMF
0039.WMF
0040.WMF
0041.WMF
0042.WMF
0043.WMF
0044.WMF
0045.WMF
0046.WMF
0047.WMF
0048.WMF
0049.WMF
0050.WMF
0051.WMF
0052.WMF
0053.WMF
0054.WMF
0057.WMF
0058.WMF
0072.WMF
0086.WMF
0107.WMF
0118.WMF
0184.WMF
0185.WMF
0187.WMF
0188.WMF
0430.WMF
0433.WMF
0531.WMF
0532.WMF
0533.WMF
0534.WMF
0539.WMF
0540.WMF
0777.WMF
1088BIGC.WMF
1HAPPY_C.WMF
2HAPPY_C.WMF
3062.WMF
3064.WMF
ACROBAT.WMF
ACROBT1.WMF
ACROBT2.WMF
ANTICMN1.WMF
ARLEKIN.WMF
ARLEKIN2.WMF
BALL.WMF
BALL1.WMF
BALLERN.WMF
BALLOONS.WMF
BALLS.WMF
BEAR.WMF
BICA011J.WMF
BICA024J.WMF
BICA027J.WMF
BIG_TOP1.WMF
BIG
TOP
BIG_TOP2.WMF
BLACKBOX.WMF
BOOTH.WMF
BOW.WMF
BUMP_CAR.WMF
C20789.WMF
C20796.WMF
CAR.WMF
CARNIVAL.WMF
CAROUSEL.WMF
CC11.WMF
CC12.WMF
CC13.WMF
CC14.WMF
CC15.WMF
CC16.WMF
CIRCUS.WMF
CIRCUSEL.WMF
CIRCUSWA.WMF
CLOWN.WMF
CLOWN01.WMF
CLOWN02.WMF
CLOWN03.WMF
CLOWN04.WMF
CLOWN05.WMF
CLOWN06.WMF
CLOWN07.WMF
CLOWN1.WMF
CLOWN2.WMF
CLOWN3.MF
CLOWN3.WMF
CLOWN34.WMF
CLOWN4.WMF
CLOWN5.WMF
CLOWN6.WMF
CLOWN7.WMF
CLOWN_WI.WMF
CLOWNDOG.WMF
CLOWNERY.WMF
CLOWNFAT.WMF
CLOWNIN1.WMF
CLOWNON1.WMF
CLOWNSKA.WMF
CLOWNSWC.WMF
CLOWNWB1.WMF
CLOWNWIC.WMF
CLOWNY.WMF
CLWN01M.WMF
CLWNBLN.WMF
COBRA.WMF
COBRA1.WMF
CRCSARN.WMF
CROCODIL.WMF
CRTN062.WMF
CRTN063.WMF
CRTN064.WMF
CRTN065.WMF
CRTN066.WMF
CRTN067.WMF
CRTN068.WMF
CRTN069.WMF
CRTN070.WMF

CRTN071.WMF
CRTN072.WMF
CRTN073.WMF
CRTN155.WMF
CRTN164.WMF
CRTN165.WMF
CTMISC64.WMF
CURTAIN.WMF
CURTN1.WMF
DOG.WMF
DOGTRIK1.WMF
DOGTRIK2.WMF
DOLL.WMF
DOLL1.WMF
DONKEY__.WMF
DRUM.WMF
DRUMMER.WMF
DUALAIRB.WMF
ELEPHAN_.WMF
ELEPHANT.WMF
ELEPHNT.WMF
ENCA012J.WMF
ENCA014D.WMF
ENCA019D.WMF
ENGC001J.WMF
ENGC002J.WMF
ENGC003J.WMF
ENGC004J.WMF
ENGC005J.WMF
ENGC025D.WMF
ENGC026D.WMF
ENGC041D.WMF
ENGC042D.WMF
ENGC043D.WMF
ENGC044D.WMF
ENGC045D.WMF
ENGC046D.WMF
ENGC047D.WMF
FERISWHL.WMF
FIGHTER.WMF
FIGHTER1.WMF
FIGHTER2.WMF
FIRERNG.WMF
FIREWRK.WMF
FLAMINGH.WMF
FOCUS.WMF
FOCUS1.WMF
FOCUS2.WMF
FSW004A.WMF
FSW004B.WMF
FSW004D.WMF
FSW004E.WMF
FWN001A.WMF
FWN005A.WMF
FWN005B.WMF
FWN005C.WMF
FWN008A.WMF
FWN025A.WMF
FWN025B.WMF
FWN025C.WMF
FWN037A.WMF
FWN037B.WMF
FWN044A.WMF
FWN045A.WMF
GARLAND.WMF
GASI028D.WMF
GREASPNT.WMF
GRESPNT1.WMF
GRIMACE.WMF
GYMNAST.WMF
GYMNAST1.WMF
GYMNST1.WMF
HAN023.WMF
HAT.WMF
HAT1.WMF
HHBO026J.WMF
HIPPOPT.WMF
HLDAY024.WMF
HLDAY025.WMF
HORN.WMF
HORSE.WMF
HORSEMAN.WMF
JUGGLE.WMF
JUGGLER.WMF
JUGGLER1.WMF
JUGGLER8.WMF
KIDSATFA.WMF
LION.WMF
LION1.WMF
LOGFLUME.WMF
MAGICIN.WMF
MAGICIN1.WMF
MAGICIN2.WMF
MANONTIG.WMF
MARCHING.WMF
MASK.WMF
MASK1.WMF
MASK2.WMF
MASK3.WMF
MASK4.WMF
MISC062.WMF
MONKEY.WMF
MONKEY1.WMF
NOSE.WMF
ONSTAGE3.WMF
PARROT.WMF
PERW059J.WMF
PESI123D.WMF
PESI282D.WMF
PESI283D.WMF
PIGEONS.WMF
POPCORNW.WMF
POSTER.WMF
PUPPETS2.WMF
PUPTSHW.WMF
REACHING.WMF
ROLLER.WMF
ROPE.WMF
SALUTE.WMF
SEAL.WMF

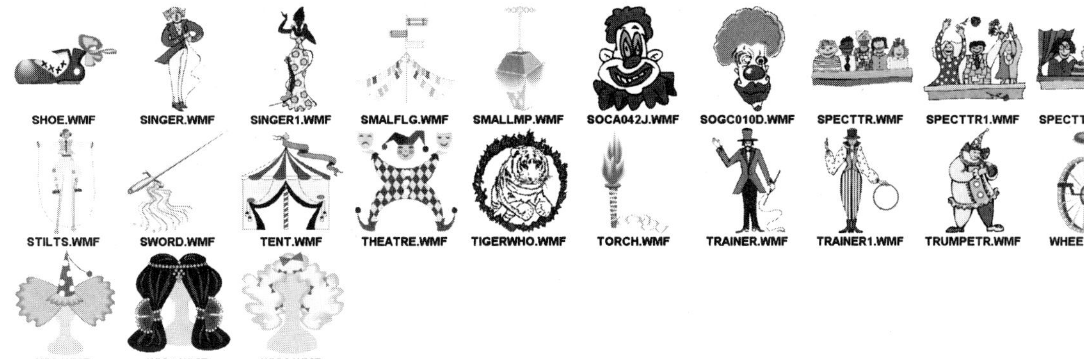
SHOE.WMF
SINGER.WMF
SINGER1.WMF
SMALFLG.WMF
SMALLMP.WMF
SOCA042J.WMF
SOGC010D.WMF
SPECTTR.WMF
SPECTTR1.WMF
SPECTTR2.WMF
STILTS.WMF
SWORD.WMF
TENT.WMF
THEATRE.WMF
TIGERWHO.WMF
TORCH.WMF
TRAINER.WMF
TRAINER1.WMF
TRUMPETR.WMF
WHEEL.WMF
WIG.WMF
WIG1.WMF
WIG2.WMF

0094.WMF
0104.WMF
0124.WMF
BALLERIN.WMF
BALLERN1.WMF
BALLET.WMF
BALLETTE.WMF
BROADWAY.WMF
CJUKEBOX.WMF
COUPLEAT.WMF
DANCE1.WMF
DANCE10.WMF
DANCE12.WMF
DANCE2.WMF
DANCE3.WMF
DANCERS.WMF
DANCING1.WMF
DANCINGB.WMF
DANCINGF.WMF
ENSI009J.WMF
ENSI044D.WMF
ENSS041D.WMF
ENSS044D.WMF
GIRLDANC.WMF
HUNGARY.WMF
MANDANCI.WMF
MINODANC.WMF
PD043YCU.WMF
PD043ZCU.WMF
PEBO012J.WMF
PEGC002J.WMF
PEGC003J.WMF
PEGC004J.WMF
PEGC027D.WMF
PERW017J.WMF
PERW036J.WMF
PRETEEND.WMF
SHOCKED1.WMF
TAP1.WMF
TAP2.WMF
TEENGIRL.WMF
YOUNGGIR.WMF
YUNGBLLT.WMF

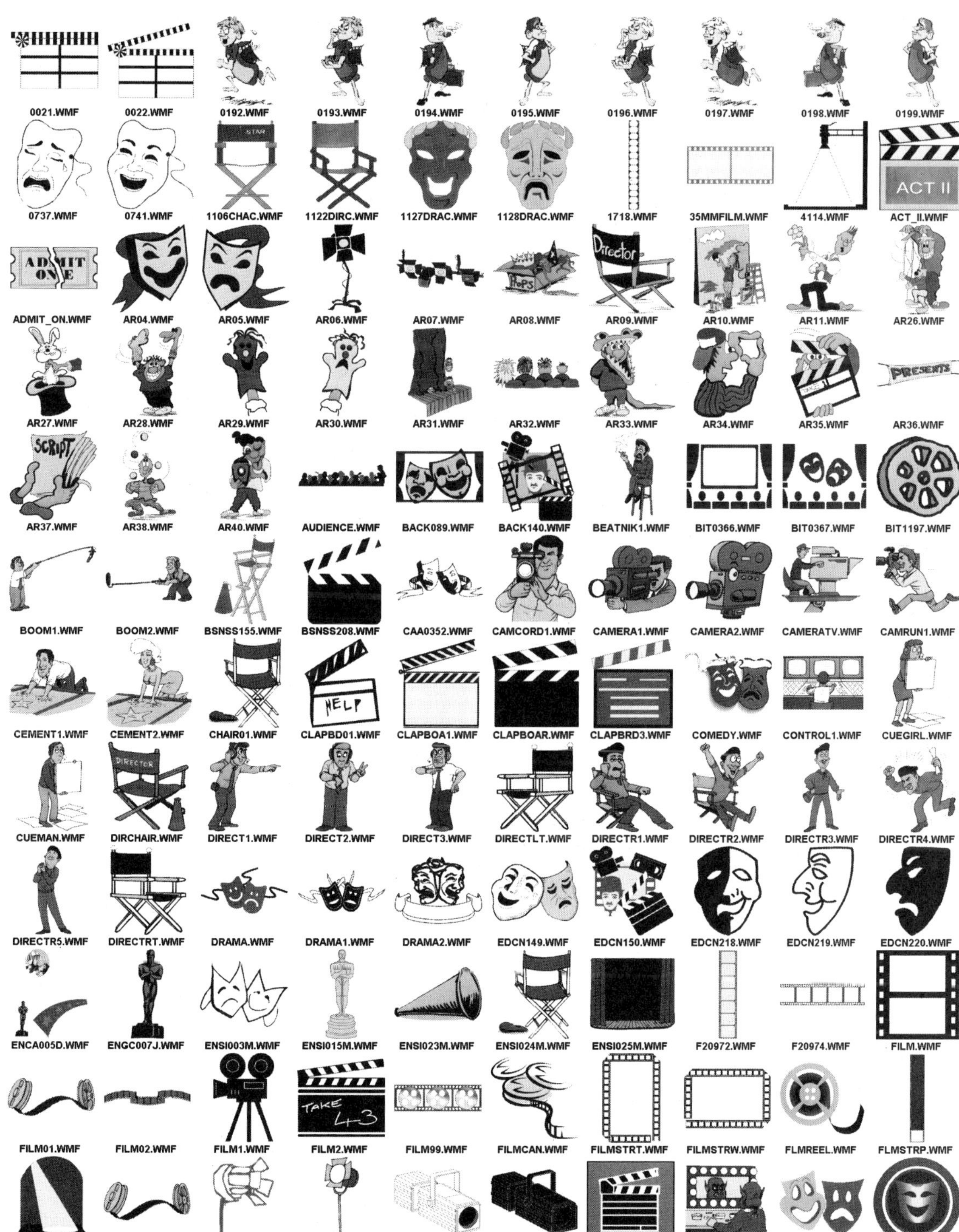
0021.WMF 0022.WMF 0192.WMF 0193.WMF 0194.WMF 0195.WMF 0196.WMF 0197.WMF 0198.WMF 0199.WMF
0737.WMF 0741.WMF 1106CHAC.WMF 1122DIRC.WMF 1127DRAC.WMF 1128DRAC.WMF 1718.WMF 35MMFILM.WMF 4114.WMF ACT_II.WMF
ADMIT_ON.WMF AR04.WMF AR05.WMF AR06.WMF AR07.WMF AR08.WMF AR09.WMF AR10.WMF AR11.WMF AR26.WMF
AR27.WMF AR28.WMF AR29.WMF AR30.WMF AR31.WMF AR32.WMF AR33.WMF AR34.WMF AR35.WMF AR36.WMF
AR37.WMF AR38.WMF AR40.WMF AUDIENCE.WMF BACK089.WMF BACK140.WMF BEATNIK1.WMF BIT0366.WMF BIT0367.WMF BIT1197.WMF
BOOM1.WMF BOOM2.WMF BSNSS155.WMF BSNSS208.WMF CAA0352.WMF CAMCORD1.WMF CAMERA1.WMF CAMERA2.WMF CAMERATV.WMF CAMRUN1.WMF
CEMENT1.WMF CEMENT2.WMF CHAIR01.WMF CLAPBD01.WMF CLAPBOA1.WMF CLAPBOAR.WMF CLAPBRD3.WMF COMEDY.WMF CONTROL1.WMF CUEGIRL.WMF
CUEMAN.WMF DIRCHAIR.WMF DIRECT1.WMF DIRECT2.WMF DIRECT3.WMF DIRECTLT.WMF DIRECTR1.WMF DIRECTR2.WMF DIRECTR3.WMF DIRECTR4.WMF
DIRECTR5.WMF DIRECTRT.WMF DRAMA.WMF DRAMA1.WMF DRAMA2.WMF EDCN149.WMF EDCN150.WMF EDCN218.WMF EDCN219.WMF EDCN220.WMF
ENCA005D.WMF ENGC007J.WMF ENSI003M.WMF ENSI015M.WMF ENSI023M.WMF ENSI024M.WMF ENSI025M.WMF F20972.WMF F20974.WMF FILM.WMF
FILM01.WMF FILM02.WMF FILM1.WMF FILM2.WMF FILM99.WMF FILMCAN.WMF FILMSTRT.WMF FILMSTRW.WMF FLMREEL.WMF FLMSTRP.WMF
GASI297M.WMF GASI362M.WMF L21193.WMF LIGHT1.WMF LIGHT16.WMF LIGHT2.WMF M21273.WMF MAKEUP.WMF MAN68.WMF MASK1.WMF

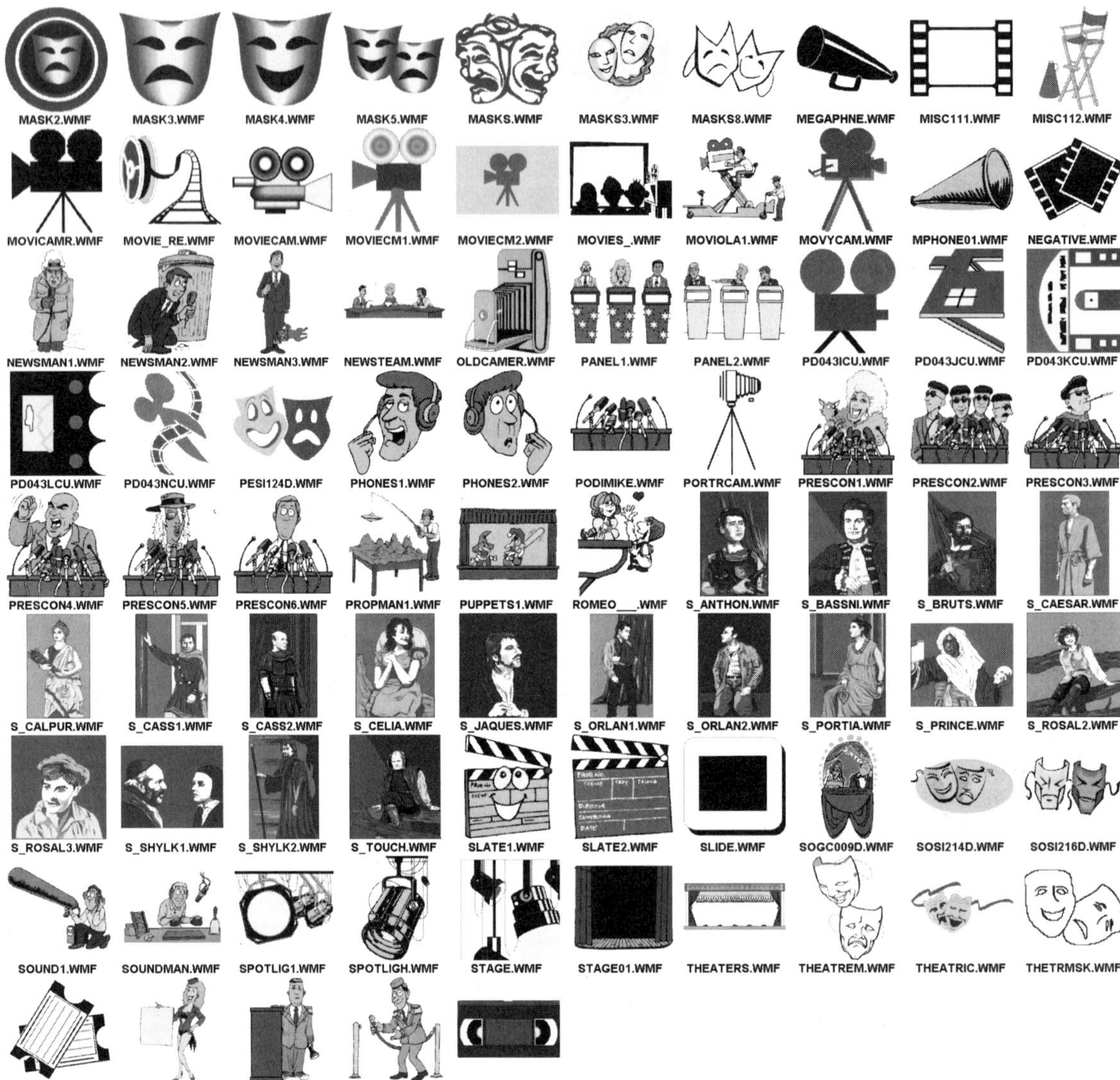
MASK2.WMF
MASK3.WMF
MASK4.WMF
MASK5.WMF
MASKS.WMF
MASKS3.WMF
MASKS8.WMF
MEGAPHNE.WMF
MISC111.WMF
MISC112.WMF
MOVICAMR.WMF
MOVIE_RE.WMF
MOVIECAM.WMF
MOVIECM1.WMF
MOVIECM2.WMF
MOVIES_.WMF
MOVIOLA1.WMF
MOVYCAM.WMF
MPHONE01.WMF
NEGATIVE.WMF
NEWSMAN1.WMF
NEWSMAN2.WMF
NEWSMAN3.WMF
NEWSTEAM.WMF
OLDCAMER.WMF
PANEL1.WMF
PANEL2.WMF
PD043ICU.WMF
PD043JCU.WMF
PD043KCU.WMF
PD043LCU.WMF
PD043NCU.WMF
PESI124D.WMF
PHONES1.WMF
PHONES2.WMF
PODIMIKE.WMF
PORTRCAM.WMF
PRESCON1.WMF
PRESCON2.WMF
PRESCON3.WMF
PRESCON4.WMF
PRESCON5.WMF
PRESCON6.WMF
PROPMAN1.WMF
PUPPETS1.WMF
ROMEO___.WMF
S_ANTHON.WMF
S_BASSNI.WMF
S_BRUTS.WMF
S_CAESAR.WMF
S_CALPUR.WMF
S_CASS1.WMF
S_CASS2.WMF
S_CELIA.WMF
S_JAQUES.WMF
S_ORLAN1.WMF
S_ORLAN2.WMF
S_PORTIA.WMF
S_PRINCE.WMF
S_ROSAL2.WMF
S_ROSAL3.WMF
S_SHYLK1.WMF
S_SHYLK2.WMF
S_TOUCH.WMF
SLATE1.WMF
SLATE2.WMF
SLIDE.WMF
SOGC009D.WMF
SOSI214D.WMF
SOSI216D.WMF
SOUND1.WMF
SOUNDMAN.WMF
SPOTLIG1.WMF
SPOTLIGH.WMF
STAGE.WMF
STAGE01.WMF
THEATERS.WMF
THEATREM.WMF
THEATRIC.WMF
THETRMSK.WMF
TICKETS.WMF
UPNEXT1.WMF
USHER1.WMF
USHER2.WMF
VIDTAPE.WMF

0701.WMF
0704.WMF
0712.WMF
0713.WMF
0714.WMF
1192.WMF
1193.WMF
1194.WMF
1195.WMF
1196.WMF
1197.WMF
1198.WMF
1199.WMF
1200.WMF
BACK192.WMF
BINGO.WMF
BISHOP.WMF
BIT0344.WMF
BIT0373.WMF
BIT0374.WMF
BIT0609.WMF
BIT0610.WMF
BIT0611.WMF
BIT0612.WMF
BIT0613.WMF
BIT0614.WMF
BIT0615.WMF
BIT0616.WMF
BIT0617.WMF
BIT0618.WMF
BIT0619.WMF
BIT0620.WMF
BIT0674.WMF
BIT0675.WMF
BIT0806.WMF
BIT0856.WMF
BLKD1.WMF
BLKD2.WMF
BLKD3.WMF
BLKD4.WMF
BLKD5.WMF
BLKD6.WMF
BLKS1.WMF
BLKS2.WMF
BLKS3.WMF
BLKS4.WMF
BLKS5.WMF
BLKS6.WMF
C20753.WMF
C20814.WMF
CHESS.WMF
CHESS10.WMF
CHESS11.WMF
CHESS12.WMF
CHESS13.WMF
CHESS14.WMF
CHESS15.WMF
CHESS16.WMF
CHESS17.WMF
CHESS18.WMF
CHESS19.WMF
CHESS20.WMF
CHESS21.WMF
CHESS22.WMF
CHESS23.WMF
CHESS24.WMF
CHESS25.WMF
CHESS26.WMF
CHESS_KN.WMF
CHESSB.WMF
CHESSB1.WMF
CHESSBRD.WMF
CHESSC.WMF
CHESSK.WMF
CHESSKG.WMF
CHESSP1.WMF
CHESSP2.WMF
CHESSP3.WMF
CHESSP4.WMF
CHESSP5.WMF
CHESSP6.WMF
CHESSP7.WMF
CHESSP8.WMF
CHESSP9.WMF
CHESSPWN.WMF
CHESSQN.WMF
CHSEGAME.WMF
DICE.WMF
DICE008.WMF
DICE01.WMF
DICE1.WMF
DICE2.WMF
DICE3.WMF
DICE50.WMF
DICE_1.WMF
DICE_2.WMF
DICE_3.WMF
DICE_4.WMF
DICE_5.WMF
DICE_6.WMF
DOMINO01.WMF
DOMINO03.WMF
DOMINO05.WMF
DOMINO07.WMF
DOMINO09.WMF
DOMINO11.WMF
DOMINO13.WMF
DOMINO15.WMF
DOMINO17.WMF
DOMINO19.WMF
DOMINO21.WMF
DOMINO23.WMF
DOMINO25.WMF
DOMINO27.WMF
DOMINO29.WMF
DOMINO31.WMF
DOMINO33.WMF
DOMINO35.WMF
DOMINO37.WMF
DOMINO39.WMF

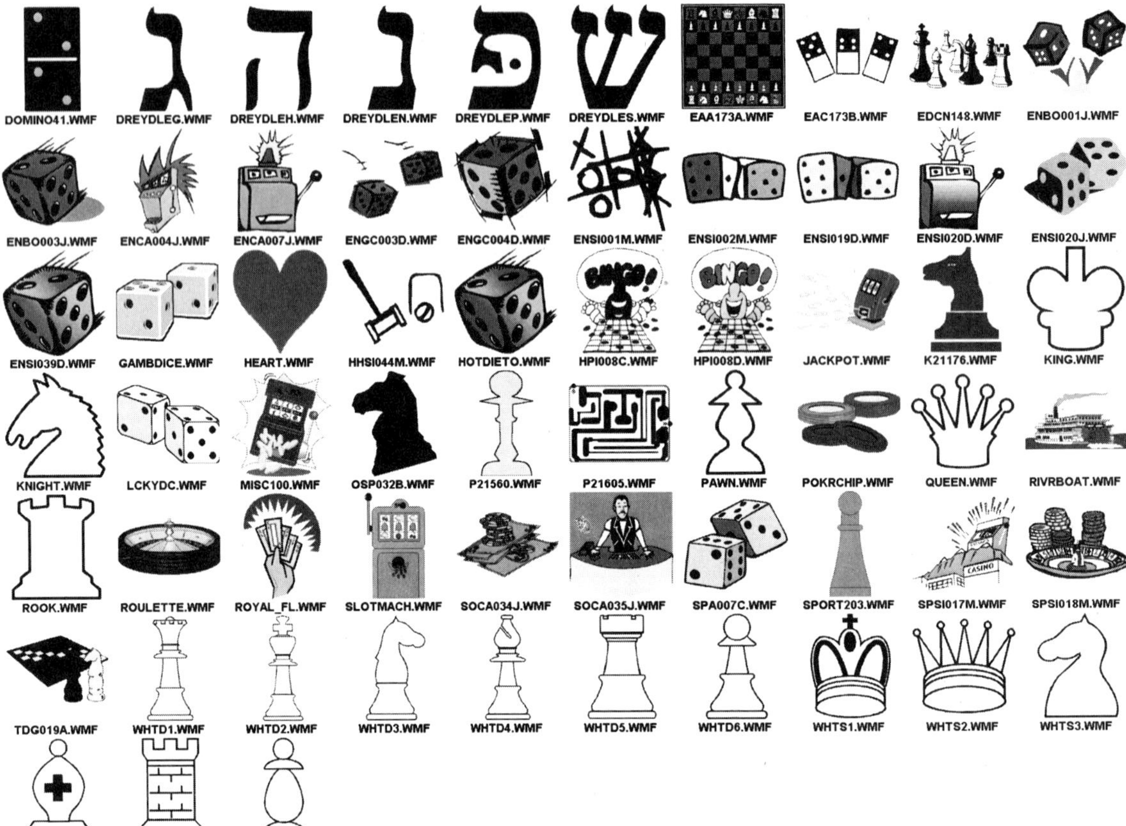
DOMINO41.WMF
DREYDLEG.WMF
DREYDLEH.WMF
DREYDLEN.WMF
DREYDLEP.WMF
DREYDLES.WMF
EAA173A.WMF
EAC173B.WMF
EDCN148.WMF
ENBO001J.WMF
ENBO003J.WMF
ENCA004J.WMF
ENCA007J.WMF
ENGC003D.WMF
ENGC004D.WMF
ENSI001M.WMF
ENSI002M.WMF
ENSI019D.WMF
ENSI020D.WMF
ENSI020J.WMF
ENSI039D.WMF
GAMBDICE.WMF
HEART.WMF
HHSI044M.WMF
HOTDIETO.WMF
HPI008C.WMF
HPI008D.WMF
JACKPOT.WMF
K21176.WMF
KING.WMF
KNIGHT.WMF
LCKYDC.WMF
MISC100.WMF
OSP032B.WMF
P21560.WMF
P21605.WMF
PAWN.WMF
POKRCHIP.WMF
QUEEN.WMF
RIVRBOAT.WMF
ROOK.WMF
ROULETTE.WMF
ROYAL_FL.WMF
SLOTMACH.WMF
SOCA034J.WMF
SOCA035J.WMF
SPA007C.WMF
SPORT203.WMF
SPSI017M.WMF
SPSI018M.WMF
TDG019A.WMF
WHTD1.WMF
WHTD2.WMF
WHTD3.WMF
WHTD4.WMF
WHTD5.WMF
WHTD6.WMF
WHTS1.WMF
WHTS2.WMF
WHTS3.WMF
WHTS4.WMF
WHTS5.WMF
WHTS6.WMF

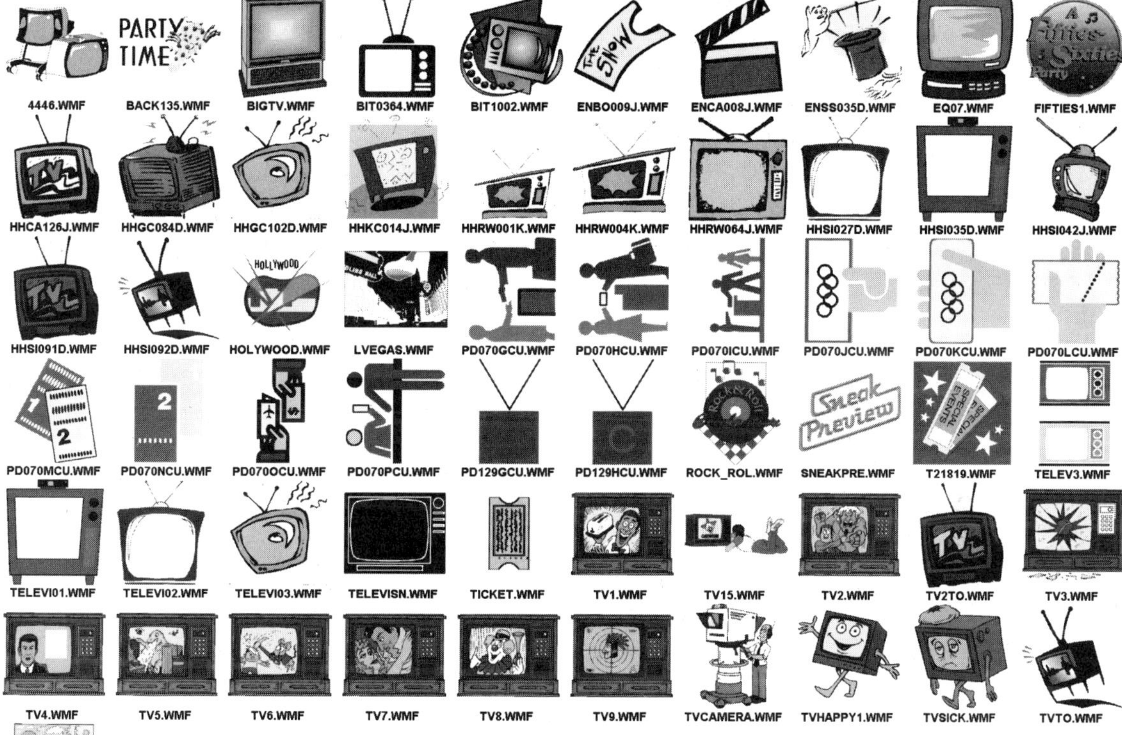
4446.WMF
PARTY TIME
BACK135.WMF
BIGTV.WMF
BIT0364.WMF
BIT1002.WMF
The Show
ENBO009J.WMF
ENCA008J.WMF
ENSS035D.WMF
EQ07.WMF
A Fifties Sixties Party
FIFTIES1.WMF
TV
HHCA126J.WMF
HHGC084D.WMF
HHGC102D.WMF
HHKC014J.WMF
HHRW001K.WMF
HHRW004K.WMF
HHRW064J.WMF
HHSI027D.WMF
HHSI035D.WMF
HHSI042J.WMF
TV
HHSI091D.WMF
HHSI092D.WMF
HOLLYWOOD
HOLYWOOD.WMF
LVEGAS.WMF
PD070GCU.WMF
PD070HCU.WMF
PD070ICU.WMF
PD070JCU.WMF
PD070KCU.WMF
PD070LCU.WMF
1
2
PD070MCU.WMF
2
PD070NCU.WMF
PD070OCU.WMF
PD070PCU.WMF
PD129GCU.WMF
PD129HCU.WMF
Rock & Roll
ROCK_ROL.WMF
Sneak Preview
SNEAKPRE.WMF
SPECIAL EVENTS
T21819.WMF
TELEV3.WMF
TELEVI01.WMF
TELEVI02.WMF
TELEVI03.WMF
TELEVISN.WMF
TICKET.WMF
TV1.WMF
TV15.WMF
TV2.WMF
TV
TV2TO.WMF
TV3.WMF
TV4.WMF
TV5.WMF
TV6.WMF
TV7.WMF
TV8.WMF
TV9.WMF
TVCAMERA.WMF
TVHAPPY1.WMF
TVSICK.WMF
TVTO.WMF

WEATHER.WMF

1998.WMF
AAL021C.WMF
ABONIM.WMF
AQCAR066.WMF
BADFAIRY.WMF
BEASTLO.WMF
BROOMCAT.WMF
CAMEL_WI.WMF
CATERPIL.WMF
CC32.WMF
CENTAUR.WMF
CHIMERA.WMF
CREATUR1.WMF
CRTN054.WMF
CYCLOPS.WMF
DEAMON.WMF
DEMONCA1.WMF
DEVILBRU.WMF
DEVILHA.WMF
DOGWWIN.WMF
DRAGON01.WMF
DRAGON02.WMF
DRAGON03.WMF
DRAGON04.WMF
DRAGON05.WMF
DRAGON06.WMF
DRAGON07.WMF
DRAGON08.WMF
DRAGON09.WMF
DRAGON10.WMF
DRAGON11.WMF
DRAGON12.WMF
DRAGON13.WMF
DRAGON14.WMF
DRAGON15.WMF
DRAGON16.WMF
DRAGON17.WMF
DRAGON18.WMF
DRAGON19.WMF
DRAGON20.WMF
DRAGON21.WMF
DRAGON22.WMF
DRAGON23.WMF
DRAGON24.WMF
DRAGON25.WMF
DRAGON26.WMF
DRAGON27.WMF
DRAGON28.WMF
DRAGON29.WMF
DRAGON30.WMF
DRAGON31.WMF
DRAGON32.WMF
DRAGON33.WMF
DRAGON34.WMF
DRYAD.WMF
EDCN206.WMF
ENCA018D.WMF
ENSI001D.WMF
ENSI009D.WMF
FAIRY01M.WMF
FBHORSE.WMF
FISHWRU.WMF
FROGPRIN.WMF
GARGOYL.WMF
GARGOYLE.WMF
GENETIC.WMF
GHOULCOL.WMF
GHOULIE.WMF
GRIFFON.WMF
HALFMAN.WMF
HATCHIN.WMF
HHW023C.WMF
HORN02.WMF
HORN03.WMF
HORN11.WMF
HORN44.WMF
HORN55.WMF
HORN66.WMF
HORN77.WMF
HORN77_1.WMF
HORN88.WMF
HORN99.WMF
JA03.WMF
JA04.WMF
LIONMAN.WMF
LOCHNESS.WMF
MASI010D.WMF
MEDUSA.WMF
MEDUSAH.WMF
MINOTAU.WMF
MINOTAU2.WMF
MINOTAUR.WMF
MORNINGM.WMF
NACA028J.WMF
NACA209J.WMF
NARW003J.WMF
NARW044J.WMF
NASI246D.WMF
ODDBEAS.WMF
OSHIP.WMF
PANWITHP.WMF
PESI057D.WMF
PESI067D.WMF
PESI069D.WMF
PESI377D.WMF
PESI378D.WMF
PHOENIX.WMF
PHOENIX3.WMF
PRIN0429.WMF
PRIN0430.WMF
PRIN0431.WMF
PRIN0432.WMF
SAC046A.WMF
SNAKEMAN.WMF
SOCA031J.WMF
SORW019J.WMF
SPA007E.WMF
SPHINX.WMF
SPIRIT.WMF
SS01.WMF

SSERPENT.WMF

T21842.WMF

U21856.WMF

WINGS01.WMF

WINGS03.WMF

WINGS04.WMF

WINGS05.WMF

WINGS06.WMF

WINGS07.WMF

WINGSO2.WMF

WOMANWR.WMF

Fantasy, Medieval & Mythology (FANTMYTH) • Cultures

DEC084E.WMF DEC084F.WMF DIVSPIR1.WMF FCP010G.WMF FCP026E.WMF FIGURE11.WMF FMI130N.WMF FMI132X.WMF FMI138G.WMF FRA008A.WMF

GARGO1.WMF GARGO10.WMF GARGO2.WMF GARGO3.WMF GARGO4.WMF GARGO5.WMF GARGO6.WMF GARGO7.WMF GARGO8.WMF GARGO9.WMF

MERCURY.WMF MOD005M.WMF MYCR106.WMF OFS070F.WMF SB31.WMF SB32.WMF SB33.WMF SPA026B.WMF SPIRIT04.WMF SPIRIT06.WMF

SPIRIT07.WMF SPIRIT08.WMF SPIRIT09.WMF SPIRIT1.WMF SPIRIT10.WMF SPIRIT11.WMF SPIRIT12.WMF SPIRIT13.WMF SPIRIT14.WMF SPIRIT15.WMF

SPIRIT16.WMF SPIRIT17.WMF SPIRIT18.WMF SPIRIT3.WMF VE24.WMF WA01.WMF WA02.WMF WA03.WMF WA06.WMF WA07.WMF

WA08.WMF WELSH DR.WMF

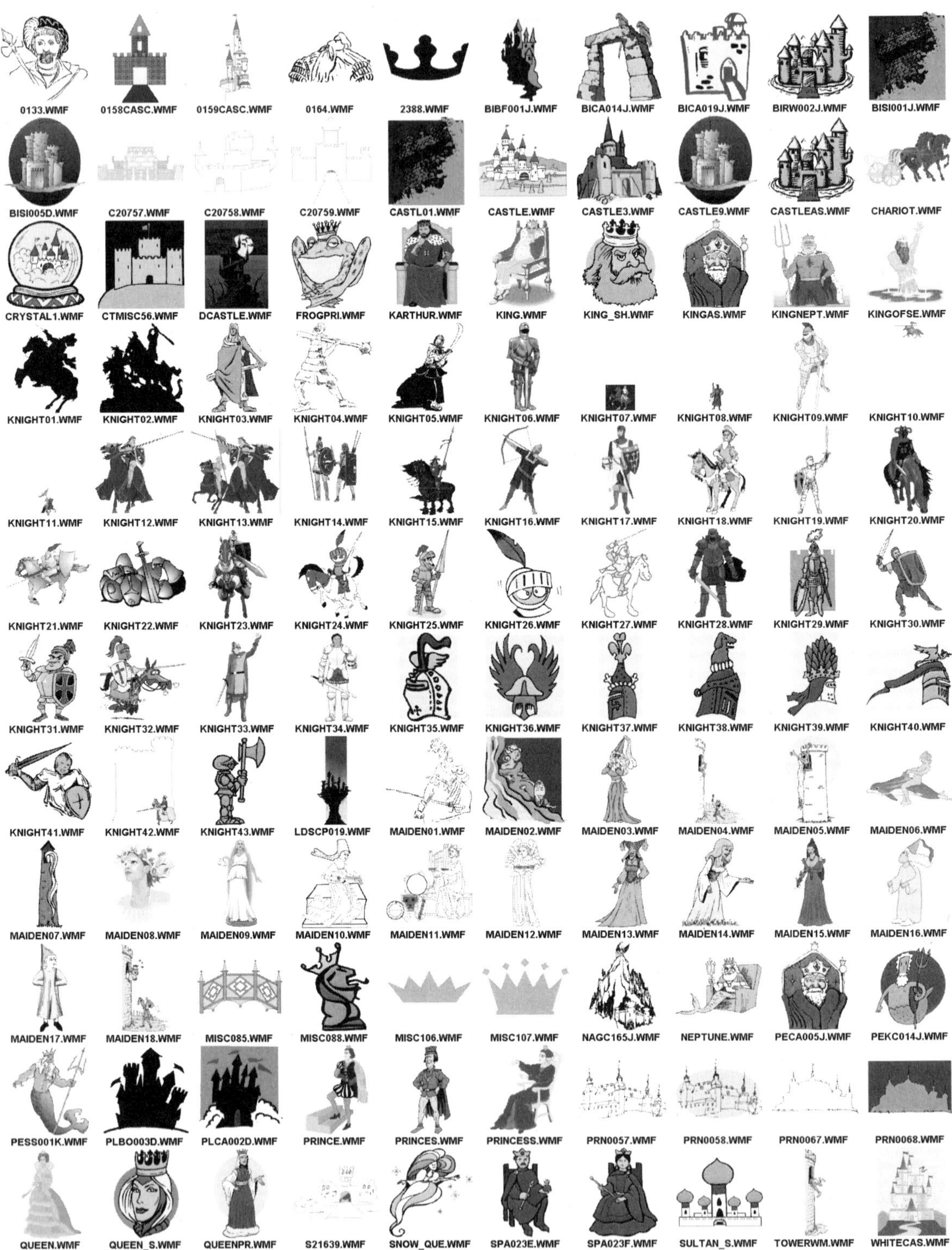
0133.WMF 0158CASC.WMF 0159CASC.WMF 0164.WMF 2388.WMF BIBF001J.WMF BICA014J.WMF BICA019J.WMF BIRW002J.WMF BISI001J.WMF
BISI005D.WMF C20757.WMF C20758.WMF C20759.WMF CASTL01.WMF CASTLE.WMF CASTLE3.WMF CASTLE9.WMF CASTLEAS.WMF CHARIOT.WMF
CRYSTAL1.WMF CTMISC56.WMF DCASTLE.WMF FROGPRI.WMF KARTHUR.WMF KING.WMF KING_SH.WMF KINGAS.WMF KINGNEPT.WMF KINGOFSE.WMF
KNIGHT01.WMF KNIGHT02.WMF KNIGHT03.WMF KNIGHT04.WMF KNIGHT05.WMF KNIGHT06.WMF KNIGHT07.WMF KNIGHT08.WMF KNIGHT09.WMF KNIGHT10.WMF
KNIGHT11.WMF KNIGHT12.WMF KNIGHT13.WMF KNIGHT14.WMF KNIGHT15.WMF KNIGHT16.WMF KNIGHT17.WMF KNIGHT18.WMF KNIGHT19.WMF KNIGHT20.WMF
KNIGHT21.WMF KNIGHT22.WMF KNIGHT23.WMF KNIGHT24.WMF KNIGHT25.WMF KNIGHT26.WMF KNIGHT27.WMF KNIGHT28.WMF KNIGHT29.WMF KNIGHT30.WMF
KNIGHT31.WMF KNIGHT32.WMF KNIGHT33.WMF KNIGHT34.WMF KNIGHT35.WMF KNIGHT36.WMF KNIGHT37.WMF KNIGHT38.WMF KNIGHT39.WMF KNIGHT40.WMF
KNIGHT41.WMF KNIGHT42.WMF KNIGHT43.WMF LDSCP019.WMF MAIDEN01.WMF MAIDEN02.WMF MAIDEN03.WMF MAIDEN04.WMF MAIDEN05.WMF MAIDEN06.WMF
MAIDEN07.WMF MAIDEN08.WMF MAIDEN09.WMF MAIDEN10.WMF MAIDEN11.WMF MAIDEN12.WMF MAIDEN13.WMF MAIDEN14.WMF MAIDEN15.WMF MAIDEN16.WMF
MAIDEN17.WMF MAIDEN18.WMF MISC085.WMF MISC088.WMF MISC106.WMF MISC107.WMF NAGC165J.WMF NEPTUNE.WMF PECA005J.WMF PEKC014J.WMF
PESS001K.WMF PLBO003D.WMF PLCA002D.WMF PRINCE.WMF PRINCES.WMF PRINCESS.WMF PRN0057.WMF PRN0058.WMF PRN0067.WMF PRN0068.WMF
QUEEN.WMF QUEEN_S.WMF QUEENPR.WMF S21639.WMF SNOW_QUE.WMF SPA023E.WMF SPA023F.WMF SULTAN_S.WMF TOWERWM.WMF WHITECAS.WMF

0790.WMF 0791.WMF 0792.WMF 1112CROC.WMF 1208SWOC.WMF BIAB004J.WMF BTLNOTE.WMF BURW010J.WMF CATACOMB.WMF CTMISC19.WMF

CTMISC61.WMF CTMISC68.WMF CTMISC69.WMF ENSI005D.WMF ENSI011M.WMF GENIE01.WMF GENIE02.WMF GENIE03.WMF GENIE04.WMF GENIE05.WMF

GENIE06.WMF GENIE07.WMF GENIE08.WMF GENIE09.WMF GENIE10.WMF GENIE11.WMF GENIE12.WMF GENIE13.WMF GENIE14.WMF GENIE15.WMF

GENIE16.WMF GENIE17.WMF GENIE18.WMF GENIE19.WMF GENIE20.WMF GENIE21.WMF GENIE22.WMF GENIE23.WMF GENIE24.WMF GENIE25.WMF

GENIE26.WMF GENIE27.WMF GOLDAPPL.WMF HLDAY022.WMF HLDAY023.WMF JESTER01.WMF JESTER02.WMF JESTER03.WMF JESTER04.WMF JESTER05.WMF

JESTER06.WMF JESTER07.WMF JESTER08.WMF JESTER09.WMF JESTER10.WMF JESTER11.WMF JESTER12.WMF JESTER13.WMF JESTER14.WMF JESTER15.WMF

JESTER16.WMF JESTER17.WMF JESTER18.WMF JESTER19.WMF JESTER20.WMF JESTER21.WMF JESTER22.WMF JESTER23.WMF JESTER24.WMF MERM01.WMF

MERM02.WMF MERM03.WMF MERM04.WMF MERM05.WMF MERM06.WMF MERM07.WMF MERM08.WMF MERM09.WMF MERM10.WMF MERM11.WMF

MERM12.WMF PIRATE01.WMF PIRATE02.WMF PIRATE03.WMF PIRATE04.WMF PIRATE05.WMF PIRATE06.WMF PIRATE07.WMF PIRATE08.WMF PIRATE09.WMF

PIRATE10.WMF PIRATE11.WMF PIRATE12.WMF PIRATE13.WMF POTOFGOL.WMF SWORDINS.WMF T21832.WMF TREASURE.WMF TRSRCHS.WMF TRUNKWIT.WMF

0177.WMF
0211.WMF
0212.WMF
0213.WMF
0214.WMF
0215.WMF
0216.WMF
0217.WMF
0218.WMF
0219.WMF
0220.WMF
0221.WMF
0222.WMF
0223.WMF
0224.WMF
0225.WMF
0226.WMF
0227.WMF
0228.WMF
0229.WMF
0230.WMF
0231.WMF
0232.WMF
0233.WMF
0234.WMF
0235.WMF
0236.WMF
A20046.WMF
ATTACKI.WMF
BISI006D.WMF
CAA0158.WMF
CAA0171.WMF
CAA0172.WMF
CAA0176.WMF
CAA0180.WMF
CAA0181.WMF
CAA0183.WMF
CRTN133.WMF
E20937.WMF
ELFPRES.WMF
ELFRIDI.WMF
ELFRIDIN.WMF
ELFWARR.WMF
ELFWBOW.WMF
ELFWITH.WMF
ENSI002D.WMF
FAIRY.WMF
FAIRYBE.WMF
FAIRYBE1.WMF
FAIRYPR.WMF
FLYINGSP.WMF
FSTV171.WMF
GNOMDIAM.WMF
GNOMEWPL.WMF
GOBLIN.WMF
GOOD_FAI.WMF
HEROLION.WMF
HOUSE.WMF
LEPRECH0.WMF
LEPRECHA.WMF
LEPRECN2.WMF
LITTLEM.WMF
LITTLEM1.WMF
LITTLEP.WMF
LITTLEP1.WMF
MACA019J.WMF
MACA020J.WMF
MACA021J.WMF
MACA024J.WMF
MARW003J.WMF
MASI001D.WMF
MESI001M.WMF
MISC003.WMF
MOTHER_G.WMF
MOUSESQ.WMF
MUSHROOM.WMF
MUSKETER.WMF
NACA021J.WMF
NYMPHNAI.WMF
ODDIMPT.WMF
PAN1.WMF
PAN2.WMF
PEBO005J.WMF
PEBO006J.WMF
PECA095J.WMF
PECA123J.WMF
PECA177D.WMF
PECA178D.WMF
PEOPL011.WMF
PEOPLE5.WMF
PEOPLE6.WMF
PEOPLE7.WMF
PEOPLE8.WMF
PEOPLE9.WMF
PESI038D.WMF
PESI092D.WMF
PESI094D.WMF
PESI193D.WMF
PESI269D.WMF
PESI278D.WMF
PESI325D.WMF
PESI356D.WMF
RIP_VAN_.WMF
SAMARAI.WMF
SORW005J.WMF
TOOLS5.WMF
TROLL.WMF
VIKINGA.WMF
VIKINGIN.WMF
VIKINGP.WMF
VIKINGSS.WMF
W21881.WMF

0202S.WMF
0205.WMF
1SORCERE.WMF
2SORCERE.WMF
BIT1059.WMF
CCROWN.WMF
COLLAGEW.WMF
CONJURIN.WMF
CRISTSPH.WMF
CRSYTBLL.WMF
CRTN128.WMF
CRYSTAL.WMF
CRYSTALB.WMF
CTMISC24.WMF
DEATH.WMF
DRUID.WMF
ENSI004M.WMF
FLUITE.WMF
MAGICBOO.WMF
MAGICCA.WMF
MAGICCA1.WMF
MAGICCAR.WMF
MAGICMI.WMF
MEGALITE.WMF
MERLIN.WMF
OLDLADY.WMF
PEBO002J.WMF
PEBO004J.WMF
PECA102D.WMF
SORCERER.WMF
SPA011F.WMF
W21883.WMF
W21884.WMF
W21885.WMF
WANDCUS.WMF
WIZARD.WMF
WIZARD00.WMF
WIZARD01.WMF
WIZARD03.WMF
WIZARD2C.WMF
WIZARDA.WMF
WIZARDAS.WMF
WIZARDB.WMF
WIZARDC.WMF
WIZARDCO.WMF
WIZARDSU.WMF
WIZARDW.WMF
WIZARDWI.WMF
WIZARDX.WMF
WIZRDAS.WMF
WIZZ_HA.WMF

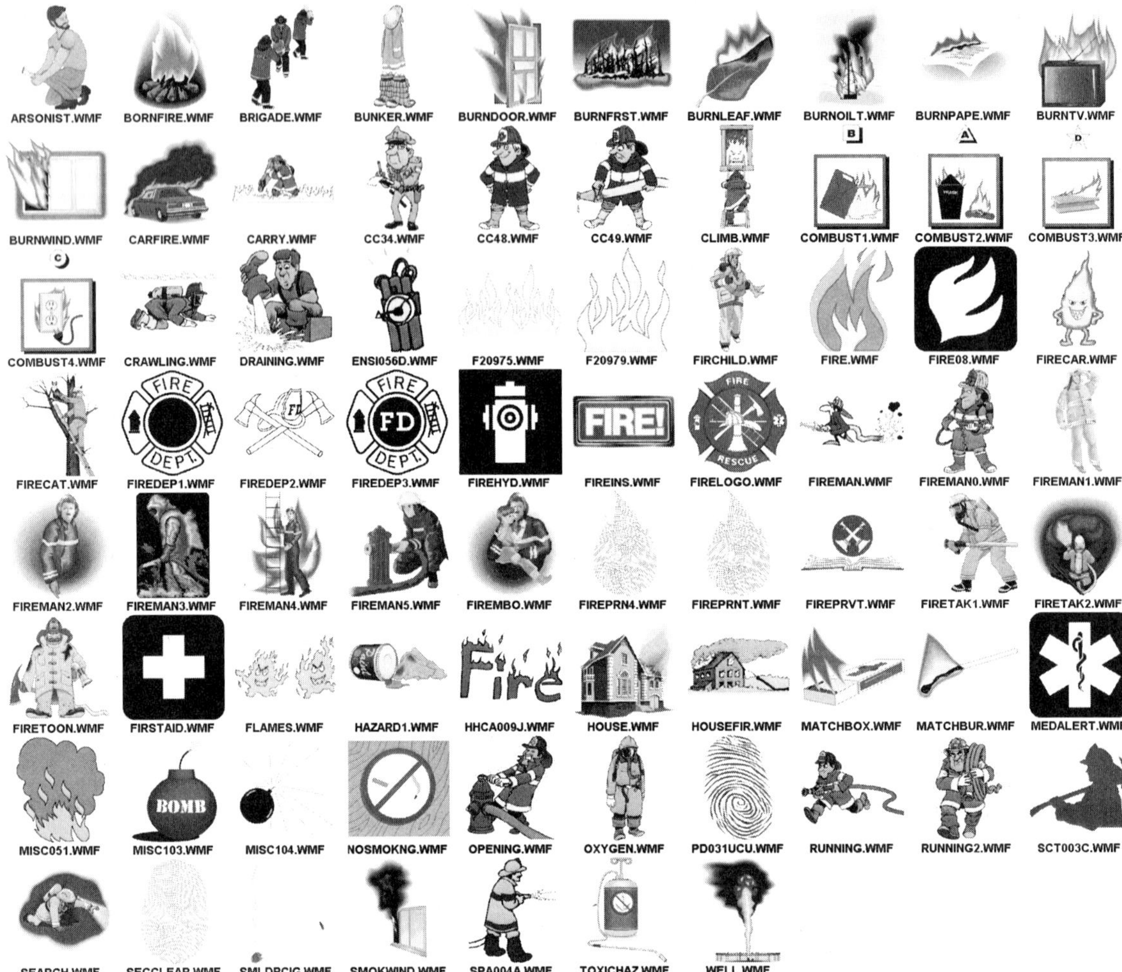
ARSONIST.WMF
BORNFIRE.WMF
BRIGADE.WMF
BUNKER.WMF
BURNDOOR.WMF
BURNFRST.WMF
BURNLEAF.WMF
BURNOILT.WMF
BURNPAPE.WMF
BURNTV.WMF
BURNWIND.WMF
CARFIRE.WMF
CARRY.WMF
CC34.WMF
CC48.WMF
CC49.WMF
CLIMB.WMF
COMBUST1.WMF
COMBUST2.WMF
COMBUST3.WMF
COMBUST4.WMF
CRAWLING.WMF
DRAINING.WMF
ENSI056D.WMF
F20975.WMF
F20979.WMF
FIRCHILD.WMF
FIRE.WMF
FIRE08.WMF
FIRECAR.WMF
FIRECAT.WMF
FIREDEP1.WMF
FIREDEP2.WMF
FIREDEP3.WMF
FIREHYD.WMF
FIREINS.WMF
FIRELOGO.WMF
FIREMAN.WMF
FIREMAN0.WMF
FIREMAN1.WMF
FIREMAN2.WMF
FIREMAN3.WMF
FIREMAN4.WMF
FIREMAN5.WMF
FIREMBO.WMF
FIREPRN4.WMF
FIREPRNT.WMF
FIREPRVT.WMF
FIRETAK1.WMF
FIRETAK2.WMF
FIRETOON.WMF
FIRSTAID.WMF
FLAMES.WMF
HAZARD1.WMF
HHCA009J.WMF
HOUSE.WMF
HOUSEFIR.WMF
MATCHBOX.WMF
MATCHBUR.WMF
MEDALERT.WMF
MISC051.WMF
MISC103.WMF
MISC104.WMF
NOSMOKNG.WMF
OPENING.WMF
OXYGEN.WMF
PD031UCU.WMF
RUNNING.WMF
RUNNING2.WMF
SCT003C.WMF
SEARCH.WMF
SECCLEAR.WMF
SMLDRCIG.WMF
SMOKWIND.WMF
SPA004A.WMF
TOXICHAZ.WMF
WELL.WMF

1040BADC.WMF 1047BURC.WMF 1073SPYC.WMF ANGRY.WMF BUGC018D.WMF BURGLAR.WMF C20771.WMF CASUAL.WMF CC21.WMF CC33.WMF

CC39.WMF CELLDR.WMF CHAIR.WMF CHOPPER1.WMF CHOPPER2.WMF CITATION.WMF CONTRAB.WMF CONTROL1.WMF CONTROL2.WMF CONVICT.WMF

COP.WMF COPBLOW.WMF CRIMERT.WMF CRIMINAL.WMF CRTN119.WMF DDRIVER.WMF DEAGENT.WMF ENSI007M.WMF ENSI010D.WMF FX02_.WMF

G21066.WMF GANG1.WMF GANG2.WMF GANG3.WMF GANG4.WMF GANG5.WMF GANGSTER.WMF HANDCUFD.WMF HOGANS.WMF HOLDUP.WMF

INTAFAIR.WMF KEYSTONE.WMF LOOTER.WMF MOUNTY.WMF MOUSEON_.WMF MUGGER.WMF OFFCTRCH.WMF OFFICSIL.WMF ONSTEPS.WMF PARADE.WMF

PATROL1.WMF PD031CU.WMF PD031ICU.WMF PD031JCU.WMF PD031KCU.WMF PD031LCU.WMF PD031MCU.WMF PD031NCU.WMF PD031OCU.WMF PD031PCU.WMF

PD031QCU.WMF PD031RCU.WMF PD031SCU.WMF PD031TCU.WMF PD031XCU.WMF PD031YCU.WMF PD031ZCU.WMF PD032ACU.WMF PD032BCU.WMF PD032CCU.WMF

PD032DCU.WMF PEGC016D.WMF PEGC017D.WMF PESI028D.WMF PESI085D.WMF PESI116D.WMF PESI135D.WMF PGX015A.WMF PGX016C.WMF PICKPOC.WMF

PLCTEEN.WMF POLCDOG2.WMF POLICCAP.WMF POLICDEP.WMF POLICDOG.WMF POLICE.WMF POLICE01.WMF POLICE02.WMF POLICE03.WMF POLICE04.WMF

POLICE05.WMF POLICE06.WMF POLICE07.WMF POLICE08.WMF POLICE09.WMF POLICE10.WMF POLICE22.WMF POLICE23.WMF POLICE24.WMF POLICE8.WMF

POLICEC.WMF POLICECH.WMF POLICEL.WMF POLICEP.WMF POLICEPG.WMF POLICINS.WMF POLICMAN.WMF POLICMN3.WMF POLICOF1.WMF POLICOF2.WMF

POLICOF3.WMF POLICOF4.WMF POLWOMAN.WMF PRANKCOL.WMF PRIVATEI.WMF RADARGUN.WMF ROBBER.WMF RUNPOL.WMF SAFECRAK.WMF SCT003A.WMF

SECURE.WMF
SECURITY.WMF
SHEBADGE.WMF
SHERFINS.WMF
SHERIFF.WMF
SHERIFF1.WMF
SHERIFF2.WMF
SHERIFF4.WMF
SHIELD2.WMF
SHOOTING.WMF
SJUMPER.WMF
SKEYS.WMF
SLEEPING.WMF
SOBRIETY.WMF
STATPOLC.WMF
STS031B.WMF
SWAT.WMF
TRAFFIC.WMF

1054HANC.WMF
1055HANC.WMF
1060JAIC.WMF
1063MAGC.WMF
1084BALC.WMF
A20012.WMF
A20013.WMF
AIRLIFT.WMF
AMBULANC.WMF
AXE.WMF
B20059.WMF
BADGE.WMF
BADGE12.WMF
BADGE2.WMF
BADGE22.WMF
BATON.WMF
BSNSS210.WMF
BSNSS211.WMF
BSNSS212.WMF
BUGC015J.WMF
BUGC019D.WMF
DIEFLAME.WMF
DOWNPOLE.WMF
EMERGEN.WMF
ENSI008J.WMF
ENSI048D.WMF
EXT01.WMF
EXTINGU1.WMF
EXTINGU2.WMF
EXTNGSHR.WMF
EXTRICAT.WMF
F20976.WMF
F20977.WMF
FHELMET.WMF
FHYD.WMF
FIRCOLLG.WMF
FIRE3.WMF
FIRE_HYD.WMF
FIREALAR.WMF
FIREAXE.WMF
FIREDOG.WMF
FIREEX.WMF
FIREEXT.WMF
FIREFGT1.WMF
FIREFGT2.WMF
FIREHYD.WMF
FIRELADD.WMF
FIRETRK.WMF
FIRETRK2.WMF
FIRETRK5.WMF
FIRETRK8.WMF
FIREXT.WMF
FIREXTB.WMF
FIRTRCK1.WMF
FIRTRUC2.WMF
FMANHAT.WMF
GASI002D.WMF
HALLIGAN.WMF
HANDCLUF.WMF
HANDCUF4.WMF
HANDCUFF.WMF
HANDSCLF.WMF
HAZARD2.WMF
HAZARDOS.WMF
HELICOP.WMF
HHCA138J.WMF
HHCA162J.WMF
HHGC017D.WMF
HHSI009J.WMF
HHSI055M.WMF
HNDCUFF2.WMF
HOOK.WMF
HOSE2.WMF
HOSE3.WMF
HOSEWATR.WMF
HSCANNER.WMF
HYDRANT.WMF
HYDRANT2.WMF
HYDRANT3.WMF
HYDRANT5.WMF
HYDRNT2.WMF
INGC001D.WMF
INGC010J.WMF
INSI003M.WMF
INSI013D.WMF
INSI036D.WMF
JAWSLIFE.WMF
LADDER.WMF
MOTORCYC.WMF
MOTRCYC3.WMF
NOZZLE.WMF
NOZZLE4.WMF
PAGER.WMF
PBADGE.WMF
PD022YCU.WMF
PESI060D.WMF
POLCAR1.WMF
POLCAR2.WMF
POLIC_CR.WMF
POLICEW.WMF
RAPPELL.WMF
REGMARK.WMF
RLADDER.WMF
SCBA.WMF
SCENE.WMF
SECURE2.WMF
SECURTY.WMF
SIREN.WMF
SIREN1.WMF
SMOKEDT.WMF
STKC001J.WMF
TRCA026J.WMF
VEST.WMF
WARRANTS.WMF
WATERRES.WMF
WILDFIRE.WMF
XTNGWSHR.WMF

0418.WMF A10.WMF A11.WMF A12.WMF A15.WMF A16.WMF A18.WMF A19_.WMF ABIL01.WMF ABIL02.WMF
ABIL03.WMF ABIL04.WMF ABIL05.WMF ABIL06.WMF ABIL07.WMF ABIL08_.WMF ABIL09.WMF ABIL10.WMF ABIL11.WMF ABIL12.WMF
ABIL13.WMF ABIL14.WMF ABIL15.WMF ABIL16.WMF ABIL17.WMF ABIL18.WMF ABIL19.WMF ABIL20.WMF ABIL21.WMF ABIL22.WMF
ABIL23.WMF ABIL24.WMF AEROBIC.WMF AEROBIC1.WMF AEROBICC.WMF AEROBICS.WMF ATH01.WMF ATH02.WMF ATH03.WMF ATH04.WMF
ATH05.WMF ATH06.WMF ATH07.WMF ATH08.WMF ATH09.WMF ATH10.WMF ATH11.WMF ATH12.WMF ATH13.WMF ATH14.WMF
ATH15.WMF ATH16.WMF ATH17.WMF ATH18.WMF ATH19.WMF ATH20.WMF ATH21.WMF ATH22.WMF ATH23.WMF ATH24.WMF
ATH25.WMF BALET1.WMF BALET1C.WMF BLLY.WMF CH01.WMF CH02.WMF CH03.WMF CH04.WMF CH05.WMF CRTN038.WMF
E44.WMF FITNES.WMF FITNES2.WMF FITNES2C.WMF FITNESC.WMF GUYRUN.WMF HLTH011.WMF HLTH014.WMF HLTH015.WMF HLTH030.WMF
HLTH046.WMF HLTH102.WMF HLTH103.WMF HLTH104.WMF HLTH105.WMF HLTH115.WMF HLTH125.WMF HLTH148.WMF HLTH149.WMF INLINE.WMF
KUNGFU1.WMF KUNGFU2.WMF KUNGFU3.WMF MUSCLES1.WMF MUSCLES2.WMF MUSCLESC.WMF PEAB006D.WMF PERW055J.WMF PESI027M.WMF RBLADER.WMF
RBLADERC.WMF SKATE1.WMF SKATE1C.WMF SPCA035J.WMF SPCA036J.WMF SPGC011D.WMF SPGC073D.WMF SPJB008J.WMF SPJB020J.WMF SPJB043J.WMF
SPJB044J.WMF SPKC005J.WMF SPSI007M.WMF SPSI017J.WMF SPSI248D.WMF SPSI289D.WMF SPSI294D.WMF SPSI295D.WMF SPSI403D.WMF SPSI404D.WMF

SPSI413D.WMF SPSI453D.WMF SPSI458D.WMF SPSI461D.WMF SPSI470D.WMF SPSI484D.WMF SPSI489D.WMF SPSI527D.WMF SPSI544D.WMF STERD1.WMF

STERD1C.WMF STERD2.WMF STERD2C.WMF STERD3.WMF STERD3C.WMF STIK01.WMF STIK02.WMF STIK03.WMF STIK04.WMF STIK05.WMF

STIK06.WMF STIK07.WMF STIK08.WMF STIK09.WMF STIK10.WMF STIK11.WMF STIK12.WMF STIK13.WMF STIK14.WMF STIK15.WMF

STIK16.WMF STIK17.WMF STIK18.WMF STIK19.WMF STIK20.WMF STIK21.WMF STIK22.WMF STIK23.WMF STIK24.WMF STIK25.WMF

STIK26.WMF STIK27.WMF STIK28.WMF STIK29.WMF STIK30.WMF STIK31.WMF STIK32.WMF STIK33.WMF STIK34.WMF STIK35.WMF

STIK36.WMF STIK37.WMF STIK38.WMF STIK39.WMF STIK40.WMF STIK41.WMF STIK42.WMF STIK43.WMF STIK44.WMF STIK45.WMF

STRONG.WMF SURFER.WMF SURFERC.WMF SURFING.WMF SYMBL10.WMF SYMBL138.WMF T502.WMF T503.WMF T505.WMF T506.WMF

T508.WMF T509.WMF T513.WMF T514.WMF T515.WMF T516.WMF T518.WMF T519.WMF T520.WMF T521.WMF

T5_01.WMF TA01.WMF TA02.WMF TA05.WMF TA06.WMF TA07.WMF TA12.WMF TA13.WMF TA14.WMF TA16.WMF

TA17.WMF TA18.WMF TA20.WMF TA21.WMF TA22.WMF TA23.WMF TA24.WMF TB25.WMF TB26.WMF TB27.WMF

TB28.WMF TB29.WMF TB31.WMF TB32.WMF TB33.WMF TB34.WMF TB35.WMF TB36.WMF TB37.WMF TB38.WMF

TB39.WMF TB40.WMF TB41.WMF TB42.WMF TB43.WMF TB44.WMF TB45.WMF TB46.WMF TB48.WMF TC49.WMF

TC50.WMF TC51.WMF TC52.WMF TC53.WMF TC54.WMF TC55.WMF TC56.WMF TC57.WMF TC58.WMF TC59.WMF
TC60.WMF TC61.WMF TC62.WMF TC63.WMF TC64.WMF TC65.WMF TC66.WMF TC67.WMF TC68.WMF TC69.WMF
TC70.WMF TC71.WMF TC72.WMF TC73.WMF TD74.WMF TD78.WMF TD79.WMF TD80.WMF TD81.WMF TD82.WMF
TD83.WMF TD84.WMF TD86.WMF TP01.WMF TP02_.WMF TP03.WMF TP04_.WMF TP05_.WMF TP06_.WMF TP07.WMF
TP08__.WMF TP09.WMF TP10_.WMF TP11_.WMF TP12.WMF TP13_.WMF TP14.WMF TP15.WMF TP16_.WMF TP17_.WMF
TP18.WMF TP19_.WMF TP20.WMF TP21_.WMF TP22.WMF TP23_.WMF TP24.WMF TRSI042D.WMF TW01.WMF TW02.WMF
TW03.WMF TW04.WMF TW05.WMF TW06.WMF TW07.WMF TW08.WMF TW09.WMF TW10.WMF TW11.WMF TW12.WMF
TW13.WMF TW14.WMF TW15.WMF TW16.WMF TW17.WMF TW18.WMF TW19.WMF TW20.WMF TW21.WMF TW22.WMF
TW23.WMF TW24.WMF TW25.WMF TZ01.WMF TZ02.WMF TZ03.WMF TZ04.WMF TZ05.WMF TZ06.WMF TZ07.WMF
TZ08.WMF TZ09.WMF TZ10.WMF TZ11.WMF TZ12.WMF TZ13.WMF TZ14.WMF TZ15.WMF TZ16.WMF TZ17.WMF
TZ18.WMF TZ19_.WMF TZ20_.WMF TZ21.WMF UNFITCOL.WMF W01.WMF W02.WMF W03.WMF W04.WMF W05.WMF
W06.WMF W07.WMF W08.WMF W09.WMF W10.WMF W11.WMF W12.WMF W13.WMF W14.WMF W15.WMF

W16.WMF W17.WMF W18.WMF W19.WMF W20.WMF W21.WMF W22.WMF W23.WMF W24.WMF W25.WMF

WALK.WMF WALKC.WMF WEIGHT.WMF WEIGHTC.WMF WORKO.WMF WORKO2.WMF WORKOUTC.WMF

Fitness • Equipment

0417.WMF 1331GYMC.WMF A15C.WMF A15CB.WMF BARBELL.WMF BARBELLS.WMF BIKINGG1.WMF BIT0145.WMF BIT0146.WMF BIT0455.WMF

CAA0361.WMF CAA0362.WMF CAA0366.WMF CAA0374.WMF CAA0380.WMF CAA0388.WMF CAA0889.WMF CAA0890.WMF CAA0891.WMF CAA0892.WMF

CAA0893.WMF CAA0894.WMF CAA0895.WMF CAA0896.WMF CAA0897.WMF CYCLIST.WMF DUMBELL.WMF HAND_BRB.WMF HLTH012.WMF HLTH016.WMF

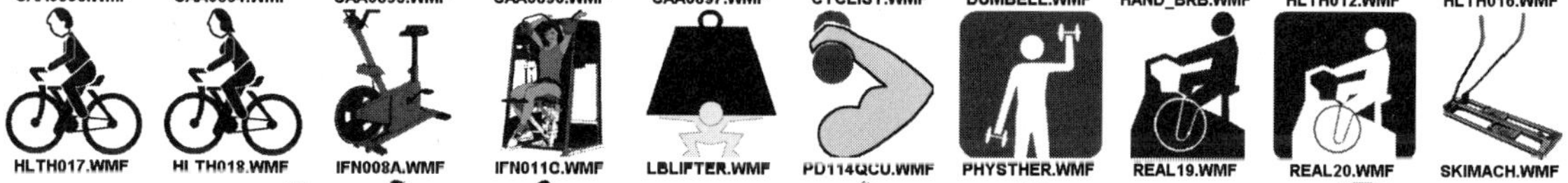

HLTH017.WMF HLTH018.WMF IFN008A.WMF IFN011C.WMF LBLIFTER.WMF PD114QCU.WMF PHYSTHER.WMF REAL19.WMF REAL20.WMF SKIMACH.WMF

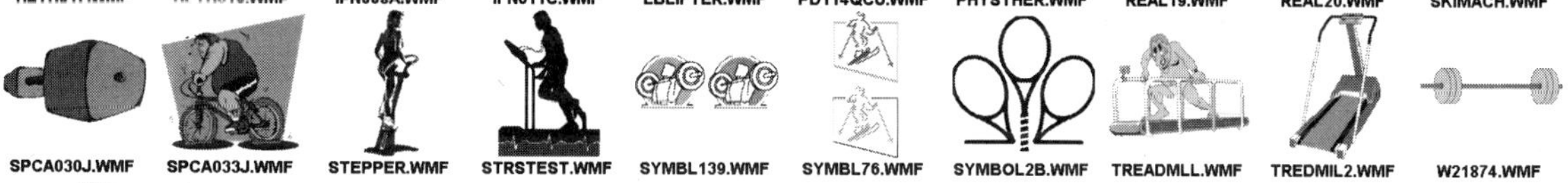

SPCA030J.WMF SPCA033J.WMF STEPPER.WMF STRSTEST.WMF SYMBL139.WMF SYMBL76.WMF SYMBOL2B.WMF TREADMLL.WMF TREDMIL2.WMF W21874.WMF

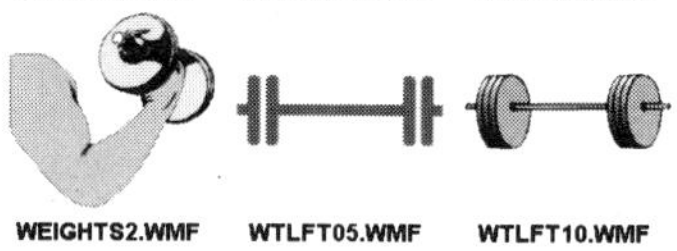

WEIGHTS2.WMF WTLFT05.WMF WTLFT10.WMF

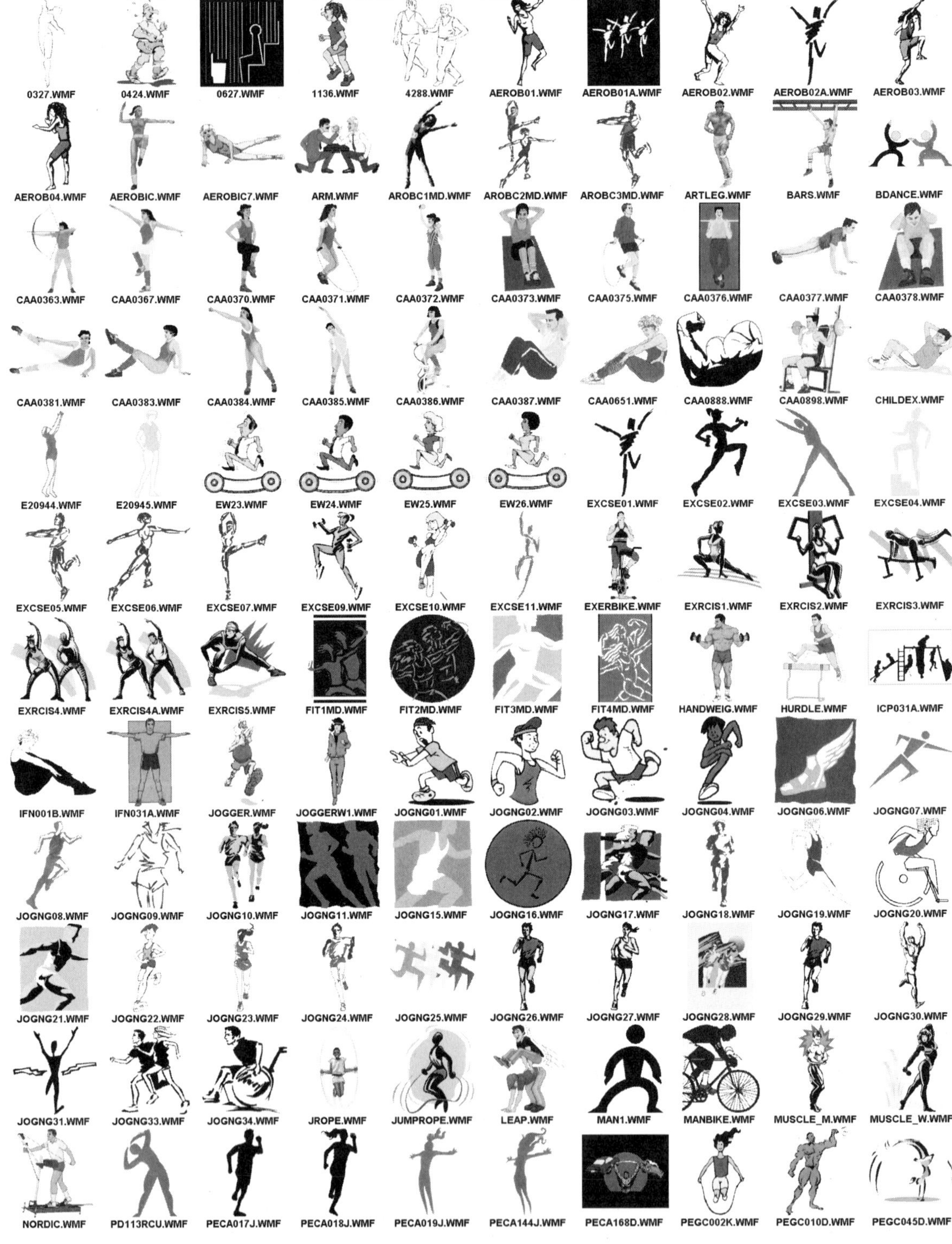
0327.WMF 0424.WMF 0627.WMF 1136.WMF 4288.WMF AEROB01.WMF AEROB01A.WMF AEROB02.WMF AEROB02A.WMF AEROB03.WMF
AEROB04.WMF AEROBIC.WMF AEROBIC7.WMF ARM.WMF AROBC1MD.WMF AROBC2MD.WMF AROBC3MD.WMF ARTLEG.WMF BARS.WMF BDANCE.WMF
CAA0363.WMF CAA0367.WMF CAA0370.WMF CAA0371.WMF CAA0372.WMF CAA0373.WMF CAA0375.WMF CAA0376.WMF CAA0377.WMF CAA0378.WMF
CAA0381.WMF CAA0383.WMF CAA0384.WMF CAA0385.WMF CAA0386.WMF CAA0387.WMF CAA0651.WMF CAA0888.WMF CAA0898.WMF CHILDEX.WMF
E20944.WMF E20945.WMF EW23.WMF EW24.WMF EW25.WMF EW26.WMF EXCSE01.WMF EXCSE02.WMF EXCSE03.WMF EXCSE04.WMF
EXCSE05.WMF EXCSE06.WMF EXCSE07.WMF EXCSE09.WMF EXCSE10.WMF EXCSE11.WMF EXERBIKE.WMF EXRCIS1.WMF EXRCIS2.WMF EXRCIS3.WMF
EXRCIS4.WMF EXRCIS4A.WMF EXRCIS5.WMF FIT1MD.WMF FIT2MD.WMF FIT3MD.WMF FIT4MD.WMF HANDWEIG.WMF HURDLE.WMF ICP031A.WMF
IFN001B.WMF IFN031A.WMF JOGGER.WMF JOGGERW1.WMF JOGNG01.WMF JOGNG02.WMF JOGNG03.WMF JOGNG04.WMF JOGNG06.WMF JOGNG07.WMF
JOGNG08.WMF JOGNG09.WMF JOGNG10.WMF JOGNG11.WMF JOGNG15.WMF JOGNG16.WMF JOGNG17.WMF JOGNG18.WMF JOGNG19.WMF JOGNG20.WMF
JOGNG21.WMF JOGNG22.WMF JOGNG23.WMF JOGNG24.WMF JOGNG25.WMF JOGNG26.WMF JOGNG27.WMF JOGNG28.WMF JOGNG29.WMF JOGNG30.WMF
JOGNG31.WMF JOGNG33.WMF JOGNG34.WMF JROPE.WMF JUMPROPE.WMF LEAP.WMF MAN1.WMF MANBIKE.WMF MUSCLE_M.WMF MUSCLE_W.WMF
NORDIC.WMF PD113RCU.WMF PECA017J.WMF PECA018J.WMF PECA019J.WMF PECA144J.WMF PECA168D.WMF PEGC002K.WMF PEGC010D.WMF PEGC045D.WMF

PEJB001J.WMF
PHYSED.WMF
PHYSED1.WMF
PHYSED3.WMF
RUNNER.WMF
RUNNERC.WMF
RUNR5MD.WMF
RUNR6MD.WMF
SITUPS.WMF
SKATE01.WMF
SKATE02.WMF
SKATE03.WMF
SKATE04.WMF
SKATE05.WMF
SKATE06.WMF
SKI_MACH.WMF
SPAB001J.WMF
SPAB018J.WMF
SPARSA00.WMF
SPBO001K.WMF
SPBO002K.WMF
SPBO011J.WMF
SPCA002J.WMF
SPCA098J.WMF
SPCA100J.WMF
SPGC010D.WMF
SPGC010J.WMF
SPGC024J.WMF
SPGC034J.WMF
SPGC035J.WMF
SPGC094D.WMF
SPJB040J.WMF
SPJB045J.WMF
SPORT086.WMF
SPORT087.WMF
SPRW060J.WMF
SPRW061J.WMF
SPRW064J.WMF
SPRW066J.WMF
SPSI004D.WMF
SPSI007D.WMF
SPSI148D.WMF
SPSI309D.WMF
SPSI356D.WMF
SPSI400D.WMF
SPSI406D.WMF
SPSI409D.WMF
SPSI435D.WMF
SPSI494D.WMF
SPSI528D.WMF
SPSI546D.WMF
SPSI565D.WMF
SPSI613D.WMF
SPSI625D.WMF
SPSI653D.WMF
SPSI660D.WMF
SPSI661D.WMF
SPSI662D.WMF
SPSI663D.WMF
TIRE_TRN.WMF
WEIGHTLI.WMF
WHEELC1.WMF
WHEELC3.WMF
WTLFT03.WMF
WTLFT08.WMF
YOGA_1.WMF
YOGA_2.WMF

1EXCERCI.WMF
4276.WMF
4277.WMF
4278.WMF
4279.WMF
4280.WMF
4281.WMF
4282.WMF
4283.WMF
4284.WMF
4285.WMF
4286.WMF
4287.WMF
A01.WMF
A02.WMF
A03.WMF
A04.WMF
A05.WMF
A06.WMF
A07.WMF
A08.WMF
A09_.WMF
A13.WMF
A14.WMF
A17.WMF
A20.WMF
A21.WMF
A22.WMF
A23.WMF
A24.WMF
AEROBICS.WMF
BIT1119.WMF
BIT1175.WMF
BIT1176.WMF
BIT1177.WMF
CAA0364.WMF
CAA0365.WMF
CAA0368.WMF
CAA0369.WMF
CAA0379.WMF
CAA0382.WMF
FITNESS.WMF
HLTH008.WMF
HLTH010.WMF
HLTH019.WMF
HLTH020.WMF
HLTH146.WMF
PEGC046D.WMF
SO01.WMF
SO02.WMF
SO03.WMF
SO04.WMF
SO05.WMF
SO06.WMF
SO07.WMF
SPGC033J.WMF
SPJB017J.WMF
SPJB018J.WMF
SPJB019J.WMF
SPORT353.WMF
SPSS008D.WMF
SPSS009D.WMF
SPSS010D.WMF
ST08.WMF
ST09.WMF
ST10.WMF
ST11.WMF
ST12.WMF
ST13.WMF
ST14.WMF
ST15.WMF
ST16.WMF
ST17.WMF
ST18.WMF
ST19.WMF
ST20.WMF
ST21.WMF
ST22.WMF
ST23.WMF
ST24.WMF
ST25.WMF
ST26.WMF
STRETCH.WMF
STRETCH5.WMF
T504.WMF
T507.WMF
T510.WMF
T511.WMF
T512.WMF
T517.WMF
TB30.WMF
TB47.WMF

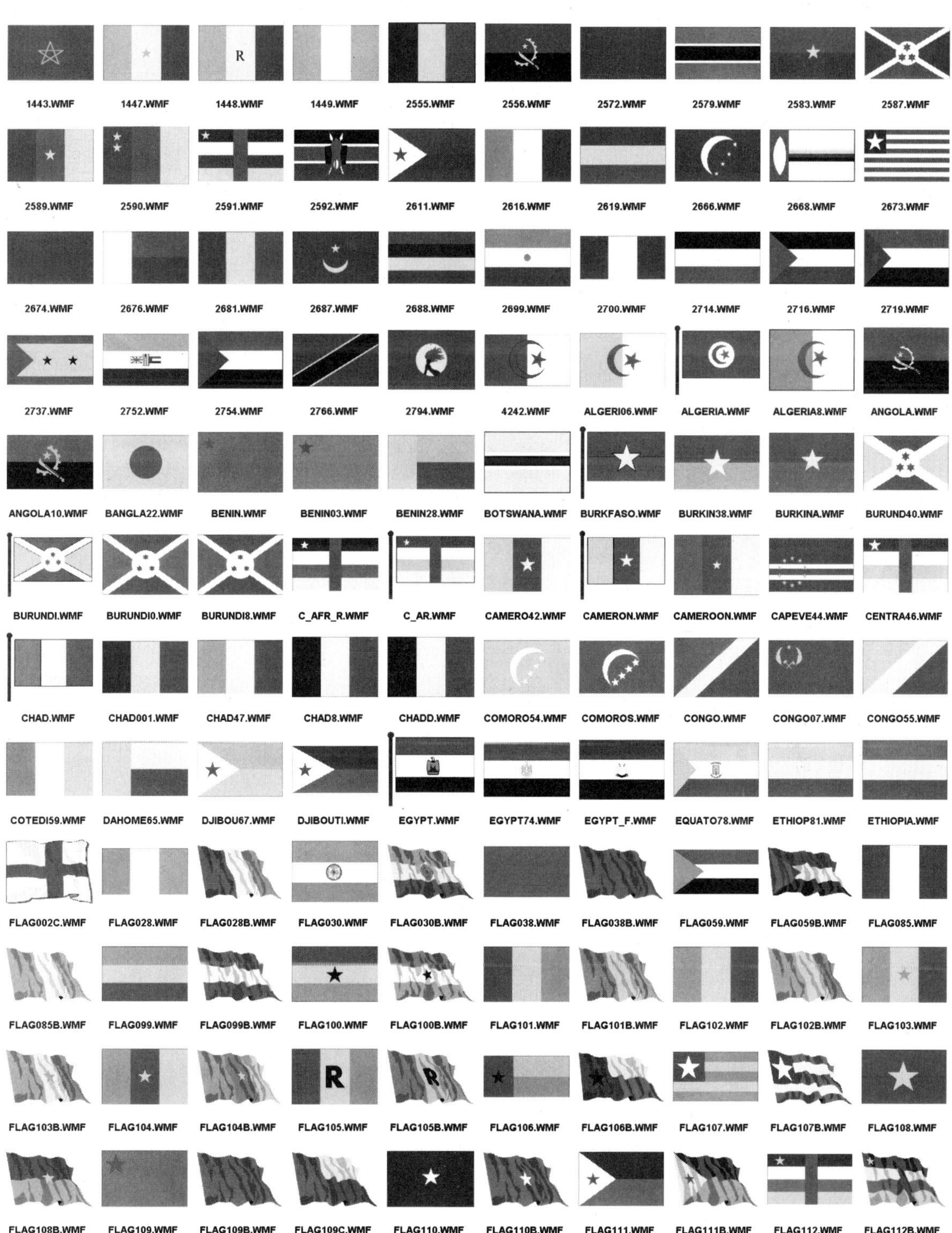
1443.WMF
1447.WMF
1448.WMF
1449.WMF
2555.WMF
2556.WMF
2572.WMF
2579.WMF
2583.WMF
2587.WMF
2589.WMF
2590.WMF
2591.WMF
2592.WMF
2611.WMF
2616.WMF
2619.WMF
2666.WMF
2668.WMF
2673.WMF
2674.WMF
2676.WMF
2681.WMF
2687.WMF
2688.WMF
2699.WMF
2700.WMF
2714.WMF
2716.WMF
2719.WMF
2737.WMF
2752.WMF
2754.WMF
2766.WMF
2794.WMF
4242.WMF
ALGERI06.WMF
ALGERIA.WMF
ALGERIA8.WMF
ANGOLA.WMF
ANGOLA10.WMF
BANGLA22.WMF
BENIN.WMF
BENIN03.WMF
BENIN28.WMF
BOTSWANA.WMF
BURKFASO.WMF
BURKIN38.WMF
BURKINA.WMF
BURUND40.WMF
BURUNDI.WMF
BURUNDI0.WMF
BURUNDI8.WMF
C_AFR_R.WMF
C_AR.WMF
CAMERO42.WMF
CAMERON.WMF
CAMEROON.WMF
CAPEVE44.WMF
CENTRA46.WMF
CHAD.WMF
CHAD001.WMF
CHAD47.WMF
CHAD8.WMF
CHADD.WMF
COMORO54.WMF
COMOROS.WMF
CONGO.WMF
CONGO07.WMF
CONGO55.WMF
COTEDI59.WMF
DAHOME65.WMF
DJIBOU67.WMF
DJIBOUTI.WMF
EGYPT.WMF
EGYPT74.WMF
EGYPT_F.WMF
EQUATO78.WMF
ETHIOP81.WMF
ETHIOPIA.WMF
FLAG002C.WMF
FLAG028.WMF
FLAG028B.WMF
FLAG030.WMF
FLAG030B.WMF
FLAG038.WMF
FLAG038B.WMF
FLAG059.WMF
FLAG059B.WMF
FLAG085.WMF
FLAG085B.WMF
FLAG099.WMF
FLAG099B.WMF
FLAG100.WMF
FLAG100B.WMF
FLAG101.WMF
FLAG101B.WMF
FLAG102.WMF
FLAG102B.WMF
FLAG103.WMF
FLAG103B.WMF
FLAG104.WMF
FLAG104B.WMF
FLAG105.WMF
FLAG105B.WMF
FLAG106.WMF
FLAG106B.WMF
FLAG107.WMF
FLAG107B.WMF
FLAG108.WMF
FLAG108B.WMF
FLAG109.WMF
FLAG109B.WMF
FLAG109C.WMF
FLAG110.WMF
FLAG110B.WMF
FLAG111.WMF
FLAG111B.WMF
FLAG112.WMF
FLAG112B.WMF

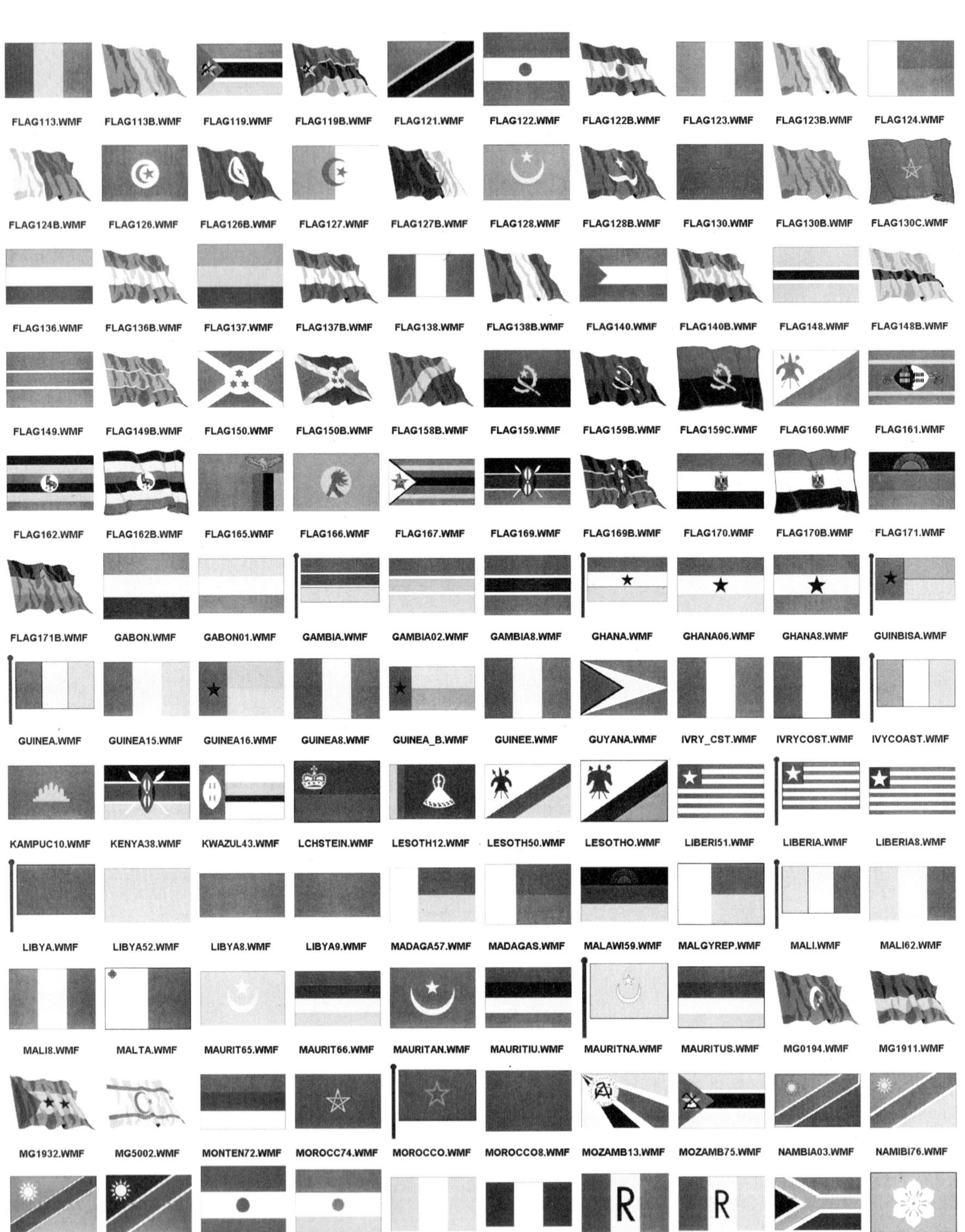
FLAG113.WMF
FLAG113B.WMF
FLAG119.WMF
FLAG119B.WMF
FLAG121.WMF
FLAG122.WMF
FLAG122B.WMF
FLAG123.WMF
FLAG123B.WMF
FLAG124.WMF
FLAG124B.WMF
FLAG126.WMF
FLAG126B.WMF
FLAG127.WMF
FLAG127B.WMF
FLAG128.WMF
FLAG128B.WMF
FLAG130.WMF
FLAG130B.WMF
FLAG130C.WMF
FLAG136.WMF
FLAG136B.WMF
FLAG137.WMF
FLAG137B.WMF
FLAG138.WMF
FLAG138B.WMF
FLAG140.WMF
FLAG140B.WMF
FLAG148.WMF
FLAG148B.WMF
FLAG149.WMF
FLAG149B.WMF
FLAG150.WMF
FLAG150B.WMF
FLAG158B.WMF
FLAG159.WMF
FLAG159B.WMF
FLAG159C.WMF
FLAG160.WMF
FLAG161.WMF
FLAG162.WMF
FLAG162B.WMF
FLAG165.WMF
FLAG166.WMF
FLAG167.WMF
FLAG169.WMF
FLAG169B.WMF
FLAG170.WMF
FLAG170B.WMF
FLAG171.WMF
FLAG171B.WMF
GABON.WMF
GABON01.WMF
GAMBIA.WMF
GAMBIA02.WMF
GAMBIA8.WMF
GHANA.WMF
GHANA06.WMF
GHANA8.WMF
GUINBISA.WMF
GUINEA.WMF
GUINEA15.WMF
GUINEA16.WMF
GUINEA8.WMF
GUINEA_B.WMF
GUINEE.WMF
GUYANA.WMF
IVRY_CST.WMF
IVRYCOST.WMF
IVYCOAST.WMF
KAMPUC10.WMF
KENYA38.WMF
KWAZUL43.WMF
LCHSTEIN.WMF
LESOTH12.WMF
LESOTH50.WMF
LESOTHO.WMF
LIBERI51.WMF
LIBERIA.WMF
LIBERIA8.WMF
LIBYA.WMF
LIBYA52.WMF
LIBYA8.WMF
LIBYA9.WMF
MADAGA57.WMF
MADAGAS.WMF
MALAWI59.WMF
MALGYREP.WMF
MALI.WMF
MALI62.WMF
MALI8.WMF
MALTA.WMF
MAURIT65.WMF
MAURIT66.WMF
MAURITAN.WMF
MAURITIU.WMF
MAURITNA.WMF
MAURITUS.WMF
MG0194.WMF
MG1911.WMF
MG1932.WMF
MG5002.WMF
MONTEN72.WMF
MOROCC74.WMF
MOROCCO.WMF
MOROCCO8.WMF
MOZAMB13.WMF
MOZAMB75.WMF
NAMBIA03.WMF
NAMIBI76.WMF
NAMIBIA.WMF
NAMIBIA8.WMF
NIGER.WMF
NIGER84.WMF
NIGERI85.WMF
NIGERIA.WMF
RWANDA.WMF
RWANDA18.WMF
SAFR001.WMF
SAGA.WMF

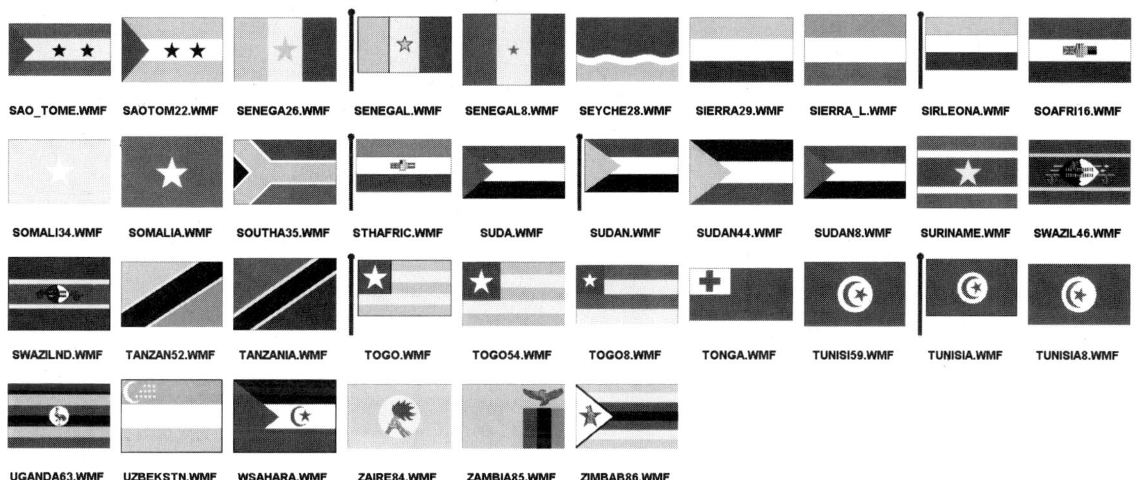
SAO_TOME.WMF
SAOTOM22.WMF
SENEGA26.WMF
SENEGAL.WMF
SENEGAL8.WMF
SEYCHE28.WMF
SIERRA29.WMF
SIERRA_L.WMF
SIRLEONA.WMF
SOAFRI16.WMF
SOMALI34.WMF
SOMALIA.WMF
SOUTHA35.WMF
STHAFRIC.WMF
SUDA.WMF
SUDAN.WMF
SUDAN44.WMF
SUDAN8.WMF
SURINAME.WMF
SWAZIL46.WMF
SWAZILND.WMF
TANZAN52.WMF
TANZANIA.WMF
TOGO.WMF
TOGO54.WMF
TOGO8.WMF
TONGA.WMF
TUNISI59.WMF
TUNISIA.WMF
TUNISIA8.WMF
UGANDA63.WMF
UZBEKSTN.WMF
WSAHARA.WMF
ZAIRE84.WMF
ZAMBIA85.WMF
ZIMBAB86.WMF

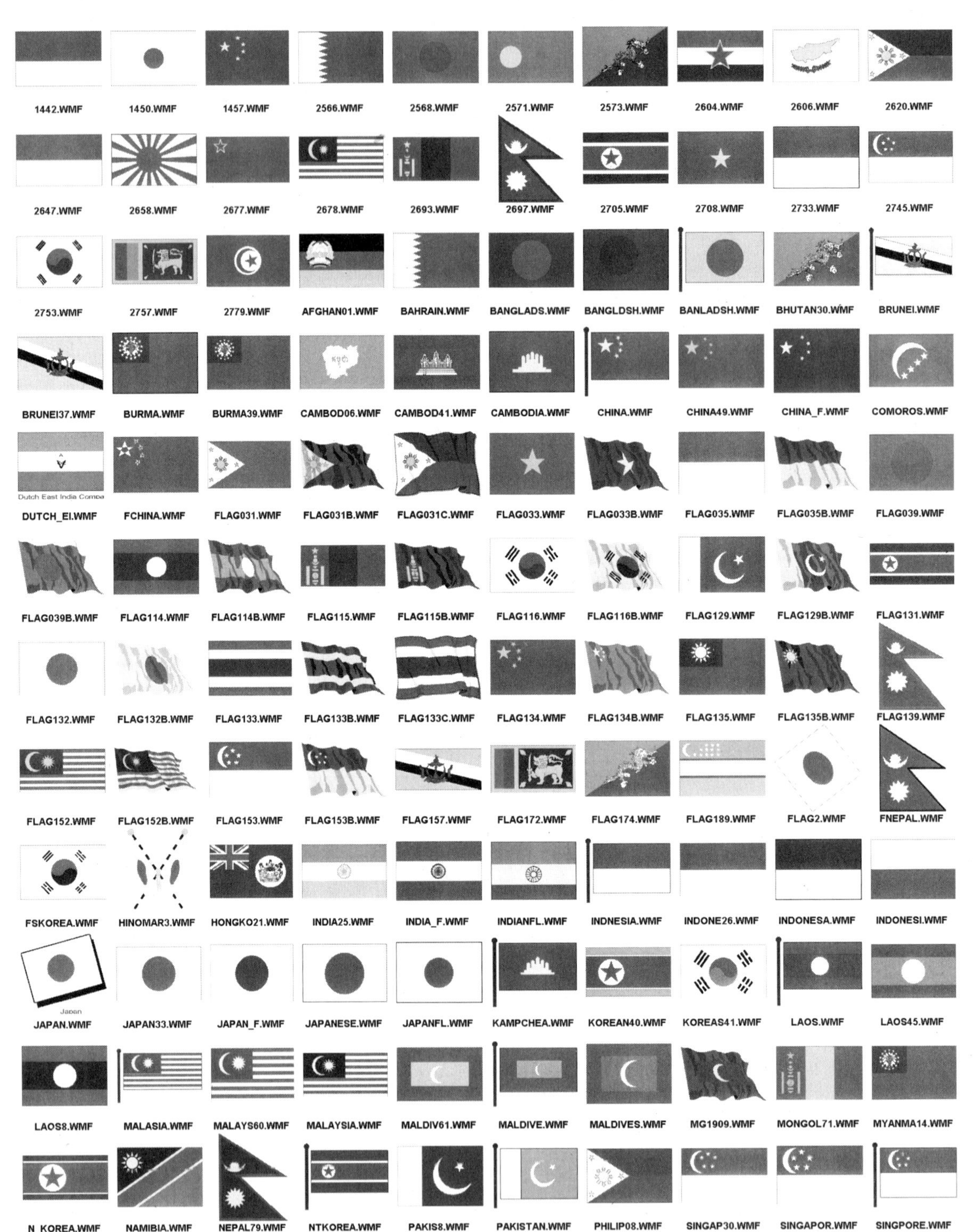
1442.WMF
1450.WMF
1457.WMF
2566.WMF
2568.WMF
2571.WMF
2573.WMF
2604.WMF
2606.WMF
2620.WMF
2647.WMF
2658.WMF
2677.WMF
2678.WMF
2693.WMF
2697.WMF
2705.WMF
2708.WMF
2733.WMF
2745.WMF
2753.WMF
2757.WMF
2779.WMF
AFGHAN01.WMF
BAHRAIN.WMF
BANGLADS.WMF
BANGLDSH.WMF
BANLADSH.WMF
BHUTAN30.WMF
BRUNEI.WMF
BRUNEI37.WMF
BURMA.WMF
BURMA39.WMF
CAMBOD06.WMF
CAMBOD41.WMF
CAMBODIA.WMF
CHINA.WMF
CHINA49.WMF
CHINA_F.WMF
COMOROS.WMF
Dutch East India Compa
DUTCH_EI.WMF
FCHINA.WMF
FLAG031.WMF
FLAG031B.WMF
FLAG031C.WMF
FLAG033.WMF
FLAG033B.WMF
FLAG035.WMF
FLAG035B.WMF
FLAG039.WMF
FLAG039B.WMF
FLAG114.WMF
FLAG114B.WMF
FLAG115.WMF
FLAG115B.WMF
FLAG116.WMF
FLAG116B.WMF
FLAG129.WMF
FLAG129B.WMF
FLAG131.WMF
FLAG132.WMF
FLAG132B.WMF
FLAG133.WMF
FLAG133B.WMF
FLAG133C.WMF
FLAG134.WMF
FLAG134B.WMF
FLAG135.WMF
FLAG135B.WMF
FLAG139.WMF
FLAG152.WMF
FLAG152B.WMF
FLAG153.WMF
FLAG153B.WMF
FLAG157.WMF
FLAG172.WMF
FLAG174.WMF
FLAG189.WMF
FLAG2.WMF
FNEPAL.WMF
FSKOREA.WMF
HINOMAR3.WMF
HONGKO21.WMF
INDIA25.WMF
INDIA_F.WMF
INDIANFL.WMF
INDNESIA.WMF
INDONE26.WMF
INDONESA.WMF
INDONESI.WMF
Japan
JAPAN.WMF
JAPAN33.WMF
JAPAN_F.WMF
JAPANESE.WMF
JAPANFL.WMF
KAMPCHEA.WMF
KOREAN40.WMF
KOREAS41.WMF
LAOS.WMF
LAOS45.WMF
LAOS8.WMF
MALASIA.WMF
MALAYS60.WMF
MALAYSIA.WMF
MALDIV61.WMF
MALDIVE.WMF
MALDIVES.WMF
MG1909.WMF
MONGOL71.WMF
MYANMA14.WMF
N_KOREA.WMF
NAMIBIA.WMF
NEPAL79.WMF
NTKOREA.WMF
PAKIS8.WMF
PAKISTAN.WMF
PHILIP08.WMF
SINGAP30.WMF
SINGAPOR.WMF
SINGPORE.WMF

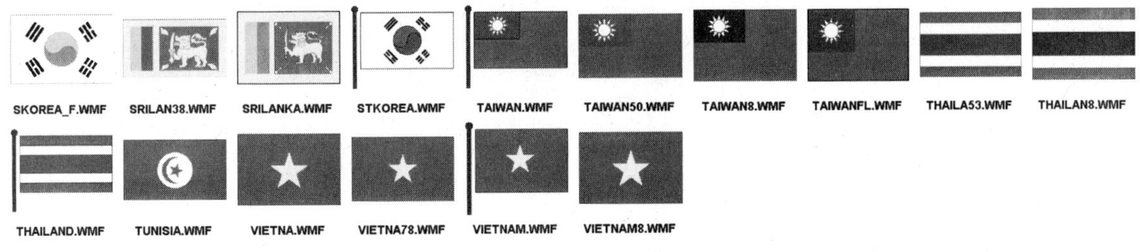

Flags • Aviation

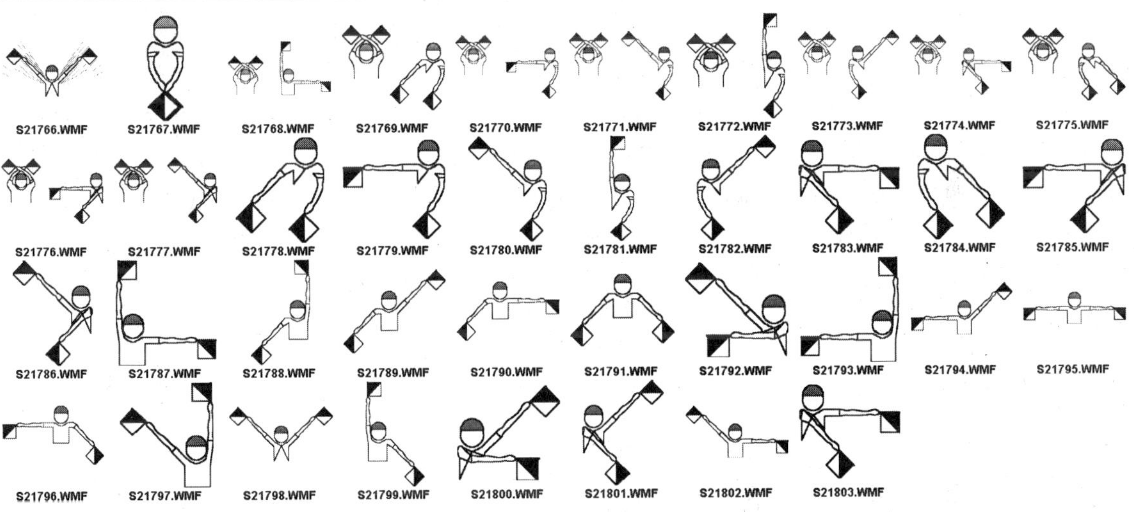

Flags • Canada

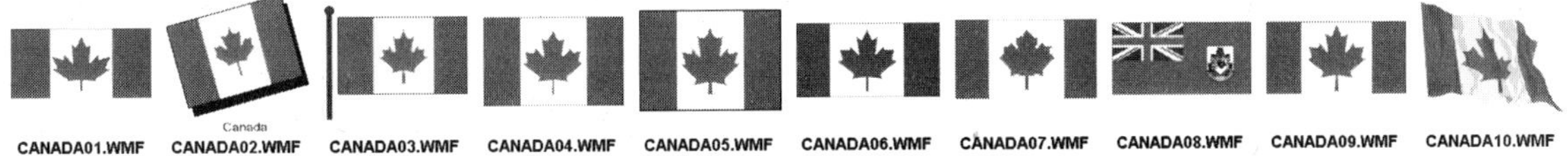

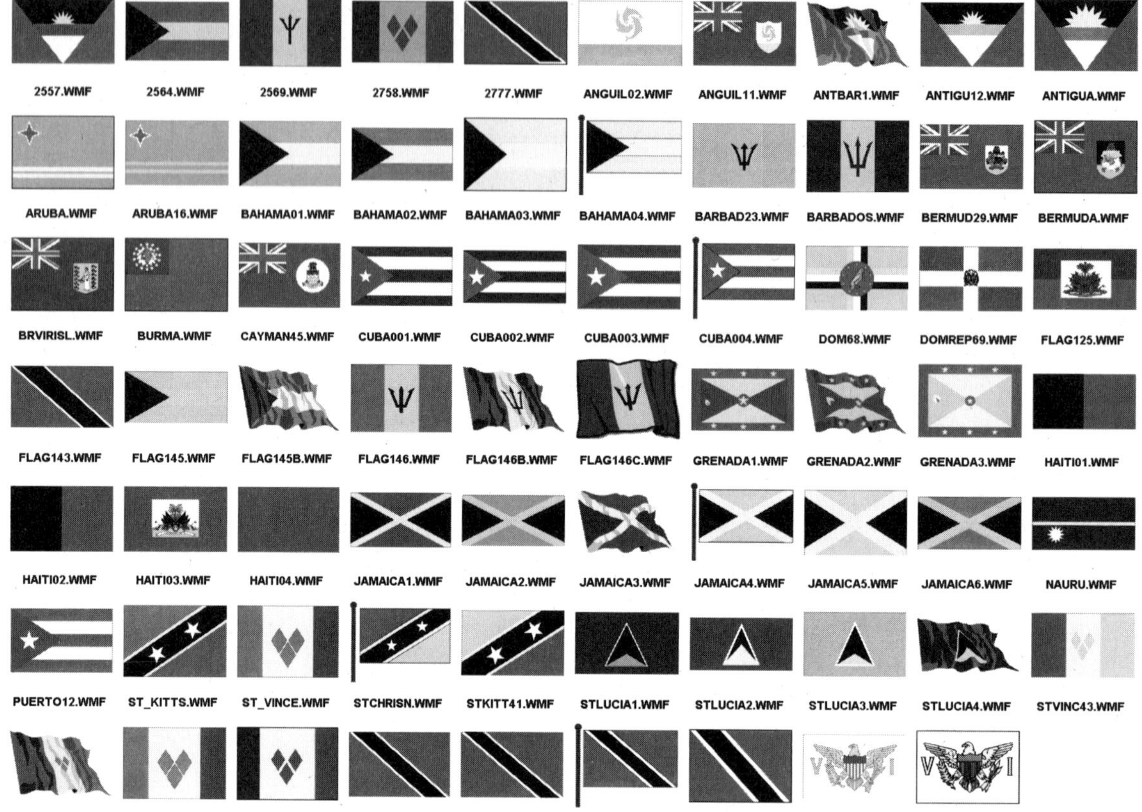
2557.WMF
2564.WMF
2569.WMF
2758.WMF
2777.WMF
ANGUIL02.WMF
ANGUIL11.WMF
ANTBAR1.WMF
ANTIGU12.WMF
ANTIGUA.WMF
ARUBA.WMF
ARUBA16.WMF
BAHAMA01.WMF
BAHAMA02.WMF
BAHAMA03.WMF
BAHAMA04.WMF
BARBAD23.WMF
BARBADOS.WMF
BERMUD29.WMF
BERMUDA.WMF
BRVIRISL.WMF
BURMA.WMF
CAYMAN45.WMF
CUBA001.WMF
CUBA002.WMF
CUBA003.WMF
CUBA004.WMF
DOM68.WMF
DOMREP69.WMF
FLAG125.WMF
FLAG143.WMF
FLAG145.WMF
FLAG145B.WMF
FLAG146.WMF
FLAG146B.WMF
FLAG146C.WMF
GRENADA1.WMF
GRENADA2.WMF
GRENADA3.WMF
HAITI01.WMF
HAITI02.WMF
HAITI03.WMF
HAITI04.WMF
JAMAICA1.WMF
JAMAICA2.WMF
JAMAICA3.WMF
JAMAICA4.WMF
JAMAICA5.WMF
JAMAICA6.WMF
NAURU.WMF
PUERTO12.WMF
ST_KITTS.WMF
ST_VINCE.WMF
STCHRISN.WMF
STKITT41.WMF
STLUCIA1.WMF
STLUCIA2.WMF
STLUCIA3.WMF
STLUCIA4.WMF
STVINC43.WMF
STVINCE1.WMF
STVINCE2.WMF
STVNCENT.WMF
TRINAD58.WMF
TRINADAD.WMF
TRINIDAD.WMF
TRINTBGO.WMF
USVIRG71.WMF
VIRGINIS.WMF

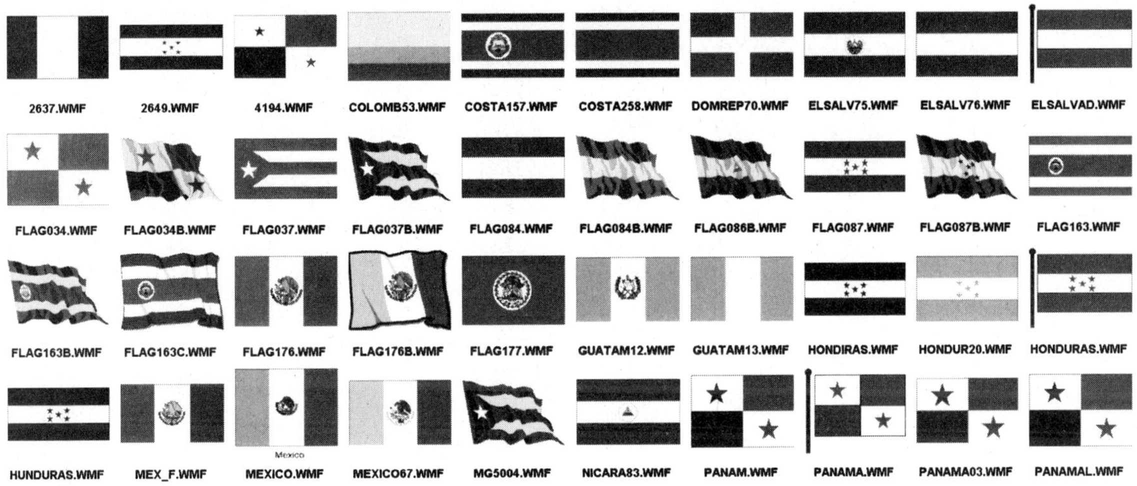
2637.WMF
2649.WMF
4194.WMF
COLOMB53.WMF
COSTA157.WMF
COSTA258.WMF
DOMREP70.WMF
ELSALV75.WMF
ELSALV76.WMF
ELSALVAD.WMF
FLAG034.WMF
FLAG034B.WMF
FLAG037.WMF
FLAG037B.WMF
FLAG084.WMF
FLAG084B.WMF
FLAG086B.WMF
FLAG087.WMF
FLAG087B.WMF
FLAG163.WMF
FLAG163B.WMF
FLAG163C.WMF
FLAG176.WMF
FLAG176B.WMF
FLAG177.WMF
GUATAM12.WMF
GUATAM13.WMF
HONDIRAS.WMF
HONDUR20.WMF
HONDURAS.WMF
HUNDURAS.WMF
MEX_F.WMF
Mexico
MEXICO.WMF
MEXICO67.WMF
MG5004.WMF
NICARA83.WMF
PANAM.WMF
PANAMA.WMF
PANAMA03.WMF
PANAMAL.WMF

XBELIZE.WMF

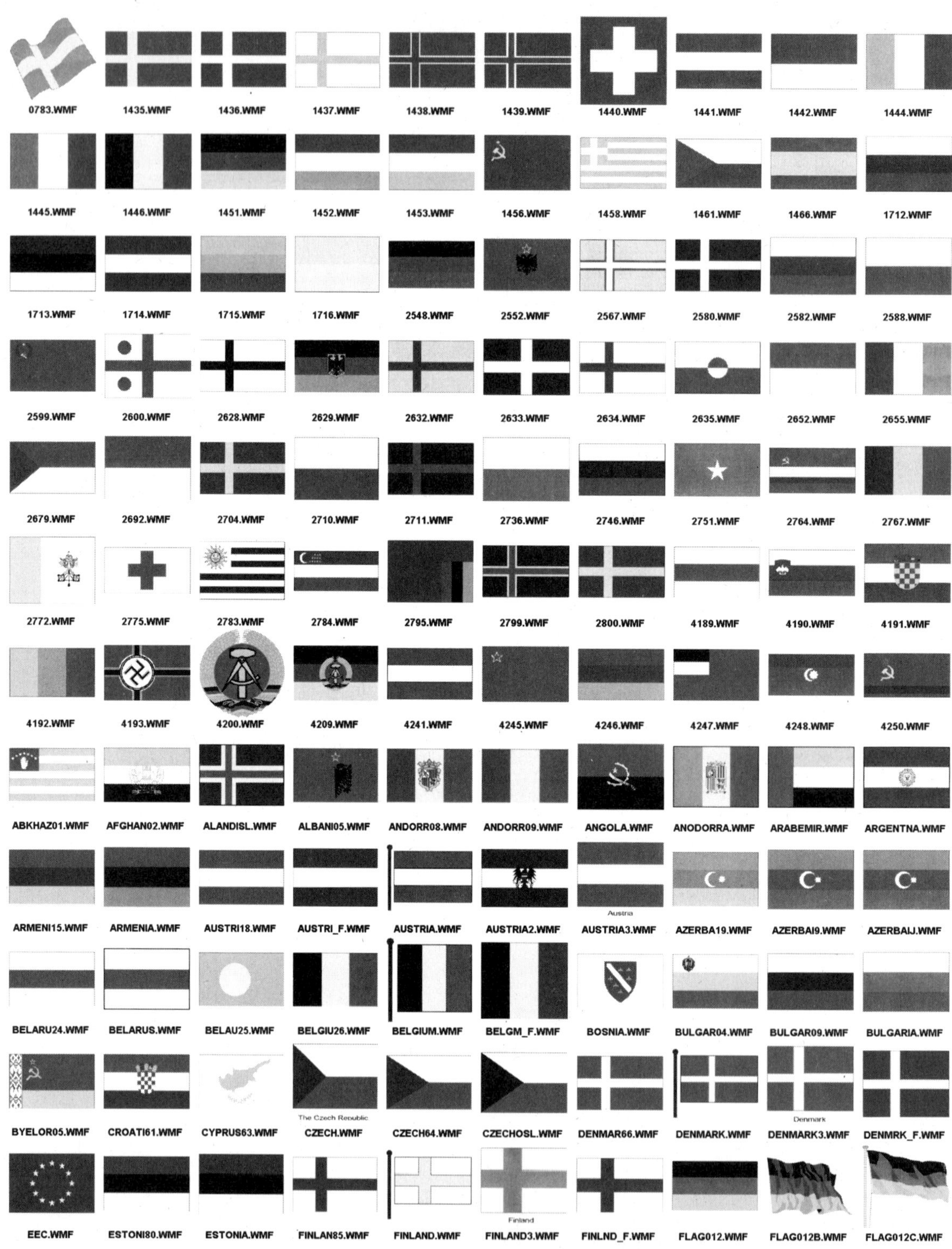
0783.WMF 1435.WMF 1436.WMF 1437.WMF 1438.WMF 1439.WMF 1440.WMF 1441.WMF 1442.WMF 1444.WMF
1445.WMF 1446.WMF 1451.WMF 1452.WMF 1453.WMF 1456.WMF 1458.WMF 1461.WMF 1466.WMF 1712.WMF
1713.WMF 1714.WMF 1715.WMF 1716.WMF 2548.WMF 2552.WMF 2567.WMF 2580.WMF 2582.WMF 2588.WMF
2599.WMF 2600.WMF 2628.WMF 2629.WMF 2632.WMF 2633.WMF 2634.WMF 2635.WMF 2652.WMF 2655.WMF
2679.WMF 2692.WMF 2704.WMF 2710.WMF 2711.WMF 2736.WMF 2746.WMF 2751.WMF 2764.WMF 2767.WMF
2772.WMF 2775.WMF 2783.WMF 2784.WMF 2795.WMF 2799.WMF 2800.WMF 4189.WMF 4190.WMF 4191.WMF
4192.WMF 4193.WMF 4200.WMF 4209.WMF 4241.WMF 4245.WMF 4246.WMF 4247.WMF 4248.WMF 4250.WMF
ABKHAZ01.WMF AFGHAN02.WMF ALANDISL.WMF ALBANI05.WMF ANDORR08.WMF ANDORR09.WMF ANGOLA.WMF ANODORRA.WMF ARABEMIR.WMF ARGENTNA.WMF
Austria
ARMENI15.WMF ARMENIA.WMF AUSTRI18.WMF AUSTRI_F.WMF AUSTRIA.WMF AUSTRIA2.WMF AUSTRIA3.WMF AZERBA19.WMF AZERBAI9.WMF AZERBAIJ.WMF
BELARU24.WMF BELARUS.WMF BELAU25.WMF BELGIU26.WMF BELGIUM.WMF BELGM_F.WMF BOSNIA.WMF BULGAR04.WMF BULGAR09.WMF BULGARIA.WMF
The Czech Republic
Denmark
BYELOR05.WMF CROATI61.WMF CYPRUS63.WMF CZECH.WMF CZECH64.WMF CZECHOSL.WMF DENMAR66.WMF DENMARK.WMF DENMARK3.WMF DENMRK_F.WMF
Finland
EEC.WMF ESTONI80.WMF ESTONIA.WMF FINLAN85.WMF FINLAND.WMF FINLAND3.WMF FINLND_F.WMF FLAG012.WMF FLAG012B.WMF FLAG012C.WMF

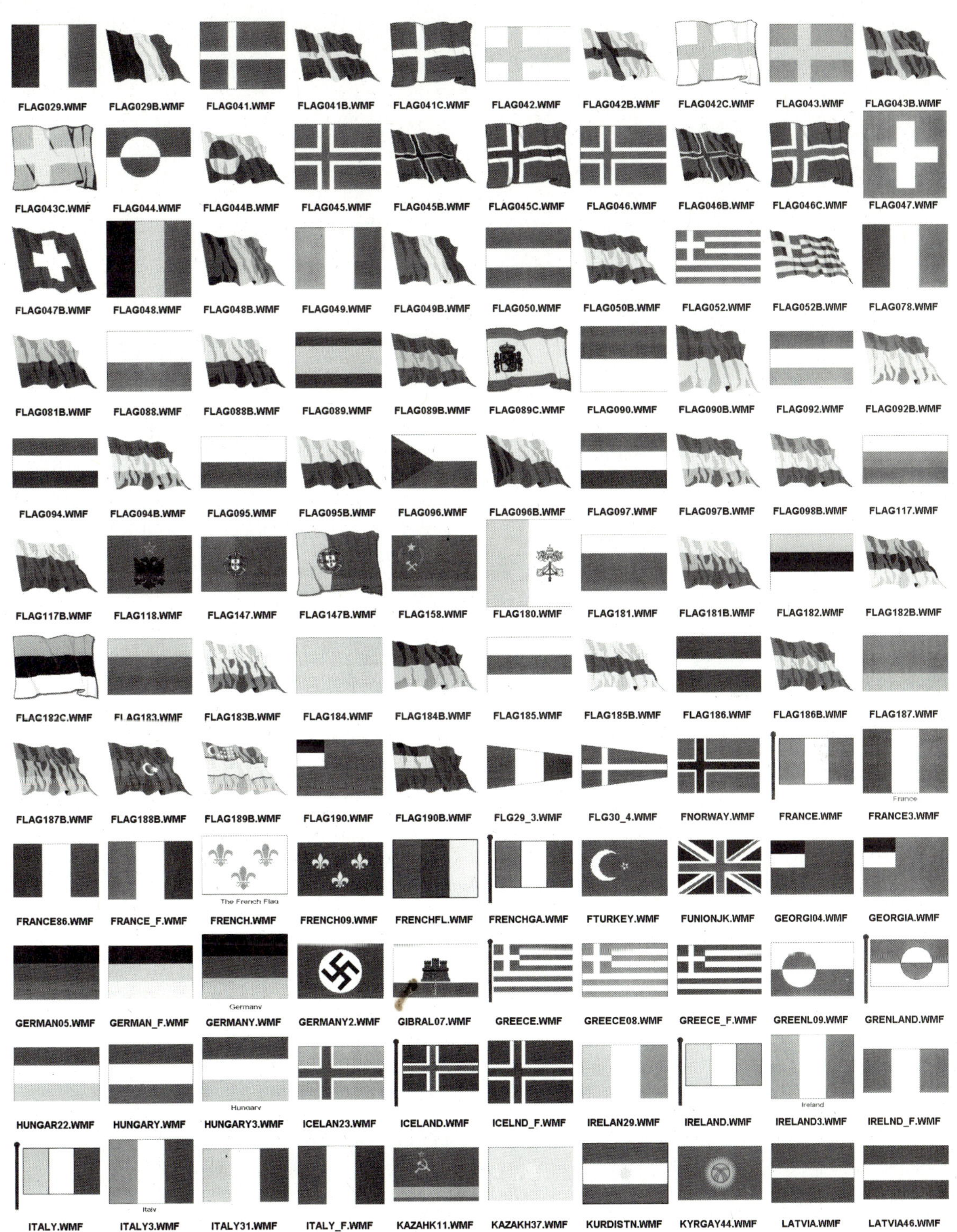
FLAG029.WMF
FLAG029B.WMF
FLAG041.WMF
FLAG041B.WMF
FLAG041C.WMF
FLAG042.WMF
FLAG042B.WMF
FLAG042C.WMF
FLAG043.WMF
FLAG043B.WMF
FLAG043C.WMF
FLAG044.WMF
FLAG044B.WMF
FLAG045.WMF
FLAG045B.WMF
FLAG045C.WMF
FLAG046.WMF
FLAG046B.WMF
FLAG046C.WMF
FLAG047.WMF
FLAG047B.WMF
FLAG048.WMF
FLAG048B.WMF
FLAG049.WMF
FLAG049B.WMF
FLAG050.WMF
FLAG050B.WMF
FLAG052.WMF
FLAG052B.WMF
FLAG078.WMF
FLAG081B.WMF
FLAG088.WMF
FLAG088B.WMF
FLAG089.WMF
FLAG089B.WMF
FLAG089C.WMF
FLAG090.WMF
FLAG090B.WMF
FLAG092.WMF
FLAG092B.WMF
FLAG094.WMF
FLAG094B.WMF
FLAG095.WMF
FLAG095B.WMF
FLAG096.WMF
FLAG096B.WMF
FLAG097.WMF
FLAG097B.WMF
FLAG098B.WMF
FLAG117.WMF
FLAG117B.WMF
FLAG118.WMF
FLAG147.WMF
FLAG147B.WMF
FLAG158.WMF
FLAG180.WMF
FLAG181.WMF
FLAG181B.WMF
FLAG182.WMF
FLAG182B.WMF
FLAG182C.WMF
FLAG183.WMF
FLAG183B.WMF
FLAG184.WMF
FLAG184B.WMF
FLAG185.WMF
FLAG185B.WMF
FLAG186.WMF
FLAG186B.WMF
FLAG187.WMF
FLAG187B.WMF
FLAG188B.WMF
FLAG189B.WMF
FLAG190.WMF
FLAG190B.WMF
FLG29_3.WMF
FLG30_4.WMF
FNORWAY.WMF
FRANCE.WMF
France
FRANCE3.WMF
FRANCE86.WMF
FRANCE_F.WMF
The French Flag
FRENCH.WMF
FRENCH09.WMF
FRENCHFL.WMF
FRENCHGA.WMF
FTURKEY.WMF
FUNIONJK.WMF
GEORGI04.WMF
GEORGIA.WMF
GERMAN05.WMF
GERMAN_F.WMF
Germany
GERMANY.WMF
GERMANY2.WMF
GIBRAL07.WMF
GREECE.WMF
GREECE08.WMF
GREECE_F.WMF
GREENL09.WMF
GRENLAND.WMF
HUNGAR22.WMF
HUNGARY.WMF
Hungary
HUNGARY3.WMF
ICELAN23.WMF
ICELAND.WMF
ICELND_F.WMF
IRELAN29.WMF
IRELAND.WMF
Ireland
IRELAND3.WMF
IRELND_F.WMF
ITALY.WMF
Italy
ITALY3.WMF
ITALY31.WMF
ITALY_F.WMF
KAZAHK11.WMF
KAZAKH37.WMF
KURDISTN.WMF
KYRGAY44.WMF
LATVIA.WMF
LATVIA46.WMF

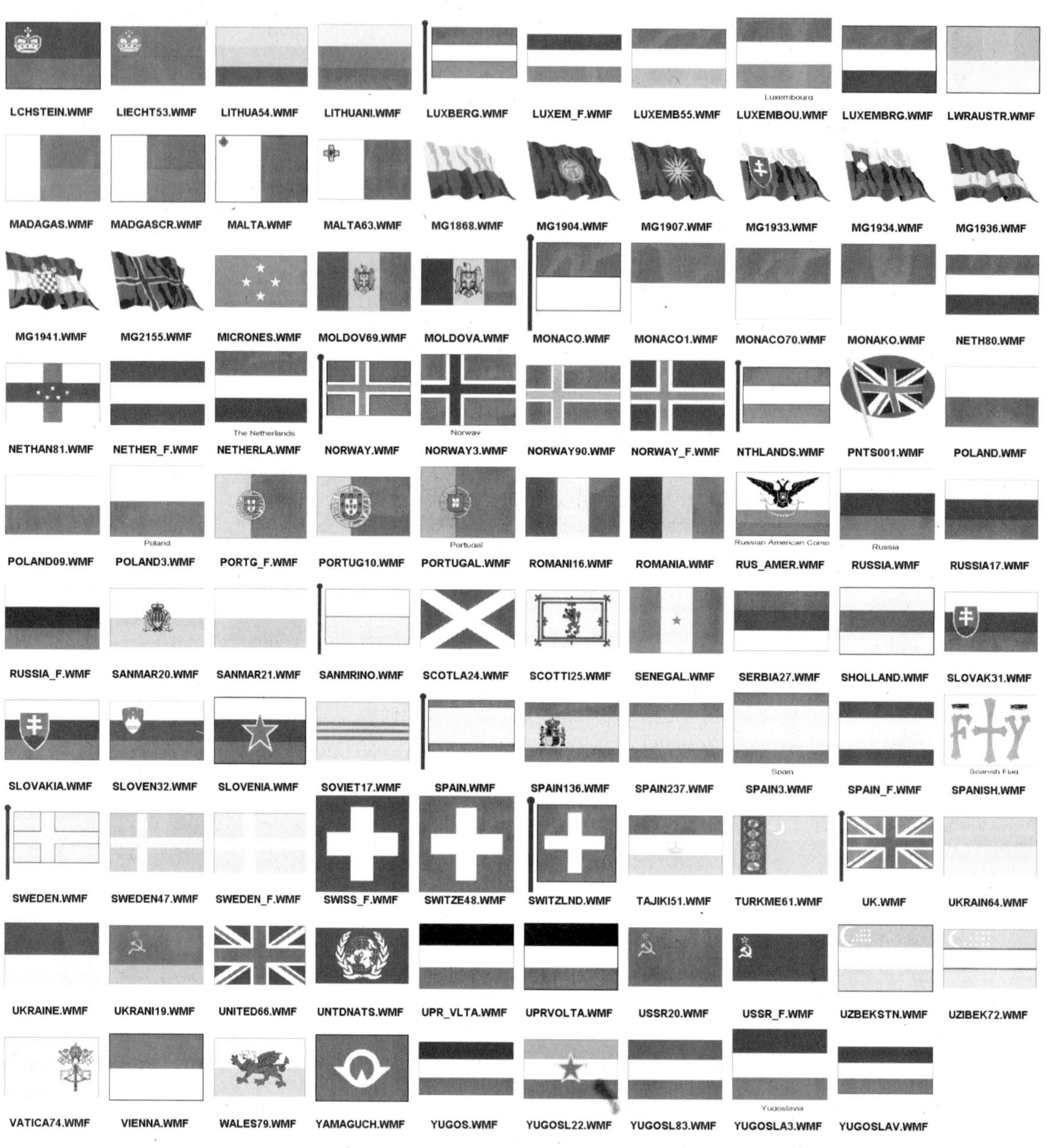
LCHSTEIN.WMF
LIECHT53.WMF
LITHUA54.WMF
LITHUANI.WMF
LUXBERG.WMF
LUXEM_F.WMF
LUXEMB55.WMF
LUXEMBOU.WMF
LUXEMBRG.WMF
LWRAUSTR.WMF
MADAGAS.WMF
MADGASCR.WMF
MALTA.WMF
MALTA63.WMF
MG1868.WMF
MG1904.WMF
MG1907.WMF
MG1933.WMF
MG1934.WMF
MG1936.WMF
MG1941.WMF
MG2155.WMF
MICRONES.WMF
MOLDOV69.WMF
MOLDOVA.WMF
MONACO.WMF
MONACO1.WMF
MONACO70.WMF
MONAKO.WMF
NETH80.WMF
NETHAN81.WMF
NETHER_F.WMF
NETHERLA.WMF
NORWAY.WMF
NORWAY3.WMF
NORWAY90.WMF
NORWAY_F.WMF
NTHLANDS.WMF
PNTS001.WMF
POLAND.WMF
POLAND09.WMF
POLAND3.WMF
PORTG_F.WMF
PORTUG10.WMF
PORTUGAL.WMF
ROMANI16.WMF
ROMANIA.WMF
RUS_AMER.WMF
RUSSIA.WMF
RUSSIA17.WMF
RUSSIA_F.WMF
SANMAR20.WMF
SANMAR21.WMF
SANMRINO.WMF
SCOTLA24.WMF
SCOTTI25.WMF
SENEGAL.WMF
SERBIA27.WMF
SHOLLAND.WMF
SLOVAK31.WMF
SLOVAKIA.WMF
SLOVEN32.WMF
SLOVENIA.WMF
SOVIET17.WMF
SPAIN.WMF
SPAIN136.WMF
SPAIN237.WMF
SPAIN3.WMF
SPAIN_F.WMF
SPANISH.WMF
SWEDEN.WMF
SWEDEN47.WMF
SWEDEN_F.WMF
SWISS_F.WMF
SWITZE48.WMF
SWITZLND.WMF
TAJIKI51.WMF
TURKME61.WMF
UK.WMF
UKRAIN64.WMF
UKRAINE.WMF
UKRANI19.WMF
UNITED66.WMF
UNTDNATS.WMF
UPR_VLTA.WMF
UPRVOLTA.WMF
USSR20.WMF
USSR_F.WMF
UZBEKSTN.WMF
UZIBEK72.WMF
VATICA74.WMF
VIENNA.WMF
WALES79.WMF
YAMAGUCH.WMF
YUGOS.WMF
YUGOSL22.WMF
YUGOSL83.WMF
YUGOSLA3.WMF
YUGOSLAV.WMF

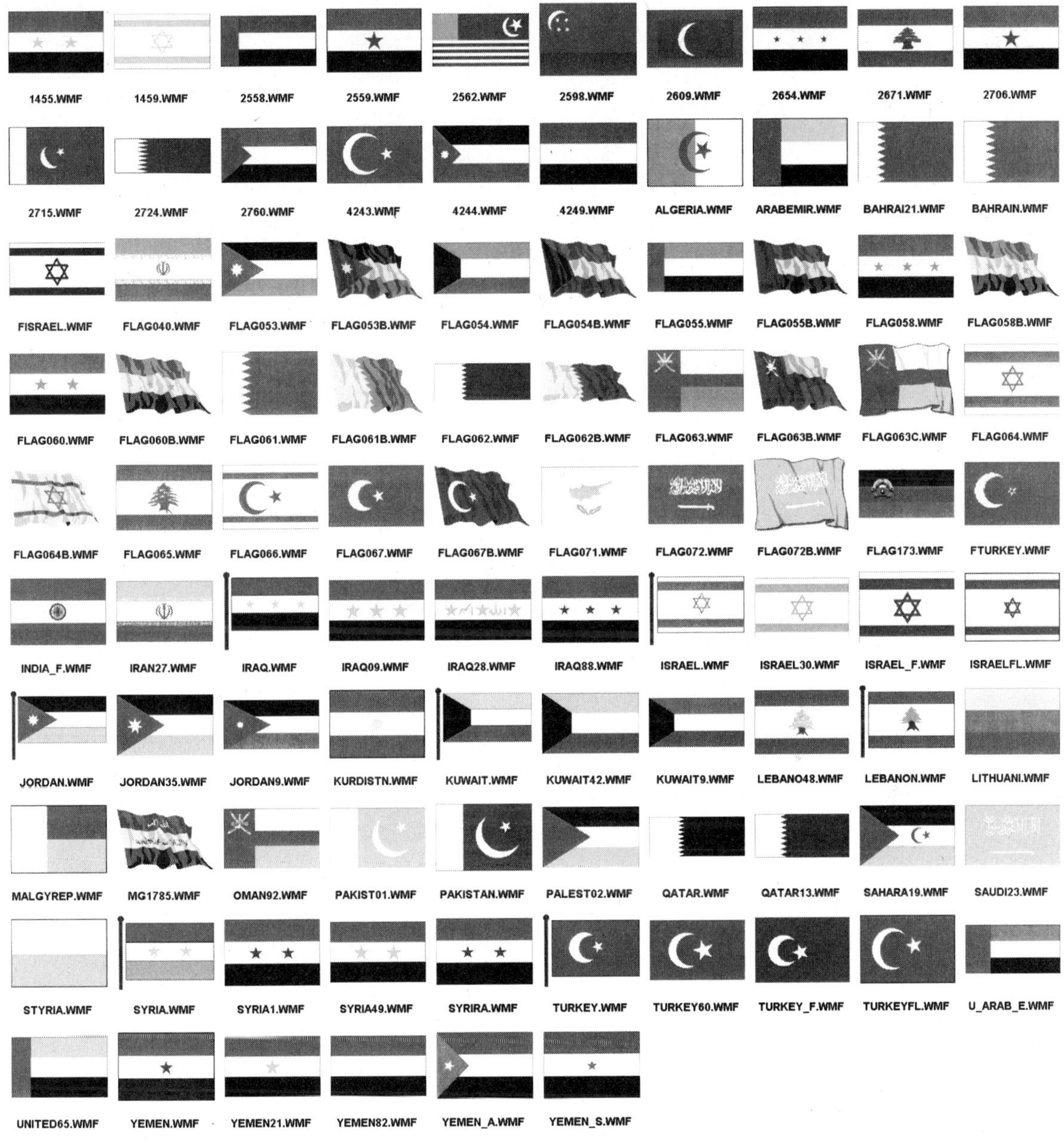
1455.WMF 1459.WMF 2558.WMF 2559.WMF 2562.WMF 2598.WMF 2609.WMF 2654.WMF 2671.WMF 2706.WMF
2715.WMF 2724.WMF 2760.WMF 4243.WMF 4244.WMF 4249.WMF ALGERIA.WMF ARABEMIR.WMF BAHRAI21.WMF BAHRAIN.WMF
FISRAEL.WMF FLAG040.WMF FLAG053.WMF FLAG053B.WMF FLAG054.WMF FLAG054B.WMF FLAG055.WMF FLAG055B.WMF FLAG058.WMF FLAG058B.WMF
FLAG060.WMF FLAG060B.WMF FLAG061.WMF FLAG061B.WMF FLAG062.WMF FLAG062B.WMF FLAG063.WMF FLAG063B.WMF FLAG063C.WMF FLAG064.WMF
FLAG064B.WMF FLAG065.WMF FLAG066.WMF FLAG067.WMF FLAG067B.WMF FLAG071.WMF FLAG072.WMF FLAG072B.WMF FLAG173.WMF FTURKEY.WMF
INDIA_F.WMF IRAN27.WMF IRAQ.WMF IRAQ09.WMF IRAQ28.WMF IRAQ88.WMF ISRAEL.WMF ISRAEL30.WMF ISRAEL_F.WMF ISRAELFL.WMF
JORDAN.WMF JORDAN35.WMF JORDAN9.WMF KURDISTN.WMF KUWAIT.WMF KUWAIT42.WMF KUWAIT9.WMF LEBANO48.WMF LEBANON.WMF LITHUANI.WMF
MALGYREP.WMF MG1785.WMF OMAN92.WMF PAKIST01.WMF PAKISTAN.WMF PALEST02.WMF QATAR.WMF QATAR13.WMF SAHARA19.WMF SAUDI23.WMF
STYRIA.WMF SYRIA.WMF SYRIA1.WMF SYRIA49.WMF SYRIRA.WMF TURKEY.WMF TURKEY60.WMF TURKEY_F.WMF TURKEYFL.WMF U_ARAB_E.WMF
UNITED65.WMF YEMEN.WMF YEMEN21.WMF YEMEN82.WMF YEMEN_A.WMF YEMEN_S.WMF

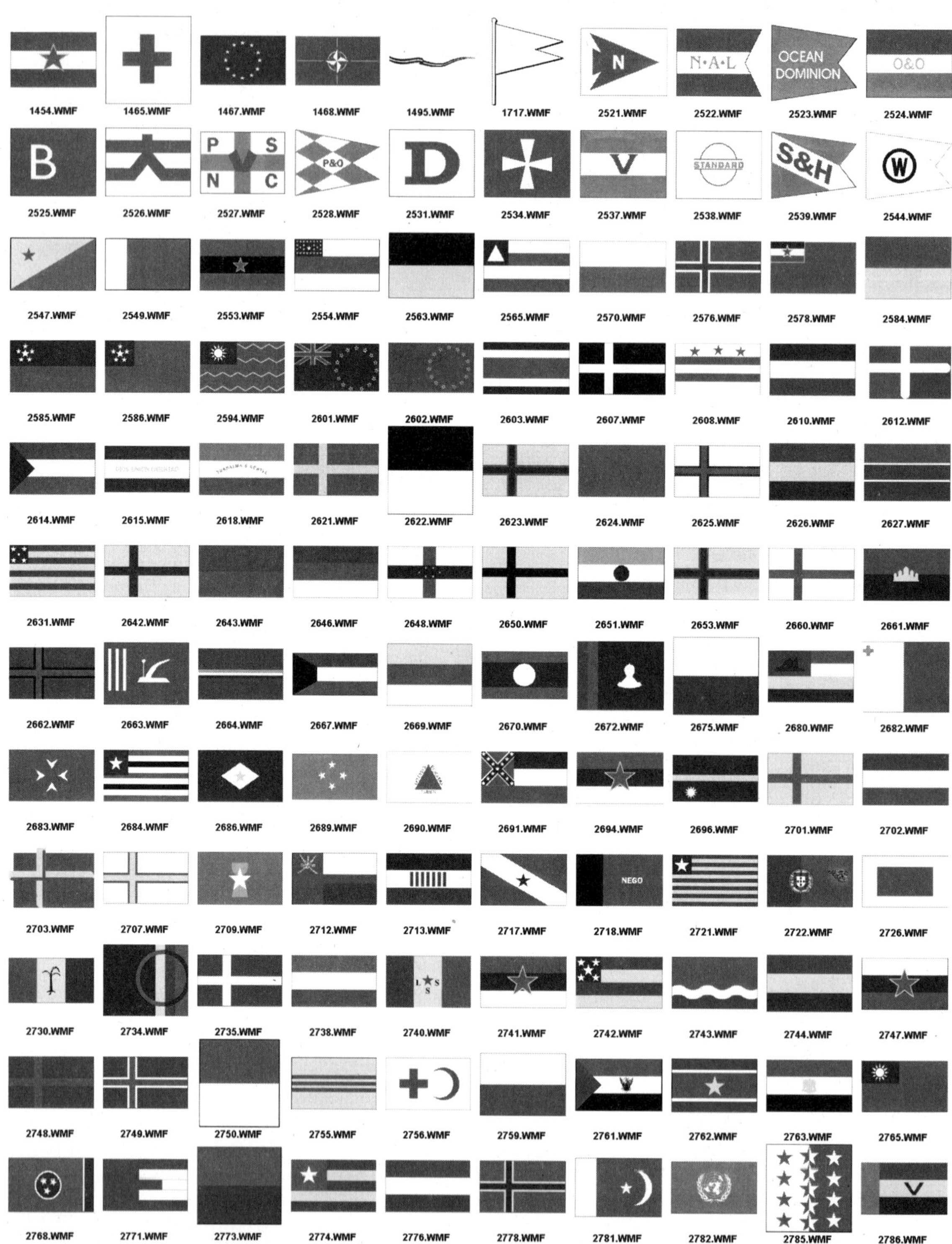

1454.WMF 1465.WMF 1467.WMF 1468.WMF 1495.WMF 1717.WMF 2521.WMF 2522.WMF 2523.WMF 2524.WMF

2525.WMF 2526.WMF 2527.WMF 2528.WMF 2531.WMF 2534.WMF 2537.WMF 2538.WMF 2539.WMF 2544.WMF

2547.WMF 2549.WMF 2553.WMF 2554.WMF 2563.WMF 2565.WMF 2570.WMF 2576.WMF 2578.WMF 2584.WMF

2585.WMF 2586.WMF 2594.WMF 2601.WMF 2602.WMF 2603.WMF 2607.WMF 2608.WMF 2610.WMF 2612.WMF

2614.WMF 2615.WMF 2618.WMF 2621.WMF 2622.WMF 2623.WMF 2624.WMF 2625.WMF 2626.WMF 2627.WMF

2631.WMF 2642.WMF 2643.WMF 2646.WMF 2648.WMF 2650.WMF 2651.WMF 2653.WMF 2660.WMF 2661.WMF

2662.WMF 2663.WMF 2664.WMF 2667.WMF 2669.WMF 2670.WMF 2672.WMF 2675.WMF 2680.WMF 2682.WMF

2683.WMF 2684.WMF 2686.WMF 2689.WMF 2690.WMF 2691.WMF 2694.WMF 2696.WMF 2701.WMF 2702.WMF

2703.WMF 2707.WMF 2709.WMF 2712.WMF 2713.WMF 2717.WMF 2718.WMF 2721.WMF 2722.WMF 2726.WMF

2730.WMF 2734.WMF 2735.WMF 2738.WMF 2740.WMF 2741.WMF 2742.WMF 2743.WMF 2744.WMF 2747.WMF

2748.WMF 2749.WMF 2750.WMF 2755.WMF 2756.WMF 2759.WMF 2761.WMF 2762.WMF 2763.WMF 2765.WMF

2768.WMF 2771.WMF 2773.WMF 2774.WMF 2776.WMF 2778.WMF 2781.WMF 2782.WMF 2785.WMF 2786.WMF

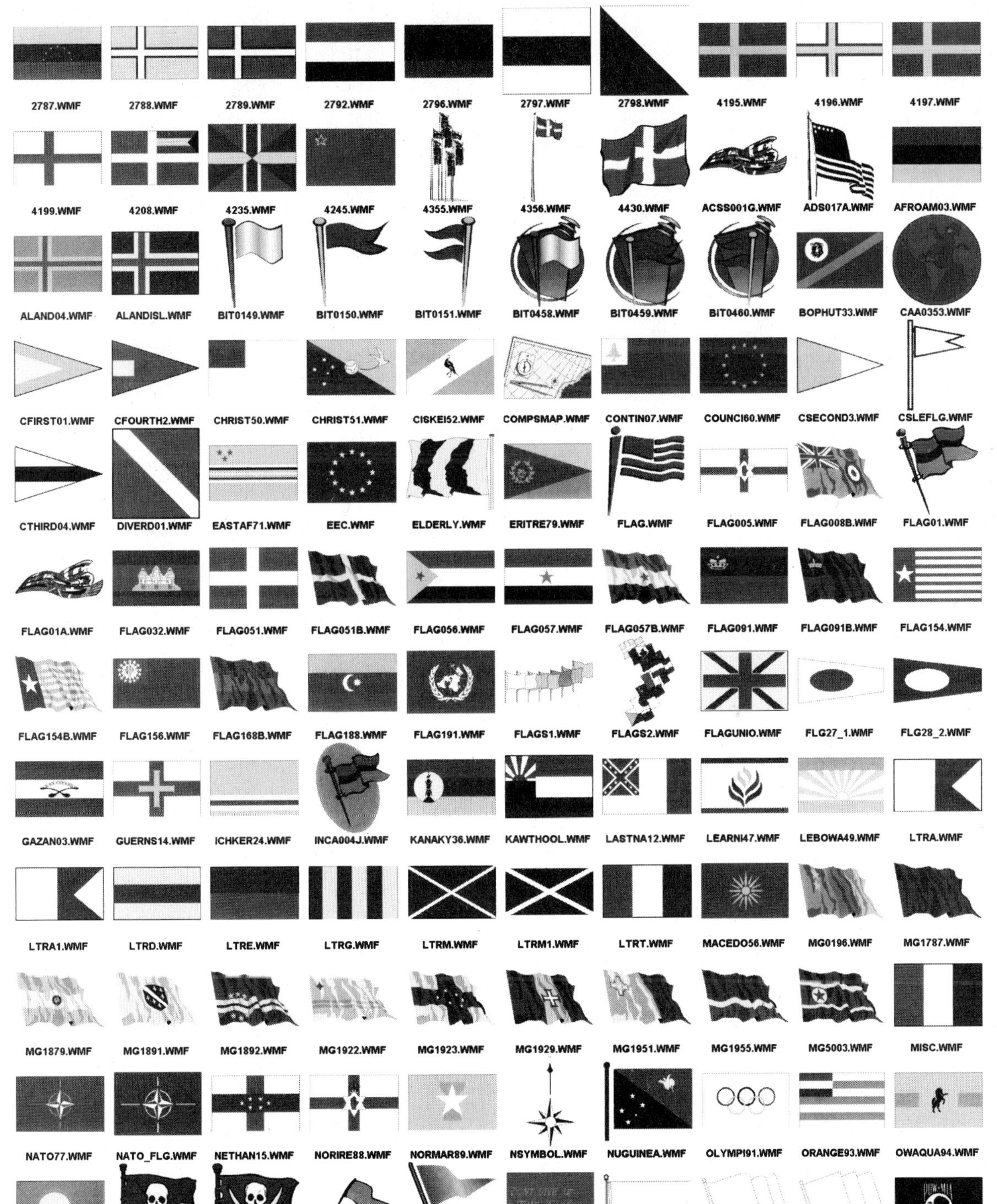
2787.WMF
2788.WMF
2789.WMF
2792.WMF
2796.WMF
2797.WMF
2798.WMF
4195.WMF
4196.WMF
4197.WMF
4199.WMF
4208.WMF
4235.WMF
4245.WMF
4355.WMF
4356.WMF
4430.WMF
ACSS001G.WMF
ADS017A.WMF
AFROAM03.WMF
ALAND04.WMF
ALANDISL.WMF
BIT0149.WMF
BIT0150.WMF
BIT0151.WMF
BIT0458.WMF
BIT0459.WMF
BIT0460.WMF
BOPHUT33.WMF
CAA0353.WMF
CFIRST01.WMF
CFOURTH2.WMF
CHRIST50.WMF
CHRIST51.WMF
CISKEI52.WMF
COMPSMAP.WMF
CONTIN07.WMF
COUNCI60.WMF
CSECOND3.WMF
CSLEFLG.WMF
CTHIRD04.WMF
DIVERD01.WMF
EASTAF71.WMF
EEC.WMF
ELDERLY.WMF
ERITRE79.WMF
FLAG.WMF
FLAG005.WMF
FLAG008B.WMF
FLAG01.WMF
FLAG01A.WMF
FLAG032.WMF
FLAG051.WMF
FLAG051B.WMF
FLAG056.WMF
FLAG057.WMF
FLAG057B.WMF
FLAG091.WMF
FLAG091B.WMF
FLAG154.WMF
FLAG154B.WMF
FLAG156.WMF
FLAG168B.WMF
FLAG188.WMF
FLAG191.WMF
FLAGS1.WMF
FLAGS2.WMF
FLAGUNIO.WMF
FLG27_1.WMF
FLG28_2.WMF
GAZAN03.WMF
GUERNS14.WMF
ICHKER24.WMF
INCA004J.WMF
KANAKY36.WMF
KAWTHOOL.WMF
LASTNA12.WMF
LEARNI47.WMF
LEBOWA49.WMF
LTRA.WMF
LTRA1.WMF
LTRD.WMF
LTRE.WMF
LTRG.WMF
LTRM.WMF
LTRM1.WMF
LTRT.WMF
MACEDO56.WMF
MG0196.WMF
MG1787.WMF
MG1879.WMF
MG1891.WMF
MG1892.WMF
MG1922.WMF
MG1923.WMF
MG1929.WMF
MG1951.WMF
MG1955.WMF
MG5003.WMF
MISC.WMF
NATO77.WMF
NATO_FLG.WMF
NETHAN15.WMF
NORIRE88.WMF
NORMAR89.WMF
NSYMBOL.WMF
NUGUINEA.WMF
OLYMPI91.WMF
ORANGE93.WMF
OWAQUA94.WMF
PALAU.WMF
PBN039B.WMF
PBN039D.WMF
PECA031J.WMF
PENNANT.WMF
PERRYS.WMF
PLNFLAG1.WMF
PLNFLAG2.WMF
PLNFLAG3.WMF
POWMIA11.WMF

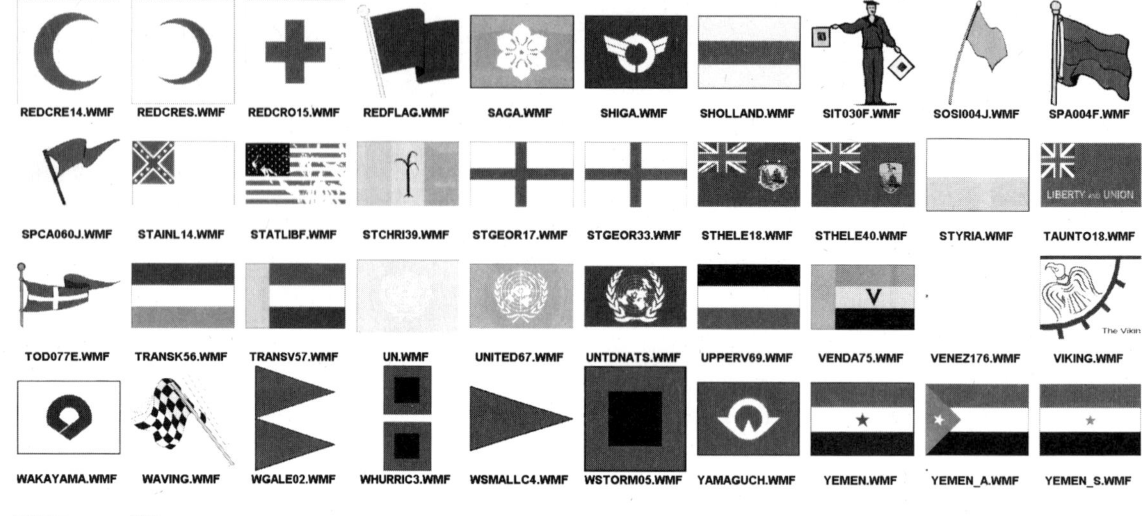

Z21946.WMF

Z21948.WMF

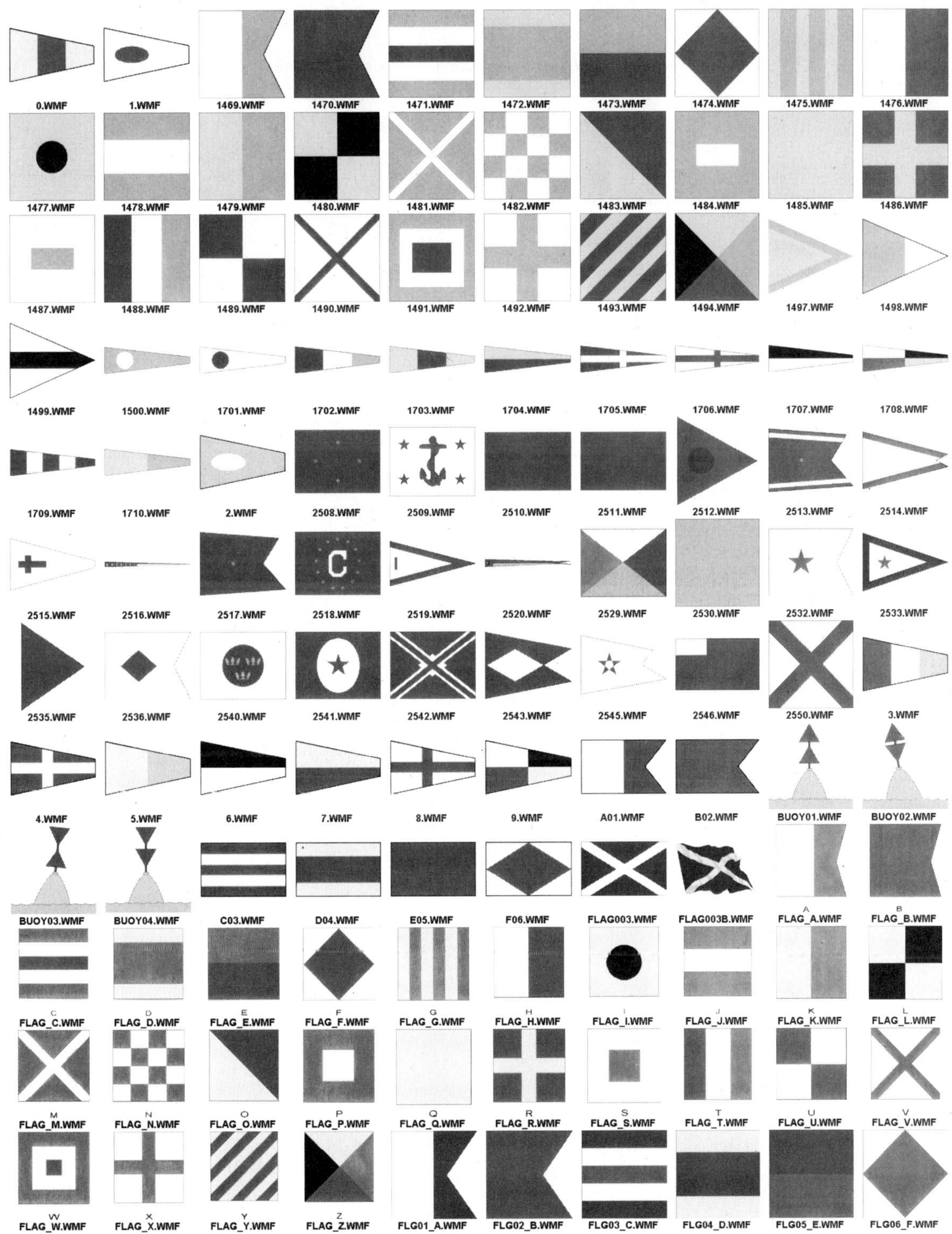

0.WMF
1.WMF
1469.WMF
1470.WMF
1471.WMF
1472.WMF
1473.WMF
1474.WMF
1475.WMF
1476.WMF
1477.WMF
1478.WMF
1479.WMF
1480.WMF
1481.WMF
1482.WMF
1483.WMF
1484.WMF
1485.WMF
1486.WMF
1487.WMF
1488.WMF
1489.WMF
1490.WMF
1491.WMF
1492.WMF
1493.WMF
1494.WMF
1497.WMF
1498.WMF
1499.WMF
1500.WMF
1701.WMF
1702.WMF
1703.WMF
1704.WMF
1705.WMF
1706.WMF
1707.WMF
1708.WMF
1709.WMF
1710.WMF
2.WMF
2508.WMF
2509.WMF
2510.WMF
2511.WMF
2512.WMF
2513.WMF
2514.WMF
2515.WMF
2516.WMF
2517.WMF
2518.WMF
2519.WMF
2520.WMF
2529.WMF
2530.WMF
2532.WMF
2533.WMF
2535.WMF
2536.WMF
2540.WMF
2541.WMF
2542.WMF
2543.WMF
2545.WMF
2546.WMF
2550.WMF
3.WMF
4.WMF
5.WMF
6.WMF
7.WMF
8.WMF
9.WMF
A01.WMF
B02.WMF
BUOY01.WMF
BUOY02.WMF
BUOY03.WMF
BUOY04.WMF
C03.WMF
D04.WMF
E05.WMF
F06.WMF
FLAG003.WMF
FLAG003B.WMF
A
FLAG_A.WMF
B
FLAG_B.WMF
C
FLAG_C.WMF
D
FLAG_D.WMF
E
FLAG_E.WMF
F
FLAG_F.WMF
G
FLAG_G.WMF
H
FLAG_H.WMF
I
FLAG_I.WMF
J
FLAG_J.WMF
K
FLAG_K.WMF
L
FLAG_L.WMF
M
FLAG_M.WMF
N
FLAG_N.WMF
O
FLAG_O.WMF
P
FLAG_P.WMF
Q
FLAG_Q.WMF
R
FLAG_R.WMF
S
FLAG_S.WMF
T
FLAG_T.WMF
U
FLAG_U.WMF
V
FLAG_V.WMF
W
FLAG_W.WMF
X
FLAG_X.WMF
Y
FLAG_Y.WMF
Z
FLAG_Z.WMF
FLG01_A.WMF
FLG02_B.WMF
FLG03_C.WMF
FLG04_D.WMF
FLG05_E.WMF
FLG06_F.WMF

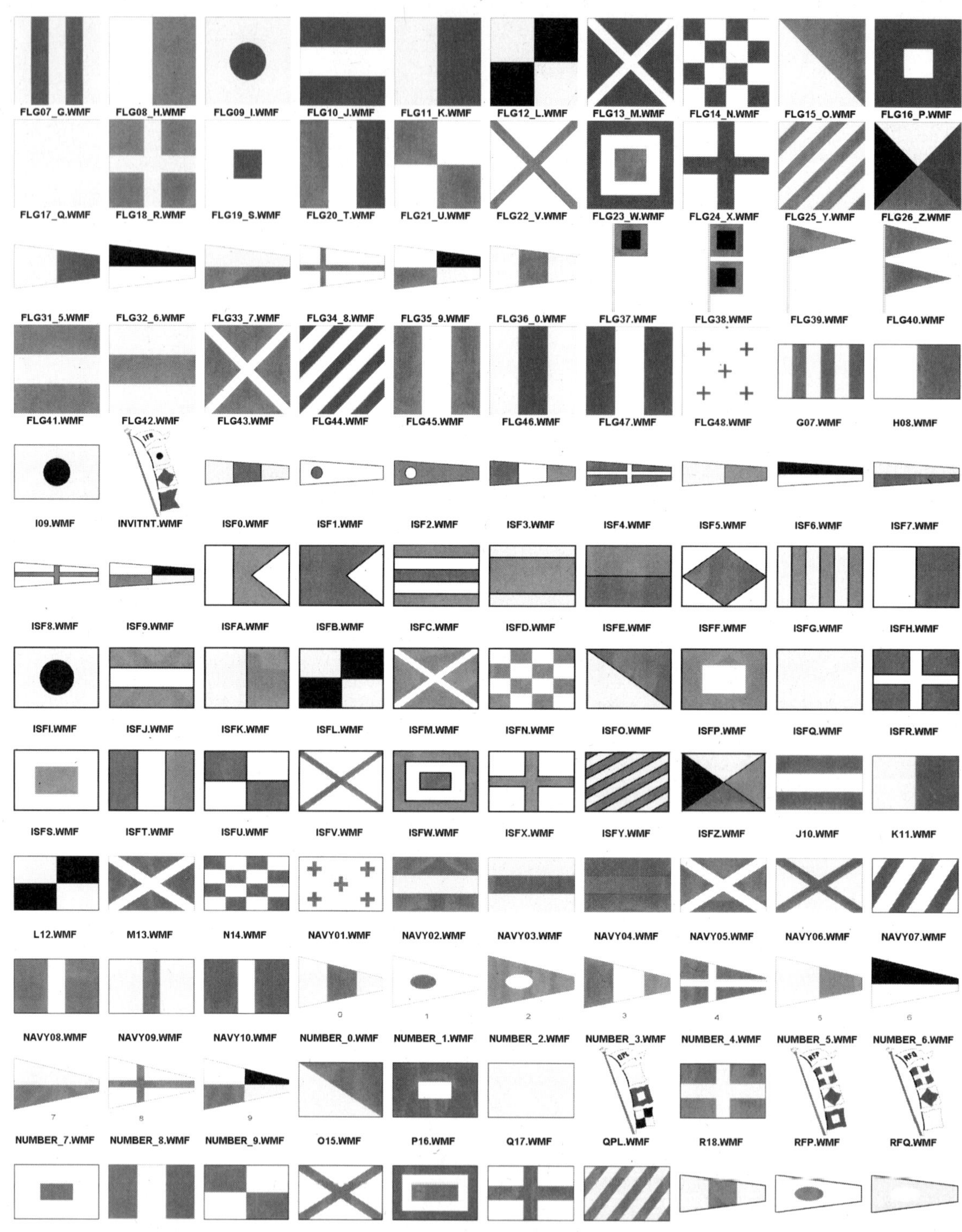
FLG07_G.WMF
FLG08_H.WMF
FLG09_I.WMF
FLG10_J.WMF
FLG11_K.WMF
FLG12_L.WMF
FLG13_M.WMF
FLG14_N.WMF
FLG15_O.WMF
FLG16_P.WMF
FLG17_Q.WMF
FLG18_R.WMF
FLG19_S.WMF
FLG20_T.WMF
FLG21_U.WMF
FLG22_V.WMF
FLG23_W.WMF
FLG24_X.WMF
FLG25_Y.WMF
FLG26_Z.WMF
FLG31_5.WMF
FLG32_6.WMF
FLG33_7.WMF
FLG34_8.WMF
FLG35_9.WMF
FLG36_0.WMF
FLG37.WMF
FLG38.WMF
FLG39.WMF
FLG40.WMF
FLG41.WMF
FLG42.WMF
FLG43.WMF
FLG44.WMF
FLG45.WMF
FLG46.WMF
FLG47.WMF
FLG48.WMF
G07.WMF
H08.WMF
I09.WMF
INVITNT.WMF
ISF0.WMF
ISF1.WMF
ISF2.WMF
ISF3.WMF
ISF4.WMF
ISF5.WMF
ISF6.WMF
ISF7.WMF
ISF8.WMF
ISF9.WMF
ISFA.WMF
ISFB.WMF
ISFC.WMF
ISFD.WMF
ISFE.WMF
ISFF.WMF
ISFG.WMF
ISFH.WMF
ISFI.WMF
ISFJ.WMF
ISFK.WMF
ISFL.WMF
ISFM.WMF
ISFN.WMF
ISFO.WMF
ISFP.WMF
ISFQ.WMF
ISFR.WMF
ISFS.WMF
ISFT.WMF
ISFU.WMF
ISFV.WMF
ISFW.WMF
ISFX.WMF
ISFY.WMF
ISFZ.WMF
J10.WMF
K11.WMF
L12.WMF
M13.WMF
N14.WMF
NAVY01.WMF
NAVY02.WMF
NAVY03.WMF
NAVY04.WMF
NAVY05.WMF
NAVY06.WMF
NAVY07.WMF
NAVY08.WMF
NAVY09.WMF
NAVY10.WMF
0
NUMBER_0.WMF
1
NUMBER_1.WMF
2
NUMBER_2.WMF
3
NUMBER_3.WMF
4
NUMBER_4.WMF
5
NUMBER_5.WMF
6
NUMBER_6.WMF
7
NUMBER_7.WMF
8
NUMBER_8.WMF
9
NUMBER_9.WMF
O15.WMF
P16.WMF
Q17.WMF
QPL.WMF
R18.WMF
RFP.WMF
RFQ.WMF
S19.WMF
T20.WMF
U21.WMF
V22.WMF
W23.WMF
X24.WMF
Y25.WMF
Z21940.WMF
Z21941.WMF
Z21942.WMF

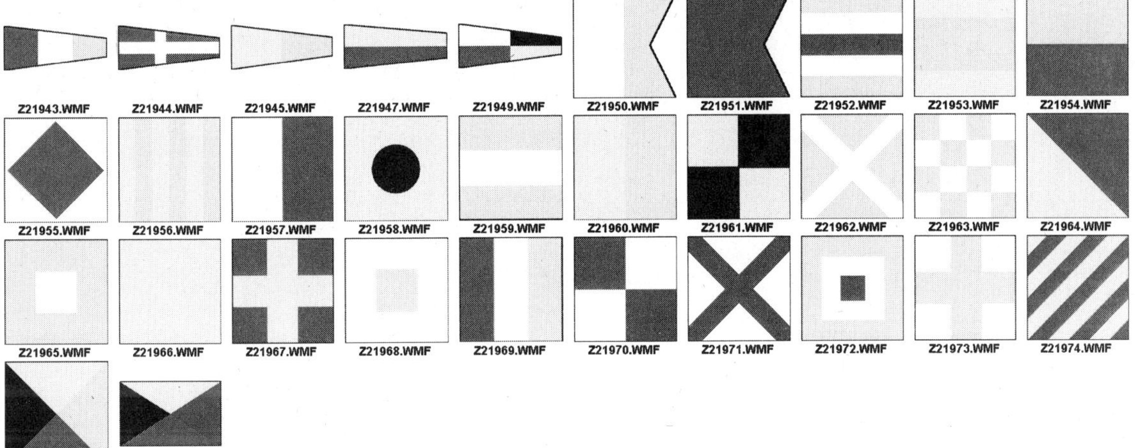

Z21943.WMF Z21944.WMF Z21945.WMF Z21947.WMF Z21949.WMF Z21950.WMF Z21951.WMF Z21952.WMF Z21953.WMF Z21954.WMF

Z21955.WMF Z21956.WMF Z21957.WMF Z21958.WMF Z21959.WMF Z21960.WMF Z21961.WMF Z21962.WMF Z21963.WMF Z21964.WMF

Z21965.WMF Z21966.WMF Z21967.WMF Z21968.WMF Z21969.WMF Z21970.WMF Z21971.WMF Z21972.WMF Z21973.WMF Z21974.WMF

Z21975.WMF Z26.WMF

Flags • Oceania

1463.WMF 1464.WMF 2561.WMF 2665.WMF 2685.WMF 2770.WMF 2780.WMF 2790.WMF AMSAMO07.WMF AUSFLAG.WMF

AUSFLAGC.WMF AUSTRA17.WMF AUSTRALA.WMF AUSTRALI.WMF AUSTRL_F.WMF AUSTRLIA.WMF CANARY43.WMF COOK56.WMF COOKISLD.WMF FAUSTRAL.WMF

FIJI84.WMF FLAG068.WMF FLAG068B.WMF FLAG069.WMF FLAG069B.WMF FLAG1.WMF FLAG155.WMF FLAG179.WMF GRANDU10.WMF GUAM11.WMF

KIRIBA39.WMF KIRIBATI.WMF MARIANAS.WMF MARSHA64.WMF MARSHALL.WMF MG1864.WMF MG1876.WMF MG1885.WMF MG1910.WMF MG1920.WMF

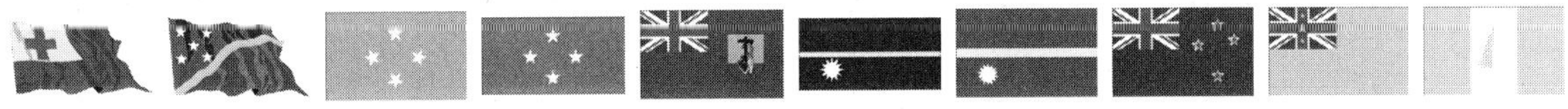

MG1938.WMF MG1956.WMF MICRON68.WMF MICRONES.WMF MONTSE73.WMF NAURU.WMF NAURU78.WMF NEWZEA82.WMF NIUE86.WMF NORFOL87.WMF

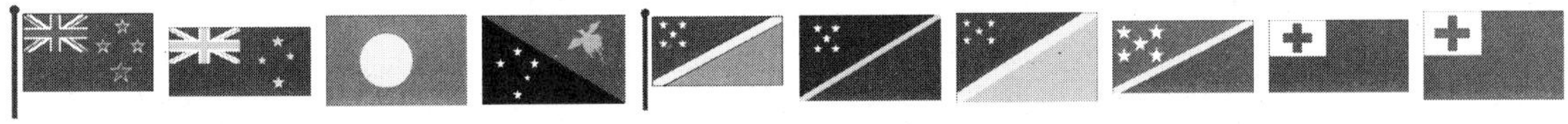

NUZELAND.WMF NZ_F.WMF PALAU.WMF PAPUA04.WMF SOLOMNIS.WMF SOLOMO01.WMF SOLOMO33.WMF SOLOMON.WMF TONGA.WMF TONGA55.WMF

TONGAAA.WMF TUVALU.WMF TUVALU62.WMF UPR_VLTA.WMF UPRVOLTA.WMF VANUAT73.WMF VANUATU.WMF W_SAMOA.WMF WALLIS80.WMF WESTSO81.WMF

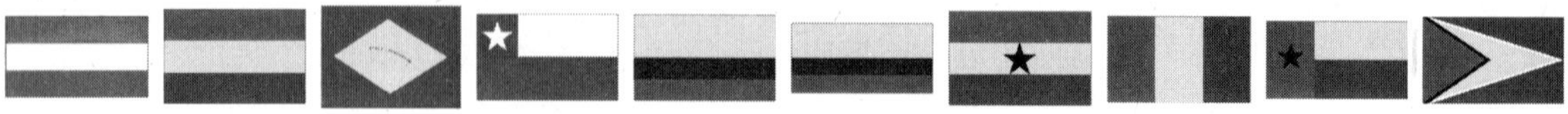

2560.WMF 2575.WMF 2581.WMF 2593.WMF 2596.WMF 2613.WMF 2630.WMF 2639.WMF 2640.WMF 2641.WMF

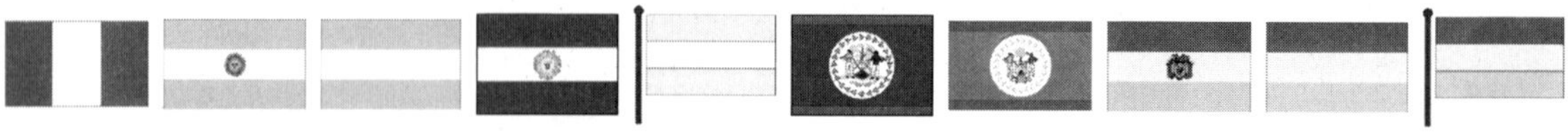

2720.WMF ARGENT13.WMF ARGENT14.WMF ARGENTNA.WMF ARGETINA.WMF BELIZE.WMF BELIZE27.WMF BOLIVI31.WMF BOLIVI32.WMF BOLIVIA.WMF

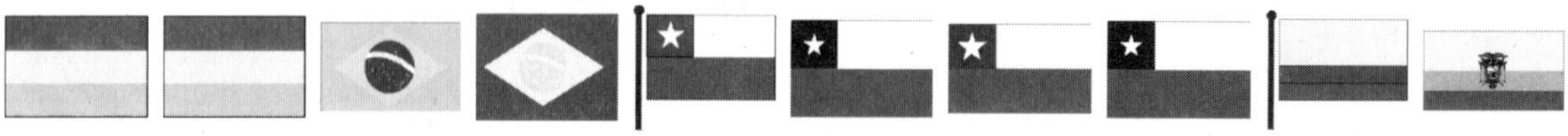

BOLIVIAA.WMF BOLIVIO.WMF BRAZIL34.WMF BRAZIL_F.WMF CHILE.WMF CHILE3.WMF CHILE48.WMF CHILI.WMF COLOMBIA.WMF ECUADO72.WMF

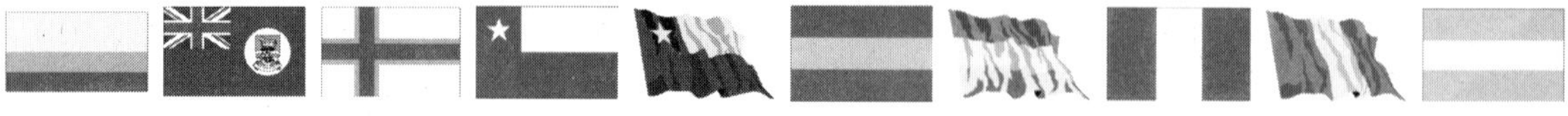

ECUADO73.WMF FALKLA82.WMF FAROES83.WMF FLAG073.WMF FLAG073B.WMF FLAG075.WMF FLAG075B.WMF FLAG076.WMF FLAG076B.WMF FLAG077.WMF

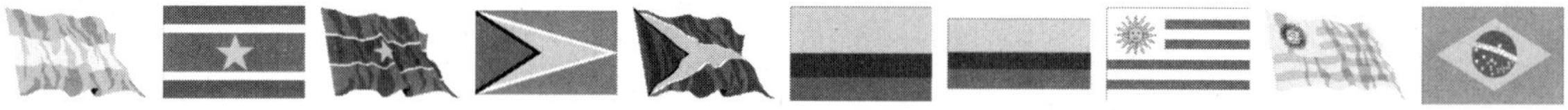

FLAG077B.WMF FLAG079.WMF FLAG079B.WMF FLAG080.WMF FLAG080B.WMF FLAG081.WMF FLAG082.WMF FLAG083.WMF FLAG083B.WMF FLAG142.WMF

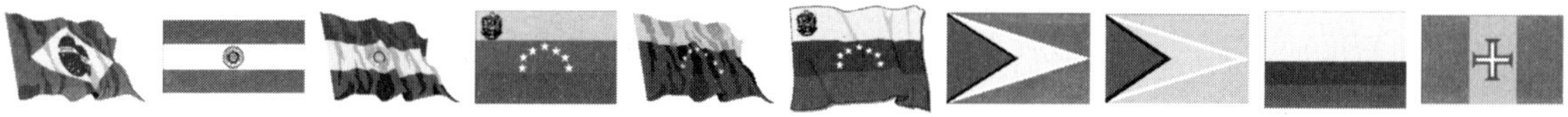

FLAG142B.WMF FLAG164.WMF FLAG164B.WMF FLAG175.WMF FLAG175B.WMF FLAG175C.WMF GUYANA.WMF GUYANA17.WMF KOLOMBIA.WMF MADEIR58.WMF

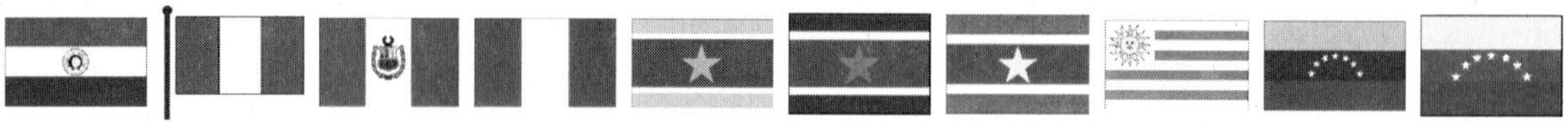

PARAGU05.WMF PERU.WMF PERU106.WMF PERU207.WMF SURINA45.WMF SURINAM.WMF SURINAME.WMF URUGUA70.WMF VENEZ277.WMF VENEZULA.WMF

Flags • United Kingdom (UK)

1462.WMF 2574.WMF 2577.WMF 2595.WMF 2617.WMF 2638.WMF 2656.WMF 2725.WMF 2727.WMF 2791.WMF

BRITNA35.WMF BRITRE04.WMF BRITVI36.WMF BRVIRISL.WMF ENGLAN77.WMF FLAG001.WMF FLAG001B.WMF FLAG001C.WMF FLAG002.WMF FLAG002B.WMF

FLAG004.WMF FLAG004C.WMF FLAG006.WMF FLAG006B.WMF FLAG007.WMF FLAG007B.WMF FLAG008.WMF FLAG009.WMF FLAG010.WMF FLAG010B.WMF

FLAG011.WMF FLAG4.WMF GR_BRIT.WMF JERSEY34.WMF KINGSC11.WMF MG2154.WMF UK_F.WMF UKFL.WMF

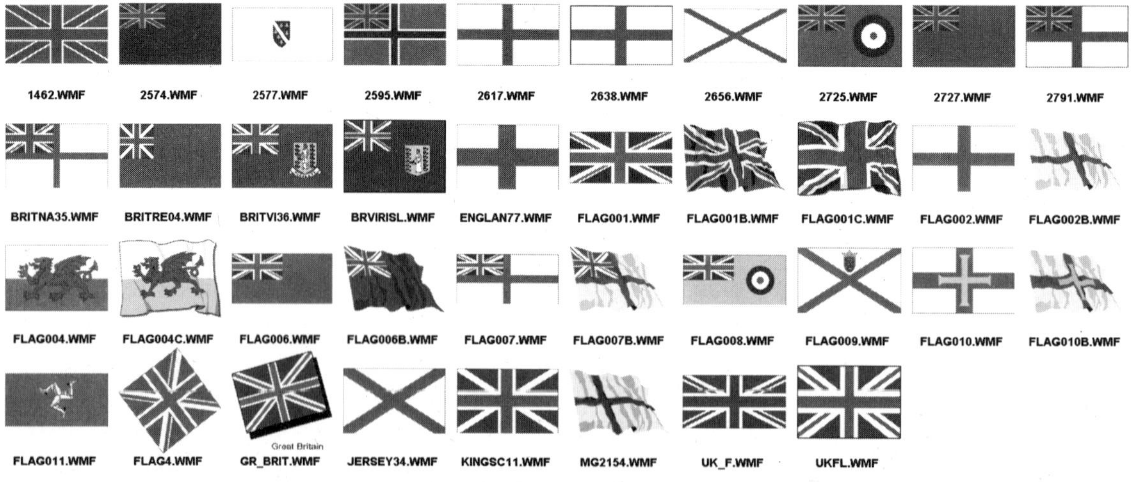

1135FLAC.WMF	1460.WMF	A20014.WMF	AMERICAN.WMF	BANNERS.WMF	CAA0348.WMF	COMICFL.WMF	F20988.WMF	F20989.WMF	F20990.WMF
F20999.WMF	FLAG0106.WMF	FLAG0207.WMF	FLAG0308.WMF	FLAG0409.WMF	FLAG0510.WMF	FLAG0611.WMF	FLAG0712.WMF	FLAG0813.WMF	FLAG0914.WMF
FLAG1015.WMF	FLAG1116.WMF	FLAG1217.WMF	FLAG1318.WMF	FLAG1419.WMF	FLAG1520.WMF	FLAG1621.WMF	FLAG1722.WMF	FLAG1924.WMF	FLAG1MD.WMF
FLAG2025.WMF	FLAG2126.WMF	FLAG2227.WMF	FLAG2328.WMF	FLAG2429.WMF	FLAG3.WMF	FSW019D.WMF	FUSA.WMF	GASI206M.WMF	HIST001.WMF
HIST002.WMF	HIST003.WMF	The Flag of 1777 HIST004.WMF	Flag of 1795 HIST005.WMF	The 48-Star Flag HIST006.WMF	HIST007.WMF	1824 HIST008.WMF	HIST009.WMF	76 HIST010.WMF	76 HIST011.WMF
HIST012.WMF	HIST013.WMF	HIST014.WMF	HIST015.WMF	HIST016.WMF	HIST017.WMF	Confederate Flag I HIST018.WMF	Confederate Flac HIST019.WMF	Confederate Flag III HIST020.WMF	HIST021.WMF
 The Continental Colors HIST022.WMF	HIST023.WMF	HIST024.WMF	HIST025.WMF	HIST026.WMF	HIST027.WMF	HIST028.WMF	HIST029.WMF	HIST030.WMF	LIBERTY HIST031.WMF
HIST032.WMF	HIST033.WMF	HIST034.WMF	LIBERTY UNION New England Flag I HIST035.WMF	76 New England Flag I HIST036.WMF	HIST037.WMF	The Other Flag of 17 HIST038.WMF	HIST039.WMF	HIST040.WMF	HIST041.WMF
HIST042.WMF	HIST043.WMF	HIST044.WMF	United States HIST045.WMF	HIST046.WMF	MADE IN USA M21212.WMF	MADE IN M21213.WMF	SOAB001J.WMF	SOBO011J.WMF	SORW039J.WMF
SOSI011J.WMF	STARS_ST.WMF	STFLG01.WMF	STFLG02.WMF	STFLG03.WMF	STFLG04.WMF	STFLG05.WMF	STFLG06.WMF	STFLG07.WMF	STFLG08.WMF
STFLG09.WMF	ARKANSAS STFLG10.WMF	STFLG11.WMF	The Bear Flag STFLG12.WMF	CALIFORNIA REPUBLIC STFLG13.WMF	STFLG14.WMF	STFLG15.WMF	STFLG16.WMF	STFLG17.WMF	STFLG18.WMF

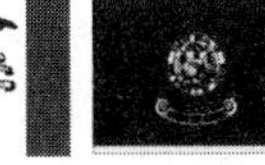
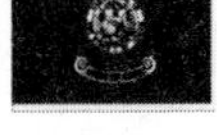

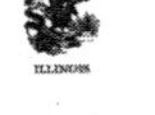

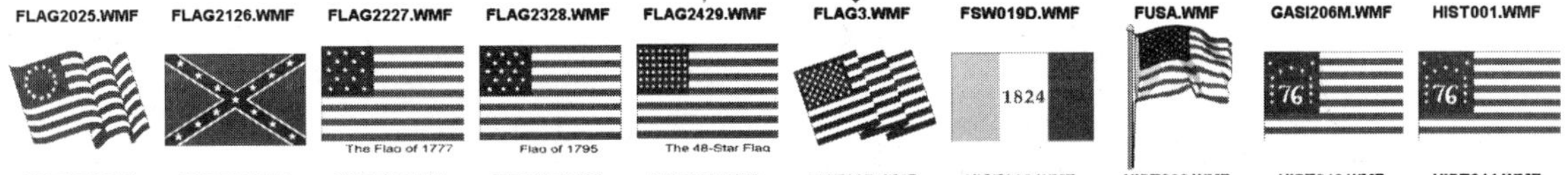

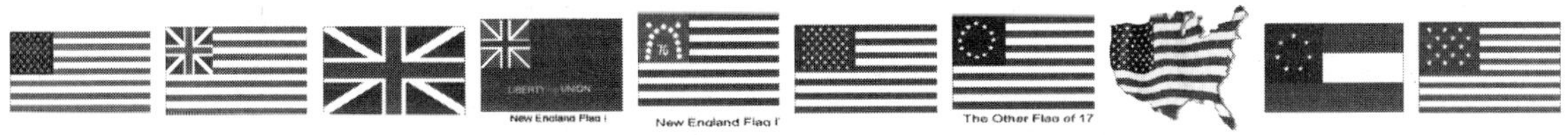

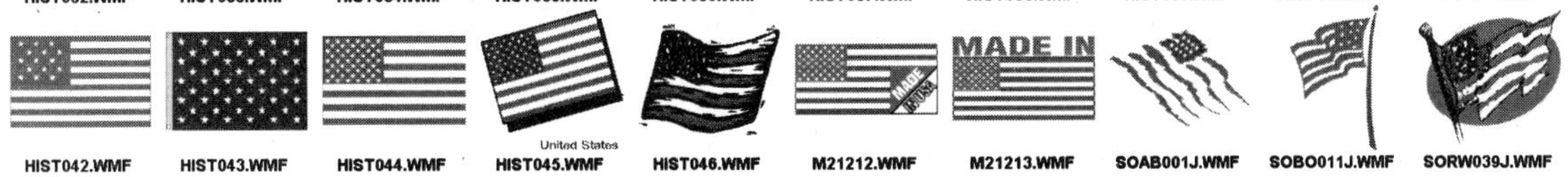

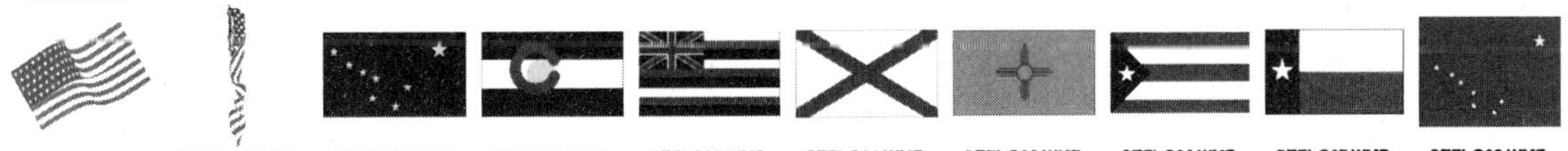

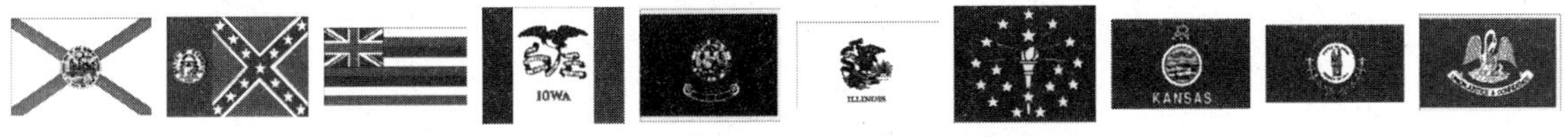

STFLG19.WMF	STFLG20.WMF	STFLG21.WMF	IOWA STFLG22.WMF	STFLG23.WMF	ILLINOIS STFLG24.WMF	STFLG25.WMF	KANSAS STFLG26.WMF	STFLG27.WMF	STFLG28.WMF

MONTANA
Texas Flag
STFLG29.WMF
STFLG30.WMF
STFLG31.WMF
STFLG32.WMF
STFLG33.WMF
STFLG34.WMF
STFLG35.WMF
STFLG36.WMF
STFLG37.WMF
STFLG38.WMF
STFLG39.WMF
STFLG40.WMF
STFLG41.WMF
STFLG42.WMF
STFLG51.WMF
TEAMWRK2.WMF
U1.WMF
U21860.WMF
UNITED34.WMF
USA1.WMF
USA2.WMF
USA3.WMF
USA_F.WMF
USA_SHLD.WMF
USFLAG1.WMF
USFLAG2.WMF
USFLAG3.WMF
USFLAG4.WMF
USFLAG5.WMF
USFLAGMD.WMF

0709.WMF 1788.WMF 1789.WMF 1816.WMF 1817.WMF 1820.WMF 1821.WMF 1822.WMF 1823.WMF 1825.WMF
1826.WMF 1827.WMF 1828.WMF 1831.WMF 1832.WMF 1834.WMF 1842.WMF 1844.WMF 1845.WMF 1846.WMF
1850.WMF 1851.WMF 1857.WMF 1858.WMF 1859.WMF 1860.WMF 1861.WMF 1863.WMF 4459.WMF 4460.WMF
ALCOHOL.WMF BARREL.WMF BARRELC.WMF BEARMUG.WMF BEER.WMF BEER001.WMF BEER2.WMF BEER_TAP.WMF BEERDRK.WMF BEERMUG.WMF
生ビール
BEERMUG2.WMF BEERTO.WMF BEV.WMF BIT0130.WMF BIT0131.WMF BIT0135.WMF BIT0136.WMF BIT0201.WMF BIT0203.WMF BIT1171.WMF
BOTBR1.WMF BOTBR2.WMF BOTTLE.WMF BOTTLE2.WMF BOTTLE77.WMF BOTTLEX.WMF BRMUG.WMF BUBBLY.WMF C20772.WMF C20809.WMF
XXX
CELEB2.WMF CHAM003.WMF CHAMPAG2.WMF CHAMPAGN.WMF CHAMPGN2.WMF CHAMPGNE.WMF CHMPNTO.WMF COCKTAIL.WMF COCKTAL.WMF COCKTAL4.WMF
COCKTALE.WMF CTMISC04.WMF DEC061B.WMF DIM075E.WMF DRIN028.WMF DRIN029.WMF DRIN030.WMF DRIN031.WMF DRIN032.WMF DRIN033.WMF
DRIN034.WMF DRIN035.WMF DRINK.WMF DRINK1.WMF DRINKAS.WMF DRINKSIL.WMF ENSI006J.WMF FD01.WMF FD02.WMF FD26.WMF
BEER
FD27.WMF FDD108B.WMF FDD111K.WMF FDD114R.WMF FDDNK005.WMF FDDNK009.WMF FDDNK034.WMF FDDNK084.WMF FDDNK104.WMF FDDNK158.WMF
FDDNK188.WMF FDDNK192.WMF FDDNK195.WMF FDDNK206.WMF FDDNK208.WMF FDDNK210.WMF FDDNK211.WMF FDDNK212.WMF FDDNK213.WMF FDDNK214.WMF
FDDNK225.WMF FDDNK227.WMF FDDNK230.WMF FDDNK231.WMF FDDNK233.WMF FDDNK234.WMF FDDNK235.WMF FDDNK238.WMF FDDNK241.WMF FDDNK242.WMF

FDDNK260.WMF FDDNK261.WMF FDDNK266.WMF FDDNK267.WMF FDDNK271.WMF FDDNK280.WMF FDDNK281.WMF FDDNK282.WMF FDDNK285.WMF FDDNK286.WMF
FOBO006J.WMF FOBO017J.WMF FOBO018J.WMF FOBO019J.WMF FOBO021J.WMF FOBO022J.WMF FOBO023J.WMF FOBO024J.WMF FOBO025J.WMF FOBO033J.WMF
FOBO034J.WMF FOBO035J.WMF FOCA001J.WMF FOCA005J.WMF FOCA010J.WMF FOCA011J.WMF FOCA012J.WMF FOCA019J.WMF FOCA020J.WMF FOCA022J.WMF
FOCA023J.WMF FOCA026J.WMF FOCA027J.WMF FOCA030J.WMF FOCA035J.WMF FOCA036J.WMF FOCA037J.WMF FOCA038J.WMF FOCA042J.WMF FOCA044J.WMF
FOCA045J.WMF FOCA046J.WMF FOCA102J.WMF FOCA104J.WMF FOCA107J.WMF FOGC001D.WMF FOGC001J.WMF FOGC002D.WMF FOGC002M.WMF FOGC003D.WMF
FOGC003M.WMF FOGC005J.WMF FOGC006D.WMF FOGC006J.WMF FOGC009J.WMF FOGC017J.WMF FOGC018J.WMF FOGC020D.WMF FOGC024J.WMF FOGC025D.WMF
FOGC028J.WMF FOGC035D.WMF FOGC037J.WMF FOGC043D.WMF FOGC044D.WMF FOGC045D.WMF FOGC046D.WMF FOGC048D.WMF FOGC049D.WMF FOKC016J.WMF
FOKC017J.WMF FOOD01M.WMF FOOD04M.WMF FOOD05M.WMF FOOD07M.WMF FOOD09.WMF FOOD10.WMF FOOD11.WMF FOOD15M.WMF FOOD16M.WMF
FOOD17.WMF FOOD17M.WMF FOOD18.WMF FOOD18M.WMF FOOD19M.WMF FOOD20.WMF FOOD21.WMF FOOD22.WMF FOOD31.WMF FOOD48.WMF
FOOD49.WMF FOOD50.WMF FOOD51.WMF FORW001J.WMF FORW003D.WMF FORW009D.WMF FORW009J.WMF FORW011J.WMF FORW029J.WMF FORW030J.WMF
FORW032J.WMF FORW041J.WMF FORW049J.WMF FORW052J.WMF FORW054J.WMF FOSI001K.WMF FOSI001M.WMF FOSI002K.WMF FOSI002M.WMF FOSI004K.WMF
FOSI008D.WMF FOSI013J.WMF FOSI017J.WMF FOSI018J.WMF FOSI026D.WMF FOSI027J.WMF FOSI028J.WMF FOSI029D.WMF FOSI029J.WMF FOSI031J.WMF

FOSI033J.WMF
FSTV176.WMF
GLASS1.WMF
GLASS2.WMF
GLSBR1.WMF
GLSBR2.WMF
GLSWN1.WMF
GRPHC078.WMF
GRPHC085.WMF
HAPPY_HR.WMF
HHSI016J.WMF
HOISTING.WMF
HPI030C.WMF
ICEC062.WMF
ICED016.WMF
INSI046D.WMF
LAC071A.WMF
LAC077G.WMF
LAC079C.WMF
LAC086C.WMF
LAC087C.WMF
LAC093B.WMF
LGTUMBLR.WMF
LIMETO.WMF
LVR032B.WMF
MARG1MD.WMF
MARTINI.WMF
MARTINI2.WMF
MARTINI3.WMF
MARTINI6.WMF
MARTINI9.WMF
MRI024B.WMF
MUGBEER.WMF
MUGBEER8.WMF
MUGBR1.WMF
MUGBR2.WMF
MUGBR3.WMF
MUGBR4.WMF
O21462.WMF
OED011E.WMF
OED014B.WMF
OED015L.WMF
OED018O.WMF
OED019G.WMF
OED027D.WMF
OED030G.WMF
PARTY1.WMF
PD047KCU.WMF
PD048ICU.WMF
PD050FCU.WMF
PD051HCU.WMF
PD051SCU.WMF
PD068QCU.WMF
PD068RCU.WMF
PD068SCU.WMF
PD068TCU.WMF
PD068UCU.WMF
PD068VCU.WMF
PD068WCU.WMF
PD068XCU.WMF
PD068ZCU.WMF
PD075MCU.WMF
PD079ACU.WMF
PD080DCU.WMF
PD081OCU.WMF
PD083TCU.WMF
PD092LCU.WMF
PD109SCU.WMF
PD117ACU.WMF
PD119HCU.WMF
PD121JCU.WMF
PD125MCU.WMF
PD129KCU.WMF
PZLBR.WMF
S21642.WMF
SPA004C.WMF
SPIRITS1.WMF
SPIRITS2.WMF
STOUTTO.WMF
SYMBL148.WMF
SYMBL21.WMF
TAP.WMF
TEQLA.WMF
TOASTING.WMF
TROPICAL.WMF
WDI028B.WMF
WHISKEY.WMF
WINE.WMF
WINE01.WMF
WINE038.WMF
WINE039.WMF
WINE2.WMF
WINE66.WMF
WINE_GLS.WMF
WINEBOTL.WMF
WINEGLA.WMF
WINEGLAS.WMF
WINGLASS.WMF

0179.WMF
0326.WMF
1094BREC.WMF
1095BREC.WMF
1096BREC.WMF
1790.WMF
1797.WMF
1801.WMF
1802.WMF
1804.WMF
1837.WMF
1845.WMF
1848.WMF
1854.WMF
1872.WMF
1878.WMF
1879.WMF
1882.WMF
1885.WMF
1898.WMF
4307.WMF
4310.WMF
4492.WMF
4502.WMF
4505.WMF
4508.WMF
4520.WMF
4525.WMF
4530.WMF
4538.WMF
4558.WMF
4576.WMF
4586.WMF
4589.WMF
4592.WMF
4602.WMF
4612.WMF
4621.WMF
4645.WMF
4656.WMF
4658.WMF
4660.WMF
4661.WMF
4665.WMF
4672.WMF
4691.WMF
4697.WMF
4704.WMF
4723.WMF
4736.WMF
4738.WMF
4739.WMF
4749.WMF
4767.WMF
4774.WMF
4784.WMF
4789.WMF
4794.WMF
B20126.WMF
BISCUIT.WMF
BISCUIT1.WMF
BISCUITS.WMF
BIT0114.WMF
BIT0115.WMF
BIT0489.WMF
BIT0490.WMF
BIT1188.WMF
BIT1191.WMF
BRD_BSKT.WMF
BRD_MFN.WMF
BRDSLIC1.WMF
BRDSLICE.WMF
BREA004.WMF
BREA005.WMF
BREA006.WMF
BREA007.WMF
BREA008.WMF
BREA009.WMF
BREA010.WMF
BREA011.WMF
BREAD
BREAD.WMF
BREAD1.WMF
BREAD2.WMF
BREAD3.WMF
BREAD4.MF
BREAD4.WMF
BREAD5.WMF
BREAD6.WMF
BREAD95.WMF
CAKE1.WMF
CEREAL
CEREAL.WMF
CORN_STA.WMF
CUPC008.WMF
DONUT.WMF
EAC046Z.WMF
FD12.WMF
FD13.WMF
FD14.WMF
FD15.WMF
FD16.WMF
FD25.WMF
FD32.WMF
FDDNK033.WMF
FDDNK062.WMF
FDDNK063.WMF
FDDNK064.WMF
FDDNK072.WMF
FDDNK086.WMF
FDDNK149.WMF
FDDNK179.WMF
FDDNK184.WMF
FDDNK245.WMF
FLOUR
FLOUR.WMF
FLOUR
FLOURS.WMF
FOAB001J.WMF
FOAB006J.WMF
FOAB007J.WMF
FOBO003J.WMF
FOBO012J.WMF
FOBO041J.WMF

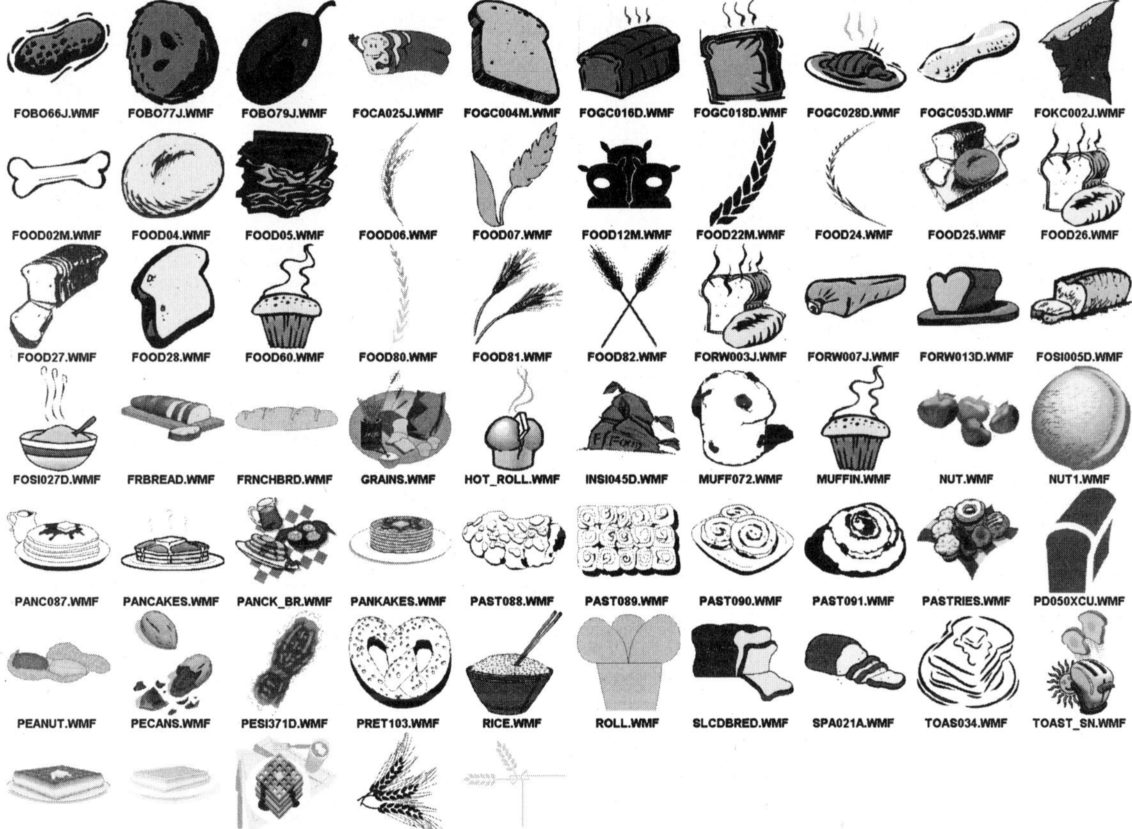
FOBO66J.WMF
FOBO77J.WMF
FOBO79J.WMF
FOCA025J.WMF
FOGC004M.WMF
FOGC016D.WMF
FOGC018D.WMF
FOGC028D.WMF
FOGC053D.WMF
FOKC002J.WMF
FOOD02M.WMF
FOOD04.WMF
FOOD05.WMF
FOOD06.WMF
FOOD07.WMF
FOOD12M.WMF
FOOD22M.WMF
FOOD24.WMF
FOOD25.WMF
FOOD26.WMF
FOOD27.WMF
FOOD28.WMF
FOOD60.WMF
FOOD80.WMF
FOOD81.WMF
FOOD82.WMF
FORW003J.WMF
FORW007J.WMF
FORW013D.WMF
FOSI005D.WMF
FOSI027D.WMF
FRBREAD.WMF
FRNCHBRD.WMF
GRAINS.WMF
HOT_ROLL.WMF
INSI045D.WMF
MUFF072.WMF
MUFFIN.WMF
NUT.WMF
NUT1.WMF
PANC087.WMF
PANCAKES.WMF
PANCK_BR.WMF
PANKAKES.WMF
PAST088.WMF
PAST089.WMF
PAST090.WMF
PAST091.WMF
PASTRIES.WMF
PD050XCU.WMF
PEANUT.WMF
PECANS.WMF
PESI371D.WMF
PRET103.WMF
RICE.WMF
ROLL.WMF
SLCDBRED.WMF
SPA021A.WMF
TOAS034.WMF
TOAST_SN.WMF
WAFFLE.WMF
WAFFLE4.WMF
WAFFLES.WMF
WHEA124.WMF
WHEAT_23.WMF

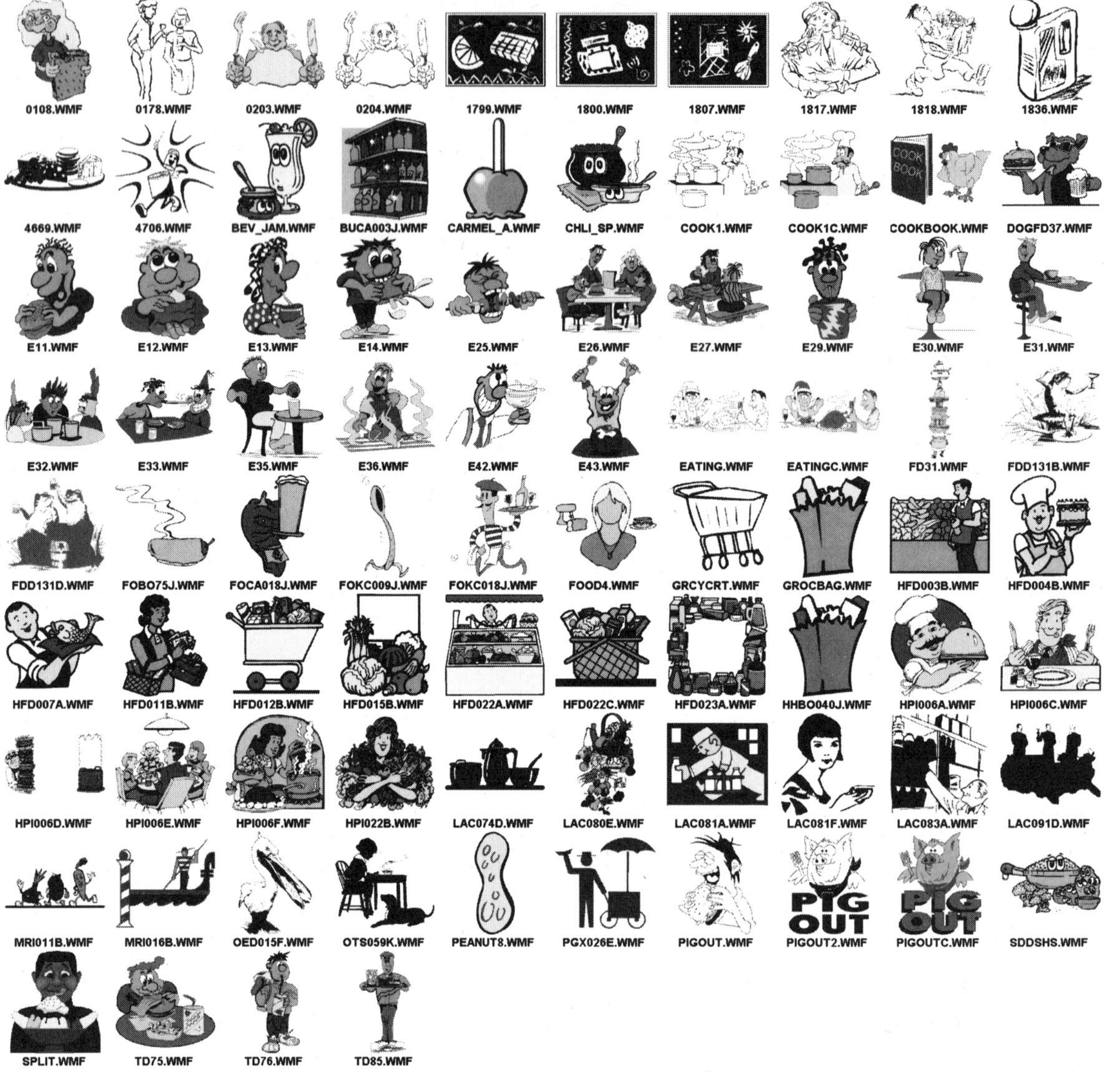
0108.WMF 0178.WMF 0203.WMF 0204.WMF 1799.WMF 1800.WMF 1807.WMF 1817.WMF 1818.WMF 1836.WMF
COOK
BOOK
4669.WMF 4706.WMF BEV_JAM.WMF BUCA003J.WMF CARMEL_A.WMF CHLI_SP.WMF COOK1.WMF COOK1C.WMF COOKBOOK.WMF DOGFD37.WMF
E11.WMF E12.WMF E13.WMF E14.WMF E25.WMF E26.WMF E27.WMF E29.WMF E30.WMF E31.WMF
E32.WMF E33.WMF E35.WMF E36.WMF E42.WMF E43.WMF EATING.WMF EATINGC.WMF FD31.WMF FDD131B.WMF
FDD131D.WMF FOBO75J.WMF FOCA018J.WMF FOKC009J.WMF FOKC018J.WMF FOOD4.WMF GRCYCRT.WMF GROCBAG.WMF HFD003B.WMF HFD004B.WMF
HFD007A.WMF HFD011B.WMF HFD012B.WMF HFD015B.WMF HFD022A.WMF HFD022C.WMF HFD023A.WMF HHBO040J.WMF HPI006A.WMF HPI006C.WMF
HPI006D.WMF HPI006E.WMF HPI006F.WMF HPI022B.WMF LAC074D.WMF LAC080E.WMF LAC081A.WMF LAC081F.WMF LAC083A.WMF LAC091D.WMF
PIG
OUT
PIG
OUT
MRI011B.WMF MRI016B.WMF OED015F.WMF OTS059K.WMF PEANUT8.WMF PGX026E.WMF PIGOUT.WMF PIGOUT2.WMF PIGOUTC.WMF SDDSHS.WMF
SPLIT.WMF TD75.WMF TD76.WMF TD85.WMF

1091BOTC.WMF 1811.WMF 1819.WMF 1827.WMF 1883.WMF 1903.WMF 1904.WMF 1905.WMF 1906.WMF 1907.WMF
1908.WMF 1909.WMF 1910.WMF 2ICECREA.WMF 3396.WMF 4519.WMF 4584.WMF 4640.WMF 4705.WMF B20131.WMF
BARREL10.WMF BEANS.WMF BEERMUG3.WMF BIT0202.WMF BIT0837.WMF BIT0838.WMF BUTRKNIF.WMF C20733.WMF CAN.WMF DEC061C.WMF
DMSTC008.WMF DRIN036.WMF DRIN037.WMF DRIN038.WMF E80.WMF E81.WMF ENKC002J.WMF EV079.WMF EV080.WMF FDD075D.WMF
FDD078B.WMF FDD080F.WMF FDD093F.WMF FDD093S.WMF FDD093T.WMF FDD093U.WMF FDDNK092.WMF FDDNK103.WMF FDDNK173.WMF FDDNK175.WMF
FDDNK177.WMF FDDNK283.WMF FDDNK284.WMF FOBO004J.WMF FOBO020J.WMF FOBO054J.WMF FOBO092J.WMF FOCA013J.WMF FOCA024J.WMF FOCA032J.WMF
FOCA033J.WMF FOCA034J.WMF FOCA039J.WMF FOCA041J.WMF FOCA100J.WMF FOGC005D.WMF FOGC014D.WMF FOGC021J.WMF FOGC022J.WMF FOGC023J.WMF
FOGC029D.WMF FOGC047D.WMF FOGC050D.WMF FOOD16.WMF FOOD20M.WMF FOOD72.WMF FORW004J.WMF FORW006J.WMF FORW035J.WMF FOSI001D.WMF
FOSI037D.WMF FOSI037J.WMF FOSI039D.WMF FOSI042D.WMF FOSI057D.WMF FOSI068D.WMF HHBO006J.WMF HHBO061J.WMF HHBO062J.WMF HHCA095J.WMF
HHCA098J.WMF HHCA102J.WMF HHCA121J.WMF HHCA133J.WMF HHCA135J.WMF HHCA169J.WMF HHCA170J.WMF HHGC011D.WMF HHGC032J.WMF HHGC088D.WMF
HHRW038J.WMF HHRW047J.WMF HHSI003J.WMF HHSI003K.WMF HHSI013M.WMF HHSI030J.WMF HHSI032J.WMF HHSI033J.WMF HHSI035J.WMF HHSI040J.WMF
HHSI051M.WMF HHSI110D.WMF INGC013D.WMF INGC018D.WMF PD050VCU.WMF PEPPER.WMF POC099BB.WMF SPSI584D.WMF SYMBL69.WMF TIN_CAN.WMF

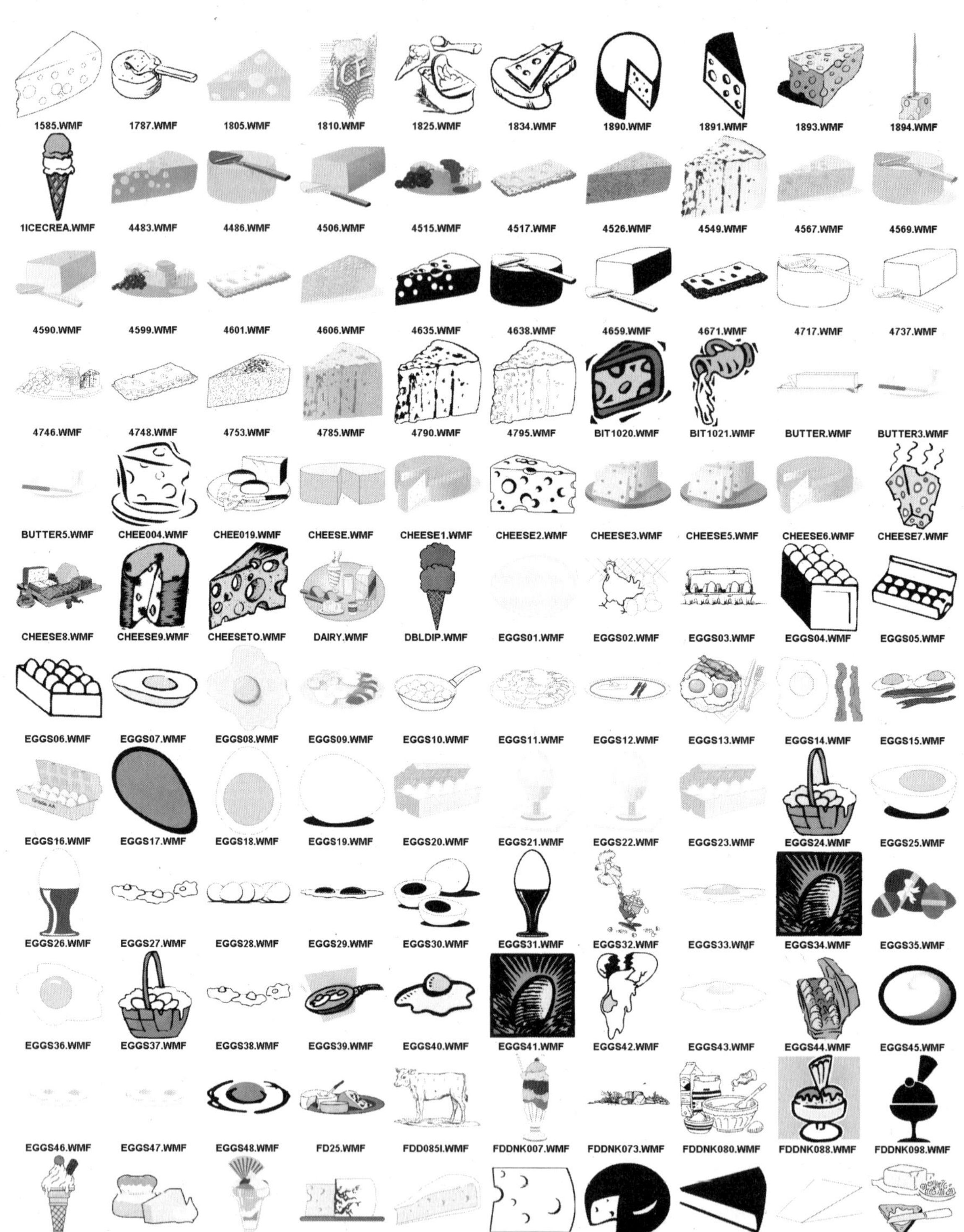
1585.WMF 1787.WMF 1805.WMF 1810.WMF 1825.WMF 1834.WMF 1890.WMF 1891.WMF 1893.WMF 1894.WMF
ICE
1ICECREA.WMF 4483.WMF 4486.WMF 4506.WMF 4515.WMF 4517.WMF 4526.WMF 4549.WMF 4567.WMF 4569.WMF
4590.WMF 4599.WMF 4601.WMF 4606.WMF 4635.WMF 4638.WMF 4659.WMF 4671.WMF 4717.WMF 4737.WMF
4746.WMF 4748.WMF 4753.WMF 4785.WMF 4790.WMF 4795.WMF BIT1020.WMF BIT1021.WMF BUTTER.WMF BUTTER3.WMF
BUTTER5.WMF CHEE004.WMF CHEE019.WMF CHEESE.WMF CHEESE1.WMF CHEESE2.WMF CHEESE3.WMF CHEESE5.WMF CHEESE6.WMF CHEESE7.WMF
CHEESE8.WMF CHEESE9.WMF CHEESETO.WMF DAIRY.WMF DBLDIP.WMF EGGS01.WMF EGGS02.WMF EGGS03.WMF EGGS04.WMF EGGS05.WMF
EGGS06.WMF EGGS07.WMF EGGS08.WMF EGGS09.WMF EGGS10.WMF EGGS11.WMF EGGS12.WMF EGGS13.WMF EGGS14.WMF EGGS15.WMF
Grade AA
EGGS16.WMF EGGS17.WMF EGGS18.WMF EGGS19.WMF EGGS20.WMF EGGS21.WMF EGGS22.WMF EGGS23.WMF EGGS24.WMF EGGS25.WMF
EGGS26.WMF EGGS27.WMF EGGS28.WMF EGGS29.WMF EGGS30.WMF EGGS31.WMF EGGS32.WMF EGGS33.WMF EGGS34.WMF EGGS35.WMF
EGGS36.WMF EGGS37.WMF EGGS38.WMF EGGS39.WMF EGGS40.WMF EGGS41.WMF EGGS42.WMF EGGS43.WMF EGGS44.WMF EGGS45.WMF
EGGS46.WMF EGGS47.WMF EGGS48.WMF FD25.WMF FDD085I.WMF FDDNK007.WMF FDDNK073.WMF FDDNK080.WMF FDDNK088.WMF FDDNK098.WMF
FDDNK127.WMF FDDNK154.WMF FDDNK186.WMF FDDNK215.WMF FDDNK216.WMF FDDNK217.WMF FDDNK218.WMF FDDNK219.WMF FDDNK220.WMF FDDNK252.WMF

FDDNK262.WMF FOGC007D.WMF FOOD15.WMF FORW002D.WMF FORW047J.WMF FRA019E.WMF FSW021B.WMF FSW021E.WMF HHCA097J.WMF ICCO058.WMF

ICCO059.WMF ICCO060.WMF ICECREA3.WMF ICECREA8.WMF ICECREAM.WMF ICECRM.WMF ICECRM4.WMF ICECRM5.WMF M21241.WMF MARGARIN.WMF

MILK.WMF MILK070.WMF MILK071.WMF MILK3.WMF MILK77.WMF MILK8.WMF MILKCART.WMF PB15.WMF SIT083A.WMF SPA022E.WMF

SWISCHES.WMF SWISS.WMF

0101.WMF
1097BUBC.WMF
1796.WMF
1809.WMF
1811.WMF
1837.WMF
1841.WMF
1876.WMF
1897.WMF
2248.WMF
4627.WMF
4677.WMF
4682.WMF
4758.WMF
APPLCAKE.WMF
BAN_SPLT.WMF
BANANSPL.WMF
BANASPL.WMF
BIT0148.WMF
BIT0457.WMF
BIT0839.WMF
BIT0848.WMF
BIT1013.WMF
BIT1022.WMF
BIT1033.WMF
BIT1035.WMF
C20745.WMF
C20782.WMF
CAKE.WMF
CAKE1.WMF
CAKE2.WMF
CAKE4ST.WMF
CAKE4WD.WMF
CAKE5.WMF
CAKE51.WMF
CAKE6CH.WMF
CAKE7BI.WMF
CAKE8COF.WMF
CAKE9.WMF
CAKE94.WMF
CAND002.WMF
CANDY.WMF
CANDY1.WMF
CANDY3.WMF
CANDY55.WMF
CANDY98.WMF
CANDYBAR.WMF
CANDYBX.WMF
CCOOKIES.WMF
CDYCANE.WMF
CHERRIES.WMF
CHESCAKE.WMF
CHOC_SUN.WMF
CHOCCAK2.WMF
CHOCCAKE.WMF
CHZCAKET.WMF
CINNROLL.WMF
CKNMLK.WMF
COOKIEM.WMF
COOKIES.WMF
COOKIES1.WMF
COOKIES2.WMF
COOKIES3.WMF
COOKIES_.WMF
COOKIEW.WMF
CPUDDING.WMF
CRT00010.WMF
CUPCAKE.WMF
CUPCAKE7.WMF
DESERT.WMF
DESSERT1.WMF
DESSERT2.WMF
DESSERT3.WMF
DESSERT4.WMF
DESSERT5.WMF
DESSERT6.WMF
DONUTS.WMF
DOUGHNUT.WMF
DSRT_TRY.WMF
FCP008G.WMF
FD40.WMF
FDDNK071.WMF
FDDNK097.WMF
FDDNK147.WMF
FDDNK250.WMF
FDDNK255.WMF
FDDNK256.WMF
FLOATTO.WMF
FOBO001J.WMF
FOBO002J.WMF
FOBO008J.WMF
FOBO011J.WMF
FOBO043J.WMF
FOBO044J.WMF
FOBO045J.WMF
FOBO046J.WMF
FOBO051J.WMF
FOBO052J.WMF
FOBO053J.WMF
FOCA003J.WMF
FOCA004J.WMF
FOCA031J.WMF
FOCA106J.WMF
FOCA112J.WMF
FOCA113J.WMF
FOGC027D.WMF
FOGC052D.WMF
FOGC066D.WMF
FOGC067D.WMF
FOKC004J.WMF
FOKC005J.WMF
FOKC010J.WMF
FOKC011J.WMF
FOOD08M.WMF
FOOD09M.WMF
FOOD17.WMF
FOOD19.WMF
FOOD67.WMF
FOOD69.WMF
FORTUNE.WMF

FORW008J.WMF FORW015J.WMF FOSI015D.WMF FOSI017D.WMF FOSI031D.WMF FOSI036D.WMF FOSI039J.WMF FOSI040J.WMF FOSI046D.WMF FOSI048D.WMF
FOSI050D.WMF FOSI058D.WMF FRA010D.WMF FRA011B.WMF FRA011E.WMF FRA030C.WMF FSW016E.WMF FSW019A.WMF FSW028E.WMF FSW032D.WMF
FWN016B.WMF FWN016C.WMF FWN016D.WMF FWN016E.WMF FWN016F.WMF FWN016G.WMF FWN016H.WMF FWN016I.WMF FWN016J.WMF FWN016K.WMF
FWN016L.WMF FWN016M.WMF FWN016N.WMF FWN016O.WMF G21044.WMF GBMAN.WMF GBMANC.WMF GINGERBO.WMF GINGERG.WMF GMBLMCHN.WMF
HC01.WMF I21135.WMF ICBA012.WMF ICCO013.WMF ICCRM_CN.WMF ICCRM_SC.WMF ICE_CREA.WMF ICEC014.WMF ICEC015.WMF ICECONE.WMF
ICECR1.WMF ICECR2.WMF ICECR3.WMF ICECR4.WMF ICECR5.WMF ICECRE_1.WMF ICECREAM.WMF ICECREM1.WMF ICECREM2.WMF ICECRM1.WMF
ICECRM51.WMF ICECRMCN.WMF IHD017B.WMF LBCAKE2.WMF LOLL017.WMF LOLLYPOP.WMF MALTED.WMF MISC113.WMF MRI004A.WMF MRI004B.WMF
MRI005B.WMF MRI009C.WMF PAST020.WMF PD117NCU.WMF PIE.WMF PIE01.WMF PIE02.WMF PIE022.WMF PIE1.WMF PIE2.WMF
PIE3.WMF PIE3PEC.WMF PIE4.WMF PIE_PLAT.WMF PIES.WMF PMPKPIE2.WMF POPCLE.WMF POPSICLE.WMF POUNDCAK.WMF QUICHE.WMF
SBERRYSH.WMF SPA011B.WMF STRAWICE.WMF SUNDAE.WMF SUNDAECR.WMF SUPRICEE.WMF SWEET.WMF SYMBOL48.WMF TAFFY_CA.WMF

0825.WMF
0826.WMF
0827.WMF
1092BOWC.WMF
1824.WMF
1829.WMF
1833.WMF
1835.WMF
1865.WMF
1867.WMF
1869.WMF
1873.WMF
1880.WMF
1882.WMF
1886.WMF
1895.WMF
4112.WMF
4252.WMF
4472.WMF
4595.WMF
4654.WMF
4747.WMF
ADS026E.WMF
BIT0412.WMF
BIT0414.WMF
BIT0415.WMF
BIT110.WMF
BIT111.WMF
BIT112.WMF
BROTH.WMF
CHILI.WMF
CONDOMTS.WMF
COUPLED1.WMF
CTMISC62.WMF
DEC060BB.WMF
DEC060T.WMF
DEC060X.WMF
DEC060Y.WMF
DEC061P.WMF
DESRTSPN.WMF
DINEOUT.WMF
EAT46.WMF
EAT47.WMF
ELEGANTD.WMF
FD38.WMF
FD39.WMF
FD40.WMF
FD42.WMF
FD43.WMF
FDD011G.WMF
FDD011K.WMF
FDD011O.WMF
FDD011T.WMF
FDD012E.WMF
FDD119R.WMF
FDDNK017.WMF
FDDNK065.WMF
FDDNK074.WMF
FDDNK075.WMF
FDDNK077.WMF
FDDNK078.WMF
FDDNK079.WMF
FDDNK093.WMF
FDDNK099.WMF
FDDNK100.WMF
FDDNK101.WMF
FDDNK102.WMF
FDDNK107.WMF
FDDNK116.WMF
FDDNK137.WMF
FDDNK142.WMF
FDDNK151.WMF
FDDNK180.WMF
FDDNK193.WMF
FDDNK194.WMF
FDDNK196.WMF
FDDNK197.WMF
FDDNK198.WMF
FDDNK199.WMF
FDDNK209.WMF
FDDNK236.WMF
FDDNK237.WMF
FDDNK244.WMF
FDDNK246.WMF
FDDNK249.WMF
FDDNK251.WMF
FDDNK265.WMF
FINEDINE.WMF
FLUTGLAS.WMF
FOBO091J.WMF
FOGC030D.WMF
FOGC036J.WMF
FOGC051D.WMF
FOGC065D.WMF
FOKC013J.WMF
FOOD06M.WMF
FORK.WMF
FORK1.WMF
FORW017J.WMF
FOSI018D.WMF
FULLDISH.WMF
GOBLET.WMF
HANDTRAY.WMF
HFD004B.WMF
HFD007A.WMF
HHGC010D.WMF
HHRW009D.WMF
HHSI046M.WMF
HONEY.WMF
HONEY5.WMF
ICONA01.WMF
JUICGLAS.WMF
KETCHUP.WMF
KNIFE.WMF
KNIFE1.WMF
KNIVES.WMF
KOTATSU.WMF
LAC070D.WMF
LAC072C.WMF
LAC072I.WMF

LAC074D.WMF	LAC074E.WMF	LAC078F.WMF	LAC093E.WMF	LUNCH.WMF	MAYONASE.WMF	MOD022J.WMF	MRI024C.WMF	MRI027C.WMF	MUSTARD.WMF
NAPKIN1.WMF	OED020C.WMF	OED023K.WMF	OED023N.WMF	OED028C.WMF	OFS066F.WMF	OFS067B.WMF	PAN1.WMF	PD043XCU.WMF	PD046XCU.WMF
PD047DCU.WMF	PD066C_1.WMF	PD066C_2.WMF	PD066C_3.WMF	PD066CU.WMF	PD067ACU.WMF	PD067BCU.WMF	PD067CCU.WMF	PD067DCU.WMF	PD067ECU.WMF
PD067FCU.WMF	PD067GCU.WMF	PD067HCU.WMF	PD067ICU.WMF	PD067JCU.WMF	PD067KCU.WMF	PD067LCU.WMF	PD067MCU.WMF	PD067NCU.WMF	PD067OCU.WMF
PD067PCU.WMF	PD067QCU.WMF	PD067RCU.WMF	PD067SCU.WMF	PD067TCU.WMF	PD075KCU.WMF	PD076HCU.WMF	PD078WCU.WMF	PD080BCU.WMF	PD081MCU.WMF
PD082QCU.WMF	PD083RCU.WMF	PD085ACU.WMF	PD086ACU.WMF	PD090CCU.WMF	PD090QCU.WMF	PD092KCU.WMF	PD094LCU.WMF	PD109QCU.WMF	PD116SCU.WMF
PD118HCU.WMF	PD118ICU.WMF	PD119FCU.WMF	PD121ICU.WMF	PD123RCU.WMF	PD123SCU.WMF	PD125LCU.WMF	PD129JCU.WMF	PGX026E.WMF	PITCHER.WMF
PLACESET.WMF	PLACET2.WMF	PLATE.WMF	PLATE1.WMF	PLATE2.WMF	PLRW005J.WMF	RLGN083.WMF	ROMDINER.WMF	SALDFORK.WMF	SALT.WMF
SALT028.WMF	SALTPEP.WMF	SERVE.WMF	SHAKER.WMF	SHUUGEN.WMF	SILVER1.WMF	SILVER2.WMF	SIT018B.WMF	SLTNPEP.WMF	SOUP.WMF
SOUP_123.WMF	SOUP_CRT.WMF	SOUPSPON.WMF	SPOON.WMF	SPOON1.WMF	SSP016D.WMF	STEAMDSH.WMF	SUGAR.WMF	SUGAR5.WMF	TABLE1.WMF
TABLE2.WMF	TABLSET1.WMF	TABLSET2.WMF	TEAPOT.WMF	TEAPTCUP.WMF	TEX12.WMF	TOKKURI.WMF	UTENSILS.WMF	WDI011B.WMF	WDI021A.WMF

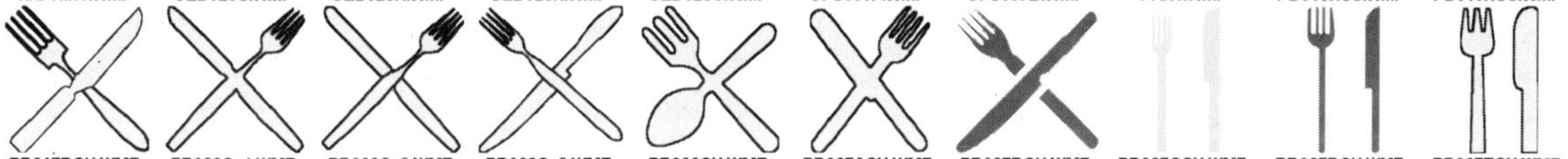

WDI026B.WMF

0132CUPC.WMF 1782.WMF 1783.WMF 1785.WMF 1786.WMF 1812.WMF 1813.WMF 1830.WMF 1831.WMF 1832.WMF

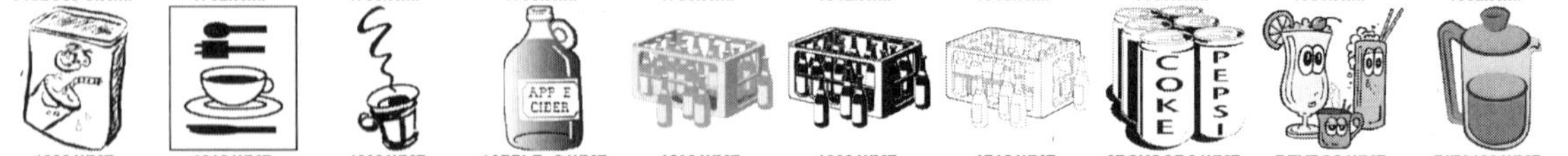

1833.WMF 1843.WMF 1868.WMF 1APPLE_C.WMF 4598.WMF 4668.WMF 4745.WMF 6PCKSODA.WMF BEVRGS.WMF BIT0123.WMF

BIT0124.WMF BIT0125.WMF BIT0434.WMF BIT0435.WMF BIT0436.WMF BIT1019.WMF BSNSS112.WMF C20815.WMF CAA0344.WMF CAN.WMF

CAN1MD.WMF CANCRSH.WMF CANS.WMF COFEECP.WMF COFF005.WMF COFF022.WMF COFF023.WMF COFFCUP.WMF COFFE.WMF COFFEE.WMF

COFFEE1.WMF COFFEE2.WMF COFFEE3.WMF COFFETO.WMF COFNDNT.WMF COKECLSC.WMF CUP.WMF CUP_A.WMF CUP_C.WMF CUP_SAUC.WMF

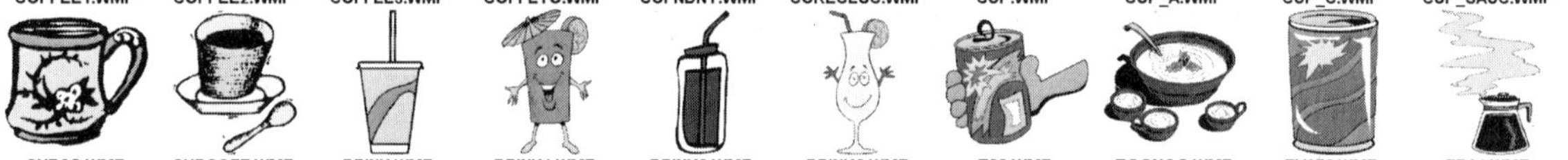

CUPAS.WMF CUPCOFF.WMF DRINK.WMF DRINK1.WMF DRINK2.WMF DRINK5.WMF E28.WMF EGGNOG.WMF EV078.WMF FD01.WMF

FD05.WMF FD06.WMF FD07.WMF FD08.WMF FD09.WMF FD10.WMF FD11.WMF FD35.WMF FDDNK001.WMF FDDNK002.WMF

FDDNK087.WMF FDDNK091.WMF FDDNK121.WMF FDDNK132.WMF FDDNK167.WMF FDDNK171.WMF FDDNK223.WMF FDDNK224.WMF FDDNK240.WMF FOCA002D.WMF

FOCA008J.WMF FOCA040J.WMF FOCA043J.WMF FOCA098J.WMF FOCA110J.WMF FOCA111J.WMF FOGC015D.WMF FOGC025J.WMF FOGC026J.WMF FOGC036D.WMF

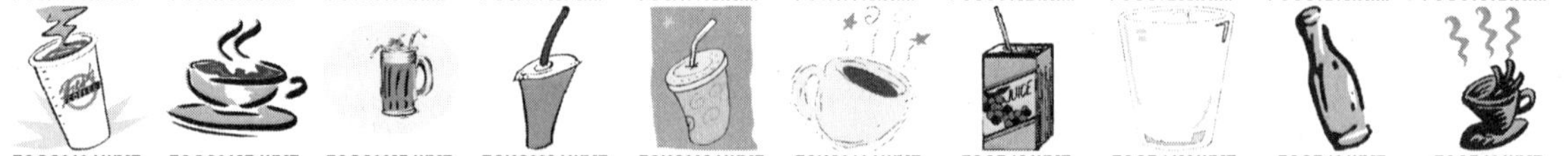

FOGC040J.WMF FOGC042D.WMF FOGC068D.WMF FOKC003J.WMF FOKC008J.WMF FOKC014J.WMF FOOD13.WMF FOOD14M.WMF FOOD19.WMF FOOD40.WMF

FOOD41.WMF FOOD61.WMF FOOD62.WMF FORW004D.WMF FORW011D.WMF FORW024J.WMF FORW025J.WMF FORW028J.WMF FORW042J.WMF FOSI030J.WMF

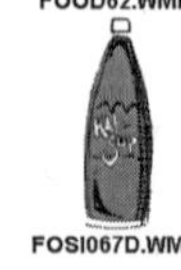

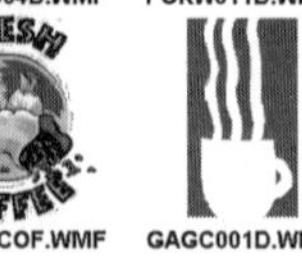

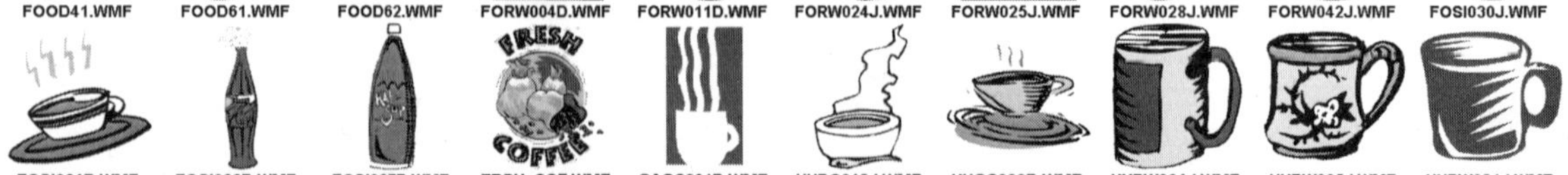

FOSI064D.WMF FOSI066D.WMF FOSI067D.WMF FRSH_COF.WMF GAGC001D.WMF HHBO042J.WMF HHGC090D.WMF HHRW004J.WMF HHRW005J.WMF HHRW031J.WMF

HHRW032J.WMF
HHRW033J.WMF
HHRW034J.WMF
HHSI004D.WMF
HHSI012D.WMF
HHSI085D.WMF
HOTCOCOA.WMF
ICDDRINK.WMF
ICE
ICE.WMF
ICECRM.WMF
ICED_TEA.WMF
ICEDTEA.WMF
ICEDTEA4.WMF
KOFFEE.WMF
LEMONADE.WMF
MART018.WMF
MINERAL
WATER
MIN_WATR.WMF
MRI024A.WMF
PD046KCU.WMF
PD046WCU.WMF
PD068YCU.WMF
PD094NCU.WMF
PD098RCU.WMF
PITC023.WMF
POP.WMF
POP_BTTL.WMF
SAKETO.WMF
SODAPO.WMF
SODAPOP.WMF
SODATO.WMF
TEA.WMF
TEA121.WMF
TEA_SERV.WMF
TEACPTO.WMF
TEAP033.WMF
WATER.WMF
WTRBTLAS.WMF

0117.WMF
0190.WMF
1152HAMC.WMF
1153HAMC.WMF
1793.WMF
1794.WMF
1795.WMF
1823.WMF
1826.WMF
1855.WMF
1900.WMF
1SUBMARI.WMF
2SUBMARI.WMF
BGRNFRY.WMF
BIT1012.WMF
BIT1014.WMF
BIT1023.WMF
BIT1027.WMF
BIT1030.WMF
BIT1034.WMF
BIT1110.WMF
BIT1192.WMF
BOWLSOUP.WMF
BUGERC.WMF
BURGER.WMF
BURGER2.WMF
BURGER28.WMF
BURGER88.WMF
BURGER9.WMF
BURGR.WMF
BURR012.WMF
BURRITOS.WMF
CANAPE.WMF
CATSUP.WMF
CHEF.WMF
COF_CRST.WMF
DAGWOOD.WMF
EDCN085.WMF
FASTFOO8.WMF
FASTFOOD.WMF
FD02.WMF
FD17.WMF
FD28.WMF
FD35.WMF
FD36.WMF
FD37.WMF
FD44.WMF
FDDNK011.WMF
FDDNK012.WMF
FDDNK013.WMF
FDDNK060.WMF
FDDNK083.WMF
FDDNK096.WMF
FDDNK109.WMF
FDDNK125.WMF
FDDNK150.WMF
FDDNK170.WMF
FDDNK258.WMF
FDDNK263.WMF
FDDNK264.WMF
FOBO001K.WMF
FOBO009J.WMF
PopCorn
FOBO014J.WMF
FOBO015J.WMF
FOBO090J.WMF
FOBO59J.WMF
FOBO60J.WMF
FOBO61J.WMF
FOCA015J.WMF
FOCA109J.WMF
FOGC019D.WMF
FOGC023D.WMF
FOGC054D.WMF
FOGC055D.WMF
FOGC056D.WMF
FOKC001J.WMF
FOOD.WMF
FOOD12.WMF
FOOD44.WMF
FOOD53.WMF
FOOD54.WMF
FOOD55.WMF
FOOD56.WMF
FOODC.WMF
FORW002J.WMF
FORW005J.WMF
FORW034J.WMF
FOSI008J.WMF
FOSI021D.WMF
FOSI036J.WMF
FOSI042J.WMF
FOSI043J.WMF
FOSI044D.WMF
FRIES.WMF
FRIES08.WMF
French Fries
FRIES8.WMF
FRNCHFRY.WMF
HALFSNDW.WMF
HAMB052.WMF
HAMB053.WMF
HAMB054.WMF
HAMBURG.WMF
HAMBURG4.WMF
HAMBURGE.WMF
HAMBURGR.WMF
HMBRGR.WMF
HOT_DOGS.WMF
HOTD011.WMF
HOTD055.WMF
HOTD056.WMF
HOTD057.WMF
HOTDOG.WMF
HOTDOG1.WMF
HOTDOG2.WMF
HOTDOG3.WMF
HOTDOG38.WMF
HOTDOG4.WMF
HOTDOG48.WMF
HOTDOG6.MF
HOTDOG9.WMF

HOTDOGC.WMF
HOTDOGO.WMF
ITALX1.WMF
ITALX19.WMF
KETCHUP.WMF
NACH019.WMF
NACH075.WMF
NACHOS.WMF
NACHOS9.WMF
NOODLTO.WMF
ONIONRIN.WMF
PD126QCU.WMF
PIZZ024.WMF
PIZZ098.WMF
PIZZ099.WMF
PIZZ100.WMF
PIZZA.WMF
PIZZA1.WMF
PIZZA9.WMF
PIZZA99.WMF
PIZZA_SL.WMF
PIZZAPAN.WMF
PIZZASLI.WMF
POPBOTTL.WMF
POPC025.WMF
POPCORN.WMF
POPCORN9.WMF
POPKORN.WMF
POPPCORN.WMF
PRETZEL.WMF
REUBEN.WMF
ROLLSNDW.WMF
SALA106.WMF
SAND107.WMF
SAND108.WMF
SANDWICH.WMF
SANWICH.WMF
SANWICH4.WMF
SNDWCH.WMF
SUBS032.WMF
SUBSNDW.WMF
TACO.WMF
TACO120.WMF
TACO9.WMF
TACOS.WMF
TEX13.WMF
TEX18.WMF
TEX19.WMF

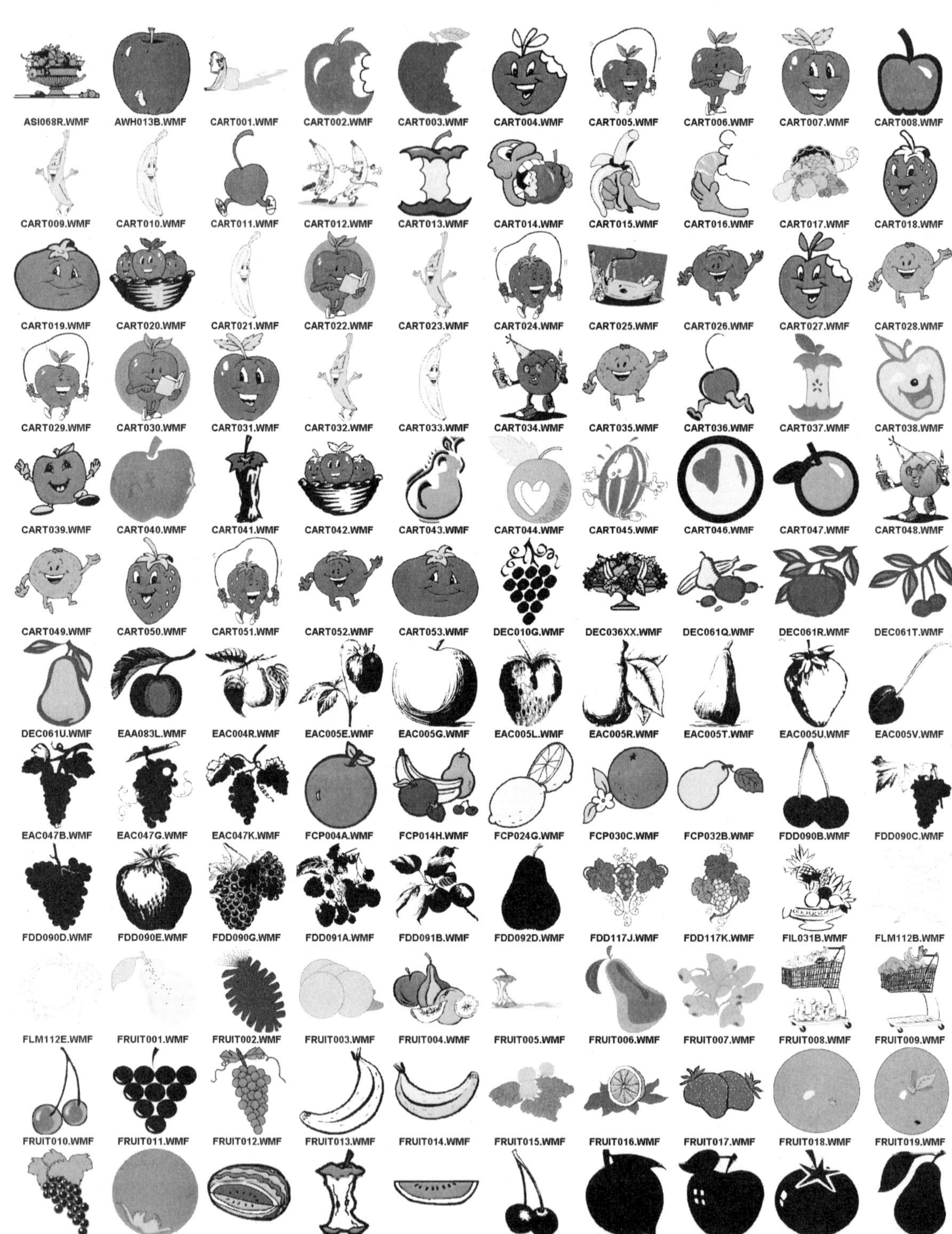
ASI068R.WMF
AWH013B.WMF
CART001.WMF
CART002.WMF
CART003.WMF
CART004.WMF
CART005.WMF
CART006.WMF
CART007.WMF
CART008.WMF
CART009.WMF
CART010.WMF
CART011.WMF
CART012.WMF
CART013.WMF
CART014.WMF
CART015.WMF
CART016.WMF
CART017.WMF
CART018.WMF
CART019.WMF
CART020.WMF
CART021.WMF
CART022.WMF
CART023.WMF
CART024.WMF
CART025.WMF
CART026.WMF
CART027.WMF
CART028.WMF
CART029.WMF
CART030.WMF
CART031.WMF
CART032.WMF
CART033.WMF
CART034.WMF
CART035.WMF
CART036.WMF
CART037.WMF
CART038.WMF
CART039.WMF
CART040.WMF
CART041.WMF
CART042.WMF
CART043.WMF
CART044.WMF
CART045.WMF
CART046.WMF
CART047.WMF
CART048.WMF
CART049.WMF
CART050.WMF
CART051.WMF
CART052.WMF
CART053.WMF
DEC010G.WMF
DEC036XX.WMF
DEC061Q.WMF
DEC061R.WMF
DEC061T.WMF
DEC061U.WMF
EAA083L.WMF
EAC004R.WMF
EAC005E.WMF
EAC005G.WMF
EAC005L.WMF
EAC005R.WMF
EAC005T.WMF
EAC005U.WMF
EAC005V.WMF
EAC047B.WMF
EAC047G.WMF
EAC047K.WMF
FCP004A.WMF
FCP014H.WMF
FCP024G.WMF
FCP030C.WMF
FCP032B.WMF
FDD090B.WMF
FDD090C.WMF
FDD090D.WMF
FDD090E.WMF
FDD090G.WMF
FDD091A.WMF
FDD091B.WMF
FDD092D.WMF
FDD117J.WMF
FDD117K.WMF
FIL031B.WMF
FLM112B.WMF
FLM112E.WMF
FRUIT001.WMF
FRUIT002.WMF
FRUIT003.WMF
FRUIT004.WMF
FRUIT005.WMF
FRUIT006.WMF
FRUIT007.WMF
FRUIT008.WMF
FRUIT009.WMF
FRUIT010.WMF
FRUIT011.WMF
FRUIT012.WMF
FRUIT013.WMF
FRUIT014.WMF
FRUIT015.WMF
FRUIT016.WMF
FRUIT017.WMF
FRUIT018.WMF
FRUIT019.WMF
FRUIT020.WMF
FRUIT021.WMF
FRUIT022.WMF
FRUIT023.WMF
FRUIT024.WMF
FRUIT025.WMF
FRUIT026.WMF
FRUIT027.WMF
FRUIT028.WMF
FRUIT029.WMF

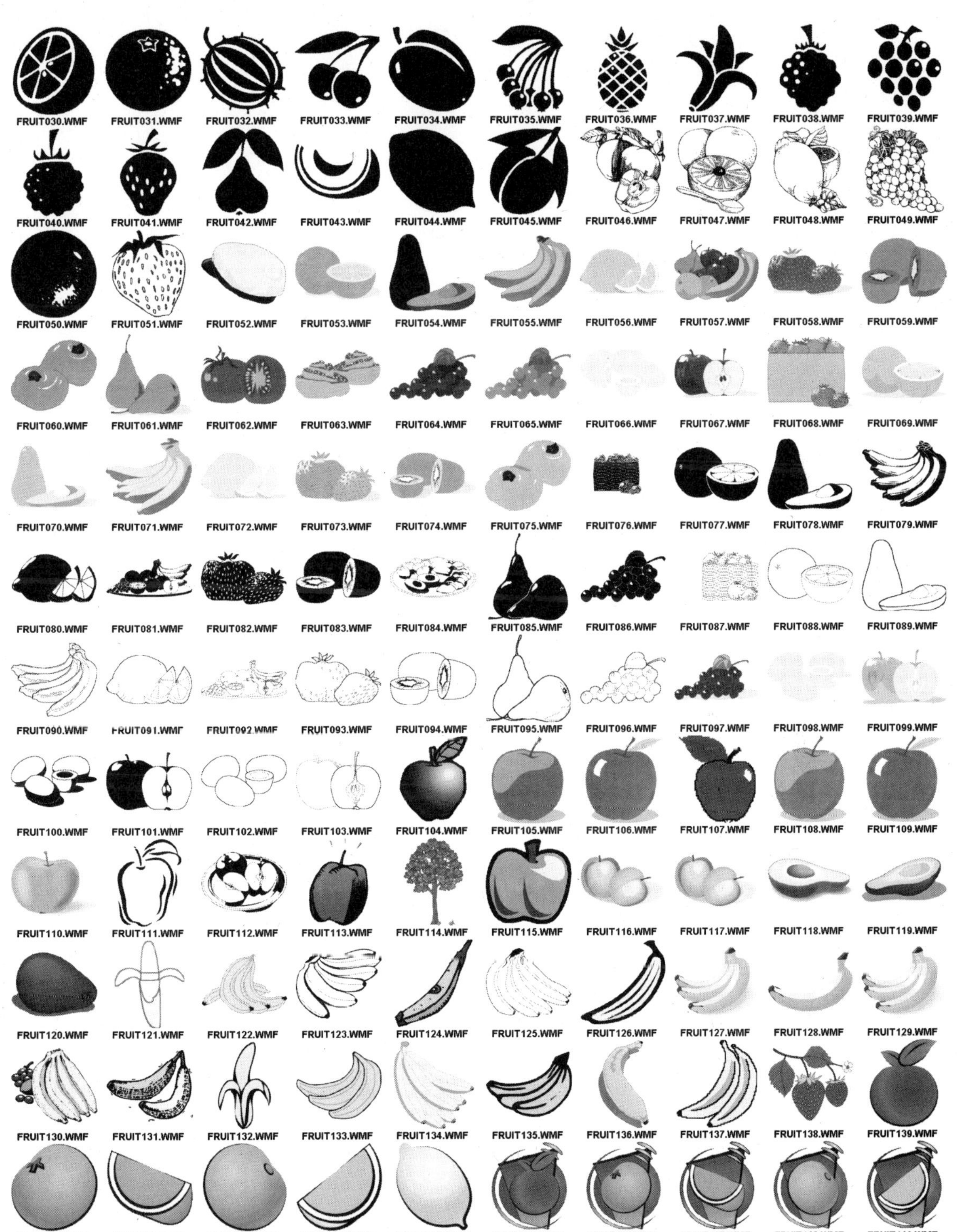
FRUIT030.WMF FRUIT031.WMF FRUIT032.WMF FRUIT033.WMF FRUIT034.WMF FRUIT035.WMF FRUIT036.WMF FRUIT037.WMF FRUIT038.WMF FRUIT039.WMF
FRUIT040.WMF FRUIT041.WMF FRUIT042.WMF FRUIT043.WMF FRUIT044.WMF FRUIT045.WMF FRUIT046.WMF FRUIT047.WMF FRUIT048.WMF FRUIT049.WMF
FRUIT050.WMF FRUIT051.WMF FRUIT052.WMF FRUIT053.WMF FRUIT054.WMF FRUIT055.WMF FRUIT056.WMF FRUIT057.WMF FRUIT058.WMF FRUIT059.WMF
FRUIT060.WMF FRUIT061.WMF FRUIT062.WMF FRUIT063.WMF FRUIT064.WMF FRUIT065.WMF FRUIT066.WMF FRUIT067.WMF FRUIT068.WMF FRUIT069.WMF
FRUIT070.WMF FRUIT071.WMF FRUIT072.WMF FRUIT073.WMF FRUIT074.WMF FRUIT075.WMF FRUIT076.WMF FRUIT077.WMF FRUIT078.WMF FRUIT079.WMF
FRUIT080.WMF FRUIT081.WMF FRUIT082.WMF FRUIT083.WMF FRUIT084.WMF FRUIT085.WMF FRUIT086.WMF FRUIT087.WMF FRUIT088.WMF FRUIT089.WMF
FRUIT090.WMF FRUIT091.WMF FRUIT092.WMF FRUIT093.WMF FRUIT094.WMF FRUIT095.WMF FRUIT096.WMF FRUIT097.WMF FRUIT098.WMF FRUIT099.WMF
FRUIT100.WMF FRUIT101.WMF FRUIT102.WMF FRUIT103.WMF FRUIT104.WMF FRUIT105.WMF FRUIT106.WMF FRUIT107.WMF FRUIT108.WMF FRUIT109.WMF
FRUIT110.WMF FRUIT111.WMF FRUIT112.WMF FRUIT113.WMF FRUIT114.WMF FRUIT115.WMF FRUIT116.WMF FRUIT117.WMF FRUIT118.WMF FRUIT119.WMF
FRUIT120.WMF FRUIT121.WMF FRUIT122.WMF FRUIT123.WMF FRUIT124.WMF FRUIT125.WMF FRUIT126.WMF FRUIT127.WMF FRUIT128.WMF FRUIT129.WMF
FRUIT130.WMF FRUIT131.WMF FRUIT132.WMF FRUIT133.WMF FRUIT134.WMF FRUIT135.WMF FRUIT136.WMF FRUIT137.WMF FRUIT138.WMF FRUIT139.WMF
FRUIT140.WMF FRUIT141.WMF FRUIT142.WMF FRUIT143.WMF FRUIT144.WMF FRUIT145.WMF FRUIT146.WMF FRUIT147.WMF FRUIT148.WMF FRUIT149.WMF

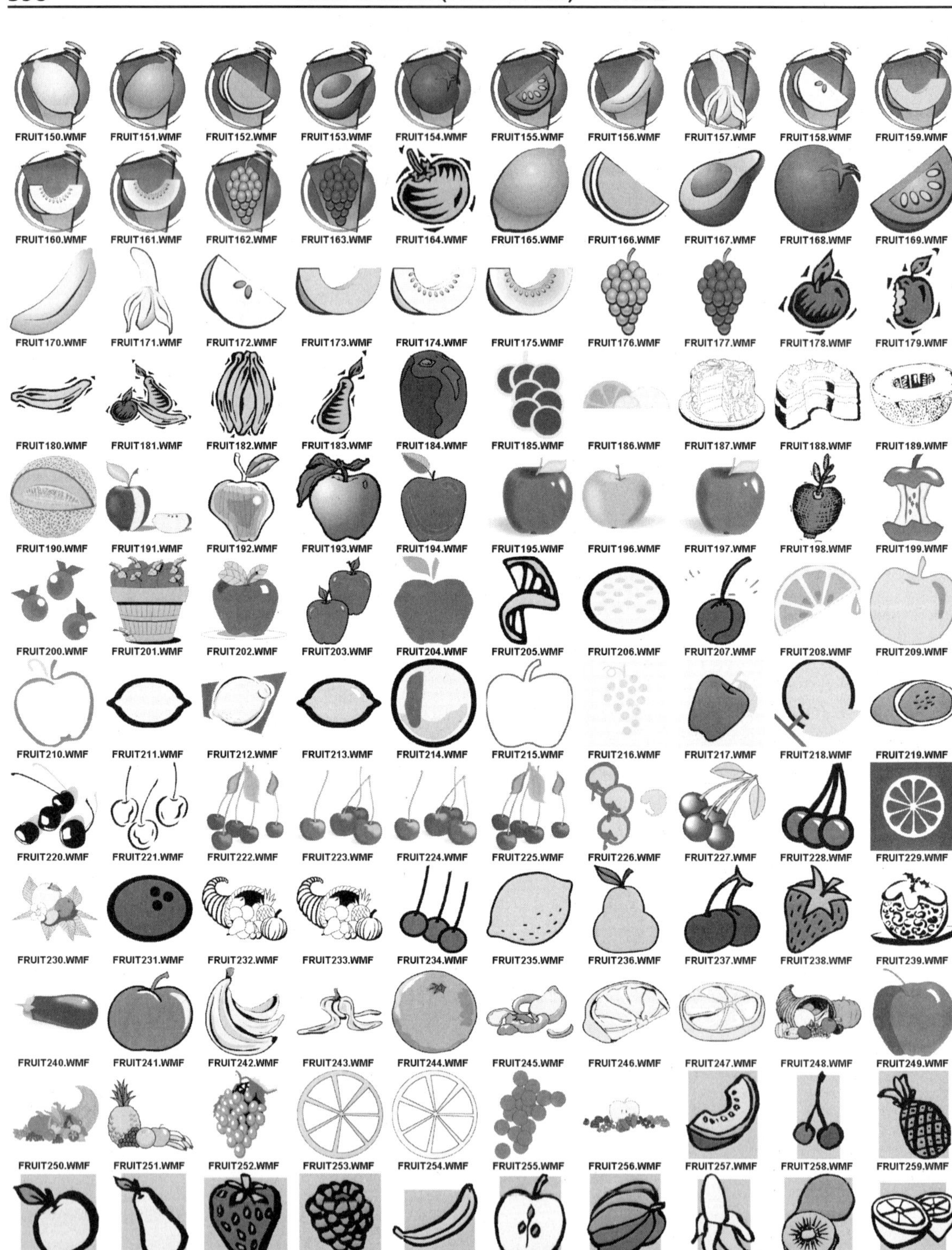
FRUIT150.WMF
FRUIT151.WMF
FRUIT152.WMF
FRUIT153.WMF
FRUIT154.WMF
FRUIT155.WMF
FRUIT156.WMF
FRUIT157.WMF
FRUIT158.WMF
FRUIT159.WMF
FRUIT160.WMF
FRUIT161.WMF
FRUIT162.WMF
FRUIT163.WMF
FRUIT164.WMF
FRUIT165.WMF
FRUIT166.WMF
FRUIT167.WMF
FRUIT168.WMF
FRUIT169.WMF
FRUIT170.WMF
FRUIT171.WMF
FRUIT172.WMF
FRUIT173.WMF
FRUIT174.WMF
FRUIT175.WMF
FRUIT176.WMF
FRUIT177.WMF
FRUIT178.WMF
FRUIT179.WMF
FRUIT180.WMF
FRUIT181.WMF
FRUIT182.WMF
FRUIT183.WMF
FRUIT184.WMF
FRUIT185.WMF
FRUIT186.WMF
FRUIT187.WMF
FRUIT188.WMF
FRUIT189.WMF
FRUIT190.WMF
FRUIT191.WMF
FRUIT192.WMF
FRUIT193.WMF
FRUIT194.WMF
FRUIT195.WMF
FRUIT196.WMF
FRUIT197.WMF
FRUIT198.WMF
FRUIT199.WMF
FRUIT200.WMF
FRUIT201.WMF
FRUIT202.WMF
FRUIT203.WMF
FRUIT204.WMF
FRUIT205.WMF
FRUIT206.WMF
FRUIT207.WMF
FRUIT208.WMF
FRUIT209.WMF
FRUIT210.WMF
FRUIT211.WMF
FRUIT212.WMF
FRUIT213.WMF
FRUIT214.WMF
FRUIT215.WMF
FRUIT216.WMF
FRUIT217.WMF
FRUIT218.WMF
FRUIT219.WMF
FRUIT220.WMF
FRUIT221.WMF
FRUIT222.WMF
FRUIT223.WMF
FRUIT224.WMF
FRUIT225.WMF
FRUIT226.WMF
FRUIT227.WMF
FRUIT228.WMF
FRUIT229.WMF
FRUIT230.WMF
FRUIT231.WMF
FRUIT232.WMF
FRUIT233.WMF
FRUIT234.WMF
FRUIT235.WMF
FRUIT236.WMF
FRUIT237.WMF
FRUIT238.WMF
FRUIT239.WMF
FRUIT240.WMF
FRUIT241.WMF
FRUIT242.WMF
FRUIT243.WMF
FRUIT244.WMF
FRUIT245.WMF
FRUIT246.WMF
FRUIT247.WMF
FRUIT248.WMF
FRUIT249.WMF
FRUIT250.WMF
FRUIT251.WMF
FRUIT252.WMF
FRUIT253.WMF
FRUIT254.WMF
FRUIT255.WMF
FRUIT256.WMF
FRUIT257.WMF
FRUIT258.WMF
FRUIT259.WMF
FRUIT260.WMF
FRUIT261.WMF
FRUIT262.WMF
FRUIT263.WMF
FRUIT264.WMF
FRUIT265.WMF
FRUIT266.WMF
FRUIT267.WMF
FRUIT268.WMF
FRUIT269.WMF

FRUIT270.WMF FRUIT271.WMF FRUIT272.WMF FRUIT273.WMF FRUIT274.WMF FRUIT275.WMF FRUIT276.WMF FRUIT277.WMF FRUIT278.WMF FRUIT279.WMF
FRUIT280.WMF FRUIT281.WMF FRUIT282.WMF FRUIT283.WMF FRUIT284.WMF FRUIT285.WMF FRUIT286.WMF FRUIT287.WMF FRUIT288.WMF FRUIT289.WMF
FRUIT290.WMF FRUIT291.WMF FRUIT292.WMF FRUIT293.WMF FRUIT294.WMF FRUIT295.WMF FRUIT296.WMF FRUIT297.WMF FRUIT298.WMF FRUIT299.WMF
FRUIT300.WMF FRUIT301.WMF FRUIT302.WMF FRUIT303.WMF FRUIT304.WMF FRUIT305.WMF FRUIT306.WMF FRUIT307.WMF FRUIT308.WMF FRUIT309.WMF
FRUIT310.WMF FRUIT311.WMF FRUIT312.WMF FRUIT313.WMF FRUIT314.WMF FRUIT315.WMF FRUIT316.WMF FRUIT317.WMF FRUIT318.WMF FRUIT319.WMF
FRUIT320.WMF FRUIT321.WMF FRUIT322.WMF FRUIT323.WMF FRUIT324.WMF FRUIT325.WMF FRUIT326.WMF FRUIT327.WMF FRUIT328.WMF FRUIT329.WMF
FRUIT330.WMF FRUIT331.WMF FRUIT332.WMF FRUIT333.WMF FRUIT334.WMF FRUIT335.WMF FRUIT336.WMF FRUIT337.WMF FRUIT338.WMF FRUIT339.WMF
FRUIT340.WMF FRUIT341.WMF FRUIT342.WMF FRUIT343.WMF FRUIT344.WMF FRUIT345.WMF FRUIT346.WMF FRUIT347.WMF FRUIT348.WMF FRUIT349.WMF
FRUIT350.WMF FRUIT351.WMF FRUIT352.WMF FRUIT353.WMF FRUIT354.WMF FRUIT355.WMF FRUIT356.WMF FRUIT357.WMF FRUIT358.WMF FRUIT359.WMF
FRUIT360.WMF FRUIT361.WMF FRUIT362.WMF FRUIT363.WMF FRUIT364.WMF FRUIT365.WMF FRUIT366.WMF FRUIT367.WMF FRUIT368.WMF FRUIT369.WMF
FRUIT370.WMF FRUIT371.WMF FRUIT372.WMF FRUIT373.WMF FRUIT374.WMF FRUIT375.WMF FRUIT376.WMF FRUIT377.WMF FRUIT378.WMF FRUIT379.WMF
FRUIT380.WMF FRUIT381.WMF FRUIT382.WMF FRUIT383.WMF FRUIT384.WMF FRUIT385.WMF FRUIT386.WMF FRUIT387.WMF FRUIT388.WMF FRUIT389.WMF

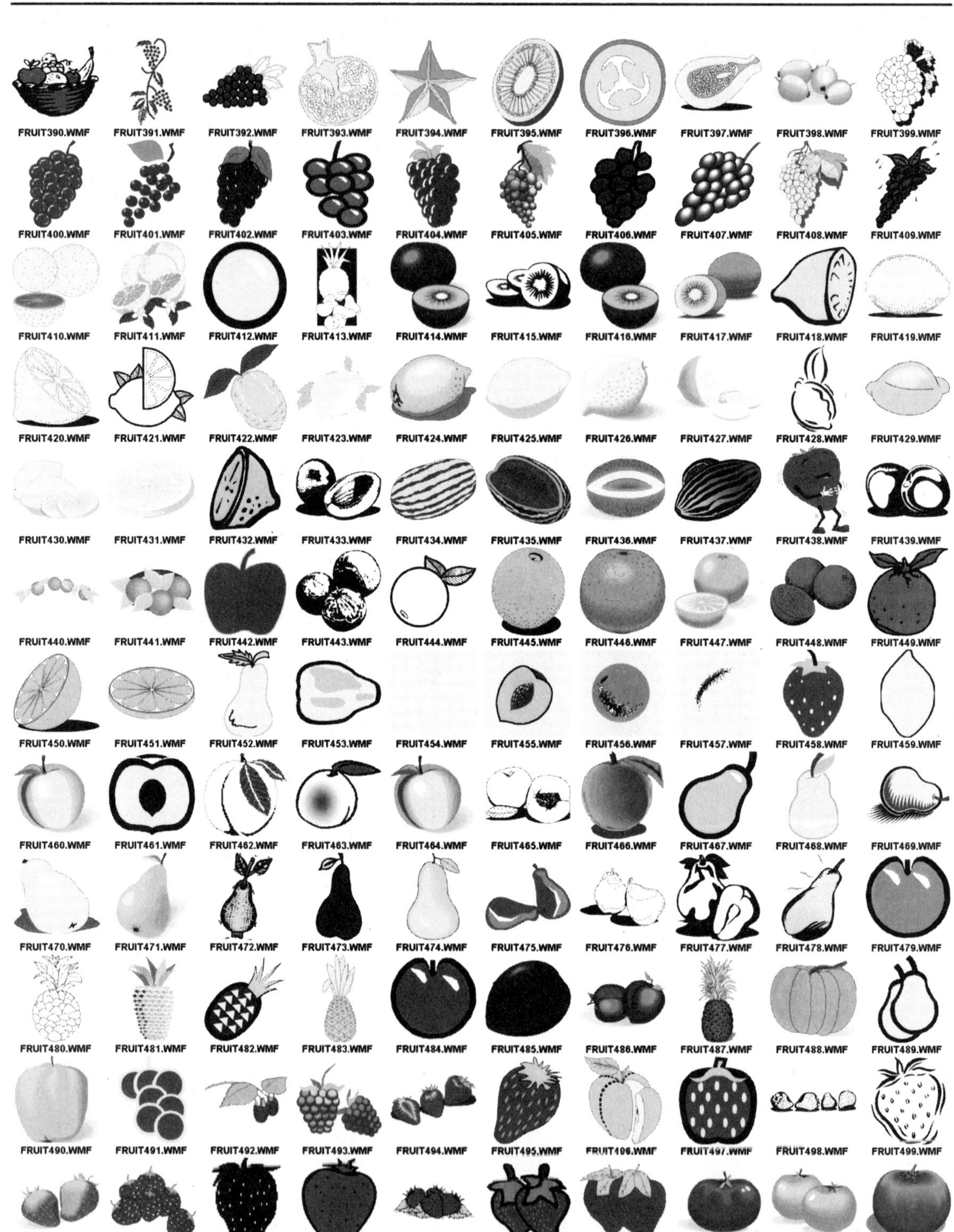
FRUIT390.WMF FRUIT391.WMF FRUIT392.WMF FRUIT393.WMF FRUIT394.WMF FRUIT395.WMF FRUIT396.WMF FRUIT397.WMF FRUIT398.WMF FRUIT399.WMF
FRUIT400.WMF FRUIT401.WMF FRUIT402.WMF FRUIT403.WMF FRUIT404.WMF FRUIT405.WMF FRUIT406.WMF FRUIT407.WMF FRUIT408.WMF FRUIT409.WMF
FRUIT410.WMF FRUIT411.WMF FRUIT412.WMF FRUIT413.WMF FRUIT414.WMF FRUIT415.WMF FRUIT416.WMF FRUIT417.WMF FRUIT418.WMF FRUIT419.WMF
FRUIT420.WMF FRUIT421.WMF FRUIT422.WMF FRUIT423.WMF FRUIT424.WMF FRUIT425.WMF FRUIT426.WMF FRUIT427.WMF FRUIT428.WMF FRUIT429.WMF
FRUIT430.WMF FRUIT431.WMF FRUIT432.WMF FRUIT433.WMF FRUIT434.WMF FRUIT435.WMF FRUIT436.WMF FRUIT437.WMF FRUIT438.WMF FRUIT439.WMF
FRUIT440.WMF FRUIT441.WMF FRUIT442.WMF FRUIT443.WMF FRUIT444.WMF FRUIT445.WMF FRUIT446.WMF FRUIT447.WMF FRUIT448.WMF FRUIT449.WMF
FRUIT450.WMF FRUIT451.WMF FRUIT452.WMF FRUIT453.WMF FRUIT454.WMF FRUIT455.WMF FRUIT456.WMF FRUIT457.WMF FRUIT458.WMF FRUIT459.WMF
FRUIT460.WMF FRUIT461.WMF FRUIT462.WMF FRUIT463.WMF FRUIT464.WMF FRUIT465.WMF FRUIT466.WMF FRUIT467.WMF FRUIT468.WMF FRUIT469.WMF
FRUIT470.WMF FRUIT471.WMF FRUIT472.WMF FRUIT473.WMF FRUIT474.WMF FRUIT475.WMF FRUIT476.WMF FRUIT477.WMF FRUIT478.WMF FRUIT479.WMF
FRUIT480.WMF FRUIT481.WMF FRUIT482.WMF FRUIT483.WMF FRUIT484.WMF FRUIT485.WMF FRUIT486.WMF FRUIT487.WMF FRUIT488.WMF FRUIT489.WMF
FRUIT490.WMF FRUIT491.WMF FRUIT492.WMF FRUIT493.WMF FRUIT494.WMF FRUIT495.WMF FRUIT496.WMF FRUIT497.WMF FRUIT498.WMF FRUIT499.WMF
FRUIT500.WMF FRUIT501.WMF FRUIT502.WMF FRUIT503.WMF FRUIT504.WMF FRUIT505.WMF FRUIT506.WMF FRUIT507.WMF FRUIT508.WMF FRUIT509.WMF

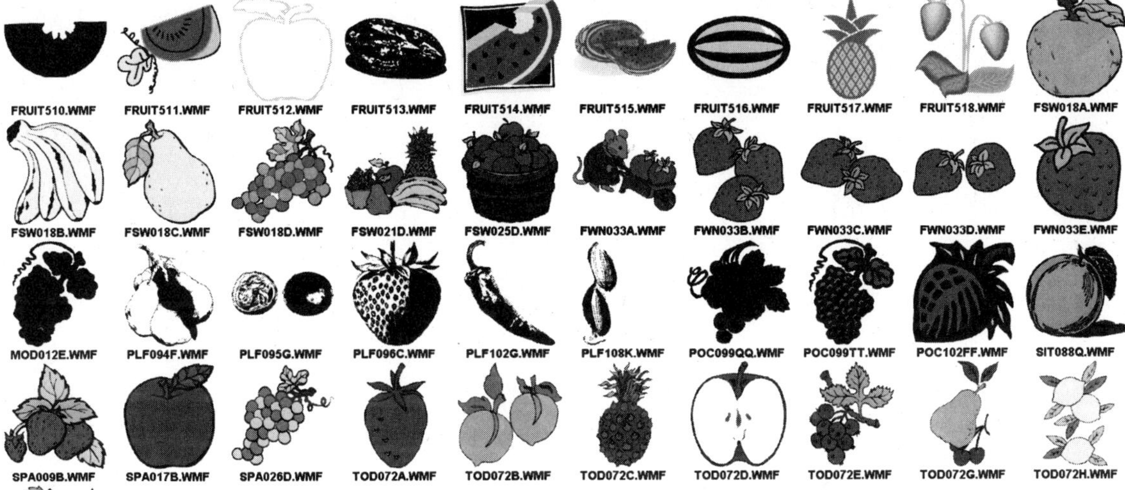
FRUIT510.WMF FRUIT511.WMF FRUIT512.WMF FRUIT513.WMF FRUIT514.WMF FRUIT515.WMF FRUIT516.WMF FRUIT517.WMF FRUIT518.WMF FSW018A.WMF
FSW018B.WMF FSW018C.WMF FSW018D.WMF FSW021D.WMF FSW025D.WMF FWN033A.WMF FWN033B.WMF FWN033C.WMF FWN033D.WMF FWN033E.WMF
MOD012E.WMF PLF094F.WMF PLF095G.WMF PLF096C.WMF PLF102G.WMF PLF108K.WMF POC099QQ.WMF POC099TT.WMF POC102FF.WMF SIT088Q.WMF
SPA009B.WMF SPA017B.WMF SPA026D.WMF TOD072A.WMF TOD072B.WMF TOD072C.WMF TOD072D.WMF TOD072E.WMF TOD072G.WMF TOD072H.WMF
TOD072P.WMF

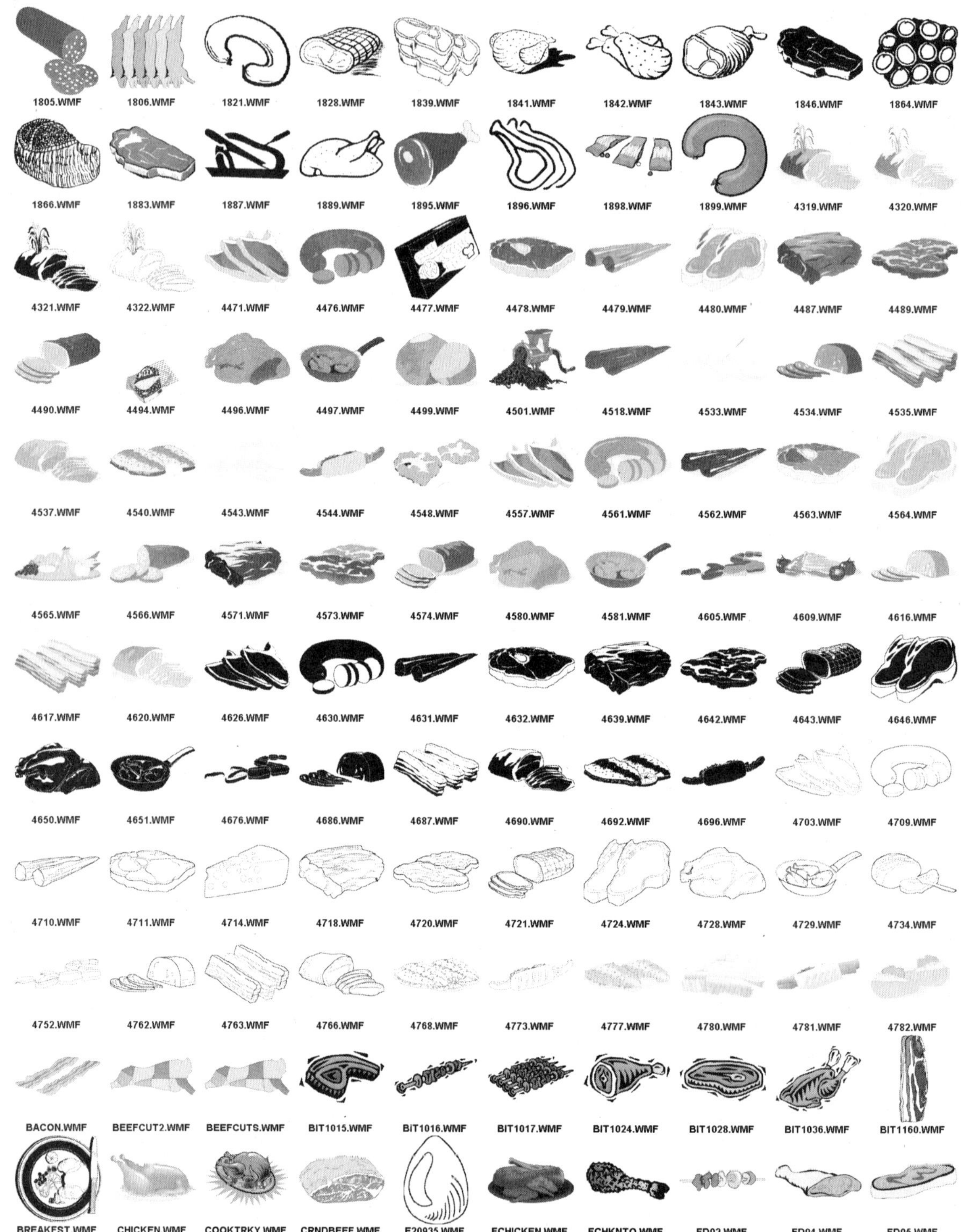
1805.WMF
1806.WMF
1821.WMF
1828.WMF
1839.WMF
1841.WMF
1842.WMF
1843.WMF
1846.WMF
1864.WMF
1866.WMF
1883.WMF
1887.WMF
1889.WMF
1895.WMF
1896.WMF
1898.WMF
1899.WMF
4319.WMF
4320.WMF
4321.WMF
4322.WMF
4471.WMF
4476.WMF
4477.WMF
4478.WMF
4479.WMF
4480.WMF
4487.WMF
4489.WMF
4490.WMF
4494.WMF
4496.WMF
4497.WMF
4499.WMF
4501.WMF
4518.WMF
4533.WMF
4534.WMF
4535.WMF
4537.WMF
4540.WMF
4543.WMF
4544.WMF
4548.WMF
4557.WMF
4561.WMF
4562.WMF
4563.WMF
4564.WMF
4565.WMF
4566.WMF
4571.WMF
4573.WMF
4574.WMF
4580.WMF
4581.WMF
4605.WMF
4609.WMF
4616.WMF
4617.WMF
4620.WMF
4626.WMF
4630.WMF
4631.WMF
4632.WMF
4639.WMF
4642.WMF
4643.WMF
4646.WMF
4650.WMF
4651.WMF
4676.WMF
4686.WMF
4687.WMF
4690.WMF
4692.WMF
4696.WMF
4703.WMF
4709.WMF
4710.WMF
4711.WMF
4714.WMF
4718.WMF
4720.WMF
4721.WMF
4724.WMF
4728.WMF
4729.WMF
4734.WMF
4752.WMF
4762.WMF
4763.WMF
4766.WMF
4768.WMF
4773.WMF
4777.WMF
4780.WMF
4781.WMF
4782.WMF
BACON.WMF
BEEFCUT2.WMF
BEEFCUTS.WMF
BIT1015.WMF
BIT1016.WMF
BIT1017.WMF
BIT1024.WMF
BIT1028.WMF
BIT1036.WMF
BIT1160.WMF
BREAKFST.WMF
CHICKEN.WMF
COOKTRKY.WMF
CRNDBEEF.WMF
E20935.WMF
FCHICKEN.WMF
FCHKNTO.WMF
FD03.WMF
FD04.WMF
FD05.WMF

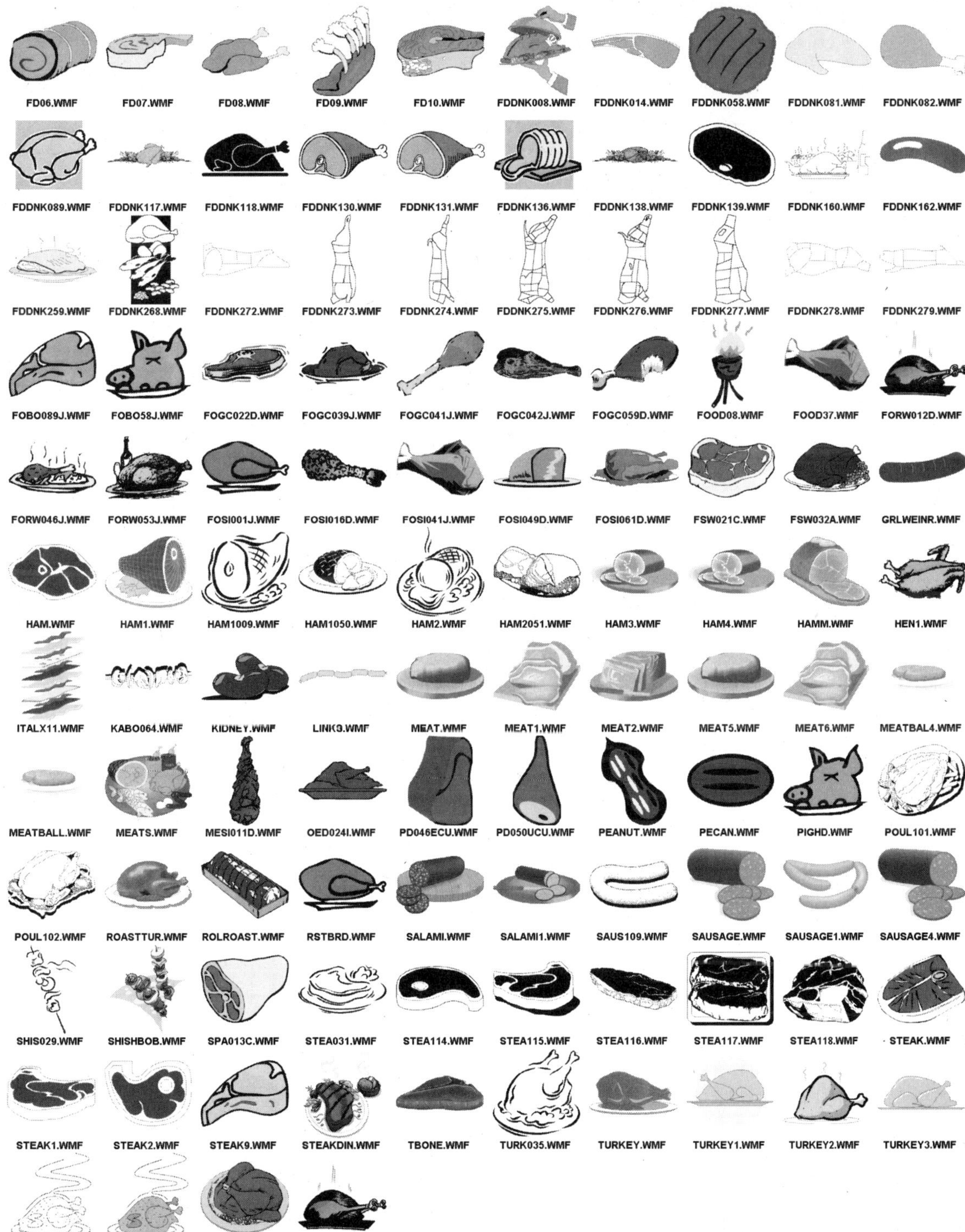
FD06.WMF
FD07.WMF
FD08.WMF
FD09.WMF
FD10.WMF
FDDNK008.WMF
FDDNK014.WMF
FDDNK058.WMF
FDDNK081.WMF
FDDNK082.WMF
FDDNK089.WMF
FDDNK117.WMF
FDDNK118.WMF
FDDNK130.WMF
FDDNK131.WMF
FDDNK136.WMF
FDDNK138.WMF
FDDNK139.WMF
FDDNK160.WMF
FDDNK162.WMF
FDDNK259.WMF
FDDNK268.WMF
FDDNK272.WMF
FDDNK273.WMF
FDDNK274.WMF
FDDNK275.WMF
FDDNK276.WMF
FDDNK277.WMF
FDDNK278.WMF
FDDNK279.WMF
FOBO089J.WMF
FOBO58J.WMF
FOGC022D.WMF
FOGC039J.WMF
FOGC041J.WMF
FOGC042J.WMF
FOGC059D.WMF
FOOD08.WMF
FOOD37.WMF
FORW012D.WMF
FORW046J.WMF
FORW053J.WMF
FOSI001J.WMF
FOSI016D.WMF
FOSI041J.WMF
FOSI049D.WMF
FOSI061D.WMF
FSW021C.WMF
FSW032A.WMF
GRLWEINR.WMF
HAM.WMF
HAM1.WMF
HAM1009.WMF
HAM1050.WMF
HAM2.WMF
HAM2051.WMF
HAM3.WMF
HAM4.WMF
HAMM.WMF
HEN1.WMF
ITALX11.WMF
KABO064.WMF
KIDNEY.WMF
LINK9.WMF
MEAT.WMF
MEAT1.WMF
MEAT2.WMF
MEAT5.WMF
MEAT6.WMF
MEATBAL4.WMF
MEATBALL.WMF
MEATS.WMF
MESI011D.WMF
OED024I.WMF
PD046ECU.WMF
PD050UCU.WMF
PEANUT.WMF
PECAN.WMF
PIGHD.WMF
POUL101.WMF
POUL102.WMF
ROASTTUR.WMF
ROLROAST.WMF
RSTBRD.WMF
SALAMI.WMF
SALAMI1.WMF
SAUS109.WMF
SAUSAGE.WMF
SAUSAGE1.WMF
SAUSAGE4.WMF
SHIS029.WMF
SHISHBOB.WMF
SPA013C.WMF
STEA031.WMF
STEA114.WMF
STEA115.WMF
STEA116.WMF
STEA117.WMF
STEA118.WMF
STEAK.WMF
STEAK1.WMF
STEAK2.WMF
STEAK9.WMF
STEAKDIN.WMF
TBONE.WMF
TURK035.WMF
TURKEY.WMF
TURKEY1.WMF
TURKEY2.WMF
TURKEY3.WMF
TURKEY4.WMF
TURKEYC.WMF
TURKEYPL.WMF
TURKYTO.WMF

Food & Drink (FOODDRNK) • Pasta

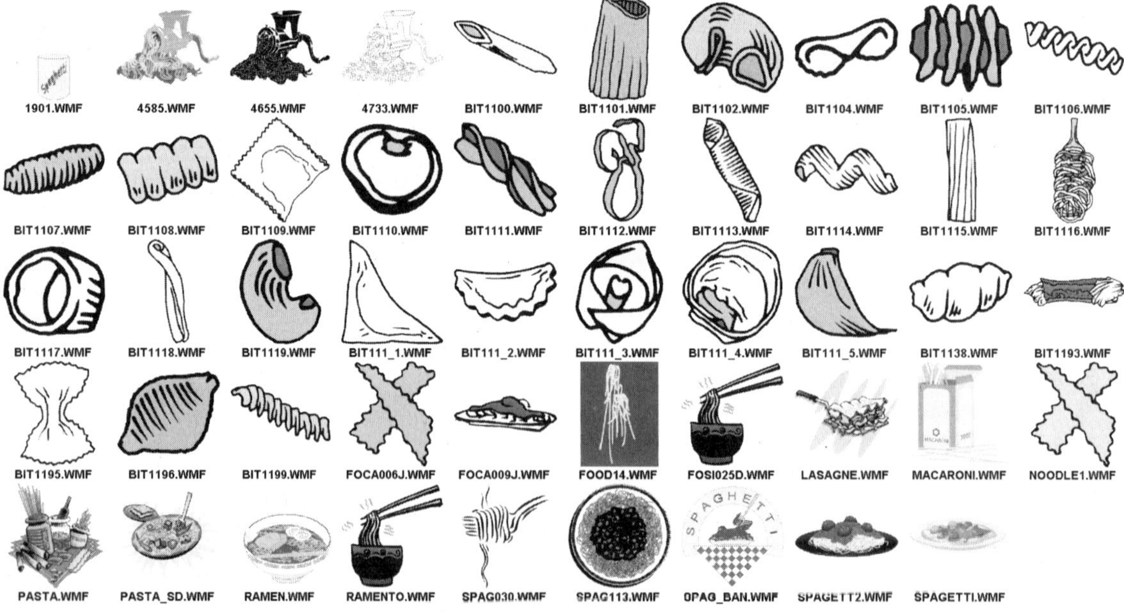

BAR-B-QUE
CHINESE FOOD
Cocktails
Country Style
FRESH FISH
ITALIAN FOOD
ITALIAN CUISINE
meXican Foods
MEXICAN RESTAURANT
Pizza
FRESH MAINE LOBSTERS
STEAK HOUSE
TAKE-OUT
WINES
DOMESTIC
FOREIGN
BARBQUE1.WMF
BARBQUE2.WMF
BARBQUE3.WMF
CHEF1.WMF
CHEF2.WMF
CHEF3.WMF
CHINDRA1.WMF
CHINDRA2.WMF
CHINFOD1.WMF
CHINFOD2.WMF
CHINFOD3.WMF
CHINFOD4.WMF
CHINFOD5.WMF
CHINFOD6.WMF
COCKTAIL.WMF
CONTRYST.WMF
DINER.WMF
DINING.WMF
FORMWEAR.WMF
FRENFOOD.WMF
FRSHFISH.WMF
INDNFOOD.WMF
ITALFOD1.WMF
ITALFOD2.WMF
ITALFOD3.WMF
ITALFOD4.WMF
JAPNFOD1.WMF
JAPNFOD2.WMF
MEXFOD1.WMF
MEXFOD2.WMF
MEXFOD3A.WMF
MEXFOD3B.WMF
MEXFOD4.WMF
PIZZA1.WMF
PIZZA2.WMF
PIZZA3.WMF
SEAFOOD1.WMF
SEAFOOD2.WMF
SEAFOOD3.WMF
SEAFOOD4.WMF
SPANISH.WMF
STEAKHS1.WMF
STEAKHS2.WMF
STEAKHS3.WMF
STEAKHS4.WMF
STEAKHS5.WMF
STRF119.WMF
TAKEOUT.WMF
WAITER1.WMF
WAITER2.WMF
WAITER3.WMF
WAITER4.WMF
WAITER5.WMF
WAITRESS.WMF
WINELST1.WMF
WINELST2.WMF

1830.WMF 1877.WMF 4484.WMF 4493.WMF 4495.WMF 4504.WMF 4513.WMF 4529.WMF 4531.WMF 4536.WMF
4539.WMF 4568.WMF 4577.WMF 4578.WMF 4579.WMF 4587.WMF 4588.WMF 4597.WMF 4611.WMF 4613.WMF
4615.WMF 4618.WMF 4619.WMF 4636.WMF 4647.WMF 4648.WMF 4649.WMF 4657.WMF 4667.WMF 4681.WMF
4683.WMF 4685.WMF 4688.WMF 4689.WMF 4695.WMF 4715.WMF 4725.WMF 4726.WMF 4727.WMF 4735.WMF
4744.WMF 4759.WMF 4761.WMF 4764.WMF 4765.WMF 4772.WMF 4776.WMF BEERCOLG.WMF BIT1025.WMF BIT1026.WMF
BIT1164.WMF BIT1173.WMF CANGOOD.WMF CANGOOD1.WMF CHNSHRMP.WMF CLAM021.WMF CLAMS.WMF CRAB006.WMF CRAB026.WMF CRAW007.WMF
EKIBEN.WMF FD11.WMF FD33.WMF FD34.WMF FDDNK090.WMF FDDNK110.WMF FDDNK111.WMF FDDNK112.WMF FDDNK113.WMF FDDNK114.WMF
FDDNK166.WMF FDDNK172.WMF FDDNK181.WMF FISH.WMF FISH045.WMF FISH046.WMF FISH047.WMF FISH1.WMF FISHPLAT.WMF FOBO047J.WMF
FOBO048J.WMF FOOD42.WMF FOSI002J.WMF KAISEKI.WMF LOBS068.WMF LOBSTER.WMF LOBSTER1.WMF LOBSTER2.WMF LOBSTER6.WMF NABEMONO.WMF
OKOLUNCH.WMF OMUSUBI.WMF SALMON.WMF SALMON3.WMF SHRI110.WMF SHRI111.WMF SHRI112.WMF SHRIMP.WMF SHRIMPS.WMF WHL_FISH.WMF

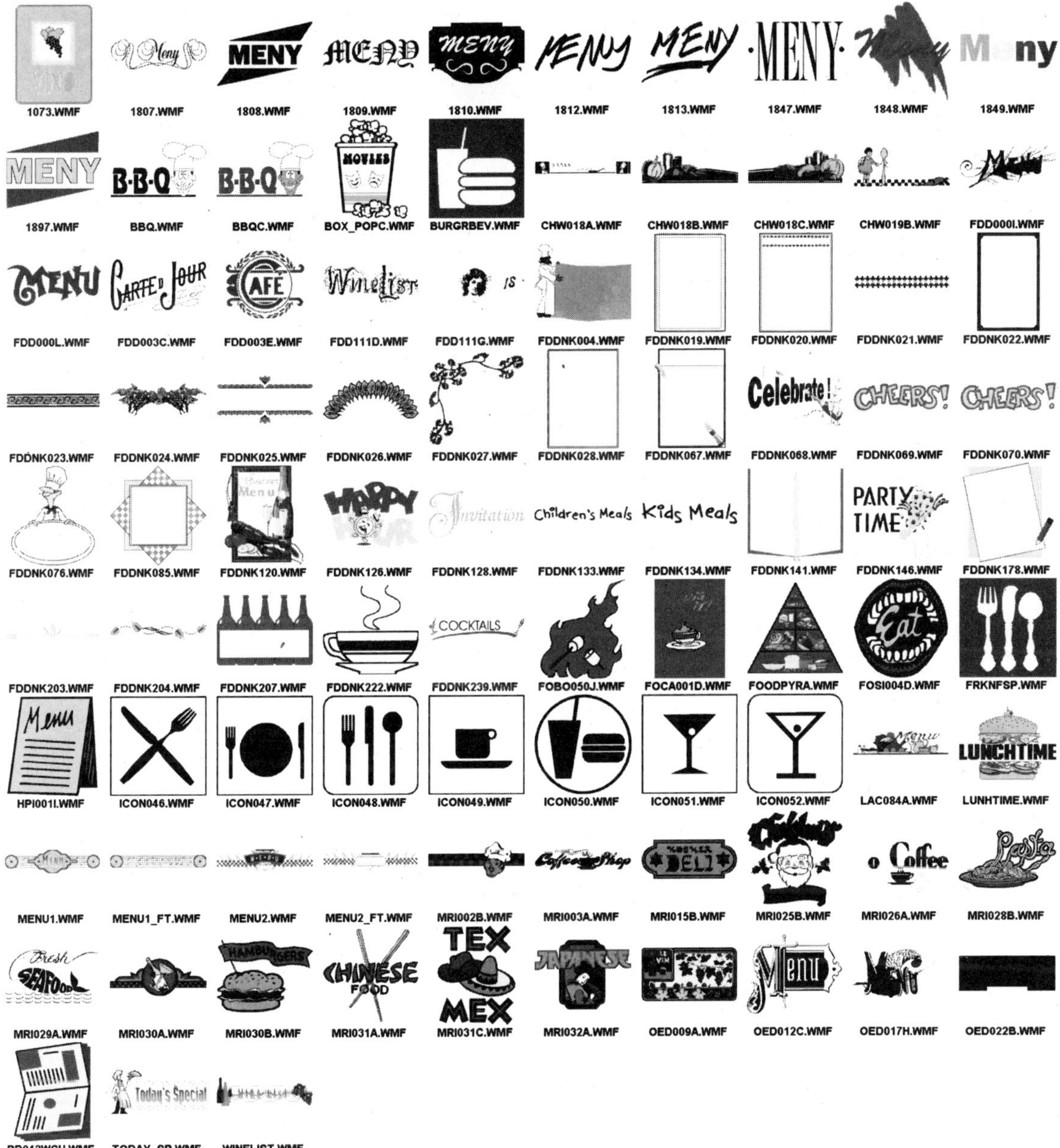

1073.WMF 1807.WMF 1808.WMF 1809.WMF 1810.WMF 1812.WMF 1813.WMF 1847.WMF 1848.WMF 1849.WMF

1897.WMF BBQ.WMF BBQC.WMF BOX_POPC.WMF BURGRBEV.WMF CHW018A.WMF CHW018B.WMF CHW018C.WMF CHW019B.WMF FDD000I.WMF

FDD000L.WMF FDD003C.WMF FDD003E.WMF FDD111D.WMF FDD111G.WMF FDDNK004.WMF FDDNK019.WMF FDDNK020.WMF FDDNK021.WMF FDDNK022.WMF

FDDNK023.WMF FDDNK024.WMF FDDNK025.WMF FDDNK026.WMF FDDNK027.WMF FDDNK028.WMF FDDNK067.WMF FDDNK068.WMF FDDNK069.WMF FDDNK070.WMF

FDDNK076.WMF FDDNK085.WMF FDDNK120.WMF FDDNK126.WMF FDDNK128.WMF FDDNK133.WMF FDDNK134.WMF FDDNK141.WMF FDDNK146.WMF FDDNK178.WMF

FDDNK203.WMF FDDNK204.WMF FDDNK207.WMF FDDNK222.WMF FDDNK239.WMF FOBO050J.WMF FOCA001D.WMF FOODPYRA.WMF FOSI004D.WMF FRKNFSP.WMF

HPI001I.WMF ICON046.WMF ICON047.WMF ICON048.WMF ICON049.WMF ICON050.WMF ICON051.WMF ICON052.WMF LAC084A.WMF LUNHTIME.WMF

MENU1.WMF MENU1_FT.WMF MENU2.WMF MENU2_FT.WMF MRI002B.WMF MRI003A.WMF MRI015B.WMF MRI025B.WMF MRI026A.WMF MRI028B.WMF

MRI029A.WMF MRI030A.WMF MRI030B.WMF MRI031A.WMF MRI031C.WMF MRI032A.WMF OED009A.WMF OED012C.WMF OED017H.WMF OED022B.WMF

PD043WCU.WMF TODAY_SP.WMF WINELIST.WMF

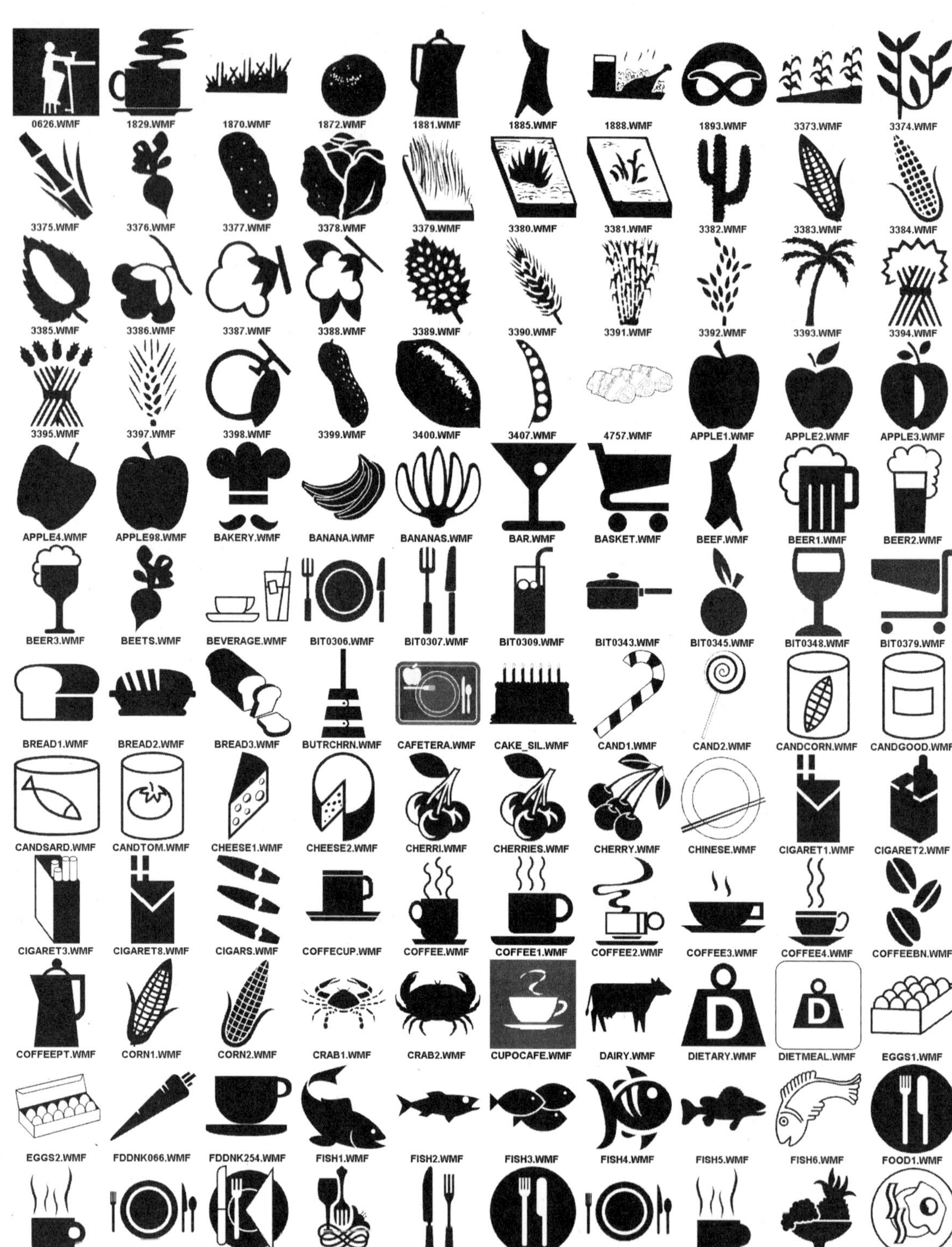
0626.WMF
1829.WMF
1870.WMF
1872.WMF
1881.WMF
1885.WMF
1888.WMF
1893.WMF
3373.WMF
3374.WMF
3375.WMF
3376.WMF
3377.WMF
3378.WMF
3379.WMF
3380.WMF
3381.WMF
3382.WMF
3383.WMF
3384.WMF
3385.WMF
3386.WMF
3387.WMF
3388.WMF
3389.WMF
3390.WMF
3391.WMF
3392.WMF
3393.WMF
3394.WMF
3395.WMF
3397.WMF
3398.WMF
3399.WMF
3400.WMF
3407.WMF
4757.WMF
APPLE1.WMF
APPLE2.WMF
APPLE3.WMF
APPLE4.WMF
APPLE98.WMF
BAKERY.WMF
BANANA.WMF
BANANAS.WMF
BAR.WMF
BASKET.WMF
BEEF.WMF
BEER1.WMF
BEER2.WMF
BEER3.WMF
BEETS.WMF
BEVERAGE.WMF
BIT0306.WMF
BIT0307.WMF
BIT0309.WMF
BIT0343.WMF
BIT0345.WMF
BIT0348.WMF
BIT0379.WMF
BREAD1.WMF
BREAD2.WMF
BREAD3.WMF
BUTRCHRN.WMF
CAFETERA.WMF
CAKE_SIL.WMF
CAND1.WMF
CAND2.WMF
CANDCORN.WMF
CANDGOOD.WMF
CANDSARD.WMF
CANDTOM.WMF
CHEESE1.WMF
CHEESE2.WMF
CHERRI.WMF
CHERRIES.WMF
CHERRY.WMF
CHINESE.WMF
CIGARET1.WMF
CIGARET2.WMF
CIGARET3.WMF
CIGARET8.WMF
CIGARS.WMF
COFFECUP.WMF
COFFEE.WMF
COFFEE1.WMF
COFFEE2.WMF
COFFEE3.WMF
COFFEE4.WMF
COFFEEBN.WMF
COFFEEPT.WMF
CORN1.WMF
CORN2.WMF
CRAB1.WMF
CRAB2.WMF
CUPOCAFE.WMF
DAIRY.WMF
DIETARY.WMF
DIETMEAL.WMF
EGGS1.WMF
EGGS2.WMF
FDDNK066.WMF
FDDNK254.WMF
FISH1.WMF
FISH2.WMF
FISH3.WMF
FISH4.WMF
FISH5.WMF
FISH6.WMF
FOOD1.WMF
FOOD11M.WMF
FOOD2.WMF
FOOD3.WMF
FOOD4.WMF
FOOD5.WMF
FOOD98.WMF
FOOD99.WMF
FOSI032J.WMF
FRUITBOL.WMF
FULBRKF.WMF

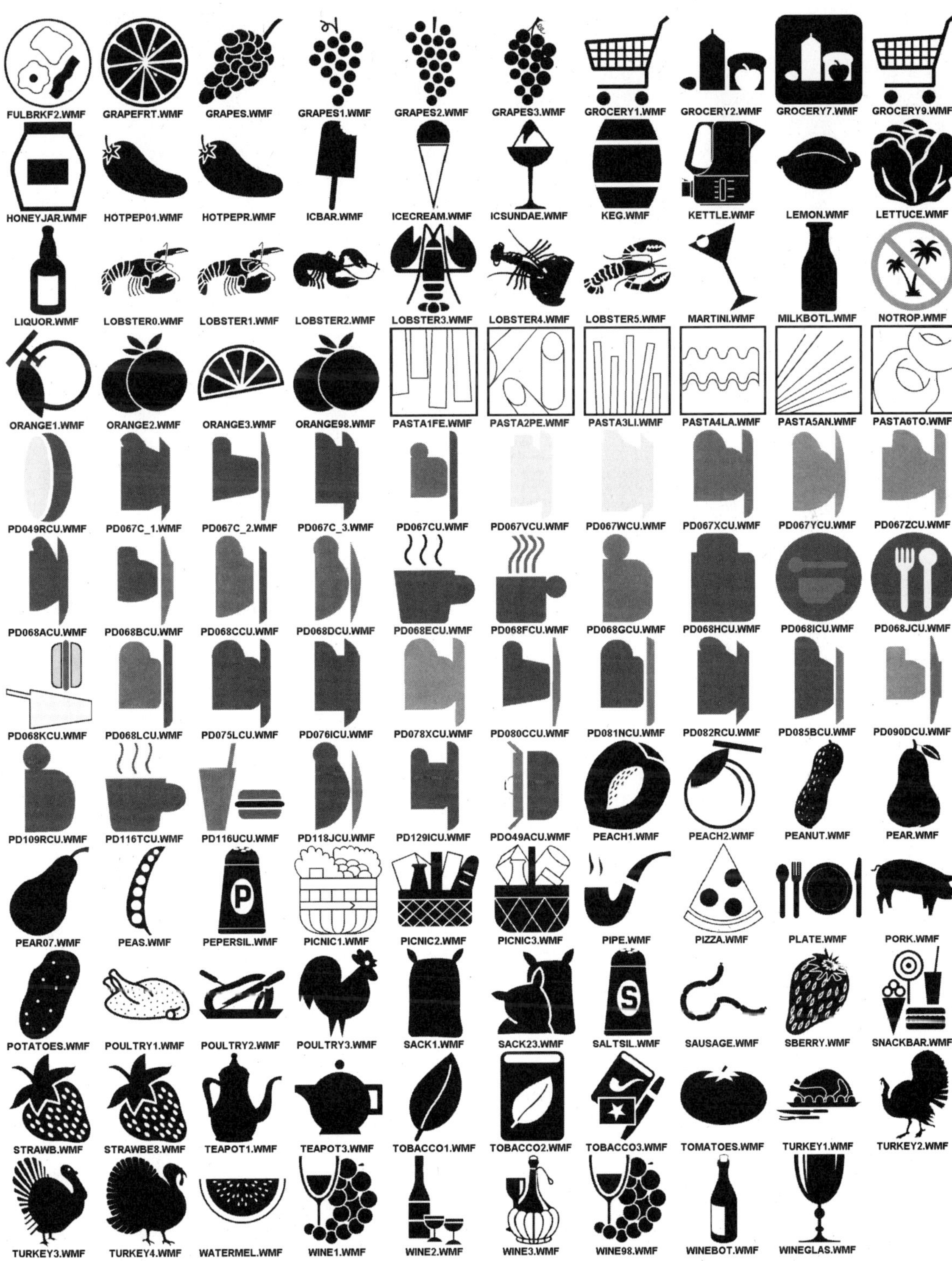
FULBRKF2.WMF GRAPEFRT.WMF GRAPES.WMF GRAPES1.WMF GRAPES2.WMF GRAPES3.WMF GROCERY1.WMF GROCERY2.WMF GROCERY7.WMF GROCERY9.WMF
HONEYJAR.WMF HOTPEP01.WMF HOTPEPR.WMF ICBAR.WMF ICECREAM.WMF ICSUNDAE.WMF KEG.WMF KETTLE.WMF LEMON.WMF LETTUCE.WMF
LIQUOR.WMF LOBSTER0.WMF LOBSTER1.WMF LOBSTER2.WMF LOBSTER3.WMF LOBSTER4.WMF LOBSTER5.WMF MARTINI.WMF MILKBOTL.WMF NOTROP.WMF
ORANGE1.WMF ORANGE2.WMF ORANGE3.WMF ORANGE98.WMF PASTA1FE.WMF PASTA2PE.WMF PASTA3LI.WMF PASTA4LA.WMF PASTA5AN.WMF PASTA6TO.WMF
PD049RCU.WMF PD067C_1.WMF PD067C_2.WMF PD067C_3.WMF PD067CU.WMF PD067VCU.WMF PD067WCU.WMF PD067XCU.WMF PD067YCU.WMF PD067ZCU.WMF
PD068ACU.WMF PD068BCU.WMF PD068CCU.WMF PD068DCU.WMF PD068ECU.WMF PD068FCU.WMF PD068GCU.WMF PD068HCU.WMF PD068ICU.WMF PD068JCU.WMF
PD068KCU.WMF PD068LCU.WMF PD075LCU.WMF PD076ICU.WMF PD078XCU.WMF PD080CCU.WMF PD081NCU.WMF PD082RCU.WMF PD085BCU.WMF PD090DCU.WMF
PD109RCU.WMF PD116TCU.WMF PD116UCU.WMF PD118JCU.WMF PD129ICU.WMF PDO49ACU.WMF PEACH1.WMF PEACH2.WMF PEANUT.WMF PEAR.WMF
P
PEAR07.WMF PEAS.WMF PEPERSIL.WMF PICNIC1.WMF PICNIC2.WMF PICNIC3.WMF PIPE.WMF PIZZA.WMF PLATE.WMF PORK.WMF
S
POTATOES.WMF POULTRY1.WMF POULTRY2.WMF POULTRY3.WMF SACK1.WMF SACK23.WMF SALTSIL.WMF SAUSAGE.WMF SBERRY.WMF SNACKBAR.WMF
STRAWB.WMF STRAWBE8.WMF TEAPOT1.WMF TEAPOT3.WMF TOBACCO1.WMF TOBACCO2.WMF TOBACCO3.WMF TOMATOES.WMF TURKEY1.WMF TURKEY2.WMF
TURKEY3.WMF TURKEY4.WMF WATERMEL.WMF WINE1.WMF WINE2.WMF WINE3.WMF WINE98.WMF WINEBOT.WMF WINEGLAS.WMF

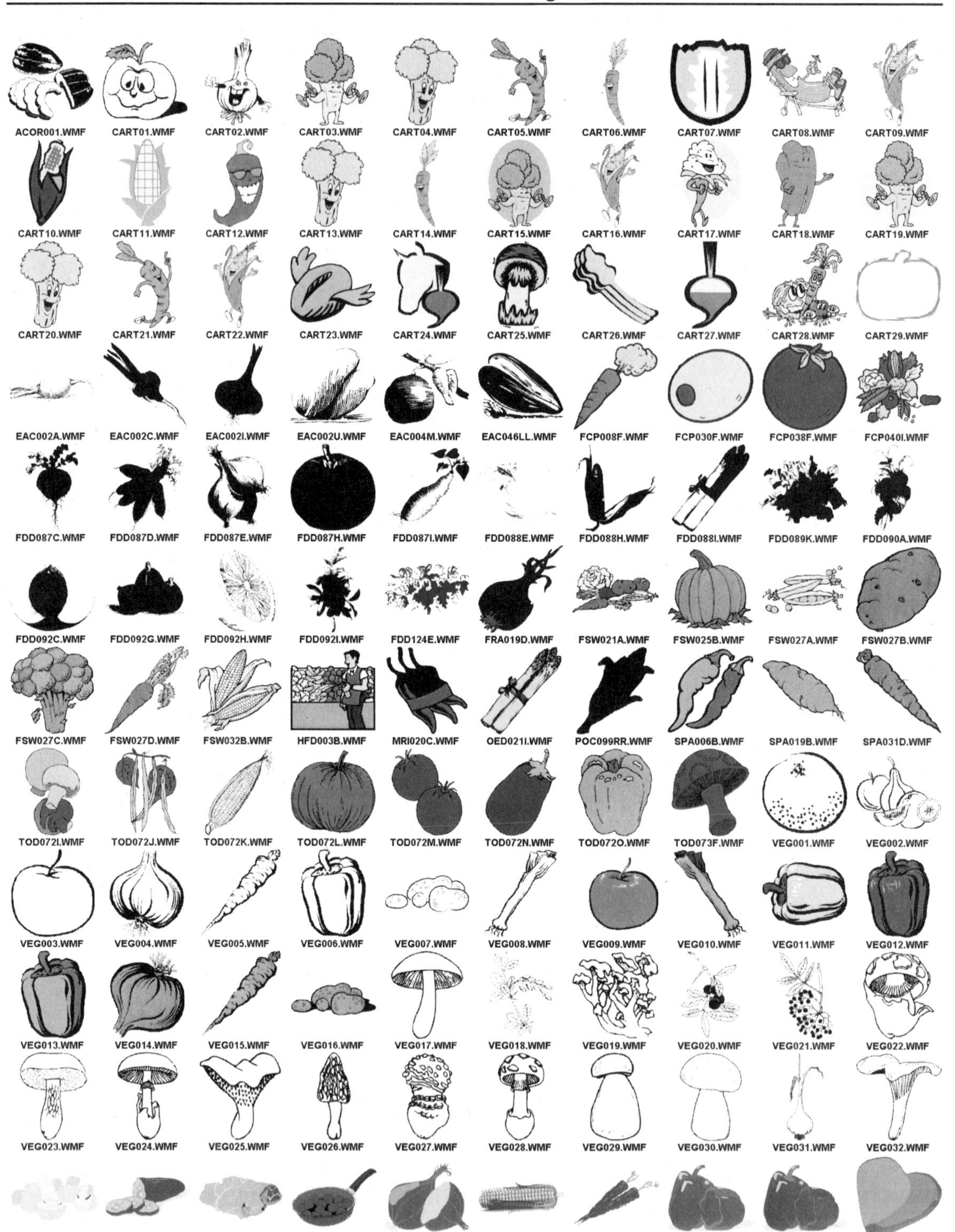
ACOR001.WMF CART01.WMF CART02.WMF CART03.WMF CART04.WMF CART05.WMF CART06.WMF CART07.WMF CART08.WMF CART09.WMF
CART10.WMF CART11.WMF CART12.WMF CART13.WMF CART14.WMF CART15.WMF CART16.WMF CART17.WMF CART18.WMF CART19.WMF
CART20.WMF CART21.WMF CART22.WMF CART23.WMF CART24.WMF CART25.WMF CART26.WMF CART27.WMF CART28.WMF CART29.WMF
EAC002A.WMF EAC002C.WMF EAC002I.WMF EAC002U.WMF EAC004M.WMF EAC046LL.WMF FCP008F.WMF FCP030F.WMF FCP038F.WMF FCP040I.WMF
FDD087C.WMF FDD087D.WMF FDD087E.WMF FDD087H.WMF FDD087I.WMF FDD088E.WMF FDD088H.WMF FDD088I.WMF FDD089K.WMF FDD090A.WMF
FDD092C.WMF FDD092G.WMF FDD092H.WMF FDD092I.WMF FDD124E.WMF FRA019D.WMF FSW021A.WMF FSW025B.WMF FSW027A.WMF FSW027B.WMF
FSW027C.WMF FSW027D.WMF FSW032B.WMF HFD003B.WMF MRI020C.WMF OED021I.WMF POC099RR.WMF SPA006B.WMF SPA019B.WMF SPA031D.WMF
TOD072I.WMF TOD072J.WMF TOD072K.WMF TOD072L.WMF TOD072M.WMF TOD072N.WMF TOD072O.WMF TOD073F.WMF VEG001.WMF VEG002.WMF
VEG003.WMF VEG004.WMF VEG005.WMF VEG006.WMF VEG007.WMF VEG008.WMF VEG009.WMF VEG010.WMF VEG011.WMF VEG012.WMF
VEG013.WMF VEG014.WMF VEG015.WMF VEG016.WMF VEG017.WMF VEG018.WMF VEG019.WMF VEG020.WMF VEG021.WMF VEG022.WMF
VEG023.WMF VEG024.WMF VEG025.WMF VEG026.WMF VEG027.WMF VEG028.WMF VEG029.WMF VEG030.WMF VEG031.WMF VEG032.WMF
VEG033.WMF VEG034.WMF VEG035.WMF VEG036.WMF VEG037.WMF VEG038.WMF VEG039.WMF VEG040.WMF VEG041.WMF VEG042.WMF

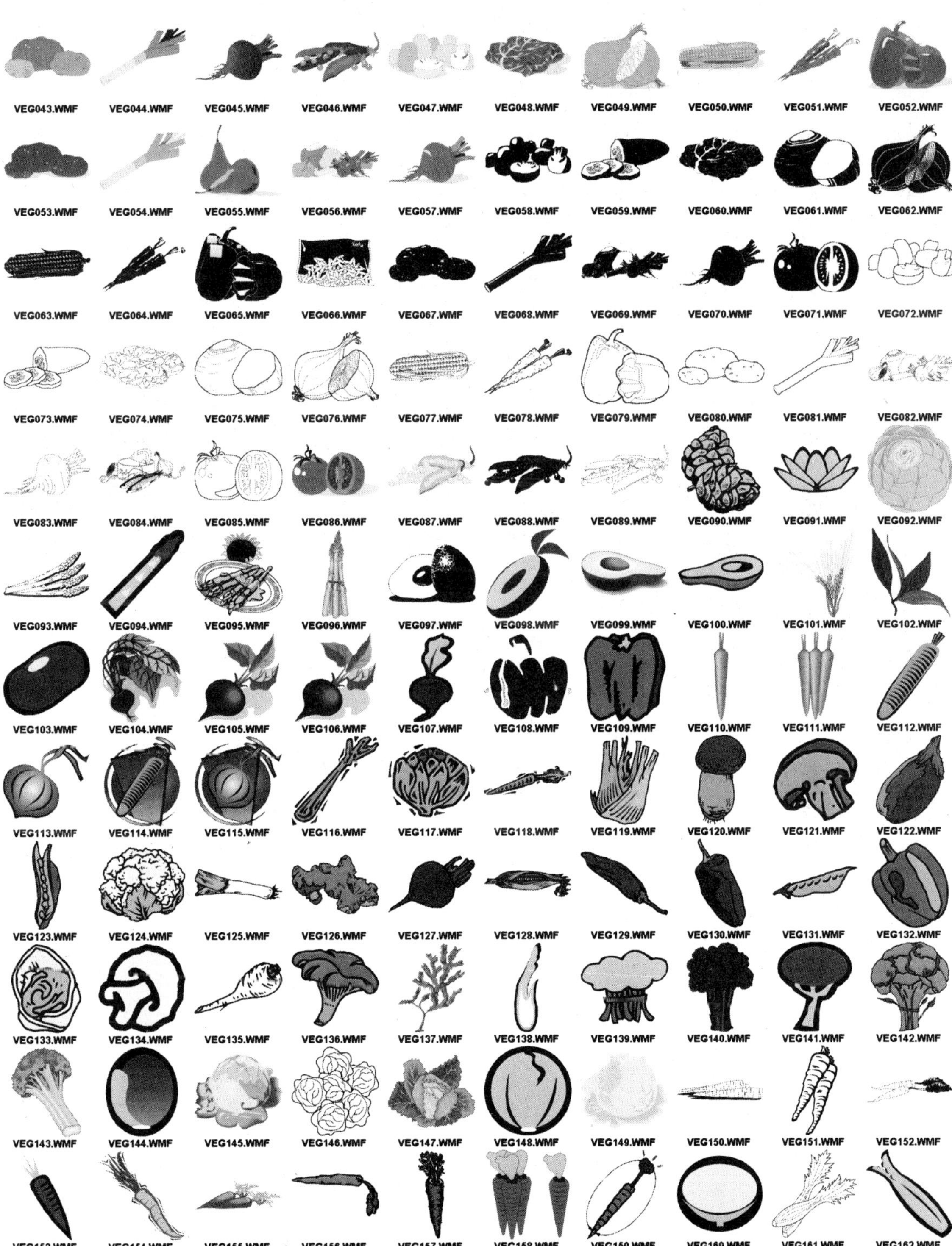
VEG043.WMF VEG044.WMF VEG045.WMF VEG046.WMF VEG047.WMF VEG048.WMF VEG049.WMF VEG050.WMF VEG051.WMF VEG052.WMF
VEG053.WMF VEG054.WMF VEG055.WMF VEG056.WMF VEG057.WMF VEG058.WMF VEG059.WMF VEG060.WMF VEG061.WMF VEG062.WMF
VEG063.WMF VEG064.WMF VEG065.WMF VEG066.WMF VEG067.WMF VEG068.WMF VEG069.WMF VEG070.WMF VEG071.WMF VEG072.WMF
VEG073.WMF VEG074.WMF VEG075.WMF VEG076.WMF VEG077.WMF VEG078.WMF VEG079.WMF VEG080.WMF VEG081.WMF VEG082.WMF
VEG083.WMF VEG084.WMF VEG085.WMF VEG086.WMF VEG087.WMF VEG088.WMF VEG089.WMF VEG090.WMF VEG091.WMF VEG092.WMF
VEG093.WMF VEG094.WMF VEG095.WMF VEG096.WMF VEG097.WMF VEG098.WMF VEG099.WMF VEG100.WMF VEG101.WMF VEG102.WMF
VEG103.WMF VEG104.WMF VEG105.WMF VEG106.WMF VEG107.WMF VEG108.WMF VEG109.WMF VEG110.WMF VEG111.WMF VEG112.WMF
VEG113.WMF VEG114.WMF VEG115.WMF VEG116.WMF VEG117.WMF VEG118.WMF VEG119.WMF VEG120.WMF VEG121.WMF VEG122.WMF
VEG123.WMF VEG124.WMF VEG125.WMF VEG126.WMF VEG127.WMF VEG128.WMF VEG129.WMF VEG130.WMF VEG131.WMF VEG132.WMF
VEG133.WMF VEG134.WMF VEG135.WMF VEG136.WMF VEG137.WMF VEG138.WMF VEG139.WMF VEG140.WMF VEG141.WMF VEG142.WMF
VEG143.WMF VEG144.WMF VEG145.WMF VEG146.WMF VEG147.WMF VEG148.WMF VEG149.WMF VEG150.WMF VEG151.WMF VEG152.WMF
VEG153.WMF VEG154.WMF VEG155.WMF VEG156.WMF VEG157.WMF VEG158.WMF VEG159.WMF VEG160.WMF VEG161.WMF VEG162.WMF

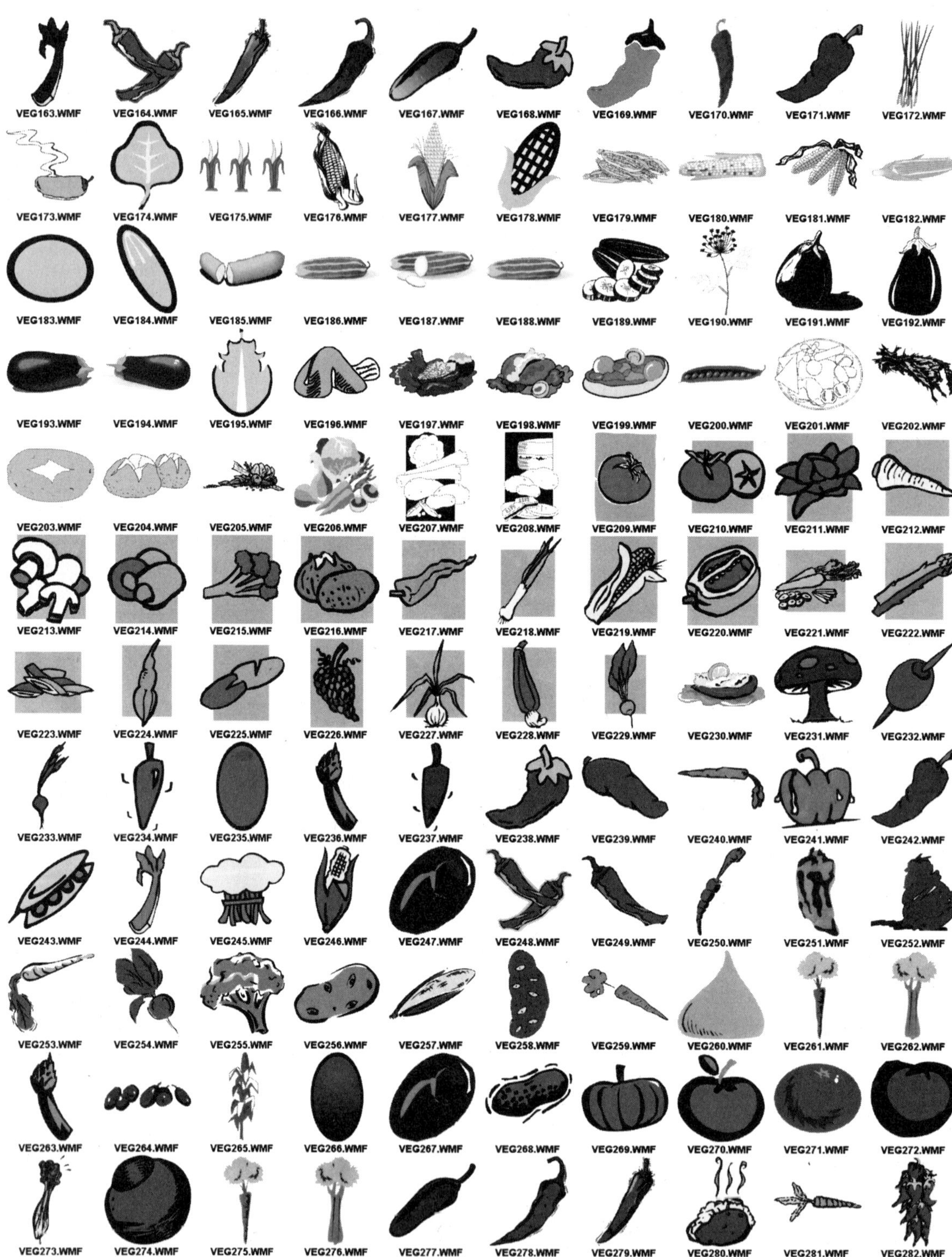
VEG163.WMF
VEG164.WMF
VEG165.WMF
VEG166.WMF
VEG167.WMF
VEG168.WMF
VEG169.WMF
VEG170.WMF
VEG171.WMF
VEG172.WMF
VEG173.WMF
VEG174.WMF
VEG175.WMF
VEG176.WMF
VEG177.WMF
VEG178.WMF
VEG179.WMF
VEG180.WMF
VEG181.WMF
VEG182.WMF
VEG183.WMF
VEG184.WMF
VEG185.WMF
VEG186.WMF
VEG187.WMF
VEG188.WMF
VEG189.WMF
VEG190.WMF
VEG191.WMF
VEG192.WMF
VEG193.WMF
VEG194.WMF
VEG195.WMF
VEG196.WMF
VEG197.WMF
VEG198.WMF
VEG199.WMF
VEG200.WMF
VEG201.WMF
VEG202.WMF
VEG203.WMF
VEG204.WMF
VEG205.WMF
VEG206.WMF
VEG207.WMF
VEG208.WMF
VEG209.WMF
VEG210.WMF
VEG211.WMF
VEG212.WMF
VEG213.WMF
VEG214.WMF
VEG215.WMF
VEG216.WMF
VEG217.WMF
VEG218.WMF
VEG219.WMF
VEG220.WMF
VEG221.WMF
VEG222.WMF
VEG223.WMF
VEG224.WMF
VEG225.WMF
VEG226.WMF
VEG227.WMF
VEG228.WMF
VEG229.WMF
VEG230.WMF
VEG231.WMF
VEG232.WMF
VEG233.WMF
VEG234.WMF
VEG235.WMF
VEG236.WMF
VEG237.WMF
VEG238.WMF
VEG239.WMF
VEG240.WMF
VEG241.WMF
VEG242.WMF
VEG243.WMF
VEG244.WMF
VEG245.WMF
VEG246.WMF
VEG247.WMF
VEG248.WMF
VEG249.WMF
VEG250.WMF
VEG251.WMF
VEG252.WMF
VEG253.WMF
VEG254.WMF
VEG255.WMF
VEG256.WMF
VEG257.WMF
VEG258.WMF
VEG259.WMF
VEG260.WMF
VEG261.WMF
VEG262.WMF
VEG263.WMF
VEG264.WMF
VEG265.WMF
VEG266.WMF
VEG267.WMF
VEG268.WMF
VEG269.WMF
VEG270.WMF
VEG271.WMF
VEG272.WMF
VEG273.WMF
VEG274.WMF
VEG275.WMF
VEG276.WMF
VEG277.WMF
VEG278.WMF
VEG279.WMF
VEG280.WMF
VEG281.WMF
VEG282.WMF

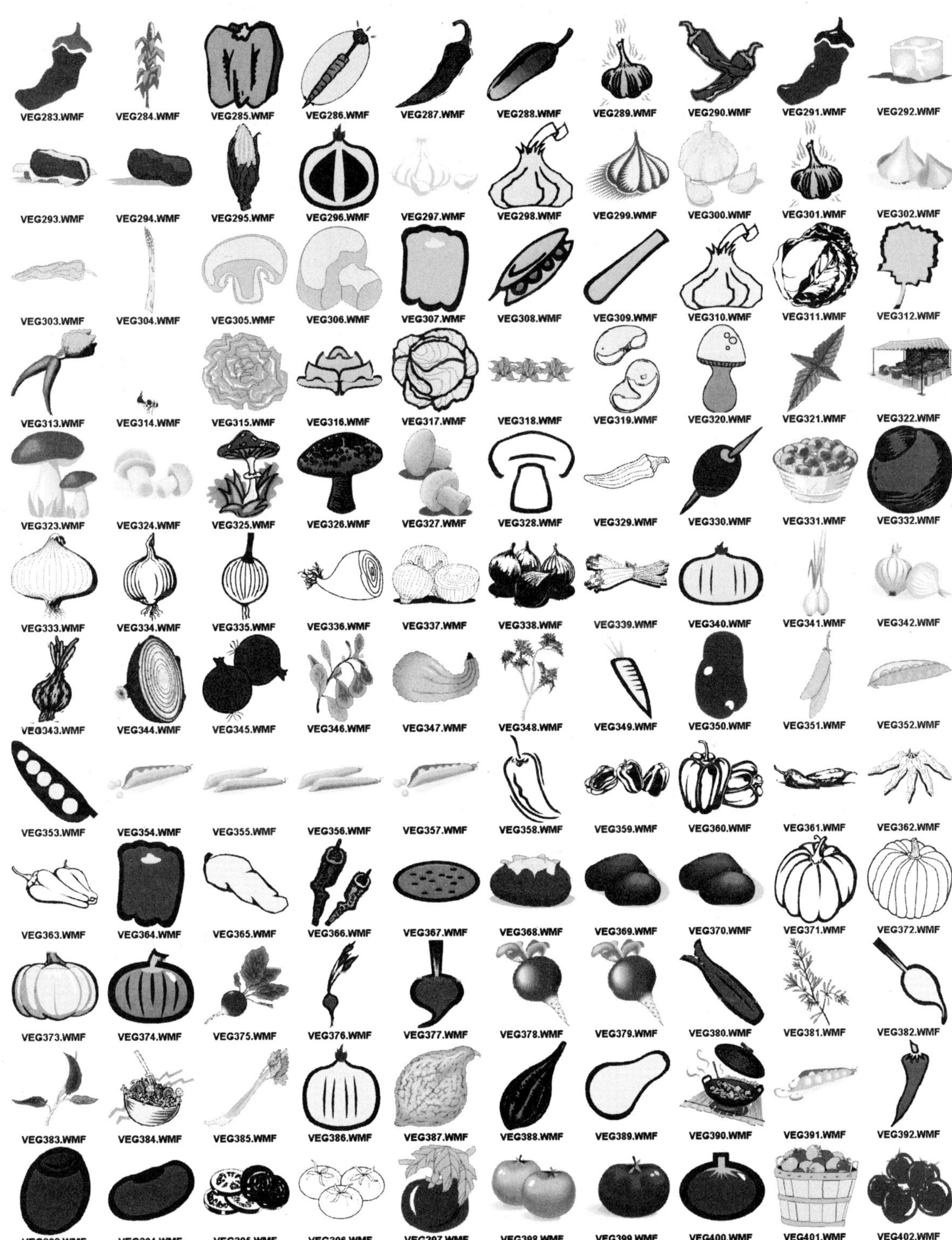
VEG283.WMF VEG284.WMF VEG285.WMF VEG286.WMF VEG287.WMF VEG288.WMF VEG289.WMF VEG290.WMF VEG291.WMF VEG292.WMF
VEG293.WMF VEG294.WMF VEG295.WMF VEG296.WMF VEG297.WMF VEG298.WMF VEG299.WMF VEG300.WMF VEG301.WMF VEG302.WMF
VEG303.WMF VEG304.WMF VEG305.WMF VEG306.WMF VEG307.WMF VEG308.WMF VEG309.WMF VEG310.WMF VEG311.WMF VEG312.WMF
VEG313.WMF VEG314.WMF VEG315.WMF VEG316.WMF VEG317.WMF VEG318.WMF VEG319.WMF VEG320.WMF VEG321.WMF VEG322.WMF
VEG323.WMF VEG324.WMF VEG325.WMF VEG326.WMF VEG327.WMF VEG328.WMF VEG329.WMF VEG330.WMF VEG331.WMF VEG332.WMF
VEG333.WMF VEG334.WMF VEG335.WMF VEG336.WMF VEG337.WMF VEG338.WMF VEG339.WMF VEG340.WMF VEG341.WMF VEG342.WMF
VEG343.WMF VEG344.WMF VEG345.WMF VEG346.WMF VEG347.WMF VEG348.WMF VEG349.WMF VEG350.WMF VEG351.WMF VEG352.WMF
VEG353.WMF VEG354.WMF VEG355.WMF VEG356.WMF VEG357.WMF VEG358.WMF VEG359.WMF VEG360.WMF VEG361.WMF VEG362.WMF
VEG363.WMF VEG364.WMF VEG365.WMF VEG366.WMF VEG367.WMF VEG368.WMF VEG369.WMF VEG370.WMF VEG371.WMF VEG372.WMF
VEG373.WMF VEG374.WMF VEG375.WMF VEG376.WMF VEG377.WMF VEG378.WMF VEG379.WMF VEG380.WMF VEG381.WMF VEG382.WMF
VEG383.WMF VEG384.WMF VEG385.WMF VEG386.WMF VEG387.WMF VEG388.WMF VEG389.WMF VEG390.WMF VEG391.WMF VEG392.WMF
VEG393.WMF VEG394.WMF VEG395.WMF VEG396.WMF VEG397.WMF VEG398.WMF VEG399.WMF VEG400.WMF VEG401.WMF VEG402.WMF

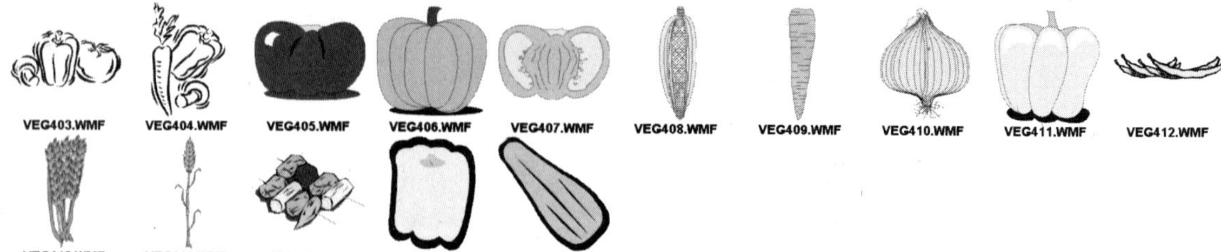

VEG403.WMF VEG404.WMF VEG405.WMF VEG406.WMF VEG407.WMF VEG408.WMF VEG409.WMF VEG410.WMF VEG411.WMF VEG412.WMF

VEG413.WMF VEG414.WMF VEG415.WMF VEG416.WMF VEG417.WMF

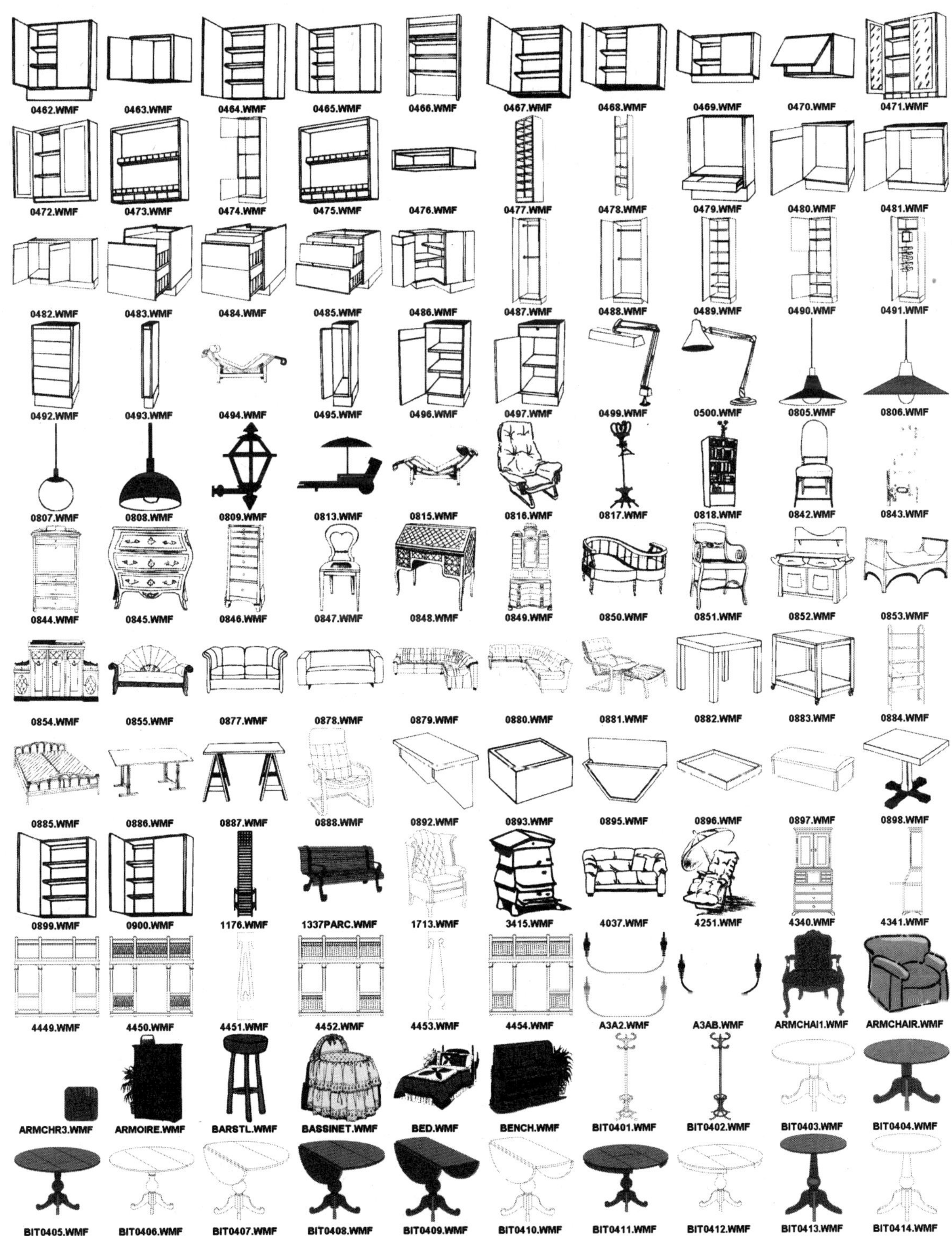
0462.WMF
0463.WMF
0464.WMF
0465.WMF
0466.WMF
0467.WMF
0468.WMF
0469.WMF
0470.WMF
0471.WMF
0472.WMF
0473.WMF
0474.WMF
0475.WMF
0476.WMF
0477.WMF
0478.WMF
0479.WMF
0480.WMF
0481.WMF
0482.WMF
0483.WMF
0484.WMF
0485.WMF
0486.WMF
0487.WMF
0488.WMF
0489.WMF
0490.WMF
0491.WMF
0492.WMF
0493.WMF
0494.WMF
0495.WMF
0496.WMF
0497.WMF
0499.WMF
0500.WMF
0805.WMF
0806.WMF
0807.WMF
0808.WMF
0809.WMF
0813.WMF
0815.WMF
0816.WMF
0817.WMF
0818.WMF
0842.WMF
0843.WMF
0844.WMF
0845.WMF
0846.WMF
0847.WMF
0848.WMF
0849.WMF
0850.WMF
0851.WMF
0852.WMF
0853.WMF
0854.WMF
0855.WMF
0877.WMF
0878.WMF
0879.WMF
0880.WMF
0881.WMF
0882.WMF
0883.WMF
0884.WMF
0885.WMF
0886.WMF
0887.WMF
0888.WMF
0892.WMF
0893.WMF
0895.WMF
0896.WMF
0897.WMF
0898.WMF
0899.WMF
0900.WMF
1176.WMF
1337PARC.WMF
1713.WMF
3415.WMF
4037.WMF
4251.WMF
4340.WMF
4341.WMF
4449.WMF
4450.WMF
4451.WMF
4452.WMF
4453.WMF
4454.WMF
A3A2.WMF
A3AB.WMF
ARMCHAI1.WMF
ARMCHAIR.WMF
ARMCHR3.WMF
ARMOIRE.WMF
BARSTL.WMF
BASSINET.WMF
BED.WMF
BENCH.WMF
BIT0401.WMF
BIT0402.WMF
BIT0403.WMF
BIT0404.WMF
BIT0405.WMF
BIT0406.WMF
BIT0407.WMF
BIT0408.WMF
BIT0409.WMF
BIT0410.WMF
BIT0411.WMF
BIT0412.WMF
BIT0413.WMF
BIT0414.WMF

BIT0415.WMF
BIT0416.WMF
BIT0417.WMF
BIT0418.WMF
BIT0419.WMF
BIT0420.WMF
BIT0421.WMF
BIT0422.WMF
BIT0423.WMF
BIT0424.WMF
BIT0425.WMF
BIT0426.WMF
BIT0427.WMF
BIT0428.WMF
BIT0429.WMF
BIT0430.WMF
BIT0431.WMF
BIT0432.WMF
BIT0502.WMF
BIT0503.WMF
BRASSBED.WMF
BUNKBEDS.WMF
BUREAU.WMF
CHAIR.WMF
CHAIR1.WMF
CHAIR2.WMF
CHAIR6.WMF
CHAIRAS.WMF
CHAIRTO.WMF
CHAIRWFO.WMF
CHAISELA.WMF
CHASLONG.WMF
COFFETBL.WMF
COMPTABL.WMF
COUCH.WMF
COUCHAS.WMF
DAYBED.WMF
DAYBED2.WMF
DESK3.WMF
DESK4.WMF
DESKCHAR.WMF
DRAFTTBL.WMF
DRESSER.WMF
DRFTTBL2.WMF
DRYBAR.WMF
DRYSINK.WMF
ENTCENTR.WMF
FLORLAMP.WMF
FRA007A.WMF
FRA024F.WMF
FTSTOL01.WMF
HHBO022J.WMF
HHBO028J.WMF
HHCA003J.WMF
HHCA093J.WMF
HHGC002D.WMF
HHGC003D.WMF
HHGC103D.WMF
HHGC130D.WMF
HHKC001J.WMF
HHKC002J.WMF
HHKC003J.WMF
HHKC004J.WMF
HHKC007J.WMF
HHRW011D.WMF
HHRW015J.WMF
HHRW042J.WMF
HHRW052J.WMF
HHRW061J.WMF
HHRW063J.WMF
HHSI015J.WMF
HHSI017M.WMF
HHSI028D.WMF
HHSI109D.WMF
HHSI122D.WMF
HHSS023J.WMF
HHSS024J.WMF
HSEHLD02.WMF
HSEHLD07.WMF
HSEHLD29.WMF
HUTCH.WMF
INSI003D.WMF
INSI015D.WMF
LAC103G.WMF
MATTRESS.WMF
MICRO.WMF
PD047ECU.WMF
PD051CCU.WMF
PD052KCU.WMF
PD052LCU.WMF
PLAN058.WMF
PLAN059.WMF
PLAN060.WMF
PLAN120.WMF
PLAN121.WMF
PLAN124.WMF
PLAN125.WMF
PLAN126.WMF
PLAN127.WMF
PLAN128.WMF
PLAN129.WMF
PLAN136.WMF
PLAN139.WMF
RATN_COU.WMF
RKNGCHAS.WMF
SEV03.WMF
SEV04.WMF
SITTING_.WMF
SOFA.WMF
SOFA6.WMF
SPA017F.WMF
SPA024D.WMF
SYMBL141.WMF
SYMBL154.WMF
TABLE.WMF
TABLE3.WMF
TBLCHAR.WMF
TRUNDBED.WMF
VACANCY.WMF
VANITY.WMF

VASE.WMF

WATERBED.WMF

WBKCHAIR.WMF

WORKSTAT.WMF

0471.WMF 1142GARC.WMF 3361.WMF 3409.WMF 3410.WMF 4362.WMF 4381.WMF 4382.WMF 4383.WMF 4391.WMF
4400.WMF AGR002.WMF BARROW.WMF BEAR_GAR.WMF BIRDBATH.WMF BIRDBTH2.WMF BIRDBTH3.WMF BIRDFEDR.WMF BIT0514.WMF BIT0515.WMF
BIT0516.WMF BIT0517.WMF BIT0522.WMF BIT0523.WMF BIT0526.WMF BIT0527.WMF BIT0528.WMF BIT0529.WMF BIT0530.WMF BIT0531.WMF
BIT0532.WMF BIT0533.WMF BIT0534.WMF BIT0535.WMF BIT0536.WMF BIT0537.WMF BIT0538.WMF BIT0539.WMF BIT0540.WMF BIT0541.WMF
BIT0542.WMF BIT0543.WMF BIT0544.WMF BIT0545.WMF BIT0546.WMF BRDEDR2.WMF BRDFED3.WMF BRDFED4.WMF BRRW.WMF BUGUMBRL.WMF
FERTILIZER
FERTILIZER
BUSHELOF.WMF BUSI016M.WMF COUNTRYG.WMF EAC006B.WMF EAC044B.WMF FERTILIZ.WMF FERTLIZ2.WMF FOBO032J.WMF FORESTS.WMF FSW025C.WMF
G21034.WMF G21035.WMF GAR01.WMF GAR02.WMF GAR03.WMF GAR04.WMF GAR05.WMF GAR06.WMF GAR14.WMF GAR15.WMF
GAR16.WMF GAR17.WMF GAR18.WMF GAR19.WMF GAR20.WMF GAR21.WMF GAR22.WMF GAR23.WMF GAR24.WMF GAR25.WMF
GAR26.WMF GAR27.WMF GARDEN2B.WMF GARDEN3.WMF GARDENCO.WMF GARDENHO.WMF GARDENPL.WMF GARDENT1.WMF GARDENTO.WMF GARDENTR.WMF
GRASS SEED
GARDNCLW.WMF GARDTOOL.WMF GAZEBO.WMF GDNCLEAV.WMF GRASSEED.WMF GRDN002.WMF GRDN003.WMF GRDN004.WMF GRDN005.WMF GRDN006.WMF
GRDN007.WMF GRDN008.WMF GRDN009.WMF GRDN010.WMF GRDN011.WMF GRDN012.WMF GRDN013.WMF GRDN014.WMF GRDN015.WMF GRDN016.WMF
GRDN017.WMF GRDN018.WMF GRDN019.WMF GRDN020.WMF GRDN021.WMF GRDN022.WMF GRDN023.WMF GRDN024.WMF GRDN025.WMF GRDN026.WMF

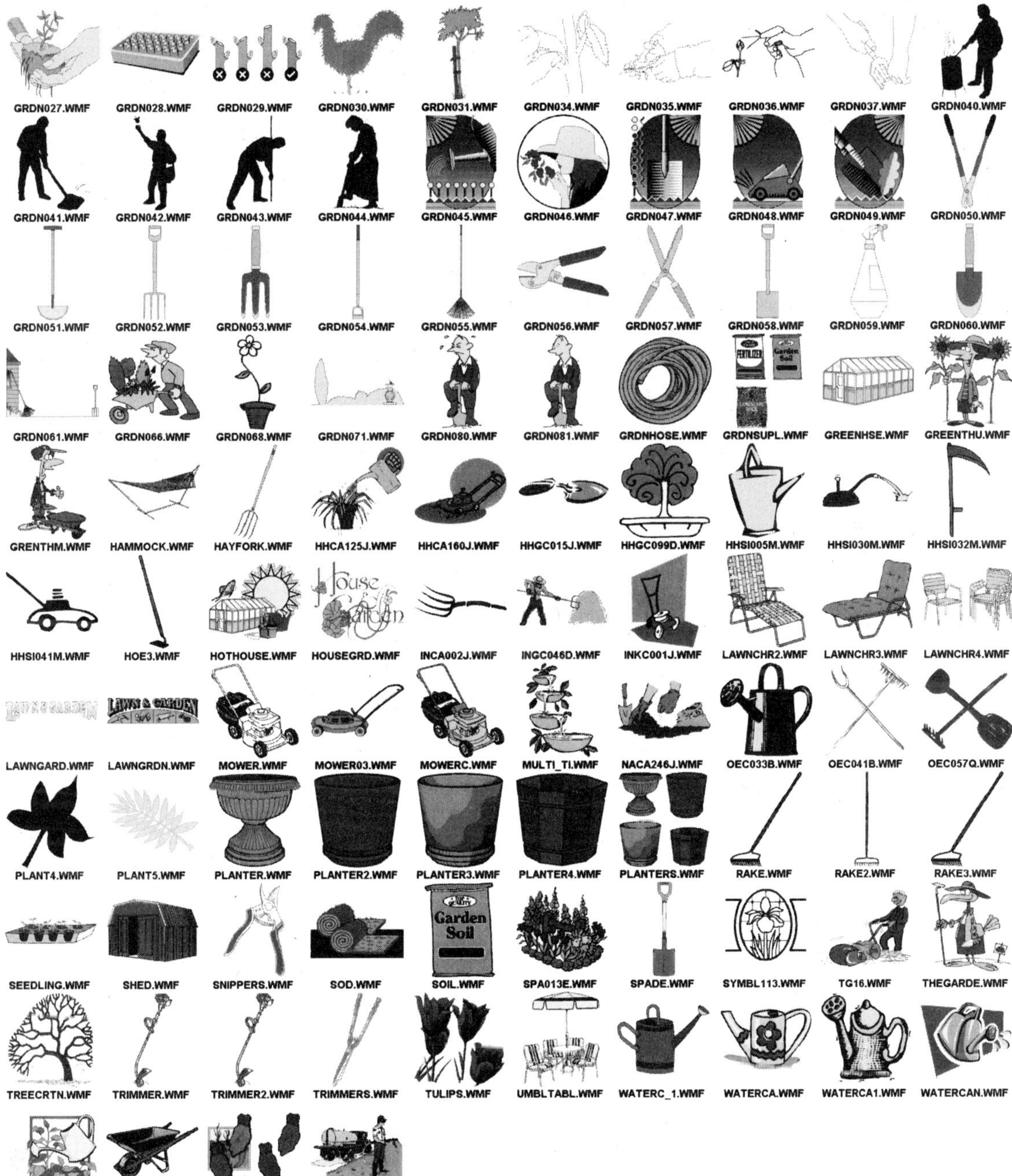

GRDN027.WMF GRDN028.WMF GRDN029.WMF GRDN030.WMF GRDN031.WMF GRDN034.WMF GRDN035.WMF GRDN036.WMF GRDN037.WMF GRDN040.WMF

GRDN041.WMF GRDN042.WMF GRDN043.WMF GRDN044.WMF GRDN045.WMF GRDN046.WMF GRDN047.WMF GRDN048.WMF GRDN049.WMF GRDN050.WMF

GRDN051.WMF GRDN052.WMF GRDN053.WMF GRDN054.WMF GRDN055.WMF GRDN056.WMF GRDN057.WMF GRDN058.WMF GRDN059.WMF GRDN060.WMF

GRDN061.WMF GRDN066.WMF GRDN068.WMF GRDN071.WMF GRDN080.WMF GRDN081.WMF GRDNHOSE.WMF GRDNSUPL.WMF GREENHSE.WMF GREENTHU.WMF

GRENTHM.WMF HAMMOCK.WMF HAYFORK.WMF HHCA125J.WMF HHCA160J.WMF HHGC015J.WMF HHGC099D.WMF HHSI005M.WMF HHSI030M.WMF HHSI032M.WMF

HHSI041M.WMF HOE3.WMF HOTHOUSE.WMF HOUSEGRD.WMF INCA002J.WMF INGC046D.WMF INKC001J.WMF LAWNCHR2.WMF LAWNCHR3.WMF LAWNCHR4.WMF

LAWNGARD.WMF LAWNGRDN.WMF MOWER.WMF MOWER03.WMF MOWERC.WMF MULTI_TI.WMF NACA246J.WMF OEC033B.WMF OEC041B.WMF OEC057Q.WMF

PLANT4.WMF PLANT5.WMF PLANTER.WMF PLANTER2.WMF PLANTER3.WMF PLANTER4.WMF PLANTERS.WMF RAKE.WMF RAKE2.WMF RAKE3.WMF

SEEDLING.WMF SHED.WMF SNIPPERS.WMF SOD.WMF SOIL.WMF SPA013E.WMF SPADE.WMF SYMBL113.WMF TG16.WMF THEGARDE.WMF

TREECRTN.WMF TRIMMER.WMF TRIMMER2.WMF TRIMMERS.WMF TULIPS.WMF UMBLTABL.WMF WATERC_1.WMF WATERCA.WMF WATERCA1.WMF WATERCAN.WMF

WATERING.WMF WHELBARL.WMF WORKGLOV.WMF YARDSERV.WMF

ACCUSE.WMF
BUDGET3.WMF
BUDGET4.WMF
CAPDOME2.WMF
DADLN.WMF
ECONPIE1.WMF
ETHICS1.WMF
IRS1.WMF
JL03.WMF
JL05.WMF
JL06.WMF
JL07.WMF
JL08.WMF
JUDGEC.WMF
JURYFITE.WMF
NOEXCUSE.WMF
PROTEST1.WMF
PROTEST2.WMF
SECRSER1.WMF
TAXES1.WMF
TAXES2.WMF
TAXES3.WMF
TAXES4.WMF
TAXES6.WMF
TAXES7.WMF
TAXPAYR1.WMF
TOLT.WMF
USADREAM.WMF
WHO ME?
WHOME.WMF

1050GAVC.WMF 1051GAVC.WMF 1069SCAC.WMF 1104CAPC.WMF 1STLADY.WMF ADMIRALT.WMF ADOPTION.WMF AGRICULT.WMF AMENDM.WMF ATTYGEN.WMF

B20088.WMF BALANCE.WMF BALANCE0.WMF BALDEAGL.WMF BANKRUPT.WMF BDGT.WMF BILL.WMF BILRIGHT.WMF BISI010M.WMF BIT1007.WMF

BLDJUST.WMF BRANCH.WMF BUDGTSYM.WMF BUGC023J.WMF BUREAU.WMF BUSI029M.WMF BUSI180D.WMF CAPDOME1.WMF CAPITOL.WMF CAPITOL2.WMF

CAPITOL3.WMF CAPITOL4.WMF CAPITOL5.WMF CIVILTRI.WMF CIVLDEFN.WMF COLLECT.WMF CONSTITU.WMF CORPLAW.WMF CORTROOM.WMF COSTANYL.WMF

COUNTY.WMF COURT.WMF COURTHO.WMF COURTHSE.WMF CPTLBLDG.WMF CRIMAPPE.WMF CRIMILAW.WMF DEPT.WMF DEPTAGRI.WMF DEPTCMRC.WMF

DEPTDEFN.WMF DEPTHOUS.WMF DEPTJUST.WMF DEPTTRAN.WMF DIVISION.WMF E20942.WMF EAGLEC.WMF ECONDEV1.WMF ESTATEPL.WMF EXECBRCH.WMF

EXECSTBR.WMF EXOFBLDG.WMF FEDAID.WMF FEDPRISN.WMF FEDSTATE.WMF FILERLY1.WMF FILERLY2.WMF FILERLY3.WMF FLAG1823.WMF GAVEL.WMF

GAVEL08.WMF GAVEL2.WMF GAVEL6.WMF GAVEL7.WMF GOVERNOR.WMF GOVTSYM2.WMF HSCHAMBR.WMF I21138.WMF IMMIGRAT.WMF INDHALL.WMF

INGC020D.WMF JEFFMEM.WMF JEFFMEM1.WMF JL04.WMF JL10.WMF JUDGE.WMF JUDGEM.WMF JUDICAL1.WMF JUDICIAL.WMF JURSDICT.WMF

JUSTICE.WMF JUSTICE2.WMF JUSTICE3.WMF KAN_CAP.WMF LABORAND.WMF LADYJUST.WMF LAW.WMF LAWSCAL1.WMF LAWSCAL2.WMF LEGLBRCH.WMF

LIBRA.WMF LINMMRL1.WMF LINMMRL2.WMF LITIGATI.WMF LOBBY.WMF LOCALGOV.WMF MEDIATI.WMF MICHMS.WMF MUNICIPL.WMF NATLGAL.WMF

OPINION1.WMF OPINION2.WMF OVALOFFC.WMF PD033C_1.WMF PD033CU.WMF PD033ZCU.WMF PD034ACU.WMF PD034BCU.WMF PD034CCU.WMF PD034DCU.WMF

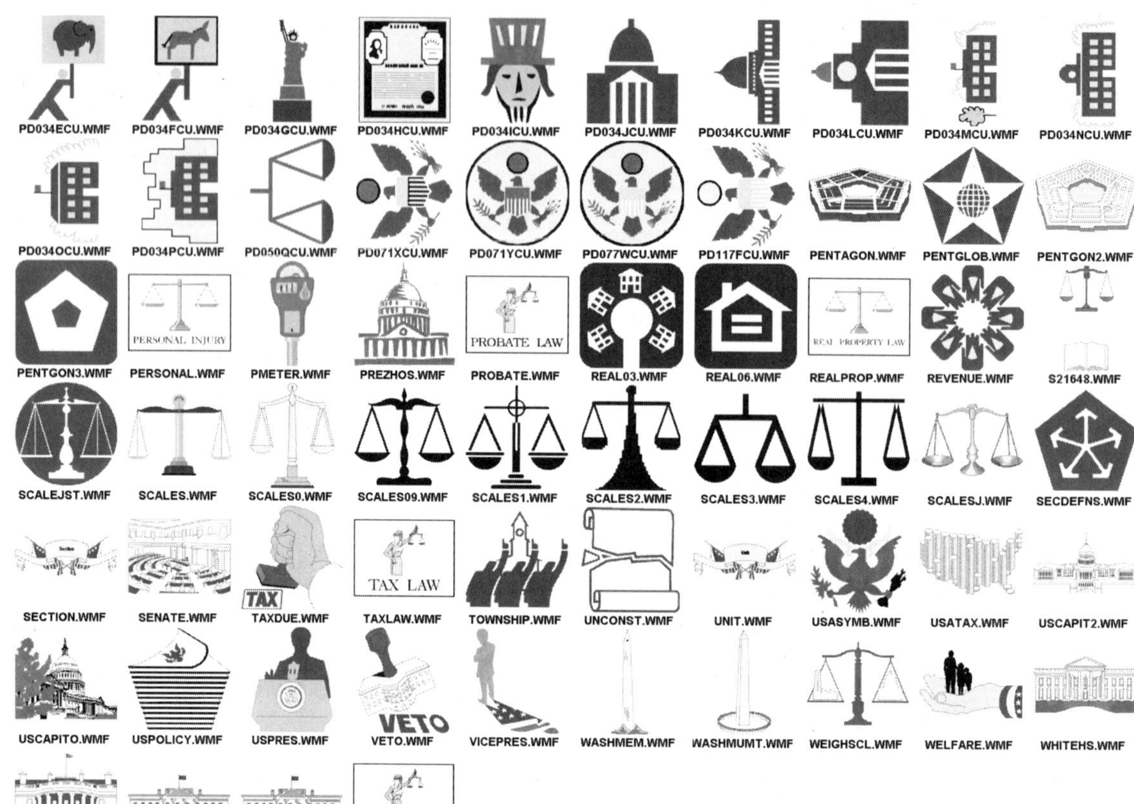
PD034ECU.WMF
PD034FCU.WMF
PD034GCU.WMF
PD034HCU.WMF
PD034ICU.WMF
PD034JCU.WMF
PD034KCU.WMF
PD034LCU.WMF
PD034MCU.WMF
PD034NCU.WMF
PD034OCU.WMF
PD034PCU.WMF
PD050QCU.WMF
PD071XCU.WMF
PD071YCU.WMF
PD077WCU.WMF
PD117FCU.WMF
PENTAGON.WMF
PENTGLOB.WMF
PENTGON2.WMF
PENTGON3.WMF
PERSONAL INJURY
PERSONAL.WMF
PMETER.WMF
PREZHOS.WMF
PROBATE LAW
PROBATE.WMF
REAL03.WMF
REAL06.WMF
REAL PROPERTY LAW
REALPROP.WMF
REVENUE.WMF
S21648.WMF
SCALEJST.WMF
SCALES.WMF
SCALES0.WMF
SCALES09.WMF
SCALES1.WMF
SCALES2.WMF
SCALES3.WMF
SCALES4.WMF
SCALESJ.WMF
SECDEFNS.WMF
SECTION.WMF
SENATE.WMF
TAX
TAXDUE.WMF
TAX LAW
TAXLAW.WMF
TOWNSHIP.WMF
UNCONST.WMF
UNIT.WMF
USASYMB.WMF
USATAX.WMF
USCAPIT2.WMF
USCAPITO.WMF
USPOLICY.WMF
USPRES.WMF
VETO
VETO.WMF
VICEPRES.WMF
WASHMEM.WMF
WASHMUMT.WMF
WEIGHSCL.WMF
WELFARE.WMF
WHITEHS.WMF
WHTHOUSE.WMF
WHTHSE.WMF
WHTHSE1.WMF
WORKERS COMPENSATION LAW
WORKCOMP.WMF

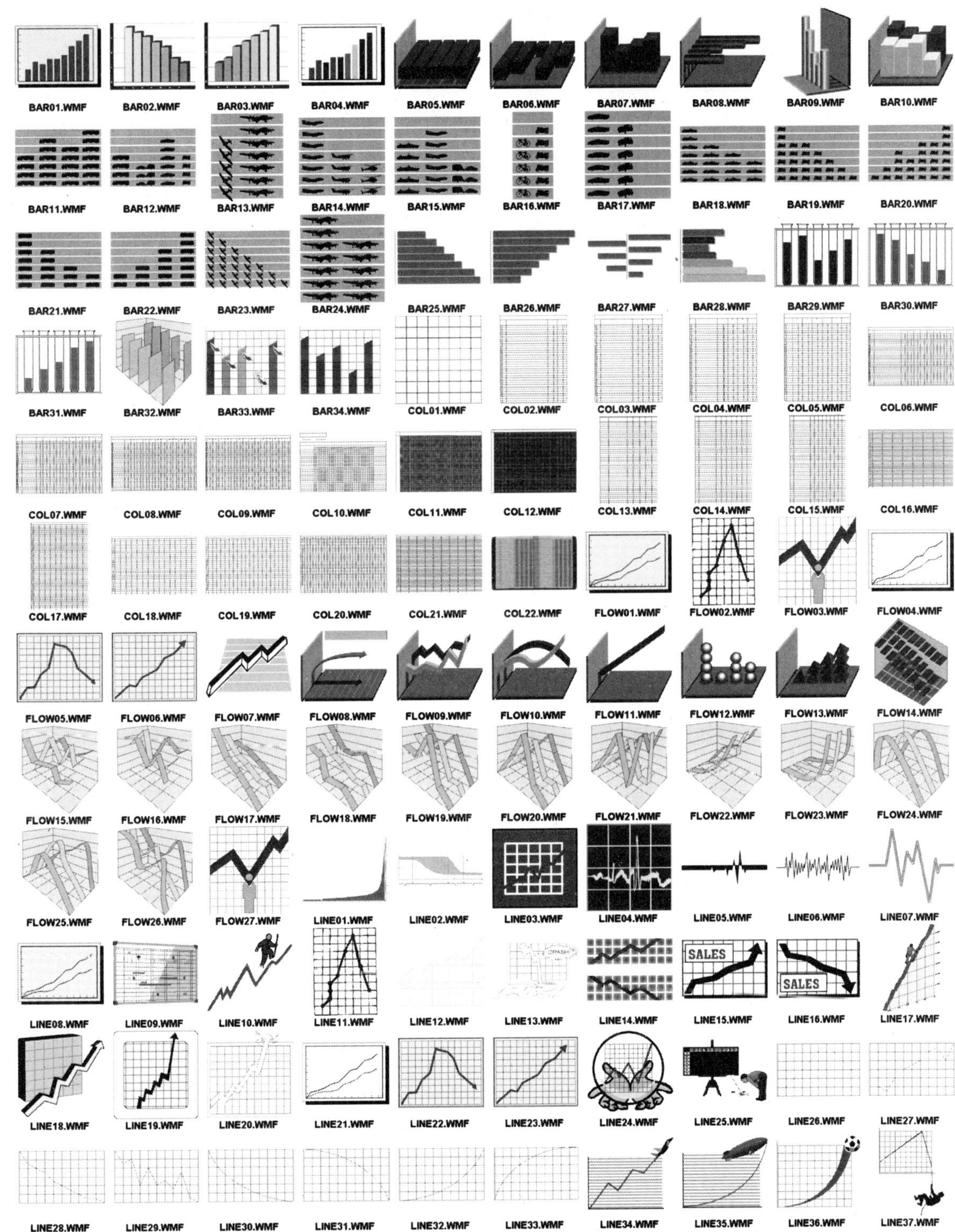
BAR01.WMF BAR02.WMF BAR03.WMF BAR04.WMF BAR05.WMF BAR06.WMF BAR07.WMF BAR08.WMF BAR09.WMF BAR10.WMF
BAR11.WMF BAR12.WMF BAR13.WMF BAR14.WMF BAR15.WMF BAR16.WMF BAR17.WMF BAR18.WMF BAR19.WMF BAR20.WMF
BAR21.WMF BAR22.WMF BAR23.WMF BAR24.WMF BAR25.WMF BAR26.WMF BAR27.WMF BAR28.WMF BAR29.WMF BAR30.WMF
BAR31.WMF BAR32.WMF BAR33.WMF BAR34.WMF COL01.WMF COL02.WMF COL03.WMF COL04.WMF COL05.WMF COL06.WMF
COL07.WMF COL08.WMF COL09.WMF COL10.WMF COL11.WMF COL12.WMF COL13.WMF COL14.WMF COL15.WMF COL16.WMF
COL17.WMF COL18.WMF COL19.WMF COL20.WMF COL21.WMF COL22.WMF FLOW01.WMF FLOW02.WMF FLOW03.WMF FLOW04.WMF
FLOW05.WMF FLOW06.WMF FLOW07.WMF FLOW08.WMF FLOW09.WMF FLOW10.WMF FLOW11.WMF FLOW12.WMF FLOW13.WMF FLOW14.WMF
FLOW15.WMF FLOW16.WMF FLOW17.WMF FLOW18.WMF FLOW19.WMF FLOW20.WMF FLOW21.WMF FLOW22.WMF FLOW23.WMF FLOW24.WMF
FLOW25.WMF FLOW26.WMF FLOW27.WMF LINE01.WMF LINE02.WMF LINE03.WMF LINE04.WMF LINE05.WMF LINE06.WMF LINE07.WMF
SALES
SALES
LINE08.WMF LINE09.WMF LINE10.WMF LINE11.WMF LINE12.WMF LINE13.WMF LINE14.WMF LINE15.WMF LINE16.WMF LINE17.WMF
LINE18.WMF LINE19.WMF LINE20.WMF LINE21.WMF LINE22.WMF LINE23.WMF LINE24.WMF LINE25.WMF LINE26.WMF LINE27.WMF
LINE28.WMF LINE29.WMF LINE30.WMF LINE31.WMF LINE32.WMF LINE33.WMF LINE34.WMF LINE35.WMF LINE36.WMF LINE37.WMF

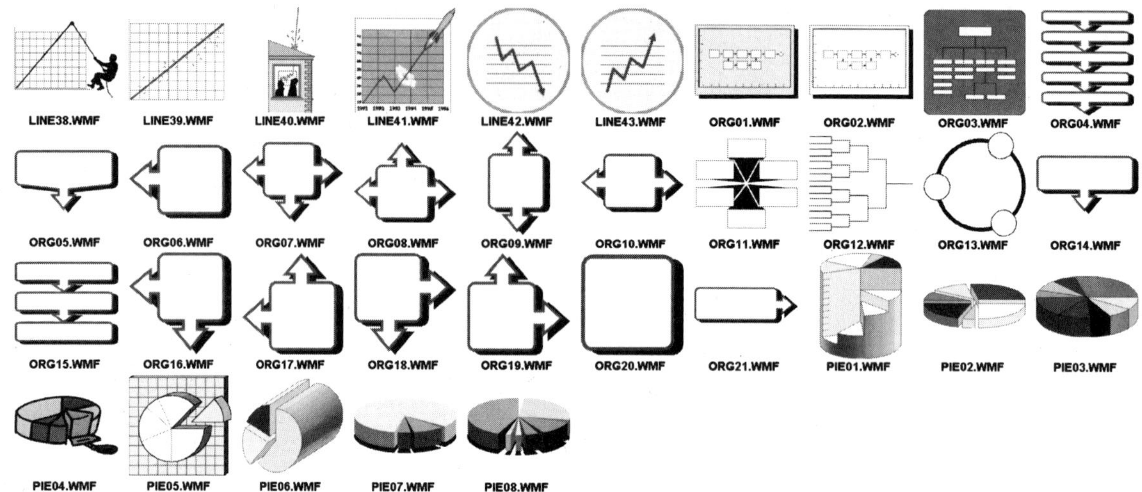

LINE38.WMF LINE39.WMF LINE40.WMF LINE41.WMF LINE42.WMF LINE43.WMF ORG01.WMF ORG02.WMF ORG03.WMF ORG04.WMF

ORG05.WMF ORG06.WMF ORG07.WMF ORG08.WMF ORG09.WMF ORG10.WMF ORG11.WMF ORG12.WMF ORG13.WMF ORG14.WMF

ORG15.WMF ORG16.WMF ORG17.WMF ORG18.WMF ORG19.WMF ORG20.WMF ORG21.WMF PIE01.WMF PIE02.WMF PIE03.WMF

PIE04.WMF PIE05.WMF PIE06.WMF PIE07.WMF PIE08.WMF

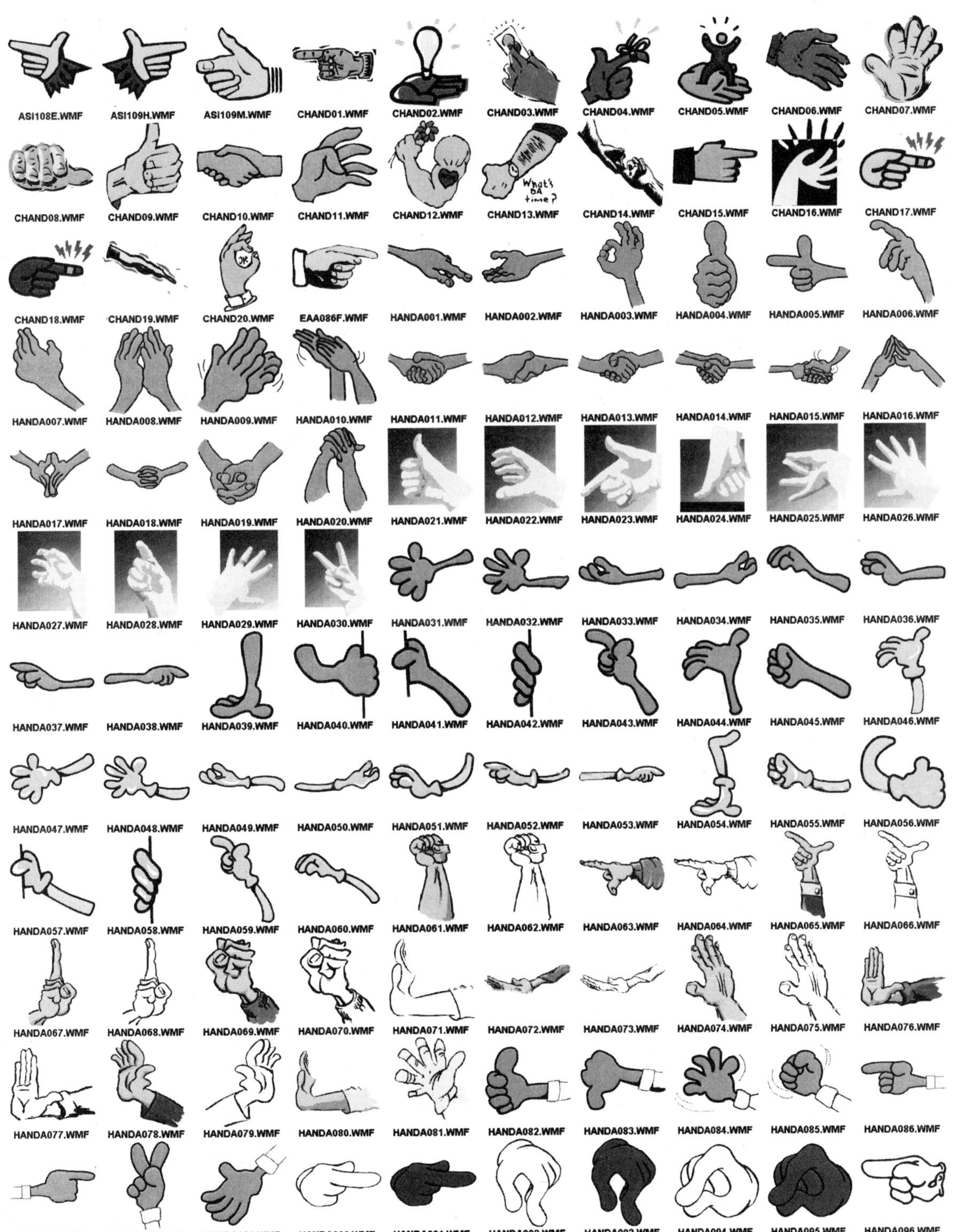

ASI108E.WMF ASI109H.WMF ASI109M.WMF CHAND01.WMF CHAND02.WMF CHAND03.WMF CHAND04.WMF CHAND05.WMF CHAND06.WMF CHAND07.WMF

CHAND08.WMF CHAND09.WMF CHAND10.WMF CHAND11.WMF CHAND12.WMF CHAND13.WMF CHAND14.WMF CHAND15.WMF CHAND16.WMF CHAND17.WMF

CHAND18.WMF CHAND19.WMF CHAND20.WMF EAA086F.WMF HANDA001.WMF HANDA002.WMF HANDA003.WMF HANDA004.WMF HANDA005.WMF HANDA006.WMF

HANDA007.WMF HANDA008.WMF HANDA009.WMF HANDA010.WMF HANDA011.WMF HANDA012.WMF HANDA013.WMF HANDA014.WMF HANDA015.WMF HANDA016.WMF

HANDA017.WMF HANDA018.WMF HANDA019.WMF HANDA020.WMF HANDA021.WMF HANDA022.WMF HANDA023.WMF HANDA024.WMF HANDA025.WMF HANDA026.WMF

HANDA027.WMF HANDA028.WMF HANDA029.WMF HANDA030.WMF HANDA031.WMF HANDA032.WMF HANDA033.WMF HANDA034.WMF HANDA035.WMF HANDA036.WMF

HANDA037.WMF HANDA038.WMF HANDA039.WMF HANDA040.WMF HANDA041.WMF HANDA042.WMF HANDA043.WMF HANDA044.WMF HANDA045.WMF HANDA046.WMF

HANDA047.WMF HANDA048.WMF HANDA049.WMF HANDA050.WMF HANDA051.WMF HANDA052.WMF HANDA053.WMF HANDA054.WMF HANDA055.WMF HANDA056.WMF

HANDA057.WMF HANDA058.WMF HANDA059.WMF HANDA060.WMF HANDA061.WMF HANDA062.WMF HANDA063.WMF HANDA064.WMF HANDA065.WMF HANDA066.WMF

HANDA067.WMF HANDA068.WMF HANDA069.WMF HANDA070.WMF HANDA071.WMF HANDA072.WMF HANDA073.WMF HANDA074.WMF HANDA075.WMF HANDA076.WMF

HANDA077.WMF HANDA078.WMF HANDA079.WMF HANDA080.WMF HANDA081.WMF HANDA082.WMF HANDA083.WMF HANDA084.WMF HANDA085.WMF HANDA086.WMF

HANDA087.WMF HANDA088.WMF HANDA089.WMF HANDA090.WMF HANDA091.WMF HANDA092.WMF HANDA093.WMF HANDA094.WMF HANDA095.WMF HANDA096.WMF

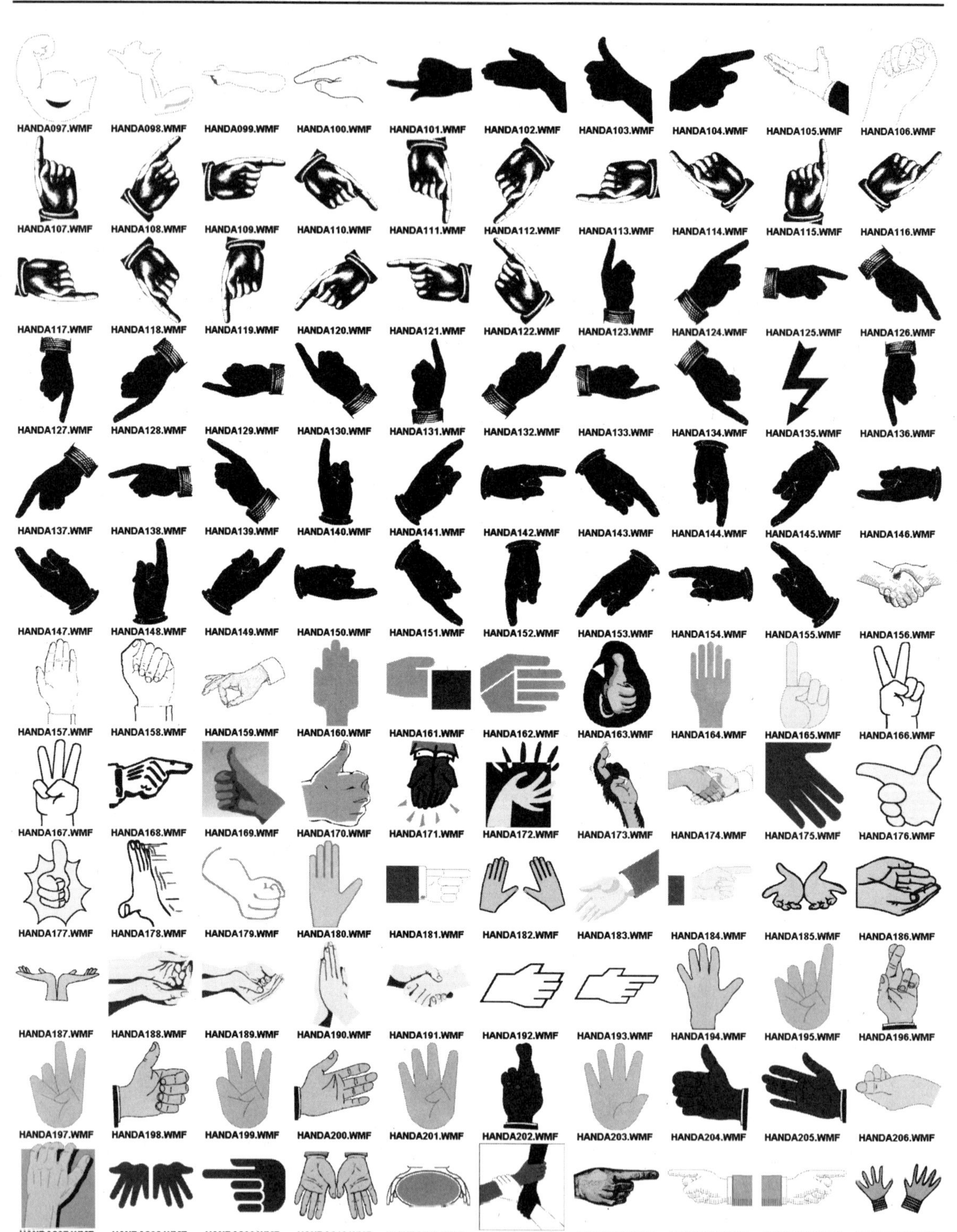
HANDA097.WMF
HANDA098.WMF
HANDA099.WMF
HANDA100.WMF
HANDA101.WMF
HANDA102.WMF
HANDA103.WMF
HANDA104.WMF
HANDA105.WMF
HANDA106.WMF
HANDA107.WMF
HANDA108.WMF
HANDA109.WMF
HANDA110.WMF
HANDA111.WMF
HANDA112.WMF
HANDA113.WMF
HANDA114.WMF
HANDA115.WMF
HANDA116.WMF
HANDA117.WMF
HANDA118.WMF
HANDA119.WMF
HANDA120.WMF
HANDA121.WMF
HANDA122.WMF
HANDA123.WMF
HANDA124.WMF
HANDA125.WMF
HANDA126.WMF
HANDA127.WMF
HANDA128.WMF
HANDA129.WMF
HANDA130.WMF
HANDA131.WMF
HANDA132.WMF
HANDA133.WMF
HANDA134.WMF
HANDA135.WMF
HANDA136.WMF
HANDA137.WMF
HANDA138.WMF
HANDA139.WMF
HANDA140.WMF
HANDA141.WMF
HANDA142.WMF
HANDA143.WMF
HANDA144.WMF
HANDA145.WMF
HANDA146.WMF
HANDA147.WMF
HANDA148.WMF
HANDA149.WMF
HANDA150.WMF
HANDA151.WMF
HANDA152.WMF
HANDA153.WMF
HANDA154.WMF
HANDA155.WMF
HANDA156.WMF
HANDA157.WMF
HANDA158.WMF
HANDA159.WMF
HANDA160.WMF
HANDA161.WMF
HANDA162.WMF
HANDA163.WMF
HANDA164.WMF
HANDA165.WMF
HANDA166.WMF
HANDA167.WMF
HANDA168.WMF
HANDA169.WMF
HANDA170.WMF
HANDA171.WMF
HANDA172.WMF
HANDA173.WMF
HANDA174.WMF
HANDA175.WMF
HANDA176.WMF
HANDA177.WMF
HANDA178.WMF
HANDA179.WMF
HANDA180.WMF
HANDA181.WMF
HANDA182.WMF
HANDA183.WMF
HANDA184.WMF
HANDA185.WMF
HANDA186.WMF
HANDA187.WMF
HANDA188.WMF
HANDA189.WMF
HANDA190.WMF
HANDA191.WMF
HANDA192.WMF
HANDA193.WMF
HANDA194.WMF
HANDA195.WMF
HANDA196.WMF
HANDA197.WMF
HANDA198.WMF
HANDA199.WMF
HANDA200.WMF
HANDA201.WMF
HANDA202.WMF
HANDA203.WMF
HANDA204.WMF
HANDA205.WMF
HANDA206.WMF
HANDA207.WMF
HANDA208.WMF
HANDA209.WMF
HANDA210.WMF
HANDA211.WMF
HANDA212.WMF
HANDA213.WMF
HANDA214.WMF
HANDA215.WMF
HANDA216.WMF

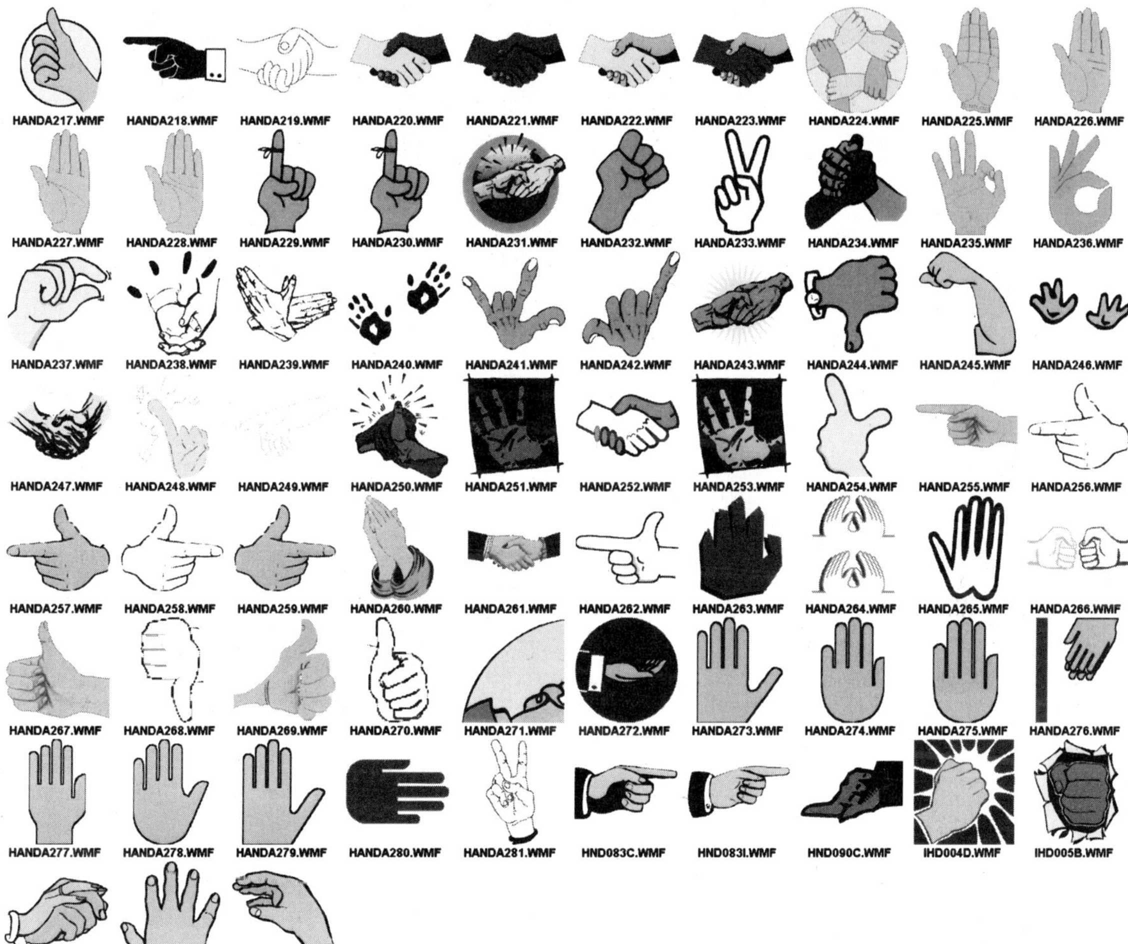
HANDA217.WMF
HANDA218.WMF
HANDA219.WMF
HANDA220.WMF
HANDA221.WMF
HANDA222.WMF
HANDA223.WMF
HANDA224.WMF
HANDA225.WMF
HANDA226.WMF
HANDA227.WMF
HANDA228.WMF
HANDA229.WMF
HANDA230.WMF
HANDA231.WMF
HANDA232.WMF
HANDA233.WMF
HANDA234.WMF
HANDA235.WMF
HANDA236.WMF
HANDA237.WMF
HANDA238.WMF
HANDA239.WMF
HANDA240.WMF
HANDA241.WMF
HANDA242.WMF
HANDA243.WMF
HANDA244.WMF
HANDA245.WMF
HANDA246.WMF
HANDA247.WMF
HANDA248.WMF
HANDA249.WMF
HANDA250.WMF
HANDA251.WMF
HANDA252.WMF
HANDA253.WMF
HANDA254.WMF
HANDA255.WMF
HANDA256.WMF
HANDA257.WMF
HANDA258.WMF
HANDA259.WMF
HANDA260.WMF
HANDA261.WMF
HANDA262.WMF
HANDA263.WMF
HANDA264.WMF
HANDA265.WMF
HANDA266.WMF
HANDA267.WMF
HANDA268.WMF
HANDA269.WMF
HANDA270.WMF
HANDA271.WMF
HANDA272.WMF
HANDA273.WMF
HANDA274.WMF
HANDA275.WMF
HANDA276.WMF
HANDA277.WMF
HANDA278.WMF
HANDA279.WMF
HANDA280.WMF
HANDA281.WMF
HND083C.WMF
HND083I.WMF
HND090C.WMF
IHD004D.WMF
IHD005B.WMF
IHD018C.WMF
SPA007B.WMF
SPA017A.WMF

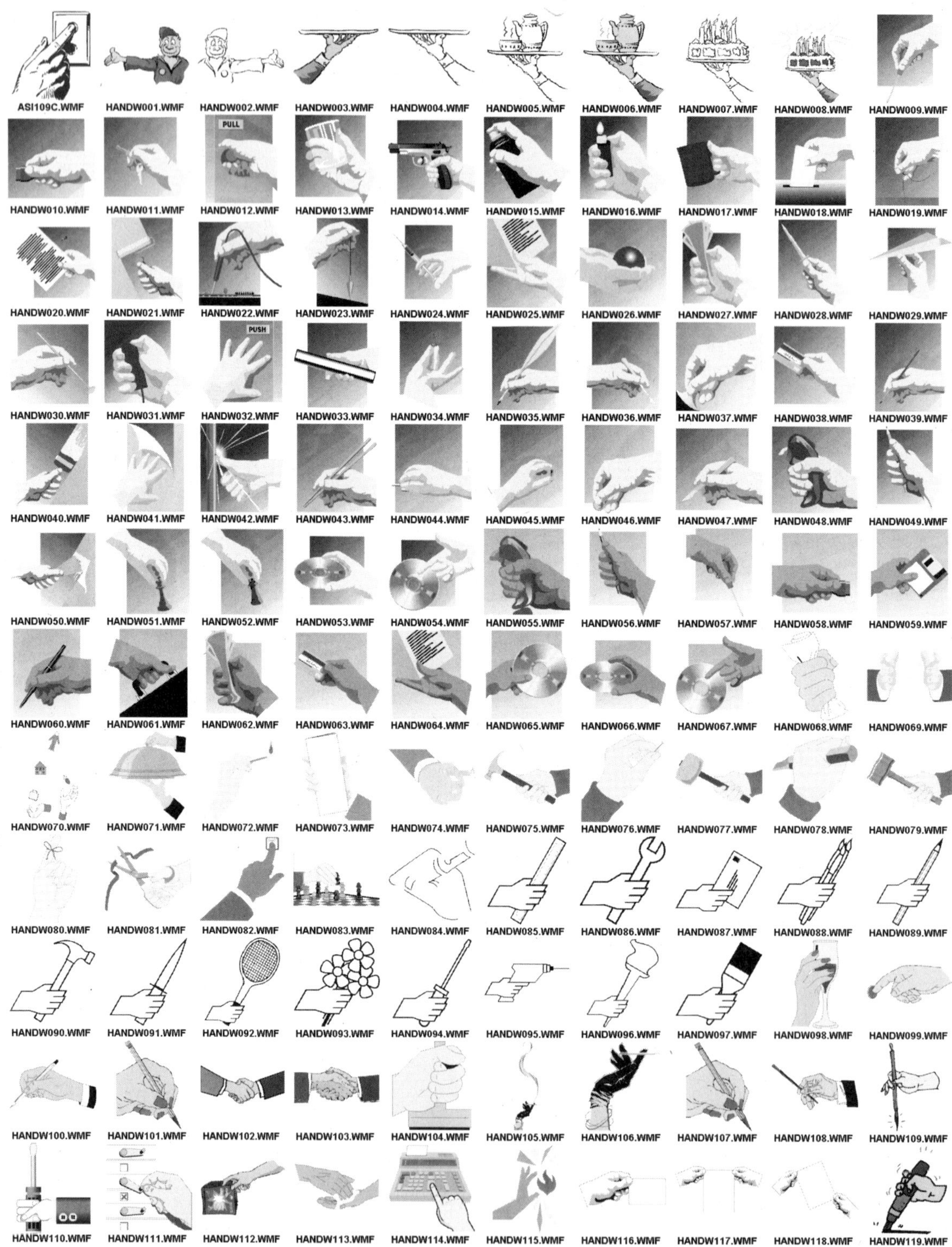
ASI109C.WMF HANDW001.WMF HANDW002.WMF HANDW003.WMF HANDW004.WMF HANDW005.WMF HANDW006.WMF HANDW007.WMF HANDW008.WMF HANDW009.WMF
PULL
HANDW010.WMF HANDW011.WMF HANDW012.WMF HANDW013.WMF HANDW014.WMF HANDW015.WMF HANDW016.WMF HANDW017.WMF HANDW018.WMF HANDW019.WMF
HANDW020.WMF HANDW021.WMF HANDW022.WMF HANDW023.WMF HANDW024.WMF HANDW025.WMF HANDW026.WMF HANDW027.WMF HANDW028.WMF HANDW029.WMF
PUSH
HANDW030.WMF HANDW031.WMF HANDW032.WMF HANDW033.WMF HANDW034.WMF HANDW035.WMF HANDW036.WMF HANDW037.WMF HANDW038.WMF HANDW039.WMF
HANDW040.WMF HANDW041.WMF HANDW042.WMF HANDW043.WMF HANDW044.WMF HANDW045.WMF HANDW046.WMF HANDW047.WMF HANDW048.WMF HANDW049.WMF
HANDW050.WMF HANDW051.WMF HANDW052.WMF HANDW053.WMF HANDW054.WMF HANDW055.WMF HANDW056.WMF HANDW057.WMF HANDW058.WMF HANDW059.WMF
HANDW060.WMF HANDW061.WMF HANDW062.WMF HANDW063.WMF HANDW064.WMF HANDW065.WMF HANDW066.WMF HANDW067.WMF HANDW068.WMF HANDW069.WMF
HANDW070.WMF HANDW071.WMF HANDW072.WMF HANDW073.WMF HANDW074.WMF HANDW075.WMF HANDW076.WMF HANDW077.WMF HANDW078.WMF HANDW079.WMF
HANDW080.WMF HANDW081.WMF HANDW082.WMF HANDW083.WMF HANDW084.WMF HANDW085.WMF HANDW086.WMF HANDW087.WMF HANDW088.WMF HANDW089.WMF
HANDW090.WMF HANDW091.WMF HANDW092.WMF HANDW093.WMF HANDW094.WMF HANDW095.WMF HANDW096.WMF HANDW097.WMF HANDW098.WMF HANDW099.WMF
HANDW100.WMF HANDW101.WMF HANDW102.WMF HANDW103.WMF HANDW104.WMF HANDW105.WMF HANDW106.WMF HANDW107.WMF HANDW108.WMF HANDW109.WMF
HANDW110.WMF HANDW111.WMF HANDW112.WMF HANDW113.WMF HANDW114.WMF HANDW115.WMF HANDW116.WMF HANDW117.WMF HANDW118.WMF HANDW119.WMF

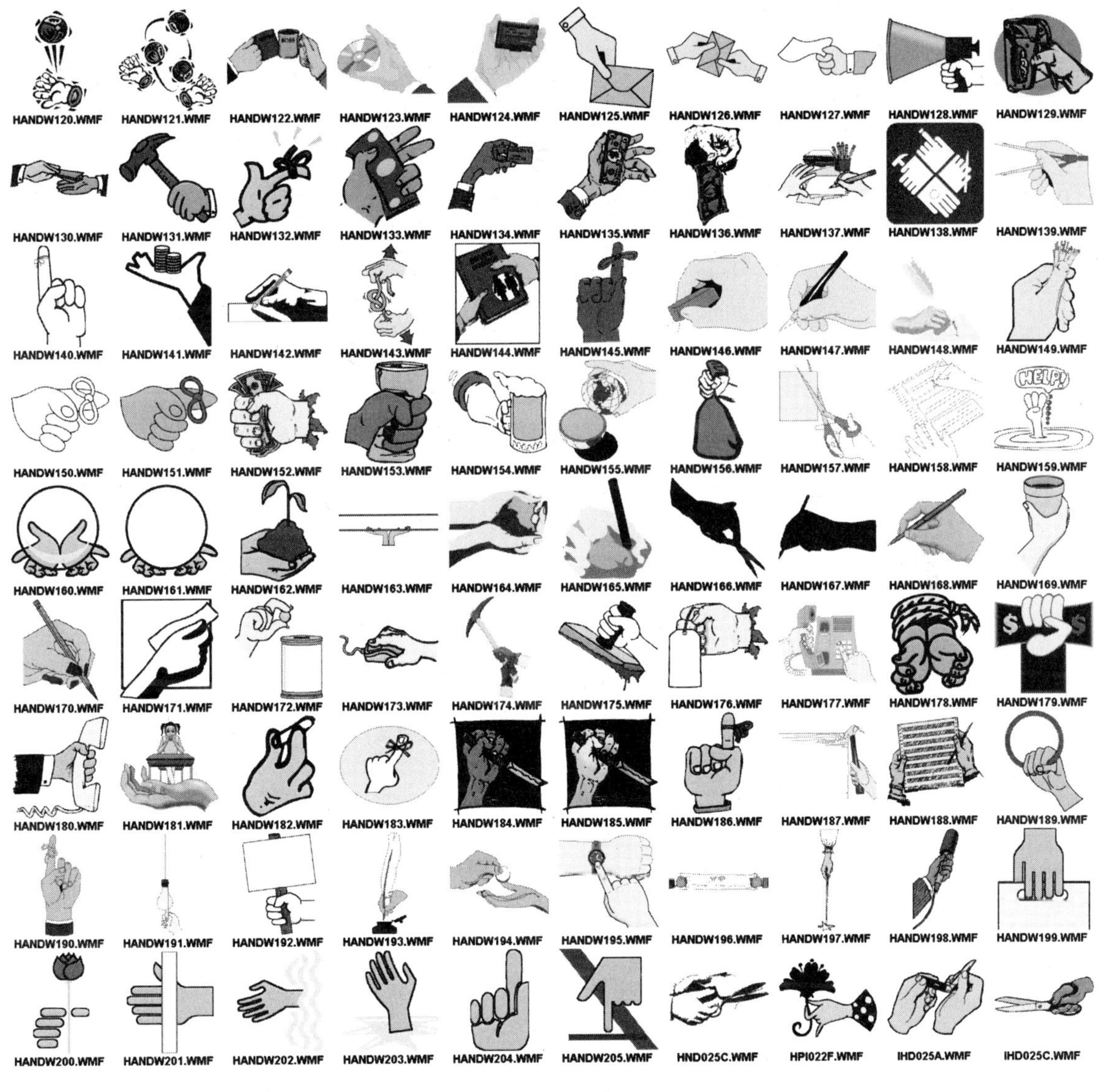
HANDW120.WMF HANDW121.WMF HANDW122.WMF HANDW123.WMF HANDW124.WMF HANDW125.WMF HANDW126.WMF HANDW127.WMF HANDW128.WMF HANDW129.WMF
HANDW130.WMF HANDW131.WMF HANDW132.WMF HANDW133.WMF HANDW134.WMF HANDW135.WMF HANDW136.WMF HANDW137.WMF HANDW138.WMF HANDW139.WMF
HANDW140.WMF HANDW141.WMF HANDW142.WMF HANDW143.WMF HANDW144.WMF HANDW145.WMF HANDW146.WMF HANDW147.WMF HANDW148.WMF HANDW149.WMF
HELP!
HANDW150.WMF HANDW151.WMF HANDW152.WMF HANDW153.WMF HANDW154.WMF HANDW155.WMF HANDW156.WMF HANDW157.WMF HANDW158.WMF HANDW159.WMF
HANDW160.WMF HANDW161.WMF HANDW162.WMF HANDW163.WMF HANDW164.WMF HANDW165.WMF HANDW166.WMF HANDW167.WMF HANDW168.WMF HANDW169.WMF
HANDW170.WMF HANDW171.WMF HANDW172.WMF HANDW173.WMF HANDW174.WMF HANDW175.WMF HANDW176.WMF HANDW177.WMF HANDW178.WMF HANDW179.WMF
HANDW180.WMF HANDW181.WMF HANDW182.WMF HANDW183.WMF HANDW184.WMF HANDW185.WMF HANDW186.WMF HANDW187.WMF HANDW188.WMF HANDW189.WMF
HANDW190.WMF HANDW191.WMF HANDW192.WMF HANDW193.WMF HANDW194.WMF HANDW195.WMF HANDW196.WMF HANDW197.WMF HANDW198.WMF HANDW199.WMF
HANDW200.WMF HANDW201.WMF HANDW202.WMF HANDW203.WMF HANDW204.WMF HANDW205.WMF HND025C.WMF HPI022F.WMF IHD025A.WMF IHD025C.WMF

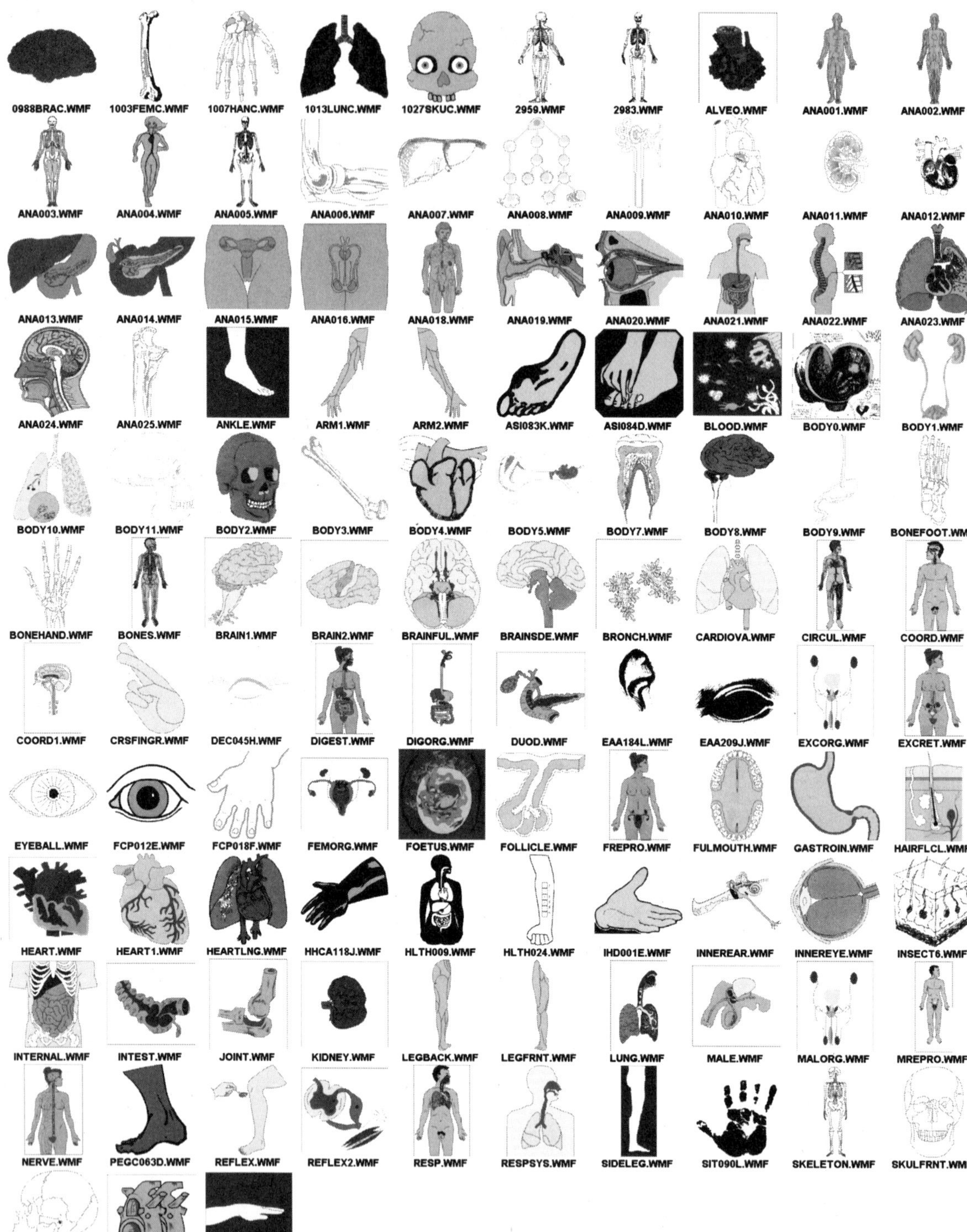
0988BRAC.WMF
1003FEMC.WMF
1007HANC.WMF
1013LUNC.WMF
1027SKUC.WMF
2959.WMF
2983.WMF
ALVEO.WMF
ANA001.WMF
ANA002.WMF
ANA003.WMF
ANA004.WMF
ANA005.WMF
ANA006.WMF
ANA007.WMF
ANA008.WMF
ANA009.WMF
ANA010.WMF
ANA011.WMF
ANA012.WMF
ANA013.WMF
ANA014.WMF
ANA015.WMF
ANA016.WMF
ANA018.WMF
ANA019.WMF
ANA020.WMF
ANA021.WMF
ANA022.WMF
ANA023.WMF
ANA024.WMF
ANA025.WMF
ANKLE.WMF
ARM1.WMF
ARM2.WMF
ASI083K.WMF
ASI084D.WMF
BLOOD.WMF
BODY0.WMF
BODY1.WMF
BODY10.WMF
BODY11.WMF
BODY2.WMF
BODY3.WMF
BODY4.WMF
BODY5.WMF
BODY7.WMF
BODY8.WMF
BODY9.WMF
BONEFOOT.WMF
BONEHAND.WMF
BONES.WMF
BRAIN1.WMF
BRAIN2.WMF
BRAINFUL.WMF
BRAINSDE.WMF
BRONCH.WMF
CARDIOVA.WMF
CIRCUL.WMF
COORD.WMF
COORD1.WMF
CRSFINGR.WMF
DEC045H.WMF
DIGEST.WMF
DIGORG.WMF
DUOD.WMF
EAA184L.WMF
EAA209J.WMF
EXCORG.WMF
EXCRET.WMF
EYEBALL.WMF
FCP012E.WMF
FCP018F.WMF
FEMORG.WMF
FOETUS.WMF
FOLLICLE.WMF
FREPRO.WMF
FULMOUTH.WMF
GASTROIN.WMF
HAIRFLCL.WMF
HEART.WMF
HEART1.WMF
HEARTLNG.WMF
HHCA118J.WMF
HLTH009.WMF
HLTH024.WMF
IHD001E.WMF
INNEREAR.WMF
INNEREYE.WMF
INSECT6.WMF
INTERNAL.WMF
INTEST.WMF
JOINT.WMF
KIDNEY.WMF
LEGBACK.WMF
LEGFRNT.WMF
LUNG.WMF
MALE.WMF
MALORG.WMF
MREPRO.WMF
NERVE.WMF
PEGC063D.WMF
REFLEX.WMF
REFLEX2.WMF
RESP.WMF
RESPSYS.WMF
SIDELEG.WMF
SIT090L.WMF
SKELETON.WMF
SKULFRNT.WMF
SKULSIDE.WMF
VERTEB.WMF
WRIST.WMF

0135.WMF 0158.WMF 0993DERC.WMF 0997.WMF 0998.WMF 235.WMF 236.WMF 237.WMF 238.WMF 239.WMF
2907.WMF AMBULAN.WMF ASI010O.WMF B20064.WMF BANDFNGR.WMF CRTN181.WMF CRTN184.WMF DCTRNRS.WMF DOC.WMF DOCCHILD.WMF
DOCPATNT.WMF DOCTOR.WMF DOCTOR_H.WMF DOCTORR.WMF DOCTORS.WMF DOCTORW.WMF DOCTRS.WMF DOCTRW.WMF DOCWSTO.WMF EYEDOC.WMF
Medical
FCP010C.WMF FCP028D.WMF FCP029A.WMF FCP044C.WMF FEMALE_D.WMF GASI105M.WMF GOOFYDOC.WMF HANDMED.WMF HEADACHE.WMF HEART.WMF
HECA001J.WMF HEGC001D.WMF HEGC001K.WMF HEGC002J.WMF HEGC003D.WMF HEGC003J.WMF HEGC004D.WMF HEGC004J.WMF HEGC005D.WMF HEGC005J.WMF
HEGC006D.WMF HEGC007D.WMF HEGC008D.WMF HEGC009D.WMF HEGC010D.WMF HEGC011D.WMF HEGC012D.WMF HEGC013D.WMF HEGC014D.WMF HEGC015D.WMF
HEGC016D.WMF HEGC018D.WMF HEGC019D.WMF HERW001J.WMF HERW002J.WMF HERW003J.WMF HERW004J.WMF HERW005J.WMF HERW006J.WMF HERW007J.WMF
HERW008J.WMF HESI003D.WMF HESI003M.WMF HHBO016J.WMF HHCA103J.WMF HLTH006.WMF HLTH021.WMF HLTH022.WMF HLTH037.WMF HLTH039.WMF
HLTH041.WMF HLTH042.WMF HLTH044.WMF HLTH045.WMF HLTH048.WMF HLTH049.WMF HLTH083.WMF HLTH095.WMF HLTH096.WMF HLTH097.WMF
HLTH098.WMF HLTH099.WMF HLTH100.WMF HLTH108.WMF HLTH139.WMF HLTH140.WMF HLTH141.WMF HLTH142.WMF HLTH143.WMF HLTH144.WMF
HLTH145.WMF HLTH147.WMF HOTWATE.WMF INGC022D.WMF INJURY.WMF INJURYC.WMF IVART.WMF JOLLYROG.WMF LAB_TECH.WMF MALE_DOC.WMF
MAN_WITH.WMF MANDENT.WMF MANORDE.WMF MD01.WMF MD13.WMF MD14.WMF MD15.WMF MD16.WMF MD17.WMF MD18.WMF

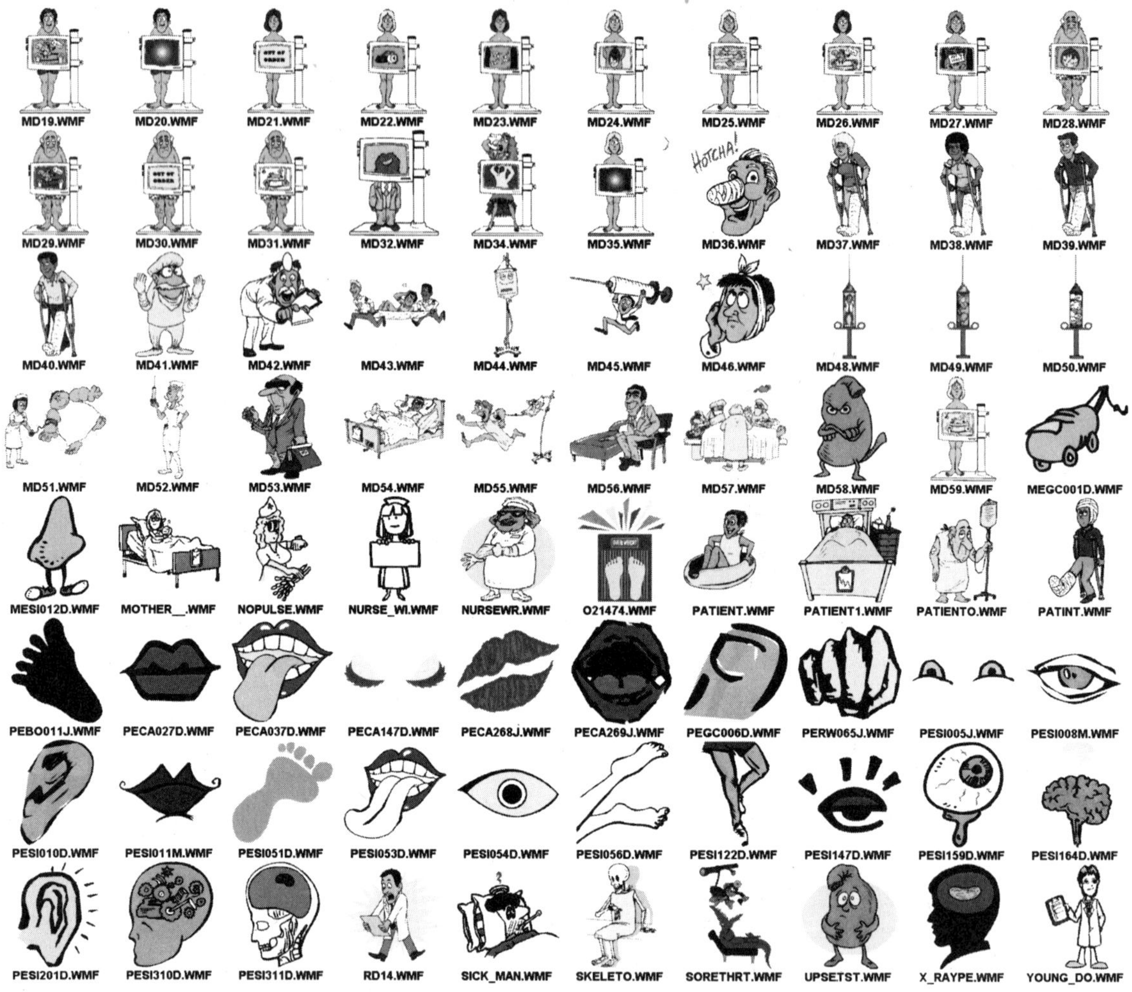
MD19.WMF MD20.WMF MD21.WMF MD22.WMF MD23.WMF MD24.WMF MD25.WMF MD26.WMF MD27.WMF MD28.WMF
HOTCHA!
MD29.WMF MD30.WMF MD31.WMF MD32.WMF MD34.WMF MD35.WMF MD36.WMF MD37.WMF MD38.WMF MD39.WMF
MD40.WMF MD41.WMF MD42.WMF MD43.WMF MD44.WMF MD45.WMF MD46.WMF MD48.WMF MD49.WMF MD50.WMF
MD51.WMF MD52.WMF MD53.WMF MD54.WMF MD55.WMF MD56.WMF MD57.WMF MD58.WMF MD59.WMF MEGC001D.WMF
MESI012D.WMF MOTHER__.WMF NOPULSE.WMF NURSE_WI.WMF NURSEWR.WMF O21474.WMF PATIENT.WMF PATIENT1.WMF PATIENTO.WMF PATINT.WMF
PEBO011J.WMF PECA027D.WMF PECA037D.WMF PECA147D.WMF PECA268J.WMF PECA269J.WMF PEGC006D.WMF PERW065J.WMF PESI005J.WMF PESI008M.WMF
PESI010D.WMF PESI011M.WMF PESI051D.WMF PESI053D.WMF PESI054D.WMF PESI056D.WMF PESI122D.WMF PESI147D.WMF PESI159D.WMF PESI164D.WMF
PESI201D.WMF PESI310D.WMF PESI311D.WMF RD14.WMF SICK_MAN.WMF SKELETO.WMF SORETHRT.WMF UPSETST.WMF X_RAYPE.WMF YOUNG_DO.WMF

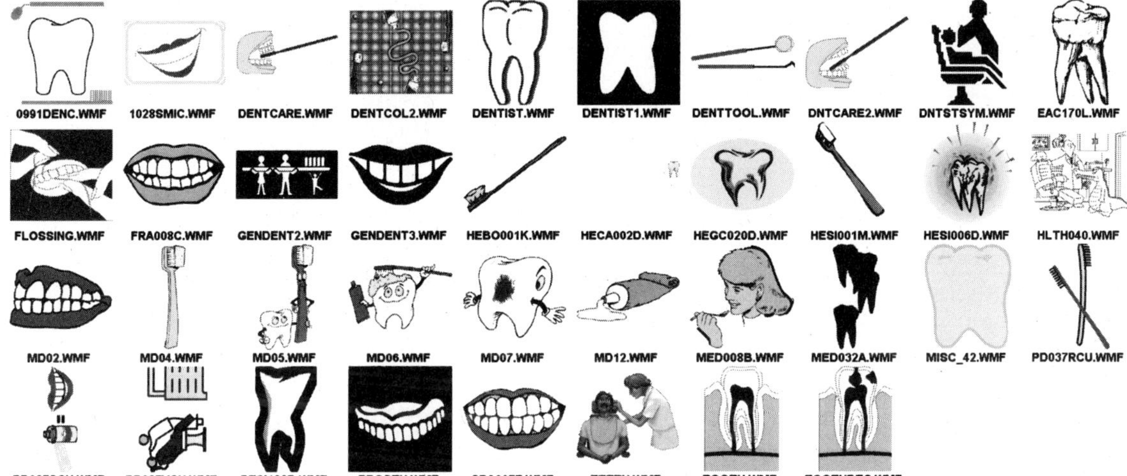
0991DENC.WMF
1028SMIC.WMF
DENTCARE.WMF
DENTCOL2.WMF
DENTIST.WMF
DENTIST1.WMF
DENTTOOL.WMF
DNTCARE2.WMF
DNTSTSYM.WMF
EAC170L.WMF
FLOSSING.WMF
FRA008C.WMF
GENDENT2.WMF
GENDENT3.WMF
HEBO001K.WMF
HECA002D.WMF
HEGC020D.WMF
HESI001M.WMF
HESI006D.WMF
HLTH040.WMF
MD02.WMF
MD04.WMF
MD05.WMF
MD06.WMF
MD07.WMF
MD12.WMF
MED008B.WMF
MED032A.WMF
MISC_42.WMF
PD037RCU.WMF
PD037SCU.WMF
PD037VCU.WMF
PESI126D.WMF
PROSTH.WMF
SPA007F.WMF
TEETH.WMF
TOOTH.WMF
TOOTHDEC.WMF

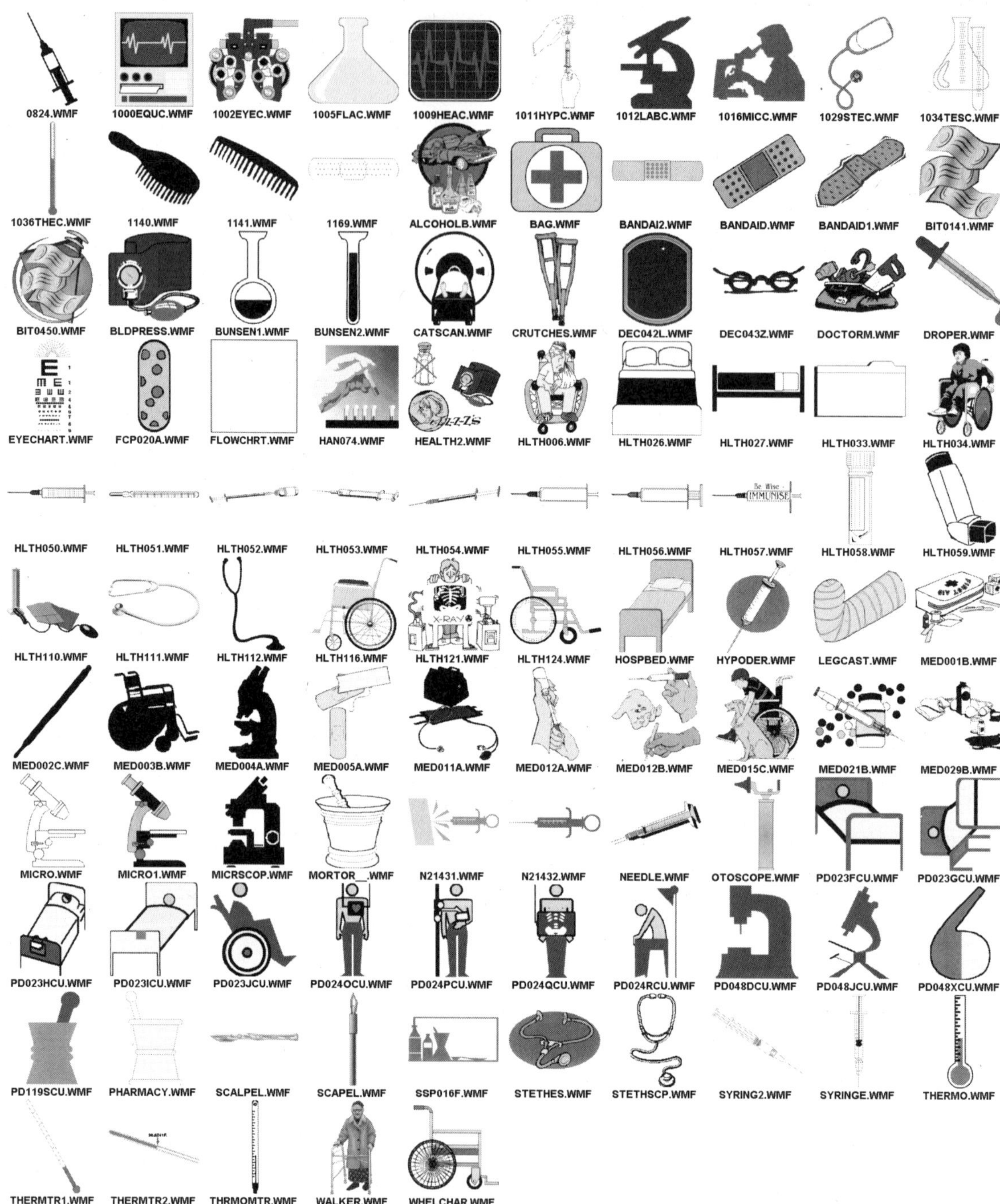

0824.WMF 1000EQUC.WMF 1002EYEC.WMF 1005FLAC.WMF 1009HEAC.WMF 1011HYPC.WMF 1012LABC.WMF 1016MICC.WMF 1029STEC.WMF 1034TESC.WMF

1036THEC.WMF 1140.WMF 1141.WMF 1169.WMF ALCOHOLB.WMF BAG.WMF BANDAI2.WMF BANDAID.WMF BANDAID1.WMF BIT0141.WMF

BIT0450.WMF BLDPRESS.WMF BUNSEN1.WMF BUNSEN2.WMF CATSCAN.WMF CRUTCHES.WMF DEC042L.WMF DEC043Z.WMF DOCTORM.WMF DROPER.WMF

EYECHART.WMF FCP020A.WMF FLOWCHRT.WMF HAN074.WMF HEALTH2.WMF HLTH006.WMF HLTH026.WMF HLTH027.WMF HLTH033.WMF HLTH034.WMF

HLTH050.WMF HLTH051.WMF HLTH052.WMF HLTH053.WMF HLTH054.WMF HLTH055.WMF HLTH056.WMF HLTH057.WMF HLTH058.WMF HLTH059.WMF

HLTH110.WMF HLTH111.WMF HLTH112.WMF HLTH116.WMF HLTH121.WMF HLTH124.WMF HOSPBED.WMF HYPODER.WMF LEGCAST.WMF MED001B.WMF

MED002C.WMF MED003B.WMF MED004A.WMF MED005A.WMF MED011A.WMF MED012A.WMF MED012B.WMF MED015C.WMF MED021B.WMF MED029B.WMF

MICRO.WMF MICRO1.WMF MICRSCOP.WMF MORTOR__.WMF N21431.WMF N21432.WMF NEEDLE.WMF OTOSCOPE.WMF PD023FCU.WMF PD023GCU.WMF

PD023HCU.WMF PD023ICU.WMF PD023JCU.WMF PD024OCU.WMF PD024PCU.WMF PD024QCU.WMF PD024RCU.WMF PD048DCU.WMF PD048JCU.WMF PD048XCU.WMF

PD119SCU.WMF PHARMACY.WMF SCALPEL.WMF SCAPEL.WMF SSP016F.WMF STETHES.WMF STETHSCP.WMF SYRING2.WMF SYRINGE.WMF THERMO.WMF

THERMTR1.WMF THERMTR2.WMF THRMOMTR.WMF WALKER.WMF WHELCHAR.WMF

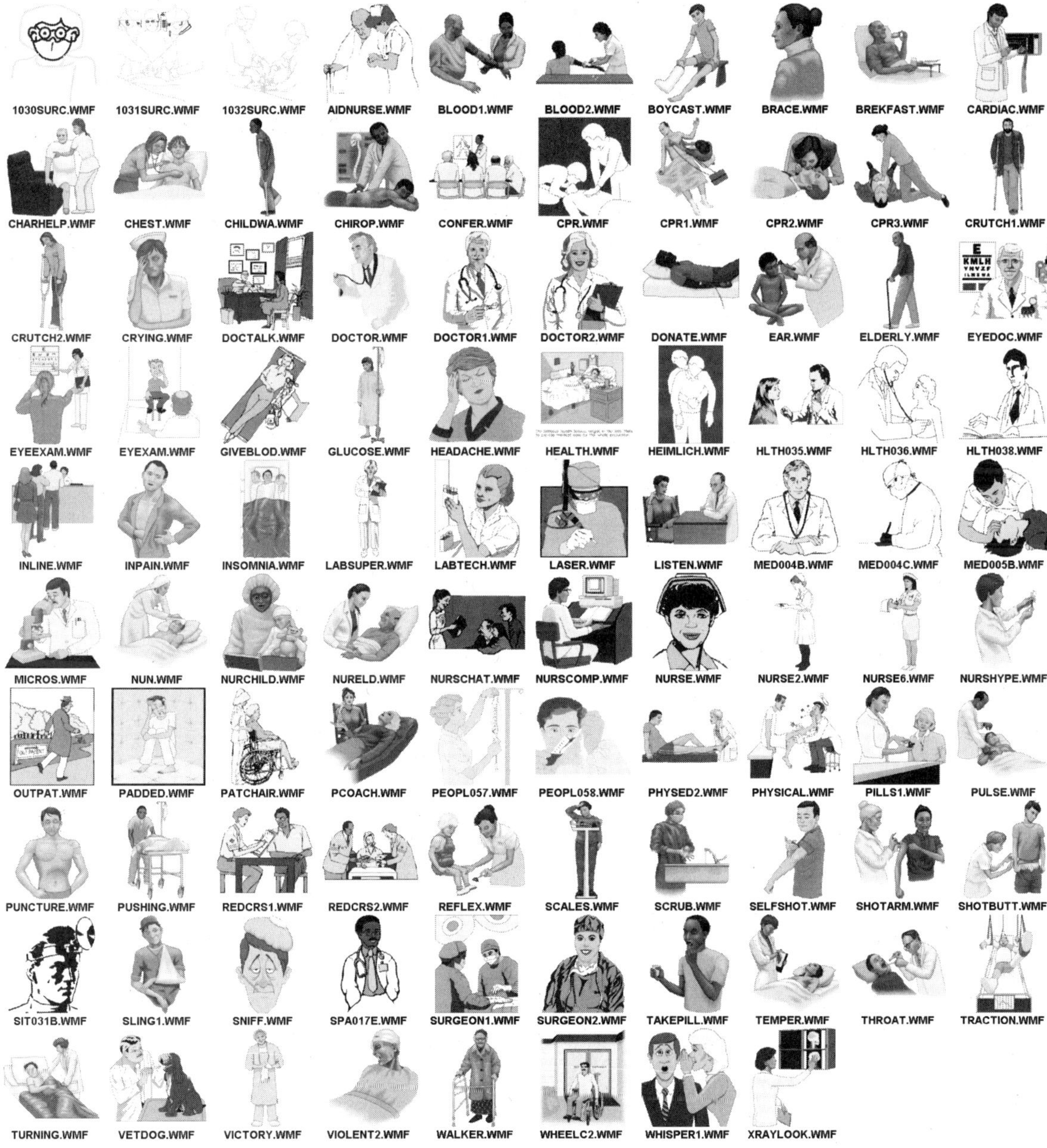
1030SURC.WMF 1031SURC.WMF 1032SURC.WMF AIDNURSE.WMF BLOOD1.WMF BLOOD2.WMF BOYCAST.WMF BRACE.WMF BREKFAST.WMF CARDIAC.WMF
CHARHELP.WMF CHEST.WMF CHILDWA.WMF CHIROP.WMF CONFER.WMF CPR.WMF CPR1.WMF CPR2.WMF CPR3.WMF CRUTCH1.WMF
CRUTCH2.WMF CRYING.WMF DOCTALK.WMF DOCTOR.WMF DOCTOR1.WMF DOCTOR2.WMF DONATE.WMF EAR.WMF ELDERLY.WMF EYEDOC.WMF
EYEEXAM.WMF EYEXAM.WMF GIVEBLOD.WMF GLUCOSE.WMF HEADACHE.WMF HEALTH.WMF HEIMLICH.WMF HLTH035.WMF HLTH036.WMF HLTH038.WMF
INLINE.WMF INPAIN.WMF INSOMNIA.WMF LABSUPER.WMF LABTECH.WMF LASER.WMF LISTEN.WMF MED004B.WMF MED004C.WMF MED005B.WMF
MICROS.WMF NUN.WMF NURCHILD.WMF NURELD.WMF NURSCHAT.WMF NURSCOMP.WMF NURSE.WMF NURSE2.WMF NURSE6.WMF NURSHYPE.WMF
OUTPAT.WMF PADDED.WMF PATCHAIR.WMF PCOACH.WMF PEOPL057.WMF PEOPL058.WMF PHYSED2.WMF PHYSICAL.WMF PILLS1.WMF PULSE.WMF
PUNCTURE.WMF PUSHING.WMF REDCRS1.WMF REDCRS2.WMF REFLEX.WMF SCALES.WMF SCRUB.WMF SELFSHOT.WMF SHOTARM.WMF SHOTBUTT.WMF
SIT031B.WMF SLING1.WMF SNIFF.WMF SPA017E.WMF SURGEON1.WMF SURGEON2.WMF TAKEPILL.WMF TEMPER.WMF THROAT.WMF TRACTION.WMF
TURNING.WMF VETDOG.WMF VICTORY.WMF VIOLENT2.WMF WALKER.WMF WHEELC2.WMF WHISPER1.WMF XRAYLOOK.WMF

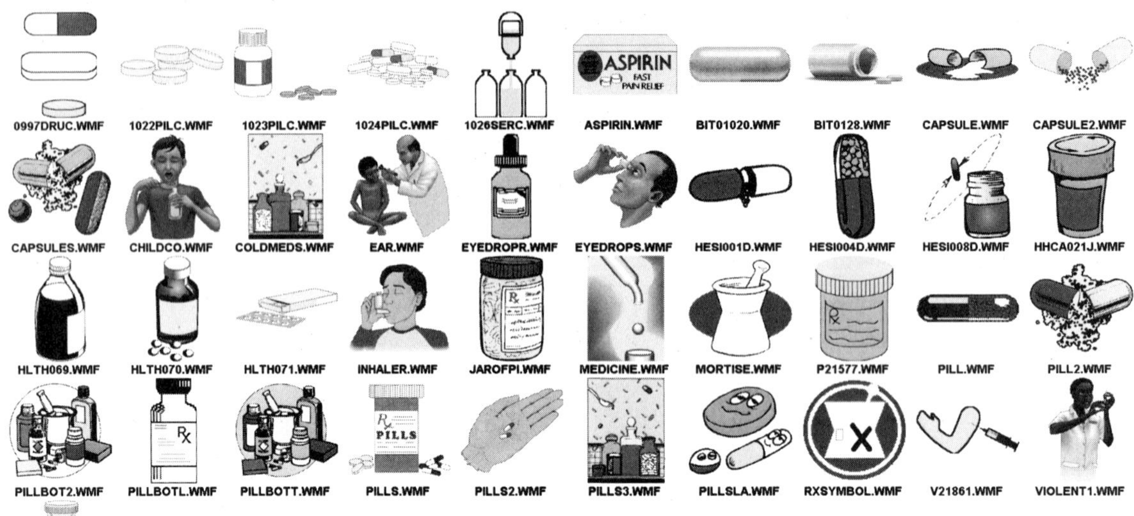

VITAMINS
VITAMINS.WMF

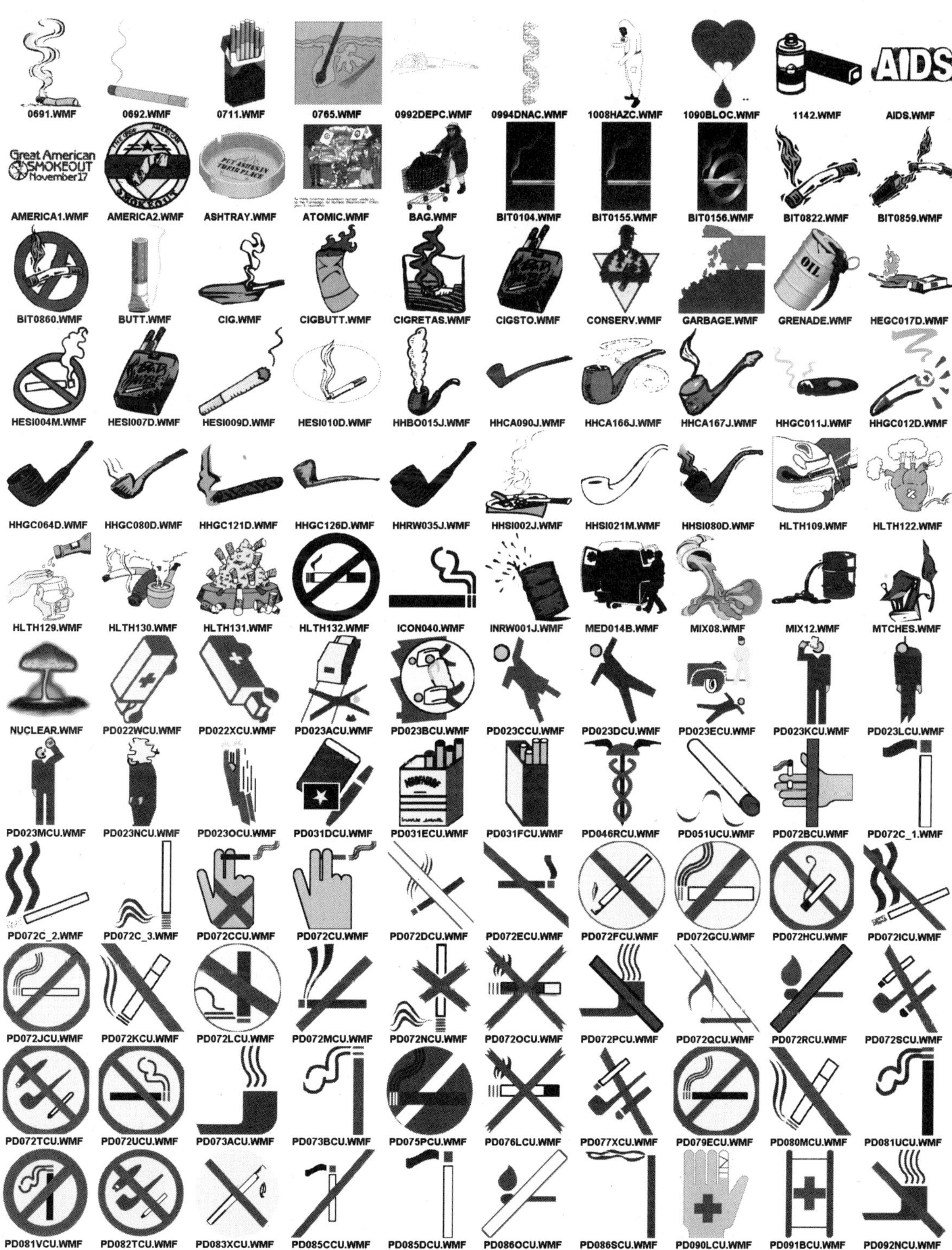
AIDS
Great American
SMOKEOUT
November 17
0691.WMF 0692.WMF 0711.WMF 0765.WMF 0992DEPC.WMF 0994DNAC.WMF 1008HAZC.WMF 1090BLOC.WMF 1142.WMF AIDS.WMF
AMERICA1.WMF AMERICA2.WMF ASHTRAY.WMF ATOMIC.WMF BAG.WMF BIT0104.WMF BIT0155.WMF BIT0156.WMF BIT0822.WMF BIT0859.WMF
BIT0860.WMF BUTT.WMF CIG.WMF CIGBUTT.WMF CIGRETAS.WMF CIGSTO.WMF CONSERV.WMF GARBAGE.WMF GRENADE.WMF HEGC017D.WMF
HESI004M.WMF HESI007D.WMF HESI009D.WMF HESI010D.WMF HHBO015J.WMF HHCA090J.WMF HHCA166J.WMF HHCA167J.WMF HHGC011J.WMF HHGC012D.WMF
HHGC064D.WMF HHGC080D.WMF HHGC121D.WMF HHGC126D.WMF HHRW035J.WMF HHSI002J.WMF HHSI021M.WMF HHSI080D.WMF HLTH109.WMF HLTH122.WMF
HLTH129.WMF HLTH130.WMF HLTH131.WMF HLTH132.WMF ICON040.WMF INRW001J.WMF MED014B.WMF MIX08.WMF MIX12.WMF MTCHES.WMF
NUCLEAR.WMF PD022WCU.WMF PD022XCU.WMF PD023ACU.WMF PD023BCU.WMF PD023CCU.WMF PD023DCU.WMF PD023ECU.WMF PD023KCU.WMF PD023LCU.WMF
PD023MCU.WMF PD023NCU.WMF PD023OCU.WMF PD031DCU.WMF PD031ECU.WMF PD031FCU.WMF PD046RCU.WMF PD051UCU.WMF PD072BCU.WMF PD072C_1.WMF
PD072C_2.WMF PD072C_3.WMF PD072CCU.WMF PD072CU.WMF PD072DCU.WMF PD072ECU.WMF PD072FCU.WMF PD072GCU.WMF PD072HCU.WMF PD072ICU.WMF
PD072JCU.WMF PD072KCU.WMF PD072LCU.WMF PD072MCU.WMF PD072NCU.WMF PD072OCU.WMF PD072PCU.WMF PD072QCU.WMF PD072RCU.WMF PD072SCU.WMF
PD072TCU.WMF PD072UCU.WMF PD073ACU.WMF PD073BCU.WMF PD075PCU.WMF PD076LCU.WMF PD077XCU.WMF PD079ECU.WMF PD080MCU.WMF PD081UCU.WMF
PD081VCU.WMF PD082TCU.WMF PD083XCU.WMF PD085CCU.WMF PD085DCU.WMF PD086OCU.WMF PD086SCU.WMF PD090LCU.WMF PD091BCU.WMF PD092NCU.WMF

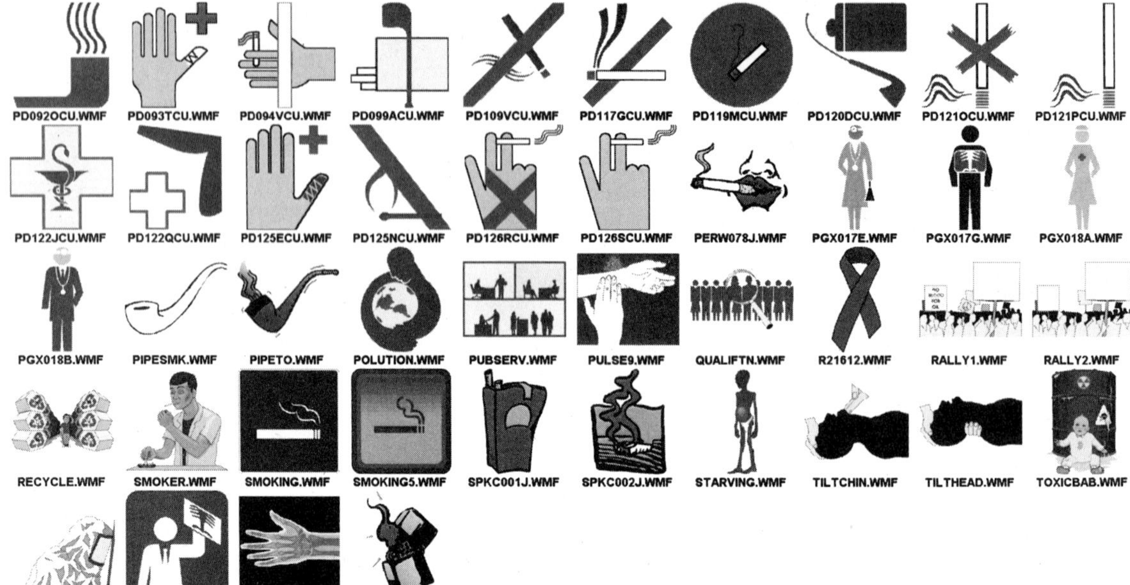
PD092OCU.WMF
PD093TCU.WMF
PD094VCU.WMF
PD099ACU.WMF
PD109VCU.WMF
PD117GCU.WMF
PD119MCU.WMF
PD120DCU.WMF
PD121OCU.WMF
PD121PCU.WMF
PD122JCU.WMF
PD122QCU.WMF
PD125ECU.WMF
PD125NCU.WMF
PD126RCU.WMF
PD126SCU.WMF
PERW078J.WMF
PGX017E.WMF
PGX017G.WMF
PGX018A.WMF
PGX018B.WMF
PIPESMK.WMF
PIPETO.WMF
POLUTION.WMF
PUBSERV.WMF
PULSE9.WMF
QUALIFTN.WMF
R21612.WMF
RALLY1.WMF
RALLY2.WMF
RECYCLE.WMF
SMOKER.WMF
SMOKING.WMF
SMOKING5.WMF
SPKC001J.WMF
SPKC002J.WMF
STARVING.WMF
TILTCHIN.WMF
TILTHEAD.WMF
TOXICBAB.WMF
TOXICWTM.WMF
XRAY.WMF
XRAYH.WMF
ZIPPOTO.WMF

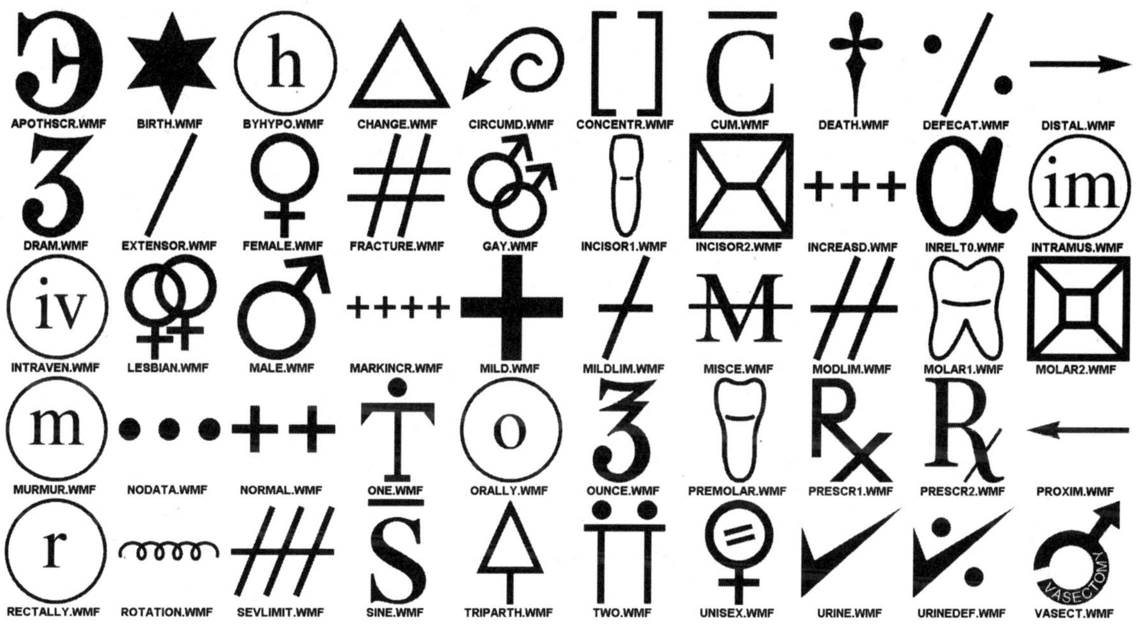

APOTHSCR.WMF
BIRTH.WMF
h
BYHYPO.WMF
CHANGE.WMF
CIRCUMD.WMF
CONCENTR.WMF
CUM.WMF
DEATH.WMF
DEFECAT.WMF
DISTAL.WMF
DRAM.WMF
EXTENSOR.WMF
FEMALE.WMF
FRACTURE.WMF
GAY.WMF
INCISOR1.WMF
INCISOR2.WMF
+++
INCREASD.WMF
INRELTO.WMF
im
INTRAMUS.WMF
iv
INTRAVEN.WMF
LESBIAN.WMF
MALE.WMF
++++
MARKINCR.WMF
MILD.WMF
MILDLIM.WMF
M
MISCE.WMF
MODLIM.WMF
MOLAR1.WMF
MOLAR2.WMF
m
MURMUR.WMF
NODATA.WMF
++
NORMAL.WMF
ONE.WMF
o
ORALLY.WMF
OUNCE.WMF
PREMOLAR.WMF
PRESCR1.WMF
PRESCR2.WMF
PROXIM.WMF
r
RECTALLY.WMF
ROTATION.WMF
SEVLIMIT.WMF
S
SINE.WMF
TRIPARTH.WMF
TWO.WMF
UNISEX.WMF
URINE.WMF
URINEDEF.WMF
VASECTOMY
VASECT.WMF

0136.WMF
ANA017.WMF
BABYBED.WMF
BABYD.WMF
BABYFEET.WMF
BABYH.WMF
BABYWDAD.WMF
BF08.WMF
BODY6.WMF
BREASTF.WMF
DELIVERY.WMF
DIAPERS.WMF
HLTH060.WMF
HLTH061.WMF
HLTH062.WMF
HLTH063.WMF
HLTH064.WMF
HLTH065.WMF
HLTH066.WMF
HLTH067.WMF
HLTH068.WMF
HLTH074.WMF
HLTH075.WMF
HLTH076.WMF
HLTH077.WMF
HLTH078.WMF
HLTH079.WMF
HLTH080.WMF
HLTH081.WMF
HLTH082.WMF
HLTH084.WMF
HLTH085.WMF
HLTH086.WMF
HLTH087.WMF
HLTH088.WMF
HLTH089.WMF
HLTH090.WMF
HLTH091.WMF
HLTH092.WMF
HLTH093.WMF
BABY
HLTH094.WMF
HLTH107.WMF
ITSAGIRL.WMF
Just for
BABY
JUSTFORB.WMF
MED005C.WMF
MED019A.WMF
CONDOM
CONDUM
MISC_13.WMF
SAFETY
FIRST
PLEASE
MISC_14.WMF
NEWBORN.WMF
OBST1.WMF
OBST2.WMF
PREMIE.WMF
STORK.WMF
STORKFLY.WMF
SYMBL135.WMF
SYMBL136.WMF
WEIGH.WMF

EAA199M.WMF
MED002D.WMF
MED023A.WMF
MED023B.WMF
MED023C.WMF
First aid
SYMB001.WMF
SYMB002.WMF
HOSPITAL
SYMB003.WMF
SYMB004.WMF
H
HOSPITAL
SYMB005.WMF
Agenda
SYMB006.WMF
APPOINTMENTS
SYMB007.WMF
LOOK
SYMB008.WMF
meeting
SYMB009.WMF
REMEMBER
SYMB010.WMF
STRESS
SYMB011.WMF
TEAMWORK
SYMB012.WMF
HEART
SYMB013.WMF
IMPORTANT NOTICES
SYMB014.WMF
SYMB015.WMF
SYMB016.WMF
SYMB017.WMF
SYMB018.WMF
SYMB019.WMF
SYMB020.WMF
SYMB021.WMF
SYMB022.WMF
SYMB023.WMF
SYMB024.WMF
SYMB025.WMF
SYMB026.WMF
SYMB027.WMF
$
SYMB028.WMF
SYMB029.WMF
SYMB030.WMF
SYMB031.WMF
SYMB032.WMF
SYMB033.WMF
SYMB034.WMF
SYMB035.WMF
SYMB036.WMF
SYMB037.WMF
SYMB038.WMF
SYMB039.WMF
SYMB040.WMF
SYMB041.WMF
SYMB042.WMF
SYMB043.WMF
SYMB044.WMF
SYMB045.WMF
SYMB046.WMF
SYMB047.WMF
SYMB048.WMF
SYMB049.WMF
SYMB050.WMF
SYMB051.WMF
SYMB052.WMF
SYMB053.WMF
SYMB054.WMF
SYMB055.WMF
SYMB056.WMF
SYMB057.WMF
SYMB058.WMF
SYMB059.WMF
SYMB060.WMF
SYMB061.WMF
SYMB062.WMF
SYMB063.WMF
SYMB064.WMF
SYMB065.WMF
EMERGENCY
SYMB066.WMF
SYMB067.WMF
SYMB068.WMF
E
F P
T O Z
SYMB069.WMF
SYMB070.WMF
SYMB071.WMF
SYMB072.WMF
SYMB073.WMF
SYMB074.WMF
SYMB075.WMF
SYMB076.WMF
SYMB077.WMF
SYMB078.WMF
SYMB079.WMF
SYMB080.WMF
SYMB081.WMF
SYMB082.WMF
SYMB083.WMF
SYMB084.WMF
SYMB085.WMF
SYMB086.WMF
H
SYMB087.WMF
SYMB088.WMF
SYMB089.WMF
SYMB090.WMF
?
SYMB091.WMF
SYMB092.WMF
SYMB093.WMF
SYMB094.WMF
SYMB095.WMF
SYMB096.WMF
SYMB097.WMF
SYMB098.WMF
SYMB099.WMF
???
SYMB100.WMF
SYMB101.WMF
SYMB102.WMF
SYMB103.WMF
SYMB104.WMF
SYMB105.WMF
SYMB106.WMF
SYMB107.WMF
SYMB108.WMF
SYMB109.WMF
SYMB110.WMF
SYMB111.WMF
SYMB112.WMF
SYMB113.WMF
SYMB114.WMF
SYMB115.WMF

SYMB116.WMF SYMB117.WMF SYMB118.WMF SYMB119.WMF SYMB120.WMF SYMB121.WMF SYMB122.WMF SYMB123.WMF SYMB124.WMF SYMB125.WMF

SYMB126.WMF SYMB127.WMF SYMB128.WMF SYMB129.WMF SYMB130.WMF SYMB131.WMF SYMB132.WMF SYMB133.WMF SYMB134.WMF SYMB135.WMF

SYMB136.WMF SYMB137.WMF SYMB138.WMF SYMB139.WMF SYMB140.WMF SYMB141.WMF SYMB142.WMF SYMB143.WMF SYMB144.WMF SYMB145.WMF

SYMB146.WMF SYMB147.WMF SYMB148.WMF SYMB149.WMF SYMB150.WMF SYMB151.WMF SYMB152.WMF SYMB153.WMF SYMB154.WMF SYMB155.WMF

SYMB156.WMF SYMB157.WMF SYMB158.WMF SYMB159.WMF SYMB160.WMF SYMB161.WMF SYMB162.WMF SYMB163.WMF SYMB164.WMF SYMB165.WMF

SYMB166.WMF SYMB167.WMF SYMB168.WMF SYMB169.WMF SYMB170.WMF SYMB171.WMF SYMB172.WMF SYMB173.WMF SYMB174.WMF SYMB175.WMF

SYMB176.WMF SYMB177.WMF SYMB178.WMF SYMB179.WMF SYMB180.WMF SYMB181.WMF SYMB182.WMF SYMB183.WMF SYMB184.WMF SYMB185.WMF

SYMB186.WMF SYMB187.WMF SYMB188.WMF SYMB189.WMF SYMB190.WMF SYMB191.WMF SYMB192.WMF SYMB193.WMF SYMB194.WMF SYMB195.WMF

SYMB196.WMF SYMB197.WMF SYMB198.WMF SYMB199.WMF SYMB200.WMF SYMB201.WMF SYMB202.WMF SYMB203.WMF SYMB204.WMF SYMB205.WMF

SYMB206.WMF SYMB207.WMF SYMB208.WMF SYMB209.WMF SYMB210.WMF SYMB211.WMF SYMB212.WMF SYMB213.WMF SYMB214.WMF SYMB215.WMF

SYMB216.WMF SYMB217.WMF SYMB218.WMF SYMB219.WMF SYMB220.WMF SYMB221.WMF SYMB222.WMF SYMB223.WMF SYMB224.WMF SYMB225.WMF

SYMB226.WMF SYMB227.WMF SYMB228.WMF SYMB229.WMF SYMB230.WMF SYMB231.WMF SYMB232.WMF SYMB233.WMF SYMB234.WMF SYMB235.WMF

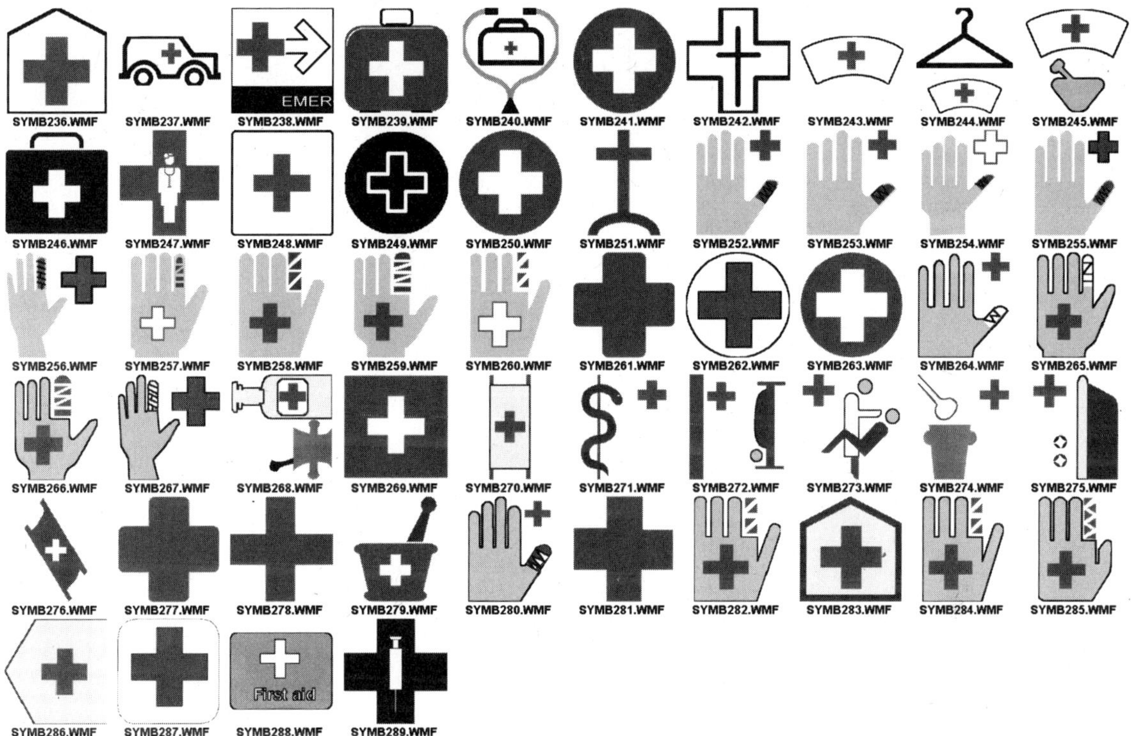
SYMB236.WMF
SYMB237.WMF
EMER
SYMB238.WMF
SYMB239.WMF
SYMB240.WMF
SYMB241.WMF
SYMB242.WMF
SYMB243.WMF
SYMB244.WMF
SYMB245.WMF
SYMB246.WMF
SYMB247.WMF
SYMB248.WMF
SYMB249.WMF
SYMB250.WMF
SYMB251.WMF
SYMB252.WMF
SYMB253.WMF
SYMB254.WMF
SYMB255.WMF
SYMB256.WMF
SYMB257.WMF
SYMB258.WMF
SYMB259.WMF
SYMB260.WMF
SYMB261.WMF
SYMB262.WMF
SYMB263.WMF
SYMB264.WMF
SYMB265.WMF
SYMB266.WMF
SYMB267.WMF
SYMB268.WMF
SYMB269.WMF
SYMB270.WMF
SYMB271.WMF
SYMB272.WMF
SYMB273.WMF
SYMB274.WMF
SYMB275.WMF
SYMB276.WMF
SYMB277.WMF
SYMB278.WMF
SYMB279.WMF
SYMB280.WMF
SYMB281.WMF
SYMB282.WMF
SYMB283.WMF
SYMB284.WMF
SYMB285.WMF
SYMB286.WMF
SYMB287.WMF
First aid
SYMB288.WMF
SYMB289.WMF

History • 1500

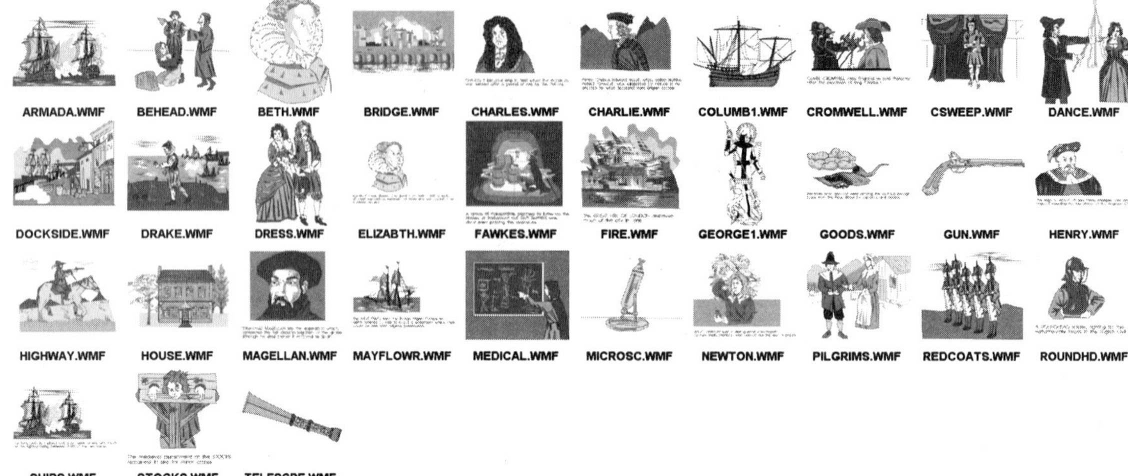

ARMADA.WMF BEHEAD.WMF BETH.WMF BRIDGE.WMF CHARLES.WMF CHARLIE.WMF COLUMB1.WMF CROMWELL.WMF CSWEEP.WMF DANCE.WMF

DOCKSIDE.WMF DRAKE.WMF DRESS.WMF ELIZABTH.WMF FAWKES.WMF FIRE.WMF GEORGE1.WMF GOODS.WMF GUN.WMF HENRY.WMF

HIGHWAY.WMF HOUSE.WMF MAGELLAN.WMF MAYFLOWR.WMF MEDICAL.WMF MICROSC.WMF NEWTON.WMF PILGRIMS.WMF REDCOATS.WMF ROUNDHD.WMF

SHIPS.WMF STOCKS.WMF TELESCPE.WMF

History • 1750

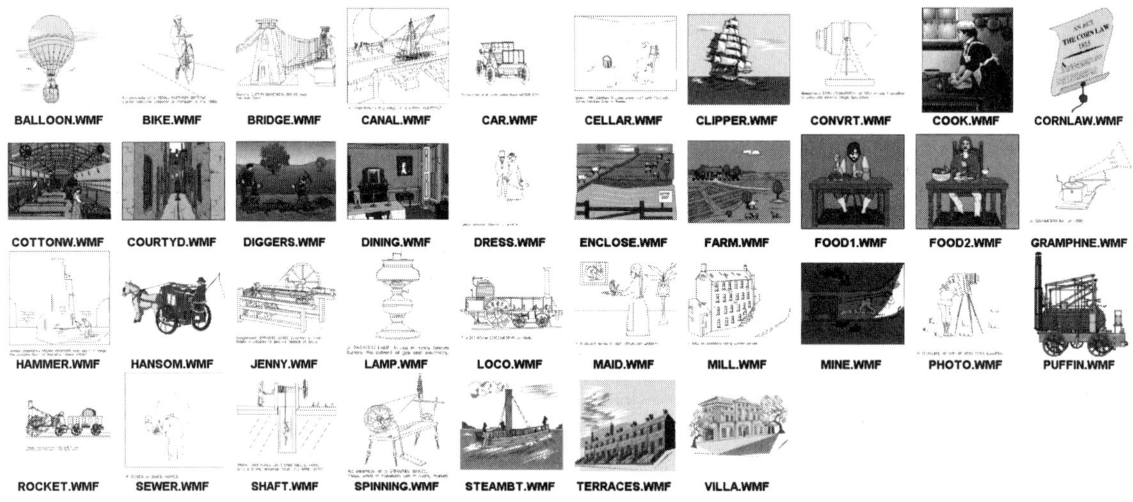

BALLOON.WMF BIKE.WMF BRIDGE.WMF CANAL.WMF CAR.WMF CELLAR.WMF CLIPPER.WMF CONVRT.WMF COOK.WMF CORNLAW.WMF

COTTONW.WMF COURTYD.WMF DIGGERS.WMF DINING.WMF DRESS.WMF ENCLOSE.WMF FARM.WMF FOOD1.WMF FOOD2.WMF GRAMPHNE.WMF

HAMMER.WMF HANSOM.WMF JENNY.WMF LAMP.WMF LOCO.WMF MAID.WMF MILL.WMF MINE.WMF PHOTO.WMF PUFFIN.WMF

ROCKET.WMF SEWER.WMF SHAFT.WMF SPINNING.WMF STEAMBT.WMF TERRACES.WMF VILLA.WMF

History • Aztecs

ART.WMF

JEWELS.WMF

SKNIFE.WMF

WEAVE.WMF

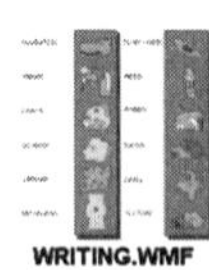

WRITING.WMF

History • Castle

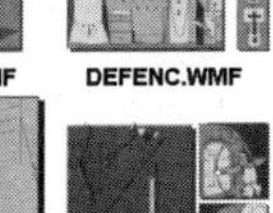

BARBIC.WMF BELFRY.WMF DEFENC.WMF HOIST.WMF LODGE.WMF MAINPC.WMF MINING.WMF MORTAR.WMF RAM.WMF RANGE.WMF

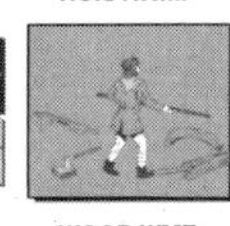

TOOLS.WMF WALL.WMF WEAPON.WMF WOOD.WMF

History • Egypt

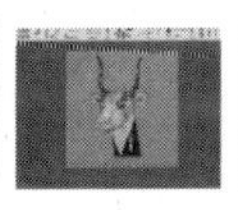

ANIMALS.WMF ANUBIS.WMF BUILDING.WMF CHAIR.WMF ECOW.WMF FIGUR2.WMF FIGURE1.WMF FIGURES.WMF GAMES.WMF HOUSE.WMF

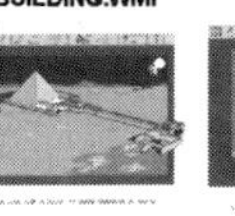

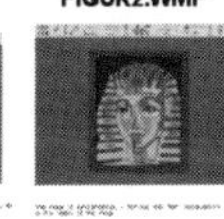

INSIDE.WMF PILLARS.WMF PYRAMID.WMF SHIP.WMF TOMB.WMF TUT.WMF

History • Explorers (EXPLORER)

BANKS.WMF BASS.WMF BOTBAY.WMF BURKE.WMF C_OVEN.WMF CANOE.WMF COOK.WMF DAGAMA.WMF DISEMB.WMF EKEHU.WMF

ENDEAV.WMF FISHBT.WMF FOUND.WMF GOVHSE.WMF MACQU.WMF MAORI.WMF MARSDN.WMF MARSHL.WMF MISSN.WMF MORIRA.WMF

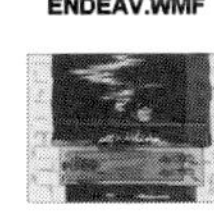
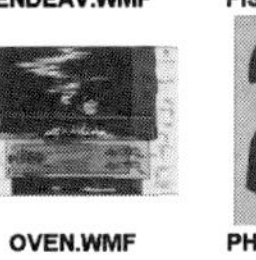

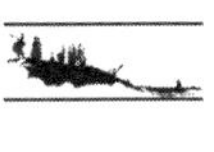

OVEN.WMF PHILLP.WMF PRSPCT.WMF SOLAND.WMF SOPHIA.WMF SQUATT.WMF TASMAN.WMF TRADEP.WMF ADS029A.WMF

History • Fossils

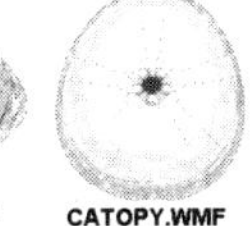

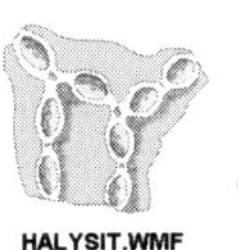
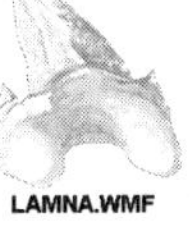
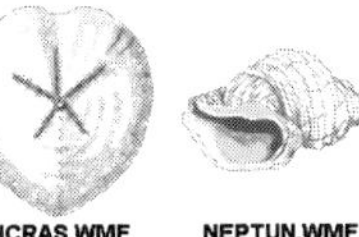
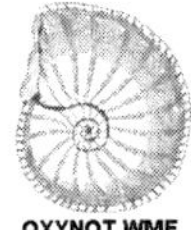

BIVALV.WMF CATOPY.WMF CYLIND.WMF GONIAT.WMF HALYSIT.WMF LAMNA.WMF MICRAS.WMF NEPTUN.WMF OXYNOT.WMF PSEUDU.WMF

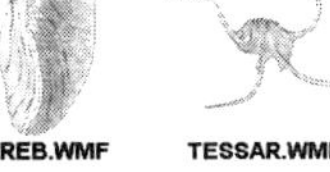

TEREB.WMF TESSAR.WMF TRINUC.WMF

ANIMALS.WMF
ARCHITEC.WMF
ATHENA.WMF
BRACELET.WMF
BRIDGE.WMF
DINNER.WMF
DRESS.WMF
DRINK.WMF
FOUNTAIN.WMF
GAMES.WMF
GOVERNMT.WMF
HOUSE.WMF
HUNTING.WMF
JAR.WMF
MASKS.WMF
MINOTAUR.WMF
MUSIC.WMF
ODYSSEY.WMF
OLIVES.WMF
ORACLE.WMF
PAINT.WMF
PARTHEN.WMF
PEGASUS.WMF
SCHOOL.WMF
SHIP.WMF
SLAVES.WMF
SOLDIER.WMF
THEATRE.WMF
TROJAN.WMF
WRESTLE.WMF

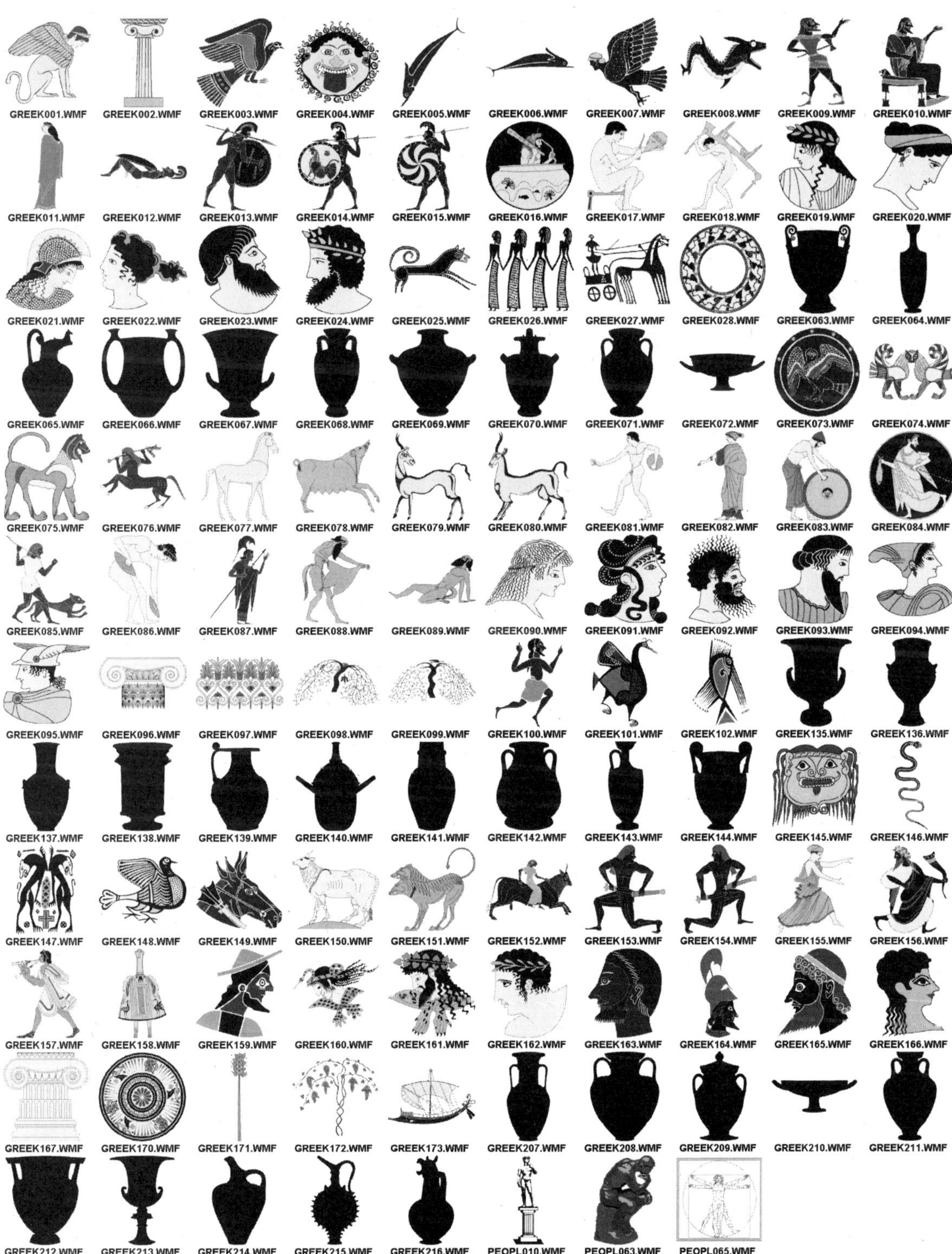
GREEK001.WMF GREEK002.WMF GREEK003.WMF GREEK004.WMF GREEK005.WMF GREEK006.WMF GREEK007.WMF GREEK008.WMF GREEK009.WMF GREEK010.WMF
GREEK011.WMF GREEK012.WMF GREEK013.WMF GREEK014.WMF GREEK015.WMF GREEK016.WMF GREEK017.WMF GREEK018.WMF GREEK019.WMF GREEK020.WMF
GREEK021.WMF GREEK022.WMF GREEK023.WMF GREEK024.WMF GREEK025.WMF GREEK026.WMF GREEK027.WMF GREEK028.WMF GREEK063.WMF GREEK064.WMF
GREEK065.WMF GREEK066.WMF GREEK067.WMF GREEK068.WMF GREEK069.WMF GREEK070.WMF GREEK071.WMF GREEK072.WMF GREEK073.WMF GREEK074.WMF
GREEK075.WMF GREEK076.WMF GREEK077.WMF GREEK078.WMF GREEK079.WMF GREEK080.WMF GREEK081.WMF GREEK082.WMF GREEK083.WMF GREEK084.WMF
GREEK085.WMF GREEK086.WMF GREEK087.WMF GREEK088.WMF GREEK089.WMF GREEK090.WMF GREEK091.WMF GREEK092.WMF GREEK093.WMF GREEK094.WMF
GREEK095.WMF GREEK096.WMF GREEK097.WMF GREEK098.WMF GREEK099.WMF GREEK100.WMF GREEK101.WMF GREEK102.WMF GREEK135.WMF GREEK136.WMF
GREEK137.WMF GREEK138.WMF GREEK139.WMF GREEK140.WMF GREEK141.WMF GREEK142.WMF GREEK143.WMF GREEK144.WMF GREEK145.WMF GREEK146.WMF
GREEK147.WMF GREEK148.WMF GREEK149.WMF GREEK150.WMF GREEK151.WMF GREEK152.WMF GREEK153.WMF GREEK154.WMF GREEK155.WMF GREEK156.WMF
GREEK157.WMF GREEK158.WMF GREEK159.WMF GREEK160.WMF GREEK161.WMF GREEK162.WMF GREEK163.WMF GREEK164.WMF GREEK165.WMF GREEK166.WMF
GREEK167.WMF GREEK170.WMF GREEK171.WMF GREEK172.WMF GREEK173.WMF GREEK207.WMF GREEK208.WMF GREEK209.WMF GREEK210.WMF GREEK211.WMF
GREEK212.WMF GREEK213.WMF GREEK214.WMF GREEK215.WMF GREEK216.WMF PEOPL010.WMF PEOPL063.WMF PEOPL065.WMF

ARCHER.WMF
ARMOUR.WMF
ASTROLB.WMF
ASTROLBE.WMF
AUMBRY.WMF
AXE.WMF
BAILEY.WMF
BAKEHOUS.WMF
BAKERY.WMF
BALLISTA.WMF
BANQUET.WMF
BARBIC2.WMF
BARGE.WMF
BARRELS.WMF
BATRAM.WMF
BATTLE.WMF
BEAUMARS.WMF
BED.WMF
BEDROOM.WMF
BELFRY.WMF
BLCKSMTH.WMF
BOAT.WMF
BOOTS.WMF
BUILDCST.WMF
BUILDER.WMF
BUTCHER.WMF
BUTTRESS.WMF
CARPENT1.WMF
CARPENT2.WMF
CARPENT3.WMF
CARPENT4.WMF
CARRIER.WMF
CARRYING.WMF
CART.WMF
CASTLE.WMF
CHALICE.WMF
CHAMBER.WMF
CHAPEL.WMF
CHEST.WMF
CHURCH.WMF
CISTERN.WMF
CLOTHES.WMF
COACH.WMF
COMPASS.WMF
CONTAIN.WMF
COOK.WMF
DEATH.WMF
DRAWBRGE.WMF
DRINKING.WMF
DUCKING.WMF
FAIR.WMF
FALCON.WMF
FIREWOOD.WMF
FISH.WMF
FLAIL.WMF
FOOD.WMF
FOOTBALL.WMF
GALLEON.WMF
GARDRBE.WMF
GATEHSE.WMF
GLITTERN.WMF
GUILD.WMF
GUN.WMF
HARLECH.WMF
HARVEST.WMF
HATS.WMF
HIGHWAY.WMF
HORSEBK.WMF
HORSECRT.WMF
HOURDING.WMF
HOUSE.WMF
INN.WMF
IRON.WMF
IRONWORK.WMF
JOUST.WMF
KITCHEN.WMF
KITCHEN2.WMF
KNGHT14C.WMF
KNIFE.WMF
KNIGHTS.WMF
KTNMAID.WMF
LABOURER.WMF
LEVELLER.WMF
LEVELTLS.WMF
LONGHSE.WMF
LOOPHOLE.WMF
MACHIOLA.WMF
MAN.WMF
MAN1.WMF
MASON.WMF
MASONTLS.WMF
MESSENG1.WMF
MESSENG2.WMF
MORTAR.WMF
MOTTE.WMF
MUGS.WMF
MUGT.WMF
PACKHRSE.WMF
PATEN.WMF
PERRIER3.WMF
PIGS.WMF
PIKE.WMF
PILGRIMS.WMF
PISCINA.WMF
PLUMBER.WMF
PROVISN.WMF
RECEIVER.WMF
RECESS.WMF
ROOM.WMF
SADDLE.WMF
SAPPER.WMF
SCROLLS.WMF
SEDILE.WMF
SETTER.WMF
SEXTANT.WMF
SHEEP.WMF
SHIPSECT.WMF
SHOP.WMF
SKILLET.WMF
SLING.WMF

SPIT.WMF

SPOON.WMF

STREET.WMF

TABLE.WMF

THEATRE.WMF

TIMER.WMF

TRANSPRT.WMF

TREBUCH1.WMF

TREBUCH2.WMF

TRENCHER.WMF

WOODBOWL.WMF

History • Pre-America (PREAMERN)

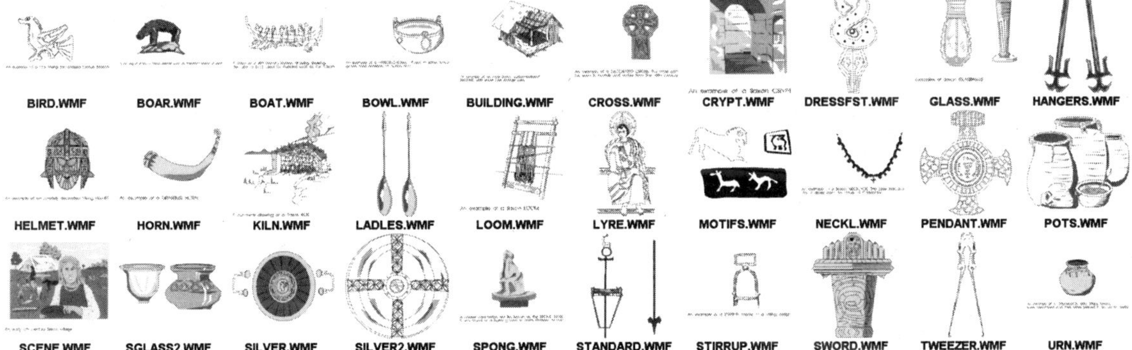
BIRD.WMF BOAR.WMF BOAT.WMF BOWL.WMF BUILDING.WMF CROSS.WMF CRYPT.WMF DRESSFST.WMF GLASS.WMF HANGERS.WMF

HELMET.WMF HORN.WMF KILN.WMF LADLES.WMF LOOM.WMF LYRE.WMF MOTIFS.WMF NECKL.WMF PENDANT.WMF POTS.WMF

SCENE.WMF SGLASS2.WMF SILVER.WMF SILVER2.WMF SPONG.WMF STANDARD.WMF STIRRUP.WMF SWORD.WMF TWEEZER.WMF URN.WMF

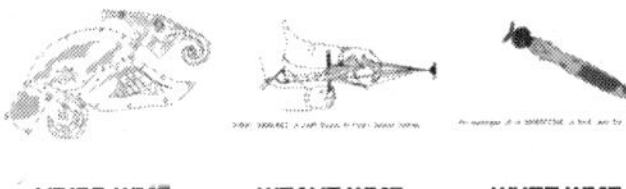
VBIRD.WMF WEAVE.WMF WHET.WMF

AQUEDUCT.WMF

ARAPACIS.WMF

AUGUSTUS.WMF

BALCONY.WMF

BALLISTA.WMF

BEDROOM.WMF

CLAUDIUS.WMF

CLOTHING.WMF

COINS.WMF

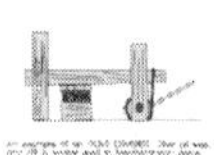
CRUSHER.WMF

DINING.WMF

EMBLEM.WMF

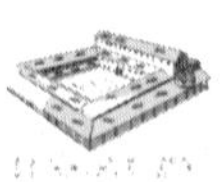
FORUM.WMF

FRESCO.WMF

GLADIATR.WMF

KILN.WMF

KITCHEN.WMF

LEGION.WMF

MULECART.WMF

MUSIC.WMF

RBATH.WMF RBRIDGE.WMF

RSHIP.WMF

SOLDIER.WMF

SPABATH.WMF

TABLE1.WMF

TABLE2.WMF

TAVERN.WMF

TROJHELM.WMF

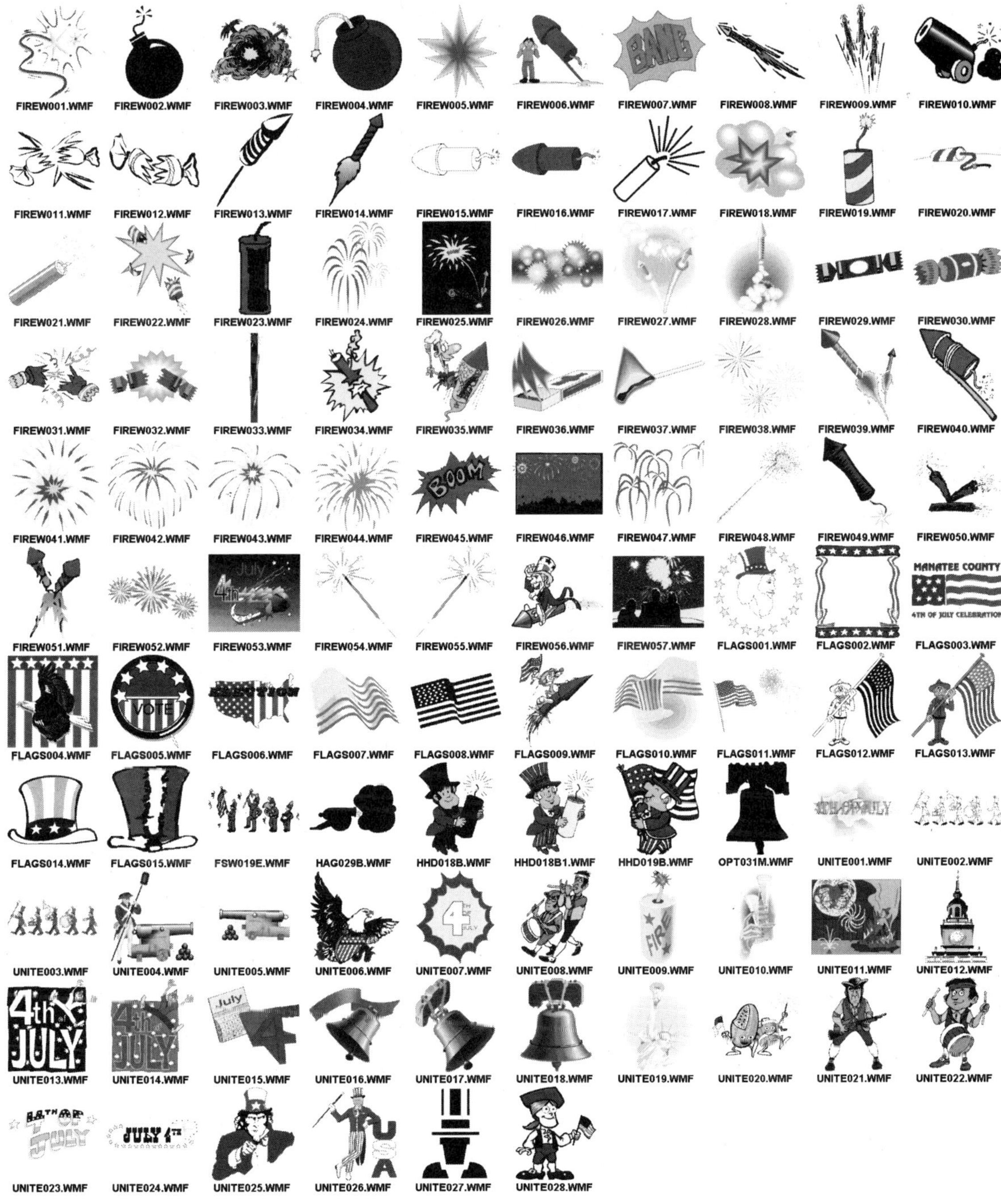
FIREW001.WMF
FIREW002.WMF
FIREW003.WMF
FIREW004.WMF
FIREW005.WMF
FIREW006.WMF
FIREW007.WMF
FIREW008.WMF
FIREW009.WMF
FIREW010.WMF
FIREW011.WMF
FIREW012.WMF
FIREW013.WMF
FIREW014.WMF
FIREW015.WMF
FIREW016.WMF
FIREW017.WMF
FIREW018.WMF
FIREW019.WMF
FIREW020.WMF
FIREW021.WMF
FIREW022.WMF
FIREW023.WMF
FIREW024.WMF
FIREW025.WMF
FIREW026.WMF
FIREW027.WMF
FIREW028.WMF
FIREW029.WMF
FIREW030.WMF
FIREW031.WMF
FIREW032.WMF
FIREW033.WMF
FIREW034.WMF
FIREW035.WMF
FIREW036.WMF
FIREW037.WMF
FIREW038.WMF
FIREW039.WMF
FIREW040.WMF
FIREW041.WMF
FIREW042.WMF
FIREW043.WMF
FIREW044.WMF
FIREW045.WMF
FIREW046.WMF
FIREW047.WMF
FIREW048.WMF
FIREW049.WMF
FIREW050.WMF
FIREW051.WMF
FIREW052.WMF
FIREW053.WMF
FIREW054.WMF
FIREW055.WMF
FIREW056.WMF
FIREW057.WMF
FLAGS001.WMF
FLAGS002.WMF
FLAGS003.WMF
FLAGS004.WMF
FLAGS005.WMF
FLAGS006.WMF
FLAGS007.WMF
FLAGS008.WMF
FLAGS009.WMF
FLAGS010.WMF
FLAGS011.WMF
FLAGS012.WMF
FLAGS013.WMF
FLAGS014.WMF
FLAGS015.WMF
FSW019E.WMF
HAG029B.WMF
HHD018B.WMF
HHD018B1.WMF
HHD019B.WMF
OPT031M.WMF
UNITE001.WMF
UNITE002.WMF
UNITE003.WMF
UNITE004.WMF
UNITE005.WMF
UNITE006.WMF
UNITE007.WMF
UNITE008.WMF
UNITE009.WMF
UNITE010.WMF
UNITE011.WMF
UNITE012.WMF
UNITE013.WMF
UNITE014.WMF
UNITE015.WMF
UNITE016.WMF
UNITE017.WMF
UNITE018.WMF
UNITE019.WMF
UNITE020.WMF
UNITE021.WMF
UNITE022.WMF
UNITE023.WMF
UNITE024.WMF
UNITE025.WMF
UNITE026.WMF
UNITE027.WMF
UNITE028.WMF

1928.WMF BELLS001.WMF BELLS002.WMF BELLS003.WMF BELLS004.WMF BELLS005.WMF BELLS006.WMF BELLS007.WMF BELLS008.WMF BELLS009.WMF

BELLS010.WMF BELLS011.WMF BELLS012.WMF BELLS013.WMF BELLS014.WMF BELLS015.WMF BELLS016.WMF BELLS017.WMF BELLS018.WMF BELLS019.WMF

BELLS020.WMF BELLS021.WMF BELLS022.WMF BELLS023.WMF BELLS024.WMF BELLS025.WMF BELLS026.WMF BELLS027.WMF BELLS028.WMF BELLS029.WMF

BELLS030.WMF BELLS031.WMF BELLS032.WMF BELLS033.WMF BELLS034.WMF BELLS035.WMF BELLS036.WMF BELLS037.WMF BELLS038.WMF BELLS039.WMF

BELLS040.WMF BELLS041.WMF BELLS042.WMF BELLS043.WMF BELLS044.WMF BELLS045.WMF BELLS046.WMF BELLS047.WMF BELLS048.WMF BELLS049.WMF

BELLS050.WMF BELLS051.WMF BELLS052.WMF BELLS053.WMF BELLS054.WMF BELLS055.WMF BELLS056.WMF BELLS057.WMF BELLS058.WMF BELLS059.WMF

BELLS060.WMF BELLS061.WMF BELLS062.WMF BELLS063.WMF BELLS064.WMF CANDL001.WMF CANDL002.WMF CANDL003.WMF CANDL004.WMF CANDL005.WMF

CANDL006.WMF CANDL007.WMF CANDL008.WMF CANDL009.WMF CANDL010.WMF CANDL011.WMF CANDL012.WMF CANDL013.WMF CANDL014.WMF CANDL015.WMF

CANDL016.WMF CANDL017.WMF CANDL018.WMF CANDL019.WMF CANDL020.WMF CANDL021.WMF CANDL022.WMF CANDL023.WMF CANDL024.WMF CANDL025.WMF

CANDL026.WMF CANDL027.WMF CANDL028.WMF CANDL029.WMF CANDL030.WMF CANDL031.WMF CANDL032.WMF CANDL033.WMF CANDL034.WMF CANDL035.WMF

CANDL036.WMF CANDL037.WMF CANDL038.WMF CANDL039.WMF CANDL040.WMF CANDL041.WMF CANDL042.WMF CANDL043.WMF CANDL044.WMF CANDL045.WMF

CANDL046.WMF CANDL047.WMF CANDL048.WMF CANDL049.WMF CANDL050.WMF CANDL051.WMF CANDL052.WMF CANDL053.WMF CANDY001.WMF CANDY002.WMF

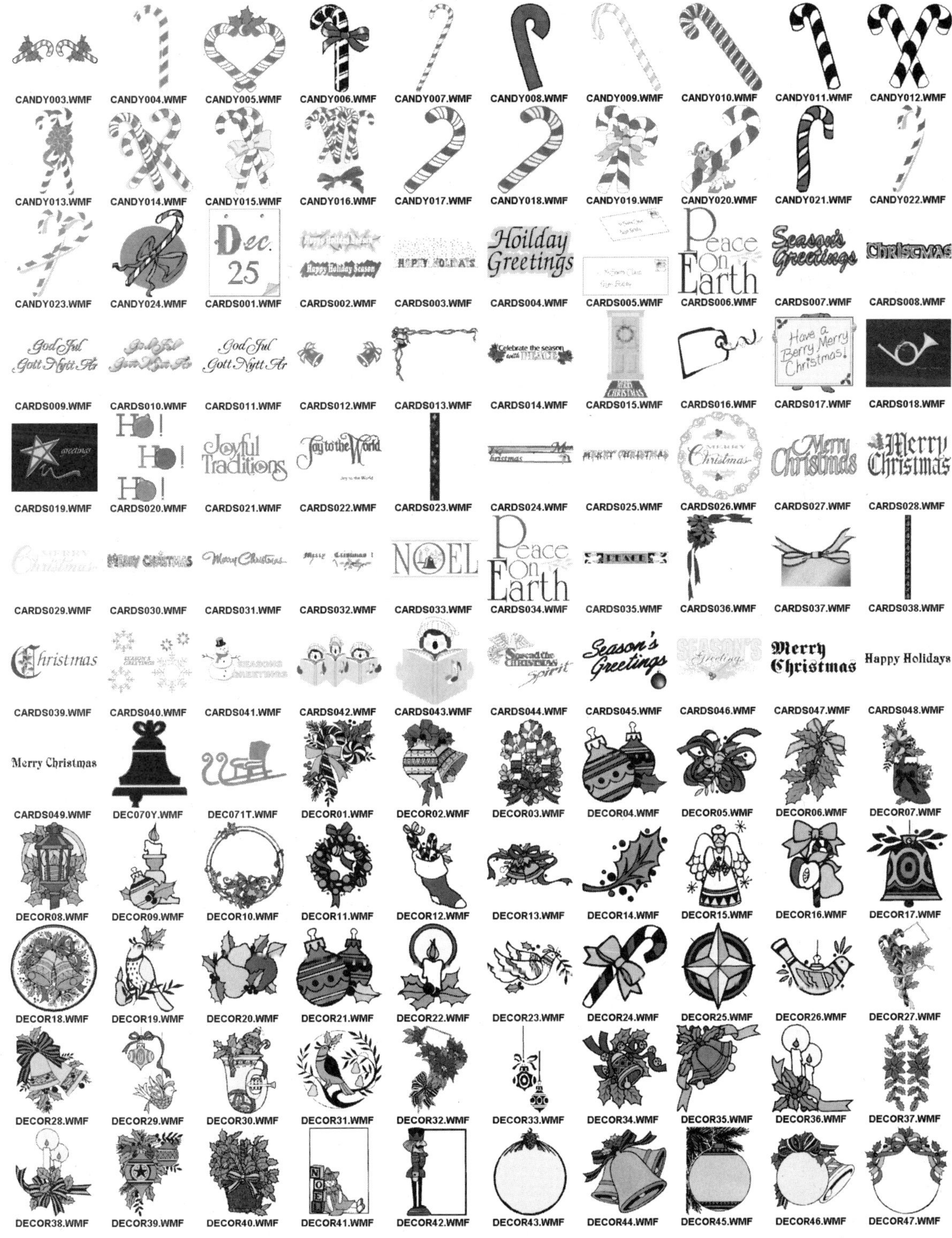

CANDY003.WMF CANDY004.WMF CANDY005.WMF CANDY006.WMF CANDY007.WMF CANDY008.WMF CANDY009.WMF CANDY010.WMF CANDY011.WMF CANDY012.WMF
CANDY013.WMF CANDY014.WMF CANDY015.WMF CANDY016.WMF CANDY017.WMF CANDY018.WMF CANDY019.WMF CANDY020.WMF CANDY021.WMF CANDY022.WMF
CANDY023.WMF CANDY024.WMF CARDS001.WMF CARDS002.WMF CARDS003.WMF CARDS004.WMF CARDS005.WMF CARDS006.WMF CARDS007.WMF CARDS008.WMF
CARDS009.WMF CARDS010.WMF CARDS011.WMF CARDS012.WMF CARDS013.WMF CARDS014.WMF CARDS015.WMF CARDS016.WMF CARDS017.WMF CARDS018.WMF
CARDS019.WMF CARDS020.WMF CARDS021.WMF CARDS022.WMF CARDS023.WMF CARDS024.WMF CARDS025.WMF CARDS026.WMF CARDS027.WMF CARDS028.WMF
CARDS029.WMF CARDS030.WMF CARDS031.WMF CARDS032.WMF CARDS033.WMF CARDS034.WMF CARDS035.WMF CARDS036.WMF CARDS037.WMF CARDS038.WMF
CARDS039.WMF CARDS040.WMF CARDS041.WMF CARDS042.WMF CARDS043.WMF CARDS044.WMF CARDS045.WMF CARDS046.WMF CARDS047.WMF CARDS048.WMF
CARDS049.WMF DEC070Y.WMF DEC071T.WMF DECOR01.WMF DECOR02.WMF DECOR03.WMF DECOR04.WMF DECOR05.WMF DECOR06.WMF DECOR07.WMF
DECOR08.WMF DECOR09.WMF DECOR10.WMF DECOR11.WMF DECOR12.WMF DECOR13.WMF DECOR14.WMF DECOR15.WMF DECOR16.WMF DECOR17.WMF
DECOR18.WMF DECOR19.WMF DECOR20.WMF DECOR21.WMF DECOR22.WMF DECOR23.WMF DECOR24.WMF DECOR25.WMF DECOR26.WMF DECOR27.WMF
DECOR28.WMF DECOR29.WMF DECOR30.WMF DECOR31.WMF DECOR32.WMF DECOR33.WMF DECOR34.WMF DECOR35.WMF DECOR36.WMF DECOR37.WMF
DECOR38.WMF DECOR39.WMF DECOR40.WMF DECOR41.WMF DECOR42.WMF DECOR43.WMF DECOR44.WMF DECOR45.WMF DECOR46.WMF DECOR47.WMF

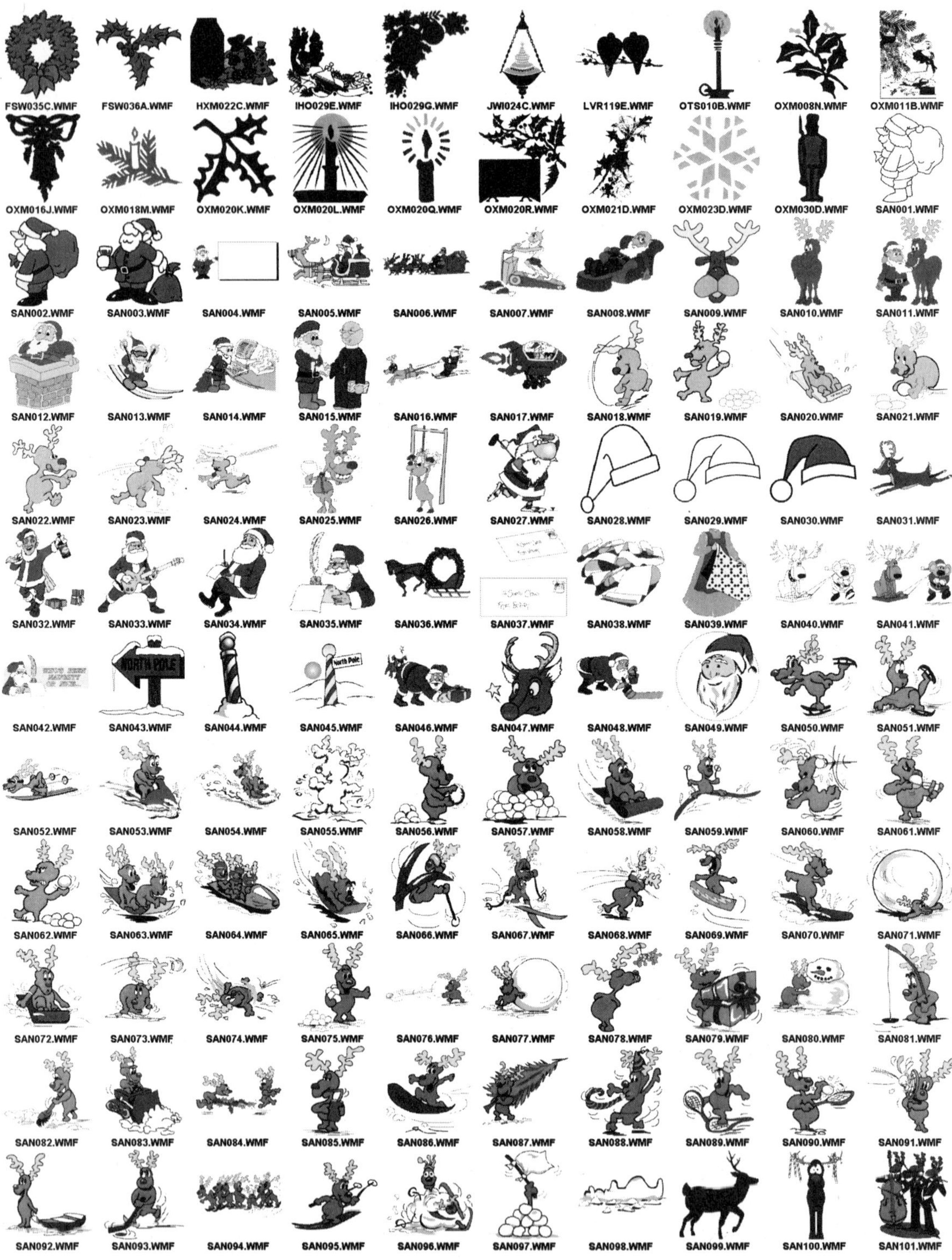
FSW035C.WMF
FSW036A.WMF
HXM022C.WMF
IHO029E.WMF
IHO029G.WMF
JWI024C.WMF
LVR119E.WMF
OTS010B.WMF
OXM008N.WMF
OXM011B.WMF
OXM016J.WMF
OXM018M.WMF
OXM020K.WMF
OXM020L.WMF
OXM020Q.WMF
OXM020R.WMF
OXM021D.WMF
OXM023D.WMF
OXM030D.WMF
SAN001.WMF
SAN002.WMF
SAN003.WMF
SAN004.WMF
SAN005.WMF
SAN006.WMF
SAN007.WMF
SAN008.WMF
SAN009.WMF
SAN010.WMF
SAN011.WMF
SAN012.WMF
SAN013.WMF
SAN014.WMF
SAN015.WMF
SAN016.WMF
SAN017.WMF
SAN018.WMF
SAN019.WMF
SAN020.WMF
SAN021.WMF
SAN022.WMF
SAN023.WMF
SAN024.WMF
SAN025.WMF
SAN026.WMF
SAN027.WMF
SAN028.WMF
SAN029.WMF
SAN030.WMF
SAN031.WMF
SAN032.WMF
SAN033.WMF
SAN034.WMF
SAN035.WMF
SAN036.WMF
SAN037.WMF
SAN038.WMF
SAN039.WMF
SAN040.WMF
SAN041.WMF
SAN042.WMF
NORTH POLE
SAN043.WMF
SAN044.WMF
SAN045.WMF
SAN046.WMF
SAN047.WMF
SAN048.WMF
SAN049.WMF
SAN050.WMF
SAN051.WMF
SAN052.WMF
SAN053.WMF
SAN054.WMF
SAN055.WMF
SAN056.WMF
SAN057.WMF
SAN058.WMF
SAN059.WMF
SAN060.WMF
SAN061.WMF
SAN062.WMF
SAN063.WMF
SAN064.WMF
SAN065.WMF
SAN066.WMF
SAN067.WMF
SAN068.WMF
SAN069.WMF
SAN070.WMF
SAN071.WMF
SAN072.WMF
SAN073.WMF
SAN074.WMF
SAN075.WMF
SAN076.WMF
SAN077.WMF
SAN078.WMF
SAN079.WMF
SAN080.WMF
SAN081.WMF
SAN082.WMF
SAN083.WMF
SAN084.WMF
SAN085.WMF
SAN086.WMF
SAN087.WMF
SAN088.WMF
SAN089.WMF
SAN090.WMF
SAN091.WMF
SAN092.WMF
SAN093.WMF
SAN094.WMF
SAN095.WMF
SAN096.WMF
SAN097.WMF
SAN098.WMF
SAN099.WMF
SAN100.WMF
SAN101.WMF

SAN102.WMF SAN103.WMF SAN104.WMF SAN105.WMF SAN106.WMF SAN107.WMF SAN108.WMF SAN109.WMF SAN110.WMF SAN111.WMF

SAN112.WMF SAN113.WMF SAN114.WMF SAN115.WMF SAN116.WMF SAN117.WMF SAN118.WMF SAN119.WMF SAN120.WMF SAN121.WMF

SAN122.WMF SAN123.WMF SAN124.WMF SAN125.WMF SAN126.WMF SAN127.WMF SAN128.WMF SAN129.WMF SAN130.WMF SAN131.WMF

SAN132.WMF SAN133.WMF SAN134.WMF SAN135.WMF SAN136.WMF SAN137.WMF SAN138.WMF SAN139.WMF SAN140.WMF SAN141.WMF

SAN142.WMF SAN143.WMF SAN144.WMF SAN145.WMF SAN146.WMF SAN147.WMF SAN148.WMF SAN149.WMF SAN150.WMF SAN151.WMF

SAN152.WMF SAN153.WMF SAN154.WMF SAN155.WMF SAN156.WMF SAN157.WMF SAN158.WMF SAN159.WMF SAN160.WMF SAN161.WMF

SAN162.WMF SAN163.WMF SAN164.WMF SAN165.WMF SAN166.WMF SAN167.WMF SAN168.WMF SAN169.WMF SAN170.WMF SAN171.WMF

SAN172.WMF SAN173.WMF SAN174.WMF SAN175.WMF SAN176.WMF SAN177.WMF SAN178.WMF SAN179.WMF SAN180.WMF SAN181.WMF

SAN182.WMF SAN183.WMF SAN184.WMF SAN185.WMF SAN186.WMF SAN187.WMF SAN188.WMF SAN189.WMF SAN190.WMF SAN191.WMF

SAN192.WMF SAN193.WMF SAN194.WMF SAN195.WMF SAN196.WMF SAN197.WMF SAN198.WMF SAN199.WMF SAN200.WMF SAN201.WMF

SAN202.WMF SAN203.WMF SAN204.WMF SAN205.WMF SAN206.WMF SAN207.WMF SAN208.WMF SAN209.WMF SAN210.WMF SAN211.WMF

SAN212.WMF SAN213.WMF SAN214.WMF SAN215.WMF SAN216.WMF SAN217.WMF SAN218.WMF SAN219.WMF SAN220.WMF SAN221.WMF

SAN222.WMF
SAN223.WMF
SAN224.WMF
SAN225.WMF
SAN226.WMF
SAN227.WMF
SAN228.WMF
SAN229.WMF
SAN230.WMF
SAN231.WMF
SAN232.WMF
SAN233.WMF
SAN234.WMF
SAN235.WMF
SAN236.WMF
SAN237.WMF
SAN238.WMF
SAN239.WMF
SAN240.WMF
SAN241.WMF
SAN242.WMF
SAN243.WMF
SAN244.WMF
SAN245.WMF
SAN246.WMF
SAN247.WMF
SAN248.WMF
SAN249.WMF
SAN250.WMF
SAN251.WMF
SAN252.WMF
SAN253.WMF
SAN254.WMF
SAN255.WMF
SAN256.WMF
SAN257.WMF
SAN258.WMF
SAN259.WMF
SAN260.WMF
SAN261.WMF
SAN262.WMF
SAN263.WMF
SAN264.WMF
SAN265.WMF
SAN266.WMF
SAN267.WMF
SAN268.WMF
SAN269.WMF
SAN270.WMF
SAN271.WMF
SAN272.WMF
SAN273.WMF
SAN274.WMF
SAN275.WMF
SAN276.WMF
SAN277.WMF
SAN278.WMF
SAN279.WMF
SAN280.WMF
SAN281.WMF
SAN282.WMF
SAN283.WMF
SAN284.WMF
SAN285.WMF
SAN286.WMF
SAN287.WMF
SAN288.WMF
SAN289.WMF
SAN290.WMF
SAN291.WMF
SAN292.WMF
SAN293.WMF
SAN294.WMF
SAN295.WMF
SAN296.WMF
SAN297.WMF
SAN298.WMF
SAN299.WMF
SAN300.WMF
SAN301.WMF
SAN302.WMF
SAN303.WMF
SAN304.WMF
SAN305.WMF
SAN306.WMF
SAN307.WMF
SAN308.WMF
SAN309.WMF
SAN310.WMF
SAN311.WMF
SAN312.WMF
SAN313.WMF
SAN314.WMF
SAN315.WMF
SAN316.WMF
SAN317.WMF
SAN318.WMF
SAN319.WMF
SAN320.WMF
SAN321.WMF
SAN322.WMF
SAN323.WMF
SAN324.WMF
SAN325.WMF
SAN326.WMF
SAN327.WMF
SAN328.WMF
SAN329.WMF
SAN330.WMF
SAN331.WMF
SAN332.WMF
SAN333.WMF
SAN334.WMF
SAN335.WMF
SAN336.WMF
SAN337.WMF
SAN338.WMF
SAN339.WMF
SAN340.WMF
SAN341.WMF

SAN342.WMF SAN343.WMF SAN344.WMF SAN345.WMF SAN346.WMF SAN347.WMF SAN348.WMF SAN349.WMF SAN350.WMF SAN351.WMF

SAN352.WMF SAN353.WMF SAN354.WMF SAN355.WMF SAN356.WMF SAN357.WMF SAN358.WMF SAN359.WMF SAN360.WMF SAN361.WMF

SAN362.WMF SAN363.WMF SAN364.WMF SAN365.WMF SAN366.WMF SAN367.WMF SAN368.WMF SAN369.WMF SAN370.WMF SAN371.WMF

SAN372.WMF SAN373.WMF SAN374.WMF SAN375.WMF SAN376.WMF SAN377.WMF SAN378.WMF SAN379.WMF SAN380.WMF SAN381.WMF

SAN382.WMF SAN383.WMF SAN384.WMF SAN385.WMF SAN386.WMF SAN387.WMF SAN388.WMF SAN389.WMF SAN390.WMF SAN391.WMF

SAN392.WMF SAN393.WMF SAN394.WMF SAN395.WMF SAN396.WMF SAN397.WMF SAN398.WMF SAN399.WMF SAN400.WMF SAN401.WMF

SAN402.WMF SAN403.WMF SAN404.WMF SAN405.WMF SAN406.WMF SAN407.WMF SAN408.WMF SAN409.WMF SAN410.WMF SAN411.WMF

SAN412.WMF SAN413.WMF SAN414.WMF SAN415.WMF SAN416.WMF SAN417.WMF SAN418.WMF SAN419.WMF SAN420.WMF SAN421.WMF

SAN422.WMF SAN423.WMF SAN424.WMF SAN425.WMF SAN426.WMF SAN427.WMF SAN428.WMF SAN429.WMF SAN430.WMF SAN431.WMF

SAN432.WMF SAN433.WMF SAN434.WMF SAN435.WMF SAN436.WMF SAN437.WMF SAN438.WMF SAN439.WMF SAN440.WMF SAN441.WMF

SAN442.WMF SAN443.WMF SAN444.WMF SAN445.WMF SAN446.WMF SAN447.WMF SAN448.WMF SAN449.WMF SAN450.WMF SAN451.WMF

SAN452.WMF SAN453.WMF SAN454.WMF SAN455.WMF SAN456.WMF SAN457.WMF SAN458.WMF SAN459.WMF SAN460.WMF SAN461.WMF

SAN462.WMF
SAN463.WMF
SAN464.WMF
SAN465.WMF
SAN466.WMF
SAN467.WMF
SAN468.WMF
SAN469.WMF
SAN470.WMF
SAN471.WMF
SAN472.WMF
SAN473.WMF
SAN474.WMF
SAN475.WMF
SAN476.WMF
SAN477.WMF
SAN478.WMF
SAN479.WMF
SAN480.WMF
SAN481.WMF
SAN482.WMF
SAN483.WMF
SAN484.WMF
SAN485.WMF
SAN486.WMF
SAN487.WMF
SAN488.WMF
SAN489.WMF
SAN490.WMF
SAN491.WMF
SAN492.WMF
SAN493.WMF
SAN494.WMF
SAN495.WMF
SAN496.WMF
SAN497.WMF
SAN498.WMF
TDG020A.WMF
TREE01.WMF
TREE02.WMF
TREE03.WMF
TREE04.WMF
VSC052A.WMF
WREATH01.WMF
WREATH02.WMF
WREATH03.WMF
WREATH04.WMF
XDN019D.WMF
XDN019E.WMF
XDN019J.WMF
XDN022A.WMF
XMC003B.WMF
XMC006B.WMF
XMC027B.WMF

3RDDAYHD.WMF 4THDAYHD.WMF 5THDAYHD.WMF 6THDAYHD.WMF 7THDAYHD.WMF 8THDAYHD.WMF 9THDAYHD.WMF ADS040E.WMF CARDS050.WMF CARTO001.WMF

CARTO002.WMF CARTO003.WMF CARTO004.WMF CARTO005.WMF CARTO006.WMF CARTO007.WMF CARTO008.WMF CARTO009.WMF CARTO010.WMF CARTO011.WMF

CARTO012.WMF CARTO013.WMF CARTO014.WMF CARTO015.WMF CARTO016.WMF CARTO017.WMF CARTO018.WMF CARTO019.WMF CARTO020.WMF CARTO021.WMF

CARTO022.WMF CARTO023.WMF CARTO024.WMF CARTO025.WMF CARTO026.WMF CARTO027.WMF CARTO028.WMF CARTO029.WMF CARTO030.WMF CARTO031.WMF

CARTO032.WMF CARTO033.WMF CARTO034.WMF CARTO035.WMF CARTO036.WMF CARTO037.WMF CARTO038.WMF CARTO039.WMF CARTO040.WMF CARTO041.WMF

CARTO042.WMF CARTO043.WMF CARTO044.WMF CARTO045.WMF CARTO046.WMF CARTO047.WMF CARTO048.WMF CARTO049.WMF CARTO050.WMF CARTO051.WMF

CARTO062.WMF CARTO053.WMF CARTO054.WMF CARTO055.WMF CARTO056.WMF CARTO057.WMF CARTO058.WMF CARTO059.WMF CARTO060.WMF CARTO061.WMF

CARTO062.WMF CARTO063.WMF CARTO064.WMF CARTO065.WMF CARTO066.WMF CARTO067.WMF CARTO068.WMF CARTO069.WMF CARTO070.WMF CARTO071.WMF

CARTO072.WMF CARTO073.WMF DEC070C.WMF HOLLY001.WMF HOLLY002.WMF HOLLY003.WMF HOLLY004.WMF HOLLY005.WMF HOLLY006.WMF HOLLY007.WMF

HOLLY008.WMF HOLLY009.WMF HOLLY010.WMF HOLLY011.WMF HOLLY012.WMF HOLLY013.WMF HOLLY014.WMF HOLLY015.WMF HOLLY016.WMF HOLLY017.WMF

HOLLY018.WMF HOLLY019.WMF HOLLY020.WMF HOLLY021.WMF HOLLY022.WMF HOLLY023.WMF HOLLY024.WMF HOLLY025.WMF HOLLY026.WMF HOLLY027.WMF

HOLLY028.WMF HOLLY029.WMF HOLLY030.WMF HOLLY031.WMF HOLLY032.WMF HOLLY033.WMF HOLLY034.WMF HOLLY035.WMF HOLLY036.WMF HOLLY037.WMF

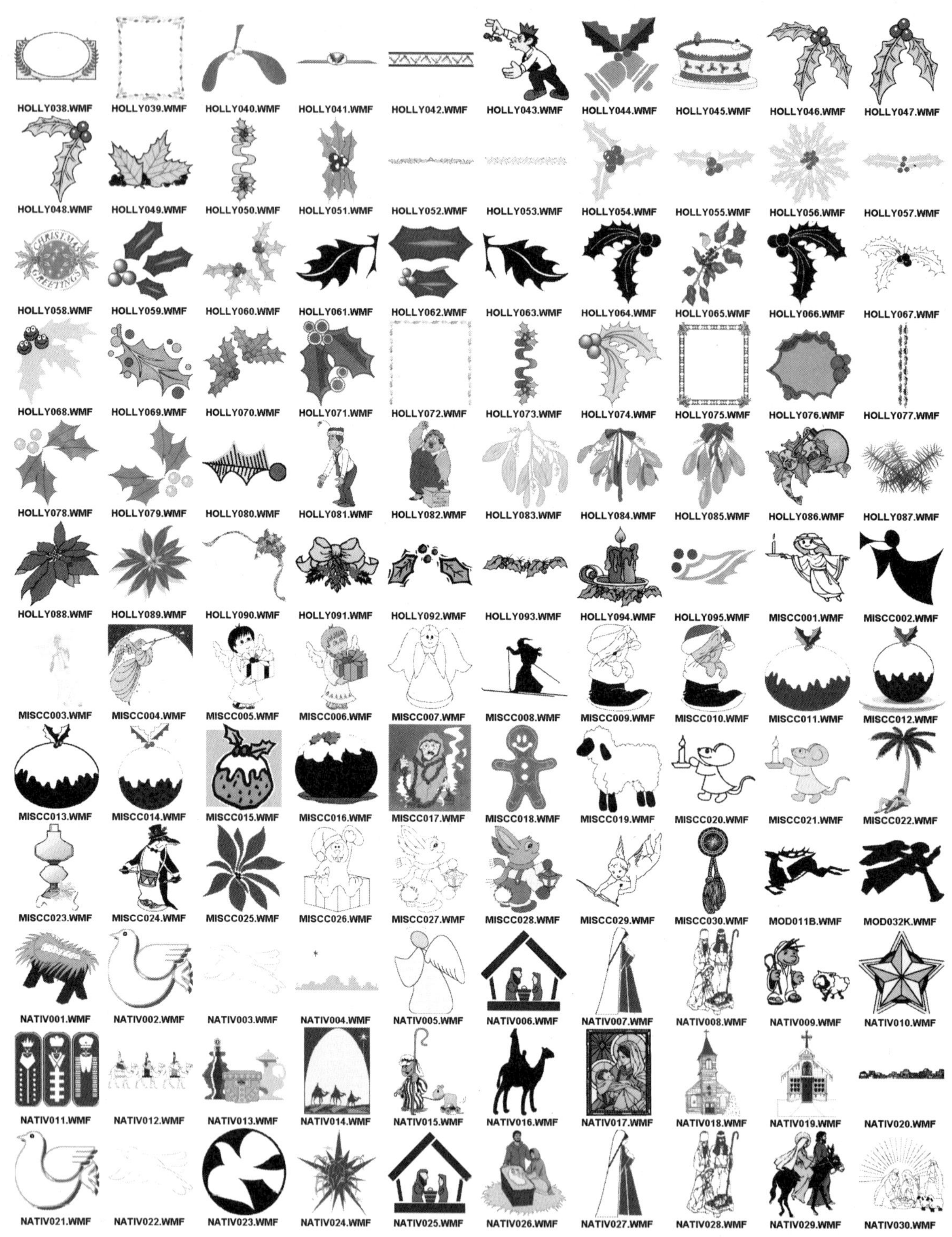

HOLLY038.WMF HOLLY039.WMF HOLLY040.WMF HOLLY041.WMF HOLLY042.WMF HOLLY043.WMF HOLLY044.WMF HOLLY045.WMF HOLLY046.WMF HOLLY047.WMF

HOLLY048.WMF HOLLY049.WMF HOLLY050.WMF HOLLY051.WMF HOLLY052.WMF HOLLY053.WMF HOLLY054.WMF HOLLY055.WMF HOLLY056.WMF HOLLY057.WMF

HOLLY058.WMF HOLLY059.WMF HOLLY060.WMF HOLLY061.WMF HOLLY062.WMF HOLLY063.WMF HOLLY064.WMF HOLLY065.WMF HOLLY066.WMF HOLLY067.WMF

HOLLY068.WMF HOLLY069.WMF HOLLY070.WMF HOLLY071.WMF HOLLY072.WMF HOLLY073.WMF HOLLY074.WMF HOLLY075.WMF HOLLY076.WMF HOLLY077.WMF

HOLLY078.WMF HOLLY079.WMF HOLLY080.WMF HOLLY081.WMF HOLLY082.WMF HOLLY083.WMF HOLLY084.WMF HOLLY085.WMF HOLLY086.WMF HOLLY087.WMF

HOLLY088.WMF HOLLY089.WMF HOLLY090.WMF HOLLY091.WMF HOLLY092.WMF HOLLY093.WMF HOLLY094.WMF HOLLY095.WMF MISCC001.WMF MISCC002.WMF

MISCC003.WMF MISCC004.WMF MISCC005.WMF MISCC006.WMF MISCC007.WMF MISCC008.WMF MISCC009.WMF MISCC010.WMF MISCC011.WMF MISCC012.WMF

MISCC013.WMF MISCC014.WMF MISCC015.WMF MISCC016.WMF MISCC017.WMF MISCC018.WMF MISCC019.WMF MISCC020.WMF MISCC021.WMF MISCC022.WMF

MISCC023.WMF MISCC024.WMF MISCC025.WMF MISCC026.WMF MISCC027.WMF MISCC028.WMF MISCC029.WMF MISCC030.WMF MOD011B.WMF MOD032K.WMF

NATIV001.WMF NATIV002.WMF NATIV003.WMF NATIV004.WMF NATIV005.WMF NATIV006.WMF NATIV007.WMF NATIV008.WMF NATIV009.WMF NATIV010.WMF

NATIV011.WMF NATIV012.WMF NATIV013.WMF NATIV014.WMF NATIV015.WMF NATIV016.WMF NATIV017.WMF NATIV018.WMF NATIV019.WMF NATIV020.WMF

NATIV021.WMF NATIV022.WMF NATIV023.WMF NATIV024.WMF NATIV025.WMF NATIV026.WMF NATIV027.WMF NATIV028.WMF NATIV029.WMF NATIV030.WMF

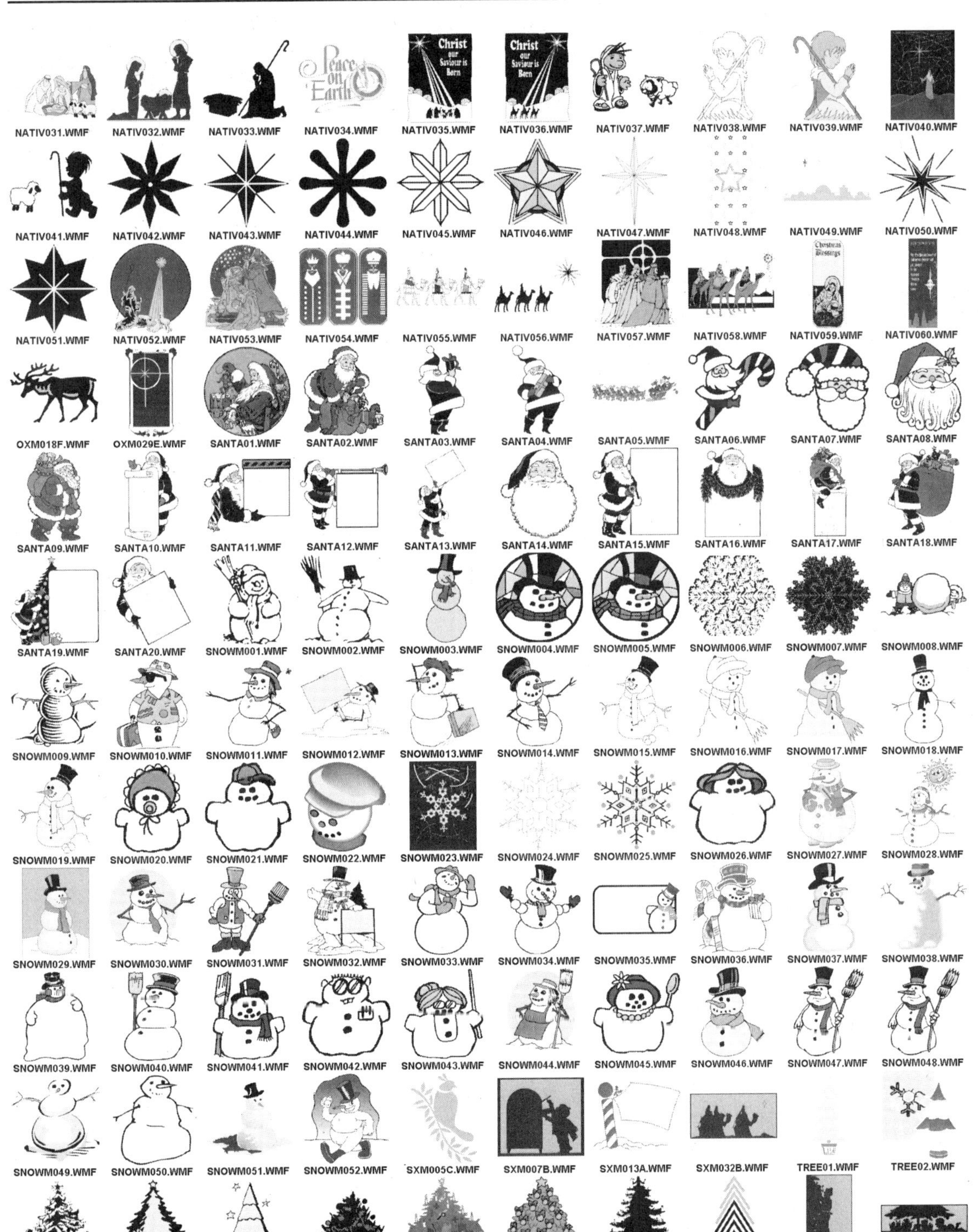
NATIV031.WMF
NATIV032.WMF
NATIV033.WMF
NATIV034.WMF
NATIV035.WMF
NATIV036.WMF
NATIV037.WMF
NATIV038.WMF
NATIV039.WMF
NATIV040.WMF
NATIV041.WMF
NATIV042.WMF
NATIV043.WMF
NATIV044.WMF
NATIV045.WMF
NATIV046.WMF
NATIV047.WMF
NATIV048.WMF
NATIV049.WMF
NATIV050.WMF
NATIV051.WMF
NATIV052.WMF
NATIV053.WMF
NATIV054.WMF
NATIV055.WMF
NATIV056.WMF
NATIV057.WMF
NATIV058.WMF
NATIV059.WMF
NATIV060.WMF
OXM018F.WMF
OXM029E.WMF
SANTA01.WMF
SANTA02.WMF
SANTA03.WMF
SANTA04.WMF
SANTA05.WMF
SANTA06.WMF
SANTA07.WMF
SANTA08.WMF
SANTA09.WMF
SANTA10.WMF
SANTA11.WMF
SANTA12.WMF
SANTA13.WMF
SANTA14.WMF
SANTA15.WMF
SANTA16.WMF
SANTA17.WMF
SANTA18.WMF
SANTA19.WMF
SANTA20.WMF
SNOWM001.WMF
SNOWM002.WMF
SNOWM003.WMF
SNOWM004.WMF
SNOWM005.WMF
SNOWM006.WMF
SNOWM007.WMF
SNOWM008.WMF
SNOWM009.WMF
SNOWM010.WMF
SNOWM011.WMF
SNOWM012.WMF
SNOWM013.WMF
SNOWM014.WMF
SNOWM015.WMF
SNOWM016.WMF
SNOWM017.WMF
SNOWM018.WMF
SNOWM019.WMF
SNOWM020.WMF
SNOWM021.WMF
SNOWM022.WMF
SNOWM023.WMF
SNOWM024.WMF
SNOWM025.WMF
SNOWM026.WMF
SNOWM027.WMF
SNOWM028.WMF
SNOWM029.WMF
SNOWM030.WMF
SNOWM031.WMF
SNOWM032.WMF
SNOWM033.WMF
SNOWM034.WMF
SNOWM035.WMF
SNOWM036.WMF
SNOWM037.WMF
SNOWM038.WMF
SNOWM039.WMF
SNOWM040.WMF
SNOWM041.WMF
SNOWM042.WMF
SNOWM043.WMF
SNOWM044.WMF
SNOWM045.WMF
SNOWM046.WMF
SNOWM047.WMF
SNOWM048.WMF
SNOWM049.WMF
SNOWM050.WMF
SNOWM051.WMF
SNOWM052.WMF
SXM005C.WMF
SXM007B.WMF
SXM013A.WMF
SXM032B.WMF
TREE01.WMF
TREE02.WMF
TREE03.WMF
TREE04.WMF
TREE05.WMF
TREE06.WMF
TREE07.WMF
TREE08.WMF
TREE09.WMF
TREE10.WMF
TREE11.WMF
TREE12.WMF

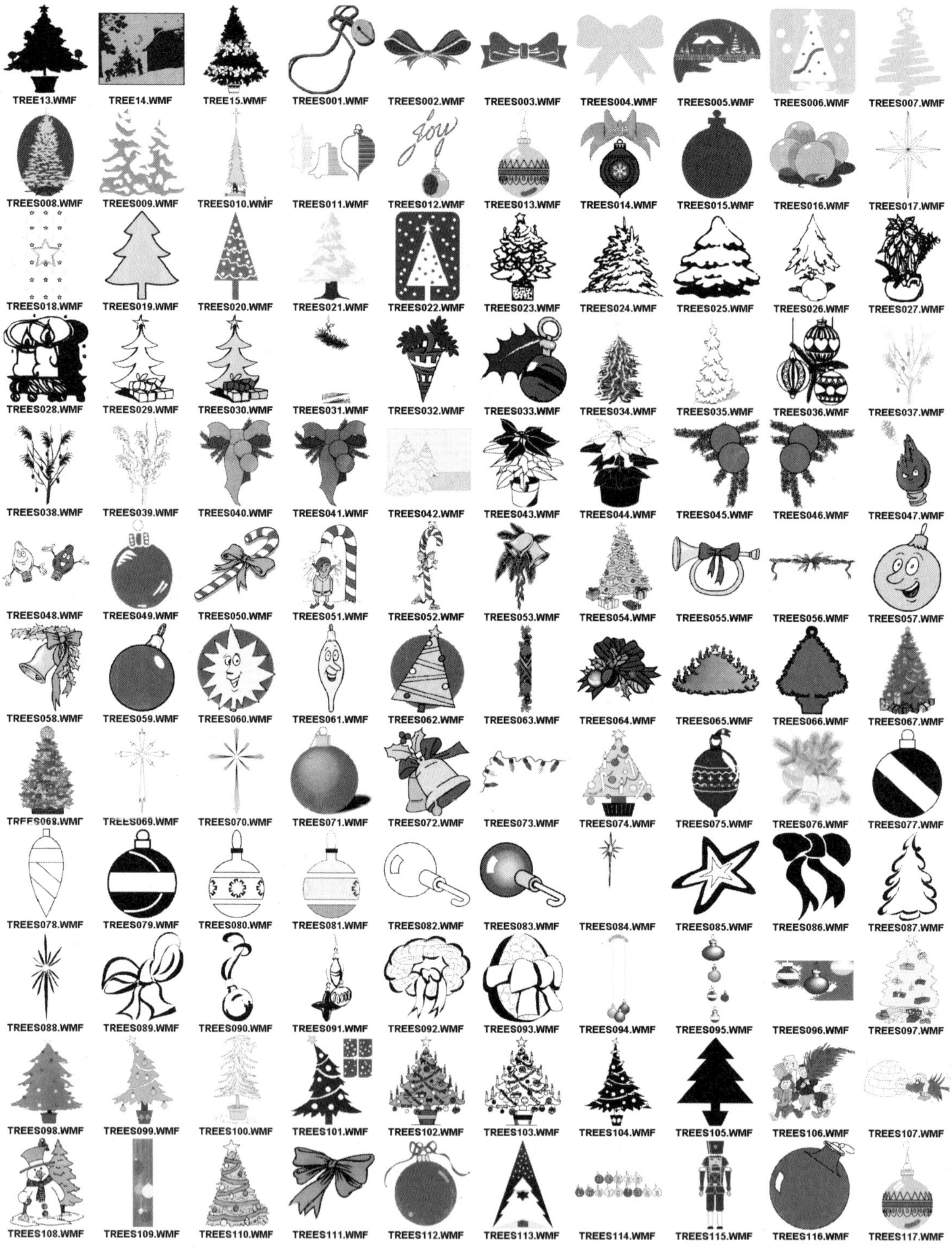
TREE13.WMF TREE14.WMF TREE15.WMF TREES001.WMF TREES002.WMF TREES003.WMF TREES004.WMF TREES005.WMF TREES006.WMF TREES007.WMF
TREES008.WMF TREES009.WMF TREES010.WMF TREES011.WMF TREES012.WMF TREES013.WMF TREES014.WMF TREES015.WMF TREES016.WMF TREES017.WMF
TREES018.WMF TREES019.WMF TREES020.WMF TREES021.WMF TREES022.WMF TREES023.WMF TREES024.WMF TREES025.WMF TREES026.WMF TREES027.WMF
TREES028.WMF TREES029.WMF TREES030.WMF TREES031.WMF TREES032.WMF TREES033.WMF TREES034.WMF TREES035.WMF TREES036.WMF TREES037.WMF
TREES038.WMF TREES039.WMF TREES040.WMF TREES041.WMF TREES042.WMF TREES043.WMF TREES044.WMF TREES045.WMF TREES046.WMF TREES047.WMF
TREES048.WMF TREES049.WMF TREES050.WMF TREES051.WMF TREES052.WMF TREES053.WMF TREES054.WMF TREES055.WMF TREES056.WMF TREES057.WMF
TREES058.WMF TREES059.WMF TREES060.WMF TREES061.WMF TREES062.WMF TREES063.WMF TREES064.WMF TREES065.WMF TREES066.WMF TREES067.WMF
TREES068.WMF TREES069.WMF TREES070.WMF TREES071.WMF TREES072.WMF TREES073.WMF TREES074.WMF TREES075.WMF TREES076.WMF TREES077.WMF
TREES078.WMF TREES079.WMF TREES080.WMF TREES081.WMF TREES082.WMF TREES083.WMF TREES084.WMF TREES085.WMF TREES086.WMF TREES087.WMF
TREES088.WMF TREES089.WMF TREES090.WMF TREES091.WMF TREES092.WMF TREES093.WMF TREES094.WMF TREES095.WMF TREES096.WMF TREES097.WMF
TREES098.WMF TREES099.WMF TREES100.WMF TREES101.WMF TREES102.WMF TREES103.WMF TREES104.WMF TREES105.WMF TREES106.WMF TREES107.WMF
TREES108.WMF TREES109.WMF TREES110.WMF TREES111.WMF TREES112.WMF TREES113.WMF TREES114.WMF TREES115.WMF TREES116.WMF TREES117.WMF

TREES118.WMF TREES119.WMF TREES120.WMF TREES121.WMF TREES122.WMF TREES123.WMF TREES124.WMF TREES125.WMF TREES126.WMF TREES127.WMF
TREES128.WMF TREES129.WMF TREES130.WMF TREES131.WMF TREES132.WMF TREES133.WMF TREES134.WMF TREES135.WMF TREES136.WMF TREES137.WMF
TREES138.WMF TREES139.WMF TREES140.WMF TREES141.WMF TREES142.WMF TREES143.WMF TREES144.WMF TREES145.WMF TREES146.WMF TREES147.WMF
TREES148.WMF TREES149.WMF TREES150.WMF TREES151.WMF TREES152.WMF TREES153.WMF TREES154.WMF TREES155.WMF TREES156.WMF TREES157.WMF
TREES158.WMF TREES159.WMF TREES160.WMF TREES161.WMF TREES162.WMF TREES163.WMF TREES164.WMF TREES165.WMF TREES166.WMF TREES167.WMF
TREES168.WMF TREES169.WMF TREES170.WMF TREES171.WMF TREES172.WMF TREES173.WMF TREES174.WMF TREES175.WMF TREES176.WMF TREES177.WMF
TREES178.WMF TREES179.WMF TREES180.WMF TREES181.WMF TREES182.WMF TREES183.WMF TREES184.WMF TREES185.WMF TREES186.WMF TREES187.WMF
TREES188.WMF TREES189.WMF TREES190.WMF TREES191.WMF TREES192.WMF TREES193.WMF TREES194.WMF TREES195.WMF TREES196.WMF TREES197.WMF
TREES198.WMF TREES199.WMF TREES200.WMF TREES201.WMF TREES202.WMF TREES203.WMF TREES204.WMF TREES205.WMF TREES206.WMF TREES207.WMF
TREES208.WMF TREES209.WMF TREES210.WMF TREES211.WMF TREES212.WMF TREES213.WMF TREES214.WMF TREES215.WMF TREES216.WMF TREES217.WMF
Days 'Til Christmas!
Days 'Til Christmas!
TREES218.WMF TREES219.WMF TREES220.WMF TREES221.WMF TWELV001.WMF TWELV002.WMF TWELV003.WMF TWELV004.WMF TWELV005.WMF TWELV006.WMF
Days 'Til Christmas!
Day 'Til Christmas!
Days 'Til Christmas!
Days 'Til Christmas!
TWELV007.WMF TWELV008.WMF TWELV009.WMF TWELV010.WMF TWELV011.WMF TWELV012.WMF TWELV013.WMF TWELV014.WMF TWELV015.WMF TWELV016.WMF

TWELV017.WMF
TWELV018.WMF
TWELV019.WMF
TWELV020.WMF
TWELV021.WMF
TWELV022.WMF
TWELV023.WMF
TWELV024.WMF
TWELV025.WMF
TWELV026.WMF
TWELV027.WMF
TWELV028.WMF
TWELV029.WMF
TWELV030.WMF
TWELV031.WMF
TWELV032.WMF
TWELV033.WMF
TWELV034.WMF
TWELV035.WMF
VSC055K.WMF
WREATH01.WMF
WREATH02.WMF
WREATH03.WMF
WREATH04.WMF
WREATH05.WMF
WREATH06.WMF
WREATH07.WMF
WREATH08.WMF
WREATH09.WMF
WREATH10.WMF
WREATH11.WMF
WREATH12.WMF
WREATH13.WMF
WREATH14.WMF
XDN031A.WMF
XMC029B.WMF

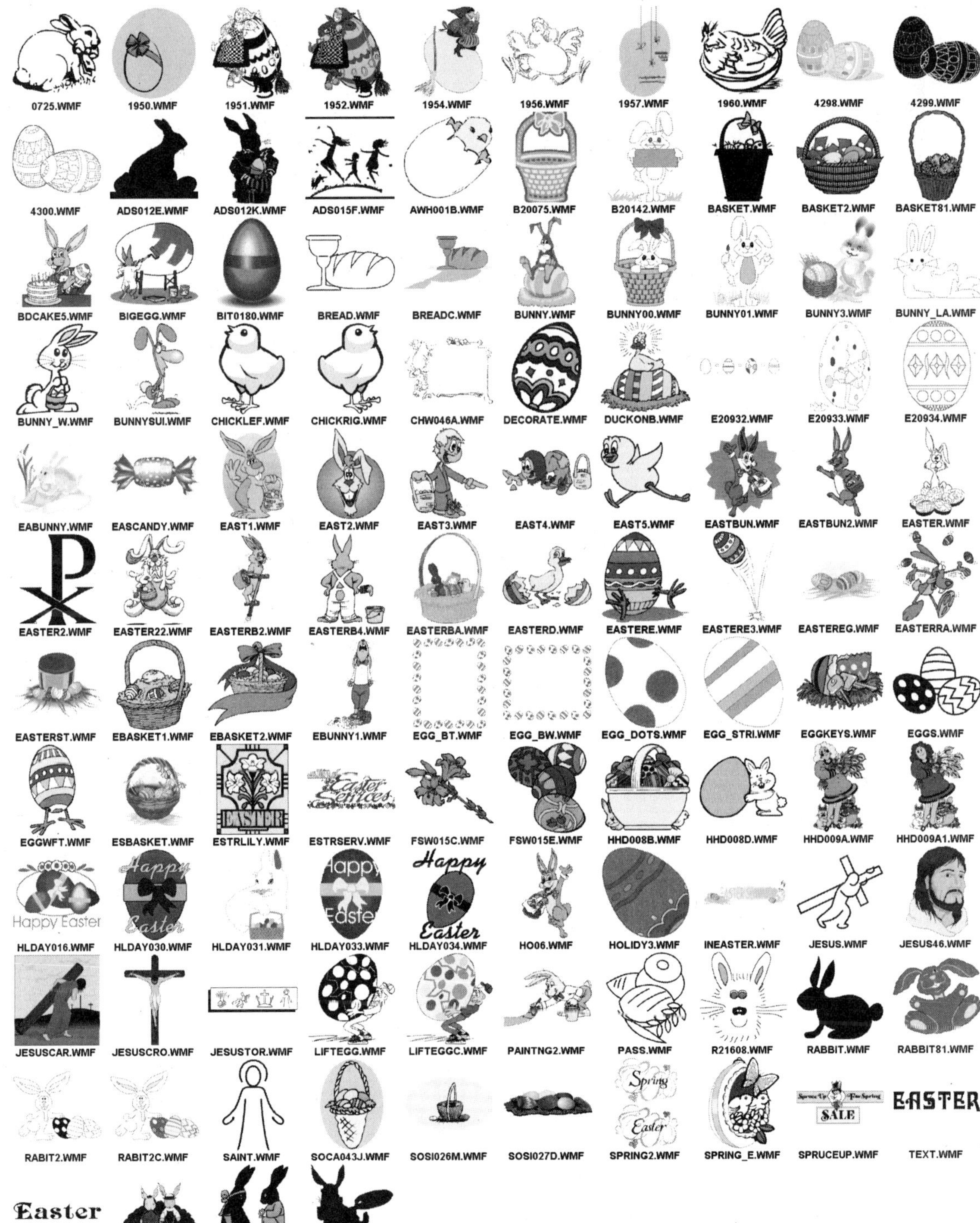
0725.WMF
1950.WMF
1951.WMF
1952.WMF
1954.WMF
1956.WMF
1957.WMF
1960.WMF
4298.WMF
4299.WMF
4300.WMF
ADS012E.WMF
ADS012K.WMF
ADS015F.WMF
AWH001B.WMF
B20075.WMF
B20142.WMF
BASKET.WMF
BASKET2.WMF
BASKET81.WMF
BDCAKE5.WMF
BIGEGG.WMF
BIT0180.WMF
BREAD.WMF
BREADC.WMF
BUNNY.WMF
BUNNY00.WMF
BUNNY01.WMF
BUNNY3.WMF
BUNNY_LA.WMF
BUNNY_W.WMF
BUNNYSUI.WMF
CHICKLEF.WMF
CHICKRIG.WMF
CHW046A.WMF
DECORATE.WMF
DUCKONB.WMF
E20932.WMF
E20933.WMF
E20934.WMF
EABUNNY.WMF
EASCANDY.WMF
EAST1.WMF
EAST2.WMF
EAST3.WMF
EAST4.WMF
EAST5.WMF
EASTBUN.WMF
EASTBUN2.WMF
EASTER.WMF
EASTER2.WMF
EASTER22.WMF
EASTERB2.WMF
EASTERB4.WMF
EASTERBA.WMF
EASTERD.WMF
EASTERE.WMF
EASTERE3.WMF
EASTEREG.WMF
EASTERRA.WMF
EASTERST.WMF
EBASKET1.WMF
EBASKET2.WMF
EBUNNY1.WMF
EGG_BT.WMF
EGG_BW.WMF
EGG_DOTS.WMF
EGG_STRI.WMF
EGGKEYS.WMF
EGGS.WMF
EGGWFT.WMF
ESBASKET.WMF
EASTER
ESTRLILY.WMF
Easter Services
ESTRSERV.WMF
FSW015C.WMF
FSW015E.WMF
HHD008B.WMF
HHD008D.WMF
HHD009A.WMF
HHD009A1.WMF
Happy Easter
HLDAY016.WMF
Happy Easter
HLDAY030.WMF
HLDAY031.WMF
Happy Easter
HLDAY033.WMF
Happy Easter
HLDAY034.WMF
HO06.WMF
HOLIDY3.WMF
INEASTER.WMF
JESUS.WMF
JESUS46.WMF
JESUSCAR.WMF
JESUSCRO.WMF
JESUSTOR.WMF
LIFTEGG.WMF
LIFTEGGC.WMF
PAINTNG2.WMF
PASS.WMF
R21608.WMF
RABBIT.WMF
RABBIT81.WMF
RABIT2.WMF
RABIT2C.WMF
SAINT.WMF
SOCA043J.WMF
SOSI026M.WMF
SOSI027D.WMF
Spring Easter
SPRING2.WMF
SPRING_E.WMF
Spruce Up For Spring
SALE
SPRUCEUP.WMF
EASTER
TEXT.WMF
Easter
TEXTORNB.WMF
VSC048C.WMF
VSC048D.WMF
VSC048E.WMF

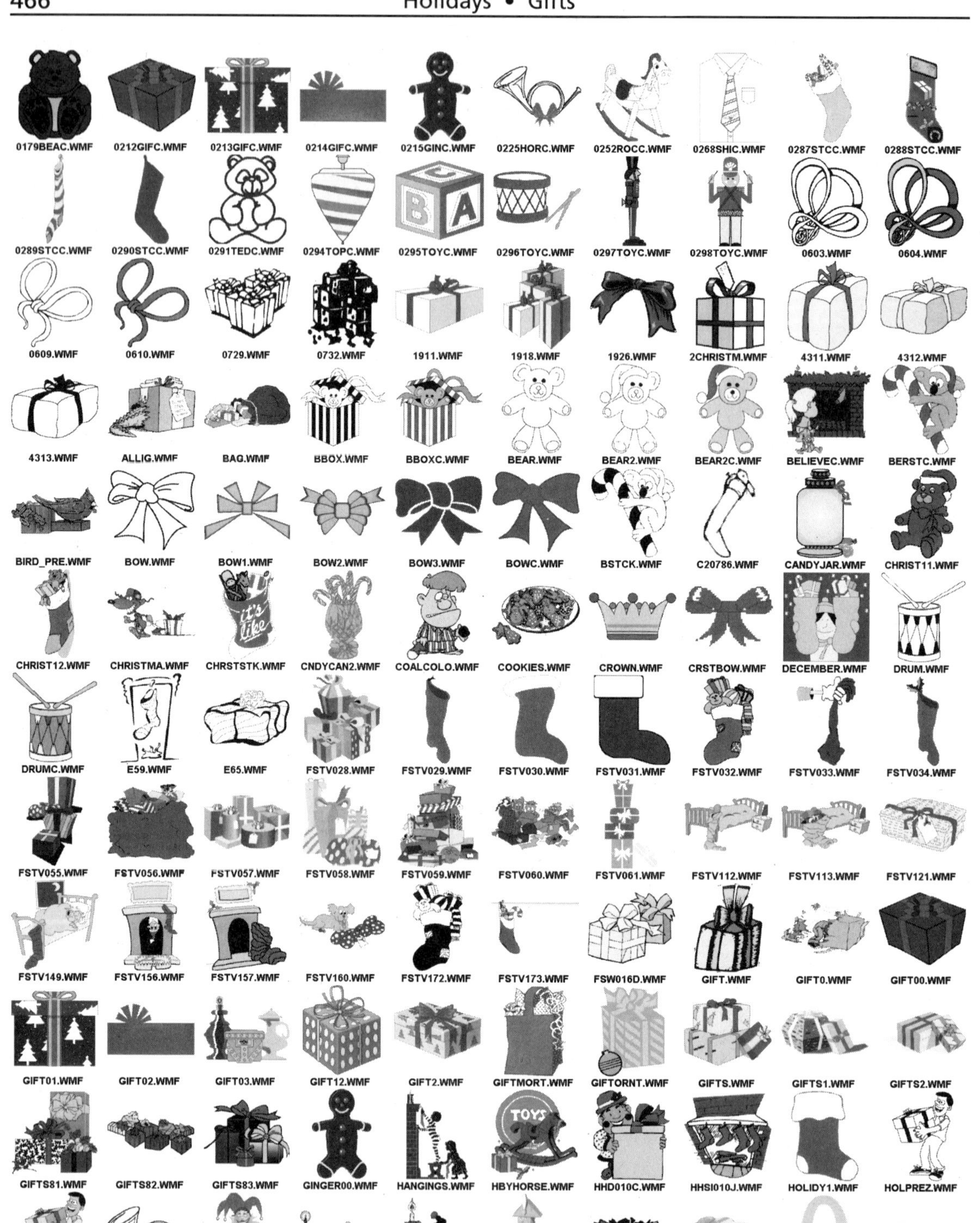
0179BEAC.WMF 0212GIFC.WMF 0213GIFC.WMF 0214GIFC.WMF 0215GINC.WMF 0225HORC.WMF 0252ROCC.WMF 0268SHIC.WMF 0287STCC.WMF 0288STCC.WMF
0289STCC.WMF 0290STCC.WMF 0291TEDC.WMF 0294TOPC.WMF 0295TOYC.WMF 0296TOYC.WMF 0297TOYC.WMF 0298TOYC.WMF 0603.WMF 0604.WMF
0609.WMF 0610.WMF 0729.WMF 0732.WMF 1911.WMF 1918.WMF 1926.WMF 2CHRISTM.WMF 4311.WMF 4312.WMF
4313.WMF ALLIG.WMF BAG.WMF BBOX.WMF BBOXC.WMF BEAR.WMF BEAR2.WMF BEAR2C.WMF BELIEVEC.WMF BERSTC.WMF
BIRD_PRE.WMF BOW.WMF BOW1.WMF BOW2.WMF BOW3.WMF BOWC.WMF BSTCK.WMF C20786.WMF CANDYJAR.WMF CHRIST11.WMF
CHRIST12.WMF CHRISTMA.WMF CHRSTSTK.WMF CNDYCAN2.WMF COALCOLO.WMF COOKIES.WMF CROWN.WMF CRSTBOW.WMF DECEMBER.WMF DRUM.WMF
DRUMC.WMF E59.WMF E65.WMF FSTV028.WMF FSTV029.WMF FSTV030.WMF FSTV031.WMF FSTV032.WMF FSTV033.WMF FSTV034.WMF
FSTV055.WMF FSTV056.WMF FSTV057.WMF FSTV058.WMF FSTV059.WMF FSTV060.WMF FSTV061.WMF FSTV112.WMF FSTV113.WMF FSTV121.WMF
FSTV149.WMF FSTV156.WMF FSTV157.WMF FSTV160.WMF FSTV172.WMF FSTV173.WMF FSW016D.WMF GIFT.WMF GIFT0.WMF GIFT00.WMF
GIFT01.WMF GIFT02.WMF GIFT03.WMF GIFT12.WMF GIFT2.WMF GIFTMORT.WMF GIFTORNT.WMF GIFTS.WMF GIFTS1.WMF GIFTS2.WMF
GIFTS81.WMF GIFTS82.WMF GIFTS83.WMF GINGER00.WMF HANGINGS.WMF HBYHORSE.WMF HHD010C.WMF HHSI010J.WMF HOLIDY1.WMF HOLPREZ.WMF
HOLPREZC.WMF HORN00.WMF JACKBOX.WMF MANTLEWS.WMF MOUSEWGI.WMF NUTCRACK.WMF OPENEDGI.WMF OPENGIFT.WMF ORNMEN6.WMF P21594.WMF

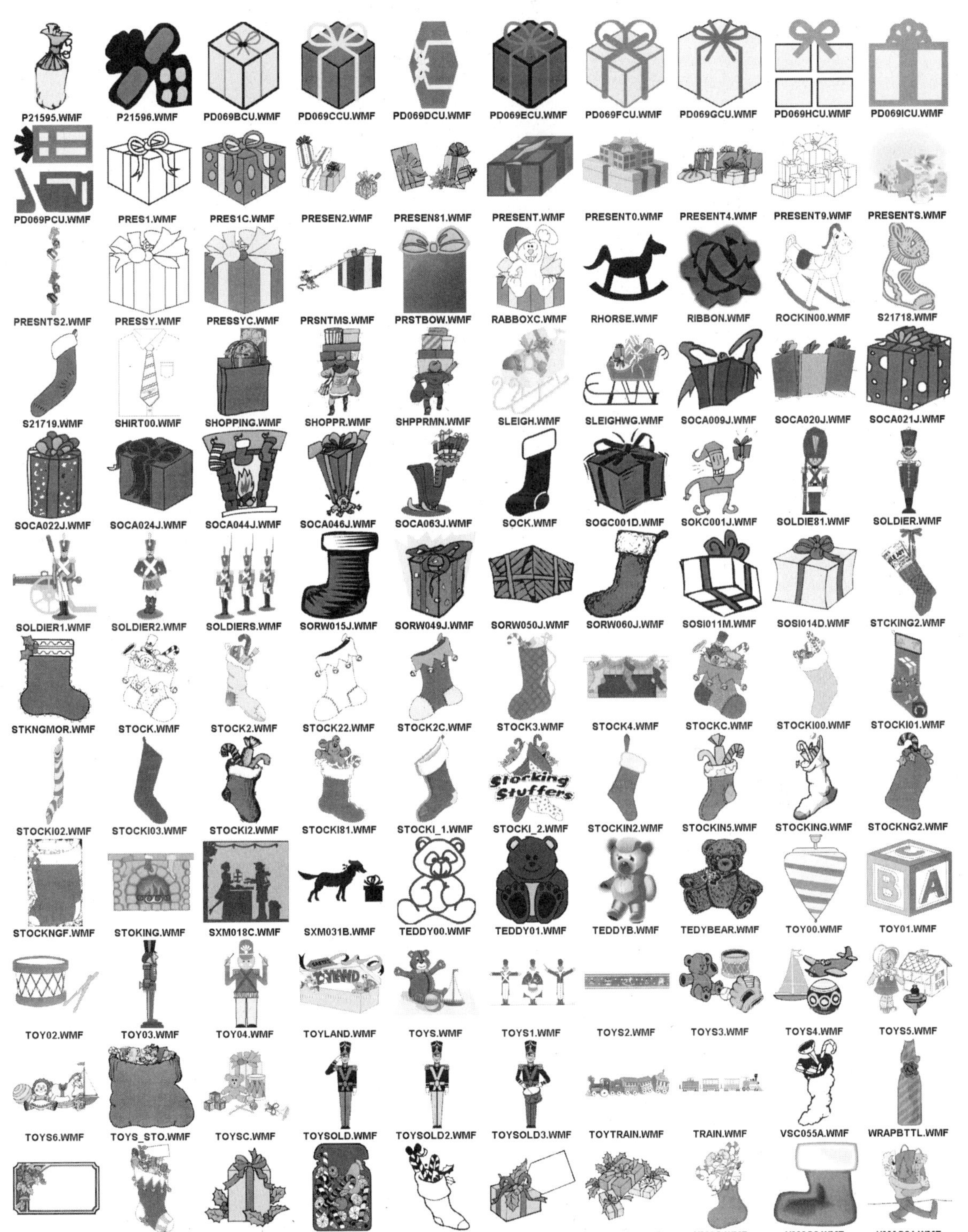
P21595.WMF
P21596.WMF
PD069BCU.WMF
PD069CCU.WMF
PD069DCU.WMF
PD069ECU.WMF
PD069FCU.WMF
PD069GCU.WMF
PD069HCU.WMF
PD069ICU.WMF
PD069PCU.WMF
PRES1.WMF
PRES1C.WMF
PRESEN2.WMF
PRESEN81.WMF
PRESENT.WMF
PRESENT0.WMF
PRESENT4.WMF
PRESENT9.WMF
PRESENTS.WMF
PRESNTS2.WMF
PRESSY.WMF
PRESSYC.WMF
PRSNTMS.WMF
PRSTBOW.WMF
RABBOXC.WMF
RHORSE.WMF
RIBBON.WMF
ROCKIN00.WMF
S21718.WMF
S21719.WMF
SHIRT00.WMF
SHOPPING.WMF
SHOPPR.WMF
SHPPRMN.WMF
SLEIGH.WMF
SLEIGHWG.WMF
SOCA009J.WMF
SOCA020J.WMF
SOCA021J.WMF
SOCA022J.WMF
SOCA024J.WMF
SOCA044J.WMF
SOCA046J.WMF
SOCA063J.WMF
SOCK.WMF
SOGC001D.WMF
SOKC001J.WMF
SOLDIE81.WMF
SOLDIER.WMF
SOLDIER1.WMF
SOLDIER2.WMF
SOLDIERS.WMF
SORW015J.WMF
SORW049J.WMF
SORW050J.WMF
SORW060J.WMF
SOSI011M.WMF
SOSI014D.WMF
STCKING2.WMF
STKNGMOR.WMF
STOCK.WMF
STOCK2.WMF
STOCK22.WMF
STOCK2C.WMF
STOCK3.WMF
STOCK4.WMF
STOCKC.WMF
STOCKI00.WMF
STOCKI01.WMF
STOCKI02.WMF
STOCKI03.WMF
STOCKI2.WMF
STOCKI81.WMF
STOCKI_1.WMF
Stocking Stuffers
STOCKI_2.WMF
STOCKIN2.WMF
STOCKIN5.WMF
STOCKING.WMF
STOCKNG2.WMF
STOCKNGF.WMF
STOKING.WMF
SXM018C.WMF
SXM031B.WMF
TEDDY00.WMF
TEDDY01.WMF
TEDDYB.WMF
TEDYBEAR.WMF
TOY00.WMF
TOY01.WMF
TOY02.WMF
TOY03.WMF
TOY04.WMF
TOYLAND.WMF
TOYS.WMF
TOYS1.WMF
TOYS2.WMF
TOYS3.WMF
TOYS4.WMF
TOYS5.WMF
TOYS6.WMF
TOYS_STO.WMF
TOYSC.WMF
TOYSOLD.WMF
TOYSOLD2.WMF
TOYSOLD3.WMF
TOYTRAIN.WMF
TRAIN.WMF
VSC055A.WMF
WRAPBTTL.WMF
XDN006C.WMF
XDN008A.WMF
XDN008B.WMF
XDN009B.WMF
XDN018C.WMF
XDN021B.WMF
XDN027B.WMF
XMAS.WMF
XMAS2.WMF
XMAS24.WMF

XMAS28.WMF
XMAS33.WMF
XMAS38.WMF
XMAS41.WMF
XMAS5.WMF
XMAS8.WMF
XMASPRS.WMF
XMASSCK.WMF
XMASTOWN.WMF
XMC011B.WMF
XMC019B.WMF
XMC023B.WMF
XMC025B.WMF
XMC028A.WMF
XMC028B.WMF
XMC029A.WMF
XMC032A.WMF

0702.WMF 0705.WMF 0706.WMF 0707.WMF 0708.WMF 0710.WMF 0742.WMF 0743.WMF 0744.WMF 0745.WMF
0746.WMF 0747.WMF 0748.WMF 0749.WMF 0750.WMF 0751.WMF 0752.WMF 0753.WMF 0754.WMF 0755.WMF
0756.WMF 0757.WMF 0758.WMF 0759.WMF 0760.WMF 0761.WMF 0762.WMF 0763.WMF 0764.WMF 0765.WMF
0766.WMF 0767.WMF 0768.WMF 0769.WMF 0770.WMF 0771.WMF 0772.WMF 0773.WMF 0774.WMF 0775.WMF
0776.WMF 0777.WMF 0778.WMF 0779.WMF 0780.WMF 0781.WMF 0782.WMF 0783.WMF 0784.WMF 0785.WMF
0786.WMF 0787.WMF 0788.WMF 0789.WMF 0790.WMF 0791.WMF 0792.WMF 0793.WMF 0794.WMF 0795.WMF
0796.WMF 0797.WMF 0798.WMF 0799.WMF 0800.WMF 1939.WMF 1941.WMF 1942.WMF 1945.WMF 1948.WMF
1961.WMF 4_HWEEKH.WMF APRILFOO.WMF APRLFOOL.WMF BELLMORT.WMF BLACKHIS.WMF BOSSDAY.WMF BUSINESS.WMF CANADAD1.WMF CHINESE.WMF
CHRISTOP.WMF CHURCHMO.WMF CINCO.WMF COLMBS.WMF COLMBSHP.WMF COLUMB81.WMF COLUMBS2.WMF COLUMBU1.WMF COLUMBU2.WMF COLUMBU3.WMF
COLUMBU5.WMF COLUMBU7.WMF COLUMBU8.WMF COLUMBUS.WMF DAIRYMON.WMF DREAMISA.WMF FIRESAF2.WMF FIRESAF3.WMF FRIDAY13.WMF FSTV094.WMF
GRNDHOG.WMF GRNDHOG2.WMF GRONDHOG.WMF GROUNDHO.WMF HAPPYHO.WMF HAPPYHO3.WMF HAPPYHO4.WMF ICECREAM.WMF INCOMETA.WMF L21190.WMF
MARDI1.WMF MARDI2.WMF MARDIGRA.WMF MARDIGRS.WMF MEMRLDY1.WMF MEMRLDY2.WMF MLK_DAY.WMF NEWSPAPE.WMF PATYDUD.WMF PATYDUDC.WMF

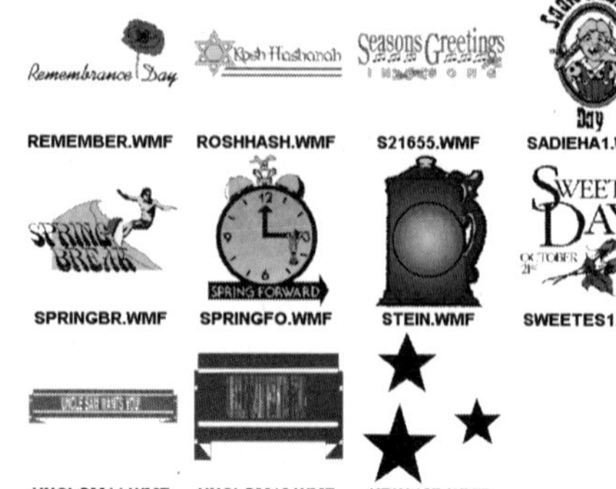

REMEMBER.WMF ROSHHASH.WMF S21655.WMF SADIEHA1.WMF SADIEHAW.WMF SADIHAWK.WMF SANTAMAR.WMF SEAFOODM.WMF SIESTA.WMF SPACEWEE.WMF

SPRINGBR.WMF SPRINGFO.WMF STEIN.WMF SWEETES1.WMF SWEETEST.WMF TAXTIMEH.WMF THANKYOU.WMF THEDREAM.WMF TIMETOWI.WMF TOPBRAS1.WMF

UNCLSM11.WMF UNCLSM12.WMF XDN015B.WMF

ADS023F.WMF ADS023H.WMF ADS024D.WMF ADS024K.WMF ADS024L.WMF ADS024O.WMF ADS025D.WMF ADS025K.WMF FSW028A.WMF FSW028AB.WMF

FSW028B.WMF FSW028BC.WMF FSW028D.WMF HHD025A.WMF HHW001A.WMF HHW001B.WMF HHW001B1.WMF HHW001C.WMF HHW002A.WMF HHW002B.WMF

HHW002C.WMF HHW002C1.WMF HHW003A.WMF HHW003B.WMF HHW003C.WMF HHW004A.WMF HHW004B.WMF HHW004C.WMF HHW005A.WMF HHW005B.WMF

HHW005C.WMF HHW006A.WMF HHW006B.WMF HHW006C.WMF HHW007A.WMF HHW007B.WMF HHW007C.WMF HHW008A.WMF HHW008B.WMF HHW008B1.WMF

HHW009A.WMF HHW009B.WMF HHW010A.WMF HHW010B.WMF HHW010C.WMF HHW011A.WMF HHW011B.WMF HHW011C.WMF HHW012A.WMF HHW012B.WMF

HHW012C.WMF HHW013A.WMF HHW013B.WMF HHW013C.WMF HHW014A.WMF HHW014B.WMF HHW014C.WMF HHW015A.WMF HHW015B.WMF HHW015C.WMF

HHW016A.WMF HHW016B.WMF HHW016C.WMF HHW017A.WMF HHW017B.WMF HHW017C.WMF HHW018A.WMF HHW018B.WMF HHW018C.WMF HHW019A.WMF

HHW019B.WMF HHW020A.WMF HHW020B.WMF HHW020C.WMF HHW021A.WMF HHW021B.WMF HHW021C.WMF HHW022A.WMF HHW022B.WMF HHW022C.WMF

HHW023A.WMF HHW023B.WMF HHW024A.WMF HHW024B.WMF HHW024C.WMF HHW025A.WMF HHW025B.WMF HHW025C.WMF HHW026A.WMF HHW026B.WMF

HHW026C.WMF HHW027A.WMF HHW027B.WMF HHW027C.WMF HHW028A.WMF HHW028B.WMF HHW028C.WMF HHW029A.WMF HHW029B.WMF HHW030A.WMF

HHW030B.WMF HHW030C.WMF HHW031A.WMF HHW031B.WMF HHW031C.WMF HHW032A.WMF HHW032B.WMF HHW032C.WMF HHW032D.WMF HHW032E.WMF

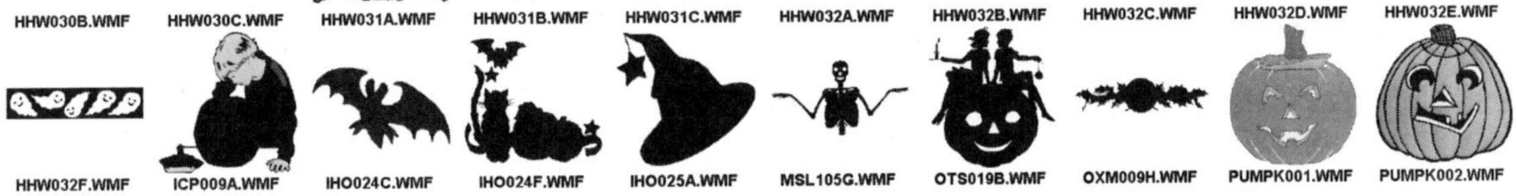

HHW032F.WMF ICP009A.WMF IHO024C.WMF IHO024F.WMF IHO025A.WMF MSL105G.WMF OTS019B.WMF OXM009H.WMF PUMPK001.WMF PUMPK002.WMF

PUMPK003.WMF PUMPK004.WMF PUMPK005.WMF PUMPK006.WMF PUMPK007.WMF PUMPK008.WMF PUMPK009.WMF PUMPK010.WMF PUMPK011.WMF PUMPK012.WMF

PUMPK013.WMF PUMPK014.WMF PUMPK015.WMF PUMPK016.WMF PUMPK017.WMF PUMPK018.WMF PUMPK019.WMF PUMPK020.WMF PUMPK021.WMF PUMPK022.WMF

PUMPK023.WMF PUMPK024.WMF PUMPK025.WMF PUMPK026.WMF PUMPK027.WMF PUMPK028.WMF PUMPK029.WMF PUMPK030.WMF PUMPK031.WMF PUMPK032.WMF

PUMPK033.WMF PUMPK034.WMF PUMPK035.WMF PUMPK036.WMF PUMPK037.WMF PUMPK038.WMF PUMPK039.WMF PUMPK040.WMF PUMPK041.WMF PUMPK042.WMF

PUMPK043.WMF PUMPK044.WMF PUMPK045.WMF PUMPK046.WMF PUMPK047.WMF PUMPK048.WMF PUMPK049.WMF PUMPK050.WMF PUMPK051.WMF PUMPK052.WMF

PUMPK053.WMF PUMPK054.WMF PUMPK055.WMF PUMPK056.WMF PUMPK057.WMF PUMPK058.WMF PUMPK059.WMF PUMPK060.WMF PUMPK061.WMF PUMPK062.WMF

PUMPK063.WMF PUMPK064.WMF PUMPK065.WMF PUMPK066.WMF PUMPK067.WMF PUMPK068.WMF SCARY001.WMF SCARY002.WMF SCARY003.WMF SCARY004.WMF

SCARY005.WMF SCARY006.WMF SCARY007.WMF SCARY008.WMF SCARY009.WMF SCARY010.WMF SCARY011.WMF SCARY012.WMF SCARY013.WMF SCARY014.WMF

SCARY015.WMF SCARY016.WMF SCARY017.WMF SCARY018.WMF SCARY019.WMF SCARY020.WMF SCARY021.WMF SCARY022.WMF SCARY023.WMF SCARY024.WMF

SCARY025.WMF SCARY026.WMF SCARY027.WMF SCARY028.WMF SCARY029.WMF SCARY030.WMF SCARY031.WMF SCARY032.WMF SCARY033.WMF SCARY034.WMF

SCARY035.WMF SCARY036.WMF SCARY037.WMF SCARY038.WMF SCARY039.WMF SCARY040.WMF SCARY041.WMF SCARY042.WMF SCARY043.WMF SCARY044.WMF

SCARY045.WMF SCARY046.WMF SCARY047.WMF SCARY048.WMF SCARY049.WMF SCARY050.WMF SCARY051.WMF SCARY052.WMF SCARY053.WMF SCARY054.WMF

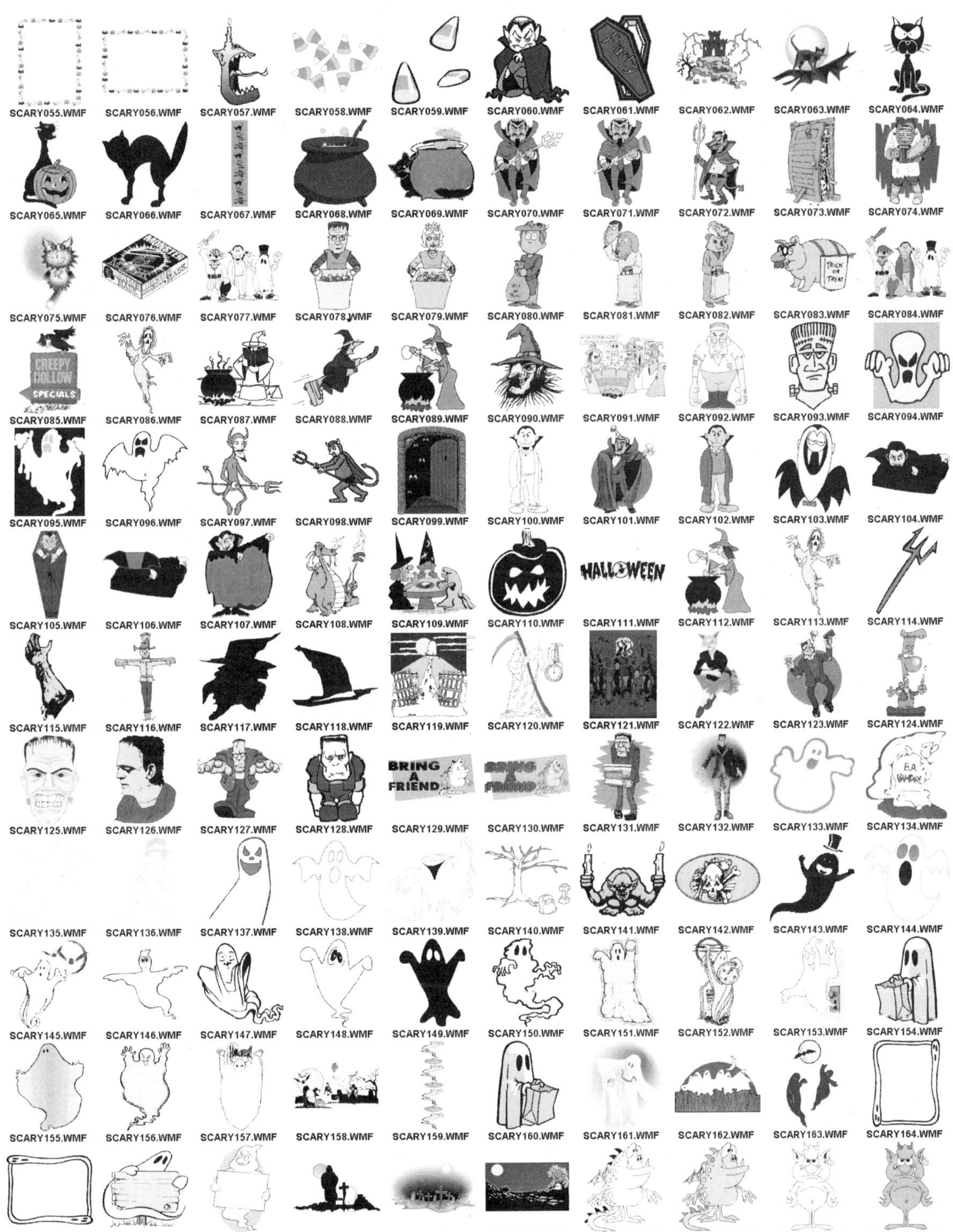

SCARY055.WMF SCARY056.WMF SCARY057.WMF SCARY058.WMF SCARY059.WMF SCARY060.WMF SCARY061.WMF SCARY062.WMF SCARY063.WMF SCARY064.WMF

SCARY065.WMF SCARY066.WMF SCARY067.WMF SCARY068.WMF SCARY069.WMF SCARY070.WMF SCARY071.WMF SCARY072.WMF SCARY073.WMF SCARY074.WMF

SCARY075.WMF SCARY076.WMF SCARY077.WMF SCARY078.WMF SCARY079.WMF SCARY080.WMF SCARY081.WMF SCARY082.WMF SCARY083.WMF SCARY084.WMF

SCARY085.WMF SCARY086.WMF SCARY087.WMF SCARY088.WMF SCARY089.WMF SCARY090.WMF SCARY091.WMF SCARY092.WMF SCARY093.WMF SCARY094.WMF

SCARY095.WMF SCARY096.WMF SCARY097.WMF SCARY098.WMF SCARY099.WMF SCARY100.WMF SCARY101.WMF SCARY102.WMF SCARY103.WMF SCARY104.WMF

SCARY105.WMF SCARY106.WMF SCARY107.WMF SCARY108.WMF SCARY109.WMF SCARY110.WMF SCARY111.WMF SCARY112.WMF SCARY113.WMF SCARY114.WMF

SCARY115.WMF SCARY116.WMF SCARY117.WMF SCARY118.WMF SCARY119.WMF SCARY120.WMF SCARY121.WMF SCARY122.WMF SCARY123.WMF SCARY124.WMF

SCARY125.WMF SCARY126.WMF SCARY127.WMF SCARY128.WMF SCARY129.WMF SCARY130.WMF SCARY131.WMF SCARY132.WMF SCARY133.WMF SCARY134.WMF

SCARY135.WMF SCARY136.WMF SCARY137.WMF SCARY138.WMF SCARY139.WMF SCARY140.WMF SCARY141.WMF SCARY142.WMF SCARY143.WMF SCARY144.WMF

SCARY145.WMF SCARY146.WMF SCARY147.WMF SCARY148.WMF SCARY149.WMF SCARY150.WMF SCARY151.WMF SCARY152.WMF SCARY153.WMF SCARY154.WMF

SCARY155.WMF SCARY156.WMF SCARY157.WMF SCARY158.WMF SCARY159.WMF SCARY160.WMF SCARY161.WMF SCARY162.WMF SCARY163.WMF SCARY164.WMF

SCARY165.WMF SCARY166.WMF SCARY167.WMF SCARY168.WMF SCARY169.WMF SCARY170.WMF SCARY171.WMF SCARY172.WMF SCARY173.WMF SCARY174.WMF

SCARY175.WMF SCARY176.WMF SCARY177.WMF SCARY178.WMF SCARY179.WMF SCARY180.WMF SCARY181.WMF SCARY182.WMF SCARY183.WMF SCARY184.WMF
SCARY185.WMF SCARY186.WMF SCARY187.WMF SCARY188.WMF SCARY189.WMF SCARY190.WMF SCARY191.WMF SCARY192.WMF SCARY193.WMF SCARY194.WMF
SCARY195.WMF SCARY196.WMF SCARY197.WMF SCARY198.WMF SCARY199.WMF SCARY200.WMF SCARY201.WMF SCARY202.WMF SCARY203.WMF SCARY204.WMF
SCARY205.WMF SCARY206.WMF SCARY207.WMF SCARY208.WMF SCARY209.WMF SCARY210.WMF SCARY211.WMF SCARY212.WMF SCARY213.WMF SCARY214.WMF
SCARY215.WMF SCARY216.WMF SCARY217.WMF SCARY218.WMF SCARY219.WMF SCARY220.WMF SCARY221.WMF SCARY222.WMF SCARY223.WMF SCARY224.WMF
SCARY225.WMF SCARY226.WMF SCARY227.WMF SCARY228.WMF SCARY229.WMF SCARY230.WMF SCARY231.WMF SCARY232.WMF SCARY233.WMF SCARY234.WMF
SCARY235.WMF SCARY236.WMF SCARY237.WMF SCARY238.WMF SCARY239.WMF SCARY240.WMF SCARY241.WMF SCARY242.WMF SCARY243.WMF SCARY244.WMF
SCARY245.WMF SCARY246.WMF SCARY247.WMF SCARY248.WMF SCARY249.WMF SCARY250.WMF SCARY251.WMF SCARY252.WMF SCARY253.WMF SCARY254.WMF
SCARY255.WMF SCARY256.WMF SCARY257.WMF SCARY258.WMF SCARY259.WMF SCARY260.WMF SCARY261.WMF SCARY262.WMF SCARY263.WMF SCARY264.WMF
SCARY265.WMF SCARY266.WMF SCARY267.WMF SCARY268.WMF SCARY269.WMF SCARY270.WMF SCARY271.WMF SCARY272.WMF SCARY273.WMF SCARY274.WMF
SCARY275.WMF SCARY276.WMF SCARY277.WMF SCARY278.WMF SCARY279.WMF SCARY280.WMF SCARY281.WMF SCARY282.WMF SCARY283.WMF SCARY284.WMF
SCARY285.WMF SCARY286.WMF SCARY287.WMF SCARY288.WMF SCARY289.WMF SCARY290.WMF SCARY291.WMF SCARY292.WMF SCARY293.WMF SCARY294.WMF

SCARY295.WMF SCARY296.WMF SCARY297.WMF SCARY298.WMF SCARY299.WMF SCARY300.WMF SCARY301.WMF SCARY302.WMF SCARY303.WMF SCARY304.WMF

SCARY305.WMF SCARY306.WMF SCARY307.WMF SCARY308.WMF SCARY309.WMF SCARY310.WMF SCARY311.WMF SCARY312.WMF SCARY313.WMF SCARY314.WMF

SCARY315.WMF SCARY316.WMF SCARY317.WMF SCARY318.WMF SCARY319.WMF SCARY320.WMF SCARY321.WMF SCARY322.WMF SCARY323.WMF SCARY324.WMF

SCARY325.WMF SCARY326.WMF SCARY327.WMF SCARY328.WMF SCARY329.WMF SCARY330.WMF SCARY331.WMF SCARY332.WMF SCARY333.WMF SCARY334.WMF

SCARY335.WMF SCARY336.WMF SCARY337.WMF SCARY338.WMF SCARY339.WMF SCARY340.WMF SCARY341.WMF SCARY342.WMF SCARY343.WMF SCARY344.WMF

SCARY345.WMF SCARY346.WMF SCARY347.WMF SCARY348.WMF SCARY349.WMF SCARY350.WMF SCARY351.WMF SCARY352.WMF SCARY353.WMF SCARY354.WMF

SCARY355.WMF SCARY356.WMF SCARY357.WMF SCARY358.WMF SCARY359.WMF SCARY360.WMF SCARY361.WMF SCARY362.WMF SCARY363.WMF SCARY364.WMF

SCARY365.WMF SCARY366.WMF SCARY367.WMF SCARY368.WMF SCARY369.WMF SCARY370.WMF SCARY371.WMF SCARY372.WMF SCARY373.WMF SCARY374.WMF

SCARY375.WMF SCARY376.WMF SCARY377.WMF SCARY378.WMF SCARY379.WMF SCARY380.WMF SCARY381.WMF SCARY382.WMF SCARY383.WMF SCARY384.WMF

SCARY385.WMF SCARY386.WMF SCARY387.WMF SCARY388.WMF SCARY389.WMF SCARY390.WMF SCARY391.WMF SCARY392.WMF SCARY393.WMF SCARY394.WMF

SCARY395.WMF SCARY396.WMF SCARY397.WMF SCARY398.WMF SCARY399.WMF SCARY400.WMF SCARY401.WMF SCARY402.WMF SCARY403.WMF SCARY404.WMF

SCARY405.WMF SCARY406.WMF SCARY407.WMF SCARY408.WMF SCARY409.WMF SCARY410.WMF SCARY411.WMF SCARY412.WMF SCARY413.WMF SCARY414.WMF

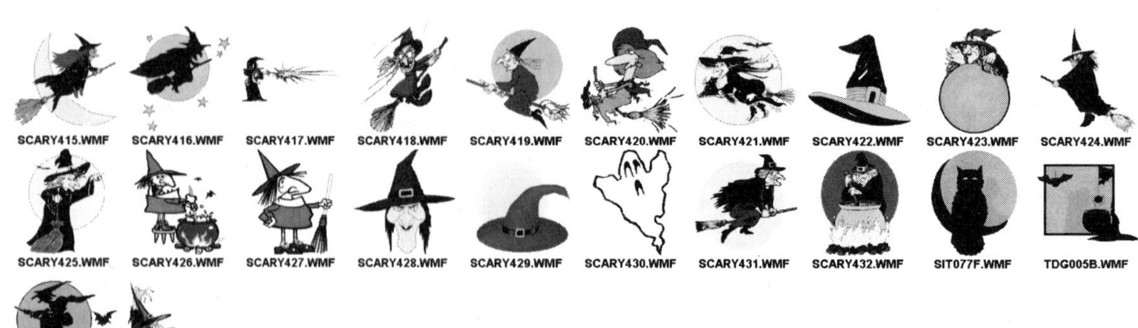

SCARY415.WMF SCARY416.WMF SCARY417.WMF SCARY418.WMF SCARY419.WMF SCARY420.WMF SCARY421.WMF SCARY422.WMF SCARY423.WMF SCARY424.WMF

SCARY425.WMF SCARY426.WMF SCARY427.WMF SCARY428.WMF SCARY429.WMF SCARY430.WMF SCARY431.WMF SCARY432.WMF SIT077F.WMF TDG005B.WMF

VSC050F.WMF WOFAC099.WMF

Holidays • Miscellaneous (MISC)

ABLIN.WMF DADDAY01.WMF DADDAY02.WMF DADDAY03.WMF DADDAY04.WMF DADDAY05.WMF DADDAY06.WMF DADDAY07.WMF DADDAY08.WMF DADDAY09.WMF

DADDAY10.WMF DADDAY11.WMF DADDAY12.WMF DADDAY13.WMF DADDAY14.WMF DADDAY15.WMF DADDAY16.WMF DADDAY17.WMF DADDAY18.WMF DADDAY19.WMF

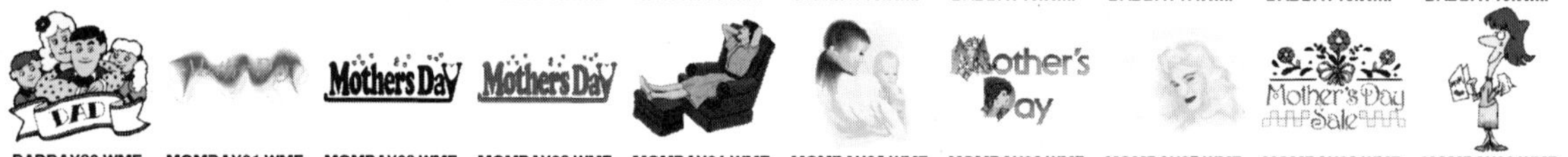

DADDAY20.WMF MOMDAY01.WMF MOMDAY02.WMF MOMDAY03.WMF MOMDAY04.WMF MOMDAY05.WMF MOMDAY06.WMF MOMDAY07.WMF MOMDAY08.WMF MOMDAY09.WMF

MOMDAY10.WMF MOMDAY11.WMF MOMDAY12.WMF MOMDAY13.WMF MOMDAY14.WMF MOMDAY15.WMF MOMDAY16.WMF MOMDAY17.WMF WORLD01.WMF WORLD02.WMF

WORLD03.WMF WORLD04.WMF WORLD05.WMF WORLD06.WMF WORLD07.WMF WORLD08.WMF WORLD09.WMF WORLD10.WMF WORLD11.WMF WORLD12.WMF

0671.WMF 1FATHER_.WMF 1HAPPY_1.WMF 1HAPPY_N.WMF 1NEW_YEA.WMF 2FATHER_.WMF 2HAPPY_N.WMF 2NEW_YEA.WMF 3NEW_YEA.WMF ADS002F.WMF

ADS006B.WMF ASHAMP.WMF BABY.WMF BALLOON8.WMF BALLOONS.WMF BTLWNE.WMF BUBBLE00.WMF CHAMPAGN.WMF CHAMPNG.WMF COCKT_H.WMF

COCLEMON.WMF COCTAIL.WMF CONFET.WMF CONFETTI.WMF DADTIME1.WMF DISCO.WMF DISCOC.WMF FATHER2.WMF FATHERIN.WMF FATHERT.WMF

FTHRTIME.WMF FTHRTM2.WMF FTHRTMB.WMF GLASSESC.WMF HAPPYMAN.WMF HAPPYNE.WMF HAPPYNE2.WMF HHD001A.WMF HLDAY018.WMF HOURGL.WMF

HOURGL00.WMF HOURGLAS.WMF HPPYNEW.WMF HPPYNWYR.WMF HPYANVRS.WMF HPYNEWYR.WMF HY02.WMF HY03.WMF HY04.WMF MOUSE1.WMF

MOUSE1C.WMF NEWYEAR.WMF NEWYEAR1.WMF NEWYEAR2.WMF NEWYEAR3.WMF NEWYEAR8.WMF NEWYEAR9.WMF NEWYEARC.WMF NEWYEARS.WMF NMAKER.WMF

NWYRBY2.WMF NWYRSDY.WMF NY1.WMF NY2.WMF OLDYEAR.WMF PARTBALN.WMF PARTMN2.WMF PARTMN2C.WMF PARTY.WMF PARTYC.WMF

PARTYGUY.WMF PARTYHAT.WMF PARTYMAN.WMF PB29.WMF RINGNWYR.WMF SIT057F.WMF SOCA003J.WMF SOCA020D.WMF SOCA039J.WMF TEXT_1B.WMF

TEXT_2B.WMF TIMEWAR.WMF WAITING_.WMF XMC001A.WMF XMC001B.WMF XMC002A.WMF XMC002B.WMF XMC003A.WMF XMC003B.WMF XMC004A.WMF

XMC006A.WMF XMC00A.WMF XMC030A.WMF

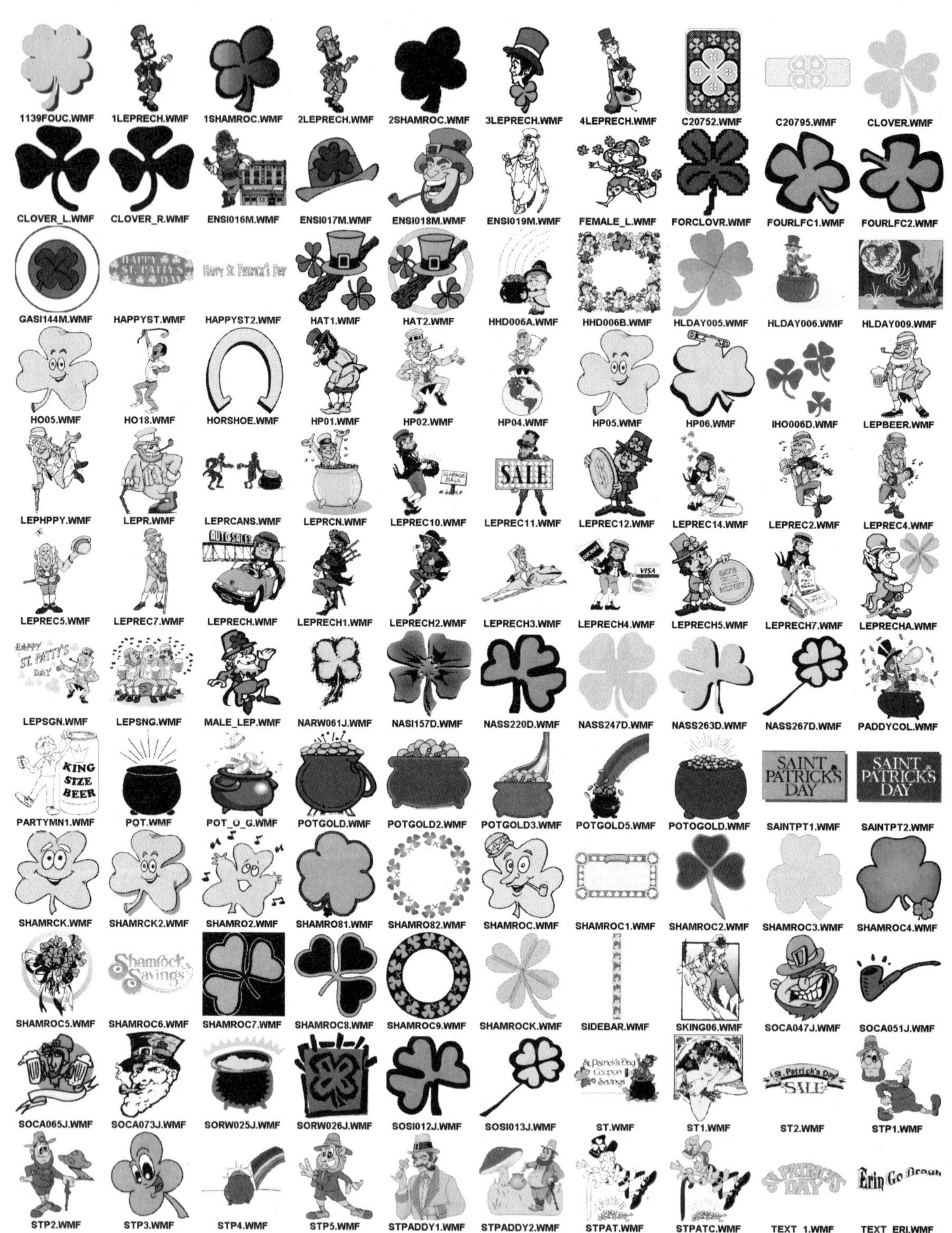
1139FOUC.WMF
1LEPRECH.WMF
1SHAMROC.WMF
2LEPRECH.WMF
2SHAMROC.WMF
3LEPRECH.WMF
4LEPRECH.WMF
C20752.WMF
C20795.WMF
CLOVER.WMF
CLOVER_L.WMF
CLOVER_R.WMF
ENSI016M.WMF
ENSI017M.WMF
ENSI018M.WMF
ENSI019M.WMF
FEMALE_L.WMF
FORCLOVR.WMF
FOURLFC1.WMF
FOURLFC2.WMF
GASI144M.WMF
HAPPYST.WMF
HAPPYST2.WMF
HAT1.WMF
HAT2.WMF
HHD006A.WMF
HHD006B.WMF
HLDAY005.WMF
HLDAY006.WMF
HLDAY009.WMF
HO05.WMF
HO18.WMF
HORSHOE.WMF
HP01.WMF
HP02.WMF
HP04.WMF
HP05.WMF
HP06.WMF
IHO006D.WMF
LEPBEER.WMF
LEPHPPY.WMF
LEPR.WMF
LEPRCANS.WMF
LEPRCN.WMF
LEPREC10.WMF
SALE
LEPREC11.WMF
LEPREC12.WMF
LEPREC14.WMF
LEPREC2.WMF
LEPREC4.WMF
LEPREC5.WMF
LEPREC7.WMF
AUTO SALES
LEPRECH.WMF
LEPRECH1.WMF
LEPRECH2.WMF
LEPRECH3.WMF
VISA
LEPRECH4.WMF
LEPRECH5.WMF
LEPRECH7.WMF
LEPRECHA.WMF
HAPPY ST. PATTY'S DAY
LEPSGN.WMF
LEPSNG.WMF
MALE_LEP.WMF
NARW061J.WMF
NASI157D.WMF
NASS220D.WMF
NASS247D.WMF
NASS263D.WMF
NASS267D.WMF
PADDYCOL.WMF
KING SIZE BEER
PARTYMN1.WMF
POT.WMF
POT_O_G.WMF
POTGOLD.WMF
POTGOLD2.WMF
POTGOLD3.WMF
POTGOLD5.WMF
POTOGOLD.WMF
SAINT PATRICK'S DAY
SAINTPT1.WMF
SAINT PATRICK'S DAY
SAINTPT2.WMF
SHAMRCK.WMF
SHAMRCK2.WMF
SHAMRO2.WMF
SHAMRO81.WMF
SHAMRO82.WMF
SHAMROC.WMF
SHAMROC1.WMF
SHAMROC2.WMF
SHAMROC3.WMF
SHAMROC4.WMF
SHAMROC5.WMF
Shamrock Savings
SHAMROC6.WMF
SHAMROC7.WMF
SHAMROC8.WMF
SHAMROC9.WMF
SHAMROCK.WMF
SIDEBAR.WMF
SKING06.WMF
SOCA047J.WMF
SOCA051J.WMF
SOCA065J.WMF
SOCA073J.WMF
SORW025J.WMF
SORW026J.WMF
SOSI012J.WMF
SOSI013J.WMF
St. Patrick's Day Coupon Savings
ST.WMF
ST1.WMF
St. Patrick's Day SALE
ST2.WMF
STP1.WMF
STP2.WMF
STP3.WMF
STP4.WMF
STP5.WMF
STPADDY1.WMF
STPADDY2.WMF
STPAT.WMF
STPATC.WMF
ST. PATRICK'S DAY
TEXT_1.WMF
Erin Go Bragh
TEXT_ERI.WMF

1915.WMF
1CORNUCO.WMF
2CORNUCO.WMF
3CORNUCO.WMF
ADS026J.WMF
ADS029G.WMF
ADS030M.WMF
ANIMAL3.WMF
AWH025H.WMF
BASKET.WMF
CHSETUK.WMF
CHSETUKC.WMF
COPIA.WMF
COPIA42.WMF
COPIACAN.WMF
CORNCOP.WMF
CORNCPIA.WMF
CORNUCOP.WMF
CORNULBK.WMF
CORNULT.WMF
CORNURBK.WMF
CORNURT.WMF
DEC088P.WMF
FEMALELB.WMF
FEMALELT.WMF
FEMALERB.WMF
FEMALERT.WMF
FOOD1.WMF
FOOD2.WMF
FORW044J.WMF
FSTV114.WMF
FSTV115.WMF
FSTV125.WMF
FSW032C.WMF
HATMOR.WMF
HMC009B.WMF
HRNMSE.WMF
IHO023D.WMF
IHO026H.WMF
IHO027A.WMF
INDIAN.WMF
JWI026C.WMF
MALELT.WMF
MALELTBK.WMF
MALERT.WMF
MALERTBK.WMF
PILGRI00.WMF
PILGRIM.WMF
PILGRIM1.WMF
PILGRIM2.WMF
PILGRIMC.WMF
PILGRIMF.WMF
PILGRIMH.WMF
PILGRIMM.WMF
PILGRIMW.WMF
PILGRIMX.WMF
PILGRIMY.WMF
PILGRIMZ.WMF
PLGMHNT.WMF
PLGMHTFT.WMF
PLGRM.WMF
PLGRMLDY.WMF
PLGRMPLT.WMF
POC100L.WMF
ROTURK.WMF
SCORNBKG.WMF
SOCA003D.WMF
SOCA050J.WMF
SORW020J.WMF
T21849.WMF
Let's Talk TURKEY
Happy Thanksgiving
Happy Thanksgiving
Happy Thanksgiving
T21850.WMF
TALKTURK.WMF
TEXT_1.WMF
TEXT_2.WMF
TEXT_3.WMF
THANKS.WMF
THANKS2.WMF
THANKS_1.WMF
THANKSG.WMF
THANKSG1.WMF
THANKSG2.WMF
THANKSG3.WMF
THANKSG4.WMF
THANKSG5.WMF
THANKSG6.WMF
THANKSG7.WMF
THANKSG8.WMF
THANKSGC.WMF
THE_FIRS.WMF
TRKYMLT.WMF
TRKYPRS.WMF
TRKYRUN.WMF
TURKEY.WMF
TURKEY00.WMF
TURKEY1.WMF
TURKEY2.WMF
TURKEY3.WMF
VEGETARIANS R US!
TURKEY4.WMF
TURKEY81.WMF
TURKEY_W.WMF
TURKEYC.WMF
TURKEYCO.WMF
TURKEYW.WMF
TURKY.WMF
VEGITABL.WMF
WMG044L.WMF
WMG044M.WMF
WMG044N.WMF

CANADIAN.WMF
CHARTCOU.WMF
CHRSMAS.WMF
CHRSMASC.WMF
CHRSTJLY.WMF
DADWANT3.WMF
DADWANTS.WMF
EASTER.WMF
EASTERC.WMF
FSTV046.WMF
FSTV047.WMF
FSTV048.WMF
FSTV049.WMF
FSTV050.WMF
FSTV051.WMF
FSTV052.WMF
FSTV053.WMF
FSTV054.WMF
FULLMOON.WMF
GHOST82.WMF
GHOSTLYB.WMF
GODBLESU.WMF
HALLOW81.WMF
HALLOWE1.WMF
HALLOWN3.WMF
HALOWEN.WMF
HALOWENC.WMF
HEARTBOR.WMF
INSCRIP.WMF
INVITE.WMF
INVITEC.WMF
MCHRIST1.WMF
MCHRIST3.WMF
MCHRST2.WMF
MCHRST2C.WMF
MCHRST4.WMF
MCHRST4C.WMF
MCHST5C.WMF
MEMORIAL.WMF
MONSTERR.WMF
MOONLIG1.WMF
MOONLIG2.WMF
MOONLIG4.WMF
MOVINGSA.WMF
NEWWORLD.WMF
NEWYEAR.WMF
NEWYEARC.WMF
OCTOBERS.WMF
PALMSUN.WMF
PALMSUNC.WMF
SANTASIZ.WMF
SEASCLR.WMF
SEASON1.WMF
SEASON2.WMF
SHAMROC1.WMF
SHAMROC2.WMF
SPOOKYSA.WMF
STPATBDR.WMF
TAKEDADT.WMF
VALENTIN.WMF
VALWORDC.WMF
VALWORDS.WMF
VETERAN1.WMF
VETERANS.WMF
WITCHBOR.WMF
WOLVES.WMF

0608HEAC.WMF 0823.WMF 0824.WMF 0833.WMF 1949.WMF 1CUTE_CU.WMF 1DINOSAU.WMF 1FLOWER_.WMF 2CUTE_CU.WMF 2DINOSAU.WMF

2FLOWER_.WMF 2HEARTS.WMF 4318.WMF ADS008K.WMF ADS010D.WMF BEMYVAL.WMF BKNHEART.WMF BLEEDHRT.WMF BONBON.WMF BONBONC.WMF

BROKEN_H.WMF C20816.WMF CANDYHE.WMF CANDYHT1.WMF CANDYHT2.WMF CARVED_H.WMF CHOC1.WMF CHOC2.WMF CHW003D.WMF CHW003E.WMF

COLDHRT.WMF COMPUTER.WMF COUPLE.WMF COUPLE1.WMF COUPLE1C.WMF COUPLEC.WMF CUPDARRW.WMF CUPID.WMF CUPID00.WMF CUPID2.WMF

CUPID3.WMF CUPID4.WMF CUPID42.WMF CUPID81.WMF CUPID9.WMF CUPID_S.WMF CUPIDBAC.WMF CUPIDBOW.WMF CUPIDBU.WMF CUPIDCOL.WMF

CUPIDLEF.WMF CUPIDON4.WMF CUPIDRT.WMF CUPIDSL1.WMF CUPIDSL2.WMF CUPIDWH2.WMF DEC062T.WMF DEC073C.WMF DEC074H.WMF DEC075W.WMF

DESSERT.WMF DOLLY.WMF FCP019C.WMF FDDNK190.WMF FILLED_1.WMF FILLED_H.WMF FLORAL_D.WMF FLORIST_.WMF FLOWERS.WMF FSD032A.WMF

FSW009A.WMF FSW009B.WMF FSW009C.WMF FSW009D.WMF GASI111M.WMF GASI142M.WMF GFYCPID.WMF GIRLHRT.WMF GRBO007J.WMF H21092.WMF

H21093.WMF H21094.WMF H21095.WMF H21096.WMF H21097.WMF H21098.WMF H21099.WMF H21100.WMF HEART.WMF HEART00.WMF

HEART01.WMF HEART02.WMF HEART03.WMF HEART04.WMF HEART1.WMF HEART11.WMF HEART12.WMF HEART13.WMF HEART19.WMF HEART2.WMF

HEART3.WMF HEART4.WMF HEART5.WMF HEART9.WMF HEART_BO.WMF HEART_ON.WMF HEARTBL.WMF HEARTEA.WMF HEARTFLL.WMF HEARTFLR.WMF

HEARTLTL.WMF HEARTLTR.WMF HEARTS.WMF HEARTS4.WMF HEARTS_I.WMF HEARTSI.WMF HEARTTLL.WMF HEARTTLR.WMF HHD002B.WMF HLDAY007.WMF

Valentine
HLDAY020.WMF HLTH126.WMF HLTH127.WMF HO15.WMF HOLLOW_H.WMF HPILLOW.WMF HRTWARRW.WMF IHO005B.WMF IHO005D.WMF ILUVU.WMF
ILUVUC.WMF INSHEART.WMF KISSING.WMF LIPSPR.WMF LITTLE_G.WMF LOVE1.WMF LOVE_CAR.WMF LOVE_TEX.WMF LOVERS.WMF LOVERS_K.WMF
LOVE
I Love You
LOVEYOUB.WMF LOVEYOUG.WMF LUV_YA_B.WMF LVR005F.WMF LVR007G.WMF LVR026I.WMF LVR075A.WMF LVR101F.WMF LVR104B.WMF LVR105G.WMF
LVR119C.WMF MISC_39.WMF MOUSE2.WMF MOUSE2C.WMF MSELUVU.WMF MSELUVUC.WMF MSL105C.WMF OCI001C.WMF OCI001E.WMF OCI001G.WMF
OCI007I.WMF OCI011H.WMF OCI014F.WMF OCI015J.WMF OCI017A.WMF OCI021H.WMF OCI029E.WMF OCI031A.WMF OTS021C.WMF PESI180D.WMF
LoVe
PRINCE.WMF PRINCESS.WMF RABBIT_W.WMF RABBITS_.WMF RINGS.WMF RLGN127.WMF ROM025K.WMF ROM026G.WMF ROM032J.WMF ROSE.WMF
ROSES.WMF SHAPE018.WMF SHAPE027.WMF SIDEDEC.WMF SIT040B.WMF SIT040H.WMF SIT040I.WMF SOBO001J.WMF SOBO015J.WMF SOBO016J.WMF
SOCA010J.WMF SOCA033J.WMF SOGC008D.WMF SORW004J.WMF SORW007J.WMF SORW017J.WMF SORW021J.WMF SORW045J.WMF SOSI014J.WMF SOSI015J.WMF
SOSI018J.WMF SOSI024J.WMF SQUIRREL.WMF SWHRT.WMF SYMBOL52.WMF TARGET.WMF TBR013A.WMF TBR031A.WMF TEDLUV.WMF TEDLUVC.WMF
BE MY VALENTINE
HAPPY VALENTINES DAY
TEXT_1.WMF TEXT_2.WMF TOD075B.WMF TOD075P.WMF TOD07B.WMF TOD07P.WMF TWOHEART.WMF VAL1.WMF VAL10.WMF VAL11.WMF
VAL12.WMF VAL13.WMF VAL14.WMF VAL15.WMF VAL17.WMF VAL2.WMF VAL25.WMF VAL3.WMF VAL35.WMF VAL4.WMF
VAL45.WMF VAL5.WMF VAL6.WMF VAL7.WMF VAL8.WMF VAL9.WMF VALDAY.WMF VALEN.WMF VALENT42.WMF VALENTIN.WMF

VALENTND.WMF

VALNTIN9.WMF

VALNTINE.WMF

VDCANDY.WMF

VL_CANDY.WMF

VSC047D.WMF

VSC047H.WMF

VSC047J.WMF

WOMAN_WI.WMF

0074.WMF
0109.WMF
0365.WMF
0672.WMF
0683.WMF
0684.WMF
0763.WMF
0773.WMF
0774.WMF
0868.WMF
0890.WMF
1137.WMF
1138.WMF
1139.WMF
4212.WMF
4213.WMF
4239.WMF
4335.WMF
4337.WMF
4338.WMF
4380.WMF
4485.WMF
4541.WMF
4570.WMF
4693.WMF
4770.WMF
4778.WMF
A47C.WMF
A47CB.WMF
A47D.WMF
A47DB.WMF
ADS068K.WMF
BEAUTY4.WMF
BEAUTY4B.WMF
BEAUTY6.WMF
BEAUTY6B.WMF
BIT0679.WMF
BIT0680.WMF
BIT0729.WMF
BIT0737.WMF
BLUSHBRS.WMF
BRUSH.WMF
BRUSH23.WMF
CHEM001.WMF
CHEM002.WMF
COMB.WMF
GARMBAG.WMF
HHBO007J.WMF
HHBO008J.WMF
HHBO009J.WMF
HHBO010J.WMF
HHBO011J.WMF
HHBO023J.WMF
HHGC028D.WMF
HHGC071D.WMF
HHGC083D.WMF
HHGC111D.WMF
HHGC112D.WMF
HHGC114D.WMF
HHGC115D.WMF
HHGC128D.WMF
HHKC006J.WMF
HHKC009J.WMF
HHRW005K.WMF
HHRW016J.WMF
HHRW049J.WMF
HHRW065J.WMF
HHSI001K.WMF
HHSI002K.WMF
HHSI003D.WMF
HHSI004K.WMF
HHSI006M.WMF
HHSI007J.WMF
HHSI018M.WMF
HHSI021D.WMF
HHSI031M.WMF
HHSI033M.WMF
HHSI034M.WMF
HHSI035M.WMF
HHSI039J.WMF
HHSI098D.WMF
HHSI107D.WMF
HHSS001K.WMF
HOUSES13.WMF
HOUSES9.WMF
HPI024F.WMF
INBEDMA.WMF
INGC047D.WMF
M21243.WMF
MIRROR1.WMF
PAPERTWL.WMF
PD037LCU.WMF
PD038ECU.WMF
PD038ICU.WMF
PD038NCU.WMF
PD038PCU.WMF
PILLOW.WMF
PLAN080.WMF
PLAN081.WMF
PLAN082.WMF
PLAN083.WMF
PLAN084.WMF
PLAN085.WMF
PLAN090.WMF
PLAN091.WMF
PLAN092.WMF
PLAN143.WMF
PLAN144.WMF
PLAN145.WMF
PLAN146.WMF
PLAN147.WMF
PLAN152.WMF
PLAN154.WMF
PLAN155.WMF
PLAN156.WMF
PLAN157.WMF
PLAN198.WMF
PLAN199.WMF
PLAN200.WMF
PLAN201.WMF

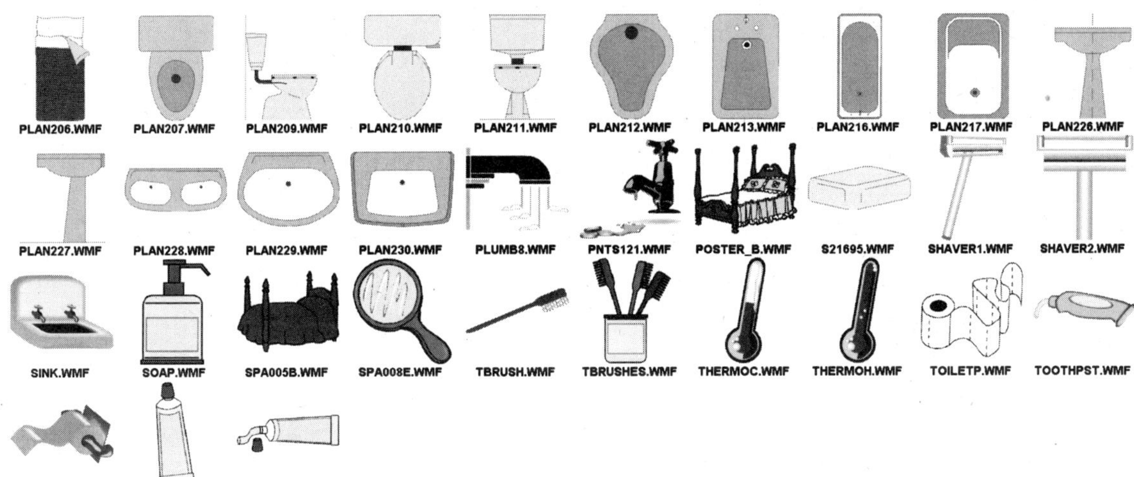
PLAN206.WMF
PLAN207.WMF
PLAN209.WMF
PLAN210.WMF
PLAN211.WMF
PLAN212.WMF
PLAN213.WMF
PLAN216.WMF
PLAN217.WMF
PLAN226.WMF
PLAN227.WMF
PLAN228.WMF
PLAN229.WMF
PLAN230.WMF
PLUMB8.WMF
PNTS121.WMF
POSTER_B.WMF
S21695.WMF
SHAVER1.WMF
SHAVER2.WMF
SINK.WMF
SOAP.WMF
SPA005B.WMF
SPA008E.WMF
TBRUSH.WMF
TBRUSHES.WMF
THERMOC.WMF
THERMOH.WMF
TOILETP.WMF
TOOTHPST.WMF
TP.WMF
TPASTE.WMF
TPASTE1.WMF

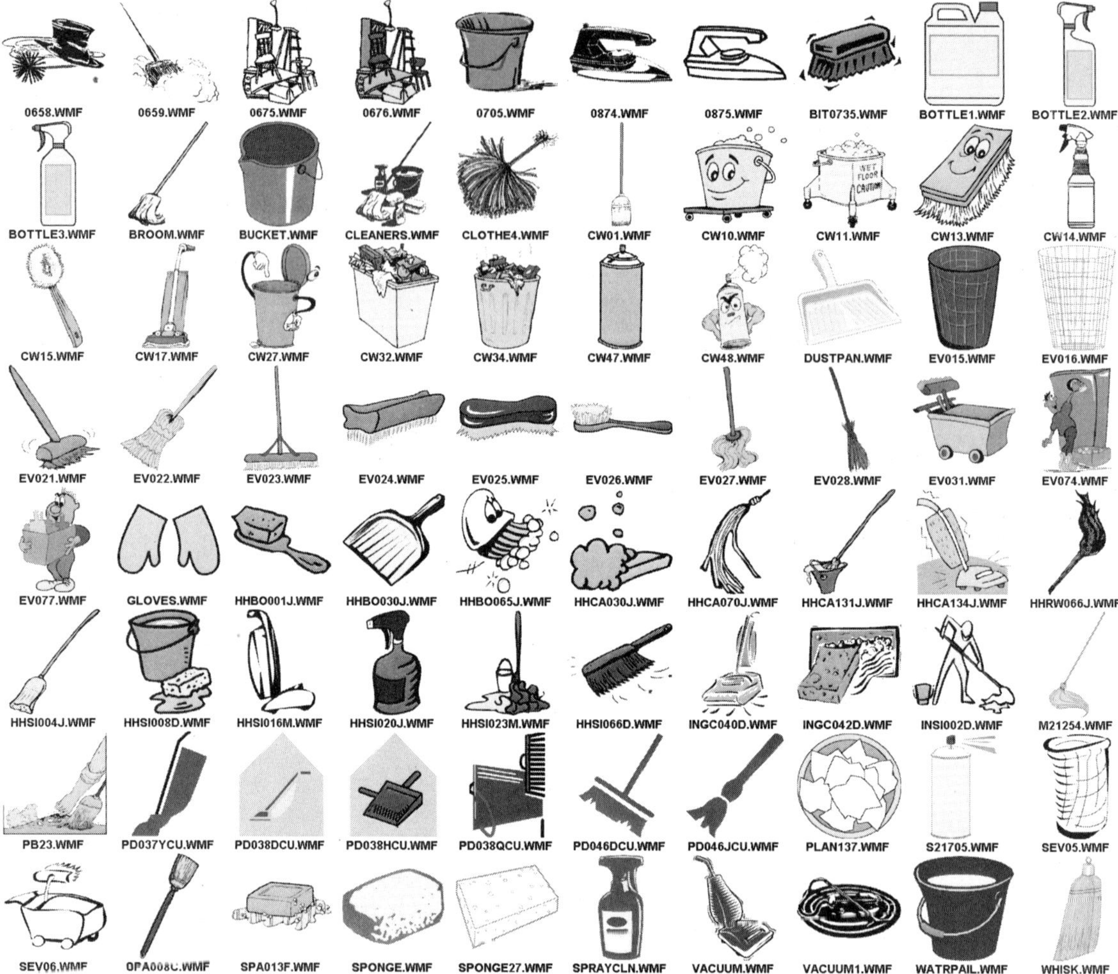
0658.WMF
0659.WMF
0675.WMF
0676.WMF
0705.WMF
0874.WMF
0875.WMF
BIT0735.WMF
BOTTLE1.WMF
BOTTLE2.WMF
BOTTLE3.WMF
BROOM.WMF
BUCKET.WMF
CLEANERS.WMF
CLOTHE4.WMF
CW01.WMF
CW10.WMF
CW11.WMF
CW13.WMF
CW14.WMF
CW15.WMF
CW17.WMF
CW27.WMF
CW32.WMF
CW34.WMF
CW47.WMF
CW48.WMF
DUSTPAN.WMF
EV015.WMF
EV016.WMF
EV021.WMF
EV022.WMF
EV023.WMF
EV024.WMF
EV025.WMF
EV026.WMF
EV027.WMF
EV028.WMF
EV031.WMF
EV074.WMF
EV077.WMF
GLOVES.WMF
HHBO001J.WMF
HHBO030J.WMF
HHBO065J.WMF
HHCA030J.WMF
HHCA070J.WMF
HHCA131J.WMF
HHCA134J.WMF
HHRW066J.WMF
HHSI004J.WMF
HHSI008D.WMF
HHSI016M.WMF
HHSI020J.WMF
HHSI023M.WMF
HHSI066D.WMF
INGC040D.WMF
INGC042D.WMF
INSI002D.WMF
M21254.WMF
PB23.WMF
PD037YCU.WMF
PD038DCU.WMF
PD038HCU.WMF
PD038QCU.WMF
PD046DCU.WMF
PD046JCU.WMF
PLAN137.WMF
S21705.WMF
SEV05.WMF
SEV06.WMF
OPA008C.WMF
SPA013F.WMF
SPONGE.WMF
SPONGE27.WMF
SPRAYCLN.WMF
VACUUM.WMF
VACUUM1.WMF
WATRPAIL.WMF
WHISK.WMF

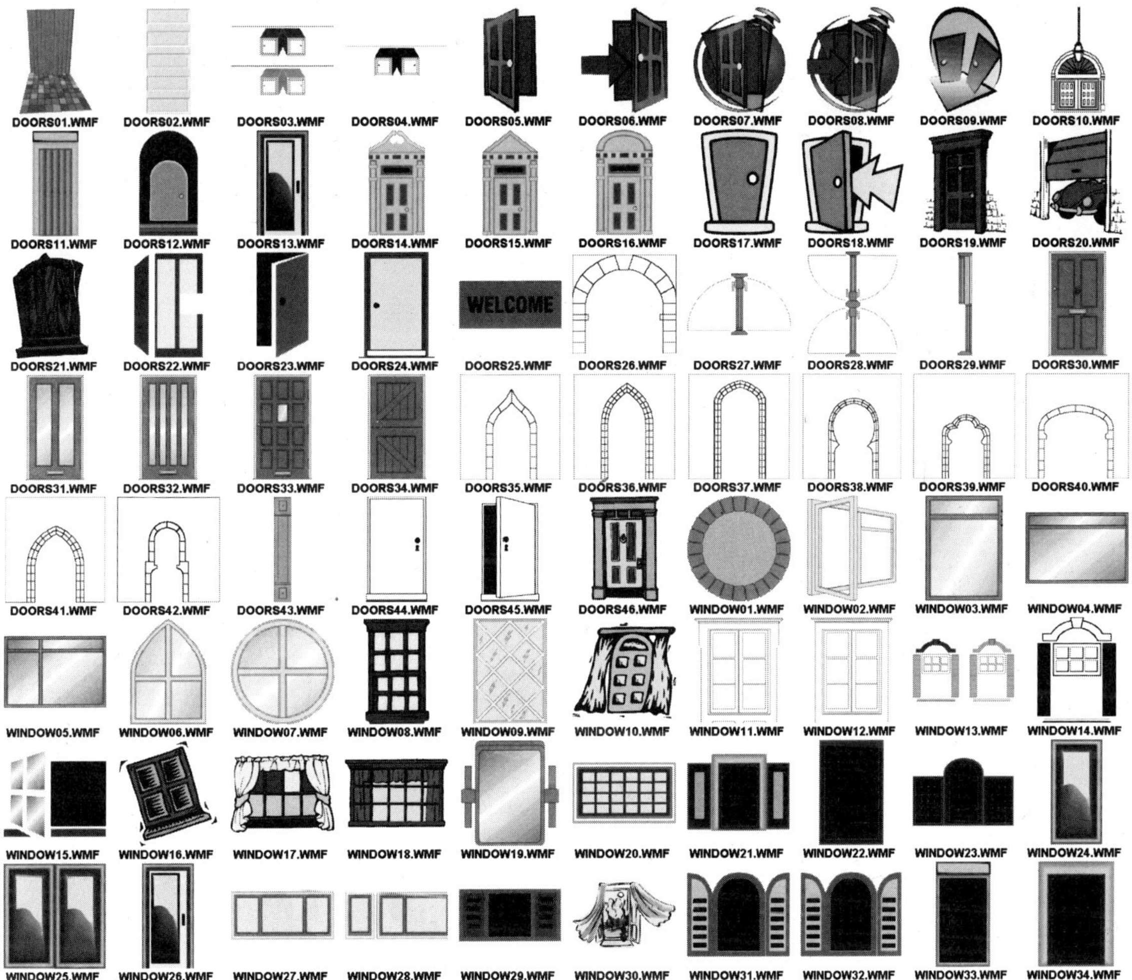
DOORS01.WMF DOORS02.WMF DOORS03.WMF DOORS04.WMF DOORS05.WMF DOORS06.WMF DOORS07.WMF DOORS08.WMF DOORS09.WMF DOORS10.WMF
DOORS11.WMF DOORS12.WMF DOORS13.WMF DOORS14.WMF DOORS15.WMF DOORS16.WMF DOORS17.WMF DOORS18.WMF DOORS19.WMF DOORS20.WMF
WELCOME
DOORS21.WMF DOORS22.WMF DOORS23.WMF DOORS24.WMF DOORS25.WMF DOORS26.WMF DOORS27.WMF DOORS28.WMF DOORS29.WMF DOORS30.WMF
DOORS31.WMF DOORS32.WMF DOORS33.WMF DOORS34.WMF DOORS35.WMF DOORS36.WMF DOORS37.WMF DOORS38.WMF DOORS39.WMF DOORS40.WMF
DOORS41.WMF DOORS42.WMF DOORS43.WMF DOORS44.WMF DOORS45.WMF DOORS46.WMF WINDOW01.WMF WINDOW02.WMF WINDOW03.WMF WINDOW04.WMF
WINDOW05.WMF WINDOW06.WMF WINDOW07.WMF WINDOW08.WMF WINDOW09.WMF WINDOW10.WMF WINDOW11.WMF WINDOW12.WMF WINDOW13.WMF WINDOW14.WMF
WINDOW15.WMF WINDOW16.WMF WINDOW17.WMF WINDOW18.WMF WINDOW19.WMF WINDOW20.WMF WINDOW21.WMF WINDOW22.WMF WINDOW23.WMF WINDOW24.WMF
WINDOW25.WMF WINDOW26.WMF WINDOW27.WMF WINDOW28.WMF WINDOW29.WMF WINDOW30.WMF WINDOW31.WMF WINDOW32.WMF WINDOW33.WMF WINDOW34.WMF

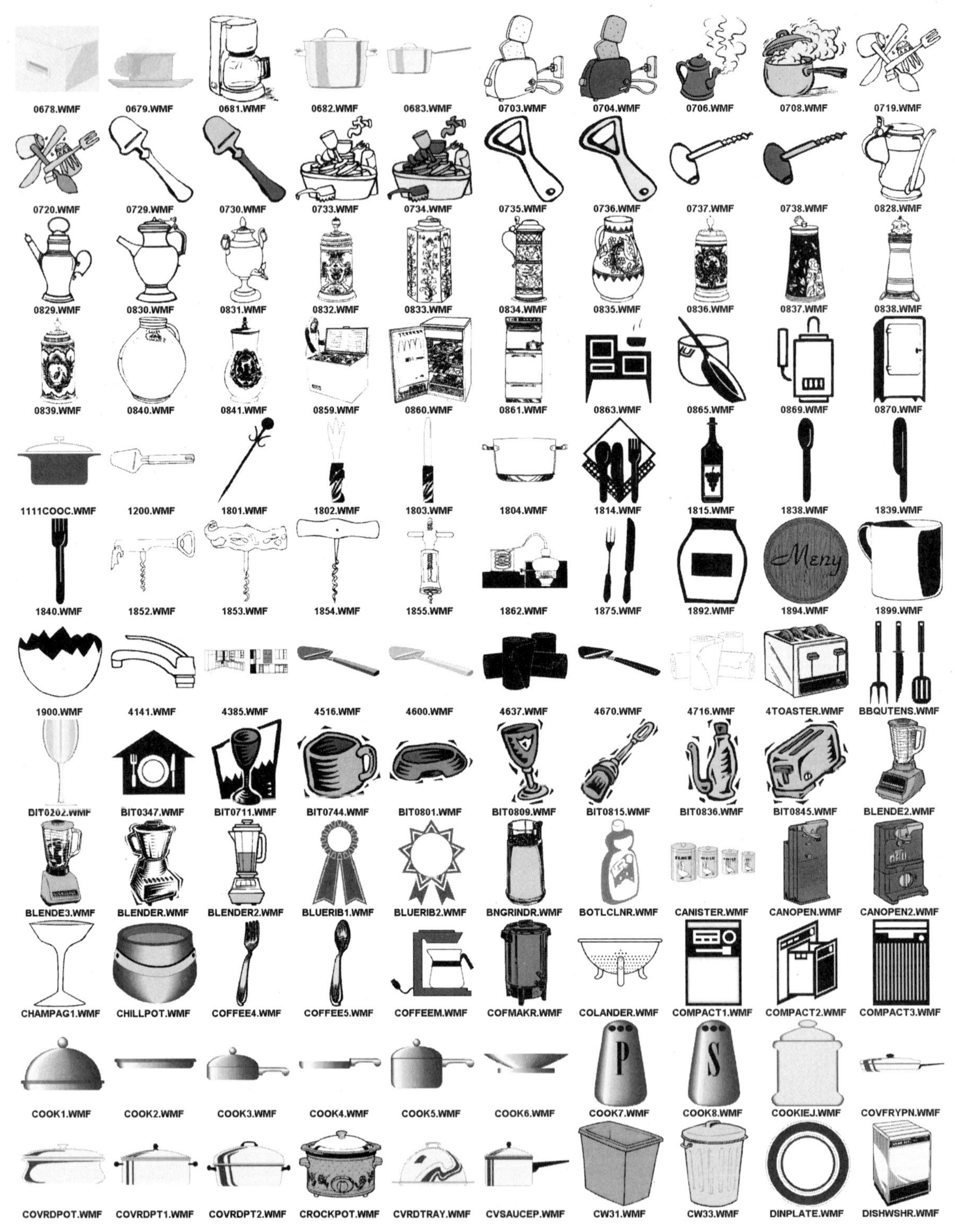
0678.WMF 0679.WMF 0681.WMF 0682.WMF 0683.WMF 0703.WMF 0704.WMF 0706.WMF 0708.WMF 0719.WMF
0720.WMF 0729.WMF 0730.WMF 0733.WMF 0734.WMF 0735.WMF 0736.WMF 0737.WMF 0738.WMF 0828.WMF
0829.WMF 0830.WMF 0831.WMF 0832.WMF 0833.WMF 0834.WMF 0835.WMF 0836.WMF 0837.WMF 0838.WMF
0839.WMF 0840.WMF 0841.WMF 0859.WMF 0860.WMF 0861.WMF 0863.WMF 0865.WMF 0869.WMF 0870.WMF
1111COOC.WMF 1200.WMF 1801.WMF 1802.WMF 1803.WMF 1804.WMF 1814.WMF 1815.WMF 1838.WMF 1839.WMF
1840.WMF 1852.WMF 1853.WMF 1854.WMF 1855.WMF 1862.WMF 1875.WMF 1892.WMF 1894.WMF 1899.WMF
1900.WMF 4141.WMF 4385.WMF 4516.WMF 4600.WMF 4637.WMF 4670.WMF 4716.WMF 4TOASTER.WMF BBQUTENS.WMF
BIT0202.WMF BIT0347.WMF BIT0711.WMF BIT0744.WMF BIT0801.WMF BIT0809.WMF BIT0815.WMF BIT0836.WMF BIT0845.WMF BLENDE2.WMF
BLENDE3.WMF BLENDER.WMF BLENDER2.WMF BLUERIB1.WMF BLUERIB2.WMF BNGRINDR.WMF BOTLCLNR.WMF CANISTER.WMF CANOPEN.WMF CANOPEN2.WMF
CHAMPAG1.WMF CHILLPOT.WMF COFFEE4.WMF COFFEE5.WMF COFFEEM.WMF COFMAKR.WMF COLANDER.WMF COMPACT1.WMF COMPACT2.WMF COMPACT3.WMF
COOK1.WMF COOK2.WMF COOK3.WMF COOK4.WMF COOK5.WMF COOK6.WMF COOK7.WMF COOK8.WMF COOKIEJ.WMF COVFRYPN.WMF
COVRDPOT.WMF COVRDPT1.WMF COVRDPT2.WMF CROCKPOT.WMF CVRDTRAY.WMF CVSAUCEP.WMF CW31.WMF CW33.WMF DINPLATE.WMF DISHWSHR.WMF

DISPOSE.WMF DNRPLATE.WMF DUTCHOV1.WMF DUTCHOV2.WMF DWASH1.WMF DWASH2.WMF ELECRNGE.WMF EQ01.WMF EQ03.WMF EQ04.WMF
FCP008B.WMF FD34.WMF FD50.WMF FD51.WMF FD73.WMF FDD094L.WMF FDD103A.WMF FDD103D.WMF FDD104C.WMF FDD123A.WMF
FDD123G.WMF FOODPROC.WMF FOODSLIC.WMF FORK.WMF FRA010E.WMF FRYPAN.WMF FRYPAN1.WMF FRYPAN2.WMF FRYPAN3.WMF FSTV161.WMF
FSW037C.WMF GASRANGE.WMF GLASS01.WMF GLASS02.WMF GLASS03.WMF GLASS04.WMF GLASS05.WMF GLASS06.WMF GLASS07.WMF GLASS08.WMF
GLASS09.WMF GLASS10.WMF GLASS11.WMF GLASS12.WMF GLASS13.WMF GLASS14.WMF GLASS15.WMF GLASS16.WMF GLASS17.WMF GLASS18.WMF
GLASS19.WMF GLASS20.WMF GLASS21.WMF GLASS22.WMF GLASS23.WMF GLASS24.WMF GLASS25.WMF GLASS26.WMF GLASS27.WMF GLASS28.WMF
GLASS29.WMF GLASS30.WMF GLASS31.WMF HANDBLEN.WMF HHBO021J.WMF HHBO029J.WMF HHBO037J.WMF HHBO038J.WMF HHBO039J.WMF HHCA019J.WMF
HHCA024J.WMF HHCA031J.WMF HHCA091J.WMF HHGC004J.WMF HHGC014J.WMF HHGC053D.WMF HHGC058D.WMF HHGC060D.WMF HHGC081D.WMF HHGC086D.WMF
HHGC116D.WMF HHGC117D.WMF HHGC118D.WMF HHGC119D.WMF HHGC127D.WMF HHGC132D.WMF HHRW027J.WMF HHRW028J.WMF HHRW067J.WMF HHSI001J.WMF
HHSI013D.WMF HHSI052D.WMF HHSI053D.WMF HHSI079D.WMF HHSI083D.WMF HHSI088D.WMF HHSI115D.WMF HONEY.WMF HPI001G.WMF HPI001H.WMF
ICCRMAK.WMF ICTEAMAK.WMF INGC019D.WMF INSI016D.WMF JJRW022J.WMF JUG.WMF JUICER.WMF KETTLE.WMF KETTLE01.WMF KETTLE1.WMF
KETTLE2.WMF KNIFE.WMF KNIFE1.WMF KNIFE2.WMF KNIFE3.WMF KNIFE4.WMF KNIFE5.WMF KNIFE6.WMF LABSAVE.WMF LAC095E.WMF

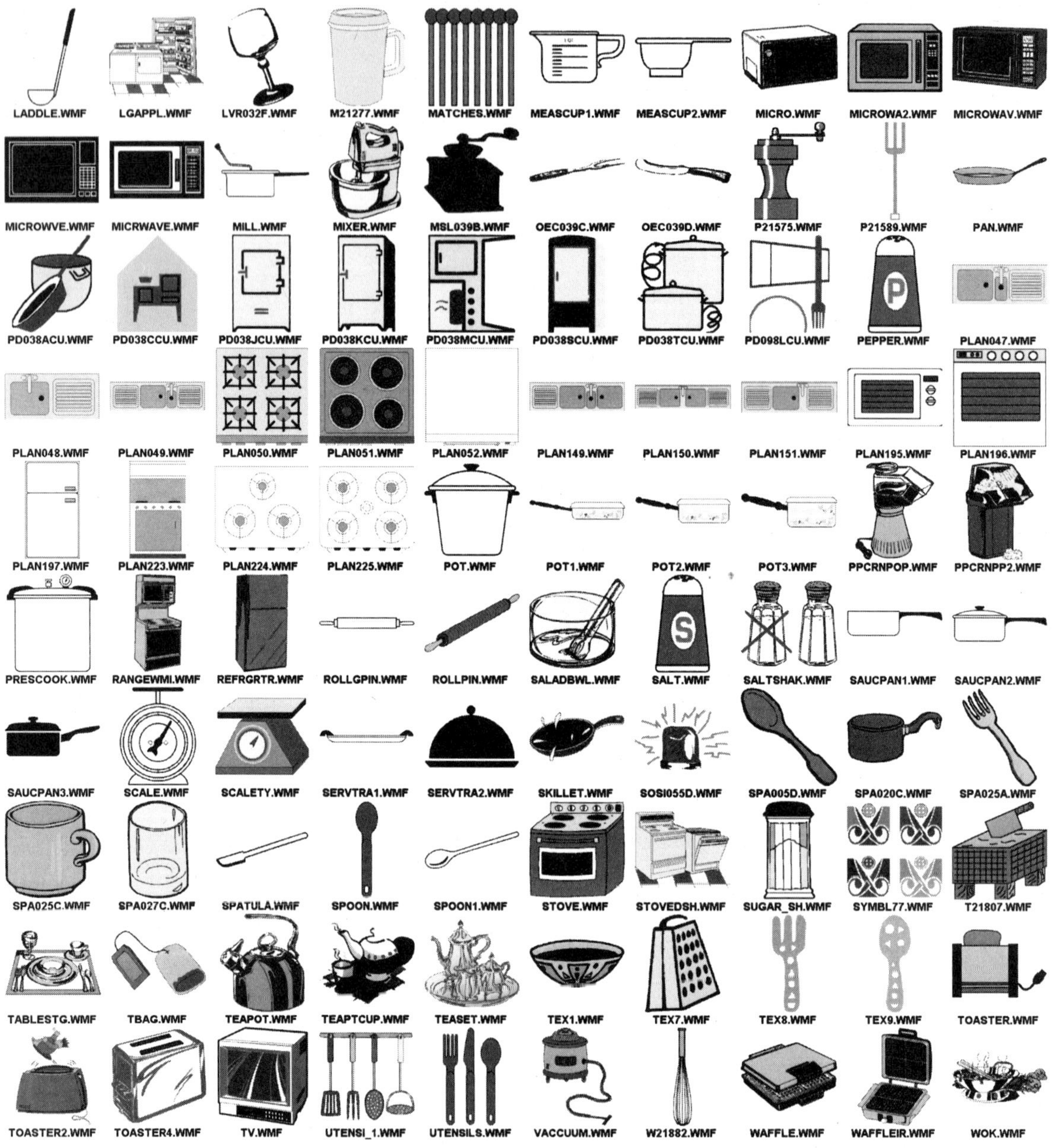
LADDLE.WMF LGAPPL.WMF LVR032F.WMF M21277.WMF MATCHES.WMF MEASCUP1.WMF MEASCUP2.WMF MICRO.WMF MICROWA2.WMF MICROWAV.WMF
MICROWVE.WMF MICRWAVE.WMF MILL.WMF MIXER.WMF MSL039B.WMF OEC039C.WMF OEC039D.WMF P21575.WMF P21589.WMF PAN.WMF
PD038ACU.WMF PD038CCU.WMF PD038JCU.WMF PD038KCU.WMF PD038MCU.WMF PD038SCU.WMF PD038TCU.WMF PD098LCU.WMF PEPPER.WMF PLAN047.WMF
PLAN048.WMF PLAN049.WMF PLAN050.WMF PLAN051.WMF PLAN052.WMF PLAN149.WMF PLAN150.WMF PLAN151.WMF PLAN195.WMF PLAN196.WMF
PLAN197.WMF PLAN223.WMF PLAN224.WMF PLAN225.WMF POT.WMF POT1.WMF POT2.WMF POT3.WMF PPCRNPOP.WMF PPCRNPP2.WMF
PRESCOOK.WMF RANGEWMI.WMF REFRGRTR.WMF ROLLGPIN.WMF ROLLPIN.WMF SALADBWL.WMF SALT.WMF SALTSHAK.WMF SAUCPAN1.WMF SAUCPAN2.WMF
SAUCPAN3.WMF SCALE.WMF SCALETY.WMF SERVTRA1.WMF SERVTRA2.WMF SKILLET.WMF SOSI055D.WMF SPA005D.WMF SPA020C.WMF SPA025A.WMF
SPA025C.WMF SPA027C.WMF SPATULA.WMF SPOON.WMF SPOON1.WMF STOVE.WMF STOVEDSH.WMF SUGAR_SH.WMF SYMBL77.WMF T21807.WMF
TABLESTG.WMF TBAG.WMF TEAPOT.WMF TEAPTCUP.WMF TEASET.WMF TEX1.WMF TEX7.WMF TEX8.WMF TEX9.WMF TOASTER.WMF
TOASTER2.WMF TOASTER4.WMF TV.WMF UTENSI_1.WMF UTENSILS.WMF VACCUUM.WMF W21882.WMF WAFFLE.WMF WAFFLEIR.WMF WOK.WMF

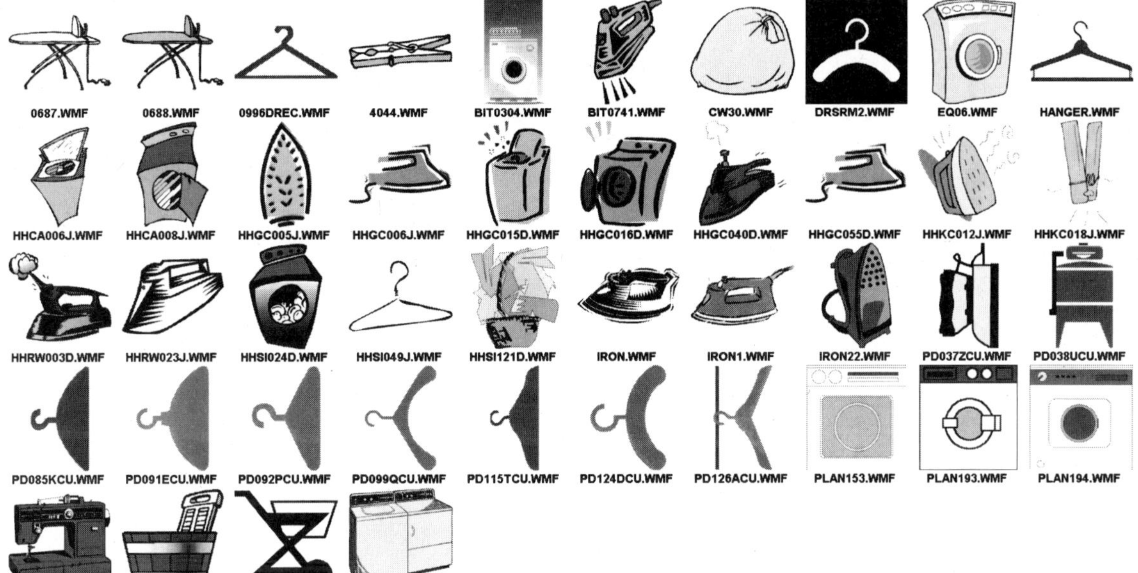
0687.WMF
0688.WMF
0996DREC.WMF
4044.WMF
BIT0304.WMF
BIT0741.WMF
CW30.WMF
DRSRM2.WMF
EQ06.WMF
HANGER.WMF
HHCA006J.WMF
HHCA008J.WMF
HHGC005J.WMF
HHGC006J.WMF
HHGC015D.WMF
HHGC016D.WMF
HHGC040D.WMF
HHGC055D.WMF
HHKC012J.WMF
HHKC018J.WMF
HHRW003D.WMF
HHRW023J.WMF
HHSI024D.WMF
HHSI049J.WMF
HHSI121D.WMF
IRON.WMF
IRON1.WMF
IRON22.WMF
PD037ZCU.WMF
PD038UCU.WMF
PD085KCU.WMF
PD091ECU.WMF
PD092PCU.WMF
PD099QCU.WMF
PD115TCU.WMF
PD124DCU.WMF
PD126ACU.WMF
PLAN153.WMF
PLAN193.WMF
PLAN194.WMF
SEWMACH.WMF
WASH_TUB.WMF
WASHTROL.WMF
WSHRDRYR.WMF

0779.WMF
4387.WMF
BIT0569.WMF
BIT0570.WMF
BIT0571.WMF
BIT0572.WMF
BIT0573.WMF
BIT0574.WMF
BIT0608.WMF
BIT0719.WMF
BIT0723.WMF
BIT0724.WMF
BIT0746.WMF
BIT0826.WMF
BIT0832.WMF
BUGC047D.WMF
BULB.WMF
BULB03.WMF
BULBMT.WMF
BUSI013D.WMF
BUSI017M.WMF
BUSI047D.WMF
BUSI159D.WMF
C20734.WMF
C20735.WMF
C20736.WMF
C20737.WMF
C20738.WMF
C20739.WMF
C20740.WMF
C20741.WMF
C20742.WMF
C20744.WMF
CANDLE.WMF
CANDLE2.WMF
CANDLE9.WMF
CANDLES.WMF
CANDLSTX.WMF
CW20.WMF
CW22.WMF
CW23.WMF
CW24.WMF
CW25.WMF
CW26.WMF
DESKLAMP.WMF
E69.WMF
ENKC004J.WMF
EQ10.WMF
GASLAMP.WMF
HAG008B.WMF
HEARTLIT.WMF
HHCA137J.WMF
HHCA161J.WMF
HHGC010J.WMF
HHGC012J.WMF
HHGC059D.WMF
HHGC079D.WMF
HHKC015J.WMF
HHRW010J.WMF
HHRW013J.WMF
HHRW014J.WMF
HHRW043J.WMF
HHRW053J.WMF
HHSI001M.WMF
HHSI011J.WMF
HHSI019D.WMF
HHSI026D.WMF
HHSI036J.WMF
HHSI036M.WMF
HHSI037J.WMF
HHSI038M.WMF
HHSI049D.WMF
HHSI059J.WMF
HHSI059M.WMF
HHSI061D.WMF
HHSI069D.WMF
HHSI076D.WMF
HHSI100D.WMF
HHSI108D.WMF
HOUSES14.WMF
I21136.WMF
IDEABULB.WMF
IDEALIT.WMF
INCA003J.WMF
INSI006M.WMF
LAMP.WMF
LAMP1.WMF
LAMP11.WMF
LAMP12.WMF
LAMP2.WMF
LAMP23.WMF
LAMP3.WMF
LIGHT1.WMF
LIGHT2.WMF
LIGHTBLB.WMF
LITBULB.WMF
LITEBULB.WMF
OBK005J.WMF
OIL_LAMP.WMF
OILY.WMF
PD038GCU.WMF
PD038OCU.WMF
PD122XCU.WMF
PLAN071.WMF
PLAN072.WMF
SOBO009J.WMF
SOCA006D.WMF
STAND_UP.WMF
STRTLAMP.WMF
SYMBL34.WMF
TBLLAMP.WMF
TBLLAMP5.WMF
TRKLITE.WMF

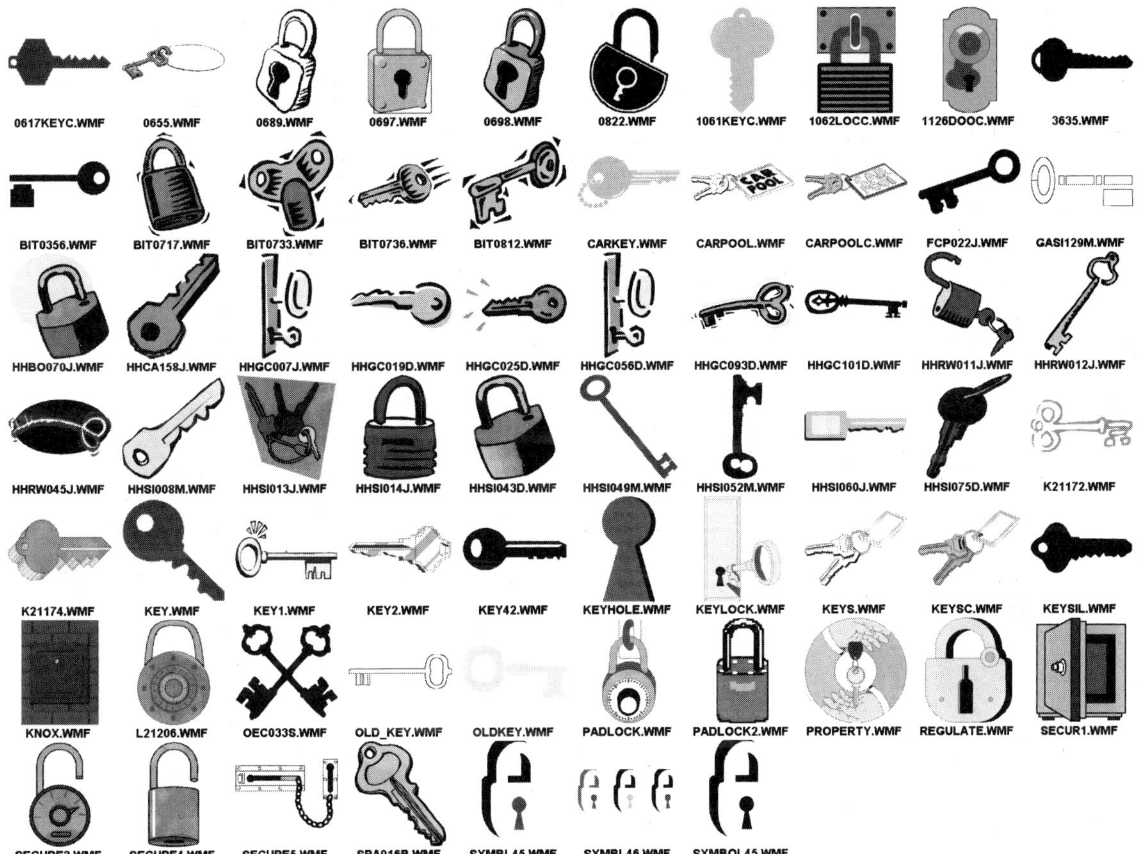
0617KEYC.WMF
0655.WMF
0689.WMF
0697.WMF
0698.WMF
0822.WMF
1061KEYC.WMF
1062LOCC.WMF
1126DOOC.WMF
3635.WMF
BIT0356.WMF
BIT0717.WMF
BIT0733.WMF
BIT0736.WMF
BIT0812.WMF
CARKEY.WMF
CARPOOL.WMF
CARPOOLC.WMF
FCP022J.WMF
GASI129M.WMF
HHBO070J.WMF
HHCA158J.WMF
HHGC007J.WMF
HHGC019D.WMF
HHGC025D.WMF
HHGC056D.WMF
HHGC093D.WMF
HHGC101D.WMF
HHRW011J.WMF
HHRW012J.WMF
HHRW045J.WMF
HHSI008M.WMF
HHSI013J.WMF
HHSI014J.WMF
HHSI043D.WMF
HHSI049M.WMF
HHSI052M.WMF
HHSI060J.WMF
HHSI075D.WMF
K21172.WMF
K21174.WMF
KEY.WMF
KEY1.WMF
KEY2.WMF
KEY42.WMF
KEYHOLE.WMF
KEYLOCK.WMF
KEYS.WMF
KEYSC.WMF
KEYSIL.WMF
KNOX.WMF
L21206.WMF
OEC033S.WMF
OLD_KEY.WMF
OLDKEY.WMF
PADLOCK.WMF
PADLOCK2.WMF
PROPERTY.WMF
REGULATE.WMF
SECUR1.WMF
SECURE3.WMF
SECURE4.WMF
SECURE5.WMF
SPA016B.WMF
SYMBL45.WMF
SYMBL46.WMF
SYMBOL45.WMF

0687.WMF
0701.WMF
0707.WMF
0766VASC.WMF
0795.WMF
0799.WMF
0801.WMF
0803.WMF
0819.WMF
0820.WMF
0823.WMF
0894.WMF
0995DREC.WMF
2.WMF
3160.WMF
3418.WMF
4371.WMF
4372.WMF
4411.WMF
4473.WMF
A37FB.WMF
AIRCLEAN.WMF
AIRCLN2.WMF
AIRCOND.WMF
AIRCOND1.WMF
AIRCOND2.WMF
ARMCHAIR.WMF
ASI093F.WMF
WE HAVE MOVED
BACK139.WMF
BIT0351.WMF
BIT0678.WMF
BIT0682.WMF
BIT0725.WMF
BIT0728.WMF
BIT0824.WMF
BIT0932.WMF
BUCKET1.WMF
BUILD10.WMF
C20754.WMF
CEILFAN.WMF
CEILFAN2.WMF
CEILFAN3.WMF
CHAIR.WMF
CHEM004.WMF
CHOLDER.WMF
CLEAN2.WMF
COFTABLE.WMF
COUNTRYM.WMF
CRKDWALL.WMF
D20881.WMF
DEHUMID.WMF
DOORKNCR.WMF
DOORKNOK.WMF
DRYER1.WMF
DRYER2.WMF
EAA116P.WMF
EDCN221.WMF
EV076.WMF
FAN.WMF
FAUCET.WMF
FIL025C.WMF
FMF098L.WMF
FMF116L.WMF
FOGC004D.WMF
FSW015B.WMF
FSW031D.WMF
FSW037B.WMF
GENKAN.WMF
GLOBE.WMF
H21117.WMF
H21127.WMF
H21128.WMF
H21131.WMF
H21132.WMF
HAMNAIL.WMF
HEATER.WMF
HEATPUMP.WMF
HESI002M.WMF
HHBO076J.WMF
HHCA099J.WMF
HHGC002J.WMF
HHGC003J.WMF
HHGC052D.WMF
HHKC016J.WMF
HHRW046J.WMF
HHRW058J.WMF
HHSI001N.WMF
HHSI006D.WMF
HHSI007M.WMF
HHSI016D.WMF
HHSI022M.WMF
HHSI024M.WMF
HHSI028M.WMF
HHSI047D.WMF
HHSI055D.WMF
HHSI072D.WMF
HHSI125D.WMF
HOUSE10.WMF
HOUSING.WMF
HUMIDIF2.WMF
HUMIDIF3.WMF
HUMIDIFR.WMF
LADDER.WMF
LEISURE.WMF
LOUNGE.WMF
M21214.WMF
M21215.WMF
MAILBOX.WMF
MATCHES.WMF
MCHNL014.WMF
MSETRAP.WMF
NEEDLE_A.WMF
O21466.WMF
O21483.WMF
P21556.WMF
PAINT01.WMF
PAINT02.WMF
PAINT03.WMF
PAINT04.WMF
PAINT05.WMF

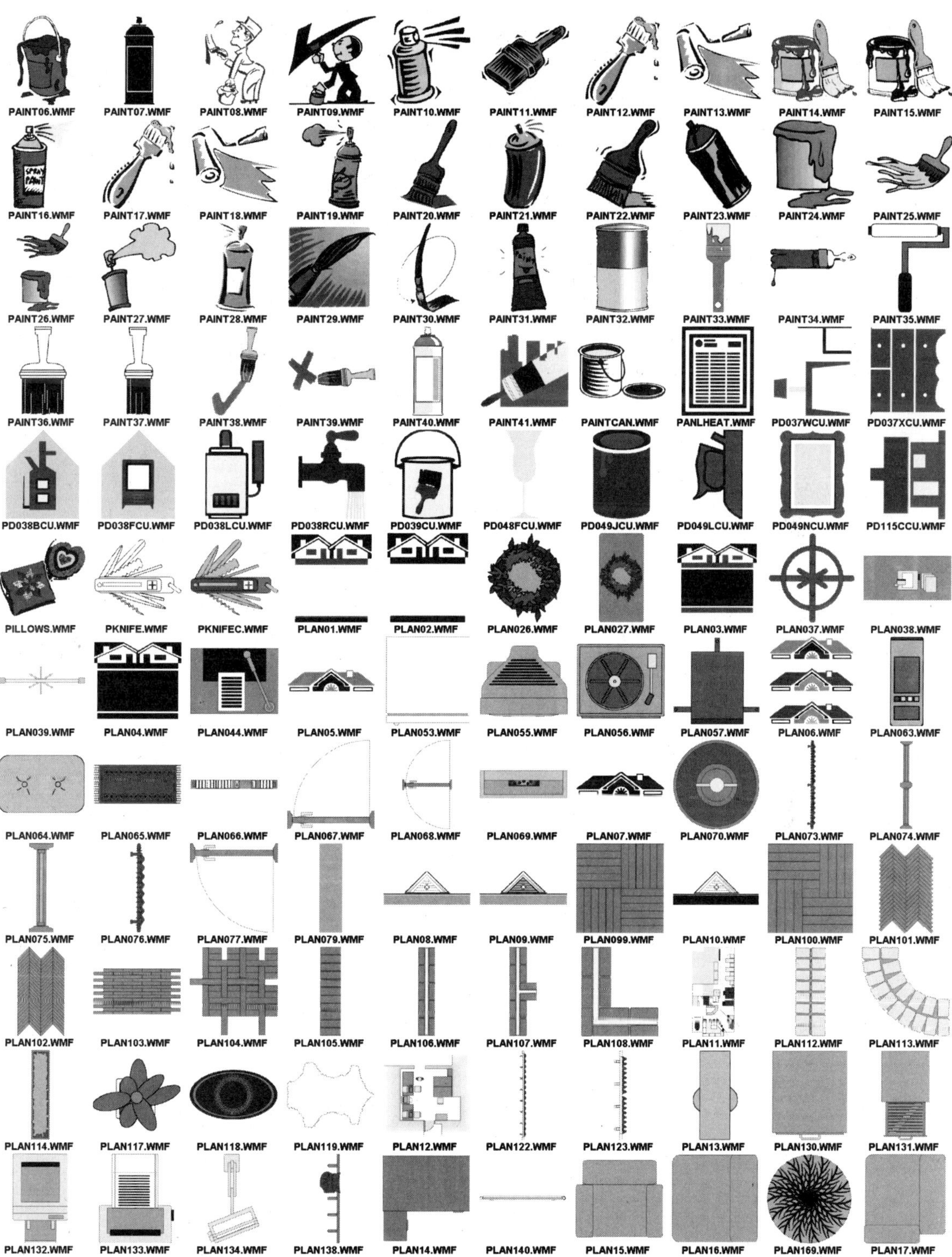
PAINT06.WMF
PAINT07.WMF
PAINT08.WMF
PAINT09.WMF
PAINT10.WMF
PAINT11.WMF
PAINT12.WMF
PAINT13.WMF
PAINT14.WMF
PAINT15.WMF
PAINT16.WMF
PAINT17.WMF
PAINT18.WMF
PAINT19.WMF
PAINT20.WMF
PAINT21.WMF
PAINT22.WMF
PAINT23.WMF
PAINT24.WMF
PAINT25.WMF
PAINT26.WMF
PAINT27.WMF
PAINT28.WMF
PAINT29.WMF
PAINT30.WMF
PAINT31.WMF
PAINT32.WMF
PAINT33.WMF
PAINT34.WMF
PAINT35.WMF
PAINT36.WMF
PAINT37.WMF
PAINT38.WMF
PAINT39.WMF
PAINT40.WMF
PAINT41.WMF
PAINTCAN.WMF
PANLHEAT.WMF
PD037WCU.WMF
PD037XCU.WMF
PD038BCU.WMF
PD038FCU.WMF
PD038LCU.WMF
PD038RCU.WMF
PD039CU.WMF
PD048FCU.WMF
PD049JCU.WMF
PD049LCU.WMF
PD049NCU.WMF
PD115CCU.WMF
PILLOWS.WMF
PKNIFE.WMF
PKNIFEC.WMF
PLAN01.WMF
PLAN02.WMF
PLAN026.WMF
PLAN027.WMF
PLAN03.WMF
PLAN037.WMF
PLAN038.WMF
PLAN039.WMF
PLAN04.WMF
PLAN044.WMF
PLAN05.WMF
PLAN053.WMF
PLAN055.WMF
PLAN056.WMF
PLAN057.WMF
PLAN06.WMF
PLAN063.WMF
PLAN064.WMF
PLAN065.WMF
PLAN066.WMF
PLAN067.WMF
PLAN068.WMF
PLAN069.WMF
PLAN07.WMF
PLAN070.WMF
PLAN073.WMF
PLAN074.WMF
PLAN075.WMF
PLAN076.WMF
PLAN077.WMF
PLAN079.WMF
PLAN08.WMF
PLAN09.WMF
PLAN099.WMF
PLAN10.WMF
PLAN100.WMF
PLAN101.WMF
PLAN102.WMF
PLAN103.WMF
PLAN104.WMF
PLAN105.WMF
PLAN106.WMF
PLAN107.WMF
PLAN108.WMF
PLAN11.WMF
PLAN112.WMF
PLAN113.WMF
PLAN114.WMF
PLAN117.WMF
PLAN118.WMF
PLAN119.WMF
PLAN12.WMF
PLAN122.WMF
PLAN123.WMF
PLAN13.WMF
PLAN130.WMF
PLAN131.WMF
PLAN132.WMF
PLAN133.WMF
PLAN134.WMF
PLAN138.WMF
PLAN14.WMF
PLAN140.WMF
PLAN15.WMF
PLAN16.WMF
PLAN169.WMF
PLAN17.WMF

PLAN170.WMF
PLAN18.WMF
PLAN19.WMF
PLAN20.WMF
PLAN202.WMF
PLAN203.WMF
PLAN204.WMF
PLAN205.WMF
PLAN21.WMF
PLAN214.WMF
PLAN215.WMF
PLAN218.WMF
PLAN219.WMF
PLAN22.WMF
PLAN220.WMF
PLAN221.WMF
PLAN222.WMF
PLAN23.WMF
PLAN24.WMF
PLAN25.WMF
PLAN26.WMF
PLAN27.WMF
PLAN28.WMF
PLAN29.WMF
PLAN30.WMF
PLAN31.WMF
PLAN32.WMF
PLMBNG10.WMF
PLUMB10.WMF
PLUMB2.WMF
PLUMB3.WMF
PLUMB5.WMF
POC103K.WMF
PTBRUSH.WMF
PTBRUSH6.WMF
REAL09.WMF
ROOF2.WMF
ROOF2B.WMF
SAW.WMF
SAW3.WMF
SEAT.WMF
SEWMACH.WMF
SHUTERS2.WMF
SHUTTER2.WMF
SHUTTER3.WMF
SIT092I.WMF
SPA009D.WMF
SPIN_.WMF
SRI031B.WMF
STADIUMB.WMF
SYMBL29.WMF
SYMBL31.WMF
SYMBL32.WMF
SYMBL71.WMF
SYMBOL29.WMF
SYMBOL31.WMF
SYMBOL32.WMF
TABLE.WMF
TDG022B.WMF
TOKONOMA.WMF
TOOLBOX.WMF
TRASH01.WMF
TRASH02.WMF
TRASH03.WMF
TRASH04.WMF
TRASH05.WMF
TRASH06.WMF
WASTE
TRASH07.WMF
TRASH08.WMF
TRASH09.WMF
TRASH10.WMF
TRASH11.WMF
TRASH12.WMF
TRASH13.WMF
TRASH14.WMF
TRASH15.WMF
TV.WMF
UMBREL.WMF
UMBRELC.WMF
VIDEO1.WMF
VIDEO2.WMF
VSC036F.WMF
W21869.WMF
W21879.WMF
W21880.WMF
W21912.WMF
WASHER1.WMF
WASHER2.WMF
WASHER3.WMF
WATRFACT.WMF
WATRHEAT.WMF
WHELBARO.WMF
WINDOW.WMF
WINDOW4.WMF
WINDOW4B.WMF

0008BUTC.WMF
1427.WMF
1428.WMF
ADMIRAL.WMF
ANIM017.WMF
ANIM018.WMF
ANIM019.WMF
ANMO8.WMF
APOLLO.WMF
ARCTKAJA.WMF
ATLAS.WMF
AWH010D.WMF
AWH018E.WMF
AWP031D.WMF
B20145.WMF
B20146.WMF
B20147.WMF
B20148.WMF
B20149.WMF
B20150.WMF
BATTRFLY.WMF
BIGNACRE.WMF
BIT1137.WMF
BTTRFLY1.WMF
BTTRFLY2.WMF
BTTRFLYL.WMF
BTTRFLYR.WMF
BUTERFLY.WMF
BUTRFLY.WMF
BUTRFLY3.WMF
BUTRFLY4.WMF
BUTTER1.WMF
BUTTERF1.WMF
BUTTERFL.WMF
BUTTFLY.WMF
BUTTFLYC.WMF
BUTTRF_1.WMF
BUTTRFL.WMF
BUTTRFLY.WMF
C25.WMF
C26.WMF
CALERIO.WMF
CALIFDOG.WMF
CATOCALA.WMF
CLEOPATR.WMF
CLOUDEDY.WMF
CLOUDYEL.WMF
DCS011A.WMF
DEC084L.WMF
DEC084V.WMF
DEC086AA.WMF
DEC087W.WMF
DEC088C.WMF
DEC088D.WMF
DILOBA.WMF
DRAGONF1.WMF
EAA153J.WMF
EAC029B.WMF
EAC029D.WMF
EAC029J.WMF
EAC029M.WMF
EAC029Q.WMF
EUCHLOE.WMF
FBI007B.WMF
FIREFLY.WMF
FRA020A.WMF
FWN01.WMF
FWN014A.WMF
FWN014B.WMF
FWN014C.WMF
FWN014D.WMF
FWN014E.WMF
FWN014F.WMF
FWN014G.WMF
FWN014H.WMF
FWN014I.WMF
FWN014J.WMF
FWN014K.WMF
FWN014L.WMF
FWN01D.WMF
GRASHOP.WMF
GTIGER.WMF
HELICON.WMF
INACHIS.WMF
INSECT0.WMF
LGEMOTH.WMF
LGEWHITE.WMF
MAAKA.WMF
MACHAON.WMF
MONARCH.WMF
MONARCHB.WMF
MOONMOTH.WMF
MOURCLC.WMF
NABO001J.WMF
NACA323J.WMF
NAKC001J.WMF
NASI231D.WMF
PASHA.WMF
PBUTTER.WMF
PIERIS.WMF
POC102T.WMF
REDADMRL.WMF
SAC039A.WMF
SAC040A.WMF
SAC041B.WMF
SATURNIA.WMF
SPA017D.WMF
SWALLOWT.WMF
TELEA.WMF
TOD071M.WMF
TOD093P.WMF
WHITEADM.WMF
ZBUTTER.WMF

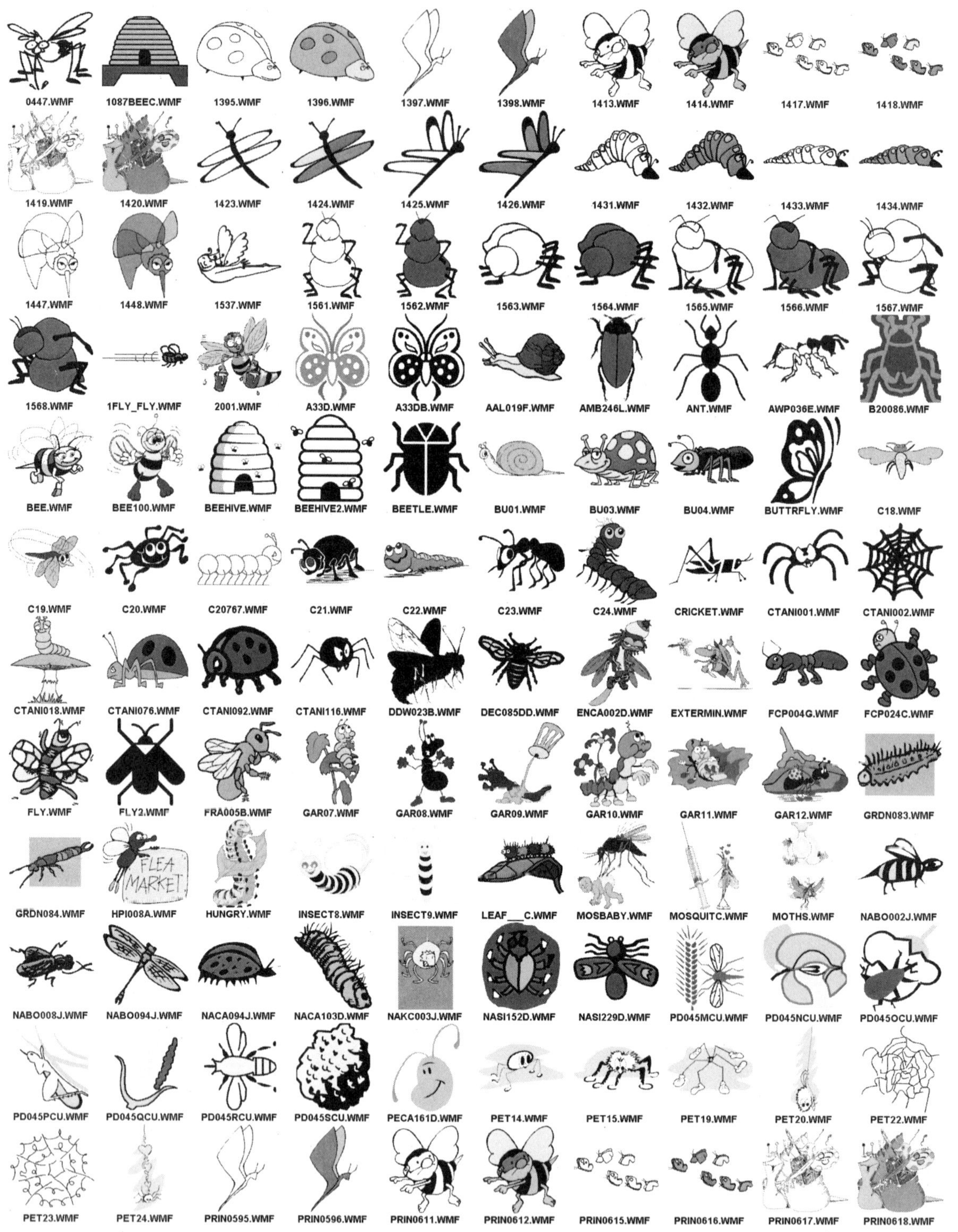
0447.WMF
1087BEEC.WMF
1395.WMF
1396.WMF
1397.WMF
1398.WMF
1413.WMF
1414.WMF
1417.WMF
1418.WMF
1419.WMF
1420.WMF
1423.WMF
1424.WMF
1425.WMF
1426.WMF
1431.WMF
1432.WMF
1433.WMF
1434.WMF
1447.WMF
1448.WMF
1537.WMF
1561.WMF
1562.WMF
1563.WMF
1564.WMF
1565.WMF
1566.WMF
1567.WMF
1568.WMF
1FLY_FLY.WMF
2001.WMF
A33D.WMF
A33DB.WMF
AAL019F.WMF
AMB246L.WMF
ANT.WMF
AWP036E.WMF
B20086.WMF
BEE.WMF
BEE100.WMF
BEEHIVE.WMF
BEEHIVE2.WMF
BEETLE.WMF
BU01.WMF
BU03.WMF
BU04.WMF
BUTTRFLY.WMF
C18.WMF
C19.WMF
C20.WMF
C20767.WMF
C21.WMF
C22.WMF
C23.WMF
C24.WMF
CRICKET.WMF
CTANI001.WMF
CTANI002.WMF
CTANI018.WMF
CTANI076.WMF
CTANI092.WMF
CTANI116.WMF
DDW023B.WMF
DEC085DD.WMF
ENCA002D.WMF
EXTERMIN.WMF
FCP004G.WMF
FCP024C.WMF
FLY.WMF
FLY2.WMF
FRA005B.WMF
GAR07.WMF
GAR08.WMF
GAR09.WMF
GAR10.WMF
GAR11.WMF
GAR12.WMF
GRDN083.WMF
GRDN084.WMF
FLEA
MARKET
HPI008A.WMF
HUNGRY.WMF
INSECT8.WMF
INSECT9.WMF
LEAF___C.WMF
MOSBABY.WMF
MOSQUITC.WMF
MOTHS.WMF
NABO002J.WMF
NABO008J.WMF
NABO094J.WMF
NACA094J.WMF
NACA103D.WMF
NAKC003J.WMF
NASI152D.WMF
NASI229D.WMF
PD045MCU.WMF
PD045NCU.WMF
PD045OCU.WMF
PD045PCU.WMF
PD045QCU.WMF
PD045RCU.WMF
PD045SCU.WMF
PECA161D.WMF
PET14.WMF
PET15.WMF
PET19.WMF
PET20.WMF
PET22.WMF
PET23.WMF
PET24.WMF
PRIN0595.WMF
PRIN0596.WMF
PRIN0611.WMF
PRIN0612.WMF
PRIN0615.WMF
PRIN0616.WMF
PRIN0617.WMF
PRIN0618.WMF

PRIN0621.WMF
PRIN0622.WMF
PRIN0623.WMF
PRIN0624.WMF
PRIN0625.WMF
PRIN0626.WMF
PRIN0627.WMF
PRIN0628.WMF
PRIN0629.WMF
PRIN0630.WMF
PRIN0631.WMF
PRIN0632.WMF
PRIN0645.WMF
PRIN0646.WMF
S21693.WMF
S21699.WMF
S21700.WMF
S21701.WMF
SLUG.WMF
SPA003C.WMF
SPA003D.WMF
SPA011C.WMF
SPA012F.WMF
SPA020F.WMF
SYMBL66.WMF
SYMBL67.WMF
SYMBL68.WMF
SYMBOL66.WMF
SYMBOL67.WMF
SYMBOL68.WMF
W21896.WMF
W21897.WMF
W21898.WMF
W21900.WMF

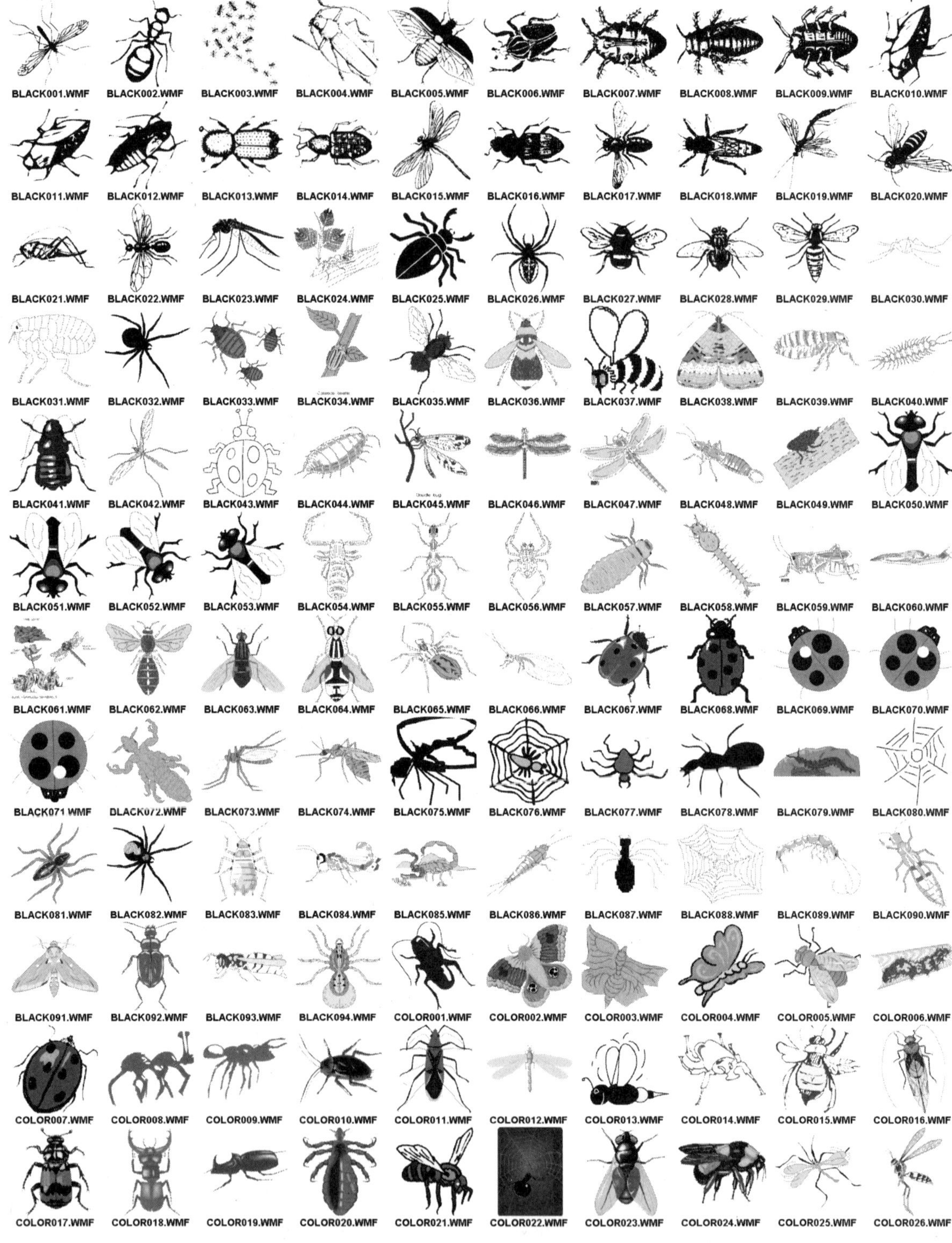
BLACK001.WMF BLACK002.WMF BLACK003.WMF BLACK004.WMF BLACK005.WMF BLACK006.WMF BLACK007.WMF BLACK008.WMF BLACK009.WMF BLACK010.WMF
BLACK011.WMF BLACK012.WMF BLACK013.WMF BLACK014.WMF BLACK015.WMF BLACK016.WMF BLACK017.WMF BLACK018.WMF BLACK019.WMF BLACK020.WMF
BLACK021.WMF BLACK022.WMF BLACK023.WMF BLACK024.WMF BLACK025.WMF BLACK026.WMF BLACK027.WMF BLACK028.WMF BLACK029.WMF BLACK030.WMF
BLACK031.WMF BLACK032.WMF BLACK033.WMF BLACK034.WMF BLACK035.WMF BLACK036.WMF BLACK037.WMF BLACK038.WMF BLACK039.WMF BLACK040.WMF
BLACK041.WMF BLACK042.WMF BLACK043.WMF BLACK044.WMF BLACK045.WMF BLACK046.WMF BLACK047.WMF BLACK048.WMF BLACK049.WMF BLACK050.WMF
BLACK051.WMF BLACK052.WMF BLACK053.WMF BLACK054.WMF BLACK055.WMF BLACK056.WMF BLACK057.WMF BLACK058.WMF BLACK059.WMF BLACK060.WMF
BLACK061.WMF BLACK062.WMF BLACK063.WMF BLACK064.WMF BLACK065.WMF BLACK066.WMF BLACK067.WMF BLACK068.WMF BLACK069.WMF BLACK070.WMF
BLACK071.WMF BLACK072.WMF BLACK073.WMF BLACK074.WMF BLACK075.WMF BLACK076.WMF BLACK077.WMF BLACK078.WMF BLACK079.WMF BLACK080.WMF
BLACK081.WMF BLACK082.WMF BLACK083.WMF BLACK084.WMF BLACK085.WMF BLACK086.WMF BLACK087.WMF BLACK088.WMF BLACK089.WMF BLACK090.WMF
BLACK091.WMF BLACK092.WMF BLACK093.WMF BLACK094.WMF COLOR001.WMF COLOR002.WMF COLOR003.WMF COLOR004.WMF COLOR005.WMF COLOR006.WMF
COLOR007.WMF COLOR008.WMF COLOR009.WMF COLOR010.WMF COLOR011.WMF COLOR012.WMF COLOR013.WMF COLOR014.WMF COLOR015.WMF COLOR016.WMF
COLOR017.WMF COLOR018.WMF COLOR019.WMF COLOR020.WMF COLOR021.WMF COLOR022.WMF COLOR023.WMF COLOR024.WMF COLOR025.WMF COLOR026.WMF

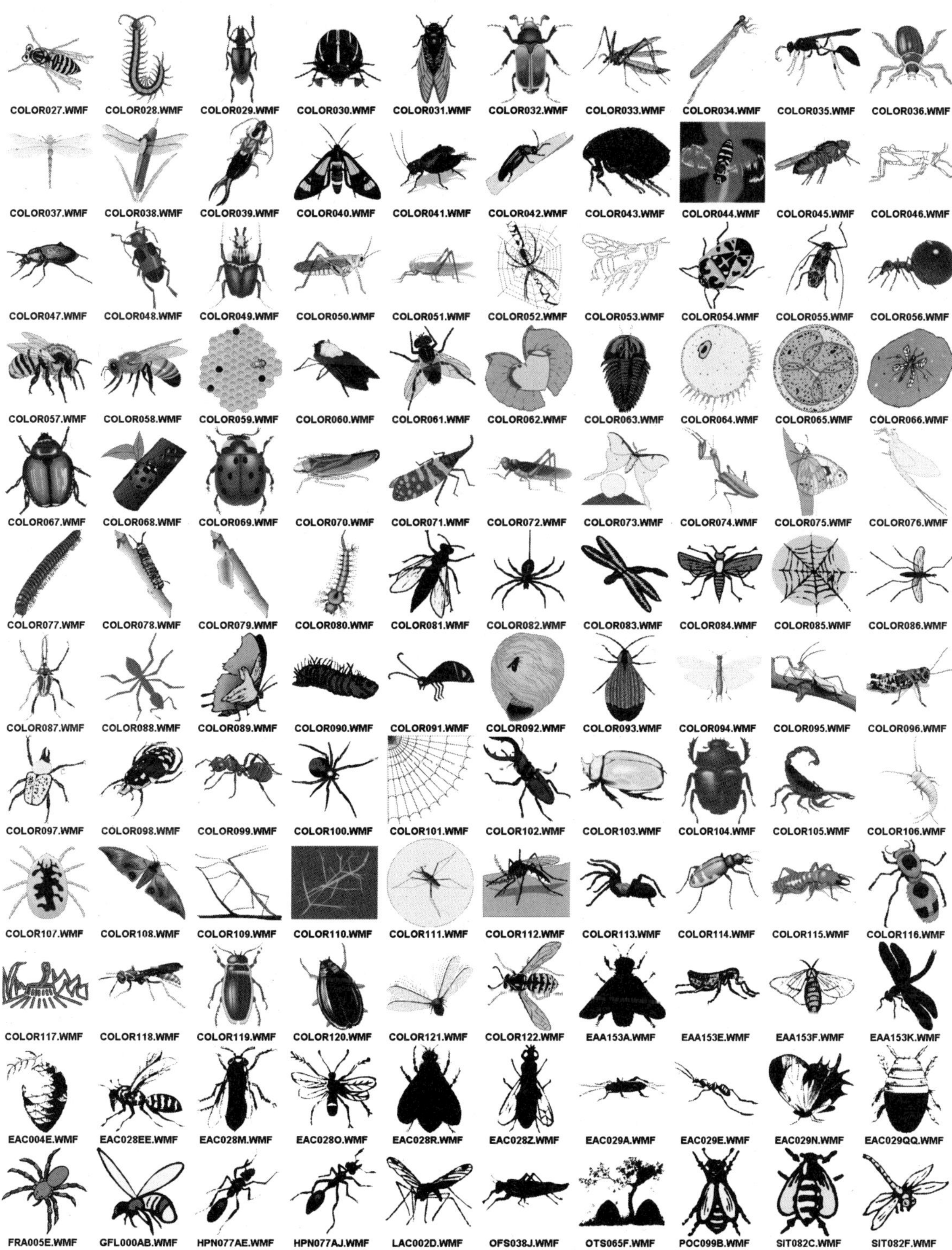
COLOR027.WMF COLOR028.WMF COLOR029.WMF COLOR030.WMF COLOR031.WMF COLOR032.WMF COLOR033.WMF COLOR034.WMF COLOR035.WMF COLOR036.WMF
COLOR037.WMF COLOR038.WMF COLOR039.WMF COLOR040.WMF COLOR041.WMF COLOR042.WMF COLOR043.WMF COLOR044.WMF COLOR045.WMF COLOR046.WMF
COLOR047.WMF COLOR048.WMF COLOR049.WMF COLOR050.WMF COLOR051.WMF COLOR052.WMF COLOR053.WMF COLOR054.WMF COLOR055.WMF COLOR056.WMF
COLOR057.WMF COLOR058.WMF COLOR059.WMF COLOR060.WMF COLOR061.WMF COLOR062.WMF COLOR063.WMF COLOR064.WMF COLOR065.WMF COLOR066.WMF
COLOR067.WMF COLOR068.WMF COLOR069.WMF COLOR070.WMF COLOR071.WMF COLOR072.WMF COLOR073.WMF COLOR074.WMF COLOR075.WMF COLOR076.WMF
COLOR077.WMF COLOR078.WMF COLOR079.WMF COLOR080.WMF COLOR081.WMF COLOR082.WMF COLOR083.WMF COLOR084.WMF COLOR085.WMF COLOR086.WMF
COLOR087.WMF COLOR088.WMF COLOR089.WMF COLOR090.WMF COLOR091.WMF COLOR092.WMF COLOR093.WMF COLOR094.WMF COLOR095.WMF COLOR096.WMF
COLOR097.WMF COLOR098.WMF COLOR099.WMF COLOR100.WMF COLOR101.WMF COLOR102.WMF COLOR103.WMF COLOR104.WMF COLOR105.WMF COLOR106.WMF
COLOR107.WMF COLOR108.WMF COLOR109.WMF COLOR110.WMF COLOR111.WMF COLOR112.WMF COLOR113.WMF COLOR114.WMF COLOR115.WMF COLOR116.WMF
COLOR117.WMF COLOR118.WMF COLOR119.WMF COLOR120.WMF COLOR121.WMF COLOR122.WMF EAA153A.WMF EAA153E.WMF EAA153F.WMF EAA153K.WMF
EAC004E.WMF EAC028EE.WMF EAC028M.WMF EAC028O.WMF EAC028R.WMF EAC028Z.WMF EAC029A.WMF EAC029E.WMF EAC029N.WMF EAC029QQ.WMF
FRA005E.WMF GFL000AB.WMF HPN077AE.WMF HPN077AJ.WMF LAC002D.WMF OFS038J.WMF OTS065F.WMF POC099B.WMF SIT082C.WMF SIT082F.WMF

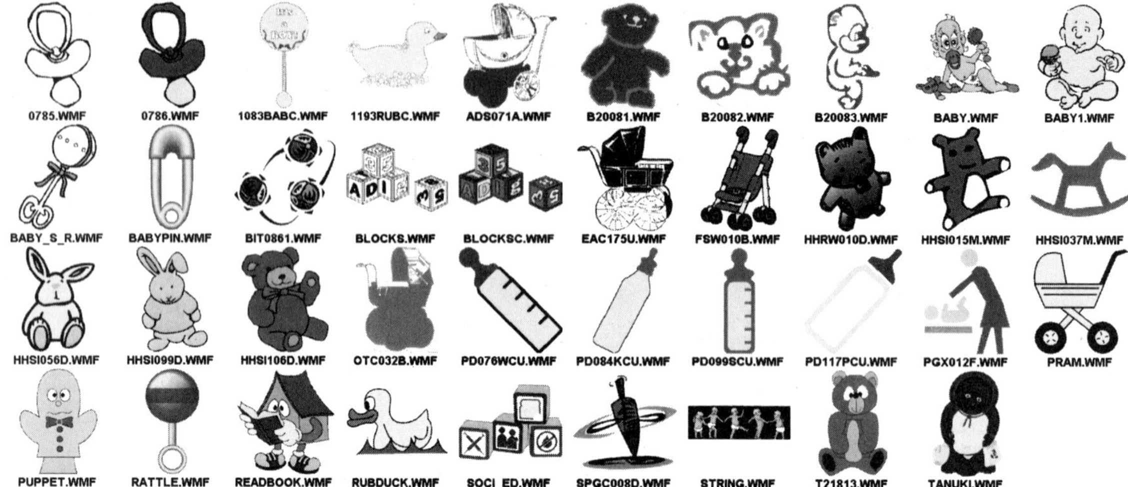
0785.WMF
0786.WMF
1083BABC.WMF
1193RUBC.WMF
ADS071A.WMF
B20081.WMF
B20082.WMF
B20083.WMF
BABY.WMF
BABY1.WMF
BABY_S_R.WMF
BABYPIN.WMF
BIT0861.WMF
BLOCKS.WMF
BLOCKSC.WMF
EAC175U.WMF
FSW010B.WMF
HHRW010D.WMF
HHSI015M.WMF
HHSI037M.WMF
HHSI056D.WMF
HHSI099D.WMF
HHSI106D.WMF
OTC032B.WMF
PD076WCU.WMF
PD084KCU.WMF
PD099SCU.WMF
PD117PCU.WMF
PGX012F.WMF
PRAM.WMF
PUPPET.WMF
RATTLE.WMF
READBOOK.WMF
RUBDUCK.WMF
SOCI_ED.WMF
SPGC008D.WMF
STRING.WMF
T21813.WMF
TANUKI.WMF

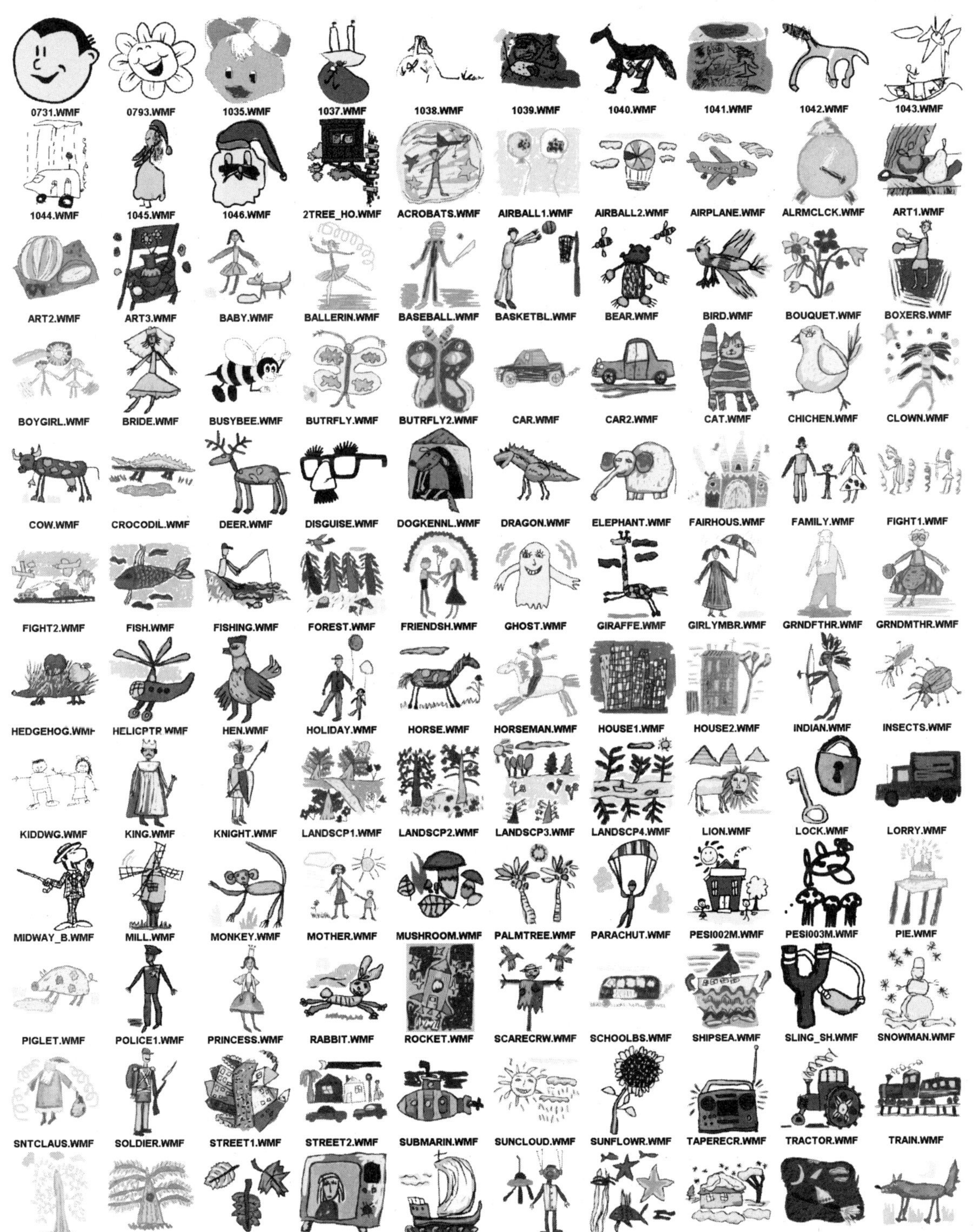
0731.WMF 0793.WMF 1035.WMF 1037.WMF 1038.WMF 1039.WMF 1040.WMF 1041.WMF 1042.WMF 1043.WMF
1044.WMF 1045.WMF 1046.WMF 2TREE_HO.WMF ACROBATS.WMF AIRBALL1.WMF AIRBALL2.WMF AIRPLANE.WMF ALRMCLCK.WMF ART1.WMF
ART2.WMF ART3.WMF BABY.WMF BALLERIN.WMF BASEBALL.WMF BASKETBL.WMF BEAR.WMF BIRD.WMF BOUQUET.WMF BOXERS.WMF
BOYGIRL.WMF BRIDE.WMF BUSYBEE.WMF BUTRFLY.WMF BUTRFLY2.WMF CAR.WMF CAR2.WMF CAT.WMF CHICHEN.WMF CLOWN.WMF
COW.WMF CROCODIL.WMF DEER.WMF DISGUISE.WMF DOGKENNL.WMF DRAGON.WMF ELEPHANT.WMF FAIRHOUS.WMF FAMILY.WMF FIGHT1.WMF
FIGHT2.WMF FISH.WMF FISHING.WMF FOREST.WMF FRIENDSH.WMF GHOST.WMF GIRAFFE.WMF GIRLYMBR.WMF GRNDFTHR.WMF GRNDMTHR.WMF
HEDGEHOG.WMF HELICPTR.WMF HEN.WMF HOLIDAY.WMF HORSE.WMF HORSEMAN.WMF HOUSE1.WMF HOUSE2.WMF INDIAN.WMF INSECTS.WMF
KIDDWG.WMF KING.WMF KNIGHT.WMF LANDSCP1.WMF LANDSCP2.WMF LANDSCP3.WMF LANDSCP4.WMF LION.WMF LOCK.WMF LORRY.WMF
MIDWAY_B.WMF MILL.WMF MONKEY.WMF MOTHER.WMF MUSHROOM.WMF PALMTREE.WMF PARACHUT.WMF PESI002M.WMF PESI003M.WMF PIE.WMF
PIGLET.WMF POLICE1.WMF PRINCESS.WMF RABBIT.WMF ROCKET.WMF SCARECRW.WMF SCHOOLBS.WMF SHIPSEA.WMF SLING_SH.WMF SNOWMAN.WMF
SNTCLAUS.WMF SOLDIER.WMF STREET1.WMF STREET2.WMF SUBMARIN.WMF SUNCLOUD.WMF SUNFLOWR.WMF TAPERECR.WMF TRACTOR.WMF TRAIN.WMF
TREE1.WMF TREE2.WMF TREELEAF.WMF TVSET.WMF VESSEL.WMF VISITOR.WMF WATRWRLD.WMF WINTER.WMF WITCH.WMF WOLF.WMF

0163GIRC.WMF 0168PIGC.WMF 0180.WMF 0728.WMF ACORNS.WMF ADS064D.WMF AIRBALL.WMF ALICE_IN.WMF ANGEL.WMF ANGELL.WMF

APPLE.WMF ARK.WMF ASI047I.WMF B20090.WMF BABY.WMF BABYCAR.WMF BAKER.WMF BALARM.WMF BALOON.WMF BAT.WMF

BBYBTTL.WMF BEARART.WMF BEARF.WMF BEARHOL.WMF BEARMTHR.WMF BEARP.WMF BFLOWERS.WMF BIT0802.WMF BODS.WMF BONNET.WMF

BOOKBAG.WMF BOOKBOY.WMF BOOT.WMF BOW.WMF BOY.WMF BOY___YO.WMF BOY_WITH.WMF BTRFLLY.WMF BUGLER.WMF BUGLERC.WMF

BULLRIDE.WMF BUNNY.WMF BUNNYC.WMF BUNW.WMF CANDIES.WMF CAROUSEL.WMF CARROTS.WMF CATERPIL.WMF CATS.WMF CHASING.WMF

CHICKEN.WMF CHILD1.WMF CHILD2.WMF CHILDREN.WMF CHRISTC.WMF CHRISTT.WMF CLOWN.WMF COALLA.WMF COP.WMF CORNUCOP.WMF

COW.WMF CROCOD.WMF CUPID.WMF DARUMA2.WMF DEER.WMF DOG.WMF DOLL.WMF DOLL2.WMF DOLL42.WMF DONKEY.WMF

DUCKPON.WMF ELEPHANT.WMF ENSI012M.WMF FAMLY025.WMF FAMLY026.WMF FCP004B.WMF FCP022I.WMF FISH.WMF FLAG.WMF FLOWERS.WMF

FROG.WMF FRUITS.WMF FSW001A.WMF FSW007B.WMF FSW007C.WMF FSW009A.WMF FSW011A.WMF FSW011C.WMF FSW011D.WMF FSW014D.WMF

FSW016C.WMF FSW019C.WMF FUNNY__1.WMF FUNNY_FA.WMF FWN006A.WMF FWN006B.WMF FWN006E.WMF FWN006F.WMF FWN013A.WMF FWN020A.WMF

FWN021A.WMF FWN023A.WMF FWN024A.WMF FWN028A.WMF FWN030A.WMF FWN031A.WMF FWN034A.WMF FWN034B.WMF FWN038A.WMF FWN039A.WMF

FWN040A.WMF FWN041A.WMF FWN046A.WMF FWN046B.WMF FWN047A.WMF GDSTDNT.WMF GERLSMR.WMF GERLSPR.WMF GERLWNT.WMF GFATHER.WMF

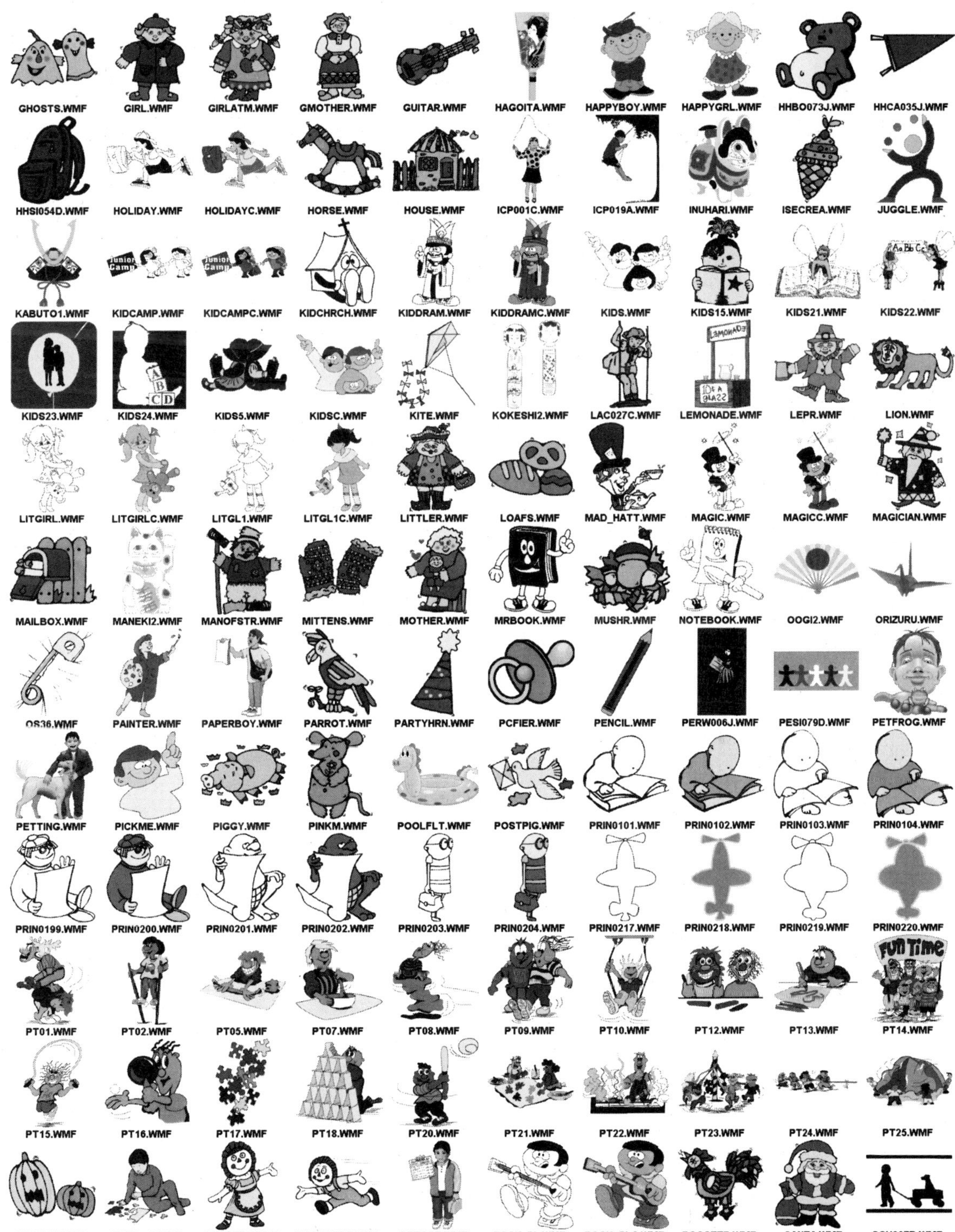
GHOSTS.WMF
GIRL.WMF
GIRLATM.WMF
GMOTHER.WMF
GUITAR.WMF
HAGOITA.WMF
HAPPYBOY.WMF
HAPPYGRL.WMF
HHBO073J.WMF
HHCA035J.WMF
HHSI054D.WMF
HOLIDAY.WMF
HOLIDAYC.WMF
HORSE.WMF
HOUSE.WMF
ICP001C.WMF
ICP019A.WMF
INUHARI.WMF
ISECREA.WMF
JUGGLE.WMF
KABUTO1.WMF
KIDCAMP.WMF
KIDCAMPC.WMF
KIDCHRCH.WMF
KIDDRAM.WMF
KIDDRAMC.WMF
KIDS.WMF
KIDS15.WMF
KIDS21.WMF
KIDS22.WMF
KIDS23.WMF
KIDS24.WMF
KIDS5.WMF
KIDSC.WMF
KITE.WMF
KOKESHI2.WMF
LAC027C.WMF
LEMONADE.WMF
LEPR.WMF
LION.WMF
LITGIRL.WMF
LITGIRLC.WMF
LITGL1.WMF
LITGL1C.WMF
LITTLER.WMF
LOAFS.WMF
MAD_HATT.WMF
MAGIC.WMF
MAGICC.WMF
MAGICIAN.WMF
MAILBOX.WMF
MANEKI2.WMF
MANOFSTR.WMF
MITTENS.WMF
MOTHER.WMF
MRBOOK.WMF
MUSHR.WMF
NOTEBOOK.WMF
OOGI2.WMF
ORIZURU.WMF
OS36.WMF
PAINTER.WMF
PAPERBOY.WMF
PARROT.WMF
PARTYHRN.WMF
PCFIER.WMF
PENCIL.WMF
PERW006J.WMF
PESI079D.WMF
PETFROG.WMF
PETTING.WMF
PICKME.WMF
PIGGY.WMF
PINKM.WMF
POOLFLT.WMF
POSTPIG.WMF
PRIN0101.WMF
PRIN0102.WMF
PRIN0103.WMF
PRIN0104.WMF
PRIN0199.WMF
PRIN0200.WMF
PRIN0201.WMF
PRIN0202.WMF
PRIN0203.WMF
PRIN0204.WMF
PRIN0217.WMF
PRIN0218.WMF
PRIN0219.WMF
PRIN0220.WMF
PT01.WMF
PT02.WMF
PT05.WMF
PT07.WMF
PT08.WMF
PT09.WMF
PT10.WMF
PT12.WMF
PT13.WMF
PT14.WMF
PT15.WMF
PT16.WMF
PT17.WMF
PT18.WMF
PT20.WMF
PT21.WMF
PT22.WMF
PT23.WMF
PT24.WMF
PT25.WMF
PUMPKIN.WMF
PUZZL_1.WMF
RAGGEDY.WMF
RAGGEDY2.WMF
REPORT.WMF
ROCK_RL.WMF
ROCK_RLC.WMF
ROOSTER.WMF
SANTA.WMF
SCH007B.WMF

SCH010B.WMF
SCH016A.WMF
SCH018A.WMF
SCH022B.WMF
SCT027A.WMF
SHEEP.WMF
SHELL.WMF
SHELTER.WMF
SHERIFF.WMF
SHIP.WMF
SHOE.WMF
SIT036I.WMF
SIT086G.WMF
SKTBEAR.WMF
SKTEBORD.WMF
SLIDE.WMF
SLING2.WMF
SNDCSTL.WMF
SNEAKERS.WMF
SNOWM.WMF
SOCKS.WMF
SPCA029J.WMF
SPSI614D.WMF
STRAWB.WMF
STROLLER.WMF
STUDNT4.WMF
STUDY3.WMF
SUNFLWER.WMF
SUNRAIN.WMF
SUNSHADE.WMF
SWING.WMF
TD01.WMF
TD03.WMF
TD04.WMF
TD05.WMF
TD07.WMF
TD08.WMF
TD09.WMF
TD10.WMF
TD11.WMF
TD13.WMF
TD14.WMF
TD15.WMF
TD17.WMF
TD18.WMF
TD21.WMF
TD22.WMF
TD23.WMF
TD25.WMF
TEA_1.WMF
TEDDY.WMF
TOD071A.WMF
TOD071L.WMF
TOD071M.WMF
TOD071W.WMF
TOY.WMF
TOYBOY.WMF
TRAMPOLN.WMF
TREE.WMF
TS16.WMF
UMBRLGRL.WMF
VIOLINST.WMF
WATER.WMF
WHIRLIG.WMF
WITCH.WMF
WMG053D.WMF
WREATHC.WMF
XRAYCRTN.WMF
YTHNEWS1.WMF

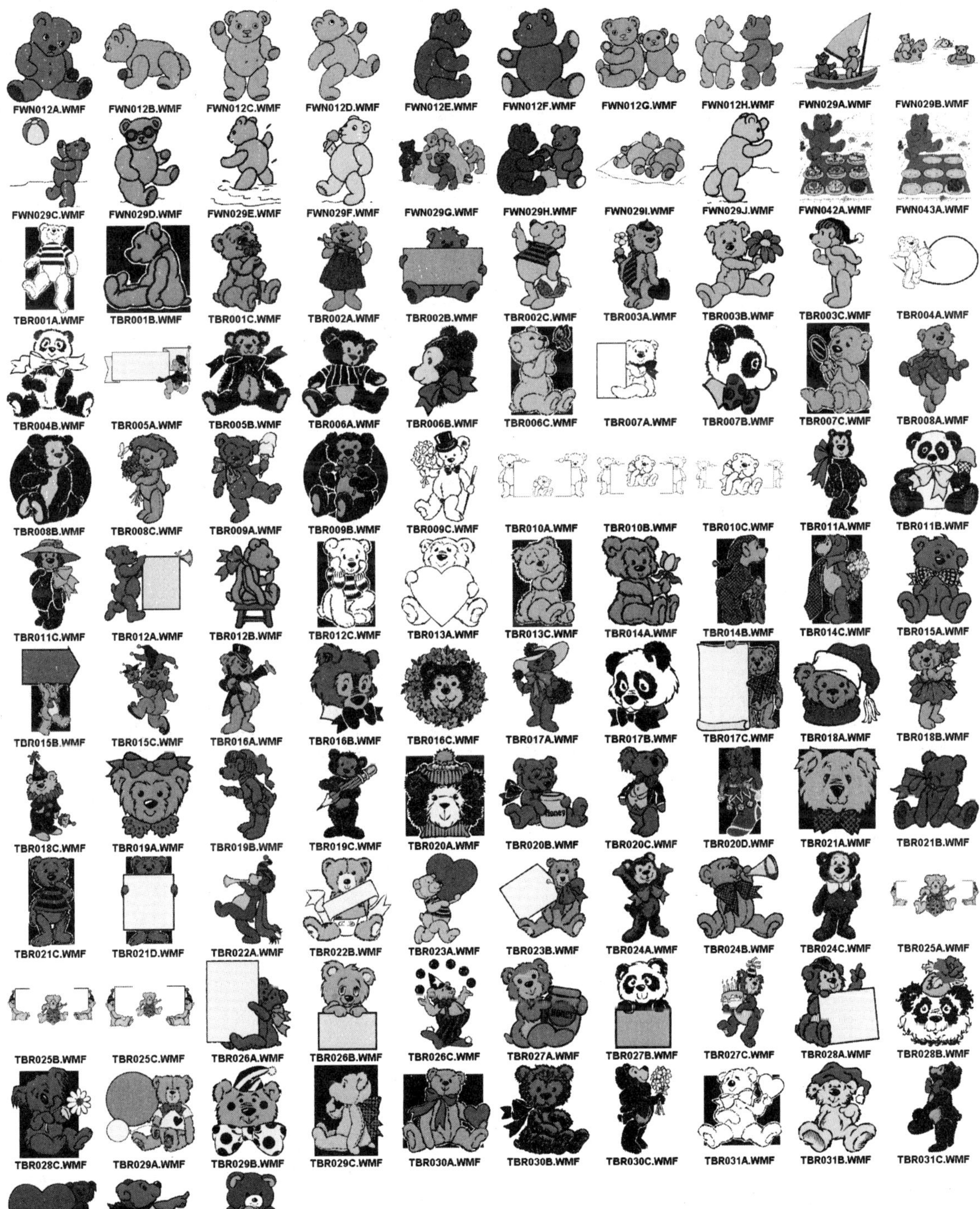
FWN012A.WMF
FWN012B.WMF
FWN012C.WMF
FWN012D.WMF
FWN012E.WMF
FWN012F.WMF
FWN012G.WMF
FWN012H.WMF
FWN029A.WMF
FWN029B.WMF
FWN029C.WMF
FWN029D.WMF
FWN029E.WMF
FWN029F.WMF
FWN029G.WMF
FWN029H.WMF
FWN029I.WMF
FWN029J.WMF
FWN042A.WMF
FWN043A.WMF
TBR001A.WMF
TBR001B.WMF
TBR001C.WMF
TBR002A.WMF
TBR002B.WMF
TBR002C.WMF
TBR003A.WMF
TBR003B.WMF
TBR003C.WMF
TBR004A.WMF
TBR004B.WMF
TBR005A.WMF
TBR005B.WMF
TBR006A.WMF
TBR006B.WMF
TBR006C.WMF
TBR007A.WMF
TBR007B.WMF
TBR007C.WMF
TBR008A.WMF
TBR008B.WMF
TBR008C.WMF
TBR009A.WMF
TBR009B.WMF
TBR009C.WMF
TBR010A.WMF
TBR010B.WMF
TBR010C.WMF
TBR011A.WMF
TBR011B.WMF
TBR011C.WMF
TBR012A.WMF
TBR012B.WMF
TBR012C.WMF
TBR013A.WMF
TBR013C.WMF
TBR014A.WMF
TBR014B.WMF
TBR014C.WMF
TBR015A.WMF
TBR015B.WMF
TBR015C.WMF
TBR016A.WMF
TBR016B.WMF
TBR016C.WMF
TBR017A.WMF
TBR017B.WMF
TBR017C.WMF
TBR018A.WMF
TBR018B.WMF
TBR018C.WMF
TBR019A.WMF
TBR019B.WMF
TBR019C.WMF
TBR020A.WMF
TBR020B.WMF
TBR020C.WMF
TBR020D.WMF
TBR021A.WMF
TBR021B.WMF
TBR021C.WMF
TBR021D.WMF
TBR022A.WMF
TBR022B.WMF
TBR023A.WMF
TBR023B.WMF
TBR024A.WMF
TBR024B.WMF
TBR024C.WMF
TBR025A.WMF
TBR025B.WMF
TBR025C.WMF
TBR026A.WMF
TBR026B.WMF
TBR026C.WMF
TBR027A.WMF
TBR027B.WMF
TBR027C.WMF
TBR028A.WMF
TBR028B.WMF
TBR028C.WMF
TBR029A.WMF
TBR029B.WMF
TBR029C.WMF
TBR030A.WMF
TBR030B.WMF
TBR030C.WMF
TBR031A.WMF
TBR031B.WMF
TBR031C.WMF
TBR032A.WMF
TBR032B.WMF
TDG029B.WMF

0162CRAC.WMF
0696.WMF
0710.WMF
1251CRAC.WMF
1629.WMF
1630.WMF
1631.WMF
1632.WMF
1633.WMF
1634.WMF
1GUM_MAC.WMF
1SHINY_B.WMF
1TREE_HO.WMF
2GUM_MAC.WMF
2SHINY_B.WMF
4_WHEELJ.WMF
4_WHEELT.WMF
AIRPLANE.WMF
ANESAMA.WMF
BABYBLOC.WMF
BABYBOW.WMF
BABYBOW8.WMF
BABYCARG.WMF
BABYCLO.WMF
BABYCLOK.WMF
BABYDOLL.WMF
BABYUM.WMF
BABYUMBR.WMF
BALL.WMF
BALL216.WMF
BALLOONS.WMF
BALOON55.WMF
BALOONS.WMF
BARBIDOL.WMF
BASEBALL.WMF
BAT.WMF
BEAR_PLA.WMF
BELL.WMF
BELL36.WMF
BICYC2.WMF
BICYCLE.WMF
BICYCLES.WMF
BIKEWTRA.WMF
BIT1002.WMF
BLOCKT.WMF
BLOCKTOY.WMF
BOAT.WMF
BROKENPI.WMF
CAROUSEL.WMF
CART.WMF
CHOOCHOO.WMF
CLOWN.WMF
CLOWN55.WMF
COALA.WMF
COLORPEN.WMF
COW.WMF
CRAYONS.WMF
CRSLHORS.WMF
DICE.WMF
DOG.WMF
DOLL.WMF
DOLL1.WMF
DOLL2.WMF
DOLL3.WMF
DOLL4.WMF
DOLL5.WMF
DOLL6.WMF
DOLLGLAS.WMF
DOLLS.WMF
DRUM.WMF
DRUM2.WMF
DRUM22.WMF
DUMPTRUC.WMF
ELEPHANT.WMF
ELEPHNT2.WMF
ENCA002J.WMF
ENCA018J.WMF
ENSI033D.WMF
FCP004F.WMF
FCP008E.WMF
FCP018C.WMF
FCP034H.WMF
FIREENGI.WMF
FIRERESC.WMF
FOOTBALL.WMF
FOX.WMF
FRA006A.WMF
FROG.WMF
FSW010C.WMF
FSW010D.WMF
FSW012B.WMF
FSW014A.WMF
FSW014B.WMF
FSW014C.WMF
FSW015D.WMF
FSW016B.WMF
FSW036C.WMF
FWN024B.WMF
FWN024C.WMF
FWN024D.WMF
FWN024E.WMF
FWN024F.WMF
FWN024G.WMF
FWN024H.WMF
FWN024I.WMF
GANTRICK.WMF
GIFTANGL.WMF
GIRAFFE.WMF
HAMMT56.WMF
HAMMTOP.WMF
HDC124E.WMF
HEDGEHOG.WMF
HELICOPT.WMF
HIPPO.WMF
HOBBYHOR.WMF
HPSCOTCH.WMF
JACK_IN_.WMF
JACKBO61.WMF
JACKBOX1.WMF
JACKBOX2.WMF

JACKNBO2.WMF JACKNBOX.WMF JUNGLE.WMF KITE.WMF KITE2.WMF KOMA1.WMF LEPRECHN.WMF LILTRAIN.WMF LION.WMF LUNCHBOX.WMF
MACHINE.WMF MAGICIAN.WMF MARBLE_B.WMF MASHINE1.WMF MERRYGO.WMF MOUSE.WMF OFSS003K.WMF ORNAME35.WMF ORNAMENT.WMF PANDA.WMF
PARTYHAT.WMF PENCIL35.WMF PENCILS.WMF PENGUIN.WMF PIG.WMF PIG2.WMF PIGGBANK.WMF PINKRABT.WMF PLAYHORS.WMF PLAYHOUS.WMF
PT06.WMF PT11.WMF PT19.WMF PUMPKIN.WMF PUPPET.WMF PUZLPIEC.WMF RABBIT.WMF RABBIT1.WMF RATTLE1.WMF RATTLE13.WMF
RATTLE2.WMF RATTLE23.WMF RINGTOY.WMF RINGTOY2.WMF ROBOT.WMF ROCKET.WMF ROCKHO2.WMF ROCKHORS.WMF ROCKINGH.WMF ROOSTER.WMF
SANDBOX.WMF SANDBOX2.WMF SCOOTER.WMF SEESAW.WMF SHIP1.WMF SHIP135.WMF SHIP2.WMF SHOEBA35.WMF SHOEBABY.WMF SLIDE.WMF
SMR004N.WMF SOLDIER.WMF SOLDIER2.WMF SOSI019D.WMF SPA013D.WMF SPA030D.WMF STOCKING.WMF STUFDANM.WMF SWING.WMF TD02.WMF
TD06.WMF TD16.WMF TD19A.WMF TD20.WMF TD24_.WMF TDG001A.WMF TDG002B.WMF TDG004B.WMF TDG005A.WMF TDG011A.WMF
TDG012A.WMF TDG012C.WMF TDG022A.WMF TDG022C.WMF TDG023E.WMF TDG029A.WMF TEDBE2.WMF TEDBE3.WMF TEDBE35.WMF TEDBE4.WMF
TEDBE5.WMF TEDBEAR.WMF TEDBEAR1.WMF TEDBEAR2.WMF TEDBEAR3.WMF TEDBEAR4.WMF TEDBEAR5.WMF TEDDY.WMF TEDDYB2.WMF TEDDYBEA.WMF
TEDDYBR.WMF TEDYBER2.WMF TIGER.WMF TIRE_SWI.WMF TORTOISE.WMF TOYBORD1.WMF TOYCOMPT.WMF TOYCOO2.WMF TOYCOO35.WMF TOYCOOKW.WMF
TOYLAND SPECIALS
TOYHOR35.WMF TOYHORN.WMF TOYLAND2.WMF TOYLANDS.WMF TOYPA35.WMF TOYPAIL.WMF TOYPHONE.WMF TOYS.WMF TOYS2.WMF TOYS3.WMF

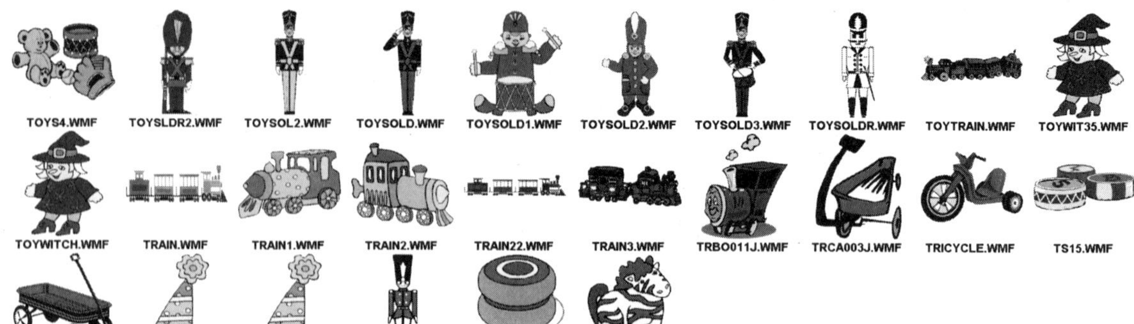
TOYS4.WMF
TOYSLDR2.WMF
TOYSOL2.WMF
TOYSOLD.WMF
TOYSOLD1.WMF
TOYSOLD2.WMF
TOYSOLD3.WMF
TOYSOLDR.WMF
TOYTRAIN.WMF
TOYWIT35.WMF
TOYWITCH.WMF
TRAIN.WMF
TRAIN1.WMF
TRAIN2.WMF
TRAIN22.WMF
TRAIN3.WMF
TRBO011J.WMF
TRCA003J.WMF
TRICYCLE.WMF
TS15.WMF
WAGON.WMF
WIZRDH35.WMF
WIZRDHAT.WMF
WOODEN_S.WMF
YOYO.WMF
ZEBRA.WMF

CART001.WMF CART002.WMF CART003.WMF CART004.WMF CART005.WMF CART006.WMF CART007.WMF CART008.WMF CART009.WMF CART010.WMF

CART011.WMF CART012.WMF CART013.WMF CART014.WMF CART015.WMF CART016.WMF CART017.WMF CART018.WMF CART019.WMF CART020.WMF

CART021.WMF CART022.WMF CART023.WMF CART024.WMF CART025.WMF CART026.WMF CART027.WMF CART028.WMF CART029.WMF CART030.WMF

CART031.WMF CART032.WMF CART033.WMF CART034.WMF CART035.WMF CART036.WMF CART037.WMF CART038.WMF CART039.WMF CART040.WMF

LANDSC01.WMF LANDSC02.WMF LANDSC03.WMF LANDSC04.WMF LANDSC05.WMF LANDSC06.WMF LANDSC07.WMF LANDSC08.WMF LANDSC09.WMF LANDSC10.WMF

LANDSC11.WMF LANDSC12.WMF LANDSC13.WMF LANDSC14.WMF LANDSC15.WMF LANDSC16.WMF LANDSC17.WMF LANDSC18.WMF LANDSC19.WMF LANDSC20.WMF

LANDSC21.WMF LANDSC22.WMF LANDSC23.WMF LANDSC24.WMF LANDSC25.WMF LANDSC26.WMF LANDSC27.WMF LANDSC28.WMF LANDSC29.WMF LANDSC30.WMF

LANDSC31.WMF LANDSC32.WMF LANDSC33.WMF LANDSC34.WMF LANDSC35.WMF LANDSC36.WMF LANDSC37.WMF LANDSC38.WMF LANDSC39.WMF LANDSC40.WMF

LANDSC41.WMF LANDSC42.WMF LANDSC43.WMF LANDSC44.WMF LANDSC45.WMF LANDSC46.WMF LANDSC47.WMF LANDSC48.WMF LANDSC49.WMF LANDSC50.WMF

LANDSC51.WMF LANDSC52.WMF LANDSC53.WMF LANDSC54.WMF LANDSC55.WMF LANDSC56.WMF LANDSC57.WMF LANDSC58.WMF LANDSC59.WMF LANDSC60.WMF

LANDSC61.WMF LANDSC62.WMF LANDSC63.WMF LANDSC64.WMF LANDSC65.WMF LANDSC66.WMF LANDSC67.WMF LANDSC68.WMF LANDSC69.WMF LANDSC70.WMF

LANDSC71.WMF LANDSC72.WMF LANDSC73.WMF LANDSC74.WMF LANDSC75.WMF LANDSC76.WMF LANDSC77.WMF NATUR001.WMF NATUR002.WMF NATUR003.WMF

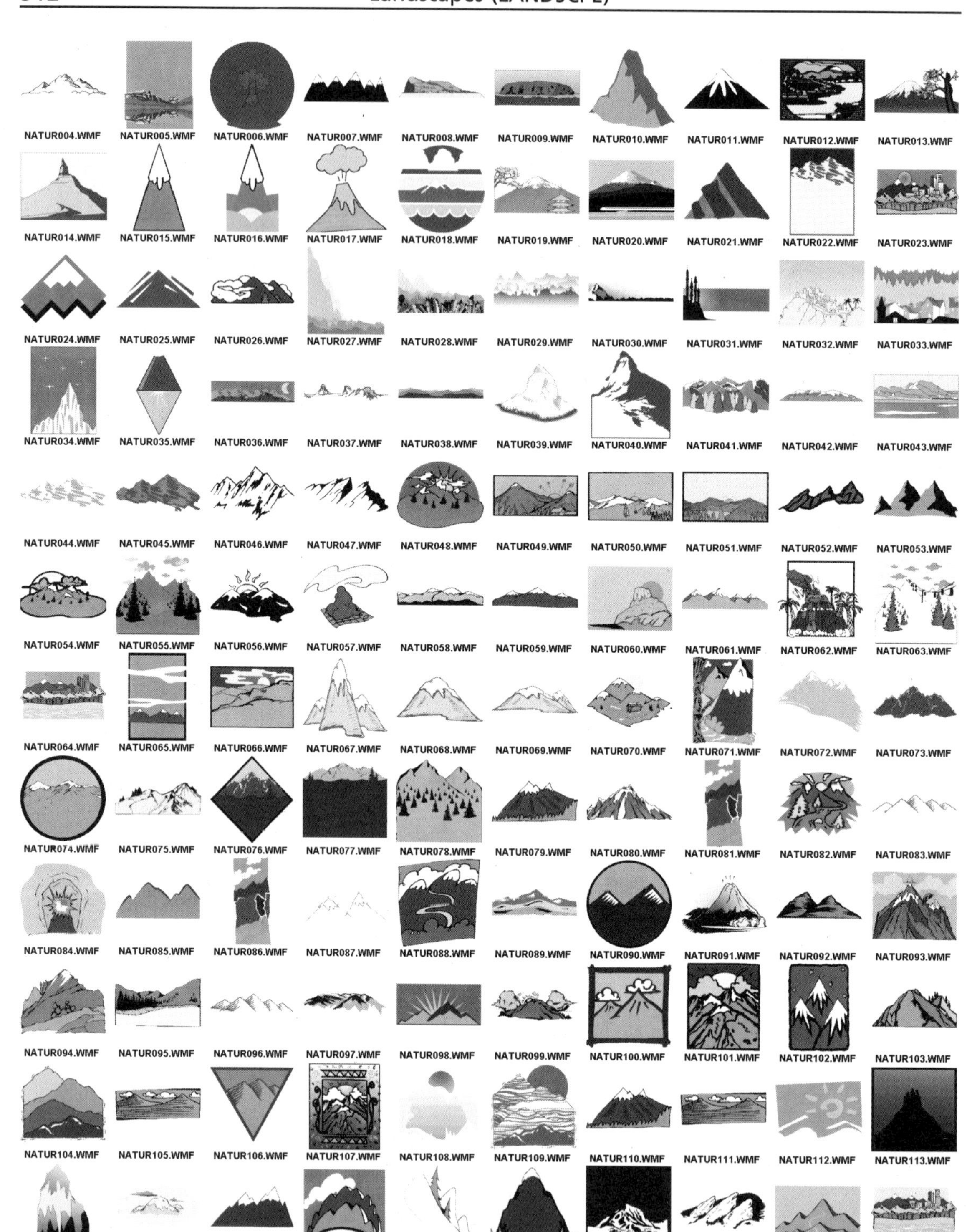

NATUR004.WMF
NATUR005.WMF
NATUR006.WMF
NATUR007.WMF
NATUR008.WMF
NATUR009.WMF
NATUR010.WMF
NATUR011.WMF
NATUR012.WMF
NATUR013.WMF
NATUR014.WMF
NATUR015.WMF
NATUR016.WMF
NATUR017.WMF
NATUR018.WMF
NATUR019.WMF
NATUR020.WMF
NATUR021.WMF
NATUR022.WMF
NATUR023.WMF
NATUR024.WMF
NATUR025.WMF
NATUR026.WMF
NATUR027.WMF
NATUR028.WMF
NATUR029.WMF
NATUR030.WMF
NATUR031.WMF
NATUR032.WMF
NATUR033.WMF
NATUR034.WMF
NATUR035.WMF
NATUR036.WMF
NATUR037.WMF
NATUR038.WMF
NATUR039.WMF
NATUR040.WMF
NATUR041.WMF
NATUR042.WMF
NATUR043.WMF
NATUR044.WMF
NATUR045.WMF
NATUR046.WMF
NATUR047.WMF
NATUR048.WMF
NATUR049.WMF
NATUR050.WMF
NATUR051.WMF
NATUR052.WMF
NATUR053.WMF
NATUR054.WMF
NATUR055.WMF
NATUR056.WMF
NATUR057.WMF
NATUR058.WMF
NATUR059.WMF
NATUR060.WMF
NATUR061.WMF
NATUR062.WMF
NATUR063.WMF
NATUR064.WMF
NATUR065.WMF
NATUR066.WMF
NATUR067.WMF
NATUR068.WMF
NATUR069.WMF
NATUR070.WMF
NATUR071.WMF
NATUR072.WMF
NATUR073.WMF
NATUR074.WMF
NATUR075.WMF
NATUR076.WMF
NATUR077.WMF
NATUR078.WMF
NATUR079.WMF
NATUR080.WMF
NATUR081.WMF
NATUR082.WMF
NATUR083.WMF
NATUR084.WMF
NATUR085.WMF
NATUR086.WMF
NATUR087.WMF
NATUR088.WMF
NATUR089.WMF
NATUR090.WMF
NATUR091.WMF
NATUR092.WMF
NATUR093.WMF
NATUR094.WMF
NATUR095.WMF
NATUR096.WMF
NATUR097.WMF
NATUR098.WMF
NATUR099.WMF
NATUR100.WMF
NATUR101.WMF
NATUR102.WMF
NATUR103.WMF
NATUR104.WMF
NATUR105.WMF
NATUR106.WMF
NATUR107.WMF
NATUR108.WMF
NATUR109.WMF
NATUR110.WMF
NATUR111.WMF
NATUR112.WMF
NATUR113.WMF
NATUR114.WMF
NATUR115.WMF
NATUR116.WMF
NATUR117.WMF
NATUR118.WMF
NATUR119.WMF
NATUR120.WMF
NATUR121.WMF
NATUR122.WMF
NATUR123.WMF

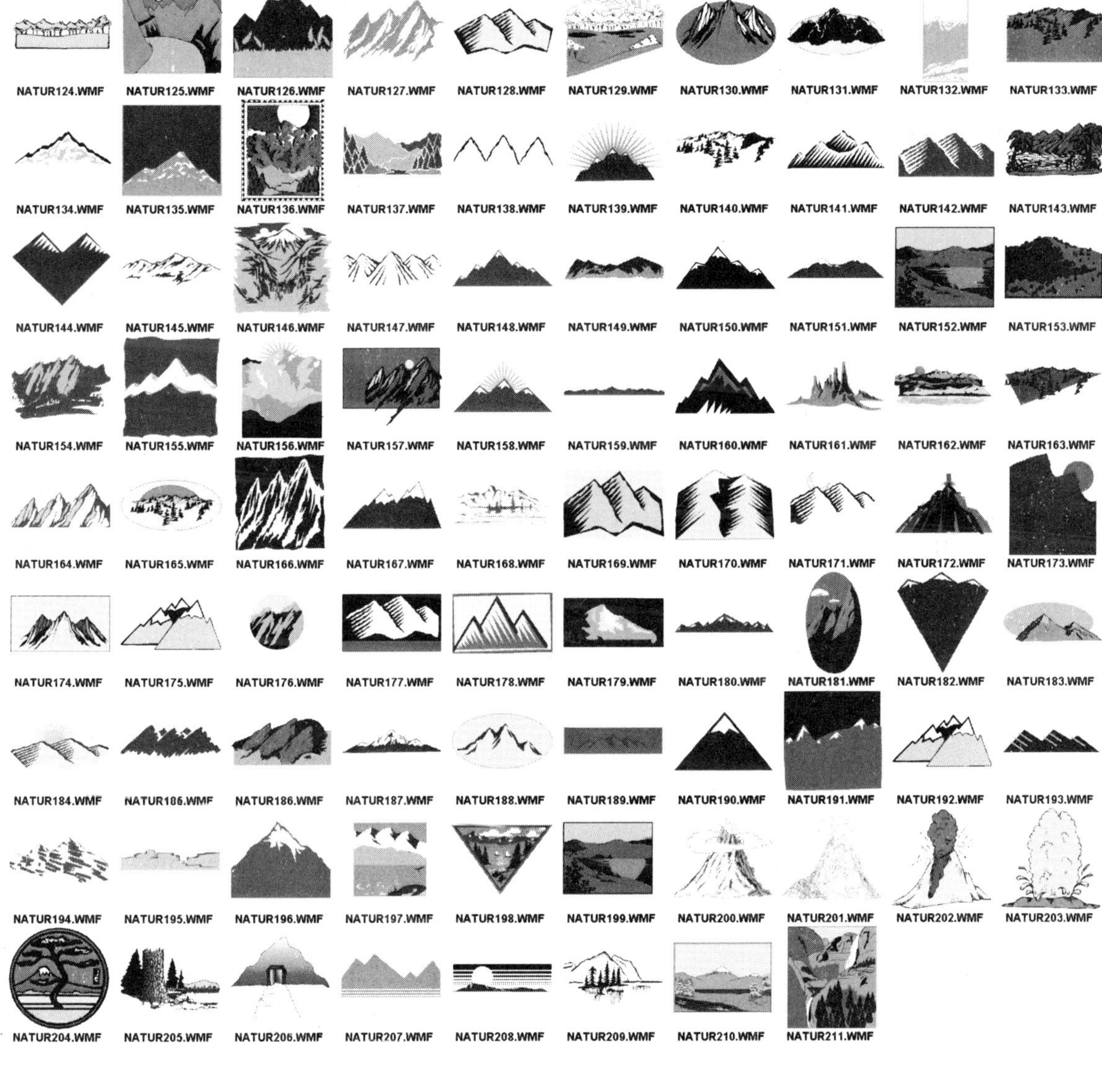
NATUR124.WMF
NATUR125.WMF
NATUR126.WMF
NATUR127.WMF
NATUR128.WMF
NATUR129.WMF
NATUR130.WMF
NATUR131.WMF
NATUR132.WMF
NATUR133.WMF
NATUR134.WMF
NATUR135.WMF
NATUR136.WMF
NATUR137.WMF
NATUR138.WMF
NATUR139.WMF
NATUR140.WMF
NATUR141.WMF
NATUR142.WMF
NATUR143.WMF
NATUR144.WMF
NATUR145.WMF
NATUR146.WMF
NATUR147.WMF
NATUR148.WMF
NATUR149.WMF
NATUR150.WMF
NATUR151.WMF
NATUR152.WMF
NATUR153.WMF
NATUR154.WMF
NATUR155.WMF
NATUR156.WMF
NATUR157.WMF
NATUR158.WMF
NATUR159.WMF
NATUR160.WMF
NATUR161.WMF
NATUR162.WMF
NATUR163.WMF
NATUR164.WMF
NATUR165.WMF
NATUR166.WMF
NATUR167.WMF
NATUR168.WMF
NATUR169.WMF
NATUR170.WMF
NATUR171.WMF
NATUR172.WMF
NATUR173.WMF
NATUR174.WMF
NATUR175.WMF
NATUR176.WMF
NATUR177.WMF
NATUR178.WMF
NATUR179.WMF
NATUR180.WMF
NATUR181.WMF
NATUR182.WMF
NATUR183.WMF
NATUR184.WMF
NATUR186.WMF
NATUR186.WMF
NATUR187.WMF
NATUR188.WMF
NATUR189.WMF
NATUR190.WMF
NATUR191.WMF
NATUR192.WMF
NATUR193.WMF
NATUR194.WMF
NATUR195.WMF
NATUR196.WMF
NATUR197.WMF
NATUR198.WMF
NATUR199.WMF
NATUR200.WMF
NATUR201.WMF
NATUR202.WMF
NATUR203.WMF
NATUR204.WMF
NATUR205.WMF
NATUR206.WMF
NATUR207.WMF
NATUR208.WMF
NATUR209.WMF
NATUR210.WMF
NATUR211.WMF

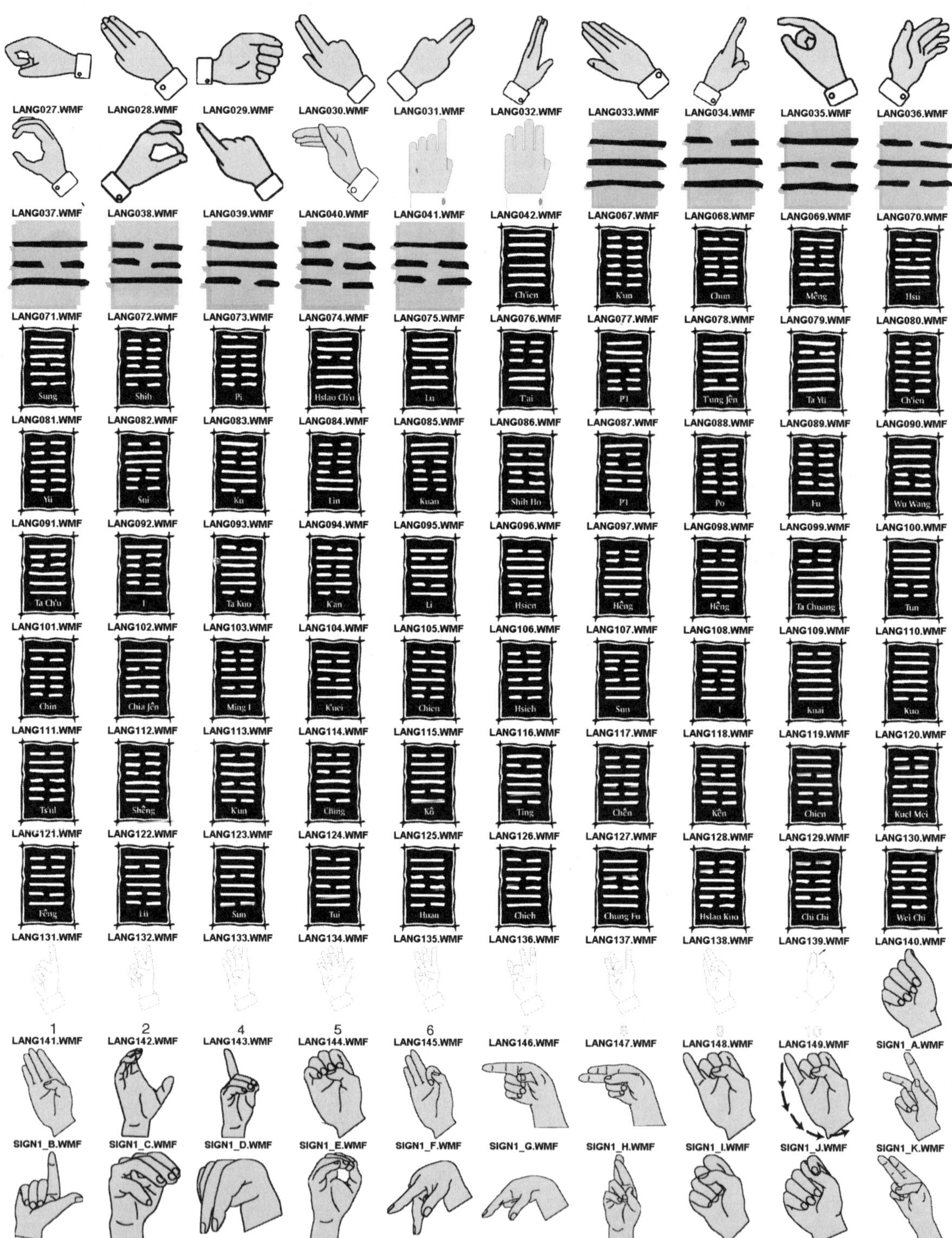
LANG027.WMF
LANG028.WMF
LANG029.WMF
LANG030.WMF
LANG031.WMF
LANG032.WMF
LANG033.WMF
LANG034.WMF
LANG035.WMF
LANG036.WMF
LANG037.WMF
LANG038.WMF
LANG039.WMF
LANG040.WMF
LANG041.WMF
LANG042.WMF
LANG067.WMF
LANG068.WMF
LANG069.WMF
LANG070.WMF
LANG071.WMF
LANG072.WMF
LANG073.WMF
LANG074.WMF
LANG075.WMF
LANG076.WMF
LANG077.WMF
LANG078.WMF
LANG079.WMF
LANG080.WMF
LANG081.WMF
LANG082.WMF
LANG083.WMF
LANG084.WMF
LANG085.WMF
LANG086.WMF
LANG087.WMF
LANG088.WMF
LANG089.WMF
LANG090.WMF
LANG091.WMF
LANG092.WMF
LANG093.WMF
LANG094.WMF
LANG095.WMF
LANG096.WMF
LANG097.WMF
LANG098.WMF
LANG099.WMF
LANG100.WMF
LANG101.WMF
LANG102.WMF
LANG103.WMF
LANG104.WMF
LANG105.WMF
LANG106.WMF
LANG107.WMF
LANG108.WMF
LANG109.WMF
LANG110.WMF
LANG111.WMF
LANG112.WMF
LANG113.WMF
LANG114.WMF
LANG115.WMF
LANG116.WMF
LANG117.WMF
LANG118.WMF
LANG119.WMF
LANG120.WMF
LANG121.WMF
LANG122.WMF
LANG123.WMF
LANG124.WMF
LANG125.WMF
LANG126.WMF
LANG127.WMF
LANG128.WMF
LANG129.WMF
LANG130.WMF
LANG131.WMF
LANG132.WMF
LANG133.WMF
LANG134.WMF
LANG135.WMF
LANG136.WMF
LANG137.WMF
LANG138.WMF
LANG139.WMF
LANG140.WMF
1
LANG141.WMF
2
LANG142.WMF
4
LANG143.WMF
5
LANG144.WMF
6
LANG145.WMF
LANG146.WMF
LANG147.WMF
LANG148.WMF
LANG149.WMF
SIGN1_A.WMF
SIGN1_B.WMF
SIGN1_C.WMF
SIGN1_D.WMF
SIGN1_E.WMF
SIGN1_F.WMF
SIGN1_G.WMF
SIGN1_H.WMF
SIGN1_I.WMF
SIGN1_J.WMF
SIGN1_K.WMF
SIGN1_L.WMF
SIGN1_M.WMF
SIGN1_N.WMF
SIGN1_O.WMF
SIGN1_P.WMF
SIGN1_Q.WMF
SIGN1_R.WMF
SIGN1_S.WMF
SIGN1_T.WMF
SIGN1_U.WMF

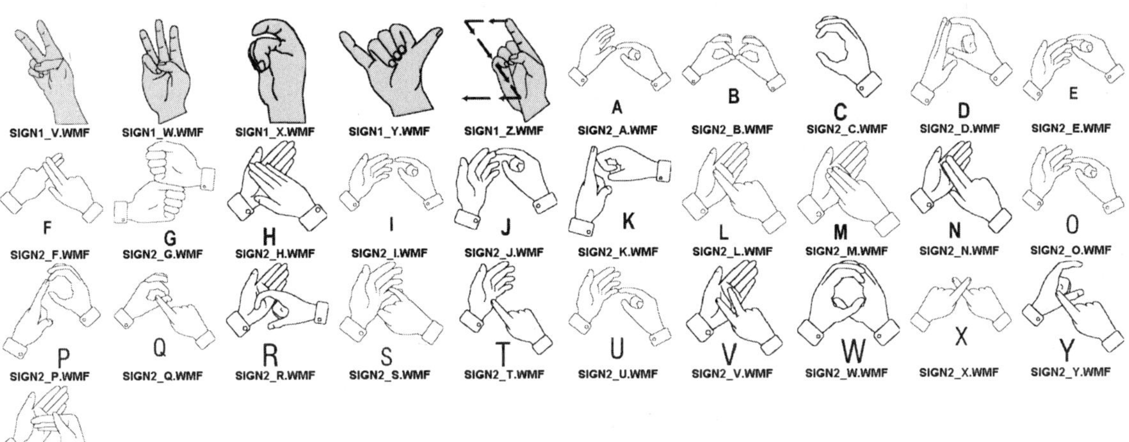
SIGN1_V.WMF
SIGN1_W.WMF
SIGN1_X.WMF
SIGN1_Y.WMF
SIGN1_Z.WMF
A
SIGN2_A.WMF
B
SIGN2_B.WMF
C
SIGN2_C.WMF
D
SIGN2_D.WMF
E
SIGN2_E.WMF
F
SIGN2_F.WMF
G
SIGN2_G.WMF
H
SIGN2_H.WMF
I
SIGN2_I.WMF
J
SIGN2_J.WMF
K
SIGN2_K.WMF
L
SIGN2_L.WMF
M
SIGN2_M.WMF
N
SIGN2_N.WMF
O
SIGN2_O.WMF
P
SIGN2_P.WMF
Q
SIGN2_Q.WMF
R
SIGN2_R.WMF
S
SIGN2_S.WMF
T
SIGN2_T.WMF
U
SIGN2_U.WMF
V
SIGN2_V.WMF
W
SIGN2_W.WMF
X
SIGN2_X.WMF
Y
SIGN2_Y.WMF
Z
SIGN2_Z.WMF

0136EQUC.WMF 1238FEMC.WMF 1501.WMF 1502.WMF 1503.WMF 1504.WMF 1505.WMF 1506.WMF 1507.WMF 1508.WMF

1509.WMF 1510.WMF 1511.WMF 1512.WMF 1513.WMF 1514.WMF 1516.WMF 1517.WMF 1518.WMF 1519.WMF

1520.WMF 1521.WMF 1522.WMF 1523.WMF 1524.WMF 1525.WMF 1526.WMF 1527.WMF 1528.WMF 1529.WMF

1530.WMF 1531.WMF 1532.WMF 1533.WMF 1534.WMF 1535.WMF 1536.WMF 1537.WMF 1538.WMF 1539.WMF

1540.WMF 1541.WMF 1543.WMF 1544.WMF 1548.WMF 1551.WMF 1552.WMF 1553.WMF 1554.WMF 1556.WMF

1557.WMF 1558.WMF 1560.WMF 1561.WMF 1562.WMF 2217.WMF 4047.WMF 4048.WMF 4117.WMF 4119.WMF

4120.WMF 4123.WMF 4124.WMF 4125.WMF 4126.WMF 4127.WMF 4134.WMF 4135.WMF 4136.WMF 4153.WMF

4156.WMF 4183.WMF RAMADAN.WMF

Logos • U.S.

0142FEDC.WMF 1110COMC.WMF 1114CUBC.WMF 1123DICC.WMF 1515.WMF 1542.WMF 1545.WMF 1546.WMF 1547.WMF 1549.WMF

1550.WMF 1555.WMF 1559.WMF 2231.WMF 4121.WMF 4131.WMF 4143.WMF AMEX.WMF AMEXSIGN.WMF CRTEBLNH.WMF

DINNERS1.WMF DINNERS2.WMF DISCOV_1.WMF DISCOVER.WMF MASTER.WMF MASTRCRD.WMF VISA.WMF VISA12.WMF

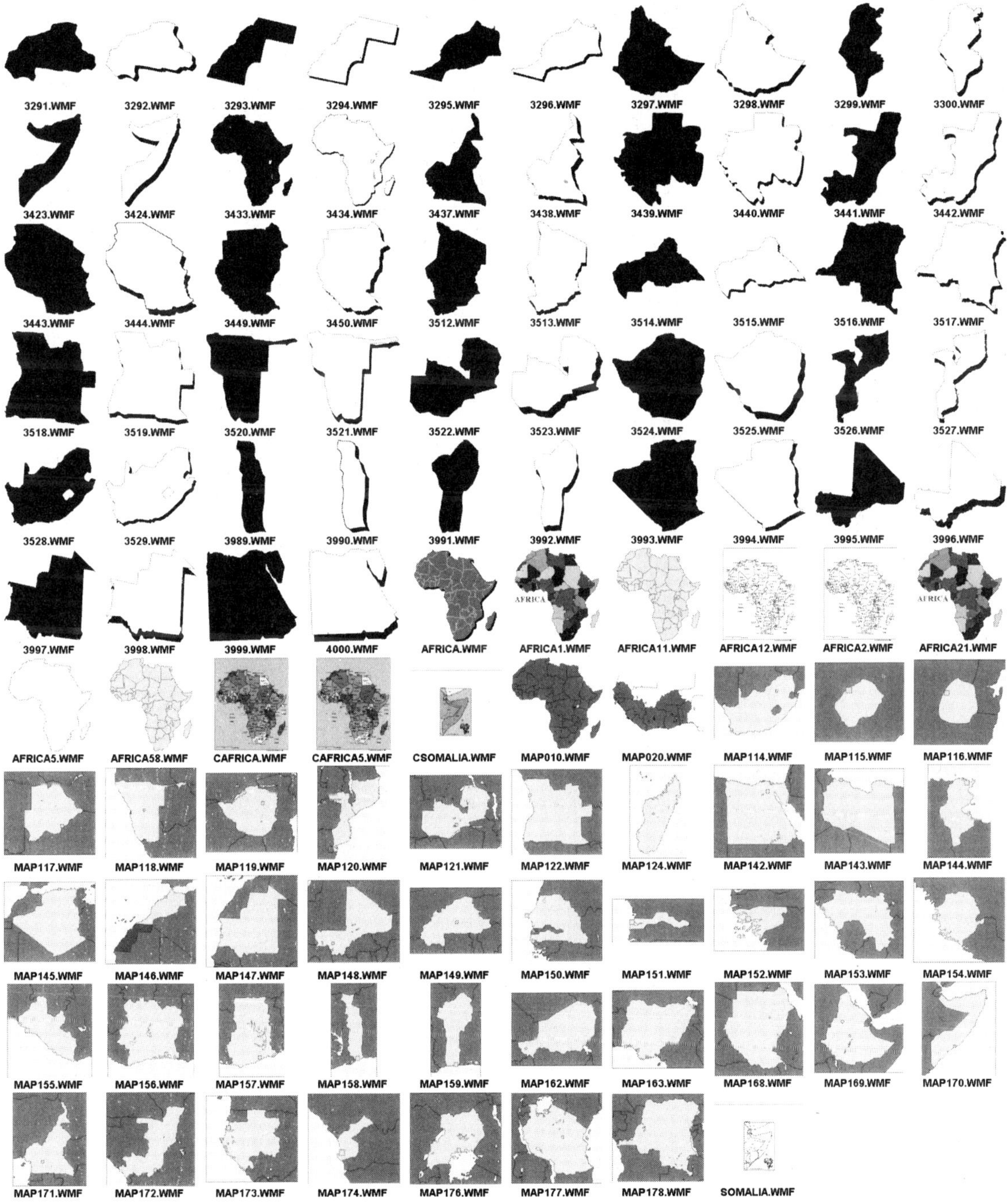
3291.WMF 3292.WMF 3293.WMF 3294.WMF 3295.WMF 3296.WMF 3297.WMF 3298.WMF 3299.WMF 3300.WMF
3423.WMF 3424.WMF 3433.WMF 3434.WMF 3437.WMF 3438.WMF 3439.WMF 3440.WMF 3441.WMF 3442.WMF
3443.WMF 3444.WMF 3449.WMF 3450.WMF 3512.WMF 3513.WMF 3514.WMF 3515.WMF 3516.WMF 3517.WMF
3518.WMF 3519.WMF 3520.WMF 3521.WMF 3522.WMF 3523.WMF 3524.WMF 3525.WMF 3526.WMF 3527.WMF
3528.WMF 3529.WMF 3989.WMF 3990.WMF 3991.WMF 3992.WMF 3993.WMF 3994.WMF 3995.WMF 3996.WMF
3997.WMF 3998.WMF 3999.WMF 4000.WMF AFRICA.WMF AFRICA1.WMF AFRICA11.WMF AFRICA12.WMF AFRICA2.WMF AFRICA21.WMF
AFRICA5.WMF AFRICA58.WMF CAFRICA.WMF CAFRICA5.WMF CSOMALIA.WMF MAP010.WMF MAP020.WMF MAP114.WMF MAP115.WMF MAP116.WMF
MAP117.WMF MAP118.WMF MAP119.WMF MAP120.WMF MAP121.WMF MAP122.WMF MAP124.WMF MAP142.WMF MAP143.WMF MAP144.WMF
MAP145.WMF MAP146.WMF MAP147.WMF MAP148.WMF MAP149.WMF MAP150.WMF MAP151.WMF MAP152.WMF MAP153.WMF MAP154.WMF
MAP155.WMF MAP156.WMF MAP157.WMF MAP158.WMF MAP159.WMF MAP162.WMF MAP163.WMF MAP168.WMF MAP169.WMF MAP170.WMF
MAP171.WMF MAP172.WMF MAP173.WMF MAP174.WMF MAP176.WMF MAP177.WMF MAP178.WMF SOMALIA.WMF

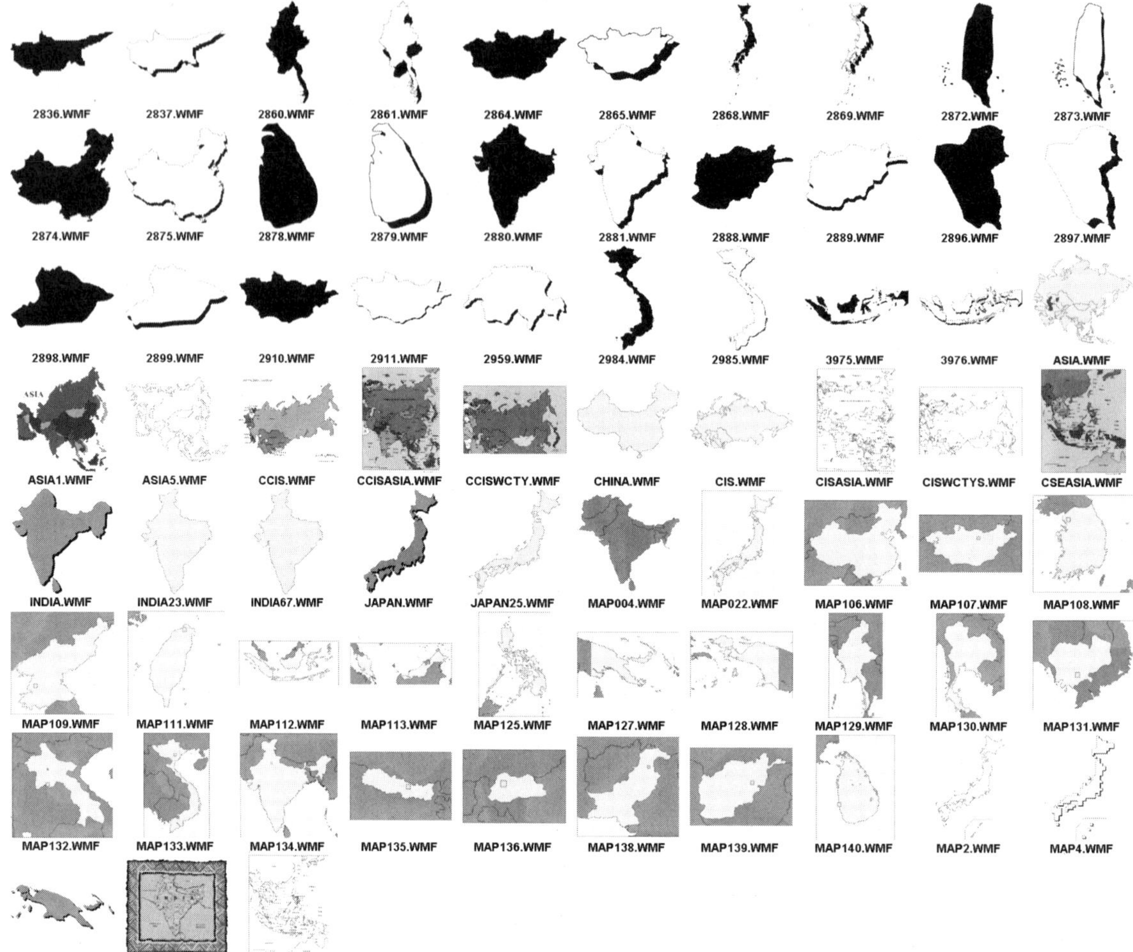
2836.WMF
2837.WMF
2860.WMF
2861.WMF
2864.WMF
2865.WMF
2868.WMF
2869.WMF
2872.WMF
2873.WMF
2874.WMF
2875.WMF
2878.WMF
2879.WMF
2880.WMF
2881.WMF
2888.WMF
2889.WMF
2896.WMF
2897.WMF
2898.WMF
2899.WMF
2910.WMF
2911.WMF
2959.WMF
2984.WMF
2985.WMF
3975.WMF
3976.WMF
ASIA.WMF
ASIA1.WMF
ASIA5.WMF
CCIS.WMF
CCISASIA.WMF
CCISWCTY.WMF
CHINA.WMF
CIS.WMF
CISASIA.WMF
CISWCTYS.WMF
CSEASIA.WMF
INDIA.WMF
INDIA23.WMF
INDIA67.WMF
JAPAN.WMF
JAPAN25.WMF
MAP004.WMF
MAP022.WMF
MAP106.WMF
MAP107.WMF
MAP108.WMF
MAP109.WMF
MAP111.WMF
MAP112.WMF
MAP113.WMF
MAP125.WMF
MAP127.WMF
MAP128.WMF
MAP129.WMF
MAP130.WMF
MAP131.WMF
MAP132.WMF
MAP133.WMF
MAP134.WMF
MAP135.WMF
MAP136.WMF
MAP138.WMF
MAP139.WMF
MAP140.WMF
MAP2.WMF
MAP4.WMF
NWGUINEA.WMF
PLRW002J.WMF
SEASIA.WMF

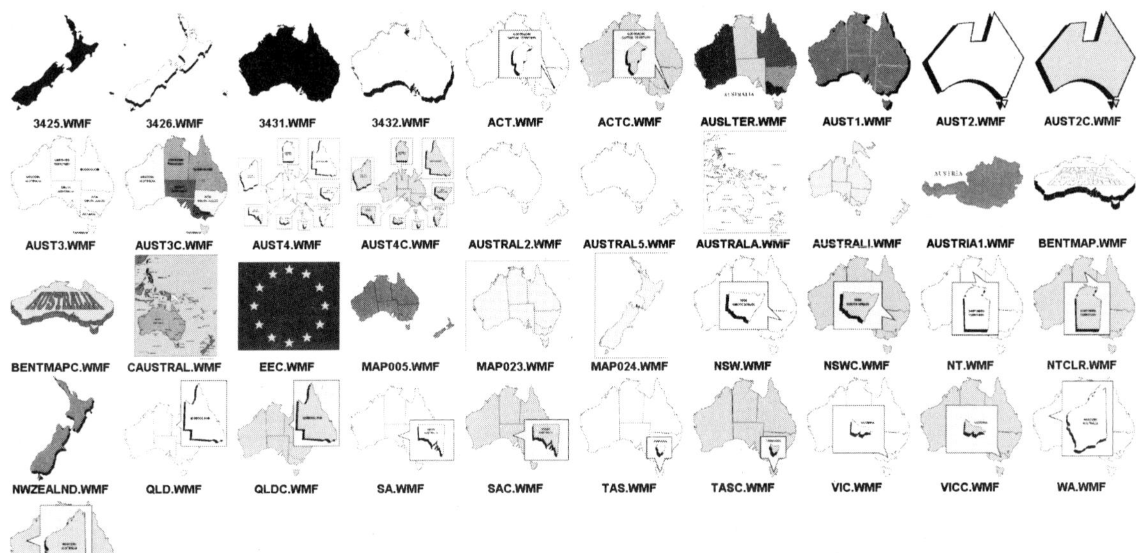

3425.WMF 3426.WMF 3431.WMF 3432.WMF ACT.WMF ACTC.WMF AUSLTER.WMF AUST1.WMF AUST2.WMF AUST2C.WMF

AUST3.WMF AUST3C.WMF AUST4.WMF AUST4C.WMF AUSTRAL2.WMF AUSTRAL5.WMF AUSTRALA.WMF AUSTRALI.WMF AUSTRIA1.WMF BENTMAP.WMF

BENTMAPC.WMF CAUSTRAL.WMF EEC.WMF MAP005.WMF MAP023.WMF MAP024.WMF NSW.WMF NSWC.WMF NT.WMF NTCLR.WMF

NWZEALND.WMF QLD.WMF QLDC.WMF SA.WMF SAC.WMF TAS.WMF TASC.WMF VIC.WMF VICC.WMF WA.WMF

WAC.WMF

Maps • Canada

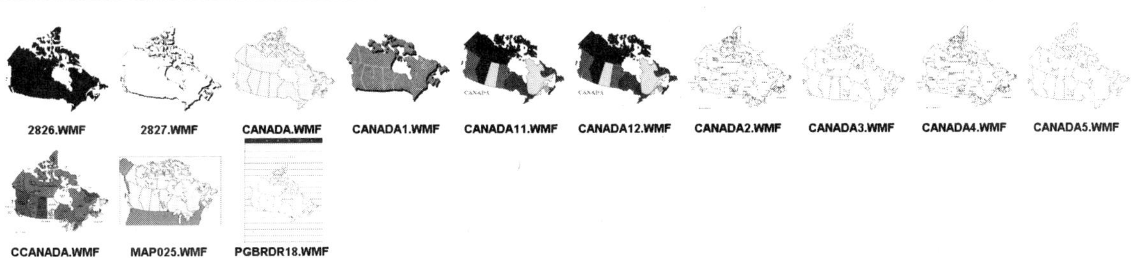

2826.WMF 2827.WMF CANADA.WMF CANADA1.WMF CANADA11.WMF CANADA12.WMF CANADA2.WMF CANADA3.WMF CANADA4.WMF CANADA5.WMF

CCANADA.WMF MAP025.WMF PGBRDR18.WMF

Maps • Caribbean (CARIBEAN)

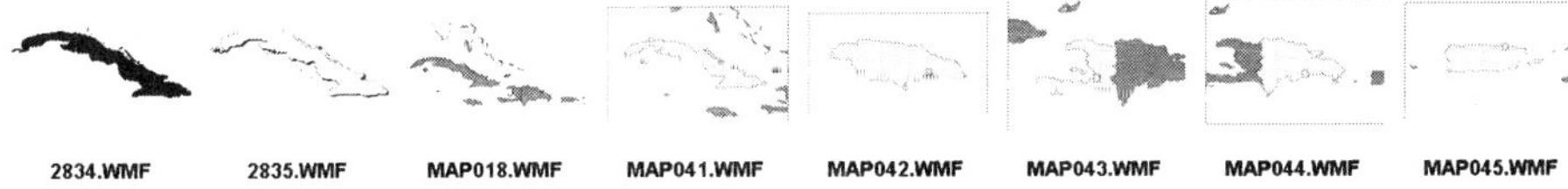

2834.WMF 2835.WMF MAP018.WMF MAP041.WMF MAP042.WMF MAP043.WMF MAP044.WMF MAP045.WMF

Maps • Central America (CAMERICA)

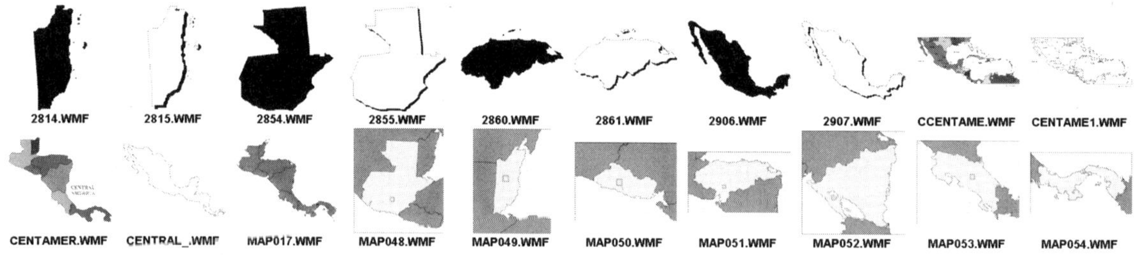

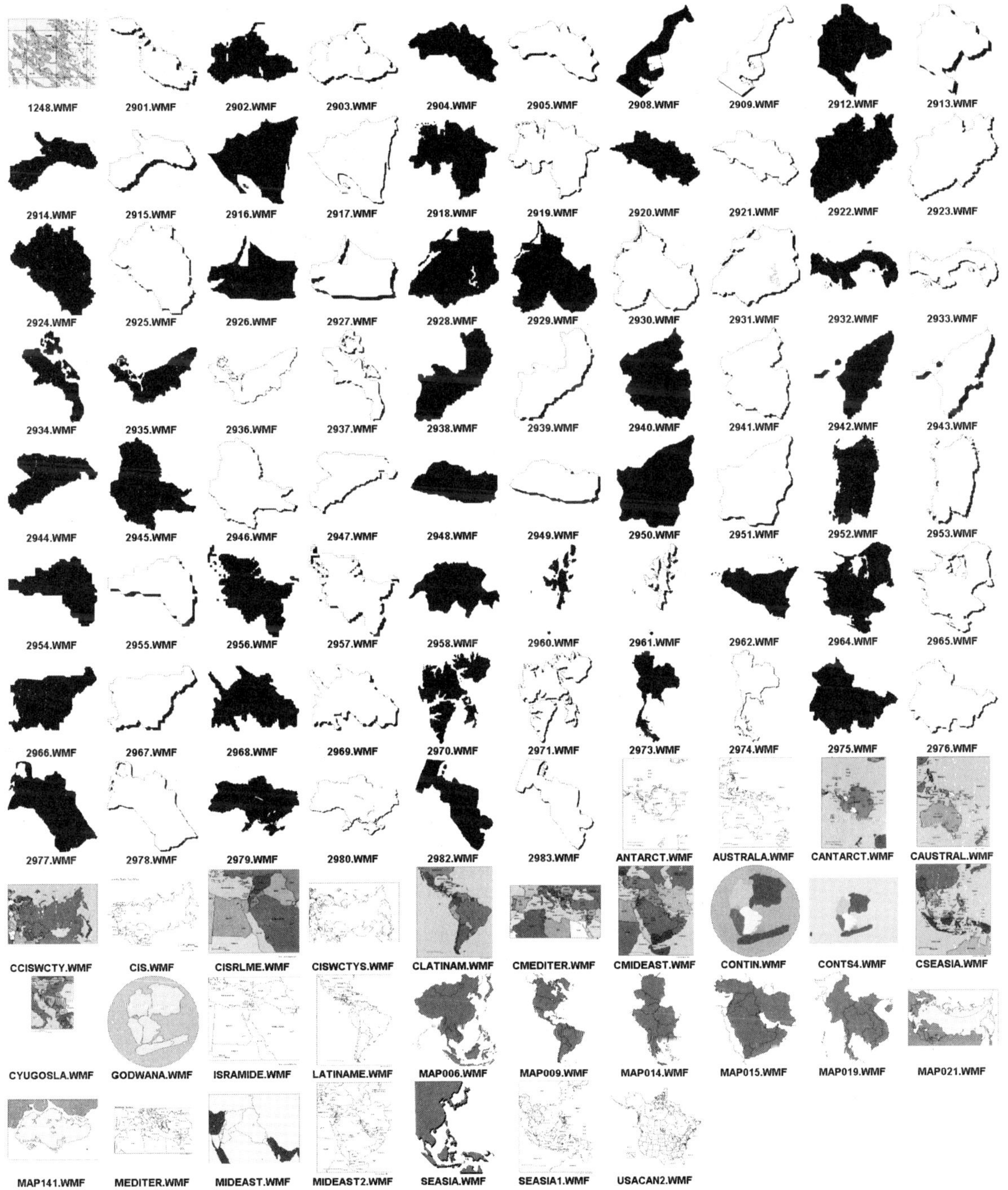

1248.WMF 2901.WMF 2902.WMF 2903.WMF 2904.WMF 2905.WMF 2908.WMF 2909.WMF 2912.WMF 2913.WMF
2914.WMF 2915.WMF 2916.WMF 2917.WMF 2918.WMF 2919.WMF 2920.WMF 2921.WMF 2922.WMF 2923.WMF
2924.WMF 2925.WMF 2926.WMF 2927.WMF 2928.WMF 2929.WMF 2930.WMF 2931.WMF 2932.WMF 2933.WMF
2934.WMF 2935.WMF 2936.WMF 2937.WMF 2938.WMF 2939.WMF 2940.WMF 2941.WMF 2942.WMF 2943.WMF
2944.WMF 2945.WMF 2946.WMF 2947.WMF 2948.WMF 2949.WMF 2950.WMF 2951.WMF 2952.WMF 2953.WMF
2954.WMF 2955.WMF 2956.WMF 2957.WMF 2958.WMF 2960.WMF 2961.WMF 2962.WMF 2964.WMF 2965.WMF
2966.WMF 2967.WMF 2968.WMF 2969.WMF 2970.WMF 2971.WMF 2973.WMF 2974.WMF 2975.WMF 2976.WMF
2977.WMF 2978.WMF 2979.WMF 2980.WMF 2982.WMF 2983.WMF ANTARCT.WMF AUSTRALA.WMF CANTARCT.WMF CAUSTRAL.WMF
CCISWCTY.WMF CIS.WMF CISRLME.WMF CISWCTYS.WMF CLATINAM.WMF CMEDITER.WMF CMIDEAST.WMF CONTIN.WMF CONTS4.WMF CSEASIA.WMF
CYUGOSLA.WMF GODWANA.WMF ISRAMIDE.WMF LATINAME.WMF MAP006.WMF MAP009.WMF MAP014.WMF MAP015.WMF MAP019.WMF MAP021.WMF
MAP141.WMF MEDITER.WMF MIDEAST.WMF MIDEAST2.WMF SEASIA.WMF SEASIA1.WMF USACAN2.WMF

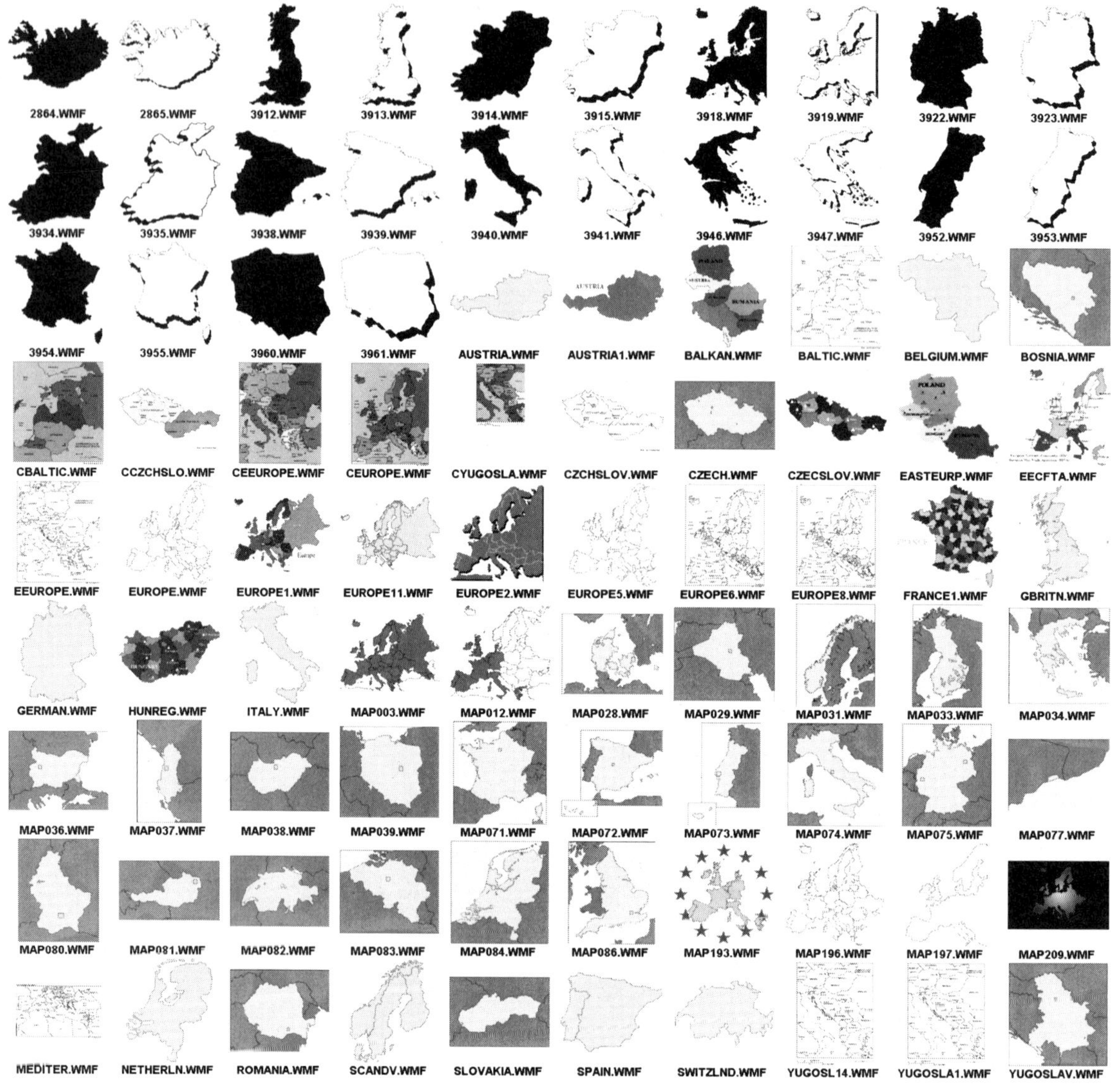
2864.WMF
2865.WMF
3912.WMF
3913.WMF
3914.WMF
3915.WMF
3918.WMF
3919.WMF
3922.WMF
3923.WMF
3934.WMF
3935.WMF
3938.WMF
3939.WMF
3940.WMF
3941.WMF
3946.WMF
3947.WMF
3952.WMF
3953.WMF
3954.WMF
3955.WMF
3960.WMF
3961.WMF
AUSTRIA.WMF
AUSTRIA1.WMF
BALKAN.WMF
BALTIC.WMF
BELGIUM.WMF
BOSNIA.WMF
CBALTIC.WMF
CCZCHSLO.WMF
CEEUROPE.WMF
CEUROPE.WMF
CYUGOSLA.WMF
CZCHSLOV.WMF
CZECH.WMF
CZECSLOV.WMF
EASTEURP.WMF
EECFTA.WMF
EEUROPE.WMF
EUROPE.WMF
EUROPE1.WMF
EUROPE11.WMF
EUROPE2.WMF
EUROPE5.WMF
EUROPE6.WMF
EUROPE8.WMF
FRANCE1.WMF
GBRITN.WMF
GERMAN.WMF
HUNREG.WMF
ITALY.WMF
MAP003.WMF
MAP012.WMF
MAP028.WMF
MAP029.WMF
MAP031.WMF
MAP033.WMF
MAP034.WMF
MAP036.WMF
MAP037.WMF
MAP038.WMF
MAP039.WMF
MAP071.WMF
MAP072.WMF
MAP073.WMF
MAP074.WMF
MAP075.WMF
MAP077.WMF
MAP080.WMF
MAP081.WMF
MAP082.WMF
MAP083.WMF
MAP084.WMF
MAP086.WMF
MAP193.WMF
MAP196.WMF
MAP197.WMF
MAP209.WMF
MEDITER.WMF
NETHERLN.WMF
ROMANIA.WMF
SCANDV.WMF
SLOVAKIA.WMF
SPAIN.WMF
SWITZLND.WMF
YUGOSL14.WMF
YUGOSLA1.WMF
YUGOSLAV.WMF

AIRPORT.WMF BATTFILD.WMF CASTLE.WMF CATHCHUR.WMF CEMETERY.WMF CHRMISS.WMF COALMINE.WMF COLLEGE.WMF COMPAS1.WMF COMPAS2.WMF

CONIFTRE.WMF DOWN.WMF ELEV.WMF EXPWRECK.WMF FACTORY.WMF GOLFCOUR.WMF GRAVPIT.WMF HEALCLIN.WMF HIGHEST.WMF HISTSITE.WMF

HYDROPLT.WMF LARGHOSP.WMF LEFT.WMF LODGING.WMF MARSH.WMF MILINST.WMF MINE1.WMF MINE2.WMF MINSPR.WMF MOHMOSQ.WMF

NATLREEF.WMF NONCONTR.WMF NUCLPWWR.WMF OASIS.WMF OIL1.WMF OIL2.WMF PAGODA.WMF POINTINT.WMF PWRPL.WMF RANGRSTA.WMF

REDWOOD.WMF RIGHT.WMF RUINS.WMF SCHOOL.WMF SEAPORT.WMF SYNAGOG.WMF TANK.WMF TELECOMM.WMF TOURIST.WMF UP.WMF

WINDMILL.WMF

Maps • Mideast

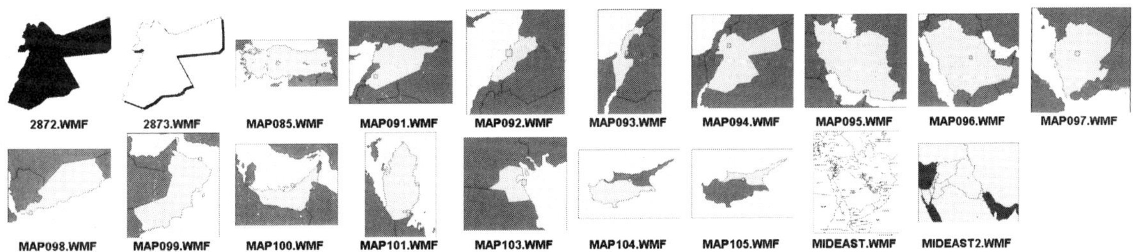

2872.WMF 2873.WMF MAP085.WMF MAP091.WMF MAP092.WMF MAP093.WMF MAP094.WMF MAP095.WMF MAP096.WMF MAP097.WMF

MAP098.WMF MAP099.WMF MAP100.WMF MAP101.WMF MAP103.WMF MAP104.WMF MAP105.WMF MIDEAST.WMF MIDEAST2.WMF

1722.WMF
1731.WMF
1732.WMF
2802.WMF
2803.WMF
2804.WMF
2805.WMF
2806.WMF
2807.WMF
2808.WMF
2809.WMF
2810.WMF
2811.WMF
2812.WMF
2813.WMF
2815.WMF
2816.WMF
2817.WMF
2818.WMF
2819.WMF
2820.WMF
2821.WMF
2822.WMF
2823.WMF
2824.WMF
2825.WMF
2828.WMF
2829.WMF
2830.WMF
2831.WMF
2832.WMF
2833.WMF
2837.WMF
2838.WMF
2839.WMF
2844.WMF
2845.WMF
2846.WMF
2847.WMF
2848.WMF
2849.WMF
2850.WMF
2851.WMF
2852.WMF
2853.WMF
2856.WMF
2856A.WMF
2857.WMF
2858.WMF
2859.WMF
2862.WMF
2862A.WMF
2863.WMF
2863A.WMF
2866.WMF
2866A.WMF
2867.WMF
2867A.WMF
2868.WMF
2869.WMF
2870.WMF
2870A.WMF
2871.WMF
2871A.WMF
2874.WMF
2875.WMF
2876.WMF
2876A.WMF
2877.WMF
2877B.WMF
2878.WMF
2879.WMF
2880.WMF
2881.WMF
2882.WMF
2882A.WMF
2883.WMF
2883A.WMF
2884.WMF
2884A.WMF
2885.WMF
2885A.WMF
2886.WMF
2886A.WMF
2887.WMF
2887A.WMF
2888.WMF
2889.WMF
2890.WMF
2891.WMF
2892.WMF
2892A.WMF
2893.WMF
2893A.WMF
2894.WMF
2894A.WMF
2895.WMF
2895A.WMF
2896.WMF
2897.WMF
2898.WMF
2899.WMF
2900.WMF
2900A.WMF
2963.WMF
2989.WMF
2990.WMF
2991.WMF
2992.WMF
3170.WMF
3289.WMF
3290.WMF
3429.WMF
3430.WMF
3435.WMF
3436.WMF
3445.WMF
3446.WMF
3447.WMF
3448.WMF

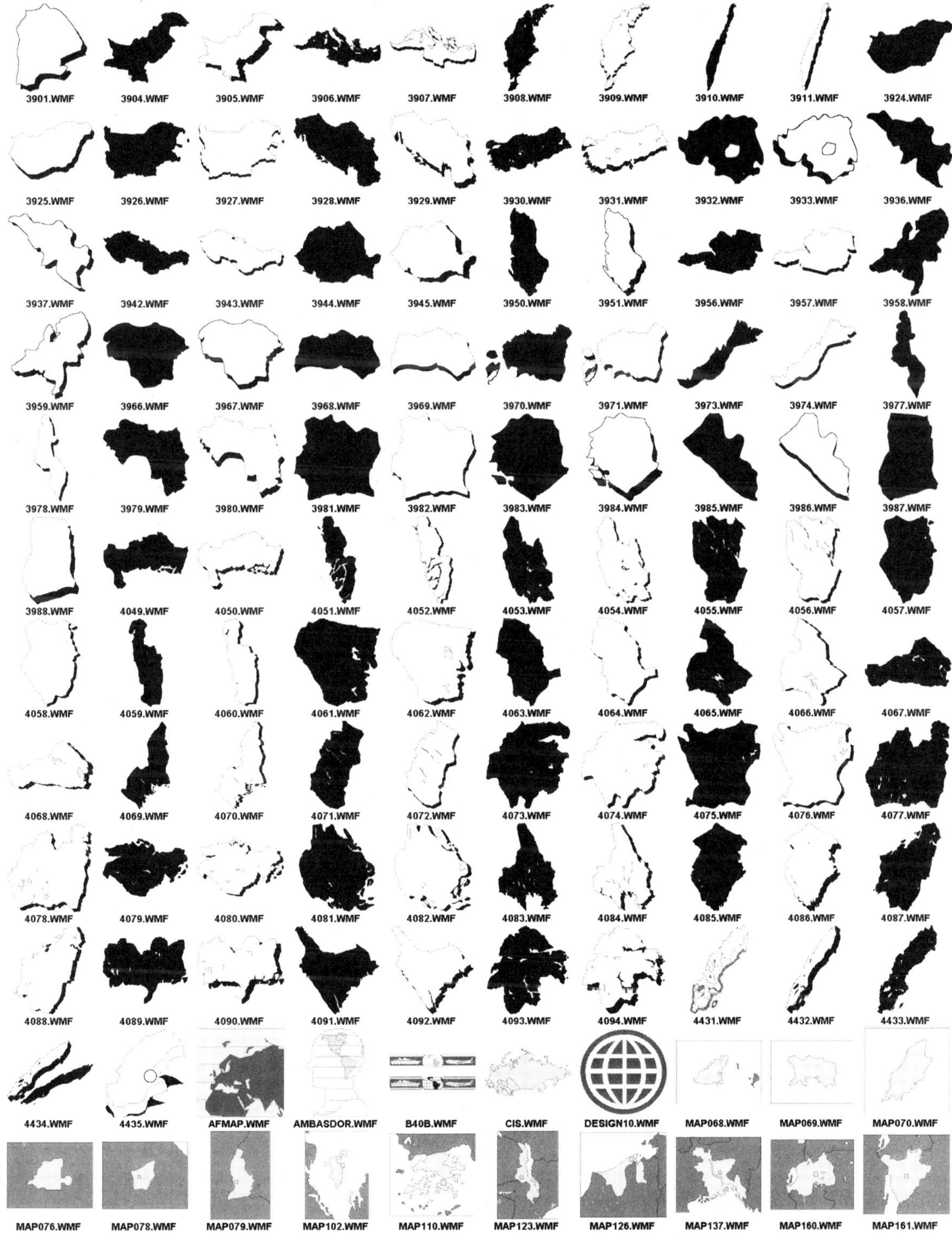
3901.WMF
3904.WMF
3905.WMF
3906.WMF
3907.WMF
3908.WMF
3909.WMF
3910.WMF
3911.WMF
3924.WMF
3925.WMF
3926.WMF
3927.WMF
3928.WMF
3929.WMF
3930.WMF
3931.WMF
3932.WMF
3933.WMF
3936.WMF
3937.WMF
3942.WMF
3943.WMF
3944.WMF
3945.WMF
3950.WMF
3951.WMF
3956.WMF
3957.WMF
3958.WMF
3959.WMF
3966.WMF
3967.WMF
3968.WMF
3969.WMF
3970.WMF
3971.WMF
3973.WMF
3974.WMF
3977.WMF
3978.WMF
3979.WMF
3980.WMF
3981.WMF
3982.WMF
3983.WMF
3984.WMF
3985.WMF
3986.WMF
3987.WMF
3988.WMF
4049.WMF
4050.WMF
4051.WMF
4052.WMF
4053.WMF
4054.WMF
4055.WMF
4056.WMF
4057.WMF
4058.WMF
4059.WMF
4060.WMF
4061.WMF
4062.WMF
4063.WMF
4064.WMF
4065.WMF
4066.WMF
4067.WMF
4068.WMF
4069.WMF
4070.WMF
4071.WMF
4072.WMF
4073.WMF
4074.WMF
4075.WMF
4076.WMF
4077.WMF
4078.WMF
4079.WMF
4080.WMF
4081.WMF
4082.WMF
4083.WMF
4084.WMF
4085.WMF
4086.WMF
4087.WMF
4088.WMF
4089.WMF
4090.WMF
4091.WMF
4092.WMF
4093.WMF
4094.WMF
4431.WMF
4432.WMF
4433.WMF
4434.WMF
4435.WMF
AFMAP.WMF
AMBASDOR.WMF
B40B.WMF
CIS.WMF
DESIGN10.WMF
MAP068.WMF
MAP069.WMF
MAP070.WMF
MAP076.WMF
MAP078.WMF
MAP079.WMF
MAP102.WMF
MAP110.WMF
MAP123.WMF
MAP126.WMF
MAP137.WMF
MAP160.WMF
MAP161.WMF

Maps • Miscellaneous (MISC)

MAP164.WMF

MAP165.WMF

MAP166.WMF

MAPDOG.WMF

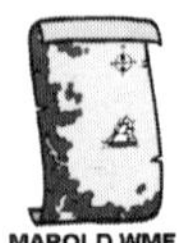
MAPOLD.WMF

MAPTREAS.WMF

Maps • North America (NAMERICA)

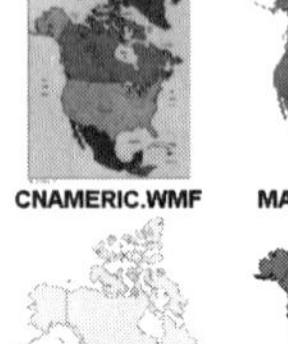
CNAMERIC.WMF

MAP008.WMF

MAP046.WMF

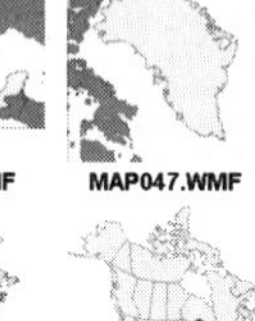
MAP047.WMF

MAP208.WMF

MEXICO.WMF

NAMER2.WMF

NAMER3.WMF

NAMERIC1.WMF

NAMERICA.WMF

NORTHAMR.WMF

NTHAM.WMF

NTHAMC.WMF

US_CANDA.WMF

USACAN2.WMF

USMAP.WMF

Maps • Russia

2890.WMF

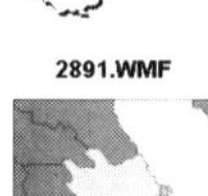
2891.WMF

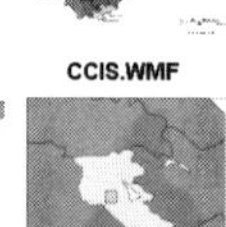
CCIS.WMF

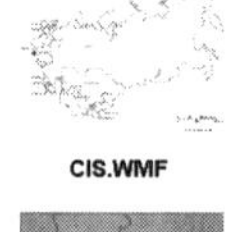
CIS.WMF

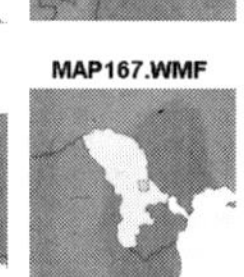
MAP167.WMF

MAP175.WMF

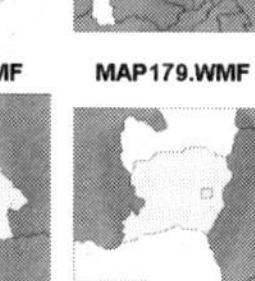
MAP179.WMF

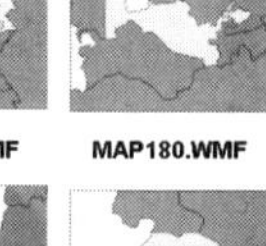
MAP180.WMF

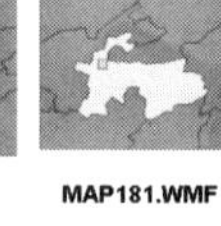
MAP181.WMF

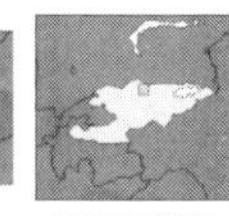
MAP182.WMF

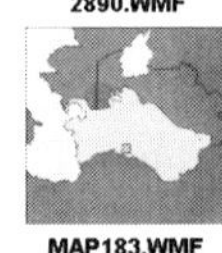
MAP183.WMF

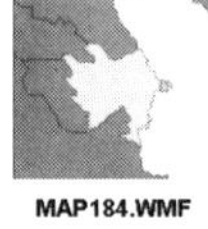
MAP184.WMF

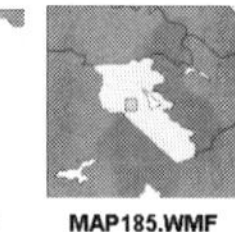
MAP185.WMF

MAP186.WMF

MAP187.WMF

MAP188.WMF

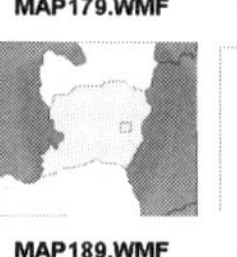
MAP189.WMF

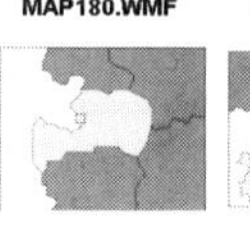
MAP190.WMF

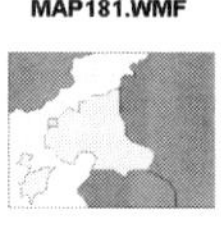
MAP191.WMF

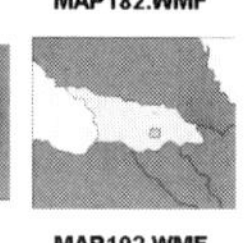
MAP192.WMF

MOLDOVA.WMF

Maps • Scandinavia (SCAN)

2972.WMF

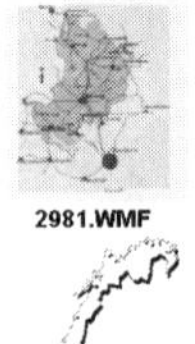
2981.WMF

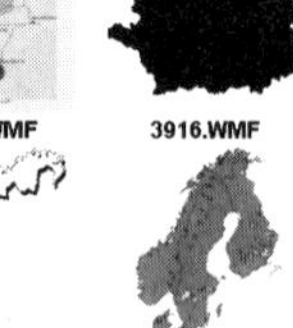
3916.WMF

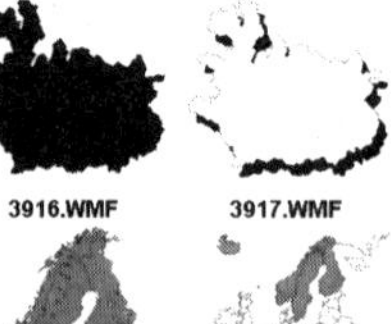
3917.WMF

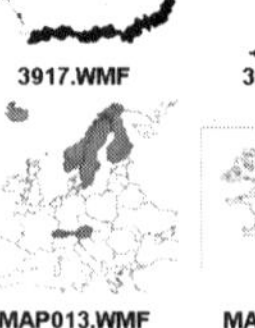
3920.WMF

3921.WMF

3948.WMF

3949.WMF

3962.WMF

3963.WMF

3964.WMF

3965.WMF

MAP011.WMF

MAP013.WMF

MAP027.WMF

MAP032.WMF

SCANDV.WMF

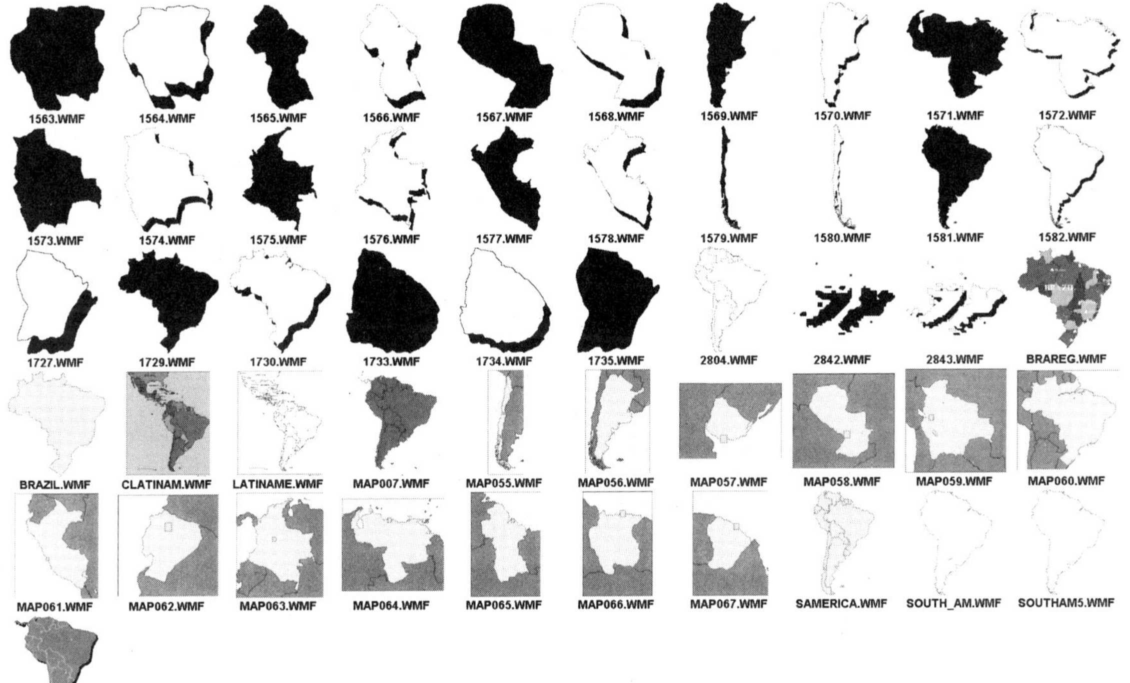

Maps • United Kingdom (UK)

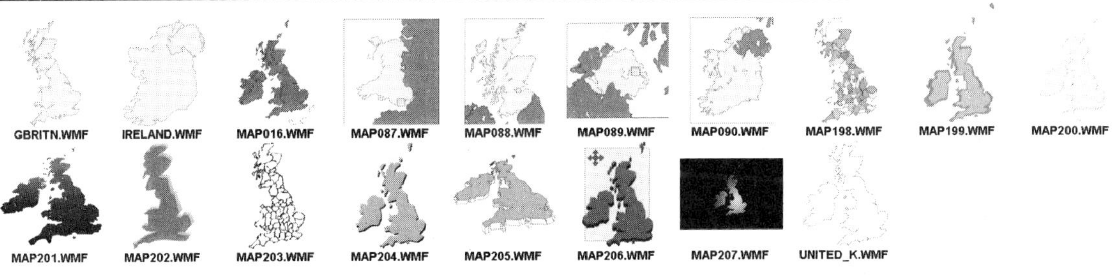

Maps • USA - Cities (USCITIES)

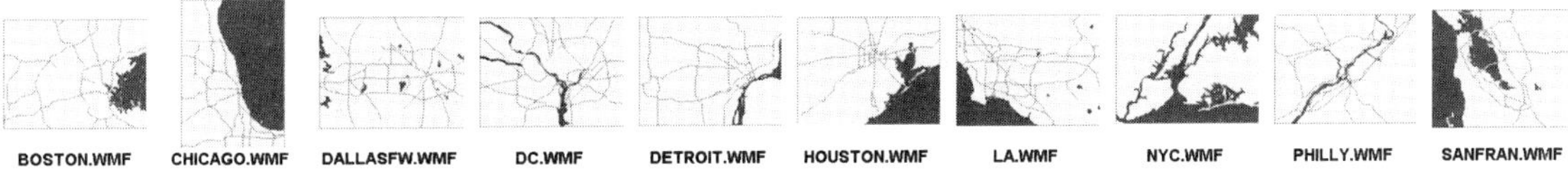

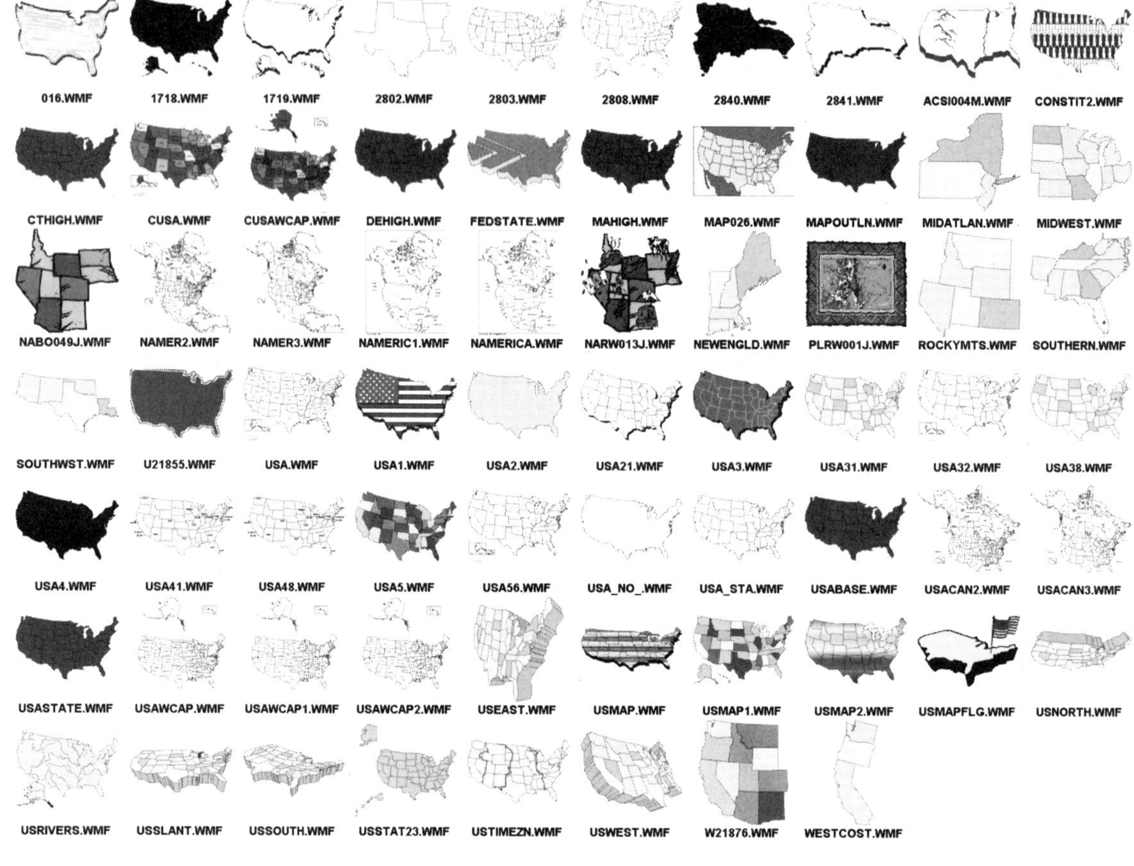
016.WMF
1718.WMF
1719.WMF
2802.WMF
2803.WMF
2808.WMF
2840.WMF
2841.WMF
ACSI004M.WMF
CONSTIT2.WMF
CTHIGH.WMF
CUSA.WMF
CUSAWCAP.WMF
DEHIGH.WMF
FEDSTATE.WMF
MAHIGH.WMF
MAP026.WMF
MAPOUTLN.WMF
MIDATLAN.WMF
MIDWEST.WMF
NABO049J.WMF
NAMER2.WMF
NAMER3.WMF
NAMERIC1.WMF
NAMERICA.WMF
NARW013J.WMF
NEWENGLD.WMF
PLRW001J.WMF
ROCKYMTS.WMF
SOUTHERN.WMF
SOUTHWST.WMF
U21855.WMF
USA.WMF
USA1.WMF
USA2.WMF
USA21.WMF
USA3.WMF
USA31.WMF
USA32.WMF
USA38.WMF
USA4.WMF
USA41.WMF
USA48.WMF
USA5.WMF
USA56.WMF
USA_NO_.WMF
USA_STA.WMF
USABASE.WMF
USACAN2.WMF
USACAN3.WMF
USASTATE.WMF
USAWCAP.WMF
USAWCAP1.WMF
USAWCAP2.WMF
USEAST.WMF
USMAP.WMF
USMAP1.WMF
USMAP2.WMF
USMAPFLG.WMF
USNORTH.WMF
USRIVERS.WMF
USSLANT.WMF
USSOUTH.WMF
USSTAT23.WMF
USTIMEZN.WMF
USWEST.WMF
W21876.WMF
WESTCOST.WMF

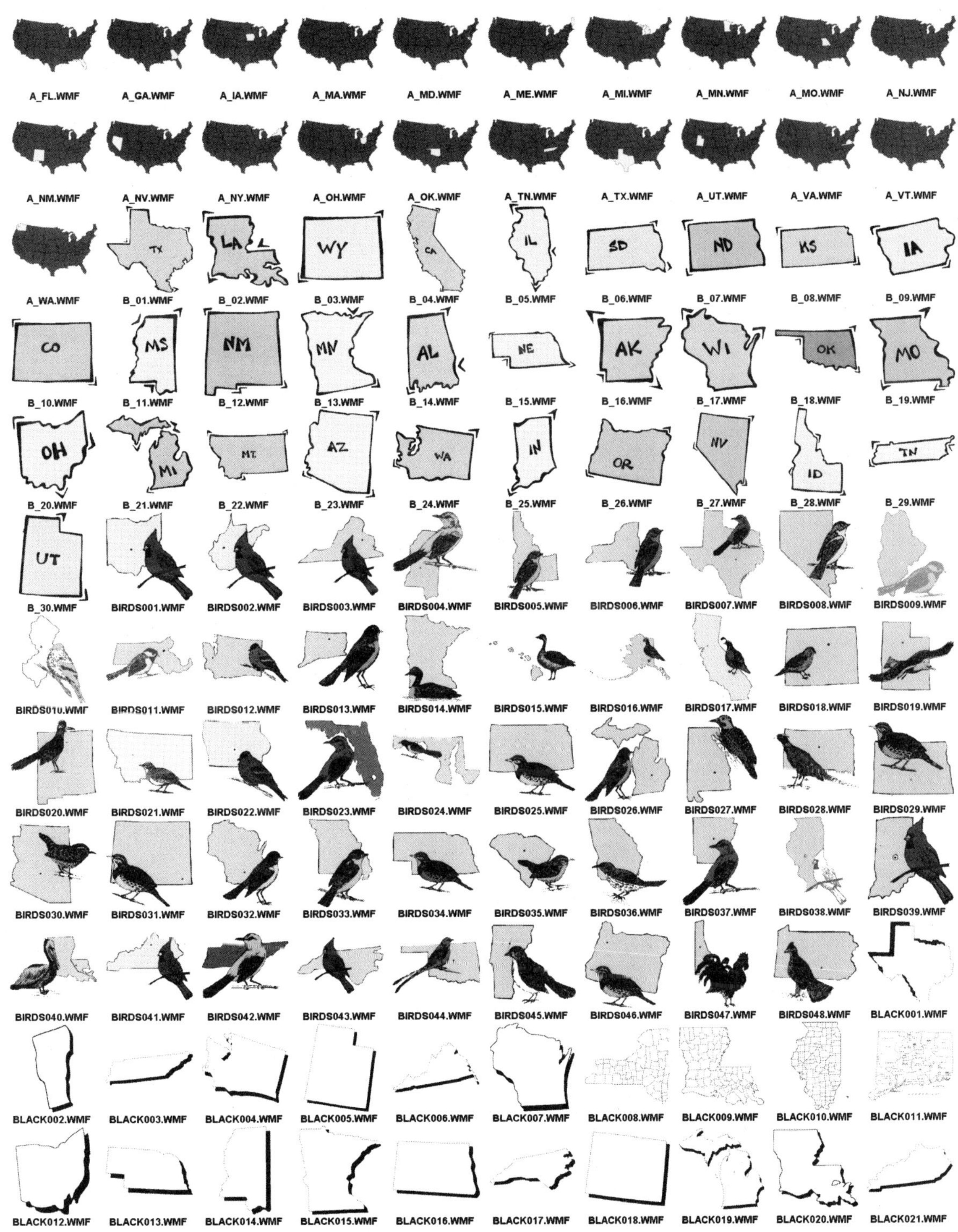

A_FL.WMF A_GA.WMF A_IA.WMF A_MA.WMF A_MD.WMF A_ME.WMF A_MI.WMF A_MN.WMF A_MO.WMF A_NJ.WMF

A_NM.WMF A_NV.WMF A_NY.WMF A_OH.WMF A_OK.WMF A_TN.WMF A_TX.WMF A_UT.WMF A_VA.WMF A_VT.WMF

A_WA.WMF B_01.WMF B_02.WMF B_03.WMF B_04.WMF B_05.WMF B_06.WMF B_07.WMF B_08.WMF B_09.WMF

B_10.WMF B_11.WMF B_12.WMF B_13.WMF B_14.WMF B_15.WMF B_16.WMF B_17.WMF B_18.WMF B_19.WMF

B_20.WMF B_21.WMF B_22.WMF B_23.WMF B_24.WMF B_25.WMF B_26.WMF B_27.WMF B_28.WMF B_29.WMF

B_30.WMF BIRDS001.WMF BIRDS002.WMF BIRDS003.WMF BIRDS004.WMF BIRDS005.WMF BIRDS006.WMF BIRDS007.WMF BIRDS008.WMF BIRDS009.WMF

BIRDS010.WMF BIRDS011.WMF BIRDS012.WMF BIRDS013.WMF BIRDS014.WMF BIRDS015.WMF BIRDS016.WMF BIRDS017.WMF BIRDS018.WMF BIRDS019.WMF

BIRDS020.WMF BIRDS021.WMF BIRDS022.WMF BIRDS023.WMF BIRDS024.WMF BIRDS025.WMF BIRDS026.WMF BIRDS027.WMF BIRDS028.WMF BIRDS029.WMF

BIRDS030.WMF BIRDS031.WMF BIRDS032.WMF BIRDS033.WMF BIRDS034.WMF BIRDS035.WMF BIRDS036.WMF BIRDS037.WMF BIRDS038.WMF BIRDS039.WMF

BIRDS040.WMF BIRDS041.WMF BIRDS042.WMF BIRDS043.WMF BIRDS044.WMF BIRDS045.WMF BIRDS046.WMF BIRDS047.WMF BIRDS048.WMF BLACK001.WMF

BLACK002.WMF BLACK003.WMF BLACK004.WMF BLACK005.WMF BLACK006.WMF BLACK007.WMF BLACK008.WMF BLACK009.WMF BLACK010.WMF BLACK011.WMF

BLACK012.WMF BLACK013.WMF BLACK014.WMF BLACK015.WMF BLACK016.WMF BLACK017.WMF BLACK018.WMF BLACK019.WMF BLACK020.WMF BLACK021.WMF

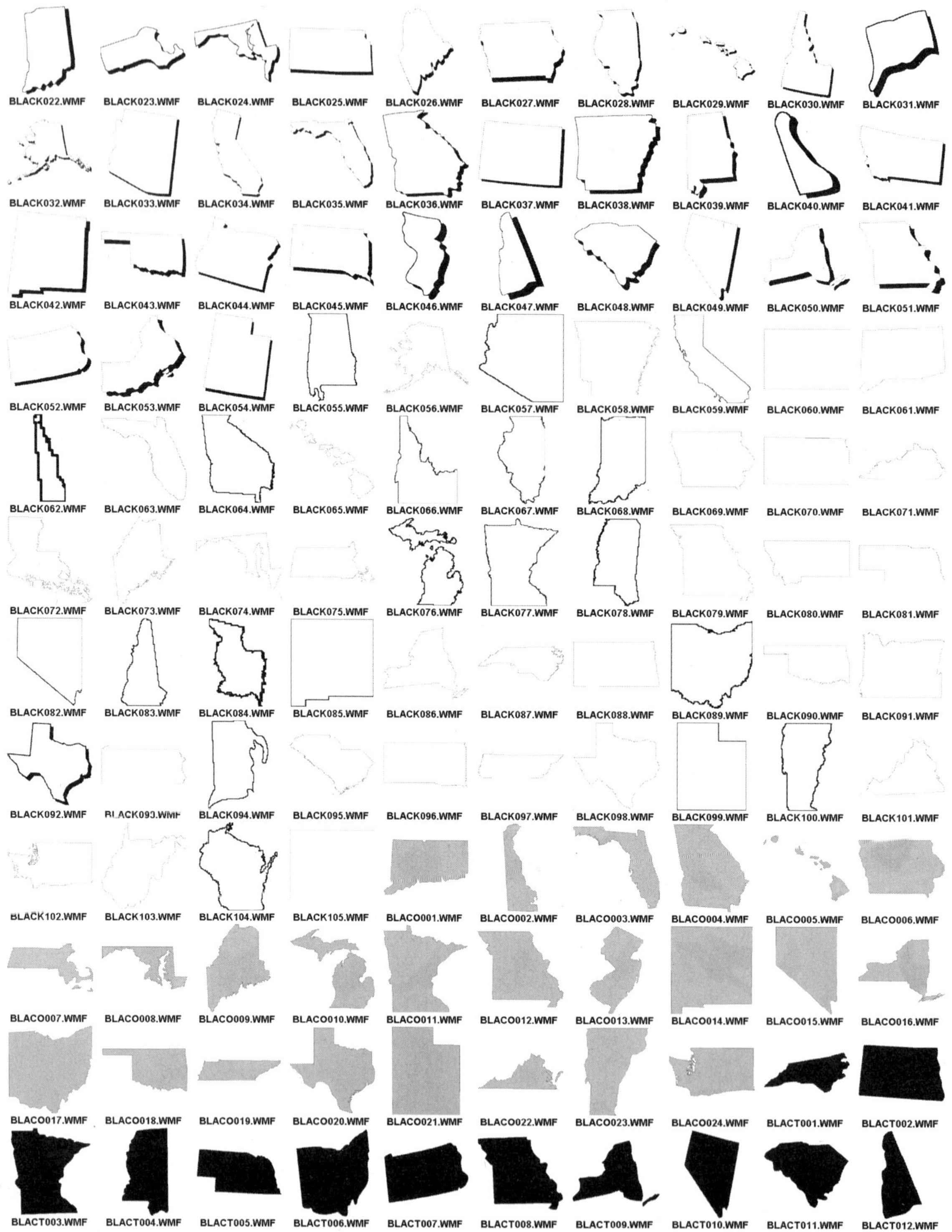
BLACK022.WMF
BLACK023.WMF
BLACK024.WMF
BLACK025.WMF
BLACK026.WMF
BLACK027.WMF
BLACK028.WMF
BLACK029.WMF
BLACK030.WMF
BLACK031.WMF
BLACK032.WMF
BLACK033.WMF
BLACK034.WMF
BLACK035.WMF
BLACK036.WMF
BLACK037.WMF
BLACK038.WMF
BLACK039.WMF
BLACK040.WMF
BLACK041.WMF
BLACK042.WMF
BLACK043.WMF
BLACK044.WMF
BLACK045.WMF
BLACK046.WMF
BLACK047.WMF
BLACK048.WMF
BLACK049.WMF
BLACK050.WMF
BLACK051.WMF
BLACK052.WMF
BLACK053.WMF
BLACK054.WMF
BLACK055.WMF
BLACK056.WMF
BLACK057.WMF
BLACK058.WMF
BLACK059.WMF
BLACK060.WMF
BLACK061.WMF
BLACK062.WMF
BLACK063.WMF
BLACK064.WMF
BLACK065.WMF
BLACK066.WMF
BLACK067.WMF
BLACK068.WMF
BLACK069.WMF
BLACK070.WMF
BLACK071.WMF
BLACK072.WMF
BLACK073.WMF
BLACK074.WMF
BLACK075.WMF
BLACK076.WMF
BLACK077.WMF
BLACK078.WMF
BLACK079.WMF
BLACK080.WMF
BLACK081.WMF
BLACK082.WMF
BLACK083.WMF
BLACK084.WMF
BLACK085.WMF
BLACK086.WMF
BLACK087.WMF
BLACK088.WMF
BLACK089.WMF
BLACK090.WMF
BLACK091.WMF
BLACK092.WMF
BLACK093.WMF
BLACK094.WMF
BLACK095.WMF
BLACK096.WMF
BLACK097.WMF
BLACK098.WMF
BLACK099.WMF
BLACK100.WMF
BLACK101.WMF
BLACK102.WMF
BLACK103.WMF
BLACK104.WMF
BLACK105.WMF
BLACO001.WMF
BLACO002.WMF
BLACO003.WMF
BLACO004.WMF
BLACO005.WMF
BLACO006.WMF
BLACO007.WMF
BLACO008.WMF
BLACO009.WMF
BLACO010.WMF
BLACO011.WMF
BLACO012.WMF
BLACO013.WMF
BLACO014.WMF
BLACO015.WMF
BLACO016.WMF
BLACO017.WMF
BLACO018.WMF
BLACO019.WMF
BLACO020.WMF
BLACO021.WMF
BLACO022.WMF
BLACO023.WMF
BLACO024.WMF
BLACT001.WMF
BLACT002.WMF
BLACT003.WMF
BLACT004.WMF
BLACT005.WMF
BLACT006.WMF
BLACT007.WMF
BLACT008.WMF
BLACT009.WMF
BLACT010.WMF
BLACT011.WMF
BLACT012.WMF

BLACT013.WMF BLACT014.WMF BLACT015.WMF BLACT016.WMF BLACT017.WMF BLACT018.WMF BLACT019.WMF BLACT020.WMF BLACT021.WMF BLACT022.WMF
BLACT023.WMF BLACT024.WMF BLACT025.WMF BLACT026.WMF BLACT027.WMF BLACT028.WMF BLACT029.WMF BLACT030.WMF BLACT031.WMF BLACT032.WMF
BLACT033.WMF BLACT034.WMF BLACT035.WMF BLACT036.WMF BLACT037.WMF BLACT038.WMF BLACT039.WMF BLACT040.WMF BLACT041.WMF BLACT042.WMF
BLACT043.WMF BLACT044.WMF BLACT045.WMF BLACT046.WMF BLACT047.WMF BLACT048.WMF CALABAMA.WMF CALASKA.WMF CARIZONA.WMF CARKANSA.WMF
CCALIF.WMF CCOLORAD.WMF CCONN.WMF CDELAWAR.WMF CFLORIDA.WMF CGEORGIA.WMF CHAWAII.WMF CIDAHO.WMF CILLINOI.WMF CINDIANA.WMF
CIOWA.WMF CKANSAS.WMF CKENTUCY.WMF CLOUISIA.WMF CMAINE.WMF CMARYLAN.WMF CMASS.WMF CMICHIGA.WMF CMINN.WMF CMISS.WMF
CMISSOUR.WMF CMONTANA.WMF CNCAROLI.WMF CNDAKOTA.WMF CNEBRASK.WMF CNEVADA.WMF CNEWHAMP.WMF CNEWJERS.WMF CNEWMEX.WMF CNEWYORK.WMF
COHIO.WMF COKLAHOM.WMF COREGON.WMF COUNC001.WMF COUNC002.WMF COUNC003.WMF COUNC004.WMF COUNC005.WMF COUNC006.WMF COUNC007.WMF
COUNC008.WMF COUNC009.WMF COUNC010.WMF COUNC011.WMF COUNC012.WMF COUNC013.WMF COUNC014.WMF COUNC015.WMF COUNC016.WMF COUNC017.WMF
COUNC018.WMF COUNC019.WMF COUNC020.WMF COUNC021.WMF COUNC022.WMF COUNC023.WMF COUNC024.WMF COUNC025.WMF COUNC026.WMF COUNC027.WMF
COUNC028.WMF COUNC029.WMF COUNC030.WMF COUNC031.WMF COUNC032.WMF COUNC033.WMF COUNC034.WMF COUNC035.WMF COUNC036.WMF COUNC037.WMF
COUNC038.WMF COUNC039.WMF COUNC040.WMF COUNC041.WMF COUNC042.WMF COUNC043.WMF COUNC044.WMF COUNC045.WMF COUNC046.WMF COUNC047.WMF

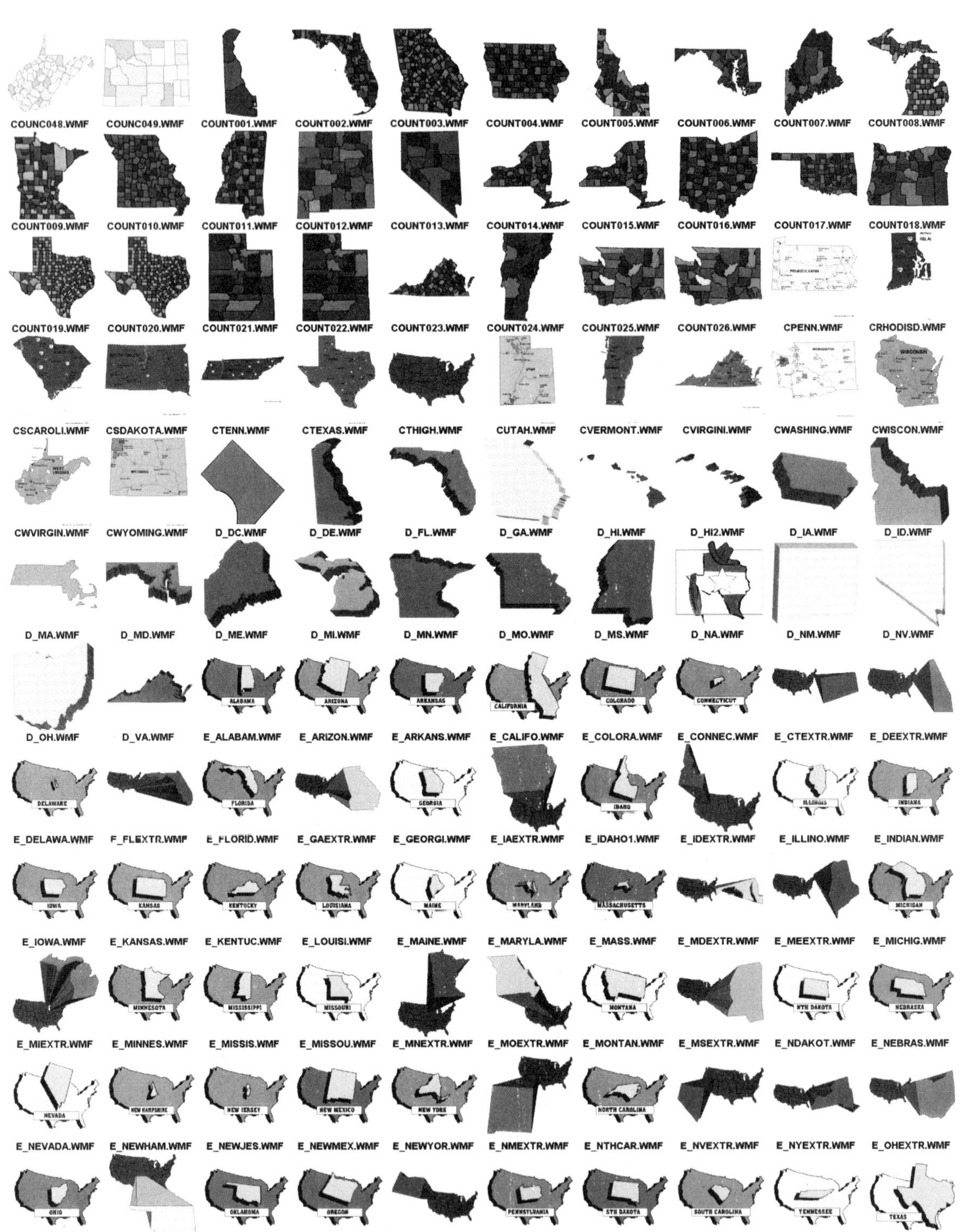

COUNC048.WMF COUNC049.WMF COUNT001.WMF COUNT002.WMF COUNT003.WMF COUNT004.WMF COUNT005.WMF COUNT006.WMF COUNT007.WMF COUNT008.WMF
COUNT009.WMF COUNT010.WMF COUNT011.WMF COUNT012.WMF COUNT013.WMF COUNT014.WMF COUNT015.WMF COUNT016.WMF COUNT017.WMF COUNT018.WMF
COUNT019.WMF COUNT020.WMF COUNT021.WMF COUNT022.WMF COUNT023.WMF COUNT024.WMF COUNT025.WMF COUNT026.WMF CPENN.WMF CRHODISD.WMF
CSCAROLI.WMF CSDAKOTA.WMF CTENN.WMF CTEXAS.WMF CTHIGH.WMF CUTAH.WMF CVERMONT.WMF CVIRGINI.WMF CWASHING.WMF CWISCON.WMF
CWVIRGIN.WMF CWYOMING.WMF D_DC.WMF D_DE.WMF D_FL.WMF D_GA.WMF D_HI.WMF D_HI2.WMF D_IA.WMF D_ID.WMF
D_MA.WMF D_MD.WMF D_ME.WMF D_MI.WMF D_MN.WMF D_MO.WMF D_MS.WMF D_NA.WMF D_NM.WMF D_NV.WMF
D_OH.WMF D_VA.WMF E_ALABAM.WMF E_ARIZON.WMF E_ARKANS.WMF E_CALIFO.WMF E_COLORA.WMF E_CONNEC.WMF E_CTEXTR.WMF E_DEEXTR.WMF
E_DELAWA.WMF F_FLEXTR.WMF E_FLORID.WMF E_GAEXTR.WMF E_GEORGI.WMF E_IAEXTR.WMF E_IDAHO1.WMF E_IDEXTR.WMF E_ILLINO.WMF E_INDIAN.WMF
E_IOWA.WMF E_KANSAS.WMF E_KENTUC.WMF E_LOUISI.WMF E_MAINE.WMF E_MARYLA.WMF E_MASS.WMF E_MDEXTR.WMF E_MEEXTR.WMF E_MICHIG.WMF
E_MIEXTR.WMF E_MINNES.WMF E_MISSIS.WMF E_MISSOU.WMF E_MNEXTR.WMF E_MOEXTR.WMF E_MONTAN.WMF E_MSEXTR.WMF E_NDAKOT.WMF E_NEBRAS.WMF
E_NEVADA.WMF E_NEWHAM.WMF E_NEWJES.WMF E_NEWMEX.WMF E_NEWYOR.WMF E_NMEXTR.WMF E_NTHCAR.WMF E_NVEXTR.WMF E_NYEXTR.WMF E_OHEXTR.WMF
E_OHIO.WMF E_OKEXTR.WMF E_OKLAHO.WMF E_OREGON.WMF E_OREXTR.WMF E_PENNSY.WMF E_SDAKOT.WMF E_STHCAR.WMF E_TENNES.WMF E_TEXAS.WMF

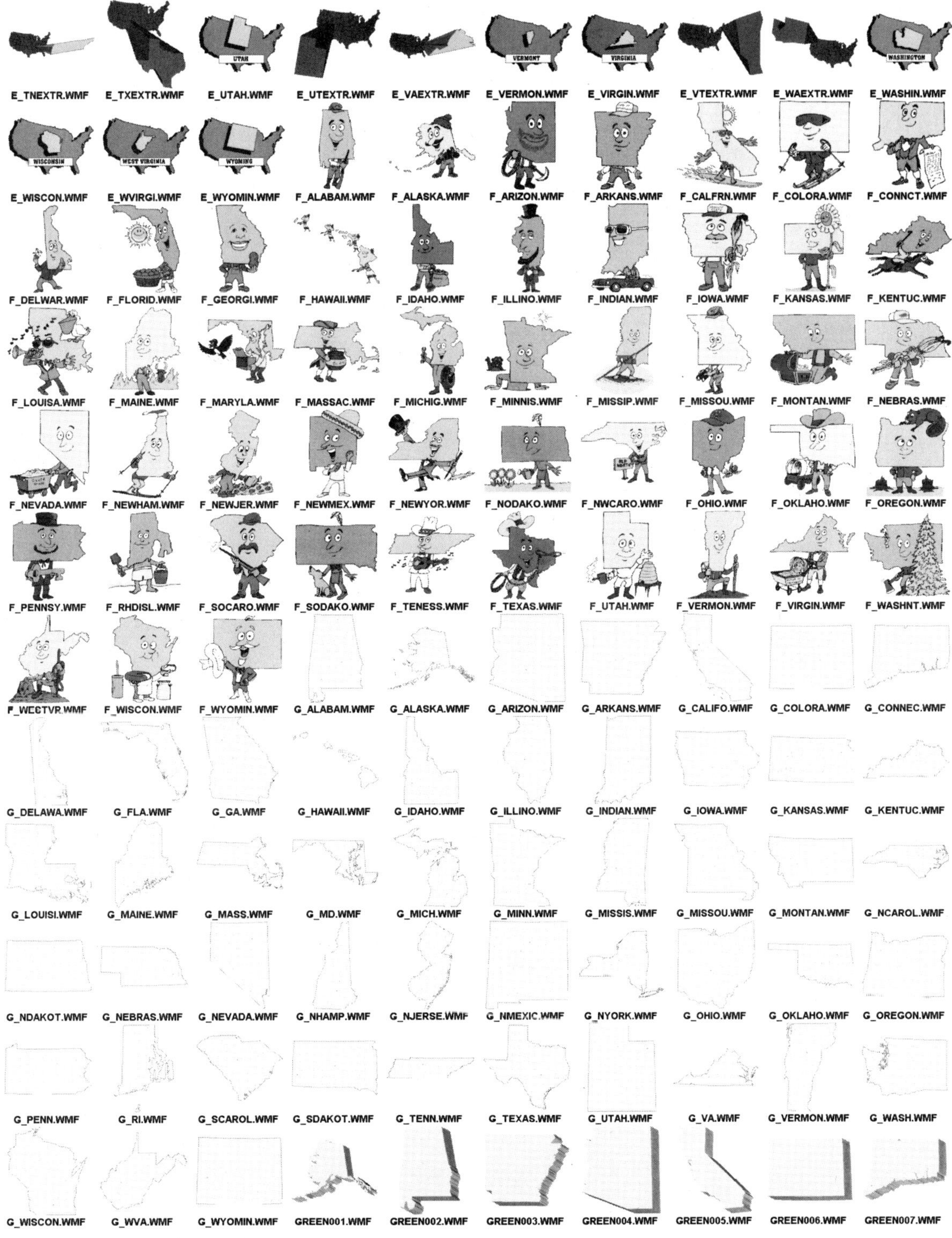

E_TNEXTR.WMF E_TXEXTR.WMF E_UTAH.WMF E_UTEXTR.WMF E_VAEXTR.WMF E_VERMON.WMF E_VIRGIN.WMF E_VTEXTR.WMF E_WAEXTR.WMF E_WASHIN.WMF

E_WISCON.WMF E_WVIRGI.WMF E_WYOMIN.WMF F_ALABAM.WMF F_ALASKA.WMF F_ARIZON.WMF F_ARKANS.WMF F_CALFRN.WMF F_COLORA.WMF F_CONNCT.WMF

F_DELWAR.WMF F_FLORID.WMF F_GEORGI.WMF F_HAWAII.WMF F_IDAHO.WMF F_ILLINO.WMF F_INDIAN.WMF F_IOWA.WMF F_KANSAS.WMF F_KENTUC.WMF

F_LOUISA.WMF F_MAINE.WMF F_MARYLA.WMF F_MASSAC.WMF F_MICHIG.WMF F_MINNIS.WMF F_MISSIP.WMF F_MISSOU.WMF F_MONTAN.WMF F_NEBRAS.WMF

F_NEVADA.WMF F_NEWHAM.WMF F_NEWJER.WMF F_NEWMEX.WMF F_NEWYOR.WMF F_NODAKO.WMF F_NWCARO.WMF F_OHIO.WMF F_OKLAHO.WMF F_OREGON.WMF

F_PENNSY.WMF F_RHDISL.WMF F_SOCARO.WMF F_SODAKO.WMF F_TENESS.WMF F_TEXAS.WMF F_UTAH.WMF F_VERMON.WMF F_VIRGIN.WMF F_WASHNT.WMF

F_WESTVR.WMF F_WISCON.WMF F_WYOMIN.WMF G_ALABAM.WMF G_ALASKA.WMF G_ARIZON.WMF G_ARKANS.WMF G_CALIFO.WMF G_COLORA.WMF G_CONNEC.WMF

G_DELAWA.WMF G_FLA.WMF G_GA.WMF G_HAWAII.WMF G_IDAHO.WMF G_ILLINO.WMF G_INDIAN.WMF G_IOWA.WMF G_KANSAS.WMF G_KENTUC.WMF

G_LOUISI.WMF G_MAINE.WMF G_MASS.WMF G_MD.WMF G_MICH.WMF G_MINN.WMF G_MISSIS.WMF G_MISSOU.WMF G_MONTAN.WMF G_NCAROL.WMF

G_NDAKOT.WMF G_NEBRAS.WMF G_NEVADA.WMF G_NHAMP.WMF G_NJERSE.WMF G_NMEXIC.WMF G_NYORK.WMF G_OHIO.WMF G_OKLAHO.WMF G_OREGON.WMF

G_PENN.WMF G_RI.WMF G_SCAROL.WMF G_SDAKOT.WMF G_TENN.WMF G_TEXAS.WMF G_UTAH.WMF G_VA.WMF G_VERMON.WMF G_WASH.WMF

G_WISCON.WMF G_WVA.WMF G_WYOMIN.WMF GREEN001.WMF GREEN002.WMF GREEN003.WMF GREEN004.WMF GREEN005.WMF GREEN006.WMF GREEN007.WMF

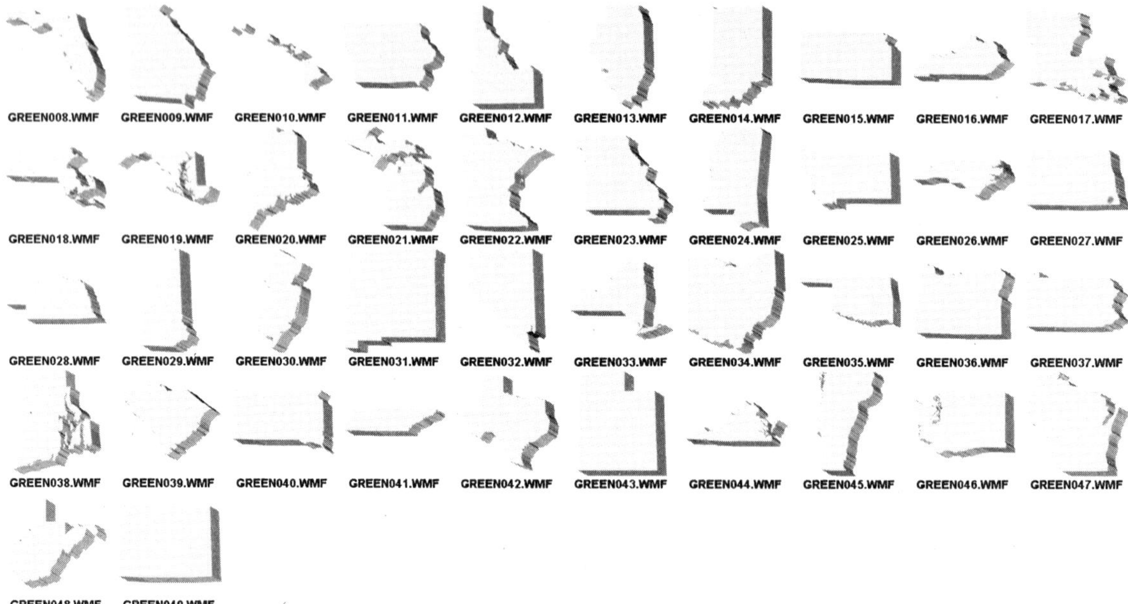
GREEN008.WMF
GREEN009.WMF
GREEN010.WMF
GREEN011.WMF
GREEN012.WMF
GREEN013.WMF
GREEN014.WMF
GREEN015.WMF
GREEN016.WMF
GREEN017.WMF
GREEN018.WMF
GREEN019.WMF
GREEN020.WMF
GREEN021.WMF
GREEN022.WMF
GREEN023.WMF
GREEN024.WMF
GREEN025.WMF
GREEN026.WMF
GREEN027.WMF
GREEN028.WMF
GREEN029.WMF
GREEN030.WMF
GREEN031.WMF
GREEN032.WMF
GREEN033.WMF
GREEN034.WMF
GREEN035.WMF
GREEN036.WMF
GREEN037.WMF
GREEN038.WMF
GREEN039.WMF
GREEN040.WMF
GREEN041.WMF
GREEN042.WMF
GREEN043.WMF
GREEN044.WMF
GREEN045.WMF
GREEN046.WMF
GREEN047.WMF
GREEN048.WMF
GREEN049.WMF

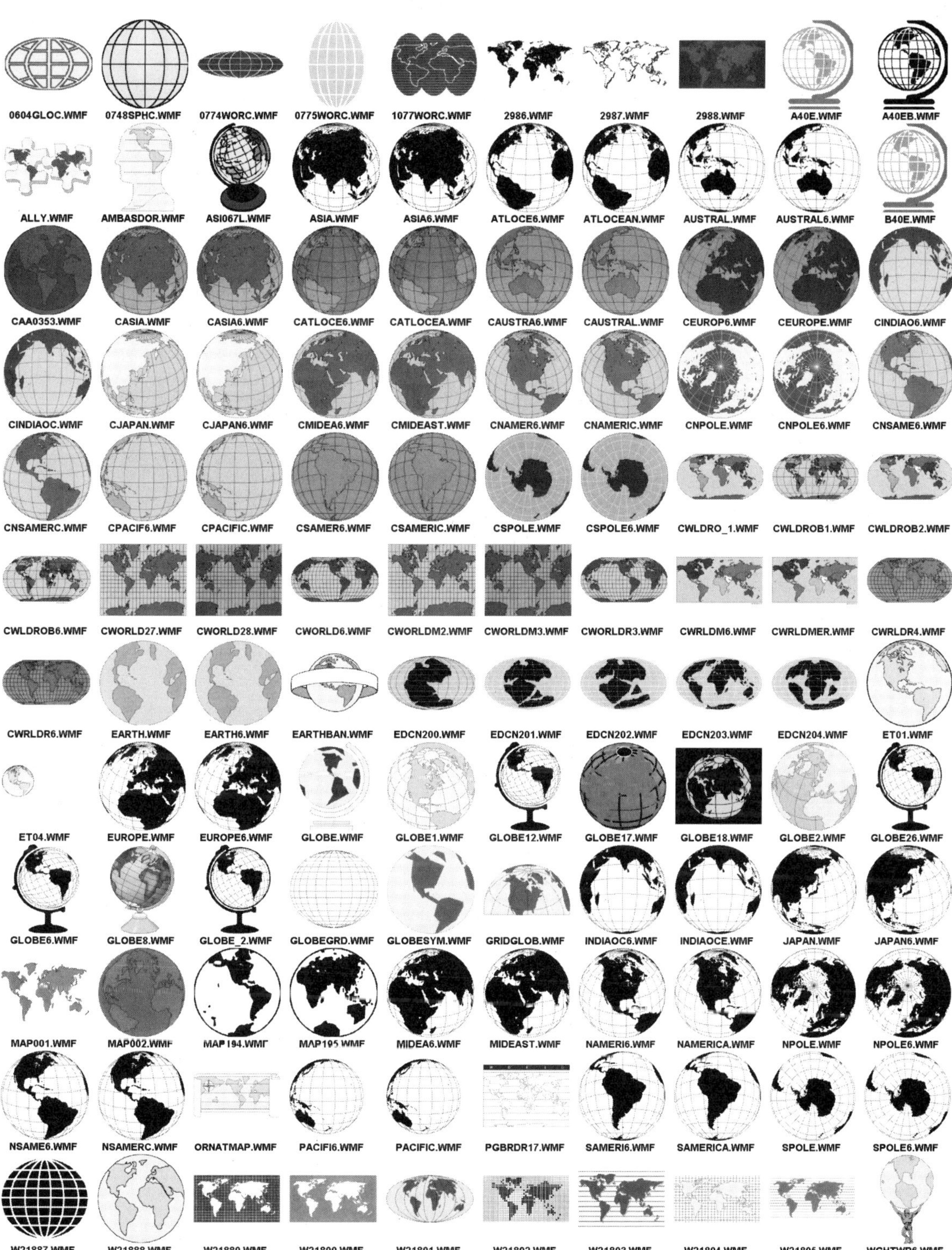

0604GLOC.WMF 0748SPHC.WMF 0774WORC.WMF 0775WORC.WMF 1077WORC.WMF 2986.WMF 2987.WMF 2988.WMF A40E.WMF A40EB.WMF

ALLY.WMF AMBASDOR.WMF ASI067L.WMF ASIA.WMF ASIA6.WMF ATLOCE6.WMF ATLOCEAN.WMF AUSTRAL.WMF AUSTRAL6.WMF B40E.WMF

CAA0353.WMF CASIA.WMF CASIA6.WMF CATLOCE6.WMF CATLOCEA.WMF CAUSTRA6.WMF CAUSTRAL.WMF CEUROP6.WMF CEUROPE.WMF CINDIAO6.WMF

CINDIAOC.WMF CJAPAN.WMF CJAPAN6.WMF CMIDEA6.WMF CMIDEAST.WMF CNAMER6.WMF CNAMERIC.WMF CNPOLE.WMF CNPOLE6.WMF CNSAME6.WMF

CNSAMERC.WMF CPACIF6.WMF CPACIFIC.WMF CSAMER6.WMF CSAMERIC.WMF CSPOLE.WMF CSPOLE6.WMF CWLDRO_1.WMF CWLDROB1.WMF CWLDROB2.WMF

CWLDROB6.WMF CWORLD27.WMF CWORLD28.WMF CWORLD6.WMF CWORLDM2.WMF CWORLDM3.WMF CWORLDR3.WMF CWRLDM6.WMF CWRLDMER.WMF CWRLDR4.WMF

CWRLDR6.WMF EARTH.WMF EARTH6.WMF EARTHBAN.WMF EDCN200.WMF EDCN201.WMF EDCN202.WMF EDCN203.WMF EDCN204.WMF ET01.WMF

ET04.WMF EUROPE.WMF EUROPE6.WMF GLOBE.WMF GLOBE1.WMF GLOBE12.WMF GLOBE17.WMF GLOBE18.WMF GLOBE2.WMF GLOBE26.WMF

GLOBE6.WMF GLOBE8.WMF GLOBE_2.WMF GLOBEGRD.WMF GLOBESYM.WMF GRIDGLOB.WMF INDIAOC6.WMF INDIAOCE.WMF JAPAN.WMF JAPAN6.WMF

MAP001.WMF MAP002.WMF MAP194.WMF MAP195.WMF MIDEA6.WMF MIDEAST.WMF NAMERI6.WMF NAMERICA.WMF NPOLE.WMF NPOLE6.WMF

NSAME6.WMF NSAMERC.WMF ORNATMAP.WMF PACIFI6.WMF PACIFIC.WMF PGBRDR17.WMF SAMERI6.WMF SAMERICA.WMF SPOLE.WMF SPOLE6.WMF

W21887.WMF W21888.WMF W21889.WMF W21890.WMF W21891.WMF W21892.WMF W21893.WMF W21894.WMF W21895.WMF WGHTWR6.WMF

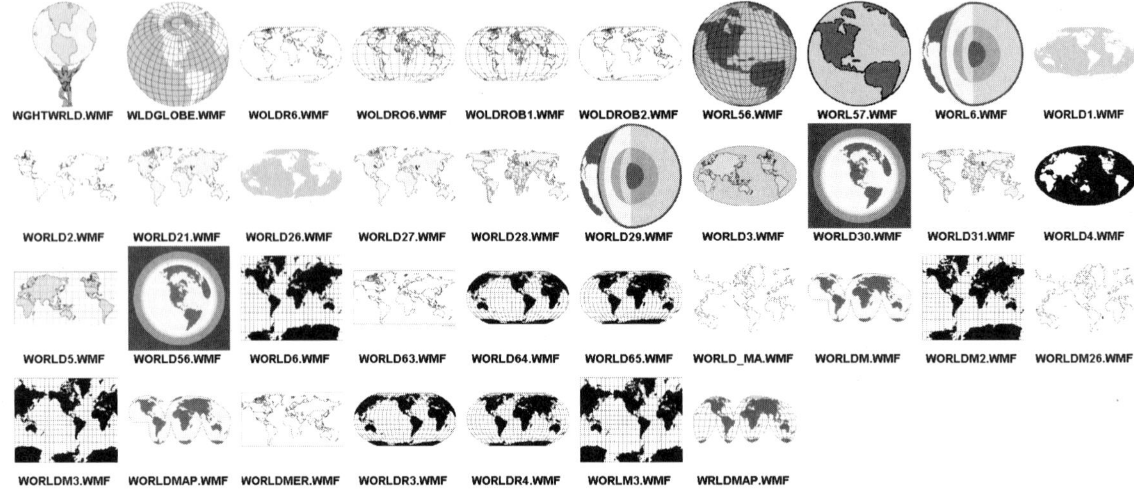
WGHTWRLD.WMF
WLDGLOBE.WMF
WOLDR6.WMF
WOLDRO6.WMF
WOLDROB1.WMF
WOLDROB2.WMF
WORL56.WMF
WORL57.WMF
WORL6.WMF
WORLD1.WMF
WORLD2.WMF
WORLD21.WMF
WORLD26.WMF
WORLD27.WMF
WORLD28.WMF
WORLD29.WMF
WORLD3.WMF
WORLD30.WMF
WORLD31.WMF
WORLD4.WMF
WORLD5.WMF
WORLD56.WMF
WORLD6.WMF
WORLD63.WMF
WORLD64.WMF
WORLD65.WMF
WORLD_MA.WMF
WORLDM.WMF
WORLDM2.WMF
WORLDM26.WMF
WORLDM3.WMF
WORLDMAP.WMF
WORLDMER.WMF
WORLDR3.WMF
WORLDR4.WMF
WORLM3.WMF
WRLDMAP.WMF

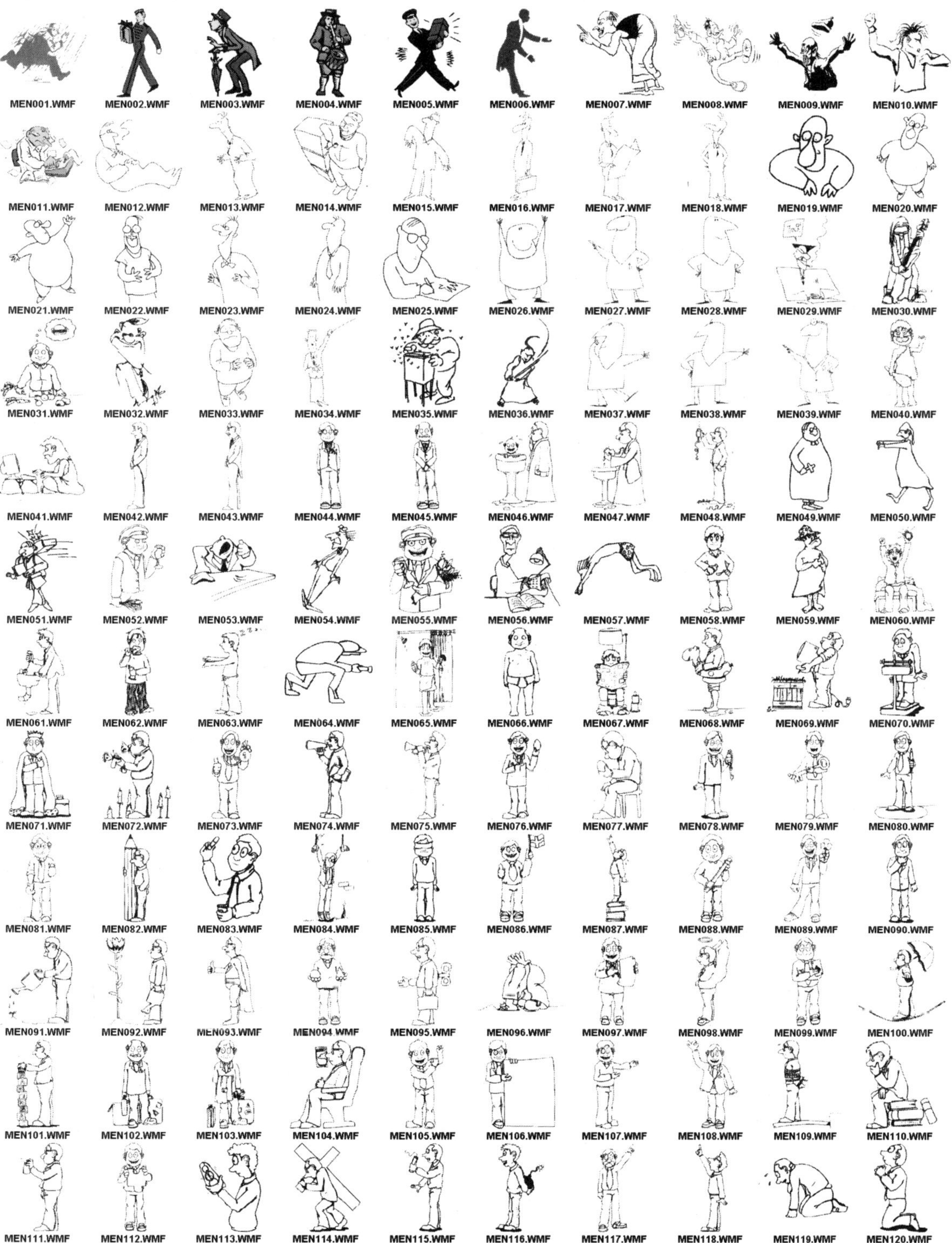
MEN001.WMF MEN002.WMF MEN003.WMF MEN004.WMF MEN005.WMF MEN006.WMF MEN007.WMF MEN008.WMF MEN009.WMF MEN010.WMF
MEN011.WMF MEN012.WMF MEN013.WMF MEN014.WMF MEN015.WMF MEN016.WMF MEN017.WMF MEN018.WMF MEN019.WMF MEN020.WMF
MEN021.WMF MEN022.WMF MEN023.WMF MEN024.WMF MEN025.WMF MEN026.WMF MEN027.WMF MEN028.WMF MEN029.WMF MEN030.WMF
MEN031.WMF MEN032.WMF MEN033.WMF MEN034.WMF MEN035.WMF MEN036.WMF MEN037.WMF MEN038.WMF MEN039.WMF MEN040.WMF
MEN041.WMF MEN042.WMF MEN043.WMF MEN044.WMF MEN045.WMF MEN046.WMF MEN047.WMF MEN048.WMF MEN049.WMF MEN050.WMF
MEN051.WMF MEN052.WMF MEN053.WMF MEN054.WMF MEN055.WMF MEN056.WMF MEN057.WMF MEN058.WMF MEN059.WMF MEN060.WMF
MEN061.WMF MEN062.WMF MEN063.WMF MEN064.WMF MEN065.WMF MEN066.WMF MEN067.WMF MEN068.WMF MEN069.WMF MEN070.WMF
MEN071.WMF MEN072.WMF MEN073.WMF MEN074.WMF MEN075.WMF MEN076.WMF MEN077.WMF MEN078.WMF MEN079.WMF MEN080.WMF
MEN081.WMF MEN082.WMF MEN083.WMF MEN084.WMF MEN085.WMF MEN086.WMF MEN087.WMF MEN088.WMF MEN089.WMF MEN090.WMF
MEN091.WMF MEN092.WMF MEN093.WMF MEN094.WMF MEN095.WMF MEN096.WMF MEN097.WMF MEN098.WMF MEN099.WMF MEN100.WMF
MEN101.WMF MEN102.WMF MEN103.WMF MEN104.WMF MEN105.WMF MEN106.WMF MEN107.WMF MEN108.WMF MEN109.WMF MEN110.WMF
MEN111.WMF MEN112.WMF MEN113.WMF MEN114.WMF MEN115.WMF MEN116.WMF MEN117.WMF MEN118.WMF MEN119.WMF MEN120.WMF

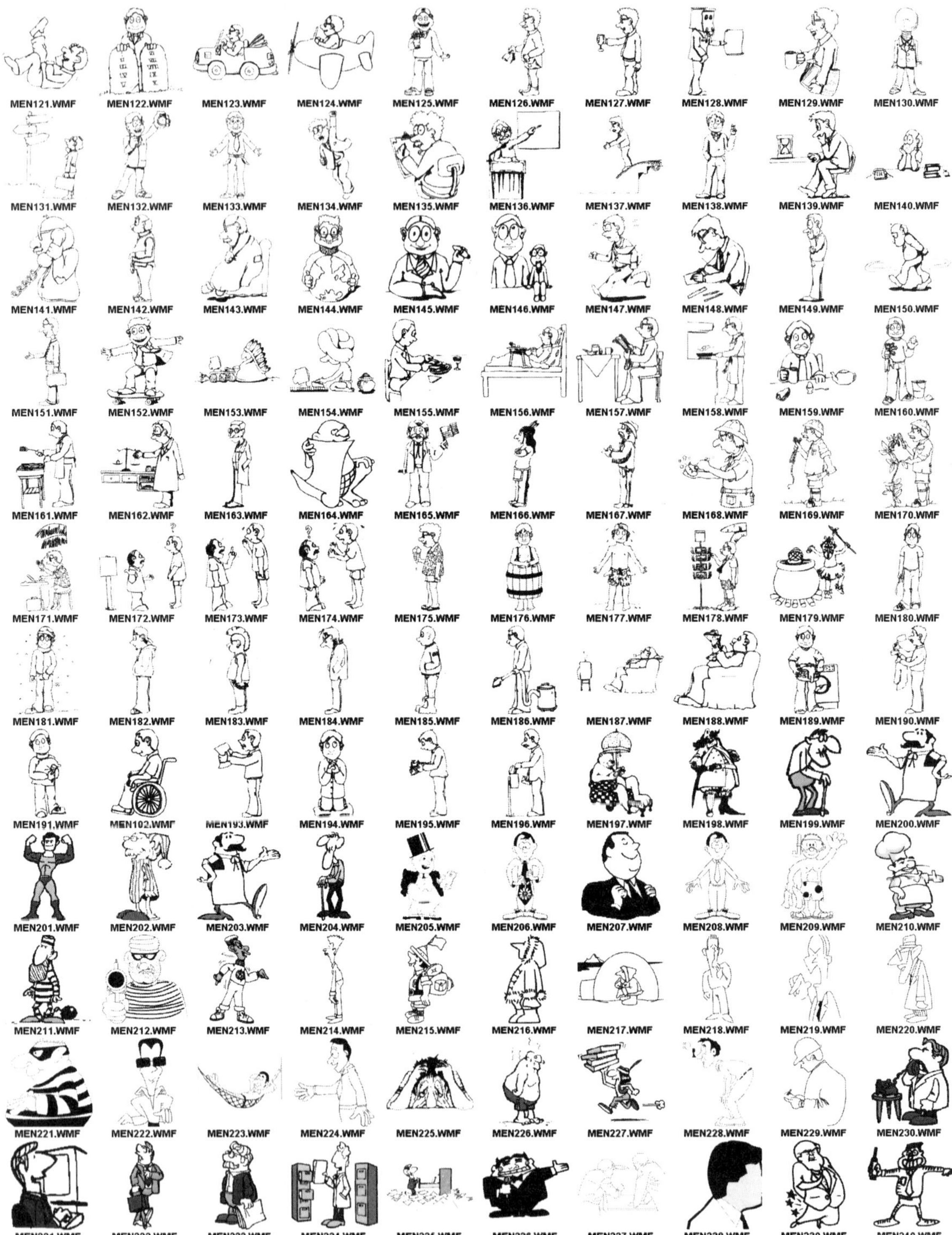
MEN121.WMF
MEN122.WMF
MEN123.WMF
MEN124.WMF
MEN125.WMF
MEN126.WMF
MEN127.WMF
MEN128.WMF
MEN129.WMF
MEN130.WMF
MEN131.WMF
MEN132.WMF
MEN133.WMF
MEN134.WMF
MEN135.WMF
MEN136.WMF
MEN137.WMF
MEN138.WMF
MEN139.WMF
MEN140.WMF
MEN141.WMF
MEN142.WMF
MEN143.WMF
MEN144.WMF
MEN145.WMF
MEN146.WMF
MEN147.WMF
MEN148.WMF
MEN149.WMF
MEN150.WMF
MEN151.WMF
MEN152.WMF
MEN153.WMF
MEN154.WMF
MEN155.WMF
MEN156.WMF
MEN157.WMF
MEN158.WMF
MEN159.WMF
MEN160.WMF
MEN161.WMF
MEN162.WMF
MEN163.WMF
MEN164.WMF
MEN165.WMF
MEN166.WMF
MEN167.WMF
MEN168.WMF
MEN169.WMF
MEN170.WMF
MEN171.WMF
MEN172.WMF
MEN173.WMF
MEN174.WMF
MEN175.WMF
MEN176.WMF
MEN177.WMF
MEN178.WMF
MEN179.WMF
MEN180.WMF
MEN181.WMF
MEN182.WMF
MEN183.WMF
MEN184.WMF
MEN185.WMF
MEN186.WMF
MEN187.WMF
MEN188.WMF
MEN189.WMF
MEN190.WMF
MEN191.WMF
MEN192.WMF
MEN193.WMF
MEN194.WMF
MEN195.WMF
MEN196.WMF
MEN197.WMF
MEN198.WMF
MEN199.WMF
MEN200.WMF
MEN201.WMF
MEN202.WMF
MEN203.WMF
MEN204.WMF
MEN205.WMF
MEN206.WMF
MEN207.WMF
MEN208.WMF
MEN209.WMF
MEN210.WMF
MEN211.WMF
MEN212.WMF
MEN213.WMF
MEN214.WMF
MEN215.WMF
MEN216.WMF
MEN217.WMF
MEN218.WMF
MEN219.WMF
MEN220.WMF
MEN221.WMF
MEN222.WMF
MEN223.WMF
MEN224.WMF
MEN225.WMF
MEN226.WMF
MEN227.WMF
MEN228.WMF
MEN229.WMF
MEN230.WMF
MEN231.WMF
MEN232.WMF
MEN233.WMF
MEN234.WMF
MEN235.WMF
MEN236.WMF
MEN237.WMF
MEN238.WMF
MEN239.WMF
MEN240.WMF

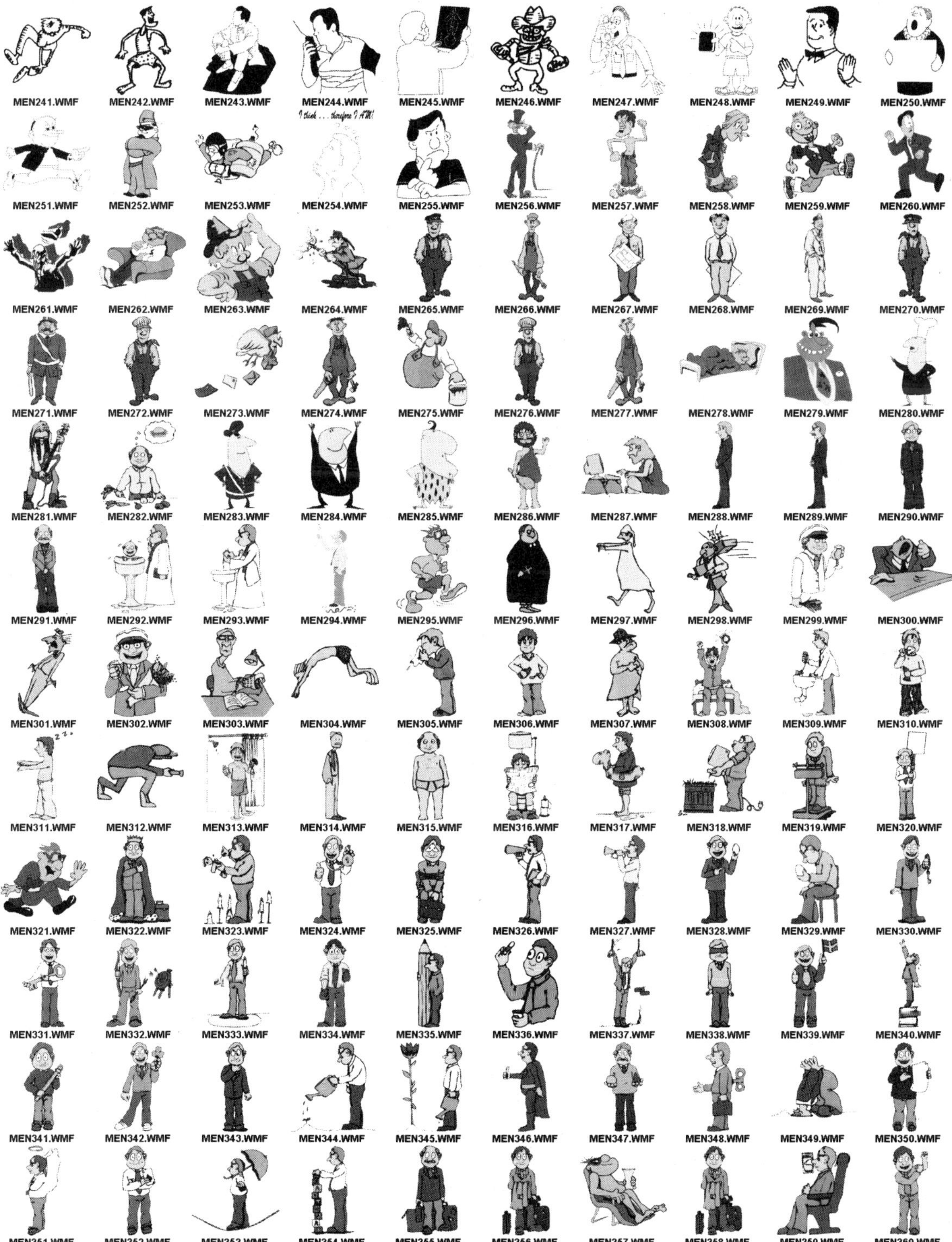

MEN241.WMF MEN242.WMF MEN243.WMF MEN244.WMF MEN245.WMF MEN246.WMF MEN247.WMF MEN248.WMF MEN249.WMF MEN250.WMF

MEN251.WMF MEN252.WMF MEN253.WMF MEN254.WMF MEN255.WMF MEN256.WMF MEN257.WMF MEN258.WMF MEN259.WMF MEN260.WMF

MEN261.WMF MEN262.WMF MEN263.WMF MEN264.WMF MEN265.WMF MEN266.WMF MEN267.WMF MEN268.WMF MEN269.WMF MEN270.WMF

MEN271.WMF MEN272.WMF MEN273.WMF MEN274.WMF MEN275.WMF MEN276.WMF MEN277.WMF MEN278.WMF MEN279.WMF MEN280.WMF

MEN281.WMF MEN282.WMF MEN283.WMF MEN284.WMF MEN285.WMF MEN286.WMF MEN287.WMF MEN288.WMF MEN289.WMF MEN290.WMF

MEN291.WMF MEN292.WMF MEN293.WMF MEN294.WMF MEN295.WMF MEN296.WMF MEN297.WMF MEN298.WMF MEN299.WMF MEN300.WMF

MEN301.WMF MEN302.WMF MEN303.WMF MEN304.WMF MEN305.WMF MEN306.WMF MEN307.WMF MEN308.WMF MEN309.WMF MEN310.WMF

MEN311.WMF MEN312.WMF MEN313.WMF MEN314.WMF MEN315.WMF MEN316.WMF MEN317.WMF MEN318.WMF MEN319.WMF MEN320.WMF

MEN321.WMF MEN322.WMF MEN323.WMF MEN324.WMF MEN325.WMF MEN326.WMF MEN327.WMF MEN328.WMF MEN329.WMF MEN330.WMF

MEN331.WMF MEN332.WMF MEN333.WMF MEN334.WMF MEN335.WMF MEN336.WMF MEN337.WMF MEN338.WMF MEN339.WMF MEN340.WMF

MEN341.WMF MEN342.WMF MEN343.WMF MEN344.WMF MEN345.WMF MEN346.WMF MEN347.WMF MEN348.WMF MEN349.WMF MEN350.WMF

MEN351.WMF MEN352.WMF MEN353.WMF MEN354.WMF MEN355.WMF MEN356.WMF MEN357.WMF MEN358.WMF MEN359.WMF MEN360.WMF

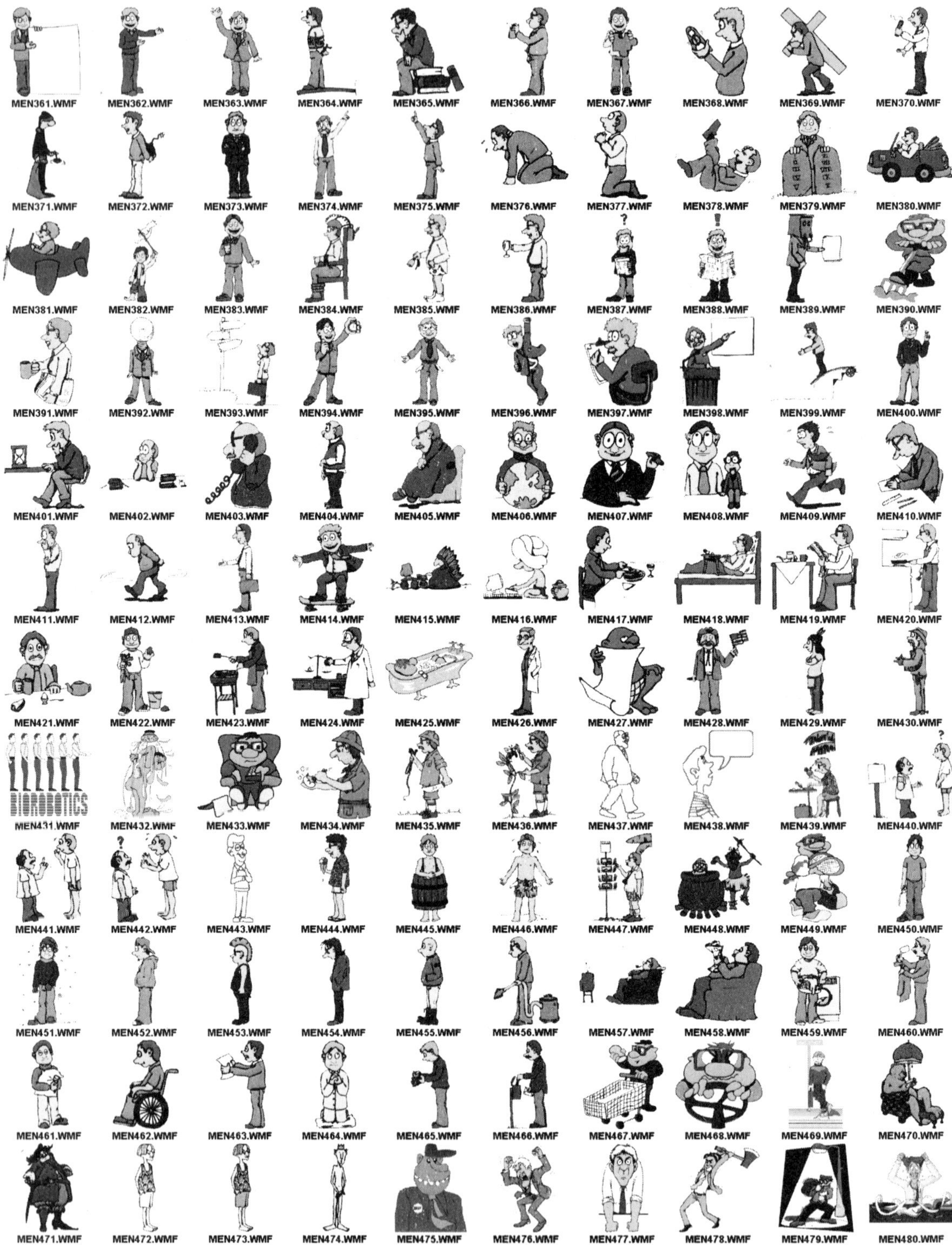
MEN361.WMF
MEN362.WMF
MEN363.WMF
MEN364.WMF
MEN365.WMF
MEN366.WMF
MEN367.WMF
MEN368.WMF
MEN369.WMF
MEN370.WMF
MEN371.WMF
MEN372.WMF
MEN373.WMF
MEN374.WMF
MEN375.WMF
MEN376.WMF
MEN377.WMF
MEN378.WMF
MEN379.WMF
MEN380.WMF
MEN381.WMF
MEN382.WMF
MEN383.WMF
MEN384.WMF
MEN385.WMF
MEN386.WMF
MEN387.WMF
MEN388.WMF
MEN389.WMF
MEN390.WMF
MEN391.WMF
MEN392.WMF
MEN393.WMF
MEN394.WMF
MEN395.WMF
MEN396.WMF
MEN397.WMF
MEN398.WMF
MEN399.WMF
MEN400.WMF
MEN401.WMF
MEN402.WMF
MEN403.WMF
MEN404.WMF
MEN405.WMF
MEN406.WMF
MEN407.WMF
MEN408.WMF
MEN409.WMF
MEN410.WMF
MEN411.WMF
MEN412.WMF
MEN413.WMF
MEN414.WMF
MEN415.WMF
MEN416.WMF
MEN417.WMF
MEN418.WMF
MEN419.WMF
MEN420.WMF
MEN421.WMF
MEN422.WMF
MEN423.WMF
MEN424.WMF
MEN425.WMF
MEN426.WMF
MEN427.WMF
MEN428.WMF
MEN429.WMF
MEN430.WMF
BIOROBOTICS
MEN431.WMF
MEN432.WMF
MEN433.WMF
MEN434.WMF
MEN435.WMF
MEN436.WMF
MEN437.WMF
MEN438.WMF
MEN439.WMF
MEN440.WMF
MEN441.WMF
MEN442.WMF
MEN443.WMF
MEN444.WMF
MEN445.WMF
MEN446.WMF
MEN447.WMF
MEN448.WMF
MEN449.WMF
MEN450.WMF
MEN451.WMF
MEN452.WMF
MEN453.WMF
MEN454.WMF
MEN455.WMF
MEN456.WMF
MEN457.WMF
MEN458.WMF
MEN459.WMF
MEN460.WMF
MEN461.WMF
MEN462.WMF
MEN463.WMF
MEN464.WMF
MEN465.WMF
MEN466.WMF
MEN467.WMF
MEN468.WMF
MEN469.WMF
MEN470.WMF
MEN471.WMF
MEN472.WMF
MEN473.WMF
MEN474.WMF
MEN475.WMF
MEN476.WMF
MEN477.WMF
MEN478.WMF
MEN479.WMF
MEN480.WMF

MEN481.WMF MEN482.WMF MEN483.WMF MEN484.WMF MEN485.WMF MEN486.WMF MEN487.WMF MEN488.WMF MEN489.WMF MEN490.WMF

MEN491.WMF MEN492.WMF MEN493.WMF MEN494.WMF MEN495.WMF MEN496.WMF MEN497.WMF MEN498.WMF MEN499.WMF MEN500.WMF

MEN501.WMF MEN502.WMF MEN503.WMF MEN504.WMF MEN505.WMF MEN506.WMF MEN507.WMF MEN508.WMF MEN509.WMF MEN510.WMF

MEN511.WMF MEN512.WMF MEN513.WMF MEN514.WMF MEN515.WMF MEN516.WMF MEN517.WMF MEN518.WMF MEN519.WMF MEN520.WMF

MEN521.WMF MEN522.WMF MEN523.WMF MEN524.WMF MEN525.WMF MEN526.WMF MEN527.WMF MEN528.WMF MEN529.WMF MEN530.WMF

MEN531.WMF MEN532.WMF MEN533.WMF MEN534.WMF MEN535.WMF MEN536.WMF MEN537.WMF MEN538.WMF MEN539.WMF MEN540.WMF

MEN541.WMF MEN542.WMF MEN543.WMF MEN544.WMF MEN545.WMF MEN546.WMF MEN547.WMF MEN548.WMF MEN549.WMF MEN550.WMF

MEN551.WMF MEN552.WMF MEN553.WMF MEN554.WMF MEN555.WMF MEN556.WMF MEN557.WMF MEN558.WMF MEN559.WMF MEN560.WMF

MEN561.WMF MEN562.WMF MEN563.WMF MEN564.WMF MEN565.WMF MEN566.WMF MEN567.WMF MEN568.WMF MEN569.WMF MEN570.WMF

MEN571.WMF MEN572.WMF MEN573.WMF MEN574.WMF MEN575.WMF MEN576.WMF MEN577.WMF MEN578.WMF MEN579.WMF MEN580.WMF

MEN581.WMF MEN582.WMF MEN583.WMF MEN584.WMF MEN585.WMF MEN586.WMF MEN587.WMF MEN588.WMF MEN589.WMF MEN590.WMF

MEN591.WMF MEN592.WMF MEN593.WMF MEN594.WMF MEN595.WMF MEN596.WMF MEN597.WMF MEN598.WMF MEN599.WMF

FACES001.WMF
FACES002.WMF
FACES003.WMF
FACES004.WMF
FACES005.WMF
FACES006.WMF
FACES007.WMF
FACES008.WMF
FACES009.WMF
FACES010.WMF
FACES011.WMF
FACES012.WMF
FACES013.WMF
FACES014.WMF
FACES015.WMF
FACES016.WMF
FACES017.WMF
FACES018.WMF
FACES019.WMF
FACES020.WMF
FACES021.WMF
FACES022.WMF
FACES023.WMF
FACES024.WMF
FACES025.WMF
FACES026.WMF
FACES027.WMF
FACES028.WMF
FACES029.WMF
FACES030.WMF
FACES031.WMF
FACES032.WMF
FACES033.WMF
FACES034.WMF
FACES035.WMF
FACES036.WMF
FACES037.WMF
FACES038.WMF
FACES039.WMF
FACES040.WMF
FACES041.WMF
FACES042.WMF
FACES043.WMF
FACES044.WMF
FACES045.WMF
FACES046.WMF
FACES047.WMF
FACES048.WMF
FACES049.WMF
FACES050.WMF
FACES051.WMF
FACES052.WMF
FACES053.WMF
FACES054.WMF
FACES055.WMF
FACES056.WMF
FACES057.WMF
FACES058.WMF
FACES059.WMF
FACES060.WMF
FACES061.WMF
FACES062.WMF
FACES063.WMF
FACES064.WMF
FACES065.WMF
FACES066.WMF
FACES067.WMF
FACES068.WMF
FACES069.WMF
FACES070.WMF
FACES071.WMF
FACES072.WMF
FACES073.WMF
FACES074.WMF
FACES075.WMF
FACES076.WMF
FACES077.WMF
FACES078.WMF
FACES079.WMF
FACES080.WMF
FACES081.WMF
FACES082.WMF
FACES083.WMF
FACES084.WMF
FACES085.WMF
FACES086.WMF
FACES087.WMF
FACES088.WMF
FACES089.WMF
FACES090.WMF
FACES091.WMF
FACES092.WMF
FACES093.WMF
FACES094.WMF
FACES095.WMF
FACES096.WMF
FACES097.WMF
FACES098.WMF
FACES099.WMF
FACES100.WMF
FACES101.WMF
FACES102.WMF
FACES103.WMF
FACES104.WMF
FACES105.WMF
FACES106.WMF
FACES107.WMF
FACES108.WMF
FACES109.WMF
FACES110.WMF
FACES111.WMF
FACES112.WMF
FACES113.WMF
FACES114.WMF
FACES115.WMF
FACES116.WMF
FACES117.WMF
FACES118.WMF
FACES119.WMF
FACES120.WMF

FACES121.WMF FACES122.WMF FACES123.WMF FACES124.WMF FACES125.WMF FACES126.WMF FACES127.WMF FACES128.WMF FACES129.WMF FACES130.WMF

FACES131.WMF FACES132.WMF FACES133.WMF FACES134.WMF FACES135.WMF FACES136.WMF FACES137.WMF FACES138.WMF FACES139.WMF FACES140.WMF

FACES141.WMF FACES142.WMF FACES143.WMF FACES144.WMF FACES145.WMF FACES146.WMF FACES147.WMF FACES148.WMF FACES149.WMF FACES150.WMF

FACES151.WMF FACES152.WMF FACES153.WMF FACES154.WMF FACES155.WMF FACES156.WMF FACES157.WMF FACES158.WMF FACES159.WMF FACES160.WMF

FACES161.WMF FACES162.WMF FACES163.WMF FACES164.WMF FACES165.WMF FACES166.WMF FACES167.WMF FACES168.WMF FACES169.WMF FACES170.WMF

FACES171.WMF FACES172.WMF FACES173.WMF FACES174.WMF FACES175.WMF FACES176.WMF FACES177.WMF FACES178.WMF FACES179.WMF FACES180.WMF

FACES181.WMF FACES182.WMF FACES183.WMF FACES184.WMF FACES185.WMF FACES186.WMF FACES187.WMF FACES188.WMF FACES189.WMF FACES190.WMF

FACES191.WMF FACES192.WMF FACES193.WMF FACES194.WMF FACES195.WMF FACES196.WMF FACES197.WMF FACES198.WMF FACES199.WMF FACES200.WMF

FACES201.WMF FACES202.WMF FACES203.WMF FACES204.WMF FACES205.WMF FACES206.WMF FACES207.WMF FACES208.WMF FACES209.WMF FACES210.WMF

FACES211.WMF FACES212.WMF FACES213.WMF FACES214.WMF FACES215.WMF FACES216.WMF FACES217.WMF FACES218.WMF FACES219.WMF FACES220.WMF

FACES221.WMF FACES222.WMF FACES223.WMF FACES224.WMF FACES225.WMF FACES226.WMF FACES227.WMF FACES228.WMF FACES229.WMF FACES230.WMF

FACES231.WMF FACES232.WMF FACES233.WMF FACES234.WMF FACES235.WMF FACES236.WMF FACES237.WMF FACES238.WMF FACES239.WMF FACES240.WMF

FACES241.WMF FACES242.WMF FACES243.WMF FACES244.WMF FACES245.WMF FACES246.WMF FACES247.WMF FACES248.WMF FACES249.WMF FACES250.WMF
FACES251.WMF FACES252.WMF FACES253.WMF FACES254.WMF FACES255.WMF FACES256.WMF FACES257.WMF FACES258.WMF FACES259.WMF FACES260.WMF
FACES261.WMF FACES262.WMF FACES263.WMF FACES264.WMF FACES265.WMF FACES266.WMF FACES267.WMF FACES268.WMF FACES269.WMF FACES270.WMF
FACES271.WMF FACES272.WMF FACES273.WMF FACES274.WMF MEN600.WMF MEN601.WMF MEN602.WMF MEN603.WMF MEN604.WMF MEN605.WMF
MEN606.WMF MEN607.WMF MEN608.WMF MEN609.WMF MEN610.WMF MEN611.WMF MEN612.WMF MEN613.WMF MEN614.WMF MEN615.WMF
MEN616.WMF MEN617.WMF MEN618.WMF MEN619.WMF MEN620.WMF MEN621.WMF MEN622.WMF MEN623.WMF MEN624.WMF MEN625.WMF
MEN626.WMF MEN627.WMF MEN628.WMF MEN629.WMF MEN630.WMF MEN631.WMF MEN632.WMF MEN633.WMF MEN634.WMF MEN635.WMF
MEN636.WMF MEN637.WMF MEN638.WMF MEN639.WMF MEN640.WMF MEN641.WMF MEN642.WMF MEN643.WMF MEN644.WMF MEN645.WMF
MEN646.WMF MEN647.WMF MEN648.WMF MEN649.WMF MEN650.WMF MEN651.WMF MEN652.WMF MEN653.WMF MEN654.WMF MEN655.WMF
MEN656.WMF MEN657.WMF MEN658.WMF MEN659.WMF MEN660.WMF MEN661.WMF MEN662.WMF MEN663.WMF MEN664.WMF MEN665.WMF
MEN666.WMF MEN667.WMF MEN668.WMF MEN669.WMF MEN670.WMF MEN671.WMF MEN672.WMF MEN673.WMF MEN674.WMF MEN675.WMF
MEN676.WMF MEN677.WMF MEN678.WMF MEN679.WMF MEN680.WMF MEN681.WMF MEN682.WMF MEN683.WMF MEN684.WMF MEN685.WMF

MEN686.WMF MEN687.WMF MEN688.WMF MEN689.WMF MEN690.WMF MEN691.WMF MEN692.WMF MEN693.WMF MEN694.WMF MEN695.WMF
MEN696.WMF MEN697.WMF MEN698.WMF MEN699.WMF MEN700.WMF MEN701.WMF MEN702.WMF MEN703.WMF MEN704.WMF MEN705.WMF
MEN706.WMF MEN707.WMF MEN708.WMF MEN709.WMF MEN710.WMF MEN711.WMF MEN712.WMF MEN713.WMF MEN714.WMF MEN715.WMF
MEN716.WMF MEN717.WMF MEN718.WMF MEN719.WMF MEN720.WMF MEN721.WMF MEN722.WMF MEN723.WMF MEN724.WMF MEN725.WMF
MEN726.WMF MEN727.WMF MEN728.WMF MEN729.WMF MEN730.WMF MEN731.WMF MEN732.WMF MEN733.WMF MEN734.WMF MEN735.WMF
MEN736.WMF MEN737.WMF MEN738.WMF MEN739.WMF MEN740.WMF MEN741.WMF MEN742.WMF MEN743.WMF MEN744.WMF MEN745.WMF
MEN746.WMF MEN747.WMF MEN748.WMF MEN749.WMF MEN750.WMF MEN751.WMF MEN752.WMF MEN753.WMF MEN754.WMF MEN755.WMF
MEN756.WMF MEN757.WMF MEN758.WMF MEN759.WMF MEN760.WMF MEN761.WMF MEN762.WMF MEN763.WMF MEN764.WMF MEN765.WMF
MEN766.WMF MEN767.WMF MEN768.WMF MEN769.WMF MEN770.WMF MEN771.WMF MEN772.WMF MEN773.WMF MEN774.WMF MEN775.WMF
MEN776.WMF MEN777.WMF MEN778.WMF MEN779.WMF MEN780.WMF MEN781.WMF MEN782.WMF MEN783.WMF MEN784.WMF MEN785.WMF
MEN786.WMF MEN787.WMF MEN788.WMF MEN789.WMF MEN790.WMF MEN791.WMF MEN792.WMF MEN793.WMF MEN794.WMF MEN795.WMF
MEN796.WMF MEN797.WMF MEN798.WMF MEN799.WMF MEN800.WMF MEN801.WMF MEN802.WMF MEN803.WMF MEN804.WMF MEN805.WMF

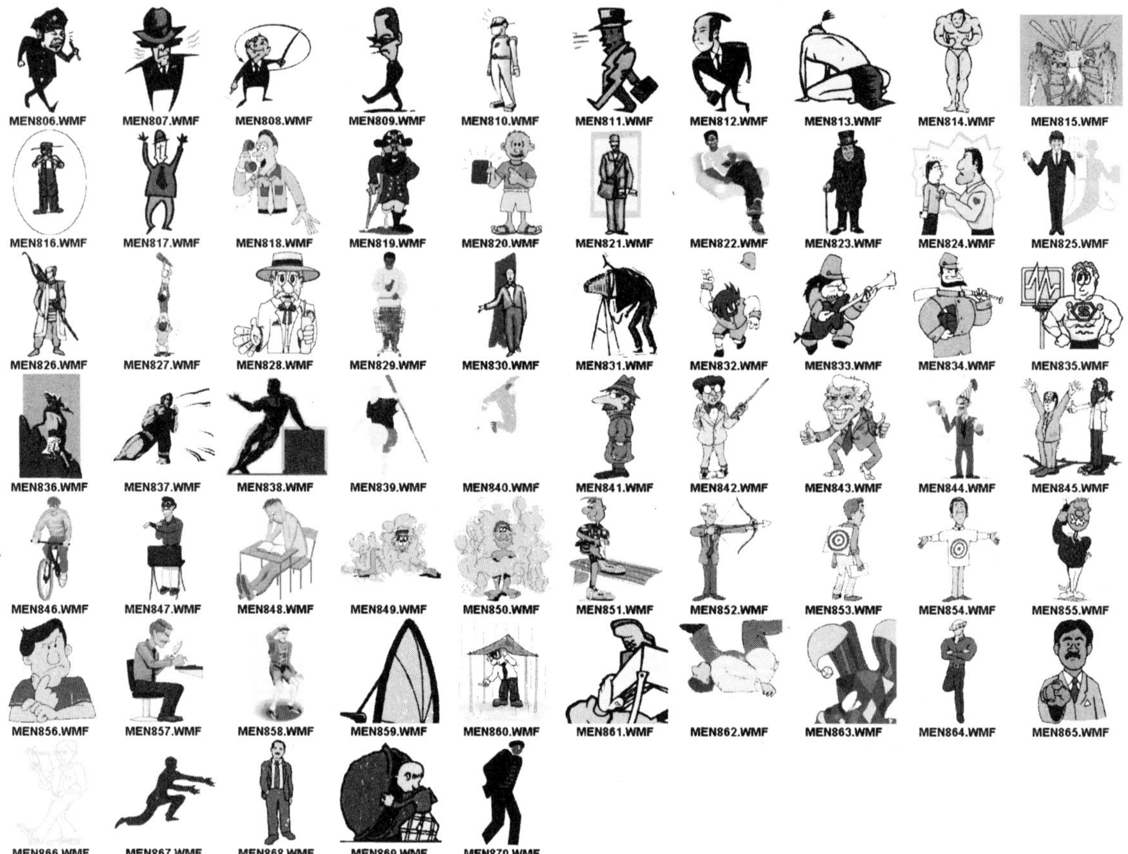
MEN806.WMF
MEN807.WMF
MEN808.WMF
MEN809.WMF
MEN810.WMF
MEN811.WMF
MEN812.WMF
MEN813.WMF
MEN814.WMF
MEN815.WMF
MEN816.WMF
MEN817.WMF
MEN818.WMF
MEN819.WMF
MEN820.WMF
MEN821.WMF
MEN822.WMF
MEN823.WMF
MEN824.WMF
MEN825.WMF
MEN826.WMF
MEN827.WMF
MEN828.WMF
MEN829.WMF
MEN830.WMF
MEN831.WMF
MEN832.WMF
MEN833.WMF
MEN834.WMF
MEN835.WMF
MEN836.WMF
MEN837.WMF
MEN838.WMF
MEN839.WMF
MEN840.WMF
MEN841.WMF
MEN842.WMF
MEN843.WMF
MEN844.WMF
MEN845.WMF
MEN846.WMF
MEN847.WMF
MEN848.WMF
MEN849.WMF
MEN850.WMF
MEN851.WMF
MEN852.WMF
MEN853.WMF
MEN854.WMF
MEN855.WMF
MEN856.WMF
MEN857.WMF
MEN858.WMF
MEN859.WMF
MEN860.WMF
MEN861.WMF
MEN862.WMF
MEN863.WMF
MEN864.WMF
MEN865.WMF
MEN866.WMF
MEN867.WMF
MEN868.WMF
MEN869.WMF
MEN870.WMF

0239.WMF 02491.WMF 02571.WMF 02581.WMF 2926.WMF 2995.WMF 4210.WMF 4363.WMF 4799.WMF 4800.WMF
4801.WMF 4803.WMF 4805.WMF 4806.WMF 4807.WMF 4808.WMF 4809.WMF 4810.WMF 4811.WMF 4813.WMF
4814.WMF 4815.WMF 4816.WMF 4817.WMF 4818.WMF 4819.WMF 4821.WMF 4822.WMF 4823.WMF 4824.WMF
4825.WMF 4826.WMF 4828.WMF 4829.WMF 4830.WMF 4831.WMF 4832.WMF 4833.WMF 4834.WMF 4835.WMF
4836.WMF 4837.WMF 4839.WMF 4841.WMF 4843.WMF 4844.WMF 4845.WMF 4846.WMF 4847.WMF 4848.WMF
4849.WMF 4851.WMF 4852.WMF 4853.WMF 4854.WMF 4855.WMF 4857.WMF 4858.WMF 4859.WMF 4860.WMF
4862.WMF 4863.WMF 4864.WMF 4865.WMF 4866.WMF 4867.WMF 4868.WMF 4869.WMF 4870.WMF 4871.WMF
4873.WMF 4874.WMF 4876.WMF 4877.WMF 4878.WMF 4879.WMF 4880.WMF 4881.WMF 4882.WMF 4883.WMF
4884.WMF 4885.WMF 4886.WMF 4887.WMF 4888.WMF 4889.WMF 4890.WMF 4891.WMF 4892.WMF 4893.WMF
4894.WMF 4895.WMF 4896.WMF 4897.WMF 4898.WMF 4899.WMF 4900.WMF 4901.WMF 4902.WMF 4904.WMF
4905.WMF 4906.WMF 4907.WMF 4908.WMF 4909.WMF 4910.WMF 4912.WMF 4914.WMF 4915.WMF 4916.WMF
4917.WMF 4918.WMF 4919.WMF 4922.WMF 4923.WMF 4925.WMF 4926.WMF 4927.WMF 4928.WMF 4929.WMF

4930.WMF 4931.WMF 4932.WMF 4933.WMF 4934.WMF 4935.WMF 4936.WMF 4937.WMF 4938.WMF 4939.WMF

4940.WMF 4941.WMF 4942.WMF 4943.WMF 4944.WMF 4946.WMF 4947.WMF 4948.WMF 4949.WMF 4950.WMF

4951.WMF 4952.WMF 4953.WMF 4954.WMF 4955.WMF 4956.WMF 4957.WMF 4958.WMF 4959.WMF 4960.WMF

4961.WMF 4962.WMF 4963.WMF 4964.WMF 4965.WMF 4966.WMF 4967.WMF 4968.WMF 4969.WMF 4970.WMF

4972.WMF 4973.WMF 4974.WMF 4975.WMF 4976.WMF 4977.WMF 4978.WMF 4979.WMF 4980.WMF 4981.WMF

4982.WMF 4983.WMF 4985.WMF 4986.WMF 4987.WMF 4988.WMF 4989.WMF 4990.WMF 4991.WMF 4992.WMF

4993.WMF 4994.WMF 4995.WMF 4996.WMF 4997.WMF 4999.WMF 5000.WMF ADS052J.WMF ARMSTRNG.WMF CAPONE.WMF

CAVEND.WMF CHARLIEC.WMF CPARR.WMF DHLAWRNC.WMF DRAKE.WMF EINSTEIN.WMF ELVIS.WMF ENSS036D.WMF FACE23.WMF FACE25.WMF

FACE26.WMF FROBISHR.WMF GALILEO.WMF HENRY8.WMF J21150.WMF J21151.WMF MARTIN.WMF MLKING.WMF NEWTON.WMF PEBF001K.WMF

PEKC028J.WMF PEKC029J.WMF PEKC030J.WMF PEKC031J.WMF PEKC032J.WMF PEKC033J.WMF PEKC034J.WMF PEKC035J.WMF PEKC036J.WMF PEKC037J.WMF

PEKC038J.WMF PEKC039J.WMF PEKC040J.WMF PEKC041J.WMF PEOPL001.WMF PEOPL002.WMF PEOPL004.WMF PEOPL014.WMF PESI105D.WMF SHAKESPR.WMF

2PILGRIM.WMF
3PILGRIM.WMF
ADS052S.WMF
ASI101C.WMF
AUGUSTUS.WMF
BCODY1.WMF
BCODY2.WMF
BENITOMU.WMF
BIT1046.WMF
BIT1049.WMF
BIT1051.WMF
BIT1053.WMF
BIT1056.WMF
BIT1102.WMF
BIT1104.WMF
BIT1106.WMF
BOOKERTW.WMF
BRUTUS.WMF
CAESAR1.WMF
CAESAR2.WMF
CASTRO1.WMF
CASTRO2.WMF
CASTRO3.WMF
CC17.WMF
CC27.WMF
CC54.WMF
CHURCHIL.WMF
COLMBUS2.WMF
COLUMBUS.WMF
CORONADO.WMF
CORTEZ.WMF
CUSTER1.WMF
CUSTER2.WMF
CUSTER3.WMF
CUSTER4.WMF
CZARNICK.WMF
DBOONE1.WMF
DBOONE2.WMF
DBOONE3.WMF
DEGAULLE.WMF
EDISON1.WMF
EDISON2.WMF
ELEANORR.WMF
EMC2.WMF
EMC2B.WMF
EVITA.WMF
FACE11.WMF
FACE13.WMF
FACE14.WMF
FACE15.WMF
FRANKLN1.WMF
FRANKLN2.WMF
FREUD.WMF
GANDHI.WMF
GANDHI1.WMF
GANDHI2.WMF
GANDHI3.WMF
GORBY.WMF
GORBY2.WMF
GUEVARA.WMF
GWCARVER.WMF
HENRY8.WMF
HITLER.WMF
HITLER1.WMF
HITLER2.WMF
HITLER3.WMF
HTUBMAN.WMF
JESUS.WMF
KARLMARX.WMF
KTCARSON.WMF
LAWYER1.WMF
LENIN.WMF
LENIN2.WMF
LINDBERG.WMF
LUTHER.WMF
MAO.WMF
MAO1.WMF
MBEGIN.WMF
MLKING.WMF
MOTHERT1.WMF
MOTHERT2.WMF
MOTHERT3.WMF
MTWAIN1.WMF
MTWAIN2.WMF
NAPOLEO1.WMF
NAPOLEON.WMF
NERO1.WMF
NERO2.WMF
NEWTON1.WMF
NEWTON2.WMF
OJSIMPSN.WMF
PECA084D.WMF
PECA135J.WMF
PEJB002D.WMF
PEOPL006.WMF
PLATO.WMF
POLICMAN.WMF
POPEJPII.WMF
PREZ.WMF
PTBARNUM.WMF
RASPUTN1.WMF
RASPUTN2.WMF
REVKING.WMF
RURIK.WMF
SANTHONY.WMF
SHAKESP1.WMF
SHAKESP2.WMF
SOCRATES.WMF
STALIN.WMF
STALIN2.WMF
VOTES FOR WOMEN
SUFRAJET.WMF
TAILOR.WMF
TROTSKY.WMF
UNCLESA.WMF
UNCLESA2.WMF
UNCSAM1.WMF
UNCSAM2.WMF
UNCSAM3.WMF
UNCSAM4.WMF
UNCSAM5.WMF

UNCSAM6.WMF

UNCSAM7.WMF

UNCSAM8.WMF

UNCSAM9.WMF

Men • Realistic (REALISTC)

RFACE001.WMF	RFACE002.WMF	RFACE003.WMF	RFACE004.WMF	RFACE005.WMF	RFACE006.WMF	RFACE007.WMF	RFACE008.WMF	RFACE009.WMF	RFACE010.WMF
RFACE011.WMF	RFACE012.WMF	RFACE013.WMF	RFACE014.WMF	RFACE015.WMF	RFACE016.WMF	RFACE017.WMF	RFACE018.WMF	RFACE019.WMF	RFACE020.WMF
RFACE021.WMF	RFACE022.WMF	RFACE023.WMF	RFACE024.WMF	RFACE025.WMF	RFACE026.WMF	RFACE027.WMF	RFACE028.WMF	RFACE029.WMF	RFACE030.WMF
RFACE031.WMF	RFACE032.WMF	RFACE033.WMF	RFACE034.WMF	RFACE035.WMF	RFACE036.WMF	RFACE037.WMF	RFACE038.WMF	RFACE039.WMF	RFACE040.WMF
RFACE041.WMF	RFACE042.WMF	RFACE043.WMF	RFACE044.WMF	RFACE045.WMF	RFACE046.WMF	RFACE047.WMF	RFACE048.WMF	RFACE049.WMF	RFACE050.WMF
RFACE051.WMF	RFACE052.WMF	RFACE053.WMF	RFACE054.WMF	RFACE055.WMF	RFACE056.WMF	RFACE057.WMF	RFACE058.WMF	RFACE059.WMF	RFACE060.WMF
RFACE061.WMF	RFACE062.WMF	RFACE063.WMF	RFACE064.WMF	RFACE065.WMF	RFACE066.WMF	RFACE067.WMF	RFACE068.WMF	RFACE069.WMF	RFACE070.WMF
RFACE071.WMF	RFACE072.WMF	RFACE073.WMF	RFACE074.WMF	RFACE075.WMF	RFACE076.WMF	RFACE077.WMF	RFACE078.WMF	RFACE079.WMF	RFACE080.WMF

RFACE081.WMF
RFACE082.WMF
RFACE083.WMF
RFACE084.WMF
RFACE085.WMF
RFACE086.WMF
RFACE087.WMF
RFACE088.WMF
RFACE089.WMF
RFACE090.WMF
RFACE091.WMF
RFACE092.WMF
RMEN001.WMF
RMEN002.WMF
RMEN003.WMF
RMEN004.WMF
RMEN005.WMF
RMEN006.WMF
RMEN007.WMF
RMEN008.WMF
RMEN009.WMF
RMEN010.WMF
RMEN011.WMF
RMEN012.WMF
RMEN013.WMF
RMEN014.WMF
RMEN015.WMF
RMEN016.WMF
RMEN017.WMF
RMEN018.WMF
RMEN019.WMF
RMEN020.WMF
RMEN021.WMF
RMEN022.WMF
RMEN023.WMF
RMEN024.WMF
RMEN025.WMF
RMEN026.WMF
RMEN027.WMF
RMEN028.WMF
RMEN029.WMF
RMEN030.WMF
RMEN031.WMF
RMEN032.WMF
RMEN033.WMF
RMEN034.WMF
RMEN035.WMF
RMEN036.WMF
RMEN037.WMF
RMEN038.WMF
RMEN039.WMF
RMEN040.WMF
RMEN041.WMF
RMEN042.WMF
RMEN043.WMF
RMEN044.WMF
RMEN045.WMF
RMEN046.WMF
RMEN047.WMF
RMEN048.WMF
RMEN049.WMF
RMEN050.WMF
RMEN051.WMF
RMEN052.WMF
RMEN053.WMF
RMEN054.WMF
RMEN055.WMF
RMEN056.WMF
RMEN057.WMF
RMEN058.WMF
RMEN059.WMF
RMEN060.WMF
RMEN061.WMF
RMEN062.WMF
RMEN063.WMF
RMEN064.WMF
RMEN065.WMF
RMEN066.WMF
RMEN067.WMF
RMEN068.WMF
RMEN069.WMF
RMEN070.WMF
RMEN071.WMF
RMEN072.WMF
RMEN073.WMF
RMEN074.WMF
RMEN075.WMF
RMEN076.WMF
RMEN077.WMF

2725.WMF 2726.WMF 2727.WMF 2744.WMF 2749.WMF 2750.WMF 2751.WMF 2752.WMF 2753.WMF 2754.WMF
2755.WMF 2756.WMF 2757.WMF 2758.WMF 2759.WMF 2760.WMF 2761.WMF 2762.WMF 2763.WMF 2764.WMF
4221.WMF A10TBOLT.WMF AIRFORC.WMF AIRSTRIK.WMF APACHE.WMF ASI048J.WMF BIT0301.WMF BOMBERS1.WMF BOMBERS2.WMF BOMBERS3.WMF
BOMBERS4.WMF C130HERC.WMF C5AGALX.WMF COMNDRHO.WMF COPTER.WMF DFNC016.WMF DFNC018.WMF DFNC019.WMF DFNC020.WMF DFNC022.WMF
DFNC023.WMF DFNC024.WMF DFNC025.WMF DFNC026.WMF DFNC027.WMF DFNC028.WMF DFNC029.WMF DFNC030.WMF DFNC031.WMF DFNC032.WMF
DFNC033.WMF DFNC034.WMF DFNC035.WMF DFNC036.WMF DFNC037.WMF DFNC038.WMF DFNC039.WMF DFNC040.WMF DFNC041.WMF DFNC042.WMF
DFNC043.WMF DFNC044.WMF DFNC045.WMF DFNC046.WMF EAGLSYM.WMF FIGHTER1.WMF FIGHTER2.WMF FIGHTER3.WMF FIGHTER4.WMF FIGHTER5.WMF
FIGHTER6.WMF FIGHTER7.WMF HAWKER.WMF JET1.WMF JET2.WMF MISSLE2.WMF PD019ACU.WMF PD019BCU.WMF PD019CCU.WMF PD019DCU.WMF
PD019ECU.WMF PD019FCU.WMF PD019GCU.WMF PD019HCU.WMF PD019ICU.WMF PD019JCU.WMF PITTSPEC.WMF PLANES.WMF SENTRY.WMF SPITFIRE.WMF
STEALTH.WMF STRW006D.WMF STSI004D.WMF STSI005D.WMF STSI006D.WMF STSI007D.WMF STSI008D.WMF STSI019D.WMF STSI031D.WMF TRSI030D.WMF
TRSI054D.WMF TRSI057D.WMF TRSI059D.WMF USAFACAD.WMF V1.WMF WPLANE.WMF ZZZ01.WMF ZZZ02.WMF ZZZ03.WMF ZZZ04.WMF
ZZZ05.WMF ZZZ06.WMF ZZZ07.WMF ZZZ08.WMF ZZZ09.WMF ZZZ10.WMF ZZZ11.WMF ZZZ12.WMF ZZZ13.WMF ZZZ14.WMF

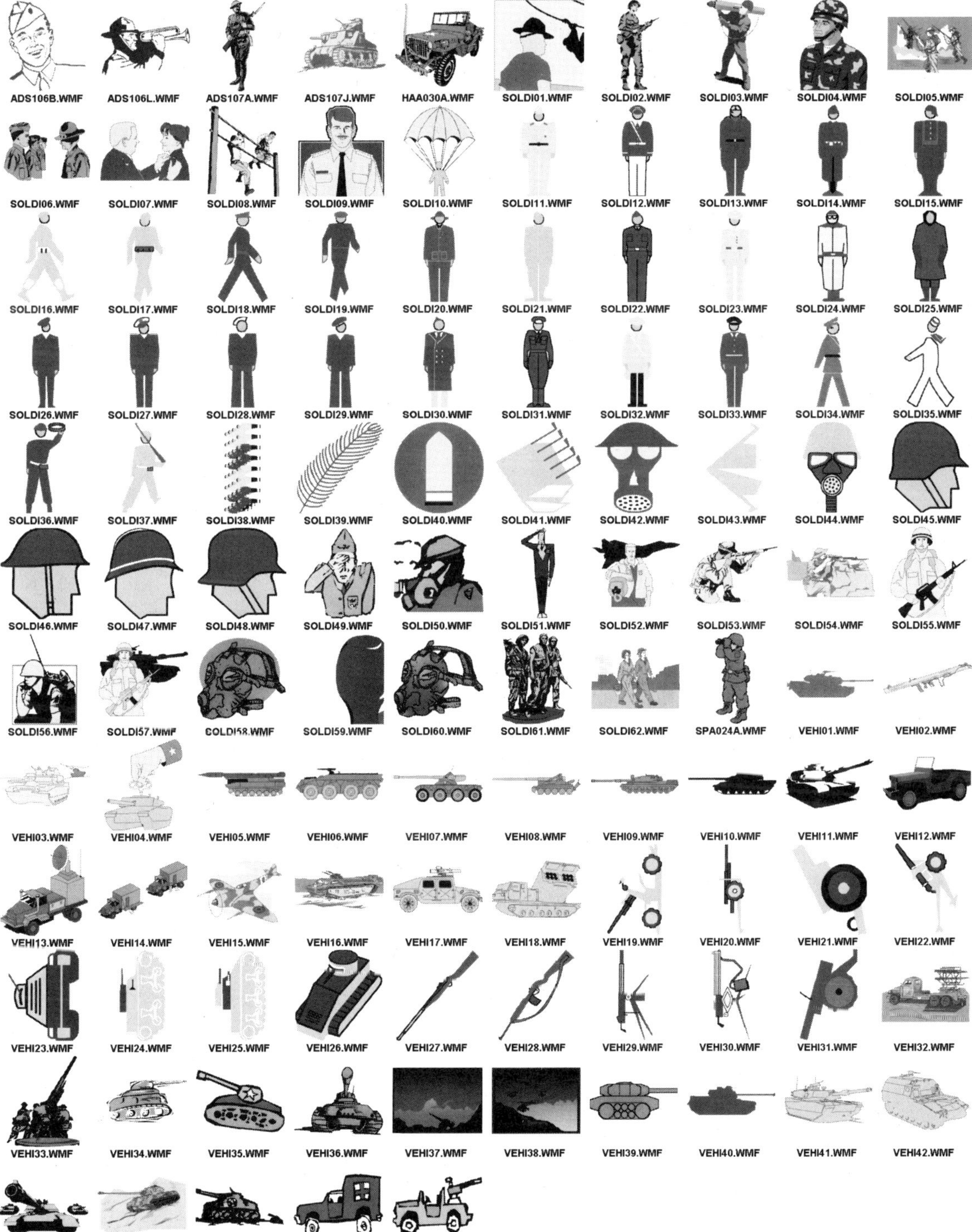

ADS106B.WMF ADS106L.WMF ADS107A.WMF ADS107J.WMF HAA030A.WMF SOLDI01.WMF SOLDI02.WMF SOLDI03.WMF SOLDI04.WMF SOLDI05.WMF

SOLDI06.WMF SOLDI07.WMF SOLDI08.WMF SOLDI09.WMF SOLDI10.WMF SOLDI11.WMF SOLDI12.WMF SOLDI13.WMF SOLDI14.WMF SOLDI15.WMF

SOLDI16.WMF SOLDI17.WMF SOLDI18.WMF SOLDI19.WMF SOLDI20.WMF SOLDI21.WMF SOLDI22.WMF SOLDI23.WMF SOLDI24.WMF SOLDI25.WMF

SOLDI26.WMF SOLDI27.WMF SOLDI28.WMF SOLDI29.WMF SOLDI30.WMF SOLDI31.WMF SOLDI32.WMF SOLDI33.WMF SOLDI34.WMF SOLDI35.WMF

SOLDI36.WMF SOLDI37.WMF SOLDI38.WMF SOLDI39.WMF SOLDI40.WMF SOLDI41.WMF SOLDI42.WMF SOLDI43.WMF SOLDI44.WMF SOLDI45.WMF

SOLDI46.WMF SOLDI47.WMF SOLDI48.WMF SOLDI49.WMF SOLDI50.WMF SOLDI51.WMF SOLDI52.WMF SOLDI53.WMF SOLDI54.WMF SOLDI55.WMF

SOLDI56.WMF SOLDI57.WMF SOLDI58.WMF SOLDI59.WMF SOLDI60.WMF SOLDI61.WMF SOLDI62.WMF SPA024A.WMF VEHI01.WMF VEHI02.WMF

VEHI03.WMF VEHI04.WMF VEHI05.WMF VEHI06.WMF VEHI07.WMF VEHI08.WMF VEHI09.WMF VEHI10.WMF VEHI11.WMF VEHI12.WMF

VEHI13.WMF VEHI14.WMF VEHI15.WMF VEHI16.WMF VEHI17.WMF VEHI18.WMF VEHI19.WMF VEHI20.WMF VEHI21.WMF VEHI22.WMF

VEHI23.WMF VEHI24.WMF VEHI25.WMF VEHI26.WMF VEHI27.WMF VEHI28.WMF VEHI29.WMF VEHI30.WMF VEHI31.WMF VEHI32.WMF

VEHI33.WMF VEHI34.WMF VEHI35.WMF VEHI36.WMF VEHI37.WMF VEHI38.WMF VEHI39.WMF VEHI40.WMF VEHI41.WMF VEHI42.WMF

VEHI43.WMF VEHI44.WMF VEHI45.WMF VEHI46.WMF VEHI47.WMF

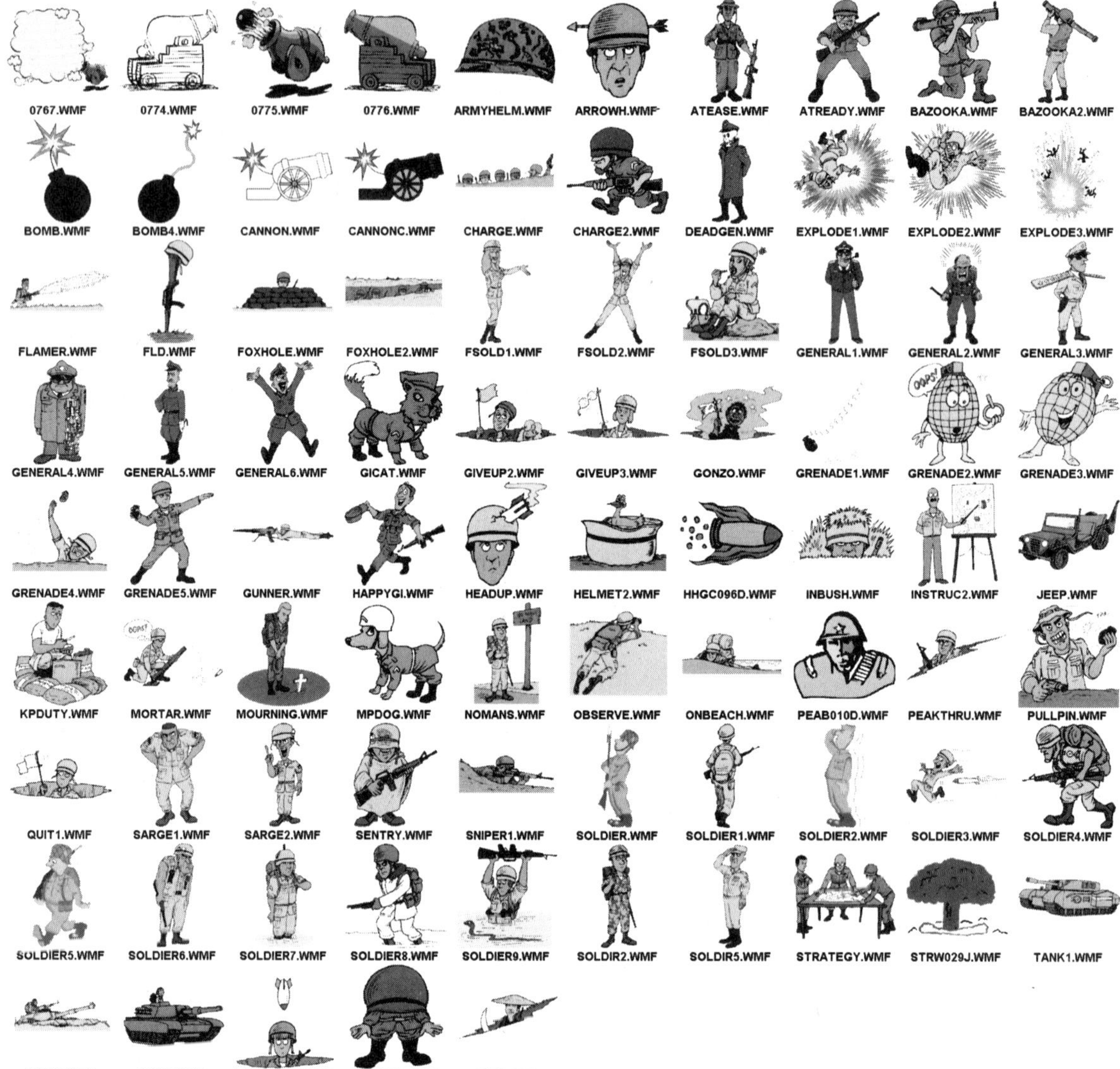
0767.WMF
0774.WMF
0775.WMF
0776.WMF
ARMYHELM.WMF
ARROWH.WMF
ATEASE.WMF
ATREADY.WMF
BAZOOKA.WMF
BAZOOKA2.WMF
BOMB.WMF
BOMB4.WMF
CANNON.WMF
CANNONC.WMF
CHARGE.WMF
CHARGE2.WMF
DEADGEN.WMF
EXPLODE1.WMF
EXPLODE2.WMF
EXPLODE3.WMF
FLAMER.WMF
FLD.WMF
FOXHOLE.WMF
FOXHOLE2.WMF
FSOLD1.WMF
FSOLD2.WMF
FSOLD3.WMF
GENERAL1.WMF
GENERAL2.WMF
GENERAL3.WMF
GENERAL4.WMF
GENERAL5.WMF
GENERAL6.WMF
GICAT.WMF
GIVEUP2.WMF
GIVEUP3.WMF
GONZO.WMF
GRENADE1.WMF
OOPS!
GRENADE2.WMF
GRENADE3.WMF
GRENADE4.WMF
GRENADE5.WMF
GUNNER.WMF
HAPPYGI.WMF
HEADUP.WMF
HELMET2.WMF
HHGC096D.WMF
INBUSH.WMF
INSTRUC2.WMF
JEEP.WMF
KPDUTY.WMF
OOPS!
MORTAR.WMF
MOURNING.WMF
MPDOG.WMF
NOMANS.WMF
OBSERVE.WMF
ONBEACH.WMF
PEAB010D.WMF
PEAKTHRU.WMF
PULLPIN.WMF
QUIT1.WMF
SARGE1.WMF
SARGE2.WMF
SENTRY.WMF
SNIPER1.WMF
SOLDIER.WMF
SOLDIER1.WMF
SOLDIER2.WMF
SOLDIER3.WMF
SOLDIER4.WMF
SOLDIER5.WMF
SOLDIER6.WMF
SOLDIER7.WMF
SOLDIER8.WMF
SOLDIER9.WMF
SOLDIR2.WMF
SOLDIR5.WMF
STRATEGY.WMF
STRW029J.WMF
TANK1.WMF
TANK2.WMF
TANK3.WMF
THEGONER.WMF
TIGHTLID.WMF
VIET.WMF

BIT1008.WMF GASI075M.WMF GEOSTAR.WMF GRBO004J.WMF GSTAR.WMF JETPATCH.WMF MARINCOR.WMF MEDAL.WMF MEDAL2.WMF MEDALSIL.WMF

NAVYACAD.WMF PD018C_1.WMF PD018CU.WMF PD018PCU.WMF PD018QCU.WMF PD018RCU.WMF PD018SCU.WMF PD018TCU.WMF PD018UCU.WMF PD018VCU.WMF

PD018WCU.WMF PD018XCU.WMF PD018YCU.WMF PD018ZCU.WMF SERGEANT.WMF STRW028J.WMF

Military • General

0214.WMF ADS104J.WMF ADVANCE.WMF ARMY.WMF AWRDHAND.WMF DEPTSTAT.WMF EUROFORC.WMF EVZONE.WMF FTSHTR.WMF GUARDSMN.WMF

IRA.WMF JETARGET.WMF JETPEACE.WMF MARINES.WMF MILITARY.WMF MINUTEMN.WMF MISSILE6.WMF NATLGARD.WMF NATLGRD2.WMF NAVY.WMF

R21624.WMF R21625.WMF RECRUIT.WMF RIFLES.WMF RUNWAY.WMF SGRENADE.WMF SHELTER.WMF SOLDIER3.WMF STGC008D.WMF STRATEGC.WMF

STRATGY.WMF STRETCHR.WMF STSI022D.WMF SURENDER.WMF TERRISM.WMF TRIDENT.WMF USPOWER.WMF VETERANS.WMF VETSALUT.WMF WAR.WMF

WESTPNT.WMF

WESTPONT.WMF

AIRRAID.WMF
ALLOTMNT.WMF
ANTIAIR.WMF
B24.WMF
CAMPS.WMF
CARRIER.WMF
CEMETRY.WMF
CHURCHLL.WMF
EDCN138.WMF
EDCN139.WMF
EDCN140.WMF
EDCN141.WMF
EDCN196.WMF
EVACUATE.WMF
FASHION.WMF
GASMASK.WMF
GUARDSMN.WMF
HIROSHMA.WMF
HITLER.WMF
IDCARD.WMF
MARINES.WMF
MONTY.WMF
MUSKETER.WMF
PD016CCU.WMF
PD016DCU.WMF
PD016ECU.WMF
PD016FCU.WMF
PD016GCU.WMF
PD016HCU.WMF
PD016ICU.WMF
PD016JCU.WMF
PD016KCU.WMF
PD016LCU.WMF
PD016MCU.WMF
PD016NCU.WMF
SAMURAI.WMF
TEA.WMF
VEDAY.WMF
VETERAN1.WMF
VIETNAM.WMF
VIETNAMM.WMF
YANKEE.WMF

ADS106C.WMF
ADS106D.WMF
ASI045M.WMF
PLANE01.WMF
PLANE02.WMF
PLANE03.WMF
PLANE04.WMF
PLANE05.WMF
PLANE06.WMF
PLANE07.WMF
SAILO01.WMF
SAILO02.WMF
SAILO03.WMF
SAILO04.WMF
SAILO05.WMF
SAILO06.WMF
SAILO07.WMF
SAILO08.WMF
SAILO09.WMF
SAILO10.WMF
SAILO11.WMF
SAILO12.WMF
SAILO13.WMF
SAILO14.WMF
SAILO15.WMF
SAILO16.WMF
SAILO17.WMF
SAILO18.WMF
SHIPS01.WMF
SHIPS02.WMF
SHIPS03.WMF
SHIPS04.WMF
SHIPS05.WMF
SHIPS06.WMF
SHIPS07.WMF
SHIPS08.WMF
SHIPS09.WMF
SHIPS10.WMF
SHIPS11.WMF
SHIPS12.WMF
SHIPS13.WMF
SHIPS14.WMF
SHIPS15.WMF
SHIPS16.WMF
SHIPS17.WMF
SHIPS18.WMF
SHIPS19.WMF
SHIPS20.WMF
SHIPS21.WMF
SHIPS22.WMF
SHIPS23.WMF
SHIPS24.WMF
SHIPS25.WMF
SHIPS26.WMF
SHIPS27.WMF
SHIPS28.WMF
SHIPS29.WMF
SHIPS30.WMF
SHIPS31.WMF
SHIPS32.WMF
SHIPS33.WMF
SHIPS34.WMF
SHIPS35.WMF
SHIPS36.WMF
SHIPS37.WMF
SHIPS38.WMF
SHIPS39.WMF

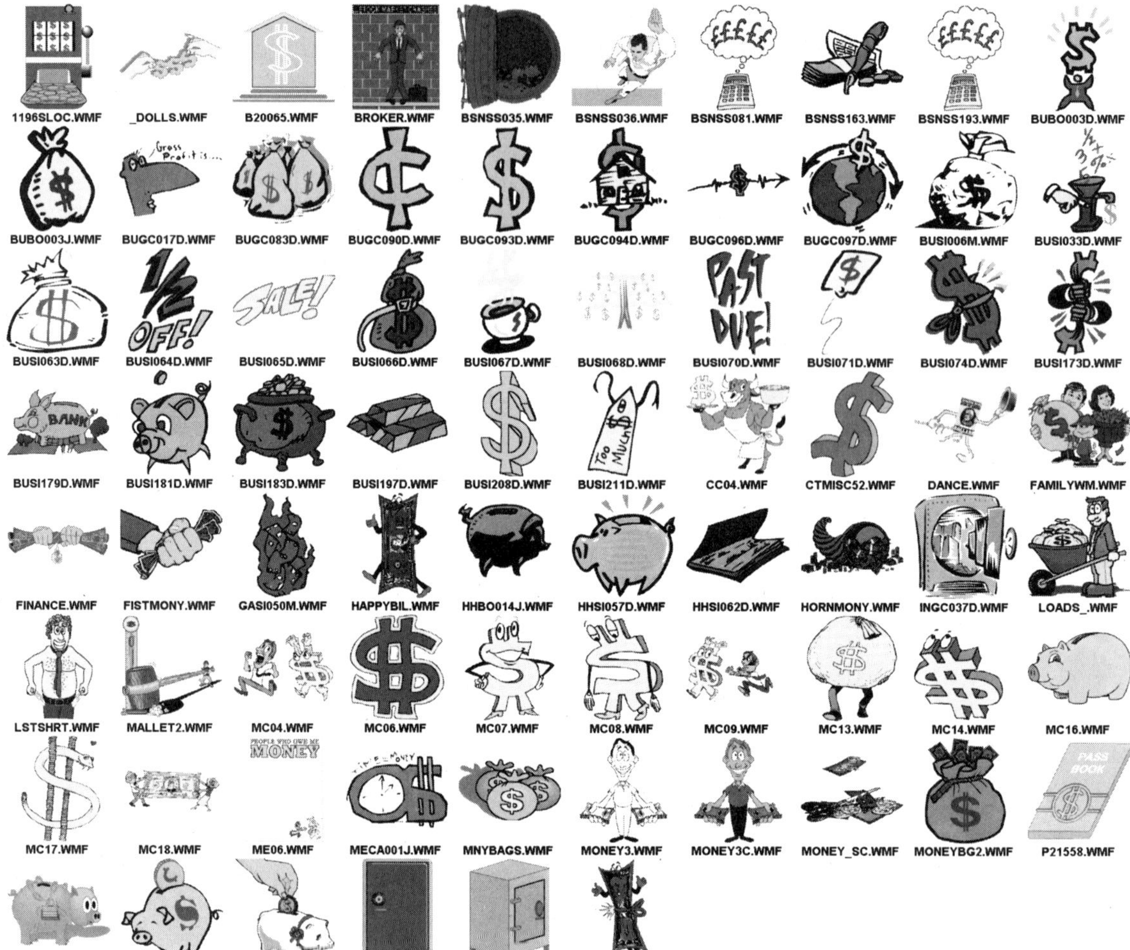
1196SLOC.WMF
_DOLLS.WMF
B20065.WMF
BROKER.WMF
BSNSS035.WMF
BSNSS036.WMF
BSNSS081.WMF
BSNSS163.WMF
BSNSS193.WMF
BUBO003D.WMF
BUBO003J.WMF
BUGC017D.WMF
BUGC083D.WMF
BUGC090D.WMF
BUGC093D.WMF
BUGC094D.WMF
BUGC096D.WMF
BUGC097D.WMF
BUSI006M.WMF
BUSI033D.WMF
BUSI063D.WMF
BUSI064D.WMF
BUSI065D.WMF
BUSI066D.WMF
BUSI067D.WMF
BUSI068D.WMF
BUSI070D.WMF
BUSI071D.WMF
BUSI074D.WMF
BUSI173D.WMF
BUSI179D.WMF
BUSI181D.WMF
BUSI183D.WMF
BUSI197D.WMF
BUSI208D.WMF
BUSI211D.WMF
CC04.WMF
CTMISC52.WMF
DANCE.WMF
FAMILYWM.WMF
FINANCE.WMF
FISTMONY.WMF
GASI050M.WMF
HAPPYBIL.WMF
HHBO014J.WMF
HHSI057D.WMF
HHSI062D.WMF
HORNMONY.WMF
INGC037D.WMF
LOADS_.WMF
LSTSHRT.WMF
MALLET2.WMF
MC04.WMF
MC06.WMF
MC07.WMF
MC08.WMF
MC09.WMF
MC13.WMF
MC14.WMF
MC16.WMF
MC17.WMF
MC18.WMF
ME06.WMF
MECA001J.WMF
MNYBAGS.WMF
MONEY3.WMF
MONEY3C.WMF
MONEY_SC.WMF
MONEYBG2.WMF
P21558.WMF
PIGBANK.WMF
PIGGYBNK.WMF
PIGYBANK.WMF
S21631.WMF
S21632.WMF
TIEDBILL.WMF

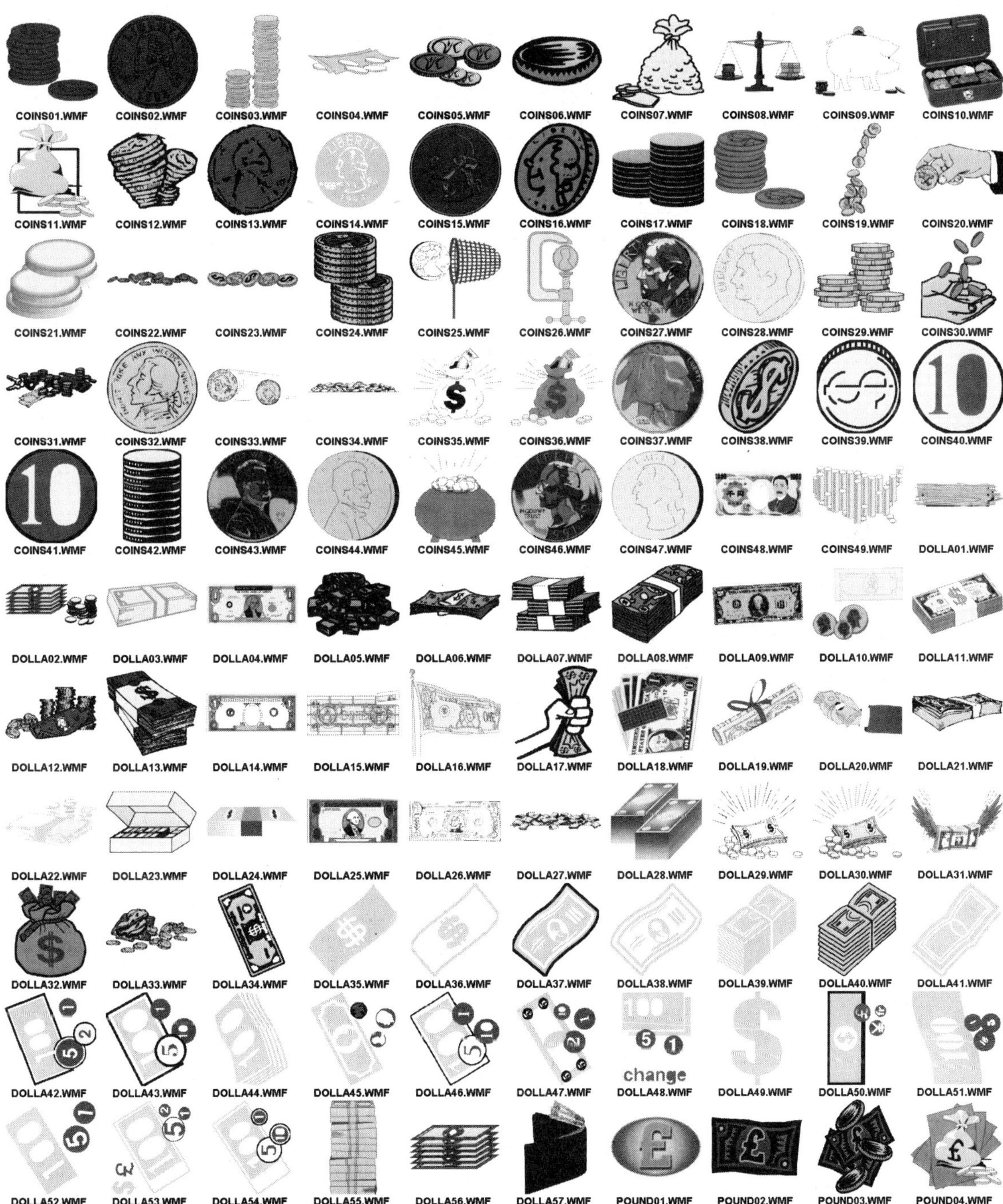

COINS01.WMF COINS02.WMF COINS03.WMF COINS04.WMF COINS05.WMF COINS06.WMF COINS07.WMF COINS08.WMF COINS09.WMF COINS10.WMF

COINS11.WMF COINS12.WMF COINS13.WMF COINS14.WMF COINS15.WMF COINS16.WMF COINS17.WMF COINS18.WMF COINS19.WMF COINS20.WMF

COINS21.WMF COINS22.WMF COINS23.WMF COINS24.WMF COINS25.WMF COINS26.WMF COINS27.WMF COINS28.WMF COINS29.WMF COINS30.WMF

COINS31.WMF COINS32.WMF COINS33.WMF COINS34.WMF COINS35.WMF COINS36.WMF COINS37.WMF COINS38.WMF COINS39.WMF COINS40.WMF

COINS41.WMF COINS42.WMF COINS43.WMF COINS44.WMF COINS45.WMF COINS46.WMF COINS47.WMF COINS48.WMF COINS49.WMF DOLLA01.WMF

DOLLA02.WMF DOLLA03.WMF DOLLA04.WMF DOLLA05.WMF DOLLA06.WMF DOLLA07.WMF DOLLA08.WMF DOLLA09.WMF DOLLA10.WMF DOLLA11.WMF

DOLLA12.WMF DOLLA13.WMF DOLLA14.WMF DOLLA15.WMF DOLLA16.WMF DOLLA17.WMF DOLLA18.WMF DOLLA19.WMF DOLLA20.WMF DOLLA21.WMF

DOLLA22.WMF DOLLA23.WMF DOLLA24.WMF DOLLA25.WMF DOLLA26.WMF DOLLA27.WMF DOLLA28.WMF DOLLA29.WMF DOLLA30.WMF DOLLA31.WMF

DOLLA32.WMF DOLLA33.WMF DOLLA34.WMF DOLLA35.WMF DOLLA36.WMF DOLLA37.WMF DOLLA38.WMF DOLLA39.WMF DOLLA40.WMF DOLLA41.WMF

DOLLA42.WMF DOLLA43.WMF DOLLA44.WMF DOLLA45.WMF DOLLA46.WMF DOLLA47.WMF DOLLA48.WMF DOLLA49.WMF DOLLA50.WMF DOLLA51.WMF

DOLLA52.WMF DOLLA53.WMF DOLLA54.WMF DOLLA55.WMF DOLLA56.WMF DOLLA57.WMF POUND01.WMF POUND02.WMF POUND03.WMF POUND04.WMF

POUND05.WMF

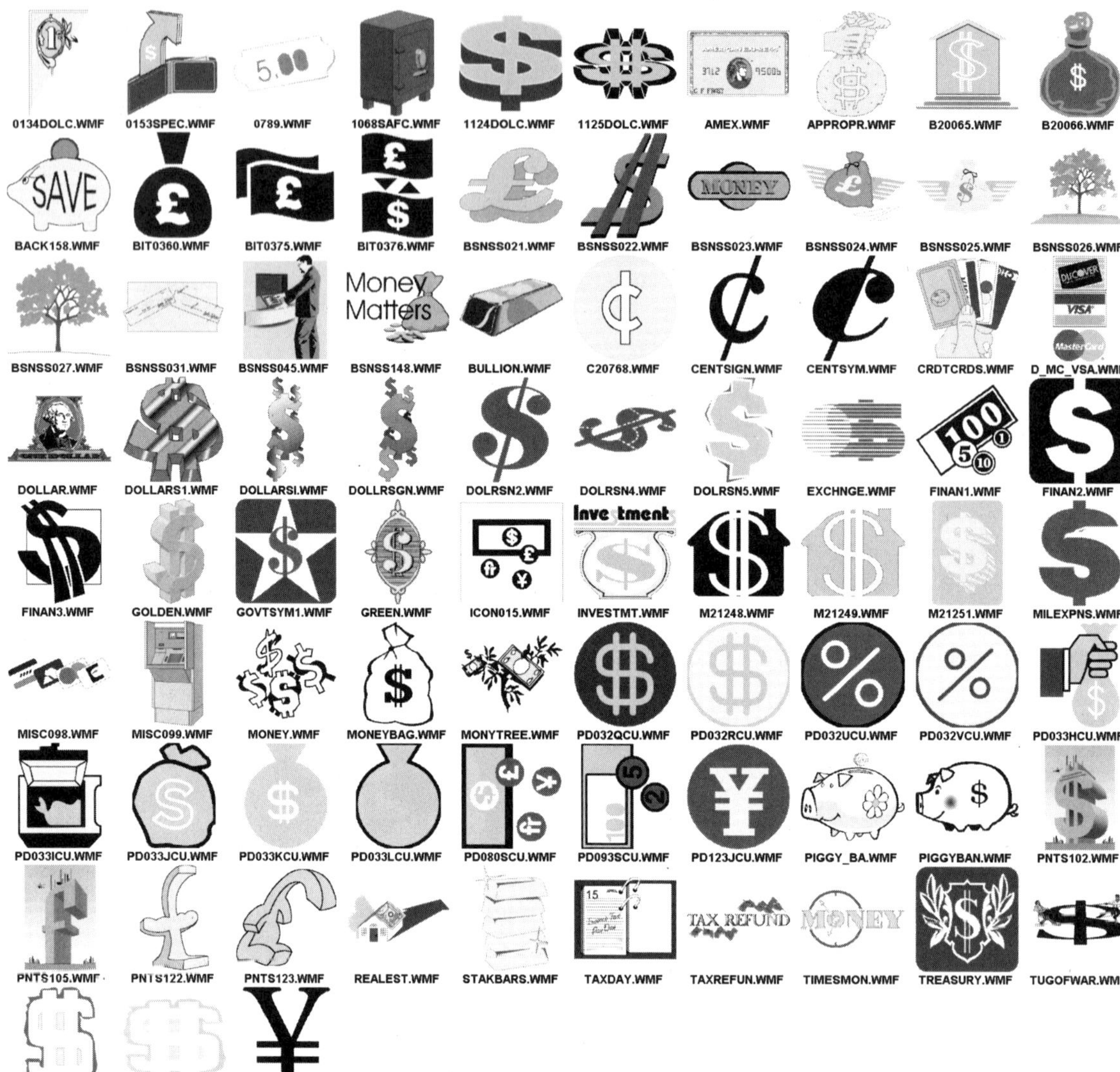
0134DOLC.WMF
0153SPEC.WMF
0789.WMF
1068SAFC.WMF
1124DOLC.WMF
1125DOLC.WMF
AMEX.WMF
APPROPR.WMF
B20065.WMF
B20066.WMF
BACK158.WMF
BIT0360.WMF
BIT0375.WMF
BIT0376.WMF
BSNSS021.WMF
BSNSS022.WMF
BSNSS023.WMF
BSNSS024.WMF
BSNSS025.WMF
BSNSS026.WMF
BSNSS027.WMF
BSNSS031.WMF
BSNSS045.WMF
BSNSS148.WMF
BULLION.WMF
C20768.WMF
CENTSIGN.WMF
CENTSYM.WMF
CRDTCRDS.WMF
D_MC_VSA.WMF
DOLLAR.WMF
DOLLARS1.WMF
DOLLARSI.WMF
DOLLRSGN.WMF
DOLRSN2.WMF
DOLRSN4.WMF
DOLRSN5.WMF
EXCHNGE.WMF
FINAN1.WMF
FINAN2.WMF
FINAN3.WMF
GOLDEN.WMF
GOVTSYM1.WMF
GREEN.WMF
ICON015.WMF
INVESTMT.WMF
M21248.WMF
M21249.WMF
M21251.WMF
MILEXPNS.WMF
MISC098.WMF
MISC099.WMF
MONEY.WMF
MONEYBAG.WMF
MONYTREE.WMF
PD032QCU.WMF
PD032RCU.WMF
PD032UCU.WMF
PD032VCU.WMF
PD033HCU.WMF
PD033ICU.WMF
PD033JCU.WMF
PD033KCU.WMF
PD033LCU.WMF
PD080SCU.WMF
PD093SCU.WMF
PD123JCU.WMF
PIGGY_BA.WMF
PIGGYBAN.WMF
PNTS102.WMF
PNTS105.WMF
PNTS122.WMF
PNTS123.WMF
REALEST.WMF
STAKBARS.WMF
TAXDAY.WMF
TAXREFUN.WMF
TIMESMON.WMF
TREASURY.WMF
TUGOFWAR.WMF
W21909.WMF
W21910.WMF
YEN.WMF

AR18.WMF
AR19.WMF
AR20.WMF
AR22.WMF
AR23.WMF
AR24.WMF
AR25.WMF
AR39.WMF
AR41.WMF
BRNHLD.WMF
E21.WMF
E22.WMF
E23.WMF
E24.WMF
E37.WMF
ENBO002J.WMF
PEACE
ENCA011J.WMF
ENCA013D.WMF
ENCA015D.WMF
ENGC029D.WMF
ENGC030D.WMF
ENGC031D.WMF
ENGC032D.WMF
ENGC033D.WMF
ENGC034D.WMF
ENGC035D.WMF
ENGC036D.WMF
ENGC037D.WMF
ENKC003J.WMF
ENKC005J.WMF
ENKC007J.WMF
ENRW002J.WMF
ENSI023D.WMF
ENSI034D.WMF
ENSS010D.WMF
ENSS021D.WMF
ENSS028D.WMF
ENSS029D.WMF
ENSS030D.WMF
ENSS031D.WMF
ENSS040D.WMF
FLUTEP.WMF
HPI008D.WMF
MUSICALR.WMF
PEBO015J.WMF
VKNG.WMF

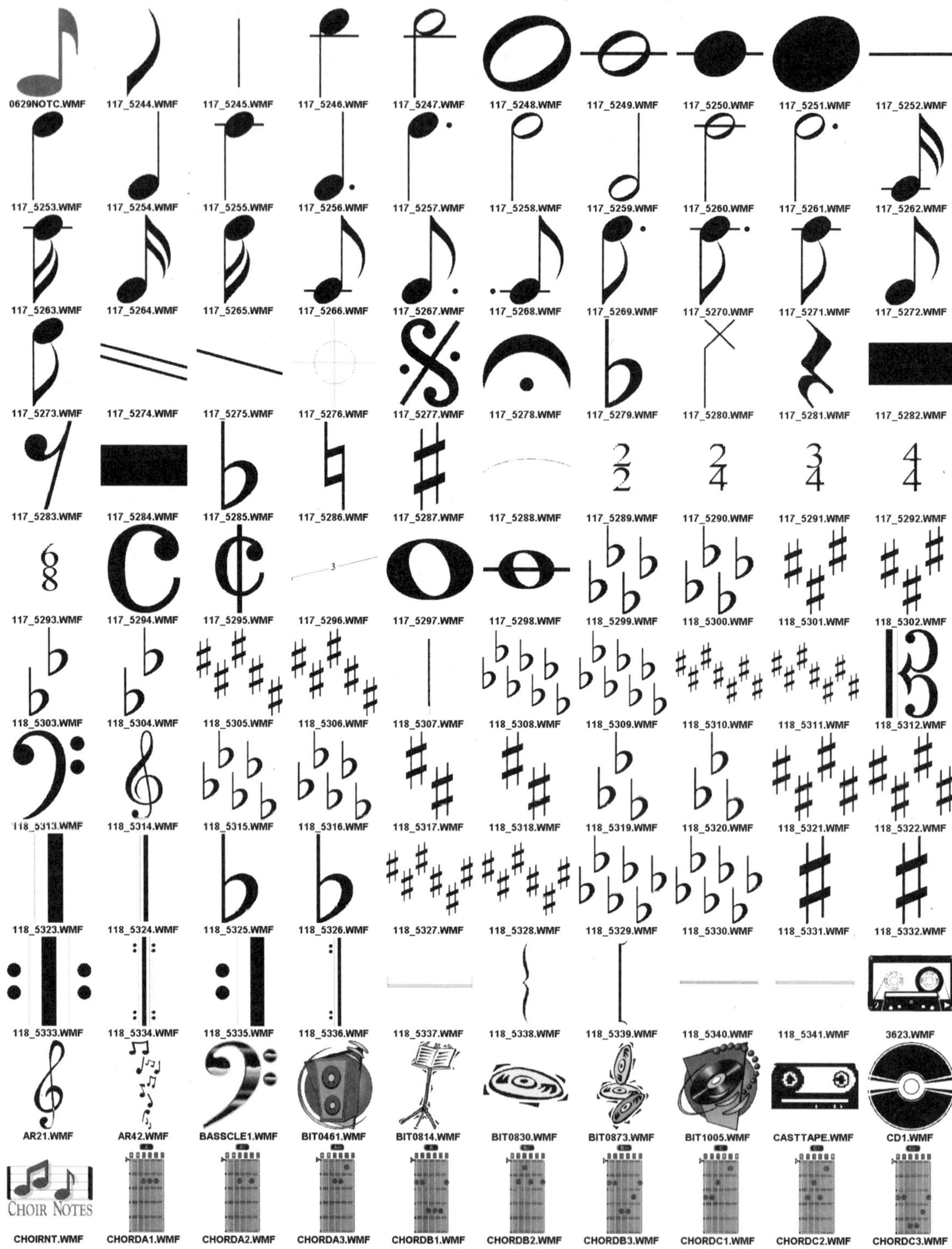
0629NOTC.WMF
117_5244.WMF
117_5245.WMF
117_5246.WMF
117_5247.WMF
117_5248.WMF
117_5249.WMF
117_5250.WMF
117_5251.WMF
117_5252.WMF
117_5253.WMF
117_5254.WMF
117_5255.WMF
117_5256.WMF
117_5257.WMF
117_5258.WMF
117_5259.WMF
117_5260.WMF
117_5261.WMF
117_5262.WMF
117_5263.WMF
117_5264.WMF
117_5265.WMF
117_5266.WMF
117_5267.WMF
117_5268.WMF
117_5269.WMF
117_5270.WMF
117_5271.WMF
117_5272.WMF
117_5273.WMF
117_5274.WMF
117_5275.WMF
117_5276.WMF
117_5277.WMF
117_5278.WMF
117_5279.WMF
117_5280.WMF
117_5281.WMF
117_5282.WMF
117_5283.WMF
117_5284.WMF
117_5285.WMF
117_5286.WMF
117_5287.WMF
117_5288.WMF
117_5289.WMF
117_5290.WMF
117_5291.WMF
117_5292.WMF
117_5293.WMF
117_5294.WMF
117_5295.WMF
117_5296.WMF
117_5297.WMF
117_5298.WMF
118_5299.WMF
118_5300.WMF
118_5301.WMF
118_5302.WMF
118_5303.WMF
118_5304.WMF
118_5305.WMF
118_5306.WMF
118_5307.WMF
118_5308.WMF
118_5309.WMF
118_5310.WMF
118_5311.WMF
118_5312.WMF
118_5313.WMF
118_5314.WMF
118_5315.WMF
118_5316.WMF
118_5317.WMF
118_5318.WMF
118_5319.WMF
118_5320.WMF
118_5321.WMF
118_5322.WMF
118_5323.WMF
118_5324.WMF
118_5325.WMF
118_5326.WMF
118_5327.WMF
118_5328.WMF
118_5329.WMF
118_5330.WMF
118_5331.WMF
118_5332.WMF
118_5333.WMF
118_5334.WMF
118_5335.WMF
118_5336.WMF
118_5337.WMF
118_5338.WMF
118_5339.WMF
118_5340.WMF
118_5341.WMF
3623.WMF
AR21.WMF
AR42.WMF
BASSCLE1.WMF
BIT0461.WMF
BIT0814.WMF
BIT0830.WMF
BIT0873.WMF
BIT1005.WMF
CASTTAPE.WMF
CD1.WMF
CHOIR NOTES
CHOIRNT.WMF
CHORDA1.WMF
CHORDA2.WMF
CHORDA3.WMF
CHORDB1.WMF
CHORDB2.WMF
CHORDB3.WMF
CHORDC1.WMF
CHORDC2.WMF
CHORDC3.WMF

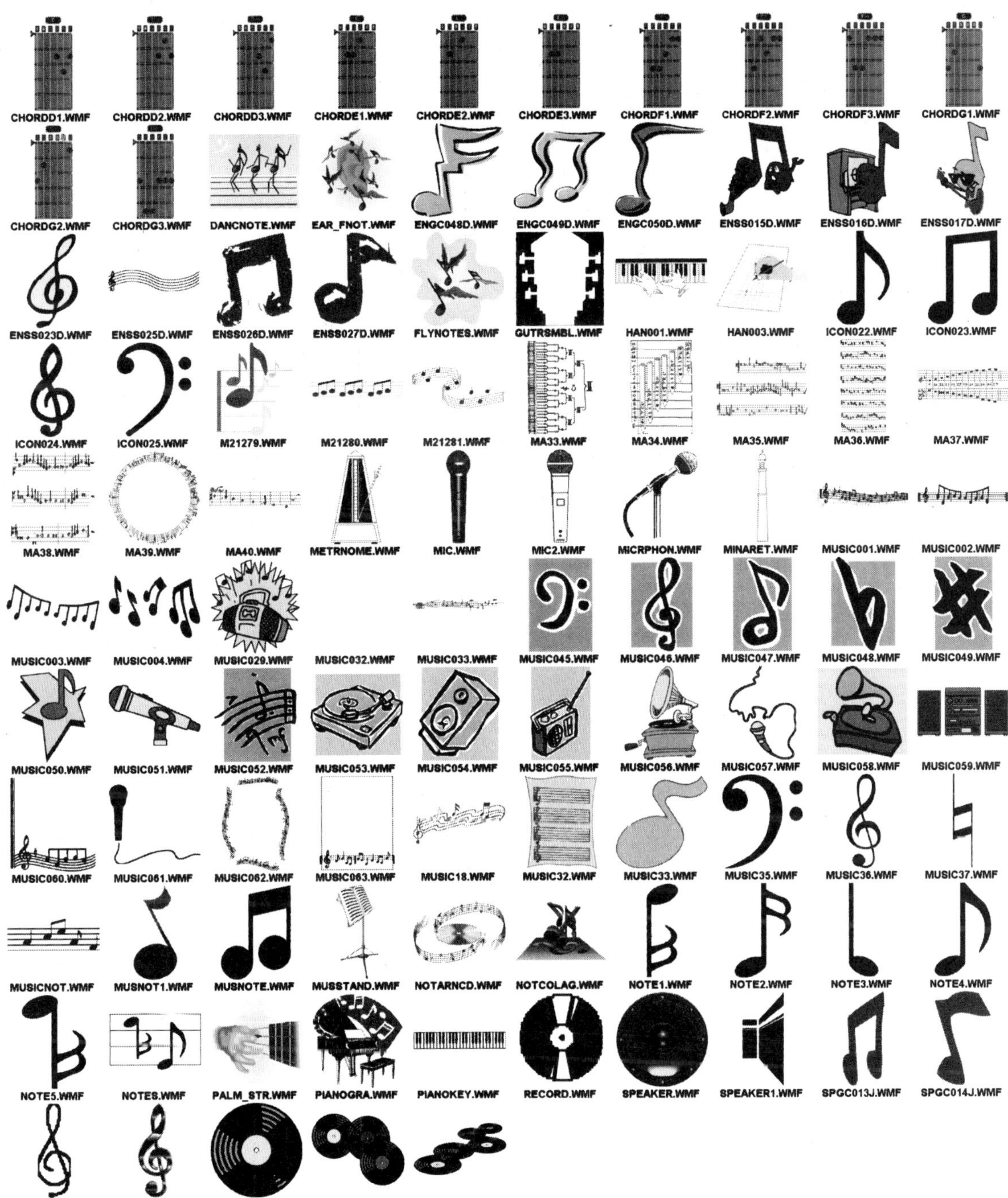
CHORDD1.WMF
CHORDD2.WMF
CHORDD3.WMF
CHORDE1.WMF
CHORDE2.WMF
CHORDE3.WMF
CHORDF1.WMF
CHORDF2.WMF
CHORDF3.WMF
CHORDG1.WMF
CHORDG2.WMF
CHORDG3.WMF
DANCNOTE.WMF
EAR_FNOT.WMF
ENGC048D.WMF
ENGC049D.WMF
ENGC050D.WMF
ENSS015D.WMF
ENSS016D.WMF
ENSS017D.WMF
ENSS023D.WMF
ENSS025D.WMF
ENSS026D.WMF
ENSS027D.WMF
FLYNOTES.WMF
GUTRSMBL.WMF
HAN001.WMF
HAN003.WMF
ICON022.WMF
ICON023.WMF
ICON024.WMF
ICON025.WMF
M21279.WMF
M21280.WMF
M21281.WMF
MA33.WMF
MA34.WMF
MA35.WMF
MA36.WMF
MA37.WMF
MA38.WMF
MA39.WMF
MA40.WMF
METRNOME.WMF
MIC.WMF
MIC2.WMF
MICRPHON.WMF
MINARET.WMF
MUSIC001.WMF
MUSIC002.WMF
MUSIC003.WMF
MUSIC004.WMF
MUSIC029.WMF
MUSIC032.WMF
MUSIC033.WMF
MUSIC045.WMF
MUSIC046.WMF
MUSIC047.WMF
MUSIC048.WMF
MUSIC049.WMF
MUSIC050.WMF
MUSIC051.WMF
MUSIC052.WMF
MUSIC053.WMF
MUSIC054.WMF
MUSIC055.WMF
MUSIC056.WMF
MUSIC057.WMF
MUSIC058.WMF
MUSIC059.WMF
MUSIC060.WMF
MUSIC061.WMF
MUSIC062.WMF
MUSIC063.WMF
MUSIC18.WMF
MUSIC32.WMF
MUSIC33.WMF
MUSIC35.WMF
MUSIC36.WMF
MUSIC37.WMF
MUSICNOT.WMF
MUSNOT1.WMF
MUSNOTE.WMF
MUSSTAND.WMF
NOTARNCD.WMF
NOTCOLAG.WMF
NOTE1.WMF
NOTE2.WMF
NOTE3.WMF
NOTE4.WMF
NOTE5.WMF
NOTES.WMF
PALM_STR.WMF
PIANOGRA.WMF
PIANOKEY.WMF
RECORD.WMF
SPEAKER.WMF
SPEAKER1.WMF
SPGC013J.WMF
SPGC014J.WMF
TREBCLEF.WMF
TREBLECL.WMF
VINYL01.WMF
VINYL02.WMF
VINYL03.WMF

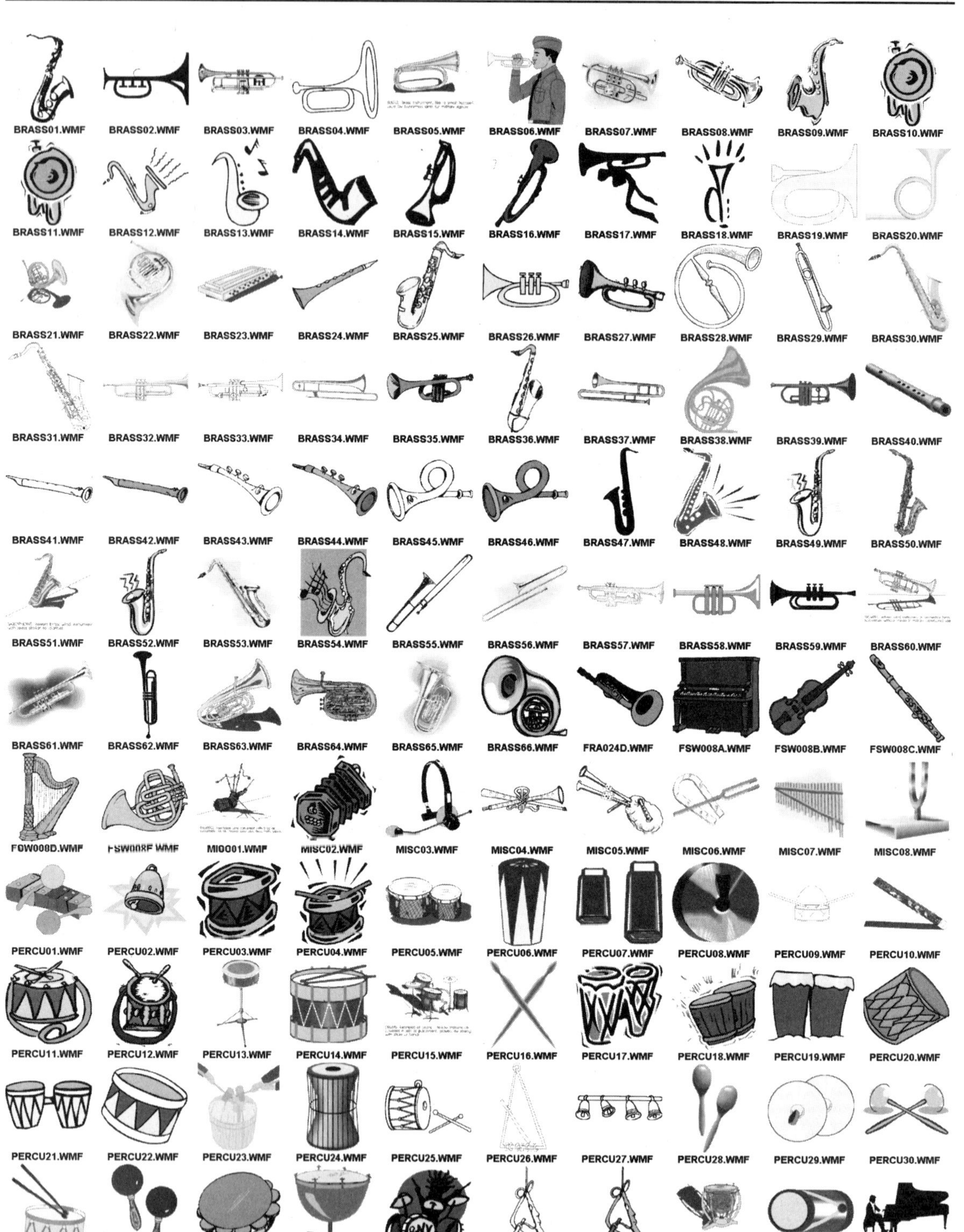

BRASS01.WMF BRASS02.WMF BRASS03.WMF BRASS04.WMF BRASS05.WMF BRASS06.WMF BRASS07.WMF BRASS08.WMF BRASS09.WMF BRASS10.WMF
BRASS11.WMF BRASS12.WMF BRASS13.WMF BRASS14.WMF BRASS15.WMF BRASS16.WMF BRASS17.WMF BRASS18.WMF BRASS19.WMF BRASS20.WMF
BRASS21.WMF BRASS22.WMF BRASS23.WMF BRASS24.WMF BRASS25.WMF BRASS26.WMF BRASS27.WMF BRASS28.WMF BRASS29.WMF BRASS30.WMF
BRASS31.WMF BRASS32.WMF BRASS33.WMF BRASS34.WMF BRASS35.WMF BRASS36.WMF BRASS37.WMF BRASS38.WMF BRASS39.WMF BRASS40.WMF
BRASS41.WMF BRASS42.WMF BRASS43.WMF BRASS44.WMF BRASS45.WMF BRASS46.WMF BRASS47.WMF BRASS48.WMF BRASS49.WMF BRASS50.WMF
BRASS51.WMF BRASS52.WMF BRASS53.WMF BRASS54.WMF BRASS55.WMF BRASS56.WMF BRASS57.WMF BRASS58.WMF BRASS59.WMF BRASS60.WMF
BRASS61.WMF BRASS62.WMF BRASS63.WMF BRASS64.WMF BRASS65.WMF BRASS66.WMF FRA024D.WMF FSW008A.WMF FSW008B.WMF FSW008C.WMF
FSW008D.WMF FSW008E.WMF MISC01.WMF MISC02.WMF MISC03.WMF MISC04.WMF MISC05.WMF MISC06.WMF MISC07.WMF MISC08.WMF
PERCU01.WMF PERCU02.WMF PERCU03.WMF PERCU04.WMF PERCU05.WMF PERCU06.WMF PERCU07.WMF PERCU08.WMF PERCU09.WMF PERCU10.WMF
PERCU11.WMF PERCU12.WMF PERCU13.WMF PERCU14.WMF PERCU15.WMF PERCU16.WMF PERCU17.WMF PERCU18.WMF PERCU19.WMF PERCU20.WMF
PERCU21.WMF PERCU22.WMF PERCU23.WMF PERCU24.WMF PERCU25.WMF PERCU26.WMF PERCU27.WMF PERCU28.WMF PERCU29.WMF PERCU30.WMF
PERCU31.WMF PERCU32.WMF PERCU33.WMF PERCU34.WMF PERCU35.WMF PERCU36.WMF PERCU37.WMF PERCU38.WMF PERCU39.WMF PIANO01.WMF

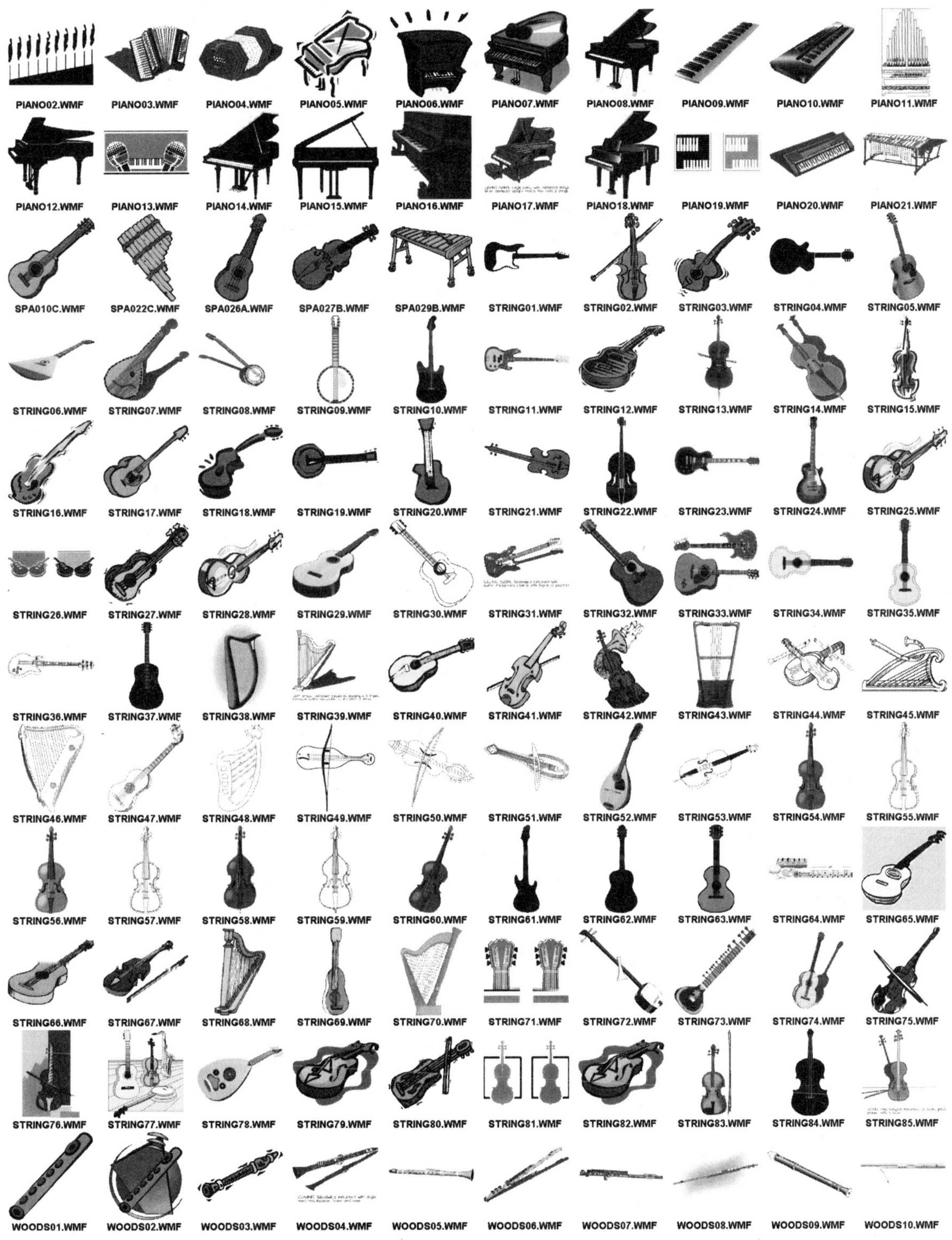
PIANO02.WMF
PIANO03.WMF
PIANO04.WMF
PIANO05.WMF
PIANO06.WMF
PIANO07.WMF
PIANO08.WMF
PIANO09.WMF
PIANO10.WMF
PIANO11.WMF
PIANO12.WMF
PIANO13.WMF
PIANO14.WMF
PIANO15.WMF
PIANO16.WMF
PIANO17.WMF
PIANO18.WMF
PIANO19.WMF
PIANO20.WMF
PIANO21.WMF
SPA010C.WMF
SPA022C.WMF
SPA026A.WMF
SPA027B.WMF
SPA029B.WMF
STRING01.WMF
STRING02.WMF
STRING03.WMF
STRING04.WMF
STRING05.WMF
STRING06.WMF
STRING07.WMF
STRING08.WMF
STRING09.WMF
STRING10.WMF
STRING11.WMF
STRING12.WMF
STRING13.WMF
STRING14.WMF
STRING15.WMF
STRING16.WMF
STRING17.WMF
STRING18.WMF
STRING19.WMF
STRING20.WMF
STRING21.WMF
STRING22.WMF
STRING23.WMF
STRING24.WMF
STRING25.WMF
STRING26.WMF
STRING27.WMF
STRING28.WMF
STRING29.WMF
STRING30.WMF
STRING31.WMF
STRING32.WMF
STRING33.WMF
STRING34.WMF
STRING35.WMF
STRING36.WMF
STRING37.WMF
STRING38.WMF
STRING39.WMF
STRING40.WMF
STRING41.WMF
STRING42.WMF
STRING43.WMF
STRING44.WMF
STRING45.WMF
STRING46.WMF
STRING47.WMF
STRING48.WMF
STRING49.WMF
STRING50.WMF
STRING51.WMF
STRING52.WMF
STRING53.WMF
STRING54.WMF
STRING55.WMF
STRING56.WMF
STRING57.WMF
STRING58.WMF
STRING59.WMF
STRING60.WMF
STRING61.WMF
STRING62.WMF
STRING63.WMF
STRING64.WMF
STRING65.WMF
STRING66.WMF
STRING67.WMF
STRING68.WMF
STRING69.WMF
STRING70.WMF
STRING71.WMF
STRING72.WMF
STRING73.WMF
STRING74.WMF
STRING75.WMF
STRING76.WMF
STRING77.WMF
STRING78.WMF
STRING79.WMF
STRING80.WMF
STRING81.WMF
STRING82.WMF
STRING83.WMF
STRING84.WMF
STRING85.WMF
WOODS01.WMF
WOODS02.WMF
WOODS03.WMF
WOODS04.WMF
WOODS05.WMF
WOODS06.WMF
WOODS07.WMF
WOODS08.WMF
WOODS09.WMF
WOODS10.WMF

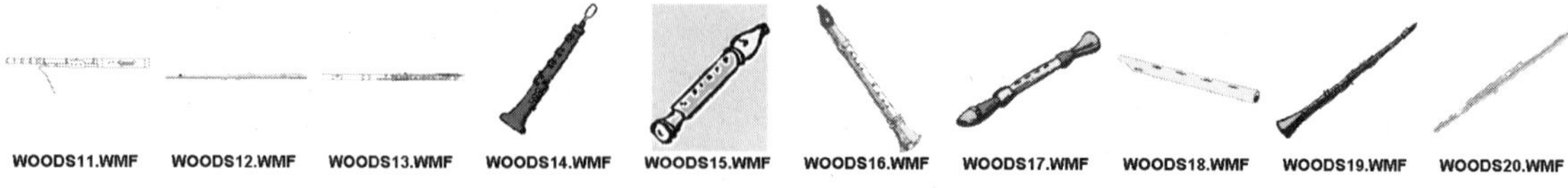

WOODS11.WMF WOODS12.WMF WOODS13.WMF WOODS14.WMF WOODS15.WMF WOODS16.WMF WOODS17.WMF WOODS18.WMF WOODS19.WMF WOODS20.WMF

WOODS21.WMF

Music • Miscellaneous (MISC)

1623.WMF 2201.WMF 2203.WMF 2204.WMF 2205.WMF 2206.WMF 2207.WMF A17BB.WMF A17DB.WMF A18EB.WMF

A20AB.WMF A20FB.WMF A20GB.WMF BSNSS185.WMF BSNSS186.WMF CHOIRNWS.WMF CHORNTE1.WMF COMM039.WMF ENJOYTHE.WMF ENSS022D.WMF

EV037.WMF GRAMPHON.WMF GRMAPHN.WMF HHCA069J.WMF JUKEBOX.WMF MICROPHO.WMF MUSIC027.WMF MUSIC028.WMF MUSIC030.WMF MUSIC064.WMF

MUSIC1.WMF MUSIC18.WMF MUSIC2.WMF MUSICFRA.WMF MUSICHEA.WMF OFFICE32.WMF PD043CU.WMF PD043MCU.WMF PD043OCU.WMF PD043VCU.WMF

RECORD.WMF REEL5.WMF SPGC114D.WMF SYMBL100.WMF SYMBL110.WMF SYMBL111.WMF SYMBL112.WMF TAPE.WMF TAPE1.WMF

0155.WMF
0167MANC.WMF
1235CHIC.WMF
1236CONC.WMF
1243MANC.WMF
1245PLAC.WMF
1246PLAC.WMF
1247SINC.WMF
1617.WMF
1620.WMF
1621.WMF
1622.WMF
2988.WMF
2989.WMF
2992.WMF
2993.WMF
2994.WMF
2997.WMF
2998.WMF
4426.WMF
ART003A.WMF
BACH.WMF
BAND01.WMF
BAND02.WMF
BAND03.WMF
BAND04.WMF
BAND05.WMF
BAND06.WMF
BAND07.WMF
BAND08.WMF
BAND09.WMF
BAND10.WMF
BAND11.WMF
BANDLEAD.WMF
BANJOPLY.WMF
BASSPLAY.WMF
BEETHOVN.WMF
BIZET.WMF
BNJOPLYR.WMF
CC28.WMF
CHOPIN.WMF
CONDUCT.WMF
CONDUCTO.WMF
CONDUCTR.WMF
DRUMCOLO.WMF
ELGAR.WMF
ENSS002J.WMF
FA10.WMF
GUITPLR.WMF
HM02.WMF
HM04.WMF
HM05.WMF
HM06.WMF
HM07.WMF
HM08.WMF
HM09.WMF
HM10.WMF
HM11.WMF
JA07.WMF
JAZZPLAY.WMF
LUTE.WMF
MANWCYMB.WMF
MONKEYW_.WMF
MUSIC034.WMF
MUSIC035.WMF
MUSIC036.WMF
MUSIC037.WMF
MUSIC038.WMF
MUSIC039.WMF
MUSIC040.WMF
ONSTAGE1.WMF
ONSTAGE2.WMF
ONSTAGE4.WMF
ONSTAGE5.WMF
ONSTAGE9.WMF
ONSTAGEA.WMF
ONSTAGEB.WMF
ONSTAGEC.WMF
OPERA.WMF
OPERA1.WMF
ORCHSILH.WMF
PLAYHARP.WMF
PLAYPIAN.WMF
ROCKER.WMF
SHOWMAN.WMF
SINGER.WMF
SINGER2.WMF
SINGRFM.WMF
SINGRMAL.WMF
STRAUSS.WMF
SX.WMF
TRIO.WMF
TRUMPETP.WMF
TRUMPLR.WMF
VIOLINST.WMF
VOLN.WMF

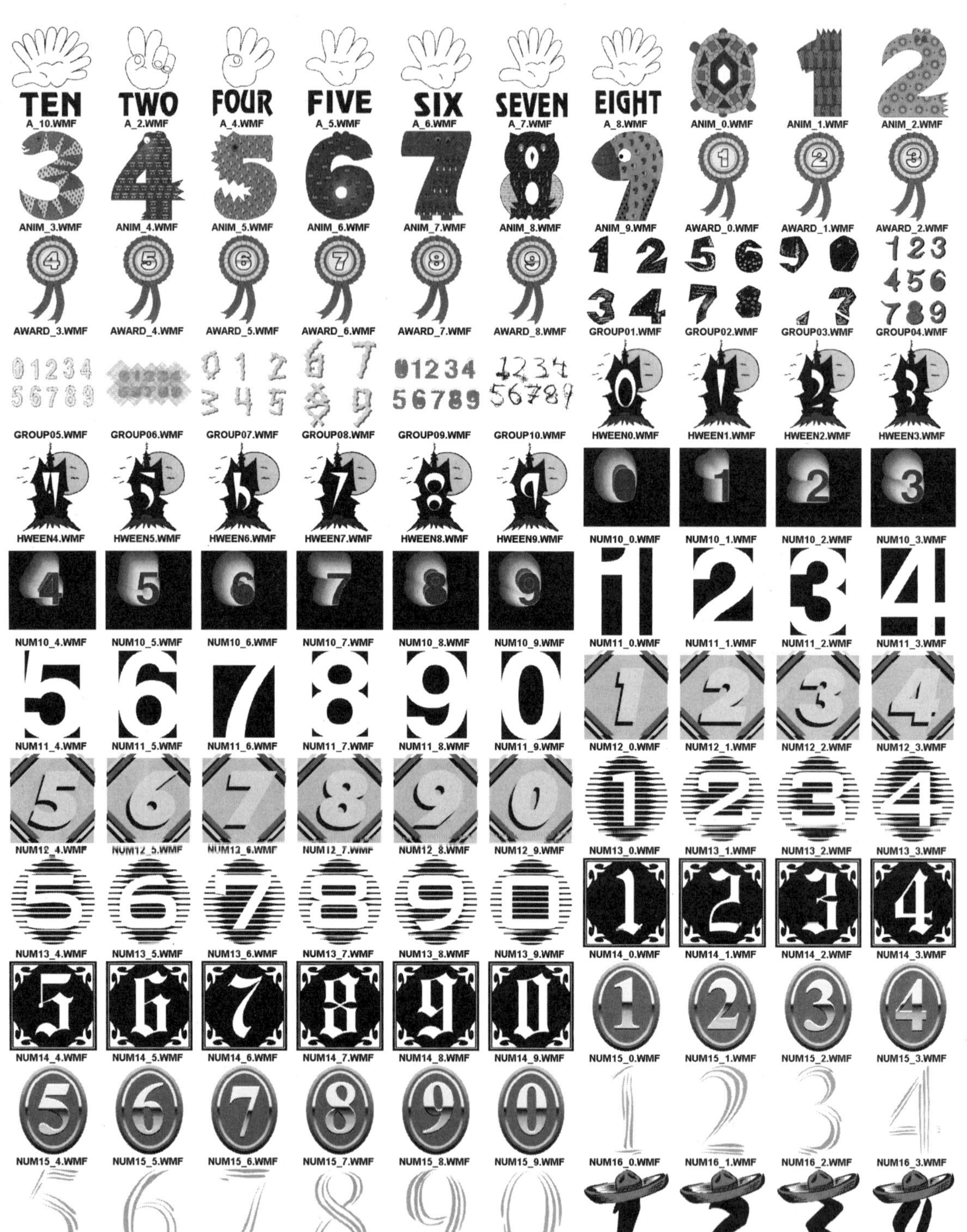
TEN
A_10.WMF
TWO
A_2.WMF
FOUR
A_4.WMF
FIVE
A_5.WMF
SIX
A_6.WMF
SEVEN
A_7.WMF
EIGHT
A_8.WMF
ANIM_0.WMF
ANIM_1.WMF
ANIM_2.WMF
ANIM_3.WMF
ANIM_4.WMF
ANIM_5.WMF
ANIM_6.WMF
ANIM_7.WMF
ANIM_8.WMF
ANIM_9.WMF
AWARD_0.WMF
AWARD_1.WMF
AWARD_2.WMF
AWARD_3.WMF
AWARD_4.WMF
AWARD_5.WMF
AWARD_6.WMF
AWARD_7.WMF
AWARD_8.WMF
GROUP01.WMF
GROUP02.WMF
GROUP03.WMF
GROUP04.WMF
GROUP05.WMF
GROUP06.WMF
GROUP07.WMF
GROUP08.WMF
GROUP09.WMF
GROUP10.WMF
HWEEN0.WMF
HWEEN1.WMF
HWEEN2.WMF
HWEEN3.WMF
HWEEN4.WMF
HWEEN5.WMF
HWEEN6.WMF
HWEEN7.WMF
HWEEN8.WMF
HWEEN9.WMF
NUM10_0.WMF
NUM10_1.WMF
NUM10_2.WMF
NUM10_3.WMF
NUM10_4.WMF
NUM10_5.WMF
NUM10_6.WMF
NUM10_7.WMF
NUM10_8.WMF
NUM10_9.WMF
NUM11_0.WMF
NUM11_1.WMF
NUM11_2.WMF
NUM11_3.WMF
NUM11_4.WMF
NUM11_5.WMF
NUM11_6.WMF
NUM11_7.WMF
NUM11_8.WMF
NUM11_9.WMF
NUM12_0.WMF
NUM12_1.WMF
NUM12_2.WMF
NUM12_3.WMF
NUM12_4.WMF
NUM12_5.WMF
NUM12_6.WMF
NUM12_7.WMF
NUM12_8.WMF
NUM12_9.WMF
NUM13_0.WMF
NUM13_1.WMF
NUM13_2.WMF
NUM13_3.WMF
NUM13_4.WMF
NUM13_5.WMF
NUM13_6.WMF
NUM13_7.WMF
NUM13_8.WMF
NUM13_9.WMF
NUM14_0.WMF
NUM14_1.WMF
NUM14_2.WMF
NUM14_3.WMF
NUM14_4.WMF
NUM14_5.WMF
NUM14_6.WMF
NUM14_7.WMF
NUM14_8.WMF
NUM14_9.WMF
NUM15_0.WMF
NUM15_1.WMF
NUM15_2.WMF
NUM15_3.WMF
NUM15_4.WMF
NUM15_5.WMF
NUM15_6.WMF
NUM15_7.WMF
NUM15_8.WMF
NUM15_9.WMF
NUM16_0.WMF
NUM16_1.WMF
NUM16_2.WMF
NUM16_3.WMF
NUM16_4.WMF
NUM16_5.WMF
NUM16_6.WMF
NUM16_7.WMF
NUM16_8.WMF
NUM16_9.WMF
NUM17_0.WMF
NUM17_1.WMF
NUM17_2.WMF
NUM17_3.WMF

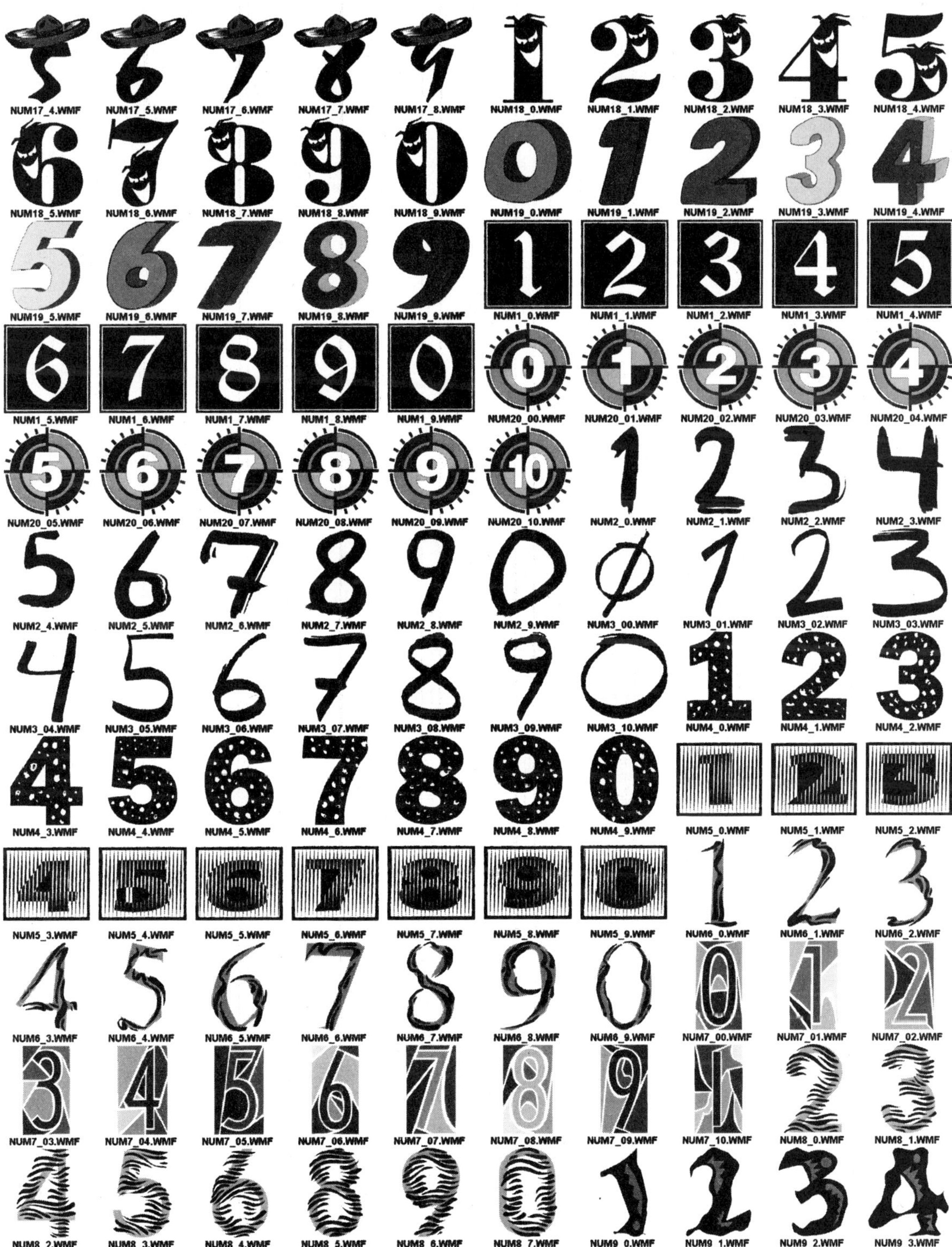
NUM17_4.WMF NUM17_5.WMF NUM17_6.WMF NUM17_7.WMF NUM17_8.WMF NUM18_0.WMF NUM18_1.WMF NUM18_2.WMF NUM18_3.WMF NUM18_4.WMF
NUM18_5.WMF NUM18_6.WMF NUM18_7.WMF NUM18_8.WMF NUM18_9.WMF NUM19_0.WMF NUM19_1.WMF NUM19_2.WMF NUM19_3.WMF NUM19_4.WMF
NUM19_5.WMF NUM19_6.WMF NUM19_7.WMF NUM19_8.WMF NUM19_9.WMF NUM1_0.WMF NUM1_1.WMF NUM1_2.WMF NUM1_3.WMF NUM1_4.WMF
NUM1_5.WMF NUM1_6.WMF NUM1_7.WMF NUM1_8.WMF NUM1_9.WMF NUM20_00.WMF NUM20_01.WMF NUM20_02.WMF NUM20_03.WMF NUM20_04.WMF
NUM20_05.WMF NUM20_06.WMF NUM20_07.WMF NUM20_08.WMF NUM20_09.WMF NUM20_10.WMF NUM2_0.WMF NUM2_1.WMF NUM2_2.WMF NUM2_3.WMF
NUM2_4.WMF NUM2_5.WMF NUM2_6.WMF NUM2_7.WMF NUM2_8.WMF NUM2_9.WMF NUM3_00.WMF NUM3_01.WMF NUM3_02.WMF NUM3_03.WMF
NUM3_04.WMF NUM3_05.WMF NUM3_06.WMF NUM3_07.WMF NUM3_08.WMF NUM3_09.WMF NUM3_10.WMF NUM4_0.WMF NUM4_1.WMF NUM4_2.WMF
NUM4_3.WMF NUM4_4.WMF NUM4_5.WMF NUM4_6.WMF NUM4_7.WMF NUM4_8.WMF NUM4_9.WMF NUM5_0.WMF NUM5_1.WMF NUM5_2.WMF
NUM5_3.WMF NUM5_4.WMF NUM5_5.WMF NUM5_6.WMF NUM5_7.WMF NUM5_8.WMF NUM5_9.WMF NUM6_0.WMF NUM6_1.WMF NUM6_2.WMF
NUM6_3.WMF NUM6_4.WMF NUM6_5.WMF NUM6_6.WMF NUM6_7.WMF NUM6_8.WMF NUM6_9.WMF NUM7_00.WMF NUM7_01.WMF NUM7_02.WMF
NUM7_03.WMF NUM7_04.WMF NUM7_05.WMF NUM7_06.WMF NUM7_07.WMF NUM7_08.WMF NUM7_09.WMF NUM7_10.WMF NUM8_0.WMF NUM8_1.WMF
NUM8_2.WMF NUM8_3.WMF NUM8_4.WMF NUM8_5.WMF NUM8_6.WMF NUM8_7.WMF NUM9_0.WMF NUM9_1.WMF NUM9_2.WMF NUM9_3.WMF

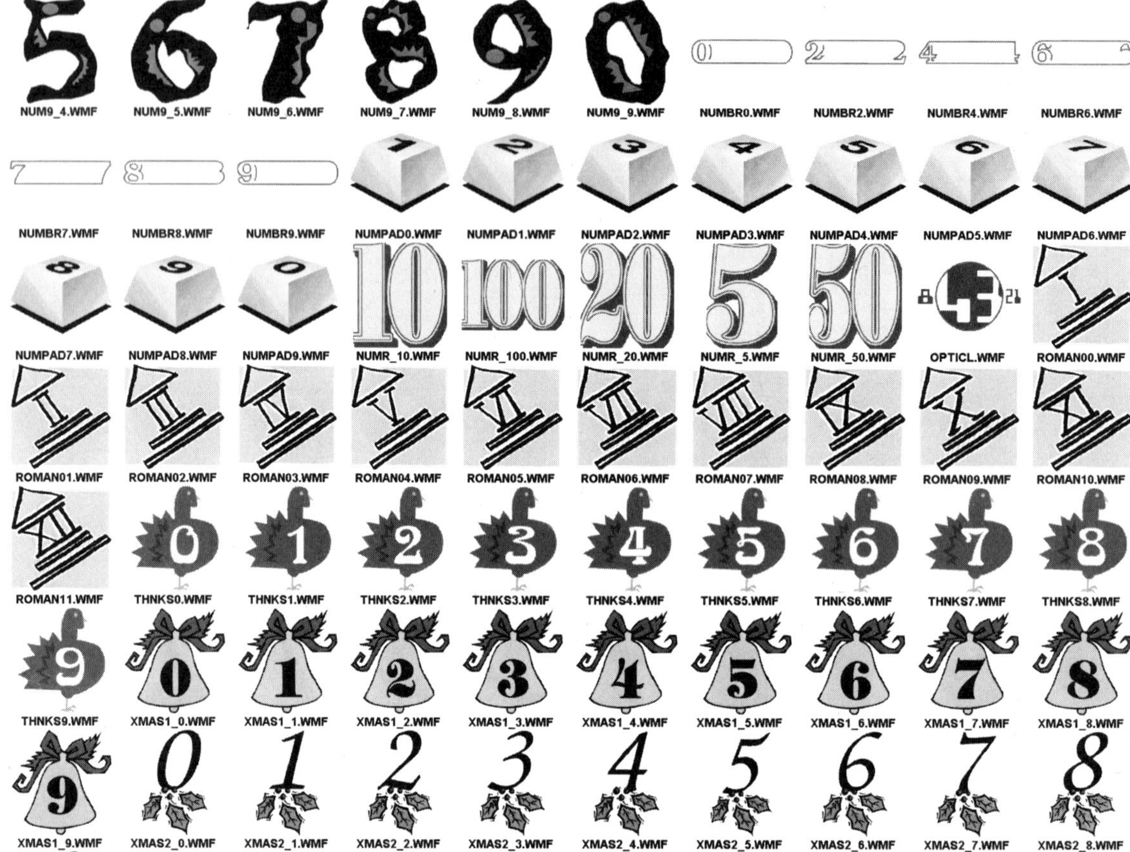
NUM9_4.WMF
NUM9_5.WMF
NUM9_6.WMF
NUM9_7.WMF
NUM9_8.WMF
NUM9_9.WMF
NUMBR0.WMF
NUMBR2.WMF
NUMBR4.WMF
NUMBR6.WMF
NUMBR7.WMF
NUMBR8.WMF
NUMBR9.WMF
NUMPAD0.WMF
NUMPAD1.WMF
NUMPAD2.WMF
NUMPAD3.WMF
NUMPAD4.WMF
NUMPAD5.WMF
NUMPAD6.WMF
NUMPAD7.WMF
NUMPAD8.WMF
NUMPAD9.WMF
NUMR_10.WMF
NUMR_100.WMF
NUMR_20.WMF
NUMR_5.WMF
NUMR_50.WMF
OPTICL.WMF
ROMAN00.WMF
ROMAN01.WMF
ROMAN02.WMF
ROMAN03.WMF
ROMAN04.WMF
ROMAN05.WMF
ROMAN06.WMF
ROMAN07.WMF
ROMAN08.WMF
ROMAN09.WMF
ROMAN10.WMF
ROMAN11.WMF
THNKS0.WMF
THNKS1.WMF
THNKS2.WMF
THNKS3.WMF
THNKS4.WMF
THNKS5.WMF
THNKS6.WMF
THNKS7.WMF
THNKS8.WMF
THNKS9.WMF
XMAS1_0.WMF
XMAS1_1.WMF
XMAS1_2.WMF
XMAS1_3.WMF
XMAS1_4.WMF
XMAS1_5.WMF
XMAS1_6.WMF
XMAS1_7.WMF
XMAS1_8.WMF
XMAS1_9.WMF
XMAS2_0.WMF
XMAS2_1.WMF
XMAS2_2.WMF
XMAS2_3.WMF
XMAS2_4.WMF
XMAS2_5.WMF
XMAS2_6.WMF
XMAS2_7.WMF
XMAS2_8.WMF
XMAS2_9.WMF

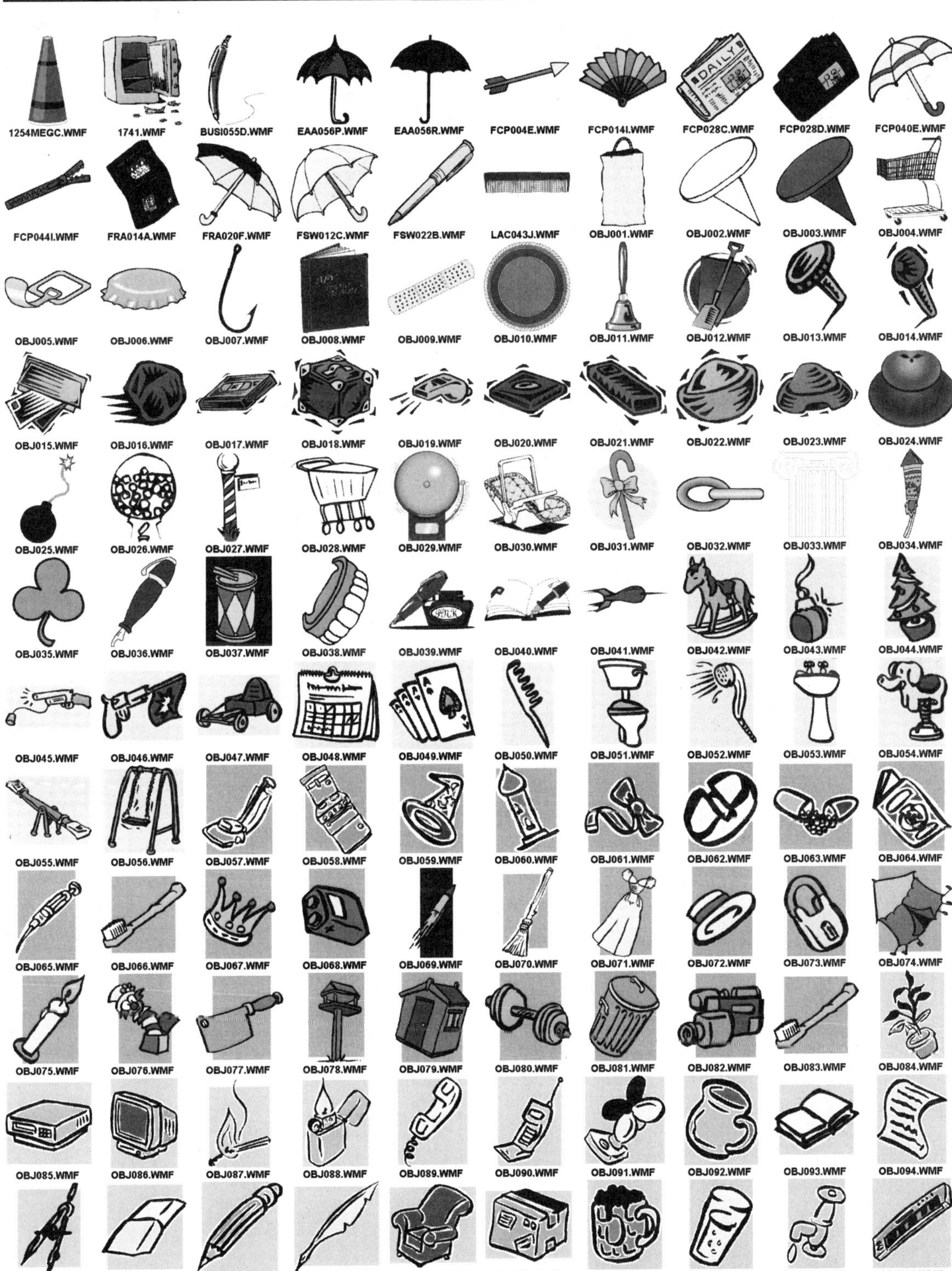

1254MEGC.WMF 1741.WMF BUSI055D.WMF EAA056P.WMF EAA056R.WMF FCP004E.WMF FCP014I.WMF FCP028C.WMF FCP028D.WMF FCP040E.WMF

FCP044I.WMF FRA014A.WMF FRA020F.WMF FSW012C.WMF FSW022B.WMF LAC043J.WMF OBJ001.WMF OBJ002.WMF OBJ003.WMF OBJ004.WMF

OBJ005.WMF OBJ006.WMF OBJ007.WMF OBJ008.WMF OBJ009.WMF OBJ010.WMF OBJ011.WMF OBJ012.WMF OBJ013.WMF OBJ014.WMF

OBJ015.WMF OBJ016.WMF OBJ017.WMF OBJ018.WMF OBJ019.WMF OBJ020.WMF OBJ021.WMF OBJ022.WMF OBJ023.WMF OBJ024.WMF

OBJ025.WMF OBJ026.WMF OBJ027.WMF OBJ028.WMF OBJ029.WMF OBJ030.WMF OBJ031.WMF OBJ032.WMF OBJ033.WMF OBJ034.WMF

OBJ035.WMF OBJ036.WMF OBJ037.WMF OBJ038.WMF OBJ039.WMF OBJ040.WMF OBJ041.WMF OBJ042.WMF OBJ043.WMF OBJ044.WMF

OBJ045.WMF OBJ046.WMF OBJ047.WMF OBJ048.WMF OBJ049.WMF OBJ050.WMF OBJ051.WMF OBJ052.WMF OBJ053.WMF OBJ054.WMF

OBJ055.WMF OBJ056.WMF OBJ057.WMF OBJ058.WMF OBJ059.WMF OBJ060.WMF OBJ061.WMF OBJ062.WMF OBJ063.WMF OBJ064.WMF

OBJ065.WMF OBJ066.WMF OBJ067.WMF OBJ068.WMF OBJ069.WMF OBJ070.WMF OBJ071.WMF OBJ072.WMF OBJ073.WMF OBJ074.WMF

OBJ075.WMF OBJ076.WMF OBJ077.WMF OBJ078.WMF OBJ079.WMF OBJ080.WMF OBJ081.WMF OBJ082.WMF OBJ083.WMF OBJ084.WMF

OBJ085.WMF OBJ086.WMF OBJ087.WMF OBJ088.WMF OBJ089.WMF OBJ090.WMF OBJ091.WMF OBJ092.WMF OBJ093.WMF OBJ094.WMF

OBJ095.WMF OBJ096.WMF OBJ097.WMF OBJ098.WMF OBJ099.WMF OBJ100.WMF OBJ101.WMF OBJ102.WMF OBJ103.WMF OBJ104.WMF

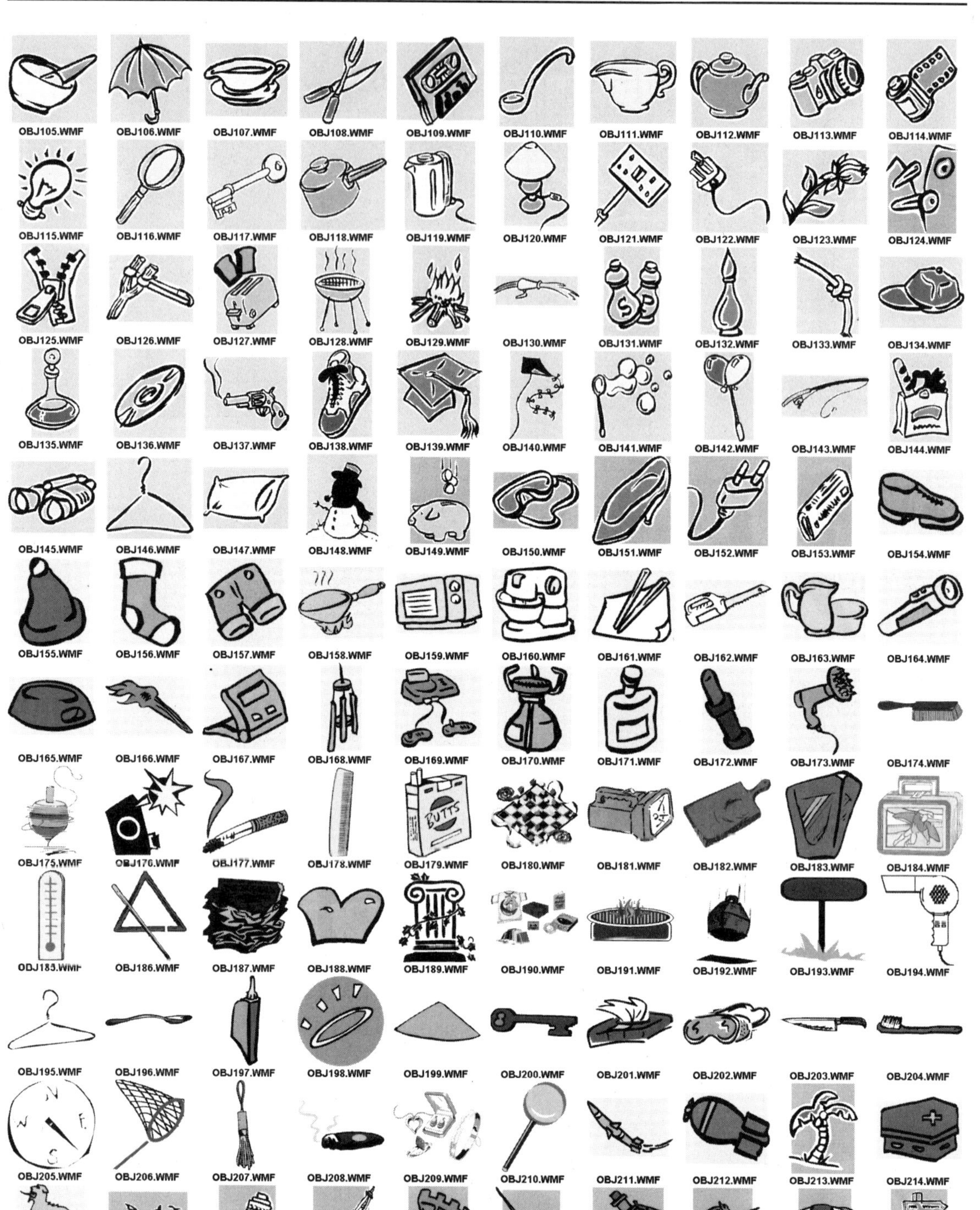
OBJ105.WMF OBJ106.WMF OBJ107.WMF OBJ108.WMF OBJ109.WMF OBJ110.WMF OBJ111.WMF OBJ112.WMF OBJ113.WMF OBJ114.WMF
OBJ115.WMF OBJ116.WMF OBJ117.WMF OBJ118.WMF OBJ119.WMF OBJ120.WMF OBJ121.WMF OBJ122.WMF OBJ123.WMF OBJ124.WMF
OBJ125.WMF OBJ126.WMF OBJ127.WMF OBJ128.WMF OBJ129.WMF OBJ130.WMF OBJ131.WMF OBJ132.WMF OBJ133.WMF OBJ134.WMF
OBJ135.WMF OBJ136.WMF OBJ137.WMF OBJ138.WMF OBJ139.WMF OBJ140.WMF OBJ141.WMF OBJ142.WMF OBJ143.WMF OBJ144.WMF
OBJ145.WMF OBJ146.WMF OBJ147.WMF OBJ148.WMF OBJ149.WMF OBJ150.WMF OBJ151.WMF OBJ152.WMF OBJ153.WMF OBJ154.WMF
OBJ155.WMF OBJ156.WMF OBJ157.WMF OBJ158.WMF OBJ159.WMF OBJ160.WMF OBJ161.WMF OBJ162.WMF OBJ163.WMF OBJ164.WMF
OBJ165.WMF OBJ166.WMF OBJ167.WMF OBJ168.WMF OBJ169.WMF OBJ170.WMF OBJ171.WMF OBJ172.WMF OBJ173.WMF OBJ174.WMF
BUTTS
OBJ175.WMF OBJ176.WMF OBJ177.WMF OBJ178.WMF OBJ179.WMF OBJ180.WMF OBJ181.WMF OBJ182.WMF OBJ183.WMF OBJ184.WMF
OBJ183.WMF OBJ186.WMF OBJ187.WMF OBJ188.WMF OBJ189.WMF OBJ190.WMF OBJ191.WMF OBJ192.WMF OBJ193.WMF OBJ194.WMF
OBJ195.WMF OBJ196.WMF OBJ197.WMF OBJ198.WMF OBJ199.WMF OBJ200.WMF OBJ201.WMF OBJ202.WMF OBJ203.WMF OBJ204.WMF
N W E S
OBJ205.WMF OBJ206.WMF OBJ207.WMF OBJ208.WMF OBJ209.WMF OBJ210.WMF OBJ211.WMF OBJ212.WMF OBJ213.WMF OBJ214.WMF
OBJ215.WMF OBJ216.WMF OBJ217.WMF OBJ218.WMF OBJ219.WMF OBJ220.WMF OBJ221.WMF OBJ222.WMF OBJ223.WMF OBJ224.WMF

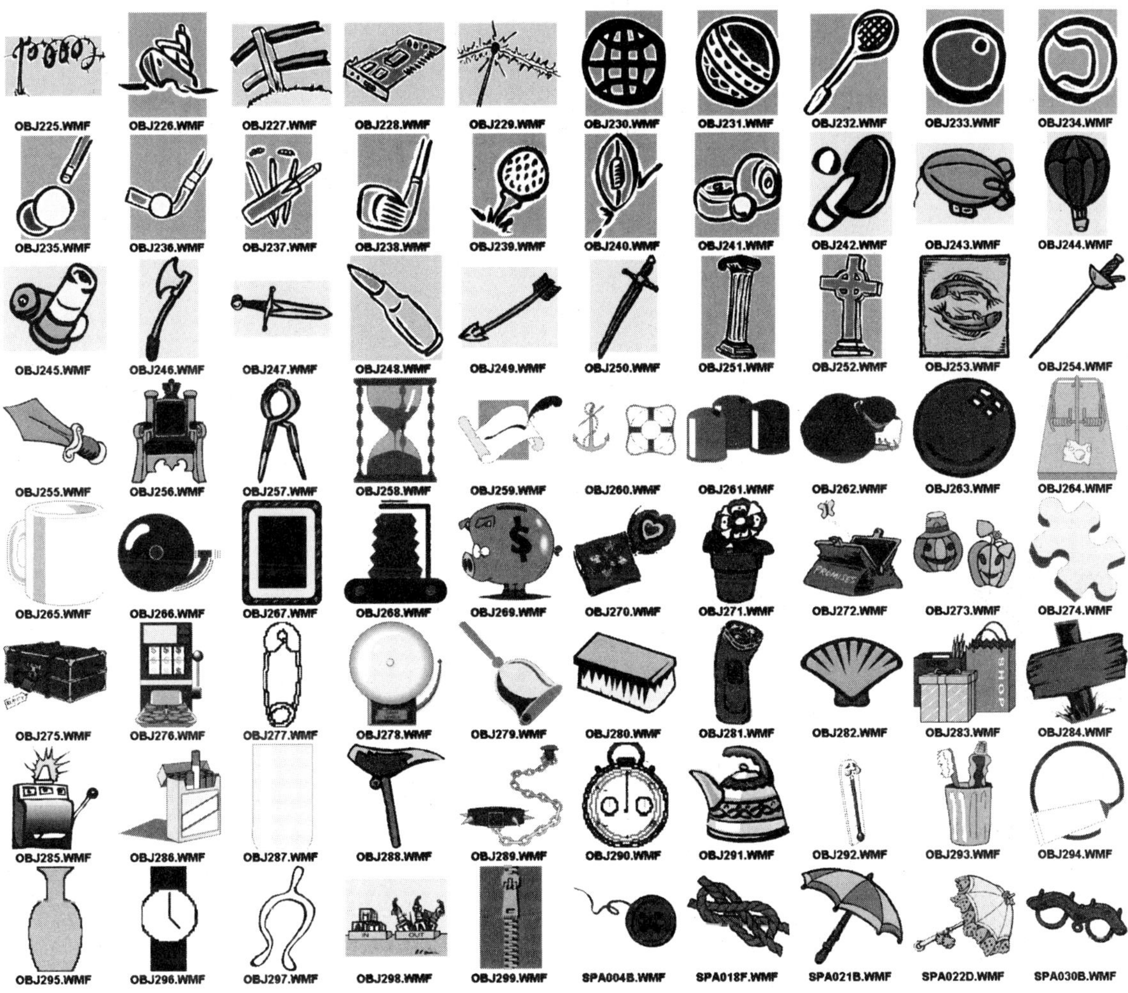
OBJ225.WMF
OBJ226.WMF
OBJ227.WMF
OBJ228.WMF
OBJ229.WMF
OBJ230.WMF
OBJ231.WMF
OBJ232.WMF
OBJ233.WMF
OBJ234.WMF
OBJ235.WMF
OBJ236.WMF
OBJ237.WMF
OBJ238.WMF
OBJ239.WMF
OBJ240.WMF
OBJ241.WMF
OBJ242.WMF
OBJ243.WMF
OBJ244.WMF
OBJ245.WMF
OBJ246.WMF
OBJ247.WMF
OBJ248.WMF
OBJ249.WMF
OBJ250.WMF
OBJ251.WMF
OBJ252.WMF
OBJ253.WMF
OBJ254.WMF
OBJ255.WMF
OBJ256.WMF
OBJ257.WMF
OBJ258.WMF
OBJ259.WMF
OBJ260.WMF
OBJ261.WMF
OBJ262.WMF
OBJ263.WMF
OBJ264.WMF
OBJ265.WMF
OBJ266.WMF
OBJ267.WMF
OBJ268.WMF
OBJ269.WMF
OBJ270.WMF
OBJ271.WMF
OBJ272.WMF
OBJ273.WMF
OBJ274.WMF
OBJ275.WMF
OBJ276.WMF
OBJ277.WMF
OBJ278.WMF
OBJ279.WMF
OBJ280.WMF
OBJ281.WMF
OBJ282.WMF
OBJ283.WMF
OBJ284.WMF
OBJ285.WMF
OBJ286.WMF
OBJ287.WMF
OBJ288.WMF
OBJ289.WMF
OBJ290.WMF
OBJ291.WMF
OBJ292.WMF
OBJ293.WMF
OBJ294.WMF
OBJ295.WMF
OBJ296.WMF
OBJ297.WMF
OBJ298.WMF
OBJ299.WMF
SPA004B.WMF
SPA018F.WMF
SPA021B.WMF
SPA022D.WMF
SPA030B.WMF

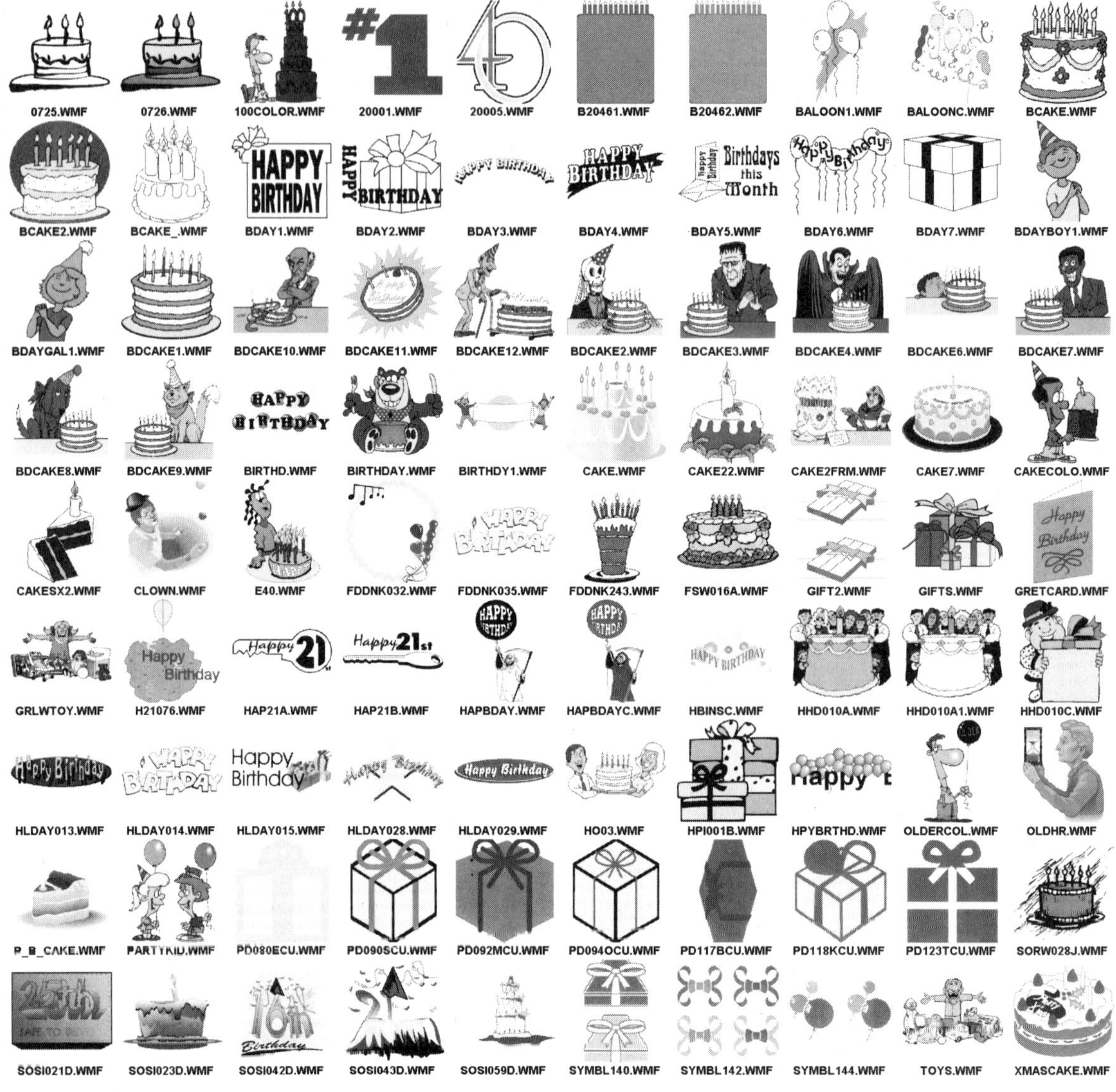
0725.WMF
0726.WMF
100COLOR.WMF
20001.WMF
20005.WMF
B20461.WMF
B20462.WMF
BALOON1.WMF
BALOONC.WMF
BCAKE.WMF
BCAKE2.WMF
BCAKE_.WMF
BDAY1.WMF
BDAY2.WMF
BDAY3.WMF
BDAY4.WMF
BDAY5.WMF
BDAY6.WMF
BDAY7.WMF
BDAYBOY1.WMF
BDAYGAL1.WMF
BDCAKE1.WMF
BDCAKE10.WMF
BDCAKE11.WMF
BDCAKE12.WMF
BDCAKE2.WMF
BDCAKE3.WMF
BDCAKE4.WMF
BDCAKE6.WMF
BDCAKE7.WMF
BDCAKE8.WMF
BDCAKE9.WMF
BIRTHD.WMF
BIRTHDAY.WMF
BIRTHDY1.WMF
CAKE.WMF
CAKE22.WMF
CAKE2FRM.WMF
CAKE7.WMF
CAKECOLO.WMF
CAKESX2.WMF
CLOWN.WMF
E40.WMF
FDDNK032.WMF
FDDNK035.WMF
FDDNK243.WMF
FSW016A.WMF
GIFT2.WMF
GIFTS.WMF
GRETCARD.WMF
GRLWTOY.WMF
H21076.WMF
HAP21A.WMF
HAP21B.WMF
HAPBDAY.WMF
HAPBDAYC.WMF
HBINSC.WMF
HHD010A.WMF
HHD010A1.WMF
HHD010C.WMF
HLDAY013.WMF
HLDAY014.WMF
HLDAY015.WMF
HLDAY028.WMF
HLDAY029.WMF
HO03.WMF
HPI001B.WMF
HPYBRTHD.WMF
OLDERCOL.WMF
OLDHR.WMF
P_B_CAKE.WMF
PARTYKID.WMF
PD080ECU.WMF
PD090SCU.WMF
PD092MCU.WMF
PD094OCU.WMF
PD117BCU.WMF
PD118KCU.WMF
PD123TCU.WMF
SORW028J.WMF
SOSI021D.WMF
SOSI023D.WMF
SOSI042D.WMF
SOSI043D.WMF
SOSI059D.WMF
SYMBL140.WMF
SYMBL142.WMF
SYMBL144.WMF
TOYS.WMF
XMASCAKE.WMF

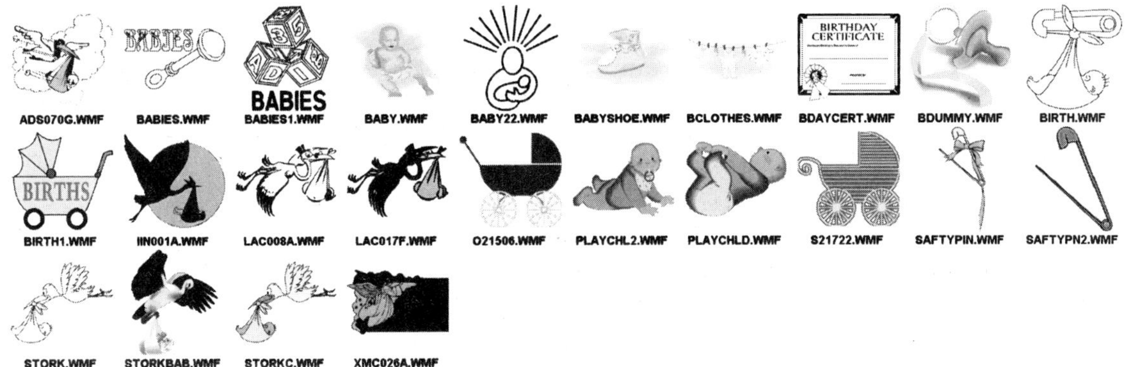

Occasions (OCCASION) • Other

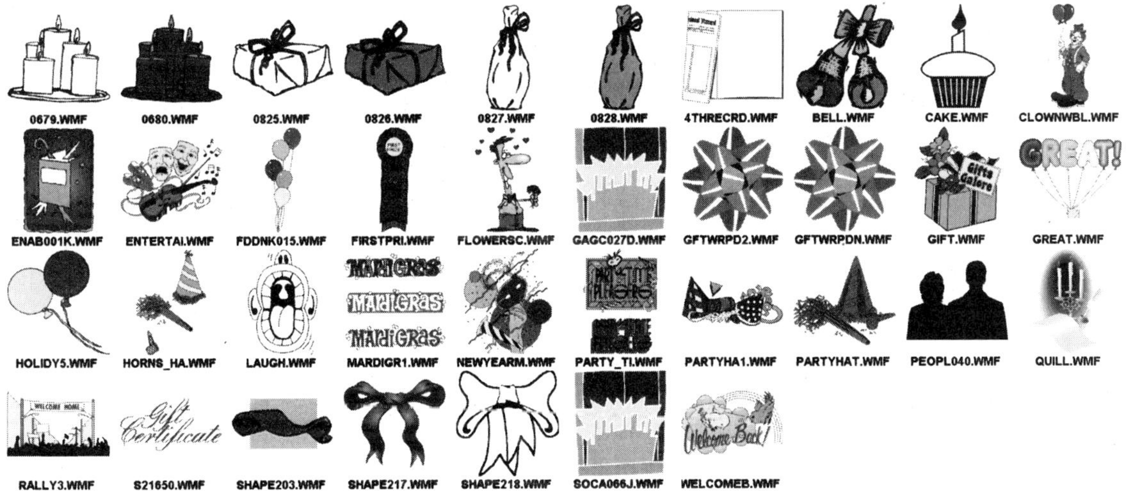

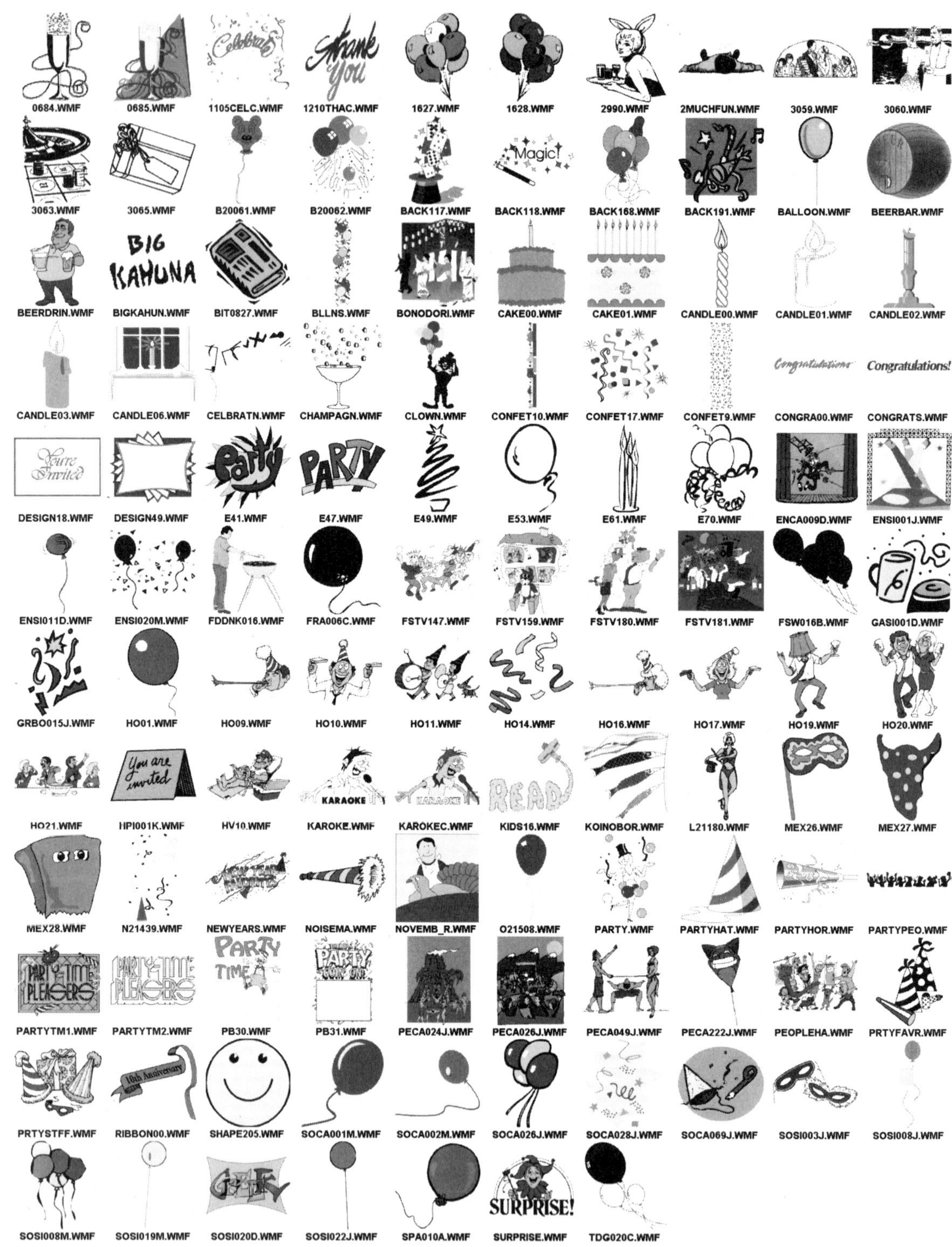
0684.WMF 0685.WMF 1105CELC.WMF 1210THAC.WMF 1627.WMF 1628.WMF 2990.WMF 2MUCHFUN.WMF 3059.WMF 3060.WMF
3063.WMF 3065.WMF B20061.WMF B20062.WMF BACK117.WMF BACK118.WMF BACK168.WMF BACK191.WMF BALLOON.WMF BEERBAR.WMF
BEERDRIN.WMF BIGKAHUN.WMF BIT0827.WMF BLLNS.WMF BONODORI.WMF CAKE00.WMF CAKE01.WMF CANDLE00.WMF CANDLE01.WMF CANDLE02.WMF
CANDLE03.WMF CANDLE06.WMF CELBRATN.WMF CHAMPAGN.WMF CLOWN.WMF CONFET10.WMF CONFET17.WMF CONFET9.WMF CONGRA00.WMF CONGRATS.WMF
DESIGN18.WMF DESIGN49.WMF E41.WMF E47.WMF E49.WMF E53.WMF E61.WMF E70.WMF ENCA009D.WMF ENSI001J.WMF
ENSI011D.WMF ENSI020M.WMF FDDNK016.WMF FRA006C.WMF FSTV147.WMF FSTV159.WMF FSTV180.WMF FSTV181.WMF FSW016B.WMF GASI001D.WMF
GRBO015J.WMF HO01.WMF HO09.WMF HO10.WMF HO11.WMF HO14.WMF HO16.WMF HO17.WMF HO19.WMF HO20.WMF
HO21.WMF HPI001K.WMF HV10.WMF KAROKE.WMF KAROKEC.WMF KIDS16.WMF KOINOBOR.WMF L21180.WMF MEX26.WMF MEX27.WMF
MEX28.WMF N21439.WMF NEWYEARS.WMF NOISEMA.WMF NOVEMB_R.WMF O21508.WMF PARTY.WMF PARTYHAT.WMF PARTYHOR.WMF PARTYPEO.WMF
PARTYTM1.WMF PARTYTM2.WMF PB30.WMF PB31.WMF PECA024J.WMF PECA026J.WMF PECA049J.WMF PECA222J.WMF PEOPLEHA.WMF PRTYFAVR.WMF
PRTYSTFF.WMF RIBBON00.WMF SHAPE205.WMF SOCA001M.WMF SOCA002M.WMF SOCA026J.WMF SOCA028J.WMF SOCA069J.WMF SOSI003J.WMF SOSI008J.WMF
SOSI008M.WMF SOSI019M.WMF SOSI020D.WMF SOSI022J.WMF SPA010A.WMF SURPRISE.WMF TDG020C.WMF

0055.WMF
25TH.WMF
50TH.WMF
ADS020F.WMF
ADS020I.WMF
ADS020Q.WMF
ADS021I.WMF
ANIVRSRY.WMF
ANNIVER1.WMF
ANNIVER2.WMF
ASYOUBEG.WMF
BALLOON.WMF
BELLS.WMF
BELLS1.WMF
BOUQUET.WMF
BOUQUET1.WMF
BRIDAL.WMF
BRIDALFL.WMF
BRIDALRE.WMF
BRIDALSH.WMF
BRIDE.WMF
BRIDE01A.WMF
BRIDE01B.WMF
BRIDE02.WMF
BRIDE03.WMF
BRIDE04.WMF
BRIDE05.WMF
BRIDE06.WMF
BRIDE07.WMF
BRIDE08.WMF
BRIDE09.WMF
BRIDE10.WMF
BRIDE11.WMF
BRIDE12.WMF
BRIDE13.WMF
BRIDEACC.WMF
BRIDES19.WMF
CAKE.WMF
CANDLAB.WMF
CANDLES.WMF
CHAMPAGN.WMF
CHERUB1.WMF
CHERUB2.WMF
CHILDREN.WMF
CHURCH.WMF
DANCING1.WMF
DANCING2.WMF
DOVES.WMF
DOVOLIVE.WMF
ENSI003D.WMF
FCP034E.WMF
FDDNK200.WMF
FDDNK201.WMF
FORMAL.WMF
FSW023A.WMF
FSW023B.WMF
FSW023C.WMF
FSW023D.WMF
FSW023E.WMF
GARTER.WMF
GOBLETS.WMF
GRDN075.WMF
GROMBRID.WMF
GROOM.WMF
HAPPY.WMF
HAPPYCOU.WMF
HEART1.WMF
HEART2.WMF
HEART3.WMF
HEART4.WMF
HHCA014J.WMF
HHCA063J.WMF
HHSI025J.WMF
HHSS006J.WMF
IHO019F.WMF
IWD006A.WMF
IWD030A.WMF
IWD030B.WMF
IWD031A.WMF
IWD031B.WMF
JUSTMARR.WMF
KEKKON3.WMF
LILY.WMF
LIMO1.WMF
LIMO2.WMF
MANWIFE1.WMF
MANWIFE2.WMF
MANWIFE3.WMF
MANWIFE4.WMF
MANWIFE5.WMF
MANWIFE6.WMF
MARRIAGE.WMF
MGLASES.WMF
OURWED.WMF
PD006ABW.WMF
PGX027F.WMF
PGX032C.WMF
RING.WMF
RINGS1.WMF
RLGN163.WMF
RLGN187.WMF
RLGN188.WMF
RLGN189.WMF
RLGN190.WMF
RLGN191.WMF
RLGN192.WMF
ROSE1.WMF
ROSE2.WMF
ROSE3.WMF
ROSE4.WMF
ROSE5.WMF
ROSE6.WMF
ROSE7.WMF
ROSE8.WMF
ROSE9.WMF
VALCOLAG.WMF
VSC054D.WMF
WCAKE.WMF
WED1.WMF
WED2.WMF

WED3.WMF

WED4.WMF

WEDDING1.WMF

WEDDING3.WMF

WEDDING4.WMF

WEDDINGB.WMF

WEDDINGC.WMF

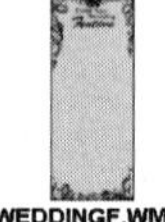
WEDDINGF.WMF

WEDDINGR.WMF

WEDRINGS.WMF

WHITELAC.WMF

YOUREINV.WMF

1400.WMF
1402.WMF
1404.WMF
1406.WMF
1408.WMF
1410.WMF
1412.WMF
1414.WMF
1416.WMF
1418.WMF
1420.WMF
1422.WMF
1424.WMF
1430.WMF
1432.WMF
1434.WMF
1436.WMF
1438.WMF
1440.WMF
1442.WMF
1444.WMF
1446.WMF
1448.WMF
1450.WMF
1452.WMF
1454.WMF
1456.WMF
1458.WMF
1460.WMF
1462.WMF
1464.WMF
1466.WMF
1468.WMF
1470.WMF
1472.WMF
1474.WMF
1476.WMF
1478.WMF
1480.WMF
1482.WMF
1484.WMF
1486.WMF
1488.WMF
1490.WMF
1492.WMF
1494.WMF
1496.WMF
1498.WMF
1502.WMF
1504.WMF
1506.WMF
1508.WMF
2POSTMAN.WMF
ACCOUN2.WMF
ACCOUNT.WMF
ACCOUNT2.WMF
ACCOUNTA.WMF
ACHASER.WMF
ASI097D.WMF
ASTRONOM.WMF
AUTOMECH.WMF
BABALPLA.WMF
BAGOMNY.WMF
BALET1C.WMF
BALET2C.WMF
BALLETCO.WMF
BANKER.WMF
BARBER.WMF
BELLHOP.WMF
BIKERCOL.WMF
BILLCOLL.WMF
BMAN01.WMF
BMAN01CR.WMF
BRGLR.WMF
BSNSS060.WMF
BSNSS061.WMF
BSNSS062.WMF
BSNSS063.WMF
BULLRIDE.WMF
BURGLARC.WMF
BWMANC.WMF
CACH.WMF
CARPENT.WMF
CARPENT9.WMF
CARPENTE.WMF
CARWASH.WMF
CC35.WMF
CC36.WMF
CC42.WMF
CC43.WMF
CC46.WMF
CC47.WMF
CC50.WMF
CC51.WMF
CC52.WMF
CHAINSW.WMF
CHEF2.WMF
CHEF24.WMF
CHEF3.WMF
CHEF314.WMF
CHEF55.WMF
CHEFCOLO.WMF
CHEFSTI.WMF
CHEMIST.WMF
CHF.WMF
CHINESEC.WMF
CMPTRRT.WMF
CMRMN.WMF
COMPART.WMF
CONSTR2.WMF
CONSTR4.WMF
CONSTRU.WMF
CONSTRUC.WMF
COUCHPOT.WMF
COWGIRLC.WMF
COWPOKEC.WMF
CROSWALK.WMF
CRPNTR.WMF
CRTN035.WMF
CRTN061.WMF

CRTN080.WMF
CUSTODIN.WMF
CW02.WMF
CW03.WMF
CW04.WMF
CW05.WMF
CW06.WMF
CW07.WMF
CW08.WMF
CW09.WMF
CW28.WMF
CW29.WMF
CW35.WMF
CW36.WMF
CW38.WMF
CW39.WMF
CW40.WMF
CW41.WMF
CW42.WMF
CW44.WMF
CW45.WMF
CW46.WMF
DANCER.WMF
DEC048X.WMF
DELIVERY.WMF
DENTISTC.WMF
DOORDOOR.WMF
DRIVERCO.WMF
ELECTRIC.WMF
EW15.WMF
EW19.WMF
EW21.WMF
EXCTVMAN.WMF
EXCTVWMN.WMF
FD29.WMF
FD30.WMF
FD44.WMF
FILLING.WMF
FIREMAN.WMF
FLATLNR.WMF
FMANC.WMF
FORTUNET.WMF
FSW024C.WMF
FSW030A.WMF
FSW030B.WMF
FSW030C.WMF
FSW030E.WMF
GARBAG.WMF
GARBAGE.WMF
GASSTAT.WMF
GROCER.WMF
GTPLAYC.WMF
GUNSLING.WMF
HANDYMA2.WMF
HANDYMAN.WMF
HANDYWOM.WMF
HG10.WMF
HN03.WMF
HOI014C.WMF
HOI015B.WMF
HOST1.WMF
HOUSES5.WMF
HPPE.WMF
HPPE2.WMF
HTS001C.WMF
HTS002B.WMF
HTS004A.WMF
HTS009C.WMF
HTS012A.WMF
HTS015C.WMF
HTS017A.WMF
HTS018A.WMF
HTS019A.WMF
HTS020B.WMF
HTS023B.WMF
HTS025C.WMF
HTS027B.WMF
HTS028A.WMF
HTS029C.WMF
HUNTER.WMF
KIDARTIS.WMF
KIDBUSI1.WMF
KIDBUSIN.WMF
KIDCHEF.WMF
KIDCONST.WMF
KIDCOP.WMF
KIDDOCTO.WMF
KIDFIREF.WMF
KIDNURSE.WMF
KIDOPERA.WMF
LADYWRES.WMF
LWYR.WMF
LWYR2.WMF
MAIL.WMF
MAILMAN.WMF
MANWWHE.WMF
MCHNC.WMF
MECH1C.WMF
MECH2C.WMF
MECHANI1.WMF
MECHANI2.WMF
MECHANI3.WMF
MECHANI5.WMF
MECHANI6.WMF
MECHANIC.WMF
MINERIN.WMF
MINERLO.WMF
NEWS.WMF
NEWSANN.WMF
NEWSBOYC.WMF
NEWSREPO.WMF
NURSE.WMF
NURSING.WMF
ONSTAGE7.WMF
ONSTAGE8.WMF
PAINTERC.WMF
PAINTR.WMF
PAINTR9.WMF
PAN.WMF
PHOTOGRA.WMF

PHROH.WMF
PILOT.WMF
PIZZA_MN.WMF
PIZZAGUY.WMF
PLUMBER8.WMF
PLUMBERC.WMF
POLICEMN.WMF
PRFSSR.WMF
PRMDC.WMF
PROF_1.WMF
PROF_2.WMF
PROST.WMF
PRT.WMF
PS08.WMF
PSTMN.WMF
R21626.WMF
RADIO1.WMF
RADIO2.WMF
RD11.WMF
RD13.WMF
RD15.WMF
RD17.WMF
RD18.WMF
RD19.WMF
RD20.WMF
RD22.WMF
RD23.WMF
RD24.WMF
RD25.WMF
REFEREEC.WMF
REPAIRMA.WMF
ROCKINGC.WMF
SALESDES.WMF
SALESMAN.WMF
SCENTST.WMF
SCHOOLT.WMF
SCIENTIS.WMF
SECRETA.WMF
SECTARC.WMF
SEEDPLA.WMF
SHOPPERC.WMF
SIGN.WMF
SIL015F.WMF
SIT052M.WMF
SOLDIERC.WMF
SRSPNDR.WMF
SS06.WMF
SS07.WMF
SS08.WMF
STARGAZ.WMF
STARGAZE.WMF
STKCWBY.WMF
STOCK.WMF
STOCKC.WMF
STORECL.WMF
SUMO.WMF
TAILOR.WMF
TALKRADI.WMF
TASTERCO.WMF
TAXID.WMF
TILEFLO.WMF
TMR.WMF
TNTDUDE.WMF
TOURIST.WMF
TRAINCOL.WMF
TRAPPER.WMF
UNDRFRE.WMF
WAITER.WMF
WAITER2.WMF
WAITERCO.WMF
WAITR.WMF
WAITRES.WMF
WINDOWWA.WMF
NOMANMED.WMF

AGENTC.WMF
ASI092D.WMF
ASI100F.WMF
BAKERC.WMF
BLOCKS.WMF
BRICKYC.WMF
BUTCHERC.WMF
CAPENTRC.WMF
CHEFC.WMF
CLEANERC.WMF
CONSTRC.WMF
DATAPROC.WMF
DOCTORC.WMF
EAA182D.WMF
EAC163T.WMF
EAC163U.WMF
ELECTRON.WMF
ENGINERC.WMF
GARDENRC.WMF
HND026B.WMF
LIBRARNC.WMF
MECHANC.WMF
MINERC.WMF
PAINTER7.WMF
PD024DCU.WMF
PD024ECU.WMF
PD024FCU.WMF
PD024GCU.WMF
PD024HCU.WMF
PD024ICU.WMF
PD024JCU.WMF
PD024KCU.WMF
PD024LCU.WMF
PD024MCU.WMF
PD024NCU.WMF
PD024SCU.WMF
PD024TCU.WMF
PD024UCU.WMF
PD024VCU.WMF
PD024WCU.WMF
PD024XCU.WMF
PD024YCU.WMF
PD024ZCU.WMF
PD025ACU.WMF
PD025BCU.WMF
PD025CCU.WMF
PD025DCU.WMF
PD025ECU.WMF
PD025FCU.WMF
PD025GCU.WMF
PD025HCU.WMF
PD025ICU.WMF
PD025JCU.WMF
PD025KCU.WMF
PD025LCU.WMF
PD025MCU.WMF
PD026NCU.WMF
PD026OCU.WMF
PD026PCU.WMF
PD026QCU.WMF
PD026RCU.WMF
PD026SCU.WMF
PD026TCU.WMF
PD026UCU.WMF
PD026VCU.WMF
PD027ACU.WMF
PD027BCU.WMF
PD027CCU.WMF
PD027DCU.WMF
PHOTOGC.WMF
PHSIOC.WMF
POC111D.WMF
POLITIC.WMF
PREACHRC.WMF
SPAINTC.WMF
SURVEYC.WMF
TEACHERC.WMF
TECHNOL.WMF
WORKERC.WMF

1399.WMF 1401.WMF 1403.WMF 1405.WMF 1407.WMF 1409.WMF 1411.WMF 1413.WMF 1415.WMF 1417.WMF

1419.WMF 1421.WMF 1423.WMF 1429.WMF 1431.WMF 1433.WMF 1435.WMF 1437.WMF 1439.WMF 1441.WMF

1443.WMF 1445.WMF 1447.WMF 1449.WMF 1451.WMF 1453.WMF 1455.WMF 1457.WMF 1459.WMF 1461.WMF

1463.WMF 1465.WMF 1467.WMF 1469.WMF 1471.WMF 1473.WMF 1475.WMF 1477.WMF 1479.WMF 1481.WMF

1483.WMF 1485.WMF 1487.WMF 1489.WMF 1491.WMF 1493.WMF 1495.WMF 1497.WMF 1501.WMF 1503.WMF

1505.WMF 1507.WMF 1BALLERI.WMF 1BALLET_.WMF 1POSTMAN.WMF 1TRACTOR.WMF 2BALLERI.WMF 2BALLET_.WMF 2TRACTOR.WMF AGENT.WMF

ASI090B.WMF ASI091M.WMF ASI092I.WMF ASI092L.WMF ASI093H.WMF ASI093L.WMF ASI093O.WMF ASI093Q.WMF ASI098F.WMF ASTRONAU.WMF

BAKER.WMF BALET1.WMF BALET2.WMF BEE_KEEP.WMF BRICKY.WMF BUGLER2.WMF BUTCHER.WMF BUTTERFL.WMF BWMAN.WMF CAPENTR.WMF

CHEF.WMF CLEANER.WMF COAL.WMF CONSTR.WMF CRTN157.WMF DEC052EE.WMF DETECTIV.WMF DIRECTOR.WMF DOCTOR.WMF ENGINEER.WMF

ENGINER.WMF FMAN.WMF FRENCH_C.WMF GARDENR.WMF GTPLAY.WMF LAC010K.WMF LIBRARN.WMF LUMBERJA.WMF MAID.WMF MECH1.WMF

MECH2.WMF MECHAN.WMF MINER.WMF MOD024I.WMF MSL005A.WMF MSL050A.WMF PAINTER.WMF PAINTER2.WMF PANNING_.WMF PGX019G.WMF

PGX020A.WMF PGX020B.WMF PGX020C.WMF PGX020D.WMF PGX020E.WMF PGX021F.WMF PGX025C.WMF PGX032A.WMF PHOTOG.WMF PHSIO.WMF

POLITI.WMF
PREACHR.WMF
RAD2.WMF
SCT002B.WMF
SECTAR.WMF
SOLDIER.WMF
SPAINT.WMF
STS001A.WMF
STS002A.WMF
STS002B.WMF
STS003A.WMF
STS003B.WMF
STS004A.WMF
STS004B.WMF
STS005A.WMF
STS005B.WMF
STS005C.WMF
STS007A.WMF
STS007B.WMF
STS009B.WMF
STS009C.WMF
STS011A.WMF
STS012B.WMF
STS013B.WMF
STS014B.WMF
STS015A.WMF
STS016A.WMF
STS017B.WMF
STS019A.WMF
STS019B.WMF
STS025A.WMF
STS026B.WMF
SURVEY.WMF
TEACHER.WMF
A+B
TRAVELIN.WMF
UNDERTAK.WMF
WOOD_CAR.WMF
WORKER.WMF

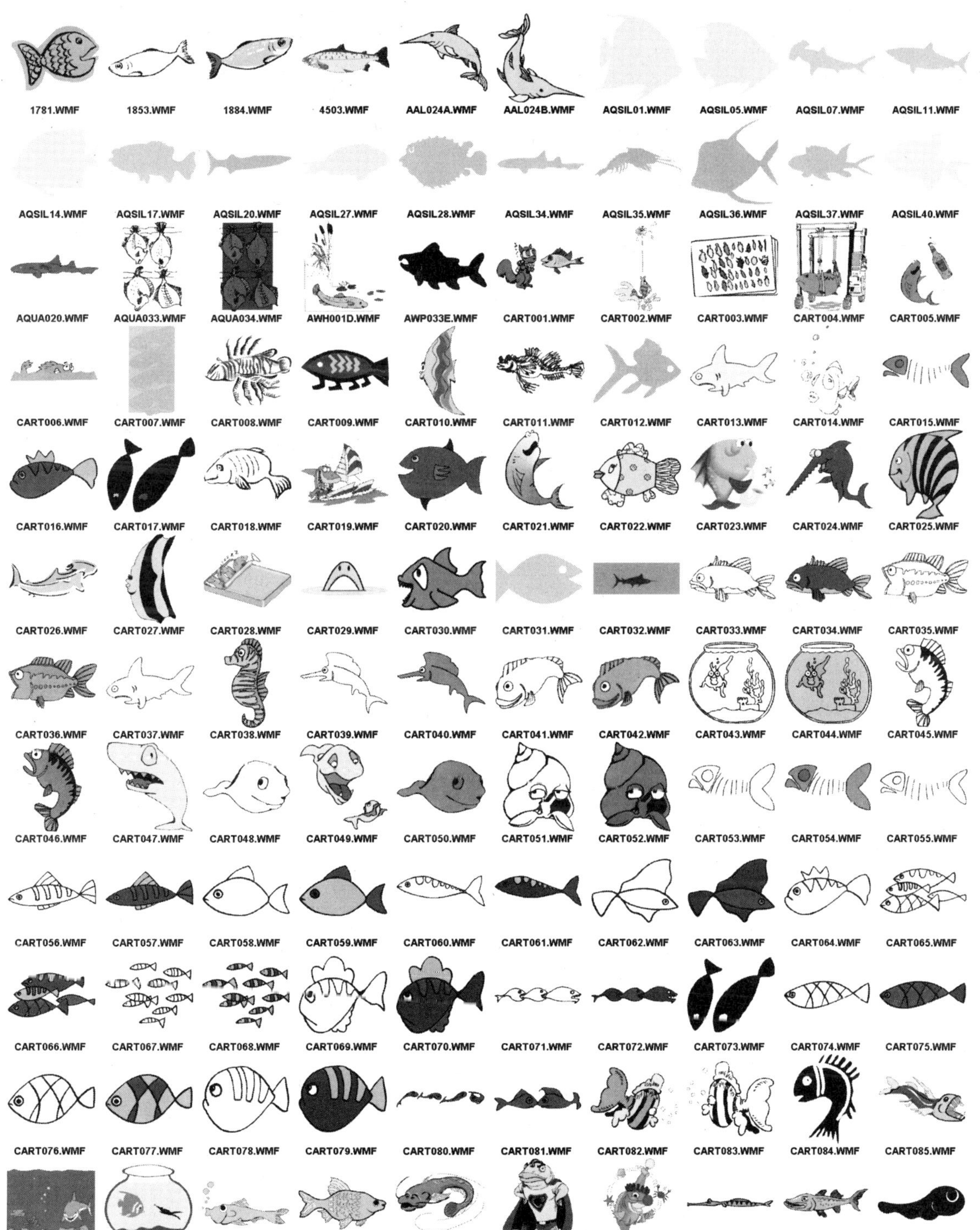

1781.WMF 1853.WMF 1884.WMF 4503.WMF AAL024A.WMF AAL024B.WMF AQSIL01.WMF AQSIL05.WMF AQSIL07.WMF AQSIL11.WMF

AQSIL14.WMF AQSIL17.WMF AQSIL20.WMF AQSIL27.WMF AQSIL28.WMF AQSIL34.WMF AQSIL35.WMF AQSIL36.WMF AQSIL37.WMF AQSIL40.WMF

AQUA020.WMF AQUA033.WMF AQUA034.WMF AWH001D.WMF AWP033E.WMF CART001.WMF CART002.WMF CART003.WMF CART004.WMF CART005.WMF

CART006.WMF CART007.WMF CART008.WMF CART009.WMF CART010.WMF CART011.WMF CART012.WMF CART013.WMF CART014.WMF CART015.WMF

CART016.WMF CART017.WMF CART018.WMF CART019.WMF CART020.WMF CART021.WMF CART022.WMF CART023.WMF CART024.WMF CART025.WMF

CART026.WMF CART027.WMF CART028.WMF CART029.WMF CART030.WMF CART031.WMF CART032.WMF CART033.WMF CART034.WMF CART035.WMF

CART036.WMF CART037.WMF CART038.WMF CART039.WMF CART040.WMF CART041.WMF CART042.WMF CART043.WMF CART044.WMF CART045.WMF

CART046.WMF CART047.WMF CART048.WMF CART049.WMF CART050.WMF CART051.WMF CART052.WMF CART053.WMF CART054.WMF CART055.WMF

CART056.WMF CART057.WMF CART058.WMF CART059.WMF CART060.WMF CART061.WMF CART062.WMF CART063.WMF CART064.WMF CART065.WMF

CART066.WMF CART067.WMF CART068.WMF CART069.WMF CART070.WMF CART071.WMF CART072.WMF CART073.WMF CART074.WMF CART075.WMF

CART076.WMF CART077.WMF CART078.WMF CART079.WMF CART080.WMF CART081.WMF CART082.WMF CART083.WMF CART084.WMF CART085.WMF

CART086.WMF CART087.WMF CART088.WMF CART089.WMF CART090.WMF CART091.WMF CART092.WMF CART093.WMF CART094.WMF CART095.WMF

CART096.WMF CART097.WMF CART098.WMF CART099.WMF CART100.WMF CART101.WMF CART102.WMF CART103.WMF CART104.WMF CART105.WMF

CART106.WMF CART107.WMF CART108.WMF CART109.WMF CART110.WMF CART111.WMF CART112.WMF CART113.WMF CART114.WMF CART115.WMF

CART116.WMF CART117.WMF CART118.WMF CART119.WMF CART120.WMF CART121.WMF CART122.WMF CART123.WMF CART124.WMF CART125.WMF

CART126.WMF CART127.WMF CART128.WMF CART129.WMF CART130.WMF CART131.WMF CART132.WMF CART133.WMF CART134.WMF CART135.WMF

CART136.WMF CART137.WMF CART138.WMF CART139.WMF CART140.WMF CART141.WMF CART142.WMF CART143.WMF CART144.WMF CART145.WMF

CART146.WMF CART147.WMF CART148.WMF CART149.WMF CART150.WMF CART151.WMF CART152.WMF CART153.WMF CART154.WMF CART155.WMF

CART156.WMF CART157.WMF CART158.WMF CART159.WMF CART160.WMF CART161.WMF CART162.WMF CART163.WMF CART164.WMF CART165.WMF

CART166.WMF CART167.WMF CART168.WMF CART169.WMF CART170.WMF CART171.WMF CART172.WMF CART173.WMF CART174.WMF CART175.WMF

CART176.WMF CART177.WMF CART178.WMF CART179.WMF CART180.WMF CART181.WMF CART182.WMF CART183.WMF CART184.WMF CART185.WMF

CART186.WMF CART187.WMF CART188.WMF CART189.WMF CART190.WMF CART191.WMF CART192.WMF CART193.WMF CART194.WMF CART195.WMF

CART196.WMF CART197.WMF CART198.WMF CART199.WMF CART200.WMF CART201.WMF CART202.WMF CART203.WMF CART204.WMF CART205.WMF

CART206.WMF CART207.WMF DEC086B.WMF DEC086G.WMF DEC088I.WMF EAA154D.WMF EAA154H.WMF EAC027D.WMF EAC027J.WMF FD30.WMF

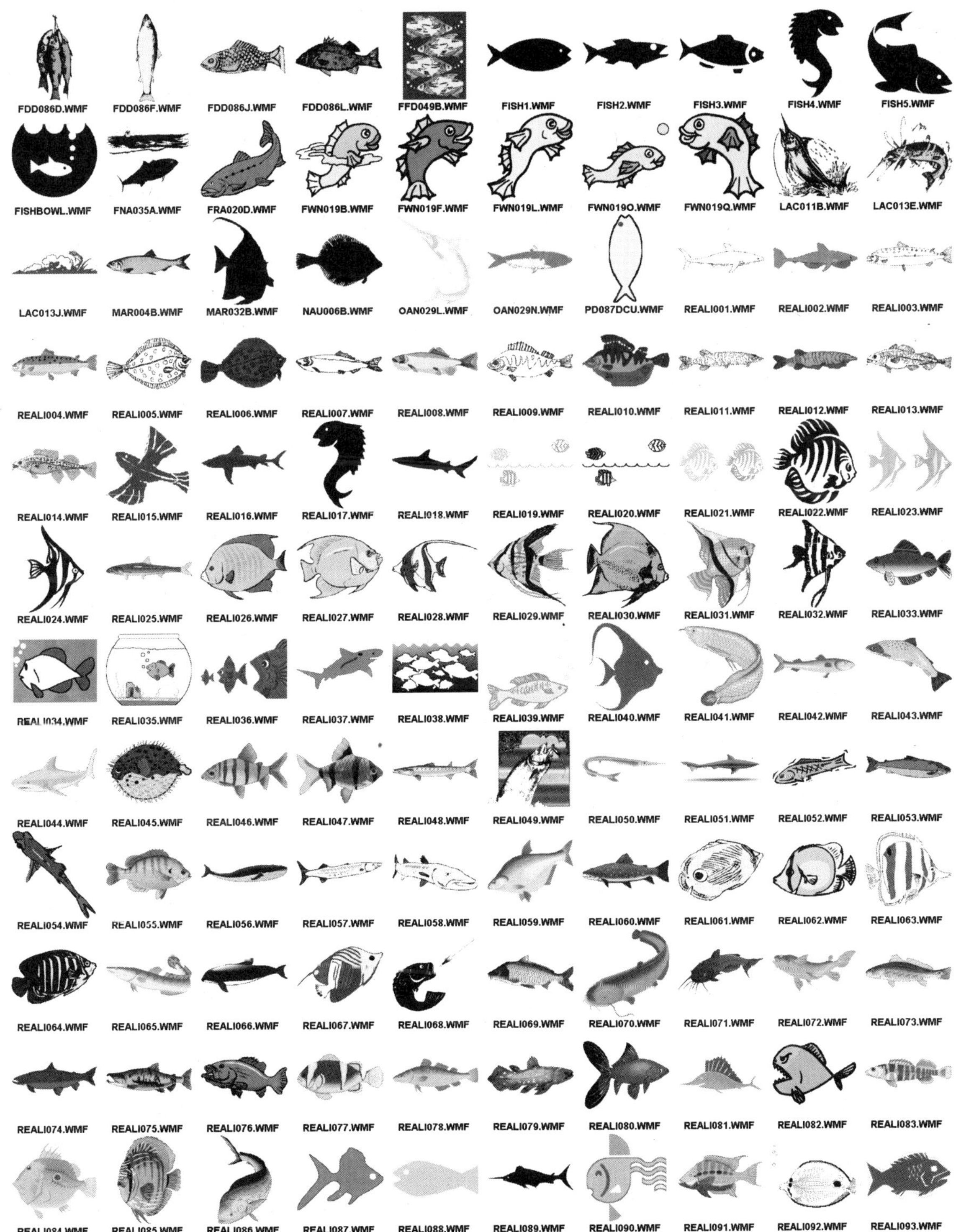
FDD086D.WMF
FDD086F.WMF
FDD086J.WMF
FDD086L.WMF
FFD049B.WMF
FISH1.WMF
FISH2.WMF
FISH3.WMF
FISH4.WMF
FISH5.WMF
FISHBOWL.WMF
FNA035A.WMF
FRA020D.WMF
FWN019B.WMF
FWN019F.WMF
FWN019L.WMF
FWN019O.WMF
FWN019Q.WMF
LAC011B.WMF
LAC013E.WMF
LAC013J.WMF
MAR004B.WMF
MAR032B.WMF
NAU006B.WMF
OAN029L.WMF
OAN029N.WMF
PD087DCU.WMF
REALI001.WMF
REALI002.WMF
REALI003.WMF
REALI004.WMF
REALI005.WMF
REALI006.WMF
REALI007.WMF
REALI008.WMF
REALI009.WMF
REALI010.WMF
REALI011.WMF
REALI012.WMF
REALI013.WMF
REALI014.WMF
REALI015.WMF
REALI016.WMF
REALI017.WMF
REALI018.WMF
REALI019.WMF
REALI020.WMF
REALI021.WMF
REALI022.WMF
REALI023.WMF
REALI024.WMF
REALI025.WMF
REALI026.WMF
REALI027.WMF
REALI028.WMF
REALI029.WMF
REALI030.WMF
REALI031.WMF
REALI032.WMF
REALI033.WMF
REALI034.WMF
REALI035.WMF
REALI036.WMF
REALI037.WMF
REALI038.WMF
REALI039.WMF
REALI040.WMF
REALI041.WMF
REALI042.WMF
REALI043.WMF
REALI044.WMF
REALI045.WMF
REALI046.WMF
REALI047.WMF
REALI048.WMF
REALI049.WMF
REALI050.WMF
REALI051.WMF
REALI052.WMF
REALI053.WMF
REALI054.WMF
REALI055.WMF
REALI056.WMF
REALI057.WMF
REALI058.WMF
REALI059.WMF
REALI060.WMF
REALI061.WMF
REALI062.WMF
REALI063.WMF
REALI064.WMF
REALI065.WMF
REALI066.WMF
REALI067.WMF
REALI068.WMF
REALI069.WMF
REALI070.WMF
REALI071.WMF
REALI072.WMF
REALI073.WMF
REALI074.WMF
REALI075.WMF
REALI076.WMF
REALI077.WMF
REALI078.WMF
REALI079.WMF
REALI080.WMF
REALI081.WMF
REALI082.WMF
REALI083.WMF
REALI084.WMF
REALI085.WMF
REALI086.WMF
REALI087.WMF
REALI088.WMF
REALI089.WMF
REALI090.WMF
REALI091.WMF
REALI092.WMF
REALI093.WMF

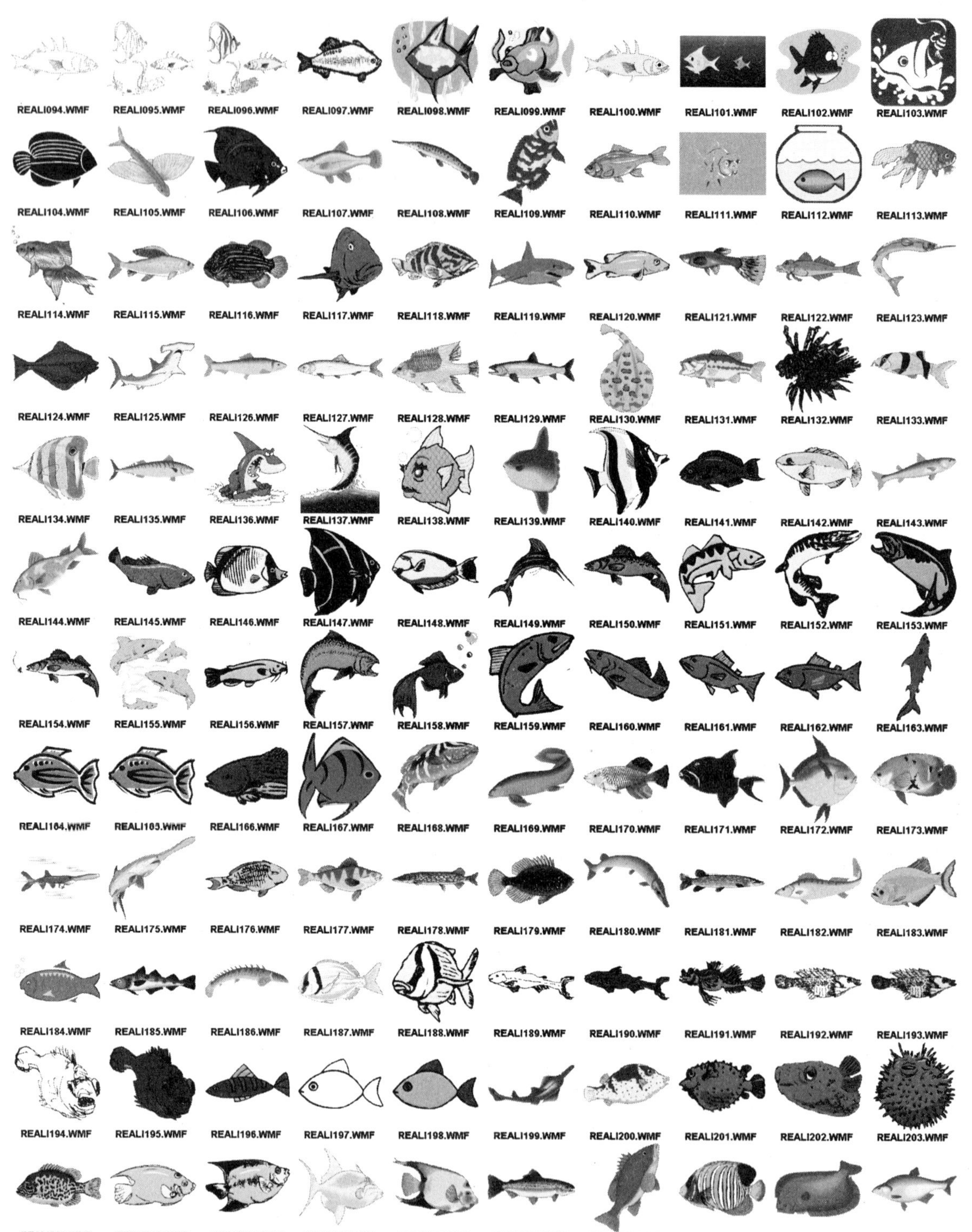
REALI094.WMF
REALI095.WMF
REALI096.WMF
REALI097.WMF
REALI098.WMF
REALI099.WMF
REALI100.WMF
REALI101.WMF
REALI102.WMF
REALI103.WMF
REALI104.WMF
REALI105.WMF
REALI106.WMF
REALI107.WMF
REALI108.WMF
REALI109.WMF
REALI110.WMF
REALI111.WMF
REALI112.WMF
REALI113.WMF
REALI114.WMF
REALI115.WMF
REALI116.WMF
REALI117.WMF
REALI118.WMF
REALI119.WMF
REALI120.WMF
REALI121.WMF
REALI122.WMF
REALI123.WMF
REALI124.WMF
REALI125.WMF
REALI126.WMF
REALI127.WMF
REALI128.WMF
REALI129.WMF
REALI130.WMF
REALI131.WMF
REALI132.WMF
REALI133.WMF
REALI134.WMF
REALI135.WMF
REALI136.WMF
REALI137.WMF
REALI138.WMF
REALI139.WMF
REALI140.WMF
REALI141.WMF
REALI142.WMF
REALI143.WMF
REALI144.WMF
REALI145.WMF
REALI146.WMF
REALI147.WMF
REALI148.WMF
REALI149.WMF
REALI150.WMF
REALI151.WMF
REALI152.WMF
REALI153.WMF
REALI154.WMF
REALI155.WMF
REALI156.WMF
REALI157.WMF
REALI158.WMF
REALI159.WMF
REALI160.WMF
REALI161.WMF
REALI162.WMF
REALI163.WMF
REALI164.WMF
REALI165.WMF
REALI166.WMF
REALI167.WMF
REALI168.WMF
REALI169.WMF
REALI170.WMF
REALI171.WMF
REALI172.WMF
REALI173.WMF
REALI174.WMF
REALI175.WMF
REALI176.WMF
REALI177.WMF
REALI178.WMF
REALI179.WMF
REALI180.WMF
REALI181.WMF
REALI182.WMF
REALI183.WMF
REALI184.WMF
REALI185.WMF
REALI186.WMF
REALI187.WMF
REALI188.WMF
REALI189.WMF
REALI190.WMF
REALI191.WMF
REALI192.WMF
REALI193.WMF
REALI194.WMF
REALI195.WMF
REALI196.WMF
REALI197.WMF
REALI198.WMF
REALI199.WMF
REALI200.WMF
REALI201.WMF
REALI202.WMF
REALI203.WMF
REALI204.WMF
REALI205.WMF
REALI206.WMF
REALI207.WMF
REALI208.WMF
REALI209.WMF
REALI210.WMF
REALI211.WMF
REALI212.WMF
REALI213.WMF

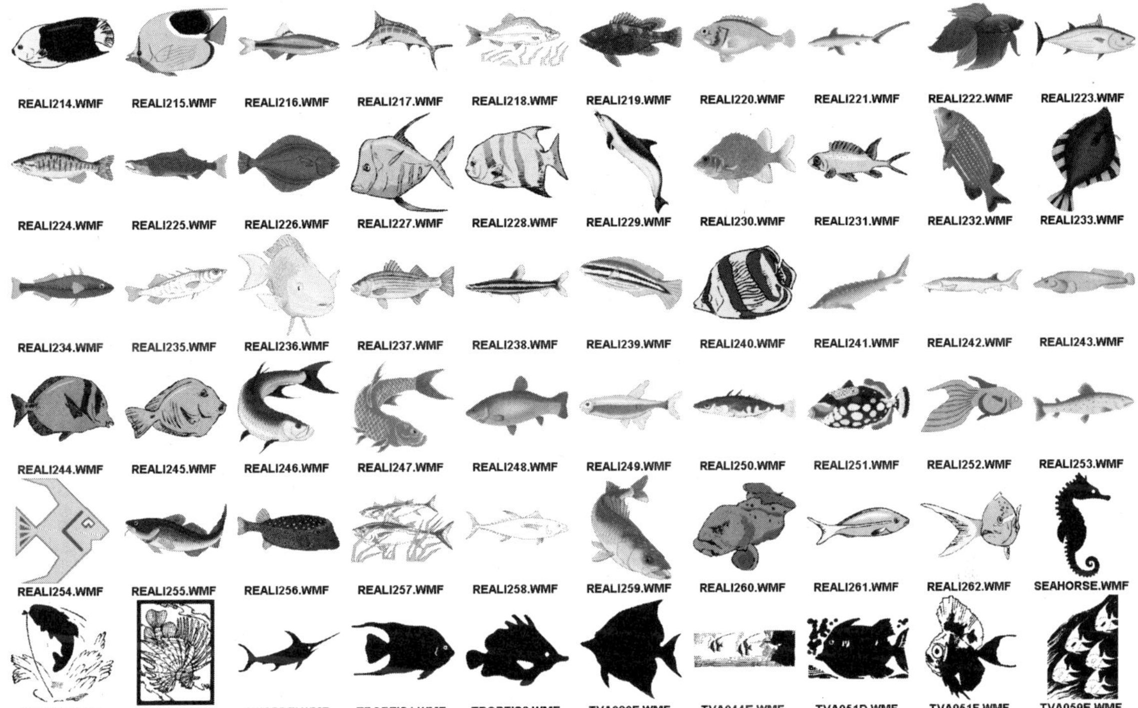
REALI214.WMF
REALI215.WMF
REALI216.WMF
REALI217.WMF
REALI218.WMF
REALI219.WMF
REALI220.WMF
REALI221.WMF
REALI222.WMF
REALI223.WMF
REALI224.WMF
REALI225.WMF
REALI226.WMF
REALI227.WMF
REALI228.WMF
REALI229.WMF
REALI230.WMF
REALI231.WMF
REALI232.WMF
REALI233.WMF
REALI234.WMF
REALI235.WMF
REALI236.WMF
REALI237.WMF
REALI238.WMF
REALI239.WMF
REALI240.WMF
REALI241.WMF
REALI242.WMF
REALI243.WMF
REALI244.WMF
REALI245.WMF
REALI246.WMF
REALI247.WMF
REALI248.WMF
REALI249.WMF
REALI250.WMF
REALI251.WMF
REALI252.WMF
REALI253.WMF
REALI254.WMF
REALI255.WMF
REALI256.WMF
REALI257.WMF
REALI258.WMF
REALI259.WMF
REALI260.WMF
REALI261.WMF
REALI262.WMF
SEAHORSE.WMF
SIT073C.WMF
SLG001A.WMF
SWORDFI.WMF
TROPFIS1.WMF
TROPFIS2.WMF
TVA029F.WMF
TVA044E.WMF
TVA051D.WMF
TVA051F.WMF
TVA059E.WMF

A_01.WMF
A_02.WMF
A_03.WMF
A_04.WMF
A_05.WMF
A_06.WMF
A_07.WMF
A_08.WMF
A_09.WMF
A_10.WMF
A_11.WMF
A_12.WMF
A_13.WMF
A_14.WMF
A_15.WMF
A_16.WMF
A_17.WMF
A_18.WMF
A_19.WMF
A_20.WMF
A_21.WMF
A_22.WMF
A_23.WMF
A_24.WMF
A_25.WMF
AOD076E.WMF
AOD077A.WMF
AOD077D.WMF
ASI040C.WMF
ASI041K.WMF
EAA159J.WMF
EQUIP01.WMF
EQUIP02.WMF
EQUIP03.WMF
EQUIP04.WMF
EQUIP05.WMF
EQUIP06.WMF
EQUIP07.WMF
EQUIP08.WMF
EQUIP09.WMF
EQUIP10.WMF
EQUIP11.WMF
EQUIP12.WMF
EQUIP13.WMF
EQUIP14.WMF
EQUIP15.WMF
EQUIP16.WMF
EQUIP17.WMF
EQUIP18.WMF
EQUIP19.WMF
EQUIP20.WMF
EQUIP21.WMF
EQUIP22.WMF
EQUIP23.WMF
EQUIP24.WMF
EQUIP25.WMF
EQUIP26.WMF
EQUIP27.WMF
EQUIP28.WMF
EQUIP29.WMF
EQUIP30.WMF
EQUIP31.WMF
EQUIP32.WMF
NAU000B.WMF
OEC039I.WMF
SIT089D.WMF
TOD076E.WMF
TOD077A.WMF
TOD077D.WMF
TOD077E.WMF

AQSIL08.WMF AQSIL10.WMF AQSIL19.WMF AQSIL22.WMF AQSIL24.WMF AQSIL26.WMF AQSIL30.WMF AQSIL31.WMF AQSIL38.WMF AQUA003.WMF
AQUA015.WMF AQUA031.WMF AQUA032.WMF AQUA035.WMF AQUA043.WMF AQUA044.WMF AQUA047.WMF AQUA048.WMF AQUA057.WMF AQUA067.WMF
AQUA078.WMF AQUA083.WMF AQUA084.WMF AQUA085.WMF AQUA086.WMF AQUA098.WMF AQUA099.WMF AQUA103.WMF AQUA104.WMF AQUA116.WMF
AQUA140.WMF AQUA141.WMF AQUA142.WMF AQUA143.WMF AQUA144.WMF AQUA145.WMF AQUA152.WMF AQUA154.WMF BLACK01.WMF BLACK02.WMF
BLACK03.WMF BLACK04.WMF BLACK05.WMF BLACK06.WMF BLACK07.WMF BLACK08.WMF BLACK09.WMF BLACK10.WMF BLACK11.WMF BLACK12.WMF
BLACK13.WMF BLACK14.WMF BLACK15.WMF BLACK16.WMF BLACK17.WMF BLACK18.WMF BLACK19.WMF BLACK20.WMF BLACK21.WMF BLACK22.WMF
BLACK23.WMF BLACK24.WMF BLACK25.WMF CART001.WMF CART002.WMF CART003.WMF CART004.WMF CART005.WMF CART006.WMF CART007.WMF
CART008.WMF CART009.WMF CART010.WMF CART011.WMF CART012.WMF CART013.WMF CART014.WMF CART015.WMF CART016.WMF CART017.WMF
CART018.WMF CART019.WMF CART020.WMF CART021.WMF CART022.WMF CART023.WMF CART024.WMF CART025.WMF CART026.WMF CART027.WMF
CART028.WMF CART029.WMF CART030.WMF CART031.WMF CART032.WMF CART033.WMF CART034.WMF COLOR001.WMF COLOR002.WMF COLOR003.WMF
COLOR004.WMF COLOR005.WMF COLOR006.WMF COLOR007.WMF COLOR008.WMF COLOR009.WMF COLOR010.WMF COLOR011.WMF COLOR012.WMF COLOR013.WMF
COLOR014.WMF COLOR015.WMF COLOR016.WMF COLOR017.WMF COLOR018.WMF COLOR019.WMF COLOR020.WMF COLOR021.WMF COLOR022.WMF COLOR023.WMF

COLOR024.WMF	COLOR025.WMF	COLOR026.WMF	COLOR027.WMF	COLOR028.WMF	COLOR029.WMF	COLOR030.WMF	COLOR031.WMF	COLOR032.WMF	COLOR033.WMF
COLOR034.WMF	COLOR035.WMF	COLOR036.WMF	COLOR037.WMF	COLOR038.WMF	COLOR039.WMF	COLOR040.WMF	COLOR041.WMF	COLOR042.WMF	COLOR043.WMF
COLOR044.WMF	COLOR045.WMF	COLOR046.WMF	COLOR047.WMF	COLOR048.WMF	COLOR049.WMF	COLOR050.WMF	COLOR051.WMF	COLOR052.WMF	COLOR053.WMF
COLOR054.WMF	COLOR055.WMF	COLOR056.WMF	COLOR057.WMF	COLOR058.WMF	COLOR059.WMF	EAC027GG.WMF	FCP030B.WMF	FDD086C.WMF	LOBSTR.WMF
MAR002C.WMF	MAR004C.WMF	MAR009B.WMF	MAR016A.WMF	MAR022A.WMF	MAR030A.WMF	MOD009D.WMF	NAU015A.WMF	SHI027A.WMF	SHI027B.WMF
SHR016M.WMF	SHR016N.WMF	SHR017C.WMF	SHR017D.WMF	SHR032C.WMF	SWA002A.WMF				

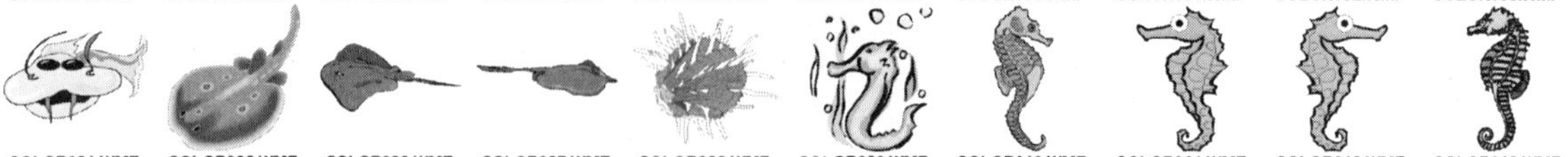

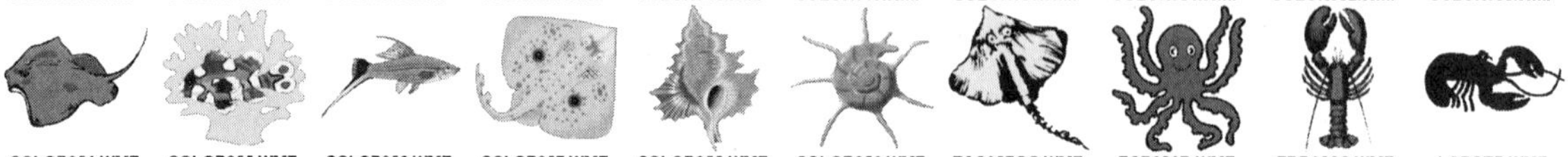

Ocean • Shells

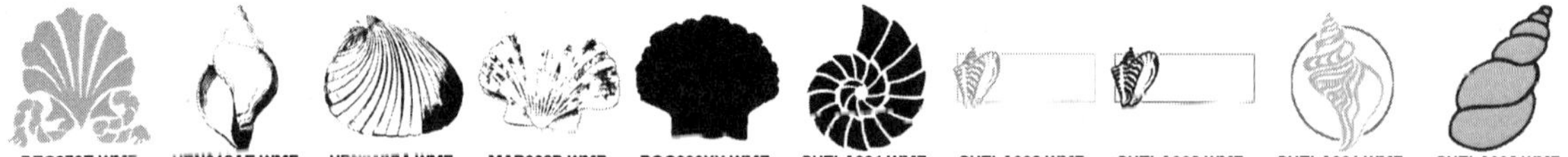

DEC079T.WMF	HPN042AE.WMF	HPN042CA.WMF	MAR002B.WMF	POC099XX.WMF	SHELA001.WMF	SHELA002.WMF	SHELA003.WMF	SHELA004.WMF	SHELA005.WMF
SHELA006.WMF	SHELA007.WMF	SHELA008.WMF	SHELA009.WMF	SHELA010.WMF	SHELA011.WMF	SHELA012.WMF	SHELA013.WMF	SHELA014.WMF	SHELA015.WMF
SHELA016.WMF	SHELA017.WMF	SHELA018.WMF	SHELA019.WMF	SHELA020.WMF	SHELA021.WMF	SHELB001.WMF	SHELB002.WMF	SHELB003.WMF	SHELB004.WMF
SHELB005.WMF	SHELB006.WMF	SHELB007.WMF	SHELB008.WMF	SHELB009.WMF	SHELB010.WMF	SHELB011.WMF	SHELB012.WMF	SHELB013.WMF	SHELB014.WMF
SHELB015.WMF	SHELB016.WMF	SHELB017.WMF	SHELB018.WMF	SHELB019.WMF	SHELB020.WMF	SHELB021.WMF	SHELB022.WMF	SHELB023.WMF	SHELB024.WMF

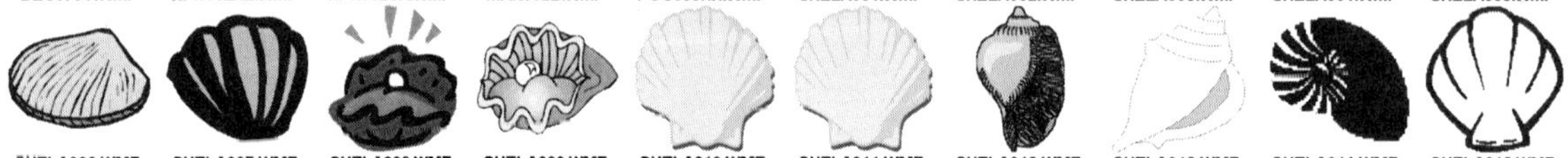

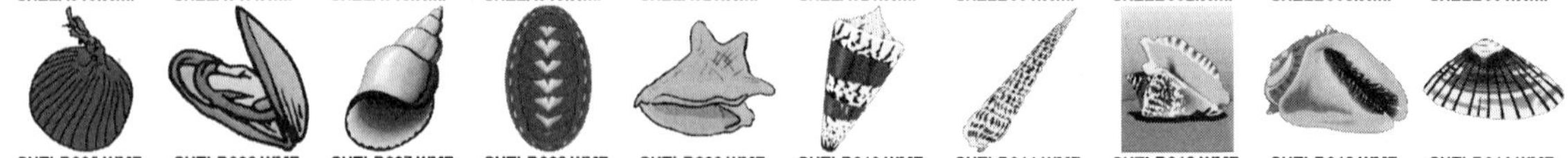

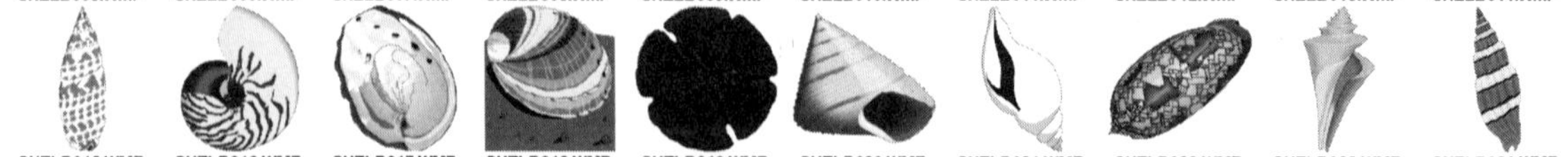

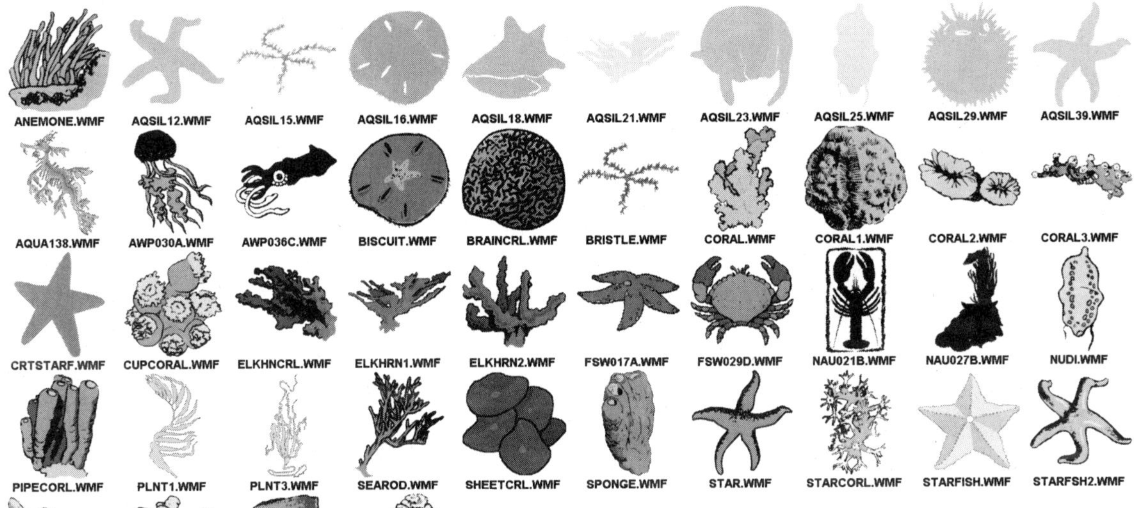
ANEMONE.WMF
AQSIL12.WMF
AQSIL15.WMF
AQSIL16.WMF
AQSIL18.WMF
AQSIL21.WMF
AQSIL23.WMF
AQSIL25.WMF
AQSIL29.WMF
AQSIL39.WMF
AQUA138.WMF
AWP030A.WMF
AWP036C.WMF
BISCUIT.WMF
BRAINCRL.WMF
BRISTLE.WMF
CORAL.WMF
CORAL1.WMF
CORAL2.WMF
CORAL3.WMF
CRTSTARF.WMF
CUPCORAL.WMF
ELKHNCRL.WMF
ELKHRN1.WMF
ELKHRN2.WMF
FSW017A.WMF
FSW029D.WMF
NAU021B.WMF
NAU027B.WMF
NUDI.WMF
PIPECORL.WMF
PLNT1.WMF
PLNT3.WMF
SEAROD.WMF
SHEETCRL.WMF
SPONGE.WMF
STAR.WMF
STARCORL.WMF
STARFISH.WMF
STARFSH2.WMF
STGHNCRL.WMF
TUBESPNG.WMF
VASECORL.WMF
WORM.WMF

0680.WMF
0716.WMF
BARBECU4.WMF
BARBECUE.WMF
BBQGRILL.WMF
BBQMAN.WMF
BIT0847.WMF
BIT0849.WMF
BIT0854.WMF
BIT0855.WMF
COOLER.WMF
FDDNK059.WMF
FDDNK257.WMF
FSW017E.WMF
FSW019B.WMF
HFSI003D.WMF
HHBO019J.WMF
HHBO020J.WMF
HHCA120J.WMF
HHGC075D.WMF
HHGC091D.WMF
HHGC124D.WMF
HHSI050D.WMF
HHSI051D.WMF
HHSI077D.WMF
HHSI097D.WMF
HHSI127D.WMF
MANGRILL.WMF
MANWCHAR.WMF
MANWPLAT.WMF
PCNC.WMF
PICBSKT2.WMF
PICNCBSK.WMF
PICNCGRP.WMF
PICNIC.WMF
PICNIC76.WMF
PICNICB2.WMF
PICNICCO.WMF
PORTABL1.WMF
SPCA017D.WMF
TDG024C.WMF

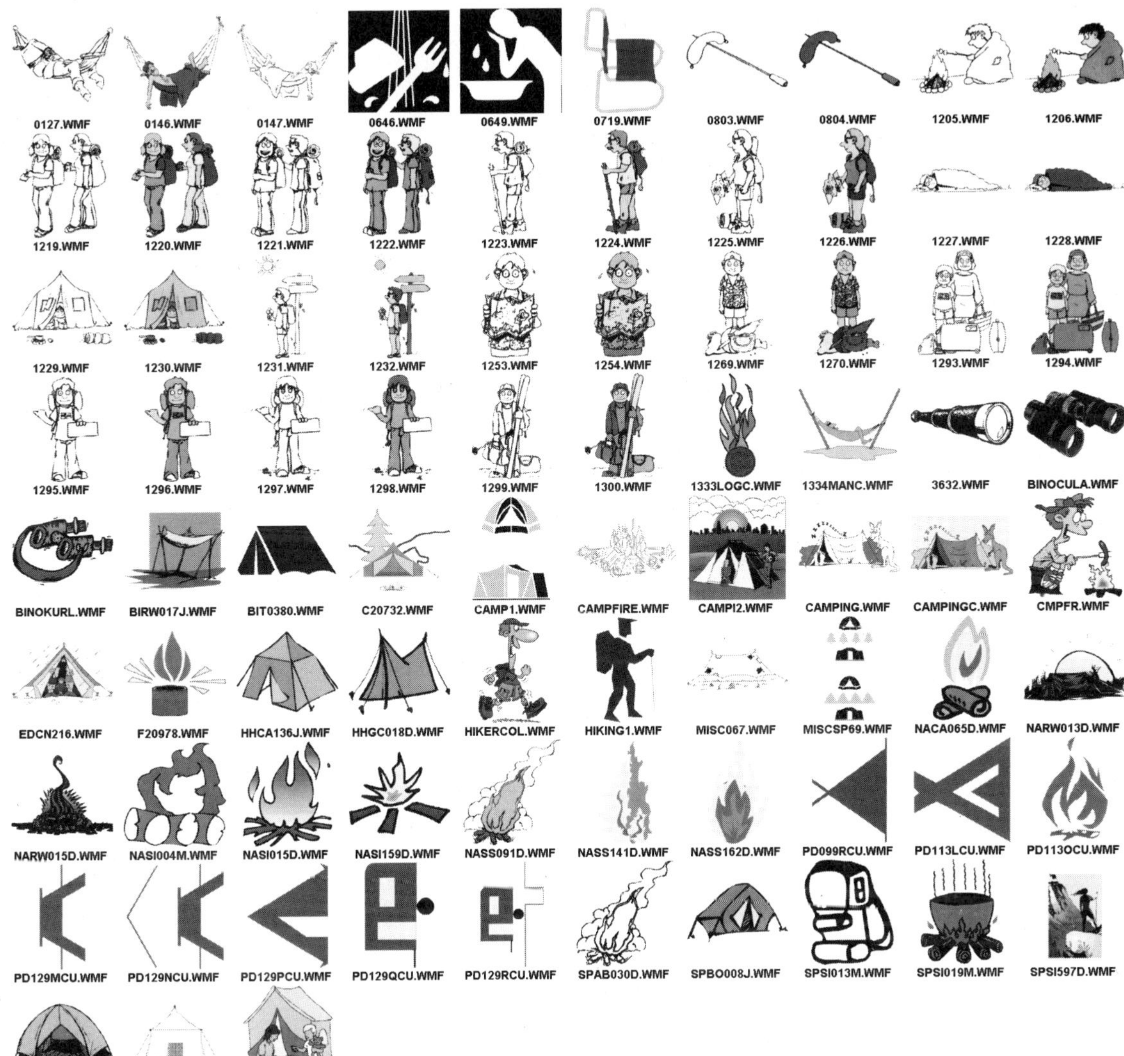
0127.WMF
0146.WMF
0147.WMF
0646.WMF
0649.WMF
0719.WMF
0803.WMF
0804.WMF
1205.WMF
1206.WMF
1219.WMF
1220.WMF
1221.WMF
1222.WMF
1223.WMF
1224.WMF
1225.WMF
1226.WMF
1227.WMF
1228.WMF
1229.WMF
1230.WMF
1231.WMF
1232.WMF
1253.WMF
1254.WMF
1269.WMF
1270.WMF
1293.WMF
1294.WMF
1295.WMF
1296.WMF
1297.WMF
1298.WMF
1299.WMF
1300.WMF
1333LOGC.WMF
1334MANC.WMF
3632.WMF
BINOCULA.WMF
BINOKURL.WMF
BIRW017J.WMF
BIT0380.WMF
C20732.WMF
CAMP1.WMF
CAMPFIRE.WMF
CAMPI2.WMF
CAMPING.WMF
CAMPINGC.WMF
CMPFR.WMF
EDCN216.WMF
F20978.WMF
HHCA136J.WMF
HHGC018D.WMF
HIKERCOL.WMF
HIKING1.WMF
MISC067.WMF
MISCSP69.WMF
NACA065D.WMF
NARW013D.WMF
NARW015D.WMF
NASI004M.WMF
NASI015D.WMF
NASI159D.WMF
NASS091D.WMF
NASS141D.WMF
NASS162D.WMF
PD099RCU.WMF
PD113LCU.WMF
PD113OCU.WMF
PD129MCU.WMF
PD129NCU.WMF
PD129PCU.WMF
PD129QCU.WMF
PD129RCU.WMF
SPAB030D.WMF
SPBO008J.WMF
SPSI013M.WMF
SPSI019M.WMF
SPSI597D.WMF
TENT.WMF
TENT2.WMF
TENTKIDS.WMF

AD01.WMF
AD02.WMF
AD03.WMF
AD04.WMF
AD05.WMF
AD06.WMF
AD07.WMF
AD08.WMF
AD09.WMF
AD10.WMF
AD11.WMF
AD12.WMF
AD13.WMF
AD14.WMF
AD15.WMF
AD16.WMF
AD17.WMF
AD18.WMF
AD19.WMF
AD20.WMF
AD21.WMF
AD22.WMF
AD23.WMF
AD24.WMF
AD25.WMF
AD26.WMF
C01.WMF
C02.WMF
C03.WMF
C04.WMF
C05.WMF
C06.WMF
C07.WMF
C08.WMF
C09.WMF
C10.WMF
C11.WMF
C12.WMF
C13.WMF
C14.WMF
C15.WMF
C42.WMF
C44.WMF
E15.WMF
HAMMOCK2.WMF
HOTTUB.WMF
TD77.WMF

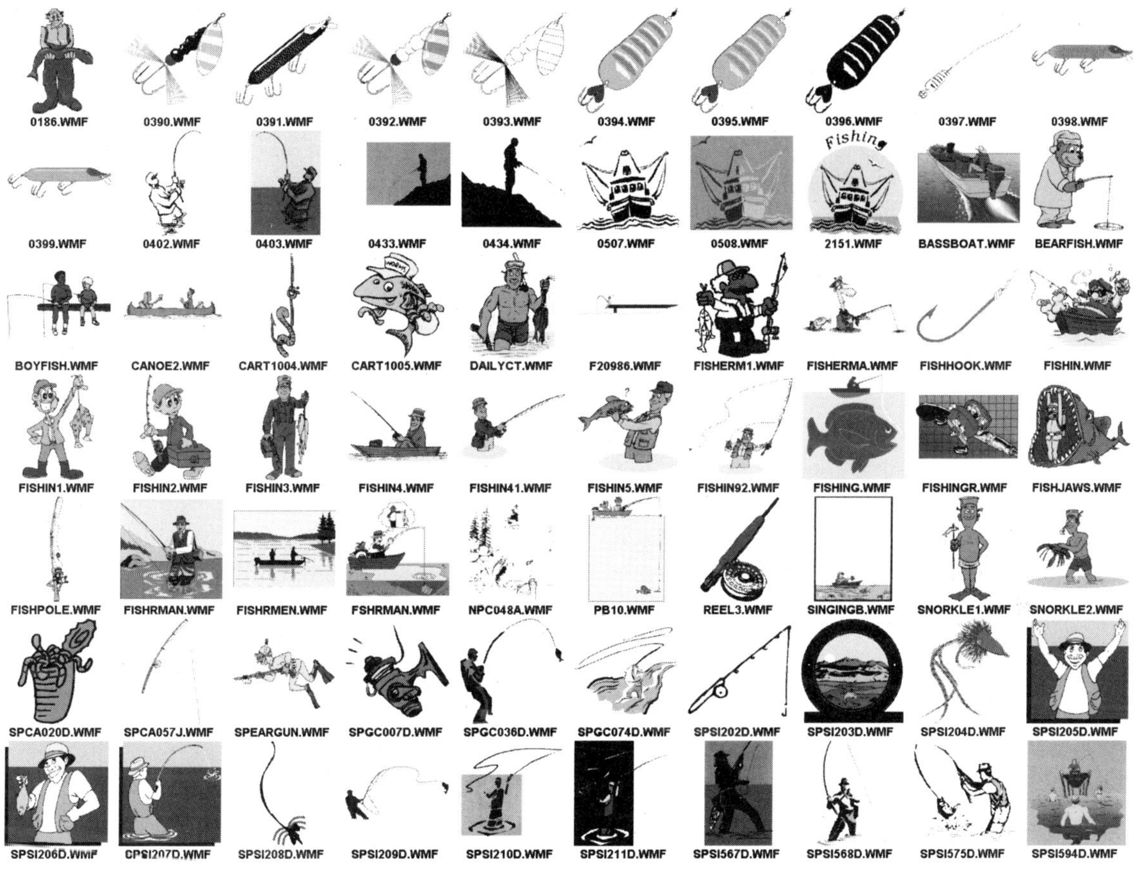
0186.WMF
0390.WMF
0391.WMF
0392.WMF
0393.WMF
0394.WMF
0395.WMF
0396.WMF
0397.WMF
0398.WMF
0399.WMF
0402.WMF
0403.WMF
0433.WMF
0434.WMF
0507.WMF
0508.WMF
Fishing
2151.WMF
BASSBOAT.WMF
BEARFISH.WMF
BOYFISH.WMF
CANOE2.WMF
CART1004.WMF
CART1005.WMF
DAILYCT.WMF
F20986.WMF
FISHERM1.WMF
FISHERMA.WMF
FISHHOOK.WMF
FISHIN.WMF
FISHIN1.WMF
FISHIN2.WMF
FISHIN3.WMF
FISHIN4.WMF
FISHIN41.WMF
FISHIN5.WMF
FISHIN92.WMF
FISHING.WMF
FISHINGR.WMF
FISHJAWS.WMF
FISHPOLE.WMF
FISHRMAN.WMF
FISHRMEN.WMF
FSHRMAN.WMF
NPC048A.WMF
PB10.WMF
REEL3.WMF
SINGINGB.WMF
SNORKLE1.WMF
SNORKLE2.WMF
SPCA020D.WMF
SPCA057J.WMF
SPEARGUN.WMF
SPGC007D.WMF
SPGC036D.WMF
SPGC074D.WMF
SPSI202D.WMF
SPSI203D.WMF
SPSI204D.WMF
SPSI205D.WMF
SPSI206D.WMF
SPSI207D.WMF
SPSI208D.WMF
SPSI209D.WMF
SPSI210D.WMF
SPSI211D.WMF
SPSI567D.WMF
SPSI568D.WMF
SPSI575D.WMF
SPSI594D.WMF

Outdoors • Water Activities (WATER)

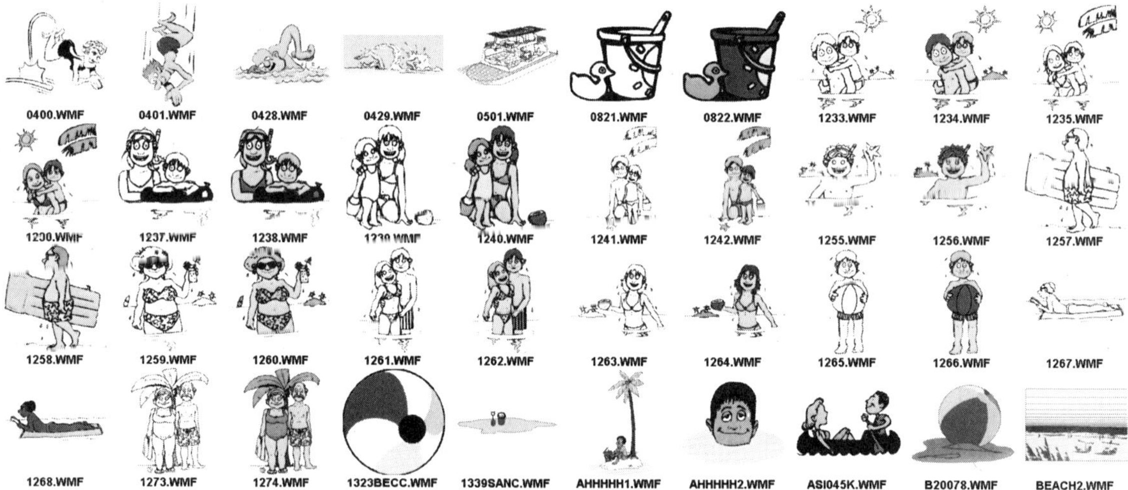

BEACHBA1.WMF
BEACHBAL.WMF
BEACHBOY.WMF
BEACHDES.WMF
BEACHGAL.WMF
BEACHGRL.WMF
BEACHMAN.WMF
BEACHTOY.WMF
BIT0816.WMF
BRELLA1.WMF
CANOE01M.WMF
CANOE1.WMF
CANOEIN3.WMF
CANOEING.WMF
CARIBEAN.WMF
CTMISC20.WMF
DEEPSEA.WMF
DETECTOR.WMF
DIVERCOL.WMF
ENCA010J.WMF
FCP020H.WMF
FISHERMA.WMF
FLOATING.WMF
FRA015A.WMF
FSW031A.WMF
FSW031B.WMF
FSW031C.WMF
GIRLATPO.WMF
HAMMOCK1.WMF
HHCA053J.WMF
HHCA111J.WMF
HSP002C.WMF
I21139.WMF
ICP031B.WMF
IHO013E.WMF
ISLAND.WMF
JULY.WMF
L21181.WMF
L21194.WMF
LIGHTHOU.WMF
LOTION1.WMF
MEGC002D.WMF
MSL046E.WMF
OSP023A.WMF
OSP023B.WMF
OSP023C.WMF
OTC030M.WMF
PD039MCU.WMF
PD099UCU.WMF
PGX001E.WMF
POL.WMF
POOL.WMF
POOLCHEM.WMF
RAFTING.WMF
RELAX1.WMF
RELAX2.WMF
RELAX3.WMF
ROW.WMF
ROWC.WMF
SAND_CAS.WMF
SANDBURY.WMF
SANDCSTL.WMF
SHELL1.WMF
SHELL2.WMF
SKER.WMF
SKJT.WMF
SPA028D.WMF
SPSI001M.WMF
SPSI588D.WMF
SPSI589D.WMF
SUNBAKE.WMF
SUNBAKEC.WMF
SUNBURN5.WMF
SUNBURN6.WMF
SURFERCO.WMF
SWIMMING.WMF
SWM.WMF
SWM2.WMF
TANNING1.WMF
TANNING2.WMF
TANNING3.WMF
THEPLUNG.WMF
TOASTIN1.WMF
TOASTIN2.WMF
TOWEL.WMF
TREASURE.WMF
UPTHECRE.WMF
W21872.WMF
WATERSKI.WMF

PECA176J.WMF
PECA177J.WMF
PECA179J.WMF
PECA180J.WMF
PECA181J.WMF
PECA182J.WMF
PECA183J.WMF
PECA185J.WMF
PECA186J.WMF
PECA187J.WMF
PECA188J.WMF
PECA189J.WMF
PECA190J.WMF
PECA193J.WMF
PECA194J.WMF
PECA197J.WMF
PECA198J.WMF
PECA199J.WMF
PECA200J.WMF
PECA201J.WMF
PECA202J.WMF
PECA203J.WMF
PECA204J.WMF
PECA205J.WMF
PECA206J.WMF
PECA207J.WMF
PECA208J.WMF
PECA209J.WMF
PECA210J.WMF
PECA211J.WMF
PECA212J.WMF
PECA213J.WMF
PECA214J.WMF
PECA215J.WMF
PECA236J.WMF
PECA237J.WMF
PECA238J.WMF
PECA239J.WMF
PECA240J.WMF
PECA241J.WMF
PECA242J.WMF
PECA243J.WMF
PECA244J.WMF
PECA245J.WMF

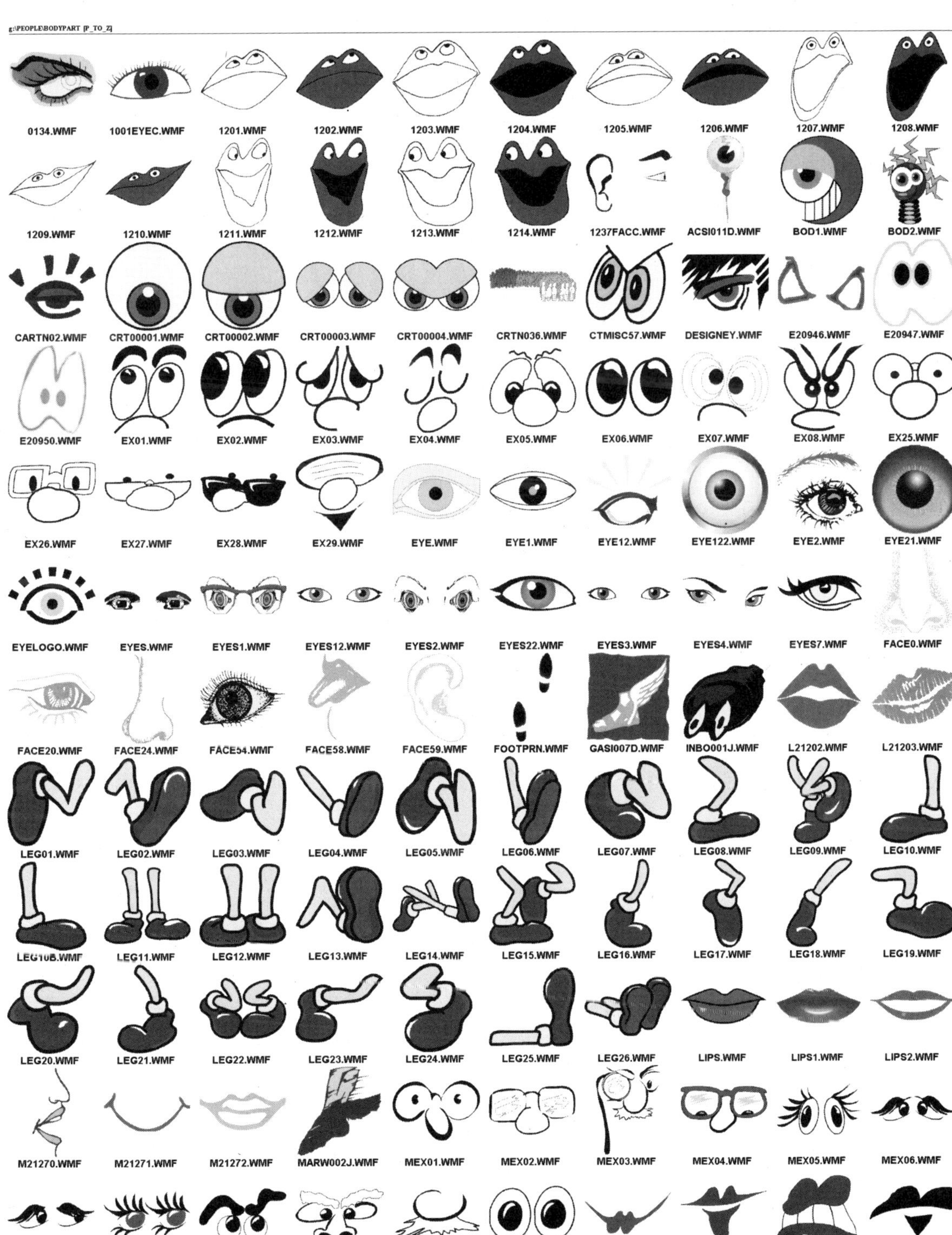
g:\PEOPLE\BODYPART [P_TO_Z]
0134.WMF
1001EYEC.WMF
1201.WMF
1202.WMF
1203.WMF
1204.WMF
1205.WMF
1206.WMF
1207.WMF
1208.WMF
1209.WMF
1210.WMF
1211.WMF
1212.WMF
1213.WMF
1214.WMF
1237FACC.WMF
ACSI011D.WMF
BOD1.WMF
BOD2.WMF
CARTN02.WMF
CRT00001.WMF
CRT00002.WMF
CRT00003.WMF
CRT00004.WMF
CRTN036.WMF
CTMISC57.WMF
DESIGNEY.WMF
E20946.WMF
E20947.WMF
E20950.WMF
EX01.WMF
EX02.WMF
EX03.WMF
EX04.WMF
EX05.WMF
EX06.WMF
EX07.WMF
EX08.WMF
EX25.WMF
EX26.WMF
EX27.WMF
EX28.WMF
EX29.WMF
EYE.WMF
EYE1.WMF
EYE12.WMF
EYE122.WMF
EYE2.WMF
EYE21.WMF
EYELOGO.WMF
EYES.WMF
EYES1.WMF
EYES12.WMF
EYES2.WMF
EYES22.WMF
EYES3.WMF
EYES4.WMF
EYES7.WMF
FACE0.WMF
FACE20.WMF
FACE24.WMF
FACE54.WMF
FACE58.WMF
FACE59.WMF
FOOTPRN.WMF
GASI007D.WMF
INBO001J.WMF
L21202.WMF
L21203.WMF
LEG01.WMF
LEG02.WMF
LEG03.WMF
LEG04.WMF
LEG05.WMF
LEG06.WMF
LEG07.WMF
LEG08.WMF
LEG09.WMF
LEG10.WMF
LEG10B.WMF
LEG11.WMF
LEG12.WMF
LEG13.WMF
LEG14.WMF
LEG15.WMF
LEG16.WMF
LEG17.WMF
LEG18.WMF
LEG19.WMF
LEG20.WMF
LEG21.WMF
LEG22.WMF
LEG23.WMF
LEG24.WMF
LEG25.WMF
LEG26.WMF
LIPS.WMF
LIPS1.WMF
LIPS2.WMF
M21270.WMF
M21271.WMF
M21272.WMF
MARW002J.WMF
MEX01.WMF
MEX02.WMF
MEX03.WMF
MEX04.WMF
MEX05.WMF
MEX06.WMF
MEX07.WMF
MEX08.WMF
MEX09.WMF
MEX10.WMF
MEX11.WMF
MEX12.WMF
MEX13.WMF
MEX14.WMF
MEX15.WMF
MEX16.WMF

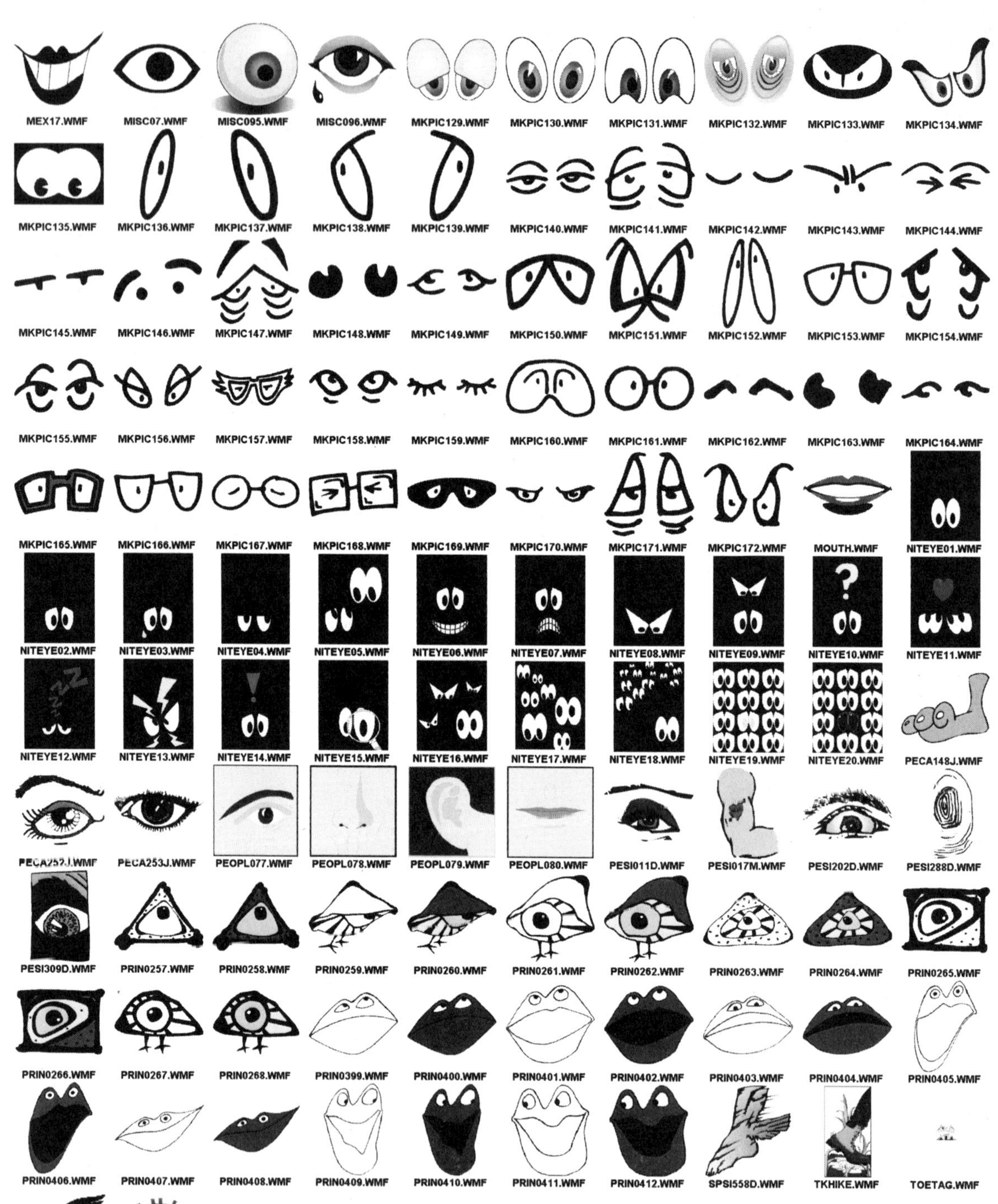
MEX17.WMF
MISC07.WMF
MISC095.WMF
MISC096.WMF
MKPIC129.WMF
MKPIC130.WMF
MKPIC131.WMF
MKPIC132.WMF
MKPIC133.WMF
MKPIC134.WMF
MKPIC135.WMF
MKPIC136.WMF
MKPIC137.WMF
MKPIC138.WMF
MKPIC139.WMF
MKPIC140.WMF
MKPIC141.WMF
MKPIC142.WMF
MKPIC143.WMF
MKPIC144.WMF
MKPIC145.WMF
MKPIC146.WMF
MKPIC147.WMF
MKPIC148.WMF
MKPIC149.WMF
MKPIC150.WMF
MKPIC151.WMF
MKPIC152.WMF
MKPIC153.WMF
MKPIC154.WMF
MKPIC155.WMF
MKPIC156.WMF
MKPIC157.WMF
MKPIC158.WMF
MKPIC159.WMF
MKPIC160.WMF
MKPIC161.WMF
MKPIC162.WMF
MKPIC163.WMF
MKPIC164.WMF
MKPIC165.WMF
MKPIC166.WMF
MKPIC167.WMF
MKPIC168.WMF
MKPIC169.WMF
MKPIC170.WMF
MKPIC171.WMF
MKPIC172.WMF
MOUTH.WMF
NITEYE01.WMF
NITEYE02.WMF
NITEYE03.WMF
NITEYE04.WMF
NITEYE05.WMF
NITEYE06.WMF
NITEYE07.WMF
NITEYE08.WMF
NITEYE09.WMF
NITEYE10.WMF
NITEYE11.WMF
NITEYE12.WMF
NITEYE13.WMF
NITEYE14.WMF
NITEYE15.WMF
NITEYE16.WMF
NITEYE17.WMF
NITEYE18.WMF
NITEYE19.WMF
NITEYE20.WMF
PECA148J.WMF
PECA252J.WMF
PECA253J.WMF
PEOPL077.WMF
PEOPL078.WMF
PEOPL079.WMF
PEOPL080.WMF
PESI011D.WMF
PESI017M.WMF
PESI202D.WMF
PESI288D.WMF
PESI309D.WMF
PRIN0257.WMF
PRIN0258.WMF
PRIN0259.WMF
PRIN0260.WMF
PRIN0261.WMF
PRIN0262.WMF
PRIN0263.WMF
PRIN0264.WMF
PRIN0265.WMF
PRIN0266.WMF
PRIN0267.WMF
PRIN0268.WMF
PRIN0399.WMF
PRIN0400.WMF
PRIN0401.WMF
PRIN0402.WMF
PRIN0403.WMF
PRIN0404.WMF
PRIN0405.WMF
PRIN0406.WMF
PRIN0407.WMF
PRIN0408.WMF
PRIN0409.WMF
PRIN0410.WMF
PRIN0411.WMF
PRIN0412.WMF
SPSI558D.WMF
TKHIKE.WMF
TOETAG.WMF
WINGFOOT.WMF
YMISC494.WMF

g:\PEOPLE\CARTOONS [P_TO_Z]
CARTA001.WMF CARTA002.WMF CARTA003.WMF CARTA004.WMF CARTA005.WMF CARTA006.WMF CARTA007.WMF CARTA008.WMF CARTA009.WMF CARTA010.WMF
CARTA011.WMF CARTA012.WMF CARTA013.WMF CARTA014.WMF CARTA015.WMF CARTA016.WMF CARTA017.WMF CARTA018.WMF CARTA019.WMF CARTA020.WMF
CARTA021.WMF CARTA022.WMF CARTA023.WMF CARTA024.WMF CARTA025.WMF CARTA026.WMF CARTA027.WMF CARTA028.WMF CARTA029.WMF CARTA030.WMF
CARTA031.WMF CARTA032.WMF CARTA033.WMF CARTA034.WMF CARTA035.WMF CARTA036.WMF CARTA037.WMF CARTA038.WMF CARTA039.WMF CARTA040.WMF
CARTA041.WMF CARTA042.WMF CARTA043.WMF CARTA044.WMF CARTA045.WMF CARTA046.WMF CARTA047.WMF CARTA048.WMF CARTA049.WMF CARTA050.WMF
CARTA051.WMF CARTA052.WMF CARTA053.WMF CARTA054.WMF CARTA055.WMF CARTA056.WMF CARTA057.WMF CARTA058.WMF CARTA059.WMF CARTA060.WMF
CARTA061.WMF CARTA062.WMF CARTA063.WMF CARTA064.WMF CARTA065.WMF CARTA066.WMF CARTA067.WMF CARTA068.WMF CARTA069.WMF CARTA070.WMF
CARTA071.WMF CARTA072.WMF CARTA073.WMF CARTA074.WMF CARTA075.WMF CARTA076.WMF CARTA077.WMF CARTA078.WMF CARTA079.WMF CARTA080.WMF
CARTA081.WMF CARTA082.WMF CARTA083.WMF CARTA084.WMF CARTA085.WMF CARTA086.WMF CARTA087.WMF CARTA088.WMF CARTA089.WMF CARTA090.WMF
CARTA091.WMF CARTA092.WMF CARTA093.WMF CARTA094.WMF CARTA095.WMF CARTA096.WMF CARTA097.WMF CARTA098.WMF CARTA099.WMF CARTA100.WMF
CARTA101.WMF CARTA102.WMF CARTA103.WMF CARTA104.WMF CARTA105.WMF CARTA106.WMF CARTA107.WMF CARTA108.WMF CARTA109.WMF CARTA110.WMF
CARTA111.WMF CARTA112.WMF CARTA113.WMF CARTA114.WMF CARTA115.WMF CARTA116.WMF CARTA117.WMF CARTA118.WMF CARTA119.WMF CARTA120.WMF

CARTA121.WMF
CARTA122.WMF
CARTA123.WMF
CARTA124.WMF
CARTA125.WMF
CARTA126.WMF
CARTA127.WMF
CARTA128.WMF
CARTA129.WMF
CARTA130.WMF
CARTA131.WMF
CARTA132.WMF
CARTA133.WMF
CARTA134.WMF
CARTA135.WMF
CARTA136.WMF
CARTA137.WMF
CARTA138.WMF
CARTA139.WMF
CARTA140.WMF
CARTA141.WMF
CARTA142.WMF
CARTA143.WMF
CARTA144.WMF
CARTA145.WMF
CARTA146.WMF
CARTA147.WMF
CARTA148.WMF
CARTA149.WMF
CARTA150.WMF
CARTA151.WMF
CARTA152.WMF
CARTA153.WMF
CARTA154.WMF
CARTA155.WMF
CARTA156.WMF
CARTA157.WMF
CARTA158.WMF
CARTA159.WMF
CARTA160.WMF
CARTA161.WMF
CARTA162.WMF
CARTA163.WMF
CARTA164.WMF
CARTA165.WMF
CARTA166.WMF
CARTA167.WMF
CARTA168.WMF
CARTA169.WMF
CARTA170.WMF
CARTA171.WMF
CARTA172.WMF
CARTA173.WMF
CARTA174.WMF
CARTA175.WMF
CARTA176.WMF
CARTA177.WMF
CARTA178.WMF
CARTA179.WMF
CARTA180.WMF
CARTA181.WMF
CARTA182.WMF
CARTA183.WMF
CARTA184.WMF
CARTA185.WMF
CARTA186.WMF
CARTA187.WMF
CARTA188.WMF
CARTA189.WMF
CARTA190.WMF
CARTA191.WMF
CARTA192.WMF
CARTA193.WMF
CARTA194.WMF
CARTA195.WMF
CARTA196.WMF
CARTA197.WMF
CARTA198.WMF
CARTA199.WMF
CARTA200.WMF
CARTA201.WMF
CARTA202.WMF
CARTA203.WMF
CARTA204.WMF
CARTA205.WMF
CARTA206.WMF
CARTA207.WMF
CARTA208.WMF
CARTA209.WMF
CARTA210.WMF
CARTA211.WMF
CARTA212.WMF
CARTA213.WMF
CARTA214.WMF
CARTA215.WMF
CARTA216.WMF
CARTA217.WMF
CARTA218.WMF
CARTA219.WMF
CARTA220.WMF
CARTA221.WMF
CARTA222.WMF
CARTA223.WMF
CARTA224.WMF
CARTA225.WMF
CARTA226.WMF
CARTA227.WMF
CARTA228.WMF
CARTA229.WMF
CARTA230.WMF
CARTA231.WMF
CARTA232.WMF
CARTA233.WMF
CARTA234.WMF
CARTA235.WMF
CARTA236.WMF
CARTA237.WMF
CARTA238.WMF
CARTA239.WMF
CARTA240.WMF

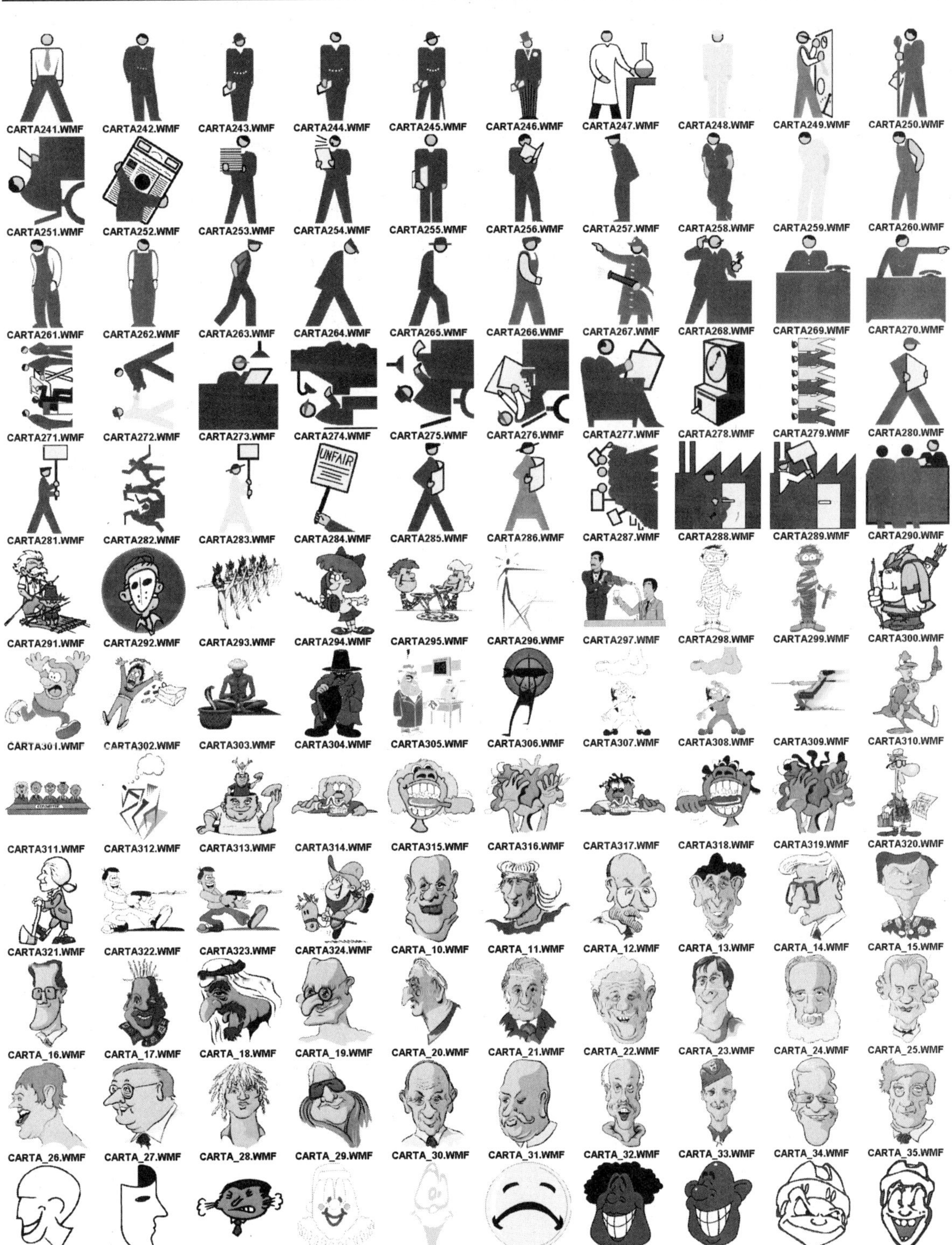
CARTA241.WMF CARTA242.WMF CARTA243.WMF CARTA244.WMF CARTA245.WMF CARTA246.WMF CARTA247.WMF CARTA248.WMF CARTA249.WMF CARTA250.WMF
CARTA251.WMF CARTA252.WMF CARTA253.WMF CARTA254.WMF CARTA255.WMF CARTA256.WMF CARTA257.WMF CARTA258.WMF CARTA259.WMF CARTA260.WMF
CARTA261.WMF CARTA262.WMF CARTA263.WMF CARTA264.WMF CARTA265.WMF CARTA266.WMF CARTA267.WMF CARTA268.WMF CARTA269.WMF CARTA270.WMF
CARTA271.WMF CARTA272.WMF CARTA273.WMF CARTA274.WMF CARTA275.WMF CARTA276.WMF CARTA277.WMF CARTA278.WMF CARTA279.WMF CARTA280.WMF
UNFAIR
CARTA281.WMF CARTA282.WMF CARTA283.WMF CARTA284.WMF CARTA285.WMF CARTA286.WMF CARTA287.WMF CARTA288.WMF CARTA289.WMF CARTA290.WMF
CARTA291.WMF CARTA292.WMF CARTA293.WMF CARTA294.WMF CARTA295.WMF CARTA296.WMF CARTA297.WMF CARTA298.WMF CARTA299.WMF CARTA300.WMF
CARTA301.WMF CARTA302.WMF CARTA303.WMF CARTA304.WMF CARTA305.WMF CARTA306.WMF CARTA307.WMF CARTA308.WMF CARTA309.WMF CARTA310.WMF
CARTA311.WMF CARTA312.WMF CARTA313.WMF CARTA314.WMF CARTA315.WMF CARTA316.WMF CARTA317.WMF CARTA318.WMF CARTA319.WMF CARTA320.WMF
CARTA321.WMF CARTA322.WMF CARTA323.WMF CARTA324.WMF CARTA_10.WMF CARTA_11.WMF CARTA_12.WMF CARTA_13.WMF CARTA_14.WMF CARTA_15.WMF
CARTA_16.WMF CARTA_17.WMF CARTA_18.WMF CARTA_19.WMF CARTA_20.WMF CARTA_21.WMF CARTA_22.WMF CARTA_23.WMF CARTA_24.WMF CARTA_25.WMF
CARTA_26.WMF CARTA_27.WMF CARTA_28.WMF CARTA_29.WMF CARTA_30.WMF CARTA_31.WMF CARTA_32.WMF CARTA_33.WMF CARTA_34.WMF CARTA_35.WMF
CARTA_36.WMF CARTA_37.WMF CARTA_38.WMF CARTA_39.WMF CARTA_40.WMF CARTA_41.WMF CARTA_42.WMF CARTA_43.WMF CARTA_44.WMF CARTA_45.WMF

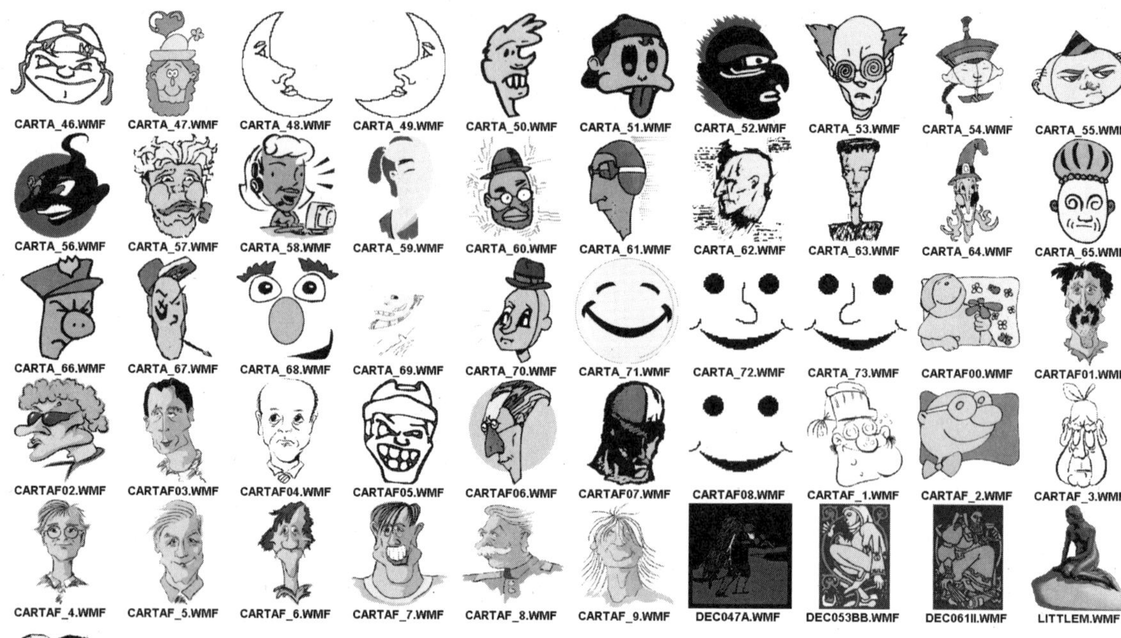

PESI199D.WMF

g:\PEOPLE\COUPLES [P_TO_Z]

0689.WMF
0690.WMF
0987.WMF
0988.WMF
ASI065C.WMF
FAMHAP.WMF
FAMILY.WMF
FAMILY1B.WMF
FAMLY010.WMF
FAMLY017.WMF
FAMLY_41.WMF
FAMLY_42.WMF
FAMLY_43.WMF
FAMLY_44.WMF
FATHER__.WMF
FATHER_D.WMF
FML002.WMF
HELPING.WMF
HHD015A.WMF
HPI014B.WMF
HPI020A.WMF
HPI020E.WMF
HPI020F.WMF
HPI028B.WMF
HTS030B.WMF
JAPANESE.WMF
KIDPARTY.WMF
MOTHER_R.WMF
MOTHSON.WMF
MUMBAB7.WMF
OTS052A.WMF
OYAKO3.WMF
PD006ECU.WMF
PD006FCU.WMF
PD006GCU.WMF
PD006HCU.WMF
PD006ICU.WMF
PD006JCU.WMF
PD006KCU.WMF
PD006LCU.WMF
PD006MCU.WMF
PD006NCU.WMF
PD006OCU.WMF
PD006PCU.WMF
PD006QCU.WMF
PD006RCU.WMF
PD006VCU.WMF
PD006XCU.WMF
PD007ACU.WMF
PD007BCU.WMF
PD007GCU.WMF
PECA021D.WMF
PECA060D.WMF
PEOPL035.WMF
PEOPL12.WMF
PEOPL12C.WMF
PEOPL13.WMF
PEOPL13C.WMF
PEOPL3.WMF
PEOPL3C.WMF
PESI262D.WMF
PGX031A.WMF
SLH102B.WMF
SUPERDAD.WMF
TD87.WMF
WMG049F.WMF

g:\PEOPLE\HBEANS [P_TO_Z]
4X4BEAN.WMF
ANGRYBEA.WMF
ARGHBEA.WMF
ARMYBEAN.WMF
BABYBEAN.WMF
BALLERIN.WMF
BARBQB.WMF
BASKETBE.WMF
BATTERBE.WMF
BEANDINN.WMF
BEANSKEL.WMF
BEEKERBE.WMF
BEERBEAN.WMF
BIKERBEA.WMF
BODYBEAN.WMF
BUSINESS.WMF
CAMPERBE.WMF
CARPENTE.WMF
CAVEBEAN.WMF
CHARTBEA.WMF
CHILIBEA.WMF
COFFEEBE.WMF
COMPUTE0.WMF
COMPUTE1.WMF
COMPUTE2.WMF
COMPUTE3.WMF
COMPUTER.WMF
COWBOYBE.WMF
CRYINGBE.WMF
DANCINGB.WMF
DR.WMF
DRAWINGB.WMF
EASTERBE.WMF
FARMERBE.WMF
FIREBEAN.WMF
FISHINGB.WMF
FLOWERSB.WMF
FOOTBEAN.WMF
FORSALEB.WMF
FRANKENB.WMF
FRIZBEEB.WMF
GARDENBE.WMF
GATORBEA.WMF
GIRLBEAN.WMF
GOLFBEAN.WMF
GRADUATE.WMF
GUITARBE.WMF
HOCKEYBE.WMF
HOTDOGBE.WMF
HUNTERBE.WMF
INSPECTO.WMF
IRONWORK.WMF
JOGGERBE.WMF
LEPRICON.WMF
LUMBERBE.WMF
MAGICBEA.WMF
MOMMYBEA.WMF
MOTOBEAN.WMF
MOUNTAIN.WMF
MOVIEBEA.WMF
OFFICERB.WMF
PHONEBEA.WMF
PHOTOBEA.WMF
PILGRAMB.WMF
PIRATEBE.WMF
PITCHERB.WMF
PIZZABEA.WMF
PLANEBEA.WMF
POKERBEA.WMF
RACECARB.WMF
RAQUETBE.WMF
READINGB.WMF
ROLLERBE.WMF
SAILBEAN.WMF
SANTABEA.WMF
SECRETAR.WMF
SHYBEAN.WMF
SINGINGB.WMF
SIRBEAN.WMF
SKATERBE.WMF
SKIBEAN.WMF
SOCCERBE.WMF
SPAGHETT.WMF
SPOCKBEA.WMF
STUDENTB.WMF
SUNTANBE.WMF
TEDDYBEA.WMF
TENNISBE.WMF
TRAINBEA.WMF
TRUCKERB.WMF
TVBEAN.WMF
UNCLEBEA.WMF
VALENTIN.WMF
WALLBEAN.WMF
WHISTLIN.WMF
WHITEWAT.WMF
WITCHBEA.WMF
WIZARDBE.WMF
YELLINGB.WMF
YIPPIBEA.WMF

ADS059J.WMF
ADS075F.WMF
ADS079C.WMF
ADS091J.WMF
DEC056T.WMF
MSL001H.WMF
MSL001K.WMF
MSL004G.WMF
MSL005C.WMF
MSL006J.WMF
MSL015C.WMF
MSL026A.WMF
MSL028I.WMF
MSL038H.WMF
MSL045A.WMF
MSL048A.WMF
MSL055B.WMF
MSL068G.WMF
MSL080C.WMF
MSL084E.WMF
MSL098A.WMF
MSL098C.WMF
MSL103A.WMF
OFS006A.WMF
OFS018D.WMF
OFS049A.WMF
OTS018B.WMF
OTS025G.WMF
OTS028A.WMF
OTS028J.WMF
OTS028L.WMF
OTS060H.WMF
SAC012A.WMF
SCH001B.WMF
SCT019A.WMF
SIT024F.WMF
SLH069J.WMF
SMR015D.WMF
SMR030N.WMF
SSP028D.WMF
TVA033H.WMF
VSC062D.WMF
WMG006D.WMF
WMG006K.WMF
WMG017E.WMF

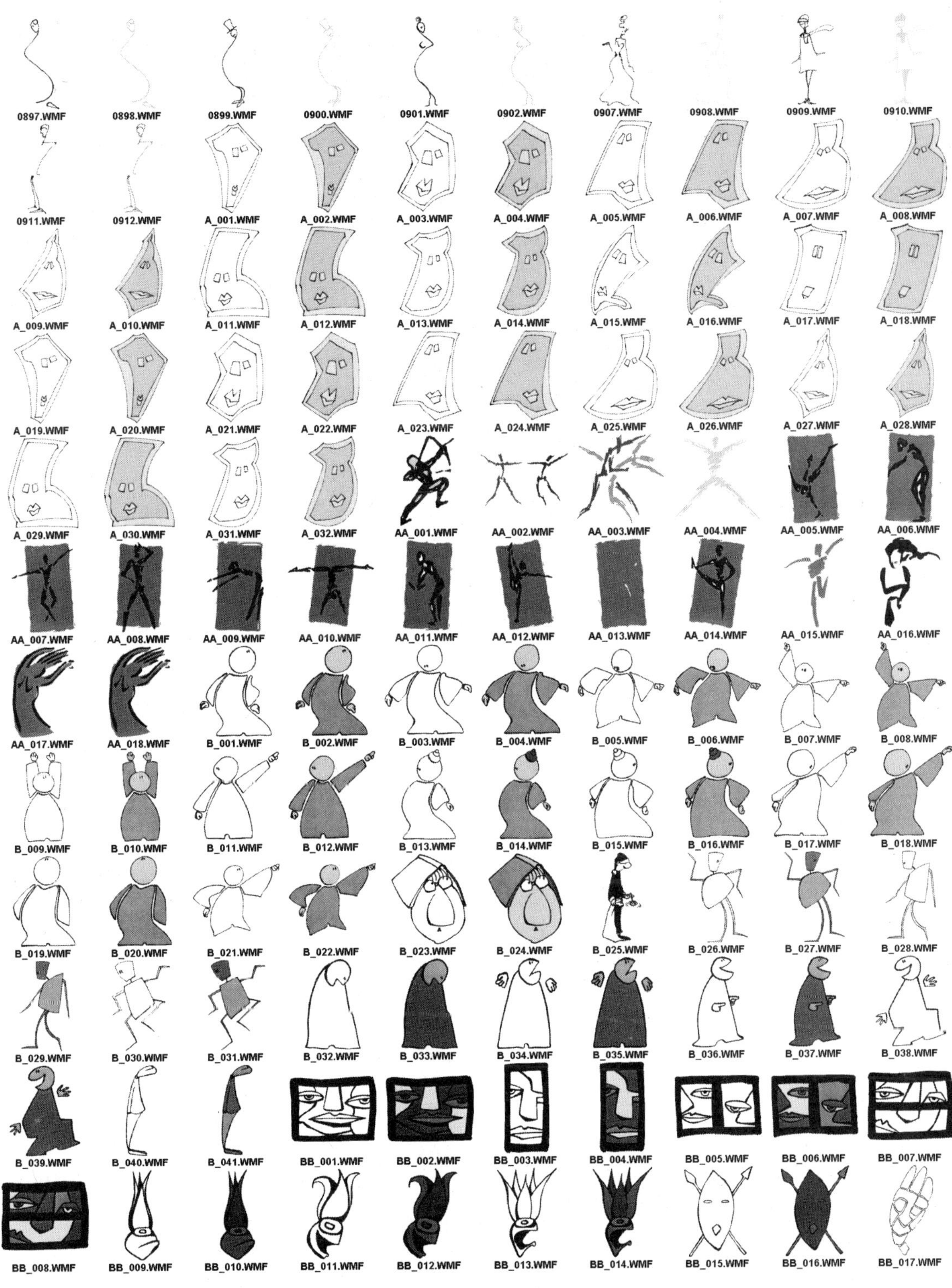
0897.WMF 0898.WMF 0899.WMF 0900.WMF 0901.WMF 0902.WMF 0907.WMF 0908.WMF 0909.WMF 0910.WMF
0911.WMF 0912.WMF A_001.WMF A_002.WMF A_003.WMF A_004.WMF A_005.WMF A_006.WMF A_007.WMF A_008.WMF
A_009.WMF A_010.WMF A_011.WMF A_012.WMF A_013.WMF A_014.WMF A_015.WMF A_016.WMF A_017.WMF A_018.WMF
A_019.WMF A_020.WMF A_021.WMF A_022.WMF A_023.WMF A_024.WMF A_025.WMF A_026.WMF A_027.WMF A_028.WMF
A_029.WMF A_030.WMF A_031.WMF A_032.WMF AA_001.WMF AA_002.WMF AA_003.WMF AA_004.WMF AA_005.WMF AA_006.WMF
AA_007.WMF AA_008.WMF AA_009.WMF AA_010.WMF AA_011.WMF AA_012.WMF AA_013.WMF AA_014.WMF AA_015.WMF AA_016.WMF
AA_017.WMF AA_018.WMF B_001.WMF B_002.WMF B_003.WMF B_004.WMF B_005.WMF B_006.WMF B_007.WMF B_008.WMF
B_009.WMF B_010.WMF B_011.WMF B_012.WMF B_013.WMF B_014.WMF B_015.WMF B_016.WMF B_017.WMF B_018.WMF
B_019.WMF B_020.WMF B_021.WMF B_022.WMF B_023.WMF B_024.WMF B_025.WMF B_026.WMF B_027.WMF B_028.WMF
B_029.WMF B_030.WMF B_031.WMF B_032.WMF B_033.WMF B_034.WMF B_035.WMF B_036.WMF B_037.WMF B_038.WMF
B_039.WMF B_040.WMF B_041.WMF BB_001.WMF BB_002.WMF BB_003.WMF BB_004.WMF BB_005.WMF BB_006.WMF BB_007.WMF
BB_008.WMF BB_009.WMF BB_010.WMF BB_011.WMF BB_012.WMF BB_013.WMF BB_014.WMF BB_015.WMF BB_016.WMF BB_017.WMF

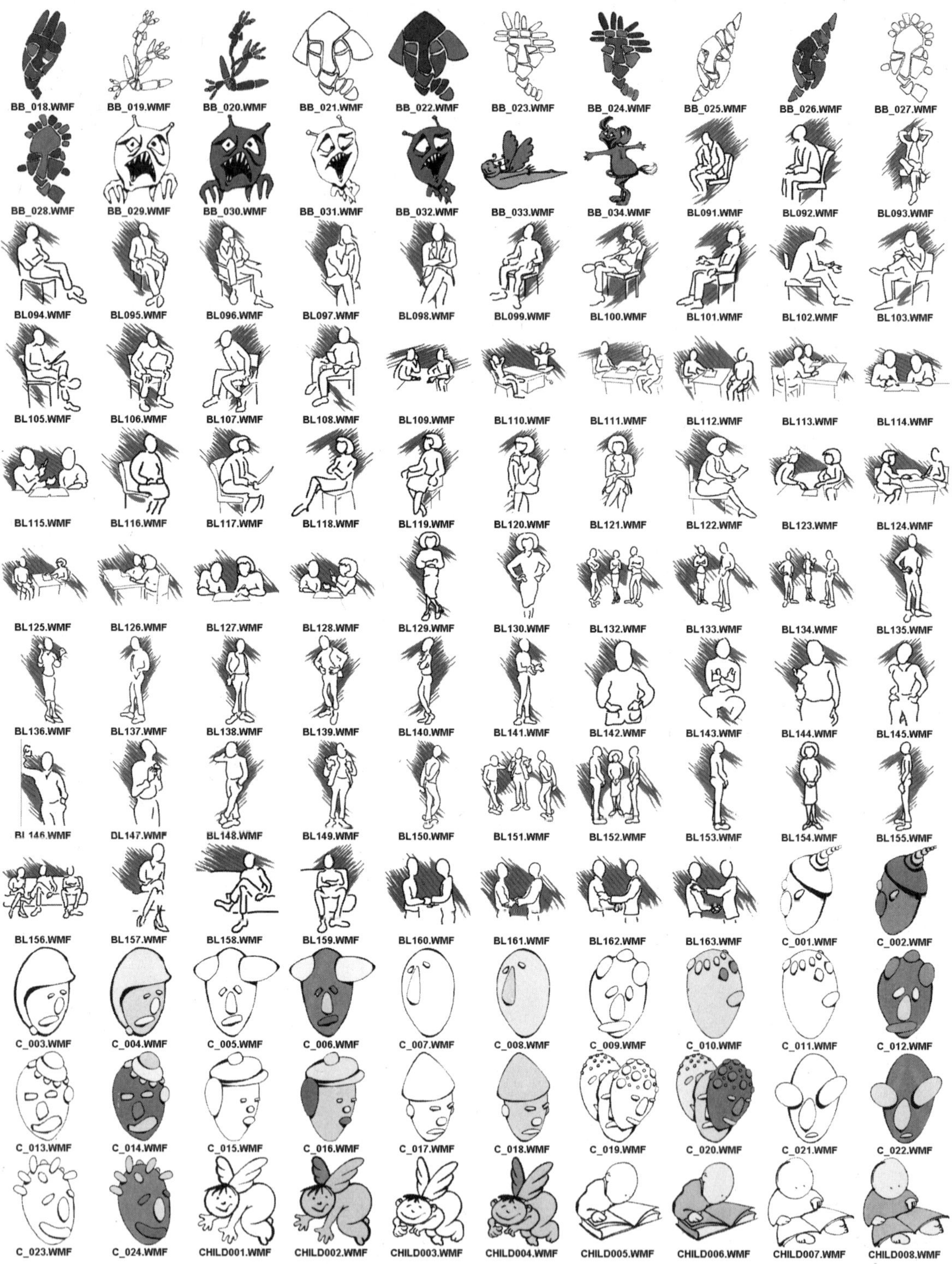

BB_018.WMF
BB_019.WMF
BB_020.WMF
BB_021.WMF
BB_022.WMF
BB_023.WMF
BB_024.WMF
BB_025.WMF
BB_026.WMF
BB_027.WMF
BB_028.WMF
BB_029.WMF
BB_030.WMF
BB_031.WMF
BB_032.WMF
BB_033.WMF
BB_034.WMF
BL091.WMF
BL092.WMF
BL093.WMF
BL094.WMF
BL095.WMF
BL096.WMF
BL097.WMF
BL098.WMF
BL099.WMF
BL100.WMF
BL101.WMF
BL102.WMF
BL103.WMF
BL105.WMF
BL106.WMF
BL107.WMF
BL108.WMF
BL109.WMF
BL110.WMF
BL111.WMF
BL112.WMF
BL113.WMF
BL114.WMF
BL115.WMF
BL116.WMF
BL117.WMF
BL118.WMF
BL119.WMF
BL120.WMF
BL121.WMF
BL122.WMF
BL123.WMF
BL124.WMF
BL125.WMF
BL126.WMF
BL127.WMF
BL128.WMF
BL129.WMF
BL130.WMF
BL132.WMF
BL133.WMF
BL134.WMF
BL135.WMF
BL136.WMF
BL137.WMF
BL138.WMF
BL139.WMF
BL140.WMF
BL141.WMF
BL142.WMF
BL143.WMF
BL144.WMF
BL145.WMF
BL146.WMF
BL147.WMF
BL148.WMF
BL149.WMF
BL150.WMF
BL151.WMF
BL152.WMF
BL153.WMF
BL154.WMF
BL155.WMF
BL156.WMF
BL157.WMF
BL158.WMF
BL159.WMF
BL160.WMF
BL161.WMF
BL162.WMF
BL163.WMF
C_001.WMF
C_002.WMF
C_003.WMF
C_004.WMF
C_005.WMF
C_006.WMF
C_007.WMF
C_008.WMF
C_009.WMF
C_010.WMF
C_011.WMF
C_012.WMF
C_013.WMF
C_014.WMF
C_015.WMF
C_016.WMF
C_017.WMF
C_018.WMF
C_019.WMF
C_020.WMF
C_021.WMF
C_022.WMF
C_023.WMF
C_024.WMF
CHILD001.WMF
CHILD002.WMF
CHILD003.WMF
CHILD004.WMF
CHILD005.WMF
CHILD006.WMF
CHILD007.WMF
CHILD008.WMF

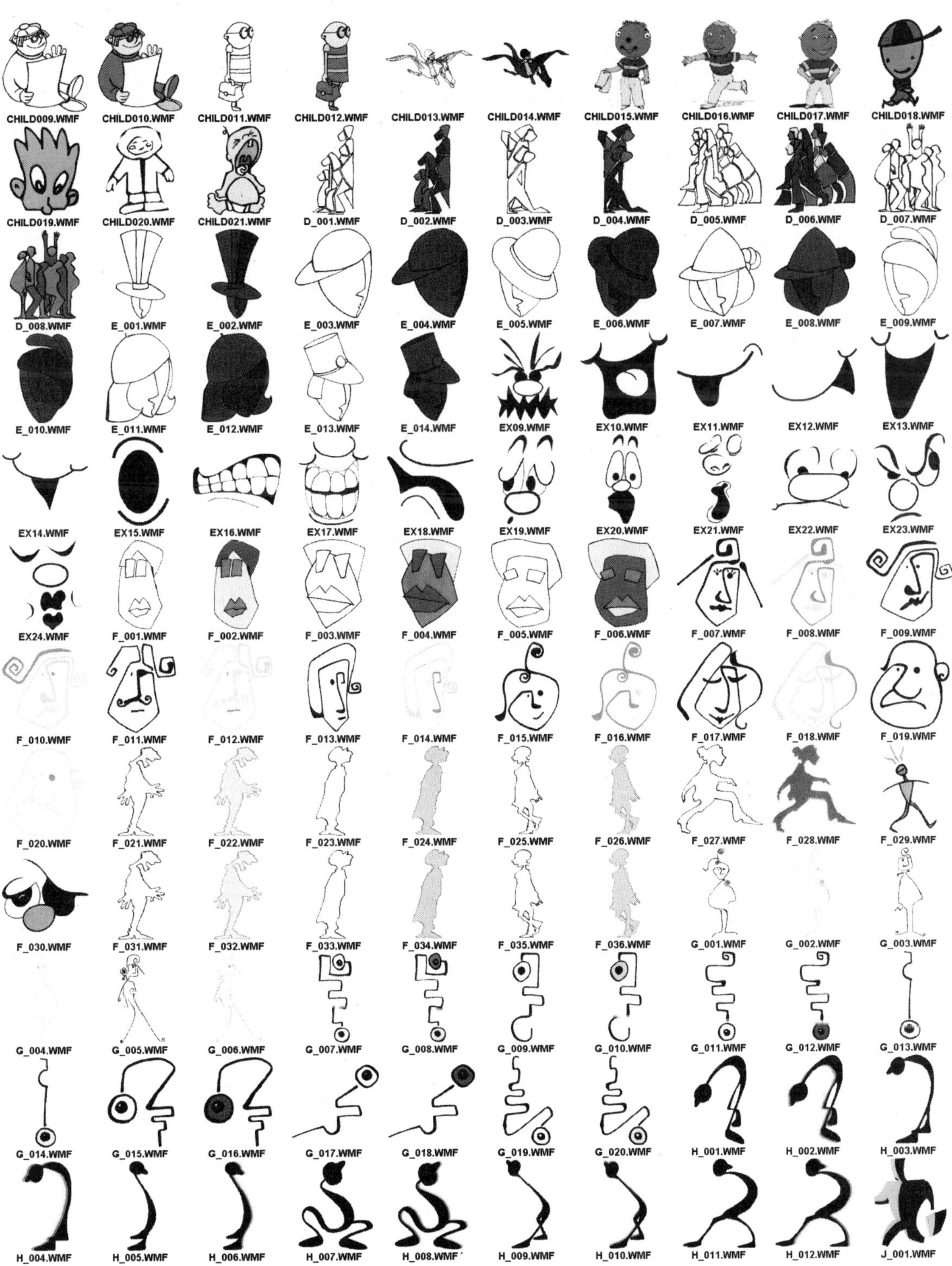
CHILD009.WMF CHILD010.WMF CHILD011.WMF CHILD012.WMF CHILD013.WMF CHILD014.WMF CHILD015.WMF CHILD016.WMF CHILD017.WMF CHILD018.WMF
CHILD019.WMF CHILD020.WMF CHILD021.WMF D_001.WMF D_002.WMF D_003.WMF D_004.WMF D_005.WMF D_006.WMF D_007.WMF
D_008.WMF E_001.WMF E_002.WMF E_003.WMF E_004.WMF E_005.WMF E_006.WMF E_007.WMF E_008.WMF E_009.WMF
E_010.WMF E_011.WMF E_012.WMF E_013.WMF E_014.WMF EX09.WMF EX10.WMF EX11.WMF EX12.WMF EX13.WMF
EX14.WMF EX15.WMF EX16.WMF EX17.WMF EX18.WMF EX19.WMF EX20.WMF EX21.WMF EX22.WMF EX23.WMF
EX24.WMF F_001.WMF F_002.WMF F_003.WMF F_004.WMF F_005.WMF F_006.WMF F_007.WMF F_008.WMF F_009.WMF
F_010.WMF F_011.WMF F_012.WMF F_013.WMF F_014.WMF F_015.WMF F_016.WMF F_017.WMF F_018.WMF F_019.WMF
F_020.WMF F_021.WMF F_022.WMF F_023.WMF F_024.WMF F_025.WMF F_026.WMF F_027.WMF F_028.WMF F_029.WMF
F_030.WMF F_031.WMF F_032.WMF F_033.WMF F_034.WMF F_035.WMF F_036.WMF G_001.WMF G_002.WMF G_003.WMF
G_004.WMF G_005.WMF G_006.WMF G_007.WMF G_008.WMF G_009.WMF G_010.WMF G_011.WMF G_012.WMF G_013.WMF
G_014.WMF G_015.WMF G_016.WMF G_017.WMF G_018.WMF G_019.WMF G_020.WMF H_001.WMF H_002.WMF H_003.WMF
H_004.WMF H_005.WMF H_006.WMF H_007.WMF H_008.WMF H_009.WMF H_010.WMF H_011.WMF H_012.WMF J_001.WMF

J_002.WMF J_003.WMF J_004.WMF J_005.WMF J_006.WMF J_007.WMF J_008.WMF J_009.WMF J_010.WMF J_011.WMF
J_012.WMF J_013.WMF J_014.WMF J_015.WMF J_016.WMF L_001.WMF L_002.WMF L_003.WMF L_004.WMF L_005.WMF
L_006.WMF L_007.WMF L_008.WMF L_009.WMF L_010.WMF L_011.WMF L_012.WMF L_013.WMF L_014.WMF L_015.WMF
L_016.WMF L_017.WMF L_018.WMF LL_001.WMF LL_002.WMF LL_003.WMF LL_004.WMF LL_005.WMF LL_006.WMF LL_007.WMF
LL_008.WMF LL_009.WMF LL_010.WMF LL_011.WMF LL_012.WMF LL_013.WMF LL_014.WMF LL_015.WMF LL_016.WMF LL_017.WMF
LL_018.WMF M_001.WMF M_002.WMF M_003.WMF M_004.WMF M_005.WMF M_006.WMF M_007.WMF M_008.WMF M_009.WMF
M_010.WMF M_011.WMF M_012.WMF M_013.WMF M_014.WMF MEN001.WMF MEN002.WMF MEN003.WMF MEN004.WMF MEN005.WMF
MEN006.WMF MEN007.WMF MEN008.WMF MEN009.WMF MEN010.WMF MEN011.WMF MEN012.WMF MEN013.WMF MEN014.WMF MEN015.WMF
MEN016.WMF MEN017.WMF MEN018.WMF MEN019.WMF MEN020.WMF MEN021.WMF MEN022.WMF MEN023.WMF MEN024.WMF MEN025.WMF
MEN026.WMF MEN027.WMF MEN028.WMF MEN029.WMF MEN030.WMF MEN031.WMF MEN032.WMF MEN033.WMF MEN034.WMF MEN035.WMF
MEN036.WMF MEN037.WMF MEN038.WMF MEN039.WMF MEN040.WMF MEN041.WMF MEN042.WMF MEN043.WMF MEN044.WMF MEN045.WMF
MEN046.WMF MEN047.WMF MEN048.WMF MEN049.WMF MEN050.WMF MEN051.WMF MEN052.WMF MEN053.WMF MEN054.WMF MEN055.WMF

MEN056.WMF MEN057.WMF MEN058.WMF MEN059.WMF MEN060.WMF MEN061.WMF MEN062.WMF MEN063.WMF MEN064.WMF MEN065.WMF
MEN066.WMF MEN067.WMF MEN068.WMF MEN069.WMF MEN070.WMF MEN071.WMF MEN072.WMF MEN073.WMF MEN074.WMF MEN075.WMF
MEN076.WMF MEN077.WMF MEN078.WMF MEN079.WMF MEN080.WMF MEN081.WMF MEN082.WMF MEN083.WMF MEN084.WMF MEN085.WMF
MEN086.WMF MEN087.WMF MEN088.WMF MEN089.WMF MEN090.WMF MEN091.WMF MEN092.WMF MEN093.WMF MEN094.WMF MEN095.WMF
MEN096.WMF MEN097.WMF MEN098.WMF MEN099.WMF MEN100.WMF MEN101.WMF MEN102.WMF MEN103.WMF MEN104.WMF MEN105.WMF
MEN106.WMF MEN107.WMF MEN108.WMF MEN109.WMF MEN110.WMF MEN111.WMF MEN112.WMF MEN113.WMF MEN114.WMF MEN115.WMF
MEN116.WMF MEN117.WMF MEN118.WMF MEN119.WMF MEN120.WMF MEN121.WMF MEN122.WMF MEN123.WMF MEN124.WMF MISC001.WMF
MISC002.WMF MISC003.WMF MISC004.WMF MISC005.WMF MISC006.WMF MISC007.WMF MISC008.WMF MISC009.WMF MISC010.WMF MISC011.WMF
MISC012.WMF MISC013.WMF MISC014.WMF MISC015.WMF MISC016.WMF MISC017.WMF MISC018.WMF MISC019.WMF MISC020.WMF MISC021.WMF
MISC022.WMF MISC023.WMF MISC024.WMF MISC025.WMF MISC026.WMF MISC027.WMF MISC028.WMF MISC029.WMF MISC030.WMF MISC031.WMF
MISC032.WMF MISC033.WMF MISC034.WMF MISC035.WMF MISC036.WMF MISC037.WMF MISC038.WMF MISC039.WMF MISC040.WMF MISC041.WMF
MISC042.WMF MISC043.WMF MISC044.WMF MISC045.WMF MISC046.WMF MISC047.WMF MISC048.WMF MISC049.WMF MISC050.WMF MISC051.WMF

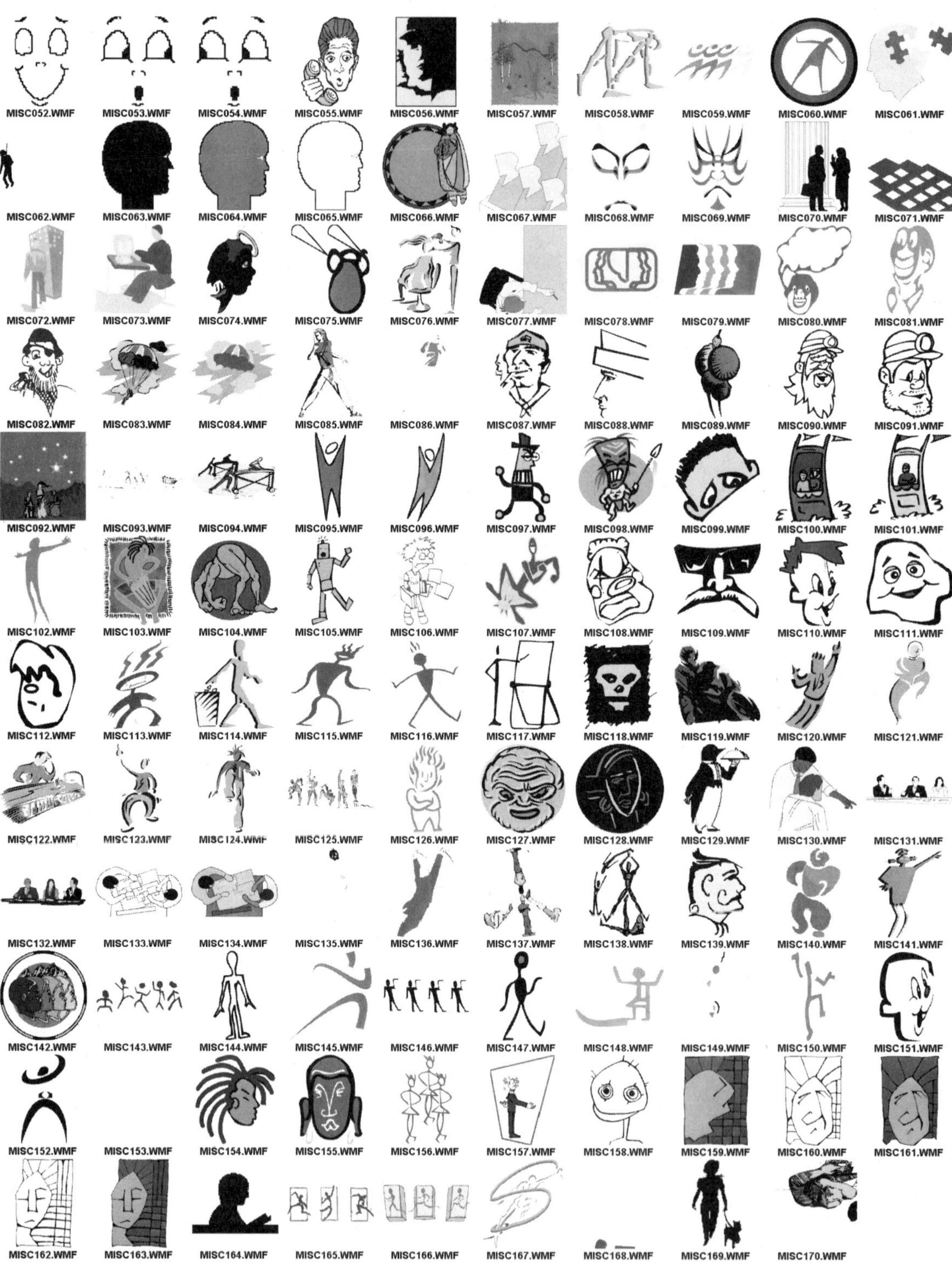

MISC052.WMF MISC053.WMF MISC054.WMF MISC055.WMF MISC056.WMF MISC057.WMF MISC058.WMF MISC059.WMF MISC060.WMF MISC061.WMF

MISC062.WMF MISC063.WMF MISC064.WMF MISC065.WMF MISC066.WMF MISC067.WMF MISC068.WMF MISC069.WMF MISC070.WMF MISC071.WMF

MISC072.WMF MISC073.WMF MISC074.WMF MISC075.WMF MISC076.WMF MISC077.WMF MISC078.WMF MISC079.WMF MISC080.WMF MISC081.WMF

MISC082.WMF MISC083.WMF MISC084.WMF MISC085.WMF MISC086.WMF MISC087.WMF MISC088.WMF MISC089.WMF MISC090.WMF MISC091.WMF

MISC092.WMF MISC093.WMF MISC094.WMF MISC095.WMF MISC096.WMF MISC097.WMF MISC098.WMF MISC099.WMF MISC100.WMF MISC101.WMF

MISC102.WMF MISC103.WMF MISC104.WMF MISC105.WMF MISC106.WMF MISC107.WMF MISC108.WMF MISC109.WMF MISC110.WMF MISC111.WMF

MISC112.WMF MISC113.WMF MISC114.WMF MISC115.WMF MISC116.WMF MISC117.WMF MISC118.WMF MISC119.WMF MISC120.WMF MISC121.WMF

MISC122.WMF MISC123.WMF MISC124.WMF MISC125.WMF MISC126.WMF MISC127.WMF MISC128.WMF MISC129.WMF MISC130.WMF MISC131.WMF

MISC132.WMF MISC133.WMF MISC134.WMF MISC135.WMF MISC136.WMF MISC137.WMF MISC138.WMF MISC139.WMF MISC140.WMF MISC141.WMF

MISC142.WMF MISC143.WMF MISC144.WMF MISC145.WMF MISC146.WMF MISC147.WMF MISC148.WMF MISC149.WMF MISC150.WMF MISC151.WMF

MISC152.WMF MISC153.WMF MISC154.WMF MISC155.WMF MISC156.WMF MISC157.WMF MISC158.WMF MISC159.WMF MISC160.WMF MISC161.WMF

MISC162.WMF MISC163.WMF MISC164.WMF MISC165.WMF MISC166.WMF MISC167.WMF MISC168.WMF MISC169.WMF MISC170.WMF

N_001.WMF N_002.WMF N_003.WMF N_004.WMF N_005.WMF N_006.WMF N_007.WMF N_008.WMF N_009.WMF N_010.WMF
N_011.WMF N_012.WMF N_013.WMF N_014.WMF N_015.WMF N_016.WMF N_017.WMF N_018.WMF N_019.WMF N_020.WMF
N_021.WMF N_022.WMF N_023.WMF N_024.WMF N_025.WMF N_026.WMF N_027.WMF N_028.WMF N_029.WMF N_030.WMF
N_031.WMF N_032.WMF N_033.WMF N_034.WMF N_035.WMF N_036.WMF N_037.WMF N_038.WMF N_039.WMF N_040.WMF
N_041.WMF N_042.WMF N_043.WMF N_044.WMF N_045.WMF N_046.WMF N_047.WMF N_048.WMF N_049.WMF N_050.WMF
N_051.WMF N_052.WMF N_053.WMF N_054.WMF N_055.WMF N_056.WMF N_057.WMF N_058.WMF N_059.WMF N_060.WMF
N_061.WMF N_062.WMF N_063.WMF N_064.WMF N_065.WMF N_066.WMF N_067.WMF N_068.WMF N_069.WMF N_070.WMF
N_071.WMF N_072.WMF N_073.WMF N_074.WMF N_075.WMF N_076.WMF N_077.WMF N_078.WMF N_079.WMF N_080.WMF
N_081.WMF N_082.WMF N_083.WMF N_084.WMF N_085.WMF N_086.WMF N_087.WMF N_088.WMF N_089.WMF N_090.WMF
N_091.WMF N_092.WMF N_093.WMF N_094.WMF N_095.WMF N_096.WMF N_097.WMF N_098.WMF N_099.WMF N_100.WMF
N_101.WMF N_102.WMF N_103.WMF N_104.WMF N_105.WMF N_106.WMF N_107.WMF N_108.WMF N_109.WMF N_110.WMF
N_111.WMF N_112.WMF N_113.WMF N_114.WMF N_115.WMF N_116.WMF N_117.WMF N_118.WMF N_119.WMF N_120.WMF

N_121.WMF N_122.WMF N_123.WMF N_124.WMF N_125.WMF N_126.WMF N_127.WMF N_128.WMF N_129.WMF N_130.WMF
N_131.WMF N_132.WMF N_133.WMF N_134.WMF N_135.WMF N_136.WMF N_137.WMF N_138.WMF N_139.WMF N_140.WMF
N_141.WMF N_142.WMF N_143.WMF N_144.WMF N_145.WMF N_146.WMF N_147.WMF N_148.WMF N_149.WMF N_150.WMF
N_151.WMF N_152.WMF N_153.WMF N_154.WMF N_155.WMF N_156.WMF N_157.WMF N_158.WMF N_159.WMF N_160.WMF
N_161.WMF N_162.WMF N_163.WMF N_164.WMF N_165.WMF N_166.WMF N_167.WMF N_168.WMF N_169.WMF N_170.WMF
N_171.WMF N_172.WMF N_173.WMF N_174.WMF N_175.WMF N_176.WMF N_177.WMF N_178.WMF N_179.WMF N_180.WMF
N_181.WMF N_182.WMF N_183.WMF N_184.WMF N_185.WMF N_186.WMF N_187.WMF N_188.WMF N_189.WMF N_190.WMF
N_191.WMF N_192.WMF N_193.WMF N_194.WMF N_195.WMF N_196.WMF N_197.WMF N_198.WMF N_199.WMF N_200.WMF
N_201.WMF N_202.WMF N_203.WMF N_204.WMF N_205.WMF N_206.WMF N_207.WMF N_208.WMF N_209.WMF N_210.WMF
N_211.WMF N_212.WMF N_213.WMF N_214.WMF P_001.WMF P_002.WMF P_003.WMF P_004.WMF P_005.WMF P_006.WMF
P_007.WMF P_008.WMF PRIN0099.WMF PRIN0100.WMF PRIN0106.WMF PRIN0108.WMF PRIN0109.WMF PRIN0110.WMF Q_001.WMF Q_002.WMF
Q_003.WMF Q_004.WMF Q_005.WMF Q_006.WMF Q_007.WMF Q_008.WMF Q_009.WMF Q_010.WMF R_001.WMF R_002.WMF

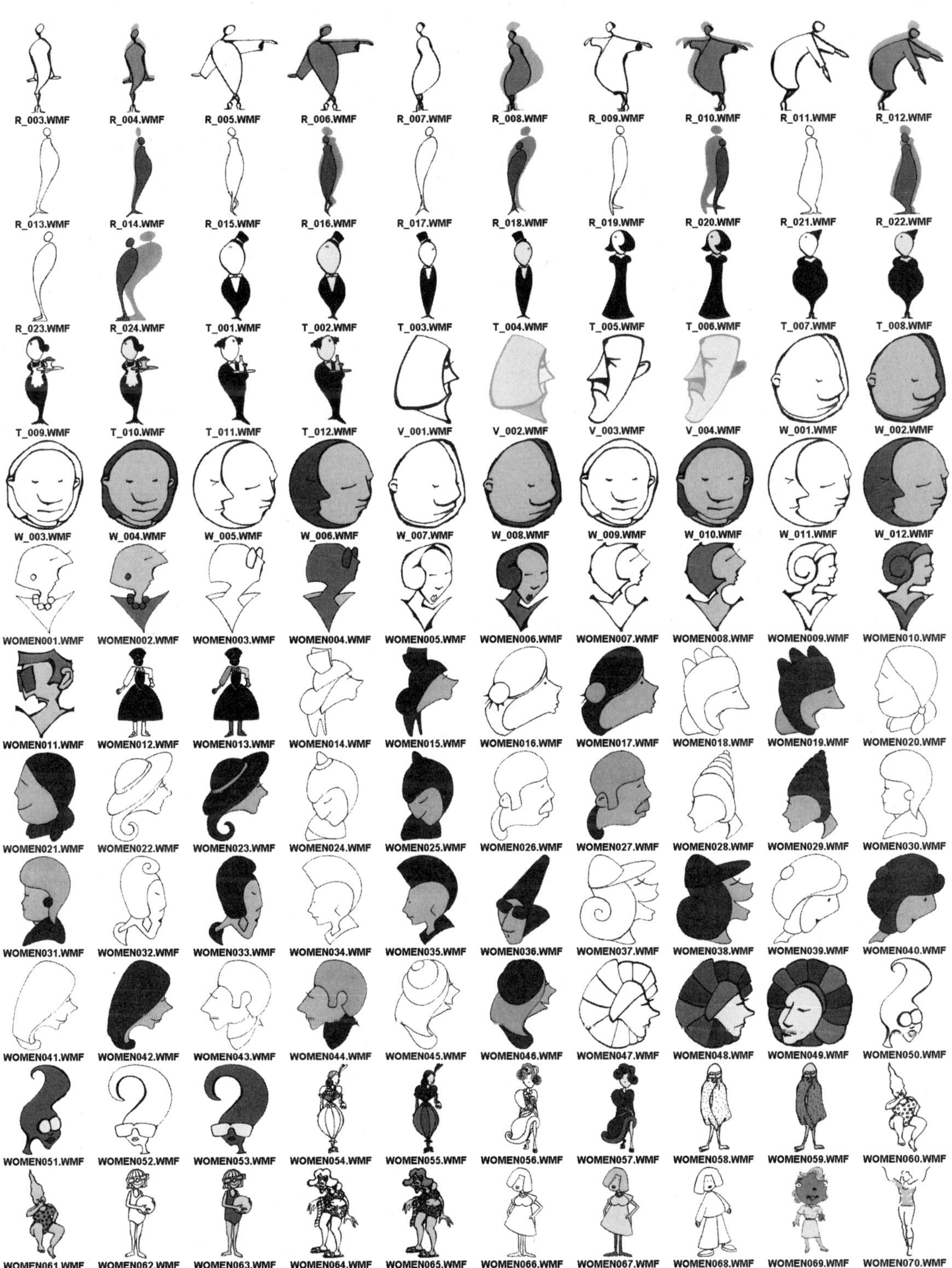
R_003.WMF
R_004.WMF
R_005.WMF
R_006.WMF
R_007.WMF
R_008.WMF
R_009.WMF
R_010.WMF
R_011.WMF
R_012.WMF
R_013.WMF
R_014.WMF
R_015.WMF
R_016.WMF
R_017.WMF
R_018.WMF
R_019.WMF
R_020.WMF
R_021.WMF
R_022.WMF
R_023.WMF
R_024.WMF
T_001.WMF
T_002.WMF
T_003.WMF
T_004.WMF
T_005.WMF
T_006.WMF
T_007.WMF
T_008.WMF
T_009.WMF
T_010.WMF
T_011.WMF
T_012.WMF
V_001.WMF
V_002.WMF
V_003.WMF
V_004.WMF
W_001.WMF
W_002.WMF
W_003.WMF
W_004.WMF
W_005.WMF
W_006.WMF
W_007.WMF
W_008.WMF
W_009.WMF
W_010.WMF
W_011.WMF
W_012.WMF
WOMEN001.WMF
WOMEN002.WMF
WOMEN003.WMF
WOMEN004.WMF
WOMEN005.WMF
WOMEN006.WMF
WOMEN007.WMF
WOMEN008.WMF
WOMEN009.WMF
WOMEN010.WMF
WOMEN011.WMF
WOMEN012.WMF
WOMEN013.WMF
WOMEN014.WMF
WOMEN015.WMF
WOMEN016.WMF
WOMEN017.WMF
WOMEN018.WMF
WOMEN019.WMF
WOMEN020.WMF
WOMEN021.WMF
WOMEN022.WMF
WOMEN023.WMF
WOMEN024.WMF
WOMEN025.WMF
WOMEN026.WMF
WOMEN027.WMF
WOMEN028.WMF
WOMEN029.WMF
WOMEN030.WMF
WOMEN031.WMF
WOMEN032.WMF
WOMEN033.WMF
WOMEN034.WMF
WOMEN035.WMF
WOMEN036.WMF
WOMEN037.WMF
WOMEN038.WMF
WOMEN039.WMF
WOMEN040.WMF
WOMEN041.WMF
WOMEN042.WMF
WOMEN043.WMF
WOMEN044.WMF
WOMEN045.WMF
WOMEN046.WMF
WOMEN047.WMF
WOMEN048.WMF
WOMEN049.WMF
WOMEN050.WMF
WOMEN051.WMF
WOMEN052.WMF
WOMEN053.WMF
WOMEN054.WMF
WOMEN055.WMF
WOMEN056.WMF
WOMEN057.WMF
WOMEN058.WMF
WOMEN059.WMF
WOMEN060.WMF
WOMEN061.WMF
WOMEN062.WMF
WOMEN063.WMF
WOMEN064.WMF
WOMEN065.WMF
WOMEN066.WMF
WOMEN067.WMF
WOMEN068.WMF
WOMEN069.WMF
WOMEN070.WMF

WOMEN071.WMF WOMEN072.WMF WOMEN073.WMF WOMEN074.WMF WOMEN075.WMF WOMEN076.WMF WOMEN077.WMF WOMEN078.WMF WOMEN079.WMF WOMEN080.WMF

WOMEN081.WMF WOMEN082.WMF WOMEN083.WMF WOMEN084.WMF WOMEN085.WMF WOMEN086.WMF WOMEN087.WMF WOMEN088.WMF WOMEN089.WMF WOMEN090.WMF

WOMEN091.WMF WOMEN092.WMF WOMEN093.WMF WOMEN094.WMF WOMEN095.WMF WOMEN096.WMF WOMEN097.WMF WOMEN098.WMF WOMEN099.WMF WOMEN100.WMF

WOMEN101.WMF WOMEN102.WMF WOMEN103.WMF WOMEN104.WMF WOMEN105.WMF WOMEN106.WMF WOMEN107.WMF WOMEN108.WMF WOMEN109.WMF WOMEN110.WMF

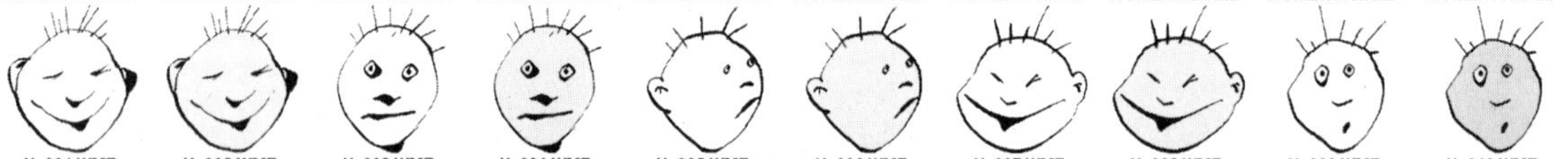

X_001.WMF X_002.WMF X_003.WMF X_004.WMF X_005.WMF X_006.WMF X_007.WMF X_008.WMF X_009.WMF X_010.WMF

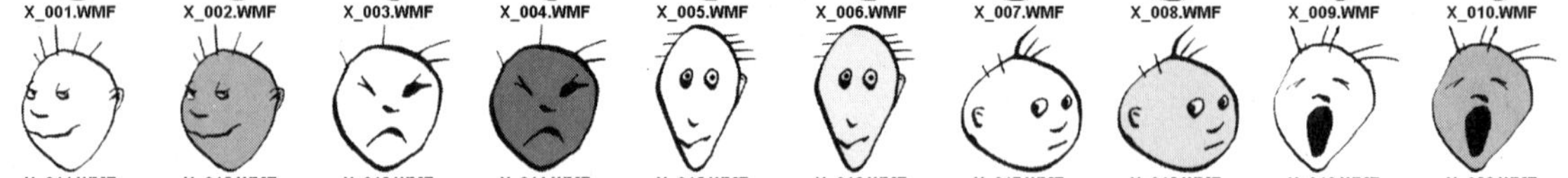

X_011.WMF X_012.WMF X_013.WMF X_014.WMF X_015.WMF X_016.WMF X_017.WMF X_018.WMF X_019.WMF X_020.WMF

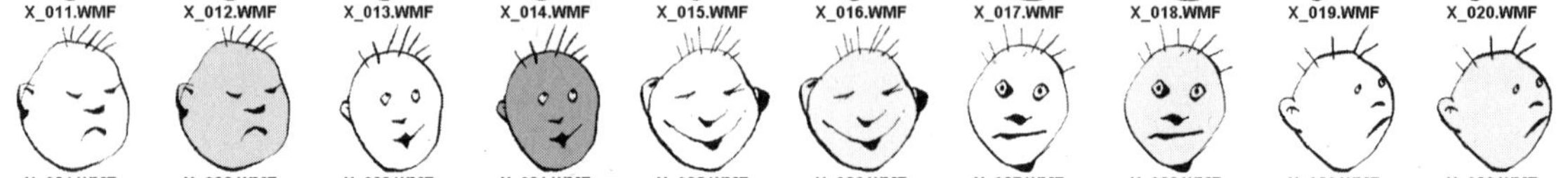

X_021.WMF X_022.WMF X_023.WMF X_024.WMF X_025.WMF X_026.WMF X_027.WMF X_028.WMF X_029.WMF X_030.WMF

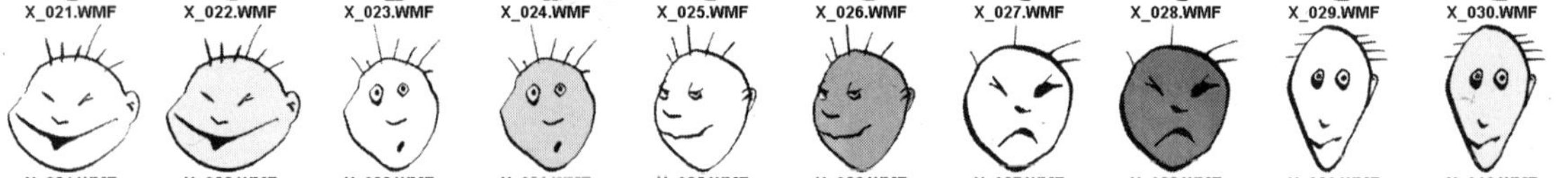

X_031.WMF X_032.WMF X_033.WMF X_034.WMF X_035.WMF X_036.WMF X_037.WMF X_038.WMF X_039.WMF X_040.WMF

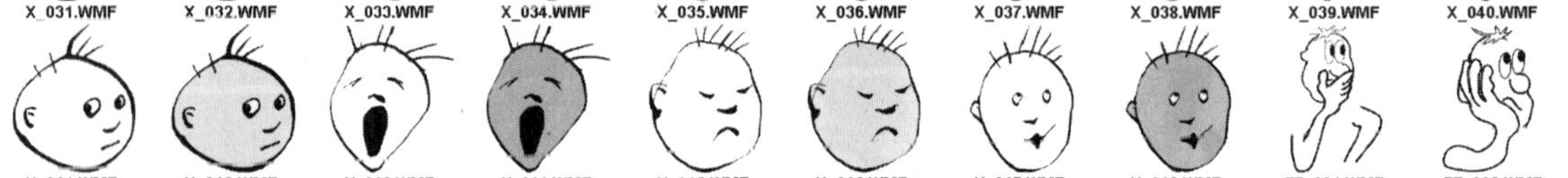

X_041.WMF X_042.WMF X_043.WMF X_044.WMF X_045.WMF X_046.WMF X_047.WMF X_048.WMF ZZ_001.WMF ZZ_002.WMF

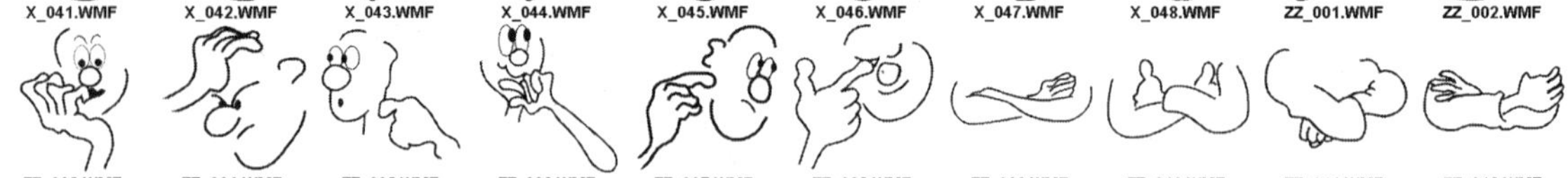

ZZ_003.WMF ZZ_004.WMF ZZ_005.WMF ZZ_006.WMF ZZ_007.WMF ZZ_008.WMF ZZ_009.WMF ZZ_010.WMF ZZ_011.WMF ZZ_012.WMF

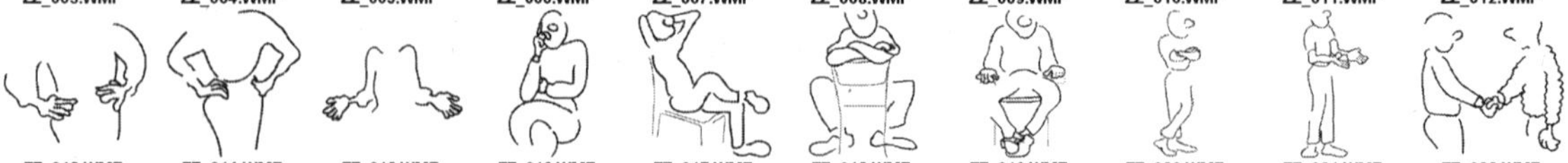

ZZ_013.WMF ZZ_014.WMF ZZ_015.WMF ZZ_016.WMF ZZ_017.WMF ZZ_018.WMF ZZ_019.WMF ZZ_020.WMF ZZ_021.WMF ZZ_022.WMF

ZZ_023.WMF

WORLD001.WMF WORLD002.WMF WORLD003.WMF WORLD004.WMF WORLD005.WMF WORLD006.WMF WORLD007.WMF WORLD008.WMF WORLD009.WMF WORLD010.WMF

WORLD011.WMF WORLD012.WMF WORLD013.WMF WORLD014.WMF WORLD015.WMF WORLD016.WMF WORLD017.WMF WORLD018.WMF WORLD019.WMF WORLD020.WMF

WORLD021.WMF WORLD022.WMF WORLD023.WMF WORLD024.WMF WORLD025.WMF WORLD026.WMF WORLD027.WMF WORLD028.WMF WORLD029.WMF WORLD030.WMF

WORLD031.WMF WORLD032.WMF WORLD033.WMF WORLD034.WMF WORLD035.WMF WORLD036.WMF WORLD037.WMF WORLD038.WMF WORLD039.WMF WORLD040.WMF

WORLD041.WMF WORLD042.WMF WORLD043.WMF WORLD044.WMF WORLD045.WMF WORLD046.WMF WORLD047.WMF WORLD048.WMF WORLD049.WMF WORLD050.WMF

WORLD051.WMF WORLD052.WMF WORLD053.WMF WORLD054.WMF WORLD055.WMF WORLD056.WMF WORLD057.WMF WORLD058.WMF WORLD059.WMF WORLD060.WMF

WORLD061.WMF WORLD062.WMF WORLD063.WMF WORLD064.WMF WORLD065.WMF WORLD066.WMF WORLD067.WMF WORLD068.WMF WORLD069.WMF WORLD070.WMF

WORLD071.WMF WORLD072.WMF WORLD073.WMF WORLD074.WMF WORLD075.WMF WORLD076.WMF WORLD077.WMF WORLD078.WMF WORLD079.WMF WORLD080.WMF

WORLD081.WMF WORLD082.WMF WORLD083.WMF WORLD084.WMF WORLD085.WMF WORLD086.WMF WORLD087.WMF WORLD088.WMF WORLD089.WMF WORLD090.WMF

WORLD091.WMF WORLD092.WMF WORLD093.WMF WORLD094.WMF WORLD095.WMF WORLD096.WMF WORLD097.WMF WORLD098.WMF WORLD099.WMF WORLD100.WMF

WORLD101.WMF WORLD102.WMF WORLD103.WMF WORLD104.WMF WORLD105.WMF WORLD106.WMF WORLD107.WMF WORLD108.WMF WORLD109.WMF WORLD110.WMF

WORLD111.WMF WORLD112.WMF WORLD113.WMF WORLD114.WMF WORLD115.WMF WORLD116.WMF WORLD117.WMF WORLD118.WMF WORLD119.WMF WORLD120.WMF

WORLD121.WMF
WORLD122.WMF
WORLD123.WMF
WORLD124.WMF
WORLD125.WMF
WORLD126.WMF
WORLD127.WMF
WORLD128.WMF
WORLD129.WMF
WORLD130.WMF
WORLD131.WMF
WORLD132.WMF
WORLD133.WMF
WORLD134.WMF
WORLD135.WMF
WORLD136.WMF
WORLD137.WMF
WORLD138.WMF
WORLD139.WMF
WORLD140.WMF
WORLD141.WMF
WORLD142.WMF
WORLD143.WMF
WORLD144.WMF
WORLD145.WMF
WORLD146.WMF
WORLD147.WMF
WORLD148.WMF
WORLD149.WMF
WORLD150.WMF
WORLD151.WMF
WORLD152.WMF
WORLD153.WMF
WORLD154.WMF
WORLD155.WMF
WORLD156.WMF
WORLD157.WMF
WORLD158.WMF
WORLD159.WMF
WORLD160.WMF
WORLD161.WMF
WORLD162.WMF
WORLD163.WMF
WORLD164.WMF
WORLD165.WMF
WORLD166.WMF
WORLD167.WMF
WORLD168.WMF
WORLD169.WMF
WORLD170.WMF
WORLD171.WMF
WORLD172.WMF
WORLD173.WMF
WORLD174.WMF
WORLD175.WMF
WORLD176.WMF
WORLD177.WMF
WORLD178.WMF
WORLD179.WMF
WORLD180.WMF
WORLD181.WMF
WORLD182.WMF
WORLD183.WMF
WORLD184.WMF

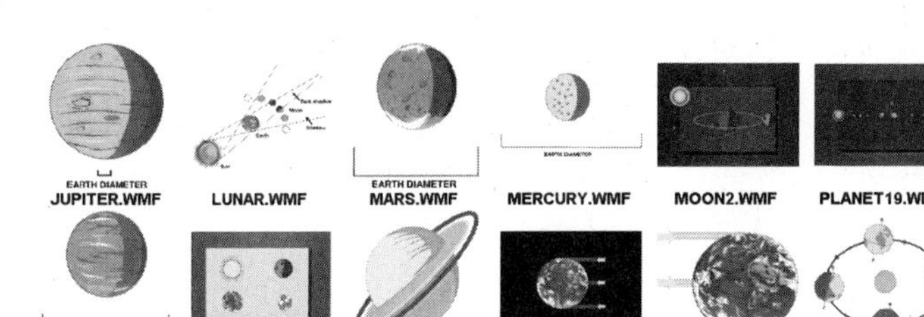

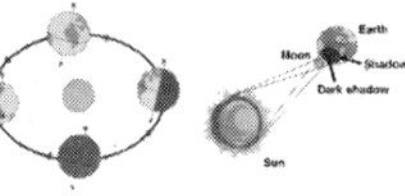

JUPITER.WMF LUNAR.WMF MARS.WMF MERCURY.WMF MOON2.WMF PLANET19.WMF PLANET20.WMF PLANET23.WMF PLANET31.WMF PLANET32.WMF

PLANET33.WMF PLANET35.WMF PLANET38.WMF PLANET39.WMF PLANET41.WMF SEASON2.WMF SOLAR.WMF

Planets • Planets

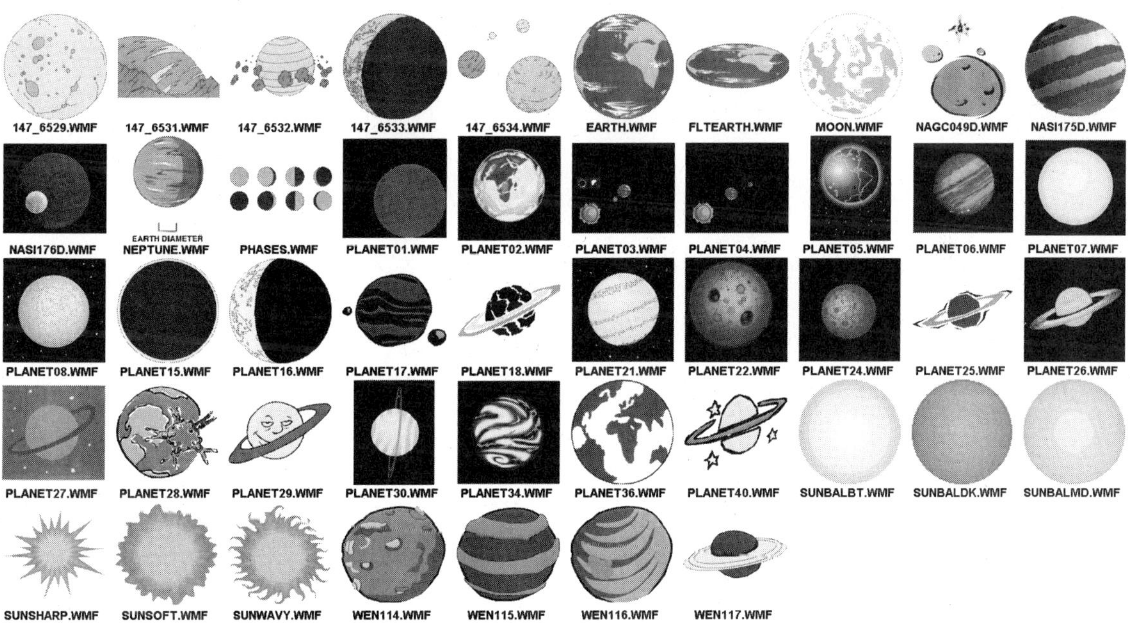

147_6529.WMF 147_6531.WMF 147_6532.WMF 147_6533.WMF 147_6534.WMF EARTH.WMF FLTEARTH.WMF MOON.WMF NAGC049D.WMF NASI175D.WMF

NASI176D.WMF NEPTUNE.WMF PHASES.WMF PLANET01.WMF PLANET02.WMF PLANET03.WMF PLANET04.WMF PLANET05.WMF PLANET06.WMF PLANET07.WMF

PLANET08.WMF PLANET15.WMF PLANET16.WMF PLANET17.WMF PLANET18.WMF PLANET21.WMF PLANET22.WMF PLANET24.WMF PLANET25.WMF PLANET26.WMF

PLANET27.WMF PLANET28.WMF PLANET29.WMF PLANET30.WMF PLANET34.WMF PLANET36.WMF PLANET40.WMF SUNBALBT.WMF SUNBALDK.WMF SUNBALMD.WMF

SUNSHARP.WMF SUNSOFT.WMF SUNWAVY.WMF WEN114.WMF WEN115.WMF WEN116.WMF WEN117.WMF

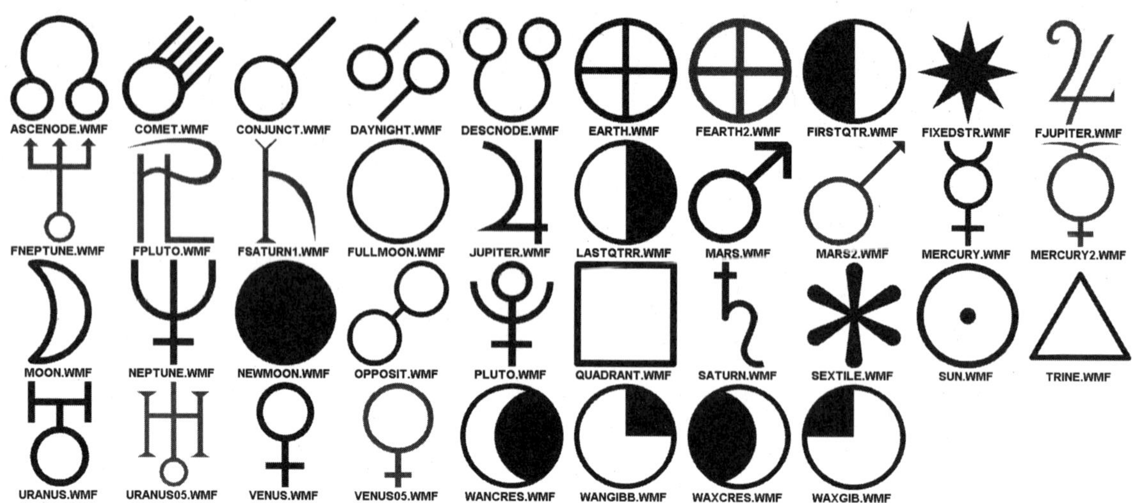
ASCENODE.WMF
COMET.WMF
CONJUNCT.WMF
DAYNIGHT.WMF
DESCNODE.WMF
EARTH.WMF
FEARTH2.WMF
FIRSTQTR.WMF
FIXEDSTR.WMF
FJUPITER.WMF
FNEPTUNE.WMF
FPLUTO.WMF
FSATURN1.WMF
FULLMOON.WMF
JUPITER.WMF
LASTQTRR.WMF
MARS.WMF
MARS2.WMF
MERCURY.WMF
MERCURY2.WMF
MOON.WMF
NEPTUNE.WMF
NEWMOON.WMF
OPPOSIT.WMF
PLUTO.WMF
QUADRANT.WMF
SATURN.WMF
SEXTILE.WMF
SUN.WMF
TRINE.WMF
URANUS.WMF
URANUS05.WMF
VENUS.WMF
VENUS05.WMF
WANCRES.WMF
WANGIBB.WMF
WAXCRES.WMF
WAXGIB.WMF

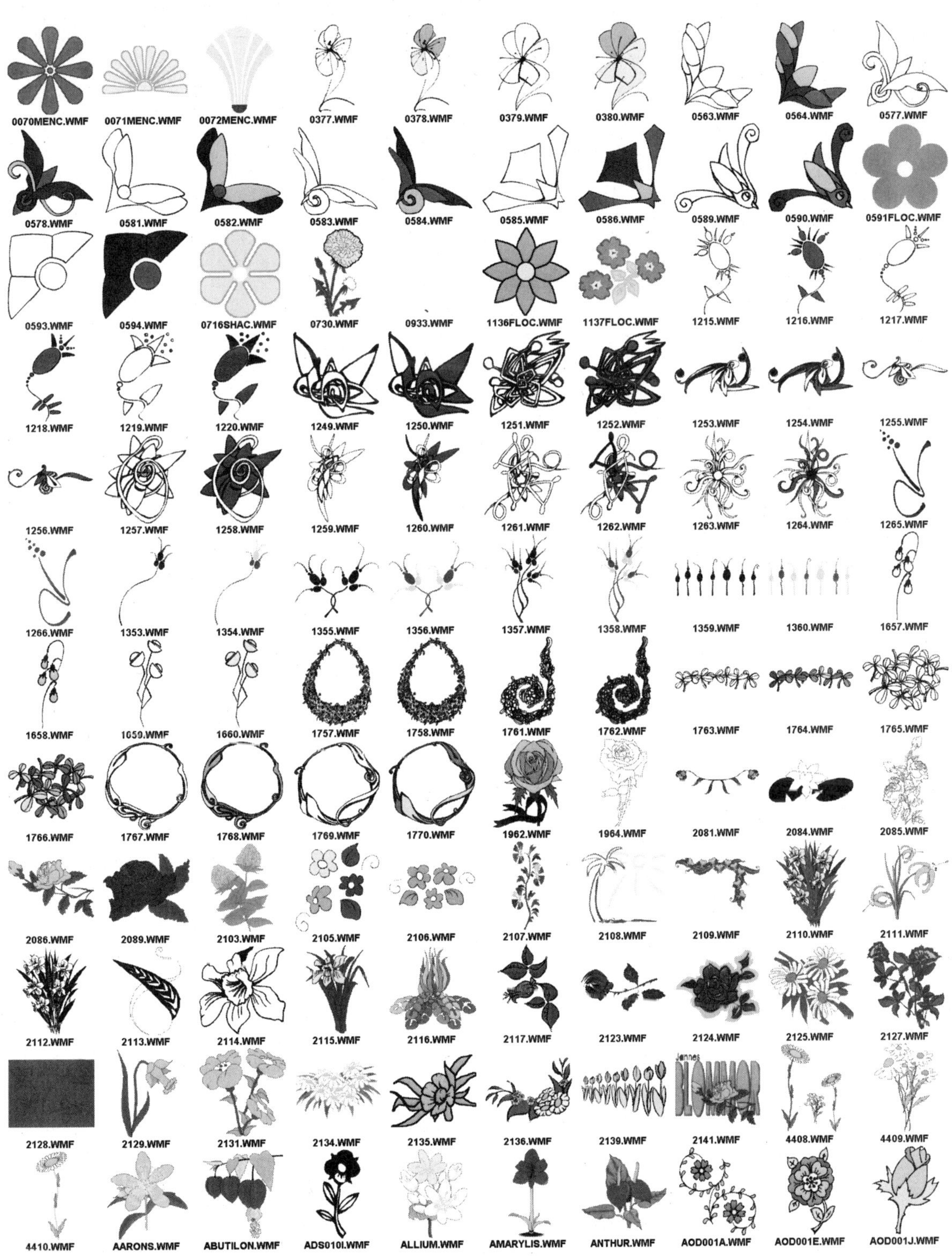
0070MENC.WMF
0071MENC.WMF
0072MENC.WMF
0377.WMF
0378.WMF
0379.WMF
0380.WMF
0563.WMF
0564.WMF
0577.WMF
0578.WMF
0581.WMF
0582.WMF
0583.WMF
0584.WMF
0585.WMF
0586.WMF
0589.WMF
0590.WMF
0591FLOC.WMF
0593.WMF
0594.WMF
0716SHAC.WMF
0730.WMF
0933.WMF
1136FLOC.WMF
1137FLOC.WMF
1215.WMF
1216.WMF
1217.WMF
1218.WMF
1219.WMF
1220.WMF
1249.WMF
1250.WMF
1251.WMF
1252.WMF
1253.WMF
1254.WMF
1255.WMF
1256.WMF
1257.WMF
1258.WMF
1259.WMF
1260.WMF
1261.WMF
1262.WMF
1263.WMF
1264.WMF
1265.WMF
1266.WMF
1353.WMF
1354.WMF
1355.WMF
1356.WMF
1357.WMF
1358.WMF
1359.WMF
1360.WMF
1657.WMF
1658.WMF
1659.WMF
1660.WMF
1757.WMF
1758.WMF
1761.WMF
1762.WMF
1763.WMF
1764.WMF
1765.WMF
1766.WMF
1767.WMF
1768.WMF
1769.WMF
1770.WMF
1962.WMF
1964.WMF
2081.WMF
2084.WMF
2085.WMF
2086.WMF
2089.WMF
2103.WMF
2105.WMF
2106.WMF
2107.WMF
2108.WMF
2109.WMF
2110.WMF
2111.WMF
2112.WMF
2113.WMF
2114.WMF
2115.WMF
2116.WMF
2117.WMF
2123.WMF
2124.WMF
2125.WMF
2127.WMF
2128.WMF
2129.WMF
2131.WMF
2134.WMF
2135.WMF
2136.WMF
2139.WMF
2141.WMF
4408.WMF
4409.WMF
4410.WMF
AARONS.WMF
ABUTILON.WMF
ADS010I.WMF
ALLIUM.WMF
AMARYLIS.WMF
ANTHUR.WMF
AOD001A.WMF
AOD001E.WMF
AOD001J.WMF

AOD001N.WMF
AOD002B.WMF
AOD002D.WMF
AOD004L.WMF
AOD004M.WMF
AOD004P.WMF
AOD005A.WMF
AOD005J.WMF
AOD007D.WMF
AOD007E.WMF
AOD007H.WMF
AOD009A.WMF
AOD011A.WMF
APLBLSSM.WMF
AQUILEG.WMF
ASTER.WMF
ASTER5.WMF
ASTERS.WMF
AYAME2.WMF
AZALEA.WMF
AZTEC.WMF
BACHELOR.WMF
BBONNET.WMF
BEAVRTLC.WMF
BEGON2.WMF
BEGONIA.WMF
BELLFLOW.WMF
BEYESUSN.WMF
BFLOWER.WMF
BIRD_OF.WMF
BIRDOF.WMF
BIT0727.WMF
BIT0926.WMF
BIT0927.WMF
BIT1128.WMF
BIT1129.WMF
BIT1131.WMF
BIT_ROOT.WMF
BITTROOT.WMF
BLACKEYE.WMF
BLEEDING.WMF
BLOODROO.WMF
BLUEBONN.WMF
BOTTLEBR.WMF
BOUQU2.WMF
BOUQUET.WMF
BOUQUET2.WMF
BOUQUET3.WMF
BOUQUET4.WMF
BRHODNRN.WMF
BROADWIL.WMF
BUNCH_OF.WMF
CALLALIL.WMF
CAMELIA.WMF
CAMELLIA.WMF
CAPEMARI.WMF
CARNATIN.WMF
CARNATON.WMF
CART01.WMF
CART02.WMF
CART03.WMF
CART04.WMF
CART05.WMF
CART06.WMF
CART07.WMF
CART08.WMF
CART09.WMF
CART10.WMF
CART11.WMF
CART12.WMF
CART13.WMF
CART14.WMF
CART15.WMF
CART16.WMF
CART17.WMF
CART18.WMF
CART19.WMF
CART20.WMF
CART21.WMF
CART22.WMF
CART23.WMF
CART24.WMF
CDS003B.WMF
CHEROSE.WMF
CHINAROS.WMF
CHINESEL.WMF
CHRYSAN1.WMF
CHRYSAN2.WMF
CHRYSANT.WMF
CINERAR.WMF
CIRCLEMU.WMF
CLANTERN.WMF
CLEMATIS.WMF
CLOVER.WMF
COLUMBIN.WMF
CONEFLW.WMF
CONVOLV.WMF
CORNERRO.WMF
CORSAGE.WMF
CORSAGE2.WMF
COSMOS.WMF
COTTON.WMF
CROCUS.WMF
CROCUS5.WMF
CS54_.WMF
CS55_.WMF
CS56_.WMF
CS57_.WMF
CS58_.WMF
CS59_.WMF
CS60_.WMF
CYCLAME5.WMF
CYCLAMEN.WMF
CYELJASM.WMF
DAFFOD5.WMF
DAFFODI4.WMF
DAFFODIL.WMF
DAHLIA.WMF
DAISY.WMF
DAISY13.WMF

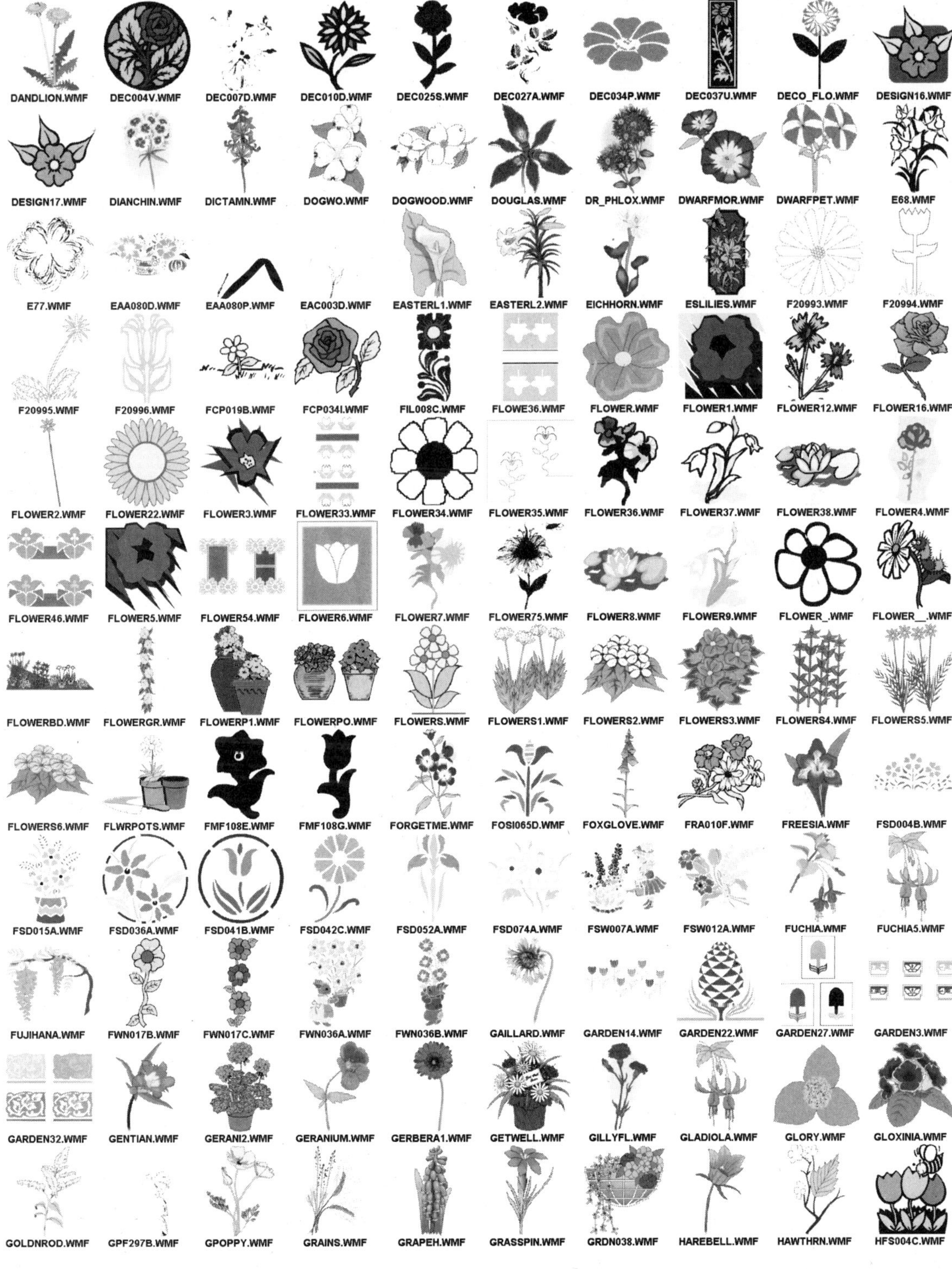
DANDLION.WMF
DEC004V.WMF
DEC007D.WMF
DEC010D.WMF
DEC025S.WMF
DEC027A.WMF
DEC034P.WMF
DEC037U.WMF
DECO_FLO.WMF
DESIGN16.WMF
DESIGN17.WMF
DIANCHIN.WMF
DICTAMN.WMF
DOGWO.WMF
DOGWOOD.WMF
DOUGLAS.WMF
DR_PHLOX.WMF
DWARFMOR.WMF
DWARFPET.WMF
E68.WMF
E77.WMF
EAA080D.WMF
EAA080P.WMF
EAC003D.WMF
EASTERL1.WMF
EASTERL2.WMF
EICHHORN.WMF
ESLILIES.WMF
F20993.WMF
F20994.WMF
F20995.WMF
F20996.WMF
FCP019B.WMF
FCP034I.WMF
FIL008C.WMF
FLOWE36.WMF
FLOWER.WMF
FLOWER1.WMF
FLOWER12.WMF
FLOWER16.WMF
FLOWER2.WMF
FLOWER22.WMF
FLOWER3.WMF
FLOWER33.WMF
FLOWER34.WMF
FLOWER35.WMF
FLOWER36.WMF
FLOWER37.WMF
FLOWER38.WMF
FLOWER4.WMF
FLOWER46.WMF
FLOWER5.WMF
FLOWER54.WMF
FLOWER6.WMF
FLOWER7.WMF
FLOWER75.WMF
FLOWER8.WMF
FLOWER9.WMF
FLOWER_.WMF
FLOWER__.WMF
FLOWERBD.WMF
FLOWERGR.WMF
FLOWERP1.WMF
FLOWERPO.WMF
FLOWERS.WMF
FLOWERS1.WMF
FLOWERS2.WMF
FLOWERS3.WMF
FLOWERS4.WMF
FLOWERS5.WMF
FLOWERS6.WMF
FLWRPOTS.WMF
FMF108E.WMF
FMF108G.WMF
FORGETME.WMF
FOSI065D.WMF
FOXGLOVE.WMF
FRA010F.WMF
FREESIA.WMF
FSD004B.WMF
FSD015A.WMF
FSD036A.WMF
FSD041B.WMF
FSD042C.WMF
FSD052A.WMF
FSD074A.WMF
FSW007A.WMF
FSW012A.WMF
FUCHIA.WMF
FUCHIA5.WMF
FUJIHANA.WMF
FWN017B.WMF
FWN017C.WMF
FWN036A.WMF
FWN036B.WMF
GAILLARD.WMF
GARDEN14.WMF
GARDEN22.WMF
GARDEN27.WMF
GARDEN3.WMF
GARDEN32.WMF
GENTIAN.WMF
GERANI2.WMF
GERANIUM.WMF
GERBERA1.WMF
GETWELL.WMF
GILLYFL.WMF
GLADIOLA.WMF
GLORY.WMF
GLOXINIA.WMF
GOLDNROD.WMF
GPF297B.WMF
GPOPPY.WMF
GRAINS.WMF
GRAPEH.WMF
GRASSPIN.WMF
GRDN038.WMF
HAREBELL.WMF
HAWTHRN.WMF
HFS004C.WMF

HHGC016J.WMF HHGC063D.WMF HIBISCUS.WMF HOLLYHOC.WMF HORIZONT.WMF HPI001C.WMF HPI022C.WMF HPI022E.WMF HYACENTH.WMF HYACIN5.WMF
HYACINTH.WMF ICHO.WMF IHO026C.WMF IKEBANA.WMF IPAINTBR.WMF IRIS.WMF IRIS1.WMF IRIS2.WMF IRIS3.WMF JASMINE.WMF
LADYSLPR.WMF LAVENDER.WMF LEWISIA.WMF LILAC.WMF LILAC4.WMF LILACS.WMF LILY_R.WMF LILY_V.WMF MAGNOLIA.WMF MIMOSA.WMF
MOD004F.WMF MOD006L.WMF MOD010J.WMF MOD013G.WMF MOD015B.WMF MOD015E.WMF MOD016M.WMF MOD017D.WMF MOD018G.WMF MOD018J.WMF
MOD019N.WMF MOD019P.WMF MOD025L.WMF MOD027E.WMF MOD032G.WMF MOTHRDAY.WMF NACA015J.WMF NACA254J.WMF NACA255J.WMF NACA256J.WMF
NACA257J.WMF NACA259J.WMF NACA312J.WMF NACA313J.WMF NACA314J.WMF NACA334J.WMF NACA335J.WMF NAGC006J.WMF NAGC031D.WMF NARCISS.WMF
NARROW.WMF NARW002D.WMF NASI005D.WMF NASI006K.WMF NASI124D.WMF NASI125D.WMF NASI132D.WMF NASS025D.WMF NASS055D.WMF NASS062D.WMF
NASS136D.WMF NASS198D.WMF NASS199D.WMF NASS202D.WMF NASS211D.WMF NASS212D.WMF NASS221D.WMF NASS225D.WMF NASS226D.WMF NASS229D.WMF
NASS230D.WMF NASS235D.WMF NASS236D.WMF NASS237D.WMF NASS264D.WMF NASS266D.WMF NASS273D.WMF NASTUR.WMF NASTURT.WMF NATR028.WMF
NATR029.WMF NATR030.WMF NATR031.WMF NATR032.WMF NATR033.WMF NATR034.WMF NATR035.WMF NATR036.WMF NATR037.WMF NATR038.WMF
NATR039.WMF NATR040.WMF NATR041.WMF NATR042.WMF NATR043.WMF NATR044.WMF NATR045.WMF NATR046.WMF NATR047.WMF NATR048.WMF
NATR049.WMF NATR050.WMF NATR072.WMF NATR073.WMF NATR074.WMF NATR077.WMF NATR078.WMF NATR079.WMF NATR080.WMF NATR081.WMF

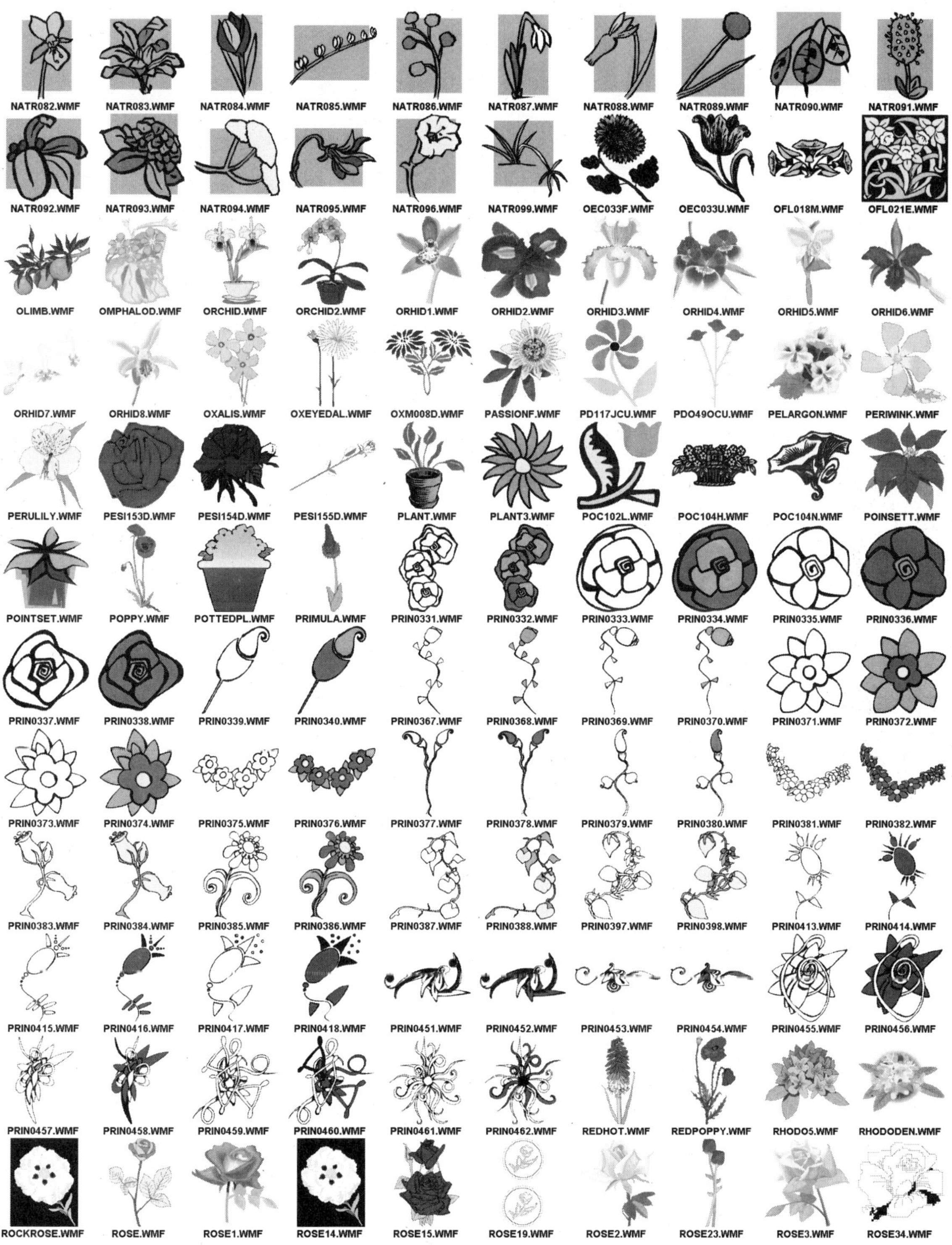
NATR082.WMF NATR083.WMF NATR084.WMF NATR085.WMF NATR086.WMF NATR087.WMF NATR088.WMF NATR089.WMF NATR090.WMF NATR091.WMF
NATR092.WMF NATR093.WMF NATR094.WMF NATR095.WMF NATR096.WMF NATR099.WMF OEC033F.WMF OEC033U.WMF OFL018M.WMF OFL021E.WMF
OLIMB.WMF OMPHALOD.WMF ORCHID.WMF ORCHID2.WMF ORHID1.WMF ORHID2.WMF ORHID3.WMF ORHID4.WMF ORHID5.WMF ORHID6.WMF
ORHID7.WMF ORHID8.WMF OXALIS.WMF OXEYEDAL.WMF OXM008D.WMF PASSIONF.WMF PD117JCU.WMF PDO49OCU.WMF PELARGON.WMF PERIWINK.WMF
PERULILY.WMF PESI153D.WMF PESI154D.WMF PESI155D.WMF PLANT.WMF PLANT3.WMF POC102L.WMF POC104H.WMF POC104N.WMF POINSETT.WMF
POINTSET.WMF POPPY.WMF POTTEDPL.WMF PRIMULA.WMF PRIN0331.WMF PRIN0332.WMF PRIN0333.WMF PRIN0334.WMF PRIN0335.WMF PRIN0336.WMF
PRIN0337.WMF PRIN0338.WMF PRIN0339.WMF PRIN0340.WMF PRIN0367.WMF PRIN0368.WMF PRIN0369.WMF PRIN0370.WMF PRIN0371.WMF PRIN0372.WMF
PRIN0373.WMF PRIN0374.WMF PRIN0375.WMF PRIN0376.WMF PRIN0377.WMF PRIN0378.WMF PRIN0379.WMF PRIN0380.WMF PRIN0381.WMF PRIN0382.WMF
PRIN0383.WMF PRIN0384.WMF PRIN0385.WMF PRIN0386.WMF PRIN0387.WMF PRIN0388.WMF PRIN0397.WMF PRIN0398.WMF PRIN0413.WMF PRIN0414.WMF
PRIN0415.WMF PRIN0416.WMF PRIN0417.WMF PRIN0418.WMF PRIN0451.WMF PRIN0452.WMF PRIN0453.WMF PRIN0454.WMF PRIN0455.WMF PRIN0456.WMF
PRIN0457.WMF PRIN0458.WMF PRIN0459.WMF PRIN0460.WMF PRIN0461.WMF PRIN0462.WMF REDHOT.WMF REDPOPPY.WMF RHODO5.WMF RHODODEN.WMF
ROCKROSE.WMF ROSE.WMF ROSE1.WMF ROSE14.WMF ROSE15.WMF ROSE19.WMF ROSE2.WMF ROSE23.WMF ROSE3.WMF ROSE34.WMF

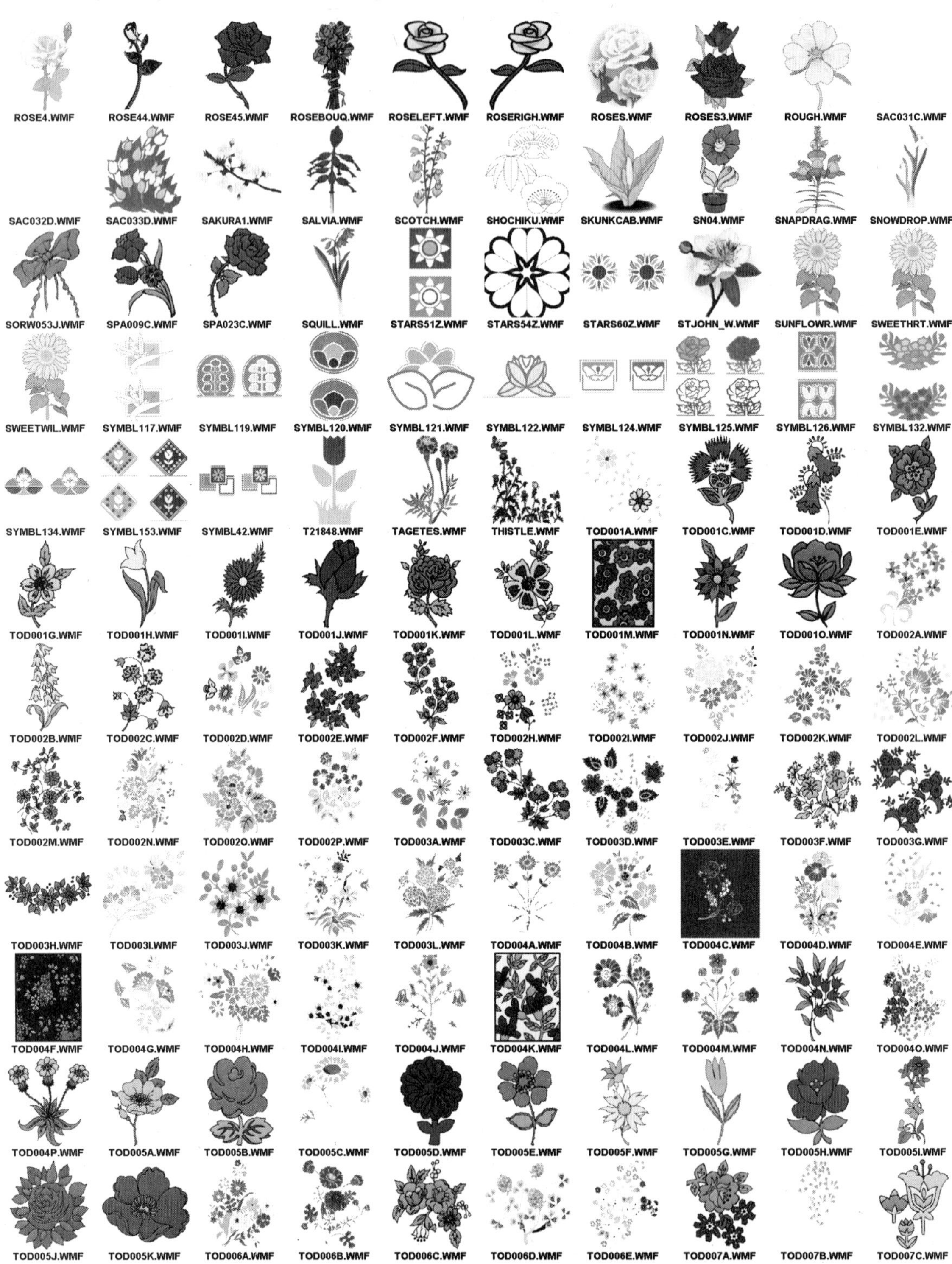
ROSE4.WMF
ROSE44.WMF
ROSE45.WMF
ROSEBOUQ.WMF
ROSELEFT.WMF
ROSERIGH.WMF
ROSES.WMF
ROSES3.WMF
ROUGH.WMF
SAC031C.WMF
SAC032D.WMF
SAC033D.WMF
SAKURA1.WMF
SALVIA.WMF
SCOTCH.WMF
SHOCHIKU.WMF
SKUNKCAB.WMF
SN04.WMF
SNAPDRAG.WMF
SNOWDROP.WMF
SORW053J.WMF
SPA009C.WMF
SPA023C.WMF
SQUILL.WMF
STARS51Z.WMF
STARS54Z.WMF
STARS60Z.WMF
STJOHN_W.WMF
SUNFLOWR.WMF
SWEETHRT.WMF
SWEETWIL.WMF
SYMBL117.WMF
SYMBL119.WMF
SYMBL120.WMF
SYMBL121.WMF
SYMBL122.WMF
SYMBL124.WMF
SYMBL125.WMF
SYMBL126.WMF
SYMBL132.WMF
SYMBL134.WMF
SYMBL153.WMF
SYMBL42.WMF
T21848.WMF
TAGETES.WMF
THISTLE.WMF
TOD001A.WMF
TOD001C.WMF
TOD001D.WMF
TOD001E.WMF
TOD001G.WMF
TOD001H.WMF
TOD001I.WMF
TOD001J.WMF
TOD001K.WMF
TOD001L.WMF
TOD001M.WMF
TOD001N.WMF
TOD001O.WMF
TOD002A.WMF
TOD002B.WMF
TOD002C.WMF
TOD002D.WMF
TOD002E.WMF
TOD002F.WMF
TOD002H.WMF
TOD002I.WMF
TOD002J.WMF
TOD002K.WMF
TOD002L.WMF
TOD002M.WMF
TOD002N.WMF
TOD002O.WMF
TOD002P.WMF
TOD003A.WMF
TOD003C.WMF
TOD003D.WMF
TOD003E.WMF
TOD003F.WMF
TOD003G.WMF
TOD003H.WMF
TOD003I.WMF
TOD003J.WMF
TOD003K.WMF
TOD003L.WMF
TOD004A.WMF
TOD004B.WMF
TOD004C.WMF
TOD004D.WMF
TOD004E.WMF
TOD004F.WMF
TOD004G.WMF
TOD004H.WMF
TOD004I.WMF
TOD004J.WMF
TOD004K.WMF
TOD004L.WMF
TOD004M.WMF
TOD004N.WMF
TOD004O.WMF
TOD004P.WMF
TOD005A.WMF
TOD005B.WMF
TOD005C.WMF
TOD005D.WMF
TOD005E.WMF
TOD005F.WMF
TOD005G.WMF
TOD005H.WMF
TOD005I.WMF
TOD005J.WMF
TOD005K.WMF
TOD006A.WMF
TOD006B.WMF
TOD006C.WMF
TOD006D.WMF
TOD006E.WMF
TOD007A.WMF
TOD007B.WMF
TOD007C.WMF

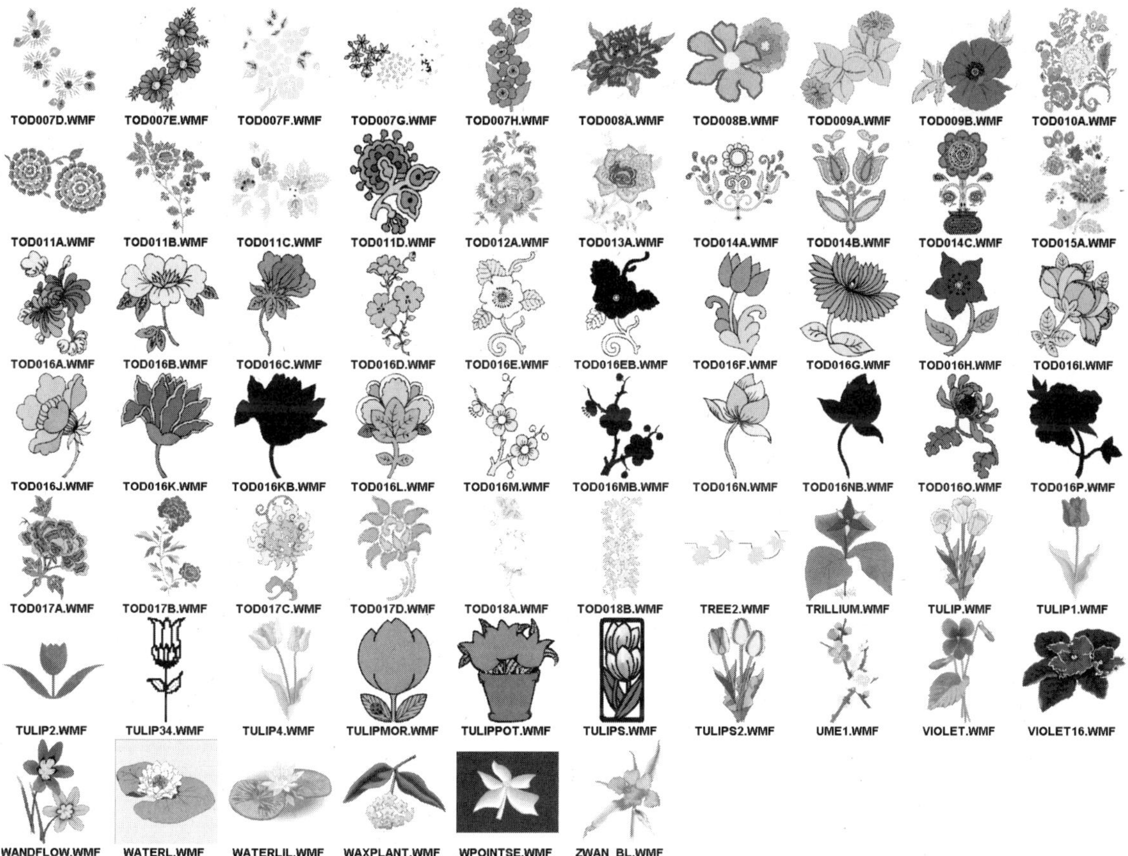
TOD007D.WMF
TOD007E.WMF
TOD007F.WMF
TOD007G.WMF
TOD007H.WMF
TOD008A.WMF
TOD008B.WMF
TOD009A.WMF
TOD009B.WMF
TOD010A.WMF
TOD011A.WMF
TOD011B.WMF
TOD011C.WMF
TOD011D.WMF
TOD012A.WMF
TOD013A.WMF
TOD014A.WMF
TOD014B.WMF
TOD014C.WMF
TOD015A.WMF
TOD016A.WMF
TOD016B.WMF
TOD016C.WMF
TOD016D.WMF
TOD016E.WMF
TOD016EB.WMF
TOD016F.WMF
TOD016G.WMF
TOD016H.WMF
TOD016I.WMF
TOD016J.WMF
TOD016K.WMF
TOD016KB.WMF
TOD016L.WMF
TOD016M.WMF
TOD016MB.WMF
TOD016N.WMF
TOD016NB.WMF
TOD016O.WMF
TOD016P.WMF
TOD017A.WMF
TOD017B.WMF
TOD017C.WMF
TOD017D.WMF
TOD018A.WMF
TOD018B.WMF
TREE2.WMF
TRILLIUM.WMF
TULIP.WMF
TULIP1.WMF
TULIP2.WMF
TULIP34.WMF
TULIP4.WMF
TULIPMOR.WMF
TULIPPOT.WMF
TULIPS.WMF
TULIPS2.WMF
UME1.WMF
VIOLET.WMF
VIOLET16.WMF
WANDFLOW.WMF
WATERL.WMF
WATERLIL.WMF
WAXPLANT.WMF
WPOINTSE.WMF
ZWAN_BL.WMF

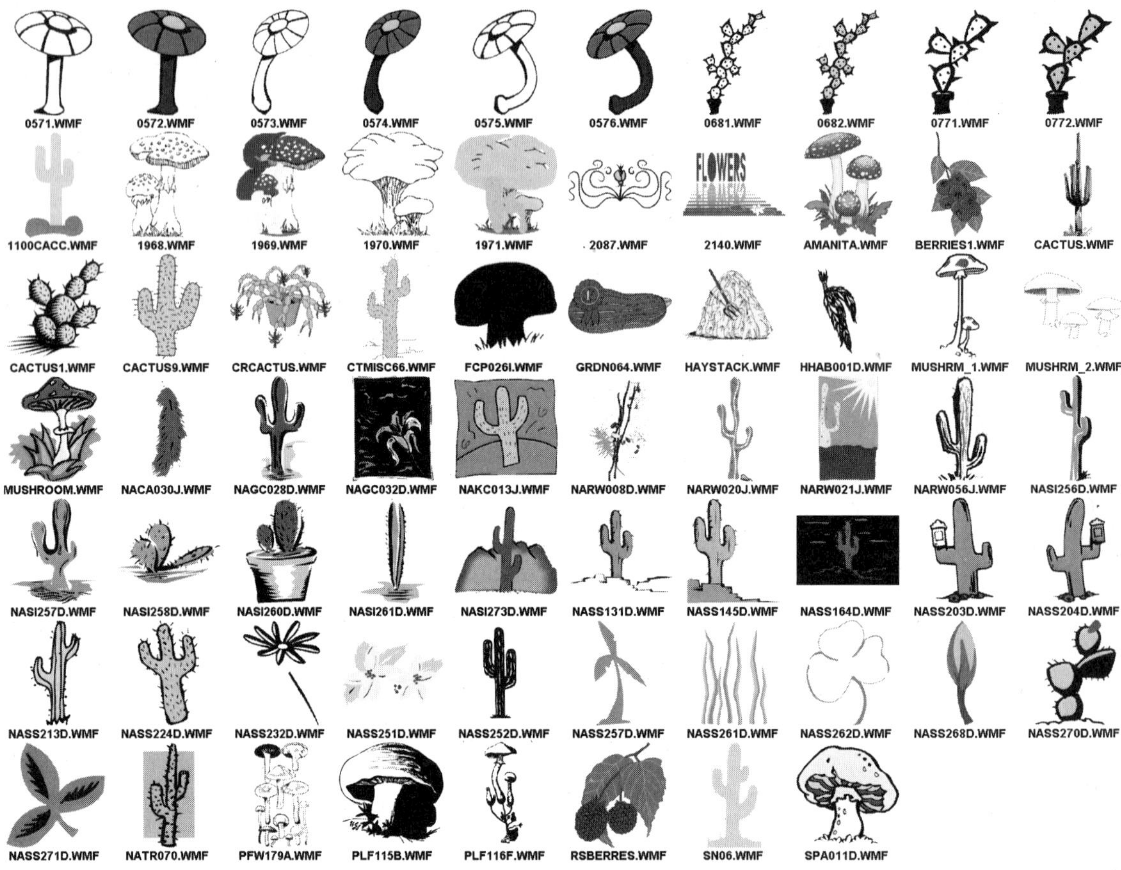
0571.WMF
0572.WMF
0573.WMF
0574.WMF
0575.WMF
0576.WMF
0681.WMF
0682.WMF
0771.WMF
0772.WMF
1100CACC.WMF
1968.WMF
1969.WMF
1970.WMF
1971.WMF
2087.WMF
FLOWERS
2140.WMF
AMANITA.WMF
BERRIES1.WMF
CACTUS.WMF
CACTUS1.WMF
CACTUS9.WMF
CRCACTUS.WMF
CTMISC66.WMF
FCP026I.WMF
GRDN064.WMF
HAYSTACK.WMF
HHAB001D.WMF
MUSHRM_1.WMF
MUSHRM_2.WMF
MUSHROOM.WMF
NACA030J.WMF
NAGC028D.WMF
NAGC032D.WMF
NAKC013J.WMF
NARW008D.WMF
NARW020J.WMF
NARW021J.WMF
NARW056J.WMF
NASI256D.WMF
NASI257D.WMF
NASI258D.WMF
NASI260D.WMF
NASI261D.WMF
NASI273D.WMF
NASS131D.WMF
NASS145D.WMF
NASS164D.WMF
NASS203D.WMF
NASS204D.WMF
NASS213D.WMF
NASS224D.WMF
NASS232D.WMF
NASS251D.WMF
NASS252D.WMF
NASS257D.WMF
NASS261D.WMF
NASS262D.WMF
NASS268D.WMF
NASS270D.WMF
NASS271D.WMF
NATR070.WMF
PFW179A.WMF
PLF115B.WMF
PLF116F.WMF
RSBERRES.WMF
SN06.WMF
SPA011D.WMF

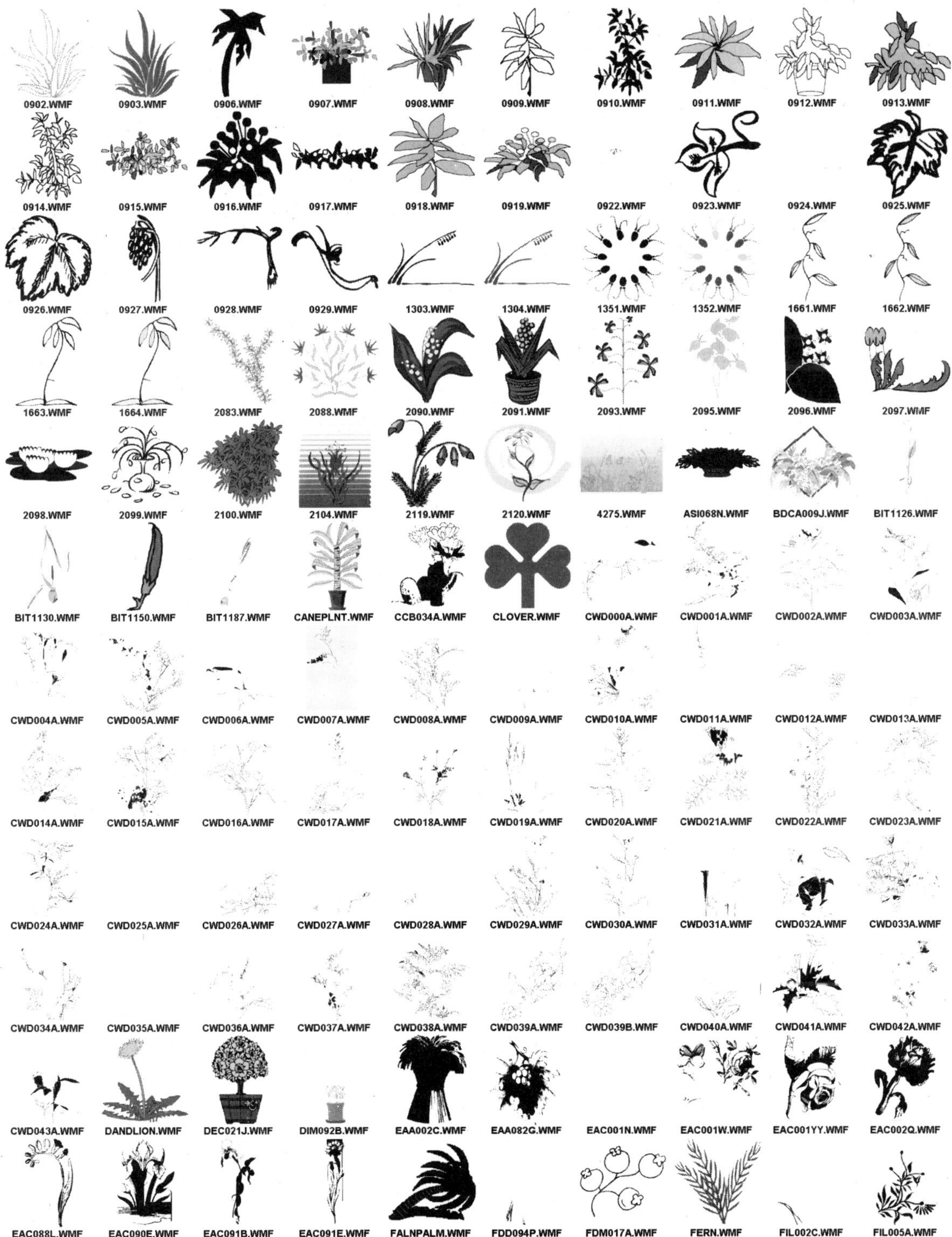

0902.WMF 0903.WMF 0906.WMF 0907.WMF 0908.WMF 0909.WMF 0910.WMF 0911.WMF 0912.WMF 0913.WMF
0914.WMF 0915.WMF 0916.WMF 0917.WMF 0918.WMF 0919.WMF 0922.WMF 0923.WMF 0924.WMF 0925.WMF
0926.WMF 0927.WMF 0928.WMF 0929.WMF 1303.WMF 1304.WMF 1351.WMF 1352.WMF 1661.WMF 1662.WMF
1663.WMF 1664.WMF 2083.WMF 2088.WMF 2090.WMF 2091.WMF 2093.WMF 2095.WMF 2096.WMF 2097.WMF
2098.WMF 2099.WMF 2100.WMF 2104.WMF 2119.WMF 2120.WMF 4275.WMF ASI068N.WMF BDCA009J.WMF BIT1126.WMF
BIT1130.WMF BIT1150.WMF BIT1187.WMF CANEPLNT.WMF CCB034A.WMF CLOVER.WMF CWD000A.WMF CWD001A.WMF CWD002A.WMF CWD003A.WMF
CWD004A.WMF CWD005A.WMF CWD006A.WMF CWD007A.WMF CWD008A.WMF CWD009A.WMF CWD010A.WMF CWD011A.WMF CWD012A.WMF CWD013A.WMF
CWD014A.WMF CWD015A.WMF CWD016A.WMF CWD017A.WMF CWD018A.WMF CWD019A.WMF CWD020A.WMF CWD021A.WMF CWD022A.WMF CWD023A.WMF
CWD024A.WMF CWD025A.WMF CWD026A.WMF CWD027A.WMF CWD028A.WMF CWD029A.WMF CWD030A.WMF CWD031A.WMF CWD032A.WMF CWD033A.WMF
CWD034A.WMF CWD035A.WMF CWD036A.WMF CWD037A.WMF CWD038A.WMF CWD039A.WMF CWD039B.WMF CWD040A.WMF CWD041A.WMF CWD042A.WMF
CWD043A.WMF DANDLION.WMF DEC021J.WMF DIM092B.WMF EAA002C.WMF EAA082G.WMF EAC001N.WMF EAC001W.WMF EAC001YY.WMF EAC002Q.WMF
EAC088L.WMF EAC090E.WMF EAC091B.WMF EAC091E.WMF FALNPALM.WMF FDD094P.WMF FDM017A.WMF FERN.WMF FIL002C.WMF FIL005A.WMF

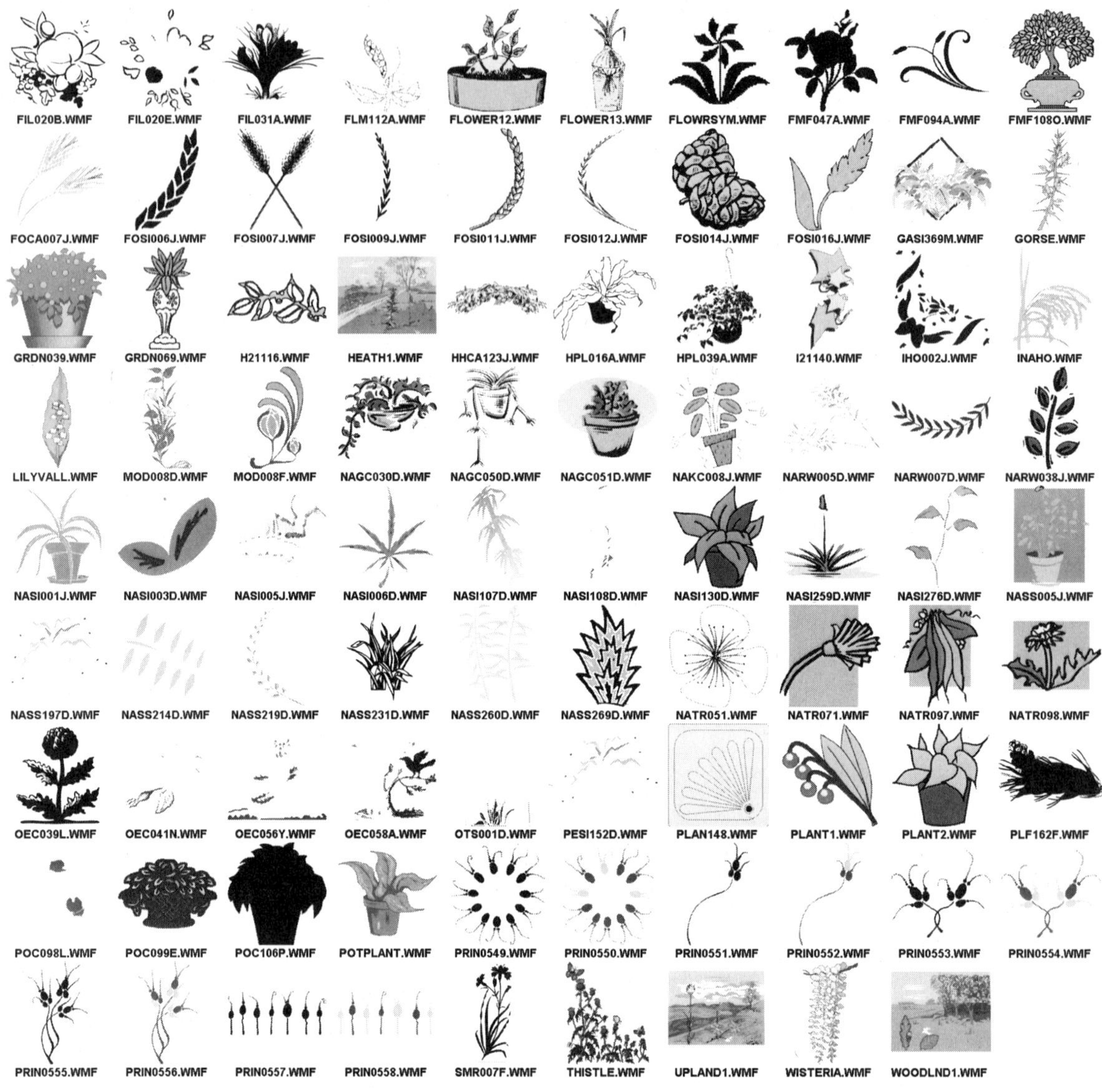
FIL020B.WMF
FIL020E.WMF
FIL031A.WMF
FLM112A.WMF
FLOWER12.WMF
FLOWER13.WMF
FLOWRSYM.WMF
FMF047A.WMF
FMF094A.WMF
FMF108O.WMF
FOCA007J.WMF
FOSI006J.WMF
FOSI007J.WMF
FOSI009J.WMF
FOSI011J.WMF
FOSI012J.WMF
FOSI014J.WMF
FOSI016J.WMF
GASI369M.WMF
GORSE.WMF
GRDN039.WMF
GRDN069.WMF
H21116.WMF
HEATH1.WMF
HHCA123J.WMF
HPL016A.WMF
HPL039A.WMF
I21140.WMF
IHO002J.WMF
INAHO.WMF
LILYVALL.WMF
MOD008D.WMF
MOD008F.WMF
NAGC030D.WMF
NAGC050D.WMF
NAGC051D.WMF
NAKC008J.WMF
NARW005D.WMF
NARW007D.WMF
NARW038J.WMF
NASI001J.WMF
NASI003D.WMF
NASI005J.WMF
NASI006D.WMF
NASI107D.WMF
NASI108D.WMF
NASI130D.WMF
NASI259D.WMF
NASI276D.WMF
NASS005J.WMF
NASS197D.WMF
NASS214D.WMF
NASS219D.WMF
NASS231D.WMF
NASS260D.WMF
NASS269D.WMF
NATR051.WMF
NATR071.WMF
NATR097.WMF
NATR098.WMF
OEC039L.WMF
OEC041N.WMF
OEC056Y.WMF
OEC058A.WMF
OTS001D.WMF
PESI152D.WMF
PLAN148.WMF
PLANT1.WMF
PLANT2.WMF
PLF162F.WMF
POC098L.WMF
POC099E.WMF
POC106P.WMF
POTPLANT.WMF
PRIN0549.WMF
PRIN0550.WMF
PRIN0551.WMF
PRIN0552.WMF
PRIN0553.WMF
PRIN0554.WMF
PRIN0555.WMF
PRIN0556.WMF
PRIN0557.WMF
PRIN0558.WMF
SMR007F.WMF
THISTLE.WMF
UPLAND1.WMF
WISTERIA.WMF
WOODLND1.WMF

0080.WMF 1776.WMF 1BUNTING.WMF 1FAN_BUN.WMF 1FLAG_RI.WMF 1STARRED.WMF 1STRIPED.WMF 2BUNTING.WMF 2FAN_BUN.WMF 2FLAG_RI.WMF

2STARRED.WMF 2STRIPED.WMF A18A.WMF A18AA.WMF A18AB.WMF A18B.WMF A18BA.WMF A18BB.WMF AMENDMTS.WMF AMERICA.WMF

BALLOT.WMF BALLOT1.WMF BALLOTB1.WMF BANNER01.WMF BANNER02.WMF BANNER03.WMF BANNER04.WMF BANNER05.WMF BANNER06.WMF BANNER07.WMF

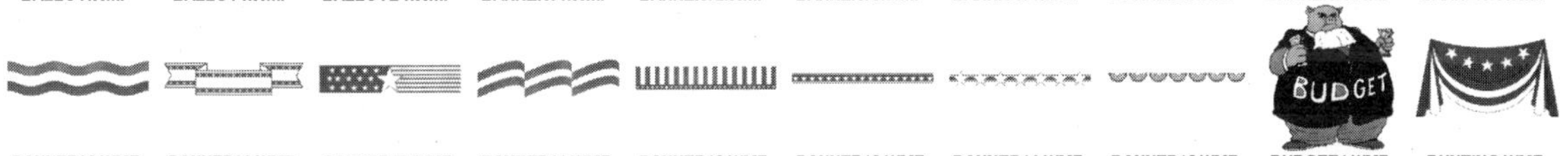

BANNER08.WMF BANNER09.WMF BANNER10.WMF BANNER11.WMF BANNER12.WMF BANNER13.WMF BANNER14.WMF BANNER15.WMF BUDGET1.WMF BUNTING.WMF

C20748.WMF CAMPAIGN.WMF CAPDOME3.WMF CAPDOME4.WMF CAPDOME5.WMF CAPITOL1.WMF CAPITOL3.WMF CAPITOL4.WMF CHECKBO1.WMF CHECKBO2.WMF

CHECKMA1.WMF CHECKMA2.WMF CHECKMA3.WMF CHECKMA4.WMF CHECKMA5.WMF CIVLSERV.WMF CONGBILL.WMF DELEGAT1.WMF DELEGAT2.WMF DELEGAT3.WMF

DELEGAT4.WMF DELEGAT7.WMF DELEGAT8.WMF DELEGATE.WMF DEMOCRAT.WMF DRUMFIFE.WMF EAGLE01.WMF EAGLE02.WMF EAGLE03.WMF EAGLE04.WMF

EAGLE05.WMF EAGLE06.WMF EAGLE07.WMF EAGLE08.WMF EAGLE09.WMF EAGLE10.WMF EAGLE11.WMF EAGLE12.WMF EAGLE13.WMF EAGLE14.WMF

EAGLE_OR.WMF ELECTDAY.WMF ELECTIO1.WMF ELECTION.WMF ELECTSYM.WMF FATCAT.WMF FIRECRA1.WMF FIRECRA2.WMF FIREWOR1.WMF FIREWOR2.WMF

FLAG_ORN.WMF FOUNDING.WMF FREEDOM_.WMF HANDSHAK.WMF INAGURAT.WMF INAUGURA.WMF INDENDA.WMF LADYLIB.WMF LEGISLAT.WMF LIBERTY1.WMF

LIBERTYB.WMF LINCOLN1.WMF LINCOLN2.WMF LINCOLN3.WMF MEMORIAL.WMF MISC101.WMF MISC102.WMF NO.WMF PAT.WMF PATRIOT1.WMF

PATRIOT2.WMF PLEATEDF.WMF PLEATEDH.WMF POLIT.WMF POLITSYM.WMF PRO.WMF RD2WHTHS.WMF REFEREND.WMF REGISTRA.WMF REVOLUTI.WMF

ROLLCALL.WMF
SEN_EAGL.WMF
SHIELD1.WMF
SHIELD2.WMF
SHIELD3.WMF
SIGNS1.WMF
SOAPBOX1.WMF
SOAPBOX2.WMF
SOLDIER.WMF
SPEECH.WMF
STAR01.WMF
STAR02.WMF
STAR03.WMF
STAR04.WMF
STAR05.WMF
STAR06.WMF
STAR07.WMF
STAR08.WMF
STAR09.WMF
STAR10.WMF
STAR11.WMF
STARS.WMF
STARSST1.WMF
STARSST2.WMF
STARSST3.WMF
STATUE1.WMF
STATUE2.WMF
STATUE_O.WMF
SYMBL108.WMF
SYMBL13.WMF
SYMBOL13.WMF
TAXES5.WMF
U21858.WMF
UNCLESA1.WMF
UNCLESA2.WMF
UNCLESA3.WMF
US_ROCKE.WMF
USA.WMF
USAMCAP.WMF
USASYMB.WMF
USCAP1.WMF
USCAP2.WMF
USMAP1.WMF
USMAP2.WMF
USPRES.WMF
VBOOTH1.WMF
VBOOTH2.WMF
VBOOTH3.WMF
VBOOTH4.WMF
VBOOTH5.WMF
VBOOTH6.WMF
VBOOTH7.WMF
VICEPRES.WMF
VOTE.WMF
VOTE1.WMF
VOTE11.WMF
VOTE2.WMF
VOTE21.WMF
VOTE22.WMF
VOTE3.WMF
VOTE_BUT.WMF
VOTING_B.WMF
WASH1.WMF
WASH2.WMF
WESTPNT.WMF
WHITEHS.WMF
YES.WMF

2PARTY1.WMF
DELEGAT5.WMF
DELEGAT6.WMF
DEM1.WMF
DEM10.WMF
DEM11.WMF
DEM12.WMF
DEM2.WMF
DEM3.WMF
DEM4.WMF
DEM5.WMF
DEM6.WMF
DEM7.WMF
DEM8.WMF
DEM9.WMF
DEMCUT1.WMF
DEMOCR01.WMF
DEMOCR02.WMF
DEMOCR03.WMF
DEMOCR04.WMF
DEMOCR05.WMF
DEMOCR06.WMF
DEMOCR07.WMF
DEMOCR08.WMF
DEM
DEMOCR09.WMF
DEMOCR10.WMF
DEMOCRA2.WMF
DEMOCRAT
DEMOCRAT.WMF
DONKEY_S.WMF
ELEPHAN_.WMF
ELEPHANT.WMF
FA16.WMF
FA17.WMF
GOP1.WMF
GOP10.WMF
GOP11.WMF
GOP12.WMF
GOP2.WMF
GOP3.WMF
GOP4.WMF
GOP5.WMF
GOP6.WMF
GOP7.WMF
GOP8.WMF
GOP9.WMF
GOPCUT1.WMF
GOPDEMS.WMF
INDEPENDENT
INDEPEND.WMF
JA01.WMF
JA02.WMF
POLITI.WMF
POLITIC2.WMF
REPUB.WMF
REPUBL1.WMF
REPUBL2.WMF
REPUBL3.WMF
REPUBL4.WMF
REPUBL5.WMF
GOP
REPUBL6.WMF
REPUBL7.WMF
REPUBLCN.WMF
REPUBLICAN
REPUBLIC.WMF

g:\PRESIDNT [P_TO_Z]
0143GEOC.WMF
ABE.WMF
ABE_LINC.WMF
ABRAHAML.WMF
ADS018A.WMF
ADS018D.WMF
ADS018I.WMF
FDR1.WMF
GEORGE.WMF
GEORGE_W.WMF
GEORGEW1.WMF
GEORGEW2.WMF
GEORGEW3.WMF
GEORGEWA.WMF
GWASHNGT.WMF
JFK.WMF
LINCOL00.WMF
LINCOLN.WMF
LINCOLN1.WMF
LINCOLN2.WMF
LINCOLN3.WMF
LINCOLNX.WMF
NIXON1.WMF
NIXON2.WMF
NIXON3.WMF
OFS020F.WMF
OPT006A.WMF
PDENTS.WMF
PEAB001J.WMF
PEARY1.WMF
PEARY2.WMF
PEOPL024.WMF
PEOPL025.WMF
PERW002J.WMF
PERW004J.WMF
PERW008J.WMF
PERW009J.WMF
PERW010J.WMF
PERW012J.WMF
PERW013J.WMF
PERW027J.WMF
PESI001G.WMF
POPFCE0.WMF
POPFCE1.WMF
POPFCE10.WMF
POPFCE11.WMF
POPFCE12.WMF
POPFCE13.WMF
POPFCE14.WMF
POPFCE15.WMF
POPFCE16.WMF
POPFCE17.WMF
POPFCE18.WMF
POPFCE19.WMF
POPFCE2.WMF
POPFCE20.WMF
POPFCE21.WMF
POPFCE22.WMF
POPFCE23.WMF
POPFCE24.WMF
POPFCE25.WMF
POPFCE26.WMF
POPFCE27.WMF
POPFCE28.WMF
POPFCE29.WMF
POPFCE3.WMF
POPFCE30.WMF
POPFCE31.WMF
POPFCE32.WMF
POPFCE33.WMF
POPFCE34.WMF
POPFCE35.WMF
POPFCE36.WMF
POPFCE37.WMF
POPFCE38.WMF
POPFCE39.WMF
POPFCE4.WMF
POPFCE40.WMF
POPFCE5.WMF
POPFCE6.WMF
POPFCE7.WMF
POPFCE8.WMF
POPFCE9.WMF
REAGAN1.WMF
REAGAN2.WMF
SB01.WMF
SORW040J.WMF
SORW046J.WMF
TEDDYR1.WMF
TEDDYR2.WMF
TEDDYR3.WMF
WASHING.WMF
WASHING2.WMF
WASHTON1.WMF

g:\REALESTA [P_TO_Z]
01FRAME.WMF 02FRAME.WMF 03FRAME.WMF 04FRAME.WMF 05FRAME.WMF 06AFRAME.WMF 06BFRAME.WMF 06CFRAME.WMF 07FRAME.WMF 08FRAME.WMF
09AFRAME.WMF 09BFRAME.WMF 09CFRAME.WMF 10FRAME.WMF 11AFRAME.WMF 11BFRAME.WMF 12FRAME.WMF 13FRAME.WMF 14FRAME.WMF 15FRAME.WMF
16AFRAME.WMF 16BFRAME.WMF 16CFRAME.WMF 17AFRAME.WMF 17BFRAME.WMF 19FRAME.WMF 20FRAME.WMF 21AFRAME.WMF 21BFRAME.WMF 22AFRAME.WMF
22BFRAME.WMF AUCTION1.WMF BUILDG1.WMF BUILDG3.WMF BUILDG4.WMF CITYSCP2.WMF CIYSCP1.WMF COMM1.WMF COMM2.WMF COMM3.WMF
COMPUTR.WMF CONDO.WMF DOORKNOK.WMF FARM.WMF FARMSCP.WMF FORENT1.WMF FORENT2.WMF FORLEASE.WMF FORSALE.WMF FORSALE0.WMF
FORSALE1.WMF FORSALE2.WMF FORSALE3.WMF FORSALE4.WMF FORSALE5.WMF FORSALE6.WMF FORSALE7.WMF FORSALE8.WMF FORSALE9.WMF HOME.WMF
HOME0005.WMF HOUSE.WMF HPI002B.WMF HPI002D.WMF HPI002E.WMF HPI020I.WMF INDUSTR.WMF JUDGE.WMF KEY1.WMF KEY2.WMF
KEY3.WMF LAWYER.WMF OPENHOUS.WMF OPENHSE.WMF OPENHSE1.WMF OPNHOUS.WMF REALEST1.WMF REALESTA.WMF REALTOR.WMF RENTAL1.WMF
RENTAL2.WMF RESID01.WMF RESID02.WMF RESID03.WMF RESID04.WMF RESID05.WMF RESID06.WMF RESID07.WMF RESID08.WMF RESID09.WMF
RESID10.WMF RESID11.WMF RESID12.WMF RESID13.WMF ROOFTOP1.WMF ROOFTOP2.WMF ROOFTOP3.WMF SCHOLHSE.WMF SEASCAPE.WMF SIGN1.WMF
SIGN2.WMF SIGN3.WMF SIGN5.WMF SOLD.WMF SOLD1.WMF SOLD2.WMF SOLD3.WMF SOLD4.WMF STORFRT1.WMF STORFRT2.WMF
UNDCONST.WMF UNDDEP.WMF USMAP.WMF WAREHOUS.WMF

A20015.WMF A20016.WMF A20017.WMF ANGEL.WMF ANGEL00.WMF ANGEL001.WMF ANGEL01.WMF ANGEL01M.WMF ANGEL05.WMF ANGEL1.WMF

ANGEL11.WMF ANGEL12.WMF ANGEL2.WMF ANGEL21.WMF ANGEL22.WMF ANGEL23.WMF ANGEL24.WMF ANGEL25.WMF ANGEL26.WMF ANGEL27.WMF

ANGEL28.WMF ANGEL29.WMF ANGEL30.WMF ANGEL31.WMF ANGELA.WMF ANGELAFR.WMF ANGELB.WMF ANGELBL.WMF ANGLEKO.WMF DEVIL.WMF

DEVIL01.WMF DEVIL01A.WMF DEVIL01M.WMF DEVIL03.WMF DEVIL04.WMF DEVIL05.WMF DEVIL06.WMF DVLBOYTO.WMF DVLFORK.WMF FSW036B.WMF

GLASS.WMF MOD009C.WMF MUSICAGL.WMF OXM028B.WMF OXM028C.WMF OXM029F.WMF RLGN071.WMF SPA007A.WMF SXM002A.WMF TANGEL01.WMF

TANGEL02.WMF TANGEL03.WMF TANGEL04.WMF TANGEL05.WMF TANGEL06.WMF TANGEL07.WMF TANGEL08.WMF WMG046H.WMF WMG046J.WMF

Religion • Biblical Scenes (BIBSCENE)

BABTOW.WMF BREADWIN.WMF CREATING.WMF DONKEY.WMF DONKEYC.WMF EDCN137.WMF EVA.WMF EZEKIEL.WMF J21149.WMF N21427.WMF

N21428.WMF NOAHARK.WMF RLGN002.WMF RLGN010.WMF RLGN011.WMF RLGN012.WMF RLGN014.WMF RLGN069.WMF RLGN089.WMF RLGN108.WMF

RLGN113.WMF RLGN114.WMF RLGN115.WMF RLGN116.WMF RLGN117.WMF RLGN119.WMF RLGN132.WMF RLGN135.WMF RLGN146.WMF RLGN147.WMF

RLGN153.WMF RLGN157.WMF RLGN168.WMF RLGN170.WMF RLGN178.WMF RLGN198.WMF RLGN199.WMF RLGN200.WMF RLGN201.WMF STAINED.WMF

XBLESS.WMF XSACRIF.WMF

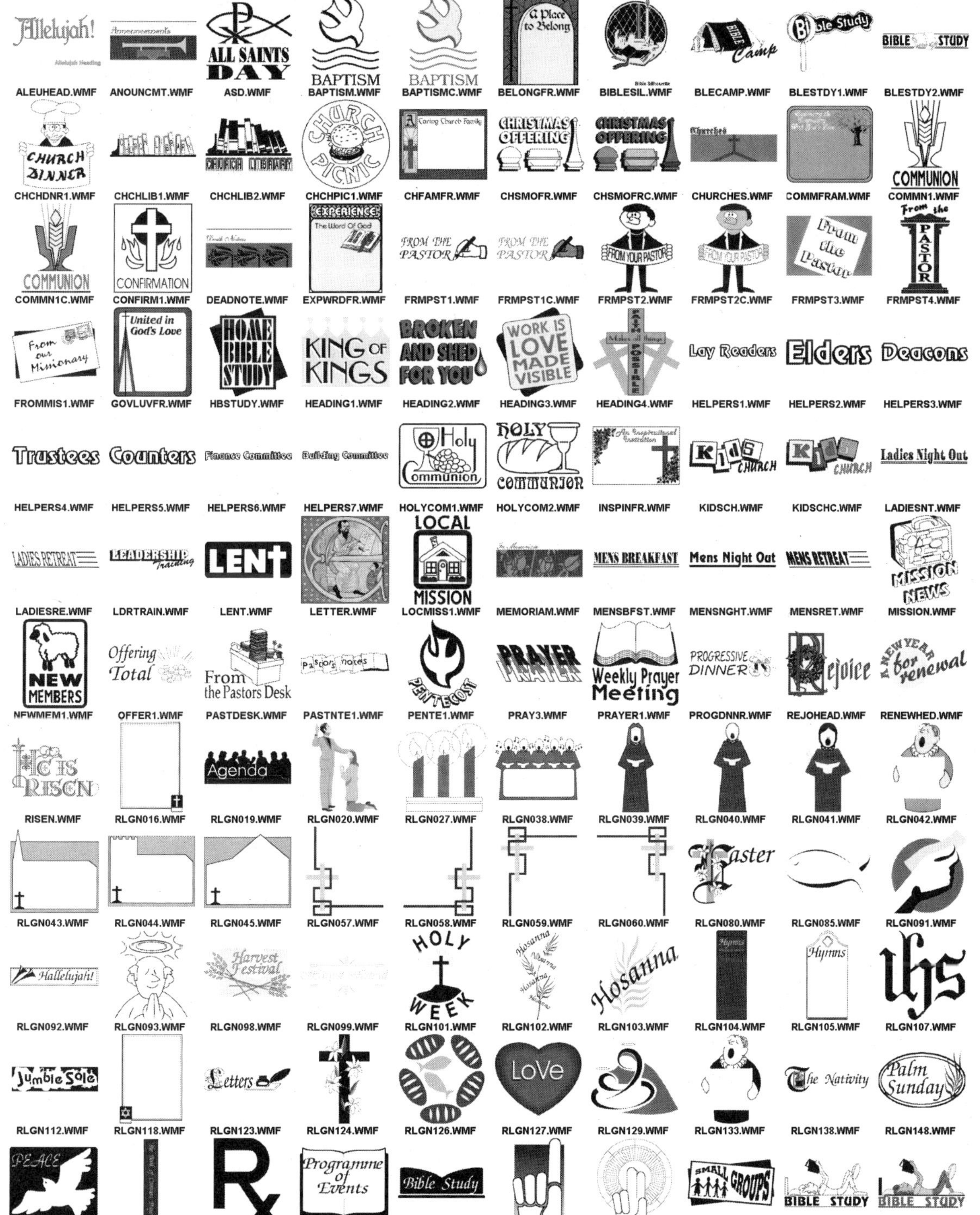

ALEUHEAD.WMF ANOUNCMT.WMF ASD.WMF BAPTISM.WMF BAPTISMC.WMF BELONGFR.WMF BIBLESIL.WMF BLECAMP.WMF BLESTDY1.WMF BLESTDY2.WMF

CHCHDNR1.WMF CHCHLIB1.WMF CHCHLIB2.WMF CHCHPIC1.WMF CHFAMFR.WMF CHSMOFR.WMF CHSMOFRC.WMF CHURCHES.WMF COMMFRAM.WMF COMMN1.WMF

COMMN1C.WMF CONFIRM1.WMF DEADNOTE.WMF EXPWRDFR.WMF FRMPST1.WMF FRMPST1C.WMF FRMPST2.WMF FRMPST2C.WMF FRMPST3.WMF FRMPST4.WMF

FROMMIS1.WMF GOVLUVFR.WMF HBSTUDY.WMF HEADING1.WMF HEADING2.WMF HEADING3.WMF HEADING4.WMF HELPERS1.WMF HELPERS2.WMF HELPERS3.WMF

HELPERS4.WMF HELPERS5.WMF HELPERS6.WMF HELPERS7.WMF HOLYCOM1.WMF HOLYCOM2.WMF INSPINFR.WMF KIDSCH.WMF KIDSCHC.WMF LADIESNT.WMF

LADIESRE.WMF LDRTRAIN.WMF LENT.WMF LETTER.WMF LOCMISS1.WMF MEMORIAM.WMF MENSBFST.WMF MENSNGHT.WMF MENSRET.WMF MISSION.WMF

NEWMEM1.WMF OFFER1.WMF PASTDESK.WMF PASTNTE1.WMF PENTE1.WMF PRAY3.WMF PRAYER1.WMF PROGDNNR.WMF REJOHEAD.WMF RENEWHED.WMF

RISEN.WMF RLGN016.WMF RLGN019.WMF RLGN020.WMF RLGN027.WMF RLGN038.WMF RLGN039.WMF RLGN040.WMF RLGN041.WMF RLGN042.WMF

RLGN043.WMF RLGN044.WMF RLGN045.WMF RLGN057.WMF RLGN058.WMF RLGN059.WMF RLGN060.WMF RLGN080.WMF RLGN085.WMF RLGN091.WMF

RLGN092.WMF RLGN093.WMF RLGN098.WMF RLGN099.WMF RLGN101.WMF RLGN102.WMF RLGN103.WMF RLGN104.WMF RLGN105.WMF RLGN107.WMF

RLGN112.WMF RLGN118.WMF RLGN123.WMF RLGN124.WMF RLGN126.WMF RLGN127.WMF RLGN129.WMF RLGN133.WMF RLGN138.WMF RLGN148.WMF

RLGN149.WMF RLGN152.WMF RLGN158.WMF RLGN160.WMF RLGN177.WMF RLGN185.WMF RLGN186.WMF SMLGRPS.WMF STUDY1.WMF STUDY1C.WMF

SUNMORN.WMF SUNNIGHT.WMF SUNSCHL.WMF SUNSCHLC.WMF TITHES.WMF WELCOME.WMF WOMNCIR.WMF WOMNCIRC.WMF WRLDMIS.WMF WRLDMISC.WMF

YTHSTDY.WMF

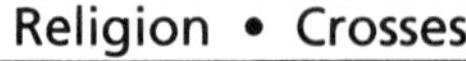

Religion • Crosses

0500.WMF 0501.WMF 0502.WMF 0503.WMF 0504.WMF 0505.WMF 0506.WMF 0507.WMF 0508.WMF 0509.WMF

0510.WMF 0511.WMF 0512.WMF 0513.WMF 0514.WMF 0515.WMF 0516.WMF 0517.WMF 0518.WMF 0519.WMF

0520.WMF 0521.WMF 0522.WMF 0523.WMF 0524.WMF 0525.WMF 0526.WMF 0527.WMF 0528.WMF 0529.WMF

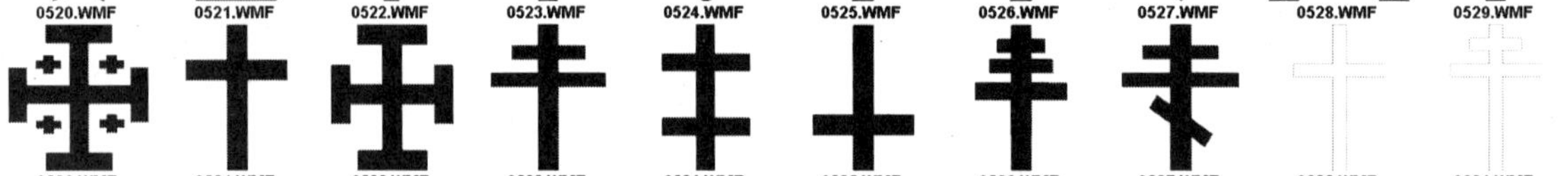

0530.WMF 0531.WMF 0532.WMF 0533.WMF 0534.WMF 0535.WMF 0536.WMF 0537.WMF 0632.WMF 0634.WMF

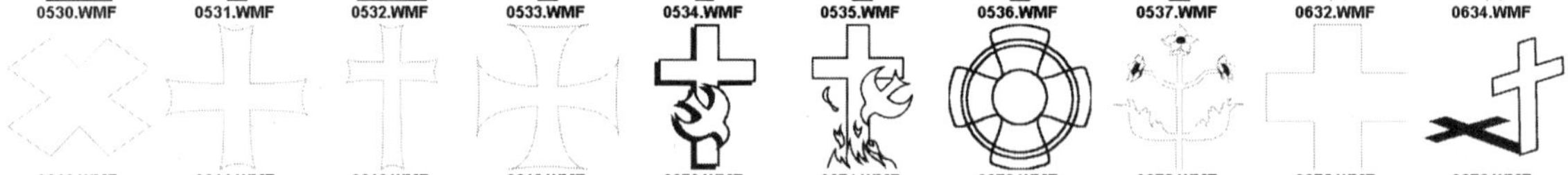

0640.WMF 0644.WMF 0646.WMF 0648.WMF 0670.WMF 0671.WMF 0672.WMF 0673.WMF 0675.WMF 0676.WMF

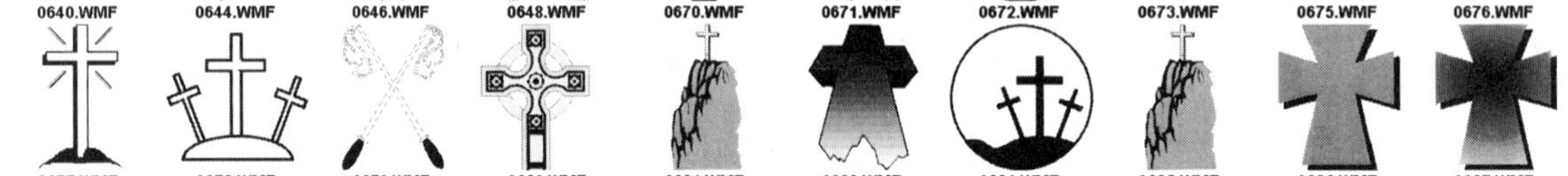

0677.WMF 0678.WMF 0679.WMF 0680.WMF 0681.WMF 0682.WMF 0684.WMF 0685.WMF 0686.WMF 0687.WMF

0841.WMF 0867.WMF ANCROSS1.WMF ANCROSS2.WMF ANCROSS3.WMF ANCROSS4.WMF AVELLAN.WMF BARBEE.WMF BEZANT.WMF BOTTONEE.WMF

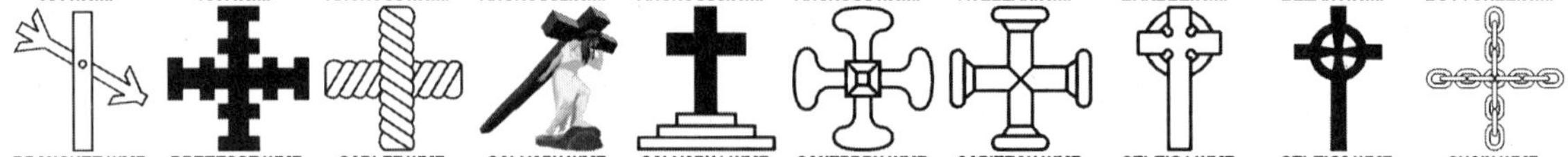

BRANCHEE.WMF BRETESSE.WMF CABLEE.WMF CALVARY.WMF CALVARY1.WMF CANTRBRY.WMF CAPITEAU.WMF CELTIC1.WMF CELTIC2.WMF CHAIN.WMF

CHRISVIC.WMF CLECHEE.WMF CRAMPONE.WMF CROISSAN.WMF CROSLILY.WMF CROSS005.WMF CROSS008.WMF CROSS01.WMF CROSS05.WMF CROSS06.WMF

CROSS08.WMF CROSS1.WMF CROSS2.WMF CROSS3.WMF CROSS4.WMF CROSS5.WMF CROSS6.WMF CROSS_1.WMF CROSS_3.WMF CROSS_A.WMF

CROSS_B.WMF CROSS_C.WMF CROSSLET.WMF CROSSORD.WMF CRSSLIL.WMF CRUCIFI.WMF CRUCIFIX.WMF DEMISARC.WMF DOVETAIL.WMF EARLCRS1.WMF

EARLCRS2.WMF EASDAY.WMF EASTER.WMF EASTERN.WMF ENGRAILD.WMF ENTRAILD.WMF FICHEE.WMF FITCHEE.WMF FLEURETT.WMF FLEURY.WMF

FORMEE.WMF FOURCHEE.WMF FRETTEE.WMF FUSILS.WMF G21064.WMF GREEK.WMF HFRW001J.WMF INSPINFR.WMF INTERLAC.WMF LAMBEAU.WMF

LATIN.WMF LORRAINE.WMF LOTHRING.WMF MALTESE.WMF MASCLY.WMF METHODIS.WMF MILLRINE.WMF MOUSSUE.WMF NEBULEE.WMF OTHDOX.WMF

PAPAL.WMF PATERNOS.WMF PATRIARC.WMF PERRONNE.WMF PHEONS.WMF POMMEE.WMF POTENT.WMF QUADRATE.WMF RAGULY.WMF RCROSS.WMF

REMBRNCE.WMF RLGN013.WMF RLGN024.WMF RLGN055.WMF RLGN056.WMF RLGN061.WMF RLGN062.WMF RLGN063.WMF RLGN079.WMF RLGN094.WMF

RLGN096.WMF RLGN097.WMF RLGN124.WMF RLGN134.WMF RLGN136.WMF RLGN159.WMF RLGN184.WMF ROSARY01.WMF ROSARY02.WMF SOSI212D.WMF

SOSS002D.WMF SOSS003D.WMF STANDREW.WMF STCLEMEN.WMF STJAMES.WMF STJULIAN.WMF STPETER.WMF TAU.WMF TIUMPH.WMF TRONONNE.WMF

URDEE.WMF WAVY.WMF

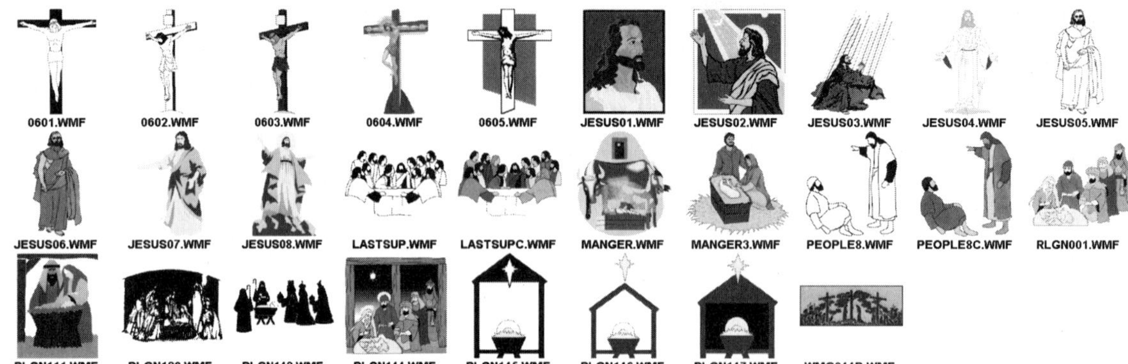
0601.WMF
0602.WMF
0603.WMF
0604.WMF
0605.WMF
JESUS01.WMF
JESUS02.WMF
JESUS03.WMF
JESUS04.WMF
JESUS05.WMF
JESUS06.WMF
JESUS07.WMF
JESUS08.WMF
LASTSUP.WMF
LASTSUPC.WMF
MANGER.WMF
MANGER3.WMF
PEOPLE8.WMF
PEOPLE8C.WMF
RLGN001.WMF
RLGN111.WMF
RLGN139.WMF
RLGN142.WMF
RLGN144.WMF
RLGN145.WMF
RLGN146.WMF
RLGN147.WMF
WMG044B.WMF

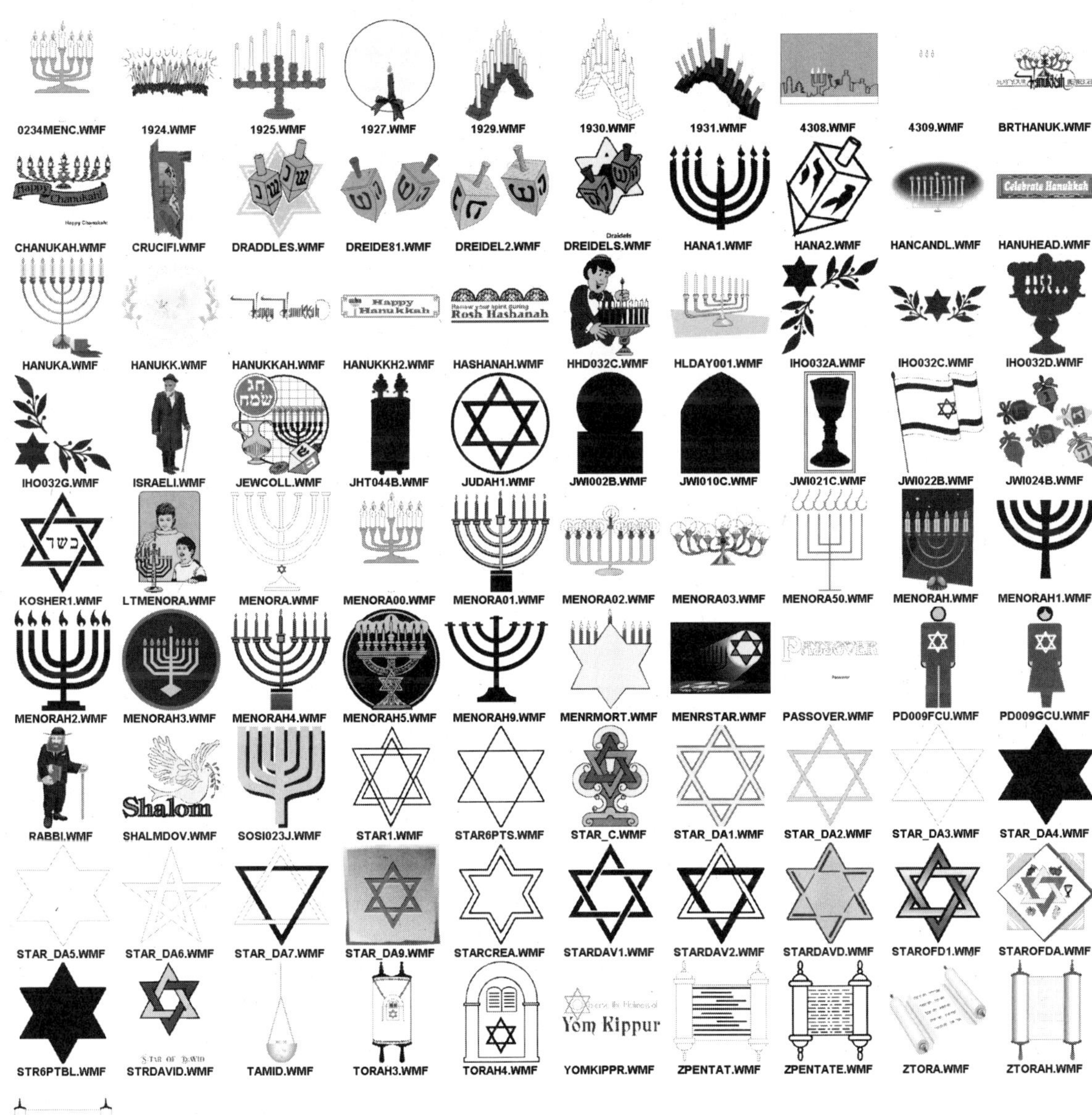

0234MENC.WMF 1924.WMF 1925.WMF 1927.WMF 1929.WMF 1930.WMF 1931.WMF 4308.WMF 4309.WMF BRTHANUK.WMF

CHANUKAH.WMF CRUCIFI.WMF DRADDLES.WMF DREIDE81.WMF DREIDEL2.WMF DREIDELS.WMF HANA1.WMF HANA2.WMF HANCANDL.WMF HANUHEAD.WMF

HANUKA.WMF HANUKK.WMF HANUKKAH.WMF HANUKKH2.WMF HASHANAH.WMF HHD032C.WMF HLDAY001.WMF IHO032A.WMF IHO032C.WMF IHO032D.WMF

IHO032G.WMF ISRAELI.WMF JEWCOLL.WMF JHT044B.WMF JUDAH1.WMF JWI002B.WMF JWI010C.WMF JWI021C.WMF JWI022B.WMF JWI024B.WMF

KOSHER1.WMF LTMENORA.WMF MENORA.WMF MENORA00.WMF MENORA01.WMF MENORA02.WMF MENORA03.WMF MENORA50.WMF MENORAH.WMF MENORAH1.WMF

MENORAH2.WMF MENORAH3.WMF MENORAH4.WMF MENORAH5.WMF MENORAH9.WMF MENRMORT.WMF MENRSTAR.WMF PASSOVER.WMF PD009FCU.WMF PD009GCU.WMF

RABBI.WMF SHALMDOV.WMF SOSI023J.WMF STAR1.WMF STAR6PTS.WMF STAR_C.WMF STAR_DA1.WMF STAR_DA2.WMF STAR_DA3.WMF STAR_DA4.WMF

STAR_DA5.WMF STAR_DA6.WMF STAR_DA7.WMF STAR_DA9.WMF STARCREA.WMF STARDAV1.WMF STARDAV2.WMF STARDAVD.WMF STAROFD1.WMF STAROFDA.WMF

STR6PTBL.WMF STRDAVID.WMF TAMID.WMF TORAH3.WMF TORAH4.WMF YOMKIPPR.WMF ZPENTAT.WMF ZPENTATE.WMF ZTORA.WMF ZTORAH.WMF

ZTORAH1.WMF

10COM.WMF BIBLE.WMF BIBLE009.WMF BIBLE1.WMF BIBLE12.WMF BIBLE2.WMF BIBLE3.WMF BIBLE5.WMF BIBLE9.WMF BIBLE_1.WMF

BIBLE_2.WMF CMMNDMNT.WMF DESCEN.WMF DOVE005.WMF DOVE1.WMF DOVE2.WMF DOVESUN.WMF DOVESUNB.WMF EDCN231.WMF OEC041S.WMF

PD043DCU.WMF PEACE1.WMF PEACEBNR.WMF RLGN017.WMF RLGN018.WMF RLGN021.WMF RLGN054.WMF RLGN074.WMF RLGN075.WMF RLGN076.WMF

RLGN077.WMF RLGN078.WMF RLGN202.WMF RLGN203.WMF SXM009B.WMF TENCOMM.WMF

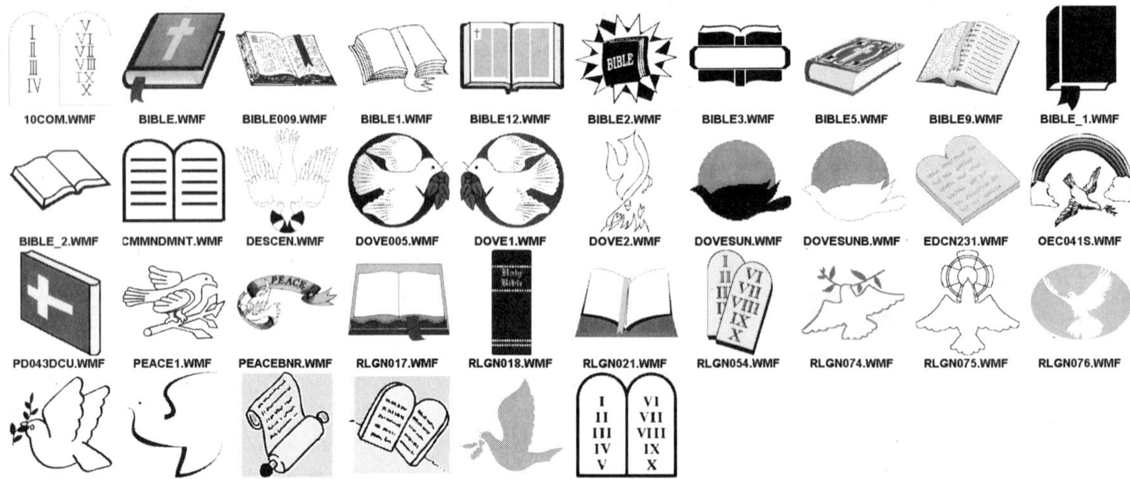

Religion • Objects

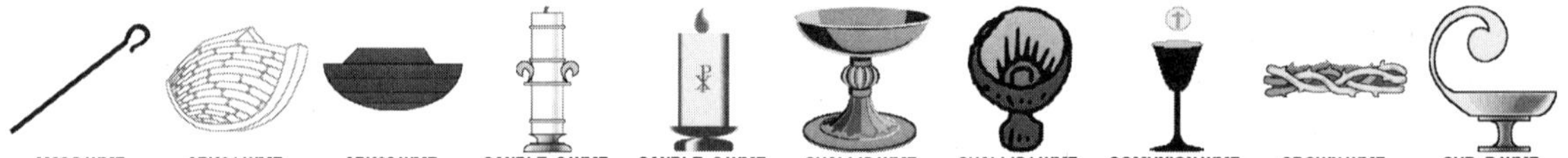

AMOS.WMF ARK01.WMF ARK02.WMF CANDLE_2.WMF CANDLE_3.WMF CHALLIS.WMF CHALLIS1.WMF COMUNION.WMF CROWN.WMF CUP_B.WMF

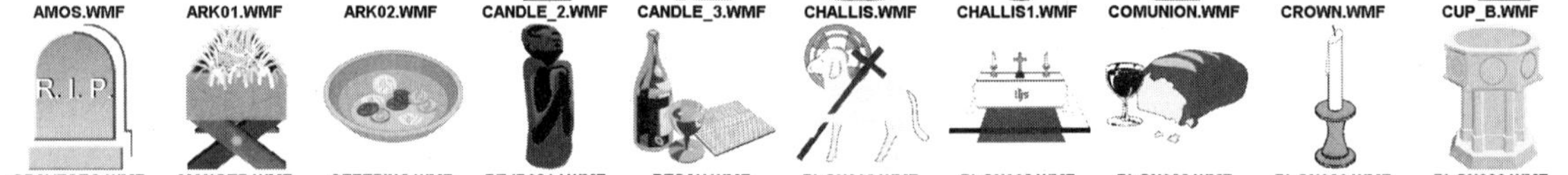

GRAVESTO.WMF MANGER.WMF OFFERING.WMF PEJB021J.WMF PESAH.WMF RLGN003.WMF RLGN008.WMF RLGN022.WMF RLGN029.WMF RLGN090.WMF

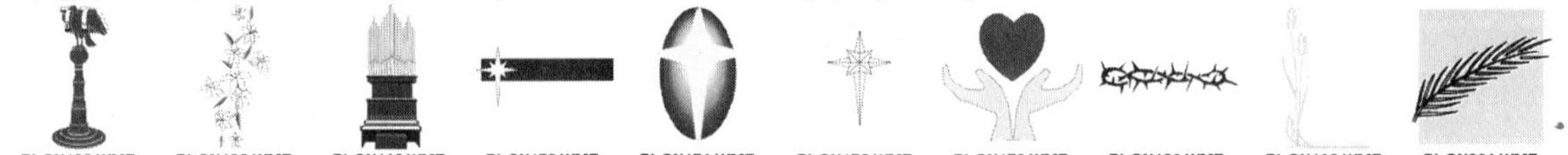

RLGN122.WMF RLGN125.WMF RLGN145.WMF RLGN173.WMF RLGN174.WMF RLGN175.WMF RLGN179.WMF RLGN180.WMF RLGN193.WMF RLGN204.WMF

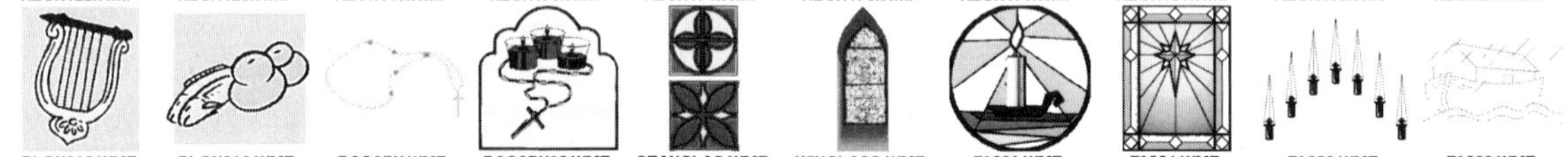

RLGN205.WMF RLGN206.WMF ROSARY.WMF ROSARY05.WMF STANGLAS.WMF WINGLASS.WMF Z0550.WMF Z0551.WMF Z0552.WMF Z0553.WMF

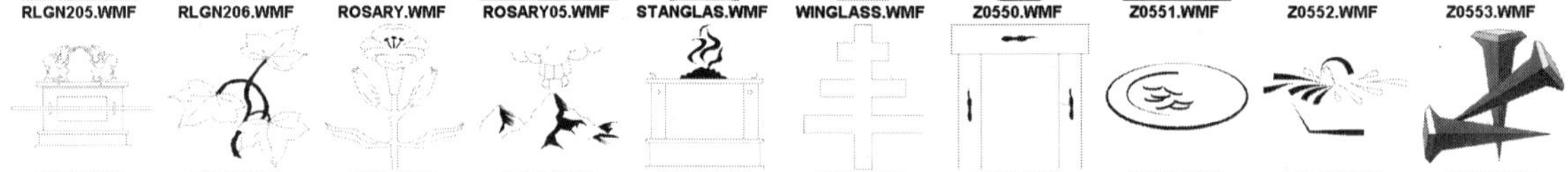

Z0554.WMF Z0555.WMF Z0556.WMF Z0557.WMF Z0558.WMF Z0559.WMF Z0560.WMF Z0561.WMF Z0562.WMF Z0563.WMF

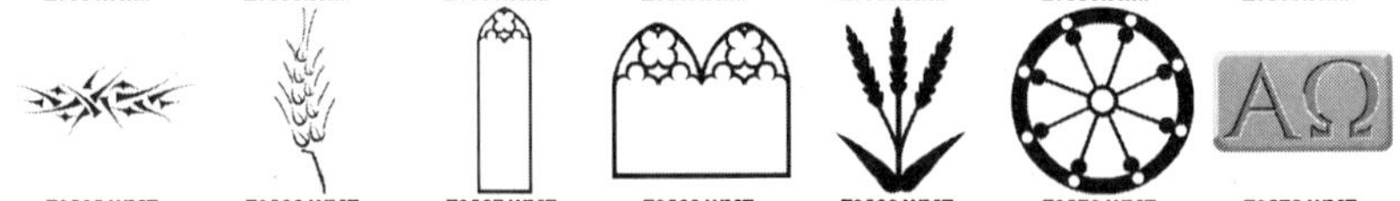

Z0565.WMF Z0566.WMF Z0567.WMF Z0568.WMF Z0569.WMF Z0570.WMF Z0572.WMF

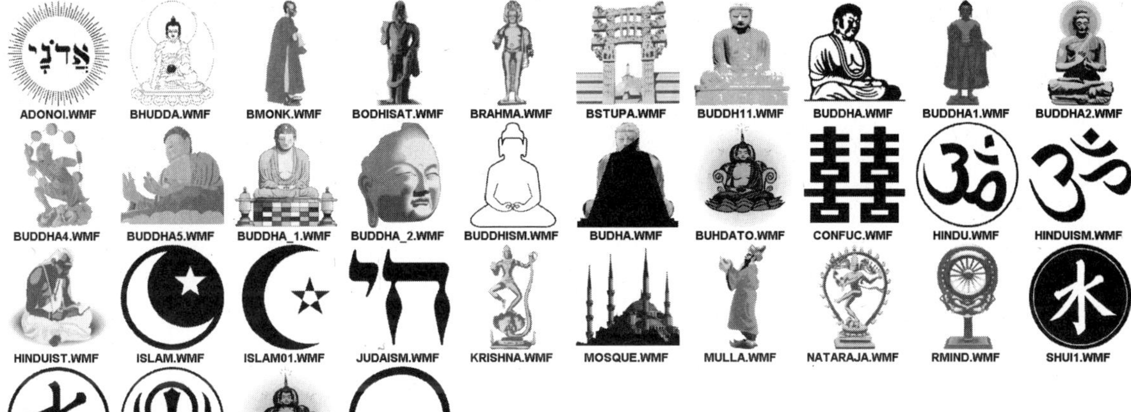

ADONOI.WMF BHUDDA.WMF BMONK.WMF BODHISAT.WMF BRAHMA.WMF BSTUPA.WMF BUDDH11.WMF BUDDHA.WMF BUDDHA1.WMF BUDDHA2.WMF

BUDDHA4.WMF BUDDHA5.WMF BUDDHA_1.WMF BUDDHA_2.WMF BUDDHISM.WMF BUDHA.WMF BUHDATO.WMF CONFUC.WMF HINDU.WMF HINDUISM.WMF

HINDUIST.WMF ISLAM.WMF ISLAM01.WMF JUDAISM.WMF KRISHNA.WMF MOSQUE.WMF MULLA.WMF NATARAJA.WMF RMIND.WMF SHUI1.WMF

SHUI2.WMF SIKH.WMF SOSI005D.WMF ZEN.WMF

Religion • People

1425.WMF 1426.WMF 1427.WMF 1428.WMF HOLYWRIT.WMF LUTHER.WMF MONKWR.WMF MOTHERT.WMF MUDRACD.WMF MUDRAGD.WMF

MUDRALSC.WMF MUDRASHM.WMF MUDRASV.WMF OXM029H.WMF PD009CCU.WMF PD009DCU.WMF PD009ECU.WMF PEOPLE1.WMF PEOPLE1C.WMF PEOPLE2.WMF

PEOPLE2C.WMF PEOPLE3.WMF PEOPLE3C.WMF PEOPLE4.WMF PEOPLE4C.WMF PEOPLE5.WMF PEOPLE5C.WMF PEOPLE6.WMF PEOPLE6C.WMF PEOPLE7.WMF

PEOPLE7C.WMF PGX027E.WMF POPE.WMF PRAYER51.WMF PRAYHND.WMF PRAYHND1.WMF PRIEST.WMF PRIEST01.WMF RLGN047.WMF RLGN120.WMF

RLGN121.WMF RLGN128.WMF RLGN151.WMF RLGN154.WMF RLGN155.WMF RLGN156.WMF RLGN166.WMF RLGN167.WMF RLGN184.WMF WATCHING.WMF

0838.WMF
10DISCIP.WMF
12TRIBE.WMF
4POINTED.WMF
ABRAHA.WMF
ALISEE.WMF
ALLSEE.WMF
ANCHR.WMF
ASCENS.WMF
BIT0762.WMF
BIT0763.WMF
BIT0764.WMF
BIT0774.WMF
BIT0776.WMF
BIT0777.WMF
BIT0778.WMF
BIT0779.WMF
BIT0780.WMF
CHAPEL.WMF
CHIRHO1.WMF
CHIRHO2.WMF
CHIRHO3.WMF
CROSPORT.WMF
CRUCIF.WMF
CRUX.WMF
DANIEL.WMF
DAVID.WMF
DIIS.WMF
EPIPH.WMF
EPISCOP.WMF
EUCHAR.WMF
EXPEL.WMF
FAITH.WMF
FISH.WMF
FISH01.WMF
FISH1.WMF
FISH2.WMF
FOUNT.WMF
GAMMAD.WMF
GRACE.WMF
HANDOF.WMF
HANDS.WMF
HOLYSPRT.WMF
HOPE.WMF
IMMCON.WMF
KING.WMF
KIRPAN.WMF
L21208.WMF
LAMB.WMF
MANDALA.WMF
MONO.WMF
MOON.WMF
PALMSU.WMF
PD128SCU.WMF
PD128UCU.WMF
PEACE.WMF
PEACE2.WMF
PENTEC.WMF
PHOENI.WMF
RLGN004.WMF
RLGN005.WMF
RLGN006.WMF
RLGN037.WMF
RLGN046.WMF
RLGN065.WMF
RLGN066.WMF
RLGN067.WMF
RLGN068.WMF
RLGN084.WMF
RLGN086.WMF
RLGN087.WMF
RLGN088.WMF
RLGN106.WMF
RLGN150.WMF
RLGN161.WMF
RLGN162.WMF
RLGN171.WMF
RLGN172.WMF
RLGN182.WMF
RLGN183.WMF
RLGN209.WMF
ROSE.WMF
SACREDFI.WMF
SAMARI.WMF
SATAN.WMF
SHINTO.WMF
SIN.WMF
SJAMES.WMF
SOULS.WMF
SOVERE.WMF
STARBETH.WMF
STARD.WMF
STARREG.WMF
STJOHN.WMF
STJUDE.WMF
STMARY.WMF
STPETE.WMF
SWORD.WMF
TEMPT.WMF
TRIFOIL.WMF
TRIFTRI.WMF
TRINTY.WMF
TRIQUER1.WMF
TRIQUER2.WMF
VATICAN.WMF
VESICA.WMF
VIRGIN.WMF
X_FISH.WMF
YINYANG.WMF
YINYANG1.WMF

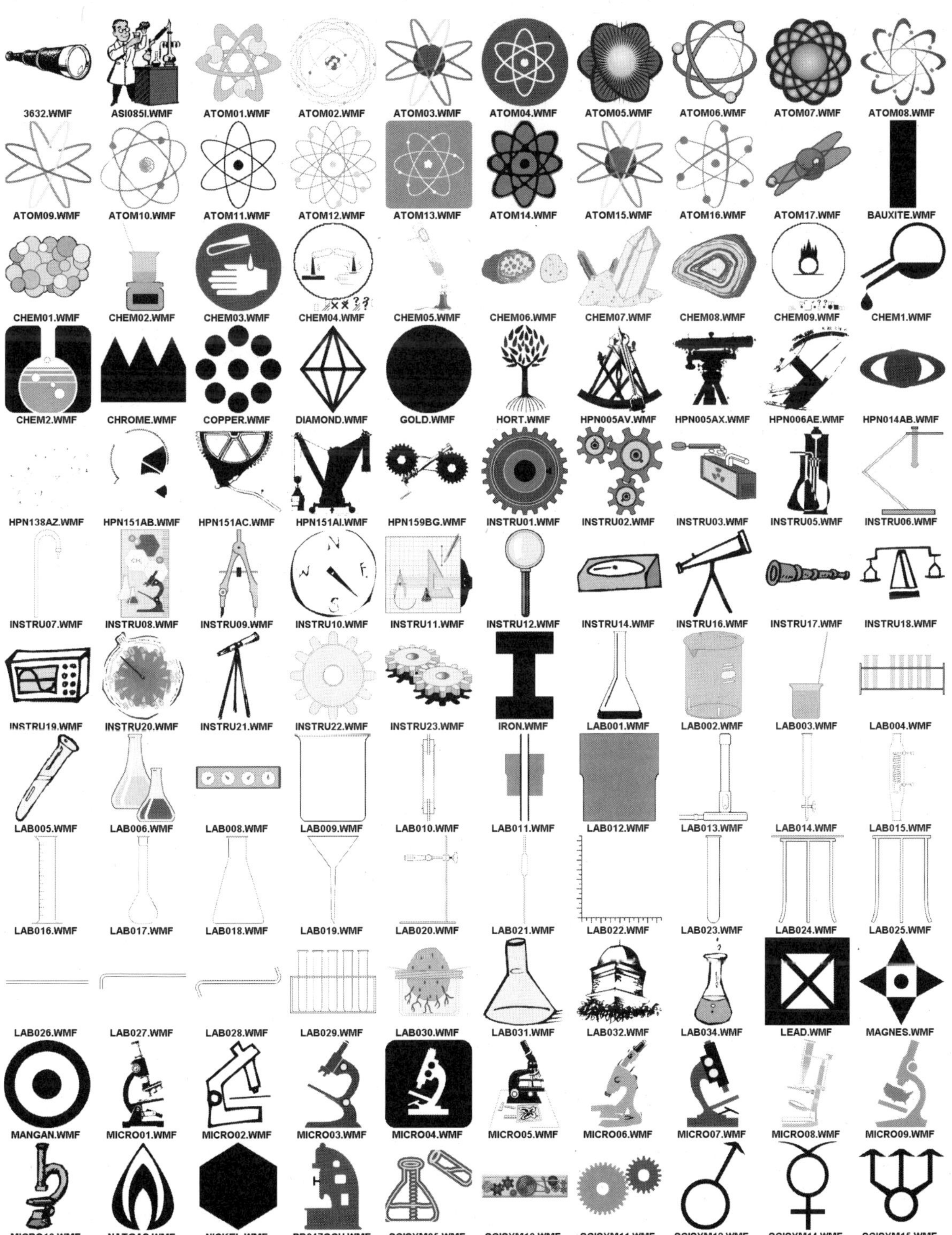
3632.WMF
ASI085I.WMF
ATOM01.WMF
ATOM02.WMF
ATOM03.WMF
ATOM04.WMF
ATOM05.WMF
ATOM06.WMF
ATOM07.WMF
ATOM08.WMF
ATOM09.WMF
ATOM10.WMF
ATOM11.WMF
ATOM12.WMF
ATOM13.WMF
ATOM14.WMF
ATOM15.WMF
ATOM16.WMF
ATOM17.WMF
BAUXITE.WMF
CHEM01.WMF
CHEM02.WMF
CHEM03.WMF
CHEM04.WMF
CHEM05.WMF
CHEM06.WMF
CHEM07.WMF
CHEM08.WMF
CHEM09.WMF
CHEM1.WMF
CHEM2.WMF
CHROME.WMF
COPPER.WMF
DIAMOND.WMF
GOLD.WMF
HORT.WMF
HPN005AV.WMF
HPN005AX.WMF
HPN006AE.WMF
HPN014AB.WMF
HPN138AZ.WMF
HPN151AB.WMF
HPN151AC.WMF
HPN151AI.WMF
HPN159BG.WMF
INSTRU01.WMF
INSTRU02.WMF
INSTRU03.WMF
INSTRU05.WMF
INSTRU06.WMF
INSTRU07.WMF
INSTRU08.WMF
INSTRU09.WMF
INSTRU10.WMF
INSTRU11.WMF
INSTRU12.WMF
INSTRU14.WMF
INSTRU16.WMF
INSTRU17.WMF
INSTRU18.WMF
INSTRU19.WMF
INSTRU20.WMF
INSTRU21.WMF
INSTRU22.WMF
INSTRU23.WMF
IRON.WMF
LAB001.WMF
LAB002.WMF
LAB003.WMF
LAB004.WMF
LAB005.WMF
LAB006.WMF
LAB008.WMF
LAB009.WMF
LAB010.WMF
LAB011.WMF
LAB012.WMF
LAB013.WMF
LAB014.WMF
LAB015.WMF
LAB016.WMF
LAB017.WMF
LAB018.WMF
LAB019.WMF
LAB020.WMF
LAB021.WMF
LAB022.WMF
LAB023.WMF
LAB024.WMF
LAB025.WMF
LAB026.WMF
LAB027.WMF
LAB028.WMF
LAB029.WMF
LAB030.WMF
LAB031.WMF
LAB032.WMF
LAB034.WMF
LEAD.WMF
MAGNES.WMF
MANGAN.WMF
MICRO01.WMF
MICRO02.WMF
MICRO03.WMF
MICRO04.WMF
MICRO05.WMF
MICRO06.WMF
MICRO07.WMF
MICRO08.WMF
MICRO09.WMF
MICRO10.WMF
NATGAS.WMF
NICKEL.WMF
PD047QCU.WMF
SCISYM05.WMF
SCISYM10.WMF
SCISYM11.WMF
SCISYM13.WMF
SCISYM14.WMF
SCISYM15.WMF

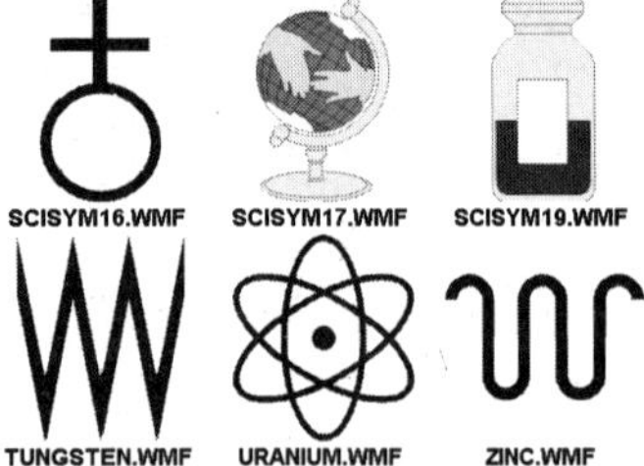

SCISYM16.WMF SCISYM17.WMF SCISYM19.WMF SCISYM25.WMF

SCISYM26.WMF SCISYM31.WMF

SILVER.WMF

SPA012C.WMF

SULFUR.WMF

TIN.WMF

TUNGSTEN.WMF URANIUM.WMF ZINC.WMF

0491.WMF 0492.WMF 066.WMF 147_6507.WMF ALIEN.WMF ALIEN1.WMF ALIEN2.WMF ALIENEGG.WMF ALIENLRD.WMF ALINFACE.WMF

ALNSPRNT.WMF APEPRSNT.WMF BLNKSIGN.WMF BODYPOD.WMF BURNGRND.WMF CARTOON.WMF CONTRLMA.WMF CONTROLS.WMF CRTN167.WMF CTMISC85.WMF

CTMISC86.WMF DANCING.WMF DINOSOLD.WMF ENGC024D.WMF ENSI031D.WMF ENSI041D.WMF ENSI058D.WMF ENSI060D.WMF ENSI061D.WMF ENSI063D.WMF

ENSI064D.WMF ENSI065D.WMF ENSI066D.WMF ENSI067D.WMF ENSI068D.WMF EXPLORER.WMF FEMSOLD.WMF FLY1.WMF FLY2.WMF GIANTWRM.WMF

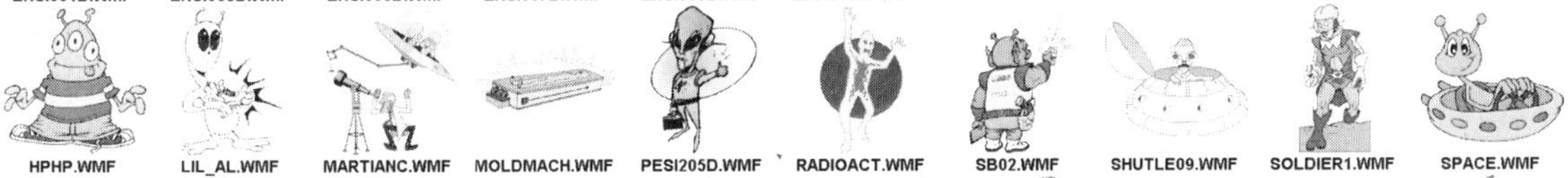

HPHP.WMF LIL_AL.WMF MARTIANC.WMF MOLDMACH.WMF PESI205D.WMF RADIOACT.WMF SB02.WMF SHUTLE09.WMF SOLDIER1.WMF SPACE.WMF

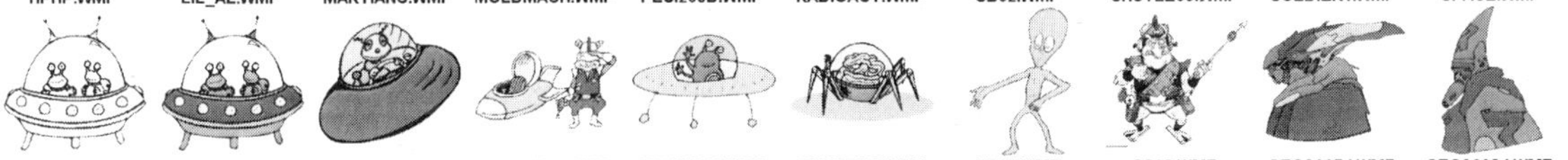

SPCSHP01.WMF SPCSHP02.WMF SPCSHP04.WMF SPCSHP06.WMF SPCSHP15.WMF SPIDERBO.WMF SS01.WMF SS02.WMF STCA007J.WMF STCA008J.WMF

STCA009J.WMF T21843.WMF TELESCOP.WMF TRANSPOR.WMF TRANSPRT.WMF UFO.WMF XRAY.WMF

Science Fiction (SCIFI) • Miscellaneous (MISC)

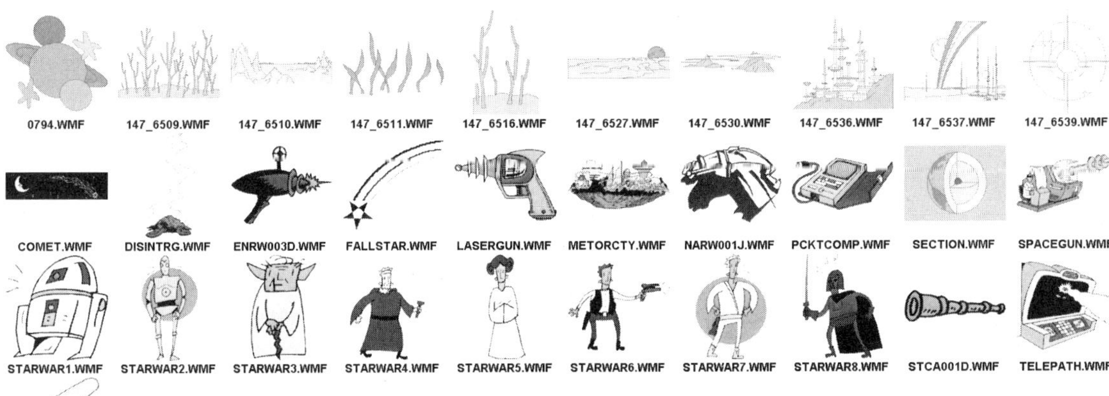

0794.WMF 147_6509.WMF 147_6510.WMF 147_6511.WMF 147_6516.WMF 147_6527.WMF 147_6530.WMF 147_6536.WMF 147_6537.WMF 147_6539.WMF

COMET.WMF DISINTRG.WMF ENRW003D.WMF FALLSTAR.WMF LASERGUN.WMF METORCTY.WMF NARW001J.WMF PCKTCOMP.WMF SECTION.WMF SPACEGUN.WMF

STARWAR1.WMF STARWAR2.WMF STARWAR3.WMF STARWAR4.WMF STARWAR5.WMF STARWAR6.WMF STARWAR7.WMF STARWAR8.WMF STCA001D.WMF TELEPATH.WMF

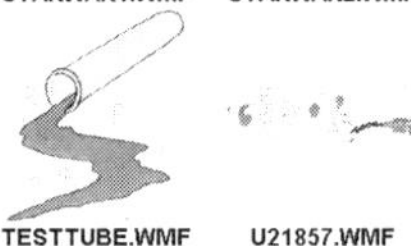

TESTTUBE.WMF U21857.WMF

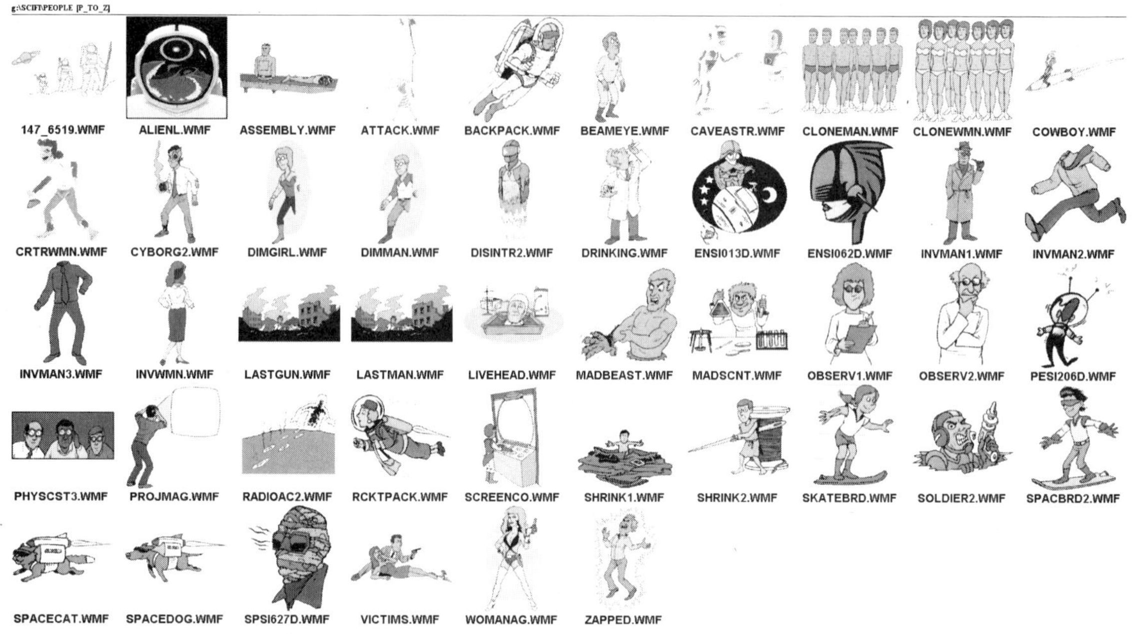

Science Fiction (SCIFI) • Robots

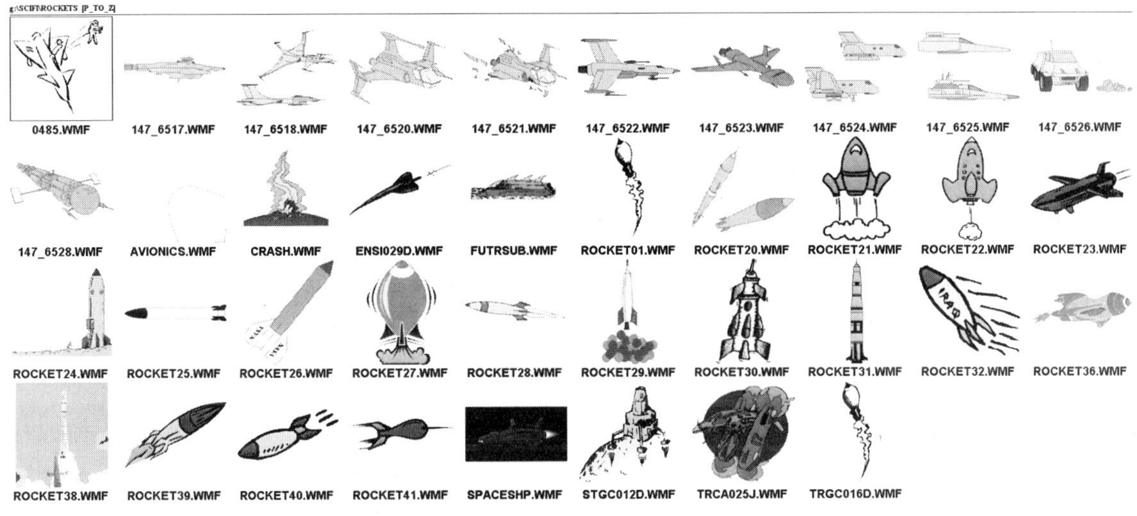

Science Fiction (SCIFI) • Saucers

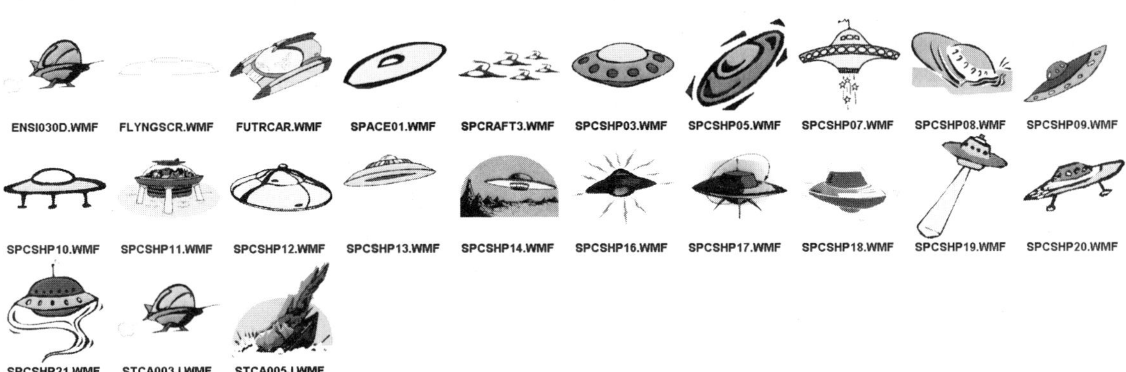

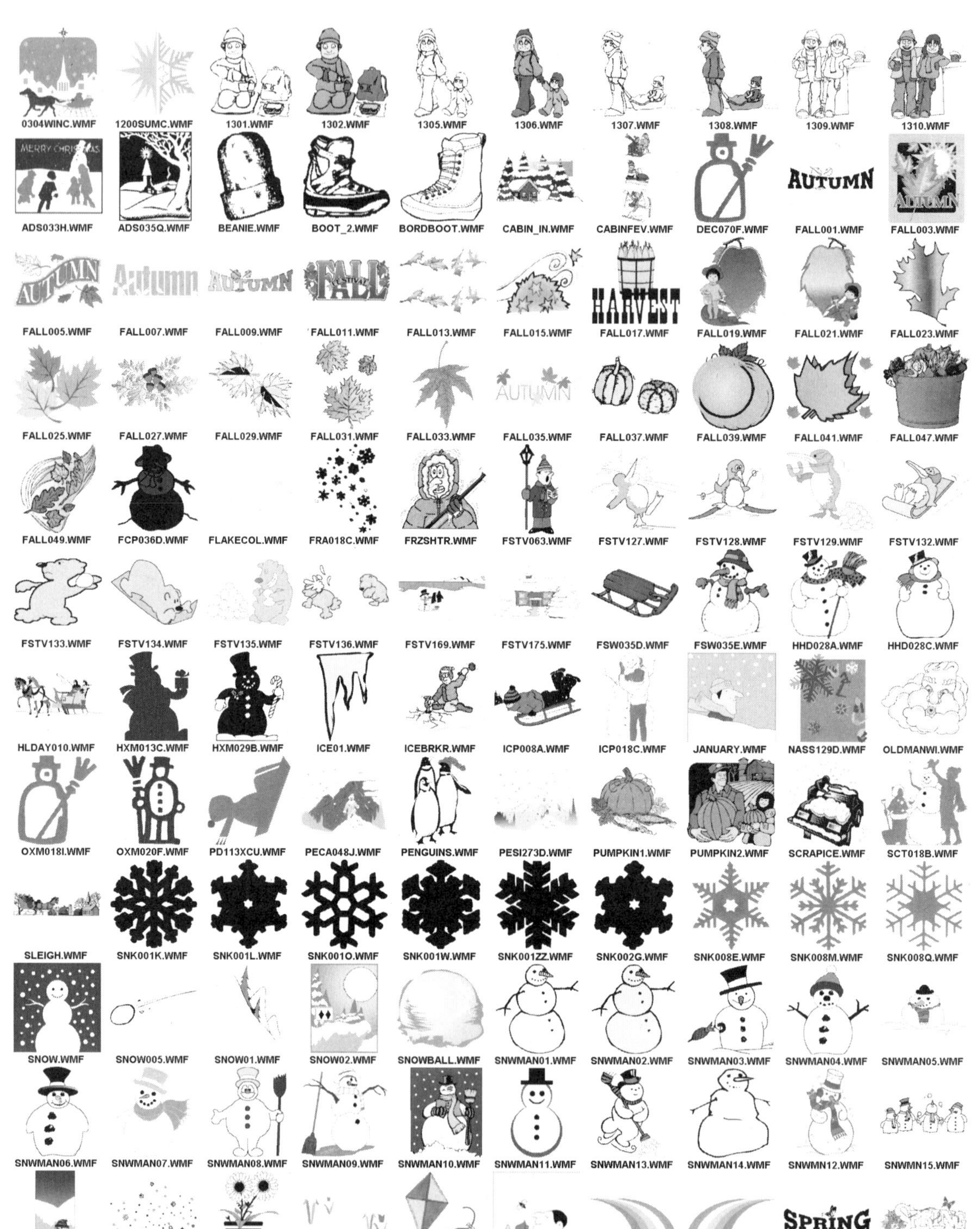
0304WINC.WMF 1200SUMC.WMF 1301.WMF 1302.WMF 1305.WMF 1306.WMF 1307.WMF 1308.WMF 1309.WMF 1310.WMF
ADS033H.WMF ADS035Q.WMF BEANIE.WMF BOOT_2.WMF BORDBOOT.WMF CABIN_IN.WMF CABINFEV.WMF DEC070F.WMF FALL001.WMF FALL003.WMF
FALL005.WMF FALL007.WMF FALL009.WMF FALL011.WMF FALL013.WMF FALL015.WMF FALL017.WMF FALL019.WMF FALL021.WMF FALL023.WMF
FALL025.WMF FALL027.WMF FALL029.WMF FALL031.WMF FALL033.WMF FALL035.WMF FALL037.WMF FALL039.WMF FALL041.WMF FALL047.WMF
FALL049.WMF FCP036D.WMF FLAKECOL.WMF FRA018C.WMF FRZSHTR.WMF FSTV063.WMF FSTV127.WMF FSTV128.WMF FSTV129.WMF FSTV132.WMF
FSTV133.WMF FSTV134.WMF FSTV135.WMF FSTV136.WMF FSTV169.WMF FSTV175.WMF FSW035D.WMF FSW035E.WMF HHD028A.WMF HHD028C.WMF
HLDAY010.WMF HXM013C.WMF HXM029B.WMF ICE01.WMF ICEBRKR.WMF ICP008A.WMF ICP018C.WMF JANUARY.WMF NASS129D.WMF OLDMANWI.WMF
OXM018I.WMF OXM020F.WMF PD113XCU.WMF PECA048J.WMF PENGUINS.WMF PESI273D.WMF PUMPKIN1.WMF PUMPKIN2.WMF SCRAPICE.WMF SCT018B.WMF
SLEIGH.WMF SNK001K.WMF SNK001L.WMF SNK001O.WMF SNK001W.WMF SNK001ZZ.WMF SNK002G.WMF SNK008E.WMF SNK008M.WMF SNK008Q.WMF
SNOW.WMF SNOW005.WMF SNOW01.WMF SNOW02.WMF SNOWBALL.WMF SNWMAN01.WMF SNWMAN02.WMF SNWMAN03.WMF SNWMAN04.WMF SNWMAN05.WMF
SNWMAN06.WMF SNWMAN07.WMF SNWMAN08.WMF SNWMAN09.WMF SNWMAN10.WMF SNWMAN11.WMF SNWMAN13.WMF SNWMAN14.WMF SNWMN12.WMF SNWMN15.WMF
SNWMN16.WMF SPA018B.WMF SPRING01.WMF SPRING04.WMF SPRING07.WMF SPRING10.WMF SPRING13.WMF SPRING16.WMF SPRING19.WMF SPRING22.WMF

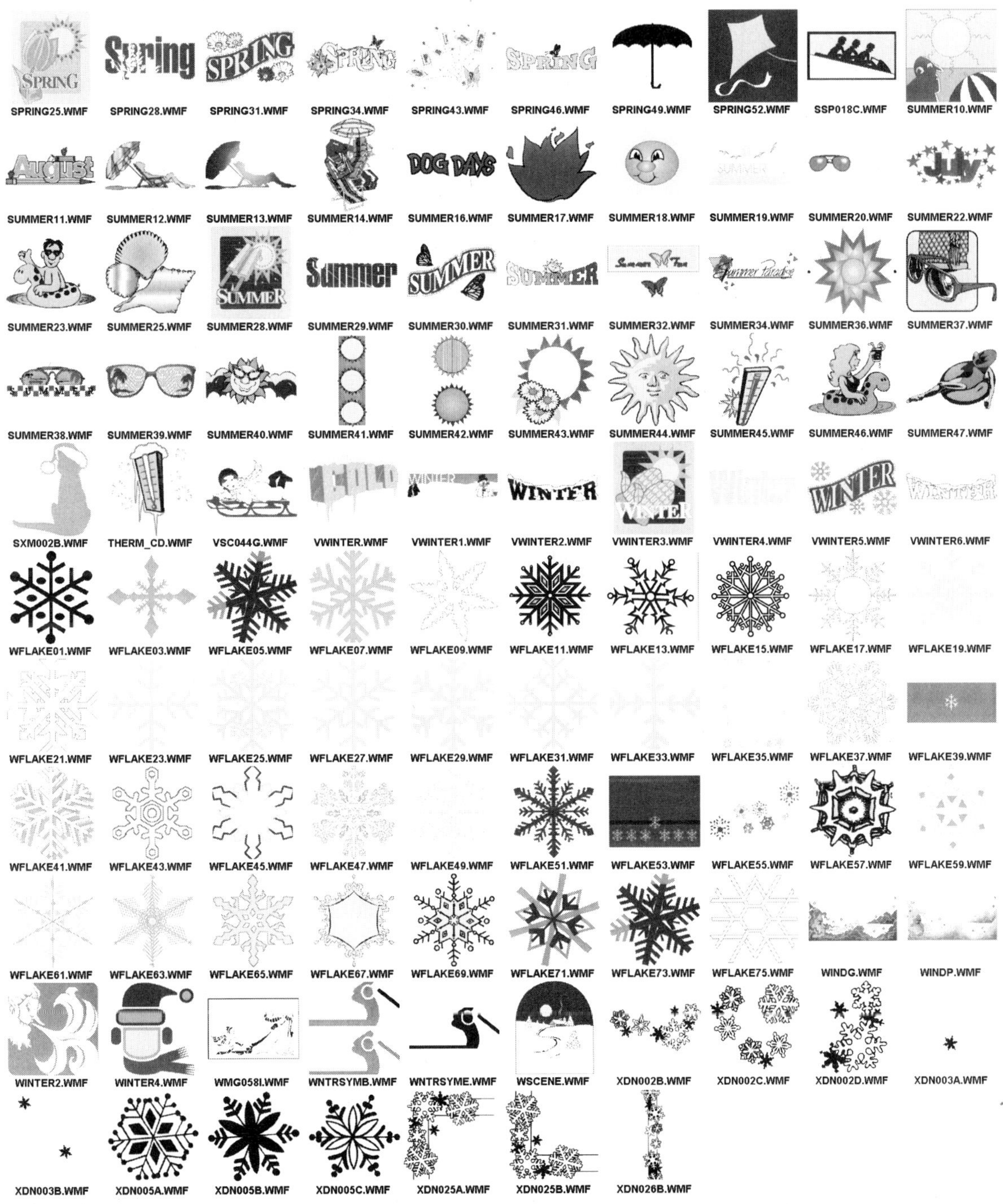
SPRING25.WMF SPRING28.WMF SPRING31.WMF SPRING34.WMF SPRING43.WMF SPRING46.WMF SPRING49.WMF SPRING52.WMF SSP018C.WMF SUMMER10.WMF
SUMMER11.WMF SUMMER12.WMF SUMMER13.WMF SUMMER14.WMF SUMMER16.WMF SUMMER17.WMF SUMMER18.WMF SUMMER19.WMF SUMMER20.WMF SUMMER22.WMF
SUMMER23.WMF SUMMER25.WMF SUMMER28.WMF SUMMER29.WMF SUMMER30.WMF SUMMER31.WMF SUMMER32.WMF SUMMER34.WMF SUMMER36.WMF SUMMER37.WMF
SUMMER38.WMF SUMMER39.WMF SUMMER40.WMF SUMMER41.WMF SUMMER42.WMF SUMMER43.WMF SUMMER44.WMF SUMMER45.WMF SUMMER46.WMF SUMMER47.WMF
SXM002B.WMF THERM_CD.WMF VSC044G.WMF VWINTER.WMF VWINTER1.WMF VWINTER2.WMF VWINTER3.WMF VWINTER4.WMF VWINTER5.WMF VWINTER6.WMF
WFLAKE01.WMF WFLAKE03.WMF WFLAKE05.WMF WFLAKE07.WMF WFLAKE09.WMF WFLAKE11.WMF WFLAKE13.WMF WFLAKE15.WMF WFLAKE17.WMF WFLAKE19.WMF
WFLAKE21.WMF WFLAKE23.WMF WFLAKE25.WMF WFLAKE27.WMF WFLAKE29.WMF WFLAKE31.WMF WFLAKE33.WMF WFLAKE35.WMF WFLAKE37.WMF WFLAKE39.WMF
WFLAKE41.WMF WFLAKE43.WMF WFLAKE45.WMF WFLAKE47.WMF WFLAKE49.WMF WFLAKE51.WMF WFLAKE53.WMF WFLAKE55.WMF WFLAKE57.WMF WFLAKE59.WMF
WFLAKE61.WMF WFLAKE63.WMF WFLAKE65.WMF WFLAKE67.WMF WFLAKE69.WMF WFLAKE71.WMF WFLAKE73.WMF WFLAKE75.WMF WINDG.WMF WINDP.WMF
WINTER2.WMF WINTER4.WMF WMG058I.WMF WNTRSYMB.WMF WNTRSYME.WMF WSCENE.WMF XDN002B.WMF XDN002C.WMF XDN002D.WMF XDN003A.WMF
XDN003B.WMF XDN005A.WMF XDN005B.WMF XDN005C.WMF XDN025A.WMF XDN025B.WMF XDN026B.WMF

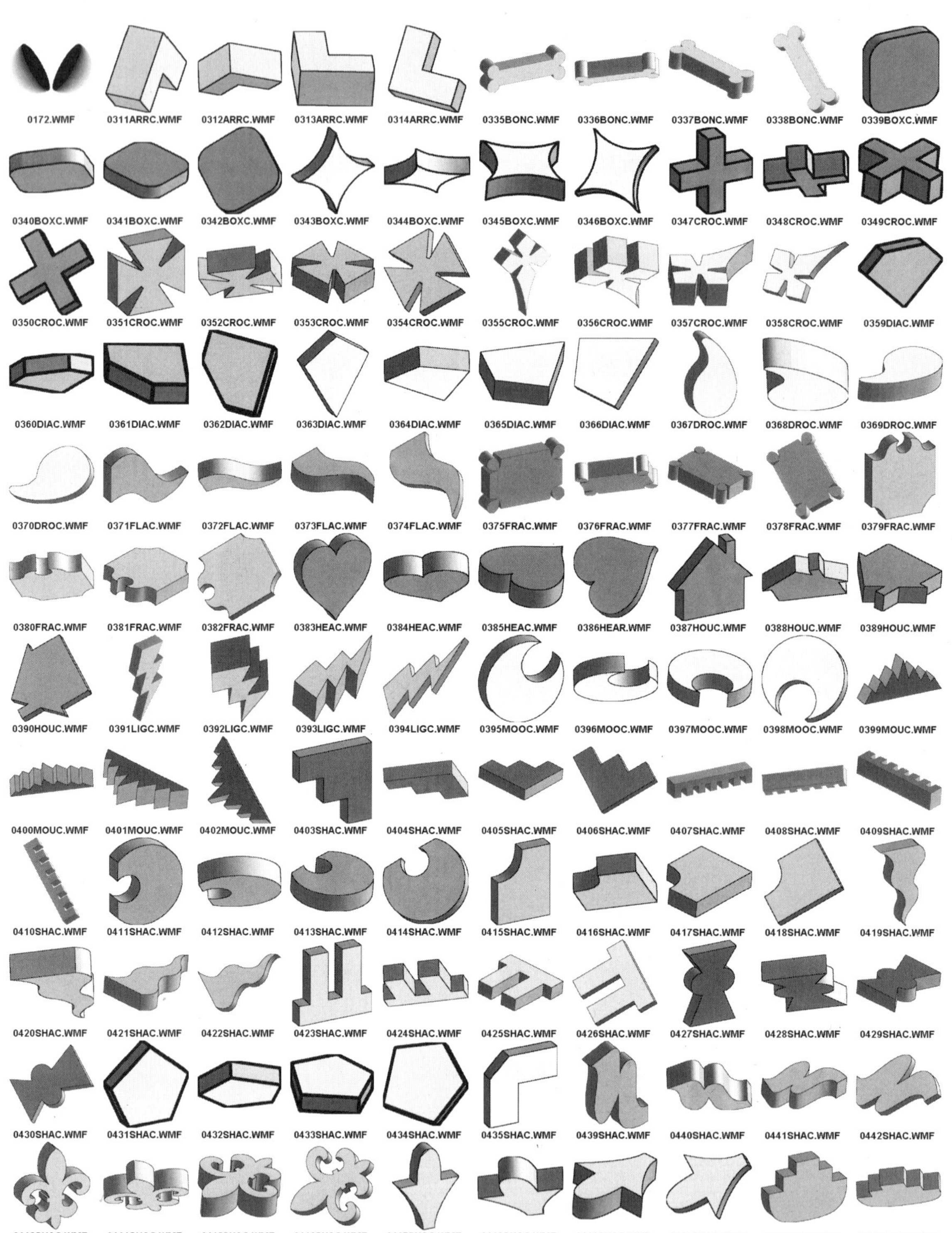
0172.WMF 0311ARRC.WMF 0312ARRC.WMF 0313ARRC.WMF 0314ARRC.WMF 0335BONC.WMF 0336BONC.WMF 0337BONC.WMF 0338BONC.WMF 0339BOXC.WMF
0340BOXC.WMF 0341BOXC.WMF 0342BOXC.WMF 0343BOXC.WMF 0344BOXC.WMF 0345BOXC.WMF 0346BOXC.WMF 0347CROC.WMF 0348CROC.WMF 0349CROC.WMF
0350CROC.WMF 0351CROC.WMF 0352CROC.WMF 0353CROC.WMF 0354CROC.WMF 0355CROC.WMF 0356CROC.WMF 0357CROC.WMF 0358CROC.WMF 0359DIAC.WMF
0360DIAC.WMF 0361DIAC.WMF 0362DIAC.WMF 0363DIAC.WMF 0364DIAC.WMF 0365DIAC.WMF 0366DIAC.WMF 0367DROC.WMF 0368DROC.WMF 0369DROC.WMF
0370DROC.WMF 0371FLAC.WMF 0372FLAC.WMF 0373FLAC.WMF 0374FLAC.WMF 0375FRAC.WMF 0376FRAC.WMF 0377FRAC.WMF 0378FRAC.WMF 0379FRAC.WMF
0380FRAC.WMF 0381FRAC.WMF 0382FRAC.WMF 0383HEAC.WMF 0384HEAC.WMF 0385HEAC.WMF 0386HEAR.WMF 0387HOUC.WMF 0388HOUC.WMF 0389HOUC.WMF
0390HOUC.WMF 0391LIGC.WMF 0392LIGC.WMF 0393LIGC.WMF 0394LIGC.WMF 0395MOOC.WMF 0396MOOC.WMF 0397MOOC.WMF 0398MOOC.WMF 0399MOUC.WMF
0400MOUC.WMF 0401MOUC.WMF 0402MOUC.WMF 0403SHAC.WMF 0404SHAC.WMF 0405SHAC.WMF 0406SHAC.WMF 0407SHAC.WMF 0408SHAC.WMF 0409SHAC.WMF
0410SHAC.WMF 0411SHAC.WMF 0412SHAC.WMF 0413SHAC.WMF 0414SHAC.WMF 0415SHAC.WMF 0416SHAC.WMF 0417SHAC.WMF 0418SHAC.WMF 0419SHAC.WMF
0420SHAC.WMF 0421SHAC.WMF 0422SHAC.WMF 0423SHAC.WMF 0424SHAC.WMF 0425SHAC.WMF 0426SHAC.WMF 0427SHAC.WMF 0428SHAC.WMF 0429SHAC.WMF
0430SHAC.WMF 0431SHAC.WMF 0432SHAC.WMF 0433SHAC.WMF 0434SHAC.WMF 0435SHAC.WMF 0439SHAC.WMF 0440SHAC.WMF 0441SHAC.WMF 0442SHAC.WMF
0443SHAC.WMF 0444SHAC.WMF 0445SHAC.WMF 0446SHAC.WMF 0447SHAC.WMF 0448SHAC.WMF 0449SHAC.WMF 0450SHAC.WMF 0451SHAC.WMF 0452SHAC.WMF

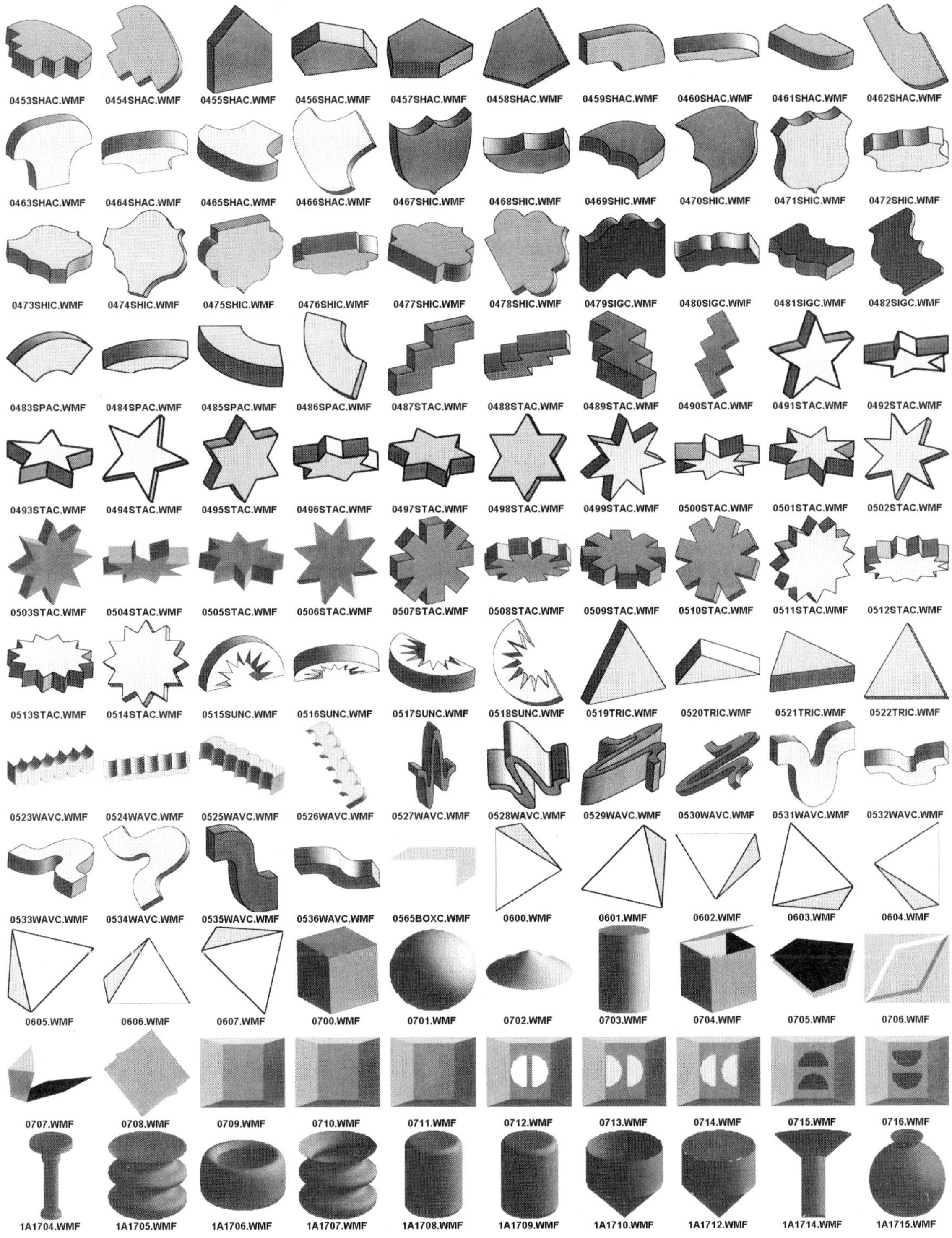
0453SHAC.WMF
0454SHAC.WMF
0455SHAC.WMF
0456SHAC.WMF
0457SHAC.WMF
0458SHAC.WMF
0459SHAC.WMF
0460SHAC.WMF
0461SHAC.WMF
0462SHAC.WMF
0463SHAC.WMF
0464SHAC.WMF
0465SHAC.WMF
0466SHAC.WMF
0467SHIC.WMF
0468SHIC.WMF
0469SHIC.WMF
0470SHIC.WMF
0471SHIC.WMF
0472SHIC.WMF
0473SHIC.WMF
0474SHIC.WMF
0475SHIC.WMF
0476SHIC.WMF
0477SHIC.WMF
0478SHIC.WMF
0479SIGC.WMF
0480SIGC.WMF
0481SIGC.WMF
0482SIGC.WMF
0483SPAC.WMF
0484SPAC.WMF
0485SPAC.WMF
0486SPAC.WMF
0487STAC.WMF
0488STAC.WMF
0489STAC.WMF
0490STAC.WMF
0491STAC.WMF
0492STAC.WMF
0493STAC.WMF
0494STAC.WMF
0495STAC.WMF
0496STAC.WMF
0497STAC.WMF
0498STAC.WMF
0499STAC.WMF
0500STAC.WMF
0501STAC.WMF
0502STAC.WMF
0503STAC.WMF
0504STAC.WMF
0505STAC.WMF
0506STAC.WMF
0507STAC.WMF
0508STAC.WMF
0509STAC.WMF
0510STAC.WMF
0511STAC.WMF
0512STAC.WMF
0513STAC.WMF
0514STAC.WMF
0515SUNC.WMF
0516SUNC.WMF
0517SUNC.WMF
0518SUNC.WMF
0519TRIC.WMF
0520TRIC.WMF
0521TRIC.WMF
0522TRIC.WMF
0523WAVC.WMF
0524WAVC.WMF
0525WAVC.WMF
0526WAVC.WMF
0527WAVC.WMF
0528WAVC.WMF
0529WAVC.WMF
0530WAVC.WMF
0531WAVC.WMF
0532WAVC.WMF
0533WAVC.WMF
0534WAVC.WMF
0535WAVC.WMF
0536WAVC.WMF
0565BOXC.WMF
0600.WMF
0601.WMF
0602.WMF
0603.WMF
0604.WMF
0605.WMF
0606.WMF
0607.WMF
0700.WMF
0701.WMF
0702.WMF
0703.WMF
0704.WMF
0705.WMF
0706.WMF
0707.WMF
0708.WMF
0709.WMF
0710.WMF
0711.WMF
0712.WMF
0713.WMF
0714.WMF
0715.WMF
0716.WMF
1A1704.WMF
1A1705.WMF
1A1706.WMF
1A1707.WMF
1A1708.WMF
1A1709.WMF
1A1710.WMF
1A1712.WMF
1A1714.WMF
1A1715.WMF

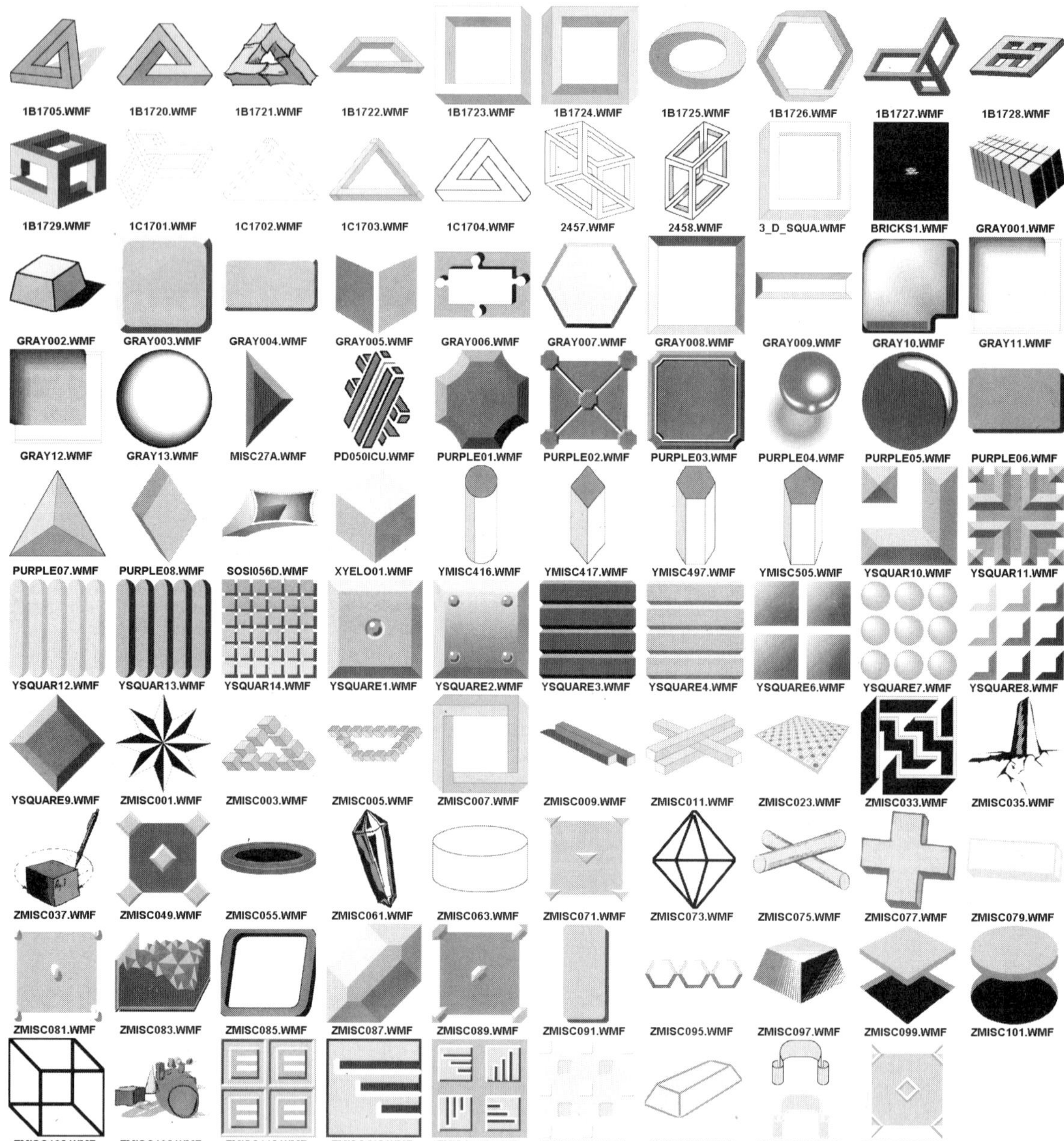
1B1705.WMF
1B1720.WMF
1B1721.WMF
1B1722.WMF
1B1723.WMF
1B1724.WMF
1B1725.WMF
1B1726.WMF
1B1727.WMF
1B1728.WMF
1B1729.WMF
1C1701.WMF
1C1702.WMF
1C1703.WMF
1C1704.WMF
2457.WMF
2458.WMF
3_D_SQUA.WMF
BRICKS1.WMF
GRAY001.WMF
GRAY002.WMF
GRAY003.WMF
GRAY004.WMF
GRAY005.WMF
GRAY006.WMF
GRAY007.WMF
GRAY008.WMF
GRAY009.WMF
GRAY10.WMF
GRAY11.WMF
GRAY12.WMF
GRAY13.WMF
MISC27A.WMF
PD050ICU.WMF
PURPLE01.WMF
PURPLE02.WMF
PURPLE03.WMF
PURPLE04.WMF
PURPLE05.WMF
PURPLE06.WMF
PURPLE07.WMF
PURPLE08.WMF
SOSI056D.WMF
XYELO01.WMF
YMISC416.WMF
YMISC417.WMF
YMISC497.WMF
YMISC505.WMF
YSQUAR10.WMF
YSQUAR11.WMF
YSQUAR12.WMF
YSQUAR13.WMF
YSQUAR14.WMF
YSQUARE1.WMF
YSQUARE2.WMF
YSQUARE3.WMF
YSQUARE4.WMF
YSQUARE6.WMF
YSQUARE7.WMF
YSQUARE8.WMF
YSQUARE9.WMF
ZMISC001.WMF
ZMISC003.WMF
ZMISC005.WMF
ZMISC007.WMF
ZMISC009.WMF
ZMISC011.WMF
ZMISC023.WMF
ZMISC033.WMF
ZMISC035.WMF
ZMISC037.WMF
ZMISC049.WMF
ZMISC055.WMF
ZMISC061.WMF
ZMISC063.WMF
ZMISC071.WMF
ZMISC073.WMF
ZMISC075.WMF
ZMISC077.WMF
ZMISC079.WMF
ZMISC081.WMF
ZMISC083.WMF
ZMISC085.WMF
ZMISC087.WMF
ZMISC089.WMF
ZMISC091.WMF
ZMISC095.WMF
ZMISC097.WMF
ZMISC099.WMF
ZMISC101.WMF
ZMISC103.WMF
ZMISC105.WMF
ZMISC113.WMF
ZMISC115.WMF
ZMISC117.WMF
ZMISC121.WMF
ZMISC125.WMF
ZMISC127.WMF
ZMISC129.WMF

1301.WMF 1302.WMF 73STAR.WMF 74STAR.WMF 78STAR.WMF ABSTRC06.WMF ABSTRC07.WMF ABSTRCT1.WMF ABSTRCT2.WMF ABSTRCT3.WMF

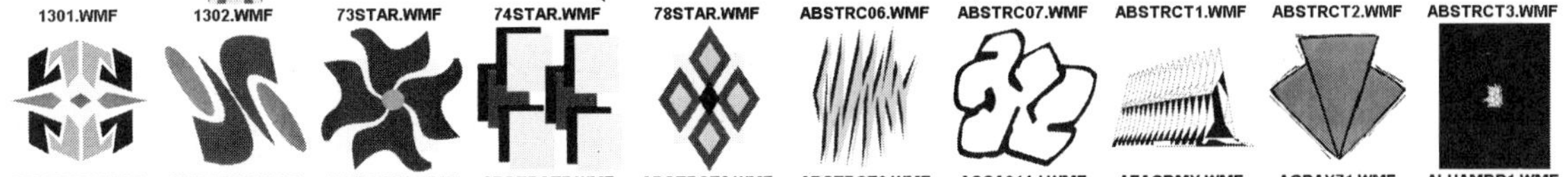

ABSTRCT4.WMF ABSTRCT5.WMF ABSTRCT6.WMF ABSTRCT7.WMF ABSTRCT8.WMF ABSTRCT9.WMF ACCA014J.WMF AFACDMY.WMF AGRAY71.WMF ALHAMBR1.WMF

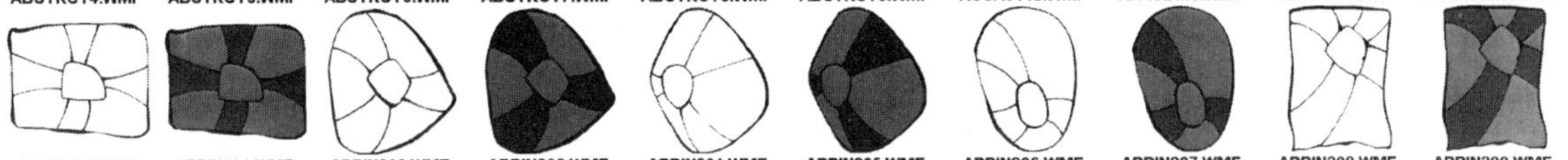

APRIN200.WMF APRIN201.WMF APRIN202.WMF APRIN203.WMF APRIN204.WMF APRIN205.WMF APRIN206.WMF APRIN207.WMF APRIN208.WMF APRIN209.WMF

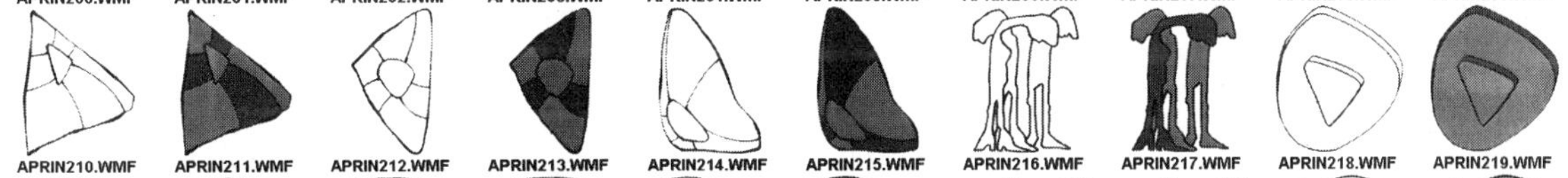

APRIN210.WMF APRIN211.WMF APRIN212.WMF APRIN213.WMF APRIN214.WMF APRIN215.WMF APRIN216.WMF APRIN217.WMF APRIN218.WMF APRIN219.WMF

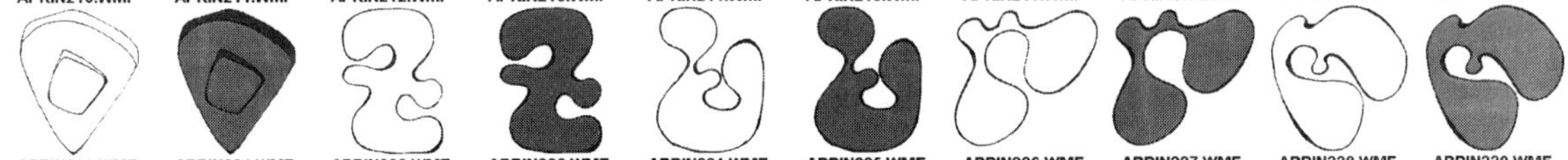

APRIN220.WMF APRIN221.WMF APRIN222.WMF APRIN223.WMF APRIN224.WMF APRIN225.WMF APRIN226.WMF APRIN227.WMF APRIN228.WMF APRIN229.WMF

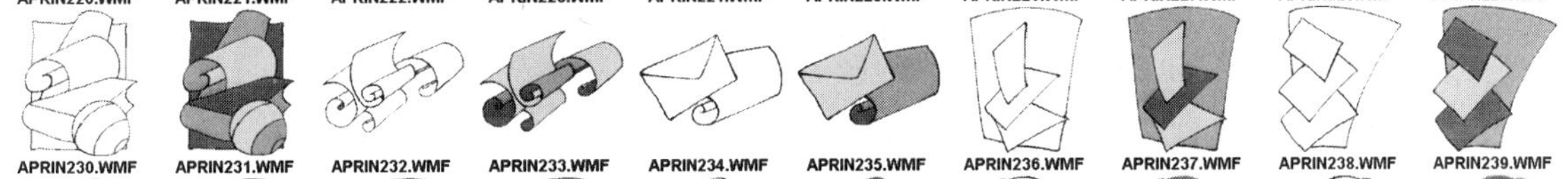

APRIN230.WMF APRIN231.WMF APRIN232.WMF APRIN233.WMF APRIN234.WMF APRIN235.WMF APRIN236.WMF APRIN237.WMF APRIN238.WMF APRIN239.WMF

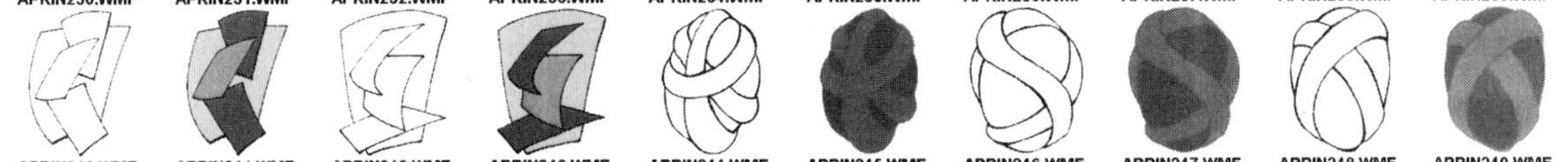

APRIN240.WMF APRIN241.WMF APRIN242.WMF APRIN243.WMF APRIN244.WMF APRIN245.WMF APRIN246.WMF APRIN247.WMF APRIN248.WMF APRIN249.WMF

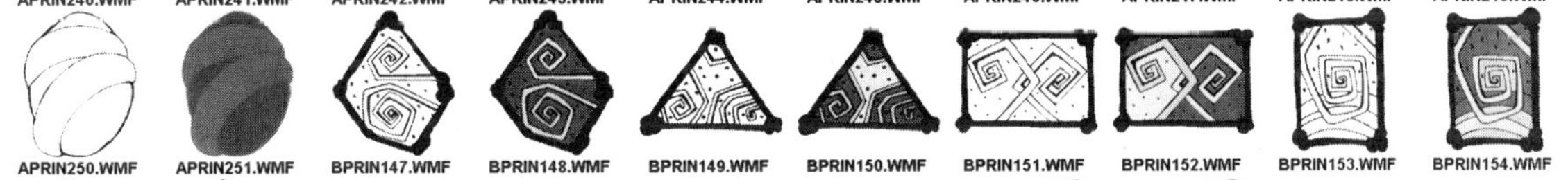

APRIN250.WMF APRIN251.WMF BPRIN147.WMF BPRIN148.WMF BPRIN149.WMF BPRIN150.WMF BPRIN151.WMF BPRIN152.WMF BPRIN153.WMF BPRIN154.WMF

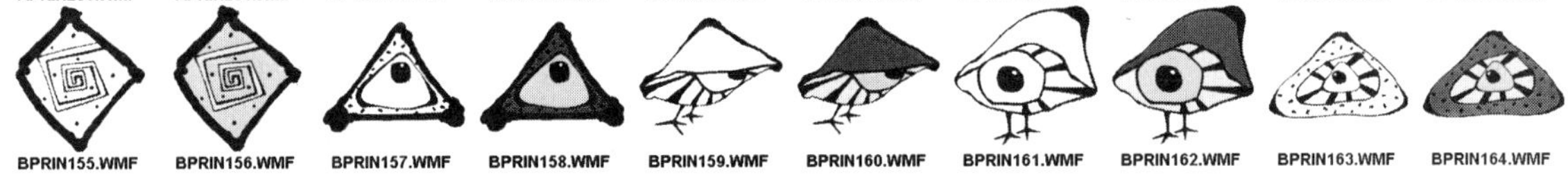

BPRIN155.WMF BPRIN156.WMF BPRIN157.WMF BPRIN158.WMF BPRIN159.WMF BPRIN160.WMF BPRIN161.WMF BPRIN162.WMF BPRIN163.WMF BPRIN164.WMF

BPRIN165.WMF BPRIN166.WMF BPRIN167.WMF BPRIN168.WMF BPRIN169.WMF BPRIN170.WMF BPRIN171.WMF BPRIN172.WMF BPRIN190.WMF BPRIN191.WMF

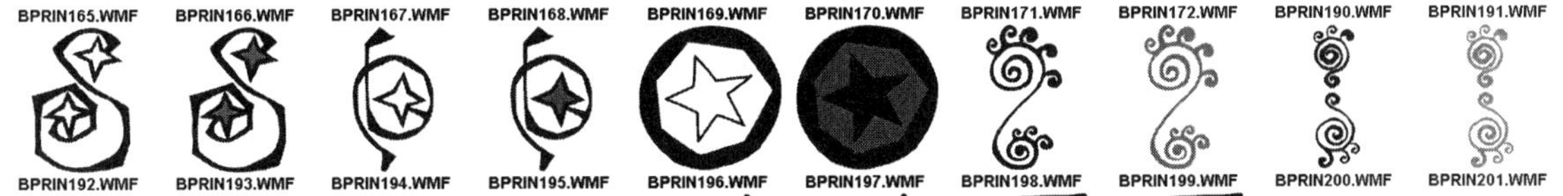

BPRIN192.WMF BPRIN193.WMF BPRIN194.WMF BPRIN195.WMF BPRIN196.WMF BPRIN197.WMF BPRIN198.WMF BPRIN199.WMF BPRIN200.WMF BPRIN201.WMF

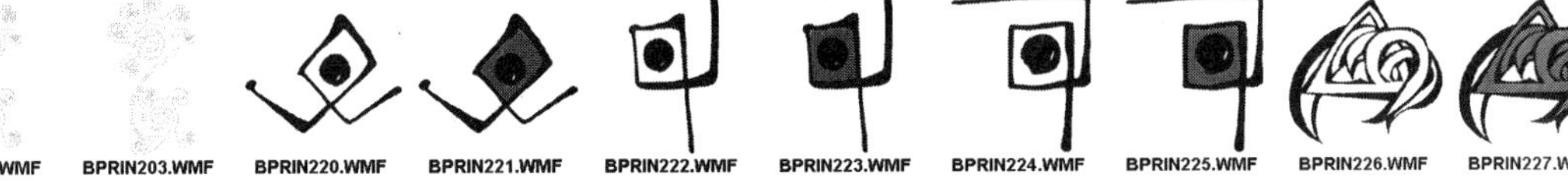

BPRIN202.WMF BPRIN203.WMF BPRIN220.WMF BPRIN221.WMF BPRIN222.WMF BPRIN223.WMF BPRIN224.WMF BPRIN225.WMF BPRIN226.WMF BPRIN227.WMF

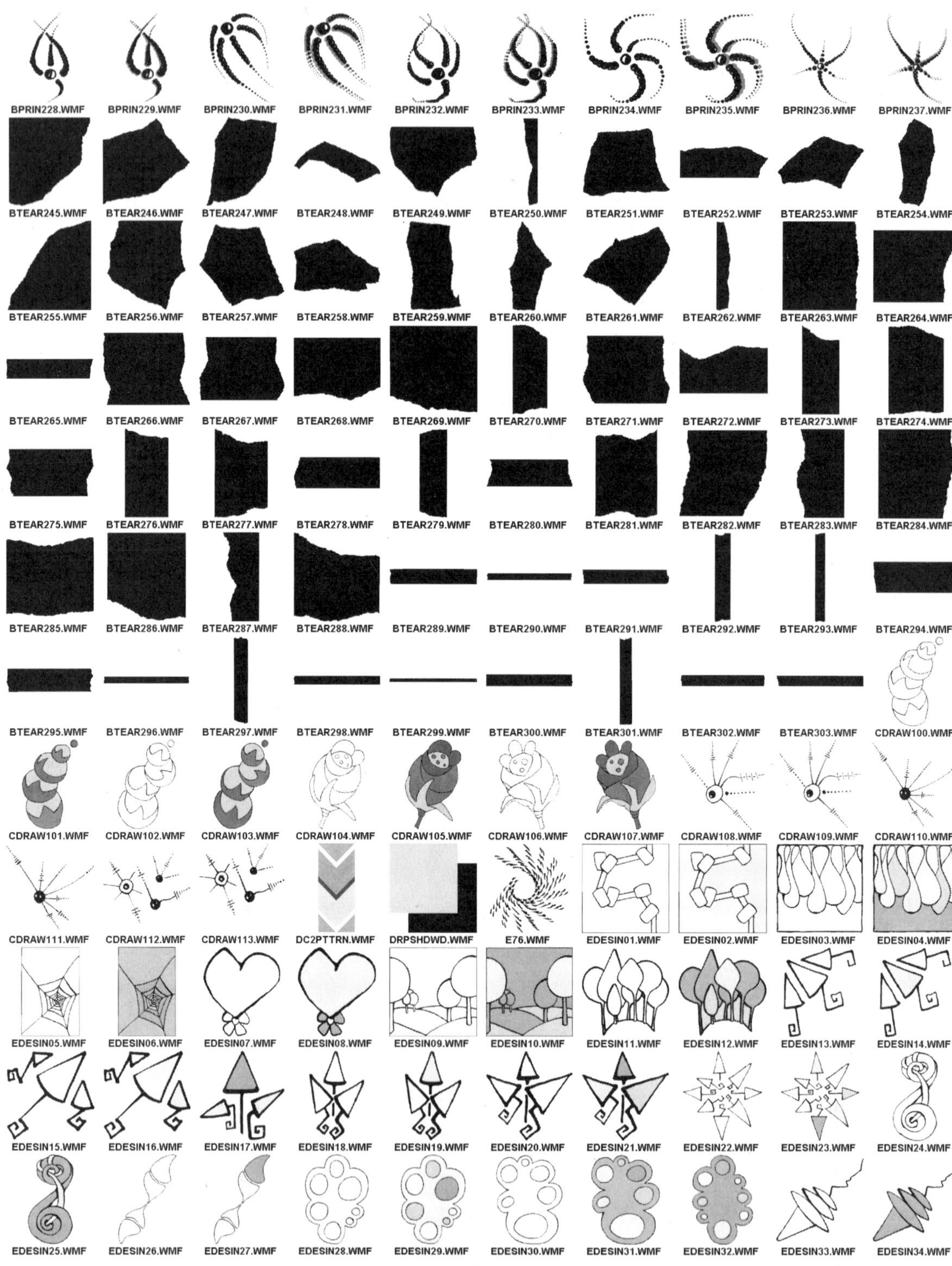
BPRIN228.WMF
BPRIN229.WMF
BPRIN230.WMF
BPRIN231.WMF
BPRIN232.WMF
BPRIN233.WMF
BPRIN234.WMF
BPRIN235.WMF
BPRIN236.WMF
BPRIN237.WMF
BTEAR245.WMF
BTEAR246.WMF
BTEAR247.WMF
BTEAR248.WMF
BTEAR249.WMF
BTEAR250.WMF
BTEAR251.WMF
BTEAR252.WMF
BTEAR253.WMF
BTEAR254.WMF
BTEAR255.WMF
BTEAR256.WMF
BTEAR257.WMF
BTEAR258.WMF
BTEAR259.WMF
BTEAR260.WMF
BTEAR261.WMF
BTEAR262.WMF
BTEAR263.WMF
BTEAR264.WMF
BTEAR265.WMF
BTEAR266.WMF
BTEAR267.WMF
BTEAR268.WMF
BTEAR269.WMF
BTEAR270.WMF
BTEAR271.WMF
BTEAR272.WMF
BTEAR273.WMF
BTEAR274.WMF
BTEAR275.WMF
BTEAR276.WMF
BTEAR277.WMF
BTEAR278.WMF
BTEAR279.WMF
BTEAR280.WMF
BTEAR281.WMF
BTEAR282.WMF
BTEAR283.WMF
BTEAR284.WMF
BTEAR285.WMF
BTEAR286.WMF
BTEAR287.WMF
BTEAR288.WMF
BTEAR289.WMF
BTEAR290.WMF
BTEAR291.WMF
BTEAR292.WMF
BTEAR293.WMF
BTEAR294.WMF
BTEAR295.WMF
BTEAR296.WMF
BTEAR297.WMF
BTEAR298.WMF
BTEAR299.WMF
BTEAR300.WMF
BTEAR301.WMF
BTEAR302.WMF
BTEAR303.WMF
CDRAW100.WMF
CDRAW101.WMF
CDRAW102.WMF
CDRAW103.WMF
CDRAW104.WMF
CDRAW105.WMF
CDRAW106.WMF
CDRAW107.WMF
CDRAW108.WMF
CDRAW109.WMF
CDRAW110.WMF
CDRAW111.WMF
CDRAW112.WMF
CDRAW113.WMF
DC2PTTRN.WMF
DRPSHDWD.WMF
E76.WMF
EDESIN01.WMF
EDESIN02.WMF
EDESIN03.WMF
EDESIN04.WMF
EDESIN05.WMF
EDESIN06.WMF
EDESIN07.WMF
EDESIN08.WMF
EDESIN09.WMF
EDESIN10.WMF
EDESIN11.WMF
EDESIN12.WMF
EDESIN13.WMF
EDESIN14.WMF
EDESIN15.WMF
EDESIN16.WMF
EDESIN17.WMF
EDESIN18.WMF
EDESIN19.WMF
EDESIN20.WMF
EDESIN21.WMF
EDESIN22.WMF
EDESIN23.WMF
EDESIN24.WMF
EDESIN25.WMF
EDESIN26.WMF
EDESIN27.WMF
EDESIN28.WMF
EDESIN29.WMF
EDESIN30.WMF
EDESIN31.WMF
EDESIN32.WMF
EDESIN33.WMF
EDESIN34.WMF

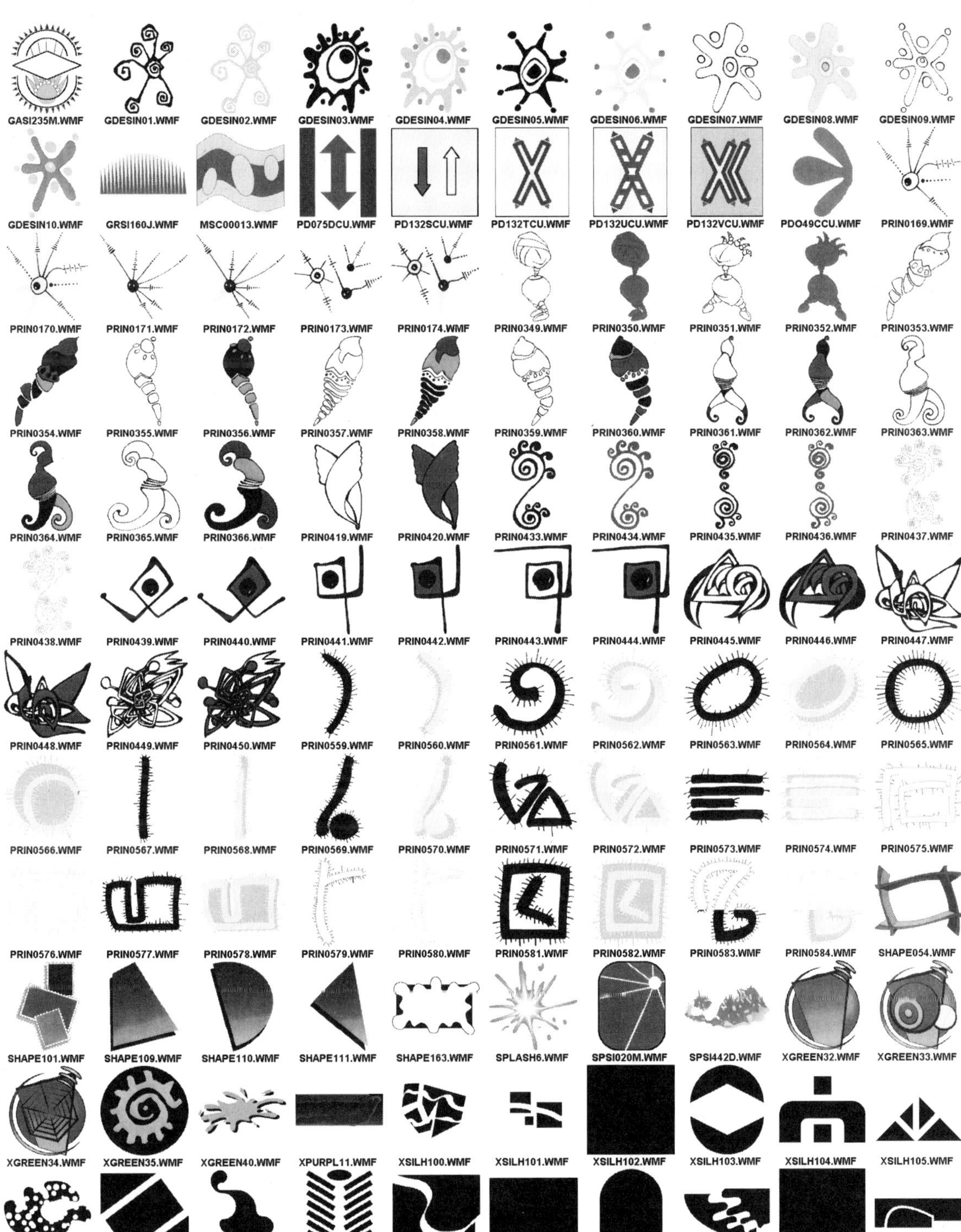
GASI235M.WMF
GDESIN01.WMF
GDESIN02.WMF
GDESIN03.WMF
GDESIN04.WMF
GDESIN05.WMF
GDESIN06.WMF
GDESIN07.WMF
GDESIN08.WMF
GDESIN09.WMF
GDESIN10.WMF
GRSI160J.WMF
MSC00013.WMF
PD075DCU.WMF
PD132SCU.WMF
PD132TCU.WMF
PD132UCU.WMF
PD132VCU.WMF
PDO49CCU.WMF
PRIN0169.WMF
PRIN0170.WMF
PRIN0171.WMF
PRIN0172.WMF
PRIN0173.WMF
PRIN0174.WMF
PRIN0349.WMF
PRIN0350.WMF
PRIN0351.WMF
PRIN0352.WMF
PRIN0353.WMF
PRIN0354.WMF
PRIN0355.WMF
PRIN0356.WMF
PRIN0357.WMF
PRIN0358.WMF
PRIN0359.WMF
PRIN0360.WMF
PRIN0361.WMF
PRIN0362.WMF
PRIN0363.WMF
PRIN0364.WMF
PRIN0365.WMF
PRIN0366.WMF
PRIN0419.WMF
PRIN0420.WMF
PRIN0433.WMF
PRIN0434.WMF
PRIN0435.WMF
PRIN0436.WMF
PRIN0437.WMF
PRIN0438.WMF
PRIN0439.WMF
PRIN0440.WMF
PRIN0441.WMF
PRIN0442.WMF
PRIN0443.WMF
PRIN0444.WMF
PRIN0445.WMF
PRIN0446.WMF
PRIN0447.WMF
PRIN0448.WMF
PRIN0449.WMF
PRIN0450.WMF
PRIN0559.WMF
PRIN0560.WMF
PRIN0561.WMF
PRIN0562.WMF
PRIN0563.WMF
PRIN0564.WMF
PRIN0565.WMF
PRIN0566.WMF
PRIN0567.WMF
PRIN0568.WMF
PRIN0569.WMF
PRIN0570.WMF
PRIN0571.WMF
PRIN0572.WMF
PRIN0573.WMF
PRIN0574.WMF
PRIN0575.WMF
PRIN0576.WMF
PRIN0577.WMF
PRIN0578.WMF
PRIN0579.WMF
PRIN0580.WMF
PRIN0581.WMF
PRIN0582.WMF
PRIN0583.WMF
PRIN0584.WMF
SHAPE054.WMF
SHAPE101.WMF
SHAPE109.WMF
SHAPE110.WMF
SHAPE111.WMF
SHAPE163.WMF
SPLASH6.WMF
SPSI020M.WMF
SPSI442D.WMF
XGREEN32.WMF
XGREEN33.WMF
XGREEN34.WMF
XGREEN35.WMF
XGREEN40.WMF
XPURPL11.WMF
XSILH100.WMF
XSILH101.WMF
XSILH102.WMF
XSILH103.WMF
XSILH104.WMF
XSILH105.WMF
XSILH106.WMF
XSILH107.WMF
XSILH108.WMF
XSILH109.WMF
XSILH110.WMF
XSILH111.WMF
XSILH112.WMF
XSILH113.WMF
XSILH114.WMF
XSILH115.WMF

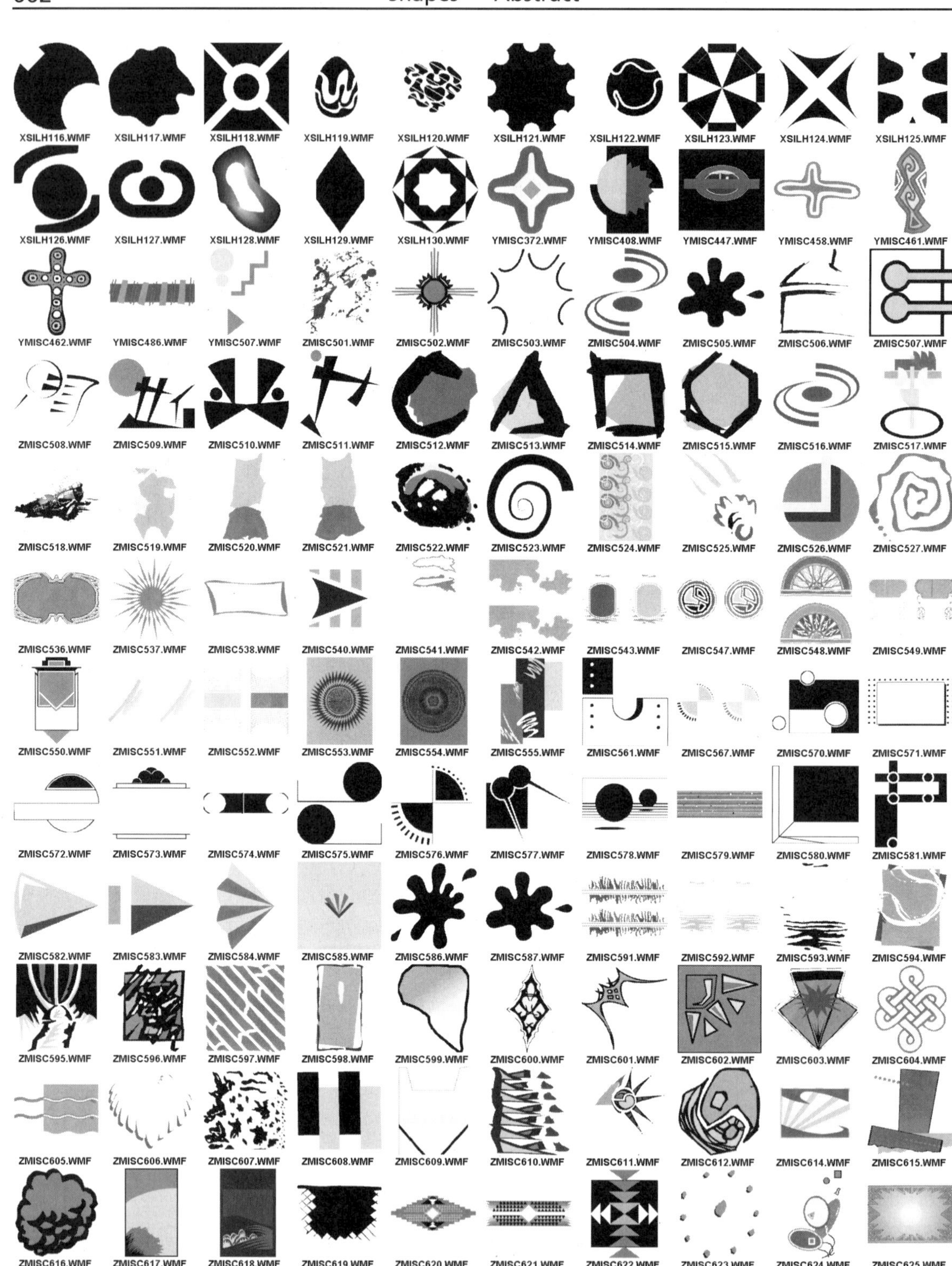

XSILH116.WMF
XSILH117.WMF
XSILH118.WMF
XSILH119.WMF
XSILH120.WMF
XSILH121.WMF
XSILH122.WMF
XSILH123.WMF
XSILH124.WMF
XSILH125.WMF
XSILH126.WMF
XSILH127.WMF
XSILH128.WMF
XSILH129.WMF
XSILH130.WMF
YMISC372.WMF
YMISC408.WMF
YMISC447.WMF
YMISC458.WMF
YMISC461.WMF
YMISC462.WMF
YMISC486.WMF
YMISC507.WMF
ZMISC501.WMF
ZMISC502.WMF
ZMISC503.WMF
ZMISC504.WMF
ZMISC505.WMF
ZMISC506.WMF
ZMISC507.WMF
ZMISC508.WMF
ZMISC509.WMF
ZMISC510.WMF
ZMISC511.WMF
ZMISC512.WMF
ZMISC513.WMF
ZMISC514.WMF
ZMISC515.WMF
ZMISC516.WMF
ZMISC517.WMF
ZMISC518.WMF
ZMISC519.WMF
ZMISC520.WMF
ZMISC521.WMF
ZMISC522.WMF
ZMISC523.WMF
ZMISC524.WMF
ZMISC525.WMF
ZMISC526.WMF
ZMISC527.WMF
ZMISC536.WMF
ZMISC537.WMF
ZMISC538.WMF
ZMISC540.WMF
ZMISC541.WMF
ZMISC542.WMF
ZMISC543.WMF
ZMISC547.WMF
ZMISC548.WMF
ZMISC549.WMF
ZMISC550.WMF
ZMISC551.WMF
ZMISC552.WMF
ZMISC553.WMF
ZMISC554.WMF
ZMISC555.WMF
ZMISC561.WMF
ZMISC567.WMF
ZMISC570.WMF
ZMISC571.WMF
ZMISC572.WMF
ZMISC573.WMF
ZMISC574.WMF
ZMISC575.WMF
ZMISC576.WMF
ZMISC577.WMF
ZMISC578.WMF
ZMISC579.WMF
ZMISC580.WMF
ZMISC581.WMF
ZMISC582.WMF
ZMISC583.WMF
ZMISC584.WMF
ZMISC585.WMF
ZMISC586.WMF
ZMISC587.WMF
ZMISC591.WMF
ZMISC592.WMF
ZMISC593.WMF
ZMISC594.WMF
ZMISC595.WMF
ZMISC596.WMF
ZMISC597.WMF
ZMISC598.WMF
ZMISC599.WMF
ZMISC600.WMF
ZMISC601.WMF
ZMISC602.WMF
ZMISC603.WMF
ZMISC604.WMF
ZMISC605.WMF
ZMISC606.WMF
ZMISC607.WMF
ZMISC608.WMF
ZMISC609.WMF
ZMISC610.WMF
ZMISC611.WMF
ZMISC612.WMF
ZMISC614.WMF
ZMISC615.WMF
ZMISC616.WMF
ZMISC617.WMF
ZMISC618.WMF
ZMISC619.WMF
ZMISC620.WMF
ZMISC621.WMF
ZMISC622.WMF
ZMISC623.WMF
ZMISC624.WMF
ZMISC625.WMF

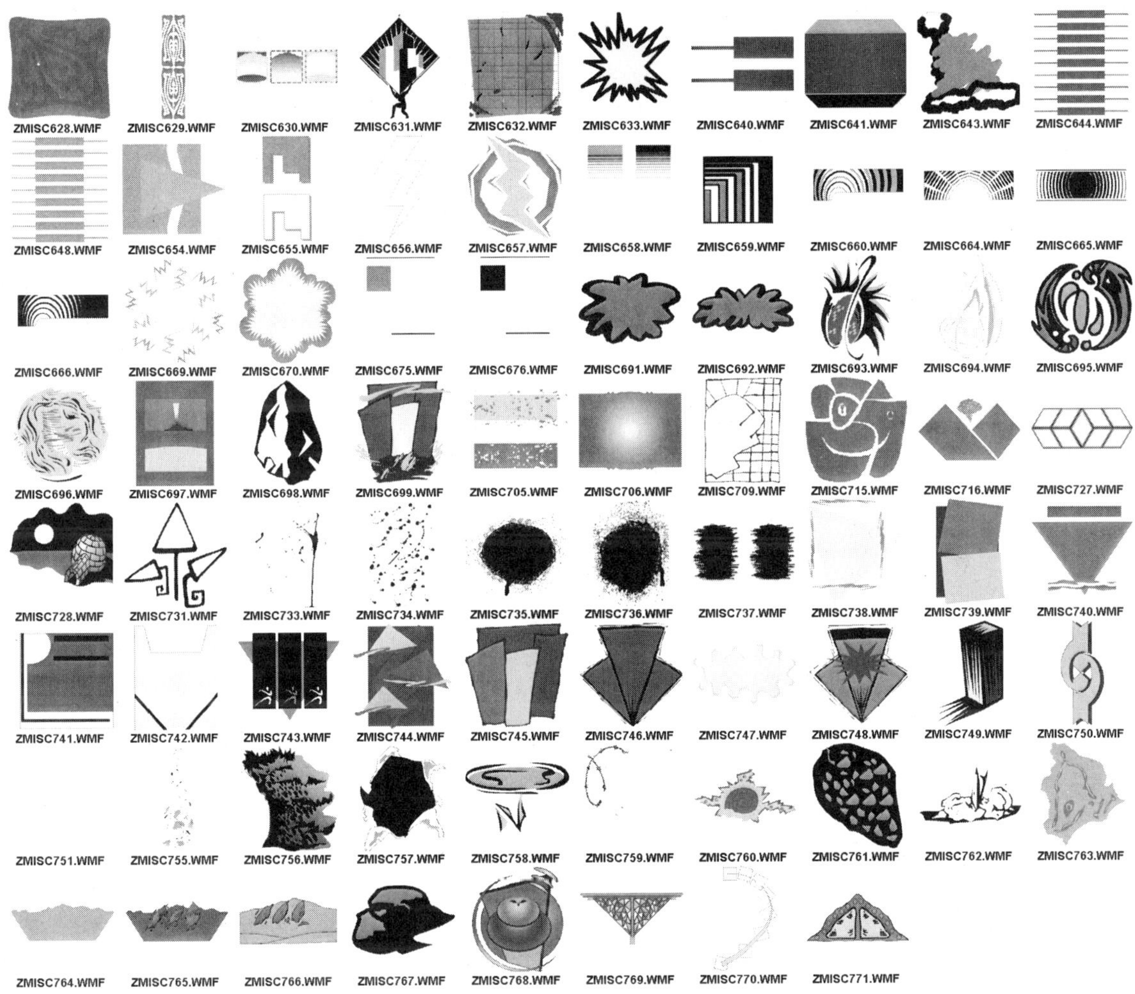
ZMISC628.WMF ZMISC629.WMF ZMISC630.WMF ZMISC631.WMF ZMISC632.WMF ZMISC633.WMF ZMISC640.WMF ZMISC641.WMF ZMISC643.WMF ZMISC644.WMF
ZMISC648.WMF ZMISC654.WMF ZMISC655.WMF ZMISC656.WMF ZMISC657.WMF ZMISC658.WMF ZMISC659.WMF ZMISC660.WMF ZMISC664.WMF ZMISC665.WMF
ZMISC666.WMF ZMISC669.WMF ZMISC670.WMF ZMISC675.WMF ZMISC676.WMF ZMISC691.WMF ZMISC692.WMF ZMISC693.WMF ZMISC694.WMF ZMISC695.WMF
ZMISC696.WMF ZMISC697.WMF ZMISC698.WMF ZMISC699.WMF ZMISC705.WMF ZMISC706.WMF ZMISC709.WMF ZMISC715.WMF ZMISC716.WMF ZMISC727.WMF
ZMISC728.WMF ZMISC731.WMF ZMISC733.WMF ZMISC734.WMF ZMISC735.WMF ZMISC736.WMF ZMISC737.WMF ZMISC738.WMF ZMISC739.WMF ZMISC740.WMF
ZMISC741.WMF ZMISC742.WMF ZMISC743.WMF ZMISC744.WMF ZMISC745.WMF ZMISC746.WMF ZMISC747.WMF ZMISC748.WMF ZMISC749.WMF ZMISC750.WMF
ZMISC751.WMF ZMISC755.WMF ZMISC756.WMF ZMISC757.WMF ZMISC758.WMF ZMISC759.WMF ZMISC760.WMF ZMISC761.WMF ZMISC762.WMF ZMISC763.WMF
ZMISC764.WMF ZMISC765.WMF ZMISC766.WMF ZMISC767.WMF ZMISC768.WMF ZMISC769.WMF ZMISC770.WMF ZMISC771.WMF

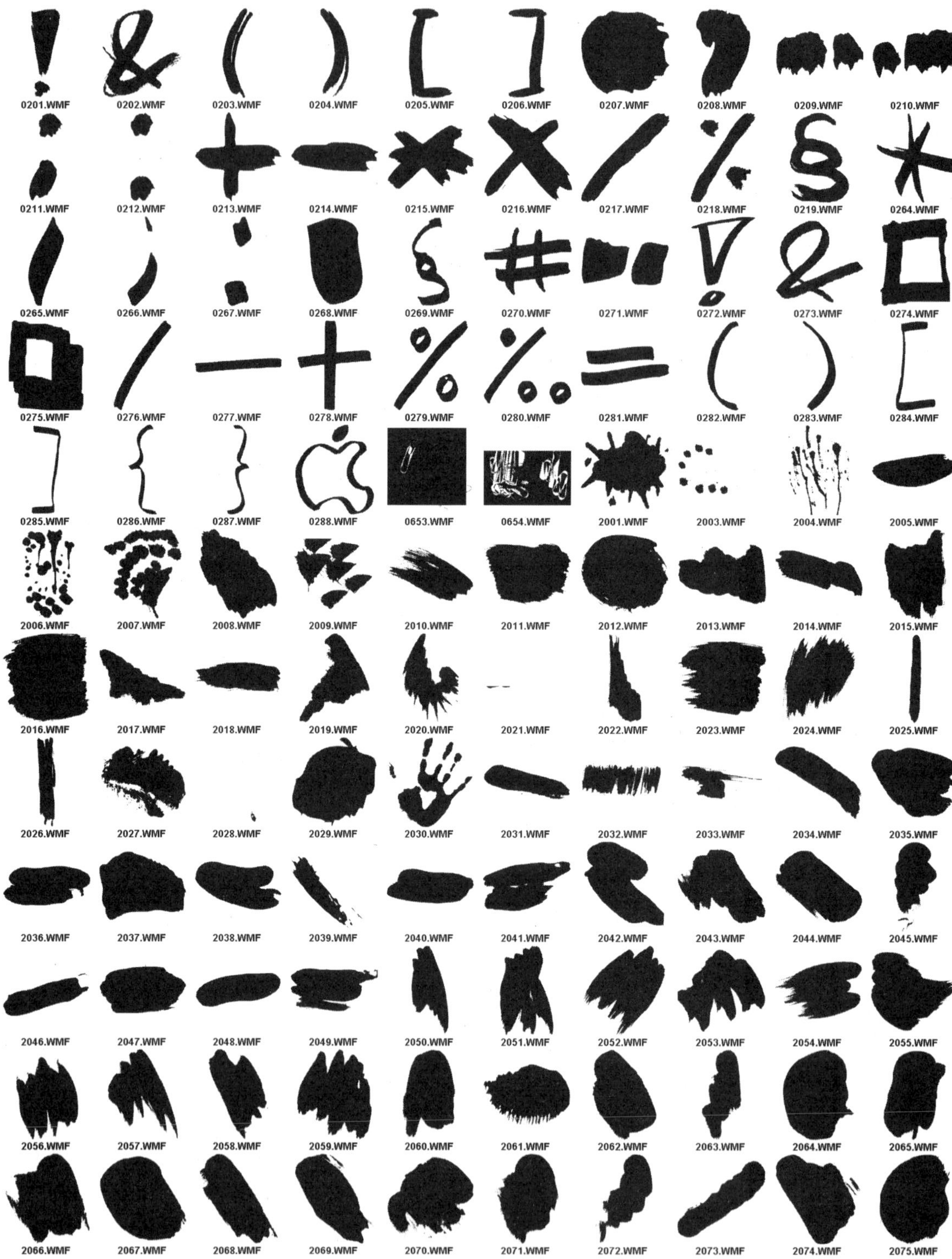
0201.WMF
0202.WMF
0203.WMF
0204.WMF
0205.WMF
0206.WMF
0207.WMF
0208.WMF
0209.WMF
0210.WMF
0211.WMF
0212.WMF
0213.WMF
0214.WMF
0215.WMF
0216.WMF
0217.WMF
0218.WMF
0219.WMF
0264.WMF
0265.WMF
0266.WMF
0267.WMF
0268.WMF
0269.WMF
0270.WMF
0271.WMF
0272.WMF
0273.WMF
0274.WMF
0275.WMF
0276.WMF
0277.WMF
0278.WMF
0279.WMF
0280.WMF
0281.WMF
0282.WMF
0283.WMF
0284.WMF
0285.WMF
0286.WMF
0287.WMF
0288.WMF
0653.WMF
0654.WMF
2001.WMF
2003.WMF
2004.WMF
2005.WMF
2006.WMF
2007.WMF
2008.WMF
2009.WMF
2010.WMF
2011.WMF
2012.WMF
2013.WMF
2014.WMF
2015.WMF
2016.WMF
2017.WMF
2018.WMF
2019.WMF
2020.WMF
2021.WMF
2022.WMF
2023.WMF
2024.WMF
2025.WMF
2026.WMF
2027.WMF
2028.WMF
2029.WMF
2030.WMF
2031.WMF
2032.WMF
2033.WMF
2034.WMF
2035.WMF
2036.WMF
2037.WMF
2038.WMF
2039.WMF
2040.WMF
2041.WMF
2042.WMF
2043.WMF
2044.WMF
2045.WMF
2046.WMF
2047.WMF
2048.WMF
2049.WMF
2050.WMF
2051.WMF
2052.WMF
2053.WMF
2054.WMF
2055.WMF
2056.WMF
2057.WMF
2058.WMF
2059.WMF
2060.WMF
2061.WMF
2062.WMF
2063.WMF
2064.WMF
2065.WMF
2066.WMF
2067.WMF
2068.WMF
2069.WMF
2070.WMF
2071.WMF
2072.WMF
2073.WMF
2074.WMF
2075.WMF

2076.WMF
2077.WMF
2078.WMF
2079.WMF
2080.WMF
2081.WMF
2082.WMF
2083.WMF
2084.WMF
2085.WMF
2086.WMF
2087.WMF
2088.WMF
2089.WMF
2090.WMF
2091.WMF
2092.WMF
2093.WMF
2094.WMF
2095.WMF
2096.WMF
2097.WMF
2098.WMF
2099.WMF
2100.WMF
2358.WMF
2359.WMF
2360.WMF
2361.WMF
2362.WMF
2363.WMF
2364.WMF
2365.WMF
2401.WMF
2402.WMF
2403.WMF
2404.WMF
2405.WMF
2406.WMF
2407.WMF
2408.WMF
2409.WMF
2410.WMF
2411.WMF
2412.WMF
2413.WMF
2414.WMF
2415.WMF
2416.WMF
2417.WMF
2418.WMF
2419.WMF
2420.WMF
2421.WMF
2422.WMF
2423.WMF
2424.WMF
2425.WMF
2426.WMF
2427.WMF
2428.WMF
2429.WMF
2430.WMF
2431.WMF
2432.WMF
2433.WMF
2434.WMF
2435.WMF
2436.WMF
2437.WMF
2438.WMF
2439.WMF
2440.WMF
2441.WMF
2442.WMF
2443.WMF
2444.WMF
2445.WMF
2446.WMF
2447.WMF
2448.WMF
2449.WMF
2450.WMF
2451.WMF
2452.WMF
2453.WMF
2454.WMF
2455.WMF
2456.WMF
2457.WMF
2458.WMF
2459.WMF
2460.WMF
2461.WMF
2462.WMF
2463.WMF
2464.WMF
2465.WMF
2470.WMF
2472.WMF
2473.WMF
2475.WMF
2476.WMF
2993.WMF
2999.WMF
3000.WMF
69STAR.WMF
APURPL1.WMF
APURPL10.WMF
APURPL11.WMF
APURPL12.WMF
APURPL17.WMF
APURPL18.WMF
APURPL2.WMF
APURPL21.WMF
APURPL22.WMF
APURPL23.WMF
APURPL24.WMF
APURPL25.WMF
APURPL26.WMF

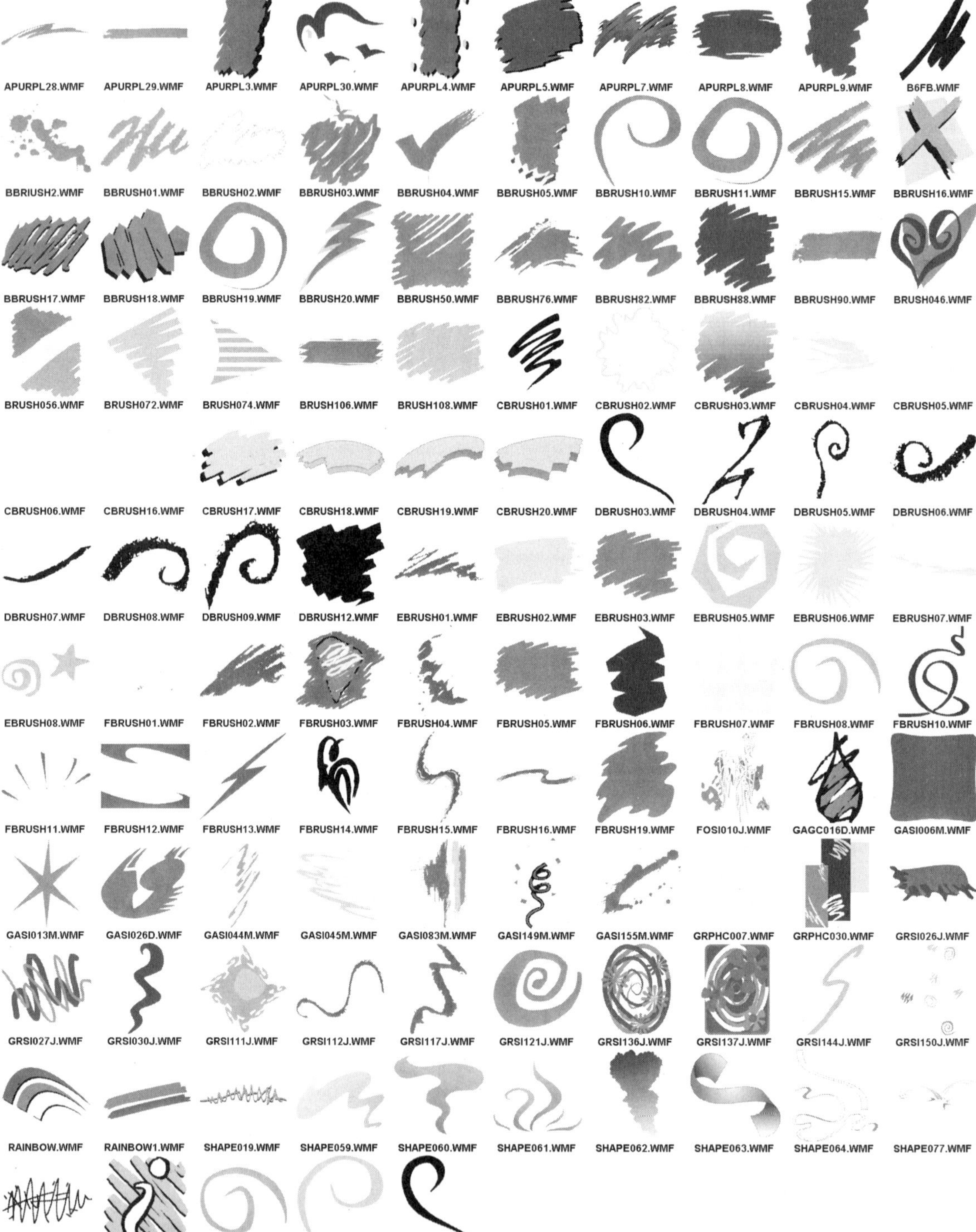
APURPL28.WMF
APURPL29.WMF
APURPL3.WMF
APURPL30.WMF
APURPL4.WMF
APURPL5.WMF
APURPL7.WMF
APURPL8.WMF
APURPL9.WMF
B6FB.WMF
BBRIUSH2.WMF
BBRUSH01.WMF
BBRUSH02.WMF
BBRUSH03.WMF
BBRUSH04.WMF
BBRUSH05.WMF
BBRUSH10.WMF
BBRUSH11.WMF
BBRUSH15.WMF
BBRUSH16.WMF
BBRUSH17.WMF
BBRUSH18.WMF
BBRUSH19.WMF
BBRUSH20.WMF
BBRUSH50.WMF
BBRUSH76.WMF
BBRUSH82.WMF
BBRUSH88.WMF
BBRUSH90.WMF
BRUSH046.WMF
BRUSH056.WMF
BRUSH072.WMF
BRUSH074.WMF
BRUSH106.WMF
BRUSH108.WMF
CBRUSH01.WMF
CBRUSH02.WMF
CBRUSH03.WMF
CBRUSH04.WMF
CBRUSH05.WMF
CBRUSH06.WMF
CBRUSH16.WMF
CBRUSH17.WMF
CBRUSH18.WMF
CBRUSH19.WMF
CBRUSH20.WMF
DBRUSH03.WMF
DBRUSH04.WMF
DBRUSH05.WMF
DBRUSH06.WMF
DBRUSH07.WMF
DBRUSH08.WMF
DBRUSH09.WMF
DBRUSH12.WMF
EBRUSH01.WMF
EBRUSH02.WMF
EBRUSH03.WMF
EBRUSH05.WMF
EBRUSH06.WMF
EBRUSH07.WMF
EBRUSH08.WMF
FBRUSH01.WMF
FBRUSH02.WMF
FBRUSH03.WMF
FBRUSH04.WMF
FBRUSH05.WMF
FBRUSH06.WMF
FBRUSH07.WMF
FBRUSH08.WMF
FBRUSH10.WMF
FBRUSH11.WMF
FBRUSH12.WMF
FBRUSH13.WMF
FBRUSH14.WMF
FBRUSH15.WMF
FBRUSH16.WMF
FBRUSH19.WMF
FOSI010J.WMF
GAGC016D.WMF
GASI006M.WMF
GASI013M.WMF
GASI026D.WMF
GASI044M.WMF
GASI045M.WMF
GASI083M.WMF
GASI149M.WMF
GASI155M.WMF
GRPHC007.WMF
GRPHC030.WMF
GRSI026J.WMF
GRSI027J.WMF
GRSI030J.WMF
GRSI111J.WMF
GRSI112J.WMF
GRSI117J.WMF
GRSI121J.WMF
GRSI136J.WMF
GRSI137J.WMF
GRSI144J.WMF
GRSI150J.WMF
RAINBOW.WMF
RAINBOW1.WMF
SHAPE019.WMF
SHAPE059.WMF
SHAPE060.WMF
SHAPE061.WMF
SHAPE062.WMF
SHAPE063.WMF
SHAPE064.WMF
SHAPE077.WMF
SHAPE165.WMF
SHAPE282.WMF
YMISC427.WMF
YMISC428.WMF
YMISC430.WMF

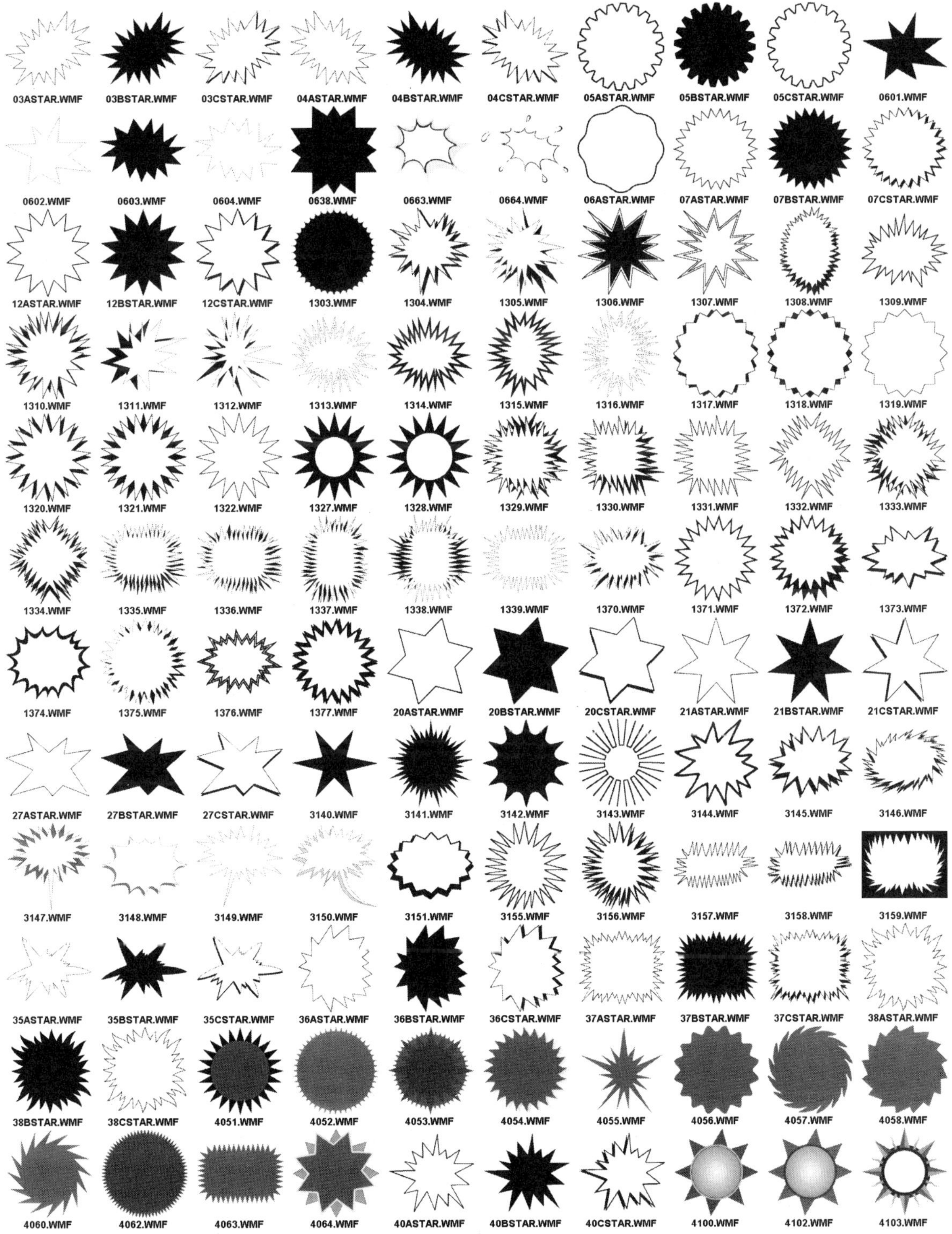
03ASTAR.WMF 03BSTAR.WMF 03CSTAR.WMF 04ASTAR.WMF 04BSTAR.WMF 04CSTAR.WMF 05ASTAR.WMF 05BSTAR.WMF 05CSTAR.WMF 0601.WMF
0602.WMF 0603.WMF 0604.WMF 0638.WMF 0663.WMF 0664.WMF 06ASTAR.WMF 07ASTAR.WMF 07BSTAR.WMF 07CSTAR.WMF
12ASTAR.WMF 12BSTAR.WMF 12CSTAR.WMF 1303.WMF 1304.WMF 1305.WMF 1306.WMF 1307.WMF 1308.WMF 1309.WMF
1310.WMF 1311.WMF 1312.WMF 1313.WMF 1314.WMF 1315.WMF 1316.WMF 1317.WMF 1318.WMF 1319.WMF
1320.WMF 1321.WMF 1322.WMF 1327.WMF 1328.WMF 1329.WMF 1330.WMF 1331.WMF 1332.WMF 1333.WMF
1334.WMF 1335.WMF 1336.WMF 1337.WMF 1338.WMF 1339.WMF 1370.WMF 1371.WMF 1372.WMF 1373.WMF
1374.WMF 1375.WMF 1376.WMF 1377.WMF 20ASTAR.WMF 20BSTAR.WMF 20CSTAR.WMF 21ASTAR.WMF 21BSTAR.WMF 21CSTAR.WMF
27ASTAR.WMF 27BSTAR.WMF 27CSTAR.WMF 3140.WMF 3141.WMF 3142.WMF 3143.WMF 3144.WMF 3145.WMF 3146.WMF
3147.WMF 3148.WMF 3149.WMF 3150.WMF 3151.WMF 3155.WMF 3156.WMF 3157.WMF 3158.WMF 3159.WMF
35ASTAR.WMF 35BSTAR.WMF 35CSTAR.WMF 36ASTAR.WMF 36BSTAR.WMF 36CSTAR.WMF 37ASTAR.WMF 37BSTAR.WMF 37CSTAR.WMF 38ASTAR.WMF
38BSTAR.WMF 38CSTAR.WMF 4051.WMF 4052.WMF 4053.WMF 4054.WMF 4055.WMF 4056.WMF 4057.WMF 4058.WMF
4060.WMF 4062.WMF 4063.WMF 4064.WMF 40ASTAR.WMF 40BSTAR.WMF 40CSTAR.WMF 4100.WMF 4102.WMF 4103.WMF

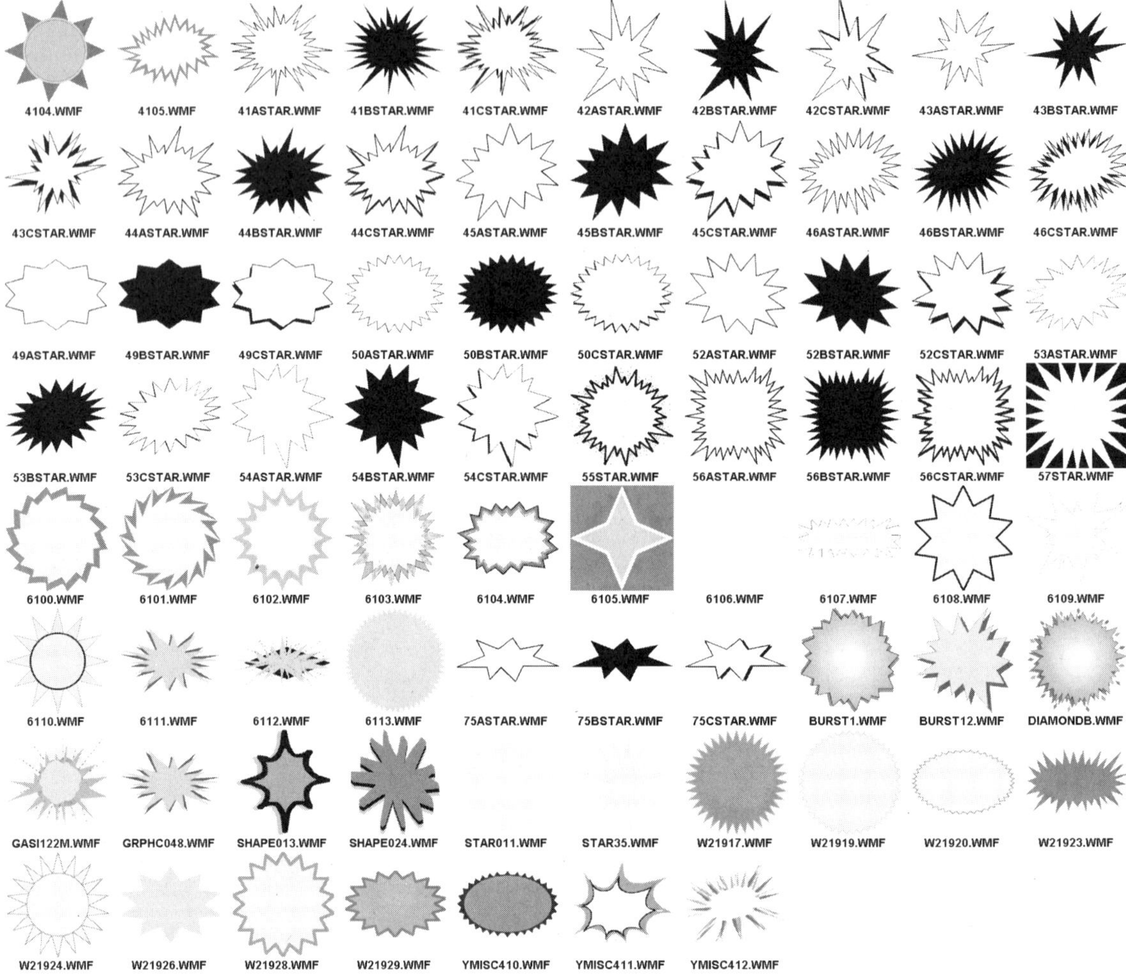
4104.WMF
4105.WMF
41ASTAR.WMF
41BSTAR.WMF
41CSTAR.WMF
42ASTAR.WMF
42BSTAR.WMF
42CSTAR.WMF
43ASTAR.WMF
43BSTAR.WMF
43CSTAR.WMF
44ASTAR.WMF
44BSTAR.WMF
44CSTAR.WMF
45ASTAR.WMF
45BSTAR.WMF
45CSTAR.WMF
46ASTAR.WMF
46BSTAR.WMF
46CSTAR.WMF
49ASTAR.WMF
49BSTAR.WMF
49CSTAR.WMF
50ASTAR.WMF
50BSTAR.WMF
50CSTAR.WMF
52ASTAR.WMF
52BSTAR.WMF
52CSTAR.WMF
53ASTAR.WMF
53BSTAR.WMF
53CSTAR.WMF
54ASTAR.WMF
54BSTAR.WMF
54CSTAR.WMF
55STAR.WMF
56ASTAR.WMF
56BSTAR.WMF
56CSTAR.WMF
57STAR.WMF
6100.WMF
6101.WMF
6102.WMF
6103.WMF
6104.WMF
6105.WMF
6106.WMF
6107.WMF
6108.WMF
6109.WMF
6110.WMF
6111.WMF
6112.WMF
6113.WMF
75ASTAR.WMF
75BSTAR.WMF
75CSTAR.WMF
BURST1.WMF
BURST12.WMF
DIAMONDB.WMF
GASI122M.WMF
GRPHC048.WMF
SHAPE013.WMF
SHAPE024.WMF
STAR011.WMF
STAR35.WMF
W21917.WMF
W21919.WMF
W21920.WMF
W21923.WMF
W21924.WMF
W21926.WMF
W21928.WMF
W21929.WMF
YMISC410.WMF
YMISC411.WMF
YMISC412.WMF

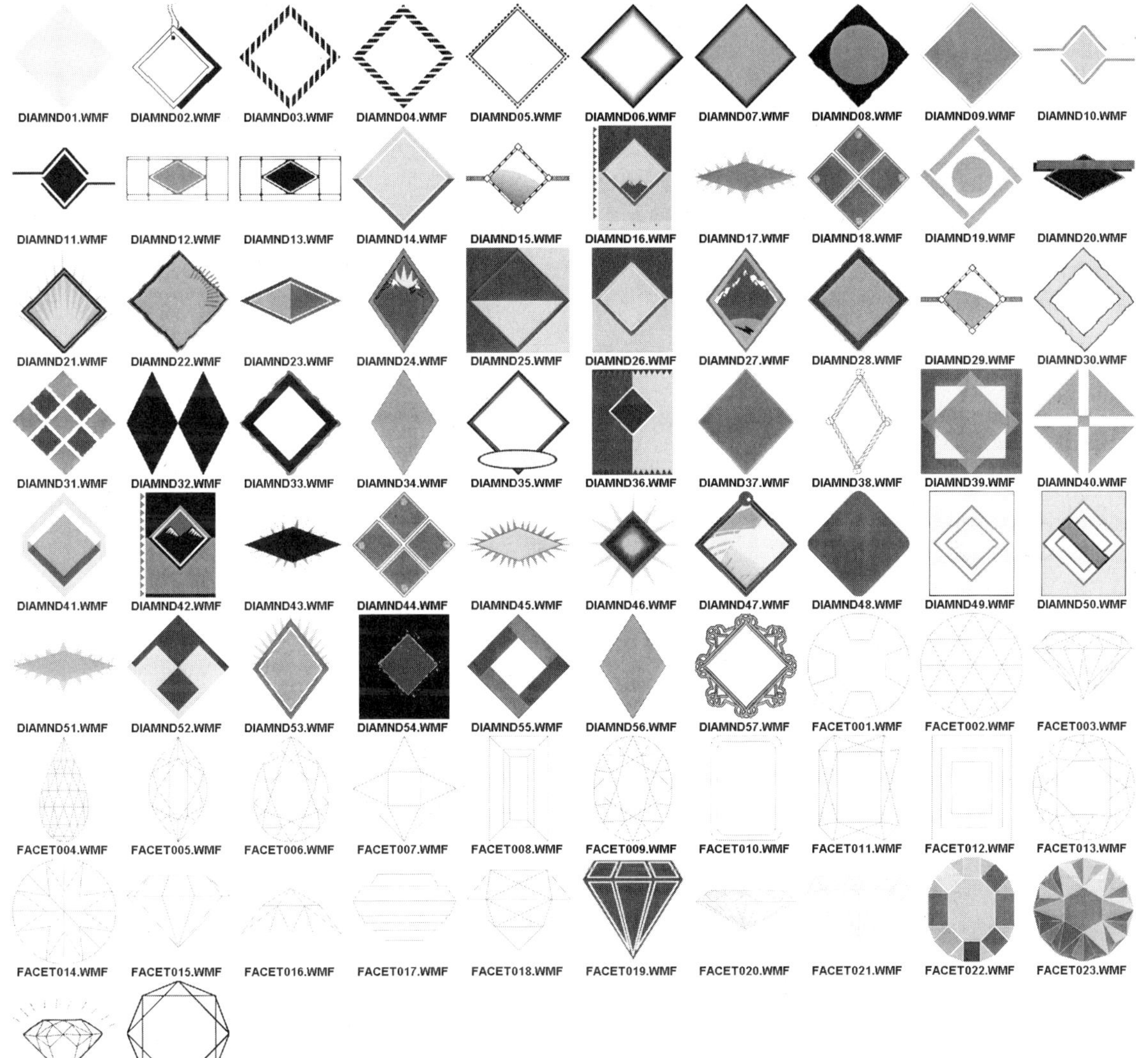
DIAMND01.WMF
DIAMND02.WMF
DIAMND03.WMF
DIAMND04.WMF
DIAMND05.WMF
DIAMND06.WMF
DIAMND07.WMF
DIAMND08.WMF
DIAMND09.WMF
DIAMND10.WMF
DIAMND11.WMF
DIAMND12.WMF
DIAMND13.WMF
DIAMND14.WMF
DIAMND15.WMF
DIAMND16.WMF
DIAMND17.WMF
DIAMND18.WMF
DIAMND19.WMF
DIAMND20.WMF
DIAMND21.WMF
DIAMND22.WMF
DIAMND23.WMF
DIAMND24.WMF
DIAMND25.WMF
DIAMND26.WMF
DIAMND27.WMF
DIAMND28.WMF
DIAMND29.WMF
DIAMND30.WMF
DIAMND31.WMF
DIAMND32.WMF
DIAMND33.WMF
DIAMND34.WMF
DIAMND35.WMF
DIAMND36.WMF
DIAMND37.WMF
DIAMND38.WMF
DIAMND39.WMF
DIAMND40.WMF
DIAMND41.WMF
DIAMND42.WMF
DIAMND43.WMF
DIAMND44.WMF
DIAMND45.WMF
DIAMND46.WMF
DIAMND47.WMF
DIAMND48.WMF
DIAMND49.WMF
DIAMND50.WMF
DIAMND51.WMF
DIAMND52.WMF
DIAMND53.WMF
DIAMND54.WMF
DIAMND55.WMF
DIAMND56.WMF
DIAMND57.WMF
FACET001.WMF
FACET002.WMF
FACET003.WMF
FACET004.WMF
FACET005.WMF
FACET006.WMF
FACET007.WMF
FACET008.WMF
FACET009.WMF
FACET010.WMF
FACET011.WMF
FACET012.WMF
FACET013.WMF
FACET014.WMF
FACET015.WMF
FACET016.WMF
FACET017.WMF
FACET018.WMF
FACET019.WMF
FACET020.WMF
FACET021.WMF
FACET022.WMF
FACET023.WMF
FACET024.WMF
FACET025.WMF

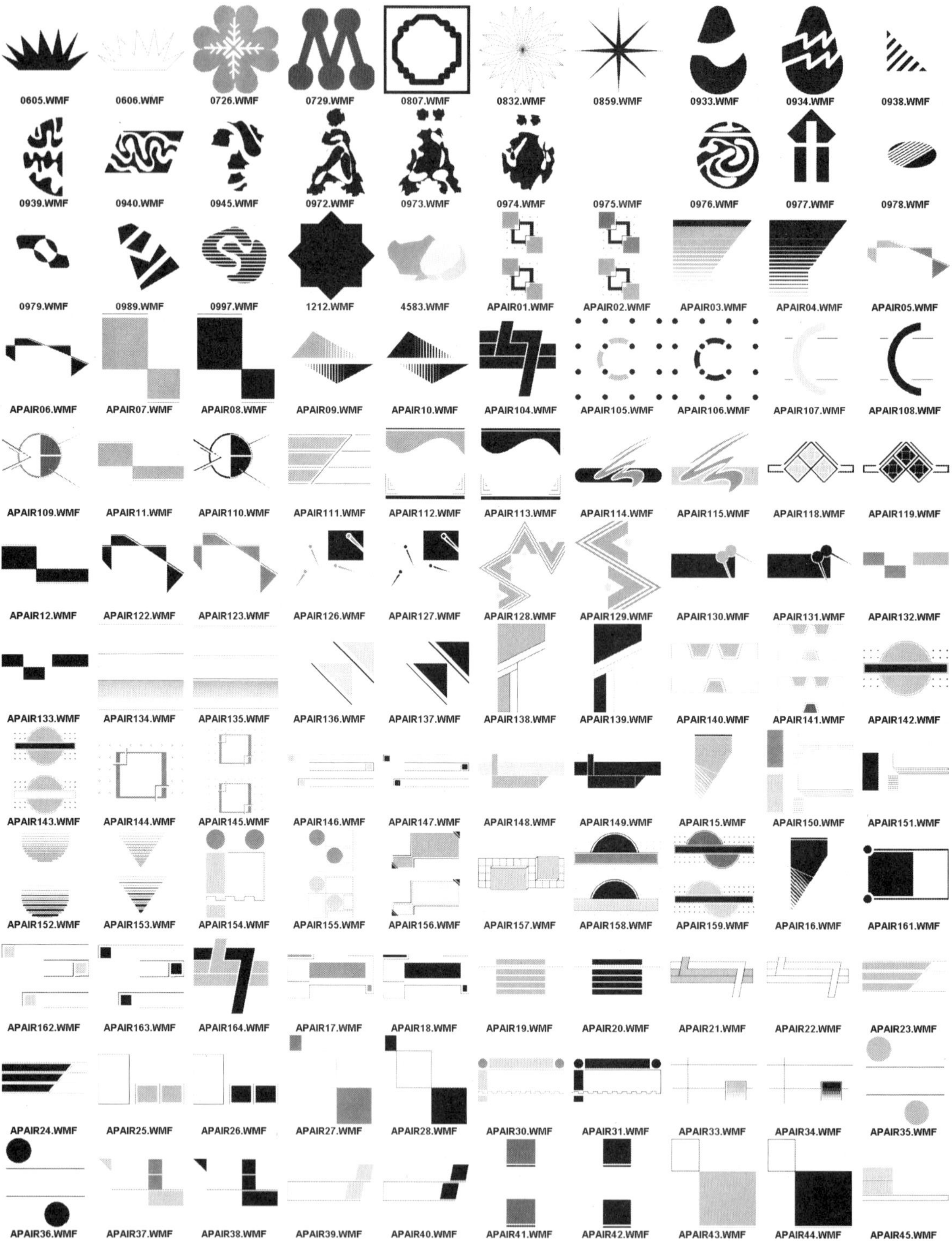
0605.WMF 0606.WMF 0726.WMF 0729.WMF 0807.WMF 0832.WMF 0859.WMF 0933.WMF 0934.WMF 0938.WMF
0939.WMF 0940.WMF 0945.WMF 0972.WMF 0973.WMF 0974.WMF 0975.WMF 0976.WMF 0977.WMF 0978.WMF
0979.WMF 0989.WMF 0997.WMF 1212.WMF 4583.WMF APAIR01.WMF APAIR02.WMF APAIR03.WMF APAIR04.WMF APAIR05.WMF
APAIR06.WMF APAIR07.WMF APAIR08.WMF APAIR09.WMF APAIR10.WMF APAIR104.WMF APAIR105.WMF APAIR106.WMF APAIR107.WMF APAIR108.WMF
APAIR109.WMF APAIR11.WMF APAIR110.WMF APAIR111.WMF APAIR112.WMF APAIR113.WMF APAIR114.WMF APAIR115.WMF APAIR118.WMF APAIR119.WMF
APAIR12.WMF APAIR122.WMF APAIR123.WMF APAIR126.WMF APAIR127.WMF APAIR128.WMF APAIR129.WMF APAIR130.WMF APAIR131.WMF APAIR132.WMF
APAIR133.WMF APAIR134.WMF APAIR135.WMF APAIR136.WMF APAIR137.WMF APAIR138.WMF APAIR139.WMF APAIR140.WMF APAIR141.WMF APAIR142.WMF
APAIR143.WMF APAIR144.WMF APAIR145.WMF APAIR146.WMF APAIR147.WMF APAIR148.WMF APAIR149.WMF APAIR15.WMF APAIR150.WMF APAIR151.WMF
APAIR152.WMF APAIR153.WMF APAIR154.WMF APAIR155.WMF APAIR156.WMF APAIR157.WMF APAIR158.WMF APAIR159.WMF APAIR16.WMF APAIR161.WMF
APAIR162.WMF APAIR163.WMF APAIR164.WMF APAIR17.WMF APAIR18.WMF APAIR19.WMF APAIR20.WMF APAIR21.WMF APAIR22.WMF APAIR23.WMF
APAIR24.WMF APAIR25.WMF APAIR26.WMF APAIR27.WMF APAIR28.WMF APAIR30.WMF APAIR31.WMF APAIR33.WMF APAIR34.WMF APAIR35.WMF
APAIR36.WMF APAIR37.WMF APAIR38.WMF APAIR39.WMF APAIR40.WMF APAIR41.WMF APAIR42.WMF APAIR43.WMF APAIR44.WMF APAIR45.WMF

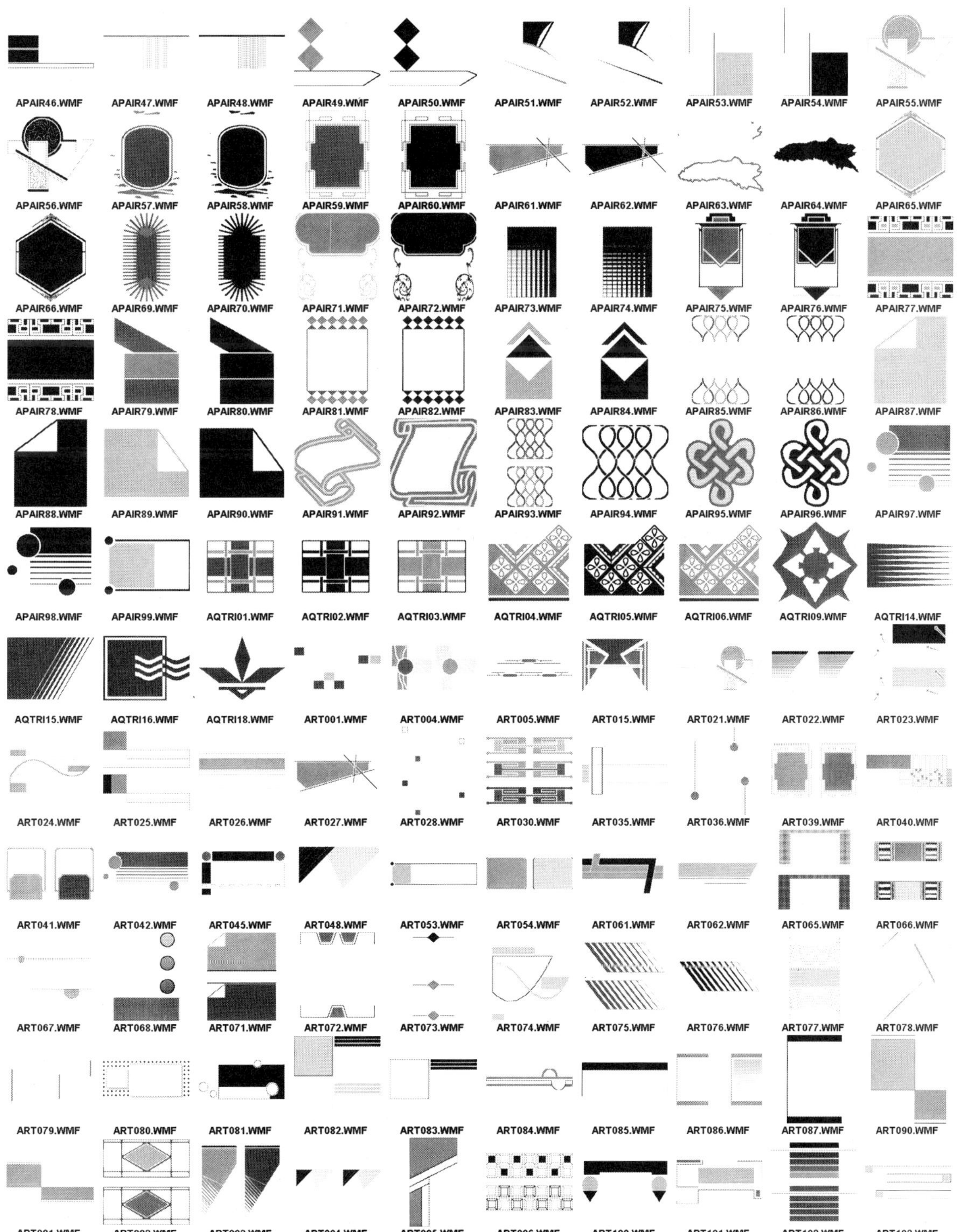
APAIR46.WMF APAIR47.WMF APAIR48.WMF APAIR49.WMF APAIR50.WMF APAIR51.WMF APAIR52.WMF APAIR53.WMF APAIR54.WMF APAIR55.WMF
APAIR56.WMF APAIR57.WMF APAIR58.WMF APAIR59.WMF APAIR60.WMF APAIR61.WMF APAIR62.WMF APAIR63.WMF APAIR64.WMF APAIR65.WMF
APAIR66.WMF APAIR69.WMF APAIR70.WMF APAIR71.WMF APAIR72.WMF APAIR73.WMF APAIR74.WMF APAIR75.WMF APAIR76.WMF APAIR77.WMF
APAIR78.WMF APAIR79.WMF APAIR80.WMF APAIR81.WMF APAIR82.WMF APAIR83.WMF APAIR84.WMF APAIR85.WMF APAIR86.WMF APAIR87.WMF
APAIR88.WMF APAIR89.WMF APAIR90.WMF APAIR91.WMF APAIR92.WMF APAIR93.WMF APAIR94.WMF APAIR95.WMF APAIR96.WMF APAIR97.WMF
APAIR98.WMF APAIR99.WMF AQTRI01.WMF AQTRI02.WMF AQTRI03.WMF AQTRI04.WMF AQTRI05.WMF AQTRI06.WMF AQTRI09.WMF AQTRI14.WMF
AQTRI15.WMF AQTRI16.WMF AQTRI18.WMF ART001.WMF ART004.WMF ART005.WMF ART015.WMF ART021.WMF ART022.WMF ART023.WMF
ART024.WMF ART025.WMF ART026.WMF ART027.WMF ART028.WMF ART030.WMF ART035.WMF ART036.WMF ART039.WMF ART040.WMF
ART041.WMF ART042.WMF ART045.WMF ART048.WMF ART053.WMF ART054.WMF ART061.WMF ART062.WMF ART065.WMF ART066.WMF
ART067.WMF ART068.WMF ART071.WMF ART072.WMF ART073.WMF ART074.WMF ART075.WMF ART076.WMF ART077.WMF ART078.WMF
ART079.WMF ART080.WMF ART081.WMF ART082.WMF ART083.WMF ART084.WMF ART085.WMF ART086.WMF ART087.WMF ART090.WMF
ART091.WMF ART092.WMF ART093.WMF ART094.WMF ART095.WMF ART096.WMF ART100.WMF ART101.WMF ART102.WMF ART103.WMF

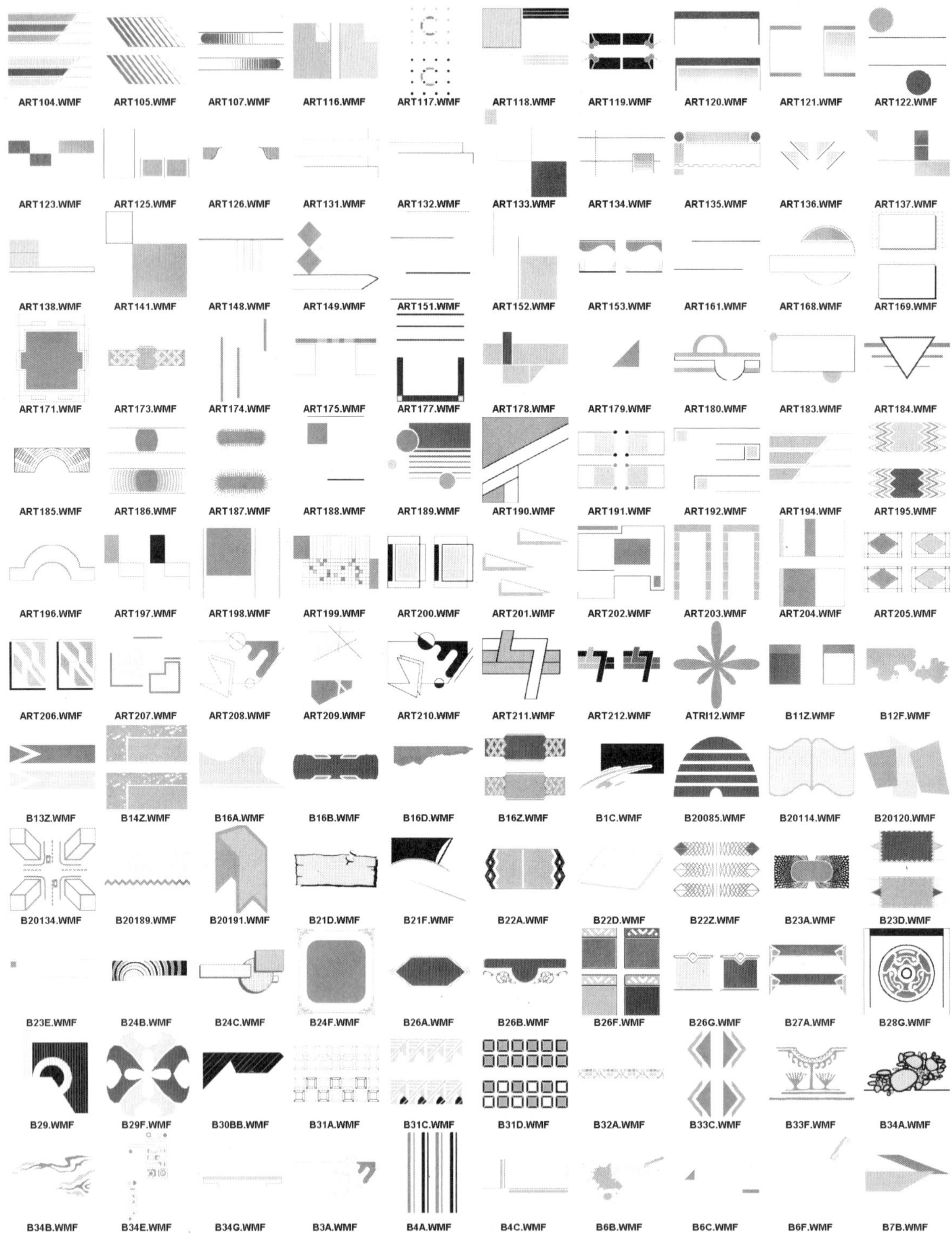
ART104.WMF
ART105.WMF
ART107.WMF
ART116.WMF
ART117.WMF
ART118.WMF
ART119.WMF
ART120.WMF
ART121.WMF
ART122.WMF
ART123.WMF
ART125.WMF
ART126.WMF
ART131.WMF
ART132.WMF
ART133.WMF
ART134.WMF
ART135.WMF
ART136.WMF
ART137.WMF
ART138.WMF
ART141.WMF
ART148.WMF
ART149.WMF
ART151.WMF
ART152.WMF
ART153.WMF
ART161.WMF
ART168.WMF
ART169.WMF
ART171.WMF
ART173.WMF
ART174.WMF
ART175.WMF
ART177.WMF
ART178.WMF
ART179.WMF
ART180.WMF
ART183.WMF
ART184.WMF
ART185.WMF
ART186.WMF
ART187.WMF
ART188.WMF
ART189.WMF
ART190.WMF
ART191.WMF
ART192.WMF
ART194.WMF
ART195.WMF
ART196.WMF
ART197.WMF
ART198.WMF
ART199.WMF
ART200.WMF
ART201.WMF
ART202.WMF
ART203.WMF
ART204.WMF
ART205.WMF
ART206.WMF
ART207.WMF
ART208.WMF
ART209.WMF
ART210.WMF
ART211.WMF
ART212.WMF
ATRI12.WMF
B11Z.WMF
B12F.WMF
B13Z.WMF
B14Z.WMF
B16A.WMF
B16B.WMF
B16D.WMF
B16Z.WMF
B1C.WMF
B20085.WMF
B20114.WMF
B20120.WMF
B20134.WMF
B20189.WMF
B20191.WMF
B21D.WMF
B21F.WMF
B22A.WMF
B22D.WMF
B22Z.WMF
B23A.WMF
B23D.WMF
B23E.WMF
B24B.WMF
B24C.WMF
B24F.WMF
B26A.WMF
B26B.WMF
B26F.WMF
B26G.WMF
B27A.WMF
B28G.WMF
B29.WMF
B29F.WMF
B30BB.WMF
B31A.WMF
B31C.WMF
B31D.WMF
B32A.WMF
B33C.WMF
B33F.WMF
B34A.WMF
B34B.WMF
B34E.WMF
B34G.WMF
B3A.WMF
B4A.WMF
B4C.WMF
B6B.WMF
B6C.WMF
B6F.WMF
B7B.WMF

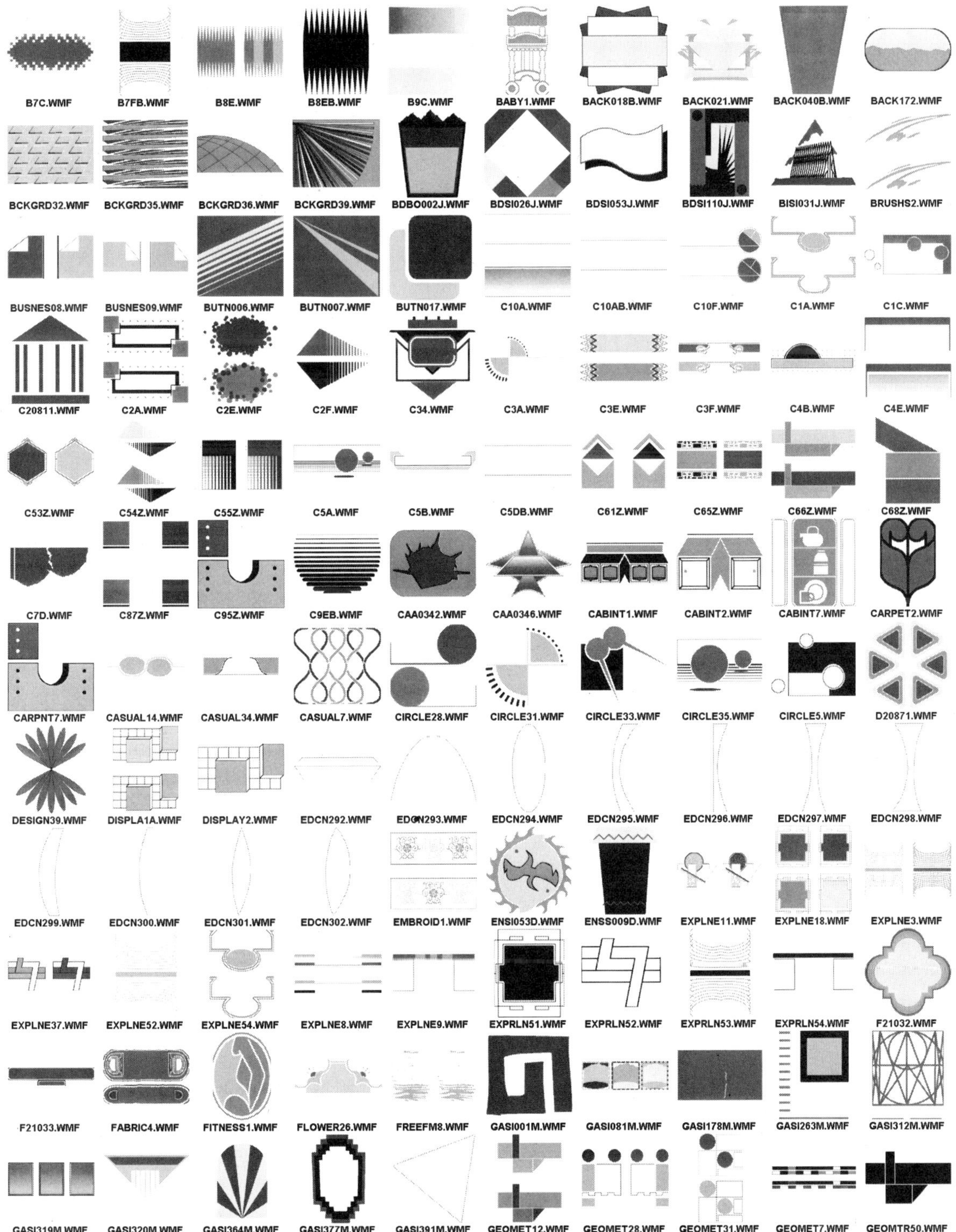

B7C.WMF B7FB.WMF B8E.WMF B8EB.WMF B9C.WMF BABY1.WMF BACK018B.WMF BACK021.WMF BACK040B.WMF BACK172.WMF

BCKGRD32.WMF BCKGRD35.WMF BCKGRD36.WMF BCKGRD39.WMF BDBO002J.WMF BDSI026J.WMF BDSI053J.WMF BDSI110J.WMF BISI031J.WMF BRUSHS2.WMF

BUSNES08.WMF BUSNES09.WMF BUTN006.WMF BUTN007.WMF BUTN017.WMF C10A.WMF C10AB.WMF C10F.WMF C1A.WMF C1C.WMF

C20811.WMF C2A.WMF C2E.WMF C2F.WMF C34.WMF C3A.WMF C3E.WMF C3F.WMF C4B.WMF C4E.WMF

C53Z.WMF C54Z.WMF C55Z.WMF C5A.WMF C5B.WMF C5DB.WMF C61Z.WMF C65Z.WMF C66Z.WMF C68Z.WMF

C7D.WMF C87Z.WMF C95Z.WMF C9EB.WMF CAA0342.WMF CAA0346.WMF CABINT1.WMF CABINT2.WMF CABINT7.WMF CARPET2.WMF

CARPNT7.WMF CASUAL14.WMF CASUAL34.WMF CASUAL7.WMF CIRCLE28.WMF CIRCLE31.WMF CIRCLE33.WMF CIRCLE35.WMF CIRCLE5.WMF D20871.WMF

DESIGN39.WMF DISPLA1A.WMF DISPLAY2.WMF EDCN292.WMF EDCN293.WMF EDCN294.WMF EDCN295.WMF EDCN296.WMF EDCN297.WMF EDCN298.WMF

EDCN299.WMF EDCN300.WMF EDCN301.WMF EDCN302.WMF EMBROID1.WMF ENSI053D.WMF ENSS009D.WMF EXPLNE11.WMF EXPLNE18.WMF EXPLNE3.WMF

EXPLNE37.WMF EXPLNE52.WMF EXPLNE54.WMF EXPLNE8.WMF EXPLNE9.WMF EXPRLN51.WMF EXPRLN52.WMF EXPRLN53.WMF EXPRLN54.WMF F21032.WMF

F21033.WMF FABRIC4.WMF FITNESS1.WMF FLOWER26.WMF FREEFM8.WMF GASI001M.WMF GASI081M.WMF GASI178M.WMF GASI263M.WMF GASI312M.WMF

GASI319M.WMF GASI320M.WMF GASI364M.WMF GASI377M.WMF GASI391M.WMF GEOMET12.WMF GEOMET28.WMF GEOMET31.WMF GEOMET7.WMF GEOMTR50.WMF

GEOMTR51.WMF
GEOMTR52.WMF
GEOMTR53.WMF
GRSI016J.WMF
GRSI019J.WMF
GRSI095J.WMF
HUMNSRV2.WMF
I21137.WMF
ITALX8.WMF
J21153.WMF
L21179.WMF
LINEBL18.WMF
M21350.WMF
M21351.WMF
MET006.WMF
MET007.WMF
MET008.WMF
MET009.WMF
MET010.WMF
MET011.WMF
MET012.WMF
MET013.WMF
MET014.WMF
MET017.WMF
MET018.WMF
MET019.WMF
MET020.WMF
MET021.WMF
MET022.WMF
MET023.WMF
MET024.WMF
MET025.WMF
MET026.WMF
MET027.WMF
MET036.WMF
MET037.WMF
MET038.WMF
MET039.WMF
MET040.WMF
MET041.WMF
MIS0021A.WMF
MISC_11.WMF
MODERN8.WMF
MONUMNTS.WMF
N21441.WMF
O21538.WMF
OIRI.WMF
ORNATE14.WMF
P21552.WMF
REAL01.WMF
REAL13.WMF
REAL14.WMF
S21667.WMF
S21676.WMF
S21707.WMF
S21712.WMF
S21733.WMF
SHAPE019.WMF
SHAPE020.WMF
SHAPE082.WMF
SHAPE097.WMF
SHAPE114.WMF
SHAPE130.WMF
SHAPE141.WMF
SHAPE143.WMF
SHAPE161.WMF
SHAPE288.WMF
SHELF4.WMF
SILVERSE.WMF
SPSI022M.WMF
SQRCTG26.WMF
SUN18.WMF
SYMBL143.WMF
SYMBL17.WMF
SYMBL22.WMF
SYMBL32.WMF
SYMBL33.WMF
SYMBL44.WMF
SYMBL59.WMF
SYMBOL42.WMF
SYMBOL53.WMF
SYMBOL54.WMF
SYMBOL57.WMF
TARGET02.WMF
TILE5.WMF
TILE8.WMF
TRINGE10.WMF
TRINGE14.WMF
TRINGE15.WMF
TRINGE2.WMF
TRINGE4.WMF
TRINGE6.WMF
TRINGE8.WMF
TRINGLE4.WMF
TRINGLE9.WMF
TRNGLS15.WMF
TRNGLS4B.WMF
TRNGLS8B.WMF
W21907.WMF
WAKABA.WMF
YUUBIN.WMF
ZMISC01.WMF
ZMISC02.WMF
ZMISC04.WMF
ZMISC05.WMF
ZMISC06.WMF
ZMISC07.WMF
ZMISC667.WMF
ZMISC668.WMF
ZMISC700.WMF
ZMISC701.WMF
ZMISC702.WMF
ZMISC708.WMF

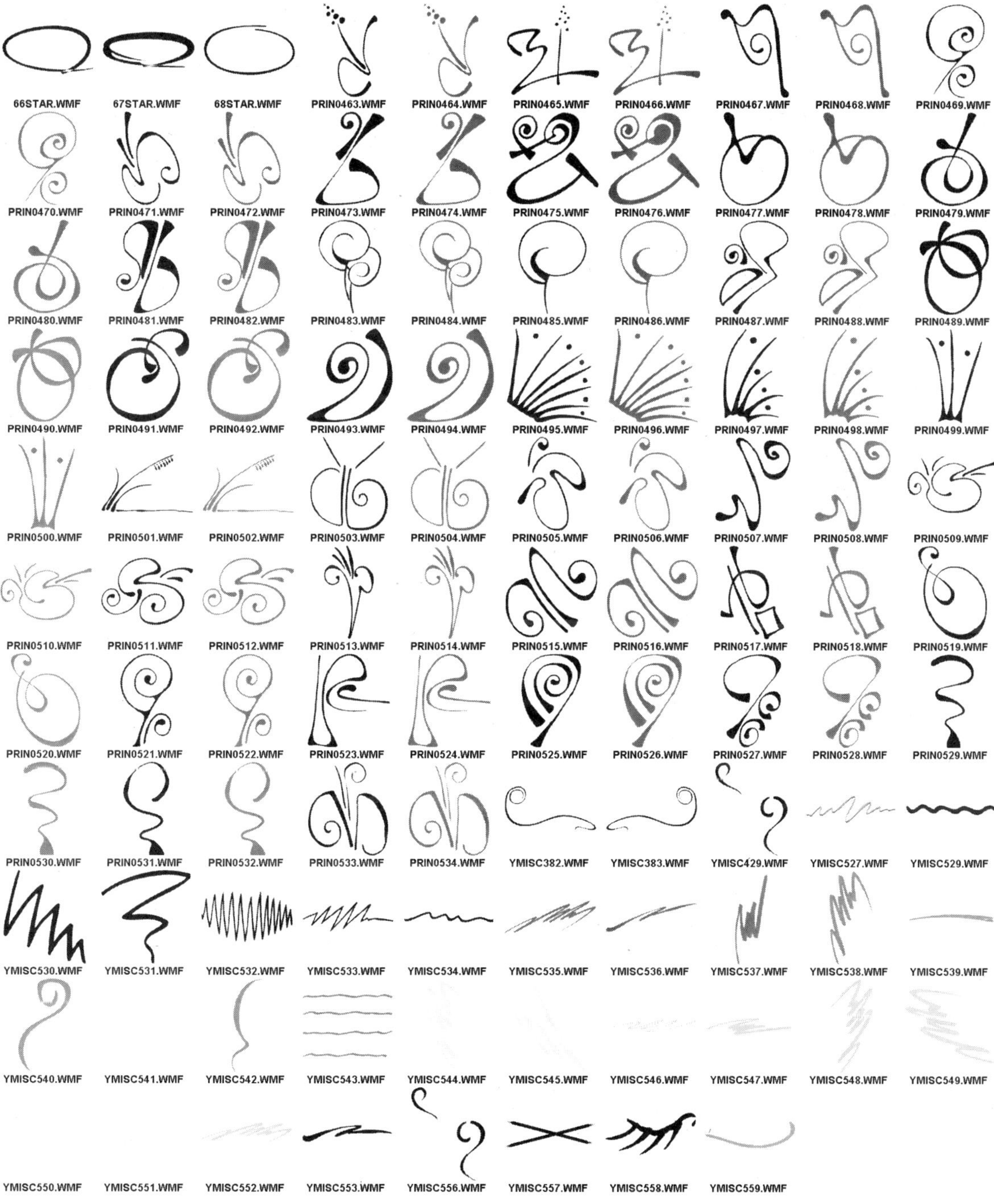
66STAR.WMF
67STAR.WMF
68STAR.WMF
PRIN0463.WMF
PRIN0464.WMF
PRIN0465.WMF
PRIN0466.WMF
PRIN0467.WMF
PRIN0468.WMF
PRIN0469.WMF
PRIN0470.WMF
PRIN0471.WMF
PRIN0472.WMF
PRIN0473.WMF
PRIN0474.WMF
PRIN0475.WMF
PRIN0476.WMF
PRIN0477.WMF
PRIN0478.WMF
PRIN0479.WMF
PRIN0480.WMF
PRIN0481.WMF
PRIN0482.WMF
PRIN0483.WMF
PRIN0484.WMF
PRIN0485.WMF
PRIN0486.WMF
PRIN0487.WMF
PRIN0488.WMF
PRIN0489.WMF
PRIN0490.WMF
PRIN0491.WMF
PRIN0492.WMF
PRIN0493.WMF
PRIN0494.WMF
PRIN0495.WMF
PRIN0496.WMF
PRIN0497.WMF
PRIN0498.WMF
PRIN0499.WMF
PRIN0500.WMF
PRIN0501.WMF
PRIN0502.WMF
PRIN0503.WMF
PRIN0504.WMF
PRIN0505.WMF
PRIN0506.WMF
PRIN0507.WMF
PRIN0508.WMF
PRIN0509.WMF
PRIN0510.WMF
PRIN0511.WMF
PRIN0512.WMF
PRIN0513.WMF
PRIN0514.WMF
PRIN0515.WMF
PRIN0516.WMF
PRIN0517.WMF
PRIN0518.WMF
PRIN0519.WMF
PRIN0520.WMF
PRIN0521.WMF
PRIN0522.WMF
PRIN0523.WMF
PRIN0524.WMF
PRIN0525.WMF
PRIN0526.WMF
PRIN0527.WMF
PRIN0528.WMF
PRIN0529.WMF
PRIN0530.WMF
PRIN0531.WMF
PRIN0532.WMF
PRIN0533.WMF
PRIN0534.WMF
YMISC382.WMF
YMISC383.WMF
YMISC429.WMF
YMISC527.WMF
YMISC529.WMF
YMISC530.WMF
YMISC531.WMF
YMISC532.WMF
YMISC533.WMF
YMISC534.WMF
YMISC535.WMF
YMISC536.WMF
YMISC537.WMF
YMISC538.WMF
YMISC539.WMF
YMISC540.WMF
YMISC541.WMF
YMISC542.WMF
YMISC543.WMF
YMISC544.WMF
YMISC545.WMF
YMISC546.WMF
YMISC547.WMF
YMISC548.WMF
YMISC549.WMF
YMISC550.WMF
YMISC551.WMF
YMISC552.WMF
YMISC553.WMF
YMISC556.WMF
YMISC557.WMF
YMISC558.WMF
YMISC559.WMF

0017BASC.WMF
0070.WMF
0071.WMF
0072.WMF
0073.WMF
0074.WMF
0075.WMF
0076.WMF
0077.WMF
0078.WMF
0079.WMF
0080.WMF
0081.WMF
0569.WMF
0578.WMF
0579.WMF
06BSTAR.WMF
06CSTAR.WMF
0844.WMF
0935.WMF
0936.WMF
0937.WMF
0941.WMF
0942.WMF
0983.WMF
0984.WMF
0986.WMF
0987.WMF
0988.WMF
0990.WMF
0991.WMF
0992.WMF
0993.WMF
0995.WMF
0996.WMF
0998.WMF
0999.WMF
09ASTAR.WMF
09BSTAR.WMF
09CSTAR.WMF
09STAR.WMF
10ASTAR.WMF
10BSTAR.WMF
11ASTAR.WMF
11BSTAR.WMF
11CSTAR.WMF
11DSTAR.WMF
1229.WMF
1230.WMF
1239.WMF
1240.WMF
14ASTAR.WMF
14BSTAR.WMF
15ASTAR.WMF
15BSTAR.WMF
15CSTAR.WMF
16ASTAR.WMF
16BSTAR.WMF
1PURPLE9.WMF
22ASTAR.WMF
22BSTAR.WMF
22CSTAR.WMF
24STAR.WMF
25ASTAR.WMF
25BSTAR.WMF
25CSTAR.WMF
29ASTAR.WMF
29BSTAR.WMF
29CSTAR.WMF
30ASTAR.WMF
30BSTAR.WMF
30CSTAR.WMF
32STAR.WMF
33ASTAR.WMF
33BSTAR.WMF
34ASTAR.WMF
34BSTAR.WMF
39ASTAR.WMF
39BSTAR.WMF
39CSTAR.WMF
39DSTAR.WMF
47ASTAR.WMF
47BSTAR.WMF
47CSTAR.WMF
48ASTAR.WMF
48BSTAR.WMF
48CSTAR.WMF
59STAR.WMF
61ASTAR.WMF
61BSTAR.WMF
62ASTAR.WMF
62BSTAR.WMF
62CSTAR.WMF
70STAR.WMF
76STAR.WMF
81STAR.WMF
AGRAY008.WMF
AGRAY009.WMF
AGRAY010.WMF
AGRAY013.WMF
AGRAY014.WMF
AGRAY015.WMF
AGRAY016.WMF
AGRAY017.WMF
AGRAY018.WMF
AGRAY019.WMF
AGRAY020.WMF
AGRAY021.WMF
AGRAY022.WMF
AGRAY023.WMF
AGRAY032.WMF
AGRAY033.WMF
AGRAY034.WMF
AGRAY035.WMF
AGRAY036.WMF
AGRAY037.WMF
AGRAY038.WMF
AGRAY039.WMF
AGRAY040.WMF
AGRAY041.WMF

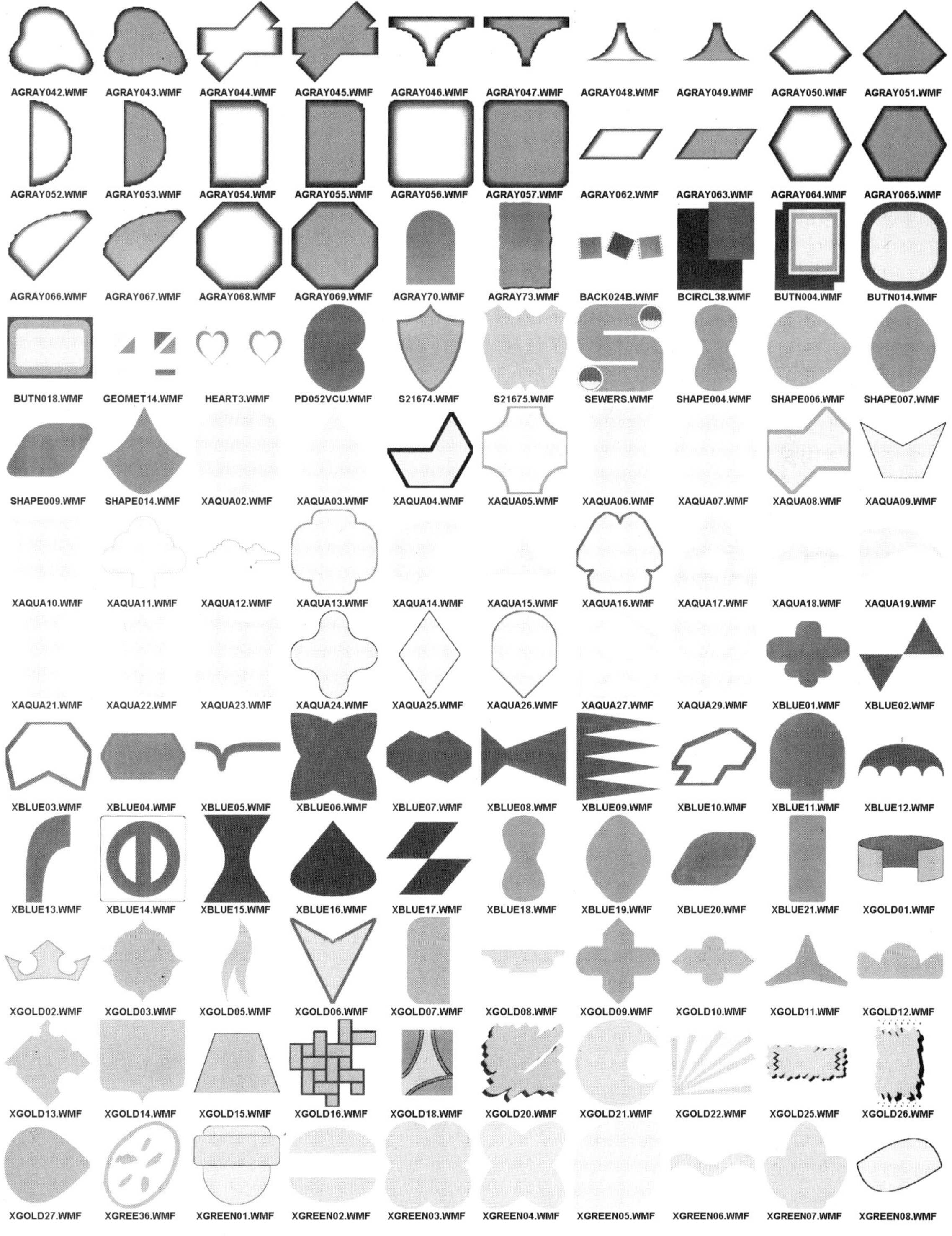
AGRAY042.WMF
AGRAY043.WMF
AGRAY044.WMF
AGRAY045.WMF
AGRAY046.WMF
AGRAY047.WMF
AGRAY048.WMF
AGRAY049.WMF
AGRAY050.WMF
AGRAY051.WMF
AGRAY052.WMF
AGRAY053.WMF
AGRAY054.WMF
AGRAY055.WMF
AGRAY056.WMF
AGRAY057.WMF
AGRAY062.WMF
AGRAY063.WMF
AGRAY064.WMF
AGRAY065.WMF
AGRAY066.WMF
AGRAY067.WMF
AGRAY068.WMF
AGRAY069.WMF
AGRAY70.WMF
AGRAY73.WMF
BACK024B.WMF
BCIRCL38.WMF
BUTN004.WMF
BUTN014.WMF
BUTN018.WMF
GEOMET14.WMF
HEART3.WMF
PD052VCU.WMF
S21674.WMF
S21675.WMF
SEWERS.WMF
SHAPE004.WMF
SHAPE006.WMF
SHAPE007.WMF
SHAPE009.WMF
SHAPE014.WMF
XAQUA02.WMF
XAQUA03.WMF
XAQUA04.WMF
XAQUA05.WMF
XAQUA06.WMF
XAQUA07.WMF
XAQUA08.WMF
XAQUA09.WMF
XAQUA10.WMF
XAQUA11.WMF
XAQUA12.WMF
XAQUA13.WMF
XAQUA14.WMF
XAQUA15.WMF
XAQUA16.WMF
XAQUA17.WMF
XAQUA18.WMF
XAQUA19.WMF
XAQUA21.WMF
XAQUA22.WMF
XAQUA23.WMF
XAQUA24.WMF
XAQUA25.WMF
XAQUA26.WMF
XAQUA27.WMF
XAQUA29.WMF
XBLUE01.WMF
XBLUE02.WMF
XBLUE03.WMF
XBLUE04.WMF
XBLUE05.WMF
XBLUE06.WMF
XBLUE07.WMF
XBLUE08.WMF
XBLUE09.WMF
XBLUE10.WMF
XBLUE11.WMF
XBLUE12.WMF
XBLUE13.WMF
XBLUE14.WMF
XBLUE15.WMF
XBLUE16.WMF
XBLUE17.WMF
XBLUE18.WMF
XBLUE19.WMF
XBLUE20.WMF
XBLUE21.WMF
XGOLD01.WMF
XGOLD02.WMF
XGOLD03.WMF
XGOLD05.WMF
XGOLD06.WMF
XGOLD07.WMF
XGOLD08.WMF
XGOLD09.WMF
XGOLD10.WMF
XGOLD11.WMF
XGOLD12.WMF
XGOLD13.WMF
XGOLD14.WMF
XGOLD15.WMF
XGOLD16.WMF
XGOLD18.WMF
XGOLD20.WMF
XGOLD21.WMF
XGOLD22.WMF
XGOLD25.WMF
XGOLD26.WMF
XGOLD27.WMF
XGREE36.WMF
XGREEN01.WMF
XGREEN02.WMF
XGREEN03.WMF
XGREEN04.WMF
XGREEN05.WMF
XGREEN06.WMF
XGREEN07.WMF
XGREEN08.WMF

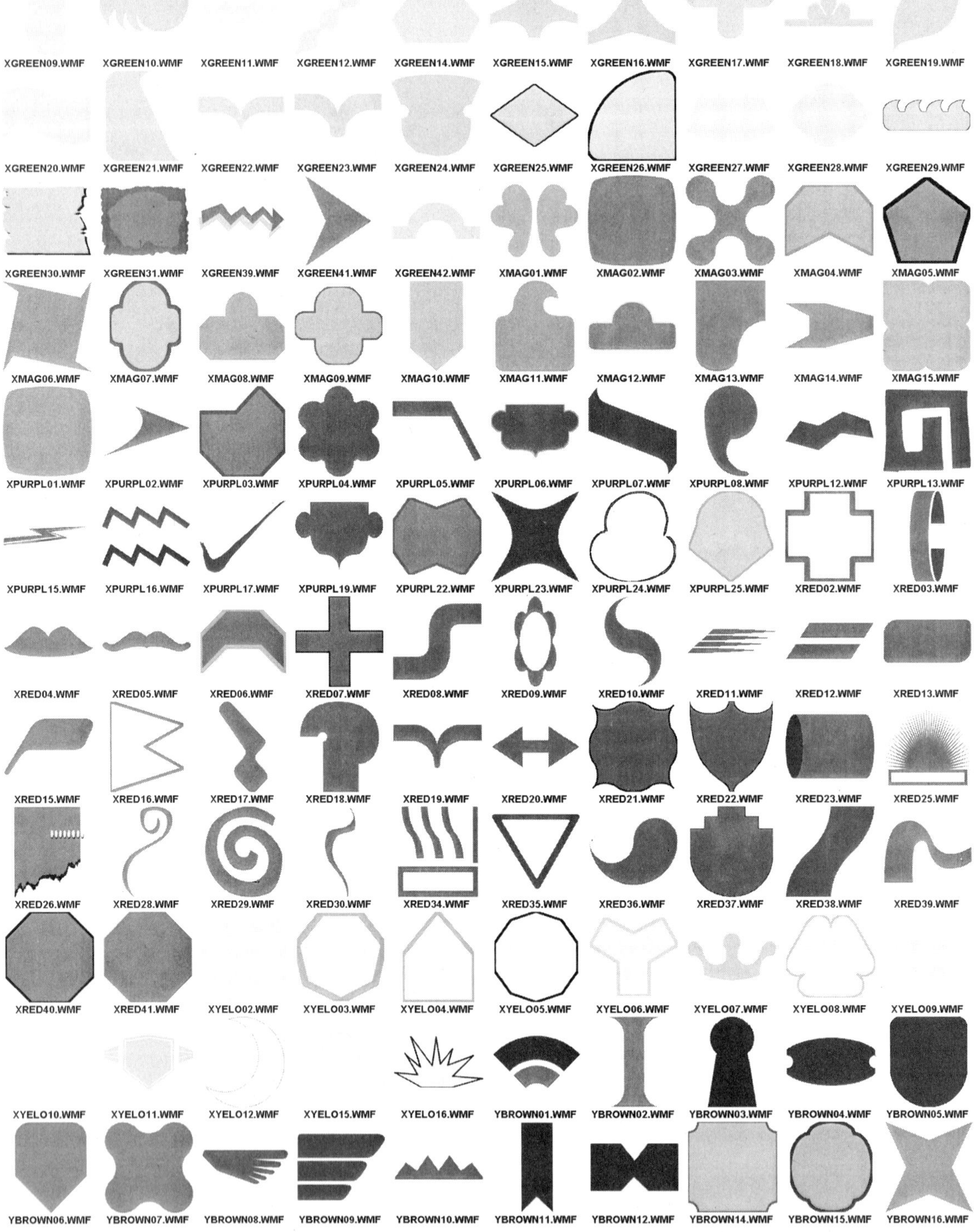
XGREEN09.WMF
XGREEN10.WMF
XGREEN11.WMF
XGREEN12.WMF
XGREEN14.WMF
XGREEN15.WMF
XGREEN16.WMF
XGREEN17.WMF
XGREEN18.WMF
XGREEN19.WMF
XGREEN20.WMF
XGREEN21.WMF
XGREEN22.WMF
XGREEN23.WMF
XGREEN24.WMF
XGREEN25.WMF
XGREEN26.WMF
XGREEN27.WMF
XGREEN28.WMF
XGREEN29.WMF
XGREEN30.WMF
XGREEN31.WMF
XGREEN39.WMF
XGREEN41.WMF
XGREEN42.WMF
XMAG01.WMF
XMAG02.WMF
XMAG03.WMF
XMAG04.WMF
XMAG05.WMF
XMAG06.WMF
XMAG07.WMF
XMAG08.WMF
XMAG09.WMF
XMAG10.WMF
XMAG11.WMF
XMAG12.WMF
XMAG13.WMF
XMAG14.WMF
XMAG15.WMF
XPURPL01.WMF
XPURPL02.WMF
XPURPL03.WMF
XPURPL04.WMF
XPURPL05.WMF
XPURPL06.WMF
XPURPL07.WMF
XPURPL08.WMF
XPURPL12.WMF
XPURPL13.WMF
XPURPL15.WMF
XPURPL16.WMF
XPURPL17.WMF
XPURPL19.WMF
XPURPL22.WMF
XPURPL23.WMF
XPURPL24.WMF
XPURPL25.WMF
XRED02.WMF
XRED03.WMF
XRED04.WMF
XRED05.WMF
XRED06.WMF
XRED07.WMF
XRED08.WMF
XRED09.WMF
XRED10.WMF
XRED11.WMF
XRED12.WMF
XRED13.WMF
XRED15.WMF
XRED16.WMF
XRED17.WMF
XRED18.WMF
XRED19.WMF
XRED20.WMF
XRED21.WMF
XRED22.WMF
XRED23.WMF
XRED25.WMF
XRED26.WMF
XRED28.WMF
XRED29.WMF
XRED30.WMF
XRED34.WMF
XRED35.WMF
XRED36.WMF
XRED37.WMF
XRED38.WMF
XRED39.WMF
XRED40.WMF
XRED41.WMF
XYELO02.WMF
XYELO03.WMF
XYELO04.WMF
XYELO05.WMF
XYELO06.WMF
XYELO07.WMF
XYELO08.WMF
XYELO09.WMF
XYELO10.WMF
XYELO11.WMF
XYELO12.WMF
XYELO15.WMF
XYELO16.WMF
YBROWN01.WMF
YBROWN02.WMF
YBROWN03.WMF
YBROWN04.WMF
YBROWN05.WMF
YBROWN06.WMF
YBROWN07.WMF
YBROWN08.WMF
YBROWN09.WMF
YBROWN10.WMF
YBROWN11.WMF
YBROWN12.WMF
YBROWN14.WMF
YBROWN15.WMF
YBROWN16.WMF

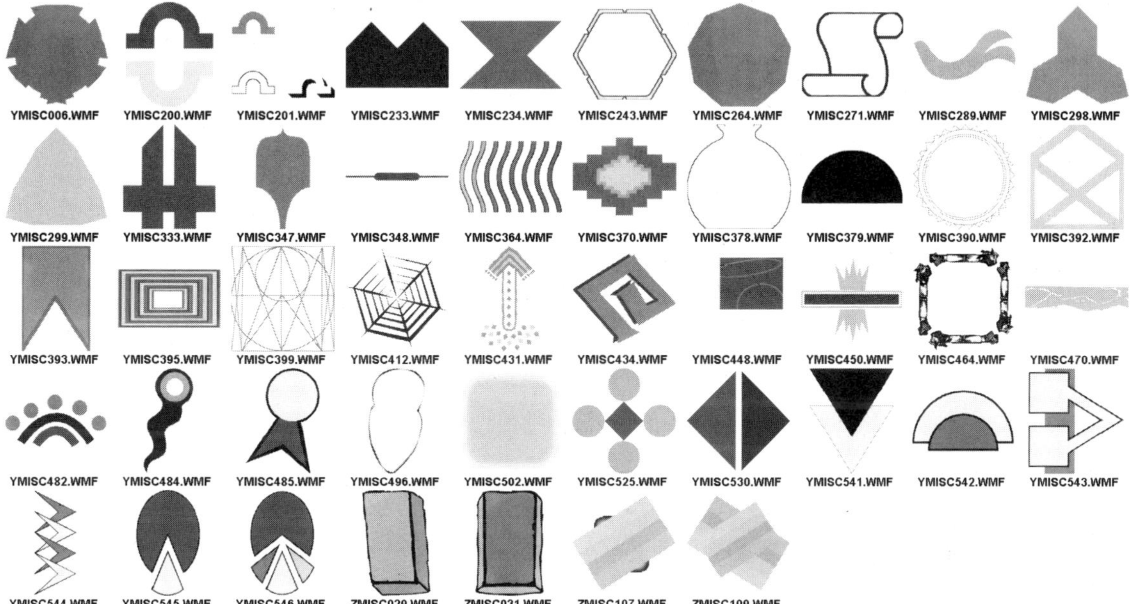
YMISC006.WMF
YMISC200.WMF
YMISC201.WMF
YMISC233.WMF
YMISC234.WMF
YMISC243.WMF
YMISC264.WMF
YMISC271.WMF
YMISC289.WMF
YMISC298.WMF
YMISC299.WMF
YMISC333.WMF
YMISC347.WMF
YMISC348.WMF
YMISC364.WMF
YMISC370.WMF
YMISC378.WMF
YMISC379.WMF
YMISC390.WMF
YMISC392.WMF
YMISC393.WMF
YMISC395.WMF
YMISC399.WMF
YMISC412.WMF
YMISC431.WMF
YMISC434.WMF
YMISC448.WMF
YMISC450.WMF
YMISC464.WMF
YMISC470.WMF
YMISC482.WMF
YMISC484.WMF
YMISC485.WMF
YMISC496.WMF
YMISC502.WMF
YMISC525.WMF
YMISC530.WMF
YMISC541.WMF
YMISC542.WMF
YMISC543.WMF
YMISC544.WMF
YMISC545.WMF
YMISC546.WMF
ZMISC029.WMF
ZMISC031.WMF
ZMISC107.WMF
ZMISC109.WMF

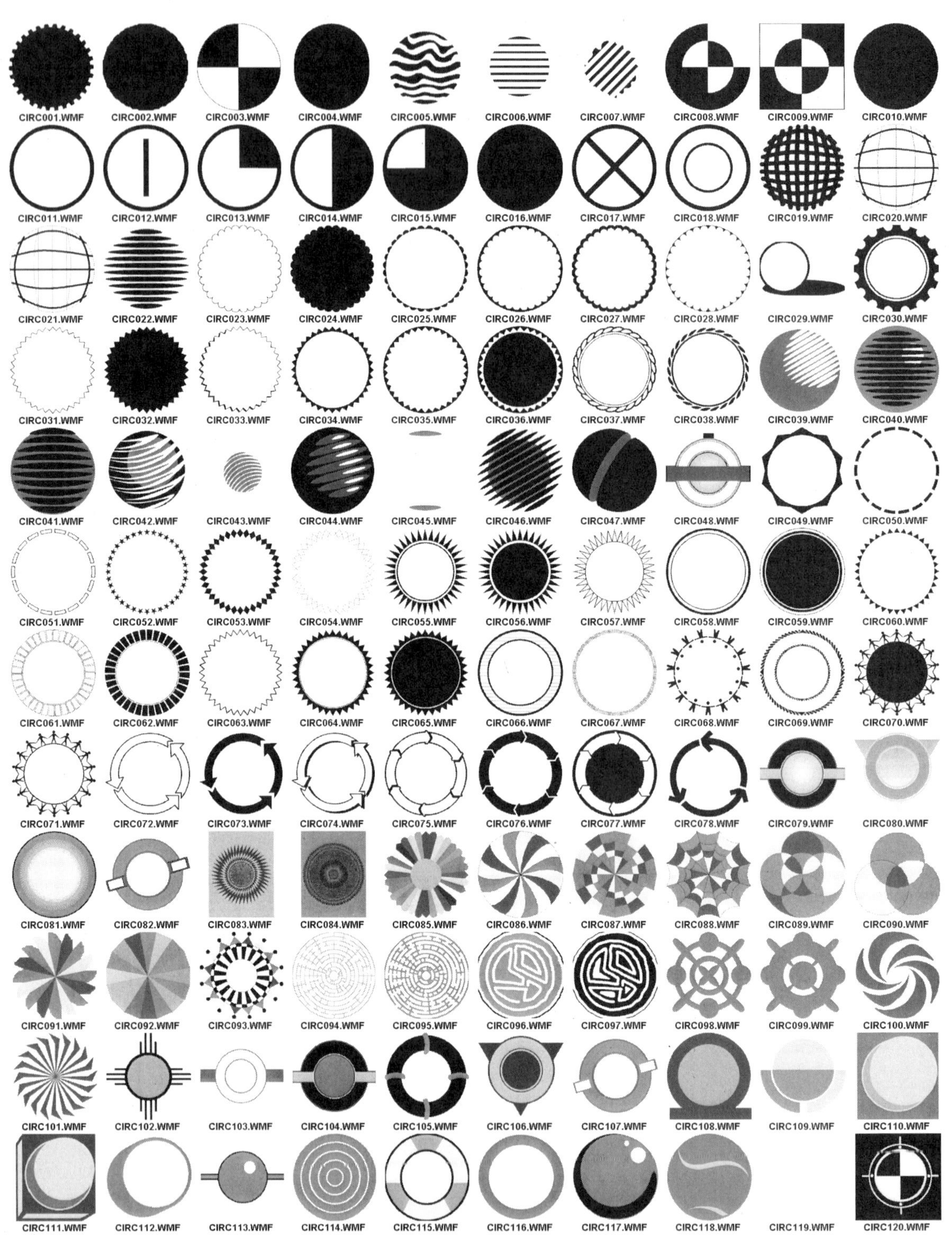
CIRC001.WMF CIRC002.WMF CIRC003.WMF CIRC004.WMF CIRC005.WMF CIRC006.WMF CIRC007.WMF CIRC008.WMF CIRC009.WMF CIRC010.WMF
CIRC011.WMF CIRC012.WMF CIRC013.WMF CIRC014.WMF CIRC015.WMF CIRC016.WMF CIRC017.WMF CIRC018.WMF CIRC019.WMF CIRC020.WMF
CIRC021.WMF CIRC022.WMF CIRC023.WMF CIRC024.WMF CIRC025.WMF CIRC026.WMF CIRC027.WMF CIRC028.WMF CIRC029.WMF CIRC030.WMF
CIRC031.WMF CIRC032.WMF CIRC033.WMF CIRC034.WMF CIRC035.WMF CIRC036.WMF CIRC037.WMF CIRC038.WMF CIRC039.WMF CIRC040.WMF
CIRC041.WMF CIRC042.WMF CIRC043.WMF CIRC044.WMF CIRC045.WMF CIRC046.WMF CIRC047.WMF CIRC048.WMF CIRC049.WMF CIRC050.WMF
CIRC051.WMF CIRC052.WMF CIRC053.WMF CIRC054.WMF CIRC055.WMF CIRC056.WMF CIRC057.WMF CIRC058.WMF CIRC059.WMF CIRC060.WMF
CIRC061.WMF CIRC062.WMF CIRC063.WMF CIRC064.WMF CIRC065.WMF CIRC066.WMF CIRC067.WMF CIRC068.WMF CIRC069.WMF CIRC070.WMF
CIRC071.WMF CIRC072.WMF CIRC073.WMF CIRC074.WMF CIRC075.WMF CIRC076.WMF CIRC077.WMF CIRC078.WMF CIRC079.WMF CIRC080.WMF
CIRC081.WMF CIRC082.WMF CIRC083.WMF CIRC084.WMF CIRC085.WMF CIRC086.WMF CIRC087.WMF CIRC088.WMF CIRC089.WMF CIRC090.WMF
CIRC091.WMF CIRC092.WMF CIRC093.WMF CIRC094.WMF CIRC095.WMF CIRC096.WMF CIRC097.WMF CIRC098.WMF CIRC099.WMF CIRC100.WMF
CIRC101.WMF CIRC102.WMF CIRC103.WMF CIRC104.WMF CIRC105.WMF CIRC106.WMF CIRC107.WMF CIRC108.WMF CIRC109.WMF CIRC110.WMF
CIRC111.WMF CIRC112.WMF CIRC113.WMF CIRC114.WMF CIRC115.WMF CIRC116.WMF CIRC117.WMF CIRC118.WMF CIRC119.WMF CIRC120.WMF

CIRC121.WMF
CIRC122.WMF
CIRC123.WMF
CIRC124.WMF
CIRC125.WMF
CIRC126.WMF
CIRC127.WMF
CIRC128.WMF
CIRC129.WMF
CIRC130.WMF
CIRC131.WMF
CIRC132.WMF
CIRC133.WMF
CIRC134.WMF
CIRC135.WMF
CIRC136.WMF
CIRC137.WMF
CIRC138.WMF
CIRC139.WMF
CIRC140.WMF
CIRC141.WMF
CIRC142.WMF
CIRC143.WMF
CIRC144.WMF
CIRC145.WMF
CIRC146.WMF
CIRC147.WMF
CIRC148.WMF
CIRC149.WMF
CIRC150.WMF
CIRC151.WMF
CIRC152.WMF
CIRC153.WMF
CIRC154.WMF
CIRC155.WMF
CIRC156.WMF
CIRC157.WMF
CIRC158.WMF
CIRC159.WMF
CIRC160.WMF
CIRC161.WMF
CIRC162.WMF
CIRC163.WMF
CIRC164.WMF
CIRC165.WMF
CIRC166.WMF
CIRC167.WMF
CIRC168.WMF
CIRC169.WMF
CIRC170.WMF
CIRC171.WMF
CIRC172.WMF
CIRC173.WMF
CIRC174.WMF
CIRC175.WMF
CIRC176.WMF
CIRC177.WMF
CIRC178.WMF
CIRC179.WMF
CIRC180.WMF
CIRC181.WMF
CIRC182.WMF
CIRC183.WMF
CIRC184.WMF
CIRC185.WMF
CIRC186.WMF
CIRC187.WMF
CIRC188.WMF
CIRC189.WMF
CIRC190.WMF
CIRC191.WMF
CIRC192.WMF
CIRC193.WMF
OVAL01.WMF
OVAL02.WMF
OVAL03.WMF
OVAL04.WMF
OVAL05.WMF
OVAL06.WMF
OVAL07.WMF
OVAL08.WMF
OVAL09.WMF
OVAL10.WMF
OVAL11.WMF
OVAL12.WMF
OVAL13.WMF
OVAL14.WMF
OVAL15.WMF
OVAL16.WMF
OVAL17.WMF
OVAL18.WMF
OVAL19.WMF
OVAL20.WMF
OVAL21.WMF
OVAL22.WMF
RECT01.WMF
RECT02.WMF
RECT03.WMF
RECT04.WMF
RECT05.WMF
RECT06.WMF
RECT07.WMF
RECT08.WMF
RECT09.WMF
RECT10.WMF
RECT11.WMF
RECT12.WMF
RECT13.WMF
RECT14.WMF
RECT15.WMF
RECT16.WMF
RECT17.WMF
RECT18.WMF
RECT19.WMF
RECT20.WMF
RECT21.WMF
RECT22.WMF
RECT23.WMF
RECT24.WMF
RECT25.WMF

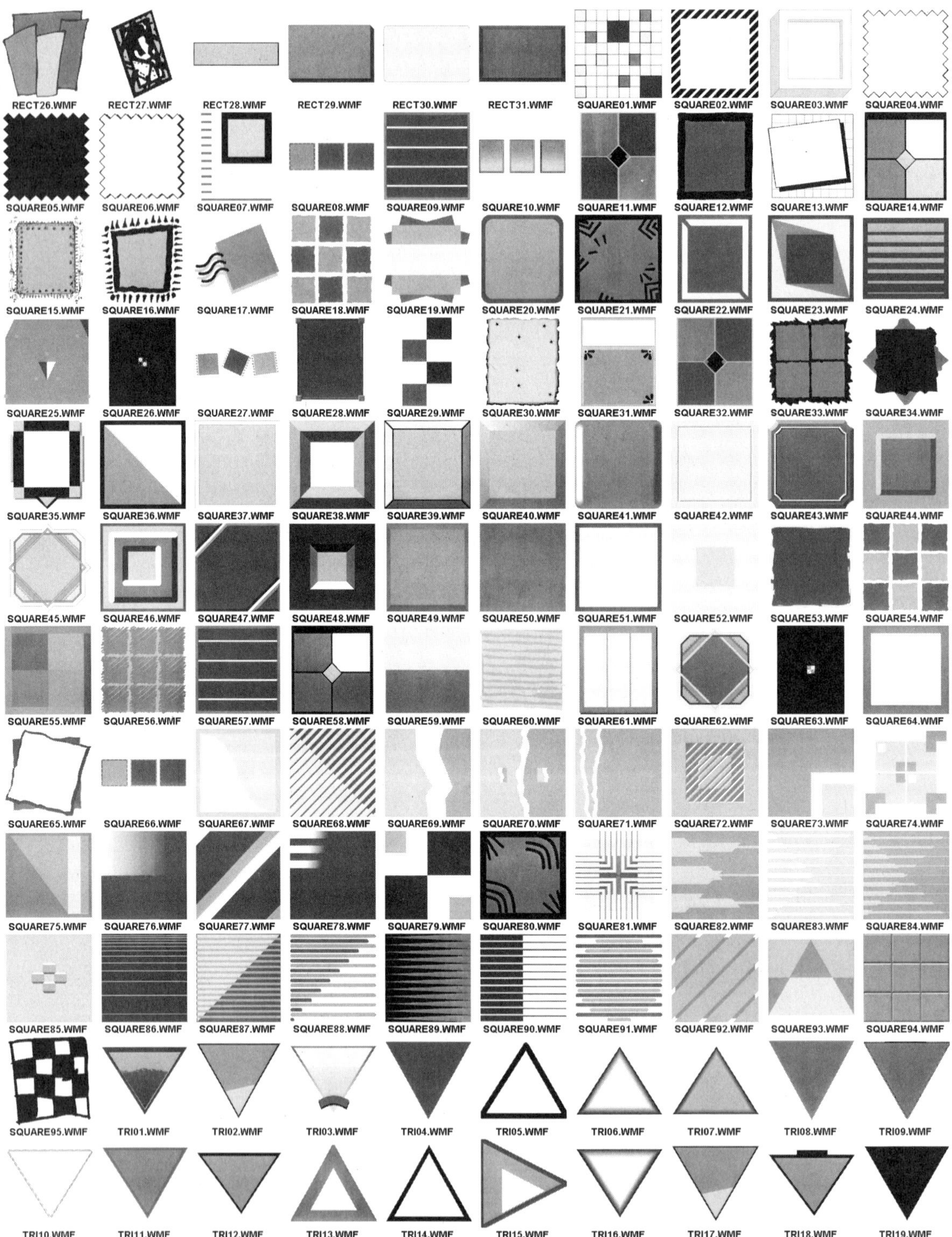
RECT26.WMF RECT27.WMF RECT28.WMF RECT29.WMF RECT30.WMF RECT31.WMF SQUARE01.WMF SQUARE02.WMF SQUARE03.WMF SQUARE04.WMF
SQUARE05.WMF SQUARE06.WMF SQUARE07.WMF SQUARE08.WMF SQUARE09.WMF SQUARE10.WMF SQUARE11.WMF SQUARE12.WMF SQUARE13.WMF SQUARE14.WMF
SQUARE15.WMF SQUARE16.WMF SQUARE17.WMF SQUARE18.WMF SQUARE19.WMF SQUARE20.WMF SQUARE21.WMF SQUARE22.WMF SQUARE23.WMF SQUARE24.WMF
SQUARE25.WMF SQUARE26.WMF SQUARE27.WMF SQUARE28.WMF SQUARE29.WMF SQUARE30.WMF SQUARE31.WMF SQUARE32.WMF SQUARE33.WMF SQUARE34.WMF
SQUARE35.WMF SQUARE36.WMF SQUARE37.WMF SQUARE38.WMF SQUARE39.WMF SQUARE40.WMF SQUARE41.WMF SQUARE42.WMF SQUARE43.WMF SQUARE44.WMF
SQUARE45.WMF SQUARE46.WMF SQUARE47.WMF SQUARE48.WMF SQUARE49.WMF SQUARE50.WMF SQUARE51.WMF SQUARE52.WMF SQUARE53.WMF SQUARE54.WMF
SQUARE55.WMF SQUARE56.WMF SQUARE57.WMF SQUARE58.WMF SQUARE59.WMF SQUARE60.WMF SQUARE61.WMF SQUARE62.WMF SQUARE63.WMF SQUARE64.WMF
SQUARE65.WMF SQUARE66.WMF SQUARE67.WMF SQUARE68.WMF SQUARE69.WMF SQUARE70.WMF SQUARE71.WMF SQUARE72.WMF SQUARE73.WMF SQUARE74.WMF
SQUARE75.WMF SQUARE76.WMF SQUARE77.WMF SQUARE78.WMF SQUARE79.WMF SQUARE80.WMF SQUARE81.WMF SQUARE82.WMF SQUARE83.WMF SQUARE84.WMF
SQUARE85.WMF SQUARE86.WMF SQUARE87.WMF SQUARE88.WMF SQUARE89.WMF SQUARE90.WMF SQUARE91.WMF SQUARE92.WMF SQUARE93.WMF SQUARE94.WMF
SQUARE95.WMF TRI01.WMF TRI02.WMF TRI03.WMF TRI04.WMF TRI05.WMF TRI06.WMF TRI07.WMF TRI08.WMF TRI09.WMF
TRI10.WMF TRI11.WMF TRI12.WMF TRI13.WMF TRI14.WMF TRI15.WMF TRI16.WMF TRI17.WMF TRI18.WMF TRI19.WMF

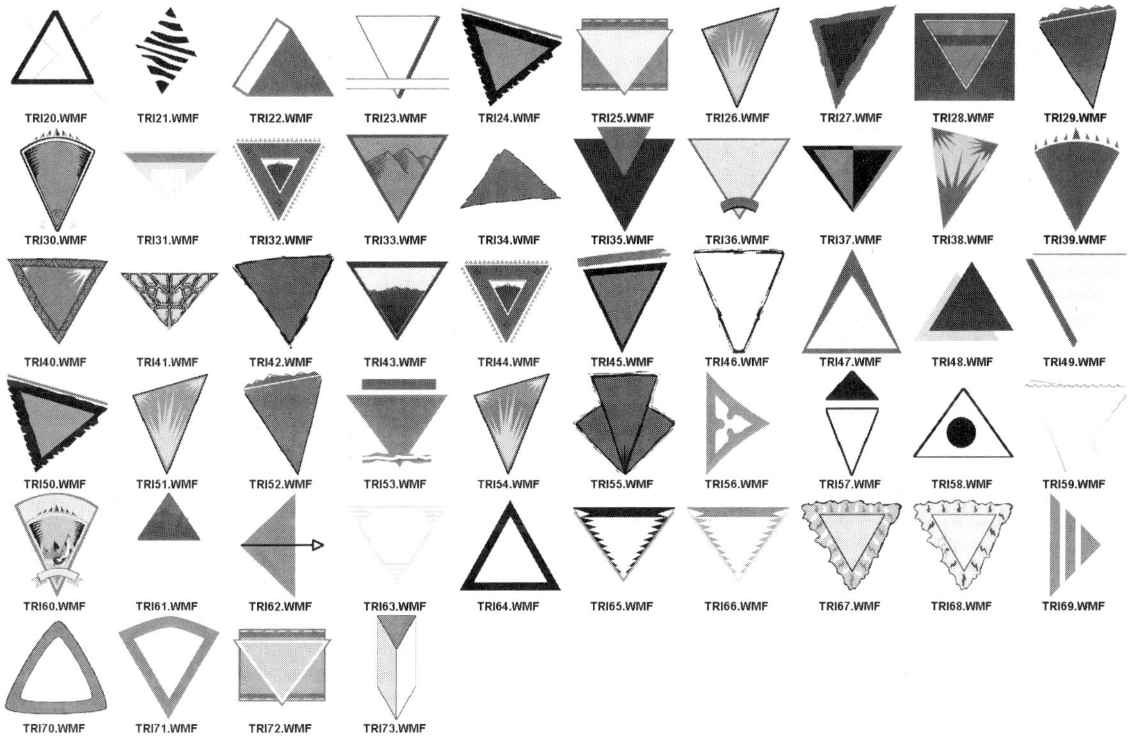
TRI20.WMF
TRI21.WMF
TRI22.WMF
TRI23.WMF
TRI24.WMF
TRI25.WMF
TRI26.WMF
TRI27.WMF
TRI28.WMF
TRI29.WMF
TRI30.WMF
TRI31.WMF
TRI32.WMF
TRI33.WMF
TRI34.WMF
TRI35.WMF
TRI36.WMF
TRI37.WMF
TRI38.WMF
TRI39.WMF
TRI40.WMF
TRI41.WMF
TRI42.WMF
TRI43.WMF
TRI44.WMF
TRI45.WMF
TRI46.WMF
TRI47.WMF
TRI48.WMF
TRI49.WMF
TRI50.WMF
TRI51.WMF
TRI52.WMF
TRI53.WMF
TRI54.WMF
TRI55.WMF
TRI56.WMF
TRI57.WMF
TRI58.WMF
TRI59.WMF
TRI60.WMF
TRI61.WMF
TRI62.WMF
TRI63.WMF
TRI64.WMF
TRI65.WMF
TRI66.WMF
TRI67.WMF
TRI68.WMF
TRI69.WMF
TRI70.WMF
TRI71.WMF
TRI72.WMF
TRI73.WMF

0012BASC.WMF
0574.WMF
0634OCTC.WMF
0749STAC.WMF
0750STAC.WMF
0751STAC.WMF
0752STAC.WMF
0753STAC.WMF
0754STAC.WMF
0837.WMF
1198STAC.WMF
1199STAC.WMF
1213.WMF
1253.WMF
13ASTAR.WMF
13BSTAR.WMF
13CSTAR.WMF
1954.WMF
28ASTAR.WMF
28BSTAR.WMF
63ASTAR.WMF
63BSTAR.WMF
63CSTAR.WMF
AGRAY024.WMF
AGRAY025.WMF
AGRAY026.WMF
AGRAY027.WMF
AGRAY028.WMF
AGRAY029.WMF
AGRAY030.WMF
AGRAY031.WMF
AQTRI10.WMF
AQTRI11.WMF
BIT0163.WMF
BIT1004.WMF
BIT1057.WMF
BIT1058.WMF
BUTN012.WMF
COMPASS.WMF
DESIGN21.WMF
DESIGN22.WMF
FLASH.WMF
GRPHC001.WMF
GRPHC133.WMF
GRPHC135.WMF
GRPHC136.WMF
GRPHC137.WMF
GRSO038J.WMF
LASERLIT.WMF
MISC_12.WMF
NABO034J.WMF
PRIN0421.WMF
PRIN0422.WMF
PRIN0423.WMF
PRIN0424.WMF
PRIN0425.WMF
PRIN0426.WMF
PRIN0427.WMF
PRIN0428.WMF
S21656.WMF
S21682.WMF
S21683.WMF
S21684.WMF
S21709.WMF
S21710.WMF
S21711.WMF
S21716.WMF
S21717.WMF
SHAPE001.WMF
SHAPE005.WMF
SHAPE006.WMF
SHAPE007.WMF
SHAPE080.WMF
SHAPE081.WMF
SHAPE106.WMF
SHAPE115.WMF
SHAPE144.WMF
SHAPE151.WMF
SHAPE156.WMF
SHAPE164.WMF
SHAPE276.WMF
SHAPE287.WMF
STAR.WMF
STAR001.WMF
STAR002.WMF
STAR004.WMF
STAR005.WMF
STAR012.WMF
STAR013.WMF
STAR014.WMF
STAR015.WMF
STAR017.WMF
STAR018.WMF
STAR019.WMF
STAR041.WMF
STAR042.WMF
STAR043.WMF
STAR044.WMF
STAR045.WMF
STAR046.WMF
STAR048.WMF
STAR051.WMF
STAR052.WMF
STAR056.WMF
STAR34.WMF
STAR37.WMF
STAR4.WMF
STAR5PTS.WMF
STAR_B.WMF
STARBRST.WMF
STARBURB.WMF
STARFAD1.WMF
STARS.WMF
STARS060.WMF
STARS2.WMF
STARS50Z.WMF
STARS52Z.WMF
STARS53Z.WMF
STARS55Z.WMF
STARS56Z.WMF

STARS57Z.WMF
STARS58Z.WMF
STARS59Z.WMF
STARS61Z.WMF
STARS_EX.WMF
STARSYMB.WMF
W21922.WMF
XGOLD17.WMF
XGOLD19.WMF
YMISC425.WMF
YMISC433.WMF
YMISC473.WMF
YMISC483.WMF
YMISC490.WMF
YMISC491.WMF
YMISC492.WMF
YMISC504.WMF
ZMISC111.WMF

CAUSGN44.WMF CAUSGN46.WMF CAUSGN48.WMF CAUSGN50.WMF CAUSGN52.WMF CAUTAG01.WMF CAUTAG03.WMF CAUTAG05.WMF CAUTAG07.WMF CAUTAG09.WMF

CAUTAG11.WMF CAUTAG13.WMF CAUTAG15.WMF CAUTAG17.WMF CAUTION2.WMF EXPLOSIV.WMF FLAMGAS1.WMF FLAMGAS2.WMF FLAMSO1.WMF FLAMSO2.WMF

HARMFUL.WMF SIGN008.WMF SIGN046.WMF SIGN047.WMF SIGN048.WMF SIGN051.WMF SIGN052.WMF SIGN053.WMF SIGN054.WMF SIGN055.WMF

SIGN056.WMF SIGN057.WMF SIGN058.WMF SIGN059.WMF SIGN060.WMF SIGN067.WMF SIGN068.WMF SIGN069.WMF SIGN070.WMF SIGN071.WMF

SIGN072.WMF SIGN080.WMF SIGN081.WMF SIGN082.WMF

Signs • Danger

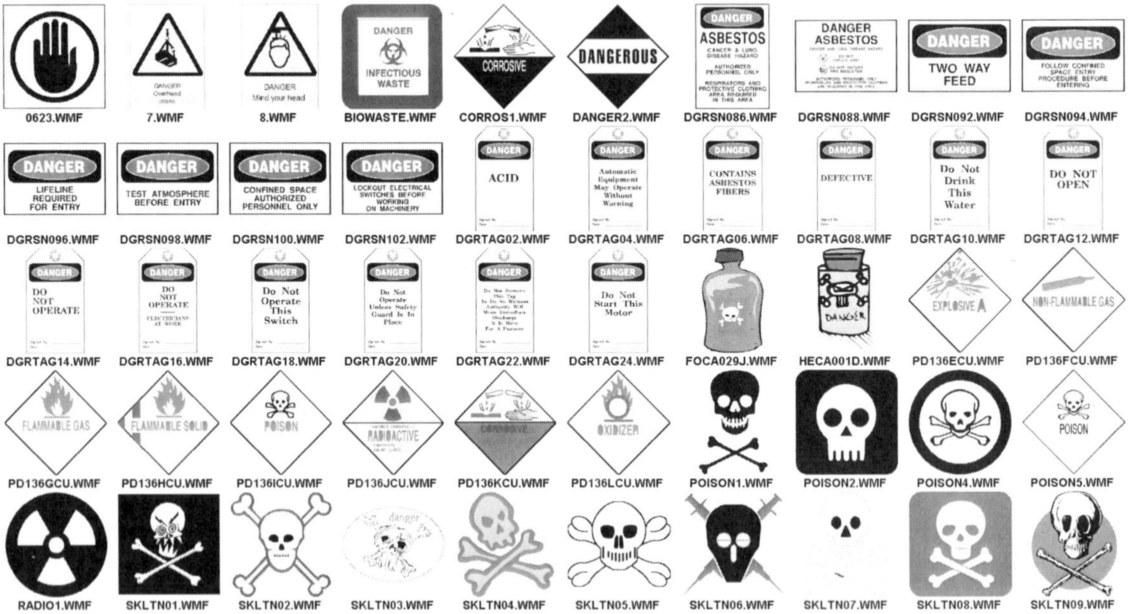

0623.WMF 7.WMF 8.WMF BIOWASTE.WMF CORROS1.WMF DANGER2.WMF DGRSN086.WMF DGRSN088.WMF DGRSN092.WMF DGRSN094.WMF

DGRSN096.WMF DGRSN098.WMF DGRSN100.WMF DGRSN102.WMF DGRTAG02.WMF DGRTAG04.WMF DGRTAG06.WMF DGRTAG08.WMF DGRTAG10.WMF DGRTAG12.WMF

DGRTAG14.WMF DGRTAG16.WMF DGRTAG18.WMF DGRTAG20.WMF DGRTAG22.WMF DGRTAG24.WMF FOCA029J.WMF HECA001D.WMF PD136ECU.WMF PD136FCU.WMF

PD136GCU.WMF PD136HCU.WMF PD136ICU.WMF PD136JCU.WMF PD136KCU.WMF PD136LCU.WMF POISON1.WMF POISON2.WMF POISON4.WMF POISON5.WMF

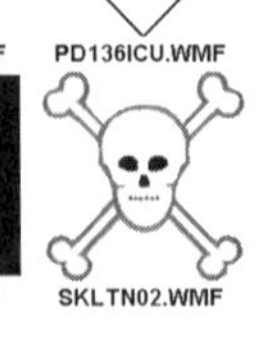

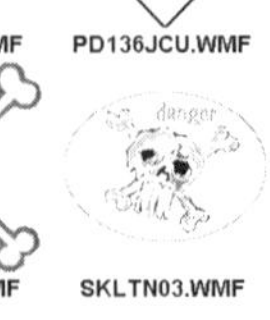

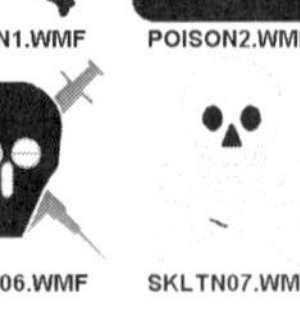

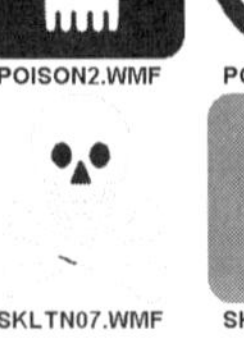

RADIO1.WMF SKLTN01.WMF SKLTN02.WMF SKLTN03.WMF SKLTN04.WMF SKLTN05.WMF SKLTN06.WMF SKLTN07.WMF SKLTN08.WMF SKLTN09.WMF

01RECYC.WMF
02RECYC.WMF
03RECYC.WMF
04RECYC.WMF
RECYCLE
05RECYC.WMF
0618.WMF
06RECYC.WMF
07RECYC.WMF
08RECYC.WMF
09RECYC.WMF
10RECYC.WMF
11RECYC.WMF
12RECYC.WMF
13RECYC.WMF
14RECYC.WMF
15RECYC.WMF
16RECYC.WMF
17RECYC.WMF
RECYCLE
18RECYC.WMF
19RECYC.WMF
20RECYC.WMF
ACIDFREE.WMF
AIR.WMF
AMERICA RECYCLES
AMERRECY.WMF
ARROCIRC.WMF
CANS
CANRECEP.WMF
ENVIRONMENTALLY SAFE
ENVIRSAF.WMF
fight litter
RECYCLE
FIGHTLIT.WMF
GLASS RECYCLES
GLASREC1.WMF
Glass Recycles
GLASREC2.WMF
GLASS
GLASRECP.WMF
GLOBE1.WMF
GLOBE2.WMF
GLOBE3.WMF
HHCA101J.WMF
ICON005.WMF
ICON006.WMF
ICON007.WMF
ICON009.WMF
ICON026.WMF
ICON029.WMF
ICON031.WMF
ICON052.WMF
LAND.WMF
NOISE.WMF
Oil
OILRECY.WMF
CONTAINS NO PROPELIANT ALLEGED TO DAMAGE OZONE
OZSAFE1.WMF
CONTAINS NO PROPELLANT ALLEGED TO DAMAGE OZONE
OZSAFE2.WMF
OZONE FRIENDLY NO CFC'S
OZSAFE3.WMF
No CFC's Environmentally Safe
OZSAFE4.WMF
PAPER
PAPERCPT.WMF
Pitch In!
PITCHIN1.WMF
Pitch-In
PITCHIN2.WMF
POPULATN.WMF
Read Then Recycle.
READRECY.WMF
recyclable aluminum
RECYALUM.WMF
RECYCLABLE BIODEGRADABLE RENEWABLE RESOURCE
RECYCBL1.WMF
100% RECYCLABLE BIODEGRADABLE
RECYCBL2.WMF
RECYCBL3.WMF
RECYCL01.WMF
RECYCL04.WMF
RECYCL05.WMF
RECYCL06.WMF
RECYCL07.WMF
RECYCL08.WMF
GENUINE RECYCLED PAPER 10 INCLUDES 10% POST-CONSUMER WASTE
RECYCL10.WMF
RECYCL11.WMF
RECYCL13.WMF
RECYCL16.WMF
RECYCL18.WMF
PLASTIC
RECYCL20.WMF
PAPER
RECYCL21.WMF
CANS
RECYCL22.WMF
RECYCL23.WMF
RECYCL24.WMF
recycle
RECYCL25.WMF
RECYCL26.WMF
RECYCLD1.WMF
DER GRÜNE PUNKT
RECYCLD2.WMF
MADE FROM RECYCLED MATERIALS
RECYCMAT.WMF
Corrugated Recycles
RECYCORR.WMF
Printed on recyclable paper
RECYCPAP.WMF
RECYCLE SOFT DRINK PLASTIC
RECYCPLA.WMF
RECYCLED PAPER
RECYDPAP.WMF
RECYCLED POLYSTYRENE
RECYDPOL.WMF
Steel the recycled material
RECYDST1.WMF
STEEL
RECYDST2.WMF
RECYCLABLE A RENEWABLE RESOURCE
RENEWRES.WMF
SAVE-A-TREE
SAVATREE.WMF
1
PETE
SPI1.WMF
2
HDPE
SPI2.WMF
3
V
SPI3.WMF
4
LDPE
SPI4.WMF
5
PP
SPI5.WMF
6
PS
SPI6.WMF
7
Other
SPI7.WMF
SUN1.WMF
SUN2.WMF
TONERECH.WMF
TRASH
TRASHRCT.WMF
TREE.WMF
PRINTED WITH VEGETABLE BASED INK ENVIRONMENTALLY SAFE
VEGINK.WMF
WATER.WMF
WE CAN MAKE A WORLD OF DIFFERENCE
WRLDDIFF.WMF

DIRFIRE.WMF EXIT001.WMF EXIT003.WMF EXIT005.WMF EXIT007.WMF EXIT009.WMF EXIT011.WMF EXIT013.WMF FIRE001.WMF FIRE002.WMF

FIRE003.WMF FIRE004.WMF FIRE005.WMF FIRE006.WMF FIRE007.WMF FIRE008.WMF FIRE009.WMF FIRE010.WMF FIRE011.WMF FIRE012.WMF

FIREALM3.WMF FIREHOS1.WMF FIREHOS2.WMF FIRESCP1.WMF FIRESCP2.WMF FIRXTNG1.WMF FIRXTNG2.WMF PD095BCU.WMF PD095CCU.WMF PD096ECU.WMF

Signs • Handicapped (HANDICAP)

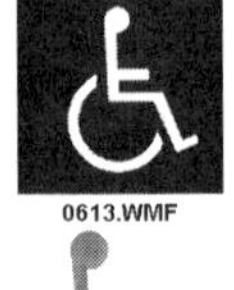

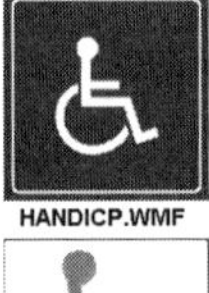
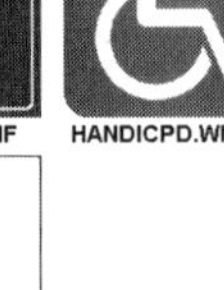

0613.WMF 1787.WMF DISABLED.WMF FORESCP3.WMF HANDCAP1.WMF HANDICAP.WMF HANDICP.WMF HANDICPD.WMF HNDICPD2.WMF ICON068.WMF

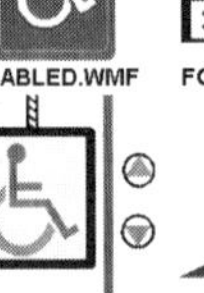
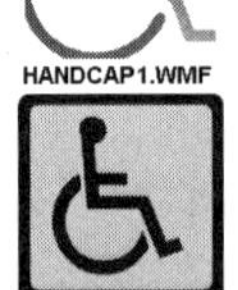

PD082BCU.WMF PD100ICU.WMF PD120BCU.WMF REAL08.WMF SIGN077.WMF WHELCHR1.WMF WHELCHR2.WMF

Signs • Hazardous Materials (HAZMAT)

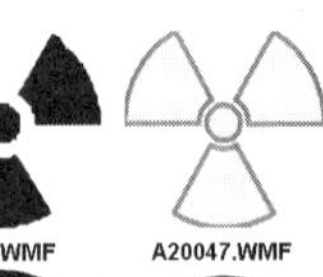

0601.WMF 0818.WMF A20047.WMF BIOHAZ1.WMF BIOHAZ2.WMF BIOHAZD.WMF DGRSN090.WMF FALSHTR.WMF HAZWASTE.WMF ICON089.WMF

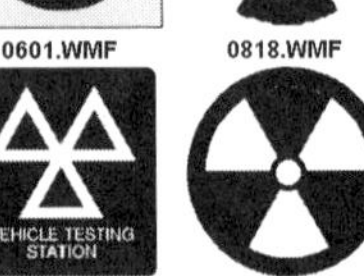

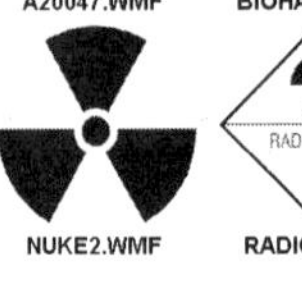

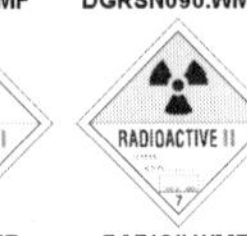

ICON091.WMF NUKE1.WMF NUKE2.WMF RADIO2.WMF RADIOACT.WMF RADIOI.WMF RADIOII.WMF RADIOIII.WMF SIGN007.WMF SIGN049.WMF

SIGN066.WMF STGC014D.WMF

BLSQ01.WMF BLSQ02.WMF BLSQ03.WMF BLSQ04.WMF BLSQ05.WMF BLSQ06.WMF BLSQ07.WMF BLSQ08.WMF BLSQ09.WMF BLSQ10.WMF
BLSQ11.WMF BLSQ12.WMF BLSQ13.WMF BLSQ14.WMF BLSQ15.WMF BLSQ16.WMF BLSQ17.WMF BLSQ18.WMF BLSQ19.WMF BLSQ20.WMF
BLSQ21.WMF BLSQ22.WMF BLSQ23.WMF BLSQ24.WMF BLSQ25.WMF BLUICO01.WMF BLUICO02.WMF BLUICO03.WMF BLUICO04.WMF BLUICO05.WMF
BLUICO06.WMF BLUICO07.WMF BLUICO08.WMF BLUICO09.WMF BLUICO10.WMF BLUICO11.WMF BLUICO12.WMF BLUICO13.WMF BLUICO14.WMF BLUICO15.WMF
BLUICO16.WMF CLOSING.WMF FRAGILE1.WMF FRAGILE5.WMF HANDCAR1.WMF ICONS01.WMF ICONS02.WMF ICONS03.WMF ICONS04.WMF ICONS05.WMF
ICONS06.WMF ICONS07.WMF ICONS08.WMF ICONS09.WMF ICONS10.WMF ICONS11.WMF ICONS12.WMF ICONS13.WMF ICONS14.WMF ICONS15.WMF
ICONS16.WMF ICONS17.WMF ICONS18.WMF ICONS19.WMF ICONS20.WMF ICONS21.WMF ICONS22.WMF ICONS23.WMF ICONS24.WMF ICONS25.WMF
ICONS26.WMF ICONS27.WMF ICONS28.WMF INSURANC.WMF KPDRY1.WMF PGX017A.WMF SIGN4.WMF SQR01.WMF SQR02.WMF SQR03.WMF
SQR04.WMF SQR05.WMF SQR06.WMF SQR07.WMF SQR08.WMF SQR09.WMF SQR10.WMF SQR11.WMF SQR12.WMF SQR13.WMF
Pitch In!
SQR14.WMF SQR15.WMF SQR16.WMF SQR17.WMF SQR18.WMF SQR19.WMF SQR20.WMF SQR21.WMF SQR22.WMF SQR23.WMF
SQR24.WMF SQR25.WMF SQR26.WMF SQR27.WMF SQR28.WMF SQR29.WMF SQR30.WMF SQR31.WMF SQR32.WMF SQR33.WMF
SQR34.WMF SQR35.WMF SQR36.WMF SQR37.WMF SQR38.WMF SQR39.WMF SQR40.WMF SQR41.WMF

BLUE01.WMF BLUE02.WMF BLUE03.WMF BLUE04.WMF BLUE05.WMF BLUE06.WMF BLUE07.WMF BLUE08.WMF BLUE09.WMF BLUE10.WMF
BLUE11.WMF BLUE12.WMF BLUE13.WMF BLUE14.WMF BLUE15.WMF BLUE16.WMF BLUE17.WMF BLUE18.WMF BWSQ01.WMF BWSQ02.WMF
P
P
BWSQ03.WMF BWSQ04.WMF BWSQ05.WMF BWSQ06.WMF BWSQ07.WMF BWSQ08.WMF BWSQ09.WMF BWSQ10.WMF BWSQ11.WMF BWSQ12.WMF
WC
BWSQ13.WMF BWSQ14.WMF BWSQ15.WMF BWSQ16.WMF BWSQ17.WMF BWSQ18.WMF BWSQ19.WMF BWSQ20.WMF BWSQ21.WMF BWSQ22.WMF
SIGHTSEEING
BWSQ23.WMF BWSQ24.WMF BWSQ25.WMF BWSQ26.WMF BWSQ27.WMF BWSQ28.WMF BWSQ29.WMF BWSQ30.WMF BWSQ31.WMF ENTER01.WMF
RESTAURANTS
NIGHT LIFE
SERVICES
SHOPPING
SPORTS & REC
Informatie
INFORMATION
ENTER02.WMF ENTER03.WMF ENTER04.WMF ENTER05.WMF ENTER06.WMF ENTER07.WMF I01.WMF I02.WMF I03.WMF I04.WMF
INFORMATION
Informatie
INFORMATION
INFORMATION
I05.WMF I06.WMF I07.WMF I08.WMF I09.WMF MISC01.WMF MISC02.WMF MISC03.WMF MISC04.WMF MISC05.WMF
WC
MISC06.WMF MISC07.WMF MISC08.WMF MISC09.WMF MISC10.WMF MISC11.WMF MISC12.WMF MISC13.WMF MISC14.WMF MISC15.WMF
WC
MISC16.WMF MISC17.WMF MISC18.WMF MISC19.WMF MISC20.WMF MISC21.WMF MISC22.WMF MISC23.WMF MISC24.WMF MISC25.WMF
Police
WC
RESERVATION
RESERVATION
RESERVATION
RESERVATION
MISC26.WMF MISC27.WMF MISC28.WMF MISC29.WMF MISC30.WMF MISC31.WMF MISC32.WMF PD095MCU.WMF PD095NCU.WMF PD095OCU.WMF
PD095PCU.WMF QUEST01.WMF QUEST02.WMF QUEST03.WMF QUEST04.WMF QUEST05.WMF QUEST06.WMF QUEST07.WMF QUEST08.WMF QUEST09.WMF
QUEST10.WMF QUEST11.WMF QUEST12.WMF QUEST13.WMF QUEST14.WMF QUEST15.WMF QUEST16.WMF QUEST17.WMF QUEST18.WMF QUEST19.WMF

QUEST20.WMF
QUEST21.WMF
QUEST22.WMF
QUEST23.WMF
ROUND01.WMF
ROUND02.WMF
ROUND03.WMF
ROUND04.WMF
ROUND05.WMF
ROUND06.WMF
ROUND07.WMF
ROUND08.WMF
ROUND09.WMF
ROUND10.WMF
ROUND11.WMF
ROUND12.WMF
ROUND13.WMF
ROUND14.WMF
ROUND15.WMF
ROUND16.WMF
ROUND17.WMF
ROUND18.WMF
ROUND19.WMF
ROUND20.WMF
ROUND21.WMF
ROUND22.WMF
ROUND23.WMF
ROUND24.WMF
ROUND25.WMF
ROUND26.WMF
ROUND27.WMF
ROUND28.WMF
ROUND29.WMF
ROUND30.WMF
ROUND31.WMF
ROUND32.WMF
ROUND33.WMF

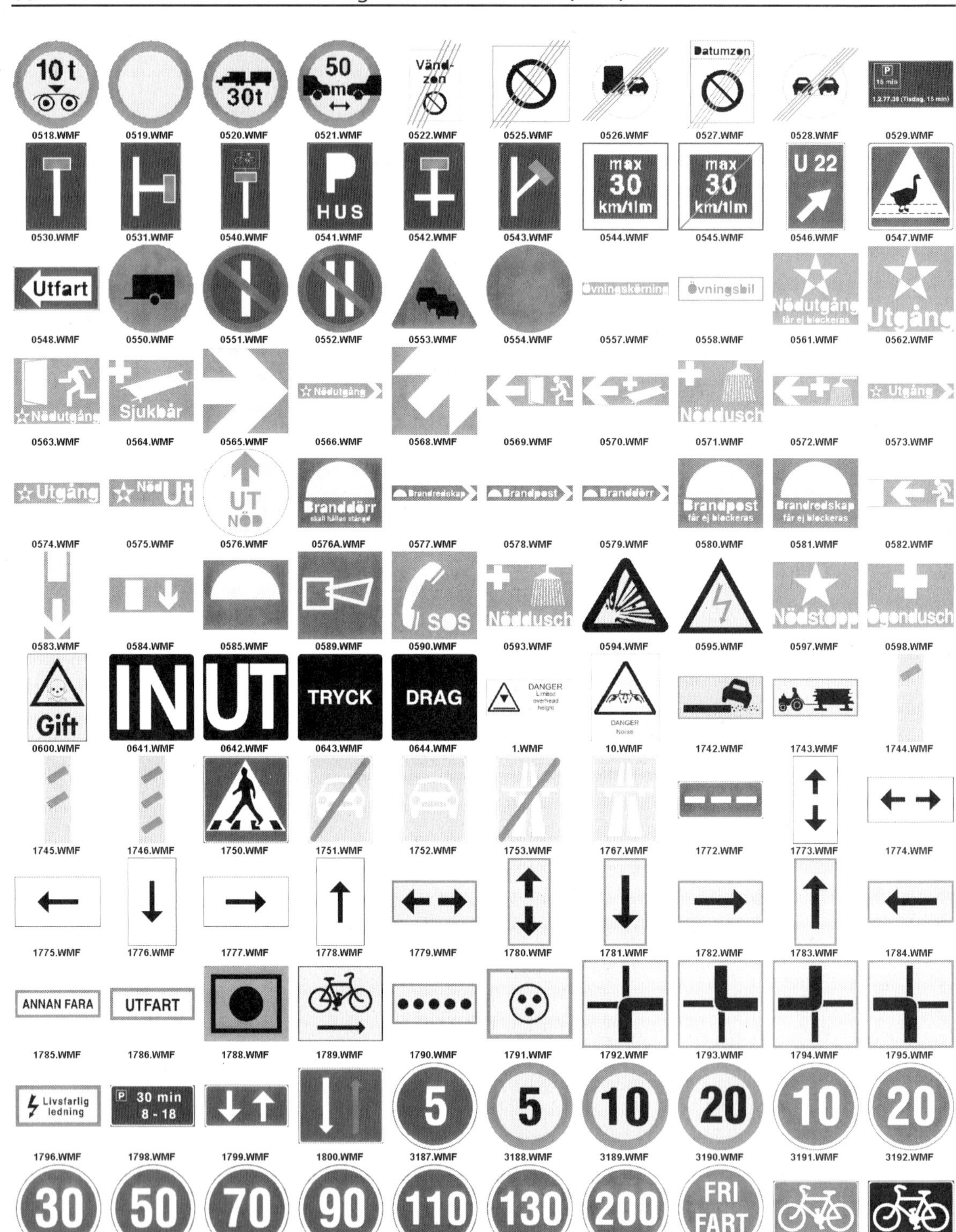
0518.WMF 0519.WMF 0520.WMF 0521.WMF 0522.WMF 0525.WMF 0526.WMF 0527.WMF 0528.WMF 0529.WMF
0530.WMF 0531.WMF 0540.WMF 0541.WMF 0542.WMF 0543.WMF 0544.WMF 0545.WMF 0546.WMF 0547.WMF
0548.WMF 0550.WMF 0551.WMF 0552.WMF 0553.WMF 0554.WMF 0557.WMF 0558.WMF 0561.WMF 0562.WMF
0563.WMF 0564.WMF 0565.WMF 0566.WMF 0568.WMF 0569.WMF 0570.WMF 0571.WMF 0572.WMF 0573.WMF
0574.WMF 0575.WMF 0576.WMF 0576A.WMF 0577.WMF 0578.WMF 0579.WMF 0580.WMF 0581.WMF 0582.WMF
0583.WMF 0584.WMF 0585.WMF 0589.WMF 0590.WMF 0593.WMF 0594.WMF 0595.WMF 0597.WMF 0598.WMF
0600.WMF 0641.WMF 0642.WMF 0643.WMF 0644.WMF 1.WMF 10.WMF 1742.WMF 1743.WMF 1744.WMF
1745.WMF 1746.WMF 1750.WMF 1751.WMF 1752.WMF 1753.WMF 1767.WMF 1772.WMF 1773.WMF 1774.WMF
1775.WMF 1776.WMF 1777.WMF 1778.WMF 1779.WMF 1780.WMF 1781.WMF 1782.WMF 1783.WMF 1784.WMF
1785.WMF 1786.WMF 1788.WMF 1789.WMF 1790.WMF 1791.WMF 1792.WMF 1793.WMF 1794.WMF 1795.WMF
1796.WMF 1798.WMF 1799.WMF 1800.WMF 3187.WMF 3188.WMF 3189.WMF 3190.WMF 3191.WMF 3192.WMF
3193.WMF 3194.WMF 3195.WMF 3196.WMF 3197.WMF 3198.WMF 3199.WMF 3200.WMF 3651.WMF 3652.WMF

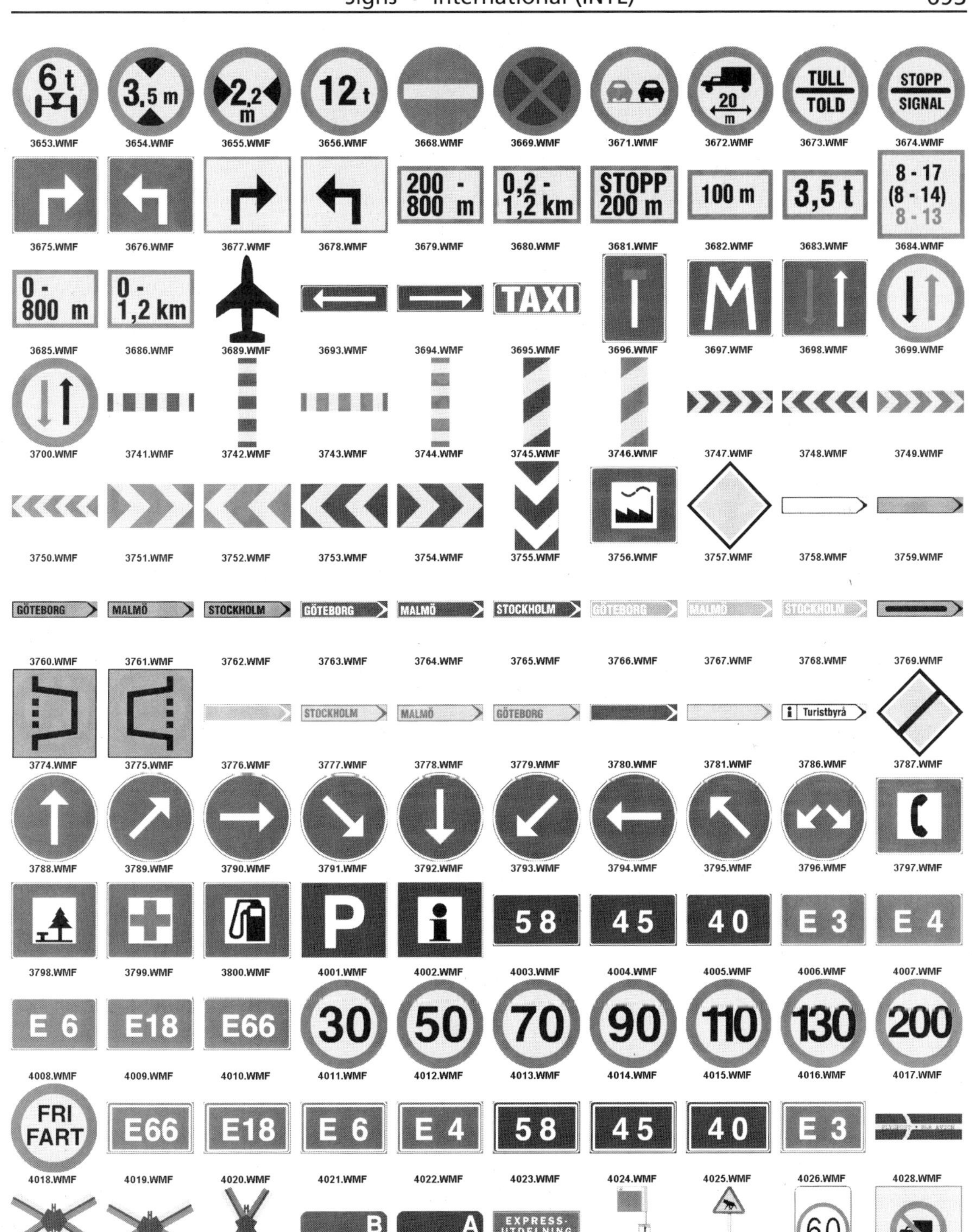

3653.WMF 3654.WMF 3655.WMF 3656.WMF 3668.WMF 3669.WMF 3671.WMF 3672.WMF 3673.WMF 3674.WMF

3675.WMF 3676.WMF 3677.WMF 3678.WMF 3679.WMF 3680.WMF 3681.WMF 3682.WMF 3683.WMF 3684.WMF

3685.WMF 3686.WMF 3689.WMF 3693.WMF 3694.WMF 3695.WMF 3696.WMF 3697.WMF 3698.WMF 3699.WMF

3700.WMF 3741.WMF 3742.WMF 3743.WMF 3744.WMF 3745.WMF 3746.WMF 3747.WMF 3748.WMF 3749.WMF

3750.WMF 3751.WMF 3752.WMF 3753.WMF 3754.WMF 3755.WMF 3756.WMF 3757.WMF 3758.WMF 3759.WMF

3760.WMF 3761.WMF 3762.WMF 3763.WMF 3764.WMF 3765.WMF 3766.WMF 3767.WMF 3768.WMF 3769.WMF

3774.WMF 3775.WMF 3776.WMF 3777.WMF 3778.WMF 3779.WMF 3780.WMF 3781.WMF 3786.WMF 3787.WMF

3788.WMF 3789.WMF 3790.WMF 3791.WMF 3792.WMF 3793.WMF 3794.WMF 3795.WMF 3796.WMF 3797.WMF

3798.WMF 3799.WMF 3800.WMF 4001.WMF 4002.WMF 4003.WMF 4004.WMF 4005.WMF 4006.WMF 4007.WMF

4008.WMF 4009.WMF 4010.WMF 4011.WMF 4012.WMF 4013.WMF 4014.WMF 4015.WMF 4016.WMF 4017.WMF

4018.WMF 4019.WMF 4020.WMF 4021.WMF 4022.WMF 4023.WMF 4024.WMF 4025.WMF 4026.WMF 4028.WMF

4029.WMF 4030.WMF 4031.WMF 4236.WMF 4237.WMF 4238.WMF 4339.WMF 4458.WMF 60K.WMF A0540.WMF

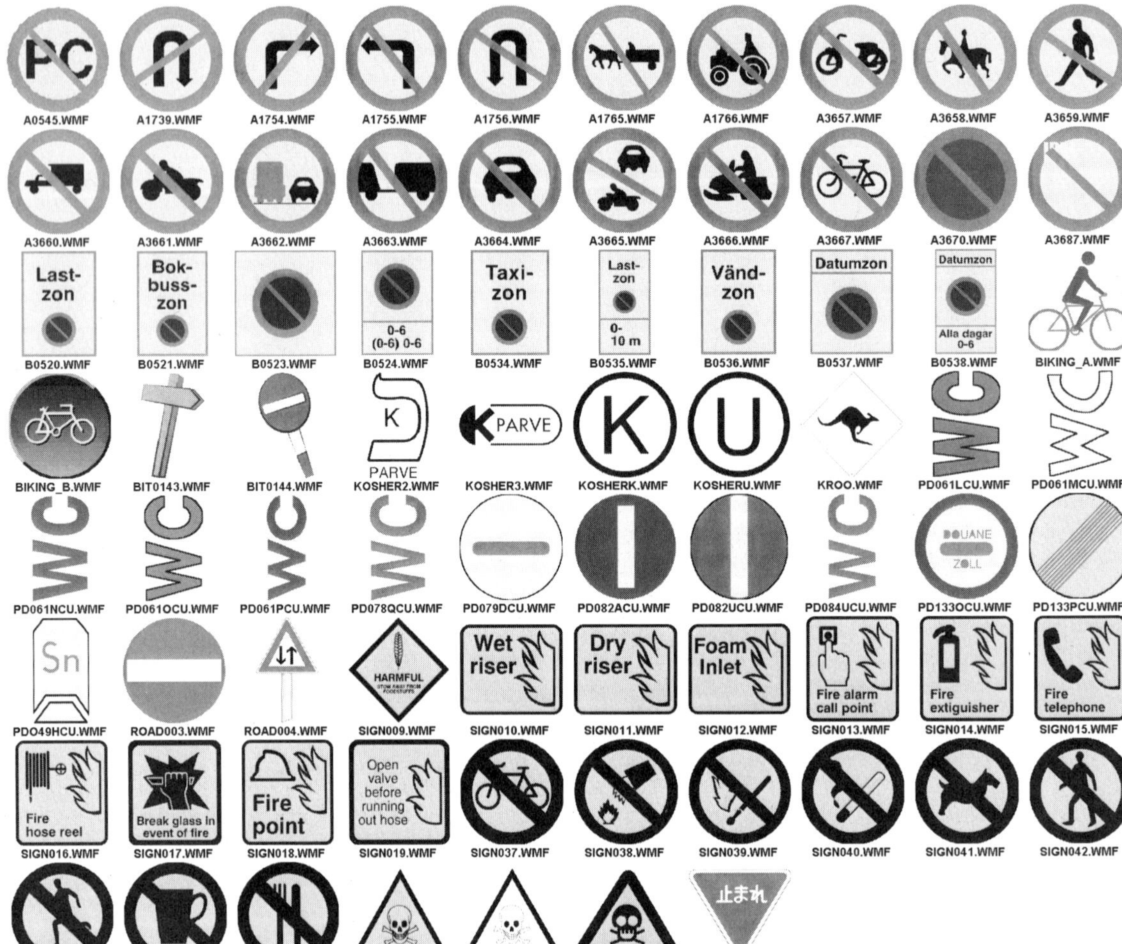
PC
A0545.WMF
A1739.WMF
A1754.WMF
A1755.WMF
A1756.WMF
A1765.WMF
A1766.WMF
A3657.WMF
A3658.WMF
A3659.WMF
A3660.WMF
A3661.WMF
A3662.WMF
A3663.WMF
A3664.WMF
A3665.WMF
A3666.WMF
A3667.WMF
A3670.WMF
A3687.WMF
Last-zon
B0520.WMF
Bok-buss-zon
B0521.WMF
B0523.WMF
0-6 (0-6) 0-6
B0524.WMF
Taxi-zon
B0534.WMF
Last-zon 0-10 m
B0535.WMF
Vänd-zon
B0536.WMF
Datumzon
B0537.WMF
Datumzon Alla dagar 0-6
B0538.WMF
BIKING_A.WMF
BIKING_B.WMF
BIT0143.WMF
BIT0144.WMF
K PARVE
KOSHER2.WMF
PARVE
KOSHER3.WMF
K
KOSHERK.WMF
U
KOSHERU.WMF
KROO.WMF
WC
PD061LCU.WMF
WC
PD061MCU.WMF
WC
PD061NCU.WMF
WC
PD061OCU.WMF
WC
PD061PCU.WMF
WC
PD078QCU.WMF
PD079DCU.WMF
PD082ACU.WMF
PD082UCU.WMF
WC
PD084UCU.WMF
DOUANE ZOLL
PD133OCU.WMF
PD133PCU.WMF
Sn
PDO49HCU.WMF
ROAD003.WMF
ROAD004.WMF
HARMFUL
SIGN009.WMF
Wet riser
SIGN010.WMF
Dry riser
SIGN011.WMF
Foam Inlet
SIGN012.WMF
Fire alarm call point
SIGN013.WMF
Fire extiguisher
SIGN014.WMF
Fire telephone
SIGN015.WMF
Fire hose reel
SIGN016.WMF
Break glass in event of fire
SIGN017.WMF
Fire point
SIGN018.WMF
Open valve before running out hose
SIGN019.WMF
SIGN037.WMF
SIGN038.WMF
SIGN039.WMF
SIGN040.WMF
SIGN041.WMF
SIGN042.WMF
SIGN043.WMF
SIGN044.WMF
SIGN045.WMF
SIGN050.WMF
SIGN062.WMF
SIGN065.WMF
止まれ
TOMARE.WMF

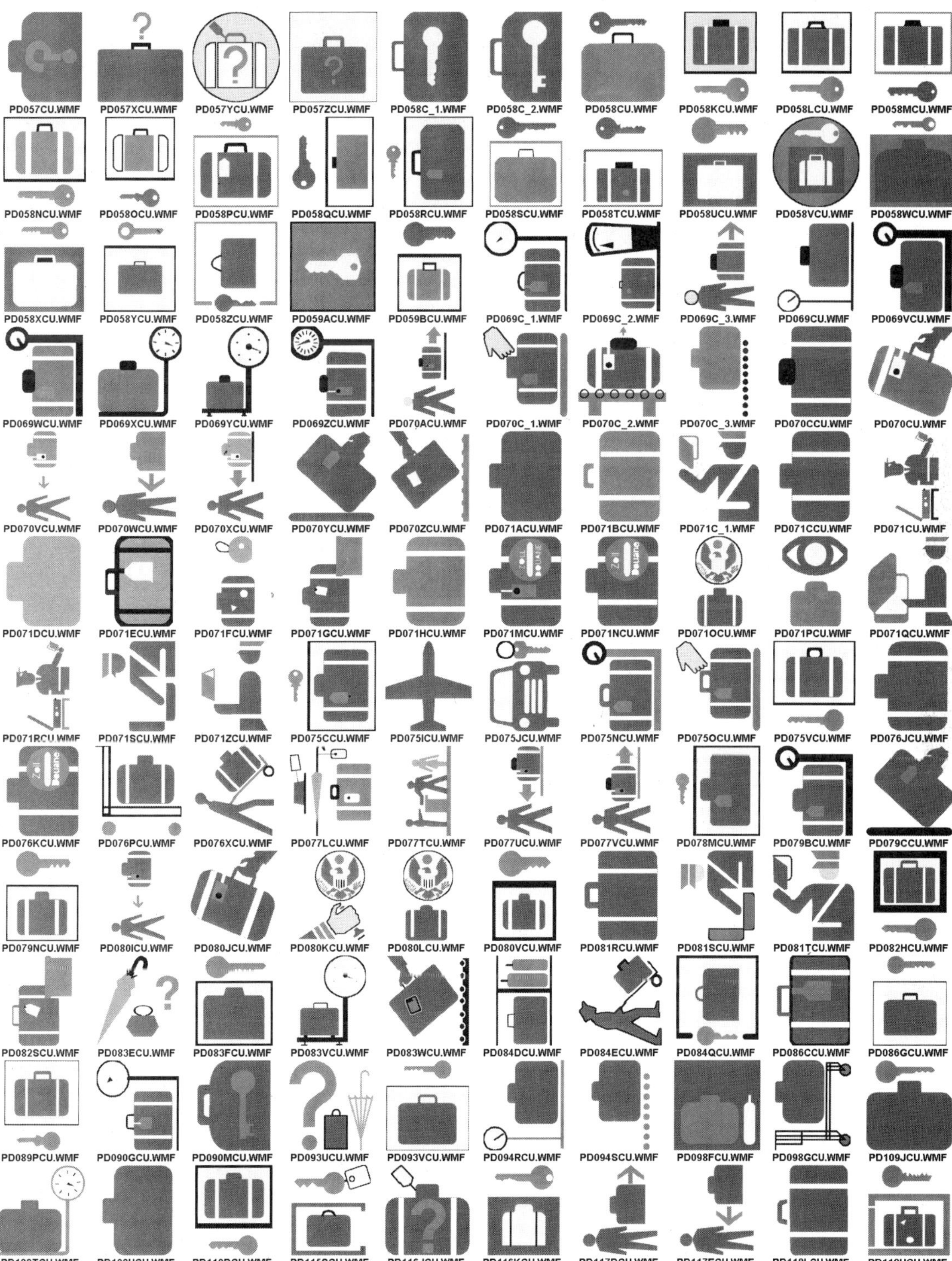
PD057CU.WMF PD057XCU.WMF PD057YCU.WMF PD057ZCU.WMF PD058C_1.WMF PD058C_2.WMF PD058CU.WMF PD058KCU.WMF PD058LCU.WMF PD058MCU.WMF
PD058NCU.WMF PD058OCU.WMF PD058PCU.WMF PD058QCU.WMF PD058RCU.WMF PD058SCU.WMF PD058TCU.WMF PD058UCU.WMF PD058VCU.WMF PD058WCU.WMF
PD058XCU.WMF PD058YCU.WMF PD058ZCU.WMF PD059ACU.WMF PD059BCU.WMF PD069C_1.WMF PD069C_2.WMF PD069C_3.WMF PD069CU.WMF PD069VCU.WMF
PD069WCU.WMF PD069XCU.WMF PD069YCU.WMF PD069ZCU.WMF PD070ACU.WMF PD070C_1.WMF PD070C_2.WMF PD070C_3.WMF PD070CCU.WMF PD070CU.WMF
PD070VCU.WMF PD070WCU.WMF PD070XCU.WMF PD070YCU.WMF PD070ZCU.WMF PD071ACU.WMF PD071BCU.WMF PD071C_1.WMF PD071CCU.WMF PD071CU.WMF
PD071DCU.WMF PD071ECU.WMF PD071FCU.WMF PD071GCU.WMF PD071HCU.WMF PD071MCU.WMF PD071NCU.WMF PD071OCU.WMF PD071PCU.WMF PD071QCU.WMF
PD071RCU.WMF PD071SCU.WMF PD071ZCU.WMF PD075CCU.WMF PD075ICU.WMF PD075JCU.WMF PD075NCU.WMF PD075OCU.WMF PD075VCU.WMF PD076JCU.WMF
PD076KCU.WMF PD076PCU.WMF PD076XCU.WMF PD077LCU.WMF PD077TCU.WMF PD077UCU.WMF PD077VCU.WMF PD078MCU.WMF PD079BCU.WMF PD079CCU.WMF
PD079NCU.WMF PD080ICU.WMF PD080JCU.WMF PD080KCU.WMF PD080LCU.WMF PD080VCU.WMF PD081RCU.WMF PD081SCU.WMF PD081TCU.WMF PD082HCU.WMF
PD082SCU.WMF PD083ECU.WMF PD083FCU.WMF PD083VCU.WMF PD083WCU.WMF PD084DCU.WMF PD084ECU.WMF PD084QCU.WMF PD086CCU.WMF PD086GCU.WMF
PD089PCU.WMF PD090GCU.WMF PD090MCU.WMF PD093UCU.WMF PD093VCU.WMF PD094RCU.WMF PD094SCU.WMF PD098FCU.WMF PD098GCU.WMF PD109JCU.WMF
PD109TCU.WMF PD109UCU.WMF PD110DCU.WMF PD115SCU.WMF PD116JCU.WMF PD116KCU.WMF PD117DCU.WMF PD117ECU.WMF PD118LCU.WMF PD118UCU.WMF

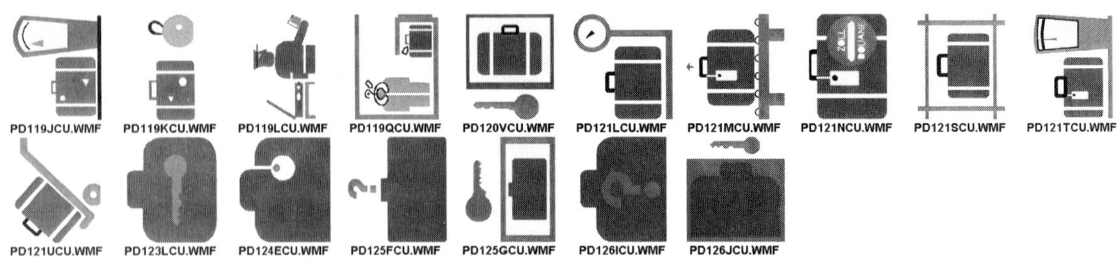
PD119JCU.WMF
PD119KCU.WMF
PD119LCU.WMF
PD119QCU.WMF
PD120VCU.WMF
PD121LCU.WMF
PD121MCU.WMF
ZOLL
DOUANE
PD121NCU.WMF
PD121SCU.WMF
PD121TCU.WMF
PD121UCU.WMF
PD123LCU.WMF
PD124ECU.WMF
PD125FCU.WMF
PD125GCU.WMF
PD126ICU.WMF
PD126JCU.WMF

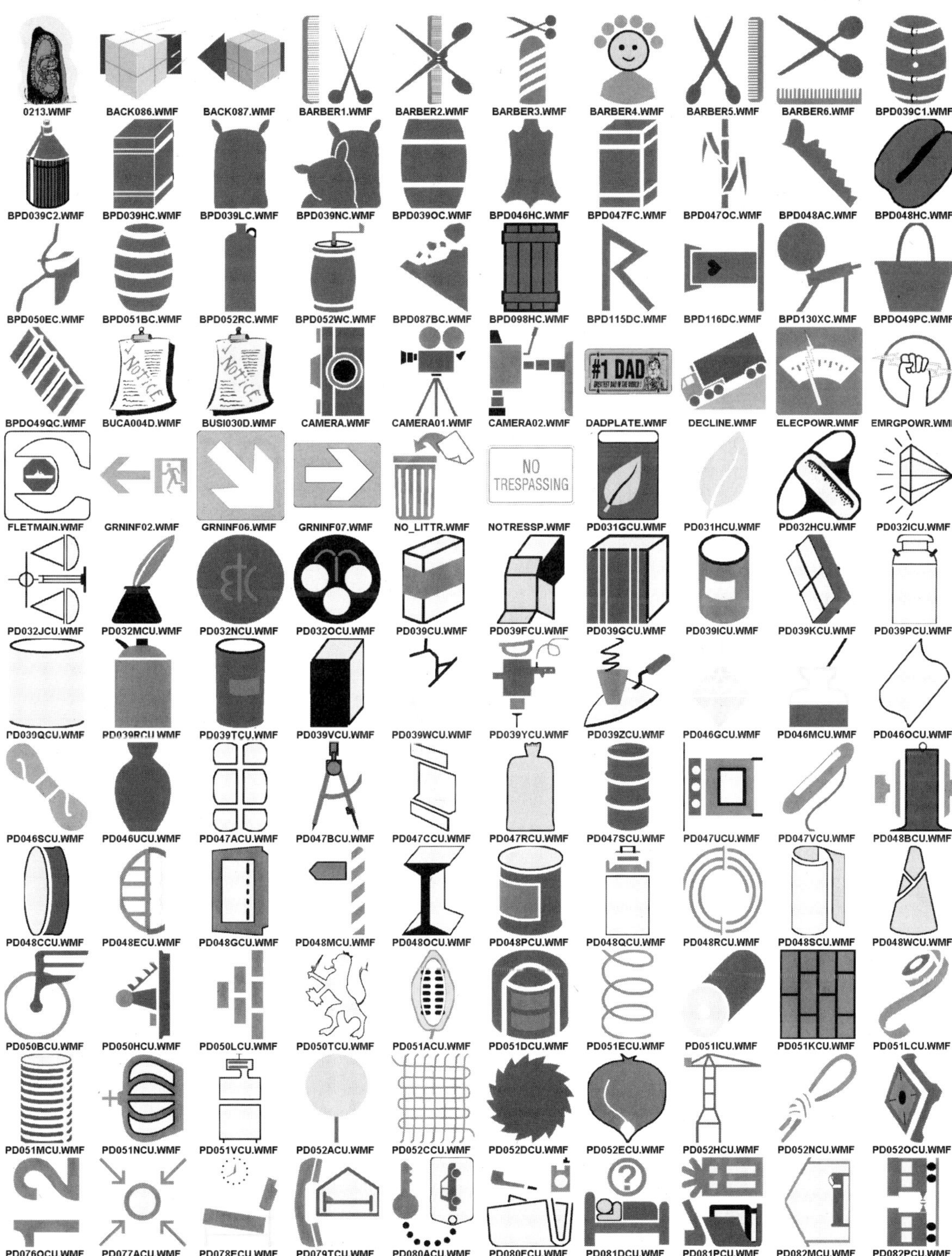

#1 DAD
NO
TRESPASSING
0213.WMF BACK086.WMF BACK087.WMF BARBER1.WMF BARBER2.WMF BARBER3.WMF BARBER4.WMF BARBER5.WMF BARBER6.WMF BPD039C1.WMF
BPD039C2.WMF BPD039HC.WMF BPD039LC.WMF BPD039NC.WMF BPD039OC.WMF BPD046HC.WMF BPD047FC.WMF BPD047OC.WMF BPD048AC.WMF BPD048HC.WMF
BPD050EC.WMF BPD051BC.WMF BPD052RC.WMF BPD052WC.WMF BPD087BC.WMF BPD098HC.WMF BPD115DC.WMF BPD116DC.WMF BPD130XC.WMF BPDO49PC.WMF
BPDO49QC.WMF BUCA004D.WMF BUSI030D.WMF CAMERA.WMF CAMERA01.WMF CAMERA02.WMF DADPLATE.WMF DECLINE.WMF ELECPOWR.WMF EMRGPOWR.WMF
FLETMAIN.WMF GRNINF02.WMF GRNINF06.WMF GRNINF07.WMF NO_LITTR.WMF NOTRESSP.WMF PD031GCU.WMF PD031HCU.WMF PD032HCU.WMF PD032ICU.WMF
PD032JCU.WMF PD032MCU.WMF PD032NCU.WMF PD032OCU.WMF PD039CU.WMF PD039FCU.WMF PD039GCU.WMF PD039ICU.WMF PD039KCU.WMF PD039PCU.WMF
PD039QCU.WMF PD039RCU.WMF PD039TCU.WMF PD039VCU.WMF PD039WCU.WMF PD039YCU.WMF PD039ZCU.WMF PD046GCU.WMF PD046MCU.WMF PD046OCU.WMF
PD046SCU.WMF PD046UCU.WMF PD047ACU.WMF PD047BCU.WMF PD047CCU.WMF PD047RCU.WMF PD047SCU.WMF PD047UCU.WMF PD047VCU.WMF PD048BCU.WMF
PD048CCU.WMF PD048ECU.WMF PD048GCU.WMF PD048MCU.WMF PD048OCU.WMF PD048PCU.WMF PD048QCU.WMF PD048RCU.WMF PD048SCU.WMF PD048WCU.WMF
PD050BCU.WMF PD050HCU.WMF PD050LCU.WMF PD050TCU.WMF PD051ACU.WMF PD051DCU.WMF PD051ECU.WMF PD051ICU.WMF PD051KCU.WMF PD051LCU.WMF
PD051MCU.WMF PD051NCU.WMF PD051VCU.WMF PD052ACU.WMF PD052CCU.WMF PD052DCU.WMF PD052ECU.WMF PD052HCU.WMF PD052NCU.WMF PD052OCU.WMF
PD076OCU.WMF PD077ACU.WMF PD078ECU.WMF PD079TCU.WMF PD080ACU.WMF PD080FCU.WMF PD081DCU.WMF PD081PCU.WMF PD082MCU.WMF PD082PCU.WMF

PD083LCU.WMF PD083SCU.WMF PD084ICU.WMF PD085LCU.WMF PD085MCU.WMF PD085PCU.WMF PD085QCU.WMF PD086KCU.WMF PD086RCU.WMF PD086VCU.WMF
PD086WCU.WMF PD087ACU.WMF PD087CCU.WMF PD090FCU.WMF PD090HCU.WMF PD090OCU.WMF PD090RCU.WMF PD091CCU.WMF PD092CCU.WMF PD092JCU.WMF
PD092RCU.WMF PD094CCU.WMF PD094KCU.WMF PD094MCU.WMF PD094QCU.WMF PD094TCU.WMF PD094UCU.WMF PD094WCU.WMF PD094XCU.WMF PD095ACU.WMF
PD095QCU.WMF PD095SCU.WMF PD096DCU.WMF PD096FCU.WMF PD096LCU.WMF PD096MCU.WMF PD096NCU.WMF PD097OCU.WMF PD097PCU.WMF PD097UCU.WMF
PD097VCU.WMF PD098BCU.WMF PD098NCU.WMF PD098OCU.WMF PD099ECU.WMF PD099FCU.WMF PD099NCU.WMF PD099OCU.WMF PD110BCU.WMF PD110ICU.WMF
PD110JCU.WMF PD110NCU.WMF PD110OCU.WMF PD110PCU.WMF PD110QCU.WMF PD111KCU.WMF PD111OCU.WMF PD111PCU.WMF PD115FCU.WMF PD115GCU.WMF
PD115HCU.WMF PD115LCU.WMF PD115MCU.WMF PD115NCU.WMF PD115PCU.WMF PD115VCU.WMF PD116ECU.WMF PD116LCU.WMF PD117CCU.WMF PD117MCU.WMF
PD117OCU.WMF PD117QCU.WMF PD117TCU.WMF PD119BCU.WMF PD119GCU.WMF PD119RCU.WMF PD119UCU.WMF PD119VCU.WMF PD119WCU.WMF PD119XCU.WMF
PD120ACU.WMF PD120CCU.WMF PD120ECU.WMF PD120HCU.WMF PD120ICU.WMF PD120KCU.WMF PD120PCU.WMF PD121KCU.WMF PD122SCU.WMF PD122VCU.WMF
PD123BCU.WMF PD123CCU.WMF PD123ECU.WMF PD123FCU.WMF PD123GCU.WMF PD123OCU.WMF PD124PCU.WMF PD125SCU.WMF PD125VCU.WMF PD126CCU.WMF
PD126VCU.WMF PD126WCU.WMF PD126XCU.WMF PD127BCU.WMF PD127CCU.WMF PD127DCU.WMF PD128PCU.WMF PD128QCU.WMF PD128RCU.WMF PD128TCU.WMF
PD128VCU.WMF PD129ACU.WMF PD129BCU.WMF PD129CCU.WMF PD129LCU.WMF PD129OCU.WMF PD129UCU.WMF PD130QCU.WMF PD130RCU.WMF PD130SCU.WMF

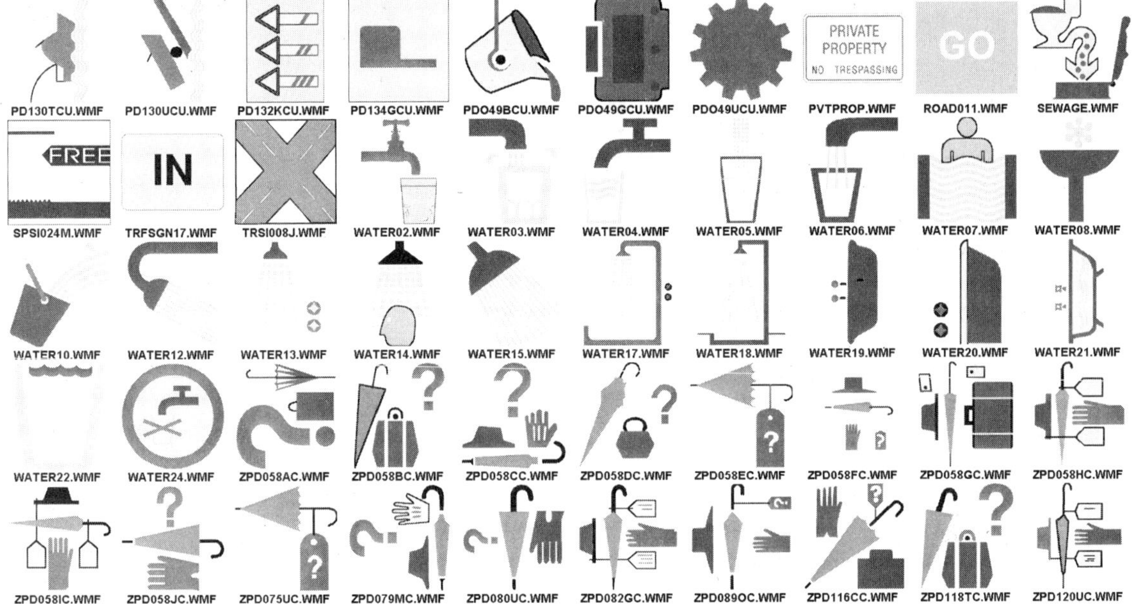

PD130TCU.WMF PD130UCU.WMF PD132KCU.WMF PD134GCU.WMF PDO49BCU.WMF PDO49GCU.WMF PDO49UCU.WMF PVTPROP.WMF ROAD011.WMF SEWAGE.WMF

SPSI024M.WMF TRFSGN17.WMF TRSI008J.WMF WATER02.WMF WATER03.WMF WATER04.WMF WATER05.WMF WATER06.WMF WATER07.WMF WATER08.WMF

WATER10.WMF WATER12.WMF WATER13.WMF WATER14.WMF WATER15.WMF WATER17.WMF WATER18.WMF WATER19.WMF WATER20.WMF WATER21.WMF

WATER22.WMF WATER24.WMF ZPD058AC.WMF ZPD058BC.WMF ZPD058CC.WMF ZPD058DC.WMF ZPD058EC.WMF ZPD058FC.WMF ZPD058GC.WMF ZPD058HC.WMF

ZPD058IC.WMF ZPD058JC.WMF ZPD075UC.WMF ZPD079MC.WMF ZPD080UC.WMF ZPD082GC.WMF ZPD089OC.WMF ZPD116CC.WMF ZPD118TC.WMF ZPD120UC.WMF

0548.WMF 0595.WMF 0596.WMF 0607.WMF 0619.WMF 1HWYSG_1.WMF 1HWYSGN4.WMF 1NO_CAMP.WMF 1NO_FOOD.WMF 1NO_LEFT.WMF
1NO_PICN.WMF 1NO_RIGH.WMF 1NO_SMOK.WMF 1NO_TRUC.WMF 1NO_UTUR.WMF 2.WMF 3.WMF 4.WMF 5.WMF A0001.WMF
A0002.WMF A0003.WMF A0004.WMF A0005.WMF A0006.WMF A0007.WMF A0008.WMF A0009.WMF A0010.WMF A0011.WMF
A0012.WMF A0013.WMF A0014.WMF A0015.WMF BIT0381.WMF BIT0382.WMF BIT0383.WMF BIT0384.WMF BIT0385.WMF BIT0386.WMF
BIT0387.WMF BIT0388.WMF DIGSAFE.WMF DONOTFRZ.WMF DONOTRL1.WMF DONOTST.WMF DONOTUM1.WMF DONOTUM2.WMF DONOTUM3.WMF DONTDR.WMF
DONTEXT1.WMF DONTEXT2.WMF DONTLUBE.WMF DONTSTRT.WMF DONTUSHD.WMF FOOD0.WMF FOOD1.WMF FOOD2.WMF FOOD27.WMF FOOD3.WMF
HEAVY.WMF ICON004.WMF ICON041.WMF ICON066.WMF KPDRY4.WMF NOBAREFT.WMF NOBZPILL.WMF NOENTRY.WMF NOFOOD1.WMF NOFOOD2.WMF
NOLARD.WMF NOOPENFL.WMF NOPARKIN.WMF NOPASSWO.WMF NOPEDEST.WMF NOPETS.WMF NOPWR.WMF NOPWRAN.WMF NORAZOR.WMF NOREDTAP.WMF
NORIGHT.WMF NOSMOKE.WMF NOSMOKE1.WMF NOSMOKE2.WMF NOSMOKE5.WMF NOSMOKIN.WMF NOSMOKNG.WMF NOSPADE.WMF NOTROP.WMF NOUTURN.WMF
NOUTURNS.WMF PD120JCU.WMF PD123WCU.WMF PD133HCU.WMF PD133JCU.WMF PD133KCU.WMF PISTOL.WMF RESTRICT.WMF SHOTGUN.WMF SHRTPARK.WMF
SIGN002.WMF STRANGER.WMF

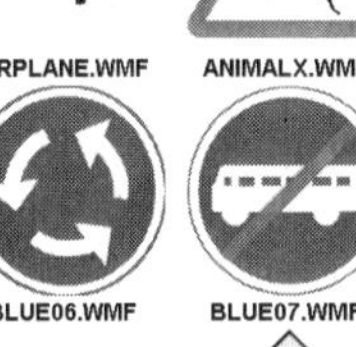
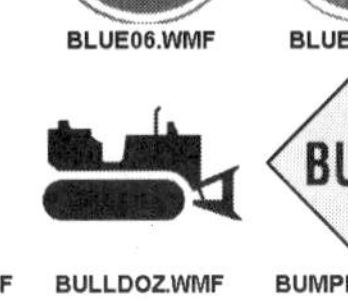

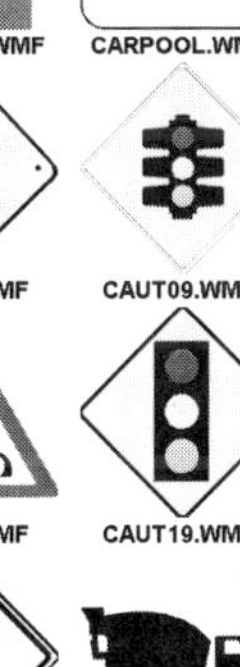

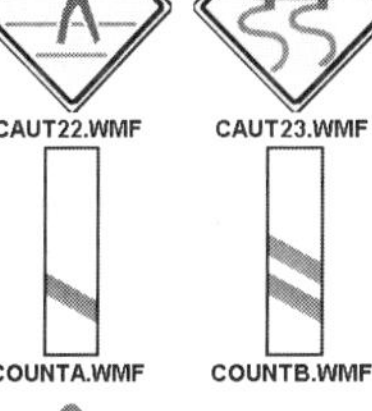

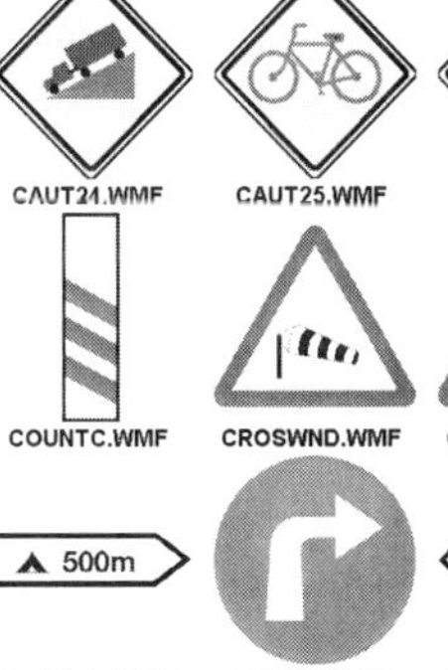

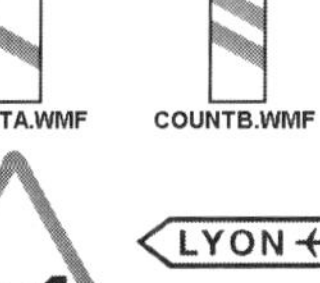

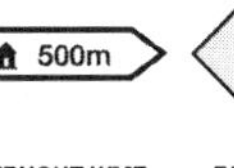

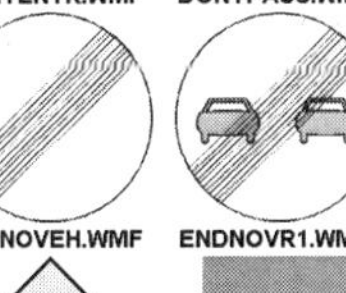

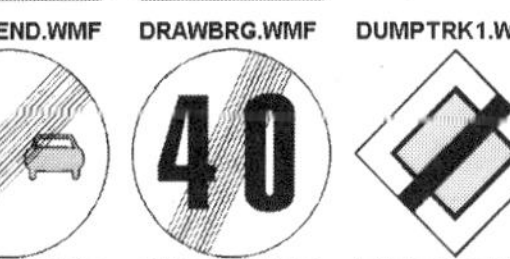
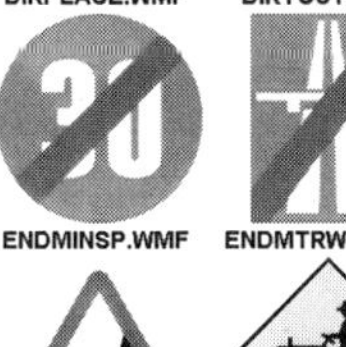
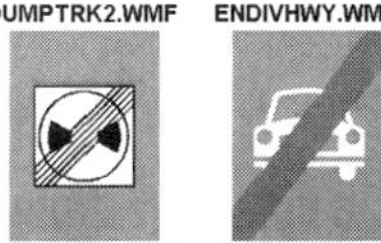

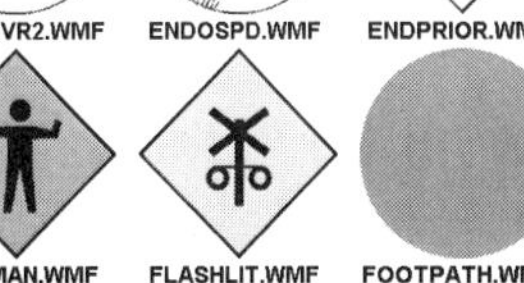
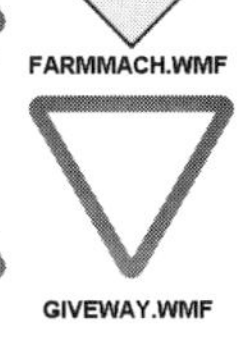

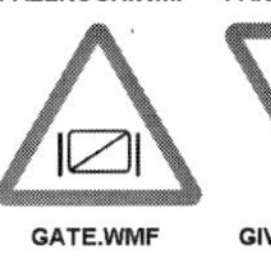

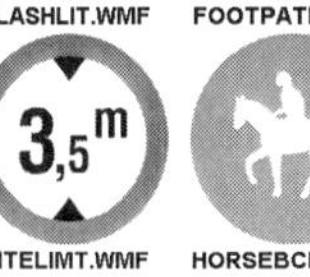

1WAY01.WMF 1WAY02.WMF 1WAY03.WMF 1WAY04.WMF 1WAY05.WMF 1WAY06.WMF 4WAY.WMF AIRFIELD.WMF AIRPLANE.WMF ANIMALX.WMF

AXLELIM.WMF BACKHOE.WMF BIKEXING.WMF BLUE01.WMF BLUE02.WMF BLUE03.WMF BLUE04.WMF BLUE05.WMF BLUE06.WMF BLUE07.WMF

BLUE08.WMF BLUE09.WMF BLUE10.WMF BLUE11.WMF BLUE12.WMF BLUE13.WMF BLUE14.WMF BREAKDWN.WMF BULLDOZ.WMF BUMPEPS.WMF

BUS.WMF BUSSTOP.WMF CAMPER.WMF CAMPGSIT.WMF CAMPSITE.WMF CARPOOL.WMF CATLXING.WMF CAUT01.WMF CAUT02.WMF CAUT03.WMF

CAUT04.WMF CAUT05.WMF CAUT06.WMF CAUT07.WMF CAUT08.WMF CAUT09.WMF CAUT10.WMF CAUT11.WMF CAUT12.WMF CAUT13.WMF

CAUT14.WMF CAUT15.WMF CAUT16.WMF CAUT17.WMF CAUT18.WMF CAUT19.WMF CAUT20.WMF CAUT21.WMF CAUT22.WMF CAUT23.WMF

CAUT24.WMF CAUT25.WMF CAUT26.WMF CAUT27.WMF CAUT28.WMF CEMENTMX.WMF CHILDREN.WMF COFFEE.WMF COUNTA.WMF COUNTB.WMF

COUNTC.WMF CROSWND.WMF CYCLISTS.WMF CYCLTRK.WMF DANGBEND.WMF DEERXING.WMF DELTRUCK.WMF DETOUR.WMF DIP.WMF DIRAIRFL.WMF

DIRCAMP.WMF DIRFILO.WMF DIRPLACE.WMF DIRYOUT.WMF DIVHWY.WMF DONTENTR.WMF DONTPASS.WMF DOUBBEND.WMF DRAWBRG.WMF DUMPTRK1.WMF

DUMPTRK2.WMF ENDIVHWY.WMF ENDMINSP.WMF ENDMTRWY.WMF ENDNOPRK.WMF ENDNOVEH.WMF ENDNOVR1.WMF ENDNOVR2.WMF ENDOSPD.WMF ENDPRIOR.WMF

ENDPWRSC.WMF ENDROAD.WMF FALLROCK.WMF FARMMACH.WMF FARMTRAC.WMF FIREDEPT.WMF FIRSTAID.WMF FLAGMAN.WMF FLASHLIT.WMF FOOTPATH.WMF

FORKLIFT.WMF FUEL.WMF GATE.WMF GIVEWAY.WMF GONDOLA.WMF GRADX.WMF GRADXGAT.WMF HIGHSHIE.WMF HITELIMT.WMF HORSEBCK.WMF

HORSXING.WMF HOSPITAL.WMF HOTEL.WMF INTERS1.WMF INTERS2.WMF INTERS3.WMF INTERS4.WMF KEEPRT1.WMF KEEPRT2.WMF LANEPRES.WMF

LEFTBEND.WMF LEVELX1.WMF LEVELX2.WMF LITESIGL.WMF LOOSGRAV.WMF LOWCLER1.WMF LOWCLER2.WMF LOWFLY.WMF MENWORK.WMF MERGE.WMF

MERGTRAF.WMF MINSPD.WMF MOTORWAY.WMF MOTRGAT.WMF NARRBR.WMF NARRSTR.WMF NOANIMAL.WMF NOANIMVE.WMF NOAUDIB.WMF NOBIKES.WMF

NOBOTH.WMF NOBUSES.WMF NOCARS.WMF NOENT.WMF NOENTPED.WMF NOENTRY.WMF NOHNDCRT.WMF NOLEFT.WMF NOLORRIE.WMF NOMOPEDS.WMF

NOMOTORC.WMF NOOVER.WMF NOPARANY.WMF NOPARBUS.WMF NOPARCOR.WMF NOSTND.WMF NOTHRU1.WMF NOTHRU2.WMF NOTRACTS.WMF NOTRAIL1.WMF

NOTRAIL2.WMF NOTRKS.WMF NOVEHEXP.WMF NOVERTAK.WMF NOVERTLO.WMF NOWTRPOL.WMF OILTRUCK.WMF ONEWAY.WMF OTHRDANG.WMF PARK01.WMF

PARK02.WMF PARK03.WMF PARK04.WMF PARK05.WMF PARK06.WMF PARK07.WMF PARK08.WMF PARK09.WMF PARK10.WMF PARK11.WMF

PARK12.WMF PARK13.WMF PARK14.WMF PARK15.WMF PARK16.WMF PARK17.WMF PARK18.WMF PARK19.WMF PARK20.WMF PARK21.WMF

PARK22.WMF PARK23.WMF PARK24.WMF PARK25.WMF PARK26.WMF PARK27.WMF PARK28.WMF PARK29.WMF PARK30.WMF PARK31.WMF

PARK32.WMF PARK33.WMF PARK34.WMF PARK35.WMF PARK36.WMF PARK37.WMF PARK38.WMF PARK39.WMF PARKALT.WMF PARKCLOK.WMF

PARKDISC.WMF PARKEVEN.WMF PARKING.WMF PARKODD.WMF PASSCARE.WMF PASSTHIS.WMF PAVENARO.WMF PEDCROSS.WMF PEDEXING.WMF PEDXING.WMF

PICSITE.WMF PLAYGRND.WMF PRIORITY.WMF PRIOROAD.WMF PRIOROUT.WMF PULPTRUK.WMF RAILXING.WMF REDSPEED.WMF RESTAUR.WMF RIDGE.WMF

RIGHTBND.WMF	RIVERBNK.WMF	ROADCLOS.WMF	ROADENTR.WMF	ROADMTR.WMF	ROADNAR1.WMF	ROADNAR2.WMF	ROADNARO.WMF	ROADOPEN.WMF	ROADWORK.WMF
ROUNDAB.WMF	ROUNDABO.WMF	ROUSHIEL.WMF	SAILBOAT.WMF	SATARTPT.WMF	SCHOOL.WMF	SCHOOLX.WMF	SCHOONER.WMF	SLIPPERY.WMF	SLIPROAD.WMF
SLOWMOV.WMF	SNOWCHNS.WMF	SNOWXING.WMF	SPEED01.WMF	SPEED02.WMF	SPEED03.WMF	SPEED04.WMF	SPEED05.WMF	SPEEDLIM.WMF	SPORTSCR.WMF
STEEPAS1.WMF	STEEPAS2.WMF	STEEPASC.WMF	STEEPD1.WMF	STEEPD2.WMF	STEEPDE1.WMF	STEEPDE2.WMF	STOP04.WMF	STOP05.WMF	STOP06.WMF
STOP07.WMF	STOP08.WMF	STOP09.WMF	STOP10.WMF	STOP11.WMF	STOP12.WMF	STOP13.WMF	STOP14.WMF	STOP15.WMF	STOP16.WMF
STOP17.WMF	STOP18.WMF	STOP19.WMF	STOP20.WMF	STOP21.WMF	STOPAHED.WMF	STOPHED1.WMF	STOPHED2.WMF	STOPHED3.WMF	STOPSIGN.WMF
STR101.WMF	STR102.WMF	STR103.WMF	STR104.WMF	STR105.WMF	STR106.WMF	STR107.WMF	STR108.WMF	STR109.WMF	STR110.WMF
STR111.WMF	STR112.WMF	STR113.WMF	STR114.WMF	STR115.WMF	STR116.WMF	STR117.WMF	STR118.WMF	STR119.WMF	STR120.WMF
STR201.WMF	STR202.WMF	STR203.WMF	STR204.WMF	STR205.WMF	STR206.WMF	STR207.WMF	STR208.WMF	STR209.WMF	STR210.WMF
STR211.WMF	STR212.WMF	STR213.WMF	STR214.WMF	STR215.WMF	STR216.WMF	STR217.WMF	STR218.WMF	STR219.WMF	STR220.WMF
STR221.WMF	STR501.WMF	STR502.WMF	STR503.WMF	STR504.WMF	STR505.WMF	STR506.WMF	STR507.WMF	STR508.WMF	STR509.WMF
STR510.WMF	STR511.WMF	STR512.WMF	STR513.WMF	STR514.WMF	STR515.WMF	TELEPHON.WMF	TOURINFO.WMF	TOWAWAY.WMF	TRACTRA.WMF

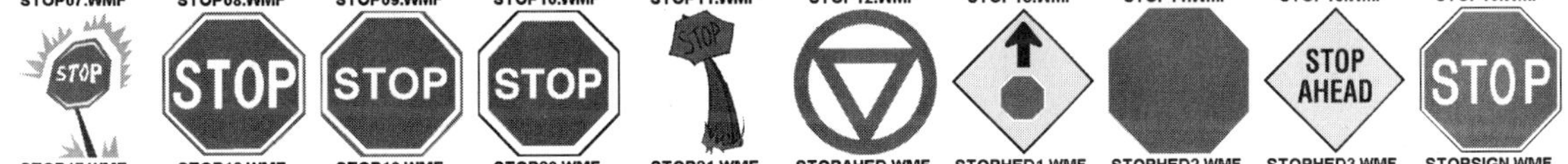

TRAF.WMF
TRAFSIG1.WMF
TRAFSIG2.WMF
TRAFSIG3.WMF
TRAMWYST.WMF
TRAVEL.WMF
TRI01.WMF
TRI02.WMF
TRI03.WMF
TRI04.WMF
TRI05.WMF
TRI06.WMF
TRI07.WMF
TRI08.WMF
TRI09.WMF
TRI10.WMF
TRI11.WMF
TRI12.WMF
TRI13.WMF
TRI14.WMF
TRI15.WMF
TRI16.WMF
TRI17.WMF
TRI18.WMF
TRI19.WMF
TRI20.WMF
TRI21.WMF
TRI22.WMF
TRI23.WMF
TRI24.WMF
TRI25.WMF
TRI26.WMF
TRI27.WMF
TRI28.WMF
TRI29.WMF
TRI30.WMF
TRI31.WMF
TRI32.WMF
TRI33.WMF
TRI34.WMF
TRI35.WMF
TRI36.WMF
200m
TRI37.WMF
TRI38.WMF
TRI39.WMF
TRI40.WMF
TRI41.WMF
TRI42.WMF
TRI43.WMF
TRI44.WMF
TRI45.WMF
TRI46.WMF
TRI47.WMF
TRI48.WMF
TRI49.WMF
TRI50.WMF
TRI51.WMF
TRI52.WMF
TRI53.WMF
TRI54.WMF
TRI55.WMF
TRI56.WMF
TRI57.WMF
TRI58.WMF
TRI59.WMF
TRI60.WMF
TRI61.WMF
TRI62.WMF
TRI63.WMF
TRI64.WMF
TRI65.WMF
TRI66.WMF
TRI67.WMF
10%
TRI68.WMF
TRI69.WMF
TRKXING.WMF
TRLRSITE.WMF
TWOWAY.WMF
UNEVEN.WMF
VAN.WMF
WEARBL1.WMF
WEAR SAFETY BELTS
WEARBLT2.WMF
2m
WIDTLIM1.WMF
10 m
WIDTLIM2.WMF
YIELD
YIELD.WMF
YIELD
YIELD04.WMF
YIELD05.WMF
YIELD
YIELD06.WMF
YIELD
YIELD07.WMF
YIELD08.WMF
YIELD
YIELD09.WMF
YIELD
YIELD10.WMF
YIELD
YIELD11.WMF
YOUTHSTL.WMF

11.WMF 12.WMF 13.WMF 14.WMF 15.WMF 16.WMF 17.WMF 18.WMF 9.WMF AUTHPERS.WMF

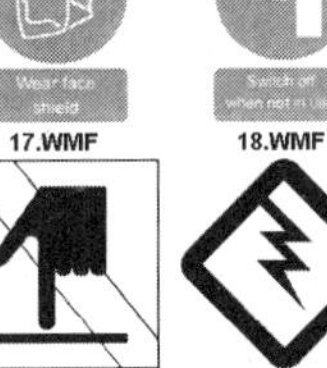

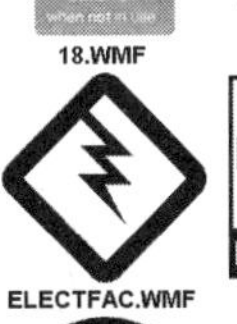
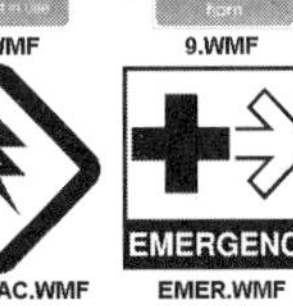

AVISO.WMF CANCRHAZ.WMF CAUTION1.WMF CUIDADO.WMF DANGER.WMF DIAL911.WMF DONTTOUC.WMF ELECTFAC.WMF EMER.WMF EMEREXIT.WMF

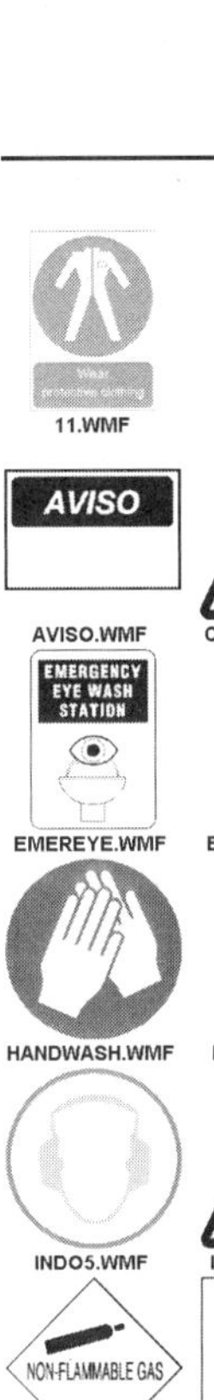
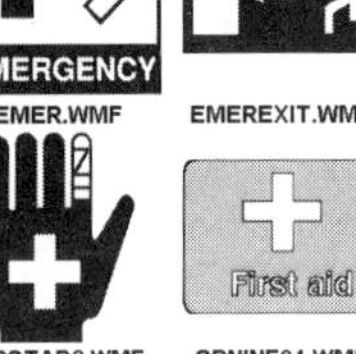

EMEREYE.WMF EMERSHW.WMF EMERSHWR.WMF FALLOBJ.WMF FIREALM1.WMF FIREALM2.WMF FIREPROT.WMF FIRSTAD1.WMF FIRSTAD2.WMF GRNINF04.WMF

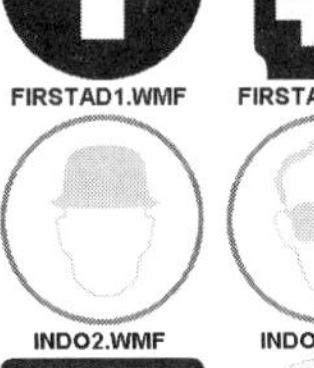
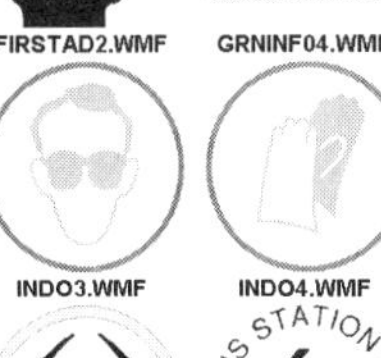

HANDWASH.WMF HAZAREA.WMF HAZSPIL.WMF HIGHVOL1.WMF HIGHVOL2.WMF HOT.WMF INDO1.WMF INDO2.WMF INDO3.WMF INDO4.WMF

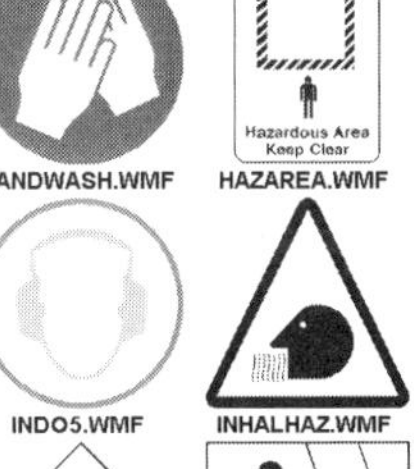
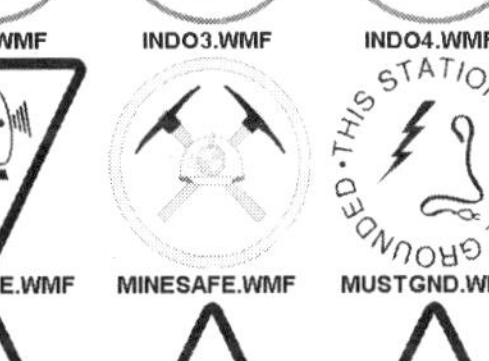

INDO5.WMF INHALHAZ.WMF KEEPCHIL.WMF LASBEAM1.WMF LASBEAM2.WMF MACHHAZ.WMF MAGNET2.WMF MICRWAVE.WMF MINESAFE.WMF MUSTGND.WMF

NONFLAM1.WMF NOSIT.WMF NOSMOKE1.WMF NOSMOKE3.WMF NOSMOKE4.WMF NOSTAND.WMF NOTICE.WMF OPENPIT.WMF OVERCRN1.WMF OVERCRN2.WMF

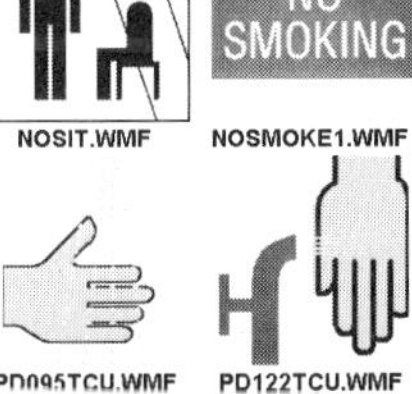

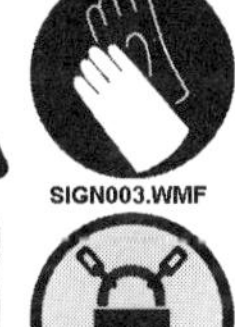

OXIDIZR1.WMF PD095TCU.WMF PD122TCU.WMF PELIGRO.WMF SAFETY.WMF SAFETY1.WMF SAFETY2.WMF SAFETYEQ.WMF SHARP.WMF SIGN003.WMF

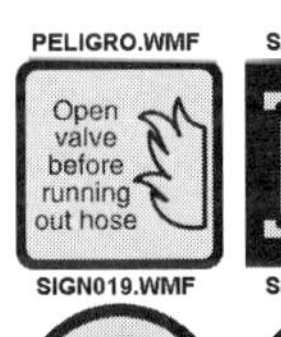

SIGN006.WMF SIGN017.WMF SIGN018.WMF SIGN019.WMF SIGN020.WMF SIGN021.WMF SIGN022.WMF SIGN023.WMF SIGN024.WMF SIGN025.WMF

SIGN026.WMF SIGN027.WMF SIGN028.WMF SIGN029.WMF SIGN030.WMF SIGN031.WMF SIGN032.WMF SIGN033.WMF SIGN034.WMF SIGN035.WMF

SIGN036.WMF SIGN037.WMF SIGN080.WMF SIGN081.WMF SIGN082.WMF SIGN083.WMF SIGN084.WMF SLIPERY1.WMF SLIPERY2.WMF WARNING1.WMF

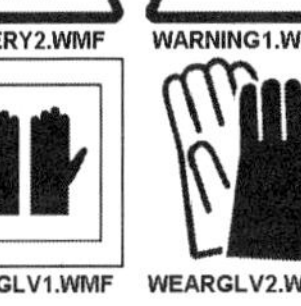

WARNING2.WMF WATCHAND.WMF WATCHFRK.WMF WATCHSTP.WMF WEARBOT1.WMF WEAREAR1.WMF WEAREAR2.WMF WEARGAS.WMF WEARGLV1.WMF WEARGLV2.WMF

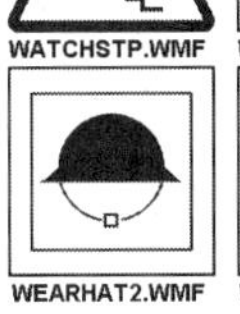
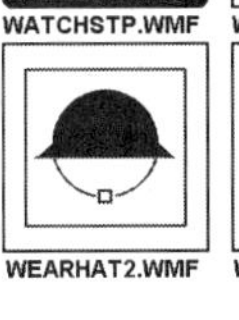

WEARGOG1.WMF WEARGOG2.WMF WEARHAT1.WMF WEARHAT2.WMF WEARPBLT.WMF WEARPC.WMF WETFLOOR.WMF WETPAINT.WMF

AD
AD.WMF
AHEADARR.WMF
AIRPORT1.WMF
AIRPORT2.WMF
AIRTRANS.WMF
AMPHITH.WMF
ARRIVING.WMF
ATVTRAIL.WMF
AUDIO DESCRIPTION
AUDIODES.WMF
AUTO.WMF
AUTOBANK.WMF
AUTOS.WMF
BAGCART.WMF
BAGCLAIM.WMF
BAGLOCK.WMF
BAGLOCKR.WMF
BAGUNCL.WMF
BALLET.WMF
BAND.WMF
BANK.WMF
BAOTLAUN.WMF
BAR.WMF
BARBBEAU.WMF
BARBER.WMF
BEACH1.WMF
BEACH2.WMF
BEARVIEW.WMF
BEAUTY.WMF
BIKETRL.WMF
BOATACC.WMF
BOATTOUR.WMF
Braille
BRAILLE.WMF
BUS.WMF
BUSCTR.WMF
BUSSTOP.WMF
CABLETV.WMF
CAMPERTR.WMF
CAMPFIRE.WMF
CAMPGRND.WMF
CARFERRY.WMF
CARRENT.WMF
CARRYNO.WMF
CARTRENT.WMF
CARWASH.WMF
CAUTDEEP.WMF
CAUTROCK.WMF
CAVERNS.WMF
CHAPEL.WMF
CC
CLOSECAP.WMF
COATCHEK.WMF
COFFSHOP.WMF
CONFLITE.WMF
100
5
10
CURREXCH.WMF
CUSTOMS.WMF
DAM.WMF
DANCING.WMF
DEERVIEW.WMF
DEPFLIGH.WMF
DIRARROW.WMF
DRESSRM.WMF
DRINKFT.WMF
DRINKWTR.WMF
DROWNFIR.WMF
DUTYFREE.WMF
ELEVATR1.WMF
ELEVATR2.WMF
ENTERTAN.WMF
ENVSTDY.WMF
ESCALATR.WMF
EXIT.WMF
FALLROCK.WMF
FIREARMS.WMF
FIREEXT.WMF
FIREWOOD.WMF
FIRSTAID.WMF
FISHATCH.WMF
FISHLADR.WMF
FLITINFO.WMF
FOOD.WMF
FUEL.WMF
D
FUELDIES.WMF
FULBRKFS.WMF
GAS.WMF
GIFTSHP1.WMF
GIFTSHP2.WMF
GROCERY.WMF
GROUNDTR.WMF
GRPCMPG.WMF
GRTRINFO.WMF
GUIDEDOG.WMF
HANDICAP.WMF
HEARIMP1.WMF
HEARIMP2.WMF
HELIPORT.WMF
HIKINGTR.WMF
HORSETR1.WMF
HORSETR2.WMF
HORSETR3.WMF
H
HOSPITAL.WMF
HOSTEL.WMF
HOTEL1.WMF
HOTEL2.WMF
HOTELINF.WMF
IMMIGRA.WMF
INFO.WMF
INTAUTTR.WMF
INTTRAIL.WMF
JEEPTRL.WMF
KENNEL.WMF
Large
Print
LARGEPRT.WMF
LAUNDRY.WMF
LEFTARRO.WMF
LEFTBAG.WMF
LIBRARY.WMF
LIFEJCKT.WMF
LIGHTHSE.WMF
LITTER.WMF
LODGING.WMF
LOOKOUT.WMF
LOSTFND.WMF

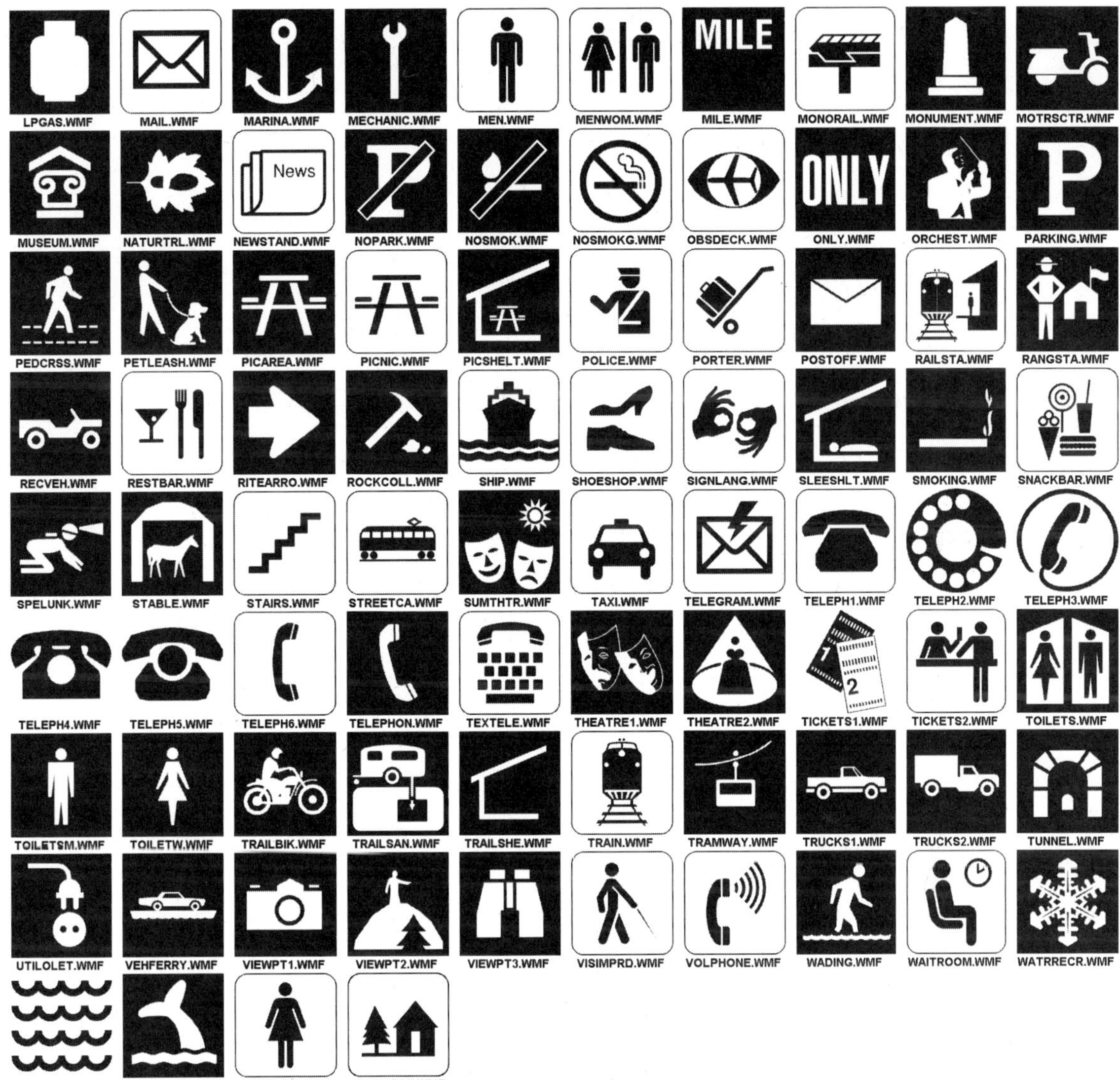
MILE
LPGAS.WMF
MAIL.WMF
MARINA.WMF
MECHANIC.WMF
MEN.WMF
MENWOM.WMF
MILE.WMF
MONORAIL.WMF
MONUMENT.WMF
MOTRSCTR.WMF
News
ONLY
P
MUSEUM.WMF
NATURTRL.WMF
NEWSTAND.WMF
NOPARK.WMF
NOSMOK.WMF
NOSMOKG.WMF
OBSDECK.WMF
ONLY.WMF
ORCHEST.WMF
PARKING.WMF
PEDCRSS.WMF
PETLEASH.WMF
PICAREA.WMF
PICNIC.WMF
PICSHELT.WMF
POLICE.WMF
PORTER.WMF
POSTOFF.WMF
RAILSTA.WMF
RANGSTA.WMF
RECVEH.WMF
RESTBAR.WMF
RITEARRO.WMF
ROCKCOLL.WMF
SHIP.WMF
SHOESHOP.WMF
SIGNLANG.WMF
SLEESHLT.WMF
SMOKING.WMF
SNACKBAR.WMF
SPELUNK.WMF
STABLE.WMF
STAIRS.WMF
STREETCA.WMF
SUMTHTR.WMF
TAXI.WMF
TELEGRAM.WMF
TELEPH1.WMF
TELEPH2.WMF
TELEPH3.WMF
1
2
TELEPH4.WMF
TELEPH5.WMF
TELEPH6.WMF
TELEPHON.WMF
TEXTELE.WMF
THEATRE1.WMF
THEATRE2.WMF
TICKETS1.WMF
TICKETS2.WMF
TOILETS.WMF
TOILETSM.WMF
TOILETW.WMF
TRAILBIK.WMF
TRAILSAN.WMF
TRAILSHE.WMF
TRAIN.WMF
TRAMWAY.WMF
TRUCKS1.WMF
TRUCKS2.WMF
TUNNEL.WMF
UTILOLET.WMF
VEHFERRY.WMF
VIEWPT1.WMF
VIEWPT2.WMF
VIEWPT3.WMF
VISIMPRD.WMF
VOLPHONE.WMF
WADING.WMF
WAITROOM.WMF
WATRRECR.WMF
WATRSPRT.WMF
WHALWTCH.WMF
WOMEN.WMF
YOUTHOST.WMF

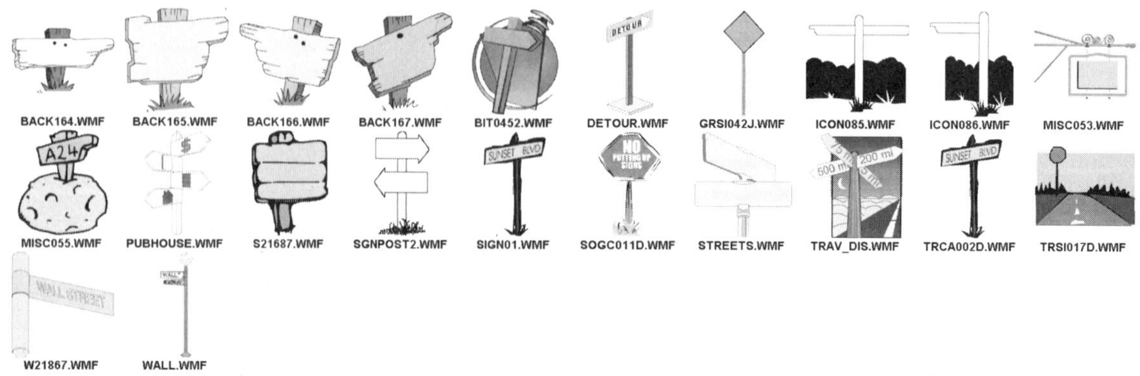

BACK164.WMF BACK165.WMF BACK166.WMF BACK167.WMF BIT0452.WMF DETOUR.WMF GRSI042J.WMF ICON085.WMF ICON086.WMF MISC053.WMF
MISC055.WMF PUBHOUSE.WMF S21687.WMF SGNPOST2.WMF SIGN01.WMF SOGC011D.WMF STREETS.WMF TRAV_DIS.WMF TRCA002D.WMF TRSI017D.WMF
W21867.WMF WALL.WMF

Signs • Stylized

27.WMF 28.WMF 29.WMF BALLROLL.WMF BYHAND.WMF CALLME.WMF COMEIN.WMF DAYNITE.WMF FACEIT.WMF FIRST.WMF
FLIGHT.WMF FOOTNOTE.WMF GEAR.WMF HANDSON.WMF HANGON.WMF HUGKISS.WMF IGNORE.WMF INTOUCH.WMF ITSME.WMF LEANONME.WMF
LOCKEDUP.WMF LOOKBACK.WMF MISTAKES.WMF NESTEGG.WMF PAGEDOWN.WMF PAGEUP.WMF PAUSE.WMF PERFECT.WMF PICTURE.WMF PLEASE.WMF
PUTALID.WMF REFLECT.WMF SINKSWIM.WMF STOCKEX.WMF STOP.WMF SURPRISE.WMF THISWAY.WMF TIEDUP.WMF TIMETOGO.WMF TURNPAGE.WMF
WRITEIT.WMF

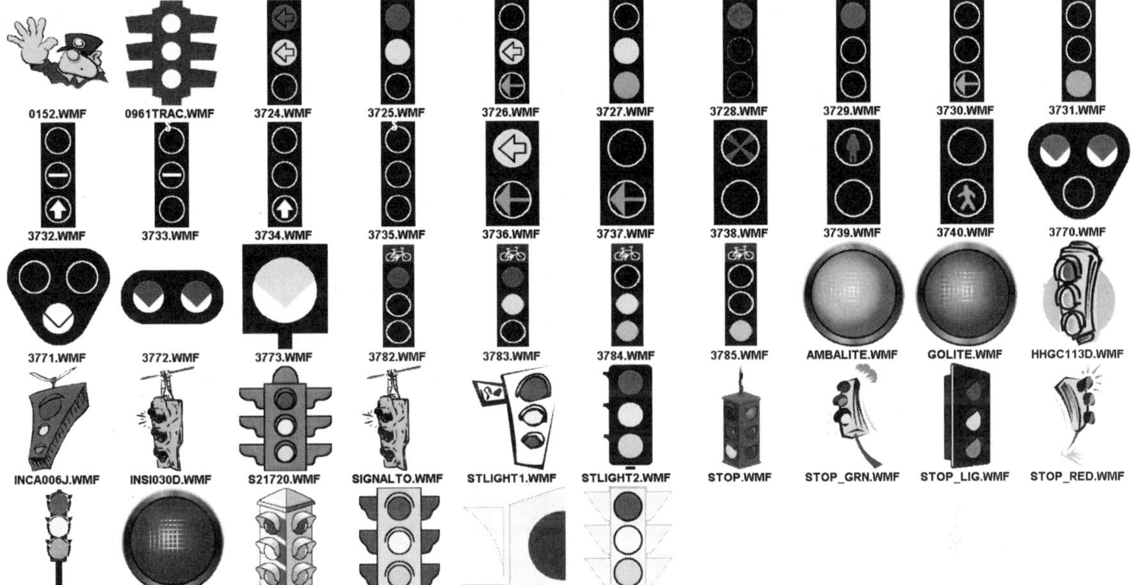
0152.WMF
0961TRAC.WMF
3724.WMF
3725.WMF
3726.WMF
3727.WMF
3728.WMF
3729.WMF
3730.WMF
3731.WMF
3732.WMF
3733.WMF
3734.WMF
3735.WMF
3736.WMF
3737.WMF
3738.WMF
3739.WMF
3740.WMF
3770.WMF
3771.WMF
3772.WMF
3773.WMF
3782.WMF
3783.WMF
3784.WMF
3785.WMF
AMBALITE.WMF
GOLITE.WMF
HHGC113D.WMF
INCA006J.WMF
INSI030D.WMF
S21720.WMF
SIGNALTO.WMF
STLIGHT1.WMF
STLIGHT2.WMF
STOP.WMF
STOP_GRN.WMF
STOP_LIG.WMF
STOP_RED.WMF
STOPLGHT.WMF
STOPLITE.WMF
TRAF_SIG.WMF
TRAFFICL.WMF
TRAFSGN2.WMF
TRAFSIGN.WMF

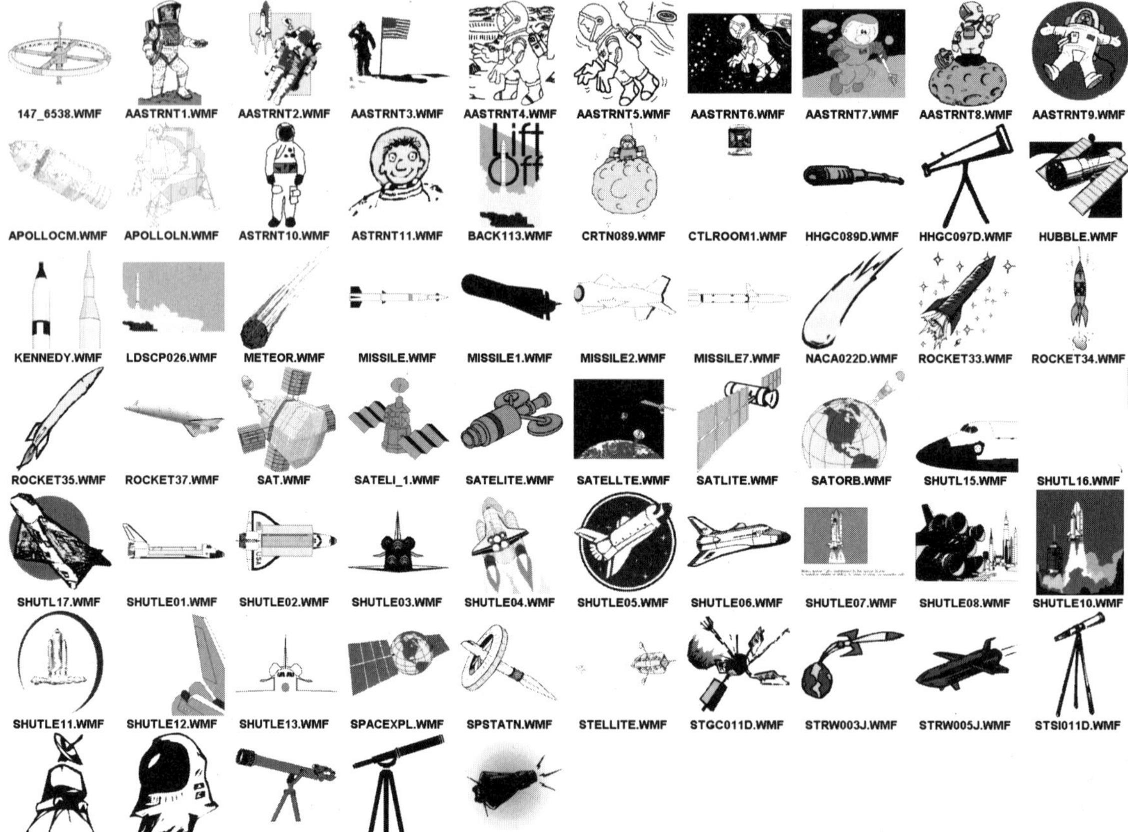
147_6538.WMF
AASTRNT1.WMF
AASTRNT2.WMF
AASTRNT3.WMF
AASTRNT4.WMF
AASTRNT5.WMF
AASTRNT6.WMF
AASTRNT7.WMF
AASTRNT8.WMF
AASTRNT9.WMF
Lift Off
APOLLOCM.WMF
APOLLOLN.WMF
ASTRNT10.WMF
ASTRNT11.WMF
BACK113.WMF
CRTN089.WMF
CTLROOM1.WMF
HHGC089D.WMF
HHGC097D.WMF
HUBBLE.WMF
KENNEDY.WMF
LDSCP026.WMF
METEOR.WMF
MISSILE.WMF
MISSILE1.WMF
MISSILE2.WMF
MISSILE7.WMF
NACA022D.WMF
ROCKET33.WMF
ROCKET34.WMF
ROCKET35.WMF
ROCKET37.WMF
SAT.WMF
SATELI_1.WMF
SATELITE.WMF
SATELLTE.WMF
SATLITE.WMF
SATORB.WMF
SHUTL15.WMF
SHUTL16.WMF
SHUTL17.WMF
SHUTLE01.WMF
SHUTLE02.WMF
SHUTLE03.WMF
SHUTLE04.WMF
SHUTLE05.WMF
SHUTLE06.WMF
SHUTLE07.WMF
SHUTLE08.WMF
SHUTLE10.WMF
SHUTLE11.WMF
SHUTLE12.WMF
SHUTLE13.WMF
SPACEXPL.WMF
SPSTATN.WMF
STELLITE.WMF
STGC011D.WMF
STRW003J.WMF
STRW005J.WMF
STSI011D.WMF
STSI012D.WMF
STSI013D.WMF
TELESCOP.WMF
TELSCOPE.WMF
TRRW003D.WMF

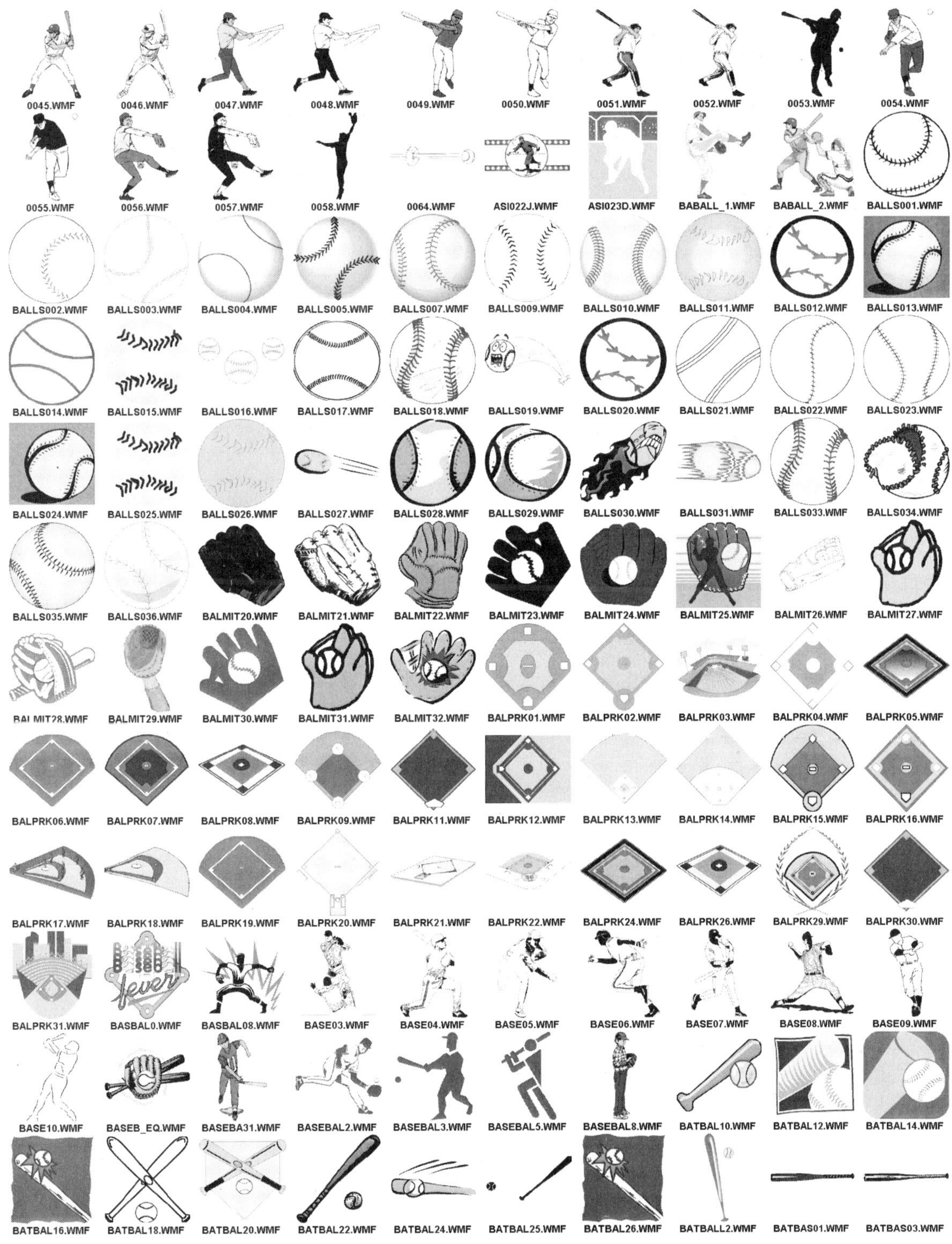
0045.WMF
0046.WMF
0047.WMF
0048.WMF
0049.WMF
0050.WMF
0051.WMF
0052.WMF
0053.WMF
0054.WMF
0055.WMF
0056.WMF
0057.WMF
0058.WMF
0064.WMF
ASI022J.WMF
ASI023D.WMF
BABALL_1.WMF
BABALL_2.WMF
BALLS001.WMF
BALLS002.WMF
BALLS003.WMF
BALLS004.WMF
BALLS005.WMF
BALLS007.WMF
BALLS009.WMF
BALLS010.WMF
BALLS011.WMF
BALLS012.WMF
BALLS013.WMF
BALLS014.WMF
BALLS015.WMF
BALLS016.WMF
BALLS017.WMF
BALLS018.WMF
BALLS019.WMF
BALLS020.WMF
BALLS021.WMF
BALLS022.WMF
BALLS023.WMF
BALLS024.WMF
BALLS025.WMF
BALLS026.WMF
BALLS027.WMF
BALLS028.WMF
BALLS029.WMF
BALLS030.WMF
BALLS031.WMF
BALLS033.WMF
BALLS034.WMF
BALLS035.WMF
BALLS036.WMF
BALMIT20.WMF
BALMIT21.WMF
BALMIT22.WMF
BALMIT23.WMF
BALMIT24.WMF
BALMIT25.WMF
BALMIT26.WMF
BALMIT27.WMF
BALMIT28.WMF
BALMIT29.WMF
BALMIT30.WMF
BALMIT31.WMF
BALMIT32.WMF
BALPRK01.WMF
BALPRK02.WMF
BALPRK03.WMF
BALPRK04.WMF
BALPRK05.WMF
BALPRK06.WMF
BALPRK07.WMF
BALPRK08.WMF
BALPRK09.WMF
BALPRK11.WMF
BALPRK12.WMF
BALPRK13.WMF
BALPRK14.WMF
BALPRK15.WMF
BALPRK16.WMF
BALPRK17.WMF
BALPRK18.WMF
BALPRK19.WMF
BALPRK20.WMF
BALPRK21.WMF
BALPRK22.WMF
BALPRK24.WMF
BALPRK26.WMF
BALPRK29.WMF
BALPRK30.WMF
BALPRK31.WMF
BASBAL0.WMF
BASBAL08.WMF
BASE03.WMF
BASE04.WMF
BASE05.WMF
BASE06.WMF
BASE07.WMF
BASE08.WMF
BASE09.WMF
BASE10.WMF
BASEB_EQ.WMF
BASEBA31.WMF
BASEBAL2.WMF
BASEBAL3.WMF
BASEBAL5.WMF
BASEBAL8.WMF
BATBAL10.WMF
BATBAL12.WMF
BATBAL14.WMF
BATBAL16.WMF
BATBAL18.WMF
BATBAL20.WMF
BATBAL22.WMF
BATBAL24.WMF
BATBAL25.WMF
BATBAL26.WMF
BATBALL2.WMF
BATBAS01.WMF
BATBAS03.WMF

BATBAS05.WMF
BATBAS07.WMF
BATBAS09.WMF
BATBAS11.WMF
BATBAS13.WMF
BATBAS15.WMF
BATBAS17.WMF
BATBAS19.WMF
BATBAS21.WMF
BATBAS23.WMF
BATBAS25.WMF
BATGLOVE.WMF
BATTER01.WMF
BATTER02.WMF
BATTER12.WMF
BATTER2.WMF
BATTERA.WMF
BATTERAB.WMF
BATTERSW.WMF
BBALL01.WMF
BSBAL03.WMF
BSBAL05.WMF
BSBAL06.WMF
BSBAL07.WMF
BSBAL08.WMF
BSBAL09.WMF
BSBAL13.WMF
BSBAL14.WMF
BSBAL15.WMF
BSBAL17.WMF
BSBAL18.WMF
BSBAL19.WMF
BSBAL22.WMF
BSBAL25.WMF
BSBAL26.WMF
BSBAL32.WMF
BSBAL33.WMF
BSBAL34.WMF
BSBAL35.WMF
BSBAL36.WMF
BSBAL37.WMF
BSBAL38.WMF
BSBAL39.WMF
BSBAL40.WMF
BSBAL41.WMF
BSBAL42.WMF
BSBAL47.WMF
BSBAL51.WMF
BSBAL56.WMF
BSBAL60.WMF
BSBAL64.WMF
BSBAL67.WMF
BSBAL68.WMF
BSBAL69.WMF
BSBAL70.WMF
BSBL_PLY.WMF
BSEBAL03.WMF
BSEBAL06.WMF
BSEBAL09.WMF
CAA0437.WMF
CAA0438.WMF
CAA0439.WMF
CAA0442.WMF
CAA0443.WMF
CAA0445.WMF
CAA0446.WMF
CAA0447.WMF
CAA0448.WMF
CAA0453.WMF
CAA0455.WMF
CAA0456.WMF
CAA0459.WMF
CAA0465.WMF
CAA0468.WMF
CAA0469.WMF
CAA0470.WMF
CAA0471.WMF
CAA0472.WMF
CAA0764.WMF
CAA0765.WMF
CAA0766.WMF
CAA0767.WMF
CAA0768.WMF
CAA0769.WMF
CAA0771.WMF
CAA0772.WMF
CAA0773.WMF
CAA0774.WMF
CAA0775.WMF
CAA0776.WMF
CAA0777.WMF
CATCHER.WMF
CATCHER5.WMF
COACH.WMF
CTCH_UMP.WMF
DEC066G.WMF
DEC066J.WMF
DEC066P.WMF
DEC069E.WMF
EQUIP.WMF
FIELDER.WMF
FSW012D.WMF
FSW020A.WMF
FSW020B.WMF
FSW020C.WMF
FSW020D.WMF
GBATTER.WMF
GIRLSOFT.WMF
GIRLSSOF.WMF
HPI010C.WMF
HSP014B.WMF
HSP015A.WMF
IBS001C.WMF
IBS003A.WMF
IBS008C.WMF
IBS010B.WMF
IBS017C.WMF
IBS018C.WMF
IBS023B.WMF
IBS024A.WMF

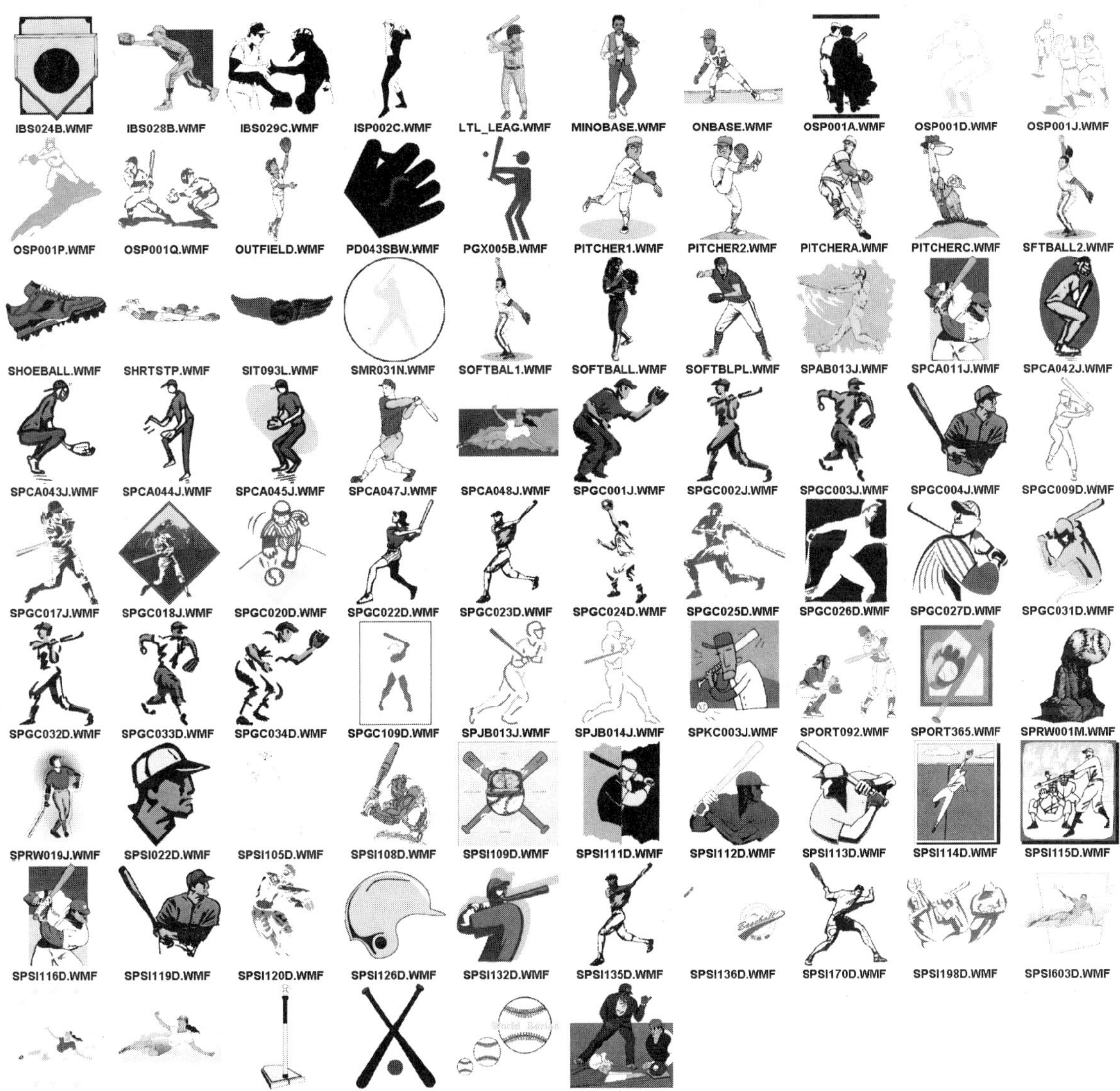

IBS024B.WMF IBS028B.WMF IBS029C.WMF ISP002C.WMF LTL_LEAG.WMF MINOBASE.WMF ONBASE.WMF OSP001A.WMF OSP001D.WMF OSP001J.WMF

OSP001P.WMF OSP001Q.WMF OUTFIELD.WMF PD043SBW.WMF PGX005B.WMF PITCHER1.WMF PITCHER2.WMF PITCHERA.WMF PITCHERC.WMF SFTBALL2.WMF

SHOEBALL.WMF SHRTSTP.WMF SIT093L.WMF SMR031N.WMF SOFTBAL1.WMF SOFTBALL.WMF SOFTBLPL.WMF SPAB013J.WMF SPCA011J.WMF SPCA042J.WMF

SPCA043J.WMF SPCA044J.WMF SPCA045J.WMF SPCA047J.WMF SPCA048J.WMF SPGC001J.WMF SPGC002J.WMF SPGC003J.WMF SPGC004J.WMF SPGC009D.WMF

SPGC017J.WMF SPGC018J.WMF SPGC020D.WMF SPGC022D.WMF SPGC023D.WMF SPGC024D.WMF SPGC025D.WMF SPGC026D.WMF SPGC027D.WMF SPGC031D.WMF

SPGC032D.WMF SPGC033D.WMF SPGC034D.WMF SPGC109D.WMF SPJB013J.WMF SPJB014J.WMF SPKC003J.WMF SPORT092.WMF SPORT365.WMF SPRW001M.WMF

SPRW019J.WMF SPSI022D.WMF SPSI105D.WMF SPSI108D.WMF SPSI109D.WMF SPSI111D.WMF SPSI112D.WMF SPSI113D.WMF SPSI114D.WMF SPSI115D.WMF

SPSI116D.WMF SPSI119D.WMF SPSI120D.WMF SPSI126D.WMF SPSI132D.WMF SPSI135D.WMF SPSI136D.WMF SPSI170D.WMF SPSI198D.WMF SPSI603D.WMF

SPSI604D.WMF SPSI605D.WMF TBALL.WMF TDG026B.WMF WORLDSER.WMF YEROUT.WMF

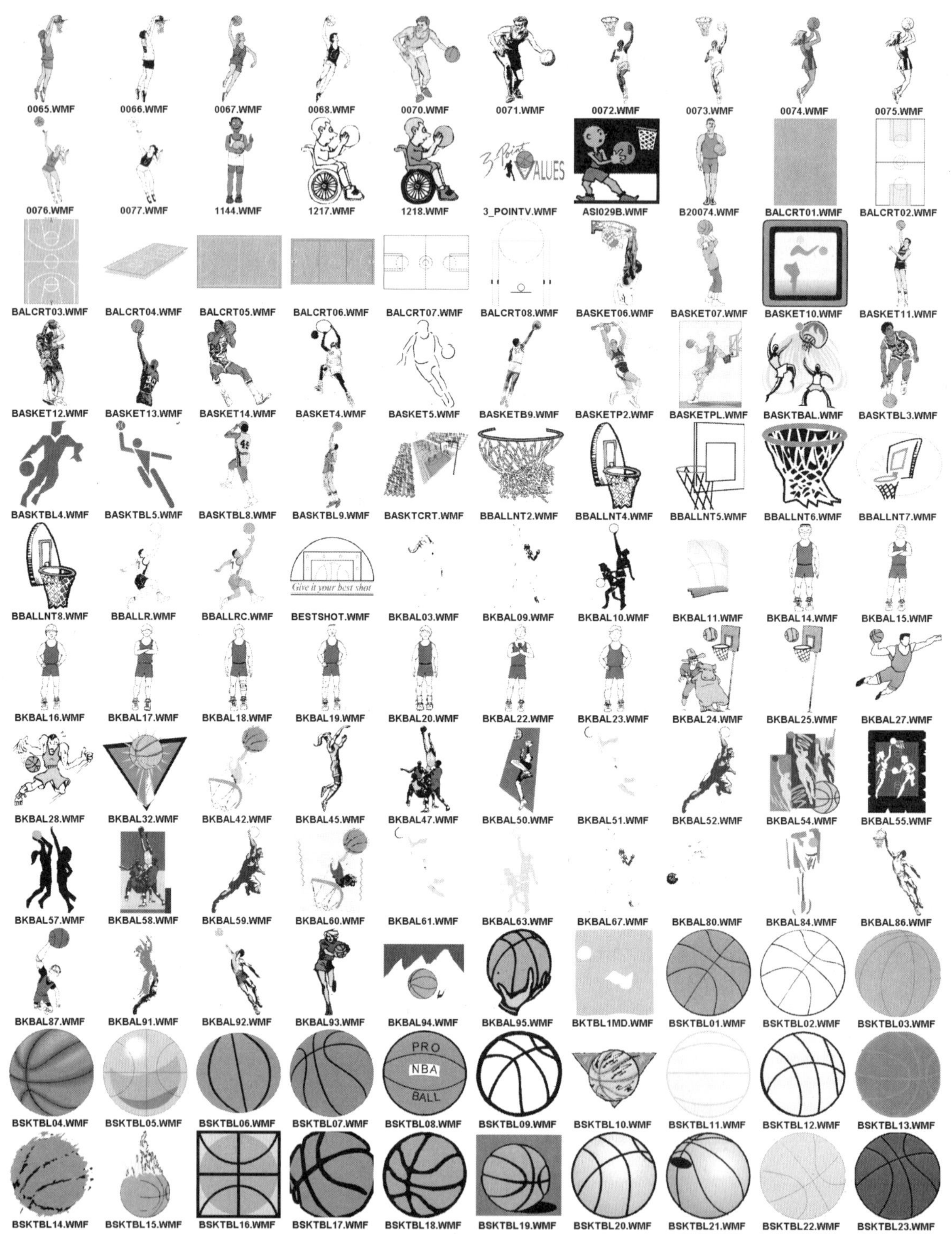

0065.WMF 0066.WMF 0067.WMF 0068.WMF 0070.WMF 0071.WMF 0072.WMF 0073.WMF 0074.WMF 0075.WMF

0076.WMF 0077.WMF 1144.WMF 1217.WMF 1218.WMF 3_POINTV.WMF ASI029B.WMF B20074.WMF BALCRT01.WMF BALCRT02.WMF

BALCRT03.WMF BALCRT04.WMF BALCRT05.WMF BALCRT06.WMF BALCRT07.WMF BALCRT08.WMF BASKET06.WMF BASKET07.WMF BASKET10.WMF BASKET11.WMF

BASKET12.WMF BASKET13.WMF BASKET14.WMF BASKET4.WMF BASKET5.WMF BASKETB9.WMF BASKETP2.WMF BASKETPL.WMF BASKTBAL.WMF BASKTBL3.WMF

BASKTBL4.WMF BASKTBL5.WMF BASKTBL8.WMF BASKTBL9.WMF BASKTCRT.WMF BBALLNT2.WMF BBALLNT4.WMF BBALLNT5.WMF BBALLNT6.WMF BBALLNT7.WMF

BBALLNT8.WMF BBALLR.WMF BBALLRC.WMF BESTSHOT.WMF BKBAL03.WMF BKBAL09.WMF BKBAL10.WMF BKBAL11.WMF BKBAL14.WMF BKBAL15.WMF

BKBAL16.WMF BKBAL17.WMF BKBAL18.WMF BKBAL19.WMF BKBAL20.WMF BKBAL22.WMF BKBAL23.WMF BKBAL24.WMF BKBAL25.WMF BKBAL27.WMF

BKBAL28.WMF BKBAL32.WMF BKBAL42.WMF BKBAL45.WMF BKBAL47.WMF BKBAL50.WMF BKBAL51.WMF BKBAL52.WMF BKBAL54.WMF BKBAL55.WMF

BKBAL57.WMF BKBAL58.WMF BKBAL59.WMF BKBAL60.WMF BKBAL61.WMF BKBAL63.WMF BKBAL67.WMF BKBAL80.WMF BKBAL84.WMF BKBAL86.WMF

BKBAL87.WMF BKBAL91.WMF BKBAL92.WMF BKBAL93.WMF BKBAL94.WMF BKBAL95.WMF BKTBL1MD.WMF BSKTBL01.WMF BSKTBL02.WMF BSKTBL03.WMF

BSKTBL04.WMF BSKTBL05.WMF BSKTBL06.WMF BSKTBL07.WMF BSKTBL08.WMF BSKTBL09.WMF BSKTBL10.WMF BSKTBL11.WMF BSKTBL12.WMF BSKTBL13.WMF

BSKTBL14.WMF BSKTBL15.WMF BSKTBL16.WMF BSKTBL17.WMF BSKTBL18.WMF BSKTBL19.WMF BSKTBL20.WMF BSKTBL21.WMF BSKTBL22.WMF BSKTBL23.WMF

BSKTBL24.WMF BSKTBL25.WMF BSKTBL26.WMF BSKTBL27.WMF BSKTBL28.WMF BSKTBL29.WMF BSKTBL30.WMF BSKTBL31.WMF BSKTBL32.WMF BSKTBL33.WMF
BSKTBL34.WMF BSKTBL35.WMF BSKTBL36.WMF BSKTBL37.WMF BSKTBL38.WMF BSKTBL39.WMF BSKTBL40.WMF BSKTBL41.WMF BSKTBL42.WMF BSKTBL43.WMF
BSKTBL44.WMF BSKTBL45.WMF BSKTBL46.WMF BSKTPLYR.WMF CAA0501.WMF CAA0502.WMF CAA0503.WMF CAA0504.WMF CAA0505.WMF CAA0506.WMF
CAA0507.WMF CAA0508.WMF CAA0509.WMF CAA0520.WMF CAA0522.WMF CAA0523.WMF CAA0525.WMF CAA0526.WMF CAA0527.WMF CAA0529.WMF
Jump
CAA0877.WMF CAA0878.WMF DRIBBLER.WMF DRIBBLR5.WMF DUNK3.WMF FADEAWAY.WMF FREETHR9.WMF FREETHRW.WMF GETAJUMP.WMF GIRL_BSK.WMF
GOAL01.WMF GOAL02.WMF GOAL03.WMF GOAL04.WMF GOAL05.WMF GOAL06.WMF GOAL07.WMF GOAL08.WMF HOOKS.WMF HPI024C.WMF
HSP016A.WMF HSP017D.WMF IHD023A.WMF JUMPBALL.WMF JUMPSHOT.WMF LAY_UP.WMF MNSTR2MD.WMF MNSTR3MD.WMF NTBALL01.WMF NTBALL02.WMF
NTBALL06.WMF NTBALL07.WMF NTBALL10.WMF NTBALL11.WMF NTBALL12.WMF NTBALL13.WMF NTBALL14.WMF NTBALL15.WMF NTBALL16.WMF NTBALL17.WMF
NTBALL18.WMF NTBALL19.WMF NTBALL20.WMF NTBALL21.WMF NTBALL22.WMF NTBALL23.WMF NTBALL24.WMF NTBALL25.WMF NTBALL26.WMF NTBALL27.WMF
NTBALL28.WMF NTBALL29.WMF NTBALL30.WMF NTBALL32.WMF NTBALL33.WMF NTBALL34.WMF NTBALL35.WMF NTBALL36.WMF NTBALL38.WMF NTBALL39.WMF
Slam-DunK
SPECIALS
NTBALL40.WMF NTBALL45.WMF PD091UCU.WMF SLAM_DN2.WMF SLAM_DUN.WMF SPAB002D.WMF SPAB003D.WMF SPCA027J.WMF SPCA039J.WMF SPGC013D.WMF
SPGC015D.WMF SPGC016D.WMF SPGC017D.WMF SPGC018D.WMF SPGC039J.WMF SPORT048.WMF SPORT113.WMF SPRW016J.WMF SPRW017J.WMF SPSI065D.WMF

SPSI072D.WMF SPSI074D.WMF SPSI075D.WMF

SPSI078D.WMF SPSI080D.WMF

SPSI087D.WMF

SPSI579D.WMF

SPSI621D.WMF

SPSI665D.WMF

SPSS005J.WMF

WHLCH_BB.WMF WMBSKTBL.WMF

0388.WMF
0389.WMF
0514.WMF
0515.WMF
0516.WMF
0517.WMF
BICYCLE.WMF
BICYCLE1.WMF
BICYCLE2.WMF
BIKE001.WMF
BIKE002.WMF
BIKE003.WMF
BIKE004.WMF
BIKE005.WMF
BIKE006.WMF
BIKE007.WMF
BIKE008.WMF
BIKE009.WMF
BIKE010.WMF
BIKER2MD.WMF
BIKER3MD.WMF
BIKER4MD.WMF
BIKERACE.WMF
BIKETOUR.WMF
CAA0473.WMF
CAA0474.WMF
CAA0475.WMF
CAA0476.WMF
CAA0477.WMF
CAA0478.WMF
CAA0479.WMF
CAA0480.WMF
CAA0481.WMF
CYCLE05.WMF
CYCLE06.WMF
CYCLE07.WMF
CYCLE08.WMF
CYCLE09.WMF
CYCLE11.WMF
CYCLE12.WMF
CYCLE13.WMF
CYCLE14.WMF
CYCLE15.WMF
CYCLE18.WMF
CYCLE19.WMF
CYCLE20.WMF
CYCLE21.WMF
CYCLE22.WMF
CYCLE23.WMF
CYCLE24.WMF
CYCLE25.WMF
CYCLE27.WMF
CYCLE28.WMF
CYCLE29.WMF
CYCLE30.WMF
CYCLE31.WMF
CYCLE32.WMF
CYCLING.WMF
CYCLING1.WMF
CYCLING2.WMF
CYCLING3.WMF
CYCLING4.WMF
CYCLING5.WMF
CYCLING9.WMF
CYCLIST.WMF
CYCLIST1.WMF
CYCLIST2.WMF
CYCLISTC.WMF
DEC068J.WMF
EAC072N.WMF
IFN023C.WMF
OFS055H.WMF
PD091LCU.WMF
SCH003A.WMF
SPAB003K.WMF
SPAB050D.WMF
SPAC001D.WMF
SPCA038J.WMF
SPGC001D.WMF
SPGC001M.WMF
SPGC012D.WMF
SPGC036J.WMF
SPGC037J.WMF
SPGC071D.WMF
SPGC078D.WMF
SPGC106D.WMF
SPGC110D.WMF
SPGC111D.WMF
SPGC112D.WMF
SPGC123D.WMF
SPGC124D.WMF
SPJB009J.WMF
SPJB010J.WMF
SPORT050.WMF
SPORT095.WMF
SPRW014J.WMF
SPRW015J.WMF
SPSI008D.WMF
SPSI010D.WMF
SPSI011D.WMF
SPSI011J.WMF
SPSI012J.WMF
SPSI018D.WMF
SPSI020J.WMF
SPSI021D.WMF
SPSI024D.WMF
SPSI543D.WMF
SPSI611D.WMF
SPSI615D.WMF
SPSI636D.WMF
TEN_SPEE.WMF

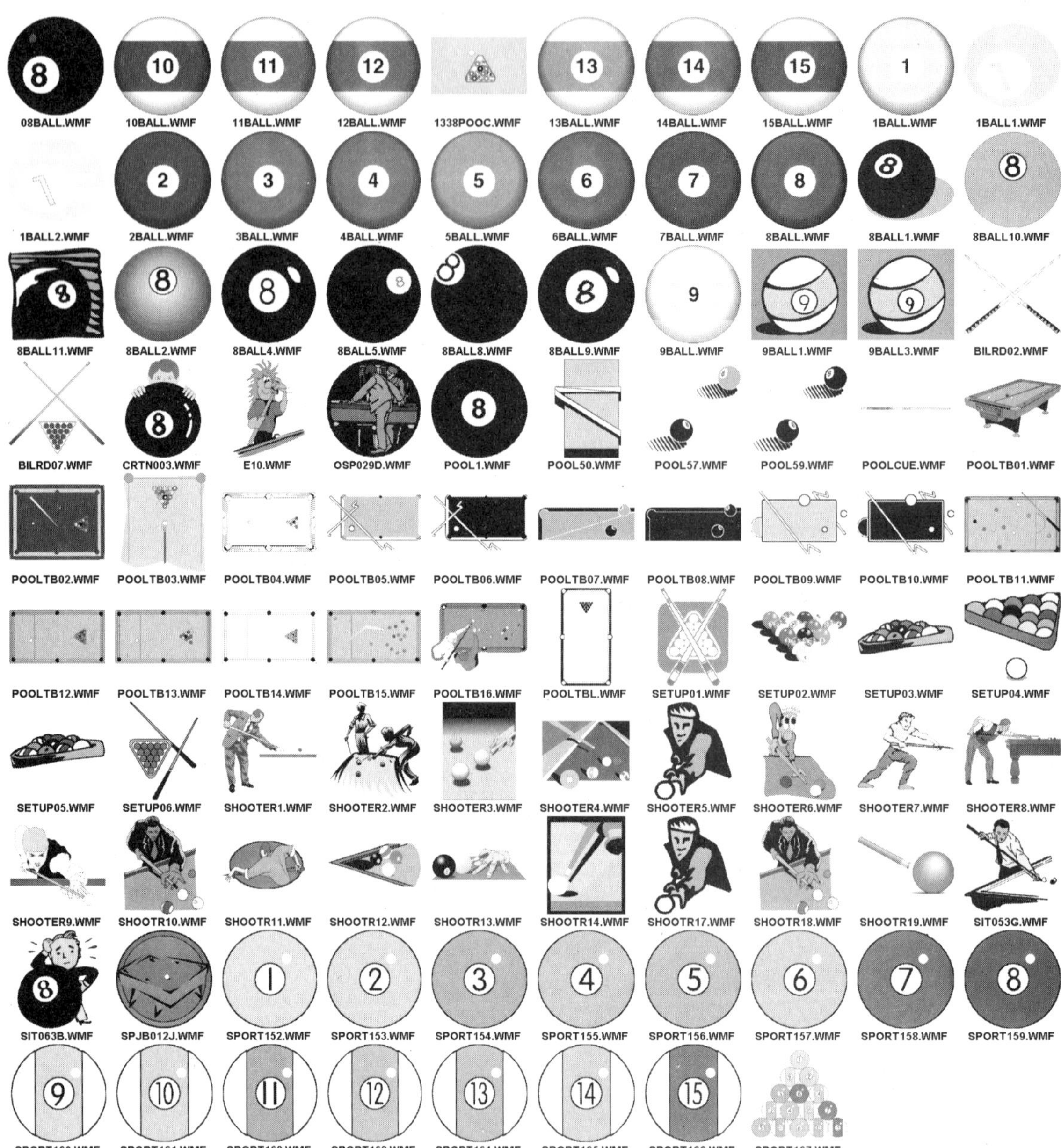

08BALL.WMF 10BALL.WMF 11BALL.WMF 12BALL.WMF 1338POOC.WMF 13BALL.WMF 14BALL.WMF 15BALL.WMF 1BALL.WMF 1BALL1.WMF

1BALL2.WMF 2BALL.WMF 3BALL.WMF 4BALL.WMF 5BALL.WMF 6BALL.WMF 7BALL.WMF 8BALL.WMF 8BALL1.WMF 8BALL10.WMF

8BALL11.WMF 8BALL2.WMF 8BALL4.WMF 8BALL5.WMF 8BALL8.WMF 8BALL9.WMF 9BALL.WMF 9BALL1.WMF 9BALL3.WMF BILRD02.WMF

BILRD07.WMF CRTN003.WMF E10.WMF OSP029D.WMF POOL1.WMF POOL50.WMF POOL57.WMF POOL59.WMF POOLCUE.WMF POOLTB01.WMF

POOLTB02.WMF POOLTB03.WMF POOLTB04.WMF POOLTB05.WMF POOLTB06.WMF POOLTB07.WMF POOLTB08.WMF POOLTB09.WMF POOLTB10.WMF POOLTB11.WMF

POOLTB12.WMF POOLTB13.WMF POOLTB14.WMF POOLTB15.WMF POOLTB16.WMF POOLTBL.WMF SETUP01.WMF SETUP02.WMF SETUP03.WMF SETUP04.WMF

SETUP05.WMF SETUP06.WMF SHOOTER1.WMF SHOOTER2.WMF SHOOTER3.WMF SHOOTER4.WMF SHOOTER5.WMF SHOOTER6.WMF SHOOTER7.WMF SHOOTER8.WMF

SHOOTER9.WMF SHOOTR10.WMF SHOOTR11.WMF SHOOTR12.WMF SHOOTR13.WMF SHOOTR14.WMF SHOOTR17.WMF SHOOTR18.WMF SHOOTR19.WMF SIT053G.WMF

SIT063B.WMF SPJB012J.WMF SPORT152.WMF SPORT153.WMF SPORT154.WMF SPORT155.WMF SPORT156.WMF SPORT157.WMF SPORT158.WMF SPORT159.WMF

SPORT160.WMF SPORT161.WMF SPORT162.WMF SPORT163.WMF SPORT164.WMF SPORT165.WMF SPORT166.WMF SPORT167.WMF

SKATEBO.WMF
SKTBRD01.WMF
SKTBRD03.WMF
SKTBRD05.WMF
SKTBRD07.WMF
SKTBRD09.WMF
SKTBRD11.WMF
SKTBRD13.WMF
SKTBRD15.WMF
SKTBRD17.WMF
SKTBRD19.WMF
SKTBRD21.WMF
SKTBRD23.WMF
SKTBRD25.WMF
SKTBRD27.WMF
SKTBRD29.WMF
SKTBRD31.WMF
SKTBRD33.WMF
SKTBRD35.WMF
SKTBRD37.WMF
SKTBRD39.WMF
SKTBRD41.WMF
SKTBRD43.WMF
SKTBRD45.WMF
SKTBRD47.WMF
SKTBRD49.WMF
SKTBRD51.WMF
SKTBRD53.WMF
SKTBRD55.WMF
SKTBRD57.WMF
SKTBRD59.WMF
SNWBRD01.WMF
SNWBRD02.WMF
SNWBRD03.WMF
SNWBRD04.WMF
SNWBRD05.WMF
SNWBRD06.WMF
SNWBRD07.WMF
SNWBRD08.WMF
SNWBRD09.WMF
SNWBRD10.WMF
SNWBRD11.WMF
SNWBRD12.WMF
SNWBRD13.WMF
SNWBRD14.WMF
SNWBRD15.WMF
SNWBRD16.WMF
SNWBRD17.WMF
SNWBRD18.WMF
SNWBRD19.WMF
SNWBRD20.WMF
SNWBRD21.WMF
SNWBRD22.WMF
SNWBRD23.WMF
SNWBRD24.WMF
SNWBRD25.WMF
SNWBRD26.WMF
SNWBRD27.WMF
SNWBRD28.WMF
SNWBRD29.WMF
SNWBRD30.WMF
SNWBRD31.WMF
SNWBRD32.WMF
SNWBRD33.WMF
SNWBRD34.WMF
SNWBRD36.WMF
SNWBRD37.WMF
SNWBRD38.WMF
SNWBRD39.WMF
SNWBRD40.WMF
SNWBRD41.WMF
SNWBRD42.WMF
SNWBRD43.WMF
SNWBRD44.WMF
SNWBRD45.WMF
SNWBRD46.WMF
SNWBRD47.WMF
SRFBD001.WMF
SRFBD002.WMF
SRFBD003.WMF
SRFBD004.WMF
SRFBD005.WMF
SRFBD006.WMF
SRFBD007.WMF
SRFBD008.WMF
SRFBD009.WMF
SRFBD010.WMF
SRFBD012.WMF
SRFBD015.WMF
SRFBD016.WMF
SRFBD017.WMF
SRFBD018.WMF
SRFBD022.WMF
SRFBD023.WMF
SRFBD024.WMF
SRFBD025.WMF
SRFBD026.WMF
SRFBD027.WMF

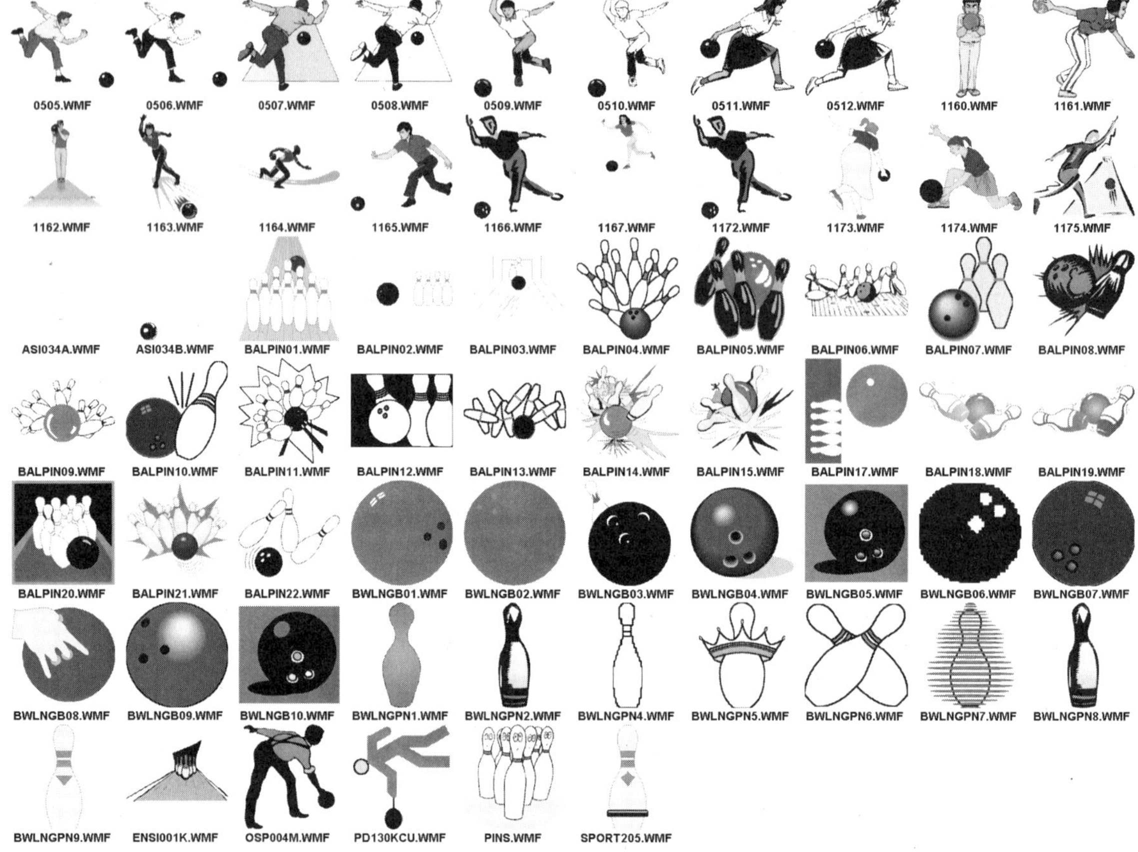
0505.WMF
0506.WMF
0507.WMF
0508.WMF
0509.WMF
0510.WMF
0511.WMF
0512.WMF
1160.WMF
1161.WMF
1162.WMF
1163.WMF
1164.WMF
1165.WMF
1166.WMF
1167.WMF
1172.WMF
1173.WMF
1174.WMF
1175.WMF
ASI034A.WMF
ASI034B.WMF
BALPIN01.WMF
BALPIN02.WMF
BALPIN03.WMF
BALPIN04.WMF
BALPIN05.WMF
BALPIN06.WMF
BALPIN07.WMF
BALPIN08.WMF
BALPIN09.WMF
BALPIN10.WMF
BALPIN11.WMF
BALPIN12.WMF
BALPIN13.WMF
BALPIN14.WMF
BALPIN15.WMF
BALPIN17.WMF
BALPIN18.WMF
BALPIN19.WMF
BALPIN20.WMF
BALPIN21.WMF
BALPIN22.WMF
BWLNGB01.WMF
BWLNGB02.WMF
BWLNGB03.WMF
BWLNGB04.WMF
BWLNGB05.WMF
BWLNGB06.WMF
BWLNGB07.WMF
BWLNGB08.WMF
BWLNGB09.WMF
BWLNGB10.WMF
BWLNGPN1.WMF
BWLNGPN2.WMF
BWLNGPN4.WMF
BWLNGPN5.WMF
BWLNGPN6.WMF
BWLNGPN7.WMF
BWLNGPN8.WMF
BWLNGPN9.WMF
ENSI001K.WMF
OSP004M.WMF
PD130KCU.WMF
PINS.WMF
SPORT205.WMF

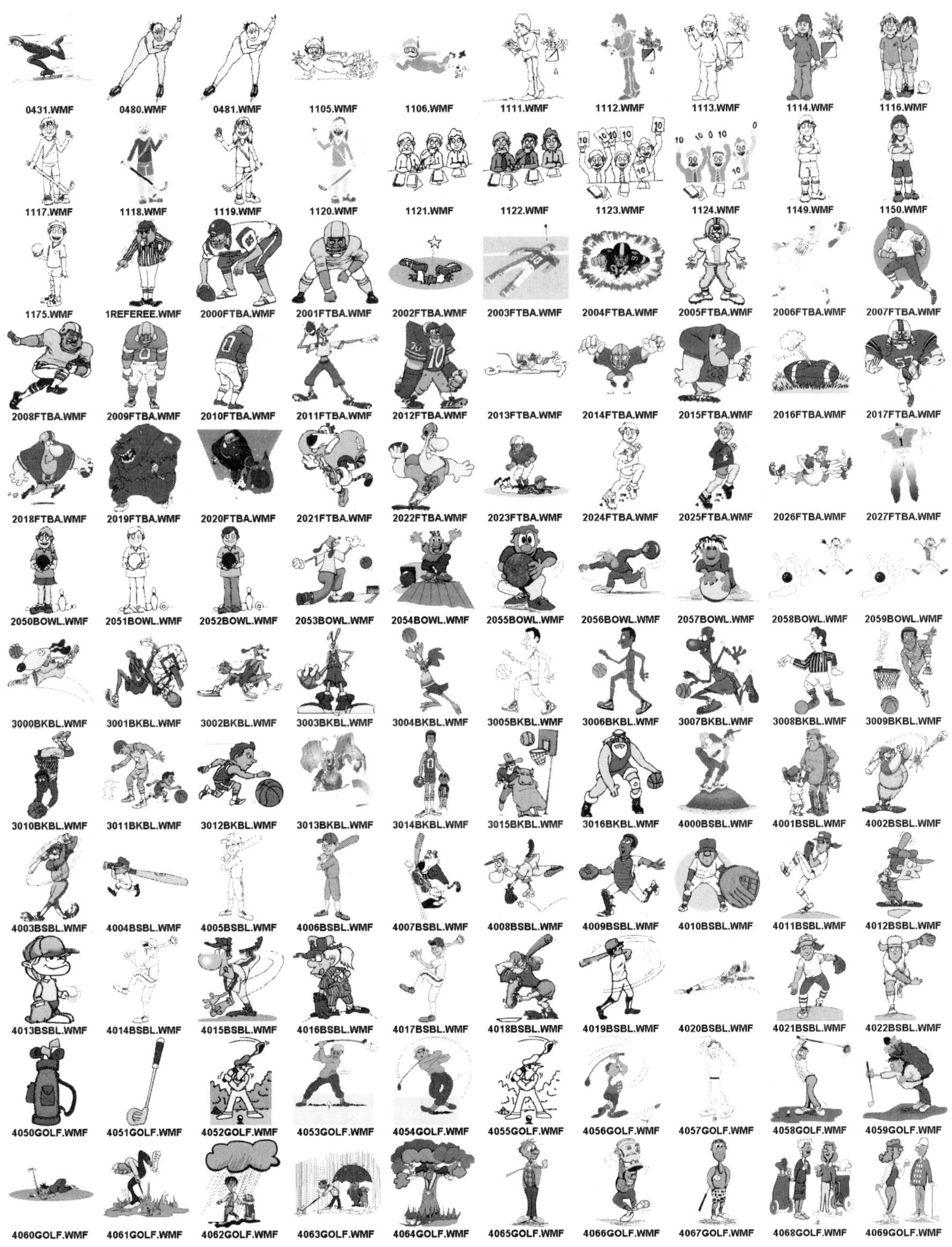

0431.WMF 0480.WMF 0481.WMF 1105.WMF 1106.WMF 1111.WMF 1112.WMF 1113.WMF 1114.WMF 1116.WMF
1117.WMF 1118.WMF 1119.WMF 1120.WMF 1121.WMF 1122.WMF 1123.WMF 1124.WMF 1149.WMF 1150.WMF
1175.WMF 1REFEREE.WMF 2000FTBA.WMF 2001FTBA.WMF 2002FTBA.WMF 2003FTBA.WMF 2004FTBA.WMF 2005FTBA.WMF 2006FTBA.WMF 2007FTBA.WMF
2008FTBA.WMF 2009FTBA.WMF 2010FTBA.WMF 2011FTBA.WMF 2012FTBA.WMF 2013FTBA.WMF 2014FTBA.WMF 2015FTBA.WMF 2016FTBA.WMF 2017FTBA.WMF
2018FTBA.WMF 2019FTBA.WMF 2020FTBA.WMF 2021FTBA.WMF 2022FTBA.WMF 2023FTBA.WMF 2024FTBA.WMF 2025FTBA.WMF 2026FTBA.WMF 2027FTBA.WMF
2050BOWL.WMF 2051BOWL.WMF 2052BOWL.WMF 2053BOWL.WMF 2054BOWL.WMF 2055BOWL.WMF 2056BOWL.WMF 2057BOWL.WMF 2058BOWL.WMF 2059BOWL.WMF
3000BKBL.WMF 3001BKBL.WMF 3002BKBL.WMF 3003BKBL.WMF 3004BKBL.WMF 3005BKBL.WMF 3006BKBL.WMF 3007BKBL.WMF 3008BKBL.WMF 3009BKBL.WMF
3010BKBL.WMF 3011BKBL.WMF 3012BKBL.WMF 3013BKBL.WMF 3014BKBL.WMF 3015BKBL.WMF 3016BKBL.WMF 4000BSBL.WMF 4001BSBL.WMF 4002BSBL.WMF
4003BSBL.WMF 4004BSBL.WMF 4005BSBL.WMF 4006BSBL.WMF 4007BSBL.WMF 4008BSBL.WMF 4009BSBL.WMF 4010BSBL.WMF 4011BSBL.WMF 4012BSBL.WMF
4013BSBL.WMF 4014BSBL.WMF 4015BSBL.WMF 4016BSBL.WMF 4017BSBL.WMF 4018BSBL.WMF 4019BSBL.WMF 4020BSBL.WMF 4021BSBL.WMF 4022BSBL.WMF
4050GOLF.WMF 4051GOLF.WMF 4052GOLF.WMF 4053GOLF.WMF 4054GOLF.WMF 4055GOLF.WMF 4056GOLF.WMF 4057GOLF.WMF 4058GOLF.WMF 4059GOLF.WMF
4060GOLF.WMF 4061GOLF.WMF 4062GOLF.WMF 4063GOLF.WMF 4064GOLF.WMF 4065GOLF.WMF 4066GOLF.WMF 4067GOLF.WMF 4068GOLF.WMF 4069GOLF.WMF

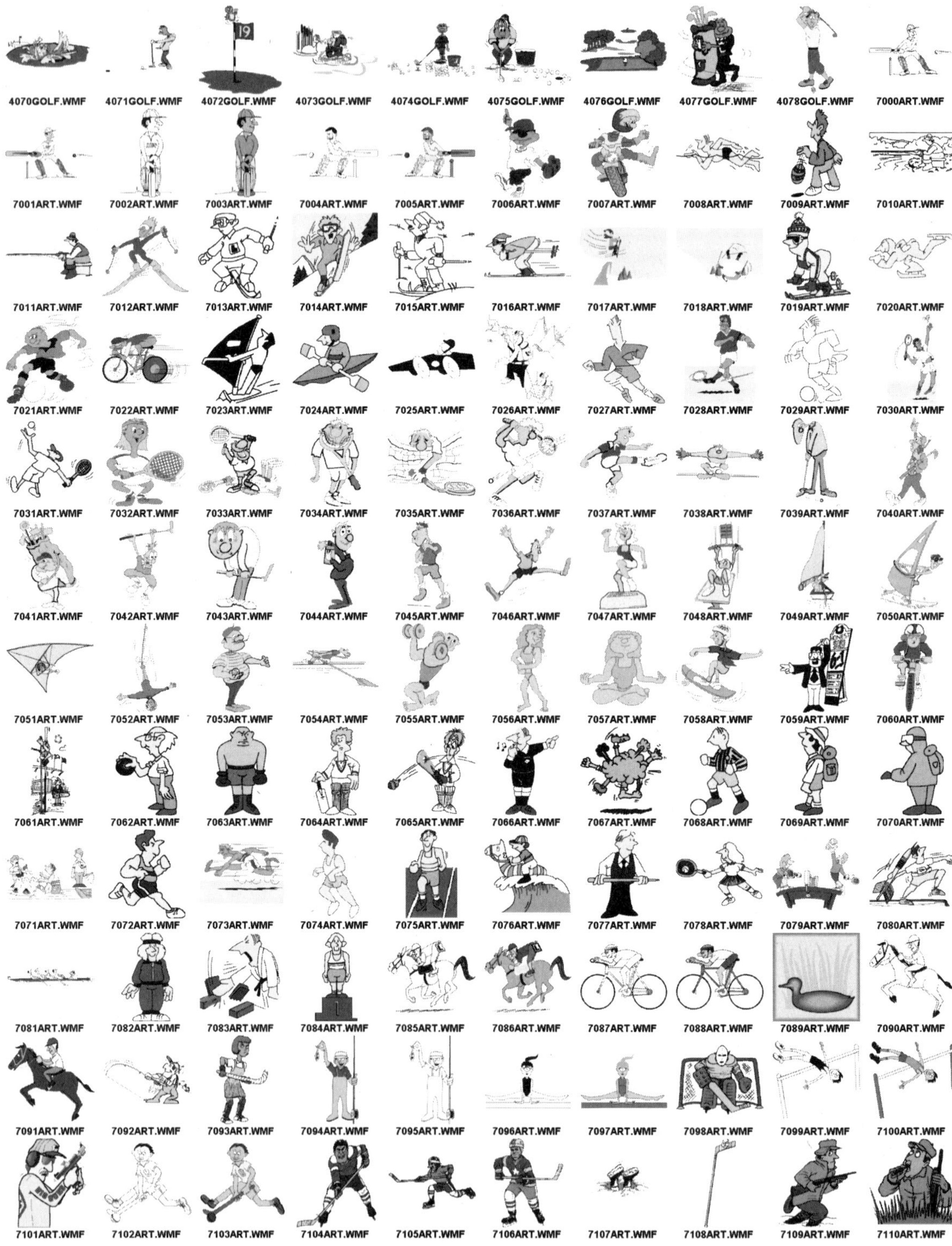
4070GOLF.WMF 4071GOLF.WMF 4072GOLF.WMF 4073GOLF.WMF 4074GOLF.WMF 4075GOLF.WMF 4076GOLF.WMF 4077GOLF.WMF 4078GOLF.WMF 7000ART.WMF
19
7001ART.WMF 7002ART.WMF 7003ART.WMF 7004ART.WMF 7005ART.WMF 7006ART.WMF 7007ART.WMF 7008ART.WMF 7009ART.WMF 7010ART.WMF
7011ART.WMF 7012ART.WMF 7013ART.WMF 7014ART.WMF 7015ART.WMF 7016ART.WMF 7017ART.WMF 7018ART.WMF 7019ART.WMF 7020ART.WMF
7021ART.WMF 7022ART.WMF 7023ART.WMF 7024ART.WMF 7025ART.WMF 7026ART.WMF 7027ART.WMF 7028ART.WMF 7029ART.WMF 7030ART.WMF
7031ART.WMF 7032ART.WMF 7033ART.WMF 7034ART.WMF 7035ART.WMF 7036ART.WMF 7037ART.WMF 7038ART.WMF 7039ART.WMF 7040ART.WMF
7041ART.WMF 7042ART.WMF 7043ART.WMF 7044ART.WMF 7045ART.WMF 7046ART.WMF 7047ART.WMF 7048ART.WMF 7049ART.WMF 7050ART.WMF
7051ART.WMF 7052ART.WMF 7053ART.WMF 7054ART.WMF 7055ART.WMF 7056ART.WMF 7057ART.WMF 7058ART.WMF 7059ART.WMF 7060ART.WMF
7061ART.WMF 7062ART.WMF 7063ART.WMF 7064ART.WMF 7065ART.WMF 7066ART.WMF 7067ART.WMF 7068ART.WMF 7069ART.WMF 7070ART.WMF
7071ART.WMF 7072ART.WMF 7073ART.WMF 7074ART.WMF 7075ART.WMF 7076ART.WMF 7077ART.WMF 7078ART.WMF 7079ART.WMF 7080ART.WMF
7081ART.WMF 7082ART.WMF 7083ART.WMF 7084ART.WMF 7085ART.WMF 7086ART.WMF 7087ART.WMF 7088ART.WMF 7089ART.WMF 7090ART.WMF
7091ART.WMF 7092ART.WMF 7093ART.WMF 7094ART.WMF 7095ART.WMF 7096ART.WMF 7097ART.WMF 7098ART.WMF 7099ART.WMF 7100ART.WMF
7101ART.WMF 7102ART.WMF 7103ART.WMF 7104ART.WMF 7105ART.WMF 7106ART.WMF 7107ART.WMF 7108ART.WMF 7109ART.WMF 7110ART.WMF

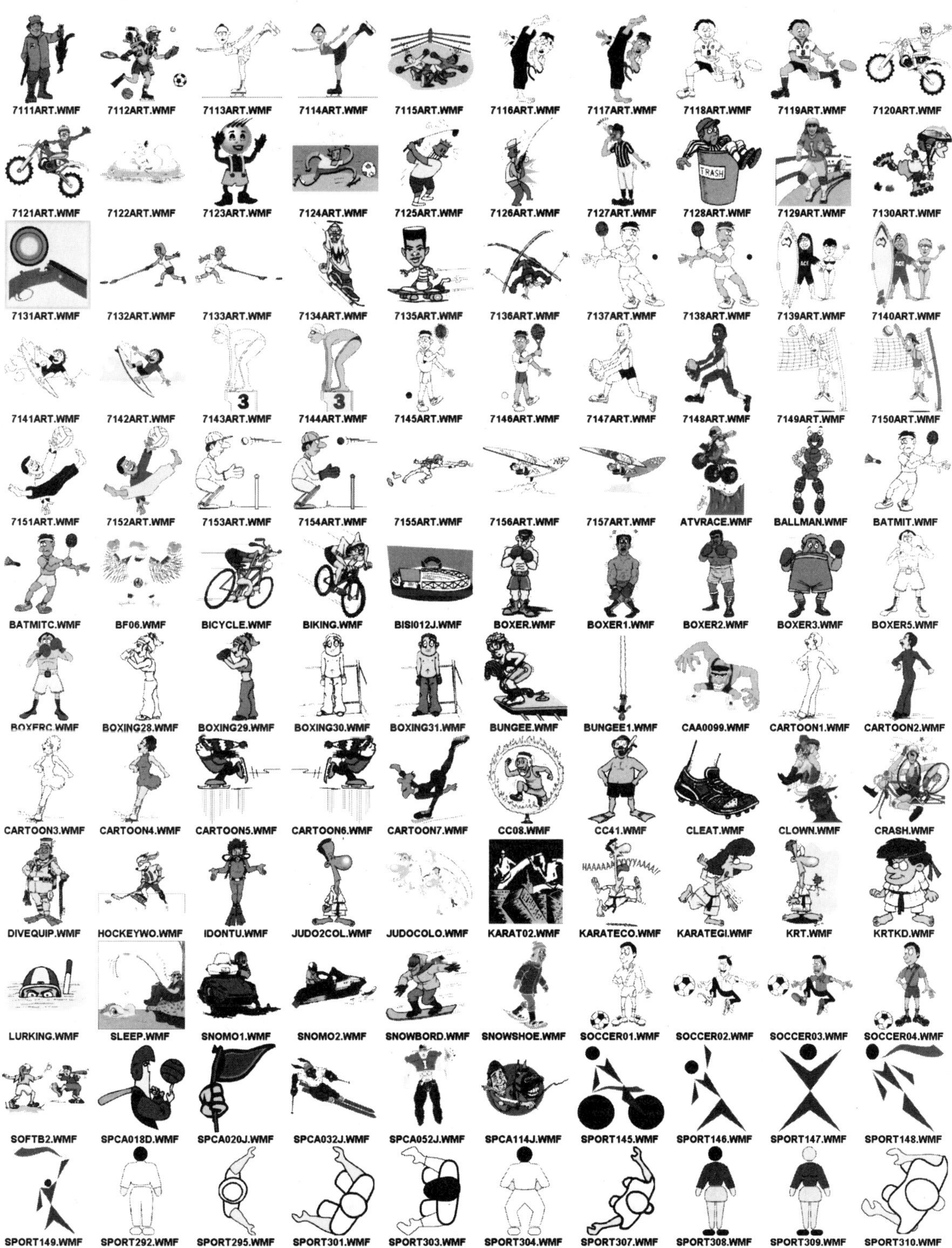
7111ART.WMF 7112ART.WMF 7113ART.WMF 7114ART.WMF 7115ART.WMF 7116ART.WMF 7117ART.WMF 7118ART.WMF 7119ART.WMF 7120ART.WMF
7121ART.WMF 7122ART.WMF 7123ART.WMF 7124ART.WMF 7125ART.WMF 7126ART.WMF 7127ART.WMF 7128ART.WMF 7129ART.WMF 7130ART.WMF
TRASH
7131ART.WMF 7132ART.WMF 7133ART.WMF 7134ART.WMF 7135ART.WMF 7136ART.WMF 7137ART.WMF 7138ART.WMF 7139ART.WMF 7140ART.WMF
3
3
7141ART.WMF 7142ART.WMF 7143ART.WMF 7144ART.WMF 7145ART.WMF 7146ART.WMF 7147ART.WMF 7148ART.WMF 7149ART.WMF 7150ART.WMF
7151ART.WMF 7152ART.WMF 7153ART.WMF 7154ART.WMF 7155ART.WMF 7156ART.WMF 7157ART.WMF ATVRACE.WMF BALLMAN.WMF BATMIT.WMF
BATMITC.WMF BF06.WMF BICYCLE.WMF BIKING.WMF BISI012J.WMF BOXER.WMF BOXER1.WMF BOXER2.WMF BOXER3.WMF BOXER5.WMF
BOXERC.WMF BOXING28.WMF BOXING29.WMF BOXING30.WMF BOXING31.WMF BUNGEE.WMF BUNGEE1.WMF CAA0099.WMF CARTOON1.WMF CARTOON2.WMF
CARTOON3.WMF CARTOON4.WMF CARTOON5.WMF CARTOON6.WMF CARTOON7.WMF CC08.WMF CC41.WMF CLEAT.WMF CLOWN.WMF CRASH.WMF
HAAAAAAYYYYYAAAA!!
DIVEQUIP.WMF HOCKEYWO.WMF IDONTU.WMF JUDO2COL.WMF JUDOCOLO.WMF KARAT02.WMF KARATECO.WMF KARATEGI.WMF KRT.WMF KRTKD.WMF
LURKING.WMF SLEEP.WMF SNOMO1.WMF SNOMO2.WMF SNOWBORD.WMF SNOWSHOE.WMF SOCCER01.WMF SOCCER02.WMF SOCCER03.WMF SOCCER04.WMF
SOFTB2.WMF SPCA018D.WMF SPCA020J.WMF SPCA032J.WMF SPCA052J.WMF SPCA114J.WMF SPORT145.WMF SPORT146.WMF SPORT147.WMF SPORT148.WMF
SPORT149.WMF SPORT292.WMF SPORT295.WMF SPORT301.WMF SPORT303.WMF SPORT304.WMF SPORT307.WMF SPORT308.WMF SPORT309.WMF SPORT310.WMF

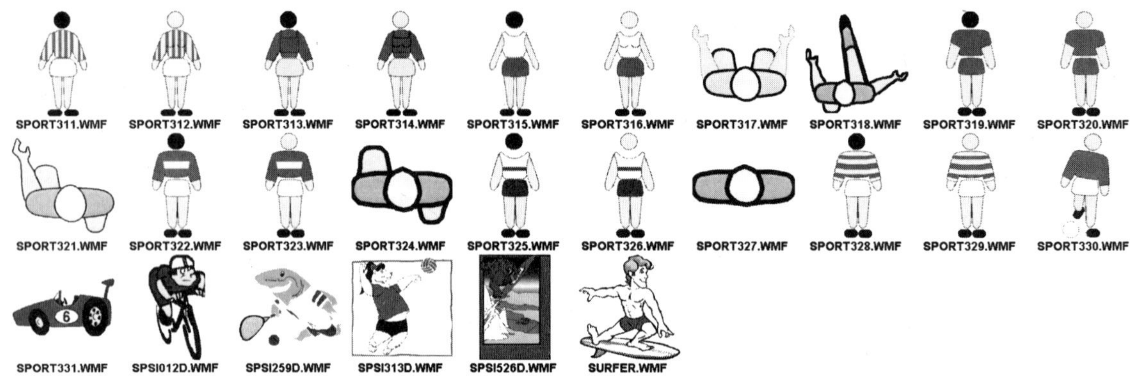
SPORT311.WMF
SPORT312.WMF
SPORT313.WMF
SPORT314.WMF
SPORT315.WMF
SPORT316.WMF
SPORT317.WMF
SPORT318.WMF
SPORT319.WMF
SPORT320.WMF
SPORT321.WMF
SPORT322.WMF
SPORT323.WMF
SPORT324.WMF
SPORT325.WMF
SPORT326.WMF
SPORT327.WMF
SPORT328.WMF
SPORT329.WMF
SPORT330.WMF
SPORT331.WMF
SPSI012D.WMF
SPSI259D.WMF
SPSI313D.WMF
SPSI526D.WMF
SURFER.WMF

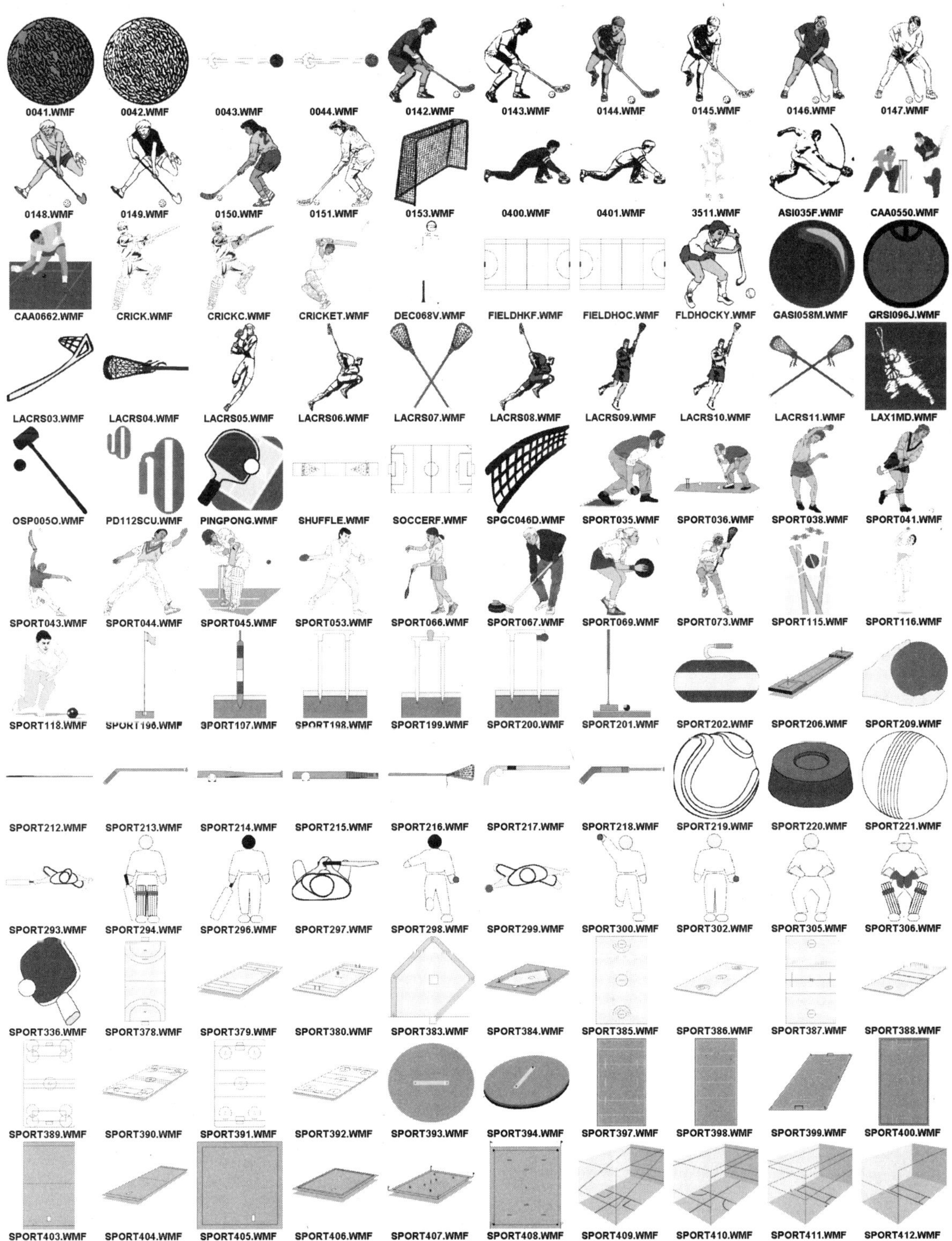

0041.WMF 0042.WMF 0043.WMF 0044.WMF 0142.WMF 0143.WMF 0144.WMF 0145.WMF 0146.WMF 0147.WMF

0148.WMF 0149.WMF 0150.WMF 0151.WMF 0153.WMF 0400.WMF 0401.WMF 3511.WMF ASI035F.WMF CAA0550.WMF

CAA0662.WMF CRICK.WMF CRICKC.WMF CRICKET.WMF DEC068V.WMF FIELDHKF.WMF FIELDHOC.WMF FLDHOCKY.WMF GASI058M.WMF GRSI096J.WMF

LACRS03.WMF LACRS04.WMF LACRS05.WMF LACRS06.WMF LACRS07.WMF LACRS08.WMF LACRS09.WMF LACRS10.WMF LACRS11.WMF LAX1MD.WMF

OSP005O.WMF PD112SCU.WMF PINGPONG.WMF SHUFFLE.WMF SOCCERF.WMF SPGC046D.WMF SPORT035.WMF SPORT036.WMF SPORT038.WMF SPORT041.WMF

SPORT043.WMF SPORT044.WMF SPORT045.WMF SPORT053.WMF SPORT066.WMF SPORT067.WMF SPORT069.WMF SPORT073.WMF SPORT115.WMF SPORT116.WMF

SPORT118.WMF SPORT196.WMF SPORT197.WMF SPORT198.WMF SPORT199.WMF SPORT200.WMF SPORT201.WMF SPORT202.WMF SPORT206.WMF SPORT209.WMF

SPORT212.WMF SPORT213.WMF SPORT214.WMF SPORT215.WMF SPORT216.WMF SPORT217.WMF SPORT218.WMF SPORT219.WMF SPORT220.WMF SPORT221.WMF

SPORT293.WMF SPORT294.WMF SPORT296.WMF SPORT297.WMF SPORT298.WMF SPORT299.WMF SPORT300.WMF SPORT302.WMF SPORT305.WMF SPORT306.WMF

SPORT336.WMF SPORT378.WMF SPORT379.WMF SPORT380.WMF SPORT383.WMF SPORT384.WMF SPORT385.WMF SPORT386.WMF SPORT387.WMF SPORT388.WMF

SPORT389.WMF SPORT390.WMF SPORT391.WMF SPORT392.WMF SPORT393.WMF SPORT394.WMF SPORT397.WMF SPORT398.WMF SPORT399.WMF SPORT400.WMF

SPORT403.WMF SPORT404.WMF SPORT405.WMF SPORT406.WMF SPORT407.WMF SPORT408.WMF SPORT409.WMF SPORT410.WMF SPORT411.WMF SPORT412.WMF

SPORT413.WMF
SPORT414.WMF
SPORT416.WMF
SPORT417.WMF
SPRTGOOD.WMF
SPSI199D.WMF
SPSI200D.WMF
SPSI201D.WMF
SPSI235D.WMF
SPSI237D.WMF
SPSI238D.WMF
SPSI241D.WMF
SPSI242D.WMF
VSC046B.WMF

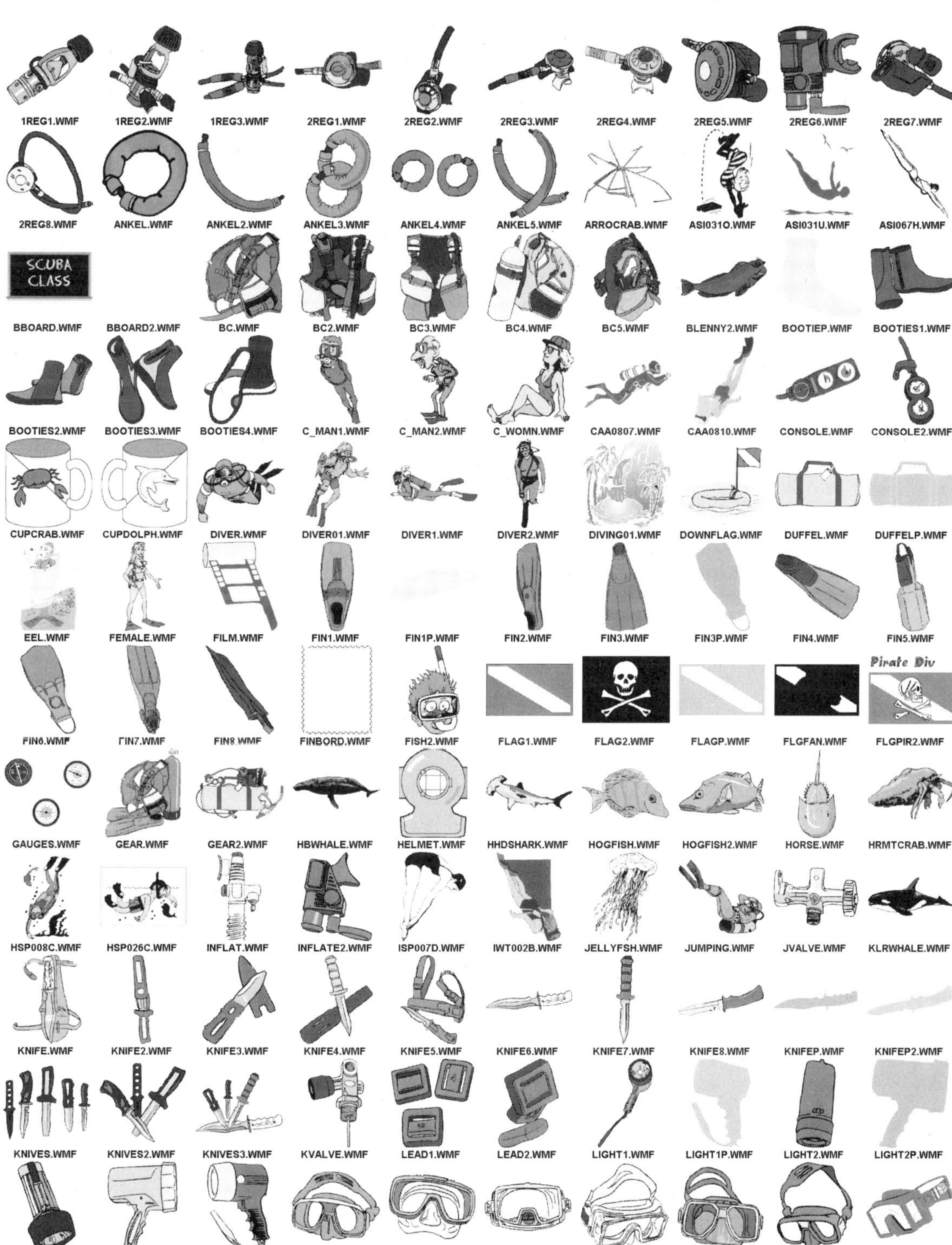
1REG1.WMF
1REG2.WMF
1REG3.WMF
2REG1.WMF
2REG2.WMF
2REG3.WMF
2REG4.WMF
2REG5.WMF
2REG6.WMF
2REG7.WMF
2REG8.WMF
ANKEL.WMF
ANKEL2.WMF
ANKEL3.WMF
ANKEL4.WMF
ANKEL5.WMF
ARROCRAB.WMF
ASI031O.WMF
ASI031U.WMF
ASI067H.WMF
SCUBA CLASS
BBOARD.WMF
BBOARD2.WMF
BC.WMF
BC2.WMF
BC3.WMF
BC4.WMF
BC5.WMF
BLENNY2.WMF
BOOTIEP.WMF
BOOTIES1.WMF
BOOTIES2.WMF
BOOTIES3.WMF
BOOTIES4.WMF
C_MAN1.WMF
C_MAN2.WMF
C_WOMN.WMF
CAA0807.WMF
CAA0810.WMF
CONSOLE.WMF
CONSOLE2.WMF
CUPCRAB.WMF
CUPDOLPH.WMF
DIVER.WMF
DIVER01.WMF
DIVER1.WMF
DIVER2.WMF
DIVING01.WMF
DOWNFLAG.WMF
DUFFEL.WMF
DUFFELP.WMF
EEL.WMF
FEMALE.WMF
FILM.WMF
FIN1.WMF
FIN1P.WMF
FIN2.WMF
FIN3.WMF
FIN3P.WMF
FIN4.WMF
FIN5.WMF
FIN6.WMF
FIN7.WMF
FIN8.WMF
FINBORD.WMF
FISH2.WMF
FLAG1.WMF
FLAG2.WMF
FLAGP.WMF
FLGFAN.WMF
Pirate Div
FLGPIR2.WMF
GAUGES.WMF
GEAR.WMF
GEAR2.WMF
HBWHALE.WMF
HELMET.WMF
HHDSHARK.WMF
HOGFISH.WMF
HOGFISH2.WMF
HORSE.WMF
HRMTCRAB.WMF
HSP008C.WMF
HSP026C.WMF
INFLAT.WMF
INFLATE2.WMF
ISP007D.WMF
IWT002B.WMF
JELLYFSH.WMF
JUMPING.WMF
JVALVE.WMF
KLRWHALE.WMF
KNIFE.WMF
KNIFE2.WMF
KNIFE3.WMF
KNIFE4.WMF
KNIFE5.WMF
KNIFE6.WMF
KNIFE7.WMF
KNIFE8.WMF
KNIFEP.WMF
KNIFEP2.WMF
KNIVES.WMF
KNIVES2.WMF
KNIVES3.WMF
KVALVE.WMF
LEAD1.WMF
LEAD2.WMF
LIGHT1.WMF
LIGHT1P.WMF
LIGHT2.WMF
LIGHT2P.WMF
LIGHT3.WMF
LIGHT4.WMF
LIGHT5.WMF
MASK1.WMF
MASK2.WMF
MASK3.WMF
MASK4.WMF
MASK5.WMF
MASK6.WMF
MASK66.WMF

MASKP.WMF
MASKP2.WMF
MASKS1.WMF
MASKS2.WMF
MASKS3.WMF
MASKS4.WMF
PD114NBW.WMF
PD114NCU.WMF
PHOTOGR.WMF
REG1.WMF
S21654.WMF
SCUBA.WMF
SCUBA005.WMF
SCUBA01.WMF
SCUBA03.WMF
SCUBA_DI.WMF
SCUBADIV.WMF
SCUBAEQP.WMF
SCUBAFIN.WMF
SCUBATNK.WMF
SEI028B.WMF
SHARK.WMF
SHR016H.WMF
SNORK1.WMF
SNORK2.WMF
SNORK3.WMF
SNORKLER.WMF
SNORKP.WMF
SOCA032J.WMF
SOFT.WMF
SONAR.WMF
SPGC068D.WMF
SPGC075D.WMF
SPGC077D.WMF
STROBE.WMF
STSI010D.WMF
SUIT1.WMF
SUITP.WMF
SVEST.WMF
TANK1.WMF
TANK2.WMF
TANK3.WMF
TANKJ.WMF
TANKK.WMF
TANKK2.WMF
TANKP.WMF
TANKS.WMF
WTBELT.WMF

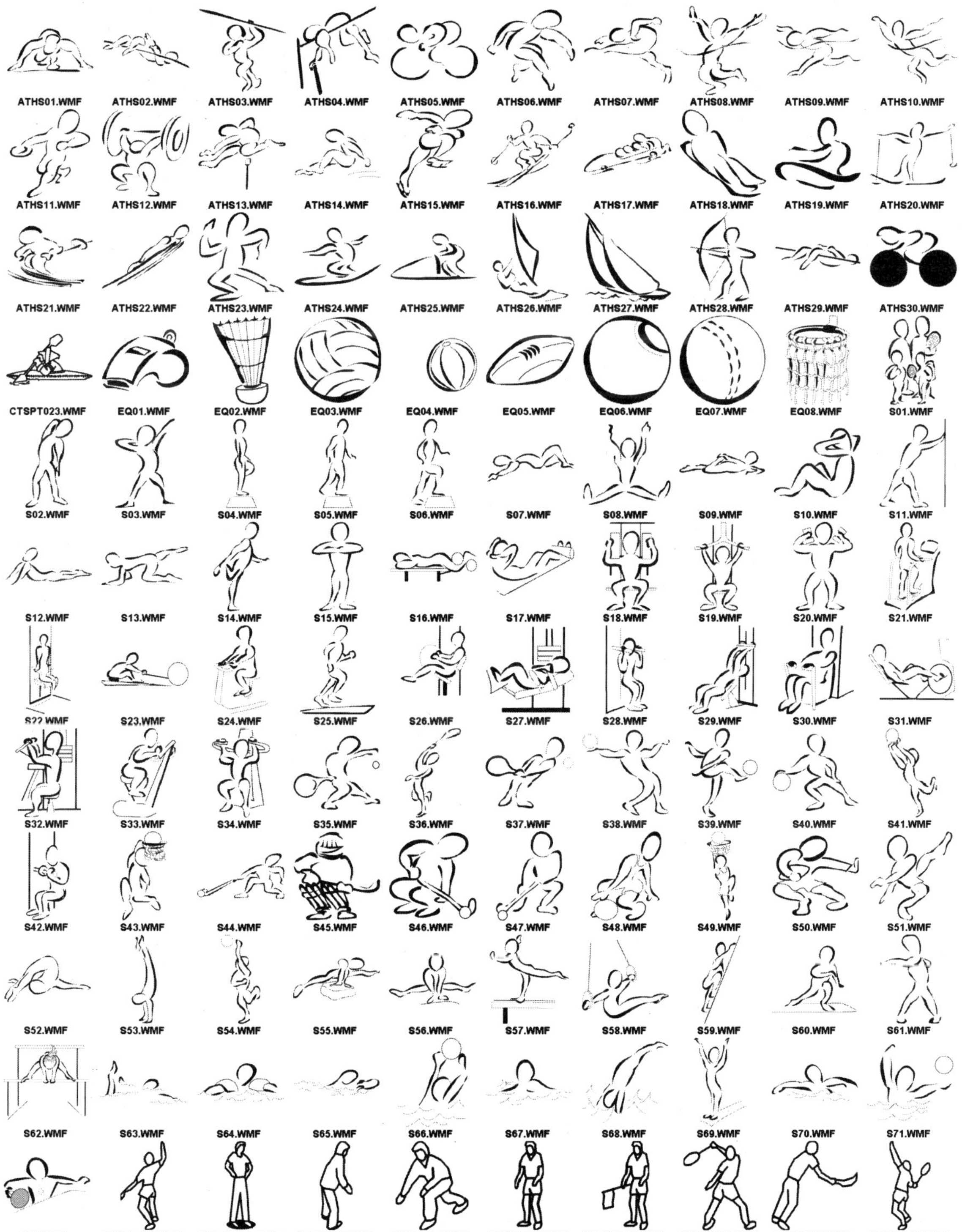
ATHS01.WMF ATHS02.WMF ATHS03.WMF ATHS04.WMF ATHS05.WMF ATHS06.WMF ATHS07.WMF ATHS08.WMF ATHS09.WMF ATHS10.WMF
ATHS11.WMF ATHS12.WMF ATHS13.WMF ATHS14.WMF ATHS15.WMF ATHS16.WMF ATHS17.WMF ATHS18.WMF ATHS19.WMF ATHS20.WMF
ATHS21.WMF ATHS22.WMF ATHS23.WMF ATHS24.WMF ATHS25.WMF ATHS26.WMF ATHS27.WMF ATHS28.WMF ATHS29.WMF ATHS30.WMF
CTSPT023.WMF EQ01.WMF EQ02.WMF EQ03.WMF EQ04.WMF EQ05.WMF EQ06.WMF EQ07.WMF EQ08.WMF S01.WMF
S02.WMF S03.WMF S04.WMF S05.WMF S06.WMF S07.WMF S08.WMF S09.WMF S10.WMF S11.WMF
S12.WMF S13.WMF S14.WMF S15.WMF S16.WMF S17.WMF S18.WMF S19.WMF S20.WMF S21.WMF
S22.WMF S23.WMF S24.WMF S25.WMF S26.WMF S27.WMF S28.WMF S29.WMF S30.WMF S31.WMF
S32.WMF S33.WMF S34.WMF S35.WMF S36.WMF S37.WMF S38.WMF S39.WMF S40.WMF S41.WMF
S42.WMF S43.WMF S44.WMF S45.WMF S46.WMF S47.WMF S48.WMF S49.WMF S50.WMF S51.WMF
S52.WMF S53.WMF S54.WMF S55.WMF S56.WMF S57.WMF S58.WMF S59.WMF S60.WMF S61.WMF
S62.WMF S63.WMF S64.WMF S65.WMF S66.WMF S67.WMF S68.WMF S69.WMF S70.WMF S71.WMF
S72.WMF SPORT231.WMF SPORT232.WMF SPORT233.WMF SPORT234.WMF SPORT235.WMF SPORT236.WMF SPORT237.WMF SPORT238.WMF SPORT239.WMF

SPORT240.WMF
SPORT241.WMF
SPORT242.WMF
SPORT243.WMF
SPORT244.WMF
SPORT245.WMF
SPORT246.WMF
SPORT247.WMF
SPORT248.WMF
SPORT249.WMF
SPORT250.WMF
SPORT251.WMF
SPORT252.WMF
SPORT253.WMF
SPORT254.WMF
SPORT255.WMF
SPORT256.WMF
SPORT257.WMF
SPORT258.WMF
SPORT259.WMF
SPORT260.WMF
SPORT261.WMF
SPORT262.WMF
SPORT263.WMF
SPORT264.WMF
SPORT265.WMF
SPORT266.WMF
SPORT267.WMF
SPORT268.WMF
SPORT269.WMF
SPORT270.WMF
SPORT271.WMF
SPORT272.WMF
SPORT273.WMF
SPORT274.WMF
SPORT275.WMF
SPORT276.WMF
SPORT277.WMF
SPORT278.WMF
SPORT279.WMF
SPORT280.WMF
SPORT281.WMF
SPORT282.WMF
SPORT283.WMF
SPORT284.WMF
SPORT285.WMF
SPORT286.WMF
SPORT287.WMF
SPORT288.WMF
SPORT289.WMF
SPORT290.WMF
SPORT291.WMF

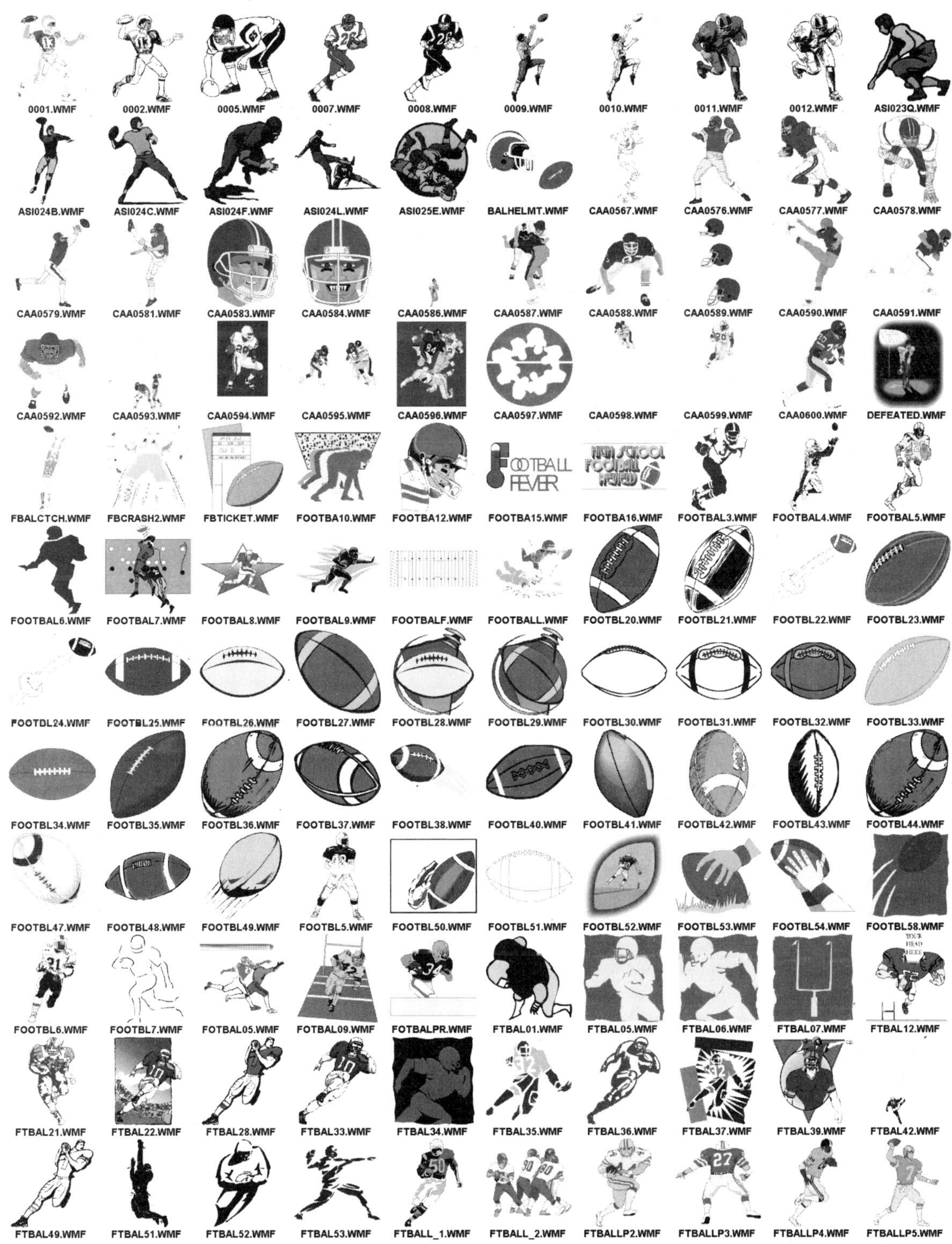

0001.WMF 0002.WMF 0005.WMF 0007.WMF 0008.WMF 0009.WMF 0010.WMF 0011.WMF 0012.WMF ASI023Q.WMF
ASI024B.WMF ASI024C.WMF ASI024F.WMF ASI024L.WMF ASI025E.WMF BALHELMT.WMF CAA0567.WMF CAA0576.WMF CAA0577.WMF CAA0578.WMF
CAA0579.WMF CAA0581.WMF CAA0583.WMF CAA0584.WMF CAA0586.WMF CAA0587.WMF CAA0588.WMF CAA0589.WMF CAA0590.WMF CAA0591.WMF
CAA0592.WMF CAA0593.WMF CAA0594.WMF CAA0595.WMF CAA0596.WMF CAA0597.WMF CAA0598.WMF CAA0599.WMF CAA0600.WMF DEFEATED.WMF
FBALCTCH.WMF FBCRASH2.WMF FBTICKET.WMF FOOTBA10.WMF FOOTBA12.WMF FOOTBA15.WMF FOOTBA16.WMF FOOTBAL3.WMF FOOTBAL4.WMF FOOTBAL5.WMF
FOOTBAL6.WMF FOOTBAL7.WMF FOOTBAL8.WMF FOOTBAL9.WMF FOOTBALF.WMF FOOTBALL.WMF FOOTBL20.WMF FOOTBL21.WMF FOOTBL22.WMF FOOTBL23.WMF
FOOTBL24.WMF FOOTBL25.WMF FOOTBL26.WMF FOOTBL27.WMF FOOTBL28.WMF FOOTBL29.WMF FOOTBL30.WMF FOOTBL31.WMF FOOTBL32.WMF FOOTBL33.WMF
FOOTBL34.WMF FOOTBL35.WMF FOOTBL36.WMF FOOTBL37.WMF FOOTBL38.WMF FOOTBL40.WMF FOOTBL41.WMF FOOTBL42.WMF FOOTBL43.WMF FOOTBL44.WMF
FOOTBL47.WMF FOOTBL48.WMF FOOTBL49.WMF FOOTBL5.WMF FOOTBL50.WMF FOOTBL51.WMF FOOTBL52.WMF FOOTBL53.WMF FOOTBL54.WMF FOOTBL58.WMF
FOOTBL6.WMF FOOTBL7.WMF FOTBAL05.WMF FOTBAL09.WMF FOTBALPR.WMF FTBAL01.WMF FTBAL05.WMF FTBAL06.WMF FTBAL07.WMF FTBAL12.WMF
FTBAL21.WMF FTBAL22.WMF FTBAL28.WMF FTBAL33.WMF FTBAL34.WMF FTBAL35.WMF FTBAL36.WMF FTBAL37.WMF FTBAL39.WMF FTBAL42.WMF
FTBAL49.WMF FTBAL51.WMF FTBAL52.WMF FTBAL53.WMF FTBALL_1.WMF FTBALL_2.WMF FTBALLP2.WMF FTBALLP3.WMF FTBALLP4.WMF FTBALLP5.WMF

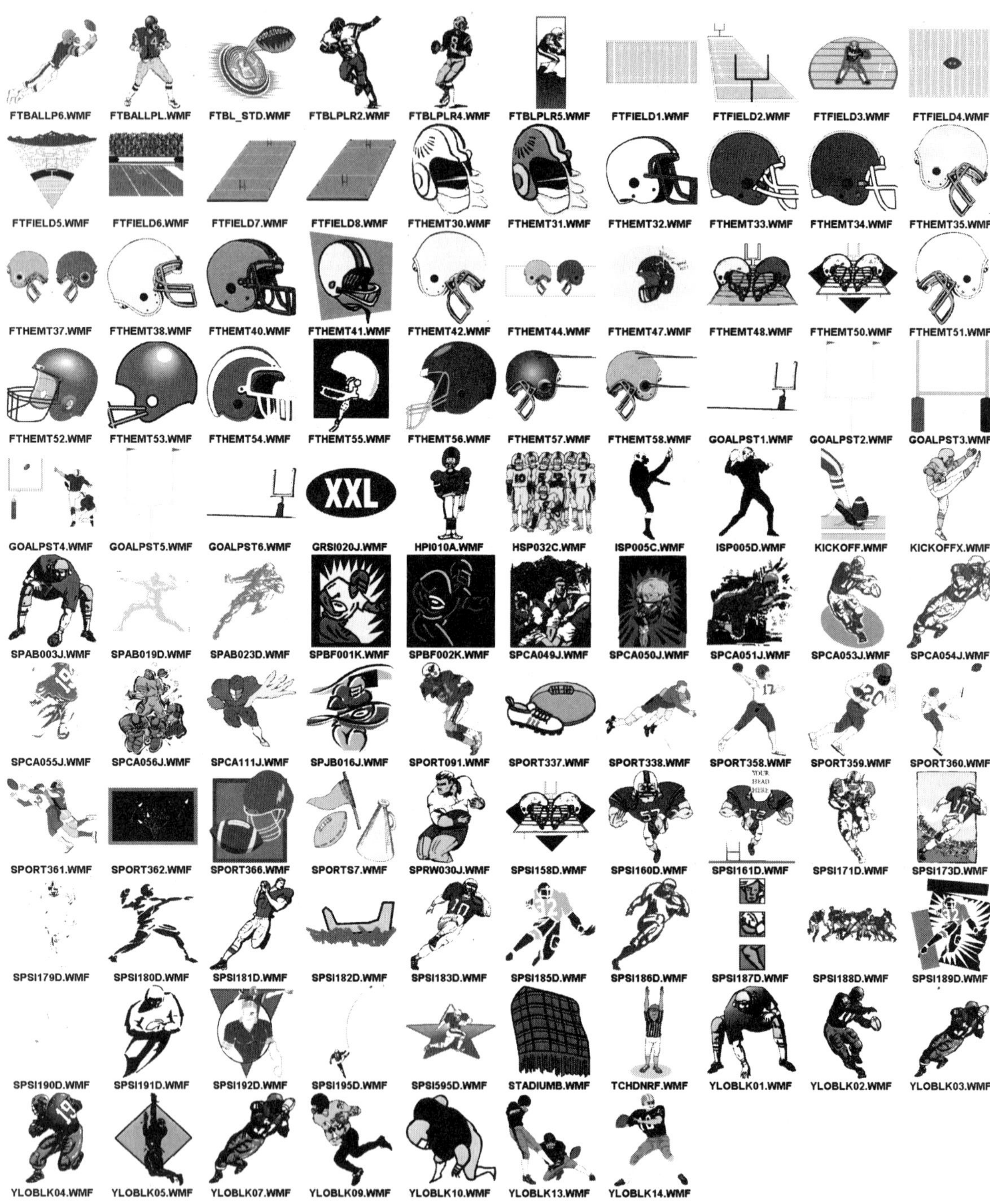

FTBALLP6.WMF FTBALLPL.WMF FTBL_STD.WMF FTBLPLR2.WMF FTBLPLR4.WMF FTBLPLR5.WMF FTFIELD1.WMF FTFIELD2.WMF FTFIELD3.WMF FTFIELD4.WMF

FTFIELD5.WMF FTFIELD6.WMF FTFIELD7.WMF FTFIELD8.WMF FTHEMT30.WMF FTHEMT31.WMF FTHEMT32.WMF FTHEMT33.WMF FTHEMT34.WMF FTHEMT35.WMF

FTHEMT37.WMF FTHEMT38.WMF FTHEMT40.WMF FTHEMT41.WMF FTHEMT42.WMF FTHEMT44.WMF FTHEMT47.WMF FTHEMT48.WMF FTHEMT50.WMF FTHEMT51.WMF

FTHEMT52.WMF FTHEMT53.WMF FTHEMT54.WMF FTHEMT55.WMF FTHEMT56.WMF FTHEMT57.WMF FTHEMT58.WMF GOALPST1.WMF GOALPST2.WMF GOALPST3.WMF

GOALPST4.WMF GOALPST5.WMF GOALPST6.WMF GRSI020J.WMF HPI010A.WMF HSP032C.WMF ISP005C.WMF ISP005D.WMF KICKOFF.WMF KICKOFFX.WMF

SPAB003J.WMF SPAB019D.WMF SPAB023D.WMF SPBF001K.WMF SPBF002K.WMF SPCA049J.WMF SPCA050J.WMF SPCA051J.WMF SPCA053J.WMF SPCA054J.WMF

SPCA055J.WMF SPCA056J.WMF SPCA111J.WMF SPJB016J.WMF SPORT091.WMF SPORT337.WMF SPORT338.WMF SPORT358.WMF SPORT359.WMF SPORT360.WMF

SPORT361.WMF SPORT362.WMF SPORT366.WMF SPORTS7.WMF SPRW030J.WMF SPSI158D.WMF SPSI160D.WMF SPSI161D.WMF SPSI171D.WMF SPSI173D.WMF

SPSI179D.WMF SPSI180D.WMF SPSI181D.WMF SPSI182D.WMF SPSI183D.WMF SPSI185D.WMF SPSI186D.WMF SPSI187D.WMF SPSI188D.WMF SPSI189D.WMF

SPSI190D.WMF SPSI191D.WMF SPSI192D.WMF SPSI195D.WMF SPSI595D.WMF STADIUMB.WMF TCHDNRF.WMF YLOBLK01.WMF YLOBLK02.WMF YLOBLK03.WMF

YLOBLK04.WMF YLOBLK05.WMF YLOBLK07.WMF YLOBLK09.WMF YLOBLK10.WMF YLOBLK13.WMF YLOBLK14.WMF

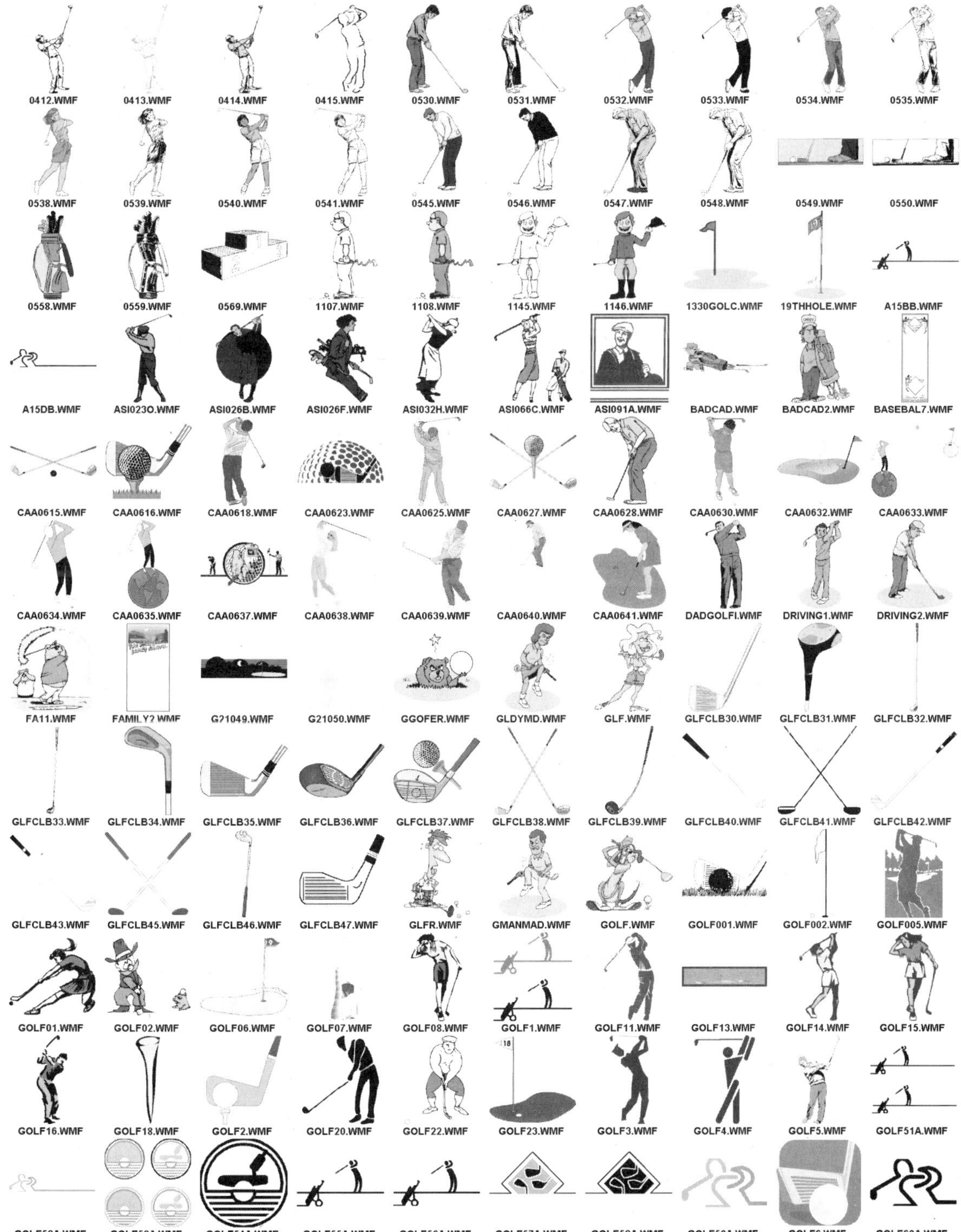
0412.WMF
0413.WMF
0414.WMF
0415.WMF
0530.WMF
0531.WMF
0532.WMF
0533.WMF
0534.WMF
0535.WMF
0538.WMF
0539.WMF
0540.WMF
0541.WMF
0545.WMF
0546.WMF
0547.WMF
0548.WMF
0549.WMF
0550.WMF
0558.WMF
0559.WMF
0569.WMF
1107.WMF
1108.WMF
1145.WMF
1146.WMF
1330GOLC.WMF
19THHOLE.WMF
A15BB.WMF
A15DB.WMF
ASI023O.WMF
ASI026B.WMF
ASI026F.WMF
ASI032H.WMF
ASI066C.WMF
ASI091A.WMF
BADCAD.WMF
BADCAD2.WMF
BASEBAL7.WMF
CAA0615.WMF
CAA0616.WMF
CAA0618.WMF
CAA0623.WMF
CAA0625.WMF
CAA0627.WMF
CAA0628.WMF
CAA0630.WMF
CAA0632.WMF
CAA0633.WMF
CAA0634.WMF
CAA0635.WMF
CAA0637.WMF
CAA0638.WMF
CAA0639.WMF
CAA0640.WMF
CAA0641.WMF
DADGOLFI.WMF
DRIVING1.WMF
DRIVING2.WMF
FA11.WMF
FAMILY2.WMF
G21049.WMF
G21050.WMF
GGOFER.WMF
GLDYMD.WMF
GLF.WMF
GLFCLB30.WMF
GLFCLB31.WMF
GLFCLB32.WMF
GLFCLB33.WMF
GLFCLB34.WMF
GLFCLB35.WMF
GLFCLB36.WMF
GLFCLB37.WMF
GLFCLB38.WMF
GLFCLB39.WMF
GLFCLB40.WMF
GLFCLB41.WMF
GLFCLB42.WMF
GLFCLB43.WMF
GLFCLB45.WMF
GLFCLB46.WMF
GLFCLB47.WMF
GLFR.WMF
GMANMAD.WMF
GOLF.WMF
GOLF001.WMF
GOLF002.WMF
GOLF005.WMF
GOLF01.WMF
GOLF02.WMF
GOLF06.WMF
GOLF07.WMF
GOLF08.WMF
GOLF1.WMF
GOLF11.WMF
GOLF13.WMF
GOLF14.WMF
GOLF15.WMF
GOLF16.WMF
GOLF18.WMF
GOLF2.WMF
GOLF20.WMF
GOLF22.WMF
GOLF23.WMF
GOLF3.WMF
GOLF4.WMF
GOLF5.WMF
GOLF51A.WMF
GOLF52A.WMF
GOLF53A.WMF
GOLF54A.WMF
GOLF55A.WMF
GOLF56A.WMF
GOLF57A.WMF
GOLF58A.WMF
GOLF59A.WMF
GOLF6.WMF
GOLF60A.WMF

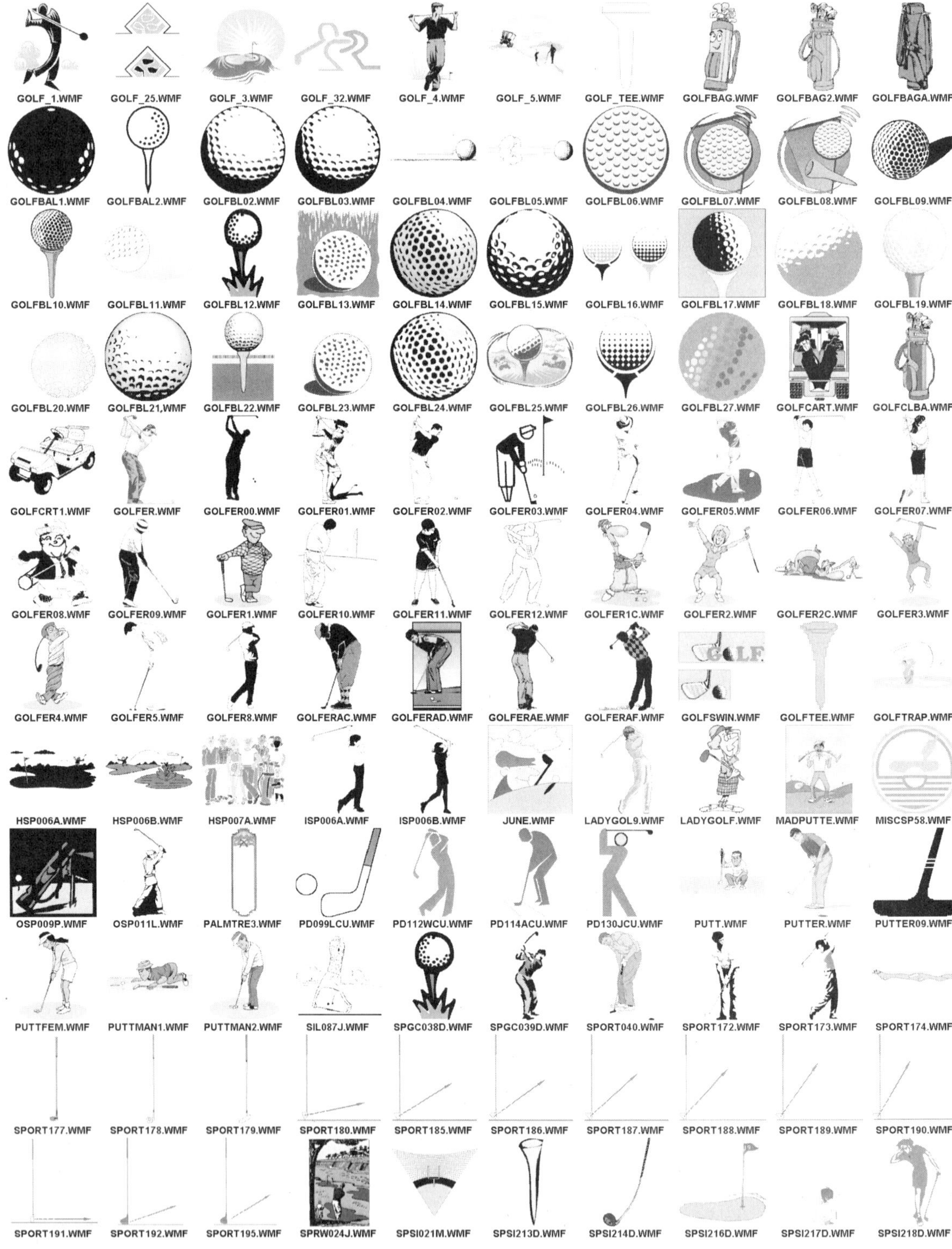
GOLF_1.WMF
GOLF_25.WMF
GOLF_3.WMF
GOLF_32.WMF
GOLF_4.WMF
GOLF_5.WMF
GOLF_TEE.WMF
GOLFBAG.WMF
GOLFBAG2.WMF
GOLFBAGA.WMF
GOLFBAL1.WMF
GOLFBAL2.WMF
GOLFBL02.WMF
GOLFBL03.WMF
GOLFBL04.WMF
GOLFBL05.WMF
GOLFBL06.WMF
GOLFBL07.WMF
GOLFBL08.WMF
GOLFBL09.WMF
GOLFBL10.WMF
GOLFBL11.WMF
GOLFBL12.WMF
GOLFBL13.WMF
GOLFBL14.WMF
GOLFBL15.WMF
GOLFBL16.WMF
GOLFBL17.WMF
GOLFBL18.WMF
GOLFBL19.WMF
GOLFBL20.WMF
GOLFBL21.WMF
GOLFBL22.WMF
GOLFBL23.WMF
GOLFBL24.WMF
GOLFBL25.WMF
GOLFBL26.WMF
GOLFBL27.WMF
GOLFCART.WMF
GOLFCLBA.WMF
GOLFCRT1.WMF
GOLFER.WMF
GOLFER00.WMF
GOLFER01.WMF
GOLFER02.WMF
GOLFER03.WMF
GOLFER04.WMF
GOLFER05.WMF
GOLFER06.WMF
GOLFER07.WMF
GOLFER08.WMF
GOLFER09.WMF
GOLFER1.WMF
GOLFER10.WMF
GOLFER11.WMF
GOLFER12.WMF
GOLFER1C.WMF
GOLFER2.WMF
GOLFER2C.WMF
GOLFER3.WMF
GOLFER4.WMF
GOLFER5.WMF
GOLFER8.WMF
GOLFERAC.WMF
GOLFERAD.WMF
GOLFERAE.WMF
GOLFERAF.WMF
GOLFSWIN.WMF
GOLFTEE.WMF
GOLFTRAP.WMF
HSP006A.WMF
HSP006B.WMF
HSP007A.WMF
ISP006A.WMF
ISP006B.WMF
JUNE.WMF
LADYGOL9.WMF
LADYGOLF.WMF
MADPUTTE.WMF
MISCSP58.WMF
OSP009P.WMF
OSP011L.WMF
PALMTRE3.WMF
PD099LCU.WMF
PD112WCU.WMF
PD114ACU.WMF
PD130JCU.WMF
PUTT.WMF
PUTTER.WMF
PUTTER09.WMF
PUTTFEM.WMF
PUTTMAN1.WMF
PUTTMAN2.WMF
SIL087J.WMF
SPGC038D.WMF
SPGC039D.WMF
SPORT040.WMF
SPORT172.WMF
SPORT173.WMF
SPORT174.WMF
SPORT177.WMF
SPORT178.WMF
SPORT179.WMF
SPORT180.WMF
SPORT185.WMF
SPORT186.WMF
SPORT187.WMF
SPORT188.WMF
SPORT189.WMF
SPORT190.WMF
SPORT191.WMF
SPORT192.WMF
SPORT195.WMF
SPRW024J.WMF
SPSI021M.WMF
SPSI213D.WMF
SPSI214D.WMF
SPSI216D.WMF
SPSI217D.WMF
SPSI218D.WMF

Sports • Golf

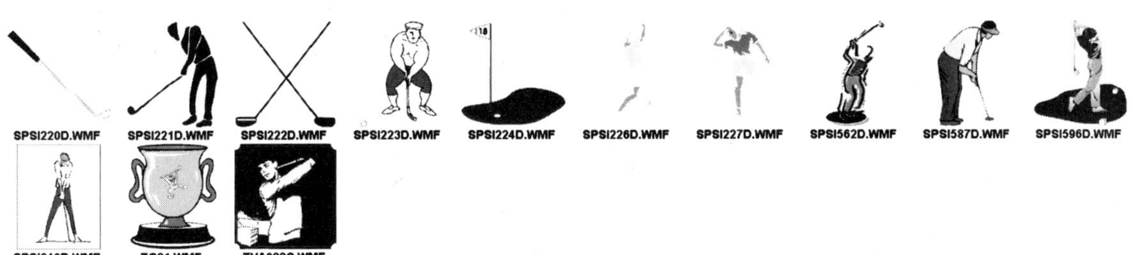

SPSI220D.WMF SPSI221D.WMF SPSI222D.WMF SPSI223D.WMF SPSI224D.WMF SPSI226D.WMF SPSI227D.WMF SPSI562D.WMF SPSI587D.WMF SPSI596D.WMF
SPSI640D.WMF TG21.WMF TVA022C.WMF

Sports • Gymnastics (GYMNASTC)

BARS001.WMF BARS002.WMF BARS003.WMF BARS004.WMF BARS005.WMF BARS006.WMF CAA0661.WMF FLOOR001.WMF FLOOR010.WMF FLOOR011.WMF
FLOOR012.WMF FLOOR02.WMF FLOOR03.WMF FLOOR04.WMF FLOOR05.WMF FLOOR06.WMF FLOOR07.WMF FLOOR08.WMF FLOOR09.WMF FSW004C.WMF
GYMANST4.WMF GYMNSTC.WMF HORSE001.WMF HORSE002.WMF HORSE003.WMF HORSE004.WMF HORSE005.WMF HORSE006.WMF HORSE007.WMF HORSE008.WMF
HORSE009.WMF HORSE010.WMF HORSE011.WMF HORSE012.WMF ISP011D.WMF PD091JCU.WMF RINGS001.WMF RINGS002.WMF RINGS003.WMF RINGS004.WMF
RINGS005.WMF RINGS006.WMF RINGS007.WMF SPCA012J.WMF SPGC080D.WMF SPGC084D.WMF SPORT088.WMF SPORT117.WMF

0028.WMF
0029.WMF
0031.WMF
0032.WMF
0033.WMF
0034.WMF
0035.WMF
0036.WMF
0037.WMF
0038.WMF
0039.WMF
0040.WMF
0154.WMF
0155.WMF
0156.WMF
0366.WMF
0380.WMF
0402.WMF
0403.WMF
0404.WMF
0405.WMF
0406.WMF
0407.WMF
0408.WMF
0409.WMF
0410.WMF
0411.WMF
0412.WMF
0413.WMF
0414.WMF
0415.WMF
0416.WMF
0417.WMF
0419.WMF
0420.WMF
0421.WMF
0422.WMF
0423.WMF
0424.WMF
0425.WMF
0426.WMF
0427.WMF
0428.WMF
0433.WMF
0434.WMF
0435.WMF
0436.WMF
0437.WMF
0438.WMF
0442.WMF
ICE
ICE
BABY
1332HOCC.WMF
ASI023U.WMF
ASI037O.WMF
CAA0668.WMF
CAA0670.WMF
CAA0672.WMF
CAA0673.WMF
CAA0674.WMF
CAA0675.WMF
CAA0676.WMF
CAA0677.WMF
CAA0678.WMF
CAA0679.WMF
CAA0680.WMF
CAA0681.WMF
CAA0682.WMF
CAA0683.WMF
FSW033C.WMF
FSW033D.WMF
FSW033E.WMF
GOAL1MD.WMF
GOALIE.WMF
GOALTEND.WMF
H21102.WMF
H21103.WMF
H21104.WMF
H21105.WMF
H21106.WMF
H21107.WMF
H21112.WMF
H21113.WMF
H21114.WMF
H21115.WMF
HHSI033D.WMF
HOCK_1.WMF
HOCK_GLV.WMF
HOCKEY.WMF
HOCKEY07.WMF
HOCKEY08.WMF
HOCKEY09.WMF
HOCKEY2.WMF
HOCKEY3.WMF
HOCKEY4.WMF
HOCKEY5.WMF
HOCKEY_1.WMF
HOCKEY_2.WMF
HOCKEY_3.WMF
HOCKEY_4.WMF
HOCKEYCO.WMF
HOCKEYG.WMF
HOCKEYLA.WMF
HOCKEYPL.WMF
HOCKEYR.WMF
HOCKEYSK.WMF
HOCKSTK1.WMF
HOCKSTK2.WMF
HOCKSTK3.WMF
HOCKSTK4.WMF
HOCKSTK5.WMF
HOCKSTK6.WMF
HOCKSTK7.WMF
HOCKSTK8.WMF
HOCKSTK9.WMF
HOCKY01.WMF
HOCKY03.WMF
HOCKY04.WMF
HOCKY05.WMF
HOCKY06.WMF
HSP030C.WMF
ICEHCKY.WMF

IWS017A.WMF OTS004K.WMF PD091NCU.WMF PD093DCU.WMF PD112KCU.WMF PD112XCU.WMF PD124XCU.WMF PGX005A.WMF PUCK01.WMF PUCK02.WMF

PUCK03.WMF PUCK04.WMF PUCK05.WMF PUCK06.WMF PUCK07.WMF PUCK08.WMF PUCK09.WMF PUCK10.WMF SCT020B.WMF SPGC085D.WMF

SPGC086D.WMF SPORT002.WMF SPORT135.WMF SPORT367.WMF SPSI228D.WMF SPSI229D.WMF SPSI230D.WMF SPSI231D.WMF SPSI386D.WMF SPSI641D.WMF

YOUTHHOC.WMF

0294.WMF
0295.WMF
0296.WMF
0297.WMF
0298.WMF
0299.WMF
0301.WMF
0302.WMF
0303.WMF
0304.WMF
0305.WMF
0306.WMF
0307.WMF
0308.WMF
0311.WMF
0312.WMF
0313.WMF
0314.WMF
0315.WMF
0316.WMF
1147.WMF
1148.WMF
3507.WMF
ASI023V.WMF
ASI036R.WMF
CAA0561.WMF
CAA0564.WMF
CAA0565.WMF
CHURCHHL.WMF
EAC019C.WMF
EQSTRIAN.WMF
EQUESTRI.WMF
GUNHORSE.WMF
HDC010D.WMF
HDC027D.WMF
HDC047C.WMF
HDC048E.WMF
HDC057E.WMF
HDC059A.WMF
HDC059F.WMF
HDC061C.WMF
HDC061F.WMF
HORSE.WMF
HORSE1.WMF
HORSERAC.WMF
HORSRAC1.WMF
HORSRAC2.WMF
HRSE01.WMF
HRSE02.WMF
HRSE03.WMF
JOCKTOON.WMF
MSL100B.WMF
OFS056G.WMF
OSP012E.WMF
OTS069B.WMF
PD091WCU.WMF
PD093MCU.WMF
RACEHORS.WMF
RACEHOS2.WMF
RACEHRSE.WMF
RECEHRS1.WMF
SIL093A.WMF
SIL093C.WMF
SIL093E.WMF
SIL094B.WMF
SMR013A.WMF
SMR016O.WMF
SMR030D.WMF
SPCA064J.WMF
SPGC040D.WMF
SPORT047.WMF
SPORT072.WMF
SPORT075.WMF
SPORT127.WMF
SPORT133.WMF
STSI002D.WMF

0443.WMF
0444.WMF
0445.WMF
0446.WMF
0447.WMF
0448.WMF
0449.WMF
0450.WMF
0477.WMF
0478.WMF
0479.WMF
ASI037N.WMF
CAA0711.WMF
CAA0712.WMF
CAA0715.WMF
CAA0716.WMF
CAA0717.WMF
CAA0718.WMF
CAA0719.WMF
CAA0720.WMF
CAA0721.WMF
CAA0722.WMF
CAA0724.WMF
CAA0726.WMF
CAA0728.WMF
CAA0729.WMF
CAA0732.WMF
CAA0733.WMF
CAA0734.WMF
FIG_SKT.WMF
FIGSKAT.WMF
ICE_SKAT.WMF
ICEKTNG1.WMF
ICESKAT4.WMF
ICESKATE.WMF
ICESKT1.WMF
ICESKT2.WMF
ICESKT3.WMF
ICESKT4.WMF
ICESKT5.WMF
ICESKT6.WMF
ICESKT7.WMF
ICESKTS.WMF
ISP031E.WMF
IWS001B.WMF
PD113BCU.WMF
PD124VCU.WMF
PD124WCU.WMF
SKATER05.WMF
SKATER1.WMF
SKATER2.WMF
SPD_SKAT.WMF
SPDSKTNG.WMF
SPEEDSK1.WMF
SPEEDSK2.WMF
SPEEDSKT.WMF
SPORT006.WMF
SPORT008.WMF
SXM001B.WMF

AEROBICS.WMF
ARCHERY1.WMF
ARCHERY2.WMF
AUTORACE.WMF
BASEBA1.WMF
BASEBAL2.WMF
BASKET1.WMF
BASKET2.WMF
BIATHLON.WMF
BICYLING.WMF
BILLIARD.WMF
BOATING.WMF
BOBSLIEG.WMF
BOWLING.WMF
BOXING1.WMF
BOXING2.WMF
CANOE1.WMF
CANOE2.WMF
CANOE3.WMF
CLIMBING.WMF
COMBSKI.WMF
CRSCTRY1.WMF
CRSCTRY2.WMF
CURLING.WMF
DIVING.WMF
DOWNHILL.WMF
EQUEST1.WMF
EQUEST2.WMF
FENCING.WMF
FIELDHOK.WMF
FIGSKAT.WMF
FISHING1.WMF
FISHING2.WMF
FISHING3.WMF
FITNESS1.WMF
FITNESS2.WMF
FOOTBALL.WMF
GIANSLAL.WMF
GOLF1.WMF
GOLF2.WMF
GOLF3.WMF
GOLF4.WMF
GYMN1.WMF
GYMN2.WMF
HIKING.WMF
HUNTING.WMF
ICEHOCKY.WMF
INLINE.WMF
JOGGING.WMF
JUDO.WMF
LACROSS.WMF
LITTLELG.WMF
LUGE.WMF
MUSHING.WMF
PENTATH.WMF
PINGPONG.WMF
PLAYGND1.WMF
PLAYGND2.WMF
RAFTING.WMF
ROCKCLIM.WMF
ROWING.WMF
RUNNING.WMF
SAILING1.WMF
SAILING2.WMF
SCUBA.WMF
SHUFFLE.WMF
SKATEBD.WMF
SKIBOBB.WMF
SLALOM.WMF
SLEDDING.WMF
SLIJUMP.WMF
SNOWMOB.WMF
SNOWSHOE.WMF
SOCCER.WMF
SOFTBALL.WMF
SPEEDSKT.WMF
SURFING.WMF
SWIM1.WMF
SWIM2.WMF
TARGET.WMF
TENNIS1.WMF
TENNIS2.WMF
TENNIS3.WMF
TENNIS4.WMF
TRACK1.WMF
TRACK2.WMF
VOLLEY1.WMF
VOLLEY2.WMF
VOLLEY3.WMF
WALKING.WMF
WATPOLO1.WMF
WATPOLO2.WMF
WATSKI.WMF
WEIGHT1.WMF
WEIGHT2.WMF
WINDSRF2.WMF
WINSRF1.WMF
WRESTLNG.WMF

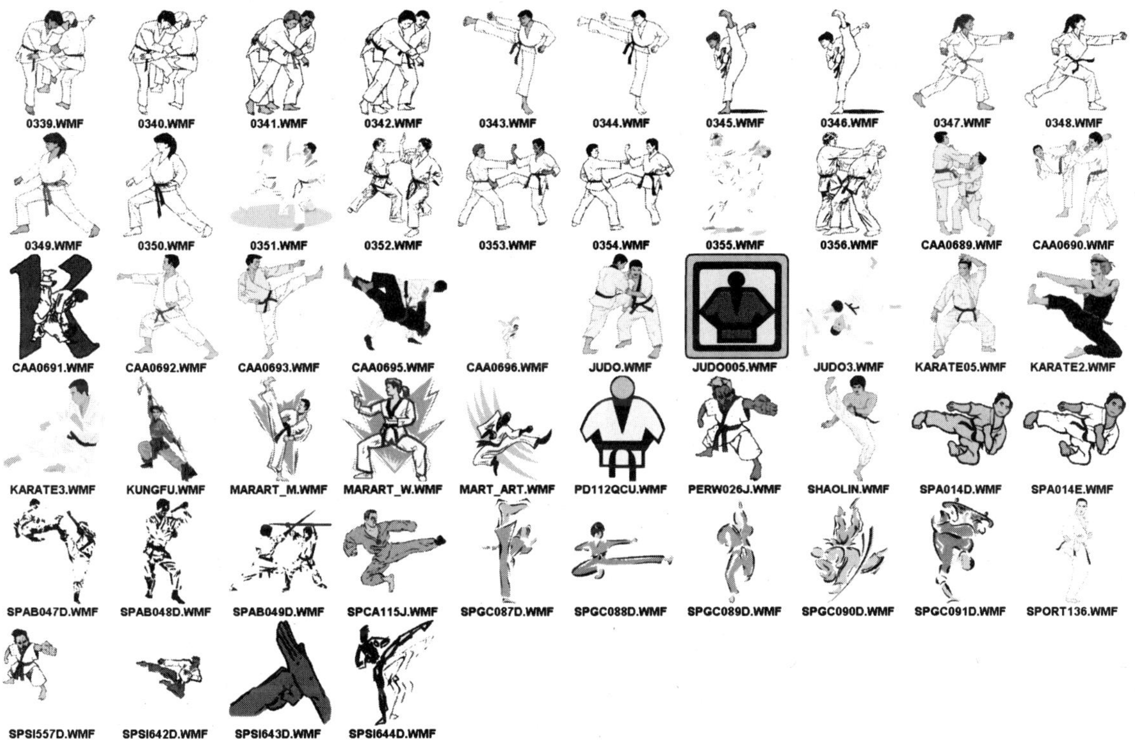
0339.WMF
0340.WMF
0341.WMF
0342.WMF
0343.WMF
0344.WMF
0345.WMF
0346.WMF
0347.WMF
0348.WMF
0349.WMF
0350.WMF
0351.WMF
0352.WMF
0353.WMF
0354.WMF
0355.WMF
0356.WMF
CAA0689.WMF
CAA0690.WMF
CAA0691.WMF
CAA0692.WMF
CAA0693.WMF
CAA0695.WMF
CAA0696.WMF
JUDO.WMF
JUDO005.WMF
JUDO3.WMF
KARATE05.WMF
KARATE2.WMF
KARATE3.WMF
KUNGFU.WMF
MARART_M.WMF
MARART_W.WMF
MART_ART.WMF
PD112QCU.WMF
PERW026J.WMF
SHAOLIN.WMF
SPA014D.WMF
SPA014E.WMF
SPAB047D.WMF
SPAB048D.WMF
SPAB049D.WMF
SPCA115J.WMF
SPGC087D.WMF
SPGC088D.WMF
SPGC089D.WMF
SPGC090D.WMF
SPGC091D.WMF
SPORT136.WMF
SPSI557D.WMF
SPSI642D.WMF
SPSI643D.WMF
SPSI644D.WMF

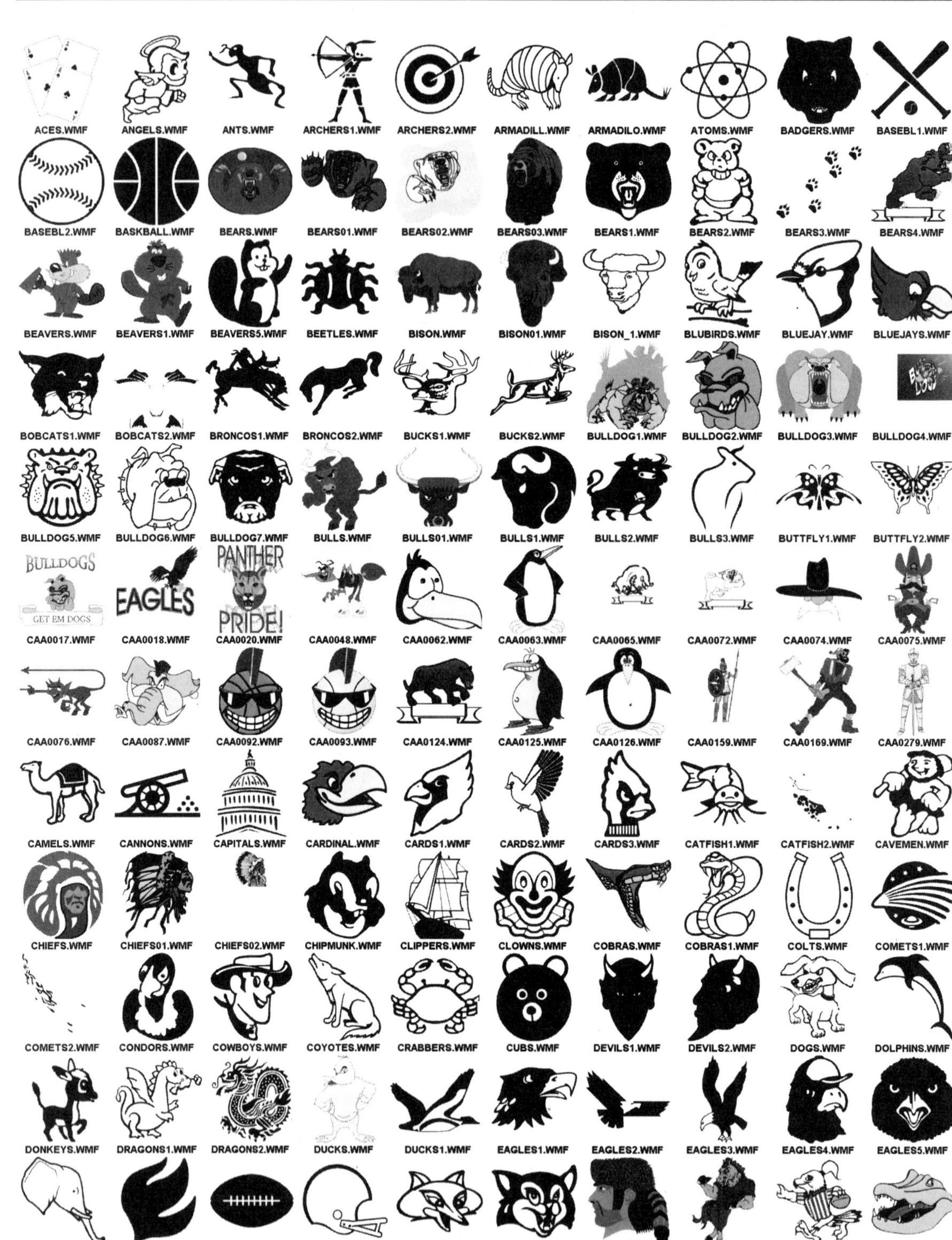
ACES.WMF
ANGELS.WMF
ANTS.WMF
ARCHERS1.WMF
ARCHERS2.WMF
ARMADILL.WMF
ARMADILO.WMF
ATOMS.WMF
BADGERS.WMF
BASEBL1.WMF
BASEBL2.WMF
BASKBALL.WMF
BEARS.WMF
BEARS01.WMF
BEARS02.WMF
BEARS03.WMF
BEARS1.WMF
BEARS2.WMF
BEARS3.WMF
BEARS4.WMF
BEAVERS.WMF
BEAVERS1.WMF
BEAVERS5.WMF
BEETLES.WMF
BISON.WMF
BISON01.WMF
BISON_1.WMF
BLUBIRDS.WMF
BLUEJAY.WMF
BLUEJAYS.WMF
BOBCATS1.WMF
BOBCATS2.WMF
BRONCOS1.WMF
BRONCOS2.WMF
BUCKS1.WMF
BUCKS2.WMF
BULLDOG1.WMF
BULLDOG2.WMF
BULLDOG3.WMF
BULLDOG4.WMF
BULLDOG5.WMF
BULLDOG6.WMF
BULLDOG7.WMF
BULLS.WMF
BULLS01.WMF
BULLS1.WMF
BULLS2.WMF
BULLS3.WMF
BUTTFLY1.WMF
BUTTFLY2.WMF
BULLDOGS
GET EM DOGS
CAA0017.WMF
EAGLES
CAA0018.WMF
PANTHER
PRIDE!
CAA0020.WMF
CAA0048.WMF
CAA0062.WMF
CAA0063.WMF
CAA0065.WMF
CAA0072.WMF
CAA0074.WMF
CAA0075.WMF
CAA0076.WMF
CAA0087.WMF
CAA0092.WMF
CAA0093.WMF
CAA0124.WMF
CAA0125.WMF
CAA0126.WMF
CAA0159.WMF
CAA0169.WMF
CAA0279.WMF
CAMELS.WMF
CANNONS.WMF
CAPITALS.WMF
CARDINAL.WMF
CARDS1.WMF
CARDS2.WMF
CARDS3.WMF
CATFISH1.WMF
CATFISH2.WMF
CAVEMEN.WMF
CHIEFS.WMF
CHIEFS01.WMF
CHIEFS02.WMF
CHIPMUNK.WMF
CLIPPERS.WMF
CLOWNS.WMF
COBRAS.WMF
COBRAS1.WMF
COLTS.WMF
COMETS1.WMF
COMETS2.WMF
CONDORS.WMF
COWBOYS.WMF
COYOTES.WMF
CRABBERS.WMF
CUBS.WMF
DEVILS1.WMF
DEVILS2.WMF
DOGS.WMF
DOLPHINS.WMF
DONKEYS.WMF
DRAGONS1.WMF
DRAGONS2.WMF
DUCKS.WMF
DUCKS1.WMF
EAGLES1.WMF
EAGLES2.WMF
EAGLES3.WMF
EAGLES4.WMF
EAGLES5.WMF
ELEPHANT.WMF
FLAMES.WMF
FOOTBAL1.WMF
FOOTBAL2.WMF
FOX1.WMF
FOX2.WMF
FRONTIER.WMF
FTBAL08.WMF
FTBAL09.WMF
GATORS.WMF

GATORS01.WMF GATORS1.WMF GOLF.WMF GREYHNDS.WMF GRIFFIN1.WMF GRIFFIN2.WMF HAWKS.WMF HAWKS01.WMF HOCKEY.WMF HOOTERS.WMF

HORNETS.WMF HORNETS1.WMF HORNETS2.WMF HORNETS3.WMF HORNETS5.WMF HORNETS6.WMF HORNETS8.WMF HOUNDOGS.WMF HUSKIES.WMF INDIANS.WMF

INDIANS1.WMF INDIANS2.WMF INDIANS3.WMF IRISH1.WMF IRISH2.WMF IRISH3.WMF JAGUARS.WMF JESTER.WMF JETS.WMF KILLRWHL.WMF

KINGS.WMF KNIGHTS.WMF LADYBUGS.WMF LANCERS.WMF LEOPARDS.WMF LIGHTNGS.WMF LIONS.WMF LIONS01.WMF LIONS1.WMF LIONS2.WMF

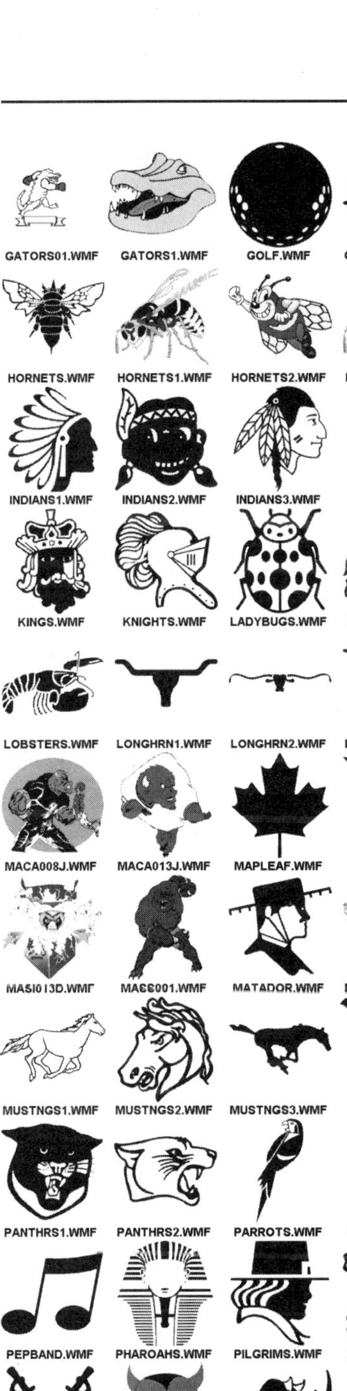

LOBSTERS.WMF LONGHRN1.WMF LONGHRN2.WMF LONGHRN3.WMF LONGHRN4.WMF LONGHRN5.WMF LUMBRJCK.WMF MACA004D.WMF MACA004J.WMF MACA005J.WMF

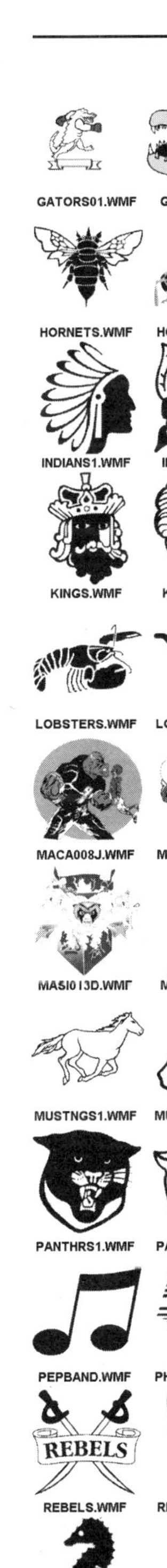

MACA008J.WMF MACA013J.WMF MAPLEAF.WMF MARINR1.WMF MARINR2.WMF MARINR3.WMF MARLINS.WMF MASI003D.WMF MASI007D.WMF MASI008D.WMF

MASI013D.WMF MASS001.WMF MATADOR.WMF MERMAIDS.WMF MINERS.WMF MINERS01.WMF MONARCH1.WMF MONARCH2.WMF MOUNTIES.WMF MOUNTNER.WMF

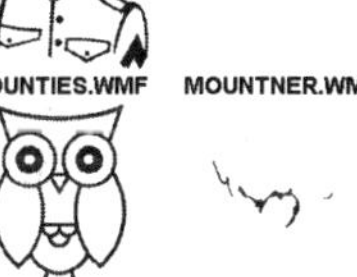

MUSTNGS1.WMF MUSTNGS2.WMF MUSTNGS3.WMF NINJAS.WMF OCTOPUS.WMF OILERS.WMF ORIOLES.WMF OWLS1.WMF OWLS2.WMF OWLS3.WMF

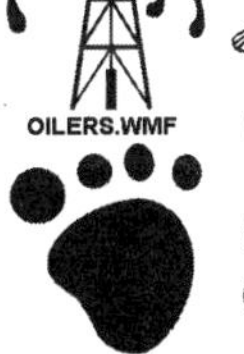

PANTHRS1.WMF PANTHRS2.WMF PARROTS.WMF PATRIOT1.WMF PATRIOT2.WMF PAW1.WMF PAW2.WMF PEGASUS.WMF PELICANS.WMF PENGUINS.WMF

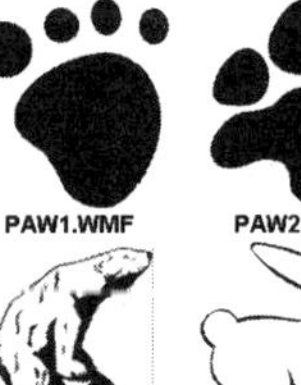

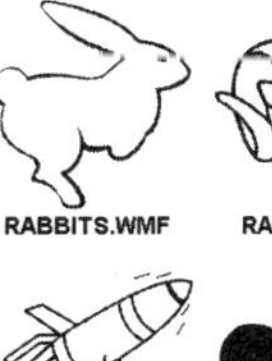

PEPBAND.WMF PHAROAHS.WMF PILGRIMS.WMF PIRATES1.WMF PIRATES2.WMF POLARBR.WMF RABBITS.WMF RAMS1.WMF RAMS2.WMF RATTLRS.WMF

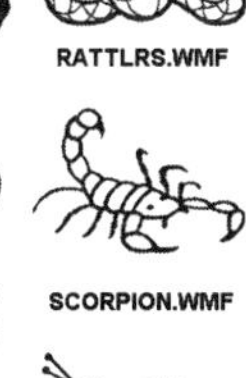

REBELS.WMF REDDEVIL.WMF RHINOS.WMF ROADRNR1.WMF ROADRNR2.WMF ROADRNR3.WMF ROCKETS.WMF SAINTS1.WMF SAINTS2.WMF SCORPION.WMF

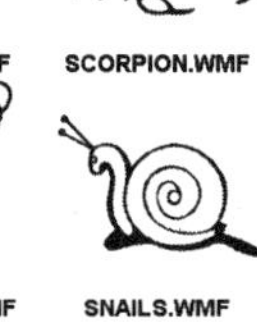

SEAHORSE.WMF SEALIONS.WMF SEALS.WMF SEATURTL.WMF SHARKS.WMF SHARKS01.WMF SHARKS1.WMF SHARKS2.WMF SHARKS3.WMF SNAILS.WMF

SOCCER.WMF
SOLDIERS.WMF
SOONERS.WMF
SPARTANS.WMF
SPIDERS.WMF
STALIONS.WMF
STALLION.WMF
STARS1.WMF
STARS2.WMF
STARS3.WMF
STINGRAY.WMF
STORM1.WMF
STORM2.WMF
SUNS1.WMF
SUNS2.WMF
SWANS.WMF
THUNDBR1.WMF
THUNDBR2.WMF
TIGERS1.WMF
TIGERS2.WMF
TIGERS3.WMF
TOADS.WMF
TORCH.WMF
TORNADO1.WMF
TORNADO2.WMF
TORTOISE.WMF
TRKFLD.WMF
TROJAN1.WMF
TROJAN2.WMF
TROJANS.WMF
TROJANS1.WMF
UNICORN1.WMF
UNICORN2.WMF
VAMPIRES.WMF
VIKINGS.WMF
VIKINGS1.WMF
VIKINGS2.WMF
VIKINGS5.WMF
VIKINGS9.WMF
VOLYBALL.WMF
WARTHOGS.WMF
WHALERS.WMF
WLDCAT01.WMF
WLDCAT02.WMF
WLDCAT03.WMF
WLDCAT04.WMF
WLDCAT05.WMF
WLDCAT06.WMF
WLDCAT07.WMF
WLDCAT08.WMF
WLDCAT10.WMF
WLDCAT11.WMF
WLDCAT12.WMF
WLDCAT14.WMF
WLDCAT15.WMF
WOLVES.WMF
WOLVES1.WMF
WOLVES2.WMF
ZEBRAS.WMF

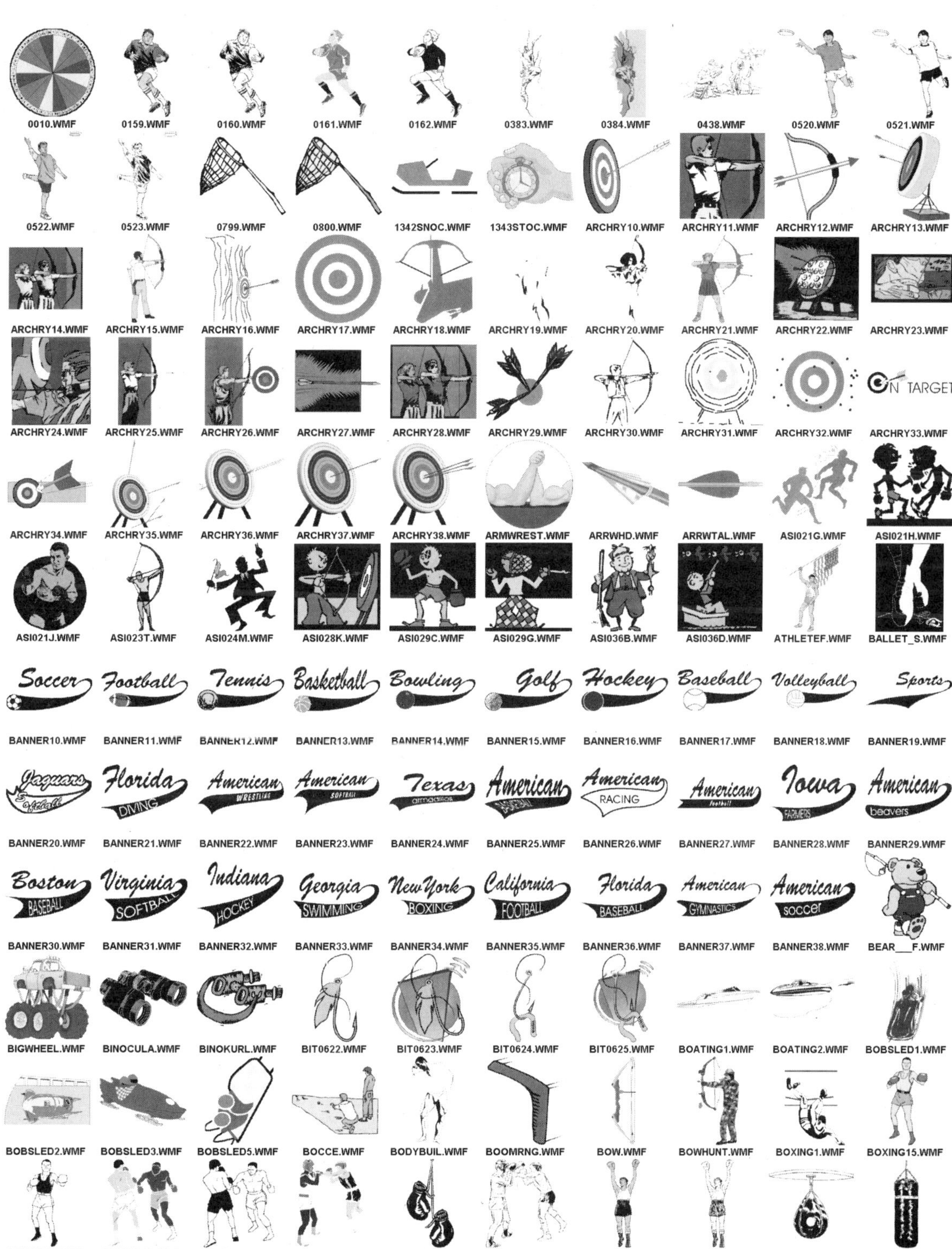

0010.WMF 0159.WMF 0160.WMF 0161.WMF 0162.WMF 0383.WMF 0384.WMF 0438.WMF 0520.WMF 0521.WMF

0522.WMF 0523.WMF 0799.WMF 0800.WMF 1342SNOC.WMF 1343STOC.WMF ARCHRY10.WMF ARCHRY11.WMF ARCHRY12.WMF ARCHRY13.WMF

ARCHRY14.WMF ARCHRY15.WMF ARCHRY16.WMF ARCHRY17.WMF ARCHRY18.WMF ARCHRY19.WMF ARCHRY20.WMF ARCHRY21.WMF ARCHRY22.WMF ARCHRY23.WMF

ARCHRY24.WMF ARCHRY25.WMF ARCHRY26.WMF ARCHRY27.WMF ARCHRY28.WMF ARCHRY29.WMF ARCHRY30.WMF ARCHRY31.WMF ARCHRY32.WMF ARCHRY33.WMF

ARCHRY34.WMF ARCHRY35.WMF ARCHRY36.WMF ARCHRY37.WMF ARCHRY38.WMF ARMWREST.WMF ARRWHD.WMF ARRWTAL.WMF ASI021G.WMF ASI021H.WMF

ASI021J.WMF ASI023T.WMF ASI024M.WMF ASI028K.WMF ASI029C.WMF ASI029G.WMF ASI036B.WMF ASI036D.WMF ATHLETEF.WMF BALLET_S.WMF

BANNER10.WMF BANNER11.WMF BANNER12.WMF BANNER13.WMF BANNER14.WMF BANNER15.WMF BANNER16.WMF BANNER17.WMF BANNER18.WMF BANNER19.WMF

BANNER20.WMF BANNER21.WMF BANNER22.WMF BANNER23.WMF BANNER24.WMF BANNER25.WMF BANNER26.WMF BANNER27.WMF BANNER28.WMF BANNER29.WMF

BANNER30.WMF BANNER31.WMF BANNER32.WMF BANNER33.WMF BANNER34.WMF BANNER35.WMF BANNER36.WMF BANNER37.WMF BANNER38.WMF BEAR___F.WMF

BIGWHEEL.WMF BINOCULA.WMF BINOKURL.WMF BIT0622.WMF BIT0623.WMF BIT0624.WMF BIT0625.WMF BOATING1.WMF BOATING2.WMF BOBSLED1.WMF

BOBSLED2.WMF BOBSLED3.WMF BOBSLED5.WMF BOCCE.WMF BODYBUIL.WMF BOOMRNG.WMF BOW.WMF BOWHUNT.WMF BOXING1.WMF BOXING15.WMF

BOXING16.WMF BOXING17.WMF BOXING18.WMF BOXING19.WMF BOXING2.WMF BOXING20.WMF BOXING21.WMF BOXING22.WMF BOXING23.WMF BOXING24.WMF

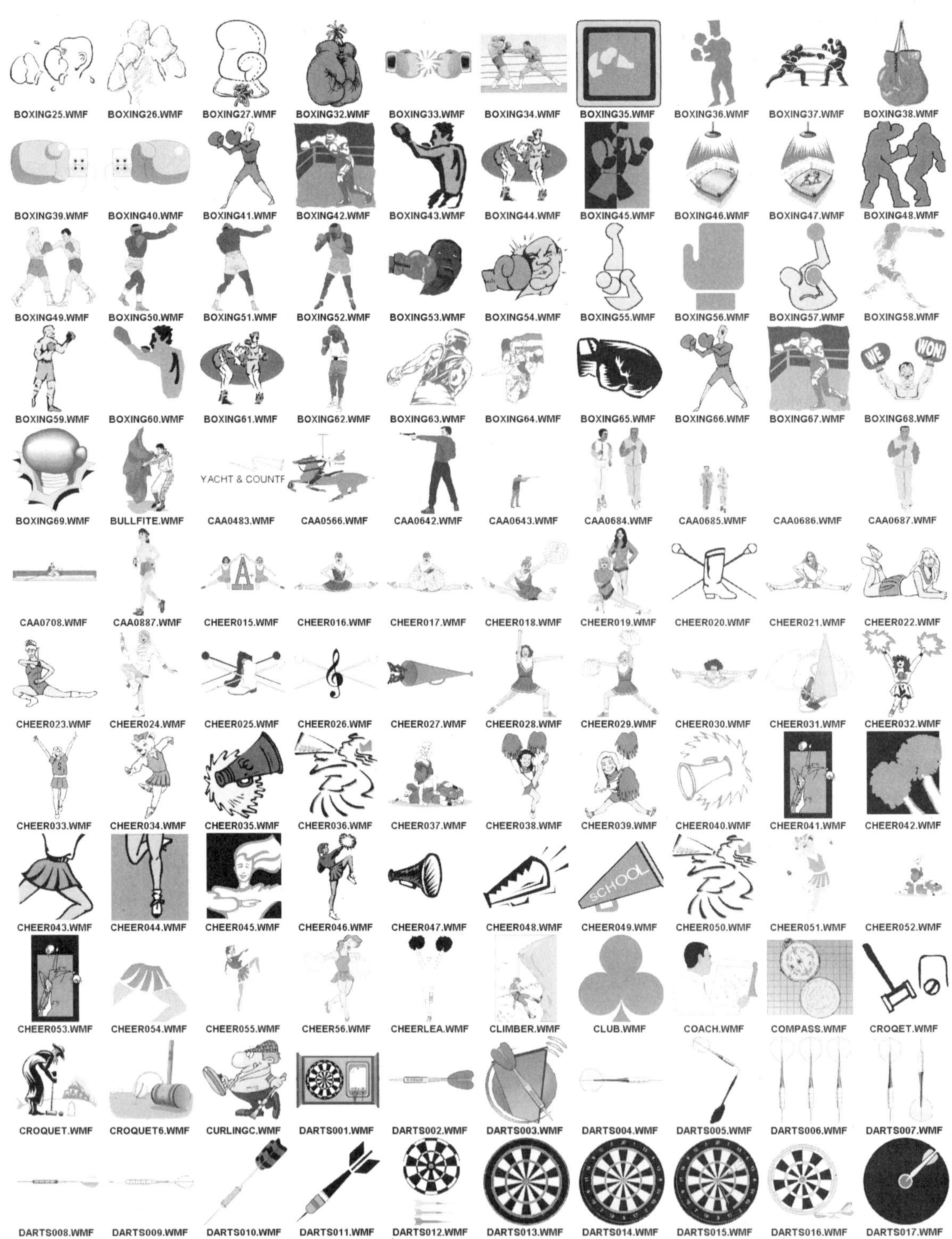

BOXING25.WMF BOXING26.WMF BOXING27.WMF BOXING32.WMF BOXING33.WMF BOXING34.WMF BOXING35.WMF BOXING36.WMF BOXING37.WMF BOXING38.WMF

BOXING39.WMF BOXING40.WMF BOXING41.WMF BOXING42.WMF BOXING43.WMF BOXING44.WMF BOXING45.WMF BOXING46.WMF BOXING47.WMF BOXING48.WMF

BOXING49.WMF BOXING50.WMF BOXING51.WMF BOXING52.WMF BOXING53.WMF BOXING54.WMF BOXING55.WMF BOXING56.WMF BOXING57.WMF BOXING58.WMF

BOXING59.WMF BOXING60.WMF BOXING61.WMF BOXING62.WMF BOXING63.WMF BOXING64.WMF BOXING65.WMF BOXING66.WMF BOXING67.WMF BOXING68.WMF

BOXING69.WMF BULLFITE.WMF CAA0483.WMF CAA0566.WMF CAA0642.WMF CAA0643.WMF CAA0684.WMF CAA0685.WMF CAA0686.WMF CAA0687.WMF

CAA0708.WMF CAA0887.WMF CHEER015.WMF CHEER016.WMF CHEER017.WMF CHEER018.WMF CHEER019.WMF CHEER020.WMF CHEER021.WMF CHEER022.WMF

CHEER023.WMF CHEER024.WMF CHEER025.WMF CHEER026.WMF CHEER027.WMF CHEER028.WMF CHEER029.WMF CHEER030.WMF CHEER031.WMF CHEER032.WMF

CHEER033.WMF CHEER034.WMF CHEER035.WMF CHEER036.WMF CHEER037.WMF CHEER038.WMF CHEER039.WMF CHEER040.WMF CHEER041.WMF CHEER042.WMF

CHEER043.WMF CHEER044.WMF CHEER045.WMF CHEER046.WMF CHEER047.WMF CHEER048.WMF CHEER049.WMF CHEER050.WMF CHEER051.WMF CHEER052.WMF

CHEER053.WMF CHEER054.WMF CHEER055.WMF CHEER56.WMF CHEERLEA.WMF CLIMBER.WMF CLUB.WMF COACH.WMF COMPASS.WMF CROQET.WMF

CROQUET.WMF CROQUET6.WMF CURLINGC.WMF DARTS001.WMF DARTS002.WMF DARTS003.WMF DARTS004.WMF DARTS005.WMF DARTS006.WMF DARTS007.WMF

DARTS008.WMF DARTS009.WMF DARTS010.WMF DARTS011.WMF DARTS012.WMF DARTS013.WMF DARTS014.WMF DARTS015.WMF DARTS016.WMF DARTS017.WMF

DARTS018.WMF DARTS019.WMF DARTS020.WMF DARTS021.WMF DARTS022.WMF DARTS023.WMF DARTS024.WMF DARTS025.WMF DARTS026.WMF DARTS027.WMF

DARTS028.WMF DARTS029.WMF DARTS030.WMF DEC069DD.WMF DOGSLED.WMF EDCN120.WMF FANCOLOR.WMF FENCER.WMF FENCNG01.WMF FENCNG02.WMF

FENCNG03.WMF FENCNG04.WMF FENCNG05.WMF FENCNG06.WMF FENCNG07.WMF FENCNG08.WMF FENCNG09.WMF FENCNG10.WMF FENCNG11.WMF FENCNG12.WMF

FENCNG13.WMF FENCNG14.WMF FENCNG15.WMF FENCNG16.WMF FENCNG17.WMF FENCNG18.WMF FENCNG19.WMF FENCNG20.WMF FENCNG21.WMF FENCNG22.WMF

FENCNG23.WMF FENCNG24.WMF FENCNG25.WMF FENCNG26.WMF FENCNG27.WMF FENCNG28.WMF FIELDHK.WMF FINISH.WMF FISHING3.WMF FISHING4.WMF

FNSHLINE.WMF FOOTY.WMF FOOTY1.WMF FOOTY1C.WMF FOOTYC.WMF FRISBEE.WMF GONEFISH.WMF HANG_GLI.WMF HANGGLI1.WMF HANGGLID.WMF

HANGLID2.WMF HANGLIDE.WMF HIKER.WMF HIKER01.WMF HORSHOE.WMF HPI010B.WMF HPI010E.WMF HRSESHOE.WMF HUNTING1.WMF HUNTING2.WMF

HUNTING3.WMF HUNTING4.WMF HUNTING5.WMF HUNTING6.WMF HYDROPLA.WMF IGB027C.WMF IGB027F.WMF IOD014A.WMF IOD017D.WMF IOD026C.WMF

IOD031A.WMF ISP010C.WMF ISP031A.WMF IWS003C.WMF IWS004C.WMF IWS007B.WMF IWS019A.WMF IWS026A.WMF IWS032B.WMF JUJITSU.WMF

KENDO.WMF KENDO2.WMF KYAKING.WMF LUGE.WMF LUGE001.WMF LUGE002.WMF LUGE003.WMF LUGE004.WMF MAN_FISH.WMF MATADOR.WMF

MATADOR1.WMF MISCSP50.WMF MISCSP51.WMF MISCSP52.WMF MISCSP53.WMF MISCSP67.WMF MISCSP68.WMF MISCSP74.WMF MSL001B.WMF MSL044A.WMF

MSL044D.WMF MSL044E.WMF MTCLIMB1.WMF MTCLIMB2.WMF OFS028C.WMF OFS030G.WMF OLD_FASH.WMF OLYMPC01.WMF OLYMPC02.WMF OLYMPC03.WMF

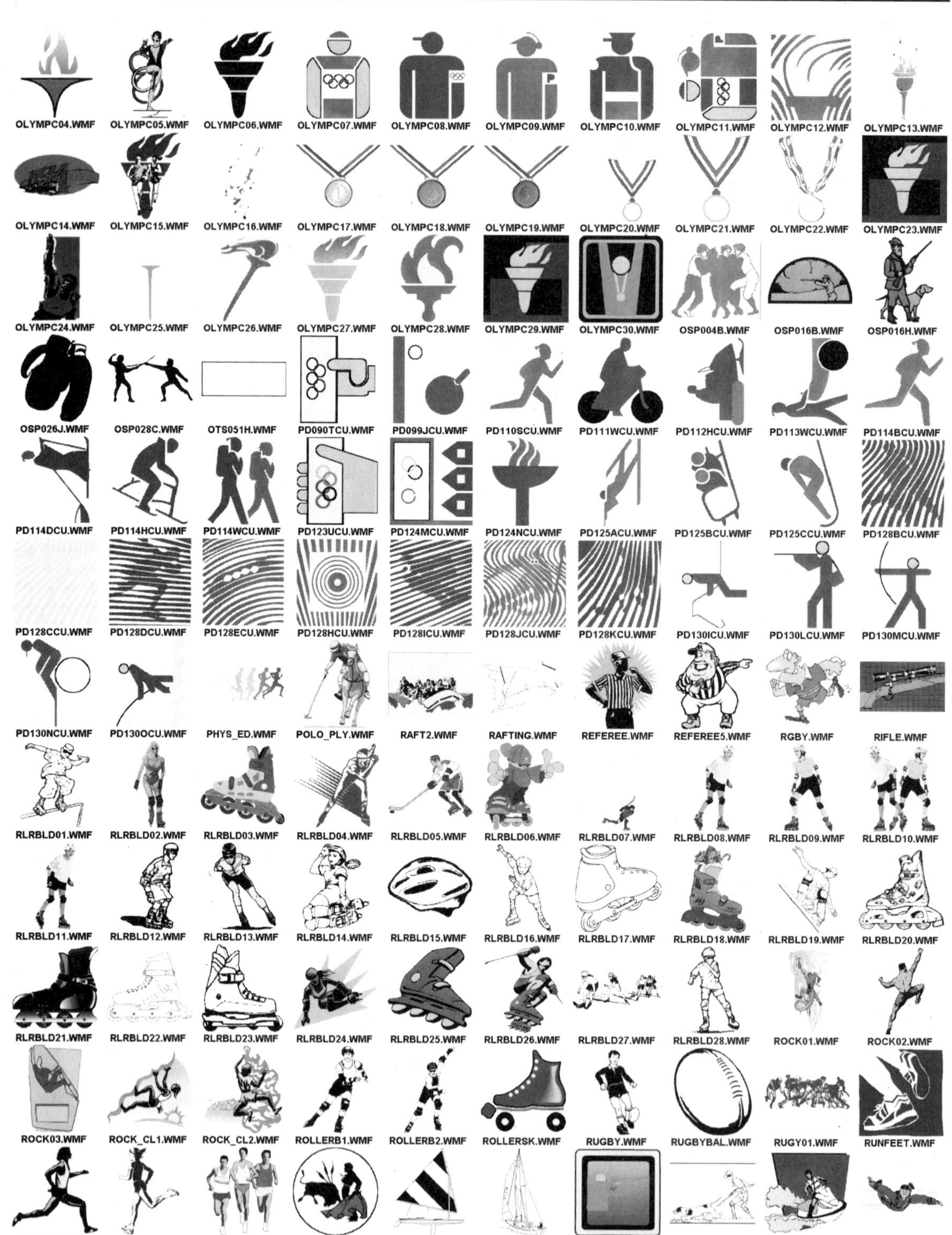
OLYMPC04.WMF OLYMPC05.WMF OLYMPC06.WMF OLYMPC07.WMF OLYMPC08.WMF OLYMPC09.WMF OLYMPC10.WMF OLYMPC11.WMF OLYMPC12.WMF OLYMPC13.WMF
OLYMPC14.WMF OLYMPC15.WMF OLYMPC16.WMF OLYMPC17.WMF OLYMPC18.WMF OLYMPC19.WMF OLYMPC20.WMF OLYMPC21.WMF OLYMPC22.WMF OLYMPC23.WMF
OLYMPC24.WMF OLYMPC25.WMF OLYMPC26.WMF OLYMPC27.WMF OLYMPC28.WMF OLYMPC29.WMF OLYMPC30.WMF OSP004B.WMF OSP016B.WMF OSP016H.WMF
OSP026J.WMF OSP028C.WMF OTS051H.WMF PD090TCU.WMF PD099JCU.WMF PD110SCU.WMF PD111WCU.WMF PD112HCU.WMF PD113WCU.WMF PD114BCU.WMF
PD114DCU.WMF PD114HCU.WMF PD114WCU.WMF PD123UCU.WMF PD124MCU.WMF PD124NCU.WMF PD125ACU.WMF PD125BCU.WMF PD125CCU.WMF PD128BCU.WMF
PD128CCU.WMF PD128DCU.WMF PD128ECU.WMF PD128HCU.WMF PD128ICU.WMF PD128JCU.WMF PD128KCU.WMF PD130ICU.WMF PD130LCU.WMF PD130MCU.WMF
PD130NCU.WMF PD130OCU.WMF PHYS_ED.WMF POLO_PLY.WMF RAFT2.WMF RAFTING.WMF REFEREE.WMF REFEREE5.WMF RGBY.WMF RIFLE.WMF
RLRBLD01.WMF RLRBLD02.WMF RLRBLD03.WMF RLRBLD04.WMF RLRBLD05.WMF RLRBLD06.WMF RLRBLD07.WMF RLRBLD08.WMF RLRBLD09.WMF RLRBLD10.WMF
RLRBLD11.WMF RLRBLD12.WMF RLRBLD13.WMF RLRBLD14.WMF RLRBLD15.WMF RLRBLD16.WMF RLRBLD17.WMF RLRBLD18.WMF RLRBLD19.WMF RLRBLD20.WMF
RLRBLD21.WMF RLRBLD22.WMF RLRBLD23.WMF RLRBLD24.WMF RLRBLD25.WMF RLRBLD26.WMF RLRBLD27.WMF RLRBLD28.WMF ROCK01.WMF ROCK02.WMF
ROCK03.WMF ROCK_CL1.WMF ROCK_CL2.WMF ROLLERB1.WMF ROLLERB2.WMF ROLLERSK.WMF RUGBY.WMF RUGBYBAL.WMF RUGY01.WMF RUNFEET.WMF
RUNNER.WMF RUNNER1.WMF RUNNERS.WMF SAC020D.WMF SAILING3.WMF SAILING4.WMF SHOOTING.WMF SIL092B.WMF SKING04.WMF SKYDIVER.WMF

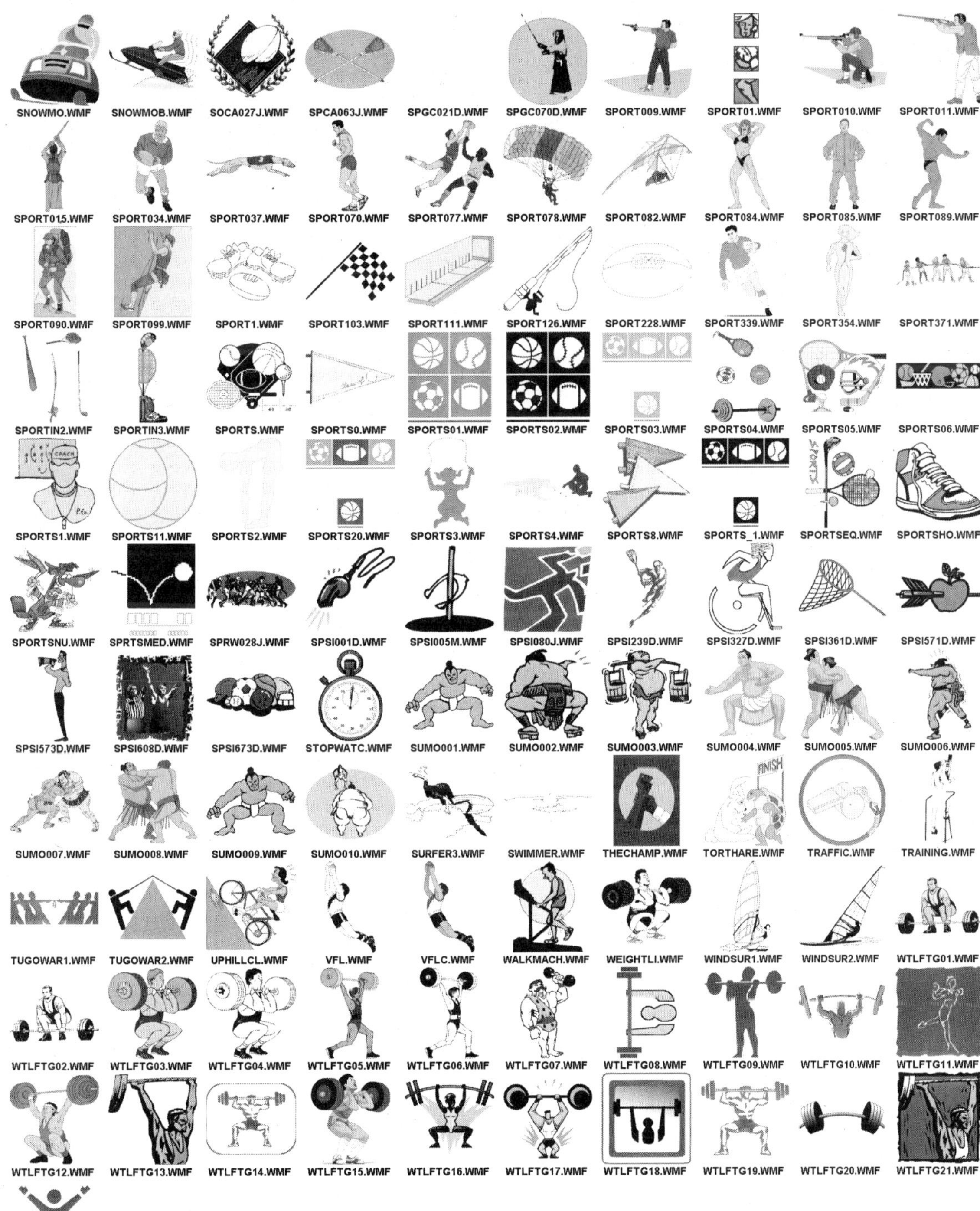
SNOWMO.WMF
SNOWMOB.WMF
SOCA027J.WMF
SPCA063J.WMF
SPGC021D.WMF
SPGC070D.WMF
SPORT009.WMF
SPORT01.WMF
SPORT010.WMF
SPORT011.WMF
SPORT015.WMF
SPORT034.WMF
SPORT037.WMF
SPORT070.WMF
SPORT077.WMF
SPORT078.WMF
SPORT082.WMF
SPORT084.WMF
SPORT085.WMF
SPORT089.WMF
SPORT090.WMF
SPORT099.WMF
SPORT1.WMF
SPORT103.WMF
SPORT111.WMF
SPORT126.WMF
SPORT228.WMF
SPORT339.WMF
SPORT354.WMF
SPORT371.WMF
SPORTIN2.WMF
SPORTIN3.WMF
SPORTS.WMF
SPORTS0.WMF
SPORTS01.WMF
SPORTS02.WMF
SPORTS03.WMF
SPORTS04.WMF
SPORTS05.WMF
SPORTS06.WMF
SPORTS1.WMF
SPORTS11.WMF
SPORTS2.WMF
SPORTS20.WMF
SPORTS3.WMF
SPORTS4.WMF
SPORTS8.WMF
SPORTS_1.WMF
SPORTSEQ.WMF
SPORTSHO.WMF
SPORTSNU.WMF
SPRTSMED.WMF
SPRW028J.WMF
SPSI001D.WMF
SPSI005M.WMF
SPSI080J.WMF
SPSI239D.WMF
SPSI327D.WMF
SPSI361D.WMF
SPSI571D.WMF
SPSI573D.WMF
SPSI608D.WMF
SPSI673D.WMF
STOPWATC.WMF
SUMO001.WMF
SUMO002.WMF
SUMO003.WMF
SUMO004.WMF
SUMO005.WMF
SUMO006.WMF
SUMO007.WMF
SUMO008.WMF
SUMO009.WMF
SUMO010.WMF
SURFER3.WMF
SWIMMER.WMF
THECHAMP.WMF
TORTHARE.WMF
TRAFFIC.WMF
TRAINING.WMF
TUGOWAR1.WMF
TUGOWAR2.WMF
UPHILLCL.WMF
VFL.WMF
VFLC.WMF
WALKMACH.WMF
WEIGHTLI.WMF
WINDSUR1.WMF
WINDSUR2.WMF
WTLFTG01.WMF
WTLFTG02.WMF
WTLFTG03.WMF
WTLFTG04.WMF
WTLFTG05.WMF
WTLFTG06.WMF
WTLFTG07.WMF
WTLFTG08.WMF
WTLFTG09.WMF
WTLFTG10.WMF
WTLFTG11.WMF
WTLFTG12.WMF
WTLFTG13.WMF
WTLFTG14.WMF
WTLFTG15.WMF
WTLFTG16.WMF
WTLFTG17.WMF
WTLFTG18.WMF
WTLFTG19.WMF
WTLFTG20.WMF
WTLFTG21.WMF
XFIGURE.WMF

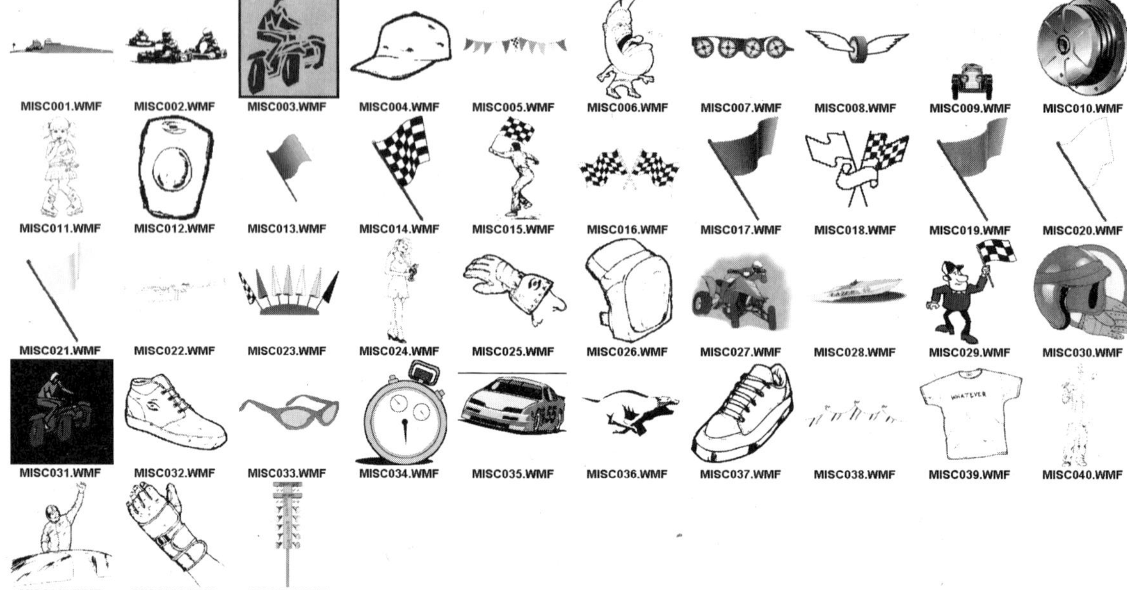

MISC001.WMF MISC002.WMF MISC003.WMF MISC004.WMF MISC005.WMF MISC006.WMF MISC007.WMF MISC008.WMF MISC009.WMF MISC010.WMF

MISC011.WMF MISC012.WMF MISC013.WMF MISC014.WMF MISC015.WMF MISC016.WMF MISC017.WMF MISC018.WMF MISC019.WMF MISC020.WMF

MISC021.WMF MISC022.WMF MISC023.WMF MISC024.WMF MISC025.WMF MISC026.WMF MISC027.WMF MISC028.WMF MISC029.WMF MISC030.WMF

MISC031.WMF MISC032.WMF MISC033.WMF MISC034.WMF MISC035.WMF MISC036.WMF MISC037.WMF MISC038.WMF MISC039.WMF MISC040.WMF

MISC041.WMF MISC042.WMF MISC043.WMF

0366.WMF 0367.WMF 1ST_2ND.WMF 2_59S.WMF 2INTURN.WMF 2LATE.WMF 2MODS.WMF 2NEWCUPS.WMF 2PROCOMP.WMF 2PROS.WMF

2SLIDIN.WMF 2TRUCKS.WMF AAFCRACE.WMF AAFUELER.WMF AAR_SIDE.WMF ALTERED.WMF AUTORACI.WMF AWESOME.WMF BAAACKIN.WMF BANKING.WMF

BEAST.WMF BENZRACE.WMF BIGCOMP.WMF BIGRED.WMF BIGSPRIN.WMF BIGWINGS.WMF BKERAC01.WMF BKERAC02.WMF BKERAC03.WMF BKERAC04.WMF

BKERAC05.WMF BKERAC06.WMF BKERAC07.WMF BKERAC08.WMF BKERAC09.WMF BKERAC10.WMF BKERAC11.WMF BKERAC12.WMF BKERAC13.WMF BKERAC14.WMF

BKERAC15.WMF BKERAC16.WMF BKERAC17.WMF BKERAC18.WMF BKERAC19.WMF BKERAC20.WMF BKERAC21.WMF BKERAC22.WMF BKERAC23.WMF BKERAC24.WMF

BKERAC25.WMF BKERAC26.WMF BKERAC27.WMF BKERAC28.WMF BKERAC29.WMF BKERAC30.WMF BKERAC31.WMF BKERAC32.WMF BKERAC33.WMF BKERAC34.WMF

BKERAC35.WMF BKERAC36.WMF BKERAC37.WMF BKERAC38.WMF BKERAC39.WMF BLASTOFF.WMF BOMBER.WMF BONUS_1.WMF BONUS_10.WMF BONUS_11.WMF

BONUS_12.WMF BONUS_13.WMF BONUS_15.WMF BONUS_16.WMF BONUS_18.WMF BONUS_21.WMF BONUS_24.WMF BONUS_25.WMF BONUS_3.WMF BONUS_6.WMF

BONUS_8.WMF BONUS_9.WMF BTOPMIDG.WMF BYE_BYE.WMF CAA0389.WMF CAA0390.WMF CAA0391.WMF CAA0395.WMF CAA0396.WMF CAA0397.WMF

CAA0398.WMF CAA0399.WMF CAA0400.WMF CAA0404.WMF CAA0408.WMF CAA0410.WMF CAA0416.WMF CAA0419.WMF CAA0421.WMF CAA0422.WMF

CAMERO.WMF CAMVSVET.WMF CARTER.WMF CHEVPONT.WMF CHUTE.WMF CLEAN.WMF COLRFUEL.WMF COLRFUNY.WMF COLRIMCA.WMF DEPLOY.WMF

DIGGERS.WMF DIRTERS.WMF DIRTIN.WMF DIRTLATE.WMF DIRTMOD.WMF DIRTSTOC.WMF DODGE.WMF DOINK.WMF DOWNBAR.WMF DRAGGER.WMF

DRAGSTER.WMF
DRIVER.WMF
DUELING.WMF
DWRFRACE.WMF
EARLY60.WMF
EARLY80S.WMF
EASTMOD.WMF
EDMOD.WMF
ENDURO.WMF
F1.WMF
F1CAR.WMF
F_1.WMF
FASTFLIP.WMF
FENDERS.WMF
FERRARI.WMF
FORMV.WMF
FRONT.WMF
FUNLSIDE.WMF
FUNNYCAR.WMF
FUNRSIDE.WMF
FUNSTER.WMF
FVRAIL.WMF
GASSER.WMF
GOCART01.WMF
GRANPRIX.WMF
HAVTAMP.WMF
HEAD_ON.WMF
HEAVYS.WMF
HELMET.WMF
HELMET05.WMF
HOTGAS.WMF
IGNITE.WMF
IMCARACE.WMF
IMCATURN.WMF
INDYCAR.WMF
INDYCAR2.WMF
IRL.WMF
ISP026B.WMF
JRDRAG.WMF
JRG_MID.WMF
JRGGOLD.WMF
JRGRAIL.WMF
JRGTOWER.WMF
K71_.WMF
KABOOM.WMF
KARTER.WMF
KARTING.WMF
KARTRACE.WMF
KK_CAM.WMF
KKTURNS.WMF
L_SIDE.WMF
LATEMOD.WMF
LATETOW.WMF
LAYDOWN.WMF
LEAVIN.WMF
LEAVING.WMF
LEGEND.WMF
LEGENDS.WMF
LILBLUE.WMF
LONGALTR.WMF
LSIDE_SP.WMF
LUMINA.WMF
MFRONT.WMF
MIDSLIDE.WMF
MIDV4.WMF
MINIRAIL.WMF
MINISPRI.WMF
MOD_2.WMF
MOD_TURN.WMF
MONTE.WMF
MONTE7.WMF
MONTELM.WMF
MOTORCRS.WMF
MOTORCY1.WMF
MOTORCY2.WMF
NASCMOD.WMF
NASCPONT.WMF
NEAT_4.WMF
NEMODS.WMF
NEWBIRD.WMF
NEWCHMP.WMF
NEWDWARF.WMF
NEWMIDG.WMF
NO_WING.WMF
OLD_40.WMF
OLD_51.WMF
OLDCOUPE.WMF
OLDIE.WMF
OLDSFUN.WMF
OLDSLATE.WMF
OLDVPONT.WMF
OPENLID.WMF
OUTLAW.WMF
OUTLAW2.WMF
PAVE2.WMF
PAVE_SP.WMF
PAVEMOD.WMF
PIT_STOP.WMF
PITSTOP.WMF
PLYM.WMF
PONTIAC.WMF
POUNDERS.WMF
PROSTK.WMF
PSLSIDE.WMF
PSRSIDE.WMF
PULLIN57.WMF
QUART.WMF
R_SIDE.WMF
RACE01.WMF
RACE02.WMF
RACE03.WMF
RACE04.WMF
RACECAR.WMF
RACECAR1.WMF
RACECAR2.WMF
RACECAR5.WMF
RACECAR8.WMF
RACECARA.WMF
RACECARR.WMF
RACEIMCA.WMF

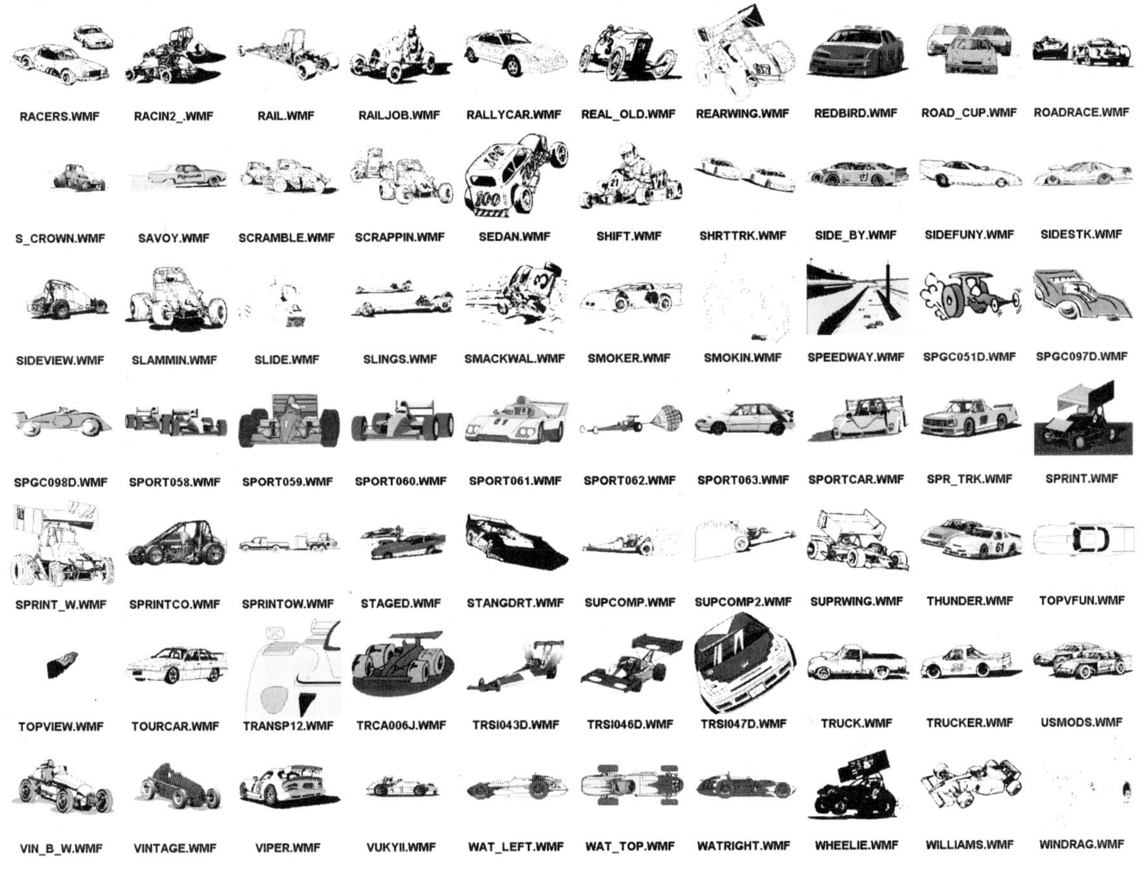

RACERS.WMF RACIN2_.WMF RAIL.WMF RAILJOB.WMF RALLYCAR.WMF REAL_OLD.WMF REARWING.WMF REDBIRD.WMF ROAD_CUP.WMF ROADRACE.WMF

S_CROWN.WMF SAVOY.WMF SCRAMBLE.WMF SCRAPPIN.WMF SEDAN.WMF SHIFT.WMF SHRTTRK.WMF SIDE_BY.WMF SIDEFUNY.WMF SIDESTK.WMF

SIDEVIEW.WMF SLAMMIN.WMF SLIDE.WMF SLINGS.WMF SMACKWAL.WMF SMOKER.WMF SMOKIN.WMF SPEEDWAY.WMF SPGC051D.WMF SPGC097D.WMF

SPGC098D.WMF SPORT058.WMF SPORT059.WMF SPORT060.WMF SPORT061.WMF SPORT062.WMF SPORT063.WMF SPORTCAR.WMF SPR_TRK.WMF SPRINT.WMF

SPRINT_W.WMF SPRINTCO.WMF SPRINTOW.WMF STAGED.WMF STANGDRT.WMF SUPCOMP.WMF SUPCOMP2.WMF SUPRWING.WMF THUNDER.WMF TOPVFUN.WMF

TOPVIEW.WMF TOURCAR.WMF TRANSP12.WMF TRCA006J.WMF TRSI043D.WMF TRSI046D.WMF TRSI047D.WMF TRUCK.WMF TRUCKER.WMF USMODS.WMF

VIN_B_W.WMF VINTAGE.WMF VIPER.WMF VUKYII.WMF WAT_LEFT.WMF WAT_TOP.WMF WATRIGHT.WMF WHEELIE.WMF WILLIAMS.WMF WINDRAG.WMF

WINSCUP.WMF

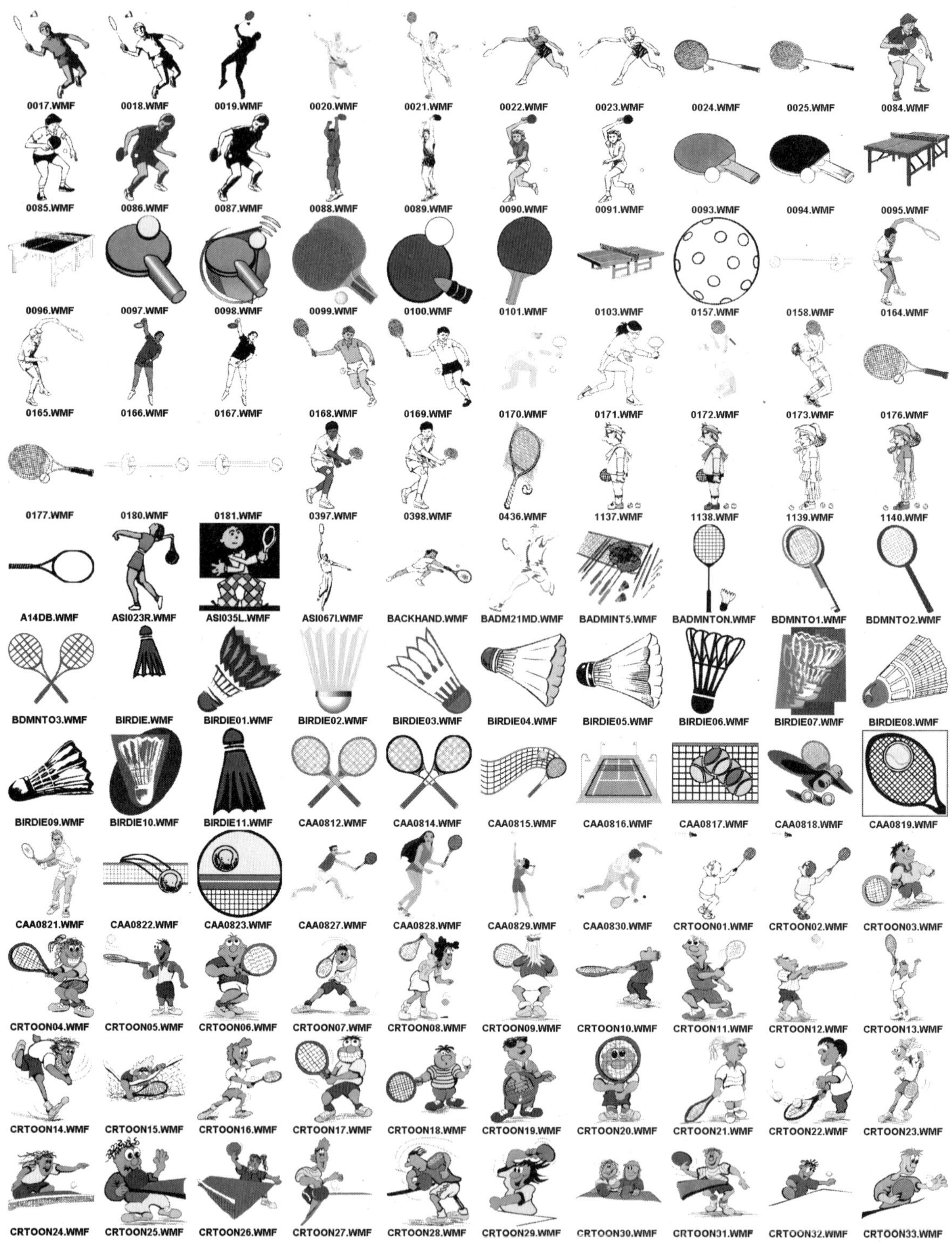
0017.WMF 0018.WMF 0019.WMF 0020.WMF 0021.WMF 0022.WMF 0023.WMF 0024.WMF 0025.WMF 0084.WMF
0085.WMF 0086.WMF 0087.WMF 0088.WMF 0089.WMF 0090.WMF 0091.WMF 0093.WMF 0094.WMF 0095.WMF
0096.WMF 0097.WMF 0098.WMF 0099.WMF 0100.WMF 0101.WMF 0103.WMF 0157.WMF 0158.WMF 0164.WMF
0165.WMF 0166.WMF 0167.WMF 0168.WMF 0169.WMF 0170.WMF 0171.WMF 0172.WMF 0173.WMF 0176.WMF
0177.WMF 0180.WMF 0181.WMF 0397.WMF 0398.WMF 0436.WMF 1137.WMF 1138.WMF 1139.WMF 1140.WMF
A14DB.WMF ASI023R.WMF ASI035L.WMF ASI067I.WMF BACKHAND.WMF BADM21MD.WMF BADMINT5.WMF BADMNTON.WMF BDMNTO1.WMF BDMNTO2.WMF
BDMNTO3.WMF BIRDIE.WMF BIRDIE01.WMF BIRDIE02.WMF BIRDIE03.WMF BIRDIE04.WMF BIRDIE05.WMF BIRDIE06.WMF BIRDIE07.WMF BIRDIE08.WMF
BIRDIE09.WMF BIRDIE10.WMF BIRDIE11.WMF CAA0812.WMF CAA0814.WMF CAA0815.WMF CAA0816.WMF CAA0817.WMF CAA0818.WMF CAA0819.WMF
CAA0821.WMF CAA0822.WMF CAA0823.WMF CAA0827.WMF CAA0828.WMF CAA0829.WMF CAA0830.WMF CRTOON01.WMF CRTOON02.WMF CRTOON03.WMF
CRTOON04.WMF CRTOON05.WMF CRTOON06.WMF CRTOON07.WMF CRTOON08.WMF CRTOON09.WMF CRTOON10.WMF CRTOON11.WMF CRTOON12.WMF CRTOON13.WMF
CRTOON14.WMF CRTOON15.WMF CRTOON16.WMF CRTOON17.WMF CRTOON18.WMF CRTOON19.WMF CRTOON20.WMF CRTOON21.WMF CRTOON22.WMF CRTOON23.WMF
CRTOON24.WMF CRTOON25.WMF CRTOON26.WMF CRTOON27.WMF CRTOON28.WMF CRTOON29.WMF CRTOON30.WMF CRTOON31.WMF CRTOON32.WMF CRTOON33.WMF

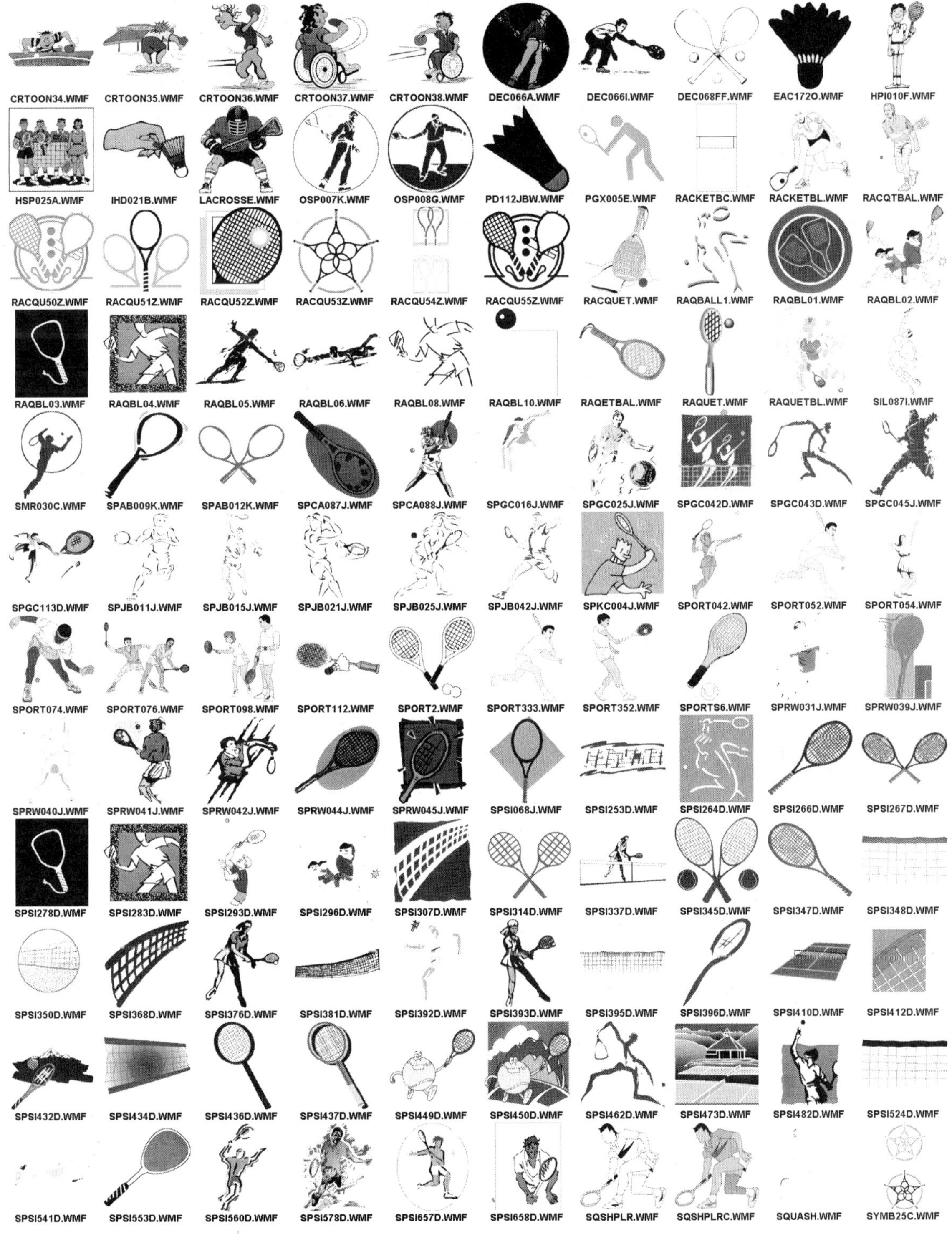
CRTOON34.WMF CRTOON35.WMF CRTOON36.WMF CRTOON37.WMF CRTOON38.WMF DEC066A.WMF DEC066I.WMF DEC068FF.WMF EAC172O.WMF HPI010F.WMF
HSP025A.WMF IHD021B.WMF LACROSSE.WMF OSP007K.WMF OSP008G.WMF PD112JBW.WMF PGX005E.WMF RACKETBC.WMF RACKETBL.WMF RACQTBAL.WMF
RACQU50Z.WMF RACQU51Z.WMF RACQU52Z.WMF RACQU53Z.WMF RACQU54Z.WMF RACQU55Z.WMF RACQUET.WMF RAQBALL1.WMF RAQBL01.WMF RAQBL02.WMF
RAQBL03.WMF RAQBL04.WMF RAQBL05.WMF RAQBL06.WMF RAQBL08.WMF RAQBL10.WMF RAQETBAL.WMF RAQUET.WMF RAQUETBL.WMF SIL087I.WMF
SMR030C.WMF SPAB009K.WMF SPAB012K.WMF SPCA087J.WMF SPCA088J.WMF SPGC016J.WMF SPGC025J.WMF SPGC042D.WMF SPGC043D.WMF SPGC045J.WMF
SPGC113D.WMF SPJB011J.WMF SPJB015J.WMF SPJB021J.WMF SPJB025J.WMF SPJB042J.WMF SPKC004J.WMF SPORT042.WMF SPORT052.WMF SPORT054.WMF
SPORT074.WMF SPORT076.WMF SPORT098.WMF SPORT112.WMF SPORT2.WMF SPORT333.WMF SPORT352.WMF SPORTS6.WMF SPRW031J.WMF SPRW039J.WMF
SPRW040J.WMF SPRW041J.WMF SPRW042J.WMF SPRW044J.WMF SPRW045J.WMF SPSI068J.WMF SPSI253D.WMF SPSI264D.WMF SPSI266D.WMF SPSI267D.WMF
SPSI278D.WMF SPSI283D.WMF SPSI293D.WMF SPSI296D.WMF SPSI307D.WMF SPSI314D.WMF SPSI337D.WMF SPSI345D.WMF SPSI347D.WMF SPSI348D.WMF
SPSI350D.WMF SPSI368D.WMF SPSI376D.WMF SPSI381D.WMF SPSI392D.WMF SPSI393D.WMF SPSI395D.WMF SPSI396D.WMF SPSI410D.WMF SPSI412D.WMF
SPSI432D.WMF SPSI434D.WMF SPSI436D.WMF SPSI437D.WMF SPSI449D.WMF SPSI450D.WMF SPSI462D.WMF SPSI473D.WMF SPSI482D.WMF SPSI524D.WMF
SPSI541D.WMF SPSI553D.WMF SPSI560D.WMF SPSI578D.WMF SPSI657D.WMF SPSI658D.WMF SQSHPLR.WMF SQSHPLRC.WMF SQUASH.WMF SYMB25C.WMF

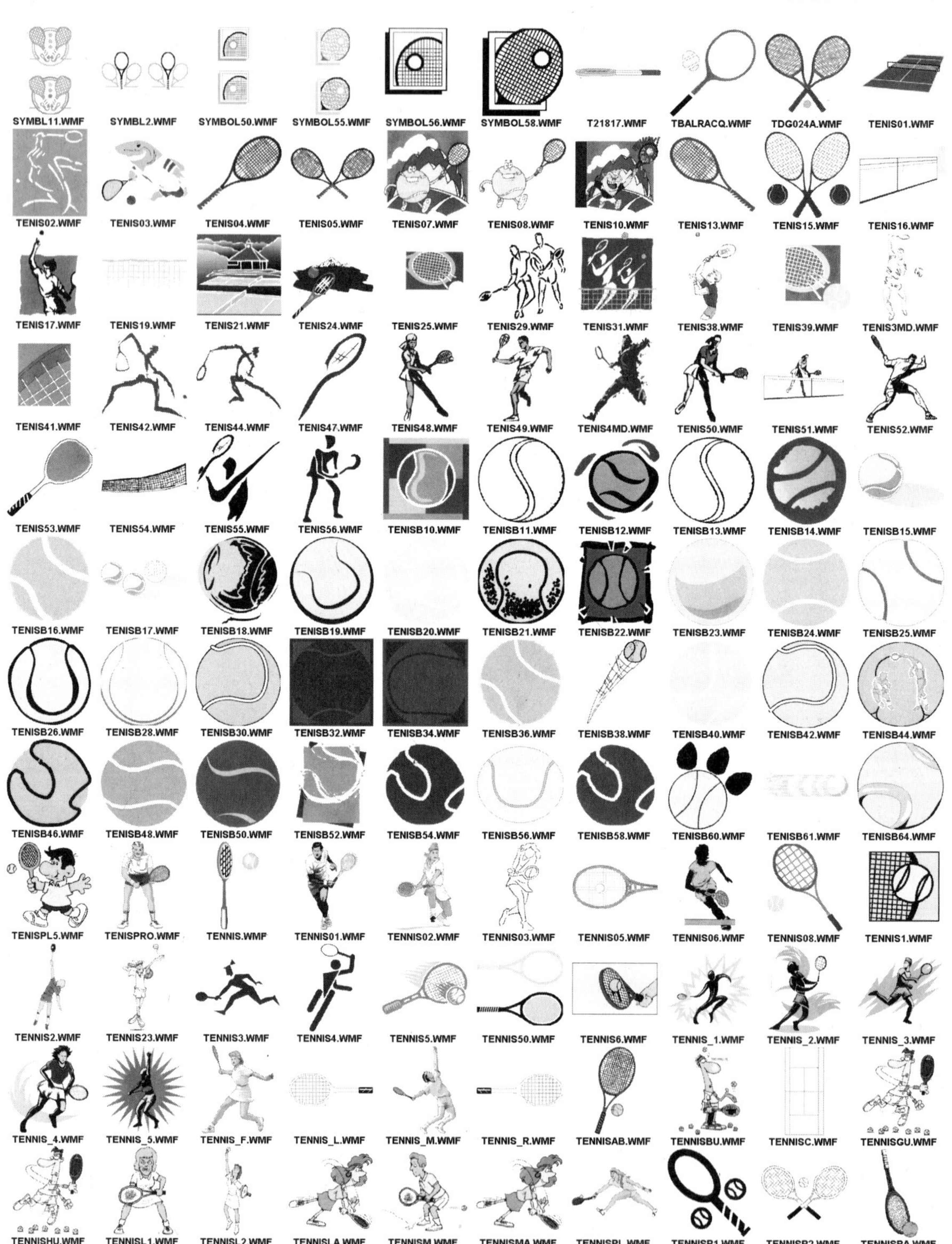
SYMBL11.WMF
SYMBL2.WMF
SYMBOL50.WMF
SYMBOL55.WMF
SYMBOL56.WMF
SYMBOL58.WMF
T21817.WMF
TBALRACQ.WMF
TDG024A.WMF
TENIS01.WMF
TENIS02.WMF
TENIS03.WMF
TENIS04.WMF
TENIS05.WMF
TENIS07.WMF
TENIS08.WMF
TENIS10.WMF
TENIS13.WMF
TENIS15.WMF
TENIS16.WMF
TENIS17.WMF
TENIS19.WMF
TENIS21.WMF
TENIS24.WMF
TENIS25.WMF
TENIS29.WMF
TENIS31.WMF
TENIS38.WMF
TENIS39.WMF
TENIS3MD.WMF
TENIS41.WMF
TENIS42.WMF
TENIS44.WMF
TENIS47.WMF
TENIS48.WMF
TENIS49.WMF
TENIS4MD.WMF
TENIS50.WMF
TENIS51.WMF
TENIS52.WMF
TENIS53.WMF
TENIS54.WMF
TENIS55.WMF
TENIS56.WMF
TENISB10.WMF
TENISB11.WMF
TENISB12.WMF
TENISB13.WMF
TENISB14.WMF
TENISB15.WMF
TENISB16.WMF
TENISB17.WMF
TENISB18.WMF
TENISB19.WMF
TENISB20.WMF
TENISB21.WMF
TENISB22.WMF
TENISB23.WMF
TENISB24.WMF
TENISB25.WMF
TENISB26.WMF
TENISB28.WMF
TENISB30.WMF
TENISB32.WMF
TENISB34.WMF
TENISB36.WMF
TENISB38.WMF
TENISB40.WMF
TENISB42.WMF
TENISB44.WMF
TENISB46.WMF
TENISB48.WMF
TENISB50.WMF
TENISB52.WMF
TENISB54.WMF
TENISB56.WMF
TENISB58.WMF
TENISB60.WMF
TENISB61.WMF
TENISB64.WMF
TENISPL5.WMF
TENISPRO.WMF
TENNIS.WMF
TENNIS01.WMF
TENNIS02.WMF
TENNIS03.WMF
TENNIS05.WMF
TENNIS06.WMF
TENNIS08.WMF
TENNIS1.WMF
TENNIS2.WMF
TENNIS23.WMF
TENNIS3.WMF
TENNIS4.WMF
TENNIS5.WMF
TENNIS50.WMF
TENNIS6.WMF
TENNIS_1.WMF
TENNIS_2.WMF
TENNIS_3.WMF
TENNIS_4.WMF
TENNIS_5.WMF
TENNIS_F.WMF
TENNIS_L.WMF
TENNIS_M.WMF
TENNIS_R.WMF
TENNISAB.WMF
TENNISBU.WMF
TENNISC.WMF
TENNISGU.WMF
TENNISHU.WMF
TENNISL1.WMF
TENNISL2.WMF
TENNISLA.WMF
TENNISM.WMF
TENNISMA.WMF
TENNISPL.WMF
TENNISR1.WMF
TENNISR2.WMF
TENNISRA.WMF

TENSPLYR.WMF

TR21.WMF

TR22.WMF

TR23.WMF

TR24.WMF

TT01.WMF

TT17.WMF

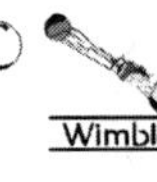

WIMBLDON.WMF

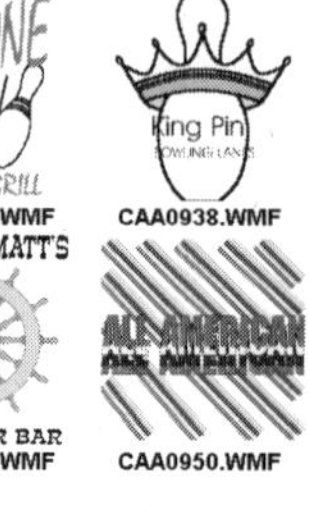

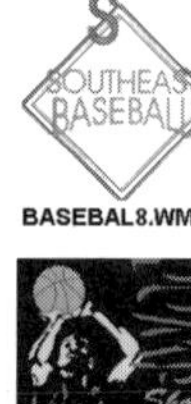
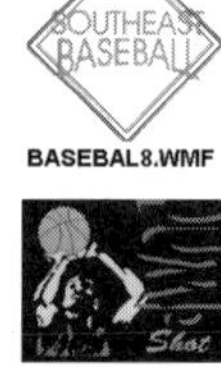

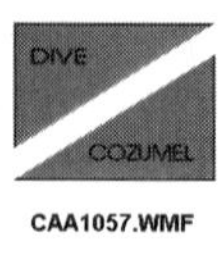

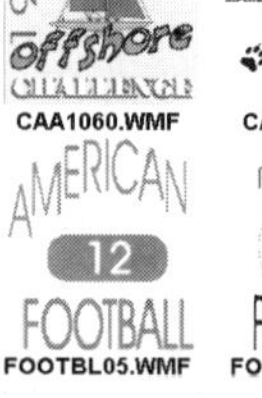

BASEBAL1.WMF	BASEBAL2.WMF	BASEBAL3.WMF	BASEBAL4.WMF	BASEBAL5.WMF	BASEBAL6.WMF	BASEBAL7.WMF	BASEBAL8.WMF	BASEBAL9.WMF	BASEBL10.WMF
BASEBL11.WMF	BASEBL12.WMF	BASKTBAL.WMF	BSKTBAL1.WMF	BSKTBAL2.WMF	BSKTBAL3.WMF	BSKTBAL4.WMF	BSKTBAL5.WMF	BSKTBAL6.WMF	CAA0931.WMF
CAA0933.WMF	CAA0935.WMF	CAA0936.WMF	CAA0937.WMF	CAA0938.WMF	CAA0939.WMF	CAA0940.WMF	CAA0942.WMF	CAA0944.WMF	CAA0945.WMF
CAA0946.WMF	CAA0947.WMF	CAA0948.WMF	CAA0949.WMF	CAA0950.WMF	CAA0951.WMF	CAA0952.WMF	CAA0953.WMF	CAA0954.WMF	CAA0955.WMF
CAA0956.WMF	CAA0957.WMF	CAA0958.WMF	CAA0959.WMF	CAA0960.WMF	CAA0961.WMF	CAA0962.WMF	CAA0963.WMF	CAA0964.WMF	CAA0965.WMF
CAA0966.WMF	CAA0967.WMF	CAA0968.WMF	CAA0972.WMF	CAA0973.WMF	CAA0974.WMF	CAA0975.WMF	CAA0976.WMF	CAA0979.WMF	CAA0981.WMF
CAA0984.WMF	CAA0987.WMF	CAA0989.WMF	CAA0993.WMF	CAA0994.WMF	CAA0995.WMF	CAA1000.WMF	CAA1002.WMF	CAA1003.WMF	CAA1005.WMF
CAA1006.WMF	CAA1007.WMF	CAA1008.WMF	CAA1009.WMF	CAA1010.WMF	CAA1011.WMF	CAA1012.WMF	CAA1014.WMF	CAA1016.WMF	CAA1018.WMF
CAA1019.WMF	CAA1020.WMF	CAA1021.WMF	CAA1024.WMF	CAA1027.WMF	CAA1028.WMF	CAA1029.WMF	CAA1030.WMF	CAA1031.WMF	CAA1034.WMF
CAA1035.WMF	CAA1036.WMF	CAA1038.WMF	CAA1039.WMF	CAA1040.WMF	CAA1041.WMF	CAA1043.WMF	CAA1044.WMF	CAA1045.WMF	CAA1047.WMF
CAA1049.WMF	CAA1052.WMF	CAA1053.WMF	CAA1055.WMF	CAA1056.WMF	CAA1057.WMF	CAA1058.WMF	CAA1059.WMF	CAA1060.WMF	CAA1061.WMF
CAA1062.WMF	CAA1063.WMF	CAA1064.WMF	CAA1065.WMF	FOOTBL01.WMF	FOOTBL02.WMF	FOOTBL03.WMF	FOOTBL04.WMF	FOOTBL05.WMF	FOOTBL06.WMF

FOOTBL07.WMF

FOOTBL08.WMF

FOOTBL09.WMF

VOLLEY01.WMF

VOLLEY02.WMF

VOLLEY03.WMF

VOLLEY04.WMF

VOLLEY05.WMF

0003.WMF
0006.WMF
0030.WMF
0069.WMF
0092.WMF
0111.WMF
0135.WMF
0152.WMF
0163.WMF
0174.WMF
0175.WMF
0184.WMF
0191.WMF
0202.WMF
0211.WMF
0220.WMF
0227.WMF
0234.WMF
0245.WMF
0246.WMF
0259.WMF
0260.WMF
0267.WMF
0274.WMF
0275.WMF
0282.WMF
0287.WMF
0288.WMF
0293.WMF
0300.WMF
0309.WMF
0310.WMF
0317.WMF
0324.WMF
0325.WMF
0338.WMF
0357.WMF
0358.WMF
0359.WMF
0374.WMF
0385.WMF
0396.WMF
0399.WMF
0418.WMF
0451.WMF
0452.WMF
0467.WMF
0472.WMF
0482.WMF
0491.WMF
0498.WMF
0513.WMF
0518.WMF
0519.WMF
0524.WMF
0529.WMF
0536.WMF
0537.WMF
0542.WMF
0543.WMF
0544.WMF
0568.WMF
0630.WMF
0969VOLC.WMF
0970VOLC.WMF
0971VOLC.WMF
0972WADC.WMF
0974WATC.WMF
0975WATC.WMF
0977WEIC.WMF
0978WEIC.WMF
0979WEIC.WMF
0981WREC.WMF
0982WREC.WMF
1341SKIC.WMF
3509.WMF
3510.WMF
AEROB050.WMF
AEROB051.WMF
AEROBIC1.WMF
AEROBIC2.WMF
AEROBIC3.WMF
AEROBIC4.WMF
BALPLAYR.WMF
BASBAL2.WMF
BASEBAL1.WMF
BASEBAL2.WMF
BASEBAL3.WMF
BASEBAL4.WMF
BASEBAL5.WMF
BASEBAL6.WMF
BASEDIAM.WMF
BASEGLOV.WMF
BASKET1.WMF
BASKET2.WMF
BASKET3.WMF
BASKETB1.WMF
BASKETB2.WMF
BBALPLYR.WMF
BKBAL02.WMF
BKBAL06.WMF
BKBAL56.WMF
BONUS_22.WMF
BONUS_23.WMF
BOWLING1.WMF
BOWLING2.WMF
BOWLING6.WMF
BOXING.WMF
BSBAL62.WMF
CAA0444.WMF
CAA0449.WMF
CAA0451.WMF
CAA0452.WMF
CAA0454.WMF
CAA0464.WMF
CAA0493.WMF
CAA0495.WMF
CAA0535.WMF
CAA0558.WMF
CAA0608.WMF

CAA0609.WMF CAA0610.WMF CAA0619.WMF CAA0620.WMF CAA0629.WMF CAA0631.WMF CAA0644.WMF CAA0649.WMF CAA0652.WMF CAA0658.WMF

CAA0688.WMF CAA0694.WMF CAA0697.WMF CAA0713.WMF CAA0714.WMF CAA0725.WMF CAA0727.WMF CAA0730.WMF CAA0731.WMF CAA0778.WMF

CAA0791.WMF CAA0792.WMF CAA0808.WMF CAA0820.WMF CAA0834.WMF CAA0844.WMF CANOE1.WMF CANOE2.WMF CHRLD01.WMF CYCLIST1.WMF

CYCLIST2.WMF DANCE1.WMF DANCE2.WMF DANCE3.WMF DARTS.WMF DING1.WMF DING2.WMF DING3.WMF DINGBAT1.WMF DINGBAT2.WMF

DINGBAT3.WMF DINGBT1.WMF DINGBT2.WMF DINGBT3.WMF DISCUS.WMF EDCN119.WMF EQUESTR.WMF EQUESTRI.WMF FENCING.WMF FENCING5.WMF

FISHING1.WMF FISHING2.WMF FOOTBAL1.WMF FOOTBAL2.WMF FOOTBAL3.WMF FOOTY.WMF GASI018D.WMF GASI019D.WMF GASI020D.WMF GOLFER2.WMF

GOLFER3.WMF GOLFER4.WMF GOLFER5.WMF GYMNAST1.WMF GYMNAST2.WMF GYMNAST3.WMF GYMNAST4.WMF GYMNAST5.WMF GYMNAST6.WMF GYMNSTCS.WMF

HANDPLNT.WMF HANGGLI2.WMF HIGHDIV1.WMF HIGHDIV2.WMF HIGHJUMP.WMF HIJUMP.WMF HIKER.WMF HOCKEY1.WMF HOCKEY2.WMF HORSE1.WMF

HORSERA1.WMF HORSERA2.WMF HORSERA3.WMF HORSERAC.WMF HOTAIRBA.WMF HUNT1.WMF HUNT2.WMF HUNTING1.WMF HUNTING2.WMF HUNTING3.WMF

ICESKAT1.WMF ICESKAT2.WMF ICESKAT3.WMF JAVELIN.WMF KARAT03.WMF KARATE.WMF KARATE1.WMF KARATE2.WMF KARATE3.WMF KAYAK1.WMF

LONGJUMP.WMF MBIKE.WMF MISCSP59.WMF MISCSP60.WMF MISCSP64.WMF MOTOCROS.WMF MOTORCY.WMF MTBIKE.WMF PD091GCU.WMF PD091MCU.WMF

PD091VCU.WMF PD091XCU.WMF PD092BCU.WMF PD092SCU.WMF PD092VCU.WMF PD093CCU.WMF PD093GCU.WMF PD093HCU.WMF PD093NCU.WMF PD093PCU.WMF

PD112MCU.WMF
PD112UCU.WMF
PD113ACU.WMF
PD113CCU.WMF
PD113DCU.WMF
PD113ECU.WMF
PD113FCU.WMF
PD113HCU.WMF
PD113JCU.WMF
PD113KCU.WMF
PD113MCU.WMF
PD113NCU.WMF
PD113PCU.WMF
PD113QCU.WMF
POLEVAU.WMF
POLO.WMF
POOL2.WMF
PUSHBIKE.WMF
RACEFG.WMF
RACKETB.WMF
RAQBL09.WMF
RECEHRS2.WMF
REVERSE.WMF
ROCKCLI1.WMF
ROCKCLI2.WMF
RODEO.WMF
RODEO1.WMF
ROWING1.WMF
ROWING2.WMF
ROWING3.WMF
RUNNER1.WMF
RUNNER2.WMF
RUNNER3.WMF
RUNNER5.WMF
SAILING1.WMF
SAILING2.WMF
SCUBA1.WMF
SCUBA2.WMF
SKATEBOA.WMF
SKIER05.WMF
SKIER1.WMF
SKIER2.WMF
SKIER3.WMF
SKIER4.WMF
SKIER5.WMF
SKIER6.WMF
SKIER7.WMF
SKYDIVER.WMF
SNORKLR.WMF
SNOWBOAR.WMF
SNOWMOB1.WMF
SNOWMOB2.WMF
SOCCER1.WMF
SOCCER2.WMF
SOCCER3.WMF
SPAB007K.WMF
SPAB008K.WMF
SPAB009J.WMF
SPAB011J.WMF
SPAB012D.WMF
SPAB013D.WMF
SPAB014D.WMF
SPAB015D.WMF
SPAB015J.WMF
SPAB016J.WMF
SPAB017D.WMF
SPAB017J.WMF
SPAB024D.WMF
SPBF001J.WMF
SPCA001K.WMF
SPCA104J.WMF
SPEEDSKA.WMF
SPGC004D.WMF
SPGC005J.WMF
SPGC006D.WMF
SPGC006J.WMF
SPGC007J.WMF
SPGC008J.WMF
SPGC009J.WMF
SPGC037D.WMF
SPJB006J.WMF
SPJB007J.WMF
SPJB026J.WMF
SPJB030J.WMF
SPJB031J.WMF
SPJB032J.WMF
SPJB033J.WMF
SPJB034J.WMF
SPORT057.WMF
SPORT142.WMF
SPRTSIL1.WMF
SPRTSIL2.WMF
SPRTSIL3.WMF
SPRTSIL4.WMF
SPRTSIL5.WMF
SPSI004J.WMF
SPSI005D.WMF
SPSI005J.WMF
SPSI009M.WMF
SPSI011M.WMF
SPSI013J.WMF
SPSI014J.WMF
SPSI019D.WMF
SPSI061J.WMF
SPSI062D.WMF
SPSI062J.WMF
SPSI063J.WMF
SPSI067D.WMF
SPSI067J.WMF
SPSI070J.WMF
SPSI071.WMF
SPSI072J.WMF
SPSI073D.WMF
SPSI073J.WMF
SPSI075J.WMF
SPSI076J.WMF
SPSI077J.WMF
SPSI078J.WMF
SPSI079J.WMF
SPSI082J.WMF

SPSI083D.WMF
SPSI084J.WMF
SPSI085J.WMF
SPSI089D.WMF
SPSI130D.WMF
SPSI131D.WMF
SPSI234D.WMF
SPSI236D.WMF
SPSI240D.WMF
SPSI246D.WMF
SPSI247D.WMF
SPSI260D.WMF
SPSI261D.WMF
SPSI419D.WMF
SPSI420D.WMF
SPSI421D.WMF
SPSI433D.WMF
SPSI465D.WMF
SPSI467D.WMF
SPSI468D.WMF
SPSI472D.WMF
SPSI478D.WMF
SPSI481D.WMF
SPSI513D.WMF
SPSI542D.WMF
SPSI616D.WMF
SPSI617D.WMF
SPSI618D.WMF
SPSI628D.WMF
SPSS003J.WMF
SPSS005D.WMF
SPSS006D.WMF
SPSS007D.WMF
SPSS009J.WMF
SPSS011D.WMF
SPSS100D.WMF
SURFER1.WMF
SURFER2.WMF
TENNIS1.WMF
TENNIS2.WMF
VOLLEYB.WMF
VOLLEYB1.WMF
VOLLEYB2.WMF
VYBAL64.WMF
VYBAL65.WMF
WATERSKI.WMF
WEIGHTL.WMF
WINDSURF.WMF

0390.WMF
0391.WMF
0392.WMF
0393.WMF
0394.WMF
0395.WMF
0430.WMF
0432.WMF
0435.WMF
0455.WMF
0456.WMF
0457.WMF
0458.WMF
0459.WMF
0460.WMF
0461.WMF
0462.WMF
0463.WMF
0464.WMF
0465.WMF
0466.WMF
0468.WMF
0469.WMF
0470.WMF
0471.WMF
0473.WMF
0474.WMF
0475.WMF
0476.WMF
0485.WMF
0486.WMF
0487.WMF
0488.WMF
0489.WMF
0490.WMF
0499.WMF
0500.WMF
0501.WMF
0502.WMF
0503.WMF
0504.WMF
1169.WMF
1170.WMF
1171.WMF
1172.WMF
1173.WMF
1174.WMF
1303.WMF
1304.WMF
3504.WMF
3505.WMF
ASI036H.WMF
ASI037E.WMF
ASI037J.WMF
CAA0735.WMF
CAA0736.WMF
CAA0738.WMF
CAA0739.WMF
CAA0740.WMF
CAA0741.WMF
CAA0742.WMF
CAA0743.WMF
CAA0744.WMF
CAA0745.WMF
CAA0746.WMF
CAA0747.WMF
CAA0748.WMF
DEC069F.WMF
DOWNHILL.WMF
DOWNSKI.WMF
DOWNSKI1.WMF
DOWNSKI2.WMF
DWNHILL5.WMF
FEML_SKI.WMF
FSW035B.WMF
HPI010G.WMF
HSP012A.WMF
HSP012C.WMF
ICP003B.WMF
IOD026B.WMF
ISP029A.WMF
ISP029B.WMF
IWS011A.WMF
IWS023A.WMF
IWS023B.WMF
IWS030A.WMF
IWS032C.WMF
LONGJUMP.WMF
MALE_SKI.WMF
MISCSP72.WMF
OFS054I.WMF
OSP019D.WMF
PD110TCU.WMF
PD110UCU.WMF
PD111RCU.WMF
PD112ICU.WMF
PD114JCU.WMF
PD114KCU.WMF
PD114MCU.WMF
PD114OCU.WMF
PD114RCU.WMF
PD124QCU.WMF
PD124RCU.WMF
PD124SCU.WMF
PD124TCU.WMF
PD124UCU.WMF
PD128FCU.WMF
PD128GCU.WMF
PD130HCU.WMF
PGX006B.WMF
ROWING.WMF
SKI050.WMF
SKI051.WMF
SKI052.WMF
SKI053.WMF
SKIBOOTS.WMF
SKIER.WMF
SKIER005.WMF
SKIER08.WMF
SKIER1.WMF

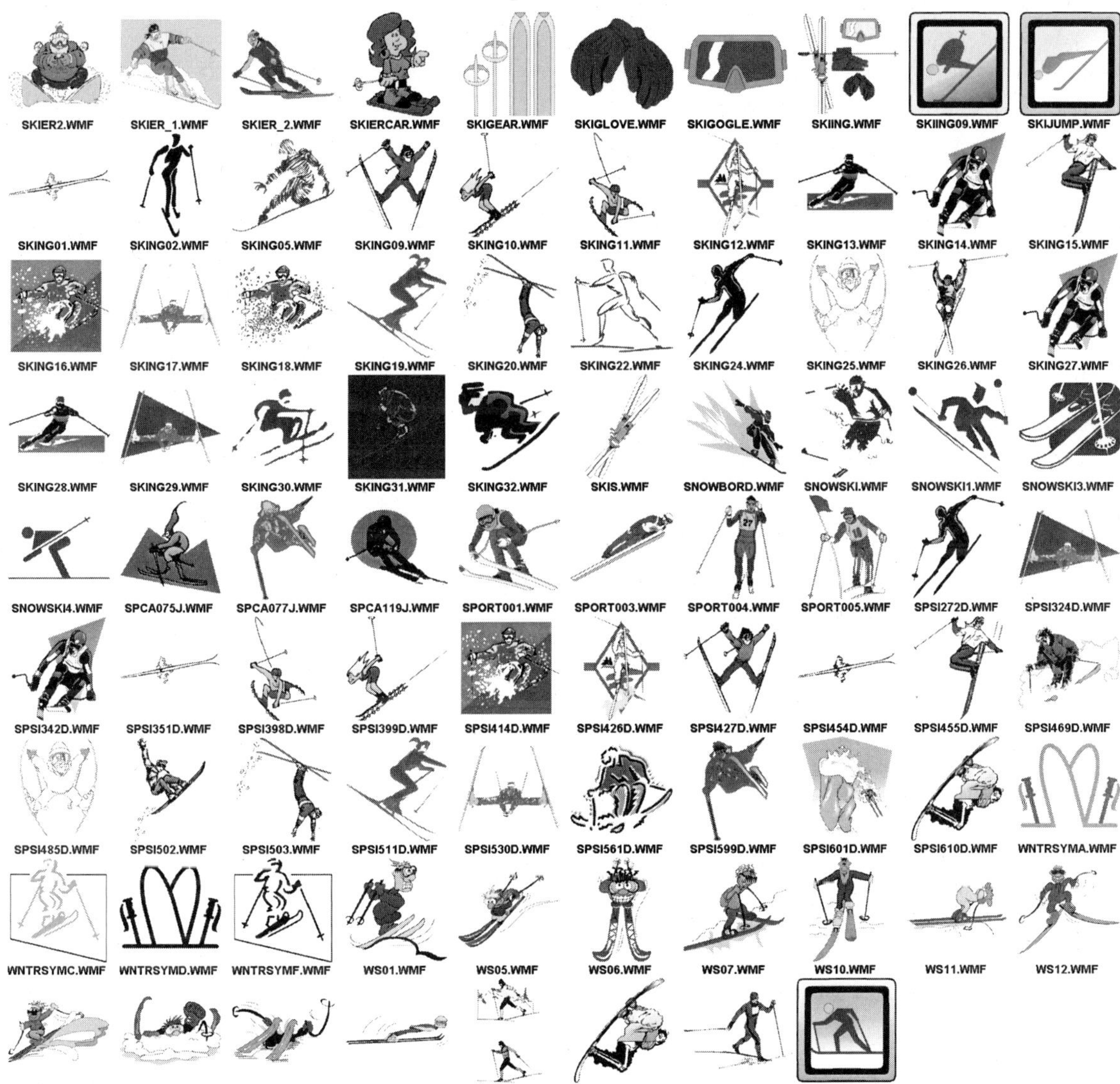
SKIER2.WMF
SKIER_1.WMF
SKIER_2.WMF
SKIERCAR.WMF
SKIGEAR.WMF
SKIGLOVE.WMF
SKIGOGLE.WMF
SKIING.WMF
SKIING09.WMF
SKIJUMP.WMF
SKING01.WMF
SKING02.WMF
SKING05.WMF
SKING09.WMF
SKING10.WMF
SKING11.WMF
SKING12.WMF
SKING13.WMF
SKING14.WMF
SKING15.WMF
SKING16.WMF
SKING17.WMF
SKING18.WMF
SKING19.WMF
SKING20.WMF
SKING22.WMF
SKING24.WMF
SKING25.WMF
SKING26.WMF
SKING27.WMF
SKING28.WMF
SKING29.WMF
SKING30.WMF
SKING31.WMF
SKING32.WMF
SKIS.WMF
SNOWBORD.WMF
SNOWSKI.WMF
SNOWSKI1.WMF
SNOWSKI3.WMF
SNOWSKI4.WMF
SPCA075J.WMF
SPCA077J.WMF
SPCA119J.WMF
SPORT001.WMF
SPORT003.WMF
SPORT004.WMF
SPORT005.WMF
SPSI272D.WMF
SPSI324D.WMF
SPSI342D.WMF
SPSI351D.WMF
SPSI398D.WMF
SPSI399D.WMF
SPSI414D.WMF
SPSI426D.WMF
SPSI427D.WMF
SPSI454D.WMF
SPSI455D.WMF
SPSI469D.WMF
SPSI485D.WMF
SPSI502.WMF
SPSI503.WMF
SPSI511D.WMF
SPSI530D.WMF
SPSI561D.WMF
SPSI599D.WMF
SPSI601D.WMF
SPSI610D.WMF
WNTRSYMA.WMF
WNTRSYMC.WMF
WNTRSYMD.WMF
WNTRSYMF.WMF
WS01.WMF
WS05.WMF
WS06.WMF
WS07.WMF
WS10.WMF
WS11.WMF
WS12.WMF
WS13.WMF
WS14.WMF
WS15.WMF
WS16.WMF
X_COUNT1.WMF
XRAYBRD2.WMF
XXSKIER.WMF
XXSKIING.WMF

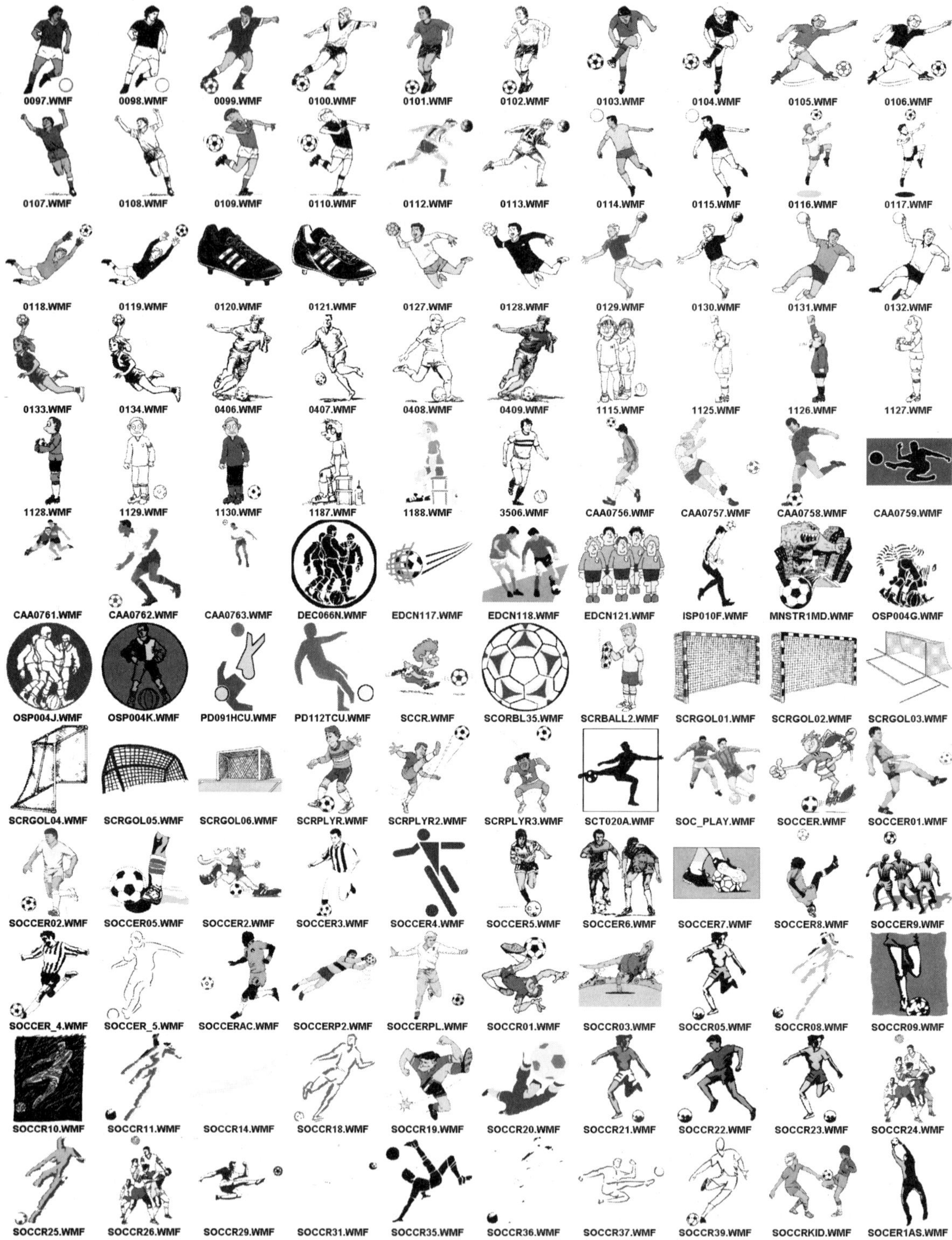
0097.WMF
0098.WMF
0099.WMF
0100.WMF
0101.WMF
0102.WMF
0103.WMF
0104.WMF
0105.WMF
0106.WMF
0107.WMF
0108.WMF
0109.WMF
0110.WMF
0112.WMF
0113.WMF
0114.WMF
0115.WMF
0116.WMF
0117.WMF
0118.WMF
0119.WMF
0120.WMF
0121.WMF
0127.WMF
0128.WMF
0129.WMF
0130.WMF
0131.WMF
0132.WMF
0133.WMF
0134.WMF
0406.WMF
0407.WMF
0408.WMF
0409.WMF
1115.WMF
1125.WMF
1126.WMF
1127.WMF
1128.WMF
1129.WMF
1130.WMF
1187.WMF
1188.WMF
3506.WMF
CAA0756.WMF
CAA0757.WMF
CAA0758.WMF
CAA0759.WMF
CAA0761.WMF
CAA0762.WMF
CAA0763.WMF
DEC066N.WMF
EDCN117.WMF
EDCN118.WMF
EDCN121.WMF
ISP010F.WMF
MNSTR1MD.WMF
OSP004G.WMF
OSP004J.WMF
OSP004K.WMF
PD091HCU.WMF
PD112TCU.WMF
SCCR.WMF
SCORBL35.WMF
SCRBALL2.WMF
SCRGOL01.WMF
SCRGOL02.WMF
SCRGOL03.WMF
SCRGOL04.WMF
SCRGOL05.WMF
SCRGOL06.WMF
SCRPLYR.WMF
SCRPLYR2.WMF
SCRPLYR3.WMF
SCT020A.WMF
SOC_PLAY.WMF
SOCCER.WMF
SOCCER01.WMF
SOCCER02.WMF
SOCCER05.WMF
SOCCER2.WMF
SOCCER3.WMF
SOCCER4.WMF
SOCCER5.WMF
SOCCER6.WMF
SOCCER7.WMF
SOCCER8.WMF
SOCCER9.WMF
SOCCER_4.WMF
SOCCER_5.WMF
SOCCERAC.WMF
SOCCERP2.WMF
SOCCERPL.WMF
SOCCR01.WMF
SOCCR03.WMF
SOCCR05.WMF
SOCCR08.WMF
SOCCR09.WMF
SOCCR10.WMF
SOCCR11.WMF
SOCCR14.WMF
SOCCR18.WMF
SOCCR19.WMF
SOCCR20.WMF
SOCCR21.WMF
SOCCR22.WMF
SOCCR23.WMF
SOCCR24.WMF
SOCCR25.WMF
SOCCR26.WMF
SOCCR29.WMF
SOCCR31.WMF
SOCCR35.WMF
SOCCR36.WMF
SOCCR37.WMF
SOCCR39.WMF
SOCCRKID.WMF
SOCER1AS.WMF

SOCER2.WMF SOCERPL.WMF SOCRBL10.WMF SOCRBL11.WMF SOCRBL13.WMF SOCRBL14.WMF SOCRBL15.WMF SOCRBL16.WMF SOCRBL17.WMF SOCRBL18.WMF

SOCRBL19.WMF SOCRBL20.WMF SOCRBL21.WMF SOCRBL22.WMF SOCRBL23.WMF SOCRBL24.WMF SOCRBL25.WMF SOCRBL27.WMF SOCRBL28.WMF SOCRBL29.WMF

SOCRBL30.WMF SOCRBL31.WMF SOCRBL32.WMF SOCRBL33.WMF SOCRBL34.WMF SOCRBL36.WMF SOCRBL37.WMF SOCRBL38.WMF SOCRBL39.WMF SOCRBL40.WMF

SOCRBL41.WMF SOCRBL42.WMF SOCRBL43.WMF SOCRBL44.WMF SOCRBL45.WMF SOCRBL46.WMF SOCRBL47.WMF SOCRBL48.WMF SOCRBL49.WMF SOCRBL50.WMF

SOCRBL51.WMF SOCRBL52.WMF SOCRBL53.WMF SOCRBL54.WMF SOCRBL55.WMF SOCRBL56.WMF SOCRBL57.WMF SOCRBL58.WMF SOCRBL59.WMF SOCRBL60.WMF

SOCRBL61.WMF SOCRBL62.WMF SOCRBL63.WMF SOCRBL64.WMF SOCRBL65.WMF SOCRBL66.WMF SOCRBL67.WMF SOCRBL68.WMF SOCRSHOE.WMF SPAB005J.WMF

SPAB006K.WMF SPAB007J.WMF SPAB020J.WMF SPAB026D.WMF SPAB042D.WMF SPCA027D.WMF SPCA069J.WMF SPCA072J.WMF SPGC043J.WMF SPGC092D.WMF

SPGC118D.WMF SPGC119D.WMF SPGC120D.WMF SPGC121D.WMF SPGC122D.WMF SPORT033.WMF SPORT129.WMF SPORT332.WMF SPORT346.WMF SPORT347.WMF

SPORT348.WMF SPORT349.WMF SPORT369.WMF SPRW032J.WMF SPRW033J.WMF SPRW034J.WMF SPRW035J.WMF SPRW036J.WMF SPRW037J.WMF SPRW051J.WMF

SPRW052J.WMF SPSI243D.WMF SPSI274D.WMF SPSI338D.WMF SPSI362D.WMF SPSI383D.WMF SPSI387D.WMF SPSI391D.WMF SPSI424D.WMF SPSI456D.WMF

SPSI474D.WMF SPSI483D.WMF SPSI529D.WMF SPSI539D.WMF SPSI545D.WMF SPSI566D.WMF SPSS001J.WMF SPSS002J.WMF SPSS008J.WMF TEENBOYS.WMF

TGR.WMF WCUP.WMF

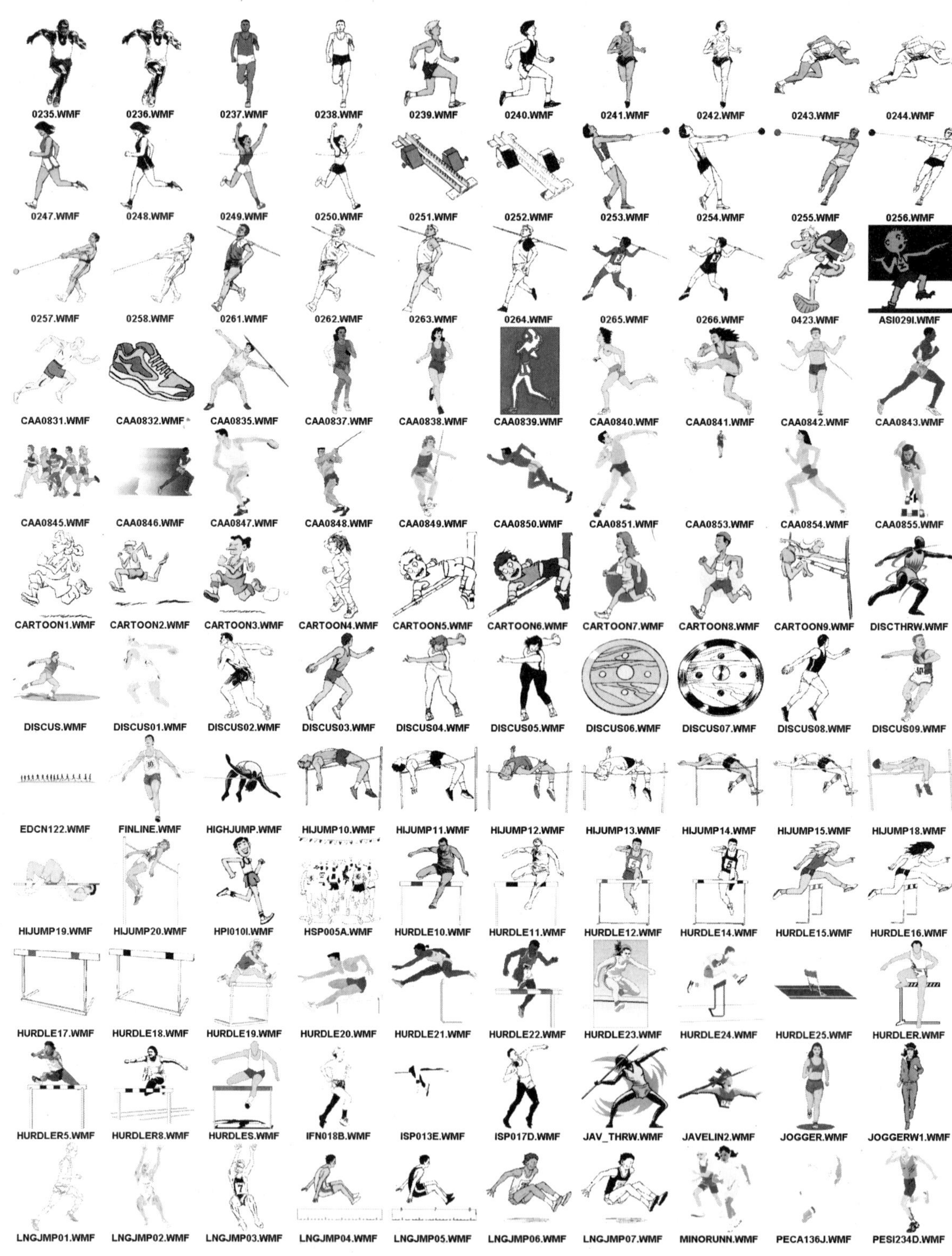
0235.WMF
0236.WMF
0237.WMF
0238.WMF
0239.WMF
0240.WMF
0241.WMF
0242.WMF
0243.WMF
0244.WMF
0247.WMF
0248.WMF
0249.WMF
0250.WMF
0251.WMF
0252.WMF
0253.WMF
0254.WMF
0255.WMF
0256.WMF
0257.WMF
0258.WMF
0261.WMF
0262.WMF
0263.WMF
0264.WMF
0265.WMF
0266.WMF
0423.WMF
ASI029I.WMF
CAA0831.WMF
CAA0832.WMF
CAA0835.WMF
CAA0837.WMF
CAA0838.WMF
CAA0839.WMF
CAA0840.WMF
CAA0841.WMF
CAA0842.WMF
CAA0843.WMF
CAA0845.WMF
CAA0846.WMF
CAA0847.WMF
CAA0848.WMF
CAA0849.WMF
CAA0850.WMF
CAA0851.WMF
CAA0853.WMF
CAA0854.WMF
CAA0855.WMF
CARTOON1.WMF
CARTOON2.WMF
CARTOON3.WMF
CARTOON4.WMF
CARTOON5.WMF
CARTOON6.WMF
CARTOON7.WMF
CARTOON8.WMF
CARTOON9.WMF
DISCTHRW.WMF
DISCUS.WMF
DISCUS01.WMF
DISCUS02.WMF
DISCUS03.WMF
DISCUS04.WMF
DISCUS05.WMF
DISCUS06.WMF
DISCUS07.WMF
DISCUS08.WMF
DISCUS09.WMF
EDCN122.WMF
FINLINE.WMF
HIGHJUMP.WMF
HIJUMP10.WMF
HIJUMP11.WMF
HIJUMP12.WMF
HIJUMP13.WMF
HIJUMP14.WMF
HIJUMP15.WMF
HIJUMP18.WMF
HIJUMP19.WMF
HIJUMP20.WMF
HPI010I.WMF
HSP005A.WMF
HURDLE10.WMF
HURDLE11.WMF
HURDLE12.WMF
HURDLE14.WMF
HURDLE15.WMF
HURDLE16.WMF
HURDLE17.WMF
HURDLE18.WMF
HURDLE19.WMF
HURDLE20.WMF
HURDLE21.WMF
HURDLE22.WMF
HURDLE23.WMF
HURDLE24.WMF
HURDLE25.WMF
HURDLER.WMF
HURDLER5.WMF
HURDLER8.WMF
HURDLES.WMF
IFN018B.WMF
ISP013E.WMF
ISP017D.WMF
JAV_THRW.WMF
JAVELIN2.WMF
JOGGER.WMF
JOGGERW1.WMF
LNGJMP01.WMF
LNGJMP02.WMF
LNGJMP03.WMF
LNGJMP04.WMF
LNGJMP05.WMF
LNGJMP06.WMF
LNGJMP07.WMF
MINORUNN.WMF
PECA136J.WMF
PESI234D.WMF

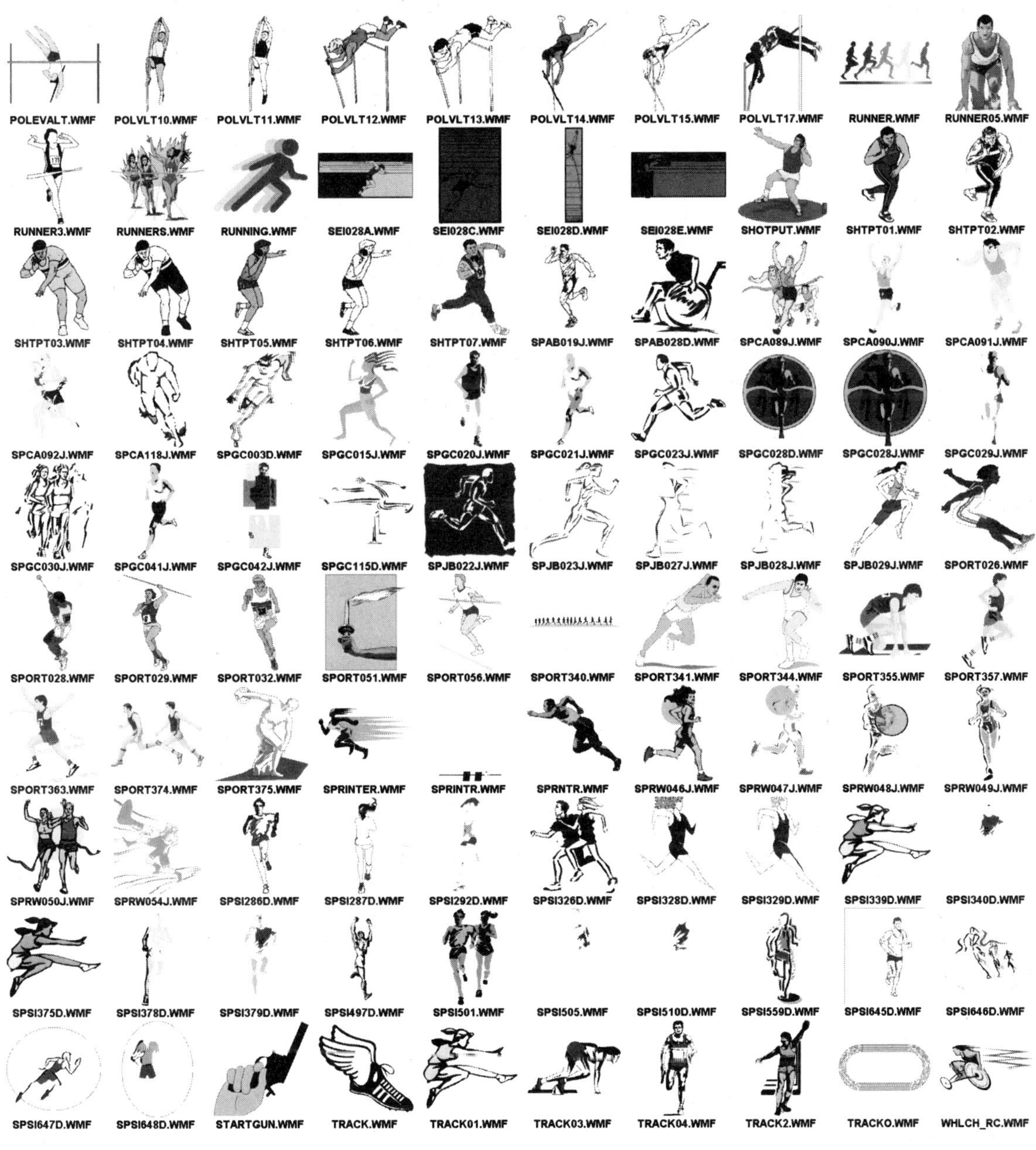
POLEVALT.WMF
POLVLT10.WMF
POLVLT11.WMF
POLVLT12.WMF
POLVLT13.WMF
POLVLT14.WMF
POLVLT15.WMF
POLVLT17.WMF
RUNNER.WMF
RUNNER05.WMF
RUNNER3.WMF
RUNNERS.WMF
RUNNING.WMF
SEI028A.WMF
SEI028C.WMF
SEI028D.WMF
SEI028E.WMF
SHOTPUT.WMF
SHTPT01.WMF
SHTPT02.WMF
SHTPT03.WMF
SHTPT04.WMF
SHTPT05.WMF
SHTPT06.WMF
SHTPT07.WMF
SPAB019J.WMF
SPAB028D.WMF
SPCA089J.WMF
SPCA090J.WMF
SPCA091J.WMF
SPCA092J.WMF
SPCA118J.WMF
SPGC003D.WMF
SPGC015J.WMF
SPGC020J.WMF
SPGC021J.WMF
SPGC023J.WMF
SPGC028D.WMF
SPGC028J.WMF
SPGC029J.WMF
SPGC030J.WMF
SPGC041J.WMF
SPGC042J.WMF
SPGC115D.WMF
SPJB022J.WMF
SPJB023J.WMF
SPJB027J.WMF
SPJB028J.WMF
SPJB029J.WMF
SPORT026.WMF
SPORT028.WMF
SPORT029.WMF
SPORT032.WMF
SPORT051.WMF
SPORT056.WMF
SPORT340.WMF
SPORT341.WMF
SPORT344.WMF
SPORT355.WMF
SPORT357.WMF
SPORT363.WMF
SPORT374.WMF
SPORT375.WMF
SPRINTER.WMF
SPRINTR.WMF
SPRNTR.WMF
SPRW046J.WMF
SPRW047J.WMF
SPRW048J.WMF
SPRW049J.WMF
SPRW050J.WMF
SPRW054J.WMF
SPSI286D.WMF
SPSI287D.WMF
SPSI292D.WMF
SPSI326D.WMF
SPSI328D.WMF
SPSI329D.WMF
SPSI339D.WMF
SPSI340D.WMF
SPSI375D.WMF
SPSI378D.WMF
SPSI379D.WMF
SPSI497D.WMF
SPSI501.WMF
SPSI505.WMF
SPSI510D.WMF
SPSI559D.WMF
SPSI645D.WMF
SPSI646D.WMF
SPSI647D.WMF
SPSI648D.WMF
STARTGUN.WMF
TRACK.WMF
TRACK01.WMF
TRACK03.WMF
TRACK04.WMF
TRACK2.WMF
TRACKO.WMF
WHLCH_RC.WMF

0182.WMF 0183.WMF 0185.WMF 0186.WMF 0187.WMF 0188.WMF 0189.WMF 0190.WMF CAA0865.WMF CAA0868.WMF
CAA0869.WMF CAA0870.WMF CAA0871.WMF CAA0872.WMF CAA0873.WMF CAA0874.WMF CAA0875.WMF CAA0876.WMF CAA0879.WMF CARTOON1.WMF
CARTOON2.WMF CARTOON3.WMF CARTOON4.WMF CARTOON5.WMF CARTOON6.WMF CARTOON7.WMF CARTOON8.WMF CARTOON9.WMF CRTOON10.WMF CRTOON11.WMF
CRTOON12.WMF CRTOON13.WMF CRTOON15.WMF CRTOON16.WMF CRTOON18.WMF CRTOON19.WMF CRTOON20.WMF ISP004B.WMF PD091SCU.WMF PGX004F.WMF
SPAB008J.WMF SPCA093J.WMF SPCA094J.WMF SPCA105J.WMF SPGC031J.WMF SPGC049D.WMF SPGC108D.WMF SPJB001J.WMF SPJB002J.WMF SPJB035J.WMF
SPJB036J.WMF SPSI276D.WMF SPSI277D.WMF SPSI297D.WMF SPSI352D.WMF SPSI365D.WMF SPSI369D.WMF SPSI422D.WMF SPSI425D.WMF SPSI439D.WMF
SPSI440D.WMF SPSI445D.WMF SPSI475D.WMF SPSI476D.WMF SPSI491D.WMF SPSI492D.WMF SPSI496D.WMF SPSI498D.WMF SPSI540D.WMF SPSI659D.WMF
VOLLEY.WMF VOLLEY01.WMF VOLLEYBL.WMF VOLLY.WMF VOLLY005.WMF VOLLYBAL.WMF VOLYBA_1.WMF VOLYBAL3.WMF VOLYBAL4.WMF VOLYBALL.WMF
VOLYBL12.WMF VOLYBL13.WMF VOLYBL14.WMF VOLYBL15.WMF VOLYBL16.WMF VOLYBL17.WMF VOLYBL18.WMF VOLYBL19.WMF VOLYBL20.WMF VOLYBL21.WMF
VOLYBL22.WMF VOLYBL23.WMF VOLYBL24.WMF VOLYBL25.WMF VOLYBL26.WMF VOLYBL27.WMF VOLYBL28.WMF VOLYBL29.WMF VOLYBL30.WMF VOLYBL31.WMF
VOLYBL32.WMF VOLYBL33.WMF VOLYBL34.WMF VOLYBL35.WMF VOLYBL36.WMF VOLYBL37.WMF VOLYBL38.WMF VOLYBL39.WMF VOLYBL40.WMF VOLYBL41.WMF
VOLYBL42.WMF VOLYBL43.WMF VOLYBL44.WMF VOLYBL45.WMF VOLYBL46.WMF VOLYBL47.WMF VOLYBL48.WMF VOLYBL49.WMF VOLYBL50.WMF VOLYBL51.WMF

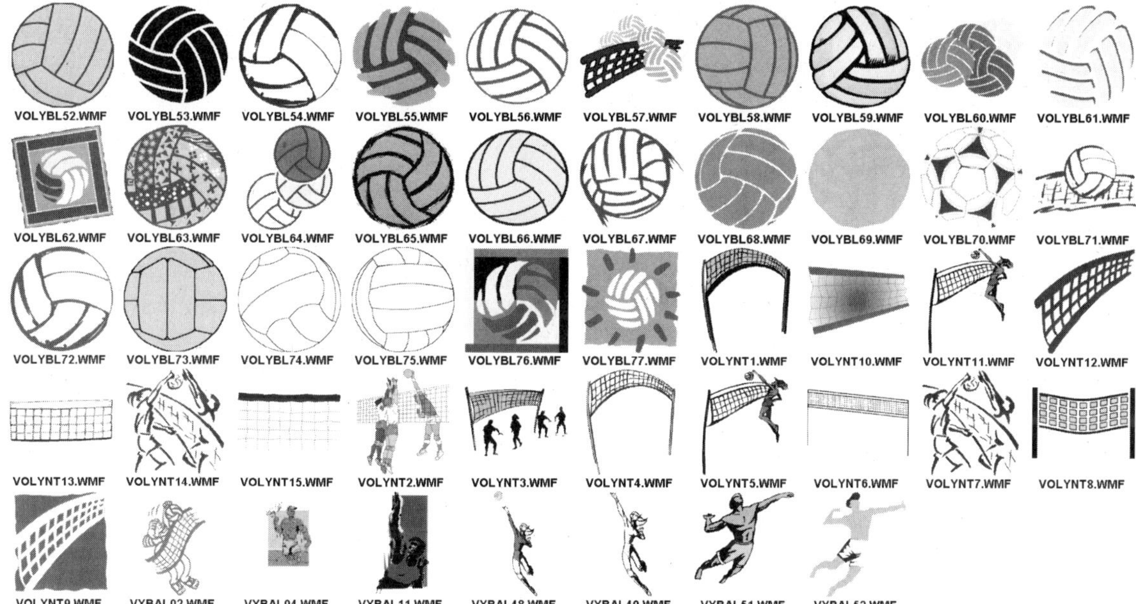
VOLYBL52.WMF
VOLYBL53.WMF
VOLYBL54.WMF
VOLYBL55.WMF
VOLYBL56.WMF
VOLYBL57.WMF
VOLYBL58.WMF
VOLYBL59.WMF
VOLYBL60.WMF
VOLYBL61.WMF
VOLYBL62.WMF
VOLYBL63.WMF
VOLYBL64.WMF
VOLYBL65.WMF
VOLYBL66.WMF
VOLYBL67.WMF
VOLYBL68.WMF
VOLYBL69.WMF
VOLYBL70.WMF
VOLYBL71.WMF
VOLYBL72.WMF
VOLYBL73.WMF
VOLYBL74.WMF
VOLYBL75.WMF
VOLYBL76.WMF
VOLYBL77.WMF
VOLYNT1.WMF
VOLYNT10.WMF
VOLYNT11.WMF
VOLYNT12.WMF
VOLYNT13.WMF
VOLYNT14.WMF
VOLYNT15.WMF
VOLYNT2.WMF
VOLYNT3.WMF
VOLYNT4.WMF
VOLYNT5.WMF
VOLYNT6.WMF
VOLYNT7.WMF
VOLYNT8.WMF
VOLYNT9.WMF
VYBAL02.WMF
VYBAL04.WMF
VYBAL11.WMF
VYBAL48.WMF
VYBAL49.WMF
VYBAL51.WMF
VYBAL52.WMF

0368.WMF 0369.WMF 0370.WMF 0371.WMF 0372.WMF 0373.WMF 0375.WMF 0376.WMF 0377.WMF 0378.WMF
0379.WMF 0380.WMF 0381.WMF 0382.WMF 0383.WMF 0384.WMF 0386.WMF 0387.WMF 0388.WMF 0389.WMF
0493.WMF 0494.WMF 0495.WMF 0497.WMF 0498.WMF 1WATER_S.WMF 2WATER_S.WMF ASI033E.WMF BOATING2.WMF BOY_DIVI.WMF
BOY_SWIM.WMF BOYWATER.WMF BUOY.WMF BYPOOL.WMF CAA0787.WMF CAA0788.WMF CAA0789.WMF CAA0790.WMF CAA0793.WMF CAA0794.WMF
CAA0795.WMF CAA0796.WMF CAA0797.WMF CAA0798.WMF CAA0799.WMF CAA0800.WMF CAA0801.WMF CAA0802.WMF CAA0803.WMF CAA0804.WMF
CAA0805.WMF CAA0806.WMF CAA0809.WMF CAA0811.WMF CANOE.WMF DIVER05.WMF DIVER1.WMF DIVER6.WMF DIVING.WMF EDCN123.WMF
FCP028B.WMF HPI010D.WMF HSP002A.WMF HSP031A.WMF IFN028D.WMF IHO013H.WMF IWT015C.WMF JET_SKI.WMF JETSKI.WMF JETSKIER.WMF
KAYAK2.WMF KAYAKART.WMF KAYAKER.WMF KAYAKING.WMF L21192.WMF LIFGUAR.WMF MISCSP66.WMF OCTOPUS.WMF PD091ICU.WMF PD091PCU.WMF
PD091TCU.WMF PD092ACU.WMF PD092UCU.WMF PD093FCU.WMF PD093JCU.WMF PD093LCU.WMF PD093OCU.WMF PD099ICU.WMF PD113SCU.WMF PD113TCU.WMF
PD113VCU.WMF PD114GCU.WMF PD114UCU.WMF PD114XCU.WMF PD115ACU.WMF PGX002F.WMF PRESERVE.WMF RAFTING1.WMF ROWERS.WMF ROWING.WMF
S21738.WMF SAILBOA1.WMF SAILBOA3.WMF SAILBOAT.WMF SAILING.WMF SCT020C.WMF SCT021C.WMF SEADO.WMF SKING03.WMF SKING33.WMF
Perfect Entry
SOSI022D.WMF SPA028B.WMF SPAB027D.WMF SPCA078J.WMF SPCA081J.WMF SPCA083J.WMF SPCA084J.WMF SPCA085J.WMF SPCA086J.WMF SPCA101J.WMF

SPCA117J.WMF SPGC002D.WMF SPGC050D.WMF SPGC052D.WMF SPGC093D.WMF SPGC105D.WMF SPJB024J.WMF SPORT018.WMF SPORT019.WMF SPORT020.WMF
SPORT021.WMF SPORT022.WMF SPORT068.WMF SPORT071.WMF SPORT080.WMF SPORT093.WMF SPORT342.WMF SPORT343.WMF SPORT351.WMF SPORT418.WMF
SPORT419.WMF SPORT420.WMF SPORT421.WMF SPORT422.WMF SPORT423.WMF SPORT424.WMF SPORT425.WMF SPSI275D.WMF SPSI291D.WMF SPSI315D.WMF
SPSI330D.WMF SPSI341D.WMF SPSI358D.WMF SPSI372D.WMF SPSI377D.WMF SPSI389D.WMF SPSI390D.WMF SPSI408D.WMF SPSI451D.WMF SPSI452D.WMF
SPSI459D.WMF SPSI460D.WMF SPSI508D.WMF SPSI512D.WMF SPSI554D.WMF SPSI593D.WMF SPSI600D.WMF SPSI606D.WMF SPSI649D.WMF SPSI650D.WMF
SPSI651D.WMF SPSI652D.WMF STARFISH.WMF STEPAERO.WMF SURFER.WMF SURFER05.WMF SWIM005.WMF SWIM03.WMF SWIM04.WMF SWIM05.WMF
SWIM08.WMF SWIM1005.WMF SWIM12.WMF SWIM13.WMF SWIM14.WMF SWIM15.WMF SWIM16.WMF SWIM17.WMF SWIM18.WMF SWIM20.WMF
SWIM21.WMF SWIM24.WMF SWIM25.WMF SWIM27.WMF SWIM28.WMF SWIM29.WMF SWIM30.WMF SWIM32.WMF SWIM33.WMF SWIM34.WMF
SWIM35.WMF SWIM36.WMF SWIM37.WMF SWIM38.WMF SWIM41.WMF SWIM42.WMF SWIMER5.WMF SWIMING.WMF SWIMMER.WMF SWIMMER5.WMF
SWIMMER_.WMF SWIMMING.WMF SWIMPOOL.WMF SWMMNG.WMF TA03.WMF TA04.WMF TA15.WMF TE95.WMF TE96.WMF TE97.WMF
TE98.WMF THISWAY.WMF TURTLE.WMF TVA046B.WMF W21878.WMF WATERPOL.WMF WATERSK1.WMF WATERSK2.WMF WATERSKI.WMF WATR_SKI.WMF
WATRPOLO.WMF WATRSKI.WMF WATRSKI5.WMF WETSKI1.WMF WETSKI2.WMF WETSKI3.WMF WHITEWAT.WMF WHWTR_RF.WMF WINDSU_1.WMF WINDSURF.WMF

WNDSRF5.WMF

WNDSURF5.WMF

WOMANONW.WMF

WTRSPR50.WMF

WTRSPR54.WMF

WTRSPR55.WMF

X_COUNT1.WMF

XXSKIER.WMF

YACHTING.WMF

Sports • Wrestling (WRESTLE)

0330.WMF 0331.WMF 0332.WMF 0333.WMF 0334.WMF 0335.WMF 0336.WMF 0337.WMF ASI023S.WMF CAA0880.WMF

CAA0881.WMF CAA0882.WMF CAA0883.WMF CAA0884.WMF CAA0885.WMF CAA0886.WMF DEC066O.WMF ISP018B.WMF OSP027O.WMF PD091QCU.WMF

PD112PCU.WMF SPBO012J.WMF SPCA097J.WMF SPCA099J.WMF SPGC046J.WMF SPJB039J.WMF SPORT017.WMF SPSI249D.WMF SPSI268D.WMF SPSI284D.WMF

SPSI357D.WMF SPSI495D.WMF SPSI506.WMF SPSS006J.WMF WRES1MD.WMF WRES2MD.WMF WRES3MD.WMF WRESTL1.WMF WRESTL2.WMF WRESTL_2.WMF

WRESTLE.WMF WRESTLER.WMF WRESTLRS.WMF WRSTLING.WMF WRTLG01.WMF WRTLG02.WMF WRTLG03.WMF WRTLG04.WMF WRTLG05.WMF WRTLG06.WMF

WRTLG07.WMF WRTLG08.WMF WRTLG09.WMF WRTLG10.WMF

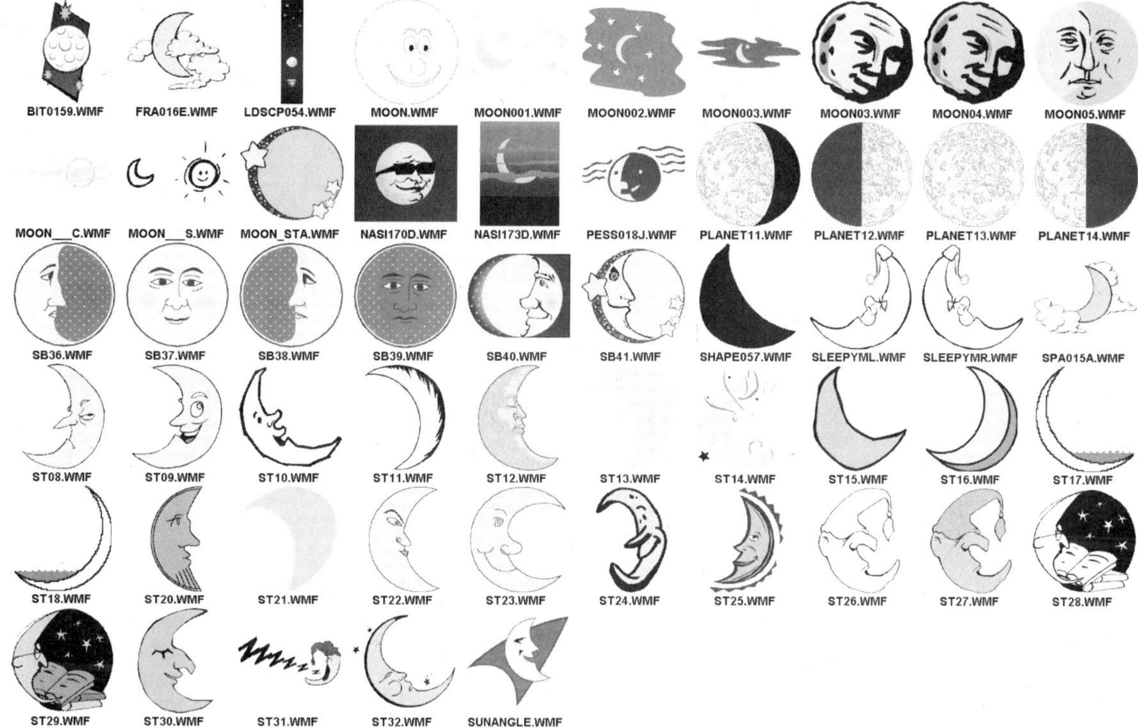
BIT0159.WMF
FRA016E.WMF
LDSCP054.WMF
MOON.WMF
MOON001.WMF
MOON002.WMF
MOON003.WMF
MOON03.WMF
MOON04.WMF
MOON05.WMF
MOON___C.WMF
MOON___S.WMF
MOON_STA.WMF
NASI170D.WMF
NASI173D.WMF
PESS018J.WMF
PLANET11.WMF
PLANET12.WMF
PLANET13.WMF
PLANET14.WMF
SB36.WMF
SB37.WMF
SB38.WMF
SB39.WMF
SB40.WMF
SB41.WMF
SHAPE057.WMF
SLEEPYML.WMF
SLEEPYMR.WMF
SPA015A.WMF
ST08.WMF
ST09.WMF
ST10.WMF
ST11.WMF
ST12.WMF
ST13.WMF
ST14.WMF
ST15.WMF
ST16.WMF
ST17.WMF
ST18.WMF
ST20.WMF
ST21.WMF
ST22.WMF
ST23.WMF
ST24.WMF
ST25.WMF
ST26.WMF
ST27.WMF
ST28.WMF
ST29.WMF
ST30.WMF
ST31.WMF
ST32.WMF
SUNANGLE.WMF

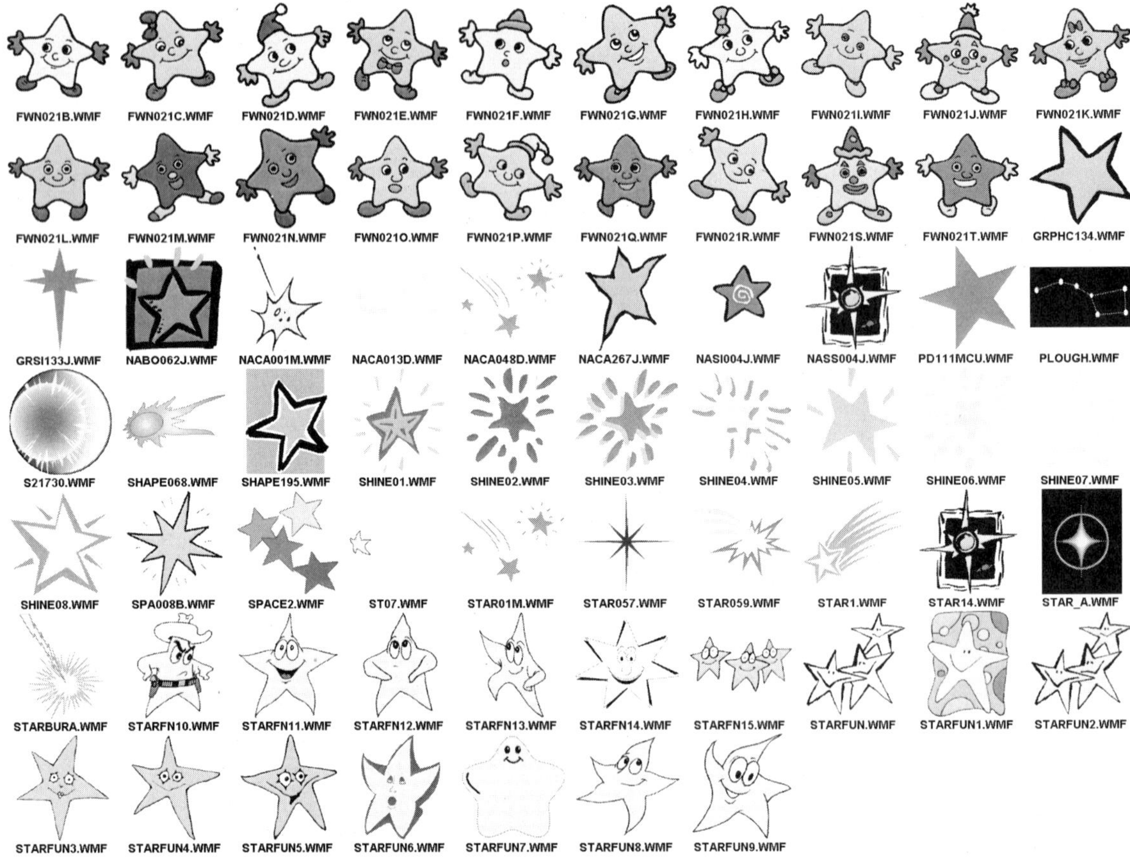
FWN021B.WMF
FWN021C.WMF
FWN021D.WMF
FWN021E.WMF
FWN021F.WMF
FWN021G.WMF
FWN021H.WMF
FWN021I.WMF
FWN021J.WMF
FWN021K.WMF
FWN021L.WMF
FWN021M.WMF
FWN021N.WMF
FWN021O.WMF
FWN021P.WMF
FWN021Q.WMF
FWN021R.WMF
FWN021S.WMF
FWN021T.WMF
GRPHC134.WMF
GRSI133J.WMF
NABO062J.WMF
NACA001M.WMF
NACA013D.WMF
NACA048D.WMF
NACA267J.WMF
NASI004J.WMF
NASS004J.WMF
PD111MCU.WMF
PLOUGH.WMF
S21730.WMF
SHAPE068.WMF
SHAPE195.WMF
SHINE01.WMF
SHINE02.WMF
SHINE03.WMF
SHINE04.WMF
SHINE05.WMF
SHINE06.WMF
SHINE07.WMF
SHINE08.WMF
SPA008B.WMF
SPACE2.WMF
ST07.WMF
STAR01M.WMF
STAR057.WMF
STAR059.WMF
STAR1.WMF
STAR14.WMF
STAR_A.WMF
STARBURA.WMF
STARFN10.WMF
STARFN11.WMF
STARFN12.WMF
STARFN13.WMF
STARFN14.WMF
STARFN15.WMF
STARFUN.WMF
STARFUN1.WMF
STARFUN2.WMF
STARFUN3.WMF
STARFUN4.WMF
STARFUN5.WMF
STARFUN6.WMF
STARFUN7.WMF
STARFUN8.WMF
STARFUN9.WMF

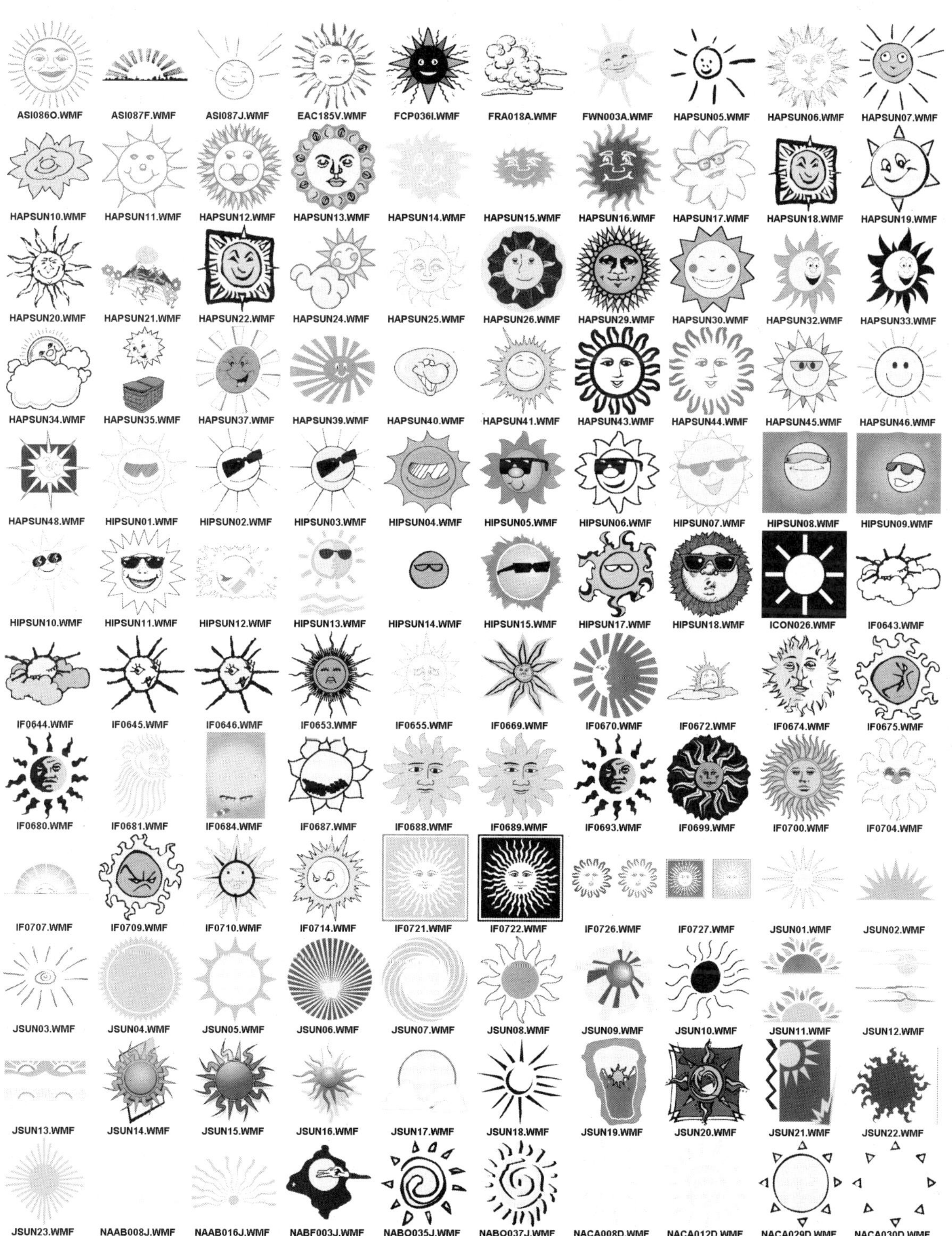
ASI086O.WMF ASI087F.WMF ASI087J.WMF EAC185V.WMF FCP036I.WMF FRA018A.WMF FWN003A.WMF HAPSUN05.WMF HAPSUN06.WMF HAPSUN07.WMF
HAPSUN10.WMF HAPSUN11.WMF HAPSUN12.WMF HAPSUN13.WMF HAPSUN14.WMF HAPSUN15.WMF HAPSUN16.WMF HAPSUN17.WMF HAPSUN18.WMF HAPSUN19.WMF
HAPSUN20.WMF HAPSUN21.WMF HAPSUN22.WMF HAPSUN24.WMF HAPSUN25.WMF HAPSUN26.WMF HAPSUN29.WMF HAPSUN30.WMF HAPSUN32.WMF HAPSUN33.WMF
HAPSUN34.WMF HAPSUN35.WMF HAPSUN37.WMF HAPSUN39.WMF HAPSUN40.WMF HAPSUN41.WMF HAPSUN43.WMF HAPSUN44.WMF HAPSUN45.WMF HAPSUN46.WMF
HAPSUN48.WMF HIPSUN01.WMF HIPSUN02.WMF HIPSUN03.WMF HIPSUN04.WMF HIPSUN05.WMF HIPSUN06.WMF HIPSUN07.WMF HIPSUN08.WMF HIPSUN09.WMF
HIPSUN10.WMF HIPSUN11.WMF HIPSUN12.WMF HIPSUN13.WMF HIPSUN14.WMF HIPSUN15.WMF HIPSUN17.WMF HIPSUN18.WMF ICON026.WMF IF0643.WMF
IF0644.WMF IF0645.WMF IF0646.WMF IF0653.WMF IF0655.WMF IF0669.WMF IF0670.WMF IF0672.WMF IF0674.WMF IF0675.WMF
IF0680.WMF IF0681.WMF IF0684.WMF IF0687.WMF IF0688.WMF IF0689.WMF IF0693.WMF IF0699.WMF IF0700.WMF IF0704.WMF
IF0707.WMF IF0709.WMF IF0710.WMF IF0714.WMF IF0721.WMF IF0722.WMF IF0726.WMF IF0727.WMF JSUN01.WMF JSUN02.WMF
JSUN03.WMF JSUN04.WMF JSUN05.WMF JSUN06.WMF JSUN07.WMF JSUN08.WMF JSUN09.WMF JSUN10.WMF JSUN11.WMF JSUN12.WMF
JSUN13.WMF JSUN14.WMF JSUN15.WMF JSUN16.WMF JSUN17.WMF JSUN18.WMF JSUN19.WMF JSUN20.WMF JSUN21.WMF JSUN22.WMF
JSUN23.WMF NAAB008J.WMF NAAB016J.WMF NABF003J.WMF NABO035J.WMF NABO037J.WMF NACA008D.WMF NACA012D.WMF NACA029D.WMF NACA030D.WMF

NACA040J.WMF
NACA044D.WMF
NACA046D.WMF
NACA049D.WMF
NACA050D.WMF
NACA051D.WMF
NACA052D.WMF
NACA057D.WMF
NACA264J.WMF
NAGC026D.WMF
NARW021D.WMF
NASS001D.WMF
NASS002D.WMF
NASS003D.WMF
NASS006D.WMF
NASS008D.WMF
NASS008J.WMF
NASS033D.WMF
NASS060D.WMF
NASS098D.WMF
NASS169D.WMF
NATURE0.WMF
NATURE16.WMF
NATURE17.WMF
O21537.WMF
S21727.WMF
SHAPE067.WMF
SHAPE070.WMF
SHAPE072.WMF
SHAPE216.WMF
SPA024B.WMF
SPA024C.WMF
ST11.WMF
SUN.WMF
SUN001.WMF
SUN01.WMF
SUN01M.WMF
SUN02.WMF
SUN02M.WMF
SUN03.WMF
SUN05.WMF
SUN06.WMF
SUN07.WMF
SUN08.WMF
SUN11.WMF
SUN12.WMF
SUN2AS.WMF
SUN50.WMF
SUN51.WMF
SUN52.WMF
SUN_HEAT.WMF
SUNAS.WMF
SUNMORT1.WMF
SUNMORTI.WMF
SUNNY.WMF
SUNRISE.WMF
SUNSET.WMF
SUNSET_B.WMF
SUNSET_G.WMF
SUNSYM.WMF
SYMBL201.WMF
SYMBL202.WMF
SYMBL203.WMF
SYMBL206.WMF
SYMBOL86.WMF
SYMBOL87.WMF
SYMBOL90.WMF
SYMBOL91.WMF
SYMBOL94.WMF
SYMBOL97.WMF

001DING.WMF
002DING.WMF
003DING.WMF
004DING.WMF
005DING.WMF
006DING.WMF
007DING.WMF
008DING.WMF
009DING.WMF
010DING.WMF
011DING.WMF
012DING.WMF
013DING.WMF
014DING.WMF
015DING.WMF
016DING.WMF
017DING.WMF
018DING.WMF
019DING.WMF
020DING.WMF
021DING.WMF
022DING.WMF
023DING.WMF
024DING.WMF
025DING.WMF
026DING.WMF
027DING.WMF
028DING.WMF
029DING.WMF
030DING.WMF
031DING.WMF
032DING.WMF
033DING.WMF
034DING.WMF
035DING.WMF
036DING.WMF
037DING.WMF
038DING.WMF
039DING.WMF
040DING.WMF
041DING.WMF
042DING.WMF
043DING.WMF
044DING.WMF
045DING.WMF
046DING.WMF
047DING.WMF
048DING.WMF
049DING.WMF
050DING.WMF
051DING.WMF
052DING.WMF
053DING.WMF
054DING.WMF
055DING.WMF
056DING.WMF
0572CHCC.WMF
057DING.WMF
058DING.WMF
059DING.WMF
060DING.WMF
061DING.WMF
062DING.WMF
063DING.WMF
064DING.WMF
065DING.WMF
066DING.WMF
067DING.WMF
068DING.WMF
069DING.WMF
070DING.WMF
071DING.WMF
072DING.WMF
073DING.WMF
074DING.WMF
075DING.WMF
076DING.WMF
077DING.WMF
078DING.WMF
079DING.WMF
080DING.WMF
081DING.WMF
082DING.WMF
083DING.WMF
084DING.WMF
085DING.WMF
086DING.WMF
087DING.WMF
088DING.WMF
089DING.WMF
090DING.WMF
091DING.WMF
092DING.WMF
093DING.WMF
094DING.WMF
095DING.WMF
096DING.WMF
097DING.WMF
098DING.WMF
099DING.WMF
100DING.WMF
101DING.WMF
102DING.WMF
103DING.WMF
104DING.WMF
105DING.WMF
106DING.WMF
107DING.WMF
108DING.WMF
109DING.WMF
110DING.WMF
111DING.WMF
112DING.WMF
113DING.WMF
114DING.WMF
ASI011AA.WMF
CCB031A.WMF
DEC016D.WMF
DEC021H.WMF
DEC022Z.WMF

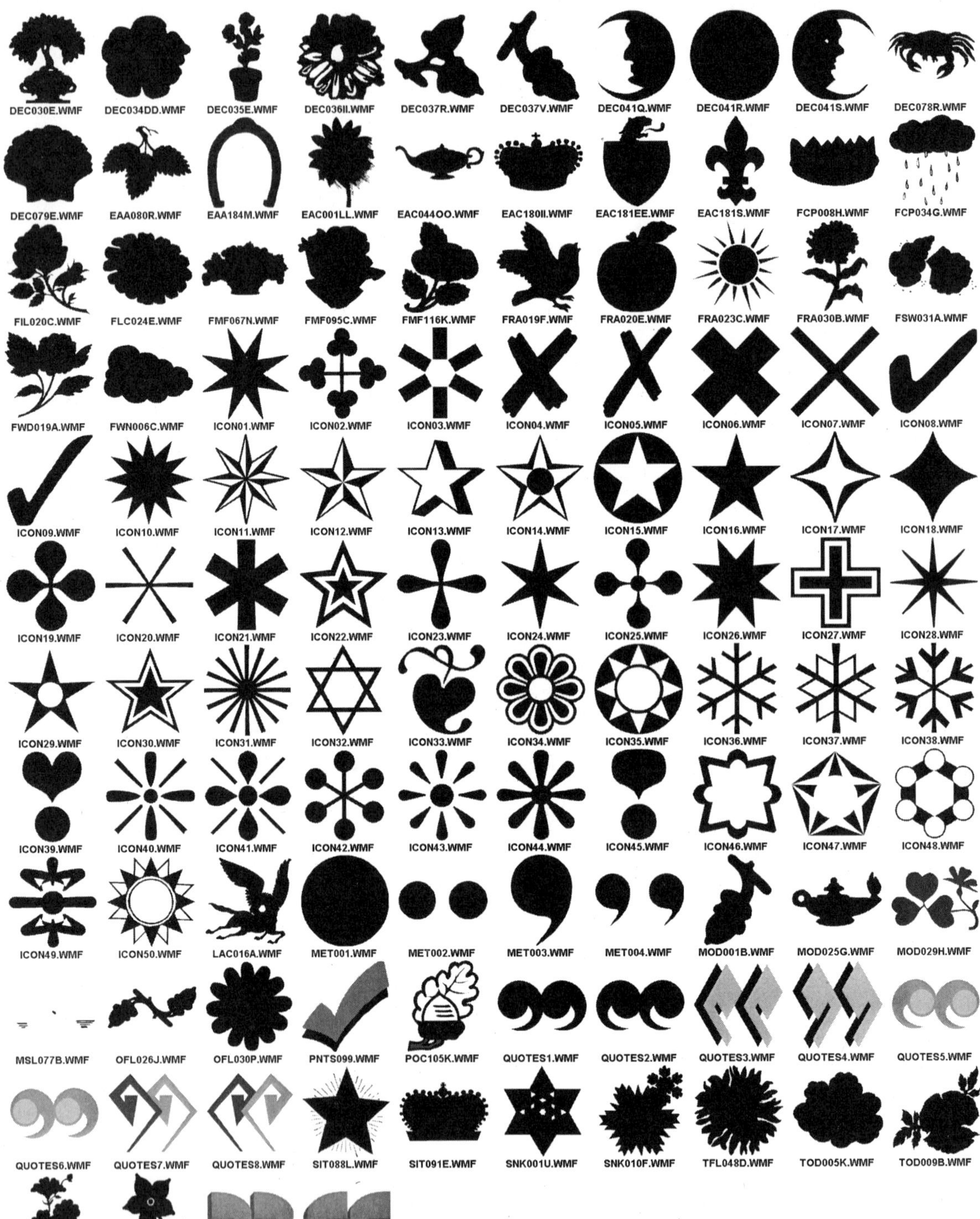
DEC030E.WMF
DEC034DD.WMF
DEC035E.WMF
DEC036II.WMF
DEC037R.WMF
DEC037V.WMF
DEC041Q.WMF
DEC041R.WMF
DEC041S.WMF
DEC078R.WMF
DEC079E.WMF
EAA080R.WMF
EAA184M.WMF
EAC001LL.WMF
EAC044OO.WMF
EAC180II.WMF
EAC181EE.WMF
EAC181S.WMF
FCP008H.WMF
FCP034G.WMF
FIL020C.WMF
FLC024E.WMF
FMF067N.WMF
FMF095C.WMF
FMF116K.WMF
FRA019F.WMF
FRA020E.WMF
FRA023C.WMF
FRA030B.WMF
FSW031A.WMF
FWD019A.WMF
FWN006C.WMF
ICON01.WMF
ICON02.WMF
ICON03.WMF
ICON04.WMF
ICON05.WMF
ICON06.WMF
ICON07.WMF
ICON08.WMF
ICON09.WMF
ICON10.WMF
ICON11.WMF
ICON12.WMF
ICON13.WMF
ICON14.WMF
ICON15.WMF
ICON16.WMF
ICON17.WMF
ICON18.WMF
ICON19.WMF
ICON20.WMF
ICON21.WMF
ICON22.WMF
ICON23.WMF
ICON24.WMF
ICON25.WMF
ICON26.WMF
ICON27.WMF
ICON28.WMF
ICON29.WMF
ICON30.WMF
ICON31.WMF
ICON32.WMF
ICON33.WMF
ICON34.WMF
ICON35.WMF
ICON36.WMF
ICON37.WMF
ICON38.WMF
ICON39.WMF
ICON40.WMF
ICON41.WMF
ICON42.WMF
ICON43.WMF
ICON44.WMF
ICON45.WMF
ICON46.WMF
ICON47.WMF
ICON48.WMF
ICON49.WMF
ICON50.WMF
LAC016A.WMF
MET001.WMF
MET002.WMF
MET003.WMF
MET004.WMF
MOD001B.WMF
MOD025G.WMF
MOD029H.WMF
MSL077B.WMF
OFL026J.WMF
OFL030P.WMF
PNTS099.WMF
POC105K.WMF
QUOTES1.WMF
QUOTES2.WMF
QUOTES3.WMF
QUOTES4.WMF
QUOTES5.WMF
QUOTES6.WMF
QUOTES7.WMF
QUOTES8.WMF
SIT088L.WMF
SIT091E.WMF
SNK001U.WMF
SNK010F.WMF
TFL048D.WMF
TOD005K.WMF
TOD009B.WMF
TOD016D.WMF
TOD016H.WMF
ZMISC067.WMF
ZMISC069.WMF

0801.WMF 0810.WMF 0811.WMF 0812.WMF 0813.WMF 0814.WMF 0815.WMF 0816.WMF 0827.WMF 0829.WMF
0830.WMF 0831.WMF 0833.WMF 0836.WMF 0842.WMF 0843.WMF 0845.WMF 0846.WMF 0847.WMF 0848.WMF
0849.WMF 0852.WMF 0853.WMF 0854.WMF 0855.WMF 0856.WMF 0857.WMF 0962TRAC.WMF 0963TRAC.WMF 0964TRCC.WMF
0965TRCC.WMF 0966TUNC.WMF 0967TUNC.WMF 0968UNLC.WMF 0973WATC.WMF 0976WATC.WMF 1069.WMF 1085.WMF 1086.WMF 1087.WMF
1088.WMF 1090.WMF 1092.WMF 1586.WMF 1955.WMF 2456.WMF 3608.WMF 3609.WMF BIT0628.WMF BIT0629.WMF
BIT0630.WMF BIT0631.WMF BIT0632.WMF BIT0633.WMF BIT0634.WMF BIT0635.WMF BIT0636.WMF BIT0637.WMF BIT0638.WMF BIT0639.WMF
BIT0640.WMF BIT0641.WMF BIT0642.WMF BIT0643.WMF BIT0644.WMF BIT0645.WMF BIT0646.WMF BIT0647.WMF BIT0648.WMF BIT0649.WMF
BIT0650.WMF BIT0651.WMF BIT0652.WMF BIT0653.WMF BIT0654.WMF BIT0655.WMF BIT0656.WMF BIT0657.WMF BIT0658.WMF BIT0659.WMF
BIT0660.WMF BIT0661.WMF BIT0662.WMF BIT0663.WMF BIT0664.WMF BIT0665.WMF BLUERIB.WMF BROKHART.WMF CACTUS.WMF CDROM.WMF
CHECKMRK.WMF CONFFLAG.WMF CROWN.WMF CROWN2.WMF DARK.WMF DEC078E.WMF DEC078GG.WMF DEC078H.WMF DOWN.WMF EAA006P.WMF
EAGSALAD.WMF EMPTY.WMF FASTFWD.WMF FLEUR.WMF FULL.WMF HAMRSIKL.WMF HANDSHAK.WMF HAPPY.WMF HEARING.WMF HERMAPHR.WMF
HOURGLAS.WMF ICON036.WMF ICON038.WMF ICON039.WMF ICON042.WMF ICON043.WMF ICON044.WMF ICON045.WMF ICON046.WMF ICON054.WMF

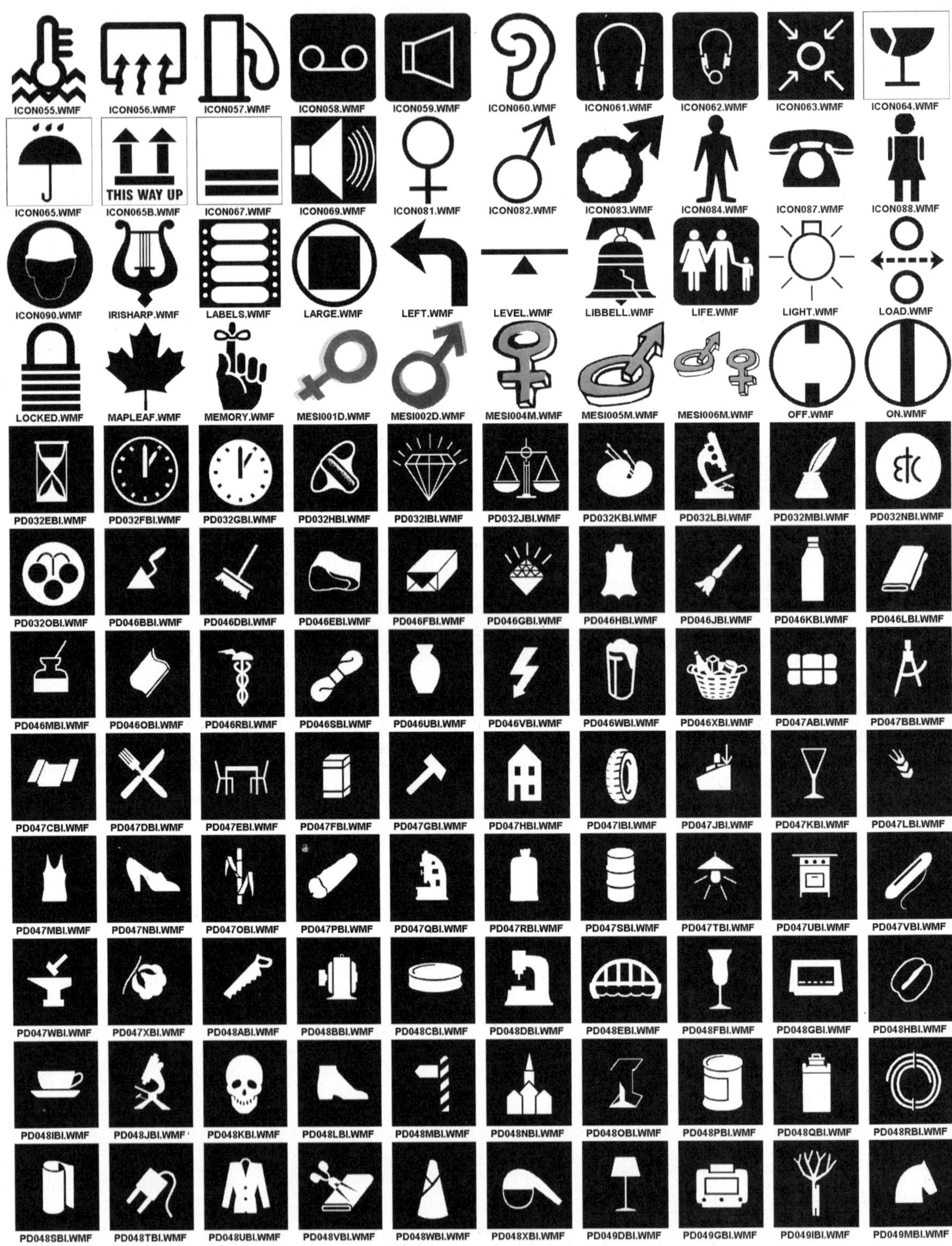
ICON055.WMF
ICON056.WMF
ICON057.WMF
ICON058.WMF
ICON059.WMF
ICON060.WMF
ICON061.WMF
ICON062.WMF
ICON063.WMF
ICON064.WMF
THIS WAY UP
ICON065.WMF
ICON065B.WMF
ICON067.WMF
ICON069.WMF
ICON081.WMF
ICON082.WMF
ICON083.WMF
ICON084.WMF
ICON087.WMF
ICON088.WMF
ICON090.WMF
IRISHARP.WMF
LABELS.WMF
LARGE.WMF
LEFT.WMF
LEVEL.WMF
LIBBELL.WMF
LIFE.WMF
LIGHT.WMF
LOAD.WMF
LOCKED.WMF
MAPLEAF.WMF
MEMORY.WMF
MESI001D.WMF
MESI002D.WMF
MESI004M.WMF
MESI005M.WMF
MESI006M.WMF
OFF.WMF
ON.WMF
PD032EBI.WMF
PD032FBI.WMF
PD032GBI.WMF
PD032HBI.WMF
PD032IBI.WMF
PD032JBI.WMF
PD032KBI.WMF
PD032LBI.WMF
PD032MBI.WMF
PD032NBI.WMF
PD032OBI.WMF
PD046BBI.WMF
PD046DBI.WMF
PD046EBI.WMF
PD046FBI.WMF
PD046GBI.WMF
PD046HBI.WMF
PD046JBI.WMF
PD046KBI.WMF
PD046LBI.WMF
PD046MBI.WMF
PD046OBI.WMF
PD046RBI.WMF
PD046SBI.WMF
PD046UBI.WMF
PD046VBI.WMF
PD046WBI.WMF
PD046XBI.WMF
PD047ABI.WMF
PD047BBI.WMF
PD047CBI.WMF
PD047DBI.WMF
PD047EBI.WMF
PD047FBI.WMF
PD047GBI.WMF
PD047HBI.WMF
PD047IBI.WMF
PD047JBI.WMF
PD047KBI.WMF
PD047LBI.WMF
PD047MBI.WMF
PD047NBI.WMF
PD047OBI.WMF
PD047PBI.WMF
PD047QBI.WMF
PD047RBI.WMF
PD047SBI.WMF
PD047TBI.WMF
PD047UBI.WMF
PD047VBI.WMF
PD047WBI.WMF
PD047XBI.WMF
PD048ABI.WMF
PD048BBI.WMF
PD048CBI.WMF
PD048DBI.WMF
PD048EBI.WMF
PD048FBI.WMF
PD048GBI.WMF
PD048HBI.WMF
PD048IBI.WMF
PD048JBI.WMF
PD048KBI.WMF
PD048LBI.WMF
PD048MBI.WMF
PD048NBI.WMF
PD048OBI.WMF
PD048PBI.WMF
PD048QBI.WMF
PD048RBI.WMF
PD048SBI.WMF
PD048TBI.WMF
PD048UBI.WMF
PD048VBI.WMF
PD048WBI.WMF
PD048XBI.WMF
PD049DBI.WMF
PD049GBI.WMF
PD049IBI.WMF
PD049MBI.WMF

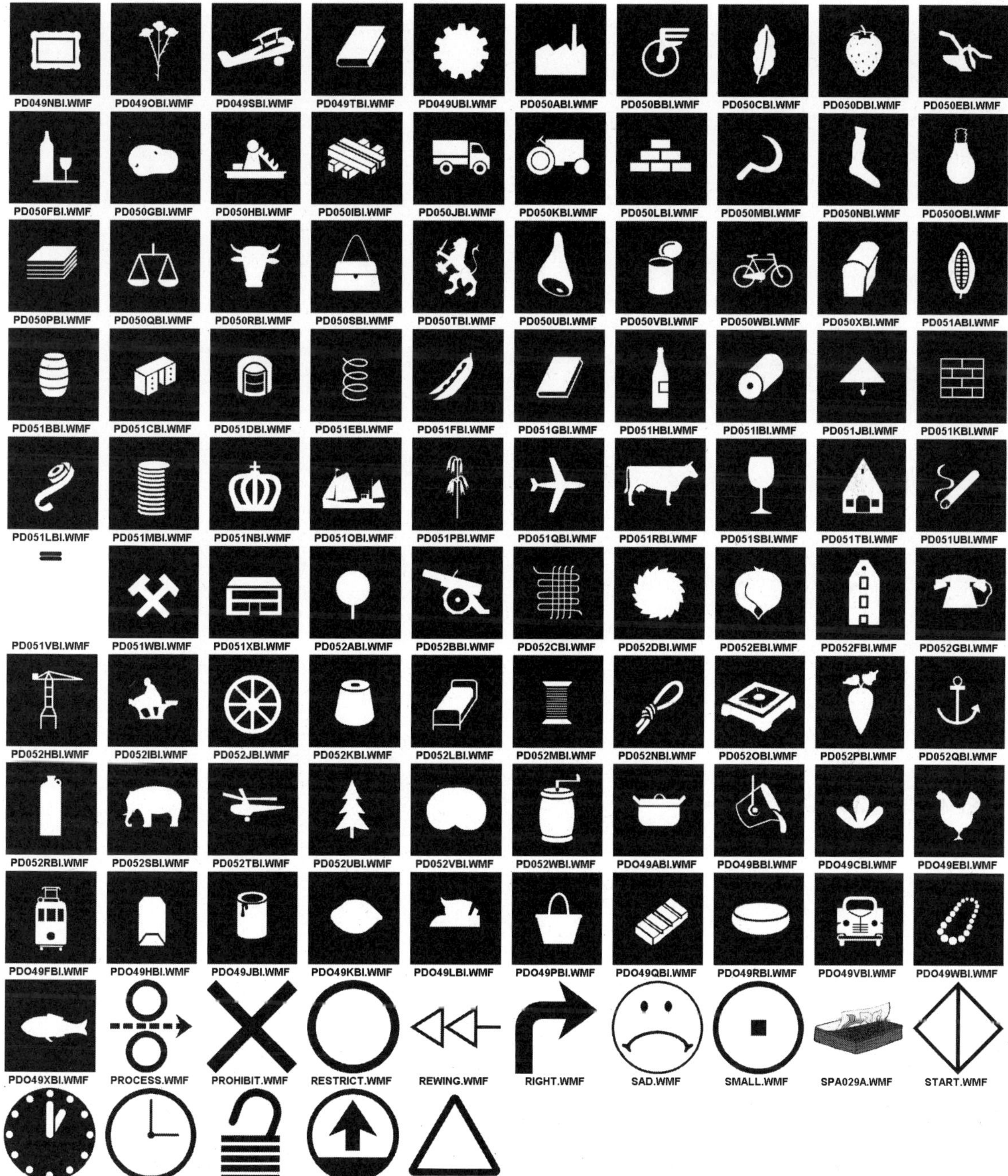
PD049NBI.WMF
PD049OBI.WMF
PD049SBI.WMF
PD049TBI.WMF
PD049UBI.WMF
PD050ABI.WMF
PD050BBI.WMF
PD050CBI.WMF
PD050DBI.WMF
PD050EBI.WMF
PD050FBI.WMF
PD050GBI.WMF
PD050HBI.WMF
PD050IBI.WMF
PD050JBI.WMF
PD050KBI.WMF
PD050LBI.WMF
PD050MBI.WMF
PD050NBI.WMF
PD050OBI.WMF
PD050PBI.WMF
PD050QBI.WMF
PD050RBI.WMF
PD050SBI.WMF
PD050TBI.WMF
PD050UBI.WMF
PD050VBI.WMF
PD050WBI.WMF
PD050XBI.WMF
PD051ABI.WMF
PD051BBI.WMF
PD051CBI.WMF
PD051DBI.WMF
PD051EBI.WMF
PD051FBI.WMF
PD051GBI.WMF
PD051HBI.WMF
PD051IBI.WMF
PD051JBI.WMF
PD051KBI.WMF
PD051LBI.WMF
PD051MBI.WMF
PD051NBI.WMF
PD051OBI.WMF
PD051PBI.WMF
PD051QBI.WMF
PD051RBI.WMF
PD051SBI.WMF
PD051TBI.WMF
PD051UBI.WMF
PD051VBI.WMF
PD051WBI.WMF
PD051XBI.WMF
PD052ABI.WMF
PD052BBI.WMF
PD052CBI.WMF
PD052DBI.WMF
PD052EBI.WMF
PD052FBI.WMF
PD052GBI.WMF
PD052HBI.WMF
PD052IBI.WMF
PD052JBI.WMF
PD052KBI.WMF
PD052LBI.WMF
PD052MBI.WMF
PD052NBI.WMF
PD052OBI.WMF
PD052PBI.WMF
PD052QBI.WMF
PD052RBI.WMF
PD052SBI.WMF
PD052TBI.WMF
PD052UBI.WMF
PD052VBI.WMF
PD052WBI.WMF
PDO49ABI.WMF
PDO49BBI.WMF
PDO49CBI.WMF
PDO49EBI.WMF
PDO49FBI.WMF
PDO49HBI.WMF
PDO49JBI.WMF
PDO49KBI.WMF
PDO49LBI.WMF
PDO49PBI.WMF
PDO49QBI.WMF
PDO49RBI.WMF
PDO49VBI.WMF
PDO49WBI.WMF
PDO49XBI.WMF
PROCESS.WMF
PROHIBIT.WMF
RESTRICT.WMF
REWING.WMF
RIGHT.WMF
SAD.WMF
SMALL.WMF
SPA029A.WMF
START.WMF
TIME1.WMF
TIME2.WMF
UNLOCKED.WMF
UP.WMF
WARNING.WMF

3610.WMF
3611.WMF
3612.WMF
3615.WMF
3618.WMF
4105.WMF
4106.WMF
4107.WMF
4118.WMF
4142.WMF
AIR FREIGHT
&
4LEAF.WMF
AIRFRT.WMF
AMPRSAND.WMF
AUDIOCAS.WMF
AUTUMN.WMF
BAL1.WMF
BAL2.WMF
BASKET.WMF
BASSCLEF.WMF
BIT0308.WMF
BIT0338.WMF
BIT0346.WMF
BIT0349.WMF
BIT0350.WMF
BIT0370.WMF
BIT0377.WMF
BIT0378.WMF
BIT0627.WMF
Clamp
CLAMP.WMF
CONTLTR.WMF
CORROS2.WMF
CORROS3.WMF
DANGER1.WMF
DAY.WMF
DIMENS.WMF
DONOTRL2.WMF
Fork
FORKLIFT.WMF
FRAGILE2.WMF
FRAGILE
FRAGILE3.WMF
FRAGILE4.WMF
FRAGILE6.WMF
FRAGILE7.WMF
FRIDAY.WMF
GROSSWT.WMF
HANDCAR2.WMF
Hand
HANDTRK.WMF
HEAVYWT1.WMF
HEAVYWT2.WMF
HIGHTOX.WMF
HOUR.WMF
IRRADIAT.WMF
KPDRY2.WMF
KPFMCLD2.WMF
keep from heat
KPFMHT3.WMF
KPFMHT4.WMF
LIFTHER1.WMF
LIFTHER2.WMF
Made In America
MADEAMER.WMF
MADE IN CANADA
MADECAN1.WMF
MADE IN
CANADA
MADECAN2.WMF
MAGNET1.WMF
MARINE POLLUTANT
MARPOLL.WMF
MONDAY.WMF
MONTH.WMF
MUSIC1.WMF
MUSIC2.WMF
NETWT.WMF
NEUTER.WMF
NONFLAM2.WMF
NOXIOUS.WMF
OPENHERE.WMF
OXIDIZR2.WMF
PACKED WITH PRIDE
IN THE U.S.A.
PACKEDUS.WMF
PEACE.WMF
PEACE01.WMF
PEACE02.WMF
PEACE03.WMF
PEACE04.WMF
PEACE05.WMF
PEACE06.WMF
PEACE07.WMF
PEACE08.WMF
PERFUME.WMF
PERISH1.WMF
PERISHABLE
RUSH
PERISH2.WMF
PETROL.WMF
POISON3.WMF
PULL.WMF
RADIO.WMF
RAMPLION.WMF
REAL02.WMF
REGMARK.WMF
RUSH
SHIPMENT
RUSH1.WMF
RUSH
RUSH2.WMF
SATURDAY.WMF
SEXTANT.WMF
SHAMROCK.WMF
SLINGHER.WMF
SPRING.WMF
12
STAKLIM.WMF
STAR.WMF
STATIC1.WMF
STATIC2.WMF
STATIC3.WMF
SUMMER.WMF
SUNDAY.WMF
TARGET.WMF
THISUP1.WMF
THISUP2.WMF
THISUP3.WMF
THISUP4.WMF
UP
FRAGILE
THISUP5.WMF
THURSDAY.WMF
TOPHEAV1.WMF
CAUTION
TOP HEAVY
TOPHEAV2.WMF
TOXIC.WMF
TRIDENT.WMF
TUESDAY.WMF
UMBRELLA.WMF
USEAGLE.WMF

USENOHK1.WMF

USENOHK2.WMF

USFLAG.WMF

USMAP.WMF

WATCH.WMF

WEDNESDA.WMF

WEEK.WMF

WHEELLAW.WMF

WINTER.WMF

YEAR.WMF

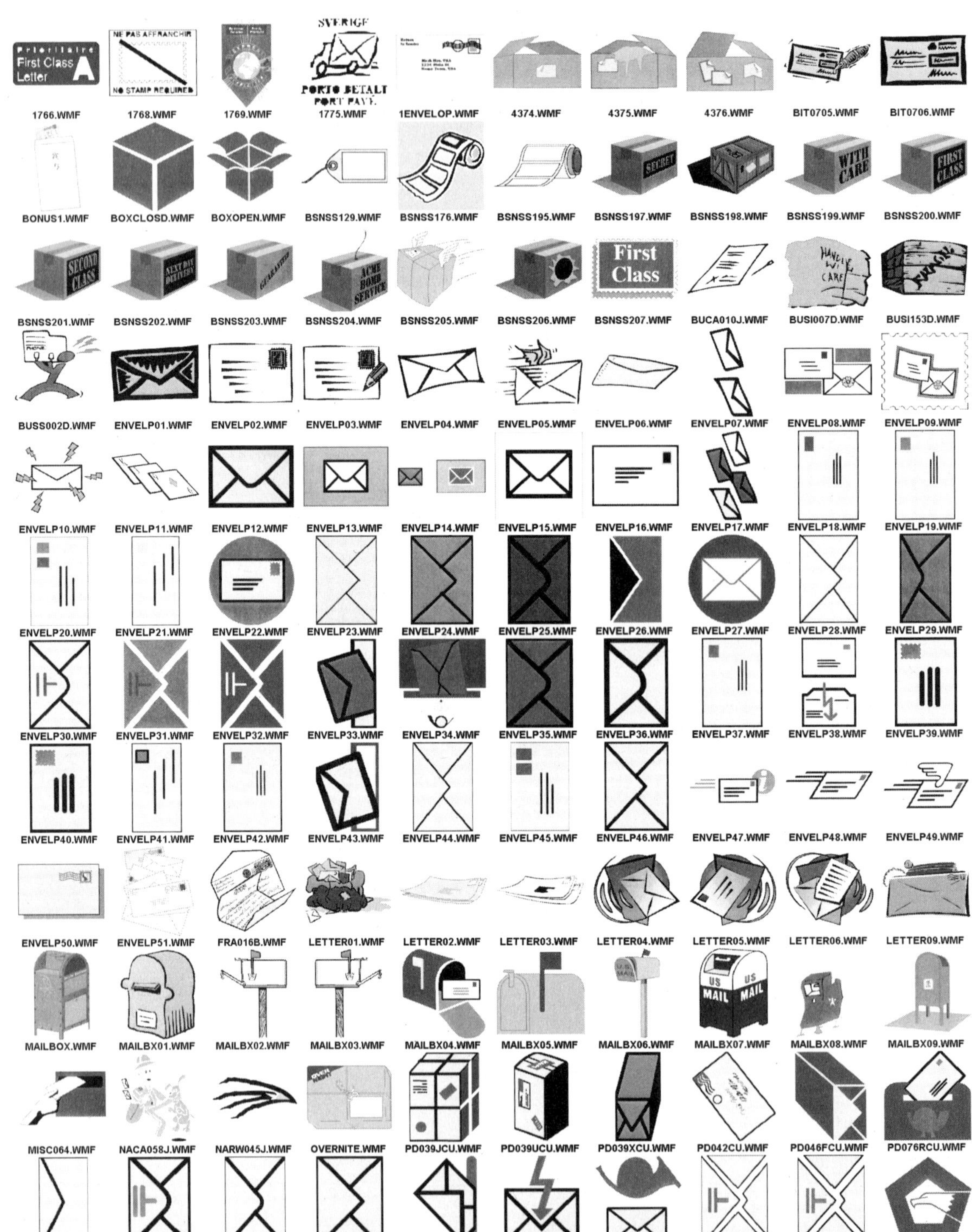
1766.WMF
1768.WMF
1769.WMF
1775.WMF
1ENVELOP.WMF
4374.WMF
4375.WMF
4376.WMF
BIT0705.WMF
BIT0706.WMF
BONUS1.WMF
BOXCLOSD.WMF
BOXOPEN.WMF
BSNSS129.WMF
BSNSS176.WMF
BSNSS195.WMF
BSNSS197.WMF
BSNSS198.WMF
BSNSS199.WMF
BSNSS200.WMF
BSNSS201.WMF
BSNSS202.WMF
BSNSS203.WMF
BSNSS204.WMF
BSNSS205.WMF
BSNSS206.WMF
BSNSS207.WMF
BUCA010J.WMF
BUSI007D.WMF
BUSI153D.WMF
BUSS002D.WMF
ENVELP01.WMF
ENVELP02.WMF
ENVELP03.WMF
ENVELP04.WMF
ENVELP05.WMF
ENVELP06.WMF
ENVELP07.WMF
ENVELP08.WMF
ENVELP09.WMF
ENVELP10.WMF
ENVELP11.WMF
ENVELP12.WMF
ENVELP13.WMF
ENVELP14.WMF
ENVELP15.WMF
ENVELP16.WMF
ENVELP17.WMF
ENVELP18.WMF
ENVELP19.WMF
ENVELP20.WMF
ENVELP21.WMF
ENVELP22.WMF
ENVELP23.WMF
ENVELP24.WMF
ENVELP25.WMF
ENVELP26.WMF
ENVELP27.WMF
ENVELP28.WMF
ENVELP29.WMF
ENVELP30.WMF
ENVELP31.WMF
ENVELP32.WMF
ENVELP33.WMF
ENVELP34.WMF
ENVELP35.WMF
ENVELP36.WMF
ENVELP37.WMF
ENVELP38.WMF
ENVELP39.WMF
ENVELP40.WMF
ENVELP41.WMF
ENVELP42.WMF
ENVELP43.WMF
ENVELP44.WMF
ENVELP45.WMF
ENVELP46.WMF
ENVELP47.WMF
ENVELP48.WMF
ENVELP49.WMF
ENVELP50.WMF
ENVELP51.WMF
FRA016B.WMF
LETTER01.WMF
LETTER02.WMF
LETTER03.WMF
LETTER04.WMF
LETTER05.WMF
LETTER06.WMF
LETTER09.WMF
MAILBOX.WMF
MAILBX01.WMF
MAILBX02.WMF
MAILBX03.WMF
MAILBX04.WMF
MAILBX05.WMF
MAILBX06.WMF
MAILBX07.WMF
MAILBX08.WMF
MAILBX09.WMF
MISC064.WMF
NACA058J.WMF
NARW045J.WMF
OVERNITE.WMF
PD039JCU.WMF
PD039UCU.WMF
PD039XCU.WMF
PD042CU.WMF
PD046FCU.WMF
PD076RCU.WMF
PD086ECU.WMF
PD090KCU.WMF
PD092DCU.WMF
PD093RCU.WMF
PD095XCU.WMF
PD096ACU.WMF
PD121WCU.WMF
PD123ICU.WMF
PD126FCU.WMF
PENTGON4.WMF

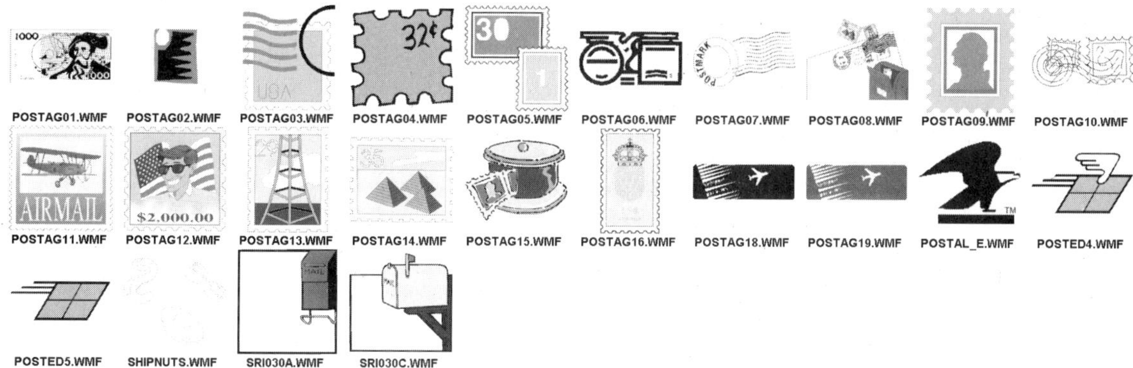

POSTAG01.WMF POSTAG02.WMF POSTAG03.WMF POSTAG04.WMF POSTAG05.WMF POSTAG06.WMF POSTAG07.WMF POSTAG08.WMF POSTAG09.WMF POSTAG10.WMF

POSTAG11.WMF POSTAG12.WMF POSTAG13.WMF POSTAG14.WMF POSTAG15.WMF POSTAG16.WMF POSTAG18.WMF POSTAG19.WMF POSTAL_E.WMF POSTED4.WMF

POSTED5.WMF SHIPNUTS.WMF SRI030A.WMF SRI030C.WMF

Technology & Communication (TECHCOMM) • Technology & Communication (TECHCOMM)

0121.WMF 0172.WMF 0693.WMF 0694.WMF 0695.WMF 0696.WMF 0697.WMF 2212.WMF 249.WMF 250.WMF

4443.WMF BIT0702.WMF BSNSS046.WMF BSNSS047.WMF BSNSS064.WMF BSNSS089.WMF BSNSS161.WMF COMM006.WMF COMM007.WMF COMM008.WMF

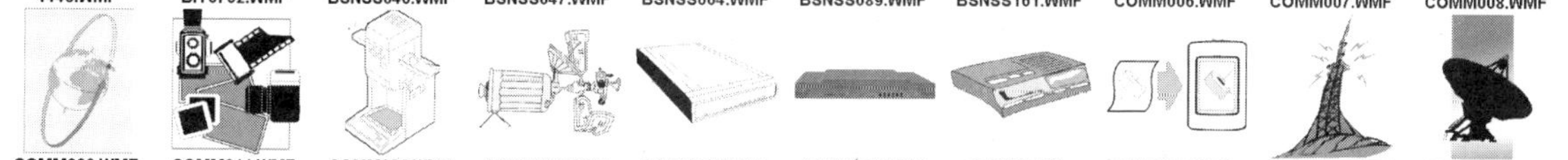

COMM009.WMF COMM011.WMF COMM026.WMF COMM032.WMF COMM037.WMF COMM038.WMF EQ08.WMF IMAGING.WMF INGC016D.WMF LDSCP037.WMF

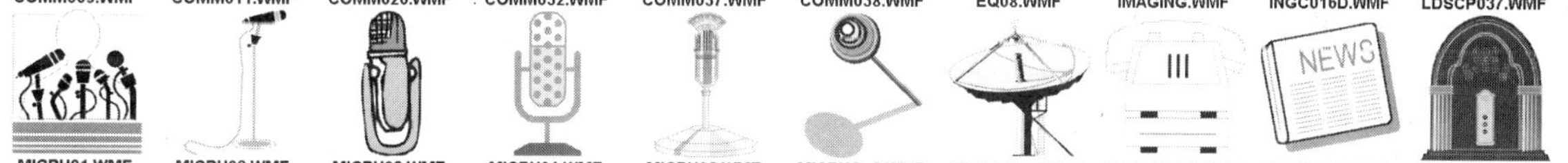

MICPH01.WMF MICPH02.WMF MICPH03.WMF MICPH04.WMF MICPH05.WMF MICPHO_2.WMF MICROWAV.WMF MODMPHON.WMF NEWSPPR.WMF OFRADIO.WMF

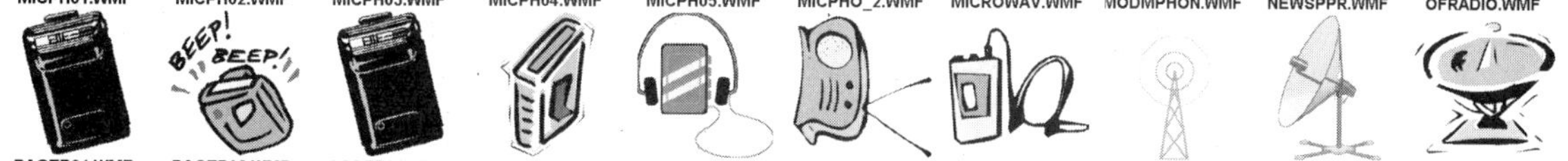

PAGER01.WMF PAGER02.WMF PAGER03.WMF PAGER04.WMF POR_RDIO.WMF RADIO01.WMF RADIO02.WMF RADIO_TW.WMF SATDISH.WMF SATDISH1.WMF

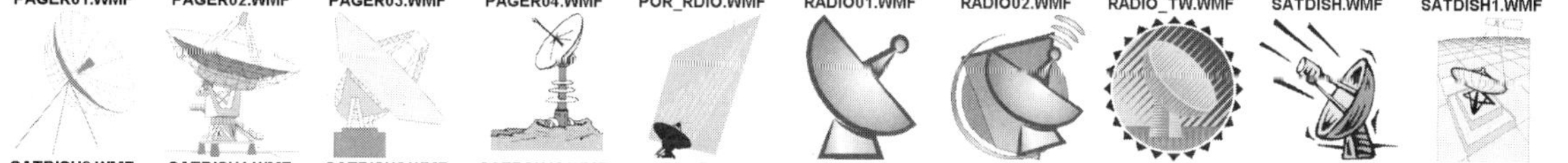

SATDISH3.WMF SATDISH4.WMF SATDISH5.WMF SATDSH12.WMF SATELIT1.WMF SATELIT2.WMF SATELIT3.WMF SATELIT4.WMF SATELIT5.WMF SATELIT6.WMF

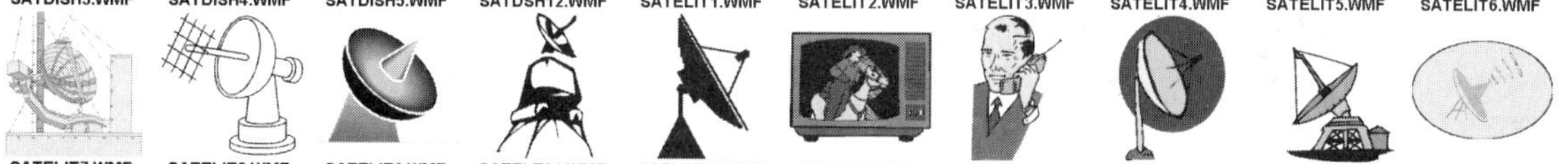

SATELIT7.WMF SATELIT8.WMF SATELIT9.WMF SATELT01.WMF SATLDISH.WMF SPA028A.WMF STGC002D.WMF STRW030J.WMF STSI018D.WMF STSI029D.WMF

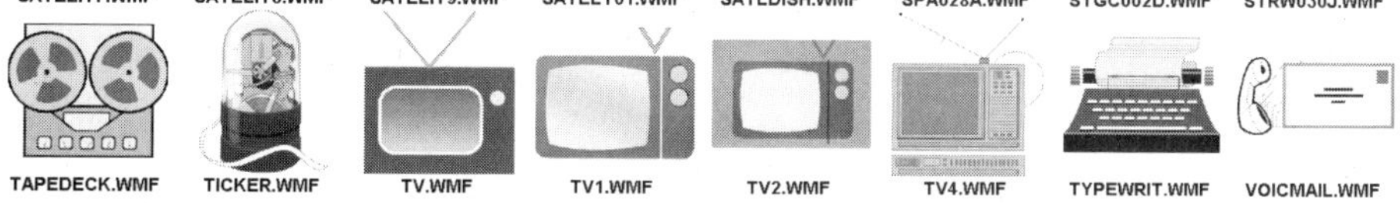

TAPEDECK.WMF TICKER.WMF TV.WMF TV1.WMF TV2.WMF TV4.WMF TYPEWRIT.WMF VOICMAIL.WMF

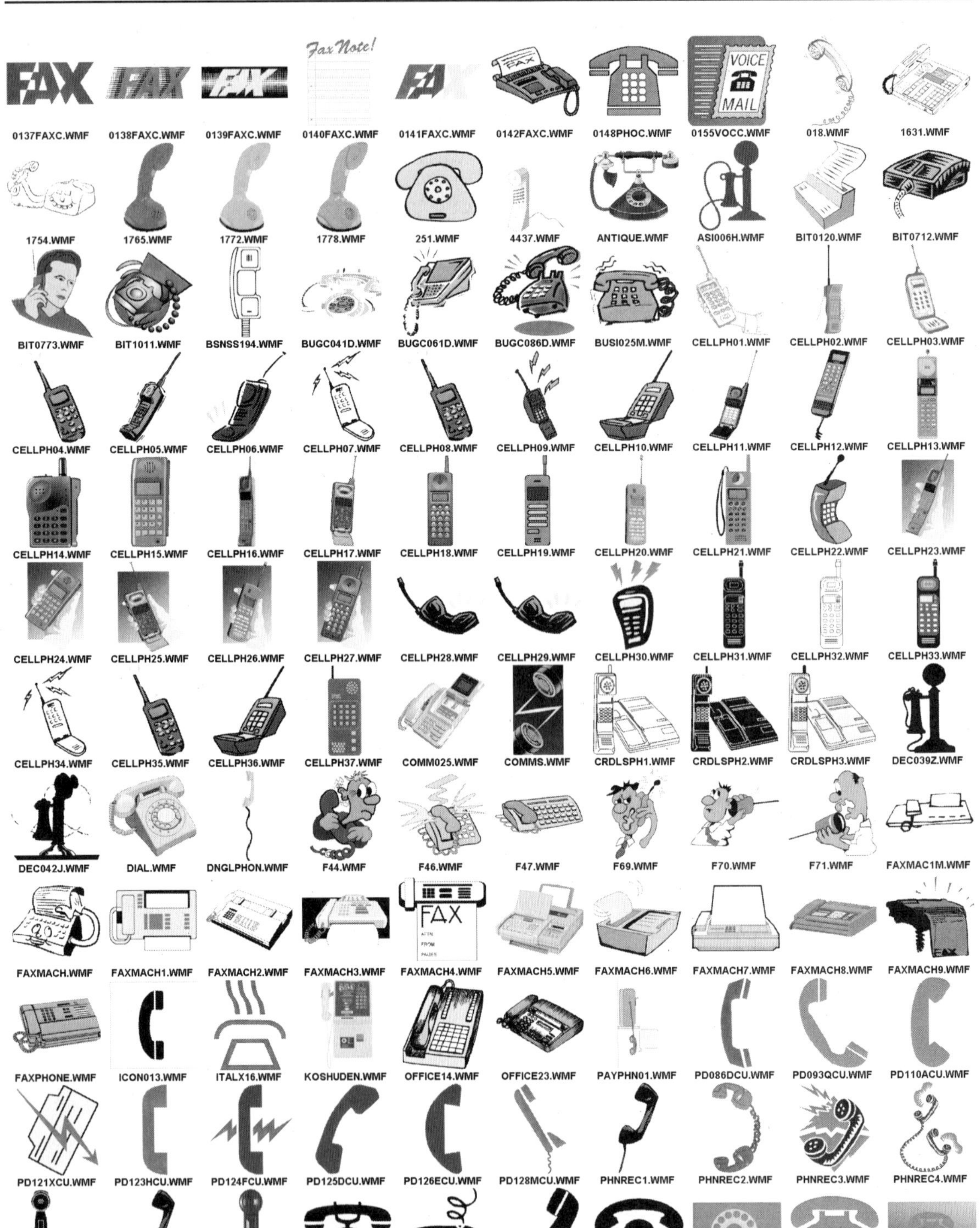
0137FAXC.WMF 0138FAXC.WMF 0139FAXC.WMF 0140FAXC.WMF 0141FAXC.WMF 0142FAXC.WMF 0148PHOC.WMF 0155VOCC.WMF 018.WMF 1631.WMF
1754.WMF 1765.WMF 1772.WMF 1778.WMF 251.WMF 4437.WMF ANTIQUE.WMF ASI006H.WMF BIT0120.WMF BIT0712.WMF
BIT0773.WMF BIT1011.WMF BSNSS194.WMF BUGC041D.WMF BUGC061D.WMF BUGC086D.WMF BUSI025M.WMF CELLPH01.WMF CELLPH02.WMF CELLPH03.WMF
CELLPH04.WMF CELLPH05.WMF CELLPH06.WMF CELLPH07.WMF CELLPH08.WMF CELLPH09.WMF CELLPH10.WMF CELLPH11.WMF CELLPH12.WMF CELLPH13.WMF
CELLPH14.WMF CELLPH15.WMF CELLPH16.WMF CELLPH17.WMF CELLPH18.WMF CELLPH19.WMF CELLPH20.WMF CELLPH21.WMF CELLPH22.WMF CELLPH23.WMF
CELLPH24.WMF CELLPH25.WMF CELLPH26.WMF CELLPH27.WMF CELLPH28.WMF CELLPH29.WMF CELLPH30.WMF CELLPH31.WMF CELLPH32.WMF CELLPH33.WMF
CELLPH34.WMF CELLPH35.WMF CELLPH36.WMF CELLPH37.WMF COMM025.WMF COMMS.WMF CRDLSPH1.WMF CRDLSPH2.WMF CRDLSPH3.WMF DEC039Z.WMF
DEC042J.WMF DIAL.WMF DNGLPHON.WMF F44.WMF F46.WMF F47.WMF F69.WMF F70.WMF F71.WMF FAXMAC1M.WMF
FAXMACH.WMF FAXMACH1.WMF FAXMACH2.WMF FAXMACH3.WMF FAXMACH4.WMF FAXMACH5.WMF FAXMACH6.WMF FAXMACH7.WMF FAXMACH8.WMF FAXMACH9.WMF
FAXPHONE.WMF ICON013.WMF ITALX16.WMF KOSHUDEN.WMF OFFICE14.WMF OFFICE23.WMF PAYPHN01.WMF PD086DCU.WMF PD093QCU.WMF PD110ACU.WMF
PD121XCU.WMF PD123HCU.WMF PD124FCU.WMF PD125DCU.WMF PD126ECU.WMF PD128MCU.WMF PHNREC1.WMF PHNREC2.WMF PHNREC3.WMF PHNREC4.WMF
PHNREC5.WMF PHNREC6.WMF PHNREC7.WMF PHNSGN01.WMF PHNSGN02.WMF PHNSGN03.WMF PHNSGN04.WMF PHNSGN49.WMF PHONE1.WMF PHONE2.WMF

WOLDWIDE.WMF

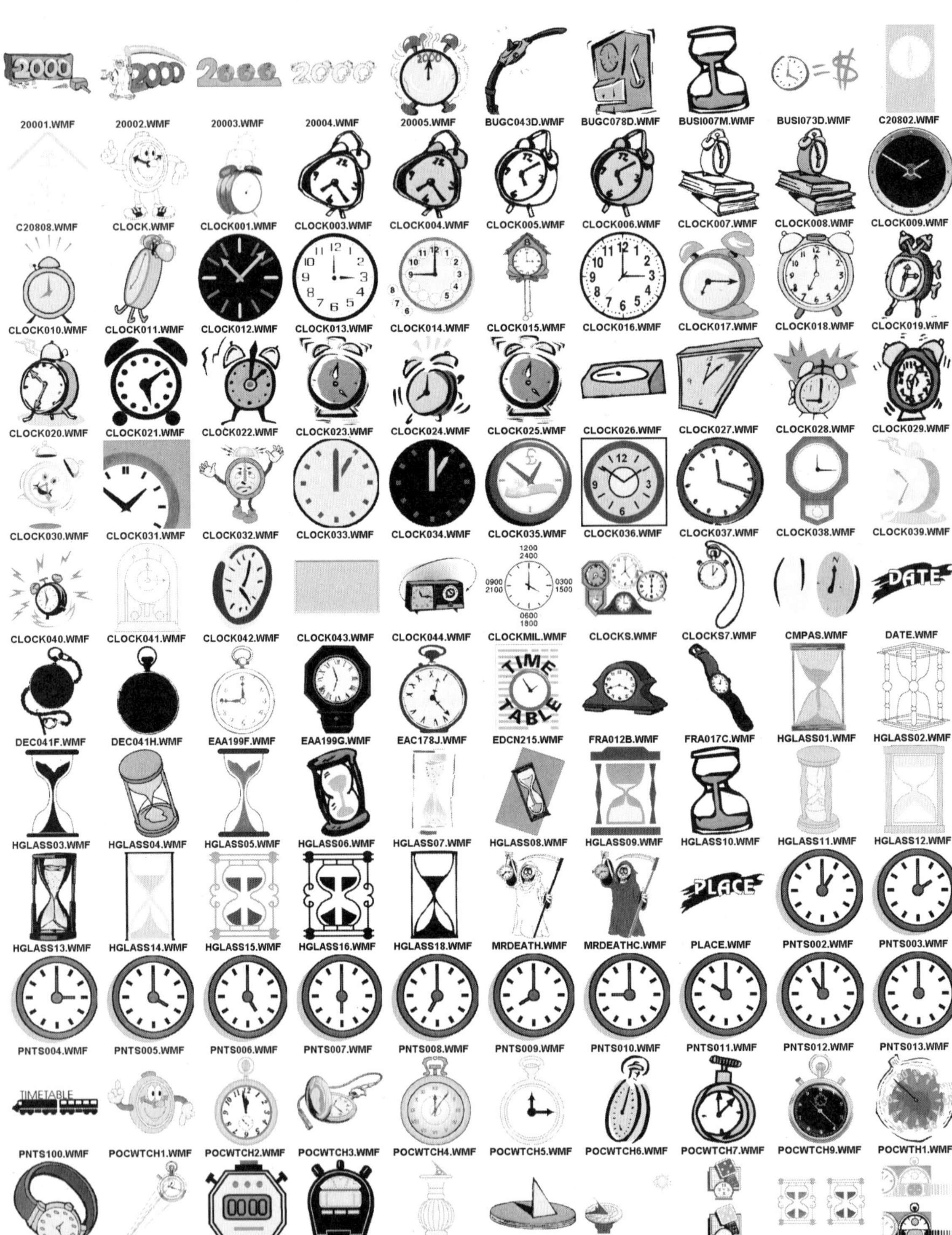
20001.WMF
20002.WMF
20003.WMF
20004.WMF
20005.WMF
BUGC043D.WMF
BUGC078D.WMF
BUSI007M.WMF
BUSI073D.WMF
C20802.WMF
C20808.WMF
CLOCK.WMF
CLOCK001.WMF
CLOCK003.WMF
CLOCK004.WMF
CLOCK005.WMF
CLOCK006.WMF
CLOCK007.WMF
CLOCK008.WMF
CLOCK009.WMF
CLOCK010.WMF
CLOCK011.WMF
CLOCK012.WMF
CLOCK013.WMF
CLOCK014.WMF
CLOCK015.WMF
CLOCK016.WMF
CLOCK017.WMF
CLOCK018.WMF
CLOCK019.WMF
CLOCK020.WMF
CLOCK021.WMF
CLOCK022.WMF
CLOCK023.WMF
CLOCK024.WMF
CLOCK025.WMF
CLOCK026.WMF
CLOCK027.WMF
CLOCK028.WMF
CLOCK029.WMF
CLOCK030.WMF
CLOCK031.WMF
CLOCK032.WMF
CLOCK033.WMF
CLOCK034.WMF
CLOCK035.WMF
CLOCK036.WMF
CLOCK037.WMF
CLOCK038.WMF
CLOCK039.WMF
CLOCK040.WMF
CLOCK041.WMF
CLOCK042.WMF
CLOCK043.WMF
CLOCK044.WMF
CLOCKMIL.WMF
CLOCKS.WMF
CLOCKS7.WMF
CMPAS.WMF
DATE.WMF
DEC041F.WMF
DEC041H.WMF
EAA199F.WMF
EAA199G.WMF
EAC178J.WMF
EDCN215.WMF
FRA012B.WMF
FRA017C.WMF
HGLASS01.WMF
HGLASS02.WMF
HGLASS03.WMF
HGLASS04.WMF
HGLASS05.WMF
HGLASS06.WMF
HGLASS07.WMF
HGLASS08.WMF
HGLASS09.WMF
HGLASS10.WMF
HGLASS11.WMF
HGLASS12.WMF
HGLASS13.WMF
HGLASS14.WMF
HGLASS15.WMF
HGLASS16.WMF
HGLASS18.WMF
MRDEATH.WMF
MRDEATHC.WMF
PLACE.WMF
PNTS002.WMF
PNTS003.WMF
PNTS004.WMF
PNTS005.WMF
PNTS006.WMF
PNTS007.WMF
PNTS008.WMF
PNTS009.WMF
PNTS010.WMF
PNTS011.WMF
PNTS012.WMF
PNTS013.WMF
PNTS100.WMF
POCWTCH1.WMF
POCWTCH2.WMF
POCWTCH3.WMF
POCWTCH4.WMF
POCWTCH5.WMF
POCWTCH6.WMF
POCWTCH7.WMF
POCWTCH9.WMF
POCWTH1.WMF
SPA023B.WMF
STOPWATC.WMF
STOPWTCH.WMF
STPWTCH.WMF
SUNDIAL.WMF
SUNDIAL1.WMF
SUNDIAL5.WMF
SYMBL14.WMF
SYMBL15.WMF
SYMBOL50.WMF

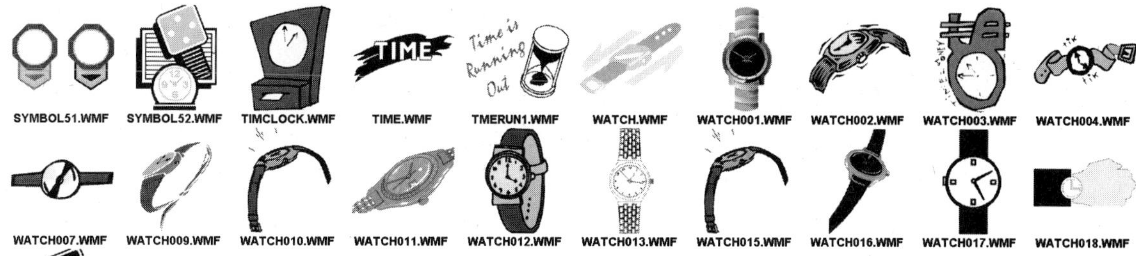

SYMBOL51.WMF SYMBOL52.WMF TIMCLOCK.WMF TIME.WMF TMERUN1.WMF WATCH.WMF WATCH001.WMF WATCH002.WMF WATCH003.WMF WATCH004.WMF

WATCH007.WMF WATCH009.WMF WATCH010.WMF WATCH011.WMF WATCH012.WMF WATCH013.WMF WATCH015.WMF WATCH016.WMF WATCH017.WMF WATCH018.WMF

WATCHES.WMF

10THDAY.WMF
1109COMC.WMF
11THDAY.WMF
12THDAY.WMF
1STDAYHD.WMF
2NDDAYHD.WMF
ACTION.WMF
AIRMAIL.WMF
AMENDM.WMF
AND.WMF
ASAP.WMF
ATTENTIO.WMF
BACK085.WMF
BACK095.WMF
BACK114.WMF
BACK120.WMF
BACK145.WMF
BACK157.WMF
BACK270.WMF
BENIFITS.WMF
BORD059.WMF
BULDFUND.WMF
BUSHEL.WMF
BUT3A.WMF
BUT3B.WMF
BUT3C.WMF
BUT3D.WMF
BUT3E.WMF
BUT3F.WMF
BUT3G.WMF
BUT3H.WMF
CAA0012.WMF
CAA0013.WMF
CALENDBL.WMF
CALENDSH.WMF
CELEBRAT.WMF
CHALLNGE.WMF
CLASSFID.WMF
COFTIMEC.WMF
CONCLUDE.WMF
CONFDNT1.WMF
CONFIDEN.WMF
CONFIDNT.WMF
CONGRATS.WMF
CUSTOMER.WMF
CUTOUT1.WMF
CUTOUT1C.WMF
DBELATE.WMF
DESIGN4.WMF
DODONT.WMF
E48.WMF
ENSS038D.WMF
EVENINGC.WMF
FACTS.WMF
FACTS_.WMF
FACTS_C.WMF
FIRST_CL.WMF
FREE_HOR.WMF
FSTRATED.WMF
GRAD.WMF
GRDOPEN.WMF
HEARD11.WMF
HELP.WMF
HELP_1.WMF
HEY.WMF
HEY1.WMF
HIGHLITE.WMF
HOMES.WMF
IMPOTANT.WMF
INSTRUCT.WMF
INVOLVED.WMF
ISSUE.WMF
JOINUS.WMF
JOY.WMF
KICK_OFF.WMF
LIBERTY.WMF
MAKEPLN.WMF
MARKDTE.WMF
MARKDTEC.WMF
MENONLY.WMF
MERCHNDS.WMF
MICRABLE.WMF
MISC_25.WMF
MONEYBAG.WMF
NAILTHIS.WMF
NCUA.WMF
NOCHOL1.WMF
NOCHOL2.WMF
OBJECTVE.WMF
OF.WMF
ORGANIZE.WMF
PD096KCU.WMF
PHOTOMAT.WMF
PINUP1.WMF
PINUP1C.WMF
PLAN.WMF
PLSPHON_.WMF
PLSPHONE.WMF
PNTS033.WMF
PNTS039.WMF
PNTS040.WMF
PNTS113.WMF
PNTS114.WMF
PNTS115.WMF
PNTS127.WMF
POLL.WMF
PROJECT.WMF
PROPOSE.WMF
QUALITY.WMF
QUESANSW.WMF
R21622.WMF
RAD.WMF
RADC.WMF
REASONS.WMF
RESPONSE.WMF
RESULTS.WMF
ROSHASH.WMF
RUSH.WMF
SALE_EXC.WMF
SALE_FIL.WMF

Titles • General

Titles • Miscellaneous (MISC)

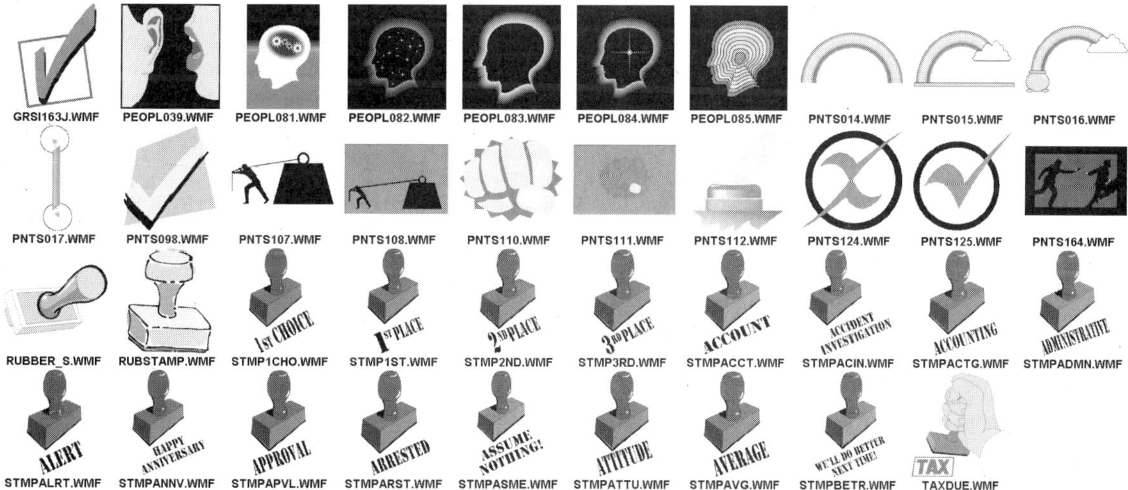

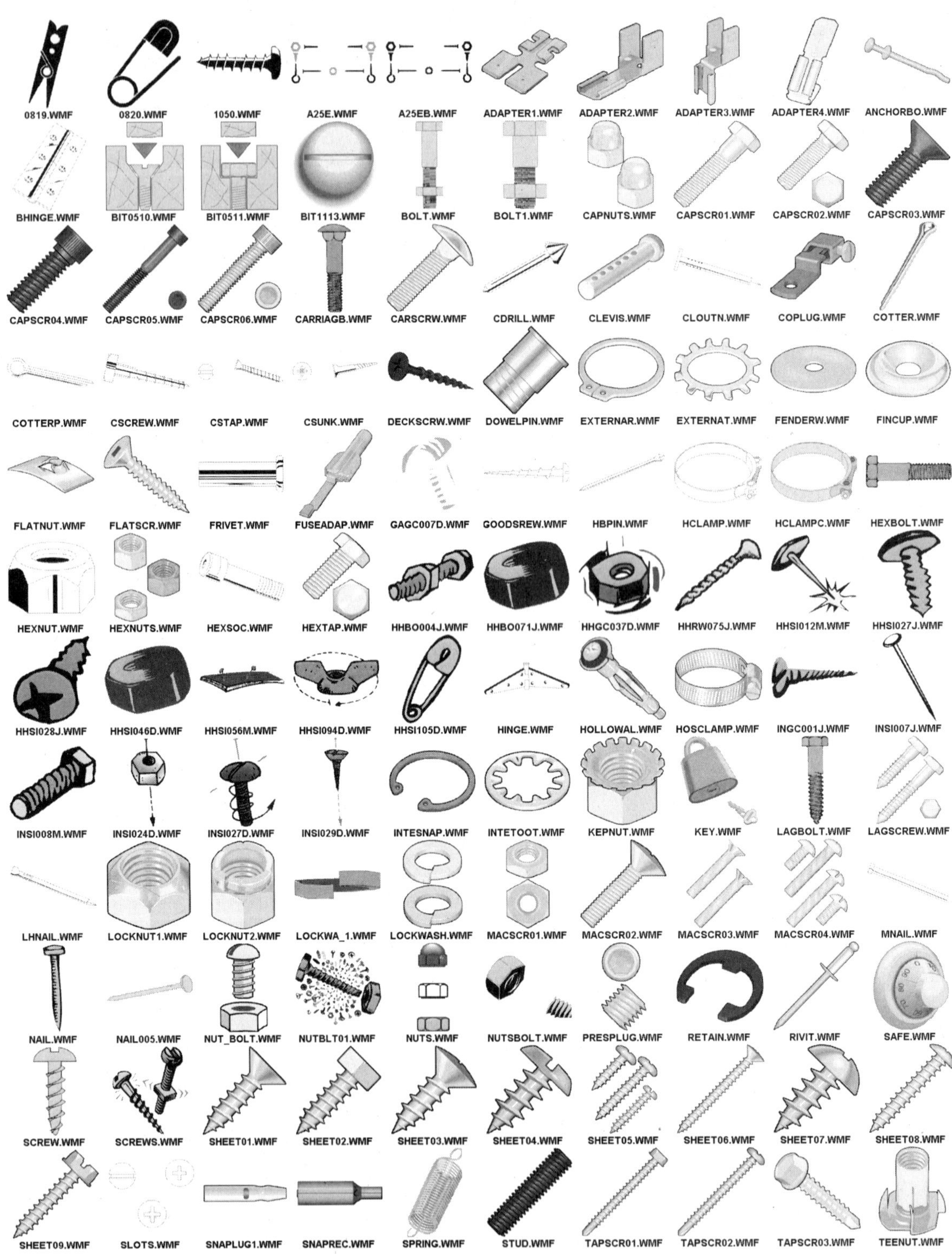
0819.WMF
0820.WMF
1050.WMF
A25E.WMF
A25EB.WMF
ADAPTER1.WMF
ADAPTER2.WMF
ADAPTER3.WMF
ADAPTER4.WMF
ANCHORBO.WMF
BHINGE.WMF
BIT0510.WMF
BIT0511.WMF
BIT1113.WMF
BOLT.WMF
BOLT1.WMF
CAPNUTS.WMF
CAPSCR01.WMF
CAPSCR02.WMF
CAPSCR03.WMF
CAPSCR04.WMF
CAPSCR05.WMF
CAPSCR06.WMF
CARRIAGB.WMF
CARSCRW.WMF
CDRILL.WMF
CLEVIS.WMF
CLOUTN.WMF
COPLUG.WMF
COTTER.WMF
COTTERP.WMF
CSCREW.WMF
CSTAP.WMF
CSUNK.WMF
DECKSCRW.WMF
DOWELPIN.WMF
EXTERNAR.WMF
EXTERNAT.WMF
FENDERW.WMF
FINCUP.WMF
FLATNUT.WMF
FLATSCR.WMF
FRIVET.WMF
FUSEADAP.WMF
GAGC007D.WMF
GOODSREW.WMF
HBPIN.WMF
HCLAMP.WMF
HCLAMPC.WMF
HEXBOLT.WMF
HEXNUT.WMF
HEXNUTS.WMF
HEXSOC.WMF
HEXTAP.WMF
HHBO004J.WMF
HHBO071J.WMF
HHGC037D.WMF
HHRW075J.WMF
HHSI012M.WMF
HHSI027J.WMF
HHSI028J.WMF
HHSI046D.WMF
HHSI056M.WMF
HHSI094D.WMF
HHSI105D.WMF
HINGE.WMF
HOLLOWAL.WMF
HOSCLAMP.WMF
INGC001J.WMF
INSI007J.WMF
INSI008M.WMF
INSI024D.WMF
INSI027D.WMF
INSI029D.WMF
INTESNAP.WMF
INTETOOT.WMF
KEPNUT.WMF
KEY.WMF
LAGBOLT.WMF
LAGSCREW.WMF
LHNAIL.WMF
LOCKNUT1.WMF
LOCKNUT2.WMF
LOCKWA_1.WMF
LOCKWASH.WMF
MACSCR01.WMF
MACSCR02.WMF
MACSCR03.WMF
MACSCR04.WMF
MNAIL.WMF
NAIL.WMF
NAIL005.WMF
NUT_BOLT.WMF
NUTBLT01.WMF
NUTS.WMF
NUTSBOLT.WMF
PRESPLUG.WMF
RETAIN.WMF
RIVIT.WMF
SAFE.WMF
SCREW.WMF
SCREWS.WMF
SHEET01.WMF
SHEET02.WMF
SHEET03.WMF
SHEET04.WMF
SHEET05.WMF
SHEET06.WMF
SHEET07.WMF
SHEET08.WMF
SHEET09.WMF
SLOTS.WMF
SNAPLUG1.WMF
SNAPREC.WMF
SPRING.WMF
STUD.WMF
TAPSCR01.WMF
TAPSCR02.WMF
TAPSCR03.WMF
TEENUT.WMF

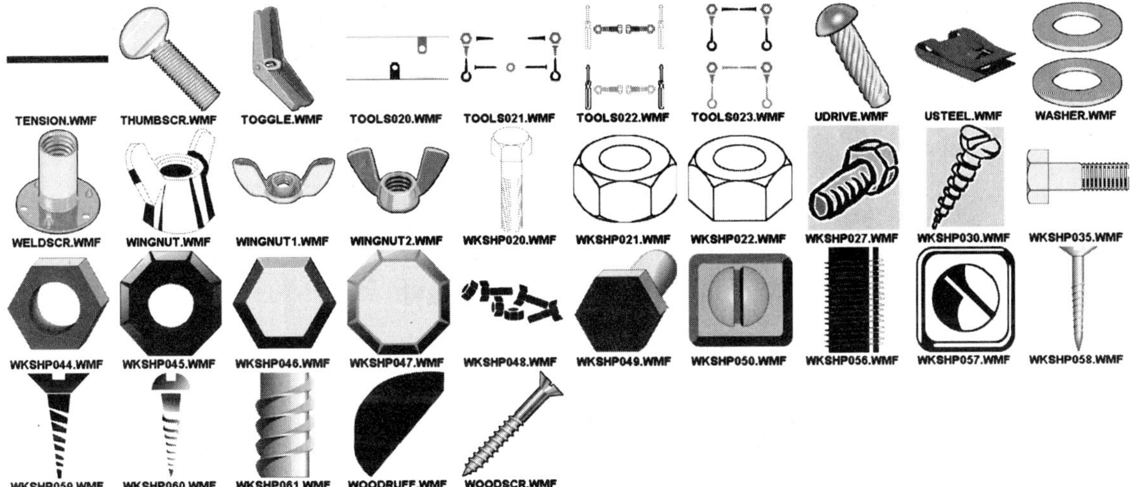
TENSION.WMF
THUMBSCR.WMF
TOGGLE.WMF
TOOLS020.WMF
TOOLS021.WMF
TOOLS022.WMF
TOOLS023.WMF
UDRIVE.WMF
USTEEL.WMF
WASHER.WMF
WELDSCR.WMF
WINGNUT.WMF
WINGNUT1.WMF
WINGNUT2.WMF
WKSHP020.WMF
WKSHP021.WMF
WKSHP022.WMF
WKSHP027.WMF
WKSHP030.WMF
WKSHP035.WMF
WKSHP044.WMF
WKSHP045.WMF
WKSHP046.WMF
WKSHP047.WMF
WKSHP048.WMF
WKSHP049.WMF
WKSHP050.WMF
WKSHP056.WMF
WKSHP057.WMF
WKSHP058.WMF
WKSHP059.WMF
WKSHP060.WMF
WKSHP061.WMF
WOODRUFF.WMF
WOODSCR.WMF

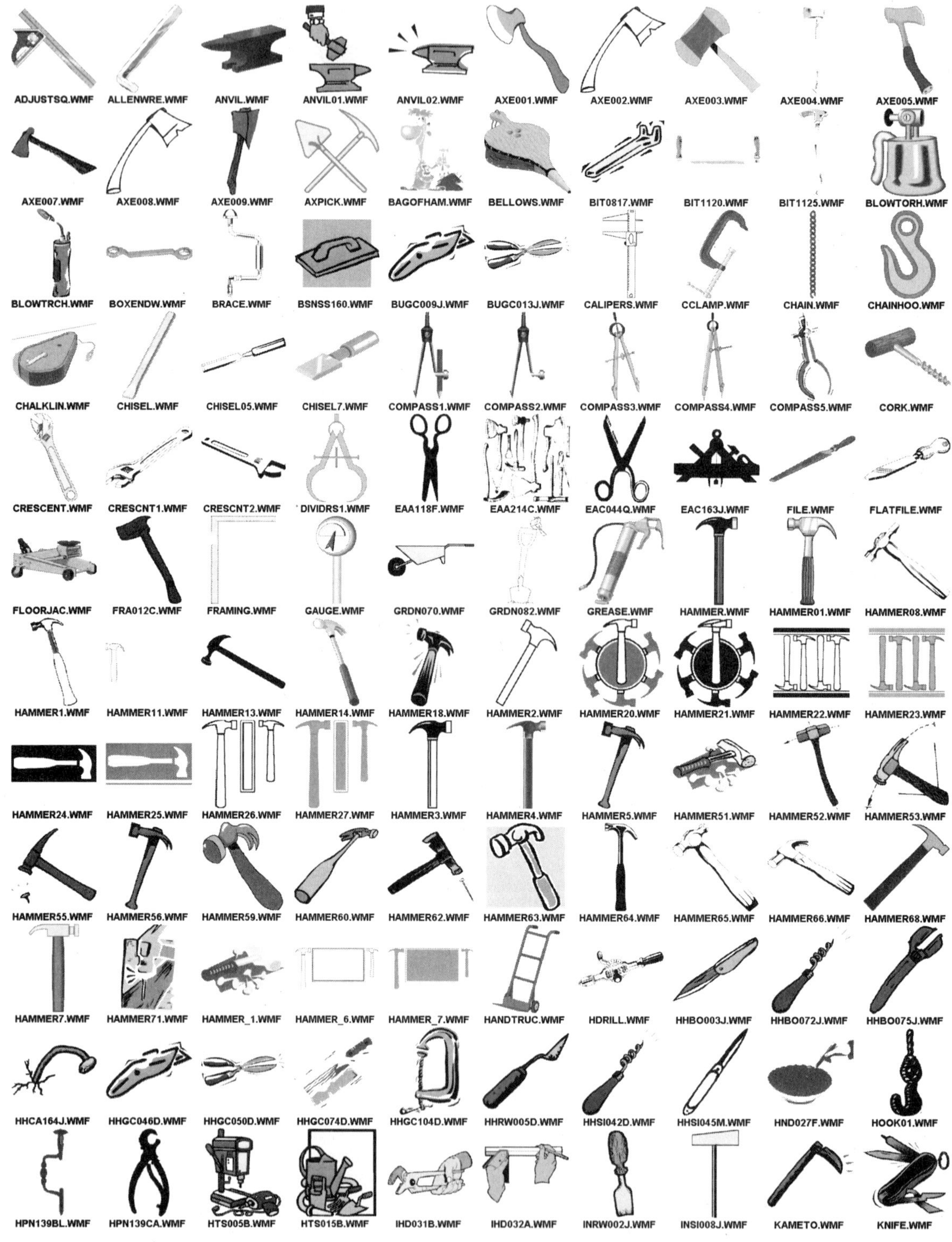
ADJUSTSQ.WMF
ALLENWRE.WMF
ANVIL.WMF
ANVIL01.WMF
ANVIL02.WMF
AXE001.WMF
AXE002.WMF
AXE003.WMF
AXE004.WMF
AXE005.WMF
AXE007.WMF
AXE008.WMF
AXE009.WMF
AXPICK.WMF
BAGOFHAM.WMF
BELLOWS.WMF
BIT0817.WMF
BIT1120.WMF
BIT1125.WMF
BLOWTORH.WMF
BLOWTRCH.WMF
BOXENDW.WMF
BRACE.WMF
BSNSS160.WMF
BUGC009J.WMF
BUGC013J.WMF
CALIPERS.WMF
CCLAMP.WMF
CHAIN.WMF
CHAINHOO.WMF
CHALKLIN.WMF
CHISEL.WMF
CHISEL05.WMF
CHISEL7.WMF
COMPASS1.WMF
COMPASS2.WMF
COMPASS3.WMF
COMPASS4.WMF
COMPASS5.WMF
CORK.WMF
CRESCENT.WMF
CRESCNT1.WMF
CRESCNT2.WMF
DIVIDRS1.WMF
EAA118F.WMF
EAA214C.WMF
EAC044Q.WMF
EAC163J.WMF
FILE.WMF
FLATFILE.WMF
FLOORJAC.WMF
FRA012C.WMF
FRAMING.WMF
GAUGE.WMF
GRDN070.WMF
GRDN082.WMF
GREASE.WMF
HAMMER.WMF
HAMMER01.WMF
HAMMER08.WMF
HAMMER1.WMF
HAMMER11.WMF
HAMMER13.WMF
HAMMER14.WMF
HAMMER18.WMF
HAMMER2.WMF
HAMMER20.WMF
HAMMER21.WMF
HAMMER22.WMF
HAMMER23.WMF
HAMMER24.WMF
HAMMER25.WMF
HAMMER26.WMF
HAMMER27.WMF
HAMMER3.WMF
HAMMER4.WMF
HAMMER5.WMF
HAMMER51.WMF
HAMMER52.WMF
HAMMER53.WMF
HAMMER55.WMF
HAMMER56.WMF
HAMMER59.WMF
HAMMER60.WMF
HAMMER62.WMF
HAMMER63.WMF
HAMMER64.WMF
HAMMER65.WMF
HAMMER66.WMF
HAMMER68.WMF
HAMMER7.WMF
HAMMER71.WMF
HAMMER_1.WMF
HAMMER_6.WMF
HAMMER_7.WMF
HANDTRUC.WMF
HDRILL.WMF
HHBO003J.WMF
HHBO072J.WMF
HHBO075J.WMF
HHCA164J.WMF
HHGC046D.WMF
HHGC050D.WMF
HHGC074D.WMF
HHGC104D.WMF
HHRW005D.WMF
HHSI042D.WMF
HHSI045M.WMF
HND027F.WMF
HOOK01.WMF
HPN139BL.WMF
HPN139CA.WMF
HTS005B.WMF
HTS015B.WMF
IHD031B.WMF
IHD032A.WMF
INRW002J.WMF
INSI008J.WMF
KAMETO.WMF
KNIFE.WMF

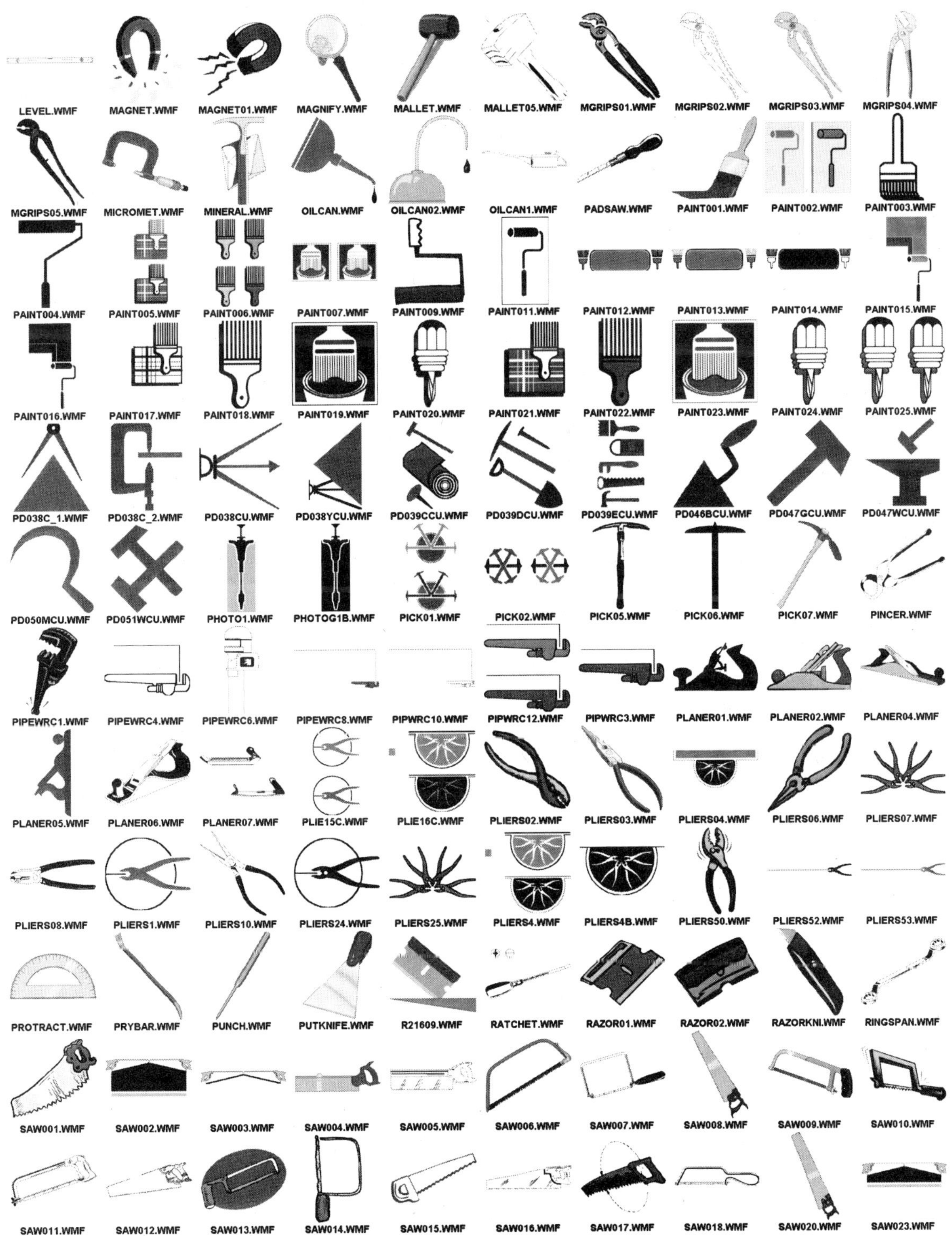
LEVEL.WMF
MAGNET.WMF
MAGNET01.WMF
MAGNIFY.WMF
MALLET.WMF
MALLET05.WMF
MGRIPS01.WMF
MGRIPS02.WMF
MGRIPS03.WMF
MGRIPS04.WMF
MGRIPS05.WMF
MICROMET.WMF
MINERAL.WMF
OILCAN.WMF
OILCAN02.WMF
OILCAN1.WMF
PADSAW.WMF
PAINT001.WMF
PAINT002.WMF
PAINT003.WMF
PAINT004.WMF
PAINT005.WMF
PAINT006.WMF
PAINT007.WMF
PAINT009.WMF
PAINT011.WMF
PAINT012.WMF
PAINT013.WMF
PAINT014.WMF
PAINT015.WMF
PAINT016.WMF
PAINT017.WMF
PAINT018.WMF
PAINT019.WMF
PAINT020.WMF
PAINT021.WMF
PAINT022.WMF
PAINT023.WMF
PAINT024.WMF
PAINT025.WMF
PD038C_1.WMF
PD038C_2.WMF
PD038CU.WMF
PD038YCU.WMF
PD039CCU.WMF
PD039DCU.WMF
PD039ECU.WMF
PD046BCU.WMF
PD047GCU.WMF
PD047WCU.WMF
PD050MCU.WMF
PD051WCU.WMF
PHOTO1.WMF
PHOTOG1B.WMF
PICK01.WMF
PICK02.WMF
PICK05.WMF
PICK06.WMF
PICK07.WMF
PINCER.WMF
PIPEWRC1.WMF
PIPEWRC4.WMF
PIPEWRC6.WMF
PIPEWRC8.WMF
PIPWRC10.WMF
PIPWRC12.WMF
PIPWRC3.WMF
PLANER01.WMF
PLANER02.WMF
PLANER04.WMF
PLANER05.WMF
PLANER06.WMF
PLANER07.WMF
PLIE15C.WMF
PLIE16C.WMF
PLIERS02.WMF
PLIERS03.WMF
PLIERS04.WMF
PLIERS06.WMF
PLIERS07.WMF
PLIERS08.WMF
PLIERS1.WMF
PLIERS10.WMF
PLIERS24.WMF
PLIERS25.WMF
PLIERS4.WMF
PLIERS4B.WMF
PLIERS50.WMF
PLIERS52.WMF
PLIERS53.WMF
PROTRACT.WMF
PRYBAR.WMF
PUNCH.WMF
PUTKNIFE.WMF
R21609.WMF
RATCHET.WMF
RAZOR01.WMF
RAZOR02.WMF
RAZORKNI.WMF
RINGSPAN.WMF
SAW001.WMF
SAW002.WMF
SAW003.WMF
SAW004.WMF
SAW005.WMF
SAW006.WMF
SAW007.WMF
SAW008.WMF
SAW009.WMF
SAW010.WMF
SAW011.WMF
SAW012.WMF
SAW013.WMF
SAW014.WMF
SAW015.WMF
SAW016.WMF
SAW017.WMF
SAW018.WMF
SAW020.WMF
SAW023.WMF

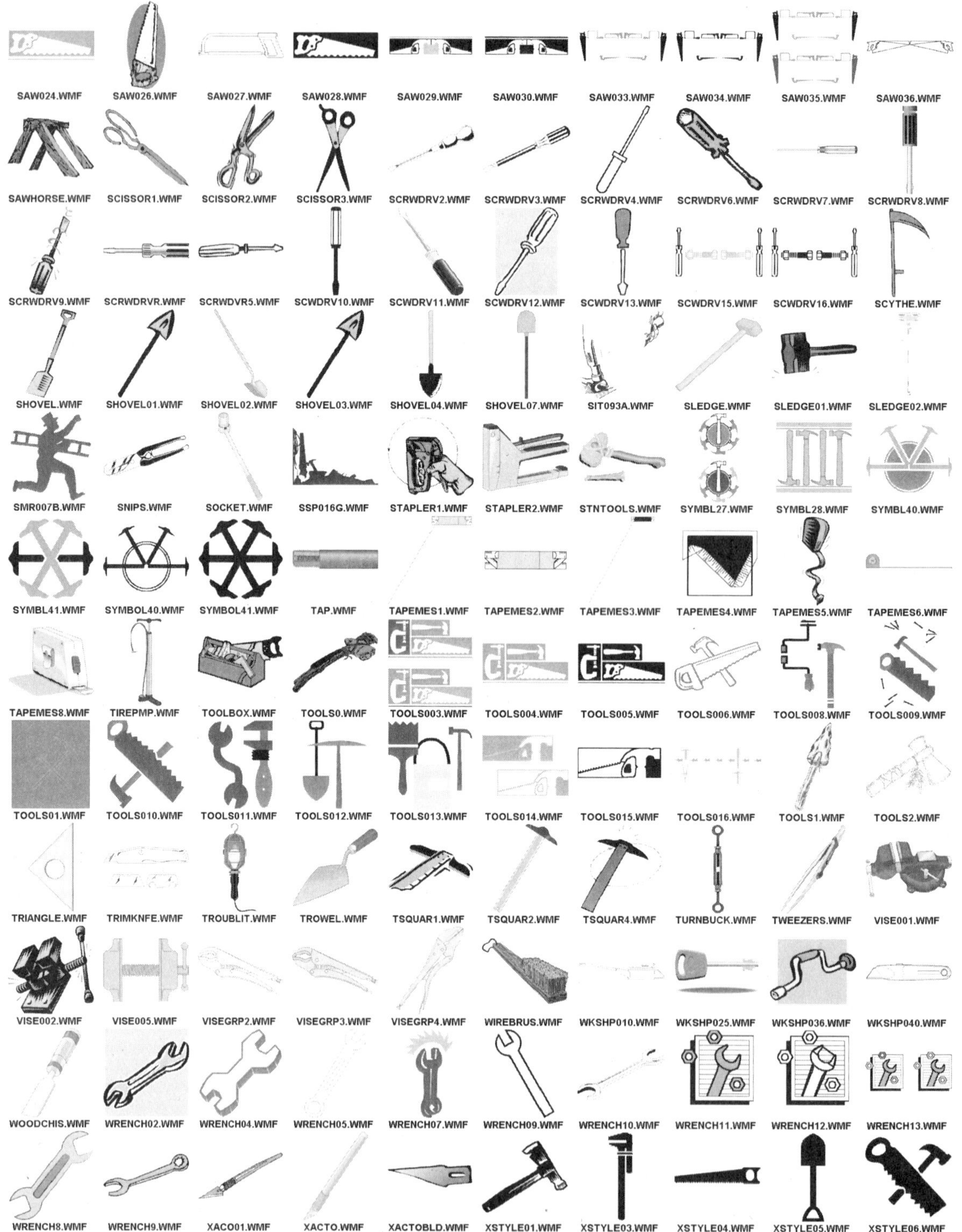
SAW024.WMF SAW026.WMF SAW027.WMF SAW028.WMF SAW029.WMF SAW030.WMF SAW033.WMF SAW034.WMF SAW035.WMF SAW036.WMF
SAWHORSE.WMF SCISSOR1.WMF SCISSOR2.WMF SCISSOR3.WMF SCRWDRV2.WMF SCRWDRV3.WMF SCRWDRV4.WMF SCRWDRV6.WMF SCRWDRV7.WMF SCRWDRV8.WMF
SCRWDRV9.WMF SCRWDRVR.WMF SCRWDVR5.WMF SCWDRV10.WMF SCWDRV11.WMF SCWDRV12.WMF SCWDRV13.WMF SCWDRV15.WMF SCWDRV16.WMF SCYTHE.WMF
SHOVEL.WMF SHOVEL01.WMF SHOVEL02.WMF SHOVEL03.WMF SHOVEL04.WMF SHOVEL07.WMF SIT093A.WMF SLEDGE.WMF SLEDGE01.WMF SLEDGE02.WMF
SMR007B.WMF SNIPS.WMF SOCKET.WMF SSP016G.WMF STAPLER1.WMF STAPLER2.WMF STNTOOLS.WMF SYMBL27.WMF SYMBL28.WMF SYMBL40.WMF
SYMBL41.WMF SYMBOL40.WMF SYMBOL41.WMF TAP.WMF TAPEMES1.WMF TAPEMES2.WMF TAPEMES3.WMF TAPEMES4.WMF TAPEMES5.WMF TAPEMES6.WMF
TAPEMES8.WMF TIREPMP.WMF TOOLBOX.WMF TOOLS0.WMF TOOLS003.WMF TOOLS004.WMF TOOLS005.WMF TOOLS006.WMF TOOLS008.WMF TOOLS009.WMF
TOOLS01.WMF TOOLS010.WMF TOOLS011.WMF TOOLS012.WMF TOOLS013.WMF TOOLS014.WMF TOOLS015.WMF TOOLS016.WMF TOOLS1.WMF TOOLS2.WMF
TRIANGLE.WMF TRIMKNFE.WMF TROUBLIT.WMF TROWEL.WMF TSQUAR1.WMF TSQUAR2.WMF TSQUAR4.WMF TURNBUCK.WMF TWEEZERS.WMF VISE001.WMF
VISE002.WMF VISE005.WMF VISEGRP2.WMF VISEGRP3.WMF VISEGRP4.WMF WIREBRUS.WMF WKSHP010.WMF WKSHP025.WMF WKSHP036.WMF WKSHP040.WMF
WOODCHIS.WMF WRENCH02.WMF WRENCH04.WMF WRENCH05.WMF WRENCH07.WMF WRENCH09.WMF WRENCH10.WMF WRENCH11.WMF WRENCH12.WMF WRENCH13.WMF
WRENCH8.WMF WRENCH9.WMF XACO01.WMF XACTO.WMF XACTOBLD.WMF XSTYLE01.WMF XSTYLE03.WMF XSTYLE04.WMF XSTYLE05.WMF XSTYLE06.WMF

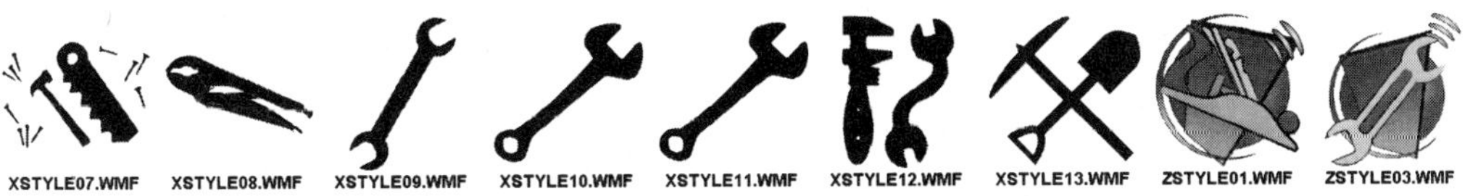

XSTYLE07.WMF XSTYLE08.WMF XSTYLE09.WMF XSTYLE10.WMF XSTYLE11.WMF XSTYLE12.WMF XSTYLE13.WMF ZSTYLE01.WMF ZSTYLE03.WMF

Tools & Hardware (TOOLS) • Other

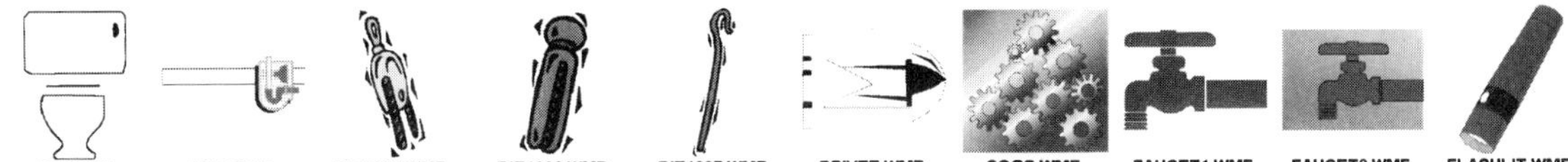

0864.WMF A41C.WMF BIT0841.WMF BIT1006.WMF BIT1007.WMF BRIVET.WMF COGS.WMF FAUCET1.WMF FAUCET2.WMF FLASHLIT.WMF

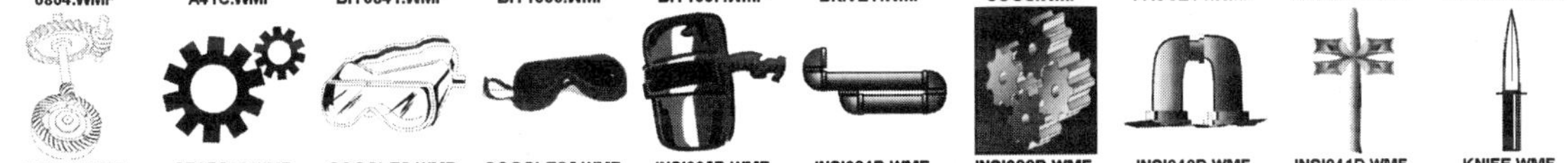

GEARS.WMF GEARS05.WMF GOGGLES.WMF GOGGLES5.WMF INSI005D.WMF INSI034D.WMF INSI038D.WMF INSI040D.WMF INSI041D.WMF KNIFE.WMF

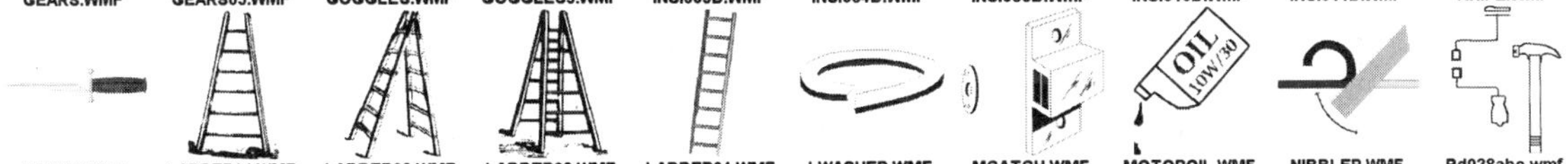

KNIFE1.WMF LADDER01.WMF LADDER02.WMF LADDER03.WMF LADDER04.WMF LWASHER.WMF MCATCH.WMF MOTOROIL.WMF NIBBLER.WMF Pd038abo.wmf

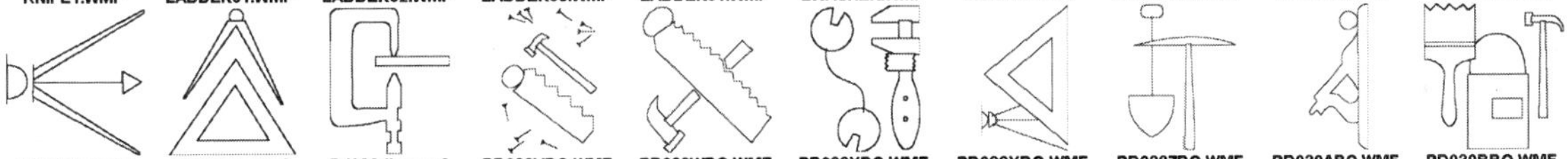

Pd038bbo.wmf Pd038cbo.wmf Pd038dbo.wmf PD038VBO.WMF PD038WBO.WMF PD038XBO.WMF PD038YBO.WMF PD038ZBO.WMF PD039ABO.WMF PD039BBO.WMF

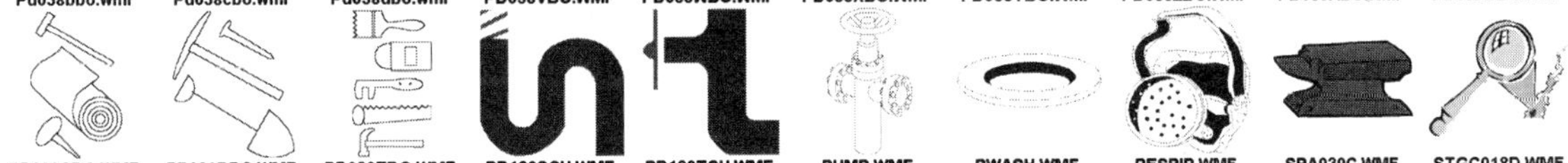

PD039CBO.WMF PD039DBO.WMF PD039EBO.WMF PD129SCU.WMF PD129TCU.WMF PUMP.WMF PWASH.WMF RESPIR.WMF SPA030C.WMF STGC018D.WMF

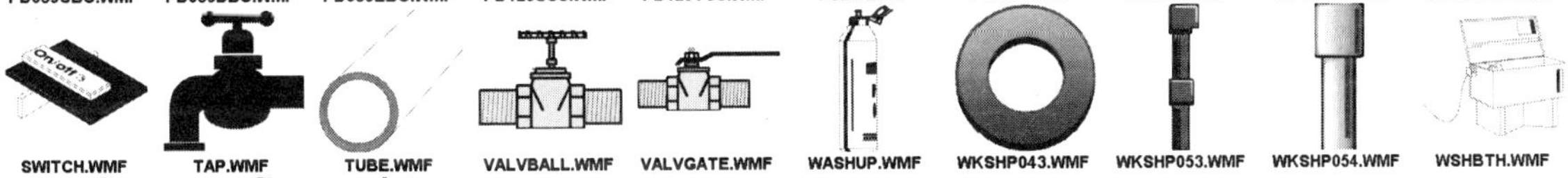

SWITCH.WMF TAP.WMF TUBE.WMF VALVBALL.WMF VALVGATE.WMF WASHUP.WMF WKSHP043.WMF WKSHP053.WMF WKSHP054.WMF WSHBTH.WMF

ZSTYLE02.WMF ZSTYLE04.WMF ZSTYLE05.WMF

1734.WMF BIT0504.WMF BIT0505.WMF BIT0506.WMF BIT0507.WMF BIT0508.WMF BIT0509.WMF BIT0512.WMF BIT0555.WMF BIT0602.WMF

BIT0604.WMF BIT0605.WMF BIT0606.WMF BIT0607.WMF CEMENT.WMF COMPRES.WMF COMPRESC.WMF DRILL.WMF DRILLBIT.WMF DRILPRES.WMF

ELECSAND.WMF FIRE.WMF GLUEGUN.WMF GLUEGUN5.WMF HANDRL8.WMF HNDDRILL.WMF HNDRIL02.WMF HNDRIL10.WMF HNDRIL11.WMF HNDRIL12.WMF

HNDRIL2.WMF HNDRIL4.WMF HNDRIL5.WMF HNDRIL6.WMF HNDRIL7.WMF HNDRIL8.WMF HNDRIL9.WMF HNDRL3.WMF HOTWIRE.WMF INGC015D.WMF

INGC039D.WMF INSI006D.WMF INSI008D.WMF INSI017D.WMF INSI043D.WMF JACK.WMF LANTERN.WMF ROUTER.WMF SAW001A.WMF SAW002A.WMF

SAW003A.WMF SAW004A.WMF SAW005A.WMF SAW006A.WMF SAW007A.WMF SAW008A.WMF SAW009A.WMF SAW010A.WMF SAW011A.WMF SAW012A.WMF

SAW013A.WMF SAW014A.WMF SOLDGUN.WMF SOLDIRON.WMF STRW021J.WMF TABLESAW.WMF WINCH.WMF WKSHP019.WMF WKSHP032.WMF ZSTYLE06.WMF

ZSTYLE07.WMF

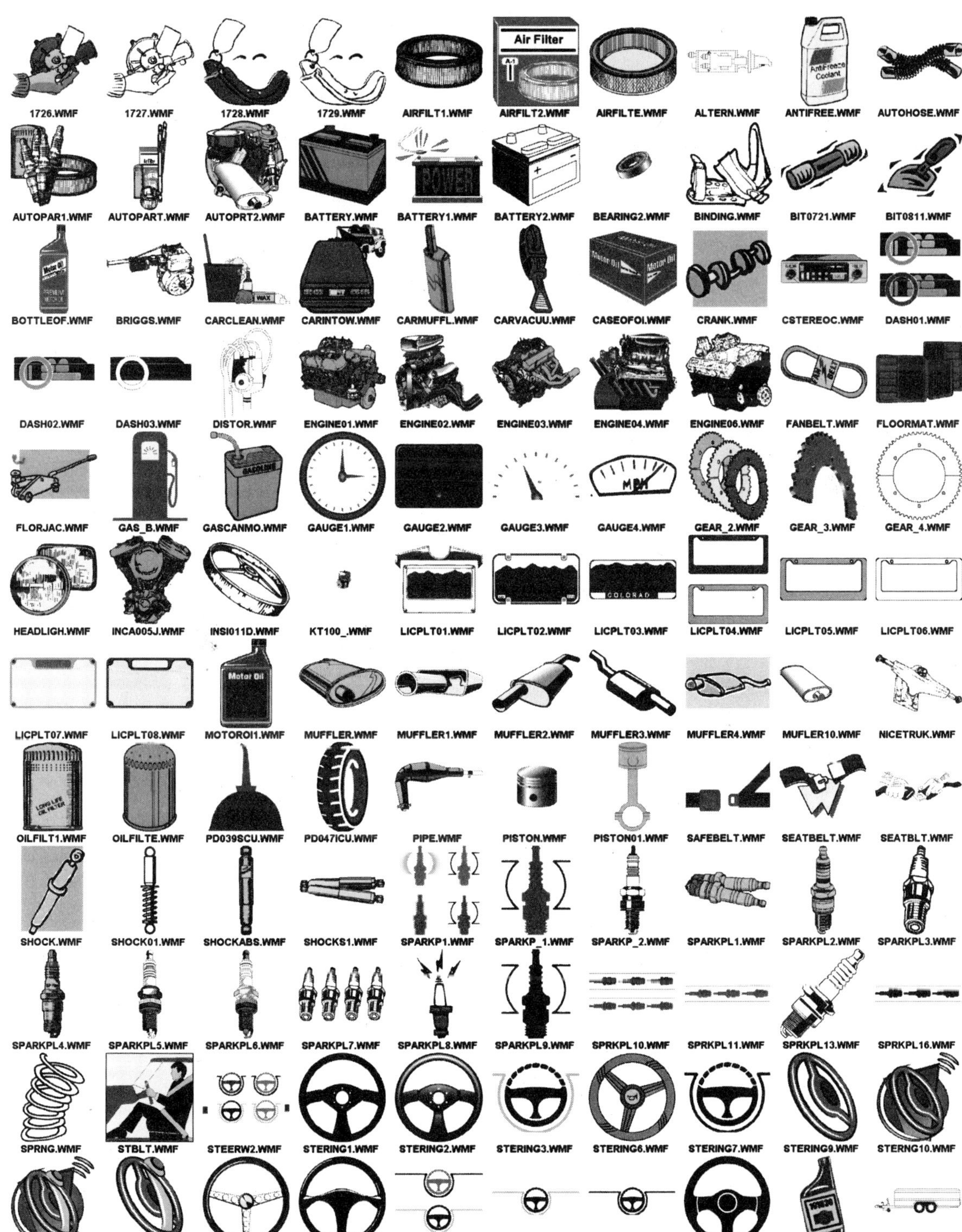

1726.WMF 1727.WMF 1728.WMF 1729.WMF AIRFILT1.WMF AIRFILT2.WMF AIRFILTE.WMF ALTERN.WMF ANTIFREE.WMF AUTOHOSE.WMF

AUTOPAR1.WMF AUTOPART.WMF AUTOPRT2.WMF BATTERY.WMF BATTERY1.WMF BATTERY2.WMF BEARING2.WMF BINDING.WMF BIT0721.WMF BIT0811.WMF

BOTTLEOF.WMF BRIGGS.WMF CARCLEAN.WMF CARINTOW.WMF CARMUFFL.WMF CARVACUU.WMF CASEOFOI.WMF CRANK.WMF CSTEREOC.WMF DASH01.WMF

DASH02.WMF DASH03.WMF DISTOR.WMF ENGINE01.WMF ENGINE02.WMF ENGINE03.WMF ENGINE04.WMF ENGINE06.WMF FANBELT.WMF FLOORMAT.WMF

FLORJAC.WMF GAS_B.WMF GASCANMO.WMF GAUGE1.WMF GAUGE2.WMF GAUGE3.WMF GAUGE4.WMF GEAR_2.WMF GEAR_3.WMF GEAR_4.WMF

HEADLIGH.WMF INCA005J.WMF INSI011D.WMF KT100_.WMF LICPLT01.WMF LICPLT02.WMF LICPLT03.WMF LICPLT04.WMF LICPLT05.WMF LICPLT06.WMF

LICPLT07.WMF LICPLT08.WMF MOTOROI1.WMF MUFFLER.WMF MUFFLER1.WMF MUFFLER2.WMF MUFFLER3.WMF MUFFLER4.WMF MUFLER10.WMF NICETRUK.WMF

OILFILT1.WMF OILFILTE.WMF PD039SCU.WMF PD047ICU.WMF PIPE.WMF PISTON.WMF PISTON01.WMF SAFEBELT.WMF SEATBELT.WMF SEATBLT.WMF

SHOCK.WMF SHOCK01.WMF SHOCKABS.WMF SHOCKS1.WMF SPARKP1.WMF SPARKP_1.WMF SPARKP_2.WMF SPARKPL1.WMF SPARKPL2.WMF SPARKPL3.WMF

SPARKPL4.WMF SPARKPL5.WMF SPARKPL6.WMF SPARKPL7.WMF SPARKPL8.WMF SPARKPL9.WMF SPRKPL10.WMF SPRKPL11.WMF SPRKPL13.WMF SPRKPL16.WMF

SPRNG.WMF STBLT.WMF STEERW2.WMF STERING1.WMF STERING2.WMF STERING3.WMF STERING6.WMF STERING7.WMF STERING9.WMF STERNG10.WMF

STERNG11.WMF STERNG12.WMF STERNG14.WMF STERNG15.WMF STERNG16.WMF STERNG17.WMF STERNG18.WMF STERNG19.WMF STSI004J.WMF TRAN163.WMF

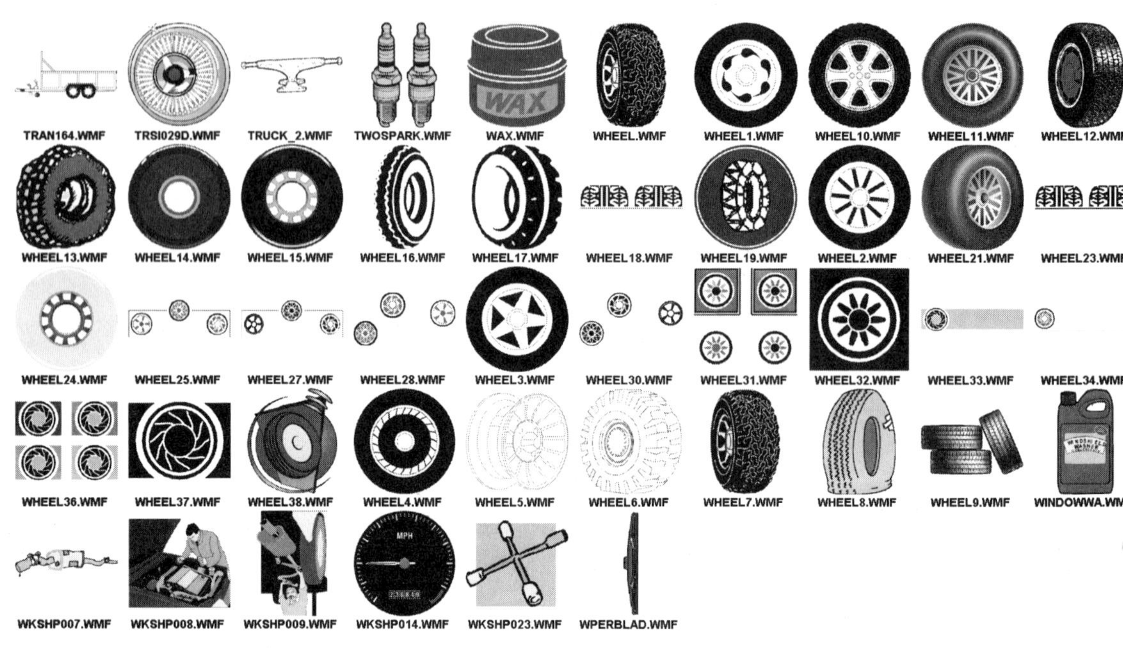
TRAN164.WMF
TRSI029D.WMF
TRUCK_2.WMF
TWOSPARK.WMF
WAX.WMF
WHEEL.WMF
WHEEL1.WMF
WHEEL10.WMF
WHEEL11.WMF
WHEEL12.WMF
WHEEL13.WMF
WHEEL14.WMF
WHEEL15.WMF
WHEEL16.WMF
WHEEL17.WMF
WHEEL18.WMF
WHEEL19.WMF
WHEEL2.WMF
WHEEL21.WMF
WHEEL23.WMF
WHEEL24.WMF
WHEEL25.WMF
WHEEL27.WMF
WHEEL28.WMF
WHEEL3.WMF
WHEEL30.WMF
WHEEL31.WMF
WHEEL32.WMF
WHEEL33.WMF
WHEEL34.WMF
WHEEL36.WMF
WHEEL37.WMF
WHEEL38.WMF
WHEEL4.WMF
WHEEL5.WMF
WHEEL6.WMF
WHEEL7.WMF
WHEEL8.WMF
WHEEL9.WMF
WINDOWWA.WMF
WKSHP007.WMF
WKSHP008.WMF
WKSHP009.WMF
WKSHP014.WMF
WKSHP023.WMF
WPERBLAD.WMF

0157CARC.WMF
0441.WMF
0442.WMF
0443.WMF
0444.WMF
0446.WMF
0448.WMF
0449.WMF
0450.WMF
0451.WMF
0452.WMF
0453.WMF
0454.WMF
0455.WMF
0456.WMF
0457.WMF
0458.WMF
0459.WMF
0463.WMF
0465.WMF
0474.WMF
0475.WMF
0481.WMF
0484.WMF
116.WMF
121.WMF
122.WMF
1957BUIC.WMF
1BUG_CAR.WMF
2766.WMF
2768.WMF
2775.WMF
2776.WMF
2778.WMF
2779.WMF
2780.WMF
2781.WMF
2782.WMF
2783.WMF
2784.WMF
2785.WMF
2786.WMF
2787.WMF
2788.WMF
2789.WMF
2790.WMF
2791.WMF
2792.WMF
2793.WMF
2794.WMF
2795.WMF
2BUG_CAR.WMF
30FORDA.WMF
32FORD.WMF
34DEUSE.WMF
35BENT.WMF
35MERZ.WMF
36CAD.WMF
36CORD.WMF
3720.WMF
3723.WMF
39CITRO.WMF
39FORD.WMF
39MERZ.WMF
39PACK.WMF
4254.WMF
4415.WMF
4416.WMF
4417.WMF
4461.WMF
4462.WMF
4463.WMF
4464.WMF
47CADI.WMF
47JAG.WMF
47VWBUG.WMF
48JAG120.WMF
48LINC.WMF
48MBTC.WMF
48TUCK.WMF
50CADI.WMF
50CHEV.WMF
50FORD.WMF
52STUDE.WMF
53HUDSON.WMF
55CHEV.WMF
55FORD.WMF
55MG.WMF
56CHEVY.WMF
56CORV.WMF
56FORD.WMF
56MERC.WMF
56OLDS.WMF
57_CHEV.WMF
57CHEVY.WMF
57STUDE.WMF
57VETTE.WMF
59_FORD.WMF
59IMPALA.WMF
60CHRYS.WMF
60LESABR.WMF
63CORV.WMF
64AVANTI.WMF
64CONT.WMF
64PONT.WMF
65MUSTNG.WMF
66CHEVEL.WMF
66MUST.WMF
66SHELBY.WMF
66TORO.WMF
67PONT.WMF
68CHARG.WMF
68ELDO.WMF
68OLDS.WMF
69CAMERO.WMF
69CORV.WMF
69GTO.WMF
69MUST.WMF
72PONT.WMF
79JAGUAR.WMF

814DELOR.WMF
82VETTE.WMF
85CAMERO.WMF
A20058.WMF
A22A.WMF
A22AB.WMF
A22B.WMF
A22B2.WMF
A22BB.WMF
A22D2.WMF
A22E.WMF
A22E2.WMF
A22EB.WMF
ACURLEG.WMF
ACURVIG.WMF
ALFASPID.WMF
ANT_CAR.WMF
ASI050I.WMF
ASI051H.WMF
ASI051L.WMF
ASI052D.WMF
ASI052G.WMF
ASI052M.WMF
ASI054J.WMF
AUDI100.WMF
AUSTIN7.WMF
AUTO02.WMF
AUTO10.WMF
AUTO11.WMF
AUTO12M.WMF
AUTO17.WMF
AUTO17B.WMF
AUTO19.WMF
AUTO19B.WMF
AUTO2.WMF
AUTOONSL.WMF
AUTOTO.WMF
BACK174.WMF
BEETLE.WMF
BIT1045.WMF
BIT1048.WMF
BLKCARTO.WMF
BMW.WMF
BMW5.WMF
BUBBLE.WMF
BUICKCEN.WMF
BUICKESS.WMF
BUICKSAB.WMF
CADELDO.WMF
CADIET.WMF
CAMARO.WMF
CAPRI.WMF
CAPRIC.WMF
CAR.WMF
CAR1.WMF
CAR12.WMF
CAR5.WMF
CAR_1.WMF
CAR_SHOP.WMF
CAR_SYM.WMF
CAR_WASH.WMF
CARC.WMF
CARCLUNK.WMF
CARFOUR.WMF
CARFRONT.WMF
CARS.WMF
CHEVBE.WMF
CHEVBLA.WMF
CHEVCAMA.WMF
CHEVCAMB.WMF
CHEVCORV.WMF
CHEVIE.WMF
CHEVLUM.WMF
CHEVPKUP.WMF
CHEVS10.WMF
CHEVSUBU.WMF
CHRYLABA.WMF
CHRYSLER.WMF
CLASSCAR.WMF
COMMOD.WMF
COMMODC.WMF
CONVERT.WMF
CORVET01.WMF
CRASH01.WMF
CRASH03.WMF
CRASH05.WMF
CRASH06.WMF
CRASH08.WMF
CRASHED.WMF
CRUSER.WMF
CTP012A.WMF
CTP012C.WMF
CTP012D.WMF
CTP014A.WMF
CTP014B.WMF
CTP016A.WMF
CTP016B.WMF
CTP017A.WMF
CTP017B.WMF
CTP018A.WMF
CTP018B.WMF
CTP018C.WMF
CTP019A.WMF
CTP019B.WMF
CTP019C.WMF
CTP020A.WMF
CTP020B.WMF
CTP020C.WMF
CTP021A.WMF
CTP021B.WMF
CTP021C.WMF
CTP022A.WMF
CTP022B.WMF
CTP023A.WMF
CTP023B.WMF
CTP023C.WMF
DEC080Q.WMF
DODGERAM.WMF
DODGEVIP.WMF
DODYNAST.WMF

DOMINIVA.WMF DOSTEALT.WMF DOSUNDAN.WMF DRAGSTER.WMF DUPONT.WMF EAGLE.WMF EBFALCO.WMF EBFALCOC.WMF EBTAXI.WMF EBTAXIC.WMF
EDCAR.WMF EDSEL.WMF ENSI024D.WMF FAST_CAR.WMF FER456G.WMF FER512TR.WMF FERF40.WMF FERRARI.WMF FERRARI1.WMF FERTESTA.WMF
FIAT500.WMF FIREBIRD.WMF FORDC.WMF FORDCLUB.WMF FORDESCO.WMF FORDEXPL.WMF FORDF1.WMF FORDF2.WMF FORDMUST.WMF FORDTBRD.WMF
FORDTGL.WMF FORDTLX.WMF FORDTWAG.WMF FORDWIND.WMF FORM1A.WMF FORM1B.WMF FOURWDRI.WMF FSW010A.WMF FSW026C.WMF GEOMETRO.WMF
GEOSTORM.WMF GMCPKUP.WMF HAA029A.WMF HAA033A.WMF HAA035A.WMF HANDIVAN.WMF HMC028B.WMF HONDACCA.WMF HONDACCB.WMF HONDCIV.WMF
HOTROD.WMF HPI018H.WMF HTS025A.WMF HYUNDAI.WMF IMPALATO.WMF INDY500C.WMF INFIG20.WMF INFIQ45.WMF INGC009D.WMF ISUZU.WMF
JAGUAR.WMF JAGXK.WMF JEEP00.WMF JEEP01.WMF JEEP02.WMF JEEP03.WMF JEEP04.WMF JEEP06.WMF JEEP07.WMF JEEPCHER.WMF
JEEPWRAN.WMF JETCARTO.WMF JRGMONST.WMF LAMBO.WMF LASER.WMF LASERC.WMF LEMANSGT.WMF LEXUS.WMF LIMOA.WMF LIMOB.WMF
LINCCONT.WMF LINCMK8A.WMF LINCMK8B.WMF LOTUS.WMF MAZMIA.WMF MAZMX3.WMF MAZRX762.WMF MAZRX7A.WMF MAZRX7B.WMF MERCCAPR.WMF
MERCED.WMF MERCEDES.WMF MERCMARQ.WMF MERCVILL.WMF MERCXR7.WMF MERZ190.WMF MERZ300.WMF MERZ_E.WMF MINI.WMF MINIVAN.WMF
MOD031G.WMF MODELT.WMF MONSTRK.WMF MTCABCAR.WMF MUSTANG.WMF MUSTANG1.WMF NASCAR.WMF NICECAR.WMF NISS300.WMF NISS4X4.WMF
NISSANPA.WMF NISSMA.WMF NISWAG.WMF NISWAGC.WMF NOVASS.WMF OFS042I.WMF OLD_CAR.WMF OLD_PICK.WMF OLDSACH.WMF OLDSCAL.WMF

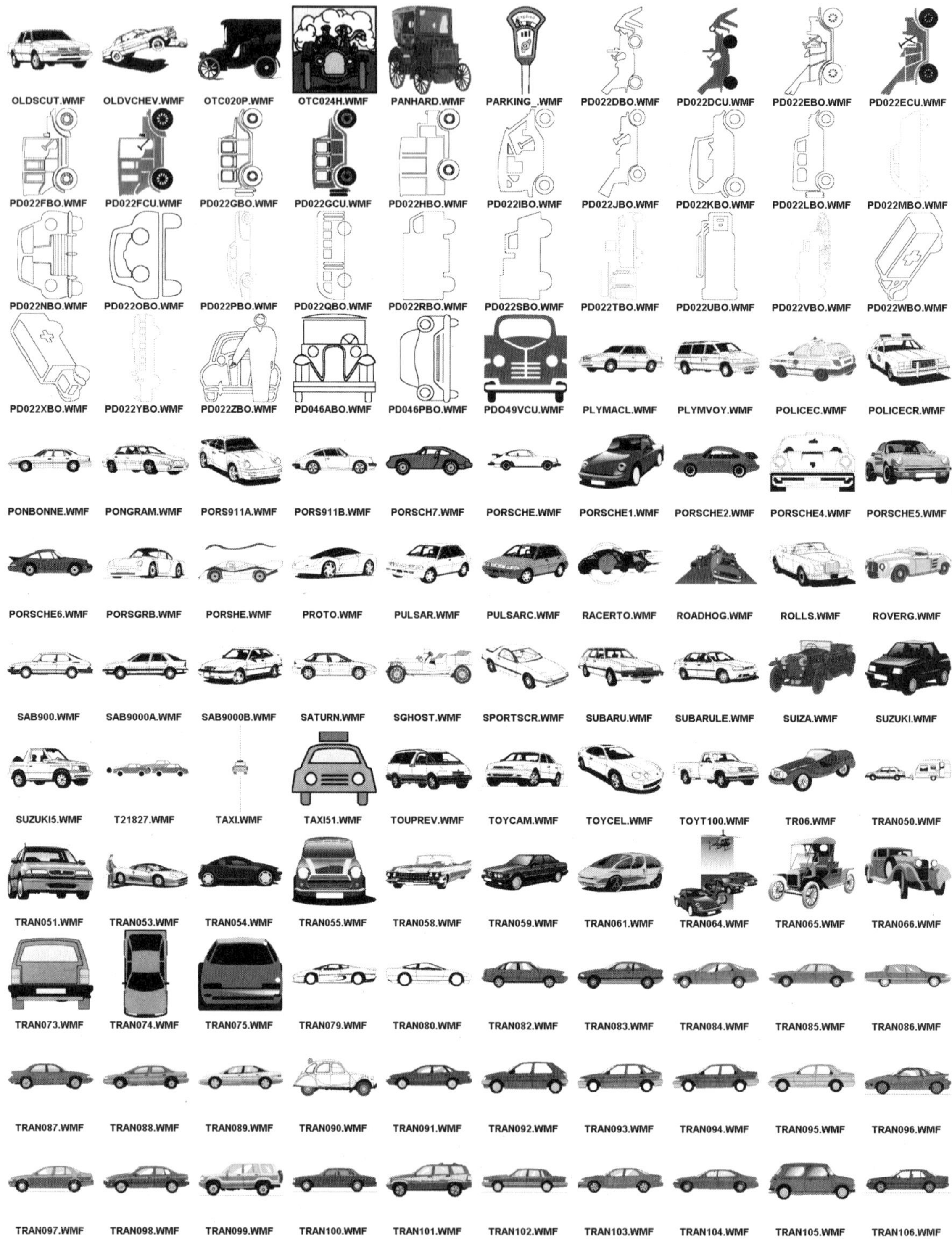

OLDSCUT.WMF OLDVCHEV.WMF OTC020P.WMF OTC024H.WMF PANHARD.WMF PARKING_.WMF PD022DBO.WMF PD022DCU.WMF PD022EBO.WMF PD022ECU.WMF

PD022FBO.WMF PD022FCU.WMF PD022GBO.WMF PD022GCU.WMF PD022HBO.WMF PD022IBO.WMF PD022JBO.WMF PD022KBO.WMF PD022LBO.WMF PD022MBO.WMF

PD022NBO.WMF PD022OBO.WMF PD022PBO.WMF PD022QBO.WMF PD022RBO.WMF PD022SBO.WMF PD022TBO.WMF PD022UBO.WMF PD022VBO.WMF PD022WBO.WMF

PD022XBO.WMF PD022YBO.WMF PD022ZBO.WMF PD046ABO.WMF PD046PBO.WMF PDO49VCU.WMF PLYMACL.WMF PLYMVOY.WMF POLICEC.WMF POLICECR.WMF

PONBONNE.WMF PONGRAM.WMF PORS911A.WMF PORS911B.WMF PORSCH7.WMF PORSCHE.WMF PORSCHE1.WMF PORSCHE2.WMF PORSCHE4.WMF PORSCHE5.WMF

PORSCHE6.WMF PORSGRB.WMF PORSHE.WMF PROTO.WMF PULSAR.WMF PULSARC.WMF RACERTO.WMF ROADHOG.WMF ROLLS.WMF ROVERG.WMF

SAB900.WMF SAB9000A.WMF SAB9000B.WMF SATURN.WMF SGHOST.WMF SPORTSCR.WMF SUBARU.WMF SUBARULE.WMF SUIZA.WMF SUZUKI.WMF

SUZUKI5.WMF T21827.WMF TAXI.WMF TAXI51.WMF TOUPREV.WMF TOYCAM.WMF TOYCEL.WMF TOYT100.WMF TR06.WMF TRAN050.WMF

TRAN051.WMF TRAN053.WMF TRAN054.WMF TRAN055.WMF TRAN058.WMF TRAN059.WMF TRAN061.WMF TRAN064.WMF TRAN065.WMF TRAN066.WMF

TRAN073.WMF TRAN074.WMF TRAN075.WMF TRAN079.WMF TRAN080.WMF TRAN082.WMF TRAN083.WMF TRAN084.WMF TRAN085.WMF TRAN086.WMF

TRAN087.WMF TRAN088.WMF TRAN089.WMF TRAN090.WMF TRAN091.WMF TRAN092.WMF TRAN093.WMF TRAN094.WMF TRAN095.WMF TRAN096.WMF

TRAN097.WMF TRAN098.WMF TRAN099.WMF TRAN100.WMF TRAN101.WMF TRAN102.WMF TRAN103.WMF TRAN104.WMF TRAN105.WMF TRAN106.WMF

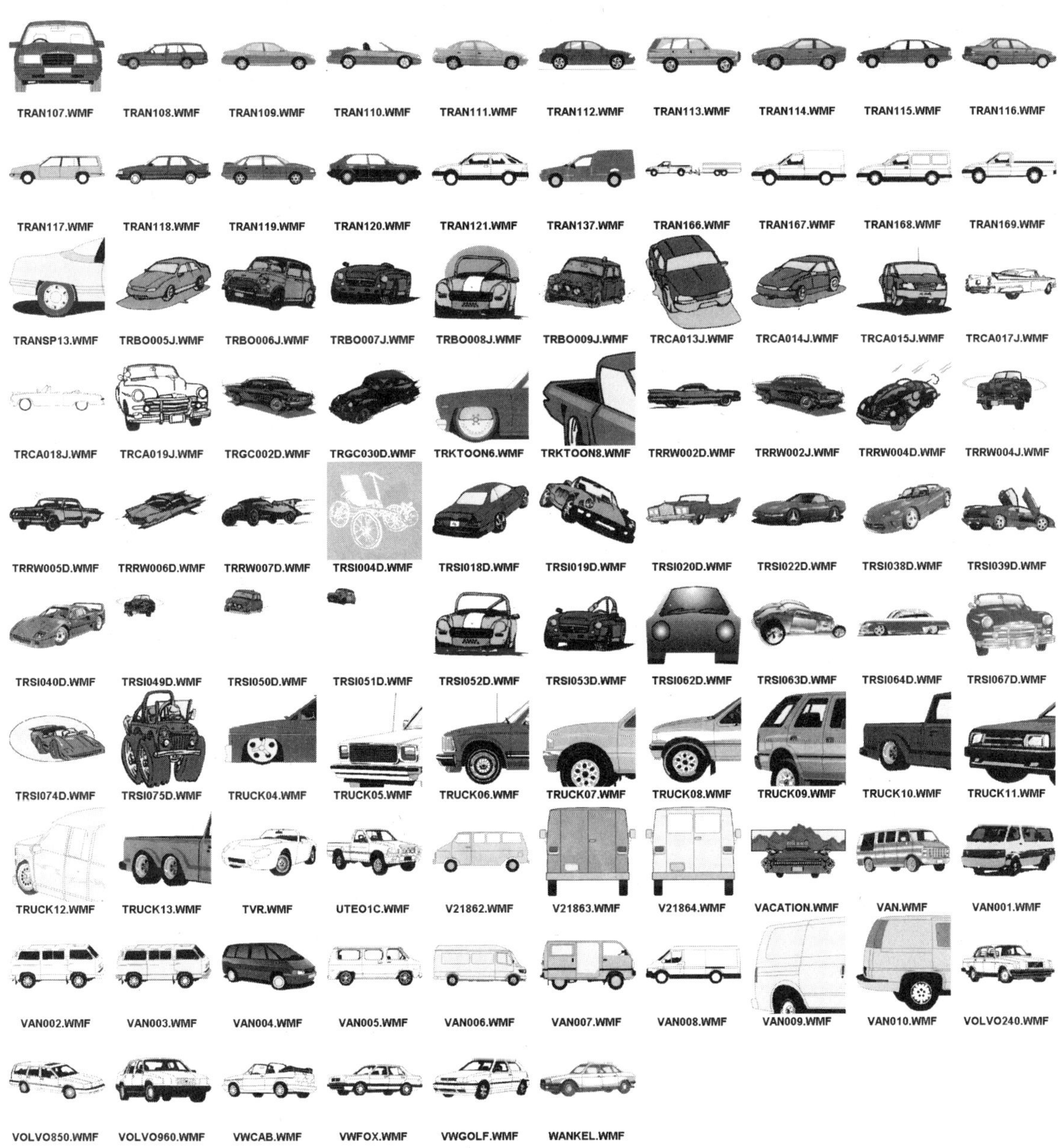
TRAN107.WMF TRAN108.WMF TRAN109.WMF TRAN110.WMF TRAN111.WMF TRAN112.WMF TRAN113.WMF TRAN114.WMF TRAN115.WMF TRAN116.WMF
TRAN117.WMF TRAN118.WMF TRAN119.WMF TRAN120.WMF TRAN121.WMF TRAN137.WMF TRAN166.WMF TRAN167.WMF TRAN168.WMF TRAN169.WMF
TRANSP13.WMF TRBO005J.WMF TRBO006J.WMF TRBO007J.WMF TRBO008J.WMF TRBO009J.WMF TRCA013J.WMF TRCA014J.WMF TRCA015J.WMF TRCA017J.WMF
TRCA018J.WMF TRCA019J.WMF TRGC002D.WMF TRGC030D.WMF TRKTOON6.WMF TRKTOON8.WMF TRRW002D.WMF TRRW002J.WMF TRRW004D.WMF TRRW004J.WMF
TRRW005D.WMF TRRW006D.WMF TRRW007D.WMF TRSI004D.WMF TRSI018D.WMF TRSI019D.WMF TRSI020D.WMF TRSI022D.WMF TRSI038D.WMF TRSI039D.WMF
TRSI040D.WMF TRSI049D.WMF TRSI050D.WMF TRSI051D.WMF TRSI052D.WMF TRSI053D.WMF TRSI062D.WMF TRSI063D.WMF TRSI064D.WMF TRSI067D.WMF
TRSI074D.WMF TRSI075D.WMF TRUCK04.WMF TRUCK05.WMF TRUCK06.WMF TRUCK07.WMF TRUCK08.WMF TRUCK09.WMF TRUCK10.WMF TRUCK11.WMF
TRUCK12.WMF TRUCK13.WMF TVR.WMF UTEO1C.WMF V21862.WMF V21863.WMF V21864.WMF VACATION.WMF VAN.WMF VAN001.WMF
VAN002.WMF VAN003.WMF VAN004.WMF VAN005.WMF VAN006.WMF VAN007.WMF VAN008.WMF VAN009.WMF VAN010.WMF VOLVO240.WMF
VOLVO850.WMF VOLVO960.WMF VWCAB.WMF VWFOX.WMF VWGOLF.WMF WANKEL.WMF

0095.WMF 0469.WMF 0472.WMF 0479.WMF 0480.WMF 0511.WMF 0513.WMF 0514.WMF 0781.WMF 0782.WMF
AIRPL01.WMF AIRPL02.WMF AIRPL03.WMF AIRPL04.WMF AIRPL05.WMF AIRPL06.WMF AIRPL07.WMF AIRPL08.WMF AIRPL09.WMF ASI045H.WMF
ASI047K.WMF AUTO01.WMF AUTO03.WMF BGTRUCK3.WMF BIGFISH1.WMF BLIMP001.WMF BLIMP002.WMF BUGC008D.WMF BUGC020J.WMF BUGC021J.WMF
BUSI148D.WMF C20749.WMF C43.WMF CAR001.WMF CAR002.WMF CAR003.WMF CAR004.WMF CAR005.WMF CAR006.WMF CAR007.WMF
Car Rally
Car Rally
CAR008.WMF CAR009.WMF CAR010.WMF CAR011.WMF CAR012.WMF CAR015.WMF CAR016.WMF CAR017.WMF CAR018.WMF CAR019.WMF
CAR020.WMF CAR021.WMF CAR022.WMF CAR023.WMF CAR024.WMF CAR025.WMF CAR026.WMF CAR030.WMF CAR031.WMF CAR034.WMF
CAR035.WMF CAR036.WMF CAR037.WMF CAR038.WMF CAR040.WMF CAR042.WMF CAR043.WMF CAR044.WMF CAR15.WMF CAR2.WMF
CAR22.WMF CARGUY.WMF CARPOOL.WMF CARTRUBL.WMF CRTN018.WMF CRTN022.WMF CRTN045.WMF CRTN198.WMF CTMISC26.WMF CTMISC58.WMF
CTMISC82.WMF DEC080Q.WMF DRAW01.WMF DRAW02.WMF DRAW03.WMF DRAW04.WMF DRAW05.WMF DRAW06.WMF DRAW07.WMF DRAW08.WMF
TAXI
DRAW09.WMF DRAW10.WMF DRAW11.WMF DRAW13.WMF DRAW15.WMF DRAW16.WMF DRAW17.WMF DRAW19.WMF DRIVER.WMF E18.WMF
E20.WMF EAA091E.WMF ENCA013J.WMF EV033.WMF F38.WMF F39.WMF FCP038B.WMF FCP038J.WMF FLATTIRE.WMF FRA024E.WMF
FSW026C.WMF FSW026D.WMF GETAWYTO.WMF GREMLINS.WMF HELICP21.WMF HELICP25.WMF HELICP26.WMF HG03.WMF HMC028A.WMF HMC028B.WMF

HMC029A.WMF HMC029B.WMF HOT_AIR_.WMF HV03.WMF INJURY01.WMF MANDRIVI.WMF MECHANIC.WMF MENORAH2.WMF MISC087.WMF MOD031G.WMF
MOVINGVL.WMF MOVINGVR.WMF OLD_TAXI.WMF OLDCARAS.WMF OTC011K.WMF OTC024H.WMF P21553.WMF PAPRPLAN.WMF PLNTOON1.WMF PLNTOON2.WMF
PLNTOON3.WMF PLNTOON4.WMF PLSI007D.WMF PLTOON20.WMF PLTOON21.WMF PLTOON22.WMF PLTOON23.WMF PLTOON24.WMF PLTOON25.WMF PLTOON26.WMF
PLTOON28.WMF PLTOON29.WMF PLTOON30.WMF PLTOON31.WMF PLTOON32.WMF PLTOON33.WMF PLTOON34.WMF PLTOON35.WMF PLTOON36.WMF PLTOON37.WMF
PLTOON38.WMF PLTOON39.WMF PRTYCAR.WMF PRTYCAR1.WMF PRTYCAR2.WMF PRTYCAR5.WMF SLEDKID.WMF SPA031A.WMF SPSI311D.WMF SPSI405D.WMF
SPSI564D.WMF STATION.WMF SUB001.WMF SUB002.WMF SUB003.WMF SUB004.WMF SUB005.WMF SUB006.WMF TA19.WMF TR07.WMF
TR08.WMF TRAIN.WMF TRAIN001.WMF TRAINSMO.WMF TRAN016.WMF TRAN018.WMF TRAN043.WMF TRAN140.WMF TRAN141.WMF TRAN176.WMF
TRAN179.WMF TRAN183.WMF TRAN198.WMF TRAN205.WMF TRAN206.WMF TRBO004J.WMF TRBO012J.WMF TRCA024J.WMF TRGC007D.WMF TRGC010D.WMF
TRGC015D.WMF TRGC037D.WMF TRGC039D.WMF TRGC041D.WMF TRGC042D.WMF TRGC043D.WMF TRGC044D.WMF TRGC048D.WMF TRKC002J.WMF TRKC003J.WMF
TRKTOON2.WMF TRKTOON3.WMF TRKTOON5.WMF TRRW007J.WMF TRRW008J.WMF TRRW010D.WMF TRRW013J.WMF TRRW019J.WMF TRSI010D.WMF TRSI076D.WMF
TRUCK.WMF WT01.WMF WT02.WMF WT03.WMF WT04.WMF WT05.WMF WT06.WMF WT07.WMF WT08.WMF WT09.WMF
WT10.WMF WT11.WMF WT12.WMF WT13.WMF WT14.WMF WT15.WMF WT16.WMF WT17.WMF

10TONTRK.WMF 2767.WMF 2769.WMF 2777.WMF 5TONTRUK.WMF A20031.WMF AMBLANCE.WMF AMBULANC.WMF AMBULNC1.WMF AMBULNCE.WMF

ARMSCARY.WMF BGTRUCK1.WMF BGTRUCK2.WMF BIGRIG.WMF BULLDOZ1.WMF BULLDOZ2.WMF BUS.WMF BUS001.WMF BUS003.WMF BUS005.WMF

BUS007.WMF BUS009.WMF BUS010.WMF BUS011.WMF BUS015.WMF BUS019.WMF BUS021.WMF BUS023.WMF BUS025.WMF BUS027.WMF

BUS029.WMF BUS031.WMF BUS033.WMF BUS037.WMF BUS039.WMF BUS400.WMF CAB_OVER.WMF CAR3.WMF CARCARR.WMF CEMENT.WMF

CTP022C.WMF CTP024A.WMF CTP024B.WMF CTP026A.WMF CTP026B.WMF CTP027A.WMF CTP027B.WMF CTP030A.WMF CTP030B.WMF CTP030C.WMF

CTP031C.WMF DECKER01.WMF DECKER02.WMF DECKER03.WMF DELIVERY.WMF DELIVTRK.WMF DOUBDECK.WMF DUMPTRK.WMF DUSTCART.WMF FARMTRAC.WMF

FCP038J.WMF FEDEX.WMF FIRETRK.WMF FLATBED.WMF FORKLIFT.WMF FRNTLOAD.WMF HAG027A.WMF HAULER.WMF HAULER_1.WMF HLTH002.WMF

INGC043D.WMF LDSCP028.WMF LORRY1.WMF LORRY2.WMF MACK.WMF MACKC.WMF MAILTRUC.WMF PD022HCU.WMF Pd063abo.wmf Pd063bbo.wmf

Pd063cbo.wmf Pd063dbo.wmf PD063JBO.WMF PD063VBO.WMF PD063WBO.WMF PD063XBO.WMF PD063YBO.WMF PD063ZBO.WMF PD064ABO.WMF PD064BBO.WMF

PD064CBO.WMF PD064DBO.WMF PD064EBO.WMF PD064FBO.WMF PD064GBO.WMF PD064HBO.WMF PD064IBO.WMF PD064JBO.WMF PD064KBO.WMF PD064LBO.WMF

PD064MBO.WMF PD064NBO.WMF PD064OBO.WMF PD064PBO.WMF PD075HCU.WMF PD076DCU.WMF PD077BCU.WMF PD077QCU.WMF PD077RCU.WMF PD078SCU.WMF

PD078TCU.WMF PD079UCU.WMF PD079VCU.WMF PD081ECU.WMF PD081FCU.WMF PD082NCU.WMF PD082OCU.WMF PD083MCU.WMF PD083NCU.WMF PD083OCU.WMF

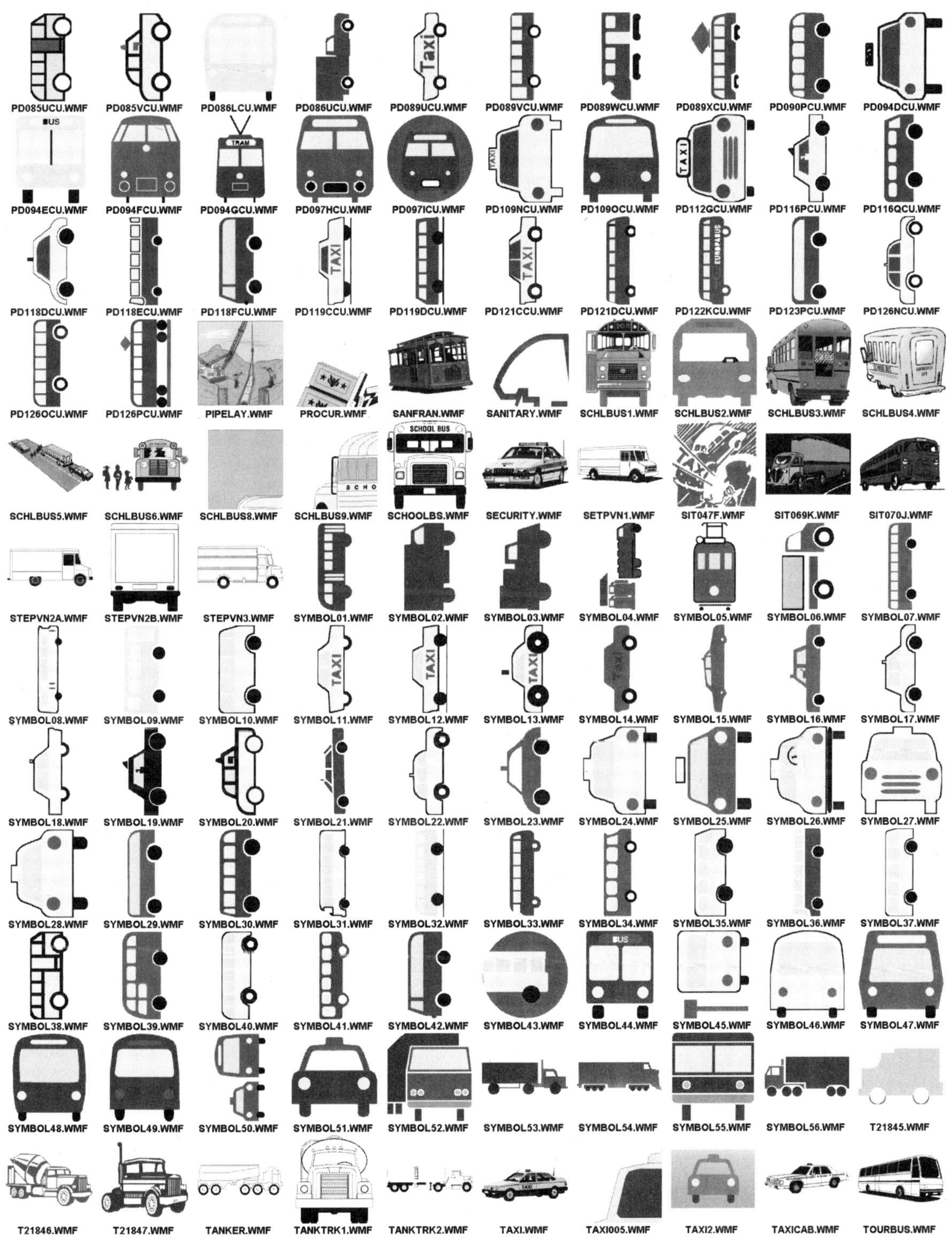
PD085UCU.WMF PD085VCU.WMF PD086LCU.WMF PD086UCU.WMF PD089UCU.WMF PD089VCU.WMF PD089WCU.WMF PD089XCU.WMF PD090PCU.WMF PD094DCU.WMF
PD094ECU.WMF PD094FCU.WMF PD094GCU.WMF PD097HCU.WMF PD097ICU.WMF PD109NCU.WMF PD109OCU.WMF PD112GCU.WMF PD116PCU.WMF PD116QCU.WMF
PD118DCU.WMF PD118ECU.WMF PD118FCU.WMF PD119CCU.WMF PD119DCU.WMF PD121CCU.WMF PD121DCU.WMF PD122KCU.WMF PD123PCU.WMF PD126NCU.WMF
PD126OCU.WMF PD126PCU.WMF PIPELAY.WMF PROCUR.WMF SANFRAN.WMF SANITARY.WMF SCHLBUS1.WMF SCHLBUS2.WMF SCHLBUS3.WMF SCHLBUS4.WMF
SCHLBUS5.WMF SCHLBUS6.WMF SCHLBUS8.WMF SCHLBUS9.WMF SCHOOLBS.WMF SECURITY.WMF SETPVN1.WMF SIT047F.WMF SIT069K.WMF SIT070J.WMF
STEPVN2A.WMF STEPVN2B.WMF STEPVN3.WMF SYMBOL01.WMF SYMBOL02.WMF SYMBOL03.WMF SYMBOL04.WMF SYMBOL05.WMF SYMBOL06.WMF SYMBOL07.WMF
SYMBOL08.WMF SYMBOL09.WMF SYMBOL10.WMF SYMBOL11.WMF SYMBOL12.WMF SYMBOL13.WMF SYMBOL14.WMF SYMBOL15.WMF SYMBOL16.WMF SYMBOL17.WMF
SYMBOL18.WMF SYMBOL19.WMF SYMBOL20.WMF SYMBOL21.WMF SYMBOL22.WMF SYMBOL23.WMF SYMBOL24.WMF SYMBOL25.WMF SYMBOL26.WMF SYMBOL27.WMF
SYMBOL28.WMF SYMBOL29.WMF SYMBOL30.WMF SYMBOL31.WMF SYMBOL32.WMF SYMBOL33.WMF SYMBOL34.WMF SYMBOL35.WMF SYMBOL36.WMF SYMBOL37.WMF
SYMBOL38.WMF SYMBOL39.WMF SYMBOL40.WMF SYMBOL41.WMF SYMBOL42.WMF SYMBOL43.WMF SYMBOL44.WMF SYMBOL45.WMF SYMBOL46.WMF SYMBOL47.WMF
SYMBOL48.WMF SYMBOL49.WMF SYMBOL50.WMF SYMBOL51.WMF SYMBOL52.WMF SYMBOL53.WMF SYMBOL54.WMF SYMBOL55.WMF SYMBOL56.WMF T21845.WMF
T21846.WMF T21847.WMF TANKER.WMF TANKTRK1.WMF TANKTRK2.WMF TAXI.WMF TAXI005.WMF TAXI2.WMF TAXICAB.WMF TOURBUS.WMF

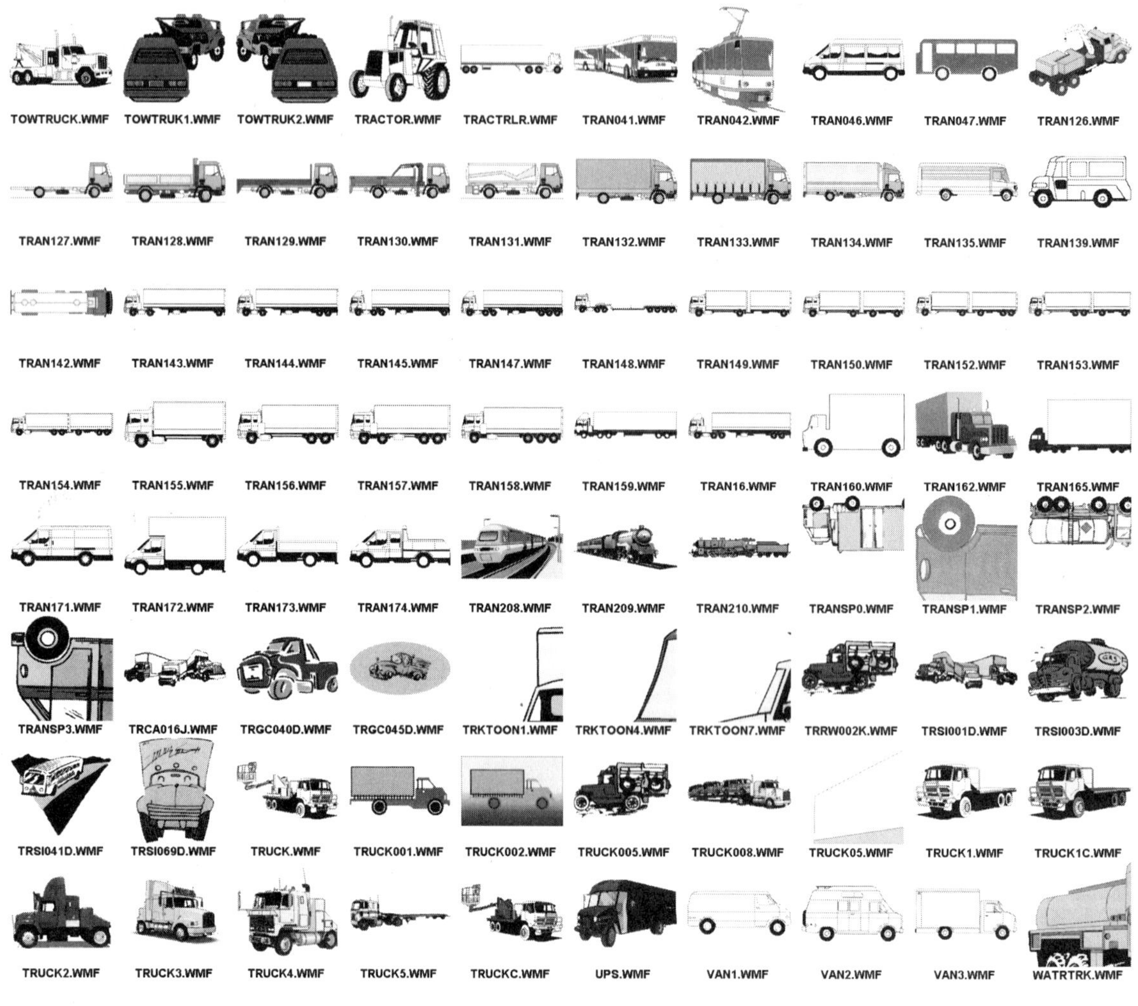
TOWTRUCK.WMF
TOWTRUK1.WMF
TOWTRUK2.WMF
TRACTOR.WMF
TRACTRLR.WMF
TRAN041.WMF
TRAN042.WMF
TRAN046.WMF
TRAN047.WMF
TRAN126.WMF
TRAN127.WMF
TRAN128.WMF
TRAN129.WMF
TRAN130.WMF
TRAN131.WMF
TRAN132.WMF
TRAN133.WMF
TRAN134.WMF
TRAN135.WMF
TRAN139.WMF
TRAN142.WMF
TRAN143.WMF
TRAN144.WMF
TRAN145.WMF
TRAN147.WMF
TRAN148.WMF
TRAN149.WMF
TRAN150.WMF
TRAN152.WMF
TRAN153.WMF
TRAN154.WMF
TRAN155.WMF
TRAN156.WMF
TRAN157.WMF
TRAN158.WMF
TRAN159.WMF
TRAN16.WMF
TRAN160.WMF
TRAN162.WMF
TRAN165.WMF
TRAN171.WMF
TRAN172.WMF
TRAN173.WMF
TRAN174.WMF
TRAN208.WMF
TRAN209.WMF
TRAN210.WMF
TRANSP0.WMF
TRANSP1.WMF
TRANSP2.WMF
TRANSP3.WMF
TRCA016J.WMF
TRGC040D.WMF
TRGC045D.WMF
TRKTOON1.WMF
TRKTOON4.WMF
TRKTOON7.WMF
TRRW002K.WMF
TRSI001D.WMF
TRSI003D.WMF
TRSI041D.WMF
TRSI069D.WMF
TRUCK.WMF
TRUCK001.WMF
TRUCK002.WMF
TRUCK005.WMF
TRUCK008.WMF
TRUCK05.WMF
TRUCK1.WMF
TRUCK1C.WMF
TRUCK2.WMF
TRUCK3.WMF
TRUCK4.WMF
TRUCK5.WMF
TRUCKC.WMF
UPS.WMF
VAN1.WMF
VAN2.WMF
VAN3.WMF
WATRTRK.WMF

1OLD_FAS.WMF
2OLD_FAS.WMF
BICYCLE.WMF
BIKE01.WMF
BIKE03.WMF
BIKE05.WMF
BIKE07.WMF
BIKE09.WMF
BIKE11.WMF
BIKE13.WMF
BIKE15.WMF
BIKE17.WMF
BIKE19.WMF
BIKE21.WMF
BIKE23.WMF
BIKE25.WMF
BIKE27.WMF
BIKE29.WMF
BIKENGAS.WMF
BIKERCOL.WMF
CTP031E.WMF
CTP032A.WMF
CTP032B.WMF
CTP032C.WMF
CTP032D.WMF
CYCLE01.WMF
CYCLE02.WMF
CYCLE03.WMF
CYCLE04.WMF
CYCLE05.WMF
CYCLE06.WMF
CYCLE07.WMF
CYCLE08.WMF
CYCLE09.WMF
CYCLE10.WMF
CYCLE11.WMF
CYCLE12.WMF
CYCLE13.WMF
CYCLE14.WMF
CYCLE15.WMF
CYCLE16.WMF
CYCLE17.WMF
CYCLE18.WMF
CYCLE19.WMF
CYCLE20.WMF
CYCLE21.WMF
CYCLE22.WMF
CYCLE24.WMF
CYCLE26.WMF
CYCLE28.WMF
MOTORCRS.WMF
MOTRCYC1.WMF
MOTRCYC2.WMF
MOTRSCTR.WMF
MTNBIKE.WMF
OTC008A.WMF
OTC009M.WMF
PD111BCU.WMF
PD111VCU.WMF
PD112DCU.WMF
SCOOTER.WMF
SYMBL155.WMF
TRBF004J.WMF
TRSI008D.WMF
UNICYCLE.WMF

HELICOP.WMF HELICOPT.WMF HELICP01.WMF HELICP02.WMF HELICP03.WMF HELICP04.WMF HELICP05.WMF HELICP06.WMF HELICP07.WMF HELICP08.WMF

HELICP09.WMF HELICP10,WMF HELICP11.WMF HELICP12.WMF HELICP13.WMF HELICP14.WMF HELICP15.WMF HELICP16.WMF HELICP17.WMF HELICP18.WMF

HELICP19.WMF HELICP22.WMF HELICP23.WMF HELICP24.WMF HELICP27.WMF HELICP28.WMF HELICP29.WMF HELICP30.WMF HELICP31.WMF PD052TCU.WMF

PD065CU.WMF PD065VCU.WMF PD065WCU.WMF PD065XCU.WMF PD065YCU.WMF PD065ZCU.WMF PD076FCU.WMF PD079XCU.WMF PD081JCU.WMF PD083PCU.WMF

PD094ICU.WMF PD110LCU.WMF PLTOON27.WMF TRANSP10.WMF TRANSP11.WMF TRANSP9.WMF

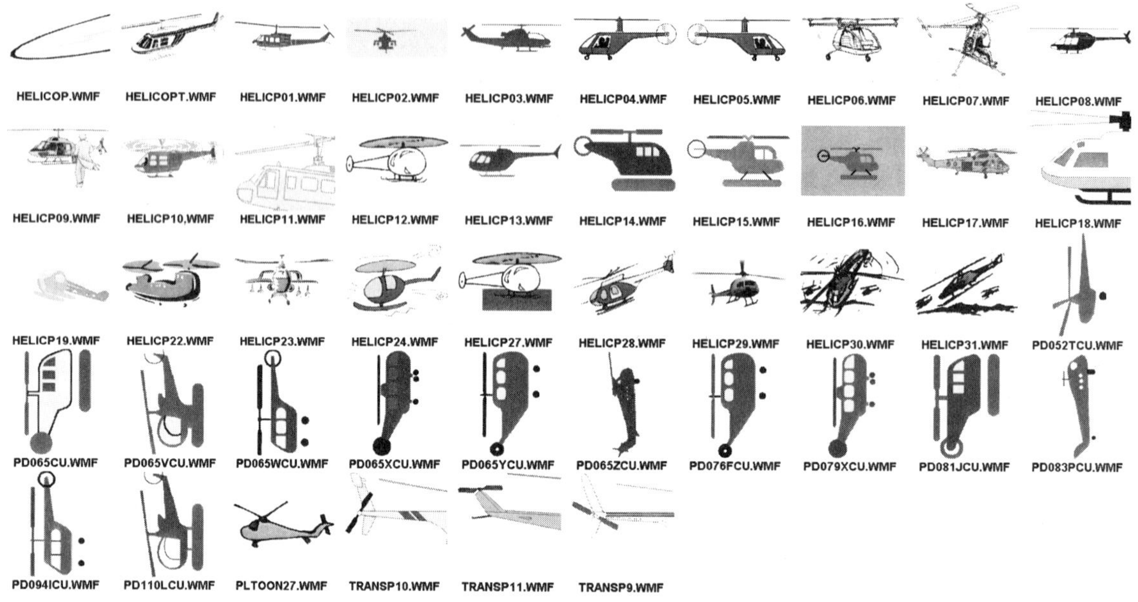

Transportation (TRANSPRT) • Other Air (OTHERAIR)

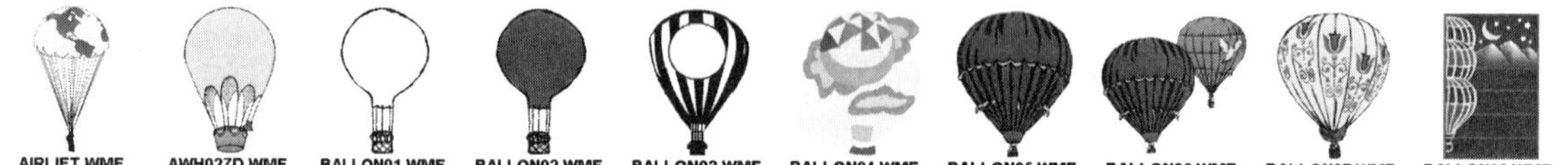

AIRLIFT.WMF AWH027D.WMF BALLON01.WMF BALLON02.WMF BALLON03.WMF BALLON04.WMF BALLON05.WMF BALLON06.WMF BALLON07.WMF BALLON08.WMF

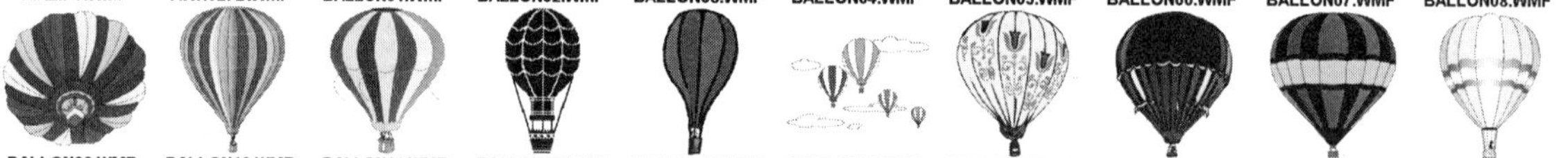

BALLON09.WMF BALLON10.WMF BALLON11.WMF BALLON12.WMF BALLON13.WMF BALLON14.WMF BALLON16.WMF BALLON18.WMF BALLON19.WMF BALLON20.WMF

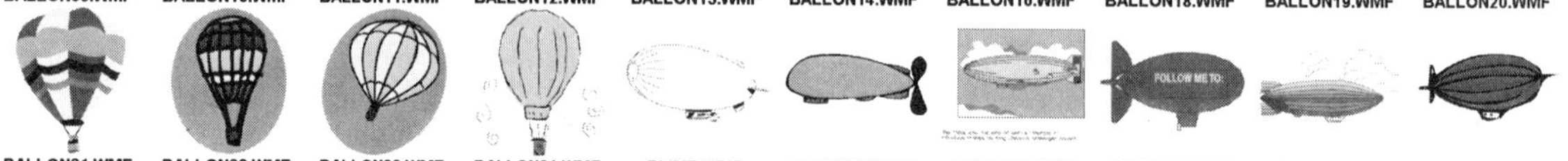

BALLON21.WMF BALLON22.WMF BALLON23.WMF BALLON24.WMF BLIMP.WMF BLIMP001.WMF BLIMP002.WMF BLIMP003.WMF BLIMP004.WMF BLIMP005.WMF

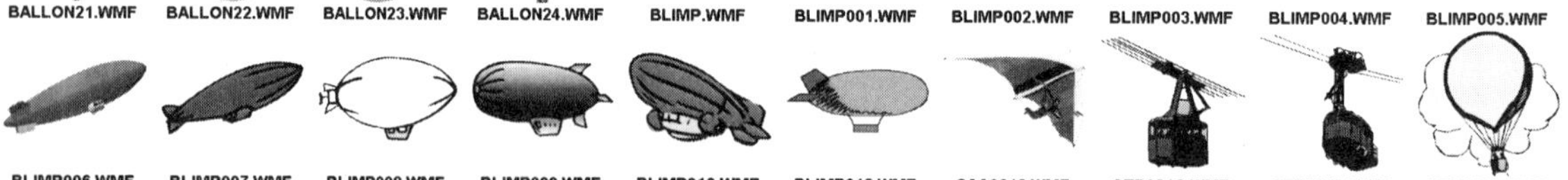

BLIMP006.WMF BLIMP007.WMF BLIMP008.WMF BLIMP009.WMF BLIMP010.WMF BLIMP012.WMF CAA0612.WMF CTP031C.WMF CTP031D.WMF DEC081D.WMF

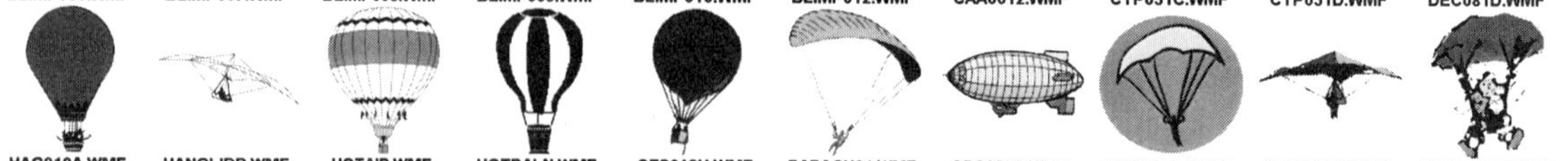

HAG019A.WMF HANGLIDR.WMF HOTAIR.WMF HOTBALN.WMF OFS043H.WMF PARACH01.WMF SPA031A.WMF SPBO004J.WMF SPCA113J.WMF SPGC069D.WMF

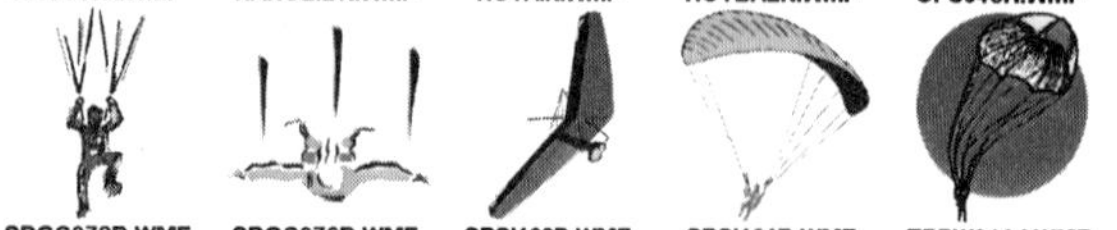

SPGC072D.WMF SPGC076D.WMF SPSI463D.WMF SPSI464D.WMF TRRW014J.WMF

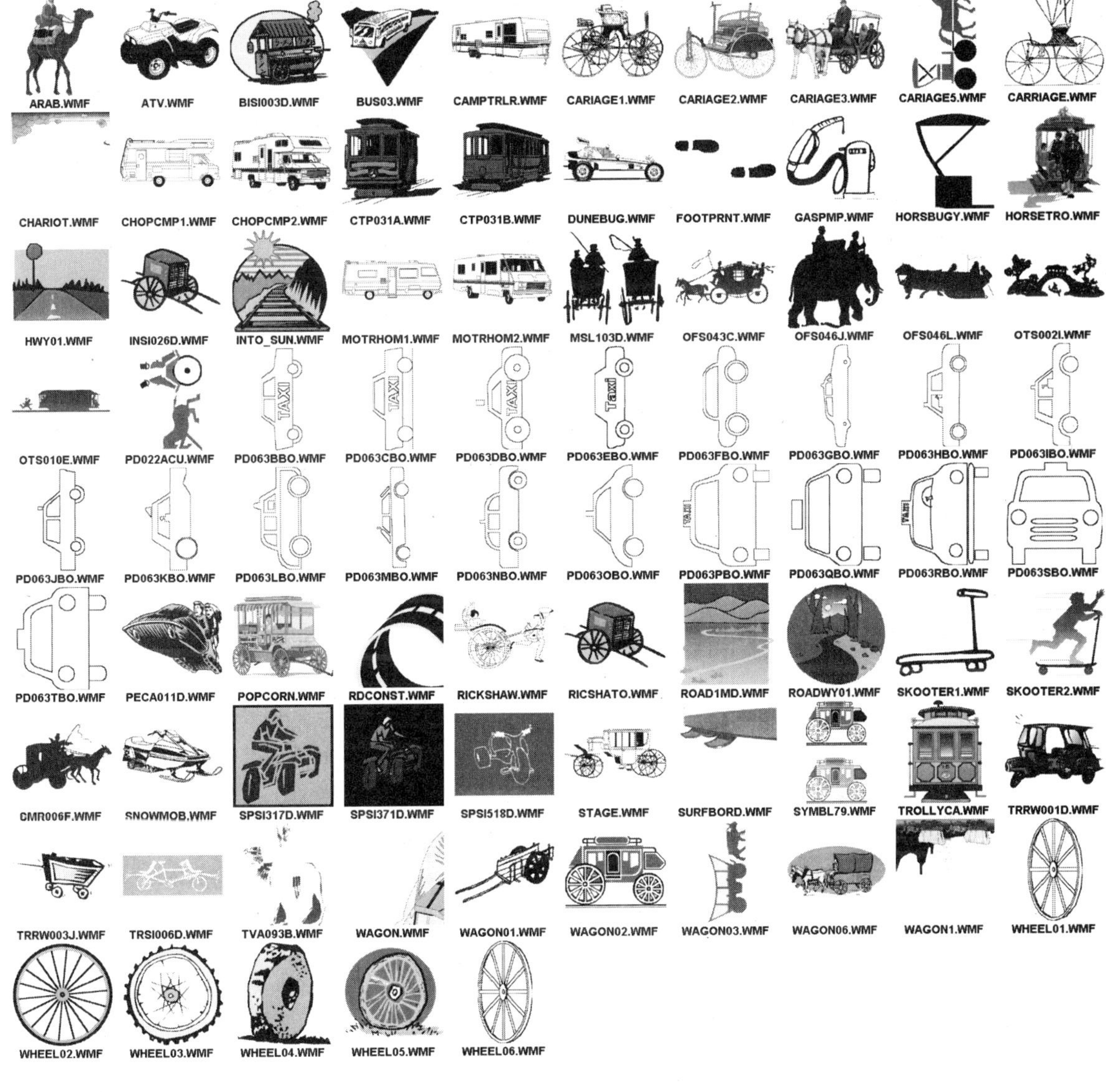

ARAB.WMF
ATV.WMF
BISI003D.WMF
BUS03.WMF
CAMPTRLR.WMF
CARIAGE1.WMF
CARIAGE2.WMF
CARIAGE3.WMF
CARIAGE5.WMF
CARRIAGE.WMF
CHARIOT.WMF
CHOPCMP1.WMF
CHOPCMP2.WMF
CTP031A.WMF
CTP031B.WMF
DUNEBUG.WMF
FOOTPRNT.WMF
GASPMP.WMF
HORSBUGY.WMF
HORSETRO.WMF
HWY01.WMF
INSI026D.WMF
INTO_SUN.WMF
MOTRHOM1.WMF
MOTRHOM2.WMF
MSL103D.WMF
OFS043C.WMF
OFS046J.WMF
OFS046L.WMF
OTS002I.WMF
OTS010E.WMF
PD022ACU.WMF
PD063BBO.WMF
PD063CBO.WMF
PD063DBO.WMF
PD063EBO.WMF
PD063FBO.WMF
PD063GBO.WMF
PD063HBO.WMF
PD063IBO.WMF
PD063JBO.WMF
PD063KBO.WMF
PD063LBO.WMF
PD063MBO.WMF
PD063NBO.WMF
PD063OBO.WMF
PD063PBO.WMF
PD063QBO.WMF
PD063RBO.WMF
PD063SBO.WMF
PD063TBO.WMF
PECA011D.WMF
POPCORN.WMF
RDCONST.WMF
RICKSHAW.WMF
RICSHATO.WMF
ROAD1MD.WMF
ROADWY01.WMF
SKOOTER1.WMF
SKOOTER2.WMF
SMR006F.WMF
SNOWMOB.WMF
SPSI317D.WMF
SPSI371D.WMF
SPSI518D.WMF
STAGE.WMF
SURFBORD.WMF
SYMBL79.WMF
TROLLYCA.WMF
TRRW001D.WMF
TRRW003J.WMF
TRSI006D.WMF
TVA093B.WMF
WAGON.WMF
WAGON01.WMF
WAGON02.WMF
WAGON03.WMF
WAGON06.WMF
WAGON1.WMF
WHEEL01.WMF
WHEEL02.WMF
WHEEL03.WMF
WHEEL04.WMF
WHEEL05.WMF
WHEEL06.WMF

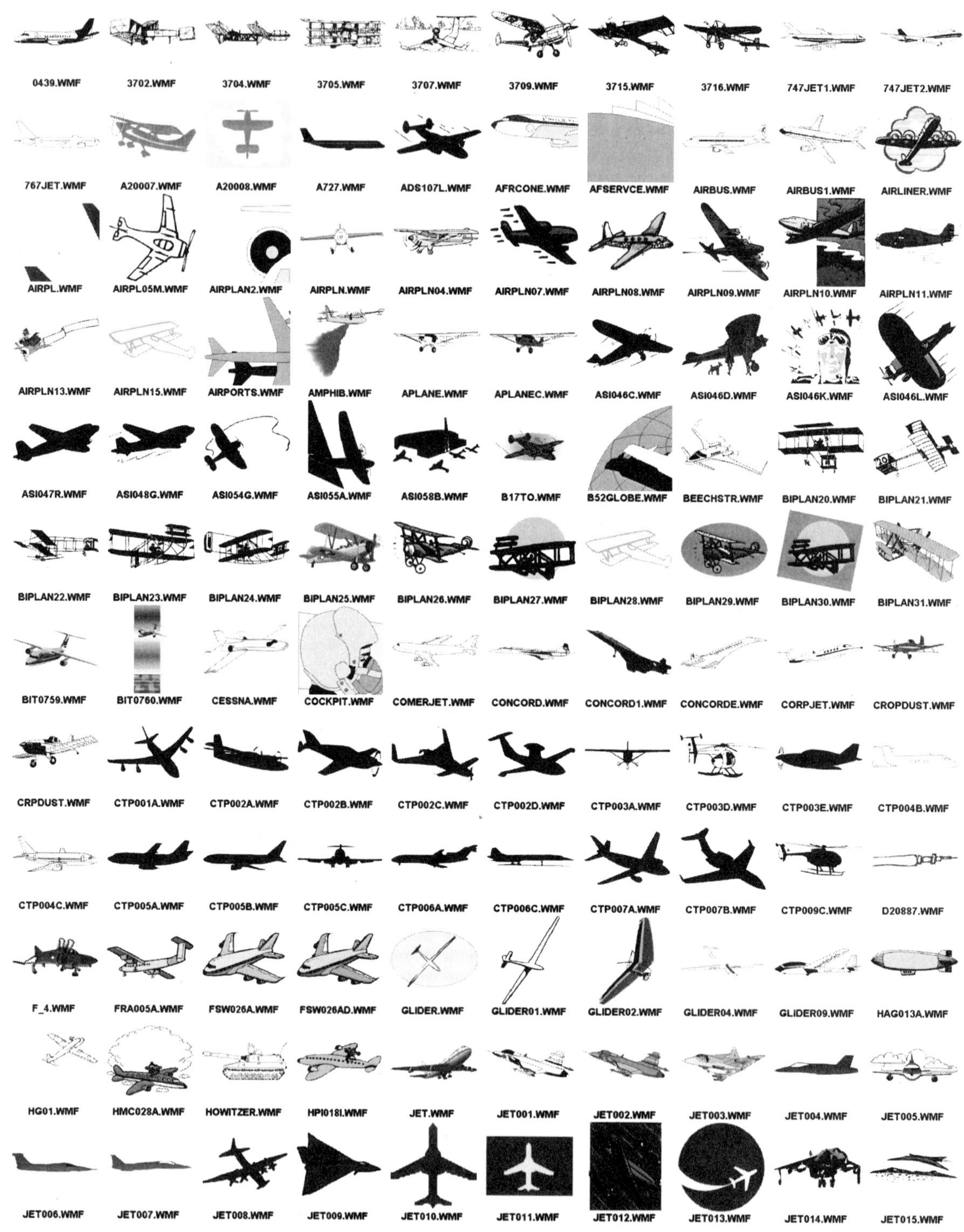
0439.WMF 3702.WMF 3704.WMF 3705.WMF 3707.WMF 3709.WMF 3715.WMF 3716.WMF 747JET1.WMF 747JET2.WMF
767JET.WMF A20007.WMF A20008.WMF A727.WMF ADS107L.WMF AFRCONE.WMF AFSERVCE.WMF AIRBUS.WMF AIRBUS1.WMF AIRLINER.WMF
AIRPL.WMF AIRPL05M.WMF AIRPLAN2.WMF AIRPLN.WMF AIRPLN04.WMF AIRPLN07.WMF AIRPLN08.WMF AIRPLN09.WMF AIRPLN10.WMF AIRPLN11.WMF
AIRPLN13.WMF AIRPLN15.WMF AIRPORTS.WMF AMPHIB.WMF APLANE.WMF APLANEC.WMF ASI046C.WMF ASI046D.WMF ASI046K.WMF ASI046L.WMF
ASI047R.WMF ASI048G.WMF ASI054G.WMF ASI055A.WMF ASI058B.WMF B17TO.WMF B52GLOBE.WMF BEECHSTR.WMF BIPLAN20.WMF BIPLAN21.WMF
BIPLAN22.WMF BIPLAN23.WMF BIPLAN24.WMF BIPLAN25.WMF BIPLAN26.WMF BIPLAN27.WMF BIPLAN28.WMF BIPLAN29.WMF BIPLAN30.WMF BIPLAN31.WMF
BIT0759.WMF BIT0760.WMF CESSNA.WMF COCKPIT.WMF COMERJET.WMF CONCORD.WMF CONCORD1.WMF CONCORDE.WMF CORPJET.WMF CROPDUST.WMF
CRPDUST.WMF CTP001A.WMF CTP002A.WMF CTP002B.WMF CTP002C.WMF CTP002D.WMF CTP003A.WMF CTP003D.WMF CTP003E.WMF CTP004B.WMF
CTP004C.WMF CTP005A.WMF CTP005B.WMF CTP005C.WMF CTP006A.WMF CTP006C.WMF CTP007A.WMF CTP007B.WMF CTP009C.WMF D20887.WMF
F_4.WMF FRA005A.WMF FSW026A.WMF FSW026AD.WMF GLIDER.WMF GLIDER01.WMF GLIDER02.WMF GLIDER04.WMF GLIDER09.WMF HAG013A.WMF
HG01.WMF HMC028A.WMF HOWITZER.WMF HPI018I.WMF JET.WMF JET001.WMF JET002.WMF JET003.WMF JET004.WMF JET005.WMF
JET006.WMF JET007.WMF JET008.WMF JET009.WMF JET010.WMF JET011.WMF JET012.WMF JET013.WMF JET014.WMF JET015.WMF

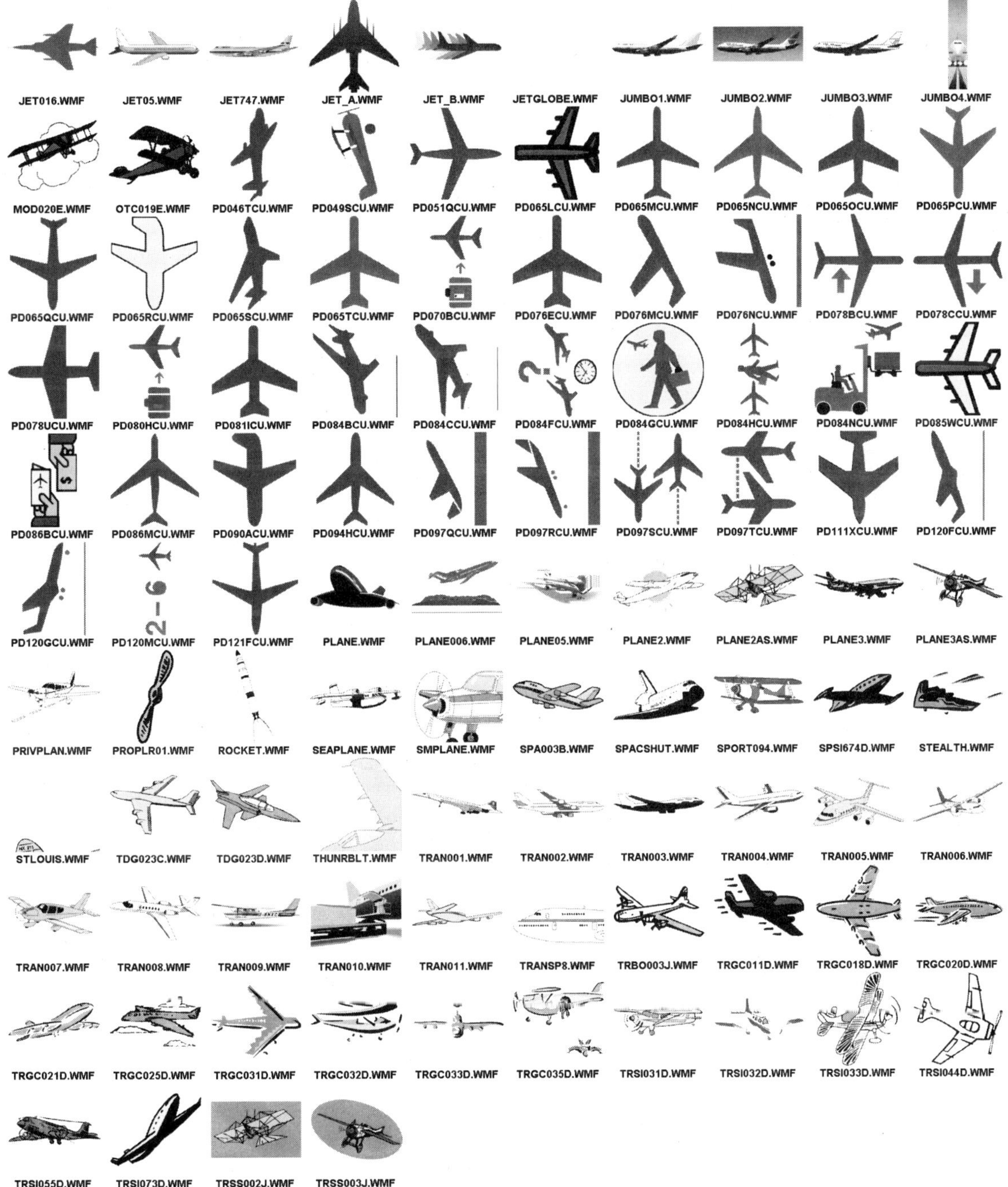
JET016.WMF
JET05.WMF
JET747.WMF
JET_A.WMF
JET_B.WMF
JETGLOBE.WMF
JUMBO1.WMF
JUMBO2.WMF
JUMBO3.WMF
JUMBO4.WMF
MOD020E.WMF
OTC019E.WMF
PD046TCU.WMF
PD049SCU.WMF
PD051QCU.WMF
PD065LCU.WMF
PD065MCU.WMF
PD065NCU.WMF
PD065OCU.WMF
PD065PCU.WMF
PD065QCU.WMF
PD065RCU.WMF
PD065SCU.WMF
PD065TCU.WMF
PD070BCU.WMF
PD076ECU.WMF
PD076MCU.WMF
PD076NCU.WMF
PD078BCU.WMF
PD078CCU.WMF
PD078UCU.WMF
PD080HCU.WMF
PD081ICU.WMF
PD084BCU.WMF
PD084CCU.WMF
PD084FCU.WMF
PD084GCU.WMF
PD084HCU.WMF
PD084NCU.WMF
PD085WCU.WMF
PD086BCU.WMF
PD086MCU.WMF
PD090ACU.WMF
PD094HCU.WMF
PD097QCU.WMF
PD097RCU.WMF
PD097SCU.WMF
PD097TCU.WMF
PD111XCU.WMF
PD120FCU.WMF
PD120GCU.WMF
PD120MCU.WMF
PD121FCU.WMF
PLANE.WMF
PLANE006.WMF
PLANE05.WMF
PLANE2.WMF
PLANE2AS.WMF
PLANE3.WMF
PLANE3AS.WMF
PRIVPLAN.WMF
PROPLR01.WMF
ROCKET.WMF
SEAPLANE.WMF
SMPLANE.WMF
SPA003B.WMF
SPACSHUT.WMF
SPORT094.WMF
SPSI674D.WMF
STEALTH.WMF
STLOUIS.WMF
TDG023C.WMF
TDG023D.WMF
THUNRBLT.WMF
TRAN001.WMF
TRAN002.WMF
TRAN003.WMF
TRAN004.WMF
TRAN005.WMF
TRAN006.WMF
TRAN007.WMF
TRAN008.WMF
TRAN009.WMF
TRAN010.WMF
TRAN011.WMF
TRANSP8.WMF
TRBO003J.WMF
TRGC011D.WMF
TRGC018D.WMF
TRGC020D.WMF
TRGC021D.WMF
TRGC025D.WMF
TRGC031D.WMF
TRGC032D.WMF
TRGC033D.WMF
TRGC035D.WMF
TRSI031D.WMF
TRSI032D.WMF
TRSI033D.WMF
TRSI044D.WMF
TRSI055D.WMF
TRSI073D.WMF
TRSS002J.WMF
TRSS003J.WMF

0477.WMF
1672.WMF
3721.WMF
AFPLANE.WMF
AIRCARR.WMF
AIRPLN01.WMF
AIRPLN02.WMF
AIRPLN03.WMF
AIRPLN04.WMF
AIRPLN05.WMF
AIRPLN06.WMF
AIRPLN07.WMF
AIRPLN08.WMF
AIRPLN09.WMF
AIRPLN10.WMF
AIRPLN11.WMF
AIRPLN12.WMF
AIRPLN13.WMF
AIRPLN14.WMF
AIRPLN15.WMF
AIRPLN16.WMF
AIRPLN17.WMF
AIRPLN18.WMF
AIRPLN19.WMF
AIRPORT.WMF
ANCHOR.WMF
ASI051H.WMF
ATV1.WMF
ATV2.WMF
AUTO1.WMF
AUTO2.WMF
AUTO3.WMF
AUTO4.WMF
AUTO400.WMF
AUTO5.WMF
AUTO6.WMF
AUTO_1.WMF
AUTOACC.WMF
AUTOBODY.WMF
AUTOREPR.WMF
BACK111.WMF
BACKHOE.WMF
BARGE.WMF
BATSHIP1.WMF
BATSHIP2.WMF
BATSHIP3.WMF
BATTERY.WMF
BIT0150.WMF
BIT0352.WMF
BIT0359.WMF
BIT0362.WMF
BIT0363.WMF
BOATSIL.WMF
BRAKEDIS.WMF
BRAKEOIL.WMF
BRAKESDR.WMF
BULLDZR.WMF
BUS.WMF
BUS1.WMF
BUS2.WMF
BUS3.WMF
CAMPER1.WMF
CAMPER2.WMF
CAMPER3.WMF
CAMPER4.WMF
CAMPER5.WMF
CANOE.WMF
CARAUDIO.WMF
CARAVAN.WMF
CHOPPER.WMF
CIGLIGHT.WMF
CMNTMXR.WMF
CONTASB.WMF
COPTER1.WMF
COVWGN.WMF
CREEPER.WMF
CS84_.WMF
DDG51SHP.WMF
DRAGSIL.WMF
ELS007B.WMF
EV109.WMF
EXCAVSIL.WMF
FIRETRK.WMF
FORKLFT.WMF
FORKLIFT.WMF
FORWARD.WMF
FUEL.WMF
GONDOLA.WMF
GRADER.WMF
HELICOP1.WMF
HELICOP2.WMF
HELICOP3.WMF
HELICOP4.WMF
HIRANGE.WMF
HORSBUG1.WMF
HORSBUG2.WMF
HOTAIR.WMF
IGNITION.WMF
KAYAK.WMF
LIGHTS.WMF
LIMOUSIN.WMF
LOWRANGE.WMF
MECHANIC.WMF
MONORAIL.WMF
MOTRCYC1.WMF
MOTRCYC2.WMF
MOTRCYC3.WMF
MUFFLER.WMF
NASI178D.WMF
NEUTRAL.WMF
OFS038K.WMF
OFS042I.WMF
OFS042J.WMF
OFS046G.WMF
OILCHG.WMF
OTS002L.WMF
OTS010E.WMF
PD022ICU.WMF
PD022JCU.WMF
PD022KCU.WMF

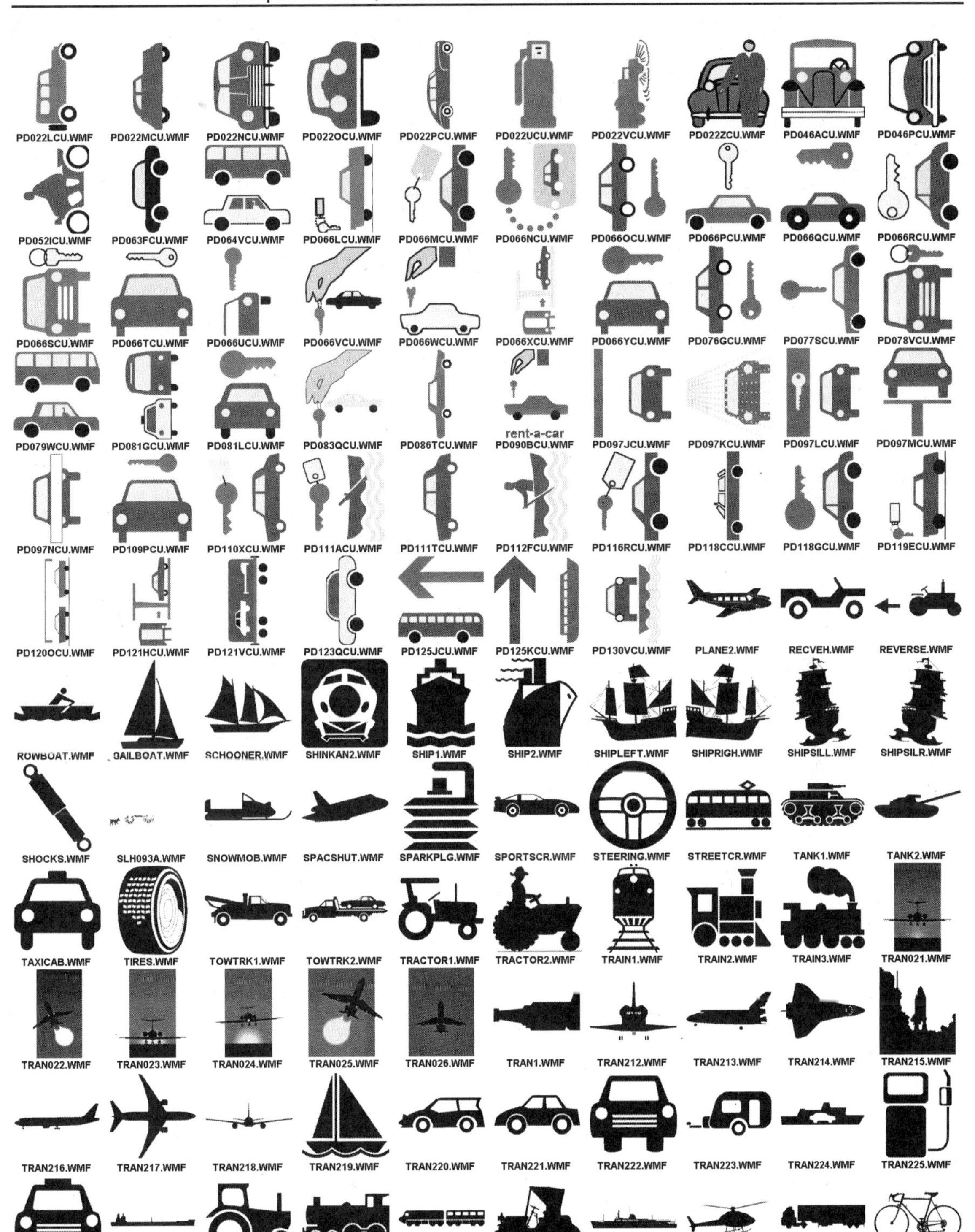
PD022LCU.WMF
PD022MCU.WMF
PD022NCU.WMF
PD022OCU.WMF
PD022PCU.WMF
PD022UCU.WMF
PD022VCU.WMF
PD022ZCU.WMF
PD046ACU.WMF
PD046PCU.WMF
PD052ICU.WMF
PD063FCU.WMF
PD064VCU.WMF
PD066LCU.WMF
PD066MCU.WMF
PD066NCU.WMF
PD066OCU.WMF
PD066PCU.WMF
PD066QCU.WMF
PD066RCU.WMF
PD066SCU.WMF
PD066TCU.WMF
PD066UCU.WMF
PD066VCU.WMF
PD066WCU.WMF
PD066XCU.WMF
PD066YCU.WMF
PD076GCU.WMF
PD077SCU.WMF
PD078VCU.WMF
PD079WCU.WMF
PD081GCU.WMF
PD081LCU.WMF
PD083QCU.WMF
PD086TCU.WMF
rent-a-car
PD090BCU.WMF
PD097JCU.WMF
PD097KCU.WMF
PD097LCU.WMF
PD097MCU.WMF
PD097NCU.WMF
PD109PCU.WMF
PD110XCU.WMF
PD111ACU.WMF
PD111TCU.WMF
PD112FCU.WMF
PD116RCU.WMF
PD118CCU.WMF
PD118GCU.WMF
PD119ECU.WMF
PD120OCU.WMF
PD121HCU.WMF
PD121VCU.WMF
PD123QCU.WMF
PD125JCU.WMF
PD125KCU.WMF
PD130VCU.WMF
PLANE2.WMF
RECVEH.WMF
REVERSE.WMF
ROWBOAT.WMF
SAILBOAT.WMF
SCHOONER.WMF
SHINKAN2.WMF
SHIP1.WMF
SHIP2.WMF
SHIPLEFT.WMF
SHIPRIGH.WMF
SHIPSILL.WMF
SHIPSILR.WMF
SHOCKS.WMF
SLH093A.WMF
SNOWMOB.WMF
SPACSHUT.WMF
SPARKPLG.WMF
SPORTSCR.WMF
STEERING.WMF
STREETCR.WMF
TANK1.WMF
TANK2.WMF
TAXICAB.WMF
TIRES.WMF
TOWTRK1.WMF
TOWTRK2.WMF
TRACTOR1.WMF
TRACTOR2.WMF
TRAIN1.WMF
TRAIN2.WMF
TRAIN3.WMF
TRAN021.WMF
TRAN022.WMF
TRAN023.WMF
TRAN024.WMF
TRAN025.WMF
TRAN026.WMF
TRAN1.WMF
TRAN212.WMF
TRAN213.WMF
TRAN214.WMF
TRAN215.WMF
TRAN216.WMF
TRAN217.WMF
TRAN218.WMF
TRAN219.WMF
TRAN220.WMF
TRAN221.WMF
TRAN222.WMF
TRAN223.WMF
TRAN224.WMF
TRAN225.WMF
TRAN226.WMF
TRAN227.WMF
TRAN228.WMF
TRAN229.WMF
TRAN230.WMF
TRAN231.WMF
TRAN232.WMF
TRAN233.WMF
TRAN234.WMF
TRAN235.WMF

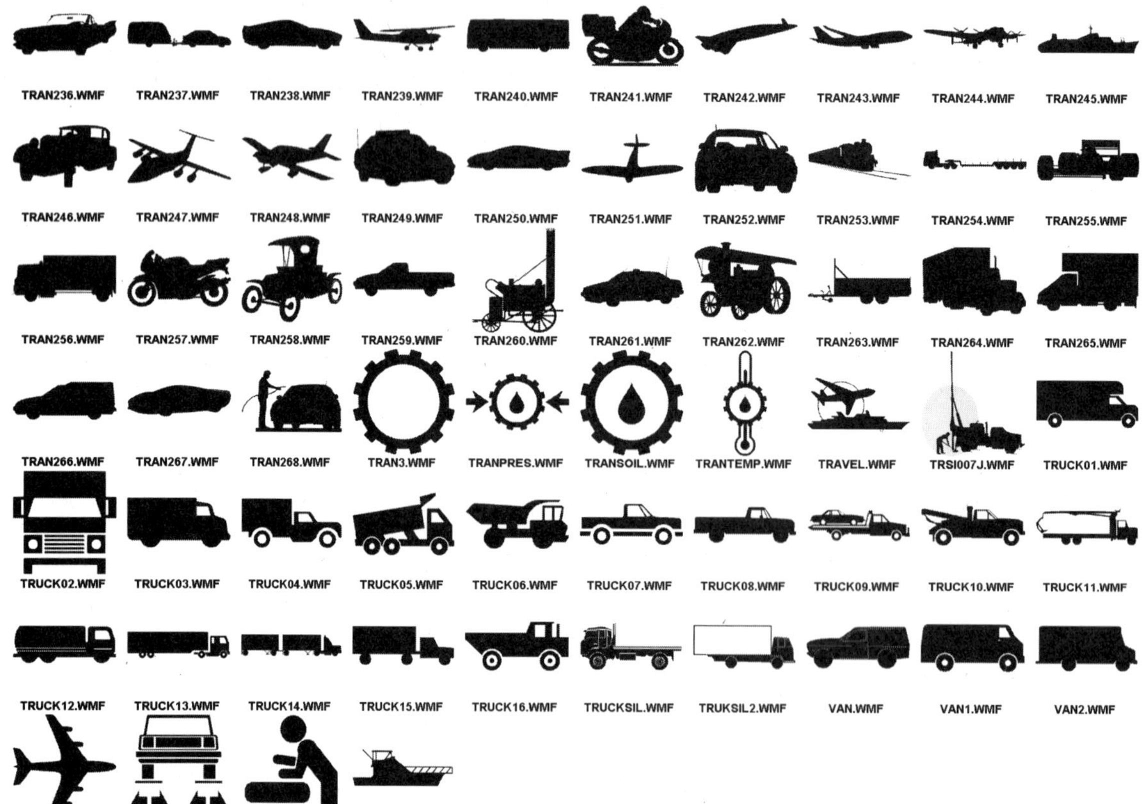
TRAN236.WMF
TRAN237.WMF
TRAN238.WMF
TRAN239.WMF
TRAN240.WMF
TRAN241.WMF
TRAN242.WMF
TRAN243.WMF
TRAN244.WMF
TRAN245.WMF
TRAN246.WMF
TRAN247.WMF
TRAN248.WMF
TRAN249.WMF
TRAN250.WMF
TRAN251.WMF
TRAN252.WMF
TRAN253.WMF
TRAN254.WMF
TRAN255.WMF
TRAN256.WMF
TRAN257.WMF
TRAN258.WMF
TRAN259.WMF
TRAN260.WMF
TRAN261.WMF
TRAN262.WMF
TRAN263.WMF
TRAN264.WMF
TRAN265.WMF
TRAN266.WMF
TRAN267.WMF
TRAN268.WMF
TRAN3.WMF
TRANPRES.WMF
TRANSOIL.WMF
TRANTEMP.WMF
TRAVEL.WMF
TRSI007J.WMF
TRUCK01.WMF
TRUCK02.WMF
TRUCK03.WMF
TRUCK04.WMF
TRUCK05.WMF
TRUCK06.WMF
TRUCK07.WMF
TRUCK08.WMF
TRUCK09.WMF
TRUCK10.WMF
TRUCK11.WMF
TRUCK12.WMF
TRUCK13.WMF
TRUCK14.WMF
TRUCK15.WMF
TRUCK16.WMF
TRUCKSIL.WMF
TRUKSIL2.WMF
VAN.WMF
VAN1.WMF
VAN2.WMF
WARPLANE.WMF
WHALIGN.WMF
WHBAL.WMF
YACHT.WMF

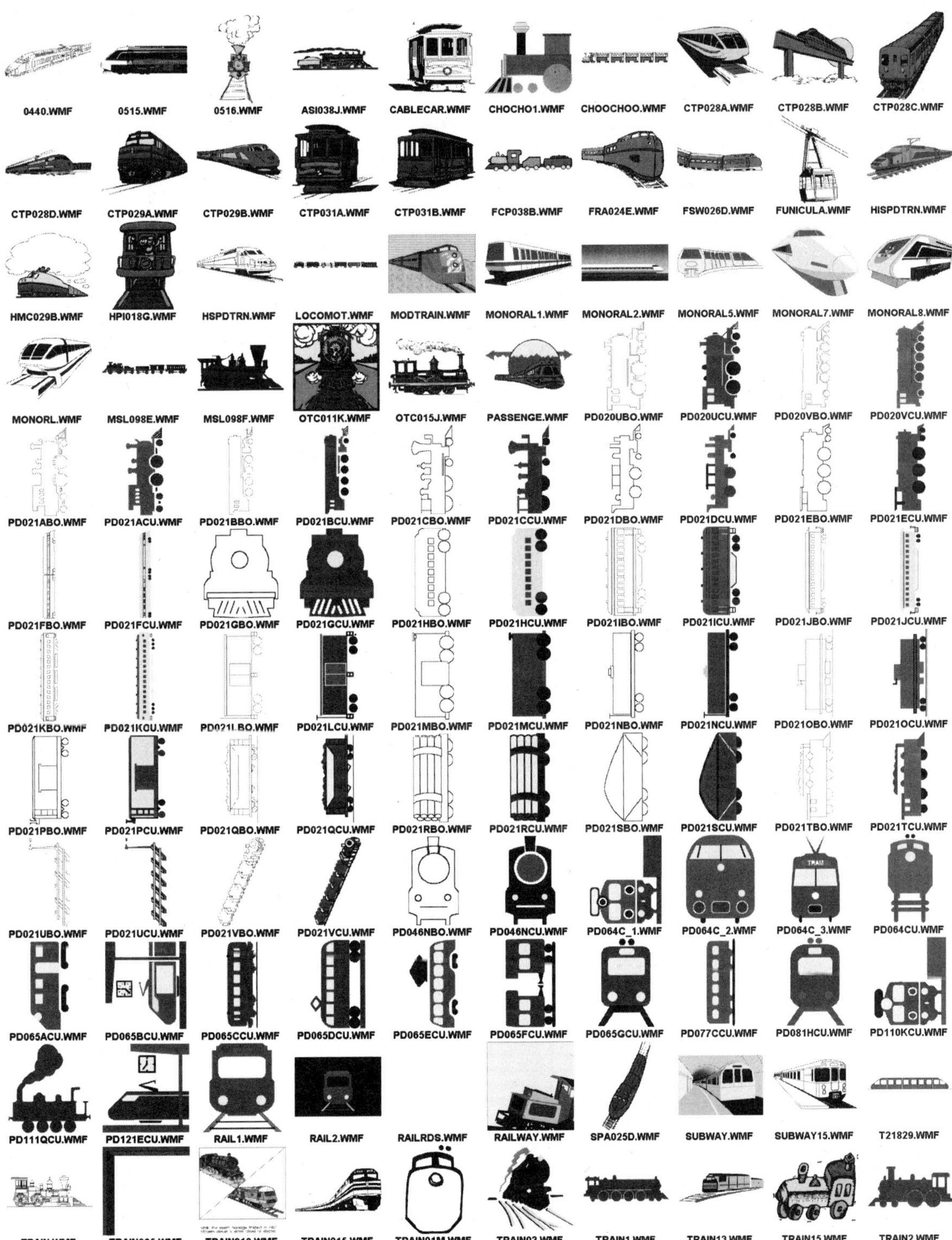
0440.WMF 0515.WMF 0516.WMF ASI038J.WMF CABLECAR.WMF CHOCHO1.WMF CHOOCHOO.WMF CTP028A.WMF CTP028B.WMF CTP028C.WMF
CTP028D.WMF CTP029A.WMF CTP029B.WMF CTP031A.WMF CTP031B.WMF FCP038B.WMF FRA024E.WMF FSW026D.WMF FUNICULA.WMF HISPDTRN.WMF
HMC029B.WMF HPI018G.WMF HSPDTRN.WMF LOCOMOT.WMF MODTRAIN.WMF MONORAL1.WMF MONORAL2.WMF MONORAL5.WMF MONORAL7.WMF MONORAL8.WMF
MONORL.WMF MSL098E.WMF MSL098F.WMF OTC011K.WMF OTC015J.WMF PASSENGE.WMF PD020UBO.WMF PD020UCU.WMF PD020VBO.WMF PD020VCU.WMF
PD021ABO.WMF PD021ACU.WMF PD021BBO.WMF PD021BCU.WMF PD021CBO.WMF PD021CCU.WMF PD021DBO.WMF PD021DCU.WMF PD021EBO.WMF PD021ECU.WMF
PD021FBO.WMF PD021FCU.WMF PD021GBO.WMF PD021GCU.WMF PD021HBO.WMF PD021HCU.WMF PD021IBO.WMF PD021ICU.WMF PD021JBO.WMF PD021JCU.WMF
PD021KBO.WMF PD021KCU.WMF PD021LBO.WMF PD021LCU.WMF PD021MBO.WMF PD021MCU.WMF PD021NBO.WMF PD021NCU.WMF PD021OBO.WMF PD021OCU.WMF
PD021PBO.WMF PD021PCU.WMF PD021QBO.WMF PD021QCU.WMF PD021RBO.WMF PD021RCU.WMF PD021SBO.WMF PD021SCU.WMF PD021TBO.WMF PD021TCU.WMF
PD021UBO.WMF PD021UCU.WMF PD021VBO.WMF PD021VCU.WMF PD046NBO.WMF PD046NCU.WMF PD064C_1.WMF PD064C_2.WMF PD064C_3.WMF PD064CU.WMF
PD065ACU.WMF PD065BCU.WMF PD065CCU.WMF PD065DCU.WMF PD065ECU.WMF PD065FCU.WMF PD065GCU.WMF PD077CCU.WMF PD081HCU.WMF PD110KCU.WMF
PD111QCU.WMF PD121ECU.WMF RAIL1.WMF RAIL2.WMF RAILRDS.WMF RAILWAY.WMF SPA025D.WMF SUBWAY.WMF SUBWAY15.WMF T21829.WMF
TRAIN.WMF TRAIN005.WMF TRAIN010.WMF TRAIN015.WMF TRAIN01M.WMF TRAIN03.WMF TRAIN1.WMF TRAIN13.WMF TRAIN15.WMF TRAIN2.WMF

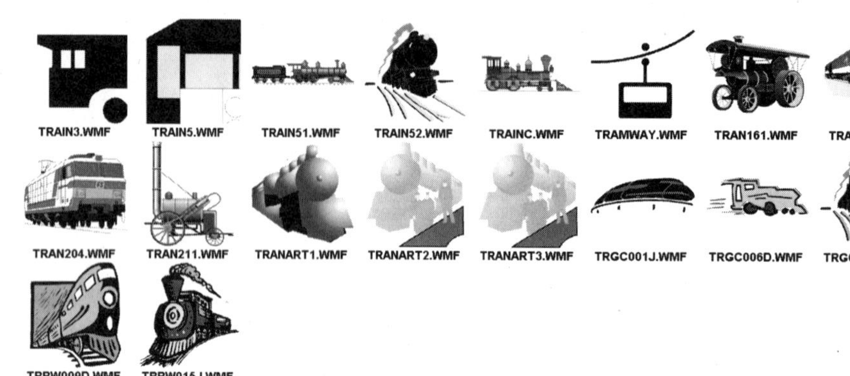
TRAIN3.WMF
TRAIN5.WMF
TRAIN51.WMF
TRAIN52.WMF
TRAINC.WMF
TRAMWAY.WMF
TRAN161.WMF
TRAN199.WMF
TRAN200.WMF
TRAN201.WMF
TRAN204.WMF
TRAN211.WMF
TRANART1.WMF
TRANART2.WMF
TRANART3.WMF
TRGC001J.WMF
TRGC006D.WMF
TRGC008D.WMF
TRGC014D.WMF
TRGC038D.WMF
TRRW009D.WMF
TRRW015J.WMF

0487.WMF 0492.WMF 0502.WMF 0503.WMF 0504.WMF 0509.WMF 0510.WMF 1079ANCC.WMF 1STEAM_S.WMF 2772.WMF

2STEAM_S.WMF 3722.WMF 4420.WMF 4421.WMF AERIALBR.WMF AIRBOAT.WMF AIRCARR.WMF ANCHOR.WMF ANCHOR01.WMF ANCHOR02.WMF

ANCHOR03.WMF ANCHOR04.WMF ANCHOR05.WMF ANCHORSA.WMF AOD076C.WMF AOD076D.WMF ARC017.WMF ASI042L.WMF ASI042M.WMF ASI043K.WMF

ASI044I.WMF ASI045B.WMF ASI045H.WMF ASI055F.WMF ASI058K.WMF ASI061K.WMF B45D.WMF B45G.WMF B45GB.WMF BATTLESH.WMF

BISMRK.WMF BOAT002.WMF BOAT01.WMF BOAT02.WMF BOAT03.WMF BOAT04.WMF BOAT05.WMF BOAT06.WMF BOAT07.WMF BOAT08.WMF

BOAT09.WMF BOAT1.WMF BOAT10.WMF BOAT11.WMF BOAT12.WMF BOAT13.WMF BOAT14.WMF BOAT15.WMF BOAT17.WMF BOAT18.WMF

BOAT19.WMF BOAT2.WMF BOAT20.WMF BOAT21.WMF BOAT22.WMF BOAT23.WMF BOATAS.WMF BOATING.WMF BUSI028D.WMF BUSI139D.WMF

C20803.WMF CAA0482.WMF CABCRUSE.WMF CANOE.WMF CANOE005.WMF CANOE01.WMF CANOE02.WMF CANOE03.WMF CANOE6.WMF CARGO.WMF

CARGO01.WMF CAT.WMF CAT01.WMF CATFERRY.WMF CATMARAN.WMF CHIKATET.WMF CLIPERSH.WMF CLIPPER.WMF CLIPPER1.WMF CLIPPER2.WMF

CLIPPER4.WMF CLIPPER5.WMF CLIPPER6.WMF CLIPPER8.WMF CLIPPER9.WMF CLIPPR.WMF COBRASHP.WMF COLLR.WMF CRUISE.WMF CRUISE01.WMF

CRUISE05.WMF CRUISE1.WMF CRUISE2.WMF CRUISE50.WMF CRUISESH.WMF CRUISSHP.WMF CTP008B.WMF CTP009A.WMF CTP010C.WMF CTP011B.WMF

DAYSLR.WMF DCS075A.WMF DEC079EE.WMF DEC079L.WMF DEC079U.WMF DESTR.WMF DHOW.WMF DOUBLEHU.WMF DRIFT.WMF DRIFTER.WMF

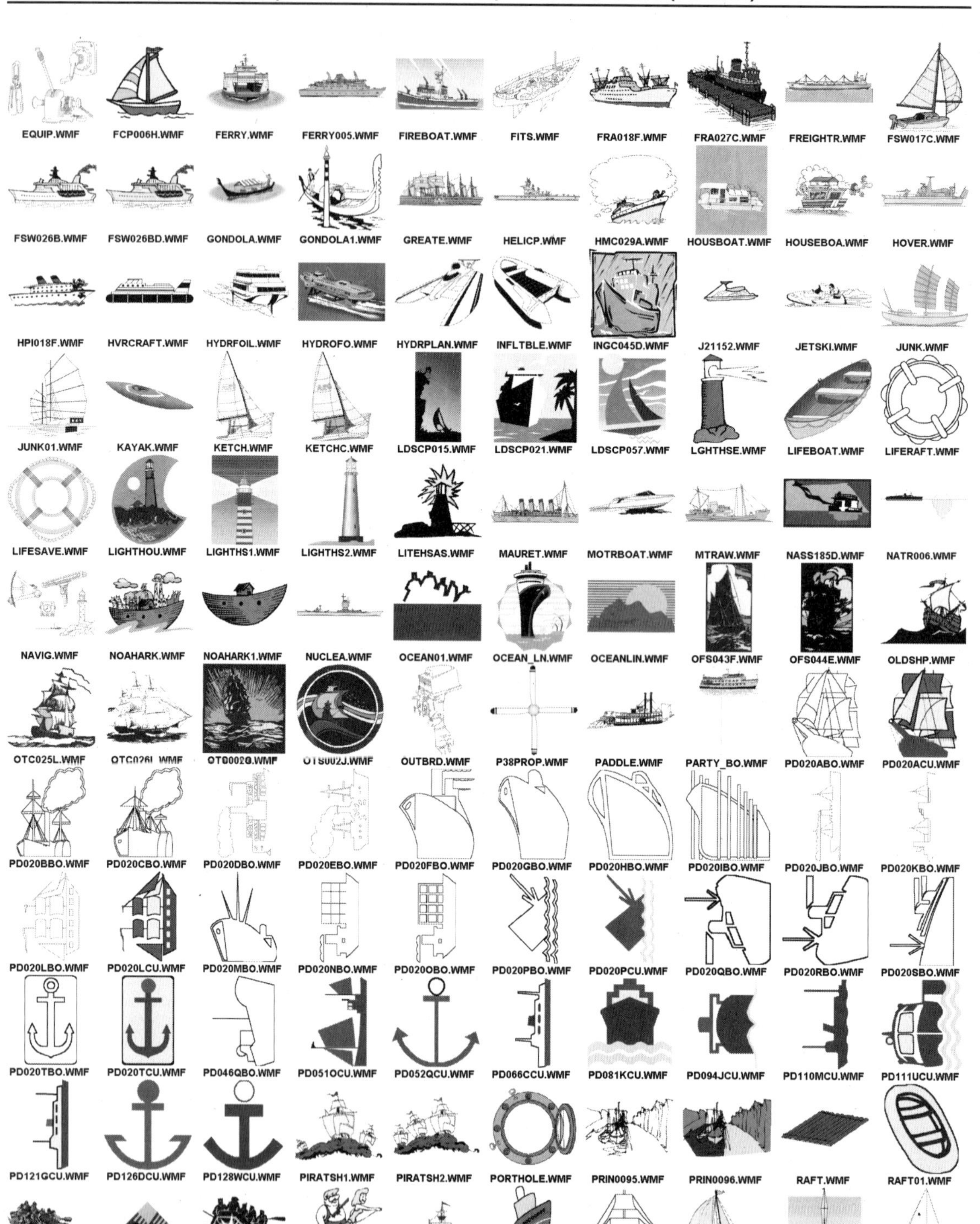
EQUIP.WMF FCP006H.WMF FERRY.WMF FERRY005.WMF FIREBOAT.WMF FITS.WMF FRA018F.WMF FRA027C.WMF FREIGHTR.WMF FSW017C.WMF
FSW026B.WMF FSW026BD.WMF GONDOLA.WMF GONDOLA1.WMF GREATE.WMF HELICP.WMF HMC029A.WMF HOUSBOAT.WMF HOUSEBOA.WMF HOVER.WMF
HPI018F.WMF HVRCRAFT.WMF HYDRFOIL.WMF HYDROFO.WMF HYDRPLAN.WMF INFLTBLE.WMF INGC045D.WMF J21152.WMF JETSKI.WMF JUNK.WMF
JUNK01.WMF KAYAK.WMF KETCH.WMF KETCHC.WMF LDSCP015.WMF LDSCP021.WMF LDSCP057.WMF LGHTHSE.WMF LIFEBOAT.WMF LIFERAFT.WMF
LIFESAVE.WMF LIGHTHOU.WMF LIGHTHS1.WMF LIGHTHS2.WMF LITEHSAS.WMF MAURET.WMF MOTRBOAT.WMF MTRAW.WMF NASS185D.WMF NATR006.WMF
NAVIG.WMF NOAHARK.WMF NOAHARK1.WMF NUCLEA.WMF OCEAN01.WMF OCEAN_LN.WMF OCEANLIN.WMF OFS043F.WMF OFS044E.WMF OLDSHP.WMF
OTC025L.WMF OTC026L.WMF OTS002G.WMF OTS002J.WMF OUTBRD.WMF P38PROP.WMF PADDLE.WMF PARTY_BO.WMF PD020ABO.WMF PD020ACU.WMF
PD020BBO.WMF PD020CBO.WMF PD020DBO.WMF PD020EBO.WMF PD020FBO.WMF PD020GBO.WMF PD020HBO.WMF PD020IBO.WMF PD020JBO.WMF PD020KBO.WMF
PD020LBO.WMF PD020LCU.WMF PD020MBO.WMF PD020NBO.WMF PD020OBO.WMF PD020PBO.WMF PD020PCU.WMF PD020QBO.WMF PD020RBO.WMF PD020SBO.WMF
PD020TBO.WMF PD020TCU.WMF PD046QBO.WMF PD051OCU.WMF PD052QCU.WMF PD066CCU.WMF PD081KCU.WMF PD094JCU.WMF PD110MCU.WMF PD111UCU.WMF
PD121GCU.WMF PD126DCU.WMF PD128WCU.WMF PIRATSH1.WMF PIRATSH2.WMF PORTHOLE.WMF PRIN0095.WMF PRIN0096.WMF RAFT.WMF RAFT01.WMF
RAFT04.WMF RAFT05.WMF RAFT06.WMF RAFT07.WMF S21677.WMF S21678.WMF S21679.WMF SAIL.WMF SAILBO_A.WMF SAILBOAT.WMF

SAILBOT0.WMF
SAILBOT1.WMF
SAILBOT3.WMF
SAILBOT4.WMF
SAILBOT5.WMF
SAILBOT6.WMF
SAILBOT7.WMF
SAILBOT8.WMF
SAILBOT9.WMF
SAILBT.WMF
SALBOATS.WMF
SANPAN.WMF
SATLITE2.WMF
SHICHIFU.WMF
SHIP008.WMF
SHIP01.WMF
SHIP010.WMF
SHIP02.WMF
SHIP03.WMF
SHIP04.WMF
SHIP05.WMF
SHIP1.WMF
SHIP12.WMF
SHIP2.WMF
SHIP5.WMF
SHIP51.WMF
SHIP52.WMF
SHIP_1.WMF
SHIPAC.WMF
SHIPCART.WMF
SHIPMORT.WMF
SHIPWTYP.WMF
SIGNAL.WMF
SIT070M.WMF
SMR018D.WMF
SMR020E.WMF
SPA018D.WMF
SPA030E.WMF
SPEEDBT.WMF
SPORT.WMF
SPRW029J.WMF
SPSI270D.WMF
SPSI612D.WMF
SPSI622D.WMF
SPSI624D.WMF
SPSS004D.WMF
STEAMBOA.WMF
STEAMBT.WMF
STEAMSHP.WMF
SUB.WMF
SUBMARIN.WMF
SUBMARN.WMF
SUNSET_S.WMF
SUPER.WMF
SUPERT.WMF
SUPRTANK.WMF
SYMBL12.WMF
SYMBL205.WMF
SYMBL206.WMF
SYMBL50.WMF
OYMBOL02.WMF
SYMBOL03.WMF
SYMBOL04.WMF
SYMBOL05.WMF
SYMBOL06.WMF
SYMBOL07.WMF
SYMBOL08.WMF
SYMBOL09.WMF
SYMBOL10.WMF
SYMBOL11.WMF
SYMBOL12.WMF
SYMBOL13.WMF
SYMBOL14.WMF
SYMBOL15.WMF
SYMBOL16.WMF
SYMBOL17.WMF
SYMBOL18.WMF
SYMBOL19.WMF
SYMBOL20.WMF
SYMBOL21.WMF
SYMBOL22.WMF
SYMBOL23.WMF
SYMBOL24.WMF
TALLSHIP.WMF
TDG026C.WMF
TOD076B.WMF
TOD076C.WMF
TRAN175.WMF
TRAN178.WMF
TRAN180.WMF
TRAN181.WMF
TRAN182.WMF
TRAN184.WMF
TRAN185.WMF
TRAN186.WMF
TRAN187.WMF
TRAN188.WMF
TRAN189.WMF
TRAN190.WMF
TRAN191.WMF
TRAN192.WMF
TRAN193.WMF
TRAN194.WMF
TRAN195.WMF
TRAN196.WMF
TRAN197.WMF
TRANS10.WMF
TRANSP5.WMF
TRAWL.WMF
TRAWLER.WMF
TRCA011J.WMF
TRCA020J.WMF
TRCA021J.WMF
TRGC013D.WMF
TRSI009D.WMF
TRSI009J.WMF
TRSI012D.WMF
TRSI037D.WMF
TRSI060D.WMF
TUG.WMF

TUG005.WMF

TUGBOAT.WMF

TUGBOAT1.WMF

TUGBOAT2.WMF

TUGBOAT8.WMF

TVA070E.WMF

TVA070F.WMF

TVL013A.WMF

VICALB.WMF

VICTRY.WMF

VIKING.WMF

VIKING02.WMF

VIKING1M.WMF

VIKNGSHP.WMF

WINDSOC1.WMF

WINDSRFR.WMF

YACHT.WMF

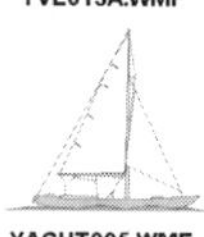
YACHT005.WMF

YACHT01.WMF

YOURSHIP.WMF

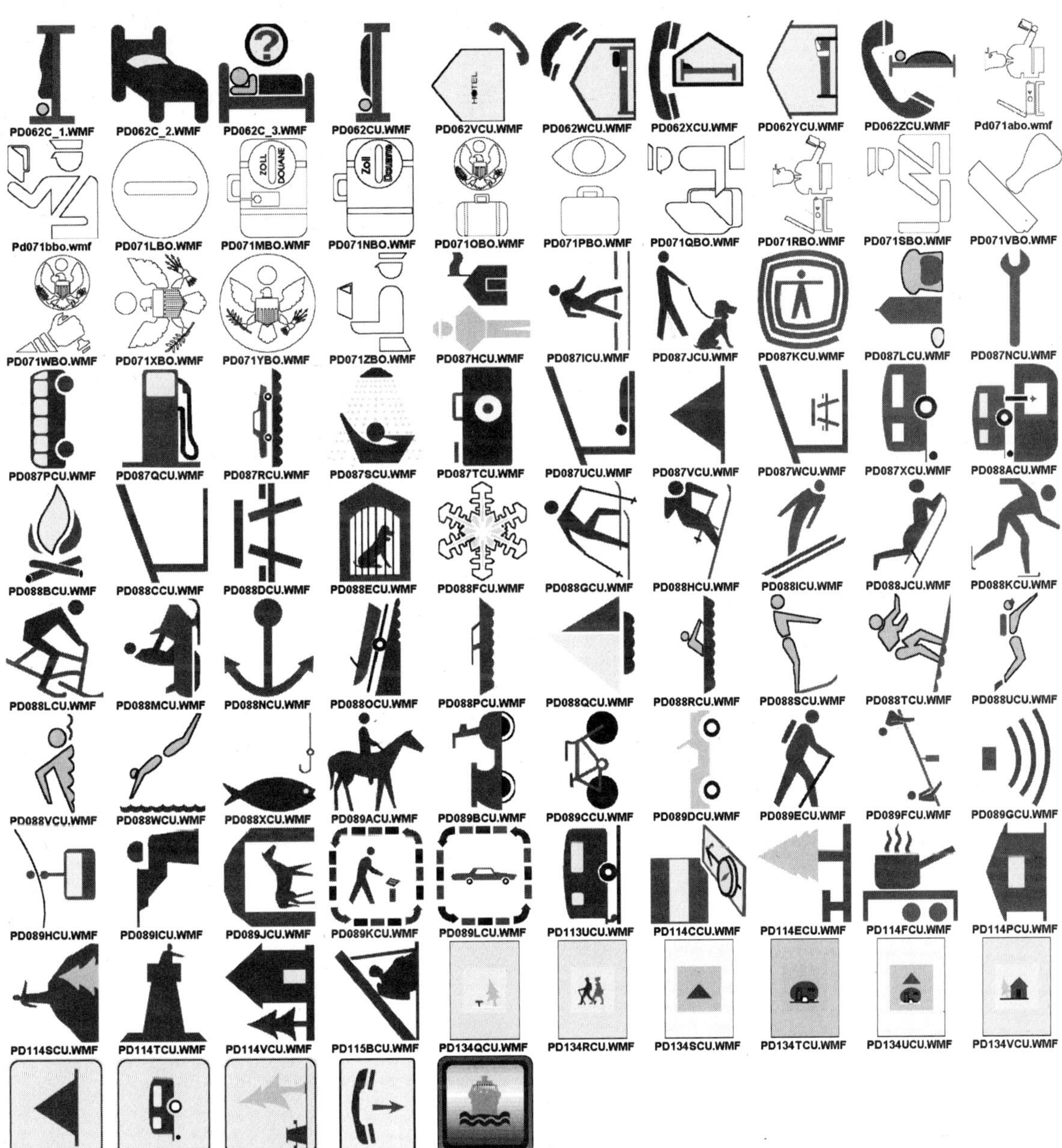
PD062C_1.WMF
PD062C_2.WMF
PD062C_3.WMF
PD062CU.WMF
HOTEL
PD062VCU.WMF
PD062WCU.WMF
PD062XCU.WMF
PD062YCU.WMF
PD062ZCU.WMF
Pd071abo.wmf
Pd071bbo.wmf
PD071LBO.WMF
ZOLL
DOUANE
PD071MBO.WMF
Zoll
Douane
PD071NBO.WMF
PD071OBO.WMF
PD071PBO.WMF
PD071QBO.WMF
PD071RBO.WMF
PD071SBO.WMF
PD071VBO.WMF
PD071WBO.WMF
PD071XBO.WMF
PD071YBO.WMF
PD071ZBO.WMF
PD087HCU.WMF
PD087ICU.WMF
PD087JCU.WMF
PD087KCU.WMF
PD087LCU.WMF
PD087NCU.WMF
PD087PCU.WMF
PD087QCU.WMF
PD087RCU.WMF
PD087SCU.WMF
PD087TCU.WMF
PD087UCU.WMF
PD087VCU.WMF
PD087WCU.WMF
PD087XCU.WMF
PD088ACU.WMF
PD088BCU.WMF
PD088CCU.WMF
PD088DCU.WMF
PD088ECU.WMF
PD088FCU.WMF
PD088GCU.WMF
PD088HCU.WMF
PD088ICU.WMF
PD088JCU.WMF
PD088KCU.WMF
PD088LCU.WMF
PD088MCU.WMF
PD088NCU.WMF
PD088OCU.WMF
PD088PCU.WMF
PD088QCU.WMF
PD088RCU.WMF
PD088SCU.WMF
PD088TCU.WMF
PD088UCU.WMF
PD088VCU.WMF
PD088WCU.WMF
PD088XCU.WMF
PD089ACU.WMF
PD089BCU.WMF
PD089CCU.WMF
PD089DCU.WMF
PD089ECU.WMF
PD089FCU.WMF
PD089GCU.WMF
PD089HCU.WMF
PD089ICU.WMF
PD089JCU.WMF
PD089KCU.WMF
PD089LCU.WMF
PD113UCU.WMF
PD114CCU.WMF
PD114ECU.WMF
PD114FCU.WMF
PD114PCU.WMF
PD114SCU.WMF
PD114TCU.WMF
PD114VCU.WMF
PD115BCU.WMF
PD134QCU.WMF
PD134RCU.WMF
PD134SCU.WMF
PD134TCU.WMF
PD134UCU.WMF
PD134VCU.WMF
PD136ACU.WMF
PD136BCU.WMF
PD136CCU.WMF
PD136DCU.WMF
SHIP.WMF

1289.WMF
1290.WMF
1291.WMF
1292.WMF
CAMRAGUY.WMF
DRINKS.WMF
GIFTSHOP.WMF
GUIDE1.WMF
HIKER.WMF
JUICEBAR.WMF
LUGGAGE2.WMF
LUGGAGE3.WMF
MAPBOARD.WMF
MUSEUM.WMF
OOPS1.WMF
POSTCARD.WMF
RDTRIP.WMF
READING.WMF
RESTING.WMF
SHOPPING.WMF
SLUSHDAN.WMF
TOURIS_1.WMF
TOURIST.WMF
TOURIST1.WMF
TOURIST2.WMF
TOURIST3.WMF
TOURIST4.WMF
TOURIST5.WMF
TOURIST6.WMF
TOURIST7.WMF
TOURIST8.WMF
TOURIST9.WMF
TOURISTA.WMF
TOURISTB.WMF
TOURISTS.WMF
TRAVELI0.WMF
TRIPPIC1.WMF
TRIPPIC2.WMF
TRIPPIC3.WMF
TURIST08.WMF
VACPHOTO.WMF
VIDEOTAP.WMF
WRITING.WMF

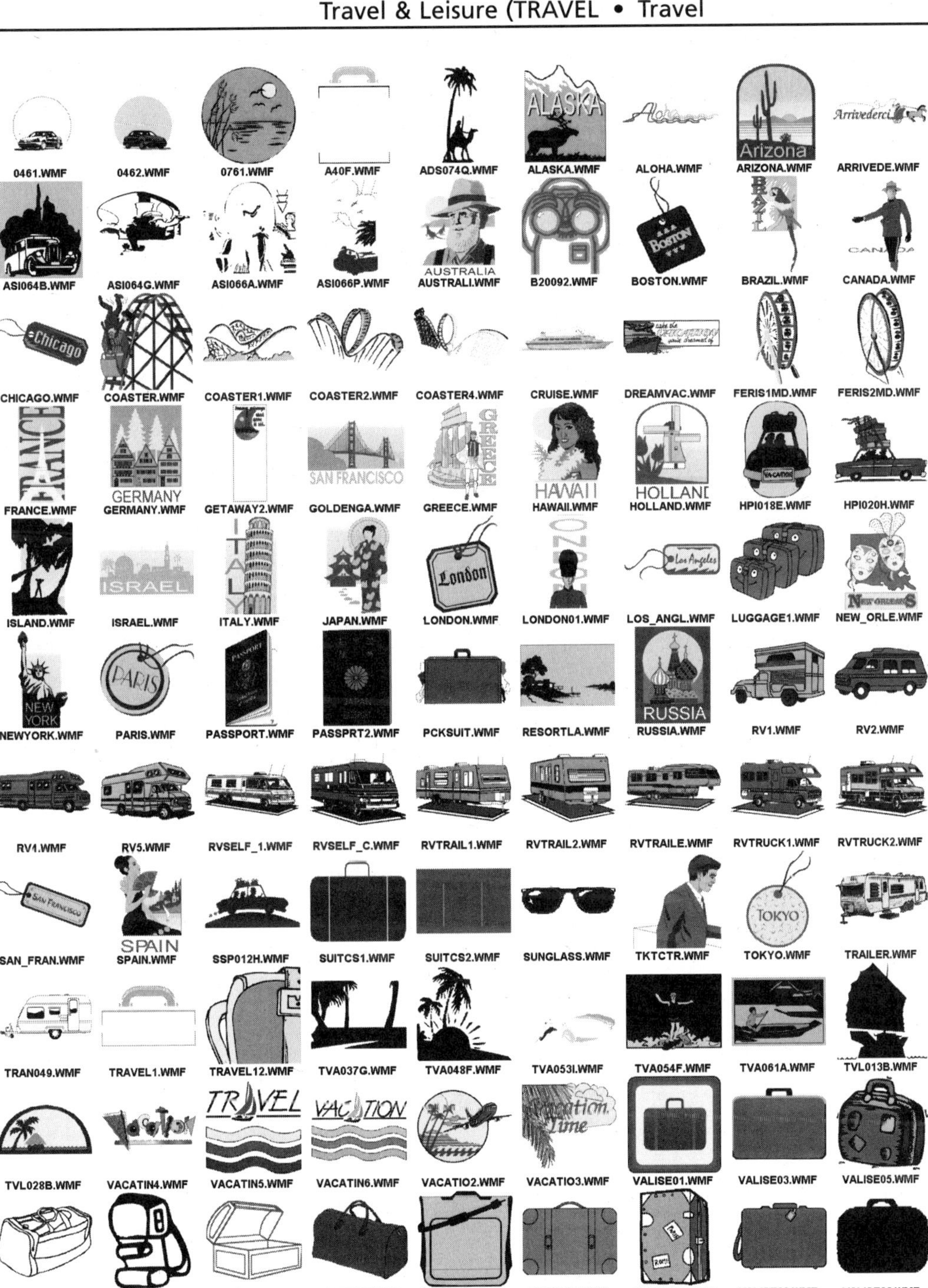

0461.WMF 0462.WMF 0761.WMF A40F.WMF ADS074Q.WMF ALASKA.WMF ALOHA.WMF ARIZONA.WMF ARRIVEDE.WMF ASI064A.WMF
ASI064B.WMF ASI064G.WMF ASI066A.WMF ASI066P.WMF AUSTRALI.WMF B20092.WMF BOSTON.WMF BRAZIL.WMF CANADA.WMF CELEB01.WMF
CHICAGO.WMF COASTER.WMF COASTER1.WMF COASTER2.WMF COASTER4.WMF CRUISE.WMF DREAMVAC.WMF FERIS1MD.WMF FERIS2MD.WMF FLORIDA.WMF
FRANCE.WMF GERMANY.WMF GETAWAY2.WMF GOLDENGA.WMF GREECE.WMF HAWAII.WMF HOLLAND.WMF HPI018E.WMF HPI020H.WMF IRELAND.WMF
ISLAND.WMF ISRAEL.WMF ITALY.WMF JAPAN.WMF LONDON.WMF LONDON01.WMF LOS_ANGL.WMF LUGGAGE1.WMF NEW_ORLE.WMF NEW_YORK.WMF
NEWYORK.WMF PARIS.WMF PASSPORT.WMF PASSPRT2.WMF PCKSUIT.WMF RESORTLA.WMF RUSSIA.WMF RV1.WMF RV2.WMF RV3.WMF
RV4.WMF RV5.WMF RVSELF_1.WMF RVSELF_C.WMF RVTRAIL1.WMF RVTRAIL2.WMF RVTRAILE.WMF RVTRUCK1.WMF RVTRUCK2.WMF RVTRUCK3.WMF
SAN_FRAN.WMF SPAIN.WMF SSP012H.WMF SUITCS1.WMF SUITCS2.WMF SUNGLASS.WMF TKTCTR.WMF TOKYO.WMF TRAILER.WMF TRAILER6.WMF
TRAN049.WMF TRAVEL1.WMF TRAVEL12.WMF TVA037G.WMF TVA048F.WMF TVA053I.WMF TVA054F.WMF TVA061A.WMF TVL013B.WMF TVL020C.WMF
TVL028B.WMF VACATIN4.WMF VACATIN5.WMF VACATIN6.WMF VACATIO2.WMF VACATIO3.WMF VALISE01.WMF VALISE03.WMF VALISE05.WMF VALISE07.WMF
VALISE09.WMF VALISE11.WMF VALISE13.WMF VALISE15.WMF VALISE17.WMF VALISE19.WMF VALISE21.WMF VALISE23.WMF VALISE25.WMF VALISE27.WMF
VALISE29.WMF VALISE33.WMF VALISE35.WMF VALISE37.WMF VALISE39.WMF VENICE.WMF

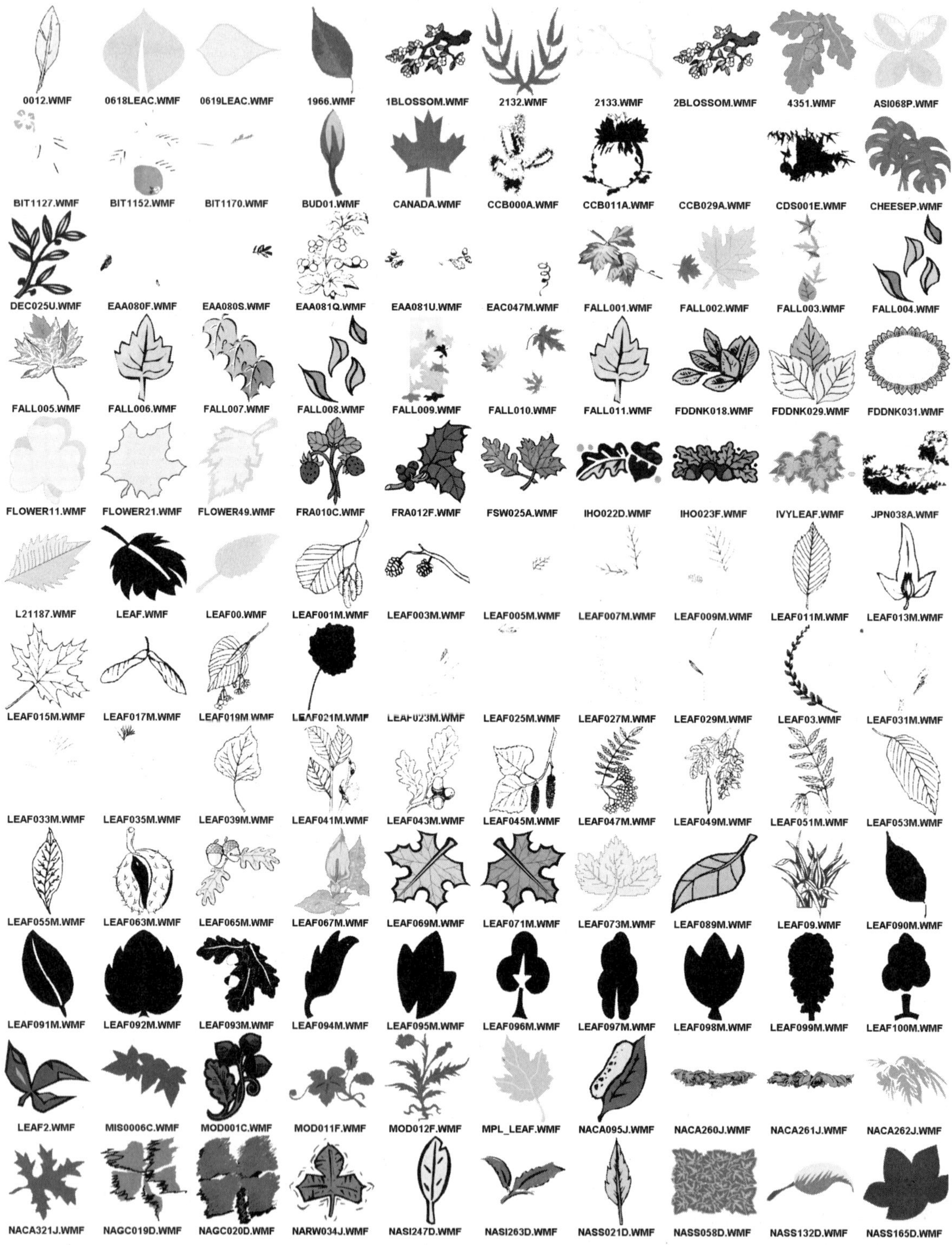
0012.WMF 0618LEAC.WMF 0619LEAC.WMF 1966.WMF 1BLOSSOM.WMF 2132.WMF 2133.WMF 2BLOSSOM.WMF 4351.WMF ASI068P.WMF
BIT1127.WMF BIT1152.WMF BIT1170.WMF BUD01.WMF CANADA.WMF CCB000A.WMF CCB011A.WMF CCB029A.WMF CDS001E.WMF CHEESEP.WMF
DEC025U.WMF EAA080F.WMF EAA080S.WMF EAA081Q.WMF EAA081U.WMF EAC047M.WMF FALL001.WMF FALL002.WMF FALL003.WMF FALL004.WMF
FALL005.WMF FALL006.WMF FALL007.WMF FALL008.WMF FALL009.WMF FALL010.WMF FALL011.WMF FDDNK018.WMF FDDNK029.WMF FDDNK031.WMF
FLOWER11.WMF FLOWER21.WMF FLOWER49.WMF FRA010C.WMF FRA012F.WMF FSW025A.WMF IHO022D.WMF IHO023F.WMF IVYLEAF.WMF JPN038A.WMF
L21187.WMF LEAF.WMF LEAF00.WMF LEAF001M.WMF LEAF003M.WMF LEAF005M.WMF LEAF007M.WMF LEAF009M.WMF LEAF011M.WMF LEAF013M.WMF
LEAF015M.WMF LEAF017M.WMF LEAF019M.WMF LEAF021M.WMF LEAF023M.WMF LEAF025M.WMF LEAF027M.WMF LEAF029M.WMF LEAF03.WMF LEAF031M.WMF
LEAF033M.WMF LEAF035M.WMF LEAF039M.WMF LEAF041M.WMF LEAF043M.WMF LEAF045M.WMF LEAF047M.WMF LEAF049M.WMF LEAF051M.WMF LEAF053M.WMF
LEAF055M.WMF LEAF063M.WMF LEAF065M.WMF LEAF067M.WMF LEAF069M.WMF LEAF071M.WMF LEAF073M.WMF LEAF089M.WMF LEAF09.WMF LEAF090M.WMF
LEAF091M.WMF LEAF092M.WMF LEAF093M.WMF LEAF094M.WMF LEAF095M.WMF LEAF096M.WMF LEAF097M.WMF LEAF098M.WMF LEAF099M.WMF LEAF100M.WMF
LEAF2.WMF MIS0006C.WMF MOD001C.WMF MOD011F.WMF MOD012F.WMF MPL_LEAF.WMF NACA095J.WMF NACA260J.WMF NACA261J.WMF NACA262J.WMF
NACA321J.WMF NAGC019D.WMF NAGC020D.WMF NARW034J.WMF NASI247D.WMF NASI263D.WMF NASS021D.WMF NASS058D.WMF NASS132D.WMF NASS165D.WMF

NASS201D.WMF
NATR027.WMF
NATR052.WMF
NATR053.WMF
NATR054.WMF
NATR055.WMF
NATR056.WMF
NATR057.WMF
NATR058.WMF
NATR059.WMF
NATR060.WMF
NATR061.WMF
NATR062.WMF
NATR063.WMF
NATR064.WMF
NATR065.WMF
NATR066.WMF
NATR067.WMF
NATR068.WMF
NATR069.WMF
NATR075.WMF
NATR076.WMF
NATR100.WMF
NATR102.WMF
NATR103.WMF
NATR104.WMF
NATR105.WMF
NATR106.WMF
NATR107.WMF
OFL005I.WMF
OFL016B.WMF
OXM006E.WMF
PLF166F.WMF
POC104P.WMF
POC105I.WMF
POC105M.WMF
SHW000A.WMF
SLH129C.WMF
SMR015E.WMF
SOR242A.WMF
SOR242C.WMF
SPA011E.WMF
SPA011F.WMF

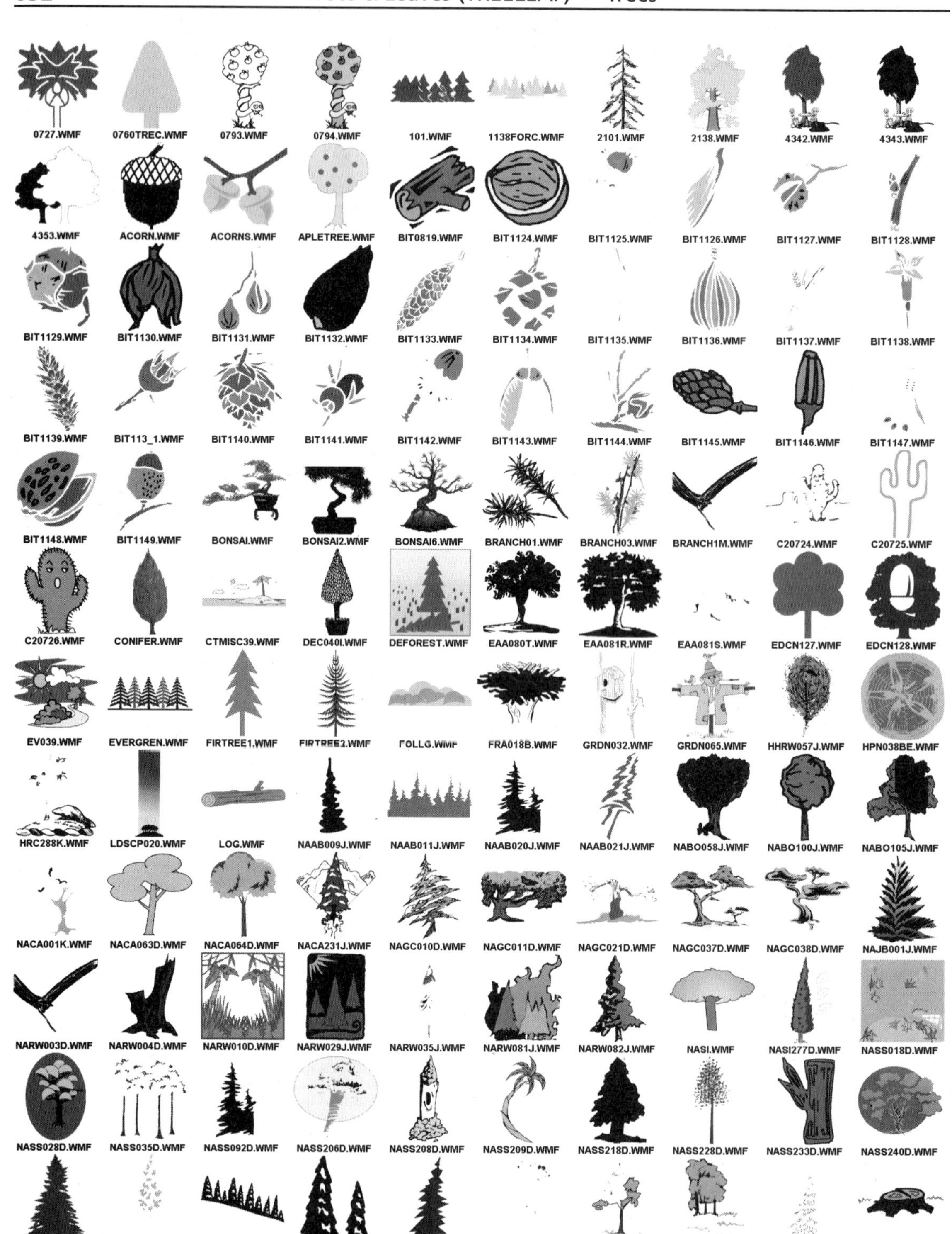
0727.WMF
0760TREC.WMF
0793.WMF
0794.WMF
101.WMF
1138FORC.WMF
2101.WMF
2138.WMF
4342.WMF
4343.WMF
4353.WMF
ACORN.WMF
ACORNS.WMF
APLETREE.WMF
BIT0819.WMF
BIT1124.WMF
BIT1125.WMF
BIT1126.WMF
BIT1127.WMF
BIT1128.WMF
BIT1129.WMF
BIT1130.WMF
BIT1131.WMF
BIT1132.WMF
BIT1133.WMF
BIT1134.WMF
BIT1135.WMF
BIT1136.WMF
BIT1137.WMF
BIT1138.WMF
BIT1139.WMF
BIT113_1.WMF
BIT1140.WMF
BIT1141.WMF
BIT1142.WMF
BIT1143.WMF
BIT1144.WMF
BIT1145.WMF
BIT1146.WMF
BIT1147.WMF
BIT1148.WMF
BIT1149.WMF
BONSAI.WMF
BONSAI2.WMF
BONSAI6.WMF
BRANCH01.WMF
BRANCH03.WMF
BRANCH1M.WMF
C20724.WMF
C20725.WMF
C20726.WMF
CONIFER.WMF
CTMISC39.WMF
DEC040I.WMF
DEFOREST.WMF
EAA080T.WMF
EAA081R.WMF
EAA081S.WMF
EDCN127.WMF
EDCN128.WMF
EV039.WMF
EVERGREN.WMF
FIRTREE1.WMF
FIRTREE2.WMF
FOLLG.WMF
FRA018B.WMF
GRDN032.WMF
GRDN065.WMF
HHRW057J.WMF
HPN038BE.WMF
HRC288K.WMF
LDSCP020.WMF
LOG.WMF
NAAB009J.WMF
NAAB011J.WMF
NAAB020J.WMF
NAAB021J.WMF
NABO058J.WMF
NABO100J.WMF
NABO105J.WMF
NACA001K.WMF
NACA063D.WMF
NACA064D.WMF
NACA231J.WMF
NAGC010D.WMF
NAGC011D.WMF
NAGC021D.WMF
NAGC037D.WMF
NAGC038D.WMF
NAJB001J.WMF
NARW003D.WMF
NARW004D.WMF
NARW010D.WMF
NARW029J.WMF
NARW035J.WMF
NARW081J.WMF
NARW082J.WMF
NASI.WMF
NASI277D.WMF
NASS018D.WMF
NASS028D.WMF
NASS035D.WMF
NASS092D.WMF
NASS206D.WMF
NASS208D.WMF
NASS209D.WMF
NASS218D.WMF
NASS228D.WMF
NASS233D.WMF
NASS240D.WMF
NASS241D.WMF
NASS243D.WMF
NASS244D.WMF
NASS245D.WMF
NASS246D.WMF
NASS248D.WMF
NASS258D.WMF
NASS259D.WMF
NASS265D.WMF
NASS272D.WMF

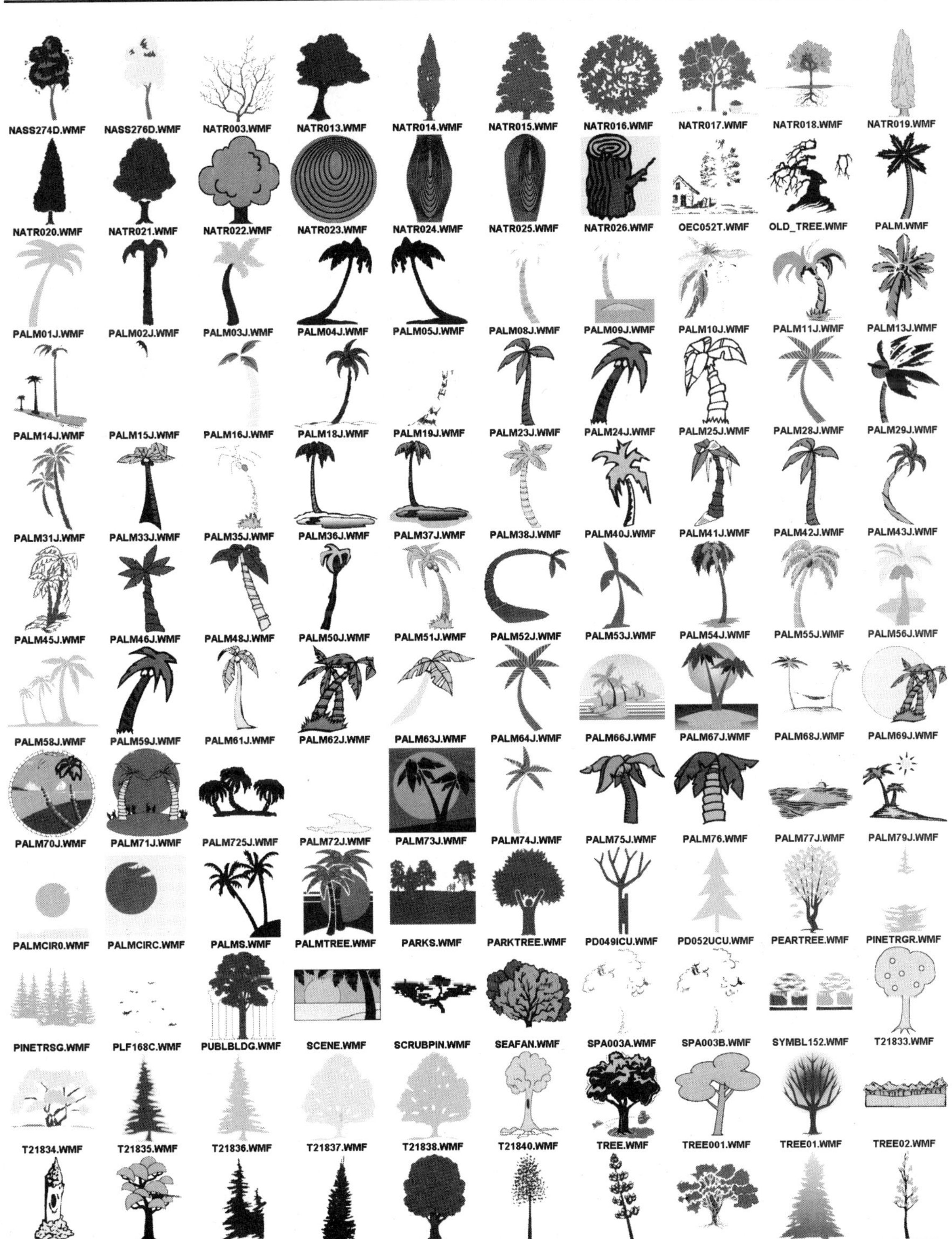
NASS274D.WMF
NASS276D.WMF
NATR003.WMF
NATR013.WMF
NATR014.WMF
NATR015.WMF
NATR016.WMF
NATR017.WMF
NATR018.WMF
NATR019.WMF
NATR020.WMF
NATR021.WMF
NATR022.WMF
NATR023.WMF
NATR024.WMF
NATR025.WMF
NATR026.WMF
OEC052T.WMF
OLD_TREE.WMF
PALM.WMF
PALM01J.WMF
PALM02J.WMF
PALM03J.WMF
PALM04J.WMF
PALM05J.WMF
PALM08J.WMF
PALM09J.WMF
PALM10J.WMF
PALM11J.WMF
PALM13J.WMF
PALM14J.WMF
PALM15J.WMF
PALM16J.WMF
PALM18J.WMF
PALM19J.WMF
PALM23J.WMF
PALM24J.WMF
PALM25J.WMF
PALM28J.WMF
PALM29J.WMF
PALM31J.WMF
PALM33J.WMF
PALM35J.WMF
PALM36J.WMF
PALM37J.WMF
PALM38J.WMF
PALM40J.WMF
PALM41J.WMF
PALM42J.WMF
PALM43J.WMF
PALM45J.WMF
PALM46J.WMF
PALM48J.WMF
PALM50J.WMF
PALM51J.WMF
PALM52J.WMF
PALM53J.WMF
PALM54J.WMF
PALM55J.WMF
PALM56J.WMF
PALM58J.WMF
PALM59J.WMF
PALM61J.WMF
PALM62J.WMF
PALM63J.WMF
PALM64J.WMF
PALM66J.WMF
PALM67J.WMF
PALM68J.WMF
PALM69J.WMF
PALM70J.WMF
PALM71J.WMF
PALM725J.WMF
PALM72J.WMF
PALM73J.WMF
PALM74J.WMF
PALM75J.WMF
PALM76.WMF
PALM77J.WMF
PALM79J.WMF
PALMCIR0.WMF
PALMCIRC.WMF
PALMS.WMF
PALMTREE.WMF
PARKS.WMF
PARKTREE.WMF
PD049ICU.WMF
PD052UCU.WMF
PEARTREE.WMF
PINETRGR.WMF
PINETRSG.WMF
PLF168C.WMF
PUBLBLDG.WMF
SCENE.WMF
SCRUBPIN.WMF
SEAFAN.WMF
SPA003A.WMF
SPA003B.WMF
SYMBL152.WMF
T21833.WMF
T21834.WMF
T21835.WMF
T21836.WMF
T21837.WMF
T21838.WMF
T21840.WMF
TREE.WMF
TREE001.WMF
TREE01.WMF
TREE02.WMF
TREE02M.WMF
TREE03.WMF
TREE06.WMF
TREE07.WMF
TREE1.WMF
TREE10.WMF
TREE11.WMF
TREE12.WMF
TREE13.WMF
TREE14.WMF

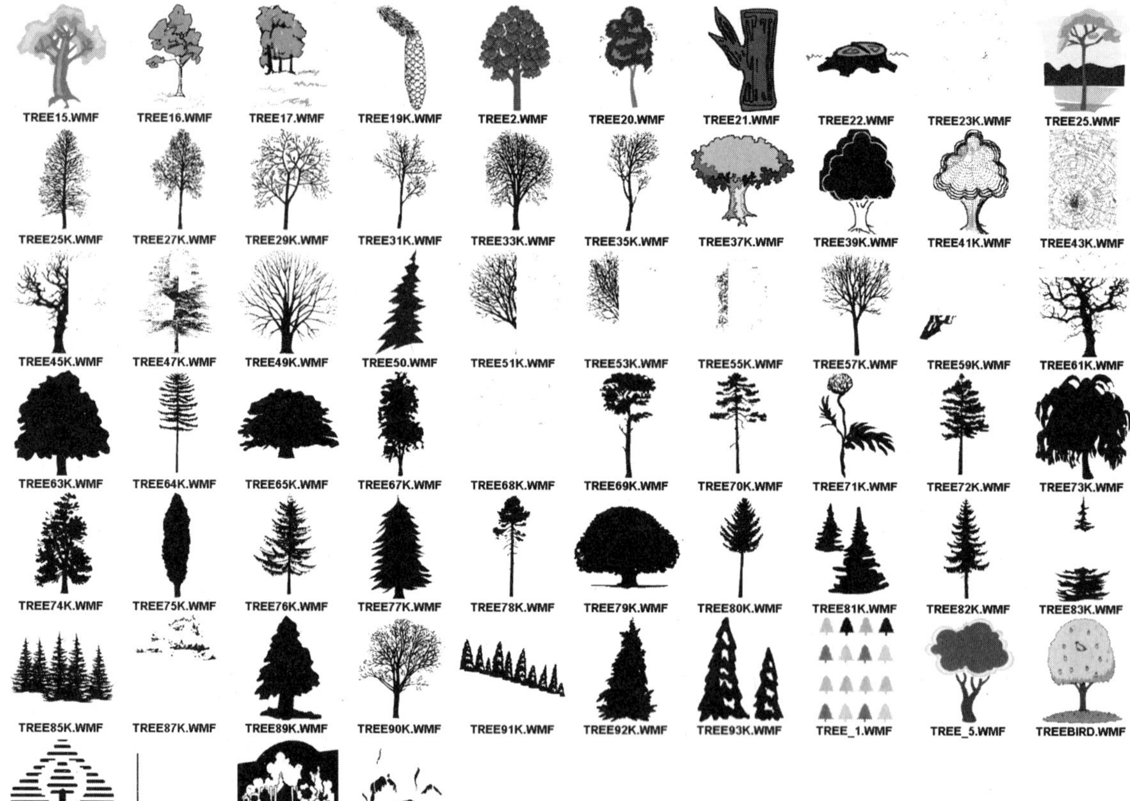
TREE15.WMF
TREE16.WMF
TREE17.WMF
TREE19K.WMF
TREE2.WMF
TREE20.WMF
TREE21.WMF
TREE22.WMF
TREE23K.WMF
TREE25.WMF
TREE25K.WMF
TREE27K.WMF
TREE29K.WMF
TREE31K.WMF
TREE33K.WMF
TREE35K.WMF
TREE37K.WMF
TREE39K.WMF
TREE41K.WMF
TREE43K.WMF
TREE45K.WMF
TREE47K.WMF
TREE49K.WMF
TREE50.WMF
TREE51K.WMF
TREE53K.WMF
TREE55K.WMF
TREE57K.WMF
TREE59K.WMF
TREE61K.WMF
TREE63K.WMF
TREE64K.WMF
TREE65K.WMF
TREE67K.WMF
TREE68K.WMF
TREE69K.WMF
TREE70K.WMF
TREE71K.WMF
TREE72K.WMF
TREE73K.WMF
TREE74K.WMF
TREE75K.WMF
TREE76K.WMF
TREE77K.WMF
TREE78K.WMF
TREE79K.WMF
TREE80K.WMF
TREE81K.WMF
TREE82K.WMF
TREE83K.WMF
TREE85K.WMF
TREE87K.WMF
TREE89K.WMF
TREE90K.WMF
TREE91K.WMF
TREE92K.WMF
TREE93K.WMF
TREE_1.WMF
TREE_5.WMF
TREEBIRD.WMF
TREESYMB.WMF
TVL030B.WMF
WMG025L.WMF
WMG026D.WMF

1698.WMF
ADS016H.WMF
ADS017F.WMF
ADS017H.WMF
ADS017I.WMF
ADS034A.WMF
ADS034B.WMF
ADS108C.WMF
ALAMO.WMF
ALAMO1.WMF
ARC011.WMF
ARCH01.WMF
ARCH02.WMF
ARCH03.WMF
ARCH04.WMF
CAA0258.WMF
CONSTIT2.WMF
DEC086T.WMF
DEC089X.WMF
EDUCATN.WMF
DENVER
EMPIREST.WMF
FLAG08.WMF
GDNGTBRG.WMF
GGBRIDGE.WMF
GRCANYON.WMF
HLLYWD.WMF
HOLLYWOO
HLLYWD01.WMF
HLLYWD02.WMF
INDHALL.WMF
INDPHALL.WMF
IOWA_CAP.WMF
LIBELL01.WMF
LIBELL02.WMF
LIBELL03.WMF
LIBELL04.WMF
LIBELL05.WMF
LIBELL06.WMF
LIBELL07.WMF
LIBELL08.WMF
LIBELL09.WMF
LIBELL10.WMF
LIBELL11.WMF
LIBELL12.WMF
LIBELL13.WMF
LIBERTY3.WMF
LIBRTY01.WMF
LIBRTY02.WMF
LIBRTY03.WMF
LIBRTY04.WMF
LIBRTY05.WMF
LIBRTY06.WMF
LIBRTY07.WMF
LIBRTY08.WMF
LIBRTY09.WMF
LIBRTY10.WMF
LIBRTY11.WMF
LIBRTY12.WMF
LIBRTY13.WMF
LIBRTY14.WMF
LIBRTY15.WMF
MADE IN U.S.A.
MADE IN
U. S. A.
PROUDLY
MADE IN THE USA
LIBRTY16.WMF
LIBRTY17.WMF
LIGHTHOU.WMF
LINCOLNM.WMF
MACKINAC.WMF
MADEUSA1.WMF
MADEUSA2.WMF
MADEUSA3.WMF
MADEUSA4.WMF
MARINMEM.WMF
MCHENRY.WMF
NEWYRK.WMF
NORLEANS.WMF
OPT023N.WMF
OPT032F.WMF
PEARLHBR.WMF
PORTLAND.WMF
RI_3.WMF
RSHMORE1.WMF
RSHMORE2.WMF
RUSHMOR.WMF
RUSHMOR1.WMF
RUSHMORE.WMF
SEATTLE.WMF
SETOOHAS.WMF
SKYSCRAP.WMF
SPCENDLE.WMF
SPCNEEDL.WMF
STATCRTS.WMF
STONEMTN.WMF
TOWER1MD.WMF
TVL002B.WMF
TVL003A.WMF
TVL003B.WMF
UNCLE01.WMF
UNCLESAM.WMF
UNCLESM.WMF
UNCSAM.WMF
UNCSMHAT.WMF
USA1.WMF
WAITING.WMF
WASH_MON.WMF
WRIGHT.WMF

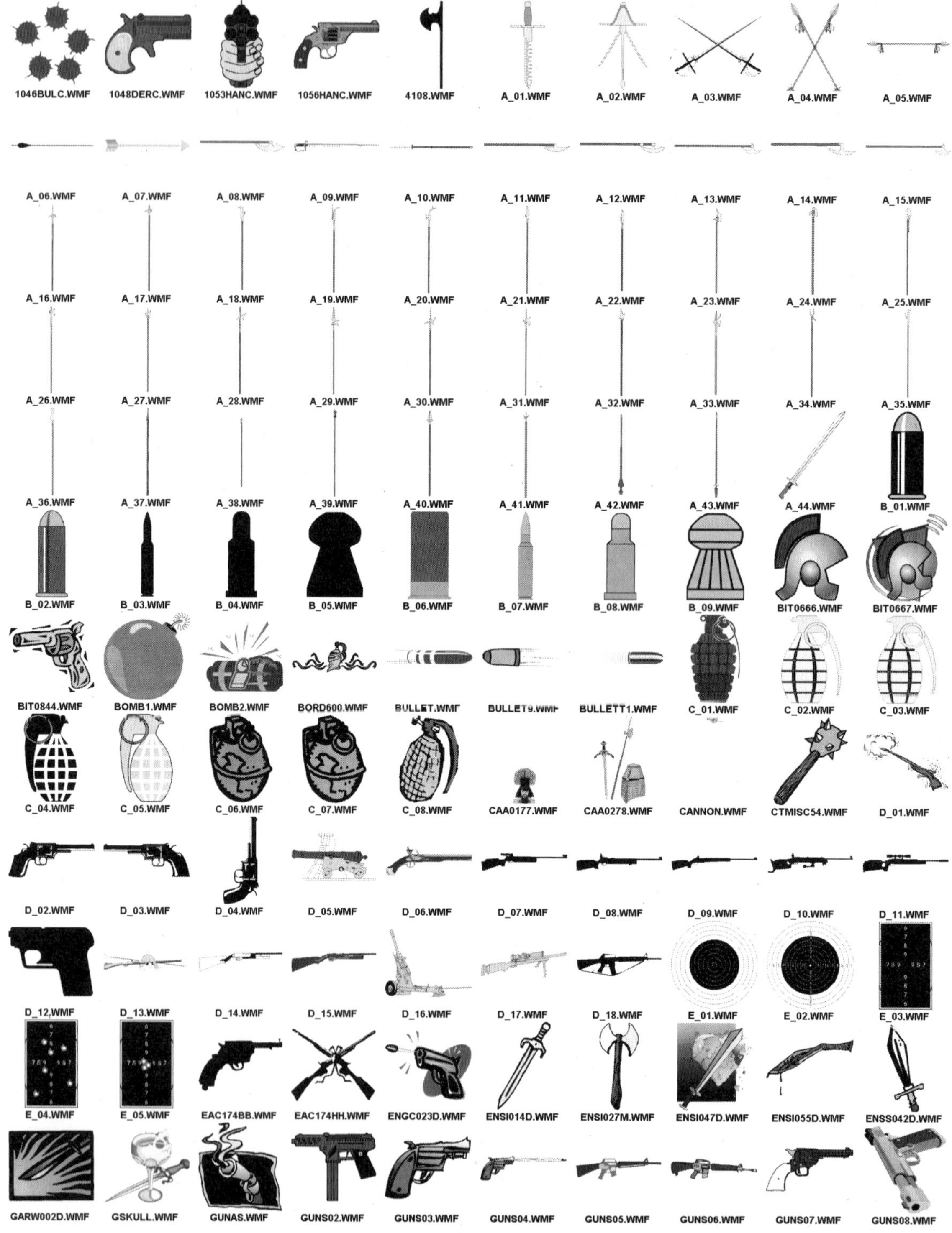
1046BULC.WMF 1048DERC.WMF 1053HANC.WMF 1056HANC.WMF 4108.WMF A_01.WMF A_02.WMF A_03.WMF A_04.WMF A_05.WMF
A_06.WMF A_07.WMF A_08.WMF A_09.WMF A_10.WMF A_11.WMF A_12.WMF A_13.WMF A_14.WMF A_15.WMF
A_16.WMF A_17.WMF A_18.WMF A_19.WMF A_20.WMF A_21.WMF A_22.WMF A_23.WMF A_24.WMF A_25.WMF
A_26.WMF A_27.WMF A_28.WMF A_29.WMF A_30.WMF A_31.WMF A_32.WMF A_33.WMF A_34.WMF A_35.WMF
A_36.WMF A_37.WMF A_38.WMF A_39.WMF A_40.WMF A_41.WMF A_42.WMF A_43.WMF A_44.WMF B_01.WMF
B_02.WMF B_03.WMF B_04.WMF B_05.WMF B_06.WMF B_07.WMF B_08.WMF B_09.WMF BIT0666.WMF BIT0667.WMF
BIT0844.WMF BOMB1.WMF BOMB2.WMF BORD600.WMF BULLET.WMF BULLET9.WMF BULLETT1.WMF C_01.WMF C_02.WMF C_03.WMF
C_04.WMF C_05.WMF C_06.WMF C_07.WMF C_08.WMF CAA0177.WMF CAA0278.WMF CANNON.WMF CTMISC54.WMF D_01.WMF
D_02.WMF D_03.WMF D_04.WMF D_05.WMF D_06.WMF D_07.WMF D_08.WMF D_09.WMF D_10.WMF D_11.WMF
D_12.WMF D_13.WMF D_14.WMF D_15.WMF D_16.WMF D_17.WMF D_18.WMF E_01.WMF E_02.WMF E_03.WMF
E_04.WMF E_05.WMF EAC174BB.WMF EAC174HH.WMF ENGC023D.WMF ENSI014D.WMF ENSI027M.WMF ENSI047D.WMF ENSI055D.WMF ENSS042D.WMF
GARW002D.WMF GSKULL.WMF GUNAS.WMF GUNS02.WMF GUNS03.WMF GUNS04.WMF GUNS05.WMF GUNS06.WMF GUNS07.WMF GUNS08.WMF

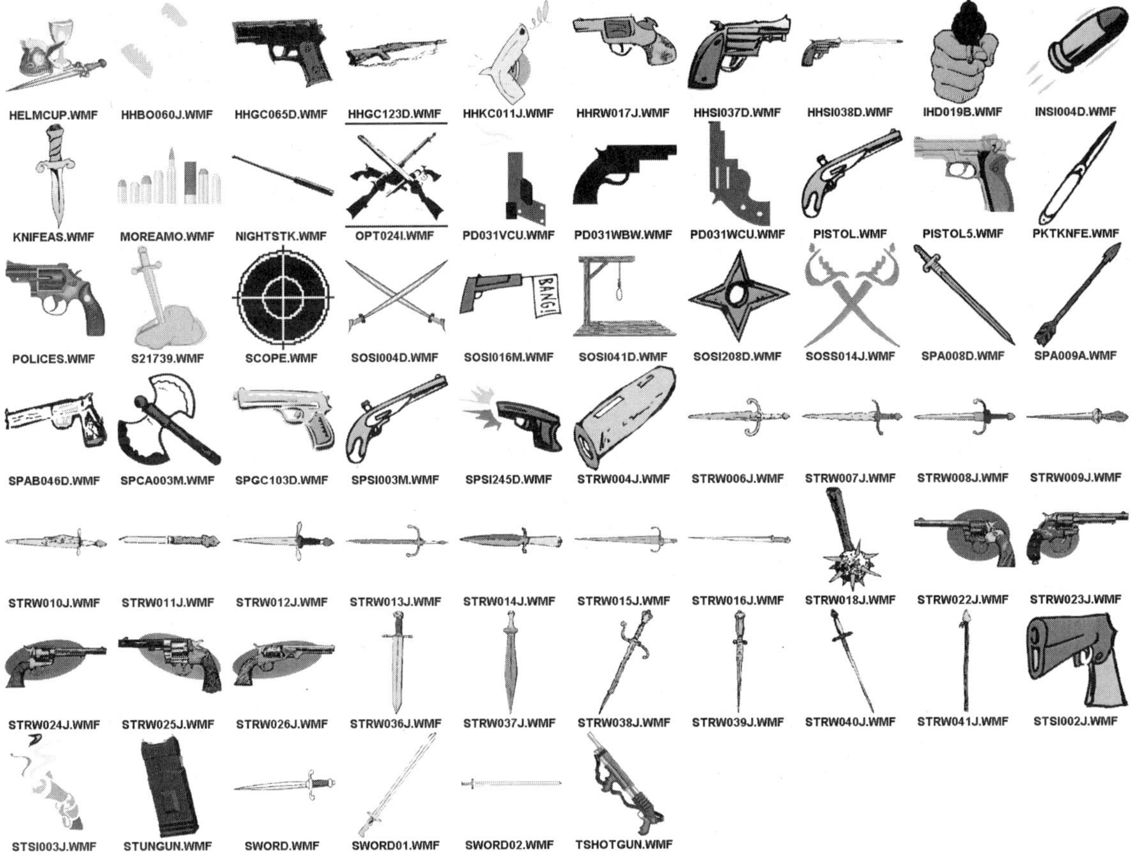
HELMCUP.WMF
HHBO060J.WMF
HHGC065D.WMF
HHGC123D.WMF
HHKC011J.WMF
HHRW017J.WMF
HHSI037D.WMF
HHSI038D.WMF
IHD019B.WMF
INSI004D.WMF
KNIFEAS.WMF
MOREAMO.WMF
NIGHTSTK.WMF
OPT024I.WMF
PD031VCU.WMF
PD031WBW.WMF
PD031WCU.WMF
PISTOL.WMF
PISTOL5.WMF
PKTKNFE.WMF
POLICES.WMF
S21739.WMF
SCOPE.WMF
SOSI004D.WMF
BANG!
SOSI016M.WMF
SOSI041D.WMF
SOSI208D.WMF
SOSS014J.WMF
SPA008D.WMF
SPA009A.WMF
SPAB046D.WMF
SPCA003M.WMF
SPGC103D.WMF
SPSI003M.WMF
SPSI245D.WMF
STRW004J.WMF
STRW006J.WMF
STRW007J.WMF
STRW008J.WMF
STRW009J.WMF
STRW010J.WMF
STRW011J.WMF
STRW012J.WMF
STRW013J.WMF
STRW014J.WMF
STRW015J.WMF
STRW016J.WMF
STRW018J.WMF
STRW022J.WMF
STRW023J.WMF
STRW024J.WMF
STRW025J.WMF
STRW026J.WMF
STRW036J.WMF
STRW037J.WMF
STRW038J.WMF
STRW039J.WMF
STRW040J.WMF
STRW041J.WMF
STSI002J.WMF
STSI003J.WMF
STUNGUN.WMF
SWORD.WMF
SWORD01.WMF
SWORD02.WMF
TSHOTGUN.WMF

0114.WMF
0115.WMF
0656.WMF
0784.WMF
179_8737.WMF
3625.WMF
ALTCUMTR.WMF
ALTOSTOP.WMF
ALTOSTRA.WMF
ALTOSTRU.WMF
ANEMOM.WMF
ASI011U.WMF
ATCUMOP.WMF
BACK224.WMF
BAROMETR.WMF
BIT0158.WMF
BIT0159.WMF
BIT0160.WMF
BIT0161.WMF
BIT0162.WMF
CLOUDBW3.WMF
CLOUDY.WMF
CULUFRAC.WMF
CUMCALVU.WMF
CUMCAPIL.WMF
CUMCONG.WMF
CUMHUML.WMF
DRIZZLE.WMF
DUSTWHL.WMF
EDCN132.WMF
EDCN133.WMF
ENERGY.WMF
EV106.WMF
EV108.WMF
FALL1.WMF
FALL2.WMF
FCP042H.WMF
FREEZING.WMF
FWN006C.WMF
FWN006D.WMF
HAIL.WMF
HLTH118.WMF
HLTH119.WMF
HURRICAN.WMF
KPDRY3.WMF
KPFMCLD1.WMF
40°C
104°F
KPFMHT1.WMF
+50°
KPFMHT2.WMF
KPFMHT5.WMF
LAC047I.WMF
MAXMIN.WMF
MODICING.WMF
MODTURB.WMF
NARW020D.WMF
NARW032J.WMF
NASI183D.WMF
NASI184D.WMF
NASS190D.WMF
NASS191D.WMF
NATURE22.WMF
NATURE5.WMF
1/1
1/2
PD122RCU.WMF
PD136MBO.WMF
PD136MCU.WMF
PD136NDO.WMF
PD136NCU.WMF
PD136OBO.WMF
PD136OCU.WMF
PD136PBO.WMF
PD136PCU.WMF
PD136SBO.WMF
PD136SCU.WMF
PD136TBO.WMF
PD136TCU.WMF
PD136UBO.WMF
PD136UCU.WMF
PD136VBO.WMF
PD136VCU.WMF
PD136WBO.WMF
PD136WCU.WMF
PD136XBO.WMF
PD136XCU.WMF
PD137ABO.WMF
PD137ACU.WMF
PD137BBO.WMF
PD137BCU.WMF
PTCLOUDY.WMF
RAIN.WMF
RAINBOW1.WMF
RAINBOW2.WMF
RAINBOW3.WMF
RAINBOW4.WMF
RAINBOW5.WMF
RAINPRED.WMF
RAINYDAY.WMF
SANDSTRM.WMF
SHOWERS.WMF
SNOW.WMF
SNOW008.WMF
SPA016A.WMF
SPRING1.WMF
SPRING2.WMF
SQUALL.WMF
STRATOC.WMF
STRUTUS.WMF
SUMMER1.WMF
SUMMER2.WMF
SUNCLD01.WMF
SUNCLD02.WMF
SUNCLD03.WMF
SUNCLD04.WMF
SUNCLD05.WMF
SUNCLD06.WMF
SUNCLD07.WMF
SUNCLD08.WMF
SUNMETER.WMF
SUNNY.WMF
SVICING.WMF
SVTURB.WMF

THERMOME.WMF
THUNDERS.WMF
TORN.WMF
TORNADO.WMF
TROPSTOR.WMF
UMB001.WMF
UMB002.WMF
UMB003.WMF
UMB004.WMF
UMB005.WMF
UMB006.WMF
UMB007.WMF
UMB008.WMF
UMB009.WMF
UMB010.WMF
UMB011.WMF
UMB020.WMF
WEATHER2.WMF
WINTER1.WMF
WINTER2.WMF
WMG031K.WMF
XLIGHT01.WMF
XLIGHT03.WMF
XLIGHT05.WMF
XLIGHT07.WMF
XLIGHT09.WMF
XLIGHT11.WMF
XLIGHT13.WMF
XLIGHT15.WMF
XLIGHT17.WMF
XLIGHT19.WMF
XLIGHT21.WMF
XLIGHT23.WMF
XLIGHT25.WMF
XLIGHT27.WMF
XLIGHT31.WMF
XLIGHT33.WMF
XLIGHT35.WMF
XLIGHT37.WMF
XLIGHT39.WMF
XLIGHT41.WMF
XLIGHT45.WMF
XLIGHT47.WMF
XLIGHT49.WMF
XLIGHT51.WMF
XLIGHT53.WMF
YRAIN01.WMF
YRAIN03.WMF
YRAIN05.WMF
YRAIN07.WMF
YRAIN09.WMF
YRAIN11.WMF
YRAIN13.WMF
YRAIN15.WMF
YRAIN17.WMF
YRAIN19.WMF
YRAIN21.WMF
YRAIN23.WMF
YRAIN24.WMF
YRAIN25.WMF
YRAIN27.WMF
YRAIN29.WMF
YRAIN31.WMF
YRAIN33.WMF
ZCLOUD03.WMF
ZCLOUD05.WMF
ZCLOUD07.WMF
ZCLOUD09.WMF
ZCLOUD11.WMF
ZCLOUD13.WMF
ZCLOUD15.WMF
ZCLOUD17.WMF
ZCLOUD19.WMF
ZCLOUD21.WMF
ZCLOUD23.WMF
ZCLOUD25.WMF
ZCLOUD27.WMF
ZCLOUD29.WMF
ZCLOUD31.WMF
ZCLOUD33.WMF
ZCLOUD35.WMF
ZCLOUD37.WMF
ZCLOUD39.WMF
ZCLOUD41.WMF
ZCLOUD43.WMF
ZCLOUD45.WMF
ZCLOUD47.WMF
ZCLOUD49.WMF
ZCLOUD51.WMF
ZCLOUD53.WMF
ZCLOUD55.WMF
ZCLOUD57.WMF
ZCLOUD59.WMF
ZCLOUD61.WMF
ZCLOUD63.WMF
ZCLOUD65.WMF
ZCLOUD66.WMF
ZCLOUD67.WMF
ZCLOUD68.WMF
ZCLOUD69.WMF
ZCLOUD70.WMF
ZCLOUD71.WMF
ZCLOUD72.WMF

BARRELRA.WMF
BOOTS_HA.WMF
BRAND.WMF
BRONC.WMF
BULLRIDR.WMF
CAA0560.WMF
CAA0562.WMF
CAA0563.WMF
CALFROPR.WMF
CART001.WMF
CART002.WMF
CART003.WMF
CART004.WMF
CART005.WMF
CART006.WMF
CART007.WMF
CART008.WMF
CART009.WMF
CART010.WMF
CART011.WMF
CART012.WMF
CART013.WMF
CART014.WMF
CART015.WMF
CART016.WMF
CBOYFBAL.WMF
CC19.WMF
CC20.WMF
COWBOY.WMF
COWBOY01.WMF
COWBOY02.WMF
COWBOY03.WMF
COWBOY05.WMF
COWBOY06.WMF
COWBOY07.WMF
COWBOY08.WMF
COWBOY1.WMF
COWBOY12.WMF
COWBOYRO.WMF
COWBY01.WMF
FIXFENCE.WMF
FSW030D.WMF
HDC074B.WMF
NAGC172J.WMF
NARW064J.WMF
OLDWEST.WMF
RODEO.WMF
RODEO2.WMF
SIT055H.WMF
SPA027F.WMF
STEERW.WMF
TROPERS.WMF
TRSI068D.WMF
TWOGUN.WMF
UPFACE.WMF
WGN.WMF

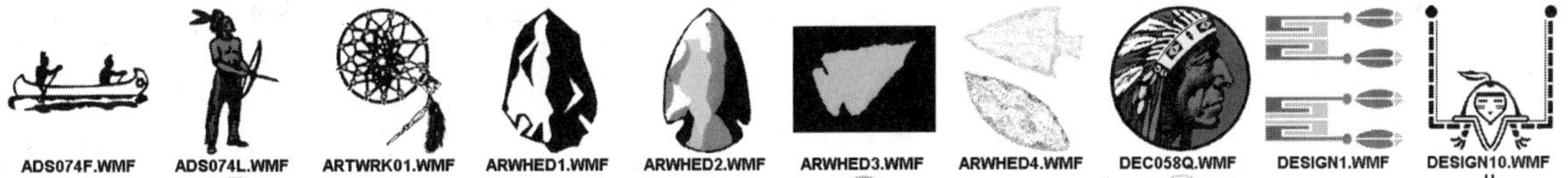

ADS074F.WMF ADS074L.WMF ARTWRK01.WMF ARWHED1.WMF ARWHED2.WMF ARWHED3.WMF ARWHED4.WMF DEC058Q.WMF DESIGN1.WMF DESIGN10.WMF

DESIGN11.WMF DESIGN12.WMF DESIGN13.WMF DESIGN14.WMF DESIGN15.WMF DESIGN16.WMF DESIGN17.WMF DESIGN19.WMF DESIGN2.WMF DESIGN20.WMF

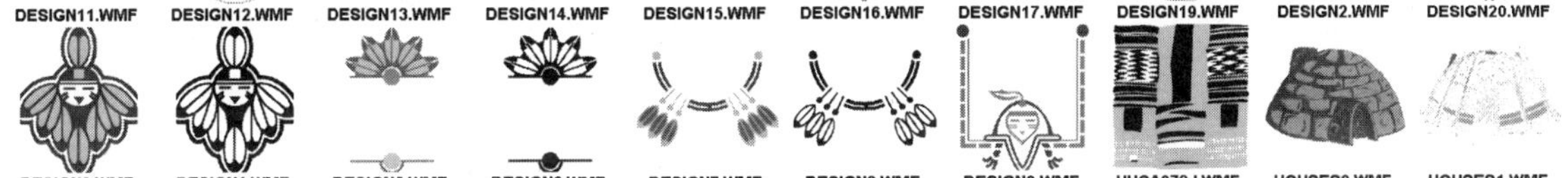

DESIGN3.WMF DESIGN4.WMF DESIGN5.WMF DESIGN6.WMF DESIGN7.WMF DESIGN8.WMF DESIGN9.WMF HHCA072J.WMF HOUSES0.WMF HOUSES1.WMF

HOUSES2.WMF HOUSES3.WMF HOUSES4.WMF INDIAN01.WMF INDIAN02.WMF INDIAN03.WMF INDIAN04.WMF INDIAN05.WMF INDIAN06.WMF INDIAN07.WMF

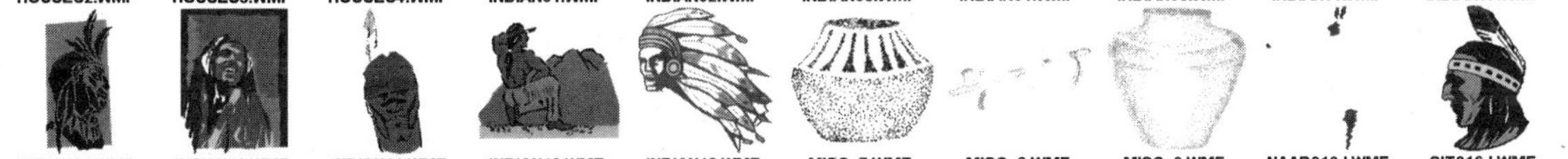

INDIAN08.WMF INDIAN10.WMF INDIAN11.WMF INDIAN12.WMF INDIAN13.WMF MISC_7.WMF MISC_8.WMF MISC_9.WMF NAAB019J.WMF SIT016J.WMF

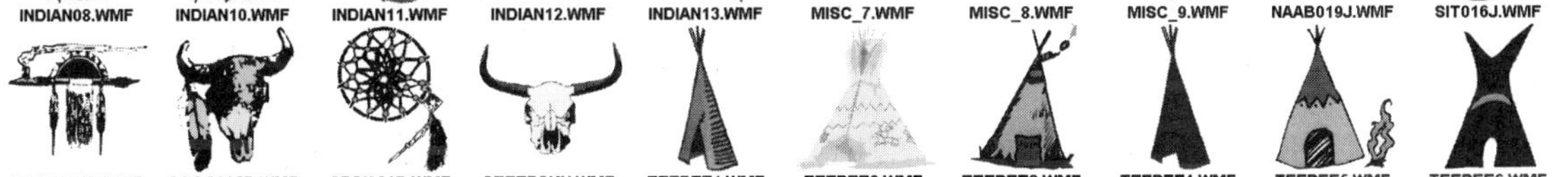

SOGC004D.WMF SOGC005D.WMF SPSI334D.WMF STEERSKU.WMF TEEPEE1.WMF TEEPEE2.WMF TEEPEE3.WMF TEEPEE4.WMF TEEPEE5.WMF TEEPEE6.WMF

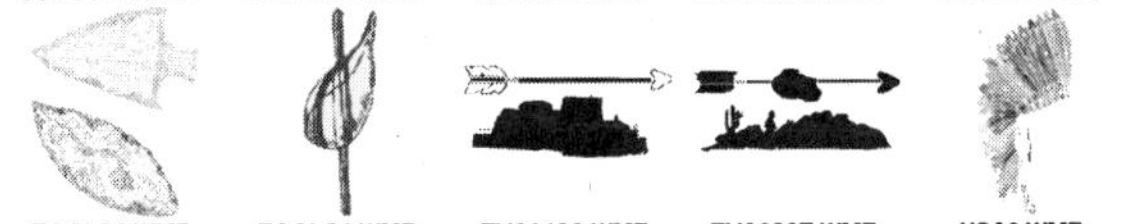

TOOLS3.WMF TOOLS4.WMF TVA018A.WMF TVA026E.WMF USA0.WMF

Western • Western

1192RODC.WMF A2A.WMF A2AB.WMF B20070.WMF B20133.WMF CAA0325.WMF CACTSBKG.WMF DESERT.WMF DESERTCA.WMF GHOSTTOW.WMF

H21123.WMF H21124.WMF HHSI047M.WMF HORSECRT.WMF NASS010J.WMF RODEOHEA.WMF S21708.WMF SMOKINGG.WMF SYMBL80.WMF SYMBOL80.WMF

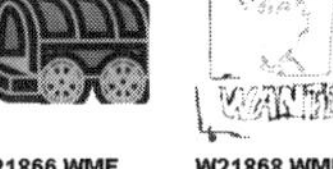

W21866.WMF W21868.WMF

03WOMEN.WMF 04WOMEN.WMF ADS047H.WMF DEC048V.WMF JPN032A.WMF OTS025F.WMF PGX024F.WMF SBS016B.WMF SIT005H.WMF SIT006A.WMF
SPA017C.WMF SPA024C.WMF SPA024E.WMF TVA040F.WMF WOBOD001.WMF WOBOD002.WMF WOBOD003.WMF WOBOD004.WMF WOBOD005.WMF WOBOD006.WMF
WOBOD007.WMF WOBOD008.WMF WOBOD009.WMF WOBOD010.WMF WOBOD011.WMF WOBOD012.WMF WOBOD013.WMF WOBOD014.WMF WOBOD015.WMF WOBOD016.WMF
WOBOD017.WMF WOBOD018.WMF WOBOD019.WMF WOBOD020.WMF WOBOD021.WMF WOBOD022.WMF WOBOD023.WMF WOBOD024.WMF WOBOD025.WMF WOBOD026.WMF
WOBOD027.WMF WOBOD028.WMF WOBOD029.WMF WOBOD030.WMF WOBOD031.WMF WOBOD032.WMF WOBOD033.WMF WOBOD034.WMF WOBOD035.WMF WOBOD036.WMF
WOBOD037.WMF WOBOD038.WMF WOBOD039.WMF WOBOD040.WMF WOBOD041.WMF WOBOD042.WMF WOBOD043.WMF WOBOD044.WMF WOBOD045.WMF WOBOD046.WMF
WOBOD047.WMF WOBOD048.WMF WOBOD049.WMF WOBOD050.WMF WOBOD051.WMF WOBOD052.WMF WOBOD053.WMF WOBOD054.WMF WOBOD055.WMF WOBOD056.WMF
WOBOD057.WMF WOBOD058.WMF WOBOD059.WMF WOBOD060.WMF WOBOD061.WMF WOBOD062.WMF WOBOD063.WMF WOBOD064.WMF WOBOD065.WMF WOBOD066.WMF
WOBOD067.WMF WOBOD068.WMF WOBOD069.WMF WOBOD070.WMF WOBOD071.WMF WOBOD072.WMF WOBOD073.WMF WOBOD074.WMF WOBOD075.WMF WOBOD076.WMF
WOBOD077.WMF WOBOD078.WMF WOBOD079.WMF WOBOD080.WMF WOBOD081.WMF WOBOD082.WMF WOBOD083.WMF WOBOD084.WMF WOBOD085.WMF WOBOD086.WMF
WOBOD087.WMF WOBOD088.WMF WOBOD089.WMF WOBOD090.WMF WOBOD091.WMF WOBOD092.WMF WOBOD093.WMF WOBOD094.WMF WOBOD095.WMF WOBOD096.WMF
WOBOD097.WMF WOBOD098.WMF WOBOD099.WMF WOBOD100.WMF WOBOD101.WMF WOBOD102.WMF WOBOD103.WMF WOBOD104.WMF WOBOD105.WMF WOBOD106.WMF

WOBOD107.WMF WOBOD108.WMF WOBOD109.WMF WOBOD110.WMF WOBOD111.WMF WOBOD112.WMF WOBOD113.WMF WOBOD114.WMF WOBOD115.WMF WOBOD116.WMF

WOBOD117.WMF WOBOD118.WMF WOBOD119.WMF WOBOD120.WMF WOBOD121.WMF WOBOD122.WMF WOBOD123.WMF WOBOD124.WMF WOBOD125.WMF WOBOD126.WMF

WOBOD127.WMF WOBOD128.WMF WOBOD129.WMF WOBOD130.WMF WOBOD131.WMF WOBOD132.WMF WOBOD133.WMF WOBOD134.WMF WOBOD135.WMF WOBOD136.WMF

WOBOD137.WMF WOBOD138.WMF WOBOD139.WMF WOBOD140.WMF WOBOD141.WMF WOBOD142.WMF WOBOD143.WMF WOBOD144.WMF WOBOD145.WMF WOBOD146.WMF

WOBOD147.WMF WOBOD148.WMF WOBOD149.WMF WOBOD150.WMF WOBOD151.WMF WOBOD152.WMF WOBOD153.WMF WOBOD154.WMF WOBOD155.WMF WOBOD156.WMF

WOBOD157.WMF WOBOD158.WMF WOBOD159.WMF WOBOD160.WMF WOBOD161.WMF WOBOD162.WMF WOBOD163.WMF WOBOD164.WMF WOBOD165.WMF WOBOD166.WMF

WOBOD167.WMF WOBOD168.WMF WOBOD169.WMF WOBOD170.WMF WOBOD171.WMF WOBOD172.WMF WOBOD173.WMF WOBOD174.WMF WOBOD175.WMF WOBOD176.WMF

WOBOD177.WMF WOBOD178.WMF WOBOD179.WMF WOBOD180.WMF WOBOD181.WMF WOBOD182.WMF WOBOD183.WMF WOBOD184.WMF WOBOD185.WMF WOBOD186.WMF

WOBOD187.WMF WOBOD188.WMF WOBOD189.WMF WOBOD190.WMF WOBOD191.WMF WOBOD192.WMF WOBOD193.WMF WOBOD194.WMF WOBOD195.WMF WOBOD196.WMF

WOBOD197.WMF WOBOD198.WMF WOBOD199.WMF WOBOD200.WMF WOBOD201.WMF WOBOD202.WMF WOBOD203.WMF WOBOD204.WMF WOBOD205.WMF WOBOD206.WMF

WOBOD207.WMF WOBOD208.WMF WOBOD209.WMF WOBOD210.WMF WOBOD211.WMF WOBOD212.WMF WOBOD213.WMF WOBOD214.WMF WOBOD215.WMF WOBOD216.WMF

WOBOD217.WMF WOBOD218.WMF WOBOD219.WMF WOBOD220.WMF WOBOD221.WMF WOBOD222.WMF WOBOD223.WMF WOBOD224.WMF WOBOD225.WMF WOBOD226.WMF

WOBOD227.WMF
WOBOD228.WMF
WOBOD229.WMF
WOBOD230.WMF
WOBOD231.WMF
WOBOD232.WMF
WOBOD233.WMF
WOBOD234.WMF
WOBOD235.WMF
WOBOD236.WMF
WOBOD237.WMF
WOBOD238.WMF
WOBOD239.WMF
WOBOD240.WMF
WOBOD241.WMF
WOBOD242.WMF
WOBOD243.WMF
WOBOD244.WMF
WOBOD245.WMF
WOBOD246.WMF
WOBOD247.WMF
WOBOD248.WMF
WOBOD249.WMF
WOBOD250.WMF
WOBOD251.WMF
WOBOD252.WMF
WOBOD253.WMF
WOBOD254.WMF
WOBOD255.WMF
WOBOD256.WMF
WOBOD257.WMF
WOBOD258.WMF
WOBOD259.WMF
WOBOD260.WMF
WOBOD261.WMF
WOBOD262.WMF
WOBOD263.WMF
WOBOD264.WMF
WOBOD265.WMF
WOBOD266.WMF
WOBOD267.WMF
WOBOD268.WMF
WOBOD269.WMF
WOBOD270.WMF
WOBOD271.WMF
WOBOD272.WMF
WOBOD273.WMF
WOBOD274.WMF
WOBOD275.WMF
WOBOD276.WMF
WOBOD277.WMF
WOBOD278.WMF
WOBOD279.WMF
WOBOD280.WMF
WOBOD281.WMF
WOBOD282.WMF
WOBOD283.WMF
WOBOD284.WMF
WOBOD285.WMF
WOBOD286.WMF
WOBOD287.WMF
WOBOD288.WMF
WOBOD289.WMF
WOBOD290.WMF
WOBOD291.WMF
WOBOD292.WMF
WOBOD293.WMF
WOBOD294.WMF
WOBOD295.WMF
WOBOD296.WMF
WOBOD297.WMF
WOBOD298.WMF
WOBOD299.WMF
WOBOD300.WMF
WOBOD301.WMF
WOBOD302.WMF
WOBOD303.WMF
WOBOD304.WMF
WOBOD305.WMF
WOBOD306.WMF
WOBOD307.WMF
WOBOD308.WMF
WOBOD309.WMF
WOBOD310.WMF
WOBOD311.WMF
WOBOD312.WMF
WOBOD313.WMF
WOBOD314.WMF
WOBOD315.WMF
WOBOD316.WMF
WOBOD317.WMF
WOBOD318.WMF
WOBOD319.WMF
WOBOD320.WMF
WOBOD321.WMF
WOBOD322.WMF
WOBOD323.WMF
WOBOD324.WMF
WOBOD325.WMF
WOBOD326.WMF
WOBOD327.WMF
WOBOD328.WMF
WOBOD329.WMF
WOBOD330.WMF
WOBOD331.WMF
WOBOD332.WMF
WOBOD333.WMF
WOBOD334.WMF
WOBOD335.WMF
WOBOD336.WMF
WOBOD337.WMF
WOBOD338.WMF
WOBOD339.WMF
WOBOD340.WMF
WOBOD341.WMF
WOBOD342.WMF
WOBOD343.WMF
WOBOD344.WMF
WOBOD345.WMF
WOBOD346.WMF

WOBOD347.WMF
WOBOD348.WMF
WOBOD349.WMF
WOBOD350.WMF
WOBOD351.WMF
WOBOD352.WMF
WOBOD353.WMF
WOBOD354.WMF
WOBOD355.WMF
WOBOD356.WMF
WOBOD357.WMF
WOBOD358.WMF
WOBOD359.WMF
WOBOD360.WMF
WOBOD361.WMF
WOBOD362.WMF
WOBOD363.WMF
WOBOD364.WMF
WOBOD365.WMF
WOBOD366.WMF
WOBOD367.WMF
WOBOD368.WMF
WOBOD369.WMF
WOBOD370.WMF
WOBOD371.WMF
WOBOD372.WMF
WOBOD373.WMF
WOBOD374.WMF
WOBOD375.WMF
WOBOD376.WMF
WOBOD377.WMF
WOBOD378.WMF
WOBOD379.WMF
WOBOD380.WMF
WOBOD381.WMF
WOBOD382.WMF
WOBOD383.WMF
WOBOD384.WMF
WOBOD385.WMF
WOBOD386.WMF
WOBOD387.WMF
WOBOD388.WMF
WOBOD389.WMF
WOBOD390.WMF
WOBOD391.WMF
WOBOD392.WMF
WOBOD393.WMF
WOBOD394.WMF
WOBOD395.WMF
WOBOD396.WMF
WOBOD397.WMF
WOBOD398.WMF
WOBOD399.WMF
WOBOD400.WMF
WOBOD401.WMF
WOBOD402.WMF
WOBOD403.WMF
WOBOD404.WMF
WOBOD405.WMF
WOBOD406.WMF
WOBOD407.WMF
WOBOD408.WMF
WOBOD409.WMF
WOBOD410.WMF
WOBOD411.WMF
WOBOD412.WMF
WOBOD413.WMF
WOBOD414.WMF
WOBOD415.WMF
WOBOD416.WMF
WOBOD417.WMF
WOBOD418.WMF
WOBOD419.WMF
WOBOD420.WMF
WOBOD421.WMF
WOBOD422.WMF
WOBOD423.WMF
WOBOD424.WMF
WOFAC001.WMF
WOFAC002.WMF
WOFAC003.WMF
WOFAC004.WMF
WOFAC005.WMF
WOFAC006.WMF
WOFAC007.WMF
WOFAC008.WMF
WOFAC009.WMF
WOFAC010.WMF
WOFAC011.WMF
WOFAC012.WMF
WOFAC013.WMF
WOFAC014.WMF
WOFAC015.WMF
WOFAC016.WMF
WOFAC017.WMF
WOFAC018.WMF
WOFAC019.WMF
WOFAC020.WMF
WOFAC021.WMF
WOFAC022.WMF
WOFAC023.WMF
WOFAC024.WMF
WOFAC025.WMF
WOFAC026.WMF
WOFAC027.WMF
WOFAC028.WMF
WOFAC029.WMF
WOFAC030.WMF
WOFAC031.WMF
WOFAC032.WMF
WOFAC033.WMF
WOFAC034.WMF
WOFAC035.WMF
WOFAC036.WMF
WOFAC037.WMF
WOFAC038.WMF
WOFAC039.WMF
WOFAC040.WMF
WOFAC041.WMF
WOFAC042.WMF

WOFAC043.WMF WOFAC044.WMF WOFAC045.WMF WOFAC046.WMF WOFAC047.WMF WOFAC048.WMF WOFAC049.WMF WOFAC050.WMF WOFAC051.WMF WOFAC052.WMF

WOFAC053.WMF WOFAC054.WMF WOFAC055.WMF WOFAC056.WMF WOFAC057.WMF WOFAC058.WMF WOFAC059.WMF WOFAC060.WMF WOFAC061.WMF WOFAC062.WMF

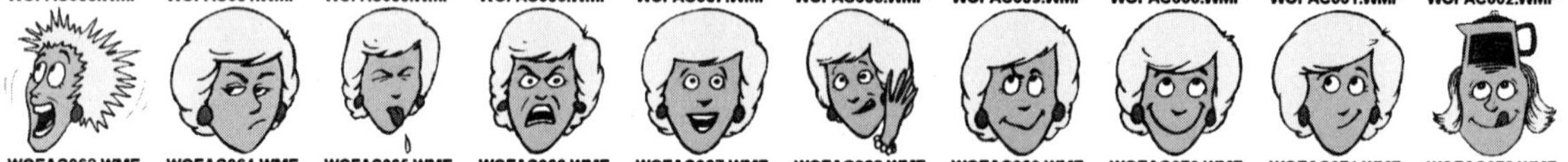

WOFAC063.WMF WOFAC064.WMF WOFAC065.WMF WOFAC066.WMF WOFAC067.WMF WOFAC068.WMF WOFAC069.WMF WOFAC070.WMF WOFAC071.WMF WOFAC072.WMF

WOFAC073.WMF WOFAC074.WMF WOFAC075.WMF WOFAC076.WMF WOFAC077.WMF WOFAC078.WMF WOFAC079.WMF WOFAC080.WMF WOFAC081.WMF WOFAC082.WMF

WOFAC083.WMF WOFAC084.WMF WOFAC085.WMF WOFAC086.WMF WOFAC087.WMF WOFAC088.WMF WOFAC089.WMF WOFAC090.WMF WOFAC091.WMF WOFAC092.WMF

WOFAC093.WMF WOFAC094.WMF WOFAC095.WMF WOFAC096.WMF WOFAC097.WMF WOFAC098.WMF WOFAC100.WMF WOFAC101.WMF WOFAC102.WMF WOFAC103.WMF

WOFAC104.WMF

Women • Historical (HISTORIC)

01WOMEN.WMF
02WOMEN.WMF
05WOMEN.WMF
06WOMEN.WMF
07WOMEN.WMF
08WOMEN.WMF
09WOMEN.WMF
10WOMEN.WMF
11WOMEN.WMF
12WOMEN.WMF
13WOMEN.WMF
14WOMEN.WMF
15WOMEN.WMF
16WOMEN.WMF
17WOMEN.WMF
18WOMEN.WMF
19WOMEN.WMF
20WOMEN.WMF
21WOMEN.WMF
22WOMEN.WMF
23WOMEN.WMF
24WOMEN.WMF
25WOMEN.WMF
26WOMEN.WMF
27WOMEN.WMF
28WOMEN.WMF
29WOMEN.WMF
30WOMEN.WMF
31WOMEN.WMF
32WOMEN.WMF
33WOMEN.WMF
34WOMEN.WMF
35WOMEN.WMF
36WOMEN.WMF
37WOMEN.WMF
38WOMEN.WMF
39WOMEN.WMF
40WOMEN.WMF
41WOMEN.WMF
42WOMEN.WMF
43WOMEN.WMF
44WOMEN.WMF
45WOMEN.WMF
46WOMEN.WMF
47WOMEN.WMF
48WOMEN.WMF
49WOMEN.WMF
50WOMEN.WMF
REALB001.WMF
REALB002.WMF
REALB003.WMF
REALB004.WMF
REALB005.WMF
REALB006.WMF
REALB007.WMF
REALB008.WMF
REALB009.WMF
REALB010.WMF
REALB011.WMF
REALB012.WMF
REALB013.WMF
REALB014.WMF
REALB015.WMF
REALB016.WMF
REALB017.WMF
REALB018.WMF
REALB019.WMF
REALB020.WMF
REALB021.WMF
REALB022.WMF
REALB023.WMF
REALB024.WMF
REALB025.WMF
REALB026.WMF
REALB027.WMF
REALB028.WMF
REALB029.WMF
REALB030.WMF
REALB031.WMF
REALB032.WMF
REALB033.WMF
REALB034.WMF
REALB035.WMF
REALB036.WMF
REALB037.WMF
REALB038.WMF
REALB039.WMF
REALB040.WMF
REALB041.WMF
REALB042.WMF
REALB043.WMF
REALB044.WMF
REALB045.WMF
REALB046.WMF
REALB047.WMF
REALB048.WMF
REALB049.WMF
REALB050.WMF
REALB051.WMF
REALB052.WMF
REALB053.WMF
REALB054.WMF
REALB055.WMF
REALB056.WMF
REALB057.WMF
REALB058.WMF
REALB059.WMF
REALB060.WMF
REALB061.WMF
REALB062.WMF
REALB063.WMF
REALB064.WMF
REALB065.WMF
REALB066.WMF
REALB067.WMF
REALB068.WMF
REALB069.WMF
REALB070.WMF
REALB071.WMF
REALB072.WMF

REALB073.WMF REALB074.WMF REALB075.WMF REALB076.WMF REALB077.WMF REALB078.WMF REALB079.WMF REALB080.WMF REALB081.WMF REALB082.WMF
REALB083.WMF REALB084.WMF REALB085.WMF REALB086.WMF REALB087.WMF REALB088.WMF REALB089.WMF REALB090.WMF REALB091.WMF REALB092.WMF
REALB093.WMF REALB094.WMF REALB095.WMF REALB096.WMF REALB097.WMF REALB098.WMF REALB099.WMF REALB100.WMF REALB101.WMF REALB102.WMF
REALB103.WMF REALB104.WMF REALB105.WMF REALB106.WMF REALB107.WMF REALB108.WMF REALB109.WMF REALB110.WMF REALB111.WMF REALB112.WMF
REALB113.WMF REALB114.WMF REALB115.WMF REALB116.WMF REALB117.WMF REALB118.WMF REALB119.WMF REALB120.WMF REALB121.WMF REALB122.WMF
REALB123.WMF REALB124.WMF REALB125.WMF REALB126.WMF REALB127.WMF REALB128.WMF REALB129.WMF REALB130.WMF REALB131.WMF REALB132.WMF
REALB133.WMF REALB134.WMF REALB135.WMF REALB136.WMF REALB137.WMF REALB138.WMF REALB139.WMF REALB140.WMF REALB141.WMF REALB142.WMF
REALB143.WMF REALB144.WMF REALB145.WMF REALB146.WMF REALB147.WMF REALB148.WMF REALB149.WMF REALB150.WMF REALB151.WMF REALB152.WMF
REALB153.WMF REALB154.WMF REALB155.WMF REALB156.WMF REALB157.WMF REALB158.WMF REALB159.WMF REALB160.WMF REALB161.WMF REALB162.WMF
REALB163.WMF REALB164.WMF REALB165.WMF REALB166.WMF REALB167.WMF REALB168.WMF REALB169.WMF REALB170.WMF REALB171.WMF REALB172.WMF
REALB173.WMF REALB174.WMF REALB175.WMF REALB176.WMF REALB177.WMF REALB178.WMF REALB179.WMF REALB180.WMF REALB181.WMF REALB182.WMF
REALB183.WMF REALF001.WMF REALF002.WMF REALF003.WMF REALF004.WMF REALF005.WMF REALF006.WMF REALF007.WMF REALF008.WMF REALF009.WMF

REALF010.WMF
REALF011.WMF
REALF012.WMF
REALF013.WMF
REALF014.WMF
REALF015.WMF
REALF016.WMF
REALF017.WMF
REALF018.WMF
REALF019.WMF
REALF020.WMF
REALF021.WMF
REALF022.WMF
REALF023.WMF
REALF024.WMF
REALF025.WMF
REALF026.WMF
REALF027.WMF
REALF028.WMF
REALF029.WMF
REALF030.WMF
REALF031.WMF
REALF032.WMF
REALF033.WMF
REALF034.WMF
REALF035.WMF
REALF036.WMF
REALF037.WMF
REALF038.WMF
REALF039.WMF
REALF040.WMF
REALF041.WMF
REALF042.WMF
REALF043.WMF
REALF044.WMF
REALF045.WMF
REALF046.WMF
REALF047.WMF
REALF048.WMF
REALF049.WMF
REALF050.WMF
REALF051.WMF
REALF052.WMF
REALF053.WMF
REALF054.WMF
REALF055.WMF
REALF056.WMF
REALF057.WMF
REALF058.WMF
REALF059.WMF
REALF060.WMF
REALF061.WMF
REALF062.WMF
REALF063.WMF
REALF064.WMF
REALF065.WMF
REALF066.WMF
REALF067.WMF
REALF068.WMF
REALF069.WMF
REALF070.WMF
REALF071.WMF
REALF072.WMF
REALF073.WMF
SMR016M.WMF
SMR021H.WMF

2049.WMF ABORIG.WMF ANZAC.WMF ANZACC.WMF AUSTDAY.WMF AUSTRALI.WMF AUSTSIL.WMF BIT1003.WMF BOOMRANG.WMF ENCA003J.WMF

SYDNEY.WMF SYDNEY01.WMF SYDNEY04.WMF SYDNEY05.WMF SYDNEY06.WMF SYDNEY07.WMF SYDNEY08.WMF SYDNEY09.WMF SYDNEY10.WMF SYDNEY11.WMF

SYDNEY12.WMF

World • Country Signs (COUNTRY)

1401.WMF 1402.WMF 1403.WMF 1404.WMF 1405.WMF 1406.WMF 1407.WMF 1408.WMF 1409.WMF 1410.WMF

1411.WMF 1412.WMF 1413.WMF 1414.WMF 1415.WMF 1416.WMF 1417.WMF 1418.WMF 1419.WMF 1420.WMF

1421.WMF 1422.WMF 1423.WMF 1424.WMF 1425.WMF 1426.WMF 1427.WMF 1428.WMF 1429.WMF 1430.WMF

1431.WMF 1432.WMF 1433.WMF 1434.WMF

ANUBIS.WMF ARC022.WMF BACK029.WMF BISI004M.WMF BIT0513.WMF BORD027.WMF CAA0175.WMF COLUMN02.WMF EGLSYMBL.WMF FIGURE05.WMF

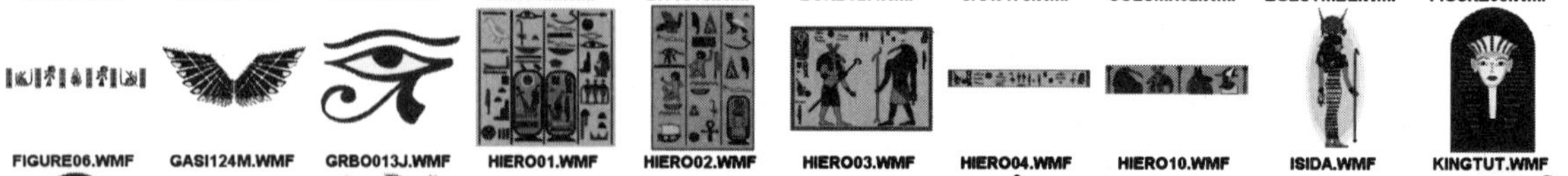

FIGURE06.WMF GASI124M.WMF GRBO013J.WMF HIERO01.WMF HIERO02.WMF HIERO03.WMF HIERO04.WMF HIERO10.WMF ISIDA.WMF KINGTUT.WMF

KWEENEF.WMF NASI007M.WMF NINGODNS.WMF OSIRIS.WMF PECA005D.WMF PECA006D.WMF PECA172J.WMF PECA173J.WMF PECA180D.WMF PERW045J.WMF

PERW046J.WMF PERW047J.WMF PESI001D.WMF PESI002D.WMF PESS037J.WMF PLSI001D.WMF PYRAMD01.WMF PYRAMID.WMF PYRAMIDS.WMF SLCA001M.WMF

SPHYNX.WMF SPINX.WMF SPIRIT19.WMF SPIRIT2.WMF SPIRIT20.WMF SPIRIT21.WMF SPIRIT22.WMF SPIRIT23.WMF THRONE.WMF TOT.WMF

TRAVEL10.WMF TRAVEL3.WMF TUTMASK.WMF

World • France

0050.WMF 1682.WMF ARC029.WMF ARC039.WMF ARC040.WMF ARCDETRI.WMF ARCH.WMF ASI066J.WMF BIKC003J.WMF EIFFEL.WMF

EIFFEL1.WMF EIFFEL2.WMF EIFFEL_1.WMF EIFFELTO.WMF FENCING.WMF FRANCE.WMF PARISHEA.WMF TVL012D.WMF

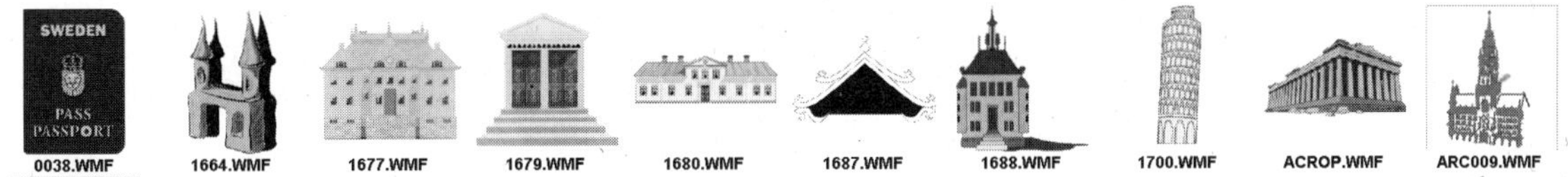

0038.WMF 1664.WMF 1677.WMF 1679.WMF 1680.WMF 1687.WMF 1688.WMF 1700.WMF ACROP.WMF ARC009.WMF

ARC010.WMF ARC012.WMF ARC013.WMF ARC014.WMF ARC018.WMF ARC021.WMF ARC026.WMF ARC030.WMF ARC031.WMF ARC032.WMF

ARC035.WMF ARC036.WMF ARC043.WMF ARC044.WMF ARC045.WMF ARC047.WMF ARC048.WMF ARC049.WMF AZTEC.WMF BASILS.WMF

BEJIING.WMF BIGBEN1.WMF BIGBEN2.WMF CANTER.WMF COLLOS.WMF EASTERIS.WMF EQUAGOD.WMF GR_WALL.WMF GREATWAL.WMF JAGUARG.WMF

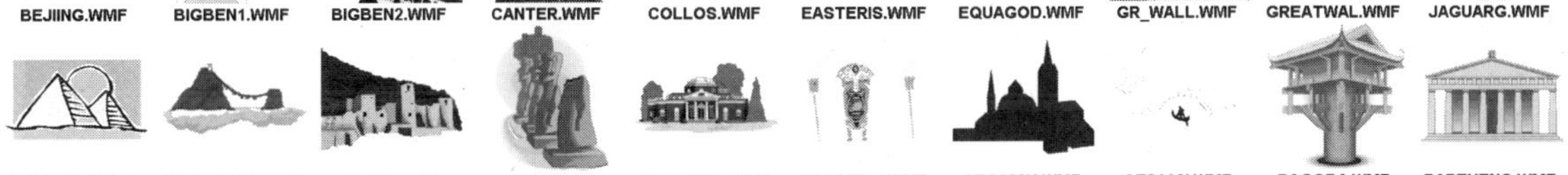

LDSCP052.WMF MEOTOIWA.WMF MESA.WMF MOAI.WMF MONTICEL.WMF NACA230J.WMF OEC052K.WMF OTS002I.WMF PAGODA.WMF PARTHENO.WMF

PILLAR01.WMF PISA.WMF PISA20.WMF RIO.WMF RMCOL01M.WMF RUSSIA.WMF SMTHINST.WMF SOGC003D.WMF SPHYNX20.WMF TAIKOBAS.WMF

TORII.WMF TVA091F.WMF TVL008A.WMF TVL010A.WMF TVL010B.WMF TVL012A.WMF

World • United Kingdom (UK)

ARC034.WMF ASI066B.WMF ASI066D.WMF ASI066I.WMF BAGPIPER.WMF BIGBEN.WMF BIGBEN05.WMF BIT0668.WMF BIT0669.WMF BOBBY.WMF

BODIAM.WMF BRITISH.WMF PALACE.WMF PIPER.WMF STONE.WMF STONEHEN.WMF STONEHNG.WMF

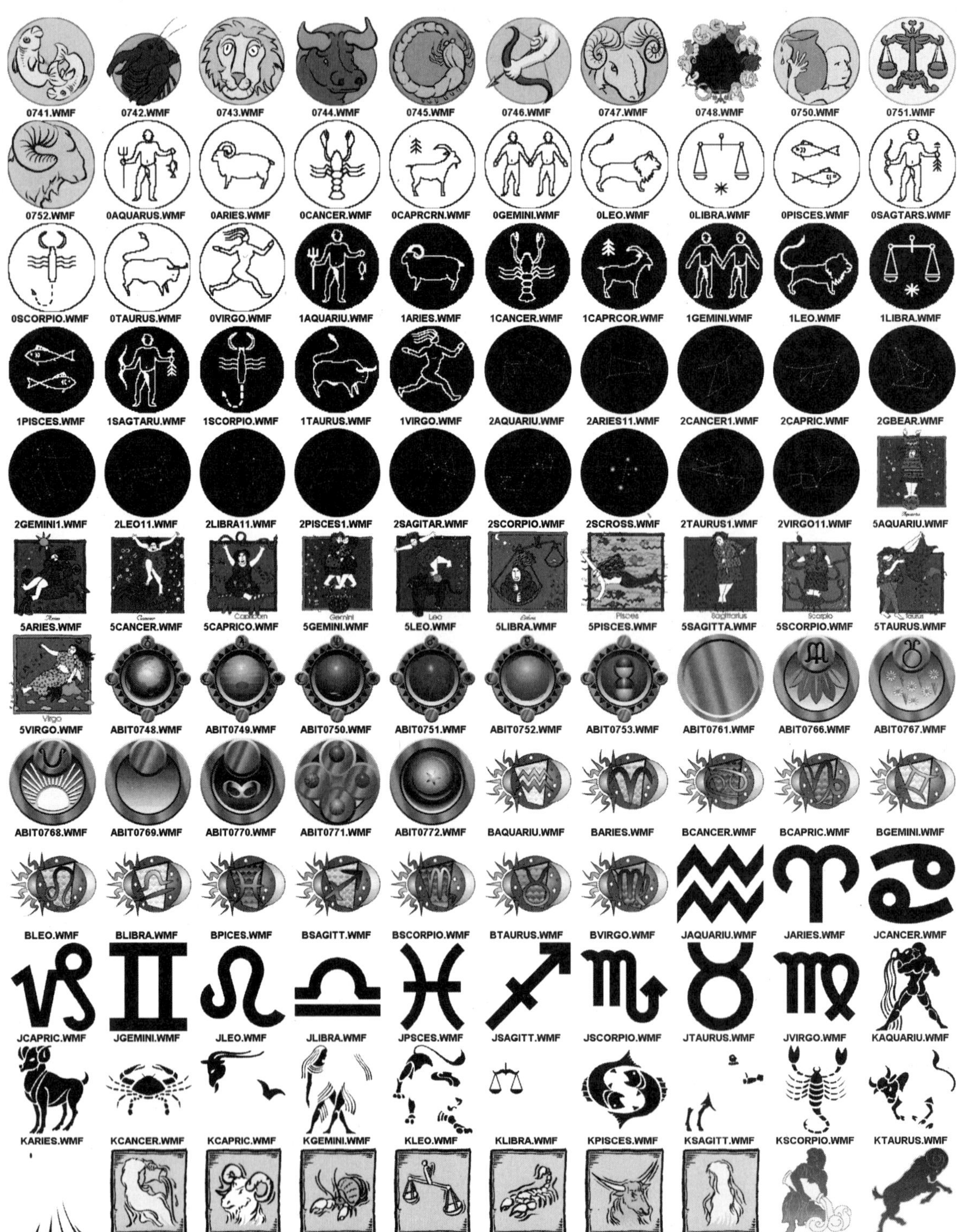
0741.WMF
0742.WMF
0743.WMF
0744.WMF
0745.WMF
0746.WMF
0747.WMF
0748.WMF
0750.WMF
0751.WMF
0752.WMF
0AQUARUS.WMF
0ARIES.WMF
0CANCER.WMF
0CAPRCRN.WMF
0GEMINI.WMF
0LEO.WMF
0LIBRA.WMF
0PISCES.WMF
0SAGTARS.WMF
0SCORPIO.WMF
0TAURUS.WMF
0VIRGO.WMF
1AQUARIU.WMF
1ARIES.WMF
1CANCER.WMF
1CAPRCOR.WMF
1GEMINI.WMF
1LEO.WMF
1LIBRA.WMF
1PISCES.WMF
1SAGTARU.WMF
1SCORPIO.WMF
1TAURUS.WMF
1VIRGO.WMF
2AQUARIU.WMF
2ARIES11.WMF
2CANCER1.WMF
2CAPRIC.WMF
2GBEAR.WMF
2GEMINI1.WMF
2LEO11.WMF
2LIBRA11.WMF
2PISCES1.WMF
2SAGITAR.WMF
2SCORPIO.WMF
2SCROSS.WMF
2TAURUS1.WMF
2VIRGO11.WMF
5AQUARIU.WMF
5ARIES.WMF
5CANCER.WMF
5CAPRICO.WMF
5GEMINI.WMF
5LEO.WMF
5LIBRA.WMF
5PISCES.WMF
5SAGITTA.WMF
5SCORPIO.WMF
5TAURUS.WMF
5VIRGO.WMF
ABIT0748.WMF
ABIT0749.WMF
ABIT0750.WMF
ABIT0751.WMF
ABIT0752.WMF
ABIT0753.WMF
ABIT0761.WMF
ABIT0766.WMF
ABIT0767.WMF
ABIT0768.WMF
ABIT0769.WMF
ABIT0770.WMF
ABIT0771.WMF
ABIT0772.WMF
BAQUARIU.WMF
BARIES.WMF
BCANCER.WMF
BCAPRIC.WMF
BGEMINI.WMF
BLEO.WMF
BLIBRA.WMF
BPICES.WMF
BSAGITT.WMF
BSCORPIO.WMF
BTAURUS.WMF
BVIRGO.WMF
JAQUARIU.WMF
JARIES.WMF
JCANCER.WMF
JCAPRIC.WMF
JGEMINI.WMF
JLEO.WMF
JLIBRA.WMF
JPSCES.WMF
JSAGITT.WMF
JSCORPIO.WMF
JTAURUS.WMF
JVIRGO.WMF
KAQUARIU.WMF
KARIES.WMF
KCANCER.WMF
KCAPRIC.WMF
KGEMINI.WMF
KLEO.WMF
KLIBRA.WMF
KPISCES.WMF
KSAGITT.WMF
KSCORPIO.WMF
KTAURUS.WMF
KVIRGO.WMF
MAQUARIU.WMF
MARIES.WMF
MCANCER.WMF
MLIBRA.WMF
MSCORPIO.WMF
MTAURUS.WMF
MVIRGO.WMF
QAQUARIU.WMF
QARIES5.WMF

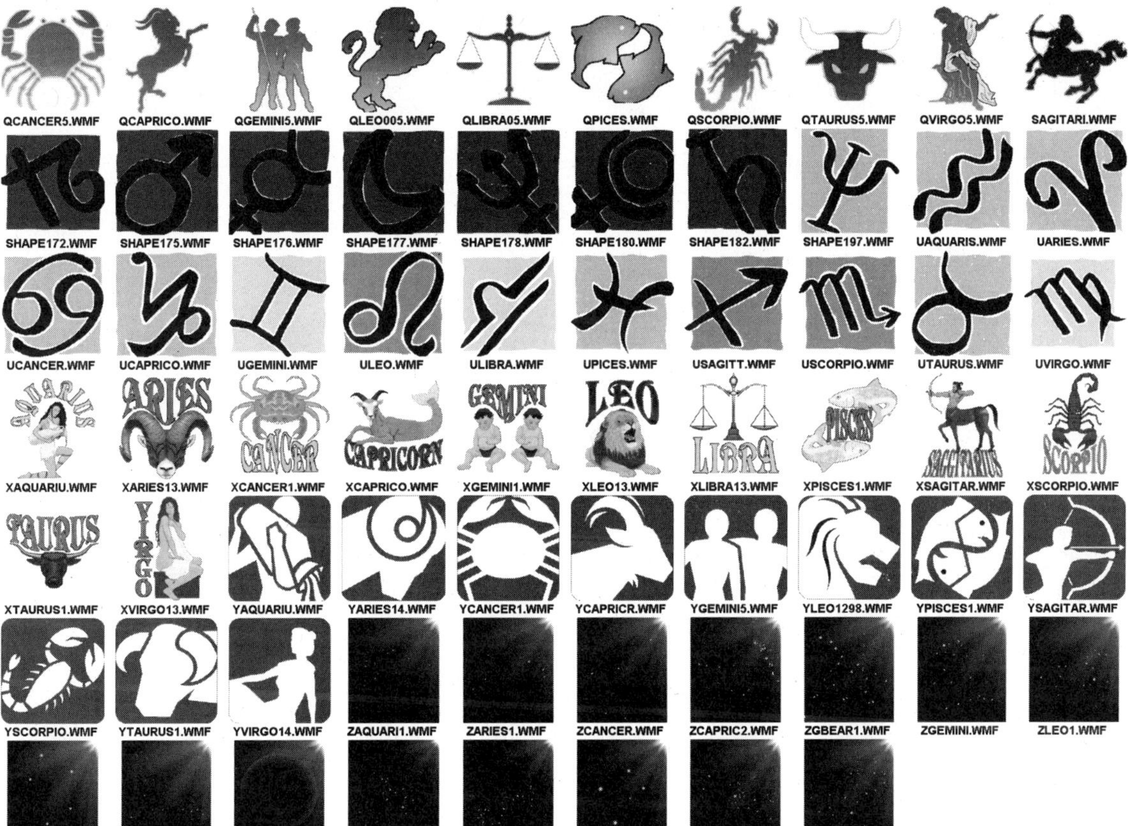
QCANCER5.WMF
QCAPRICO.WMF
QGEMINI5.WMF
QLEO005.WMF
QLIBRA05.WMF
QPICES.WMF
QSCORPIO.WMF
QTAURUS5.WMF
QVIRGO5.WMF
SAGITARI.WMF
SHAPE172.WMF
SHAPE175.WMF
SHAPE176.WMF
SHAPE177.WMF
SHAPE178.WMF
SHAPE180.WMF
SHAPE182.WMF
SHAPE197.WMF
UAQUARIS.WMF
UARIES.WMF
UCANCER.WMF
UCAPRICO.WMF
UGEMINI.WMF
ULEO.WMF
ULIBRA.WMF
UPICES.WMF
USAGITT.WMF
USCORPIO.WMF
UTAURUS.WMF
UVIRGO.WMF
XAQUARIU.WMF
XARIES13.WMF
XCANCER1.WMF
XCAPRICO.WMF
XGEMINI1.WMF
XLEO13.WMF
XLIBRA13.WMF
XPISCES1.WMF
XSAGITAR.WMF
XSCORPIO.WMF
XTAURUS1.WMF
XVIRGO13.WMF
YAQUARIU.WMF
YARIES14.WMF
YCANCER1.WMF
YCAPRICR.WMF
YGEMINI5.WMF
YLEO1298.WMF
YPISCES1.WMF
YSAGITAR.WMF
YSCORPIO.WMF
YTAURUS1.WMF
YVIRGO14.WMF
ZAQUARI1.WMF
ZARIES1.WMF
ZCANCER.WMF
ZCAPRIC2.WMF
ZGBEAR1.WMF
ZGEMINI.WMF
ZLEO1.WMF
ZLIBRA1.WMF
ZPISCES1.WMF
ZPLANET.WMF
ZSAGITAR.WMF
ZSCORPIO.WMF
ZSCROSS1.WMF
ZTAURUS1.WMF
ZVIRGO1.WMF